INTELLECTUAL PROPERTY:

PATENTS, COPYRIGHT, TRADE MARKS AND ALLIED RIGHTS

Seventh Edition

By

WILLIAM CORNISH

Formerly Herchel Smith Professor of Intellectual Property Law, University of Cambridge

and

DAVID LLEWELYN

Professor, King's College London
External Director, IP Academy Singapore
Of Counsel, White & Case LLP (Singapore)

and

TANYA APLIN

Reader in Intellectual Property Law, King's College London

SWEET & MAXWELL

THOMSON REUTERS

First Edition 1981
Second Impression 1982
Third Impression 1984
Second Edition 1989
Second Impression 1990
Third Impression 1991
Fourth Impression 1993
Fifth Impression 1994
Sixth Impression 1995
Third Edition 1996
Second Impression 1997
Third Impression 1998
Fourth Edition 1999
Second Impression 2000
Third Impression 2001
Fifth Edition 2003
Sixth Edition 2007
Seventh Edition 2010

Published by
Sweet & Maxwell Limited
100 Avenue Road
Swiss Cottage
London, NW3 3PF
www.sweetandmaxwell.co.uk

Typeset by
YHT Ltd, London
Printed in the UK by
CPI William Clowes, Beccles NR34 7TL

British Library Cataloguing in Publication Data
Cornish, W. R. (William Rodolph), 1937—
Intellectual property: patents, copyright,
trade marks and allied rights.—2nd ed.
1. Great Britain, Intellectual property Law
I. Title
334'1064'8

ISBN 978 1847039231 (pb)

PREFACE TO THE SEVENTH EDITION

Intellectual Property used to be regarded by most judges, lawyers, industrialists, politicians, journalists, civil servants and individual inventors and creators as a recondite specialism that was best left to small bands of people who knew what it was about. Today it is too important and too controversial for such casualness to pass muster. The reach of the various types of protection—by patents, copyright, trademarks and so on—has expanded and at the same time the relevant law has become far more complex than before. Legislation—primary and secondary—streams forth. The decisions of courts form a rising tide. Keeping our readership up to date necessitates a Seventh Edition on the heels of the Sixth. To cope with the flood of new material William Cornish and David Llewelyn are very pleased now to be joined by Dr Tanya Aplin. She becomes the specialist in the team responsible for matters of copyright and design law.

The book deals with IP issues arising under the law of the United Kingdom. The subject has to be surveyed at the levels of purely national law, European Law and international law. Over the last four decades, the Europeanisation of IP law has been striking, for all that the fundamental structures given to the different types of IP have varied in critical respects. Not least remarkable has been the active pursuit by the institutions of the European Union of rights that extend to the whole Internal Market, and the harmonisation of equivalent rights under the laws of Member States, despite the absence of explicit constitutional power to intervene in the IP field. Only under the Lisbon Treaty of 2008 has this been rectified by Article 118 of the Treaty on the Functioning of the European Union. Evolving operative schemes from the legal and administrative experience of European states has involved many compromises, and some of them are ripe for reconsideration, according to important interest groups. Yet what has emerged in Europe so far has provided a model for legislation in the field across the globe. Since most countries around the world are members of the World Trade Organisation, and are obliged therefore to comply with the high-level standards of its Agreement on Trade-related Aspects of Intellectual Property rights (TRIPs), the European models have had a timely significance.

Concerning the patent systems in Europe, for decades it had been thought politically intractable to secure amendments to the European Patent Convention of 1973. However, "EPC 2000", which does provide for a limited number of changes, was finally given effect on December 13, 2007. The London Agreement, also of 2000, which concerns the language regimes applying to European patents, also gained assent. But the hope of finally securing a Community Patent under a regime prescribed by an EU Regulation has so far remained elusive, largely because of disagreements about whether it is necessary to translate such a patent into the EU's 23 official languages.

As to basic doctrine, attention in recent years has shifted away from differences in the courts of EPC states over the proper approach to determining the scope of patents, towards the criteria of validity. The requirements have been the subject of major decisions from the House of Lords or the Court of Appeal, which restate with considerable subtlety the criteria by which the requirements for patentable subject-matter, novelty, inventive step, industrial capability, adequate disclosure and the proportionality between description and claims fall to be judged. Some of these decisions go to the adaptation of the law to meet the demands for patents upon biotechnological and digital inventions. As we go to press, the Enlarged Board of Appeal of the European Patent Office has published its self-regarding opinion that the decisions of its Boards of Appeal have not treated the exclusion of computer programs from the patent sphere inconsistently. Accordingly, there is nothing for the Enlarged Board to set right. Our first regret about this curious decision is that in this edition we have not been able to deal with its contentions at any length.

In relation to copyright, the harmonisation achieved by the InfoSoc Directive is beginning to be tested, with an ever-increasing number of references to the ECJ concerning the scope of the rights of reproduction and communication to the public and the meaning of "fair compensation" when it comes to the private copying exception. Such rulings will inevitably make the impact of harmonisation more pronounced. An incipient jurisprudence has also started to develop around the Resale Royalty Right Directive and a handful of rulings on the Database Directive have confirmed the extent of *sui generis* protection for databases. Meanwhile, national courts continue to struggle with the issue of originality for copyright databases, particularly for functional yet highly commercial compilations of data. The battle at the EU level to extend the term of protection for performers and producers of sound recordings, so vehemently fought over since 2008, has been temporarily stayed while the Commission assesses the potential impact on audiovisual performers. Internet piracy, particularly of films and music, continues to cause much anxiety amongst rightholders and ISPs have been at first cajoled and later forced into the role of policeman. The national frameworks for encouraging or obliging ISPs to intervene, such as that introduced in the UK by the Digital Economy Act 2010, have been hotly contested. Finally, the ambitious agenda set by the Gowers Review for reform of UK copyright exceptions has rapidly declined into a more modest set of proposals, favouring mostly libraries, archives and educational institutions. Parodists and private users have been abandoned, as have users of orphan works, during the last minute rush to pass the Digital Economy Act 2010.

Concerning designs, we have seen an emerging clarity on the notional informed user as well as the relationship between validity requirements and infringement provisions. However, quirks remain between the multi-layered systems of designs protection, such as the availability of financial remedies for innocent infringement of UK registered designs, but not for Community designs. In the unique area of UK unregistered designs attempts to broaden protection to include design concepts have been (quite rightly) rejected by the courts.

As to the ever-burgeoning law on trade marks and unfair competition, the flood of cases before national and EU courts has continued unabated since the last edition. The ECJ has tried valiantly to give guidance to national courts. Occasionally this has been a success; but more frequently the result has been even more confusion and complexity. What is clear is that trade marks have become much easier, and cheaper, to obtain (and maintain) and the scope protection has expanded considerably. It remains to be seen whether this position will survive the ongoing review of the overall functioning of the EU trade mark system being carried out by the Max Planck Institute in Munich at the behest of the EU Commission; but there are growing signs of disquiet at the profusion of trade marks and their capacity to derail what most neutral observers would regard to be legitimate competition.

WRC
DLl
TA

June, 2010

CONTENTS

TABLE OF CASES

ICI/Pyridine Herbicides (T206/83) [1986] E.P.O.R. 232 5–18
ICOS/Transmembrane receptor [200] O.J. EPO 275 21–08
IDA Ltd v University of Southampton sub nom: University of Southampton's Patent Applications [2006] EWCA Civ 145; [2006] R.P.C. 21; (2006) 29(5) I.P.D. 29038 .... 4–07, 7–02
IG Farbenindustrie AG's Patents (1930) 47 R.P.C. 289 5–23
IGT/Electronic multi-play poker (T336/07) [2008] E.P.O.R. 18 20–31
IHT Internationale Heiztechnik GmbH v Ideal Standard GmbH (C-9/93) [1994] E.C.R. I-2789; [1994] 3 C.M.L.R. 857; [1995] F.S.R. 59 ....18–121, 19–06, 19–20
IMH Investments Ltd v Trinidad Home Developers Ltd [1994] F.S.R. 616 7–25
IMS Health Inc v Commission of the European Communities (T-184/01 R) (No.2) [2001] E.C.R. II-3193; [2002] 4 C.M.L.R. 2 ....19–16, 20–43
IN Newman Ltd v Adlem [2005] EWCA Civ 741; [2006] F.S.R. 16; (2005) 28(8) I.P.D. 28059 17–13
INS case, 248 U.S. 215 (1918) SC (US) 17–35
IPC Magazines Ltd v MGN Ltd [1998] F.S.R. 431 18–105
IPC Media Ltd v Highbury Leisure Publishing Ltd (No.2) [2004] EWHC 2985 (Ch); [2005] F.S.R. 20; (2005) 28(2) I.P.D. 28006 12–06
IPC Media Ltd v News Group Newspapers Ltd [2005] EWHC 317 (Ch); [2005] E.M.L.R. 23; [2005] F.S.R. 35; (2005) 28(5) I.P.D. 28038 12–41
ITS Rubber's Application [1979] R.P.C. 318 5–57
IceTV Pty Ltd v Nine Netwoek Australia Pty Ltd [2009] H.C.A. 14 Aust 11–10, 12–06, 12–07, 12–13
Ide Line AG v Philips Electronics NV [1997] E.T.M.R. 377 ....18–19, 18–43
Ifejika v Ifejika Joined Cases: Ifejika v Lens Care Ltd [2009] EWHC 3343 (Pat); [2010] F.S.R. 7; (2010) 33(3) I.P.D. 33019 15–22
Illinois Tools Works Inc v Autobars Co (Services) Ltd [1972] F.S.R. 67; [1974] R.P.C. 337 ....4–09, 5–40
Illustrated Newspapers Ltd v Publicity Services (London) Ltd 96 [1938] Ch. 414; (1938) 55 R.P.C. 172 17–37
Imaginarium TM [2004] R.P.C. 594 18–71
Imperial Group Plc v Philip Morris Ltd [1984] R.P.C. 293 17–28
Imperial Tobacco Ltd v Berry Bros & Rudd [2001] All E.R. (D) 447 17–17
Imperial Tobacco Co of India Ltd v Bonnan [1924] A.C. 755; (1924) 41 R.P.C. 441 JC 17–19
Import of Spirituous Drinks, Re (C2/78) sub nom: Commission of European Communities v Belgium (C2/78) [1979] E.C.R. 1761; [1980] 1 C.M.L.R. 216 1–52
Impro Licensing's Sarl Patent [2006] R.P.C. 517 2–11
Improver Corp v Remington Consumer Products Ltd [1990] F.S.R. 181 6–04
Imutran Ltd v Uncaged Campaigns Ltd: [2001] 2 All E.R. 385; [2001] C.P. Rep. 28; [2001] E.C.D.R. 16; [2001] E.M.L.R. 21; [2001] H.R.L.R. 31; [2002] F.S.R. 2; (2001) 24(5) I.P.D. 24031 8–44
Indata Equipment Supplies Ltd (t/a Autofleet) v ACL Ltd [1998] 1 B.C.L.C. 412; [1998] F.S.R. 248; (1997) 141 S.J.L.B. 216 ....2–16, 18–23, 18–47
Independent Television Publications Ltd v Time Out Ltd and Elliott Joined Cases: BBC v Time Out Ltd and Elliott [1984] F.S.R. 64 11–05
Independiente Ltd v Music Trading On-Line (HK) Ltd [2007] EWHC 533 (Ch); [2007] E.M.L.R. 25; [2007] F.S.R. 21; (2007) 30(4) I.P.D. 30028 12–27
India TV Independent News Service PVT Ltd v India Broadcast Live LLC [2008] F.S.R. 2 2–79
Indupak [2002] E.O.P.R. 81 4–28
Industrial Furnaces v Reaves [1970] R.P.C. 605 ....2–37, 8–20, 8–40, 12–03, 12–17
Industrie Diensten Groep BV v JA Beele Handelmaatschappij BV (C6/81) [1982] E.C.R. 707; [1982] 3 C.M.L.R. 102; [1983] F.S.R. 119 19–11
Infabrics Ltd v Jaytex Ltd (No.1) sub nom: Infabrics Ltd v Jaytex Shirt Fabrics Ltd [1982] A.C. 1; [1981] 2 W.L.R. 646; [1981] 1 All E.R. 1057; [1981] E.C.C. 405; [1981] F.S.R. 261; [1984] R.P.C. 405; (1981) 125 S.J. 257 ....12–27, 12–29
Infamous Nut Co Ltd v Percy Dalton (Holdings) Ltd [2003] R.P.C. 7 18–65
Infopaq International A/S v Danske Dagblades Forening (C-5/08) [2009] E.C.D.R. 16 12–06
Inhale Therapeutic Systems Inc v Quadrant Healthcare Plc [2002] R.P.C. 21; (2001) 24(11) I.P.D. 24075 ....5–18, 6–11

* *this reference is to the hardback edition.*

TABLE OF STATUTES

References are to para. number

* *this reference is to the hardback edition.*

TABLE OF STATUTORY INSTRUMENTS

** this reference is to the hardback edition.*

TABLE OF EUROPEAN AND INTERNATIONAL LEGISLATION

Regulations

Decisions

* *this reference is to the hardback edition.*

TABLE OF INTERNATIONAL TREATIES, CONVENTIONS AND AGREEMENTS

** this reference is to the hardback edition.*

Part I

COMMON GROUND

Chapter 1

STARTING POINTS

1. General

(1) "Intellectual property"

Patents give temporary protection to technological inventions and design rights to the appearance of mass-produced goods; copyright gives longer lasting rights in, for instance, literary, artistic and musical creations; trade marks are protected against imitation so long at least as they continue to be employed in trade. These and similar rights in UK law are the subject-matter of this book. There is no single generic term that satisfactorily covers them all. "Industrial property" is not infrequently used in the common law world, but many would hold this to exclude copyright, particularly if they want to emphasise the special importance and vulnerability of the creative artist. **1–01**

"Intellectual property" is the term used in this book for the whole field. The term scarcely describes trade marks and similar marketing devices; but it has now acquired international acceptance.[1] "IP" or "IPR" is indeed becoming a fashionable description of research results and other original ideas, whether or not they fall within the ambit of what the law protects as intellectual property or intellectual property rights. The abbreviations are convenient and we will adopt them. For one thing, they help to deflate the grandiloquence inherent in "intellectual property". While this is a branch of the law which protects some of the finer manifestations of human achievement, it also shields much that is trivial and ephemeral. The ultimate art in shaping of IP policy lies in securing outcomes that are proportionate to the aim of that protection. The various aspects of the subject differ in purpose and in detailed rule. Nonetheless there is good sense in studying them together. Each is concerned with marking out, by means of legal definition, types of conduct which may not be pursued without the consent of the right-owner. The rights thus delimited are enforced in similar ways[2] and all are dealt with by broad analogy to property rights in tangible movables.[3] Frequently the objective of controlling the activities of competitors and licensees is achieved by use of a number of forms of intellectual property conjointly. Where their deployment comes in conflict with other policies, such as has happened under the impact of European Union ("EU") law, comparisons between the different forms of intellectual property need to be made.[4]

(2) Organisation of the material

1–02 The main branches of intellectual property each have a part devoted to them in the course of the book. Those concerned with the protection of ideas and information—patents, breach of confidence, copyright and designs—are treated before those which deal with trade marks, trade names and the like. Before reaching this stage, however, there are a number of themes that can usefully be pursued in common and they are explored in this introductory part.

In the remainder of this chapter, four distinct topics are raised: the roles of national, regional and international law in the development of intellectual property law; the use of statute and judicial decision as a means of defining intellectual property rights and the interrelation between these two sources of law; basic economic considerations underlying the objectives of the law; and certain relevant principles of the European Union. Chapter 2 deals with

[1] As in the title of the UN organ, World Intellectual Property Organisation (WIPO); and in the Agreement on Trade-Related Intellectual Property Rights including Trade in Counterfeit Goods (TRIPS), which forms part of the GATT Round completed in April 1994. In older Continental usage, intellectual property referred to the protection of works of authorship.

[2] See below, Ch.2.

[3] An analogy that nonetheless is not straightforward: see, e.g. the discussion of damages for breach of confidence below, in para.8–47.

[4] See further, below, paras 1–51—1–57, and the references given there to other parts of this book.

matters more immediately practical: the remedies and procedures generally available in the enforcement of intellectual property rights.

The subject has grown in a variety of directions over recent years. Its increasing economic significance for countries with any degree of industrial development is making it both more international and more complex. To contain it within a single book has called for a considerable measure of selection. This has involved a number of strategic choices, which it is worth listing at the outset: **1–03**

(1) Each of the subjects has spawned enough detailed law to merit very substantial texts for specialist practitioners.[5] This book does not try to cover all the detailed points of statute, case law or practice to be found in them. Beyond this the reader in search of all the available knowledge must be prepared to refer to them without explicit guidance from this book. In particular, the account here tends to concentrate on substantive rules rather than on matters of procedure, both in the acquiring and the enforcement of rights.

(2) The major statutes on British intellectual property have been subject to very substantial revision in the last two decades.[6] Of particular importance have been the Patents Act 1977, the Copyright, Designs and Patents Act 1988 and the Trade Marks Act 1994; and there is a continuing stream of further measures, the most significant of which today come from the European Union and include the major amendments to the system of registered designs. At the same time, the EU has begun to achieve its long-term goal of creating unitary IP regimes for the whole of its ever-growing territory, now comprising 27 countries. The Community Trade Mark (CTM) has been operative since 1996, the Community Registered Design (CRD) came on stream in 2003.[7] Each is governed by direct EU legislation, administered in part by a Community granting office and in part through national courts. These forms of Community IPR operate as alternatives to those arising under national law for each EU State. Complicated choices ensue.

(3) Of the lesser intellectual property regimes, the protection of registered and unregistered designs is closely entwined with artistic copyright and the 1988 Act regime in the field is dealt with in Ch.15. That discussion also extends to the special protection given to semiconductor chip topographies.[8] Public lending right and artists' resale

[5] Most are referred to in abbreviated forms: see the Table of Abbreviations.

[6] These statutes apply throughout the UK, and most of the case law is applicable in each of the British jurisdictions. See however, MacQueen in Vaver and Bently, Ch.4.

[7] See below, paras 15–08, 16–16; and for the Community Plant Variety Right, para.A3–01. In contrast, the plan for a Community Patant has rested on the stocks of non-implementation since 1975: paras 3–26 et seq.

[8] See below, paras 15–53—15–56.

right are treated as adjuncts of copyright.[9] Plant variety rights, however, are assigned to Appendix 3.

(4) With membership of the European Union, the rules of competition and allied principles in the Union Treaty have come to play a prominent role in the whole subject. This difficult and often imprecise field of law deserves study on its own. Here all that can be examined is the impact of competition and free movement rules on the different types of intellectual property. To this end: (a) the rules are outlined in this introductory part[10]; (b) the impact of the policies embodied in them (together with certain provisions of British statute law) is discussed in the parts on patents, copyright and trade marks and then in a separate chapter[11]; (c) Appendix 1 gives some further crucial clues to the administration of EU competition policy; and (d) the same appendix says something about British competition law, which now has a parallel impact within the United Kingdom.

(5) The law contained in this book is largely based on statutes applicable to the United Kingdom as a whole. By contrast, most of the case law has been decided in English courts. Nonetheless there are three separate jurisdictions to which litigants may on occasion resort. While the procedures and remedies available in Northern Ireland closely resemble those of England and Wales, the Scottish system is often distinct in substance or in nomenclature. The special characteristics of Scottish litigation, however, are not pursued here.

(6) For readers who come to this subject without much legal background, it is important also to say that knowledge of the general structure of both the English legal system and that of the EC (within the EU) is assumed.

2. Types of Intellectual Property[12]

1–04 Intellectual property protects applications of ideas and information that are of commercial value. The subject is growing in importance, to the advanced industrial countries in particular, as the fund of exploitable ideas becomes more sophisticated and as their hopes for a successful economic future come to depend increasingly upon their superior corpus of new knowledge and fashionable conceits. There has recently been a great deal of political and legal activity designed to assert and strengthen the various types of protection for ideas.

[9] See below, paras 14–45—14–46.

[10] See below, paras 1–48—1–59. There is also a brief introduction to Community law-making below, in paras 1–26, 1–29.

[11] See below, paras 7–33—7–39, 13–59—13–62, 18–120, 18–122; Ch.19, passim.

[12] For the evolution of the concept, see Ladas, *Patents, Trade Marks and Related Rights*, Vols I, II (1975); Sherman and Bently, *The Making of Modern Intellectual Property Law* (1999).

One characteristic shared by all types of IPR is that they are essentially negative: they are rights to stop others doing certain things—rights, in other words, to stop pirates, counterfeiters, imitators and even in some cases third parties who have independently reached the same ideas, from exploiting them without the licence of the right-owner. Some aspects of intellectual property confer positive entitlements, such as the right to be granted a patent or to register a trade mark upon fulfilling the requisite conditions; but these are essentially ancillary.

The fact that intellectual property gives a right to control the activities of others has a number of implications, often inadequately understood. The right-owner does not need the right in order to exploit a market for its goods or services: a patent is not a pre-condition to exploiting one's own invention. By way of corollary, the right gives no liberty to ignore the rights of other individuals (including their IPRs) or to override public liabilities: a trade mark registration does not justify its use to advertise illegal goods. Nor does intellectual property confer on the right-owner's products any privileged position in international trade, rendering them exempt from prohibitions or quotas which a country would otherwise apply to them: the fact that films embody copyright does not mean that they cannot be the subject of programming limitations designed to favour national culture. Of course, it would be possible to adopt a new approach to these matters, and arguments for doing so are made from time to time. However, if they were ever to succeed, fundamental assumptions about the role and purpose of intellectual property would also shift, with consequences which might be very hard to predict.

Apart from this shared characteristic, the three central types of intellectual property right—patents for inventions, copyright for literary and artistic works and associated products, and trade marks and names for the goodwill attaching to marketing symbols—cover distinct subject-matter and have different objectives. The law on each accordingly varies in strategic ways and these need to be compared at the outset.

(1) Patents (Chs 3–7, 21)

Patents are granted in respect of inventions, i.e. technological improvements, great and small, which contain at least some scintilla of inventiveness over what is previously known. To take the standards now operating in much of Europe, they are typified by the following: **1–05**

- they issue from a state or regional patent office after a substantial examination of their validity;
- they last for a maximum of 20 years from application; and
- they require that the invention be publicly described in the patent specification.

The right which they accord is to prevent all others—not just imitators, but even independent devisers of the same idea—from using the invention for the duration of the patent. That core conception reveals a great deal about why invention patents are the most basic, the most valuable, and, to competitors, potentially the most dangerous, of all intellectual property—the category which demands to be studied above all others.[13]

The practical applications of scientific knowledge which make up "technology" are rooted in objective information. Inventions are discoveries about the inherent capacities of matter, and in a sense are waiting to be made. Inventors may proceed by all sorts of routes, but those addressing the same problem are after essentially the same knowledge. A first discovery in a particular field may well be followed by further research results which all competitors in an industry will need to embody in their products if they are to keep in the market.

A stage will be reached where further inventions produce both advantages and disadvantages over other ways of making and doing things, at which point product developers will have alternatives to hand. But whether a patent is for a primary breakthrough or for some subsequent development, it will only have industrial value to the extent that it covers all embodiments of its inventive concept. Otherwise there will be ways of taking the idea over without infringing the right and any patent will be good only against simple imitators. A patent system must above all strive to ensure that it gives rights over all applications of the invention revealed but over no more than this—a balance which can be remarkably difficult to achieve.[14]

The special potential of a patent is accordingly that it may be used to prevent all others from including any form of the invention in their products and services; and where real breakthroughs are patented this potential is occasionally so considerable as to render the competition obsolete. More regularly, a patent poses serious difficulties for competitors. This is why patents are not freely available for all industrial improvements, but only for what is judged to qualify as a "patentable invention" by comparison with what is already known in an industry.

(2) Copyright (Chs 10–14, 20)

1–06 Copyright, by contrast, is a right given against the copying of defined types of cultural, informational and entertainment productions. Classically, these have been (in international jargon) "literary and artistic works"—the

[13] Elements of personal, even arbitrary, choice may enter the design of embodiments of the invention and some of these may come to define industrial standards—the gauge of railway track, the dimensions of couplings and other interfaces; but these are not usually part of the invention itself.

[14] See below, paras 6–28—6–31.

creations of authors, playwrights, composers, artists and film directors.[15] At least the outstanding works in each of these categories are marked by their individuality—that distinctness which results from the creator's myriad choices made in the course of constructing the work in the chosen medium. Because aesthetic productions are endlessly different, and therefore the protection, quite properly, operates only against copying, the right has come to have a very substantial duration: typically, the author's life and 50 years thereafter—or 70 years as it has now become in the European Union and the United States.[16]

In this century, the range of copyright has been complicated by the addition of certain analogous rights given to performers and to the producers of sound recordings, films, broadcasters and other entrepreneurs, for somewhat shorter periods (sometimes labelled "related" or "neighbouring" rights as distinct from "authors' rights"). At this introductory stage it can be taken that these rights share many of the characteristics of the authors' copyright. They are, however, somewhat closer to industrial property in the relative shortness of their duration.

The basis of copyright lies in the personal character of the subject-matter in issue. It is the particular expression making up a work which is protected, rather than the idea behind it. It is Shaw's *St Joan* or Honegger's *Jeanne d'Arc au bûcher* which is copyright, rather than any play or oratorio on the historical story of Joan of Arc. Copyright law must strive, therefore, to give meaning and a sense of proportion to the often amorphous distinction between "expression" and "idea". It is a difficulty which becomes acute when copyright is extended to utilitarian subject-matter and nowhere more so than in treating computer programs as "literary works" within copyright.[17] Yet without some such distinction, the right would be of unconstrained breadth. It would then be very difficult to justify the long term attached to it.

(3) Trade marks and names (Chs 16–18)

Trade marks and related aspects of trading goodwill (get-up, trade names of **1–07** businesses, etc.) are protected as symbols needed by consumers to distinguish between competing products and services in a market economy. As long as they continue to be used in trade these signs are a prominent part of goodwill and rights in them cannot be subject to any maximum duration. In the British and many other systems, rights are conferred either by virtue of

---

[15] While the work of film directors is included within the Berne Convention on Literary and Artistic Works (for which see below, para.10–24), it is only recently that it has been given direct recognition in British copyright law: for the complex development, see below, paras 11–23—11–25.

[16] See below, paras 11–43 et seq.

[17] See below, paras 20–04—20–25.

formal registration or else because of a reputation generated by actual trading (mainly through the action against passing off).

By association with a successful product or service, or by persistent advertising or even the vagaries of fashion, a mark may be built into an asset of prime value to a business; witness the household names of five continents—Levis for jeans, Mercedes for cars, Panasonic for televisions, Outspan for oranges, Fosters for lager. Nonetheless, marks do not by themselves have the capacity to prevent a competitor from entering any market with his own products or services; they merely prevent him from annexing the protected mark in order to facilitate his market entry. Accordingly there is no policy reason for imposing any limit on the duration of rights of this type. At least, this will remain so provided that marks are not allowed to become barriers in the way of marketing products or services themselves.

(4) Other aspirants

1–08 These three types of intellectual property may be regarded as setting the models to which aspirants will turn for the protection of other ideas, information and "trade values". Throughout the period of industrialisation there have been claimants who seek either to fit a new subject-matter within one of the model systems or else to have a new regime created to protect it.

(a) *Industrial designs (Ch.15)*

1–09 The longest standing of these has concerned the design of industrial products. Legal responses remain as much a problematic hybrid today as they have long been. Many countries have a design registration system, but they differ in the extent to which the right granted is akin to patent protection (in the form of a full monopoly) or to copyright (requiring copying). Some use artistic copyright itself to give protection of the designs of industrial products, often with some modification of its scope. This may raise awkward questions about whether the two types of protection can be cumulative. Others again may add a right that is sui generis, as the United Kingdom did in 1988 with its unregistered design right for the shape of products, both technical and non-technical.[18]

(b) *Trade secrets and other confidential information (Chs 8 and 9)*

1–10 Over much the same period, there have been claims to rights over secret business information—technological know-how (whether inventive or not), ideas for new products and markets, commercial information about customers, finance, employment and many other things. To this countries have responded in various ways, some confining protection to general civil remedies affecting contract, tort, property and perhaps unjust enrichment; some

[18] See below, paras 15–38 et seq.; and for the purely transitional Community Unregistered Design Right, para.15–31.

building specific provisions into their law of unfair competition; some (notably common law jurisdictions) generating a form of sui generis protection that is akin to but is not quite a form of property right. Countries in this last tradition, such as the United Kingdom, have tended to place the protection of trade secrets in a broader conceptual frame which also encompasses governmental secrets and personal confidences and indeed the privacy of individuals.[19] This approach avoids the need to define limited categories, but it means that cases which may demand very different responses will fall to be considered under a single rubric. However the protection of secrets is formulated, the rights given are likely to be unlimited in time and also to be effective against unjustified uses and disclosures of all kinds. Hence the reluctance to give them the absolute character of "property".

(c) *Further demands*

In more recent times, an increasing number of countries have thought that industry needs a system of short-term rights protecting minor technical advances, which supplements the patent system and is particularly valuable where know-how cannot be kept secret. Known variously as petty patents, short-term patents and utility models, they depend upon an official grant of rights for a term of six to 10 years. The basis on which they are granted, the subject-matter they may cover and numerous other elements vary from country to country. The case for this form of protection has so far been rejected in Britain.[20] **1–11**

To turn to more specific fields, there have been claims from breeders of new plant varieties which numerous countries have now met with patent or sui generis protection. Latterly they are being followed by the developers of new animal breeds. Both spheres now work partly by genetic manipulation techniques and their activities are one aspect of a whole complex of issues about the future of intellectual property in the sphere of biotechnology.[21]

For more than a century, new technology has constantly invaded the copyright worlds of culture, education and entertainment, bringing in succession sound recording, film, broadcasting, cable and satellite transmission and the modern wonders of copying technology.

All these have created immense pressure for expansion of copyright, the creation of "neighbouring rights", and the protection of entertainment ideas, as well as for the improvement of the legal machinery against piracy and the collective administration of rights.[22] The arrival of the computer, and the demand for protection of programs, electronic databases and

[19] Ch.9 is largely devoted to the impact of the European Convention on Human Rights, arts 8 and 10, on civil rights of action under English law for the protection of privacy since effect was given in 2000 to the Human Rights Act 1998.

[20] The European Commission has proposed possible systems for the whole Community: see below, paras 3–29 et seq.

[21] See below, paras 5–70 et seq.

[22] See below, Chs 11, 14, 20 and 21.

computer output, at least against copying, have imposed very considerable strains on traditional conceptions of intellectual property. Indeed, the current coalescence of computer technology and advanced systems of telecommunication is causing a multi-media revolution which may wear down current notions of intellectual property beyond serviceable endurance. Alongside these developments of central economic significance have run an unending miscellany of other claims: for type-faces; folk-songs and other indigenous culture; traditional knowledge about the medicinal properties of plants; the format of media game-shows; "look-alikes" to products and their get-up; character merchandising; merchandising of sport, exhibitions, festivals, universities and film sites; the use of personal characteristics (name, voice, appearance) in publicity—and these are but examples.

3. Pressures for Development

1–12 Much of this book is concerned with the extent to which these demands have been met. The position varies from country to country and our attention will be centred on the United Kingdom as a core within the wider frame set by the EU.

Virtually no country favours conferring on the creator of an idea a perpetual property in it against imitators. The political and economic implications of such a privilege would be remarkable. Instead a set of limited forms of protection are fashioned against some types of exploitation by others. The root issue is whether the balance achieved by this approach is broadly appropriate to the economic needs of the country and to the prevailing sense of what is just. While the legal protection that is provided varies for the different types of subject-matter, there are some useful preliminary points to make; about the way, historically, that developments have occurred; about the kinds of justification for adopting one or other course of action; and about the foundations from which arguments about ends and means ought to proceed. These are taken up in what follows.

(1) Specific rights and unfair competition

1–13 As a regime is developed for protecting a form of intellectual property, a number of basic decisions have to be made: What types of subject-matter are to be included? Is the right to be conferred only upon application to a government office? How long is it to last? Is it to be a right good only against imitators (as with copyright and unregistered designs), or is it a "full monopoly" that even affects independent devisers of the same idea (as with patents for inventions, registered designs and trade marks)? The operative rules vary because each type of subject-matter calls for a different balance of public and private interests—the interests of the society as a whole in its economic and cultural development, and the interest of the individual to secure a "fair" value for his intellectual effort or investment of capital or labour.

The marked tendency under modern conditions is to reach answers about the proper scope of protection by political decision expressed primarily in legislation. Partly this is because the interest groups concerned are expected to make out their case sufficiently to a responsible body; and partly because a complex set of rules is required which cannot satisfactorily be fashioned from the vagaries of litigation.

Hence, in Britain, the majority of intellectual property rights have a **1–14** statutory basis. The patent system had its origins in royal grants under the prerogative, which, from the Statute of Monopolies 1624 onwards, came to be conditioned by legislation.[23] In the complex evolution of the copyright system a strategic decision was reached in 1774: to the extent that Parliament had entered the field, copyright under the Statute of Anne 1710 was not to be supplemented by more embracing common law rights.[24] And in the modern period, the ability to adhere to the principle of legislative creation has been much enhanced by the willingness of Parliament to use "copyright" as a catch-all for the protection of new subject-matter, such as records, films, broadcasts, published format, computer programs and databases, and to act with expedition enough for the judges to reserve their creative urges mainly for ancillary matters, such as remedies.[25]

But this is not the unvarying history. In the early industrial period the judges fashioned the tort of passing off to meet an evident commercial need; and when Parliament did introduce a system for registering trade marks this was regarded as a supplement, and not a displacement, of common law rights.[26] More recently the courts have extended the action against breach of confidence unassisted by legislative intervention and in response to another strong demand that the law should act against certain kinds of unacceptable business practice.[27]

In all these developments there are distinctively British characteristics, **1–15** which are the product of a particular economic development and political history. What is perhaps most striking of all, however, is the absence of any basic conception that "unfair competition" or the "misappropriation of trade values" should be treated as an underlying principle of liability by which the judges can extend protection to new types of subject-matter and business relationships as they see fit.

In 1918 a majority of the US Supreme Court in principle adopted a misappropriation doctrine. The well-known *INS* case[28] arose out of the

[23] See below, paras 3–04—3–11.
[24] *Donaldson v Beckett* (1774) 2 Bro. P.C. 129.
[25] See below, para.10–11.
[26] See below, paras 16–08, 17–36 et seq.
[27] See below, paras 10–04, 10–05.
[28] *International News Service v Associated Press*, 248 US 215 (1918). See further, below, paras 17–36 et seq.

French government's refusal to allow facilities to the Hearst press to report the war in Europe. So one way in which the Hearst news agency procured its war reports was from first editions of Associated Press's newspapers on the American East Coast. It telegraphed the information to its West Coast papers in time for reports to appear in competition with Associated Press newspapers there. This keen bit of acquisition was held a tortious form of competition even though it lay outside the confines of statutory copyright. Noting that "the news has an exchange value to one who can misappropriate it", Pitney J. characterised the defendant's conduct thus:

> "Stripped of all disguises, the process amounts to an unauthorised interference with the normal business operation of complainant's legitimate business precisely at the point where the profit is to be reaped, in order to divert a material portion of the profit from those who have earned it to those who have not; with the special advantage to defendant in the competition because of the fact that it is not burdened with any part of the expense of gathering the news."[29]

Significantly, however, Holmes J. would have restricted relief so that it covered only the implied misrepresentation that the news was Hearst's own (through failure to acknowledge source); and Brandeis J. insisted that legislation alone was the proper medium for fashioning new legal rights in information.

1–16 Some years later Dixon J. of the Australian High Court summarised developments elsewhere in the common law world in a way that showed a close affinity to Brandeis J.'s position:

> "[The courts] have not in British jurisdictions thrown the protection of an injunction around all the intangible elements of value, that is value in exchange, which may flow from the exercise by an individual of his powers or resources whether in the organisation of a business or undertaking or in the use of ingenuity, knowledge, skill or labour. This is sufficiently evidenced by the history of the law of copyright and by the fact that the exclusive right to invention, trade marks, designs, trade names and reputation are dealt with in English law as special heads of protected interests and not under a wide generalisation."[30]

The evidence for this lay in a succession of decisions. For instance, the House of Lords had refused to subject untruths in comparative advertisements to the discipline of civil action, save in extreme cases of malicious

---

[29] 248 US 215 at 240 (1918).

[30] *Victoria Park Racing v Taylor* (1937) 58 C.L.R. 479 at 509, firmly reiterated in *Moorgate Tobacco v Philip Morris* [1985] R.P.C. 219 at 236–240, per Deane J., HC (Aust.); cf. Ricketson and Macchi [1997] E.I.P.R. 128.

falsehood.[31] Another of its decisions apparently prevented misrepresentation about the quality of one competitor's goods from being actionable at the suit of a rival.[32] In the case being discussed by Dixon J., it was no tort for a broadcasting station to run a commentary on a race meeting from a stand erected outside the course but looking onto it.[33]

The contrast lay not only with the emergent misappropriation doctrine in the United States (which did not prosper, particularly in its early years) but also with most countries of Western Europe. There, starting either from general provisions on tortious liability in civil codes[34] or from separate proscriptions of unfair competition,[35] the judges tended to develop a broadening series of precedents concerning unfair business practices in the marketplace.[36] Under such a rubric, advertisements that made, or even implied, comparisons were treated as actionable; and various types of seller's enticements, such as additional "gifts", were treated as unfair ploys. There was also some tendency to consider slavish copying of the details of products as a form of actionable misappropriation—notably when new technology, such as the apparatus which made it possible to copy records and broadcasts, allowed piracy that fell outside the scope of existing copyright laws.[37] Protection against the direct imitation of products began to assume the character of a sub-species of intellectual property. **1–17**

Whenever this occurred, the ability of competitors to copy a novel product or service after "reverse engineering", it was proportionately diminished. Yet one of the most fundamental assumptions about a competitive economy has been that once a producer enters a market, exactly that type of imitation needs to be present, at least as a potentiality. For no other

[31] *White v Mellin* [1895] A.C. 154 HL. See also *Hubbuck v Wilkinson* [1899] 1 Q.B. 86 CA; *Alcott v Millar's Karri* (1904) 21 T.L.R. 30 CA; and generally, below, paras 17–48 et seq. These cases put a stop to the more generous attitude suggested in *Western Counties Manure v Lawes* (1874) L.R. 9 Ex. 218.

[32] *Native Guano v Sewage Manure* (1891) 8 R.P.C. 125 (alleged representation that "native guano"—human excreta converted into a fertiliser—was made by the plaintiff's process, when it was not). See also *Cambridge U.P. v University Tutorial Press* (1928) 45 R.P.C. 335. The decision in the *Guano* case has now been deprived of much of its effect by remarks upon it in the *"Advocaat"* case [1980] R.P.C. 31 at 408–409, 418.

[33] See above, n.30. This, however, was one of the earlier instances of "misappropriation" admitted in the US, under the INS doctrine: *Pittsburgh Athletic Club v K.Q.V. Broadcasting*, 24 F.Supp. 490 (1938).

[34] As in the case of France: see, e.g. Krasser, *Répression de la concurrence déloyale: France* (1972); Plaisant [1979] J.B.L. 83; Kaufmann, *Passing Off and Misappropriation* (1986).

[35] As in the case of Germany: see, e.g. Reimer, *Répression de la concurrence déloyale en Allemagne* (1978); Kaufmann (above, n.34); Fammier [1994] E.I.P.R. 448; Steckler [1996] E.I.P.R. 390.

[36] It remains a deep desire of some Continental experts that Britain should be obliged to adopt a general unfair competition law by means of an EU Directive on the subject. For a recent project, Henning-Bodewig and Schricker [2002] E.I.P.R. 271. See also Henning-Bodewig, *Unfair Competition Law: European Union and Member States* (2006).

[37] Unfair competition doctrine in the US expanded for the same reason and at much the same time: e.g. *Waring v WDAS*, 327 Pa. 433 (1937); *Jackson v Universal*, 36 Cal. (2d) 116 (1950); *Metropolitan Opera v Wagner-Nichols*, 199 Misc. 786 (1950); *Capitol v Mercury*, 221 F. (2d) 657 (1955).

mechanism will so efficiently secure the welfare of consumers as the prospect of such competition. The intellectual property rights in ideas (patents, copyright, etc.) exist by way of limited exception in order to encourage the mental effort and productive investment which will procure new products and services. To add to their range a right against misappropriation or unfair imitation is to place an amorphous further impediment in the way of competition by imitation and that is an inherently controversial step. It is important for the law to preserve a freedom to engage in reverse engineering unless there are convincing reasons against it. The issue will recur at numerous points throughout this book, for many people now consider that they have exactly such reasons.

1–18 It is worth trying to divine why British common lawyers resisted a demand from business litigants that was being met in comparable countries—places indeed whose industrial and commercial development had only followed the British. A complex set of justifications and underlying motives seem to have been at work. To have adopted a broad principle such as "unfair competition" would have been foreign to the traditional caution of the common law courts. Their preference for development only by close and necessary analogy had long been expressed through the forms of action, and even the abandonment of that technique in the judicature reforms of the 1850s and 1870s had done little to modify the basic attitude.[38] The nineteenth century had given flesh to one great (indeed over-broad) generalisation, the concept of contract. But the sanctity of bargains, so much a part of the Victorian *Zeitgeist*, was inimical to legal obligations imposed *ab extra*, as distinct from those reached by voluntary agreement. Large generalisations about rights—unjust enrichment, the right to privacy and unfair competition, just as much as the duty to one's neighbour to take care—found little favour.

1–19 Another recurrent fear was of a flood of litigation[39]—a matter of serious concern to a court system (with its underlying professional structure) in which a small number of superior judges held the power to make law through precedents. In the case of unfair competition, this threat was linked with a concern that the courts should not become a forum for justifying the advertising claims of one business competitor against those of another.[40] At the same time, the emergence of parliamentary democracy provided new reason for the judges to appear as objective administrators of established law, rather than as wholesale makers of new principle; the more so in the

[38] With the conjoint system of judicial administration introduced by the Judicature Act 1873 rather more contact came about between the traditions of common law and equity. But where equity's penchant for large moral generalisations produced results that would make "mercantile men cry out" (Lord Bramwell, *Derry v Peek* (1889) 14 App. Cas. 337 at 350), its excesses were curbed. For our purposes, note the tendency to confine breach of confidence to liability in contract: below, paras 8–06, 8–07.

[39] See, e.g. *White v Mellin* [1895] A.C. 154 at 164 HL.

[40] *White v Mellin* (above, n.39).

various fields of intellectual property where the legislature was increasingly active.

How far, then, were the judges also expressing a clearly reasoned preference for freedom to compete, even if it involved making use of the ideas or goodwill of others? Did they, in particular, consider that the public interest in an improved economic future was best served by as little legal interference as possible, and that accordingly rights of intellectual property should be confined to the exceptional categories marked out in the existing law? Whatever their ultimate motives may have been, it is hard to find evidence that they worked out their decisions explicitly from such a premise. If they had felt strongly the need to encourage competition they ought to have been active in turning the law against a different form of unfair business practice from the "excessive" competition in which we are primarily interested. They should have been ready to refuse to enforce agreements amongst competitors not to compete but rather to link together in cartels and other restrictive agreements that would preserve to each his existing market share. **1–20**

Yet in a succession of judgments, they showed considerable reluctance to intervene.[41] The watchword was provided by Fry L.J.: "to draw a line between fair and unfair competition, between what is reasonable and unreasonable, passes the power of the courts".[42] In truth, in the quarter century before the First World War, free-trade Britain, facing the growing competition of protectionist Germany and America, had reason to think that there was competition enough.[43] Her judges could afford to place themselves apart for the sorts of motive mentioned earlier. In a world that was having to accept enterprises of the size and strength of the modern business corporation, they showed little desire to become embroiled in the obviously political business of settling the rules of competition.

Over recent decades there has been some modification of the courts' approach; but when compared with developments of unfair competition doctrine in parts of Western Europe and the United States,[44] the continuing **1–21**

[41] See especially *British United Shoe v Somervell* (1906) 95 LT. 711; *USM Canada v Brunet* [1909] A.C. 330 JC; *Attorney-General for the Commonwealth v Adelaide Steamship* [1913] A.C. 781 JC; *North Western Salt v Electrolytic Alkali* [1914] A.C. 461 HL; *English Hop Growers v Dering* [1928] 2 K.B. 174 CA; cf. *Evans v Heathcote* [1918] 1 K.B. 418 CA; *McEllistrim v Ballymacelligott Coop.* [1919] A.C. 548 HL. Note also the refusal to hold tortious a cartel's indirect pressure upon an outsider: *Mogul Steamship v McGregor Gow* [1892] A.C. 25.

[42] *Mogul SS v McGregor Gow* (1889) 23 Ch.D. 598 at 625–626 CA.

[43] Attitudes in Britain, France and Germany contrasted strongly with those in the US: see Cornish in *Law and the Big Enterprises in the 19th and early 20th Centuries* (Horn and Kocka (eds), 1979), p.280.

[44] But in the US, there was a significant "liberal" reaction against uses of the misappropriation doctrine: see *Sears-Roebuck v Stiffel*, 376 US 225; *Compco v Daybrite*, 376 US, 234 (1964). Argument centred upon the constitutional power of state legislatures and courts, but it carried more general overtones. In turn the full effect of this has been tempered: see especially *Goldstein v California*, 412 US 546 (1973); *Kewanee v Bicron*, 416 US 470 (1974). The pendulous movement continued: cf. *Bonito Boats v Thunder Craft Boats*, 103 L. (2d) 118 (1989).

attraction of late-Victorian attitudes remains apparent. Most developed economies have responded to "consumerism" and the fear of business coalitions by introducing anti-trust laws which draw considerably on the American inspiration. Likewise they have tried to improve the standards of information and legal protection that traders must meet in advertising and selling goods and services. In some countries,[45] it has been possible to adapt the action for unfair competition so as to allow competitors and consumer groups equally to enforce these standards. The particular advantage of these civil proceedings is that they make available the potent weapon of injunctive relief.

In Britain, as we shall see, over much of the field, criminal law sanctions and administrative enforcement alone perform the same tasks. Civil obligation has expanded only fitfully. On the one hand, in its *"Advocaat"* decision,[46] the House of Lords offered some encouragement towards a broader conception of unfair competition.[47] At the same time, that very decision, with its emphasis on the need to show damage, underscored the limits of tort law. Cases soon followed which conveyed a lively concern for the dangers of "monopoly" inherent in extensions of exclusive trading rights.[48] The judges of the 1980s and 1990s proved as sensitive on the issue as their predecessors a century before.[49] In deciding *Douglas v Hello!* in favour of one "celebrity" magazine against its main rival, because of the way in which the latter reduced the commercial value of the former's exclusive rights to photographs of the Michael Douglas/Catherine Zeta-Jones wedding, the House of Lords may have set the law on an interventionist track which had until then been eschewed.[50]

1–22 The first parliamentary interventions in the creation of intellectual property—the Statute of Monopolies 1624, the Copyright Act 1710 and their successors—left much for the courts to work out in terms of principle. Over the past century, as legislation has become broader in range and more complete in content, judicial influence has increasingly been felt through the interpretation of statute. In earlier decades of last century, the attitudes of the judges have much in common with their caution towards the creation of new common law rights. The preference for taking the meaning of a statute

[45] Germany is a significant example. For harmonisation of unfair competition law at the European level, see Henning-Bodewig (above, n.35); cf. Wadlow [2006] E.I.P.R. 433, 469.

[46] *Erven Warnink v Townend* [1980] R.P.C. 31; cf. *Moorgate* [1985] R.P.C. 219.

[47] See below, para.17–03.

[48] Three of the most striking, since affected by legislative changes, were *"Holly Hobbie" T.M.* [1984] R.P.C. 329 HL (registration of a mark for merchandising not permitted); *Coca-Cola T.Ms* [1986] 421 HL (bottle shape not a trade mark); *British Leyland v Armstrong* [1986] R.P.C. 279 HL (copyright in car exhausts not assertable against spare parts).

[49] Recently, however, English courts have shown some willingness to accord direct effect to specific EU legislation, even to the extent of recognising an intent to give one competitor a right against another who is in breach of the legislation: see below, para.2–22. For the need to develop a general doctrine of unfair competition in English law, see Dworkin in Vaver and Bently, Ch.12.

[50] [2008] AC 1; see below, para.2–16, 9–19.

apparently expressed by Parliament, rather than searching for some "true" intent; the refusal to fill in gaps in legislation; the readiness to insist that it is for Parliament to remedy unsatisfactory results—these are all part of an approach which abjures obvious intervention in the political process.

It is an approach in no way peculiar to intellectual property, and its consequences in this field have, as we shall see, been varied. What should be appreciated is the effect of the general approach upon the style of statutory draftsmanship practised in the United Kingdom and countries which follow its lead. The tendency to proliferate detail and to make complicated cross-references has a long history. It is rooted in the assumption that the judges cannot, will not or should not, work out the implications of statutory directives for themselves. We shall have occasion enough to wrestle with provisions that neglect the statement of general principle in favour of dealing elaborately with relatively special circumstances.[51]

Today, however, there are influences at work—and nowhere more so than in the intellectual property field—that are inducing change.[52] To these we shall return under the next heading.

(2) Enhancement of intellectual property

(a) *Demands for greater protection*

The expansion of trade competition since 1950 has brought ever-increasing **1–23**
advantages to those in the van of innovation. Intellectual property rights, which help to sustain the lead of those with technical know-how, with successful marketing schemes, with new fetishes for pop culture, have come to foster immense commercial returns. The increasing numbers of patents granted and trade marks registered, in industrial countries and rapidly developing economies, and the upsurge of publishing, record-producing, film-making and broadcasting, stand as some measure of this development. But in some of these fields particularly, success has been accompanied by advances in copying techniques which make piracy possible on a scale that is just as new. The resources of existing legal techniques are under considerable strain. This is one reason why today there is a profusion of different demands, some for new and some for improved rights.

The growth of international organisations, particularly within the frame of the UN, has provided one forum for the discussion of such claims. In particular, the World Intellectual Property Organisation (WIPO) (situated in Geneva) administers and fosters the Paris Convention on Industrial Property, the Patent Co-operation Treaty, the Berne and Rome

[51] Lord Diplock found occasion to remark upon the "unhappy legacy of this judicial attitude" (*Fothergill v Monarch Airlines* [1980] 2 All E.R. 696 at 705). See further, below, para.6–03, n.8.

[52] Their influence gave both the Copyright, Designs and Patents Act 1988 and the Trade Marks Act 1994 a novel clarity of organisation and expression.

Conventions on copyright and neighbouring rights and the Madrid Agreements on trade mark registration, as well as various others, which are in existence or in the making.[53]

Beyond this there is a separate development. The General Agreement on Tariffs and Trade (GATT—not a UN organ), in completing its Uruguay Round in April 1994, created the World Trade Organisation (WTO) (also situated in Geneva) which, among other things, administers a highly significant instrument, the Agreement on Trade-related Aspects of Intellectual Property Rights, including Trade in Counterfeit Goods (TRIPS). Most states have joined WTO, including the People's Republic of China. The increasingly global condition of world trade makes it a necessity. Under TRIPS, states become bound to a mutual recognition of intellectual property rights at a high level of protection, in various respects going beyond the range of international obligation achieved in the Conventions mentioned in the previous paragraph. The ramifications of TRIPS are considerable and we accordingly return to them later in this chapter.[54]

1–24 Industries and professional experts have produced a plethora of interest groups which seek to further their own political ambitions at the national and international level. At the same time, other pressures for change have been at work. The expansion of bureaucracies, such as national and regional patent offices, has brought in its train plans for rationalising their activities. Partly this goes to standardising procedures such as classification for indexing purposes, but it also aims to reduce overlaps in the work that they do.[55] Thus it is a basic object of the Patent Co-operation Treaty that the acceptance, searching and even examination stages of applying for a patent should be conducted on an international basis before proceeding to the grant of national patents.[56]

In Western Europe it has been possible to link this desire to eliminate repetitious waste with the movement to strengthen the bonds of the Economic Community and associated free trade area (now together entitled the European Economic Area—EEA). One result has been the opening of the European Patent Office, another the Convention for a unified Community patent, latterly in gestation as a draft EU Regulation.[57] In the field of trade marks, the drive by EU authorities to eliminate distortions in the EU has resulted in a Community-wide system of registration.[58] Harmonisation of copyright within the EU, which is proceeding step-wise, has now been the subject of successive Directives of very considerable importance, most

[53] See below, paras 1–30—1–32. In addition, UNESCO administers the Universal Copyright Convention. For the role of UNCTAD, see below, para.3–17.

[54] See below, para.1–31.

[55] The urge to rationalise is all the greater when budgetary overseers notice that an office is being run as a service below cost.

[56] See below, paras 3–01, 3–19—3–22.

[57] See below, paras 3–01, 3–23—3–29.

[58] See below, paras 16–16—16–18.

recently in relation to the internet.[59] A Community Plant Varieties Office has been instituted and a Community designs regime is in place, together with Directive on the harmonisation of national designs law being already in place.[60] There has already been Community legislation on semiconductor chip design, supplementary protection for pharmaceutical and like inventions, industrial design, misleading and comparative advertising, databases; and, after long and acrid debates, biotechnological patents.[61] The plan for a Directive on Utility Model protection remains in abeyance.[62]

(b) *Sources of UK law: legislation and interpretation*

The end product of much of this will be domestic legislation, particularly **1–25** given the rule which requires the authority of a parliamentary act to turn the international obligations of the United Kingdom into municipal law. This may be done either by re-enacting a convention in a paraphrase which a British draftsman deems suitable for legislation here, or it may be done by making the convention text itself part of UK law. It is the latter technique which is applied to the EU Treaty of Rome 1957 and EU legislation under it in the form of regulations.[63] The British enabling statute is then no more than a conduit pipe for texts which will likely have been drafted with a Continental preference for the statement of general principle—relatively uncomplicated in language, but more or less indeterminate in scope. The former technique may be adopted at least partly in the belief that British courts must be provided with more specific guidance than the convention text affords.[64] If not, they may be led by their traditional approaches to interpretation into destructive readings that would do little for comity between the contracting states concerned.

The fear is not without foundation. The court's preference for literal interpretation in the past gave rise to the rule of construction that, unless a British statute is ambiguous, its meaning must be accepted, however much this results in inconsistency with the convention from which it derives.[65] But the point at which ambiguity is considered to arise is itself a matter of

[59] See below, paras 10–17—10–19.

[60] See below, paras 4–26, 5–82 et seq., 14–50—14–52, 15–52—15–55, 18–107.

[61] See below, paras 15–48—15–50, 15–26.

[62] See below, para.15–27. For the difficulties in achieving implementation of the Directive on artists' resale rights, see below, paras 14–45 et seq.

[63] Under the European Communities Act 1972. For specific examples, see PA 1977 s.86 (CPC); TMA 1994 ss.51, 52 (CTM); Designs Regulations 2003 (CRD).

[64] In taking over principles of the PCT and EPC, the PA 1977 provides numerous examples of this approach. This seems particularly curious in an Act which (see previous note) also adopts an EU convention in virgin form.

[65] *Ellerman Lines v Murray* [1931] A.C. 126 HL; *Soloman v Commrs. of Customs and Excise* [1967] 2 Q.B. 116 at 143, per Lord Diplock; *Warwick Films v Eisinger* [1969] 1 Ch. 508; cf. *Buchanan (James) v Babco Forwarding* [1978] A.C. 141 at 153, per Lord Wilberforce. But note also the tendency to stress that, if there is room for manoeuvre, a court will strive to achieve consistency between statute and convention: e.g. *Post Office v Estuary Radio* [1968] 2 Q.B. 740; *The Jade* [1976] 1 All E.R. 920 at 924, per Lord Diplock; *Smith Kline and French v Harbottle* [1980] R.P.C. 363; *E's Applications* [1983] R.P.C. 231.

judgment. Certainly once the meaning of a provision is deemed uncertain, the courts have shown a new willingness to resort to the convention text (or texts, if more than one language has been used).[66] In searching for the most acceptable meaning in such a case, the House of Lords has indorsed the adoption of a purposive approach to interpretation, rather than a literal one.[67] Equally, the House is willing to take account of the decisions of foreign courts on the Convention's meaning, the writings of experts on the subject and even (with caution) the *travaux préparatoires* which led to the agreement of the final text, at least if they have been published[68] and were intended to resolve doubts about its meaning.

Indeed, as part of the shift in perception, the House of Lords has ruled that, in certain limited circumstances, judges should take account of explanations offered in the course of British parliamentary proceedings about the intended meaning of a particular provision, if to the court it appears ambiguous, obscure or absurd. This allows reference to be made to any clear statement by the Minister or other promoter of the Bill, if it discloses the mischief aimed at or the legislative intention.[69] Purposive interpretation and the aids to it are evidently important in dealing with law that comes from the EU. British courts heed the European Court of Justice's approach to the interpretation of legislative texts. This is characterised by Lord Diplock as teleological rather than historical, seeking "to give effect to what the Court conceives to be the spirit rather than the letter of the treaties; sometimes, indeed, it may seem to the exclusion of the letter".[70] This, as we shall see, is likely to be equally important whether the text has become UK law in its original form, or whether it has been adapted to the purpose by the British draftsman.[71]

---

[66] The House of Lords has refused to accept that a foreign text may only be referred to if expert evidence about its meaning is led; there are no precise rules and a judge may rely on his own knowledge of the foreign language, dictionaries or expert opinion, when it is appropriate to do so: see Lord Wilberforce, *Buchanan* [1978] A.C. 126 at 152 HL; Lord Fraser of Tullybelton, *Fothergill* (below, n.65) at 709–710.

[67] *Fothergill v Monarch Airlines* [1980] 2 All E.R. 696.

[68] In enacting measures, the EU Council and Commission may record Minutes of Understanding. Though often in circulation they used not to be public documents. They could, therefore, be cited as guides to interpretation in an English court: *Wagamama v City Centre Restaurants* [1995] F.S.R. 713. For access, where no confidentiality is in issue today, see Council Decisions 93/731, 96/705, 2000/23, Bull. UE 10/95, 1.9.1.

[69] *Pepper v Hart* [1993] A.C. 593. This draws counsel into careful monitoring of *Hansard*, a task which, in relation to modern intellectual property statutes, can be formidable. Hundreds of amendments stood in the paths through the legislature of the Patents Bill 1977, the Copyright, Designs and Patents Bill 1988 and the Trade Marks Bill 1994. Even before this development, the courts were prepared to consider the reports of official commissions and committees with the same end in view: *Fothergill* case (above, n.64) at 705–706. For the implementation of EU directives, see below, para.1–27.

[70] *R. v Henn and Darby* [1980] 2 All E.R. 166 at 196.

[71] Note, in particular, the appreciation of the need to bring uniform interpretation to the EPC and its national derivatives, demonstrated on the "second medical use" question: see below, paras 5–74 et seq.

(c) *Sources of European Union law: general*

Since EU law is now the most fecund source for change in British intellectual property law, the status of its legal acts—and in particular of regulations and directives—deserves to be outlined.[72] The Treaty of Rome 1957, established the European Economic Community and alterations to the constitutional arrangements of what has since become the European Union, which have amended it and added Member States to the EU (the Single European Act (1985), the Maastricht Treaty (1992), the Amsterdam Treaty (1997), the Nice Treaty (2001), the Lisbon Treaty (2009)) have had a considerable effect. The Amsterdam Treaty created the Treaty Establishing the European Community (TEC). The Lisbon Treaty provided the latest revision, which involves a bifurcation into the Treaty of the European Union (TEU) and the Treaty on the Functioning of the European Union (TFEU). None of these documents has conferred a specific power on European Union institutions to enact laws relating to intellectual property rights. Only Lisbon has conferred a power on the Council and Parliament, which is limited to the context of the internal market, allowing them to establish measures for European intellectual property rights that provide uniform protection of those rights throughout the EU, together with centralised Union-wide authorisation, coordination and supervision arrangements.[73] This amounts only to an ex-post facto recognition of what has already been achieved under the general legislative powers described next.[74] **1–26**

Under arts 288–92 TFEU (ex-249 TEC), the Council, together with the European Parliament,[75] has power to make regulations having general application and to issue directives to Member States.[76] Regulations by their very nature are directly applicable in all Member States, both in relations between individuals and the Member States and, where appropriate, in relations one with another. This consequence is secured in UK law by the terms of s.2 of the European Communities Act 1972.

---

72 See generally, e.g. Horspool and Humphreys, *European Union Law* 5th edn (2008) Ch.4. For procedures, and for the current status of interventions in intellectual property matters, see each month's issue of the E.I.P.R.

73 TFEU, art.118. The Article reserves to the Council (by unanimous vote, and after consulting the EP) the right to establish language arrangements for each European IPR. Intellectual property remains unlisted in the general powers of exclusive or shared competence in TFEU art.4, 5.

74 The provision preserving the system of property rights in Member States (TFEU art.345 ex-295 TEC) has not been permitted to inhibit the creation of Community IPRs. However, the ECJ refused to allow the adoption of criminal sanctions for infringement of IP rights under the pre-Lisbon constitutional arrangements: *European Commission v EU Council* (C176-03) [2005] E.C.R. I-

75 When acting under art.352 TFEU (ex-308 TEC), the Council has only to consult the European Parliament, but when acting under art.114 TFEU (ex-95 TEC), the co-decision procedure instituted under art.294 TFEU (ex-251 TEC) must be followed.

76 Of the other law-making powers of Community institutions, we should note the Commission's power to issue decisions, particularly in implementation of the Rules of Competition, and equally the power of the Community Trade Mark and Designs Office (OHIM) in dealing with applications for rights.

A Regulation under art.352 TFEU (ex-308 TEC) has, for instance, been the means of establishing the EU's own Community trade mark and the Office in Alicante which operates as its registry.[77] Article 352 is the residual provision which empowers the Council to take appropriate measures, over and above those provided for in the Treaty, which are "necessary to attain, in the course of the operation of the common market, one of the objectives of the Community".[78]

1–27 As the name implies, a Directive binds the Member States which it addresses but gives them a choice as to implementation and indeed sometimes as to extent. In our context, of particular significance is the power of the Council and the Parliament under art.114 TFEU (ex-95 TEC) to issue directives "for the approximation of the provisions laid down by law, regulation or administrative action in Member States which have as their object the establishment and functioning of the internal market".[79]

Under this Article, Directives have now required the partial harmonisation of both national copyright and national trade mark law.[80] Incorporation of their contents into national law necessarily varies because the relevant legislation differs from country to country. A Directive requirement may already be part of national law by legislative statement or case law and so will not need restatement. Directives can also include non-mandatory provisions, which accordingly leave an express choice to the Member States.[81] This is an important procedure when otherwise it would not be clear whether a Directive was, or was not, intended to preclude a Member State from (say) giving additional rights to those provided by EU law.[82] Whether a state has adequately implemented a Directive can ultimately be tested by proceedings before the European Court of Justice, brought either by a Member State or the Commission.[83]

A Directive, being addressed to Member States, does not have the same direct effect on the rights and obligations of individuals which may follow

[77] See below, para.16–16. Regulations have introduced the Community Plant Variety Right (below, paras A3–02 et seq.); the Supplementary Protection Certificate for pharmaceutical and similar inventions (below, para.4–26), and the Community Registered Design (below, paras 15–08 et seq.). The Community Patent, originally negotiated as a separate convention, will be introduced through an EC Regulation (below, para.3–27).

[78] The consequential effect of adopting a treaty obligation with external states under art.218 TFEU (ex-300 TEC) is discussed in relation to TRIPS: below, para.1–31.

[79] The Commission must propose, the Economic and Social Committee must be consulted; and (in the post-Maastricht world) the Council, if it is to act by qualified majority, must obtain the assent of the European Parliament under art.251. Despite formal conciliation arrangements, this procedure led in 1994 to rejection of the politically sensitive Directive on Patent Rights in Biotechnology. It was only enacted four years later (see below, paras 21–06 et seq.).

[80] Also the protection of semi-conductor chip layouts (see below, paras 15–52—15–55) and databases (see below, paras 20–37 et seq.). See generally Ullrich in Vaver and Bently, Ch.2.

[81] Whether there is then power under the European Communities Act 1972 to take up this permission by delegated legislation is doubtful.

[82] See, e.g. the scope of rights permitted in national trade mark laws: below, para.16–17.

[83] Under TFEU, arts 257, 258 (ex-226, 227 TEC).

from a regulation, but, in certain circumstances, it may be relied upon against a state which has failed to implement it (but not against an individual).[84] This, for instance, can occur if a state fails to enact a provision relating to the invalidity of a trade mark under the relevant harmonisation directive.[85] If on the other hand, non-implementation means that one person has been deprived of a right against another, it would be for the state which was in default to make good the injury by compensation—a principle introduced by the Court of Justice in *Francovich v Italy*[86]—out of despair at the inability of some Member States to implement directives timeously. This, however, is only so where: (1) the Directive itself is intended to grant a right to individuals, (2) it defines the content of the right, and (3) there is a causal link between breach of the state's obligation and the damage suffered.[87]

Beyond this, a Directive may also have an indirect effect, in that its terms are to be applied, where relevant, in resolving ambiguities in the interpretation of national law. In its controversial *Marleasing* decision,[88] the European Court of Justice held that this principle can even affect the law operative in a state before the directive is due for implementation. The better view[89] is that it does so only as a principle of preferable interpretation when the previous law is unsettled; and this ambiguity may arise either because statutory wording is unclear, or because case law is in conflict or is of uncertain scope. In other words it is not a rule which *requires* the old law to be overridden retrospectively.

(d) *The EU Treaty and intellectual property*

Regulations on Community intellectual property rights and directives for the harmonisation of national rights have in practice to be made under the non-specific provisions of arts 352 and 114 (ex-308, 95). Proposals and legislative texts accordingly begin with a recital of the grounds for intervention which are considered to justify reliance upon the relevant provision. **1–28**

---

84 *Marshall v Southampton Area Health Authority* [1986] E.C.R. 723. See generally, Horspool and Humphreys, *European Union Law* 5th edn (2008) Ch.7.

85 *"Mister Long" T.M.* [1998] R.P.C. 401; and for the supremacy of a Community Directive over a contradictory national law: *Konsumentombudsmannen v De Agnostini* [1998] 1 C.M.L.R. 32 ECJ. See the limitations imposed in *Van Gend en Loos v Nederlandse Belastingensadministratie* [1963] E.C.R. 1, and developed in subsequent case law.

86 [1991] E.C.R. I-5357; *Faccini Dori v Recreb* [1995] 1 C.M.L.R. 665.

87 The long drawn-out proceedings brought or instigated by the British Recording Collection Agency and Phonographic Performance Ltd against the UK government for failing to implement the Rental Directive (92/100) have included a *Francovich* claim against the Department of Trade and Industry: see below para.12–32.

88 *Marleasing v Comercial International de Alimentacion* [1990] I E.C.R. 4135; *Wagner Miret v Fondo de Garantia Salarial* [1993] E.C.R. I-6911; *Silhouette v Hartlauer* [1998] I E.C.R. 729 at 737 ECJ; and see *Webb v EMO Cargo* [1995] 4 All E.R. 577 HL.

89 See, e.g. Horspool and Humphreys, *European Union Law* (5th edn (2008) Ch.8. For an application in relation to EU Directives in the field of copyright, see *Murphy v Media Protection Services* [2008] F.S.R. 15. Note also *Football Association v QC Leisure* [2008] F.S.R. 22.

In respect of intellectual property, the assertions of EU need most frequently refer to the efficiencies of having an EU-wide right or to the need to eliminate differences of national law which may have a consequential effect on the free flow of goods within the internal market.[90] These assertions result from the lobbying for legislative change from sectors of European industry and the consultations which the Commission, the European Parliament and other institutions make in the course of responding to such pressure. They remain no more than assertions. As a new proposal makes its way forward, questions have often enough been raised about the legal authority for it. This was particularly true during the course of the Community Trade Mark Regulation, since it set up a completely new Community organ—the eventual Office for Harmonisation in the Internal Market (Trade Marks and Designs) (OHIM), whose cumbrous title reflects the constitutional sensitivities.[91]

The issue has occasionally been raised before the European Court of Justice. An EC Regulation provided a mechanism for extending the term of pharmaceutical and agro-chemical patents, where Government testing has delayed commercial introduction of the invention.[92] Previously the term of patents had been a matter for national law, as harmonised in a separate Convention between EU states. Spain objected that the EU Council had no power to create such a Regulation, relying most fundamentally upon the guarantee of "systems of property ownership" in Member States.[93] Whatever the scope and purpose of this provision,[94] the court refused to employ it in order to invalidate the Regulation. A general consequence appears predictable. Only in most unusual cases will the court find that the enhancement of intellectual property on an EU-wide basis cannot be justified. On most essential issues of legal policy in the field, the Union is empowered to pursue its unifying and harmonising objectives as it may decide.[95]

(e) *European Convention on Human Rights*

1–29 The European Convention on Human Rights (ECHR) was first established in 1950. So far as the United Kingdom was concerned, until enactment of

[90] For their use in the interpretation of Community legislation, see, e.g. *Green Land Products v PMS International* [2009] F.S.R. 28 at [12].

[91] See below, para.16–16.

[92] Below, para.4–20.

[93] *Spain v EU Council* [1996] E.C.R. I-1985. The Spanish government also argued that, by requiring Member States to grant extensions, the Community was introducing a tool which might be used only in some states and so might increase the barriers to movement between Member States. But some states had already introduced their own extensions of patent term, and there was a much greater risk of differential treatment if no uniform provision were made across the EU, a counter-argument which the court had no difficulty in justifying under what was then art.295 TEC.

[94] One view is that art.345 TFEU (ex-295 TEC) exists to prevent the EU from compelling Member States to adjust their particular apportionments of public and private ownership.

[95] Thus the court upheld the Directive on the Legal Protection of Biotechnological Inventions (98/44) against a Dutch challenge to its content on various ethical and legal grounds: below para.21–08.

the Human Rights Act 1998 the Convention had direct application only at an international level. The fundamental standards prescribed by the Convention are the closest that most European countries come to prescribing basic guarantees of intellectual property rights.[96] In particular, the First Protocol of the ECHR, art.1, requires Member States to ensure the peaceful enjoyment of property, and therefore to limit deprivations of possession, while allowing controls over property in the general interest. In addition, the Convention's guarantees of privacy and freedom of expression,[97] often in direct conflict with one another, have caused our judges to admit civil actions in favour of the right to private life of individuals into English law. This striking new development is passing rapidly beyond the bridgehead provided by the action for breach of confidence. The privacy right is dealt with in Ch.9. As to enforcement of the Convention itself, it is the subject of rulings by the European Court of Human Rights (ECtHR) in Strasbourg and can include proceedings by individuals against Member States as well as proceedings between those states. The ECtHR has accepted that the First Protocol covers intellectual property rights, once granted.[98] But it has refused to hold that an application to secure a grant creates legitimate expectations that are within the Protocol.[99]

(f) *Legal issues across state boundaries; international conventions*

Intellectual property rights have been introduced by nation states in response to economic demands and ideas of moral value which have focused particularly on their own territories and nationals. The rights accordingly arise primarily under national law. Obligations between states in this field, whether regional or wholly international, operate to shape and condition national laws, but not for the most part to displace them. **1–30**

One strain within the moral arguments for intellectual property is universalist in character, stressing the peculiar value to mankind of invention and aesthetic creation.[100] But attractive as such notions may be, they have to be set against the high levels of jealousy and suspicion which are all too readily generated when industries of one country demand intellectual

[96] For the case that IPRs should receive direct constitutional guarantees see Geiger (2006) 37 I.I.C. 371.

[97] Under arts 8 and 10 respectively.

[98] See, e.g. *Melnychuk v Ukraine* ECtHR 2005-IX; and cf. *LeviStrauss v Tesco Stores* [2003] R.P.C. 18.

[99] *Anheuser-Busch v Portugal*, Applicn 73049/01 (January 11, 2007). The European Patent Convention is a treaty between national states of Europe, to which the EU is not a contracting party. An attempt to argue before the ECtHR that it had jurisdiction to consider whether the opposition procedures under the EPC failed to meet the Convention's guarantees of fair procedures in litigation led that court to doubt whether it could consider the issue; but it went on nonetheless to indicate its view that there was no breach of the Convention: *Rambus v Germany* (2010) 41 I.I.C. 99.

[100] For strong expression of the contrary view—that countries should adopt IPRs only to the extent judged by them to be politically and economically appropriate: Vaver (2002) 25 Dalhousie L.J. 1.

property protection for their trading and licensing activities in other countries. Such tensions run high in the relations between the great producer countries and developing countries. However, they can be equally acute between the largest economies, particularly where one country believes that over decades it has been the subject of sophisticated and highly successful imitation by another (which is a common attitude of Americans towards Japan). Moreover, as the 1994 re-negotiation of the GATT has shown, intellectual property has become one important factor in the demand for greater mutual access to markets in international trade.

One way of expressing the close association of national policy and legal right lies in the principle of "territoriality". While this characteristic is often attributed to the major forms of intellectual property, there is less accord on its implications. The territorial nature of the rights *may* be treated as having at least four potential ramifications:

(1) The right in each country is determined by the law of that country and is independent of equivalent rights governing the same subject-matter (invention, work, trade mark, etc.) in other countries and neither stands nor falls with them.
(2) The right only affects activities undertaken by others within the geographical territory for which it is granted. This area is normally defined by the boundaries of the state concerned, with possible extensions for cross-border, sea, air and space activities connected to it.
(3) The right may be asserted only by nationals of the country for which it is granted and such others as the law also includes.
(4) The right may be asserted only in the courts of the country for which it is granted.

Civil rights of action in general (concerning tort, property, contract, etc.) are not considered to have such wide-ranging associations with territoriality, though they are likely to have some, particularly in relation to the first two attributes just mentioned. Most rights of action are not restricted by reference to the plaintiff's nationality, domicile or residence. Moreover, as we shall note later, in most countries there is a principle of private international law allowing actions to be brought for torts committed abroad in accordance with certain jurisdictional and choice of law rules.[101]

A good measure of the peculiarly territorial character of intellectual property is this: it is conceivable that nations would agree to treat inventors and authors as having personal rights to patents or copyright which are determined by their country of origin. In principle, then, they would be able to carry their rights thus defined to other countries and demand recognition and enforcement there. Under such a principle an author from country A

[101] See below, paras 2–71—2–87.

which gives copyright for the author's life and 70 years would be able to demand that period of protection in country B, even though its local law is limited to a copyright of (say) 56 years. The same would be true of the range of material protected and the scope of the rights granted. In the early period of industrialisation, the political unacceptability of this approach was soon enough appreciated and instead the territorial character of intellectual property became widely accepted during the nineteenth century.

Thanks to the third aspect of territoriality, states have needed to negotiate reciprocal recognition of rights for their citizens. By the late nineteenth century, they were devising multilateral conventions, which became early versions of the international instruments now administered by WIPO. In them each state undertakes to accord intellectual property rights to the nationals of the other participants: **1–31**

— In the sphere of industrial property, which includes patents for inventions, industrial design rights, trade marks and names and unfair competition protection, there has since 1883 been a basic international agreement, the Paris Convention for the Protection of Industrial Property (PIP).[102] Beside it have developed a host of further initiatives, notably on international applications for patents and trade marks; on micro-organism deposits for patents; on design registration; appellations of origin; and semiconductor chips. They have succeeded in varying degrees; the United Kingdom is not party to them all. Beyond them there are agreements at regional level (the United Kingdom having particular interests in those for the EU and Europe more generally) and bi-lateral accords, often as part of wider trade negotiations.

— In the sphere of copyright, authors' rights have since 1886 been the subject of the Berne Convention for the Protection of Literary and Artistic Works (Berne), and to a lesser extent to the Universal Copyright Convention of 1952 (UCC); while so-called "neighbouring" or "related" rights are partly covered by the Rome Convention for the Protection of Performers, Phonograms and Broadcasting Organisations of 1961 (Rome).[103] As with industrial property there is a phalanx of further international, regional and bi-lateral arrangements of various kinds and degrees of success.

— In the 1994 Accord finalising the Uruguay Round of the General Agreement on Tariffs and Trade (GATT) there is an Agreement on

[102] In 2007 the Paris Convention had 171 contracting states. For the history, see Bodenhausen, *Guide to the Paris Convention for Industrial Property* (1968); Ladas, *Patents, Trademarks and Related Rights* (1975).

[103] In 2007, the Berne Union comprised 163 States. See Ricketson and Ginsburg, *International Copyright and Neighbouring Rights* (2006); Geller and Nimmer, *International Copyright Law and Practice* (1987 et seq.); Nordemann, Vinck, Hertin and Meyer, *International Copyright and Neighbouring Rights Law* (1990); Sterling, *World Copyright Law* (2003).

Trade-Related Aspects of Intellectual Property Rights including Trade in Counterfeited Goods (TRIPS), which adds significantly to all previous international arrangements by including provisions on all the major forms of right. The World Trade Organisation (WTO), established by the 1994 Accord, administers TRIPS.[104]
Most States (in 2008, 153 in all, including China) are WTO members and therefore must comply with TRIPS in accordance with its timetables. TRIPS expressly incorporates requirements of the Paris and Berne Conventions and that has one directly significant effect. The states party to the earlier conventions could nominally require other parties to comply with their obligations by reference of disputes to the International Court of Justice. While there have long been allegations enough of non-compliance, this never led to such cumbrous proceedings. Under TRIPS, however, breach by a state may lead to the WTO dispute settlement procedure and, if necessary, to sanctions withdrawing WTO advantages.[105] These could include the suspension of concessions in the same sector or even cross-retaliatory measures such as the imposition of quotas or other exclusions on a country's export of goods or services.[106] In one significant proceeding to date concerning TRIPS obligations, exceptions in the US Copyright Act, s.110(5), which allowed for free use of music and drama in homestead relays, was held to be in contravention of the performance right obligations introduced into TRIPS from the Berne Convention art.11(1).[107] TRIPS thus has a potency of a novel order in the international relations of IPRs.[108] Only WTO states are able to use its procedures, but governments may well be willing to help their major industries, or even individual firms, by acting against other states which can be held responsible for a TRIPS breach. On occasion this may provide an alternative mode of attack when actions to enforce individual rights have given no satisfaction.

---

[104] For the significance of TRIPs within the WTO system: Drahos (1995) 13 Prometheus 6; Gervais, *The TRIPS Agreement* 2nd edn (2003); Correa and Yusof (eds)), *Intellectual Property and International Trade* (1998); Reichman (1996) 29 Vand. J. Trans. L. 345; Correa, *IPRs, the WTO and Developing Countries* (2000); Drahos and Mayne (eds), *International Intellectual Property Rights* (2002); Matthews, *Globalising IPRs: the TRIPs Agreement* (2002); Blakeney in Vaver and Bently, Ch.1.

[105] For the constitution and work of the Panels under the GATT Dispute Settlement Understanding, see Geuze and Wager (1999) J. Int.Ec.L. 347; Jackson, *Jurisprudence of GATT and the WTO* (2000); Weiler, *The Rule of Lawyers and the Ethos of Diplomats* (2000).

[106] There are evident difficulties in withdrawing intellectual property rights by way of sanction against other GATT breaches, since the rights are conferred on individuals; see Cottier (1992) 79 Aussenwirtschaft 97, 100–102. Helfer (1999) E.I.P.R. 8.

[107] See Goldmann (2001) 32 I.I.C. 412; Kennedy and Wager, *ALAI Proceedings* (2002); Burke (2002) 20 Cop. Rep. 176; Senftleben (2006) 37 I.I.C. 407; Geiger, ibid, 683.

[108] So exorbitant are its demands that only 35 states were bound from the start by its requirements; others are permitted transitional delays of 5 or 10 years, which in some respects have been extended by the Doha Declaration of 2001.

All these Conventions seek to achieve reciprocity, while at the same time allowing for the fact that national laws may differ in scope. The main technique for accommodating differences between laws is the principle of national treatment which operates as a ground rule of Paris, Berne and the UCC, and now in TRIPS[109]: each Member State is obliged to grant nationals of the other members the same rights as it accords to its own nationals.[110] National treatment is thus the corollary of the territoriality of intellectual property rights. **1–32**

In addition, where reciprocity is considered vital, as occurs particularly with copyright, the Conventions strive to set minimum standards which all members must meet. They may also introduce exceptions to national treatment, such as the "rule of the lesser term" in Berne.[111] Where reciprocity is not of the same order of significance, as with patents, some Convention States may not even limit the right to apply for protection to persons of any particular nationality.[112]

(g) *International treaties: authority and applicability*

In accordance with the general principle of English law, an international instrument ratified by the UK Government is not itself part of municipal law. Parliament must first enact its provisions. This is the position with the Paris Convention and the other agreements mentioned in previous paragraphs. However, many countries, including civil law systems within Europe, do not insist on so strict a dualism between international law and the national legal order. If an obligation under an international treaty is intended to affect the legal relations of individuals, in such a country it may well be found to be of "direct effect", and this may give one of the individuals a right enforceable against the other through process in a national court. **1–33**

What then of international obligations assumed by the European Union? Above all in relation to intellectual property, what is the position concerning the provisions of the TRIPs Agreement of the WTO? Given that protection of intellectual property is not specified to be an object of the European Union, two factors have been identified as giving powers in the field to its institutions.[113] One is the responsibility for the common commercial policy of the Union, which can be advanced, for example, by reaching **1–34**

[109] PIP, arts 2, 3; Berne, art.5; UCC, art.2; Rome, arts 2, 4–6; TRIPS, art.2; Evans [1996] E.I.P.R. 149.

[110] The TRIPS Agreement (art.3) also requires most-favoured-nation treatment. This is the result of certain bi-lateral agreements with the US which offer US nationals better treatment than home nationals (notably the so-called "pipeline" provisions to secure future patent rights once a national office is established for present inventions). It may have unintended consequences: see below, para.11–56.

[111] See below, para.10–25.

[112] As, for instance, with the European Patent Convention: below, para.4–06.

[113] See *Spain v EU Council* (above, n.90). On the intricate constitutional issues mentioned in the following paragraphs, see Drexl in Beier and Schricker, *From GATT to TRIPs* (1996) 18; Govaere in Drexl et al. (eds), *Technology and Competition* (2009) 699.

international agreements with non-member states. There are numerous such agreements which impose mutual responsibilities to respect aspects of IPRs—but because they cover other subject-matter they are labelled "mixed agreements".[114] The other lies in the powers of the Union to further the internal market by enacting a regulation under art.308 or a directive under art.95.[115]

The European Commission, eager to by-pass national objections that IPRs at root remain fields for Member State law alone, first sought to persuade the ECJ that the commercial policy power conferred on the institutions of the Union charge over the whole of intellectual property, internally as well as externally. This applied both to the legislative development and administration of TRIPs provisions, and to their interpretation in law, as being within the competence of the EU courts. The Court of Justice, however, showed greater political sensibility. First, it asserted jurisdiction to decide all questions of competence between the EU and Member States—for the good reason that it alone could reach decisions binding in the whole EU order. Then, turning attention to different types of IPR, it held that where an aspect of intellectual property law had been substantially covered by EU law, that law alone governed its content. So it became with trade marks, once the Community trade mark was brought into operation, having at its side the Harmonisation Directive on national trade mark systems. The occupation of the field was in essence complete since these enactments define both the scope of protectable subject-matter and infringement of the right. The court has held that a provision such as TRIPS art.50, which imposes specific requirements for the procedures involved in enforcing a registered mark, will have direct effect, to the extent that this is so under EU law.[116] But, perhaps out of some vestigial respect for the fact that Member States have very different traditions over the direct effectiveness of international obligations, the court's view takes a nuanced form. It is for a national court to interpret its national procedural rules "as far as possible in the light of the wording and purpose of Article 50".[117]

This should equally be the case with the EU law on industrial designs; also with the Regulation establishing Supplementary Protection Certificates, which has the effect of extending the term of certain pharmaceutical and agricultural patents.[118] Conversely, if there had been no direct enactment of EU law, a matter would remain for the Member States individually. So it was with the initial term of a patent, which TRIPs art.33 requires to be for a maximum of 20 years. The courts of a Member State may choose to give

---

114 *EC Commission v Ireland* [2002] E.C.R. I-2943 is an example.

115 See above, paras 1–26, 1–27.

116 *Hermès International v FHT Marketing* [1998] E.C.R. I-3603; cf. *Lenzing AG's European Patent* [1997] R.P.C. 245.

117 *Christian Dior v Tuk Consultancy* [2001] E.T.M.R. 277 at [47, 49]; and see *Schieving-Nijstad v Groeneveld* [2001] E.C.R. I-5851 at [35].

118 See below, paras 15–10—15–31, 4–26.

direct effect to that international obligation (where its own term is less) because it retains "principal competence" over that issue and there has been no more general annexation of the "sphere" of patents by EU law.[119] Another instance is provided by the law of unfair competition, which to a considerable extent remains a matter for national law, either through the general law of delict or tort or by national legislation: while the TRIPs agreement contains provisions which require measures against unfair competition to be adopted

In between, however, there are "spheres" to which both EU law and national law could be applicable. With these the ECJ will decide how far an issue has become a matter of EU law, and to that extent will pronounce upon the substantive content of the issue.[120] Copyright is one instance. In the *Ireland* case, the ECJ considered that the line of EU directives on copyright have made that equally a field of EU law intervention. But the issue deserves to be reconsidered. The directives still have only a limited impact on the basic concepts of copyright law—what is a work, what kind of originality is called for, what constitutes infringement, etc. However that may be, an obligation placed on EU states by the European Economic Area Agreement to ratify the Paris Act of the Berne Copyright Convention (1973) fell to be determined by the court as a matter of EU law obligation. Ireland was accordingly found to have failed to implement this duty. When it comes to legislative and administrative matters falling in this middle ground, the Union Council and Commission on the one hand, and the governments of Member States on the other, are empowered to act in conjunction even when the latter allow themselves to be represented by the Commission in negotiating diplomatic agreements. The situation with unfair competition law led to a converse result, even though there has been considerable intervention by Community Directives in the sphere of misleading advertising and such conjoint topics as comparative advertising.

When the court first set out this stratification of jural capacities in 1994,[121] it was giving an advisory opinion on competence in relation to the TRIPs Agreement. It held that only the provisions dealing with enforcement of rights against cross-border piracy and counterfeiting had become a field exclusively governed by EU law.[122] The rest of IP law subject to TRIPs obligations—including obligations to adhere to most provisions of the Paris and Berne Conventions—was either a matter of mixed responsibility or it was the sole responsibility of Member States. Accordingly the views of those states could not simply be overridden by EU institutions, if they were at odds. The joint competence justified what happened at the diplomatic level.

[119] See *Merck Genéricos*, below, n.121; and for the EPC, below, paras 3–23—3–29.

[120] Above n.114, at [17]

[121] See *Merck Genéricos* [2007] E.C.R. I-7001 at [35] et seq.

[122] *Advisory Opinion No 1/1994* [1994] E.C.R. I-5267; see also *Commission v Council* Case (C-176/03) on criminal law provisions to give effective implementation of EU law under the EC Treaty: below, para.2–19.

The TRIPs Agreement was signed by the EU and its 15 Member States at the time.

(3) Challenges to intellectual property: political

1–35 As on the one hand the demand for increased protection has arisen, so on the other has the level of suspicion and criticism of intellectual property protection. Some of this has come from English judges specialising in intellectual property, speaking on public platforms rather than through judgments.[123] This adds significantly to a long-standing British readiness to ask whether extensions of protection are justifiable. More comes from two outside sources.

First, the developing countries, which are only beginning to exploit intellectual property of their own, have often enough found themselves with an inheritance of "protectionist" laws from colonial days. These can all too easily appear a legal pretext for foreign industry, technical and cultural, to cream off scarce resources in royalty payments. Yet in the race for development, there is a real need to acquire technology from the advanced nations and there is often strong popular demand for products bearing the allure of Western prosperity. Patent, copyright and trade mark laws therefore tend to be kept because they give the security that will continue to attract foreign enterprise. There is, however, a natural tendency to modify their operation in the national interest, just as in the past American and European legislatures have required home manufacture, or refused rights to foreign nationals or accorded protection to those who bring in the ideas of others. There have been experiments with compulsory licence requirements, curbs on the manner in which royalties may be paid, or official examination of the terms on which foreign right-owners establish their own local operations or grant licences to local enterprises.

For two decades, the developing countries strove to secure the international acceptability of such derogations from unfettered rights of "property". They based their claim upon their need for freer access to technical and educational materials and for self-sufficiency and independent initiative for national business concerns. Of this movement, which had its first major impact during the revision of the Berne Copyright Convention in Stockholm in 1967 and continued particularly at the meetings of UNCTAD, and the abortive attempts to revise the Paris Industrial Property Convention, there will be more to note at later stages.

It undoubtedly made more remarkable the counter-offensive, led by the United States, but strongly supported by the European Community and Japan, for the Uruguay Round re-negotiations of the GATT, which have

[123] Jacob [1993] E.I.P.R. 312; [1997] I.P.Q. 1; Laddie [1996] E.I.P.R. 253. See also Ricketts and Austin (eds), *International Intellectual Property and the Common Law World* (2000); Cornish, *Intellectual Property: Omnipresent, Distracting, Irrelevant?* (2002); Vaver and Bently (eds), *Intellectual Property in the New Millennium* (2004).

now seen the acceptance of TRIPS as an international guarantee of respect for intellectual property. The depth and breadth of that accord, which a decade before would have seemed the purest fantasy, became possible because of a change of attitude among developing countries. In part, unquestionably, this is the product of single-minded pressure from an America haunted by trade deficit. In part also it derived from the alluring example of the rapidly industrialising States of the Pacific Rim and more generally from the extraordinary shifts in political organisation and allegiances across the world which came with the collapse of East European communism in 1989–1990.

At least for a while, TRIPS was treated as an inevitable quid pro quo in the enhancement of free trade and access to international markets enshrined in the WTO. TRIPS placed significant limits on the ability of developing countries to give little recognition to IPRs and make no effort to see them enforced.[124] But those countries suspended their suspicion for only a few years. The operation of the patent system in the realm of health care in particular caused deep resentment.[125] Certain modifications of TRIPS had to be conceded at the Doha Meeting in November 2001 and given proper acknowledgment by the TRIPS Council. At the same time a vociferous movement to improve the chance of benefits to developing countries of IPRs and other intangible rights has gained increasing sway in international fora.[126] There has, for instance, been pressure for property like entitlements for tribes, local communities and under-developed peoples to a share in advanced developments arising out of traditional knowledge (TK). This encompasses both understandings of the medicinal qualities of natural materials (for instance, the rose periwinkle of Madagascar is the source of modern treatment for cancerous lymphomas) and the exploitation of folklore in modern music and art.[127]

At the beginning of this debate, the industrialised states, ignoring the inconvenient portions of their own IP history, showed a dismissive scorn towards the very idea, but they are moving towards grudging concession.[128] There remain considerable difficulties in the conception. These go to such matters as: Who should be entitled to claim? Who should be beneficiaries? What role should be played by a public record of potential claims? How far

[124] The US has maintained an independent right to require higher intellectual property rights than those guaranteed by TRIPs through the medium of bilateral trade agreements: see Endeshaw [2006] E.I.P.R. 374.

[125] Below, para.7–41; Matthews [2006] I.P.Q. 91; cf. Crespi [2003] E.I.P.R. 242.

[126] Thus sharp entrepreneurs have recently sought to take over the names or the product characteristics of foods such as Basmati rice and Darjeeling tea, leading to a considerable interest in plant variety rights and appellations of origin by some developing countries and their peoples: see, e.g. Commission on IPRs (UK Department for International Development), *Integrating IPRs and Development Policy* (2002) Ch.3.

[127] For a review of the current debates, see ibid., esp. Chs 2, 3, and above, n.2.

[128] An Inter-Governmental Commission of WIPO has become a major forum for studying the prospects for action at the international level; Wendland (2002) 33 I.I.C. 485; Gibson, *Community Resources* (2005) Ch.4.

should recompense be left to voluntary contracting between developers and traditional claimants? What co-ordination is needed with modern IPRs, given that they turn upon new or original creativity by individuals rather than the inherited practices of groups? How long should any claim endure? What controls should there be on associated physical material (such as the content of gene banks)? But with the right will some fulfilment of such proposals is undoubtedly possible. In the shorter term these may be found in such modifications of present IPR schemes as requiring the source of biologically based inventions to be given in patent specifications; refusing trade marks that wrongly suggest association with indigenous or traditional communities; and granting geographical indications of origin to appropriate communities.

1–36 Secondly, there remains a tendency amongst the developed capitalist states to limit the monopolistic tendencies of successful private enterprise by anti-trust laws (or competition laws as they are known in the EU). Intellectual property rights have often enough been one basis for powerful anti-competitive collaborations. Since their very purpose is to confer rights to exclude competitors, it is inevitable that they should have been combined into wider accretions of market power. Legislatures, competition authorities and courts have felt the need to impose restrictions upon at least the most evidently excessive arrangements of this kind: cartel-like patent pools, copyright collecting societies, international or regional divisions of marketing territories achieved by the splitting of rights and the suppression of the initiative and independence of licensees, remain to some extent open to attack, though it is apparent that the single-minded vigour behind these efforts in the 1960s and 1970s have now given place to a less liberal view of the inherent dangers of monopoly. Nonetheless the balance between the two requires discussion at numerous points in this book.[129]

(4) Challenges to intellectual property: technological

1–37 Intellectual property rights are constantly destabilised by technological advance. Patent law, evolving primarily around machines and chemical processes, has had to absorb the emergence of electrical engineering, computer construction, atomic energy, microbiological production techniques and now biotechnology. Copyright, initially a rather belated response to the printing press, had then to address the performance of plays and music, photography, sound recording, film, broadcasting and now the extraordinary prospects of digital recording and transmission.

As the pre-history of copyright makes plain, the demand for new forms of protection is dependent upon many factors, including the expansion and

---

[129] For an introduction, in relation to the single market policies of the EU, see below, paras 1–48—1–59. For competition law control of technology transfer licences, see below, paras 7–31 et seq.

liberation of an economy to a point where new entrants to a market can no longer be excluded by local cartels in the form of guilds and corporations. When the London stationers found in the late seventeenth century that they could no longer control what was printed and sold in the capital, they were obliged to press their authors' case for a copyright in what they published and they procured the world's first copyright statute in 1710. Their earlier position was undermined by improvements in typesetting, which cheapened the costs of imitation, and improvements in transportation, which made it possible to ship copies into the capital from around the kingdom.

In other words, it is not the initial technology so much as the technology of imitation which stimulates the strongest demands for intellectual property. The early computer industry was content with contract and secrecy as the legal weapons of its development; but the opening of mass markets made possible by micro-computer technology and its astonishing ability to copy programs, rapidly reversed such perceptions. The greater the differential between initial development costs and those of easy and accurate imitation, the more exigent the case for legal protection becomes.

Intellectual property rights are the result of idealistic and utilitarian **1–38**
perceptions. In some traditions, aesthetic and cultural values are held to justify these rights (or some of them—particularly the rights of authors, performers and inventors) quite apart from any role which they may have as incentives to production and so to economic expansion and enhanced consumer choice. These non-economic values also express the wrongness of allowing one person to take over and reap rewards from the intellectual or the marketing efforts of another. "Reaping without sowing" declare those with a strong sense of the injustice. "But the sower's seed came from the crops of others before her", answer those who would preserve a sense of moral proportion in the matter. And so the law must establish regimes which offer market exclusivity to an extent that will rectify the most evident cases of undue appropriation of intangible value, while preventing them from giving protection against the effects of competition which is quite disproportionate.

Today's great advances—in computing, telecommunications, biotechnology and so on—require very considerable investment indeed in order to be made, but are often taken over by others quickly, efficiently and cheaply. This makes the case for some intellectual property protection very hard to resist. It explains why in the 1980s the copyright system was roughly manipulated so as to provide a degree of protection for computer programs, and why semiconductor layouts acquired their own form of right. It also explains why there is currently a strong drive to protect database compilations, multi-media works, new forms of electronic distribution and even DNA structures, whether revealed in their natural state or varied by genetic engineering. Now, as perhaps never before, policy-makers are having to react to demands for new or adapted protection before there is real time to contemplate desirable conditions and qualifications. Controversies are particularly acute in relation to IPR protection on the internet and the medical prospects of genome research. That is why these technologies are explored in the two final chapters of this book, Ch.20 on Digitisation and Ch.21 on Biotechnology.

4. Property and Monopoly: Economic Approaches

1–39 No serious student of intellectual property law can today afford to ignore the economic arguments for and against the maintenance of these rights. Patents, copyright and trade marks each have a different form of economic impact, so a good deal must be reserved for later discussion.[130]

Underlying them all, however, are theoretical approaches to two matters: the justification for conferring private property rights and the nature of monopoly power in a market. Full analysis must be sought in a textbook on economics,[131] but a word of non-technical explanation may at least be suggestive.

(1) Property rights

1–40 Intellectual property operates mainly as a form of legal exclusivity in free enterprise markets. While Eastern bloc countries remained in the grip of socialist planning, patents, copyright and trade marks had only vestigial meaning in their internal economies. For them the rights acted as an ancillary attraction to foreign trade. It was during the latter stages of the great battle of economic systems, that, in the West (and hence the world), these rights came regularly to be treated as "property" and labelled "intellectual property".

At that period, economists who strove to analyse the virtues of liberal capitalism as practised in the United States, Western Europe, Japan and other newly industrialising states, were turning afresh to theories of private property rights. They argued that only with firm legal recognition of individual ownership would the full value of society's resources come to be realised. Property, with a functioning regime of contract law as its necessary corollary, would maximise exploitation. A synergy of individual transactions would enable the economy to grow and diffuse its riches to an increasing range of its population. Classic theories enjoyed new favour: John Locke's justification of property entitlements as stemming from the

[130] See especially below, paras 3–36—3–54, 10–45—10–55, 16–24 et seq.

[131] Particular help may be derived from Samuelson and Nordhaus, *Economics* 18th edn (2005), Pt III; Scherer and Ross, *Industrial Market Structure and Economic Performance* 3rd edn (1990), especially Chs 2, 14–17; Granstrand, *The Economics and Management of Intellectual Property* (2000), Chs 1–3; Landes and Posner, *The Economic Structure of Intellectual Property* (2003) Dreyfuss et al. *Expanding the Boundaries of Intellectual Property* (2007); Merges, *Economics of Intellectual Property* (2007). For a substantial collection of papers, Towse and Holzhauer, *The Economics of Intellectual Property* (2002) Pts I–IV.

labour of the person in cultivating and producing; Adam Smith's prescription for economic health in the freedom of individuals to pursue their manifold, differing self-interests. To some degree their essentially utilitarian view of the public policies in favour of at least some IP protection had to be ranked beside ideas of the great idealist philosophers and their justifications of private property as a whole.[132]

Ideas of private property have evolved around tangible things—land and movables. Their physical existence inevitably *constrains* the uses that can be made of them. If that use is to be shared—by joint or common entitlement, by successive interests in time (life interests, leases, hiring), by division up of uses (easements, profits)—each exploiter is constrained in his use by the need to preserve the interests of others. Property rights theorists argue for the efficiency of undivided, absolute ownership and have seen its vindication, first and foremost, in the collapsing Communist regimes of the 1980s. Equally the claims for property rights have been set against much less complete systems of social co-determination. Thus they underpin the current retreat across the world from governmental ownership or control of staple elements in free enterprise economies, such as power supply, transport, communications, housing, health, social protection and even education. **1–41**

A degree of theoretical adjustment is needed if intellectual property is to be fitted within the justifications for property rights in general. The information which these rights protect is not a restricted resource in the same sense as physical property. On the contrary, information which one person discovers, creates or publicises will not be lost to him because it comes to be used by others. In that sense, it is open to divided use without limit. When the law intervenes to insist, artificially, that only one person has the right to deploy categories of information in certain ways, it does so, not as a support for the physical reality of possession, but in order to create out of nothing an equivalent exclusivity. It can certainly be argued that this fencing off of intangible subject-matter fulfils an economic function equivalent to that of ownership of physical property, because otherwise the incentive to optimise the value of the information will be impaired or destroyed. Those who would be innovators will wait instead to be imitators and the dynamic processes which would have generated new ideas will disappear; in the end there will be little or nothing different to imitate.

Nonetheless, the analogy remains incomplete. If A appropriates B's invention, both remain able to use it. A does not preclude B from competing in the same measure as when he has appropriated the axe which B previously used for tree-cutting. Information has an inherent capacity to be taken over by all who can get access to it and used by them all, for **1–42**

[132] See Drahos, *A Philosophy of Intellectual Property* (1996); Harris, *Property and Justice* (1996); Waldron, *The Right to Private Property* (1988); Hughes (1988) 77 Georgetown L.J. 287; Hettinger (1989) 18 Phil. & P.A. 31; Paine (1991) 20 Phil & P.A. 247; Palmer (1989) 12 Hamline L.R. 261; Drahos (ed.), *Intellectual Property* (1999) and further, below, paras 10–42 et seq.

competitive and non-competitive purposes alike. Plainly, competition can enhance the welfare of consumers by reducing prices to them and providing greater choices; so much so that in general there is a presumption in its favour unless there is a sufficient case to the contrary.

Intellectual property rights are therefore granted to the extent that competition involving the unauthorised use of the right-holder's work or invention or mark evidently prejudices that person's exploitation of it and therefore his willingness to engage in the mental and associated activities which brought it to light in the first place. Nonetheless the greatest differences among economists over intellectual property now lie between those who would stress the virtues of conferring protection in the form of property; and those who would calculate with scrupulous care the degree of protection needed to procure new production of material. The first group adopts a relaxed view of the growth of these property rights and is ready to extend them by analogy so as to capture as much intangible value of economic activity as is not overridden by sufficient countervailing arguments. The latter regards them with suspicion and would limit the categories of protectable material, keep a tight rein on their term, introduce qualifications to reflect other basic values, such as further experimentation and freedom of expression, and ensure that they cannot be used to exert market power over and above that intended by the strictly limited nature of the right.

This book is about the ways in which the United Kingdom and the EU choose, through their law, to resolve this unending tension. Some of the arguments turn upon a degree of familiarity with economic analysis of monopoly and competition and to this we must turn.

(2) Monopolist behaviour

1–43 The typical circumstance in which monopoly power is acquired concerns a commodity which the consumer already needs or desires: a monopolist's power can be thought of in terms of his ability to restrict the supply of the commodity; this has a consequential effect on its price. Everyday experience of prices for (say) petrol, food or land suggests the effect of cutting down the quantity of such a commodity on the market. Some purchasers will be prepared to devote more of their resources to buying what there is of it. If, therefore, a supplier is in a position to reduce the quantity of something that the public wants, he will be able to effect an increase in its price: he then behaves as a monopolist. If, on the contrary, he has competitors enough it will not avail him to reduce his output, because they are likely to be able to expand their output to fill the shortfall that he would otherwise bring about. And of course to raise his prices unilaterally would be merely to invite his customers to take their business to a cheaper competitor. This is equally true whether the competitors offer precisely the same products or things more or less similar which the public will treat as substitutes. The profit that any trader makes depends upon three principal factors: the number of things sold, their price and their cost per unit to produce. Assuming that unit costs do not vary significantly, there is a relationship between number and price which is crucial to an understanding of why a monopolist may benefit from selling fewer units at higher prices. Suppose that the first producer of a video-cassette recorder is setting his price for a year in which he can expect no competition from other manufacturers. He knows that if he limits his production run to a given number, he should be able to increase his price to the level that this number of purchasers is willing to pay. (How far the level of demand will regress as price increases is something that he will have to guess from such market indicators as he can amass.) But he must appreciate that, if demand can be accurately forecast, there is an optimum number and correlated price to find. Suppose the calculation looks like this:

Number	*Price per unit*	*Cost per unit*	*Profit (total revenue less total cost)*
	£	£	000's
1,000	700	400	300
2,000	600	400	400
3,000	550	400	450
4,000	500	400	400
5,000	475	400	375
6,000	450	400	300

A rational producer under these conditions will market 3,000 at £550.

(3) The presumption against monopoly

In any economy which is to a substantial extent unplanned by government, there are good reasons for fearing the market power of the monopolist, or at least for making sure that there are countervailing justifications, general or specific. Four arguments may be mentioned: **1–44**

(1) The basic theoretical objection taken by economists concerns those who were not prepared to buy at the monopoly price, though they would have paid the competitive price or something in between. These consumers are left by the monopolist's behaviour to buy something else less valuable to them and in this sense there is a "misallocation of resources"; too little of society's resources by this criterion are being put into the production of the goods monopolised. This objection is in fact a complex argument turning upon a number of assumptions: in particular that competition, or conditions equivalent to it, prevails in the market for similar or connected goods. Such qualifications are enough to make some economists doubt the relevance of this theory to the problem of monopoly.

(2) Compare with this the common objection—socio-political rather than economic in nature—which looks rather at the position of those who do pay the monopolist's price. The latter thereby acquires his monopoly profit at their expense. A redistribution of wealth takes place which may be regarded as unjustifiable.
(3) The monopolist is able to determine factors about goods in addition to their price: the kinds of service supplied, continuity of supply, the number of different versions, the amount of research and development into future products or services. This may have deleterious effects, immediate or consequential, for the consumer.
(4) The monopolist loses the incentive to keep down costs that comes from competition. For only if his costs are constantly pared can a competitor hope to maintain or enhance his market share against those of his rivals.

Monopoly, or at least some measure of market power, nonetheless has its advocates. At one extreme lie cases where economies of scale are such that the most efficient production will be procured from a single source. Few people would argue against the advantages of this sort of "natural monopoly", but if it is to remain in private hands it may be desirable to make it in some way publicly accountable. We shall see that copyright collecting societies present a special instance of such a phenomenon.[133] More equivocal are cases where, for instance, it can be said that only with the security of monopoly profits will a firm make sufficient investment in research to secure the really advantageous breakthroughs for the future.[134] This sort of consideration becomes particularly germane to the justification of the patent system.

Advanced industrial societies engage in a continuing debate about the advisability of taking steps to curb or restrain the dangers set by monopolists, oligopolists and cartels within the private economic sector. The current growth of "anti-trust" laws is an indication of an increasing concern over the scale of profit and economic power of private enterprise. The tendency in these laws to treat certain manifestations of market power as at least prima facie unjustifiable demonstrates the force that experience gives to the theoretical objections to monopoly; equally, the provision that is made to allow firms to justify their practices is some admission that there may well be a countervailing case to be made out.

(4) Intellectual property and monopoly

1–45 All intellectual property consists in the exclusive right to perform some defined activity, in the main productive or commercial. But this is not at all

[133] See below, paras 13–51—13–62.
[134] See below, paras 3–31—3–37.

the same thing as the ability to exert monopoly power within a market.[135] A market for goods has to be conceived in terms of all the goods that consumers will treat as substitutes for one another: will they switch from one to another if, for instance, the price of the first is raised? The extent to which purchasers want the product that is the subject of intellectual property and not some alternative is often difficult to determine. It may depend on the technical advance that has been made (particularly in the field covered by patents), or upon the dictates of fashion (as with many of the most popular copyright works), or upon the effect of repeated advertising (as with well-known trade marks).

The degree of market power that may be secured in these different areas by the deployment of intellectual property is a matter that we will take up topic by topic. Here it is appropriate merely to bring out two underlying considerations.

First, the fact that much intellectual property has very little capacity to generate market power leads to considerable difficulty in arguments over the proper scope of rights. On the one hand there is the potential disadvantage of power over a market in the few really successful cases—a power which may sometimes be unjustifiably great even given the special public policies (such as the encouragement of invention) which may underlie the creation of the right in the first place. On the other hand, if the investment of resources to produce ideas or convey information is left unprotected, it will be prey to the attentions of a competitive imitator who will not be obliged to pay anything for what he takes. There will accordingly be little incentive to invest in the ideas or information and the consumer may be correspondingly the poorer. The only way out of this dilemma is, on the one hand, to make the best practicable estimate of the dangers that unjustified monopolies may produce; and, on the other hand, to assess the degree to which the claimant's investment will be open to dissipation if he is not accorded his right. **1–46**

Secondly, to the extent that intellectual property is capable of generating market power, it offers its owner (and his associates) the opportunity to reduce output and raise prices. What it does not bring about is the condition in which the monopolist behaves as though he were the only competitor on the market. Yet the more naive arguments in favour of one or other exclusive right often imply that this alone will be the effect of according the right sought. This intermediate condition can indeed be aimed at: through mechanisms such as direct price control, or through one or other of the forms of statutory or compulsory licensing. Accordingly it is no surprise to find that economists who doubt the justifiability of unconstrained **1–47**

[135] See Kitch (1986) 8 Rsch. in L. & Econs. 31; Bouckaert (1991) 13 Harv. J.L. Pub.Pol. 775; Palmer, 13 Harv. J.L. Pub.Pol. 817; MacKaay, 13 Harv. J.L. Pub.Pol. 867; Meiners and Staaf, 13 Harv. J.L. Pub.Pol. 911; Lehmann (1989) 20 I.I.C. 3.

intellectual property turn to the compulsory licence as a moderating technique.[136] In theory at least it provides machinery for obliging the right-owner to accept a return (the royalty officially set under the licence) at a rate below that which he would have accepted if left to exercise his market power unfettered (hence the need for compulsion). Whether in practice this mechanism can be made to work without creating a disproportionate run of administrative expense depends on the legal form in which it is clothed. We shall have occasion to study a number of different examples in the course of this book.[137]

5. Division of Markets and the European Economic Area

(1) Dividing markets

1–48 The European Economic Area (EEA) to which this section and later discussion refers was constituted in 1994–1995 to establish free trade obligations between the European Community and certain former European Free Trade Area States. Since Austria, Finland and Sweden joined the EC in 1995, the states in this free trade association are Iceland, Liechtenstein and Norway (Switzerland having refused to join). The principles of free movement and the rules of competition, described in the following paragraphs in their EU embodiments, now apply equally to EEA relations, though in rather complex ways.[138]

The obvious purpose of intellectual property is to give protection against rival enterprises which would otherwise sell goods or provide services in direct competition. In international trade, however, these rights have acquired a separate significance. In many cases, by adopting the appropriate legal technique, goods produced by a single organisation or associated enterprises can be prevented from moving from one territory to another; a barrier of private rights can be set up against imports or exports which is as effective as an embargo or tariff imposed by a state.[139] The procedure is often more effective than limitations on movement imposed only by contract.

Accordingly a middleman (known in EU jargon as a "parallel importer") cannot buy A's goods in cheap state No.1 and transport them to expensive state No.2 for resale at a profit. But A's ability to discriminate in his pricing between different territories is only one reason for restraining parallel

[136] Good instances are the Economic Council of Canada, *Report on Intellectual and Industrial Property* (1971), Ch.5; Penrose, *The Economics of the International Patent System* (1951). And see Scherer, *The Economic Effects of Compulsory Patent Licensing* (1977).
[137] See below, paras 7–39—7–50.
[138] See Oliver, *Free Movement of Goods in the European Community* 5th edn (2010), Ch.14.
[139] The customs authorities of a state may be used to arrest the importing of goods that infringe an intellectual property right: for the British position, see below, para.2–23.

importing. In countries other than his home territory it may be economically desirable, or sometimes legally necessary, to manufacture and sell through the medium of a local licensee, or at least to sell imported goods through a local distributor. Difficulties with the local language, local contacts or local labour relations may be overcome by such arrangements. It may, however, be hard to find a local licensee or distributor unless he can be assured of exclusive rights to market in his own territory; for he will have his own investment in promoting a foreign product to protect. An intermediate case is the transnational corporation which has reasons (often involving taxation and foreign exchange) for operating in different territories through national subsidiaries. Again, each may be given exclusive rights to restrain imports of products emanating from the others—in order to protect price differentials, or to monitor performance comparatively within the group.

(2) Exhaustion of rights

The manner in which intellectual property can be deployed to divide mar- **1–49**
kets varies with the kind of right held. The question is accordingly one to which we must return at later points.[140] But one general concept can usefully be introduced here. In every intellectual property law it is necessary to decide which steps in the chain of production and distribution of goods require the licence of the right-owner: manufacture; first sale by the manufacturer; subsequent sales and other dealings; export and import; use. In the past, legislators have often left the answer to the courts. In many cases, both in British and in foreign laws, the rights are "exhausted" after first sale by the right-owner or with his consent. But often this is confined to first sales within the territory covered by the right—it amounts to a principle of domestic, rather than international, exhaustion. Accordingly, national rights that are subject to such limitation can still be used to prevent the importation of goods sold abroad by the national right-owner or goods which come from an associated enterprise.

In Britain, the relation between rights and distribution of goods has not in the past been dealt with by any general concept of exhaustion. The approach has varied with the subject-matter. In the case of patent law (in contrast with other major patent systems), the British traditionally adopted the contrary position to "exhaustion": in principle, subsequent uses and sales continued to require the patentee's licence. This, as we shall see,[141] is an approach that is in process of being dismantled in all save exceptional cases. For this, basic policies of the EU are primarily responsible.

---

[140] The discussion of exhaustion is taken up below, at paras 6–15—6–16, 7–34—7–35 (patents), paras 12–27—12–29, 13–28—13–32 (copyright) and para.18–120 (trade marks). As regards EC law in general, see below, Ch.19.

[141] See below, paras 6–15—6–16.

(3) The idea of a common market

1–50 A common market is the product of a political decision to promote trade competition without the interposition of legal or fiscal barriers. It is a normal consequence of political unification (the United Kingdom) or federation (the United States, Canada, Australia) and it may be established by independent states that are concerned with economic integration (as originally with the European Economic Community). How far legal measures are introduced to help in achieving a common market has varied with time and place. But as far as intellectual property rights are concerned, it has been usual to work towards a unified law for the whole territory.

In the EU, the absence of political union has made any movement towards unified or harmonised laws of patents, copyright and trade marks a complex business.[142] Yet in the past, intellectual property rights have played a major role in preventing the movement of goods from one part of a common market territory to another. In the eyes of the EU authorities the need to put an end to this has correspondingly been urgent. Indeed this was initially seen as the prime reason for studying the unification of intellectual property laws.

However, action has not waited upon the outcome of these investigations. The European Court of Justice and the EU Commission have interpreted provisions of the Treaty of Rome as limiting the scope of national intellectual property laws in certain circumstances where they give rise to a conflict with policies expressed in the Treaty. Basic provisions, such as the outlawing of discrimination on the ground of nationality, may accordingly apply.[143] Beyond these, two aspects of the Treaty have had persistent importance: the elimination of restrictions upon the free movement of goods between Member States, and the establishment of a system to prevent distortions of competition in interstate trade.[144] The provisions of the Treaty which give specific content to these objectives are arts 28–30 (free movement of goods) and arts 81–86 (competition). At this stage, these provisions can be introduced in general terms, while leaving their effect upon the different types of right to later chapters. Both sets of provisions are directly enforceable and so may generate rights and obligations in individuals, as well as in Member States, which may be enforced or pleaded in defence in litigation before national courts.[145] Accordingly, it should be noted that decisions on the content of EU law may reach the ultimate court of reference, the European Court of Justice, by way of appeal from the

[142] See above, paras 1–26 et seq.

[143] Article 11 TFEU (ex-art.6 TEC). See esp. *Collins v Imtrat* [1993] 3 C.M.L.R. 773: below, para.19–01.

[144] Other policies of the Treaty—notably the freedom to provide services and the right of establishment—contain some potential for conflict with intellectual property. See below, para.1–52.

[145] For the extent to which the provision afford direct rights of action to individuals, see below, para.19–03.

Commission—for example in respect of a violation of the rules of competition; or by way of art.234 reference in the course of national litigation—as where the enforcement of an intellectual property right is allegedly in conflict with the free movement of goods policy or the rules of competition.

(4) Free movement of goods

Article 28 of the Treaty prohibits quantitative restrictions on imports "as between Member States", and all measures having equivalent effect. The European Court of Justice has held that national industrial property rights may amount to "measures having equivalent effect" when they are directed to preventing acts of importation.[146] Accordingly actions for the enforcement of such rights should not be allowed to succeed unless justified by art.30. This permits prohibitions or restrictions on imports if they are justified on various grounds, including the protection of industrial and commercial property. But this exemption itself does not apply where the "prohibitions or restrictions ... amount to a means of arbitrary discrimination [or] a disguised restriction of trade between Member States".[147] **1–51**

As we shall see, there are a wide range of circumstances in which the Court of Justice has ruled that national intellectual property rights should not be used to restrain parallel importing so as to defeat the free movement of goods policy. Article 30 has not been allowed to stand in the way, any more than has art.295 which provides that the Treaty is no way to prejudice the rules in Member States governing the system of property ownership. The court has characterised some assertions of these rights as going to their very existence (and therefore properly made), while other assertions have been labelled mere exercise of the right (and therefore not within the exemption of art.30).[148] The distinction has been made to turn upon a "definition" of the specific subject-matter of the particular right.[149] But, as with the basic dichotomy between existence and exercise, these definitions have the appearance of being formulated only in the wake of a policy decision to give preference to Community policies over some assertions of national rights. All of this may seem an exercise in legal obscurantism, but the basic intent is not hard to grasp: intellectual property rights are properly exercised when used against goods that come from independent competitors in trade; but

[146] But not when the right applies to some other action within the territory (e.g. hiring or selling), irrespective of whether the articles in question are of local manufacture or are imported from another Member State.

[147] See the final sentence of art.36 TFEU (ex-art.30 TEC); Barnard, *Substantive Law of the EU* 2nd edn (2007) Chs 5, 9.

[148] The distinction was first applied in connection with the competition policy (from the *Consten/Grundig* case onwards); but it was treated as equally relevant to free movement of goods (from the *Deutsche Grammophon* case (below, para.19–04, n.19) onwards).

[149] This refinement was first introduced, for trade marks, in the *Hag I* and *Winthrop* cases and for patents, in the *Sterling Drug* case: below, paras 19–04, 19–05.

they are not to be used against the movement from one Member State to another of goods initially connected with the right-owner.

1–52 Intellectual property is not the only form of legal embargo that can affect the free movement of goods. The Court of Justice has been equally strict in appraising other forms of legal barrier, some of which have related objectives. Thus regulations under the German Wine Act 1971, which allowed "Sekt" and "Weinbrand" to be used only on German sparkling wine and brandy, were held equivalent to a restriction on imports. In Germany, the words were not specific designations or indications of origin but simply general descriptions of types of goods, and as such not within any exemption provided by art.30.[150] One permitted ground within that Article is the protection of life and health, but still the measure must be a matter of imperative necessity.[151] A Dutch Decree which had the effect of restricting importation of a drug to the enterprise which secured its clearance from the Dutch health authorities was deemed in this respect unduly restrictive.[152]

The conjoint policy concerning the free provision of services, outlined in the TFEU arts 56–62 (ex-49–55 TEC), may also have an impact upon intellectual property rights, as for instance in the broadcasting or cable-casting of copyright material. Article 49 has required the abolition of restrictions on the freedom to provide services within the Community "in respect of nationals of Member States who are established in a State ... other than that of the person for whom the services are intended". The articles do not explicitly refer to justifiable exceptions; there is no provision equivalent to art.36 (ex-art.30 TEC). Nevertheless, the Court of Justice interprets these provisions as open to reasonable limitation.[153]

(5) Rules of competition

1–53 The Rules of Competition in the Treaty that apply to private undertakings hang upon two pegs. Article 101 TFEU (ex-81 TEC) deals with restrictive practices between enterprises, art.102 TFEU (ex-82 TEC) with abuse by one or more firms of their dominant monopolistic position. A particular commercial practice could well be prohibited under both heads. Without these rules there would be little point in lowering customs and other barriers to trade imposed by states. They are vital machinery in insisting that resources should be allocated by market forces—forces that will cause efficient firms and sectors to expand at the expense of others.

---

[150] *Re German Sparkling Wines and Brandies* [1975] 1 C.M.L.R. 340.

[151] See esp. *Rewe v Bundesmonopolverwaltung für Branntwein* [1979] E.C.R. 649 ("Cassis de Dijon"); below, paras 19–13 et seq.

[152] *Officier van Justitie v De Peijper* [1976] 2 C.M.L.R. 271. For a similar decision that regulations were unduly restrictive of parallel imports, even though their object (protecting the genuineness of "Scotch" for whisky) was proper: *Procureur du Roi v Dassonville* [1974] E.C.R. 837; [1974] 2 C.M.L.R. 436. cf. *EC Commission v Belgium* [1979] E.C.R. 1761; *EC Commission v Ireland* [1982] E.C.R. 4005 ("Buy Irish"); *Exportur v Lor* [1992] E.C.R. I-5529.

[153] In relation to copyright, see *Coditel v Ciné Vog (No. 1)* [1980] E.C.R. 881.

Article 101(1) prohibits agreements between undertakings, decisions of associations of undertakings and concerted practices "which may affect trade between Member States and the object and effect of which is to prevent, restrict or distort competition within the Common Market".[154] An agreement which falls within this prohibition may nevertheless be exempted for a limited period where it can be economically justified: if it contributes towards improving the production or distribution of goods, or towards promoting technical or economic progress, whilst allowing consumers a fair share of the resulting benefit; provided also that it does not: (1) impose on the undertakings concerned restrictions which are not indispensable to the achievement of these objectives, nor (2) afford them the possibility of eliminating competition in a substantial part of the products in question. The European Commission, which is the body chiefly charged with the enforcement of the rules of competition, has power to grant such an exemption under art.101(3), after an assessment by the parties.

In its formative decision on the impact of art.101, the Court of Justice had to consider whether the electrical manufacturers, Grundig, could divide the markets for its products among distributors which each had different Member States of the EU as their exclusive territory. As well as settling that such vertical restrictions fell within the scope of the article, the court also held it offensive to add a separate mark, "Gint", to the products and have that mark registered in each state in the name of the exclusive distributor there.[155] The special purpose of this technique was to furnish each distributor with its own intellectual property repellent against the parallel importing of genuine "Grundig" products from other countries. It could not be saved by exemption under art.101(3). **1–54**

Article 102 prohibits any abuse by one or more undertakings of a dominant position within the EU (or a substantial part of it) insofar as it may affect trade between Member States.[156] There is here no explicit power to exempt a practice for its countervailing benefits, but this is implicit in the requirement that the deployment of dominant position be abusive.

To re-emphasise: some basic points about the enforcement of the competition rules are contained in Appendix 1. Their impact upon the exploitation of the various forms of intellectual property is taken up in later parts relating to the different rights, and again in general in Ch.19.[157]

(6) Relation between the two policies

The policy of securing the free movement of goods between Member States is an objective distinct from that sought by the rules of competition. **1–55**

---

[154] A list of examples is then set out. Article 101(2) declares such agreements and decisions to be "automatically void".

[155] *Consten and Grundig v EC Commission* [1996] E.C.R. 299.

[156] Again a list of examples is attached.

[157] See below, paras 7–30—7–40, 19–14—19–16.

Accordingly there are two basic differences in the scope of the relevant provisions of the Rome Treaty which call for mention at once.

(a) *Trade between Member States*

1–56 The provisions on the free movement of goods relate specifically to the import and export of goods between one Member State and another. They do not apply where the goods are being moved between a non-Member and a Member State. In *EMI v CBS*,[158] the Court of Justice held that trade mark rights in any Member State could be used to prevent the importation of goods from the United States without offending art.34 TFEU (ex 28 TEC). But in the rules of competition, the requirement that there be an effect on trade between Member States need only be consequential. Thus, if the reason why imports of CBS's records from America could be kept out of any EU country by virtue of trade mark rights was that the various EU marks had been put into EMI's hands in pursuance of an agreement, the object and effect of that agreement would have to be examined. If it brought about a significant distortion of competition in the EU by keeping out goods that otherwise would be sold somewhere within it, art.102(1) would be offended.[159] It seems that in applying this article it is not necessary to ask for proof that the goods would, if sold in part of the market, have been purchased for resale in another part; this may instead be assumed.[160]

(b) *The economic counter-balance*

1–57 From another perspective, the free movement of goods policy, when it does apply, may be more categorical. The competition rules of arts 101 and 102 allow the economic impact of an apparently impermissible practice to be viewed as a whole, since an analysis is required of the market or markets which it affects. If there are countervailing benefits, it may nevertheless be permitted—under art.101(3) by way of exemption, by finding the deployment of dominant position not, after all, to be abusive. By contrast, the manner of reading art.34 (ex-28) that was initially developed did not take account of economic justifications for using industrial property rights in ways that may result in division of markets within the totality of the EU. More recent decisions, however, bring a greater measure of differentiation to this task. National laws of intellectual property and unfair competition are examined to see whether their application affects imports from another Member State disadvantageously in comparison with domestic products. If so there is "arbitrary discrimination" within art.34.[161] It is also asked

[158] [1976] E.C.R. 811; [1976] 2 C.M.L.R. 235, see Judgment, paras 8–12; See also *Re Tylosin* [1977] 1 C.M.L.R. 460 (West German SC); Hay and Oldekop (1977) 25 Am.J.Comp.L. 120.
[159] Judgment, paras 25–39.
[160] cf. Judgment, paras 28–29 with the observations of Warner Adv-Gen [1976] 2 C.M.L.R. 235 at 258–259.
[161] See below, paras 19–15 et seq.

whether the exploitation is a normal means of realising their economic potential.

(7) Overview of the parallel importation problem

The extent to which territorially limited intellectual property rights should be an instrument to prevent the international movement of "legitimate" goods is an issue of great political moment, yet one which is wracked with conflicting policy demands. We are concerned at various points in the coming chapters with questions of present and of future law, as well as of underlying rationale. We shall return to the position from an EU perspective in the final chapter. In the meantime, the following pointers should be absorbed. **1–58**

First, "parallel importation" normally refers to the activity of an independent entrepreneur who acquires "legitimate" goods in one country (normally the cheaper) and transports them for sale in another (normally the dearer). It is a distinct phenomenon from exclusive rights to manufacture or distribute in a particular territory. The latter is a consequence of business strategies in which the developer of products finds his best hope of market penetration in an exclusive collaborator: save at egregious extremities, there is economic advantage in leaving the developer of a product or service to choose the channels of exploitation. With parallel importation, however, the initial marketing choices have already been made and price differentials (for a host of reasons) have emerged which apparently disadvantage one group of consumers. That is why legal rules which prevent parallel importation require special justification.

Secondly, within the EEA, the policy of a unified market demands the free movement of goods and the elimination of price differentials which is part of that unification process. Accordingly intellectual property rights (and rights against unfair competition, etc.) have become subject in EU law to a wide-ranging doctrine of exhaustion. It takes effect not only upon release of relevant goods in one Member State by the right-owner itself, but equally where there is any legal or economic connection between the first marketer and the right-holder. Contracts which attempt to restrict any consequent parallel importation will be void and may lead to penalties under the rules of competition.

Thirdly, at the outer perimeter of the EEA, where parallel imports are **1–59**
being brought in from third countries, there may be no exhaustion of right. The legal position needs careful examination, since it may depend on any of the following:

(1) In the view of the ECJ, regulations and directives on particular rights, which prescribe an internal exhaustion throughout the EU necessarily imply a rule of "non-exhaustion" at the EEA's external boundaries.

(2) How far it is correct may depend upon the basic scope of the right itself. In particular, external non-exhaustion may apply to intellectual property which exists as an incentive to the creation and commercialisation of new ideas (patents, copyright, etc.). However, it may have no relevance to a trade mark or similar right. Arguably a mark which is used on genuine goods cannot be infringed, since there is then no misstatement about their origin. (What should count as "genuine goods" in this context is then a matter of dispute, and will be complicated by differences in quality between the goods put out in different countries.) If there is a rule of external exhaustion for trade marks, the policy is of general impact, since a much wider range of consumer products bear marks than embody protected inventions, works or similar subject-matter.

(3) A rule of non-exhaustion must be subject to the contrary intention of the right-holder in the country of importation. If that right-holder has marketed elsewhere (or consented to that marketing) on terms that the goods may then be moved to other countries, this ought to be determinative. However, the ECJ has ruled that a sale without express restriction on subsequent movement should not be understood as carrying authorisation to move.[162] The question ought to be treated as of secondary importance, since, if an impeding notice is required, trans-national corporations will make sure it is given. Accordingly, it is a way of introducing protection against parallel importation under partial disguise; a convenient outcome to an issue that is highly controversial.

(4) Despite the current upsurge in favour of international free trade, countries are deeply uncertain about the issue of parallel importation in relation to intellectual property. None wishes itself to introduce international exhaustion unless it can secure a reciprocal move from countries with which it trades. None relishes explaining to its own consumers why internationally available goods are less expensive in other countries; nor that this differential is maintained because intellectual property rights cut out the levelling effects of bringing in the cheaper goods.

Yet, on the other hand, industrialised countries may wish to encourage their industries to set up production in de-socialising or developing countries, and will be able to do so only if there is some guarantee against consequent parallel importation from markets that will (at least initially) be cheaper. To do this by the "private" route of intellectual property barriers, rather than a public policy of quotas, has an obvious attraction (hence the European

[162] Below, paras 18–119—18–122.

Commission's bullishness on the issue). In the end, TRIPS explicitly refrained from addressing "the issue of exhaustion of intellectual property rights".[163] If countries realised that their interests on the subject were too evidently opposed then, the matter has become even more apparent since. There is simply no prospect of a co-ordinated approach at the international level in relation to any form of IPR.

[163] Article 6—unless the issue can be dressed up as concerning national treatment or most-favoured-nation treatment (arts 3, 4). "Exhaustion" is not defined and could have various meanings: see Heath (1998) 29 I.I.C. 623; Verma (1998) 29 I.I.C. 534.

CHAPTER 2

THE ENFORCEMENT OF RIGHTS

This chapter deals with the forms of relief available to the owner of intellectual property rights and with a variety of procedural factors affecting their enforcement. Although there are variations between the different specific fields, there is enough common ground to justify treating these matters in one place: a good deal of repetition can be avoided and various comparisons made. **2–01**

There is a more basic reason for prefacing the discussion of the different rights with some consideration of how they work in practice. Most commercial law is facilitative in character. It determines the effect of consensual dealings between individuals and limits their freedom of contract only where some public policy exception overrides. Accordingly, for much of the time, commercial law provides a safety-net for the execution of contracts. When the net is needed, it is frequently the contract which provides one party with a self-help remedy. Intellectual property rights are, of course, the basis of many contractual dealings. But their fundamental characteristic is their power to constrain those who have no relationship with the right-owner. They are rights that depend for their effectiveness, to a peculiar degree, upon the speed and cheapness with which they can be enforced.[1]

[1] See Harms [2004] E.I.P.R. 483.

Intellectual property actions are likely therefore to test the procedures and remedies provided by the courts. In Britain, these are matters typically within the province of the judges, who receive only a modicum of direction from Parliament. Many of the issues raised in particular cases have large implications.

2–02 The remarkable advances in information storage and copying technology mentioned in the last chapter have made piracy and counterfeiting a major and highly unscrupulous trade in many parts of the world, as well as inducing unauthorised reproduction on a very considerable scale in enterprises, organisations and the home. The challenges to intellectual property rights at so many levels have prompted the courts to expand their repertoire of civil procedures, while Parliament has been active in increasing the range and severity of criminal law in this field.

To give one claimant a more effective method of proceeding is to give it to all who can claim to be in a comparable position. Inevitably, amongst them will be those whose claims are dubious or downright false—a particularly telling consideration where the rights are intangible and may depend on complex value judgments. Accordingly there are delicate balances to be struck in most of the issues that call for examination.

In some countries, the degree of piracy has been threatening to deprive intellectual property of any meaning at all. The music, film, computer, pharmaceutical and luxury goods trades have had to set up joint organisations dedicated to combating infringement on a commercial scale. They have had rough treks uphill—wrestling with conspiracies of silence, official disinterest, organised criminal gangs, courts unable or unwilling to understand or assist, fly-by-night copy-dens, stark thuggery—in their battles for their own rights and protection of their licensees and distributors. Much of the effort which currently goes into inter-governmental negotiation on the recognition of intellectual property is concerned with this unrefined, but critically important, aspect of the business of intellectual property exploitation and enforcement.

2–03 The TRIPS Agreement, indeed, sets out a new consensus on the measures which must exist in the legal systems of WTO countries in order to give effective meaning to substantive rights.[2] In a book on UK law it is not necessary to detail the whole set of TRIPS articles on the subject, because they read as an international ratification of so much of what this country, particularly over the last 30 years, has striven to put into place. Overall, TRIPS calls for enforcement procedures which permit effective action against intellectual property infringement, "including expeditious remedies to prevent infringements and remedies which constitute a deterrent to

[2] See Dreier in Beier and Schricker, p.248.

further infringements"; at the same time the measures must avoid being barriers to legitimate trade and provide safeguards against abuse.[3]

Under TRIPS, civil process must be provided which may lead to injunctive as well as compensatory relief and delivery up for destruction of infringing material and means for producing it.[4] It is permissible to require information about the source and distribution of infringing goods or services.[5] It is mandatory to have provisional procedures for preventing infringement of intellectual property rights and preserving relevant evidence.[6] Against the importation of counterfeit trade mark goods and pirated copyright goods, there must be arrangements for customs seizure.[7] The activities must be treated as serious criminal offences, with accompanying measures for seizure, forfeiture and destruction.[8] Responding to these obligations the EU passed the IP Enforcement Directive of April 29, 2004,[9] requiring Member States to provide fair and equitable remedies which must also be "effective, proportionate and dissuasive". Implemented by Regulations in the United Kingdom prior to the deadline of April 29, 2006,[10] the Directive has required few changes in procedures except in relation to damages. Regulation 3 incorporates verbatim the wording of art.13 of the Directive, to the effect that where the defendant knew or should have known that he was engaged in infringing activity, the court should award damages proportionate to the "actual prejudice" suffered. "Actual prejudice" is defined to include not only "negative economic consequences" but also "moral prejudice" suffered by the claimant.[11]

---

[3] TRIPS Agreement art.41, which, with arts 42, 43 and 48, specifies a number of due process requirements: fairness and equity; no undue cost, complexity, time-limits or delays; right to be heard and to give evidence; right to a prompt, reasoned, written decision; judicial review; written notice of claims; legal representation; protection of confidential information; discovery of evidence held by the other side; indemnification against undue enforcement.

[4] TRIPS Agreement arts 44–46.

[5] TRIPS Agreement art.47.

[6] TRIPS Agreement art.50, providing at the same time a set of specific safeguards against abuse: after ex parte proceedings a prompt right for the defendant to be heard, speedy procedures for determination of the allegations, compensation for unjustified relief.

[7] TRIPS Agreement arts 51–60 (and see also PIP art.9; Berne Convention art.16).

[8] TRIPS Agreement art.61. Other infringements may be the subject of criminal procedure, "in particular where they are committed wilfully and on a commercial scale".

[9] Directive 2004/48/EC; Cornish, Drexl, Hilty & Kur [2003] E.I.P.R. 447; Huniar [2006] E.I.P.R. 92. Also see the Commission's strategy for enforcement of IPRs in third countries: [2005] OJ C129/3.

[10] Intellectual Property (Enforcement, etc.) Regulations 2006 (SI 2006/1028), which also take the opportunity of effecting certain changes to UK legislation which were not required by the Directive.

[11] On the Directive generally, see Kur (2004) 35 I.I.C. 821; Massa and Strowel [2004] E.I.P.R. 244.

1. Types of Proceeding

2–04 This section takes up some basic characteristics of the different methods of protecting intellectual property. It treats in turn civil actions, criminal proceedings, administrative procedures and measures of self-help. Of these, civil actions are the most central and many additional aspects of them are dealt with elsewhere in this book. The other three categories are dealt with only in passing at later points.

(1) Civil causes of action

2–05 For the most part, the acts of infringement with which we are concerned are treated as tortious invasions of property.[12] Questions accordingly arise about which people have title to sue, whom they may proceed against and which courts they may use. These are dealt with first. Then some consideration is given to the more general economic torts, particularly where they may help claimants who otherwise have no sufficient basis for action.

(a) *Owners and licensees of intellectual property*

2–06 The obvious person to bring proceedings for infringement of one of the statutory types of intellectual property is the owner at law (or one of them). A person with a purely equitable title (under a trust or a specifically enforceable contract) is permitted to bring a motion for interim relief, but he may not proceed further without joining the legal owner.[13] A person lacking title when he institutes an action cannot cure the defect by subsequently taking an assignment.[14]

Where the right is the subject of a grant by the state, the fact that the proprietor is not registered as such may introduce complications. In the case of patents and trade marks, the true owner is entitled to sue but risks failing to secure damages or an account of profits if not registering his title (for example, by failing to register an assignment).[15]

In the case of patents, registered marks, copyright and unregistered design right, an exclusive licensee is entitled to bring the proceedings, joining the proprietor as a defendant if he will not be joined as claimant.[16] In other

[12] Breach of confidence, however, requires special consideration: see Ch.8 below. See generally, Carty, *An Analysis of the Economic Torts* (2001).

[13] *PRS v London Theatre of Varieties* [1924] A.C. 1; *Baxter International v NPLB* [1998] R.P.C. 250; but note the modern rules on the assignment of future copyright: below, para.13–12.

[14] *Mekon Israel v ABC News* [1994] E.I.P.R. D–30.

[15] PA 1977 s.68 (see below, para.7–17); TMA 1994 s.25(4).

[16] PA 1977 s.67; TMA 1994 s.31; CDPA 1988 ss.101, 102, 234, 235. The licence must exclude even the licensor and must exist when the claim form (formerly the writ) is issued: *Procter & Gamble v Peaudouce* [1989] 1 F.S.R. 180 CA. In the case of copyright and design right, it must comply with the formalities prescribed in CDPA 1988 ss.92, 225. Beyond this it is a matter of interpreting each licence to decide whether, and if so in what respect, it is exclusive: *Morton-Norwich v Intercen (No. 2)* [1981] F.S.R. 337; *Biotrading & Financing v Biohit* [1998] F.S.R. 109 CA. In each case there are provisions concerning the assessment of damages; in the case of copyright and design right these are elaborate.

cases, licensees cannot themselves sue for infringement of intellectual property,[17] but must rely upon their licensors to take action (and should ensure that the licence includes appropriate provisions requiring the licensor to do so). This can be difficult and cumbersome, particularly for an organisation which exists to provide right-owners with collective protection.

A representative action may be pursued, for instance, against a defendant who has allegedly been selling pirated tapes of copyright sound recordings. Thus the association of British record producers, British Phonographic Industries Ltd, could proceed in the name of one member, suing on behalf of itself and all other members. In the circumstances, the court would order not only an injunction but an inquiry as to damages suffered by all the members.[18] However, a representative action for passing off brought by Chocosuisse, a trade association set up to protect the interests of Swiss chocolate manufacturers, was not permitted as the association did not manufacture or sell Swiss chocolate.[19]

(b) *Defendants*

The law relating to each form of intellectual property defines the nature of the exclusive right in terms of content and business activity. For instance, the invention that is the subject of a patent is defined principally in the claims of the patent specification; it is then an infringement to make, sell or use this invention in the various ways prescribed in the Patents Act 1977.[20] A person who performs such an infringing act is liable in respect of it and anyone else who collaborates in a common design to do the act will be liable as a joint tortfeasor.[21] This is today a principle of growing importance in securing relief against all the parties involved, including those who themselves may be doing nothing within the jurisdiction.[22] A person, who, in supplying an infringing article or some essential component of it, acts solely outside the jurisdiction, will not thereby be infringing a British intellectual property right. However, if he is collaborating with a person who acts within **2–07**

[17] They may, however, be able to sustain an action for the tort of unlawful interference with trade: *PCUK v Diamond Shamrock* [1981] F.S.R. 427. For an exception, see TMA 1994 s.30.

[18] *EMI Records v Riley* [1981] F.S.R. 503. Equally an action may be pursued against a represented class in which an ex parte interim injunction and associated relief may be ordered: *EMI Records v Kaidhail* [1985] F.S.R. 36.

[19] [1999] R.P.C. 826 CA.

[20] See below, paras 6–09 et seq.

[21] A director of a company or other real person in the background will be personally liable for torts committed on the company's behalf where he has ordered or procured their commission: see *MCA Records v Charly Records* [2002] F.S.R. 401 CA; cf. *Cantor Fitzgerald v Tradition (UK)* [2000] R.P.C. 95 at para.89. For the responsibility of a subsidiary which agrees to procure adherence of an associated company to a settlement agreement: *Bargain Pages v Midland Independent Newspapers* [2004] F.S.R. 101.

[22] See above, para.1–30.

the jurisdiction, he becomes jointly liable for the latter's infringement.[23] Because of their common design, he will not merely be facilitating but will be procuring the doing of the act.[24]

2–08 In order to begin English proceedings against a defendant, the court must have jurisdiction and this is determined by complex and changing rules.[25] Provided the requirements for jurisdiction are satisfied, a defendant must respond with a defence which provides a comprehensive response to the claims made and has a real prospect of succeeding at trial.[26] Failing that, the defendant faces the prospect of an order for summary judgment, which will normally include orders of the same kind as are made after full trial of an issue: injunction, inquiry as to damages, etc.[27]

2–09 In addition, an employer is vicariously liable for torts committed by an employee in the course of his employment,[28] but a person who commissions work from an independent contractor is not normally placed under the same responsibility.[29] The distinction is often important where the production of some species of intellectual property is concerned. Many authors, composers and artists, and some inventors, work independently from those who take up their ideas for exploitation. In the field of copyright, as we shall see, the absence of vicarious liability in such cases is compensated for by other means: to "authorise" an act of infringement in that field is treated as itself amounting to infringement.[30] Although the action for breach of confidence arises in equity and not in tort, it is probable that the same principles of vicarious liability would apply.[31]

It is not always easy to determine whether a person is employed, nor whether he is acting within the course of his employment.[32] The principles of the law in general apply in the context of intellectual property rights, even where they are mentioned in particular statutes.[33] It is not therefore appropriate to give a different definition of "employment" by reference to

[23] *Unilever v Gillette* [1989] R.P.C. 583 at 608, per Mustill L.J.; *Mönlycke v Procter & Gamble* [1992] R.P.C. 21 at 29, per Dillon L.J. Cf. the case of successive infringement down a distribution chain, where nonetheless there was no common design: *Def Lepp v Stuart-Brown* [1986] R.P.C. 273. See further below, para.2–75. A parent company must engage in furthering a common design to be jointly liable for infringements committed by a subsidiary: *Mead Corp v Riverwood Multiple Packaging* [1997] F.S.R. 484.

[24] *Belegging, Lavender v Witten* [1979] F.R.S. 59 at 66, per Buckley L.J.

[25] See below, paras 2–72 et seq.

[26] Civil Procedure Rules (CPR) Pt 16.5.

[27] CPR Pt 24.

[28] Vicarious liability of the employer in no way exempts the employee from his personal liability.

[29] For the exceptional cases (not of significance to intellectual property), see *Clerk and Lindsell on Torts* 19th edn (2006), para.6–53.

[30] See below, paras 12–18—12–20; cf. "indirect" infringement of a patent, below, paras 6–17—6–19; and the general tort of incitement or procurement, below, para.2–14.

[31] *Coulthard v South Australia* (1995) 63 S.A.S.R. 531.

[32] For a detailed consideration of the case law, in the context of a design right ownership dispute, see the judgment of Waller L.J. in *Ultraframe UK Ltd v Fielding* [2004] R.P.C. 36 CA at [15–21].

[33] *Ultraframe UK v Fielding* [2004] R.P.C. 36 CA.

the context of the particular statute. Employment may be a part-time, as well as a full-time, relationship.

Traditionally the governing characteristic has been that the employer is entitled to control the work that is done in detail. But many types of work relationship are now treated as employment, even though the employee exercises managerial or professional skills under no regular supervision. In those cases other indicators are relied upon. Typical attributes of employment today are: payment of regular sums as a wage or salary, rather than lump sums for given jobs; income tax deductions under Schedule E on the PAYE basis; joint contribution to a pension scheme; and joint national insurance contributions as for an employed person.[34]

Much is accordingly determined by the relationship that the two sides set out to establish. Tribunals have to settle the issue where the practical arrangements still leave ambiguities. A composer who is obliged to supply a music publisher with one song a month will be an independent contractor if his return is to come solely from royalties and none of the other attributes of employment are present. But the contrary will likely be the case if he receives a monthly salary subject to PAYE and national insurance deductions, even though he is entitled to copyright royalties in addition. What an employee does in the course of his employment is determined by what he is employed to do. The employer may not restrict the scope of vicarious responsibility by instructing the employee not to commit torts in the course of those duties.[35] If a broadcasting organisation employs a commentator who makes a slanderous statement, the organisation remains liable however firm its rule against defamation. However, as we shall see, not everything that a journalist or business executive writes is done in his employment.[36] There must be sufficient connection between his job and what he has written.

(c) *High Court and county court*

In England and Wales civil proceedings for the enforcement of intellectual property have traditionally been brought in the Chancery Division of the High Court, patent matters being required to go before the Patents Court within that Division.[37] It is from this superior jurisdiction that claimants have been able to secure the range of interim and final relief which makes civil process their usual resort. **2–10**

At the same time the county court jurisdiction in tort, traditionally limited **2–11**

[34] On the question generally, see *Clerk and Lindsell on Torts* 19th edn (2006), paras 6.03 *et seq.*; Sweet & Maxwell's *Encyclopedia of Employment Law*, I B, Chs 1, 2.

[35] *Clerk and Lindsell*, paras 6.26 et seq.

[36] See below, paras 7–04, 13–05, 13–06. The same question arises in deciding whether intellectual property belongs to an employee or his employer.

[37] For patent infringement, revocation and related claims, see below, para.6–23 and Cornish and Llewelyn (2004) 23 I.I.C. Studies, Ch.3. The position in the jurisdictions of Scotland and Northern Ireland should be sought in specialist works on the various rights.

in amount, has been used for a few intellectual property matters.[38] This has changed over recent years in two ways, one general and the other specific:

(1) Proceedings may not be started in the High Court unless the value of the claim is more than £15,000,[39] and where issued in the High Court with an estimated value of less than £50,000 the proceedings will generally be transferred to the county court.[40] County courts in general have power to grant interim and other injunctions, though not "freezing" (formerly *Mareva*) injunctions or search (formerly *Anton Piller*) orders.[41]
(2) Having regard to the notoriously high cost of full-fledged litigation over patents and similar rights,[42] in 1989 a Patents County Court with a specialist judge was established in London. Originally this PCC had jurisdiction to try patent and design issues, and ancillary questions,[43] but this is now extended also to trade mark claims[44] (including Community trade marks).[45] The purpose of creating this court was to provide a cheaper forum for the resolution of less complex or valuable intellectual property disputes.[46] It has power to grant orders freezing assets and for the seizure of infringing articles. There are no limits on monetary awards or special restrictions on costs related to such awards.[47] The Patents County Court has sought to restrict recoverable costs and to advance the preparation of actions. Its flow

[38] e.g. for obliging pubs and restaurants to pay for performing copyright music or recordings.

[39] High Court and County Courts Jurisdiction Order 1991 (SI 1991/724), as amended in 1993, 1995, 1999, 2001 and 2005. By Practice Direction 7, a claim should be started in the High Court if the claimant believes it should be heard by a High Court judge because of its complexity or value.

[40] In special circumstances, the amount may be even more: PD 29 para.2.3. There are certain cases, such as seizure orders of material infringing copyright, designs and trade marks, where there is no jurisdictional limit in any county court.

[41] County Courts Remedies Regulations 1991 (SI 1991/1222), allowing limited transfer to the High Court for such orders.

[42] See Intellectual Property Rights and Innovation (Cmnd.9117, 1983), pp.20–22; Report of the Oulton Committee on Patent Litigation (1987).

[43] CDPA 1988 ss.288–291; Courts and Legal Services Act 1990 s.2(1); Patents County Court (Designation and Jurisdiction) Order 1994 (SI 1994/1609). On jurisdiction, see *McDonald v Graham* [1994] R.P.C. 407 CA; *Chaplin Patents v Group Lotus, The Times*, January 24, 1994, CA. See generally the Patents Court Guide, issued July 7, 2008.

[44] The High Court and County Court Jurisdiction (Amendment) Order 2005 (SI 2005/587) granted the Patents County Court jurisdiction over registered trade marks.

[45] CPR PD 63, para.24.1, states that the Patents County Court is a designated Community trade mark court under art.91(1) of the CTM Regulation, as now provided by the Community Trade Mark Regulations 2006 (SI 2006/1027). The Jackson Review of Civil Litigation Costs (2010), Pt 25 , Ch.4.5, urges that copyright claims should also be brought into the jurisdiction.

[46] In *Halliburton v Smith International* [2006] R.P.C. 2 Pumfrey J. observed: "These proceedings started life in the County Court. The hearing before me, which lasted 13 days with substantial pre-reading, revealed the subject matter of the patents was complex and more than justified the 15-day estimate that the trial ultimately received. The proceedings were not suitable for the County Court and should not have been started there." (at 37).

[47] As well as barristers and solicitors, patent attorneys have rights of audience before it.

of business enables it to act promptly. Nonetheless it continues to attract criticism from users and a recent review has recommended improvements both for small claims (for estimated values up to £5,000) and for "fast track" litigation (£5,000 to £25,000).[48] Its existence undoubtedly acted as a spur to the Patents High Court, which did much, even in advance of the general "Woolf Reforms" of April 1999, to control the course of patent and other intellectual property proceedings in the interests of efficiency,[49] including the introduction of the streamlined procedure with written evidence only, no requirement to give disclosure, no experiments, limited cross-examination and a trial normally not more than one day in duration.[50] In *Canady v Erbe Electromedizin*[51] Pumfrey J. ordered a split trial on validity and infringement, with the latter to be decided under the streamlined procedure, commenting: "[t]hose of the profession who admire the German way of doing things will be able to compare a streamline trial of the issue of infringement with the manner in which the same issue would be disposed of, let us say, in Düsseldorf and draw what one can only hope will be helpful comparisons."[52]

(d) *General torts covering economic loss*

The common law developed a number of heads of liability which are usually grouped together as economic torts. Two of these—passing off and injurious falsehood—are directly germane to our subject and are dealt with in Pt V.[53] Here, however, mention must be made of torts which may effectively broaden the range of people who can be held responsible when someone interferes with intellectual property or proposes to do so. In particular, these torts have some capacity to go beyond the rules on claimants and defendants which have just been discussed. Their general characteristics are that the defendant must be acting intentionally or recklessly; that the claimant **2–12**

[48] See the Jackson Review of Civil Litigation Costs (2010) Pt 25, Ch.4), which also proposes that further county courts should have IP jurisdiction. In connection with this, see Thambisetty [2010] E.I.P.R. 143.

[49] The TRIPS Agreement obliges WTO Member States to provide fair and equitable civil procedures (art.42), which are prescribed in considerable detail (arts 43–50): above, para.2–03.

[50] See the Patents Court Guide, issued November 12, 2003, para.10. Also, see generally the Practice Direction supplementing CPR Pt 63. In *Impro Licensing's Sarl Patent* [2006] R.P.C. 517 Pumfrey J. noted, at 525: "The decision to use the streamlined procedure is an objective one to be arrived at on all the material. There are no presumptions" (for instance, that once proposed by one party it should be used in the absence of a convincing objection from the other).

[51] [2006] F.S.R. 10.

[52] [2006] F.S.R. 10.

[53] See below, Ch.17.

must suffer damage, or must be about to suffer it; and that they will not apply if some ground of justification is open to the defendant.[54] Nevertheless, the House of Lords now considers it incorrect to regard these torts as examples of some larger generalisation, which might classify as wrongful all conduct aiming deliberately to contribute to economic injury suffered by a claimant as wrongful unless justifiable.[55] If that were indeed so, the organiser of a sporting or similar spectacle might have a right to sue outside observers who were somehow able to exploit its economic potential[56]; the exclusive licensee of a musical or dramatic performance might have a cause of action against an audience member who bootlegged the performance by undercover recording[57]; the members of a business cartel who, in seeking to damage a rival by warning potential suppliers to that rival that if they did so they risked losing future business with cartel members[58]; and so on. The refusal to adopt a general principle for business torts concentrates attention on the characteristics of each known form, as outlined in the next paragraphs.

2–13 (i) **Conspiracy.** It is tortious for two or more people to combine together with the purpose of injuring the claimant and so to cause him damage. However, the conspirators must either intend to use unlawful means (the narrow form of the tort), or else intend to act without employing any such means, but having as their predominant motive to injure the claimant, rather than to pursue their own selfish interests (the wider form).[59] Thus, under the narrow form, it is tortious for two or more people to agree to secure the commission of an infringement of intellectual property, as of other unlawful acts.[60] This may occur if one or more of the conspirators are to perform the infringing act or equally if a third party is to be induced to do so.[61]

---

[54] No attempt can be made to present a full treatment of the torts that are mentioned. Good analyses can be found, e.g. *Clerk and Lindsell on Torts* 19th edn (2006), Ch.25; Carty (2001).

[55] *Douglas v Hello! (No. 3)* [2009] A.C. 1 HL

[56] Action disallowed by the HC, Australia, in *Victoria Park Racing v Taylor* (1937) 58 C.L.R. 479; see above, para.1–16.

[57] Action by the exclusive licensee disallowed in *RCA v Pollard* [1983] Ch 135 CA and *Oren v Red Box Toy* [1999] F.S.R. 785; both firmly approved in *Douglas v Hello! (No. 3)*, above, n.55. The effect of these decisions was to confine any right of action to that given to owners of IPRs in the performances by statute.

[58] Action disallowed in *Mogul SS v McGregor Gow* [1892] A.C. 25; above, para.1–20.

[59] The wider form has no special relevance to intellectual property matters; but see *Jarman & Platt v Barget* [1977] F.S.R. 260 at 277–282 CA. In the context of the tort of interfering with economic relations by unlawful means ((v) below), the House of Lords condemned the distinction between primarily intending to advance one's own trading position and primarily intending to injure another, as amounting to no more than two sides of the same coin: see Lord Hoffmann, *Douglas v Hello!* [2008] A.C. at [134–135].

[60] For what may constitute "unlawful means", see *Clerk and Lindsell*, paras 25–121—25–124. Breach of confidence is one form: *Spermolin v Winter*, *Guardian*, June 22, 1962; such a claim failed at first instance in *Faccenda Chicken v Fowler* [1985] 1 All E.R. 724.

[61] For the application of this tort where the wrong is infringement of a patent, see below, para.6–17.

(ii) **Inciting or procuring commission of a tort.** While there has been recognition that such a basis for liability exists,[62] it appears that it is not an action appreciably wider than that of joint tortfeasance.[63] It is necessary to show more than that the defendant facilitated the doing of an act. He must, generally speaking, induce, incite or persuade a specific infringer and must procure a particular infringement.[64] In the *Amstrad* case, a company was manufacturing and selling a twin-deck tape-recorder, knowing the likelihood of its use for home-taping which would infringe copyright. The company was nonetheless not a procurer of any infringement,[65] any more than that it was a joint tortfeasor, or a person who incited the commission of crime.[66]As already mentioned, in the law of copyright there is a statutory proscription against "authorising" and "permitting" types of IP infringement[67]; and in the Patents Act 1977 there is an elaborately defined notion of "indirect" infringement.[68] In their particular fields, these are extensions of the strictly limited common law conception. They operate to benefit IP owners and, if the relevant statute goes so far, also exclusive licensees.[69] 2–14

(iii) **Inducing or procuring breach of contract.** It is tortious for a defendant, D, to induce T to break a contract which D knows he has with a claimant, C, so as to cause C loss. This could occur, for instance, where a licensee of intellectual property was persuaded to depart from the limits of his licence and so to infringe. It is also a form of liability that may apply to indirect recipients of confidential information.[70] In the twentieth century, the tort was allowed to develop so as to cover the case where D indirectly procures the breach of T and C's contract, for instance by getting S not to supply T with the materials necessary for performing T's contract with C—a situation in which T is prevented from carrying out the contract, rather than induced not to do so.[71] It was also extended to inducements to T to break the contract without realising, and to T's failure to perform it where, because of a limitation of liability in it, T will not be responsible for making good C's loss.[72] Subsequently, the House of Lords insisted that the nature of the tort 2–15

[62] *Law Debenture v Ural Caspian Oil* [1995] 1 All E.R. 157.
[63] For which, see above, para.2–07.
[64] *Lavender BV v Witten Industrial Diamonds* [1979] F.S.R. 59 at 60, per Buckley L.J.; *Dow Chemical v Spence Bryson* [1982] F.S.R. 397 CA; *Kalman v P.C.L. Packaging* [1982] F.S.R. 406; *Cadbury v Ulmer* [1988] F.S.R. 385.
[65] *CBS Songs v Amstrad* [1988] 2 All E.R. 484 at 496–497.
[66] [1988] 2 All E.R. 484 at 497.
[67] See below, paras 12–18—12–20. In the *Amstrad* case [1988] 2 All E.R. 484, the selling of the tape-recorders did not amount to "authorising" infringement.
[68] See below, paras 6–17—6–19: but there was already some authority concerning the common law tort in the patents field: ibid.
[69] See above, n.57.
[70] For its relevance in that field, see below, para.8–06.
[71] See esp. *Douglas v Hello! (No. 3)* [2009] A.C. 1 at 168–182.
[72] *National Phonograph v Edison Bell* [1908] 1 Ch.335 CA; *Merkur Island Shipping v Laughton* [1983] A.C. 570 HL; and where the claimant's loss is still potential: *Law Debenture v Ural Caspian Oil* [1995] 1 All E.R. 157 CA.

is secondary: liability cannot arise unless the third party is induced to break a contract with the claimant. Cases where the defendant has prevented T from carrying out the contract involve primary liability by the defendant: he or she must must be shown to have interfered with the claimant's economic relations by unlawful means.[73]

2–16 (iv) **Wrongfully interfering with business or other economic relations by unlawful means.** Early instances under this head involved threats to injure T physically, causing him to do business with D rather than C.[74] Subsequently, the tort also arose where D threatened to break contracts with T, for instance, by strike action.[75] Equally the liability arises if D tells T lies which induce T not to deal with C.[76] The tort is thus concerned with primary liability arising from the unlawful act of the defendant, rather than secondary liability that is characteristic of inducing breach of a contract between another (T) the claimant (C).[77] The defendant's unlawful act may consist of a tort or a breach of contract. Thus, an importer of illicit recordings of copyright music committed the tort of infringement against the copyright owner; but equally he could be sued by the collecting society which licensed legitimate recordings of the music and took a contractual commission on the licence fees.[78] It is less clear how far the unlawful means may consist of a criminal offence or breach of statutory duty. At a time when the only express protection given against the unauthorised recording of a performance was by criminal law, the Court of Appeal was prepared to hold that the consequent injury to the expectations of the performers' recording company justified interim relief.[79] However, later the same court held that it was not enough to show that a contract had been rendered less valuable because of criminal activity. The crime must be one intended by Parliament to give rise to civil responsibility to the claimant. The Performers' Protection Acts were interpreted as giving this protection to performers, but not to the recording companies with which they had exclusive contracts.[80] In *Douglas v Hello! (No.3)*,[81] Lord Hoffmann, the leading voice for the majority of the House of Lords, took as his starting point the desirability of maintaining an expansive view of what would count as

[73] See below, para.2–16.

[74] *Tarleton v McGawley* (1794) Peake 279.

[75] *Rookes v Barnard* [1964] A.C. 1129 HL.

[76] *Lonrho v Fayed* [1990] 2 Q.B. 479 CA, and see [1992] 1 A.C. 448 HL.

[77] See above, n.55. See also *Merkur Island* [1983] A.C. 570; *Indata Equipment Supplies v ACL* [1998] F.S.R. 248 CA; cf. *Lonrho v Shell* [1982] A.C. 173 HL, *Fayed* [1990] 2 Q.B. 479.

[78] *Carlin v Collins* [1979] F.S.R. 548.

[79] *Ex p. Island Records* [1978] Ch.122. See also *Gouriet v Union of Post Office Workers* [1978] A.C. 435 HL; but cf. the criticism in *Shell* [1982] A.C. 173 at 187 per Lord Diplock.

[80] *RCA v Pollard* [1983] Ch.135; *Rickless v United Artists* [1987] F.S.R. 362; for the present protection of performers, see below, paras 14–30 et seq. For a similar problem in relation to patents, see *Oren v Red Box Toy* [1999] F.S.R. 785.

[81] Above, n.55. The final appeal took the unusual course of considering the nature of the tort of causing injury by unlawful means in relation to three cases with very different facts, the other two being *OBG v Allan* and *Mainstream Properties v Young*.

"unlawful means"; a narrow approach would lead to extensions of the wrong by reference to the "intent" of the defendant, drawn along the unrealistic line between intending to improve one's own economic position and intending to injure the claimant.[82] The opposing view, adumbrated by Lord Walker, considered it desirable, and also more consistent with previous authority, to confine the concept of "unlawful means" in relation to this tort.[83] The outcome of the case turned on the circumstances in which an obligation of confidence could amount to unlawful means; and to that we return in Ch.9. [84]

(v) **Duties of care.** In addition to the discussion of intentional economic torts within the sphere of our subject, there have also been attempts to argue that failure to prevent others from infringing intellectual property amounts to the tort of negligence. They have not met with success. A printer who produced labels for a skin cream to the order of a customer without knowing or inquiring about the latter's proposed use of them, would be liable for any infringement of copyright; but he did not have an additional duty to discover whether the customer would engage in passing off skin cream as the claimant's.[85] Likewise, in the twin-deck cassette recorder case, Amstrad owed no duty to ensure that those who purchased its tape-recorders did not make infringing copies on them. Those who merely facilitate infringement by others, without controlling what they do or positively encouraging it, are not to be made liable by this route.[86] **2–17**

(2) Criminal proceedings

It is a distinctive characteristic of the English judicial system that civil and criminal modes of redress are largely kept separate.[87] In our field of interest, most claimants make use of the civil process, partly because its technique **2–18**

[82] Above, n.55 at [45–65]. Although in the result a member of the Lords' minority, Lord Nicholls adopted a similar approach to "unlawful means"; see at [141–163]. He referred to the "instrumentality" of the injury to the third party—a causative concept which he preferred to understand broadly.

[83] Above at n.55 [266–170], wondering whether Lord Hoffmann's approach, "if taken out of context, might be regarded as so flexible as to be of limited utility". Note also the CA's refusal to find the defendant liable: [2006] Q.B. 125.

[84] Below, paras 9–21—9–22.

[85] *Paterson Zochonis v Merfarken Packaging* [1983] F.S.R. 273 CA.

[86] *Amstrad* case [1988] 2 All E.R. 484 at 497–498. See also *Western Front v Vestron* [1987] F.S.R. 66.

[87] If anything this tendency became more marked from the late nineteenth century onwards. There is now some movement back. Under the Powers of Criminal Courts Act 1973 ss.35–38 (as amended by the Criminal Justice Act 1988 s.72), a court, on convicting an offender, may order him to pay compensation in respect of personal injury and other loss or damage. Magistrates' courts may order up to £1,000 compensation and a Crown Court has the alternative of making a criminal bankruptcy order (ss.39–41). Compensation orders have been made with some regularity in favour of consumers misled by false trade descriptions. In *R. v Thomson Holidays* [1974] Q.B. 592, it was held that a series of orders could be made in favour of different customers misled by the same travel brochure.

and atmosphere are appropriate to the assertion of private property rights amongst business people, and partly because the types of remedy—in particular the injunction (interim and permanent) and damages—are more useful than punishment in the name of the state.[88] The very power that civil remedies generate has been one reason for circumspection in conferring civil rights. Accordingly there are some activities on the periphery of our sphere where the relevant statutes only specify criminal sanctions.[89] This remains true of various forms of misleading advertising and labelling that may be injurious to competitors as well as consumers (and constitute offences under the Trade Descriptions Act 1968 and allied legislation).[90] In this connection it is worth noting the competence of any citizen (in England and Wales and Northern Ireland) to institute criminal proceedings.[91] Under the Trade Descriptions Act this means that in theory a competitor, who objects to a misdescription on a rival's product, may institute a prosecution, just as may a consumer, a police officer or a trading standards inspector.

There are some criminal offences that cover the same ground as rights of intellectual property. In these cases the right-owner usually prefers the civil route—for the reasons already mentioned, and because of two further factors:

(1) There is no possibility in criminal procedure of securing an interim order to desist from conduct pending the trial (which will take at least weeks or more likely months to mount); nor are there pre-trial procedures, such as disclosure of documents, for the extraction of information from a defendant.
(2) There is a high burden of proof on the prosecution in criminal proceedings: the defendant must be shown to be guilty beyond reasonable doubt, and not merely (as for most civil issues) on a balance of probabilities. This quantum of proof may be specially hard to demonstrate if the type of offence requires proof of *mens rea* on the part of the defendant, for example that he knew, or had reason to believe, that he was committing an infringing act or other offence.

(a) *Offences specifically concerning intellectual property*

2–19 Offences are most prominent in relation to infringement of trade marks and of copyright, where there is a long history of conferring special remedies

[88] The decision to prefer criminal proceedings, where they are open, remains with the right-owner, not the court: *Thames & Hudson v DACS* [1995] F.S.R. 153.
[89] For the unauthorised recording of performances, see above, para.2–17.
[90] Discussed below, in para.17–03.
[91] But some crimes are exceptional in requiring the consent of the Attorney-General or Director of Public Prosecutions. The Law Commission has expressed the view that this should apply to all prosecutions under the CDPA 1988 and any which might in future become available for wrongful use or disclosure of trade secrets: Consultation Paper No. 149 (1997); Harbottle [1998] E.I.P.R. 317.

against pirates.[92] The Copyright, Designs and Patents Act 1988 creates a series of summary offences concerning infringements of copyright. These cover the same sphere as "secondary infringement" of copyright, and in the case of the more serious instances may now be prosecuted either summarily or on indictment.[93] Likewise, the trade marks legislation now provides a similar set of offences against the counterfeiting of registered trade marks,[94] both on goods within the registration and even, in cases of improper dilution, on other goods.[95]

While such offences do not cover everything that is actionable as infringement in civil proceedings, their ambit is much wider than anything applicable to patents, registered designs or confidential information.[96] Since the first two are forms of protection which depend upon official grant or registration, there are specific offences relating to this procedure. It is in each case an offence to secure false entries in the register[97] and to make an unauthorised claim to the right.[98] However, no criminal liability attaches specifically to the activity of an infringer, as is equally the case with unregistered design right.

(b) *Conspiracy to defraud*[99]

To some extent the lacuna just noted may be filled by the general crime of conspiracy to defraud.[100] This may be committed not only where those agreeing together are proposing to acquire property dishonestly, but also when they seek to obtain some other pecuniary advantage or try to deceive a person into acting contrary to his duty. Thus in *Scott v Metropolitan Police Commissioner*[101] there was a conspiracy to defraud the owners of film copyright by bribing cinema employees to hand over films so that they could be surreptitiously copied and returned. The House of Lords confirmed that the owners were defrauded by this practice, even though no one was **2–20**

92 See below, para.10–03.
93 CDPA 1988 ss.107–110, and see below, para.12–29; also Tapper in Vaver and Bently, Ch.19.
94 *R. v Johnstone* [2003] 3 All E.R. 884 HL; Rahmatin (2004) 67 M.L.R. 670. On the TMA 1994 s.92, Lindsay and Chacksfield [2003] E.I.P.R. 388..
95 TMA 1994 ss.92 et seq. It is no longer a defence to show that other matter dispelled any potential in the mark to deceive or cause confusion; so it would now be an offence to sell a product as a "brand copy", specifying the brand. Also, a market trader who bought designer goods at low prices from an unknown person could not rely on the innocence defence in s.92(5) TMA 1994: *West Sussex CC v Kahraman* [2006] All E.R. (D).
96 As to the last, see below, paras 8–55, 8–56.
97 See PA 1977 s.109; TMA 1994 s.94; RDA 1949 s.34.
98 See PA 1977 s.110 (s.111 covers false claims to have applied for a patent); TMA 1994 s.95; RDA 1949 s.35. There are also offences connected with secrecy directions in PA 1977 ss.22(9), 23(3); RDA 1949 s.34.
99 See generally, e.g. Ashworth, *Principles of Criminal Law* 5th edn (2006) Ch.11.
100 For the preservation of this common law form of conspiracy, see Criminal Law Act 1977 s.5.
101 [1975] A.C. 819. See further Cornish (1975) 6 I.I.C. 43 at 57.

deceived by the operation.[102] The decision does not depend upon the fact that the actual copying was itself a summary offence,[103] and so it might apply if the subject-matter were some form of intellectual property other than copyright.

There is some doubt where the subject-matter is confidential information.[104] In *DPP v Withers*[105] the accused conspirators induced bank officers to provide information about their customers by pretending to be acting for another bank; they then supplied the information to their own clients. This may be chargeable as a conspiracy to defraud, either if the information is itself treated as close enough to property to be in the line of *Scott's* case, or because persons are being actively deceived into breaking a duty. However, it is not clear whether the latter approach extends beyond deceiving public officers and covers deceiving those acting for private institutions such as banks.[106]

(c) *Crimes and civil relief*

2–21 As already noted, the mere fact that a person is the victim of a crime does not entitle him to civil relief such as damages or an injunction.[107] While accepting that the Trade Descriptions Act 1968 gave no civil causes of action, Lord Diplock nevertheless encouraged the judges to look to the range of the criminal law in determining the scope of equivalent civil redress—in this instance, the extent of the tort of passing off.[108] Also there have been instances where English courts have found that a competitor may sue another for infraction of a specific EU Regulation. This depends on finding that the legislation was intended to have direct effect, which entails showing, inter alia, that the Regulation is sufficiently clear and precise. For instance, the Regulation protecting the marketing of spirits, which referred to the interests of producers and importers in its Recitals, has been held to give a competitor a right to object to a drink being marketed as "whisky" when its alcohol content fell below the required 40 per cent.[109]

---

[102] Relying upon a line of authority, especially *Welham v DPP* [1961] A.C. 103 at 123–124.

[103] Conspiracy to commit this offence was also charged: it would now rank as a statutory form of conspiracy (Criminal Law Act 1977 s.1(1)), and could only be charged with the consent of the DPP (see s.4(1)).

[104] See also below, para.8–34.

[105] [1975] A.C. 842 HL. The prosecution failed because the accused were charged with conspiracy to effect a public mischief, an offence held to be unknown to the criminal law.

[106] In *Scott* [1975] A.C. 819 HL, Lord Diplock thought that, if there was no element of economic loss, a public officer must be deceived; but other members of the House were more equivocal.

[107] See, in relation to injunctions, *Emperor of Austria v Day* (1861) 3 De G.F. & J. 217; *Springhead Spinning v Riley* (1868) L.R. 6 Eq. 551; *CBS Songs v Amstrad* [1987] R.P.C. 429 CA.

[108] *Erven Warnink v Townend* [1980] RPC 31 HL. See below, para.17–03.

[109] *Scotch Whisky Assocn v JD Vintners* [1996] Eur. L.R. 446; and see *Taittinger v Allbev* [1993] F.S.R. 641 CA; *Scotch Whisky Assocn v Glen Kella* [1997] E.T.M.R. 470. cf. *Antonio Munoz v Frumar* [1999] F.S.R. 872, where an attempt to enforce private rights under the EU Grape Regulations was rejected.

A further possibility should be noted. If the criminal offence is imposed in order to confer a "public right", the Attorney-General may secure an injunction to restrain its commission. He has an unfettered discretion over intervening, which the judges will not review; it makes no difference whether the Attorney-General considers the case upon his own motion or at the request of some interested person.[110] Thus he refused to intervene in order to protect the interests of particular performers under the Performers' Protection Acts.[111] In addition, special powers have been conferred on the Office of Fair Trading and on other regulators at the national and local level (such as weights and measures authorities and the Financial Services Authority) to issue "Stop Now orders".[112] They are used to ensure compliance with the Trade Descriptions Act and other applicable legislation.

(3) Administrative procedures

(a) *Customs prohibition*[113]

Appropriately enough, the possibility of arresting the movement of pirated and counterfeit goods[114] through the intervention of customs officials at borders has become a matter largely for EU legislation.[115] What is more, the dismantling of customs controls between Member States has meant that the main impact of such procedures is now at the external boundaries of the EU.[116] The principal legislation is contained in Council Regulation 1383/2003[117] which is implemented in the United Kingdom by the Goods Infringing Intellectual Property Rights (Customs) Regulations 2004.[118] Each state must nominate a single service within its customs authority to receive and decide on applications for border protection, and a limit is placed on the **2–22**

[110] See especially *Gouriet v Union of Post Office Workers* [1978] A.C. 435 HL. For repeated breaches of the criminal law an injunction may be granted: *Attorney-General v Harris* [1961] Q.B. 74 CA.
[111] See *Ex p. Island Records* [1978] Ch.122 CA.
[112] Enterprise Act Pt 8.
[113] See generally Wordsall and Clark, *Anti-Counterfeiting* (1998) Ch.7; Arsie (1995) 18 World Comp. 75; Clark [1998] E.I.P.R. 414.
[114] Counterfeiting adds imitation of marks and packaging to pirated copies of products, with the intention of deceiving purchasers completely.
[115] Pirating is not a term of legal art, but refers to the illicit production and marketing of products copied from a source protected by certain types of IP: as with films and records, photocopies, objects bearing designs, etc. At present, the EU regime does not extend to patented products, and there is controversy over adding them: see Clark [1998] E.I.P.R. 414.
[116] UK legislation continues to prescribe the procedure for seeking action by the Commissioners of Customs and Excise and it now forms the basis for UK implementation of the 1994 Regulation: see SI 1995/1430, 1444 and 1445; CDPA 1988 ss.111, 112; TMA 1994 ss.89–91; *Commissioners of Customs v Top High* [1998] F.S.R. 464; *Polo Lauren v PT Dividua* [2000] E.T.M.R. 535 ECJ; *Miller Brewing v Mersey Docks* [2004] F.S.R. 5. The TRIPS Agreement, arts 51–60, requires WTO states to maintain such controls of imports. The considerable detail of these provisions is satisfied in the EU and UK arrangements discussed here.
[117] [1994] OJ L341, as amended by reg.806/2003 [2003] OJ L122; Cottier and Véron (eds) *Concise International and European IP Law* (2008) 316-405; *Re Rolex* [2004] E.C.R. I-651.
[118] SI 2004/1473. See Kerly, Ch.21.

amount of information which can be demanded from right-holders. Once pirated or counterfeit goods are identified in accordance with the notification, the customs authority will refuse to release them to the importer. However, the right-holder owes the authority a duty to indemnify it against any liability or expense.

(b) *Trading standards authorities*

2–23 The measures of consumer protection that have been developed under the modern law are now enforced principally by the trading standards departments of local authorities. In particular a positive duty to act was placed upon these authorities by the Trade Descriptions Act 1968. To this end they are armed with powers to make test purchases and to seize goods and documents for the purposes of the Act.[119] The extent to which the criminal offences contained in that Act may protect competitors against unfair practices has already been noted. The executive powers of the local authorities may sometimes provide a lever in the process of securing evidence or in informally putting a stop to some relatively minor injury.

(c) *Supervision of advertising*

2–24 The content of advertising is supervised primarily by the Office of Communications (Ofcom) (for broadcast media) and the Office of Fair Trading (for non-broadcast media). To a large extent, their supervisory role and powers have been delegated to the Advertising Standards Authority, as discussed further in Ch.16 below.[120]

(d) *Advertising Standards Authority*

2–25 Outside the field of broadcasting, the advertising industry averted the creation of a public body to supervise it by setting up a voluntary organ of its own, the Advertising Standards Authority, with half of the members drawn from outside the industry.[121] The system is mentioned here in order to point out the contrast with the public institutions that work in related fields.

(4) Self-help

2–26 Those entitled to possession of chattels have a right of recaption which entitles them to take their things, using no more force than is reasonably

[119] Trade Descriptions Act 1968 s.26(1).

[120] See below, paras 16–23 et seq.

[121] As a recognised authority under the Control of Misleading Advertisements Regulations 1988 (UK) (giving effect to the Misleading Advertising Directive 84/450), the authority is subject to judicial review: *R. v Advertising Standards Authority Ex p. Ratti* [2000] E.M.L.R. 581. Its Codes of Advertising and Sales Promotion are treated as "prescribed by law".

necessary.[122] The rights in intangible property which we are discussing give rise to no equivalent remedy by self-help, with one exception. The Copyright, Designs and Patents Act 1988 creates such a power, subject to specified conditions, which is exercisable against the lowest rung in the piratical hierarchy, but only in relation to copyright and rights in performances.[123] The right-owner, or anyone he authorises, may seize and detain infringing copies that are "exposed or otherwise immediately available for sale or hire", provided, first, that a local police station is duly notified and, secondly, that the seizure is in a public place or is on public premises from a person who does not have a permanent or regular place of business there.[124] Notice of what has been seized has to be given in the prescribed form.[125] No force may be used,[126] so, if the police will not accompany, the remedy is probably only good against the feeblest suitcase-salesman. The seller will mostly be committing a relatively minor offence, which is non-arrestable. However, a police officer present may be able to use his discretionary power to arrest, on the ground, for instance, that he cannot ascertain the name, or the true name, of the offender.[127]

2. Remedies in Civil Actions

The precise value of a right must be measured in terms of the remedies available for its enforcement. The range of relief provided by civil courts for the protection of property is wide and that is one of the most significant consequences of characterising patents, copyright, trade marks and the like as property. The forms of intellectual property now embodied in statute list the forms of remedy available, and to some extent regulate the detailed law.[128] However, the subject must be approached with one eye upon history. Before the mid-nineteenth century reforms which culminated in the Judicature Acts, the award of damages (assessed by a jury) was the remedy of the courts of common law. Remedies such as the injunction, which laid constraints upon a defendant beyond the mere payment of money, were developed by the Chancellor in equity. Some causes of action arose at common law, others in equity. Each attracted the remedies available in its own court. Furthermore, while purely equitable actions could not lead to an **2–27**

[122] *Clerk and Lindsell on Torts* 19th edn (2006), para.31–12; *R. v Mitchell* [2004] Crim. L.R. 139 but note that the CCA stated that a person's entitlement to use reasonable force to recover a chattel of which he has been wrongfully deprived was not a general rule (see *Clerk and Lindsell* para.31–13).

[123] As originally introduced, the power was to have been much broader.

[124] CDPA 1988 ss.100, 196.

[125] CDPA 1988 s.100(4).

[126] CDPA 1988 s.100(3).

[127] See Police and Criminal Evidence Act 1984 s.24, as amended by s.110(1) of the Serious Organised Crime and Police Act 2005.

[128] See PA 1977 ss.61, 62; CDPA 1988 ss.96–100, 195, 229–233; TMA 1994 ss.15–19; see below, paras 6–25—6–27; 12–58—12–60.

award of common law damages, equity might supplement the relief in a common law action by granting an equitable remedy. However, Chancery judges would frequently require that the opinion of a common law court first be taken on the substance of the matter.[129]

2–28 In the 1850s, statutes began the process of making the remedies of each jurisdiction available more readily in the other. In particular: courts of common law could award equitable forms of relief including injunctions[130]; courts of equity were to grant injunctions for breach of common law rights without first requiring a common law trial[131]; and by Lord Cairns' Act 1858, damages might be awarded in a court of equity "in lieu of or in addition to" an injunction (and other equitable relief).[132] This cross-fertilisation laid a basis from which to achieve the coalescence in administering civil law that was brought about by the Judicature Acts.[133]

2–29 The main intellectual property rights, whether they arose out of statute or judicial decision, were early in their existence accepted as rights enforceable at common law. This meant that damages were available, although, as the jury was gradually dropped from the trial of civil actions,[134] their assessment fell to the judge trying the action. But as the consequence primarily desired by most right-owners was the cessation of the wrong, an injunction was commonly sought, even in the days when it was necessary to pursue the case through two courts. Only the action for breach of confidence does not conform to this straightforward pattern. It grew as a comparatively recent manifestation of equity's power to put down impropriety by means of injunction, and its exact status is still in some measure opaque. To this special case we shall return later.[135]

(1) Injunction

2–30 An injunction looks to the future. It is an order of the court directing a party to litigation to do or refrain from doing an act.[136] Wilfully to disobey is contempt of court, punishable by fine, imprisonment or sequestration of

[129] Not that the Lord Chancellor necessarily considered himself bound by the jury's verdict.

[130] Patent Law Amendment Act 1852 s.42; Common Law Procedure Act 1854 ss.79 et seq.

[131] Court of Chancery Procedure Act 1852 ss.61, 62; Chancery Regulation Act 1862 ss.1–3.

[132] The jurisdiction established by Lord Cairns' Act continues in force, though by a somewhat circuitous route: see 24 *Halsbury's Laws of England* (4th edn, reissue), para.834.

[133] But substantive rights were not in consequence expanded or altered in nature. Thus an attempt to argue that the Acts gave a house-owner a new right to an injunction to restrain his neighbour from calling his house by the same name was firmly rejected: *Day v Brownrigg* (1878) 10 Ch.D. 294.

[134] Because of the length and difficulty of patent actions, the right of a party to a jury was restricted in the latter 19th century.

[135] See below, Ch.8.

[136] The order may restrain the defendant by its directors, employees or solicitors from doing the prohibited act: the latter, and any others who deliberately engage in the conduct, will be liable in contempt: *Seaward v Paterson* [1897] 1 Ch. 545 CA; *Marengo v Daily Sketch* [1948] 1 All E.R. 406 HL; *Attorney-General v Newspaper Publishing* [1987] 3 All E.R. 276 CA; cf. *Chelsea Man v Chelsea Girl (No.2)* [1988] F.S.R. 217.

assets.[137] The law of injunctions is beset with over-general propositions that require qualification in particular areas of application. Nonetheless they are not confined to particular categories of case and may issue wherever it is appropriate to do so.[138] In the intellectual property field an injunction is almost always prohibitory (as opposed to mandatory) since it enjoins the threatened commission[139] or continuance of wrongful acts. It can be granted after a trial establishing infringement of the claimant's right, when it is called "final" or "perpetual". However, it may also be sought in "interim" form, not to enforce an established right, but to maintain the status quo until a trial of the merits can take place. A cause of action is, however, a necessary precondition of this form of relief.[140] This latter type of injunction contributes a great deal to the practical efficacy of intellectual property rights and we shall discuss it first.

(a) *Interim injunction*

(i) **Preconditions.** An interim injunction, ordering the defendant not to continue or not to embark upon a course of action until the trial of the issue with the claimant, is a rapid and relatively cheap way of procuring temporary redress.[141] Its effect against a business competitor may be to cut off for good the road to commercial success. Even without this, businesses frequently treat the outcome of the interim proceedings as settling the matter in dispute. **2–31**

Whether such an injunction should be granted has always been a matter of discretion.[142] The motion to procure it must be brought as soon as the claimant learns of the alleged infringement of his rights; even short periods of delay may debar interim relief if there is no reasonable explanation.[143] An

[137] *Director-General of Fair Trading v Smith's Concrete* [1991] 4 All E.R. 150 CA. Sequestration is the form appropriate to contempt by a company. And see *Hospital for Sick Children v Walt Disney* [1968] Ch. 52 CA.

[138] *R. v Broadmoor Hospital Authority* [2000] 2 All E.R. 727. An injunction may be against all the world: *Venables v News Group* [2000] E.M.L.R. 255 (preventing the revelation of the new identities of discharged prisoners, out of fear that they might suffer physical reprisals). In *Jobserve v Skillsite* [2004] F.S.R. 36 contempt was found by reason of breach of undertakings given to the court not to use a database of CVs to set up a rival site in the personnel recruitment businesses.

[139] An injunction may be granted *quia timet* against a proposed course of action that will infringe the claimant's rights, if there is a strong probability that harm will occur. It may include, where appropriate, an injunction concerning future rights and it may go to a person innocently dealing in infringing goods: *Coflexip v Stolt Comex* [1999] F.S.R. 473; *Microsoft v Plato Technology* [1999] F.S.R. 834; cf. *British Telecommuncations v Textcall* [2000] E.T.M.R. 943.

[140] *The Veracruz* [1992] 1 Lloyd's Rep. 353 at 357, 359 CA, abandoning Lord Denning's view to the contrary.

[141] See CPR Pt 25. Exceptionally the injunction may be mandatory, requiring action of the defendant: *Zockoll Group v Mercury Communications* [1998] F.S.R. 354 CA.

[142] *Series 5 Software v Clarke* [1996] F.S.R. 273; *A v B* [2002] 2 All E.R. 545 CA (on breach of confidence). It is a discretion difficult to challenge on appeal: *Elan Digital v Elan Computers* [1984] F.S.R. 374 at 384, 386.

[143] cf. e.g. *Bourjois v British Home Stores* (1951) 68 R.P.C. 280 CA; *Versil v Cork Asbestos* [1966] R.P.C. 76; *Quaker Oats v Alltrades* [1981] F.S.R. 9 CA.

injunction will normally be granted to a claimant, other than the Crown,[144] only if he gives a cross-undertaking to make good any damage suffered by any defendant from the injunction, should the claimant fail at the trial.[145] The intervening period will inevitably be a matter of months and, in a patent action, perhaps a year or more. The defendant's competitive losses over such a period may well be considerable. The cross-undertaking cannot be lightly given,[146] although if the interim injunction turns out to have been wrongly granted the beneficiary is not to be treated as a wrongdoer in relation to the costs of the litigation.[147]

The injunction granted is typically in the form that the defendant be restrained from infringing the claimant's right as asserted. This will cover variations of what the defendant has been doing if they too would amount to infringement.[148] It is open to the defendant to obtain a declaration that his altered product is outside the injunction; and he will protect himself better if he chooses that course rather than putting the variation on the market without telling the claimant.[149]

2–32 (ii) **Assessment:** *American Cyanamid.* Beyond this, the usual approach was, until 1975, first to consider whether the claimant has made out a prima facie case of infringement, taking account of the apparent merits of any defence that the defendant proposed to establish at the trial.[150] Each side normally supported its case with written evidence in affidavits.[151] If a prima facie case was established, the court then considered whether the balance of convenience lay in favour of restraining the defendant until the trial or in leaving the claimant to recover damages at the trial for any infringements by the defendant in the intervening period.

---

[144] The cross-undertaking will not usually be required of the Crown where it seeks the injunction to enforce the law: *Hoffmann-La Roche v Secretary for Trade* [1975] A.C. 295.

[145] Under CPR PD 25A the cross-undertaking may extend to third parties who are not defendants in the proceedings; *Smithkline Beecham v Apotex Europe (No.2)* [2005] F.S.R. 24 which held that an injunction will be withheld if the applicant is not willing to give a cross-undertaking, at [30]. The cross-undertaking does not found an independent cause of action, but is a discretionary order: *Cheltenham and Gloucester Building Society v Ricketts* [1993] 1 W.L.R. 1545.

[146] See Jacob L.J. in *Smithkline Beecham v Apotex Europe* [2007] F.S.R. 6 CA at [23–32]; *Les Laboratoires Servier v Apotex* [2009] F.S.R. 3.

[147] *SmithKline Beecham v Apotex Europe (No.2)* [2005] F.S.R. 24 CA per Jacob L.J. at [23]. The cross-undertaking does not extend to a right to claim profits made by the patentee while the injunction is in effect; but customers of the patentee who paid a monopoly price should be able to be joined as parties so that they can recover the "over-charge": *Wake Forest University v Smith & Nephew* [2009] F.S.R. 11. See also *Research in Motion v Visto* [2008] F.S.R. 20 CA; *Les Laboratoires Servier v Apotex* [2009] F.S.R. 3.

[148] This assumes that the right as alleged can be substantiated at the trial: *Spectravest v Aperknit* [1988] F.S.R. 161; but note Scott J.'s doubt whether such an assumption can properly be made: *Staver v Digitext Display* [1985] F.S.R. 512. Cf. *Video Arts v Paget Industries* [1988] F.S.R. 501.

[149] *Spectravest v Aperknit* [1988] F.S.R. 161.

[150] For an instance, see *Hubbard v Vosper* [1972] 2 Q.B. 84 CA.

[151] Witnesses were summoned to give oral evidence only when it appeared crucial to test their credibility at this preliminary stage.

In *American Cyanamid v Ethicon*,[152] the House of Lords modified this approach. It did so in patent litigation, insisting, however, that the new principles were in no way special to this field. According to Lord Diplock, the correct approach is as follows: the court must first be satisfied that there is a "serious question to be tried".[153] **2–33**

Thereafter, it should not try to assess relative merit by looking for a prima facie case in the affidavit evidence; it should instead turn at once to the balance of convenience.[154] If it appears that damages awarded at the trial will adequately compensate the claimant, and that the defendant is likely to be able to pay them,[155] interim relief should not normally be granted. If damages will not be adequate to compensate the claimant, it becomes necessary to consider whether, on the other hand, the defendant would be adequately compensated by damages upon the claimant's cross-undertaking, should the claimant not make good his claim at trial. If these damages would be adequate, the injunction is likely to be granted. Where there is doubt about the adequacy of damages to one or both,[156] any factor which may affect the balance of convenience is brought into account—in particular, whether the defendant has not yet started on his allegedly infringing course of action[157] (it being "a counsel of prudence . . . to preserve the status quo").[158] If the balance remains substantially even, some account can ultimately be taken of the relative strength of each party's case as revealed by the affidavit evidence.

> "This, however, should be done only where it is apparent upon the facts disclosed by evidence as to which there is no credible dispute that the

---

152 [1975] A.C. 396; [1975] R.P.C. 513. *The White Book 2006* notes, at para.25.1.11, that "the context within which the *American Cyanamid* rules were designed to operate has altered" with the new rules of civil procedure which mean, among other things, that delays between issue of proceedings and trial are much reduced.

153 i.e. that the claim was not "frivolous or vexatious" or that it "disclosed no real prospect of [the claimant] succeeding in his claim for a permanent injunction at the trial". Lord Diplock used all three phrases, apparently as synonyms, and subsequent courts have varied in their understanding of the standard which the claimant must satisfy: see Megarry V.C. in *Mothercare v Robson* [1979] F.S.R. 466 at 471–474, in whose view the claimant must show more than "an honest but hopelessly optimistic case". For patent infringement actions, see below, para.6–27.

154 A weakness of the judgment is that it did not deal with *Stratford v Lindley* [1965] A.C. 269 or with the *Hoffmann-La Roche* case [1975] A.C. 295, in both of which the House of Lords adopted a "prima facie" case approach: see *Series 5 Software v Clarke* [1996] F.S.R. 273. For the impact of the Human Rights Act 1998 s.12(3), see *Cream Holdings v Banerjee* [2005] 1 A.C. 253 HL.

155 See, e.g. *Belfast Ropeworks v Pixdane* [1976] F.S.R. 337 CA.

156 *Walker (John) v Rothmans* [1978] F.S.R. 357; *Combe v Scholl* [1980] R.P.C. 1.

157 See *Beecham Group v Bristol* [1967] R.P.C. 406 at 416 CA; *Beecham Group v Bristol* [1968] R.P.C. 301 HC (Aust).

158 Where there is a delay between issue of the claim form and its service, it is at the latter date that the status quo falls to be considered: *Graham v Delderfield* [1992] F.S.R. 313 CA.

strength of one party's case is disproportionate to that of the other party."[159]

2–34 How substantial a reorientation was effected by this judgment has been debated ever since.[160] Because a court has no longer to consider whether, if the case went to trial on the affidavit evidence, the claimant would probably succeed, it can cut short any invitation to evaluate rival contentions presented in elaborate affidavits.[161] Accordingly, substantial trials-before-trials can be eliminated. But short of this, because so many cases that are fought at the interim stage involve substantial uncertainties, it is difficult for the court to exclude all consideration of relative merits—the factor given such prominence in the former "prima facie case" approach. Thus some considerations that previously went to the prima facie case are given weight in deciding whether there is a serious case to be tried[162]; and they may appear equally relevant to the adequacy or otherwise of damages. Whether the defendant's trade mark or name is close enough to the claimants' to constitute passing off often affects the likelihood of damage.[163] In other cases again, because the adequacy of damages remains in doubt, some judges have taken advantage of the statement that as a last resort they may balance the merits.[164]

2–35 (iii) **Balance of convenience.** *American Cyanamid* gave greater prominence to the balance of convenience, although no appreciable change has occurred in the manner of assessing it. Three factors in particular are of recurrent importance. First is the degree to which claimant and defendant are

[159] [1975] R.P.C. 513 at 542. This cautious approach was directly challenged as unduly restrictive by Laddie J.: *Series 5 Software v Clarke* [1996] F.S.R. 273 at 285, 286; Phillips [1997] J.B.L. 486.

[160] Judges varied in their readiness to follow the changed approach religiously. Lord Denning M.R. and Pennycuick V.C. were early doubters: see *Fellowes v Fisher* [1976] Q.B. 122; *Hubbard v Pitt* [1975] 3 All E.R. 1 at 10; and see *Dunford v Johnston* [1978] F.S.R. 143 at 150. It has however stood the test of time, although Jacob J. suggested that there may come a point when the House of Lords should review its application to cases where the court is in a position to make a reasonable assessment of the prospects of both sides, in *SmithKline Beecham v Generics*, unreported judgment of October 23, 2001. The Court of Appeal has insisted that it applies both to restraint of trade and passing off cases: *Lawrence David v Ashton* [1989] F.S.R. 87; *County Sound v Ocean Sound* [1991] F.S.R. 367; cf. *Series 5 Software v Clarke* [1996] F.S.R. 273.

[161] *American Cyanamid v Ethicon* posed just this threat: see [1977] F.S.R. 593 CA.

[162] Thus an important question of law was decided under this rubric in *Revlon v Cripps & Lee* [1980] F.S.R. 85; see below, paras 18–114 et seq. See also *Mothercare v Penguin Books* [1988] R.P.C. 113; *Mail Newspapers v Express Newspapers* [1987] F.S.R. 90.

[163] *Sirdar v Mulliez* [1975] F.S.R. 309; *Walker (John) v Rothmans* [1978] F.S.R. 357; *Morning Star v Express* [1979] F.S.R. 113 DC; *Newsweek v BBC* [1979] R.P.C. 441; *Marcus Publishing v Hutton-Wild Communications* [1990] R.P.C. 576 CA; *Antec International v South Western Chicks* [1997] F.S.R. 278.

[164] *Constable v Clarkson* [1980] F.S.R. 123 CA; *Quaker Oats v Alltrades* [1981] F.S.R. 9 CA; *Mirage Studios v Counter-Feat Clothing* [1991] F.S.R. 145. If the result of the interim proceedings is likely to dispose of the dispute, the court will consider the relative chances of success: see Lord Diplock, *NWL v Woods* [1979] 3 All E.R. 614 at 625–626; applied in *Athletes Foot v Cobra Sports* [1980] R.P.C. 343; *BBC v Talbot* [1981] F.S.R. 228.

successfully established in business: for loss of market share during the interim period until trial may well be thought to have wide-ranging effects that cannot be easily quantified in damages. If the defendant has not yet set up in production, but the claimant is already on the market, the balance may well be in the latter's favour.[165] If both are marketing and the claimant is struggling to gain a foothold with a new product, again the special danger to him may lead to grant of the injunction. The contrary may well apply if he is already well-established and the defendant is unlikely to offer major competition in the interim.[166] In such cases, it is generally easier to assess the loss to the claimant from actual sales by the defendant than loss to the defendant by being enjoined from competing.[167] Secondly, if either party appears to lack the financial ability or backing to meet any ultimate liability in damages this may operate against him.[168] Thirdly, unnecessary delay on the claimant's part will weigh against him, at least if the defendant has materially altered his position in consequence.[169]

Beyond this, for all its alleged universality, the manner in which the *American Cyanamid* rule is applied needs to be separately considered in relation to particular intellectual property rights.[170] As a result of the Enforcement Directive, the Civil Procedure Rules [171] now provide that in lieu of the grant of an interim injunction the court is empowered to grant an order allowing the defendant to continue its activities subject to lodging appropriate guarantees capable of compensating the claimant if he is found at trial to be infringing.

(b) *Final injunction*

Even after the claimant has established his right at trial of the action, an injunction is said to be subject to two considerations: it lies in the discretion of the court; and it is available at the instance of a private litigant only if he has some proprietary right or interest to protect. As regards intellectual property the following can be said in amplification: **2–36**

[165] *Belfast Ropework v Pixdane* [1976] F.S.R. 337 CA; but see *Sirdar v Mulliez* [1975] F.S.R. 309.

[166] *Catnic v Stressline* [1976] F.S.R. 157 CA; cf. e.g. *Parfums Givenchy v Designer Alternatives* [1994] R.P.C. 243 CA. If the dispute is worldwide the damage to each must be considered in that context; where the claimant has been unable to secure interim protection through his patents in other countries, this may militate against a grant in England: *Polaroid v Eastman Kodak* [1977] F.S.R. 25 CA. If the effect of an injunction would be to deprive the defendant of his usual means of earning, this weighs against grant: *Raindrop Data v Systemics* [1988] F.S.R. 354. Likewise, if the effect will be to put the defendant out of business: *Cayne v Global Natural Resources* [1984] 1 All E.R. 225 CA; *Entec v Abacus Mouldings* [1992] F.S.R. 332 CA.

[167] It is no argument that failure to grant the injunction effectively licenses invasion of the right: *Hunter v Wellings* [1987] F.S.R. 83 CA.

[168] *Standex v Blades* [1976] F.S.R. 114 CA.

[169] *Sirdar v Mulliez* [1975] F.S.R. 309; *Radley Gowns v Spyrou* [1975] F.S.R. 455; cf. *Belfast Ropework* case [1976] F.S.R. 337.

[170] See below, paras 6–24—6–27, 8–41—8–43.

[171] CPR r.25(1)(p).

(1) Against proven infringement of patent, design, copyright, trade mark and any other right that has acquired the status of "property" at common law, an injunction will be granted in the absence of something special in the case—such as imminent expiry of the right, no likelihood of repetition by the defendant, or some conduct on the claimant's part that leaves him with unclean hands, such as a representation that he would not seek an injunction.[172] To leave the claimant to a remedy in damages[173] would in effect be to compel him to license his right to all comers.[174]

(2) To protect confidential information, injunctive relief is more evidently at the court's discretion. The relevant case law is discussed later.[175]

(3) There is no right to an injunction in order to protect against irrecoverable loss, e.g. loss of sales to other companies linked to the claimant only indirectly and not as subsidiaries.[176]

(4) A private party may not procure an injunction against violation of the criminal law unless he has a special interest in its enforcement greater than that of the ordinary citizen.[177] Even if he has this interest, the statute creating the offence must not have been drawn with the intention of restricting its enforcement to criminal law procedures.[178]

(2) Delivery up

2–37 In order to ensure that injunctions are properly effective, courts of equity and their successors maintain a discretion to order delivery up of infringing articles or documents for destruction, or else to require their destruction under oath by the defendant, or some equivalent step such as erasure of a trade mark.[179] In a breach of confidence case, however, the defendant was

[172] cf. *Banks v EMI Songs* [1996] E.M.L.R. 452 and *Navitaire v EasyJet Airline* [2006] R.P.C. 000 (which, in refusing the grant of a final injunction where the effect would have been oppressive, and awarding damages instead, distinguished *Banks*). An intermediate possibility is for the court to give the claimant leave to apply for an injunction should it prove necessary in future.

[173] Whether by refusing an injunction under the general discretion or under Lord Cairns' Act.

[174] "[I]f the effect of the grant of an injunction is not oppressive the defendant cannot buy his way out of it, even if the price, objectively ascertained, would be modest. My understanding of the word 'oppressive' in this context is that the effect of the grant of the injunction would be grossly disproportionate to the right protected", per Pumfrey J. in *Navitaire v EasyJet Airline* [2006] R.P.C. 3, 4; approved in *Virgin Atlantic v Premium Aircraft* [2009] EWCA Civ 1513.

[175] See below, paras 8–41 et seq.

[176] *Polaroid v Eastman Kodak* [1997] R.P.C. 379 at 394–395, 397; *Peaudouce v Kimberley-Clark* [1996] F.S.R. 680.

[177] See above, para.2–21.

[178] See above, para.2–21.

[179] See, e.g. *Mergenthaler Linotype v Intertype* (1927) 43 R.P.C. 381; *Slazenger v Feltham (No. 2)* (1889) 6 R.P.C. 531 at 538 (trade mark); *Peter Pan v Corsets Silhouette* [1963] 3 All E.R. 402. Cf. *Ocular Sciences v Aspect Vision Care* [1997] R.P.C. 289 and 420: relief refused because it would be disproportionately damaging to the defendant.

ordered to deliver up when he was not trusted to destroy under oath.[180] In the case of copyright and unregistered design right this jurisdiction is now governed by statute and extends both to infringing copies and to apparatus, etc. specifically designed to make infringing copies.[181] Here the court's discretion is wider than in general, for, in order to compensate the right-owner, it may forfeit the things to him rather than order destruction or other disposal.[182]

(3) Damages

(a) *Bases for assessment*

The normal aim of an award of damages is to compensate the claimant for the harm caused him by the legal injury.[183] In the case of breach of contract, damages generally seek to put the claimant in the position that he would have occupied had the contract been carried out; and so (subject to the exclusion of losses that are unforeseeably remote) he may recover profits that he anticipated making from the contract.[184] Damages in tort (again subject to exclusion of the unforeseeably remote)[185] aim to put the victim back to his position before the tort, the victim being able to recover for any loss which was foreseeable (i.e. not too remote), caused by the wrong and not excluded from recovery by public or social policy.[186] Generally, if a tortious action is also a breach of contract, the law allows the claim to be put on either basis; and occasionally the different assumptions for calculating damages may make this significant. **2–38**

Contrary to the older view, exemplary damages may not be awarded to punish the claimant for wrongful conduct, however aggressively or insultingly deliberate. But there is an exception where the defendant's conduct has

[180] *Industrial Furnaces v Reaves* [1970] R.P.C. 605 at 627–628.

[181] CDPA 1988 ss.99, 230. There is in general a time limit on such an order of six years from making the article. In criminal proceedings for copyright infringement similar orders may be made: CDPA 1988 s.108; and for forfeiture orders concerning trade marks, see TMA 1994 ss.97, 98.

[182] CDPA 1988, ss.114, 114A, 114B, 231. See also *Industrial Furnaces v Reaves* [1970] R.P.C. 605 at 627–628.

[183] Not from some other cause: see *United Horse Shoe v Stewart* (1888) 5 R.P.C. 260 at 267. But it is no excuse that the defendant might have injured the claimant as much by some non-infringing act: (1888) 5 R.P.C. 260.

[184] See, e.g. *Chitty on Contracts* 29th edn (2004), para.1551; *McGregor on Damages* 17th edn (2003), paras 1–021—1–040, 2–002—2–39.

[185] This concept is apparently somewhat narrower in contract than in tort: *Koufos v Czamikow* [1969] 1 A.C. 350 at 422–423 HL.

[186] *Gerber v Lectra* [1997] R.P.C. 443 CA; see further below, para.2–45; cf. also *Cambridge Water v Eastern Counties Leather* [1994] 2 A.C. 264; *Claydon Architectural Metalwork v Higgins* [1997] F.S.R. 475.

been calculated by him to make a profit for himself which may well exceed the compensation payable to him by the claimant; for "it is necessary for the law to show that it cannot be broken with impunity".[187] However, it is still open to courts to award aggravated damages, adding compensation for injury to the claimant's feelings or reputation to a sum for the breach which otherwise may only be nominal.[188]

2–39 In arriving at the measure of damages in the various fields of intellectual property, courts have to deal with recurrent circumstances. The similarities are often of broad outline rather than of detail. Accordingly statements about the proper approach to assessment provide general guidelines, not strict rules. In particular the judges resist being saddled with any single test for all cases.[189] The fact that a particular assessment is difficult and must be rather rough-and-ready is not a reason for refusing to attempt it.[190]

There are many ways in which particular copyrights and patents may be exploited. A starting point in assessing damages is accordingly to ask whether the claimant and defendant are in actual competition.[191] Where this is so, the next question is whether the defendant might have had the claimant's licence if only he had sought it. Then the measure of damages will likely be what the claimant would have charged for a licence (on the basis of the "user" principle).[192] The award for infringements already perpetrated may well be based on a royalty for each infringement.[193] However, the claimant is not normally under any compulsion to grant licences.[194] If he

---

[187] *Rookes v Barnard* [1964] A.C. 1129 at 1220–1231, per Lord Devlin. The other recognised exception concerns the acts of government servants. See also *Cassell v Broome* [1972] A.C. 1027 HL; *Morton-Norwich v Intercen (No.2)* [1981] F.S.R. 337; and see *Kuddus v Chief Constable of Leicestershire* [2002] 2 A.C. 122.

[188] e.g. for the injurious falsehood of proclaiming a former lover a prostitute: *Khodaparast v Shad* [2000] E.M.L.R. 265. Notice also the power in a copyright or unregistered design case to award additional damages: CDPA 1988 ss.97(2), 229(3); below, para.12–61. In the Directive on Enforcement of IPRs, 2004/48 of April 29, 2004, damages are to be assessed taking into account the prejudice suffered by the claimant; Recital 26 states explicitly that the aim is not to introduce punitive damages. Punitive awards of this kind (treble damages) existed under the Statute of Monopolies 1624 s.4, but have survived into modern times only in the US.

[189] *Meters v Metropolitan Gas* (1911) 28 R.P.C. 157 at 161, 163 CA; *Watson, Laidlaw v Potts Cassels* (1914) 31 R.P.C. 104 at 117–118 HL; *Interfirm Comparison v Law Society* (1975) 6 A.L.R. 445 at 446–447 S.C. (N.S.W.).

[190] *Chaplin v Hicks* [1911] 2 K.B. 786; *Watson, Laidlaw* case 31 R.P.C. 104 at 118. See also Ricketson [1980] E.I.P.R. 149.

[191] Taking account of competition by the claimant's licensees, if any.

[192] *General Tire v Firestone* [1976] R.P.C. 197 at 212 et seq. HL. In *Reed Executive v Reed Business Information* [2004] R.P.C. 20 CA, Jacob L.J. indicated that he was "by no means convinced that the 'user' principle *automatically* applies in trade mark and passing off cases, especially where the 'mark' concerned is not the sort of mark available for hire": at [165].

[193] A claimant who has fought his case to judgment may not then be bound by the royalty rate that he gave before the validity of his right was established; it depends on whether the rate was a standard one or not: *General Tire* case [1976] R.P.C. 197; and see *Caxton v Sutherland* [1939] A.C. 178 at 203 HL. If no injunction is to be granted for the future, damages may take the form of a capitalised royalty. See also *British Thomson-Houston v Naamloose* (1923) 40 R.P.C. 119 at 127–128, IH.

[194] See the possibility of compulsory licensing for patents and designs: below, paras 7–39 et seq.

would not have done so, the court will look to his losses through the defendant's competition. It is only where the claimant's and defendant's anticipated profits are the same in the same market that the defendant's gain will be the claimant's loss. To take an obvious example: the claimant may be exploiting his copyright by selling small numbers of high-priced hardback books, and the defendant may infringe with large quantities of low-priced paperbacks. The issue is the loss to the claimant, and this may include not only the lost profits on hardback sales (taking account of any price reduction forced on him by the defendant's conduct),[195] but also the damage to his future prospects—his chance of putting out paperbacks, the loss of ancillary supplies or services[196] and possibly even the fact that infringement has enabled the defendant to build up a strong position in other competitive lines.[197]

When it comes to non-competitive infringements, the courts have held that a reasonable royalty for non-competing use will be awarded upon a principle "of price or of hire".[198] Otherwise the right might be invaded with impunity.[199] A different question also goes to the nature of the "property". Suppose that the infringement (even if competing) is only one contributory factor in the profit that the defendant has made: a copyright work has been included in a larger compilation; an invention forms one part of more complex plant; or it is a machine or process that is used in making a non-patented article. In which of these cases, if any, is the claimant only entitled to some proportion of the whole amount otherwise arising under the principles just discussed? If the damages represent lost sales to the claimant[200] he is entitled to the whole lost profit.[201] Where this is not so a royalty may be the appropriate basis of calculation at a rate which takes into account the proportional contribution of the right infringed.[202] **2–40**

(b) *Innocence*

Normally, rights that rank as common law property are enforceable even against those who unwittingly interfere with them. However, this aspect of the property analogy in our field has not always appealed to Parliament and **2–41**

[195] See *Meters v Metropolitan* (1911) 28 R.P.C. 157 at 163; *Manus v Fullwood* (1954) 71 R.P.C. 243. cf. *United Horse Shoe v Stewart* (1888) 13 App.Cas. 401; 3 R.P.C. 139.

[196] *Gerber Garment v Lectra* [1997] R.P.C. 443 CA.

[197] cf. *Alexander v Henry* (1895) 12 R.P.C. 360 (trade mark); *Khawam v Chelaram* [1964] R.P.C. 337 at 342–343 PC (registered design).

[198] Lord Shaw, *Watson, Laidlaw* case, 31 R.P.C. 104 at 119–120; and see Fletcher Moulton L.J., *Meters* case, 28 R.P.C. 157 at 163–165: *Blayney v Clogau St Davids Gold Mines* [2003] F.S.R. 3 CA.

[199] "...what would have been the condition of the Plaintiff, if the Defendants had acted properly instead of acting improperly?": Page Wood V.C., *Penn v Jack* (1867) L.R. 5 Eq. 81 at 84. For the possible application of this approach to trade mark infringement, see *Dormeuil v Feraglow* [1990] R.P.C. 449.

[200] Because the claimant would have produced an end product competing with the defendant's.

[201] *United Horse Shoe v Stewart* (1888) 13 App.Cas. 401; 3 R.P.C. 139 (patented machine saved expense in making nails).

[202] cf. *Meters v Metropolitan* (1911) 28 R.P.C. 157 CA.

the courts. They have not, it is true, refused injunctions against the continuance of an infringement simply on the ground that a defendant in all innocence expended money on a production system—a change of position that will bring him loss if he is then obliged to desist. But there has been some reluctance to oblige him to pay damages for infringements committed during a period of "innocence". Thus, in the Acts relating to patents, designs and copyright it is explicitly provided that no damages are payable for a period in which the infringer did not know, and had no reasonable grounds for supposing, that the right existed.[203] However, a genuine belief that there was no infringement or that the right had been properly licensed is not an excuse.[204] The requirement of reasonableness, moreover, means that a defendant who copies a new product ought to inquire whether it is patented,[205] and one who copies a literary work or the like should look for any indications that it is in copyright.[206] Where statute has not intervened there is less certainty. Innocent infringement of a trade mark, whether registered or unregistered, gives rise to damages,[207] though a discretionary remedy such as an account might be refused.

We shall see that the uncertain status of confidential information—is it property, and if so is the property legal or equitable?—is bound up with the question whether any form of relief should be given against "innocent" defendants.[208] In this connection the comparison with the rules for the established forms of intellectual property needs to be remembered; it has sometimes been ignored in the past.

(4) Account of profits

2–42 Equity never trespassed so directly upon the prerogatives of the common law courts as to award damages for common law wrongs.[209] However, as a corollary of the injunction, it might order a defendant to account to a claimant for profits made from wrong-doing such as the infringement of an intellectual property right.[210] This is not a notional computation as with damages, but an investigation of actual accounts,[211] which may incidentally

[203] PA 1977 s.62(1); RDA 1949 s.9(1); CDPA 1988 ss.97(1), 233 (also affecting "secondary infringement").

[204] See, e.g. *Byrne v Statist* [1914] 1 K.B. 622 (belief that someone other than claimant owned copyright did not excuse).

[205] *Lancer Boss v Henley Fork-Lift* [1975] R.P.C. 307. But note the provision that (in the case of patents and registered designs) it is not enough to mark goods "patent", "registered", etc. without adding the number.

[206] *Byrne v Statist* [1914] 1 K.B. 622.

[207] *Spalding v Gamage* (1915) 32 R.P.C. 273 HL; *Gillette v Edenwest* [1994] R.P.C. 279.

[208] See below, paras 8–33 et seq.

[209] Equity did, however, order payments to rectify equitable wrongs, such as breach of trust. This jurisdiction is now being claimed as the basis for equitable damages: see below, para.8–47.

[210] This was treated as accepted by Lord Eldon, *Hogg v Kirby* (1803) 8 Ves.Jun. 215 at 223.

[211] It is thus a personal remedy against unjust enrichment: see esp. *Attorney-General v Observer* [1990] 1 A.C. 109 at 262, 265–267, 288, 293–294.

afford the claimant a sight of customers' names and other information about the defendant.[212] Nonetheless it is a laborious and expensive procedure and is infrequently resorted to. If the protected subject matter is part of the article sold, or a mark used to sell it, the claimant is entitled to the whole profit on each infringement.[213] If the defendant's wrong merely enables him to save expense in production, the claimant may only be entitled to the amount by which the saving increases the profit.[214]

In principle, the account will give a better recompense than damages when the defendant has been making profits that the claimant would not himself have made,[215] but if the case is an exceptional one, exemplary damages may achieve much the same result.[216] It used to be said that the claimant must elect either for damages or an account, upon the theory that by seeking an account the claimant adopted the defendant's acts as his own,[217] but this explanation is now dubious.[218] The better principle is merely that in respect of any one infringement the claimant should not be entitled to be both reimbursed and compensated.[219]

A modern view worth attention is that it is restitutionary in character, **2–43**
aiming to put paid to an unjust enrichment to the defendant at the claimant's expense. It is only a personal, not a proprietary, remedy, such as would give the claimant title in equity to particular funds or property representing the profit.[220] To achieve such an outcome, it would be necessary to impose a constructive trust. While equitable interests may be called in aid to give effect to the intended arrangements concerning the ownership of

[212] There is a discretion to order discovery concerning infringing acts in relation to damages as well as an account: *Smith Kline & French v Doncaster Pharmaceuticals* [1989] F.S.R. 401; and see *Minnesota Mining v Jeffries* [1993] F.S.R. 189 FC (Aust.).

[213] *Peter Pan Manufacturing Corporation v Corsets Silhouette* [1963] 3 All E.R. 402; *Potton v Yorkclose* [1990] F.S.R. 11; *Celanese Int v BP Chemicals* [1999] R.P.C. 203. In a trade mark case, the claimant is entitled to the profit on each item wrongly sold—he does not have to prove that the sale was to a deceived customer: *Lever v Goodwin* (1887) 36 Ch.D. 1 CA; if necessary the number may have to be reached by approximation: *My Kinda Town v Soll* [1982] F.S.R. 147; *House of Spring Gardens v Point Blank* [1985] F.S.R. 327 at 345. For expenditure properly deductible in calculating the defendant's costs, and the entitlement of the claimant to lost opportunity profits, see *Dart Industries v Decor* (1993) 179 C.L.R. 101 HC (Aust.); *Zupanovich v Beale* (1995) 32 I.P.R. 339.

[214] *United Horse Shoe v Stewart* (1889)5 R.P.C. 260 at 266–267. Cf. the calculation of damages on the basis of actual sales lost, where the claimant can claim the whole of his own lost profit: see above, para.2–40.

[215] As far as the innocent defendant is concerned there are curious differences: the patent infringer is protected to the same extent as he is from paying damages, whereas the opposite applies in the case of copyright and unregistered design right: *Wienerworld v Vision Video* [1998] F.S.R. 832. Since an account is discretionary, the innocence of the defendant may always be a reason for refusing it: e.g. *Seager v Copydex* (No. 1) [1967] 2 All E.R. 415, but cf. *Edelsten v Edelsten* (1863) 1 De G.J. & S. 185.

[216] For the conditions, see above, para.2–42.

[217] e.g. *Neilson v Betts* (1871) L.R. 5 HL 1; *De Vitre v Betts* (1873) L.R. 6 HL 319; *Sutherland v Caxton* [1936] Ch. 323 at 336.

[218] cf. the House of Lords' rejection as fictitious of the same theory for waiver of tort: *United Australia v Barclays Bank* [1941] A.C. 1; Street, *Law of Damages* (1962), pp.263–266.

[219] This appears to follow from the formula in PA 1977 s.61(2).

[220] And identified if necessary, by equitable tracing rules.

intellectual property (as may, for instance, be the proper implication to be drawn from a commission to create a copyright work), a trust is not imposed by way of remedy attaching to the tortious profits of infringing intellectual property. But here the equitable character of breach of confidence makes for complications. Given in particular the proximity of that obligation to fiduciary duties, it is conceivable that constructive trusts may form part of the court's remedial armoury for protecting trade and similar secrets.[221] It is hard to see why this should be so where technical know-how has been misappropriated, yet not so when a patent is infringed. The law's strongest incentives go to inventions which qualify for patents.

(5) "Franking"

2–44 Intellectual property rights relate to a series of stages in the commercial life of products—their creation and preparation for sale, their distribution down the chain to ultimate users; and in some cases also to their use, their resale second-hand, etc. The question accordingly arises whether monetary payments for infringement, paid on goods in respect of an early step in the chain, "franks" them as legitimate thereafter. It has been held, both in relation to damages and an account of profits for patent infringement, that no such legal effect is brought about. Actions may be maintained in relation to later wrongful acts.[222] Where there has been a settlement, any payment will not be understood to "frank" infringement unless this is an agreed term.[223]

(6) Remedies for acts which are not themselves infringements

2–45 Frequently the acts which infringe intellectual property have come to be defined in terms first of a primary act or acts and then secondary acts. The latter may take the form of preparation for completion of a primary act (for example, providing parts for making a patented invention)[224] or they may consist of consequential acts, for example importing or marketing goods which fall to be treated as infringements or as bearing infringing marks.[225] In those circumstances, legislation settles that the law should extend its remedies against these surrounding activities. However, in some cases there will be no liability, or remedies will be limited, unless the defendant is shown to know or to have reason to believe that infringing goods were involved.[226] Intriguing questions arise about the extent to which legal or equitable

[221] See below, para.8–52, esp. for the difficult *Lac Minerals* case.
[222] *Catnic Components v Evans* [1983] F.S.R. 401; *Codex v Racal-Milgo* [1984] F.S.R. 87.
[223] *Lewis Trusts v Bamber Stores* [1982] F.S.R. 281; *Rose Records v Motown Records* [1983] F.S.R. 361.
[224] See below, paras 6–17 et seq.
[225] See below, para.18–84.
[226] For instance, see below, para.12–29.

remedies may encompass acts or events which do not themselves constitute primary, contributory or consequential infringement.

In *Chappell v Graphophone Co*,[227] according to the law then in effect, it was infringement of musical copyright to copy sheet music but not to record the work from it. A defendant who did both these things was held liable to deliver up the records it had made for destruction. This form of relief was not confined merely to the sheet music.[228]

In *Gerber v Lectra*,[229] the infringer of a patent for automatic cutting machines was held liable (inter alia) for the "associated" damages arising from lost profits on computer-aided design systems sold with the machines, on spare parts for them, on servicing contracts, and for putting itself, through infringement, in a position to make sales after expiry of the patent.

As already noted, the latter decision was based on the concepts of foreseeability and causation, but was made subject to considerations of public and social policy.[230] Policy in intellectual property matters has always been to balance a fair scope for the right-owner against a general freedom of competitors to imitate what is not within the bounds of the right. It is this policy which should remain the governing consideration.[231] It should not become wrongful to write a non-infringing sequel to a novel by virtue merely of having made a single copy of the novel from which to work; nor wrongful to make a non-infringing variation of a patented invention by virtue merely of having made commercial use of the invention once.

A rule of law applied in a case will have an effect on later cases according to the rules of precedent, whether or not the parties are the same or different. But decisions on the application of a rule to particular facts, in litigation between different parties, where the factual evidence may differ, will not in general prevent the issue from being reconsidered. Thus questions of construction of patent specifications can depend on assessments of common general knowledge and the understanding of the skilled addressee of technical information in the specification. These are matters for evidence in each case.[232]

---

227 [1914] 2 Ch. 745 CA. See also *Crossley v Derby Gas-Lights* (1838) 3 My. & Cr. 428 (injunction); Prescott (1991) 54 M.L.R. 451.

228 cf. the decompilation of a computer program: below, paras 20–17 et seq.

229 [1997] R.P.C. 443 CA; Moss and Rogers [1997] E.I.P.R. 425. As to post-expiry damages, see also *Union Carbide v BP Chemicals* [1999] R.P.C. 409; *Generics v Smith Kline* [1997] E.C.R. I-3929 ECJ.

230 Above para.2–39.

231 As seems well recognised in cases not applied in *Gerber: Polaroid v Eastman Kodak* [1977] R.P.C. 379 at 394; *Corruplast v George Harrison Agencies* [1978] R.P.C. 761 at 764, 765; *Catnic Components v Hill & Smith* [1983] F.S.R. 512. See generally, *McGregor on Damages* 17th edn (2003), paras 40–023—40–041.

232 See, e.g., *Novartis v Dexcel-Pharma* [2009] F.S.R. 31 at 21.

3. Securing Evidence of Infringement

2–46 Intellectual property litigation is mostly governed by the general principles of civil procedure[233] and no attempt can here be made to review the whole gamut of relevant rules.[234] But given the great significance of the law's machinery in this field, two things can be attempted. In this section, attention is given to procedures developed to help the claimant in amassing evidence for his case. Often enough it is difficult for him to know whom to sue or to discover what a particular competitor or pirate is doing. In the next section we look from the opposite direction—by considering what a defendant can do against a claimant who turns litigation into a war of nerves. This section, then, is concerned with three aspects of the claimant's armoury. It concentrates particularly on recent developments designed to increase the strength of his position.

(1) Search order for inspection and other relief; formerly known as the Anton Piller order[235]

(a) *Requirements for the order*

2–47 In *Anton Piller v Manufacturing Processes*,[236] the Court of Appeal approved a procedure that is of major practical importance to some owners of intellectual property rights. The claimant applies to the High Court or Patents County Court[237] in camera without any notice to the defendant, for an order that the defendant permit him (with his solicitor) to inspect the defendant's premises[238] and to seize, copy or photograph material relevant to the alleged infringement. The defendant may be required to deliver up infringing goods,[239] keep infringing stock or incriminating papers,[240] and even to give information, for instance, about his sources of supply, or the destination of

233 It should be noted, however, that intellectual property proceedings receive their own treatment in Pt 63 of the Civil Procedure Rules (CPR).

234 Reference should be made to the standard texts on the various intellectual property rights.

235 See S. Gee, *Commercial Injunctions* 5th revised edn (2006); L.A. Sheridan, *Injunctions and Similar Orders* (1999).

236 *Anton Piller v Manufacturing Processes* [1976] Ch. 55; [1976] R.P.C. 719; approving *EMI v Pandit* [1975] 1 All E.R. 418. A slender line of earlier precedent existed: e.g. *East India Co v Kynaston* (1821) Bli.P.C. 153; *Hennessy v Bohmann* [1877] W.N. 14.

237 The jurisdiction given to all county courts in 1984 was removed in 1991: County Court Remedies Regulations 1991 (SI 1991/1222) reg.3.

238 Orders covering any premises under the defendant's control are made only in exceptional circumstances: *Protector Alarms v Maxim Alarms* [1979] F.S.R. 442. Orders have sometimes been made against those who have no premises, or whose names are not known: *EMI Records v Kudhail* [1985] F.S.R. 36; *Tony Blain v Splain* [1994] F.S.R. 497 SC (NZ); Barron [1996] E.I.P.R. 183. Against some of these, there is a self-help remedy available in copyright cases: see above, para.2–27. Being an ex parte procedure, an *Anton Piller* order is not enforceable in other EC countries under the Brussels Judgments Convention art.24: *Denilauler v Couchet Frè;res* [1981] 1 C.M.L.R. 62.

239 *Universal City v Mukhtar* [1976] F.S.R. 252.

240 *EMI v Sarwar* [1977] F.S.R. 146 CA.

stock passing through his hands. An injunction against infringement may be part of the order. The procedure, now known as a search order, is given statutory force by the Civil Procedure Act 1997 s.7,[241] and the procedure is contained in r.25.1 (1)(f) of the Civil Procedure Rules (with details set out in para.7 of the Practice Direction on Interim Injunctions).

The order will be made if the claimant: (1) provides an extremely strong prima facie case of infringement, (2) shows that the damage, actual or potential, to him is very serious, and (3) provides clear evidence that the defendant has in his possession incriminating documents or things and that there is a probability that this material will be destroyed before any application attended by both sides can be made.[242] There are certain safeguards which are said to distinguish this sort of order from a search warrant[243]: the claimant's solicitor, who is an officer of the court, must attend,[244] and so must a supervising solicitor from another firm[245]; the defendant must be given time to think and must be informed of his right to consult his own solicitor and to apply to discharge the order.[246] The claimant must also give a cross-undertaking in damages. Subject to these, the defendant's refusal to allow the inspection is contempt of court (as well as in itself being evidence against him) and will be dealt with according to the circumstances.[247]

(b) *Dangers in the process*

Search orders were a response to growing concern over the volume of sound recording, video and other copyright piracy and the counterfeiting of popular trade marks, and are still used in that field, but they are equally available, for instance, in breach of confidence cases.[248] Although the reassurance was at first given that the orders would be rare,[249] the procedure is still regularly used 30 years later. It has contributed greatly to the speed and effectiveness of the civil process in dealing with pirates and counterfeiters **2–48**

---

241 See also the Civil Procedure Rules 1998 Pt 25.

242 *Anton Piller* case [1976] R.P.C. 719.

243 Ormrod L.J., *Anton Piller* case [1976] R.P.C. 719 at 726; and see Lord Denning M.R. (at 752) who added that the inspection must do no real harm to the defendant or his case. On the basic requirements, note also the *Island Records* and *Carlin* cases (above, para.2–17).

244 *Anton Piller* case [1976] R.P.C. 719, at 724, 726; now see PD 25 para.7.

245 As provided for in para.7.2 of the Pt 25 CPR Practice Direction on Interim Remedies (text with annexed draft Orders).

246 Normally the defendant will have up to two hours during which he can prevent the search from starting (though not entry by the supervising solicitor only): Pt 25 Practice Direction, annexed example order. An ex parte application to discharge the order will not, however, be granted in the absence of strong evidence: *Hallmark Cards v Image Arts* [1977] F.S.R. 150 CA.

247 Even a defendant whose contempt is not very serious may have to pay the claimant's costs on the application on an indemnity basis: *Channel v Three Pears* [1979] F.S.R. 393; cf. the *Hallmark* case [1977] F.S.R. 150 CA.

248 *Anton Piller* itself concerned copyright and confidential information in a machine. See also *Vapormatic v Sparex* [1976] F.S.R. 461—confidential list of customers ordered to be removed.

249 Ormrod L.J., *Anton Piller* case [1976] R.P.C. 719 at 725.

and the Enforcement Directive provision was modelled on the procedure.[250] Yet it raises the spectre which in former times made the courts so fearful of the general warrant to search. The proceedings turn upon the claimant's evidence alone and they occur *in private*. If a single judge is satisfied prima facie that there is infringement and a likelihood of serious injury, the claimant through his solicitor is empowered to launch his own raid on the defendant's premises or even his house. Those executing the order are likely to believe that right is on their side and that they must put on a show of aggression if they are to secure what their client needs and deserves. In the tensions generated by the surprise service of the order, a defendant will need considerable temerity if he is to seek legal advice and challenge the basis on which the order was made. As a measure of "privatisation" the order is remarkable: a non-state agency is employed in a direct infraction of personal liberties; and, more than that, those executing the order act for the very person who can least be expected to preserve a measure of objectivity and sense of proportion.

2–49 Because of its inherent unfairness, the *Anton Piller* order became the subject of increasing concern in the later 1980s.[251] Many of the criticisms went to the undue eagerness with which it was sometimes executed. A double threat would be produced by having the police simultaneously execute a search warrant procured on suspicion of criminal conduct such as dealing in obscene material. This practice was challenged under the European Convention on Human Rights art.8, which contains a guarantee of respect for private life and the home.[252] Since art.8 allows for exceptions where public authority acts "in accordance with the law" and (inter alia) "for the protection of the rights and freedoms of others", the European Court of Human Rights found that the *Anton Piller* process was in principle justifiable, case law having substantially delimited its scope. The court was critical of the execution of the order in the particular case,[253] although it did not in the end find this "disproportionate to the legitimate aim pursued" against a commercial infringer of film copyright. Nor did it accept an argument that the order could only be legitimate if executed by, or in the presence of, a court official.

The tenor of that judgment was reflected in Hoffmann J.'s call for:

> "careful balancing of, on the one hand, the [claimant's right] to recover his property or to preserve important evidence, against, on the other

[250] COM (2003) 46 final, p.21.

[251] See esp. Scott J., *Columbia Pictures v Robinson* [1986] 3 All E.R. 331 (describing the process as "draconian and essentially unfair"); Hoffmann J., *Lock International v Beswick* [1989] 1 W.L.R. 1268 at 1281; Nichols V.C. *Universal Thermosensors v Hibben* [1992] 1 W.L.R. 840 at 854. In its first flush, some 500 *Anton Piller* orders were being made a year, but as criticism grew this number fell considerably.

[252] *Chappell v United Kingdom* [1989] F.S.R. 617.

[253] As had been the Court of Appeal on a motion for contempt of the undertakings in the *Anton Piller* order by those executing it, a motion which likewise did not on balance succeed.

hand, violation of the privacy of a defendant who has had no opportunity to put his side of the case ... To borrow a useful concept from the jurisprudence of the European Community, there must be proportionality between the perceived threat to the [claimant's] rights and the remedy granted."[254]

In 1992, Nicholls V.C. showed such concern over the effects of carrying out the order[255] that the Lord Chancellor's Department issued a Consultation Paper[256] and from this followed a Practice Direction of 1994[257]: now replaced by the CPR Practice Direction on Interim Remedies. The Direction obliges the judge making the order either to require a private watch-dog in the form of the supervising solicitor already mentioned, or else to state why this is not appropriate. The added cost which this entails was considered to be an unavoidable burden.[258] **2–50**

(c) *Challenges to the order*

Accordingly the courts strive to be watchful for claimants who go to excess, seeking, for instance, a means of shutting out the defendant from all business, legitimate as well as illegitimate. There is a mandatory return date, when the court examines the execution of the order, including the report of the supervising solicitor. The ground on which defendants have regularly challenged orders is the claimant's failure fully to disclose all material circumstances. This, it has been said, should err on the side of excess; for it is for the court, not the claimant's advisers, to decide whether the order is justified.[259] It is no answer to a charge of inadequate disclosure that enough was shown to justify the making of the order.[260] Moreover, if business records have been seized, they should not be retained until trial, but should be returned after necessary information has been extracted from them; and where infringing material has been seized it should be handed over to the defendant's solicitor, once he is on the record, upon his undertaking to keep it in safe custody and produce it, if required, at the trial.[261] **2–51**

Even if the order is open to challenge, for instance because of inadequate disclosure, it is for the court, not the defendant, to decide whether it should **2–52**

[254] *Lock International v Beswick* [1989] 1 W.L.R. 1268.

[255] *Universal Thermosensors v Hibben* [1992] 1 W.L.R. 840, which accepted the uncompromising criticisms of Dockray and Laddie (1990) 106 L.Q.R. 601, including their proposal for a supervising solicitor. See also Davenport (1992) 109 L.Q.R. 555; Russell [1992] E.I.P.R. 243.

[256] *Anton Piller* Orders (No.181, 1992).

[257] Davies [1996] Civ. Just. Q. 17. The supervising solicitor must make a report on execution, to be supplied to the applicant's solicitors who must, in turn, both serve a copy on the respondent's solicitors and file one with the court (PD on Interim Remedies, para.7.5(11)).

[258] But the role of this person is problematic: Willoughby [1999] Civ. Just. Q. 103.

[259] See esp. *Lock International* [1989] 1 W.L.R. 1268; *Naf Naf v Dickson* [1993] F.S.R. 424; *Intergraph v Solid Systems CAD Services* [1993] F.S.R. 617.

[260] *Wardle Fabrics v Myristis* [1984] F.S.R. 263.

[261] *Columbia Picture Industries v Robinson* [1986] 3 All E.R. 338 at 371. It is also wrong to procure wider seizure than the order allows without the defendant having a solicitor's advice.

be discharged.[262] One objection which the court will not accept is that if a defendant is obliged to reveal information he risks personal violence from criminal associates.[263] Accordingly it remains contempt of court to refuse to comply with the order.[264] The defendant is protected by the discretion on costs and the claimant's cross-undertaking in damages. If the order was not justified or its execution was oppressive—whether or not it is subsequently discharged—the defendant will be entitled to compensatory damages for injury to his business; and possibly also to aggravated damages for the "affront" in the way the proceedings were used against him, and even to exemplary damages. The last are justified under the special case concerning wrongs committed by government servants, given that the claimant's solicitor is acting as a court officer.[265]

(d) *Self-incrimination*

2–53 The acute difficulties of balancing efficacy against fairness have surfaced equally over the element of "instant discovery"[266] in any search (*Anton Piller*) order that requires answers on sources of supply or customers. Since these answers would in many cases furnish evidence of criminal conduct, defendants at first sought to plead in response a privilege against self-incrimination. The House of Lords upheld this plea in any case where there was more than a remote or fanciful chance that a serious charge, attracting heavy penalties, might result.[267] This meant that the privilege was available to those who ran substantial piracy operations and so were likely to be charged with conspiracy to defraud, as distinct from (say) a summary offence under the copyright or trade descriptions legislation, which might be appropriate against a street trader. Because the upshot was to offer a haven to those apparently most culpable, Parliament proved willing to intervene. Under s.72 of the Supreme Court Act 1981, in proceedings for infringement of intellectual property rights[268] or passing off, a defendant may after all be compelled to answer a question or comply with an order which would tend to expose him or her to proceedings for a related offence or recovery of a

[262] [1986] 3 All E.R. 338 at 372–375. Even if a wrongly obtained order has been executed, it will be discharged: *Booker McConnell v Plascow* [1985] R.P.C. 475 CA, unless that would amount to an empty gesture without practical effect: *Columbia Picture Industries*, at 377–379. It remains in the court's discretion to decide whether to restrain use of implicatory information wrongly obtained: *Naf Naf* case [1993] F.S.R. 424.

[263] *Coca-Cola v Gilbey* [1996] F.S.R. 23 CA.

[264] *Wardle* [1984] F.S.R. 263; *Columbia Picture Industries* [1986] 3 All E.R. 338 at 368.

[265] *Columbia Picture Industries* [1986] 3 All E.R. 338 at 379–380; *Universal Thermosensors v Hibben* [1992] 1 W.L.R. 840 at 854.

[266] Bridge L.J., *Rank Film v Video Information* [1980] 2 All E.R. 283.

[267] *Rank Film v Video Information* [1982] A.C. 380.

[268] This, the first statutory use of the term, encompasses "patent, trade mark, copyright, registered design, technical or commercial information or other intellectual property": Supreme Court Act 1981 s.73(5). The privilege may still be claimed in other cases: see *Cobra Golf v Rata (No.2)* [1997] F.S.R. 317; CPR r.25.7.9.

related penalty.[269] It is, however, not possible to use any statement or admission so procured in any equivalent criminal proceedings.[270]

With such a patchwork of exceptions, the privilege itself is not easily justified as a general rule; yet it still applies in cases of fraud outside the scope of the statutory exceptions, and notably where a defendant is likely to be prosecuted for conspiracy to defraud.[271] Where it applies, it has a perverse effect: it protects most readily when the evidence against the person concerned is really damning and is therefore likely to result in prosecution for a serious offence.[272] Either it should be restored as the general rule in a real sense, or it should be replaced by the approach now used in the exceptional cases: the incriminating answers must be given (and other facts revealed), although the information may not then be used as evidence in criminal proceedings.[273] **2–54**

(2) Freezing orders for the retention of assets: formerly known as Mareva injunctions[274]

The development of the search order coincided with another, more general evolution in interim procedure. The freezing order is directed, not to the uncovering and preserving of "fragile" evidence, but to the retention of assets belonging to the defendant which may be needed to satisfy judgment in the action, particularly if they may otherwise be removed from the jurisdiction.[275] Orders are not uncommonly made which contain both search and freezing terms.[276] These may relate to bank accounts and other financial assets.[277] Equally, there have been orders directed to the seizure of specified valuables, such as cars, in which, according to evidence, the proceeds of infringement have been invested. Just as a defendant is permitted an **2–55**

[269] The privilege is taken away more generally where proceedings are being brought against apprehended infringement, rather than against acts which have already occurred: s.73(5); *Universal City v Hubbard* [1984] R.P.C. 43 CA. But it seems that documents wrongly seized, where the privilege should still have been upheld, do not have to be returned: Cumming-Bruce L.J. at 47–48.

[270] i.e. such proceedings as are no longer a justification for upholding the privilege against incrimination by virtue of the section.

[271] *Tate Access Floors v Boswell* [1990] 3 All E.R. 303; and see *Societdad Nacional (Sonangol) v Lundqvist* [1991] 2 W.L.R. 280.

[272] See, e.g. Lord Templeman, *Istel v Tully* [1992] 3 W.L.R. 344 at 350 HL.

[273] This approach is favoured in the Lord Chancellor's Department's Consultation Papers on Self-Incrimination and *Anton Piller* Orders.

[274] Civil Procedure Rules r.25(1)(h). See S. Gee, *Commercial Injunctions* 5th revised edn (2006); Sheridan, *Injunctions and Similar Orders* (1999); Zuckermann (1992) 109 L.Q.R. 560.

[275] A number of cases have manifested a desire to aid a claimant in searching for the defendant's assets world-wide: *Babanhaft v Bassatne* [1989] 2 W.L.R. 232 CA; *Republic of Haiti v Duvalier* [1989] 2 W.L.R. 261 CA; *Derby v Weldon (No.1, Nos 3 and 4)* [1989] 2 W.L.R. 276 at 412 CA; *Grupo Torras v Sheikh Fahad Mohammed Al-Sabah* [1995] 1 Lloyd's Rep. 374 QBD. See also Collins (1989) 105 L.Q.R. 262; Capper (1991) 54 M.L.R. 329.

[276] Equally they may well contain an interim injunction.

[277] In order to ensure efficacy, the court may allow cross-examination on affidavits in defence: *House of Spring Gardens v Waite* [1985] F.S.R. 173 CA.

allowance for living expenses out of financial assets that are subject to a freezing order, so also, where the order relates to other assets, he will not be deprived of things needed for living and conducting legitimate trade.[278]

2–56 As with search orders, the courts tended to relax the requirements as they became more familiar with their use. To begin with, they required proof of an extremely strong prima facie case, but that later became a "good arguable case"[279]; the need to identify the defendant's assets in advance was bypassed, as was the need to show that he was likely deliberately to dissipate his assets.[280] There is so far no requirement that a supervising solicitor be appointed and the court does not itself supervise the continuance of the order. The effect of such an order, going as it does to the defendant's assets as a whole, and giving the applicant some real opportunity to convert an entitlement into a preferred claim, is capable of inflicting very considerable harm and judges are rightly cautious about granting them.[281]

(3) Discovery of names: Norwich Pharmacal action

2–57 Sometimes the only lead that a right-owner can pick up about infringing goods is that they are passing through the hands of some person in the course of transit. That person may, however, not be infringing and may not even know that others have infringed or are likely to do so. The court may order such a person to disclose the names of the consignors or consignees responsible, if this is necessary to dispose fairly of the claim or to save costs, in the words of r.31.17 of the Civil Procedure Rules.[282] In *Norwich Pharmacal v Commissioner of Customs and Excise*,[283] an order was made against the Commissioners of Customs and Excise to reveal the names of importers of a patented drug, which their published records showed to have been imported. The order under r.31.17 is not confined to such circumstances, but will not be granted if the result would be unduly oppressive.[284] For instance, a television company was ordered to reveal the name of a "mole" within British Steel, who was admittedly in breach of confidence in revealing how

[278] *CBS United Kingdom v Lambert* [1983] F.S.R. 123 CA.

[279] See Lord Denning M.R., *Rasu Maritima v Perusahan* [1978] 1 Q.B. 644 at 661.

[280] See *Nimenia v Trave* [1983] 1 W.L.R. 1412.

[281] Willoughby and Connal [1997] E.I.P.R. 479.

[282] *CHC Software v Hopkins & Wood* [1993] F.S.R. 241; *Ashworth Security Hospital v MGN* [2003] F.S.R. 311, disapproving Sedley L.J., *Interbrew v Financial Times* [2002] E.M.L.R. 24.

[283] [1974] A.C. 133; [1974] R.P.C. 101 HL; *Jade Engineering (Coventry) Ltd v Antiference Window Systems Ltd* [1996] F.S.R. 461. The costs of the proceedings may be recovered as damages from the infringers thus exposed: *Morton-Norwich v Intercen (No.2)* [1981] F.S.R. 337. An importing or exporting agent might equally be subject to such an order: see *Orr v Diaper* (1876) 4 Ch.D. 23; *Upmann v Forester* (1885) 24 Ch.D. 231. Information obtained against one person may be used in the pursuit of others: *Levi Strauss v Barclays* [1993] F.S.R. 179.

[284] *Sega Enterprises v Alca Electronics* [1982] F.S.R. 516; cf. *AIRC v PPL* [1993] E.M.L.R. 181 at 244; *Romeike & Curtice Ltd v Newspaper Licensing Agency* [1999] E.M.L.R. 142. It is excepted from the Data Protection Act 1998 by its s.35: *Totalise v Motley Fool* [2001] E.M.L.R. 29; and see *Re Adidas* [2000] F.S.R. 227 ECJ.

the board was acting against strikers. The purpose of the proceedings was to procure the mole's dismissal, not to sue him.[285] Where goods are involved which are still being held, an injunction restraining their removal may also be granted.[286] In *Ashworth Security Hospital v MGN*,[287] the House of Lords granted a disclosure order against a journalist to require him to reveal the intermediary who supplied confidential medical records from a prison hospital of the Moors murderer, Ian Brady. Since this raised issues of freedom of the press in the context of the Human Rights Act 1998 s.10(2), the House was careful to insist that there must be a pressing social need for the order. A court must first be apprised clearly of the alleged wrongdoing and it must place restrictions confining use of the information to achieving the purpose of the order.

(4) Disclosure, interrogatories, inspection

English courts have generally been careful to protect defendants against speculative suits that are no more than "fishing expeditions"—proceedings begun to find out what, if anything, might really be claimed.[288] Accordingly, in our field, infringement actions cannot be launched effectively unless the claimant can specify in his particulars of claim at least one act of infringement.[289] If he does not give them and does not comply with any order for further and better particulars he will be unable to defend himself on a motion to strike out pleadings or action.[290] **2–58**

Provided that he can show enough to repel attacks on his pleadings, the claimant will carry his case forward to the stage of pre-trial preparations. As in other types of civil litigation, disclosure of documents and the administration of interrogatories are steps which on occasion may provide **2–59**

[285] *British Steel v Granada* [1981] A.C. 1096.

[286] See Buckley L.J., *Norwich Pharmacal* case [1972] R.P.C. 743 at 771.

[287] *Ashworth Security Hospital v MGN* [2003] F.S.R. 311 HL.

[288] For an analysis of CPR r.31.16 (which applies to pre-action discosure) in a design right case, see the judgment of Patten J. in *BSW v Balltec* [2007] F.S.R. 1.; see also *Red Spider v Omega Completion* [2010] F.S.R. 6.

[289] Equally if a defendant ripostes with a defence or counterclaim which turns on issues of fact, he may be required to give particulars of allegations; for instance, that the claimant's alleged trade mark is in fact common to the trade. If his response in a patent suit is to seek revocation of a patent he will be obliged to give particulars of his objections to validity.

It has been said that a claimant who brings a motion for interim relief is entitled, on seeing the defendant's evidence, to apply to stand the motion over until trial of the action without costs being immediately awarded against him: *Jeffrey v Shelana* [1976] F.S.R. 54. But this may invite a form of fishing and a later court has held that the award of costs is always a matter of discretion: *Simons Records v W.E.A. Records* [1980] F.S.R. 35 at 36. See also *Rockwell v Serck* [1988] F.S.R. 187.

[290] Equally he will not be permitted to seek disclosure or deliver interrogatories: *AG für Autogene Aluminium v London Aluminium* [1919] 2 Ch. 67.

important evidence or admissions.[291] In the United States of America such steps have been inflated into a form of discovery that allows wide-ranging preliminary cross-examination of party by party.[292] That has not occurred in England and the amount of disclosure required has been reduced considerably as a result of the Woolf reforms. A party is required to disclose only: (a) those documents on which he relies, (b) documents which adversely affect his own or another's case or which support another party's case, and (c) other documents which he is required to disclose by a Practice Direction.[293] If the documents disclosed contain confidential information, the other party may be restrained from using the information for purposes such as revelations in the press[294] or further litigation.

2–60 Beyond this there are special procedures for cases involving industrial techniques. The claimant may need to discover what the defendant is doing; but the defendant may fear that inspection by him will reveal the defendant's own secrets—a fear that, in the race to get ahead, is sometimes acute. The court has power to order inspection even against this sort of objection.[295] But while it will not require first to be satisfied prima facie that the defendant is infringing,[296] it may need to be shown that there are "formidable grounds", rather than a mere suspicion.[297] It may try to alleviate the defendant's anxieties by requiring an independent expert to make the inspection.[298] If such a person could not make a properly informed inspection, then it may have to be done by the claimant and his advisers; but

---

[291] Disclosure concerning the whole of a defendant's trading operation, in order to secure evidence going purely to his credit, is oppressive and will not be allowed: *Ballatine v Dixon* [1975] R.P.C. 111; *EG Music v SF (Film Distributors)* [1978] F.S.R. 121; cf. *Mood Music v de Wolfe* [1976] Ch. 119.

[292] For the impact of this procedural development in patent actions, see *Chisum on Patents* (2006).

[293] CPR r.31.6(c). Also, para.9.1 of PD 49E exempts disclosure of documents: (a) relating to infringement of a patent by a product or process, provided that the alleged infringer serves full particulars of the product or process alleged to infringe, (b) relating to any ground on which the validity of the patent is put in issue, except documents which came into existence within the period beginning two years before the earliest claimed priority and ending two years after that date, and (c) relating to the issue of commercial success, provided that full particulars are served in a schedule directed by the court.

[294] *Distillers v Times Newspapers* [1975] 1 All E.R. 41; *Home Office v Harman* [1983] A.C. 280; *Wilden Pump Engineering Co v Fusfield* [1985] F.S.R. 159 CA. This applies equally to prejudicial material uncovered under a search (*Anton Piller*) order, which carries an implied undertaking not to use it for a collateral purpose; but the court has an ultimate jurisdiction in the matter: *Crest Homes v Marks* [1987] F.S.R. 305 HL; *CCE v Hamlin Slowe* [1986] F.S.R. 346; *Cobra Golf v Rata (No.2)* [1997] F.S.R. 317. It is proper to use the material to arrest assets in another jurisdiction: *Bayer v Winter (No.2)* [1986] F.S.R. 357; but see *Grapha Holdings v Quebecor Printing* [1996] F.S.R. 711; *Chiron v Evans Medical* [1997] F.S.R. 268.

[295] *Medway v Doublelock* [1978] 1 All E.R. 1261; *Riddick v Thames Board* [1977] 3 All E.R. 677 CA.

[296] *British Xylonite v Fibrenyle* [1959] R.P.C. 252 CA. To hold that there was a prima facie case might embarrass the trial judge.

[297] *Wahl v Buhler-Miag* [1979] F.S.R. 183; and see *Electrolux Northern v Black & Decker* [1996] F.S.R. 595.

[298] cf. *Printers & Finishers v Holloway* [1964] 3 All E.R. 54 (inspection of claimant's plant on behalf of defendant: elements claimed to be secret must be pointed out).

possibly on condition that nothing is copied or taken away and that all involved are placed under obligations to respect confidence.[299]

4. Delayed Ambush and Selective Action

In the main it is not isolated acts of infringement but actual or threatened repeat marketing or sales that provoke the owner of intellectual property rights into taking action. Accordingly, a defendant's stake is likely to be high; and it may well become higher if proceedings against him are delayed until he has established commercial production and tied himself to distribution arrangements. While there are incentives that will induce right-owners in many circumstances to move as quickly as possible (in particular, the chance to secure interim relief),[300] these may for some reason have little or no force. Not only may there be tactical advantages in delay, it may also seem more damaging to proceed not against the manufacturer who is the source of the alleged infringement, but against his wholesale or resale distributors or even the ultimate users or consumers. In all this, the legal limitations upon a claimant's freedom of action can have great importance, and the most important of these limitations, many of them matters of general law, deserve to be sketched in. **2–61**

(1) Limitation of actions

The question here is: within what period after a particular infringement has been perpetrated must a claim form be issued? The various infringement actions in our field, being tortious in character, must normally be begun within six years of the wrongful act.[301] The same applies to actions based upon breach of contract. Only the action for breach of confidence may differ (when not founded in contract) because of its equitable origin: probably the only principle is that a period of too great a delay (*laches*) must not be allowed to lapse.[302] **2–62**

An action which is commenced within the limitation period, but then allowed to stagnate, may be struck out for want of prosecution. Under the

[299] *Centri-Spray v Cera* [1979] F.S.R. 175; *Roussel Uclaf v ICI* [1990] F.S.R. 25.

[300] See above, para.2–32.

[301] Limitation Act 1980 s.2: see *Phonographic Performance Ltd v Dept of Trade and Industry* [2005] R.P.C. 152, where Morritt V.C. held that the six-year limitation period applies to a claim against the Government for failure to give effect to art.8(2) of the Rental Rights Directive, giving rise to a breach of statutory duty claim founded in tort. There are exceptions for cases of mistake and fraud: see generally, 28 *Halsbury's Laws of England* 4th edn reissue, paras 1119–1122. The provision applies to amendments alleging additional acts of infringement: *Sorata v Gardex* [1984] F.S.R. 81.

[302] See below, para.2–64. In *Mersey Care NHS Trust v Ackroyd* [2006] E.M.L.R. 12, Tugendhat J. declined to grant a *Norwich Pharmacal* order for disclosure by a journalist of a source of information because the disclosure had taken place more than six years previously and circumstances had changed, making the grant of the order not proportionate.

practice prior to the introduction of the Civil Procedure Rules (CPR), this was only done if there was real prejudice to the defendant as well as inordinate delay.[303] Such prejudice might arise if witnesses in a patent action would have to testify to the state of an art which has receded a considerable distance in time.[304] Under the CPR there is now a requirement that a party to proceedings should behave reasonably both before and after they have commenced proceedings and, under rr.1.1(2)(d) and 1.3, parties are under a duty to assist the court in ensuring that cases are dealt with expeditiously and fairly.[305]

(2) Acquiescence

2–63 Beyond the limitation periods for particular wrongs lies a further question: if a defendant has been left to pursue a course of infringement for a substantial period of time, can the right-owner be taken to have consented to its continuance? If so, no part of the defendant's activity, even the most recent, is actionable. This consent may be expressly given or it may be implied from the circumstances; it may occur before, at the time of, or after the infringing act. Conduct alone can create an implied licence in some circumstances. Where the claimant represents, expressly or impliedly, that the defendant's conduct is not an infringement, he will thereafter be estopped from asserting his right.[306] A party may not deny that which, knowingly or unknowingly, he has allowed or encouraged another to assume to his detriment.[307] In such a case there is no need to show any element of delay.

At least when the question is whether an injunction should be granted in support of a legal right, it may be enough to prove delay by itself if the delay is "inordinate"; or delay coupled with:

> "something ... to encourage the wrongdoer to believe that he does not intend to rely upon his strict legal rights, and the wrongdoer must have acted to his prejudice in that belief".[308]

---

303 *Birkett v James* [1978] A.C. 297 HL; *Compagnie Franμaise de Télévision v Thorn* [1978] R.P.C. 735 CA; *Bestworth v Wearwell* [1986] R.P.C. 527; *Department of Transport v Smaller* [1989] A.C. 1197 HL.

304 *Horstman Gear v Smiths Industries* [1979] F.S.R. 461.

305 See Lord Woolf M.R. in *Clark v University of Lincolnshire and Humberside* [2000] 1 W.L.R. 1988 at [34–36] CA,

306 Cotton L.J., *Proctor v Bennis* (1886) 36 Ch.D. 740 at 758–761.

307 Oliver J., *Taylor Fashions v Liverpool Victoria* [1982] 1 Q.B. 133; *Film Investors v Home Video Channel* [1997] E.M.L.R. 347.

308 Goff L.J., *Bulmer v Bollinger* [1978] R.P.C. 79 at 134–136, referring especially to *Electrolux v Electrix* (1954) 71 R.P.C. 23; *Cluett-Peabody v McIntyre* [1958] R.P.C. 335. In *Vine Products v Mackenzie* [1969] R.P.C. 1 at 25–26, Cross J. held that the defence might arise, even though the claimant did not appreciate that the law afforded him any civil remedy; but cf. *Willmott v Barber* (1880) 15 Ch. D. 96. For acquiescence as a reason for refusing an account of profits, see *International Scientific Communications v Pattison* [1979] F.S.R. 429.

(3) Estoppels of record (res judicata)[309]

In order to give finality and to prevent a person from repeatedly asserting either an unsubstantiable right or the freedom to act in contravention of another's right, estoppels of record may be raised against him in various circumstances. Three kinds should be distinguished. **2–64**

(a) *Judgment in rem*

Certain types of judgment bind all persons and not merely the parties to the action. In our field, an order revoking a patent, registered design or registered trade mark—the rights that depend upon grant—may be relied upon by all the world against the former right-owner. By contrast a decision that a claimant has no copyright, that a patent is valid or that a trade mark is properly registered can only have a binding effect on the other parties to the action and their privies.[310] The judgment is in personam and falls for consideration under the next headings. **2–65**

(b) *Cause of action estoppel*[311]

If A sues B, alleging a particular cause of action upon pleaded facts, and he loses, he will subsequently be estopped from suing upon the same cause of action.[312] Suppose, for instance, the action is for passing off and A fails to provide sufficient evidence that the public was likely to be deceived by the defendant's acts into believing that it was getting goods of the claimant; or he unsuccessfully claims a reputation with the public as manufacturer when he might have succeeded on a claim to be known as a distributor; or a general rule of law is held to preclude his claim. In each of these circumstances a second case based on the same facts would be precluded, if **2–66**

[309] This is a complex subject. See generally, Spencer-Bower, Turner & Handley, *The Doctrine of Res Judicata* (3rd edn. 1996); 15 *Halsbury's Laws of England* (4th edn reissue), paras 964 et seq. The term res judicata, commonly applied to one or other aspect of the subject, is here avoided because of its ambiguities.

[310] But certificates of contested validity may be granted for patents and registered designs and marks: PA 1977 s.65; RDA 1949 s.25; TMA 1994 s.73. An unsuccessful challenge subsequently risks an award of solicitor-and-client costs (designs and marks), or even solicitor-and-non-client costs (patents).

[311] In *Markem v Zipher* [2005] R.P.C. 31 CA, the Court of Appeal found it an abuse of process to bring fresh proceedings for breach of confidence after proceedings for patent entitlement involving the same issues had been resolved, referring to the judgment of Lord Bingham in *Johnson v Gore Wood* [2002] A.C. 1 at 31 where he noted: "*Henderson v Henderson* abuse of process, as now understood, although separate and distinct from cause of action estoppel and issue estoppel, has much in common with them. The underlying public interest is the same: that there should be finality in litigation and that a party should not be twice vexed in the same matter."

[312] In certain circumstances, a decision of a foreign court also can be relied upon as creating a cause of action estoppel: *Barrett v Universal-Island Records* [2006] E.M.L.R. 21.

the first judgment was final and not interim.[313] Thus, this category of estoppel may debar attempts to put the same case more persuasively, whether in point of evidence or legal argument; but it operates only where the cause of action is the same.[314] In *Special Effects Ltd v L'Oréal*[315] it was held for the purposes of a counterclaim for invalidity of a registered mark that:

> "to describe the applicant for [trade mark] registration as having a cause of action for registration would be an inappropriate and artificial use of language. The same is true of the opponent"

and therefore a cause of action estoppel did not apply to the later counterclaim for invalidity on grounds similar to those raised in the opposition.[316]

(c) *Issue estoppel*

2–67 If a court decides an issue of fact and gives a final judgment, the loser is estopped from raising the issue a second time even upon a different cause of action.[317] In the case of such an issue estoppel, both the initial parties and

[313] Decisions in the course of examining a patent application (including third-party oppositions) have been held not to be final: see *Buehler AG v Chronos Richardson Ltd*, where the relevant jurisdiction was divided between the English courts and the Opposition Division of the EPO. Similarly as regards as trade marks, there is no issue estoppel involved in applying for a declaration of invalidity after having failed in an opposition: *Special Effects v L'Oréal* [2007] EWCA Civ 1 at [52]–[72].

[314] In general, any matter is res judicata which is raised on the pleadings and falls within the terms of the order; but exceptionally, an explicit qualification in the judgment may be taken account of to limit the scope of the estoppel: *Patchett v Sterling* (1954) 71 R.P.C. 61 CA.

[315] [2007] EWCA Civ 1.

[316] [2007] EWCA Civ 1 at [49]. The court distinguished *Hormel Foods Corp v Antilles Landscape Investments* [2005] R.P.C. 28, on the ground that the latter concerned revocation in both instances (at para.[50]). At first instance, Arnold QC had reviewed the authorities in detail and concluded that "(i) a person who attacks the validity of a patent or registered design is under a duty to put his full case in support of that attack at trial; and (ii) if he is unsuccessful, he will be barred by cause of action estoppel from attacking the validity of the patent or registered design in subsequent proceedings whether on the same or similar grounds ... even if he could not have discovered those different grounds by the exercise of reasonable diligence before the first trial" (at para.86). Mr Arnold then applied this conclusion to trade marks (at paras 95–96); see Burden [2005] E.I.P.R 477.

[317] *Carl Zeiss v Rayner & Keeler (No. 2)* [1967] 1 A.C. 853; *Chiron v Organon Teknika (No. 14)* [1996] F.S.R. 701 CA; *Kirin-Amgen v Boehringer Mannheim* [1997] F.S.R: 289 CA; *Hodgkinson & Corby v Wards Mobility Services (No. 2)* [1998] F.S.R. 530 CA. Under the law before 1978, the conditional character of a decision to allow a patent application to proceed to grant despite opposition meant that it was not final (see *Bristol Myers v Beecham* [1978] F.S.R. 553 (Israel SC)). Now that a third party may challenge only after grant it may well be that an unsuccessful attack on validity before the Comptroller or in an EPO opposition would raise an estoppel. On the difficult questions which may arise when only one issue is appealed, see the *Bristol Myers* case (cf. at 562–563, 568–571). In relation to trade marks, the Court of Appeal in *Special Effects v L'Oréal* [2007] EWCA Civ 1 found that "the co-existence of the provisions for opposition and for a declaration of invalidity has the result that opposition proceedings are inherently not final": at para.71.

their privies will be bound. The range of this "privity" is not wide.[318] Where a number of enterprises are engaged in the evolution of a product from conception to marketing, and a question of (say) copyright infringement arises, the successors in title and the employees of any business will be treated as its privies, and probably also an assignee of its rights. But a design-creating firm and the manufacturer which it commissions to execute its designs are not privy.[319] In *Coflexip v Stolt Offshore (No. 2)* the Court of Appeal held that an enquiry as to damages should proceed against a party found to have infringed, despite a successful subsequent challenge to the validity of the patent. The approach also applies where a European patent (UK) is held valid and infringed in English proceedings, but remains thereafter the subject of an attack in opposition proceedings in the European Patent Office.[320] The root justification is a matter of policy. Certainty in business relations is an important goal. An IP rightholder, as much as any civil claimant, should contest his position on an issue at one time only, rather than being allowed to start over again when he thinks he has a better chance.

The manner in which issue estoppel may go further than cause of action estoppel is illustrated by this: if it were decided that A and not B is the successor in title to a business by proceedings to establish ownership, in subsequent passing-off proceedings by A against B for misappropriation of the marks of the business, B could not re-open the question of A's ownership. But the issue must have been raised and not allowed to go by default—in this respect issue estoppel is narrower. In its wider aspect, issue estoppel has special importance for intellectual property. In this sphere, defendants frequently repeat the allegedly infringing act in the course of producing or marketing goods. Each new act may give rise to a distinct cause of action, so the cause of action estoppel may be too narrow to achieve the objective that the law sets itself.[321] **2–68**

Both cause of action and issue estoppel may be raised in English proceedings upon the judgment of a foreign court.[322] As intellectual property has grown in significance as a supra-national commodity, so has the impact of this rule: litigating the same issue in several jurisdictions can be just as harassing (and expensive) as litigating it several times in one. Equally, the courts are likely to approach this form of issue estoppel with caution, taking care to ensure that the issue was a basis for the foreign decision, rather than being merely collateral or obiter, and avoiding prejudice to a party who **2–69**

[318] See Lloyd L.J. in *Special Effects v L'Oréal* [2007] EWCA Civ 1 at [81–82].

[319] *Gleeson v Wippell* [1977] F.S.R. 301, now approved by the House of Lords in *Johnson v Gore Wood & Co* [2002] A.C. 1 (a professional negligence case); see also *Kirin Amgen v Boehringer Mannheim* [1997] F.S.R: 289; *Coca-Cola Co v Ketteridge* [2004] F.S.R. 3.

[320] *Unilin Beheer v Berry Floor* [2007] F.S.R. 25; *Virgin Atlantic v Premium Aircraft* [2009] EWCA Civ 1513 CA.

[321] For an instance, see *Form Tubes v Guinness* [1989] F.S.R. 41.

[322] *Carl Zeiss v Rayner & Keeler (No. 2)* [1967] 1 A.C. 853 and *Bristol Myers v Beecham* [1978] F.S.R. 553.

found it impracticable to fight the issue properly in the foreign jurisdiction.[323]

2–70 As already noted, the main intellectual property rights are territorial in character.[324] A French judgment, therefore, on (say) infringement of a French patent or copyright cannot give rise to a cause of action estoppel between the same proprietor of the equivalent British rights and the same defendant who is performing equivalent acts in England. Whether it might found an issue estoppel is less certain: the question remains unexplored in the case law.[325] Since the actual activities must be different, the issue would be concerned with the application of the law to equivalent facts. A finding of estoppel could scarcely be made unless the court was satisfied that the same legal principle fell to be applied. Given such arrangements as the European Patent Convention, it may now be possible to meet this criterion in some circumstances (for example, on the validity of patents granted by the European route in light of a prior publication or use).

(4) Actions concerning foreign intellectual property[326]

(a) *Foreign infringements*

2–71 In the past English courts refused to hear actions based on claims for alleged IP infringement occurring in other countries. Since the subject matter stems from national policy and can easily generate suspicions of favouritism towards local parties, there was good sense in this caution. The increasingly global reach of trade and the prospects for global infringement of rights on the internet may call for some re-consideration of this tradition. However, the Court of Appeal has insisted that change should not be brought about by case law. Rather it needs careful balancing of interests in a convention between states. So far as the countries in the European Union and European Free Trade Area are concerned, this has been achieved by the Judgments Regulation of 2001 and the preceding Conventions which it replaced.[327] In relation to non-EU countries the old rules have survived in relation to all aspects of IP: entitlement, validity and infringement.

The former position was justified both by a jurisdictional rule of public policy and under the choice of law rule which called for "double actionability":

---

[323] *Carl Zeiss v Rayner & Keeler (No. 2)* [1967] 1 A.C. 853 at 917–918, per Lord Reid; and see at 948–949 (Lord Upjohn), and at 972 (Lord Wilberforce).

[324] See above, paras 1–30 et seq.

[325] The Israel SC in *Bristol Myers v Beecham* [1978] F.S.R. 553, however, assumes the possibility in appropriate circumstances.

[326] See Wadlow, *Enforcement of Intellectual Property in European and International Law* (1998); Fawcett and Torremans, *Intellectual Property and Private International Law* (1998); Ginsburg, *The Private International Law of Copyright in an Era of Technological Change* (1999); Mankowski (2001) 32 I.I.C. 390; cf. Ulmer, *Intellectual Property Rights and the Conflict of Laws* (1978). As to patents, see Stauder, von Rospatt (1998) 29 I.I.C. 497 at 504, 509.

[327] See below para.2–74.

(a) The rule of public policy (the *Moçambique* rule)[328] abrogated jurisdiction over foreign torts where their character was "local" as opposed to "transitory". The primary category of "local" rights were those pertaining to land; but increasingly intellectual property was also treated as having the same close connection with its own territory.[329]

(b) The "double actionability" rule in private international law concerned torts in general. It arose because English courts chose to apply their own tort law to wrongs occurring abroad and therefore required as a condition that the action should also be wrongful by the law of the place where it occurred.[330] While that remained the general rule, in *Red Sea Insurance v Bouygues* the Privy Council admitted an exception under which, where an issue between the parties had its most significant relationship with an occurrence in another country, then the law of that country should be applied to it.[331] This qualification was in effect transformed into the prima facie rule by the Private International Law (Miscellaneous Provisions) Act 1995 Pt III.

In *Pearce v Ove Arup*, the Court of Appeal accepted a reversal of both the traditional rules concerning actions over foreign intellectual property. At least this was so within the EU and EFTA, the action in England being concerned with a claim that in erecting his design for Rotterdam Town Hall, the Dutch architect, Rem Koolhaas, has infringed copyright in a plan drawn up by an associate in his London office.[332] The public policy rule, having already been abolished by statute in relation to land,[333] was held not to apply to intellectual property either. Alongside this, the "double actionability" rule was to be taken as abrogated by the *Red Sea* case: it was particularly appropriate to apply the local law to the foreign intellectual property wrong because of its strictly territorial reach.[334] Since *Pearce* concerned the **2–72**

[328] *British South Africa Co v Companhia de Moçambique* [1893] A.C. 602; applied in patent matters by the High Court of Australia: *Potter v Broken Hill Pty Ltd* (1906) 3 C.L.R. 479; and see *Norbert Steinhart v Meth* (1960) 105 C.L.R. 440.

[329] See esp. *Mölnlycke v Procter & Gamble* [1992] R.P.C. 21 at 21 CA, per Dillon L.J. Because of it, the Brussels and Lugano Conventions (for which see below para.2–74) were previously regarded as introducing an exception, which would operate only as between states party to the Conventions: see *Pearce v Ove Arup* [1997] F.S.R. 64 (Lloyd J.); *Coin Controls v Suzo* [1997] F.S.R. 660 (Laddie J.); *Fort Dodge Animal Health v Akzo* [1998] F.S.R. 222 at 226–227 (Laddie J.) and, by implication also the CA in that case: [1998] F.S.R. 222 at 239 et seq.

[330] *Dicey and Morris on the Conflict of Laws* 14th edn (2006) r.203, deriving from *Phillips v Eyre* (1870) L.R. 6 Q.B. 1 at 28–29; *Boys v Chaplin* [1971] A.C. 356.

[331] [1995] A.C. 190; the exception was foreshadowed in *Dicey and Morris*, r.203.

[332] [1999] F.S.R. 525.

[333] Civil Jurisdiction and Judgments Act 1982 s.2(1).

[334] The wrongful activity in the *Pearce* case occurred before the Private International Law (Miscellaneous Provisions) Act 1995 took effect: the allegation was of infringement of copyright by erecting a building in Holland in accordance with architectural plans drawn in England. Hence the court's decision was determined exclusively by the position at common law.

copyright law of The Netherlands, the impact of the judgment on IP arising in non-EU/EFTA states could at most be obiter. When faced with the latter issue directly, a later Court of Appeal insisted that the old public policy approach be maintained.[335]

Thus it has become permissible to bring an action in England in respect of the infringement abroad of foreign intellectual property rights, where the other country concerned is a Member State of the EU or of EFTA. We shall consider the position between EU/EFTA states first, since that is governed by the special arrangements of the Judgments Regulation.[336] Then we return to the present status of rules vis-à-vis non-EU/EFTA jurisdictions.[337]

(b) *Jurisdiction: the Judgments Regulation*

2–73 EC Regulation 44/2001[338] (the "Judgments Regulation") now embodies a modified version of the Brussels Convention on Jurisdiction and Enforcement of Judgments in Civil and Commercial Matters.[339] The Brussels Convention was first agreed in 1968 as a separate instrument by the six Member States of the then European Economic Community. In the case of the United Kingdom it was given effect by the Civil Jurisdiction and Judgments Act 1982.[340] The Lugano Convention of 1989 extends the same arrangements to the EFTA countries,[341] and became part of UK law through the Civil Jurisdiction and Judgments Act 1991. The transfer from separate Conventions to EU Regulation has given the Community control over its content and its reform. The purpose of the Judgments Regulation is to determine the international jurisdiction of courts in EU countries, so as to facilitate recognition of judgments and to introduce an expeditious procedure for securing their enforcement, and other instruments and court settlements. It is designed accordingly to ensure the equality and uniformity of rights, in pursuit of legal certainty, not least by reducing the scope for forum shopping.[342]

As experience with cross-territory patent actions has shown, the Regulation falls demonstrably short of this aim. The structure of the two Conventions is best understood by first looking at the three bases of jurisdiction which they allow:

---

[335] *Lucasfilm v Ainsworth* [2010] F.S.R. 10.

[336] Below, paras. 2–74—2–82.

[337] Below, paras. 2–83—2–84

[338] Effective from March 1, 2002. For the UK, see Civil Jurisdiction and Judgments Order (2001/3929).

[339] Special arrangements to accommodate Denmark have involved continuing the two Conventions in the relations between that country and the other States concerned.

[340] Note that the rule is in no way dependent on the domicile of the claimant; so it may be taken advantage of by a non-EU citizen or resident.

[341] At present, Iceland, Norway and Switzerland. Lugano follows the terms now found in the Judgments Regulation.

[342] *Duijnstee v Goderbauer* [1985] 1 C.M.L.R. 220 ECJ (a case concerned with entitlement to patents).

(1) the basic preference is for suit to be brought in the EU or EFTA state of the defendant's "domicile", where such a connection exists;
(2) additional jurisdiction arises in the place of tortious harm;
(3) but where an IPR requires registration, exclusive jurisdiction over validity and associated matters is reserved to the granting country.

Then come three further qualifying factors:

(a) the rule concerning co-defendants;
(b) the rules on priority of jurisdiction in cases of *lis pendens* and related actions; and
(c) the ability of other jurisdictions to take provisional measures.[343]

(i) **General jurisdiction: defendant's "domicile" in an EU State.** The first principle of the Regulation, specified in art.2, is that an EU defendant can be sued for a civil or commercial matter in the courts of that person's "domicile". Unless an exception arises under some other article, this is the sole basis of jurisdiction.[344] "Domicile"—a matter for the law of the relevant state[345]—in the United Kingdom means: **2–74**

(1) in the case of an individual, that he or she is resident in, and has a substantial connection with, the United Kingdom;
(2) in the case of a company, the state in which it has its seat.[346]

At one stage in the 1990s, this root provision had a dramatic effect, in particular, upon patent cases: actions for cross-border injunctions and other extra-territorial relief became regular features of life in some of the states concerned. If there is only one defendant, or if all defendants share the same domicile, the courts of that domicile have jurisdiction over an action claiming infringement in any other EU/EFTA state and the principle of territoriality will oblige them to apply the law of that other state to the question. A single court may therefore determine all such claims; hence art.2 gives the widest jurisdiction under the Conventions. Unfortunately, as we shall see, in more complex cases that desirable end is easily subverted and

[343] Save where this specific jurisdiction applies, an English court may give effect to an agreement that the scope of claims in equivalent patents held in different countries shall be determined by it: *Celltech v MedImmune* [2005] F.S.R. 21 CA, Jacob L.J. noting: "It makes sense for the parties to select a jurisdiction with a specialist, experienced court to decide matters, as I think they have done": at para.18.

[344] Note that the rule is in no way dependent on the domicile of the claimant: so it may be taken advantage of by a non-EU claimant.

[345] The original six members of the Convention used the term to mean "habitual residence": Judgments Regulation art.59.1.

[346] Judgments Regulation art.22.2. A company has its seat where it is incorporated or where it has its "central management and control".

the parties may well perceive very different advantages for themselves in having the case dealt with in one jurisdiction rather than another.

2–75 (ii) **Special jurisdiction: place of tortious harm.** An exception by way of *addition* arises under the Judgments Regulation art.5(3), which allows an action to be brought "in matters relating to tort, delict or quasi-delict, in the courts of the place where the harmful event occurred". This can embrace intellectual property infringement and threats actions, since both involve torts within the broad phraseology of the exception.[347] It thus allows jurisdiction in patent, copyright and trade mark matters in accordance with the rule which had previously been applied in English courts.[348] Difficulties may arise when, for instance, manufacturing steps are taken in one jurisdiction and commercial disposal occurs in another. The case law tends to take the place where the defendant acts as a "harmful event" forum where remedies may be granted on an international scale; whereas in a country where the consequential harm is suffered by a victim, that person's claim is limited to damage within that jurisdiction.[349] The effects of internet transmission make this potentially a global issue, which British courts have not had much chance to address so far. It has been held insufficient merely to show that a website provided abroad is accessible from a British jurisdiction[350]; but the opposite applies where the site is particularly intended to cause harm, such as trade mark infringement, in Britain. Hence a Scottish court heard an action against a cybersquatter who was living in Greece and was managing director of a Mauritius company, for incorporating the title of a Scottish newspaper, *Business AM*, into 22 domain names.[351] Where this is the basis of jurisdiction, relief is likely to be limited to infringements occurring within the jurisdiction.[352]

2–76 (iii) **Exclusive jurisdiction: registration and validity of a patent.** An *exclusionary* exception arises under the Judgments Regulation art.22(4). Regardless of "domicile", in proceedings concerned with the registration or validity of patents, trade marks, designs, or other similar rights required to be deposited or registered, jurisdiction is reserved to the courts of the

[347] *Bonnier Media v Smith* [2002] E.T.M.R. 86. It is likely also to extend to actions for declarations of non-infringement: but cf. *"Flootek"* (2001) 32 I.I.C. 231 (Sweden), criticised by Lundstedt (2001) 32 I.I.C. at 124. The broad definition would also encompass an action for relief against anti-competitive acts of collaboration or abuse of dominant position, provided that they produce effects within the jurisdiction concerned: *Scandisk v Philips Electronics* [2007] F.S.R. 22.

[348] See *Modus Vivendi v Sanmex* [1996] F.S.R. 790, a passing-off case, in which it was held that the place where the harmful event occurred was where the passing off was achieved by misleading customers. For the issue on a world basis in the context of the internet, *Gutnick v Dow Jones* [2002] H.C.A. 56.

[349] *Shevill v Presse Alliance* [1995] E.C.R. I-415 ECJ (defamation jurisdiction); *Scandisk v Philips* [2007] F.S.R. 22 (anti-competitive licence of a patent).

[350] *Euromarket Designs v Peters* [2001] F.S.R. 20; *"800-Flowers" T.M.* [2002] F.S.R. 12.

[351] *Bonnier Media v Smith* [2002] E.T.M.R. 86. For the issue on a world basis, see *Gutnick v Dow Jones* [2002] H.C.A. 56.

[352] *UVG Ambulances v Auto Conversions* [2000] E.C.D.R. 479.

contracting state in which the deposit or registration has been applied for, has taken place or is under the terms of an international convention deemed to have taken place.[353]

Thus in the realm of patents, exclusive jurisdiction applies to proceedings in national courts for revocation of the patent or similar registered right, for a declaration of validity, or for amendment of the patent specification.[354] This is also the case where the issue of validity of a patent is raised as a counterclaim or defence by the defendant to an action for its infringement.[355] Courts in The Netherlands at one stage showed a readiness to allow the infringement action to be maintained in EU countries other than that of the patent, characterising the issue of invalidity as merely an "incidental question" to be dealt with before the infringement issue. The ECJ refused to accept this, rightly holding that such a result "would multiply the risk of conflicting decisions which the Convention seeks specifically to avoid".[356] It is therefore only in relation to suits where infringement alone is in issue that the general principles of the Regulation apply, rather than the exclusion prescribed in art.22(4). **2–77**

(iv) **Co-defendants.** The principal provision of the Judgments Regulation which undermines the intention to eliminate forum shopping is art.6(1). Where there are a number of defendants, a defendant may be sued in the courts where any one of them is domiciled.[357] In Britain, when this is crossed with the new acceptance that actions may be brought for foreign infringements, applying the *lex loci delicto*,[358] a bewildering variety of circumstances may present themselves, all of which require a distracting factual investigation before jurisdiction is properly established. At one extreme, there are cases where an English domiciled defendant is allegedly infringing the British rights, and the other related defendants (typically, local subsidiaries in various EU states) are also contributing to the British infringement. At least where the English defendant is principally responsible, this must be a straightforward case for applying art.6(1).[359] At the other extreme, the English defendant may be the only infringer of the British rights, the attack **2–78**

[353] Likewise in respect of issues arising in the course of granting European Patents which are reserved to the EPO. Jurisdiction concerning Community IPRs (trademarks, designs, plant variety rights) is reserved to the tribunals designated in the Regulations establishing the rights.

[354] The exclusive jurisdiction does not cover proceedings concerning entitlement to the right: *Duijnstee v Goderbauer* [1985] 1 C.M.L.R. 220 ECJ.

[355] Counter-attacks of this nature are not available under the patent system in Germany, a structural difference which may have led to differences of opinion about the effects of art.22(4).

[356] *Gesellschaft für Antriebstechnik v LUK* [2006] F.S.R. 45 ECJ at [29].

[357] Article 6(3) provides for jurisdiction on a counterclaim arising from the same contract or facts on which the original claim was based, in the court in which the original claim is pending.

[358] Above para.2–73.

[359] So held in *Mölnlycke v Procter & Gamble (No. 4)* [1992] R.P.C. 21 CA, applying, as the test for joinder, that there be a good arguable case against each defendant.

on the other subsidiaries being that each infringes its local rights. In such a situation, the Court of Appeal has refused to allow the foreign subsidiaries to be joined, relying on the legal consequence of territoriality: there can be no danger of irreconcilable judgments because each right has effect only in its own domain.[360]

In a reference from the Dutch Supreme Court, the Court of Justice held that art.6(1) does not apply to European patent infringement proceedings involving a number of companies established in various Brussels Convention contracting states in respect of acts committed in one or more of those states, even where those companies belong to the same group and may have acted in accordance with a common policy laid down by one of them.[361]

2–79 (v) **Lis pendens.** If proceedings may be commenced on the basis of a single defendant's domicile, the domicile of any one among connected defendants or the place of infringement, conflicts of jurisdiction are an inevitable consequence. Article 27 of the Judgments Regulation gives the first court to be seized strict primacy where more than one set of proceedings involving the same cause of action and between the same parties are brought, even where a motivation for bringing proceedings in the first court is to take advantage of the slowness of its procedures and effectively "torpedoing the action".[362] Where, however, related actions, i.e. actions which risk resulting in irreconcilable judgments, are brought in courts of different states, later courts may cede precedence but, under art.28, do not have to do so.

So far as the strict rule in art.27 is concerned, actions to enforce patents for different Member States, even when they are granted for the same invention and in common form from the EPO and are asserted against equivalent acts, are not for the same cause.[363]

As to the art.28 question of related actions, the principal factor to be taken into account—the danger of irreconcilable judgments[364]—is the test which courts have also used to judge how far jurisdiction under the Regulation may be assumed upon the basis of the domicile of any one co-defendant (art.6(1)).[365] The Hague Court of Appeal has now agreed with its English counterpart that causes of action for infringement of equivalent patents in different Convention states are separate because of the

[360] *Fort Dodge Animal Health v Akzo Nobel* [1998] F.S.R. 222 at 243.

[361] *Roche Nederland v Primus, Goldenberg* [2007] F.S.R. 5 ECJ at [41].

[362] *Erich Gasser v MISAT* [2003] I-E.C.R. I-14693 ECJ; Véron (2004) 35 I.I.C. 638.

[363] Article 27 requires the later court of its own motion to stay its proceedings until such time as the jurisdiction of the court first seized is established, and thereafter to decline jurisdiction. The discretion given by art.28 to the later court is to stay proceedings for a related action while proceedings at first instance are pending in the court first seized. For its basis, see *The Tatry* [1994] E.C.R. 1-5439.

[364] The factor is explicitly mentioned in art.28(3); cf. art.6(1).

[365] In *Abcko Music v Jodorowski* [2003] E.C.D.R. 13, the very different approaches of French and English law to initial ownership of copyright was a principal reason for refusing a stay of English proceedings under art.28. See also *Research in Motion vVisto* [2008] F.S.R. 20; *Independent News Service v India Broadcast* [2008] F.S.R. 2 SC, (India).

territorially distinct nature of each patent.[366] On this strict view, judgments from two contracting state courts, relating to the patent for the same invention in each of their jurisdictions, would not be treated as irreconcilable and the later court would not be called upon to decide whether to stay the action before it. That is a rather unsatisfactory outcome since it precludes a court from considering what is the appropriate outcome in a case which alleges only parallel infringements. In relation to patent actions in particular, the "torpedo" tactic of a defendant rapidly commencing proceedings for a declaration of non-infringement in a country, such as Belgium or Italy, where an inexperienced court could leave the case on the shelf for years, has caused considerable indignation—a gross example of the forum shopping which the Regulation aims to preclude.[367]

(vi) **Provisional and Protective Measures.** Article 31 of the Judgments **2–80** Regulation provides that a court which does not have jurisdiction over the substantive matter may nonetheless impose provisional or protective measures. In the view of The Hague Court of Appeal, these can only relate to activities occurring within the jurisdiction of the court hearing the matter and not to foreign infringements.[368] This additional jurisdiction is conferred because the local court is best placed to judge the circumstances of the application[369]; it should not therefore employ the Conventions to grant cross-border injunctions or preservation orders relating to events beyond its territory.

(c) *Recognition and Enforcement: the Regulation and the Conventions*

A judgment given in accordance with the Judgments Regulation in one **2–81** contracting state is to be recognised in others without further proceedings; and (after registration, so far as the United Kingdom is concerned) such terms as require it are to be enforced.[370] It may be for an injunction as well as for monetary relief.[371] It is not to be recognised if (inter alia) it conflicts with art.22(4)[372]; nor if it is contrary to substantive public policy,[373] or is irreconcilable with a judgment given in a dispute between the same parties in the state in which recognition is sought.[374] These limitations, as already noted, are not adequate to deal with all conflicts which may arise between

[366] cf. Fawcett and Torremans, *Intellectual Property and Private International Law* (1998), at pp.36–37, proclaiming the court's view "old-fashioned".
[367] Franzosi [1997] E.I.P.R. 382; (2002) 33 I.I.C. 154.
[368] *Expandable Grafts v Boston Scientific* [1999] F.S.R. 352.
[369] *Denilauler v Couchet Frères* [1980] E.C.R. 1553.
[370] Articles 33, 40.
[371] For interim relief, see *Encyc. P.L.*, para.10–505.
[372] Article 28, first sentence.
[373] Articles 27(1)(a), 28, third sentence. It is no sufficient reason not to enforce that the judgment is for infringement of design rights in spare car parts in the country giving the judgment, whereas no equivalent right existed in the country where enforcement is sought, that being the country where the products originated: *Renault v Maxicar* [2001] E.C.R. I-2973.
[374] Article 27(3).

judgments finding infringement and judgments finding invalidity or ordering revocation. In the end, the Regulation will be made to apply satisfactorily to the range of disputes that can arise over patents only if courts engage in some highly purposive interpretation of its text.

(d) *Foreign defendant from outside EU and EFTA*

2–82 The Judgments Regulation, as we have just seen, lays down a series of rules that not merely entitle, but require, the courts of a given country to assume jurisdiction. One object was to leave these courts no power to refuse to hear a case because some other more suitable jurisdiction was being sought by one of the parties. Unlike the United Kingdom and Ireland, other European countries had not adopted this doctrine of *forum non conveniens*. The desire for certainty which underlies the continental European approach means that a court may not sidestep the Regulation's paths in order to reach a fair solution in complex cases. The Regulation in consequence stipulates which court in an EU or EFTA state will decide questions of infringement arising in any of the contracting states—it being assumed that it will do so in accordance with the law of the state where the wrong occurred. When, however, the issue for an English court is whether it has jurisdiction over a dispute as to intellectual property rights in a non-EU/EFTA state, the question is one for common law rules. In the last quarter-century, some decisions continued to take the view that there was no jurisdiction to do so. On the other hand, there were cases, culminating in the Court of Appeal's judgment in *Pearce v Ove Arup*, which could be read as favouring a surrender of the common law's former caution, particularly in relation to actions for infringement.[375] However, the Court of Appeal has since ruled, in *Lucasfilm v Ainsworth,*[376] that the Regulation does not by implication impose any equivalent rules on disputes in which parties belong to a non-European state. Nor does it alter the previous approach which treats both the law applicable to infringements occurring in a non-European state as the law of that place and confers jurisdiction exclusively on the courts of that place. The justification for intellectual property rights, whether under a system of registration or not, is seen as lying in the economic policy of the state conferring them.The issue arose in English litigation between the US owners of rights in the helmets worn by characters in the first *Star Wars* film and the British plastics firm which produced the helmet design for manufacture. For many years the helmets were sold internationally as playthings for children. By the time of the litigation, copyright in the helmets still existed under US copyright law, but the UK copyright had expired because of the time limitations in the Copyright, etc Act 1988 ss.51 and 52.[377] At first instance Mann J. held himself entitled to decide whether infringements of the US

[375] *Pearce v Ove Arup* [1999] F.S.R. 525 CA; for critical scrutiny, Fentiman, in Nuyts (ed.) *International Litigation in Intellectual Property and Information Technology* Ch.8.
[376] [2010] F.S.R. 10.
[377] For the copyright aspects of the decision, see below, paras 16–11—16–14.

copyright had occurred in California. As a preliminary issue, he could determine that under US law the American copyright in the design of the helmets belonged to the film producer, because that enterprise had provided drawings and a model to the defendant from which to work. However, in the Court of Appeal's categorical view, English courts had no jurisdiction to consider either issue of US law, since the US was not a country within the Judgments Regulation of the EU. All the main forms of intellectual property—patents, registered and unregistered designs, copyright, and registered trade marks—were treated as instruments of public policy. As such they varied from state to state and could be sued upon only in the courts of the state where infringing acts had occurred.

As already outlined, actions limited in this way are characterised under the *Moçambique*[378] decision of 1893 as "local" rather than "transitory" , the instance in that case being an action for trespass to land. A line of decisions over the ensuing century mostly confirmed that intellectual property disputes should be so treated.[379] The *Lucasfilm* judgment must now be treated as making intellectual property a case a fortiori to that of rights in land, first because in the United Kingdom the *Moçambique* rule has, in relation to land, been modified by statute[380]; and secondly because *Lucasfilm* is stated to apply to all rights that "exclude others", i.e. not just the statutory forms of intellectual property but to passing off and unfair competition.[381] No distinction exists between rights that depend on a form of official registration and those that do not.[382] Nor does the fact that the action is primarily to establish who is entitled to the intellectual property, whether the right is valid, or whether it has been infringed.[383] The justification for so comprehensive a classification of intellectual property disputes as "local" is, in the Court of Appeal's view, necessitated by the variations of policy embodied in different national laws,[384] and also by the considerable opportunities for forum shopping that otherwise arise; by the difficult issues about which of competing fora should be treated as most convenient; and by the absence of international conventions dealing with the matter.[385] This keeps English law

[378] *British South Africa Co. v Compahnia de Moçambique* [1893] A.C. 602, building upon American precedent.

[379] *Potter v Broken Hill Pty* (1906) 3 C.L.R. 479

[380] See the Civil Jurisdiction and Judgments Act 1982 s.30.

[381] [2010] F.S.R. 10 at [181 (iv)]]. Protection of trade secrets is not mentioned specifically, though many countries treat under it the general rubric of unfair competition: see above, paras 1–13 et seq.

[382] Were it otherwise, it could be relevant to consider whether or not registration is subject to substantive examination: at [181 (v)] Above all else, therefore, the rule relates to copyright.

[383] At [181 (ii)]. It is pointed out both that validity and infringement can often be intertwined, and that what in one system is treated as giving rise to no right in others may be classed as a defence to infringement.

[384] As was evident in the issues at stake in *Lucasfilm* itself: at [176]. So equally with *Tyburn v Conan Doyle* [1991] Ch. 75, which sought from an English court a declaratory judgment that US copyright law contained a right to prevent sequel adventures of literary characters (in the instance, Sherlock Holmes). The attempt failed.

[385] See below, para.2–84.

abstemious. Its courts cannot generally be used to determine issues arising in relation to what are allegedly equivalent infringements of a right in different countries or involve equivalent attacks on validity of essentially the same rights. At the same time, a discretion exists under which English courts may decide that they are most conveniently placed to dispose of an issue in the round This is the concept of *forum conveniens* that is treated with such suspicion in civilian systems. Conceivably this could be used in "non-Regulation" cases to secure disposal of a case where equivalent infringements are allegedly occurring , thanks to a flourishing export trade. But where there are real issues about the comparative scope of the rights across borders the "local" character of the right is likely to put a stop to the English action.

2–83 The common law principle governing the recognition and enforcement of a foreign judgment, where neither the Judgments Regulation nor any international agreement between states applies, is that these steps will be allowed only where the judgment debtor is present in the jurisdiction granting the relief when the proceedings were instituted there. While this presence can be a temporary connection short of residence, it is not enough merely to deliver goods there. In the case of a company it must have a fixed place of business there from which it or its agent operates. When the defendant does business in a country only by means of the internet the judgment from the courts of that country is unlikely to be enforceable in England. [386]

(e) *An International Recognition and Enforcement Convention?*

2–84 In 1999 the Hague Conference on Private International Law adopted a preliminary draft Convention which aimed to provide a fully international equivalent to the EU/EFTA Conventions in their European sphere. The stimulus came from certain practitioners in the United States and elsewhere whose expertise extended to cross-border litigation. The draft was then discussed at a Diplomatic Conference. While it aims to embrace jurisdictional questions affecting all civil and commercial matters, its probable impact upon patent and other intellectual property litigation has proved particularly contentious. It is not difficult to appreciate that the spread of information across the internet, and more generally the rapid growth of world trade, may extend IP disputes across many borders. Yet there remains a widespread scepticism about the competence of courts in other countries to deal with such cases swiftly and fairly. In addition, it is accepted as a political necessity that the validity of registered rights should remain solely in the competence of the courts of the country which grants the rights. That would lead to undesirable fragmentation of IP litigation, and to new forms of delay and expense as the court seized with jurisdiction referred the validity question to each of the countries in question. The Hague proposal has not come to fruition. The American Law Institute has adopted a

[386] *Lucasfilm v Ainsworth* [2010] F.S.R. 10 at [193–194].

statement concerning private international law issues affecting intellectual property. It was drafted by Professors Dreyfuss, Dessemontet and Ginsburg. It finds that national courts should have jurisdiction over this subject matter in foreign territories.[387] However, not until the problems of solving multi-state litigation country by country have become widespread and debilitating is the movement for a generally improved ordering of international litigation likely to succeed.

(f) *Foreign transactions*[388]

Intellectual property acquires its value partly through the pursuit of infringers but even more through voluntary transactions.[389] These are contractual agreements which incorporate within them the grant of a proprietary interest or licence and they raise their own issues of private international law.[390] To formal questions concerning assignment and licensing, the law of the country of grant will be applicable.[391] To questions of the interpretation and execution of agreed terms, English law will apply its rule for contractual conflicts, which normally refers the issue to the proper law, that is the law of the country with which the contract has most connection, if it has not been expressly selected.[392] Many difficulties can, however, arise. Only two of them can be identified here. **2–85**

First, the right to grant an assignment or licence may turn on an issue of ownership of the intellectual property. Notions of territoriality would lead one to expect that ownership of a right will be determined in accordance with local law. In each jurisdiction, this law may be complex, varying sometimes from right to right, and certainly varying country by country. Yet those dealing with a set of national rights in the same invention, work or other subject matter need the security of knowing that they have accomplished the proprietary grants which are the whole purpose of their dealing. There is accordingly a pressing need, unless very strong policy interests **2–86**

[387] American Law Institute, *Principles governing Jurisdiction, Choice of Law and Judgments in Transnational Disputes* (2008).

[388] See Wadlow, *Enforcement of Intellectual Property in European and International Law* (1998), Ch.7; Fawcett and Torremans, *Intellectual Property and Private International Law* (1998), Ch.11; *Dicey and Morris on the Conflict of Laws* 14th edn (2006) r.205.

[389] See, e.g. Kur [2002] E.I.P.R. 175; Guibault and Hugenholtz, *Study on the Conditions applicable to Contracts relating to IP in the EU* (2002); Westkamp (2006) 37 I.I.C. 637.

[390] So far as concerns jurisdiction in litigation, the principles of the Brussels Regulation and Lugano Convention may be applicable. An outline of those principles has been given in relation to infringement claims (above, para.2–73); note also the jurisdiction based on place of performance of a contract; art.5(1). Any valid jurisdiction clause in an agreement will prevail in an action as to the validity and enforcement of the contract: art.17; *Benincasa v Dentalkit* [1997] E.T.M.R. 447.

[391] The Court of Appeal held that a person commissioned in England by a US filmmaker to produce plastic helmets for costumes was subject to an implied condition that copyrights in the helmet designs would pass to the filmmaker:—it being likely that English Law governed the contract to assign: *Lucasfilm v Ainsworth* [2009] EWCA Civ 1328 at [196–208].

[392] As now modified to some extent by the Contracts (Applicable Law) Act 1990, implementing the Rome Convention 1980, with its Brussels Protocol giving interpretative jurisdiction to the ECJ: see *Dicey and Morris*, r.202, esp. at pp.1541–1560.

dictate to the contrary, to ensure that a single law settles substantive questions of entitlement, for instance, between employer and employee or between commissioner and person commissioned. The uniform answer which that solution provides could well be adopted as a general rule in relation to IP ownership around the world and has been adopted for copyright in the US.[393] The ownership of a European patent for an employee's invention will be determined in European Patent Convention countries by reference to the law of the country of employment, thanks to art.60 of the Convention.[394] In *Celltech (Adair's) US Patent*[395] the Court of Appeal applied US patent law to a term of an English law governed patent licence agreement which required payment of royalties if the product sold was covered by a valid claim in a particular US patent; this involved an analysis of the *Festo* principles on the doctrine of equivalence.[396]

2–87 Secondly, where the proper law is not that of the country where the relevant rights arise, that country may have a rule of public policy limiting freedom of contract. This is particularly apparent in the field of copyright, where countries in the European tradition of authors' rights may have rules highly protective of authors. It will be necessary to examine the rule to determine whether it is mandatory for all transactions affecting the local right, or is only a rule affecting contracts governed by local law or affecting persons with a personal attachment to that country.[397] It will be necessary to examine whether in the place of performance executing the contract would be unlawful; and if that place is England, whether it would be contrary to any public policy.[398]

2–88 It has been held, for instance, that the proper law alone determines whether an ex-employee's undertaking to respect trade secrets and otherwise refrain from competition is enforceable, so that it is irrelevant what the law of, for instance, the forum is; likewise, the question whether a trade mark dispute can be settled by a binding undertaking not subsequently to attack the validity of the registration.[399] By contrast, where the British patents legislation rendered a patent unenforceable so long as an agreement existed under which a licensee was obliged to obtain starting material from the

[393] *Itar-Tass v Russian Kurier*, 153 F.3d 82 (2d Cir., 1998): ownership of copyright in Russian journalist's work determined by Russian law; infringement occurring in the US by US law. Torremans [1999] I.P.Q. 372. In *Griggs Group v Evans (No. 2)* [2004] F.S.R. 48, after a wide-ranging consideration of relevant conflict rules the court ordered one of the defendants to transfer the copyright in various foreign countries to the claimant which it had found was the owner in equity of them all.

[394] See below, paras 4–08 and 7–08 et seq.

[395] *Celltech (Adair's) US Patent* [2004] F.S.R. 35 CA.

[396] *Festo v Shoketsu Kinzoku* [2004] F.S.R. 11, US CA for FC.

[397] See further below, paras 12–79, 13–26 et seq.

[398] See *Dicey and Morris*, r.205.

[399] *Apple Corp v Apple Computer* [1992] F.S.R. 431.

patentee, that principle prevailed in Britain; it was irrelevant that the proper law of the licence did not prohibit such a tying arrangement.[400]

(5) Making others responsible

A defendant to an action who wishes to establish the responsibility of another solely or jointly for the alleged wrong may do so by issuing him with a third-party notice.[401] If two or more defendants in an action are liable in respect of the same damage, and one meets the liability, he will have a claim to contribution from the others.[402] The same is true where the second and subsequent persons have not been sued by the victim of the tort.[403] The amount of contribution due is that found to be just and equitable having regard to the person in question's responsibility for the damage.[404] **2–89**

A contract to indemnify for loss suffered through legal liability will displace this principle. These indemnities are common in intellectual property dealings: for instance, where an inventor assigns the rights in what he claims to be his invention, or where an author, in entering a publishing agreement, undertakes that he infringes no one else's rights. The obligation to indemnify is indeed implied in some contracts. If a person purchases a machine and is then obliged to pay damages for its use because it infringes a patent, the vendor will be in breach of his implied warranty of quiet possession[405] and accordingly obliged to make good the loss. Where one person commissions another to carry out work for him and the other thereby unwittingly commits a patent or copyright infringement, there is arguably a similar implied undertaking to indemnify for any loss through liability; but the matter has never been decided. **2–90**

(6) Establishing freedom from liability

A person who fears that he will be sued can only have the issue brought to a head if: (1) he has some countervailing right, (2) a procedure exists for annulling the right on which the other party may eventually claim, or (3) the claim against him is imminent. In the case of patents and other registered **2–91**

[400] *Chiron v Organon Teknika (No. 2)* [1993] F.S.R. 567 CA; the rule itself was abolished for the future by the Competition Act 1998.
[401] CPR Pt 20. Equally a manufacturer may intervene in proceedings against his customer under CPR r.19.4.
[402] Civil Liability (Contribution) Act 1978 s.1. The legal basis of liability may be tort, contract, trust or otherwise: s.6(1).
[403] When the victim's action against the others has become time-barred the payer may still seek contribution: Civil Liability (Contribution) Act 1978 s.(3). But there is also a limitation period for the contribution claim: see Limitation Act 1980 s.10. For the subject in detail, see, e.g. Goff and Jones, *Law of Restitution* 7th edn (2007), Ch.14 and para.43–008; *Clerk and Lindsell on Torts* 19th edn (2006), Ch.4.
[404] Law Reform (Married Women and Tortfeasors) Act 1935 s.6(2).
[405] Sale of Goods Act 1979 s.12(2)(b). But to the extent that this obligation is limited in accordance with s.12(3) and (5), the responsibility will be reduced.

rights, statutory procedures exist for attacking the validity of the right, and these are open to competitors and others with sufficient interest to bring them.[406] Even then, the question whether a person is infringing lies outside these procedures: the alleged infringer must proceed by way of an action for a declaration that he is not doing so.

In intellectual property litigation generally, the possibility of seeking a declaration of freedom from liability is a relatively recent development.[407] In the case of patents, special provision was made earlier. A person may apply in writing to a patentee[408] for an acknowledgment that a particular act does not infringe the patent.[409] If this acknowledgment is not forthcoming he may seek a declaration from the court to the same effect.[410] In the course of the proceedings questions of the patent's validity, as well as of infringement, may be raised.

(7) Threats to sue[411]

2–92 If a potential claimant chooses to do what damage he can merely by threatening to sue, again those affected may find it difficult to force his hand. Apart from instituting revocation or rectification proceedings in the cases mentioned under the last heading, a person who suffers by the threats may not be able to prevent them, save in exceptional cases. In general the common law has not limited the freedom to institute claims or to threaten that they will be begun. Rather it insists that those who choose to succumb to a claim instead of fighting must abide by the consequences of their faint-heartedness. If the claim was in fact groundless, they are not in general permitted to re-open the controversy by having the settlement rescinded, by claiming back money paid or by suing for loss suffered because of their submission.[412]

The same approach applies in general even where the threats cause injury indirectly. For instance, A, a promotion firm, imported toy bricks to be used as free gifts in a campaign being organised for a client, B. C threatened B with an action for infringement of rights in their design if the campaign went ahead. In consequence B refused to participate, leaving A with the stock of

---

406 See e.g. PA 1977 s.72.

407 In *Vine Products v Mackenzie* [1969] R.P.C. 1, it was assumed somewhat unrealistically that, after an exchange of letters before action, the person threatened with liability could himself institute the proceedings for a declaration of freedom from liability. *Bulmer v Bollinger* [1978] R.P.C. 79 CA, followed the same course.

408 Or exclusive licensee.

409 He is not obliged to show the alleged infringement to the patentee, only to describe it: *Plasticisers v Pixdane* [1979] R.P.C. 327.

410 PA 1977 s.71.

411 For a comparative study from civil and common law perspectives, see Brack (2006) 37 I.I.C. 1.

412 For these rules and exceptions to them, see, e.g. Goff and Jones, *Law of Restitution* 7th edn (2007), esp. paras 4–029—4–031.

toys on its hands. An action by A against C for wrongful interference with contractual relations was struck out as disclosing no cause of action.[413]

2–93 However, the tort of injurious falsehood will lie for the malicious statement that a right of action exists and will be sued upon.[414] Malice will be present if the threatener knows that his claim is groundless; likewise, if he draws attention to his success in proceedings against another defendant without saying that the court stayed the injunction pending an appeal.[415] Nonetheless the requirement of malice severely limits this form of tortious relief.

2–94 In the case of patents, where the expense and uncertainty of infringement and validity proceedings is acute and the threat to sue is accordingly grave, an exception has long existed by statute, although the formulation in the Patents Act 1977 s.70 has recently been amended by the Patents Act 2004 to make it more amenable to those making the threats.[416] A person aggrieved by the threat that he himself or someone else (such as a customer) will be sued for patent infringement may claim relief in civil proceedings in the form of a declaration that the threats are unjustifiable, an injunction against their continuance and/or damages for any loss that they cause (for example because a customer switches his orders to the threatener).[417] But threats relating either to making or importing a product for disposal, or to using a process, are outside the scope of this special provision[418] Similar provisions have also been introduced in relation to registered and unregistered design rights, and most recently in relation to registered trade marks.[419] The result is an odd patchwork, still leaving out copyright, confidential information and those marks and names protected only at common law through passing off or injurious falsehood. Since copyrights are often administered by powerful collecting societies there is a strong case for extending into that field protection against threats.

2–95 To avoid liability the threatener may show either that what he said did not amount to a threat, or that the threat was justified,[420] or if he proves that at the time of making the threats he did not know, or have reason to believe, that the patent was invalid in the respect shown by the claimant.[421] The

[413] *Granby Marketing v Interlego* [1984] R.P.C. 209.

[414] The scope of injurious falsehood is discussed in detail, below, paras 17–48—17–56.

[415] *Mentmore v Fomento* (1955) 72 R.P.C. 157 CA.

[416] Roberts [2004] E.I.P.R. 393.

[417] PA 1977 s.70 as amended by the Patents Act 2004. For orders restraining the institution of vexatious proceedings against customers, see *Landi den Hartog v Sea Bird* [1976] F.S.R. 489; *Jacey v Norton* [1977] F.S.R. 475.

[418] PA 1977 s.70(4) as amended by the Patents Act 2004 now extends exemption from the threats provision, to threats made to such a maker, importer or user (of a process) in relation to any subsequent dealings with such a product.

[419] RDA 1949 s.26; CDPA 1988 s.253; TMA 1994 s.21. For the threats which are not caught: see RDA 1949 s.26(2A); CDPA 1988 s.253(3); TMA 1994 s.21(1) cf. *Prince v Prince Sports Group* [1998] F.S.R. 21.

[420] e.g. he may show that the threat concerned infringement of a valid patent. But the patent must have been granted: *Brain v Ingledew (No. 2)* [1997] F.S.R. 271.

[421] PA 1977 s.70(2A), inserted by the Patents Act 2004 s.12(2).

patentee is entitled to draw attention to the existence of his patent or provide purely factual information about it.[422] In addition, he may make appropriate enquiries to ascertain whether there has been primary infringement and, if so, who by, making assertions about the patent for such purpose. If he has used his best endeavours to discover the identity of a primary infringer and has failed, the patentee may then threaten an alleged secondary infringer provided he explains the abortive efforts made to identify the primary infringer.[423] To go further is still to court danger.[424] It is actionable, for instance, for a patentee to say to a competitor's customers that he is going to apply for an injunction against the competitor and that the customers are to see that there are no further infringements.[425] In the case of circulars to customers or notices in trade journals (common ways of giving notice of rights claimed) a person suing for threats must show that potential customers of his would understand the circular or notice to be referring to his goods.[426]

A threat can be justified only if the threatener shows that the acts of which he complains do constitute infringement of some patent (or other right), and the person suffering by the threats cannot establish that the relevant patent claim is invalid.[427] Thus, in the case of a serious fight, the threat gives the alleged infringer a springboard equivalent to an action for a declaration of non-infringement from which to launch the contest and require the right owner to "put up or shut up" by deciding whether to counterclaim for infringement or not.

On the rather peculiar facts of *Quads 4 Kids v Colin Campbell*[428] Pumfrey J. granted an interim injunction against the repetition of threats of infringement of a Community design which the judge considered were made by way of a VeRO (Verified Rights Owner) notice to auction site eBay, noting "[i]t is entirely wrong for owners of intellectual property rights to attempt to assert them without litigation, or without the threat of litigation, in reply".[429]

---

[422] PA 1977 s.70(5) as amended by the Patent Act 2004 and see RDA 1949 s.26(3); CDPA 1988 s.253(4); TMA 1994 s.21(4).

[423] PA 1977 s.70(6), added by the Patents Act 2004 s.12(5).

[424] There is a threat if an ordinary recipient would so treat it: *L'Oreal v Johnson & Johnson* [2000] F.S.R. 686. A solicitor's letter before action can frequently amount to a threat. However, once a claim form is actually issued, consequential losses are normally attributed to it rather than the preceding threat: *Carflow v Linwood Securities* [1998] F.S.R. 691; *Symonds Cider v Showerings* [1997] E.T.M.R. 238 (Irish HC).

[425] *Berkeley & Young v Stillwell* (1940) 57 R.P.C. 291. Note, however, the obligation under the CPR to set out claims and defences fully in pre-action correspondence: *Unilever v Procter & Gamble* [1999] F.S.R. 849.

[426] *Reymes-Cole v Elite Hosiery* [1965] R.P.C. 102 at 120 CA.

[427] Frequently these issues are raised by counterclaim for infringement and counter-counterclaim for revocation of the patent.

[428] *Quads 4 Kids v Colin Campbell* [2006] EWHC 2482 (ChD).

[429] *Quads 4 Kids* [2006] EWHC 2482 (ChD), at para.24. The case arose from the surprising fact that, under the Design Regulation 6/2002, the validity of a Community design cannot be raised in proceedings for a declaration of non-infringement but can be under the domestic law provided by reg.2(3) of the Community Design Regulations 2005 (SI 2005/2339).

Part II

PATENTS

CHAPTER 3

GROWTH AND PURPOSE OF PATENTS

1. THE NEW DEAL OF 1978

From the enactment of s.6 of the Statute of Monopolies 1624 onwards, the **3–01** legal basis of the patent system in Britain was statutory; even though its brief terms left a great deal to be settled by officers of the Crown and the judges.[1] With the current legislation, the Patents Act 1977, the British patent system received the largest culture shock in its history. The Act introduced machinery for collaborating in three supra-national ventures:

(1) Since June 1, 1978, it has been possible to secure a patent for the United Kingdom either by the traditional route of an application to the UK Intellectual Property Office or by applying to the European Patent Office (EPO), established under the European Patent Convention 1973 (EPC). The EPC is an international agreement between its contracting national states in Europe, which include EU Members States and also states of the European Free Trade Area and others which are aspirants to become members of the EU. The EU is accordingly not as yet party to the EPC.[2] The EPO grants a bundle of national patents in common form, of which one may be a European

[1] The basic importance of this has recently been emphasised in leading judgments: see, esp, Lord Walker, *Synthon v SmithKline Beecham* [2006] R.P.C. at [57–58]

[2] See below, para.3–25.

patent (UK).[3] The EPO's headquarters are in Munich, its Search Branch in The Hague.

(2) From the same date it has been possible to initiate international patent applications in a number of countries throughout the world by a "one-stop" procedure under the Patent Cooperation Treaty 1970 (PCT). The PCT system provides for a single application and search, and in some cases a single preliminary examination; but thereafter it transmits applications to national offices for them to decide upon the grant of a patent for their territories.[4] It is administered by the World Intellectual Property Organisation (WIPO) in Geneva.

(3) From a date still to be fixed, an application to the EPO for a patent in an EU country may mature into a single EU patent covering the whole EU of 27 Member States. The main provisions of this scheme were contained in the Community Patent Convention 1975 (CPC), which has since been the subject of much wrangling. In 2000 another proposal for a Community patent was put forward by the European Commission which would be introduced in the form of an EU Regulation and would come therefore within the corpus of EU law.[5] Despite initial high hopes, the project has also run into the sand. A decision of the EU's Competitiveness Council of December 4, 2009 endorsed the case for an EU patent and for a unified patent litigation system in Europe. The decision proposes a "general approach" which will settle a basic text, but delay decisions on such controversial issues as languages and translation, renewal fees, enhanced partnership and the EU accession to the EPC. Resolution of language issues is to continue to require the unanimous vote of Member States; but other questions will be decided by qualified majority; and the co-decision procedure with the European Parliament will apply. At the same time work will continue on the Unified Patent Litigation System (UPLS), for which the political momentum comes from the European Commission. A rival litigation scheme, having the support of the EPO and voicing the position of interests in the Member States, is known as the European Patent Litigation Agreement (EPLA). The former proposes a hierarchy of patent courts in which the first instance is either a local or regional institution in which judges with patent experience, legal or technical, will come mainly from the particular country or region but will sit with a judge from another state and drawn from a central pool. The Appeal Court, however, will have one site and will serve the whole EU. Even by British standards, this procedural structure will be a grand affair, and therefore an expense that will have to be met by fees paid by litigants or governmental revenue from taxpayers.

[3] See below, paras 3–23—3–25, 4–01—4–05.
[4] See below, paras 3–19—3–22, 4–02.
[5] See below, paras 3–26—3–30.

In addition to all this, the substantive and procedural law governing patents for the United Kingdom was extensively altered by the 1977 Act. This was for various reasons. The EPC arrangements require each contracting state to treat a European Patent granted by the EPO for that territory in accordance with standard rules on basic matters such as term, validity and scope of protection. There was a strong case for subjecting patents granted by the national system to the same substantive regime and for modelling the application procedure on similar lines to the European granting system.[6] At the level of legislative texts, the process of "parallelisation" has been carried a very considerable way. But still the scheme has a fundamental legal flaw in that there is no keystone court which can establish precedents for the system as a whole. On the one hand the EPO has a structure of tribunals with its own apex in the form of the Enlarged Board of Appeal to which litigants nonetheless have no *right* of access. On the other hand, national courts deal exclusively with issues of infringement and may also rule on questions of validity once the patent is granted. It is the final jurisdictions of appeal in those states which have the ultimate power to rule on patent issues, whether the patent for their territory has been granted by the national office or the EPO. In the early decades of the European system of 1977 a degree of suspicion at the national level sometimes appeared to combine with beliefs in the virtue of inherited national rules. In Britain today a greater willingness has emerged to recognise that the development of law through decisions of the EPO tribunals must, in the interests of clarity, common purpose and legal certainty, give them a position of special respect, at least when they settle a consistent line of approach.[7] There is no inclination in the United Kingdom, however, to allow respect to harden into binding obligation. One basic reason is that the EPO is concerned only with the granting of patents and so with their validity at the formative stage. National courts deal with infringement as well as validity, often at a maturer stage when the patent has shown a commercial value worth fighting about. That process is likely to offer greater opportunities to see the interworkings of the whole construction that is the patent system,. **3–02**

The resulting edifice is byzantine in complexity. At least it can be said that the building blocks from which it is built are not themselves a novelty. These have been formed out of the experience of national patents; and in their turn national systems are a characteristic by-product of a country's transformation from an agrarian to an industrial economy. In capitalist economies a patent system represents a judicious compromise. On the one hand, it is a recognition that technological innovation, which is seen as the key to economic growth and social prosperity, cannot be left to the stimulus of market competition alone. On the other, it leaves the added incentives to be **3–03**

[6] See below, paras 4–01, 5–01.

[7] See esp. Mustill LJ, *Genentech v Wellcome* [1989] R.P.C. 147 at 266; *Activas v Merck* [2008] EWCA Civ 444.

determined by demands of the market rather than by the apparatus of the state through rewards or grants of some kind. But because the idea is a compromise in a vital area, it has long been the subject of controversy—particularly in the mid-nineteenth century and again in our own time. Indeed, the arguments today are a part of much larger questions: about the possibility and desirability of pursuing innovation, and the need to avert its more damaging consequences for people and their environment.

This chapter accordingly contains, first, an historical sketch of the British patent system and its relations with those of other countries. An account follows of the international developments that stood behind the 1977 Act. Finally, there is an introduction to the range of current debate about patent systems; national and international.

2. The British Patent System: Historical Development

(1) Beginnings[8]

3–04 The idea of conferring a market monopoly as an incentive to innovate has old roots.[9] In England, as in other parts of Europe, it emerged as one minor form of state patronage.[10] James I was partial to rewarding his political creditors with trading monopolies granted by letters patent. For this there were precedents enough from the illustrious hand of Elizabeth I.[11] But James lacked her force and in 1624 Parliament sought to declare these exercises of royal prerogative void.[12]

3–05 The Statute of Monopolies which it enacted suggests not only the growing significance of trade in the country's economy and the beginnings of the long political campaign to favour competition at the expense of monopoly,[13] it

[8] The growth of the British system is reviewed in greater depth by Cornish in Cornish *et al.*, *Oxford History of the Laws of England*, XIII (2010) Pt V, Ch III. See also the considerable learning in two unpublished theses: Van Zyl Smit, *Social Creation of a Legal Reality* (Edinburgh University, 1981); Duncan, *From Privileges to the Paris Convention* (Monash University, 1997).

[9] The growth of guilds and boroughs with exclusive trading privileges was to some extent connected with the desire to introduce and support new industries: see, e.g. Fox, *Monopolies and Patents* (1947), Ch.2; Davenport, *The United Kingdom Patent System* (1979).

[10] A Venetian law of 1474 went so far as to establish a positive system for granting 10-year privileges to inventors of new arts and machines: Mandich/Prager (1948) 30 J.P.O.S. 166; (1960) 42 J.P.O.S. 378. See generally, Penrose, *The Economics of the International Patent System* (1951), pp.2 et seq.; Phillips [1983] E.I.P.R. 41.

[11] Even she, at the end of her reign, had to face considerable pressure which led to her issuing the Proclamation concerning Monopolies of 1601. Subsequent litigation declared the invalidity at common law of a patented monopoly granted by her in playing cards; expediently, the case was not brought to judgment until after her death: *Darcy v Allin* (1602) 11 Co.Rep. 846. See also Fox (above, n.9), Chs 7, 8; Davies (1938) 48 L.Q.R. 398.

[12] This was the culmination of a battle on the subject that ran throughout James's reign and continued against his successor, Charles I: see Fox, Chs 8–10.

[13] The idea is more completely expressed in the case of the *Cloth Workers of Ipswich* (1615) Godb. R. 252. See further, Fox, pp.219–232.

also shows the readiness of the political forces represented in Parliament to challenge policies of convenience to the Crown. In its own way it reflects some of the conditions which gradually coalesced to make England the first country to leap forward into industrial production.

Section 6 of the Statute of Monopolies, which exceptionally allowed patent monopolies for 14 years upon "any manner of new manufacture" within the realm to the "true and first inventor", had its own character. The English were already feeling their relative technical backwardness—in comparison with France and Holland—and an "inventor" was accordingly understood to cover not only the deviser of the invention but also one who imported it from abroad. The appeal of patent systems to countries that aim to catch up in the race for technology is a continuing one and one that makes the international aspects of patents, if anything, more important than domestic considerations.

Section 6 also expressed the desire to impose some limitations to the system in the name of higher public interests. The protected manufactures were not to be "contrary to the law nor mischievous to the State, by raising prices of commodities at home, or hurt of trade, or generally inconvenient". The difficulty of finding either criteria or language that could more precisely curb excesses in the system remains as perplexing today. More generally the terms of the section make it plain that an act of economic policy was intended: the objectives were the encouragement of industry, employment and growth, rather than justice to the "inventor" for his intellectual percipience. The patentee's "consideration" for the grant was that he would put the invention to use and the 14-year period represented two cycles of 7-year apprenticeships. At least until the latter eighteenth century patents were, in the language of the formal letters of grant, a matter of royal condescension, not of private right. But the force of this discretionary element gradually dissipated. It was replaced by rules enunciated in case law that determined whether the invention in question warranted the grant sought or made.[14]

(2) The coming of industrialisation

The seventeenth century provided no more than a germ of a functioning **3–06**
patent system.[15] Even the patent specification, the kernel of today's practice, made its appearance only in the early eighteenth century. Then patentees started to enrol (or, in today's terminology, register) descriptions of their inventions with the Court of Chancery. Initially this practice may have been a device to help prove against infringers what the protected invention was.[16] A half-century later the courts were requiring the patentee to make a sufficient statement of his conception as "consideration" for the monopoly

[14] Cornish, *Oxford History*, above n.8 at pp.934–6

[15] For a detailed study of the eighteenth-century system, see McLeod, *Inventing the Industrial Revolution* (1988).

[16] Hulme (1897) 13 L.Q.R. 313; but cf. Adams and Averley (below, n.17) at 158–160.

granted to him.[17] In the pre-industrial world, the notion that patents should be used as a regular source of technical information was not an obvious one. As long as competition in international trade remained primitive, each country might hope to keep its technical advances to itself. Britain was to be first to learn the economic rewards of exporting technology, but not before she had attempted a policy of national protectionism[18] which did not fit well with the idea of patents as a source of technical information. But the requirement of an adequate description was often pressed by the judges,[19] not only because patents could then teach an industry what its liveliest members were doing, but also because it provided competitors with ammunition to attack the patent. The description of the invention in early specifications tended to be hazy and a competitor who sought to carry it out from what was revealed might well find that it did not work. Patentees after all had no natural interest in giving their ideas away.[20] There was a correlative shift in the conception of novelty which would justify the patent grant: the question had been whether anyone was already practising the invention in the country. Now another issue was added: did the trade already know of it through publication or demonstration?[21]

3–07 These changes of emphasis coincide with the first steps towards mechanised factory production and with a decisive increase in the number of patents.[22] Probably these concerned many more home-grown inventions than before, but the role of the patent system in this first remarkable stage of industrial development was somewhat tangential, if not as irrelevant as some economic historians have supposed.[23] Among the famous, Boulton and Watt secured large sums from their steam-engine patents, but these came partly from a special extending Act.[24] Arkwright's main patent on his

[17] Hulme (1902) 18 L.Q.R. 280, claiming Lord Mansfield's judgment in *Liardet v Johnson* (1778) to have been decisive; but cf. Adams and Averley (1986) 7 J.Leg.Hist. 156. See also Adams (1987) 8 J.Leg.Hist. 18.

[18] A succession of Acts (not completely repealed until 1843) forbade the export of British machinery, parts or plans and the emigration of skilled workers. Arkwright attempted to defend the obscurity of one specification by claiming that the invention was being kept from foreigners: Mantoux, *The Industrial Revolution in the Eighteenth Century* (1961), pp.227–228.

[19] As in *Arkwright's* case; see below, n.21.

[20] James Watt was one who argued that the description of the invention should be kept secret during the life of the patent: see Cornish, *Oxford History*, above n.8, at pp.936–942.

[21] A doctrine also propounded in *Liardet v Johnson* (above, n.14). Half a century later it seems to have been thought that one act of communication to a third party, without any condition of confidence, would rank as an anticipation: Select Committee (below, n.25) at p.9. This became settled law later: see below, para.5–13.

[22] In the 1750s fewer than 10 patents a year were being granted: in the 1760s that number more than doubled. By the 1810s the average was 110 p.a. and in the 1840s 458 p.a. The figures are tabulated in Boehm, *The British Patent System: 1. Administration* (1967), pp.22–23: later periods: pp.33–34.

[23] H. Dutton, *The Patent System and Inventive Activity during the Industrial Revolution 1750–1852* (1984) and C. MacLeod, *Inventing the Industrial Revolution* (1988) are each valuable assessments of the evidence.

[24] And after laborious litigation: *Boulton v Bull* (1795) 2 Hy.Bl. 463; *Hornblower v Boulton* (1799) 8 T.R. 95.

spinning mule threatened the whole industry but proved to be too obscurely drawn to survive attacks on its validity.[25] Crompton had to be given a parliamentary reward of £5,000 since he had virtually no commercial return from his spinning jenny.[26] Patents provided equally sporadic encouragement for those with less celebrated improvements.[27]

Part of the explanation must lie in the inefficiencies and uncertainties that surrounded the procedures for securing and enforcing patents.[28] Despite vociferous complaints to a Select Committee in 1829,[29] the process of patenting was to remain one of those obscure areas which were able to resist the demands of bureaucratic reform longest. Change finally came just as the Great Exhibition of 1851 marked the vast commercial success of Britain's technical pre-eminence. The reforms in the patent system were earnest of purpose rather than complacent. The rifts in industrial society were to be filled by providing the working man with every opportunity for self-improvement; and what more significant contribution could there be than to help finance his inventive schemes?[30] **3–08**

The changes to the patents system in 1852,[31] relatively cheap and simple in concept, were sought by some protagonists in order to attract capital for the small ventures being generated on the fringes of industry as much as at its centre. For reasonable fees,[32] an applicant could in effect secure grant merely by registering his specification; and he might take advantage of the new arrangement allowing him first to file a provisional, and then within 12 months, a complete specification, thus gaining time to work out his ideas more fully. The amount of patenting activity at once increased markedly.[33] Perhaps it was invention at a relatively minor level that was particularly encouraged—it has often enough been said that this is the point where the system has most impact. **3–09**

But easier patenting had other, less happy consequences. Patent litigation had always been notably protracted and costly. This might deter the genuine

[25] See *R. v Arkwright* (1785) 1 W.P.C. 64. Subsequently, Arkwright considered publishing all the details of his machine so that foreigners could have it as well: Fitton and Wadsworth, *The Strutts and the Arkwrights* 1758–1830 (1958), p.88.

[26] See Mantoux (above, n.18), pp.237–238.

[27] See Boehm (above, n.22), pp.22–26.

[28] Separate patents had to be secured for England, Ireland and Scotland (until 1852) and a large number of officials had to give their approval. There were some (inevitably) who thought this disincentive a useful filter, but active reform groups kept up agitation. Dickens provided some telling parodies of the inventor's lot (*A Poor Man's Tale of a Patent; Little Dorrit*). See Dutton (above, n.23), Chs 2, 3; Phillips, *Charles Dickens and the "Poor Man's Tale of a Patent"* (1984).

[29] P.P. 1829 (332) III; Cornish, *Oxford History*, above, n.8 at pp.951–956.

[30] The same motivation impelled a contemporaneous movement for companies with limited liability.

[31] Introduced by the Patent Law Amendment Act 1852; and see the Report of the Select Committee on Patents, P.P. 1851 (486) XVIII.

[32] The initial cost of securing UK protection was reduced from some £300 to £25, with additional fees being charged during the life of the patent.

[33] Number of patents sealed: 1852–891; 1854–2113: see Boehm (above, n.22).

inventor from seeking protection from the courts, but it left the swashbuckler plenty of room to brandish dubious patents, hoping that competitors would find it simpler to treat shadow as if it were substance. In the high age of economic liberalism, one school of thought reacted by demanding abolition of the whole system, another by proposing that the alleged invention should, at least in some measure, be the subject of an official examination before any patent was granted.[34]

3–10 Even so, change only came slowly. In 1883,[35] the modern Patent Office replaced the Commissioners of 1852 and it began to examine applications, mainly for formal defects and for sufficiency of description.[36] Successive governments remained reluctant to create a bureaucracy that would search the prior literature and examine against the search results; and this despite the fact that the United States Patent Office had done so since 1836. It was not until 1901, when the Fry Committee demonstrated that 40 per cent or more of the patents granted were for inventions already described in earlier British specifications, that the change became irresistible.[37] In 1905 the Office began to search British specifications of the previous 50 years,[38] but the examination (unlike the US example) was confined to the issue of novelty. From this point on, novelty is generally to be understood in its limited modern sense—as separate from any inquiry into the obviousness of the alleged invention. But equally, it is by this time accepted that a patent once granted might be attacked for its obviousness or lack of inventive step.[39] This additional criterion, which casts such a miasma of uncertainty

[34] The critics had opportunities to put their cases before a Royal Commission (P.P. 1864 [3419] XXIX) and then a Select Committee (P.P. 1871 (368) X, 1872 (193) XI); and a bill imposing very severe constraints on the system was even passed by the House of Lords, though it did not become law: see Batzel [1982] Bus. Hist. 189; Oppenheim [1998] I.P.R. 400. A similar anti-patent movement arose elsewhere in Western Europe. It soon enough lost headway in face of the movement for international patent co-operation, and also the adoption in 1877 of the Patent Law of the German Reich: see Duncan, above n.8, Ch.3; cf. Machlup and Penrose (1950) 10 J.Econ.Hist. 1; Fisher [2005] I.P.Q. 1, who treat the anti-patent movement in Britain as a serious threat.

[35] Patents, Designs and Trade Marks Act 1883. Again the initial fees were reduced and the number of patents granted rose from under 4,000 p.a. to some 9,000 p.a.: Boehm (above, n.22); Cornish, *Oxford History* (above, n.8) at pp.963–964.

[36] The new Comptroller-General was also given a limited power to hear third-party oppositions to applications for patents, a jurisdiction somewhat expanded in 1902. Right of appeal was to the Solicitor-General and Attorney-General until 1932, when the Patents Appeal Tribunal (consisting of a Chancery Division judge) was established.

[37] P.P. 1901 [Cd 506, Cd 530] XXIII.

[38] See Patents Act 1902.

[39] Fox (above, n.9). Part II traces the beginnings of this doctrine (which it is his object to denounce) to *Crane v Price* (1842) 1 W.P.C. 393 at 411. By the end of the century Brett M.R. could treat it "generally with amused contempt" (*Edison Bell v Smith* (1894) 11 R.P.C. 389 at 398; and see him also in *Hayward v Hamilton* (1879–81) Griff P.C. 115 at 121). But thereafter the doctrine was looked at with suspicion, e.g. by Fletcher Moulton L.J. in *British Westinghouse v Braulik* (1910) 27 R.P.C. 209.

around patents, is one result of concern over the consequences of making patents "too easy" to obtain.[40]

Two other changes in 1883 are linked: juries were effectively excluded from trials of patent actions in favour of a single judge[41]; and patentees were obliged to include in their specifications at least one claim delineating the scope of their monopoly.[42] The question whether the defendant was infringing, so often marginal in contested cases, ceased to be weighed upon a private moral balance in the jury-room and was instead subjected to that nice form of linguistic inquiry so natural to the Chancery mind. Buoyed up by a certain suspicion of monopoly grants, the judges soon insisted that claims marked out the full range of protection: alternative embodiments outside the scope of the words used in the claims were not covered,[43] nor were the separate parts of machines claimed as mechanical combinations.[44] As we shall see, this use of claims as "fence-posts", rather than as "guide-lines", has many consequences in the basic law of patents. It is a development which has not been followed or paralleled in some other important industrial countries. Even today, when defining claims are much more the norm, there are still crucial differences of attitude towards their significance.[45] **3–11**

With these developments, the essential features of the modern system were settled in a way that was not to be disturbed until the events of the 1970s. The statutory revisions of 1907, 1919, 1932 and, above all, 1949, put the law more in the form of a code and altered it in many details, but attempted nothing drastic. Apart from certain international considerations dealt with below, events worth recording were the restrictions upon claims to chemical substances introduced in 1919 and removed again in 1949 as having little real value[46]; and the introduction in 1949 of obviousness as a ground of pre-grant opposition—an objection which, however, proved very difficult to substantiate in pre-grant proceedings.[47] **3–12**

[40] Obviousness secured an earlier foothold in US law (see *Hotchkiss v Greenwood*, 52 US 248 (1850)), but patents were then more readily available in that country.

[41] Complaints about the difficulty of presenting technical matters to juries can be found in the various parliamentary investigations. The practice of trial by judge alone gained legislative support only in the Patents and Designs Act 1907.

[42] Patents, Designs and Trade Marks Act 1883 s.5(5): "a distinct statement of the invention claimed". On the evolution of claims, see Brennan [2005] I.P.Q. 261.; Cornish, *Oxford History* (above, n.8) at pp.964–972.

[43] *Nobel v Anderson* (1895) 12 R.P.C. 164 HL.

[44] *British United Shoe Manufacturers v Fussell* (1908) 25 R.P.C. 631 CA.

[45] See below, paras 4–45 et seq.

[46] See below, paras 4–47—4–48.

[47] See below, paras 5–39 et seq.

3. The "International" Patent System

(1) Foreign impact upon national systems

3–13 Many countries have been attracted to introduce a patent system by the hope that it will act as a lure to foreign technology. The same concern has induced them to open their systems to foreign applications. The United States, for instance, allowed foreigners to apply for patents well before it offered copyright to foreign authors.[48] Equally, the patenting countries of the nineteenth century were led to a modest union, under the Paris Industrial Property Convention of 1883,[49] which guaranteed the nationals of each country of the union the same treatment in the others as was given to their own nationals.[50] The union also established the system of Convention priority, under which an application in one of the contracting countries gave a period (eventually 12 months) in which to pursue an application in any of the others; this would bear the same priority date as the first.[51]

3–14 In the second half of the twentieth century, the international exchange of technology became the chief point of maintaining patent systems in countries whose socialist or communist economies provided little reason for offering market power as a reward to domestic inventors. Within a planned economy it was logical to encourage innovation by systems of state rewards.[52]

3–15 As in seventeenth-century England, any country which offers patents to foreigners will want the invention to be exploited to the advantage of its own economy. It may indeed take measures to make the patent more than a cover protecting the import of foreign-made goods. If it has a domestic industry that competes with the foreign patentee there may be particular cause for jealousy. This certainly was the reason for the introduction into the British system of provisions allowing the grant of compulsory licences

---

[48] In 1836 and 1891 respectively. The British, having greater interest in securing rights for themselves abroad, were in both fields prepared to extend protection to foreigners; even so, in copyright it took reciprocal agreement to establish that publication in another country could found British copyright: see below, paras 10–06—10–08.

[49] Subsequently revised in 1900 (Brussels), 1911 (Washington), 1925 (The Hague), 1934 (London), 1958 (Lisbon) and 1967 (Stockholm), and amended in 1979. The UK ratified the latest version in 1969. For the debates leading to the Convention, see Ladas, *The International Protection of Industrial Property* (1930); Penrose, *The Economics of the International Patent System* (1951), Ch.3; Duncan (above, n.8) Ch.6. In 2008, the Convention had 173 members of its Union.

[50] The point of this formula was that countries without a patent law could join the Union and get benefits for their own nationals abroad. On this basis the Netherlands and Switzerland joined and the strategy proved useful in getting them to adopt patent systems of their own. The present provisions (arts 2, 3) provide equal treatment on a basis of domicile and place of business as well as nationality.

[51] See below, paras 4–10—4–13.

[52] For such inventors' certificates see Hamson, *Patent Rights for Scientific Discoveries* (1930); Soltysinski (1969) 32 M.L.R. 408; Boguslavski (1979) 18 Ind.Prop. 113. They have disappeared from the current patent laws of Central and Eastern Europe.

on the ground that the invention was not being worked domestically[53]; the success of the German and Swiss chemical industries in the late nineteenth century was built to a substantial degree on the holding of key patents.[54]

The French originally went even further, making revocation of the patent the penalty for importing patented articles from abroad; lifting this draconian sanction was made a precondition of membership of the Paris Convention.[55] The majority of patenting countries now have some form of compulsory working requirement,[56] which the Paris Convention allows to be sanctioned by compulsory licensing once three years have elapsed from grant[57]; and by revocation if compulsory licensing fails after two years to produce the required result.[58] Provisions of this kind in national law are not only offensive to notions of international comity supposedly underlying the Convention; they are also economically unsound in any case where efficiencies of scale demand production in one place for international markets. Despite this, the TRIPs Agreement now sets out in art.31 the limits which Member States should apply to such licensing. However, art.31(f) which provides that such use should be authorised "predominantly for the supply of the domestic market", has been the subject of considerable controversy in relation to drugs for the treatment of HIV/AIDS and has been qualified by the Doha Declaration of 2001, a WTO Council Decision of 2003 and an EU Regulation permitting compulsory licences for export to developing countries.[59]

(2) Hostility to patents

Countries which are well enough organised to bargain hard for the foreign technology that they buy, and technically advanced enough to further develop what they learn, are generally satisfied with what they get out of the international "patent bargain". Before 1990, by keeping their patent systems alive, East European countries created some sense of security for Western enterprises selling them technology. To some extent they appreciated that the system has a potential for underpinning the transfer of technology. If technology recipients are adept in building upon their local strengths, they may secure access to industrial development in ways denied to state economic planning and expropriation. Today, countries such as China have come to appreciate the same message. **3–16**

[53] Tentatively introduced in 1883 without reference to foreign working, the provisions were made much more specific in 1907. As elsewhere, they did not lead to frequent applications: see below, paras 7–40—7–43.

[54] Haber, *The Chemical Industry during the Nineteenth Century* (1971), pp.166–167, 198–204.

[55] See Penrose (above, n.45), pp.74–77; PIP, art.5A(1).

[56] But the US has always, by geography and economic position, been able to remain aloof from this sort of requirement.

[57] Or four years from application if this is longer.

[58] PIP art.5A(2)–(5).

[59] Regulation 816/2006.

It was in countries where the patent system is part of an unplanned or partly planned economy that its effects upon the international trade of the state have been more persistently called into question. To take two very different examples among common law countries: in Canada in the early 1970s, the patent system came under careful but sceptical scrutiny from a team of economists.[60] To them it seemed to operate largely as a shield for the imported products of foreign owners (mainly from the United States), while doing very little to encourage the development of home-based industry. However, plans drastically to curtail the scope of the patent monopoly in the wake of these criticisms met with a hostile reception from industry there and abroad—some measure at least of the very considerable value that substantial owners do attach to patents.[61] Around the same time in India, where the Government became intent on rapid intervention in industrial ownership and policy, wide powers were actually taken to grant compulsory licences on "reasonable" terms.[62] One result was a marked reduction in the amount of patenting by foreign enterprises in that country. In 2005 the old system was abandoned and, in particular, pharmaceutical patents were introduced.

3–17 For countries less advanced, the disadvantages may seem still graver. Yet they have been under indomitable pressure from industrialised countries and transnational enterprises to have a patent system, whether or not one has been inherited from a colonial past. In the 1970s and 1980s developing countries were searching for a happy medium by which they could use patents to attract foreign technology, while at the same time influencing by bureaucratic intervention the terms on which their own firms collaborated with foreign enterprises. In the 1970s a number of experiments were made in domestic legislation, particularly in Central and South America.[63] In international circles there was increasing discussion about acceptable models.

This focused particularly on two negotiations: one was the formulation of UNCTAD's Code of Conduct for the Transfer of Technology, which was a practical expression of the search for a New International Economic Order. The other was the Revision Conference of the Paris Convention, which also grew out of UNCTAD criticisms of the current operation of patent systems internationally. The Transfer of Technology Code was by 1980 taken to a point where detailed drafts existed; but it was a point of high controversy, with different versions being preferred by the Group of 77 (developing

[60] Economic Council of Canada, *Report on Intellectual and Industrial Property* (1971) (with additional background studies); Firestone, *Economic Implications of Patents* (1972). For a similar appraisal in Australia, see Manderville, et al. (below, para.3–36, n.19).

[61] Working Paper on Patent Law Reform (1976).

[62] Patents Act 1970 (India); Vedaraman (1972) 3 I.I.C. 39; Kunz-Hallstein (1975) 4 I.I.C. 427 at 438–440.

[63] Following, in particular, resolutions of the Andean Pact countries in 1970 and the Argentine law on technology transfer of the same year: see, e.g. Soberanis (1977) 7 Georgia J.Int.L. 17 (on Mexico).

countries), the industrial countries and the socialist countries.[64] It was never settled whether any final form of the Code would have legal effect or would be regarded as a voluntary code of good practice. Immediately after this, the Revision Conference of the Paris Convention held three sessions, but then adjourned sine die in 1982. The eventual sticking point proved to be demands from the Group of 77, for example, that their countries have power to impose *exclusive* compulsory licences on patentees in respect of failure to work the invention in the national territory.[65]

Against such revisions, the United States took a particularly strong **3–18**
position, urging the importance at the least of maintaining the Convention's existing standards of protection.[66] The stalemate incited the United States to take intellectual property into the frame of inter-governmental trade negotiation, making it a prominent part of bilateral agreements with countries such as Korea and Brazil and using its Trade Act powers to block imports into its territory where a country did not come up to scratch on the intellectual property front. In the field of inventions, the greatest pressure has been to secure the extension of patent systems to chemical and/or pharmaceutical products per se.[67] The success of the tactic has led to the incorporation of intellectual property protection in the new GATT as the TRIPS Agreement (to which we come back under the next heading). The United States is by no means content with the remarkable bouleversement of the state of affairs a decade ago. Alongside TRIPS and its dispute settlement procedures, the United States' Government, through its Trade Representative, has continued pursuing individual countries with import sanctions, wherever they offend its view on what is proper in intellectual property matters, as well as pursuing a policy of bilateral free trade agreements requiring the other country to introduce so-called TRIPS-Plus intellectual property regimes even more protective than that of the United States itself.

[64] For these developments, see, e.g. Anderfelt, *International Patent Legislation and Developing Countries* (1971); Vaitsos (1972) 9 J.Dev. Studies; Penrose (1973) Econ.J. 768; Lall (1976) 10 J. World Trade Law 1; Kunz-Hallstein (n.57, above); Laird (1980) 9 CIPA 276; Wilner and Fikentscher in *Legal Problems of Codes of Conduct for Multinational Enterprises* (Horn ed., 1980), pp.177, 189; Fikentscher, *The Draft International Code of Conduct on the Transfer of Technology* (1980); Cabanellas, *Antitrust and Direct Regulation of International Transfer of Technology Transactions* (1984); Blakeney, *Legal Aspects of the Transfer of Technology to Developing Countries* (1989).

[65] On this particular campaign compare, PA 1977 s.49(3), now quietly removed by CDPA 1988 Sch.5 para.13.

[66] It stood alone in resisting demands that the present unanimity rule for amending the Convention become a qualified majority rule.

[67] In some cases this treatment was offered preferentially to Americans, and it was this which led to the Most-Favoured-Nation provision in TRIPS; for which, see above, para.1–31.

(3) Co-operation in patenting: worldwide linkages

3–19 Before 1977, there was nothing that could be called an international patent system, at least in legal and organisational terms. The Paris Convention (PIP) was largely restricted to basic principles for securing readier access to the national systems maintained by the different contracting countries.[68] It made no arrangements, beyond its priority system, for standardising or simplifying the process of applying for patents and it required the substantive law to conform to its standards only on such collateral matters as the compulsory licensing requirements.[69]

The experience of many industrialised countries has been that unexamined patents lead to nuisance. The answer to this was to institute some form of pre-grant examination of the substantive merits of the application in the light of a search of earlier technical literature. Serious examination is not cheap; and, as the number of countries demanding an examination rose, so did the cost. The applicant seeking a patent in several countries saw his case processed in a roughly similar way, but subjected to a search of a varying range of literature and judged according to varying criteria, in a series of offices operating independently. Accordingly, patentees (whatever the interests of their patent departments and professional advisers) and governments (whatever the bureaucratic pretensions of their patent offices) began to appreciate that "internationalising" the patenting process might increase efficiency and reduce costs.

3–20 On a worldwide basis,[70] the system of international patent applications under the Patent Co-operation Treaty (PCT) (Washington, 1970) was put into effect from June 1, 1978, its central administration being provided by WIPO in Geneva.[71] The Treaty is of interest to any country which is not content to have a pure registration system but instead opts for some form of examination. Its main chapters provide for two things, after the submission of a single international application designating the PCT countries in which patents are wanted.[72] Chapter I creates an international search conducted by one of a handful of international search authorities (the Australian, Japanese, Russian and United States Patent Offices, the European Patent Office and, to a more limited extent, the Swedish and Austrian Offices)[73]; Chapter II establishes an International Preliminary Examination. Participating states

[68] On the principle of national treatment as it affects patents, see Evans [1996] E.I.P.R. 149. In 2006 there were 169 PIP States.

[69] See above, para.3–15.

[70] Another collaboration of importance is the Strasbourg Convention concerning the International Patent Classification 1971 (not yet ratified by the UK).

[71] Records of the Diplomatic Conference are published. See generally Pfanner (1979) 1 E.I.P.R. 98. In 2006 there were 128 PCT States.

[72] National or regional patent offices are appointed receiving offices for applications from given countries.

[73] The range of material open to search is broadly defined: PCT art.15(2), Rules under Patent Co-operation Treaty r.33; but each search authority will work upon a different body of material, depending upon its collection and linguistic capacity.

are not obliged to adhere to both chapters[74]; nor is an applicant obliged to have the Preliminary Examination.

The Treaty is not founded upon any international agreement about the grounds of validity for a patent. However, since January 2004 the International Search Report by the international search authority provides a written opinion on patentability, in accordance with criteria that are defined only generally in the Treaty.[75] Nevertheless, for countries that have no examining system, the report may provide a basis upon which a national patent office, applying its own law, can decide whether or not to grant a patent. In the hope of opening this opportunity to developing countries, it was hastily decided to introduce the second chapter along with the first in 1978.[76] **3–21**

Apart from this, the main advantage of the Treaty is practical: it allows an applicant to make applications in numerous countries by a single procedure; and to delay his final decision to apply in a number of countries (with the official fees, agents' fees and translation costs that this entails) for a period of 30 months (whether or not an international examination is requested) after his priority date.[77] What the Treaty does not provide is an "international patent", since in the end each national office, or regional office such as the EPO, decides what patents to grant for its own territory. In 2006, 128 countries belonged to the PCT.

By way of contrast, the TRIPS Agreement standardises substantive patent law and procedures for its enforcement to a much greater extent than ever before. The influence of the EPC model on its provisions is plain, and therefore it has not required major amendment to UK or European patent law.[78] The provisions on patentable subject matter and on adequate disclosure bear a family resemblance to the EPC, though they are not always so explicit.[79] Likewise the provisions on the patent term and on the scope of rights resemble those in the European Conventions, but rights do not have to be defined by reference to claims in the patent specification.[80] There are, however, extensive provisions designed to inhibit the granting of compulsory licences, which extend to exceptions for the benefit of governments and those they authorise. The impact of these on UK law will be considered later.[81] **3–22**

---

[74] The Member States adopting Chs I and II, the search authorities and examining authorities at any time may be ascertained from the latest issue of the PCT Gazette.

[75] PCT art.33; Rules Under Patent Co-Operation Treaty r.64.

[76] Accordingly a number of developing countries from the start took advantage of both chapters.

[77] See below, para.4–10.

[78] But see McGrath [1996] E.I.P.R. 398; Verma (1996) 27 I.I.C. 331; Imam (2006) 37 I.I.C.445; Vaver and Basheer [2006] E.I.P.R. 282

[79] TRIPS arts 27, 29 and 32 (revocation). In its campaigns to exclude such exceptions from national laws, the US has used bilateral trade agreements with various countries: see Vaver and Basheer (above, n.74).

[80] TRIPS arts 28, 30, 33, 34 (reversed burden of proof).

[81] See below, para.7–42.

A current may now be running in favour of a truly international patent system. Alongside the TRIPS negotiations have been two other potentially significant discussions. A WIPO initiative for a world-wide Treaty harmonising essential substantive rules began with publication of a first draft in 1990.[82] By its side, the largest patent offices—those of the United States and Japan, together with the EPO—entered tri-partite discussions which include standardisation of application procedures. The Treaty on substantive law has made only fitful progress for it confronts both philosophical differences and professional jealousies of considerable proportions. But a Patent Law Treaty of 2000, brought into effect in 2005, aims to standardise important details of patent office practice in different countries and regions. There has been subsequent talk of a WIPO-operated "world patent". But the bowstring for that venture will need a great deal more tightening before any shooting takes place.

Meanwhile the shifting economic fortunes of the developing world have to an extent displaced the direct antagonisms of the 1970s with a more complex set of concerns. The environmental concern to preserve the diversity of natural resources is driven partly by a desire to preserve traditional forms of pre-industrial existence, but also by a desire to manage changes in production and life-style in a way which ensures that local communities benefit from new opportunities. Where, in particular, pharmaceuticals and other products are developed from plants or other resources of a particular country, there is now persistent demand for that country to benefit from the revenue stream being generated internationally, equivalent to the royalties which come from the extraction of minerals. This, however, is a claim being made on behalf of communities and other groups, mainly in traditional societies. How it can be accommodated within the individualistic scheme of reference which is the basis of intellectual property rights is a very difficult question. The answers to it can only emerge after extended debate.[83]

(4) Co-operation in patenting: Western Europe[84]

3–23 Europe's industrial renaissance after the Second World War pointed up the considerable differences that existed in the systems of patent administration in the different countries. West Germany, Holland and Switzerland, for instance, undertook extensive examination of patents before grant and permitted third-party interventions; but the first two countries had introduced arrangements allowing this to be deferred for up to seven years.[85]

[82] For a useful summary of issues and debates, see Wegner, *Patent Harmonisation* (1993). For a critical view of the prospects, see Kingston [2004] E.I.P.R. 447.

[83] Contrast, e.g. Straus [1993] 24 I.I.C. 602; Wells [1994] E.I.P.R. 111; da Costa de Silva [1995] E.I.P.R. 522; Blakeney [1997] E.I.P.R. 298; Curci, *The Protection of Biodiversity and Traditional Knowledge in International Law of Intellectual Property* (2010).

[84] Leith, *Harmonisation of Intellectual Property in Europe* (1998).

[85] See below, para.4–18.

France, Belgium and Italy had mere registration systems, though in the French Law of 1968 a search, with examiner's commentary, was introduced.[86] Britain occupied a mid-way position, providing for a limited search and examination, together with the possibility of third-party opposition on somewhat wider grounds.

It was appreciated very early in the life of the European Economic Community that patents would pose a substantial barrier to intra-Community trade in "legitimate" goods.[87] In 1959, a working group was convened to consider solving the problem by instituting an EEC patent. Its plan for the purpose[88] was put aside in the wake of Britain's first failure to secure entry to the EEC; for the desirability of having the British in such an enterprise was widely acknowledged. When, however, the United States took the lead in promoting the Patent Cooperation Treaty, France sought refuge in a revival of the Community plan. With only the beginnings of an examination system, she found reason to fear the advent of international applications for France which would carry the impress of a PCT search and preliminary examination. **3–24**

The revived negotiations now involved a double package: first, a convention for a single granting system through a European Patent Office; secondly, a convention for a Community patent which would be one product of this system. The first convention was concerned, not with freedom of EC trade, but with providing a less wasteful, but nonetheless substantial, examination of applications. It was accordingly to be open to a wider range of Western European states, including the United Kingdom. A successful applicant would secure at the end of the process a bundle of national patents, normally in common form, for such participant countries as he designated in his application. The system would only provide an alternative route to a patent in those countries, each of which would be left free to maintain its own national system.[89] On this basis the European Patent Convention (EPC) was signed at Munich in 1973.[90] That city became the headquarters of the European Patent Office (EPO),[91] which opened its doors **3–25**

[86] This "documentary report system" survived in the 1978 legislation which gave effect to the new conventions, but the opportunities for intervention have increased: Vianges (1979) 18 Ind.Prop. 220; Lecca (1979) 9 CIPA 282.

[87] See above, para.1–51.

[88] The "Haertel Draft" of 1962. This was followed by the Strasbourg Convention on The Unification of Certain Points of Substantive Patent Law (Council of Europe, 1963), which has proved of great influence in settling substantial legal principles in the EPC and CPC. Its entry into force was, however, delayed until 1980 (the UK being one of the initial ratifying states). For the history of the European Conventions, see further Van Empel (below, n.90), Ch.1; Banks Report (Cmnd.4407, 1970), Ch.3.

[89] Proceedings of the negotiations have been published and form a source which is considered in deciding how to interpret the EPC.

[90] See Van Empel, *The Granting of European Patents* (1975); Paterson, *The European Patent System* (2nd edn, 2001); Singer and Stauder, *The European Patent Convention* English 2nd edn (2003).

[91] The main sub-branch is at the Hague where the Search Division of the EPO is situated: the Office took over the former International Patent Institute there.

for applications on June 1, 1978.[92] In 28 years of operation, it has granted well over 740,000 patents, having received 2.3 million applications, of which 1.4 million required examination (a quarter for them under the PCT). In 2004, 180,662 applications were made but only 58,730 patents were granted (these being for applications made at earlier dates); in 2005 there were 193,623 applications and 53,259 patents. Slowness in the examination process has long been a complaint from users. A high proportion of the applications originate in the United States and Japan, the leading EPC state being Germany.[93] There are now 31 countries participating in the system, the 27 EU Member States, together with Switzerland, Turkey, Iceland, Monaco and Liechtenstein. Five Balkan states recognise European patents.[94] A range of revisions to the EPC were agreed in 2000 and took effect on December 13, 2007. Their incorporation into the text is known as "EPC 2000".[95]

3–26 The second part of the arrangement, the Community Patent Convention (CPC), was signed in 1975 in Luxembourg by the EC states (including, by then, the United Kingdom). Its principle is that, at the end of the European granting procedure, if a patent is sought for any EU state, a single patent for the whole EU will be granted.[96] This EU patent will thus come in the "bundle", together with national patents for such non-EU states as are also designated.

3–27 There have been various reasons for the long delay in introducing the CPC. The chief advantage of the single EU patent would be the ability to enforce it throughout the EU by a single main proceeding or to have its validity determined for that geographical area.[97] The EU Council, has committed itself to achieve an operative EU patent, with a complete structure of EU tribunals, a trial jurisdiction being given to a specialist EU court attached to the General Court of the ECJ (ex-the Court of First Instance), to which court there would be a right of appeal.[98] The proposal accepts that matters both of validity and infringement should be within the jurisdiction, since courts may have to examine largely the same factors in

---

[92] Originally the fields in which it would examine were restricted, but progress towards the complete range was completed by December 1, 1979; see EPC art.162.

[93] EPO Annual Report 2005, which contains much else by way of interest on the European system.

[94] Albania, Bosnia and Herzogovina, Croatia, the former Yugoslav Republic of Macedonia, and Serbia and Montenegro.

[95] Agreed at a Diplomatic Conference in November 2000 and implemented by Administrative Council Decision, June 28, 2001.

[96] CPC art.3. The EU patent is to be "unitary" in the sense that it can be granted, transferred, revoked or allowed to lapse only in respect of the whole EU: art.2(2). It seems, however, that an applicant will retain the right to opt for national patents: Jacob in Vaver and Bently, Ch.5.

[97] This would include the possibility of interim orders having EU-wide effect. Note, however, the possible development of cross-border judgments in national patent litigation: above, para.2–74.

[98] Statement of Presidency to Competitiveness Council: 6843/1/03. Previous proposals had advocated the use of national tribunals as courts of first instance.

both types of proceeding.[99] The system is to be embodied in an EU Regulation, which will replace the CPC as the legal medium for the new entitlement. However, it still remains to be seen whether and when the EU patent is to become a reality.[100] The transition is a stormy prospect and it may prove necessary to pass through an intermediate stage in which the leading EPC states arrange a special jurisdiction for mutual despatch of patent litigation.[101] It is an accepted standard in the court structures of democracies that there will be a final instance of appeal with authority to settle uncertainties in legal rules and in their application to facts. With the division of function between the EPO and the national jurisdictions of EPC states, the current scheme for patents in Europe fails to meet this desideratum and increasingly comes under critical fire in consequence. [102]

Other problems have been political. Because the CPC was negotiated as a **3–28**
convention distinct from the Treaty of Rome, EU organs possessed no power to impose the terms of the Convention on Member States. It was hoped that the CPC would form an element in the unified internal market of 1992 that the 1989 version of the CPC allowed its introduction first for those states wishing to join it—a step which in the circumstances would have been a wry compromise.

In the event, a majority of states insisted that upon grant an EU patent **3–29**
must be translated into their national languages.[103] This is only one instance of the Babel crisis which threatens the very future of an enlarged EU, but it is a significant illustration of it. Without limitation upon translation requirements (restricting them, for instance, to the claims of the specification), a cost saving is lost which would otherwise be a main key to the success of the EU patent. The attempt at a compromise on the question of translation has been severely criticised and this has been one reason why the EU has not after all been able to achieve a Regulation introducing the EU patent. The EPC states have also tried to take a hand in solving the question in relation to the European bundle of patents that it grants. The London Agreement reached in the European Patent Organisation in 2000 provides that countries which accept it will not require the translation of the whole specification (as distinct from just the claims) into their national language,

---

[99] The tribunal would contain one technically expert judge or make use of a technical rapporteur.

[100] See European Commission, *Promoting Innovation through Patents Com* (97) 314; Straus, *The Present State of the Patent System in the European Union* (1997); Ullrich (2002) 8 Eur. L.J. 433; cf. Bossung (2003) 34 I.I.C. 1. *The Gowers Review of Intellectual Property* (2006) supports introduction of the EU patent, just as it does the London Agreement on reducing translation costs as an interim measure: paras 5.13–5.19.

[101] For this European Patent Law Agreement (EPLA) project, Willems in A.Kur et al. (eds), *Patent Law on the Move* (2005), p.325; Luginbuehl [2003] E.I.P.R. 256; Oser [2006] 37 I.I.C. 520.

[102] See, e.g. Jacob L.J. *European Central Bank v Document Security Systems* [2008] EWCA Civ 192; *Leo Pharma v Sandoz* [2009] EWCA Civ 1188.

[103] On translation issues, see Huebner [2003] E.I.P.R. 543.

where the grant is in one of the three official languages of the EPC. This means, for instance, that France would not require the translation of a specification granted in German or English. President Sarkozy has seen to it that this concession has become a reality.

(5) A second-tier right for Europe?[104]

3–30 A separate question of unified or unitary rights within the EU has enjoyed some prominence. A number of Member States (not including the UK) supplement their patent system with a secondary form of formal protection for technical advances.[105] These go by various names—short-term patent, petty patent, utility model (an awkward translation of *Gebrauchsmuster*), *certificat d'utilité*—and may together be labelled "second-tier protection". The variety of names is a first indication of the considerable differences in these rights from country to country. Inevitably, the variations and the lack of such protection in some states, have led the EC Commission to study prospects for an EU right and/or national harmonisation.[106]

3–31 The special position of the United Kingdom lies in the distinctive route which it has followed in order to provide a second tier of protection for technical ideas: by introducing industrial copyright and then by replacing it with unregistered design right, it has provided a wholly informal means of protecting the shape of industrial articles; and at the same time it has extended this protection indiscriminately to technical and to aesthetic shapes of products.[107] The systems provided elsewhere in EU countries all adopt a formal process of some kind, making application to a national office a necessary pre-condition. It is primarily this difference which seems to put the UK unregistered design right beyond the range of possible models for a European future.[108]

---

104 See generally Reichman in Dreyfuss, Zimmerman & First, *Expanding the Boundaries of Intellectual Property* (2001) Ch.2.

105 Austria, Belgium, Czech Republic, Denmark, Estonia, Finland, France, Germany, Greece, Holland, Hungary, Ireland, Italy, Portugal, Slovakia, Slovenia and Spain. Cyprus, Latvia, Lithuania, Luxembourg, Malta and Sweden do not have such protection. Under the Paris Convention, "utility models" must be given national treatment and six months' priority. This is extended to WTO countries by TRIPS art.2(1), but the latter Agreement does not require second-tier protection—it is not part of the US world-view.

106 Green Paper on Utility Model Protection in the Common Market (July 19, 1995, COM(95) 370). In preparation the Commission obtained two Reports from the IFO-Institut which show some industrial opinion in favour of an utility-model system, but the Green Paper itself is extremely cautious. Compare the much more forthright proposal for an EC utility model by the Max Planck Institute for IP Law, Munich (1993); Kern [1994] 25 I.I.C. 627. For the position in international perspective, see Reichman in Dreyfuss et al., *Expanding the Boundaries of Intellectual Property* (2005) Ch.2.

107 See below, paras 15–38 et seq.

108 See further, below, paras 15–52 et seq.

Of the various schemes now operating in the EU, none is subject to any substantive examination of validity before grant.[109] As a balance for this relative informality (and cheapness), the rights endure for a much shorter period than a patent, ranging from six years to 10 years from application.[110] The chief differences concern two matters: the extent of subject-matter within the system; and the test of necessary advance over the prior art. **3–32**

Some variants have adopted a modest range, operating in the sphere of technical design and relating only to the functional shape of articles.[111] Such a "utility model" system became well known in Germany (where, however, it was expanded in 1990) and passed from there to Finland, Greece, Italy, Spain and Portugal, where it remains in force. In contrast, Austria, Ireland, Belgium and France all permit second-tier rights in any patentable subject matter[112]; and Germany (since its reform) permits everything save processes, as does Denmark. **3–33**

So far as the element of technical advance is concerned, almost all countries seek to lower the threshold of admissibility, compared with the inventive step requirement of modern patent law. There may be no requirement other than novelty (as in Austria, Italy and Greece) or some differentiating phrase may be adopted, such as the Spanish *superevidencia—utter obviousness*.[113]

The typical case which countries have had in mind when introducing second-tier schemes is the inventor of modest workshop improvements, perhaps in his own or some other small business which lacks the resources to engage in full-scale patenting.[114] This meritorious image has made the development a particularly attractive one recently in smaller EU states. Where the system is confined to technical design (utility model protection in the true sense), it probably fits this modest aim reasonably well. It is when the schemes are extended to all patentable subject matter, at the same time as lowering the threshold of technical advance, that real danger is to be anticipated. Patent systems, after all, were obliged to introduce the expensive and time-consuming business of substantive examination in order to cut out the belligerent claimant to a dubious invention from doing a great deal **3–34**

---

[109] There may, however, be a search before grant (e.g. in Austria, or optionally in Germany) or a search before infringement proceedings (e.g. in France and Ireland). The Japanese system used to be the best-known utility model with a patent-like examination; in 1994, however, this was dropped. The number of applications there has plummeted.

[110] In fine isolation, Portugal allows indefinite renewal.

[111] Thus at this point providing some affinity to the UK unregistered design right.

[112] In one significant respect, Austria goes further, allowing this form of protection for the logic underlying a computer program (Act of 1994 art.1(2)): this appears intended to by-pass the exclusion of computer programs as such from the patent system: below, paras 5–63 et seq.

[113] Another limitation may be that novelty takes account only of the national state of the art (at least for prior use). This may lead importers of inventions to secure second-tier protection. The Commission appears to favour a test of absolute, rather than relative, novelty in its Green Paper above, n.2). It would also want a 12-month grace period.

[114] Smaller countries with less advanced technological bases feel a natural interest in such schemes. See, e.g. Parkes (1994) 25 I.I.C. 204 (discussing the Irish short-term patent).

of damage by threatening litigation. Yet a wide-ranging second-tier right actually entitles the holder to claims of a breadth which may well not be sustainable under a patent system. He may indeed acquire this extensive, unexamined protection for his first 10 years and then, for the second decade, get a patent for as much as he can actually justify.[115]

3–35 The British have had the historical experience and commonsense to hold back from any development on such a scale, arguing instead for improved efficiency in the patent system itself.[116] At the same time, by creating the Patents County Court, and by reforming High Court procedure, they have taken steps to reduce what is often considered the enormity of patent litigation in the United Kingdom.[117]

In 1998 the European Commission published a draft directive for a moderate form of standard "utility model" to be adopted by all EU States.[118] It was proposed as a harmonising measure that would enhance competitiveness in the EU, in particular, by encouraging the innovative efforts of small and medium firms. A right would be granted for a maximum 10 years[119] without any preceding examination of the substance. The applicant would merely have the right to require a search to be conducted for prior art.[120] The right would be for an "invention", which, like a patentable invention, would have to be novel, inventive and industrially applicable.

Despite the borrowing of these concepts from patent law, on the all-important question of "inventive step", only a lower threshold would need to be satisfied: compared with the prior art, the invention must show either particular effectiveness in terms of, for example, ease of application or use; or a practical or industrial advantage.[121] This could, at the same time, establish a very low threshold of inventiveness for a utility model and push up the requirement in patent law. It could indeed herald a return to the opaque concept of the former German law which required a sufficient "level" of inventiveness in a valid patent. Because some major industries object to the inevitable insecurities that this would introduce in the kernel of protection, they would be omitted from the plan. The right would not be

---

[115] See Tootal [1994] E.I.P.R. 511; Llewelyn, *Utility Models/Second Tier Protection* (1996).

[116] The concept of a "registered patent" was fostered in the Nicholson Green Paper (Intellectual Property Rights and Innovation (Cmnd. 9117, 1983), paras 220–222) but rejected in the Government's White Paper (Cmnd.9712, 1986), paras 15–18. For attempts to keep the idea alive in the UK, see Lees [1993] CIPA 79 and subsequent report, at 150; Chartered Institute of Patent Agents, *Second Tier Protection* (1994).

[117] See above, paras 2–10—2–11; Nott [1994] E.I.P.R. 3; Jacob [1997] I.P.Q. 3.

[118] [1998] OJ C36/13.

[119] The right will be granted for six years, renewable twice for two-year periods.

[120] A Member State would be entitled to require a search before any litigation to the utility model was brought—not much comfort to a defendant already working within its bounds.

[121] Article 6. Double-talk pervades the loose drafting of this provision. It is said that the applicant has to satisfy this test "clearly and convincingly" (to what level of proof?). Since there is to be no examination, it is only a right-owner who has to do so. That is the nub of the difficulties.

available for biological inventions, chemical or pharmaceutical substances or processes, or "inventions involving computer programs".[122] That would only make the distinction between the two rights more obscure in the remaining industrial fields. The proposal accordingly made no progress. Rather the EU institutions saw to the introduction of EU registered and unregistered designs, combined with a Directive to harmonise national registered design laws.[123] Insofar as it is permissible within those schemes to protect designs that are primarily functional, this movement has provided a partial substitute for a secondary form of technological protection.

4. Justifying the Patent System

(1) Basic objectives

In the course of time, both "individual" and "public" justifications have played prominent roles in the arguments in favour of patents for invention, as for other kinds of intellectual property.[124] At various periods the idea of a patent as an instrument of justice to the inventor has proved attractive, and the power of this sort of argument is by no means exhausted.[125] **3–36**

Yet rewarding inventive ingenuity may seem little more than an incidental consequence of modern patent systems. They do not protect each inventor who conceives an invention. Only the first-comer is entitled. Indeed, in most systems, it is the first to apply for a patent, rather than the first to invent, who is given priority (and even the United States is now considering changing its law to this effect). The protection is then good not only against

[122] Article 4. Biotechnical inventions have received their own dispensation in the Biotechnology Directive 98/44, which is discussed at paras 21–13 et seq., cf. the much narrower exclusion from the patent system of computer programs as such: below, paras 5–63 et seq, 20–26 et seq.

[123] See below Ch.15.

[124] What follows builds upon the ideas introduced above at paras 1–32—1–36. The best-known detailed discussion of the justifications for patent systems, sceptical in tone, is Machlup, *An Economica Review of the Patent System* (US Senate Committee on the Judiciary, Sub-Committee on Patents, Trademarks and Copyrights, Study No.15). And see Plant (1934) 1 Economica 30; Arrow [1962] N.B. Econ. Rsch. 609; Nordhaus, *Invention, Growth and Welfare* (1969); Scherer and Ross, *Industrial Market Structure and Economic Performance* 3rd edn (1990), Ch.15; Economic Council of Canada, *Report on Intellectual and Industrial Property* (1971), Chs 3, 4; together with Hindley, *Background Study on Economic Theory*, Ch.1; and Firestone, *Economic Implications of Patents* (1971); Taylor and Silberston, *The Economic Impact of the Patent System* (1973), Ch.2; Bowman, *Patent and Anti-trust Law* (1973), Ch.2; Kitch (1977) 29 J. Law & Econ.265; Manderville, Lamberton and Bishop, *Economic Effects of the Australian Patent System* (1982); Kaufer, *Economics of the Patent System* (1989); Dam, (1994) 23 J.L.St. 247; Hall, *Innovation, Economics and Evolution* (1994); Arup, *Innovation Policy and Law* (1993); Granstrand, *The Economics and Management of Intellectual Property* (1999) Ch.2; Maskus, *Intellectual Property Rights in the Global Economy* (2000); Teece, *Managing Intellectual Capital* (2000); Landes and Posner, *The Economic Structure of Intellectual Property Law* (2003); Fisher, *Fundamentals of Patent Law* (2007).

[125] For instance, the introduction of compensation for employee-inventors reflects this attitude: see below, paras 7–08—7–09.

those who derive their information from that patentee but also against those who work it out independently. The period of protection, moreover, is relatively short compared with other forms of "property". If a major object were to give the inventor his just reward, a system more closely akin to copyright—with its "property"-like duration and its protection of all original creations, but only against copying—would seem more appropriate. In this connection, the intrusion in the United Kingdom of artistic copyright into the sphere of industrial production after 1968, and its major modification 20 years later, provides a telling comparison.[126]

3–37 Today the debate over patent systems tends to concentrate upon their role as a "public" instrument of economic policy. Patents are looked upon to provide two kinds of impetus towards the technical efficiency, and hence the growing wealth, of the community as a whole. They are intended to encourage the making of inventions and the subsequent innovative work that will put those inventions to practical use; and they are expected to procure information about the invention for the rest of the industry and the public generally, which otherwise might be withheld, at least for a period that could be crucial. These incentives and informational objectives deserve separate consideration.

(2) Patents as incentives to invent and innovate

3–38 Discussion about the efficacy of incentives has a practical, utilitarian flavour which is lacking when the argument is about the demands of justice for the individual. Even so, it is very difficult to measure or assess the effects (if any) that a patent system is producing. It is widely felt that some sort of intervention is needed if inventions are to be made and introduced at anything like an optimal rate. Whether this should be done by a patent system, rather than by giving legal protection against breach of confidence or copying, or by direct investment on the part of the state, is more controversial. If it is to be by a patent system, there are many questions about its exact nature which may affect its performance.

Modern patent systems, it should be observed, offer a standard formula to all who have "inventions" to protect. They contrast with systems of research grant and reward, whether funded by the state or private organisations.[127] These usually depend upon a decision by the paymaster to concentrate resources upon particular objectives. Assessing a patent system, accordingly, means taking a view of its effects across the board—and that

[126] See below, Ch.15.

[127] Compare the proposals for systems of "innovation patent" and "innovation warrant", both of which require a state office to play a decisive role in determining the term and other incidents of the right granted: Kronz [1983] E.I.P.R. 178, 206; Kingston (ed.), *Direct Protection of Innovation* (1987); Shavell and Van Ypersele (2001) 44 J. of Law and Econ. 525; Scherer in Dreyfuss, Zimmerman & First (eds), *Expanding the Boundaries of Intellectual Property* (2001) Ch.1.

adds considerably to the difficulty. Two aspects of its range which make useful starting points in the discussion are the types of inventor for whom today it provides its incentive; and the types of invention to which it is applied.

(a) *Types of inventor*

One persistent argument against patents in the nineteenth century controversy was: since inventions are there to be discovered, industries that have progressed to a certain point will inevitably make them, and so artificial aids are unnecessary.[128] This was a line of argument that carried some conviction when the bulk of inventions concerned relatively simple mechanical products that were often worked out as a by-product of ordinary manufacturing. In the face of increasingly systematic organisation of research and development, and the extensive process of education which precedes it, this point of view is harder to maintain. **3–39**

If anything, the development of this characteristic of modern industry turns the issue on its head: is the pertinent question now whether patents are needed to produce the optimal degree of investment in research and development organised on a "corporate" scale? It seems not. One perceptive account of the historical record suggests that the individual inventor, and the small organisation centred around individuals of outstanding quality, continue to contribute a significant, even perhaps a disproportionate, number of the most important inventions that have been made over recent decades.[129] This type of inventor certainly cannot be ignored in any assessment of patents. **3–40**

In any case, there is no clear evidence that corporations are not influenced in their research and development decisions by their chances of securing and taking advantage of patent protection.[130] Invention, and its subsequent development, still occur across the whole spectrum of industrial organisation from giant corporation to one-man band. One of the more attractive **3–41**

[128] See Machlup and Penrose above, para.3–09, n.30. Further, it could be said that there was injustice in giving the reward to the man who stumbled upon the solution first, since he probably owed a great deal to what he had learned from his precursors. Note in this connection the refusal of a patent to a genetic engineering firm because it merely won a race to a known goal by known methods: below, para.5–47.

[129] Jewkes, Sawers and Stillerman, *The Sources of Invention* 2nd edn (1969), Ch.9; Mansfield (1986) 32 J.Pol.Sc. 175; Schankerman and Pakes (1986) 96 Econ..J. 1052. It does not follow that individual inventors are necessarily spurred by the patent system. In the past academic scientists, for instance, have been moved more by the desire for knowledge and the recognition that invention may bring. That attitude is now changing, but serious tensions are the result. See Eisenberg (1987) 97 Yale L.J. 177.

[130] In this context, see the criticism by Sir Hugh Laddie of the "obvious to try" notion in the obviousness ground of invalidity: "If the reward for finding a solution to a problem and securing a monopoly for that solution is very high, then it may well be worthwhile for large players to examine all potential avenues to see if one gives the right result ... So, the more commercially attractive the solution and the more pressing the public clamour for it, the harder it will be to avoid an obviousness attack", at p.93 in Vaver & Bently (eds), *Intellectual Property in the New Millennium* (2004).

arguments for a patent system is that, because of this very diversity, a range of different incentives is desirable.[131] Patents then have their place as a technique aimed at those who feel the attraction of market rewards.[132]

(b) *Levels of invention*

3–42 Patent systems protect a wide variety of technical inventions, from basic perceptions that will found new industries, to relatively minor improvements in established products. The chance of behaving to any striking degree as a monopolist is in fact reserved to a tiny proportion of all patentees.[133] Two characteristics of the invention will determine how far this is possible: the extent to which it fulfils a demand from consumers that was previously not met at all, or met only by something much less satisfactory (television in place of sound radio); and the degree to which it is cheaper or leads to more efficient operations in comparison with the substitutes which preceded it (power-driven tool replacing one hand-operated).

Occasionally, as with a drug that had no real precursor, a patentee may be able to withhold supplies so as to charge the price which will give him the largest return from estimated demand. So also when he is able to cut costs of production so much that he can still reach this level of profit at a price below that at which competitors can sell any substitute products and stay in business. More often, however, he cannot achieve so drastic an effect. His room for manoeuvre is then limited by the need to sell at a price just enough below that of competitors to cut into their market shares.[134]

3–43 Some of the last century's most significant inventions were only put to productive use long after their discovery, which suggests the system is not always a noticeably efficient mechanism for procuring commercial innovation.[135] But equally the long gaps indicate the need for some artificial intrusion into the competitive process. The barriers that may stand in the way of introducing completely new ideas, however striking their ultimate commercial success, are numerous. The difficulties may be innovative—the investment and time needed to arrive at a viable product may be unpredictable. The problems may be financial—the cost of setting up new plant,

[131] Jewkes et al. (above, n.129).

[132] There is some evidence that the expenditure of really large firms on R & D does not produce proportionately as much invention as that of smaller firms; see esp. Kamien and Schwartz, *Market Structure and Innovation* (1982) pp.49–104. But it is hard to weigh the significance of this, since it requires an evaluation of the merits of different inventions; nor, even if it is true, has it any clear consequence for the future of patent systems. Cf. Scherer in Dreyfuss et al., *Expanding the Scope of Intellectual Property* (2005), Ch.1.

[133] See also above, paras 1–45–1–47.

[134] This puts in very summary form some crucial conclusions to be drawn from the standard economic analysis of the patent system: for which see, e.g. Baxter (1966) 76 Yale L.J. 267, 358–370 (Appendix); Kitch (1986) 8 L.R. Econ.31; Laddie in Vaver and Bently, Ch.6.

[135] Individuals or industries have an obvious motive for suppressing highly efficient inventions of the long-lasting razor-blade variety. However, there is not much evidence that this object can actually be achieved: that it can be brought about by patenting, as distinct from swearing all concerned to secrecy, seems highly unlikely, though it is sometimes suggested.

and often of writing-off old, or the cost of persuading distributors to stock and consumers to buy, may seem forbidding. The inhibitions may be organisational—the very size of an enterprise may mean that risky ideas are abandoned in face of well-reasoned argument from one or another entrenched interest.

Of course there are industries where the leading firms become seized by a determination to innovate. Pharmaceutical producers are one outstanding recent example, the computer industry another. But in others again, major technical change may be delayed until individuals with flair and determination can secure the independence (within or outside a larger organisation) that they need to override the well-meaning caution of others less adventurous. In particular, if the dominant firms in an industry are few, there is a danger of complacent sluggishness; of this a number of illustrations exist.[136]

Patent systems ought to help in lowering the psychological barriers to major innovation, particularly since the limited period of protection imposes a penalty for being dilatory. But the practical operation of the system introduces elements that diminish this impact. An innovator who is successful either demonstrates that there is a new market to be tapped, or he begins to cut substantially into the market shares of established competitors. At that stage he is obviously exposed to envious imitation. It becomes vital for competitors to examine the innovator's patents for weaknesses. Since the protection a patent gives depends primarily on the language used to define the claims in the specification, a rival may well spend a good deal on finding other ways of doing much the same thing, which the draftsman of the specification did not contemplate (and did not inadvertently manage to cover). Any determined competitor must be expected to look for methods of "inventing around" the specification.[137] **3–44**

As far as the validity of a patent is concerned, the difference between making the invention and succeeding in innovation is crucial. Before the patent was applied for, there may have been various suggestions in the literature and practice which reached more or less the same invention. Even if none of these led to successful production, they may nevertheless provide a plausible basis for attacking the patent.[138] A patentee who appreciates this when he is deciding whether to manufacture may be obliged to treat his exclusive right as a weapon that can be tested only in prolonged and expensive legal skirmishes. **3–45**

In terms of objectives, the implications are straightforward: if the patent system is to provide a useful incentive for the making and commercial **3–46**

[136] e.g. Jewkes et al. (above, n.129), pp.166–168 on the extraction of iron from laconite; Merges and Nelson (1990) 90 Col.L.R. 839, 884; David in Wallerstein et al., *Global Dimensions of Intellectual Property Rights in Science and Technology* (1993).

[137] This, and the patentee's counter-ploy of himself fencing off all alternatives, may sometimes produce valuable information. But it is hardly a rational way to allocate scarce resources: see Plant (above, n.124) at 21; Machlup (above, n.124) at 51.

[138] See further, below, para.5–27 et seq.

introduction of major inventions, it must give firm rights of clear scope. The current movement to strengthen the examination procedures of patent offices should not be allowed to slacken. If in consequence a few significant inventions are mistakenly refused protection, this should be accepted as an inevitable risk in the pursuit of a greater good. Regrettably, the creation of competing patent offices, such as has occurred in Europe, has the effect of making them "applicant friendly". While this may be a desirable reversal of the past attitude of some national offices, it can easily be carried too far.

Looking across the whole range of industry, however, a measure of doubt must continue to surround the role of patent systems in encouraging the exploitation of major inventions. Even with pharmaceutical products, where patents do appear to provide a significant amount of protection, it is evident that this strength arises from a combination of forces: in particular, the fact that many countries now require lengthy testing of new products substantially increases the "lead-time" of a novel drug over the substitutes and alternatives that competitors may then develop. It may well be that the incentive effect of patents is of more significance when it comes to marginal ideas—concepts that do not hold hope of more than minor improvements over what exists already. Although a patent cannot in such a case guarantee a major run of monopoly profits, nonetheless it offers the chance to explore and exploit free of direct imitation; and competitors may not feel the same compulsion to find equivalents or to attack validity. With major inventions, moreover, the advantage of being first in the field may well be a perfectly adequate incentive, whereas lesser improvements may well be neglected in the absence of a protective stimulus. Of course, there is no telling when something that looks small will turn out big.

3–47 One practical question which stems from such considerations is how to define the minimum inventive content that will justify the grant of a patent. Should the general patent system adopt a requirement of inventive step (or "non-obviousness"), and, if so, how should its level be set? Most modern patent systems (including the British) have such a test, and we shall discuss later the search for verbal formulae which seek to specify the elusive quality in question.[139] Here it should be emphasised that the issue creates uncertainty about the validity of many patents and is one significant cause in lowering the practical value of the system as an incentive to invention and innovation.

"Second-tier" schemes such as petty patents are sometimes advocated as a means of reducing this problem. As already suggested they may result in an even wider margin of uncertainty.

(c) *Optimum term for patents*

3–48 The consensus in the European Convention negotiations was that patents deserve to last for 20 years from filing, although one study has found that

[139] See below, para.5–30 et seq.

only 37 per cent of US patents were still in force after 12 years.[140] A single period of protection for all patents has an arbitrary appearance[141]; but the British experience of granting extensions in deserving cases demonstrated the practical hurdles in the way of introducing individual variations. If one term must be chosen as a maximum, how can the most desirable be ascertained? The answer must be given in terms of incentives, and in particular of the encouragement needed for inventions of commercial importance enough to last for the whole period. It may be that the increase in the British term from 16 to 20 years in 1978 was large enough to have real impact on the willingness to spend on invention and innovation of this potential kind. Nonetheless, the present value of a return of investment from a point so far in the future is small.[142] Additions to the term even of this magnitude can have little predictable effect on incentives. Yet each year that is added increases the social cost of having the invention available only through the channel of the patent monopoly. Certainly any further extension should be made only after most careful consideration.

(3) Patents as an information system

In Britain the policy of making the patent system a source of technical information has been deliberately pursued since the early industrial revolution.[143] For many years the results have justified treating this aspect of the system as more than a useful by-product. Patents do make available a large quantity of information about the latest technical advances, and they are regularly consulted by those concerned with developments in many industries. Nevertheless exaggerated expectations need to be avoided. If the inventive concept is one that has to be embodied in a marketed product, the patent may give earlier access to the information and perhaps a more explicit statement of what the invention is. Only if the invention is one that need never be revealed to the rest of the industry in the course of exploiting it does the patent provide a clear long-term gain in terms of publicity. But this, of course, is the case where secrecy offers a real alternative—a route that, despite the danger of leaks, may seem simpler and cheaper to pursue. **3–49**

The disclosure side of the patent bargain is not a policy that is easy to implement.[144] There is an obvious temptation for any patentee to omit from **3–50**

[140] Lemley (2001) 95 Northwestern University L.R. 1495 at 1504, using 1998 data.

[141] Hence the successful campaign of the pharmaceutical and agricultural industries for an additional term of protection (in the EU through the Supplementary Protection Certificate) to compensate for the delay imposed by official testing of novel drugs and crop products: see below, para.4–26.

[142] For a technical demonstration of this, see Machlup (above, n.124) at 66–73; cf. Nordhaus (above, n.19); Scherer (1977) 62 Am.Ec.R. 422; Priest (1986) 8 Rsch. in L. &. Econ.19.

[143] See above, para.3–06.

[144] See generally, Beier and Straus (1977) 8 I.I.C. 387; Eisenschitz and Oppenheim in Phillips (ed.), *Patents in Perspective* (1985) Chs 5, 6; Koenig (1983) 12 Res. Pol. 15; Mansfield (1985) 34 J. Ind. Econ. 217.

his specification information that may seem incidental but is in fact useful or important to commercial success. When this effect can be achieved, the patent system is reduced to an index of sources from which further information may be had on application and payment. This leaves the policy-maker, whether legislator, patent office administrator or judge, with a choice: either to recognise that the system cannot hope to provide more information, or to insist that it should by declaring such patents invalid. Countries with examining offices have arrived at rather varied results in their approach to this dilemma. The typical American specification is noteworthy for its dogged attention to pedestrian detail; a German specification may be hazy about practical steps but is more likely to reveal basic concepts. One decision of the English Court of Appeal leans in the former direction: it holds that a specification about basic ideas in a new technology should teach its principles to second-rank technicians rather than to leading researchers in the field.[145] This sort of insistence carries with it the danger that really significant developments may be the subject of invalid patents. Yet to give up any real effort to police the disclosure requirement may be to surrender the one public advantage of the patent system that remains relatively uncontroversial.

3–51 The notion of patent collections as an index of where to apply for more information at least gives some clue to the businessman's continuing interest in the patent system. Of course, specifications are read by competitors who are at roughly the same stage of advance and who then seek licences in order to avoid impediments in the way of their own development work. But a great deal of licensing is of an information package to a firm which lacks the background to set up production for itself. In this sort of case the basic concept is frequently patented, while much crucial incident exists only as know-how that has to be transmitted under terms of confidence. For this sort of case, the patent system may alert potential licensees about people who have interesting ideas on offer; and the licensor will be interested in having a patent, not only for the publicity that may follow but also because it may provide a measure of security. If his only protection lies in confidence obligations, he has to ensure that all personnel have given adequate undertakings and he may well have to contemplate proceedings against them if they appear to be in breach. Resources ought not to be devoted to ensuring that people keep their bargains whenever this can be avoided.

(4) Adapting the patent system: new technology

3–52 The emergence of each major technology requires adjustments in the patent system and is, therefore, likely to stir up arguments about underlying rationales and specific policy objectives. The coming of computers, as already noted, first activated symptoms of denial, with a series of moves to

[145] *Valensi v British Radio* [1973] R.P.C. 337; and see generally, below, para.5–90.

place computer programs beyond the reach of the system; latterly, there has been growing industrial pressure to take the opposite position.[146] Over a much longer period, resistance to the idea of a monopoly over something as fundamental as a chemical substance (particularly where it is a pharmaceutical) has gradually given way.[147] A set of rules on the disclosure requirement have enabled claims of commercially significant breadth to be made; but at the same time, where necessary, biological material has to be made available to others through culture collections.[148]

Almost half a century after Crick and Watson's uncoiling of living structures, genetic knowledge and techniques of genetic manipulation have undergone a series of remarkable advances. Once revealed, each procedure has been rapidly taken over by laboratories everywhere, spawning quantities of competitive research. In particular medical applications of biotechnology have attracted a rash of new businesses, often spinning out of academic research. There have been rushes to patent, accompanied by demands for very wide claims modelled on those of the initial master patents by now familiar in organic chemistry. Courts in the United Kingdom have shown a tendency to react slowly and cautiously to this.[149] Patent offices, by contrast, have been ready to embrace the new technologies. In Europe that attitude has been encouraged by the fact that there are competing routes to patent protection. However, over the last 15 years, they have faced a growing barrage of objection, which, as we shall see, has made the issues far more prominent and is leading to a somewhat more critical attitude towards what should fall within the patent system and under what conditions.[150]

As the consequences for medical diagnosis and treatment of the mapping of the human genome become more apparent, these issues are likely to become even sharper. There are of course those for whom the very idea that a state-supported incentive such as a patent system should be offered to commercialise the benefits of genetic knowledge is abhorrent. But by their side are more specific objections, couched in terms of how the major requirements for patent protection (invention, industrial application, inventive step, disclosure and claims limited so as to relate to that disclosure) should apply. At this stage, it can be said that arguments for wide rights at early stages of discovery (analogous to mining licences) are losing ground to views favouring limiting the rights proportionate only to what is shown to have been discovered.

The experience with biotechnology underscores how the justifications for **3–53**
the patent system are not independent. Rather they are cumulative, and each imposes its limitations. From competition in the production of goods and

[146] The subject, together with other forms of IP protection, is reserved for detailed discussion, below, at paras 20–26 et seq.
[147] The TRIPS Agreement marks a strategic triumph: see above, para.3–22.
[148] See below, para.5–87.
[149] See further below, paras 21–15—21–17.
[150] Below, paras 21–01 et seq.

services, consumers benefit from the range of alternatives presented to them and the resultant capping effect on prices. Even to encourage the generation and commercialisation of new products, patent rights are limited to technological invention, and the rights ought to preclude competitors in proportion to the scale of that invention. In order to measure that scale, the invention must be described, and thus the disclosure requirement is not just an economic benefit in opening up vital information. It is an essential element in determining whether and what there is that deserves state-supported curtailment of competition at a point where competition is likely to be intense.

The justification for this balance is largely economic. The system seeks to offer incentives to invent and then to innovate at a level which secures a considerable measure of action, while providing the industry concerned with highly useful information and some chance to stay in the technology by making improvements and variations.[151] At the same time, there is no denying that an underlying sense of justice insists that invention alone justifies any reward by exclusive right, and then only a proportional reward. To depart from this root impulse—for instance, by saying that the commercial development of any novelty should be the basis for exclusivity—will replace the incentives with other, probably less desirable alternatives. It will also be felt to lead to unfair preferences which could ultimately return us to the backlash that resulted in the early seventeenth century from Queen Elizabeth's patent over playing cards.

5. The Patents Act 1977: Structure and Interpretation

3–54 This chapter ends with a bridge passage. The international and European antecedents of the Patents Act 1977 make it a complex measure which needs a more technical outline than has yet been given. Part I sets out the domestic law. So far as this is concerned with the making and processing of applications, it only affects applications to the British Patent Office as such[152]; European applications are governed by the EPC so long as they are being dealt with by the EPO (that is, up to grant and during post-grant opposition before the EPO). The other main provisions apply to British patents granted by either route. These concern patentability,[153] term, restoration and surrender[154]; property rights and employees' inventions[155]; abuse of monopoly

[151] See esp. Merges and Nelson (above, n.136).

[152] See PA 1977 ss.14–21; to this s.13(3) is an exception. The provisions on secrecy (ss.22, 23) can affect European and foreign applications generally.

[153] PA 1977 ss.1–6.

[154] PA 1977 ss.24–29.

[155] PA 1977 ss.30–43.

and Crown use[156]; infringement, revocation and associated issues[157]; and amendment.[158]

Part II provides the incorporative machinery for the EPC, CPC and PCT. International applications under the PCT may evolve into applications to the British Office under the Act by virtue of s.89. By s.77, European patents which designate the United Kingdom fall to be treated as patents under the 1977 Act from publication of the mention of grant in the *European Patent Bulletin*; and there follow a number of consequential provisions on European applications, authentic texts, conversion into a national application, jurisdiction over the right to apply for a European patent, professional representation and evidence for EPO proceedings.[159] **3–55**

By contrast, if and when the CPC takes effect, as is likely under an EU Regulation, EU patents will be governed by that legislation.[160]. Thus infringement of an EU patent will be determined by the Regulation's provisions, not the Act's[161]; and the rules on patentability will be the relevant articles in the EPC since these will be incorporated into the Regulation. But because there is still no immediate prospect of the EU patent being introduced, the law governing EU patents will be mentioned only incidentally in the following chapters.[162]

Part III deals with a variety of general matters: legal proceedings, including the creation of the Patents Court within the frame of the Chancery Division[163]; criminal offences[164]; patent agents[165]; administrative provisions[166]; the power to make Patent Rules[167]; a provision attempting to elucidate what is meant by the scope of a patented invention (taking account of the Protocol to the EPC art.69)[168]; and interpretation.[169] **3–56**

Some parts of the domestic law have been inspired in a general way by legal developments elsewhere. Thus the restructured application system in the British Patent Office is to a considerable extent modelled on the arrangements for the PCT and the EPO. Yet the derivation is not direct, in the sense that provisions of the Patents Act do not use the same language as the international and European conventions. Yet strangely s.130(7) of the **3–57**

156 PA 1977 ss.44–59.
157 PA 1977 ss.60–74.
158 PA 1977 ss.75, 76.
159 PA 1977 ss.78–85.
160 The Patents Act 2004 repealed PA 1977 s.86 and 87, which made provisional arrangements for the introduction of the Community Patent.
161 cf. the *Harbottle* case, below, para.6–12, n.72.
162 PA 1977 Pt II also provides machinery for declaring countries to be Convention countries for the purpose of the Paris Convention arrangements on priority (s.90(1)) and on evidence, judicial notice and other matters in relation to the more recent conventions (ss.91–95).
163 PA 1977 ss.96–108.
164 PA 1977 ss.109–113.
165 PA 1977 ss.114–115.
166 PA 1977 ss.116–123.
167 PA 1977 s.124.
168 PA 1977 s.125.
169 PA 1977 s.130.

1977 Act declares that they are "so framed as to have, as nearly as practicable, the same effects in the United Kingdom as do the corresponding provisions" of the EPC, CPC and PCT in the territories to which they apply.[170] Where an issue arises which is governed by the UK counterpart of an EPC or CPC provision within s.130(7), an English court will, so far as possible, treat the Convention provision directly. For one thing, this aids an understanding of the decision in other jurisdictions.[171] With the forthcoming revisions under EPC 2000 the 1977 Act will in some respects follow EPC wording much more closely.

3–58 There have now been numerous occasions on which the terms of s.130(7) have been used in order to reach an interpretation of the Act which is considered consistent with a convention text.[172] More than 20 years ago, Whitford J. remarked that:

> "it is of the greatest importance that in this jurisdiction we should take note of the decisions of the EPO and that, so far as may be possible in all those countries which are now bound by the common interest created by the Convention, an attempt should be made to give the same meaning to relevant provisions, whichever the jurisdiction which is being invoked".[173]

That spirit of co-operation is currently fostered by biennial meetings of judges concerned with patent matters from the EPC States, which began in 1982.

The significance of the remark by Whitford J. lies in the fact that there is no ultimate Court of Appeal to which questions of interpretation can be referred for final settlement. Within the EU this will to a large extent be rectified when eventually the EU patent takes effect, since this is likely to create a coherent court structure with an ultimate appeal court.[174] But even so, there will still be no unified jurisdiction for the whole network of authorities established through the Conventions, since these bodies would deal with the validity and infringement of EU patents once granted, but would not act as final appellate body from decisions of the EPO taken in the course of its granting procedure. These will continue to go to the EPO Boards of Appeal, with ultimate reference to the Enlarged Board of Appeal.[175] The need for a single ultimate tribunal as the keystone in the

[170] These provisions concern: patentability and the requirements for description and claims of the specification; revocation at the behest of the person properly entitled to grant; non-working as a ground for granting a compulsory licence; infringement and the extent of monopoly; grounds of revocation; and certain supplemental provisions.

[171] Jacob L.J., *Aerotel v Telco; Macrossan's Applcn* [2007] R.P.C. 7 at [6].

[172] e.g. *Smith Kline v Harbottle* [1980] R.P.C. 363; *Schering's and Wyeth's Applications* [1985] R.P.C. 545.

[173] *B & R Relay's Application* [1985] R.P.C. 1 at 6.

[174] See above, para.3–27.

[175] EPC arts 106–112; Paterson, Ch.2. Arrangements have now been instituted for national patent judges to sit on the Enlarged Board where appropriate.

European patent arch is reinforced by the difficulties which currently exist in securing reforms in the governing Convention texts. Although EPC 2000 was agreed and it was thereby shown that the Convention was not always to be preserved in the same aspic, amendment remains a cumbersome procedure. The European Commission aspires to take the whole structure over, but whether it will succeed remains to be seen.

CHAPTER 4

THE PATENT: GRANT AND CONTENT

1. OBTAINING A PATENT

(1) General

(a) *Parallel routes*

A patent may now be secured for the United Kingdom either through the British Office (the UKIPO) or the EPO; with the additional possibility of entering either system by means of an international application under the PCT. In 1977, domestic British procedures were substantially remodelled to resemble the new granting system introduced by the European Patent Convention. Accordingly the major steps through which an application proceeds to the stage of grant in each office can be represented in a common diagram (see p.164). **4–01**

A European patent designating the United Kingdom falls to be treated as a patent under the Patents Act 1977 as if it had been granted by the British Office.[1] For a variety of purposes the European application ranks as if it were a British application.[2] But there remains one significant difference: the European patent as a whole is open for a limited period to opposition proceedings before the EPO, and the European patent (UK) will be subject to revocation proceedings before British tribunals throughout its life.

[1] PA 1977 s.77.
[2] PA 1977 s.78.

Obviously a patent granted by the British Office can be subject only to the latter form of attack.[3]

(b) *Competition between the systems*

4–02 The international arrangements have provided a measure of competition which has benefited patenting industries. The greater efficiency that is their chief attraction turns on a number of variables. As far as the PCT is concerned much depends on the trust that is accorded to the international search.[4] The EPO has proved a popular office in which to pursue PCT applications through their various stages, because of the reliability of its search and preliminary examination. Such has been the pressure upon it that it has had to acquire power to limit its processing of PCT applications from countries which have their own PCT offices (notably the United States and Japan). Currently it will not handle such applications in the fields of biotechnology, telecommunications and business methods.[5]

4–03 Within the EPC states the choice between application routes is complex. For the applicant with a strong case, confirmed perhaps by a private search in advance, the single procedure before the EPO will look more attractive if protection is wanted in three or four participant countries (or more). It is at this point that the considerable fees and other expenses of a European application begin to fall below the cost of national fees and the other costs of separate applications.[6] But if the expenditure of patenting is justified at all, it is worth paying for the course that is more likely to give the desired protection. The EPO route, moreover, has an all-or-nothing outcome in terms of geographical coverage. The EPO examines applications in a reasonably helpful spirit.[7]

The choice may well turn on the countries for which protection is most needed: thus the possibility of deferring examination in the Netherlands and Germany for seven years may in some cases be important, or the absence of any examination in Belgium or Italy or of a power of rejection in France. In some cases, it will be considered worthwhile pursuing both European and national patents. The only consequence of trying to protect an invention to the same extent by both procedures, as far as the United Kingdom is

---

[3] See below, paras 4–27 et seq.

[4] Rules Under Patent Co-Operation Treaty r.34 lays down the minimum documentation that an international search authority must cover.

[5] The arrangement is made through the EPO's Tripartite links with the US and Japanese Patent Offices and by amendment of the WIPO/EPO Treaty: see [2001] OJ EPO 601.

[6] Notably the costs of professional representation and translation: for the latter, see below, paras 4–04—4–05.

[7] The aim has been to achieve a standard mid-way between the severity of the Dutch and the lenience of the Austrian and British approaches: the German standard was thought to be "about right": Van Benthem and Wallace (1978) 9 I.I.C. 297 at 298; see also Pagenberg (1978) 9 I.I.C. 121; Casalonga (1979) 10 I.I.C. 412.

concerned, is that the Comptroller-General of Patents must then revoke the patent granted by the British Office.[8]

(c) *Languages*

One particular advantage offered by the international conventions concerns languages. This is not just a matter of saving translation costs, considerable though these often are. In an art so tied to linguistic skills, every translation is fraught with dangers of error and inaccuracy. What the PCT provides is the longest chance to delay the preparation of translations during the crucial months after an initial application has been lodged.[9] The international application must be in the appropriate PCT language[10]; but translations are not needed until the application is transferred into the national (or regional) offices: normally after 30 months from the priority date.[11] **4–04**

In the EPO an applicant may proceed in any of the official languages, English, French, or German.[12] When his application is published, he will need to translate the claims, as they then stand, into the languages of his designated states if he wants to secure protection from then until grant[13]; and when his patent is accepted for grant he must translate the claims into the other official languages.[14] Most participant states require translation of the whole specification into their own language.[15] The authentic text remains that of the language of the proceedings before the EPO; but some protection is provided for a person misled by a narrower translation.[16] **4–05**

(2) Persons entitled to grant

The Paris Industrial Property Convention ensures that nationals of any one Union country have the same right to secure patents in each other Union **4–06**

[8] PA 1977 s.73(2) (as amended by CDPA 1988 Sch.5 para.19). The British patent must be "directed to the same invention": see *Maag Gear's Patent* [1985] R.P.C. 572; *Marley Roof's Patent* [1994] R.P.C. 231 CA.

[9] See below, nn.11 and 12.

[10] i.e. the language that is used by the international search authority to which an application from the particular receiving office will be referred: English, French, or German where the EPO will search, English for the US Patent Office, Japanese for the Japanese Patent Office and so on. The search report and abstract will be translated into English, if in another language: Rules Under Patent Co-Operation Treaty r.48.3.

[11] See the extension of period introduced by amendment of the PCT arts 22(1) and 39(1) from April 2002.

[12] EPC art.14(1). Nationals of states (such as Italy) which do not have English, French, or German as an official language are entitled to file in their own language and supply a translation, the original document being treated as the document filed, in cases of variance: see art.14(2), (4) and further, Ency. P.L., paras 11–301—11–304.

[13] If this is not done, states are permitted to treat the application as not giving rise to any intermediate rights: EPC art.67(3). Most have done so, but not so far the UK (note the power given by PA 1977 s.78(7), (8)).

[14] EPC art.97(5); EPC Rules r.51(4).

[15] EPC art.65 leaves the matter optional. Power to require this translation is to be found in PA 1977 s.77(6)–(9) and was exercised in 1987. Under the London Agreement of 2000, however, this is likely to change.

[16] See PA 1977 s.80; EPC art.70.

country as do nationals of the latter.[17] Both the United Kingdom and the EPC systems go further, making access open to all without consideration of nationality, residence or other status.[18]

In the British system, the right to be granted a patent is given to the inventor or the inventors[19] unless: (1) at the time when the invention is made a general rule of law or an enforceable agreement gives that right to someone else[20]; or (2) the person entitled when the invention was made (under heading (1)) later assigns his right, or it has been otherwise disposed of to a successor in title (through death, bankruptcy, winding up, etc.).[21] Under heading (1) the most likely person to supersede the inventor by virtue of a rule of law is his employer[22]; this is a matter treated more fully in Ch.7.[23]

4–07 The 1977 Act creates a presumption that the applicant or applicants are the persons entitled to be granted the patent.[24] But it provides channels through which someone else may claim to be properly entitled—alleging, for instance, that he revealed it to the applicant without transferring any right to secure grant of a patent or that they made the invention together.[25] Such questions of proprietary right can always be raised in declaratory or other proceedings in the High Court.[26] In addition the Comptroller is given special jurisdiction to decide upon the right to be granted not only the British patent, but also European and foreign patents and allied rights, provided

[17] PIP art.2(1).

[18] See EPC art.58; cf. PCT art.9: Rules Under Patent Co-Operation Treaty r.18 (resident or national). There was a stage in the EPC negotiations when the exclusion of foreign nationals was seriously contemplated. This was intended as retaliation against the US: foreign applicants there were considered to suffer certain disadvantages in comparison with domestic applicants. Nobler sentiments prevailed: see Van Empel, *The Granting of European Patents* (1975), pp.72–80.

[19] i.e. the actual deviser of the invention: PA 1977 s.7(3). The hallowed notion of the importer of an idea as inventor (see above, para.3–05) finally disappeared with the 1977 Act. Its only recent value had been in overcoming formal difficulties that could affect applications from abroad.

[20] But "the whole of the property (other than equitable interests)" must be given to the preferred person; which may lead to complications where there are joint inventors.

[21] PA 1977 s.7(2). But the applicable rule may arise by foreign law, treaty or convention (s.7(2)(b)), because this is the appropriate rule to apply by virtue of the private international law of the British jurisdiction invoked.

[22] PA 1977 s.39.

[23] See below, paras 7–03 et seq.

[24] PA 1977 s.7(4).

[25] See Laddie J. in *University of Southampton's Applications* [2005] R.P.C. 11 at 234: "First, it is necessary to identify the inventive concept or concepts in the patent or application. Secondly, it is necessary to identify who came up with the inventive concept or concepts. He or they are the inventors. Thirdly, a person is not an inventor merely because he 'contributes to a claim'.".

[26] PA 1977 s.72(1)(b) and (2) together permit a patent to be revoked, at the behest of such a claimant, on the ground that it was granted to a person not entitled. The jurisdiction appears to have been limited in curious ways by s.74(4). But, given the equivalent provisions in the EPC art.138(1) and CPC art.56(1), these sections have been read so as to allow such claims to be made either where an exclusive entitlement or a shared entitlement is in issue: *Henry Bros v Ministry of Defence* [1997] R.P.C. 693.

that the question is referred to him before the relevant patent is granted.[27] He can also entertain references concerning the right to be granted the UK patent even after its grant (by either route).[28] Neither the court nor the Comptroller may resolve a dispute concerning rights in a granted patent by revoking it, unless the proceedings were begun within two years of grant, or a person registered was shown to know of the defective title at grant or on assignment to him.[29]

If a challenger shows that he has a proper entitlement in the patent, for all or some part of the subject-matter covered by the specification,[30] the tribunal has a wide discretion to do what it thinks fit.[31] The proper claimant may be allowed to join in, or take over, the existing application[32]; or, if the patent has already been granted, to be registered as proprietor. Or he may be allowed to start afresh, taking for himself the date of filing of the displaced application (provided that he does not add to its disclosure),[33] but after grant this course is open only if proceedings are begun within two years.[34] There is also power to grant and transfer licences, and to register transactions and instruments relied upon by the claimant.[35] **4–08**

As far as European applications are concerned, the EPO does not undertake investigations of entitlement[36]; that is left to national tribunals.[37] So long as the EPO has not granted the European patent, the proper forum

[27] PA 1977 ss.8, 12; see, e.g., *University of Southampton's Applcn* [2006] R.P.C. 21 CA. Note that the question can be raised before any application has been made, leading to a declaration over entitlement to grant, and to consequential arrangements such as the grant of an exclusive licence: *Goddin and Rennie's Application* [1996] R.P.C. 141 Ct of Sess.

[28] PA 1977 s.37 (as amended by CDPA 1988 Sch.5 para.9). A reference received before grant by the UK office is treated as continuing under this section: PA 1977 s.9. The Comptroller may refuse to act on the ground that the court is a more suitable tribunal: ss.8(7), 12(2), 37(8).

[29] PA 1977 ss.37(5), 37(9), 72(2); but cf. s.37(8). For amendment within the permitted time limit, see *Yeda Research v Rhone Poulenc* [2008] R.P.C. 1 HL.

[30] The jurisdiction conferred on the Comptroller also allows him to deal with disputes where one co-applicant is objecting to the transfer or granting of any right to any other person. In addition, there is a separate power to give directions to joint applicants if they cannot agree upon how a British application is to proceed: PA 1977 s.10.

[31] For examples of how the jurisdiction has been exercised, see Ency. P.L., paras 8–107A, 8–107B.

[32] Where the rights of licensees may be affected, they are afforded at least some measure of protection: see PA 1977 ss.11, 38.

[33] It appears that he may not also annexe any earlier priority claimed for the original: *Georgia Pacific's Application* [1984] R.P.C. 469.

[34] See PA 1977 ss.8(2), (3), 37(2), 37(9). In the case of "non-British" applications—apart from the special cases dealt with in s.12(6)—the Comptroller is left to determine the question as far as he is able and makes such order as he thinks fit: see s.12(1): *Markem v Zipher (No. 3)* [2005] R.P.C. 3. The court's jurisdiction and the jurisdiction to order revocation on the ground that the patent was granted to a person not entitled are similarly limited in time: ss.37(9), 72(1)(b) (as amended by CDPA 1988 Sch.5 para.18), PA 1977 s.72(2); *Dolphin Showers v Farmiloe* [1989] F.S.R. 1; Thorley [1995] C.I.P.A. 104.

[35] PA 1977 s.37(5).

[36] EPC art.60(3); see Ency. P.L. para.13–102.

[37] In the EPO the application will, on request and subject to limitations, be stayed: see EPC Rules rr.13, 14. British applications are not stayed in the same way: see above, n.28.

for deciding who is entitled to the grant is dealt with in a special protocol to the EPC.[38] Once the patents have been granted, however, the question is one for each designated country. Where a challenge is successfully made to a European application, the challenger may, in appropriate circumstances, continue the application, have it withdrawn, or file his own application (as to the whole or a part), with a claim to the earlier priority date if he is adding nothing of substance.[39]

(3) Patent specification

4–09 It should by now be plain that the crucial document in the whole process of securing and relying upon a patent is the specification. In the British and European systems it has two main parts[40]: the description (which may be accompanied by diagrams or drawings) and the claims. The former must disclose the invention sufficiently for it to be performed by an appropriately skilled person, the latter will mark out the scope of monopoly rights.[41] Where the invention involves use of a micro-organism, it may be necessary to deposit a sample with a recognised culture collection.[42] There will be a good deal to say about both aspects of the specification. The reader who has not had an opportunity to study specifications should look at a representative sample.[43] In particular, it is useful to note how far the draftsman has referred to the "prior art" in an effort to bring out the character of the invention; the degree to which specific examples are used to give explicit description of how the invention can be performed; the generalisations used in the claims (particularly the broadest); and the manner in which a succession of claims cover increasingly specific areas (for fear that the wider may prove invalid).

---

38 This Protocol on Jurisdiction and Recognition gives jurisdiction first to the contracting state agreed by the disputants; if not agreed, then, in employer–employee disputes, to the state where employed (see art.60); and in other cases, to the applicant's state; or otherwise to the claimant's state; and if none of these tests provides a contracting State, then to Germany. PA 1977 s.82 (jurisdiction) and s.83 (recognition) give effect in the UK to this Protocol. See further Ency. P.L. para.8–111; *Kakkar v Szelke* [1989] F.S.R. 225 CA.

39 EPC art.61.

40 It must also have a title and name the inventor. The abstract, which is used for patent office search purposes and to notify the public at once of the fact and nature of the application, is separate: this notification is made in the issues of abstracts that accompany the British Patent Office Journal, the EPO Bulletin, or the PCT Gazette.

41 The claims must be separately identified; they are not to be found simply in the body of the description: *ex p. Knight* [2007] EWHC 2264 (Admin).

42 See below, para.5–87.

43 If no other source is available, the reported case law often sets out in full the specification in dispute. Good examples for beginners: *Carroll v Tomado* [1971] R.P.C. 401 at 402–404 (clothes horse); *Reeves v Standard Fabrics* [1972] R.P.C. 47 at 48–62 (bonding polyurethane foam); *Bugges Insecticide v Herbon* [1972] R.P.C. 197 at 198–202 (weedkiller); *Minnesota Mining v Bondina* [1973] R.P.C. 491 at 493–503 (scouring pads); *Illinois Tool v Autobars* [1974] R.P.C. 337 at 339–351 (nestable cups for vending machines); *Procter & Gamble v Peaudouce* [1989] F.S.R. 180 CA (nappy holders).

(4) Priority

Today more than ever, those engaged in research may be competing to solve a scientific or technical problem. The "first-to-file" basis of most patent systems exacerbates the pressure to reach the patent office as soon as feasible.[44] It may be necessary to file a series of applications as, on the one hand, more is discovered about how the invention works, and, on the other, more is appreciated about alternatives that might be deployed by competitors outside the scope of the initial application. On top of this, the question of which foreign patents to pursue imposes its own pressures, since foreign applications often involve collaboration with patent agents abroad and the making of translations. **4–10**

This brings us to the initiatory steps on the Table (p.164). It has long been recognised that an applicant should have some room for manoeuvre in these matters. Within one year, he is given a limited opportunity to amplify his application without losing his priority. Equally, through the machinery of the Paris Convention, he is able to keep the priority of his first application for other applications filed within a year in or for other Convention countries.[45] Most countries of any industrial significance belong to this Convention and the European system is also within its net.[46] To secure this advantage, the earlier "informal" application need only satisfy the basic requirements for a filing date: an indication that a patent is sought, identification of the application, a description of the invention, and, for a European or international application, at least one claim and the designation of at least one state.[47] **4–11**

The "priority date" of a patent is the date on which it is tested against "the state of the art"[48]; and it is the date on which it becomes part of the art, when assessing the novelty (but not the obviousness) of later applications.[49] This crucial date will be the filing date of the application unless the date of an earlier application in the United Kingdom, the EPO, or a Paris Convention country is claimed.[50] The earlier application must have been made within the previous 12 months and it must "support" the invention in the **4–12**

[44] The EPC regimen takes a severer attitude than ever before on the need to reach the patent office without prior publication, yet with an application complete enough to support the eventual patent: the elements that are compounded in this attitude are considered together below, in paras 6–28—6–31. On the comparison with a "first to invent" system, see Nicolai (1972) 3 I.I.C. 103; Kingston [1992] E.I.P.R. 223.

[45] For the tendency nonetheless to favour national applicants at the expense of Convention applicants in some Member States, see Wieczorek (1975) 6 I.I.C. 135; Gansser (1980) II I.I.C. 1.

[46] For the relation of the EPC to PIP, see Paterson, Ch.8B.

[47] PA 1977 s.15(1); EPC art.80; PCT art.11. For the full requirements of a "formal" application, see below, para.4–16. It is possible to claim priority from a utility model or utility certificate; but not from a registered design application: *Agfa-Gevaert's (Engelsmann) Application* [1982] R.P.C. 441 CA; *Arenhold* [1981] OJ EPO 213.

[48] See below, para.5–03.

[49] See below, paras 5–14, 5–15.

[50] PA 1977 s.5(1), (2); EPC art.7(1)–(3), and note art.89.

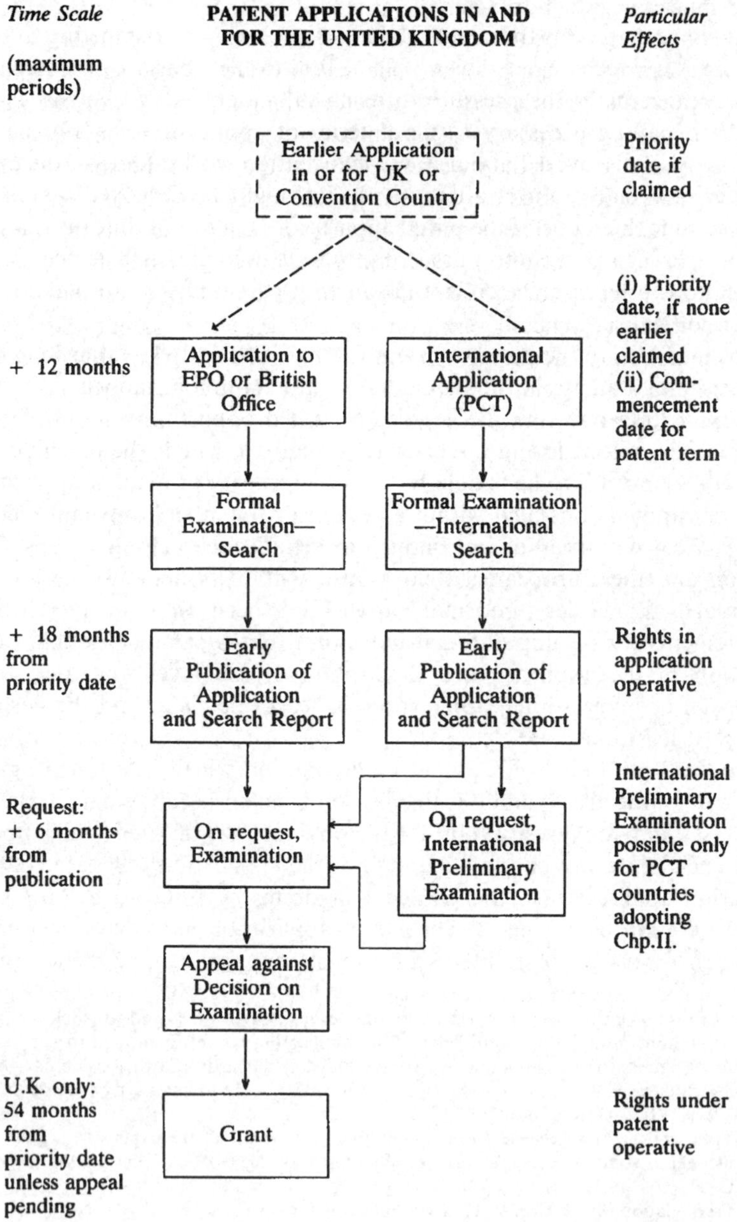
Time Scale
(maximum periods)
PATENT APPLICATIONS IN AND FOR THE UNITED KINGDOM
Particular Effects
Earlier Application in or for UK or Convention Country
Priority date if claimed
+ 12 months
Application to EPO or British Office
International Application (PCT)
(i) Priority date, if none earlier claimed
(ii) Commencement date for patent term
Formal Examination—Search
Formal Examination—International Search
+ 18 months from priority date
Early Publication of Application and Search Report
Early Publication of Application and Search Report
Rights in application operative
Request: + 6 months from publication
On request, Examination
On request, International Preliminary Examination
International Preliminary Examination possible only for PCT countries adopting Chp.II.
Appeal against Decision on Examination
U.K. only: 54 months from priority date unless appeal pending
Grant
Rights under patent operative

later application by the matter it discloses.[51] In other words, no additional feature must be added to what is disclosed in the priority document.[52] Generally also it must be the applicant's first disclosure of the invention in a patent application.[53] So, a priority issue may involve examining the content of applications made both during and before the relevant 12-month period.

In either case, the question is essentially the same: has there been an "enabling disclosure" of the invention? Would the skilled person to whom the description is addressed have been able to perform it without engaging in independent invention? The previous, looser practice looked only at whether there had been a description. The new rigour has had beneficial effects throughout the corpus of the law. This is because the same test also determines whether an earlier description has anticipated a patent claim and settles whether an applicant has made a sufficient disclosure of the invention for which the patent claims protection.[54] The House of Lords so held, finding that the terms of a claim may be used to amplify the expressed or implicit meaning of descriptive matter, but cannot stand in place of that description.

The case in point, *Asahi KK's Application*,[55] which raised interrelated questions of priority and novelty, concerned the effect of an application for the protein, human tissue necrosis factor (HTNF), when produced by genetic engineering. It gave the DNA-structure of HTNF but did not disclose how to make it, at a time when it was exactly this problem that competitors were seeking to overcome.[56] It could not, therefore, confer the priority necessary to cause one application to anticipate another. The date for determining whether an enabling disclosure has been made in a patent

[51] EPC art.87 has been similarly read by the EPO Enlarged BA: *Priority Interval* (G 01/91) [1994] E.P.O.R. 521. That case settles that the EPC creates one particular difficulty for an eager applicant: suppose he puts in a first application, publishes the content and then makes a second application from the first but cannot sustain his priority; his second application will be anticipated. It has been held that the same must apply in UK law, despite PA 1977 s.6: *Beloit v Valmet* [1995] R.P.C. 705.

[52] *Meiji Milk v Nestlé/Priority of the "same invention"* (T92/98) [2001] OJ EPO 413.

[53] Disclosures in a first application can be disregarded only if that application was unconditionally withdrawn, abandoned or refused without having been made available to the public before filing of a second application from which it is sought to derive priority and the first was not the basis of any claim to priority: PA 1977 s.5(3); EPC art.87(4), giving effect to PIP art.4C(4); cf. Beier and Straus (1990) 21 I.I.C. 593; Wegner (1992) 23 I.I.C. 184; Harden (1993) 24 I.I.C. 729.

[54] For these issues, see below, paras 5–18, 5–84.

[55] [1991] R.P.C. 485. See also *Biogen v Medeva* [1997] R.P.C. 1 HL; *Chiron v Murex Diagnostics* [1996] F.S.R. 153 CA; *Evans Medical's Patent* [1998] R.P.C. 517. Cf. the distinction concerning enablement as it applies to novelty and adequate disclosure made in *Synthon v SmithKline Beecham* [2006] R.P.C. 10 HL, below paras. 5–18, 5–85, 5–86. This conclusion is in line with EPC art.88(4), despite its different wording. PA 1977 s.130(3), which makes reference to the content of claims as well as description, does not alter this. For the same approach in the EPO, see GO2/98 "*Same Invention*" [2002] E.P.O.R. 167, Enlarged BA; *Unilin v Berry Floor* [2005] F.S.R. 6 CA.

[56] The case concerned anticipation by a prior unpublished application, under the special conditions of PA 1977 s.2(3), for which see below, paras 5–14, 5–15.

specification is that at which priority is claimed, not the date at which that specification is later published.[57]

4–13 The 1977 Act allows an applicant to claim multiple priorities, based on different earlier applications, not only for different claims but even for different aspects of a single claim.[58] If, for example, a first document discloses molten metal cathodes, a second document other cathodes and the application or suit in one claim refers to the two classes separately, then the different priority dates can easily be assigned. But if the cathodes are claimed only in general the claim must be split into separate parts.[59]

The system of priorities eases the pressure on an applicant to decide whether in Europe to proceed in the EPO or in national offices, since he may use an application in any one office to give priority in the others. It is not necessary to designate (say) the United Kingdom in a European application in order to secure priority for a subsequent national application in the United Kingdom.[60]

(5) Secrecy: national interest

4–14 Applications under the EPC and PCT may be lodged with the UK Patent Office. One purpose of this arrangement is to allow the national office, in collaboration with the Ministry of Defence, the Atomic Energy Authority and other government departments, to vet applications in the interests of national security and public safety. British residents, indeed, are obliged (under criminal law sanction) to lodge applications with the British Office six weeks before applying abroad.[61] If the Comptroller considers that any application contains information prejudicial to the defence of the realm[62] or the safety of the public he may make a secrecy direction.[63] So long as it remains, the application cannot be sent on through the EPC or PCT routes,[64] and foreign applications may be made only through restricted arrangements, for instance within NATO.[65] It may be processed in the British Office, but without any publication, to the point where it is ready for

[57] *Biogen v Medeva* [1997] R.P.C. 1 HL; *Pharmacia v Merck* [2002] R.P.C. 41 at [96, 97, 101].

[58] PA 1977 s.25(2); EPC art.88(2), (3). This reverses the restrictive approach concerning convention applications apparently adopted in *Union Carbide's Application* [1968] R.P.C. 371; and see *SCM's Application* [1979] R.P.C. 341 CA.

[59] For the requirement of unity of inventive concept, see below, para.4–15, and *Biogen v Medeva*, below, para.5–82.

[60] It would in practice be unusual to use a European application in order to secure priority for national applications.

[61] PA 1977 s.23; the Comptroller's permission may be sought to file abroad without filing first in Britain. See generally, Ency. P.L., paras 6–118—6–120.

[62] By reference to a list of subject-matter supplied by the Ministry of Defence.

[63] PA 1977 s.22(1); and for the muddled and muddy history, see O'Dell, *Inventions and Official Secrecy* (1994).

[64] Provided that the UK is a designated country, an EPC application may be converted into a British application; a PCT application is similarly treated: see EPC arts 75(2), 77(4), (5); PCT arts 11(3), 12(3); PA 1977 s.81(1)(b).

[65] PA 1977 s.23(1)(b).

grant. No patent will be granted, but the applicant is entitled to compensation for any Crown use[66]; and—as a matter of departmental favour—he may also be compensated for hardship resulting from the secrecy direction: taking account, for instance, of lost commercial opportunities and foreign patent rights.[67] The government department involved must review the need for secrecy from time to time.[68]

(6) Unity and division

Two patents are not to be had for the price of one. One invention per patent, moreover, simplifies the classification of specifications and the process of searching which is the reason for classifying. Accordingly, as the EPC has it, an application must "relate to one invention only or to a group of inventions so linked as to form a single general inventive concept".[69] It is possible to have claims for a process, the apparatus to operate it and its products; or for products, processes for making them and use of the products.[70] Beyond this what will be allowed is a matter of judgment, and one that is left to the examiner(s) of the patent office in question.[71] **4–15**

An applicant may cope with an objection that he is seeking to patent more than one invention by dividing his single application into two (or more). Provided that he adds no new matter and keeps to the prescribed time schedule, he may keep his priority date for the "new" applications.[72] Division is permitted even where there is no objection to unity: it may be requested, for instance, where new claims are wanted which might give rise to an objection to unity.[73]

---

[66] Following the general rules: see below, paras 7–49—7–50.

[67] PA 1977 s.22(7).

[68] PA 1977 s.22(5): i.e. on the making of the secrecy direction, then at least at the ninth month from the filing date and annually thereafter.

[69] EPC art.82; PA 1977 s.14(5)(d) (omitting "general"). See, e.g. *Kennedy Institute of Rheumatology* [2005] E.P.O.R. 51 .

[70] EPC Rules r.30; PA 1977 Rules r.22.

[71] In the past the Appeal Tribunal in Britain has been exceedingly reluctant to interfere with the British Office's discretion. And it is no objection to a granted patent that it lacks unity: PA 1977 s.26. In the EPO, where Search and Examining Divisions are separate, and only the latter may refuse an application, the Search Division may require a second fee to search parts of an application which it considers separate; with power in the Examining Division to remit the fee if it finds unity: EPC Rules r.46 (note also r.45; search not possible, as a whole or in part).

[72] For EPO practice, see *Ex p. Advanced Semiconductor Products* [1995] E.P.O.R. 97 (Enlarged BA).

[73] For time limits, see Ency. P.L., paras 6–111, 14–202. For problems abour priority in relation to divisional applications see, e.g. *Brother* [2006] E.P.O.R. 33; *Seiko* [2006] E.P.O.R. 34; *Microsoft/clipboard formats II* [2006] E.P.O.R. 40.

(7) Formal examination

4–16 If the applicant does not ask for a preliminary examination and search, the only value of an application will be that it may found priority for a later application. But, once the request is made (and fee paid), the office will make its preliminary examination to ensure that there is a request for grant; a description and one or more claims; any drawings referred to; identification of the applicant(s); identification of the inventor(s); an abstract of the invention described; and compliance with various formalities.[74] In the EPC, the states for which a patent is sought have also to be designated: these designations may afterwards be withdrawn but never added to.[75] An application will, of course, normally be drawn to meet the much more stringent standards of the substantive examination, and these will be discussed later.

The inventor or inventors must be named as a matter of "moral right".[76] Now that employee-inventors are entitled on occasion to "compensation", there may be considerable evidential value in being named as an inventor.[77]

The abstract is required as an aid to those conducting searches, giving them preliminary assistance in deciding whether a specification is relevant to their investigation. Its terms may ultimately be settled by the patent office concerned, and it is disregarded when treating the specification as part of the art. Probably it is not to be used in interpreting the claims.[78]

(8) Search and examination

(a) *Introductory*

4–17 At the heart of the European and the British systems lies a compulsory examination before grant, not only of the novelty but also of the inventiveness of the alleged invention. To this there are three important preliminaries: (1) a substantial search; (2) "early publication" of the application in the form that it has by then reached; and (3) the opportunity within a short period after that for the applicant to decide whether or not he wants his application to proceed to examination.

British practice under the 1949 Act was very different: the Patent Office's examination only went to novelty and prior claiming, judged against a

---

[74] PA 1977 ss.14(1)–(3A), 17(1)–(3); EPC arts 78, 90, 91. Only in relation to drawings is there a special rule in effect allowing post-dating. If drawings referred to are not provided, reference to them can be deleted; or they may be filed within a limited time, the date of filing being postponed until this is done.

[75] EPC art.79. A mistaken failure to designate may, however, be remedied under EPC Rules r.88: [1980] OJ EPO 293.

[76] PA 1977 s.13; PA 1977 Rules rr.14, 15; EPC arts 62, 81; EPC Rules rr.17–19 in implementation of PIP art.4. For the concept of "inventor", above, para.4–06. See *Nippon Piston Ring's Application* [1987] R.P.C. 120.

[77] See below, paras 7–08—7–14.

[78] PA 1977 s.14(2); PA 1977 Rules r.19; EPC art.85; EPC Rules r.33.

search of British specifications for the previous 50 years. It took place without the applicant's first considering the search result and before the industry was acquainted with the content of the specification. The detailed content could be kept dark for as much as four years from the priority date. Before grant, obviousness could only be brought in issue by an outside party in separate opposition proceedings, but upon whatever prior art he put to the tribunal. However, this ground of opposition was narrower than that available in post-grant attacks on the validity of the patent before the High Court; and the same restriction applied in "belated oppositions" launched before the office within one year of grant.

Under the EPC approach, both the UKIPO and the EPO examine for obviousness as a matter of course in proceedings before grant that are ex parte.

Neither the European nor the British system of 1977 adopted the technique of deferred examination. This was introduced into the "full examination" systems of the Netherlands, West Germany and Japan in order to lift some of the burden on their patent offices in the great patenting boom of the 1960s. Quite apart from bureaucratic considerations, this arrangement has one advantage. Many patents that are applied for prove to have no lasting commercial value; even if granted they would be allowed to lapse. Delaying examination for up to seven years, while allowing a provisional form of protection after publication of the application, means that this swill of unwanted patents can filter away without wasting resources on examining the applications.[79] **4–18**

In the councils where the EPO was negotiated, however, a different principle triumphed. The importance of trying to ensure that an industry was saddled only with valid patents was held to require a rapid pre-grant examination.[80] Accordingly, the applicant was given only six months from early publication in which to decide whether to seek examination. It should be noted, however, that neither the Dutch nor the Germans abandoned deferred examination in their own systems. This remains one factor which may attract an applicant in Europe to the national systems, particularly if he is not sure how he will fare under examination or if he doubts the commercial potential of the patent.

(b) *Search*

A search undertaken by one of the PCT authorities, or by the EPO for itself, will cover a considerable body of patents from major patenting countries and a range of the most important technical literature.[81] If the UKIPO is **4–19**

---

[79] See, e.g. Hoffmann (1972) 3 I.I.C. 423; Webman (1995) 77 J.P.T.O.S. 921.

[80] The Banks Committee's firm rejection of deferment was influential: Cmnd.4407, 1970, paras 100 et seq.

[81] For the range covered by the EPO, see its Guidelines B IX.

searching for itself, the material covered is narrower,[82] even though the British system now is concerned with the prior art throughout the world .[83]

(c) *Early publication of application*

4–20 The new systems aim to publish the application, for the benefit of outsiders, 18 months from the priority date.[84] References to the prior art cited in the search report are also published.[85] From this point in time the patent-office file (subject to a variety of exceptions) falls open to inspection[86]: outsiders may thus trace how an applicant has reacted to the results of the search and objections that examiners may subsequently put.[87]

If at this point an applicant using the PCT does not opt for the International Preliminary Examination,[88] his application must pass into the national systems (or the EPO).[89]

(d) *Amending during prosecution*

4–21 In the successful prosecution of an application, much may turn on the degree to which a specification and claims originally filed can be amended and the points in time at which this can be done. The applicant is offered his largest opportunity in the period after receiving the search report and in his response to the first report of the examiner; thereafter, amendments require leave.[90] Even when making amendments of his own volition, however, the applicant is constrained by general rules. As far as the description of the invention is concerned, he may not add to his original disclosure; if he does, the examiner may reject the amendment, or subsequently (even if the examiner allows it) the patent, once granted, may be revoked.[91]

Equally with claims: although they may be broadened in the course of prosecution, they must continue to be supported by the description—as well as being clear and concise. As we shall see, objections to claims can be raised

[82] It is still largely confined to prior British specifications.

[83] See below, para.5–03.

[84] PA 1977 s.16; PA 1977 Rules rr.27, 28; EPC art.93; EPC Rules rr.48–50; PCT art.21; Rules Under Patent Co-Operation Treaty, r.48. Until publication, the application may be withdrawn without jeopardising the novelty of its contents. In the UK Office, this may be done until allotment to a printing contractor and collection: *Intera's Application* [1986] R.P.C. 459 CA.

[85] In the European system, if the search report is not available at the date of early publication, it may be published later; in which case the time for requesting examination is extended: EPC art.93(2); cf. Rules Under Patent Co-Operation Treaty r.48.2(g).

[86] PA 1977 s.118; PA 1977 Rules rr.92–96; EPC art.128; EPC Rules rr.92–95; PCT art.30 (but note art.38—confidential nature of International Preliminary Examination).

[87] For the significance of this, see below, para.4–45.

[88] Or cannot do so, because a country has not ratified Ch. II.

[89] PCT art.20; PA 1977 s.89 (requiring a translation into English if necessary); EPC art.158 (requiring a version in one of the three official languages). For supplementary search in the EPO, see above, para.4–02.

[90] PA 1977 s.19; PA 1977 Rules r.36; EPC art.123(1); EPC Rules r.86; PCT arts 19, 28; Rules Under Patent Co-Operation Treaty rr.46, 52.

[91] Amendment is considered further below, at paras 4–30—4–35.

after grant, but subject to rather imprecise limits.[92] So examiners ought to take this requirement particularly seriously. But without the stimulus of third-party objections before grant, it may be tempting for them to let the applicant's drafting stand.

(e) *The course of examination*

The purpose of the examination is to decide whether the application meets all the criteria for the grant of a patent: whether the subject-matter is within the patentable field; whether, in the light of the search report, the invention is novel and inventive; whether there is a sufficient description and the claims meet the criteria mentioned above. Examining the application in the light of the search report proceeds with relative informality. The examiner in charge sets forth any objections in a letter and states the time within which amendments may be submitted in order to overcome the objections. If applicant and examiner cannot agree, the issue may be raised in a formal hearing—in the UK Office before a senior examiner, in the EPO before the full Examining Division[93]; in either case, with a right of appeal.[94] Formal proceedings at this stage are infrequent in the British system, even with obviousness on the agenda.[95] **4–22**

Although outsiders have no right to present a case in opposition to grant before it takes place, they may make observations on patentability, drawing attention to prior art or even prior use which may not be known to the office.[96] Even though there are opportunities for competitors to monitor the progress of applications after early publication,[97] this remains an occasional strategy. Its tactical disadvantage is that the competitor cannot put a case on how the information should be regarded.[98]

(f) *Time-limits*

The EPO and the British Office and courts have seen a procession of cases about failure to comply with the requirements of the application system **4–23**

[92] See below, para.5–91—5–93.

[93] i.e. three examiners of whom one has been primarily responsible, from the outset.

[94] i.e. in the British Office, to the Patents Court and in some cases to the Court of Appeal (PA 1977 s.97); in the EPO, to a Board of Appeals: EPC arts 106(1), 21(3); Paterson [1987] E.I.P.R. 221; Stephens-Ofner [1990] E.I.P.R. 215.

[95] Unless an appeal is pending, the period for completing the examination in the British Office is 4½ years from priority: PA 1977 s.20; PA 1977 Rules r.34. The EPO has no such prescribed limit. The price of the EPO's success has been a serious backlog, which has attracted harsh criticism. Statistically at least, performance is now improving: see above, para.3–25; Dent [2006] E.I.P.R. 381.

[96] PA 1977 s.21; EPC art.115; it is a substantial procedural violation for the examiners to ignore the observations: *Anotio* [2006] E.P.O.R. (35) 390.

[97] See above, para.4–20.

[98] The *Gowers Review of Intellectual Property* (2006, Rec. 22) considers that more use of this procedure should be made in an effort to improve the efficacy of examination; but it offers no incentive to potential opponents to intervene at this stage.

within the prescribed time limits. The fact that such errors occur with frequency is one measure of the complexity of the whole structure.[99] Thus a noticeable proportion of those arising in Britain have concerned the process of converting an international application under the PCT into a national application, either after search or after preliminary international examination.[100] Where the default is in part a consequence of a failure in communication from the patent office concerned, the tendency has been to discount it.[101] In the EPO there may be further help under the arrangements for restitution of an out-of-time application where due care has been observed.[102] However, there are some dates crucial to the whole procedure—such as the six-month period for requesting examination—to which that special concession does not apply. These require the most scrupulous watching.

(9) Grant and renewal

4–24 The patent grant is formally effective from the date when notice of it is officially published.[103] The maximum term for which it may last is 20 years from the filing date,[104] the effective period for a claim to damages running from the date of early publication.[105] Grant is also the point at which the European application matures into a bundle of patents for the designated contracting States (including, once the CPC is brought into operation, a Community patent).

4–25 A patent continues for the full 20 years only upon payment of the annual renewal fees. In the United Kingdom these start with the fifth year and increase with age: the one official price of success. The fees may be paid up to six months late under penalty.[106] After that time the patent will lapse for non-payment, but may be restored within a further prescribed period subject to a measure of protection for those who in the meantime begin in good

[99] For details, see, e.g. Ency. P.L., paras 6–002, 13–005. For the duty of good faith required of the EPO, see G02/97, *Unilever* [2000] E.P.O.R. 73 Enl.B.A.

[100] See, e.g. *E's Applications* [1983] R.P.C. 231 HL; *Mitsui's Application* [1984] R.P.C. 471; *Matsuda's Application* [1987] R.P.C. 37; and see also PA 1977 ss.89, 89A, 89B (as amended by CDPA 1988 Sch.5 paras 24, 25). For equivalent questions in the EPO, see Gall [1984] E.I.P.R. 302.

[101] See PA 1977 Rules r.100; *M's Application* [1985] R.P.C. 249 CA; *Mills' Application* [1985] R.P.C. 339 CA; *Université Laval* [1995] OJ EPO 831.

[102] EPC art.122. If the mistake is made by a professional representative, he must show that it was an isolated error in a normally satisfactory system: *Motorola* [1987] OJ EPO 362; see Paterson, paras 6–20—6–42.

[103] When the patent is in order, the fees due must be paid; in the case of the EPO, the Examining Division has also to notify the applicant of the final terms of the grant. Translations of the claims into other official languages have to be filed; see EPC art.97(5); EPC Rules r.51(4); Teschemacher [1986] E.I.P.R. 149.

[104] See above, para.4–10. This is the term now required by the TRIPS Agreement art.33.

[105] EPC art.63; PA 1977 s.25(1). The EPC allows general extensions on account of a state of war or similar emergency conditions; and the 1977 Act gives a rule-making power that would include such cases.

[106] PA 1977 s.25(3)–(5), Sch.1; PA 1977 Rules r.39.

faith to work within the patent.[107] If the Comptroller finds it proper, a patentee may formally surrender his patent.[108] He may also secure a 50 per cent reduction of renewal fees if he has the patent indorsed "licences of right"[109]; in which case he must license all comers on terms which, if they cannot be agreed, will be fixed by the Comptroller.

Patented pharmaceuticals cannot today be marketed until there has been substantial safety testing by government authorities. So their introduction may be delayed for years during which time the patent is in force. Intensive lobbying by the drug industry procured it a form of patent extension,[110] the "supplementary protection certificate" (SPC). This cumbrous name indicates the convoluted networking of legislation which creates the right. The power to grant SPCs lies with national patent authorities.[111] So far as concerns EU countries, these authorities are required by a Council Regulation of 1992[112] to grant SPCs for patented products which have been authorised for marketing as a medicine under control procedures.[113] In the United Kingdom at least, an SPC is governed by the existing patent legislation.[114] The scheme is relatively straightforward to administer, though there are certain grounds on which a grant can be challenged by outsiders.[115] **4–26**

The term of an SPC depends upon the period of delay between the date of patent grant (that is the date of filing the application) and the date of authorisation.[116] A delay of six years gives a right to a year's supplement; and each additional year's delay gives a further year's supplement up to a

[107] PA 1977 ss.28, 28A. The liberalising amendments introduced by CDPA 1988 Sch.5 paras 6, 7, were a response to a set of difficult cases about failure to renew on time.

[108] PA 1977 s.29. The surrender would likely not be accepted if it prejudiced a licensee; cf. CPC, art.50.

[109] PA 1977 s.46, which contains further conditions.

[110] The first country to allow an extension of term was the United States.

[111] Where the patent was originally granted by the EPO, the EPC art.63 (by amendment: [1992] OJ EPO 1) confers this authority.

[112] 1768/92: After considerable debate, extended to agro-chemicals by Regulation 1610/96; (and see UK SI 1992/3091, SI 1996/1320). Later an additional six-month term for medicines within the Paediatric Regulation was added by Regulation 1901/2006 (for which see *Du Pont v UKIPO* [2009] EWCA Civ 966; Reese et al. [2010] E.I.P.R. 146). There is a consolidating Regulation for the SPC system: 469/2009. For the validity of the scheme under EU law, see above para.1–28.

[113] Thus it applies to national patents granted either by the EPO or the national office. See further, *Biogen v Smithkline Beecham* [1998] R.P.C. 833; *Yamanouchi v Comptroller-General* [1998] R.P.C. 844.

[114] See the Patents (Supplementary Protection Certificates for Medicinal Products) Regulations 1992 (SI 1992/3091) reg.5. No special provision regulates licences during the extended period. Grant may be subject to authorisation to market the product: *Yamanouchi Pharmaceutical v Comptroller-General of Patents* [1997] E.C.R. I–3251 ECJ.

[115] For persons entitled to apply, see *Chiron and Novo Nordisk's Application* [2005] R.P.C. (24) 587. The EPO and some national patent offices (including the British) take the view that the legislation covers the case where the patent is for a compound in its acid form and the medicine licence is for one of its esters or salts: see Adams [1995] E.I.P.R. 277. It does not apply to new formulations of known drugs: *Draco's Application* [1996] R.P.C. 417; *Haas v BIE* [2002] R.P.C. GET ECJ.

[116] For the precise date of authorisation, see *Novartis v Comptroller-General* [2005] R.P.C. 22 ECJ.

maximum of five years. Thus a delay of 10 or more years qualifies for a five-year SPC. Hostility from patient groups and drug imitators put an end to the demand for a maximum of 10 or more additional years of protection.

(10) Objections to validity after grant[117]

4–27 The EPC, drawing inspiration from "belated oppositions" in the former British procedure, allows an outsider to launch an opposition in the EPO within nine months of grant.[118] Objections may be taken on three grounds[119]—unpatentable subject matter,[120] inadequate disclosure[121] and unallowable amendment.[122] If it succeeds, the whole "bundle" of European patents will be revoked, or granted only in amended form, save in exceptional cases.[123] So the procedure offers an outsider a unique chance of attack and is therefore being used with some frequency. However, because of the thorough consideration now provided during examination before grant, an opposition based on the material in the search report and nothing else is not likely to succeed.

4–28 Contrary to the British "accusatorial" tradition, which applied as much to oppositions as to court proceedings, Opposition Divisions of the EPO are expected to play a more active part in resolving issues raised before them—deciding what evidence to take, and possibly securing information from sources not nominated by the parties, appointing experts to give opinions and conducting inspections.[124] Even if an opponent withdraws, the Opposition Division should continue where it is convinced that the patent cannot be supported, at least in its granted form.[125] British proceedings allow

---

[117] See generally, Roberts [1999] I.P.Q. 304; and for an investigation of the appellate boards of the EPO, Leith [2001] I.P.Q. 50.

[118] EPC arts 99 et seq. The opponent need establish no special interest to oppose. Jacob L.J. has suggested that abolishing the time limit would lead to a dramatic fall in the number of oppositions: see Vaver & Bently (eds), *Intellectual Property in the New Millennium* (2004), at p.83 n.17. Even after the time for launching an opposition has expired, any person who has been sued or threatened with infringement proceedings personally may intervene in an opposition: art.105. See generally, *Indupak* [2002] E.O.P.R. 81; *Cairnstores v Hassle* [2002] F.S.R. 35; *Oystertec's Patent* [2003] R.P.C. 29.

[119] EPC art.100.

[120] See below, paras 5–54—5–81.

[121] See below, paras 5–84—5–97.

[122] i.e. that the amendment extends the subject-matter beyond the application as filed: see below, para.4–31—4–33.

[123] If the state of the art differs for different States, because prior applications do not designate them all (as to which see below, para.5–14), a patent may be available only in some; alternatively, it may be granted subject to amendment for some. Or if proprietors differ, amendments may vary from state to state.

[124] But adequate notice of them must be given as a matter of due process: *Atotech* [1998] E.P.O.R. 135. See further, Gall (1983) 14 I.I.C. 229; Stephens-Ofner [1997] E.I.P.R. 167.

[125] ICI [1989] OJ EPO 412. An opponent may not add new grounds during an appeal: see, e.g. G1/95 and G7/95 [1996] OJ EPO 615 at 626 Enl.BA. Nice questions can arise about the extent to which an opposition appeal can be allowed to result in placing the appellant in a worse position than if he had no appealed (*reformatio in peius*): see G4/93 and G1/99 (both Enl. BA).

questions of infringement and validity to be tried together, so that their interrelation can be assessed. Nowhere does the absence of a single court hierarchy within the EPC system appear more ungainly than in this scheme. Even within the EPO, the various Technical Boards of Appeal, which have jurisdiction at the examination and the opposition stages, form the final stage of process, the parties having no right of appeal to the Enlarged Board of Appeal.[126] Yet under the legislative scheme of the EPC an EPO decision to uphold a patent even after opposition still leaves it open to a national court to find the European patent void for its territory. An English court has a broad discretion to order a stay of its own proceedings and may well, in these special conditions, do so pending an EPO opposition, although there is no simple presumption that it should do so. Unfortunately EPO oppositions can be long-drawn-out—a factor which may result in an order permitting the English proceedings to continue. To make such an order may result in wasteful competition between the parties, but the Court of Appeal has made clear the core significance of seeking 'some commercial certainty somewhat sooner' where there are predictable time differences concerning the proceedings; and because a commercial party resisting an order to stay the English proceedings generally has good reasons for making that choice .[127]

The British system continues to offer the outside party an opportunity of attacking a patent[128] by a largely documentary procedure originating in the Patent Office[129]; this is intended to be cheaper and more expeditious than a challenge to validity in the Patents County Court or the High Court.[130] This chance does not arise until after grant, but it is then available throughout the life of the patent and the grounds are the same as those on which an attack may be launched in court proceedings. It is an alternative to the latter, rather than an intermediate course.[131] Accordingly the applicant for revocation ought not to face any specially high standard of proof, although he must still make out his case. **4–29**

---

[126] For the limited circumstances in which a BA or the President of the EPO may refer a question of law to the Enlarged Board, see EPC, art.112; and below, para.20–31.

[127] See esp. *Beloit v Valmet* [1996] F.S.R. 715 CA; *Unilever v Procter & Gamble* [2000] F.S.R. 235 CA; *Kimberley-Clark Worldwide v Procter & Gamble* [2000] R.P.C. 422 CA; *Unilin Beheer v Berry Floor* [2007] EWCA 364 CA. In *Glaxo v Genentech* [2008] F.S.R. 18 , Mummery L.J. provided an extensive account of how the Patents Court should approach exercise of the discretion. *Eli Lilly v Human Genome Sciences* [2010] EWCA Civ.33 demonstrates a new willingness of the EPO and the English CA to co-operate in setting timetables for the hearing of proceedings concerning the validity of a European Patent.

[128] Including, of course, a European patent (UK). If the patent is also being opposed in the EPO, the British proceedings are likely to be stayed: see Ency P.L., para.12–102.

[129] PA 1977 s.72; as to amendments in such proceedings, see below, paras 4–31—4–34.

[130] See Ency. P.L., paras 6–201 et seq.

[131] As indicated by this: if the Comptroller refuses to revoke, the applicant may apply to the court only with leave: PA 1977 s.72(6). The Comptroller may always certify that the case would be more suitably determined by the court: s.72(7). The court will in its discretion decide whether proceedings before it ought to be stayed in favour of those in the British Office: *Hawker Siddeley v Real Time* [1985] R.P.C. 395; cf. *Gen Set v Mosarc* [1985] F.S.R. 302.

A particular question of issue estoppel can arise in this connection. An objection may be raised to an application: for instance, the invention may be said not to be novel, or to involve no inventive step, on the basis of particular documents which contain relevant prior art. A decision during the application stage (including in this an EPO opposition) may determine the issue in favour of the applicant and the patent is granted. In Britain, however, decisions on the application have traditionally not been treated as involving a final judgment, and the Court of Appeal has held that this applies to UK patents granted under the 1977 Act.[132] The patentee may thus be left to face the same battle twice. The approach has been thought justified because the true assessment of such issues deserves to be tested with the full evidence that can be presented in a challenge to the validity of the granted patent (above all on issues of inventive step). It is conceivable that, if in future the national and European patent offices gain real standing, at least a cause of action estoppel might arise from the initial decision to allow the patent.[133]

More generally, some have argued that there is too great an imbalance between the position of the patentee and that of competitors who challenge validity. If a patent applicant fails to survive Office examination and loses on appeal, he has no subsequent opportunity to justify his case; yet if he then succeeds he may still face third-party objections at the opposition stage, and equally thereafter. The fact remains, however, that it is patentees and not opponents who are seeking exclusive rights. An improvement in the "balance" could arguably be achieved if procedures in the EPO, both during examination and opposition, were capable of final appeal to a highly experienced court which was plainly positioned outside the Office.[134]

2. Amendment

(1) Introductory

4–30 The fact that a specification may be amended adds finesse to the art of patenting. In the course of securing the grant, the description, the claims or both may be substantially rewritten, either to take account of prior art or some other objection to validity, or to reflect the growing understanding of the invention by those prosecuting the application. Nevertheless, amendments have to comply with important ground rules and these can conveniently be set out here. Some illustrations of what can be achieved by amendment will, however, be found in the discussion of validity in Ch.5, below.

[132] *Buehler v Chronos Richardson* [1998] R.P.C. 609 CA.

[133] i.e. an estoppel between the same parties on the same allegation: see above paras 2–67, 2–68.

[134] See Von Morzé and Van Zant [1998] I.P.Q. 117; and, for an interim proposal, Jacob [1997] E.I.P.R. 224; Brinkhof [1997] E.I.P.R. 226.

The legal provisions in point distinguish two cases: (1) alterations that are intended to introduce new ideas, or at least new expressions of existing ideas; and (2) corrections that remove mistakes in expressing what was originally intended. The bulk of amendments, proposed and allowed, are of the first kind. But the two categories are not always easy to distinguish, and there may be advantages in trying to justify a change under the second head. This is discussed below.

(2) Amendment: general

(a) *Legal requirements*[135]

The rules governing amendment distinguish between alterations in the description of the invention and in the claims. The description must not be amended so as to introduce matter extending beyond that disclosed in the specification as filed.[136] This applies whether the amendment is sought during the application or after.[137] If such an amendment is improperly allowed after grant, this may ground a suit for revocation of the patent, in whole or in part.[138] **4–31**

If the claims are amended during application, they must not notionally add something new to the description in the body of the specification. Thus, a claim including a "mechanical compression spring" was not allowed to be changed to a "mechanical spring", because this added a whole range of springs not included in the previous unambiguous language.[139] Moreover, the amended claims have still to satisfy the basic rules that they must be clear and concise, be supported by the description and satisfy the requirement of unity of invention. But it is primarily for the patent office concerned to see that this principle is observed.[140] Amendments that are themselves sought after grant[141] may not alter the claims so as to extend the scope of

---

[135] See generally Ency. P.L., Ch.7; Paterson, Ch.5; Wheeler, Laddie, Brinkhof, Rogge (1997) 28 I.I.C. 822 et seq.

[136] PA 1977 s.76(2) (as amended by CDPA 1988 Sch.5 para.20); EPC art.123(2); Opinion 93/89 [1993] OJ EPO 117. For circumstances in which cross-referencing is permissible, see *Raychem/Event detector* [1993] OJ EPO 616. See also *Hsiung's Patent* [1992] R.P.C. 497 CA.

[137] PA 1977 ss.19, 27, 75; and see above para.4–30.

[138] PA 1977 s.72(1)(d); EPC art.100(c); *Liversidge v British Telecommunications* [1991] R.P.C. 219. The content of the claims constitutes a distinct disclosure: PA 1977 s.130(3); *Southco v Dzus Fastener* [1990] R.P.C. 587; *Edwards v Acme Signs* [1992] R.P.C. 131 CA.

[139] *Protoned's Application* [1983] F.S.R. 110.

[140] How far the content of the claims is open to challenge after grant is considered below, in paras 5–92—5–99.

[141] Either in the course of proceedings for infringement or revocation (PA 1977 s.75); or, if none are pending, in an application to the Comptroller to amend (s.27); or in opposition proceedings before the EPO (EPC art.123(2), (3)); see *Decision G1/93* [1994] OJ EPO 169. Section 75 jurisdiction will prevail over that of the EPO so far as concerns the British patent: *Petrolite Holdings v Dyno Oil* [1998] F.S.R. 190; but cf. *Palmaz's European Patents* [1999] R.P.C. 47.

protection; if wrongly admitted, they may provide cause for revocation.[142] If they are proper, they have a retroactive effect.[143] In the course of seeking amendments after grant, the patentee cannot be required to amend his original claims so as to render them fairly based on the description.[144]

4–32 In many cases the aim of an amendment is to cut down the scope of what is claimed, because a piece of prior art is discovered which makes the original claim cover unjustifiably broad territory. Sometimes this can be achieved by amending the claims alone: the broadest may have to be deleted; or features of subsidiary claims may have to be added to it; or claims for different aspects of the invention may have to be coalesced. In a classic example,[145] the broadest claim originally related to a tool for crimping together electrical wires and connectors, which had a ratchet and pawl device to prevent premature release of the tool before crimping was complete. In order to sidestep prior art, the patentee was allowed to add to this a device that was mentioned in the description incidentally as an additional feature—a stop designed to prevent crimping from going too far. Within this general principle, it is permissible to change a product claim to a claim to its use.[146]

4–33 If the description must also be amended, the issue may be more difficult. In the crimping tool case,[147] if the stop device had not originally been mentioned, to add it by amendment would in most circumstances be barred as "extending" the matter disclosed. The same would probably apply if originally a particular kind of stop was mentioned and the amendment sought to refer to all kinds of stop. Again, suppose that stops were mentioned in general and the amendment sought to refer to one particular kind of stop. It may be objected that this is to give prominence to something not previously pointed up in the description. If so the proposed amendment will be classed as an "intermediate generalisation" and disallowed as a departure from the governing principle that the patentee must disclose the essential features of his invention from the application onwards.[148] The test overall is whether the skilled man would learn from the amended specification anything about the invention which he could not learn from the unamended specification.[149]

---

[142] PA 1977 s.72(1)(e) and see EPC arts 123(3), 138(1)(d): *Raychem's Application* [1986] R.P.C. 521.

[143] PA 1977 ss.27(3), 75(3).

[144] *Chiron v Organon Teknika (No. 11)* [1995] F.S.R. 589 CA—a decision related to a more general problem, discussed below, at para.5–86.

[145] *Amp v Hellerman* [1962] R.P.C. 55 HL; and see *Edwards v Acme Signs* (above n.138); *Mölnlycke v Procter & Gamble (No. 5)* [1994] R.P.C. 49 CA; *LG Philips v Tatung* [2007] R.P.C. 21 CA.

[146] *Advanced Semiconductor Products* (G1/93) [1995] E.P.O.R. 97 EnlBA; *PPG/Disclaimer* (G1/03) [2004] OJ EPO 413 EnlBA.

[147] *Amp v Hellerman* [1962] R.P.C. 55 HL.

[148] See *Ward's Application* [1986] R.P.C. 54; *Pharmacia v Merck* [2002] R.P.C. 41 CA; *Zipher v Markem* [2009] F.S.R. 1. In *LG Philips v Tatung* (above n.145) an argument that "intermediate generalization" was an unacceptable development in case law that had no foundation in the EPC was rejected, notably in light of *Advanced SemiconductorProducts,* above, n.146

[149] Jacob L.J., *Vector v Glatt Air* [2007] EWCA 805; *Napp v Sandoz* [2009] R.P.C. 18.

(b) *The discretion*

Amendment in the course of application is frequent; after grant, much less so. But if leave to amend is sought from the Comptroller or the court after grant, not only must the applicant show that it is within the legal requirements just discussed; he must also satisfy the tribunal that it should in its discretion allow the amendment to be made.[150] **4–34**

In the past, the discretion has been used to subject the patentee's conduct to critical scrutiny. This contrasts with the approach to most other issues, where the applicant or patentee is obliged to meet specific requirements but not in addition to show that he has behaved properly, honestly and candidly.[151] Patentees who delayed their application to amend for long periods after appreciating the need, or who insisted first in maintaining an invalid claim, were denied leave to amend.[152] Seeking to ensure that the British approach to amendment falls into line with the practice of the EPO, it was enacted that from December 13, 2007 the court or Comptroller should exercise the discretion having regard to any relevant principles under the EPC.[153] Case law has indicated that the old consideration of whether the patentee's conduct has been reprehensible is no longer correct. But it would seem that where public interest, rather than moral condemnation, justifies it, the discretion may still be used against a proposed amendment. If the application is merely to delete, it will almost always be granted.[154] But when seeking an amendment to alter the content of description or claims, the applicant must put the whole story of why the amendment is needed.[155] Moreover the interest of competitors is likely to suffer if an unduly wide claim has deliberately left to stand. The discretion accordingly still has a role to play, even though it must now be exercised in a way that strikes a proportional balance: on the one hand, there will be a case for maintaining those parts of a patent that are valid; on the other there should be a deterrent against acting as the patentee did where the conduct is a serious failing. [156] On the other hand when the patent is held invalid at trial and then amendments are proposed to a claim not under attack at the trial, the amendments are unlikely to be allowed if their effect would be to provoke a

[150] PA 1977 ss.27(1), 75(1); leave to amend may be conditional, requiring possibly that no proceedings be brought for past infringement. See Krasser (1992) 23 I.I.C. 467.

[151] But cf. the duties associated with the requirement of disclosure: see below, paras 5–86 et seq.

[152] For examples, see Ency. P.L., para.7–205.

[153] See now PA 1977 ss.27(6) and 75(5) inserted by PA 2004 s.2.

[154] *Kirin-Amgen v Transkaryotic Therapies* [2003] R.P.C. 3; *Synthon v Smithkline Beecham* [2003] All E.R. (D) 208. Hence neither this factor nor the fact that damages may not ultimately be available against an innocent defendant (PA 1977 s.62(3)) are reasons for refusing to grant an interim injunction: *Smithkline Beecham v Apotex Europe* [2003] F.S.R. 31.

[155] *SCM Corp's Application* [1979] R.P.C. 341 CA; *Smith Kline & French v Evans* [1989] F.S.R. 561 CA; *Kimberly-Clark v Procter & Gamble* [2000] F.S.R. 235 CA; cf. *Instance v CCL Label* [2002] F.S.R. 8.

[156] See *Vector v Glatt Air Techniques* [2007] R.P.C. 12; *Zipher v Markem* [2009] F.S.R. 1.

second trial on validity. In the first trial the challenger must put forward the whole of his case on validity.[157]

(3) Correction of errors

4–35 The British Office and the EPO each has power itself to correct errors of translation, transcription, clerical errors and mistakes in all documents.[158] But in the case of specifications, the correction has to be obvious in the sense that it is immediately evident that nothing else would have been intended than what is offered as the correction. This is a severe limitation. The Enlarged EPO Board of Appeal requires that a skilled person be able to appreciate the true intention directly and unambiguously from the document itself and common general knowledge, without additional evidence. Moreover, errors in the description, drawings or claims can be altered only if there is in consequence no extension to them over the subject-matter originally filed.[159]

4–36 Errors of translation are particularly liable to occur. However, the rule seems to allow little scope for their correction, since so often translations leave obscure what the original must have meant. Only in the case of European patent applications may a special rule apply. If the United Kingdom at any time requires the claims of the published application and the whole of the granted patent to be translated from French or German into English,[160] these can be corrected so as to achieve the meaning of the original.[161] There is, however, intermediate protection for those who rely on the earlier version.[162] Claims of the European patent have to be translated into the other official languages; but it is the original which governs[163] and in this case there is no special protection for a person who relies on a more narrowly formulated translation.

3. Claims

(1) Claims and infringement: an introduction

4–37 In Britain, the United States and countries which have taken their patent laws from these sources, the purpose of claims in the patent specification is

---

[157] See Ency PL, para.7–205.

[158] PA 1977 s.117; PA 1977 Rules r.91(2); EPC Rules r.88. In the EPO there must first be a request (though not necessarily from the proprietor of the patent).

[159] *Opinions G3/89 and 11/91* [1993] OJ EPO 117; and see *VEB Kombinat's Application* [1987] R.P.C. 405; *Holtite v Jost* [1979] R.P.C. 81 HL.

[160] i.e. making use of powers in PA 1977 ss.77(6), 78(7); see above, para.4–04.

[161] PA 1977 s.80, following EPC art.70(3), (4).

[162] PA 1977 s.80(3), (4).

[163] PA 1977 s.80(1), following EPC art.70(1).

to delimit the scope of the monopoly.[164] "Fence-posts" are set up, most often by the use of words, but commonly also by chemical and mathematical symbols; sometimes by reference to drawings. Activities within the territory thus defined require the patentee's consent if they are not to infringe.[165] Whether activities which for all practical purposes fall within the area also infringe has been the subject of some flux in British case law. There was a period in the 1960s when the House of Lords seemed intent on keeping the patentee strictly to his claim, at least when the invention consisted only of a modest improvement over what was already known.[166] During the European Convention negotiations, this undoubtedly aroused a mistrust of the British way of doing things. Using the claims in this way has two crucial consequences. First, draftsmen must perfect the art of legitimate generalisation—in part this is an exercise in imagining alternative forms for the inventive idea, in part in finding descriptions that will cover all the variants concisely. Secondly, disputes about the interpretation of claims become of central significance, both in deciding what constitutes infringement and in determining the validity of the patent itself.[167]

"Fence-post" claiming is to be distinguished from the "sign-post" **4–38** claiming which has been favoured by some patent systems. "Sign-post" claims aim to specify the essential inventive concept in the specification: an important part of this accordingly is to distinguish what is new from what is old, and the claims are generally put into a form which is designed to achieve this.[168] The relation between claim and protected territory is then less direct: to some extent it is left to the court to work out the proper scope of the monopoly from the description of the invention, the claims merely showing what the patentee considers is his inventive step. In the more extreme applications of this approach the court is in effect deciding whether, given the description of the invention, a "fence-post" claim could have been written that would cover the alleged infringement.

With the introduction of the EPC and PCT examining arrangements, this **4–39** difference of emphasis suddenly became something much more immediate than an occasional trap in patenting across a spectrum of countries.[169] For it affects not only infringement but also questions of validity. In the European system, so far as statutory texts go, the "fence-post" approach has been preferred. By art.69(1) of the EPC, the extent of protection is determined by "the terms of the claims", using the description and drawings to interpret

[164] Generally, see Brennan [2005] I.P.Q. 361–399.
[165] The concept of infringement is dealt with in detail below, in paras 6–01 et seq.
[166] For these cases, see below, para.6–03.
[167] For the general principles of construction, see below, paras 4–41—4–42.
[168] The influence of this thinking is to be found in the form that European patent claims are to be given "wherever appropriate": the features shared with the prior art must first be described, and then the inventive additions emphasised in a phrase starting "characterised by . . .": EPC Rules r.29(1).
[169] See Stenvik and Franzosi (2001) 32 I.I.C. 1 and 113, respectively.

them; and this formula is in effect repeated for UK patents in s.125 of the 1977 Act.

4–40 Even so, qualification looms, in the ungainly form of the Protocol on the Interpretation of Article 69.[170] This requires art.69 to be read as defining a middle position which combines a fair protection for the patentee with a reasonable degree of certainty for third parties. Two extremes are disapproved: using the strict, literal meaning of the claims to define the scope of protection, with resort to description and drawings only to resolve ambiguities (a caricature of the former British approach); and using the claims only as a guideline, the scope of protection covering "what, from a consideration of the description and drawings a person skilled in the art, the patentee has contemplated" (an exaggeration perhaps of the old German approach). While the Protocol has not had explicit effect on British attitudes to interpretation,[171] there has come in the last few years to be a new emphasis on "purposive construction" which seems in result to honour its objective.[172]

If it achieves anything at all, the Protocol may help courts in other countries to realise that they ought not to mark out their own bounds for the monopoly; and it may stimulate patent draftsmen in other countries into imagining alternatives and drafting claims to cover them. If Britain or another EPC country with a similar approach to claims is among those designated for a European patent, the claims must be drawn to meet their more exacting standards.

(2) Interpretation of specifications

4–41 Since the claims are the principal determinant of the scope of the monopoly, how they are to be interpreted is frequently the nub of a dispute. In so far as this goes to infringement, the patentee will generally be arguing for a wide construction. However, if it goes to validity, he may well want a narrow reading. Sometimes he finds himself caught in a dilemma: the defendant will allege that what he is doing is something anticipated in the prior art or obvious from it. In which case, if the claim covers the activity, it is bad; if not, there is no infringement.[173]

The construction of claims is not something that can be considered in isolation from the rest of the specification. Claims are intended to be pithy delineations of the scope of monopoly, and they are drafted in light of the

---

[170] The Protocol is set out in para.6–02. See also PA 1977 s.125(1), (3). On the whole question, see now Chisum et al., *International Perspectives on the Legal Interpretation of Patent Claims* (1995); Pagenberg and Cornish, *Interpretation of Patents in Europe: Application of Article 69 EPC* (2006).

[171] See below, para.6–08.

[172] For this notion, see below, para.6–05.

[173] This is the so-called "Gillette" defence, after Lord Moulton in *Gillette v Anglo-American Trading* (1913) 30 R.P.C. 465 at 480. It requires strict proof: *Hickman v Andrews* [1983] R.P.C. 147.

much more detailed text of the description.[174] A specification must always be read as a whole, just as any other document is.[175] It must moreover be read as having been addressed to a person acquainted with the technology in question. So it must take account of that person's state of knowledge at the time. Terms which then have a special meaning in the art, or are given a special definition by the specification, will be read in their particular sense. Otherwise they will be understood in their ordinary meaning.[176] There is no principle requiring that patent specifications be interpreted in favour of validity, where an ambiguity arises.[177]

The direction in art.69 of the EPC that description and drawings are to be **4–42** used to interpret the claims[178] simply reflects British practice. It has not been proper to construe claims in isolation unless and until some ambiguity emerges in the course of doing so. What British courts have insisted on is that the claims are there to mark out the monopolised territory; art.69 says the same. If they clearly do mean one thing, arguments that they nevertheless mean something else will be rejected. It is in this sense alone that Lord Russell of Killowen's well-known dictum is to be understood:

> "I know of no canon or principle which will justify one in departing from the unambiguous and grammatical meaning of a claim and narrowing or extending its scope by reading into it words which are not in it; or will justify one in using stray phrases in the body of the specification for the purpose of narrowing or widening the boundaries of the monopoly fixed by the plain words of a claim."[179]

As will be emphasised later, claims are to be construed purposively, seeking to determine how they would be understood by those skilled in the relevant art as indications of the scope of monopoly claimed.[180] This modern approach is apposite not only when the question is whether the claim is infringed, or where an issue of validity arises, such as novelty, inventive step or adequate disclosure.[181]

[174] See Lord Russell in *EMI v Lissen* (1939) 56 R.P.C. 23 at 40–41 HL.
[175] See *EMI v Lissen* (1939) 56 R.P.C. 23 at 40–41 HL; and *Ransburg v Aerostyle* [1968] R.P.C. 287 at 297 HL.
[176] See Lord Russell, above, n.71.
[177] *SmithKline Beecham's (Paroxetine Anhydrate) Patent* [2003] R.P.C. (49) 855 at paras 10, 98–103 CA.
[178] See above, para.4–40.
[179] See above, n.71.
[180] *Catnic v Hill & Smith* [1981] F.S.R. 60.
[181] See *Dow Chemical v Spence Bryson* [1982] F.S.R. 397 CA; *Van der Lely v Ruston's Engineering* [1985] R.P.C. 461 CA; *Warin Pipe v Hepworth Iron* [1984] F.S.R. 32.

(3) The addressee of the specification

4–43 The complexity of some modern technologies, and the fact that some fields—notably organic chemistry[182]—have lost the precision of earlier, simpler days, makes the task of interpreting specifications increasingly difficult. Some assumption, however, has to be made about the persons to whom it is addressed. As we shall see, essentially the same question arises when assessing whether the invention is obvious and whether the disclosure is adequate,[183] though in those cases there is likely to be more concern over what conclusions the reader would draw from what he is told, and whether he would likely be misled by positive misstatements and misleading implications.

4–44 In *Valensi v British Radio*,[184] the Court of Appeal felt constrained by venerable authority to hold that, even in a new and still experimental field (colour television in 1939), a specification must be looked upon as addressed to skilled technicians, rather than to leading experts (that is, those in the few research teams then tackling the problem) or to manual workers. The court did find that such an intermediate group must have existed in fact and that it would have included representatives from the different technical fields whose knowledge was being pooled in the research.[185] If specialist and highly skilled workers are the only ones who exist at the priority date, the specification may, it seems, be treated as addressed to them.[186] The judges have been careful to preserve the general rule that it is they who interpret the words of a document.[187] However, expert witnesses may be asked what technical words, phrases and even sentences mean in context to them.[188] It is the general responsibility of the judge, before he construes the claim, to acquaint himself with the art concerned as it would have been understood by the notional addressee at the priority date.[189]

---

182 See Satchell (1970) 1 I.I.C. 179, on the serious practical problem of defining inventions in macro-molecular chemistry. See also *Fernholz's Application* [1984] OJ EPO 555; *Bayer's (Wegner) Application* [1982] OJ EPO 149.

183 See below, paras 5–39 et seq., 5–89.

184 *Valensi v British Radio* [1973] R.P.C. 337. See further below, paras 5–90 et seq., below.

185 *Valensi* [1973] R.P.C. 337 at 375–377.

186 *American Cyanamid v Ethicon* [1979] R.P.C. 215 at 245–246; for an application of this high standard in the technology of synchronising signals in mobile phones, see *Nokia v IPCom* [2009] EWHC 3482 (Pat).

187 See especially Lord Tomlin in *British Celanese v Courtaulds* (1935) 52 R.P.C. 171 at 196; *Glaverbel v British Coal* [1993] R.P.C. 90; [1994] R.P.C. 443. In origin, construction of documents was a matter for literate judges, not jurors of uncertain education. The same attitude is not maintained in respect of drawings and photographs: *Van der Lely v Bamfords* [1961] R.P.C. 296 at 306 CA; [1963] R.P.C. 61 at 71 HL.

188 *American Cyanamid v Ethicon* [1979] R.P.C. 215 at 251–255.

189 *Boyd v Horrocks* (1892) 9 R.P.C. 77 at 82 HL; *British Dynamite v Krebs* (1896) 13 R.P.C. 190 at 192 HL; but it has been firmly denied that the specification should be construed specifically in the light of an alleged anticipation in the prior art, with an eye to avoiding it: *Dudgeon v Thomson* (1877) 3, App.Cas. 34 at 53–54 HL; *Molins v Industrial Machinery* (1938) 55 R.P.C. 31 at 39 CA. Equally, no account is taken of the alleged infringement: *Dudgeon v Thomson* (above); *Nobel v Anderson* (1894) 11 R.P.C. 519 at 523 CA.

(4) The application file

In the course of prosecuting an application, substantial amendments are frequently made.[190] Before 1978, outsiders were not entitled to inspect the official file and so could not know of amendments before publication.[191] Since then they may do so at the EPO and the British Office.[192] This may well provide evidence, for instance, of why a claim was limited in a particular way, or what construction the applicant said ought to be put upon a claim when he persuaded the examiner to drop an objection. Such "file-wrapper" estoppels are used as an aid to the construction of claims in the United States.[193] It has also been accepted in English proceedings that if an applicant relied on a narrow meaning of a term in order to secure grant, he cannot subsequently argue for a wide view of the same term.[194] **4–45**

(5) Types of claim

(a) *General*

In modern patent systems a certain amount turns on the kind of claim in question. The basic distinction is between, on the one hand, product or substance claims and, on the other, process, method or use claims. The first of these categories comprises claims to things. Such claims are infringed primarily by making, selling or using the things claimed. The second category concerns procedures for conducting activities. Here infringement consists primarily of performing the activity. There are overlaps. Consider a claim to an article which is some form of mechanical apparatus: since the monopoly includes using the apparatus, it must cover a process. Conversely, we shall see that a process claim may be infringed by dealing in its products in certain circumstances.[195] Between these in the past has lain a "product-by-process" claim which was treated as giving a monopoly in the specified product only when made by the defined process. But such claims generally appear superfluous. The European Patent Office has adopted the view that a "product-by-process" claim should be treated as a claim to the product however made. The inclusion of reference to a process of production should be understood as a means of defining that product. Accordingly a product-by-process claim should only be permitted where there is no other adequate way of defining the product. This may occur, for instance, with the **4–46**

190 See above, paras 4–31—4–32.
191 Publication previously took place after examination and acceptance by the British Office.
192 EPC art.128; EPC Rules rr.93–95; PA 1977 s.118; PA 1977 Rules rr.93–95. There are various exceptions and procedural requirements.
193 See *Festo Corp. v Shoketsu*, 535 U.S. 772 (2002); Chisum, *Patents* paras 18.02(3), 18.02(6); the judges have differed in their willingness to look beyond amendments to the reasons for requiring, proposing or resisting them.
194 *Fürr v CD Truline* [1985] F.S.R. 553.
195 See below, para.6–14.

production of highly complex new chemicals with a molecular structure still to be identified.[196] The House of Lords has now accepted the criticism of the older British practice and has agreed that the practice under the EPC should now be followed.[197] The older British practice of allowing a claim to a known substance by requiring it to be made by a new method is not permitted. Since the substances remains unchanged it remains not novel, despite the new method of manufacture.

(b) *Chemical inventions*

4–47 The distinction just made is particularly important in the application of the patent system to chemical inventions—rather more so than in the case of mechanical inventions. Indeed, the adaptation of the patent system so as to accommodate the various branches of the chemical industry has proved a difficult matter, and one on which some international consensus has been slow to emerge.[198] Speaking very broadly, inventive activity in the chemical field sometimes consists of making or analysing compounds whose existence could not even have been theoretically predicted in advance. More often it involves devising ways of making substances more successfully or cheaply. But the largest part of the ground is concerned with searching for the values that substances may have in use. This sort of work is frequently concerned either with substances which are new (in the sense of never having been made before) but can be made from known starting materials by known methods; or with substances which are known, either as laboratory playthings or as functional products, and which are then tested for initial or further practical uses.

4–48 The first difficulty in the chemical field is whether patents should ever be granted for a chemical substance itself. Substances may prove to have a variety of useful applications: well-known examples are dyestuffs which prove to have valuable pharmaceutical properties.[199] (By contrast, mechanical things less readily assume new functions, at least without adaptation.) Accordingly, many systems have at some time required chemical claims to be for "substance-by-process". The British system contained such a constraint between 1919 and 1949.[200] But it was found, as in other countries, that this only introduced a game of seeing whether the patentee could think of all the possible processes for producing the substance and therefore claim them. This still left him with the difficulty of showing that the defendant was using one of them.

In Britain from 1949 onwards, and now elsewhere as TRIPS art.27(1)

196 *International Flavours & Fragrances* [1984] OJ EPO 309.

197 *Kirin-Amgen v Hoechst Marion Roussel* [[2005] R.P.C 9 at 9[86–101].

198 cf., e.g. the papers by Satchell (1970) 1 I.I.C. 179, and Robinson and Nastelski (1972) 3 I.I.C. 139, 267; Lawrence (1973) 2 CIPA 385; Gaumont (1982) 13 I.I.C. 457; Klöpsch (1982) 13 I.I.C. 457.

199 See for instance the adventures of the phenothiazines: *Olin Mathieson v Biorex* [1970] R.P.C. 157 at 185 et seq.

200 See Final Report of the Swan Committee (Cmd.7206, 1947) paras 92–95.

takes effect,[201] it has been accepted that claims to chemical substances of all kinds, including pharmaceuticals, are admissible. It seems that they may be validly granted whenever the substance itself is not part of the prior art.[202] This is then treated as any other article claim: the patentee's permission is needed to make the article for any purpose. If a second use for the substance is found during the life of his patent, his permission is needed just as much to make, sell and use for that purpose as for the purpose that he worked out. This is not so overbearing as it may sound, because there are ways in which the second inventor can secure patents, by means of use claims or through the special rules for "selection".[203] If the first patentee wishes to use second invention he will need a licence under it; while, so long as the first patent remains in force, the second patentee and any of its licensees will also need a licence from the first patentee.[204] The effect may be the growth of a patent thicket which could have deterrent effects on the development of a whole technology. The relation between intellectual property constraints and general rules of competition law in such cases can be remarkably difficult to determine. One way of avoiding the worst effects may be the establishment of technical standards with associated patent licences open to an industry as a whole. But these can be costly to construct and maintain. Competition authorities will wish to ensure that the standard does not contain catches that enable leading players after all to exclude competitors unfairly.[205]

A second problem concerns the breadth of monopoly allowable.[206] Much **4–49**
investigation into the properties of organic substances involves testing a few substances in a family of compounds that may have thousands or millions of members. The basic structure of the family has a defined molecular form which can be varied by attaching atoms or chains at particular positions of the molecule. Experience shows that in many cases, the whole group of compounds will have similar characteristics, though in different degrees and with different consequences. The dilemma then is this: if the patentee is restricted to claims upon the substances that he has used in his experiments, his rival is free to take up the next nearest in imitation. If, however, he is given a claim to the whole family of compounds, his monopoly may appear unduly wide. Authorities in different countries have reacted with greater or less caution in seeking some compromise, looking primarily at the degree of certainty with which it can be predicted that the whole class will share the discovered advantages. On a strict view, for instance, it can be insisted that either end of a range of compounds be tested, together with a representative sample of those in between. But it is difficult to reach a formula like this

[201] Requiring patents to be available in all fields of technology.
[202] But see below, further paras 5–94—5–94.
[203] See below, paras 5–23—5–25.
[204] Should he obstruct exploitation of the second invention by refusing to license his patent, a compulsory licence could be secured: see below, para.7–39.
[205] See further below, paras 7–32 et seq, 19–16.
[206] See Roberts [1994] E.I.P.R. 371; Brandi-Dohrn [1994] I.I.C. 648; Wibbelmann [1997] E.I.P.R. 515; Domeij [2001] E.I.P.R. 321; and see below para.21–16.

which seems reasonable in every case.[207] In Britain, by contrast, it has been held that it is enough, in the absence of positive proof that some members of the class do not work at all,[208] to base a claim to the class simply upon a sound prediction that all members will show the advantageous property in some degree.[209] The test finds a place in the EPO Guidelines[210]; and it has been espoused by the Supreme Court of Canada in place of an earlier, more grudging approach.[211]

4–50 Chemical patents present a number of other difficulties. With the macromolecular substances that play such a part in plastics and other chemistry, there are major obstacles to finding a sufficiently clear description for a claim.[212] There is a problem when the substance claimed has itself no use but may prove a useful intermediate in the production of something that does turn out to be valuable.[213] The continued preclusion of patents for methods of human and animal treatment poses problems which are growing with the expansion of biotechnology.[214] These are particular difficulties which can be left for later discussion. But they are symptomatic of a larger truth.

---

[207] An attempt by the German Patent Office to require this was rejected by the courts: see Nastelski (1972) 2 I.I.C. 267.

[208] Although it should be noted that inutility is no longer a distinct ground of objection to validity: see below, para.5–51.

[209] Graham J., *Olin Mathieson* case (above, n.199) at 193: see below, para.5–95 et seq.

[210] EPO Guidelines, CIII 6.2; *AgrEvo/triazoles* (T939/92) [1996] E.O.P.R. 171; below, para.5–48.

[211] *Monsanto's (Coran and Kerwood) Application* [1980] F.S.R. 50.

[212] See above, para.4–43, and see Dack and Cohen (2001) 32 I.I.C. 485.

[213] See below, para.5–54.

[214] See below, paras 5–76 et seq, Ch.21.

CHAPTER 5

VALIDITY

This chapter investigates the substantive law of validity of patents. A number of ideas introduced in the last chapter form an essential background. First, the challenges that may be made to validity, and the persons who may make them, differ for applications and granted patents. Secondly, if a patentee seeks to enforce his rights, he may be met by the defence that his patent is invalid or by a counterclaim for its revocation. Thirdly, the claims, which define the monopoly, are the starting point of various issues about validity. **5–01**

European patents must meet the criteria of validity specified in the EPC; but a national State for which a European patent is granted may not add further requirements by its own law.[1] The Patents Act 1977 accordingly adopts the EPC grounds of invalidity for UK patents whether granted by the European or the British Office.[2] But to some extent the language of the EPC is revamped, with attendant uncertainties.[3] In outline the grounds are these:

There must be an "invention" (a concept which is not defined)[4] and that invention must be patentable; that is:

---

[1] One basic limb of the so-called "maximum" approach adopted in drafting the Convention: see EPC art.138. For a comparison of interpretations of the provisions by national courts of EPC states, see Tilmann (2006) 37 I.I.C.62.

[2] PA 1977 s.72.

[3] These difficulties are, if anything, compounded by PA 1977 s.130(7): see above, para.3–58.

[4] Following the terms of TRIPS art.27(1), the EPC 2000 art.52(1) specifies that patents are available for inventions in all fields of technology. See also below, para.5–52 et seq.

(1) it must be novel (or not "anticipated");
(2) it must involve an inventive step (thus escaping the taint of "obviousness");
(3) it must be capable of industrial application; and
(4) it must not fall within any of the categories of subject-matter specifically excluded or made subject to exception.[5]

The specification must satisfy the "internal" requirement of adequate disclosure,[6] which also ensures that the claims meet a number of standards.[7]

There are certain other objections relating to the right to grant and to unallowable amendments.[8] The grounds of invalidity are formulated in general terms. Yet the issues that are hardest fought often lie at their perimeters. There remains much for the courts and other tribunals to do in determining the precise application of law to particular cases.

5–02 There is now a considerable body of case law, from national courts and even more from the EPO Boards of Appeal which interpret the provisions of the Patents Act 1977, other national legislation and the articles of the EPC from which they derive.[9] Decisions under the former British law must be treated as suggestive rather than authoritative, for they were concerned with statutory texts that were differently formulated.

An important objective of the present regime is that patents should be granted only after a more extensive examination than previously. The former British approach deliberately and rather indiscriminately set a low standard for applicants to satisfy before grant: if doubt existed about an objection it was to be resolved in the applicant's favour, full investigation being reserved for proceedings after grant.[10] We shall see that there are inherent reasons for taking a cautious approach to some objections, notably obviousness, at an early stage in the life of an invention. But a firmer hand may be applied at that stage to other questions, such as whether categories of subject-matter (computer programs, micro-organisms, etc.) fall within the system or not. For these are issues of policy and interpretation that do not depend on evidence in the particular case.[11] We shall, however, reserve consideration of them until we have dealt with novelty and obviousness.

---

[5] EPC arts 52(2)–(4), 53; PA 1977 ss.1(2)–(4), 4(2)–(3). See below, paras 5–52 et seq, 20–26—20–34; 21–06—21–13.
[6] EPC arts 83, 100(b); PA 1977 ss.14(3), 72(1)(c), below, paras 5–84—5–92.
[7] See below, paras 5–90—5–97.
[8] See above, paras 4–30—4–36.
[9] If and when the EU Patent Regulation takes effect, the European Court of Justice and the proposed Community Patent Appeal Court will also have jurisdiction.
[10] The approach stemmed from the *R. v PAT Ex p. Swift* [1962] R.P.C. 37 DC.
[11] For examples, see below, paras 5–52—5–81.

1. Novelty[12]

(1) Introduction

No system grants valid patents for inventions that are already known: that would be to encumber industry with constraints upon the use of information without any sufficient return. Accordingly, the present law requires a patented invention to be new in the sense of forming no part of the state of the art, that is it must not be found at the priority date in any "matter (whether a product, a process, information about either, or anything else) which has at any time been made available to the public (whether in the United Kingdom or elsewhere) by written or oral description, by use, or in any other way".[13] **5–03**

This concept draws no distinction between information published by the inventor and by someone unconnected with him: if the inventor were protected from prejudicing himself, he might delay his patent until it was commercially most advantageous to apply.[14]

In most cases the assessment of novelty is relatively straightforward.[15] Here are a few examples which illustrate the nature of the inquiry and point towards some of the problems requiring further discussion. **5–04**

(1) (*Van der Lely v Bamford*[16]: mechanical product.) The patentee claimed a hayraking machine in which the rake-wheels were turned not by an engine but by contact with the ground. The patent was held to have been anticipated by a photograph in a journal which showed a hayrake with this feature. (The issue was whether the photograph was clear enough to reveal the invention to a person skilled in the art. It was found to do so.)

(2) (*Fomento v Mentmore*[17]: mechanical process/product). The patentee claimed a ball-point pen in which the housing around the ball had a groove running in a ring below the equatorial plane of the ball; this produced a smooth flow of ink. One alleged anticipation (a patent specification)[18] was found to describe a method of enclosing the housing around the ball by "peining", that is by hitting the open

[12] See Rogge (1997) 28 I.I.C. 443; Crespi (1997) 28 I.I.C. 603.

[13] PA 1977 s.1(1)(a), s.2(1), (2), based upon EPC arts 52, 54. For the special problem of prior patent applications subsequently published (PA 1977 s.2(3), EPC art.54(3)), see below, paras 5–14—5–15.

[14] But see below, para.5–07.

[15] Because the standard is relatively precise, an appellate court can consider the question of novelty without first finding that the lower court has erred in principle: *Technip France's Patent* [2004] R.P.C. 46 CA.

[16] *Van der Lely v Bamfords* [1963] R.P.C. 61 HL. For anticipation in a drawing, see, e.g. *Charbonnages/Venturi* (T204/83)' [1985] E.P.O.R. 1.

[17] *Fomento v Mentmore* [1956] R.P.C. 87 CA.

[18] In which at least one plaintiff had an interest.

housing with a tool shaped like a candle-snuffer. Before there could be anticipation, however, it was necessary to show that peining would inevitably produce the desired ring-like groove in the correct position; and the earlier document, it was held, only gave instructions that "might well" produce this effect.[19]

(3) (*Opinion: Availability to the Public*[20]: chemical combination.) A chemical composition was marketed before the priority date of a patent claiming that substance. It could be analysed and reproduced by a person with the appropriate skills. The claim was therefore anticipated.

5–05 From these examples it may be seen that novelty involves an essentially factual investigation: has the same invention already been made public? There is comparatively little room for the sort of evaluation that arises where the issue is obviousness: is the step over what is already known significant enough to be called inventive? There are circumstances in which, if an anticipation cannot be shown, there is no room for an attack on the grounds of obviousness. Equally, "what is hidden may still be obvious".[21] It is therefore important to know what counts as lack of novelty. It is worth introducing some of the problems in historical and comparative terms.

(2) Disclosure through description and use

5–06 The British patent system originally treated prior use as the principal objection to the validity of a patent, the first purpose of the system being to encourage the introduction of inventions into British manufacture.[22] Even when prior publication evolved as a distinct ground of objection, prior use kept its independent status—for instance, in the principle that even a secret use was in some circumstances a ground of invalidity; and in the rule that a prior use which did not reveal the invention to the world but which involved no deliberate secrecy could found an objection under the general provision relating to novelty, rather than the more limited secret use provision.[23]

5–07 In the current law, use has lost its independent status as an objection to validity. An invention is new if it does not form part of the state of the art; and the state of the art comprises all matter made available to the public before the priority date of the invention "by written or oral description, by use or in any other way".[24] Use founds an attack on novelty if it effects a public release—which covers documentary publication but also other

[19] There was also a prior use point: below, para.5–13.
[20] (G01/92) [1993] E.P.O.R. 241 Enlarged BA.
[21] *Mobil/Friction-reducing additive* (G02/88) [1990] E.P.O.R. 73.
[22] See above, paras 3–04, 3–05.
[23] See PA 1949 s.32(1)(c), (e); Frost [1996] E.I.P.R. 18; Aüz Castro (1996) 27 I.I.C. 190; Törnroth (1997) 28 I.I.C. 800.
[24] There is no distinction between the two forms of anticipation: *Availability to the Public: Opinion G1/92* [1993] E.P.O.R. 241 Enlarged BA; *Quantel v Spaceward* [1990] R.P.C. 83.

situations. The issue is whether a skilled worker, by observation or analysis, could discover and reproduce the invention.[25] But to make batches of one chemical substance that are then mixed with others so as to be undetectable when the mixture is sold[26] would not be to "publish" the substance. Under the new law, novelty is concerned with the patent system as a source of information, not as a stimulus to use nor as protection to those who have already used the invention.[27] The prior user who does not reveal his invention is confined to a limited measure of protection against being held an infringer.[28]

While prior use was a distinct objection, it was not open to an inventor of a secret process first to use it until it became a success and then to patent it at the most advantageous moment. If he can do so, the patent system suffers as an incentive to early revelation in the very case where it ought to have greatest effect. However, the devisers of the EPC chose not to provide separately against this danger. Certainly in a system which is strictly "first to file", an inventor who intends to patent can risk delay only if he sees no serious hazard of others publishing or applying for a patent before he does. **5–08**

(3) Material available for consideration

Under both the 1949 and the 1977 Acts, for there to be an obstacle to novelty in the prior art an "enabling disclosure" must be shown. The expression captures the essence of basic authorities under the old law, notably *Hill v Evans*[29] and *General Tire v Firestone Tyre*.[30] As explained in relation to the priority of claims, it came to particular prominence in *Asahi's Application*.[31] The concept was later divided by the House of Lords, in *Synthon v SmithKline Beecham (No.2) (Paroxetine Methanesulfonate)*[32] into two distinct elements, that of disclosure and that of enablement. **5–09**

Disclosure requires information to be provided about actions which, if performed after grant of the contested patent without the patentee's authority, would virtually always infringe it. The disclosure must be complete in itself, without taking account of what a skilled worker might achieve by trial and error. Enablement calls for instructions to the person skilled in the art, but takes account of what he could find out by experiments using

[25] *Stahlwerk Becker's Patent* (1919) 36 R.P.C. 13 HL, held that to market a steel was to publish its composition, since this could be deduced by chemical analysis. See also Opinion (above, n.24).

[26] As in *Bristol Myers' (Johnson) Application* [1975] R.P.C. 127 HL.

[27] For difficulties in applying this principle, see below, para.5–20.

[28] See below, paras 6–21, 6–22.

[29] *Hill v Evans* (1862) 31 LJ(NS) 457 at 463 *per* Lord Westbury.

[30] *General Tire v Firestone Tyre* [1972] R.P.C. 457 at 485–486 CA: The last sentence has been much repeated: " The prior inventor must be clearly shown to have planted his flag at the precise destination before the patentee".

[31] *Asahi's Application* [1991] R.P.C. 485 HL.

[32] *Synthon v SmithKline Beecham (No.2) (Paroxetine Methanesulfonate)* [2006] R.P.C. 10 per Lords Hoffmann and Walker. Applied in *Apotex v Sanofi-Synthelabo* [2009] F.S.R. 5 (SC, Canada)

common general knowledge, in order to get the idea to work. The separate role of enablement as part of the concept of anticipation provides an equivalent to the sufficiency requirement placed upon a patentee to make an adequate disclosure of the invention in the patent specification.[33] In both cases of enablement the law aims to support the public interest in learning what the invention is, rather than an interest in having the invention made in the first place.[34]

In addition, the law employs broad criteria relating to time, place and form. Each element can be separately considered:

(a) *Temporal factors*

5–10 The British system has long taken the priority date of the patent as the point in time for deciding whether there has been an anticipation[35] and this continues to be the rule: there is no general grace period. Periods of grace pertaining to material published by the patentee (or deriving from him) are to be found in various systems, notably that of the United States.[36] It is difficult, above all in academic environments, to hold back researchers from openly discussing their latest results until the necessary patent applications have been made.[37] A period of six or 12 months after the priority date, during which publicising would not count, would do much to relieve this pressure.[38] The price would be that patent agents and other investigators for industry would have a more complex and costly task. They would have to monitor the research output of actual and potential rivals in greater detail in order to work out which publications would count against a patent. That is why the relative simplicity of a cut-off at the priority date continues to attract many patent professionals. The special difficulty created by applications with earlier priority, which are published only after the later priority date of another application, receives new treatment as far as British law is concerned: the earlier specification is added to the state of the art for purposes of novelty but not obviousness. To the problems that this may cause, we return subsequently.[39]

[33] For sufficiency, see below, paras 5–82—5–89.

[34] See Jacob J. [1995] R.P.C. 705 at 730; Laddie J., *University of Southampton's Applications* [2005] R.P.C. at [46]; *Availability to the Public* (G1/92) [1993] E.P.O.R. 241 at [1.4].

[35] For the present exceptions, see below, para.5–16. Under the 1949 Act no account was taken of the content of patent specifications more than 50 years old, but that limitation does not apply under the 1977 Act.

[36] See Chisum, *Patents I*, paras 3.04–3.07. Wegner, *Patent Harmonization* (1993), Ch.9. Famously, Calder and Boyers took advantage of the US grace period in securing the American patent on their invention of the basic technique for recombinant DNA technology. They were not able to obtain equivalent European patents.

[37] See European Commission, SEC (2002) 50.

[38] For the argument that the EPC should admit a grace period, above all because other countries have done so, Straus, *Grace Period and the European and International Patent Law* (2001).

[39] See below, para.5–14.

(b) *Territorial factors*

Traditionally the British system, with its emphasis on the encouragement of national industry, only looked at anticipations within the United Kingdom.[40] Other countries have taken greater account of the growing internationalism of technical knowledge. But in the various solutions adopted, there has been some tendency to distinguish between anticipations by documentary publication and by use: in some systems the former is considered upon a worldwide purview, while the latter has to take place within the territory.[41] **5–11**

The EPC and the 1977 Act pursue an uninhibited internationalism in the matter, apparently imposing no territorial constraints at all. The British Act refers specifically to material "made available to the public (whether in the United Kingdom or elsewhere)".[42] But this liberality offers temptations to the unscrupulous to produce instances of anticipation from highly obscure foreign sources. If a British court or tribunal has doubts about the genuineness of the evidence, it may find that the attacker has not sufficiently proved his case. Alternatively, it may be attracted to hold that the anticipation must have been made available to a public which includes at least some persons from British industry. Certainly on this basis material could be disregarded which, because of a legal embargo in a foreign country, could not be consulted by a British technician or research scientist; more doubtfully in the case of material which could only be obtained by such a person after laborious and expensive persistence.

(c) *Form*

In the past, prior publication of an invention has normally been found in a document, while prior use has required proof that the use has taken place. The current law admits prior matter irrespective of its form. It may be made available to the public "by written or oral description, by use or in any other way".[43] While this makes clear that the essential inquiry is the same in respect of publications and actual embodiments or uses, the very fact that in the latter category the information has to be capable of discovery by some means other than reading does pose additional considerations, to which we come below.[44] **5–12**

[40] See above, paras 3–04, 3–05.

[41] For countries which prefer this "relative" novelty, those which allow "absolute" novelty and those which adopt the "local" novelty formerly found in British law, see Baxter, *World Patent Law and Practice*, paras 4.01, 4.02.

[42] PA 1977 s.2(2). The EPC art.54(2) has nothing equivalent to the phrase in brackets.

[43] See EPO Guidelines, D V 3 1. Demonstrating in specialist training courses or on television are given as examples of "other ways".

[44] See below, para. 5–19. Arguably the obligation to keep information secret stretches to information that is acquired from another without there being any prior assumption of a confidential relationship; for which development of the breach of confidence action, see below, para.8–34.

(d) *Degree of dissemination*

5–13 Underlying the rules about place and form is a general question of degree. How far must information have been communicated, or at least put at the disposal of others, before it can be said to be available to the public, and in particular to a person skilled in the relevant art? As under the previous British law, availability to the public calls only for a minimum that is unquestionably artificial. It is enough that information about the invention (or the means of discovering it from a concrete embodiment) is put into the hands of a single person who may use it as he or she likes, free from obligations of confidence and similar duties.[45] Likewise it suffices that a document was placed in a library or other place in the United Kingdom for consultation as of right by any person with or without paying a fee.[46] If a device is used in a public place, it does not matter that no observer actually saw the details of how it worked.[47]

When a version of the invention is kept on private premises, a more discriminating examination of the alleged revelation is likely to take place. Thus where two outsiders visited a factory—one a government minister, the other a newspaper photographer—and they assumed no obligations of confidence, it was relevant to investigate what they could reasonably be supposed to have learned about the claimed invention from seeing a test mechanism which embodied it. On the balance of probabilities, it was held unlikely that they would have inspected the test unit, let alone that they would have learned how to construct a stair according to the claim. There was therefore no "making available to the public".[48] Since the evidence of what happened can by very difficult to assess in such circumstances, the EPO has been firm in insisting that proof by the person asserting the anticipation through use must be beyond reasonable doubt.[49]

---

[45] *Humpherson v Syer* (1887) 4 R.P.C. 407 at 413–414 CA; *Fomento v Mentmore* (above, n.17) at 99; *Monsanto's (Brignac) Application* [1971] R.P.C. 127; *Quantel v Spaceward* [1990] R.P.C. 83 at 127; *PLG v Ardon* [1993] F.S.R. 197 at 225–226; *Télémechanique/Power supply unit* (T482/89) [1993] E.P.O.R. 259; *Cayla/Pre-fading* (T165/96) [2002] E.P.O.R. 59. Claims that a communication was not confidential will be critically examined: *AT & T/prior publication* (T750/94) [1997] E.P.O.R. 509. Private conversations between scientists are likely to be treated as a secret: *Visx v Nidex* [1999] F.S.R. 406.

[46] PA 1949 s.101(1); PA 1977 s.130(1) "published"; *Woolard's Application* [2002] R.P.C. 19. Display on the same day anticipates; but mere proof of posting beforehand does not suffice: *IBM/Ion etching* (T534/88) [1991] E.P.O.R. 18; nor does a mere contract to publish: *Bilfinger/Sealing screen* (T842/91)[1999] E.P.O.R. 192.

[47] *Lux v Pike* [1993] R.P.C. 107 at 132–135 (field trials of prototype traffic lights made the invention part of the state of the art); *Kavanagh Balloons v Cameron Balloons* [2004] R.P.C. 5.

[48] *Folding Attic Stairs v Loft Stairs* [2009] F.S.R. 24 at [81]–[90].

[49] See e.g. *Sekisu/Shrinkable sheet* 472/92 [1998] E.P.O.R. 432; *Documotion Research/tamper-evident form* before [2009] (T354/05) [2007] E.P.O.R. 29 at [15]: "proof up to the hilt".

(e) *Matter in prior specifications*

If competitors make the same invention at much the same time (by no means an uncommon phenomenon in today's race for innovation) there is a special aspect of the principle under which the first to secure a priority date is preferred. Once the earlier applicant has his specification published, it becomes part of the state of the art. But without special provision it would not have that character in the period between securing the priority date and publication of the specification. Yet if nothing is done, "double patenting" may result, and that has long been thought unacceptable. Previously, British law sought to deal with the problem in the way that would least jeopardise the chances of the later patentee: by preventing him from also claiming protection for inventions within the claims of the earlier patent, provided that they were valid. But under the 1949 Act this process of comparing claims in order to exclude overlap bred highly recondite judicial decisions and the drafters of the EPC in the main preferred the whole contents approach.[50] **5–14**

Instead, the material in a patent specification is now given a priority date, which is determined in the same way as the priority date of a claim. Provided that it is subsequently published, it is treated as having formed part of the state of the art in the intervening period for the purpose of assessing the novelty of later inventions[51]; but not, let it be stressed, for ascertaining inventive step.[52] In applications to the British Office this applies to the contents of prior applications for the United Kingdom[53]; in the EPO to the contents of prior European applications, but only to the extent that the same states are designated in the earlier and later applications[54] (hence the European patents granted for various states may differ in content). Correspondingly, after grant of a British patent by either route, the Comptroller or court must take account of earlier applications for UK patents by either route.[55] It is not required of applications that they must mature into granted patents, a pre-condition which would conjure echoes of "prior claiming".[56]

This "whole contents" approach applies not only between rival applicants **5–15**

[50] For the debate, see the Banks Report (Cmnd.4407, 1970), Ch.10; Rogge (1997) 28 I.I.C. 794.

[51] The general tests of anticipation apply here: *Synthon v SmithKline Beecham* [2006] R.P.C. 10 H.L.

[52] PA 1977 s.2(3); EPC art.54(3). The Banks Committee had proposed the contrary (Ch.11) but this was not accepted for the EPC or the PA 1977.

[53] As far as the PA 1977 is concerned (see s.78(1), (2)), this could also include prior European applications designating the UK. A third-party "observation", however (see above, para.4–22) could provide the notification.

[54] EPC art.54(3), (4). The limitation to cases where the same States have been designated is to be removed by EPC 2000.

[55] PA 1977 ss.2(3), 78(1), (2). This is a matter for national law: see EPC art.139. PA 1977 s.73(1) gives the Comptroller special power to revoke upon his own initiative, in order to take account in particular of late information about prior European patents (UK). Under s.73(2) and (3), a British-granted patent will be revoked if a European patent (UK) for the same invention bears the same priority date.

[56] See now PA 1977, s.78(5A), inserted by CDPA 1988 Sch.5 para.22.

but also to successive applications by the same person. Hence the danger of "self-collision", which is particularly apparent in the case of mechanical inventions. In that field, one piece of research may produce a succession of broadly interrelated inventions, each of which calls for a separate application either as a matter of tactics or because of the requirement of "unity of invention".[57] Each application will need a sufficient description and this may well call for mention of the other parts of the whole concept. If the applications are not filed on the same day, it is only too easy for the first to describe matter for which the second seeks protection. It was just this hazard that the old "prior claiming" approach avoided; but by making the earlier material part of the art only for novelty and not for obviousness (until it is actually published) the danger is to some extent reduced.

(f) Special exclusions

5–16 A patentee faces the risk of anticipation from two sources: from independent inventors and from those whose information comes from the same inventive source as his own. In a modern business organisation risks of the latter kind may arise because its research staff are eager for recognition, because an employee has turned disloyal, or because an outsider to whom the invention was revealed in confidence breaks his undertaking. Against such hazards as these, the 1977 Act affords some measure of protection, but it is more limited than under the old law. For instance, inventors are no longer free to describe the invention in a paper to a learned society.[58] So it is crucial to keep their natural desire to share ideas with colleagues under rein until all relevant priority dates have been secured.[59] Now that academic researchers are driven increasingly to contemplate the commercial prospects of their work, these severe requirements cause considerable aggravation. The case for a general grace period of, say, six months continues to be hotly debated.[60]

In two circumstances, according to the British Act, a disclosure does not count in determining novelty for a period of six months after it is made[61]:

(1) if the information was obtained unlawfully or in breach of confidence; or if it was disclosed in breach of confidence[62];

---

[57] See above, para.4–15.

[58] As in *Palmaz's European Patents* [1999] R.P.C. 47 at 83. Cf. PA 1949 s.51(2)(d) and note the other exceptions in ss.50, 51.

[59] Because of the equivalent position under the EPC, PA 1977 s.6, provides no effective protection for the applicant who is not able to maintain expected priority and publishes in the interim: above, para.4–12.

[60] Above, para.5–10.

[61] The six months run between disclosure and the actual filing date, not the priority date: *University Patents* (G03/98) [2001] E.P.O.R. 249 Enlarged BA.

[62] PA 1973 s.2(4)(a), (b). This abbreviates highly elaborate provisions, covering various possible situations. On the burden of proof, see *Dunlop's Application* [1979] R.P.C. 523 CA.

(2) if the disclosure resulted from display by the inventor at a prescribed "international exhibition" and the applicant files proper notification of this.[63] Only exhibitions to educate the public (not trade fairs) are within the exception and they must last between three and 26 weeks and must occur no more than once in every 20 years.[64]

These exceptions do not follow the equivalent EPC provisions,[65] apparently because "it will not do"[66] to have English judges wrestle with the Convention's vague language ("evident abuse in relation to the applicant or his legal predecessor"). One consequent difference is that the British provisions appear to exempt the disclosure of an invention even if it has also been made by an inventor who is quite independent of the applicant or his predecessor, and the information comes from this separate source.

(4) Relations between anticipation and invention in suit

(a) *The comparison*

Novelty involves a comparison between the invention, in any of its embodiments, and the thing that is revealed by the prior publication or use. The question is whether anything within the claims has already been published or used. Or, standing the question on its head: would the earlier thing fall within the later claims for purposes of infringement (assuming that other conditions for infringement were fulfilled)?[67] For instance, in *Van der Lely v Bamfords*,[68] if a competitor had made the photographed hayrake in the United Kingdom after publication of the patent application, would it fall within the scope of any claim? If it would, then the photograph was an anticipation. Given the new emphasis on the purposive construction of claims, the result may be a correspondingly enlarged scope for anticipation.[69] Thus a claim to a windsurfer of the familiar modern type of board included as one element, "a pair of arcuate booms", by which was meant the wishbone-shaped grip held by the surfer. An earlier model made by a young **5–17**

---

[63] PA 1977 s.2(4)(c). The exhibition has to be one within the Convention on International Exhibitions 1928: see PA 1977 s.130(1), (2). For the notification required, see PA 1977 Rules r.5; EPC Rules r.23.
[64] Unlike the more generous provisions in the previous law: see Ency. P.L., para.5–122; [1979] OJ EPO 159; Vitoria [1978] October E.I.P.R. 29; note the attempt to read in an additional "common law" exception for reasonable public experimentation: *Prout v British Gas* [1992] F.S.R. 428, dismissed by Jacob [1993] E.I.P.R. 312 at 315; and see *Lux v Pike* [1993] R.P.C. 107.
[65] EPC art.55; Paterson, paras 9–22—9–30.
[66] J. C. H. Ellis, in Vitoria (ed.) *The Patents Act 1977*, p.23.
[67] See, e.g. *Harwood v GNR* (1865) 11 H.L.C. 654 at 681; *General Tire v Firestone Tyre* [1972] R.P.C. 457 at 486, 496 CA; *Synthon v Smithkline Beecham* [2006] R.P.C. 10 at [22].
[68] See above, para.5–04, example (1).
[69] See above, para.4–41.

amateur and used publicly, had a pair of straight booms. Since in use these deformed flexibly into arcs, they were held to anticipate.[70]

(b) *The anticipation: clarity and sufficiency of a document*

5–18 Not infrequently a question of anticipation centres on whether the prior document does sufficiently disclose the later invention. This may be so when the alleged anticipation is "unintentional"[71]; but the issue is by no means confined to such cases. For instance, in *Fomento v Mentmore*,[72] actual examples were put in evidence of pens produced according to the allegedly anticipatory instructions. Virtually all showed the crucial deformation of the housing of the ball that constituted the claimed invention. Yet the Court of Appeal still found, on the evidence as a whole, that, while this "might well" occur from following the instructions, yet it would not do so "necessarily", or "inevitably", or "in 99 cases out of a hundred".[73] The earlier description has, accordingly, to be of acts or things which must (not may) fall within the claim. If they do, it is then irrelevant that a misleading description of their scientific nature is given. Thus the description of a new variant of a pharmaceutical anti-depressant was in this sense disclosed, even though it was said to have different crystalline forms, when it had only one. The question whether the skilled worker was not enabled to make the invention is a separate issue which may depend on the general knowledge and understanding of that notional person.[74]

This then is the test: if the claim is for a method of use or a process, the anticipation must give "clear and unmistakeable directions to do what the patentee claims to have invented".[75] If it is for an article, apparatus or substance, the qualified reader must be enabled "at once to perceive and

[70] *Windsurfing International v Tabur Marine* [1985] R.P.C. 59 CA. See also *Dow Chemical v Spence Bryson* [1982] F.S.R. 397 CA.

[71] This has been called an invention "by happenstance". "The earlier proposal when carried out just happened to fall within the later claim, even though the earlier inventor had some different idea." *Inhale Therapeutic Systems v Quadrant Healthcare* [2002] R.P.C. 21; *SmithKline Beecham's Patent (No.2)* [2003] R.P.C. 33.

[72] See above, para.5–04, example (2).

[73] A statement, later shown to be incorrect, that something would not work can scarcely be an anticipation: see *Nestle's Application* [1970] R.P.C. 88; but a statement that something has been tried and did not work is more doubtful; a statement that something works for a purpose when it does not anticipate a claim to the thing, even though it is found to have a different advantage: *Shell's Patent* [1960] R.P.C. 35; but see below, paras 5–26, 5–27.

[74] *Synthon v SmithKline Beecham* [2006] R.P.C. 10 HL; Sharples and Curley [2006] E.I.P.R. 308; see further below, paras 5–58, 5–86.

[75] Parker J., *Flour Oxidising v Carr* (1908) 25 R.P.C. 428 at 457. Subsequently much cited, e.g. Lord Dunedin, *Metropolitan Vickers v British Thomson-Houston* (1927) 45 R.P.C. 1 at 22–23; *Beecham Group's (Amoxycillin) Application* [1980] R.P.C. 261; *Evans Medical's Patent* [1998] R.P.C. 517 at 560–561 CA. "A signpost, however clear, upon the road to the patentee's invention will not suffice. The prior inventor must be clearly shown to have planted his flag at the precise destination before the patentee": Sachs L.J., *General Tire v Firestone Tyre* [1972] R.P.C. 457 at 486.

understand and be able practically to apply the discovery without the necessity of making further experiments".[76] If instructions are given for carrying out a chemical process with such precision that a particular substance must result, there cannot thereafter be a claim for that substance; it makes no difference that the later work establishes more information about its structure or other characteristics.[77] Instructions or descriptions may, however, anticipate even if they fall short of the detailed description that would be needed to support a valid patent.[78] But—and here obviousness must be distinguished—it is not permissible to read two documents together if one does not positively cross-refer to the other.[79]

In the case of a publication describing a new substance but not how to make it, if common general knowledge in the industry would not permit a skilled person to select or secure the starting material or make intermediate products, there has been no sufficient description of the invention and accordingly there is no anticipation. To satisfy these criteria, there must be an enabling disclosure in the sense required by the House of Lords in *Asahi KK's Application*.[80] Not least in its biotechnological context, this case has imposed a significant constraint on attempts at pre-emptive patenting where analysis has run ahead of practical production.

(c) *The anticipation: appreciation of significance of an embodiment*

For a prior use of the invention to constitute anticipation, it is only **5–19**
necessary for another person (not under any obligation of confidence)[81] to be able to secure, from the thing or the process, the knowledge necessary to make or perform it himself. But in what sense must it have been possible to carry out the necessary observation or analysis? Must there have been some indicator which would induce a skilled worker to undertake the analysis? Would his analysis have revealed the advantage which the subsequent patentee has demonstrated?

The Enlarged Board of Appeal (EPO) requires that a skilled person must have been able to discover the composition or the internal structure of a

---

[76] Lord Westbury, *Hill v Evans* (1862) 4 De G. F. & J. 288 at 300; cited in *Van der Lely v Bamfords* [1963] R.P.C. 61 at 71 HL.

[77] *Bayer/Diastereomers* (T12/81) [1982] E.P.O.R B308; *Mobil Oil/Friction-reducing additive* (G02/88) [1990] E.P.O.R. 73; cf. *Du Pont/Copolymers* (T124/87) [1989] E.P.O.R. 33.

[78] Lord Watson, *King Brown v Anglo American Brush* (1892) 9 R.P.C. 313 at 320; cited *Ransburg v Aerostyle* [1968] R.P.C. 287 at 299 HL.

[79] See below, para.5–40. For an example of what suffices in the law of novelty, *Actelion/glucosylceramile* (T1391/05) [2009] E.P.O.R. 6.

[80] *Asahi KK's Application* [1991] R.P.C. 485 H.L; see above, para.4–12—a test deriving from *ICI/Pyridine herbicides* (T206/83) [1986] E.P.O.R. 232 and *Collaborative/Preprorennin* (T81/87) [1990] E.P.O.R. 361. Applied subsequently, e.g. in *Lux v Pike* [1993] R.P.C. 107 and *Merrell Dow v Norton* (below n.88); and see *Genentech Human t-PA* (T923/92) [1996] E.P.O.R. 275; *Synthon v SmithKline Beecham* [2006] R.P.C. 10.

[81] As to which, see above, para.5–13.

product and also to reproduce it "without undue burden".[82] A particular DNA sequence could, in principle, be made public if deposited in an appropriate gene bank; but it is not enough to show that it was there in a "library" of fragments and could only be detected by probing tens of thousands of samples.[83]

As to the likelihood or otherwise of the analysis being carried out, some EPO decisions required that there must be sufficient reason to conduct the analysis, including consideration of whether it was financially worthwhile. However, the Enlarged Board has rejected these.[84] It has preferred the relatively mechanical and straightforward approach to the question, long followed in the United Kingdom,[85] which inquires only into the feasibility and not the likelihood of the investigation. As a consequence, some anticipations have an entirely notional character: but straightforward advice can be given on the matter.

As to knowledge of advantages, we reach difficult and shifting terrain which will take some considerable exploration. At the outset, let us note that the former law took a plain attitude: if a thing or a process had been used or described publicly, then it could not be claimed again, even when an important new purpose was found for it. A way would have to be sought for claiming something that was physically different.

In *Molins v Industrial Machinery*[86] the patent concerned a way of ensuring an even distribution of tobacco in cigarettes formed on a high-speed machine: the trick lay in giving the tobacco a preliminary push in the same direction as the paper in which it would be wrapped. Bonsack's much earlier specification, dealing with a low-speed machine, described a device which would give this movement. Accordingly it anticipated, although it was not directed to solving the patentee's problem.

There may well be a way of respecting this principle while allowing an amended claim which will give adequate protection to the later discovered advantage. In the *Molins* case, an amendment restricted the claim to high-speed machines, leaving a process which was not obvious in light of Bonsack's patent.

5–20 If the rule on anticipation were otherwise, there could be further patents for discovering how something which is already known to work actually does so. The result would be a form of double patenting, and if both patents were obtained by the same applicant it would become an unacceptable

[82] *Availability to the Public* (G01/92) [1993] E.P.O.R. 241; applied in *Merrell Dow v Norton* (below n.88). "Without undue burden" relates only to the ability to reproduce the subject-matter: *Packard/Supersolve* [1995] OJ EPO 755.

[83] *Biogen/Alpha-interferons* (T301/87) [1990] E.P.O.R. 190.

[84] Opinion, above, n.77; not following, e.g. *Hoechst/polyvinyl ester dispersion* (T93/89) [1992] E.P.O.R. 155; *Heidelberger Drueckmaschinen/Microchip* (T461/88) [1993] E.P.O.R. 529.

[85] See above, para.5–07.

[86] *Molins v Industrial Machinery* (1938) 55 R.P.C. 31 CA.

means of "evergreening" protection.[87] In *Merrell Dow v Norton*,[88] the House of Lords refused to contemplate such a prospect. The plaintiff had already benefited considerably from a patented antihistamine drug, terfenadine. Before expiry of the first patent, the plaintiff discovered that in the liver terfenadine was metabolised to produce an acid metabolite of terfenadine. This was a previously unidentified, chemically distinct, substance which was largely responsible for the drug's effectiveness in the treatment of asthmatic disorders. By patenting the acid metabolite, the plaintiff extended its overall period of protection substantially.[89] The first patent, which clearly disclosed use of the substance claimed, terfenadine, in order to treat the conditions also covered in the acid metabolite patent, was held to anticipate the second; its claim would include the metabolite as produced in the liver, and the steps necessary to produce the metabolite had been described in the first patent even though the nature of the chemical reaction had not then been identified.[90] The House of Lords would not rule out a claim to the metabolite, when made outside the human body, because that would be physically different from the state of the art.[91] Equally, it distinguished the case where a new advantage is discovered for a known thing, a matter on which the EPO has recently shown a novel generosity. This we must reserve for later consideration.[92]

In *Merrell Dow*, the House refused to find anticipation from actual administration of the drug to patients, as distinct from publishing the specification which disclosed doing so. It is perhaps hard to see why doing and describing the same thing should be differently treated in the law of novelty. The House, however, considered that it must give some scope to the 1977 change which prevented account any longer being taken of prior unwitting use or prior secret use. In *Evans Medical's Patent*[93] Laddie J. was at pains to stress the special application of doctrine which arose on the facts of *Merrell Dow*: the person taking terfenadine was not put in a position to conduct an analysis which would reveal the substance subsequently patented—the metabolite. The actual giving of terfenadine itself to a patient did not provide the means of discovering the invention claimed in the second patent. The case was therefore different from one in which an article capable of analysis in order to discover the invention was placed in a third party's

[87] As to which, see Rothstein J., *Apotex v Sanofi Synthelabo* [2009] F.S.R. 5 (SC, Canada) at [98–100].

[88] *Merrell Dow v Norton* [1996] R.P.C. 76; Karet [1996] E.I.P.R. 97.

[89] A competitor marketing terfenadine was alleged to be infringing "indirectly" by supplying "essential means" for making the acid metabolite (see below, para.6–17.

[90] Both patents had to be for the pharmaceuticals, since use claims could have been excluded as methods of medical treatment (see below, paras 5–65 et seq.). It made no difference whether the two patents were held by the same or by quite separate patentees. Had there only been use, and not disclosure, of terfenadine, by itself this would not have constituted anticipation, and the user could have been stopped from doing what he had already done.

[91] The patent was later amended to this effect.

[92] See below, paras 5–24, 5–25.

[93] *Evans Medical's Patent* [1998] R.P.C. 517 at 573–568.

hands in non-confidential circumstances. The latter continues to be a form of anticipation.

(5) Things and their uses

(a) *New thing with an advantage*

5–21 It has long been a basic assumption of our own and many other patent systems that the discovery of a use for a previously unknown thing or substance may found claims to the thing or substance itself, whatever it is subsequently used for.[94] As justification it has been asserted that, if product per se claims could only be enforced in relation to uses known at the time of the patent application, much of the incentive to invest in original research would disappear.[95]

How far this is true is guesswork. There are many who are obliged by the existence of prior art to settle for mere use claims. It is pure conjecture that they are less willing to undertake research because they will not enjoy the benefits of later, unsuspected inventions.

The present approach is nonetheless acceptable for its simplicity, so long as one assumes that for the most part first discoveries represent the most important breakthroughs. About this, however, there are now serious doubts. In medical and other biotechnology, the initial description and discovery of use for a gene or some smaller sequence of DNA is comparatively straightforward. The real difficulties lie in subsequent work on the stimulation and control of externally created genes and their operation in the circumstances of actual treatment. Some sources, particularly in Italy, have suggested that the European patent system should adopt a more discriminating approach either to the drafting or the interpretation of claims to the first use of a substance or thing.[96] The issue deserves most careful monitoring in the coming years.

The next paragraphs consider the ways in which consequential inventions can in general be claimed. At this juncture, we should note that the field of pharmaceuticals forms a special case, which we will deal with after we have taken account of the special exclusionary principle, which places outside the system claims to methods of medical treatment of humans and animals.[97]

---

[94] Indeed, if a phrase of the type "for use as ..." is added this will be interpreted as meaning that the thing is suitable for that use; but the exclusive right extends to production, distribution or use for any purpose.

[95] Armitage and Ellis [1990] E.I.P.R. 119. Drawing on the Kitch metaphor (above, para.3–53, n.46), they add: "It is rather like asking someone investing in a gold mine to limit his return to what he knows about at the time of the investment and to forgo any additional benefit if the mine later struck it rich." Certainly he should have the rewards from gold-findings, even if unexpectedly large. But also from diamonds, if they turn up unbeknownst? At least, beware metaphor.

[96] See Marsico [1990] E.I.P.R. 397; cf. Armitage and Ellis (above, n.95); Jacob, Paterson (1996) 27 I.I.C. 170 at 179.

[97] Below, paras 5–65 et seq.

(b) *New use of an old thing*

The principle, that once a thing has been made public no one may have a patent for it, must be understood as a ground rule to which a number of qualifications are admitted. These certainly go some way towards giving patentees a monopoly commensurate with the novelty of their invention. But not in every case; for the system does not aim to reward merely for creative effort. **5–22**

Many of the difficulties in the basic rules arise from the fact that an inventor may discover a new use for something already known. He may, for instance, discover that a well-known chemical can be added to water in a boiler so as to reduce scaling. To allow him to claim the chemical as a substance would give him a monopoly over all its uses, not just in boilers; this would be more than he is entitled to. But if no one has found a use for the chemical in boilers before, he is entitled to claim "a method for preventing scale in boilers in which ...". Such a claim limits his monopoly to what he has discovered: only those who use the chemical in this way, or who induce its use, will infringe.[98]

(c) *Patents for selected improvements or variants*

In certain types of case, mainly concerned with chemical substances and mixtures,[99] special treatment has long been accorded to "selection patents".[100] Where a class of things is already known from a general description in the prior art, it has been held that a claim may be made to specific substances, mixtures or things within that class, provided that these latter are shown to have an advantage over the class as a whole. That approach applies equally to a claim to a sub-class of the whole.[101] The rules turned on a crucial presupposition. This was that, in order to provide a patent (particularly one for chemical substances) with breadth enough to prevent competitors from simply choosing some related alternative to that on which the patentee had actually worked, it was necessary to permit claims to all the members of a class, or a list of related substances, on which only some had been specifically shown to have an advantage. This was allowed whenever it could be predicted that all members of the class would have a similar medical or other technical effect in some degree. It then became an infringement for an unauthorised third party to make or use any of the things included in the claim. At the same time, if no evidence was **5–23**

[98] The exclusion of methods of medical treatment (see n.97), limits the possibility of using use claims in pharmaceutical and veterinary patents. That is why special techniques developed to expand their scope: below, esp. paras 5–33, 5–67.

[99] Only occasionally is selection possible in a mechanical case.

[100] The EPO, sometimes with knotty convolution, has accepted a similar approach: Paterson, paras 10–55—10–57; Spangenberg (1997) 28 I.I.C. 808.

[101] It was never firmly settled whether the selection patent rules applied to the assessment of obviousness, as well as novelty, though was authority for the view that they applied only to novelty: *Ranbaxy UK v Warner-Lambert* [2006] F.S.R. 14; upheld in [2007] R.P.C. 44.

provided in the first patent that a substance or sub-class of substances later selected for a second patent actually had the advantage claimed for it in the second patent, then that second patent, restricted to its selection, would be treated as novel.

This "selection patent" rule was given classical formulation by Maugham J. in *IG Farbenindustrie's Patent,* which required that the new advantage should be present in all the class selected and that it should be peculiar to the class.[102] In *Du Pont's (Witesiepe) Application*[103] the House of Lords gave its authority to these rules on selection patents in a case arising under the Patents Act 1949. The patent application in suit claimed as one ingredient for a plastic a chemical that improved its hardening quality. An earlier application had disclosed a plastic with an enhanced capacity for absorbing dyes in which the equivalent chemical was named as one of nine substances from which the maker would need to choose. While the same chemical was named in the hardening plastic application, it was not said in the dye-absorption patent to have been used in actual experimentation and so was simply a paper proposal. To make it the centrepiece of the later application in which it was treated as inventive for a different purpose was taken by the House of Lords to amount to a selection which conferred novelty on that invention.[104] The essence of this aspect of selections is followed equally by the EPO Boards of Appeal, which refer to "selection inventions".[105] According to *Hemosol/haemoglobin complexes*,[106] "it is required that an effect can be shown for the selected subject-matter which is not present outside the selection". The same qualification had been introduced as a qualification into the selection patent rules in the United Kingdom, but was sometimes doubted afterwards.[107]

It may well be that British courts will in future move away from their traditional selection patent rules,[108] because in any case they are absorbing aspects of them into modern notions of what explanations in a specification can justify claims for new substances and other things (as distinct from claims to methods of making them); and, by way of balance, for determining what information falls to be treated as giving rise to an anticipation or a

---

102 (1930) 47 R.P.C. 289 at 321. Subsequent decisions cast some doubt on how far the two conditions must be strictly satisfied.

103 *Du Pont's (Wibesiepe) Application* [1983] F.S.R. 303 HL.

104 The decision may be viewed as a precursor of the House of Lords decision on the requirement of disclosure in *Asahi's Applcn* [1991] R.P.C. 485 above, para.5–09.

105 See the discussion of the case law in *Singer/Stauder* I, art.54 at [68]–[82].

106 *Hemesol/haemoglobin complexes* (T445/07) [2009] E.P.O.R. 2 at [25].

107 The selection patent rules were applied by the CA in one decision under the PA 1977, *Mentor v Hollister* [1993] R.P.C. 7.

108 The view that the mainly pre-1977 Act selection rules should now be treated as history, rather than the living law, was put resiliently by Jacob L.J. in *Dr Reddy's Laboratories v Eli Lilly* [2009] EWCA Civ 1362 at [35–39], and rather more circumspectly by Lord Neuberger MR at [95, 104]. See Cole (2010) 39 CIPA 105.

finding of obviousness. In each case, what is coming to be required is a plausible foundation, based on technological knowledge, and not an unsupported guess at what could prove to be a practical result.[109] This distinction arises not only in deciding what is an anticipation or an obvious precursor in relation to novelty and inventive step, but also in respect of industrial applicability and adequate disclosure. Plausible foundation can be used to support the applicant/patentee's case laid out in his specification; equally its lack may sustain the opponent/revoker's case in relation to the prior art or the inadequacies of the description.

Whether a seismic shift in the balance of patent law is about to occur is hard to predict. It has become reasonably clear in European law that a claim to a class does not amount to an anticipation of its individual members when a new or improved use for them is patented later. If such thinking is carried far it could be used to challenge the assumption that the initial revealer of a use for a large class is entitled to a patent for all its member instances on the basis of a prediction of similar qualities. To the consequences of that in respect of infringement we will return in the next chapter, remarking here only that the parity between what is an anticipation before the priority date and what is infringement after the patent grant may have to be revised.[110]

(d) *New Advantage of Old Thing*

5–24

In *Mobil Oil/Friction-reducing additive*,[111] the Enlarged Board of Appeal upheld a claim to the use of a specified lubricant for the reduction of friction in engines, even though it has previously been used in engines as a rust inhibitor. Likewise a claim was allowed for a given compound as a regulator of plant growth, when previously it had been used as an insectide[112] In both cases, the physical acts within the claims would be exactly the same as the steps taken during the previous use. The circumstances thus differ from the new use of an old thing, where the earlier use can continue unobstructed by the later patent because it is not within the new claim. The EBA considered the distinction nonetheless to be artificial and so one that ought no longer to

[109] In relation to sufficient basis for a product claim, see esp. *Conor Medsystems v Angiotech*, below, para.5–000.

[110] For this parity, see, e.g. Lord Hoffmann in *Synthon v SmithKline Beecham* [2006] R.P.C. 10 at [22].

[111] (G02/88): [1990] OJ EPO 93; G 6/88: *Bayer/Plant growth regulating agent* [1990] OJ EPO 114; Paterson, paras 9–72—9–77; Doble [1996] E.I.P.R. 511.

[112] G6/88: *Bayer/Plant growth regulating agent* [1990] OJ EPO 114. Both this decision and that in *Mobil Oil* were severely criticised by Floyd [1996] E.I.P.R. 480; and some doubt about the step was expressed by Lord Hoffmann in *Merrell Dow v Norton Baker* [1995] R.P.C. 76. However in *Actavis UK v Merck* [2008] EWCA Civ 444, Jacob L.J., speaking for the Court, gave strong support to *Mobil Oil,* suggesting that it made only for "Byzantine logic" to treat *Mobil* claims as bad, while maintaining that those for second medical uses were good: see at [30]; and below, para.5–67.

be drawn. Subsequent decisions of the EPO have at least stressed that there must be a new purpose and not merely the demonstration of a novel technical effect.[113] This seems in line with the concern of the House of Lords in *Merrell Dow v Norton*[114] that the provision of further information about the function of an invention should not become the basis for re-patenting.

5–25 Being solely a granting office, the EPO does not have to decide what activities will constitute direct or indirect infringement of a claim to use a thing for a new purpose, as distinct from use by a new physical act. To anticipate the issue on that front: if the scope of the right can be limited so as to cover only the making, using and commercial supply of the thing (or its essential elements) specifically for the new purpose, then the freedom of other users can be to some degree assured.[115]

Even so—and despite the virtues of comity within the ranks of EPC countries—national courts may yet consider that the Enlarged Board is wrong to introduce distinction of purpose into the law of novelty in the way that it has. As we have seen, the House of Lords indignantly rejected what looked like an attempt to obtain a second patent monopoly on a drug for having found out more about how it worked.[116] That may be a special and distinguishable case, but it shows the difficulties of the way ahead. Some of these the EPO is having to face for itself.

Two components were known for use in an agent which would sequester the ions of certain elements. It was not permissible to reclaim them for this same use purely on the basis of showing that they were together more effective than the use of either component by itself.[117]

A substance was first described as a food additive for flavour control and as a thickening agent; it was subsequently claimed as an emulsion stabiliser. If this last effect had previously been hidden, it could, according to the Technical Board of Appeal, be found novel.[118]

(6) Exclusion by amendment

5–26

Where one of the alternatives covered by a claim is anticipated by a previous description, it may be possible to save the rest if the particular case is disclaimed by amendment. Such an amendment, giving what is often referred to as an "n–1" claim, is available as an exceptional remedy. It will

---

[113] e.g. *Dow chemical/sequestering agent* (T958/90) [1994] E.P.O.R. 1; *American Cyanamid/melamine derivatives* (T297/93) [1999] E.P.O.R. 88; applied in *Actavis v Janssen Pharmaceutica* [2009] F.S.R. 35

[114] Above, para.5–20, n.88.

[115] See above, para.4–40 and below, para.6–20.

[116] See above, n.80.

[117] *Dow/Sequestering agent* (T958/90) [1994] E.P.O.R. 1.

[118] *Mars II/Glucomannan* (T112/92) [1994] E.P.O.R. 249 (although "hidden", the invention was nonetheless found obvious).

[1] *Beloit/Digester* (T37/96) [2002] E.P.O.R. 308; *Eastman Kodak/Dispersed Filter Dye* (T917/94) [2002] E.P.O.R. 341; *Beecham/Toothbrush* (T725/00) [2005] E.P.O.R. 2; *Rohm & Haas/Poliner* (T500/00) [2005] E.P.O.R. 3.

not be allowed in order to save subject matter that is in any case obvious.[119] In most cases, if one alternative has been described, others are likely to be held obvious. If the earlier description covered the later only by chance and not as a result of an effort to solve the same problem, the objection of obviousness will not arise: hence the amendments allowed in such examples as *Molins*. A disclaimer may be allowable in order to restore novelty by delimiting a claim against the state of the art; or in order to restore novelty by delimiting a claim against an accidental anticipation, such an anticipation which is unrelated to and remote from the claimed invention. The person skilled in the art would never have taken it into consideration when making the invention necessary to restore novelty or remove non-technical subject matter.[120]

2. Inventive Step

(1) Introduction

Patents are constantly sought for inventions which vary from the known **5–27**
only in some more or less minor detail. For instance, when a new kind of material is put on the market, claims will likely follow which attempt to patent the making of well-known articles out of the material (plastics, for instance, provided a welter of examples).[121] Likewise, the alleged invention may be said to consist purely in putting two known articles together to make a single product.[122] Sometimes at the outset the applicant will know that he is seeking protection for a thing that is not greatly different from what is known already. Sometimes he is pushed into that position by the unearthing of prior art which he did not appreciate. The difficulty is increased by the need to mark out broad "fence-post" claims, since there must be an inventive step in each of them.[123]

It is in order to draw a line excluding some claims of this kind that many patent systems have come to require the presence of an inventive step.[124] In the EPC and the 1977 Act, an inventive step[125] is considered to be present if, having regard to the state of the art, the invention is not obvious to a person skilled in the art.[126] The state of the art is the same broad conception that

[120] *Genetic Systems/Disclaimer* (G1/03) [2004] E.P.O.R. 33 (Enl BA); for an instance of disclaimer refused, *University of British Columbia/NSAID for dementia* (T739/01) [2006] E.P.O.R. 25.

[121] See below, para.5–47.

[122] *Williams v Nye* (1890) 7 R.P.C. 62 CA; *Sabaf v MFI Furniture* [2005] R.P.C. 10 HL.

[123] *Procter & Gamble/Liabase* (T848/04) [2006] E.P.O.R. 27.

[124] See above, para.3–10.

[125] Which is a requisite of "patentability": EPC art.52(1); PA 1977 s.1(1). See generally, Beier (1986) 17 I.I.C. 301.

[126] EPC art.56; PA 1977 s.3.

operates in assessing novelty,[127] save that no account is taken of any prior specifications subsequently published.

5–28 The evaluative issue that this introduces is the largest single cause of uncertainty about the validity of patents and hence a frequent inflator of the scale and length of patent disputes. The assessment it calls for is often labelled a jury question[128]; which means, amongst other things, that firm rules (such as define the factual comparison called for in determining novelty) are replaced by a vaguer, qualitative yardstick. Kitchin J.'s stress upon the evaluative nature of the exercise has recently been much quoted:

> "The question of obviousness must be considered on the facts of each case. The court must consider the weight to be attached to any particular factor in the light of all the relevant circumstances. These may include such matters as the motive to find a solution to the problem the patent addresses, the number and extent of the possible avenues of research, the effort involved in pursuing them and the expectation of success."[129]

Measuring inventive step involves the four "stages" identified by Oliver L.J. in *Windsurfing International v Tabur Marine*[130] and subsequently re-ordered by Jacob L.J. in *Pozzoli v BDMO*.[131] In this newer version they are as follows:

(1) (a) Identify the notional "person skilled in the art"; and (b) identify the relevant common general knowledge of that person.
(2) Identify the inventive concept of the claim in question or, if that cannot readily be done, construe it.
(3) Identify what, if any, differences exist between the matter cited as forming part of the "state of the art" and the inventive concept of the claim or the claim as construed.
(4) Viewed without any knowledge of the alleged invention as claimed, do those differences constitute steps which would have been obvious to the person skilled in the art or do they require any degree of invention?

---

[127] See above, para.5–03. The exclusions (PA 1977 s.2(4); EPC art.55) probably apply to inventive step as well.
[128] e.g. Jenkins L.J., *Allmänna Elektriska v Burntisland Shipbuilding* (1952) 69 R.P.C. 63 at 69; *Johns Manville's Patent* [1967] R.P.C. 179 at 491, 496 CA.
[129] *Generics (UK) v Lundbeck* [2007] R.P.C. 32 at [72].
[130] *Windsurfing International v Tabur Marine* [1985] R.P.C. 59. Oliver L.J.'s approach became the foundation of all subsequent discussions of obviousness under PA 1977 s.3.
[131] *Pozzoli v BDMO* [2007] F.S.R. 37 at [23].

In seeking to describe in more detail how this strategy is to be applied, we must first take a number of introductory points.[132] With them in position, we can then turn to the essence of the inquiry.[133]

(a) *Terminology*

It has become customary to treat "inventive subject-matter" and "non-obviousness" as largely synonymous with "inventive step". But cases occur where what the patentee is suggesting is pointless (at least at the time). If there is no reason for it, the step is scarcely an obvious one to take: yet if nothing useful is being added to the sum of human knowledge there ought to be no inventive step.[134] **5–29**

(b) *Paraphrases*

The *Polozzi* steps are essentially a procedural strategy; they do not attempt any verbal paraphrase of the concept of "obviousness" or "inventive step". It is currently accepted that verbal variations of these expressions generate heat, rather than light.[135] In particular, phrases which suggest that the addition to knowledge has only to be slight—such as "very plain" or "lacking a scintilla of invention"—are no longer considered helpful. The same is true of the question, does the patent disclose something sufficiently inventive to deserve the grant of a monopoly?[136] **5–30**

But paraphrase is difficult to keep entirely at bay. The Court of Appeal has looked to see if the inventor has produced "a novel insight or discovery".[137] This has been linked with another phrase which has some tendency to raise the standard of an inventive step: would a person versed in the art assess the likelihood of success as sufficient to warrant actual trial?[138] Was it, in this limited sense, "obvious to try"? In the EPO, where legal tests are devised in order to instruct a large staff of examiners across the whole range of technology, the question is: would the skilled worker be likely to use it, as distinct from could he have done so (the "would ... could" test)?[139] That test has the merit of keeping some content in the concept of inventive step, so long as it is confined (as it is during the application stage) to considering the technical advance in question. But it has been objected in the

[132] See below, paras 5–31—5–35.

[133] See below, paras 5–36—5–50.

[134] cf. Lord Shaw, *British Thomson-Houston v Duram* (1918) 35 R.P.C. 161 at 184; Jenkins J., *May & Baker v Ciba* (1948) 65 R.P.C. 255 at 281; Lloyd-Jacob J., *Anxionnaz v Rolls-Royce* [1967] R.P.C. 419 at 467. In *Conor Medsystems v Angiotech* [2009] R.P.C. 28, Lord Hoffmann talks of such cases as "obvious": see below, para.5–50.

[135] *Mölnlycke v Procter & Gamble* [1994] R.P.C. 49 CA at 112; *PLG Research v Ardon* [1995] R.P.C. 236.

[136] *Mölnlycke* (above, n.135) at 112.

[137] *Biogen v Medeva* [1995] F.S.R. 4 at 56.

[138] Lord Diplock, *Johns-Manville's Patent* [1967] R.P.C. 479 at 494 (at the same time warning against the dangers of general paraphrases; and see at 496); Lord Reid, *Technograph v Mills & Rockley* [1972] R.P.C. 346 at 356; *Genentech/Human t-PA* (T923/92) [1996] E.P.O.R. 275.

[139] See Paterson, para.10–30; *Toshiba/IC Card* (T273/02) [2005] E.P.O.R.(52).

United Kingdom that "would" directs attention to commercial, rather than technical, considerations, and that can be important after the patent grant, especially when searching for legal grounds that will justify an appeal.[140]

It will be apparent from this how difficult it is to establish a consistent line on the degree of severity which is to be brought to the testing of inventive step. Amongst the countries now collaborating in the EPC, a particularly stringent test of "inventiveness" seems previously to have prevailed in the Netherlands and Switzerland; while in Germany talk of a "level of invention", together with the separate protection of utility models (a form of petty patent) that in theory at least need not reach the same inventive level, creates an impression that there too rather more has been required.[141] The EPO has indicated that it aims for a middle level (roughly equivalent to that of German practice), rather than the particularly favourable attitude towards applicants that characterised British pre-grant procedure under the 1949 Act.[142]

(c) *Objective test*

5–31 The comparison called for is between two objective conditions: the state of the art and what the patentee claims to have invented. It is not an inquiry into how easy or difficult it was for him personally to take the step. The patent system makes no attempt to exclude protection for accidental, lucky or sudden inventions.[143] Equally it is of no relevance to consider whether the person responsible thought that he had made an invention.[144] He may well have worked out independently what was public knowledge already. Nonetheless it is relevant to the ultimate assessment to know how the alleged inventor reached his result and accordingly discovery may be ordered of notes and other documents concerning his research. This may assist the defendant in cross-examining the inventor and other witnesses, in obtaining expert evidence of what a skilled man would or should have done, and in comparing what was actually done with the state of the art at the priority date.[145]

(d) *Advance in the art*

5–32 There is no distinct requirement in the new law, any more than in the old, that an invention should show "technical progress" over the prior art, that

---

[140] *Pharmacia v Merck* [2002] R.P.C. 775 CA, paras 122–128. See further, below, paras 5–47, 5–48.

[141] On the nuances that may attach to EPC art.56 in its various linguistic versions, see Pagenberg (1974) 5 I.I.C. 157.

[142] See above, para.5–02, below, para.5–35.

[143] *Crane v Price* (1842) 1 W.P.C. 393 at 411. See further below, paras 5–40, 5–41.

[144] Fletcher Moulton L.J., *British United Shoe Manufacturers v Fussell* (1908) 25 R.P.C. 631 at 652; *Allmänna Elektriska v Burntisland* (1952) 69 R.P.C. 63 at 70.

[145] *SKM v Wagner Spraytech* [1982] R.P.C. 497 CA; *Hoechst Celanese v BP Chemicals* [1997] F.S.R. 547.

is, that it should in some practical sense be a better way of doing things.[146] However, considerations of technical advance, as of commercial value, become points of reference in the search for an inventive step. For if the idea is a real step forward in technique, yet it is an obvious one, why was it not made before?[147] And in the case of "selection" from a larger class, the particular advantage which the specification must describe, and which alone avoids the objection of anticipation, must also be one that is not obvious: the selection must be more than a mere verification that particular properties would be found in the sub-group.[148]

"Technical progress", which was previously a requirement of German patent law and which has been actively debated in the United States, in fact involves two sorts of consideration: substantive (whether there is any advance at all, whether it is so large that there must be invention), and formal (whether the specification must describe the advance). Accordingly it is an issue to which we turn again when discussing sufficiency of description.[149]

(e) *New advantage and new use*

The discovery of a new advantage in a thing already known does not in general save it from objection.[150] So equally a thing that it is obvious to make for one purpose should not become the less so just because a further, unexpected, advantage is subsequently discovered.[151]A patentee claimed a self-pulling type of corkscrew in which the screw element had a non-stick coating of the kind commonly found on saucepans. The coating produced a surprising improvement in extracting the cork. Because it was predictable that the coating would help to insert the screw, it was obvious to add it even before the effect on extraction of the cork was appreciated; whether there was any commercial merit in doing so was not relevant.[152] The additional advantage could only become the subject of a valid patent if it could be claimed as a new use or as a selection.[153] In this way, the patentee could be confined to a monopoly proportionate to his real invention. **5–33**

[146] But cf. Warrington L.J.: "a step which is useful and not merely one which results in some immaterial and futile improvement": *Teste v Coombes* (1923) 41 R.P.C. 88 at 104 CA.

[147] See, e.g. *British Vacuum v LSWR* (1912) 29 R.P.C. 309 at 328–330, 333. In *Moulinage de Chavonoz's Application* [1961] R.P.C. 279 at 295, Lloyd Jacob J. distinguishes between the perception of the advance in the art and its evaluation in terms of inventive ingenuity. The former, being "susceptible of reasonably precise expression" is more readily open to review on appeal.

[148] For the rules concerning selection patents, see above, paras 5–23—5–25. They need to be considered not only in relation to obviousness but also in relation to sufficient disclosure: see next note.

[149] See below, paras 5–90—5–94.

[150] See also above, paras 5–22—5–28.

[151] *Degussa-Huls v Copmptroller-General* [2005] R.P.C. 29.

[152] *Hallen v Brabantia* [1991] R.P.C. 195 CA; but cf. *Cleveland Graphite v Glacier Metal* (1930) 67 R.P.C. 149 HL.

[153] A new use claim was not open in the "corkscrew" case; equally the patent had not been drafted as a selection: [1991] R.P.C. 195 at 217–218.

(f) *Perception of problem*

5–34 The inventive step may lie in seeing that a particular solution to a problem should be adopted: it does not have to be found in the technical means that are then employed.[154] Consider, for instance:

> "the problem of indicating to the driver of a motor vehicle at night the line of the road ahead by using the light from the vehicle itself. As soon as the problem is stated in this form the technical solution, *viz.* the provision of reflective markings along the road surface, appears simple and obvious."[155]

(g) *Onus of proof*

5–35 Since obviousness has become a matter for patent office examiners to judge upon the material arising from the search (and their own general knowledge), much is likely to turn on the onus and quantum of proof employed during the examination stage. The past practice of the British Office and tribunals was to resolve doubts about an inventive step in the applicant's favour,[156] because, although these proceedings had to arise out of the opposition of an outside party, the evidence was not tested as thoroughly as it would be in court, where oral witnesses would be examined as a matter of course.[157] In the new law this procedural difference remains in essence, even when the legal tests have become the same.

(2) Assessing obviousness[158]

(a) *The notional skilled worker*

5–36 The tribunal assessing obviousness is expected to trace out the mental processes of a determinedly prosaic individual—one who, according to British case law, has the following characteristics:[159]

(1) He is a skilled technician who is well acquainted with workshop techniques. "Technician" may probably be contrasted both with the

[154] *Hickton's Patent Syndicate v Patents & Machine Improvements* (1909) 26 R.P.C. 339 CA (inventive to see that a process of "shogging", already used in net machines, could be used in lace machines for the purpose, there important, of equalising the bobbin threads).

[155] EPO Guidelines, C IV 9.4(i). The whole chapter is full of useful examples.

[156] See above, para.5–02. "At this stage in the lifetime of an application there exists in addition to the two verdicts, so to speak, of obviousness and non-obviousness, an interim stage of non-proven": Lloyd-Jacob J. *Bakelite's Application* [1958] R.P.C. 152 at 160.

[157] *General Electric's Applications* [1964] R.P.C. 413 at 452–453, treating the differently worded standards of obviousness before and after grant (PA 1949 ss.14(1)(e), 32(1)(f)) as merely reflecting the difference of approach necessitated by the different procedures. The 1977 Act no longer draws this verbal distinction but that is not the governing consideration.

[158] See generally, Asquith (1978) 8 CIPA 19; Reid, pp.34–48.

[159] See Lord Reid, *Technograph v Mills & Rockley* [1972] R.P.C. 346 at 355; followed in *General Tire v Firestone* [1972] R.P.C. 457 at 504.

highly-qualified research staff who in industry today are set to solve many of the more complex technical problems; and also with the "ordinary workmen" who frequented the earlier case law.

(2) He will read the relevant literature carefully,[160] showing an unlimited capacity to assimilate it but none in making even a "scintilla" of invention from it.[161] Such indefatigable but uninspired individuals do not wittingly give evidence themselves; for the most part, tribunals are left to make their own assessment after hearing what cleverer people have to say.[162]

(3) Where research is normally conducted by a team—as typically today in much pharmaceutical and biotechnological work—a notional group will replace a single individual as the court's starting-point.[163] Where it is obvious to call in special expertise, the notional skilled workman will have it.[164]

(b) *The uninventive technician's knowledge*

Like novelty, obviousness is judged by the state of the art, excluding, it must **5–37** be supposed, the same material published in breach of confidence and at international exhibitions.[165] Accordingly, the notional technician will be taken to have in mind, first, the common general knowledge of his art at the priority date and, secondly whatever he would learn from the existing literature when seeking an answer to the problem at issue. Frequently a case of obviousness is built up by referring to specific documents (such as patent specifications, learned articles, and items in the general press) and to specific instances of use; and generally these belong to the second category. Common general knowledge (which may be shown from such sources as standard texts and use throughout an industry)[166] is then used to explain

[160] See below, paras 5–37—5–42.

[161] He bears considerable resemblance to the ordinary skilled worker by whose powers of comprehension the adequacy of disclosure is tested: see below, para.5–44. But it has been doubted whether, in determining obviousness, his powers of perception must be regarded as quite so limited: *Genentech v Wellcome Foundation* [1989] R.P.C. 147 per Mustill L.J., at 280.

[162] Jacob L.J.'s recent characterisation of the unimaginative skilled worker as a "nerd . . . but not a complete android" has not found universal acceptance: *Technip France's Patent* [2004] R.P.C. 46 at [6–15]; cf. Pill L.J., para.135.

[163] *Boehringer Mannheim v Genzyme* [1993] R.P.C. 716 at 727.

[164] *Fives-Cail Babcock/Conveyor cleaner* (T32/81) [1982] E.P.O.R. B377; *Jalon/Luminescent security fibres* (T422/93) [1999] E.P.O.R. 486; cf. *Richardson-Vick's Patent* [1997] R.P.C. 888 CA.

[165] This is not made explicit in the relevant provisions; see above, para.5–16.

[166] Common general knowledge is what is generally known and regarded as a good basis for further action by the bulk of those who are engaged in the particular art: Luxmoore J., *British Acoustic Films v Nettlefold* (1936) 53 R.P.C. 221 at 250, as modified in *General Tire v Firestone* (above n.51); and see *Beloit v Valmet* [1997] R.P.C. 489 CA; *Buhler v Satake* [1997] R.P.C. 232; *Union Carbide v BP Chemicals* [1998] R.P.C. 1; *Raychem's Patent* [1998] R.P.C. 31; *Wheatley v Drillsafe* [2001] R.P.C. 7 CA.

why it would be obvious to take the patentee's step from the specific sources that have been cited.[167]

5–38 In one instance,[168] the patent was for a steel tip to a shoe heel so made that the bottom of the heel fitted the tip, thus solving the problem of aligning the two parts. At the time, this seemed inventive to shoe repairers. But shoe manufacturers were already using very similar heels, which were thus part of the trade's general knowledge. In addition, some of these heels were illustrated in cited documents. The attack might well have succeeded even if one or other class of evidence had not been available. Note, however, that the general knowledge arose from actual use of the interlinking tips. It is much more difficult to show that a "mere paper proposal" is part of the ordinary technician's standard mental equipment. Even as specific citations, unworked proposals—mere "laboratory toys"—are treated with suspicion.[169] Occasionally they may form the basis for a finding of obviousness, perhaps because they come very close to being an anticipation.[170] But they demand answers to the standard questions: Are they addressed to the same problem which the patentee solved? If so, why did they not lead to earlier discovery of his solution?

5–39 Now that patent offices regularly examine the question of an inventive step, it is important to step back from the applicant's view of what he has invented. The specification is likely to have been drafted in light of the prior art known to the applicant. The question to be addressed, however, is whether objectively there is an inventive step over the prior art produced by the search. The EPO has accordingly favoured a "problem-and-solution" approach in which the examiners, having identified the closest prior art, formulate the technical problem to be solved in reaching the claimed invention and then judge whether that solution is obvious.[171] The viewpoint must be forward from the prior art, not backward from the invention, otherwise the judgment will be infected by hindsight. As with the "would/could" test, "problem/solution" is a guideline of the type needed to secure a certain homogeneity of approach among a large body of examiners. British criticisms of it tend to relate not to the processing of the application but to attacks on the granted UK patent where there is heavy concentration on the

[167] Common general knowledge is not pleaded: *Holliday v Heppenstall* (1889) 6 R.P.C. 320; *British Thomson-Houston v Stonebridge* (1916) 33 R.P.C. 166. Since the state of the art is not limited to what is known and used in the UK, common general knowledge should be similarly judged: cf. *Lucas v Chloride Batteries* [1979] F.S.R. 322 Fed.Ct. (Aust.).

[168] *Colburn v Ward* (1950) 67 R.P.C. 73. See also *Fives-Cail Babcock's Application* (T32/81) [1982] E.P.O.R. B377: if a problem concerning a suitable substitute material for making scrapers would have been put to a materials specialist, the issue must be judged from his perspective.

[169] Basic scientific principles may attract rather different treatment: *Sonotone v Multitone* (below, n.194).

[170] See below, paras 5–44, 5–45.

[171] *Bayer/Carbonless Copying Paper* (T1/80) [1982] E.P.O.R. 250; *BASF/Metal Refining* (T24/81) [1982] E.P.O.R. 354; Paterson, paras 10–04 et seq.; Szabo (1995) 26 I.I.C. 457; but cf. *Alcan* [1996] OJ EPO 32; Cole [1998] E.I.P.R. 214 at 267.

particular instance at stake. Then there is likely to be lengthy investigation into what the notional skilled worker could be expected to know at the priority date and so into common general knowledge and the role alongside it of particular citations. Evidence from experts has to be judged in the round. Hence the fear of over-emphasis that can follow from picking out just one citation for comparison.[172]

In this connection, Buckley L.J drew a useful distinction.[173] There will be the situation where the uninventive but skilled man has a particular problem or need in mind, in which case the testing carried out by him may amount to no more than obvious verification. On the other hand it could be inventive if the result is unexpected in kind rather than degree. Equally there will be the case where the skilled man has no particular problem or need in mind. Then, selecting a particular course for further research which provides unexpected results is likely to be inventive, for he is then on "a voyage of discovery" rather than "a mere exercise of ingenuity". In *Beecham Group's (Amoxycillin) Application*,[174] Buckley and Browne L.JJ. were prepared to classify the case before them as falling within the second of these categories, since though the prior art indicated that work should be done on six further substances in the search for better semi-synthetic penicillins. Nonetheless the applicant was entitled to a patent for one of them, upon making the anticipated discovery of its outstanding ability for absorption into the blood-stream.[175]

(c) *"Mosaicing"*

Obviousness is judged by viewing the invention as a whole[176] against the state of the art as a whole.[177] Cited documents do not have to be treated in isolation (as normally they would be when assessing novelty). They may be read in the light of one another—but only if it is obvious to do so.[178] Even so, James L.J. disparagingly called this making a "mosaic of extracts",[179] **5–40**

[172] For a sceptical assessment of 'problem/solution' and the 'would/could' test, see Jacob L.J., *Actavis v Novartis* [2010] EWCA Civ 82 at [25–50].

[173] *Beecham* [1980] R.P.C. 261 at 291; and see *Pfizer/Sertraline* (T158/96) [1999] E.P.O.R. 286.

[174] *Beecham Group's (Amoxycillin) Application* [1980] R.P.C. 261; and similarly in New Zealand: [1982] F.S.R. 218.

[175] Contrast the assessments of later Courts of Appeal in the *Genentech* and *Biogen* cases: below, para.5–50.

[176] A combination should not be picked apart into its components: Lord Romer, *Non-Drip v Strangers* (1943) 60 R.P.C. 135 at 145 HL; *Technip France's Patent* [2004] R.P.C. 46 CA.

[177] Lord Simonds, *Martin v Millwood* [1956] R.P.C. 125 at 133–134; *Illinois Tool v Autobars* [1974] R.P.C. 337.

[178] "... a mosaic which can be put together by an unimaginative man with no inventive capacity": Lord Reid, *Technograph v Mills & Rockley* [1972] R.P.C. 346 at 355; and see *GE/Polycarbonate compound* (T184/90) [1997] E.P.O.R. 341.

[179] *Von Heyden v Neustadt* (1880) 50 L.J. Ch. 126 at 128; and see Fletcher Moulton L.J., *British Westinghouse v Braulik* (1910) 27 R.P.C. 209 at 230. In the EPO, where there tends to be less reliance on common general knowledge, there is greater willingness to read documents together. Sometimes this is done in order to show a trend pointing away from the invention: see, e.g. *BASF* (n.58, above); *Solva/Olefins* [1985] OJ EPO 166; *Britax* (T142/84) [1987] E.P.O.R. 148.

and it remains difficult to build up such a case. Again doubts surface which can be hard to refute. Why, if it is obvious to combine two pieces of knowledge, has no one done so before? Is the case not one where the precursors were able to think out everything except the crucial bridge from failure to success? It is in this context that some judges have been particularly hard on paper proposals.[180]

(d) *Obscure sources: publication*

5–41 Obviousness calls for inquiry into whether the invention in suit could have been straightforwardly derived from what was already known. Accordingly, difficult problems are set by the fact that a prior publication or use would have been hard for the average skilled worker to find, or understand.

On the difficulties of unearthing sources: on the one hand it is possible to treat the state of the art as being the same for obviousness as it is for novelty (save for the special case of subsequently published specifications)—that is, anything made freely available to even a single person will be treated as published.[181] On the other hand it is possible to limit the state of the art for obviousness to whatever a diligent searcher would have uncovered.

In the case law on the 1949 Act each approach had its adherents, Lord Diplock emerging as protagonist of the former, Lord Reid of the latter.[182] The former approach had the merit of not attributing different meanings to the same statutory formula.[183] It also eliminates one dimension of evaluative judgment—a dimension which it may be particularly difficult for patent office examiners to handle on a regular basis. The latter approach aims to make the inquiry into the activities of the unimaginative technician somewhat more realistic; but it may be doubted whether, even on its own terms, it helps much. For the diligent searcher still has to be treated as having found some things that in reality would have been unlikely to have reached him by the priority date: for instance a description in a patent specification published only a few days before[184]; or, given the definition of "the state of the art", a use which has occurred only in a remote place. There seems little

---

[180] cf. *Gratwick* (1972) 88 L.Q.R. 349; Blanco White (1973) 89 L.Q.R. 16. But in *Allmänna Elektriska v Burntisland* (1952) 69 R.P.C. 63 at 68–69, the Court of Appeal refused to hold that there could never be a mosaic of documents, as distinct from actual uses; and proceeded (surprisingly) to read together descriptions different in date and language.

[181] See above, para.5–13.

[182] *Technograph v Mills & Rockley* [1972] R.P.C. 346 at 355, 361. In the Court of Appeal [1969] R.P.C. 395 at 408, Sachs L.J. even suggested that the searcher might confine his reading of prior specifications to the claims and perhaps the drawings; Lord Diplock specifically disapproved this and certainly Lord Reid did not go so far. See also *General Tire v Firestone* [1972] R.P.C. 457 at 499 CA; *ICI's (Pointer) Application* [1977] F.S.R. 434.

[183] i.e. previously "known or used ... in the United Kingdom"; now "the state of the art", as defined.

[184] As in *Du Pont's (Holland) Application* [1971] R.P.C. 7.

point in striving to decide what revelations are so exceedingly remote that they should be discounted.[185]

(e) *Obscure sources: comprehension*

In *Woven Plastics v British Ropes*, it was accepted by counsel that utility model specifications, available only in Japanese and apparently never worked, were to be treated as known. Harman L.J. regretted that such "recondite" publications should have to be brought into account.[186] In the new world of supra-national patenting, however, the notional technician presumably has acquired, at least passively, the gift of tongues. **5–42**

Language difficulties aside, the notional technician's reading of the literature will be "careful".[187] If after this it appears that a document expresses its ideas obscurely, it is unlikely that obvious inferences are to be drawn from it. But there is the further case where, although (with hindsight, particularly) a highly suggestive reference can be found in a prior document, it is for some reason masked, perhaps by the abundance of other documentation, or by prevailing opinion that other avenues of inquiry would be much more hopeful. These are factors which have weighed against a finding of obviousness.[188] Thus, even if it is proper to treat the technician as having read everything in the state of the art,[189] these further considerations may modify the effect of particular documents.

(3) The basic comparison

We may now return to the crux of the issue: was it for practical purposes obvious to the appropriate skilled technician, armed with all the specific information and general knowledge deemed relevant, that he could or should do what the patent proposes?[190] Part of the answer may depend on the proximity of the idea to the prior art, part on the extent to which the **5–43**

[185] Consider, for instance, the prior patent specification that has been inadequately indexed. In *Asea's Application* [1978] F.S.R. 115, this was held to be no reason for disregarding it when assessing obviousness. See also *Beecham/Pharmaceutical composition* (T69/94) [2000] E.P.O.R. 179 para.5.

[186] [1970] F.S.R. 47 at 48; and Widgery L.J. said that it went "beyond the bounds of reason" (at 58).

[187] See *Johns Manville* [1967] R.P.C. 479 and *Technograph* [1972] R.P.C. 346. It will, however, be by a person "oriented towards practicalities" who may only see narrower implications than would an inventor: *Boehringer/Diagnostic Agent* (T99/85) [1987] E.P.O.R. 337.

[188] See, e.g. Whitford J., *ICI's (Pointer) Application* [1977] F.S.R. 434 at 454.

[189] i.e. accepting Lord Diplock's view (above, n.182), cf. Whitford J. (previous note) who, despite a nod in Lord Diplock's direction, appears in substance to favour Lord Reid's approach.

[190] This derives from the "Cripps question", first formulated by Sir Strafford Cripps (as counsel) in *Sharpe & Dohme v Boots* (1928) 45 R.P.C. 153 at 173 CA, and reformulated in subsequent judgments (above, para.5–28). The question does not allow for two cases: (1) where it was allegedly obvious to do the thing for a different purpose (see above, para.5–35); (2) where at the date of the prior art, what was proposed in it had allegedly no usefulness at all (as in *Killick v Pye* [1958] R.P.C. 366 CA). See further, Ency. P.L., para.5–213.

idea is a technical or a commercial success. Each of these factors deserves exploration.

(a) *Proximity to the prior art*

5–44 Novelty and inventive step are different questions. Even so, the fact that an idea escapes being anticipated only by the shortest remove will often jeopardise the chances of its being found inventive. Indeed, if the claimed invention is a "mere collocation"—where two known devices are to be placed side-by-side without any working interrelationship—it will be more likely to be treated as a claim to discrete things separately anticipated.[191] The traditional example of such a case is the "sausage-machine patent": a claim to a known cutting-machine and a known filling-machine placed in juxtaposition.[192] Another example is a pill containing two known therapeutic substances which have no interactive or heightened effect when taken together.[193]

5–45 Beyond this point, "near anticipations" have to be considered for inventive step.[194] They may well fail the test, being discounted under one of the following axioms:

(1) There can be no patent for the analogous use of a thing or process; or, as it is sometimes put, for the mere new use of an old thing. For instance, it was held unpatentable to coat boot eyelets with celluloid when this was already done to hooks and studs[195]; or to keep drinks hot or cold in vacuum flasks when they had already been used for liquids in laboratories.[196]

(2) There can be no patent for the mere application of a known principle to a use or subject-matter admittedly within its scope. Thus, there was no invention in applying a basic principle of electrical amplification to bone-conducting hearing aids, even though this had not previously been suggested in the considerable period since the principle's first formulation.[197]

---

191 *Sabaf v MFI Furniture* [2005] R.P.C. 10 HL.

192 *Williams v Nye* (1890) 7 R.P.C. 62: in fact there was just enough interrelation of parts for the CA to deal with the question as one of inventive step. See also, e.g. *Abbott Laboratories/Controlled release formulation* (T453/01) [2005] E.P.O.R. 30.

193 *Prendergast's Applcn* [2000] R.P.C. 446 (reducing trauma symptoms from military service in war);*Ancare NZ's Patent* [2002] R.P.C. (8) 136 JC (curing tapeworm in sheep); cf. also *Beecham Group's (Amoxycillin) Application* [1980] R.P.C. 261 (selected substance not anticipated (or obvious) when claimed as a pharmaceutical composition).

194 A typical example is *Seller's Application* [1970] R.P.C. 103: toy bells—the new version differing from its predecessors only in a minor detail of construction which could amount only to a theoretical scientific advantage bearing no practical relationship to the purpose for which the invention was intended.

195 *Riekmann v Thierry* (1897) 14 R.P.C. 105 HL.

196 *Thermos v Isola* (1910) 27 R.P.C. 388.

197 *Sonotone v Multitone* (1955) 72 R.P.C. 131, CA; but cf. *BASF/Triazole derivates* (T231/85) [1989] E.P.O.R. 2934.

(3) There can be no patent merely for verifying previous predictions. Where it was already known that polyesters for electrical insulation could be made from reagents that were members of a chemical series, it was not inventive to demonstrate that satisfactory results ensued from substituting other members of the same series.[198] The particular choice "would sooner or later inevitably have attracted attention" and no unexpected result was demonstrated which might have justified a selection. Likewise in genetic engineering: where the substance to be made is known through its occurrence in the human body, and the relevant procedures of recombinant DNA technology are also known, there is nothing inventive in working them through, even though this involves considerable labour by specialists in a new field, and specific knowledge is procured in the course of the work. The person or team which first produces a successful result has only won a race down an established track to a known goal.[199]

These should be regarded today as no more than ways of stating emphatically that no inventive step has been taken. Like most such aphorisms, they have their counter-propositions—for use in cases that are considered to fall on the other side of the evaluative line. Thus, a use is not a mere analogy, or the mere application of a principle, if it calls for some ingenuity to overcome a practical difficulty in the adaptation or application.[200] For instance, to adapt a suction pump for the purpose of supplying petrol in an engine from fuel tank to carburettor was held to involve more than merely putting a well-known thing to a new use.[201] Likewise, a patent covers more than mere verification if others have been able to do everything except take the last crucial step. **5–46**

(b) *Obvious to try: chemical and biotechnological inventions*

The test, "was it obvious to try?" the claimed invention, may be invoked by tribunals in many situations where pre-existing information falls only a little short of what is claimed to be inventive.[202] However, in its turn it demands an assessment of how compelling the case for investigation must seem, and on what grounds. There must be an expectation of achieving a good result, and not merely a hope of success.[203] In the search for novel pharmaceuticals, a breakthrough with a new class of drugs, by working on one or a few of the **5–47**

[198] *General Electric's Application* [1964] R.P.C. 413 at 436 CA.

[199] *Genentech v Wellcome Foundation* [1989] R.P.C. 147 CA.

[200] See especially Lindley L.J., *Gadd v Mayor of Manchester* (1892) 9 R.P.C. 516 at 524; cf. *Lister's Patent* [1966] R.P.C. 30 at 35–37 DC; *Mutoh's Application* [1984] R.P.C. 85.

[201] [1956] R.P.C. 125 HL.

[202] For its acceptance in the EPO, see Paterson, *The European Patent System* 2nd edn (2001) para.12–42a.

[203] *Lilly Icos v Pfizer* [2002] F.S.R. 54 at [57] CA. The EPO applies the same test: e.g. *Schako Metallwarenfabrick/air-conditioning nozzles* (T196/93); *Monsanto/chimeric genes* (T387/94).

large range within the class, may make further investigation a relatively straightforward choice of one out of a number of laborious paths.[204]

At least in some circumstances it may be equally obvious to try them all. Laddie J. took such a view in respect of an industry (aerosol production) where whatever research there was took simple trial-and-error paths branching off from known techniques.[205] That is likely to be so with technology that can be characterised as mere workshop variants,[206] but the test is not confined to such cases.[207] If there was nothing to mark out the line of research actually pursued by the patentee as the path to follow first, a case of inventive step may well be sustained. Thus Graham J. asked:

> "Would the notional research group at the relevant date, in all the circumstances ... directly be led as a matter of course to try [the particular alternative selected by the patentee] in the expectation that it might well produce a useful alternative to or better drug than [the previously known substance] or a body useful for any other purpose?"[208]

In any case the test is relevant only where those in the art have a particular problem in mind.[209] A finding of obviousness can arise whether or not there is a reason to take the step from the prior art.[210] If it is obvious to try a thing for other reasons, there need be no super-added requirement that there should be some expectation of success.[211]

5–48 The median thus struck proved an acceptable dividing line in the pharmaceutical industry as it developed in the post-1945 decades. As applied to biotechnological work, however, the test has proved much more controversial. The work of microbiologists, geneticists and cell biologists has advanced the manipulative techniques of biotechnology in a series of remarkable leaps. Yet after each bound it has been possible to apply the new technique to all sorts of subject-matter without more than a degree of persistence and luck. Where patents are sought on successful results of such work, English courts have adopted a sceptical attitude towards claims of an inventive step. They have taken the view that, once the desired objective is

[204] Note Lord Diplock's willingness to accord patents for the "mere exercise of proficiency and practice" in laborious and costly business of isolating and adapting microorganisms for therapeutic ends, because of the need to give some security to the investment involved: *American Cyanamid (Dann's) Patent* [1971] R.P.C. 147 at 241.

[205] *Brugger v Medicaid* [1996] R.P.C. 635 at 661; and see Pumfrey J., *Monsanto v Merck* [2000] R.P.C. 709 at [139].

[206] *Hoechst Celanese v BP Chemicals* [1997] F.S.R. 547; *Unilin v Berry Floor* [2004] F.S.R. 14.

[207] *Pharmacia v Merck* [2002] R.P.C. 41 at [123–124].

[208] Graham J., *Olin Mathieson v Biorex* [1970] R.P.C. 157 at 187; and see *American Cyanamid v Ethicon* [1979] R.P.C. 215 at 266–267. "A mere speculation on the lines of 'You will find out something more and something may turn up' does not exclude an inventive step": *St Gobain v Fusion Provida* [2005] EWCA Civ 117.

[209] *Beecham's (Amoxycillin) Application* [1980] R.P.C. 261 at 290.

[210] *Pharmacia v Merck* [2002] R.P.C. 41 at [124]

[211] *Glaxo Group's Patent* [2004] R.P.C. 43.

known, and standard techniques are applied to test whether a particular route will reach it, it is merely a commercial decision whether to take the chance of success. Mustill L.J. likened the choice to a bet on a race.[212] Later, however, Lord Hoffmann contemplated the possibility that there could be invention in such research by attempting something which a man less skilled in the art might have regarded as obvious, but which the expert would have thought so beset by obstacles as to be not worth trying.[213]

In *Conor Medsystems v Angiotech*,[214] the House of Lords tackled a problem which arises when the patentee's description of his invention in the specification as at the priority date contains no account of why it works and offers no experimental evidence to show that it does work. The claim was to a stent (a well-known piece of surgical piping) coated with taxol—by that date a known substance of value in chemotherapy against cancer. However, the taxol-coated stent was a novel product. Stents are inserted at the end of an operation to widen an artery in order to keep it open. The object of the taxol coating is then to stop the growth of new tissue around the stent which would otherwise narrow its effect ("restenosis"). The lower courts considered that there was no inventive step where a patent merely asserted that a new product, such as the coated stent, would produce a beneficial medical result (later this was shown to be the case with the stent and the device became a considerable success). In order to conclude that there was no inventive step these courts characterised the patent as disclosing as its inventive step the proposal to test the device to see if it worked. The consequence, said Lord Hoffmann in the House of Lords, was to replace the claimed invention, which was to the coated stent, with a "vague paraphrase based on the extent of [the patentee's] disclosure".[215] The test of obviousness did not function in this way but had to be judged by reference to what was actually claimed. If a hypothesis turns out to work (as this one did), no explanation was required and no medical proof had to be adduced by way of example.

What the inventor must provide, but the ordinary skilled man must not already know, or be able to work out, from the state of the art at the priority date, is information which makes it *plausible* to expect that the invention will work for the purpose described in the specification. Only then can claims be allowed for the novel end-product—in *Angiotech* the taxol-coated stent. In that case, the inventors had carried out an assay which, in the House of Lords' view of the scientific evidence, pointed strongly towards taxol being *the* stent-coating to use against restenosis; but that result was not known to

212 *Genentech's Patent* [1989] R.P.C. 147 at 281.

213 *Biogen v Medeva* [1997] R.P.C. 1: in the event, he assumed an inventive step and found against validity for lack of disclosure: see below, para.5–94.

214 [2008] R.P.C. 28; and see *Dyson Technology v Samsung Gwangju* [2009] F.S.R. 15.

215 *Dyson* at [19]. Lord Hoffmann then repudiated the approach of Pumfrey J. at first instance which led to a finding of obviousness if a skilled man would test or screen taxol without any expectation of success—an approach characterised as "oxymoronic".

others seeking to solve the problem.[216] If the evidence of plausibility had not been present, the specification would have lacked any contribution to human knowledge that would show that it involved an inventive step. Merely tentative speculation is not enough. The House of Lords thus defined the degree of sufficient research progress that will entitle one competitor to gain protection for an important invention still in need of further testing. In doing so, much reliance was placed upon decisions of EPO tribunals that have insisted upon this principle in other circumstances. Thus *AgrEvo/Triazoles*[217] addressed the recurrent problem of allowing a whole class of chemical substances to be claimed, when one member of the class, itself novel and inventive, had been shown to have a particular property. The claim to the class could be permitted only when there was evidence—for instance from scientists able to predict—that all members of the class would have the same property in some measure.[218] In *AgrEvo* the compound on which experiments had been conducted showed it to be an effective herbicide. Because there was no evidence to suggest that this quality would also be present in other members of the class, the claim to the class as a whole was rejected. Likewise in *Johns Hopkins/GDF-9 activity*,[219] a claim was disallowed to a specific DNA sequence which the applicant was testing to see if it coded for a protein to deal with growth deficiency. The specification could offer only speculation about the potential use of the sequence. The decision was important for its insistence that this lack of explanation could not be made good from later positive research results.[220] If that were possible the issue of inventive step could alter over time and with it the question of validity. All three cases indicate that for the future what is claimed by the patentee about the likely successful development of a substance into a useful product will be more carefully examined for a plausible basis than has perhaps been the case in the past.[221] Once the patentee is found to satisfy that requirement, assessment of whether by the priority date it was obvious to try his claimed invention turns on whether there was a reasonable expectation of success from that notional trial.[222]

---

[216] Their attempt to do so on other evidence failed to convince the Lords.

[217] (T939/92) [1996] E.P.O.R. 171.

[218] For the emergence of this standard in UK and EPC law, see above, para.4–49; below, para.5–95. Note Jacob L.J.'s and Neuberger M.R.'s doubts about the reality of proving such predictions: *Dr Reddy's Laboratories v Eli Lilly*, above, n.108.

[219] (T1329/04).

[220] See also *Labatorios Almirall v Boehringer Ingelheim* [2009] F.S.R. 12.

[221] Cf. the doubts about the old British approach to broad class claims and to selections from earlier classes, expressed by Neuberger M.R. and Jacob L.J. in *Dr. Reddy's Laboratories v Eli Lilly* (above, n.108). By implication these suggest that patentees have been too generously treated in the claims that have been allowed in the past.

[222] Lord Hoffmann [2008] R.P.C. 28 at [42–43], accepting this standard formula as the view of Jacob L.J. below ([2007] EWCA Civ 5): "The obvious to try test really only works where it is more or less self-evident that what is being tested ought to work" (and see his earlier judgment in *St Gobain v Fusion Provida* [2005] EWCA Civ 177). This view of the test aimed to prevent inventive step from becoming the ready-wrecker of a great many patents.

(c) *Technical advantage and commercial success*

Patents that provoke litigation concern successful ideas—novelties which apparently generate substantial demand because of their technical superiority or their propensity to cut costs. Where an idea is proving to attract business, it impels the question, why was so desirable a thing not discovered and introduced before? Indeed in such circumstances, if the solution is disarmingly simple, this tends to confirm its inventive character.[223] **5–49**

Commercial success can help to demonstrate inventive character only if the invention is the cause of the success. There may well be other explanations: in *Martin v Millwood* the success of the patentee's ball-point pens was found to turn not upon the patented nib construction but upon the discovery of an adequate ink reservoir, which was not the subject of the patent[224]; in *Parkes v Crocker* the patentee's clip device became a sudden success some 11 years after the patent grant because all the railway companies agreed to adopt it and more than a million were then sold.[225]

Because other causes may exist, courts have said that they will take account of commercial success only if the need for the patentee's invention has long been felt, "so that men's minds were likely to have been engaged upon a mode of remedying" the pre-existing defect. The vigour with which Lord Herschell makes this point in *Longbottom v Shaw*[226] would suggest that the person attacking validity is not obliged to show some other explanation of the patentee's commercial success so long as the latter has not clearly demonstrated the "long-felt want" to which his invention is the answer.[227]

Such caution continues to be much in the mind of today's courts. Primary evidence on the issue of inventive step comes from properly qualified experts[228]: **5–50**

> "who will say whether or not in their opinions the relevant step would have been obvious to a skilled man having regard to the state of the art. All other evidence is secondary ... [T]he importance, or weight, to be

[223] *BASF/Triazole derivatives* (T231/85) [1989] E.P.O.R. 293; and see *Southco v Dzus* [1990] R.P.C. 587 at 619, dealing with the situation where the inventor and the skilled technician both have the same "tool box of knowledge"; if the former discovers a commercially successful solution it is probably not obvious. Similarly, *Haberman v Jackel International* [1999] F.S.R. 683.

[224] [1956] R.P.C. 125 at 139.

[225] (1929) 46 R.P.C. 241 CA.

[226] *Longbottom v Shaw* (1891) 8 R.P.C. 333 at 336 HL.

[227] cf. the balanced version of the same idea propounded by Tomlin J. in *Parkes v Crocker*: "... once it has been found ... that the problem has waited solution for many years, and that the device is in fact novel and superior to what had gone before, and has been widely used, and used in preference to alternative devices, it is, I think, practically impossible to say that there is not present that scintilla of invention necessary to support the Patent": (1929) 46 R.P.C. 241 at 248.

[228] Note that, in Aldous J.'s view, the evidence of a Nobel prize winner, especially one not working in the relevant field at the priority date, may not provide much clue to the state of the appropriate skilled worker's mind at the time: *Chiron v Organon* [1994] F.S.R. 202.

> attached to it will vary from case to case. However, such evidence must be kept firmly in its place. It must not be permitted, by reason of its volume and complexity, to obscure the fact that it is no more than an aid in assessing the primary evidence."[229]

That is a salutary attitude in a world where high-powered teams compete to solve similar problems, and the granting of a wide patent to one of them, therefore, needs clear justification. The others should not be put out of business upon loose assumptions that the patentee must have invented something important because it captured a striking market share.[230] At the stage of application (when today patent offices must examine for an inventive step in every case) there will rarely be decisive evidence of commercial success. Not surprisingly the EPO has tended to stress technical assessment rather than market reaction.[231]

The relevance of commercial success must be distinguished from commercial reasons for not previously exploring the solution claimed to be inventive. The latter may well explain why people in the art were prejudiced against doing so, and if the prejudice was strong enough, the research that overcame it could be inventive.[232]

3. Industrial Application

5–51 The requirement that a patentable invention be "susceptible" or "capable" of industrial application had no direct counterpart in previous British statutes.[233] In part, the concept is concerned with the categories of subject-matter that fall within the sphere of the patent system.[234] It is used in the EPC text to indicate that agriculture is an industry for patent purposes; and to exclude methods of medically treating humans and animals.[235] The fact

229 *Mölnlycke v Procter & Gamble* [1994] R.P.C. 49 at 113.

230 Note the tendency of some recent US decisions to move in this direction, strongly criticised by Merges (1988) 76 Calif. L.R. 805.

231 See Paterson, paras 10–31—10–34.

232 *Union Carbide v BP Chemicals* [1998] R.P.C. 1 at 13; *Dyson Appliances v Hoover* [2002] R.P.C. (22) 465 at [88, 97]; *Ivax Pharmaceuticals v Akzo Nobel (No. 2)* [2007] R.P.C. 3; *Pozzoli v BDMO* [2007] F.S.R. 37; *Buhler v Spamax* [2008] F.S.R. 27 at [47].

233 EPC art.52(1) ("susceptible of industrial application"); PA 1977 s.1(1)(c) ("capable of industrial application").

234 This was apparently considered its main function during the drafting of the EPC; for this and its origins in German law, see Ullrich, *Standards of Patentability in European Inventions* (1977), pp.7–9.

235 EPC arts 52(4), 57; PA 1977 s.4(1); *Wellcome/Pigs 1* (T116/85) [1988] E.P.O.R. 1. In contrast, other ways of treating humans and animals (weight-reduction, cosmetic improvement) are industrially applicable: *Du Pont/Appetite suppressant* (T144/83) [1987] E.P.O.R. 6. The EC Directive on Biotechnological Inventions ([1998] OJ L213/13) requires that products containing biological material, and associated processes, be treated as susceptible of industrial application: art.3. Likewise with new genetic information about, for instance, an orphan drug (i.e. a pharmaceutical that will aid an illness that occurs too rarely to make it commercially viable to sell): *ZymoGenetics* (T898/05) at [8].

that they concern a product consisting of or containing biological material, or a process by means of which biological material is a product is not of itself a reason for finding no industrial application.[236] To these factors we shall return in the next section.[237]

With the advent of biotechnology in particular, industrial application has become a vital consideration in determining the validity of some types of patent. The following basic characteristics were accepted by the Court of Appeal in *Eli Lilly v Human Genome Sciences*.[238]

(1) The concept is construed broadly to include all manufacturing, extracting and processing activities of enterprises that are carried out continuously, and for commercial gain.
(2) The person skilled in the art must be able to learn from the specification a practical way of exploiting the invention in at least one field of industrial activity.
(3) The issue falls to be judged at the priority date, the document being read together with common general knowledge of the field at that point in time.
(4) There must be a sound and concrete basis for recognising that the contribution could lead to practical application in industry.
(5) The purpose of the invention must be disclosed in definite technical terms, showing how it can be used to solve a given technical problem.
(6) A real prospect of exploitation must be derivable directly from the specification, if this is not already obvious from the nature of the invention or the background art. "Directly" here means in a straightforward manner, without undertaking further research—an idea implanted in the test of adequate disclosure in general.[239]
(7) As it is now frequently expressed, what is disclosed must make it *plausible* that the invention claimed will result in practical exploitation in an industry.

Plausible is a pliable adjective, but decisions have made it plain that in this context it means more than "not impossible". It refers to a real likelihood that the conclusions are true. "Plausibility" has equally been taken as the touchstone of inventive step, when the issue is whether the patentee asserts that there is a basis in technical evidence for the prediction in the specification of a practically successful result, rather than just an identification of a

[236] Biotechnology Directive 98/44 art.3(1). Nor is a patent excluded for biological material, if it has been isolated or produced by a technical process, merely because it previously occurred in nature: art.3(2).
[237] See below, paras 5–62 et seq.
[238] *Eli Lilly v Human Genome Sciences* [2010] EWCA 33 (leading judgment by Jacob L.J., approving Kitchin J.'s summary at first instance of the law stated by TBAs in numerous decisions).
[239] See below, paras 5–82, 21–17.

hypothesis that deserves testing.[240] As we have seen, it is this key which turns speculation into an inventive perception. The *Eli Lilly v HGS* decision draws on jurisprudence of the EPO relating particularly to genetic inventions, and is discussed in that context below.[241]

It will be apparent from these statements that questions of industrial application arise when what is at stake is identifying the point at which research has gone far enough down the road towards commercial exploitation to justify giving a patent over that goal even before its practical success has been confirmed by further work. The criterion aims to prevent patents for interesting research results that may in the end have some industrial application, when what that might be is still speculative. Patents are not granted in order to reserve an unexplored field for the applicant. To do so would be to give one researcher unwarranted control over competitors who might otherwise investigate the same subject-matter and find a way of actually exploiting it.

The capacity of an invention for industrial application raises other questions. Can objections that used to be dealt with under the notion of inutility[242] instead be treated as showing lack of industrial applicability? The EPO uses the concept for the purpose of excluding some aspects of the lunatic fringe: attempts to patent ideas which evidently do not achieve the claimed ends, such as machines to produce perpetual motion.[243] In the past the British system, partly because of its approach to claims, found occasion to deploy inutility much more extensively. The objection arose not only when the patentee's basic idea did not work, but also when one of the variants specifically pointed to in a claim proved ineffective. This sanction was rejected in the 1977 Act as unduly severe[244]; after all a claim to something unusable does not directly incommode anyone else.

Nevertheless there is one important sense in which the patent system ought to be constricted: it ought not to apply to scientific information for which there are no practical applications as yet ascertained. The Court of Appeal has now so held. A claim could not be sustained to an almost infinite number of polypeptides, mostly without any known purpose or use. Only some among them would encode the hepatitis C virus or the antigenetic determinant to the antibodies produced by exposure to that virus.[245]

---

240 *Generics v Lundbeck* [2009] R.P.C. 13.

241 See below, para.21–17.

242 For this objection under the 1949 Act, see Blanco White, paras 4–401 et seq.

243 EPO Guidelines, C IV 4.1. Note the connection with inadequate disclosure: a claim to the machine without reference to its purpose would be disallowed by the EPO on this latter ground, which is discussed below, in paras 5–90—5–94.

244 It was not included in the EPC and it was rejected by the Banks Committee: Report (Cmnd.4407, 1970) para.376.

245 *Chiron v Murex Diagnostics* [1996] F.S.R. 153 at 176–178. For the significance of this, see below, para.21–08.

4. Patentable Subject-Matter

Patent law has to define the types of subject matter to which it accords protection. The issues of policy involved are varied. Nice distinctions seem unavoidable. Decisions in particular cases have to be left to the courts and patent offices. But there is still the question, how far can they be guided by general propositions laid down in legislation or case law? **5–52**

In Britain, before the 1977 Act, the judges dealt with the matter, guided only by the Jacobean catch-phrase, "manner of new manufacture".[246] In the 1977 Act, following the EPC, arts 52 and 53, there are two lists of things which are not to be treated as inventions or are not to be granted patents.[247] The first list extends to the following:

(1) a discovery, scientific theory or mathematical method;
(2) a literary, dramatic, musical or artistic work or any other aesthetic creation whatsoever;
(3) a scheme, rule or method for performing a mental act, playing a game or doing business, or a program for a computer;
(4) the presentation of information;

but in each case only to the extent that the patent relates to that thing as such.[248]

The second list excludes patents for:

(a) inventions the commercial exploitation of which would be contrary to "ordre public" or morality;
(b) plant or animal varieties, other than microbiological processes or products;
(c) methods of human or animal treatment.[249]

In the Divisions and Appeal Boards of the EPO, a mantra was often recited proclaiming that exceptions to the scope of what was patentable were to be construed narrowly, particularly in decisions where there were other reasons for extending the range of the patent system. In England, however, the Court of Appeal made clear that the legislative exceptions are a heterogenous set of cases, not expressing underlying concepts of greater generality. In consequence they are not to be construed narrowly as exceptions to a policy favouring the grant of patents.[250] Narrow construction may, on the other hand, be appropriate to other factors which more clearly take the form

246 See generally, Ricketson [2003] I.P.Q. 79.
247 PA 1977, s.1(2) (with power to extend by order: s.1(5)), ss.1(3), (4), 4A. The EPC provisions were re-ordered to some extent in EPC 2000. For their history, see Pila (2005) 36 I.I.C. 755.
248 EPC 2000 art.52(2), (3); PA 1977 s.1(2
249 EPC 2000 art.53; PA 1977 s.4A.
250 *Aerotel v Telco*; *Macrossan's Application* [2007] R.P.C. 4 at [6–22].

of special exceptions—notably those relating to inventions contrary to public policy or morality, animal and plant varieties and related biological claims and methods of medical treatment.[251] In 2010 the Enlarged Board of Appeal of the EPO altered tack by subscribing to the same viewpoint. In construing the exception for medical treatment by surgery, the Board could find no basis in the Vienna Convention on Treaties supporting a general presumption limiting the range of exceptions to entitlements. At best, the Convention, art.31, required interpretation to be in good faith in accordance with the ordinary meaning to be given to the terms of the document in their context and in the light of its object and purposes.[252]

The Act does not define "invention".[253] According to one view, an idea may be found not to be an "invention" on a ground distinct from those set out in the specific exclusions just mentioned.[254] A majority of the House of Lords, however, has taken the view that no such cases would in practice arise.[255] The possibility should not perhaps be entirely forgotten. As the patent system sails towards the wild seas of genetics and digitised systems of novel kinds, courts may feel it necessary to have an ultimate power of control over its scope.

5–53 Two main ideas recur in distinguishing the categories of subject matter that may and may not be patented. One is that intellectual conceptions become patentable only to the extent that they have been embodied in technical applications. The other is that techniques which relate to living organisms, animal or vegetable, may call for special treatment: either because the public interest demands that their use should not be restricted or because a special legislative regime is needed for their protection. We shall first consider the specific cases associated with these two ideas, and then turn to general issues of moral and social value.

(1) Intellectual conceptions

(a) *Discoveries*

5–54 The list of things excluded from invention in the 1977 Act starts with discoveries, scientific theories and mathematical methods[256]; but these are excluded only to the extent that the patent relates to the conception "as such". The distinction is well known in many patent systems: discovery is the unearthing of causes, properties or phenomena already existing in

---

[251] PA 1977 ss.1(3), (4), 4(2)(3), Sch.A para.3(f).

[252] *Medi-Physics/ Surgical methods* (G1/07); see below, para.5–71, n.328.

[253] Under the future EPC 2000 amendments, inventions in all fields of technology will be included, following TRIPS art.27(1).

[254] See Mustill L.J., *Genentech v Wellcome* [1989] R.P.C. 147 at 262; *Biogen v Medeva* [1997] R.P.C. 1.

[255] See Lord Hoffmann, *Biogen v Medeva* [1997] R.P.C. 1.

[256] For the evolution of this in the EPC, see Kolle (1974) 5 I.I.C. 140 at 147–148; *IBM/ Document retrieval* (T22/85) [1990] E.P.O.R. 98

nature; invention is the application of such knowledge to the satisfaction of social needs.[257] For instance, in an internal combustion engine, the idea of putting a cushion of air in the cylinder between the fuel and the piston in order to cushion the explosive effect of ignition was said not in itself to be patentable; but a machine devised to do so was.[258] The distinction has become a matter of great controversy in relation to genetic research and we return to it in that context.

At this point we meet a question of interpretation that is strategic for all the exclusions discussed under this head: must the excluded subject matter be disregarded in assessing whether there is invention in a claim involving an application of it in (say) a production process or a machine. In relation to a claim for an application of a computer program, Falconer J. held that invention must be found in some aspect of the application apart from the program.[259] However, in *Genentech v Wellcome Foundation* the Court of Appeal ruled that approach to be incorrect.[260] Discoveries concerning the structure of the DNA of a given protein could contribute the element of inventiveness in a claim to the employment of that knowledge in producing the protein by genetic engineering: patentability of the discoveries was excluded only "to the extent that" they were claimed "as such". The House of Lords has held that disclosing the structure of a DNA strand amounts to discovery in this sense. It cannot itself be the subject of a patent claim.[261]

In chemical research the matter raises an issue of general importance: is it **5–55**
more than discovery to make a substance without also finding a use for it? It might be said that to give a new thing to the world is in itself sufficiently useful to merit protection; and that argument will doubtless seem stronger where technical difficulties are overcome in order to produce it.[262] Moreover, if mere making is not invention, yet discovery of one use allows a patentee to claim the substance itself in all its uses, an evident imbalance results: only if the first identifier of a use can patent for that use alone would it seem

[257] Kolle (above, n.256). And see Buckley L.J., *Reynolds v Smith* (1913) 20 R.P.C. 123 at 126: "Discovery adds to the amount of human knowledge, but it does so ... only by disclosing something ... Invention necessarily involves also the suggestion of an act to be done." Cf. also the use of "mere discovery" to preclude from patentability the discovery of a new advantage for an old thing: above, paras 5–26, 5–27.

[258] Jessel M.R. *Otto v Linford* (1882) 46 L.T. (N.S.) 35 at 39.

[259] *Merrill Lynch's Application* [1988] R.P.C. 1 at 12.

[260] [1989] R.P.C. 147; repeated in the *Merrill Lynch* case on appeal [1989] R.P.C. 561 and reaffirmed in *Chiron v Murex Diagnostics* [1996] F.S.R. 153. Both decisions were in line with the EPO's approach (adopted just before) in *Vicom* (below, para.20–29).

[261] See below, paras 21–07—21–08.

[262] It may also seem stronger where the substance is an intermediate which may be useful in making further substances, even though they are at the time of unknown usefulness. Cf. *Smith's Applications* [1971] R.P.C. 31, where it was said that the question of the value of the ultimate products was irrelevant to the assessment of obviousness; but the more fundamental issue was not addressed.

reasonable to deny any protection to the first maker of the substance.[263] This too is now giving rise to major arguments in the field of biotechnology.[264]

5–56 In the bulk of cases where discovery and invention can be distinguished, the two stages are part of a single development by one person or team. Even so, as invention has become less the product of trial and error on the job and more a matter of systematic research, the possibility of the two steps being taken by different people has increased. It is likely to have practical consequences, first between individuals, since only "inventors" are entitled to an employee's rights in an invention[265]; and secondly, between commercial rivals, as in the case where one is first to discover but only second to invent.

The case in favour of treating the conceptual stages in research and development as involving "invention", rather than "discovery", is broadly that these are the points at which the system should do more: by encouraging "pure" rather than "applied" work and by affording early protection that will stimulate the investment for innovation.[266] But unless all theoretical work is to lead to patents for whatever practical uses may subsequently be found for it, the approach raises formidable difficulties. How would it be possible to characterise information coming close enough to practical application to be patentable? And unless further requirements were built into the system, it might result in information about practical applications never being made publicly available.[267]

(b) *Schemes for performing mental acts; business methods; presentation of information*

5–57 Similar in essence to the previous category is the exclusion "as such" of schemes, rules or methods for performing mental acts, playing games or doing business; likewise presentations of information.[268] There have been many instances of attempts to patent ideas which involve some association between a technical device and the collation, interpretation or deployment

---

263 See also above, para.5–51.

264 See below, para.21–15.

265 For which, see below, paras 7–07—7–15.

266 See Neumeyer (1975) 14 Ind. Prop. 348; Beier (1975) 6 I.I.C. 367; cf. Kitch (1977) 20 J. Law & Econ. 265 at 288; Beier and Moufang (1994) 43 Revista di Diritto Industriale 340.

267 As to this cf. the US Supreme Court's requirement that there be "specific utility" before scientific information is patentable: *Brenner v Manson* 383 U.S. 519 (1966). Douglas J. (at 534): "Until the process claim ... has been reduced to production of a product shown to be useful, the metes and bounds of that monopoly are not capable of precise delineation. It may engross a vast, unknown and perhaps unknowable area. Such a patent may confer power to block off whole areas of scientific development without compensating benefit to the public." See also, below, para.21–08.

268 PA 1977 s.1(2)(c), (d); EPC art.52(2) (c), (d). "Presentations of information" comes from Rules Under Patent Co-Operation Treaty, rr.39.1(v) and 67.2(v) and should therefore be read in a limited sense: according to Kolle (above, n.256) at 152–153; *Merrill Lynch's Application* (below, n.71). For board games see Doble [1997] E.I.P.R. 587.

of information.[269] In such cases the usual inquiry has been whether the novelty or usefulness lies in the former or the latter aspect.[270] If the latter, the idea is likely to be labelled a "mere scheme or plan" and placed outside what is patentable.

Contrast the following[271]: colouring fertilisers in order to distinguish them from one another (unpatentable),[272] and colouring a squashball a particular shade of blue to make it specially visible (prima facie patentable)[273]; a system of marking buoys in a channel in order to show ships where to go (unpatentable),[274] and a system of devices on vehicles which would co-operate on approach to avoid dazzle (patentable)[275]; the rules of a new game (unpatentable), and new card-packs and similar equipment for a game (patentable)[276]; a record on which the music is new (unpatentable), and a new way of forming grooves on a record so as to transmit stereophonic sound (patentable)[277]; printed forms for a "home shopping club" (unpatentable),[278] and a new way of printing a newspaper so that it could be folded crossways as well as longways (patentable).[279] On the whole, British decisions have looked to the essence of the matter, not taking account of the form in which the invention is claimed. Experience in the EPO has been varied.[280]

Mostly the judicial decisions that distinguish between novelty in schemes **5–58**
and novelty in means offer by way of explanation the merely reiterative statement that the concern of the patent system is with technical advances alone.[281] The real justification for the distinction seems to lie partly (as with "discoveries") in concern lest monopoly powers of potentially great scope may be conferred, partly in the belief that the encouragement of industry through a market monopoly is an effective medium only in the sphere of industrial production, and partly in a fear that it would be difficult to determine what constitutes anticipation and infringement if the range of the system were broadened.[282]

---

[269] Cases where there is no technical aspect are clearly not patentable: for instance, methods of musical notation (*C's Application* (1920) 37 R.P.C. 247) or of learning a language (see EPO Guidelines, C IV 2.1); cf. however *Pitman's Application* [1969] R.P.C. 646 (material printed in a form suitable for use in a reading machine).

[270] The distinction is common to most patent systems: Kolle (above, n.256) at 150.

[271] For the many other examples, see Ency. P.L., para.5–234.

[272] *Johnson's Application* (1930) 47 R.P.C. 361.

[273] *ITS Rubber's Application* [1979] R.P.C. 318.

[274] *W's Application* (1914) 31 R.P.C. 141; cf. *de Beers' Application* [1979] F.S.R. 72 CA.

[275] *FMM's Application* (1941) 58 R.P.C. 115.

[276] See Official Ruling 1926 (A) 43 R.P.C. 1; *Cobianchi's Application* (1953) 70 R.P.C. 199.

[277] See EPO Guidelines, C IV 2.1.

[278] *Littlewood's Application* (1954) 71 R.P.C. 185.

[279] *Cooper's Application* (1902) 19 R.P.C. 53; and see *Fishburn's Application* (1940) 57 R.P.C. 245.

[280] For the grave difficulties over the application of the distinction to computer programs, performing mental acts and business methods, see below, paras 20–26—20–34.

[281] Formerly this was expressed in the proposition that a "manner of manufacture" required the making, improvement or repair of a "vendible product", an approach in effect abandoned after the *NRDC* case [1961] R.P.C. 134.

[282] See on these factors, Lloyd Jacob J., *Rolls-Royce's Application* [1963] R.P.C. 251 at 255.

In an urge to extend the patent system to all kinds of productive novelties, US courts have concluded that the patent system there is open to business methods and a great flood of applications have been pursued on this basis. The merits or otherwise of this sudden extension of the system are hotly debated in many parts of the world, and not least in order to settle the policy of the EPO and European countries more generally. One view of the US developments is that business method patents can usually be justified only when a technical element is provided by the use of computerised processing of information. Thus the issue is intimately linked with the extent to which computer programs themselves are patentable and it is in that context that we discuss the exclusion of methods of business "as such".[283]

(c) *Aesthetic creations*

5–59 The exclusion "as such" of literary, dramatic, musical and artistic works and any other aesthetic creations[284] can be justified by the existence of copyright and industrial designs protection.[285] The kinds of distinction already discussed pertain equally here. Where the element of creativity lies in the aesthetic ideas expressed there is no room for patent protection.[286] Thus, it was not patentable to claim disk jackets the only novelty of which lay in the colours given to them.[287] The contrary will apply where a new technical process or article is devised for its pleasurable appeal—for instance, a new method of making candles,[288] building materials incorporating stained-glass-like artwork[289] or a novel perfume.

(d) *Computer programs*[290]

5–60 The electronic hardware of computing technology is a natural subject for patentable invention and from its inception the industry has been sustained by such patents. Software, however, poses considerable problems.[291] In 1973, it was decided, in line with the pleas of some interest groups,

[283] Below, paras 21–26—21–34.

[284] PA 1977 s.1(2)(b); EPC art.52(2)(b); cf. *Tetra Molectric's Application* [1977] R.P.C. 290 CA.

[285] There has been much recent discussion of the extent to which technical designs should be protected by copyright (see below, Ch.15) but none of whether the patent system should offer protection to the essentially aesthetic. The registered design system, however, offers comparable monopoly protection; cf. the US, where the same kind of protection is actually incorporated within the patent system.

[286] Where they take the form of instructions (plays, music) they are methods of performing mental acts in the sense discussed in the previous paragraph.

[287] *Fuji/Disk Jacket* (T267/88) [1990] E.P.O.R. 168.

[288] cf. the German decision to this effect: 1972 Mitt. 235 BGH.

[289] *Hettling-Denker/Translucent mateials* (T686/90) [2004] E.P.O.R. 5.

[290] See Bandey, *Intellectual Property in Computer Program Technology* (1996); Blakemore [November 1995] Pat. Wld. 21; Rau and Watkin (1996) 27 I.I.C. 447; Van Raden [1996] E.I.P.R. 384; Hart (1997) 13 C.L. & S.R. 147; Newman [1997] E.I.P.R. 701; Davies [1998] E.I.P.R. 429; Harris [1999] CIPA 214.

[291] For copyright in programs and associated instructions, see below, paras 20–04—20–25.

specifically to exclude programs for computers "as such" from the ambit of what is patentable under the EPC.[292] "Computer program" is a term that may describe a wide range of phenomena, from basic algorithms capable of application in an indefinite number of more specific uses[293] to detailed instructions for the solution of particular problems. A different complication is this: the result of actually using a programmed computer is to produce information which may be taken for itself, or may immediately be put to some further use, as where a computer controls a step in the operation of a production process.[294] To add to the complexities, there is, for instance, the possibility that principles which might be written into programs are instead given expression in the circuitry of the computer, and the possibility of writing programs that will bring about the co-operation of a network of computers.

A computer uses mathematical instructions to select information from "input" data and, frequently, to perform mathematical manipulations with what is selected. It goes through processes that could theoretically be undertaken by the human brain unaided. If what is claimed to be patentable is a way of making a known machine operate upon data to produce desired results, then in essence it seems that nothing other than an instruction about how to perform intellectual tasks is being given. But the case is not a precise analogy to the instruction to the pilot to fly a plane in a certain way in order to reduce noise.[295] For no human interprets the instructions each time a computer uses its program. Computer programs accordingly lie exactly at the boundary of what previously has been thought to separate the patentable from the non-patentable: to some, even the most detailed operational programs remain nothing else than instructions for performing intellectual exercises; to others, the conversion of the operation into a technical process capable of constant repetition carries it over into the patentable sphere. We reserve detailed discussion of the case law which attempts to keep this line in place to the chapter on digitisation.[296] It is under constant pressure, not least from the example of the United States. There inventive programming has become generally patentable. **5–61**

(2) Biological subject-matter

The boundaries of the patent system are re-drawn (almost always by widening) as industries which are used to working with patents extend their **5–62**

[292] EPC art.52(2)(c); hence PA 1977 s.1(2)(c) to the same effect. For the evolution, Kolle (above, n.256) at 150–152.

[293] Some of the earliest cases to test the patentability of programs involved ideas of this type: *Slee & Harris's Applications* [1966] R.P.C. 194 (claim to computer as programmed accepted in the UK); [1968] F.S.R. 272 (refused in Australia). Cf. *Gottschalk v Benson* 409 U.S. 63 (1972) (algorithm for conversion of binary code into pure binary: refused).

[294] This at least is more than a computer program "as such".

[295] Held unpatentable in *Rolls-Royce's Application* [1963] R.P.C. 251.

[296] Below, paras 20–26—20–34.

ambit of operation. In their campaigns for novel patents, they are likely to succeed except where they meet persistent and implacable opposition from some other interest group. The pragmatic nature of this expansive process is nowhere better illustrated than in relation to patents which involve living matter.

Some "industrial" processes have traditionally used the capacities of living matter to make products, as with yeasts in brewing and baking. At least in Britain there has accordingly never been a general embargo on patents which involve living matter. Yet, for a long period, agriculture was not thought to be a proper sphere for patenting. Eventually, in the decades after 1945, agriculture, horticulture and animal production adopted increasingly artificial procedures, in which natural growth was affected by chemical additives, such as fertilisers and herbicides, and to special physical conditions, such as alterations of light, temperature and humidity. It was only then that the courts began to accommodate these techniques within the patent system. At the same time, plant breeders won a special regime of plant variety rights.[297]

Advances in microbiology were introducing production techniques for pharmaceuticals and other substances which depended upon the use of micro-organisms in controlled reactions. In Britain their patentability was accepted with little argument.[298] The question of a deposit system for new strains proved of greater concern. The EPC and the 1977 Act, created a special system to deal with the latter and thereby confirmed the place of this technology within the patent firmament.[299]

5–63 In the United States the basic issue had to be taken to the Supreme Court because for a period there had been an embargo on patents for things found in nature. That court's decision to give up such a scruple, *Diamond v Chakrabarty*,[300] made the sweeping generalisation that "anything under the sun made by man", apart from a human being, should be regarded as patentable. Accordingly it permitted a patent for a genetically engineered micro-organism which was claimed to disperse oil-slicks. The decision, steeped in the values of property rights theory, sent a crucial signal to the world that patenting must be made available in any country which sought to join the race for commercial returns on biotechnological research.

To this there has been a complex set of reactions, not least in Western Europe, where the EPC has set particular puzzles for those who would advance the patent frontiers in this field. The campaigns of these advocates have in their turn brought determined opposition, which gives expression to a whole range of ethical and environmental disquiets. In particular, the

[297] See below, paras 5–79 and App.3 (Hardback edn).
[298] *American Cyanamid v Berk Pharmaceuticals* [1976] R.P.C. 231.
[299] See below, paras 5–82, 5–89. Preceding this development, had been the 1949 extension of the system as a whole to cover chemical (including, above all, pharmaceutical) substances per se: see above, paras 4–47, 4–50.
[300] 65 Law Ed. (2d) 144 (1980).

attempt to re-mould the EPC formulae by the curious expedient of a Biotechnology Directive, dealing with the content of *national* patent laws in EU countries, was halted for three years in 1995 and only became law in modified form in 1998.[301] The main discussion of these issues is in Ch.21 on Biotechnology. Here, as part of the general description of the limits of the patent system, attention is drawn to the rather detailed provisions of the EPC which set the agenda for discussion in terms which seemed appropriate in 1973. Since then, an immense amount has been achieved in the relevant sciences, much of it involving forefront changes in medicine, food and agriculture—matters of fundamental importance to human well-being in the developing as well as the developed world.

There are three exclusions from patentable subject-matter which in the Patents Act 1977 derive directly from the EPC: (1) methods of treating the human and animal body; (2) plant and animal varieties and essentially biological methods for their creation; and (3) inventions contrary to *ordre public* or morality. Each will be treated in turn. **5–64**

(a) *Methods of treating the human or animal body*[302]

An invention that has to be claimed as a "method of treating the human or animal body by surgery or therapy or of diagnosis practised on the human or animal body" is unpatentable.[303] The 1977 Act deemed these activities to be incapable of industrial application,[304] but a new textual version taken from EPC 2000 repeats the exclusion in order to recognise the medical practitioner's freedom to treat his patients as he decides for its value to public health.[305] In Britain such claims have long been refused.[306] In the prevailing view, the patent system should not intrude into the realm of a leading liberal profession where expectations of renown and reward have traditionally taken quite different forms from those which flow from exclusive rights over commercialisation.[307] The spectre of a single doctor reserving the performance of the most satisfactory, possibly life-saving, operation to his or her own team and extracting therefrom monopoly profits **5–65**

301 Directive on the Legal Protection of Biotechnological Inventions [1998] OJ L213/13; Llewelyn [1997] E.I.P.R. 115; Nott [1998] E.I.P.R. 455; Bostyn [1999] I.P.Q. 1. Its constitutional validity has been accepted by the ECJ: below, para.21–14.

302 See Ventose [2010] E.I.P.R. 120.

303 PA 1977 s.4(A)(1) (amended in 2004); EPC 2000 art.53(3). For the history in Europe and an argument against continuance, see Moufang (1993) 24 I.I.C. 18; Visser in Kur et al., *Patent Law on the Move* (2005) p.469. Common law jurisdictions which have abandoned the exclusion include Israel (*Wellcome v Plantex* [1974] R.P.C. 514) and Australia (*Anaesthetic Supplies v Rescare* (1994) 50 F.C.R. 1; *Bristol-Myers Squibb v Faulding* (2000) 97 F.C.R. 524; Van Caenegem (2002) 13 Aust. I.P.J. 41). In the US, the law has recently shifted in the opposite direction thanks to the introduction of a defence to infringement open to those giving medical treatment directly to patients: see *Chisum on Patents*, para.1.03[3].

304 See above, para.5–51.

305 See *Wellcome/Pigs I* (T116/85) [1988] E.P.O.R. 1; *Visx v Nidex* [1999] F.S.R. 406 at 465.

306 See *Upjohn's (Robert) Application* [1977] R.P.C. 94, CA. The exclusion of animal treatment was new in 1977 so far as the UK was concerned.

307 Hence the reformulation in EPC 2000.

on the scale of a successful pop star seemed to put the matter beyond argument.

With the movement in medicine towards drug therapies, however, this abstemious approach has had to confront pharmaceutical producers avid for patent protection. In the second half of the twentieth century, patent law in every industrial state had to develop in ways which mediated this conflict. A mixture of legislation and litigation gave the pharmaceutical industry much of the protection which it has sought (though by no means all). One question which now hangs in the air is whether an exclusion of "methods of medical treatment", such as is to be found in the present European laws, makes any real sense. We shall return to that question after reviewing the ways in which, as a legal concept, the exclusion has been kept in confinement.

5–66 The legal limitation of the exception turns upon the technical distinction between types of claim which we have already met in general terms in considering novelty: a new substance or composition—one that has had no previously known use—may be claimed "as such". It, therefore, does not come with the exclusion of *methods* of medical treatment. The same applies to the selection of a specific substance or composition from a generally known class, because the discovery of a special quality justifies a claim to that thing.

It is only with a thing already known to have a use that claims must be confined to a method and the exclusion of medical treatment begins to bite. The first demand of the pharmaceutical industry has been for patents covering newly constituted substances and on the success of such patents the profitability of leading producers has depended. Here at least the system has worked in archetypal fashion. The monopoly profits of one patented success have allowed extensive research to be supported in the hope of finding a further winner which can come on stream in time to continue the flow of revenue.

Because of this crucial significance of patenting to pharmaceutical production, the case for further concessions was diligently pursued and politicians have listened with some sympathy. It is hard to see why work on a new substance, including one specially selected, should bring a patent, while work on the properties of things already known should not be patentable in the sphere of medical and veterinary application. Inventions of the latter kind may be relatively hard or relatively easy to achieve. If they are excluded from patenting, then the industry must feel itself directed to investigate new substances. Yet it cannot be claimed that, as a category, research of that kind is necessarily of greater human benefit than work to improve existing products.

5–67 Thinking on these lines led to an important exception in the EPC and its derivatives to the law of novelty as it had previously applied. An invention consisting of a substance or composition for use in an excluded method of medical treatment remains novel, despite the fact that the substance or composition is itself known, "provided that its use in any [such] method ... is not comprised in the state of the art".[308] The natural meaning of this special exception is that only for the first discovery of a medical use for a known product can a claim be made to it for that use which will be regarded as novel. So, left to itself, would the Patents Court have read it.[309] But the Enlarged Board of Appeal of the EPO, faced with numerous applications for second and subsequent discoveries of medical use, showed its determination to confine the medical treatment exception strictly to what it described as "non-commercial and non-industrial medical and veterinary activities".[310] In *Eisai's and other Applications*,[311] it decided that in addition to the exception for first medical use, it was legitimate to recognise claims to use of a substance for making up a medicament for pharmaceutical administration in pursuit of a subsequently discovered use of that substance,[312] provided that the new treatment has been tried and tested.[313] Claims of this kind were called "Swiss form" because the Swiss Patent Office was the first in Europe to accept them. In the interests of common progress, the UK Patents Appeal Tribunal proceeded to accept the same "praetorian" analogy.[314] EPC 2000 has now amended the Convention to allow claims for substances for their subsequent medical uses without the need to resort to the "Swiss form".

The potency of the *Eisai* decision was soon enough realised.[315] However, it was not at once clear how far the "Swiss form" claim could be taken. In particular, did it allow the patenting of a more efficient or less harmful dosage in the use of a drug already known for its value in treating a particular disease or condition. In *Bristol-Myers Squibb v Baker Norton*,[316] the Court of Appeal refused to allow a claim for a medicament so formulated that it would release the anti-cancer drug, taxol, over three hours instead of 24, thus reducing its side-effects. The decision reflected some skepticism over the *Eisai* decision itself, as well as over the difficulty of determining what **5–68**

[308] PA 1977 s.3(6); EPC art.54(5).

[309] See *Schering and Wyeth* (below, n.90).

[310] This language reflected the original drafting of the EPC which placed the exclusion of medical treatment under the concept of industrial applicability. This "fiction" was averted in EPC 2000 by making the exclusion self-standing.

[311] *Eisai's and other Applications* (G05/83) [1983] E.P.O.R. B241; and see *Duphar/Pigs II* (T19/86) [1989] E.P.O.R. 10.

[312] This is known as "the Swiss form of claim", the Swiss Patent Office being the first perspicacious enough to appreciate its potential; *cf.* the earlier, wider decision of the German Supreme Court (*Hydropiridine* [1984] OJ EPO 26) which was not followed. For different Swiss claim formulations, see *Thérapeutiques Substitutives* (T958/94) [1997] E.P.O.R. 417.

[313] *McManus' Application* [1994] F.S.R. 558. There is no need to show a new manufacturing process: *MAI/Trigonelline* (T143/94) [1996] E.O.P.R. 613.

[314] *Schering's and Wyeth's Applications* [1985] R.P.C. 545 (in banc).

[315] As already indicated, the EPO's Enlarged Board of Appeal went on to hold valid a claim to a known article for a novel *non-medical* purpose, even where the new purpose involved only a physical activity that is already known: see above, paras 5–26, 5–27. However, there is no explicit statutory provision to which that development could be allied, whereas in relation to medical treatment there is.

[316] *Bristol-Myers Squibb v Baker Norton* [2001] R.P.C. 1

would constitute infringement of the new dosage claim. EPO Boards of Appeal, Legal as well as Technical, reached the contrary view—not surprisingly, given that *Eisai* was decided by its Enlarged Board. *Eisai* provided a way of patenting a known active ingredient for the treatment of a different condition from that already known.[317] Acknowledging the importance that attaches to the EPO's "centralising" function in arriving at the rules of European patent law, a later Court of Appeal decision, *Activas UK v Merck*,[318] has accepted that *Bristol-Myers Squibb* should no longer be followed. No only did the later Court find reasons for distinguishing the earlier case restrictively on its facts; it also proposed a new exception to the rule in *Young v Bristol Aeroplane*,[319] which in most circumstances makes a prior Court of Appeal decision binding for later decisions of that Court concerned with the same legal issue. The new exception would in effect acknowledge the greater value as a precedent of case law expounded by a judicial authority of the regional or international type exemplified by the EPO. As to the policy issue itself, the *Activas* court was of opinion that concerns over what would constitute infringing use of the "Swiss form" claim to a new dosage were exaggerated in relation to medicaments, since for the most part their supplier was required by law to give detailed instructions about their uses. And equally, the court considered that although for the present the law lays down an exception relating to methods of medical treatment, its essential purpose was directed to the activities of doctors and other medical staff when physically treating patients: in conventional language, these actions were characterised as "non-commercial and non-industrial".[320] In any case, applications that are subject to EPC 2000 no longer turn on any distinction between first and subsequent medical or veterinary uses, as the revised version of EPC art.54(5) makes clear.[321] .

5–69 At the margins there are certain possibilities of avoiding the prohibition. If the method can be shown not to constitute surgery, therapy or diagnosis it will not be caught. Therapy covers non-surgical treatment designed to cure, alleviate, remove or lessen the symptom of, or prevent or reduce the possibility of contracting any malfunction of, the human or animal body.[322] If the method claimed has a number of steps, one of which is a therapy, the whole claim cannot stand in that form.[323] Before the 1977 Act, the view was taken in England that oral administration of known substances in reduced dosages in order to prevent conception was not *medical* treatment and is the

[317] See esp. *Genentech/administration of IFG-1* (T1020/03) [2006] E.P.O.R. 9; applied, e.g. in *Exoxemis/haloperoxide* (T292/04); *Praecis/GnRH antagonists* (T380/05); *Sepracor/descarboethoxylovatadine* (T230/01).

[318] *Activas UK v Merck* [2008] EWCA Civ 444 at [18]–[31]

[319] *Young v Bristol Aeroplane* [1944] K.B. 718.

[320] [2008] EWCA Civ. 444 at [29], quoting *Eisai.*

[321] Now transposed into PA 1977 s.4A(4). Any application which has not been completed before February 13, 2010 falls under the new provision.

[322] *Salminen/Pigs III* (T58/87) [1989] E.P.O.R. 125.

[323] See *MediPhysics/Surgical method,* below, n.328.

position taken under the new law.[324] The EPO has accepted claims to treatment for a cosmetic or other non-therapeutic purpose, such as an appetite suppressant (for slimming).[325] But these did not include the removal of plaque from teeth because it was a way of preventing dental decay. Nor can the prohibition be side-stepped by showing an additional non-medical advantage.[326]

By way of complement to this, surgery has been taken to refer to physical interventions in medical or veterinary treatment which go beyond a minimal level, such as giving injections under the skin surface or taking blood samples. Surgical interventions typically have as their prime justification the maintaining of the life or health of the patient.[327] The decision of the Enlarged Board in *Medi-Physics/surgical method* [328] adds little of substance to this definition, the Board being unable to propound a formula that will meet all cases. But it makes clear that if one step in a claimed procedure falls within this concept, then the claim as a whole cannot stand unless it can be amended so as to remove it—as is the case with therapeutic methods. The case before it concerned a "contrast agent" that must be put into a patient's body before a magnetic resonance imager can show conditions in his heart or lungs. The patent claim was for a method of positioning a particular contrast agent by injection into, for instance, the heart. This was considered clearly to be a surgical procedure, and it made no difference that the step was being taken in order to gain information for a further operation, for therapy or for diagnosis, all of which were likely uses. As earlier, the Board found it too difficult to limit surgery to steps that a member of a medical profession alone could carry out, mainly because of differences in professional regulation between EPC states. The Board was pressed to introduce the legal equivalent of the altered law in the United States, which now merely grants exemption to a professional carrying out a treatment procedure so as to protect him from infringement of any relevant patent. In the Board's view, the terms of the EPC, in its 2000 version were deliberately left unchanged and therefore did not allow case law to establish any such alteration. By 2010, the Board was willing to give the methods of medical treatment exception an independent evaluation, rather than squeezing it as far as possible dry of content. This may cause some doubt about the Board's

[324] *Schering's Application* [1971] R.P.C. 337; *General Hospital* [1995] E.P.O.R. 446; *Baxter/blood extraction* (T329/94) [1998] E.P.O.R. 363. See also *Joos v Commissioner of Patents* [1973] R.P.C. 59 HC (Aust.) (treatment to improve condition of nails and hair); *General Health's Application/optical radiation* [2005] OJ EPO L59;cf. *Wellcome/Pigs I* (T116/85) [1988] E.P.O.R. 1 (treatment of pig mange caused by parasites: unpatentable); *Telectronics/Pacers* (T82/93) [1996] E.P.O.R. 409.

[325] *Du Pont/Appetite suppressant* (T144/83) [1987] E.P.O.R. 6; see Paterson, paras 7–30—7–42.

[326] *General Hospital* (above, n.324) (therapeutic as well as contraceptive treatment). A disclaimer of the medical treatment may save a twin-purpose claim: *Moufang* (above, n.320). If one element in a course of action is a method of treatment, the whole is not patentable: *Georgetown University/Pericardial treatment* (T35/99) [2001] E.P.O.R. 21 .

[327] Referred to obiter in *Diagnostic measures*, below n.329.

[328] G1/07, decided February 19, 2010.

earlier decision concerning what constitutes diagnosis. In *Cygnus/diagnostic method*,[329] the Enlarged Board identified the essential purpose of the whole exception as being a matter of public health policy: the practice of medicine by various professionals needed to be carried on without having to consider whether a patent licence was necessary for any method of treatment.[330] Diagnosis was characterised as a four-step procedure: (i) examining the body to collect data; (ii) comparing the data with standard values; (iii) finding whether any variation is significant enough to be a symptom; and (iv) attributing that symptom to a clinical condition—the final medical or veterinary deduction. Applying a narrow approach to the exclusion, the Board held that only a procedure which includes all these steps is to be treated as diagnosis,[331] even though the final step does not have to be one that only a qualified medical or veterinary expert must take. On this basis, preliminary tests, providing results which may be taken into account in reaching a diagnosis, are not excluded from patenting, unless they fall within the definition of therapy or surgery and that becomes the reason for disallowing the claim.[332]

5–70 Under the 1949 Act, the Patent Appeals Tribunal once allowed a "pack claim" as a way of patenting the discovery of an improved dosage: the claim was for a pack giving the daily dosages of two pharmaceuticals (oral contraceptives) together with instructions about the days on which each should be taken in relation to the female menstrual cycle.[333] The need to convey this specific information was held to justify a claim to the particular type of packaging. It can, however, be said that the pack only conveyed information designed to direct the course of human conduct; certainly the Court of Appeal has prevented the proliferation of "pack claims" where the method of display does not help particularly in transmitting the new information.[334]

5–71 To return to less marginal issues: the exception covering methods of medical treatment may be regarded as a last redoubt against the sweep of the patent system into the territory of health care. Previously many countries precluded patenting for chemical substances as a whole, or pharmaceutical substances. The obligation in the TRIPS Agreement to allow such

[329] *Diagnostic measures* (G1/04) [2006] E.P.O.R. 15, which followed upon the broader TBA decision in *Cygnus/diagnostic method* (T964/99) [2002] E.P.O.R. 26.

[330] This plain speaking is in line with the treatment of the exception as self-standing, by virtue of EPC 2000.

[331] For the analytical difficulties of the solution, see Moufang (1993) 24 I.I.C. 18. Ventose, above n.302.

[332] *Bruker/Non-invasive measurement* (T385/86) [1988] E.P.O.R. 357—the leading decision before *Cygnus*.

[333] *Organon's Application* [1970] R.P.C. 574; *Blendax-Werke's Application* [1980] R.P.C. 491; cf. *L'Oréal's Application* [1970] R.P.C. 565, where a reason (putting creases in material) existed for wanting to combine the two chemicals which the applicant claimed in a pack for a different purpose (treating human hair); accordingly the claim was refused.

[334] *Ciba-Geigy's (Dürr) Application* [1977] R.P.C. 83; and see *Wellcome Foundation's Application* [1981] F.S.R. 72 HC (Aust.). The importance of "pack claims" in catching infringers has been reduced with the introduction of indirect infringement: see below, paras 6–17, 6–19.

patents demonstrates the lobbying power of leading pharmaceutical producers in much of the world.[335]

Now only the procedures followed by doctors and veterinary surgeons are beyond the range of a patent claim; but in the EPC countries that exception is fixed in the legislation and so is not just a matter of judicial determination.[336] While it may no longer make much sense to exclude the patent system from this one rather limited area of medical and health practice, it is not likely that the EPC will be amended so as to remove the provision. There is a considerable lobby against the "patenting of life". This emotive but vague expression certainly covers procedures (including DNA manipulation) directly involving the human body; and for many protesters, the animal body as well. Since the patenting of medical procedures would also generate considerable mistrust among professionals and health administrators, the exception is unlikely to be dislodged. If there were ever to be a change, there would be a strong case for subjecting medical treatment patents to compulsory licensing. **5–72**

These current sensitivities are acknowledged in the TRIPS text: it requires patents to be available in all fields of technology. But it has allowed developing countries a 10-year transitional period in which to achieve this for product patents—a period since extended by the Doha Declaration of 2001[337]; and it allows the exception under discussion to be maintained in all systems, alongside exclusions "necessary to protect *ordre public* and morality, including to protect human, animal or plant life or health or to avoid serious prejudice to the environment". **5–73**

(b) *Plant and animal varieties; certain processes for their production*

The field of "industrial application" includes agriculture and under the Biotechnology Directive includes products containing biological material and associate processes.[338] In consequence, the scope of such patents are both extended and, as with the "farmers' exception", limited.[339] Thus patents continue to be granted for those uses of chemical substances in the production of plants and animals for commercial purposes which were first given patentable status in the 1960s.[340] There is, however, a restricted exception which excludes patents for plant and animal varieties, and **5–74**

---

[335] See above, para.3–22.

[336] cf. above, para.5–67.

[337] This Declaration by the WTO took cognizance of developing countries' concerns over the international impact of patents on prices for anti-HIV and other drugs of major importance to developing countries, which had been given great prominence by the wide compulsory licensing powers introduced in South Africa. The TRIPS Council has since taken on a further review of the subject. See also CIPR, *Integrating IPRs and Development Policy* (2002) Ch.2.

[338] PA 1977 s.4(1); EPC art.57; Biotechnology Directive 98/44 art.3.

[339] See below para.6–14.

[340] A leading example was *NRDC's Application* [1961] R.P.C. 134 (use of chemical as weedkiller).

essentially biological processes for the production of plants and animals other than micro-biological processes and the products thereof.[341]

Such a tangle of words needs dividing. We shall consider separately its three main concepts—"variety", "macro-biological process" and "micro-biological process"—while bearing in mind that each may have a different impact in relation to plants and to animals. In each case the legal issue starts from the type of claim. A claim to a living thing raises the question, is this a "variety"? A claim to a procedure for making live material raises the question, is this a biological process? If so, does it concern macro- or micro-biology?

5–75 (i) **"Variety".** In the 1950s and 1960s various countries (including Great Britain) introduced a special plant variety right (PVR). At least in Western Europe, PVRs were designed to cover the production of new varieties by standard methods such as cross-pollination, hybridisation and grafting.[342] The regime was open to adaptation for different species, and (for instance in the UK system) rights were available only where a scheme had been set up for a species. Twenty-eight PVR schemes were carefully shaped to give exclusive rights in particular species of plant and it controlled the names for each variety.[343] In 1994, a Community PVR was introduced to give protection across the EU on the same basis.[344]

The notion of a plant variety is not unproblematic, but the system as practised in West Europe involves official testing to determine that an alleged new variety is sufficiently distinctive in its detailed characteristics (shape, height, colour, habit, etc.) and was also homogenous and stable. The characterising of varieties thus became an established procedure. While the rights were limited in scope, at the same time they side-stepped requirements of patent systems, such as inventiveness and adequate disclosure. They were considered by the plant breeding industry to leave no room for patents as an alternative; hence the exclusion in the EPC.[345]

5–76 By contrast, no such regime applies to the production of new animal breeds and the exclusion of "animal varieties" from patenting seems merely to have reflected traditional expectations. The expression "animal varieties" is an artificial one in any EPC language; and indeed the term in German may well refer to an entire animal species, but in French and English only to a sub-species.[346] The exclusion was adopted without animal breeders having

[341] PA 1977 s.1(3)(b); EPC art.53(b); and see Biotechnology Directive art.4(1), 4(3).

[342] See further below, App.3 (hardback edition); Greengrass (1989) 20 I.I.C. 622; Byrne, *The Scope of Intellectual Property Protection for Plants and Other Life Forms* (1989); Christie [1989] E.I.P.R. 394; Crespi (1992) 23 I.I.C. 168; Moufang (1992) 23 I.I.C. 328.

[343] The UK system now operates under the Plant Varieties Act 1997.

[344] Regulation 2100/94. See Llewelyn and Adcock, *European Plant Intellectual Property* (2006).

[345] The exclusion was originally formulated in the Strasbourg Harmonisation Convention of 1963 art.2.

[346] See *Harvard/Oncomouse* [1990] E.P.O.R. 4.

experience of exclusive rights of any kind. This helps to explain the curious drafting.

The increasingly artificial manipulation of plant and animal forms, from recombination of genetic elements in DNA upwards, has been a striking characteristic of industrial development in the decades since the EPC was written. The new techniques may yield much larger quantities of a substance, having a purity and uniformity which are very hard to achieve by extraction from nature. These products moreover have uses not only in farming and horticulture but in other forms of food production, medical diagnosis and therapy and indeed in other spheres. In a broad sense, the techniques arouse images and understandings of technology, and that makes it harder to say that it is still a sphere from which patent incentives should be debarred wholesale.

After a decade of operation, the EPO was called upon to decide the scope **5–77** of the exclusions of plant and animal varieties, and the other factors in art.53(b). One principled view was that, despite the reference to varieties, the provision operates to prevent patents for plants or animals in a general sense. A claim relating to all the plants of (say) a genus, can be regarded as a claim to each of the members of the class (and hence to all the varieties)—just as with a claim to a class of chemical substances. This would leave the sphere of plants to the PVR system, and that of animals free of any intellectual property incentive.

At first, in relation to animals, one Examining Division took this line, but then other counsels prevailed. Based upon the unspecific proposition that any exception to the range of the EPC system should be narrowly construed, the following plant patents were granted:

(1) *Ciba-Geigy/propagating material*[347]: a claim to seed of any kind dressed with a defined chemical in order to make it resistant to certain weedkillers;
(2) *Lubrizol/hybrid plants*[348]: a claim to hybrids produced in accordance with a staged sequence of selection of parent plants (one of which had to be heterozygous) and then of cross-testing, evaluation, and further multiplication;
(3) *Harvard/Oncomouse*[349]: a claim to a mouse or other non-human mammal genetically manipulated so as to insert an activated oncogene, which could then be used in cancer research, was held not to be in respect of an animal variety.

[347] *Ciba-Geigy/propagating material* (T49/83) [1985] E.P.O.R. 758.
[348] *Lubrizol/hybrid plants* (T320/87) [1990] E.P.O.R. 173.
[349] *Harvard/Oncomouse* (T19/90) [1990] E.P.O.R. 501; for the disclosure issue, below, para.5–89. For the acceptance of animal patents in US law, see *Ex p. Allen*, 2 U.S.P.Q. (2d) 1425 (polypoid oysters); and their refusal for higher life forms, such as mice in Canada: *Canada v Harvard College* [2002] S.C.C. 76. On the questions raised by animal patents, see: Lesser (ed.), *Animal Patents* (1989); Moufang (1989) 20 I.I.C. 823; Peace and Christic [1996] E.I.P.R. 213; Kinkeldy (1993) 24 I.I.C. 777; Di Cerbo (1993) 24 I.I.C. 788.

5–78 In the first two cases, Boards of Appeal confined the exclusion of "plant varieties" to claims to individually characterised plants which would have the detailed differences of taxonomy and the reproductive capacity which is required in general for a PVR. In *Oncomouse*, "animal variety" was taken to refer to a particular sub-species and nothing more general. Thereafter, Boards of Appeal reverted to the more principled stance, refusing to allow claims to all plants which (in lay terms) have been transformed by genetic engineering so as to contain foreign DNA capable of negating the effect of certain weedkillers. Eventually the conflict was referred to the Enlarged Board. It came down firmly in favour of admitting claims to technical teachings that can be implemented in the indefinite number of plant varieties. Only the identification of special varieties was left for PVR systems to protect.[350] This piece of judicial legislation was by then already confirmed through enactment. The EC's Biotechnology Directive of 1998 imposed the same approach on the patent systems of EU states; and the EPC Implementing Regulations were brought into line with this.[351] Patents are available for inventions which concern plants or animals, provided that the claims are not technically confined to a single plant or animal variety.[352] The resultant admixture of systems is a curiosity that can be explained only in historical terms.

5–79 (ii) **"Macro-biological process".** The exclusion of essentially biological processes (other than micro-biological) for the production of plants and animals is evidently related to the exclusion of varieties. Claims to methods occur alongside those to their products in the examples just considered. However, the exclusion of processes is in terms stated to apply to the production of plants and animals, and not mere varieties of them. This appears to introduce a significant distinction, given the restricted interpretation now imposed upon "variety".

The process exception was drafted in an age before biotechnology. The intended difference was probably between steps which rely upon natural development and those which involve artificial human intervention. Under the 1949 Act, it was, for instance, held that a method of improving the breeding of poinsettias by subjecting them to artificial regimes of light and dark was not patentable. Production of the plants still depended substantially on processes of growth.

However, in its *Lubrizol* decision,[353] the EPO held that intervention in breeding processes, such as the steps there specified of selection, crossing and re-crossing, could be the subject of valid claims to the method of proceeding. There was said to be enough human intervention to count as

[350] *Novartis II* (G1/980 [2000] OJ EPO 111.
[351] Directive 98/44 [1998] OJ L312/13, rec. 9, art.4.2; EPC 2000 Regulations Ch.5.
[352] Article 4(2) and see Recitals 29–33. Article 12 provides for compulsory cross-licensing in consequence.
[353] (T320/87) [1990] E.P.O.R. 173 above, n.248.

technical alteration of natural occurrences. This carried it beyond "known biological and classical breeders' processes" and so it was no longer "essentially biological". The difference from ordinary plant breeding was nonetheless only in the complexity of sequence, not in the nature of what was done.

On the animal front: in the case of the *Oncomouse*, the process involved an intervention in the ordinary workings of the animal's biological system. The oncogene had to be inserted artificially into a vector, and this was then micro-injected into the recipient foetus animal for incorporation in its genome. Claims to this process, therefore, avoided the prohibition. In addition claims to animals which had been subject to the treatment were held not to be caught by the exclusion of essentially biological processes because they were product-by-process, rather than process, claims.[354] But if that is correct, the prohibition on essentially biological processes would appear to have evaporated, since it could generally be subverted through a product-by-process claim.

(iii) **Micro-biological process.** Even if claims are made to an essentially biological process for the production of plants or animals, they are patentable if the process is micro-biological. This counter-exception acknowledges that micro-biological production techniques have been so long within the patent fold that, even when used for plant and animal production, they must be treated as patentable. That may have been a rough assumption for three decades, but its meaning is opaque, since there is no scientific line between micro- and macro-biology. In consequence an EPO Board of Appeal decided that a genetically manipulated plant variety is not as a whole the product of a microbiological process, where the insertion of DNA (itself micro-biological) is followed by the breeding of plants containing the genetic insertion.[355] **5–80**

(c) *"Ordre public" and morality*

There is a provision that was long thought to be of purely marginal relevance but which, in the tide of environmental concerns, was suddenly washed mid-stream. The 1977 Act excludes the patenting of inventions the commercial exploitation of which would be contrary to public policy or morality Both the European Union and the United Kingdom have a number of regulatory bodies which determine directly whether scientific, technical or medical practice or research should be prohibited in the interests of ethical, health, safety or environmental concerns, or should be carried out only according to specific standards, or in limited amounts, or under controlled **5–81**

[354] The Board of Appeal gave this answer, so as not to have to address a difficult issue: the product-by-process claims covered both the originally injected mice and subsequent generations which inherited the oncogene. It was argued that the latter were produced by the essentially biological process of reproduction. Even so the Board of Appeal indicated an unwillingness to accept this argument on its merits.

[355] See above n.350.

conditions. This is one factor in the intense controversy surrounding the patenting of biotechnological inventions which go to their inherent desirability and their potential dangers. It remains a subject at the nerve centre of concern about the relationship of the patent incentive to both research and subsequent applications of the results in diagnosis and therapy for humans and animals and in the realm of genetically manipulated crops. We will return to it in our discussion of biotechnology and IPRs.[356]

5. Clear and Complete Disclosure

(1) General

5–82 The specification must disclose the invention clearly enough and completely enough for it to be performed by a person skilled in the art.[357] There must be the same "enabling disclosure" as that which forms one part of the justification for a claim to priority and for an anticipation.[358] It is not enough to specify one necessary step or condition in making the invention if other requirements are not spelled out.[359] It must do so at the date of filing, not when the application is first published.[360] It is this requirement that aims to extract the essential "consideration" for the patent grant—revelation of the invention for the information of the rest of industry and any others interested. When the invention consists of a step forward that then needs only routine development to make it a commercial success, the question of disclosure is usually straightforward. But where a succession of inventions is needed, as in the evolution of most new technologies, the issue is more complex. Obviously it would be wrong to reserve the patent for the person lucky enough to take the last step towards the most successful version of the article or process. Witness to the contrary the long-settled practice of granting patents for "basic" inventions and then for improvements upon them and selections within their range. But if there are to be patents for inventions on the road to ultimate success, they must be kept for steps that are not only non-obvious, but also which work well enough to contribute something useful to what is already known; and this the instructions for performance must reveal. How the law seeks to do this we consider under the next sub-heading.

356 Below, paras 21–09 et seq.

357 PA 1977 ss.14(3), 72(1)(c); EPC arts 83, 100(b) (ground of opposition).

358 See above, paras 4–12, 5–18, referring in particular to *Asahi's Application* [1991] R.P.C. 485; and to the distinction between disclosure of the invention and enablement of its performance brought out in *Synthon v SmithKline Beecham* [2006] R.P.C. 10 HL.

359 *Kirin-Amgen v Hoechst Marion Roussel* [2005] R.P.C. 9 [116].

360 *Biogen v Medeva* [1997] R.P.C. 1 HL: in that case, the tardiness of the EPO procedure meant that there were seven years between the two dates and common general knowledge had progressed the all-important distance in the interim. At the earlier date the specification was insufficient.

Beside these considerations two associated problems arise. First, is the patentee to be bound by obligations of good faith—bound for instance to reveal the best way of performing his invention at the time of his application? It is by no means clear how far this is a requirement of the present law.[361] Secondly, how much broader may the claims be than the specific examples of the invention that are described, given the special function of claims in the specification? This relationship we shall consider when we turn in the next section to the criteria governing claims.[362] **5–83**

The former law contained a number of specific requirements covering the sorts of issues just mentioned: sufficient and fair description, utility, disclosure of best known method, fair basis for claims.[363] Now, after grant, the only relevant objection, apart from those going to amendment,[364] is absence of complete and clear disclosure. However, this provision is to be read in a broad sense, covering much of the former range of objection within its ambit.[365]

(2) Making the disclosure

In the case of mechanical contrivances, the patentee normally seeks to fulfil his obligation of disclosure by describing at least one embodiment of his concept, giving details about how it is to be made wherever that is not obvious. He may, of course, resort to such abbreviations as "any suitable material" or "general methods", whenever these will be readily understood by addressees. Likewise in a chemical case he will provide at least one example of the procedures involved in his invention. One embodiment may suffice if it contains a feature present in one or other of all the claims. Where alternatives are claimed, other examples may well be necessary.[366] **5–84**

In his examples, the patentee will often use specific measures: of size, weight, volume temperature and so forth. But in cases where nothing turns on finite limits, he may confine his description to general relationships between component parts. This is permissible if it will take only simple experiments for someone else to carry out the invention successfully. In the classic case, the invention was a "smokeless ashtray" consisting of a receptacle with a tube at the top and a deflector at the bottom, so placed that butts would give off smoke only into the enclosed space above. This was

[361] See below, para.88.
[362] See below, para.90.
[363] See especially PA 1949 s.32(1)(g)(i).
[364] See above, paras 4–30 et seq.
[365] See below, paras 5–91—5–94.
[366] It has never been an absolute requirement of British practice that even one example be provided. In the case, for instance, where the invention consists in discovering a use for a new material that is made from known materials by known methods, an example to illustrate its making may be superfluous. But in the EPO detailed description of at least one way of performing the invention is required, and more examples may be needed in many cases claiming a broad field: EPC Rules r.27(1).

properly described in terms of interrelationships that would produce the desired result (and claims in equivalent terms were also allowed).[367]

The danger inherent in such descriptions and their attendant claims is that they will merely state *desiderata*; that they will, in other words, disguise problems still awaiting solution and pre-empt the chances of those who later find the answers. Recently, in the rush to procure wide claims for techniques of biotechnology, the courts have found reason to be suspicious of sanguine generalisations. Thus, both the EPO and the House of Lords have come to insist that it is not necessarily enough to describe in detail one embodiment of the invention claimed; there must be sufficient information for the skilled addressee in essence to perform everything within a claim without himself having to invent anything.[368]

What if a patentee makes a mistaken assertion about the way of performing the invention? In one instance, a novel derivative of the well-known anti-depressant, paroxetine, was said, in Example 1 of the specification, to be obtainable by crystallisation using ethanol as a solvent. This proved not to work, but the evidence was that a skilled worker who discovered this would as a matter of course try others that were mentioned in the body of the description. The House of Lords upheld the trial judge's conclusion that there was a sufficient enablement.[369]

5–85 Whether disclosure is sufficient has always been treated as a question of fact.[370] A court must judge the issue from evidence about how the skilled addressee would have understood the specification at its date of filing.[371] The purpose is not to instruct the uninitiated in the whole art. Those who have been working in a field soon build up a web of assumptions and understandings about how things can be made to work which will not be shared by outsiders. Their common general knowledge does not have to be rehearsed in the specification.[372]

A typical issue about disclosure concerns the failure to specify a limiting condition that is crucial to success. For instance, suppose that a chemical reaction will work only in an iron autoclave, but this the patent fails to require.[373] In such a case, the patentee will seek to argue that the notional addressee would have known to use the right vessel; the objector to the patent will claim that there was no such understanding. He will, moreover, emphasise any passages which appear to suggest that any autoclave will do; for positive suggestions that something can be done which will in fact not

---

367 *No-Fume v Pitchford* (1935) 52 R.P.C. 231 CA.

368 See below, para.5–86.

369 *Synthon v SmithKline Beechamt*, above n.30.

370 *British Dynamite v Krebs* (1896) 13 R.P.C. 190 at 192, HL.

371 See above, para.5–82.

372 Lloyd L.J., *Mentor v Hollister* [1993] R.P.C. 7 at 10; *Chiron v Organon Tekniko* [1996] R.P.C. 535 CA.

373 Example drawn from *Badische Anilin v Usines de Rhône* (1898) 15 R.P.C. 359 CA, where the patentee did not in fact appreciate the significance of iron to the reaction; even so, the instructions were held insufficient.

work are likely to be fatal.[374] Since patent office examiners and patent agents tend to share a similar level of expertise, they are likely to take much the same view of what can be assumed and what must be spelled out.

It is when the matter goes into court (and particularly before non-specialist judges on appeal) that this sort of issue becomes chancy. Much may depend on the court's picture of the proper addressee. It was in considering sufficiency of description that the Court of Appeal held a "pioneer" patent in the field of colour television to be addressed to skilled technicians rather than to members of leading research teams. What is more, those technicians could not be expected to make "prolonged study of matters which present some initial difficulty".[375] These are high standards which pursue a categorical view of the patent system's informational role. In other circumstances, courts have treated specifications as addressed to leading research teams who are taken to have the most advanced apparatus.[376] **5–86**

(3) Micro-organism deposit

A special scheme deals with the disclosure requirement for a micro-biological process or its product, if it involves the use of a micro-organism which is not available to the public and cannot be described so as to enable a skilled person to carry out the invention. The scheme requires the deposit of a sample of the micro-organism with a recognised culture collection.[377] The deposit must be of all the micro-organisms needed to perform the alternatives included in the claim.[378] **5–87**

Most of these depositories operate under the Budapest Treaty of 1977 on the subject.[379] Samples have then to be made available to outsiders from the date of early publication of the application.[380] It is the only case where a competitor, in addition to receiving such information about the state of

[374] Likewise, positive suggestions that a selected sub-group has a particular advantage (subject to *de minimis* exceptions). For the requirement that a selection patent should state as part of its disclosure the special advantage involved, see above, paras 5–23—5–25. However, an erroneous explanation of why an invention works will not be objectionable, unless it is misleading to someone trying to achieve performance: *"Z" Electric v Marples* (1910) 27 R.P.C. 737 CA.

[375] *Valensi v British Radio* [1973] 3 R.P.C. 337 at 377 CA. Cf. *Genentech's Patent* [1989] R.P.C. 147 at 215 (in an advanced technology the skilled addressee has "a degree of inventiveness"). If technicians with different skills are addressed, it is assumed that they will work together: *"Z" Electric* case (above, n.37). See generally, above, paras 4–43, 4–44, 5–82.

[376] *Genentech's Patent* [1989] R.P.C. 147.

[377] PA 1977 s.125A; Patents Rules 1995 r.17, App.2; EPC Implementing Regulations, rr.31–34. These establish elaborate procedures aiming to prevent outsiders from obtaining samples in order to put them to their own use, rather than to check the validity of the patent in respect of which they are deposited.

[378] *Weyershaeuser/Cellulose* (T727/95) [2001] E.P.O.R. 35.

[379] Treaty on the International Recognition of the Deposit of Micro-organisms for the Purposes of Patent Procedure 1977. For the collections, see EPC Rules r.28. For equivalent rules in the British Patent Office see PA 1977 s.125A; Patents Rules 1995 r.17, Sch.2.

[380] For excusal by the EPO of temporary failures to make available, see Paterson, paras 3–48—3–52.

an application, also becomes entitled to starting material for performing the claimed invention. Since this possibility becomes available before the applicant knows whether or not he will succeed in securing his patent, the procedure is highly controversial. Contrast it with the US approach, where there is no early publication of applications, and release of deposited strains can occur only upon grant.

Until the application is withdrawn, refused or granted, any requester of a sample must undertake not to transfer it to others and only to use it for experimental purposes. In order further to modify the risk to the applicant, the EPO has added an "expert option". Under it the applicant may insist that during the same period, the disclosure be to a nominated expert—that is, a person approved either by the applicant or by the President of the EPO.[381] It is striking testimony to the demand for pharmaceutical and related patents that, in relation to material which might well found a secret production process, many prefer to take the risks inherent in the European type of deposit.

(4) Good faith in disclosing

5–88 It is only to be expected that some patentees may try to secure effective patent cover and at the same time keep to themselves crucial pieces of information about how the invention works best. How to make a patentee describe his invention sufficiently was a preoccupation of the early case law, and pronouncements that he must act in utmost good faith, that he must be "fair, honest and open" have been repeated often enough.[382] This attitude used to be reflected in the statute law, which required the description to be fair and to disclose the best method known to the patentee.[383] Now all that is called for is that the disclosure be clear and complete.

To prove an objection that the best method had been withheld was never easy. But, given the necessary proof, how would a court now react? If it found that the disguising had taken the form of deliberately obscure passages in the description, it would doubtless hold the disclosure insufficiently clear or complete.[384]

In *Hakoune*,[385] a European applicant claimed a step of etching stone by cathode bombardment. It was not known how to do this in the art, and the applicant admitted that it had not described the necessary steps in order to prevent them from being copied from the specification. There was found to be no sufficient description.

[381] The Biotechnology Directive 98/44, requires all Member State patent systems to adopt an "Expert Option": see arts 13, 14.

[382] See, e.g. *Morgan v Seaward* (1836) 1 W.P.C. 170 at 174; *Vidal Dyes v Levinstein* (1912) 29 R.P.C. 245 at 269 CA; *Raleigh v Miller* (1948) 65 R.P.C. 141 at 147 HL.

[383] PA 1949 s.32(1)(h).

[384] See *Biogen v Medeva* [1995] R.P.C. 25 at 86–87.

[385] *Hakoune* (T219/85) [1987] E.P.O.R. 30.

But suppose that the description leads to a perfectly acceptable, but not necessarily optimal, version of the invention, and the patentee knew this at the date of the application. The current law allows him to do just this.

Arguably, under conditions of modern research, patentees can no longer be expected necessarily to give full instructions for performance. Instead it should be enough if they indicate clearly the problem to which they have found some solution, and upon which they are likely to be pursuing further research; the patent then names the person to whom application can be made for further information and the patentee is left free to keep his extra knowledge for his own "head-start" or to sell it as know-how.[386] This modification has a certain attraction if one thinks in terms of a single technological leader and a circle of dependant exploiters. However, as the disturbing conditions of biotechnology have so forcibly shown, the patent system operates in competitive conditions and exists to heighten them. A system which does not insist upon adequate disclosure (as well as upon demonstration of a technical effect and of an inventive step) risks rewarding not those who win the race but those who jump first into the water.[387] Accordingly recent case law has been much concerned with disclosure and in particular—as explored under the next heading—the symbiotic relationship between the information provided about the invention and the claims to which this can properly lend support. **5–89**

6. Requirements for Claims

(1) Claims and disclosure

The claims of the specification, so crucial to the whole patenting process under a "fence-post" regime, must comply with four criteria: they must: (1) define the protected matter: (2) be clear and concise: (3) be supported by the description: and (4) be related to one invention.[388] **5–90**

During the application stage, the examiner must consider all these. Unity of invention has always been a matter which cannot afterwards be brought in question.[389] It is required in the interests of orderly classification and it is something which has simply to be settled one way or other at an early stage. But the other requirements are fundamental. Under the former British law, they could be raised throughout the life of a patent on the discrete ground that the claims were not fairly based on the description. That ground of objection was not contained in the EPC, either in relation to EPO oppositions or subsequent invalidity proceedings in national courts, and the British

386 On this see above, paras 5–58, 5–59, esp. the arguments of Beier and Kitch (above, para.5–56, n.266); Brandi-Dohrn (1994) 25 I.I.C. 648; Barton (1995) 26 I.I.C. 105.

387 cf. Beier and Moufang (1994) 43 Revista di Diritto Ind. 340, with Beier (previous note).

388 PA 1977 s.14(5); EPC art.84.

389 See above, para.4–15.

Act of 1977 was in the same terms.[390] Accordingly our courts at first considered, with considerable misgiving, that the proper scope of claims was not a matter that could be raised after grant.[391] However, the House of Lords has now said that at least an issue can be raised as to the adequacy of the disclosure, because of the requirement that claims be supported by the description.[392] The EPO now adopts the same approach.[393]

5–91 Thus the crucial issue has become what is a sufficient description to justify a given claim—and the answer has to be guided by the requirement of a disclosure which enables the invention to be performed to the full extent of the monopoly claimed.[394] Through a series of evolutionary decisions, both the EPO and British courts have reached the following propositions:

(1) If there is a single invention in a straightforward sense, then a description of how to perform one instance of it will suffice to support a claim to other instances in which predictably it will work. Thus, where a patent claimed a general principle for enabling plasmids to control the expression of polypeptides in bacteria, and there was no reason to believe that it would not work equally well in any plasmid, bacterium or polypetide, there was sufficient disclosure[395];

(2) In such a case, it will not be enough to attack such a claim that a few marginal instances cannot be made to work[396];

(3) The contrary will be so, if a substantial proportion of the claimed embodiments do not work or cannot be made to work merely by reliance on common general knowledge and routine trial[397];

[390] EPC arts 100, 138(1); PA 1977 s.72(1).

[391] *Genentech v Wellcome Foundation* [1989] R.P.C. 147.

[392] *Biogen v Medeva* [1997] R.P.C. 1; Colston [1997] I.P.Q. 521; Cripps [1997] C.L.J. 262; Spence (1997) 113 L.Q.R. 368; Warren [1997] J.B.L. 575; McInerney [1998] E.I.P.R. 14. After grant it is not possible directly to raise issues about the clarity or concision of the claims: *Kirin-Amgen v Transkaryotic Therapies* [2003] R.P.C. 31 at [88, 91].

[393] *Genentech/t-PA* (T923/92) [1996] E.P.O.R. 275; *Mycogen/Modified plant cells* (T694/92) [1998] E.P.O.R. 114.

[394] *Biogen v Medeva* [1997] R.P.C. 1 at 48 HL; *Kirin-Amgen v Transkaryotic Therapies* [2003] R.P.C. 31 CA.

[395] *Genentech I/Polypeptide expression* (T292/84) [1989] E.P.O.R. 1; and see *Quantel v Spaceward* [1990] R.P.C. 275; Morritt J., *Mölnlycke v Procter & Gamble* [1994] R.P.C. 49 at 99. For the distinction between classical insufficiency, Biogen insufficiency, and insufficiency through ambiguity, see *Zipher v Markem* [2009] F.S.R. 1 at [28–33]; cf. *Kirin Amgen v Transkaryotic Therapies* [2003] R.P.C. 31 at [71], where it is said that Biogen insufficiency is not a separate category.

[396] *Genentech v Wellcome Foundation* [1989] R.P.C. 147; this avoids the former strict notion of inutility, whereby a claim which covered any non-workable instance was bad (as in *Mineral Separations v Noranda* (1952) R.P.C. 81 at 95 JC).

[397] *Agrevo/Triazole sulphonamides* (T939/92) [1996] E.P.O.R. 171; *Hymo/Water-soluble polymer dispersion* (T583/93) [1997] E.P.O.R. 129; *Evans Medical's Patent* [1998] R.P.C. 517; *Pharmacia v Merck* [2002] R.P.C. 41 at [50, 56, 89, 90].

(4) In consequence, if a claim covers a number of discrete methods or products, it may be necessary to provide the skilled addressee with sufficient instructions in respect of each of them[398];

(5) Equally, if a general claim is to a product, irrespective of how it is made, the specification reveals only one way of making it and there is evidence that there probably will be other ways, the description will not be regarded as adequate to support the general claim.

Proposition 5 is an apparent ratio decidendi of *Biogen v Medeva* in the House of Lords.[399] The crucial claims were to genetically engineered DNA molecules containing an insert needed to produce a crucial protein for a vaccine against the hepatitis B virus. The virus itself consisted of an outer protein envelope (the surface antigen), an inner protein core (the core antigen) and DNA within the core. Because of this, DNA molecules had to be constructed with inserts for the surface antigen and the core antigen. The House, led by Lord Hoffmann, was satisfied that there was an adequate description of one procedure for achieving this difficult task. Subsequently, it had become clear that there were other routes which could be followed.[400] In relation at least to the claim being made in comparison with the state of the art, the patent's contribution to the art lay in solving the problem of producing the vaccine by one recombinant DNA technique. The House of Lords, led by Lord Hoffmann, held it impermissible to retain a claim that was to all ways of doing so. **5–92**

In *Generics v Lundbeck*,[401] the courts were called upon to decide the scope of the *Biogen* decision in relation to the path to the separate enantiomers of a racemate that is already known to have a pharmaceutical effect. Molecules of this type have mirror-image chemical structures referred to as the (+) and (-) enantiomers; and the racemate is a mixture of the two. It is to be expected that each form will have differing pharmaceutical effects. The one may be the major contributor to the health benefit, the other may be of little value and may even have a retarding effect. It is often difficult to find a technique for separating the two enantiomers from the racemate mixture so that each **5–93**

[398] *Biogen v Medeva* [1997] R.P.C. 1; and see generally *Mycogen* (T694/92) [1998] E.P.O.R. 114; *Procter & Gamble/Lipase* (T848/04) [2006] E.P.O.R. 27. In *Biogen* the CA's view of the facts (for which see the next paragraph) provided a pertinent illustration of this proposition: the court found that the claimed vaccine required the production of both a "surface" antigen and a "core" antigen; and that there were instructions only for making the former and not the latter—hence insufficiency. With this finding the HL disagreed.

[399] *Biogen v Medeva* [1997] R.P.C. 1.

[400] The House was careful to stress that this distinguished the case from *Genentech/Polypeptide expression* (T292/85) [1989] E.P.O.R. 1.

[401] *Generics v Lundbeck* [2009] UKHL 12; Leung [2010] E.I.P.R. 165.

can be medically tested.[402] The anti-depressant, citalopram, was a racemate that was covered by patent during the years when it became a worldwide market leader. Towards the end of that patent's life its producer's researchers eventually found a way of separating the (+) enantiomer (labelled escitalopram) and were able to show that it provided most of the pharmaceutical activity. It was accordingly advantageous to use it alone in administration to humans and it was patented as a chemical substance.

At first instance, Kitchin J. held, on the authority of *Biogen v Medeva,* that a person who discovered one way of making a previously "unenabled" molecule was not entitled to a product claim, which would thereby monopolise all ways of making it. Neither the Court of Appeal (where Lord Hoffmann sat, delivering the first judgment) nor the House of Lords considered this correct and the product claim was allowed to stand. It was for these courts to make the distinction from *Biogen* apparent. Lord Hoffmann found the difference in this: the patentee in *Biogen* was not able simply to claim the DNA molecule which could express the antigens of the hepatitis B virus in a host cell because it existed naturally in people suffering from hepatitis B. Nor could it claim to have invented the molecule isolated outside the human body, since that had already been done by purifying samples of the infective agent. The invention was accordingly restricted to finding the way of making it by recombinant DNA techniques. Where this was so, only a claim to that particular process of production could be allowed—a product-by-process claim, not a claim to all ways of making the substance. In *Lundbeck* by contrast the single molecular form was a thing not previously known, and finding out how to separate it from the racemate was an inventive step over the prior art. Accordingly a claim to all ways of making it was justified. This analysis was supported in the House of Lords. Further rationalisation was supplied, first by the distinction between product and process claims to be found in the EPC's provisions relating to infringement.[403] However, Lord Mance indicated that the distinction drawn in order to define different types of infringement provided no satisfactory reason why it should be used to draw a dividing line between what was, and was not, "industrially applicable".[404] In reality the House faced an issue which had not undergone any real consideration by the legislative bodies which enacted that requirement. Lord Mance was surely also right to point out that there could be arguments of principle or philosophy or from a utilitarian viewpoint that could justify confining the permissible claims by reference to what

[402] Since the racemate is a molecule already known, a first question is whether it stands in the way of the separate anentioners being regarded as novel. English courts have refused to countenance that objection. So have EPO tribunals (see *Exxon/Fuel Oils* (T409/91) [1994] OJ EPO 653) and courts elsewhere. (In the German litigation on the equivalent patent to that in issue in the UK *Lundbeck* case, however, the appeal court held the opposite and had to be corrected by the Bundesgerichtshof.) In *Lundbeck* before the HL, Lord Scott had initial doubts about the novelty of the antiomer: see above, n.401 at [1].

[403] See PA 1977 s.60(1), itself derived from the CPC art.25.

[404] *Generics v Lundbeck* (above, n.401) at [53].

the patentee had contributed to human knowledge—which was a way to produce escitalopram—or to justify allowing a product claim to a substance which was itself novel and which involved an inventive step over the prior art.[405]

In *Biogen*, Lord Hoffmann had sought to distinguish the cases where the wider entitlement was justified as being cases of the discovery of a principle, as distinct from those where the invention lay in an unexpected improvement of technique.[406] In *Lundbeck*, Lord Walker adumbrated a further distinction—that between "inventive concepts", which justify claims to products themselves, and "technical contribution to the art" which is the focus of attention in a process or method claim.[407] Looking to the incentive function of the patent system, it is arguable that the monopoly over a product, covering all ways of making it and all uses to which it may be put, should be particularly embracing where a new form of innovation is being launched. This could sustain the belief in industry that the market profits on the most saleable products should be screwed up high by the exclusive opportunity provided by a wide and deep patent. After all, the level of the possible prizes in any lottery determines the number of bidders and the size of their bets. But it has to be questioned whether the invention in *Lundbeck* deserved a place in the special category of principles or inventive concepts. For better or worse, the decision draws a line between patents for individual novel substances of pharmaceutical value and those for large classes of known substances for which a laboratory technique of manufacture has been worked out. In between there will doubtless be many halfway instances with which courts and tribunals will still have to deal. They will include cases where a patentee, if tied simply to his own technique, or indeed to the one new substance on which he has experimented, will be entitled to a patent of very little or no commercial value. But the measure of certainty provided by selecting only unknown products for special treatment will retain a certain usefulness. Law has often to draw what seem rather casuistic distinctions out of a feeling that opening floodgates wide will devastate in ways that a controlled use of weirs will avoid. **5–94**

(2) Ambiguous claims

The requirement that the claims define the invention and that they be clear should be read in the same sense as the similar objection under the old law.[408] The essence of the rule is disciplinary; it insists that the draftsman should not use language that is avoidably obscure and ambiguous. While this is supposed to apply whether the obscurity was deliberate, careless or **5–95**

---

405 *Generics v Lundbeck* above n.404 at [45].

406 *Biogen v Medeva* (above, n.399) at 48–49; and see *Kirin-Amgen v Hoechst Marion-Roussel* [2005] R.P.C. 9 at [112–117].

407 *Generics v Lundbeck* (above, n.404 at [29–30].

408 PA 1949 s.32(1)(i).

simply the result of lack of skill, a court is most likely to take offence at attempts unnecessarily "to puzzle a student and frighten men of business into taking out a licence".[409] The advance of science has brought increasing difficulties of definition. The old precision with which chemical formulae could be used to define the structure of substances, for instance, can no longer always be used for the macro-molecules of today.[410] Where the difficulty is genuine, a draftsman who does the best the case admits of will not be penalised.[411]

5–96 The courts have not insisted, in the name of precision, that patentees adopt strict dimensional and other limits, if to do so would likely offer competitors a simple route around the patent and they will not be seriously embarrassed in trying to decide whether or not they are performing within the claims. Thus, claims limited by result (such as for the "smokeless ashtray" mentioned in connection with sufficient disclosure)[412] are allowed if only simple experiments with the feature called for by the claim will determine what works. In similar vein, patentees may be permitted to use general words, that are comparative in import, like "large". Thus, in *British Thomson-Houston v Corona*,[413] a claim to a new type of electric light filament was held valid even though one characteristic required in the relevant claim was that the filament should be "of large diameter". This was read in the light of knowledge about filaments previously in use and was sufficiently clear to allow an informed worker to know when he was achieving the invention.

5–97 Judges have not been unanimous about how hard to strain in the search for definite meaning in a claim. On the whole, modern courts have proved readier to find some meaning rather than none, and indeed to prefer meanings that will avoid absurd results.[414] This will not necessarily rebound in the patentee's favour: for if he is trying to make his case by having his claims read in an unexpected sense (by virtue perhaps of some passage in the body of the specification) he may find the "plain" meaning preferred.[415] Altogether it has proved more difficult than in the past to sustain an attack based on the ambiguity of claims. There is no reason to suppose that this reflects a rise in standards of draftsmanship; indeed, the current readiness to be accommodating positively invites imprecision. Rather it is that patents are no longer looked upon with that suspicion of monopoly which underlay all the insistence upon accuracy in claiming.

---

[409] See especially Lord Loreburn, *Natural Colour Kinematograph v Bioschemes* (1915) 32 R.P.C. 256 at 266, 269; *Lubrizol v Esso Petroleum* [1997] R.P.C. 195 at 206.

[410] For the considerable difficulty that these present, see above, para.4–50; for a simpler instance, *Nihon Nohyakul/Lower alkyl* (T337/95) [1998] E.P.O.R. 333.

[411] For the assorted dicta, see Blanco White, para.4–702.

[412] See above, n.367.

[413] *British Thomson Houston v Naamloose* (1922) 39 R.P.C. 49.

[414] See especially, *Henriksen v Tallon* [1965] R.P.C. 434 HL (claim to ball-point pens with "jumbo" and "capillary" tubes read so as to exclude variants that would not work).

[415] See, e.g. *Mineral Separations v Noranda* (1952) 69 R.P.C. 81 at 93–94 JC; *Scanvaegt v Pelcombe* [1998] F.S.R. 786 at 797.

CHAPTER 6

SCOPE OF MONOPOLY

1. INFRINGEMENT

(1) Introduction[1]

Two sorts of patent infringer may be regarded as typical: the enterprise which through ignorance or stupidity, imitates the patentee's own product and so falls within the core of the monopoly; and the firm which, because of its independent effort or a determination to find a way round the patent, works (if at all) only in the penumbra of the claims. A patent which does not provide substantial protection against the second kind of infringer is generally not worth much. Yet if it is for an invention of real value, its precise scope is likely to be the subject of constant questioning. Hence the importance, in a system of patent law, of how this question of the scope of the right is determined. **6–01**

The British law before the 1977 Act, with its "fence-post" approach to the definition of monopoly, in fact combined scrupulousness over the question of who was infringing with a wide view of the scope of the rights affecting acts that did fall within the claims. The initial scrupulousness was found in the rule that, primarily but not quite exclusively, the monopoly was determined by the scope of the claims; and equally in the rule that a person who only contributed towards infringement could not for that alone be held liable. The subsequent breadth was to be found particularly in the principle that all sales and uses of patented goods required the patentee's licence; so

[1] See Heath and Petit (eds), *Patent Enforcement Worldwide* (2005), esp. Cornish and Llewelyn at pp.87 et seq.

that if he himself sold goods on terms restricting their resale or use, those who knowingly broke the conditions would infringe.

This highly individual blend of severity and generosity has been substantially changed in the European deal. A contributor may now be held responsible for "indirect infringement"; and a doctrine of exhaustion of rights will in future curb the possibilities of limited licensing. Both of these changes we shall discuss in due course.[2] At the same time, somewhat more interstitially, the former British approach to the question of what constitutes "direct infringement" has altered, and this must be the first subject for investigation.

(2) The role of the claims

6–02 The "fence-post" approach of the British system to the claims of the specification expresses a preference for certainty, however arbitrary it may sometimes seem, over the inevitably vaguer merits of "fair" protection to the patentee in the light of his disclosure. It is the approach that in principle has been accepted in EPC art.69,[3] and accordingly no radical redirection of British practice has been called for. The essential question over the scope of the monopoly remains whether an activity falls within the scope of a claim. This continues to make extent turn upon construction of the claim, in accordance with the rules already mentioned.[4] An article with the attributes called for in the claim remains an infringement, even if further things are added to it and even if those things make it more successful. Likewise it remains an infringement even though further work by the infringer enables him to select the best version of all the alternatives covered by the claim.[5] But a thing will cease to be within a claim if one or more of the essential elements is omitted or substituted by something different—something which does not fall within the description used in the claim.[6]

Accordingly, the question often in doubt is whether a defendant who is acting in the shadows of meaning on the periphery of a claim still falls within it. In answering this, recent decisions have responded, for the most part cautiously, to the injunction not to take too severe an interpretative

[2] See below, paras 6–15—6–19.

[3] But while the original English version says that extent is to be determined by the "terms" of the claims, the other versions use words ("teneur", "Inhalt") which may well convey a looser idea to those likely to use the French or German. When EPC 2000 comes into force, the extent is to be determined simply by "the claims".

[4] See above, paras 4–37 et seq.

[5] Even if the selector secures his own patent for his selection, this gives him no right to ignore a still subsisting patent for the wider class from which he selects: see above, paras 5–23—5–25.

[6] See, e.g. *Birmingham Sound Reproducers v Collaro* [1956] R.P.C. 232 at 245 CA; *Van der Lely v Bamfords* [1963] R.P.C. 61 HL; *Rodi & Wienenberger v Showell* [1969] R.P.C. 367 HL.

approach, which is one element in the Protocol to EPC art.69.[7] The "third way" set forth in that Protocol is this:

> "Article 69 should not be interpreted in the sense that the extent of the protection conferred by a European patent is to be understood as that defined by the strict, literal meaning of the wording used in the claims, the description and drawings being employed only for the purpose of resolving an ambiguity found in the claims. Neither should it be interpreted in the sense that the claims serve only as a guideline and that the actual protection conferred may extend to what, from a consideration of the description and drawings by a person skilled in the art, the patentee has contemplated. On the contrary, it is to be interpreted as defining a position between these extremes which combines a fair protection for the patentee with a reasonable degree of certainty for third parties."[8]

Before the 1977 Act, English case law did not in fact insist that a person was free to perform any act which did not fall exactly within the language of a patent claim properly construed. It was always law, as the recent leading cases have emphasised, that while an infringer must take each and every one of the essential integers of a claim, "non-essential" integers may be omitted or replaced by mechanical equivalents.[9] That oddly mixed metaphor—taking the "pith and marrow" of the invention—was to be understood in this sense and not as introducing some broader catch-net.[10] There was, however, considerable argument over what differences could be ignored as "insubstantial", "immaterial", "non-essential" (the three adjectives appeared interchangeable).

In the 1960s the House of Lords decided two cases concerning mechanisms where invention lay merely in a new combination of known parts. Both ideas were useful, but not major advances of technology. In *Van der Lely v Bamfords*,[11] the claim in issue was for a mechanical hay-rake with given characteristics in which the hindmost set of rakewheels could be moved forward in parallel with the foremost rakewheels, so as to cover wider areas **6–03**

[7] See also above, para.4–40; Pagenberg and Cornish, *Interpretation of Patents in Europa: Application of Article 69 EPC* (2006); Park [2005] E.I.P.R. 237; Hölder (2006) 37 E.I.P.R. 662.

[8] See also above, para.4–40. For the additional injunction "to take account of any element which is equivalent to an element in the claims", which was added by EPC 2000 see below, para.6–08.

[9] Parker J., *Marconi v British Radio* (1911) 28 R.P.C. 181 at 217; and see the cases cited above, n.6.

[10] The phrase was used by Lord Cairns in *Clark v Adie* (1877) 2 App.Cas. 315 at 320; and see Lord Reid, *Van der Lely* case (above, n.5) at 75; Lord Upjohn, *Rodi* case (above, n.6) at 391.

[11] See above, n.6. The plaintiff was reduced to relying upon this subsidiary claim because the main claims were anticipated (see above, para.5–04). The first filing was in the Netherlands where less exacting standards prevailed towards claims. The case was an object lesson to those charged with British applications to use greater imagination in thinking through obvious alternatives.

of ground in some operations. The defendant's hay-rake had means for moving its foremost rake-wheels back in line with the rearmost, which produced no different effect; but a majority of the Court refused to consider this infringement: if a claim stated that an integer should have a given characteristic, then this was essential because the patentee had chosen so to describe it.[12] Similarly in *Rodi & Wienenberger v Showell*[13] an expandable watch-strap was required by the claim to have two layers of links which were connected on each side by "U-shaped" bows. The defendant instead used "C-shaped" bows which extended from one side of the strap to the other, thus amounting to a combination of two U-shaped bows. A bare majority of the House of Lords took the view that there was no infringement in this substitution, inclining to the opinion that some material change in function had been introduced.[14]

However, in *Beecham Group v Bristol Laboratories*, a claim to a semi-synthetic penicillin was infringed by importation and sale of a chemical substance which did not have the claimed formula but which would nevertheless be converted in the human blood-stream into the claimed substance. The defendant's "bio-precursor" was treated as being the claimed substance "temporarily masked" and therefore an infringement.[15] In this case the patented invention was of basic importance, the result of a major research initiative. There was moreover no apparent advantage in using the defendant's bio-precursor form (though in other cases, administration of a drug through a bio-precursor may reduce harmful side-effects).[16]

If this suggested that some liberalisation over the attitude of the 1960s was beginning, it was confirmed by subsequent events. In the last leading case under the 1949 Act, *Catnic v Hill & Smith*,[17] the House of Lords, speaking through Lord Diplock, shifted emphasis in the construction of patent claims. True, his speech first insisted that interpretation is the sole issue, and that there is no separate question of "non-textual infringement". Equally he underscored the importance of "purposive", rather than "purely literal" construction. He disapproved of "the kind of meticulous verbal analysis in which lawyers are too often tempted by their training to indulge" and preferred the understanding of "persons with practical knowledge and experience of the kind of work in which the invention was intended to be used". Would they read a particular descriptive word or phrase as making

---

[12] Particularly where the claim was a subsidiary one, relating to something more specific than what had gone before: see Lord Radcliffe at 78; Romer L.J. *Submarine Signal v Hughes* (1932) 40 R.P.C. 149 at 175; Buckley L.J. *Catnic v Hill & Smith* [1979] F.S.R. 619 at 633.

[13] See above, n.6.

[14] And see below, n.19.

[15] *Beecham Group v Bristol Laboratories* [1978] R.P.C. 153 esp. at 200, 202.

[16] The discovery of this fact in an appropriate case could give rise to a separate patent: cf. *Beecham Group's Application* [1977] F.S.R. 565.

[17] *Catnic v Hill & Smith* [1982] R.P.C. 183. Attacked by Turner [1999] E.I.P.R. 531.

strict compliance an essential element, excluding any variant, even though it could have no material effect upon the way the invention worked?[18]

The case concerned a lintel for placing over doors and windows in the construction of buildings. It was made of reinforced steel plates formed into a box girder with a hollow inside. By replacing solid joists made of concrete and other materials, this invention provided a lighter, more manipulable substitute and was accordingly an immense success. The issue in infringement proceedings came to turn on a single adverb, "vertically". The claim required that one of the pieces of steel extend vertically down one side of the lintel. Following expert advice, the defendant's product varied the angle of the relevant piece, so that it ran either 6 per cent or 8 per cent from the vertical. This produced no known advantage of its own and it was held still to infringe: a builder would treat the side as vertical for his purposes; and the specification was addressed to him, not to a geometer.

Lord Diplock's approach was applied equally to cases arising under the **6–04**
1977 Act which involved such variants from a strict interpretation of a claim; and in *Improver v Remington*,[19] Hoffmann J. restated the issues systematically. As a preliminary it was necessary to decide whether a feature in an alleged infringement fell outside the primary, literal or a-contextual meaning of a descriptive word or phrase in the claim, and so constituted a variant. In order to decide whether the claims should be construed as covering this variant, three questions should then be asked:

> "(1) Does the variant have a material effect upon the way the invention works? If yes, the variant is outside the claim.[20] If no—
> (2) Would this (i.e. that the variant had no material effect) have been obvious at the date of publication of the patent to a reader skilled in the art.[21] If no, the variant is outside the claim. If yes—
> (3) Would the reader skilled in the art nevertheless have understood from the language of the claim that the patentee intended that strict compliance with the primary meaning was an essential requirement of the invention. If yes, the variant is outside the claim."[22]

As in *Catnic*, the *Improver* case turned on the meaning of a single expression. The invention, the "Epilady", was a popular gadget for removing body hair

[18] *Catnic* [1982] R.P.C. 183 at 242–243. For dislike of undue meticulousness, see also Lords Reid and Pearce, dissenting in *Rodi* case (above, n.6) at 378, 388.

[19] *Improver v Remington* [1990] F.S.R. 181 at 189.

[20] For instances where such differences led to a finding of non-infringement, see *Heath v Unwin* (1800) 2 W.P.C. 296; *Deere v Harrison McGregor* [1965] R.P.C. 461 HL; *Rodi* case (above, n.6), particularly as regards the second allegation of infringement in that case.

[21] This does not raise any inquiry into whether the variant was itself obvious. The question is whether the absence of any material difference in effect was obvious.

[22] Rubbing in the grammatical niceties of the exercise, for inclusion of a non-literal meaning within claim language, Hoffmann J. would require the use of an expression as synecdoche (part for a whole: "face in the crowd") or metonymy (attribute for a thing: "the Crown").

which used an electric motor to spin a coiled spring while it was bent. The spring thus opened and shut rapidly, trapping hairs and pulling them out. The defendant's "Smooth & Silky" substituted for the spring a rubber tube with a series of cuts going through almost from one side to the other—rather as if it were a comb. This was said to avoid the plaintiff's claim, which called for a "helical spring". Reaching his third question, Hoffmann J. agreed, finding that a skilled reader would expect there to be a spring, not some substitute for it that would operate in the same manner.

6–05 This litigation provided a striking test of the meaning to be attached to the EPC art.69, Protocol, since similar actions on "Epilady" patents, all deriving from a single EPO grant, were brought in several other participant countries. Both in Germany and Holland, the claimant went as far as trial and succeeded.[23] In those countries the courts followed precedents which required the wording of the claims to be taken as the "decisive basis" of protection, rather than to "what the patentee has contemplated". Nonetheless, approaching the matter from an opposite tradition to the British, the courts found that the defendant was infringing because it employed the patentee's inventive concept through a variant equivalent to what had actually been claimed.[24] This point was put in some cases in convoluted phraseology,[25] and in others in simple terms.[26] Either way, there seemed less room for the linguistic scruple which is the essential point of Hoffmann J.'s third question.[27]

For 15 years, the first instance courts and the Court of Appeal in Britain almost always strove to work through the *Catnic-Epilady* questions, or *Protocol* questions as they came latterly to be labelled.[28] The most

---

[23] For the principal "Epilady" decisions, see (1993) 24 I.I.C. 803 at 823.

[24] Note also the leading German decisions, *Formstein* [1991] R.P.C. 24; *Ion Analysis* (1991) 22 I.I.C. 249; and the Dutch decision, *Meyn v Stork* (1992) 23 I.I.C. 529—first brought to common law attention in the Hong Kong "Epilady" proceedings: [1990] 1 H.K.L.R. 33. The German law has since been developed by the German Supreme Court particularly in the "Quintet" of cases analysed by Meier-Beck and commented on by Lord Hoffmann in the *Kirin-Amgen* decision (below n.30) at para.75 The Dutch Supreme Court has continued to insist upon broad "interpretation" of the claims: *Van Bentum v Kool* [2003] BIE 99. For the position in these and other Continental jurisdictions, see Pagenberg and Cornish (above, n.7) esp. pp.73–102 (Keukenschrijver); 105–98 (Brinkhof)). For comparison with the US approach, see Chisum in *Vaver and Bently* (2004) Ch.7.

[25] As when the German Supreme Court asks whether "the average person skilled in the art would have been able to discover the embodiment deviating from the wording and literal sense of the patent claim by proceeding from the invention as it is defined in the patent claim": *Handle Cord for Battery* (1991) 22 I.I.C. 104.

[26] See above, n.24.

[27] The purpose of formulating the test differs with the nature of the adjudication. In Germany and other countries which rely for scientific advice on experts, the test forms the crucial instruction to those experts. In the US they are part of instructions to juries. But in other common law jurisdictions they form part of the judge's own rationalisation of his decision of the case.

[28] In *PLG Research v Ardon International* [1995] R.P.C. 287, the Court of Appeal indicated that the *Catnic* test should be "left to legal historians" and the matter approached purely by reference to the Protocol. The judgment made substantial reference to German case-law cited above (in nn.24, 25). But subsequently this was treated as an aberration.

perplexing issue that they raised was this: at the outset it was necessary to decide that the infringement did not fall within the primary, literal or a-contextual meaning of the claim. The three questions could then be asked about the variant. But after deciding that the variant had no material effect and that this would have been obvious, the third question asked a different question, which took the court back to interpretation: would the patentee nonetheless be understood by the notional skilled reader to be using the crucial term in its primary meaning, and not in any extended sense that would include the variant? It became evident, as variations in the meaning of the three specific tests emerged in English judgments, and criticisms continued to be raised by experts in other European jurisdictions, that the law was becoming repetitious and confusing.[29]

How to interpret patent claims in a system that remained reluctant to admit any distinct doctrine of equivalence was raised in the House of Lords in *Kirin-Amgen v Hoechst Marion Roussel*.[30] Erythropoietin ("Epo") is the protein that occurs naturally in the human body in tiny amounts to stimulate the production of red blood cells. Only through recombinant DNA technology could Epo be created in sufficient quantities to treat blood deficiencies, such as anaemia and kidney failure. Both the patentee and the alleged infringer, TKT, used techniques by which DNA was inserted into host cells so as to affect their content, but the DNA was different and it was employed at different stages. The patentee did so "downstream" by inserting a DNA sequence which is itself encoded for Epo and so caused the expression of Epo. The defendant adopted a technique that was unknown when the patentee's specification was published. This involved inserting a "control" DNA sequence "upstream". The sequence had the effect of switching on DNA encoding for Epo that was already present in the cell, but not "connected". The two claims on which the patentee relied were interpreted in the litigation as referring literally only to the downstream technique, not to the upstream.

Lord Hoffmann, in the leading judgment, insisted that the *Catnic* **6–06**
requirement of purposive interpretation was precisely in line with the Protocol, and that the Protocol set the one question that in law required to be answered. The additional questions about variants formulated in the *Catnic/Improver* questions were to be treated only as guidelines which would be more appropriate to follow in some circumstances than others. Where the real question was the understanding that the skilled observer would reasonably have of the claim, then the *Catnic/Improver* questions added nothing, since the third question tended to bring back the same issues as asking what the literal, non-contextual meaning of the claim was, simply because it is often very difficult to strip the meaning of a word or phrase of

[29] See further, Cornish and Llewelyn in Kur et al. (eds), *Patent Law on the Move* (2005) 115.

[30] *Kirin-Amgen v Hoechst Marion Roussel* [2005] R.P.C. 9 H.L. at [27–35]. See Hölder (2006) 37 I.I.C.662.

its context. So in the case before the House, it was held that claims drafted to cover the "downstream" approach could not be read as extending to any act of incorporating DNA, including the "upstream" technique. It has been noticeable that in applying *Kirin-Amgen*, subsequent courts have gratefully turned to its simplified approach.[31]

It is possible to think of circumstances where *Catnic/Improver* will still be useful, not least now that the provision concerning equivalence added to the Protocol in EPC 2000 takes effect.[32] Cases where a measurement or defined category of substance or treatment is given an outer limit in a claim, and the alleged infringement goes just outside that limit—of which *Catnic* itself was a plain example—may benefit from asking whether the variant works in the same way, and whether this would be obvious to those skilled in the field.[33] The same approach might allow a generous "reading" of a claim, contrary to that in *Van der Lely v Bamfords*.[34] There the defendant adopted the obverse arrangement to that claimed (aligning foremost rake wheels with the rearmost), which made no functional difference; yet the House of Lords found the claim not infringed.

The context may also raise issues of general policy about the scope of the patent system in relation to the subject matter of the patent claim. This was so in *Kirin-Amgen*. At first instance, Neuberger J. held that TKT had after all infringed the two claims relied upon by finding that the essence of the invention lay in disclosing the DNA structures that would encode for Epo. Disclosing the structures, however, amounted only to revealing scientific knowledge. So it was discovery as such, rather than invention, and a claim that went so far as to cover that was precluded by EPC art.52(2)(a).[35] It must be correct that, however the Protocol is read, it cannot justify treating as infringement an activity that could not be patentable subject-matter.

6–07 There is also an important relationship with the requirement of adequate disclosure as a means of controlling overbroad claiming. *American Home Products v Novartis Pharmaceuticals*[36] concerned a patent claiming rapamycin, a complex antibiotic molecule, for its properties as an immuno-suppressant which inhibited rejection of the new tissue in transplant surgery.[37] The

[31] See, e.g. *Ultraframe v Eurocell* [2005] R.P.C. 36 CA.

[32] For which, see above, para.6–02 n.8; below, para.6–08.

[33] In a "quintet" of cases concerned with alleged infringements that side-stepped numerical limits in claims, the German Supreme Court held that there cannot be infringement by equivalence: substitutes that clearly leave the claim behind; substitutes replace an essential feature with means that do not satisfy the purpose of the invention; substitutes that use additional means intentionally avoided by the claimed invention; substitutes which it was the main purpose of the invention to avoid. These limitations were considered by Lord Hoffmann in *Kirin-Amgen* to address the same question as in the British approach: what would a person skilled in the art have thought the patentee was using the language of the claim to mean? See [2005] R.P.C. 9 at [75].

[34] Above, n.6.

[35] *Kirin-Amgen* [2005] R.P.C. 9 at [76–77].

[36] *American Home Products v Novartis Pharmaceuticals* [2001] R.P.C. 8 CA.

[37] Since the molecule was already known for a different medical use, the claim was in "Swiss form", for which, see above, para.5–69.

claimant's specification referred to the many derivatives of rapamycin and predicted that some of them would have an equal or better effect in the therapy, but the claim was restricted to rapamycin itself because at the time there was no way of knowing which derivatives would prove to be effective alternatives or improvements. The defendant's variant derivative was discovered only after substantial further research. At first instance Laddie J. found infringement, essentially because the truly significant invention was in discovering the new property of rapamycin. What followed was mere improvement; but if the claimant's patent did not extend to the variant, it would in practice be valueless. At first instance, much in the manner of the first instance decision in *Kirin-Amgen*, the Court of Appeal rejected this view, refusing to find it obvious that the variant would work in the same way as the claimed molecule. The court thus insisted upon giving certainty for third parties its due under the Protocol. Showing some discomfort nonetheless, the court pointed out that the time lag that accompanies further progress in most medical research enables the patentee to reap benefits from its claim, even when confined to what its claim says.

One method of investigating how the claim should be interpreted is to look at the course of examining the patent application in order to see whether the applicant conceded limitations to the wording. The prior art revealed by the search might well have made this necessary in order to avert an objection of lack of novelty or obviousness. In the United States, the course of the application is regularly examined for evidence that would create a "file wrapper estoppel".[38] English courts have shown a marked reluctance to start down this often obscure path. Thus in *STEP v Emson*,[39] Hoffmann L.J. refused to look into purposes "buried in the prior art" or any other reason the patentee may have had for the limitation (which can embrace mistakes and misapprehensions on the part of the patent drafter). **6–08**

As the *Kirin-Amgen* and *Rapamycin* decisions demonstrated, British courts continue to insist that the issue is one of interpretation and they thereby avoid over-extended arguments for infringement by equivalence. While the Protocol in its EPC 2000 version requires "due account" to be taken of equivalence, it will remain true that certainty for third parties must continue also to be weighed. In *Virgin Atlantic v Premium Aircraft* the Court of Appeal, led by Jacob L.J., has insisted that in consequence there is no separate, preemptive doctrine of equivalence. The crucial question remains, what in the circumstances is the meaning to be attached to the claims? The price of this evaluation is that sometimes the patentee who makes the truly

[38] For the present intricacies, see *Festo v Shoketsu Kinzoku* 122 S.Ct. 1831 (2002). The rule is attacked by Thomas (1999) 47 UCLA L.R. 183; for a comparison with the UK position, Fox [2004] E.I.P.R. 528; Garde [2005] E.I.P.R. 365.

[39] *STEP v Emson* [1993] R.P.C. 513 at 522; Walker L.J. *Rohm & Haas v Collag* [2002] F.S.R. 28 CA; cf. Jacob J. *Bristol-Myers Squibb v Baker Norton* [1999] R.P.C. 253 at 274, accepting the possibility of considering the claims in the public application and perhaps also referring to statements against the patentee's interest in subsequent correspondence with the Patent Office.

significant breakthrough will not obtain a claim that is good against a further researcher whose later contribution is in comparative terms much less striking. Judges will continue to seek solutions which, within the current constraints, place the second at least in a position where it must take a licence from the first for an exploitation involving both inventions.[40]

(3) Types of infringing activity[41]

6–09 A defendant infringes only if he performs certain kinds of activity, normally industrial or commercial. These are now defined in s.60 of the Patents Act 1977, which draws upon the original CPC arts 25–28, but does not always say the same thing.[42] The bulk of patents are concerned with things manufactured or processes of manufacture; accordingly the prohibited acts may usefully be considered under three heads: acts performed during manufacture, acts after and acts before. These are rough divisions and have to be related to the type of claim which the patentee has been able to obtain. Bear in mind that in general a claim to a product (a machine, a substance, a compound) is first infringed directly at the moment when a product is made which contains all the essential features claimed; while a claim to a process (manufacturing procedure; use of a known substance) is first infringed directly when the complete process is carried out.

6–10 In all cases there are three qualifications to observe:

(1) *Territoriality*: a British patent is infringed only by acts done in the United Kingdom, its territorial waters and "designated" continental shelf.[43] A patentee who wishes to sue for acts done in (say) France must sue upon a French patent and will normally bring the action in French courts.[44]

(2) *Licence*: nothing done with the patentee's consent is an infringement; the act is then licensed. With one exception "direct" infringement occurs even where the user of the invention does not know of the invention, believes the use to fall outside the claims or believes that there is a sufficient licence.[45] Occasionally the question may arise

[40] One school of thought in the US treats this as the very case where a doctrine of equivalence should survive: see, e.g. Rader J. in *Johnson & Johnston v RE Service*, 285 F.3d 1046 (2002).

[41] See, in particular, Benyamini (1993).

[42] But remember the injunction to conform contained in PA 1977 s.130(7): see, e.g. *Smith Kline & French v Harbottle* (below, n.72).

[43] The UK includes the Isle of Man but not the Channel Islands. For the designation of seabeds, important in an age of off-shore extractions, see the Continental Shelf Act 1964; cf. generally, Stauder (1976) 7 I.I.C. 470; Benyamini, Ch.10. There is now developing a need to provide for the patenting of inventions in space, e.g. on satellites: see Beier and Stauder, *Space Stations* (1985); Meyer (1988) 70 JPTOS 332.

[44] For jurisdiction to sue for foreign infringements, see above, paras 2–72 et seq.

[45] The exception is the case of offering a process: below, para.6–17. Indirect infringement also has a knowledge requirement: below, para.6–18.

whether the patentee in effect consents either by standing by in silence or by some positive misstatement to the defendant: delay, acquiescence and estoppel have been discussed already.[46]

(3) *Additional liability at common law*: while the statute now specifies activities which constitute both "direct" and "indirect" infringement, the general law of tort can give additional aid. A patentee may be able to proceed against persons whose auxiliary activities fall beyond the range of the statutory acts: liability as a joint tortfeasor, or tortious liability for conspiracy or for inducement to wrongdoing—conceptions which often overlap—may provide this additional legal armoury.[47] In addition, there is old authority favouring the grant of an injunction against persons, such as warehousers, prohibiting them from handling infringing goods, even though they themselves would not be tortiously liable for doing so.[48]

(a) *Infringement during manufacture*

Making a patented product and using a patented process head the list of infringing acts.[49] Most of the problems here concern the issue already discussed: is the defendant's activity within the terms of the claims (or some extension beyond them allowed by law)? Suppose that a patented device (a windsurfer, to take a much litigated example) is claimed to comprise an assembly of four distinct elements. Is it "direct" infringement within s.60(1) of the Patents Act 1977 to supply a complete kit of the parts which can be assembled without difficulty by a purchaser? Occasionally courts have so held.[50] If one of the claimed elements is left out, a patentee is thrown back into the more limited realm of an action for preliminary, "indirect" infringement (under s.60(2)), for liability as a joint infringer, or for a common law tort, such as conspiracy or inducing commission of a tort.[51] **6–11**

A different borderland is reached over repairs and replacement of parts.[52] A person who obtains a patented product from a legitimate source may

---

46 See above, paras 2–63—2–71.

47 See above, paras 2–12 et seq.

48 *Washburn v Cunard Steamship* (1889) 6 R.P.C. 398 at 403. For declarations of non-infringement, see above, para.2–90.

49 PA 1977 s.60(1); original CPC art.25; Benyamini Chs 6, 7.1.

50 e.g. *Rotocrop International v Genbourne* [1982] F.S.R. 241 at 257–260; but see the doubts expressed in *Lacroix v Kwikform* [1998] F.S.R. 493.

51 See below, paras 6–17—6–19.

52 The same considerations apply, if the issue is considered as indirect infringement under PA 1977 s.60(2). Previously this was regarded as turning on the extent of the patentee's licence to use the invention, which was to be implied from unconditional sale. In future it may be better regarded as a limit upon the scope of the doctrine of exhaustion (see below, para.6–15); and consider also the doctrine of non-derogation from grant; see below, para.15–06.

repair it or have it repaired; but he may not go so far as to make the product anew.[53]

The Act creates exceptions to the range of infringing acts: two of these are general, the rest particular.[54] The general exceptions cover:

(1) *Private use*: acts done privately and for purposes which are not commercial.[55] Note the conjunctive "and": activities of governmental, educational and charitable organisations may not be commercial, but they are not likely to be private.

(2) *Experimental use*: acts done for experimental purposes relating to the subject-matter of the invention.[56] This exception has proved increasingly controversial in connection with patents over successful pharmaceutical products. Many systems traditionally admitted such an exception for the non-commercial activities of the research scientist in a university or government laboratory. Recent developments in the EPC countries show that the exception may also apply to commercial research. This appears to follow from placing the exception after the separate exemption of private, non-commercial research. Nonetheless a distinction has to be drawn between work which seeks to improve or modify the invention and other activities. It is not justifiable to use the invention for experiments on unrelated subject-matter. If for instance, a medium is wanted in order to grow a particular microorganism, and the medium is patented, then a licence for its use will be necessary.[57] Nor does it cover trials to see whether a person can produce commercially according to the patent.[58]

Three situations on the borderline may be identified:

[53] *Solar Thomson v Barton* [1977] R.P.C. 537 (design right may present a different problem); *Sirdar Rubber v Wallington* (1906) 22 R.P.C. 257 at 266; (1907) 24 R.P.C. 539 at 543; *United Wire v Screen Repair Services* [2001] R.P.C. 24 HL; *Schütz v Werit* [2010] EWHC 1623 (Pat) at [170 et seq.] Note the discussion of three recent decisions of the German Supreme Court. A person who supplies replacement parts for an infringing article may well be an indirect infringer: see below, para.6–18. A person who merely carries such repairs out, although he helps to prolong the article's life, is less likely to be caught (but does he "keep" the invention—s.60(1)(a)?). cf. *Aro Mfg v Convertible Top*, 377 U.S. 476 (1964).

[54] See generally, Benyamini Ch.11. Amongst the particular exceptions, the one relating to manufacture covers "extemporaneous" preparations by pharmacists from prescriptions: s.60(5)(c), cf original CPC art.27(c). There are also "farming use" exceptions in line with the Biotechnology Directive 98/44 EC art.11, reg.47 and see Council Regulation 2100/94.

[55] PA 1977 s.60(5)(a); original CPC art.27(a). This includes an experiment for legal proceedings: *Smith Kline v Evans* [1989] R.P.C. 513. It must be permissible to test a specification for the adequacy of its instructions. Cf. the extremely limited view of such use under US patent law: *Madey v Duke University* 307 F 3d 1351 (Fed Cir 2002); Sampson [2004] E.I.P.R. 1.

[56] PA 1977 s.60(5)(b); original CPC art.27(b). See in particular, Gilat, *Experimental Use and Patents* (1995); Eisenberg (1989) 56 U. Chi. L.R. 1017; Grossman (1990) 30 Idea 243; Cornish (1998) 29 I.I.C. 735; Cook [2006] I.P.Q. 193; Australian Council on *IP, Patents and Experimental Use* (2005).

[57] For another example, see the *SmithKline* case (above, n.55).

[58] *Inhale Therapeutic v Quadrant Healthcare* [2002] R.P.C. 21.

(i) *Testing by a defendant to procure authority to market a pharmaceutical or agro-chemical product already marketed by the patentee.* Towards the end of a successful patent's life, generic producers will be preparing to enter the market as quickly as possible and securing regulatory authority in these fields is a requirement which patentees have no wish to see speeded up. In Europe it is almost universally accepted that the experimental use defence does not permit such testing to take place in advance of expiry.[59]

(ii) *Testing by a defendant in the wake of its independent discovery of beneficial properties of a substance which falls within the plaintiff's patent but which differs from the product marketed by the plaintiff.* In this case, experiments genuinely to discover further information about the properties of the defendant's substance will be permissible, whereas tests to provide further evidence of already known qualities will not. In *Monsanto v Stauffer*,[60] the Court of Appeal allowed a defendant in such a situation to continue its in-house experiments, but disallowed external field tests because they sought only to reaffirm what was known. They had the twin purposes of satisfying regulatory authorities and demonstrating advantages to customers;

(iii) *Testing for new uses and further information about properties of a patented product, including conduct of clinical trials with patients.* This situation has yet to be considered in the United Kingdom. In Germany, two leading judgments have held that such trials fall within the exception, provided either that they have, as one real motivation, a search for further medical applications or for more information about the effects and the tolerability of a drug which incorporates the patented substance.[61] The decisions are firmly based upon the public interest in ensuring that the patent system does not act as a block on genuine research developments—the cases arose because patentees were not prepared to grant licences for the work.[62] In 2004, the EU decided to go even further.[63] It introduced an extension of the

[59] See esp. *Ethofumesate* (1991) 22 I.I.C. 541 BGH; *Auchinloss v Agricultural and Veterinary Supplies* [1999] R.P.C. 397 CA; *Generics v Smith Kline & French* [1997] R.P.C. 801 per Jacobs Adv.Gen, ECJ. In the US, the Hatch-Waxman Act has reversed this approach, to the fury of major pharmaceutical producers, who consider that the extension period allowed for delays in commercialisation because of medical certification are inadequate. Cf. the *Clinical Trials III* decision of the Japanese SC, April 16, 1999: (1999) 30 I.I.C. 448.

[60] *Monsanto v Stauffer* [1985] R.P.C. 515; and see [1984] F.S.R. 559; [1987] F.S.R. 57. See also *Corevalve v Edwards Lifesciences* [2009] F.S.R. 8.

[61] *Klinische Versuche I (Interferon-gamma)* [1997] R.P.C. 623 BGH; *Klinische Versuche II (Erythropoietin)* [1998] R.P.C. 423 BGH. Of course, there will be reason to hope that the tests will also cure or improve the condition of the subject patients. There will come a point where the breadth of the testing means that the research objective seems wholly secondary.

[62] Indeed, in the second case, the defendant had (quite exceptionally) procured a German compulsory licence to market the drug. See further, below, paras 21–19 et seq.

[63] Directive 2004/27, amending Directive 2001/83: OJ L136/34. This was in contrast with its earlier decision to bring WTO panel proceedings against Canada for introducing a similar provision: WT/DS114/R (2001).

experimental use exception to cover experimental testing for the purpose of seeking regulatory approval, thus bringing the position into line with that under US legislation.[64] For this the quid pro quo was that there is a term of protection for the data relating to approved pharmaceutical products, which runs from the date of approval. This applies to undisclosed data submitted to the authority regulating marketing of the drug.[65] In conjunction with this, third parties can file for approval of their own version of the patented drug eight years from approval, but cannot get authorisation until the 10th year—with an additional year in the case of some drugs having a "significant clinical benefit in comparison with existing clinical therapies".[66]

Particularly in the realm of biotechnology, basic research and practical applications of it are not easily distinguishable. Experimentation to further general understanding must continue in this rapidly advancing science. The importance of keeping this process to some degree free of patent constraints is expressed by the experimental use exception. It is hard to judge whether it now sets a satisfactory dividing line. Gilat suggests as a touchstone that the exception should only operate in those cases where licences of the existing patent are unlikely to be given—as where a patentee is seeking to monopolise further experimentation. That at the very least should fall within the exception.[67]

(b) *Infringement after manufacture: general provisions*

6–12 The list of infringing acts also covers: disposing of, offering to dispose of, using, importing, and even keeping for disposal or otherwise, either the patented product or a product "obtained directly by means of a patented process".[68] The range of defendants made possible by this extensive list is considerable. Where infringing goods pass down a chain of distributors each person becomes liable: as a "keeper", then as a "disposer". Even the ultimate recipient may be a "keeper", if he is not a "user".[69] A person who acquires or imports goods for the purpose of exporting them to sell abroad

---

[64] Hatch-Waxman Act 1984.

[65] This implements the requirement of TRIPs art.39(3).

[66] See Vaver and Basheer [2006] E.I.P.R. 282.

[67] The *Gowers Review* (2006) recommends an expansion of the scope of the research exemption, following the lines of current Swiss law: see paras 4.4–4.12.

[68] PA 1977 s.60(1); note that there are a number of trying variations here from the language of original CPC art.25: for instance, the former uses "disposes of", etc. in place of "puts on the market"; and see the following footnotes. When EU patents are eventually introduced, their precise scope may differ somewhat from UK patents.

[69] In contrast with (1) the previous law (see e.g. *British United Shoe Manufacturers v Collier* (1910) 27 R.P.C. 567); and (2) original CPC art.25—to which the old authorities on "use" seem relevant (see Ency. P.L., para.3–216).

will thus infringe, as he did under the previous law.[70] Both sides to a simple hiring agreement will in turn be "keepers".[71] But a mere carrier has not been treated as a keeper.[72] However, a person who negotiates with a view to selling an article after expiry of a patent covering it "offers to dispose" of it.[73]

Again, in addition to the licensing by the patentee of "acts", there are exceptions. For instance, the exclusion from infringement of private, non-commercial acts and experimental acts[74] apply in this post-manufacture phase, but only to protect those who perform the specified acts. The exceptions do not give cover for subsequent "acts" that would otherwise infringe: if infringing apparatus is sold once in a purely private sale, this does not justify its resale in a business deal.[75]

Where the chain of distribution originates abroad, a person who completes a sale by transferring property in the products in another country does not infringe (because of the restriction to acts done in the United Kingdom), but the subsequent importer will.[76] Even if the foreign exporter at some stage writes to the British purchaser about an order, he will not thereby be offering to dispose.[77] However, if he positively solicits orders from British customers, he is likely to be infringing on this ground, or as joint tortfeasor or as one who procures infringement.[78] **6–13**

It is in such cases that infringement of a process patent by dealing in its *direct* product becomes specially important.[79] The commercial value of a process patent can obviously be impaired if the process can be carried out abroad (where there may be no patent) and the product sold in competition **6–14**

---

[70] Here the different language of PA 1977 s.60 and original CPC art.25, seems to lead to the same result. And see *Hoffmann-La Roche v Harris* [1977] F.S.R. 200; *British Motor v Taylor* (1900) 17 R.P.C. 723.

[71] Under the original CPC, hiring out is covered, if at all, by "putting on the market". This phrase is also used in the CPC's definition of exhaustion of rights: see arts 28, 76. It is a common assumption that if something is hired out a patentee can continue to control its use: but that may be open to question, once this version of exhaustion takes effect. See below, paras 6–15, 6–16.

[72] *Smith, Kline & French v Harbottle* [1980] R.P.C. 363; *McDonald v Graham* [1994] R.P.C. 409 CA.

[73] *Gerber Garment v Lectra* [1995] R.P.C. 383; *Tanglass v Luowang North Glass (No. 2)* [2006] F.S.R 32.

[74] PA 1977 s.60(6). See above, para.6–11.

[75] For special exceptions covering uses connected with land, sea and air craft, see PA 1977 s.60(5) (d)–(f); original CPC art.27(d)–(f); *Stena Rederi v Irish Ferries* [2003] R.P.C. 36 CA.

[76] *Sabaf v MFI Furniture* [2005] R.P.C. 7 HL. See above, para.6–10.

[77] *Kalman v PCL Packaging* [1982] F.S.R. 406; *Badische Anilin v Johnson* (1897) 14 R.P.C. 919. Not all European countries take so restrictive a view; so the issue may have to be reconsidered: see Benyamini pp.251–257.

[78] See above, paras 2–07, 2–13.

[79] Note that the EPO will grant "product-by-process" claims only where the product is itself novel: *BICC/Radiation processing* [1986] OJ EPO 261. This does not, however, apply to a process which improves a thing (e.g. tenderising meat): *Mobil Oil/Friction reducing additive* [1990] OJ EPO 93; Paterson, paras 9–58, 9–59.

in Britain.[80] In the pre-1977 law, English courts had gone some distance in holding a claim to a process to be infringed by the importation of the subsequent product, requiring not that the product be the immediate result of the process (for there might be intermediate steps in which the first product changed its composition or other attributes)[81] but only that the contribution of the process to the final product be important (the "Saccharin" doctrine).[82]

Under the EPC and the 1977 Act, however, the connection between process and product must be "direct", or in another word, "immediate".[83] *Pioneer Electronics v Warner Music*[84] holds that this precludes infringement where there are intervening steps which deprive the first product of its essential characteristics. So in the production of compact discs, a process for producing the so-called "father" disc at a particular pressure was not infringed by importing the final discs; in between there had to be conversion into "mothers", then to "sons" and then, by injection moulding, into discs. This limited interpretation has implications both for the production of pharmaceuticals by standard techniques and through genetic manipulation.[85]

The Biotechnology Directive seeks to expand the scope of protection given to product claims in that one field so as to cover material derived by propagation or multiplication.[86] What effect this will have is hard to predict. So too with the provision concerning patents on products containing genetic information, which extends to all material in which the products are incorporated, save (it seems) the human body.[87] Thanks to the long disputed "farmer's exception", these provisions do not apply to his own use of seed or breeding of animals.[88]

---

[80] It is possible, of course, to take the strict view of the Banks Committee (Cmnd.4407, 1970), para.297, that if a patentee wants appropriate cover he must secure a product-by-process claim; which is all very well if he knows all the relevant products when he applies for his patent. This approach has not been adopted in the 1977 Act.

[81] *Saccharin Corp v Anglo-Continental Chemical* (1900) 17 R.P.C. 307.

[82] Tomlin J. *Wilderman v Berk* (1925) 42 R.P.C. 79 at 86; *Beecham Group v Bristol Laboratories* [1978] R.P.C. 153 at 201, 203, 204.

[83] Pumfrey J., *Monsanto v Cargill* [2008] F.S.R. 7 at [35].

[84] *Pioneer Electronics v Warner Music* [1997] R.P.C. 757 CA; Hurdle [1997] E.I.P.R. 322. The wording derives from Germany, and British courts have paid attention to one view from that country: Bruchhausen [1979] GRUR 743 (who is critical of more liberal German authority). Cf. Van Benthem in Pennington (ed.), *European Patents at the Crossroads* (1976) pp.125–126; Benyamini Ch.8.

[85] For the importance of the issue in biotechnology, see *Monsanto v Cargill* (above, n.83); Byrne (1985) 16 I.I.C. 1; Beier and Straus (1986) 25 Ind. Prop. 447 at 456; Christie [1989] E.I.P.R. 394 at 402.

[86] Directive 98/44 art.8 and note the movement exception in art.10. There will be no problem where a claim has been allowed to the derivative product. Although the EPC will not itself be altered by the Directive, the EPO will doubtless take account of its change in deciding what claims are justifiable.

[87] Articles 9, 10.

[88] See art.11. Where a farmer produces crops or animals from patented biological material supplied by a patentee or licensee, he is entitled to use his product for multiplication or propagation. In the case of certain crops, however, a large farmer is obliged to pay equitable remuneration for doing so: see PA 1977, Sch A1, A2.

(c) *After manufacture: exhaustion of rights*[89]

Patents used to be the field of intellectual property where in British law no notion of exhaustion of rights applied. As noted already, even when the patentee made or authorised a sale of patented goods, restrictions on their further sale or use could still be imposed as part of the patent right: these would bind not only another contracting party but all recipients of the goods with notice of the restrictions.[90] It is, however, necessary to show not only that the first recipient, but all those who precede a defendant, had the requisite knowledge, otherwise the necessary chain is broken.[91] This may create a considerable obstacle for the patentee. **6–15**

Where the British patentee himself markets patented goods abroad he will be able to prevent their import into Britain only if he attached a clear and express embargo.[92] Where, however, the sale abroad is by a licensee under the foreign patent, the goods cannot enter Britain unless there is a licence (express or implied) from the British patentee.[93]

This principle, which began to be modified by legislation such as the Resale Prices Act 1964, is now in the process of virtual annihilation. Two stages are involved: **6–16**

(1) *Limitation by the Treaty of Rome*. Until the CPC takes effect by Regulation, the former British principle continues in operation. But as well as the qualifications upon it in British legislation, it has been affected since 1973 by the twin doctrines of the Treaty of Rome: the free movement of goods and the rules of competition. Thus in 1972 it was held that where patented drugs were sold on condition that they were not to be exported from the United Kingdom, a sub-purchaser who knew of the restriction could be enjoined from infringing by exporting.[94] So far as such a condition applied to exporting to other

[89] On this important and difficult subject in relation to patents, see esp. Demaret, *Patents, Territorial Restrictions and EEC Law* (1978); Benyamini Ch.12; Rothnie Ch.3. Compare the position in respect of copyright: below, para.12–15.

[90] A fortiori, where the claim is to an intermediate "indirect" product, as distinct from an intermediate process. Even in the *Beecham* case, the House of Lords were doubtful about the former: (above, n.82) at 200–204. Any subsequent taker who knows that conditions exist will be bound: *Dunlop v Longlife* [1958] R.P.C. 473; and see *Goodyear v Lancashire Batteries* (1958) L.R. 1 R.P. 22 at 35 CA.

[91] *Roussel-Uclaf v Hockley International* [1996] R.P.C. 4431; but cf. *Gillette Industries v Bernstein* [1942] Ch. 45 CA; Wilkinson [1997] E.I.P.R. 319.

[92] *Betts v Willmott* (1871) L.R. 6 Ch. 239; *Smith Kline v Salim* [1989] F.S.R. 407, HC (Malaysia); attacked as illogical by Walton and Laddie, *Patent Laws of Europe and the UK* (1979) paras 948–950; cf. Laddie et al., *Modern Law of Copyright and Designs* 3rd edn (2000) para.18.19.

[93] *Beecham v International Products* [1968] R.P.C. 129; *Minnesota Mining v Geerpres* [1973] F.S.R. 113. These cases rely heavily on *S.A. des Glaces v Tilghmann* (1883) 25 Ch.D. 1 CA, even though it is concerned with direct exportation to the UK by a foreign licensee. Its strong emphasis on territoriality seems essentially at odds with *Betts v Willmott*: Rothnie, *Parallel Imports* (1994), pp.125–142.

[94] *Sterling Drug v Beck* [1973] R.P.C. 915.

Common Market countries, it would now be bad; the same would be true of a condition that the goods could be exported only to part of the Common Market.[95] Each of these constraints inhibits the free movement of goods within the EU.[96] But the old British principle upholds restrictions preventing exports to non-EU countries; likewise with a condition attached to a sale in a non-EU country that goods are not to be imported into the United Kingdom. To these the free movement of goods policy has no application[97] and the question is whether any aspect of the EU's competition rules is offended.

(2) *The future Community Patent regime*. If and when the CP Regulation is put into effect, it will introduce a specific doctrine of exhaustion affecting both Community and national patents within the EU.[98] This provides that once patented goods have been put on the market in any part of the EU by the patentee or with his express consent,[99] the rights conferred by the patent or other national patents within the EU can no longer extend to them, unless EU law admits some special exception. If the ownership of national patents for the same invention has been divided up among patentees economically associated, so that a different legal person must license the initial sale in the different countries, the rights will still be treated as exhausted.[100]

Because these principles of EU law, current and anticipated, directly affect the scope of patent infringement they are mentioned here in brief. But they need to be seen in broader context. This has been introduced in general already and its impact on patent deployment and licensing is dealt with in the next chapter.

We should note that the scope of "exhausted" rights is not free from doubt. Suppose X has a patent claiming: (1) chemical Y; and (2) the use of Y in process Z. If X or a licensee sells Y, X ought arguably to be able to control the use of Y in process Z: but, if the two claims are in the same patent, a literal reading of the exhaustion rule suggests that he cannot.[101]

---

[95] For the evolution of the whole doctrine, see below, Ch.19.

[96] Accordingly they would constitute a measure equivalent to a quantitative restriction on imports (Treaty of Rome art.30) which, as a "mere exercise" of industrial property rights operating as a disguised restriction upon intra-Community trade, could not be absolved by art.30: see below, para.1–51, paras 19–04 et seq.

[97] See *EMI v CBS*, above, para.1–56.

[98] CPC arts 28, 76; with specific exception for the case where the goods are first marketed by a compulsory licensee (including in Britain someone within the Crown use exemption): arts 45(1), 76(3); PA 1977 s.60(4) makes this the rule that will govern UK patents.

[99] For the significance of "express" consent, see below, para.19–07.

[100] Article 76(2); see further, below, paras 19–02 et seq.

[101] Perhaps "Community law" would admit an exception for this case: see arts 28, 76. It ought to do so, unless the arrangement is part of some larger anti-competitive agreement and in Vaver and Bently Ch.8.

(d) *Before manufacture: "indirect" and other infringement*[102]

6–17 The former law showed great reluctance to treat as a "contributory infringer" someone who assisted in preparations for acts within the claims, but did not himself perform the acts. Only if the "assister" ordered the full performance,[103] or participated in a conspiracy or common design to secure performance,[104] or knowingly induced another person to perform,[105] would any liability in tort be imposed. In other cases, the courts' caution obliged the patentee to proceed against the actual performer.[106] For one thing he might well deny infringement, claim that the patent was invalid, or claim a licence or Crown authority. The approach had some attraction, particularly where the patentee was attacking a small "assister" who supplied to a larger "performer".[107] But in the contrary case of a large "assister" supplying materials towards infringement by small "performers", the patentee could be placed in considerable difficulty.

Following other patent systems and the CPC provisions, the 1977 Act introduced general principles of contributory infringement.[108] As one special case of "direct" infringement, it is impermissible to offer a process for use, knowing that the user will have no licence from the patentee and that the use will be an infringement.[109] In strictly territorial vein, both offer and use must be in the United Kingdom[110]; and the offeror's knowledge is judged objectively, taking account of what is "obvious to a reasonable person in the circumstances".

6–18 It has also become "indirect" infringement to supply (or to offer to supply) "means relating to an essential element of the invention, for putting the invention into effect" to someone not licensed or authorised to work it, knowing that the "means" are suitable for putting, and are intended to put,

---

102 Benyamini Chs 7, 9.

103 *Sykes v Howarth* (1879) 12 Ch.D. 826.

104 *Morton-Norwich v Intercen* [1976] F.S.R. 513.

105 *Innes v Short* (1898) 15 R.P.C. 449; *Belegging Lavender v Witten* [1979] F.S.R. 59 at 66–67 CA; and see generally above, paras 2–12 et seq.

106 *Dunlop v Moseley* (1904) 21 R.P.C. 274 CA.

107 A good illustration is provided by *Slater Steel v Payer* (1968) 55 C.P.R. 61 Ex Ct (Canada).

108 The expression, "indirect infringement", is used in the original CPC art.26.

109 A paraphrase of PA 1977 s.60(1)(b); cf. original CPC art.25(b). Neither is happily drafted. The offeror must know (objectively) that use of the patent without the proprietor's consent would be infringement. This may excuse the offeror: (1) who could not have known of the patent; or (2) who could not have known that the process would be used in an infringing way; or (3) who could not have known that the user did not have the licensee's consent or other authority. The last does not easily fit the language used, but would probably be read in; cf. s.60(2), below, para.6–18. It is not within this provision to direct use in a non-infringing way when it would not be obvious to use the process in an infringing way: *Fürr v CJ Truline* [1985] F.S.R. 553; see also *Kalman v PCL Packaging* [1982] F.S.R. 406.

110 But see *Menashe Business Mercantile v William Hill* [2003] 1 All E.R. 279 CA: claim to a particular network of computers, part of which was supplied abroad. In such a case, if the effect of this supply of means was produced in the UK, this would constitute indirect infringement. Otherwise there was a danger that the patent would not be infringed in this manner anywhere.

it into effect.[111] Again the supplier is treated as knowing what is obvious to a reasonable person in the circumstances.[112] Clearly, this type of infringement may arise in cases where the "means" have non-infringing as well as infringing uses. If, accordingly, they constitute a staple commercial product, there is no infringement unless the supply is for the purpose of inducing the person supplied to infringe directly.[113]

For there to be indirect infringement, both the place of supply and the place where it is intended to carry out the invention must be in the United Kingdom. This excludes the foreign supplier of materials or parts which are brought into Britain by the "direct" infringer; and also the British manufacturer who makes up kits of the parts needed for completing manufacture or operating a process abroad.[114] Arguably, in the latter case, a doctrine of indirect infringement ought to cover such an obvious way of assisting towards infringement that is so essentially connected with production in the United Kingdom.[115] But to treat it as a common law tort, such as conspiracy or inducement,[116] would be to subvert an apparent limitation in s.60(2) of the 1977 Act and art.30(1) of the original CPC.

6–19 The former British approach made it important to secure claims, where possible, to parts of mechanical combinations, to intermediates in chemical production, and to the substances that would be applied in methods and processes. There are marks of this upon the inherited law of novelty, obviousness and patentable subject-matter.[117] Under the new law focus shifts to the question, have the conditions for "indirect" infringement been fulfilled? Whether material or apparatus is a "staple commercial product" is likely to depend on whether there exists at least one alternative way in which the product as sold could ordinarily be used. Far-fetched or purely

---

111 PA 1977 s.60(2), original CPC art.26(1). Not every person supplied has to use the thing in an infringing way: *Chapman v McAnulty* (1996, unreported). One person does not escape being an "indirect" infringer by supplying essential means to another who acts within the exceptions for private use, experiment or pharmaceutical preparation: PA 1977 s.60(6)—a most surprising limitation: Benyamini pp.182–185. The provision presumably does not apply to a person who collaborates in the direct infringement, for instance, by helping to set up clinical trials.

112 Presumably the reasonable person (who is mentioned specifically only in the PA 1977 text) is someone in the supplier's position: see Ency. P.L., para.4–204.

113 PA 1977 s.60(3); original CPC art.26(2). Where the enterprise supplied knows, or must be taken to know, the patent position and makes its decision to act as it does independently of anything that the supplier does (as, e.g. in the *Slater* case (above, n.99)), there would be neither inducement nor conspiracy: cf. *Fürr v Truline* [1986] F.S.R. 533.

114 These limitations do not apply if what is done constitutes direct infringement: for the kit-of-parts question, see above, para.6–11.

115 cf. Stauder (1972) 4 I.I.C. 491; Kerr (1974) 26 Stanford L.R. 893; and see *University of Queensland v Siemens Magnet* [2007] EWHC 2258.

116 See above, paras 2–13, 2–14.

117 For instance in the importance attaching to article claims, as distinct from method-of-use claims (above, paras 4–46 et seq.), and in the attempts to secure "pack" claims (above, para.5–70).

experimental alternatives will doubtless be discounted.[118] On the question of whether a supplier ought to have known that "means" would be put to an infringing use, consider the case where a client orders a particular part to be made up from his specifications. The maker may well not be in a position to know how the part will be used. It is presumably his (objective) state of mind that is relevant, not that of his client.[119]

Indirect infringement (together with additional tortious liability) strengthens the patentee's position by giving rights against those who are essentially involved, in a preliminary way, in bringing about complete infringement within the claims. These forms of liability delimit the extent to which a patentee can legitimately require a licence to be taken by those who supply things which are not in themselves infringing. Beyond their bounds, a licensor is in the territory of restrictive "tie-ins" and may face the strictures of EU competition law.[120]

(e) *New medical and other applications of known substances*

A substance may be claimed for its first known medical use and a composition including it may be claimed for subsequently discovered medical uses.[121] Moreover the EPO has decided to make claims in such form available to non-medical subject-matter.[122] If the claim covers the substance or composition "for" its medical use then only those who administer it or who make or market it for its medical purpose would infringe. If a claim has been allowed to the substance *puro*, proof of the earlier knowledge ought either to cut down the claim's scope so as to confine it to use in or towards the medical purpose, or amendment by the addition of a "for" phrase ought to be required.[123] If claims are in this instance to be read as limited by the discovered use, why not in other cases? Should claims to entirely new things also be read as limited by the useful application described for them in the specification? This would be one solution to the nagging problem posed by *Mullard v Philco*.[124] **6–20**

118 US patent law contains a similar distinction (Patents Act s.271(c)) and much case law to this effect: see Chisum, *Patents* (1978) IV, para.17.03 [3]. Thus if the alternative use calls for sale in much larger quantities than the defendant is putting on the market, his commodity will not be treated as staple: *Johnson v Gore*, 195 U.S.P.Q. 487 (1977).

119 PA 1977 s.60(2) leaves the matter uncertain; cf. above, para.6–17.

120 For which see below, para.7–36.

121 See above, para.5–69.

122 For this still contentious development, see above, para.5–26; Vossius [1998] Bio-Sc.L.R. 19.

123 Whether suppliers would be direct or indirect infringers is unclear, and could be important; for if "indirect" and the product is a "staple", the limitations in PA 1977 s.60(3) will apply.

124 It has never been suggested in English courts that the doctrine of equivalents could be used to cut down the apparent scope of claims: cf. *Graver v Linde*, 339 U.S. 605 at 608–609 (1950).

(4) Prior use and commencement of infringement[125]

6–21 If a person uses an invention in a way that makes it public before the priority date of a patent for it, his anticipation will render the patent invalid.[126] As well as this, he has a defence against infringement, should he continue to use the invention after the patentee's rights take effect.[127] This defence is also open to people who have not provided material for attacking the patent's validity—prior users whose activities have not made the invention available to the public,[128] and those who have in good faith made effective and serious preparations to use the invention (or to do some other act in the list of infringements).[129] The preparations must be so far advanced that the infringing acts are about to be done.[130] The defence, however, is limited: the act done or prepared for before the priority date may be continued[131] or done afterwards by the person concerned, a partner of his or an assignee of the relevant business,[132] but not by a "licensee".[133] While the person concerned may not expand into other products, he is not confined to making things which are absolutely identical or to following a process to the letter. He can go on doing what in substance he was doing before.[134]

6–22 The earliest point in time at which infringement can occur is the date of publishing the application—normally some 18 months from the priority date. But proceedings for the period between then and the grant can only be brought after grant; and the defendant's act must infringe not only the claims finally included but those in the published application.[135] There is the difficulty, however, that the claims of the early publication may be clearly objectionable. A potential infringer may have no idea whether the application will ever pass examination so as to leave claims that he will infringe.

---

[125] Monotti [1997] E.I.P.R. 351.

[126] See above, para.5–19.

[127] PA 1977 s.64 as substituted by CPDA 1988 Schs 5, 17; the original CPC art.38, follows whatever national law allows for national patents: see *Østerborg* (1981) 12 I.I.C. 447.

[128] Formerly, if their use was "secret", in certain circumstances this formed a ground for attacking validity. Now the principle is that an anticipation must be made public rather than merely used: see above, paras 5–06—5–08.

[129] Previously such people went unprotected.

[130] *Lubrizol v Esso Petroleum* [1998] R.P.C. 727 at 770 CA.

[131] Although the wording is not completely clear, this must include the ability to continue repeating a production process.

[132] PA 1977 s.64(2). Articles thus produced may be dealt with as if disposed of by the patentee: s.64(3).

[133] i.e. anyone to whom the prior user attempts to transfer or license his freedom to continue doing the act, without assigning the business.

[134] *Lubrizol* (above, n.10) at 770. He does not have a general licence to alter a process from what he was doing before.

[135] PA 1977 s.69(1), (2); Benyamini Ch.11. An account of profits is available: *Spring Form v Toy Brokers* [2002] F.S.R. 17.

If it would not have been reasonable to expect this outcome, the court or Comptroller is given a discretion to reduce damages.[136]

In the period between priority date and publication of a patent application, it is possible for another person to start his preparations and production of something in the claims. Not only will his production after publication be actionable; equally articles which he has made before this date will infringe if sold, used or kept by himself or another person after the date. In these circumstances, a seller will then be in breach of his contractual warranty either that he has the right to sell or that his buyer will enjoy quiet possession.[137] These rules constitute a fortuitous hazard, which scarcely seems necessary, to the patent system.

(5) Proceedings concerning the infringement and validity of patents[138]

Proceedings for infringement, revocation and such associated matters as relief from threats to sue for infringement and declarations of non-infringement,[139] are brought either in the Patents Court,[140] the Patents County Court,[141] or, in certain cases, before the Comptroller (with appeal first to the Patents Court).[142] The Comptroller's jurisdiction in revocation proceedings is now co-terminous with that of the Patents Courts.[143] This marks a considerable extension of his powers. Formerly he could entertain a belated opposition to the grant of the patent only on limited grounds, provided that it was commenced within 12 months of grant.[144] But the nature of the proceedings has not changed, the Comptroller's decision is still normally upon documentary evidence, with lower scales of fees.[145] Attackers who want an exhaustive investigation of the merits, with oral examination **6–23**

---

136 PA 1977 s.69(3). This is somewhat more precise than the alternative allowed by EPC art.67(2) under which compensation reasonable in the circumstances may be provided for in national legislation.

137 *Microbeads v Vinhurst Road Markings* [1976] R.P.C. 19 CA. The warranty now arises under Sale of Goods Act 1979 s.12, which allows for the undertaking to be given in conditional form. Apart from this, liability cannot be excluded: Unfair Contract Terms Act 1977 s.6(1).

138 For a comparison (Germany, France, Italy, England): see Stauder (1983) 14 I.I.C. 793; and for patent enforcement in five EU States, the US and Japan, see (2000) 31 I.I.C. 627–770. The authors of this book wrote the UK contribution.

139 For these, see above, paras 2–90—2–94.

140 Created as a part of the Chancery Division of the High Court by PA 1977 s.96; for Scottish equivalents, see ss.97(4), (5), 98. The Patents Court consists of one or more patents judges (ss.96(2), 97(2)) and there is power to appoint scientific advisers (s.96(4); RSC Ord 104 r.11). In the past this was not used: but the appellate courts now do so under equivalent powers.

141 For which, see above, paras 2–10, 2–11.

142 PA 1977 s.97(1); further appeal only lies in certain cases to the Court of Appeal: s.97(3).

143 PA 1977 s.72. The Comptroller also has certain powers to revoke upon his own initiative; see above, para.4–29.

144 See PA 1949 s.33. The Banks Committee recommended that the Comptroller be given wider jurisdiction: (Cmnd.4407, 1970), paras 181–188.

145 i.e. lower fees for both initial proceedings and any appeal to the Patents Court.

of witnesses, should still bring proceedings in court.[146] Questions of infringement can be referred to the Comptroller only by the agreement of both parties[147]; but his power to grant declarations of non-infringement is not conditioned in this way.[148]

6–24 We have already noted some general techniques that exist in intellectual property actions to preserve or elicit evidence of what the defendant has been doing. When, however, the patent is for a process, and the alleged infringements are imported, there may be no means of discovering or inspecting how they are made. In such a case it may be that a court will find against a defendant who refuses to explain himself, upon proof of a bare prima facie case of infringement.[149] There is also a statutory presumption that a new product is made by an infringing process.[150] But "new product" can only mean one not previously known for novelty purposes; and in such cases, product claims are allowed. So the provision appears to cope with a spectral difficulty.

6–25 In proceedings for infringement, the validity of the patent can be put in issue.[151] This may be done purely as a matter of defence, or by way of a counterclaim for revocation: the former will save expense, the latter is more final.[152] There are cases when the two questions are closely related: as where the defendant alleges that what he is doing is anticipated or obvious.[153] And more generally there is a feeling that a broadly just outcome can be reached only if what the plaintiff has tried to annex is set against how the defendant has acted, whether with the patent in mind or in ignorance of it.

But this traditional approach is controversial. Two EU countries—Germany and the Netherlands, each with strong examining offices—generally require validity to be raised before specialist tribunals, while leaving infringement to ordinary civil courts.[154] For EU patents, the draft CPC originally adopted this division of functions; there was a fear that non-expert tribunals in some countries would not handle revocation questions satisfactorily. But in the light of British objections, the revised version of the Convention will allow the practice to continue without limit of time and it

---

[146] The difference is marked by the rule that the Comptroller's decision creates no issue estoppel against subsequent court proceedings: PA 1977 s.72(5), but note s.72(6).

[147] PA 1977 s.61(3)–(6). He has no jurisdiction over threats.

[148] In each case, invalidity may be raised as a defence: PA 1977 s.74(1). If revocation is sought under s.72, the proceedings would be heard at the same time. See also above, para.4–29.

[149] See above, para.2–59.

[150] PA 1977 s.100; there is a saving clause protecting defendants against "unreasonable" disclosure of secrets. See *Eli Lilly v Neolab* [2009] F.S.R. 25.

[151] Likewise both issues may be raised in actions for threats and for declarations of non-infringements; and invalidity may also be raised in disputes about Crown use: see PA 1977 s.74.

[152] Even if there is no counterclaim the Court probably has power to order revocation in the public interest: Whitford J. *Norprint v SPJ Labels* [1979] F.S.R. 126.

[153] See above, para.4–41.

[154] For the German position, see Pakuscher (1979) 10 I.I.C. 671; cf. *Formstein* [1991] R.P.C. 24.

will be available in the centralised jurisdiction now being proposed for enforcing the EU patent.[155]

The length, complexity and cost of patent infringement actions have long been notorious. One consequence has been the introduction of special procedures for the protection of potential defendants—the action for a declaration of non-infringement and the action against threats, which were dealt with in Ch.2.[156] Other aspects of procedure and remedies affecting patent suits are dealt with there, and the reader is reminded particularly of the guidelines that are used to assess damages and the problems of apportionment that may arise where the infringement contributes to the making of a loss or profit for which damages are being awarded or an account taken.[157]

The one issue that deserves special comment at this stage is the availability **6–26**
of interim injunctions in patent infringement suits. Because of the grave implications of deciding to carry an action to its full term, much of the real effectiveness of a patent may turn on whether the court will intervene at this early stage. Before *American Cyanamid v Ethicon*,[158] the patentee could rarely hope to succeed. He had to make out a prima facie case and against this the defendant could usually set up a sufficient barrier by averring the invalidity of the patent, particularly on the ground of obviousness. On such an issue it is intrinsically hazardous to form a preliminary view. Accordingly, success was reserved to patents for exceptionally significant or widely acknowledged inventions.[159]

The *Ethicon* case, however, has transferred emphasis to the balance of **6–27**
convenience.[160] This means that the substantive dispute between the parties is demoted and prime weight is given to their relative commercial positions, with particular stress on the use that each is making, or is intending to make, of the invention covered (actually or allegedly) by the patent. Either party will boost his case, for instance, by showing that this is most or all of his business.[161] A patentee will make ground out of showing that he is struggling to secure a market position for the invention and would be impeded by the

[155] See original CPC arts 56–63, 68–73, 78, 90.

[156] See above, paras 2–86—2–90. Note also PA 1977 s.61(1), (2).

[157] See above, paras 2–39—2–46.

[158] [1975] A.C. 396; [1975] R.P.C. 513 HL. For the new approach to the granting of interim relief established by this case and for its application to intellectual property cases in general, see above, paras 2–32—2–36.

[159] See Blanco White (1974), para.12–113.

[160] See above, paras 2–35—2–37. The claimant's need first to show a serious case to be tried. In a patent case, they should accordingly provide sufficiently precise evidence to show that each of the features of the patent claim were present in the alleged infringement: *Novartis v Dexcel-Pharma* [2008] F.S.R. 31 at [25]. See *Cole* [1979] E.I.P.R. 71.

[161] e.g. *Netlon v Bridport-Gundry* [1979] F.S.R. 530 CA; *Potters-Ballotini v Weston-Baker* [1977] R.P.C. 202 CA (breach of confidence). The counter-argument that the defendant started production knowing that he was likely to be sued may weigh against him: *Belfast Ropework v Pixdane* [1976] F.S.R. 337 CA. But the argument that, even if a defendant is enjoined, he will be able to open up other lines of business has been discounted: *Condor v Hibbing* (1978) [1984] F.S.R. 312 CA.

defendant's direct competition.[162] A defendant will fall back if he has not yet started manufacturing and has not expended much in preparations for doing so,[163] or if he only imports and so has not committed capital to production plant.[164]

A defendant in a small way, moreover, may have difficulty in showing his ability to pay any damages ultimately awarded.[165] One line of argument that may well be to a defendant's advantage, however, is that, if he is allowed to continue, his sales will normally form a reasonable basis for assessing competitive losses to the plaintiff,[166] whereas if he is stopped, what he might have made will remain speculative.[167] There are, of course, many other such considerations which may affect the outcome of particular cases.[168]

The danger of the *Ethicon* approach is that a particular patent's value comes to depend too much on commercial position.[169] Statistically at least, the chance of securing interim relief has undoubtedly improved under the new principles. This is likely to foster the general impression that patents in Britain have become more damaging weapons in competitive industry than was previously the case.

2. The Specification in Light of the Legal Requirements

6–28 Patent specifications are drawn to deal with conflicts. Even where they form the basis for licensing, their real significance arises only when the collaboration begins to turn sour. A specification must strive to provide protection against those looking for ways of side-stepping it; at the same time, it must not break any of the validity rules. The basic principles, which we have now looked at in some detail, interact in a complex manner. We have reached the point where it is useful to summarise some crucial points in these interrelations.

---

162 cf. *Catnic v Stressline* [1976] F.S.R. 157 CA. If a patent is nearing the end of its life, the Court of Appeal has been reluctant to refuse an injunction where to do so would provide the defendant with a bridgehead against both the patentee and other competitors: *Corruplast v Harrison* [1978] R.P.C. 761 at 766.

163 *Hepworth Plastics v Naylor*, CA (see above, Cole, n.160) at 13.

164 *Belfast Ropework v Pixdane* [1976] F.S.R. 337 CA.

165 e.g. *Belfast Ropework* case (above, n.164), where even a bank guarantee of £15,000 was not enough to satisfy the Court of Appeal.

166 Refusal of an injunction may "snowball" by inducing other competitors to follow the defendant: but the Court of Appeal has been reluctant to take this into account: *Condor v Hibbing* (above, n.161).

167 *Polaroid v Eastman Kodak* [1977] R.P.C. 379 CA; *Brupat v Sandor Marine* [1983] R.P.C. 61 CA; cf. *SKM v Spraytech* [1982] R.P.C. 497.

168 Particular difficulties arise with patented pharmaceuticals. The patentee may argue that doctors and patients may be seriously put out if, after learning to use the defendant's product, they see it removed from the market after the trial: *American Cyanamid v Ethicon* [1975] R.P.C. 513. But if there is some difference between the plaintiff's and defendant's products the latter may argue that the public should not be deprived of his version, particularly if it could be life-saving: *Roussel-Uclaf v Searle* [1977] F.S.R. 125.

169 See above, Cole, n.160.

(1) The description

There are a variety of pressures upon the draftsman to include in his description of the invention a fair amount of detail, going beyond the minimum that may satisfy the requirement of a complete and clear disclosure: **6–29**

(1) There is the danger that if particular versions of the invention are not mentioned, room may be left for a competitor to secure an improvement or selection patent at the very point where the patentee wants himself to operate; whereas specific description will put paid to this possibility from the moment that the application is filed, provided that the application (or one claiming priority from it) is later published.[170]
(2) There is the need (at least before the patent office) to show support in the description for the claims, particularly the broadest.[171]
(3) A case must be developed to support the presence of an inventive step; where the subject-matter is an improvement over known art, rather than a breakthrough with a mechanical principle, chemical substance, or new micro-organism, this means spelling out the advantage that gives inventive character.[172]
(4) The limitations upon amendment condition the possibility of introducing changes during prosecution of the application[173]; the governing rule that there must be no new disclosure over the contents of the specification originally filed makes it crucial to start with all that may later be needed. It is important to put enough into any "informal" application to ground priority round the world.[174]

(2) The claims

The aim is to cover all imaginable alternatives, while avoiding the inclusion of things that are anticipated or obvious. In the United Kingdom in the past, this has meant that if, for instance, the inventor has found a way of making a material that is then used in a production process, it has been desirable to include claims for making the material, the material itself, and its use in the subsequent process. To some extent, the introduction of "indirect" infringement[175] has reduced the importance of doing this. However, it is more secure to cover the matter directly. At the other end, the rule **6–30**

[170] See above, paras 5–14, 5–15.
[171] See above, paras 5–90—5–94.
[172] In the case of a selection, advantage is also necessary to disclose what makes the invention novel; see above, paras 5–14, 5–15.
[173] See above, paras 4–31—4–34.
[174] See above, paras 4–10—4–13.
[175] See above, paras 6–17—6–19.

that a process claim covers only its direct products[176] is stricter than the former British approach; so where, for instance, a series of chemical syntheses are involved, it is important to cover those at the end as well as those at the beginning.

(3) Pitfalls of saying too much

6–31 So much for the pressures to be as complete as possible: now consider the dangers inherent in this course.

A would-be patentee may endanger his own chances by any sort of publicity: we have already noted the severity of the new European concordat in the matter of "periods of grace".[177] Equally there are dangers that one of his specifications will prejudice others that come later, whether they are attempts to cope more successfully with what is essentially the same invention or they deal with some distinct improvement. It is worth drawing together the points at which earlier applications tell against later:

(1) The arrangements for according priority are limited by the requirement that the later application or applications be made within 12 months of the first application to disclose the invention. The only exception discounts earlier applications that are totally abnegated without having been published.[178]

(2) If an application is made for patent protection in the United Kingdom (to either the British Office or the EPO) and the application reaches the stage of being published, its content is treated for novelty purposes as forming part of the art from the priority date claimed. So before the applicant allows this publication to take place, he must consider whether he is prejudicing any of his own later applications, not claiming the same priority, which attempt to patent any invention disclosed in the published form of the application. Gone is the confinement of this issue to a question of prior claiming. But it does not, for this interim period, matter that the later invention is obvious in the light of the earlier.

(3) Once an application is published,[179] like any other publication, it joins the state of the art for all purposes. Improvements that are obvious in the light of its revelation cannot be patented. No longer is there the old patent of addition, which allowed the engrafting of improvements even though they marked no inventive step over the main patent.

---

[176] See above, para.6–12.
[177] See above, para.5–16.
[178] See above, para.4–12.
[179] As to this, see Burnside (1980) 9 CIPA 266.

All in all the patent system calls for acute awareness of the hazards and the highest attention to getting the whole thing right from the outset. More than ever, it is a game that only the highly trained professional can hope to play with much success.

CHAPTER 7

PROPERTY RIGHTS AND EXPLOITATION

This chapter draws together a number of themes concerned with the ownership of patent rights and the exploitation of those rights through consensual dealings. The question of initial entitlement to a patent arises from the making of the invention onwards. It may be important before any application is made, during the application and after grant. The person or persons thus entitled may deal with their rights, disposing of them by assignment or permitting others to act within the scope of the monopoly, by giving them a licence to do so. These two aspects of property rights in patents are considered in the first part of this chapter. The second part deals more specifically with the content of patent and allied licences and takes account of the competition law criteria which they must now meet, particularly the requirements of EU law. The third part is closely related to this, since it deals with the application of EU law to the importation of patented products. The last two parts move on to other public policy considerations—the provisions seeking to correct under-exploitation by allowing for the grant of compulsory licences, and the provisions which allow for Crown use upon payment of compensation. **7–01**

1. Initial Entitlement and Property Dealings

(1) The right to grant: general

7–02 In contrast with the former law, the 1977 Act allows anyone to apply for a patent but restricts those to whom a patent may be granted.[1] At the moment of invention, s.7(2) confers the right to be granted a patent upon one of three categories of persons: (1) the inventor or co-inventor; or (2) the employer of the inventor when the invention is made during employment[2]; or (3) where foreign law[3] applies by virtue of private international law rules,[4] the person entitled by that law.[5] Whoever is given this initial entitlement to the patent can assign it; or it may devolve upon a successor because of death, or a form of insolvency. Assignees or successors are then entitled to the same share in the grant as were their predecessors. The right to an assignment may be implied from the circumstances in which an invention was made.[6]

The inventor is the person who actually devises the invention.[7] There may be more than one inventor. In such a case, to find out who ranks as inventor, a court does not set out to discover the separate contributions to the end result. Rather it identifies the inventive concept—the "heart" of what is disclosed. Then it ascertains who came up with that concept. It is not enough for a claimant to show that in some way he contributes to an eventual claim in the specification.[8] If, for instance, he gives an initial prompt without which the invention might never have been made, but he had no idea whether or not it would work, he is not an inventor. But he will be if he comes up with all the elements in the claim, even though at that stage the claim was just an idea.[9] The challenger is not obliged also to show

[1] PA 1977 s.7(1), following EPC arts 58, 60(1); PA 1949 s.1, by contrast, defined the classes of persons entitled to apply.

[2] An employer who is only entitled to a share in the property right—for instance, because his employee has worked with an outsider to make the invention—should, it appears from PA 1977 s.7(2)(b), take an assignment from his employee so as to acquire a right under s.7(2)(c).

[3] Including rights created in foreign law by treaties or conventions (in countries where, contrary to English law, international obligations may take effect directly upon ratification).

[4] This could be the law of the place of invention, or that governing the inventor's contract of employment. Such a question has never been explored in English private international law; but see below, para.7–11.

[5] The mention in PA 1977 s.7(2)(b) of entitlement by virtue of a "pre-invention" agreement seems meaningless, as far as English law is concerned, since such an agreement can only be to assign future property rights and that can at most create an equitable interest: yet the paragraph specifically excludes equitable interests.

[6] *Goddin and Rennie's Application* [1996] R.P.C. 141 (Ct of Sess); *Hartington Conway's Applications* [2004] R.P.C. 5 at 6.

[7] PA 1977 s.7(3); for modes by which a person claiming to be the inventor, or one of them, can challenge an application or patent, see paras above, 4–06—4–08.

[8] *Henry Bros v Ministry of Defence* [1997] R.P.C. 693; [1999] R.P.C. 442 CA; *Collag v Merck* [2003] F.S.R. 16; *Markem v Zipher (No.1)* [2005] R.P.C. 31 CA.; *University of Southampton's Applications* [2006] R.P.C. 17 CA; See Carter and Ayrton [2006] E.I.P.R. 51; Hull [2007] E.I.P.R. 6.

[9] *Stanelco v Fibre Optics* [2005] R.P.C. 15.

that the patent applicant or grantee had acted in a manner which constituted a legal or equitable wrong against the person challenging the application or grant. Thus in *Yeda Research v Rhone-Poulenc*, which took the form of s.37 proceedings before the Comptroller,[10] the challenger asserted that its scientists were the inventors of a new chemotherapy drug for cancer treatment. They had informed a former colleague, S, of their invention and his name was given as sole inventor that through whom the patentee—a pharmaceutical company—had claimed its entitlement.[11] The latter sought to withstand the proceeding against it, by asserting that the challenger had to demonstrate that S was in breach of some independent obligation, for example, a contractual or fiduciary obligation to keep the information for its benefit, and that it had not done so. Lying behind this supposed limitation was the belief that otherwise inventors who had played no part in subsequent development of a marketable product could gain disproportionately. The House of Lords, overruling the courts below,[12] insisted that no such additional requirement arose in determining who were inventors. Such questions of obligation could be germane in determining the prior art against which to judge novelty, particularly in relation to the "first-to-file" rule; but they had no role in determining inventorship in relation to entitlement. If it was thought that the challenger was getting an unfair advantage, this could be dealt with under the general law of proprietary estoppel.

(2) The right to grant: employees[13]

(a) *Common law rules*

In free-market economies it is an assumption, by now largely unremarked, that the products of labour belong to the owner of the business. Even so, it took some time for the first industrial countries to apply this assumption to intellectual property rights without some measure of reserve. In England it was left to Lord Simonds, in the age of corporate capitalism, to declare that: **7–03**

[10] *Yeda Research v Rhone-Poulenc* [2008] R.P.C. 1 HL. For the s.37 jurisdiction and other procedures for challenge, together with the limitations upon them, see above para.4-07.

[11] The referral under s.37 initially sought recognition of the challenger's scientists as joint inventors. Subsequently, outside the period of two years from grant prescribed in the section, an amendment by the challenger asserted that its scientists were sole inventors. This amendment was allowed: see *Yeda Research v Rhone Poulenc* (above n.10).

[12] In particular, the Court of Appeal's earlier decision in *Markem v Zipher* [2005] R.P.C. 31 CA.

[13] See also Cornish in Vitoria (ed.), *The Patents Act 1977* (1978), p.79 and [1992] E.I.P.R. 13; J. Phillips and M. Hoolahan, *Employees' Inventions in the United Kingdom* (1982); J. Phillips (ed.), *Employees' Inventions: A Comparative Study* (1981); Leistner (2004) 35 I.I.C. 859.

> "it is an implied term in the contract of service of any workman that what he produces by the strength of his arm or the skill of his hand or the exercise of his inventive faculty shall become the property of his employer".[14]

Before that, emphasis tended to be placed on the need to show either a positive contract in the employer's favour or an implied duty of trust.[15] Indeed, it was said that the invention might be the employee's even though made in the employer's time and with his materials.[16] The tendency to increase the presumption in favour of his employer probably grew as cases arose in which employees were trying to stop their employer from using the invention in his own business. The implied term adopted by English courts may be contrasted with the handling of similar problems by US courts. There, in cases where the employer's claim to entitlement is doubtful, he is given only a "shop right": he is entitled to a free licence to use himself, but has no general power to stop the employee from licensing his invention to others.[17]

7–04 In English law, there have been two kinds of case in which, commonly, an employee has been obliged to hold his invention for his employer. First, where the employee was employed to use his skill and inventive ingenuity to solve a technical problem—where he was "employed to invent". Thus an engineering draftsman who was instructed to design an unlubricated crane-brake was obliged to hold a resulting patent on trust for his employer.[18] An assistant engineer employed to design linings for colliery tunnels was sent at his own request to a particular colliery and in consequence produced an inventive solution to its problem: the arrangement of the visit was held to place him under a duty to make over the consequent patent.[19] But a man employed purely as manager to sell valves and to deal with customer problems in the first instance was not obliged to hold an invention concerning the valves for his employers. They referred serious difficulties to the Swiss firm from whom they acquired the technology.[20] Equally, a hospital registrar employed by a health authority to treat patients was held to be under no

---

[14] *Patchett v Sterling* (1955) 72 R.P.C. 50. Who is an employer in this context is left to be judged by common law tests, which are discussed in connection with copyright: below, paras 13–05, 13–06. An express agreement not to treat a person as an employee is binding: *SID Engineering v Baruch Sharon* [1994] E.I.P.R. D-51.

[15] See *Marshall and Naylor's Patent* (1900) 17 R.P.C. 553 at 555; *Edisonia v Forse* (1908) 25 R.P.C. 546 and 549, both citing *Frost on Patents*.

[16] *Worthington v Moore* (below, n.23) at 48; *Mellor v Beardmore* (1927) 44 R.P.C. 175 at 191 IH.

[17] See Stedman in Neumeyer, *The Employed Inventor in the United States* (1971) Ch.2. An attempt to introduce an apportionment of benefits into the same "grey area" (PA 1949 s.56(2)) was held to have no effect in the absence of a contractual agreement to divide: *Patchett v Sterling* [1955] 72 R.P.C. 50.

[18] *British Reinforced Concrete v Lind* (1917) 34 R.P.C. 101.

[19] *Adamson v Kenworthy* (1932) 49 R.P.C. 57.

[20] *Harris' Patent* [1985] R.P.C. 19 (decided under PA 1977 s.39; and see *Spirroll v Putti* (1976) 64 D.L.R. (3d) 280.

duty to his employer to devise improvements to ophthalmic equipment. It made no difference that, in doing so, he was using associated university facilities in pursuit of an academic career.[21]

Secondly, where the employee occupied a senior managerial position and so owed a general duty of fidelity to his employer.[22] Thus, in *Worthington v Moore*, an American pump manufacturing corporation put a man in charge of its English business at a high salary and commission and made him a vice-president of the corporation; he was held liable under an obligation of good faith to account for patents relating to developments in pumps.[23] More recently, an employee who was a chief technician, employed inter alia to give technical advice on the design and development of soda syphons, but not to design the particular kind of syphon that he actually invented, was held accountable.[24] But the manager of a lampshade business (not a director of the concern) was held entitled to keep a patent for a method of coating wire frames, an idea which amongst other uses could be applied to lampshades.[25]

The employee's duty under either head applied to rights in the invention from its conception onwards. Until a patent application had been filed, his obligation coincided with his duty to keep confidential any information about his employment which was more than mere general knowledge and skill.[26]

The common law principle operated as a presumption within a regime of **7–05** free contract; express agreement could alter its operation. Recently, however, to exclude it there had to be a positive contract and not a mere "understanding".[27] One common practice was for employers, both industrial and governmental, to require employees to give over rights in all inventions made during the time of the employment, rather than just in its course, at least if the invention related to the employer's business. But such a term has been held ineffective as being in unreasonable restraint of trade: a vacuum cleaner company could not require a senior storekeeper to

---

[21] *Greater Glasgow Health Board's Application* [1996] R.P.C. 207; Chandler [1997] E.I.P.R. 262.

[22] Not easily distinguished in scope from the duties imposed in equity upon fiduciaries, such as company directors, to account for profits where there has been a conflict of personal interest and duty: see now *Canadian Aero v O'Malley* (1973) 40 D.L.R. (3d) 371 SC (Canada); and as to the duty of a managing director to exploit all new opportunities: *Fine Industrial Commodities v Powling* (1954) 71 R.P.C. 254 at 258.

[23] (1903) 20 R.P.C. 41. Note that there was evidence that the defendant was patenting the work of other employees.

[24] *British Syphon Co v Homewood* [1956] R.P.C. 225 at 231: "Now, would it be consistent with good faith, as between master and servant, that he should in that position be entitled to make some invention in relation to a matter concerning a part of the Plaintiff's business and either keep it from his employer, if and when asked about the problem, or even sell it to a rival, and say: 'Well, yes, I know the answer to your problem, but I have already sold it to your rival!'?" Roxburgh J. held not.

[25] *Selz's Application* (1954) 71 R.P.C. 158. It was emphasised that the manager had not tried to keep knowledge of the invention or patent application from his employer.

[26] See below, para.8–30.

[27] *Patchett v Sterling* (above, n.14).

surrender rights in an invention made at home, even though it consisted of an adapter for vacuum cleaner bags.[28]

One sphere in which attitudes have changed concerns inventions that are the product of academic research in higher education institutions.[29] Before the 1980s, most British universities did not seek to assert rights over inventions made by their staff. It was by and large assumed that commercialisation of results was not part of their role as bodies sustained by government grants and student fees. As financial pressures built up upon them, however, they began to set up technology transfer offices to assist in extracting revenue from the work, and soon enough thereafter to assertions that patent rights and other forms of intellectual property belonged to them as employers. While both steps were on balance beneficial in cases where the academics involved were not interested in the business of exploitation, it engendered conflict with those who had a personal interest in supplementing relatively meagre salaries or who considered that they knew better than the university's officers how to secure the best return (or both).

Each university sought its own resolution of the controversial issue by specific terms in employment contracts and these vary in content. Typically the university claims patent and associated rights from their grant onwards, but then offers inventors (and perhaps others) a considerable share in earnings.[30] These rates of compensation often appear generous to researchers employed in industry or government establishments; but there may well be salary differentials to be brought into consideration. The terms may differ where grants by other bodies (industrial, governmental or charitable) are a condition of financial support for the research. Where the grants contain explicit obligations about commercialisation and its returns they are likely to govern the situation.

If the matter has not been settled by such a contract,[31] the legal solution can be reached only by a court considering whether there is an implied term giving ownership to the university rather than its inventive scientists. In Australia, a knowledgeable judgment of the Full Federal Court of Appeal, *University of Western Australia v Gray*,[32] has ruled that, in the circumstances before it, no such term needed to be implied *in fact* in order to give business efficacy to the contract of employment; nor could it be implied *in*

[28] *Electrolux v Hudson* [1977] F.S.R. 312. The Banks Committee (Cmnd.4407, 1970) had recommended legislation to similar effect: Ch.16; see now PA 1977 s.42(2), below, para.7–12.

[29] See Cornish [1992] E.I.P.R. 13; Monotti and Ricketson, *Universities and Intellectual Property* (2003); Deazley [2005] E.I.P.R. 97; Hull [2007] E.I.P.R. 6.

[30] It is not uncommon for the inventors to have a joint share in a third of the revenue; or else there is a graded scale giving them the major share of the first earnings but reducing their proportion thereafter. In many cases the inventors' own department or research project gains a similar portion.

[31] Where a university sets up an arbitral body to determine shares but then fails to implement the arrangement it thereby renders the express term inoperable: see *University of Western Australia v Gray*, below, n.32.

[32] [2009] FCAFC 116; Hull and Toutoungi [2010] E.I.P.R. 43.

law, since no general policy considerations made it appropriate to do so.[33] While it was true that the researchers' contracts required them to do research themselves and to encourage others to do so, they were not obliged to follow particular lines of inquiry of the kind to which a research scientist in industry is usually committed. Moreover, it was the researchers who decided when to make their findings public, and who sought out governmental and industrial funding for aspects of the project. This meant that, in the absence of an express obligation to keep the information confidential until patent applications were made, none could be implied in the university's favour. Though not in issue in the case, it was also assumed that each researcher would be free to take his results with him if he moved to other employment. All these factors were taken to derive from the ideal of academic freedom, which flowed from an appreciation that the academics were both employees of their university and members of it.[34]

(b) *The changes in the 1977 Act*

If the only purpose of the patent system in a free-enterprise economy is to stimulate that economy, it may be logical to exclude employed inventors from the benefits of employment patents: one has simply to accept that the incentives—towards instituting research, development and publication—will only affect the employer. In other words, the bait of a patent or patent share is unlikely to incite the employed inventor to greater effort. As an assumption this may seem more or less plausible. However, the shift of opinion in the employee's favour has not turned upon this sort of psychological calculation. Rather it expresses a resurgent feeling for the demands of natural justice—a belief that an inventor should not go unrewarded for the fruits of his intellectual endeavour. This inspiration has coalesced with the recent tendency to cast legal protection around contracting parties who as a class may well not appreciate the unfavourable consequences of their bargains. **7–06**

The "new deal" in the 1977 Act is, however, a strictly limited concession to the demand for fairness towards the inventor. Just what has been given is in any case still obscure, since much of the hard decision-making is left to the courts and the Comptroller.[35] What the Act does is to lay out a framework of rights, which can nevertheless be replaced if certain provisions of the scheme are observed.

---

33 This distinct aspect of the law of implied terms stems from British decisions in *Lister v Romford Ice* [1957] A.C. 555, HL: *Liverpool CC v Irwin* [1977] A.C. 239 at 254, per Lord Wilberforce; *Shell UK v Lostock Garages* [1977] 2 All E.R. 461; and *Scally v Southern HSSB* [1992] 1 A.C. 294, as well as a number of Australian authorities.

34 The broad range of these considerations, led to a comparison with the position over copyright in an academic's writings where equally the court commented that if the university owned that copyright, it could be used as an instrument of censorship: for which see below, paras 13–05—13–07.

35 This is in striking contrast with the statutory scheme in Germany, whose detailed regulations lay down methods of weighting and calculation. From these there is much of interest to be learnt: see, e.g. Leistner, above, n.13.

(c) *Basic entitlement under the 1977 Act*

7–07 Section 39 in effect departs only marginally from the common law principles which determine whether employer or employee is initially entitled to an invention.[36]

The employer takes the invention: (1) when made either in the course of the employee's normal or his specifically assigned duties, provided that an invention might reasonably be expected from carrying them out[37]; and (2) where the employee has a special obligation to further the interests of the employer's undertaking "because of the nature of his duties and the particular responsibilities arising from the nature of his duties".[38] This reflects the two types of case where the decisions held employers entitled, and they are likely guides to future decisions. In all other cases the employee has the initial rights in his own invention.

(d) *Compensation and employers' inventions*

7–08 Where the invention belongs to the employer, the inventor may nevertheless have a statutory right under s.40 to what is called "compensation", that is a special bonus. This arises when: (1) the invention or the patent for it is of outstanding benefit to the employer[39]; and (2) it is just that compensation should be awarded; in assessing which, tribunals are under the ambiguous instruction to have regard, among other things, to the size and nature of the employer's business.[40] An outstanding benefit implies a superlative and so means more than just a significant advantage.[41] Whether the invention is of outstanding benefit falls to be assessed "having regard among other things to the size and nature of the employer's undertaking". This inherently ambiguous proposition remains mysterious. Does the fact that a company is

[36] But see *Harris' Patent* [1985] R.P.C. 19; *Pinkava v Liffe Administration* [2007] R.P.C. 31, where emphasis is laid on the statutory scheme rather than the earlier case law.

[37] PA 1977 s.39(1). A specifically assigned duty has to be demonstrated by evidence. But normal duties are to be judged not only by an original job description but also by the manner in which the employment was afterwards allowed to develop: *Pinkava v Liffe Administration* [2007] R.P.C. 31.

[38] PA 1977 s.39(2). By amendment in 1988 (s.39(3)), in order to pursue a patent application, an employee entitled to a patent vis-à-vis his employer may make use of copyright or design materials relating to the invention, even though the rights in these are the employer's; the same applies to any person performing or working the invention.

[39] Until amended in 2004, s.40 referred only to outstanding benefit to the employer *from the patent*. Since a patentee needs no licence to exploit his own patent, this phraseology may have limited what can be treated as part of the "outstanding benefit". It is only to patents applied for after January 1, 2005, that the broader language applies, so it will begin to have an effect only gradually. *Kelly and Chiu* (below, n.43) is a decision on the unamended law. "Outstanding" implies a superlative, and so means more than significant: *Memco-Med's Patent* [1992] R.P.C. 403. The onus is in general on the employee, which makes the test hard indeed to satisfy: *Memco*, cf. *GEC Avionics' Patent* [1992] R.P.C. 107; *British Steel's Patent* [1992] R.P.C. 117.

[40] PA 1977 s.40(1).

[41] *Memco-Med's Patent* [1992] R.P.C. 403; *Kelly and Chiu* (below, n.43). The onus is in general on the employee, which makes the test hard to satisfy: ibid., cf. *GEC Avionics' Patent* [1992] R.P.C. 107; *British Steel's Patent* [1992] R.P.C. 117.

small make it more or less likely that a contribution to its turnover from the invention will be regarded as an "outstanding benefit"?

Once this basic test is satisfied, the 1977 Act directs that the assessment of compensation is to allow the employee "a fair share (having regard to all the circumstances)", treating for the purpose dealings between the employer and a person connected with him as if an "arm's-length dealing" had taken place between them.[42] A number of factors are specified to which the tribunal must have regard, but only among other things: (1) the employee's duties, remuneration and other advantages from employment or "in relation to" the invention; (2) the employee's effort and skill; (3) the effort and skill of others—co-inventors, whether employees or not, other employees who give advice and assistance; and (4) the employer's contribution—by the provision of advice, facilities and other assistance, the provision of opportunities, and managerial and commercial skill and activities

(e) *Applying the compensation scheme*

It took more than a quarter-century for a court to consider the compensation provisions in the context of a highly successful patent to which the employer of the inventors was initially entitled. In *Kelly and Chiu v GE Healthcare,*[43] the patents were for a radioactive agent ("Myoview") which was given to patients undergoing imaging techniques that explored their internal organs without an operation. Myoview was based on a novel compound that was invented partly by two chemist-employees. Their employer was the company that afterwards developed the agent and secured its clearance as medically safe for ingestion by humans. The success of the drug contributed significantly to the financial buoyancy of the employer-patentee, when later it was taken over. The assignee sought to resist the inventors' claims to compensation under s.40(1) by a set of arguments which laid stress on the *ex ante* position—the situation before the market success was secured. Thus it was submitted that, for compensation to be available, the inventors had to demonstrate that they suffered a financial injury—for instance, by being employed at an unfairly low rate. Likewise, in showing that there was an outstanding benefit. An approach should be used that stressed the risks being taken at the outset by the enterprise; and in assessing what was a fair share for the inventors, attention should focus on the risks and uncertainties assumed by the employer in developing the drug. Floyd J., however, rightly characterised the statutory scheme thus: **7–09**

> "What is being compensated for by both limbs of section 40 is the disparity between the benefits received by the employee and the benefits received by the employer. In the section 40(2) case, this is particularly

[42] PA 1977, s.41; and note, in PA 1977, s.41(3), the further provision governing free licences by the Crown and Research Councils.

[43] *Kelly and Chiu* [2009] R.P.C. 12. See Howell [2010] J.B.L.41.

clear—one benefit is 'inadequate in relation to' the other. The inadequacy has arisen after the event, and in the light of the disparity between the benefit to the employer and the benefit to the employee. There may have been nothing unfair about the contract assigning the patent at the time it was made: but with the benefit of hindsight it has become so. In section 40(1) the concept of compensation would be expected to be, and in my judgment is, the same: what is different is that it will only be awarded in a case where the invention is of outstanding benefit, that is to say in a case where, again with the benefit of hindsight, the disparity in benefit between employer and employee is extreme."[44]

In applying the scheme to the case before him, the judge concluded, first, that there was an outstanding benefit to the employer, which he put at £52 million. He evaluated the fair share due in all the circumstances to the two inventors at 3 per cent of that sum. Given their different employment histories he awarded one £1million and the other £500,000. These are substantial awards which are likely to encourage other inventors of major products and processes to press for statutory compensation.[45] This in turn may make employers readier to seek a general contractual arrangement which may make the calculation of the bonus to the employee more straightforward, and may also award extra payments to employees who have not ranked as inventors but who have done much to bring the innovation to the market.[46]

(f) *Compensation and inventions to which an employed inventor is entitled*

7–10 Where the patent is the employee's, the employer will be entitled to use the invention only if he has acquired rights from the employee by assignment or licence. "Compensation" falls to be paid by the employer when the consideration for this transaction is inadequate in comparison with the benefit derived by the employer from the patent or the invention, and it is just that it should be paid.[47] The general principles for the assessment of compensation are the same as those for employers' inventions. But the list of factors to be brought into account differs somewhat: while account must be taken of the contribution of any co-inventor and the employer, the employee's own employment is not relevant; but conditions in licences (granted, presumably, by the employer) are.[48]

---

[44] *Kelly and Chiu*, above, n.43 at [52].

[45] Note the different positions of researchers in universities and in industry, mentioned above in para.7–05.

[46] For the power to do this by "collective agreement", see below, para.7–12—7–13.

[47] PA 1977 s.40(2). Section 41(2) side-steps attempts by the employer to reduce the benefits to him by passing rights to a connected person at an undervalue: see *Shanks v Unilever* [2009] EWHC Civ 3164.

[48] PA 1977 s.41(5).

(g) *Scope of the provisions*

The compensation provisions apply to inventions[49] made after June 1, 1978[50] by a person who is an employee[51] mainly employed in the United Kingdom.[52] They appear to apply only between the employer and the employee at the time of making the invention—something that is likely to cause difficulty, given the lapse of time before a claim is made.[53] They do require that benefits received under foreign patents and equivalent protection be brought into account.[54] **7–11**

(h) *By-passing the Act: collective agreements*

A collective agreement may replace the statutory scheme for compensation if it is made by or on behalf of a trade union to which the employee belongs and by an employer or an employer's association to which the employer belongs and the agreement is in existence at the time of making the invention.[55] The agreement does not have to procure any particular level of benefit to the employee in order to be effective. The broad definition of "trade union" allows a temporary group (for example a research team) to negotiate a collective agreement. This possibility may enable a shop agreement to be reached where (as may well be the case) the research employees are not members of a regular union.[56] With the spread of white-collar unionism, such collective agreements may become commoner. They may well seek to spread bonus moneys amongst all the staff concerned with the development and marketing of the invention. **7–12**

(i) *By-passing the Act: individual agreements*

As with the latter-day extension of the public policy considerations in common law doctrine,[57] the Act renders unenforceable contractual terms which diminish an "employee's rights in inventions . . . or in or under patents for those inventions or applications for such patents".[58] The contracts **7–13**

---

[49] i.e. "inventions for the purposes of this Act", and so not the "things" in PA 1977 s.1(2).
[50] For the question, when is an invention made? see *Dupont's Patent* [1961] R.P.C. 336 CA; *Bristol Myers v Beecham* [1978] R.P.C. 521.
[51] Not an independent contractor, nor a director without a service contract: e.g. *Parsons v Parsons* [1979] F.S.R. 254 CA; see above, paras 2–07—2–09.
[52] Or if not mainly employed anywhere, or it is not possible to determine where he is employed, but he is attached to a UK place of business of the employer: PA 1977 s.43(2). This follows the formula in EPC art.60(2) for determining which national law shall decide employer-employee questions over European patents. If such a connection does not exist with the UK, but (exceptionally) English law applies to the question, the common law rules will apply.
[53] Benefits to the personal representatives of the employer must be brought into account; and the personal representatives of the employee may claim in his shoes: PA 1977 s.43(4), (5); but these exceptions serve to show that other substitutions are not to be made.
[54] PA 1977 s.43(4).
[55] PA 1977 s.40(3), (6).
[56] The definition of "trade union" is that in the Trade Union and Labour Relations Act 1974: see ss.28, 29.
[57] See *Electrolux v Hudson* (above, n.28).
[58] PA 1977 s.42(2).

covered are those that he makes with his employer or any third party at the employer's request or in pursuance of the contract of employment, before the date on which the invention was made.[59] This provision is beset with uncertainty, but, given the extension of common law doctrine, it may well be generously construed. It clearly applies to a provision in an employment contract requiring an employee in advance to give up his rights of initial ownership where there is no distinct consideration for this.[60] But if (say) a reasonable sum is to be paid for these rights, it might well be held that they were not "diminished" (if the sum to be paid were an undervalue, it could in any case be the subject of "compensation").[61]

More importantly, can the inventor make a pre-invention contract to surrender his rights to compensation when the patent belongs initially to the employer? The Act says he may not, if by doing so, he diminishes his rights "under" the patent; and arguably this is the case. A contract made after the invention is not affected by the statute and so by implication would seem a matter of free bargaining. Certainly, if the invention belongs to the employee he cannot make a contract with his employer, before or after the invention, which deprives him of "compensation" which would adjust the price paid to him.[62]

(j) *By-passing the Act by not patenting*

7–14 Where the employer has initial ownership of the invention under s.39 of the 1977 Act and chooses not to patent it, it would seem that the employee is deprived of any right to "compensation". The only hope of arguing to the contrary is by way of a generous construction of the reference in s.43(4) to "other protection": if this were to include the protection of the invention as confidential information or through design right, the result might be achieved.[63] A court might be tempted into such a construction if faced with an employer who had set out deliberately to do his employee down by not patenting.

[59] PA 1977 s.42(1), (2). Duties of confidentiality owed by employee to employer must be respected: s.42(3).

[60] Equally, an employer could not require the employee to seek his consent to any patent application. However, it would not diminish the employee's rights if he were required to notify the employer of the invention and any patent application.

[61] PA 1977 s.40(4).

[62] PA 1977 s.40(4).

[63] The "other protection" would be likely to include protection of designs through utility models, registered and unregistered designs and copyright in technical material (notably computer programs); and arguably confidential information. In *Kelly and Chiu* (above, n.43) Floyd J. held that Regulatory Data Exclusivity (RDE), is not "other protection". RDE is part of the regime for obtaining authority to market a pharmaceutical. While a drug remains under patent, data submitted by the patentee or a licensee to justify its safety is not available to generic companies which intend to put out a version of the drug; once it expires they may rely on that evidence in making their own application for a sales licence.

(k) *Administration*

Issues between employer and employee—over ownership or "compensation"—can be heard by the Patents County Court or the High Court or upon a reference to the Comptroller. They may order "compensation" in the form of a lump sum or periodic payments.[64] 7–15

Obviously the scope for disputes is very considerable. This potential can only be reduced if at all stages an acceptable record of events is kept concerning: (1) who instituted the research; (2) the making of the invention; and (3) its subsequent development and commercial exploitation.[65] At the same time the definition of duties in the contract and employment needs to be clear and to be kept under review.

(3) Dealing in rights

A patent is a right of personal property; so is an application.[66] Both can be dealt with by assignment, mortgage, licence and the like. The 1977 Act indeed provides a code of basic rules about such dealings, introducing at the same time certain modifications of the pre-existing law. 7–16

(a) *Formalities*

The grant of a licence is not required to be in any particular form. "Licence" covers everything from occasional permission to exclusive licence, and it is only right that an informal oral licence should be legally effective.[67] However, assignments or mortgages of patents, applications and rights in patents (including, for example assignments of patent licences) are in law void unless in writing signed by or on behalf of the parties (not just the right-giver).[68] 7–17

(b) *The Register*

In the 1977 Act, the system of maintaining a register of all legal interests in a patent is carried over from the previous law, but with some differences. There is no statutory obligation to register transactions and the like, and 7–18

[64] See PA 1977 ss.8, 12, 37, 41(6), (8). There is also power to vary, discharge, revive or suspend the order and to hear an application despite previous lack of success: see s.41(7), (9)–(11).

[65] Where research is successful and patents are obtained the records should be kept at least for the life of the patent.

[66] PA 1977 s.30(1). They are not however, things in action; though why not, is a mystery.

[67] See PA 1977 s.30; and for Scots law, s.31. Note that even an exclusive licence does not have to be in writing in order to give the licensee his entitlement to sue for infringement: see ss.67, 69 and also note s.58.

[68] See PA 1977 s.30(6). A written assignment signed only by the assignor has been treated as an agreement to transfer which in equity entitles the assignee, as equitable proprietor, to institute infringement proceedings, provided that the assignor is later made a party: *Baxter International v NPLB* [1998] R.P.C. 250.

indeed, registration only provides prima facie evidence of the things registered.[69] There are two sanctions for failure to register which are intended to provide greater incentive to do so than in fact has been the case in the past:

(1) The person with the unregistered right may lose priority to the holder of an inconsistent later right.[70] Where, for instance, the proprietor executes assignments of his title to different people, or the proprietor grants an exclusive licence and then assigns his title, the rule is that the person taking under the later of the grants is to be preferred unless at that time the earlier was already registered (or notified to the Comptroller in the case of an unpublished application) or the person taking the later right knew of the earlier.[71] This varies the rule which otherwise would have applied to legal proprietary rights in patents: that once granted they would be good against all who take later interests even in all innocence.[72]
(2) A proprietor or exclusive licensee who does not register within six months cannot, save exceptionally, be awarded costs or expenses for infringements between his entitlement and registration.[73]

The relationship between equitable interests and the requirement to register is not clear. The Comptroller is not to enter notice of trusts—express, implied or constructive—on the register.[74] Where, therefore, the legal owner of a patent is constituted trustee of the beneficial interest for others,[75] it would seem that the ordinary rules relating to equitable interests apply: their interests are enforceable against all save a person who acquires an inconsistent right in good faith for valuable consideration without actual or constructive notice. But where a contract is made to transfer a legal interest in property and is supported by consideration, this also creates an immediate equitable interest in the property. In the case of patents, such an interest has in the past been held registrable.[76]

[69] PA 1977 ss.32(2)(b), 35(1); PA 1977 Rules r.46; *Brown's Application* [1996] S.T.C. 483; Karet [1996] E.I.P.R. 404.
[70] PA 1977 s.3.
[71] Probably each joint assignee falls to be considered separately.
[72] PA 1977 s.33 deals only ambiguously with cases where subsequent dealings follow the inconsistent transactions; as where A assigns to B, and subsequently assigns to C; then B assigns to D; is D entitled to rely upon being the latest in time, or can C claim under the later of the initial transactions? See Ency. P.L., para.8–103.
[73] PA 1977 s.68 as amended from April 28, 2006. The former provision applies to earlier periods of time: *Siemens Schweiz v Thorn Security* [2008] R.P.C. 4. It has long been the practice, in order to avoid revealing the scope and extent of an entire commercial transaction, to follow an agreement which inter alia assigned patents with a second shortform assignment of the patents alone for the purpose of registration. This practice may set a trap for the patentee: *Coflexip Stena's Patent* [1997] R.P.C. 179 at 194.
[74] PA 1977 s.32(3).
[75] For instance, where an employee secures a patent to which his employer has the better right under PA 1977 s.39 (see above, para.7–07), or vice versa.
[76] *Stewart v Casey* (1892) 9 R.P.C. 9 CA.

(4) Co-ownership[77]

Joint entitlement to ownership of a patent can arise either initially (where there are co-inventors) or through subsequent dealings.[78] Joint owners are each entitled to operate under the patent by themselves or by their agents[79]; but they may not transfer, mortgage or license their interest to third parties without seeking the consent of other co-owners.[80] A co-owner who has the capacity to set up as a manufacturer himself is thus in a comparatively strong position.[81] He may have an outside business supply him with components for a thing covered by the patent without the outsider becoming liable as an indirect infringer to other co-patentees,[82] and, more generally, he may act together with agents in a non-technical sense.[83] He may also use and deal with patented articles made by him as if he had been the sole proprietor, though he may not supply parts for others to use in completing manufacture.[84] He is under no liability to share with his co-patentee what he earns from permissible exploitation. By contrast a co-owner without any manufacturing capacity can only import and sell.[85] **7–19**

2. Licences of Patents and Allied Rights[86]

(1) Traditional approach

In obeisance to freedom of contract, English courts have generally left the parties to patent licences and assignments to determine the scope and extent of obligations by mutual agreement between themselves. Whatever they included in their contract the courts would enforce, resolving any **7–20**

[77] See Marchese [1999] E.I.P.R. 364.

[78] Where a patent is granted to two or more persons, they are entitled, in the absence of contrary agreement, to equal undivided shares—i.e. they take as tenants in common, rather than as joint tenants. So the interests of each survive his death as part of his estate: PA 1977 s.36(1). See also *Florey's Patent* [1962] R.P.C. 186 at 188.

[79] This covers any "home use", but not the licensing of a third party: *Henry v Ministry of Defence* [1999] R.P.C. 442 at 450 CA.

[80] PA 1977 s.36(2), (3). If one alone is registered as proprietor, he must accept registration of the other, rather than, say, seeking revocation: *Henry v Ministry of Defence* [1999] R.P.C. 442 CA. This constraint is subject to the jurisdiction conferred by s.37 to grant a commercial licence in order to break a deadlock between co-owners: *Hughes v Paxman* [2007] R.P.C. 2 CA.

[81] The Crown's power in such a situation is particularly wide—an unsatisfactory position: *Henry v Ministry of Defence* (above, n.80) at 450.

[82] PA 1977 s.36(4).

[83] *Henry v Ministry of Defence* [1997] R.P.C. 694.

[84] Note the provisions concerning infringement suits by a co-patentee: PA 1977 s.66; for disputes between joint applicants and patentees, see ss.8, 10, 12, 37; Ency. P.L., para.8–203.

[85] Purchasers and others who acquire patented products, directly or indirectly, from one co-owner are treated as having acquired from a sole registered proprietor. PA 1977 s.36(5).

[86] For technical treatment of this complex subject, see e.g. Melville, *Forms and Agreements on Intellectual Property and International Licensing*, 3rd edn, Ch.2.

ambiguities by reference to the likely intention of the parties and reading in only such additional terms as might be reasonably necessary to give the agreement business efficacy. In 1875 it was held that the assignor of a patent must honour his undertaking to assign subsequent patent rights covering improvements to the technology. Any public disadvantage in thus discouraging him from further invention was outweighed by the policy that "contracts when entered into freely and voluntarily shall be held sacred and shall be enforced by courts of justice".[87]

Accordingly, a licence gave each party what he was strong enough to demand, or canny enough to include. Because typically it concerned technical procedures that would be used with modifications over a substantial period of time, there was the chance that one or other party would find himself benefited or disadvantaged in an unanticipated fashion: for instance, because a problematic invention licensed for a modest lump sum proved unexpectedly successful; or because a licensee found himself bound not to use alternate technology. There has been no regular technique for adjusting agreements in the name of "fairness",[88] nor did statute intervene, save exceptionally,[89] to prevent abuse of monopoly.

(2) Types of licence

7–21 As a matter of law, there is only one distinction of importance between the different types of patent licence. The exclusive licence, by which the licensor undertakes voluntarily not only to grant no other licences but also not to manufacture or sell within the licensee's province himself,[90] puts the licensee in the special position of being able to sue infringers.[91] In actual business life, the terms of licences vary greatly. It is vital to understand something of this real world, not only because it forms so significant a part of the lawyer's business in industry but also because licences have to meet exacting criteria developed by competition law. Accordingly, this section first sketches the kinds of consideration that the parties to a manufacturing licence will want to cover if left to their own self-interested concerns. After this, we can turn to the constraints upon them now imposed in the name of public interest.

(a) *Interests at the start*

7–22 The value of what the licensor has to offer varies greatly from case to case. If the licensor has not already put the invention into production, the licensee

[87] Jessel M.R., *Printing and Numerical v Sampson* (1875) 19 Eq. 462 at 465. See also, *Jones v Lees* (1856) 1 H. & N. 189 (royalty payable on non-patented item); *Brownie Wireless' Application* (1929) 46 R.P.C. 457.

[88] For possible modification of this attitude, see *Schroeder Music v Macaulay* and ensuing case law (discussed below, in paras 13–30—13–34).

[89] See below, para.7–31 et seq.

[90] See PA 1977 s.130(1), which defines an exclusive licensee as one whose rights exclude all others, including the proprietor. Where both have rights, the licence is called "sole".

[91] PA 1977 s.67.

may have no sure means of judging whether the idea is commercially or even technically viable: this may well be so where he is dealing with an individual inventor or an organisation devoted to research. If the licensee is an enterprise which also has its own research and development resources, it may be keen to restrict its obligations towards an outside licensor; then its own team remains free to explore ideas beyond and to the side of the patent.

If licensor and licensee are both manufacturing organisations, the purpose of the licence may simply be to transfer rights in one direction, because the licensor alone holds the technical knowledge; but it may be that each has technology to exchange—patented or unpatented, competing or complementary. The latter circumstance may have grown out of collaboration in a joint research programme (not infrequently organised by creating a joint subsidiary for the purpose), or a mutual agreement each to conduct research only in complementary fields.[92] The pooling of patents by cross-licensing may be one consequence of a decision to deploy joint strength in the battle against outside competition. What follows is primarily concerned with "one-way" manufacturing licences, where at the outset the technology is all on one side. But it should not be forgotten that the more complex cases of cross-licensing and pooling will raise many of the same issues for the parties, and the mutual restrictions that they are likely to contain will appear more obviously anti-competitive.

(b) *Rights in the technology*

Where an invention has been worked out into a system of production, the licensor is likely to have on offer not just the invention described in his patent specification but additional information—anything from knowledge of how to adapt the invention for particular tasks to merely incidental tricks that help in putting the invention to best use. If he is selling a whole process, the licensor may collect this know-how into an operations manual; in addition he may provide technical staff to get the plant operating properly and to teach the licensee's staff how to keep it going. In such cases the know-how is likely to be imparted upon terms of confidence which will be legally binding.[93] There may be legal reasons for keeping the know-how licence separate from the licence of associated patents: the former may carry fiscal advantages or may avoid provisions directed against abuse of monopoly. But because patents and know-how are so frequently associated in licensing we shall consider aspects of both in this discussion. **7–23**

It should be added that other forms of intellectual property have often to be included also in licences: the licensee may well want the licensor's designs, whether protected by registration or through unregistered design right, and use of his trade marks. Sometimes the licensor will want to compel the

[92] Joint ventures in R & D and specialisation agreements have attracted their share of attention from the European Commission's Competition Directorate: see further Bellamy and Child Ch.5.

[93] The legal basis of breach of confidence is dealt with below, in Ch.8.

licensee to use either designs or trade marks as part of a strategy for building long-term goodwill with the public.

(c) *Exclusivity*

7–24 Particularly when the licensor is seeking to get a technical process used in a new geographical area by finding a manufacturing source there, a basic issue is likely to arise over exclusivity: whether the licensee is to be guaranteed that neither the licensor nor other licensees will manufacture or sell, directly or indirectly, in his territory. The licensee will be interested in shoring up the investment that he will have to make: on the manufacturing side, the plant that he must install and the labour that he must employ; on the selling side, the outlets that he may have to set up, the advertising that he may have to put out, the spare parts and servicing that he may have to provide. If risks such as these are heavy and the licensor is not prepared to help in shouldering them, the licensee may well hold out for complete exclusivity: protection even against potential price differences between territories and the parallel importing that these may induce.

If a licensee is given the security of exclusivity it is frequently on condition that he will respect the exclusivity of others—licensor or exclusive licensees—in their territories. Unlike the restrictions on the licensor mentioned in the previous paragraph, which must be made a term of the licence, the licensee can be kept to his own territory simply by not granting him manufacturing or sales licences under the patents of other territories.[94] This is, of course, protection only so long as the country of import neither treats a first "legitimate" sale beyond its borders as exhausting patent rights, nor assumes that sale abroad by one licensee implies a licence to export to other countries where there are parallel patents. But it has been normal for national patent laws to give the necessary protection. It may, therefore, be difficult to use rules of competition to object to this form of exclusivity, since there may be no contractual term on which they can bite. Only in the EU does the doctrine of free movement of goods[95] qualify patent law at this point. There at least contract is the sole mode of achieving the kind of limitation under discussion (and such an agreement will likely offend the competition rules).

Mutual exclusivity in sales may, of course, be achieved indirectly. If the licensor has power to dictate prices, maximum quantities of production or even the types of goods for which the technology can be used, this may in practice lead to territorial protection.

[94] But a determined competition authority such as the European Commission may treat absence of a licence as the equivalent of an undertaking not to sell in the territory concerned: see *Chemicals Wavin v TERI* [1977] F.S.R. 181 CA.

[95] Or of EU-wide exhaustion, as it will become with the introduction of the EU Patent Regulation: see above, para.6–16.

(3) Particular terms in licences

(a) *Basic obligations*

If the licensor undertakes no more than to give the licensee permission to manufacture under his patent or patents, he acquits himself by making the grant.[96] If he is to provide "know-how", then he must make available whatever information has been described in the contract. Giving an adequate description of "know-how" for this purpose can be a difficult business. Since in practice much of it may have to be made known in the course of negotiations, the wise potential licensor insists on a preliminary contract that anything revealed will be kept confidential and used only in accordance with such contract as may be agreed. If the licensee is seeking not just a chance to work under the patent or to use the know-how, but instead wants a fully operative package, he must secure undertakings from the licensor that this is what will be provided, with escape clauses leaving him free of obligation if it is not. **7–25**

Unless for some reason the licence is to be free, the licensee's first obligation will be to pay for what he has received. This will likely take the form of a lump sum, or a royalty on articles produced (normally calculated as a proportion of their net selling price) or both. If there are special risks in the project—particularly because more technical development needs to be undertaken—a profit-sharing arrangement may prove attractive.

(b) *Duration*

Equally basic will be the duration of the licence, and the definition of circumstances in which either party is to have power to terminate it. If a patent licence is properly determined while the patent remains in effect, the former licensee falls to be treated like any other stranger.[97] More difficult issues arise upon the ending of a know-how licence; for (subject to public policy) the contract between the parties will settle whether the licensee must give up his use of the information, while continuing to keep knowledge of it from outsiders. If this is provided for expressly, it may well be coupled with an obligation to return all relevant documentary information. If it is not, it will not necessarily be implied, particularly when the information was given in order to get a business established.[98] **7–26**

In the past, strong licensors have tied their licensees to long-term

---

[96] Unless he guarantees the validity of the patent expressly, the agreement will be taken to be the licence of a risk and so to survive revocation: *African Gold Recovery v Sheba* (1897) R.P.C. 660; *IMH Investments v Trinidad Home Developers* [1994] F.S.R. 616.

[97] But there may be difficulties about the obligations which one side owes to the other at the date of termination, e.g. to make over rights in improvement patents: *National Broach v Churchill Gear* [1965] R.P.C. 61.

[98] *Regina Glass Fibre v Schuller* [1972] R.P.C. 229 CA; cf. *Torrington v Smith* [1966] R.P.C. 285.

arrangements by such techniques as requiring the continuance of royalties after expiry of the patents[99]; or requiring royalties on articles whether or not made under any licensed patent; or requiring them whether or not the patent is valid.[100]

(c) *Improvements*

7–27 Since novel technology is generally subject to further development, it is important to decide whether new information is to be fed around—from licensee to licensor as well as vice versa. And if additional intellectual property rights are acquired by one, the other is likely to want at least a non-exclusive licence under these rights. It is common practice for the patentee of a basic invention to set up a net of "one-way" manufacturing licences, country by country. Since each licensee will be likely to discover improvements, traditionally the patentee has sought to keep control over the developing technology by requiring not only "feed-back" of information for distribution to the other licensees but also "grant-back" in the form of an assignment of consequent patent and allied rights acquired by the licensee; or if not this, then at least an exclusive licence, with or without power to grant sub-licences to others within the network. Each licensee will find this arrangement to its advantage only to the extent that it feels that it is getting at least as much as it is giving. Not only may it try to drag its own feet in the matter of revelations, it may not make much effort to find improvements.

(d) *Ties*

7–28 The licensor may well want to insist that the licensee acquire non-patented goods from him alone as a condition of the patent or know-how licence. If a process is being licensed, he may in particular want the exclusive right to supply the starting materials to be used in it. Sometimes there are technical reasons for this: his material alone may be good enough to make the process function satisfactorily. For one reason or another such "ties" have, traditionally, been common.[101] There may also be "ties" in distributing the licensee's product.[102] The licensor may insist that it be marketed through his own distribution channels. This may be so even though the licensed patent only contributed to the course of production and no patent rights apply to the final article.

[99] Or requiring royalties so long as any patents relating to the subject-matter of the licence are in force—including those subsequently taken out on improvements.

[100] See below, paras 7–38—7–39.

[101] Despite legislation (from 1907 onwards) treating "ties" and exclusions of competitive technology as abuses of monopoly: for repeal, see below, para.7–38. For the position in the UK under the Competition Act 1998, see Heal [1999] E.I.P.R. 414.

[102] A special case for mention here is the "sub-contracting" out of work on parts for a machine to be completed by the licensor, as to which see the EC Commission's Notice on Sub-contracting Agreements [1979] 1 C.M.L.R. 264.

(e) *Protection for the licensor*

In exclusive licences for royalties, the licensor needs particularly to ensure that the licensee gets the invention into production. If he can negotiate a minimum royalty or minimum production clause, this will give him the guarantee of specific amounts. Beyond this he may seek an undertaking that the licensee will use his best endeavours to exploit the invention. The courts read this to mean what it says, unqualified by any notion of "reasonableness",[103] but the licensor may face grave difficulties in actually establishing that the licensee has not been as assiduous as he might have been. Closely allied to this, the licensee may undertake not to employ competing technology,[104] thus explicitly surrendering one aspect of his capacity to compete to his own best advantage. **7–29**

A different hazard for the licensor is that, because the licensee becomes closely acquainted with the invention he is in a peculiarly strong position to discover weaknesses in the patent: reasons, for instance, for saying that the disclosure was inadequate or that its subject matter is obvious in the light of prior art.[105] Even if the licensee cannot mount a sure attack he may be able to cause enough trouble to secure variations of the licence in his own favour. Accordingly, it has been traditional practice for the licensor to require an undertaking that the licensee will not challenge the validity of the patent or know-how during the currency of the licence; or to require the payment of royalties, whether valid or not.[106]

(f) *Protection for the licensee*

The exclusive licensee acquires a position of some independence from his licensor.[107] The non-exclusive licensee, on the other hand, may well be concerned that he is having to pay for permission that others are getting cheaper or for nothing. Against the danger of more favourable licences, he may seek a clause which will reduce his obligations to the best terms at any time granted to any other licensee. To meet the danger that the licensor will simply fail to pursue an infringer, he may seek power to withhold royalties for any period of inaction. **7–30**

---

[103] *Terrell v Mabie Todd* (1952) 69 R.P.C. 234; *IBM v Rockware* [1980] F.S.R. 335.

[104] But see below, para.7–39.

[105] Likewise he may be able to show that know-how has become public knowledge from an independent source.

[106] An express "no challenge" clause is arguably invalid as being in unreasonable restraint of trade and so contrary to public policy: see, per Clauson J., *VD Ltd v Boston* (1935) 52 R.P.C. 303 at 331; cf. *Mouchel v Cubitt* (1907) 24 R.P.C. 194 at 200. If this is good law, it may be questioned whether there is room for any implied estoppel, based on the notion (borrowed from landlord and tenant law) that a licensor must not "approbate and reprobate".

[107] Particularly by his ability to sue infringers: PA 1977 s.67, above, para.7–20.

(4) Competition law criteria[108]

7–31 Modern business history knows examples enough of agreements amongst leading firms in an industry which uses the licensing of intellectual property rights as a basis for anti-competitive liaisons—arrangements that will keep out or drive out competition by price, by product, by advertising, or in a host of other ways. A "pool" by leading firms under which they and they alone can use inventions patented by them individually or after joint research can prove a very efficient instrument for such manifestly horizontal links. Pools may increase geometrically the potential market power of the individual patents and there is widespread agreement that competition policy should be used against such "expansions" of patent rights, especially where they cover the competing ways of making a product. Accordingly they find no special exemption from either UK[109] or EU competition law. Yet the patenting positions for telecommunications technology and similar industries today are becoming so complex that there is a new readiness to accept open pooling arrangements which constitute standards for the industry. This occurs if licences are available on equal terms to all comers. The difficulty, increasingly to the fore today, is to distinguish between standard-setting arrangements which are benign and those which use IPRs (or other barriers to entry) as disguised means of excluding some competitors from the field.[110]

Patent and know-how licences such as those described in preceding paragraphs, however, are frequently concerned with fostering the use of the licensor's technology in the competition against the same and similar products in the market. By themselves, they do not limit "inter-product" competition. If competition authorities are to subject them to critical scrutiny it is because of their inhibiting effect upon the "intra-product" competition that could otherwise exist between licensor and his licensee or licensees. But the use of competition policy to this end is controversial for an obvious reason. A patent is a decision to allow the patentee to behave as a monopolist to the extent that the market admits. When he licenses his rights, albeit on terms that limit the licensee's or his own freedom of action, he would seem prima facie to be doing no more than realising the potential of his economic power. A rational patentee will not grant licences if his best chance of extracting monopoly profits from the market lies in exploiting the

[108] See further Bellamy and Child, *Common Market Law of Competition* 6th edn (2007); Korah, *Intellectual Property Rights and the EC Competition Rules* (2006); Anderman and Kallaugher, *Technology Transfer and the New EU Competition Rules* (2006) Whish, *Competition Law* 6th edn (2008); Goyder and Albors-Llorenz *EC Competition Law* (5th edn. (2009) Chs 12–14.

[109] For their treatment in UK law, see below, App.1 (hardback edition). For comparison with US Guidelines, Fogt and Gotts Knable [1996] E.C.L.R. 327.

[110] The subject is too complex to pursue here. One type of malpractice will arise when a firm plays a lead in establishing a standard without revealing that this will require a licence under a patent which it is seeking: see Stern [2001] E.I.P.R. 495.

patent himself. Accordingly, if a term in such licensing agreements is to be regarded as invalid, there must be an acceptable explanation in economic terms of how it increases the anti-competitive effect of the initial monopoly grant beyond what was intended.

In the early years of the Common Market, "intra-product" or "vertical" competition became of great moment to those directing the EU Competition Policy. The prime importance of breaking down barriers to free marketing within EU territories made the EU Commission critical of exclusive selling rights wherever they occurred, and whether they are created directly or as a consequence of some other restriction, such as a maximum production limit in a technology licence. Accordingly, any restrictive licence having significant impact on inter-state trade within the EU was subjected to detailed regulation. **7–32**

As we shall see, this original severity has been replaced by a greater readiness to accept that vertical limitations agreed between businessmen may have a healthy impact on inter-brand competition between businesses. A new deal has been reached in the Commission Regulation for Vertical Agreements of 1999[111] and two sets of Guidelines, one on vertical restraints and the other on horizontal cooperation agreements.[112] Their emphasis is on removing legalistic straitjackets in favour of real appreciation of market impact. As we shall see, to some extent that shift is already apparent in the 1996 Regulation of technology transfers which involve patent and associated IP licences. The competition law of the United Kingdom, as developed after the Second World War, took a much less aggressive attitude towards vertical restraints in general and intellectual property licensing in particular. That law has now been substantially renovated, the Competition Act 1998 involving a transposition into terms derived from the EU's Rules of Competition. The new UK law is likely to develop in line with this regional model.[113] The Competition Act will not be separately treated here. It may be noted, however, that it repealed two isolated provisions in the Patents Act 1977 which were directed against particular "abuses" of monopoly in patent licensing.[114]

(5) Development of European Commission policy on patent licences

As early as 1962, in a non-binding notice (the "Patent Notice"),[115] the Commission reserved its position on patent pools, cross-licences and similar **7–33**

[111] 2790/1999. Regulations on Specialisation Agreements and R & D Agreements have been revised in the same spirit: OJ L2658 and 2659/2000.
[112] Respectively OJ C291/2000; OJ C3/2001.
[113] The main body of the Act came into force in 2000.
[114] PA 1977 s.44 (collateral "tie-ins") and s.45 ("tie-ups" beyond the duration of initial patents); to be repealed by Competition Act 1998 s.70.
[115] Announcement on Patent Licensing Agreements, December 24, 1962 (hence known to initiates as the "Christmas Message")—now withdrawn.

forms of mutual horizontal restraint.[116] But it indicated that it would not regard certain limiting terms in "one-way" licences as falling within the prohibition of what is now TFEU art.101 (ex-81).[117] Even so there were indications that some clauses (non-essential "tie-ins", exclusive "grant-backs", post-patent obligations) might go too far. Within a decade, the Patent Notice clauses ceased to be a reliable guide (particularly over exclusivity in manufacturing or sales, and maximum production limits). In the 1970s a number of test decisions by the Commission took a severer (and so more controversial) line.[118] Agreements that had been thought to be outside art.101(1) were instead treated as needing exemption under art.101(3); and in the matter of sales exclusivity this proved particularly difficult to justify.

In consequence of this shift, the Commission eventually, in 1984, formulated a Block Exemption on Patent Licences that specified the conditions under which a licence need not be individually justified before exemption. To some extent the industrial and governmental objections raised against the drafts of this Block Exemption[119] induced a softening in the Commission's approach, which was indicative of a more general shift away from restrictive regulation under the competition policy. This was followed four years later with a similar Block Exemption for technical know-how licences.[120]

7–34 In 1996 the two were amalgamated in a shift that contained a significant measure of deregulation.[121] In turn it has been replaced by a Technology Transfer Block Exemption (Regulation 772/2004, referred to as "TTBE").[122] This introduces new distinctions relating to the market shares of the licensor and licensee and to the position of the parties as competitors or non-competitors. Accordingly it aims to provide a greater element of economic reality, in place of formal legal tests directed at types of term in the licence. As an aid to interpretation, the Competition Directorate of the Commission has issued a very extensive set of Guidelines. As before, the TTBE applies only to licences between two parties, not to larger arrangements. The Commission retains the power to withdraw the Exemption in special cases,

---

116 In *Video Cassette Recorders Agreements* [1978] F.S.R. 376, the Commission found a patent pooling aspect of the licences in question to be restrictive of competition because any member of the pool was to surrender its rights upon leaving the pool but was obliged to allow continuing members to retain their rights in its patents.

117 For the main content of arts 101, 102 (ex-81, 82; ex-85, 86), see above, para.1–53; for a note on their implementation, App.1.

118 See especially *Raymond/Nagoya* [1972] C.M.L.R. D45; *Davidson Rubber* [1972] C.M.L.R. D52; *Burroughs/Delplanque and Geha* [1972] C.M.L.R. D72; *Kabelmetal/Luchaire* [1975] 2 C.M.L.R. D40; *Bronbemaling v Heidemaatschappij* [1975] 2 C.M.L.R. D67; *AOIP/Beyrard* [1976] 1 C.M.L.R. D14; *Vaessen v Moris* [1979] F.S.R. 259.

119 The change in attitude is easily seen by comparing the final version with the initial draft, as given in [1977] 1 C.M.L.R. D25.

120 See Regulations 2349/84 and 556/89.

121 Regulation 1996/240.

122 For a usefully annotated version cross-referring to the Guidelines, see Korah and Fatur [2004] E.I.P.R. 421.

ever where its conditions are met.[123] However, parties who do not satisfy those conditions are no longer entitled to apply for exemption under art.81(3) on an individual basis.[124]

A technology transfer agreement now extends to the licences of patents, know-how and/or software copyright, provided that the prime object is the manufacture of contract products, rather than their distribution.[125] These agreements are dealt with differently depending on: (i) whether they are *reciprocal* or not; (ii) whether the two parties are *competing* or not; and (iii) whether they have reached specified *market shares*:

(1) *reciprocity* is present when each party is licensing competing technologies to the other[126];
(2) *competition* is measured by reference both to the market for the technology and the market for contract products. The parties are competing undertakings if one party has either technology or products that are interchangeable or substitutable for the subject-matter of the agreement[127];
(3) *market share thresholds* by "market share" is meant the presence that the licensed technology has on the relevant product market, taking the products of licensor and licensee together.[128] Where the parties are competitors, the threshold is reached if their combined market share is 20 per cent or more. Where they are not, the threshold is only crossed if either of them separately has a 30 per cent share or more.[129] Carrying out market share assessments is often problematic. One difficulty with successful new technology is that its market share may move quite quickly upwards. The effect, according to the English Court of Appeal, is that the character of a licence may shift over time.[130] At least it is stated that if the agreement comes to cover market shares over the relevant levels, there is a period of two years within which to make adjustments to the agreement in order to conform to the TTBE.[131] There is also protection for parties who become competitors only after signing their agreement: they may

---

123 TTBE art.6. For an example, see *Tetra-Pak (No. 1)* [1990] II-E.C.R. 301.
124 This makes for particular difficulty for interrelated licences together having a more than 50 per cent market share that are excluded from exemption by art.7.
125 Article 1(1)(b). "Patents" includes not only patents but utility models, designs, semiconductor topographies, SPCs and plant breeders' rights, together with applications for them: art.1(1)(h). For the definition of "know-how", see art.1(1)(i).
126 Article 1(1)(c), (d).
127 Article 1(1)(j).
128 Article 3(3). "Product" includes services: art.1(1)(e).
129 Article 3, to be worked out on the basis of market sales value data, if available, otherwise other reliable information: art.8(1).
130 *Passmore v Morland* [1999] 3 All E.R. 1005.
131 TTBE art.8(2).

continue to rely on their protection as non-competitors unless they amend the agreement in a material respect.[132]

(6) Exclusivity

7–35 Exemption under art.101(3) by complying with the TTBE and its Guidelines is necessary only to the extent that the technology licence offends the basic requirements of art.101(1). In its decisions of the 1970s on patent licences, the Commission's starting point was that undertakings to ensure the exclusivity of territories were restrictive of competition in the sense of art.101(1) of the Treaty of Rome, since they necessarily involved a surrender of the freedom to enter the market of an exclusive territory.[133] This applied to the licensor's undertaking not to manufacture or sell in the licensee's territory and not to grant licences to others to do so; and it also applied to the licensee's undertaking not to manufacture or sell in a territory which the licensor reserved to himself, or was licensing to another exclusive licensee. The latter was particularly controversial since, but for the licence to him, the licensee would have no entitlement to use the patented technology at all, and so would be even more constrained. The Commission, however, considered that the ultimate objective of unifying the internal market justified treating a licence to manufacture in one country of the EU as a licence to sell in all.

After some time, the Court of Justice ruled against so embracing an application of art.101.

The proceedings concerning a licence of plant variety rights in a new form of maize seed.[134] The developer of the new variety, a French research organisation, INRA, had granted an exclusive manufacturing and sales licence for Germany to Nungesser, a German firm. The court accepted that, so far as this agreement sought to impose *absolute* territorial protection on Nungesser, by requiring that even a parallel importer should be prevented from obtaining the seed in France and exporting it to Germany, it was bad under art.101(1) and could not be saved by exemption.

The parallel importer is a prime mover in operating the EU. But so far as the agreement only secured *open* exclusivity—undertakings that neither INRA nor its French licensees would themselves export to Germany—the matter must be judged in light of the prevailing circumstances in the particular market (in American parlance, by "rule of reason").[135] Given the "specific nature of the products in question", to introduce the newly

[132] TTBE art.4(3), Guidelines 32, 68.

[133] See esp. *Davidson Rubber*, *Raymond/Nagoya*, and *Kabelmetal/Luchaire* (above, n.8). It should be remembered that in the last two of these cases, the Commission took the view that licences for manufacture outside the EU could infringe art.101(1) if they excluded a realistic prospect of the licensee selling into the EU: see also *Davide-Campari Milano's Agreement* [1978] 2 C.M.L.R. 397.

[134] *Nungesser v EC Commission* [1982] E.C.R. 2015.

[135] On the distinction between absolute and open exclusivity, see Hoffmann and O'Farrell [1984] E.I.P.R. 104.

developed seeds involved such risks in cultivating and marketing that a potential licensee might have been deterred by the prospect of direct competition in the same product from other licensees. Accordingly competition would be prejudiced by the licensor's inability to offer exclusive rights. There was accordingly no infraction of art.101(1).

The decision constituted a *via media*. Open exclusivity may be useful **7–36** where price differentials between different parts of the EU are not substantial, or where transportation costs or other factors serve to inhibit parallel importation. But there will be circumstances where the insistence that opportunities for the parallel importer be preserved may prevent the initial producer from supplying a cheap market at all with his product, to the detriment of consumers there. The court has insisted that such a risk has to be taken, both here and (as we shall see) in relation to the free movement of goods between Member States.

The "*Maize Seed*" decision undoubtedly curbed the Commission's opposition to exclusivity provisions. The subsequent Block Exemptions took an increasingly scrupulous attitude towards them. The TTBE now brings into consideration whether the parties are competitors and whether the licence is, or is not, reciprocal. So far as limitations on production by geographical areas are concerned, these will be treated as unacceptable divisions of markets where competitors enter reciprocal licences. At the other end of the scale, if non-competitors are involved in a one-way licence, the arrangement is normally permissible. In between, as in the one-way production licence aspect of "*Maize Seed*", the TTBE may well provide exemption—the more so where the licensor retains the right to product of the licensee's territory (i.e. where the licence is sole, rather than exclusive).[136]

So far as concerns restrictions on the sale of contract products, again, this is not permitted between competitors engaging in reciprocal licensing. But if their agreement is not reciprocal, they may agree not to engage in either active or passive sales in the other's territory. Active sales are the result of positive promotion, passive sales merely the response to unsolicited orders. If the arrangement is part of a set of exclusive arrangements with licensees in different Member States, only passive sales may not be excluded by agreement. The object of these various limitations is to protect risky investments by licensees who might otherwise not enter them.[137] It was that very factor which formed the basis of the "*Maize Seed*" decision.

(7) Restrictive terms

(a) *Restrictions on production and sale*

According to art.4 on Hardcore Restrictions, it is not justifiable to restrict **7–37** the licensee's freedom, or the licensor's, in reaching certain basic decisions

[136] See generally, Guidelines 162–67.
[137] See generally, Guidelines, 87–101.

about marketing products made under the licence—in particular, about sale price at which products are offered to third parties[138] or their corollary, maximum quantities of production.[139] Between competitors it is not always permissible to divide up the technical fields of use or the product markets for the licensed technology: where the agreement is reciprocal, only the licensee of a technology may undertake such restrictions; whereas if the agreement is non-reciprocal, both may become bound.[140]

It is now accepted that an exclusive licensor must be able to build in incentives to ensure himself an adequate return. He may require a minimum quantity of production by the licensee, or the payment of a minimum royalty. Equally he may impose a requirement that the licensee use his best endeavours to exploit the licensed technology, though between competitors must not go so far as directly to prohibit the licensee from exploiting its own technology or restrict either party's research and development, unless indispensable to prevent licensed know-how reaching third parties.[141]

(b) *Previous objections now lifted*

7–38 The licensor of a new technique has a legitimate interest to ensure that it is adequately used by any licensee. He may, for instance, insist that the licensee should have no power to sub-license or assign the licence to another. In *Erauw-Jacquaery v La Hesbignonne*,[142] the Court of Justice recognised the propriety of such an objective. The licensee may be placed under an obligation (a "tie-in") to procure goods or services from the licensor or his nominee; to the same end he may be placed under minimum quality specifications and have to undergo checks to see that they are observed. It is also proper for the licensor to require that products be sold under his trade mark or with his get-up.

7–39 "No challenge" clauses are no longer objectionable. Even restrictions on "grant-back" and similar clauses which require assignment of rights or information sharing concerning improvements to the licensed technology are now permitted. Little therefore remains of the Commission's attitudes in the 1970s which strove for detailed legal control over licence terms that had some potential for possible anti-competitive effects.

---

[138] TTBE for competing undertakings: art.4.1(a); for non-competing undertakings: art.4(2)(a)—allowing certain maximum price terms.

[139] TTBE, for competing undertakings only, art.4(1)(b). Even then, output limitations may be imposed on the licensee in a non-reciprocal agreement or on only one of the licensees in a reciprocal agreement.

[140] TTBE art.4(1)(c)(i), (ii).

[141] TTBE art.4(1)(d).

[142] *Erauw-Jacquaery v La Hesbignonne* [1988] E.C.R. 1919.

3. Compulsory Licences

A wholehearted patent system will contain nothing that fetters a patentee's power to act as a monopolist if the market allows it: he will be able to hold production of his invention down to the level of maximum profit. But many countries have felt the urge to qualify this full potential in the name of some other policy objective, such as local working of the invention or the satisfaction of consumer demand.[143] The technique for this is generally some form of compulsory licence, which will prevent the patentee from acting as sole producer. He will be obliged instead to face direct competition subject only to a royalty or other fee on the licensee's sales, assessed by an outside arbitrator under some criterion of reasonableness.[144] **7–40**

Pressure for this sort of curb tends to follow upon the success of particular patentees, frequently foreigners. It is likely to be at its most intense where a clear national need arises, such as defence or health care. These indeed combined in the wake of the Al Qaeda attack on New York, when there were cases of anthrax being sent through the post. The anti-anthrax drug was patented in many countries and the United States, no less, had little compunction in threatening compulsory powers in order to obtain it. This nervous reaction cast the pall of inconsistency over the campaign which US and other multi-national drug firms had been waging against South Africa. That country had enacted wide-ranging legislation which allowed it to obtain patented drugs—notably those to counteract HIV infection—from its own source.[145] Given the heat of that confrontation, it is worth recalling recent British history. A special provision was maintained in this country from 1919 to 1977, which made compulsory licences for food and drug patents available as of right save exceptionally. Even that system proved cumbersome, since the terms of the licence had still to be settled before the licensee could begin to act, and that could prove slow and expensive. The ending of the special regime came only after heightened tension between the Health Ministry and leading pharmaceutical companies, involving a Monopolies Commission Report which recommended very substantial reduction in the price of the two leading tranquillisers of the day, which were under patent.[146] The general provisions for compulsory licensing which survive in the United Kingdom are even more laborious to set in motion and that will explain why their supposed effect today is mainly *in terrorem*. **7–41**

The meetings of Paris Convention countries have long been the field for **7–42**

---

[143] For the beginnings in the UK, see above, para.3–15.

[144] "Compulsory licence" in this broad sense extends to the Crown use provisions discussed in the next section. Their similarity is stressed, for instance, in original CPC art.46(2).

[145] See Sheppard [1999] E.I.P.R. N27–28; Harms [2000] E.I.P.R. 451; May [2003] E.I.P.R. 1.

[146] Tranquillisers Report, H.C. 197, 1973. The consequent order by the Secretary of State to make the reductions in price led to the introduction of specific procedures for compulsory licensing after an adverse report by the Competition Commission. These were introduced into PA 1977 (see ss.51, 53) and into copyright and designs legislation.

exhausting battles over the principle of compulsory licensing. A stringent requirement of local working, for instance, would seem a means by which one country could give preference for its home inventors, while hoping for no corresponding handicap upon them abroad. In the industrial countries, however, what has seemed vital in an international forum has become purely token in domestic practice: compulsory licensing provisions are commonly enmeshed in such a net of procedures that it is only the threat of invoking them that carries any significant weight. Exceptionally, the compulsory licence has been used severely enough for a serious falling-off of patenting to occur. This led to the 1982 breakdown in revising the Paris Convention.[147]

7–43 The TRIPS Agreement signalled an important reversal of direction. Article 31 subjects the granting of compulsory licences (or any other use without the patentee's authorisation, including use by governments and their collaborators[148]) to a splay of conditions.[149] Each instance has to be considered individually, and must be preceded by attempts at voluntary negotiation. The scope and duration of the licence must be confined to its purpose and must be open to review when circumstances change. The licence must be non-exclusive, non-assignable and predominantly for supply of the domestic market. Adequate remuneration must be required. Any decision, whether about authorisation or remuneration, must be open to judicial review. There are further conditions where a head patent is being licensed in order to permit exploitation of a subsidiary patent. The hostility of the United States to the very idea of compulsory patent licensing lies beneath these provisions.

The confinements of this article led, soon enough, to an explosion of objections from developing countries over the effective denial of access to medicines to combat their endemic and epidemic threats to health and life from HIV and AIDs, malaria, tuberculosis and other conditions and diseases.[150] This neglect of development problems led on to related objections—for instance, that the patent system promoted research and exploitation of results into the diseases of the developed world and the ignoring of those that occurred mostly in developing countries. The objection that patented pharmaceuticals would be available only on licensing terms that were prohibitively expensive for all but a tiny layer of people in the developing world was repeated in tones of outrage. It was exacerbated by the condition in

---

[147] See above, para.3–17.

[148] For the effect of this on Crown use, see below, para.7–51.

[149] TRIPS art.30 prefaces these specificities with the "patent version" of the Three-Step Test: exceptions to exclusive rights (of which compulsory licensing is an important example) are permitted only if they do not unreasonably conflict with a normal exploitation of the patent and do not unreasonably prejudice the legitimate interests of the patent owner, taking account of the legitimate interests of third parties.

[150] See Cameron and Berger in Vaver (ed.), *Intellectual Property Rights: Critical Concepts* (2006), IV, 437; Vaver and Basheer [2006] E.I.P.R. 282; and the essays in Maskus and Reichman (eds), *International Public Goods and Transfer of Technology under a Globalized Intellectual Property Regime* (2005), Pt 3, s.1.

art.31(h) confining any compulsory licence predominantly to the domestic market of the country that granted it. This meant, for instance, that an Indian compulsory licensee could not supply an HIV drug to African states where the condition was raging. The international pharmaceutical industry offered responses.[151] These included that the root difficulty was the severe lack of structures and training to carry out medical programmes in developing countries, rather than access to certain medicines. Also came the warning that extending the rights of compulsory licensees to send their products to other developing countries would largely lead to re-exportation to developed countries—with their attractively high prices.

Despite these points, in their 2001 Doha Declaration, WTO states accepted that consideration must be given to incorporating greater concessions into TRIPS on matters of public health in developing countries than were expressed in the 1994 text.[152] By the Declaration, WTO states were entitled to take measures to protect public health and TRIPS would be interpreted and implemented in a manner supportive of this entitlement, in particular, where using the "flexible" provisions to TRIPS to the full would promote access to medicines for all. This led to further negotiations, particularly on the non-export provision in art.31(f), that were notable for their toughness. By August 2003, a temporary Decision of the WTO Council was reached that Member States could grant compulsory licences that would permit export of "any patented produce, or product manufactured through a patented process, of the pharmaceutical sector" to countries with insufficient or no manufacturing capacity without requiring licence payments in both the exporting and the importing countries. The many details that follow cannot be pursued here.[153] A country that receives such assistance is placed under an obligation to prevent the diversion of the imports back into other non-beneficiary countries. This obligation is only to take reasonable measures within their means, proportionate to their administrative capacities. Some recognition is thus accorded to the grave difficulties that least-developed countries face in addressing opportunities that for them have till now seemed to them utterly unattainable. The 2003 decision is being incorporated into TRIPS by permanent amendment.[154] In order to give effect to the changes, the EU, for its part, has enacted a Regulation.[155] It remains to be seen what contribution this adjustment to patenting will actually make to the profound problems of public health in underprivileged

[151] It also secured the initiation of WTO complaints by the US against South Africa and Brazil respecting laws said to breach in TRIPS art.31. These did not continue after the Doha Declaration.

[152] WT/MIN(01)DEC/2, esp para.6.

[153] For a full and fair account, Matthews [2006] I.P.Q. 91.

[154] See the WTO document IP/C/41 (December 6, 2005).

[155] Regulation 816/2006 on Compulsory Licensing of Patents relating to the Manufacture of Pharmaceutical Products for Export to Countries with Public Health Problems; see Vaver and Basheer, above, n.15; supported by the *Gowers Review of Intellectual Property* (2006) paras 4.49–4.66.

parts of the world, for it does not provide for any licence of right, but only for a compulsory licence, the terms of which have to be laid down in advance. Much else needs to be done.

(1) Compulsory licensing under the 1977 Act

(a) *Legal grounds*

7–44 Once a British patent has been granted for three years, the Comptroller has power[156] to grant compulsory licences under it[157] on a number of grounds. The Comptroller then settles the terms as he sees fit.[158] The procedure allows for the patentee to oppose the grant and to apply for revocation when conditions have changed.[159] The order granting the licence is then subject to review by the Patents Court.[160] The elaborate provisions first give lists of grounds, and the applicant must show a case within one or more of them. But their breadth is qualified, not simply by the fact that the Comptroller's jurisdiction is discretionary, but by the enumeration of factors which must be considered in assessing the particular case. As the result of decisions of the European Court of Justice,[161] it has also been necessary to ensure that compulsory licence rules do not result in discrimination against enterprises from other EU states which seek to export to Britain. Equally the Act has been adapted to comply with TRIPS.[162]

7–45 Three principal motives have lain behind the creation of the present powers. First, it should not be permissible to use the exclusive right of a patent to hinder the exploitation of other new technology. This could arise, for instance, where one patentee is refusing to licence a "head" patent to another who has a derivative patent for a selection or improvement.

Secondly, a patent should not be a pretext for refusing to exploit new technology at all. There is a perennial fear that inventions so efficient as to threaten the future of an industry (the long-life light-bulb or razor-blade, for instance) are patented in order to delay their introduction. But the evidence

---

156 PA 1977 s.48(1)(2). An applicant may receive a licence in his own favour and in certain circumstances also in favour of his customers (see s.49(1)). A government department may seek a licence for another.

157 Or to enter a "licences of right" indorsement upon the register—as to which, see above, para.4–25.

158 PA 1977 s.48(4). The licence may be exclusive even of the patentee and may revoke other licences: s.49(2).

159 PA 1977 s.53.

160 PA 1977 s.97; further appeal to the Court of Appeal lies only where there is a mistake of law and leave is granted.

161 *EC Commission v Italy and United Kingdom* [1992] E.C.R. I-777 at 829; and see the decisions concerning compulsory licences of right associated with extensions of patent term under the 1977 Act: *Allen & Hanbury's v Generics* (UK) [1988] E.C.R. 1245; *Generics v Smith Kline & French* [1992] E.C.R. I-5335; PA 1977 s.46(3)(c) (as amended), cf. original CPC arts 46, 77, 83. See also below, para.19–07.

162 PA 1977 s.55(5); *Allen & Hanburys v Controller of Patents* (Ireland) [1997] F.S.R. 1 ECJ.

for this ever happening is very thin. Much more likely is that the inventor will be bought off on conditions of secrecy.

Thirdly, a patent should result in the invention being worked in the United Kingdom or another EU state.[163] As the history of the Paris Convention shows, most countries have wanted to use the patent system to induce the actual working of the invention in their home territories.[164] Some countries used to provide harsh sanctions in this endeavour[165] and one role of the Convention has been to secure some moderation: by requiring that compulsory licensing should be tried before revocation, and that it should not be imposed within three years of grant.[166] For many inventions, the scale needed for cost-effective manufacture would make it absurd to expect plant to be established in each country where products are sold.

Because of TRIPS art.31, the legal grounds on which a compulsory licence can be based are more restricted where the patentee is a WTO proprietor, than when not.[167] Since a WTO proprietor is a corporation with real and effective establishment in a WTO country, including the United Kingdom, or else an individual who is a national or domiciliary of a WTO country, the other cases will be very rare. This discussion will be restricted to cases where the TRIPS conditions apply. The grounds for grant of a compulsory licence are in these cases: **7–46**

(1) that UK demand for a patented product is not being met on reasonable terms[168];
(2) that, because of unreasonable restrictions on licensing the patent, exploitation of another patented invention, which is technically and economically important is being prevented or hindered[169]; or commercial or industrial activities in the United Kingdom are being unfairly prejudiced[170];
(3) that, because of conditions imposed upon licensing the patent, or on disposal or use of the patented product or process, *either* the manufacture, use or disposal of unpatented materials[171] or commercial or

[163] See above, para.7–42.
[164] See Ladas, *The International Protection of Industrial Property* (1930); Penrose, *The Economics of the International Patent System* (1951), pp.78–87. The old notion of the "importer-inventor" reflected the same desire: see above, para.4–06.
[165] See above, para.3–15.
[166] PIP art.5A. The Convention allows revocation as a sanction if compulsory licensing is ineffective, but this has been dropped from PA 1977.
[167] The former law applies to other cases: see now PA 1977 s.48B.
[168] PA 1977 s.48A(1)(a)
[169] PA 1977 s.48A(1)(b)(i). This can only be on cross-licensing terms: s.48A(4). Any assignment has to be to a person who is acquiring both patents: s.48A(5).
[170] PA 1977 s.48A(1)9b)(ii).
[171] This provision against the "tie-in" of non-patented materials is a much milder limitation upon the practice than existed in UK law until the repeal of PA 1977 s.44, in the Competition Act 1998. See above, para.7–37.

> industrial development in the United Kingdom is unfairly prejudiced.[172]

Other TRIPS conditions apply: there must first be a reasonable attempt to procure a voluntary licence[173]; the licence must be must be non-exclusive, assignable only with the business, predominantly for supply of the UK market, subject to adequate remuneration for the patentee and limited to the purpose for which it is granted.[174] The procedure has been excluded entirely from the field of semi-conductor technology,[175] thanks to special interest lobbying.

(b) *The discretion*

7–47 Beside these grounds, the Comptroller must balance a variety of considerations in deciding whether and what licence to grant compulsorily. To some extent these make clearer what limits upon monopoly power Parliament considered that it was imposing. Thus, it is necessary to consider the nature of the invention, the time that has elapsed since grant, what the patentee or any licensee has already done to make full use of the invention and the ability of the applicant to work it to the public advantage and the risks to him.[176] This contemplates qualifying the patentee's potential market power in two ways. First, the pressure that it imposes upon him to establish manufacturing facilities in the EU may prevent him from producing where he can do so most cheaply and efficiently. Secondly, the requirement that working be to the fullest practicable extent appears to contemplate that price ought to be reduced to satisfy larger demand, even if the monopoly profits will in consequence be reduced.[177] Because the Comptroller must still leave the patentee with "adequate remuneration", the licence must not venture too far in either of these directions. The courts have had little enough opportunity to indicate how far it is proper to go. As far as manufacturing in the EU is concerned, the patentee will not protect himself against any grant at all simply by showing that present costs of foreign manufacture abroad are lower. Earlier case law shows that there must be an historical inquiry to see whether he "used his monopoly fairly as between

[172] PA 1977 s.48A(1)(c).
[173] PA 1977 s.48A(2).
[174] PA 1977 s.48A(6).
[175] PA 1977 s.48A(3).
[176] PA 1977 s.50(2). Additional factors operate in respect of non-WTO patentees: s.50(1).
[177] The unadorned case that the patentee's own prices in the UK are too high and that therefore a compulsory licence should be granted, seems rarely to have been presented: but note *Robin Electric's Petition* (1915) 32 R.P.C. 202 (minimum price clause in voluntary licence required licensee to charge higher prices in UK than abroad; held unobjectionable, since prices "not so high as to be a serious burden on the consumer or to be unreasonable"). Such an issue is examinable by the Monopolies and Mergers Commission, if the general conditions for a reference to it are satisfied. In essence such an issue was dealt with by the Commission in its report criticising the pricing by the Hoffmann-La Roche group of its tranquillisers trade-marked "Librium" and "Valium": Report on Tranquillisers (H.C. 197, 1973).

home and foreign trade". The object is to determine whether his efforts to build up foreign manufacture prejudiced the chance of doing so in the EU.[178] In today's conditions of global trading, such a case could be very difficult to make out.

As far as concerns "further markets", where the foreign patentees of copying machinery had sold to a limited field of British customers, a compulsory licence was granted to a British company upon their prediction that they could sell to an extended range of customers.[179] Even when the Comptroller decides to grant the licence, its terms (particularly the rate of royalty) will influence the licensee's decisions about selling price and hence quantity; which in turn will affect the patentee's remuneration. The royalty rate, however, is most likely to be fixed by comparison with any relevant rate charged by the patentee or others in the industry for similar licences. **7–48**

As already pointed out, a compulsory licence system which is directed at one or other form of insufficient exploitation, and which thus requires careful investigation of the circumstances before grant, is not likely to be much used. This is indeed borne out by British and other experience.[180] How far the threat of applying to the Comptroller enhances the bargaining position of would-be voluntary licensees cannot be measured. Neither can it be discounted.[181] But in many cases it will not be strong: for the licensee may also need know-how to get started: and the licensor cannot be obliged to provide that under the present rules. **7–49**

4. Crown Use

The British Government has a special exemption from the exclusive rights of patentees. The Crown may make or sanction use of a patented invention without previous licence, subject only to an obligation to pay compensation for doing so. Originally the Crown was in no sense bound by Letters Patent: **7–50**

[178] Parker J. *Hatschek's Patent* (1909) 26 R.P.C. 228 at 243; see also *Johnson's Patent* (1909) 26 R.P.C. 52; *Bremer's Patent* (1909) 26 R.P.C. 449 at 465.

[179] *Kallé's Patent* [1966] F.S.R. 112. A number of grounds were alleged by the applicant. In a case where the circumstances were rather special (*Cathro's Application* (1934) 51 R.P.C. 75) it was said that demand must be actual not potential. But the Act now refers to "a" rather than "the" demand, and other cases, including *Kallé*, making nothing of the point: see also *Boult's Patent* (1909) 26 R.P.C. 383 at 387; *Fabricmeter's Application* (1936) 53 R.P.C. 307 at 312; *Kamborian's Patent* [1961] R.P.C. 403 at 405. As to sub-licensing, see *Hilti's Patent* [1988] R.P.C. 51.

[180] Between 1959 and 1968 an average of 1.5 p.a. were applied for in the UK under the general provisions; only two were granted for the whole period; for the special food and drugs provision average applications were 4.1 p.a.; four were granted in toto: Banks Report (Cmnd. 4407, 1970), App.D(d).

[181] The Banks Committee thought there was enough indirect effect to justify retaining the provisions on compulsory licensing in general: Ch.12; but it shared the hostility of leading pharmaceutical firms towards the compulsory licensing provision (PA 1949 s.41—abandoned in PA 1977) that allowed the grant of licences save in exceptional circumstances: Bank Reports, Ch.14.

for one thing, classic theory relieved "the Crown"—not just the sovereign in person—of civil responsibility imposed by courts of justice.[182] Compensation for use of patented inventions was paid ex gratia. In 1883 came a change. In principle the Crown was made subject to patents, but was given the benefit of Crown use provisions that were the ancestors of the present law.[183] Compensation became a matter of legal entitlement; but the Crown could, of course, claim that it was not within the scope of monopoly or that the patent was invalid.[184]

The obvious justification for the Crown use provision lies in national security.[185] But central government acts in many other spheres besides defence and the wider potential of its powers were dramatically demonstrated in 1965: the House of Lords held that the Ministry of Health might authorise an importer to bring in drugs not made by the patentee for use in the NHS hospital service.[186] In the cases to which it is applicable, the Crown's ability to override the patentee's decisions on exploitation may prove a decisive counterweight to full monopoly power. Because of this, it tends to be viewed critically, particularly in the EU and other countries which do not allow their governments so wide-ranging a weapon.[187] In response, it can be said that if a government department decides to take up an invention, it may well be providing an exceptionally large market for it, one that it might take much greater effort to establish in the private sector. As an incentive to invent and innovate, therefore, the prospect of securing compensation for Crown use may in many instances be broadly as attractive as full monopoly profits from other sources. Whether this sort of justification has a sufficient basis in historical fact deserves examination: this it has never had.

7–51 The special powers of the Crown to use and then pay compensation are governed by three principal factors:

(1) the acts performed must be "for the services of the Crown".[188] They do not have to be done by a government department. Anyone authorised to act on the Crown's behalf is included,[189] but still the aim

[182] *Feather v R.* (1865) 6 B. & S.257. For the political history, O'Dell, *Inventions and Official Secrecy* (1994). Printing of bank notes for a foreign government is not a sovereign act. It may be a patent infringement justiciable in English courts: *A Ltd v B Bank* [1997] F.S.R. 165 CA.

[183] Patents, Design and Trade Marks Act 1883 s.27.

[184] Today validity may also be challenged in proceedings for compensation: PA 1977 s.74(1)(e).

[185] In times of national emergency, the Crown's powers become very wide indeed: see PA 1977 s.59.

[186] *Pfizer v Ministry of Health* [1965] A.C. 512; [1965] R.P.C. 261.

[187] See, e.g. Demaret, *Patents, Territorial Restrictions and EEC Law* (1978), pp.12–17, 87–89. Note the limitations now imposed by the TRIPS Agreement art.31.

[188] PA 1977 s.55(1).

[189] PA 1977 s.55(1). The authorisation must be in writing; but it does not have to be given until after the event: s.55(6). Normally the patentee or an exclusive licensee needs no authority, and so obtains no right to compensation; but see the exceptions in s.57(3), (4); Ency, P.L., 9–18.

must be to fulfil a Crown service, whether the benefit goes to the Crown or to members of the public. By the Crown is meant the executive Government of the United Kingdom and its services are those supplied by Crown servants under the direction of a minister.[190] This excludes services provided by other agencies of Government or supported by public finance: the industries still in public ownership, independent authorities such as the Post Office, local government, universities and so forth. It does, however, cover the supply of anything for foreign defence purposes (that is arms to foreign governments), the supply of scheduled drugs in the Health Service, and research into, and supply of, atomic energy.[191] But why, it may be asked, central government and not the rest? Which leads back to the question: apart from defence, has central government (and through it the public) such a claim to cheap inventions that the incentive device provided by the patent system deserves to be substantially qualified?

(2) not every act which would otherwise amount to infringement falls within the Crown use exemption. In particular, while acts of manufacture, use and associated activities of keeping and importing are within the exemption, selling and offering to sell fall outside, save exceptionally: as an incident of making, using or importing; in contracts to supply arms to foreign governments; in supplying scheduled medicines through the NHS pharmaceutical services; and in disposing of things no longer required.[192]

(3) the rate of compensation is not dictated by the Crown but will, if it cannot be agreed, be settled by the High Court.[193] The Crown is entitled to put itself in the position of a licensee. If it causes loss of manufacturing or other profit, it is obliged to compensate for this.[194] Other benefits from government departments have to be brought into consideration and there is a curious provision which possibly means that the patentee may have his compensation reduced if he would not accept a reasonable offer from the Crown.[195]

Where these rules cover the operation, there are a variety of provisions which override ancillary rights; terms in licences, assignments and

[190] *Pfizer v Ministry of Health* [1965] R.P.C. 261 at 295, 301, 306.

[191] PA 1977 s.56(2)–(4).

[192] PA 1977 s.55(1). Even so, it is hard to see how these distinctions satisfy the TRIPS requirement that each case be considered individually: see above, para.7–42.

[193] PA 1977 s.55(4). The obligation may run from the date of publishing the application; or, if revealed without obligation of confidence to a government department before that, from the priority date. Note that the government department concerned is under (sanctionless) obligation to notify the patentee of use, unless contrary to the public interest: s.55(7). See generally, *Henry v Ministry of Defence* [1999] R.P.C. 442 CA.

[194] CDPA 1988 Sch.5 para.16, belatedly abrogating *Patchett's Patent* [1967] R.P.C. 237 CA.

[195] PA 1977 s.58(3). There are a number of provisions limiting the right to compensation on grounds similar to those limiting claims to damages for infringment of rights in patents and applications: see s.58(6), (8), (10).

agreements restricting working or requiring payments are of no effect[196]; copyright in certain models and documents is not infringed[197]; subsequent acquirers are treated as if the Crown were the patentee.[198] In addition, the Crown is made free of all obligations not only if it has undertaken prior use but even if the invention has been merely recorded for the Crown before the priority date of the patent.[199]

[196] PA 1977 s.57(1), (2).

[197] PA 1977 s.57(1). By contrast, registered designs are subject to Crown use provisions, similar to those applying to patents: see Registered Designs Act 1949 s.12 Sch.1. Rights in confidential information cannot be overridden (PA 1977 s.55(10)), save in the cases covered by the Defence Contracts Act 1958 ss.2, 3.

[198] PA 1977 s.55(8).

[199] PA 1977 s.55(4). As to the scope of this, see Ency. P.L., para.9–019.

Part III

CONFIDENCE AND PERSONAL PRIVACY

CHAPTER 8

CONFIDENTIAL INFORMATION

1. INTRODUCTION

(1) Nature of the liability

People ought to keep secrets if they have said that they will do so. From nineteenth-century roots, English courts have translated this simple moral precept into a form of legal liability which is of considerable breadth.[1] The development has run counter to the judges' traditional reluctance to adopt broad propositions as ground rules for the imposition of liability, and they have had to face some of the difficulties inherent in their unusual course.[2] All sorts of information may be imparted or gathered in confidence; the degree of secrecy required may be partial or total. The fashioning of the law into more specific rules is accordingly difficult and much of what follows may appear as imprecise as the subject matter is ephemeral. In contrast with many other legal systems, English law has not formally distinguished between types of information that may be protected against breach of **8–01**

[1] The subject has generated a considerable literature. See esp. Finn, *Fiduciary Obligations* (1977) Ch.19 and (1984) 58 A.L.J. 497; Vaver (1979) 1 E.I.P.R. 301; English Law Commission, Report No.110, *Breach of Confidence* (Cmnd.8388, 1981); Gurry, *Breach of Confidence* (1984, new edition in preparation); Dean, *Law of Trade Secrets* (1990); Meagher, Gummow and Lehane, *Equity: Doctrines and Remedies* 4th edn (2002), Ch.41; Goff and Jones, *Law of Restitution* 6th edn (2006) Ch.34; Hull, *Commercial Secrecy* (1998); Toulson and Phipps, *Confidentiality* 2nd edn (2007). For the historical development, see Cornish et al., *Oxford History of the Laws of England* (2010) XIII, Pt V, Ch. 5.

[2] As to the moral basis of the cause of action, see *House of Spring Gardens v Point Blank* [1983] F.S.R. 213 at 253; [1985] F.S.R. 327 at 335 SC (Ir.).

confidence: technological secrets, such as chemical formulae and mechanical techniques,[3] commercial records such as customer lists and sales figures,[4] marketing, professional and managerial procedures,[5] and equally information of political significance[6] and about personal relationships, such as the Duchess of Argyll's tales to the Duke of her earlier sentimental journeys[7]—all have been treated as protectable. Indeed the action has been a surrogate for the protection of privacy, given the traditional reluctance of English judges to admit the protection of privacy into the canons of tort liability.[8] Since the passing of the Human Rights Act 1998, however, recognition of English law's obligation to confer a right of privacy that fulfils art.8 of the European Human Rights Convention (EHRC) has caused the breach of confidence action to spin off a satellite that is establishing its own orbit. This new right to personal privacy is dealt with separately in Ch.9.

On a different front, the flexibility of breach of confidence has allowed the many issues to which it is germane to be dealt with in the civil courts. As we shall see, there is considerable reluctance to introduce criminal law penalties into this sphere, for all that occasionally major abuses of confidential information are seen to go unremedied in any way because an injunction would be valueless and monetary compensation means nothing against a man without detectable assets.[9]

(2) Confidence and patents

8–02 Given the range of subject matter it is important to compare the protection of confidential information with that provided by patents and by copyright. In the realm of technical ideas confidence cannot play any long-term role unless the information can be put to commercial use without at the same time becoming public.[10] A mechanical device will almost always reveal its workings to experts once it is marketed; and, importantly, reverse engineering by a purchaser is not a breach of confidence.[11] But a process of manufacture may not be similarly detectable. In the latter case, an inventor

---

[3] Many of the cases concern this variety of "know-how", as examples below will show.

[4] e.g. *Robb v Green* [1895] 2 Q.B. 315; *Lamb v Evans* [1893] 1 Ch. 218.

[5] *Stephenson Jordan v McDonald and Evans* (1951) 68 R.P.C. 190 (but note the traditional reluctance to recognise that business management techniques deserve protection: Evershed M.R. same case (1952) 69 R.P.C. 10 at 14); *Thomas v Mould* [1968] 1 All E.R. 963; *Interfirm Comparison v Law Society of NSW* [1975] R.P.C. 137.

[6] *Fraser v Evans* [1969] 1 All E.R. 8 CA; *Att-Gen v Jonathan Cape* [1976] Q.B. 752 DC (Cabinet papers); *Att-Gen v Guardian Newspapers (No. 2)* [1990] A.C. 109 (*"Spycatcher"*).

[7] *Argyll v Argyll* [1967] Ch. 302.

[8] See below, para.9–04.

[9] See below, para.8–55.

[10] In the short term—until a patent application can be filed—obligations of confidence prevent the danger that revelation of the invention will destroy its novelty: see above, para.5–16.

[11] See below, para.8–20.

may secure a patent that gives him monopoly protection even against independent devisers of the same invention; but it is for a limited period, and on condition that the invention is sufficiently described in the specification. Accordingly, to keep this invention secret through obligations of confidence is for him an alternative, not an additional, form of protection—an alternative that is not tied to specified time periods but which is good only against those who receive the information directly or (in some cases) indirectly from him.

Many countries have accepted that this choice should be provided, however much it may detract from the incentive to publicise that is one root purpose of the patent system. Even in the United States, where the matter was extensively debated,[12] the outcome has been to permit the alternatives. It was eventually decided that industry must be assured the opportunity of conserving new technology that was not necessarily patentable by means of confidence; and to insist that patentable inventions should only be protected by patents would be to introduce a distinction that it would be difficult and cumbersome to draw.[13] In any case, in current European law, prior secret use is not an objection to a later patent on an invention.[14] A person who chooses to keep an idea confidential during his own exploitation of it runs the serious risk of someone else discovering and patenting it.

In particular the need to protect trade secrets (technical and commercial), not just as an aspect of contractual obligation but against infractions by direct and indirect recipients in non-contractual relationships, has not infrequently been neglected, even in legal systems which have the usual panoply of specific intellectual property rights.[15] Some countries have filled the void by statutory rules or a broad interpretation of unfair competition liability.

The increasing ease with which information can be despatched round the world electronically gives an urgency to pleas for greater legal security over confidential information.[16] Responding to this interest of creators and investors, the TRIPS Agreement now contains a broad provision requiring that persons who have secret information lawfully in their control be able to prevent its unauthorised disclosure, acquisition or use "in a manner

[12] In *Cadbury Schweppes v FBI Foods* (1999) 83 C.P.R. (3d) 289, the SC of Canada gives this as one reason for not elevating confidential information to the status of property.

[13] In the wake of the *Sears* and *Compco* cases (above, para.1–21) doubts about trade secrets protection were raised in *Lear v Adkins*, 395 U.S. 653 (1969), and finally disposed of by *Kewanee v Bicron*, 416 U.S. 470 (1974). Cf. *Maggbury v Hafele Australia* [2001] 53 I.P.R. 1 HC (Aust.); Lahore and Dufty in Vaver and Bently Ch.14.

[14] See above, para.5–06.

[15] Thus it took until 1990 for Japan (of all countries) to give special protection to secret know-how and the like. The uncertain status of the liability in many systems has led to calls that trade secrets should be treated as property: Soltysinski (1986) 17 I.I.C. 331.

[16] Cross-border data flows pose private international law conundrums, which have not begun to be resolved. Their solution could soon become urgent.

contrary to honest commercial practices".[17] The liability is stated to arise "in the course of ensuring effective protection against unfair competition as provided in art.10*bis* of the Paris Convention (1967)".[18] Accordingly this international obligation must be confined to abuses of trade secrets between competitors.[19]

8–03 In actual practice, patents are often secured for a central invention, while much that is learned in the process of bringing it into commercial production is tied up as secret "know-how" by means of confidence undertakings.[20] The distinction, as we have noted, is marked in licensing practice[21]—bare patent licences are very different from operational production packages. The question to be considered here is how far the non-patentable "know-how" is really capable of protection against those who seek to make use of it without consent, as distinct from those who will pay for a licence to obtain it. The problem commonly arises when managers and other employees of a concern seek to take the "know-how" off to a rival business. We shall see that the courts have been particularly reluctant to saddle ex-employees with obligations that will prevent them from disposing of their general knowledge and skill to their best advantage.[22] Against them, breach of confidence proceedings are hard to maintain, and in this way also the courts have checked the ability of breach of confidence protection to make real inroads into the territory of the patent system.

(3) Confidence and copyright

8–04 In principle copyright is capable of helping to resist invasions of privacy, but the intrusion must take the form of making at least one copy, or of giving a performance in public, or of doing one of the other acts specified as constituting infringement.[23] Coupled with this, there must be a copying of the manner of expression and not merely use of the information contained in the copyright work. The proceedings, moreover, must be brought by those with

[17] Article 39: "secret" includes what is not generally known in interested circles. Article 39(3) has a special provision on pharmaceutical and agricultural test data submitted in order to gain approval; these must be protected against "unfair commercial use". *Quaere* the position regarding the certification of rival products. See generally, Krasser in Beier and Schricker, (eds.) *From GATT to TRIPs* (1996) p.216.

[18] A footnote indicates that liability should extend at least to knowing and grossly negligent third parties.

[19] The formulation is designed to import into art.10*bis* an activity which is conspicuously absent from the examples which it gives. These relate to activities liable to mislead the public.

[20] The patent has, of course, to satisfy the requirement of sufficient disclosure: see above, paras 5–82 et seq.

[21] See above, para.7–21.

[22] Hence the fact that licensees may be willing to pay for know-how does not necessarily demonstrate that the know-how amounts to more than an employee is entitled to treat as general skill and knowledge: see *Potters-Ballotini v Weston-Baker* [1977] R.P.C. 202 CA; *Yates Circuit Foil v Electrofoils* [1976] F.S.R. 345; and see below, paras 8–24–8–30.

[23] For the "moral" right to privacy in photographs and films under the CDPA 1988 s.84, see below, paras 12–85—12–86.

title to the copyright.[24] Breach of confidence protection resembles copyright in that the information which the defendant seeks to deploy must derive from that which the plaintiff seeks to protect. But confidence protection is not generally tied to particular ways of using the material.[25] It is concerned with the information in substance and not in form,[26] and only the person to whom obligations of confidence are owed will be entitled to sue.[27]

Thus, if a secret society has rules written for it by a person, who does nothing to dispose of his copyright in them, a renegade member intent on "exposing" the society to the public may be in breach of confidential obligations to the society, however he chooses to summarise the rules. But he will infringe the author's copyright in the rules only if he substantially reproduces their content. If he pleads "public interest" in defence, the concept is probably the same in each case; but for copyright there are further statutory defences of "fair dealing" that may be apposite.[28] **8–05**

(4) Historical and doctrinal

The jurisdiction to restrain breach of confidence has its roots in equity, partly because the remedy most often sought has been the injunction, and partly because the subject-matter occupies the same moral terrain as breach of trust.[29] The scope of the modern law began to be settled around 1850 with *Prince Albert v Strange*[30] (literary material, at once royal and private, on the borders of copyright) and *Morison v Moat*[31] (recipe for a medicine). In both cases, injunctions were granted against indirect recipients of the confidential information, and the jurisdiction was said, rather prodigally, to arise by virtue of property, agreement, confidence, trust and bailment. But it was left **8–06**

[24] See below, paras 13–04 et seq.

[25] But where the confidentiality relates to the way in which ideas are expressed (e.g. in a set of precedents or a questionnaire), breach which does not result in use of the same expression may give rise only to nominal damages: *Interfirm Comparison v Law Society* [1975] R.P.C. 157.

[26] Nor does the information have to exist in recorded form: see *Printers & Finishers v Holloway (No. 2)* [1965] R.P.C. 239 at 255; *Fraser v Thames Television* [1983] 2 All E.R. 101. As to copyright protection of television formats, see Klement [2007] E.I.P.R. 52.

[27] *Fraser v Evans* [1969] 1 All E.R. 8 CA (see below, n.39). A hospital may be entitled to confidence in records of patients, just as much as the patients themselves; *Ashworth Hospital v MGN* [2001] E.M.L.R. 301 CA.

[28] For these defences, see below, paras 8–15, 12–38.

[29] The old couplet, "Three things are to be helped in Conscience, Fraud, Accident and Things of Confidence", attributed to Sir Thomas More (see *Coco v Clark* [1969] R.P.C. 41 at 46) suggests how long the connection has stood. As perhaps the latest creation of equity, it has indeed excited the protective instincts of Chancery traditionalists against modernising fusionists: see Meagher, Gummow and Lehane (above, n.1), para.4–115—4–119.

[30] (1849) 2 De G. & Sm. 652; Mac. & G. 25. Before this there had been a number of cases in which injunctions had been granted to prevent the publication of unpublished letters, plays and other literary works; these were based on a "common law right of property" that a majority of the judges found to exist in *Millar v Taylor* (1769) 4 Burr. 2303, and *Donaldson v Beckett* (1774) 2 Bro.P.C. 129; see below, para.10–03.

[31] (1851) 9 Hare 241.

uncertain then (as it remains now) in what circumstances direct and indirect recipients of information would have liability imposed upon them. In the period after the Judicature Acts, there were some attempts (typical of their time) to confine the equitable wrong to cases in which the original disclosee agreed by contract, express or implied, to respect confidence,[32] with the apparent consequence that an indirect recipient, not being privy to the contract, would be liable only if he deliberately or recklessly induced breach of that contract.[33] Contract and tort would thus subsume the whole field between them.

8–07 More recently, contract has ceased to be treated as the universal touchstone of liability (though its role in determining what obligations of confidence exist may still be crucial).[34] Starting with *Saltman v Campbell*,[35] the courts have recognised a wider equitable jurisdiction, based, it is said, "not so much on property or on contract, but rather on good faith",[36] and this approach is now reasonably well entrenched among the judiciary. As a justification for intervening, particularly at this intermediate stage of legal development, "good faith" has a certain forthrightness that is attractive. The issue is not hedged behind conceptual dogma which all too readily states legal results without properly considering their justification. But if the true measure is a simple moral yardstick, the courts have been tantalisingly vague in the matter of how it is calibrated. This casualness has excited scientifically minded jurists to a rash of disputation: in favour of working out the implications of "good faith" more exactly in accordance with the precepts of restitution[37]; in favour of a new tort of breach of confidence[38]; in favour of "equitable property" as the true basis of protection.[39]

8–08 In the account that follows we must isolate the points at which these differences of pedigree begin to matter. They are to be found at the fringes of the wrong, and concern in particular: (1) the liability of those who in

---

[32] Contractual language reaches a climax in *Vokes v Heather* (1945) 62 R.P.C. 135 CA. Cf. *British Celanese v Moncrieff* (1948) 65 R.P.C. 165 at 167 CA. The approach produced nice conundrums: see *Triplex v Scorah* (1938) 55 R.P.C. 21. But *Robb v Green* [1895] 2 Q.B. 315 CA put the jurisdiction in both contract and equity and this conceptual casualness has been echoed more recently, e.g. in *Nichrotherm v Percy* [1957] R.P.C. 207 CA, and *Ackroyds v Islington Plastics* [1962] R.P.C. 97.

[33] *British Industrial Plastics v Ferguson* [1940] 1 All E.R. 479 HL.

[34] As to this, see below, para.8–22.

[35] (1948) 65 R.P.C. 203 CA; and see *Nichrotherm v Percy* (above, n.32) at 213–214. *Peter Pan v Corsets Silhouette* [1963] R.P.C. 45 and *Cranleigh Precision v Bryant* [1966] R.P.C. 81, are both cases in which jurisdiction is put solely in equity despite the presence of contract. See further Vaver (above, n.1) at 303.

[36] Lord Denning M.R. *Fraser v Evans* [1969] 1 All E.R. 8 at 11; and also in *Seager v Copydex (No. 1)* [1967] 2 All E.R. 415 at 417. For a distinguished precursor see Holmes J. *Du Pont v Masland*, 244 U.S. 100 at 102 (1917). In *Att-Gen v Guardian Newspapers (No. 2)* (above, n.6), the House of Lords eschewed the question, while accepting that the jurisdiction in equity extended beyond contract.

[37] Jones (1970) 86 L.Q.R. 463; and see *Goff and Jones on Restitution* 6th edn (2002) Ch.34; Gordon (1992) 78 Virg. L.R.149.

[38] Law Commission, above, n.1.

[39] Ricketson (1977) 11 M.U.L.R. 223, 289.

some sense act innocently; (2) the circumstances in which damages may be awarded for breach; (3) the possibility of awarding damages for injury to feelings as distinct from economic loss; (4) the liability of indirect recipients; and (5) the effect of dealings that treat the information as property. In addition, when it comes to personal information there is the balance between privacy and freedom of expression claims which grows out of the Human Rights Act 1998 arts 8 and 10—a matter which is reserved for the next chapter.[40] The most pertinent question to ask about these problems is whether the answers so far given justify basing the jurisdiction on "good faith"; or whether one of the other explanations, although enjoying little popularity with the judges at present, is in fact truer to the results which they wish to procure.

2. Requirements for Liability

Megarry J.'s listing of the requirements for an actionable breach of confidence[41] makes a convenient starting-point for analysis: **8–09**

> "First, the information itself ... must 'have the necessary quality of confidence about it.'[42] Secondly, that information must have been imparted in circumstances importing an obligation of confidence. Thirdly, there must be an unauthorised use of that information [possibly[43]] to the detriment of the party communicating it."

Each of these heads will be treated in turn.

(1) Subject matter capable of protection

(a) *Types of information*

The breach of confidence action, as already stated, lies in respect of technical, commercial, personal and other information without distinction by subject. A general reservation has been expressed against covering "trivial tittle-tattle"[44]; and it has recently been accepted that scandalous or immoral **8–10**

---

[40] See below, para.9–16—9–18.

[41] *Coco v Clark* [1969] R.P.C. 41 at 47. Approved by the Court of Appeal in *Dunford & Elliott v Johnston* [1978] F.S.R. 143 at 148 CA; *Jarman & Platt v Barget* [1977] F.S.R. 260 at 276–277; and relied upon in many other cases.

[42] This expression is Lord Greene M.R.'s: *Saltman v Campbell* (1948) 65 R.P.C. 203 at 215.

[43] For Megarry J.'s doubt about detriment, see below, para.8–39.

[44] Megarry J. *Coco v Clark* [1969] R.P.C. 41 at 48; *McNichol v Sportsman's Book Stores* (1928–30) Mac. C.C. 116. But trivia worth money are different: see *Argyll v Argyll* (above, n.7); cf. *Church of Scientology v Kaufman* [1973] R.P.C. 635. The information may be purely oral: *De Maudsley v Palumbo* [1996] F.S.R. 447.

material may be disqualified from protection, just as it is not accorded copyright.[45]

An idea for something yet to be elaborated may attract legal protection as confidential information where there is nothing that generates copyright. Thus, the idea for a television series about a female pop-group, which would draw upon the backgrounds and histories of three actresses intended for the parts, was held capable of protection. The requirements of copyright law to show specific expression of the idea in scenarios or scripts, in writing or other recorded form, were held not necessary in the law of confidence. It was enough that "the content of the idea was clearly identifiable, original, of potential commercial attractiveness and capable of being realised in actuality".[46] This recognises the considerable value that such initial inspirations may now have. Again, technical information does not have to be novel or attain any level of inventiveness[47]:

> "it is perfectly possible to have a confidential document, be it a formula, a plan, a sketch, or something of that kind, which is the result of work done by the maker on materials which may be available for the use of anybody; but what makes it confidential is the fact that the maker of the document has used his brain and thus produced a result which can only be reached by somebody who goes through the same process."[48]

Secrets may be embodied in a physical object, as, for example, the budwood of a new plant variety.[49] But if the object is available on the open market and an obtainer is able to analyse it in order to find out its secret content, no right of action lies. That is so even where one person supplies another, in confidence, with a chemical that can be analysed and which turns out to contain partly public and partly private information. The publicly available information may be used by a third party.[50]

---

[45] *Stephens v Avery* [1988] F.S.R. 510. However, a lesbian relationship is no longer so unmentionable a subject that it cannot be protected in confidence: *Stephens v Avery*.

[46] *Fraser v Thames Television* [1983] 2 All E.R. 101; applying *Talbot v General Television* [1981] R.P.C. 1 (SC, Victoria)—where the particular twist to the idea was merely that a programme series about millionaires would include interviews with particular exemplars. Cf. *De Maudsley v Palumbo* [1996] F.S.R. 447: "a considerable degree of particularity in a definite product needs to be shown ... That of course does not exclude simplicity ... Vagueness and simplicity are not the same", per Knox J. See also Laddie J. *Ocular Sciences v Aspect Vision* [1997] R.P.C. 289 at 360.

[47] But see *Nichrotherm v Percy* [1957] R.P.C. 207 at 209 CA, where stating the technical problem that called for solution was treated as not protectable.

[48] Lord Greene M.R. *Saltman v Campbell* (1948) 65 R.P.C. 203 at 215; and see *Ansell Rubber v Allied Rubber* [1967] V.R. 37.

[49] *Franklin v Giddens* [1978] Qld. R. 72.

[50] *EPI v Symphony Plastic* [2005] F.S.R. 22; *Crowson Fabrics v Rider* [2008] F.S.R. 17; and see below, paras 8–12—8–14.

(b) *Information and observation*

Typically, the subject of protection exists as information before the obligation of confidence is assumed. Some cases, however, have concerned events which the person bound by confidence has observed for himself.[51] The courts showed no inclination to treat the two cases differently and indeed to do so would be highly artificial. The consequence was, however, to broaden the role of the confidence action in protecting sensitive personal information—a significant driver in the movement towards a separate privacy right.[52] **8–11**

(c) *Public knowledge*

If information has been made freely and entirely public, either before it was given to the defendant in confidence, or else in the interval between that time and the trial of the action, then in many cases nothing protectable will remain,[53] at least if the defendant's breach of confidence is not the cause.[54] (The possibility of publication occurring after the court's order goes to the scope of remedies and is discussed below.)[55] **8–12**

Where the revelation is by the defendant himself, he has been held to remain liable.[56] However, this problem has yet to receive the full judicial analysis it deserves. It may well be that even in this situation no subject-matter then subsists which can subsequently be the subject of obligation.[57] But there still remains the question of liability arising from the act of revelation, which is itself a breach. It will be seen later that relief may be granted against wrongful use quite independently of wrongful disclosure,[58]

[51] This was the character of much of the information which the pop-stars were attempting to keep out of the press in *Woodward v Hutchins* [1977] 2 All E.R. 751. The plaintiffs failed for other reasons: see n.81, below. See also *Printers & Finishers v Holloway* (below, para.8–29, n.138).

[52] See below, para.9–12.

[53] See *Saltman v Campbell* (1948) 65 R.P.C. 203 at 215; *John Zink v Lloyds Bank* [1975] R.P.C. 385 at 389; *Harrison v Project & Design* [1978] F.S.R. 81 (information becoming public); *Ocular Sciences v Aspect Vision Care* [1997] R.P.C. 289 (information from public sources listed without selection). Note the readiness to take up this sort of explanation in an "unappetising" personal scandal case: *Lennon v News Group* [1978] F.S.R. 573 CA; cf. *Argyll v Argyll* (above, n.7); and below, para.9–09.

[54] If the publicity comes from the defendant, he may well be enjoined from making further or different disclosures of it: *Creation Records v News Group* [1997] E.M.L.R. 444. The defendant's action may make an injunction purposeless, but damages and other remedies ought to be available. In *Harrison v Project & Design* (above, n.53), damages were awarded to the defendant for his production during a period of time until the information became public; it is not clear how this publicity came about, if it was not through the defendant's own activity.

[55] See below, para.8–46.

[56] *Speed Seal v Paddington* [1986] 1 All E.R. 91 CA.

[57] Lord Goff (*Att-Gen v Guardian Newspapers (No. 2)* [1990] A.C. 109) at 285–286, criticised the *Speed Seal* case, particularly for its reliance on the view that only revelation by the plaintiff renders confidential information no longer open to protection—for which see below, n.69.

[58] See below, para.8–37.

and accordingly an injunction to prevent future use may be appropriate. In addition, any pecuniary relief by way of damages, account or constructive trust should bring in the continuing consequences of the unjustified revelation.[59] When it comes to personal privacy, it is already clear that rights to protection may survive limited publicity in order to prevent further spread.[60]

8–13 The issue is difficult when the relevation is in some sense only partial. If not all the relevant information has been made public, the rest (if it can be adequately specified) remains capable of protection.[61] If the information has been given to some of those interested but not to others, there may remain some "relative secrecy"[62]; whether a court will grant any form of relief in such cases seems to depend on the circumstances as a whole.

In this context, the "springboard" metaphor has enjoyed a vogue:

> "A person who has obtained information in confidence is not allowed to use it as a springboard for activities detrimental to the person who made the confidential communication, and springboard it remains even when all the features have been published or can be ascertained by actual inspection by any member of the public ... The possessor of the confidential information still has a long start over any member of the public."[63]

8–14 This is not an invariable rule which takes no account of subsequent developments and other circumstances: the "springboard does not last for ever".[64] Among other factors that a court is likely to take into account are the following[65]:

(1) How truly did the information become public? Formal tests of publication drawn from patent law are not used.[66] Nor is it enough to

---

[59] *Ocular, Sciences v Aspect Vision Centre* [1997] R.P.C. 289.

[60] Below, para.9–12.

[61] Thus, in *Mustad v Allcock and Dosen* (below, n.67) the House of Lords only refused protection after noting that, on the evidence, the plaintiff's invention had been completely revealed in its patent specification; see also *EPI v Symphony Plastic* [2005] F.S.R. 22; above, n.50. The need to define what is protectable as a secret is crucial where it must be specified in an injunction: see Ricketson (1977) 11 Melb. U.L.R. 223 at 289. The fact that a mixture of public and private information has been taken may lead to an award of damages rather than an injunction: *Seager v Copydex (No. 1)* [1967] 2 All E.R. 415 at 417 CA.

[62] Cross J. *Franchi v Franchi* [1967] R.P.C. 149; cf. *Dunford & Elliott v Johnston* [1978] F.S.R. 143 at 148 CA, where the extent of revelation is given as one reason for refusing interim relief. Note also *Foster v Mountford* [1978] F.S.R. 582 (aboriginal tribal secrets); and the case law below, in n.70.

[63] Roxburgh J. *Terrapin v Builders Supply* [1967] R.P.C. 375 at 392; first approved in the Court of Appeal, *Seager v Copydex (No.1)* (above, n.61) at 417. See also, e.g. *Cranleigh v Bryant* (n.70, below) and *Ackroyds v Islington Plastics* [1962] R.P.C. 97.

[64] Lord Denning M.R. *Potters-Ballotini v Weston-Baker* [1977] R.P.C. 202 at 205: *Harrison v Project & Design* (above, n.53) at 87. See generally, Barclay (1978) 26 U.C.L.A. Law R. 203.

[65] cf. the list in the American Restatement of Torts art.757, referred to in a number of Australian decisions; see Ricketson (above, n.61) at 228.

[66] cf. above, para.5–13; *Yates v Electrofoils* [1976] F.S.R. 345 at 387; *Interfirm Comparison v Law Society* [1975] R.P.C. 137.

show that a product has been marketed which, if dismantled or analysed, would reveal the information.[67] On the other hand, if the plaintiff includes all the information in a patent specification, he is taken to have made it public.[68]

(2) How likely was it that the defendant would in any event have discovered the information without impropriety, had he not received it in confidence from the plaintiff?[69] If it is in fact available in a third party's patent specification, the issue ought to be whether the defendant would have been likely to search for and discover that specification.[70]

(3) Did the plaintiff believe that he would be injured by release of the information, and that it was not yet in the public domain? According to Megarry J., if this belief was reasonable, the plaintiff ought to be entitled to protect it.[71] This approach may commend itself to future courts for dealing with cases where information has already got into a limited number of hands. There is some danger, however, that it will unduly favour plaintiffs.

(d) *Public interest*[72]

Until the Human Rights Act 1998 took effect,[73] free speech and freedom for the media were not directly guaranteed as fundamental legal rights under English law.[74] They were proudly maintained as political freedoms which had gradually overcome systems of censorship and then of taxes on the press. They remain circumscribed by such limits as the law of defamation, the Official Secrets Act, the Data Protection Act, proscriptions upon contempt of court and now the wrong of invading privacy.[75] Beyond these issues **8–15**

[67] See *Saltman v Campbell* (above, n.42) at 215; *Terrapin v Builders Supply* (above, n.63) at 26; *Conveyor v Cameron* [1973] 2 N.Z.L.R. 38.

[68] *Mustad v Allcock and Dosen* (1928) [1963] 3 All E.R. 416n. HL. See also *Lysnar v Gisborne* [1924] N.Z.L.R. 13.

[69] On this problem, see especially Megarry J., *Coco v Clark* [1969] R.P.C. 41 at 49–50.

[70] In *Cranleigh Precision v Bryant* [1966] R.P.C. 81 and *Franchi v Franchi* (above, n.62), it was said that the publication in a third party's patent specification should not be treated as bringing obligations of confidence to an end. But that seems too indiscriminate an approach. The former case, in particular, did not need to go so far; there were obvious breaches of fiduciary duty. The reasoning in the cases was criticised by Lord Goff: *Att-Gen v Guardian Newspapers (No. 2)* [1990] A.C. 109 at 661–662.

[71] *Marshall (Thomas) (Exports) v Guinle* [1978] 3 All E.R. 193 at 209–210. Particular usage of a trade or industry might also make the information protectable.

[72] See Cripps, *The Legal Implications of Disclosure in the Public Interest* 2nd edn (1995); Stuckey-Clarke in Clarke (above, n.1), Ch.8. See also the Public Interest Disclosure Act 1998, which adds a Pt IVA to the Employment Rights Act 1996. This seeks to protect employees who blow the whistle on their employers from being victimised in consequence. It is to be interpreted broadly: *Cream Holdings v Banerjee* [2005] 1 A.C. 253, HL.

[73] See above, para.8–01.

[74] The European Convention (see below, para.9–02), guarantees the right of freedom of speech subject, inter alia, to the preservation of confidence: art.10. In *Att-Gen v Guardian Newspapers* (above, n.70), Lords Griffiths and Goff considered the qualification discussed under this head to be in conformity with the article: at 652 and at 660.

[75] See below, Ch.9; and generally Cripps (above, n.72).

there are wider questions of the public's interest in knowing certain information. It is well settled that "there can be no confidence which can be relied on to restrain a disclosure of inquity",[76] and in this context "inquity" probably covers criminal, tortious and other legally wrongful conduct, at least if it is serious and is likely to occur in future.[77] Some judges consider that, save where the information concerns "misdeeds of a serious nature and importance to the country", they should intervene to preserve confidential obligations.[78] One way of expressing this inclination is by holding that public interest is nothing other than a consideration of the extent of the obligation to respect confidence itself.[79]

8–16 There is now a broader approach which treats "iniquity" as merely one instance of just cause for allowing confidence to be broken in the public interest. Lord Denning M.R., a principal proponent of this view,[80] held that, where pop-stars have deliberately promoted a glamorous image of themselves, it is permissible to present the less savoury truth about their life-style to the public, even if confidence has very plainly been broken in the process.[81] His view has now been reiterated in the Human Rights Act era.[82] It is an approach that has much in common with the freedom of speech defence to invasions of privacy in the United States: that by putting herself forward as a public figure, a celebrity must be prepared to suffer the exposure of truths about her personal life.

8–17 Other circumstances in which public interest may justify at least limited publication to an appropriate person to take action might include matters of public safety and the due administration of justice. Thus, in *Lion Laboratories v Evans*,[83] a newspaper came by a confidential report that a breathalyser used by the police on suspected drunken drivers gave inaccurate

---

[76] *Gartside v Outram* (1856) 26 L.J. Ch. 113.

[77] But note Bankes L.J. *Weld-Blundell v Stephens* [1919] 1 K.B. 520 at 527; cf. *Butler v Board of Trade* [1971] Ch. 680; cf. *Hellewell v Chief Constable of Derbyshire* [1995] 1 W.L.R. 804: police justified in showing known criminal's photograph to shopkeepers; *Bunn v BBC* [1999] F.S.R. 70: accused's confession to police confidential but only until revealed in open court.

[78] Ungoed Thomas J. *Beloff v Pressdram* [1973] 1 All E.R. 241 at 260–261 (copyright proceedings, treated as subject to the same public interest considerations); and see Megaw L.J. *Hubbard v Vosper* [1972] 2 Q.B. 84 at 100–101. Revelation of an agreement registrable under the Restrictive Trade Practices Act 1956 (*Initial Services v Putterill* [1968] 1 Q.B. 396) could well fall within this restricted view of public interest. Cf. also *British Steel v Granada* [1982] A.C. 1096.

[79] See esp. Gummow J. *Smith, Kline & French v Department of Health* [1990] F.S.R. 617 (FC Aust.); Simon Brown L.J. *R. v Department of Health Ex p. Source Informatics* [2001] Q.B. 424 at 443, 444. For the position in copyright, see below, para.12–38.

[80] *Initial Services v Putterill* (above, n.78) at 405; *Fraser v Evans* [1969] 1 Q.B. 349 at 11; *Hubbard v Vosper* (above, n.78) at 95–96; *Norwich Pharmacal v Commissioners of Customs* [1972] R.P.C. 743 at 766 CA.

[81] *Woodward v Hutchins* [1977] 2 All E.R. 751; Lawton and Bridge L.JJ. were equally convinced. Cf. *Argyll v Argyll* [1967] Ch.302 at 331–333; Wacks (1978) 41 M.L.R. 67.

[82] See below para.9–18.

[83] *Lion Laboratories v Evans* [1985] Q.B. 526 CA; and see *Ex p. Smith Kline & French* [1989] F.S.R. 11 CA; *Price Waterhouse v BCCI Holdings* [1992] B.C.L.C. 583; cf. *X Health Authority v Y* [1988] R.P.C. 379 (confidence in hospital records of doctors with AIDS outweighed public interest in knowing that there were doctors with the disease).

readings. It was held proper for the newspaper to publish this generally, because merely reporting the information to the police or the Home Office might well have led to suppression of the information. However, across the field of breach of confidence as a whole, English courts do not readily accept that there is a sufficient public interest, particularly to justify publication through the media. Even a "whistle-blower" from inside an organisation who is moved by moral outrage and who may well be jeopardising a career without seeking any payment in return may have difficulty in making a sufficient case.[84]

In every case, whether the basis is "iniquity" or some other ground, the court has to balance the competing interests. taking account of the proportionality of the restraint upon freedom of expression.[85] For instance, the Court of Appeal restrained a newspaper from publishing allegations about a leading jockey's involvement in misleading the Jockey Club because the information had been obtained by private and unauthorised wire-tapping of a telephone conversation: the dissemination would be too wide, the breach of confidence too serious.[86] It is clear that Peter Wright could never have justified his "treacherous" breaches of confidence about his service in MI5 by the public having an interest in knowing that he and other officers attempted to prevent Harold Wilson's re-election and other unscrupulous operations.[87] In principle it is not relevant whether or not a defendant knew of the "iniquity" at the time of revealing the information. Nonetheless it has been held that the courts will not allow the press to make outrageous allegations and then go on the hunt for evidence in support.[88] **8–18**

Many cases to do with newsworthy information are founded in copyright as well as confidence. The defence of public interest has a statutory basis in the CDPA 1988 s.171(3). In England, there is now a tendency to treat public interest as having less scope where the complaint is that copyrighted text has been taken. As we shall also see, in copyright there are other relevant

[84] Different attitudes have been expressed about the degree to which the moral scruples of the revealer are relevant in judging public interest: cf. esp. Lord Denning M.R.'s view that the use made of it by a person receiving the information is relevant, with Lord Fraser's rejection of that position: *British Steel v Granada Television* [1981] A.C. 1096 at 1202. Even a professional may be entitled to break confidence in order to secure the safety of others: *W v Egdell* [1989] 1 All E.R. 1089 (psychiatrist disclosing violent character of patient to prison authorities). In relation to personal privacy, see now, below para.9–16.

[85] The guarantee of freedom of expression in the ECHR art.10, as amplified in the Human Rights Act 1998 s.12, has application beyond the bounds of personal privacy: see, e.g. *London Regional Transport v Mayor of London* [2003] E.M.L.R. 88 CA.

[86] *Francome v Mirror Group* [1984] 2 All E.R. 408 CA; and see *Camelot Group v Centaur Communications* [1998] E.M.L.R. 1 CA.

[87] This is made plain in *Att-Gen v Guardian Newspapers (No. 2)* [1990] A.C. 109 HL. Note the Court of Appeal's remarkable refusal to grant interim relief to a newspaper which had bought the serial rights in Lady Thatcher's Downing Street memoirs when another paper was about to get in ahead with the main revelations: *Times Newspapers v Mirror Group* [1993] E.M.L.R. 442. The descriptions were said to include current events of public interest, and anyway they were intended for publication and so could not be confidential: see Nyman (1994) 3 Ent. L.R. 83.

[88] *Harrods v Times Newspaper* [2006] E.M.L.R. 13.

defences provided by statute.[89] Where they set the bounds of exemption, public interest is unlikely to add further scope for ignoring copyright.[90]

(e) *Government secrets*

8–19 An opposite public interest arises when government seeks to protect confidential information. For although it is relying on a private right, it does not have the same personal interest as an individual in preventing information from being released or used. It must show—and carries the burden of proof—that the public has an interest in the protection sought,

> "because in a free society there is a continuing public interest that the workings of Government should be open to scrutiny and criticism".[91]

Whether there is a sufficient public interest of this sort will depend on all the circumstances. Where the former minister, Richard Crossman, proposed to reveal Cabinet discussions recorded in his diaries, his publishers were not enjoined: the desirability of mutual confidence in Cabinet deliberations was not a sufficient interest when 10 years had elapsed in the interim.[92] Where, apparently through a leak from a civil servant, Australian Government documents concerning its relations with Indonesia over the East Timor crisis were about to be published, no sufficient reason for restraining their appearance could be found in national security, relations with foreign countries or the ordinary business of government.[93]

In one celebrated cause, the *Guardian* and the *Observer* published accounts of applications in Australia to stop the publication of Peter Wright's *Spycatcher*, in which they disclosed some of Wright's allegations about wrongdoing in Britain's MI5. These publications did not amount to actionable breaches of confidence, even though they came through leaks of the book's contents at a time when it had been published nowhere.[94] Equally, once *Spycatcher* was published in the United States, Australia and elsewhere, many copies and accounts entered Britain. In consequence even the *Sunday Times*, which held "serial rights" to the book by "grant" from Wright's publishers,[95] could not be restrained from publishing it. Wright's allegations had become too widely known for the Government to have any

---

[89] See below, paras 12–38 et seq.

[90] See *Associated Newspapers v Prince of Wales* [2008] Ch.57: publication of excerpts from Prince Charles' private diaries not justified as reporting current events (CDPA 1988 s.30(2)); public interest provided no further exemption.

[91] Lord Goff, *Att-Gen v Guardian Newspapers (No.2)* [1990] 1 A.C. 109 at 283. Public bodies are subject to similar considerations: *Jockey Club v Buffham* [2003] E.M.L.R. 111.

[92] *Att-Gen v Jonathan Cape* [1976] Q.B. 752.

[93] *Commonwealth of Australia v Fairfax* (1980) 32 A.L.R. 485; and see *Att-Gen v Brandon Book Publishers* [1989] F.S.R. 37.

[94] *Att-Gen v Guardian Newspapers (No.2)* [1990] A.C. 109; see Jones [1989] C.L.P. 49; Patfield [1989] E.I.P.R. 201.

[95] It seems that any such "licence" lacked subject-matter since Wright's breach of obligation left him without enforceable copyright: see below, para.12–57.

further interest to protect.[96] An attempt to show continuing damage to the operations of the Secret Services, if there could not be absolute assurance that its members would observe lifelong secrecy, was not accepted as sufficient in the circumstances.[97]

(2) Confidential obligation

(a) *Confidence in the receipt of information*

In the prime case of liability, one person supplies information to another on **8–20**
condition that he will keep it secret. Equally the obligation to do so may arise where the first person employs,[98] commissions, or even requests, the second to acquire information and hold it in confidence for him. But—and here arises the whole case for founding the jurisdiction upon the requirements of "good faith"—whether recipient or acquirer, the second is bound only if he accepts that the information is to be treated confidentially. And yet this is tested objectively.

> "If the circumstances are such that any reasonable man standing in the shoes of the recipient of the information would have realised that upon reasonable grounds the information was being given to him in confidence, then this should suffice to impose upon him the equitable obligation of confidence."[99]

Add to this that, once the obligation is assumed, it may be breached by conduct that is neither ill-motivated nor deliberate.[100] It becomes apparent that a somewhat diffuse notion of "good faith" is being employed.

In this context arises one crucially important limit that distinguishes confidence liability from patent infringement. Reverse engineering or analysis of a product or procedure that has been obtained on the market without special conditions will not in itself be treated as giving rise to any confidence. This is an attribute of ownership and applies to machinery,

---

[96] The *Sunday Times* had perpetrated an actionable breach by publishing a first episode of *Spycatcher* on the eve of US publication, for which they were liable to an account of profits. From this no payment to Wright's publishers under the supposed "licence" would be deductible: *Att-Gen v Guardian Newspapers (No. 2)* [1990] A.C. 109 per Lord Keith, esp. at 262, 263.

[97] Likewise in *Lord Advocate v Scotsman* [1989] F.S.R. 580. Note also the refusal to impose a general obligation, not related to confidential information, which would bind secret services officers (however traitorous) not to write about their service; *Att-Gen v Blake* [1996] F.S.R. 727.

[98] An instance is *Industrial Furnaces v Reaves* [1970] R.P.C. 605.

[99] Megarry J. *Coco v Clark* [1968] F.S.R. 415; and see *Yates v Electrofoils* [1976] F.S.R. 345; *Interfirm Comparison v Law Society* [1975] R.P.C. 137 at 151; *Delta Nominees v Viscount Plastic* [1979] V.R. 167 at 191; *Maccaba v Lichtenstein* [2005] E.M.L.R. 6. If evidence of subjective intent is given, the court should also bring it into account: *Carflow Products v Linwood Securities* [1996] F.S.R. 424; Clark [1996] E.I.P.R. 632.

[100] See below, para.8–38.

apparatus, the chemical composition of a thing, whether it is inorganic, organic or living tissue, or the electronic content of digitised material, such as an encryption program implanted in a vending machine.[101] Its policy justification lies in the economic value which comes from constant emulation of what competitors are doing in any particular market. An innovator who wants protection for an industrial novelty against all others, must show a patentable invention and reveal its nature so that the rest of the industry can know its essence. From this it can be claimed that there is a complementary balance between the two forms of protection.[102] Indeed, there will be arguments that the balance should not be disturbed by contractual terms rendering reverse engineering of products sold or licensed a breach. These have been frequent with computer programming, and to a limited extent they have been rendered unenforceable in EU law.[103]

8–21 There is no need to search for an implied contract, if none has been reached expressly. Matrimonial and other personal confidences may give rise to obligations[104]; so equally when one party gives another information during negotiations towards a commercial agreement that is never reached[105]; or in circumstances where statute negates the existence of a contract.[106] On the other hand, it is unlikely that one person could oblige another to respect confidence by sending him unsolicited information in a letter marked "Confidential". This is a practical problem of some importance. It is even said that one enterprise may try to foist confidential material on another in order to put difficulties in the way of the latter using it (or something similar), should it be discovered independently.[107] The recipient of an unsolicited confidence should, for his own protection, return the material at once, making it plain that he regards himself as being under no obligation. If he goes on to use the information he is likely, under the objective test, to be held bound.[108]

8–22 Of course, contracts continue to be of great importance. The circumstances may be such that the reasonable man may freely use the information

---

101 *Mars v Teknowledge* [2000] E.D.C.R. 77.

102 For a justification of this balance, Cheung (1982) 20 Econ. Inquy. 40; Friedman, Landes and Posner (1991) 5 J. Econ. Perspectives (Winter) 61; but cf. for a thought-provoking criticism, Samuelson and Scotchmer (2002) 111 Yale L.J. 1575.

103 See below, paras 20–16 et seq.

104 Cf. *Argyll v Argyll* [1967] Ch. 302 at 322, a decision that still spoke (unenthusiastically) of an implied contract, but demonstrated the unreality of such language.

105 As in *Seager v Copydex (No. 1)* [1967] R.P.C. 349 CA; *Coco v Clark* (above, n.98); *AB Consolidated v Europe Strength* [1978] 2 N.Z.L.R. 520.

106 *Malone v Commissioner of Police* [1979] 2 All E.R. 620 at 645 (no contract between telephone subscriber and Post Office).

107 See Law Commission (above, para.8–01, n.1) paras 52, 72, 109–112; *Johnson v Heat and Air* (1941) 58 R.P.C. 229 was a case where the defendant could show that he already knew the information when it was revealed to him.

108 In complex situations (for instance, where businessmen are pooling private knowledge), the extent of any obligation to use the information only for the intended common purpose will depend on the particular circumstances: see *Murray v Yorkshire Fund Managers* [1998] 1 W.L.R. 951 CA.

supplied to him in the absence of an express agreement to the contrary. Thus, where a news agency provided stock-exchange and horseracing results to its subscribers, it was able to prevent the information being passed on to non-subscribers precisely because the subscription contract forbade this being done.[109] Equally, contract may prescribe the extent of the obligation.[110] The purpose of a "know-how" licence is to permit the licensee to make use of the information provided for the purposes of his own business. Normally the agreement will limit the extent to which the "know-how" can be imparted to others, and use by the licensee after termination of the licence may also be circumscribed.[111] Again, contract may settle that the plaintiff is not owed any duty of confidence, but instead owes such a duty himself to a third party; in which case he has no qualification to sue.[112] A person who owes an obligation of confidence by contract is not relieved of that obligation just because the other party affords that person justification for repudiating the contract and she repudiates it.[113]

(b) *Fiduciary duties*

The relationship between two persons may be such that equity imposes a duty **8–23**
upon one to act in the interests of the other rather than of himself. As with contract, the proof of a fiduciary relationship may be the necessary foundation of an obligation of confidence.[114] This fiduciary duty may, for instance, exist between trustee and beneficiary, agent and principal, individual partner and partnership, director and company, senior employee and employer,[115]

[109] *Exchange Telegraph v Gregory* [1896] 1 Q.B. 147; *Exchange Telegraph v Central News* [1897] 2 Ch. 48; cf. also *Paul v Southern Instruments* [1964] R.P.C. 118 CA.

[110] For instance, by limiting the period during which the defendant is not to use the information: see *Potters-Ballotini v Weston-Baker* [1977] R.P.C. 202.

[111] *National Broach v Churchill* [1965] R.P.C. 61; *Torrington v Smith* [1966] R.P.C. 285. A plea of public interest overriding the terms of an express contract is unlikely to succeed unless the contract is about an illegal activity that would render the contract itself invalid: *Att-Gen v Parry* [2004] E.M.L.R. (13) 223 (confidence undertaking given by journalist on joining Royal Household in order to write up experiences; held binding).

[112] *Fraser v Evans* [1969] 1 All E.R. 8 CA, where the plaintiff prepared a report for the Greek Government to which he owed a duty of confidence; the defendant editor procured the report from a Greek Government source. Had it been improperly procured from the plaintiff he might have established the tort of inducing breach of his own contract of confidence. Cf. the criminal proceedings in *DPP v Withers* [1975] A.C. 842; see above, para.2–20.

[113] *Campbell v Frisbee* [2003] E.M.L.R. 3 CA: supermodel allegedly attacked personal assistant, so latter repudiated contract for her services; obligations of confidence owed to model survived.

[114] *Moorgate Tobacco v Philip Morris* [1985] R.P.C. 219 HC (Aust.).

[115] On employees, see *Canadian Aero v O'Malley* (1973) 40 D.L.R. (3d) 371 SC (Canada). Amongst the category of agents, note in particular professional advisers such as doctors, lawyers and banks. The scope of the obligations of each category is worked out in case law: for which see, e.g. *Tournier v National Provincial* [1924] 1 K.B. 461 CA (banker); *Hunter v Mann* [1974] 1 Q.B. 767 DC (doctor); *Parry-Jones v Law Society* [1969] 1 Ch. 1 CA (solicitor). For the relation between a solicitor's duty of confidence and his obligation not to reveal privileged communications in litigation without his client's consent, see *Lord Ashburton v Pape* [1913] 2 Ch. 469; *Parry-Jones v Law Society*; *Butler v Board of Trade* [1971] Ch. 680.

secret service agent and government.[116] The list of relationships is not closed; but there is a reluctance to find it in commercial relationships—for example, from franchisor to franchisee, or licensee to licensor.[117] Nor are the circumstances in which such fiduciaries are obliged to prefer the interests of their beneficiaries precisely defined.[118]

The moral impulse from which this fiduciary duty stems is very similar to that which requires confidence to be respected and often there is an overlap between the principles. But the difference needs to be observed. In the first place, a fiduciary responsibility may be the source of the duty to preserve confidence. The employee who removes a confidential report from his employer's desk will break the confidence that already exists from his duty of fidelity.[119] An outsider who did the same thing would commit a trespass, but he would probably not be in breach of confidence.[120] Again, the fiduciary duty may be wider in scope than a simple obligation to observe confidence. The fiduciary may, for example, be expected to continue using information for his beneficiary's advantage only, even after it has become public.[121] Equally he may be obliged to hold the profits of his breach on trust for his beneficiary.[122] Equity's intervention is to prevent the fiduciary from taking a personal advantage from the possible conflict of interest and duty.

(c) *Employer and employee*[123]

8–24 Where the relationship between supplier and recipient of information is that of employer and employee, a separate policy has been pursued by the judges. They have struck a balance between the desire to accord every worker the freedom to dispose of his labour where and when he pleases and the wish to give some protection to valuable pieces of information that a particular

[116] *Att-Gen v The Guardian Newspapers (No. 2)* [1990] 1 A.C. 109; it is a duty to preserve confidential information, but not a duty to remain silent about experiences in the service: *Att-Gen v Blake* (CA) (but extraordinary public law remedies were brought into play by the House of Lords in order to prevent Blake, the notorious spy for the USSR from keeping royalties due on his book of reminiscences: [2001] 1 A.C. 238).

[117] *Jirna v Mister Do-nut* (1973) 40 D.L.R. (3d) 303; *USSC v Hospital Products* (1984) 58 A.L.J.R. 587; *Moorgate Tobacco v Philip Morris* [1985] R.P.C. 219, HC Aust.; *Indata Equipment Supplies v ACL* [1998] F.S.R. 248 CA.

[118] Readers unfamiliar with this important equitable duty will find good accounts, e.g. in *Goff and Jones: Law of Restitution* 4th edn (1993) Ch.33; Finn, *Fiduciary Duties* (1977) and on company directors, Farrer et al., *Company Law* 3rd edn (1991), Chs 25, 26.

[119] As in *Jarman & Platt v Barget* [1977] F.S.R. 260 at 276 CA.

[120] On this problem, see below, paras 8–34–8–36.

[121] See *Cranleigh Precision v Bryant* [1966] R.P.C. 81. The obligation extends equally to the personal use of property and to certain competitive activities. However, tracing from information misused into property obtained by a third-party collaborator in consequence of the misuse was not permitted by the CA in *Satnam Investments v Dunlop Heywood* [1999] F.S.R. 722.

[122] See below, para.8–52.

[123] See Napier in Clarke (above, para.8–01, n.1) Ch.6. For a comparison with the position in the US, see Wilkof [1991] E.I.P.R. 269; and for Germany and other European countries, Beier in Leser and Isomura (eds), *Wege zum japanischen Recht* (1992) p.817; Chrocziel in Maclaren (ed.), *Worldwide Trade Secrets Law* (2001).

employer may possess over his competitors and which an employee might give to a competitor or use himself in competition. While he remains in employment the employee must observe his "duty of fidelity". Once he leaves his employment, the balance rests largely in favour of the employee, who is entitled to make use of all the skill and knowledge that any employee of his kind would have acquired. He is only obliged to respect two specific "interests" of his employer: in "secret processes" that are in a strict sense "trade secrets"; and in the goodwill that exists between the employer and his customers.

(i) **The employee in service.** In a contract of employment, a term will be implied (if it is not expressed) that the employee will act at all times during his service in his employer's best interests. This "duty of fidelity" embraces the protection of trade and commercial secrets, including both information which is given to the employee and that which he generates in the course of his work.[124] But it is wider than a matter of confidence and may, in some circumstances, embrace a duty not to engage, deliberately and secretly, in directly competitive work, either with another employer or on his own account. In *Hivac v Park Royal*, the plaintiff company, which produced hearing aids of advanced design, secured an interim injunction to prevent a rival company from giving jobs to some of its technicians by way of "moonlighting" after hours. Since relief was apparently granted whether or not the technicians would be likely to impart confidential "know-how", the decision went a long way; but the plaintiff was constrained by war-time legislation from simply dismissing the technicians, and this condition made it a special case.[125] **8–25**

During the continuance of employment there is certainly an obligation to keep rival research staff from access to technical secrets,[126] and a duty not to provide the employee's own trade union with the employer's commercial information relevant to wage negotiations.[127]

There is an obligation not to extract information with a view to taking it

---

[124] Employment being a contractual relationship, the implied term has been the legal device for imposing the obligation in question: see *Faccenda Chicken v Fowler* [1986] 1 All E.R. 617 at 625. But clearly it bears an affinity to the equitable duty of good faith that is imposed on fiduciaries such as trustees, agents, partners and the like (for which, see above, para.8–23). Accordingly, a tendency can be detected towards treating at least senior employees as fiduciaries: *Canadian Aero v O'Malley* [1974] 40 D.L.R. (3d) 371; in England, see *Normalec v Britton* [1983] F.S.R. 318. Cf. the position concerning patents, above, para.7–04, and copyright, above, paras 13–04—13–06.

[125] *Hivac v Park Royal* [1946] 1 All E.R. 350 CA; see also *Reading v Att-Gen* [1951] A.C. 507 HL; *Davies v Presbyterian Church of Wales* [1986] 1 All E.R. 705 HL; *Missing Link Software v Magee* [1989] F.S.R. 361. *Lancashire Fires v Lyons*, below, n.31; *Ocular Sciences v Aspect Vision Care*, ibid. While there is no duty to report his own breaches of contract, the employee is under a duty to report those of a colleague: *Sybron v Rochem* [1983] 3 W.L.R. 713 CA.

[126] e.g. *Printers & Finishers v Holloway (No. 2)* [1964] 3 All E.R. 731.

[127] *Bents Brewery v Hogan* [1945] 2 All E.R. 570 (where the covenant was express). See also below, paras 8–27 et seq. on the special problem of preparing to leave employment.

away on departure, as for instance by copying it out or deliberately memorising it.[128] But information which would naturally be remembered, including even the names and addresses of customers, may be taken.[129] There is no general duty not to plan post-departure activities in advance.[130]

8–26 (ii) **The ex-employee.** In *Faccenda Chicken v Fowler*,[131] the Court of Appeal contrasted the extensive duty owed during the continuance of employment with the more limited responsibility after termination. The principle that the employer may only seek to protect two interests—in his trade secrets and in the goodwill existing with his customers—was developed first in connection with express covenants. Undertakings by the employee that he will not, upon leaving the employment, set up or join a competitive business, solicit former customers or disclose or use trade secrets, are enforceable only if reasonably necessary to protect the employer; otherwise they are an undue restraint of trade and so are void as contrary to public policy. Such covenants by employees are scrupulously tested; they must be no wider in scope (taking account of the types of business excluded, duration and area of operation) than is reasonably necessary to give the employer protection of the relevant interest.[132]

Much detailed law has developed around this basic rule and it is easy to overstep the mark that it sets.[133] Nonetheless managerial, professional, sales and research staff are often required to enter such covenants. Not only does a covenant make the position a matter of express agreement (with attendant psychological effects) but it may give wider protection than if the employer seeks to rely upon rights arising by operation of the general law. Breach of a covenant not to compete is usually easier to establish than breach of an undertaking not to disclose or use confidential information: it is relatively easy to show that an ex-employee has joined a competitor or set up in business.

8–27 The employer who is not protected by covenant is not entirely without remedy. If, for instance, he keeps a list of customers, he is entitled to stop an employee from deliberately memorising it or copying it out in order to make use of it himself once his employment ceases. This, indeed, is an aspect of the employee's implied duty of fidelity during his term of employment.[134] But he

[128] *Baker v Gibbons* [1972] 2 All E.R. 759.

[129] *Johnson & Bloy v Wolstenholme Rink* [1989] F.S.R. 135 CA.

[130] *Balston v Headline Filters* [1990] F.S.R. 385; *Ixora Trading v Jones* [1990] F.S.R. 385.

[131] [1986] 1 All E.R. 617; *Lancashire Fires v Lyons* [1996] F.S.R. 629 CA; *Ocular Sciences v Aspect Vision Care* [1997] R.P.C. 289. See Hull, *Commercial Secrecy* (1998) Chs 7, 8.

[132] Certain doubts about the scope of this doctrine, resulting from the *Faccenda Chicken* case, were not accepted in *Lancashire Fires* (above, n.15); and see *Cantor Fitzgerald v Tradition* (UK) [2000] R.P.C. 95; but cf. *AT Poeton v Horton* [2001] F.S.R. 14 CA.

[133] There is no room to review this important doctrine here. See especially Heydon, *The Restraint of Trade Doctrine* (1972) and, for an economic analysis, M.J. Trebilcock, *The Common Law of Restraint of Trade* (1986).

[134] See, e.g. *Robb v Green* [1985] 2 Q.B. 315; *Baker v Gibbons* [1972] 2 All E.R. 759; *Diamond Stylus v Bauden* [1973] R.P.C. 675. It is difficult to prove the case if the defendant has not removed a copy of the list.

cannot stop an ex-employee from soliciting his customers in circumstances where the ex-employee merely remembers the customers' names in the ordinary course of events. If he had a valid express covenant, then he could.[135]

If there could not be an effective covenant, then, a fortiori, the law of confidence cannot be relied upon. For this general law to apply, so the *Faccenda Chicken* case emphasises, a court must be convinced that the employee has departed with information that he ought not to take advantage of.[136] It is not enough to show that this special element was something that the employee was bound to keep "confidential" during his employment. He must have acquired "trade secrets or their equivalent". In investigating this, account will be taken of various factors: (i) the nature of the employment (for example whether confidential information was regularly handled); (ii) the nature of the information at issue; (iii) the degree to which the employer impressed its secrecy on the employees; and (iv) the ease with which it can be isolated from other, unprotectable information; (v) the extent to which it is already in the public domain; and (vi) the likely damage from use or disclosure.[137] **8–28**

Chemical formulae, details of technical processes, and hard commercial information, such as prices, are considered examples of what, in the light of circumstances, may continue to be protected even after the determination of the job.[138] But within this category, a distinction is drawn between the discrete "trade secret", which any honest person of average intelligence would regard as such; and more incidental features or expedients, which were peculiar to the former employer's process or factory, but which are not to be separated from general knowledge and acquired skill.[139] While information of the first kind continues to be protectable under the general obligation of confidence, that of the second calls for an express covenant. If a covenant has been taken, it is justifiable within the rule of public policy (provided that it is no wider than warranted by the ex-employer's interest).[140] Moreover, if a covenant is taken but it proves to be too widely drawn, there may still be a breach of general obligation to respect confidence if a sufficiently significant **8–29**

135 e.g. *Coral Index v Regent Index* [1970] R.P.C. 147.

136 See also *GD Searle v Celltech* [1982] F.S.R. 92 CA.

137 *Faccenda Chicken v Fowler* [1986] 1 All E.R. 617; *FSS Travel v Johnson* [1999] F.S.R. 505 CA; *AT Poeton v Horton* [2001] F.S.R. 14 CA.

138 *Printers & Finishers v Holloway (No. 2)* [1965] R.P.C. 239; and see *Under Water Welders v Street* [1968] R.P.C. 498; *United Sterling v Felton* [1974] R.P.C. 162; *Harvey Tiling v Rodomac* [1977] R.P.C. 399 SC (SA); *Yates v Electrofoils* [1976] F.S.R. 345.

139 In *Faccenda Chicken* (above, n.37) the Court of Appeal appears to have doubted whether this intermediate category exists, but that position was not maintained, e.g. in *Lancashire Fires* [1996] F.S.R. 629. But some courts still ignore it as, e.g. *FSS Travel* (above, n.137).

140 This proposition in *Printers & Finishers* is accepted in *Balston v Headline Filters* [1987] F.S.R. 330 and *Lancashire Fires v Lyons*, above, n.131.

trade secret is at issue.[141] Nothing, therefore, is lost by taking an express covenant. If it proves valid, there is much that may be gained.

8–30 A principle which distinguishes between discrete technical secrets (protectable even in the absence of covenant), incidental information known only to the ex-employee (protectable only by covenant) and general skill and knowledge (unprotectable), places a heavy burden of proof on any previous employer who seeks to rely upon a general obligation of confidence falling within the first of these categories. It is not enough, for instance, to show that others are prepared to pay for a package of know-how and associated rights. The defendant must be taking a similar package to his new employer.[142] The courts insist, both at the interlocutory and the final stage of proceedings, upon clear evidence of what the information was (so as to be able to decide that it warranted protection) and that it was given over in confidence.[143] The ex-employer also risks revealing, by his own pleadings and evidence, significant details which the defendant may not previously have appreciated.[144] Yet the courts can offer only limited help towards preserving the secrecy of what the claimant is obliged to reveal.[145]

(d) *Government departments and agencies*

8–31 Government authorities—central, local and special—receive a mass of information, much of it, at least by implication, for limited purposes only. So far, the equity of confidence appears to apply to them as it would to other disclosees.[146] There may, however, be special reasons for allowing them to disclose or use the information in pursuit of some public interest, such as the enforcement of the civil or criminal law.[147] In this context the impact of the Official Secrets Acts and of the Freedom of Information Act 2000 should not be forgotten.[148]

---

[141] *Wessex Dairies v Smith* (1935) 2 K.B. 80 CA; *Triplex v Scorah* (1938) 55 R.P.C. 21; *Marshall (Thomas) (Exports) v Guinle* (above, n.71).

[142] Thus evidence that visitors were not restricted in their inspections, or that the employee was never informed of the secrecy is likely to tell against the employer: see e.g. *United Sterling v Felton* [1974] R.P.C. 162; *Aveley/Cybervox v Boman* [1975] F.S.R. 139 at 144.

[143] e.g. *CMI-Centers v Phytopharm* [1999] F.S.R. 235.

[144] See *Yates v Electrofoils* (above, n.22) at 394–395; and see *Potters-Ballotini v Weston-Baker* [1977] R.P.C. 202 at 206.

[145] In lieu of particulars, the court may order that an independent expert be appointed to inspect the plaintiff's plant on condition that he reveals his findings only to the defendant's legal advisers and destroys any notes; in this procedure it is for the plaintiff to point out to the expert the features that he regards as secret: *Printers & Finishers v Holloway (No.2)* [1965] R.P.C. 239 at 248. See also *Terrapin v Tecton* (1968) 64 W.W.R. 129.

[146] This seems to be accepted, e.g. in *Butler v Board of Trade* [1971] Ch. 680; *Norwich Pharmacal v CCE* [1974] A.C. 133.

[147] As in *Butler* and *Norwich Pharmacal* (see n.146).

[148] See 11 *Halsbury's Laws of England* (4th edn), paras 899 et seq.; Cripps (above, n.72), pp.148–170.

(e) *The indirect recipient*[149]

If A gives B information in confidence and B passes it to C, C—the indirect recipient—may take it knowing that it is confidential; or the circumstances may be such that he ought to have known of the confidence; or he may receive it without this knowledge, actual or imputed, only to be informed subsequently of the true position. In this last case, he may initially have purchased it or he may have had it as a gift. The courts undoubtedly wish to protect confidence to the extent of making indirect recipients liable in some of these circumstances; but which? It is here that doubts are thickest and doctrinal differences headiest. **8–32**

The deliberate or reckless recipient would in many circumstances be liable under the general law of tort: for inducing or procuring breach of contract, unjustifiably interfering with business relations or conspiracy[150]; if not, his bad faith would easily justify equity's intervention.[151] Other recipients, who at most have only been negligent, are not themselves usually regarded as acting in bad faith. However, obligations of confidence are apparently imposed on direct recipients under an objective test and this may perhaps be justified by saying that it is too much to expect the plaintiff always to establish fraud.[152] The same approach might equally be applied to the indirect recipient. But if the non-negligent recipient is ever to be held liable, it cannot be because of his own default. It must either be because confidential information has been dignified with the status of "property", or else the court's intervention is to secure the information against breach of the obligation of good faith originally assumed by the first recipient.

Judgments touching trade secrets with commercial value seem prepared to impose liability on an innocent recipient from the time when he is informed of the breach of confidence.[153] In *Wheatley v Bell* one defendant acquired confidential knowledge about franchising local business guides and proceeded to sell it to other defendants as franchisees in a different place. The latter, though initially innocent, were enjoined.[154] Assuming that it is the proper approach, then relief ought not to extend to damages for past innocent use. It would be open to a court to refuse or limit any injunction in **8–33**

[149] See Stuckey (1981) 4 U.N.S.W.L.R. 73; for the costs of policing secrecy, see Anderson, *Technology* (1996).

[150] For these torts, see above, paras 2–12 et seq. and esp. *British Industrial Plastics v Ferguson* [1940] 1 All E.R. 479 HL.

[151] Thus in *Prince Albert v Strange* (above, n.30) stress is at one point laid on the duplicity of the indirect recipient: see 1 Mac. & G. 25 at 44. It is a breach of confidence knowingly to import products produced using the confidential information or through theft of documentary material: *Union Carbide v Naturin* [1987] F.S.D. 538; *Beecham Group v Norton Health Care* [1997] F.S.R. 81.

[152] See above, para.8–20.

[153] *Stephenson Jordan v MacDonald & Evans* (1951) 68 R.P.C. 190 at 195; *Printers & Finishers v Holloway (No. 2)* [1964] 3 All E.R. 731 at 253 (liability of Vita-Tex); *Malone v Commissioner of Police* [1979] Ch. 344 at 634; *PSM International v Whitehouse* [1992] F.S.R. 489 CA; *Cadbury Schweppes v FBI Foods* (1999) 167 D.L.R. (4th) 577 SC Canada.

[154] *Wheatley v Bell* [1984] F.S.R. 16 SC (NSW).

light of the extent to which the indirect recipient would be disadvantaged. So account could be taken not only of whether he paid a purchase price, but whether he could be reimbursed for that expenditure and any consequential investment intended to exploit the information.[155]

However, breaches of confidence may result from infractions of duty by fiduciaries. In that context liability of third parties arises only if they knowingly assist in the breach of trust or equitable obligation. There would seem to be a strong case that the same principle should apply to breaches of commercial confidence which arise beyond the limits of fiduciary duties.[156] This may well prove to be a matter on which invasion of privacy becomes subject to separate limitations.[157]

If it is correct to treat confidential information as property,[158] it is either property at common law which all must respect (save to the extent that the innocent are to be excused damages for past injuries)[159]; or it is property in equity, in which case the bona fide purchaser bears no responsibility but the innocent volunteer does. The difficulty with these stereotypes is that they each take a rather inflexible view of the defendant's circumstances. There is very little indication that English courts wish to apply either theory to subject matter of such varying character as is currently protectable in the name of confidence.[160]

(f) *Absence of any relationship*

8–34 In *Malone v Commissioner of Police*,[161] an unsuccessful attack was made on the propriety of official wire-tapping (under the Home Secretary's warrant) in order to detect crime.[162] Megarry V.C. took the view in principle that if one person told a second something in confidence, but a third overheard it, the last was under no legal liability to preserve the confidence. This is a point, so it was held, at which the moral constraints upon an honourable

[155] See Jones (1970) 86 L.Q.R. 463 at 477–478; and note Evershed M.R. in the *Stephenson Jordan* case (1952) 69 R.P.C. 10 at 16.

[156] Toulson and Phipps, *Confidentiality* (2007) para.3.075. For the state of knowledge required of the third party for liability, see *Royal Brunei Airlines v Tan* [1995] 2 A.C. 378, HL, and *Twinsectra v Yardley* [2002] 2 W.L.R. 802 HL.

[157] Below, para.9–14.

[158] For the basic issue, see below, para.8–50—8–54.

[159] Even if we are dealing with a new form of intellectual "property", the tendency to preclude such damages in other instances must be remembered: above, para.2–41.

[160] On the analogy to the tort of conversion as one method of assessing damages for breach of confidence (*Seager v Copydex (No.2)* [1969] R.P.C. 250) gives implied support to the common law property approach. Certainly in *Morison v Moat* ((1851) 9 Hare 241), the bona fide purchaser was treated as exempt, but the proposition has not found clear echoes in England (cf. the cases above, in n.153, which tend the other way). However, the bona fide purchaser has been treated as protected in Canada (*International Tools v Kollar* (1968) 67 D.L.R. (2d) 386 at 391; *Tenatronics v Hauf* (1972) 23 D.L.R. (3d) 60; cf. *Polyresins v Skin-Hall* (1972) 25 D.L.R. (3d) 152).

[161] *Malone v Commissioner of Police* [1979] 2 All E.R. 620. See generally Wei (1992) 12 Leg. St. 302.

[162] The case reviews critically the present arrangement for supervising telephone tapping in Britain: "a subject which cries out for legislation": [1979] 2 All E.R. 620 at 649.

man outstrip those imposed by law. For this the only reason offered was that people (particularly those who use the telephone) know that they risk being overheard.[163] If the decision is followed strictly, only the recipient of the communication and those to whom he passes it directly or indirectly can be the subject of this equity. It cannot stretch to any form of surreptitious intervention by eavesdropping or other snooping, natural or technically aided.

Other courts have been readier to extend the scope of the equitable principle. In *Francome v Mirror Group*,[164] held that where a person had tapped a telephone, privately and without official authority, in order to get discreditable information about a leading jockey, the action would in principle lie. Apparently, a phone-user does not anticipate that form of bugging, whatever he may have to put up with from the police. In the Queensland case of *Franklin v Giddings*,[165] one fruit-farmer stole budwood for a new variety of nectarine from his neighbour's orchard, built up his own stock of trees and then went into competitive marketing. His conduct was condemned as "unconscionable" and actionable in equity; destruction of his orchard was ordered.[166]

The most significant indication that confidence liability would be broadened came from Lord Goff of Chieveley in the "*Spycatcher*" case, who said:

> "A duty of confidence arises when confidential information comes to the knowledge of a person ... in circumstances where he has notice, or is held to have agreed, that the information is confidential, with the effect that it would be just in all the circumstances that he should be precluded from disclosing the information to others."[167]

Accordingly the need to show "that information must have been imparted in circumstances importing an obligation of confidence" (Megarry J.'s second requirement[168]) does not confine the action to cases where there was a prior undertaking to keep information secret. It was enough that the person acquiring the knowledge ought to have known that he ought not to disclose it. The "*Spycatcher*" case concerned government secrets and its lead was followed in cases of surreptitious photography of film sets and of materials

---

[163] *Malone* (above, n.161) at 645–646. It is remarkable that this is the first occasion on which the general issue has been aired in a modern British case.

[164] *Francome v Mirror Group* [1984] 2 All E.R. 208 CA (see also above, para.8–18); see also *Exchange Telegraph v Howard* (1906) 22 T.L.R. 375.

[165] *Franklin v Giddings* [1978] Qd R. 72.

[166] There has been held to be a breach of confidence where a journalist is allowed to remain on private premises on condition that he does not take photographs, yet he covertly proceeds to do so: *Shelley Films v Rex Features* [1994] E.M.L.R. 134; *Creation Records v News Group* [1997] E.M.L.R. 444. While there was a prior relationship in these instances, could a wholly evasive intrusion be differently treated? Cf. instances of confrontational invasions, such as *Kaye v Robertson* [1991] F.S.R. 62 CA; below, para.9–04.

[167] *Att-Gen v Guardian Newspapers (No. 2)* [1990] 1 A.C. 109 at 281.

[168] *Coco v Clark*, above, para.8–09.

set out for picturing on a record sleeve—both entirely commercial situations with corporations as claimants.[169] Rather remarkably, as we shall see, courts in the 1990s were reluctant to show the same generosity where the claimant was alleging an invasion of personal privacy.[170]

8–35 The Younger Committee on Privacy and the Law Commission both favoured the creation of a separate form of civil liability which would encompass some activities of industrial and news spies. There were differences of view, however, about whether the improper conduct should be defined relatively specifically (for instance, by limiting only the use of technical devices)[171]; or whether some more general expression (such as "surreptitious obtaining") ought to be used, leaving more to be settled by the courts.[172] On so sensitive a matter, there is great virtue in being as specific as possible.[173] In the *Malone* case, Megarry V.C. clearly appreciated the embarrassments that some all-embracing principle of liability might pose for official investigators.[174] Equally there are non-governmental interest groups (such as the press) who can justifiably demand specific guidance upon what they remain free to do. One important indication of what remains permissible is found in *Australian Broadcasting Corp v Lenah GameMeats*.[175] Animal rights activists secretly filmed the slaughter of possums at an abbatoir. The practice was legal and no attempt was being made to prevent outsiders from knowing what was going on. The material came into the hands of a major broadcaster, which, so far as concerns breach of confidence, was not enjoined from transmitting the material, because it was not being kept secret.[176] It made no difference that the filming had been undertaken surreptitiously.[177]

8–36 If no liability can arise in equity for any form of spying or eavesdropping

[169] *Shelley Films v Rex Features* [1993] E.M.L.R. 134; *Creation Records v News Group* [1997] E.M.L.R. 444.

[170] Below, para.9–04.

[171] The Younger Committee (Cmnd.5012, 1972) favoured the creation of criminal offences relating to surreptitious surveillance by means of a technical device (paras 560–563) and that civil liability should depend upon proof of an unlawful act (para.632).

[172] The Law Commission put up the alternatives for further discussion (Working Paper No. 58, paras 135–140).

[173] Note the warning against "wide and indefinite rights" in the *Malone* case (above, n.161) at 643.

[174] Note however his criticism of the present administrative practice governing wire-tapping, and his plea for legislation.

[175] (2002) 185 A.L.R. 1 HC (Aust). For the impact of the case on the right to privacy, see below, para.9–09.

[176] cf. *Shelley Films v Rex Features* [1994] E.M.L.R. 134; *Creation Records v News Group* [1997] R.P.C. 444.

[177] cf. the dictum of Swinfen Eady L.J. (*Ashburton v Pape* [1913] 2 Ch. 469 at 475): Chancery grants relief against "the publication of confidential information improperly or surreptitiously obtained or of information imparted in confidence which ought not to be divulged". The reference to surreptitious conduct was probably to subversive activities by indirect recipients of information received initially under a contract to conserve confidence. The case, moreover was concerned with the special issue of the extent of professional privilege in litigation.

the criminal law may impose its own form of sanction and from this may arise liability in tort. If there is a combination to procure information of economic value, it may well amount to a criminal conspiracy to defraud.[178] If pecuniary damage can be shown to follow, the conduct will amount to a conspiracy actionable in tort.[179]

(3) Unauthorised use

(a) *Wrongful acts*

The acts that constitute infringement of a patent or copyright are, in different ways, limited by relatively precise criteria: in the case of patents, by confining infringement to certain kinds of industrial use and commercial exploitation within the scope of the claims defining the monopoly[180]; in the case of copyright, by the requirements of reproduction or performance, copying of the manner in which ideas are expressed and the taking of a substantial part of the work.[181] The notion of breach of confidence is by comparison loosely defined. It may consist in any disclosure or use which contravenes the limited purpose of the revelation.[182] If the question is one of misuse, it does not matter that the use will not disclose the information to further recipients.[183] Not all the information taken has to be used or disclosed before breach occurs, though doubtless the deployment of insubstantial amounts might be disregarded.[184] The information used must come from that disclosed in confidence and not from some other source. This may raise similar difficulties of proof to those arising in copyright; and, as there, courts may want to infer derivation of the idea from the similarity of end products.[185] **8–37**

The conflicts which today may arise over the wish to keep information of many kinds from undue disclosure leads courts increasingly to consider

[178] Persons who combined to make surreptitious copies of films in breach of copyright were held to be conspiring to defraud the copyright owner, even though no one was deceived: *Scott v Metropolitan Police Commissioner* [1975] A.C. 819; cf. *DPP v Withers* [1975] A.C. 842. See above, para.2–20. In this context it should be remembered that to borrow a copy of a film (in order to copy it) is not theft: *R. v Lloyd* [1986] F.S.R. 138 CA. For the development of criminal sanctions against misuse of trade secrets in the US and discussions in Canada, see Coleman (above, para.8–01, n.1), Ch.7.

[179] For this tort, see above, para.2–13; and note the other possibilities there canvassed.

[180] See above, para.6–02.

[181] See below, paras 12–03—12–20.

[182] But not where the information is no more than the knowledge, skill and experience that an employee must acquire in the course of his duties: *United Indigo v Robinson* (1932) 49 R.P.C. 178 at 189; and more generally, *Worsley v Cooper* [1939] 1 All E.R. 290 at 306–310.

[183] *Ocular Sciences v Aspect Vision Care* [1997] R.P.C. 289: if the information contributes towards making of a product, the contribution must be sufficiently extensive and important: see at 401, 404.

[184] In *Amber Size v Menzel* [1913] 2 Ch. 239 the defendant was restrained from misusing the whole or any material part of the plaintiff's secret process. Contrast the patent law principle which requires all essential integers of the claimed invention to be taken: above, para.6–02.

[185] See below, para.12–03.

carefully just what will amount to breach. One important field is that of health informatics. An information business sought to acquire information from pharmacists (for a fee) about the prescribing habits of general practitioners—information of considerable commercial value to drug manufacturers. The patient's identity would not be disclosed in the procedure. It held that there would be no breach of confidence involved, and that accordingly the Department of Health could not issue a policy document against the practice.[186] When the information is collected by one public authority and it is sought by another, the family law solution of requiring a court order which would take account of all the circumstances is being extended to other situations: for instance, where a person has made a damaging statement to the police and it is wanted by a professional body.[187]

(b) *The defendant's state of mind*

8–38 The liability of a defendant may turn upon his state of mind both at the time when he receives the information and when he uses or discloses it. The former has already been discussed, since it goes to the question whether an obligation of confidence has been assumed or is to be imposed.[188] When it comes to breach, it appears not to matter that the defendant acts out of some misguided or well-meaning motive,[189] that he does not appreciate the confidentiality of a document from which he takes the information[190] or that he has forgotten the source of the information and thinks he has thought of it himself. *Seager v Copydex*[191] was treated by the Court of Appeal as involving subconscious copying of this last kind: the defendant's employees were found to have worked out how to make a carpet grip embodying a basic idea which they had forgotten being shown by the plaintiff. An Australian decision,[192] however, applied the notion of subconscious copying only with some reluctance. It must remain doubtful whether the law—particularly if it is based upon an obligation of "good faith"—needs to go so far.

---

186 *R. v Department of Health Ex p. Health Informatics* [2001] Q.B. 424 CA.

187 *Woolgar v Chief Constable of Sussex* [1999] 3 All E.R. 604; cf. *Bunn v BBC* [1998] 3 All E.R. 552.

188 See above, paras 8–20, 8–32.

189 *Nichrotherm v Percy* [1956] R.P.C. 272 at 281.

190 *National Broach v Churchill Gear* [1965] R.P.C. 61.

191 *Seager v Copydex (No. 1)* [1967] 2 All E.R. 415 at 418; cf. "subsconscious copying" in copyright: below, para.12–04.

192 *Talbot v General Television* [1981] R.P.C. 1. See also Ricketson (1980) 2 E.I.P.R. 149.

(c) *Detriment to the plaintiff*

In *Coco v Clark*,[193] Megarry J. questioned whether the plaintiff must show that he has or will suffer detriment by the breach of confidence. The variety of information that may be the subject of confidence makes this a complex and difficult issue and one that remains unresolved. The motive for protecting technical and commercial information is normally to preserve its economic value for the plaintiff. In these cases is the plaintiff's interest like property[194] in the sense that he is entitled to decide if another may make use of it, whether or not he exploits the information himself? Or may he object only to misuses or disclosures of the information that injure him in trade competition?[195] The motive for protecting personal information may well be to prevent distress or embarrassment; though some people want privacy largely so that they can turn it to their own financial advantage.[196] In these cases, if there must be detriment, it may perhaps lie in the need to prove that the plaintiff's sensibilities will be disturbed—an issue to which we return in the next chapter.[197] When it comes to government secrets, it is necessary to show a sufficient public interest in their protection,[198] and this may be expressed as the need to show detriment.[199] **8–39**

It is tempting to say that liability ought to follow simply upon the breaking of the confidence without looking also for detriment.[200] But one should remember that a very wide range of subject matter is involved. Likewise there is always some public interest in the freedom to use information. Restriction of that freedom accordingly requires sufficient reason. In this connection it should be remembered that most economic torts are actionable only upon proof of damage[201]; and the tort of defamation is confined to statements which tend to lower the plaintiff in the eyes of right-thinking members of the public—an approach which imposes objective standards.

[193] *Coco v Clark* [1969] R.P.C. 41 at 48; *Dunford v Johnston* [1978] F.S.R. 143 at 148; and *Jarman Platt v Barget* [1977] F.S.R. 260 at 277, assume that detriment is necessary. Later cases do not demand it or find it necessarily to flow from the breach: *X Health Authority v Y* [1988] R.P.C. 379 at 391; *Federal Bank of the Middle East v Hodkinson* [2000] 2 All E.R. 395 at 413; *CMI v Phytopharm* [1999] F.S.R. 235 at 257.

[194] Talk of property may not seem very helpful in this context. Cf. the discussion of whether passing off protected the property in a trade mark or only in the goodwill of the business in which it was used: see below, paras 16–05, 16–07.

[195] If the latter is the rule, what of the case where he wants to exploit a rival invention that he has also devised? *Seager v Copydex* was such a case.

[196] Consider, e.g. *Lennon v News Group* [1978] F.S.R. 573 CA.

[197] Below, para.9–22.

[198] See above, para.8–19.

[199] So Lord Keith put the matter in *Att-Gen v Guardian Newspapers (No. 2)* [1990] A.C. 109 at 258; and see Mason J. *Commonwealth of Australia v Fairfax* (1980) 32 A.L.R. 485 at 492–493.

[200] Some judges accept this, e.g. *Federal Bank v Hadkinson* [2002] 2 All E.R. 375 at [413] CA.

[201] See above, paras 2–12—2–18.

3. Remedies[202]

(1) Injunction and other equitable remedies

8–40 The remedies available for infringement of intellectual property rights have been applied to breach of confidence without much difficulty, save in the case of damages.[203] Typically claimants hope to contain the confidence before it has escaped; hence the importance of injunctions. There has been no doctrinal impediment to awarding equity's ancillary forms of relief—account of profits[204] and delivery up or destruction on oath[205]—in appropriate cases.

To the general discussion of these equitable remedies[206] a number of supplemental points may here be added.

(a) *Interim injunctions*

8–41 In cases where a defendant is seeking to stop general publication in the media, the courts have long considered that special policies will apply. Interim injunctions are not granted in proceedings for defamation if the defendant proposes to justify his statements (that is establish their truth) or to plead fair comment[207]; the press is thus left free to publish at risk of paying damages.[208] In *Woodward v Hutchins*,[209] the Court of Appeal considered that the alleged breaches of confidence were inextricably linked with defamation (though defamation was not pleaded) and so it refused to halt a newspaper story. The claimant must show a reasonable prospect of succeeding at trial, if an interim injunction restraining freedom of expression is to be granted.[210]

8–42 In other circumstances, protection of confidence may override the preservation of free expression. In *Schering v Falkman*,[211] for instance, a man who had been hired to assist a drug company in countering adverse publicity

---

[202] Wei [2005] Singapore L.J. 108.

[203] See below, paras 8–47, 8–49.

[204] As in *Peter Pan Mfg v Corsets Silhouette* [1963] R.P.C. 45.

[205] As in *Industrial Furnaces v Reaves* [1970] R.P.C. 605, where the defendant was not trusted to destroy on oath.

[206] See above, paras 2–30, 2–36.

[207] *Bonnard v Perryman* [1891] 2 Ch. 269; *Fraser v Evans* [1969] 1 All E.R. 8 at 10 CA. Where the claim is partly for infraction of personal privacy and partly for defamation, the court may grant interim relief if it is satisfied that there is a genuine issue of privacy at stake: *RST V UVW* [2010] E.M.L.R. 13: *Terry and Persons Unknown* [2010] E.M.L.R. 16. For circumstances in which the application may itself be subject t privacy considerations, such as anonymity orders: *re Guardian News' Application* [2010] E.M.L.R. 15, HL; *G v Wikimedia Foundation* [2010] E.M.L.R. 14.

[208] Where the defendant claims a public interest in publication, the claimant has no right to see what is proposed before it appears: *Tillery Valley Foods v Channel 4 TV* [2004] EWHC; Hull [2004] E.I.P.R. 515.

[209] [1977] 2 All E.R. 751 CA; and see *Service Corp v Channel Four* [1999] E.M.L.R. 83.

[210] *Cream Holdings v Banerjee* [2005] 1 A.C. 253; *Att-Gen v Parry* [2004] E.M.L.R.13.

[211] *Schering v Falkman* [1982] Q.B. 1.

about one of its products, Primodos, had subsequently become a journalist. He and a television company were about to show a programme in which the old controversy over the drug was resurrected. The idea came from his association with the company, though the material had mainly been recovered from public sources. The majority of the Court of Appeal gave interim relief restraining the showing in terms which displayed their distaste for the journalist's lack of moral scruple in taking advantage of his earlier connection with the company. Only Lord Denning M.R. dissenting, gave higher value to the need to free the press and other media from prior restraint.[212] His position deserves to be remembered.

In the *"Spycatcher"* case, high indignation against the breaches of secrecy by the former MI5 officer, Wright, led a majority of the House of Lords to continue and to strengthen interim injunctions against three newspapers,[213] requiring them not to publish extracts or accounts from Wright's memoirs, even after publication abroad had made their contents widely known in Britain.[214] The object of this was to leave to the Attorney-General the practical possibility at the trial of arguing that general injunctions against further revelations by Wright or other confidential government officers should be granted in order to preserve the morale of the secret services.[215] In similar proceedings, shortly before the publication abroad, other newspapers had been obliged to respect the injunctions or risk liability for contempt.[216] **8–43**

When the issue is one of freedom of expression by the media, the Human Rights Act 1998 s.12, affects the extent to which revelation of information in future may be enjoined. This provision has no direct counterpart in the EHCR itself, which refers only to general qualifications upon the right to private life and to freedom of expression, leading to the requirement that each of the rights must be balanced against the other.[217] Section 12 became part of the UK Act at the behest of media interests which sought to curb any unnecessary tendency to grant interim injunctions in order to respect individual privacy. The section requires a court, in considering an application for interim relief, to have particular regard to the Convention right to freedom of expression. Accordingly it must be satisfied that the applicant is **8–44**

---

212 He referred to a fine passage of Blackstone (*Commentaries*, IV, 151–152) on the subject, and to modern developments of the theme, including the European Convention on Human Rights art.10, its interpretation in the *Sunday Times* case ((1979–1980) 2 E.H.R.R. 245), and the view of Lord Scarman in *Att-Gen v BBC* [1980] 3 All E.R. 161 at 183.

213 They were strengthened by removing exceptions pertaining in part to reporting the contemporaneous proceedings in Australia.

214 *Att-Gen v Guardian Newspapers (No. 1)* [1987] 3 All E.R. 316. See also *Att-Gen v Turnaround Distribution* [1989] 1 F.S.R. 169.

215 An argument which ultimately failed: see above, para.8–19.

216 *Att-Gen v Newspaper Publishing* [1987] 3 All E.R. 276; and ultimately *Att-Gen v Times Newspapers* [1992] 1 A.C. 191 HL; Oliver (1989) 23 Israel L.R. 409; Cripps (above, n.72) at 244–253. See also *Att-Gen v Punch* [2001] E.M.L.R. 24 CA.

217 For the relation of s.12 to the European Convention, see below, para.9–21.

likely to succeed at trial of the action.[218] And where the material is journalistic, literary or artistic, the court must take account of whether it has become available to the public or is about to do so, the extent of public interest in that publication, and to any relevant privacy code. So far as concerns newspaper publishing this last factor will include reference to the Code of Conduct of the Press Complaints Commission.[219]

8–45 Section 12 affects breach of confidence claims whether or not the applicant is asserting rights of personal privacy in implementation of art.8 of the ECHR. In a case not involving art.8 rights, the injunction sought was to prevent an ex-employee and a newspaper from publicising confidential documents which the ex-employee alleged to show corruption in the activities of the applicant, a company running nightclubs, dance festivals and so on. The defendants argued that, thanks to art.12(3), the court must be convinced on a balance of probabilities that the applicant would be likely to succeed at trial before considering how to exercise its discretion. The House of Lords refused to put so high a burden on the applicant, but held nevertheless that the standard was somewhat higher than "the arguable case" standard set by the general *American Cyanamid* principles.[220] It also accepted that in applying s.12 there could be special cases where the applicant might only satisfy a lower standard.[221] In the case before it, the House held that the applicant company had not shown that it was more likely to succeed than fail at trial. Discussion of circumstances requiring a balance between art.8 and art.10 rights is taken up in the next chapter.[222]

(b) *Discretion to grant injunction*

8–46 Courts consider a wider range of factors in deciding whether to grant a final injunction in a breach of confidence case than in patent or copyright cases.[223] Some judges have seen difficulties in imposing constraints on the defendant when the circumstances, particularly those arising after the confidential disclosure, make it unfair to go so far. In *Seager v Copydex (No. 1)*,[224] the

---

[218] This, however, has been treated as being only slightly higher in the scale than the usual obligation to show a reasonable prospect of success (for which, see above, para.2–32): *Imutran v Uncaged Campaigns* [2001] 2 All E.R. 385 at [17]; *A v B* [2002] 2 All E.R. 545 at 552 CA; but see *Cream Holdings v Banerjee*, below, n.220; Smith [2004] C.L.J. 4.

[219] Referred to explicitly in *A v B* [2002] 2 All ER 545 at 556 CA. Decisions of the Commission itself are subject to judicial review, but they will be allowed a margin of discretion in applying its Code of Practice: *R. v Press Complaints Commission* [2002] E.M.L.R. 95.

[220] *Cream Holdings v Banerjee* [2005] 1 A.C. 253 , HL; and see above, paras 2–33—2–36.

[221] Referring to *Re H (Minors: Sexual Abuse)* [1996] A.C. 563; *Re Harris Symons* [1989] 1 W.L.R. 368; *Re Primlaks* [1989] B.C.L.C. 734.

[222] Below, para.9–16.

[223] *Cadbury-Schweppes v FBI Foods* (1999) 167 D.L.R. (4th) 577, SC Canada.

[224] See above, n.191.

Court of Appeal refused an injunction and left the defendant to relief in damages; in *Coco v Clark*,[225] Megarry J. speculated upon a number of circumstances in which it might be appropriate to make the defendant pay only for what he had taken. A list of factors militating against an injunction might include: (1) the fact that the defendant was copying only subconsciously or for some reason innocently; (2) the gratuitous manner of the plaintiff's communication; (3) the fact that he was not himself utilising the idea but was rather pursuing an alternative in collaboration with another producer; (4) the extent of the defendant's own contribution to the design of a successful product; (5) whether the information was economic or personal; (6) the relatively mundane or subsidiary character of what was taken; (7) the fact that the information had become public; (8) possibly even the patentable nature of the idea—thus requiring the plaintiff who wants a full right of property to apply for a patent.[226] It would be possible for a court to limit the period of an injunction: for instance where it only wanted to deprive the defendant of his head start, or it wanted to leave the defendant free to use the information once it was put into the public domain.[227]

(2) Damages and other monetary relief[228]

Where a breach of confidence is also a breach of contract or a general tort **8–47**
such as inducing breach of contract, there is no difficulty in awarding damages in accordance with the normal principles applying to these common law wrongs.[229] Where the liability arises only in equity, damages may be awarded "in lieu of or in addition to an injunction", in accordance with the principle of Lord Cairns' Act 1858, "against the commission or continuance of the wrongful act".[230] In other fields, the courts have shown little inclination to read this power in a limited way: such damages lie: (1) where the wrongful act is purely equitable; and (2) whether the injury has already been

[225] *Coco v Clark* [1969] R.P.C. 41 at 50. The learned Judge's remarks are linked to the question of the extent of liability under the "springboard" doctrine: see above, paras 8–13—8–14. He shows some inclination to regard the liability as being to pay for information used, rather than not to use it. Cf. *Terrapin v Builders Supply* [1960] R.P.C. 128 at 135.

[226] Factors (1)–(4) and possibly (7) were relevant to the refusal of the injunction in *Seager v Copydex*. Concerning (5), Megarry J. considered that personal information might be protectable by injunction, even if industrial or commercial secrets were not. Factor (7), which is speculative, relates to the counter-policy of the patent system: above, para.8–03.

[227] Recognised in *Potters-Ballotini v Weston-Baker* [1977] R.P.C. 202 CA; *Roger Bullivant v Ellis* [1987] F.S.R. 174; and see *International Tools v Kollar* (1968) 67 D.L.R. (2d) 386 CA Ont.; *AB Consolidated v Europe Strength* [1978] 2 N.Z.L.R. 520; *Talbot v General Television* [1981] R.P.C. 1 SC Vict.

[228] Gummow in Youdan (ed.), *Equity, Fiduciaries and Trusts* (1989), p.57; Davies in Waters (ed.), *Equity, Fiduciaries and Trusts 1993* (1993), p.297; Rickett and Gardner (1994) 24 Vict U. Well. L.R. 19.

[229] *Indata Equipment v ACL* [1998] F.S.R. 248 CA.

[230] *Saltman v Campbell* (1948) 65 R.P.C. 203 CA.

committed or will be committed in the absence of an injunction.[231] There are also breach of confidence cases where damages were held available for injuries already caused, in addition to an injunction for the future.[232] But if the only likely breach has already occurred, it continues to be doubted whether damages under the Act can be given: there is then no case for the injunction to which the damages may be a substitute or addition.[233] One way of side-stepping such a narrowly historical view may be to rely on Chancery's inherent jurisdiction on a "money bill" to award compensation for an equitable wrong.[234] Where there is a pre-existing fiduciary duty, a constructive trust may be imposed on the fiduciary in appropriate circumstances.[235]

8–48 If damages are being given for future injuries in lieu of an injunction, it is said, in *Seager v Copydex (No. 2)*, that their assessment depends upon whether the information could have been acquired by employing a competent consultant. In that case his fee would be an appropriate measure.[236] If, however, the information was special—for instance, inventive—then, by analogy to the tort of conversion, the sum should represent its price between willing seller and buyer.[237] In the latter case, however, a "sale" of all the rights (including the right to apply for a patent)[238] may not always be appropriate. Where the plaintiff is exploiting the information himself, or licensing others, a royalty, as if for a non-exclusive licence, may be the appropriate measure. Altogether, the analogy to damages for misappropriation of a single tangible article is inept, given in particular the more obvious comparison to patents and copyright and the more flexible approach to damages which applies to their infringement.[239] Damages are awarded to put the plaintiff in the position that he would have been in, but for the breach of confidence. A person who loses his idea for a television series, because someone else misappropriates it, is entitled to a substantial sum even where his chances of having it taken up were uncertain.[240] So too

[231] For a full review, see Jolowicz (1975) 34 C.L.J. 24. See also *Elsley v Collins* (1978) 83 D.L.R. (3d) 1 at 13 SC (Canada); *Talbot v General Television* [1981] R.P.C. 1 SC Vict.

[232] e.g. *Peter Pan v Corsets Silhouette* [1963] R.P.C. 45.

[233] *Proctor v Bayley* (1889) 42 Ch.D. 390 at 401; *Nichrotherm v Percy* [1957] R.P.C. 207 at 213–214; *Malone v Commissioner of Police* [1979] 2 All E.R. 620 at 633.

[234] See Tettenborn (1987) 3 I.P.J. 183; Plibersek [1991] E.I.P.R. 283; Capper (1994) 14 Leg. St. 313.

[235] *Ocular Sciences v Aspect Vision Care* [1997] R.P.C. 289, relying inter alia on *Lac Minerals* (below, para.8–52); cf. *Satnam Investments v Dunlop Heywood* [1999] F.S.R. 722. And for the prospect of restitutionary damages, see above, para.2–43; *Att-Gen v Blake* [2001] 1 A.C. 268).

[236] [1969] 1 W.L.R. 809; but only if the information is for sale: *Dowson & Mason v Potter* [1986] 2 All E.R. 418 CA.

[237] [1969] R.P.C. 250; followed in *Interfirm Comparison v Law Society* [1975] R.P.C. 137 at 158.

[238] *Seager v Copydex (No. 2)* (above, n.191). The case has been treated as laying down no general principle: *Talbot v General Television* (above, n.192).

[239] cf. *Aquaculture Corp v New Zealand Green Mussel* [1990] 3 N.Z.L.R. 299 CA (NZ).

[240] *Talbot v General Television* [1981] R.P.C. 1. A plaintiff is entitled to fair compensation, but not to every potentially attributable loss: *Universal Thermosensors v Hibben* [1992] F.S.R. 361.

for a person whose business secret loses its commercial value because the defendant uses it irresponsibly.[241]

There remains the question whether damages for injury to feelings are available for breach of confidence, as they are for defamation and copyright infringement.[242] This is an issue of considerable importance to the novel variant of the breach of confidence action which gives force to art.8 of the European Human Rights Convention. Discussion is accordingly reserved until the next chapter.[243] Confidential Information as "Property" **8–49**

4. CONFIDENTIAL INFORMATION AS "PROPERTY"[244]

The willingness of the courts to hold indirect recipients responsible shows that the obligation to respect confidence is not purely personal to the initial giver of the undertaking. Is it then, in any meaningful sense, "property"? The root difficulty of such a question is the flexibility of the property notion in English law and the many ends to which it is employed.[245] Clearly, those who deal in technical know-how often treat it as such. While noting this common usage, Lord Upjohn nevertheless denied that confidential information was "property in any normal sense, but equity will restrain its transmission to another if in breach of some confidential relationship".[246] This now predominant view is used by judges to support consequential conclusions in a variety of situations. These instances, taken as a whole, suggest the wisdom of shaping the obligation over such disparate and ephemeral subject-matter by reference to the requirements of conscientious behaviour, rather than by disposing of issues simply by attaching a "property" label. **8–50**

First, property rights characteristically give the owner the power not only to license others to use the subject-matter but also to transfer ownership and engage in other transactions such as charging for loans. For established types of intellectual property, such as patents, copyright and trade marks, these basic powers are accepted and defined in the governing statutes.[247] The **8–51**

[241] *Aquaculture* case (above, n.239). The court also accepted that exemplary damages might be awarded in an appropriate case.

[242] In *Cornelius v De Taranto* [2001] E.M.L.R. 329, such a claim was approved, citing remarks in earlier editions of this book; see also *Campbell v Frisbee* [2003] E.M.L.R. 76.

[243] See further below, para.9–22.

[244] See above, para.8–32; on the issue generally, *cf.* Ricketson (1977) 11 M.U.L.R. 223, 289; Stuckey (1981) 9 Syd.L.R. 402; Roberts (1987) 3 I.P.J. 209, Palmer in Clarke (above, para.8–01, n.1), Ch.5.

[245] Thus in the *Boardman* case (below, n.246), one question was whether a fiduciary broke his equitable obligation by using his principal's property (in information) to his own advantage.

[246] *Boardman v Phipps* [1967] 2 A.C. 46 at 128 HL; *FBI Foods v Cadbury Schweppes* (1999) 167 D.L.R. (4th) 577 (SC Canada). But cf. *Goddard v Nationwide* [1987] Q.B. 670 at 685; *Att-Gen v Guardian Newspapers* [1987] 3 All E.R. 316 at 337–338; *English and American Insurance v Herbert Smith* [1988] F.S.R. 685.

[247] See above, paras 7–15 et seq., 13–11 et seq., 18–12 et seq.

licensing of technological and commercial know-how is frequent, and equally there are occasions where know-how is assigned. What the legal consequences of such an assignment are has received very little attention from courts. In *Mustad v Allcock*,[248] the assignee of manufacturing secrets was held entitled to sue for breach of confidence, but that may well be a limited case, since the know-how was part of the sale of a business. In cases of assignment of the know-how by itself it may be that the assignor remains the only person entitled to sue an outsider for misuse of it (apart from any contractual terms that there may be between the assignee and the misuser). If that is so, a crucial aspect of a property right will be lacking. As we shall see, when it comes to the right to prevent invasion of privacy, the question is of front-rank importance and the Court of Appeal has refused to accord this proprietary characteristic.[249]

Secondly, the central significance given to the undertaking to respect confidence makes liability turn on that initial personal obligation. This means that information otherwise obtained will not be protected just because it is in some sense private, and so a scrupulous respect for freedom of information and expression is maintained.[250] It means, moreover, that if a person with (say) technical know-how "assigns" it or "licenses" it exclusively to two different people in inconsistent dealings, the recipients are each left to their rights against the provider of the know-how, subject to any rights which may independently arise in law or equity directly against the other[251] (for an economic tort, or breach of fiduciary duty). Instead of the arbitrary rule that, as between owners of equitable interests, the first in time prevails, courts are enabled to reach a resolution of a difficult three-cornered dispute which takes account of all the particular circumstances.

8–52 Thirdly, if confidential information is per se classified as equitable property, when it is misused so as to make a profit, the profit ought to be recoverable not just by the personal remedies of account or damages but by the proprietary remedy of a constructive trust in any traceable assets constituting the profit. In *Lac Minerals v International Corona Resources*[252] the Supreme Court of Canada imposed this form of relief in a breach of confidence case. One gold-mining company had learned from another, during negotiations about collaboration on mining prospect No.1, that the chances on No. 2 were good. The recipient of the information thereupon secured

---

[248] (1928) [1963] 3 All E.R. 416n. HL.

[249] See below, para.9–20.

[250] See above, para.8–02.

[251] So held in *De Beer v Graham* (1891) 12 L.R. N.S.W. Eq. 144, stressing that the obligation is one of good faith. But if the information provider undertakes to the first recipient not to give it to anyone else, the second recipient is liable to respect his breach of good faith once informed of it.

[252] (1989) 61 D.L.R. (4th) 14.

No.2 behind the informant's back, developed the mine and was obliged to hold it for the informant,[253] not merely to pay damages.

The decision is, however, difficult to interpret as a precedent, since a majority of the court considered that the two parties were not in a fiduciary relationship, but a different majority favoured imposing a constructive trust.[254] A view which would better fit the hierarchy of intellectual property rights would confine the constructive trust to infractions of fiduciary relationship which are more than the mere receipt of confidential information.[255] At least it can be said that the court was divided about the particular outcome because its concern was with the consequences of a breach of good faith. On a property basis, the trust would have been imposed simply as a corollary.

Fourthly, when test material is submitted to a government authority for the licensing of a pharmaceutical product, can the authority take the information into account when considering the case of a rival submission relating to a generic version of the same drug? If it is property, this may of itself determine that the information may not be used for the second purpose. In an important Australian judgment, Gummow J. refused to uphold this line of argument and would have imposed liability only if in the circumstances the recipient authority had undertaken not to use the information in this way.[256] The same general approach is to be found in the *Source Informatics* decision of the English Court of Appeal, which held the Department of Health entitled to authorise general practitioners and pharmacists to pass information about the prescribing of specific drugs to drug producers, provided that it was "anonymised" so as to avoid a breach of patients' confidence. The patients enjoyed no greater property right in either the prescription form or the information that it contained.[257] **8–53**

Fifthly, if a person deliberately extracts confidential information and gains an advantage from it, the conduct is not theft within the Theft Act 1968.[258] This may be thought a disadvantage of refusing to accept that **8–54**

---

[253] Subject to being reimbursed for development costs. Damages would have been assessed at approximately one-quarter of the site value.

[254] Lamer J. found no fiduciary relationship, but held the undertaking of confidence enough to create a trust: see Hayhurst [1990] E.I.P.R. 30.

[255] See above, para.8–23.

[256] *Smith Kline & French v Department of Health* [1990] F.S.R. 617; Cornish in Leser and Isomura (eds), *Wege zum japanischen Recht* (1992), pp.843–850. In England, a public officer (of the Health and Safety Executive) was held entitled to pass information about the deceptive marking of a pharmaceutical product to the mark-owner, as a person to whom it was of mutual interest and concern: *Hoechst UK v Chemiculture* [1993] F.S.R. 270; and see *Process Development v Hogg* [1996] F.S.R. 45 CA.

[257] *R. v Department of Health Ex p. Health Informatics* [2001] 1 Q.B. 424 CA.

[258] *Oxford v Moss* (1979) 68 Cr.App.R. 183: the defendant temporarily extracted an examination paper in order to learn its content; followed in *R. v Absolom* (cited in Coleman (above, para.8–01, n.1) at 96), where an employee attempted to sell off highly valuable oil exploration results. The same view was taken in Scotland (*Grant v Procurator Fiscal* [1988] R.P.C. 41) and, after much argument, by the Supreme Court of Canada (*R. v Stewart* (1988) 50 D.L.R. (4th) 1). See also Alderson (1992) 7 I.P.J. 1.

information can be property. Certainly deliberate spying and unscrupulous conduct of the kind in the *Lac Minerals* case[259] can be immensely damaging and industrialists argue that criminal sanctions are badly needed. But, as English decisions on the subject have emphasised, it is not enough for theft that the information be characterised as property. There must also be an intention permanently to deprive the person entitled, and that cannot occur unless the sole record of the information is taken for good. If breach of confidence is to be made criminal, it should be by legislation which addresses the particular problem and defines the scope of the liability.[260]

5. Trade Secret Misuse: Criminal Responsibility

8–55 Flagrant abuses of confidential commercial information can occur where the wrongdoer lets out the secret and then proves to have no assets. Civil liability can have no impact on such a situation. Accordingly the Law Commission published a Discussion Paper on the desirability of making misuse of trade secrets a discrete criminal offence.[261] To do so would bring Britain broadly in line with Federal and much state law in the United States, and also with the law in many Continental countries.[262]

The paper demonstrates the complexity which such a law would have to assume. It is not able to propose any preferred definition of a "trade secret". Must the "owner" have indicated that it is to be kept secret? Is it to include professional and academic secrets? Or personal secrets? When will the information have come into the public domain? What will constitute the mens rea of the offence? What will be excluded? The Law Commission's Paper referred to the employee's and independent contractor's personal knowledge, skill and experience; information acquired independently, by reverse engineering and from a third party. Publication which is justified in the public interest would presumably be exempt.

The discussion in the Paper reflects the difficulties that the civil law has faced in reaching reasonably clear limits to the scope of liability for breach of confidence. Those who remain doubtful about the prospect of specific criminal sanctions appreciate the bitter self-justification often exhibited by each side in a breach of confidence dispute—not least in that familiar situation of employees who leave to further their own future. The danger of criminal sanctions—particularly if the offence is solely by indictment[263]—is

[259] Above, n.252.

[260] As it is in numerous American States, and equally on the European continent (where in some states, by a good mercantilist twist, sending the information abroad is an aggravated offence): see Coleman (above, para.8–01, n.1), Ch.7.

[261] i.e. an offence other than conspiracy to defraud or theft (when some physical record is misappropriated): Misuse of Trade Secrets—Paper 150, 1997; see Hull [1998] Crim. L.R. 246.

[262] See Paper 150, App.B; and Coleman, *The Legal Protection of Trade Secrets* (1992), Ch.7.

[263] As is proposed: Paper 150, para.5.11.

that it unduly weights the balance in favour of the person asserting the misuse of a secret. The Law Commission sought to deflect such criticism by limiting prosecutions to those brought by the Director of Public Prosecutions, or with his approval.[264] That at the least would be a necessary qualification. In the event the issue divided informed opinion to such an extent that the matter was not taken further.

The issue is, however, likely to become the subject of Community law. In **8–56**
April 2006, the Commission put forward a revised draft Directive on criminal measures to ensure enforcement of IPRs on a harmonised basis.[265] If enacted, Member States will have to provide, for all intentional infringements, penalties that include custodial sentences, fines, confiscation and various other measures. Is the protection of trade, commercial and possibly other types of confidential information to be regarded as "intellectual property" within this legislation? An answer that the ECJ might well give is that the TRIPS Agreement treats the protection of undisclosed information as one of the forms of intellectual property to which it applies[266]; and that a EU instrument should be construed likewise. If this becomes law, there could be considerable difficulties in deciding what constitutes an intentional infringement of trade secret liability.

264 Para.5.15.

265 COM(2006) 168, applying to all "intellectual property". This draft derives authority from the decision of the ECJ (*Commission v Council*, C176/03): criminal measures enacted by the Parliament and Council are competent where they are required for the effective implementation of Community law, this instance being cited as an example.

266 See arts 1(2), 39; and note in the latter the reference to the Paris Industrial Property Convention, art.10*bis* on unfair competition.

CHAPTER 9

PERSONAL PRIVACY

1. PRIVACY AND CONFIDENCE

(1) Independence for privacy claims

Privacy is, first and foremost, the desire of an individual to be free of intrusion. At least for the fortunate, modern life has improved the chances of solitude and intimacy, while swelling the means by which they may be broken into. Invasions of privacy may involve personal confrontation, surreptitious spying, regular surveillance, interference with personal property, entry onto private premises, or simply the acquisition and revelation of information. The variety of situations in which one person may seek to secure privacy against another can depend upon so many factors that there is great difficulty in deciding when the law should provide an instrument of protection.[1] **9–01**

As already indicated in the previous chapter, a form of liability for

[1] For reviews of a long debate, Beverley-Smith, *Commercial Appropriation of Personality* (2002), Pt III; Tugendhat and Christie (eds), *The Law of Privacy and the Media* (2002); Fenwick and Phillipson, *Media Freedom under the Human Rights Act* 2nd edn (2006); Aplin [2007] I.P.Q. 19.

invasion of privacy has detached itself from the equitable action for breach of confidence. Strands between the two remain in place, just as there have long been certain ties between confidence liability and fiduciary duty, contractual obligation, personality and economic torts such as defamation and injurious falsehood, and statutory duties such as those arising under data protection legislation.[2]

The undogmatic cast of civil liability in a common law system results in different categories of duty being formulated at levels of medium generality. It is assumed that, save where there is strong reason to the contrary, the various heads will operate in cumulative fashion. Claims may be pursued as alternatives, a single set of facts giving rise to more than one cause of action, though only for remedies appropriate to the situation as a whole.[3] Such generosity, however, cannot be allowed to create glaring inconsistencies. The Court of Appeal considers that the emergent action for breach of privacy lies whether the private information is true or not.[4] If it is untrue, as an alternative an action for the tort of defamation may lie. The jurisprudence of defamation is both elaborate and curious. Co-ordination with an action for privacy may raise many nice points. What, for instance, of the defences of fair comment and privilege?[5]

(2) The European Convention

9–02 The European Convention on Human Rights of 1950 stipulates that "everyone has the right to respect for his private and family life, his home and his correspondence" (art.8(1)). This right is subject to interference by a public authority, so far as necessary in a democratic society in the interests of national security, public safety or the economic well-being of the country, for the prevention of disorder or crime, for the protection of health or morals, or for the protection of the rights and freedoms of others; but the interference must be "according to law" (art.8(2)).[6] One countervailing right in the Convention is to freedom of expression, including freedom to hold opinions and to receive and impart information and ideas without interference by public authority and regardless of frontiers (art.10(1)).[7] Here likewise, there can be restrictions for the same necessities as those arising under art.8(2), and also for territorial integrity, preventing the disclosure of information received in confidence and maintaining the authority and

[2] For the last, see below, para.9–23.

[3] See, for instance, damages for injury to feelings, below, para.9–22.

[4] *McKennitt v Ash* [2008] Q.B. 73 at [78–80] (concerning the dispute over property transactions in that case).

[5] cf. *Culnane v Morris* [2006] E.M.L.R. 7.

[6] For interference according to law, see e.g. *Sciacca v Italy* (2005) (C–50774/99), below, at [9–17].

[7] Broadcasting, television and cinema licensing is permitted: art.10(1). A related policy requires access to information held by a public body: Freedom of Information Act 2000 and related Regulations.

impartiality of the judiciary (see art.10(2)). The United Kingdom, an original signatory of the Convention, for decades treated it only as imposing international law obligations on the Government. However its incorporation into British law in various ways by the Human Rights Act 1998 marked an important shift, not least in respect of civil litigation relating to the two Convention rights, which guarantee on the one hand, personal privacy, and on the other, freedom of expression.

In addition to the Convention requirements, s.12(4) of the 1998 Act elaborates upon the circumstances in which alone a court can impose a prior restraint on journalistic material in order to prevent its publication (normally by interim injunction). To the somewhat limited impact of s.12(4) we return when discussing remedies for invasions of personal privacy.[8]

The Convention itself (ECHR) provides a jurisdiction, currently exercised by the European Court of Human Rights (ECtHR) in Strasbourg, to which allegations that a Contracting State is not meeting one of its Convention obligations can be brought.[9] If a state is found wanting, either because of the provisions of its national law, or because of the actions or neglects of its authorities or its policies, it is for the Government of that state to remedy the situation by executive action or legal change. There is by now a considerable body of findings, in European Human Rights law, on the application of arts 8 and 10 of the Convention. Three deserve particular mention in the present context.

In *Spencer (Earl) v United Kingdom*, the Convention's Commission **9–03**
accepted that the breach of confidence action in English law had developed adequately as a method of protecting personal privacy.[10] Accordingly proceedings against the British Government for inadequate implementation of art.8 could not be brought until the complainants had exhausted their rights under municipal law. However, in *Peck v United Kingdom*,[11] the ECtHR took a much less accommodating view. A man suffering from acute mental distress was captured on a local authority's CCTV walking confusedly down a high street carrying a knife. Soon afterwards he used it to attempt suicide. The authority released their recorded shots to television stations which broadcast them. The release was intended to publicise the usefulness of CCTV not just to record criminal acts and to spot suspicious behaviour, but to watch out for people not able to look after themselves . The man's family

[8] Below, para.9–21. Sedley L.J. considered that s.12(4) must create a direct responsibility to give effect in private litigation to the Convention's freedom of expression right: *Douglas v Hello! (No. 1)* [2001] Q.B. 967. See further below, para.9–06.

[9] On this and other aspects of the functioning of the Convention and its relation to English law, see, e.g. Feldman, *Civil Liberties and Human Rights in England and Wales* 2nd edn (2002); Barendt, *Freedom of Speech* 2nd edn (2005); Fenwick and Phillipson, *Media Freedom under the Human Rights Act* (2006).

[10] *Spencer (Earl) v United Kingdom* (1998) 25 E.H.R.R. C.D. 113. In consequence the English right of action had first to be exhausted. The case concerned press revelations of Countess Spencer's admission to a medical clinic. The functions of the Commission have since been incorporated into those of the ECtHR.

[11] *Peck v United Kingdom* [2003] E.M.L.R.15.

and friends identified him because his face was not pixelated, and were distressed. There had been judicial review by an English court which had upheld the authority's release of the shots, but the ECtHR found that the standard applied was too low; and that there was no realistic prospect of an action for breach of confidence succeeding on the then state of English law. Accordingly the United Kingdom was providing no adequate protection of the man's privacy and was in breach of the Convention. As with decisions on other Convention rights, the ECtHR used to allow a margin of appreciation to national authorities; and in the context of freedom of expression there has been some readiness in the past to leave the media and others their own measure of choice in determining how to place material before the public.

Peck is one example in the balance between protectable privacy and permissible free expression, where the Court is insisting upon its own standards.[12] Another is *von Hannover v Germany*,[13] in which Princess Caroline of Monaco, married to the Prince von Hannover, raised a complaint before the ECtHR about being unrelentingly photographed by paparazzi when going about her ordinary life in public streets, shops, restaurants and the like. She complained that German law did not consider her art.8 rights to be invaded by specific examples of this surveillance, and asserted that Germany was in breach of the Convention. Finding in her favour, the Strasbourg Court held that the Convention obliged Member States, through legislation or court decision, to provide a right of action against a person who breached the privacy of other individuals in the manner that the Princess alleged.

Particularly after *Peck*, British judges have expanded the scope of privacy considerations in a number of circumstances, including actions in equity for breach of confidence.[14] Once the Human Rights Act 1998, in its special way, drew the art.8 and art.10 rights in the Convention into account in UK law, the question has arisen whether, in addition to directly affecting the liabilities of the Government in relation to private litigants, these provisions have a form of horizontal effect—direct or indirect—between private citizens. A direct (or "strong") horizontal effect would require that courts of Convention countries accord rights as between those citizens by virtue of the Convention itself. An indirect (or "weak") horizontal effect will only oblige those courts to have regard to the values enshrined in the Convention in determining the scope of their national law as it applies between individuals. To date most British judges have proved reluctant to accept that the

[12] Other prominent examples include the court's conclusions in the *Princess Caroline* and *Mitterand* cases: below, paras 9–03 and 9–12.

[13] *von Hannover v Germany* [2004] E.M.L.R. 21. The substantive allegations are considered in more detail, below, para.9–17.

[14] See further, Fenwick and Phillipson, *Media Freedom under the Human Rights Act* (2006); Barendt, *Freedom of Speech* 2nd edn (2005); Beverley-Smith, *The Commercial Appropriation of Personality* (2002), pp.214–224; and for comparative approaches, Beverley-Smith, Ohly and Lucas-Schloetter, *Privacy, Property and Personality* (2005).

Convention has a strong horizontal effect.[15] Given the inevitably controversial nature of the subject, this is scarcely surprising.[16] In *Campbell v MGN*, the House of Lords accepted that English law would in some circumstances treat photography of an individual in a public street without that person's assent as an actionable tort giving rise to damages and/or injunctive relief for subsequent publication of the picture. The celebrity supermodel, Naomi Campbell, had previously denied that she had a drug addiction, but photographs in the *Daily Mirror* showed her leaving a session at Narcotics Anonymous which she was attending in an order to cure her habit. By a bare majority, the House held that these particular circumstances did justify extending the scope of English tort law so far in order to recognise the "privacy" values immured in art.8.[17] The majority of their Lordships identified particular factors that gave rise to a reasonable expectation of privacy, despite the fact that the photographing took place in a public street. Nonetheless the House of Lords appear to keep legal liability more scrupulously constrained than did the ECtHR in *von Hannover*. For the present *Campbell* is the leading authority on the subject in English law and it is one that the Supreme Court is unlikely to overrule in a field where the national laws of Convention states each form their own meshes. Compare, for instance, the elaborate structure of German privacy law—as reviewed in *von Hannover*—with the now distinct actions under English law for breach of confidence and for invasion of privacy.

(3) Privacy: the English tradition

The historical background preceding this change needs to be appreciated. In **9–04**
1972, the Younger Committee considered that a general right of privacy should not be introduced into English law: it might be used too readily to trespass upon the freedom to receive and make use of information and to express opinions.[18] The Committee called instead for an examination of the scope of breach of confidence, which subsequently the English Law Commission undertook.[19] Its report proposed that the liability be expressed as a

[15] One of the first to advocate the strong approach was Wade (2000) 116 L.Q.R. 217; and some reflection of that approach can be seen, e.g., in *Douglas v Hello! (No.1)* [2001] Q.B. 967 at 1011, 1012 per Keene L.J. and at 1002 per Sedley LJ; in *A v B plc* [2003] Q.B. 195 at 202 per Woolf MR; in *Campbell v MGN* [2004] 2 A.C. 457 at 494 per Lady Hale; and in *McKennitt v Ash* [2008] Q.B. 73 per Buxton L.J.

[16] See, e.g. *Campbell v MGN* [2004] 2 A.C. 457 at 465 per Lord Nicholls and 472 per Lord Hoffmann; Lester and Pannick (2000) 116 L.Q.R. 380, 383; Clayton and Tomlinson, *Privacy and Freedom of Expression* (2010 2nd edn), para.12.166; Hare (2001) Eur HRLR 526, 533; Phillipson (2003) 66 M.L.R. 726, 729.

[17] For details of the factors taken into account, see below, para.9–18.

[18] Cmnd.5012, 1972. App.K quoted extensively from those who have sought to define privacy, starting with Judge Cooley's "the right to be left alone".

[19] Report No. 110 Breach of Confidence (Cmnd.8388, 1981).

statutory duty, couched in the concepts and language of tortious wrong. There would be, first of all, a duty to preserve confidence arising initially out of a confidential relationship, and extending to indirect recipients once they knew the true position. There would also be a duty to respect confidence in information acquired in seven other specified circumstances. These included: unauthorised interference with anything containing the information, being in a place without authority, using devices for surreptitious surveillance and the like. Hostility from the media meant that the Report was shelved. Tabloid and broadsheet newspapers alike continued to compete for readers by revealing the secrets of the mighty, the adulated and the humble, without count for the misery it would bring to its victims. Later the internal, voluntary regulator of the industry, which had evolved into the Press Complaints Commission, was found wanting. It was recommended that instead there should be a statutory tribunal with powers of investigation, injunction, fining and compensation; criminal penalties against various forms of physical intrusion for the purpose of obtaining personal information; and, once more, further consideration of a tort of invasion of privacy.[20] But no government was prepared to intervene so directly and Britain was left with the Press Complaints Commission and its self-enforced Privacy Code.

The courts showed very little inclination to fill the gap, so far as personal privacy was concerned.[21] In *Kaye v Robertson*[22] reporters from the *Sunday Sport* invaded the hospital room of a well-known actor who had been seriously injured, photographed him and published an "interview" with him that he was scarcely capable of comprehending. The Court of Appeal nonetheless held that no cause of action for infraction of privacy existed on which he could rely. In *Wainwright v Home Office*,[23] prison staff conducted a strip-search of relatives wanting to visit a prisoner, under regulations designed to keep out drugs, weapons and the like. But in doing so the naked visitors could be seen by people in another building. The House of Lords confirmed that no liability could arise at common law, short of the tort of intentionally inflicting nervous shock or other harm (for which the root authority is *Wilkinson v Downton*).[24] Since the officers had allowed the danger of nervous shock to arise only through their neglect and insensitivity,

[20] This was the eventual upshot of two official investigations for the Government by Sir David Calcutt: Cm.1102, 1990 (giving the press one last chance to get its house in order) and Cm.3215, 1993 (recommending legislative intervention).

[21] Contrast the expansion of confidence liability when the subject-matter was a business or government secret, as illustrated by the "*Spycatcher*" case and other decisions discussed above, in para.8–35.

[22] *Kaye v Robertson* [1991] F.S.R. 62 CA.

[23] *Wainwright v Home Office* [2003] 3 W.L.R. 1137.

[24] *Wilkinson v Downton* [1897] 2 Q.B. 57 CA. It was also essential to show sufficient causal connection between action and injury. Even if the tort had been made out, damages would be confined to compensation for physical injury or a recognised form of psychological disturbance.

there was no liability that could be attributed vicariously to the Home Office. The officers had not deliberately arranged a peep-show.[25]

In the United States, a right of privacy was famously conjured out of common law precedents (including breach of confidence) by Warren and Brandeis.[26] The underbelly of privacy is publicity. It seems that all but the most unremittingly secretive can be induced to reveal home truths at some price. Accordingly in the course of a century, the American right of privacy in turn bred a right of publicity, which gave celebrities the power to prevent unauthorised third parties from making commercial use of their names, endorsements, images, voices and other attributes of personality.[27] In defining such a right, American courts have had to separate what is commercially unacceptable conduct from what is desirable free speech. It has also been important to settle the duration of such rights, which come close to being a form of intellectual property.[28] These legal developments are part of an American willingnessto confer property rights upon value-generating activity, whatever its form.

By denying any distinct role to a right to privacy, English courts did not have to tackle the consequential questions surrounding publicity and its price. It left publicity arrangements very largely to the law of contract, supported by public law protections against misleading advertising and voluntary codes of conduct in the media, which included complaints procedures.

(4) Jurisdictions concerned with privacy

In the twentieth century, questions of privacy protection were largely formulated as actions for an injunction or damages arising out of a broad interpretation of the action for breach of confidence. This has particularly been so where the issue goes to the right of a media outlet to publicise true information about an individual. In the 1990s, however, there was an increasing number of actions under family law provisions concerning wardship, adoption, fostering or care provision for children and minors for orders that information of varying kinds be not made public.[29] By analogy, **9–05**

[25] The House refused to found liability on the fact that the visitors to the prison had been obliged to submit to the strip-search in order to gain admission, since they nonetheless consented to it. There could be cases where there was no consent at all to what happened, as for instance in a case of harassment (for which, see now the Protection from Harassment Act 1997). Even if the element of intent (including reckless indifference to the harm) had been satisfied, the victim would recover only if he or she suffered a recognised form of psychiatric disturbance: this could be established in the case of the son, not the mother. For an instance where the tort was made out, *C v D* [2006] EWHC 166.

[26] (1890) 4 Harv. L.R. 193; developed by Prosser, esp. in (1960) 48 Calif. L.R. 383.

[27] See McCarthy, *The Rights of Publicity and Privacy* (2000); and below, para.17–34.

[28] Various States have imposed statutory duration periods among other regulations of the right of publicity. See also below, paras 17–35–17–38.

[29] See below, paras 9–11, 9–17.

those responsible for the care of the mentally disabled have also been able to protect their charges from undue revelations about their private lives.[30]

Judicial review proceedings of executive decisions may also turn on a conflict between the right to private life, freedom of expression and the various public policies that can legitimately restrict privacy. For instance, are youths who receive Anti-Social Behaviour Orders because of their havoc on a housing estate entitled to prevent the police from afterwards publicising their names and photographs in their attempts to restore order and peace? A Divisional Court refused judicial review of the Police Commissioner's decision to make the defendants recognisable in the area. The publicity was justified by the very purpose of the ASBOs.[31] Is the Governor of a prison properly applying a regulation when he refuses to permit a particular prisoner to receive written material? In a case where the Governor's action was upheld, the Court of Appeal refused a review sought by the notorious killer, Dennis Nilsen, who was trying to get sight of a draft of his own autobiography which he had already sent out to an associate. Whatever the basis on which the question comes before an English court, the current tendency is to treat it as falling within its "human rights jurisdiction" growing out of the ECHR and the Human Rights Act 1998.[32] Our major concern is with the civil wrong of invasion of privacy, as it has grown from the action for breach of confidence and already appears to extend to a right of publicity. But we cannot neglect the occurrence of human rights issues across the range of personal concerns with which our courts now wrestle.

(5) Emergence of personal privacy action from breach of confidence

9–06 Within a short space, the courts have redefined breach of confidence so as to form it into a cause of action against invasions of the privacy of an individual. As the previous chapter has shown, confidence liability has long arisen where there is a discrete piece of information which a recipient has agreed to keep confidential for the provider. The action extends to situations where there is an agreement that work undertaken for a person which results in the generation of information shall be kept confidential by the person who does the work. Now there is also a right of action where the information is about how a person is or has been acting and this has been garnered by another who is a self-interested outside observer. He or she will be treated as a confidant because the information is of a kind that a reasonable person would know not to use or disclose. The precedents for this expansion of liability began to form in the 1990s in relation to government

[30] See, e.g. *Re a Local Authority* [2004] 1 W.L.R. 926.

[31] *R. (Stanley, Marshall and Kelly) v Metropolitan Police Commissioner* [2005] E.M.L.R. 3.

[32] For advantages of this broad approach in the family jurisdiction over publicity affecting children, see *Clayton v Clayton* [2007] E.M.L.R. 3. For a successful claim by corporations, *Société Colas Est v France* [2002] E.C.H.R. 421.

and business secrets.[33] Now in consequence of the Human Rights Act 1998, the same cause of action has been held to apply to personal information where that is needed to ensure "respect for ; his private and family life, his home and his correspondence". The crucial shift was first signalled by Sedley L.J. in *Douglas v Hello!(No. 1)*,[34] and affirmed by the Court of Appeal in *A v B and C*.[35] The House of Lords gave its *imprimatur* in *Campbell v MGN* and the Court of Appeal followed with its decision after the trial of the *Douglas* case;[36] and then in *McKennitt v Ash*,[37] *Associated Newspapers v Prince of Wales (HRH)*,[38] *Browne (Lord) v Associated Newspapers*,[39] and *Murray v Associated Newspapers*.[40]

As Lord Hoffmann has explained in *Campbell*:

> "... the new approach takes a different view of the underlying value which the law protects. Instead of a cause of action being based upon the duty of good faith applicable to confidential personal information and trade secrets alike, it focuses upon the protection of human autonomy and dignity—the right to control the dissemination of information about one's private life and the right to the esteem and respect of other people".[41]

Lord Nicholls was also clear that a new approach was being adopted. He doubted whether the liability could comfortably be related to the idea of confidence and went so far as to label it a tort.[42] This passing reference is having a domino effect on judges in subsequent cases, who accept that the change of classification is appropriate (though the Court of Appeal refused the temptation in the later *Douglas* case). Tort is after all a loose box in which many breeds of mount are kept. Which of them is the best stable-mate for the duty to respect privacy is more difficult to say. Until its own characteristics are better formed, there is something to be said for keeping it as a type of liability which approximates to that for "classic" breach of confidence. Certainly the "intense focus" that is called for when the right of privacy falls to be balanced against freedom of the media has a fluid quality that seems apposite to an equitable jurisdiction which takes all the circumstances of each case into account.[43]

[33] Above, para.8–20.
[34] [2001] Q.B. 967 at 1001 (interlocutory proceedings: for later stages, see below, para.9–20).
[35] [2003] Q.B. 195.
[36] *Douglas v Hello! (No.3)* [2006] Q.B. 125 CA; (but for its treatment by the HL as a simple breach of confidence, see below, para.9-20)
[37] [2008] Q.B. 73 (see below, para.9–18).
[38] [2008] Ch. 57 (see below, para.9–12).
[39] [2008] Q.B.103 (see below, para.9–18).
[40] [2008] E.C.D.R. 12.
[41] [2004] 2 A.C. 457. Lord Nicholls and Lord Hoffmann put the change more strongly than other members of the House. They were, however, the two dissentients on the facts of the case who favoured a finding for the defendant newspaper: see below, para.9–16.
[42] See generally, Schreiber [2006] I.P.Q. 160.
[43] See below, n.83.

In search of what may count as "human autonomy and dignity", rights language has become increasingly fecund. The ECtHR has stated that the right conferred by art.8 covers both the right of an individual to live as he or she chooses and the right to establish and develop social relationships, flowing from the human capacity to think and communicate.[44] Adorned with poetical quotation and philosophical reference, this is leading to such conclusions as:

> "Article 8 thus embraces both the right to maintain one's privacy and, if this is what one prefers, not merely the right to waive that privacy but also the right to share what would otherwise be private with others or, indeed, with the world at large. So the right to communicate one's story to one's fellow beings is protected not merely by Art.10 but also by Art.8."[45]

9–07 This breadth of conception seems intended to reinforce the claim to legal support for the individual with only a minimum of qualification or counterbalance. What this treatment achieves is much debated, for it has characteristics that associate it with the reluctance in breach of confidence law to admit a defence or limitation of "public interest" save in very clear cases.[46] At the same time, it would appear to confer the right to exploit one's image and information about oneself as one chooses and accordingly to commercialise it. That links closely to a typical feature of traditional breach of confidence—that the action is frequently used to keep information secret to the extent best calculated for maximum return to the claimant.

2. Constituent Elements of Privacy Claims

9–08 Invasion of privacy may arouse strong feelings of repugnance and legal intervention may well be an appropriate response. But the scope of any liability needs to be given more precise definition. The following characteristics form a basis for analysis:

(1) The right arises where the claimant had a reasonable expectation that information about an individual or individuals (the "privacy subjects"), or other act done in relation to them, will remain private.
(2) The claimant may be the privacy subject or a carer for that person or persons. The right of action is purely personal and may not be assigned or licensed to other persons, so as to allow the latter to

[44] *Niemetz v Germany* (1993) 16 E.H.R.R. 97 at [29]; *Botta v Italy* (1998) 26 E.H.R.R. 241 para.32; *Bensaid v United Kingdom* (2001) 33 E.H.R.R. 205 at [46–47]; *Pretty v United Kingdom* (2002) 35 E.H.R.R. 1 at [61], where an individual's "right to self-determination" is hazarded.

[45] Munby J. *Re Roddy* [2004] E.M.L.R. 8 at [31–32]; see also *Re X and Y* [2004] E.M.L.R. 29.

[46] See above, paras 8–15 et seq.

enforce it in their own interest. It is doubtful whether a corporate body or other commercial, financial or governmental entity is itself entitled to privacy by virtue of ECHR art.8, which would give it a right of action.

(3) The right may continue after there has been some revelation of the information, but it is questionable how far it may survive the person's death.

(4) The right is breached by misuse or disclosure of the private information but other acts invading privacy may in themselves constitute the wrong.

(5) To be liable the defendant must know, or ought to know, about the expectation of privacy.

(6) The defendant is not liable where sufficient justification for the invasion of privacy can be made out.

(7) Where that justification arises by virtue of the human right of free expression guaranteed in the ECHR, art.10, neither party bears the onus of establishing or overriding the justification; instead the court strikes a balance by weighing all the considerations itself.

(8) A person's right of privacy may have effect even when he or she intends to exploit the information commercially or as a presentation to the public.

(1) Reasonable expectation of privacy

In the leading authority on liability for breach of personal privacy, *Campbell v MGN*, Lord Nicholls expressed the prime criterion thus: **9–09**

> "Essentially the touchstone of private life is whether in respect of the disclosed facts the person in question has a reasonable expectation of privacy."[47]

The test has been put by Gleeson C.J. of the Australian High Court in more elaborate, and much quoted, terms:

> "An activity is not private simply because it is not done in public ... Certain kinds of information about a person, such as information relating to health, personal relationships, or finances, may be easy to identify as private, as may certain kinds of activity which a reasonable person, applying contemporary standards of morals and behaviour, would understand to be meant to be unobserved. The requirement that disclosure or observation of information or conduct would be highly

[47] *Campbell v MGN* [2004] A.C. 457 at [21], also stated by other members of the House at paras 85, 134, 165 (Lord Hope, Lady Hale, Lord Carswell).

offensive to a reasonable person of ordinary sensibilities is in many circumstances a useful practical test of what is private."[48]

The standard of what is "highly offensive" derives in particular from Dean Prosser's well-known advocacy of a right of privacy in US law.[49] It has been to some extent criticised by members of the House of Lords in the *Campbell* case as setting too high a standard for a claimant to satisfy.[50] But if the last sentence is read, as it should be, together with that preceding it, which points out that much that is private is easily identified, or derives from accepted standards, it does not appear exaggerated.[51] Inevitably there will be pressure to extend the boundaries of the new wrong beyond situations that fall within the core of liability. What for instance of advertising that uses a celebrity's image or voice without permission, or worse still, brings in an impersonator to play the person? Are such acts an invasion of individual autonomy whenever they occur, or only when there is a special aggravation or hurt in the circumstances? Can a photograph of a "non-celebrity" in a public place, snapped without permission, be forbidden for any commercial purpose or only when it would cause special embarrassment or other disadvantage?[52] Is it justified to order a newspaper not to reveal the sites of existing and intended homes for disturbed children in its locality because the interests of the children deserve to prevail over that of residents who object to the homes in their backyards?[53]

9–10 In recent decades British society has become rather more plural in its moral values. Accordingly it is highly desirable for judges not to be swayed by their personal value systems. If they do, their attitudes will vary and palm tree justice will prevail. In the twentieth century, when privacy claims had to be formulated in terms of breach of confidence, protection was granted to

48 *Australian Broadcasting Corp v Lenah Game Meats* (2001) 185 A.L.R. 1 at [14]. In Commonwealth jurisdictions where no guarantee of the human right to privacy is expressed in law, courts have become more active in pursuing the protection of privacy, partly as a reflection of recent developments in the United Kingdom. In Australia, as the *Lenah* case shows, the tendency has been to extend the scope of breach of confidence liability. In New Zealand, by contrast, the common law is treated as admitting a claim to personal privacy as a separate wrong—as occurred in *Hosking v Runting* (below, n.52).

49 Prosser (1960) 48 Calif. L.R. 383, 396–97.

50 Above, n.35, paras 22, 135–136 (Lord Nicholls, Lady Hale).

51 See [2004] A.C. 457 at paras 93–94, 116 (Lords Hope and Carswell). Note also, Lord Walker *M v Secretary for Work and Pensions* [2006] 2 A.C. 91 at [83].

52 When the subject is a young child, and any celebrity attaches only to its parent or parents, the Court of Appeal has held that the child has reasonable expectation of privacy against intrusive photography in a public place: *Murray v Express Newspapers* [2008] ECDR 12 (see below, n.101). The New Zealand CA in *Hosking v Runting* [2005] 1 N.Z.L.R. 1, reached the same result on very similar facts, but in rather more qualified terms.

53 In *Green Corns v Claverley Group* [2005] E.M.L.R. 31, this relief was granted to an organisation which ran such homes, at a time when the issue was being debated among people of the area. Would the same apply to probation or bail hostels or halfway houses for the mentally ill?

information that a person was in a homosexual relationship or had a sexually transmitted disease, where there was no special case justifying its revelation.[54] In the Human Rights Act era, the same non-judgmental attitudes have continued, for instance, when granting privacy rights over a person's treatment for drug addiction.[55] At the same time, courts emphasise the need to examine all the facts, particularly where a defendant maintains that the populace as a whole had a sufficient interest to know the truth about people in the public eye.

Once a legal system starts comparing aspects of conduct relatively, it is often difficult to separate general value systems from judgments about the motivation of individuals before the court. In *CD v BB*, the claimant was a husband who had had an affair with the defendant's wife. When the defendant threatened to get revenge by exposing the liaison, the claimant sought and obtained an interlocutory injunction against publication. It was an important part of the decision in his favour that it was not for the Court to condemn adultery as an affront to matrimony.[56] On the other hand the defendant was stigmatised for making plain that he was out for the claimant's notional blood through a press story. Against him as the cuckold, the moral appeared to be that, however upset or annoyed, thou should have turned the other cheek. Whereas in favour of the lover: thou shalt not be exposed for committing adultery, at least if it has been non-casual and you both "want to move on".

To look at another boundary, what if the protection that is being sought concerns an individual's activities in employment or other economic activity? Certainly, one's salary and tax return have been treated as part of private affairs by the ECtHR.[57] A journalist who practised the refined art of exposure by entrapment, tried to inveigle George Galloway MP into indiscretions, but the disguise he used did not succeed. By way of riposte, Galloway's political party, Respect, put the journalist's photo on its website in order to expose his activities. He duly objected, claiming that his method of catching the unscrupulous out involved adopting various personae; to make his appearance known therefore destroyed the privacy essential to his modus operandi. He was refused interim relief because he was unlikely to establish a case at trial that any right to private life was involved in turning the tables on him—a matter on which, arguably, Mr Galloway's right of free expression was in any case the stronger claim.[58] Likewise over allegations that a very senior executive of British Petroleum had used his position to

[54] See *Stephens v Avery* [1988] F.S.R. 510 (lesbian relationship); *H v Associated Newspapers* [2002] E.M.L.R. 23 (information for patients).

[55] As in the *Campbell* case, above, n.16.

[56] Relying on *Stephens v Avery* (above, n.54) where an order was made protecting against revelation of a lesbian relationship).

[57] *Fressoz and Roire v France* (2001) 31 E.H.R.R. 2 (the fact that a car factory boss was receiving a large earnings increase at a time when his workers were on strike was properly published as a matter of public interest).

[58] *Mahmood v Galloway* [2006] E.M.L.R. 26.

provide financial benefits to his (then) homosexual partner—again a case where the public had an interest in knowing about this behaviour that was not just a desire for newsworthy gossip.[59] Insisting upon detailed evaluation of all the facts renders the trial judge's assessment hard to attack in appellate proceedings; the case must show that the judge has fallen into error that was in some sense "a matter of principle".

These formulations of the test stress its objective nature. That should be advantageous in cases where the court suspects that the claimant is exaggerating his or her sense of outrage.[60] It will also help in a case such as *Kaye v Robertson*,[61] where the hospitalised actor was in no condition to decide anything about an interview with reporters, but a reasonable person would undoubtedly conclude that it should not take place without permission. It would supply a basis for action in English law that the ECtHR found wanting in the sad circumstances of *Peck v Home Office*.[62] As that case shows, a court should be cautious in taking account of the reactions that other people (notably family and friends) may have to disclosure of the private information. In most cases this should be relevant only in so far as it supplies a reason why the data subject could reasonably want to keep the information private.[63] When the separate privacy of all concerned has to be considered, the result can only be confusion.

(2) Claimants: data subjects and carers; legal persons and similar entities

9–11 An invasion of privacy results in an action personal to the victim of the breach. However, the powers of courts to protect children, the mentally disabled and others impeded from looking after themselves may be invoked by those who assume responsibility for them. They may raise questions in relation to specific statutory restrictions, such as those which govern the reporting of criminal trials, or they may call upon general supervisory jurisdictions. The range of interests that can arise in cases of this kind may be considerable. We shall consider several situations in relation to balancing rights of privacy against those of free expression.[64] Here it is important to distinguish the role of carers and the like from those who claim a right in the data subject's privacy by a property-like transfer from that person.[65]

One issue which goes to the relationship between the ECHR, art.8, and legal rights and responsibilities under the laws of Convention states concerns whether the right to privacy ordained by art.8 applies in any sense to

[59] *Browne (Lord) v Associated Newspapers* [2008] Q.B. 103.
[60] For instance, Sir Elton John failed to gain interlocutory relief after a journalist snapped him coming out of his house, despite the latter's unlikely story of being there quite by chance: *John v Associated Newspapers* [2006] E.M.L.R. 27.
[61] Above, n.22.
[62] Above, n.11.
[63] See further below, para.9–23.
[64] Below, paras 9–16 et seq.
[65] This separate issue is discussed below, para.9–22.

legal persons, such as corporations and statutory bodies. In its English version, art.8(1) uses concepts which seem to link its objective to the personality of individuals: "private and personal life ... home ... correspondence." It was this restricted sense that Lord Mustill espoused, in saying that a corporate body could suffer no affront to the personality, because it "has no sensitivities to wound, and no selfhood to protect"; accordingly any claim to protection of privacy that it might have would arise beyond the bounds of art.8.[66] The ECtHR, however, has once held that a legal person may fall within the compass of the Article. In *Société Colas Est v France*,[67] the French authority investigating breaches of the country's rules of competition executed a raid on three companies in the construction industry. Letters were obtained showing the firms to be engaging in unlawful concerted practices and for this they were fined in French proceedings. On the complaint under the Convention, the ECtHR ruled that art.8 could in certain circumstances be understood to include a right to respect for a company's registered office, branches and other business premises.[68] Since the French competition legislation contained no restraints on searches, it was held to be disproportionate and therefore could not be excused under art.8(2) as being "in accordance with the law". In *Varec v Belgium,* the European Court of Justice had occasion, when dealing with the procedure for reviewing the award of a public procurement contract, to conclude that art.8 conferred its fundamental human right on a legal, as well as a natural person, in order to protect its trade secrets.[69] However, in any national system (such as now the English) which has developed a cause of action to protect the confidentiality associated with such secrets, how far the Convention adds anything to the national position remains obscure.[70] In the sphere of business activities, whether conducted by corporations or individuals, it makes sense to express liability in terms that relate to the commercial value of information as such, and that is what such national laws achieve.[71]

---

[66] *R v Broadcasting Standards Commission Ex p. BBC* [2001] Q.B. 892. Hale L.J. also doubted whether the BSC, as a statutory body, could have art.8 rights, finding rather that legal protection of its private activities (such as its board meetings) was to be found, expressly or impliedly, in the UK statute which created it.

[67] *Société Colas Est v France*(2004) 39 EHRR 97. See Emberland (2003) 25 Mich J Int L 77.

[68] The court accordingly ordered France to pay modest awards of "just compensation" under the ECHR art.41.

[69] *Varec v Belgium,* [2008] C.M.L.R. 24, reversing its earlier position in *Hoechst v European Commission* [1991] 4 C.M.L.R. 410. See Oliver [2009] C.M.Law Rev. 1443.

[70] In *Varec,* the nub of the case concerned how far the Belgian Conseil d'Etat, in reviewing the award, should keep the contents of the winning competitor's contract from the loser, because of the trade secrets in it. Weasel-fashion, the ECJ left it to that court to decide how to balance the conflicting interests that thereby arose.

[71] An individual acting in a business capacity may still be accorded art.8 protection—perhaps an awkward distinction, but one that it is better to accept: see *Niemetz v Germany* (1992) 16 E.H.R.R. 97; Ford [2002] Ind.L.J. 135.

(3) Duration of the claim

9–12 In the modern law of *confidence* it has been held that the obligation cannot continue once the information in question becomes publicly available, at least through a source unconnected with the defendant. Thereafter it loses its capacity to be confidential subject-matter.[72] But that is not necessarily the case when the claim is based on personal privacy. Individuals have been permitted to claim that their private life is invaded when more people learn revealing facts about them than those to whom they passed the information in confidence. Thus in *Associated Newspapers v Prince of Wales (HRH)*,[73] one of the Prince's staff fed to a newspaper a diary kept by the Prince when attending the handover ceremony of Hong Kong to China. It apparently contained Wodehouse-ish aspersions on other participants, and his staff in dealing with it were under clear obligations of confidence, both by express contract and as part of their relationship. As was his custom, he had this diary circulated to friends (perhaps numbering 50–75), marked "Private and Confidential". In finding that the obligation of confidence remained even after that, the Court of Appeal held it to be enough that the person possessing the information did not intend that it should become available to others or imparted to the public.[74] There remained a privacy interest, which, when measured against the newspaper's right of free expression, was held to prevail.[75]

Even if a person entitled to privacy dies, it may be that their family members have their own claim to protection against disclosures that will cause them emotional upset. The ECtHR has accepted that President Mitterand's family could object to publication of details of his medical history, which had been given out in evident breach of confidence by his doctor immediately after his death. These showed that throughout his terms of office Mitterand suffered in secret from prostate cancer and lied about it. In this instance, when it came to weighing the competing rights, the distress of relatives could only override the evident public interest in the subject-matter for some three months. Thereafter, according to the ECtHR, the French courts should have lifted the injunction against publication.[76]

(4) Defendant's breach

9–13 The core subject matter involved in most invasions of personal privacy is information and the wrong consists in misusing it. The wrong is therefore complete only at the place of misuse, such as publication. That may confer

[72] See above, para.8–12.
[73] *Associated Newspapers v Prince of Wales (HRH)* [2008] Ch. 57.
[74] *Associated Newspapers* [2008] Ch. 57 at [33], relying on *Douglas v Hello (No.3)* [2006] Q.B. 125 at [55, 83] CA.
[75] For this subsequent step, see below, para.9–16.
[76] *Editions Plon v France* (2006) 42 E.H.R.R. 36; and see below, n.87.

jurisdiction on the courts of that place to hear an action for the invasion of privacy, and may determine the applicable law pertaining to it.[77] What will constitute that misuse is ultimately to be determined by the court judging the issue. Entering a contractual relationship requiring confidence over personal information or activity does not of itself increase the scope of what is protected. If nonetheless the term of a contract defines what uses are not permitted and they fall within the range of the law's protection, the term is likely to set the boundary of legal protection for the private material.

What then of conduct against privacy subjects which does not follow the "breach of confidence" pattern where information is gained and only then exploited? Since the Convention right includes respect for private and family life and home, it can scarcely be limited to the misuse of discrete information. In the *Wainwright* case—decided before the Human Rights Act took effect—the family members wanting to visit a prisoner were searched naked in a position where outsiders might see them.[78] That degrading incident of itself surely lacked respect for private life and that would appear now to fall within art.8(1). But whether the cause of action lies in respect of conduct that is not deliberate and/or which gives rise to no specific psychological disturbance are separate questions to which we return below.

(5) The defendant's state of mind

We have seen that the action of breach of confidence lies against a recipient **9–14**
of the secret information, direct or indirect, even when he receives it without knowing of the breach. He may be enjoined from misusing it from the time that he is told that the information is confidential.[79] It is that moment, so it seems, that imposes the obligation to behave in good faith on the recipient. This may be a just outcome for at least some cases where there is a time lag between receipt of the information and use of it (although the extent of protection is open to criticism). But what of the case where the initial invasion is itself the wrong, as in the *Wainwright* illustration? In that case at common law tortious harm would occur only if the defendant's conduct was deliberately aimed at injuring the privacy subject so as to cause medically recognised injury. The House of Lords demonstrated their belief that these limitations were justified as necessary barriers against the unremitting spread of tortious liability for causing emotional distress. At least until the ECtHR rules plainly otherwise, it is for British courts to settle the legal limits upon restraint against privacy invasions and recovery for their occurrence. The confinement of damage awards in *Wainwright* should not be abandoned for situations not involving communication of information

[77] See, in general, above, paras 2–74 et seq. The issue was crucial in the *Douglas* case, since the initial invasion of privacy occurred at the New York wedding but the improper publication by *Hello!* was in England.

[78] See above, para.9–04, n.23.

[79] See above, para.8–38.

without most careful consideration. When it comes to communicative uses, the limits of the right can be addressed by countervailing considerations of public interest and perhaps by limiting the range of cases that give rise to a claim for monetary relief, rather than just an injunction against future conduct. These factors are discussed in the next paragraphs.

(6) Justifiable disclosures: general

9–15 The principles governing breach of confidence in English law have developed limitations which allow the disclosure of information where there is a public interest to know, provided that the extent of the disclosure is proportionate to the need.[80] Where the claim to protection arises from an invasion of personal privacy, this notion is being adapted to cover, for example, a legitimate counter-interest of the person who obtains the information. The nature of personal material claimed to be confidential may provide just cause for revealing it in the way that has happened or is proposed. This will particularly be so where the material is iniquitous.[81] In *D v L*,[82] for instance, a woman, whose long-term relationship with a man was breaking down, secretly recorded conversations with him in order to procure evidence for domestic violence proceedings. The man sought an injunction, in proceedings concerning their interests in their house, requiring passages to be removed from the tapes which referred to a particular aspect of his sexual proclivities (as the report describes it). The Court of Appeal agreed that the injunction should not be granted. Waller L.J.'s judgment measured the man's right to privacy against the woman's own right of expression. Her right prevailed. She was not proposing to make any use of the tapes except in the violence proceedings. The case was therefore not one in which the media's freedom of expression was in issue. There had already been statements in court and in the media about the sexual proclivities of both, so that further revelations would not be particularly damaging. Threatening behaviour by the man meant that he did not have clean hands. A highly equitable balancing of what is just in the particular circumstances is thus the mark of this jurisdiction.

(7) Justifiable disclosures: freedom of expression in the media

9–16 The right of free expression, guaranteed by the EHRC in art.10(1), is qualified by necessary counter-considerations laid down in art.10(2). Nonetheless its high significance as a fundamental principle of a democratic state is much emphasised by the ECtHR, as well as by courts of the United

[80] See above, paras 8–15—8–18.

[81] *Maccaba v Lichtenstein* [2005] E.M.L.R. 6: the claimant had written passionate poems and other things to another man's wife, which the defendant sought to use in persuading him to moderate his conduct. The claimant's own conduct was too quixotic for any hope of relief.

[82] *D v L* [2004] E.M.L.R. 1 CA.

Kingdom and other Member States. Even the expression of antagonism towards groups on grounds of race, colour, gender, religion or sexual orientation has, in large measure, to be permitted. The concern of this chapter, however, is not with the limits to such tolerance but with public expressions that involve the identification of individuals and concern their right to private and family life, home or correspondence. Not therefore with articles or pamphlets that denounce a minority group as terrorists or leeches, but with material that picks on the behaviour of one person or family in order to demonstrate loathing of them or their kind.

In the majority of cases raising privacy rights, art.8 protection has to be weighed against art.10 freedom. English courts hold that there is no inherent preference of the right to private life or the right to free expression in their interpretations of the two articles. Given that each right is itself subject to the limitations expressed in the EHRC, the courts apply no presumptions or burdens of proof. As Lord Steyn expresses it:

> "First, neither Article has as such precedence over the other. Secondly, where the values under the two articles are in conflict, an intense focus on the comparative importance of the specific rights being claimed in the individual case is necessary. Thirdly, the justifications for interfering with or restricting each right must be applied to each. Finally, the proportionality test must be applied to each."[83]

Particularly when interlocutory relief is being sought, the proportionality of what each side seeks from the court is likely to be much emphasised.[84] On the one hand, the claimant's right to protection will vary the nature of the private information; on the other, the defendant will be claiming freedom to expose the information to a range of recipients who may be an individual, a limited group or the general public. These and other considerations will provide parameters in what may be a complex evaluation. Similar thinking has been apparent in the law of confidence ever since courts began to assess whether a countervailing public interest justified the disclosure of otherwise secret information.[85]

Where the two rights are in opposition to one another, the right of **9–17** expression is likely to be limited to information of genuine public interest or concern, as distinct from material simply of interest to the public.[86] A striking example of the former, already mentioned, was the cover-up of Président Mitterand's failing health on which the ECtHR ruled in *Editions*

---

[83] *Re S (FC)* [2005] 1 A.C. 593 HL. For earlier English case law of the same type, see Lord Steyn, at para.22. The speeches of both majority and minority in *Campbell v MGN* [2004] 2 A.C. 457, are the source from which this epitome is distilled.

[84] See especially, *A v B Plc*, below, n.119.

[85] See above, paras 8–15 and 8–18.

[86] *Prince of Wales v Associated Newspapers* [2008] Ch. 73 at [50].

Plon v France.[87] As to the latter, the photographers who tracked the daily life of Princess Caroline were merely providing the stuff of public gossip. The case for her privacy claim was accordingly enhanced, as it was also by the fact that she performed no public role for the Principality of Monaco.[88] In earlier decisions on the balance as it affected journalists pursuing celebrities, it was considered that a line must be drawn between what happened on private property and in public places, the latter being free territory for paparazzi. The German law to which she objected drew a line of this type. The ECtHR refused to accept it. But what degree of press hounding is now legally impermissible, in a case where there is not the added element of uncovering a truth previously denied, cannot at present be defined—an uncertainty which itself puts media freedom in splints. In the case itself, the evidence was of unending persistence by numerous press organs, some of which were defendants in the German proceedings. It is far from clear, under English legal procedure, how the activities of an informal, highly competitive, group of pursuers should be brought into account in orders against any one of them. The issuing of injunctions against the world is a step that should be adopted only in extreme cases.[89]

If the publicity about a person comes from an official source, the infraction of private life may be justified as falling within one of the necessary public purposes laid down in art.8(2). But not only is it necessary to fit the case within one of the specified purposes; the breach must be "in accordance with the law". The ECtHR found that where a prosecution office followed its practice of releasing to the press its identification photograph of a person arrested on suspicion of serious crime, the art.8(1) invasion could not be justified as there was no law regulating the practice.[90]

9–18 If there is a pre-existing undertaking to respect confidence, protection against publication is often enhanced. This was clearly so with Prince Charles' application for an injunction to protect the diary sent to the press by a disloyal secretary on his staff.[91] Likewise when Niema Ash, an admirer and confidante of the Canadian folk-singer, Loreena McKennitt, spilled stories of their acquaintance in a book which went into intimate details, by no means all of them true. Before setting off on a tour together, Ms McKennitt's agent had presented Ms Ash with a contract containing a confidentiality clause, but Ms Ash did not sign it until much later. Nonetheless the circumstances at the outset of the tour showed that Ms Ash clearly understood that confidence was to prevail.[92]

---

[87] *Editions Plon v France* (2006) 42 E.H.R.R. 36; see also *Fressoz and Roire v France* (2001) 31 E.H.R.R. 2. Neither decision left room for appreciation of the situation by the national courts involved.

[88] See above, n.13.

[89] As to how far an English court would follow *von Hannover* see the cautious appreciation by Buxton L.J. in *McKennitt v Ash* [2008] Q.B. 73 at [37–42], [58–59].

[90] *Sciacca v Italy* (2005) Case 50774/99.

[91] [2008] Ch. 75.

[92] *McKennitt v Ash* [2008] Q.B. 73 CA.

In the moral maze thus entered, judges may run up different alleys, some of them blind. The *Campbell* case concerned a tempestuous claimant who had persistently denied any addiction to drugs. The *Daily Mirror* exposed this as a lie in an article built around photos of her in the street in order to attend a group therapy session at Narcotics Anonymous. Paparazzi got the pictures thanks to a leak from Ms Campbell's staff or from within NA. The article commended her for seeking treatment. For the majority of the Lords, the degree of distress to her in her fragile condition, enhanced by the immediacy of the photographs, carried the intrusion well beyond the permissible. The minority stressed that some of her unhappiness stemmed from being shown to be a liar, and pointed out that the photos were simply of her smiling in a public street. So they considered that what was published and the comment upon it was within the realm of editorial discretion. In their view the claim should not have succeeded. This difference of opinion is not just over the result to be reached on these particular facts. It shows a variation of view about the impact of visual images in the media. And it suggests considerable differences in attitude towards the degree to which courts should enter into criticism of how the press chooses to tell its story in detail. Certainly there have been decisions of the ECtHR that advocate leaving the details of presentation to the press.[93] Otherwise there is the very real danger that the imprimatur of a court will be required before there can be any publication, despite the limits to prior restraint laid down in the Human Rights Act s.12.[94] That in itself would be a considerable threat to media freedom to report and comment.

Particular values that have been emphasised in striking the balance between privacy and free expression include the following:

(1) Publicity of proceedings in a criminal trial is itself an important value in the panoply of human rights, protecting against secrecy and absence of public scrutiny in the administration of justice.[95] The extent to which a court is empowered to take steps to prevent such reporting is to a considerable extent governed by specific statutory provisions.[96] Further prohibitions, deriving from the general principles of arts 8(1) and 10(2) of the EHRC, accordingly need clear justification. In *Re S (FC)*, a mother was being tried for murder of her elder son by poisoning. On her younger son's behalf, an application

[93] *Jersild v Denmark* (1994) 19 E.H.R.R. 1 para.31; *Fressoz and Roire v France* (2001) 31 E.H.R.R. 2.

[94] See below, para.9–21.

[95] ECHR art.6; Human Rights Act 1998 s.6. See, e.g. *Axen v Germany* (1983) 6 E.H.R.R. 195; *Diennet v France* (1995) 21 E.H.R.R. 554; and for long recognition of the same principle in the UK, *Scott v Scott* [1913] A.C. 417 HL.

[96] Where the child is the victim of the crime, as where a father organised the rape of his 11-year-old daughter by another paedophile while he was watching, any non-publicity order concerning her is governed by the Children and Young Persons Act 1933 s.39, and its bounds should not be overstepped: *Ex p. Gazette Media* [2005] E.M.L.R. 34

was made to prevent the publication of any information from which he could be identified, including his name and address and that of his school, and any photograph of him or either parent.[97] The trial judge's balance in favour of no restriction on such identification was affirmed in the House of Lords, who emphasised the need for reporting that was not disembodied and could occur in timely fashion without having to go before a court for approval. The view to the contrary taken by the Court of Appeal was not accepted, criticism being offered of Hale L.J.'s view that the need for full reporting of criminal trials was greater when there was a conviction than an acquittal.[98] There remains a distinction to be drawn between the reporting of the trial and other publicity concerning the victims or their relatives. A local authority secured an order against publishing information about a six-year-old girl whose father was accused of murdering her mother, but the order created an exception for reporting his trial.[99]

(2) By way of contrast, in the notorious case of the murder of the two-year-old James Bulger by two 10-year-olds, it was decided that the two young convicts would, on release from custody, be given new identities. Butler-Sloss P. ordered against the world that their anonymity should be strictly respected.[100]

(3) The immaturity or disability of children may be a special reason for their parents or carers seeking to protect them from distress that would flow from others learning what they looked like or private truths about them. Hence it shattered the privacy of JK Rowling's son to photograph him in his pushchair being wheeled by his parents.[101] Particularly difficult are cases where a young person who has engaged in anti-social conduct or been involved in distressing circumstances wishes to make money later out of the story, but other family members wish still to preserve their own privacy or carers think the publicity inadvisable. In *Re Roddy*, it was held that if the child was sufficiently mature to decide for herself whether she wanted to make her private affairs public, her decision must be respected, however undesirable it might appear to her parents or other carers.[102] This was said to follow from the controversial construction of art.8(1)

[97] The application was made under the inherent jurisdiction exercised by the Family Division, legislative provisions on the restriction of reporting in relation to juveniles being inapplicable to the case of a non-witness brother of the victim.

[98] [2005] E.M.L.R. at [30].

[99] *A Local Authority v PD* [2005] E.M.L.R. 35.

[100] *Venables and Thompson v News Group* [2001] 1 All E.R. 908.

[101] *Murray v Associated Newspapers* [2008] E.C.D.R. 12

[102] *Re Roddy* [2004] E.M.L.R. 8; and for a similar approach to an adult with mental disability, the onus being on the carer to show that the person did not have capacity to make the decision: *Re A Local Authority* [2004] Fam. 96. As to the position of expert witnesses in such cases, see *British Broadcasting Corporation v Rochdale MBC* [2006] E.M.L.R. 6.

as itself giving an individual the right to build relationships with others.[103] Equivalent concerns arise in respect of those under official supervision because of their mental impairment.[104]

(4) There may be a pressing need to make a limited disclosure to others, where their health comes in issue. In *H v Associated Newspapers and N Health Authority*,[105] a health authority discovered that one of its doctors was HIV positive. It therefore needed to conduct a "look-back exercise" in which patients treated by the doctor were informed so that they could receive further treatment or counselling. To what extent, could the doctor object to the revelation of his name or even his field of medical speciality in the authority's own notifications or in press coverage? In a breach of confidence action before publication, the Court of Appeal made a detailed order to deal with these difficult circumstances. It instructed the authority what it should and should not do; and it allowed the newspaper defendant to publish the specialism but not the name of the doctor.[106] Here can be seen both the extent to which the remedy in the privacy action can be adapted to fit particular circumstances and the virtues of weighing numerous factors to resolve a situation of great delicacy and concern.

(8) The data subject's interest: continued secrecy or exploitation

To what extent have the new decisions acknowledged that the data subject's interest can be protected when their primary motivation is to take commercial advantage of the information by their own publicising of it? In other words, is the right as much to publicity as to privacy? In *Douglas v Hello! (No. 3)*,[107] the film stars' wedding, a categorically private event, was at the same time being milked by them for its value. Each had signed a contract for US $500,000 with the magazine, *OK!* (the direct rival of the defendant, *Hello!*) giving *OK!* the exclusive right to publish photos of the wedding. The photographs were, however, commissioned by the Douglases and they were to decide which would appear. The Court of Appeal held that these financial arrangements did not prevent *their* claim from arising. In ordinary breach of confidence claims, the right often serves to protect commercial value and the court considered that the same should apply to invasion of privacy. Moreover, the contracts led to the security arrangements to exclude 9–19

[103] See above, para.9–06.

[104] *E v Channel Four* [2005] E.M.L.R. 30.

[105] *H v Associated Newspapers and N Health Authority* [2002] EWCA Civ 195. Cf. *Selisto v Finland* [2005] E.M.L.R. 8: Press comment referred to an unnamed surgeon who, allegedly while drunk, caused the death of a named patient. A majority of ECtHR held that the newpaper should not have been fined for defamation by a Finnish court because the discussion was on a matter of public importance and so "necessary in a democratic society" within art.10(2).

[106] cf. *X Health Authority v Y* [1988] R.P.C. 379; and see *W v Edgell* [1990] Ch. 359, CA; above, at para.8–17.

[107] *Douglas v Hello! (No. 3)* [2006] Q.B. 125.

paparazzi. Privacy was therefore an essential part of the arrangements. The control that the pair kept over which photographs would be given to *OK!* was designed to ensure that they appeared only in best bloom. Their real objection to the photographs secretly taken by the paparazzo was that they were of poor quality and showed Mrs Douglas in less than flattering moments.[108] Hence they were entitled in particular to damages for the injury to their feelings and (so it would appear) for damage that may have been done to their own promotion of themselves as film-stars.[109]

9–20 How far, if at all, the general right to confidence can be regarded as proprietary in the same sense as discrete intellectual property was discussed in the previous chapter, where it was noted that answers to that question remain obscure.[110] With the emerging right to privacy, data subjects (and carers who act to protect them) have purely personal rights and cannot assign the right to another, as was held by the Court of Appeal in *Douglas v Hello (No. 3)*.[111] *OK!*, the magazine which had purchased exclusive rights to publish the Douglas's wedding photos, joined in the suit as a claimant in its own right, seeking damages because *Hello!'s* rapid publication of the rival, surreptitious photos obliged *OK!* to bring its own photo-spreads forward at speed, and *Hello!'s* "spoiler" lost it considerable sales in the neck-and-neck race. The Douglases had such a claim, which led to a modest award of damages. *OK!*, intent on publishing the photos taken and selected by the Douglases, did not. In the House of Lords, however, it was accepted that the magazine did have a claim for breach of confidence that lasted until the information became public.[112] The confidence lay, not just in the "Douglas" photographs but in any photographic information about the wedding if it was used to decrease the profitability of the exclusive rights to wedding pictures which *OK!* had purchased so expensively. Since *Hello!* was plainly aware of the exclusivity and the likely commercial damage to *OK!* that would follow from their activities, it was liable at a level which was assessed by the trial judge at over £1 million. As to when this confidence claim expired, the members of the court divided, each side suggesting that the other had lost touch with reality. Lords Nicholls and Walker were of the opinion that because *Hello's* six photos appeared only as *OK!'s* publication hit the streets, the information lost its confidential quality and its action therefore failed. Lord Hoffmann, Lord Brown and Lady Hale, however, considered that in the circumstances this narrow understanding of the action was unacceptable.

---

[108] Had *Hello!* instead got hold of copies of the official photographs, the person owning copyright in them would have had a cause of action. On that basis, Paddy Ashdown, former leader of the Liberal party, stopped publication of his own memorandum of a meeting with Tony Blair, when it had been retrieved by a scavenger from a solicitor's dustbin: see *Ashdown v Telegraph Group* [2002] Ch. 149.

[109] For the measure of damages, see below, para.9–22.

[110] See above, para.8–50—8–54.

[111] Above, n.41.

[112] [2008] A.C. 1.

The breach of confidence by *Hello!* therefore retained a role in relation to personal information distinct from infraction of privacy, and this in the circumstances proved all important to the outcome. *OK!* also based its claim on the general economic tort of unlawful interference with its business.[113] After a substantial analysis of case law and writings, the House of Lords confirmed that the "unlawful means" required by this tort should be interpreted broadly.[114] Because *Hello!* was found to owe *OK!* an obligation not to publish "non-Douglas" photos in competition with *OK!'s* release of "Douglas" photos, even though it had not induced their taking by Thorpe, it had adopted unlawful means. For the future, this tort may provide the common law a basis for action against types of "unfair competition" between economic rivals that previously it did not admit within the pantheon of civil liability. How far it will be allowed to override the former resistance to such developments must remain in question. On the evidence, the trial judge had found that *Hello!* did have the requisite intention deliberately to injure and so *OK!*'s claim succeeded.[115]

3. Consequential Issues

(1) Rapid response: prior restraint

The Human Rights Act s.12, which imposes special conditions on prior **9–21** restraints that affect the right to freedom of expression, has already been discussed in relation to breaches of confidence in general.[116] By s.12(1)–(3), in any application to restrain publication before trial of material that might affect the Convention right of freedom of expression, the applicant must be "likely to establish that publication should not be allowed". The House of Lords has ruled that, in consequence, the first factor in determining whether interim relief curtailing that freedom can be granted, is normally whether the applicant has made out a case that is likely on the balance of probabilities to succeed at trial—a return in this instance to the old "prima facie case" rule for interim relief.[117] Where the applicant for an injunction is relying on an art.8 infraction of the right to private life, he must provide evidence that the probable revelations will be a real invasion of privacy. This

[113] See above, paras 2–14 and 2–18 and the references there given. There were also claims for conspiracy in the narrow and the extended forms, and for inducing breach of contract, but these were not considered to take *OK!'s* case further.

[114] Lord Hoffmann, at [135].

[115] The damages awarded to *OK!* were reinstated by the Lords on appeal from the contrary decision of the CA.

[116] Above, para.8–44. In the context of personal revelations, s.12(4) gives added protection to journalistic activities. That sub-section is not to be averted by seeking an injunction against the revealer of the private information and then serving it on the press organ before it can publish: see *A v B, C and D* [2005] EWHC 1651.

[117] *Cream Holdings v Banerjee* [2005] E.M.L.R. 1 1. See also above, paras 2–32 et seq.

may well be difficult in any case where the claimant has himself revealed much to his discredit about his previous conduct. The court will not assist by requiring a publisher-defendant to produce its material in advance.[118] If it did, it would indeed become a line-by-line censor of the media. Likewise, once a claimant has made public statements about one zone of his life, the court will be reluctant to restrain a defendant from contributing her own revelations about that zone.[119]

Section 12 affects many of the cases involving a balancing of privacy and freedom-of-expression interests, and courts have not attached overriding importance in favour, in particular, of the media. Where the material in question is "journalistic, literary or artistic", s.12(4) requires the court to give particular regard to freedom of expression, including the extent of publication that has already occurred, the public interest in publication and any relevant privacy code (such as that of the Press Complaints Commission[120]). But that is no way conclusive in favour of free expression.[121] Much emphasis is given to the proportionality of the competing claims, for that is a characteristic of the rules for the grant of interlocutory relief in general.[122] In *A v B Plc*,[123] the claimant, a Premier League footballer, had had casual sex with two women (C and D) but wanted to stop them telling all in a press story, because his wife did not know (hence all the initials). The Court of Appeal offered general guidance on applying the section in any case where the claimant's one chance of keeping his privacy stands against the freedom of the press, a value which is distinct from the public's interest in knowing the information. In particular, where the private matter bears closely on a personal relationship, the stability of that relationship and the special status of marriage should be given weight. A public figure must expect comment on behaviour that would not be acceptable in a private person. In the case before it, the court refused to restrain publication in part because leading footballers tend to become role models for young people and therefore should not set bad examples.[124] The fact that C and D wished to publish was also brought into account against an injunction.[125] In *Douglas v Hello!*

[118] *A v B, C and D* [2005] EWHC 1651.

[119] *A v B, C and D* [2005] EWHC 1651. It could be different if the admissions and allegations were clearly separable.

[120] See *A v B Plc* [2002] 2 All E.R. 545 CA.

[121] Sedley L.J., *Douglas v Hello! (No. 1)* [2001] QB 967 at 1004.

[122] See in this context Lord Nicholls, *Campbell v Mirror Group* [2004] 2 A.C 457 at [20–21].

[123] [2002] 2 All E.R. 545 CA. In a rather similar case, an actor had been photographed *in flagellante* at a whipping parlour. The Court stressed that he had been a wholesome presenter of children's television and also that he was given to boasting to the press about his less degrading sexual exploits. It refused an order suppressing the whole story, though in a Solomonic moment it did stop the photos from being used: *Theakston v MGN* [2002] E.M.L.R. 22 .

[124] Whether super-models have this quality has yet to be decided. Not, surely, when it comes to cadaverous slimming?

[125] In *McKennitt v Ash* [2008] Q.B. 73 at [30], however, the CA pointed out that a recipient of confidences who was not otherwise a participant in the private information had no Convention right to publish it.

(No. 1),[126] the Court of Appeal had refused interim relief over pictures of the Douglas/Zeta-Jones wedding because authorised wedding photos were about to appear in an authorised version in a rival magazine. However, that decision turned upon doubts at the time whether the claimants had a right of privacy as a matter of general principle, and also whether it arose where they were trading on its publicity value. When a later Court of Appeal, hearing the appeal after trial of the action, chose to indicate that the refusal of interim relief had been wrong in both these respects,[127] it went further by holding that there was no special public interest in seeing the unauthorised, poor quality, photos in *Hello!* in addition to the authorised, carefully shot, photos that appeared at the same time in *OK!*[128]

(2) Compensation after disclosure

For the hurt feelings suffered by a person, like Naomi Campbell, who only **9–22** wanted the information about her drug treatment kept quiet, a substantial sum may be awarded, representing the court's view of the real suffering. The award in that case was a modest £2,500, with an additional £1,000 as aggravated damages for a later, vituperative attack on her for launching the proceedings.[129] Injury to feelings cannot be measured by objective tests, so the judge's quantification in that case began the business of setting typical standards.

In a right of publicity case, the matter is likely to be more complex. As already noted, in *Douglas v Hello! (No. 3)*,[130] once it was decided that only the Douglases personally had a right of action against the defendant magazine for publishing the duplicit guest's photos, the question of damages to their interest in commercialising their wedding pictures fell away; they had been very well paid by *OK!* The fact that they had opted for publicity also reduced very substantially any award for injury to their feelings, which was restricted to £3,500 each, with £3,750 each as compensation for having to rush their own selection of photos for *OK!* ahead of the timetable in their agreements. *Hello!* was found not to have made any profit from buying the surreptitious photos. If they had, that amount could have been recovered through an account of profits. It is in relation to remedial relief that a line may be drawn between true privacy and publicity interests. The assessment

[126] *Douglas* [2001] Q.B. 967.
[127] By then it was established that *Hello!* had seriously misled the first Court of Appeal in various respects.
[128] *Douglas v Hello! (No. 3)* [2006] QB 125 at [251–59] CA, where the points were also taken that the damages awarded after trial, reasonable in themselves, were nevertheless inadequate compensation in deciding whether to grant interim relief, and that they were little deterrent to an eager interloper with sale to the press as his motive. Cf. the outcome of the appeal to the HL, above, para.9–20.
[129] *Campbell v MGN* [2002] E.M.L.R. 30 at [130–170]. See also *A v B plc* [2002] 2 All E.R. 545 at [555–556]; *Archer v Williams* [2003] E.M.L.R. 38.
[130] *Douglas* [2006] Q.B. 125.

will vary depending on the circumstances. If what is spoiled is the prospect of an exclusive sale of a personal story or private event, there could be an award for substantial economic loss which will bring into account the likelihood or otherwise of any deal coming off. A sinner's confession that he or she misled the public by earlier denials of the fault, where the confession is made in order to profit from an exclusive revelation, could scarcely lead to an award for injury to feelings; but it might leave open some claim to economic loss.

(3) Data protection compensation[131]

9–23 At first instance, Naomi Campbell not only secured moderate damages for the breach of confidence but also for misuse by the paper of her personal data, contrary to the Data Protection Act 1998. Under that Act she was a "data subject" and the paper a "data controller". The Act, giving effect to two EU Directives on the subject,[132] substantially strengthened the weaponry of the Information Commissioner over the previous law.[133] It is his duty to ensure that personal data held on individuals in automatic equipment or another filing system is not disclosed, contrary to the principles enshrined in the Act. An unjustified invasion of privacy is a contravention and so the legislation provides a separate route through which to claim legal protection. A data subject who finds information about her being used for journalistic, artistic or literary purposes in breach of the data protection principles will, thanks to s.32, have to overcome various hurdles which particularly affect these "special purposes". They reflect similar concerns to those enshrined in the Human Rights Act and give substantial protection to the media, but not total clearance. If an individual suffers from infraction of a data protection right, she is entitled to compensation under s.13 for, inter alia, the distress caused by the unauthorised disclosure.

The Court of Appeal in the *Campbell* case had to decide whether the special protection given to the media by s.32, apparently in order to ensure that there would be no undue prior restraints, also applied to a subsequent claim for compensation if instead the material had appeared. The court held that this must logically be so.[134] On questions of media liability for investigative journalism which reports on celebrities, it is likely that liability for breach of confidence, invasion of privacy and lack of data protection will be treated as co-terminous.[135]

---

[131] See also Liddell (2005) 6 Bio-Science L.R. 215.

[132] 95/46/EC; 97/66/EC.

[133] The preceding legislation, the Data Protection Act 1984, called this executive the Data Protection Registrar.

[134] [2003] Q.B. 633.

[135] So apparently concluded Lindsay J. at first instance in *Douglas v Hello! (No. 2)* [2003] EWHC 786, though the interpretation he gives of the Data Protection Act 1998 s.13, is difficult to follow.

Part IV

COPYRIGHT AND DESIGNS

CHAPTER 10

RANGE AND AIMS OF COPYRIGHT

1. HISTORICAL INTRODUCTION

(1) The emergence of copyright[1]

The notion that an author should have an exclusive "copyright" in his creation took firm shape at the beginning of the eighteenth century. It derived from a confusion of earlier strains and there was still a major evolutionary conflict to come before its modern form was finally fixed. **10–01**

From the early years of the first copying industry—printing—a pattern of exploitation had been developing: an entrepreneur, whose calling was typically that of "stationer", became the principal risk-taker; he acquired the work from its author (if he was not reprinting a classic) and organised its

[1] The evolution of copyright has attracted scholars of formidable polish. The sketch that follows relies particularly on Scrutton, *Law of Copyright* (1883), Ch.4; Birrell, *Seven Lectures on Copyright* (1898); Holdsworth, *History of English Law*, Vol.VI, 2nd edn (1957) pp.360–379; Kaplan, *An Unhurried View of Copyright* (1967), pp.1–25; Patterson, *Copyright in Historical Perspective* (1968); Feather, *A History of British Publishing* (1988); Feather (1989) 25 Pub. Hist. 45, and (1992) 10 Cardozo A.L.L.J. 455; Tompson [1992] Jur. Rev. 18; Saunders, *Authorship and Copyright* (1992); Ginsburg in Sherman and Strowel (eds), *Of Authors and Origins* (1994), p.131; Rose in ibid., p.23; Rose, *Authors and Owners* (1993); Sherman and Bently, *The Making of Modern Intellectual Property Law* (1999); Seville, *Literary Copyright Reform in Early Victorian England* (1999) and *The Internationalisation of Copyright Law* (2006); McClean and Schubert, *Dear Images* (2002); Davies, *Copyright and the Public Interest* 2nd edn (2003); Burkitt [2001] I.P.Q. 146; Deazley, *On the Origin of the Right to Copy* (2004) and *Rethinking Copyright* (2006); Ricketson and Ginsburg, *International Copyright and Neighbouring Rights* (2006); Ricketson in Vaver and Bently, Ch.15; Gómez-Arostegui (2008) 81 S.Calif. L.R. 1197; Alexander, *Copyright Law and the Public Interest in the Nineteenth Century* (2010); and see Cornish in the *Oxford History of the Laws of England* XIII (2010) Pt. V, Ch.2.

printing and sale. The stationers (forefathers of the modern publisher) were the chief proponents of exclusive rights against copiers. Certainly their own practices—their guild rules and the terms on which they dealt with authors—insisted upon this exclusivity; their regime for "insiders" became a source of trade customs from which general rights against "outsiders" might be distilled.[2]

10–02 In this objective the stationers early found an ally in the Crown. In 1534 they secured protection against the importation of foreign books; and in 1556, Mary, with her acute concern about religious opposition, granted the Stationers' Company a charter. This gave a power, in addition to the usual supervisory authority over the craft, to search out and destroy books printed in contravention of statute or proclamation. The company was thus enabled to organise what was in effect a licensing system by requiring lawfully printed books to be entered in its register. The right to make an entry was confined to company members, this being germane to the very purpose of the charter. The system of control was equally satisfying to Elizabeth and her Stuart successors, who supervised it through the Star Chamber and the heads of the established Church.[3] Governments determined to censor heterodoxy made concert with the established order of the publishing trade.

The royal predilection for granting special privileges might interfere with the interests of the stationers. Not only was the sole privilege to print Bibles, prayer books and laws claimed under the royal prerogative; much wider privileges—not confined to particular, or even new, works—were also granted by letters patent. In the long term, it was not the fact of individual grants which mattered,[4] but their cumulative effect. For they might bear the inference that, as with exclusive rights in technical inventions, it needed special authority from the Crown to secure legal protection against imitators.

So long as the licensing system survived, this line of argument was of no great significance. And Stationers' Company licensing had considerable vitality. It outlived the ignominy into which the Star Chamber fell, being kept up by the Long Parliament and confirmed in 1662 after Charles II's restoration. But he allowed it to lapse in 1679; and, while James II revived it for seven years in 1685, it could not last long in the political climate of his dethronement. Parliament finally refused to renew it in 1694. The stationers, who had argued forcefully against their loss of protection, were left with such claim to "copy-right" as they could make out of their own customary practices surrounding registration. As they also lost their search and seizure powers, and equity had not yet begun to grant injunctions to protect any

[2] See Birrell, Lecture 3; Holdsworth, pp.363–364 (both accounts being based on Arber, *A Transcript of the Stationers' Registers* (1875)).

[3] The regulatory system was brought under a comprehensive Star Chamber decree of 1586; of this there was a new version in 1637.

[4] Many of the publishing patents naturally came into the hands of Stationers' Company members.

interest that they might establish, their only hope was in common law and this they put to no decisive test.[5] Their needs were equally for definite substantive rights and for effective procedures to enforce them and these needs were reflected in the legislation that they secured in the reign of Anne, the Copyright Act of 1710.[6]

The "sole right and liberty of printing books" that the Act conferred was **10–03** given to authors and their assigns; but it stemmed nonetheless from commercial exploitation rather than literary creation pure and simple.[7] Enforcing the right depended upon registering the book's title before publication with the Stationers' Company, "as hath been usual"; and likewise it was enforceable by seizure and penalties.[8] The right lasted for 14 years from first publication "and no longer"; but if the author was still living at the end, the right was "returned" to him for another 14 years.[9] Other "copy-rights" were expressed to be unaffected by the Act. It was not difficult to argue that an author ought to have some protection over his work before it was published. Since this went uncovered by the Act, it could only lie in a right of literary property at common law.[10] But much more absorbing was the question whether any common law right survived in perpetuity the act of publication.

At first, in the view of a majority of judges, history and policy demanded the recognition of this complete property right.[11] The Act of Anne was treated as providing supplemental remedies during the period when unfair competition could most readily injure the first publisher.[12] In the end, the great case of *Donaldson v Beckett*[13] narrowly settled the issue the other way: the statute was taken to delimit the scope of rights after publication

[5] Later judges and authors would engage in speculation disguised as assertion over "common law copyright" in this period: see, e.g. Scrutton, (above, n.1) pp.89–94.

[6] See Ransom, *The First Copyright Statute* (1956); Feather (1980) 8 Pub. History 19.

[7] See Copyright Act 1710 s.1. Booksellers and printers were named as falling among the author's assigns.

[8] Copyright Act 1710 ss.1, 2.

[9] Copyright Act 1710 s.11. For books already printed on April 10, 1710, the period was 21 years from that date: s.1.

[10] The question was not actually decided before *Donaldson v Beckett* (below, n.13). But then, all but one of the judges had no doubt about its existence.

[11] Especially in *Millar v Taylor* (1769) 4 Burr. 2303, where Lord Mansfield, a great champion of authors, led the majority. But the same assumption had been made in the 1730s when Chancery began to grant interim injunctions concerning books no longer within the fold of the statute. And the booksellers found some favour from the King's Bench judges in an action (collusive and so ultimately abortive) begun in 1760. The tale is ebulliently told by Birrell (above, n.1), Lecture 4; and see Walters (1974) 29 Library 290; Abrams (1983) 29 Wayne L.R. 1119; Feather (1987) 22 Pub. Hist. 5; Rose and Tompson (above, n.1); Deazley, *Origin* (above, n.1); Cornish in O'Donovan and Rubin, *Human Rights and Legal History* (2000), Ch.10.

[12] There were other ways in which the Statute was read as protecting only the most serious invasions of the publisher's interests: thus neither translations nor "fair" abridgements at this stage constituted infringements: *Burnett v Chetwood* (1720) 2 Mer. 441; *Gyles v Wilcox* (1740) 2 Atk. 141, 3 Atk. 269; *Dodsley v Kinnersley* (1761) Amb. 403. For the relation of these decisions to the scope of the common law right, see Kaplan (above, n.1).

[13] *Donaldson v Beckett* (1774) 2 Bro. P.C. 129, 4 Burr. 2408, 17 Hansard Parl. Hist. 953. Lord Mansfield's failure to participate in the Lords suggests a dark secret: Tompson (above, n.1).

absolutely. It was a most strategic victory for those who would insist that claims to trading exclusivity must be balanced against public interest in the freedom to exploit.[14] Had the case gone the other way, protection for other forms of intellectual endeavour against "misappropriation" would have been pressed in a host of analogies. Given *Donaldson v Beckett*, new forms of protection had to be secured from the legislature; and even if a lobby succeeded, the most that could be hoped for would be an exclusive right of limited duration.[15]

(2) Additions to copyright: nineteenth-century experience

10–04 That process had indeed already begun. The engravers had succeeded in 1734 and 1766.[16] Textile designers secured some very temporary protection by statutes which were the precursors of the present registered design system.[17] In 1798 and 1814, sculptures were protected[18]; and eventually—as the technical possibilities for reproducing artistic works expanded—the Fine Arts Copyright Act 1862 brought in paintings, drawings and photographs.[19]

In 1814 the term of the statutory right in published books was extended to 28 years or the author's life, whichever was longer.[20] But Sergeant Talfourd's attempts to have it again extended—for a period of perhaps the author's life and 60 years—ran into the shoal of "economical" argument, put in particularly telling form by T. B. Macaulay.[21] His view of copyright as "a tax on readers for the purpose of giving a bounty to authors" meant that in 1842 the period was extended only to 42 years or the author's life and 7 years, whichever was longer.[22] That compromise was to last until international pressures obliged Parliament to revise its views in Talfourd's direction.[23]

---

[14] Its tone found sympathetic resonances in the century to come. A notable reiteration came in *Jeffreys v Boosey* (1854) 4 H.L.C. 815. Here the issue took the form: if statute did not allow copyright to a foreign author, was he nonetheless protected at common law? On consulting the judges the House of Lords found that a majority of them favoured the common law right. But the Lords unanimously agreed with Pollock C.B.'s positivist view of copyright as "altogether an artificial right, not naturally and necessarily arising out of the social rules that ought to prevail among mankind, but .... a creature of the municipal laws of each country, to be enjoyed for such time and under such regulation as the law of each State may direct": at 935.

[15] See below para.10–04.

[16] Engraving Copyright Acts 1734 and 1766 (and further enactments in 1777 and 1836). The term was 28 years.

[17] An Act of 1787 gave protection against the printing, working or copying of an original pattern for certain types of textile. It lasted only for two months from publication (in 1794 extended to three)—giving at most a bare head-start.

[18] These Acts extended only to sculptures, etc. of the human figure; the term was 14 years from publication, with a further 14 years for authors who were living and had kept the copyright themselves.

[19] Here the term was the author's life and seven years. See Bently in McClean and Schubert, *Dear Images* (2002), pp.331–344.

[20] Copyright Act 1814 s.4.

[21] Macaulay, *Speeches* (1866), pp.109–122.

[22] Literary Copyright Act 1842 s.3.

[23] See below, para.10–06.

The commercial interests of book publishers had called for a "copyright"[24]; and much the same applied to artistic works. But in the arts of drama and music, exploitation occurred as much through performance as through the sale of copies. Playwrights, composers and their commercial associates sought a "use" right upon each public performance of the work. In 1833 this distinct performing right was given in dramatic works[25] and in 1842 extended to musical works.[26] Despite the nature of the performing right, the wider term, "author's right", was never introduced into English usage, as it was in most other languages, in place of "copyright". The difference reflects the accretive historical process by which the UK law developed. But equally it carries another overtone: a change to "author's right" might well symbolise some preference for creator over entrepreneur. That is something which has rarely attracted much ardour in Britain. **10–05**

The same point is underscored in another way. The relation between author and exploiter offers many opportunities for tension and disagreement. In Continental Europe the need to safeguard the artistic integrity of the author in the course of such relations was eloquently argued, particularly in the latter nineteenth century; and in many copyright laws the author was accorded moral rights which were entrenched by making inoperative any surrender of the rights in advance of the time when the author might want to rely upon them. These typically might include: the right to decide to make the work public; the right to be named as author; the right to object to revisions affecting honour or reputation. Some systems have gone to the extent of adding a right to have the work withdrawn upon payment of compensation; and the right to object to destruction.[27] In Britain, this sort of demand seems scarcely to have surfaced at all. Instead, in the high age of contractual freedom, relations were left to be determined by agreement, supported by such terms as the court might imply in the name of business efficacy and subject to the torts of defamation, injurious falsehood and passing off.[28]

(3) International relations and the Act of 1911

Britain could not however afford to reject entirely the ideals of those for whom copyright was a practical expression of reverence for the act of artistic **10–06**

[24] There had been no difficulty in extending the Act of Anne to sheet music: *Bach v Longman* (1777) 2 Cowp. 623. As for maps, see *Sayre v Moore* (1785) 1 East 361n.

[25] Dramatic Copyright Act 1833; for its history, see McFarlane, *Copyright: the Development and Exercise of the Performing Right* (1980), Chs 3–5; Peacock and Weir, *The Computer in the Market Place* (1975). Lectures in public were specially treated by the Lectures Copyright Act 1835.

[26] Literary Copyright Act 1842 s.20; see further McFarlane (above, n.25); Seville (above, n.1 1999).

[27] See below, para.12–64.

[28] There is no mention of the subject, for instance, in the Reports of the Royal Commission of 1875–1878 and the Committee of 1909.

creation. Her commercial position made her a considerable exporter of copyright material and she had a strong interest in reciprocal copyright arrangements with other countries and their colonies. On the question of protecting foreign works it was possible to take a number of attitudes: the French, for instance, at first granted protection to all authors of works published in France and to works of Frenchmen published anywhere. The Americans, by contrast, underlined their independence from Britain by confining copyrights to citizens and residents; and, a century later, while conceding some place to foreign authors, country by country, Congress required all legitimate copies of various types of work to be produced in the United States (under the controversial "manufacturing clause").[29] The British, true to their own tradition of giving first consideration to home publishers, admitted foreign authors to copyright upon condition that the work was first published within the country.[30]

10–07 With protectionist America, the hope of satisfactory mutual arrangements was slender; but with Continental Europe and elsewhere the prospects were brighter. A number of bilateral arrangements were worked out.[31] Then, by the Berne Convention of 1886, a multi-national system evolved, under which either the personal connection of the author with a Member State, or first publication in a Member State, was to secure copyright in the other, under the principle of national treatment,[32] but this in turn raised questions about the scope of rights offered in each State. At the Berlin Revision of the Convention in 1908, Britain was obliged to accept the majority consensus on two matters: protection was to arise out of the act of creation itself, without any condition of registration or other formality—which obliged Britain to abandon even the traditional requirement of Stationers' Company registration before suing[33]; and the period of protection for most types of work was to be at least the author's life and 50 years—that quasi-proprietary right against which Macaulay had persuaded Parliament 70 years before.

10–08 These changes were adopted in the Copyright Act 1911 ("CA 1911"), the first UK legislation to bring the various copyrights within a single text, and at the same time to put rights, even in unpublished works, on a statutory

[29] There were a series of later modifications to the manufacturing clause, see Nimmer, *Copyright* (1979 edn), paras 722–723.

[30] For parts of this story, see Nowell-Smith, *International Copyright Law and the Publisher in the Reign of Queen Victoria* (1968), Chs 1, 2

[31] See Ladas, *The International Protection of Literary and Artistic Property* (1938), I, pp.144–66.

[32] For the history of the Berne Convention, see Ricketson and Ginsburg, above, n.1, Ch.1; Cavalli, *La Genèse de la Convention de Berne* (1986). For the British role in the evolution of the Berne Convention, Bently and Sherman (2001) 48 J.Copyright Soc USA 311; Seville (above, n. 1, 2006), Ch.3. Within the British Empire, there were complicated relationships, those between the home country and Canada proving tense: see Seville (above, n.1, 2006), Ch.4.

[33] After 1842, registration was no longer required before publication, but only before suing on the copyright. Accordingly the requirement served no obvious function, and came in for a good deal of domestic criticism.

footing.[34] There was, however, some concession to public interest arguments: in the later years of the copyright in published works there were certain provisions for automatic licences.[35]

If the author gained by this intrusion of foreign ideals, the entrepreneur was by no means forgotten. The CA 1911 gave the producers of sound recordings their own exclusive right to prevent reproductions of their recordings (and, as the courts later held, also to prevent public performances of them).[36] The right was indiscriminately labelled copyright, even though it was conferred not upon the executant artist whose performance was recorded but upon the business which organised the recording. It was thus not an author's right at all, but something which Continental theory would scrupulously distinguish as a "neighbouring right". An important precedent was set for an age that was to see a great increase in the technical possibilities for artistic expression.

(4) Developments since 1945

(a) *The 1956 Act*

In the post-war period, there has been constant activity on the international scene. However, alterations in domestic law have derived more from pressures at home and these may be dealt with first. The Copyright Act 1956 was a complex piece of draftsmanship which elaborated many rules at perplexing length while neglecting to spell out basic principles in the clear order appropriate to a real code.[37] The Act was most notable for adding three new forms of entrepreneurial copyright—in cinematograph films (hereafter **10–09**

[34] Common law copyright in unpublished works was abolished: CA 1911 s.31.

[35] CA 1911 s.3, provided that, after 25 years from the death of an author of a published work, anyone might reproduce it for sale upon payment of a 10% royalty to the copyright owner. Section 4 added a special power (first introduced in 1842) to seek a licence from the Privy Council, which in fact went unused. The Gregory Committee found that this machinery played no significant part in securing cheap republications. In order to satisfy the requirements of the Berne Convention in its 1948 revision (Brussels), the Committee recommended abandonment: see Cmd.8661, paras 21–23. This was effected in 1956.

The provisions just mentioned were often linked with the reversionary interest rules introduced in 1911, though these were motivated by a concern for authors and their dependants vis-à-vis their entrepreneurs. Section 5 rendered ineffective an *inter vivos* assignment by an author of his copyright in a work, and equally his licence to publish such a work, so far as concerned the period from 25 years after his death. While this limited reversionary right was abolished after July 1, 1957, it continued to affect assignments and licences entered into before that date: CA 1956 Sch.7 para.28(3); Sch.8 para.6. Numerous musical works which have a recurrent popularity were dealt with in ways which allowed the legatees of composers (at least when moved by others to act) to claim back the last 25 years of the copyright. The precise impact of the reversionary right provision has accordingly been the subject of complex dispute: see *Redwood Music v Francis Day* [1981] R.P.C. 337 HL; Harris [1983] 30 J. Copyright Soc USA 544; *Novello v Keith Prowse Music* [2004] R.P.C. 48.

[36] CA 1911 s.19(1); *Gramophone Co v Cawardine* [1934] Ch. 450.

[37] It was used as a text-book example of how not to proceed by Dale, *Legislative Drafting* (1976) Ch.1.

"films" for short), broadcasts and the typographical format of published editions—to the 1911 copyright in sound recordings.

Equally significant in terms of new technique was the creation of a Performing Right Tribunal. In the inter-war period, it had been shown by the Performing Right Society (PRS) that joint action was a feasible method of turning the right of public performance in copyright music into something of real value[38]; and the record companies had followed suit, once they succeeded in establishing their own performing right,[39] by setting up the Phonographic Performance Ltd (PPL). The aggregation of copyrights that such organisations acquired brought a measure of power over their markets which, as the Gregory Committee found, was capable of being exercised in controversial ways: in particular PPL had been prepared to refuse or limit licences to, for instance, dance-halls, in order to sustain the employment of live musicians.[40] The Performing Right Tribunal was accordingly created to hear disputes over performing right licences from authors' collecting societies, and recording and broadcasting organisations.[41] Its services have been used on a number of important occasions and it is now being looked to as a model for controlling the activities of licensing bodies which have been or may be established to deal with reproduction rights, as distinct from performing rights.

10–10 Those who contributed to the production of recordings, films and broadcasts as performing artists gained no part in the proprietary rights of the CA 1956. It was argued that a performers' copyright would make for disproportionate complexity in the handling of rights and that they could properly be left to protect themselves by contract.[42] However, even in 1925, it had been admitted that performers deserved some form of added help against strangers who misappropriated their performances: but they were only allowed the assistance of the criminal law.[43] The same system was continued in a series of statutes somewhat extending the original range. The Performers' Protection Acts 1958–1972 established summary offences against making non-private records or films of performances, performing them in public, and broadcasting performances, without the performers' written consent. As the volume of "bootlegging" (surreptitious recording of performances) grew, this half-way house became a much less satisfactory form of protection. There were attempts to persuade courts that the Acts conferred civil rights of action. This produced only slow progress and the issue became one of the many pressures upon the Government for the

[38] In the nineteenth century, the copyright owners of dramatic works had for some time run a Dramatic Authors' Society: see McFarlane (above, n.25), pp.65 et seq.
[39] See above, n.26.
[40] See Cmd.8862, 1952, paras 140–157.
[41] CA 1956 Pt 4; see below, paras 13–54 et seq.
[42] See the Gregory Report (Cmd.8662, 1952), paras 165–176.
[43] Dramatic and Musical Performers' Protection Act 1925.

legislation which would eventually emerge as the Copyright, Designs and Patents Act 1988.[44]

(b) *International developments*

(i) **The Universal Copyright Convention (UCC).**[45] The desire to bring the United States within a general network of international copyright relations was strong. So also was the wish to maintain the basic tenets of the Berne Convention; indeed its revision at Brussels in 1948 only served to strengthen its force. After that event UNESCO took the initiative by promoting the Universal Copyright Convention of 1952. This also guaranteed the principle of national treatment, but on less stringent conditions about the term of protection, the types of work protected and the extent of protection. There was, for instance, no mention of any moral right. The United States was able to join the new Convention, while retaining her copyright term of two periods of 28 years[46] and introducing a simple requirement of notice on published works of foreign authors not first published there: the symbol, together with the name of the copyright owner and the year of first publication.[47] Subsequently, in 1973, the USSR joined the UCC and there are now a significant number of States which belong only to the less demanding of the two general Conventions.[48] **10–11**

(ii) **The Stockholm and Paris Revisions of Berne and UCC: the developing countries.** Copyright was the first field of intellectual property in which the developing countries sought to have their needs recognised as a special case. The shock waves of the initial confrontation were considerable: the concessions in favour of developing countries were originally moulded into a Protocol to the Berne Convention at the Stockholm Revision in 1967. These proved more than the traditional publishing States (led by the British) could take. The Protocol allowed developing countries to reduce the term of copyright in their national law; to authorise translations into their national languages; to authorise publishing for educational and cultural purposes and to exclude from the scope of infringement reproduction for teaching, study or research; and to limit the scope of the right to broadcast. As it became clear that the Stockholm version would not be supported, a further **10–12**

44 Morgan, *International Protection of Performers Rights* (2002).

45 See Bogsch, *Law of Copyright under the Universal Copyright Convention* 3rd edn (1972) and Makeen [2004] 44 Copyright World 20.

46 The UCC art.4(2), provided for a minimum term of the author's life and 25 years, unless a country already measured by a term of years from publication; in that case the period had to be 25 years or more.

47 This common marking is not needed to secure protection in any member State of the Berne Union, such as the UK. For the recent adherence of the US to Berne, see below, para.10–21.

48 A Berne member may not leave and then rely upon the protection flowing from the UCC, unless it is a developing country: see UCC art.27 and Appendix Declaration, as revised in 1971.

revision conference was called (in Paris, 1971).[49] This toned down the special concessions in a new Appendix to the Berne Convention.

The Stockholm text marked the introduction into international copyright law of the "three-step" test—a statement in abstract terms of the limited extent to which the right of reproduction can be subject to exceptions. The three steps that justify exceptions or limitations are: first, that they are confined to "certain special cases"; secondly that they do not conflict with a normal exploitation of the work; and thirdly that they do not unreasonably prejudice the legitimate interest of the author.[50] It will be appreciated at once that these criteria can be read in various senses according to the preferences of the reader.[51] They have, however, been reiterated in other international instruments, notably the TRIPS Agreement, where they are applied to all exclusive rights within copyright, and, in adapted form, to patent rights.[52] They may be some form of "soft" international law, but they rarely assist the hard decisions that legislatures and courts have to make in achieving the "balance" of exclusive rights against complete freedoms and forms of compulsory licensing.

10–13 The limitations which developing countries[53] are entitled to introduce into national law have been restricted to two. First, once three years have passed since first publication, a competent authority in the country may be empowered to license a national to translate a printed work into a national language,[54] and publish it, for the purpose of teaching, scholarship or research[55]; in the alternative, the country may take advantage of an older Convention provision[56] allowing the termination of the translation right, once 10 years from first publication have elapsed without the copyright owner publishing his own translation. Secondly, if the copyright owner or an associate does not publish the work in a country within a set period[57] after first publication, the competent authority can license a national to publish.[58] In both cases, the copies in both cases must be confined to the

[49] See now Masouyé, *Guide to the Berne Convention* (1978); Ricketson and Ginsburg paras 3.49–4.19, Ch.11; Goldstein, *International Copyright* (2002) para.2.1.3.

[50] See Senftleben, *Copyright Limitations and the Three-Step Test* (2004); Goldstein, *International Copyright* (2001), para.5(5); Ricketson and Ginsburg, paras 13.03–13.37.

[51] Berne Convention art.9(2).

[52] TRIPS Agreement arts 13, 30; and see the EU Directive on Copyright in the Information Society 2001/29, art.5(5).

[53] i.e. countries so regarded in UN practice: Appendix, art.1(1).

[54] i.e. one in general use there, or in use in a region or by an ethnic or governmental group or in education.

[55] Appendix art.2. See also art.2(9) allowing a similar licence to a broadcasting organisation.

[56] Convention art.30(2), Appendix art.5.

[57] These periods differ with the type of work, the period for scientific and technological works being as little as three years from first publication: Appendix art.3(3).

[58] Appendix art.3.

national market. Any licence must be upon terms of just compensation, judged by the standard of usual royalty rates between the two countries.[59]

At the same time, rather similar compromises were reached for the UCC. As far as translations are concerned, this Convention did not previously have the 10-year exception as in Berne, but instead allowed (in any country) a compulsory licence of a published "writing" after a seven-year period.[60] On top of this, the developing countries are permitted the post-three-year compulsory licence to translate as in Berne.[61] They also have equivalent rights to allow compulsory licences to reproduce.[62] **10–14**

The process of reaching an international consensus on these points has become laborious and complex. The results may do something to colour the political climate in which publishing by foreign houses is conducted in developing countries. Yet even in those countries which have set up licensing procedures in pursuance of their Convention entitlements, there is little evidence that local publishers are taking advantage of them.[63]

(iii) **Protection of performers, recorders and broadcasters.**[64] The CA 1956 strongly confirmed the United Kingdom's interest in supporting the entrepreneurs of the entertainment industry; and more guardedly the claims of performers were also acknowledged.[65] The country was accordingly a strong supporter of international collaboration against the piracy of performances, particularly through the media of records and broadcasts. A first drive resulted in the Rome Convention on the Protection of Performers, Producers of Phonograms and Broadcasting Organisations of 1961.[66] The Rome Convention requires a member to provide[67]: (1) for performers, power to prevent the fixation or broadcasting of their live performance (but not a recorded performance)[68]; (2) for record makers, the power to prevent reproduction of their records[69]; (3) for broadcasting organisations, the power to control re-broadcasting and public performance for an entrance fee (but not diffusion by wire).[70] It was indeed ambitious to try to secure **10–15**

[59] Appendix art.6; note the compromise on currency restrictions affecting compensation: art.4(6). There are a number of provisions on formalities and further qualifications; for which see Ricketson and Ginsburg Chs 13, 14.

[60] UCC art.5.

[61] UCC art.5ter.

[62] UCC art.5quater.

[63] For considerations of the future of the Berne Convention at its centennial point, see Ricketson Pt III; and the contributions of Davies, Phillips and Koumantos to (1986) 11 Columbia-VLA J.L.A. 33, 165, 225.

[64] See Morgan, *International Protection of Performers' Rights* (2002) and Arnold, *Performers' Rights* 4th edn (2008).

[65] See above, para.10–10.

[66] See Davies [1979] 1 E.I.P.R. 154; below, paras 10–29, 10–30.

[67] In each case, for the benefit of nationals of other Member States and for specified activities carried on in those States: see Convention arts 4–6.

[68] See, in full, Rome Convention arts 7–9.

[69] See Rome Convention arts 10–12.

[70] Rome Convention art.13. The term must be at least 20 years from performance, fixation or broadcast: art.14.

international protection for rights of three groups who also have such evident conflicts of interest amongst themselves. The Convention has only attracted adherents slowly.[71] It proved necessary in 1971 to sign a second "Phonograms" Convention, dealing only with mutual protection against the unauthorised commercial copying of sound recordings.[72]

10–16 In the field of broadcasting likewise, separate links have been forged, mainly through the activities of the European Broadcasting Union. In particular, the Agreement on Television Broadcasts 1960[73] goes some way in Continental Europe towards limiting the freedom to pick up broadcasts from another member country and diffuse them by cable (Britain has been able to take advantage of an exception about this).[74] The Satellites Convention (1974) seeks to deal with those (particularly "pirate" radio stations) who might otherwise take the signals of transmissions from point-to-point satellites and broadcast or diffuse them locally. For various reasons Britain has not joined this arrangement.[75]

(c) *The new activism: from 1985*

10–17 (i) **The Copyright Designs and Patents Act 1988.** Just as technological leaps began to demand international adjustments to copyright law, so the same bounds produced repercussions for national systems. Britain had been among the earliest countries to revise its Copyright Act in 1956 to meet the developments of the post-war decade. With the Copyright, Designs and Patents Act ("CDPA 1988") the format of the law was again changed and a great many details were added, some of them to cope with the digital future. Even in the 1970s it was becoming clear that if copyright was to survive the impact of modern technology—photocopying, audio and video taping and computing—adaptations of UK law and practice would be needed.[76]

In 1974 the Whitford Committee began the considerable task of reviewing the whole range of copyright and designs law in the United Kingdom. Its Report, in 1977,[77] for the most part welcomed as an important step forward, nevertheless would remain in limbo for a decade while different parts of Government produced their own views and reactions in a series of papers,[78] and the various interest groups engaged in a ferment of proposition and

[71] In 2007, it had 86 Member States, including the UK.

[72] This Convention now has 91 members. For its content, see Stewart, *International Copyright and Neighbouring Rights* 2nd edn (1989), Ch.8; Goldstein, *International Copyright* (2002).

[73] Made permanent by a Protocol of 1965. Like the Agreement on Television Films of 1958, this agreement was secured by the Council of Europe through its expert committee on broadcasting.

[74] However, the Whitford Committee (Cmnd.6732, 1977) paras 70–75, recommended that Britain should abandon this and most other exceptions that were inserted at her behest.

[75] See on this the Whitford Report paras 76–81.

[76] See below, paras 10–18 and 14–19 et seq.

[77] Copyright and Designs Law (Cmnd.6732, 1977).

[78] See esp. Green Paper, *Reform of the Law relating to Copyright, Designs and Performers' Protection* (Cmnd.8302, 1981) and White Paper, *Intellectual Property and Innovation* (Cmnd.9712, 1986).

counter-proposition. They also secured a number of specific changes: to improve the remedies against pirates,[79] to provide copyright in cable-casts and to reinforce it in its application to computer programs.

Because, thanks to the adventure over industrial design, copyright has been drawn so far into the realm of industrial production, the question of reform fell to be assessed with the intellectual property regimes considered as a whole.[80] That is why the CDPA 1988 did a number of things. It restated the statutory law of copyright, on the whole in a plainer and more logical manner than the CA 1956. At the same time it introduced a number of changes—in particular, the granting of a rental right in certain subject-matter, the creation of moral rights for authors and directors, the extension of control over collecting societies by means of a Copyright Tribunal, and the conferment of a quasi-copyright on performers and their exclusive contractors. The Act also completely revised the law affecting industrial designs.[81] Its details are the substance of the ensuing chapters.

So febrile is the condition of copyright that the CDPA 1988 is now pock-marked by subsequent alteration, giving the law a raddled physiognomy. In large measure this stems from harmonisation measures in the EU,[82] to which we turn next.

(ii) **Dirigisme from Brussels.**[83] After laying its plans for Community patents and trade marks, the Community took a decade longer to begin serious intervention in the fields of copyright and industrial designs. An important study for the Commission by Dietz, exploring the prospects for harmonising the copyright in literary and artistic works, was published in 1977.[84] At that period the differences of ideology were considered to be too firmly entrenched for practical progress to be made. But by the mid-1980s, the problems facing the traditional copyright industries—commercial piracy, home taping of recordings and films and reprography of text, music and design—were intermingling with demands to put copyright to new tasks, notably in providing coverage for mass-produced computer programs, for the design of semiconductor chips and to deal with broadcasting and recabling between Member States.[85] **10–18**

Various cases for action at Community level were rapidly increasing in strength. A Green Paper by the Commission, *Copyright and the Challenge of Technology*, discussed a programme of action at particular points on the

[79] See esp. Copyright (Amendment) Acts of 1982 and 1983; Cable and Broadcasting Act 1984, esp. Sch.5; Films Act 1985; Copyright (Computer Software) Act 1985.

[80] Note the Report of the Government Chief Scientist, *Innovation and Intellectual Property Rights* (Cmnd.9117, 1984).

[81] The Act also varied details of patent law and administration, and extended the liabilities of trade mark infringers, a process carried still further in the TMA 1994: see below, para.18–01.

[82] See below, para.10–18 below.

[83] Hilty (2004) 35. I.I.C. 760.

[84] *Copyright in the European Community* (English version, 1978); and see Dietz [1985] E.I.P.R. 215.

[85] For the impact of the case law of the ECJ, see below, para.14–28.

juddering copyright compass.[86] It was an approach directed at the economic problems of producers, and it was soon re-oriented more in favour of authors, as the prime beneficiaries of copyright protection.[87] The consequence has been an outpouring of EU Directives, which improve the position of both creators and entrepreneurs across the entire stretch of the EU.[88]

10–19 The course of EU legislation on copyright and designs will be listed here chronologically, together with a note, concerning its incorporation into UK law. The detailed contents of the Directives will take their place in the discussion of the substantive law and practice in succeeding chapters.[89]

(1) Directive on Semiconductor Topographies ("Semiconductor Directive")[90]; requiring a regime for the protection of computer circuit layouts which is at least sufficient to meet the reciprocity requirements of US legislation on the subject; implemented in the United Kingdom by Regulation, as from November 7, 1987.[91]
(2) Directive on Computer Programs ("Computer Programs Directive")[92]: requiring programs to be treated as literary works for copyright purposes and defining infringement extensively, while allowing special exceptions relevant to such novel and distinctive subject-matter among authors' rights.
(3) Directive on Rental, Lending and Related Rights ("Rental, Lending and Related Rights Directive")[93]: by way of response to the home taping problem, requiring rental rights for authors, performers and record and film producers, and in some measure, lending rights; and as a necessary precursor, introducing the three main neighbouring rights (for performers, phonogram producers and broadcasting organisations) in harmonised form throughout the EU.
(4) Directive on Satellite Broadcasting and Cable Retransmission ("Satellite and Cable Directive")[94]: dealing with the copyright aspects of a unified (and fortified) policy on broadcasting and the re-cabling of broadcasts within the EU.

---

[86] COM (88) 172 final.
[87] Acknowledged in a Commission Follow-up to the Green Paper (COM (90) 584 final). See Cohen-Jehoram (1994) 25 I.I.C. 821; Karnell (1995) 26 I.I.C. 900; Davies (1995) 26 I.I.C. 964.
[88] Policy overall was epitomised in a Council Resolution (May 14, 1992: [1992] OJ C138/1) on increased protection for copyright and neighbouring rights; cf. Laddie [1996] E.I.P.R. 253.
[89] For a searching analysis of the impact of EU legislation, Hilty (2004) 35 I.I.C. 760.
[90] Dir. 87/54; [1987] OJ L24/36, for UK implementation, SI 1987/1497; SI 1989/1100.
[91] See below, paras 15–52—15–55.
[92] Dir. 91/250; [1991] OJ L122/42; for UK implementation, SI 1992/3233.
[93] Dir. 92/100; [1992] OJ L346/61; now codified as Dir. 2006/115; OJ L376/28; for UK implementation, SI 1996/2967.
[94] Dir.93/83; [1993] OJ L248/15; for UK implementation, SI 1996/2967.

(5) Directive on Copyright Duration ("Duration Directive")[95]: in the supposed interest of unity, harmonising upwards the terms of various authors' rights and the three main neighbouring rights, to the highest factor operating in a Member State (authors, including film directors: life-plus-70 years; others: normally 50 years from exploitation). Since this goes to the essence of the economic rights, it will be discussed further in this introductory chapter.[96]
(6) Directive on the Legal Protection of Databases ("Database Directive")[97]: introducing a double form of provision, partly by copyright and for the rest by a short-term right against unauthorised extraction or re-utilisation of the contents;
(7) Directive on the Harmonisation of Designs Law: affecting, as a correlative of the EU Design Right Regulation, the national systems for registering designs.[98]
(8) Directive on Conditional Access Services ("Conditional Access Directive")[99]: extending the range of offences covering devices which decode broadcasts and "information society" services;
(9) Directive on Electronic Commerce ("E-Commerce Directive")[100]: s.4 dealing with the liability of intermediary service providers on the internet;
(10) Directive on Copyright and related rights in the Information Society ("InfoSoc Directive")[101]: affecting the application of copyright and control techniques on the internet and restricting the range of defences to copyright infringement[102];
(11) Directive on Resale Rights in Works of Art ("Resale Right Directive")[103]: requiring artists to be entitled to a share in commercial sales of the originals of artistic works.[104]

Beyond these again lie future projects: for instance, for a levy on copying **10–20**
machinery and blank tapes and other recording means; for the regulation of

[95] Dir.93/98; [1993] OJ L290/9; now codified as Dir. 2006/116 [2006] OJ L372/12; for UK implementation, SI 1995/3297; SI 1996/2967.
[96] See below, paras 10–54—10–55. See also below, paras 11–42—11–55.
[97] Dir. 96/9; [1996] OJ L77/20; for UK implementation, SI 1997/3032; below, paras 20–37—20–43.
[98] Dir. 98/71, [1998] OJ L289/28: implementation; SI 2001/3949, see below, para.15–08.
[99] Dir. 98/84: [1998] OJ L320/54. See below, para.20–77.
[100] Dir. 2000/71; [2000] OJ 1178/1. See below, paras 20–60 et seq.
[101] Dir. 2001/29; [2001] OJ L1767/10. See below, paras 20–57 et seq.
[102] The InfoSoc Directive had its genesis in the Green Paper, *Copyright and Related Rights in the Information Society* (COM(95) 382 final). This came a year after its US counterpart (*Intellectual Property and the National Information Infrastructure*, July 1994), but was much less instructive, on both the technical and the legal side.
[103] Dir. 2001/84; [2001] OJ L272/32.
[104] See below, paras 14–45—14–46.

copyright collecting societies; perhaps, even for an alignment of moral rights.[105]

10–21 (iii) **International agreements amid new technology.** By the CDPA 1988 the United Kingdom put itself in a position to ratify the Paris Revisions (1971) of the Berne Convention and the UCC. This coincided with adherence by the United States to the Berne Convention, after a century of prevarication.[106] American accession, while exhibiting a measure of grudging suspicion,[107] nonetheless put international copyright relations into new focus. Other major states also joined: among them the Chinese and the Russian Republics.[108]

10–22 Increasingly, the United States is worried by the scale and sophistication of international piracy, and it remains uncertain what a world transected by information superhighways will mean for traditional copyright industries and their earnings. It therefore continues its bullish offensive through a combination of Berne, TRIPS and its own trade legislation which imposes penal tariffs or embargoes on offending states. While not likely to go so far in the last direction, the EU will support the international initiatives, for it shares much of the basic economic concerns of US policy.[109]

10–23 Whatever comes of these further developments it is plain that both the Berne and the Rome Conventions are of increasing relevance to national copyright law, even in countries such as the United Kingdom which can at most treat the content of such Conventions as aids to the interpretation of municipal law. Accordingly, their present contents are summarised below, as are the obligations which are shafted alongside by TRIPS.

(d) *International conventions: current scope*

10–24 (i) **Berne Convention.** The Berne Union exists to protect the rights of authors in their "literary and artistic works", an expression which is illustrated by a long catalogue of examples, and then a set of further

[105] Although efforts to harmonise private copying levies has stalled. For the position on collecting societies, see Dietz (2004) 35 I.I.C. 809 and Gillièron (2006) 37 I.I.C. 939. Generally on future neighbouring rights, Kamina in Vaver and Bently (2004), Ch.19.

[106] For which, see Brown (1988) 33 J. Copyright Soc USA 196.

[107] The US refused to introduce explicit provisions on moral rights in general implementation of art.6*bis*, though it has subsequently (by the Visual Artists Rights Act of 1990) provided a measure of protection in one demanding sphere; and it has refused to extend protection to pre-accession works, despite the principle of the Berne Convention art.18.

[108] Some 20 States, members only of the WTO, now assume Berne obligations and secure Berne benefits through TRIPS.

[109] It should not be forgotten, however, that the entire GATT renegotiation nearly foundered on an argument between France, seeking to preserve its own film industry as an expression of national culture by imposing quotas on the television showing of foreign films, and the US, seeking to get unlimited access to European channels.

explications and limitations.[110] The items in these provisions arise for discussion at various points in the next chapters, so they will not be listed here in full.[111] The aesthetic creations traditionally associated with copyright are the subject-matter of the Convention, and accordingly it covers literary, dramatic, musical and artistic works and also cinematogaphic films and analogous audio-visual works.[112] The rights arise by virtue of authorship. Although the Convention eschews any statement that an author must be a human rather than a legal person, or that the work must attain any defined level of originality, both these characteristics are commonly assumed to underlie the text.[113]

Berne's first requirement is that each Member State must follow the **10–25** principle of national treatment, itself a product of the idea of territoriality.[114] This is organised through the concept of the "country of origin" of the work. Where possible this is the country of first publication, rather than that of any author's nationality or habitual residence, an approach which makes for simplicity, particularly where there is more than one author.[115] Where the country of origin is a Berne State, other members must accord to the work the same treatment as they offer their own nationals.[116] At this point, the Convention assumes that there will be differences in the scope of rights from one member to another. And copyright remains the field in which jealousies over inequality of treatment most readily ignite.[117] The Convention itself, therefore, acknowledges a number of dispensations from national treatment, which include the well-known "principle of the shorter term".[118]

---

110 The leading work on its history and scope is Ricketson and Ginsburg, (above, para.10–01, n.1). See also Masouyé, *Guide to the Berne Convention* (1978); Nordemann *et al.*, *International Copyright and Neighbouring Rights Law* (English edn, 1990), pp.3–11; Stewart (ed.), *International Copyright and Neighbouring Rights* 2nd edn (1989), Ch.5; Nimmer and Geller (ed.), *International Copyright Law and Practice* (1988 *et seq.*), Introduction; Sterling, *World Copyright Law* (3rd edn, 2008); Goldstein, *International Copyright* (2002), von Lewinski, *International Copyright Law and Policy* (2008).

111 Berne Convention arts 2, 2*bis*.

112 Adapting the Convention to the differing national approaches to copyright in cinematographic works has not been straightforward: see especially art.14*bis*.

113 cf. Ricketson and Ginsburg, paras 7.02–7.05.

114 Berne Convention arts 3–5. See below, para.11–35; Ricketson Ch.5; Nordemann et al. pp.58–81; Vaver (1986) 17 I.I.C. 577; (1985) 16 I.I.C. 575, 715.

115 Berne Convention art.5(3), which also takes account only of publication in a Member State, if there has been simultaneous publication (i.e. within 30 days—art.3(4)) also in a non-Member State. There are special rules for films and architectural works.

116 Including the rights guaranteed by the Berne Convention: art.5(1). The Convention does not impose obligations in relation to the protection of a work in its own country of origin (art.5(3)), but its requirement of national treatment applies independently of whether there is any protection in the country of origin (art.5(2)).

117 See above, paras 10–06 et seq.

118 Berne Convention art.7(8). See below, para.11–42. This represents one example of so-called material reciprocity, as distinct from the formal reciprocity provided by (for instance) national treatment. For retaliation against non-Member States in certain circumstances, see art.6.

Because of legal differences and tendencies towards mutual suspicion,[119] the Berne Convention has gone further than any other intellectual property treaty to impose minimum standards on its members. The Convention's requirements do not cover the whole field; and in any case they consist partly of mandatory requirements and partly of limits upon the potential scope of legislative measures in Member States. This exceptional movement towards standardisation of law has been of major influence upon a world made up mainly of importer, rather than exporter, countries. But, as already pointed out, the demanding nature of the Convention has made its progress uncertain throughout much of its existence, and the recent shift in its favour, supported as it is by the terms of the TRIPS Agreement,[120] is therefore the more remarkable.

10–26 What, then, does the Convention require of its members by way of legal guarantees? Since its Berlin revision, it has outlawed any form of registration as a precondition of legal right[121]; and it requires a minimum term of the author's life and 50 years thereafter.[122] It now gives some recognition to the moral rights of authors.[123] Otherwise its main substance is concerned with the scope of economic rights. Save in two exceptional cases, these are characterised as exclusive rights and not mere rights to remuneration.[124]

The right to authorise reproduction of a protected work[125] is subject to a strictly limited qualification: "in certain special cases" members may allow such copying if it "does not conflict with a normal exploitation of the work and does not unreasonably prejudice the legitimate interests of the author".[126] By implication this limitation applies equally to the Convention's guarantees of rights to translate and to adapt works.[127] The members may

[119] The British have tended to take a large view of international comity in the copyright sphere, and, therefore, do not always appreciate the longing for material reciprocity deep in hearts of other nations.

[120] See below, para.10–31.

[121] Berne Convention art.5(2). It is, however, permissible, to require fixation in a material form: art.2(2).

[122] Berne Convention art.7(1)—measured from the end of the year of the death: art.7(5); as to joint and unidentified authors, see arts 7*bis* and 7(3). There are more limited terms for films, photographic works and works of applied art: art.7(2), (4). The rule of the shorter term (art.7(8)) arises because members are free to exceed the minima (see art.7(6)). But the Convention adopts the general proposition that once a work falls into the public domain, rights in it should not thereafter be resurrected; regrettably this admirable principle is subject to overriding agreements between States: see art.18, and below, paras 10–54, 10–55. As to the retroactive effect of joining the Convention, see Gavrilov (1993) 24 I.I.C. 571.

[123] Berne Convention art.6*bis*; see below, paras 12–64 et seq.

[124] The Berne Convention avoids the word "property". The two instances of equitable remuneration which, under the Convention, members may introduce, concern: (i) the broadcasting, etc. of works (art.11*bis*(2)); and (ii) the mechanical reproduction of musical works and associated works (art.13). As an intermediate case, the Convention recognises (in a non-mandatory form) a *droit de suite* in original art works and manuscripts which, if it exists at all, is subject to national provisions on collection and actual amounts: see art.14ter: below, paras 14–45—14–46.

[125] Berne Convention art.9(1), which includes sound and visual recording: art.9(3).

[126] Berne Convention art.9(2).

[127] Berne Convention arts 8, 12; see Ricketson and Ginsburg paras 13.83–13.86.

use this power by permitting a particular use of a work to be undertaken freely or subject to payment of equitable remuneration.[128] The Convention itself contains a number of more specific exceptions.[129]

Exploitation through new technologies has brought extensions to the Convention. Thus in addition to a general right of public performance and communication,[130] there must be protection for the broadcasting of a work, its wire and wireless transmission and public communication[131]; and also of works when they are adapted into films, so as to cover both reproduction of the result and also its public performance and communication.[132] **10–27**

It is worth noting what the Convention does not cover: (1) it gives no right over the distribution and so does not address the vexed question whether copyright should be available to prevent parallel importation; (2) it attempts no legal regulation of collecting societies; (3) works of joint authorship are recognised for the purposes of duration, but nothing is said about the nature of such works (4) save in the case of films, it has nothing to say about initial entitlement to the ownership of copyright, or about other aspects of property rights; (5) the only aspect of remedies covered relates to the seizure of infringing copies; and (6) it does not touch the now significant issue of the transmission of works held in digitised form. **10–28**

(ii) **Rome Convention for the Protection of Performers, Producers of Phonograms and Broadcasting Organisations.** The Rome Convention was achieved in 1961 at what now seems an early stage in the evolution of the entertainment industries. At that time neither sound recordings nor films could be routinely copied so as to produce a version just as good. Likewise, broadcasting frequencies were strictly limited, and extensions by cabling and by satellite relay lay in the future. Broadcasters had some copyright interests of their own, but vis-à-vis performers and record producers they were major users. It was a considerable achievement that the Convention went as far as it did; and no surprise that it attracted relatively few adherents. The United States is still not a party. **10–29**

After diplomatically stating that it leaves intact and in no way affects authors' rights,[133] the Convention requires each Member State to apply national treatment in respect of the rights which it accords to performers, record producers and broadcasting organisations.[134] In addition, Member States must offer those from other States who are protected by the Convention certain minimum rights. In the case of records (phonograms), these **10–30**

[128] A logical deduction which has some express support: see Ricketson and Ginsburg paras 13.23–13.27.
[129] See below, para.14–03, n.2.
[130] Berne Convention art.11 (covering only dramatic and musical works); public recitation is separately guaranteed: art.11*ter*.
[131] Berne Convention art.11*bis*.
[132] Berne Convention art.14. Films are themselves works within the Convention: see above, para.10–24.
[133] Rome Convention art.1.
[134] See arts 2, 3.

include an exclusive right to authorise all reproductions, direct or indirect; and also a right to equitable remuneration (which under national law could alternatively be paid to performers) for the use of records in broadcasts and public playing.[135] Broadcasters are to have exclusive rights over fixation, reproduction, re-broadcasting and public communication.[136] These two industries, however, withstood pressure from the often unionised performers (actors and musicians alike) that they also should have rights to "authorise or prohibit" equivalent acts. Performers acquired only the "possibility of preventing" various specified acts, a distinction which was thought to allow the United Kingdom, in particular, to continue its approach of only protecting performers by criminal sanctions.[137] The Convention guaranteed protection for a term of 20 years, from fixation, performance or broadcast as appropriate.[138]

10–31 (iii) **TRIPS and copyright.** The starting point of the TRIPS provisions on copyright is that all members must comply with the substantive articles (1–21) of the Berne Convention, other than the provision on moral rights.[139] At crucial points, these obligations affecting the works of authors, as defined in Berne, are extended or made more explicit. Three general and two special cases deserve note:

(1) general. For the first time in an international instrument, the basic dichotomy of this branch of the law appears (in American form): "copyright protection shall extend to expressions and not to ideas, procedures, methods of operation or mathematical concepts as such".[140] This vital touchstone for balancing exclusivity against free access thus becomes part of international understanding. For all its difficulty of application, it must accordingly remain within our own law.[141]

TRIPS makes general the Berne principle restricting the extent of exceptions in national legislation to the reproduction right.[142] As to term, there is a new minimum of 50 years from the making of a work, where term is not measured by reference to a natural person's life.[143]

(2) special. Computer programs are required to be protected as literary works "under the Berne Convention"; and so are some compilations

[135] See arts 5, 10–12.
[136] See arts 6, 13.
[137] See arts 4, 7–9; and see para.10–15, above.
[138] See art.14.
[139] TRIPS arts 1–21 (omitting art.6*bis*); Correa (1994) 26 I.I.C. 543.
[140] TRIPS art.9(2); for the US version, see below, paras 20–11 et seq.
[141] cf. below, para.12–07.
[142] TRIPS art.13; and for the Berne provision (in slightly varied language) see above, para.10–26.
[143] TRIPS art.12.

of data.[144] A rental right is introduced for computer programs, and tentatively for films.[145]

By contrast, in the sphere of neighbouring rights there is no equivalent incorporation of the Rome Convention or the Phonograms Convention (though members are allowed to adopt the Rome Convention's conditions, limitations, exceptions and reservations).[146] Instead the TRIPS Agreement has its own code of obligations relating to performers, sound-recording producers and broadcasting organisations: **10–32**

(1) performers: they must be provided with an exclusive right covering fixation, reproduction, wireless broadcasting and public communication of actual performances (as distinct from recordings of them). It must last for 50 years from the performance.[147]
(2) sound-recording producers: they must have an exclusive right in the direct or indirect reproduction of their phonograms, and likewise (subject to certain limitations) to the rental of copies. It must last for 50 years from fixation.[148]
(3) broadcasters: either broadcasting organisations themselves must have an exclusive right over fixation, reproduction and re-broadcasting of their (wireless) broadcasts, and a right of public communication in the case of television broadcasts; or else equivalent rights must be given to copyright owners of material broadcast. The minimum term is 20 years from the broadcast.[149]

These provisions impose considerable changes on many countries undergoing development, far less on the industrialised world. A quarter-century ago, a discriminating view of copyright's proper function could at least command some audience. Today it stands challenged by the unremitting lobbying of the copyright industries and by authors' associations, whether they rank as collecting societies or as labour unions.[150] Pleading their fears for a future of uncontrolled perfect copying (currently posed, in particular, by the internet) they seek constantly to broaden and to intensify the grasp of copyright: by adding new subject-matter, extending the range of infringing acts, imposing liability on general distributors such as telecommunication chains, removing or limiting traditional exceptions and insisting on **10–33**

---

[144] See below, para.20–37.
[145] TRIPS art.11.
[146] See TRIPS art.14(6).
[147] TRIPS art.14(1), (5).
[148] TRIPS art.14(2), (3), (5). The record industry has long fought to have their products treated as works of authorship, with an equivalent period of protection. The case for this extension was resoundingly rejected in the UK by the *Gowers Review of Intellectual Property* (2006), paras 4.20–4.47. The lobbying will continue elsewhere.
[149] TRIPS art.14(3), (5); *quaere*, whether the term relates only to a first broadcast.
[150] For their differing functions, see below, paras 10–49 et seq.

draconian measures to support electronic management systems. Such legal changes would buttress, for instance, the Community's commitment to a strong copyright regime.[151]

The movement to enhance the position of copyright owners draws basic support from Chicago-inspired theories of property rights.[152] This approach ranks copyright indiscriminately with other commodities and claims that its value will be most efficiently realised if it is placed in the hands of a single right-holder, either by initial allocation, or by ready, legally secure, bargaining over an exclusive right, rather than a mere right to remuneration or compensation. However much the right is the consequence of creative expression, what matters is that it should be exploited by the person most prepared to assume the investment risks of so doing. This, so it is argued, is the first object lesson of copyright's history and it leads away from the liberal view that the right is only justified to the extent that it encourages authorship and its initial marketing. Rather the law should give continued protection so that a work will be made available whenever an entrepreneur is prepared to re-issue a work. Free bargaining legally enforced, is an essential element in this process and, the argument goes, it should not be constrained, save where absolutely necessary, by rules preventing a right-holder from taking more than copyright law itself allows him. There is no room, for instance, for anti-trust rules applied to vertical restraints or for defences which in any way diminish the earning potential of the property right.

10–34 The drive behind such thinking can be taken far. Rights, whether formally classified as economic or moral, should not be allowed to proliferate, so as, in particular, to exacerbate the transaction costs involved in procuring complex products such as films, databases and multi-media works and broadcasts. The law should therefore be ready to police copyright *ab initio*, not in the hands of the creator but those of the risk investor—certainly where the two are related by employment, and even where the work is otherwise "made for hire". Ultimately such thinking may sustain the case that copyright should be perpetual, like property in tangible things (taking one back to the "Battle of the Books")[153] *and* the case that the author should no longer be treated as the bearer of rights, only as their progenitor. In proclaiming the "death of the author", Turkevich, placardiste of the American record industry, found himself bearing the very banner of his Foucault-inspired denouncers.[154]

In actual practice, such extreme propositions are unlikely to hold away.

---

[151] See above, para.10–18.

[152] For the theory in general, see above, paras 1–40 et seq., in relation to copyright: Landes and Posner (1988) 18 J. Leg. St. 325; Goldstein, *Copyright's Highway* (1994); Gordon (1982) 82 Col. L.R. 1600; (1992) 21 J. Leg. St. 449; (1993) 102 Yale L.J. 1533; Cohen Jehoram (1990–1992) 144 R.I.D.A. 80.

[153] Above, para.10–03.

[154] Turkevich (1990) J. Copyright Soc USA 41.

Copyright has emerged as an amalgam of differing passions and there is some international accord about its acceptable scope and effect. The functioning systems take account of, but are not determined by, economic arguments from either pole. Two other value systems contribute to the outcome. First, the ideal values which have been placed upon the contribution of all arts to human culture, notably in Europe, have been an essential part of the rhetoric for copyright from the French Revolution onwards. In the last half-century, this has led to demands that authorship, far from being down-graded, should attract enhanced protection in law. So it is that moral rights have often been given guaranteed form in order that the author may be sure of being named and may object if its contents are deleteriously altered. So equally, in various countries, authors have been protected against the full force of "free contracting"; in some circumstances they are assured of equitable remuneration or fair compensation or protection against unconscionable bargaining.[155]

Secondly, copyright's role in underpinning the democratic process is **10–35** presented as a distinct and vital function.[156] Democracy can operate only upon a premise of free and open debate, and it is a basic element of the history which we have examined that modern copyright emerges only with the passing of a censorship run by bookseller power-brokers in league with church and State. By outlawing pirate copying in the marketplace, copyright fosters the presentation of arguments on social, political, religious and economic policy in highly significant ways. This perception gives its own emphases. It is likely to strengthen the view that copyright should last only for a limited period, since so far as possible the borrowing and exchange of ideas is itself crucial to a free society. Equally a social contribution can properly be demanded from copyright owners. In return for the valuable support which the State offers by conferring the rights, right-owners can be expected to contribute in limited ways to social policies on maintaining the stock of knowledge, fostering the processes of research and education, allowing the transmission of news and the expression of criticism and review. Hence the various exceptions for "fair dealing" which our law currently admits, in addition to the general principle that infringement requires substantial taking from a work.[157]

One step which straddles the analogue and the digital worlds has been the enactment (already mentioned) of the EU's Database Directive.[158] This defines the extent to which copyright can exist in the creation of a database and giving a distinct right (*sui generis* or neighbouring, according to taste) to the financial organiser of a database, whether "creative" or not. The model

[155] cf. Samuelson [2001] E.I.P.R. 409; Baloch [2001] E.I.P.R. 427.
[156] See, e.g. Elkin-Koren (1996) 14 Cardozo A&L.J. 215; Hamilton (1996) 49 Vand. L.R. 73; Netanel (1996) 106 Yale L.J. 283.
[157] See below, paras 12–36—12–41, 14–02 et seq.
[158] Above, para.10–19; below, paras 20–37 et seq.

has been examined in countries including the United States and in the councils of WIPO, but it has been treated with considerable suspicion.[159]

10–36 Over the last decade, the amazing potential of the internet as a source of online services for education, information, entertainment, business and government has flamed around the world and its character has changed rapidly. Parts of it are already being used to supply the stuff of the traditional copyright industries and much more is to come. The publishing, record and film industries face at least partial revolutions in their methods of delivery and they are each searching actively for secure techniques by which material can be obtained from authorised sites only on payment of a fee equivalent to the purchase or hiring of a hard copy of material. At the same time they fear the appearance of pirate sites, and the downloading and distribution of illicit copies, which, on the worst prognostications, could amount to a complete undermining of their commercial positions. However, the possibilities within the new technology for monitoring the use of material is also considerable, and many do not take such a pessimistic view of the future.[160]

Major investigations of the position of copyright material on information superhighways were launched in the United States, the EU and—internationally—at WIPO.[161] The Digital Millenium Copyright Act of 1998 introduced in the United States, and has been followed by the EU's InfoSoc Directive will be discussed in Ch.20[162] But the developments at WIPO, which establish a first base for all that follows, deserve mention here.[163] In December 1996, two international agreements were reached.

10–37 (iv) **WIPO Copyright Treaty.**[164] As well as adding a number of general provisions to the range of the Berne Convention,[165] the Treaty deals with online digital services chiefly by requiring, for works within the Convention, a right of communication to the public (by wire or wireless means) which

159 At WIPO, the issue was raised during the 1996 Meetings which resulted in the two Treaties mentioned below. At that stage, the very idea was too new to be taken far.

160 See, e.g. Goldstein, *Copyright's Highway* (1994); Crawford and Gorman, *Future Libraries* (1995).

161 For the US see the Information Infrastructure Task Force's Report, *Intellectual Property and the National Information Infrastructure* (1995), for the EU the Green Paper, *Copyright and Related Rights in the Information Society* (COM(95) 382 final).

162 Below, paras 20–57 et seq.

163 Reinbothe and von Lewinski, *The WIPO Treaties 1996* (2002); Ficsor, *Copyright and the Internet* (2001).

164 This constitutes a Special Agreement under the Berne Convention art.20 and is open for signature by any Member State of WIPO, which must comply with Berne arts 1–12 and Appendix: see arts 1, 17. Note esp. art.3, extending the basic provisions of Berne to the new rights being accorded.

165 Computer programs become literary works (art.4); databases acquire Berne protection to the extent that they constitute intellectual creations (art.5); a right of distribution is required, but not so as to affect national rules on exhaustion of right (art.6); a right of rental is created for computer programs, films and works embodied in phonograms (art.7); no special limitation is to apply to photographic works (art.9); and all national limitations and exceptions are confined by the requirements of Berne, art.9(2) (art.10).

includes the making available to the public of their works in such a way that members of the public may access these works from a place and at a time individually chosen by them.[166] Since it was not previously clear in many copyright laws that communication to the public could take place in this piecemeal fashion, the clarification makes sense.

Much more controversial, however, was the attempt to secure a right of electronic reproduction of extreme particularity. Internet placement and transmission involves constant steps of storage, some of them only transient, others more or less permanent. Right-owners hoped for a definition that would embrace them all, thus in principle making all providers of services liable for their roles in distribution. The campaign failed and no reproduction right was included in this Treaty by way of supplement to the Berne Convention art.9.[167]

Two technical questions are also addressed. First, the States concerned have to provide protection against anti-spoiler devices. This pertains to any circumvention which would allow the sidestepping of technical barriers to copying, when they are placed either in hard copy materials or in digital sites in order to restrict access and copying which is not authorised or permitted by law.[168] Surrounding this rather opaque language is a considerable controversy about the proper scope of such legislation.[169] Secondly, there is a generally accepted requirement that interference with "rights management information" (i.e. electronic identification of author, owner, terms and conditions of use, code numbering, etc.) should itself be a form of secondary infringement.[170]

(v) **WIPO Performance and Phonograms Treaty.**[171] While dealing only with the rights of audio performers and sound recording producers, this Convention makes some advances in their general protection.[172] Both performers and record producers acquire a reproduction right, a distribution right and a rental right, as well as the right to single equitable remuneration for broadcasting and communication to the public—long a divisive issue in some countries.[173] Performers also acquire rights against the bootlegging of extempore performances and acquire certain moral rights.[174] On the digital front, equivalent provisions to those in the Copyright Treaty ensure that **10–38**

[166] See art.8.

[167] An Agreed Statement to art.1(4) states that digital storage—wholly undefined—falls within the reproduction right.

[168] See art.11.

[169] See below, paras 20–76—20–87.

[170] See art.12.

[171] A separate treaty which does not derogate from the Berne or Rome Conventions for States which are members of them: see art.1.

[172] Attempts to extend the same provisions to audio-visual performances have foundered on the very different positions of the US and European film and television industries: von Lewinski [2001] E.I.P.R. 333.

[173] See arts 7–10, 11–13, 15. The power to introduce exceptions and limitations is subjected to the threefold Berne conditions: art.16.

[174] See arts 5, 6.

communication to the public occurs upon offer of access, and there must also be protection against anti-spoiler devices and of copyright management information.[175]

In the end the two Treaties made only cautious changes to the international law which will affect copyright on the Internet. That is a desirable outcome, given that the technology is still so novel and its possibilities are constantly expanding.[176] Beneath the lobbying and in-fighting, lies a complex set of claims about the most efficient ways of eliminating piratical exploitation and about who should bear the costs of organising that process: right-owner and therefore legitimate customer, or those who pay for more general services—notably the customers of telecommunications services. At the same time there is concern that changes are being sought which will interstitially improve the position of right-owners against users across the copyright spectrum. This applies in particular to those (notably scholars, students and libraries) who in the past have been able to have free access and use of material. In the past owners have accepted (or at least conceded this) as a social contribution in return for the rights granted to them.

(e) *Copyright, unfair competition and industrial design*

10–39 An exclusive right which strikes only at copying is particularly suited to claims that a person is taking something for nothing—that he is reaping fruits sown by the creativity of others. Nonetheless UK copyright law has on the whole conformed to the prescription that new rights should not be conceded without making a reasoned case and securing legislation. Indeed, statute has increasingly been used to define not only the duration of the various copyrights, but their subject-matter, the exclusive rights to which they give rise and the exceptions that may be admitted. The refusal to allow any general principle of unfair competition that will extend to the misappropriation of ideas means, however, that no limited, short-term form of liability may be imposed upon even the most parastic purveyor of other people's ideas and enterprise. Accordingly there is always some desire to press the existing concepts of copyright into service. Lord Devlin, for example, once said:

> "Free trade does not require that one should be allowed to appropriate the fruits of another's labour, whether they are tangible or intangible. The law has not found it possible to give full protection to the intangible. But it can protect the intangible in certain states, and one of them is when it is expressed in words or print. The fact that that protection is of necessity limited is no argument for diminishing it further, and it is nothing to the

[175] See arts 10, 14, 18, 19. The reproduction rights are subject to the Agreed Statement that they include digital storage as is the case in the Copyright Treaty.

[176] See Vinje [1997] E.I.P.R. 230; cf. Reinbothe et al. [1997] E.I.P.R. 171.

> point to say that either side of the protective limits a man can obtain gratis whatever his ideas of honesty permit him to pick up."[177]

But this is not an attitude which has been maintained with consistency. There has been some tendency to look upon copyright as typically concerned with established forms of aesthetic activity; and so there are decisions making it difficult to use artistic copyright against the copying of a dress design, or to claim that a suite of furniture amounts to a "work of artistic craftsmanship".[178] In line with such caution, and very significant in its impact, was a tradition (reversed surprisingly in 1968) of excluding artistic copyright from the sphere of mass-produced goods, so as to leave the registered design system as sole occupant.

In a sense, the origins of registered designs stretch back to the earliest period of industrialisation in some parts of the textile industry.[179] However, the real impetus towards the modern system came in the 1830s. The poor quality of British industrial design, particularly when compared with the achievements of the French, incited middle-class radicals to press for a system of training designers, and manufacturers to demand a more substantial legal monopoly.[180] The system of registration that evolved under statutes of 1839 and 1842 gave a form of protection particularly directed towards preserving the original design-owner's headstart; the term was short but the design was kept confidential in the registry throughout the period.[181]

As we shall see, in 1911 artistic copyright was deliberately excluded from **10–40** much of the industrial design field, and the same policy of preventing cumulative protection was pursued in 1956 under a rather more complete and satisfactory formula.[182] But the registered design system, with its patent-like preliminary examination and its requirement of novelty or originality, was too limited and cumbersome for many industries. They secured from the Johnston Departmental Committee in 1962 a recommendation of a simpler form of protection against copying. This would last for a relatively short period; but the interests of the rest of industry demanded as a prerequisite that a person claiming such a right should deposit his design in an official register.[183]

Even this balancing of interests was by-passed in the Design Copyright **10–41** Act 1968, which was meant to secure such groups as makers of jewellery, furniture and toys against the unfair competition of free copying. The

177 *Ladbroke v Hill* [1964] 1 W.L.R. 273 at 291; see further, below, para.12–06. Contrast the thrust of these remarks with the well-known dictum of Dixon J., quoted above, in para.1–16.

178 On economic and other factors affecting the protection of applied art, see Rushton [2001] I.P.Q. 255.

179 See above, para.10–04; Sherman and Bently (above, n.1) Ch.3.

180 See Prouty, *The Transformation of the Board of Trade 1830–1857* (1957), pp.18–27.

181 Copyright of Designs Act 1842 s.17; and for subsequent Acts and further details, see Johnston Committee on Industrial Designs (Cmnd. 1808, 1962), App.B.

182 See below, paras 16–03—16–05; Laddie [1996] E.I.P.R. 253.

183 Johnston Committee on Industrial Design (Cmnd. 1808, 1962), esp. paras 47–48.

particular manner in which artistic copyright was introduced into the sphere of industrial production, however, was ill thought through. So in various respects it went much beyond the apparent intentions of its sponsors. The complicated consequences must be left to be discussed later,[184] but the overall effect of allowing registered design and copyright protection to accumulate was very considerable. At least where a design originated from two-dimensional drawings or plans, to copy them (directly or indirectly) in three-dimensional products was likely to infringe copyright in them; and mostly it made no difference that shape is a consequence of function. Copyright invaded the sphere of technical design with an efficacy and simplicity that was truly dramatic.

As a form of protection against design misappropriation it was, for a number of reasons, extreme. The very substantial reduction in scope, embodied in the CDPA 1988, is largely placed outside the frame of copyright and in the separate folds of registered and unregistered design right. One point of doing this, rather than adapting copyright, has been to avoid the international obligations which attach to the latter, given that most other countries have shown no inclination towards a reciprocal form of protection. In 2002–2003 the situation has again been altered by the introduction of the EU's Registered Design and its surrogate, a short-term unregistered right. This has dictated parallel harmonisation of registered designs granted by national offices in EU States.[185]

2. Values and Interests

10–42 Copyright sustains a triangle of relationships. While industrial property tends to establish bi-polar linkages—between right-owner and user—copyright has, on the right-owner side, both creators and entrepreneurs. As against users, their interests are largely the same: to ensure that the use of works is licensed and that the returns on use are maximised. But between themselves, there will exist tensions over how works may be exploited and how returns are to be divided. This has indeed been so in every country from the moment when publishers and other investors have pressed for protection to be accorded in the name of their authors.

It is the cultural value attaching to authorship which provides such copious moral legitimacy for legal protection. Not only are authors given a longer-lasting right than could possibly be needed by way of economic incentive; entrepreneurs are also able to justify related rights which protect their own investments in cultural productions. The realm occupied by copyright is accordingly fed by society's deep desire for artistic creativity. The rights of authors in the true sense are reserved for categories—literary,

[184] See below, para.15–01.
[185] See generally Ch.15.

dramatic, musical and artistic works, and now audiovisual works—where the best productions in the genre are considered to be of central cultural value. That is why film directors have now been accorded an author's right, while sound recording engineers have not,[186] and their employers are left with only a neighbouring right of more limited scope.

Over time these values change, and modern copyright systems have considerable capacity to embody that change once it is clearly established. However, authors' rights, as we know them today, do depend upon the experience that in the main it is only works of significant intrinsic value which survive in popularity for long. Our ever-growing appetite for the cultural trivia of previous generations may in the end upset this perception. Should it ever do so to a serious degree, it ought to lead to reductions in the scale of copyright protection.

The present balance, as it is widely perceived, allows copyright to protect **10–43** both major cultural products for very substantial periods, and more ephemeral things for their temporary shelf-life. Its capacious nature also allows for the delayed appreciation of neglected figures or particular works. Likewise, through such concepts as joint authorship and copyright in adaptations, it is able to offer linked protection to those involved in complex productions—as today in films and multi-media products. This adaptable nature of copyright, which has characterised it from the outset, enables it to carry political conviction.

One commonplace has it that copyright was sired by the cult of the Romantic Author. But that makes very limited historical sense. Of course, among campaigners for copyright there have always been those who argue single-mindedly for the adequate recognition of genius. But from the Statute of Anne onwards, all concerned in shaping the law have appreciated that the demand for copyright is also directed towards protecting much more humble and transitory material from the trespasses of pirates and other free riders.[187] Copyright everywhere is open to those who cross a low threshold of creativity, and differences between national laws over the concept of originality operate only at this margin. No system reserves copyright only for those works which pass a substantial test of aesthetic merit.[188]

There are always those who are dissatisfied with prevailing views of **10–44** copyright. Today's philosophic penchant for pointing up the relativity of artistic judgment, and for showing how dependent any creator is both upon his or her own intellectual inheritance and upon the perceptions of those

[186] Much to the chagrin of those who believe in the special structure of US copyright law on the subject: this accords an author's copyright to sound recordings, and then vests that copyright from the outset in the entrepreneur who commissions it, whenever it is a work "made for hire".

[187] See esp. Ginsburg and Saunders, above, n.1. In Britain and elsewhere, an immensely valuable product at the beginnings of copyright was the almanack, an assemblage of calendar, public information and mystic prognostication. Almanacks had the desirable quality of needing annual renewal, and should be ranked as the first commercial database.

[188] See further, below, para.11–04 et seq.

who receive the work, is antagonistic to any idea of "greatness". Deconstructionist argument is among other things deployed to undermine the copyright of authors. Michel Foucault's questioning essay, "What is an Author?",[189] has sustained a school of writing about copyright and related rights which envisions a brave new world of freely co-operating writers and artists, each contributing to evolving work, each offering selfless support and accepting enlightened criticism.[190] At least in its beginnings, the internet has seemed to offer a medium peculiarly suited to such an etherial Academe. These are ideas with particular attraction in the world of computer software, which has a growing lobby, burgeoning from the Free Software Foundation, against the industry's giants and in favour of using the copyright in programs only to establish a loose structure for mutual exchange.

The uncalculating exchange of ideas has long been part of scholarship and of shared interests of many kinds. If new technology enables that process to evolve, so much the better. But to suppose that it will supplant the need for informational, educational and entertainment material which is generated upon the expectation of a market return is the stuff of dreams. Copyright will remain because it provides necessary protection for the investment of intellectual effort and capital in material which is not produced in order to be freely shared. The law may have to be somewhat adapted, but its moral mainspring—that works should not be substantially copied or otherwise taken without authority—expresses a justification for legal intervention which will remain very widely accepted.

3. Economic and Public Interest Perspectives[191]

(1) Market power and individual works

10–45 Even so brief an historical outline will suggest the range of industries that copyright now serves. Starting from the production of books, it has moved out into the modern media of instruction and entertainment—through stage performances to recordings and broadcasting; and with its incursion into the

[189] Harari (ed.), *Textual Strategies* (1979), p.141.

[190] e.g. Woodmansee and Jaszi (eds), *The Construction of Authorship* (1994); Rose, *Authors and Owners* (1993); and see Boyle, *Shamans, Software and Spleens* (1996), Chs 6, 10, 11; Bettig, *Copyrighting Culture* (1996); Lessig, *The Future of Ideas* (2001).

[191] Modern discussion of the economics of copyright began from a highly critical perspective: Plant (1934) 1 Economica 167 and *The New Commerce in Ideas and Intellectual Property* (1953); and see further Hart and Schuchman (1996) 56 Am. Econ. R. 421; Breyer (1970) 84 Harvard L.R. 281; countered by Tyerman (1971) 18 U.C.L.A. Law Rev. 1100; 19 Bull. US Cop. S. 99. See Economic Council of Canada, *Report on Intellectual and Industrial Property* (1971), the Canadian White Paper, *From Gutenberg to Telidon* (1984); Watt, *Copyright and Economic Theory* (2000); Landes and Posner (1989) 18 J.Leg.St. 325; Koboldt (1995) 19 J. Cult. Econs. 131; Lunney (1996) 49 Vand. L.R. 483; Sterk (1996) 94 Mich. L.R. 1197; D. Nimmer (2001) 23 Houston L.R. 1; Koelman (2004) I.I.C. 603; Rahmatian [2005] E.I.P.R. 371.

field of computer programs it has provided a form of "industrial property" comparable in importance to the patent system and the protection of confidence. As with patents and confidential information, copyright may provide the legal foundation upon which monopoly profits can be generated, provided always that the market contains sufficient demand for the product. The ability of patented goods and processes to produce this effect largely depends upon their technical efficiency, judged in economic terms by comparison with any alternative products that are available. But many copyright works gain their uniqueness through the dictates of fashion, as moulded by advertising and other promotion, criticism, the reputation of the author's previous works, the shortage of new material and other factors.[192]

There are examples enough of the manner in which publishers and other **10–46**
producers of copyright material have taken a monopolist's advantage of their exclusive position: the practice of publishing hard-back editions before paperbacks, for instance,[193] or that of showing films at expensive inner-city cinemas before allowing suburban release and then television showing.[194] That such practices should follow from the conferring of copyright is not of itself a ground for criticism. The first purpose of the protection is to allow recoupment for the initiative of creating the material and the investment risked in producing and marketing it. In most instances a copyist could produce a directly competing product at a much lower cost if copyright did not restrain him.[195] Nonetheless, the "tax upon the public" should be broadly commensurate with the objectives of conferring copyright. A first economic test of this is: what measure of protection is needed to bring about the creation and production of new works and other material within the copyright sphere? Since any answer must be a rough one, the issue is largely a matter of the duration of copyright. Should it last for the relatively short period for which a patent or registered design is thought to be needed as an industrial incentive? Or is there justification for the very much longer period currently allowed for copyright?

---

[192] In his 1953 lecture (above, n.191), p.33, Plant commented upon the insatiable appetite of television programmers for expensive novelties. The Economist blamed giants of entertainment industries (mainly American) for preferring the promotion of glitz to the fostering of real talent (January 11, 2003).

[193] A practice which, in one instance, brought about the intervention of the EU Commission's Competition Directorate: see Jonathan Cape—Penguin Books, "The Old Man and the Sea" [1977] 1 C.M.L.R. D121. Examples of international price discrimination built upon copyright are to be found in the old British publishing practice of producing cheaper "colonial editions"; and in the higher pricing of books in Canada (see Economic Council of Canada, n.63 above App.B) and in Australia (see the *Time-Life* case, [1978] F.S.R. 356, below, para.13–15). Sometimes the organised power of a group of buyers may lead to raised retail prices, as was at one time the case with circulating libraries: see Plant (above, n.93) pp.186–187.

[194] See *Coditel v Ciné Vog* [1980] E.C.R. 881, ECJ; which is based upon the assumption that such a system of exploitation is in principle legitimate.

[195] For examples relating to American book publishing, see Breyer (above, n.191). In film production, comparable figures would be dramatic indeed.

In seeking an answer, the original Statute of Anne has an interesting suggestiveness. As will be recalled, it first gave a copyright period that was clearly related to the entrepreneur's needs: its term of 14 years from first publication came from the analogy of patents for inventions. But the Act proceeded to distinguish a further interest of the author. It gave him a further 14 years' copyright if he was still living at the end of the first period. In subsequent statutory developments, the usual pattern has been to provide an undivided period of entitlement; and the publisher has been left free to take an exclusive assignment or licence of the whole from the author.[196]

10–47 Economists who criticise the present approach stress the disadvantages to the consumer which flow from this accretion of the distinct interests of author and entrepreneur. Plant is surely correct in suggesting that few publishers (or, for that matter, record producers or film makers) calculate how much to risk in a particular venture by reference to likely returns over more than a few years.[197] To shorten the present copyright period is accordingly unlikely to produce any noticeable effect upon the amount of copyright material which they are prepared to put out for consumption.[198] Instead, works which prove to have lasting popularity provide them with bonuses. One justification commonly offered for this is that it induces entrepreneurs to take greater risks in promoting works for which there may be no sufficient demand. That is an attractive argument so long as one restricts attention to things scholarly or acceptably cultural. However the copyright system leaves to the entrepreneur the choice of what to select from the pool of works otherwise uneconomic. A more satisfactory method of choosing what is most deserving (whatever the criteria may be) would be through some form of government or other subsidy, a technique which would prevent the cost having to be borne by the readers of successful books.[199]

10–48 The public is supplied with copyright material through the co-operation of entrepreneur and author, and it may be that there are cases where the very long period of copyright makes it worth an author's while to embark upon a particular project. But this economic calculation can scarcely have stood high amongst the jumble of motives which have led to the current legal protection offered to authors. Their case has been borne along rather by special admiration for aesthetic creativity and the associated desire (often expressed in the rhetoric of natural justice) to provide authors with fruits for their labour which have the character of inheritable property.

[196] But note the reversionary right in published works that arose under the CA 1911 s.5.

[197] Plant (1953) (above, n.191), p.15.

[198] A far more likely way of inducing a successful author to keep writing would be to reduce the tax burden on his initial returns: see Plant (1953) (above, n.191), p.13.

[199] As it is, authors themselves, or learned societies or other patrons, often underwrite publishers in the pursuit of a risky venture.

(2) Collective enforcement

So far we have considered the market power that may stem from demand for an individual copyright work. A different monopoly effect—and one that is likely to have graver impact—can arise if rights in a whole class of works come under single control. The markets for the distribution of copies of copyright works have not so far been subject to much "cornering" of this sort, at least in Britain. **10–49**

The opposite is true for performing rights, as has already been mentioned.[200] Composers of most music, and their publishers, found it impossible to enforce their performing rights, work by work, against users such as concert promoters and theatre proprietors. The only practicable system was to found a single organ—in Britain the Performing Right Society—for the collective enforcement of rights. It then became possible to organise licensing schemes for the different categories of user and to set various rates for them.

While this accumulation of rights quite properly obliges users to respect copyright, it at the same time deprives them of the opportunity to object to the licence fee for one piece of music by playing another that is cheaper. The collecting society gains not only some power to set prices high but also to discriminate between users and to demand that performances be of a particular kind—for instance, that they be live rather than recorded. For the moment it is enough to draw attention to this type of problem. We shall return subsequently to the role that the Copyright Tribunal plays in disallowing practices by collecting societies it deems to be an abuse of their market position. Equally we shall see that the Tribunal fulfils the role of arbitrator in disputes where it cannot be said that there is much difference in the bargaining power of owner and user. For instance, PRS and PPL have as substantial a concern to see that their material is broadcast by the BBC and commercial stations as the broadcasting organisations have to secure the right to do so. **10–50**

A number of developments are driving the collective administration of copyright beyond the traditional confines of musical performance rights. Photocopying technology has finally produced administrations in numerous countries which organise licensing schemes. In Britain this is now undertaken by the Copyright Licensing Agency, which is composed equally of authors' and publishers' interests.[201] In countries which have sought recompense for home audio-taping by a levy on equipment, it has again been necessary for authors to act corporately in order to organise a system for distributing the revenue collected.[202] Individual enforcement of copyright has been impossible in these cases because of the difficulty, if not the **10–51**

[200] See above, para.10–10; MacQueen and Peacock (1995) J. Cult. Econs. 157; Kretschmer [2002] E.I.P.R. 126.

[201] See below, paras 14–15 et seq.

[202] See below, para.14–20.

impossibility, of recording what material is being used. Collecting societies are obliged to offer blanket licences for the use of material in their "repertoire" and, in some cases, to make distributions of revenue to their members on the basis of sampling or other averaging techniques.

The new prospects of the internet and other such services raise difficult issues, as yet unresolved, about payment for use of copyright material. However, it is the desperate hope of the medium that by electronic tagging the service can provide records of use accurately and very cheaply, so as to side-step the difficulties of monitoring which occur with juke boxes or home copying or public lending. Indeed, the ease with which information can be provided on such a service makes it possible to contemplate offering terms for use which distinguish one work from another. Consumers may then choose individually and their payments may be attributed to the particular authors, performers and entrepreneurs concerned. In this brave new world, there will be no need to resort to the averaging which has been part of collective administration of rights as we currently conceive it. If this can be eliminated, creators and producers will see more of the available revenue, and those whose work is most popular will be able to maximise its value.

(3) Entrepreneurs and authors

10–52 Another type of collective organisation deserves to be noted. Various commercial groups in the copyright industries have associations to watch over their mutual interests.[203] In the past at least, some of these associations have agreed that members would deal with outsiders only upon terms falling within certain limits. Thus publishers might agree upon the maximum rate of royalty that each would offer authors for certain types of copyright exploitation.[204]

Until quite recently creators have not had much reason for forming groups that will negotiate with entrepreneurial associations for collective guarantees of minimum terms in contracts to publish or use works.[205] Rather, successful authors and composers have negotiated better contracts individually, in some fields using agents, such as the literary agents who are so prominent a feature of English language publishing. This kind of practice

[203] For instance, at the national level in Britain, the Publishers Association, the British Phonographic Industry Copyright Association and the Music Publishers Association; at the international level, the International Federation of the Phonographic Industry. With the growth of commercial piracy, to these have been added organisations such as the Anti-Counterfeiting Group and the Federation against Software Theft.

[204] However, under UK competition law the legitimacy of such agreements is open to challenge.

[205] Which is not to say that mutual interest groups have not existed; witness, for instance, the Society of Authors, Playwrights and Composers and the Writers' Guild of Great Britain.

probably explains why in Britain there has been relatively little demand that authors should have legal guarantees against unfair contract terms.[206]

These conditions do not, however, prevail throughout all copyright industries, and over the last 20 years, in cases involving pop music composers and artists, instances of such oppressive, harsh and fraudulent contracting and dealing in the music industry have been demonstrated to English courts that they have intervened on grounds of undue influence, unconscionability or undue restraint of trade. In Britain this has not led to general statutory protection, for instance, guaranteeing proportional remuneration to authors; whereas in France, and now in Germany, it has.[207] But EU intervention at particular junctures makes an interstitial movement in that direction, which is viewed with considerable alarm by some investors. **10–53**

To take one instance: throughout the EU performances on record which are then broadcast require the payment of a single equitable remuneration, and this must be split between the record producer and the performers in a proportion laid down, if necessary, by the Member State concerned. This is one element in conferring on performers their own exclusive right. Previously in Britain, despite the strength of performers' trade unions, performers, were reliant upon payments from the producers under contract or else ex gratia, because their own right did not extend to the broadcast of recorded performances. The change of the law to meet the EU requirement[208] has meant that a wider range of performers are beginning to receive payments and that the proportion overall going to them has increased from one-third to one-half of receipts.

To a large extent authors and executant artists will gain a market price for their services which is not dependent on the extent of exclusive rights but will represent the outcome of negotiations. In that process those who join trade unions are likely to benefit from the combined pressure on employers which can then be brought to bear. But like all markets, expectations become settled over time, and the extent of copyright and neighbouring rights may well underpin the ordering of those expectations. As the example just given suggests, if the legal framework is changed, contractual benefits may be secured which union pressure had not by itself managed to achieve. This is the real significance of arguments over who should enjoy rights and what the scope of those rights should be. If authors and artists have been short-changed in the past, their hope for the future must lie in a combination of collective labour negotiation and lobbying for legislative guarantees.

[206] In striking contrast to developments in French and German law: see, e.g. Cornish (2002) 26 Col J.L.A. 1.

[207] cf. Rushton (1998) 22 J. Cult. Econs. 15; Watt, *Copyright and Economic Theory* (2000), Ch.3; Goldstein in Vaver and Bently (2004), Ch.18; Schricker (2004) 35 I.I.C. 850.

[208] See below, paras 12–28 and 14–33.

(4) The duration of copyright

10–54 The long term given to authors by copyright law stands in stark contrast to that for patents, industrial designs and other productive subject-matter such as plant variety rights and semiconductor layouts. It is a provocative choice: why does the creativity of authors deserve this distinction? As already pointed out, the extensive term of copyright becomes possible because of the nature of what is protected and the limited scope of the rights granted. That, however, is not a sufficient explanation. The answer cannot lie in the economic incentive needed to secure the production of aesthetic work, for that is a question largely of entrepreneurial calculation and investors are concerned with returns that materialise over much shorter terms.[209] As to the authors, composers and artists themselves: it is true that they set out upon careers with high risks of failure or of only slight success in material terms. But the same can be said of inventors. Can one prognosticate that either group is likely to be much swayed into greater productivity (particularly of quality, as distinct from quantity) by the distant prospect of returns to their inheritors? Authors' advocates sometimes make the claim, but they carry little conviction beyond their own coteries. For much of the history of copyright, the great bulk of creators have been paid off with a lump sum. The benefits of the long term, in the cases where it is of any economic value, accordingly inure to the producer who buys the rights.

A rational policy concerned with such risks would look towards direct support for the most promising talent of each generation (and today much of that is provided through employment). One way of providing it, through a link to returns on production, would be to institute a *domaine public payant*—a public fund into which royalties for use of works would be paid for (say) 20 years after the expiry of normal copyright.[210] In that way, successful authorship from two generations before would support the coming generation of literary and artistic creators. Living authors would benefit, rather than whoever has come to be copyright owner through the vagaries of commercial dealing, charitable instinct or personal inheritance.

The concept is an attractive one. But the funding of creators by grant-giving rather than by market-place returns is a process which may well attract prejudice, preference, jealousy and waste. Thereby hangs a tale. A plan for a *domaine public payant* was put to the West German legislature during the copyright revision of 1965; but antagonism towards its redistributive interventionism proved intransigent. Instead, by way of deflection, the term of authors' rights was extended by 20 years to their life plus 70

---

[209] See, e.g. Plant and Breyer, above, para.10–45, n.191; Ricketson (1992) 23 I.I.C. 753; Laddie [1996] E.I.P.R. 253; Parrinder and Cherniak (eds), *Textual Monopolies* (1997); Emiliandos [2004] E.I.P.R. 538.

[210] Occasionally, the idea has found British support: but proposals to both the Gregory and the Whitford Committees were rejected: Cmd.8662, 1952, para.24; Cmnd.6732, 1977, paras 643–647.

years. Out of this side-tracking of a serious policy initiative arose the central difference in copyright terms between EU states which, 30 years later, would be thought to require a Directive extending that term by the same amount throughout the EU, and at the same time to dictate an upward levelling of the terms of the main neighbouring rights (in general to 50 years from first publication or public communication).

Upward levelling followed mainly from the need within the Common Market to have a standard term and to achieve this at once, rather than waiting half a century for expiry of rights already granted, for a longer term existing in a few EU countries (reduction of a term already granted would be an unacceptable form of expropriation). Understood in these terms, the Directive is a once-for-all standardisation which implies nothing for the future.[211] Unfortunately it was also justified by rhodomontade about a general EU policy in favour of copyright, and about the increasing longevity of EU citizens.[212] The former is in itself no argument and cannot justify whatever step pleases interest groups; the latter ignores the fact that measurement by the author's life already builds in some compensation for longevity; and that, so far as succeeding generations are concerned, what matters is whether people are having children later, rather than whether they are living longer. **10–55**

Loose assertions of the type indulged in by the EU, however, pass for adequate justification and that in itself is interesting. Politicians and other arbiters of legislative "opinion" may know little enough of the inner workings of copyright, but they appear to accept that the archetypal forms of aesthetic work—the creation of great literature, music and art—deserve a market-based reward which should stretch over a long period.[213] They seem moved by a moral desire to give creators their due—a chance of reward somehow equating with the property rights which attach to the production of material things and the making of financial gains.

4. The CDPA 1988 and Pre-Existing Works

One technical matter may serve as a link between this introductory chapter and the next. The current copyright law of the United Kingdom is now almost entirely contained in the Copyright Designs and Patents Act 1988 and the case law pertaining to it. The CDPA 1988 repealed virtually all the **10–56**

[211] The demand for immediate effectiveness had led to the unattractive notion of reviving copyright in works which have already gone into the public domain (see below, paras 11–42—11–44). As the US has imitated this approach, a very substantial constitutional challenge has been levelled against the idea, but in the end that has been rejected by a majority of the Supreme Court: *Eldred v Ashcroft*, 537 US 186 (2003).

[212] See the Duration Directive (above, para.10–19), Recs 5, 10, 11.

[213] Whether the same logic can be applied to performers and producers of sound recordings is contentious: see Hilty et al [2009] E.I.P.R. 59 discussing the proposal to extend term from 50 to 95 years, now reduced to 70 years.

CA 1956, just as that Act had repealed the CA 1911 and the CA 1911 had largely replaced the common law and statutory rights that preceded it.[214] The commencement date of the CDPA 1988 was August 1, 1989; that for the CA 1956 was June 1, 1957; that for the CA 1911 was July 1, 1912.

The three Acts introduced basic changes. In particular, each added to the bundle of rights that constituted copyright. For instance, the CA 1911 specified that literary, dramatic and musical works were infringed by making a film, record or other "contrivance" for mechanical performance,[215] while the CA 1956 introduced infringement by broadcasting and by diffusing to subscribers.[216] The CDPA 1988 created a rental right in respect of sound recordings, films and computer programs[217]; and is noteworthy in particular for its introduction of moral rights for authors.[218] Again, statutory rules about initial ownership of the copyright were changed on each occasion,[219] as were the "qualifying factors" by which foreign publication or authorship might bring about the acquisition of UK copyright.[220] Since then, the staged implementation of EU Directives has introduced alterations each of which has its own commencement.[221] Since the duration of copyright is so substantial (particularly after the extensions of 1911), there remains a range of questions about works that were in existence before commencement of the CDPA 1988, the CA 1956, or even the CA 1911. A work produced early in an author's life, which now acquires copyright until 70 years after his death, could well have a copyright life of 100 years and might last more than 120 years.[222]

10–57 The transitional arrangements in each Act for existing works must be separately considered. Both the CA 1956 and the CDPA 1988 operate upon the presumption that they apply to things in existence at commencement as they apply to things brought into existence subsequently, subject to the particular modifications specified in Sch.7 and Sch.1 respectively.[223] Thus under the CDPA 1988, the question of whether the work had copyright under the CA 1956 is not in issue.[224] To this, however, the prime exception is that subsistence of copyright in an existing work is determined by the legal position immediately before commencement.[225]

10–58 There are a considerable number of other qualifications and exceptions

[214] See CA 1956 Sch.9 and CA 1911 Sch.2.
[215] CA 1911 s.1(2)(d).
[216] See now, CDPA 1988 s.20.
[217] CDPA 1988 s.8(3), soon to be expanded, see below, para.12–28.
[218] CDPA 1988 Pt 1, Ch.4, see below, paras 12–64 et seq.
[219] See CA 1911 s.5; CA 1956 s.4; CDPA 1988 s.11, see below, paras 13–04—13–10.
[220] For "qualifying factors", see below, paras 11–36—11–37.
[221] See above, para.10–19.
[222] For the term of copyright, see below, paras 11–43 et seq.
[223] CA 1956 Sch.7 para.45; CDPA 1988 Sch.1 paras 3, 4.
[224] Under the CA 1911 s.24, subject matter that was protected immediately before its commencement received the rights substituted by that Act, and this remains the position: CDPA 1988 Sch.1 para.2(2).
[225] CDPA 1988 Sch.1 para.5. For exceptions see para.5(2).

spelled out in Sch.1. During the immediate period of transition these are of particular importance and they will be mentioned at numerous points in the next four chapters. Where the new Act introduces enhanced rights, by and large it extends them to existing works. Where it alters or cuts down rights, the position under the CA 1956 may be conserved wholly or in part. Thus although the rules on first ownership of a work have changed in both the 1956 and 1988 Acts, the issue is determined by the law in operation when the work was made.[226] Equally, where the length of protection accorded to unpublished literary, dramatic and musical works, engravings and photographs is cut down by the CDPA 1988, there are exceptions directed to eliminating any unfair prejudice to the owners of existing copyright.[227]

Transitional arrangements concerning duration are based on a loose assumption that what is good for the future must be right for the past. So far as copyright exists in the public interest of encouraging creation of works, this would seem an irrelevant consideration so far as works already in existence are concerned. Perhaps there is some justification in the encouragement of further editions and new impressions, thought it is a much weaker consideration. The most radical recommendation of the *Gowers Review of Intellectual Property* is that the term and scope of *any* intellectual property should not be altered retrospectively.[228] It would appear to follow that a wholly new type of right should apply only to material brought into existence afterwards. The principle flies in the face of most experience with intellectual property policy, but it should not be disregarded purely on that account. If it were to become the normal approach it would undoubtedly dampen the enthusiasm of many lobbyists for greater protection. They tend primarily to be after more protection for what they have already.

[226] See below, para.13–04.
[227] See below, para.13–08.
[228] *Gowers Review* paras 4.41–4.47.

CHAPTER 11

SUBSISTENCE OF COPYRIGHT

1. THE GENERAL PICTURE

The first step in studying copyright law is to distinguish the different types of copyright and to understand the essential questions surrounding them: Is the material of the kind that attracts copyright? If so, for what duration? Who initially is entitled to ownership? What acts constitute infringement? An overview is given in the Table on the following pages. This should be understood for what it is. It does no more than highlight the starting points in discovering the relevant legal rules. Some further factors (for example the various exceptions to infringement) are too complex to include conveniently. The Table must be read in conjunction with the text. **11–01**

The previous Copyright Act (of 1956) was built upon a distinction between the Pt I copyright of creators in literary, dramatic, musical and artistic works, and the Pt II copyright, given in other *subject-matter* to entrepreneurs who produced sound recordings, films, broadcasts, cablecasts and published editions.[1] This adopted a strategic division between true authors' rights and the "neighbouring" or "related" rights of investors which was in the vain for its time: German legislation, for instance, would adopt a similar pattern only in 1965. This division, however, has been obliterated in the Copyright, Designs and Patents Act 1988. Instead—for

---

[1] See above, para.10–09.

better, for worse—the two types are listed indiscriminately. In each case the copyright is in a "work" and it is granted initially in most cases to an "author" who "creates" it. All is resolved in a grossly misshapen definition of this authorial creature (see the Table, head 3). The shift is typical of that old strain of common law thought which sees no difference of kind between true creators and investors in the creations of others; and which is inclined to prefer the latter to the former.

The transformations of copyright for a digital society may have set the UK approach again in advance: that is for the future to settle.[2] In the meantime, the tensions between our "mixed" system and the worlds of "authors" and "neighbours" established in Continental Europe have still to be resolved. We shall see them reflected also in differing concepts of originality, different rules about initial ownership of rights, different attitudes to moral rights and different approaches to legally guaranteed shares in economic returns.

11–02 The Table covers the various forms of copyright which arise under Pt I of the CDPA 1988. However, it does not include the following, none of which are "copyright":

(1) the rights given to performers and those with exclusive rights in performances, which are separately treated in Pt II of the Act[3];
(2) the unregistered design right created by Pt III[4]; or
(3) the publication right in long-secreted works which has been introduced in implementation of art.4 of the Duration Directive.[5]

The Table gives a column each to the varieties of copyright "work", grouping together (a) literary, dramatic and musical works, because of the similarities in their treatment. It only summarises the law as it applies to works created now, and makes no reference to the qualifications which may affect works created under earlier rules which continue to apply to them.

11–03 Much of this chapter concerns the criteria for deciding whether a work attracts copyright. These criteria are of two principal kinds:

(1) The nature of the material (Table, head 1) and the intellectual or entrepreneurial activity that produced it (Table, head 2). These factors, in certain respects closely interwoven, are analysed together below in Sections 2 and 3.[6]

---

[2] It was this tension which set on foot an attempt to simplify the categorisation technique employed in common law systems to enumerate the types of subject-matter which attract copyright. Undertaken in Australia, it proved an interesting, but ultimately unsuccessful venture: for an account by the chief protagonist: Christie (2000) 11 Aust. I.P.J. 40.
[3] See below, paras 14–30 et seq.
[4] See below, paras 15–38 et seq.
[5] See below, para 11–28, n.155.
[6] See below, paras 11–04—11–34.

(2) The qualifying factor, which brings into account international considerations stemming from the copyright conventions and similar arrangements (Table, head 4, considered below in Section 4).[7] In part the qualifying factor depends upon what constitutes publication or making available to the public (Table, head 5, discussed below in Section 5).[8]

Public availability may also be germane to the factors considered in the final section of this chapter, the duration of the copyright term (Table, head 6).[9] The other heads of the Table are taken up in succeeding chapters: the scope of copyright (Table, head 7) is dealt with in general terms in Ch.12, and particular aspects are considered in Ch.14. Authorship (Table, head 3) and initial ownership (Table, head 8) are discussed in Ch.13.

2. The Type and Quality of Subject-Matter

(1) Original literary, dramatic, musical and artistic works

Original literary, dramatic, musical and artistic works accorded copyright **11–04** by the CDPA 1988 are further defined to some extent by statutory provisions or case law and this is discussed below. Behind this lies the root requirement that sufficient "skill, judgment and labour", or "selection, judgment and experience", or "labour, skill and capital",[10] be expended by the author in creating the work. In other words, not only must creative intellectual activity produce the right kind of work, but the input must satisfy a certain minimum standard of effort. Otherwise, there is nothing that can be treated as a work; or—closely associated with this—the work will not be regarded as "original". In the next paragraphs the application of these concepts to the four classical types of copyright work will be discussed. Another basic axiom is that copyright protects the expression of an idea rather than the idea itself. In the case of literary, dramatic and musical works this leads to difficult questions about the need to record the expression in some permanent form; these are also considered.[11]

UK copyright law requires that a creation fit within at least one of the eight categories of work and, in this sense, is less flexible than Continental systems which favour an "open list" approach to subject matter, rather than

[7] See below, paras 11–35—11–37.
[8] See below, paras 11–38—11–41.
[9] See below, paras 11–42—11–55.
[10] This last formulation, employed by Lord Atkinson in *Macmillan v Cooper* (1923) 93 L.J.P.C. 113 at 117, has particular point when facts have been amassed by "sweat of the brow": see below, para.11–06.
[11] See below, paras 11–33—11–34.

Basic Structure of Copyright under the 1988 Act

	Literary, Dramatic, Musical Work	Artistic Work	Sound Recording	Film	Broadcast	Published edition
1. Nature of work	*Literary:* work that is written, spoken or sung, not dramatic or musical; includes table, compilation, computer program creative database *Dramatic:* includes dance or mime *Musical:* work consisting of music—not associated words or actions (s.3(1)) Secondary activities (translating, editing, adapting, etc.) may attract their own copyright	(a) "graphic work", "photograph", "sculpture", collage (b) work of architecture being a "building" or model thereof (c) work of artistic craftsmanship. Only works within (a) are protected "irrespective of artistic quality" (s.4(1))	Reproducible recording of sounds or literary, dramatic or musical work (s.5(1))	Recording on any medium from which a moving image may be produced (s.5(1))	*Broadcast*: electronic transmission of visual images, sounds or other information capable of lawful public reception or transmitted for public presentation (s.6(1))	Typographical arrangement of a published edition of literary, dramatic or musical work (s.8(1))
2. Originality or Equivalent	Work must be "original" (s.1(1))	Work must be "original" (s.1(1))	No copyright in recording that is a copy (s.3(2))	No copyright in film that is a copy (s.5(2))	Copyright in repeat expires at same time as in original (s.14(2))	No copyright in reproduction of typographical arrangement of previous edition (s.8(2))
3. Author	Creator of work (s.9(1))	Creator of work (s.9(1))	Person undertaking arrangements necessary for making recording (s.9(2))	Person undertaking arrangements necessary for making film (s.9(2)); and, since 1994, principal director	Person making the broadcast	

Basic Structure of Copyright under the 1988 Act—*continued*

	Literary, Dramatic, Musical Work	Artistic Work	Sound Recording	Film	Broadcast	Published edition
4. Qualifying Factor	Unpublished work: status of Author. Published work: either country of first publication or status of author at date of first publication or, if already dead, status at death (ss.153–155)	As for literary etc. work	Status of "author" at date of making; country of first publication (ss.153–155)	Status of "author" at date of making; country of first publication (ss.153–155)	Status of "author" when broadcast; country from which broadcast or sent (ss.153, 156)	Status of "author" at date of first publication; country of first publication (ss.153–155)
5. Publication	Issue of copies to the public, making available to the public by means of an electronic retrieval system (s.175)	As for literary etc. works; construction of architectural work or incorporation of artistic work into building is equivalent to publication (s.175)	Issue of copies to the public (s.175)	Issue of copies to the public (s.175)	Issue of copies to the public (s.175)	Issue of copies to the public (s.175)
6. Duration	Until end of 70th year from author's death (special cases: computer-generated works; unknown and joint authorship; Crown, Parliamentary and international organisation copyright) (s.12)	As for literary, etc. work	End of 50th year from making; or 50th year from release if release within 50 years of making (s.13A)	End of 70th year from the death of "persons connected with the film". (s.13B)	End of 50th year from first transmission (s.14)	End of 25th year from first publication (s.15)

Basic Structure of Copyright under the 1988 Act—*continued*

	Literary, Dramatic, Musical Work	Artistic Work	Sound Recording	Film	Broadcast	Published edition
7. Scope of Monopoly (primary infringement)	(a) Copying; (reproducing in a material form, storing electronically); issuing copies to public; adapting; rental (computer programs only)	(a) Copying; issuing copies to the public; (subject to exceptions)	(a) Copying; issuing, renting copies to public	(a) Copying; issuing or renting copies to the public	(a) Copying; issuing copies to public	Making a facsimile copy of the typographical arrangement (ss.16, 17)
	(b) Performing in public; broadcasting (ss.16–21)	(b) Broadcasting (ss.16–20)	(b) Playing in public; broadcasting (ss.16–20)	(b) Playing or showing in public; broadcasting (ss.16–20)	(b) Playing or showing in public; broadcasting (ss.16–20)	
8. First Owner (subject to assignment of future copyright)	Author or, if made in course of employment, employer (ss.9, 11)	As for literary, etc. works	"Author" (ss.9, 11)	"Author" (ss.9, 11) (now including director)	"Author" (ss.9, 11)	Publisher (ss.9, 11)

a system of pigeon-holing works.[12] Also, wherever possible, UK copyright law treats the separate elements in a composite creation as having distinct copyrights: the words and music of a song are respectively literary and musical works, each with their own author and term. Particularly now that so much material may be held in digital form, distinctions of this kind are tending to elide. Yet the rights attaching to each type of work may differ. For instance, artistic works have the special advantage that they may be infringed by transposition from two into three dimensions and vice versa; yet so far as concerns industrial manufacture of the copyright in them may well be excluded, or at least limited to a 25-year period.[13] Neither of these rules apply to literary works. If, for instance, the design of some element of an industrial product is recorded partly by diagram (an artistic work) and partly in figures or language (a literary work), should the law adopt an exclusive or a cumulative approach? Should the work be placed in only one category, by reference to its main attributes?[14] Or may it always be separated into its constituents, each enjoying the relevant type of copyright to the extent allowed for that type?[15] The issue needs to be settled, not least because multi-media digital products are likely to have a considerable commercial future. That instance suggests that the cumulative solution is to be preferred.

(a) *Literary works*[16]

The expression "literary work", said Peterson J., covers: **11–05**

> "work which is expressed in print or writing, irrespective of the question whether the quality or style is high. The word literary seems to be used in a sense somewhat similar to the use of the word 'literature' in political or electioneering literature, and refers to written or printed matter."[17]

As well as works embodying the fruits of considerable creative or intellectual endeavour, copyright has been allowed in such mundane compilations of information as a timetable index,[18] trade catalogues,[19] examination

[12] For a comparison of these approaches see Aplin in Derclaye, *Research Handbook on the Future of EU Copyright* (2009) Ch 3.
[13] See below, Ch.15.
[14] The approach preferred by Laddie J. *Electronic Techniques v Critchley* [1997] F.S.R. 401 at 413.
[15] The approach preferred by Jacob J. *Anacon v Environmental Research* [1994] F.S.R. 359; and Pumfrey J. *Sandman v Panasonic* [1998] F.S.R. 651.
[16] See CDPA 1988 ss.1(1)(a), 3. The expression is defined as any work which is written, spoken or sung, other than a dramatic or musical work, which does at least distinguish the separate copyrights in the words and music of a song (see below, para.11–12). It includes tables, compilations and computer programs. For computer programs, see below, paras 20–04 et seq.
[17] *University of London Press v University Tutorial Press* [1916] 2 Ch. 601 at 608.
[18] *Blacklock v Pearson* [1915] 2 Ch, 376.
[19] *Collis v Cater* (1898) 78 L.T. 613; *Purefoy v Sykes Boxall* (1955) 72 R.P.C. 89 CA.

papers,[20] street directories,[21] football fixture lists,[22] a racing information service[23] and the listing of programmes to be broadcast.[24] The principle that there must be sufficient "skill, judgment and labour" accordingly operates as a *proviso de minimis*, excluding as insufficient only those cases where the degree of literary composition is slight. Thus in particular instances courts have refused to recognise as literary works a card containing spaces and directions for eliciting statutory information,[25] an advertisement consisting of four commonplace sentences[26] and a short series of words conveying the need for assistance.[27] In most cases, the titles of books—and equally of plays, films and the like—are treated as insufficiently substantial to attract copyright themselves.[28] The same is true of a trade mark or name. So copyright is not a means of preventing a well-known mark from being applied to an entirely different product or service.[29]

11–06 "Literary work" also covers secondary work on existing sources, provided that it in turn involves literary "skill, labour and judgment". The following may all suffice: translation,[30] editorial work that involves amendment,[31] critical annotation or explanation,[32] compilation,[33] addition to an incomplete manuscript,[34] selection and abridgment.[35] Following this logic, an author who prepares a succession of drafts for a work has a distinct copyright in each—and if one is James Joyce, each is of considerable value.[36] However, the same de minimis principle applies: gathering together existing tables for the front of a pocket diary was held insufficient in one House of Lords decision[37]; likewise the mere extraction of the time of local trains from

[20] *University of London Press* case (n.16, above); *Boyapati v Rockefeller Management Corporation* [2008] F.C.A. 995 FC Aust.

[21] e.g. *Kelly v Morris* (1866) L.R. 1 Eq. 697.

[22] *Football League v Littlewoods* [1959] Ch. 637; *Ladbroke v Wm Hill* [1964] 1 W.L.R. 273 HL.

[23] *Portway Press v Hague* [1957] R.P.C. 426.

[24] *Independent Television Publications v Time Out* [1984] F.S.R. 64.

[25] *Libraco v Shaw* (1913) 30 T.L.R. 22.

[26] *Kirk v Fleming* [1928–1935] Mac. CC 44.

[27] *State of Victoria v Pacific Technologies (Australia) Pty Ltd* (No 2) [2009] F.C.A. 737 FC Aust.

[28] See Lord Wright, *Francis Day v Twentieth Century Fox* [1940] A.C. 112 at 123; Lord Hodson, *Ladbroke* case (above, n.22) at 286. As a corollary, merely copying the title of a literary work would rarely be a substantial enough taking to constitute infringement: see generally, below, para.12–06; and for newspaper headlines on the internet: *Shetland Times v Wills* [1997] F.S.R. 604; below, para.20–65. For the relation of titles to the writing of sequels, see Seville (2003) 51 J. Copyright Soc USA 1.

[29] *Exxon v Exxon Insurance* [1982] R.P.C. 69 CA.

[30] *Byrne v Statist Co* [1914] 1 K.B. 622; *Cummins v Bond* [1927] 1 Ch. 167.

[31] e.g. an edited version of a trial transcript: *Warwick Film v Eisinger* [1969] 1 Ch. 508.

[32] *Macmillan v Cooper* (1923) 93 L.J.P.C. 113: the notes appended to a condensed text showed sufficient literary skill, taste and judgment, cf. *Cramp v Smythson*, below, n.37.

[33] e.g. the football pool cases (above, n.23); *Portway Press v Hague* (above, n.22).

[34] cf. the same concepts affecting musical copyright, below, para.11–12.

[35] *Macmillan v Cooper* (above, n.32): condensation of a single text may not be sufficient, but collecting an anthology of verse would likely be: *Sweet v Benning* (1855) 16 C.B. 459.

[36] *Sweeney v Macmillan Publishers* [2002] R.P.C. 651.

[37] *Cramp v Smythson* [1944] A.C. 329; and see *Rose v Information Services* [1987] F.S.R. 254.

a general timetable.[38] It makes no difference to the position whether the material taken from elsewhere is in or out of copyright.[39]

In deciding whether there has been sufficient skill, the courts take account not just of skill in literary expression or presentation, but also of commercial judgment. A fixed-odds football pool form attracted copyright even though it only consisted of a compilation of 16 known forms of bet. Account was taken of the skill deployed in selecting these particular forms of wager, as distinct from the simple labour of compiling them on the pool form.[40] The process was treated as analogous to that of the compiler of a selection of poetry, even though in that case there is literary skill in the selection.[41] Likewise in a random choice game in a newspaper where the only literary material comprised grids of letters printed on cards, some set out in each day's paper.[42] **11–07**

The requirement that a literary work be "original" was only added to statutory copyright law in the Act of 1911. The adjective has been read in a limited sense. It is treated as bringing out one characteristic of the requirement of "skill, labour and judgment"—that the work must originate from the author and not be copied by him from another source. In a much repeated passage, Peterson J. said: **11–08**

> "The word 'original' does not in this connection mean that the work must be the expression of original or inventive thought. Copyright Acts are not concerned with the originality of ideas, but with the expression of thought, and, in the case of 'literary work,' with the expression of thought in print or writing. The originality which is required relates to the expression of the thought. But the Act does not require that the expression must be in an original or novel form, but that the work must not be copied from another work—that it should originate from the author."[43]

This has obvious significance for works that derive in some sense from an earlier source.[44] A piece of historical writing, a news report, a street directory and a selection of poetry all attract copyright once the choice and

---

[38] *Leslie v Young* [1894] A.C. 335 HL; cf. *Blacklock v Pearson* [1913] 2 Ch. 376.

[39] *Ashmore v Douglas-Home* [1987] F.S.R. 553.

[40] The distinction drawn in *Purefoy v Sykes Boxall* (above, n.19) between the skill in selecting goods and in writing a catalogue of them needs to be read in context: the causal connection for infringement (see below, para.12–03) was at issue; cf. *Ladbroke* case (above, n.22) at 284, 287.

[41] *Ladbroke v William Hill* (above, n.22): "An anthology of saleable poems is as much entitled to protection as an anthology of beautiful poems": Lord Devlin at 290.

[42] *Express Newspapers v Liverpool Daily Post* [1985] F.S.R. 306; and see *Mirror Newspapers v Queensland Newspapers* [1982] Qd.R. 305; *Kalamazoo (Aust.) v Compact* (1985) 5 I.P.R. 213.

[43] *University of London Press* [1916] 2 Ch. 601 at 608.

[44] On derivative works in comparative perspective, Goldstein (1983) 30 J. Copyright Soc USA 209; and on the reconstruction work on the Dead Sea Scrolls, *Eisenman v Qimron* [2001] E.C.D.R. 73, Israel SC; D. Nimmer (2001) 38 Houston L.J. 1.

arrangement of source material is more than minimal.[45] If the source or sources are still in copyright and they are reproduced to a substantial extent in the final work, a number of distinct copyrights will exist in it. If the rights are owned by different people, the permission of all will be needed for reproducing it and doing the other acts within the copyrights. This approach applies equally where a work evolves through a series of distinct drafts or other formations.[46] There is no implication that the copyright in the earlier drafts will merge or be subsumed in that for the final outcome.[47]

11–09 The strictly limited level of "original" achievement that is required in order to attract literary copyright can be explained in two ways. First, it reduces to a minimum the element of subjective judgment (and attendant uncertainties) in deciding what qualifies for protection. Secondly, it allows protection for any investment of labour and capital that in some way produces a literary result: this is true equally of the compiler of mundane facts and of the deviser of a football pool form whose real effort is in the market research determining the best bets to combine. Here copyright is being used to compensate for lack of a roving concept of unfair competition.[48] It is noteworthy that in cases of this kind where copyright is found to exist, the defendant tends to be a direct business competitor. Where some other form of relief is available against the unfair competition (as in the case of titles), copyright tends to be denied.[49]

11–10 Authors' rights systems take as their starting point the intellectual act of formulating a "work" and, therefore, tend to maintain in their law some initial criterion relating to creative expression. This differs in intent from the common law test that what is not copied is original.[50] It is, moreover, an issue which does not merely divide "copyright" and "authors' rights" systems, since the US Supreme Court has been sufficiently moved by notions of "authorship" to hold that a "White Pages" telephone book cannot be copyright because it did not reflect a "minimal level of creativity".[51] The

---

[45] Rather meanly, however, an Irish court refused copyright to a child who repeated a Bible story to some degree in her own words: *Gormley v EMI Records* [2000] E.C.D.R. 31; cf. a scriptwriter extracting a version of Homer's Odyssey: *Christoffer v Posiedon Film* [2000] E.C.D.R. 487.

[46] A topical example is the production of a computer program: from algorithm, through flowchart and source code to object code: see below, paras 20–04 et seq.

[47] *Ray v Classic FM* [1998] F.S.R. 622.

[48] On which theme, note Lord Devlin, *Ladbroke* case (above, n.22).

[49] See *"Exxon"* case (above, n.29).

[50] e.g. in *Van Dale v Romme* [1991] Ned. Jur. 608 (also in Dommering and Hugenholtz (eds), *Protecting Works of Fact* (1991), p.93), the Dutch Supreme Court required the selection of words for dictionary entries to express the selector's personal views, for there to be copyright in the list. The claimant succeeded: [1994] Ned. Jur. 58. Cf. Schricker (1995) 26 I.I.C. 41.

[51] *Feist Publications v Rural Telephone*, 499 U.S. 340 (1991); Weinreb (1998) 111 Harv. L.R. 1150. See further, below, para.14–50. For a claim that the UK approach to "sweat of the brow" copyright offends the concept of originality in the Berne Convention, Gervais [2004] E.I.P.R. 78. Before that case could be made out it would be necessary to examine how far there is a difference between sufficient skill and labour in the common law view and "small coin" copyright in authors' rights laws of Germany, France and elsewhere.

Canadian Supreme Court has ruled that a creativity standard is too high,[52] but that a work resulting from an exercise in skill and judgment will be protected.[53] The Australian Federal Court has found copyright in both "White Pages" and "Yellow Pages" telephone directories, applying the inherited British approach,[54] but later courts (including the Australian High Court) have been wary of protecting compilations resulting from investment or labour alone, preferring that they demonstrate "intellectual effort".[55]

The British approach, pragmatic and practical, is regarded by advocates of authors' rights as a hostage to fortune.[56] It might, for instance, require the admission of sound recording producers into the pantheon of authorship—an American demand which has been stoutly resisted in the counsels of the WIPO. It might undermine the moral superiority of copyright over industrial property and so set in train the argument that copyright terms should be shortened, rather than lengthened. In consequence, there has been a campaign within the EU to scotch the "debased" common law test of originality in favour of a threshold that all works be the author's "own intellectual creation". As a formula, the phrase is decidedly ambiguous. It is meant to indicate that the creator has engaged in mental activity distinct from the humdrum that anyone else might produce.[57] This test was first applied to computer programs and now delimits the range of databases which may be the subject of copyright.[58] In consequence a separate sui generis right for investors in all databases, whether creative or not, has been introduced by European Directive throughout the EU.[59]

Peterson J.'s exegesis on the notion of "originality" may lead to a peculiarly British outcome, but his words demonstrate some common foundation with both Continental and American approaches. For he makes clear that copyright is concerned with "expression of thought", rather than with "originality of ideas". Because of the limited approach to "originality", efforts to distinguish between idea and expression find only occasional place when addressing questions of whether works attract copyright at all. As with other systems, however, the dichotomy of expression and idea does play a necessary (if difficult) role in settling what amounts to substantial

[52] Misconstruing the approach of the US Supreme Court in *Feist* (above, n.51) as one that requires something closer to a patent standard of novelty or non-obviousness.

[53] *CCH Canadian Ltd v Law Society of Upper Canada* [2004] 1 S.C.R. 339.

[54] *Desktop Marketing Systems v Telstra* (2002) 119 F.C.R. 491.

[55] *IceTV Pty Ltd v Nine Network Australia Pty Ltd* [2009] H.C.A. 14 HC Aust.; *Telstra Corporation Ltd v Phone Directories Company Pty Ltd* [2010] F.C.A. 44 FC Aust.

[56] For a comparison see Casas Vallés in in Derclaye, *Research Handbook on the Future of EU Copyright* (2009), ch 5.

[57] Even Germany, which tends on occasion to take a serious view of minimum creativity, also witnesses a creeping down the scale, so as to give thin protection to "small change". Judges there, as elsewhere, prefer not to pass absolute aesthetic judgments against there being any copyright at all in a work. See also the Netherlands Copyright Law, art.10, which protects non-original "writings" in limited degree.

[58] CDPA 1988 s.3A.

[59] See below, paras 11–31 and 20–37—20–43.

taking by a copier. It is accordingly in relation to infringement that we shall return to it.[60]

(b) *Dramatic works*

11–11 Dramatic works are surprisingly difficult to define. They must have movement, story or action; they cannot be purely static.[61] The coherence needed in their content excludes computer games from this category.[62] Whether they must also be capable of being physically performed—a limitation which seems to exclude cartoon films—is much more dubious.[63] The CDPA 1988 defines "dramatic work" to include a work of dance or mime. They include the scenario or script for a film, the copyright in the film itself being separate.[64] The general principles concerning literary works apply to this closely analogous category. Nice questions can arise over the copyright entitlement of those who provide "secondary" contributions to scripts written by other playwrights. In *Tate v Thomas*, for instance, a person who supplied a number of ideas, including key lines, which were to be worked out by others secured no part in the eventual copyright.[65] Similarly, in *Brighton v Jones* the director of a play who suggested changes to plot and dialogue during rehearsals, was not recognised as a joint author, largely because the playwright was wholly responsible for the rewriting.[66] Scenic effects and costumes are only the subject of copyright if they are artistic works. Like literary works, dramatic works have to be "original" in the limited sense which that adjective has acquired in this context.[67]

The exclusion of most titles from the scope of copyright applies equally here.[68] This is linked with preclusion of any copyright in the names of characters or in the typical manner in which characters behave.[69] These can only be protected if sufficient trading reputation with the public gives rise to a form of passing off.[70]

---

[60] See below, paras 12–06 et seq.

[61] *Creation Records v News Group* [1997] E.M.L.R. 444: positioning of *objets trouvés* for a pop group photo.

[62] *Nova Productions v Mazooma Games* [2006] R.P.C. 14 paras 110–119.

[63] So held in *Norowzian v Arks (No. 2)* [2000] F.S.R. 363 CA: dance sequence subsequently edited on film by "jump cutting"; held not then to be a dramatic work because no longer capable of physical performance. Stamatoudi [2000] I.P.Q. 117; Arnold [2001] I.P.Q. 10; and see generally, Kamina, *Film Copyright in the European Union* (2002), Ch.4.

[64] CDPA 1988 ss.1(1)(a), 3(1), following Berne Convention art.2(1). For this complex issue, see below, paras 11–23—11–25.

[65] [1921] 1 Ch. 503. See also *Tate v Fullbrook* [1908] 1 K.B. 821 CA; *Wiseman v George Weidenfeld & Nicolson* [1985] F.S.R. 525; *Ashmore v Douglas-Home* [1987] F.S.R. 553.

[66] [2004] E.M.L.R. 26.

[67] See above, para.11–08.

[68] See above, para.11–05.

[69] See, e.g. Maugham J. *Kelly v Cinema Houses* [1928–1935] Mac. CC 362 at 368.

[70] cf. e.g. *Samuelson v Producers' Distributing* ([1932] 1 Ch. 201, below, para.17–44); *Shaw Bros v Golden Harvest* ([1972] R.P.C. 559, below, para.17–09).

(c) *Musical works: type and quality*

The term "musical work" is defined in the Act only as a work consisting of music, exclusive of any words or action intended to be sung, spoken or performed with it.[71] It has long been accepted in UK law that where words are set to music, the two remain distinct works for copyright purposes. [72] If there is copyright in each, and lyric writer and composer are not the same person, the two copyrights will usually expire on different dates: Gilbert and Sullivan, for instance, did not die within a year of each other. In *Hyperion Records v Sawkins,* Mummery L.J. elaborated on the statutory definition of "musical work", indicating that "music" was different from "mere noise" and "is intended to produce effects of some kind on the listener's emotions and intellect". [73] **11–12**

Again general principles discussed in relation to literary and dramatic works will apply. The techniques involved in the process of composition vary greatly. Today they include the use of electronic keyboards and mixers. Again there will be questions about contributions to a collective composition, which have to be significant, rather than trivial.[74] They do not have to be of melody or harmony or bass line, but can include, for instance, percussive effects.[75] "Secondary" activities which have been held to attract their own musical copyright include arranging music (by adding accompaniments, new harmonies, new rhythms and the like), and transcribing it for different musical forces. Musical copyright extends to various "secondary" activities such as selecting and arranging older tunes or scores,[76] orchestrating[77] or making a piano reduction[78] may qualify for its own copyright. A highly knowledgeable and skilled musicologist who prepared works by the French composer Lalande (1657–1726) for modern performance by adding a missing string part figured bass and corrections had copyright in his editions. The fact that the end result sounded much like earlier versions was not allowed to deprive him of his claim.[79] But equally, there may be very little "skill and judgment" in what is claimed to be "arrangement",[80] and this may mean that the requirement of originality is not met. Contributing only to performance and interpretation at a recording of pop songs does not make

[71] CDPA 1988 ss.1(1)(a), 2(1).

[72] See, e.g., *Brown v McAsso* [2005] F.S.R. 4.

[73] [2005] R.P.C. 32, CA.

[74] See, e.g. *Hadley v Kemp* [1999] E.M.L.R. 589; *Beckingham v Hodgens* [2002] E.M.L.R. 45 Ch; [2003] E.M.L.R. 18 CA.

[75] *Bamgboye v Reed* [2004] E.M.L.R. 5.

[76] *Austin v Columbia* [1917–1923] Mac. CC 398.

[77] *Metzler v Curwen* [1928–1935] Mac CC 127; *Godfrey v Lees* [1995] E.M.L.R. 307.

[78] *Wood v Boosey* (1868) L.R. 3 Q.B. 223; *Redwood Music v Chappell* [1982] R.P.C. 109.

[79] *Sawkins v Hyperion Records* [2005] R.P.C. 32, CA; Rahmatian (2009) 40(5) I.I.C. 560.

[80] The argument that any copyright which they do attract adheres to that of the original composer runs counter to the whole development of UK law on the subject: see Cornish [1971] J.B.L. 241; cf. *Performing Right*, November 1971, p.34.

the person a co-author, but that is a sphere where the dividing line can be difficult to draw.[81]

(d) *Artistic works*[82]

11–13 (i) **General.** Here the tension between different conceptions of copyright becomes marked. Some types of work are treated as artistic only if they bear a distinctive element of aesthetic creativity, others gain protection simply because labour and capital ought not to be freely appropriable.

Artistic works must be "original",[83] but as for literary works, this contemplates only that they will not be copied. In every case, the threshold measure of labour, skill and judgment must be present. Thus where the subject matter was designs for "Lego" toy bricks, and those designs simply repeated earlier designs with indications of minor variations in words and figures (which are themselves not artistic works), the drawings did not have distinct copyright.[84] However, if artistic skill is required to make the copy, it seems that this may supply originality: as where a photograph is taken from a picture or a three-dimensional object,[85] or a coin is engraved in three dimensions from a drawing.[86]

11–14 It is not therefore the requirement of originality which brings about the differences of approach so much as the manner in which the different categories of artistic work are listed in the Act.[87] These are: (1) irrespective of artistic quality, a graphic work,[88] photograph, sculpture or collage[89]; (2) works of architecture (buildings or models of buildings)[90]; (3) works of artistic craftsmanship not within category (1) or category (2).[91]

The requisite "skill, judgment and labour" is thus affected by the meaning of the various types of work and by the fact that only category (1) secures

[81] *Fylde Microsystems v T Radio Systems* [1998] F.S.R. 449; *Hadley v Kemp* [1999] E.M.L.R. 589; Arnold [1999] E.I.P.R. 464; *cf.* Barron (2006) 15 Soc & Leg St. 25, 101.

[82] See Kearns, *The Legal Concept of Art* (1998), Ch.3, App.4; Stokes, *Art and Copyright* 2nd edn (2003); Barron [2002] I.P.Q. 369; Booton [2003] I.P.Q. 38; Cheng [2006] E.I.P.R. 276; Maclean and Schubert, *Dear Images* (2002).

[83] CDPA 1988 s.1(1)(a).

[84] *Interlego v Tyco* [1988] R.P.C. 343 JC.

[85] *Graves' Case* (1869) L.R. 4 Q.B. 715; *Antiquesportfolio.com Plc v Rodney Fitch & Co Ltd* [2001] F.S.R. 23.

[86] *Martin v Polyplas* [1969] N.Z.L.R. 1046.

[87] CDPA 1988 s.4.

[88] "Graphic works" include: (1) a painting, drawing, diagram, map, chart or plan; and (2) an engraving, etching lithograph, woodcut or similar work. "Photograph" means a recording of light or other radiation on any medium on which an image is produced (or from which it can be produced) which is not part of a film. "Sculpture" includes a cast or model made for the purposes of sculpture. Because the definition of graphic works is not exhaustive, the bitmap files in a computer game, which enable specific images to be called up on the screen by the player, have been held to fall within this category. So too with the composite frames: *Nova Productions v Mazooma Games* [2006] R.P.C. 14 paras 98–106.

[89] A collage has to be assembled for more than a few hours and has to be stuck: *Creation Records v News Group* [1997] E.M.L.R. 444.

[90] Including any fixed structure—so this may cover a bridge or a dam.

[91] The concept is not further defined.

copyright "irrespective of artistic quality".[92] In the first category, most of the decisions set the minimal level of effort low: a simple drawing of a human hand showing voters where to mark their cross on a voting card,[93] the label design for a sweet tin,[94] drawings for patchwork bedspreads,[95] the arrangement of a few decorative lines on a parcel label,[96] have all been accorded copyright. (We shall see that, by way of counterbalance, the scope of infringement is narrowly defined in such cases.)[97] There was, moreover, a tendency to give very broad scope to the categories of artistic work included under this first head, in order to eliminate any consideration of "artistic quality". Upon such an assumption, a frisbee made from plastic was held to be an engraving because of the concentric rings on its body, and a model for its body was a sculpture[98]; a plastic mould for the heating plates of a sandwich-toaster was a sculpture[99] and so on. More recently, however, interpretation has been shifting towards everyday understanding of these terms; sculpture must have its ordinary, inevitably imprecise meaning of "a three-dimensional work made by an artist's hand"[100]; it requires carving, modelling or similar activity, not merely the assemblage of things which are to be the subject of a photograph[101] and it must be intended that the object have visual appeal.[102] This greater realism is of much significance in the new law of industrial designs.[103]

As with literary works, judgment that does not go to the degree or amount of artistic skill may be brought into account in deciding whether the minimum requirement for copyright is satisfied. Even three concentric circles may suffice if they are drawn to precise measurements because they are a plan for a technical device.[104]

The British have never scrupled to place every variety of photograph **11–15** within copyright, however merely technical the procedure of pointing the camera at a subject and pressing the shutter may be in a particular instance. Authors' rights systems tend to give copyright only to "photographic works", that is the results of careful and distinctive arrangement (scene-

[92] This phrase, destined to produce unimagined consequences (below, Ch.15), was inserted as a mild protection when maps, charts and plans were reclassified in 1956 as artistic, rather than as literary, works, as recommended by the Gregory Committee: see Fellner para.1.16.

[93] *Kenrick v Lawrence* (1890) 25 Q.B.D. 99.

[94] *Tavener Rutledge v Specters* [1959] R.P.C. 355 CA.

[95] *Vermaat v Boncrest* [2001] F.S.R. 443.

[96] *Walker v British Picker* [1961] R.P.C. 57.

[97] See below, paras 12–13—12–14.

[98] *Wham-O v Lincoln* [1985] R.P.C. 127, CA (NZ); and see *Plix Products v Winstone* [1986] F.S.R. 92.

[99] *Breville Europe v Thorn EMI* (1985) [1995] F.S.R. 77; and see *Arnold v Miafern* [1980] R.P.C. 397.

[100] *Metix v Maughan* [1997] F.S.R. 718: hence it could not include industrial results for making cartridges; see also *Greenfield v Rover-Scott Bonner* (1990) 17 I.P.R. 417.

[101] *Creation Records v News Group* [1997] E.M.L.R. 444.

[102] *Lucasfilm Ltd v Ainsworth* [2009] F.S.R. 9 Ch; [2010] F.S.R. 10 CA.

[103] See below, para.15–32.

[104] *Solar Thomson v Barton* [1977] R.P.C. 537 at 558; and see *Ladbroke* case (above, n.22).

setting, lighting, angle, etc.), involving an element of aesthetic judgment which is personal to the photographer (and/or to some "director", rather than the mere cameraman).[105] Since this will exclude not only casual snapshots (which occasionally—as when they show the shooting of a President—may have great commercial potential)[106] but also press photography, some form of related right for these lesser productions may be introduced, and with it much complicated law to distinguish the different categories.[107] In an attempt to harmonise copyright protection of photographs, art.6 of the EU Duration Directive stipulates the originality standard as "author's own intellectual creation". This is a vague standard, although one that is unlikely to support the extremely generous approach taken by the British.[108]

11–16 (ii) **Architectural works and models.**[109] An architect's plans fall within category (1) above.[110] It is the actual structure or a model of it which is separately treated in the second category. By implication, some consideration must be given to artistic quality. It may well be enough to show "something apart from the common stock of ideas".[111]

11–17 (iii) **Works of artistic craftsmanship.**[112] A considerable miscellany of artefacts—jewellery, furniture, cutlery, toys, educational aids and so on—may claim to rank as "works of artistic craftsmanship" within category (3).[113] As we shall see, the scope of this category has increased in importance under the

[105] Gendreau, Nordemann and Oesch, *Copyright and Photographs* (1999); Stokes in McClean and Schubert, *Dear Images* (2002), p.208; Arnold [2005] E.I.P.R. 303. A person who organises the objects to be photographed may be a joint author of the photograph then produced, but is not an author of another photograph of the objects, taken without authority: *Creation Records v News Group* above, n.89; Garnett and Abbott [1998] E.I.P.R. 204. Some hint that the photographer needs to show some skill in arranging the subject is to be found in *Antiquesportfolio.com v Rodney Fitch* [2001] F.S.R. 345. The US decision that photographs of paintings are not the subject of copyright in UK is probably wrong: *Bridgeman Art Library v Corel* 26 F Supp. 2d 421; 36 F. Supp. 191 (1998, SDNY); Garnett [2000] E.I.P.R. 229; cf. Deazley [2001] E.I.P.R. 179.

[106] As to which, see below, para.11–48.

[107] For another aspect of this controversy, see below, para.11–47.

[108] Despite the fact that art.6, Duration Directive allows Member States to provide protection for other photographs. This would seem to require the introduction of a related right, rather than a lax interpretation of the originality standard.

[109] See Greenwood (1986) 16 Queensland L.Soc.J. 221.

[110] See above, para.11–14. Cf. *Chabot v Davies* (1936) 155 L.T. 525; *Metricon Homes Pty Ltd v Barrett Property Group Pty Ltd* [2008] F.C.A.F.C. 46 Full FC Aust.

[111] For this distinction, *Blake v Warren* [1928–1935] Mac. CC 268 (decided under the CA 1911 s.35(1) and concerned in any case with drawings); *Metricon Homes* (above, n.110: decided under the Australian Copyright Act 1968 and concerned with architectural drawings); see also below, para.12–07.

[112] See R.G. Kenny (1984) 13 U. Queensland L.J. 206; Thomson [2010] E.I.P.R. 113.

[113] See above, para.11–14. For a recent example, the sets, costumes and latex prostheses for Mary Shelley's Frankenstein: *Shelley Films v Rex Features* [1994] E.M.L.R. 134. Note that, if a three-dimensional object can be described as a "sculpture" or an "engraving", it comes within category (1): cf. n.88, above.

CDPA 1988.[114] The criteria which a court should apply in deciding whether an article earns this description were intensively canvassed in *Hensher v Restawile*[115] (where the subject matter was a prototype for a suite of furniture of distinctly low-brow appeal).[116] However, the speeches in the House of Lords display no uniformity of approach. Three factors warrant attention: (1) is it the craftsman's intention to create something artistic that counts or rather the perception by the public of artistic quality in the article; (2) what level of artistic aspiration or attainment must be shown; (3) is it for the judge to make up his own mind on the question, or is his function to weigh the relative strength of expert and other testimony given to the court?

Concerning factor (1), the House of Lords rejected the Court of Appeal's approach. This was to ask whether the public would purchase the thing for its aesthetic appeal rather than its functional utility.[117] Lord Simon of Glaisdale drew attention to the English aesthetic tradition (stemming from Ruskin, Morris and the Arts and Crafts Movement) which eschewed any dichotomy between artistic appeal and functional value, seeking rather to derive the one from the other; indeed, the admission of "works of artistic craftsmanship" into the fold of copyright had been a response to that very movement.[118] Lord Reid, however, still attached first importance to the attitude of the public: a work of craftsmanship would be artistic if a substantial section of the public admired and valued it for its appearance.[119] Lord Kilbrandon, on the other hand, laid emphasis on the conscious intention to produce a work of art,[120] and Lord Simon took a similar starting point, though he also brought into account the result achieved.[121] Less specifically Lord Morris would give primacy neither to the intent of the artist nor the priorities of an acquirer, calling instead for a detached judgment of the thing itself. Viscount Dilhorne appears to take a similar view.[122] From all this, judges have since laid stress on whether the creator had a conscious purpose of making a work of art[123]; and whether the result could be so regarded. Thus the design of a raincape and prototypes for the mass **11–18**

[114] See below, Ch.15.

[115] *Hensher v Restawile* [1975] R.P.C. 31. For an intensive examination of this area by the Australian High Court see *Burge v Swarbuck* [2007] F.S.R. 27.

[116] *Hensher* [1975] R.P.C. 31 at 62, 70, 72. There must be some craftsmanly activity, not mere assemblage: *Creation Records v News Group*, above, n.89.

[117] *Hensher* [1975] R.P.C. 31 at 47.

[118] *Hensher* [1975] R.P.C. 31 at 65–67. One purpose of Lord Simon's disquisition was to emphasise that a work could not be excluded from consideration merely because it was machine-made, rather than hand-crafted. But Lord Reid seems to disagree: cf. at 53.

[119] *Hensher* [1975] R.P.C. 31 at 54. The same approach is found, e.g. in *Cuisenaire v Reed* [1963] V.R. 719 (coloured sticks for mathematical teaching method neither craftsmanship nor artistic); cf. also *Cuisenaire v South West Imports* [1968] 1 Ex. C.R. 493.

[120] *Hensher* [1975] R.P.C. 31 at 72.

[121] *Hensher* [1975] R.P.C. 31 at 70; see also *Hay v Sloan* (1957) 16 Fox P.C. 185.

[122] *Hensher* [1975] R.P.C. 31 at 57, 62–63.

[123] Cf. *Burge v Swarbuck* [2007] F.S.R. 27 where the High Court of Australia moved away from a "conscious purpose" test in favour of assessing "the extent to which the particular work's artistic expression, in its form, is unconstrained by functional considerations" (para.83).

production of ordinary garments failed for lack of conscious purpose,[124] as did parts of the costume worn by characters in a film,[125] while designs for sample bedspreads and cushions were not works of art but only craftsmanship.[126]

11–19 Concerning factor (2), at first instance Graham J. was satisfied that the prototype furniture qualified for copyright because it had distinctive characteristics of shape, form and finish, and resulted in articles that were much more than purely utilitarian.[127] But since the House of Lords were unanimously of the opinion that it did not qualify, it seems clear that some higher level of artistic intent or attainment is necessary; this indeed is the real significance of the case. There must be sufficient craftsmanship as well as artistry. Accordingly, Lords Reid and Morris doubted whether a mere prototype, not intended to have value or permanence in itself, could count.[128]

11–20 Concerning factor (3), Lord Kilbrandon emphasised the place of the judge's own evaluation by treating the question as one of law.[129] But Viscount Dilhorne said that it was a question of fact to be decided on the evidence[130] and Lord Simon laid stress on expert evidence—from those who are acknowledged artist-craftsmen or who train such people.[131] Yet again, Lord Reid's view calls for proof that a substantial section of the public regard the article as artistic.[132] At least a person seeking to prove this form of copyright should be permitted to lead both kinds of evidence: expert and (if positive) non-expert.

11–21 One problem which the House of Lords judgment does not touch is the question whether there can be a work of artistic craftsmanship when one person supplies the artistic idea and another the craftsmanship. Clauson J. once considered that there could not then be copyright (the two people in question being the designer and the seamstress of a dress).[133] More recently other judges have shown some coolness towards this distinction.[134] Even if in itself it is a bad point, the *Hensher* decision nonetheless requires the designer's contribution to give serious aesthetic significance to the end product. This category of copyright is not a ready tool against unfair imitation.

---

[124] *Merlet v Mothercare* [1986] R.P.C. 115; *Guild v Eskander* [2001] F.S.R. 645.

[125] *Lucasfilm Ltd v Ainsworth* [2009] F.S.R. 9 (Ch).

[126] *Vermaat v Boncrest* [2001] F.S.R. 43. See further *Coogi Australia v Hysport* (1998) 157 A.L.R. 247; *Bonz Group v Cooke* [1994] 3 N.Z.L.R. 216.

[127] *Hensher* [1975] R.P.C. 31 at 40; taken by the CA to be the same test as whether there is novelty enough to secure a registered design: at 47. For this, see below, paras 15–17, 15–18.

[128] *Hensher* [1975] R.P.C. 31 at 53, 56.

[129] *Hensher* [1975] R.P.C. 31 at 72.

[130] *Hensher* [1975] R.P.C. 31 at 62–63.

[131] *Hensher* [1975] R.P.C. 31 at 69–70.

[132] See above, n.119.

[133] *Burke v Spicers Dress Designs* [1936] 1 Ch. 400; cf. Graham J., *Restawile* case [1975] 1 R.C.P. 31 at 40. And see Eder (1976) 5 CIPA 270; Gibbins and Hobbs [1979] 1 E.I.P.R. 8.

[134] e.g. Oliver J. *Spyrou v Radley Gowns* [1975] F.S.R. 455; Fox J. *Bernstein v Sydney Murray* [1981] R.P.C. 303; Walton J. *Merlet v Mothercare* [1986] R.P.C. 115 at 123–124.

(e) *Computer-generated works*

For the most part, the author of a literary, dramatic, musical or artistic work is its creator in a real sense. He or she (but not it) is the person who, by exercising labour, skill and judgment, gives expression to ideas of the appropriate kind. But even at this juncture, a certain notionalism begins to appear. For the CDPA 1988 acknowledges that works of all these types may be computer-generated; and it provides that, where the circumstances are such that there is no human author of such a work, the author shall be taken to be the person by whom the arrangements necessary for creation of the work are undertaken.[135] **11–22**

(2) Films[136]

Until the intervention of EU Directives, the copyright in a film (as distinct from copyright in any dramatic, musical or other work incorporated into the film) was dealt with on an entrepreneurial basis. Under both the 1956 and the 1988 Acts the person who undertook the arrangements necessary for the making of the film (that is, normally, the film's producer, as financial and administrative organiser) was alone accorded the copyright in it. The CDPA 1988 continues to provide the crucial definition for the present law: "film" means a recording on any medium (including, therefore, celluloid, video tape and digital recording), provided that a moving image can be produced from it.[137] Thus the film is the recording and can be reproduced only by making a copy of that film, and not by re-filming it afresh.[138] In this it is more limited a right than the dramatic work which it may embody.[139] **11–23**

However, for films made from July 1, 1994 onwards,[140] the Duration Directive requires the principal director of a film to be considered one of its authors.[141] Film-making has today acquired an irreversible status as an art form and the Directive acknowledges the clear case of directors to be treated

135 CDPA 1988 ss.9(3), 178: "computer-generated". This conception is difficult to apply. When a subscriber to a service such as "Lexis" has the results of a search printed out, is this "computer-generated", and if so by whom? See further below, paras 20–44—20–45.

136 See Kamina, *Film Copyright in the European Union* (2002) 120–129; Kamina in Derclaye, *Research Handbook on the Future of EU Copyright* (2009), ch 4; Barron (2004) 67 M.L.R. 177; Salokannel, *Ownership of Rights in Audiovisual Productions: a comparative study* (1997); Greenfield et al, *Film and the Law* (2010). As to ownership issues, European Commission Report, COM/2002/0691.

137 CDPA 1988, s.5B.

138 *Norowzian v Arks (No. 1)* [1998] F.S.R. 394.

139 See below, para.11–46.

140 Earlier films will continue to be governed by the legal regime affecting them at the time they were made: Copyright and Related Rights Regulations 1996 (SI 1995/2967) reg.36.

141 Duration Directive (above, para.10–19), arts 2(1), 10(4). Arguably, a director who adds significantly to scenario or script of an acted film during filming in any case acquires copyright in the film as a dramatic work copyright for his or her life plus 70 years: Laddie et al., para.5.26; Kamina [1994] E.I.P.R. 319. However, there are difficulties in this approach for films made under the CA 1956. Laddie et al., para.5.44, argue that the problems can be overcome.

as authors. The acceptance of their case resolves one of the major conflicts between British copyright and Continental authors' rights. The British Government has implemented this obligation by creating an admixed, author-cum-neighbour, copyright for films.[142] Copyright in a film is thus given jointly to the producer (in the above sense) and to the principal director. This must count as the ultimate hybrid among intellectual property rights, and it demonstrates a thoroughly British determination not to subscribe to the authors' rights-neighbouring rights dichotomy.

11–24 If one puts on one side the correlative enhancement of term[143] the impending change in the director's copyright status may be of greater ideological than practical consequence. In the first place, the principal director's entitlement is subject to the general rule that works created in the course of employment are prima facie the property *ab initio* of the employer[144]; and secondly, even directors who are commissioned rather than employed must normally expect to assign copyright to their producers. If they have an extraordinary reputation they may contract to do this on royalty-sharing or other special terms. The additional prestige which directors may derive from attaining the rank of author is subtle. Over time it may well contribute to their earning power as a class, but they are likely to be helped at least as much by collective action, either in the form of trade union pressure or the institution of collecting societies,[145] to enforce their rights directly against users.

11–25 Film is a field in which the law has needed to reflect highly significant technological advances. The CA 1956 was still conceived for an era of celluloid material and referred to "cinematographic films". The subsequent arrival of video taping, and now of digital recording, has added immensely to the ways in which filmed material can be produced and subsequently manipulated. The CDPA 1988 is much more up to date than its predecessor. It talks of "film", but defines it in a way which embraces audio-visual production in general, so as to include "a recording on any medium from which a moving image can be produced".[146]

Thus it would seem to cover many "multi-media" digital recordings. These may make much greater use of text, alongside visual images and a soundtrack, than a traditional film, and they may include opportunities for interactivity; nevertheless, so long as moving images are part of their make-up, they fall to be treated as films. As with other films, the material which goes into their make-up will form distinct copyright subject-matter requiring a licence for use in any case where the subject-matter is substantially

---

142 See the 1996 Regulations (above, n.140), reg.17.

143 For which, see below, paras 11–45, 11–46.

144 CDPA 1988 (as amended) s.11(2).

145 For a presumption of assignment of rental rights in embodied material, and related rights to equitable remuneration, which will follow from implementation of the Directive on Rental Rights, see its arts 2(7), (4).

146 CDPA 1988 s.5(1).

reproduced in the product. This will be true of any incorporated computer program (itself a literary work) which is needed to control interactivity, just as in a computer game.

(3) The entrepreneurial copyrights

The copyrights in sound recordings, broadcasts and typographical format, are all carried forward in updated form from the previous legislation. The sui generis database right is the product of the EU Directive on the subject[147]; and the publisher's right in long-unpublished works comes from the Duration Directive.[148] **11–26**

The subject matter in the first category has been re-defined to take account of major technological advances. "Sound recording" covers any recording of literary, dramatic or musical work or other sounds (bird-song, the noises of a motor-race, etc.),[149] regardless of medium, and so will include disc, tape, compact disc, digital audio tape and future technical developments. There is, however, no copyright in any sound recording which is a copy of another, authorised or unauthorised.[150]

"Broadcast" has also been broadened as a category to take account of cable-casting. It covers any transmission of visual images, sounds or other information by electronic means (i.e. whether wired or wireless). It must be capable of lawful reception by the public (in particular through use of decoding equipment made available through the person transmitting in encrypted form), or which is for presentation to the public.[151] But "broadcasting" does not extend to making material available on demand on an internet or similar service. The latter creates no copyright, although it is an activity which falls within the scope of copyright belonging to others (e.g. in music and films made available through this media). A broadcast may be by terrestrial and satellite transmission. This takes account of the forms of satellite broadcasting whether they are may be directly received by individuals or are re-transmitted by cable. Following the EU Satellite and Cable Directive, the place from where the signals are transmitted to the satellite (the "up-leg") is treated as the place of broadcasting.[152] Thus copyright **11–27**

[147] Database Directive; implemented by the Copyright and Rights in Databases Regulations (SI 1997/3032) ("Database Regulations").

[148] Dir.93/98/EEC, now codified as Dir. 2006/116 art.4.

[149] CDPA 1988 s.5A(1). Both examples have a commercial value. Note that film soundtrack now falls to be treated as a sound recording, rather than as part of the film, except when used to accompany the film: s.5B(2), (3), (5). The rule applies to existing and new films: Sch.1 para.8. For the technology and its legal consequences, Sterling, *Intellectual Property Rights in Sound Recordings, Film and Video* (1992), Chs 2, 3.

[150] CDPA 1988 s.5A(2).

[151] CDPA 1988 s.6(1). Broadcasts made before June 1, 1957 acquire no copyright, though later repeats do so: Sch.1 para.9.

[152] CDPA 1988 s.6(4). If the transmission is started by cable in one country and sent to a transmitter in another, then it is the first country which counts.

arises in satellite broadcasts transmitted from the United Kingdom, extended territories and those countries with Rome Convention and other reciprocal connections to the United Kingdom.[153] The notion of the "up-leg" is here used in order to identify the national system which determines whether it is copyright and accordingly to what extent. The "up-leg", as we shall see, also defines the act of broadcasting which requires a copyright licence from authors, film and record producers, other broadcasters, etc.[154]

11–28 The typographical-arrangement copyright arises in respect of a published edition of the whole or part of one or more literary, dramatic or musical (but not artistic) works, provided that it does not simply reproduce the typographical arrangement of a previous edition.[155]

11–29 As will be seen from the Table (head 3), the "creator-author" of these rights is not the person who by labour, skill and judgment puts the recording, broadcast or printed format into its particular form. He, she or (most likely) it, is the person in charge of the undertaking: the person who makes the necessary arrangements for a sound recording, the person making a broadcast, the publisher of a typographical format. Despite their guise in the CDPA 1988, these remain in truth neighbouring rights.[156] They are accorded directly in order to protect investment, not creativity, and therefore do not depend upon any level of aesthetic achievement, such as the auditory skills of a recording engineer or the creativity of an editor in publishing. If the latter provides sufficient skill and labour in, for instance, selecting material for an anthology, he or she will be the author of a "literary work" and acquire copyright in that form.

11–30 The sui generis right in a database, deriving from the Database Directive,[157] has come into UK law as a right separate from copyright (as have rights in performances). Nevertheless its subject matter is so close to authors' copyright in compilations that the two need differentiation at this stage. A compilation is capable of being an original work of authorship for copyright purposes.[158] However, most compilations will now fall within the definition of a "database":

---

[153] For several years, WIPO has been charged with developing a new international instrument governing rights in broadcasts conceived on a wide basis: see the version of the Draft Treaty at SCCR/12/2 Rev 2 (2005). The interests involved in these developments are diverse enough to make progress slow: see Akester, *UNESCO e-Copyright Bulletin*, April–June 2006.

[154] See below, paras 14–24, 14–29, which consider the impact of the EU Satellite and Cable Directive.

[155] CDPA 1988 s.8. The Duration Directive, art.5, permits Member States to create a publishers' right in critical and scientific works which have fallen into the public domain. This may last for up to 30 years from publication. The UK has not so far taken advantage of this possibility, which for the works concerned, is not limited to a right against reprography.

[156] CDPA 1988 s.9(2).

[157] Directive 96/9; above, para.10–19.

[158] Above, para.11–06, n.33.

"a collection of independent works, data or other materials which (a) are arranged in a systematic or methodical way, and (b) are individual accessible by electronic or other means".[159]

The Directive has required that, for there to be copyright (literary—or, in appropriate cases, musical or artistic) in a database, the selection or arrangement of the independent material must constitute the author's own intellectual creation.[160] This is likely to exclude from copyright the listing of mundane information such as names and addresses in street directories, and telephone and internet listings. What else will be cut away from former understandings of "originality" is hard to surmise.[161]

However that may be, the Database Right (i.e. the sui generis right), **11–31** which has been in operation for pre-existing as well as new databases of all kinds since 1998, applies without reference to any concept of originality. It is given instead to the investor who makes a substantial investment in obtaining, verifying or presenting the contents of a database.[162] It operates, at least when there has not been further investment in changing its contents, for a restricted term of 15 years from completion.[163] It thus ranks with the other entrepreneurial rights discussed under this head. The details of the right will be dealt with later.[164]

Also deserving comparison at this point is the publication right given to a person who "publishes" a work with authority for the first time after its term of copyright has expired.[165] Literary, dramatic, musical and artistic works and films are covered for 25-year term. Aimed particularly to secure the outlay on producing re-discovered manuscripts and art-works, it fills a gap which arose when in 1988 copyright in unpublished material ceased to have an indeterminate copyright.

---

159 Database Regulations, reg.6 (included in CDPA 1988 s.3A).

160 CDPA 1988 s.3A(2).

161 See below, para.20–37.

162 Database Regulations regs 13–15.

163 Database Regulations reg.17.

164 See below, paras 20–38 et seq., in particular for qualification, term and infringement.

165 Copyright etc. Regulations (SI 1996/2967) regs 16, 17. "Publication" includes, as well as making copies available to the public, renting, lending, performing, etc. in public, broadcasting, making the work available by means of an electronic retrieval system. The authority must be that of the owner of the physical record. Publication must be in the EEA or by an EEA national. Much of the detail follows provisions on copyright, including the requirement of copying for infringement. For a full account, see Copinger Ch.17, and for differences in implementation between Member States, Burrell and Haslam [1998] E.I.P.R. 210.

3. Formalities and Permanent Form

(1) Absence of formalities

11–32 Originally UK copyright law required registration of works with the Stationers' Company as a condition, first of acquiring, later of enforcing, copyright in published works. But that had to be abandoned once the Berne Convention conceived copyright as a property flowing "naturally" and without formality from the act of creation.[166] Since the 1911 Act, neither registration nor any formal notification of the claim to copyright on copies of Berne Convention works has been a prerequisite either of copyright itself or of the entitlement to institute proceedings for infringement. As already explained,[167] the "copyright notice" on published works (©, name of copyright owner, year of first publication) appears in order to attract copyright in non-Berne countries—including, until 1989, the United States—which accept this as a sufficient formality; they do so in general because they belong to the UCC which provides that this shall be sufficient.[168]

Since these Conventions only cover literary, dramatic, musical and artistic works and films, the same constraints do not apply to other copyright material. But sound recordings no longer require marking, as they did under the CA 1956, in order to attract their own copyright.

(2) Permanent form for the work[169]

11–33 Nonetheless it is an assumption of UK copyright legislation that all subject matter requires to exist in some permanent form before it gains copyright. It is possible to look upon this as a corollary of the principle that the protection goes only to the particular expression of ideas. Thus, in the case of most artistic works it is only when the particular painting, photograph or other work is executed that the idea for it is transmuted into expression; the act of creation and the "fixation" of the work are indivisible.[170]

But literary, dramatic and musical creativity admits of more stages. A man may conceive a speech in his mind and deliver it from memory without ever writing it down. Indeed, some composers, lacking musical literacy, can

166 See above, paras 10–06–10–08; and note Berne Convention art.5(2). Copyright does not depend upon the obligation of every publisher in the UK to supply a copy of a published book to the British Museum and five other libraries: see Legal Deposit Libraries Act 2003 (c. 28).
167 See above, para.10–11.
168 See UCC art.3(1).
169 Latreille in in Derclaye, *Research Handbook on the Future of EU Copyright* (2009), Ch 6.
170 Fixation and permanence can give rise to nice issues in the sphere of artistic activity. Adam Ant's face make-up did not have permanence enough for copyright: *Merchandising Corp of America v Harpbond* [1983] F.S.R. 32 CA; nor did a device containing sand and glycerine for making "sand pictures" by moving it: *Komesaroff v Mickle* [1988] R.P.C. 204.

only get their works into permanent form by performing for another to write down or recording.[171] So long as there is no fixation, they have no copyright and must seek legal protection elsewhere, particularly through performers' protection legislation and contract.[172]

The CDPA 1988 fills a previous lacuna in the statutes: it specifies that a literary, dramatic or musical work is not the subject of copyright unless and until it is recorded, in writing or otherwise (for instance, by tape recording or filming)[173]; and that it is immaterial whether the author gave permission for the recording or not.[174] It has long been accepted that a person who arranges for a stenographer to take down his speech is the author of the resulting work, for it has merely been recorded by an amanuensis.[175] What, then, of a reporter who records a politician's speech, acting on his own initiative or that of his employer? The new provision treats the politician—the creator of the words—as the author of the literary work thus generated. The provision, however, is not to affect the question whether a distinct copyright exists in the record.[176] **11–34**

If the reporter has used an audio-tape, clearly there is a sound recording that will be the subject of a separate copyright (with, however, its own limited scope, not extending to acts of transcribing the speech as a written text).[177] But if the record was the taking down of an oral version writing—for instance, by shorthand—the old case of *Walter v Lane*[178] still applies. This treated the reporter as entitled to literary copyright in the report of the speech by virtue of his skill and labour in reducing it to permanent form. That decision was reached before the statutory requirement of "originality" was included in the law. How far it remains applicable has since been questioned and a distinction suggested between one who uses an aesthetic skill to make a record (for example the folk-song hunter) and one who uses a standard technique, such as tape-recording.[179] But a journalist who recorded a long interview and then selects brief extracts for a report shows the

[171] cf. *Hadley v Kemp* [1999] E.M.L.R. 589.

[172] The copyrights in sound recordings, films and typographical format concern fixed subject-matter. Broadcasts, however, are essentially transient activities which are nevertheless protected as such.

[173] *Norowzian v Arks (No. 2)* [1999] F.S.R. 49; the recording or filming relied upon must contain the earlier work.

[174] CDPA 1988 s.3(2), (3). Previously a work was regarded as made when it was put in permanent form by writing or otherwise; choreographic works had, however, to be notated: CA 1956 s.48(1), 49(4). Accordingly, the wider scope of recording affects them in particular.

[175] Lord James of Hereford, *Walter v Lane* [1900] A.C. 539 at 554. Cf. the "ghost writer" who is the author giving expression to the teller's ideas: *Donoghue v Allied Newspapers* [1938] 1 Ch. 106; and note *Evans v Hulton* [1923–1928] Mac. C.C. 51. See also the entertaining cases on spiritual communication: *Cummins v Bond* [1927] 1 Ch. 167; *Leah v Two Worlds* [1951] Ch. 393.

[176] CDPA 1988 s.3(3).

[177] See below, para.12–26.

[178] [1900] A.C. 539; cf. the copyright in a street directory, e.g. *Black v Stacey* [1929] 1 Ch. 177; and see also *Sands & McDougall v Robinson* (1917) 23 C.L.R. 49 at 54–55 HC Aust.; *Gould v Stoddard* (1988) 80 C.P.R. 93d) 161 CA Ont; *Hager v ECW Press* [1999] 2 F.C. 287.

[179] *Roberton v Lewis* (1960) [1976] R.P.C. 169.

necessary skill and judgment.[180] Lord Oliver once suggested that a work that copies another cannot be original in a copyright sense because the end result is the same.[181] That however has been held to apply only to relatively mechanical reproduction, such as the re-creation of a technical drawing; and not to a re-creation that requires distinct literary or artistic skill and judgment, such as the editing of an old and inadequate musical score.[182]

4. Qualification

11–35 One quintessential purpose of the Berne and UCC Conventions is to secure the principle of national treatment: the works of authors connected with any one Member State are to receive the same copyright under the law of each other Member State as do the works of authors connected with the latter state.[183] The same applies to the Rome Convention and now to TRIPS. The connection may arise by virtue of the author's personal relationship to a country—his status—or because the country is the place of first publication. While a work remains unpublished, of course, the connection can only concern personal status.

Accordingly, the UK Act first prescribes the factors (of status and first publication) that will give sufficient connection with Britain, and with the few dependent territories to which the CDPA 1988 is *extended*.[184] Then, as a consequence of British participation, the Act is *applied* to works and Pt 2 subject matter, which are connected by the same factors to other Convention countries. The legal machinery for this step is found in s.32 and the Orders in Council made in implementation of it.[185]

A complication arises because countries adhere to the Conventions at different dates. If a country is only a UCC member, then works published before the country joined do not gain UK copyright.[186] But the method of the Berne Convention is partly retrospective. Once a country joins, works that are connected with it and are still in copyright under its domestic legislation acquire UK copyright. But persons who have incurred

[180] *Express Newspapers v News (UK)* [1990] F.S.R. 359.

[181] *Interlego v Tyco Industries* [1989] AC 289 JC at 371.

[182] Jacob L.J., *Sawkins v Hyperion Records* [2005] R.P.C. 32 at paras 77–83.

[183] Berne Convention arts 3–5; UCC art.2. Both Conventions cover literary, dramatic, musical and artistic works and films: see art.2(1) and art.1, respectively.

[184] These include the Isle of Man, the Channel Islands and Colonies: see CDPA 1988 s.157 and Orders in Council thereunder. Formerly the notion of extension was important since it was the foundation of "Imperial copyright" operating throughout the British Empire. But former British possessions, even if they have stayed within the Commonwealth, have not wished to preserve an essentially uniform copyright law. They are connected today only through the medium of the international Conventions, if they have become members.

[185] In the CDPA 1988, even the British have ceased to accord protection to authors who are "British Commonwealth citizens".

[186] But unpublished works already in existence may acquire copyright by virtue of personal connection with the UCC country.

expenditure or liability for reproduction or performance of such a work before this copyright took effect can be enjoined only upon payment of compensation.[187]

(1) Qualification by personal status

If the connection is directly to the United Kingdom, it is necessary to ask whether the "author" is a "qualifying person". Is he: (1) a British citizen or person within certain other categories of the British Nationality Act 1981[188]; (2) a person domiciled or resident in the United Kingdom; or (3) a body incorporated in part of the United Kingdom?[189] If the connection comes by application of the Act to Convention countries, it will be necessary to show the status, called for in the Copyright (Application to Other Countries) Order 1999, the relevant person must be a citizen or subject, domiciliary or resident, of a scheduled Convention country, or a company incorporated there.[190] **11–36**

In either case, this question has to be asked at the "material time". For unpublished literary, dramatic, musical and artistic works, that is the date of making the work. Where the work has been published, it is the author's status at the date of first publication that is in issue; or, if the author died before publication, his status at the date of his death. By way of contrast, the material time for other copyrights does not change: it is the personal status of the "author" of a sound recording or film at the time of its making, that of the broadcasting organisation at the date of transmission and, for typographical format, that of the publisher at publication.[191]

(2) Connection by publication

First publication is not only a point in time for considering personal status; it is also a connecting factor in its own right.[192] This is so both directly under the Act and through its application to the Convention countries.[193] If publication occurs in two countries within 30 days, the second may be treated as first publication, if this helps: the two are thus deemed simultaneous.[194] **11–37**

---

[187] Berne Convention art.18; Copyright (Application to Other Countries) Order 1993 (SI 1993/942) r.7(2).

[188] i.e. a British Dependent Territories citizen, a British National (Overseas), a British Overseas Citizen, a British Subject or a British Protected Person: see generally CDPA 1988 s.154(1).

[189] In the last two categories, the connection may equally be to a country to which the Act extends.

[190] CDPA 1988 s.154(2); SI 1993/942; SI 1994/263; SI 1995/2987.

[191] CDPA 1988 s.154(4), (5). For joint authors, see s.154(3).

[192] For the meaning of "publication" see the next section.

[193] CDPA 1988 s.155.

[194] CDPA 1988 s.153(3), following Berne Convention art.3(4).

In the past, when the United States and various other countries were not members of the Berne Convention, their citizens gained international protection achieved by first publication in a Convention country. In particular, Canada acted as the "Berne back-door" for the United States, and so allowed the country which was rapidly becoming the greatest copyright exporter in the world to have the advantages of the Convention without such obligations as the long minimum term and the exclusion of registration. Today, the rush to join Berne (enhanced by the Convention's incorporation into TRIPS) has deprived this routine of much significance.[195]

A different aspect of first publication under Berne should be noted here. Because it is an action which can be relatively easily proved, the Convention takes the country of first publication as the normal indicator of a work's "country of origin".[196] Only if first publication is not in a Berne Union country, will the nationality of the author determine country of origin. As we shall see, this has become important in imposing the rule of the lesser term on works originating outside the EEA.[197]

5. Publication

11–38 What amounts to publication can be significant in establishing a qualifying factor. "Publication" is also important in measuring the term of some kinds of copyright and it may occasionally be relevant at other points in the law.

In the law of defamation, "publication" means communication to any person other than the person defamed.[198] In the law of patents, it covers making information available to any person free in law and equity to use it as he wishes.[199] As a term of art in copyright law it comes closer to ordinary understanding: in general, it means issuing copies of the work to the public in quantities intended to satisfy reasonable public demand; and, in the case of literary, dramatic, musical and artistic works, it includes making the work available to the public through an electronic retrieval system.[200] The "work" means the work as a whole, so each draft or edition must be considered separately.[201] It does not include performing a literary, dramatic or musical

[195] Along with art.6 of the Berne Convention, introduced in 1914 to close the "Berne back-door".

[196] Berne Convention art.5(4). Where there is simultaneous publication in more than one Berne country, that which gives the shorter term is the country of origin; where there is simultaneous publication in a Berne and a non-Berne country, the former is the country of origin.

[197] See below, para.11–55.

[198] See, e.g. *Clerk and Lindsell on Torts* 19th edn (2005), paras 22–66 et seq.

[199] See above, paras 5–12—5–13.

[200] CDPA 1988 s.175(1). Construction of a building is the equivalent of publishing the architectural work it embodies: s.175(3). There is also a definition of "commercial publication": s.175(2).

[201] *Sweeney v Macmillan* [2002] R.P.C. 251: early version of Joyce's *Ulysses*.

work, or broadcasting it; exhibiting an artistic work; or issuing graphic works or photographs of sculptures, works of architecture or works of artistic craftsmanship. Unauthorised acts are not brought into account.[202]

All this raises technical questions at the margins. Where the requirement is that copies be issued to the public, this refers to first putting them into circulation presumably by sale, hire or gift. Publication takes place wherever the publisher invites the public to acquire copies, not where the copies are received.[203] To hold the contrary would make the country of first publication dependent on where shipments happen first to be received.[204] Whether publication is to be accounted more than "merely colourable"[205] depends primarily on the intent of the publisher at the date in question. The Court of Appeal held it enough to put six copies of the sheet music of a song on sale at a time when the song was not known—it was not necessary to promote it first.[206] Some account was taken of the publishers' readiness to fulfil demand when the song did become highly popular[207]; this is best viewed as confirmation of the original intention to supply whatever demand there was. **11–39**

We shall see that the basic forms of copyright give the right not only to stop unauthorised reproductions of the work in its original form but also in other "material" forms, and they give protection against adaptations (for example turning a book into a ballet, a novel into a play, a work in Polish into a work in English, a song into an orchestral number, a drawing into a three-dimensional object).[208] If the author, or someone with his permission, converts an unpublished work into one of these new forms and makes copies of the result available to the public, will this have the effect of publishing the original work? The Act gives no plain guidance; but the answer may well turn on the distinction between reproduction (in any material form) and adaptation,[209] publication being primarily concerned with issuing copies to the public. Thus it was held that a drawing was published by issuing three-dimensional embodiments of it to the public, because the definition of "reproduction" specifically included converting a 2D work into 3D and vice **11–40**

202 CDPA 1988 s.175(6). Joint authors, etc. are not specifically dealt with, but probably all must consent before a publication is authorised.

203 See Megarry J. *British Northrop v Texteam* [1974] R.P.C. 57 at 67.

204 See *British Northrop v Texteam* (above, n.203); *McFarlane v Hulton* [1899] 1 Ch. 884; *"Oscar" TM* [1980] F.S.R. 429.

205 The phrase is used in CDPA 1988 s.175(5) in contradistinction to an intent to fulfil the reasonable requirements of the public.

206 *Francis Day v Feldman* [1914] 2 Ch. 728 CA; and see *Bodley Head v Flegon* [1972] 1 W.L.R. 680.

207 In *Copex v Flegon, The Times*, August 18, 1967, it was argued, but not decided, that there could be no publication of a work in its original Russian where the intent was merely to secure the copyright in subsequent translations. The two purposes, however, are not incompatible.

208 The last instance is not strictly an "adaptation".

209 See the definitions below, paras 12–23, 12–25.

versa.[210] By parity of reasoning, it would seem that issuing a work on film or in any other "material" form of "reproduction" would suffice for publication.[211]

11–41 "Adaptation", which is distinguished from reproduction among the acts restricted by literary, dramatic and musical copyright, is concerned with reworking material in a manner which normally involves enough to add a further adapter's copyright. This may well constitute sufficient reason for not treating publication of the adaptation as publication of the original. If this is right, consider its impact upon translations—an important form of adaptation. If a work is written by a resident of a non-Convention country, and is then sent to (say) France for publication there in translation, only the particular translation will acquire Convention copyright. There will be nothing to prevent a British publisher from publishing a new translation from the original language.[212]

6. Term of Copyright

11–42 The question of duration is central to the justifications for authors' rights and neighbouring rights, and from that perspective the EU Duration Directive has already been critically considered.[213] Here we turn to the practical effects of that Directive, for better or worse, under the amended CDPA 1988.[214]

The term required by the Berne Convention for the classic forms of copyright is the author's life and 50 years thereafter.[215] Although this term is a minimum,[216] it formed the root of UK legislation from 1911 to 1988. Moreover, since 1956 it has been offered to nationals of other states connected with the United Kingdom by the Convention, even when their own terms of protection have been less (for example because they were only

[210] *Merchant Adventurers v Grew* [1973] R.P.C. 1 at 10; *British Northrop* case (above, n.203) at 65. This question became significant once artistic copyright in industrial designs was recognised: see para.15–05, below. Whether these decisions remain good in relation to design documents within the exclusion of CDPA 1988 s.51, is a question of great obscurity.

[211] A further historical pointer is that, before 1911, publication consisted in principle of communicating a work to the public in any manner, including even by performance. The various specific exceptions operate to reverse this old presumption.

[212] Hence the practice of publishing at least a limited edition of the original first, in order to provide a qualification through first publication for Convention copyright in it. This was the nub of the dispute in *Copex v Flegon* (above, n.207).

[213] See above, paras 10–54, 10–55.

[214] See Adams and Edenborough [1996] E.I.P.R. 590; Emilianides [2004] E.I.P.R. 538.

[215] Berne Convention art.7 (with exceptions for films, anonymous and pseudonymous works, photographs and applied art; see Ricketson and Ginsburg, Ch.9; Berne Convention art.7(5)), and in consequence the CDPA 1988 measures the duration of copyright from the end of the year in which a triggering event occurs, such as the author's death or the publication of a work or an edition. For brevity's sake, this added factor will be assumed throughout the text.

[216] Berne Convention art.7(6); and see Rome Convention art.14; Geneva Convention art.4.

members of the UCC and not of Berne).[217] In other words, in 1956 and again in 1988, the United Kingdom did not take advantage of the "lesser term" qualification in Berne,[218] which allows a country to depart from national treatment to the extent of only giving a foreign claimant the shorter term of copyright operative in the "country of origin" of the work.[219] Now, however, the Duration Directive not only requires longer periods for copyright than Berne and Rome Convention minima; it also adopts a reciprocal, "lesser term", approach to foreign claimants from outside the EEA—an issue to which we return after considering the rules for the different types of copyright.

(1) Classical works of authorship

Following the EU Directive, the general term for copyright in literary, dramatic, musical and artistic works is the author's life and 70 years thereafter.[220] If there are joint authors, then the term is measured from the death of the longest living among those who qualify for United Kingdom copyright.[221] Special exceptions concerning term are dealt with below.[222] **11–43**

The 20-year increase in term applies to works created before its introduction date (January 1, 1996) as well as to those created subsequently.[223] This has the effect not only of *extending* the protection of works which are still in UK copyright on the introduction date, but even of *reviving* copyright in works which in Britain had by then fallen into the public domain.[224] Copyright revives wherever a work is still protected in one EEA state on July 1, 1995, the most obvious point of reference being the German term of **11–44**

[217] Less includes non-existent: as for instance with snapshots, which are not protected at all in some countries, Berne's protection of "photographic works" being understood to mean only photographs which have some artistic element about them.

[218] Berne Convention art.7(8). The Convention's own presumption is in favour of the lesser term principle.

[219] For simplicity and convenience of proof, the main criterion of "country of origin" is place of first publication, rather than nationality of author or authors: Berne, art.5(4). This has an important effect in limiting the impact of the rule against discrimination on ground of nationality in the TFEU: see below, para.19–01.

[220] CDPA 1988 s.12(1). Citations in what follows are to the Act as amended by the Duration of Copyright and Rights in Performances Regulations 1995 (SI 1995/3297) (hereafter, "Duration Regulations 1995"). Note that, in line with the Berne Convention art.7(5), British terms are defined as being measured to the end of the year in which a death or other event occurs.

[221] CDPA 1988 s.13(4); cf. Duration Directive art.1(2). For joint authorship, a limited notion in UK law, see below, paras 13–19, 13–20.

[222] See below, paras 11–51—11–54.

[223] Duration Regulations 1995 reg.16. On this the European Parliament insisted, overriding the Commission's better judgment. The constitutionality of this revival of copyright was accepted by the ECJ on the basis that no person can have a legitimate expectation that it would never occur: *Butterfly Music v Carosello* [1999] E.C.R. I-3939; *Sony Music v Fallon* [2009] E.C.D.R. 12.

[224] Moral rights are likewise extended: see below, para.12–70.

the author's life plus 70 years.[225] Both extension and revival of copyright raise questions about title and other interests during the new term, which we will deal with later.[226]

The main thrust of the changes to the duration of UK copyright can be illustrated here:

— the copyright of Puccini (died 1924) expired at the end of 1974, so it remains lapsed;
— the copyright of Virginia Woolf (died 1941) expired in 1991, so it revives from January 1, 1996 until the end of 2011;
— the copyright of Picasso (died 1973) would have been due to expire in 2023, but will now extend until the end of 2043.

Since the CDPA 1988, UK copyright has lasted for the specified term, whether or not the work has been published in that time. Previously copyright law had, in many cases, protected unreleased work without limit of time (thus acting to some degree as a blanket for privacy). It had allowed the copyright term in a work to run on until 50 years from whenever posthumously it was made available for the first time.[227] That approach was, however, deemed over-scrupulous and out of the European line, and so was abandoned even before the Duration Directive.[228] But the new approach leaves publishers without real protection against copying when they first bring out long-hidden, out-of-copyright, material. This unusual risk has led to the Directive's requirement of a 25-year publication right to cover the case.

(2) Films

11–45 Article 2(1) of the Duration Directive requires the principal director of a film made after July 1, 1994 to be given a copyright equivalent to that of other true authors and that has now been done. Thus so far as initial entitlement is concerned, "old" films are those made before that date, "new" films afterwards.[229] There is a separate obligation to increase the term of film

[225] This follows the Duration Directive art.10(2). The reference to the position in other states could in certain cases prove highly complex. It may well require an investigation of how another EEA country applies its rule of the lesser term to a particular case. At least that rule cannot be applied, in relation to an EEA citizen, so as to produce a discriminatory effect against him or her. That would be contrary to the EU Treaty art.18: *Phil Collins v Imtrat* [1993] 3 C.M.L.R. 773, para.19–01 below; Cornish [1993] Y. Eur. L. 485; and *Hessen v Ricardi* [2004] 2 C.M.L.R. 20.

[226] See below, para.13–08.

[227] See, e.g. CA 1956 ss.2(3), 3(4).

[228] Works existing on August 1, 1989, which would have enjoyed the longer posthumous period of the old law and were still not released on that date, enjoy copyright for 70 years from it: CDPA 1988 Sch.1 para.12(4) (as amended).

[229] CDPA 1998 s.9(2)(ab); Copyright and Related Rights Regulations 1996 (SI 1996/2967) regs 18, 36.

copyright, previously confined to a neighbouring right period of 50 years from making or release, so as to become as 70 years from death. This operates for all films, old and new.[230] Moreover, the very considerable investment which goes into major film productions has been held to justify a special way of measuring lives. To guard against the consequences of the director's early death, the longest life among "persons connected with the film" is taken; and these include not only the principal director but the author of the screenplay, the author of the dialogue and the composer of any specifically created film score.[231] These latter are people who, according to the Directive, do not have to be given a share in the film copyright.[232] Nonetheless they will each provide original copyright material for the films and the dramatic and musical works will have a duration measured by reference to their individual lives.[233] Film-makers need to employ assiduous obituarists, and also to make sure that one or two of the listed "lives" are young, healthy and, if promiscuous, then precautionary.[234]

Because the new term of copyright applies to existing films[235] it extends the duration of those films in which copyright has not expired and revives copyright in those which have fallen into the public domain.[236] In either case the extension may be very considerable: in some cases, much more than the 20 years which is being added to authors' rights in general. **11–46**

A documentary film shot in the 1930s, which previously went out of UK copyright in the 1980s, will, as a film, gain revived copyright from November 1, 1995 until 70 years from the last death among its "connected persons".[237] A last death in 1980 would give copyright until 2050.[238] The director will not, however, become a joint author of it with the producer.

---

230 The Duration Directive art.3(3), requires that the lesser, neighbouring right, period should continue to be the period for the producer's right in the film (itself required by the Rental Directive art.7). It is hard, therefore, to see that the UK implementation complies with the Duration Directive. To the extent that the director can be regarded as already having copyright in the dramatic work made into the film (see above, para.11–23, n.141), this may have little practical significance, since the producer will normally acquire this dramatic copyright by assignment (thus aligning the UK with most other EU countries). But this argument is hard to sustain for some films.

231 CDPA 1988 s.13B(2). There can of course be more than one person in each of these categories.

232 Thus only the principal director has been given co-ownership of new films: above, para.11–23.

233 Normally the producer will have acquired their copyright by assignment or in consequence of employment and so is in any case interested in their dates of death.

234 Each of the "lives" may consist of more than one person, where there is a collaboration.

235 i.e. those existing at the date by which the Duration Directive should have been implemented: July 1, 1995.

236 See Duration Directive art.2(2).

237 A pre–CA 1956 film which was not a dramatic work could be protected only as a series of photographs—and they had copyright only for 50 years from making: see above, para.11–23; and note Duration Regulations 1995 reg.13. The increase will be equally substantial for most films made under the CA 1956; it is less so (an extra 20 years, plus whatever bonus comes from the added lives) for those which were dramatic works under the CA 1911.

238 But, being a revived copyright, the owner is entitled only to equitable remuneration: see below, para.13–09.

The current market for old films is so strong that these extensions are of prime economic importance. The risks undertaken in today's major productions are such that a studio needs a strong back-list to be sure of survival.

(3) Photographs

11–47 This type of artistic work calls for discussion because of the comparative generosity which UK law has long shown towards it.[239] Photographs have long attracted some measure of copyright protection, without the need to show that they meet any criterion of artistic quality: in contrast with the position in most systems of authors' rights, the work of the humble snapshot-taker stands in the same category as Beaton and Cartier-Bresson.

Occasionally, a casual photo will have a very considerable commercial value: it may reveal a celebrity's lies, or capture the winning goal. This continues to be the UK approach, although the Duration Directive only requires its "life-plus-70" duration to be given to photographs which are "the author's own intellectual creation".[240]

11–48 Under earlier UK law, photographs were given their own, limited term.[241] In 1988, they were placed on the level of other artistic works, by giving protection for the photographer's life and 50 years—a term which now increases to life plus 70 years.[242] While initially the increased term applied only to new photographs,[243] implementation of the Duration Directive has its general retroactive effect of both extending and reviving copyrights in existing work. As with films, the change for photographs can be very considerable:

A child's snapshot of Mrs Thatcher riding high in 1979, not published until 1985, would have enjoyed copyright until 2035, but will now have it extended until the child's death (say in 2040), plus 70 years, that is to 2110. A photograph of a society wedding in 1930 kept UK copyright until 1980, a term unaltered by either the 1956 or the 1988 Acts. Under the 1995 changes, it may re-acquire copyright from January 1, 1996 until the end of 70 years from the photographer's death. But in order to do so, it must still have been

[239] See above, para.11–15.

[240] Duration Directive art.6. Member States are left free to protect non-creative photos by some lesser right against misappropriation, as is relatively common. They are no longer allowed to reserve full copyright for photographs which measure up to some higher criterion than "own intellectual creation". Even that level of attainment is difficult to define (which is one reason for British avoidance of it). Carefully staged photography, both professional and amateur, is likely to satisfy it. But even press photography is much less easy to categorise.

[241] Under the CA 1911 s.21, this was 50 years from making; under the CA 1956 s.4, 50 years from publication.

[242] At the same time, the law abandoned a curious entrepreneurial preference. Under the CA 1956 s.48(1), the author of a photograph was deemed to be the owner of the material on which it was taken.

[243] CDPA 1988 Sch.1 para.12(2).

protected in an EEA State on July 1, 1995. This may well involve an investigation of its artistic quality under the foreign law in question.[244]

(4) Revived copyright: protection of third parties

The revival of lapsed copyright in works or films presents obvious difficulties for those who in the interim have invested in producing the work on the understanding that it was freely available. They have accordingly received some protection. First of all, anything done before January 1, 1996 cannot amount to infringement; nor can subsequent issuing of copies to the public if they were made before July 1, 1995. In addition where arrangements have been made, at a time before January 1, 1995 when the work was out of copyright, to do anything subsequently which falls within the revived copyright, the act in question is exempt from liability.[245] Moreover, if reasonable inquiry does not reveal the name and address of the person with power to license a restricted act under the revived copyright, permission is not required.[246] **11–49**

Extensions and revivals of copyright raise inevitable questions about who is to enjoy rights in them. These have been dealt with in the UK Regulations and are discussed in Ch.13.[247]

(5) "Neighbouring" copyrights

The period now conferred for other copyrights is indicated in the Table (head 6). For sound recordings this becomes 50 years from making, or if "released"[248] within that period, 50 years from release.[249] The copyright in broadcasts continues to endure for 50 years from first transmission in an EEA country.[250] That in typographical format for 25 years from first publication.[251] Computer-generated works, which are treated much like other **11–50**

[244] Because of the limitation of copyright to creative photographs (however the foreign law defines this), mentioned above, in n.105.

[245] Duration Regulations 1995 reg.23(1), (2). There is also a provision (reg.23(3)), almost impenetrable, which allows free exploitation, despite the revived copyright, of a work or film made or arranged for before July 1, 1995 which contains a copy or adaptation of the work whose copyright is revived. Thus, where a novel which went out of "old" copyright in 1990 is the subject of a film adaptation completed in June 1995, the film-maker may arrange (say) its broadcast at any time, even though it is back in copyright from 1996–2020. Not so if the film was made in August 1995.

[246] Duration Regulations 1995 reg.23(4). If there is no copyright infringement, there can be no infringement of moral rights: reg.23(5).

[247] See below, para.13–08.

[248] i.e. in an EEA country, first published, played in public or communicated to the public, provided it is not an unauthorised act.

[249] CDPA 1988 s.13A(2), following the Duration Directive art.3(2).

[250] CDPA 1988 s.14, following the Duration Directive art.3(4).

[251] CDPA 1988 s.15.

entrepreneurial copyrights, have a term of 50 years from the making of the work.[252]

(6) Special cases

11–51 From the rules so far mentioned there are a number of important variations, set out below.

(a) *Anonymous and pseudonymous works*

11–52 The Berne Convention imposes twin obligations on member countries: first, an author of a work within the Convention should be entitled to copyright in a publication while preserving anonymity.[253] This moral imperative is not easily realised in a system which measures the copyright term by the life of the author. Hence the second requirement: the publisher of an anonymous work should be able to enforce the author's rights as his deemed representative.[254]

It is no precondition of UK copyright that the author be named in any publication; and the Act includes a presumption, until the contrary is proved, that, if a work is published in the United Kingdom without attribution but with the name of a publisher, that person shall be taken to be the owner of copyright at the date of publication.[255] If someone other than the publisher then seeks to assert copyright in the publication, he must either show that his right derives from the publisher or else he must rebut the presumption. He will not succeed in the latter endeavour merely by showing an assignment from the alleged author.[256]

Moreover, as long as a literary, dramatic, musical or artistic work remains of unknown authorship,[257] its copyright is measured without reference to the author's date of death. Instead, the work enjoys copyright for 70 years from the date when it was made; or if, before that date, the work was "made available to the public", then for 70 years from this second event.[258] The duration may not be increased by revealing the author's name once the term thus measured has expired. By implication, if the name emerges before the

[252] CDPA 1988 s.12(7); for this copyright, see below, paras 20–44–20–45. For the terms of the "non-copyrights", see above, para.11–31 (publication right); and below, paras 20–38 et seq. (database right); para.14–30 (performance rights); paras 15–38—15–56 (design right).

[253] Berne Convention art.7(3). For the history of the provision, see Ricketson and Ginsburg para.9.50.

[254] Berne Convention art.15(2).

[255] CDPA 1988 s.103(4).

[256] *Warwick Film v Eisinger* [1969] 1 Ch. 508. It must be doubted whether this truly gives effect to the Berne Convention, art.15(2), since the publisher is by no means necessarily representing the author and enforcing his rights. By confining the presumption to publication in the UK, the Act may also be failing to fulfil the Convention.

[257] Once the identity of the author, or of one among joint authors, becomes known it cannot subsequently be a work of unknown authorship: CDPA 1988 s.12(3)–(5).

[258] This implements the Duration Directive art.1(3), and eliminates a curious survival of indeterminate copyright which was included in the CDPA 1988.

end of the special term, the general rule of author's life and 70 years thereafter will apply, whether this results in a longer or a shorter term overall.[259]

The position established by implemention of the Duration Directive is at least an improvement on the former indeterminate copyright in unpublished material.[260] Previously, where there was no identifiable author, a potential user might have no means of securing a licence, yet could have no exemption in law—a blight for the scholarly in particular. At least under s.57 of the CDPA 1988, a defence was introduced for the case where the author (though unknown) could be reasonably presumed dead for 50 years. That same defence continues (the period now being raised to 70 years), but it will now (with the limited periods) be applicable only in very unusual cases. **11–53**

(b) *Crown and parliamentary copyright*

The Crown has a special copyright in works made by an officer or servant of the Crown in the course of his duties, and in Acts and Measures. The Houses of Parliament have parliamentary copyright in Bills and other works prepared under their direction and control. The CDPA 1988 has introduced substantial changes on this subject which will be discussed later. Here it should be noted that Crown copyright in literary, dramatic, musical and artistic works lasts for 50 years from publication or 125 years from creation, whichever is the shorter.[261] Parliamentary copyright in Bills covers only their duration as such, but in other works of the same type, it lasts for 50 years from making.[262] **11–54**

(7) Lesser terms outside the EEA

The Duration Directive imposes its long periods of protection in favour of rightholders from within the EU. At the same time, following Berne,[263] it uses the concept of the "shorter term" to encourage other countries to adopt equivalent standards.[264] Accordingly, when the country of origin (in the Berne Convention sense)[265] and the nationality of the author lie outside the EEA, UK (and other EEA) copyright is reduced to the period of any shorter home term. Likewise with related rights, where the right-holder is not a Community national. So long as the United States grants an author's right **11–55**

[259] The Duration Directive art.1(3), specifies this result.

[260] With only limited qualifications, "existing" anonymous works continue to be governed by their original regime: see CDPA 1988 Sch.1 para.12(3), (5).

[261] For transitional arrangements, see CDPA 1988 Sch.1 paras 41, 43.

[262] Other points about Crown copyright are discussed below, in paras 14–47—14–49.

[263] Duration Directive art.7(8).

[264] Duration Directive art.7; implemented in the UK by CDPA 1988 ss.12(6), 13A(4), 13B(7), 14(3).

[265] See above, para.10–25, and CDPA 1988 s.15A: "country of origin".

of life plus 50 years, works by American citizens first published there will have only that period of copyright in the United Kingdom and other EEA countries.[266]

The TRIPS Agreement, however, adopts a most-favoured-nation (MFN) rule, as well as a requirement of national treatment, as a general basis of its obligations.[267] Moreover, the new GATT contains no explicit exception which would allow an economic union such as the Community to give preferences between its Member States, which would not be caught by the MFN requirement.[268] Nonetheless such an understanding may need to be implied. Otherwise, the United States could possibly claim under TRIPS against each EU state when that state gives a longer period of protection to other EEA nationals and "first publishers" than to those from the United States.

[266] This, however, cannot operate so as to reduce the period of existing copyrights in non-EEA works: Duration Regulations 1995 reg.15(1).

[267] See above, para.1–32, n.110.

[268] But the question is much complicated by the meaning of Exemption (d) in TRIPS art.4.

CHAPTER 12

INFRINGEMENT OF COPYRIGHT AND MORAL RIGHTS

1. INFRINGEMENT: BASIC CONCEPTS[1]

The Copyright Act defines in some detail the types of activity which constitute infringement of the various forms of copyright. As the Table (on pp.442–444) indicates (head 7), the rights of the copyright owner may be roughly classified into "reproduction" rights and "performing" rights. The more detailed statutory categories that can be placed under these heads will be considered later,[2] as will certain special forms of infringement, defences and remedies.[3] But first, there are four basic matters to discuss: copyright must be distinguished from rights in the physical embodiment of the original work; then come two aspects of the subject-matter improperly taken—the **12–01**

[1] Laddie et al. Chs 14–19; Copinger Chs 7–8.

[2] See below, paras 12–21—12–35. Note that the new law of infringement applies to existing works in respect of acts done after commencement: CDPA 1988 Sch.1 para.14. There are special provisions affecting rental rights, subsequent dealings in copies made under an exception, typefaces, reconstruction of buildings, libraries, pre–1912 dramatic and musical works, statutory recording, and licences.

[3] Partly discussed below, in paras 12–38—12–62, and partly below in Chs 14 and 20.

need to show that the defendant has misappropriated the actual work and that this has been to a substantial extent; the last concerns the infringer—the degree to which he may infringe by authorising the acts of others.

(1) Ownership of the original work

12–02 Copyright in a work gives rights that are distinct from ownership of the physical embodiment of the original work—the manuscript, letter, painting or whatever. When one person sends another a letter, he will normally be taken to intend a gift of the paper on which it is written and the recipient becomes its owner. Only if conditions of confidence exist can the author prevent it being shown, given or sold to others.[4] But sending a private letter implies no assignment or licence of the copyright in it and the recipient has no right to make copies or give performances of its content.[5] The same is true of artistic works. The artist's lack of rights in the original painting or sculpture, once he disposes of it, is often a considerable economic disadvantage and has led some legal systems to introduce a special right to share in the proceeds of certain re-sales.[6] But such a sale assigns no copyright unless this is separately expressed or can be implied from the purpose of the transaction.[7]

If the right granted is an exclusive licence of the relevant aspect of the copyright, the licensee is also entitled to sue an infringer.[8]

(2) Misappropriation

(a) *Causal connection*

12–03 The claimant must prove that, directly or indirectly, the defendant's alleged infringement is taken from the work or subject-matter in which he claims copyright.[9] This is fundamental to the whole concept of copyright, and distinguishes it from the "full" monopoly of the patent system. (Despite the very term, copyright, the legislation has, until 1988, mostly avoided reference to "copying". Now that word is used in relation to the making and marketing of reproductions. But equally there must also be copying in a

[4] See, e.g. *Pope v Curl* (1741) 2 Atk. 341; *Gee v Pritchard* (1818) 2 Swans 402; *Philip v Pennell* [1907] 2 Ch. 577; Hauhart (1984) 13 U.Balt.L.R. 244.

[5] See *Cembrit Blunn Ltd v Apex Roofing Services Ltd* [2007] E.W.H.C. 111 (Ch), paras 236–241. Cf a letter to the editor. Under a will a bequest of an unpublished manuscript or artistic work is now to be construed as including the copyright: CDPA 1988 s.89. Cf. the CA 1911 s.17(2), restrictively construed in *Re Dickens* [1935] Ch. 267 which still applies to wills that took effect before the CA 1956: CDPA 1988 Sch.1 para.29.

[6] For this *droit de suite*, see below, paras 14–45—14–46.

[7] In any case a licence (exclusive or non-exclusive, according to circumstances) may be a more reasonable implication.

[8] CDPA 1988 ss.94, 101, 102; and see below, para.13–12; *Michael O'Mara Books v Express Newspapers* [1999] F.S.R. 49.

[9] cf. the "exclusive right" and the basic statement about infringement in CDPA 1988 ss.2, 16.

general sense for infringement of the performing rights.) The owner must show that this causal connection is the explanation of the similarity between the work and the infringement—the other possibilities being that he copied from the defendant, that they both copied from a common source, or that they arrived at their results independently.[10] On the other hand, he does not have to show that the defendant knew that his copying constituted an infringement. As with other rights of property recognised at common law, the primary exclusive rights may be asserted against even the defendant who honestly believes that he purchased the right to reproduce the work.[11]

If the evidence shows that there are striking similarities between the two works, that the claimant's was the earlier in time and that the defendant had the opportunity to get to know the claimant's work, then a court may well find copying proved in the absence of any convincing explanation to the contrary by the defendant.[12] But the judges have hesitated to fetter the assessment of each case on its facts by the introduction of rules formally shifting the burden of proof from claimant to defendant at any stage of the trial.[13] Some subject matter, such as factual and historical information, may well derive from independent effort or a common source.[14] Even if there has been some copying, whether there has been a substantial taking calls for separate evaluation; this is discussed later.[15]

(b) *Subconscious copying*

Particular difficulty arises when the defendant denies any intention to copy and the Court believes him. Some judges have accepted that copying could occur subconsciously where a person reads, sees or hears a work, forgets about it but then reproduces it, genuinely believing it to be his own.[16] In such a case, proof of copying is said to depend on: **12–04**

[10] See Sargant J. *Corelli v Gray* (1913) 29 T.L.R. 116; Diplock L.J. *Francis Day* case (below, n.16) at 625. See also Learned Hand J. *Fisher v Dillingham* 298 Fed. 145 (1924) at 150.

[11] *Mansell v Valley Printing* [1908] 2 Ch. 441; *Byrne v Statist Co* [1914] 1 K.B. 622. Innocent defendants may be protected from liability for damages: see above, para.2–41.

[12] If the question is whether the defendant's work has come from the claimant's or from independent sources, the defendant may find it difficult to explain the presence of the claimant's errors or idiosyncrasies in his text: see, e.g. *Harman Pictures v Osborne* (below, n.14).

[13] See especially the *Francis Day* case (below, n.16) cf. *Stoddard International v William Lomas Carpets* [2001] F.S.R. 848.

[14] See, e.g. *Poznanski v London Film* [1937–1945] Mac. CC 107 at 108; *Harman Pictures v Osborne* [1967] 2 All E.R. 324 at 328.

[15] *Billhöfer v Dixon* [1990] F.S.R. 105; *Ibcos v Barclays Mercantile* [1994] F.S.R. 297; and see below, paras 12–06 et seq.

[16] *Rees v Melville* [1911–1916] Mac. C.C. 168; *Ricordi v Clayton & Waller* [1928–1935] Mac. C.C. 154; *Francis Day v Bron* [1963] Ch. 587 per Willmer L.J. (cf. at 622, and at 626–627, per Upjohn and Diplock L.JJ.); *Industrial Furnaces v Reaves* [1970] R.P.C. 605 at 623. The notion has actually been applied in *Sinanide v Kosmeo* (1927) 44 T.L.R. 371 and the breach of confidence cases, *Seager v Copydex* and *Talbot v General Television* ([1981] R.P.C. 1, above, para.8–38).

"a number of composite elements: The degree of familiarity (if proved at all, or properly inferred) with the plaintiff's work, the character of the work, particularly its qualities of impressing the mind and memory, the objective similarity of the defendant's work, the inherent probability that such similarity as is found could be due to coincidence, the existence of other influences on the defendant ... the quality of the defendant's ... own evidence on the presence or otherwise in his mind of the plaintiff's work."[17]

(c) *Indirect copying*

12–05 It has long been accepted that a work may be copied by imitating a copy of it: "to hold otherwise would be to open the door to indirect piracies, which I am not at all disposed to do".[18] If the claimant owns a copyright drawing and then turns it into a three-dimensional article and this is copied in three dimensions by the defendant, the "causal connection" for indirect copying of the drawing will be established.[19] Likewise if the defendant takes a photo of the claimant's three-dimensional article, or his own copy.[20] If a novel is turned into a play, which is in turn converted into a ballet, the same will apply. But the causal chain must run in the right direction. In *Purefoy v Sykes Boxall*, C made a trade catalogue with illustrations of his products and D also published a catalogue with pictures of his own products, which were copied from C's products. In this alone there was no infringement of C's catalogue, for it was not that catalogue but the products which were the starting point in the chain.[21] On the other hand, if the claimant's parts were reproductions of copyright drawings, the defendant's illustrations would derive from those drawings. But to establish the linkage is not enough. It is also necessary to show that the defendant's ultimate use is a substantial reproduction of the claimant's work—this is simply the general requirement discussed in the next section. In providing that infringement may be direct or indirect, the CDPA 1988 also renders it immaterial that any intervening act does not itself constitute infringement.[22]

---

[17] Per Wilberforce J. *Francis Day v Bron* (above, n.16) at 614 and see *Jones v London Borough of Tower Hamlets* [2001] R.P.C. 407.

[18] Lindley L.J. *Hanfstaegl v Empire Palace* [1894] 3 Ch. 109 at 127; and see, e.g. Blackburn J. *Ex p. Beal* (1868) L.R. 3 Q.B. 387 at 394. The leading modern authorities are *King Features Syndicate v Kleeman* [1941] A.C. 417; *British Leyland v Armstrong* [1986] R.P.C. 279 HL. The principle now has statutory force: CDPA 1988 s.16(3).

[19] The great significance of this example for the law of industrial design is discussed below in paras 15–03 et seq.

[20] *Dorling v Honnor Marine* [1965] Ch.1.

[21] (1954) 71 R.P.C. 227 at 232; 72 R.P.C. 89 at 99 CA, which found nonetheless against the defendant; a degree of both direct and indirect copying of the catalogue was proved.

[22] CDPA 1988 s.16(3). It might have been better to say that the act need not involve the making of anything that could be a copyright work.

(3) Substantial taking

Where there has been copying and all or virtually all of a work is taken without emendation, the proof of infringement is straightforward. Difficulties arise when this is not the case. The CDPA 1988 requires that a substantial part must have been copied.[23] This test is a major tool for giving expression to the court's sense of fair play. So "the question whether the defendant has copied a substantial part depends much more on the quality than the quantity of what he has taken".[24] The part must be measured against the whole work, not the work minus the portions that have not been copied.[25] A songwriter-performer could not sue in respect of the vocal inflections in a single phrase transferred from one of her songs into another co-written and sung by the pop-star, Madonna.[26] An objective judgment is needed to determine what the work is; one part can be treated as a distinct work only when it is reasonably separable, as with articles in magazines.[27] **12–06**

Likewise it has often enough been insisted that the copying must be of the expression of ideas, rather than just of the ideas.[28] But that is a distinction with an ill-defined boundary. Judge Learned Hand famously pointed out that, in any case which turns upon a taking of structure, rather than line-by-line (or note-by-note) detail:

> "[u]pon any work ... a great number of patterns of increasing generality will fit equally well, as more and more incident is left out. The last may perhaps be no more than the most general statement of what the [work] is about, and may at times consist only of its title; but there is a point in this series of abstractions where they are no longer protected, since otherwise the [author] could prevent the use of his 'ideas', to which, apart from their

[23] CDPA 1988 s.16(3)(a). NB: the InfoSoc Directive art.2 which refers to "reproduction in part". In *Infopaq International v Danske Dagblades Forening* [2009] E.C.D.R. 16, the ECJ ruled that "reproduction in part" could extend to copying sentences or parts of sentences, provided the extracts were original, in the sense of reflecting the author's "intellectual creation". See Alexander (2009) Camb. L.J. 520; Derclaye [2010] 32 E.I.P.R. 247.

[24] Lord Reid, *Ladbroke v William Hill* [1964] 1 W.L.R. 273 at 276; and see Lord Pearce at 293; *Designers Guild v Russell Williams* [2000] 1 W.L.R. 2416 at 2422 per Lord Hoffmann, 2425-2426 per Lord Millet and at 2431 per Lord Scott; *PCR v Dow Jones Telerate* [1998] E.M.L.R. 407. Sometimes, in view of the very limited quantity actually taken, the emphasis upon quality may seem overstretched: as in *Ludlow Music v Robbie Williams* [2001] F.S.R. 271. Where the quantity taken is large because the work itself is rather short then there is a greater likelihood that a qualitatively substantial part has been taken: see *Larrikin Music Publishing v EMI Songs Australia* [2010] FCA 29 FC Aust.

[25] *IPC Media v Highbury-Leisure Publishing* [2004] F.S.R. 20. Laddie J. warned of the danger of creating "a legal *millefeuilles*" of copyrights arising at the same time and vested in the same person.

[26] *Coffey v Warner/Chappell Music* [2005] F.S.R. 34.

[27] *Newspaper Licensing Agency v Mark & Spencer* [2003] 1 A.C. 551 HL; *Coogi Australia v Hysport* (1998) 41 I.P.R. 593 FC Australia.

[28] *Designers Guild v Russell Williams* [2000] 1 W.L.R. 2416 at 2422-2423 per Lord Hoffmann; *Baigent v Random House* [2007] F.S.R. 24 CA; *IceTV v Nine Network Australia* [2009] H.C.A. 14 HC Aust.

expression, his property never extended ... Nobody has ever been able to fix that boundary, and nobody ever can."[29]

Whether there was copying is question of a different order from whether there has been substantial taking. In *Designers Guild v Russell Williams*[30] no challenge was made on appeal to the trial judge's view that there had been copying of a textile design, despite various differences of detail introduced into the defendant's product. The House of Lords, while stressing the difference between the issues, nonetheless held that, after the finding of copying, it was almost bound to follow that enough had been taken to constitute infringement.[31] That, however, depends on how far the distinction between taking ideas and taking expression is conceived to be a part of the first question, as well as the second.[32]

12–07 The imprecision of any line between idea and expression causes some commentators to castigate the whole notion.[33] Why then does the distinction survive such disparagement? Why, indeed, is it seized on as the basis of international accord?[34] Copyright, by universal agreement, cannot be limited to straight plagiarism and there is no simple test by which to evaluate what taking, in terms of quality and quantity, is unacceptable. But courts are inevitably pressed with cases where the claimant's grievance is that he thought of the very first instance of a whole type of work (a detective story, a restaurant guide, a building of glass panels, a "style" in visual art or architecture, and so on) and wants rights over all subsequent variants. By way of answer to such claims, the "idea/expression dichotomy" restricts liability to a taking from the protected work, and not just from the type of work of which it is an exemplar. That is a highly significant limitation upon the availability of copyright to prevent unauthorised appropriation. Inevitably there will be situations in which the work as a whole seems the valuable thing to protect and others where the devil is in the detail.[35] It is hard to think of another indicator which would bring greater precision to the judgment called for.[36]

[29] *Nichols v Universal Pictures* 45 F (2d) 119 (1930)—stated with particular reference to an allegation that one play copied the plot of another. Note also, Lord Hailsham, in *LB Plastics v Swish* [1979] R.P.C. 611 at 629: "of course, as the late Professor Joad used to observe, it all depends on what you mean by 'ideas'. What the respondents in fact copied from the appellants was no mere general idea."

[30] *Designers Guild v Russell Williams* Designers Guild v Russell Williams [2000] 1 W.L.R. 2416; Deazley [2004] I.P.Q. 121.

[31] Applied by *Nouveau Fabrics v Voyage Decoration* [2004] EWHC 895.

[32] cf. the opposing view of the CA in the *Designers Guild* case: [2000] F.S.R. 121.

[33] Laddie et al., paras 3.74–3.80; Jones (1990) 10 Pace L.R. 551.

[34] TRIPS Agreement art.9(2); WIPO Copyright Treaty 1996 art.2; and see the EU Computer Programs Directive art.1(2).

[35] For Archilocus' fabulous distinction: "the fox knows many things but the hedgehog knows only one big thing", deployed with grace in this context: Lord Hoffmann, *Designers Guild v Russell Williams*, above, n.28; cf. *Jones v Tower Hamlets* [2001] R.P.C. 407.

[36] cf. below, para.20–13, suggesting that infringement of copyright in a computer program occurs where there is "over-borrowing".

Judges who incline to the view that "what is worth copying is prima facie worth protecting"[37] may well stretch the notion of "expression" a considerable way. Once convinced that the defendant unfairly cut a competitive corner by setting out to revamp the claimant's completed work, they will not easily be dissuaded that the alterations have been sufficient.[38] In this approach the taking of ideas alone is confined to cases where the defendant does not start from the completed work at all, save in the sense that he goes through a similar process of creation: as where he paints for himself the scene that the claimant painted,[39] or draws his own cartoon for the same basic joke.[40]

The assessment of each case turns a good deal on its own circumstances. But there are some general considerations which may well have a bearing on the result. These are worth illustrating.

(a) *Unaltered copying*

If the defendant has copied without additions or alterations to the part **12–08** taken, the proportion of that part to the whole of the claimant's work need not be large: a short extract from a poem, a recognisable segment of a painting, the refrain of a pop song.[41] The objective of a particular form of copyright will influence what constitutes a substantial taking in such cases. Thus the publisher's "neighbouring" copyright in typographical format has been treated by the House of Lords as protection for the publication as a whole. In the case of a newspaper, this is the whole edition, rather than each individual news item or article. A firm was therefore free to make regular collections of extracts on particular subjects for circulation to its staff.[42]

(b) *Extent of defendant's alteration*

Where the defendant has reworked the claimant's material there comes a **12–09** point beyond which the claimant has no claim. Whatever may have been the position in the past, the fact that the defendant has himself added enough by way of skill, labour and judgment to secure copyright for his effort does not, under the present law, settle the question whether he has infringed. Rather the issue is whether a substantial part of the claimant's work survives in the

---

37 Peterson J. *University of London Press* case [1916] 2 Ch. 601 at 610; quoted by Lords Reid and Pearce in the *Ladbroke* case (above, n.24) at 279, 293. Cf. *IceTV v Nine Network Australia* [2009] HCA 14 where the High Court of Australia held that a misappropriation approach was not mandated by the copyright statute. See Christie (1984) 10 Monash L.R. 175.

38 For a striking example, see *Elanco v Mandops* [1980] R.P.C. 213 CA.

39 cf. e.g. *Krisarts v Briarfine* [1977] F.S.R. 537; and see, as to indirect copying of a drawing for an object: *Ward v Richard Sankey* [1988] F.S.R. 66.

40 *McCrum v Eisner* [1917–1923] Mac. CC 14.

41 See above, para.12–06.

42 *Newspaper Licensing Agency v Marks and Spencer* [2003] 1 A.C. 551 HL; Deazley [2004] I.P.Q. 121.

defendant's so as to appear to be a copy of it.[43] It is not relevant to ask whether it is a substantial part of the defendant's work.[44]

The Gowers Review on Intellectual Property, incited by some limited evidence about hip-hop music, has taken the view that sampling from earlier recordings was being unfairly impeded by the need to secure copyright permissions. In consequence it seeks a new and general exception to infringement (which would now require an amendment to the InfoSoc Directive) for creative, transformative or derivative works. By itself that would have very considerable punch. But the punch is pulled by adding "within the parameters of the Berne Three-Step test". However, the Intellectual Property Office has not seen fit to take this particular recommendation forward.

12–10 Particular difficulty arises when the claimant's work is taken with intent to satirise—whether the butt in mind is the work itself or some quite different object.[45] In *Glyn v Weston Feature*[46] a filmed burlesque (or, in today's language, "send-up") of Elinor Glyn's once notorious novel, *Three Weeks*, was held not to infringe because very little by way of incident was taken over from novel to film. Likewise in *Joy Music v Sunday Pictorial*,[47] a song lyric had been parodied in pursuit of Prince Philip; but only one repeated phrase was taken, and that with pointed variation. Again there was no infringement. In both decisions it was asked whether the defendant had bestowed such mental labour on what he had taken and subjected it to such revision and alteration as to produce an original work.[48] This must be understood as a way of emphasising that nothing substantial must remain from the claimant's work.[49] While in the past, English judges have seemed loath to find sufficient copying in borderline parody cases,[50] they have now also to

---

43 *Redwood Music v Chappell* [1982] R.P.C. 109 (adaptation of song—generous view of difference).

44 *Designers Guild v Russell Williams* [2000] 1 W.L.R. 2416.

45 The subject is a paradise for theorists: see, e.g. Gredley and Maniatis [1997] E.I.P.R. 339; Spence (1998) 114 L.Q.R. 594. Note that the European Human Rights Convention art.10(1), guarantees the right to parody the work of another. This, however, does not justify defamation, passing off or false attribution of authorship: *Clark v Associated Newspapers* [1998] R.P.C. 261.

46 *Glyn v Weston Feature* [1916] 1 Ch. 261. The claimant's claim also failed for its "grossly immoral" tendency: see below, paras 12–57, 12–58.

47 *Joy Music v Sunday Pictorial* [1960] 2 Q.B. 60.

48 This derives from Lindley L.J. *Hanfstaengl v Empire Palace* [1894] 3 Ch. 109 at 128; and the *Glyn* case (above, n.46) at 268; *United Feature v Star Newspaper* (1980) 2 E.I.P.R. D 43, SC (NSW).

49 *Schweppes v Wellington* [1984] F.S.R. 210 ("Schlurppes" label intended as joke; claimant not amused); *Williamson Music v Pearson Partnership* [1987] F.S.R. 97; Phillips [1984] Camb. L.J. 245.

50 Younger J., in the *Glyn* case (above, n.46) at 268, notes the absence of decisions finding infringement in "burlesque" cases.

consider the moral right of integrity, which is discussed later.[51]

A rather similar difficulty relates to résumés—summarised plots of plays, abridgments of novels, headnotes of law reports, and so on. There was a tendency, at least in earlier case law, to treat a really substantial précis of contents as permissible—because it was useful or because it did not seriously interfere with the claimant's interests.[52] To this end it has been asked whether the defendant has really produced a "new work".[53] In this context the phrase seems to indicate a very substantial condensation and revision of the material. With this should be contrasted the Court of Appeal's grant of an interim injunction in *Elanco v Mandops*.[54] The defendants first copied the claimant's instruction leaflet for a weed killer and had to withdraw it; they then produced a revision giving the same detailed information in other words. This was held to create an arguable case of infringement because the defendants were not entitled to make use of the claimant's skill and judgment in securing the information. **12–11**

A nice question arises where a defendant engages in very small borrowings from a succession of the claimants works. In *Cate v Devon and Exeter Constitutional Newspaper*,[55] items of information were drawn from each day's newspaper and this was considered substantial taking, even though each extraction in isolation would not infringe. The correctness of this approach has recently been doubted: its logic dictates that the first few extractions become infringements ex post facto.[56]

(c) *Character of claimant's or defendant's work*

Certain types of work are treated as having a particular value; to appropriate this feature is accordingly of qualitative significance. This is particularly true of dramatic works and films. In periods when stock dramas made the staple of so much English theatre, there were frequent allegations of improper borrowing. After 1911, a series of cases[57] settled that: **12–12**

---

[51] See below, paras 12–76—12–83. The *Gowers Review* paras 4.89–4.90, favoured the introduction of a parody exception, such as is permitted by the InfoSoc Directive art.5(3)(k) but this has been dropped from the agenda, largely due to lack of a clear consensus on this issue: *Taking Forward the Gowers Review of Intellectual Property* (2009), paras 323–331.

[52] Cases on the subject decided before the modern notion of infringement had fully appeared must be treated with caution. But see *D'Almaine v Boosey* (1835) 1 Y. & C. Ex. 288; *Dickens v Lee* (1844) 8 Jur. 183; *Tinsley v Lacy* (1863) 1 H. & M. 747; *Valcarenghi v Gramophone* [1928–1935] Mac. CC 301.

[53] Jervis C.J. *Sweet v Benning* (1855) 16 C.B. 459 at 483.

[54] *Elanco v Mandops* [1980] R.P.C. 213; Dworkin [1979] E.I.P.R. 117.

[55] *Cate v Devon and Exeter Constitutional Newspaper* (1889) 40 Ch. D. 500; and see *Spectravest v Aperknit* [1988] F.S.R. 161. The digital sampling of pop songs provides a current example.

[56] *Electronic Techniques v Critchley* [1997] F.S.R. at 408–410.

[57] e.g. *Corelli v Gray* (1913) 30 T.L.R. 116 CA; Scrutton L.J. *Vane v Famous Players* [1928–1935] Mac. CC 6, 8 (particularly significant in the age of silent film). One earlier decision at least had required appropriation of actual dialogue: *Scholtz v Amasis* [1905–1910] Mac. CC 216; cf. also *Chatterton v Cave* (1878) 3 App. Cas. 483.

> "if the plot of a story, whether it be found in a play or in a novel, is taken bodily with or without some minor additions or subtractions for the purposes of a stage play or cinema film, there is no doubt about the case".[58]

It was not necessary to copy the actual words used to work out the plot.[59] The same approach has now been applied to non-literal copying of computer programs.[60]

This approach shows the concept of mere ideas being confined to "starting point" conceptions—it would be no more than an idea, for instance, to conceive of a play about the return of a husband who has been presumed dead.[61] Where the works are artistic, and the court is testing sufficient similarity by appeal to the eye, stress is sometimes laid upon the "feeling and artistic character" of the claimant's work,[62] an idea that can be extended to the screen displays of a computer.[63]

(d) *Nature of claimant's effort*

12–13 In some cases, the claimant's "skill, labour and judgment" form a distinct part of the whole result. This may well be so where the effort consists of such secondary work as editing, compiling or selecting material. A court will treat the whole work as the subject of copyright.[64] But whether there is substantial taking falls to be judged by reference to the claimant's contribution. In *Warwick Film v Eisinger*,[65] an author published an edited version of Oscar Wilde's trials, a transcript of which had earlier appeared. He acquired copyright in the whole by virtue of his work in selection and providing linking passages. But a defendant who took from it passages of the transcript but very little of the author's editing was held not to infringe. This neatly adjusts the scope of protection to the author's literary effort.

The same approach can be seen to apply to some cases where the real skill lies in some commercial assessment distinct from the expressive content of the work: thus in the football pool coupon cases,[66] where it is the particular

[58] Maugham J. *Kelly v Cinema Houses* [1928–1935] Mac. CC 362; *Dagnall v British Film* [1928–1935] Mac. CC 391.

[59] In *Fernald v Jay Lewis* (1953) [1975] F.S.R. 499, even the taking of one episode out of a novel for a film was held to infringe when the literary characteristics of the episode were all copied and there were some startling similarities of dialogue.

[60] See paras 20–10—20–15, below.

[61] An example given by Scrutton L.J. *Vane* case (above, n.50) at 8–9; and see *de Manduit v Gaumont British* [1936–1945] Mac. CC 292.

[62] e.g. Somervell L.J. *Bauman v Fussell* (1953) [1978] R.P.C. 485 at 487.

[63] See below, paras 20–23—20–25.

[64] *Ladbroke* case (above, n.24).

[65] *Warwick Film v Eisinger* [1969] 1 Ch. 508; see also *John Fairfax v Australian Consolidated Press* (1960) 60 S.R. (N.S.W.) 413.

[66] See above, para.11–07. See also *IceTV v Nine Network Australia* [2009] HCA 14, where the High Court of Australia held that reproduction of time and title information from weekly tv schedules did not constitute a substantial part of the compilation because the expression that was copied involved little mental effort or exertion.

selection that is so significant, protection goes to taking the selection more or less as a whole. This correlation of protection with achievement is not easily made in all such cases. Where, for instance, the skill consists in recording someone else's performance,[67] it is arguable that there should be infringement only where some considerable part of the whole is taken. The same might be said of the entrepreneurial copyrights—particularly that for typographical format, since it is not associated with the artistic execution of performers, directors or the like. But this sort of consideration awaits an answer from the ECJ.[68]

(e) *Extent of claimant's effort*

If the claimant's labour, skill and judgment have only been just enough to earn him copyright, infringement may arise only where there is exact imitation of such features as are of some individuality. In *Kenrick v Lawrence*,[69] the claimant claimed copyright in a simple drawing of a hand, made with the intention of showing voters where to register their vote on a ballot form. But it was held that only an exact copy of the drawing would infringe, if the claimant were not to be conceded a monopoly in drawings of hands for this and other purposes.[70] Through this consideration also the Court is able to take account of the overall merit of the claimant's work. **12–14**

(f) *Manner in which the defendant has taken advantage of claimant's work*

Where the claimant's work records information, the use that a defendant may make of it for his own purposes has been carefully circumscribed. The defendant is entitled to use the claimant's work as a source of ideas or information if he takes it as a starting point for his own collation of information or as a means of checking his own independent research.[71] However, he is not entitled to copy what the claimant has done as a substitute for exercising his own labour, skill and judgment. Moreover, he will not escape having his conduct so regarded merely by taking the claimant's work and checking that its contents are accurate. Thus it was improper to compile a street directory by sending out slips for checking, which contained entries from the claimant's directory.[72] Equally, it is wrong to adopt the **12–15**

[67] In so far as this is properly the subject of copyright: cf. above, para.11–34.

[68] For a similar issue concerning database right, see below, para.20–41.

[69] *Kenrick v Lawrence* (1890) 25 Q.B.D. 99; and see *Glogau v Land Transport Safety* [1999] 1 N.Z.L.R. 257 CA NZ. Contrast the cases on plays and novels: above, para.12–12.

[70] cf. *Handi-Craft v B Free World* [2007] E.C.D.R. 21 para.171.

[71] See *Jarrold v Houston* (1857) 3 K. & J. 708; *Pike v Nicholas* (1869) L.R. 5 Ch. App. 251; *Hogg v Scott* (1874) L.R. 18 Eq. 444.

[72] *Kelly v Morris* (1866) L.R. 1 Eq. 677; see also *Morris v Ashbee* (1868) L.R. 7 Eq. 34 (poacher turned gamekeeper). The Whitford Committee (Cmnd.6732, 1977), paras 862–863 considered that new versions of the Ordnance Survey would be infringed if details were systematically copied onto other maps; see also *Sands & McDougall v Robinson* (1917) 23 C.L.R. 49 HC Aust.

same quotations which have been selected for a critical edition of a Shakespeare play,[73] or an account of historical incidents which digest the available sources.[74] In such cases, a defendant who is shown to have adopted the claimant's imaginative embellishments or plain errors will be in particular jeopardy.[75] Contrast the situation where only historical facts are taken.[76]

(g) *Whether the defendant's use will seriously interfere with the claimant's exploitation of his own work*

12–16 While infringement may occur even if there is no likelihood of competition between claimant and defendant, the possibility of such competition or its absence may nevertheless be treated as a relevant factor. This factor undoubtedly played a more significant role while copyright was still in the process of acquiring its character as a full right of property, and before substantial taking was distinguished from notions of "fair use".[77] Nonetheless the factor remains a practical consideration that courts are unlikely ever entirely to discount.[78] Thus it is referred to by Farwell J. in deciding that four brief lines from a popular song did not infringe when taken as a heading for a serial story in the *Red Star Weekly*.[79]

(h) *Reproduction by the original author*

12–17 Suppose that an author creates a work, and subsequently, at a time when he does not own the copyright,[80] he reproduces it in a second work. Some concession in his favour seems called for, in order to allow him to continue doing the kind of work at which he is proficient. But across the spectrum of copyright activity it is difficult to know how far judges would accord him any greater freedom than is permitted to others. In respect of artistic works, a special compromise is embodied in legislation: the artist may make substantial reproductions, even using the same mould, sketch or similar plan, provided that the subsequent work does not repeat or imitate the main design of the earlier work.[81] Where other types of work are concerned, a similar approach might well be adopted: the relation between the two end

---

[73] Collins M.R. *Moffatt & Page v Gill* (1902) 86 L.T. 465 at 471; and see *Blackie v Lothian* (1921) 29 C.L.R. 396 HC Aust.

[74] *Harman v Osborne* [1967] 2 All E.R. 324; *Ravenscroft v Herbert* [1980] R.P.C. 193.

[75] *Harman* case above, n.71.

[76] *Baigent v Random House* [2007] F.S.R. 24 (concerning Brown's *The Da Vinci Code*).

[77] Thus initially such activities as translation and abridgment did not count as infringement.

[78] *Chappell v Thompson* [1928–1935] Mac. CC 467 at 471. Note also Parker J. *Weatherby v International Horse Agency* [1910] 1 Ch. 297 at 305: "... the nature of the two publications and the likelihood of their entering into competition with each other is not only a relevant but may even be a determining factor in the case. But ... an unfair use may be made of one book in the preparation of another, even if there is no likelihood of competition between the former and the latter. After all copyright is property...".

[79] *Chappell v Thompson* (above, n.78); and see *Ravenscroft v Herbert* [1980] R.P.C. 193.

[80] If he has given up rights by assignment, his freedom to copy the work may be governed by its express terms.

[81] CDPA 1988 s.64, based upon *Preston v Tuck* [1926] Ch. 667.

products would be considered rather than the relation between the first work and what has been copied from it. The fact that the author made his reproduction unconsciously (if he can be believed) would probably enhance any claim not to have infringed.[82]

(4) Infringement carried out by others[83]

Infringement of copyright being a tort, in the ordinary run of things an employer will be vicariously liable[84] for any infringement committed by an employee in the course of his employment and for the acts of independent contractors which he specifically requested. Under earlier law, these principles seem to have delimited the scope of one person's liability for infringements committed by another.[85] But, in contrast with the case of patents,[86] judges have more recently been ready enough to extend the scope of responsibility for the infringement of copyright committed by others. **12–18**

In this they have been assisted by the legislature, which has introduced three forms of infringement: (1) "authorising" infringement by others[87]; (2) "permitting" a place of public entertainment to be used for performance of a work[88]; and (3) providing apparatus for performing, playing or showing a work, etc.[89] (Of these, (2) and (3) are now forms of secondary infringement which require proof of the defendant's complicity in ways which will be described later.)[90]

"Authorise" has been read as bearing its dictionary meaning of "sanction, countenance or approve".[91] In line with these broad synonyms, it has been said that "indifference, exhibited by acts of commission or omission, may reach a degree from which authorisation or permission may be inferred".[92] Accordingly in a case concerning performing rights (which has been the commonest field of application for these provisions) both authorising and **12–19**

[82] On the difficulties of deciding this, see *Industrial Furnaces v Reaves* [1970] R.P.C. 605 at 623–624.

[83] See Gendreau (2001) J. Copyright Soc USA 341.

[84] For vicarious liability, see above, para.2–09. To tell a servant not to infringe will not affect this liability if he defies instructions in the course of employment: *PRS v Mitchell & Booker* [1924] 1 K.B. 762; cf. *PRS v Bradford Corp* [1917–1923] Mac. CC 309.

[85] See especially *Karno v Pathé* (1909) 100 L.T. 260—film distributor did not "cause" representation of a play in public by supplying a theatre operator with film of it; only the operator infringed. Cf. *Falcon v Famous Players* [1926] 2 K.B. 474.

[86] See above, paras 6–17—6–19.

[87] Now CDPA 1988 s.16(2).

[88] Now CDPA 1988 s.25. This relates only to literary, dramatic and musical works; a defence concerning non-profit activities has been dropped.

[89] Now CDPA 1988 s.26.

[90] See below, para.12–35.

[91] Tomlin J. *Evans v Hulton* [1923–1928] Mac. CC 51; Bankes L.J. *Falcon v Famous Players* (above, n.85) at 491; *Pensher Security Door v Sunderland County Council* [2000] R.P.C. 24.

[92] *PRS v Ciryl* [1914] 1 K.B. 1 at 9; *Moorhouse v University of NSW* (1975) 133 C.L.R. 1; [1976] R.P.C. 151 HC Aust; Catterns (1976) 23 Bull. U.S. Cop. 213; criticised as unduly protective of copyright owners in *Law Society of Upper Canada v CCH Canadian* [2004] F.S.R. 41 SC Canada.

permitting may be alleged, and they amount to much the same thing. "Permitting" performance is expressly stated to be subject to the defence of reasonable belief that there would be no infringement[93]; "authorising" is not the subject of specific exceptions, but the meaning given to the word excludes liability when the defendant could not reasonably expect that another would infringe.[94] It is also necessary to show an act of infringement which has occurred as a result of the authorisation.[95]

To take some examples: people who organise public entertainments by hiring musicians as independent contractors are likely to be authorising or permitting infringement if they simply leave the choice of music to the musicians.[96] Accordingly they ought to procure an appropriate licence from the Performing Right Society themselves or require the musicians to do so. Where the defendant is not the organiser of the entertainment, but only, for instance, the owner of the hall, he is unlikely to be held culpable if he is simply "indifferent" to the choice of music.[97]

12–20 In other fields, authorising may also occur by implication. A person who transfers the serial rights in a book authorises their publication in that form, since the specific intent is apparent.[98] An Australian university was held to have authorised infringement by allowing library readers to use its copying machine, without giving precise information about the limits to copying within the copyright legislation and without attempting any supervision to prevent infringement: the degree of indifference was too blatant to escape liability.[99] On the other hand, those who provide the copying machinery or the material for home taping will rarely be found to have the necessary control over what is then done, to be "authorised".[100] The manufacturer of a twin-deck cassette recorder did not authorise infringement of particular copyrights, even though he advertised the capabilities of his product, since he also drew attention to copyright obligations.[101]

---

[93] CDPA 1988 s.25(1).

[94] See *Ciryl* case (above, n.92). The authorisation will be caught wherever it is given, provided that it is to infringe in the UK: *Abkco v Music Collection* [1995] E.M.L.R. 449 CA.

[95] *RCA v Fairfax* [1982] R.P.C. 91 (newspaper article suggesting the possibility of home taping); *WEA International v Hanimax* (1988) 10 I.P.R. 349.

[96] *PRS v Bradford Corp* (above, n.84); *Australian PRA v Canterbury-Bankstown Club* [1964–1965] N.S.W.R. 138; *Australian PRA v Miles* [1962] N.S.W.R. 405; *Australian PRA v Koolman* [1969] N.Z.L.R. 273. Cf. *Monaghan v Taylor* (1885) 2 T.L.R. 685 (entrepreneur present); *PRS v Bray UDC* [1930] A.C. 377 (entrepreneur approved list).

[97] *Vigneux v Canadian PRS* [1945] A.C. 108 at 123. Cf. *Winstone v Wurlitzer* [1946] V.L.R. 338; *Adelaide Corp v Australian PRS* (1928) 40 C.L.R. 481 (despite knowledge that infringement likely); *Ciryl* case (above, n.92) (defendant only managing director of entrepreneur company); *Performances (NZ) v Lion Breweries* [1980] F.S.R. 1.

[98] *Evans v Hulton* [1923–1928] Mac. CC 51; and see *Falcon v Famous Players* (above, n.85).

[99] *Moorhouse* case (above, n.92); in another context, see *Standen Engineering v Spalding* [1984] F.S.R. 554.

[100] See *A & M Records v Audio Magnetics* [1979] F.S.R. 1; *CBS v Ames* [1981] R.P.C. 407.

[101] *CBS UK v Amstrad* [1988] R.P.C. 567; and see above, para.2–14.

2. Classes of Prohibited Act

The CDPA 1988 defines the "acts restricted by the copyright" in general terms, each type applying to the various categories of work unless a specific exception is given. The CA 1956, by contrast, took each category of subject-matter and listed the relevant acts of infringement. The current technique seems rather more straightforward. In the Table (head 7) (on pp.385 to 387) the restricted acts are listed in two groups, the first being concerned with making reproductions, adaptations and the like, the second with transient activities involving a performance or broadcast. **12–21**

In UK patent law, as we have seen, the monopoly right was extended to use, as well as manufacture and sale, thus enabling the patentee and his associates to exercise whatever control over their own products seemed advantageous. In UK copyright law, the same basic assumption has not been made.[102] The typical act of infringement has been the making of copies. Control over them and their contents once legitimately made has been conceded only on a case-by-case basis: the rights over public performance and broadcasting are one form of control over use; the rental right in sound recordings, films and computer programs is another.[103] Now the "de-materialisation" effected by the internet, tends to blur the two categories, since a great deal of electronic copying goes on, much of it only transient; yet at the same time the ability of the system to hold material in readiness for individual requests from users has added to controls over use. Nevertheless we retain the distinction between copying and subsequent uses as a starting point for analysis.

Often enough the various rights that make up copyright are separately assigned or made the subject of an exclusive licence.[104] The assignee or exclusive licensee is then entitled to sue only in respect of his own part and it may be necessary to decide just what his part is. If the division up has been made by reference to the different acts listed in the statute, then the question will turn on the meaning of the statutory words.[105] If some other, more specific right has been conceded (such as the right to translate into French, or the right to engrave a picture for a particular book) then the particular assignment or licence will require interpretation.

The CDPA 1988 distinguishes two broad categories of infringement: restricted acts (or primary infringement) which occur without regard to the **12–22**

---

[102] The *droit de destination* read into French and Belgian copyright law fulfils much the same function as the British patent law doctrine; it allows, for instance, a rental right to be read into the law without specific provision: see EC Commission, Green Paper, *Copyright and the Challenge of Technology* (Com. (88) 172) 146.

[103] See below, paras 12–27—12–29, and consider also the special scheme for the public lending of books: below, paras 14–41—14–44.

[104] See below, paras 13–11 et seq.

[105] See, e.g. *Chappell v Columbia* [1914] 2 Ch. 124.

defendant's state of mind[106]; and secondary infringements which are committed only if the defendant knew or had reason to believe a defined state of affairs relating to infringement. Under each of the following heads primary and secondary infringement will be considered separately.

(1) Rights concerned with reproduction and adaptation

(a) *Primary infringement: copying*

12–23 Copyright in a work may be infringed by copying it, issuing copies of it to the public, or by making an adaptation of it.[107] Copying a work, so far as concerns literary, dramatic, musical and artistic copyright, means "reproducing the work in a material form"—a formula originally introduced in the CA 1911.[108] Some of the material forms are now specifically listed. These include: (1) storing the work in any medium by electronic means—which clearly covers computer storage and presumably extends to the incorporation of the work in a record or film[109] and the transcription into digital form; and (2) converting a two-dimensional artistic work into three dimensions, and vice versa.[110] But other changes of form may also count: for instance, turning a story into a ballet,[111] copying a photograph by painting,[112] making a knitting pattern into a fabric,[113] and turning a drawing, such as a cartoon, into a revue sketch.[114] Novel analogies can be made, subject always to the need to satisfy the test of substantial taking. The scope of "copying" is stretched to its very borders by s.17(6) of the CDPA 1988 which extends liability as far as the making of copies which are transient or are incidental to some other use. Yet it is now of great practical significance in the provision of electronic data in response to individual orders: and it raises questions about the scope of rights in performances.[115]

---

[106] Thus making the deliberateness or otherwise of the defendant's conduct not relevant to the assessment of infringement: Laddie J., *Electronic Techniques v Critchley Components* [1997] F.S.R. 401 at 410; *Sony Music Entertainment v Easyinternetcafe* [2003] E.W.H.C. 62.

[107] CDPA 1988 ss.16–18, 21.

[108] CDPA 1988 s.17(2).

[109] cf. CA 1956 s.48(1) "reproduction", which specified these cases; *Ocular Sciences v Aspect Vision Care* [1997] R.P.C. at 418.

[110] CDPA 1988 s.17(3). Instructions attached to a product drawing have been treated as part of the 2D artistic work in this context: *Gleeson v Wippel* [1977] F.S.R. 301; *Vermaat & Powell v Boncrest* [2001] F.S.R. 43; cf. the cases concerning purely literary works: below, para.12–24.

[111] *Holland v Van Damm* [1936–1945] Mac. C.C. 69.

[112] *Bauman v Fussell* (1953) [1978] R.P.C. 485 CA; *Hanfstaegl v WHSmith* [1905] 1 Ch. 519.

[113] *Lerose v Hawick Jersey* [1974] R.P.C. 42; cf. *Dicks v Brooks* (1880) Ch.D. 22 (pre-1911 legislation).

[114] *Bradbury, Agnew v Day* (1916) 32 T.L.R. 349 (cf. the pre-1911 position in *Hanfstaegl v Empire Palace* [1894] 2 Ch. 1). Note the absence of a general performing right in artistic works.

[115] See below, paras 20–60 et seq. Technological ingenuity has an awkward habit of running beyond legal concepts. The Supreme Court of Canada held that a process which transferred the ink on a poster to a different backing, leaving nothing behind on the poster, was not reproduction: *Théberge v Galerie du Petit Champlain* [2002] S.C.C. 34. The three civilian members of the court dissented, holding that the author's right lay in the work.

There are other important ramifications of this crucial idea as copyright questions develop around modern electronic techniques, particularly in the field of computerised design and manufacture. On the one hand, it may seem only appropriate to extend the range of the law to embrace a new technique for copying. On the other, there is an evident danger of going too far (particularly with a right so readily conceded and long-lasting as copyright) if it were to become infringement merely to carry out another person's instructions to do something (for example bake a cake[116]). **12–24**

Although, as we shall see, the statutory provision that a 2D artistic work can be reproduced in 3D contributed crucially to the concept of copyright affecting industrial production, the courts have in the main refused to hold that a *literary* work (recipes, etc.) can be infringed by making an object in accordance with the work.[117] However, Jacob J. apparently departed from this by holding that if instructions about the component of an electrical circuit diagram (ohms for a resistor, etc.) were worked out into a "net list" and then reproduced in a circuit board without authority, there can be infringement of the literary copyright in the claimant's net list and even the literary aspects of the circuit diagram.[118] If developed, this line of thinking might provide literary copyright in structural information about the human and other genomes which would be infringed whenever the information was copied for use in genetic engineering.[119] The general issue thus raised deserves anxious consideration, taking account in particular of whether the copyright laws of other countries are in the least likely to take a similar turn.

Quite apart from this, certain acts of adaptation are separately treated as constituting infringement: turning a literary work into a dramatic work or vice versa; translating either kind of work or turning it into a picture form (such as a comic strip); arranging or transcribing a musical work (by, for instance, harmonising or orchestrating it); arranging or altering a computer program, or translating it into another computer language.[120] **12–25**

The CDPA 1988 is not so specific as its predecessor about what acts of "copying" infringe sound recording, film and broadcasting copyright. Presumably, as before, this includes making recordings or films that are **12–26**

---

[116] For some teasing on the subject, see Mout-Bouwman [1988] E.I.P.R. 234.

[117] *Brigid Foley v Elliot* [1982] R.P.C. 433 (knitting pattern for machine); *Duriron v Hugh Jennings* [1984] F.S.R. 1 CA (table of dimensions). Cf *Autospin (Oil Seals) v Beehive Spinning* [1995] R.P.C. 683 (compilation of measurements).

[118] *Anacon v Environmental Research* [1994] F.S.R. 359; Reynolds and Brownlow [1994] E.I.P.R. 399. The circuit diagram was an artistic work, but the defendant, employing a computer to obtain its own layout, did not reproduce the physical form of the diagram. Accordingly, there was no infringement of the special design right in the topography of the circuit: for which, see below, para.15–54. The line of argument has been accepted in *Sandman v Panasonic* [1998] F.S.R. 651; but doubted in *Electronic Techniques v Critchley Components* [1997] F.S.R. 401.

[119] See esp. Laddie et al. Ch.35.

[120] CDPA 1988 s.21. Section 21(5) suggests that these forms of infringement are closely related to infringement by reproduction in a material form: "No inference shall be drawn from this section as to what does or does not amount to copying the work."

substantial copies of those things. But it is not infringement of copyright to make it afresh. A film is the recording of moving images; it is not the dramatic work or other content embodied in it.[121]

Copying also includes specific cases. Making a photograph of the whole or a substantial part of any image forming part of a film, broadcast or cable programme—for instance for a post-card or poster—is such an infringement.[122] The publisher's copyright in typographical format is infringed solely by making a facsimile copy, even if it is enlarged or reduced.[123]

(b) *Primary infringement: issuing copies, rental and lending*

12–27 Issuing copies of a work to the public[124] is a form of primary infringement which relates to the first release of the copies into circulation. When originally introduced in 1988, this form of infringement did not apply to the parallel importation of products legitimately marketed in other countries.[125] Under EU law, these could normally be freely imported from other Member States.[126] From non-Member States they also might give rise to liability for secondary infringement, if the requisite state of mind could be imputed to the defendant. This is discussed below.[127]

It is the intent of EU authorities that the exclusive right of reproduction should not be treated as exhausted by any distribution of copies outside the EEA as a whole.[128] In consequence, parallel importation of such copies into the EEA from beyond its borders should become a form of primary infringement. The matter has so far been dealt with in Directives only in relation to the literary copyright in computer programs, and the related rights given to performers, record and film producers and broadcasting organisations.[129] Even in these cases, the legal proposition is oblique: the Directives state that the rights are exhausted by first authorised sale within the EU, thereby raising the implication that there is no exhaustion of the right by sale outside the EU. (The ploy avoids drawing political attention to

[121] *Norowzian v Arks (No. 1)* [1998] F.S.R. 394; cf. *(No. 2)* [2000] F.S.R. 363; and *Shree Venkatesh Film v Vipul Amritlal Shah* Civ. 219/2009, HC Calcutta, noted by Banerjee [2010] J.I.P.L.P. 17.

[122] CDPA 1988 s.17(4), giving statutory effect to *Spelling Goldberg v BPC Publishing* [1981] R.P.C. 280 CA.

[123] CDPA 1988 ss.17, 178: "facsimile copy".

[124] CDPA 1988 s.18; previously only first publication of the work constituted primary infringement: *Infabrics v Jaytex* [1982] A.C. 1 (a narrow view of the CA 1956 provision).

[125] CDPA 1988 s.18(2), which (save for computer programs) still states that issuing copies to the public is not concerned with copies previously put into circulation in the UK or elsewhere.

[126] By virtue of the TFEU arts 34 and 36: see above, paras 1–51, 1–52, below, paras 19–02 et seq.

[127] See para.12–29, below.

[128] See above, para.1–58, below, paras 19–17 et seq. For the requirement in the InfoSoc Directive that any concept of exhaustion of rights should be confined to "objects" and not extend to electronic transmissions (e.g. on the internet), see art.4; *Peek & Cloppenberg v Cassina* [2009] E.C.D.R. 9.

[129] Computer Programs Directive art.4(c); Rental, Lending and Related Rights Directive art.9(2) and note art.1(4).

the parallel import bans.) In pursuit of this interpretation, the CDPA 1988 has been amended.[130] To import and sell legitimate copies of a work from a non-EU state counts as issuing the copies to the British public and so needs to be licensed.[131]

Despite the general restriction of the primary distribution right to initial sale and other disposal, it has nevertheless been extended to cover important forms of renting copies. The object has been to secure some measure of return to copyright owners from material which is likely to be privately copied without practical redress. The CPDA 1988 introduced temporary use protection only for the rental (not the lending) of sound recordings, films and computer programs—the three cases where renting was at all widespread. The EU Directive on Rental, Lending and Related Rights, however, expands this[132] and British legislation now gives rental and lending rights in literary, dramatic and musical works,[133] most artistic works, and films and sound recordings.[134] Rental is broadly defined to cover the temporary provision of copies "for direct or indirect economic or commercial advantage", but this will be on terms that they will or may be returned—thus excluding any electronic provision. Lending relates only to loans through a publicly accessible establishment, such as a public library.[135] A protective element in the scheme requires that once authors and performers assign their rental rights in a sound recording or audio-visual work to a producer (a practice so much to be expected in the case of films that there is a statutory presumption in its favour),[136] they will remain entitled to equitable remuneration.[137] They have no power to waive their entitlement to equitable remuneration, although they can exercise it only personally or through a collecting society. This legal intervention has the merit of safeguarding the benefits of a new right which is being attached to existing works. Its long-term effects on the overall bargaining position of authors is much less easy to predict.[138] **12–28**

[130] CDPA 1988 s.18(3); Copyright and Related Rights Regulations (SI 1996/2967) reg.9(3).

[131] *Independiente v Music Trading On-Line (HK)* [2007] F.S.R. 21.

[132] Dir. 92/100 now codified as Dir. 2006/115; above, para.10–19; Reinbothe and von Lewinski, *The EC Directive on Rental and Lending Rights and on Piracy* (1993). For the constitutionality of the Directive, see, *Metronome Musik v Music Point Hokamp* [1997] E.M.L.R. 93, [1998] ECR I-1953 ECJ.

[133] i.e. other than architectural works and works of applied art.

[134] CDPA 1988 s.18A. Note that the section confers on producers of films.

[135] CDPA 1988 s.18A (2)–(6). A number of exceptions include loans for performance, for exhibition and for on-the-spot reference; inter-library loans; and lending by an educational establishment (s.36A). Public libraries which charge no more than operating costs engage in lending, not rental. Curiously, the original work is included within the notion of "copies". For the preservation of the Public Lending right scheme for books, see below, para.14–43; and for the public lending of other material, para.14–42.

[136] CDPA 1988 ss.93A, 191F.

[137] CDPA 1988 ss.93B, 93C, 191G, 191H; and see *SENA v NOS* [2003] All E.R. (D) 67 (Feb) ECJ. For the jurisdiction of the Copyright Tribunal ss.117, 124.

[138] See Towse, *Creative, Innovation, Incentive and Reward: An Economic Analysis of Copyright and Culture in the Information Age* (2001).

(c) *Secondary infringement: dealings with copies*[139]

12–29 Infringement of all forms of copyright may be committed by a defendant concerned in the commercial exploitation of copies, if he knows or has reason to believe that the copies were infringements when they were made.[140] In the case of imported copies this includes "notional infringements", that is copies that would have infringed if they had been made in Britain or would have constituted a breach of an exclusive licence agreement relating to that work.[141] The stages of exploitation in question are: importing, possessing in the course of a business, selling, letting for hire, offering or exposing for sale or hire, and exhibiting in public in the course of a business, and distributing either in the course of a business, or otherwise to an extent that prejudicially affects the copyright owner.[142]

As to the defendant's state of mind in secondary infringement, the previous law required it to be shown that the defendant had knowledge that the copies in issue were infringements.[143] But that had been read as requiring only that he had "notice of facts such as would suggest to a reasonable man that a breach of copyright was being committed".[144] The new phrase, "knew or had reason to believe", has been understood in the same sense.[145] It is no defence genuinely to believe, or to rely upon legal advice, that what is being done does not, as a matter of law, amount to copyright infringement.[146]

(2) Rights concerned with communications to the public: performance, broadcasting, internet and similar provision

(a) *Primary infringement: communication to the public*[147]

12–30 The extension of copyright from the making of copies to the giving of public performances began in 1833. With modern technology, this then grew into a bundle of related aspects of copyright loosely grouped as "performing rights": performing, playing or showing a work in public, or broadcasting it.[148] With internet usage, the category of broadcasting has been further

---

139 See Hays [2006] E.I.P.R. 617; [2007] E.I.P.R.15.

140 CDPA 1988 ss.22–24, 27. As already noted, the person who first puts copies into circulation commits the primary infringement of issuing copies to the public: above, para.12–27. For infringement by telecommunication of text, s.24(2).

141 CDPA 1988 s.27(3); see below, paras 13–14—13–18.

142 CDPA 1988 s.23. For parallel importation, see below, para.13–14.

143 CA 1956 ss.5, 16.

144 Harvey J. *Albert v Hoffnung* (1922) 22 S.R. (NSW) 75 at 81; followed by Whitford J. *Infabrics v Jaytex* [1978] F.S.R. 451 at 464–465; and see at 467: was the defendant's selector "put on inquiry"? Did he turn "a blind eye to an inquiry which he should have known he ought to have made"? Once apprised of the truth he was allowed a number of days to make his own inquiries: *Van Dusen v Kritz* [1936] 2 K.B. 176.

145 *LA Gear v Hi-Tec* [1992] F.S.R. 121 CA; *ZYX Music v King* [1997] E.M.L.R. 319 CA.

146 *Sillitoe v McGraw-Hill Books* [1993] F.S.R. 545; *ZYX Music v King*, above, n.145.

147 In international context, see esp. Ginsburg in Vaver and Bently (2004), Ch.16; and Makeen, *Copyright in a Global Information Society: The Scope of Copyright Protection Under International, US, UK and French Law* (Kluwer, 2000).

148 CDPA 1988, ss.19, 20.

generalised. Copyright works can now be infringed by any "communication to the public". In line with the WIPO Treaties of 1996 and the EU InfoSoc Directive art.3, this embraces all communications to the public by electronic transmission, i.e. not just wired and wireless broadcasting but also "on demand, interactive services available to members of the public at their chosen time and place". The ECJ has determined that, in the interests of authors, "communication to the public" must be interpreted broadly. Accordingly, a hotel which receives a broadcast through a central aerial and then communicates it to bedrooms is transmitting to the public and must obtain copyright licences to do so.[149] That, of course, would not be necessary if the set in each room received the broadcast directly.[150] Was it desirable to favour an extra charge simply by virtue of the change in reception technology? The court's answer must, as a matter of policy, remain moot.[151]

The possibilities of infringement in this field have become complex. If, for instance, a copyright musical work is performed to a public audience at the same time as being televised, both the performance and the broadcast require a licence. If the broadcast is received and shown publicly, this calls for licence of the copyright in the music, and (save where the showing is free) of that in the broadcast.[152] If the original performance was recorded this will be either in the form of a sound recording or a film with associated soundtrack (each of which will be a form of reproduction). If either the recording or the film is broadcast, this needs a licence. However, the owner of copyright in the sound recording or film (as distinct from that in the musical work) has no right in respect of free public playings or showings of the broadcast.[153]

Performance and communication to the public are too ephemeral for it to **12–31**
be easy for copyright owners to enforce their performing rights individually. Those who have copyright in musical works and associated lyrics have been leaders in establishing societies for the collective enforcement of their rights. The great proliferation in the exploitation of music through recordings and broadcasts has made this economically feasible in many countries; and an international network of performing right societies now exists.[154] Now there

---

[149] *SGAE v Rafael Hoteles* [2006] E.C.R. I-11519; [2007] E.C.D.R. 2—an interpretation of the InfoSoc Directive art.3(1). Whether performers and record producers have an equivalent right depends on the terms of the Directive art.3(2), which are more limited.

[150] See *Football Association PL v QC Leisure* [2008] C.M.L.R. 12, which suggests that simply receiving a satellite signal, decoding it and displaying in on tv is not an act of communication to the public, but rather performance in public. An ECJ ruling on this issue is awaited. See also Case 136/09 *Organismos Sillogikis v Dirani* O.J. C141 of 20.06. 2009 p.32.

[151] See Bateman [2007] E.I.P.R. 22.

[152] cf. CDPA 1988 s.72.

[153] See CDPA 1988 s.72(2), (3).

[154] For the history, particularly of the British organisation, the Performing Right Society (PRS), see Peacock and Weir, *The Composer in the Market Place* (1975); McFarlane, *Copyright: the Development and Exercise of the Performing Right* (1980), Chs 6–11. The PRS collects on behalf of foreign societies for British use of their repertoires, and it has arrangements to receive equivalent royalties from the foreign societies on its own members' behalf. The Confédération Internationale des Socìtés d'Auteurs et Compositeurs (CISAC) has played an important role in settling the terms of the international system of collection and distribution.

is a very considerable interest in extending collective enforcement to the burgeoning websites holding unauthorised recordings, films and texts. In Britain, where record companies have performing rights in their recordings, they have a separate collecting society to assert their rights.[155] In various countries, the economic power of collecting societies has become suspect: the case for public surveillance is discussed in the next chapter.[156]

(b) *Performance in public*

12–32 It has been left to the courts to draw the line between performances in public and in private. In 1884, the Court of Appeal characterised as "quasi-domestic"—and therefore private—an amateur performance of a play in Guy's Hospital to an audience of doctors and their families, nurses, attendants and students.[157] This was regarded (even in the decision itself) as marking the extreme outpost of free territory. To be in public a performance does not have to be to a paying audience or by paid performers[158]; it is enough that entertainment is being offered as an incident of some commercial activity (such as running a hotel, or even a shop that is seeking to sell the records being played)[159] or of industrial production ("music while you work").[160] Even such worthy institutions as a Women's Institute and a football club's supporters' association engage in public performance, whether they restrict audiences to their own members or allow in guests[161]; and the CDPA 1988 makes clear that a school play or other performance will not be exempt if parents or friends are present.[162] Greene M.R. laid particular stress on the need to consider the relationship of the audience to the owner of the copyright rather than to the performers.[163] This is one way of emphasising the primacy of the owner's entitlement to an economic return from his proprietary rights; the fact that an organisation is socially desirable does not normally give it a claim to free use of copyright material. A general exception in the CDPA 1988 allowed sound recordings and broadcasts (as distinct from copyright in music and words) to be played at a charitable or similar club or organisation, provided that any charge covered only the operating costs. However, to comply with EU law, the scope of each of these exceptions has since been cut back.[164]

---

155 Called Phonographic Performance Ltd (PPL). See above, para.10–50.

156 See below, para.13–53.

157 *Duck v Bates* (1884) 13 Q.B.D. 843; under the 1833 Act, the requirement was in any case that the performance be in a "place of public entertainment".

158 *PRS v Hawthornes Hotel* [1933] Ch. 855; and see *Harms v Martans Club* [1927] 1 Ch. 526 (dance club).

159 *PRS v Harlequin Record* [1979] F.S.R. 233.

160 *Ernest Turner v PRS* [1943] Ch. 167.

161 *Jennings v Stephens* [1936] Ch. 469; *PRS v Rangers Club* [1975] R.P.C. 626; *Australian PRA v Commonwealth Bank* (1992) 25 I.P.R. 157.

162 CDPA 1988 s.34(3).

163 In the *Jennings* and *Turner* cases (above, nn.160, 161).

164 See CDPA 1988 ss.67, 72 as amended; and for further issues concerning implementation of the Rental, Lending and Related Rights Directive see *PPL v ATI* [2005] R.P.C. 8.

(c) *Broadcasting*

The broadcasting and cable transmission of copyright works require authorisation.[165] However, this portion of the copyright in a sound recording (as distinct from any copyright in works recorded) is subject to a statutory licence.[166] This limitation was adopted in Britain as the result of a critical report by the Monopolies and Mergers Commission concerning the demands of the record companies' collecting society, Phonographic Performance Ltd.[167] The rate will, if necessary be set by the Copyright Tribunal in accordance with a prescribed statutory procedure.[168] **12–33**

With satellite technology and the introduction of digital formats, broadcasting has become an increasingly international medium. A country may receive many more transmissions than would be made by its own network of sound and television broadcasts. Broadcasting organisations have accordingly insisted that, in the interests of simplicity and certainty, the "up-leg" of a transmission alone should require licensing. Under the present EU approach, the licence will be under the law of the place from which or where the "up-leg" occurs, and the fee will take account of the audience size in the various countries which may feel its footprint.[169]

Broadcasting stands on the brink of a further revolution, since the medium is shifting from a purely analogue base to a digital one. It will become possible to transmit immense quantities of digital material via a single satellite, and thousands of channels may become available, some for their own programmes and others for interactive selection of material by individuals.[170] While this will change the economic structure of broadcasting, it is not at present apparent that the UK copyright law on the subject needs change to accommodate digital broadcasting, since it already carries its own copyright, as well as copyright in protected materials which it may transmit. What has to be introduced is electronic means for monitoring and recording all the myriad works which are being broadcast. **12–34**

(d) *Secondary infringement: performances*

As with dealings in copies, certain activities connected with public performances give rise to secondary infringement. These are: (1) permitting premises to be used for an infringing performance[171]; and (2) providing certain apparatus (for playing recordings, showing films and receiving broadcasts, etc.).[172] The former of these is closely linked to the concept of authorising **12–35**

[165] CDPA 1988 s.20. The one exception is the limited copyright in the format of a published edition.
[166] CDPA 1988 ss.135A–G.
[167] See below, para.13–53.
[168] For the appropriate comparisons to be made: *PPL v Virgin Retail* [2001] E.M.L.R. 139.
[169] For implementation of the Satellite and Cable Directive, see below, paras 14–24 et seq.
[170] See below, further, para.20–77.
[171] CDPA 1988 s.25.
[172] CDPA 1988 s.26.

infringement and has been mentioned in that context.[173] The latter is allied to secondary infringement involving infringing copies, and depends upon showing that a defendant knew or had reason to believe that the act in question—provision of the equipment or premises for it—is likely to lead to use involving infringement.[174]

3. "Fair Dealing" and Like Exceptions[175]

(1) Fair dealing

(a) *General*

12–36 The requirement of "substantial taking" prevents the owner of a copyright work from objecting to minor borrowings from it. And, as we have just seen, the requirement that a performance, playing or showing be in public means that his licence is unnecessary for a private performance, even of the complete work. In the modern Copyright Acts, other exceptions from the scope of copyright have been specified and the CDPA 1988 now has a lengthy list. Some of them, such as those relating to education, concern important conflicts of interest, and they will be discussed in their own context in Chs 13 and 19. In this chapter they are listed in order that they can be compared in the round.

12–37 Inspired by those copyright industries which most fear the impact of the internet upon their present rights and so their present structures, the EU used its InfoSoc Directive as the opportunity to impose constraints upon the exceptions and limitations which national legislation could contain. A primary objective being pursued in the Directive was to settle liability that could be placed upon host service providers, secondary transmitters and access providers on the internet.[176] At the same time, the InfoSoc Directive was built upon a supposedly valuable principle that the new copyright dispensations should not draw distinctions between digital and non-digital media. It was in consequence claimed that the defences to copyright liability in general must be harmonised, at least in some measure. Otherwise curious differences in protection between Member States might prevail. In previous analyses it was apparently accepted that such harmonisation could be justified only where there was plain evidence that those differences would affect trade within the internal market. In the case of photocopying, for instance, it was hard to see that case, since the practice did not result in cross-border

[173] See above, para.12–18.
[174] CDPA 1988 s.26(2), (3).
[175] Davies, *Copyright and the Public Interest* 2nd edn (2002); Burrell and Coleman: *Copyright Exceptions: the Digital Impact* (2005); Nimmer (2003) 66 L. & C.P. 263.
[176] See below, paras 12–56, 20–69, 20–70.

trading. By the time that the InfoSoc Directive was in place, little was to be seen of such scruple.

The original plan had been to make the limits strict. But Member States began to insist that particular exceptions familiar to them should be included and it became inevitable that all possibilities should be covered in the Directive's list.[177] Even so, the effect is of rough approximation only, since the list for the most part only imposes outer boundaries on the content of national copyright laws.[178] Its one overriding direction is that all defences must comply with the "Three-Step Test" deriving from the Berne Convention and TRIPS art.13,[179] that exceptions and limitations: (1) must be confined to special cases[180]; (2) must not conflict with a normal exploitation of the work; and (3) must not unreasonably prejudice the legitimate interests of the right-holder.[181] The British Government has refused to include this as a separate statutory provision, asserting that the list of exceptions in the CDPA 1988, with only occasional revisions necessitated by the Directive, comply with the test.[182] The test, being in a Directive, is aimed at the national legislature. It does not furnish grounds which can be raised in the course of private litigation in the same way as the grounds listed or referred to in the Act. Judges, in other words, are not to be furnished with any general tool for criticising the scope of the legislation. Their role is confined to interpretation of its meaning.

Turning to the current defences listed in the CDPA 1988 (as much amended), we come first to the three instances dealing with types of "fair dealing", a concept which calls for a qualitative assessment. In these cases the courts are left to judge fairness in the light of all the circumstances. The Court of Appeal has encouraged a liberal approach to what constitutes "fair dealing".[183] Before the CA 1911, the three main "fair dealing" exceptions were foreshadowed in the case law as forms of "fair use", a concept that was not clearly distinguished from "insubstantial taking". If there is substantial copying, it is a nice question today how far the use could nevertheless be **12–38**

---

[177] InfoSoc Directive art.5(2)–(4). There may nonetheless be scope for challenges to the constitutionality of some aspects of art.5.

[178] There is no obligation on a Member State to introduce an exception on the list, though it may do so at any time (save in the case of minor exceptions existing when the Directive took effect).

[179] See above, para.10–12. In Berne the test applies to the reproduction right (art.9(2)); in TRIPS it is generalised to cover all aspects of authors' rights and the principal neighbouring rights. The test played an important part in the decision of WTO Panel holding that the "homestyle" exception in the US Copyright Act of 1976 s.110(5) was inconsistent with TRIPS, save that it could apply to dramatico-musical works: see Ginsburg (2001) 187 I.I.T.A. 3; Brennan [2002] I.P.Q. 212.

[180] Whether this is to be treated as a distinct condition, and if so what it is to imply are at present keenly debated. Is the dance a three-step or only a two-step? See Ricketson and Ginsburg, paras 13.13–13.14.

[181] InfoSoc Directive art.5(5).

[182] DTI, *Consultation Paper on Implementation* (August, 2002), pp.11–12.

[183] *Pro Sieben v Carlton UK TV* [1999] E.M.L.R. 109; below, para.14–04; cf. *Hawkes v Paramount* [1934] Ch. 593 CA; and cf. attitudes to public interest, below, para.14–05.

justified for a reason beyond the confines of the statutory exceptions. Certainly this would be difficult if the case was closely analogous to one of the statutory exceptions but just outside it.[184] Nonetheless a "defence" of publication in the public interest has been recognised to exist and now has a place in the statute.[185] It is currently treated as less extensive than in a claim based on breach of confidence,[186] since there may be a case for revealing information, but not necessarily in a form which makes use of copyrighted expression.[187]

By relying almost wholly on specified statutory limitations, UK copyright law differs both from US law, where the concept of "fair use" has a scope that is both general and central, and authors' rights systems, which tend to have a general defence of private use deriving from what are now human rights criteria.[188] In UK law, while neither "fair" nor "private" use forms a general ground of excusal in relation to the reproduction and related rights, the limitation to public use is written into the very definition of the various forms of performing right. As already noted, there are difficult issues here where exploitation is through new electronic media. Significantly, it has recently been said that it may be proper to take one copy of a whole work if the purpose is to use extracts in a way that is legitimate.[189]

(b) *Research or private study*

12–39 The first fair dealing exception is that covering purposes of private study and non-commercial research,[190] which now applies to the copyright in literary, dramatic, musical and artistic works, and published editions.[191] With this must be read: (i) the more specific exceptions covering certain librarians and archivists[192]; (ii) the exception for the inclusion of short passages of

---

[184] See above, para.8–18.

[185] CDPA 1988 s.171(3), which preserves rules of law preventing or restricting the enforcement of copyright, on grounds of public interest or otherwise. See further below, paras 12–57 and 14–05. For a critical review of those who have sought to deny the existence of this defence, see Sims [2006] E.I.P.R. 335 and Burrell [2000] E.I.P.R. 188.

[186] cf. *Hubbard v Vosper* [1972] 2 Q.B. 84 CA; *Beloff v Pressdram* [1973] 1 All E.R. 241, which did not differentiate in this way.

[187] *Commonwealth of Australia v Fairfax* (1980) 147 C.L.R. 39 HC Aust; *Kennard v Lewis* [1983] F.S.R. 346 (right-wing criticism of CND pamphlet); and cf. attitudes to public interest shown in *Hyde Park Properties v Yelland* [2000] R.P.C. 604 CA, as opposed to *Ashdown v Telegraph Group* [2002] Ch.149 CA.

[188] For views of the future structure of exceptions, see Copyright Law Review Committee (Australia), *Simplification of the Copyright Act 1968, Part 1* (1988); and see Rothnie in Sherman and Saunders (eds), *From Berne to Geneva* (1997), Ch.6. For US perspectives, Gordon (1982) 82 Col. L.R. 1600; [1997] 8 J.L. & Info. Soc. 7; Netanel (1996) 106 Yale L.J. 283; Nimmer (2003) 66 L. & C.P. 263.

[189] *Pro Sieben v Carlton UK TV* [1999] E.M.L.R. 109 at 127 per Robert Walker L.J.

[190] CDPA 1988 s.29(1), (1C). In the case of research there must be sufficient acknowledgment, unless that would be impossible: s.29(1B).

[191] The present exclusion of the major neighbouring rights seems curious. The *Gowers Review* recommends extension to all copyrights: para.4.77; and this recommendation has met with support: *Taking Forward the Gowers Review of Intellectual Property* (2009).

[192] CDPA 1988 ss.37–44. Amended in line with the InfoSoc Directive to cover research only if it is non-commercial. See further the *Gowers Review*, paras 4.78–4.84.

literary and dramatic works in collections for schools,[193] and the exceptions for copying and photocopying works in the course of instruction and examination and performing, playing or showing works in certain circumstances at schools, etc.[194]; and (iii) the exception for recording broadcasts.[195] The role of these defences is particularly important in the field of education and research and it is in that context that they will be discussed in more detail.[196] What is "fair" will vary to fit each case.

It is the InfoSoc Directive that has required that the research must be for non-commercial purposes. In 1988, Parliament refused to include that limitation because it is often difficult to determine what is commercial.[197] What, for instance, of research undertaken in a university which is sponsored by an outside firm? Or by a student whom the firm subsidises? What of research in Government? In practice the change is likely to be reflected in increased charges under the block licensing arrangements made between institutions and collecting societies.

(c) *Reporting current events*

The second fair dealing exception permits all works, other than photo- **12–40** graphs, to be used for reporting current events.[198] Photographs have been differently treated in order to preserve the full value of holding a unique visual record of some person or event. To come within the exception, the event itself must be current and not the pretext for reviving historical information: the death of the Duchess of Windsor did not justify an exchange of letters between her and the Duke being published without copyright licence.[199] The dealing has also to be fair.[200] The exception must be read in conjunction with a number of cognate provisions.[201] Together they

---

193 CDPA 1988 s.33.

194 CDPA 1988 ss.32, 34, 36. These have been the subject of minor adjustments to fit the conditions allowed by the InfoSoc Directive.

195 CDPA 1988 s.35.

196 See below, paras 14–10 et seq.

197 It is unlikely to cover research undertaken by a commercial company: *HMSO v Green Amps* [2007] EWHC 2755; Derclaye [2008] 30 E.I.P.R. 162.

198 CDPA 1988 s.30(2), (3). This may be in a newspaper or magazine, in which case sufficient acknowledgement is required; or in a sound recording, film, or broadcast, where acknowledgement is not called for where this would be impossible.

199 *Associated Newspapers v News Group* [1986] R.P.C. 515; *Newspaper Licensing Agency v Marks & Spencer* [1999] E.M.L.R. 369 CA: current events do not include lifestyle articles, etc. (but case reversed on other grounds: above, para.12–08).

200 *Ashdown* case, above, n.187.

201 Especially CDPA 1988 s.31 (incidental inclusion in an artistic work, sound recording or film); s.58 (record of spoken words); s.62 (artistic works on public display). The test of what is incidental under s.31 is objective and turns on the purpose for which the image was created and whether inclusion of the copyright material was essential or not: *Football Association PL v Panini* [2004] F.S.R. 1 CA (photos of football players showing the Club badge and FAPL emblem, in which copyright was claimed: inclusion not incidental). Cf *Football Association PL v QC Leisure* [2008] C.M.L.R. 12 (inclusion of the Premier League anthem was not essential for purpose of showing the player line-up).

are of particular importance to the public-affairs media and they will be related to that field later.[202]

(d) *Criticism or review*

12–41 It is the third fair dealing exception that is most general of all, allowing publicly available works to be used for purposes of criticism or review (of themselves or another work), one precondition of fairness being that the source should be sufficiently acknowledged.[203] Despite its potential range, the defence has not been much elucidated in the case law. The Court of Appeal has held that the criticism or review may concern the ideas expressed as well as the mode of expression.[204] And the courts will not permit wholesale borrowing to be dressed up as critical quotation.[205] Nor may comparative advertising use copyright material in order to identify a rival product.[206] Lord Denning M.R.'s remarks, stressing that fair dealing is inevitably a matter of degree, can usefully be applied not only to this head but in spirit equally to the other two:

> "You must consider first the number and extent of the quotations and extracts. Are they altogether too many and too long to be fair? Then you must consider the use made of them. If they are used as a basis for comment, criticism or review, that may be a fair dealing. If they are used to convey the same information as the author, for a rival purpose, they may be unfair. Next, you must consider the proportions. To take long extracts and attach short comments may be unfair. But short extracts and long comments may be fair. Other considerations may come to mind also. But, after all is said and done, it must be a matter of impression."[207]

(2) Other exceptions

12–42 Beyond the statutory categories of "fair dealing" and the associated provisions already mentioned, there are numerous exceptions which, as a whole, are not easily classified.

---

[202] See below, paras 14–04, 14–06.

[203] CDPA 1988 s.30(1). Section 30(1A) defines public availability in broad terms, but the act of making available must be authorised. The criticism or review must appear in a work of the type specified in CDPA 1988 s.1, but copyright does not have to subsist in it: *Fraser-Woodward v BBC* [2005] F.S.R. 36 (Beckham family photos). Display of a foreign TV station's logo can suffice for acknowledgment: *Pro Sieben v Carlton* [1999] E.M.L.R. 109 CA. As to material initially published anonymously: *PCR v Dow Jones Telerate* [1998] F.S.R. 170.

[204] *Hubbard v Vosper* [1972] 2 Q.B. 84 at 94–95, 98. See also *Time Warner v Channel* 4 [1994] E.M.L.R. 1 CA; *Pro Sieben v Carlton*, above, n.203, and see further, below, paras 14–04, 14–06.

[205] *Mawman v Tegg* (1826) 2 Russ. 385; cf. Megaw L.J., *Hubbard* case (above, n.204) at 98.

[206] *IPC Media v News Group* [2005] F.S.R. 35.

[207] *Hubbard* case (above, n.204) at 94. For a recent instance, see *Fraser-Woodward v BBC* (above, n.203)—fair to use 14 photos of the Beckham family in support of the case that "Posh Spice" Beckham manipulated the press.

(a) *Exceptions designed to encourage collective licensing schemes*

As a matter of practicality, the CDPA 1988 aims to foster the administration of copyright through licensing schemes which are conducted for groups of right-owners. Of the five specific cases, three prescribe an exception to infringement which is to operate in the absence of a certified licensing scheme covering the proposed use. These are: (1) recording of broadcasts and material contained in them for the purposes of an educational establishment[208]; (2) copying and issuing copies of the published abstracts of scientific or technical articles in periodicals[209]; and (3) making and issuing copies of broadcasts with subtitling or other modifications for the special needs of the deaf and handicapped, where this is done by a body specially designated by the Minister.[210] In a fourth case—reprographic copying by educational establishments—a similar result is achieved by conferring a limited freedom to copy if no certified scheme is offered.[211] In a fifth case—the public lending right, as it applies to literary, dramatic, musical and artistic works, sound recordings and films—the Minister has power to convert the exclusive right into a right to a reasonable royalty; set, if necessary, by the Copyright Tribunal.[212] Originally the power was directed mainly at rental practices, where there was a real fear that producers might use their exclusive right to put a stop to rental outlets; but that was outlawed by the Rental, Lending and Related Rights Directive. **12–43**

(b) *Exceptions concerning artistic works*

A number of exceptions affect artistic works. Sculptures, building models and works of artistic craftsmanship, if permanently situated in public, may be represented in a graphic work, photographed, filmed or broadcast without licence; likewise buildings, wherever situate.[213] An artistic work may be copied, and those copies issued to the public, when advertising its sale—an exception important to auction houses.[214] An artist may copy his own earlier work, provided that he does not repeat or imitate its main design.[215] A building may be reconstructed without infringing copyright in it or the original drawings or plans.[216] **12–44**

In addition there are exclusions and limitations which are crucial to the scheme of protection for industrial designs, which are reserved for discussion in Ch.14.[217]

[208] CDPA 1988 s.35.
[209] CDPA 1988 s.60.
[210] CDPA 1988 s.74.
[211] CDPA 1988 s.36; see below, paras 14–15—14–16.
[212] CDPA 1988 s.66, as revised to accord with the Rental, Lending and Related Rights Directive: see below, para.14–22.
[213] CDPA 1988 s.62—extending to certain consequential acts: s.62(3).
[214] CDPA 1988 s.63—not extending to subsequent dealings for any other purpose.
[215] CDPA 1988 s.64.
[216] CDPA 1988 s.65.
[217] CDPA 1988 ss.51 and 52 which are discussed at below, paras 15–32 et seq.

It is at this juncture that one meets the strictly limited rights recognised in a typeface as a form of artistic work.[218] The copyright is restricted to making, importing and dealing in machines and other articles specifically designed or adapted for producing material in the typeface. It does not extend to using the typeface itself. The right in relation to machines lasts for 25 years from the first marketing of the machines.[219]

(c) *Broadcasts*

12–45 (i) **Re-transmission by cable.** Where a broadcast is immediately re-transmitted by cable within the area of reception for the broadcast, this action is not an infringement of the broadcast, provided that it is not encrypted or by satellite; nor is it an infringement of any work included in the broadcast.[220] This exception, in its present version limited mainly to cases where poor reception is averted by cabling, is contested by some copyright owners as a derogation from the Berne Convention obligation to accord an exclusive right in the consequent cabling of a broadcast.[221] But that obligation may be conditioned by national legislation, as it is here.

12–46 (ii) **Free public showing.** Where a broadcast is shown or played to a non-paying audience,[222] there is no infringement of copyright in the broadcast, nor in any sound recording or film contained in them.[223] This exception extends to provisions for residents or inmates of a "place" (for example a hotel, holiday camp, hospital or prison) and for members as an incident of membership of a club or society.

12–47 (iii) **Time shifting.** By way of considerable variation on the former law, a broadcast may be recorded for private and domestic use (as distinct from research and private study) in order to view it or listen to it at a more convenient time. The exception extends to the works included in the transmission as well as the transmission itself.[224] To this extent at least, UK law has introduced a private use defence equivalent to that found in many authors' rights countries and still permitted by the InfoSoc Directive, subject to the payment of adequate compensation.[225]

[218] This is assumed in the Act from *Stephenson Blake v Grant Legros* (1916) 33 R.P.C. 406.

[219] CDPA 1988 ss.54, 55. The change enables the UK to ratify the so-far inoperative Vienna Convention on Typefaces of 1973.

[220] CDPA 1988 s.73. There is also an exception in respect of material which the Cable Authority requires to be included in a cable-cast (i.e. those granted rediffusion licences), which in turn is subject to special provision on damages: s.73(3).

[221] Berne Convention art.11*bis* (1), (2); Ricketson and Ginsburg, paras 12.24–12.27.

[222] This concept is elaborately defined.

[223] CDPA 1988 s.72. Note the counter-provision on damages: s.72(4). But not the literary, dramatic or musical works contained within the broadcast, as is clear from the language of the provision: *Football Association PL v QC Leisure* [2008] 3 C.M.L.R. 12.

[224] CDPA 1988 s.70; see below, para.14–19.

[225] InfoSoc Directive art.5(2)(b), Recs. 35, 38.

(iv) **Various.** There are also provisions covering: a compulsory licence for the broadcasting of sound recordings[226]; incidental recording in the course of making a licensed broadcast of a work[227]; recordings by the supervisory bodies for the purpose of controlling broadcasting[228]; the making of private photographs from television broadcasts[229]; the sub-titling of broadcasts to the deaf, hard of hearing and handicapped[230]; provisions for the blind[231] and archival purposes.[232] **12–48**

(d) *Preservation*

The CDPA 1988 permits prescribed libraries and archives to make copies of any items in their permanent collection for preservation or replacement purposes.[233] The exception is limited to literary, musical and dramatic works, any illustrations accompanying such works and the typographical arrangement. This neglects important audio-visual material. As well, the exception does not permit format-shifting, a useful tool in the battle against obsolescence, and limits the number of copies that may be made, so that the realities of digital preservation are not catered for. Following the *Gowers Review,* the UK Intellectual Property Office has been consulting on whether to expand the exception. It has recommended that the exception apply also to artistic works, films and sound recordings; that format shifting be permitted; and that copies made for preservation purposes only should not be numerically restricted. Perhaps, most controversially, it is proposed that museums and galleries benefit from the exception, in recognition of the role that such organisations play in preserving cultural heritage.[234] **12–49**

(e) *Public administration*

The CDPA 1988 contains a much expanded list of excepted activities connected with Government. These include things done for the purpose of parliamentary and judicial proceedings, Royal Commissions and statutory inquiries,[235] and extend to direct reports of any of them. In addition various public records and other types of official information may be copied without licence in given ways. The development is a counterpart to the new restriction in scope of Crown copyright, and will be discussed further in that context.[236] **12–50**

[226] CDPA 1988 s.135A.
[227] CDPA 1988 s.68.
[228] CDPA 1988 s.69.
[229] CDPA 1988 s.71.
[230] CDPA 1988 s.74.
[231] See the Copyright (Visually Impaired Persons) Act 2003.
[232] CDPA 1988 s.75.
[233] CDPA 1988 s.42.
[234] *Taking Forward the Gowers Review of Intellectual Property* (2009), paras 256–279.
[235] CDPA 1988 ss.45, 46.
[236] CDPA 1988 ss.47–50; below, paras 14–47—14–49.

(f) *Miscellaneous defences in the CDPA 1988*

12–51 (i) **Anonymous and pseudonymous works.** There is an ultimate exception, already discussed in relation to these types of work, where it is reasonable to suppose that copyright has expired.[237]

12–52 (ii) **Extracts in recital.** A solo reading or recitation of a reasonable extract from a literary or dramatic work may be made in public with sufficient acknowledgment; and a recording or broadcast may be made of it, if mainly of material not covered by the exception.[238]

12–53 (iii) **Folksong recordings.** A designated non-profit organisation may record a song for an archive, and make copies available for private study or non-commercial research, even though there is copyright in the words or music, provided that the words are unpublished and of unknown authorship.[239]

12–54 (iv) **Copies for the visually impaired.** An Act of 2002 amended the CDPA 1988 by inserting new ss.31A–31F concerning copies made to be accessible by the blind and those with serious physical difficulties to read. Since braille versions of books would never find a commercial market, and the same has been largely true of books in large type and audio recordings, the exception allows both the impaired person and approved bodies to make such copies, and in the latter case to hold them for further similar reproduction. The provisions, drafted in great detail, are designed to ensure that they fit within the minor exceptions provision of the InfoSoc Directive and the general three-step test.[240]

12–55 (v) **Works in electronic form.** Where the purchaser of a legitimate copy of, say, a computer program is entitled himself to make further copies, he transfers this additional power when he transfers the copy to another, unless there are express conditions to the contrary.[241]

(g) *Internet transmission*

12–56 The highly important legal provisions that have now been introduced to curtail possible liabilities on internet service providers will be dealt with in detail in Ch.20.[242] Purely in outline these exempt mere conduit providers from infringing copyright; access providers who engage in caching material for users; and host service providers from liability to pay monetary compensation for infringements of copyright and other wrongful acts before being notified and required to take the material down. These provisions

[237] CDPA 1988 s.57; for joint authorship see s.57(3).
[238] CDPA 1988 s.59.
[239] CDPA 1988 s.61. This should be related to the special arrangements under s.169 for according overseas protection authorities to exercise copyright in respect of folksongs that are part of their national heritage.
[240] See art.5(3)(o), 5(5). See Bradshaw [2005] I.P.Q. 335.
[241] CDPA 1988 s.56.
[242] See below, para.20–62.

derive partly from the E-Commerce Directive,[243] and partly from the Info-Soc Directive art.5.[244]

4. Public Policy

In contradistinction to the statutorily defined defences just mentioned, the judges have kept some ultimate power to refuse protection to a copyright owner on public policy grounds,[245] and these we may divide into two kinds. **12–57**

(1) Policy against legal protection

A line of cases justifies the refusal of relief on a variety of grounds which express disapproval of the content of the work: because it is obscene, sexually immoral, defamatory, blasphemous, irreligious, or seriously deceptive of the public.[246] Thus Elinor Glyn's *Three Weeks*, however opaque its voluptuousness may seem today, was condemned in 1916 as a "glittering record of adulterous sensuality masquerading as superior virtue".[247] A trade catalogue which contained misleading statements about the claimant's patents and the size of his premises was not protected.[248] While the power to refuse the assistance of the court survives, it is likely to be exercised today only in clear cases; in particular, some of the early nineteenth-century decisions should be treated with caution.[249] **12–58**

A work which satisfies the general criterion of originality does not lose its copyright, or cease to be enforceable, because it embodies another copyright work to an extent which requires a licence and that authority has not been obtained.[250] If A translates B's copyright novel without permission, B may obtain relief against any exploitation of the translation. But in turn no one without A's authority may infringe his rights in the translation.[251] If B

243 In UK law, they are found in the Electronic Commerce (EC Directive) Regulations (2002/2013) rr.17–19.

244 For which, see CDPA 1988 s.28A.

245 See now CDPA 1988 s.171(3).

246 See Phillips (1977) 6 Anglo-Am.L.R. 138; Sims [2008] E.I.P.R. 189; and for the same factors in breach of confidence, see above, para.8–10.

247 *Glyn v Weston Feature Film* [1916] 1 Ch. 261 at 269–270; cf. *Stephens v Avery* [1988] F.S.R. 510; *Masterman's Design* [1991] R.P.C. 89.

248 *Slingsby v Bradford Patent Truck* [1906] W.N. 51 CA; and see *Wright v Tallis* (1845) 1 C.B. 863 (book passed off as the work of a well-known author; no cause of action to protect copyright in that book).

249 See Younger J., *Glyn's* case (above, n.247) at 269. During Lord Eldon's Chancellorship, this form of "negative censorship" went particularly far: as in *Murray v Benbow* (1822) Jac. 474n (Byron's "Cain" refused protection); *Lawrence v Smith* (1822) Jac. 471. Cf. also *Stockdale v Onwhyn* (1826) 5 B. & C. 173 ("memoirs" of a prostitute). For further case law, see Laddie et al., pp.117–123.

250 *Redwood v Chappell* [1982] R.P.C. 109 at 120.

251 *Ashmore v Douglas-Home* [1987] F.S.R. 553, contra, is on this matter wrong: Laddie et al., pp.123–126.

recovers monetary compensation he will be obliged to account to A for the latter's due share.[252]

(2) Policy favouring dissemination

12–59 The ability to protect confidential information, it will be recalled, is qualified by considerations of public interest.[253] The same considerations were held in *Beloff v Pressdram* to affect copyright; they created a defence arising outside the statute and based on a general common law principle.[254] In that case, the work consisted of a journalist's private memorandum to colleagues about a Cabinet Minister's view on the succession to the leadership of the Conservative Party. A narrow view was taken of what might be justified in the public interest: it was necessary to show an "iniquity" or "misdeed" and so the defence did not succeed on the facts.[255] But some of the breach of confidence cases already discussed take a broader view of the general principle.[256]

5. Actions for Infringement

12–60 Copyright infringements give rise to a range of remedies, civil, criminal and administrative as well as of self-help. These have been mentioned in the introductory chapter on the subject.[257] All are today important, particularly given the very considerable quantity of pirate copying that continues to plague the record, film and television industries; and none more so than the *Anton Piller* order for search and seizure.[258] The whole territory will not be traversed again, comment being restricted here to a number of special provisions affecting civil actions.

(1) Damages

12–61 Copyright is a property right invaded by the particularly unfair step of copying. At the same time, to some extent it serves to protect an individual's desire to keep his affairs private. The recovery is only in respect of what amounts to infringement, and so to the taking of expression as distinct from

---

252 *ZYX Music v King* [1995] E.M.L.R. 281.
253 See above, para.8–15 et seq.
254 [1973] 1 All E.R. 241 at 259; *Att-Gen v Guardian Newspapers (No 2)* [1990] 1 A.C. 109 at 294 per Lord Jauncey; *Ashdown v Telegraph Group* [2002] Ch 149 CA; and see Johnson [2005] Ent. L.R. 1.
255 [1973] 1 All E.R. 241 at 261.
256 See above, paras 8–15–8–19.
257 See above, paras 2–28 et seq.
258 See above, paras 2–47 et seq.

idea.[259] Until the CDPA 1988 the character of the right was reflected particularly in the exceptional entitlement to "conversion damages"—essentially for the value of infringing copies as property—as distinct from "infringement damages". This advantage came, however, to be considered too draconian, and conversion damages were abolished by the CDPA 1988. The Act, however, expands the possibility of claiming "additional damages" and delivery up for disposal, both of which are discussed below.[260]

The usual basis for claiming substantial damages for infringement relates to the commercial value of the work[261]: as with patents, the claim is either for compensation for lost profits—because the defendant's infringements have lost the claimant his own opportunities for sale; how far this will be assumed from the very fact of the defendant's piratical sales depends on the particular circumstances.[262] Alternatively, the claim is for the misappropriation—because the claimant has lost the chance of licensing or selling his copyright to the defendant.[263] As part of such a claim, the claimant is entitled to show the cheap or vulgar form of the defendant's piracy injured his reputation and so lost him sales,[264] indeed it has been presumed, in the absence of explanation from the defendant, that a film's lack of success was due to the existence of poor quality copies on the market.[265]

Injury to reputation may, however, have little or nothing to do with the **12–62** commercial popularity of the work; the psychological effect, the injury to feelings, may be much more significant. The CDPA 1988 allows a court to award damages "in addition to all other material considerations", having regard to the flagrancy of the infringement and any benefit to the defendant, and this is now possible without having to consider whether effective relief is otherwise available.[266] While the normal rule today is that damages must be compensatory rather than punitive,[267] "additional damages" under the Act have been held to include damages that will deprecate a defendant's "couldn't-care-less" attitude.[268] The claimant must, however, opt for an award of damages, rather than an account of profits; otherwise there is no

---

[259] *USP v London General Holdings* [2006] F.S.R. 6 CA.

[260] See Whitford Report, paras 701, 702; CDPA 1988 Sch.1 para.30(2).

[261] But this approach may not always be followed: see Bowen C.J. *Interfirm Comparison v Law Society* (1975) 6 A.L.R. 445 at 446–447.

[262] *Columbia Picture Industries v Robinson* [1986] F.S.R. 367; *Blayney v Clogau St Davids Gold Mines* [2003] F.S.R. 360 CA.

[263] See above, para.2–40. It may be an appropriate basis even in an industry where licensing is not the practice: *SPE v Professional Preparation Contractors* [2002] EWHC 881.

[264] Lord Wright M.R. *Sutherland v Caxton* [1936] Ch. 323 at 336.

[265] *Columbia Pictures* case (above, n.262).

[266] CDPA 1988 s.97(2); cf. CA 1956, s.17(3). See Michalos [2000] E.I.P.R. 470.

[267] See above, para.2–38. But cf. the position in Singapore where they have been characterised as punitive: *New Line Productions v Aglow Video* [2005] 3 S.L.R. 660. Australian courts have also emphasised the deterrent and punitive effects of additional damages: *Aristocrat Technologies Australia v DAP Services (Kempsey)* [2007] FCAFC 40 Full FC Aust.

[268] *Nottinghamshire Healthcare v News Group* [2002] R.P.C. 49.

corpus to which the further damages can be added.[269] On this basis, "additional" damages may lie against a professional photographer for supplying the press with a wedding photo which included a man subsequently murdered, without any consent from the member of the man's family who owned the copyright[270]; or against a lampooning magazine which published a confidential memorandum written by a journalist to her colleagues, thereby damaging her reputation as a parliamentary correspondent[271]; or against a person who is ordered to obtain a licence from a collecting society but fails to do so.[272]

(2) Presumptions in copyright infringement actions

12–63 It is no longer provided in the CDPA 1988 that, if the defendant wishes to dispute the subsistence of copyright or the claimant's title, he must put the matter in issue by pleading it. The question accordingly takes its place alongside all other assertions which the claimant makes and must, if necessary, prove. There are, however, statutory presumptions which throw the legal burden of proof upon the defendant to infringement proceedings. Where literary, dramatic, musical or artistic copyright is concerned these are:

(1) that a person named as author is the author of a work; and that he did not produce it in circumstances (such as in the course of employment) which would deprive him of the copyright initially.[273] If this does not apply, then:
(2) that if first publication of a work qualifies it for copyright, copyright subsists and was owned at first publication by the person named as publisher.[274] In any case:
(3) that, where the author is dead or unidentifiable when the action is brought, the work was original and was first published where and when the claimant alleges.[275]

---

[269] *Redrow Homes v Betts Brothers* [1998] R.P.C. 793 HL. The claimant is entitled to know the court's view of flagrancy before electing between damages and an account of profits: *Condé-Nast v MGN* [1998] F.S.R. 427. An award of additional damages is possible even where nominal compensatory damages have been ordered: see *Aristocrat Technologies* (above, n.267).

[270] As in *Williams v Settle* [1960] 1 W.L.R. 1072 CA, which, however, was decided as a case on exemplary damages. For ownership of copyright in these circumstances today, see below, para.13–04, and for the consequential right of privacy, see below, paras 12–86, 12–87.

[271] *Beloff v Pressdram* [1973] 1 All E.R. 241 at 264–272; but the claimant failed for want of title (below, para.13–05).

[272] *Peninsula Books v Citation* [2004] F.S.R. 17.

[273] CDPA 1988 s.104(2); and for the same presumptions in relation to each of joint authors, s.104(3).

[274] CDPA 1988 s.104(4). This affects anonymous works: see above, para.11–53.

[275] CDPA 1988 s.104(5).

As regards copyright in sound recordings, films and computer programs, there are presumptions that statements naming the copyright owner, or giving the date or place of first publication, are true.[276]

6. Moral Rights[277]

All systems of copyright protection have as their prime inspiration the cultural value of authorship. The Romantic ideal, so ardently pursued two centuries ago, claimed for the creative artist a unique sensibility and foresight, and every age continues to regard with fascination those aesthetic achievements which it treasures as special contributions to the human condition. Indeed, whatever today's scepticism over objective values and universal truths, the arts receive serious and sustained study and participation on a scale previously unknown. **12–64**

In countries where this complex social force presses urgently, it finds legal expression in a proprietary right which protects the personality of authors as expressed in their creations alongside their economic interests in exploitation. This separate element—the author's so-called moral right (from the French *droit moral*)[278]—has been progressively enhanced in Continental systems of authors' rights over the past century.[279] In the legislative schemes of French and German law and their many derivatives, moral rights rank as a category at least the equal of economic rights. The two schemes in fact differ in basic assumption, since French law renders moral rights perpetual as well as (in some sense) inalienable, thus creating a necessary duality[280]; while German law, drawing upon the Hegelian perception of the work as the fulfilled expression of the author's personality, gives both moral and economic rights the same duration and treats them monistically as branches of the same tree.

---

276 CDPA 1988 s.105. The statements are also admissible as evidence of the facts stated and may apply in relation to infringements occurring before the publication or similar act.

277 For a comprehensive survey, Adeney, *The Moral Rights of Authors* (2006), and in common law countries, see Dworkin [1994] Aust. I.P.R. 449; Anderson and Saunders (eds), *Moral Rights Protection in a Copyright System* (1992). And cf. Copyright Law Review Committee (Australia), *Moral Rights* (1988); Ricketson [1990] Ent. L.R. 76; Attorney-General's Department (Australia), *Proposed Moral Rights Legislation* (1994); Parliamentary Sub-Committee (Canada), *A Charter of Rights for Authors* (1985); Vaver (1987) 25 Osgoode Hall L.J. 749; Gibbens (1989) 15 Can. B.L.J. 441; Ginsburg [1990] Ent. L.R. 121; Nimmer [1992] Ent. L.R. 94; Stamatoudi [1997] I.P.Q. 478; Eagles (2002) 8 NZ B.L.Q. 86. For the position on the internet: de Souza and Waelde [2002] I.P.Q. 265; and for what might be said by economists, Cotter (1997) 76 N.Car.L.R. 1; Hansmann and Santilli (1997) 26 J.Leg.St. 95.

278 German law refers to the author's right of personality in his work, an expression which in English is better fitted to what is intended.

279 For a current assessment of these developments, see esp. Dietz in ALAI, *The Moral Right of the Author* (1994), p.54; for a magisterial history, Strömholm, *Le droit moral de l'auteur* (1967). For comparisons between the US and France, see Sarraute (1968) 16 Am. J. Comp. L. 465; Treece (1968) 16 Am. J. Comp. L. 487.

280 And so the heirs of a classic playwright may object to a demeaning production of his work.

In partial recognition of these developments, art.6*bis* of the Berne Convention requires Member States to provide, in principle for as long as the economic rights,[281] independent rights to claim authorship and to object to modifications or other derogatory action in relation to a work which would be prejudicial to the author's honour or reputation.[282]

12–65 Each law within the fold of authors' rights countries differs over the precise content and scope of moral rights, but they are likely to include: a right to decide upon first publication or other release[283]; a right to be named as author; a right to object to modifications of the work and to its presentation in derogatory circumstances. There may also be provision for an author to insist on completion of the original where that depends on the execution of others, to withdraw works of which he no longer approves and to object to destruction or removal of the original.[284]

One driving inspiration for moral-rights doctrine has been the belief that at least some great artists are unworldly prey to the vultures of copyright industries: the voracious among literary and music publishers, recording, stage and film producers and art dealers. Moral rights seek at least to protect the integrity of a work and the author's connection with it. But once that step is taken, it is natural also to buttress the author's economic interest against unfair deprivation, particularly by the entrepreneurs who undertake to exploit the work. There is no simple dividing line between the purely "moral" and the purely economic. For every individual who insists unflinchingly upon his artistic integrity, there are many whose insistence can be compromised at a price. Equally, the innocent author may well need more help in realising his economic potential than in protecting his essential relationship to his work. Some of the campaigning for moral rights strives to lay a platform for rules which guarantee certain minimum returns, e.g. by way of over-riding derisory lump-sum buyouts.[285]

12–66 Anglo-American tradition has manifested a certain scepticism towards claims that authors deserve special protection in law. The attitude is part of a wider reluctance to subject the bargainings of the marketplace to higher dictates of good faith, propriety and fairness. The Victorians' primary insistence upon sanctity of contract has today been to some degree modified by broader notions of fiduciary responsibility, duties of care and unconscionability. Indeed, as we shall see, this shift has been impelled particularly by sharp and harsh practices in the modern music industry. Given that shift, the question remains, what justifies a heightened protective regime for the moral rights of authors?

---

281 In the Paris Act of 1971, there is a diplomatic exception allowing some countries to limit "some" (sic) of the moral rights to a lesser period.

282 First introduced in non-compulsory form in the Rome version (1928) art.6*bis* became obligatory in the Brussels version of 1948 and was extended in the present Paris Act: Ricketson and Ginsburg, Ch.10, Plaisant (1986) 11 Col. J.L.A. 157.

283 There is a complex link here to privacy issues: Griffiths (2001) 20 Leg. St. 485.

284 See further, below, paras 12–76—12–77.

285 See further, Cornish (2003) 26 Col. J.L.A. 1.

Argument on the subject remains intense, the representative voices of authors insisting that all systems should have a structured set of rules on moral rights in place, the entrepreneurial lobbyists claiming that these rights strengthen the position of authors unduly and lead to endless complications, particularly when it comes to complex collaborations such as audio-visual works or multi-media productions. This section returns to the root issue at its conclusion.[286] First, it must trace the course of development of UK law on the subject, concentrating on those moral rights which were given explicit legislative form, very largely for the first time, in the CDPA 1988, but in a scrupulously moderate version.

(1) Protection of authors under general legal rules

The common law may not have placed authors in any special sheepfold, but it did not leave them at large in the wild. Since most of the practical problems arose between the author and those with whom he dealt in exploitation of his work, the author could provide much of what he might want by contractual stipulation. Beyond that he might be helped by the law of confidence, defamation, passing off, injurious falsehood, and the general economic torts. Thus, in *Humphreys v Thompson*,[287] a jury found an authoress to have been defamed by a newspaper serialisation of her story in which the names of the characters were simplified, passages of description were omitted and "curtains" were added at the beginning and end of each episode to whet readers' appetites. Her reputation had thus been lowered in the eyes of right-thinking members of the public. In *Samuelson v Producers Distributing*,[288] the defendant put out a film of a revue sketch, wrongly claiming it to be the claimant's. Because the claimant's piece was well-known, thanks to its inclusion in a royal variety performance, this constituted a form of passing off. **12–67**

Subsequently s.43 of the CA 1956, by creating a tort of misattribution, extended the range of such legal protection, since it eliminated the need to show any established reputation with the public.[289] Otherwise, the legislature in 1956 followed the Gregory Committee's view of *les droits moraux* as suspiciously foreign.[290] It felt no need to confer an explicit right to claim authorship or to preserve integrity, let alone to enshrine these rights, or other manifestations of the same idea, as inalienable and incapable of waiver in advance of actual publication or other use of the work. Yet the United **12–68**

---

[286] See below, paras 12–88—12–90.

[287] *Humphreys v Thompson* [1905–1910] Mac. CC 148; and see *Lee v Gibbings* (1892) 67 L.J. 263; *Frisby v BBC* [1967] Ch. 932.

[288] See below, para.17–44. For a similar case in defamation see *Ridge v English Illustrated Magazine* [1911-1916] Mac. CC 91.

[289] For the current version, see below, paras 12–84—12–85.

[290] See Cmd.8662, 1952, para.222.

Kingdom, unlike the United States at that juncture, was preparing to ratify the Brussels Act of the Berne Convention.[291]

12–69 In 1977, the Whitford Committee accepted that these moral rights should be translated into British legislation to a reasonable extent.[292] This proposal set in train the search for a formulation which would retain due respect for freedom and sanctity of contract and would protect entrepreneurs in their turn from being held to ransom as infringers of moral rights at a time when it would be difficult and expensive to rectify the wrong.[293] It was this overbearing potential in foreign laws which had for long fuelled the common law antagonism towards them.

In the upshot, the CDPA 1988 defines four distinct moral rights, the first two of which are in fulfilment of Berne obligations:

(1) the right to be identified as author or film director (the right of paternity);
(2) the right to object to derogatory treatment of a work (the right of integrity);
(3) the right against false attribution of a work; and
(4) the right to privacy in private photographs and films.[294]

Each has its own incidents, but all adopt one basic characteristic of such rights in other systems: that they are inalienable to others while being transmissible on death.[295] Where they depart from more severely protective systems, is above all in the extent to which they may be compromised in advance by waiver.

(2) Right to be identified

(a) *Entitlement and duration*

12–70 The right to be identified as author is given to the creators of literary dramatic, musical and artistic works, and also to the directors of films even though it is only for films made after July 1, 1995 that they are to enjoy copyright.[296] It is not accorded to other persons who are treated by the CDPA 1988 as "authors" for copyright purposes. Here is a first indication

[291] Later (in 1989) the US would join Berne without explicit enactment covering art.6*bis*, in reliance upon the scope of general common law and statutory provisions which were arguably more extensive than those under English law. In 1990, limited moral rights would be conferred by Federal legislation in respect of visual art alone: see Ginsburg and Kernochan (1988) 13 Columbia-VLA J.L.A. 1; Ginsburg (1990) 14 Columbia-VLA J.L.A. 121; Tannenbaum [1991] E.I.P.R. 449; Appelbaum (1992) 8 Am.U.JILP 191.

[292] Cmnd. 6732, 1977, paras 51–57, drawing attention to the Dutch law as a model.

[293] As where a minor author of a film script might object to his omission from the credits on the eve of the premiere.

[294] See further, Cornish [1989] E.I.P.R. 449; McCartney (1991) 15 Columbia-VLA J.L.A. 161.

[295] CDPA 1988 ss.94, 95.

[296] CDPA 1988 s.77(1): for joint authors and directors, see s.88(1), (5).

that the moral rights are not simply an aspect of copyright but instead fall to be treated separately. Subject to a number of exceptions, this moral right applies to works created after August 1, 1989 and also to those existing on that date in relation to publication, public exhibition and other acts done subsequently.[297]

The right inures only if the work itself is copyright—so the same qualification rules apply as for copyright. It lasts for the same period as the copyright.[298] The requirement is only satisfied if the author is identified as such, and not in some other capacity—as, for instance, as the preparer of a performing edition of a musical work.[299]

(b) *Assertion*

It is a pre-condition of the right to be identified that it be asserted. In general, this may be done as a statement in an instrument assigning copyright in the work or by any other instrument in writing signed by the author or director during the life of the right.[300] If it is made as part of an assignment, the assertion binds the assignee and anyone claiming through him, with or without notice; whereas if it is made by another instrument, it binds only those with notice of it.[301] Thus an assertion has in principle only to be made in the required form to any exploiter of the work for it to impose on him the obligation to identify the author or director; but delay in making the assertion is to be taken into account in determining whether an injunction must be granted and also, it seems, in settling damages and other relief.[302] **12–71**

Assertion is a necessary preliminary to enjoyment of the right to be named, and so is arguably inconsistent with the requirement in art.5(2) of the Berne Convention, so far as Convention nationals are concerned, that they should enjoy rights under UK law without being subject to any formality. Assertion may have been necessary in order initially to secure the enactment of this moral right. Nonetheless it is a confusing complexity which achieves little. It should certainly be abandoned in any legislative revision. The author may still, after all, waive the right to be named, and that waiver may be given expressly or implied from the circumstances.

[297] CDPA 1988 Sch.1 paras 22, 23. The main exceptions are: the work of an author dead at commencement; works whose initial copyright vested in someone other than the author; films made before commencement; and anything done in pursuance of a licence or assignment by an author-owner. Because of the complete exclusion of pre-1989 films, there is no scope for using this right to object in the UK to their colorisation if originally black-and-white.

[298] CDPA 1988 s.86(1). The extensions of copyright terms (above, paras 11–43—11–50) accordingly affect the statutory moral rights. Any assertion of the right to be named and any waiver continue to affect extended and revived copyright works: Duration Regulations 1995 (SI 1995/3297) regs 21(1), 22(2), (3), 23(6): see below, para.13–08.

[299] *Sawkins v Hyperion Records* [2005] R.P.C. 32 CA.

[300] CDPA 1988 s.78(1), (2). There are additional provisions concerning the assertion of the right in relation to public exhibition of an artistic work: s.78(3).

[301] CDPA 1988 s.78(4).

[302] CDPA 1988 s.78(5).

(c) *Preclusion*

12–72 In contradistinction with truly protective regimes of moral rights, it is possible for the person who would otherwise enjoy any of the four rights to surrender it in advance of the time when an issue actually arises—such as, for instance, a publisher's decision to exclude an author's name from a pending publication. The waiver may be by instrument in writing signed by the person giving up the right, and it may relate not only to a specific work in existence, but to a class of works or even works in general, and to future works. It may be the subject of a condition and it may be revocable.[303] Such express consent does not require contractual consideration. But an informal waiver may also be operative under general principles of contract or estoppel.[304] So conduct of an author or director on which another person relies in the belief that identification will not be insisted upon (whether or not there has already been an assertion) may well preclude any subsequent enforcement of the moral right.

(d) *Acts covered*

12–73 The occasions on which an author or director may insist upon identification are so defined as to incorporate a "disc-jockey" exception. Thus the author of most literary, dramatic and artistic works and directors of films may require identification upon copies being published commercially, copies of a sound recording or film being issued to the public, performance or showing in public, or broadcasting.[305] However, authors of musical works, and of words intended to be sung or spoken with music, do not have the right in respect of public performances or broadcasting. In each case, the identification has to be likely to bring the identity to the attention of those acquiring a copy, listening to a performance, etc.[306]

There are other special cases. In particular, although copyright itself does not extend to the public exhibition of artistic works, there is a right to be identified as artist at a public exhibition.[307] In this respect at least, protection is given to the original work itself, as well as to copies. For this purpose, moreover, the right is sufficiently asserted by attaching an identification to the work or a copy when the author or other first owner of copyright parts with possession of it, or the assertion is included in a licence to make copies of the work; in either case notice is not necessary in order to bind third parties.[308]

12–74 Equally, there is a substantial list of exceptions. There is no right of

---

303 CDPA 1988 s.87(1)–(3).

304 CDPA 1988 s.87(4).

305 CDPA 1988 s.77(2), (3).

306 See CDPA 1988 s.77(7), for a full definition of sufficient identification: and s.77(8) for the form to be adopted.

307 CDPA 1988 s.77(4)(a). For works of architecture, sculptures and works of artistic craftsmanship, see s.77(4)(c).

308 CDPA 1988 s.78(3), (4)(c), (d).

identification in computer programs, computer-generated works, or typefaces, or works which are Crown or similar copyright.[309] Where a work or film is made in the course of employment, the employer, as first owner of the copyright, is not obliged to make the identification; nor is anyone else who acts with his authority.[310] Publication in a newspaper, magazine or periodical, or in an encyclopedia or similar work, is excluded.[311] A number of the exceptions applicable to copyright also apply to the right to be identified: fair dealing for the purpose of reporting current events in a sound recording, film, or broadcast; incidental inclusion in an artistic work, sound recording, film or broadcast; the exclusion and limitation of artistic copyright in the sphere of industrial design; and other more specific cases.[312]

(e) *Impact*

The right to be identified is inherently more likely to be of importance to those who have a reputation still to establish than those whose name will attract attention on a publication or through other exploitation. The right does, however, extend not only to failure to name anyone but also to plagiarism of work under the name of another, and here even the famous may have occasion to complain. In the film and television industries, the matter of screen credits (for performers as well as creators) is considered of such importance that detailed arrangements on the matter have been reached by collective agreement—initially in the Screenwriting Credits Agreement of 1974.[313] The precision of this order is far more satisfactory than a general obligation under legislation. **12–75**

Among lesser authors and directors, it is those who provide work for others in some capacity, without becoming employees,[314] who are most likely to be aggrieved by non-identification. There will be some circumstances where by implication the right has been contractually excluded.[315] The person who is commissioned to act as ghost-writer for another would be presumed to accept the consequences. But that is not necessarily the implication between members of a research team in writing up results. Equally the photographer who supplies material for a book or a film may well have done nothing to raise the belief that he would not claim to be identified.

[309] CDPA 1988 s.79(2), (7).
[310] CDPA 1988 s.79(3).
[311] CDPA 1988 s.79(6).
[312] CDPA 1988 s.79(4).
[313] See Cotterell, *Performance* 3rd edn (1993), pp.487–488; below, para.13–48.
[314] In general, employees in any case do not have the right: above, n.310.
[315] As the CDPA 1988 is less categoric than other systems, the question of which law governs, e.g. assignments and licences, will remain important; see the French Cour d'Appel's decision in *Rowe v Walt Disney* [1987] F.S.R. 37; *Huston* case (below, n.325).

(3) Right to object to derogatory treatment[316]

(a) *Entitlement and duration*

12–76 As in the previous case, the right to object to derogatory treatment is given to authors in respect of literary, dramatic, musical and artistic works, and to directors in respect of their films, to the extent that they are the subject of, and remain in, copyright.[317] It is a right which draws upon art.6*bis* of the Berne Convention, though it is in apparently narrower terms. Objection may be raised to "derogatory treatment" of the work, which requires demonstration: (1) that the work is subject to addition, deletion, alteration or adaptation; and (2) that this "amounts to distortion or mutilation of the work or is otherwise prejudicial to the honour or reputation of the author or director".[318]

It may not be an infraction of this right to place a work in a context which subjects it to criticism or ridicule—for instance, using a painting in an exhibition deliberately to show up the superiority of other paintings or to cast aspersions on the artist's life-style. A sculptor may not even be able to object to the hanging of Christmas decorations on his work.[319] An extensive interpretation of "addition" to the work would, however, accord with the spirit and terms of art.6*bis*. It would not give an author a cause of action if his publisher also published a piece critical of him or his work[320]; but then the law ought not to subject a publisher to a special degree of dependence beyond the need to observe the law of defamation.[321] There will, of course, be borderline cases: a production of a sentimental comedy in a vein of social criticism intended to deride the genre will offend, provided that the text is altered or explicit stage instructions are defied.[322] On the other hand, it is not enough that the author objects to what is being done.[323]

---

316 See Adeney [2005] I.P.Q. 111; Goldstein (1983) 14 I.I.C. 43; Smith [1992] Ent.L.R. 26; de Werra in in Derclaye, *Research Handbook on the Future of EU Copyright* (2009), Ch 11.

317 CDPA 1988 s.80(1). For the term, see s.86(1), and above, para.11–45. As to joint authorship and direction, see s.88(2), (5).

318 CDPA 1988 s.80(2). Berne Convention art.6*bis* refers to "distortion, mutilation *or other modification of, or other derogatory action in relation to,* [the work]" (italics added). In India, complete destruction of a sculpture has been treated as mutilation of it: *Seghal v Union of India* [2005] F.S.R. 39. So much for Lady Churchill's notorious destruction of Graham Sutherland's portrait of Sir Winston.

319 Held actionable under the Canadian provision which more faithfully follows the language of the Berne Convention, art.6*bis*: *Snow v Eaton Centre* (1982) 70 C.P.R. (2d) 105.

320 A French court granted damages to the estate of Albert Camus against his publisher, when the British sub-licensee of the publishing rights produced a book which criticised not so much Camus' writing as his personal integrity: *Gallimard v Hamish Hamilton* [1985] E.C.C. 574. It is considered an extreme and isolated decision.

321 Fair dealing for purposes of criticism or review is a defence to copyright infringement: above, para.12–41. It certainly should not be that a person who has no connection with the author cannot engage in selective quotation for such purposes just because the result is in some sense derogatory. Courts should be unwilling to find a sufficient degree of derogation (and see Laddie et al. para.27.27).

322 cf. *Maske in Blau* (1971) 2 I.I.C. 209 (Germany).

323 *Pasterfield v Denham* [1999] F.S.R. 168.

Truly committed systems of moral rights may go further than the Berne Convention in extending protection beyond cases where there will be injury to honour and reputation. Notably in France the subjective reaction of the author to the alteration or use of the work is generally the governing consideration: thus a French court upheld Beckett's objections to *Waiting for Godot* being played by women; and another refused to permit the addition to a book of even a complimentary preface.[324] On the same basis the colourisation of a black-and-white film was actionable by the director's personal representatives.[325] **12–77**

So unconditional a form of integrity right inevitably acts as a considerable constraint on the freedom of others to use the work as they in turn choose, and their motives may vary considerably. For instance, parody is for the most part a form of healthy social and artistic criticism: indeed in French law there is a special exception covering it,[326] as well as other exceptions which would allow for quotation by way of criticism. The British provisions must be interpreted in a creative way which will allow a balance to be struck between the evidently conflicting interests raised by even the limited integrity right introduced in 1988.[327] In this process, decisions from other jurisdictions make interesting comparisons. But they are frequently not based on the same legislative texts or underlying principles, and they do not necessarily have an outcome which would be regarded as sensible in this country.

Indeed under such systems, there is a concern to protect the work from conception to final solution. The stages may be characterised as follow: **12–78**

(1) refusal to supply original. In an early case in France, James McNeill Whistler was held entitled not to deliver a portrait with which he was dissatisfied to its commissioner, even though he had exhibited it.[328] The circumstance might be one in which an English court of equity would make no order of specific performance, though it might award damages or repayment of an advance. It is not an issue addressed in the moral right provisions of the CDPA 1988.

[324] RIDA 1993, No. 155, 225; J.C.P. 1988 II 21062. These examples epitomise the normal approach. Occasionally, courts react against oversensitivity: as when Salvador Dali failed to prevent his ballet costume designs from being added to: D.S. 1967 555, D.S. 1968 382; and note in Italy Giorgio Chirico's failure to stop an exhibition which he claimed gave too much attention to his early work: Foro ital. 1955 I 717.

[325] *Huston v Turner Entertainment* (1992) 23 I.I.C. 702; Edelman, 23 I.I.C. 629; Gendreau (1992) 7 I.P.J. 340. So fundamental was the right adjudged, that it was applied (for France) to the John Huston film, *Asphalt Jungle*, even though it was subject to American contractual arrangements allowing the addition of colour. The decision is considered a triumph for moral rights doctrine.

[326] Intellectual Property Code art.41. Cf. the refusal in Sweden to protect a surrealist lithograph against the addition of satirical instructions and comments: *Svanberg v Eriksson* [1979] E.I.P.R. D–93.

[327] As in the suggestion that *Carry On Cleo* would not injure the honour or reputation of the director of Anthony and Cleopatra: Laddie et al. para.13.19, n.5.

[328] *Eden v Whistler* D.P. 1900 I 497; the artist had to return his fee and undertake not to exhibit the portrait himself.

(2) completion of original to the author's design. Again in France, courts have ordered the commissioner of a space sculpture and the commissioner of a television series to complete work on the author's design or script, once execution has begun.[329] The extreme character of such decisions has, however, been criticised by leading authors.[330] In England it would be rare indeed for a court to require the carrying out of a contract which would involve personal labour or extended supervision. However, if the incomplete work were publicly exhibited, there might be infraction of the moral right of integrity.[331]

(3) correction or withdrawal of a work after publication. While this is recognised in, for instance, French law,[332] it is subject to an obligation to indemnify the publisher against loss, and so appears to be exercised rarely. No such power is conferred by the CDPA 1988.

(4) maintenance of a work at a site. If there is an obligation to complete a work, it would seem that commensurately it should be maintained in the site for which it was destined.[333] But that could impose very considerable burdens of cost and stultified use on those who own the object, and courts everywhere are likely to be cautious in extending protection so far.

(5) prevention of destruction, particularly of an original artistic work. This raises an even starker conflict with the position of the owner of the physical object. Out of distaste, physical encumbrance or financial difficulty, he or she may wish to reduce it to nothing (as distinct from turning it into something else).[334] Even in French law it is not settled that the moral right extends against destruction. Under UK law, destruction leaves behind nothing which can be copied, performed or exhibited within the terms of s.80.

(b) *Exercise and preclusion*

12–79 The right to object to derogatory treatment does not depend upon any precondition, such as assertion. As with the other moral rights, it can be precluded by consent or other waiver.[335] However, those who seek to achieve this, by an advance provision in a contract of exploitation, will need to express themselves in unequivocal terms; for it is inherently unlikely that an author or director will be wishing to expose himself to alterations which are prejudicial to his honour and reputation.[336]

---

[329] *Renault v Dubuffet* [1983] E.C.C. 453 (even though the contract contained a provision for liquidated damages in case of non-performance); Affaire TF1, RIDA 1983 Apr. 172.

[330] Françon and Ginsburg (1985) 9 Columbia-VLA J.L.A. 381.

[331] cf. Laddie et al. para.27.23.

[332] Intellectual Property Code L. 121–4.

[333] This consequence was one reason for the criticism cited above, in para.12–77.

[334] As with the celebrated refrigerator, which Bernard Buffet decorated on all its panels; its owner was prevented from breaking it up in order to sell each panel separately: D. 1962 570.

[335] CDPA 1988 s.87.

[336] See, e.g. *Frisby v BBC* [1967] Ch. 932.

The integrity of a work is most readily conceived where the work is the discrete production of a single author. Difficulties are added once there is joint authorship, or the linked authorship of (say) Rogers and Hammerstein. When one reaches complex productions, such as audio-visual works, in which it is accepted that various secondary writers (of work to be adapted, scenario, script, music, etc.) will contribute to the final outcome, but that many decisions about content will be taken by the director of the production, participation in the venture must imply a considerable readiness to permit modification of a contribution. Certainly, industry agreements and practices which define the point at which a contributor either accepts the need for modification, or is paid off for work to date, must constitute operative waivers.[337] The costly process of production could not go on without such a measure of security. **12–80**

(c) *Acts covered*

In general authors and directors may object to derogatory treatment occurring in copies being published commercially, copies of a sound recording or film being made available to the public, performance, playing and showing in public, or broadcasting.[338] So far as concerns artistic works, the right also covers public exhibition and in that respect extends to the original work itself.[339] There are, however, some major exceptions and limitations. The right does not apply in relation: (1) to translation, or transposition of the key or register of a musical work[340]; (2) to computer programs or computer generated works; (3) to any work made for the purpose of reporting current events; (4) to publication in a newspaper, magazine or periodical or encyclopedia or similar work, or any unmodified subsequent publication therefrom.[341] **12–81**

In the case of a work of architecture, the architect has no right other than to have his identification as architect removed from the building.[342] In the case of works made in employment, or which are Crown or similar copyright, an author or director who is identified may only insist upon a sufficient disclaimer of association with the work as altered.[343] The broadcasting authorities also have power to make excisions and alterations in order to

[337] As, e.g. the Writers' Guild/PACT Collective Agreement for Films and Television Films, described in Cotterell, *Performance* 3rd edn (1993) pp.481–482.

[338] CDPA 1988 s.80(3)–(6); and note s.80(7) on parts of works previously treated by others.

[339] CDPA 1988 s.80(4)(a).

[340] CDPA 1988 s.80(2)(a). But "megamixing" samples from pop music sources may well offend: *Morrison Leahy v Lightbond* [1993] E.M.L.R. 144; and possibly reducing cartoons in size: *Tidy v Natural History Museum* (1995) 39 I.P.R. 501; but not adding rap lyrics to an instrumental dance track: *Confetti Records v Warner Music UK* [2003] E.C.D.R. 31; cf. also *Pasterfield v Denham* [1999] F.S.R. 168.

[341] CDPA 1988 s.81(2)–(5).

[342] CDPA 1988 s.80(5).

[343] CDPA 1988 s.82.

stop the broadcasting of anything offensive to good taste and decency, or which could encourage or incite to crime, lead to disorder or offend public feeling.[344] In the clean new world of broadcasting, this may be a provision which is relied upon with some frequency.

(d) *Impact*

12–82 Many of the recurrent circumstances in which anxiety and objection arise over derogatory treatment have been excised or anaesthetised, so far as this right is concerned, particularly through the provisions relating to employment, the press, current affairs and, above all, translation. What can do more harm to reputation than an incomprehensible or distortive rendition in another language?[345] In the past, directors of films have complained about the manner in which producers, intent on maximising the commercial potential of their investment, have compromised the artistic integrity of the film by subsequent cutting or interpolation. Doubtless in the future producers will use express stipulations to procure their ability to do the same. However, to the extent that they do not, the director will have a power of objection more readily enforced than the vestigial possibilities at common law of suing for defamation, trade libel or some form of passing off. But at the end of the day in court, he may secure no more than an order that the work be published with a disclaimer dissociating him from it.[346]

12–83 Digital technology poses threats of a new order to the integrity of works. Once they are recorded in digital form they can be shredded into components and then varied, particle by particle, with an ease inconceivable even with analogue recordings of audio and audio-visual material. These techniques are becoming the commonplace of filming, advertisements, illustration and music-mixing. The prospects are still in their infancy. Exotic locations can be added into film on demand. A few stills of an actor can be animated into an entire performance. Personalities can be given lives after death.[347]

The law will have to work towards an accommodation between originators and adapters which allows these new techniques to flourish, while still inhibiting manipulation of digital material which is evidently unfair and unacceptable. In striking this balance, two features of UK law—the fact that the integrity right is restricted to derogatory treatment, and the fact that the right may be waived in advance—are likely to be important elements in this adjustment. Above all, once an author has assented to the digital holding of his work, potential users should be able to know whether they can only use it in unaltered form, or can use it in any altered form or in an altered form of

---

[344] CDPA 1988 s.81(6) (and for the Independent Broadcasting Authority, see the Broadcasting Act 1981 s.4(1)).

[345] Accordingly actionable in, e.g. France, *Zorine v Lucernaire* [1987] E.C.C. 54.

[346] See CDPA 1988 s.103(2).

[347] Beard (1993) 8 High Tech. L.J. 101. Following the WIPO Performers and Phonograms Treaty 1996 art.5, performers are now given moral rights: see below, para.14.33.

which the author approves. The last case requires permission case by case. Digital service providers will doubtless seek to prescribe arrangements for rapid decision-making. If authors regularly prove recalcitrant, it may be necessary to consider some form of compulsory licensing to aid the process.

(4) False attribution

The right to object to a false attribution is the converse of the right to be identified. It is an amplification of rights contained in s.43 of the CA 1956. A person to whom a literary, dramatic, musical or artistic work is attributed as author, or to whom a film is attributed as director, has the right to object when that attribution is false.[348] The objection may be in relation to the issue of copies to the public, public exhibition of an artistic work (or copy of it), public performance or showing, or broadcast of a literary, dramatic or musical work or a film.[349] Here there is also a secondary wrong (requiring proof of knowledge or reason to believe that there is false attribution) which consists in possessing or dealing with a copy of the work in the course of business: also in the case of an artistic work, dealing with it in business as the unaltered work of the artist, when in fact it was altered after leaving his possession.[350] These rights enure for 20 years from the year of death of the person who is subject to the false attribution.[351] **12–84**

There is now a considerable overlap between the false attribution right and the derogatory treatment right. Before the CDPA 1988, the former was sometimes used to object to work appearing which was very largely not that of the person named. Thus the singer, Dorothy Squires, obtained damages on account of a newspaper item allegedly by her, when she actually said only about 10 per cent of it to the journalist concerned.[352] Nonetheless false attribution turns upon the inaccurate naming of a person as author, while derogatory treatment must show prejudice to honour and reputation; the inflections are slightly different. If the attribution is misleading, it is no defence that satire was intended.[353] **12–85**

(5) Right to privacy

This, the first acknowledgment in English law of any right to privacy, operates only in strictly delimited circumstances, and is a corollary of shifting the first ownership of certain artistic works from the person who commissioned them to the person who created them or his employer.[354] **12–86**

348 CDPA 1988 s.84(1); in relation to joint works, see s.88(4), (5).
349 CDPA 1988 s.84(2).
350 CDPA 1988 s.84(3).
351 CDPA 1988 s.86(2).
352 *Moore v News of the World* [1972] 1 Q.B. 441; extended in *Noah v Shuba* [1991] F.S.R. 14, to the addition of two misleading lines to the claimant's article on hygienic skin piercing.
353 *Clark v Associated Newspapers* [1998] R.P.C. 261.
354 See below, para.13–05.

Under the CDPA 1988, where a person commissions a photograph or a film for private or domestic purposes, and that work attracts copyright, he has the right to object to issuing copies to the public, public exhibition or showing, or broadcasting.[355] To this there are certain exceptions which also apply to copyright, of which the most general is incidental inclusion in an artistic work, film, or broadcast.[356]

The right lasts as long as the copyright in the photograph or film[357] and is given independently to each joint commissioner.[358] It will be of value in those cases where a wedding group or party picture contains someone who subsequently becomes newsworthy, and will be assertable both where copyright belongs to a commercial photographer or film-maker, and to a relative or friend who undertakes the task for nothing, since the commission does not here have to be for money or money's worth.

12–87 Like all rights accorded to protect privacy, it has the potential to become a right to share in the publicity value of the work; just as much as the copyright owner, the commissioner may consent to publication or other use. In a case under the CA 1956, wedding photographs of a couple were sought by newspapers when it was learned that the wife, after a brain haemorrhage, was being kept alive in order to give birth. One issue then was whether the wife was a co-commissioner of the photographs. If so, a paper seeking exclusive rights of exploitation, which it could enforce against others, would need a copyright licence from her husband and herself.[359] Under the CDPA 1988, the paper could itself get a proprietary right only from the photographer or his successor in title. But any paper which published, without waivers from the photograph's commissioners of their moral rights of privacy, could be sued by either of them individually. It is curious that this right is conferred on the commissioner, rather than the person whose image is subjected to publicity (unwanted, or wanted only at a price). It would, however, be hopelessly cumbersome to require permission of all in a group photograph, so the commissioner is put in their stead.

(6) Overall significance

12–88 The statutory moral rights, particularly the rights to be identified and to object to derogatory treatment, give the very concept a prominence which in some measure redounds to the benefit of authors. It is hard to assess how considerable this enhancement is, compared with the protection afforded in any case by contract and by torts such as defamation, injurious falsehood and passing off. At the very least the availability of these other bases of liability must not be forgotten.

355 CDPA 1988 s.85(1).
356 CDPA 1988 s.85(2).
357 i.e. the photographer's life and 70 years.
358 CDPA 1988 ss.86, 88(6).
359 *Mail Newspapers v Express Newspapers* [1987] F.S.R. 90.

The treatment of moral rights in the CDPA 1988 as interests distinct from copyright has a number of consequences: **12–89**

(1) The rights (other than that to privacy) have been accorded only to authors whose copyright rests on creativity rather than investment. The rights were extended to film directors at a time when they were not authors and it has aided their campaign for their own copyright.
(2) The rights are personal (and in that sense inalienable), but they are good against all who treat the work in a prejudicial manner falling within one of the provisions. They accordingly afford relief in circumstances which the author could scarcely control by express contract.
(3) The rights are not entirely tied to the acts of reproduction and performance which make up copyright. In particular, in the sphere of artistic works, moral rights cover public exhibition of the original as well as copying of it.[360]

In sum, the CDPA 1988 has attempted from scratch to set out detailed rules to govern complex problems, which Continental systems have been able to tackle incrementally through case law and statute in combination. Because of this, our legislation needs imaginative interpretation. For all the exceptions and limitations in our texts, the rights have a considerable range, as has just been indicated. The courts will be assisted in keeping them within bounds by criteria in the rules which call for objective evaluation—and most notably with the concept of "derogatory treatment" which must prejudice "honour and reputation". **12–90**

Because copyright endures for long periods and often covers a range of different exploitations, there is a real case for protecting the "moral" position of authors by guaranteed rights which extend beyond the potential of contractual agreement. Nonetheless, every infraction of a moral right hampers some other person's freedom of expression or freedom to do business. The rights must accordingly be confined to cases of real injury. Scope must be left for the parties concerned to reach reasonable agreements concerning moral interests, secure in the knowledge that the agreements are binding. Where this can be achieved by collective negotiation with authors' societies,[361] there is a good case for saying that an industry standard has been settled and is not open to alteration. Isolated court decisions after the event are no adequate substitute for the hammering out of rights and procedures in advance.

---

[360] See above, paras 12–73, 12–81.
[361] As in the instances cited above, in nn.313, 337.

Chapter 13

PROPERTY RIGHTS AND EXPLOITATION

The previous two chapters have been concerned with the basic rules of UK copyright law as a whole. But copyright entwines itself in the workings of several major industries in ways which are distinct to each of them. In turning to the proprietary aspects of copyright we can begin to see something of this variable impact. **13–01**

Copyright, like other intellectual property, is first and foremost an exclusionary right and the significance of that characteristic to industries faced with modern copying technology needs no reiteration at this juncture. But there are many enterprises, as well as individuals, who want to be able to take copies and develop derivative works, to give performances, to broadcast and so on. Licensing is the stuff of much copyright exploitation and devising practicable systems for it, such as the development of collecting societies, has been a distinctive characteristic of the copyright world. The challenge set by electronic information networks is the latest (and possibly most daunting) in a long train of difficulties.

At the same time copyright is unique in the extent to which its exploitation involves not uniplanar, but bi-planar, linkages. It depends for its effectiveness not just on the relationship between right-owner and user, but equally on the relationship between the creative author and the entrepreneur who undertakes exploitation of the material. From its earliest foundations, as we have noted, copyright has been the shared sword of author and entrepreneur as they march forth against potential users; at the same time each has sought to appropriate it for internal struggles over profit shares, payments for work and artistic integrity.

13–02 The ideological differences between "authors' rights" and "copyright" systems stem from opposed views of how relationships on this internal plane should be governed in law. "Authors' rights" advocates demand with rising insistence that copyright law should set minimum standards, designed to protect individual creators against the superior bargaining knowledge, skills and sheer power of entrepreneurs. Partly these should protect the copyright work, as an expression of the author's personality, against infractions of "moral rights"; but beyond this there should also be controls which assure "equitable" or "proportional" remuneration to authors.

The Anglo-American approach to copyright reflects the strong (though not exclusive) commitment of the common law systems to the virtues of free contractual bargaining. Accordingly, as we have already seen, the notion of guaranteed moral rights for authors, has found no natural and flourishing soil within these systems; art.6*bis* of the Berne Convention, is an artificial fertiliser of still uncertain effectiveness. Much of the resistance to moral rights, however, expresses a fear that they will indirectly promote the growth of restrictions over freely bargained economic rights. The building of just such a provision into the EU's rental rights for authors and performers is taken as proof of what is more generally afoot.

13–03 Authors' rights and copyright systems can exist together in an increasingly intermeshed world because they have a similar effect over the external plane of relationships with users. Yet even here the differing internal planes may produce difficulties. Users require quick and efficient systems for the acquisition of rights. If the law increases the range of individuals who can claim copyright and the territories over which they can claim it, the task of securing all the necessary licences may become intolerably burdensome. Objections of this kind have caused the EU to adopt the "up-leg" limitation on satellite broadcast licences, but that is only one case. The digitisation of information systems seems likely to force the major copyright systems into increasingly similar forms, so that multi-country uses can be accounted for on a single basis.

So much for the future. We must first consider the inherited UK law on initial ownership and then the methods of dealing by assignment and licence, before turning to questions of contracting and the impact of the law upon the different copyright fields.

1. Initial Ownership

(1) Literary, dramatic, musical and artistic works; films

(a) *Legal framework*

13–04 Because copyright arises upon creation of the work, the question of initial ownership is not complicated, as is the case with patents and registered designs, by any need to apply for a grant. But given the lack of any formal record, it may later be difficult to establish who is the copyright owner. Hence proposals from several quarters to make it easier to secure permission to use "orphan works".[1] With literary, dramatic, musical and artistic works, first ownership rests in the author or co-authors unless the exception concerning employment applies.[2] We have already discussed what a person must do towards the joint creation of a work in order to qualify as a co-author. There must be a significant contribution of "skill, labour and judgment" of the appropriate kind to its evolution.[3] This is a simpler rule than under the CA 1956 which also contained special provisions concerning employed journalists and certain artistic works made under commission.[4] It is not, however, the solution proposed by the Whitford Committee, since it allows the copyright owner to have all the rights even when an unintended exploitation of the work materialises.[5]

Now that copyright is accorded (jointly) to the principal director of a film,[6] he or she should fall to be treated like literary and other authors.[7]

(b) *Employment*

For all the types of work under consideration, an employer becomes the initial owner of the copyright if it is made by his employee in the course of the employment and in the absence of contrary agreement. What falls within the scope of the employment will depend upon the nature and terms of the job and the relation of the work to it.[8] But while it is often clear whether or not an invention relates to an employer's business, with copyright material the issue may well be obscure. A senior executive in a firm of management consultants wrote public lectures about the budgetary control of firms; he **13–05**

[1] For the UK see *Gowers Review*, paras 4.91–4.99 and proposed ss.116A–116F, CDPA contained in the Digital Economy Bill, s.43 which were dropped at the final hour. For the EU see Commission Recommendation 2006/585/EC on the digitisation and online accessibility of cultural material and digital preservation OJ L236/28; Council conclusions on the digitisation and online accessibility of cultural material and digital preservation OJ C 297/1 of 7 December 2006; and i2010: Digital Libraries High Level Expert Group—Copyright Subgroup: *Final Report on Digital Preservation, Orphan Works and Out-of-Print Works* 4/6/08. For the US see proposals emanating from the United States Copyright Office: *Report on Orphan Works: A Report of the Register of Copyrights* (January 2006) and the legislative bills HR 5889 and S 2319 introduced into Congress in 2008.

[2] CDPA 1988 s.11; and for the concept of authorship (s.9). Crown and parliamentary copyright is also subject to special rules: s.11(3); see below, paras 14–47—14–49. Co-authorship is discussed below, in paras 13–19—13–21. See generally Stephenson [1980] 2 E.I.P.R. 19.

[3] Above, paras 11–06, 11–11, 11–12 and see further, below, para.13–20.

[4] CA 1956 s.4; preserved for works made before August 1, 1989, by CDPA 1988 Sch.1 para.11.

[5] See below, further para.14–07.

[6] See above, paras 11–23—11–25, 11–46.

[7] CDPA 1988 ss.9(2)(ab), 11(1).

[8] CDPA 1988 s.11(2). The distinction is essentially similar to that concerning patent rights: see above, paras 7–03 et seq.

was held entitled to the copyright in them.[9] So also was a journalist who undertook a piece of translation and editing from the Portuguese as a special task outside his normal hours of employment; it made no difference that the piece was for an advertisement in his employer's newspapers.[10] But another journalist who wrote an internal memorandum to her colleagues about a possible article was held to be acting strictly within the course of her employment.[11]

13–06 The distinction between servants and independent contractors—between those under contracts of service and contracts for services—is a familiar part of the principles governing vicarious liability (in which context it has already been discussed)[12] and it has become increasingly important with the growing variety of labour laws. It was in the context of copyright ownership that Denning L.J. suggested that the old test of whether the person contracting for the work could exercise control over how it was done was becoming obsolete; the question ought rather to be whether the person performing it was doing so as an integral part of the business.[13]

Under the former law, the employed journalist was permitted to have copyright in exploitations of his work beyond the purpose for which it was created, and there was some case for making this a general rule.[14] Instead, amid loud cries of "anomaly" from the newspaper industry, the CDPA 1988 cut away the exception and all employees were left to bargain for special arrangements or to demonstrate that they arise by implication.

(c) *Contracts to the contrary*

13–07 Where an employer is surrendering the initial copyright given him by law, the agreement does not have to be in any particular form and may therefore be deduced from conduct and surrounding circumstances. Where, however, an author is arranging that another person (such as a commissioner of the work) shall have copyright in it, to confer that legal title he must execute an assignment which complies with the formalities required for an actual or a future work.[15] However, an informal agreement, or indeed circumstances which give rise to fiduciary obligation, may have the effect in equity that the author from the outset holds the copyright in trust. Thus, in the

[9] *Stephenson Jordan v McDonald & Evans* (1951) 69 R.P.C. 10 CA; and similarly *Noah v Shuba* [1991] F.S.R. 14 (consultant epidemiologist in government service). In the *Stephenson Jordan* case the employer was allowed copyright in a chapter written as part of an assignment for a particular client of the employer. For application of this last case by analogy in the field of patents, see *Greater Glasgow* (above, para.7–04). See generally, Monotti and Ricketson, *Universities and Intellectual Property* (2003).

[10] *Byrne v Statist Co* [1914] 1 K.B. 622.

[11] *Beloff v Pressdram* [1973] 1 All E.R. 241.

[12] See above, para.2–09.

[13] *Stephenson Jordan* (above, n.9) at 22.

[14] CA 1956 s.4(2); the Whitford Committee (Cmnd.6732, 1977), para.574, looked with favour on a scheme of "compensation" for authors, similar to that affecting inventors; for which, see above, paras 7–08 et seq.

[15] For the requirements, see below, para.13–12.

"*Spycatcher*" case, the ex-MI5 officer, who wrote memoirs in flagrant breach of confidence owed to the Crown, was said by Members of the House of Lords to be under such an obligation.[16] In another context, work by a computer programmer as a partner has been treated as impliedly assigned in equity to the partnership,[17] and a similar conclusion is often appropriate where designs are specifically commissioned.[18] Over-riding the statutory requirement of writing is an instance of the long-standing willingness of courts to qualify formalities in the interests of justice, an attitude stretching back at least to the Statute of Frauds 1677. Nevertheless, such an implication is to be made only where it is necessary. Unless the commissioner can show that he needed to exclude the author from using the work and the ability to enforce the copyright against third party, he will only have an implied licence to use for the purposes of the commission.[19]

In applying these flexible rules, it may well be important to know whether the relevant presumption can be excluded by implication. If an employed teacher writes a textbook for his subject, he may be entitled to the copyright because he is employed to teach, not to write textbooks.[20] But if writing the book is within the course of employment, he may nevertheless be able to show that an authority employing him has not claimed copyright from him in the past, or has not done so from other teachers who have written similar books. From such evidence an agreement that any copyright is to be the teacher's may be implied.[21]

(d) *Copyright extended and revived*

When the CDPA 1988 introduced the EU's life-plus-70-years term for the major copyrights, it affected both works created before July 1, 1995 which were still in copyright and those which had expired but could enjoy a revival for the remaining portion of the added term.[22] The consequent proprietary **13–08**

[16] *Att-Gen v Guardian Newspapers (No. 2)* [1988] 3 All E.R. 545 at 645 (Lord Keith), at 647 (Lord Brightman); cf. at 604 (Lord Goff); cf. *Service Corp v Channel Four* [1999] E.M.L.R. 83. Note, in the context of good faith, the moral right of privacy in certain photographs and films, above, paras 12–86, 12–87.

[17] *John Richardson v Flanders* [1993] F.S.R. 497; Lea [1994] E.I.P.R. 152.

[18] e.g. *Merchant Adventures v Grew* [1973] R.P.C. 1; *Griggs Group v Evans* [2005] F.S.R. 31 CA. (design for logo produced to order by an advertising agency).

[19] *Ray v Classic FM* [1998] F.S.R. 622.

[20] It seems that university teachers (or at least Cambridge professors) are to be so regarded: Lord Evershed M.R., *Stephenson Jordan* case (above, n.9) at 18. While today they are often employed also to undertake research, the work to be done is not specified, nor is any requirement to present the results. If copyright were to vest in the employing institution it could be used to prevent freedom of academic expression: see further, Cornish [1992] E.I.P.R. 13. The whole issue is now politicised by the interests of academic institutions in gaining rights in computer programs and in coursework and other material for use in e-learning programmes. There are many other difficulties: over joint and accumulated rights, over changes in employment, etc. See, e.g. C. McSherry, *Who Owns Academic Work*? (2001); Gordon (1993) 102 Yale L.J. 102; Waldron (1993) 68 Chic.-Kent L.R. 841; Dreyfuss (2000) 53 Vand. L.R. 1161; Craig (2000) 47 see J. Copyright Soc USA 75; Monotti [2002] E.I.P.R. 251.

[21] *Noah v Shuba* (above, n.9). See also above, paras 2–07, 7–04.

[22] See above, para.11–44.

issues were ducked by the Duration Directive and left to national provisions.[23] In the United Kingdom, ownership in the extended term of works still in copyright was given to the owner on December 31, 1995.[24] Where assignment had previously split title to different aspects of the copyright (say, mechanical reproduction as distinct from performing rights in music), each owner keeps its portion. Licences, including those imposed by the Copyright Tribunal, and assertions and waivers of moral rights are extended on a similar basis.[25]

13–09 Where copyright has run out before January 1, 1996, but there would be some part of the new term still to run, the revived copyright goes to the owner at expiry. But if that person has died or ceased to exist before the revival date, the right goes to the author or film director or their personal representatives.[26] This may be particularly important for a film produced by a one-film company which was thereafter liquidated.

With sensible circumspection, the right in revived copyright is in many cases restricted to a right to claim a reasonable royalty, set if necessary by the Copyright Tribunal. The would-be user of the work must give notice of his intention; once he does he is treated as licensed, even though the royalty is not settled until later.[27] The Directive contains nothing to preclude this solution.

(2) Entrepreneurial copyright

13–10 The copyrights in sound recordings, films, broadcasts and typographical format are conferred initially upon the "authors" who are responsible for organising production of the material (see the Table in Ch.11 (pp.377–379), heads 4 and 8). The management company for the skaters, Torvill and Dean, commissioned the recording of music for one of the pair's skating routines. The company was held to be the "maker" of the resultant sound recording, rather than the person with whom it contracted to organise the writing of the musical arrangement, the hiring of musicians and technicians and the arrangements for the studio. It was the former who took the essential initiative and investment risk.[28]

---

[23] See the Duration of Copyright and Rights in Performances Regulations 1995 (SI 1995/3297) regs 18–25; for rights in performances, see below, paras 14–30 et seq. Detailed implementation is a matter for national law: *Butterfly Music v Carosello* [1999] E.M.L.R. 847 ECJ.

[24] Duration Regulations 1995 reg.18. Where, however, the assignment is for a limited period, the extended term accrues to the owner of the reversionary interest.

[25] Duration Regulations reg.21.

[26] Duration Regulations reg.19. Pre-revival agreements to assign or grant licences in the revived term are given effect as if executed: reg.20. Earlier waivers and assertions of moral rights are revived: reg.22.

[27] Duration Regulations regs 24, 25. The major exception arises where a licensing body (for which see below, paras 13–54 et seq.) could have granted a licence, under a scheme or otherwise.

[28] *A & M Records v Video Collection* [1995] E.M.L.R. 25. The EU Database Directive Rec.41, adopts an equivalent approach in giving the maker of a database a sui generis right against extraction or reutilisation: see below, para.20–38.

2. Assignments and Licensing

(1) The distinction

The most lucrative copyright works are often exploited in a number of ways. Take a popular novel: there are the volume rights, the serial rights (in newspapers and magazines), the translation rights, the film rights, the dramatisation rights (play, opera, musical, ballet); now there will also be electronic rights to call it up from store in any one of its emanations. Add the fact that for some of these it may be desirable to split the rights of exploitation language by language; and there is the possibility of dealing with each national copyright separately. The result is an elaborate concoction of prospects. **13–11**

As far as UK copyright is concerned, the Act permits the various rights bundled together as copyright not only to be licensed but also to be assigned separately.[29] It is possible to assign for a limited term within the copyright period.[30] Often, therefore, there is a choice whether to grant rights by assignment or by exclusive licence. Provided that the contract in which the grant is made is clear about consequential matters, it makes no difference which type is used.[31] But if ambiguities are left, their resolution may be affected by the fact that an assignment is in essence a transfer of ownership (however partial), while a licence is in essence permission to do what otherwise would be infringement.[32] Thus a licensee's freedom to make alterations in the work may be more restricted than an assignee's.[33] The licensee may well not be entitled to assign or sub-license his interest,[34] while his licensor will retain the right to grant licences to others, unless he has granted exclusive rights to the licensee. A licensee must also ensure that he does not act beyond the scope of the licence.[35]

---

[29] CDPA 1988 s.90. The right assigned can be part of one head (such as the right of reproduction or of publishing) in the list of exclusive rights. Thus the right to reproduce a book in French translation may be separately assigned. Terms purporting to give exclusive rights over acts beyond the scope of copyright can take effect only in contract.

[30] CDPA 1988 s.90(2)(b)—but no longer for part of the UK: an EU influence.

[31] A not uncommon practice has been to blur the boundary by "giving" (not "granting") the exclusive right to (say) publish. It is then a question of construction to decide which is meant. Failure to use an appropriate technical word does not preclude a finding of assignment; *Chaplin v Frewin* [1966] Ch. 71 at 94 CA; and see *Orwin v Att-Gen* [1988] F.S.R. 415 CA. The use of the word "grant" rather than "assign" or "transfer", in light of the surrounding commercial context, has been held to support a licence rather than an assignment: *JHP Ltd v BBC Worldwide* [2008] F.S.R. 29.

[32] But if more than a bare permission, it will acquire some of the characteristics of a property right.

[33] See *Frisby v BBC* [1967] Ch. 932.

[34] See below, para.13–14.

[35] See *Rutter v Brookland Valley Estate* [2009] FCA 702 FC Aust.

(2) Formal requirement

(a) *Statutory provisions*

13–12 Assignments of copyright (that is the legal right of ownership) only take effect if they are in writing, signed by or on behalf of the assignor.[36] Once this is complied with the assignment is effective against all subsequent takers of conflicting interests. There is no public register of copyright transactions and any assignee takes the risk that there are no prior assignments of which he does not know. If there are, his only recourse may well be against his assignor.[37] Agreements to assign future copyright which are signed by or on behalf of the prospective owner have the effect of automatically vesting legal ownership in the assignee. However, there must be no other person with a superior equity.[38] On occasion, courts have been willing to imply an assignment in equity from the circumstances in which works have been produced to order.[39]

Licences do not in principle have to take any particular form and here too they may be implied.[40] However, an exclusive licensee will have no right to sue infringers unless the licence complies with similar formalities to those for assignments.[41] Licences bind all successors in title[42] to the licensor's interest except a purchaser in good faith for valuable consideration and without notice (actual or constructive) and those who take from such a person.[43]

(b) *Implied licences*

13–13 Licences are frequently to be implied from the circumstances in which copyright material is handed over. A commission to prepare the work may

---

[36] CDPA 1988 s.90(3); *Roban Jig v Taylor* [1979] R.P.C. 130 CA. Agreements which do not comply with the formal requirements may still be effective to transfer an equitable interest; see above, para.13–07. But an assignment of a purely equitable interest must satisfy the formal requirements of the Law of Property Act 1925 s.53(1)(c): *Roban Jig* case. Where works are incorporated into a film under agreements with the producer, the authors' rental rights are likely to be deemed assigned to the producer, subject to the guaranteed right of equitable remuneration, for which see above, para.12–28.

[37] By way of action for breach of condition of good title or for money paid upon a total failure of consideration.

[38] CDPA 1988 s.91(1), (2). The assignment probably has to be for valuable consideration; and see *Wah Sang v Takmay* [1980] F.S.R. 303 CA (HK).

[39] See, e.g. *Massine v de Basil* [1936–1945] Mac.CC 223 (ballet); *John Richardson v Flanders* [1993] F.S.R. 497 and *Ibcos Computers v Barclays Mercantile* [1994] F.S.R. 275 (both computer programs); *Griggs Group v Evans* [2005] F.S.R. 31 CA (design for logo). Cf. *Ray v Classic FM* [1998] F.S.R. 622 (classified compilation of music for radio station) and *Fisher v Brooker* [2009] 1 W.L.R. 1764 (interest in a musical work).

[40] e.g. *Durand v Molino* [2000] E.C.D.R. 320: perpetual exclusive licence by artist to restaurant owner that portrait of latter's family could be used on menus and business materials.

[41] CDPA 1988 ss.101, 102; see above, para.2–06.

[42] This does not clearly cover a later licensee, when one or other licence is exclusive; but he ought to be similarly treated.

[43] CDPA 1988 s.90 (4). Licences of future copyright are similarly treated: s.91(3).

well carry this inference, at least to the extent that is customary. In *Blair v Osborne & Tomkins*,[44] an architect was hired to prepare plans for the submission of a planning application and was paid for the work to this point. After securing permission, the landowner built in a way that reproduced the plans, and was held to have an implied licence to do so even though he had not employed the architect to supervise construction of the building. But if the architect charges a nominal fee, rather than a proportion of the full scale fee, for his work up to the planning permission stage, and he makes it clear that no licence is being conferred for actual construction, he will not be held to have conferred one (at least in the absence of further factors).[45]

There may also be an implied licence without any initial commission from the licensee. A "letter to the editor" on a theme of public interest is taken to be intended for publication[46]; so also is a submission of material to a magazine, subject to any customary royalty.[47]

(c) *Trans-national movement of goods*

Expressly or impliedly, a licence may confer authority to produce copies of copyright works in one country and then to trans-ship them to another, whatever the prohibitions in the copyright law of the second against importation. It will be recalled that in our copyright law, leaving aside the free movement requirements for the EEA, imports into the United Kingdom will infringe if, had the goods been made in Britain, they would have infringed copyright or breached an exclusive licence, to the importer's knowledge or reasonable belief.[48] Thus, provided that the goods are actually made outside Britain, it is not relevant to consider whether they were legitimately made under the copyright law of that place. **13–14**

The extensive scope of UK patent rights (which in principle cover even the subsequent resale and use of goods first marketed by the patentee) led, by way of counterbalance, to the presumption of a broad implied licence. If the patentee disposes of the goods without limiting the manner in which they may subsequently be dealt with, the implication is that there is no restriction on their circulation or use; but the contrary might be inferred from all the circumstances.[49] **13–15**

What, then, of a sale abroad of "legitimate" goods embodying copyright? Since copyright does not embrace their subsequent sale and use in any

[44] *Blair v Osborne & Tomkins* [1971] 2 Q.B. 78 CA; and see *Beck v Montana Constructions* [1964–1965] N.S.W.R. 229.

[45] *Stovin-Bradford v Volpoint* [1971] Ch. 1007 CA. Cf. also *Netupsky v Dominion Bridge* (1969) 68 W.W.R. 529; *Barnett v Cape Town Foreshore Board* (1960) [1978] F.S.R. 176.

[46] *Springfield v Thame* (1903) 89 L.T. 242; the editor may also alter such a letter in order to fit it in. See further *Roberts v Candiware* [1980] F.S.R. 352.

[47] *Hall-Brown v Illiffe* [1928–1935] Mac. CC 88; cf. *PRS v Coates* [1923–1928] Mac. CC 103; *Banks v CBS Songs* [1996] E.M.L.R. 440.

[48] CDPA 1988 ss.22, 27(3); see above, para.12–29; and for the special position of computer programs, see above, para.12–28.

[49] See above, para.6–15. For trade marks, below, para.18–122.

general way, arguably the implied permission to export is the stronger. But in *Time-Life v Interstate Parcel*[50] the High Court of Australia refused to draw this analogy. Time-Life was exploiting its Australian copyright in certain cookery books by licensing it exclusively to a Dutch subsidiary, which in turn sub-licensed an exclusive distributor in Australia. A parallel importer bought its copies in the United States which were first marketed there by Time-Life.[51] The unconditional sales in America were held to carry no implied licence to import into Australia.[52] It was not therefore necessary to show either an express limitation ("Not for sale in Australia" or the like) or surrounding circumstances (such as knowledge of the exclusive distributorship) which would negate the implied licence.

An English court might well be persuaded to draw the analogy to the patent cases which the High Court rejected.[53] Even so, it will be seen that the argument is only about implied intent and the need to give sufficient notice that goods are not to be transferred from one national market to another. It is not about public policy rules overriding the copyright owner's wish to preserve price differentials between different countries by means of copyright.[54]

13–16 Once copies have been legitimately sold within the internal market of the EEA, they must thereafter be free to circulate between Member States, following the basic requirement of free movement prescribed in arts 34 and 36 of the TFEU (ex-28 and 30 TEC). However, at the perimeter borders of the EEA as a whole, the Commission believes that intellectual property of all kinds should prevent the importation of "legitimate" goods, even though they are initially marketed outside by the internal right-owner or an associated enterprise.[55] Whatever the difficulties of principle in translating this policy into trade mark law, in respect of copyright law in the United Kingdom, the result was largely achieved in the course of implementing the Rental, Lending and Related Rights Directive. As already explained, the "distribution right"—the primary right to issue copies to the public by first putting them into circulation—is excluded from operation only where there has already been a "putting into circulation" within the EEA[56]; releasing in another country does not count.

13–17 Secondary infringement by importation for non-private or domestic use (with the requisite state of knowledge), so important and problematic a provision in the past in relation to parallel imports, now plays only a lesser

[50] *Time-Life v Interstate Parcel* [1978] F.S.R. 251.

[51] The parallel imports sold in Australia for just over half the exclusive distributors' retail price. The Australian Competition and Consumer Commission has long criticised the protection against parallel importation provided by IPRs. See, e.g. Report of Ergas Committee, 2000.

[52] An argument based upon the warranty of quiet possession got no further.

[53] For the position regarding trade marks, see below, paras 18–119 et seq.

[54] Note, however, Murphy J.'s reference to possible breaches of the Trade Practices Act 1974 (Commonwealth): [1978] F.S.R. 251 at 287–288.

[55] See below, paras 19–17 et seq.

[56] See above, para.12–27, expressing doubts about the legal effectiveness of the proposals.

role.[57] It will cover those cases where the importing is for some internal purpose of the importer or its associates, such as bringing in a film for showing in cinemas or a record for broadcasting.[58] In order to secure customs seizure against parallel imports, it will be necessary to show that the actual importation is of an infringing copy.[59] With the implementation of the Rental, Lending and Related Rights Directive, at least the primary distribution right in the entrepreneurial copyrights applies to the first sale or similar commercial act after importation. This simplifies considerably the task of those who pursue parallel importers, as well as pirates.[60]

There must remain the question, has the person entitled either to the distribution right or the importation right nonetheless consented to the importation or subsequent sale of goods initially marketed outside the EEA with that person's assent? The distribution of newspapers and magazines may well be an instance where it is natural to expect such freedom, at least if no express conditions are laid down. **13–18**

(3) Co-ownership of copyright

Co-ownership may come about in two ways: (1) because the copyright material is produced by joint authors,[61] or (2) because an interest is assigned to more than one person.[62] In each case, there are circumstances to be distinguished. Joint authorship does not arise where a creative work is compounded of parts that demand discrete forms of mental activity: the text and music for a song or opera; script, scenery and costume design for a play; an original text and a translation of it.[63] In such cases there are distinct copyrights, each with its own duration measured by relation to the life of the relevant author, each requiring for its exploitation the assent of the owner of that particular right.[64] **13–19**

Co-authorship occurs when collaborators have worked to produce **13–20**

[57] Because this is now so, the precise import of the secondary infringement provision (CDPA 1988 s.27(3)) will not be investigated. For a virtuoso discussion of the subject, see Laddie et al., paras 19–15—19–16 and Ch.32.

[58] These may give rise to difficult fringe cases, such as importation in order to use in a way that is permitted: for instance, as an ephemeral recording for a broadcast (above, para.12–48); *Albert v Fletcher* [1976] R.P.C. 615, SC (NZ).

[59] CDPA 1988 ss.111, 112.

[60] See above, para.12–28.

[61] Laches or delay will not bar a declaration of joint ownership based on joint authorship: see *Fisher v Brooker* [2009] 1 W.L.R. 1764 HL. Where there is an implied licence in favour of the other co-authors, a joint author may be estopped from revoking it: see *Godfrey v Lees* [1995] E.M.L.R. 307; cf. *Fisher v Brooker*.

[62] In the case of assignment, whether the co-owners become joint tenants or tenants in common depends on the terms of the assignment. Joint authors have interests as tenants in common: *Lauri v Renad* [1892] 3 Ch. 402; *Redwood v Feldman* [1979] R.P.C. 1.

[63] See CDPA 1988 ss.3, 10.

[64] See also above, para.11–12.

copyright work of a single kind "in prosecution of a preconcerted joint design".[65] Each must provide a significant creative input to the expression of the finished work (akin to penmanship), which is not distinct from the contributions of others.[66] It does not arise where one author writes a play, and another subsequently adds a scene to it; rather the first author brings into existence a copyright in what he has written, and likewise the second.[67] In the latter case, infringement of each copyright is a question whether there has been substantial copying of the work that each covers; neither derives advantage from the other's contribution.[68] Where the work results from a multitude of efforts, it may be particularly difficult to establish collaboration and sufficiently creative contributions.[69]

13–21 Co-ownership by assignment does not arise when different aspects of the copyright (publishing rights, performing rights, film rights, etc.) are transferred to different people: each has the exclusive right over his apportioned subject matter.[70]

In contrast with patents, it has been held that a joint owner of copyright or a part of it is not entitled to do acts within its scope without securing permission from his fellow co-owners.[71] Equally a licensee needs permission from all his owners.[72] This can cause problems when it is not clear how many authors contributed to a joint work; for one thing, nice distinctions may have to be drawn between authors who participated in actually expressing the copyright work and preliminary contributors who put up starting ideas.[73]

---

[65] *Levy v Rutley* (1871) L.R. 6 C.P. 523 at 528, 529. There does not have to be any intention to become joint authors: *Beckingham v Hodgens* [2003] All E.R. (D) 247 (Feb) CA.

[66] *Cala Homes v McAlpine (No. 1)* [1995] F.S.R. 623; *Fylde Microsystems v Key Radio* [1998] F.S.R. 449; *Ray v Classic FM* [1998] F.S.R. 623; *Brighton v Jones* [2004] E.M.L.R. 26.

[67] Note the case of correcting and editing a text in the course of its production, which is treated as producing a joint work if the editor's contribution is sufficient to attract copyright at all: *Springfield v Thame* (1903) 89 L. T. 242; cf. *Samuelson v Producers Distributing* (1931) 48 R.P.C. 580 at 586.

[68] e.g. *Warwick Films v Eisinger* (above, para.12–13).

[69] As in *Telstra Corporation Ltd v Phone Directories Company Pty Ltd* [2010] FCA 44 FC Aust.

[70] See CDPA 1988 s.90(2)(a).

[71] *Cescinsky v Routledge* [1916] 2 K.B. 325; *Cala Homes v McAlpine* [1995] F.S.R. 818; *Ray v Classic FM* [1998] F.S.R. 623. The rule is thus the opposite of that for patents (for which, see above, para.7–19). The difference may perhaps lie in the need to protect an author against an entrepreneur, when both have become co-owners.

[72] *Powell v Head* (1879) 12 Ch.D. 686; *Mail Newspapers v Express Newspapers* [1987] F.S.R. 90 (one co-owner clinically dead). As a corollary, one joint owner can sue without having to join others.

[73] e.g. if a ghost writer is commissioned to write up a celebrity's memoirs he alone is the author: *Evans v Hulton* [1923–1928] Mac. C.C. 51; and see *Kenrick v Lawrence* (1890) 285 QBD 99 (above, para.11–14); *Tate v Thomas* [1921] 1 Ch. 503. But remember now the copyright of the speaker who is recorded: above, paras 11–33, 11–34. As to film directors, see Kamina, *Film Copyright in The EU* (2002), paras 107–134; Laddie et al., paras 7.41, 7.42.

3. Dealings Based on Copyright[74]

(1) Types of dealing

The worlds of information, education and entertainment, shaped as they are by copyright and rights in performances, are growing increasingly complex. As copying, storing and replaying technologies advance, the numbers and the variety of users, commercial, public and private, splay outwards, the search for ways of tying them to licences gains energy and, in some cases, desperation. **13–22**

How then are these proprietary possibilities turned to effect? In this section, attention focuses primarily on the plane between creator and the exploiter with whom he or she collaborates. It has to be kept in mind that, thanks to advances in copying, storing and replaying technology, the plane of owners and users is often an elaborate maze. Old patterns of understanding would treat a work of (say) fiction as primarily a matter of book publication, and only secondarily as a text which might be anthologised, filmed or photocopied, but these attitudes are being replaced. A work goes forth to find its own best seeding-grounds. All prospects need to be dealt with in advance in contracts for exploitation.[75]

On this creator-exploiter plane, the terms which are set for the exploitation of a particular work derive from three principal possibilities: **13–23**

(1) *Individual negotiation.* Leading to contractual arrangements for the rights and returns upon them within the framework of an employment relationship, a commission to undertake work or an agreement to commercialise work already done. The negotiation may be by the parties themselves, or either side may use agents. The terms may be hammered out from scratch, they may be presented on a "take-it-or-leave-it" basis by an exploiter armed with standard terms, or even by a successful creator strong enough to play the field. Whatever the particular mix, the deal is struck on the basis of the individual bargaining position of each party.

(2) *Collective negotiation.* Trade union activity by creators and performers is common, particularly in the music and audio-visual industries; it may well be matched by association among entrepreneurs which aims to establish a countervailing force of equal significance. In many circumstances, the groups represent employees and employers, as in most labour relations; but even though many writers, composers and film directors operate as independent contractors, they may join

[74] See Guibault and Hugenholtz, *Study on the Conditions Applicable to Contracts Relating to IP in the EU* (2002).

[75] For German legislation of 2002 aiming to control the negotiation of copyright contracts, see Cornish (2002) 2b Col. J.L.A. 1; Schricker (2004) 35 I.I.C. 850.

guilds and associations which will negotiate terms collectively on their behalf. Following the standard pattern of British industrial practice, these collective agreements will acquire legal force to the extent that their terms are then written into individual contracts.

Between this category and category (1) lies a no-man's-land of weaker collective action, in which a creators' association promotes model terms but does not have the strength to secure undertakings from exploiters that they will always abide by them.

(3) *Collecting society action.* With a collecting society the object of the joint action shifts from the creator-exploiter plane to that of the owner-user. A typical collecting society aims to generate returns on repetitive uses of copyright material such as performances, photocopying and now electronic distribution, which it would be too costly for owners to demand on an individual basis.[76] The first field in which it was demonstrated that collecting societies were not only necessary but could be made to work—and indeed to work on the basis of international collaboration—was in the performance of music. In that field, the necessary economies of scale came from broadcasting, with its dependence on live and recorded music. With this foundation, it was possible to maintain an often dogged policing of dance and concert halls, cinemas, bars and restaurants, shops, schools and so on.

The earliest among these societies—in Britain, the Performing Right Society (PRS)[77]—had as members both composers and their publishers. It is quite possible to apply the collecting society principle to associations purely of creators, as is now occurring with film directors, or to associations purely of exploiters, as occurred once record producers were given sound recording rights, particularly when they extended to rights in performances as well as over reproduction.

One problem, which any society may have, is to prevent penetration of its ranks by users whose ultimate interest is to keep royalty rates low or otherwise undermine the society's objectives. A collecting society acquires very considerable market power by drawing together the rights in the whole repertoire of works sought by users. Another problem accordingly is to satisfy such arbiters of the public interest as competition authorities that this economic dominance is a necessity.[78] This task, which never disappears for long, is made more difficult if

[76] See Handke and Towse [2007] 38 I.I.C. 937 on the economics of collecting societies and for a sceptical view Kretschmer [2002] E.I.P.R. 126. On the future of collecting societies in the digital environment see Gilliéron [2006] 37 I.I.C. 939.

[77] See above, para.10–49.

[78] See below, para.13–53. See Ficsor [1985] Copyright 341; Kernochan [1985] Copyright 389; Freegard [1985] Copyright 443; Karnell [1986] Copyright 45; Report by the International Bureau, WIPO, *Collective Administration of Copyright and Neighboring Rights* [1989] Copyright 309; Karnell in Watt, *Copyright and Economic Theory* (2000), Ch.6.

cartels of producers seek to justify their joint economic action by posing as copyright collecting societies.

Recognising these three categories of contracting helps to explain two basic questions: why has modern copyright law tended to proliferate the number of authors' rights and neighbouring rights? And why have countries varied in their views of the extent to which the law must guarantee fair dealing between authors and their exploiters? The grandest authors, and even more, the most popular performers, are in a position to play entrepreneurs off one against another. The general run of creators, actors and musicians, are not, and this includes, of course, the famous before they become so. **13–24**

To the extent that labour relations between these two sides have become settled, it is enough for collective agreements to define the terms on which work is done, and to leave exploitation of rights against users to the production organisers. But collectivisation of this kind is far from universal. One prospect, in order for authors and performers to improve their position, is to increase their property rights. This may give them some enhanced status in the direct bargaining process, whether this is individual or collective—and at least some of them may sooner or later be able to turn this to financial account.[79] But beyond this, a distinct right may well be necessary in order to form a society which will collect directly from users. Obviously, where collective bargaining or direct arrangements with users can succeed, the case for protective legislation is reduced. **13–25**

(2) Legal controls on bargaining[80]

In the United Kingdom the Acts of 1956 and 1988 have avoided provisions designed to protect the individual author or performer when he or she bargains from a position of economic weakness or inexperience. There is no provision to revise a royalty arrangement when a work becomes a best seller, nor is there any general guarantee of an "equitable" or "proportionate" share of earnings.[81] In part that is because general contract law provides means of intervening in egregious cases,[82] and in recent years the courts have not hesitated to use this weaponry in entertainment industry cases. Both the common law public policy against restraints of trade and the equitable doctrine of undue influence have been called in play. **13–26**

[79] For an instance, following from an increase in legal rights, see above, para.10–53.
[80] See esp. Goldstein in Vaver and Bently, Ch.18.
[81] For the special case of the rental right of authors and performers, see above, para.12–28.
[82] The determination of terms orally agreed in a publishing contract may result in a decision favouring an author against a publisher: as in *Malcolm v Oxford University Press* [1994] E.M.L.R. 17 CA.

(a) *Restraint of trade*

13–27 The common law treats as unenforceable any contractual term which is in unreasonable restraint of trade, having regard both to the interests of the parties and the public interest.[83] The doctrine has been applied with some severity to covenants binding an employee not to work for a competitor or engage in competitive work once he leaves an employment; such covenants have to be strictly limited in terms of time and place if they are not to be regarded as unreasonable. The doctrine has been applied more cautiously to restraint clauses on the sale of a business, and to restrictive business agreements among competitors.[84] However, in the 1960s, alongside the development of a British system of competition control, the courts used the restraint of trade doctrine against anti-competitive arrangements operating both horizontally and vertically.

13–28 It was at this juncture, in *A Schroeder Music v Macaulay*,[85] that the House of Lords found an agreement between a young unknown pop composer and a leading music publisher to be unenforceable as being in unreasonable restraint of trade. The broader label, "unconscionable", was also used of the agreement, but there has since been some resistance against adopting this highly amorphous concept as the essential test of what is inoperative.[86] The objection in the *Schroeder* case was the evidently unbalanced character of the obligations in what was a standard term contract: by its terms a composer who generated a moderate flow of royalties (£5,000 over 5 years) was obliged to give his services exclusively to the publisher for 10 years without any escape clause. The publisher was to be granted copyright throughout the world in all songs written solely or jointly, the composer undertaking to "obey and comply with all lawful orders and directions" from the publisher. By contrast, the publisher could at any time give one month's notice of termination, and was in any case under no obligation to publish any of the songs, being merely obliged to pay royalties and to make modest advances against them. The House of Lords regarded such terms as manifestly unfair,[87] without considering the highly competitive nature of the music

[83] See generally, e.g. Treitel, *The Law of Contract* 9th edn (1995), pp.401–424, 919–920; and for further details, Bagehot & Kanaar, *Music Business Agreements* 2nd edn (1998) esp. App.3; Nelson, *Law of Entertainment and Broadcasting* (1995) Ch.5.

[84] Note especially *Printers and Numerical Registering v Sampson* (1875) L.R. 19 Eq. 462 (patent licensee's obligation to transfer rights in subsequent inventions to licensor held valid: celebrated statement of the virtues of sanctity of contract); Lord Reid, *Esso Petroleum v Harper's Garage* [1968] A.C. 269.300; *Buchanan v Alba Diagnostics* [2004] R.P.C. (34) 681 HL.

[85] *A Schroeder Music v Macaulay* [1974] 1 W.L.R. 1308; [1974] 3 All E.R. 616.

[86] See citations in Treitel (above, n.83) at pp.370–373; Goff and Jones, *Law of Restitution* 5th edn (1998), pp.343–345.

[87] In a decision which followed soon after, Lord Denning M.R., a leading protagonist of the concept of "unconscionability", condemned a similar agreement as having "some amazing provisions" which imposed a "stranglehold" on the composers concerned: *Clifford Davis Management v WEA Records* [1975] 1 All E.R. 237. See also *Zang Tumb Tuum v Johnson* [1993] E.M.L.R. 61; *Silvertone Records v Mountford* [1993] E.M.L.R. 152.

industry, with its relentless search for new talent.[88]

The prime concern of the law in intervening to end an unreasonable restraint of trade is to aid the individual who has been unduly tied. If, therefore, he is an established artist who, with professional advice, renegotiates the terms of an earlier agreement in ways that recognise his rise to stardom, he is likely to be held bound by the new agreement, even if it ties him to working for one record company exclusively for a considerable number of years.[89] There is a policy which strongly favours upholding a renegotiated arrangement because it is a compromise.[90] **13–29**

(b) *Undue influence*

In equity, relief has long been given against contracts, wills and other transactions which have been entered into under undue influence, that is in cases where the person entering the transaction is so influenced by the ideas and personality of another that he or she is unable to reach any independent decision about its desirability.[91] Indeed the courts will presume from the existence of certain relationships between two persons that undue influence affected their transaction, unless sufficient evidence is produced to show that after all there was a chance to exercise proper judgment—usually by demonstrating that independent advice was offered. **13–30**

This relief typically takes the form of an order for rescission, which seeks, where possible, to put the parties back in an equivalent position to that which they occupied before execution of the transaction. Thus a contract made under undue influence is treated as voidable upon a court order, but not void ab initio. Acts done in execution of the contract before it is avoided—and in particular where they have an effect on innocent third parties—may accordingly remain binding. **13–31**

The relationship between a pop artist and his manager has been characterised as one capable of raising a presumption of undue influence. This will be so where, for instance, a young, inexperienced and unknown composer, librettist or performer enters publishing, recording or management agreements by virtue of which the manager master-minds the subsequent success of the artist (*Gilbert O'Sullivan v Management Agency and Music*[92]; *Elton John v James*).[93] Subsequent events, such as failure to raise any timely objection, or later agreements made with independent advice, which assume that the earlier agreements are valid, may provide reasons for refusing **13–32**

[88] Hence the vigorous criticism by Trebilcock (1976) 26 U. Toronto L.J. 359. For a more realistic assessment of the economic pressures on pop music developers, see *Elton John v James* (below, n.93), esp. at 450–453.

[89] There can be acquiescence to an agreement in undue restraint of trade: *Nicholl v Ryder* [2000] E.M.L.R. 632 CA.

[90] See *Panayiotou v Sony* [1994] E.M.L.R. 229.

[91] See generally, Treitel (above, n.83), pp.377–387; Brownsword [1998] I.P.R. 311.

[92] *Gilbert O'Sullivan v Management Agency and Music* [1985] Q.B. 428; to some extent foreshadowed by Lord Denning M.R. in the *Clifford Davis* case (above, n.87) at 241.

[93] *Elton John v James* [1991] F.S.R. 397.

rescission of the contracts. Even then, if there is secrecy which leads to the artist being paid less than his entitlement, this will amount to fraud for which damages will be awarded.[94]

13–33 There are cases in which both restraint of trade and undue influence arise on the facts, in which case rescission may be ordered wherever it is appropriate. If there is only a finding of restraint of trade, it is by no means clear what effect this can have on assignments of copyright which have taken place before the court declares the contract invalid. In *Clifford Davis v WEA Records*,[95] the Court of Appeal held that, where copyright in songs was assigned under such an invalid agreement, the assignee could not assert any copyright in songs already assigned against a record company to which the composers concerned had subsequently granted rights of exploitation. But that decision arose at a very early stage in the evolution of these modern rules.

(c) *EU competition law*

13–34 Article 101 of the TFEU (ex-81 TEC) may also affect the contracts of leading artists in entertainment.[96] If they have a significant share of the market for their type of service, then the effect of exclusivity deals upon that market will be judged from the perspective of public interest in maintaining competition, rather than from considerations of fairness to the parties. Such an argument was raised in the unsuccessful attempt by George Michael to avoid his exclusive recording contract with Sony.[97] The reasons for rejecting the argument—that the market was purely national, and that the long ties were "objectively necessary"—seem inadequate, but were at least related to the particular circumstances. In another case, the rules of competition law could well apply.

(3) The main copyright industries

(a) *Publishing*

13–35 Among professional writers of fiction, biography and the like, established authors tend to have literary agents, who have an insider's view of publishing. They do much to improve the competitiveness of the market, and can guard authors against the dangers inherent in any relationship as complex as the modern publishing agreement. Significantly, it is often the agent who presents the draft contract to the publisher for negotiation.

[94] In the *Elton John* case (above, n.93) rescission was refused for delay and acquiescence, but the levying of unjustified management charges led to an award of damages. It is one of the greatest difficulties in copyright businesses for authors and artists to ensure that they are receiving accurate accounts.

[95] *Clifford Davis v WEA Records* [1975] 1 All E.R. 237.

[96] *RAI/Unitel* [1987] 3 C.M.L.R. 306.

[97] See *Panayiotou* (above, n.90); Coulthard [1995] J.B.L. 414; and generally Fine [1992] Ent. L.R. 6.

While this practice, less known in non-English language publishing, has probably retarded the growth of collective action by writers, the practice has nonetheless advanced in the last two decades. Two major associations, the Society of Authors and the Writers' Guild of Great Britain, have indeed collaborated in producing "Minimum Term Agreements" (MTAs) which they seek to have accepted by publishers. These have not yet become trade standards, though some individual firms apply a version of them.

The MTAs specify the rights which are the subject of a publishing agreement, the minimum royalties to be paid for each right within copyright, the type of right granted (exclusive licence unless there is some specific justification for an assignment), and the various forms of exploitation covered. As to the forms of exploitation, these will today cover not only the primary forms of book publication in home and overseas markets, in translation, etc. they will also include "volume subsidiary rights", such as quotation, digest, book-club, later serial, periodical, educational-edition, large-print, strip-cartoon and reprography rights; and "non-volume subsidiary rights", such as first serial, dramatisation, merchandising and—suddenly now of high significance in many cases—electronic publishing rights. It will be appreciated that in today's rapidly changing world MTAs themselves need revision as new forms of exploitation develop. **13–36**

As to the duration of the grant, the different versions of the MTA have tackled the question of a reversionary power in various ways: a maximum licence term of 20 years[98] or of a period to be fixed in the particular agreement; full- or part-term licences which in certain cases (such as cessation of production of the work) become capable of termination by the author; licences which after a specified period or in specified circumstances become capable of renegotiation.

For publishers in general, the Publishers' Association has its own voluntary Code of Practice and this acknowledges some of the claims of the MTAs.[99] Thus it calls for the clear statement of all obligations assumed by each side, with proper explanation of the terms to an author who is not professionally advised. It recommends that the publisher be granted only a licence unless there are special reasons for an assignment. There are certain reversionary arrangements and a statement that an author should have "proper opportunity to share in the success of a work" (though nothing more specific is said about the measure of this sharing). The manuscript should be handled promptly in accordance with a set timetable and the author should be informed about all important design, promotion, marketing and sub-licensing decisions. Cancellation by the publisher should occur only for sufficient reason. The author should receive regular and clear **13–37**

[98] By 1992 five publishers had been prepared to include a 20-year limitation in their MTA: *The Author* (1992) p.91.

[99] See Owen, *Clark's Publishing Agreements* 7th edn (2007) App.F.

accounting. The publisher should respect the integrity of the work and "fullest possible credit" should be accorded to the author.[100]

(b) *Music*

13–38 (i) **Composition and initial publication, recording and performances.** The writing of music is not a field in which collective negotiation has proceeded far. Composers now have an Association of Composers' Organisations, comprising representatives of the Association of Professional Composers, the Composers Guild of Great Britain and the British Academy of Songwriters, Composers and Authors. To some extent this umbrella organisation negotiates with the Music Publishers' Association, the Producers Alliance for Cinema and Television (PACT), the BBC and the PRS on rights and appropriate fee levels, but this falls short of general agreements on minimum terms. It was the absence of either composers' agents or collective protection among entrants into pop composition, coinciding with the sudden cult of the composer-performer, which 20 years ago led the courts to their resilient use of the doctrines of restraint of trade and undue influence.[101]

The consequence of this intervention has been to enhance the position of the composer. While it is still the practice for copyright to be assigned to the publisher, the transfer of rights is no longer always for the entire copyright term. There may well be clauses allowing for reversion of title in works which the publisher chooses not to promote; for termination of the agreement (including the assignment) after a limited term; for revision of royalties either in accordance with a scheme prescribed from the outset or through an obligation to renegotiate. In the past publishers have taken express power to make adaptations, arrangements and alterations to popular compositions, and to change the title. Such clauses will now constitute waivers of the composer's moral right of integrity in the circumstances to which they apply. One effect of the statutory statement of this moral right, however, may be to induce a scrupulous interpretation of any contract term which operates as a waiver.

13–39 (ii) **Consequential uses: mechanical right.** In the United Kingdom the Mechanical-Copyright Protection Society (MCPS) is the principal body through which licences to record musical works are obtained by record producers, film producers (other than for specially commissioned works), broadcasters and others from composers, lyricists and their publishers. MCPS is owned by the Music Publishers' Association and operates not as assignee of the relevant copyright but as exclusive management agent for the copyright owners. In music industry practice the composer will normally

[100] Other provisions cover: liability to third parties, author's costs of preparation, calculation of direct costs and overheads, cost of corrections, option clauses, remaindering, changes of publisher and imprint, assistance to literary estate, and co-operation in general.

[101] See above, paras 13–27 et seq.

assign copyright to the individual publisher, save for the performing rights, which go to the PRS.

MCPS offers standard terms for membership to composers and to publishers without specifying any minimum level of activity as a precondition. To the Membership Agreement is annexed the Terms and Conditions of Business, which settle the commission charged by MCPS for its services and the basis for collecting and distributing royalties. Whatever becomes due is paid to the publisher, who alone will be responsible for distributing a share to composer and lyricist, in accordance with whatever contractual arrangements exist between them.

It is part of MCPS's role that it will negotiate with groups of users and individuals and it operates three main schemes: one for manufacture and sale of sound recordings, tapes and videos; one for recordings made by broadcasting organisations, suppliers of background music and juke-box contents, etc. (these take the form of blanket licences); and one for other recordings, including synchronisation of music in films. The operation of these schemes is further clarified by codes of practice which accompany the licence terms themselves. Since the CDPA 1988 these schemes are subject to the jurisdiction of the Copyright Tribunal.[102] The same Act abolished the statutory licence for the mechanical right in musical works which imposed a set royalty on the recording company.[103] Control over excessive demands for this copyright has accordingly passed to the Tribunal.[104]

(iii) **Consequential uses: performing and related rights.**[105] The Performing Right Society acts on behalf of its two categories of members—composers and lyricists, publishers—to license the public performance,[106] broadcasting and cabling of music,[107] mainly by establishing tariffs for different categories of use.[108] These are often reached after negotiation with trade associations **13–40**

[102] See below, paras 13–54 et seq.

[103] See CA 1956 s.8; the royalty was 6.25% of the net selling price of records.

[104] For exercise of this jurisdiction, see below, para.13–58.

[105] The conclusion of the *Gowers Review* that collecting societies should adapt better to those who use "creative commons" licences, seems particularly to be directed at performing right societies: see paras 5.63–5.67.

[106] A well-established tradition leaves administration of "grand rights", i.e. the licensing of stage performances and the like of a dramatic-musical work or a ballet, to the authors or their publishers; while the "small rights" in other performances go to the PRS. The grand/small distinction is defined with some precision in the Directives of the PRS: for which, see Cotterell, *Performance* 3rd edn (1993), pp.508–510.

[107] As well as these performing rights, the PRS administers the synchronisation right in works commissioned for the soundtrack of a particular film, in order to secure royalties on cinema performances. There are provisions in its rules for the return of the rights in a work to a member in order to allow the licensing of performances in so-called "compilation shows"; see Cotterell (above, n.106), pp.511–512. The PRS has, however, resisted the not dissimilar demand from the Irish pop-group, U2, to acquire back the right to license performance of its own works in its concerts. This led to a Decision of the Irish Competition Authority criticising the PRS's refusal: Decision No. 326, May 18, 1994.

[108] There are now many standard tariffs.

and other representative bodies of user.[109] The membership rules, which respect the requirement that there must be no discrimination against those who come from or operate in the other EU countries, prescribe minimum levels of activity to qualify for provisional, associate and finally full membership.[110]

13–41 The Society requires the assignment to it of the rights it administers, a practice justified by its not infrequent need to back its system of inspection by litigation against those who refuse to take licences. Its licences are mainly granted to those who operate venues and to broadcasting organisations, rather than to performers or their agents. Information about works performed is gathered by a mixture of methods. In the case of major broadcasting, an accurate schedule is provided; but for many other circumstances (theatres, halls, clubs, cinemas, pubs, restaurants, shops, coaches, etc.) a more or less sophisticated scheme of sampling or indirect indication is used.

13–42 The revenue received (after deduction of administration expenses) is divided principally by reference to a complex points system, which takes account both of characteristics of the work performed (principally its duration) and the nature of the performance (television or sound broadcast, live performance, recorded performance, background or foreground, etc.). As between those who have a share in a particular work, there is a standard division of two-thirds to the composer and one-third to the publisher; or equal shares if there is also a lyric writer. This standard can be varied by the two sides, but never so as to allow the publisher more than half.[111]

While this distribution scheme aims to divide revenue in accordance with the actual use of works, there is a relatively minor departure which provides a measure of social benefit to older members. Those who are 50 years old or more and have completed 25 years of membership qualify for an allowance under the Earnings Equalisation Scheme.

13–43 The technology which has become available for the private copying of sound recordings has made considerable inroads into the sales of recordings of music.[112] Implementation of the Rental, Lending and Related Rights Directive has given the authors (and performers) of works recorded their own rental right. Both acquire an unwaivable right to equitable remuneration from the record producer or subsequent assignee of their rental right, to be assessed if necessary by the Copyright Tribunal. Although no contractual agreement can fix this amount so as to render it incapable of review, the payment may take the form of one lump sum paid at the time of assignment. If such a payment is made, but the rental earnings then turn out to be

---

[109] Subject ultimately to the jurisdiction of the Copyright Tribunal.

[110] For associate and full membership, the main criterion is the earning of a prescribed minimum royalty from the PRS.

[111] The PRS must be notified of the special agreement. The division must be made in twelfths. There are numerous consequential rules: see Cotterell (above, n.106), pp.513–515.

[112] Not least with P2P transfers on the internet: below, paras 20–67—20–68.

unexpectedly large, there ought to be an entitlement to more. The right is, after all, "unwaivable".[113]

(c) *Screenwriting: film, television and video*

Production of audio-visual material in Britain takes place on many levels, from feature films, through television productions, to videograms, documentaries and promotional material. Much of it is produced on an "in-house" basis, in which case, most of the writing and other copyright contributions will be made by employees. The copyright will therefore belong to the employer from the outset unless some other contractual arrangement applies. **13–44**

Production on commission is also important, particularly for television, since both the main broadcasting organisations—the British Broadcasting Corporation and the Independent Television Commission (for the two commercial channels)—are under statutory duties to commission 25 per cent of their broadcasts from independent producers. The effect of this upon the creators of material is that a production starts from a commission contract between the BBC or one of the 15 regional commercial licensees of the ITC and the outside producer.[114] It will be for the producer then to hire the writers and performers. The commissioner, as the main financier of the production, often has the right to approve the producer's selection.

The proprietary basis of the commission is that, once the film is complete and is transferred in return for final payment, all copyright is assigned to the commissioning broadcaster. This necessitates: (1) that the producer has already secured all copyright in contributions, either through the rule on employee's copyright or by assignment; and (2) that all obligations (for example, to pay royalties) which arise under the contributors' contracts are assumed by the broadcaster upon transfer of the film. Since the producer remains contractually liable on the obligations, he must take an appropriate indemnity from the commissioner.

These arrangements have in the past been made within a copyright framework in which the material in the film has been protected for the relevant author's life and 50 years, and the film itself has had a producer's copyright, normally for 50 years from release. In implementation of the Duration Directive, as already explained, much changes. Even for existing films, copyright in the contributions extends to each author's life plus 70 years and introduces the complex machinery for revival of rights. Copyright in the film itself changes, if it is made after July 1, 1994, to a right lasting for 70 years **13–45**

[113] For the meaning of the term, see Reinbothe and von Lewinski , *The EC Directive on Rental and Lending Rights and on Piracy* (1993), p.72. See also above, para.12–28.

[114] On the commercial side, what is commissioned for the ITC network is a matter for negotiation between the licensees, in itself a complex and politically sensitive matter: see Cotterell (above, n.106), pp.539–540; Nelson, *Law of Entertainment and Broadcasting* 2nd edn (2000) Ch.28.

from the last death among the four "associated lives".[115] For films made after June 30, 1994 (subject to exploitation arrangements in a contract made before November 1992), this film copyright will belong initially to the producer and chief director jointly, unless the latter is in employment. So the producer must take the necessary assignment, on such terms as may be bargained. So far as rental rights are concerned (and this affects all the authors and also performers), the guarantee of equitable remuneration will provide one protected floor in the overall negotiations.

13–46 Writers' and other creators' contracts have accordingly to be understood within larger frameworks of direct organisation and commission. The Writers' Guild of Great Britain, which is now the main representative body of screenwriters, has negotiated a range of collective agreements with UK producers of cinema films, television productions and videos. These include:

(1) for commissions from independent production companies: the Writers' Collective Agreement for Films, Television Films and Videograms; the latest version (1992) is between the Writers' Guild and the Producers Alliance for Cinema and Television (PACT). Annexed to it is the Screenwriting Credits Agreement of 1974.
(2) for commissions from the broadcasting producers for television drama: the Writers' Collective Agreements: (a) with the British Broadcasting Corporation[116]; and (b) with the 15 programme companies which have regional licences from the Independent Television Commission (ITC) for the commercial television channels.

13–47 While varying in detail these agreements cover much common ground, and the first of them, the agreement with independent production companies, will be referred to in a little detail here. Its prime object is to give structure to an arrangement by which fees will be payable as work progresses through different stages, while allowing the producer the option to reject the work and terminate the agreement. It therefore allows for a maximum of four stages: the preliminary stage of drawing a story outline; first draft script; second draft script; and principal photography script. For each stage an initial and a delivery fee are payable, which must not be below the minima prescribed. Upon completing payment for a stage, the producer becomes owner of the copyright in the work thus far written, and becomes entitled to have another person develop the writing further—a provision which operates as a waiver of the author's moral right of integrity.

On completion of the film, the rights acquired by the producer vary somewhat with the nature of the film. To take the case of a feature film: if

[115] Chief director, screenplay writer, dialogue writer, composer of commissioned music: see above, para.11–45.

[116] In an allied field, note also the Collective Agreement of 1992 between the BBC and the Writers' Guild, together with the Society of Authors, for the commissioning of original or adapted drama for radio: see Cotterell (above, n.106), pp.476–480.

the budget is over £2 million, the producer will gain all rights except those for free (that is, non-pay) television broadcasting and videograms; if the budget is in the range £750,000–£2 million, the producer has either world theatre rights or two UK network television transmissions, plus in either case strictly limited theatre rights; for budgets below this, the same applies, save that the theatre rights are excluded. Further rights must accordingly be separately acquired and the agreement specifies minimum amounts payable for a considerable range of additional uses.

There are also provisions:

(1) for re-acquiring copyright, for example where the writing is completely original and two years have elapsed without the start of filming; there can be retrieval upon repayment of half the fees received;
(2) for publishing of the script in written form;
(3) for negotiating terms covering merchandising rights.

The Credits Agreement already mentioned deals with one moral right issue at a level of detail which would scarcely be conceivable in legislation on the subject. An author becomes entitled to have his name given as main or a subsidiary writer, following specified verbal formulae. There are also requirements for contributors of source material. Placement and size are prescribed for the film itself. Main writers must also be credited in most advertising and publicity material. There is provision for the negative moral right of non-association; but a writer must request that he should not be named at the outset or within 48 hours of the rough cut of the film being shown.[117] **13–48**

(d) *Visual arts*

In the production of graphic and ceramic works, collective organisation has not yet progressed to the point of general agreements between artists and commissioners or employers. Characteristic of the field is the large number of separate associations in which artists collaborate. These distinguish between the creators of high art and the practitioners of workaday crafts (from the National Artists' Association and the Chartered Society of Designers to the Society of Picture Researchers and Editors); and equally between general and highly specific spheres of work (from the Association of Illustrators and the Association of Photographers to the Institute of Medical Illustrators and the Association of Historical and Fine Art Photographers). **13–49**

Many of these bodies are now able to offer their members support in negotiating individual contracts, at least by suggesting model forms or by

[117] See Cotterell (above, n.106), pp.487–488.

offering advice on particular terms.[118] Thus, they stress not only on the dangers of assigning or granting exclusive licences in general terms (particularly in relation to the future), but also find occasion to advise on difficult issues of privacy, permission to use a subject (particularly a person) and copyright arising from secondary activities affecting artistic works, such as retouching, collaging, incorporation into advertisements, and so on. With the coming of digital libraries of visual art works, the scope for re-use, often after some form of re-working, is hugely enhanced.

13–50 Architectural work, which often takes the form of a professional commission, is likely to follow one of the Standard Forms of Agreement of the Royal Institute of British Architects, though these may always be varied expressly. The 1992 version of the Form for Appointment of an Architect[119] states that copyright in all documents and drawings prepared by the architect remains his or her property. However, the client is licensed to reproduce the design by building on the site or part of the site to which the design relates, provided that the architect has completed the scheme design or provided detailed design and production information and has been paid as agreed. Until a scheme design is complete, the client has no right to proceed without consent; but if the architect's services are limited to making and negotiating a planning application, consent may not unreasonably be withheld.[120]

4. Control of Monopoly

(1) The CDPA 1988

13–51 As already noted, the chance of extracting monopoly profits from copyright in particular works is less likely than from a patented invention. There is no longer any rule allowing for the grant of compulsory licences of copyright in general, equivalent to those for patents,[121] nor for that matter is the Crown permitted to use on special terms. In the early stages of sound recording, it was feared that the mechanical right to record copyright music might be used extravagantly. In the CA 1911, a statutory right was given to others in certain circumstances to make their own recordings of such music upon payment of a set royalty. This was continued in 1956, but has now been

[118] Witness, for instance, British Photographers' Liaison Committee, *The ABC of Photographic Copyright* (1994), which warns against surrendering all economic and moral rights without careful consideration, cf. *Hutchinson v Hook* [1996] F.S.R. 549.

[119] Conditions of Appointment para.1.7.1.

[120] Conditions of Appointment para.2.3. The Form for Appointment of an Architect to Design and Build (para.2.3.2) provides that, even if no scheme design has been completed, consent to use is not to be unreasonably withheld.

[121] But the general provisions for control by reference to the Competition Commission apply to copyright, as they do to patents and to the design rights: CDPA 1988 s.144.

repealed, there being no sufficient case for singling out the recording of music as suitable for "equitable remuneration".[122]

The most considerable danger of monopoly in the copyright sphere comes from the collective administration of rights, because their accumulation carries an ability to cut a user off from access to much of the material that he may wish to exploit. **13–52**

After the Second World War, there was a current of resentment from major copyright users over the terms on which the performing right societies were prepared to do business. On the recommendation of the Gregory Committee,[123] the CA 1956 established a Performing Right Tribunal (PRT), specially charged with power to review the licences and schemes offered by collecting societies in this one field by reference to the criterion of "reasonableness". For this there was already a Canadian precedent; and in turn the lead was followed in other countries, for instance, Australia, the United States, and in some European countries, such as West Germany.

Now that new technology is so rapidly amplifying the ability to copy material, collective administration is spreading also to cover reproduction rights, and in turn this has raised the need for wider public interest controls. Following proposals of the Whitford Committee,[124] the PRT was converted under the CDPA 1988 into the Copyright Tribunal. Contemporaneously with the passage of the Act, the overall justification for the existence of PPL was raised before the Monopolies and Mergers Commission at the behest of local radio stations. The Commission's report, while not uncritical,[125] has recognised the economic necessity of collecting societies in the performing rights field.[126] Nonetheless it considered that PPL's exclusive right over the broadcasting of recordings gave it unjustified market power. In 1990 the right was reduced to the statutory right to remuneration already noted.[127] If a royalty rate cannot be agreed, the broadcaster may pay a self-assessed royalty until the Copyright Tribunal makes an award, which will, if necessary, be back-dated.[128] **13–53**

[122] For the abolition of the statutory licence to record a work bearing musical copyright, see CDPA 1988 Sch.1 para.21. Note, however, the sanction against abuse of rental right in s.66; para.12–43, above.

[123] See above, para.10–09.

[124] Cmnd.6732, 1977, Ch.16.

[125] Report on Collective Licensing (Cm.530, 1988).

[126] Essentially the same judgment informs the Commission's subsequent report (Performing Rights, Cm.3147, 1996) on the workings of the Performing Right Society. But the management structure and attitudes towards membership were the subject of wide-ranging criticism and a considerable measure of remedial action is now in train. Among other things, the PRS failed to justify a claim that it must administer all performing rights of all members.

[127] See above, para.12–48.

[128] CDPA 1988 s.135A, which also prevents PPL from demanding that a broadcaster limit its proportion of "needle time" broadcasts; Dietz (2005) 35 I.I.C. 809.

(2) The Copyright Tribunal[129]

13–54 The Tribunal is composed of a chairman and two deputy chairmen, who will be legally qualified, and between two and eight ordinary members.[130] It sits in panels of three and works according to rules which, more than in the past, encourage the use of written procedures.[131]

13–55 The Tribunal may consider two principal categories of case: licensing schemes and licences. A scheme sets out "the classes of case in which the operator. . .is willing to grant licences" and the terms for doing so. Licences are permissions which fall outside this definition.[132] While a tariff offered by one of the performing right societies to all dance hall proprietors is typically a scheme, being "in the nature of a standing invitation to treat",[133] it is the Government's view that the licence for reprographic copying in schools which the Copyright Licensing Agency now offers to local education authorities is not. The correctness of this assumption may one day fall to be questioned, since it is only in the case of schemes that representative bodies of users have the right to bring a case before the Tribunal.

The Tribunal's jurisdiction does not extend to all copyright licences; it would be contrary to the Berne Convention to place under public control the licences and licensing schemes offered by individual right-owners of literary, dramatic, musical and artistic works and films. Equally it has not been thought necessary to cover publishing, as distinct from copying, these works. Accordingly, in respect of these works, jurisdiction relates to licences and schemes of a licensing body—that is, a society or other organisation with a main object of negotiating or granting licences, including licences covering works of more than one author. In other cases—relating to neighbouring rights and the new rental rights—the licences and schemes do not have to be from a licensing body.[134]

13–56 The Tribunal does not act of its own motion but on a complaint by, or on behalf of, licensees, actual or potential. They may raise objections before they enter a licence, or against the refusal to grant them one, but not afterwards, save in one special case concerning expiry[135]; sanctity of contract is not to be compromised by giving an individual licensee the continuous power to seek a re-writing of his terms. As far as concerns schemes, so long as they are not yet operational, it is for a representative organisation of potential licensees to make the reference.[136] Once the scheme takes effect, the

[129] Freegard and Black, *The Decisions of the UK Performing Right and Copyright Tribunals* (1997).

[130] CDPA 1988 Pt 1 Ch.8. The Lord Chancellor will appoint the legal members, the Secretary of State the others.

[131] Some proceedings of the Copyright Tribunal were criticised as being unduly lengthy.

[132] CDPA 1988 s.117.

[133] *PRS v Workmen's Club Union* [1988] F.S.R. 586.

[134] CDPA 1988 s.116.

[135] See CDPA 1988 s.126 for this case.

[136] CDPA 1988 s.118.

right covers both such an organisation and a person claiming a licence.[137] Once an order has been made, the scheme may be referred again by its operator, a claimant for a licence or a representative organisation.[138] As regards separate licences, it is the person seeking the licence who may refer the case.[139]

In the past there have been cases concerning schemes raised before the Copyright Tribunal by organisations of dance hall proprietors, cinema operators, and bingo-hall enterprises.[140] The second kind of application has been important for broadcasting organisations and there have been references by the BBC, Manx Radio, and the Association of Independent Radio Contractors,[141] and most recently, by online music content providers and mobile phone networks.[142]

The legislation defines one main criterion by which the Tribunal is to decide whether it will confirm or vary a scheme, or vary or impose a licence—reasonableness in the circumstances. But it is obliged to take account of all relevant considerations,[143] and in every case it must have regard to the availability of schemes or the grant of licences to others in similar circumstances, and the terms offered them, exercising its power so as to prevent unreasonable discrimination in the scheme or licences of the organisation in question.[144] In various instances more specific matters are also listed for consideration: in respect of reprography licences,[145] educational taping of broadcasts,[146] conditions imposed by promoters of events,[147] payments in respect of underlying rights,[148] and works included in retransmissions.[149] **13–57**

The actual orders of the Copyright Tribunal show that it often acted in a generally similar manner to a labour arbitrator who is dealing with a conflict about future terms and conditions of employment, rather than about existing legal rights. (Indeed, in so far as the PRS represents authors rather than entrepreneurs, their role is comparable to that of a trade union in negotiating on behalf of the labour force that it represents; the comparison becomes blurred because the Society also represents music publishers.) Thus where the prime issue is a tariff—or in other words what the licensor ought

[137] CDPA 1988 s.119.
[138] CDPA 1988 s.120; but subject to limitations designed to prevent constant harassment.
[139] CDPA 1988 s.125.
[140] See Cases 1/1958, 9/1960, 11 and 12/1962, 13/1963, 21/1966, 23/1971, 27/1973 and 28/1975. On the scope of jurisdiction, see *Reditune v PRS* (PRT Cases, 30–32/1977).
[141] See Cases 17 and 18/1964, 24/1971 and 35/1978.
[142] *British Phonographic Industry Ltd v Mechanical-Copyright Protection Society Ltd* [2008] E.M.L.R. 5.
[143] CDPA 1988 s.135.
[144] CDPA 1988 s.129.
[145] CDPA 1988 s.130; below, para.14–14.
[146] CDPA 1988 s.131.
[147] CDPA 1988 s.132.
[148] CDPA 1988 s.133.
[149] CDPA 1988 s.134.

to be able to demand for its members—the Copyright Tribunal's starting point will be the difference between asking-price and offer. It will then look to see what justifications can be offered for fixing upon one point rather than another between these poles. If there has been a previous agreement, comparisons with this tariff as the "fair price" for its own time will obviously have some relevance. Equally, it may serve a purpose to compare the rates agreed with other categories of user.[150] This, after all, is often as close as the Tribunal can get to a market comparison, and even so there will be no competing sellers.[151]

13–58 A few cases have raised issues of whose interests it is legitimate for a licensor to protect; and these resemble questions about abuse of market power. Thus it was not proper for the PRS to offer film exhibitors licences at discriminatory discounts, depending on whether an exhibitor belonged to one or other trade association; the PRS got nothing in return that could justify this preference.[152] On the other hand, it was proper for PPL to impose some limit on a local radio station's proportion of "needle time" (the amount of records broadcast compared with the amount of live music): the record companies were found to have a legitimate long-term interest in the continued employment of live performers who would act as the source for their future business.[153]

(3) Dominant position in the EU[154]

13–59 The Copyright Tribunal is primarily concerned with the licensing activities of the performing right societies rather than their constitutional arrangements. Yet there are numerous ways in which a society may want to strengthen its economic position through its rules and their effect on members. Take, for instance, the record companies: they have a performing right in their own records, exploited through PPL. They have an interest to see that the authors and publishers do not secure an undue proportion of what users will pay overall for performing rights in recordings of copyright music; and they may want to protect live performers against too high a

[150] Where the circumstances are similar, availability and terms must be taken into account: CDPA 1988 s.129. For a decision that there was no sufficient similarity, see Case 38/1978 (Independent local radio/PPL).

[151] See also *PRS v British Entertainment and Dancing Association* [1993] E.M.L.R. 143; *British Phonographic Industry v MCPS* [1993] E.M.L.R. 86; *Association of Independent Radio Companies v PPL* [1994] R.P.C. 143; *AEI Rediffusion Music v PPL* [1998] R.P.C. 335; *British Sky Broadcasting v PRS* [1998] R.P.C. 467; *British Phonographic Industry Ltd v Mechanical-Copyright Protection Society Ltd* [2008] E.M.L.R. 5.

[152] Case 9/1960. Another case concerned the PRS's insistence that Southern Television pay royalties on emphemeral recordings made in the course of broadcasting despite the explicit exception of this activity from infringement (CA 1956 s.6(7)); see now above, para.12–48; the Tribunal disapproved: Case 2/1958. Cf. the practice mentioned in the Whitford Report paras 389–394.

[153] Case 18/1964; and see also Case 35/1978.

[154] Stamatoudi [1997] E.I.P.R. 289.

proportion of "needle time"—in broadcasting, dance halls or wherever. An authors-and-publishers' society like the PRS may, therefore, be significantly affected if record companies can become members of it, for instance by setting up a publishing operation. Not surprisingly, therefore, such societies tend to take counteractive steps at least to limit the rights of record company members.[155]

The European Commission, which can intervene only within the terms of its competition rules, investigated the organisational structure of the West German collecting society, GEMA,[156] and found a number of its restrictive rules and practices to constitute an abuse of its dominant position, contrary to art.102 of the TFEU (ex-86 of the Rome Treaty, ex-82 TEC).[157] The basic objectives of joint collecting societies were accepted to be legitimate—and in a later case, the ECJ has agreed.[158] It is proper for individual members (composers, associated authors and publishers) to protect their interests against major music users (such as broadcasting organisations and record companies) by assigning rights to a joint association. But nevertheless anticompetitive arrangements must not be made if they are beyond what is required "for the association to carry out its activity on the necessary scale". **13–60**

In particular, three aspects of GEMA's rules were criticised: **13–61**

(1) Rules which followed from the arrangement amongst national collecting societies that each would have only its own nationals as members were disapproved.[159] It is true that these rules limited members' ability to express dissatisfaction with their national society by joining the society of another Member State and taking whatever advantages it offered its members: the effect of such a transfer of allegiance would be to make the national society a mere collecting agency on its own territory for the foreign society which the author had joined. The Commission's decision amounts to an insistence that members should not be deprived of this measure of ultimate independence. In reality habit makes them unlikely to take advantage of such a power.[160]

---

155 Thus the PRS has rules restricting the number of directors from "user-owned" publishers and foreign publishers. For the German society, GEMA, see below, para.13–61.

156 *Re Gema (No. 1)* [1971] C.M.L.R. D35. At the same time other national collecting societies within the then EEC were investigated, but no decisions were issued. In the US, similar collecting societies have had their activities circumscribed by anti-trust proceedings.

157 For art.82 in general, see above, para.1–53.

158 *Belgische Radio v SABAM* [1974] E.C.R. 51; [1974] 2 C.M.L.R. 238. However, imposing obligations on members which are not necessary may abuse the dominant position. Note also *Greenwich Film v SACEM* [1980] 1 C.M.L.R. 629; *BEMIM v EC Commission* [1976] E.M.L.R. 97.

159 See [1971] C.M.L.R. D35 at D47; and see *Gesellschaft für Verwertung von Leistungsschutzrechten* [1983] 3 C.M.L.R. 695. The international arrangements concerning performing rights are mentioned above, in para.12–31, n.154.

160 Rules making it difficult for publishers with foreign connections to become ordinary members were criticised as tending to hinder the formation of a Community-wide market: [1971] C.M.L.R. D35 at D47–48.

(2) Since GEMA acted as licensor not only of performing rights, but also (among other things) of the mechanical right to record music, it required a transfer of exclusive rights of all aspects of copyright, at home and abroad. It accordingly had a strong interest in preventing individual authors from being drawn out of membership and into direct relationship with a user such as a record company. This objective it pursued by a variety of measures: requiring a long period for notice of withdrawal, taking the right to future works even after resignation, paying loyalty bonuses and paying out of its social fund only to members of 20 years' standing. The Commission insisted that the rules should not oblige members to assign rights for territories in which it did not act directly; nor should it take over all aspects of copyright in the territories in which it did operate.[161] Likewise it ought to be possible to resign at the end of any year—a demand which the Commission was later to soften to three years in return for further concessions on the range of rights transferable to the society.[162]

(3) GEMA had prevented record companies from acquiring influence by excluding them from membership as publishers.[163] This the Commission also objected to, while recognising that it would be proper to restrict the voting rights of such members when they had a conflict of interests (for example over the licence rate for the mechanical right to record musical compositions).[164]

A number of GEMA's commercial practices were also characterised as abusive: for example, the tariff on the mechanical right was found to discriminate in favour of German-produced records, and that on recording equipment in favour of German manufacturers[165]; and it was improper for the mechanical right fee in effect to require payments for works not under the society's control.[166]

13–62 The types of investigations that are conducted, on the one hand by the Copyright Tribunal, and on the other by the EU Commission follow from the different powers with which they are invested. The case for the UK approach is that an organised arbitral body, independent of governmental influence, provides a satisfactory means of controlling a monopoly that is in other respects efficient from the point of view of both owners and users.[167] On the other hand the likelihood that many licensing negotiations will lead to a reference or application to the Tribunal has been criticised: the extra time and expense that are used up is said to distort the ability of the licensing

161 [1971] C.M.L.R. D35 at D48–50.
162 [1971] C.M.L.R. D35 at D50; *Re Gema (No. 2)* [1972] C.M.L.R. D115.
163 cf. the rules of the PRS on the matter, mentioned above, para.10–49.
164 [1971] C.M.L.R. D35 at D51–52; and see the later negative clearance [1982] 2 C.M.L.R. 482.
165 For this special levy on equipment, see below, para.14–20.
166 [1971] C.M.L.R. D35 at D53–55.
167 Wallace (1973) 4 I.I.C. 280; see also Joliet [1973] Europarecht 17; de Freitas (1987) 34 J. Copyright Soc USA 148; Deringer and Mestmäcker [1985] Int. Bus.L. 65, 71.

societies to react to inflation, causing them to press cases earlier and harder than would probably be the case if voluntary bargaining were the sole route to settlement. The stand taken by the European Commission has shown collecting societies that the manner in which they organise their activities is not above scrutiny in the public interest.[168] In a field where conflicts of interest are complex and the stakes are considerable, this makes a great deal of political sense.

[168] Later cases have investigated, inter alia, the range of rights for which charges are separately made (*Basset v SACEM* [1997] E.C.R. 1747); royalty rates in comparison with those of other national societies—but only where this can be done objectively (*SACEM v Lucazeau* [1989] E.C.R. 2811); a refusal to licence only part of a society's repertoire (*Ministère Public v Tournier*, ibid.); remuneration models for tv broadcasts which include music (*Kanal 5 Ltd v STIM* [2009] 5 C.M.L.R. 18); and membership and territorial clauses in reciprocal representation agreements (*CISAC Agreement* [2009] 4 C.M.L.R. 12). See also 2005/737/EC Commission Recommendation on collective cross-border management of copyright and related rights for legitimate online music services L 276/54.

CHAPTER 14

COPYRIGHT: PARTICULAR CASES

More than other types of intellectual property, copyright has burgeoned into separate varieties, related but distinct. The preceding chapters have emphasised the principles that identify the species as a whole. It is important to start with these common characteristics. For one thing they focus attention on why copyright is so often the form adopted when new circumstances call for protection: a right against copying appears proof against unduly wide monopoly and it makes others accountable where the claim is most evidently justifiable. However, the point has been reached at which we must turn to the many differences of detail in the various copyrights. **14–01**

This chapter takes up a number of subjects where the impact of copyright has been significant and controversial. Section 1 deals with the role of copyright in the politically sensitive area of the news media. Then we turn to the technological advances of the late twentieth century which continue to affect the dissemination of information, culture and entertainment: visual and aural reprography (Section 2); and the diffusion of broadcasts by wire and by satellite (Section 3). Sections 4–6 concern claims to specific forms of right: by performers; by writers and others against public lending; by visual artists for a share in resale prices. Finally, in Section 7, the special position of Crown and parliamentary copyright is treated. The limited role of copyright in the protection of industrial design is discussed in the next chapter. But the largest reservation is of topics to do with digitisation: computer programs, databases, multimedia productions and the internet. Their impact on traditional forms of IPR—not just copyright in its broad sense, but patents and other technology protection, as well as rights over names and other identifiers—continues to be profoundly unsettling. The whole subject is therefore taken up in Ch.20.

1. The Media and the Public Interest in News

14–02 Producing the news of the day generates many tensions. Between rivals in the media there is constant pressure to stay in the van, and if at all possible to get ahead with a scoop—whether it is the first story or the most captivating photograph. Tit-for-tat spoiling is a pastime in some sectors of the British press which sometimes ends in litigation. A journalist may meet all sorts of difficulties in extracting information, which will cost time and money to overcome. Obligations of confidence may hinder him even when he has acquired it. We have already seen that the judges have fashioned a defence of public interest which may limit rights in confidential information.[1] By the side of this, the action to protect personal privacy involves balancing the human right to private life against that in freedom of expression. The same issues may be raised in answer to copyright claims, but their ambit is narrower.

(1) Copyright in news

14–03 There will be no copyright in news until there is a work or other subject matter capable of protection; and then only to the extent that the particular type of copyright may be infringed.[2] The first revelation of a news story may involve the copying of private documents or pictures.[3] Once a story is turned into a literary work or illustrated by a photograph or other artistic work there may be infringement in the form of reproduction in another paper or inclusion in a broadcast. This is equally so, where the literary work is the script of a news broadcast and the copyist works from the legitimate broadcast. But if a broadcast is verbatim and there is no initial work, the copyright in the broadcast may be of no help.[4] For this special copyright probably does not cover any literary or pictorial reproduction of its content

[1] See above, paras 8–15—8–19.

[2] The Brussels version of the Berne Convention (art.9(3)) allowed member countries to create exceptions from copyright for the "news of the day"; but the current Paris version does not go so far: cf. art.2*bis*(1) (political and forensic speeches), art.10(1) (fair quotation), art.10*bis* (public interest copying of media works; reporting of current events). Nor does UK law.

[3] As for example the confidential notes of a political conversation in *Ashdown v Telegraph Group*, below, para.14–05; cf. the wrongful taking of *separate* photographs in *Douglas v Hello!*, above, para.9–19.

[4] The broadcast copyright covers filming, re-broadcasting and certain types of public performance: see above, Table, pp.442 to 444, head 7.

as such[5]; and even the right to prevent re-broadcasting may well not extend to the case where the material is taken down and a different newsreader broadcasts it afresh.[6] In these cases, the broadcast copyright is clearly infringed only if the copyist has been using a recording of the original.

In the *INS* case,[7] the Supreme Court of the United States was moved to provide a remedy against the systematic and damaging misappropriation of news by one agency from the newspapers supplied by a rival. At that time the formal requirements of American copyright law made it impracticable to seek copyright protection. In any Berne Convention state, copyright arises upon the creation of a literary or artistic work and is enforceable without formalities: its potency is accordingly the greater and the need to qualify it in the public interest is the more pressing.

In England, *Walter v Steinkopff*[8] illustrates the basic approach. The *St. James' Gazette* copied a number of extracts from *The Times* almost word for word, including some two-fifths of an article by Rudyard Kipling. This was held to infringe *The Times'* copyright in its pieces. It made no difference that *The Times* had itself borrowed some of the information, that the *St. James' Gazette* was not a direct competitor (since it gave the news only later), that the source was acknowledged or that the editor of *The Times* did not at once object. North J. sought to dispel any implication that copyright might confer exclusive rights in the news itself by stressing the dichotomy between unprotectable idea and protectable expression. In other contexts, the courts have shown some willingness to treat the taking of detailed information as infringement, even when the actual expression of the ideas has been worked out afresh.[9] Given the general interest in making news available through channels on which the public relies, it may well be that copyright in news is confined to substantial reproduction of the actual language used to write it up or the actual content of a broadcast.

It is of course a sphere in which digital communication is breaking up former modes of delivery. The monolithic presentations of newspapers and broadcasting channels are being challenged by interlinkings of information on specific subjects which users may select for themselves and pursue to a depth that suits them by consulting networked files of data. How far this goes will depend, among other things, on the impregnability of electronic controls over access.[10]

---

[5] The CA 1956 clearly excluded such forms of infringement; but the CDPA 1988 refers to "copying a work" (including a broadcast), without offering further definition, save that "reproduction in a material form" is not a form of copying that apparently applies to a broadcast: see above, para.12–26.

[6] The new Act does not deal with the point specifically, nor did the old.

[7] See above, para.1–15.

[8] [1892] 3 Ch. 489.

[9] See esp. *Elanco v Mandops* [1980] R.P.C. 213; see above, para.12–11.

[10] See below, paras 20–65—20–75 et seq.

(2) Fair dealing and recorded speech

14–04 The two forms of fair dealing that are germane to the news media[11] are: (1) use of any work for purposes of criticism or review of it or another work or a performance of either[12]; and (2) use of any work other than a photograph for the purpose of reporting current events.[13] The exception for "on-the-spot" photographs reflects their peculiar value in scoops by the press.[14]

A court must consider all the circumstances of the "dealing" in the light of the purpose for which alone it is permitted.[15] The proportion of the work that has been copied is one starting point. No question of fair dealing arises unless there has been "substantial taking"; but even when this point is passed, questions of quantity may well be less significant than quality. There may be occasions upon which it is proper to take the whole work.[16]

Equally the precise manner in which the work is used for criticism, review or reporting current events will be important. Both expressions are of wide and indefinite scope, to be interpreted liberally[17]; but:

> "the nearer that any particular derivative use of copyright material comes to the boundaries, unplotted though they are, the less likely it is to make good the fair dealing defence".[18]

In *Pro Sieben Media v Carlton*,[19] Carlton TV broadcast an exposé of "cheque-book journalism", illustrated by the furore whipped up over Mandy Allwood's pregnancy of eight embryos and the exclusive publicity organised for her, showing her determination to avoid abortion. For this clips were taken from one such interview, in which the broadcasting copyright was held by the German claimant. The Court of Appeal was prepared to apply the principle that permissible criticism could extend to ideas in a work and its social or moral implications so extensively that it could cover disapproval of a general media practice, of which the material was merely one illustration. Whether the criticisms were fair depended primarily on

[11] The broadcasting media may also benefit from the exception concerning incidental inclusion: CDPA 1988 s.68; above, para.12–48.

[12] CDPA 1988 s.30(1); "sufficient acknowledgment" (see s.78) is a prerequisite: above, para.12–41.

[13] CDPA 1988 s.30(2). Again there must be "sufficient acknowledgment" save in a sound recording, film or broadcast: see Berne Convention art.10*bis*.

[14] CDPA 1988 s.30(2); cf. CA 1956 s.4.

[15] As far as criticism or review is concerned, this may relate to the content, as distinct from the style, of a literary (or other) work; as for current events, they may not be a pretext for reporting something else: see *Commonwealth of Australia v Fairfax* (1980) 147 C.L.R. 39.

[16] *Hubbard v Vosper* [1972] 2 Q.B. 84 at 98 CA; *Beloff v Pressdram* [1973] 1 All E.R. 241 at 263; *Pro Sieben v Carlton UK TV* [1999] E.M.L.R. 109 CA; *Fraser-Woodward v BBC* [2005] F.S.R. 36.

[17] See *Time Warner Entertainment v Channel Four TV* [1994] E.M.L.R. 1 CA. (Extracts from *A Clockwork Orange* used to point up criticism of decision not to release the film in Britain.)

[18] Walker L.J., *Pro Sieben* case, above, n.16.

[19] *Pro Sieben Media v Carlton* [1999] E.M.L.R. 109 CA.

their objective impact, not on the motivations of those who made them. They did not have to present a balanced view of the source from which they were derived. In this case, fair dealing was held to have been made out.

Nevertheless, courts will remain astute to prevent dressing unfair competition up as criticism or review.[20] A photograph cannot be taken in order to illustrate a news story simply by labelling it "review".[21] The contents of an interview with an ethnic poet cannot be taken in order to fill out a biography of her.[22] Following the limitations imposed by the InfoSoc Directive, the defence of fair dealing for criticism or review has been made available only where the material taken has been made public with the copyright owner's authority.[23] That is one illustration of undesirable rigidity in Directive's approach. At least the Directive does not in terms eliminate the "public interest" defence in copyright under s.171(3), which developed primarily to cover cases where a legitimate need to know outweighs the necessity for preserving privacy or confidence.[24] That section still forms part of the CDPA 1988. **14–05**

Before implementation of the Directive, in *Ashdown v Telegraph Group*,[25] the Court of Appeal expressed the clear view that public interest may be taken into account where the action arises in copyright, as well as for breach of confidence. The fact that actual expression is being taken, rather than just the information in the private material, comes into the assessment but only as a factor in the balance. But what may amount to a "public interest" in publishing is not to be confined to limited situations. In *Yelland v Hyde Park Residences*,[26] Aldous L.J. had stated that, once copyright comes into play, only in the clearest cases of "iniquity" could a defendant justify taking the actual expression. The *Ashdown* court refused to accept this narrow position.

It could be argued that the InfoSoc Directive does not allow for a public interest defence. That would be most unfortunate. It would distort the balance set by arts 8 and 10 of the European Human Rights Convention.[27] As those articles have been interpreted by English courts to date, the balance between privacy and freedom of expression can only be reached if account is taken of all relevant circumstances. The recent case law on confidence and

---

[20] Henry L.J. *Time Warner* case, above, n.17.

[21] *Banier v News Group* [1997] F.S.R. 812. Photographs are excluded from the current affairs defence: above, n.14.

[22] *Hager v ECW Press* (1998) 85 C.P.R. (3d) 289 FC Can.

[23] Previously, the private nature of the material was only a factor which might weigh against the dealing being fair.

[24] See above, paras 12–57—12–59; and generally para.8–44.

[25] *Ashdown v Telegraph Group* [2002] Ch. 149; and see above, para.12–38; Sims [2006] E.I.P.R. 335.

[26] *Yelland v Hyde Park Residences* [2000] R.P.C. 604 CA. The judgment was built upon a very limited reading of *Lion Laboratories v Evans* [1985] Q.B. 526. In *Ashdown*, the court preferred the view of Mance L.J. in *Yelland*, which did not seek to confine *Lion Laboratories* to a special view of its facts.

[27] A basis for recognising the defence in UK law could be found in art.5(3)(o) of the InfoSoc Directive, dealing with minor exceptions.

privacy has adopted the view that celebrities must expect to have their own biographical "spin" unravelled by press exposures. In the process the media may use documents and photographs which give force to the revelations, since the courts are reluctant to act as censors. The extent to which such conduct is justifiable should not be affected by the fact that the person attacked has ownership of copyright in those pieces of evidence. At least where the issue arises before publication, and an interim injunction is sought, then the conditions set by the Human Rights Act s.12 should apply. The InfoSoc Directive does not purport to limit the operation and scope of remedies under national law.

14–06 In assessing fair dealing, economic considerations will include the amount of damage that the defendant may inflict on the claimant, and the extent to which the defendant will get for nothing something which in usual business practice he would expect to have to pay for. It was not infringement for a small satellite broadcaster to include in its sports bulletins short clips (14–37 seconds in length) showing highlights of World Cup soccer games, which were taken from the BBC broadcasts of complete matches. Audiences were not thereby diverted—a very significant element in the assessment.[28] It should also be remembered that the question arises only if there has been both copying and substantial taking. The criteria tend to overlap. In relation to neighbouring right of a publisher in typographical format the House of Lords held that an enterprise was entitled to run a regular clippings service from newspapers for its employees, since there was no substantial taking from each edition of a paper treated as a whole.[29]

14–07 The express acknowledgment in the CDPA 1988 that a speaker may acquire copyright from the recording of his statement, if the result is an original work,[30] has an immediate importance to both the written and the broadcast media, since they make wide use of interviews. The media have an exception in addition to the general fair dealing provisions. Section 58 of the CDPA 1988, provides for two distinct cases: a record of spoken words that is made for reporting current events may be used for doing so; and a record made for broadcasting may be used for that purpose. It must be a direct record, which is not an infringement of any other copyright; the use must not be prohibited by the speaker; and it must be a use permitted by the possessor of the record (not a leak). In any case, most of those who make public speeches (especially politicians) must be taken to be courting the media and so impliedly to be licensing journalistic use of the material.[31]

Particular circumstances may well import further legal considerations. If a celebrity gives someone an interview about his private life (not a current

[28] *British Broadcasting Corporation v British Satellite Broadcasting* [1992] Ch. 141.

[29] *Newspaper Licensing Agency v Marks & Spencer* [2001] [2003] 1 A.C. 551 HL; and see *Television NZ v Newsmonitor* (1993) 27 I.P.R. 441; Sinclair [1997] E.I.P.R. 188.

[30] See above, para.11–34.

[31] Laddie et al., para.2.190.

event), which is recorded verbatim, the speaker becomes the owner of the copyright.[32] He or she may therefore have a moral right to object to derogatory treatment by alteration or omission, though this will not normally extend to press publication. In this latter case, he might object by demonstrating breach of the moral right against false attribution.[33]

(3) Organisation and journalist

Since most of the material supplied to newspapers and news programmes comes from employed journalists and reporters, their copyright relationship to their employer is important. Previously newspaper journalists presumptively enjoyed a special division of the copyright, which went to the employer only for press use. It was the one instance in UK law of statutory intervention, in authors' interests, to ensure that investors acquired (at least presumptively) only that part of copyright which related to the purpose of the transaction. Under severe pressure from media interests, this special case has disappeared in the CDPA 1988. The entire copyright in the work of all employed journalists now resides initially in their employers, unless they can show a contract to the contrary.[34] **14–08**

Where the material is submitted by a freelance writer or artist, the terms of any express assignment or licence of the copyright will govern. If there are none sufficient to meet the case, there will be an implied licence to publish in accordance with usual practice.[35] This would not include a licence to use the material in a new medium, such as the internet, if no custom of conferring such an entitlement can be shown to have existed at the time.[36]

Where the employer has the copyright, the employee will not enjoy the moral right to be identified.[37] Indeed, so great was the proprietors' fear of the need to name contributors that this moral right does not arise over any publication in a newspaper, magazine or similar periodical, even where the material comes from a non-employed person.[38] It does, however, apply to broadcasts, to the extent that the exception for fair dealing in reporting current events does not operate.[39] Doubtless waivers will be extracted in many cases. The moral right to object to derogatory treatment may not be claimed by an employed journalist, or by anyone else who is published in a newspaper, magazine or periodical, if the work was prepared for such a **14–09**

[32] Whether the interviewer has a recorder's copyright is a separate issue, which may turn on the recording means employed, together with editing and similar skills: *Express Newspapers v News* (UK) [1990] F.S.R. 359.

[33] See above, paras 12–84—12–85; *Moore v News of the World* [1972] 1 All E.R. 441.

[34] CA 1956 s.4(2); cf. CDPA 1988 s.11; see above, para.13–05.

[35] *Joseph v National Magazine* [1959] Ch. 14.

[36] cf. *Tasini v New York Times*, 533 U.S. (2001) SC; Radcliffe [2001] E.I.P.R. 172.

[37] CDPA 1988 s.79(3).

[38] CDPA 1988 s.79(6).

[39] CDPA 1988 s.79(4). There must in any case be an "assertion".

purpose.[40] These exemptions of the media do not apply in countries with a stronger tradition of moral rights and do not deserve a place in UK law.

Where the material being used consists of a photograph or film, it may not be sufficient to secure the licence of the copyright owner. If the work was commissioned for private and domestic purposes, then the commissioner enjoys the special right of privacy given by s.85, and may, inter alia, object to inclusion of the material in a newspaper, or broadcast.[41]

2. Reprography and Recording: Educational and Private Copying[42]

14–10 At the beginning of this century, the techniques for copying (except by hand or typewriter) were still limited to laborious and technical procedures like printing. Even photography of the printed page or picture required the subsequent intervention of a person able to develop negatives and make prints. The vast improvement of reprographic techniques for producing copies of material written and drawn has been matched by a startling advance in simple means for recording musical and dramatic performances—in sound alone or in audio-visual form. The analogue techniques of the 1950s–1980s have since been converted by digital electronics which are both immensely efficient and easy to use. In this section, we are concerned with the copyright problems which arose up to the 1990s when the internet began its transformative spread. To the latter we turn in Ch.20.

From the 1970s, the upsurge in commercial piracy of books, recordings, films, computer games and other programs directly undermined the economic interests of the producers. It required much more intensive policing of activities which for the most part constitute direct and incontrovertible imitation. Sometimes, also, as where the entire get-up and trade-marking is also counterfeited, it is a source of ready deception to consumers. In the counter-attack in Britain, the courts made a distinct contribution, as in the development of the *Anton Piller* and allied orders; and so equally have administrative officers, as where trading standards authorities have taken action under the Trade Descriptions Act 1968. The problem was, of course, worldwide, and in many countries the enforcement machinery was dogged by inefficiency, hostility and corruption. From this came a strong motive force for TRIPS and for various other pressures towards policing the international flow of pirate products.

14–11 At the same time, the new technologies bred photocopiers, dual cassette recorders, video-cassette recorders and the like for home use. Where individuals make single copies for their private use the balance of conflicting

[40] CDPA 1988 s.81(4).
[41] See above, paras 12–86—12–87.
[42] See Christie in Vaver and Bently Ch.17.

interests between copyright owners and users is much more even. Each act, at least if viewed in isolation, is only a slight threat to the copyright owner's economic concerns; and the educational or personal value of being free to copy in this way is not to be discounted as insignificant. This section is accordingly concerned primarily with the phenomenon of private copying and home taping; and with the solutions which the Government saw fit to offer in the CDPA 1988. In this, it did not adopt the same broad stance of many other European laws: no general right of personal autonomy dictated that all private copying should be excepted from copyright liability. Instead it maintained more specific exceptions, most notably for research and private study (if there was fair dealing), and for non-profit libraries which helped in those worthy activities. Home taping for pleasure was not exempt; but since it went unpoliced copyright law simply looked foolish and occasional pockets of people felt uncomfortable about it.

(1) Visual copies of literary and other material[43]

(a) *Fair dealing and other exceptions*

The world's early copyright systems naturally concentrated their fire upon the multiplication of pirated copies. In most, including the British, little attention was given to the question whether making a single copy counted as an infringement, or whether, on the contrary, a private use was an exploitation of knowledge and ideas which ought to be left free for all. In 1911, when the "fair dealing" exceptions were first spelled out in statutory terms, "private study" and "research" were included in the list of permitted purposes[44] without the problem having surfaced in previously reported litigation. Nor was there much consideration of the matter afterwards. It was held, not surprisingly, that a publisher could not justify an infringing book by saying that readers would use it for private study.[45] But otherwise the courts were not asked to say how much could be taken; nor what purposes constituted private study or research[46]; nor whether multiple copying could ever be justified under this head. **14–12**

The CA 1956 left "fair dealing for purposes of research or private study" as an exception and added provisions concerning educational instruction and examination, the making of anthologies and, above all, copying in non-profit libraries.[47] There were a number of indications within these legislative exceptions that the notion of fair dealing in this context was restricted to the

[43] See generally Kolle (1975) 6 I.I.C. 382; Kerever [1976] Copyright 188; Ricketson (1982) 10 Aust.B.L.R. 31; Nevins [1985] 7 E.I.P.R. 222.

[44] CA 1911 s.2(1)(i).

[45] *University of London Press v University Tutorial Press* [1916] 2 Ch. 601; *Sillitoe v McGraw-Hill* [1983] F.S.R. 545.

[46] Consider, for instance, copies for the professional information of businessmen or government servants.

[47] CA 1956 ss.6(1), 6(6), 7, 9(1), 41.

taking of single copies by or for individuals and did not extend to multiple copying for (say) members of a class or choir.[48] The libraries exception, moreover, indicated that copying of a single article from a periodical was permissible, but that copying of substantial extracts from books required permission of the copyright owner where that could reasonably be obtained.[49]

(b) *The reprography problem*

14–13 For a long period, publishers in the United Kingdom contemplated possible solutions to the mounting tide of photocopying without arriving at any clear policy. The prospect of finding a technical device which would prevent machines from being used to reproduce copyright work mostly looked unpromising, and in any case would have led to an undesirable embargo on something which large numbers of readers wished to do. The field was not one in which Government was likely to be persuaded that a levy on copying machines or the paper used in them should be introduced: for one thing much photocopying involves no copyright infringement.[50]

The Whitford Committee treated the question extensively and with considerable sympathy for the difficulties faced by authors and publishers, taking the view that the scholar had no better claim to the free provision of copies of intellectual material than he did to free pens and paper.[51] The Committee's solution was to propose the introduction of appropriate blanket licensing arrangements through collecting societies of right-owners. The Government would supervise the establishment and organisation of these societies, using by way of sanction the withdrawal of reprographic copyright for any sector which failed to act. Where proper licensing arrangements were in place, the fair dealing exception for research or private study would no longer avail, so that the licence would be needed for single as well as multiple copying of copyright material in all institutions, organisations, offices and even private homes. This, however, proved too aggressive a disturbance of the existing compromise to be politically acceptable.[52]

14–14 During the 1980s, publishers began to press more vigorously for licensing arrangements. Music publishers launched proceedings against a school and a local authority for substantial photocopying of scores which otherwise they would have had to purchase.[53] Book publishers proceeded against a university for multiple copying and began looking for a solution through a collecting society. It succeeded first with local education authorities and then with universities. Now it also has schemes in operation with Government

[48] Especially CA 1956 s.41.
[49] CA 1956 s.7.
[50] Such a levy exists, however, in, e.g. Germany and Spain.
[51] Cmnd.6732, 1977, Ch.4.
[52] The libraries and educational organisations offered strong resistance to the idea.
[53] The effects of photocopying have been particularly hard on the publishers of sheet music.

departments and local authority sectors and is securing co-operation from industry and the professions.[54]

The CDPA 1988 has a range of provisions designed to encourage evolution of controls over reprography with only background legislation.[55] Fair dealing for purposes of research or private study continues to be a defence and it is specified that someone other than the scholar or researcher may copy on his behalf.[56] The Act makes clear that "systematic single copying" (for instance all the members of a class requesting the same material at once) is not within the exception.[57] No more specific guidance is given on what measure of single copying is "fair" than under the previous Act.[58] **14–15**

After substantial debate in 1988, the Government agreed that those in commerce and industry who undertake research or private study could not be excluded, partly because of the difficulty of determining what was "commercial".[59] The InfoSoc Directive, however, does not approach this defence along tracks which distinguish between single and multiple copying. In Continental style it permits an exception to the reproduction rights for all copying that is "private and for ends that are neither directly nor indirectly commercial". At the same time it provides that rightholders must receive fair compensation.[60] That can be done, for example, by imposing a charge on recording equipment and media such as tapes which produces revenue for distribution among copyright interests on the basis of a sampling of use. The Directive does deal with education in one respect by allowing an exception to reproduction and communication rights for illustration for teaching or scientific research "with acknowledgment of source and to the extent justified by the non-commercial purpose to be achieved."[61] The United Kingdom has implemented these requirements simply by providing that research can be exempted only where it is for a non-commercial purpose.[62] No steps have been taken to introduce a levy that would provide fair compensation; that has to come only from collecting society enforcement relating to multiple copying, which continues to fall outside the exception. It is unlikely that the European Commission will challenge this solution. Its justification for requiring harmonisation of national copyright laws is that otherwise there is distortion between markets within the EU. In truth (as the

[54] See Owen, *Clark's Publishing Agreements* 7th edn (2007) App.E.
[55] See Laddie et al., paras 25, 10–28.
[56] CDPA 1988 s.29.
[57] CDPA 1988 s.29(3)(b); applied to the library exceptions by s.40.
[58] See above, paras 12–38—12–41.
[59] cf. the disagreement over the legitimacy of Government copying in *Williams & Wilkins v US*, 487 Fed. 2d. 1345 (1973).
[60] InfoSoc Directive art.5(2)(b). In calculating the compensation, account has to be taken of the extent to which access to digitised material has successfully been controlled by technical means. See the following pending references on art.5(2)(6): C387/09 *EGEDA v Magnatrading* OJ C312 of 19.12.2009 p.18; and C467/08 *SGAE v Padanan* OJ C19 of 24.01.2009 p.12.
[61] InfoSoc Directive art.5(3)(a).
[62] Private study can be undertaken, no matter what its purpose.

Commission used to acknowledge) there is very little inter-state trade which flows from the use of photocopiers in study and research.

The Copyright Licensing Agency (CLA), which is a joint venture between British authors and British publishers, has, rather belatedly, built up a considerable business in licensing reprography rights. As part of its activities, the Agency has reached arrangements with local education authorities, universities and colleges and other user institutions which could claim the partial protection of s.29. Licences on a block basis and for single instances are thus being granted by a collecting society and therefore fall under the supervision of the Copyright Tribunal. When the Association of University Vice-Chancellors challenged CLA's demands for increased rates under their standard agreements, the proposed annual amount *per* student was lowered and the scheme for casebooks (CLARCS) was heavily criticised by the Tribunal.[63]

Alongside the fair dealing exception for individual students and researchers, there are separate provisions concerning copying by the librarians of prescribed (that is, non-profit-making) libraries. Provided the library is supplying an individual for non-commercial research or private study at cost and in accordance with regulations, it may copy up to one article in an issue of a periodical and a reasonable extract from any other publication. In the latter case it is no longer necessary to seek permission of the copyright owner if that is reasonably obtainable.[64] These "library" arrangements are now essentially by way of supplement to the fair dealing provision, since any librarian or other person may also rely upon the fair dealing defence, when supplying a researcher or student.

14–16 So far as concerns reprography, copyright is much more likely to be infringed by multiple copying (including colourable disguises for it). Only for purposes of examination are schools and other prescribed "educational establishments"[65] entitled to copy by means of a reprographic process.[66] But in order to encourage the organisation of general licences, the Act says this: until they become available, these institutions are permitted to copy very small amounts of literary, dramatic and musical works and typographical arrangements for purposes of instruction—1 per cent *per* quarter of the year.[67] The licences have to allow at least as much copying as this. Moreover their terms are subject to the jurisdiction of the Copyright Tribunal, which is

[63] *Universities UK v Copyright Licensing Agency* [2002] R.P.C. 693.

[64] CDPA 1988 ss.38–40. See also s.41 (one library supplying, another); s.42 (replacements); and s.43 (copying by librarians and archivists of unpublished works); note also s.44 (copy necessary before export of an article of cultural or historical importance).

[65] The category may be expanded beyond schools by Ministerial order: CDPA 1988 s.174.

[66] CDPA 1988 s.32(3)—even then there is an exception in respect of musical works, because of the widespread sale of examination pieces: s.32(4).

[67] CDPA 1988 s.36; the Gowers Report (2006) has recommended modest extensions, to cover the position of distance learning in particular: see paras 4.13–4.19. These recommendations have made their way into the second stage consultation on copyright exceptions: *Taking Forward the Gowers Review of Intellectual Property* (2009) paras 92–126.

specifically directed, in all cases dealing with reprography, to have regard to: (1) the availability of the published edition; (2) the proportion being copied; and (3) the nature of the use.[68] It is not clear how far weight will be given to evidence that (say) students are unlikely to buy a book if they cannot have a photocopy of some section of it, but it is surely a highly relevant factor.

There are three other provisions which aim to assist the creation of licensing arrangements. First, reprography schemes and other licences are subject to a statutory implied indemnity by the licensor covering infringement of any work which the licence purports to cover in its "blanket" but which is in fact not within the licensor's authority to grant.[69] Secondly, in relation to instruction in educational establishments, the Secretary of State has power to order the extension of a licence or scheme to cover works which are similar and are unreasonably excluded.[70] Thirdly, also in respect of such instruction, the Secretary of State may establish an inquiry to decide whether a scheme or general licence should be established for a category of literary, dramatic, musical or artistic work not currently covered.[71] If the recommendation favours such a step, but it is not organised by right-owners within a year, a royalty free licence takes effect.[72]

(c) *Rights for publishers*

In the 1950s the publishers saw the approaching revolution in reprography and successfully lobbied for a distinct "publishers' right" to be included in the CA 1956—the copyright in typographical arrangement of a published edition of a literary, dramatic or musical work.[73] While in this first form, much was left unsaid about the scope of protection, the version to be found in the CDPA 1988 is a considerable improvement. The right is given to the publishers for 25 years from publication of any edition of a literary, dramatic, or musical work, which is not merely a re-publication.[74] It is infringed by making a facsimile copy of the typographical arrangement, but the test of substantial taking is applied in relation to the publication as a whole, rather than items within it.[75] The work that has been published does not itself have to be in copyright; indeed the particular value of the right is in relation to new editions of old works, where the publisher nonetheless has a setting cost **14–17**

[68] CDPA 1988 s.130; and see above, paras 13–54—13–58.
[69] CDPA 1988 s.136.
[70] CDPA 1988 s.137; it is necessary to find that adding the works would not conflict with normal exploitation and would not unreasonably prejudice legitimate interests. For variation, discharge and appeal, see ss.138, 139.
[71] CDPA 1988 s.140; again subject to the condition concerning normal exploitation and unreasonable prejudice.
[72] CDPA 1988 s.141.
[73] CA 1956 s.15.
[74] CDPA 1988 s.8. Artistic works are still not included, for reasons that remain obscure. Electronic publishing is probably included.
[75] *Newspaper Licensing Agency v Marks & Spencer* [2003] 1 A.C. 551 HL.

to retrieve.[76] Where there is fair dealing for purposes of research or private study, this special copyright is not infringed: and that is likewise so in respect of the acts of copying permitted by librarians.[77]

14–18 The Duration Directive requires the establishment of a publication right in works first published after copyright has expired.[78] While it is a right reserved for that special circumstance, it is broader than the British right in the format of a publication, in that it protects the work whatever its form, and not merely the particular setting in which a publisher sets it. This is an important shift of emphasis at a juncture when works are becoming reproducible with endless variations of appearance, once they are put into digital form.

Publisher's right is an entitlement separate from copyright.[79] It is given to non-nationals only on a basis of strict reciprocity, and no moral rights are added to its economic protection. Nonetheless, the rules for copyright concerning rights, permitted acts, remedies, review of licences and copy-protection circumvention for the most part apply also to this new right. The new right deals with a somewhat obscure facet of publishing. Unlike some of the pro-copyright initiatives of the Commission after 1990, it should be regarded as essentially benign. In the main it will foster the publication of historical scholarship, which might otherwise be prey to simple, under-cutting imitation.

(2) Audio and video copying

14–19 Audio, video and now dvd recorders have enjoyed a vogue as standard equipment for the home, at least in developed countries. What modest proportion of them have any idea how frequently they are infringing copyright by their copying? The legal position under the CDPA 1988 in the United Kingdom is that copying of most copyright material remains an act of primary infringement, even where it takes place in the home.

Very little home taping could be justified as fair dealing for research or private study, for that exception does not apply to sound recording or film copyright.[80] Some home taping of sound has undoubtedly deprived recording manufacturers of sales that they would otherwise have made, but it is very difficult to determine how much. The claims of the manufacturers

---

[76] Once the CDPA 1988 abandoned the indeterminate term which applied to many works before their posthumous publication, this became more important.

[77] CDPA 1988 ss.29(1), 38(1), 39(1), 41(1), 42(1).

[78] Article 4; above, para.11–31; cf. art.5, which is only permissive in form, and allows a 30-year maximum right in "critical and scientific publications of works". Presumably this may include not only original text versions of literature, music and art, but even school editions with notes.

[79] The treatment is similar to that of rights in performances and design right.

[80] See CDPA 1988 s.29(1).

and the counterclaims of blank tape manufacturers have shown stark differences of opinion.[81] The same is true of the recording of broadcasts. Rental and sale of videos, which provide substantial slices of the returns on many films. How much of their revenue is lost through home taping at present can only be guessed.

Unlike the position with audio material, until recently the technology available to the domestic user for copying audio-visual material was largely restricted to recording of broadcasts. Moreover, much of this copying involved "time-shifting" for viewing at a more convenient moment, the copier sometimes wiping the tape by recording something else. The CDPA 1988 s.70 contains a special exemption from copyright liability for a time-shifting recording of a broadcast which is private and domestic. This extends to works included in the broadcast as well as the right in the broadcast itself.[82]

Owners of copyright in audio and video material have striven to secure an actual return by a sales royalty or levy on recording equipment or tapes or both. In Britain there have been long debates about introducing such a royalty-cum-levy. In the years before the CDPA 1988, it was the copyright issue on which the British Government swung with every wind. But in the end they feared that voters would too readily see the levy as a tax for the benefit of a single interest group. Britain, therefore, has not followed Germany, Austria, France, the Iberian countries and most Scandinavian countries.[83] As with reprography, that remains the position in the United Kingdom at present, despite the provision in the InfoSoc Directive which makes any private use exception to the reproduction right subject to the provision of fair compensation to right-holders.[84] **14–20**

Unlike the case of photocopying, it can be argued that levies only in some Member States may affect the price of recording equipment and so lead to distortions in trade. Yet no EU Directive has directly required the institution of national levies on similar terms. The InfoSoc Directive does require fair compensation to right-owners only in countries which have a private use exception, and UK law has no exception couched in such broad terms. A levy therefore seems unlikely in the future. In any case, as we shall explore in Ch.20, internet opportunity is a far greater issue today for audio recordings and is fast becoming so for video, written and multi-media material. The age

[81] For the debates, see Davies, *Private Copying of Sound and Audio-Visual Recordings* (1984); Home Taping Rights Campaign Office, *The Case for Home Taping* (1987). See generally, Davies and Hung, *Music and Video Private Copying* (1993); Davies, *Copyright and the Public Interest* 2nd edn (2003).

[82] This would seem justifiable under the Berne Convention (Paris Act) art.9(2); Ricketson and Ginsburg paras 13.03–93, pp.479–489. It is not "private or domestic use" for an internet café to provide customers with a service for downloading infringing material to its servers and then make a CD of it: *Sony Music Entertainment v Easyinternetcafe* [2003] F.S.R. 48.

[83] cf. the Government's pro-levy stand in White Paper (Cmnd.9712, 1986) Ch.6. A majority of the present EU states have some levy.

[84] Article 5(2)(b).

of the copyright compensation levy is passing rapidly, at least in its old form.[85] The concept, however, remains significant to the copyright industries since it establishes the principle that where copyright cannot be directly enforced, the state is justified in imposing a charge on the purpose of hardware by way of surrogate, so as to provide some compensation in support of the property right. The next piece of hardware in the sights of the industries is, of course, the computer and, doubtless, other digitised machinery, such as mobile phones and mp3 players. That gives an underlying impetus for campaigns still to oblige the United Kingdom to fall in line on levies over cassette and CD recorders and their tapes and disks. Even so, the future relevance of levies cannot be ranked high. *The Gowers Review of Intellectual Property* (2006) has refused to propose it.[86]

14–21 On a separate front, right-owners have attempted to persuade courts that those who supply recording equipment are authorising or inciting infringement. In the *"Betamax"* case, a majority of the United States Supreme Court refused to find private recording from television, largely for "time-shifting", to be anything other than "fair use" (according to American doctrine).[87] In England, in *CBS Songs v Amstrad*, the House of Lords refused to find infringement or other wrong in marketing a twin-deck tape recorder, for all that it would in most cases be used for taping copyright music and sound recordings without licence.[88] United Kingdom law now provides an explicit defence for time-shifting of broadcasts, and the *CBS* case continues to determine that producing analogue machines such as the recorder there in issue does not make the producer liable for decisions by their future owners to infringe copyright. Any inducement to do so is too remote.

14–22 With these avenues closed, right-owners in the United Kingdom had to rest content with two provisions. The first was the introduction in 1988 of the rental right as part of the copyright.[89] It is a right against the business activity of making copies available for a payment in money (or money's

[85] On how levies may work in the new digital environment see Netanel (2003–2004) 17 Harv. J.L. & Tech. 1; Fisher, *Promises to Keep* (2004); and Dusollier and Ker in in Derclaye, *Research Handbook on the Future of EU Copyright* (2009), Ch.14.

[86] Paras 4.72–4.76. The *Gowers Review* proposed a limited private copying exception allowing for changes in the recording format. This it considers to be an exception justifiable under the InfoSoc Directive Rec.35. However, this proposal has fallen by the wayside: see *Taking Forward the Gowers Review of Intellectual Property* (2009).

[87] *Sony v Universal City Studios*, 104 US 774 (1984); Ladd (1983) J.Copyright Soc USA 421; Leete (1986) 23 Am.Bus.L.J. 551.

[88] *CBS Songs v Amstrad* [1988] R.P.C. 567. A licence was mostly necessary as a matter of law, because there is no exception for all private use in UK law. See above, para.12–20. Cf. the position of a library which supplies a photocopying machine for use by readers: *Moorhouse v University of NSW* (1975) 133 C.L.R. 1; [1976] R.P.C. 151 HC Aust.

[89] CDPA 1988 s.18(2) proviso. Originally, the rental right applied only to computer programs, sound recordings and films, but it was extended to all relevant works by virtue of the Rental, Lending and Related Rights Directive.

worth) on terms that the copies will be returned.[90] Schemes and general licences granted by right-holders over rental are subject to the jurisdiction of the Copyright Tribunal.[91] Moreover, while authors and performers are presumed to assign their rights to producers, they thereby become entitled to equitable remuneration from rental revenues, which at present form a substantial proportion of earnings of many films.

The second provision is aimed, in an era of highly efficient copying equipment, to support the incorporation of spoiler devices and digital code which will prevent the making of unauthorised copies, not least in the home. Once such techniques are adopted the problem set by the almost inevitable appearance of anti-spoiler devices and similar means. In 1988, s.296 introduced a new right to a person who issued copies of copyright works to the public with built-in "copy-protection". This was subsequently revised after implementation of the InfoSoc Directive on October 31, 2003. Under the pre-Directive version, a person was entitled to proceed against anyone who "knowingly" made, imported or marketed equipment designed to circumvent the copy-protection.[92] A civil right of action arose, which could lead to an injunction, monetary relief, delivery up and direct seizure, as with copyright piracy. But it was not necessary for the right-owner to show that his own works were likely to be copied on the defendants' machines. **14–23**

In this respect, the protection was wide.[93] It was less embracing in requiring that, for there to be "knowledge", the alleged wrongdoer must have dealt with the device or means, "knowing or having reason to believe that it will be used to make infringing copies". Nothing, in other words, was to be presumed from the fact that the thing was likely to be used in this way. This was particularly important in relation to computers, since they mostly have multiple uses and if the section were otherwise there could have been long argument over how likely infringing use would be. Thanks to the InfoSoc Directive, the original form of s.296 was amended and is now restricted to computer programs.[94] It is broader than the old s.296 in that it covers technical devices which prevent any act of infringement, not just that of unlawful copying. As well, the persons with standing to sue include the person issuing to the public copies of the computer program; the copyright owner of the computer program or his exclusive licensee; and the owner or exclusive licensee of any intellectual property right in the technical device applied to the computer program. The language is also now closer to

[90] CDPA 1988 s.179 "rental"; but the concept is extended to all lending of this material by public libraries: see above, para.12–28.

[91] See above, paras 13–54—13–58. For the extension to public lending institutions of the same liability regarding other copyright works than books, see below, para.14–44.

[92] It also extended to those who published information intended to aid or assist such circumvention.

[93] For a discussion see Aplin, *Copyright Law in the Digital Society* (2005), 225-229.

[94] Other copyright works are governed by new ss.296A et seq: see below, paras 20–76 et seq.

art.7(1)(c) of the Computer Programs Directive.[95] We return to the question of "circumvention means" in our general discussion of digitisation.[96]

3. Cable and Satellite Transmission[97]

14–24 Broadcasting by Hertzian wave opened the first great opportunity of relaying performances to truly mass audiences. The resultant copyright issues were resolved over time. First, as with public performance, broadcasting was treated as an act of infringement; and broadcasters had therefore to seek copyright licences. Secondly, in 1956, the act of broadcasting itself attracted copyright—those who relayed or re-transmitted the broadcast then needed a licence, unless they could claim some special exemption. The use of wire to distribute broadcasts from a receiving antenna or to transmit other programmes was by then sufficiently advanced for cablecasting to be made a restricted act for literary, dramatic and musical works. A European Television Agreement of 1960, sponsored by the Council of Europe, aimed to prevent a person from receiving a broadcast from another state in order then to diffuse it by cable. To this the British became parties, but subject to significant reservations.[98] A separate right in cable-casts that were not mere relays had to wait until 1984, when the technical possibilities of co-axial cable heralded a communication revolution in the United Kingdom as in other countries.[99]

14–25 Satellite transmissions now perform an increasing range of functions. In part they concern broadcasting activities. Fixed satellite service (FSS) systems operate by securing that the transmission is received from the satellite by a station and the programme is then distributed through a cable system. Direct broadcasting by satellite (DBS) systems operate to individual receivers, such as dishes, without the intervention of earth station and cable. With the development of encryption techniques, an operator can limit direct reception so that it is available only to those who have the requisite decoding receiver. Other elements discriminating between recipients can be added, such as language and advertising. At the same time, the distinction between FSS and DBS has been blurred by the possibility of receiving the same broadcast directly or through a station. Mixed systems of this kind were licensed in the United Kingdom from 1985 onwards and are the basis of the pay-TV services, now operating in Britain and elsewhere in Europe.

Cable and satellite have between them opening many communications

---

[95] Which refers now to "sole intended purpose" of facilitating the unauthorised removal or circumvention of the technical device: for a discussion see *Kabushiki Kaisha Sony Computer Entertainment v Ball* [2004] E.C.D.R. 33.

[96] See below, paras 20–76 et seq.

[97] See Makeen, *Copyright in a Global Information Society* (2000) Chs 4 and 5.

[98] Some but not all of these were withdrawn after the CDPA 1988.

[99] Cable and Broadcasting Act 1984 s.57, Sch.5 paras 6, 7. See above, para.11–27.

prospects apart from broadcasting and cable-casting, such as relaying a meeting, speech or performance to limited numbers of people in a different place or places; transmitting the content of documents so as to produce facsimiles at the point of reception; telephoning through mobile networks and satellite, and providing access to the global information prospects of the internet.

In determining how far these activities should be the subject of copyright, the 1988 legislation proceeds by reference to general precepts. The distinction between reproduction and performance rights is observed. Thus "faxing" involves copying upon reception, and a special provision makes it secondary infringement to transmit a work by telecommunication system, where the person doing so knows or has reason to believe that such a copy will result.[100] Broadcasting (including cable-casting), however, is an act of performance which accordingly requires dissemination to sufficient numbers before they are covered. Hence the definition of "broadcast", which requires a transmission by electronic means (cable or wireless) capable of being lawfully received by members of the public simultaneously. Accordingly, it includes a transmission in encrypted form,[101] but not the provision of an interactive service, for instance on the internet, which is simply available to the public on demand. **14–26**

Beyond this, there are a number of crucial provisions determining the basis on which right-owners can assert economic interests. Thus "broadcaster" is defined (so as to affect both rights and liabilities) to cover those who share responsibility for programme content, but to exclude carriers who merely provide some part of the transmission service (such as satellite access).[102] As a result of the Satellite and Cable Directive broadcasting occurs at the stage of the "up-leg" to the satellite, rather than the subsequent "down-leg" for reception—and this is so whether the primary arrangement is for FSS or DBS transmission.[103] At least for the EU, the up-leg country is that where the signals originate, rather than the country with the transmission station to the satellite.[104] Thus, if the programme is sent for

---

[100] CDPA 1988 s.24(2).

[101] CDPA 1988 s.6(1), (2) (as amended as part of compliance with the InfoSoc Directive art.3). Note the provisions designed to reinforce the position of those who supply an encrypted service: s.297 makes it a summary offence fraudulently to receive such a programme included in a broadcasting service provided from a place in the UK (on the meaning of this see *Murphy v Media Protection Services* [2008] 1 W.L.R. 1869); and s.298 gives civil remedies against a person who makes or provides equipment for fraudulent reception: see above, para.14–23. See also the provisions implementing the Conditional Access Directive which prohibit commercially dealing in unauthorised decoders: ss.297A et seq. and the ECJ reference on the scope of these provisions in *Football Association PL v QC Leisure* [2008] C.M.L.R. 12.

[102] CDPA 1988 s.6(3).

[103] CDPA 1988 s.6(4). This accepts a solution which makes for commercial convenience, and is now required by the Satellite and Cable Directive Ch.I: see above, para.10–19. The Directive has been held to apply to digital satellite television as well: Cases 431/09, 432/09 *N.V. Airfield v SABAB, AGICOA* OJ C24 30.01.2010 p.24.

[104] CDPA 1988 s.6(4).

transmission from the United Kingdom, copyright licences are needed there and should be rewarded at a rate which takes account of audiences wherever they are being reached.

This puts paid to a strongly pro-copyright "theory" that a broadcast requires authorisation not only for its transmission but also for its reception. If adopted in the European context, where much broadcasting crosses borders, it would have meant that an author or his successors could have demanded a royalty in all the countries of reception. In consequence a swarm of collecting societies for the various authorial, performer and entrepreneurial interests could have descended upon Europe, each with its own policies for collection and payment over. The up-leg solution gives clarity through desirable limits on claims. It has accordingly been proposed for global broadcasting and the licensing needed by internet sites. But while within Europe it can be assumed that each "up-leg" country will guarantee similar rights in its copyright law, internationally there are undoubtedly countries with far lower standards, or indeed, none at all. Hence for satellite broadcasting, it is already provided that in such cases, the up-leg shall be treated as instead being in the country of actual transmission, if that is in the EU; otherwise it can be an EU country, if that is where a person commissioning the broadcasting is established.[105]

14–27 The right of a copyright owner to a return in respect of the immediate retransmission of a broadcast by cable[106] within the United Kingdom is limited. In particular, diffusion service licensees in Britain do not need a separate licence of either copyright in the broadcast or in works, recordings or films transmitted, because of their statutory responsibility to carry all BBC and ITC programmes[107]; nor do those who provide cable services in the area intended for reception of the broadcast (where the object of cabling will normally be to overcome some reception difficulty).[108] In these cases, the right-owner of material broadcast must expect his return through the royalty paid by the broadcaster, subject only to an ultimate provision concerning enhanced damages for any infringement in both the broadcast and the cable re-transmission.[109]

14–28 Within the EU, broadcasting and cabling have largely remained matters of national policy. But at a relatively early stage one Community issue presented itself somewhat peremptorily. In some Member States cable

[105] CDPA 1988 s.6A. These arrangements come from the Satellite and Cable Directive Ch.I, which prescribes in Ch.II the minimum rights which the foreign system must provide.

[106] On the complexities of cable retransmission see Makeen (2010) J. Copyright Soc USA, p.56.

[107] CDPA 1988 s.72(2), (3).

[108] CDPA 1988 s.72(2), (3); but this applies only if the transmission is not by satellite and is not encrypted.

[109] See CDPA 1988 s.73(3) proviso. Right-owners have argued that this limitation is inconsistent with the Berne Convention art.11*bis*(1), which distinguishes acts of radio-diffusion and acts of communicating radio-diffusion of a work to the public, "whether over wires or not". This position has considerable strength, given the specific language of the text, but the UK Government has not agreed.

networks were building up rapidly and were being used not just for the transmission of original cable-casts and the better reception of national broadcasts but also for the re-transmission of broadcasts from other Member States.

In *Ciné Vog v Coditel (No. 1)*,[110] a national German channel transmitted the French film, *Le Boucher*. A Belgian company received it and re-transmitted it via cable to subscribers in Brussels and West Belgium. The film was licensed for broadcasting in Germany but not yet in Belgium, in accordance with standard distribution arrangements designed first to exploit the cinema market for the film. The cabling, being unlicensed, was an infringement of Belgian copyright law, but the company argued that the initial broadcast in Germany exhausted any right in the material throughout the EU; the Rome Treaty's policy of free provision of services within the EU demanded that there could be no right over such further treatment of the material as re-cabling.[111]

The Court of Justice refused to interpret the Treaty in this way, holding **14–29** instead that restrictive distribution arrangements for films were in principle a justifiable method of maximising the economic potential of the copyright. Licences tended to be on a national basis for the practical reason that broadcasting was for the most part organised nationally. What had to be examined was whether the particular restrictions in the network of distribution agreements constituted an offensive practice under art.85 of the Rome Treaty (now art.101 TFEU).[112]

This litigious history made the question of cross-frontier rights one of the factors in a wider range of broadcasting issues between Member States. The Commission accordingly intervened, first with a contentious Green Paper, *Television without Frontiers*,[113] arguing for policies which would in various ways reduce impediments to interstate broadcasting in the EU. On the acquisition of rights, it recommended that broadcasters should be able, if necessary, to obtain a statutory licence from all right-owners, including authors. This was fiercely criticised, the case being countered, in particular, by the claim that licences were already, negotiated satisfactorily through the voluntary machinery of collecting societies, or else could be. Other aspects of broadcasting, including the requirement of a minimum EU content which so exercised the French against the Americans in the last stages of the WTO

---

[110] *Ciné Vog v Coditel (No. 1)* [1980] E.C.R. 881.

[111] The thrust of the argument was that these services should be treated in the same way as goods bearing copyright material, once they were legitimately marketed in a Community country: for which see below, paras 19–04 et seq. See now the TFEU.

[112] In a second *Coditel* case ([1982] E.C.R. 3381) the court held that limited-term agreements for exclusive cinema exhibition were justifiable and did not infringe art.85(1) (now art.101 TFEU), but that other exclusive agreements for the distribution of films required to be examined to see whether their terms were artificial and unjustifiable, were for unfairly high fees or created distortions of competition within the Common Market by their geographical limitations.

[113] COM(84) 300 final.

negotiations, had to be dealt with in advance of issues about rights. But in the end they too were settled.

4. Rights in Performances[114]

14–30 Performers engage in activities which are more immediately artistic and creative than those of entrepreneurs who enjoy copyrights in sound recordings, films, and broadcasts. The greatest and the most charismatic interpreters of drama, film scripts and music attract great followings and may therefore secure more for their services than the authors they serve. Yet in the United Kingdom there was for a long period considerable reluctance to give performers an equivalent property right, and the negative campaign was largely sustained by objections from these very entrepreneurs.[115] It was claimed that performers are protected indirectly by the entrepreneurial rights, that those financially responsible are best placed to pursue imitators, and that to give copyright to all performers in a play, a film or an orchestra would lead to quite unnecessary complexity.[116] Besides, actors and musicians tend to form powerful unions; investors and authors alike therefore resisted additions to performers' armoury.

However, some right to stop the unauthorised appropriation of performances has long been needed to cover "bootlegging", that is, the covert recording of performances, which may well not be of copyright works or at least of works written by the performers; and which equally will not infringe the legitimate recording company's rights, since no copy is taken of its contemporaneous recording of the performance. This was originally achieved through the Performers Protection Acts,[117] which carefully restricted the available sanctions to criminal penalties and conferred no civil rights of action by their explicit terms.

Although the United Kingdom was a prominent proponent of the Rome Convention for the Protection of Performers, Producers of Phonograms and Broadcasting Organisations (1961), it made sure that the right guaranteed to performers in contracting states went only to the "possibility of preventing" a list of acts, and gave no "right to authorise and prohibit", as it did for sound recordings and broadcasts.[118] Thus the approach through the criminal law could continue. Eventually the courts intervened. A civil action for breach of the duties defined in the Performers Protection Acts was accorded

[114] See Arnold, *Performers' Rights* 4th edn (2008); Morgan, *International Protection of Performers' Rights* (2002); for an economic perspective, Towse (1999) 52 Kyklos 369.
[115] But it can be heard sometimes from executives of authors' collecting societies who are imbued with tunnel vision.
[116] So the Gregory Committee were persuaded: Cmd.8662, 1952, Pt 7.
[117] Initially the Musical Performers' Protection Act 1925; subsequently the Performers Protection Acts 1958–1972.
[118] cf. Rome Convention, art.7 with arts 10, 13.

to performers, though not to the recording companies with which they had exclusive contracts.[119]

Over the last three decades, the bootlegging of performances by pop stars and others has grown considerably to the great perturbation of the music industry. The Whitford Committee was convinced that performers should enjoy a civil right of action to injunction and damages. It considered that this should not amount to copyright, even though it did not indicate with any certainty what differences there should be.[120] Loyally following this recommendation, the CDPA 1988 initially created two separate rights in performances: one for performers, which was a personal, non-assignable, right[121]; and one for their exclusive recording contractors, which could be transferred by contractual assignment.[122] This created a limited range of rights, in effect giving performers no entitlement of their own, distinct from that of their recording company, except in relation to bootlegging. **14–31**

(1) The current law

The original CDPA 1988 converted rights in performances into a form of neighbouring right to copyright. Even so it has since changed substantially. The Rental, Lending and Related Rights Directive has required that performers be given transferable property rights on a more general scale;[123] the Duration Directive has added to the period of the rights;[124] while the InfoSoc Directive has expanded the rights given in relation to fixations of performances[125] and the WIPO Performances and Phonograms Treaty 1996 has mandated that performers receive moral rights protection.[126] The law is now to be found in the CDPA 1988 Pt II—as it has since been amended by the Duration of Copyright and Rights in Performances Regulations 1995,[127] the Copyright and Related Rights Regulations 1996,[128] the Copyright and Related Rights Regulations[129] and the Performances (Moral Rights) Regulations.[130] **14–32**

The result is an almost impenetrable amalgam of provisions, in large measure because the Directives required changes to the 1988 position only in

[119] Initially, the Court of Appeal enthusiastically granted *Anton Piller* orders against bootleggers (*Island Records v Corkindale* [1978] F.S.R. 505); but subsequent doubts (notably the House of Lords in *Lonrho v Shell* [1982] A.C. 173) left a trail of uncertainty until *Rickless v United Artists* [1987] F.S.R. 362 CA. Cf. *RCA v Pollard* [1983] Ch. 135 CA.

[120] Cmnd.6732, 1977, para.412.

[121] See generally, CDPA 1988 ss.181–184, 192.

[122] CDPA 1988 ss.185–188, 192.

[123] Directive, Ch.II; and see the Satellite and Cable Directive art.4(1), which applies these requirements to satellite broadcasting.

[124] Article 3(1). The TRIPS Agreement also extended the term of protection: see art.14(5).

[125] InfoSoc Directive art.2 (reproduction) and art.3 (making available to the public).

[126] Article 5.

[127] SI 1995/3297.

[128] SI 1996/2967.

[129] SI 2003/2498.

[130] SI 2006/0018.

certain respects and the UK Statutory Instruments could not take the further steps needed for a full rationalisation. That would require primary legislation. Some of the performers' rights are characterised as "proprietary", and so fully transferable, while others are "non-proprietary". The performer is not able to assign "non-proprietary rights" inter vivos, though they may be licensed and transmitted on death.[131] Differences from copyright may lead performers to make claims that they are co-authors of the songs they do. They will succeed only where they make a significant contribution to the "creation" of the song, an activity in the world of pop music that may be difficult to pin down.[132]

14–33 As a consequence, performers now have rights in four main categories:

(1) *Rights in copies*. Performers have four basic *property* rights, giving exclusive rights to: reproduction, distribution, rental and lending and making available.[133] These rights apply to a performance which is legitimately recorded but then improperly copied, and equally to copies of a recording which has been made without authority by an interloper, such as a bootlegger. These rights are equivalent to those given to literary and other authors in relation to tangible copies of their works (in contrast with the various performing rights).

As applies equally to authors, performers who transfer their rental rights to the producer of a sound recording or a film have a guaranteed right to equitable remuneration for the rental.[134] The right to remuneration is, however, qualified in character, since it may only be assigned by the performer to a collecting society which will act on the performer's behalf.[135] Here at least, it is clear that the law's intervention is paternalist, since the right to equitable remuneration cannot be abrogated by contract. Given that, in much of the EU, rental rights were a novelty, there was a strong case for bolstering the performer's entitlement to a share in the earnings which are secured by this special protection.[136]

(2) *"Non-proprietary" rights against bootlegging*. Alongside this new core of protection, the "non-property" rights introduced in 1988 in relation to bootlegging survive. These are rights given to performers: (a) in the initial fixation and the live broadcasting of performances

[131] Meanwhile, exclusive recording contractors continue to enjoy their own rights against bootlegging, mentioned in the previous paragraph.

[132] *Barrett v Universal-Island Records* [2006] E.M.L.R. 21; Barron (2006) 15 Leg & Soc St. 101.

[133] CDPA 1988 ss.182A, 182B, 182C, 182D; 191A; s.191G.

[134] CDPA s.191G. Nonetheless, the UK Act characterises this as a "property right". In truth it is neither one thing nor the other.

[135] CDPA 1988 s.191G(2). It is, however, a right which may be transmitted by testamentary disposition or operation of law; and once this occurs, a successor in title may treat it as a full right of property, ss.182, 192A.

[136] But the case was stronger for performances which were already recorded than for future performances, undertaken when the rental right was known about.

without the performer's consent; (b) in the public performance and broadcasting of a recording made without consent; and (c) in dealings in illicit recordings.[137] It was over these activities that record and other producers had no neighbouring right of their own since the sound recording right applies only to copies of their own recordings. Yet they had a real need for protection. They accordingly have their own set of rights covering the same illicit activities.[138] Since they may by contract assign their interest, it is "quasi-proprietary".

(3) Remuneration right in public uses. Where a commercially published sound recording of a performance is played in public or broadcast to the public, the performer is entitled to equitable remuneration from the owner of the copyright in the sound recording.[139] This is the special compromise in relation to performing rights for performers which the copyright producers and major users in the EU have been prepared or obliged to concede.

(4) Moral rights.[140] There is now the right to be identified where qualifying performances are given in public or broadcast live, or where a sound recording of a qualifying performance is communicated to the public or copies are issued to the public.[141] The right also extends to performers who are identified collectively as a "group". Performers must assert their right to be identified.[142] Exceptions to the right include where it is not reasonably practicable to identify the performer (or where identification of the group is permitted instead); and where the performance is given for the purpose of reporting current events or for advertising goods or services.[143] A right to object to derogatory treatment arises where a qualifying performance has been broadcast live or is played in public or communicated to the public via a sound recording with any distortion, mutilation or other modification that is prejudicial to the reputation of the performer,[144] unless the performance is given for the purpose of reporting current

[137] CDPA 1988 s.182. Since, even in 1988, "recording" was defined to include making a copy of an existing recording (s.108(2)), there was already a "reproduction right" at that stage: see *Bassey v Icon Entertainment* [1995] E.M.L.R. 596. This "non-property" right must now be regarded as merged in the new "property right"; but what a muddle!

[138] CDPA 1988 ss.185–188, 192.

[139] CDPA 1988 s.182D. For freedom of Member States to determine criteria for assessing the remuneration: *Stichting ter Exploitatie v Nederlanse Omroep Stichting* [2003] E.M.L.R. 364 ECJ.

[140] Simon [2006] E.I.P.R. 552; [2006] E.I.P.R. 600.

[141] CDPA 1988 s.205C.

[142] CDPA 1988 s.205D. The UK Government decided to perpetuate the unnecessary formality of assertion to ensure that performers were not in a better position than authors.

[143] CDPA 1988 s.205E. There are other minor exceptions to do with news reporting, incidental inclusion, things done for examination purposes and for parliamentary or judicial proceedings, Royal Commissions and statutory inquiries.

[144] CDPA 1988 s.205F. It applies also where a sound recording of a derogatorily treated performance is sold or distributed with knowledge: s.205H.

events or the modification is consistent with normal editorial practice.[145] These moral rights are not assignable, but may be transmitted on death and last for as long as the performers' economic rights.[146] Consent and waiver provisions mean that performers' moral rights can be severely undermined (as is the case with authors).[147]

14–34 In addition to these four "primary" categories of right, there are certain forms of "secondary infringement". As in copyright, secondary infringements require it to be shown that the wrongdoer knew or had reason to believe that he or she was dealing with an illicit recording.[148] The acts of dealing which may amount to secondary infringement are: showing or playing the performance in public; communicating it to the public; importing a recording or a copy (save for private and domestic use); selling, hiring, distributing or dealing in certain other ways with copies.[149]

14–35 From the introduction of performers' rights by the CDPA 1988 onwards, the entitlements have applied equally to pre-existing, as well as subsequent, performances, though subject to the limitation that no prior acts by others can amount to infringements.[150] This has led to an elaborate set of transitional provisions, particularly concerning duration (mentioned below).[151]

(2) Other characteristics

14–36 Now that in Britain performers' rights have inched so close to copyright, they are the subject of parallel conditions. A number of these may be noted:

(1) "Performance". The rights are given in dramatic performances (including dance and mime), musical performance, reading or recitation of a literary work and performance of a variety act or any similar presentation. Other activities which might be called performances, notably those of sportsmen, do not qualify for protection.[152] Some would argue that no such distinction should be drawn.[153] There

[145] CDPA 1988 s.205G. Note the exception in also s.205G(4) to do with broadcasting standards.
[146] CDPA 1988 s.205L, s.205M and s.205I.
[147] CDPA 1988 s.205J.
[148] Under ss.180(2) and 197, "illicit recording" covers recordings made without the performer's consent and includes the copying of an earlier recording, whether or not that recording was authorised.
[149] CDPA 1988 ss.183, 184.
[150] CDPA 1988 s.180(3). The same principle is applied to the further expansions of rights by the 1995, 1996 and 2003 Regulations implementing the Directives and the 2006 Regulations implementing art.5 WPPT.
[151] The searcher for UK legislation needs to know that, while Regulations implementing EU Directives make changes to the substantive provisions of the CDPA 1988 which appear in subsequent printing of the Act, transitional provisions are to be found only in the Regulations themselves.
[152] CDPA 1988 s.180(2).
[153] See, e.g. Arnold, *Performers' Rights* 4th edn (2008) para.2–19. He regards the distinction as pure snobbery.

is however no persistent lobby claiming that sports presentations cannot be adequately "commodified" under present contractual and associated arrangements.

The performance has to be a live one, although, as we have already seen, performers' rights may relate both to authorised and to unauthorised recordings of the performance. In other words, what is not protected is the use of a recorded performance in the course of another live performance.[154] The definition inevitably recognises that a single live performance may be given by more than one individual; but it seems that each individual performer gains a separate right and each must therefore assent to the use of the performance by any other person including the other performers.[155] It is the giving of the performance which brings the right into existence. No formalities of registration, deposit or notice have to be complied with.

(2) *Qualifying Performances.* A performance qualifies for protection if it is either given by a qualifying individual (a citizen, subject or resident of a qualifying country) or takes place in a qualifying country, namely EU Member States and countries party to the Rome Convention, the TRIPS Agreement and bilateral arrangements, which are designated by a specific order.[156]

(3) *Duration.* The effect of the Duration Directive on performance rights in Britain has been to extend them from a period of 50 years from the performance to a period of 50 years from the end of the calendar year in which the performance takes place, unless a recording of the performance is released during that period, in which case the rights expires 50 years from the end of the calendar year in which the recording is released.[157] In addition, the principle of the shorter term is applied in relation to performers from qualifying countries which nevertheless have a shorter term of protection.[158]

As with the further term for authors' rights, the addition to performers' rights in existing performances (i.e. those given before January 1, 1996) has required elaborate transitional provisions.[159] These likewise distinguish between extended rights (those still under

[154] CDPA 1988 s.180(2).

[155] There is no conceptual equivalent of joint authorship in copyright law.

[156] CDPA 1988 ss.206(1), 208(1). There are further definitions of what constitutes British performances and what amounts to British territory. For the TRIPS requirements concerning performers, see art.14.

[157] CDPA 1988 s.191. "Release" occurs when, with authority, the performance is first published, played or show in public broadcast.

[158] CDPA 1988 s.191(4), (5). For the impact of the principle of non-discrimination (art.18 TFEU, ex art.12 TEC), see below, para.19–01.

[159] The rights extend to performers who died prior to the enactment of the CDPA 1988 and devolve to the performers' personal representatives: *Experience Hendrix v Purple Haze Records* [2007] F.S.R. 31 CA.

protection at the beginning of 1996) and revised rights (those already out of protection but being brought back in).[160]

(4) Exceptions and limitations. Restrictions upon the scope of rights in performances[161] to a considerable degree parallel those affecting relevant aspects of copyright. They do not however coincide. There is no fair dealing defence relating to research or private study; nor is there for a private recording of a broadcast for purposes of time-shifting.[162] The vagaries of the legislative process leave such curiosities on deposit.

(3) Remedies for infringement

14–37 These include, it would seem, injunction, damages and account of profits. The rights are enforceable as breaches of statutory duty. Because this is territory where immediate remedies are needed, the right-owner is given similar powers to those conferred on copyright owners: to engage in seizure against traders without premises, to have orders which include delivery up and disposal, and to proceed by way of prosecution for a range of statutory offences.[163]

5. Public Lending Right

(1) Background

14–38 In Britain it was not the rental of copies but their lending by public libraries which provided the first breach in the "exhaustion" of rights which arose out of the limitation of infringing acts. While in general copies legitimately made in the United Kingdom or imported here could not be controlled by copyright after disposal on the market, the special Public Lending Right Scheme provided a return to some authors when copies purchased by public libraries were then lent out to readers. The Scheme, established under the Public Lending Right Act 1979, was originally conceived for books.[164] It acknowledged that organised borrowing reduces the sale of copies to some at least of the readers. So it increases the number of people who have access to the copies lent without bringing any additional return to author and publisher, over and above their earnings on the original sale.

14–39 The case was a particularly strong one in Britain because the use of public libraries is a staunch tradition, more books being borrowed in much higher

[160] SI 1995/3297 rr.27–35.

[161] For which, see CDPA 1988 Sch.2.

[162] cf. CDPA 1988 ss.29, 70.

[163] See in general, CDPA 1988 ss.194–202, 205N; and above, paras 2–18, 2–21.

[164] The campaign for PLR was eloquent, but for two decades faced stubborn resistance: see Brophy, *Guide to Public Lending Right* (1983).

proportion to population than in most European countries or the United States. Because of this social importance, the Scheme has been financed by separate funding from central Government, rather than by the libraries themselves. Accordingly, in 1979 there was no extension of authors' copyright to include public lending. Instead, those with protectable interests had to register their works with a public office, that of the PLR Registrar, which conducts sample surveys of borrowing in order to decide how to distribute the public grant. That grant, which was running at the modest rate of £5.5 million *per* annum, has been given a catch-up boost of £14.252 million in 2003 and will become £8 million thereafter.[165]

The Scheme for books thus retains a measure of common ground with copyright, both by relating entitlement to authorship and in apportioning payments, as nearly as practicable, to the lending of individual works. The Scheme is not one, for instance, in which grants are made to authors' welfare funds or in which a levy is imposed on initial sales to libraries.[166] Other countries have adopted a variety of solutions to the problem. In Germany, notably, the copyright model was adopted for the public lending of books. When pressure to extend the British Scheme to sound recordings, films and computer programs succeeded in the CDPA 1988, these cases were put on a copyright basis. Books continue to be treated in their distinct and limited way, because they are the staple of public library lending. **14–40**

Despite the different bases of their book schemes, reciprocal arrangements for payments to each other's authors exist between Germany, The Netherlands and Britain.[167] The Rental, Lending and Related Rights Directive, read in conjunction with the Duration Directive, attempts to harmonise the law on public lending in Member States.[168] In reality, in addition to the three countries mentioned, only the Scandanavian countries have any sort of scheme. In the Directive, the obligation to introduce any PLR is restricted to the need to provide equitable remuneration to authors; and even then "certain categories of establishments" may be exempted by national legislation. **14–41**

[165] Public Lending Right (Increase of Limit) Order 2003 (SI 839/2003). Administrative expenses fall to be deducted from the grant.

[166] An investigation in the 1970s found that a borrowings-based scheme would be not significantly more expensive than a sales-based scheme: Technical Information Group, Papers of 1975 and 1976.

[167] Revenue from abroad is distributed in Britain by the Authors' Licensing and Collecting Society.

[168] Rental, Lending and Related Rights Directive 92/100, now codified as Dir. 2006/115; OJ L376/28, art.2, stating that PLR shall be accorded to authors, performers, phonogram producers, audio-visual producers (but note the derogations allowed). Lending involves making copies available for limited periods and not for direct or indirect economic or commercial advantage: art.1. See Griffiths [1997] E.I.P.R. 499.

(2) The PLR scheme for books

14–42 The right created by the 1979 Act covers books lent out to the public by local library authorities[169] in the United Kingdom. It is given to the authors of the books; but it is assignable without restriction,[170] and so it is open to publishers to negotiate an interest in it. Nothing is said about employed authors, so common law principle may dictate that presumptively they hold their interest in trust for their employers, where the work is prepared in the course of employment. The entitlement lasts at most for the author's life and 70 years thereafter.[171] The EU Directives on Rental, Lending and Related Rights and Duration together make plain that the author's PLR must last for 70 years post mortem, but implementation of this requirement is still awaited.

14–43 The Scheme itself now defines "books" to which it applies as printed and bound publications, with at least one named author who is a natural person.[172] Serials, musical scores and Crown copyright works are excluded.[173] An author is a writer (including a translator or editor) or illustrator[174] and must be qualified by having his principal home in an EEA state.[175] Rights accrue from registration. They are transmissible as personal property, but only as a whole.[176]

The manner of organising samples of borrowing is elaborately defined.[177] In 2006, when just over £6.5 millions were distributed the value of each interest (whether of one or more authors)[178] was 5.57p per borrowing. The maximum on all books of any one author of in any sample year is £6,000, which prevents the whole fund being taken up by the handful of truly popular writers. Over 18,000 authors received something.

(3) Public "rental"

14–44 The CDPA 1988 created a rental right in sound recordings, films and computer programs, where the hiring is by a business for money or its equivalent.[179] By sleight-of-hand in an obscure Schedule, the Government

[169] As defined in PLRA 1979 s.5(2). The PLR Scheme is set out in App.2 of the Act.

[170] See PLRA 1979 s.1(7)(b); Scheme para.10.

[171] PLRA 1979 s.1(6), Scheme para.20. After the author's death his successors have ten years within which to register a book for the first time.

[172] PLR Scheme para.6. They must have an ISBN and have been offered for sale to the public.

[173] Separate volumes and editions are treated as distinct books.

[174] PLR Scheme para.4, which lays down precise methods for identifying authors.

[175] PLR Scheme para.2(1) as amended by the Commencement of Variation Order 2004.

[176] See the PLR Scheme paras 20–31 for details. The Registrar may remove an entry after 10 years of no payments: para.34.

[177] PLR Scheme Pt 4. Altogether administrative costs absorb some 20 per cent of the Government grant.

[178] There are specified shares for translating (30 per cent), editing (20 per cent) and illustrating (up to 50 per cent). Those jointly entitled to any share may notify the proportions of their sub-interest: PLR Scheme para.9.

[179] See above, paras 12–27—12–28.

extended this right to lendings by public libraries of these types of material, not only where a charge is made but when the loan is free.[180] So the copyright owners of this material—by definition entrepreneurs, save in the case of the occasional computer program—have protection within the framework of copyright. They may extract what they can from the libraries (who in turn must decide what charges they will pass on to borrowers), subject only to the threat of Copyright Tribunal proceedings,[181] if these demands prove too strident. As already indicated, the Rental, Lending and Related Rights Directive imposes no obligation to provide any PLR, save to authors. It is therefore open to the UK Government to continue to provide nothing for performers. The Directive does impose an obligation to give authors at least equitable remuneration for copies of their work which are subject to public lending.[182]

6. Artists' Resale Right: Droit de Suite

The special value of some artistic works lies not in the capacity to multiply copies but in the uniqueness of the original. This is true of many paintings and sculptures. As artists acquire a reputation, works of this kind accelerate in value. Their deaths may add to the element of scarcity, and the effect may be marked in the resale prices of their works. Since artists and their estates normally benefit only from the first sale of the work, they receive no return from subsequent increases in the value of the original. A *droit de suite* had been recognised in the Berne Convention from the Brussels Revision of 1948[183] and by 2000 had come to be provided by the laws of 10 EU states. The right, whatever its details, requires a proportion of the price on each resale of the original work to be paid to the artist or his successors. Since it relates to dispositions of the original it is the antithesis of "*copy*right". But to adherents of the strict authors' rights tradition, it shares the same moral justification, being a right reserved explicitly for the artist and his or her inheritors.[184] **14–45**

In the EU states with a *droit de suite*, the scope of the right varied, particularly over the types of work covered, the application to non-auction as well as auction sales and the percentage of the price to be accounted to the artist. There was thus, at least on paper, a distortion of trade within the EU. The great European centres for the sale of modern artworks are **14–46**

[180] CDPA 1988 Sch.7 paras 6, 8, amending the Public Libraries and Museums Act 1964 s.8(6), and the Public Libraries (Scotland) Act 1955 s.4.

[181] Under CDPA 1988 s.66; see above, para.12–43.

[182] Rental, Lending and Related Rights Directive art.5.

[183] Article 14*bis*. Since the convention did not require a Member State to introduce a *droit de suite*, "the effect .... was to create a sub-Union between those States which did recognise" the right: Ricketson and Ginsburg para.3–45.

[184] See generally, Price (1960) 77 Yale L.J. 1333; Plaisant (1969) 5 Copyright 15; Lahore, *Copyright and the Arts in Australia* (1974) pp.83–86.

London and Switzerland, in neither of which the artist had any title to share in resale proceeds, and where auctioneers have been adept at extracting high commissions from sellers and buyers.

This view of the EU position drove forward a harmonisation Directive, designed to impose a standard version of artists' resale right in each Member State, including those without one.[185] In Britain, where the move was seen by many as likely simply to transfer sales of modern artworks to Geneva, New York and other havens, the plan came in for aggressive attack.[186] On basic economic assumptions, the right was said to have a dampening effect on the initial price. It was characterised as one-sided, since the artist did not have to re-pay from past receipts when a picture fell in value on a re-sale. There was said to be no adequate evidence to demonstrate that dealers attract more work if they are in a state without a *droit de suite*.[187] Variations in VAT rates were said to have more impact on what the seller received than any resale right.[188] It is also evident that, in such a specialised market, much depends upon the available expertise. For this London has built up an enviable reputation, which, so the British argued, should not be weakened by temptations to move sales to non-EU states. But all these doubts only made the advocates for artists more impassioned. Much was made of the sheer injustice to the artist, as the very creator, of seeing no return from his growing fame.

In 2001, after some crumbly resistance by the British Government, the Directive was enacted[189] and has been translated into UK law by the Artists' Resale Right Regulations 2006.[190] These give the right to living artists from February 15, 2006; for those previously deceased who created works still in copyright, their successors in title will be accorded the right by 2012.[191] It applies only to the resale of works of art,[192] and not, for instance to literary

---

185 Directive 2001/84; [2001] OJ L272/32 ("Resale Right Directive").

186 Some of the argument has been decidedly woolly: see, e.g. Whitford Report (Cmnd.6732, 1977) Ch.17. Objections that the result will be higher returns for those already over-rich, apply equally to the more distasteful excesses of pop-composers, film corporations and others blessed with copyright and neighbouring rights; cf. Merryman [1997] I.P.Q. 1; Solow (1998) 22 J. Cult Econs. 209; Kawashima [2006] I.P.Q.223.

187 One sophisticated attempt to demonstrate the distortive effect of the disparities is Doutrelepont, *Droit et l'objet d'art* (1996).

188 Jacob [1997] I.P.Q. 3; Booton [1998] I.P.Q. 165; Hughes in Bently and Maniatis, *Intellectual Property and Ethics* (1998), p.147; Karashima [2006] I.P.Q. 223.

189 Resale Right Directive, above, n.185.

190 SI 2006/346; hereafter "ARR Regulations 2006"; for an admirable listing of the *lacunae* in the Regulations, see Valentin [2006] E.I.P.R. 268. For the Irish implementation see European Communities (Artist's Resale Rights) Regulations SI 312/2006 and the discussion by Gibbons [2007] E.I.P.R. 163.

191 ARR Regulations 2006 reg.17, following the requirements of Resale Right Directive arts 8(2), 10. For the resales covered and various exemptions, see ARR Regulations regs 1, 3(1), 3(5), 12(3), 12(4),

192 Widely defined to cover graphic and plastic art (sculpture), and extending to signed lithographs and the like, but not to "works of applied art" or "works of artistic craftsmanship": Resale Right Directive art.2; ARR Regulations 2006 reg.4. The explanatory memorandum to the Regulations states that sales of applied art in Britain comfortably exceed those of fine art.

manuscripts, valuable though some of them become over time. The right is given to the artist and his inheritors on death for the copyright period.[193] Thanks to the Berne Convention, a strict reciprocity applies to artists who are non-EEA nationals. They must be nationals of a country providing an equivalent right.[194]

The resale right is inalienable in the fullest sense. It cannot be transferred, charged, waived or subject to a contractual agreement to share it or pay it back.[195] Otherwise dealers might insist on an assignment to themselves, thus rendering it of no consequence. In Britain, however, collection has to be through a collecting society.[196] It applies only to sales which are conducted by an art market professional, i.e. a dealer or an auctioneer.[197] The Regulations do not state that the sale must take place in the United Kingdom. This, however, seems to be presumed in the Accompanying Memorandum, which has a considerable discussion of the likelihood of sales being diverted to non-EEA countries, which appears to assume that the right does not arise in relation to them.[198] As Valentin suggests, various questions of private international law concerning title to movables and the completion of contracts must nevertheless be expected.[199] The obligation to make the payment is placed both on the seller and his agent (or if he does not have one, on the buyer's agent, or ultimately the buyer).[200] It is to be enforced by civil proceedings.

The UK Regulations lay down standard rates to be paid.[201] The royalty starts with sales (net of tax) above 1,000 and requires payment of 4 per cent of the sale prices up to 50,000, 3 per cent for 50,000–200,000, 1 per cent for 200,000–350,000, 0.5 per cent for 350,000–500,000 and 0.25 per cent over 500,000. The maximum payment is 12,500 which, on these figures, is reached

---

[193] ARR Regulations 2006 reg.3(2), following Resale Right Directive art.8(1). Cf. the position in Ireland where the right is only given for the life of the artist: European Communities (Artist's Resale Rights) Regulations SI 312/2006 reg.10.

[194] ARR Regulations 2006 regs 7(4), 10(1)–(3) and Sch.2, listing countries which satisfy the mutuality criterion.

[195] See Resale Right Directive arts 9(1), 6(1); ARR Regulations 2006 regs 7, 8. Article 6(1) of the Directive does not preclude a provision of national law which reserves the right to heirs, to the exclusion of legatees: Case 518/08 *Salvador Dali v ADAGP* OJ C148.

[196] ARR Regulations 2006 reg.14, adopting a choice in Resale Right Directive art.6(2). This is also the case in Sweden, where the Supreme Court has found that there is no requirement for the right to be administered exclusively by one collecting society. As such competition between collecting societies may occur: *Bildkonst Upphovsratt I Sveirge v DUR* [2003] E.C.D.R. 4.

[197] ARR Regulations 2006 reg.12(3)(a). The dealer and seller are both liable for payment of the royalty: regs 1(4), 13, following a choice in Resale Right Directive art.1(4). There is an exemption for resales below 10,000 within three years of the artist's first sale: reg.12(4), following Resale Right Directive art.1(3). In Germany, an art dealer has been interpreted as anyone who involved in the sale of works of art in their own commercial interest: *Ahlers Collection* (2009) I.I.C. 604.

[198] See above, n.192.

[199] Above, n.190.

[200] ARR Regulations 2006 reg.13.

[201] ARR Regulations 2006 reg.12, relying on choices from the Resale Right Directive arts 3, 4.

with a sale after tax of almost 2,000,000. The artist has a right to obtain information about a sale of his or her work.[202]

Given the remarkable acceleration in the sale prices of the original works of artists still in copyright, there is a strong case for affording them a return that can be regarded as broadly equivalent to those of literary authors and composers for reproductions and repeated performances. Whether, in a still divided world, the actual returns from the rights will amount to anything much remains to be seen. Nevertheless the internet and telecommunications more generally make the site of the dealer's premises less significant. The Explanatory Memorandum to the Regulations refers to other factors which may effect the choice of where to sell: transport and insurance costs of valuable art works are very considerable; there is also VAT at 5 per cent payment by an EU buyer who brings his purchase back into the single market. The whole issue will deserve close study over the next decade.

7. Crown and Parliamentary Copyright

14–47 Under the CA 1956, there were sweeping provisions giving copyright in literary, dramatic, musical and artistic works to the Crown if they were either made under its direction or control, or were so first published.[203] Thus, for instance, a patent specification, drafted by a patent agent for a client, ceased to be a copyright of either and became the Crown's when the Patent Office published it. The Whitford Committee criticised the reach of these provisions, and the Crown eventually agreed to align its rights with those of employers in general.[204] In the wake of this it has been necessary to confer a separate copyright on Parliament in respect of documents and other material emerging from its proceedings[205]; and also to confer immunity from infringement where a public office or person in authority is producing information in which there is a special public interest.[206] In approaching the subject, the lawyer needs to remember that Crown and parliamentary copyright remain distinctive creatures. Among their characteristics, those concerning duration of the rights have already been mentioned.[207]

Crown copyright under the CDPA 1988 arises where a work is made by an officer or servant of the Crown in the course of his duties.[208]

[202] ARR Regulations 2006 reg.15, from Resale Right Directive art.9.

[203] CA 1956 s.39. For egregious consequences, see, e.g. *Ironside v Att-Gen* [1988] R.P.C. 197.

[204] CDPA 1988 ss.163, 164; cf. above, para.13–05. For the copyright which may by Order be conferred on international organisations, see s.168.

[205] CDPA 1988 ss.165–167.

[206] CDPA 1988 ss.47–50.

[207] See above, para.11–54.

[208] The old test (was the work made under the Crown's direction or control?) was in some respects wider. By the relevant transitional provision, it would appear that a work which was Crown copyright under the old law, but not under the new, ceases at "commencement" to be Crown copyright and becomes (presumably) that of the author, or his employer, or the assignee of either and has the duration of ordinary copyright: Sch.1 para.40.

Parliamentary copyright is, in the main, given to whichever House has, by its direction or control, had the work made; or to both, if they are jointly responsible.[209] But while the old formula of "under direction or control" is still used in respect of parliamentary copyright, Crown copyright is explicitly limited to work made by an officer or servant of the relevant House in the course of his duties, and to any sound recording, film, live broadcast or live cable-cast of proceedings.[210] It is not sufficient that a House commissions a report from an outside person, such as specialist adviser to a Select Committee. These copyrights take effect without the need to comply with the usual rules for qualification.

As regards the acts permitted in the interests of public administration,[211] **14–48**
the Crown is entitled to make copies[212] of a literary, dramatic, musical or artistic work communicated to it in the course of public business, but only when it does so for the purpose of the communication to it, and only if no breach of confidence is involved.[213] By this, the Crown recovers some of the ground which it surrendered in accepting a more limited concept of Crown copyright. But not all: in particular, in the material that no longer belongs to it, it has no proprietary right to prevent publication, politically embarrassing though that may be. This perhaps explains (while it certainly does not excuse) the recent insistence of Government departments that they be given contractual powers to decide if and when reports of research which they have commissioned shall be published.[214] The United Kingdom is not a country in which ideas of free access to, and free use of, government information flourish with any vigour.[215] Were this so, there would have developed, as in the United States,[216] much more embracing notions of public domain material in which no copyright may be claimed. As it is, in Britain, the Crown has copyright even in Acts of Parliament and Church of England Measures.[217] For these, as for delegated legislation and official reports, the Government will doubtless continue to specify by Treasury Circular how far it will countenance free copying by others.

Of particular interest is the copyright in judgments and law reports. **14–49**

---

[209] CDPA 1988 s.165, and see s.166 for the special copyright in Bills.

[210] CDPA 1988 s.165(4).

[211] Note also CDPA 1988 s.47, allowing the person duly authorised to permit copying of the content of a public register, but not for publication; similarly, under s.49, for public records; and under s.50 for acts specifically authorised by statute.

[212] And to issue the copies to the public.

[213] CDPA 1988 ss.47, 171(1)(e).

[214] Under the old law, where copyright lay in the Crown, the Department of Health and some other departments nevertheless conceded in research contract conditions that the researchers should be entitled after notice to publish. One argument in 1987 for changing this provision, was that the Crown needed to control publication in order to "protect Crown copyright". So little is the nature and purpose of copyright understood that many must have been misled by this piece of self-serving mystification.

[215] Pace Lord Goff, *Att-Gen v Guardian Newspapers (No. 2)* [1990] 1 A.C. 109 at 283; above, para.8–19.

[216] For which see, Nimmer, *Copyright*, para.5–06.

[217] CDPA 1988 s.164.

Under the previous law (which still affects judgments given before August 1989), the first test of whether they were Crown copyright was whether they were made under the direction or control of the Crown.[218] To take this view would be quite inconsistent with the independence of the judiciary. Under the CDPA 1988, the question becomes whether judges are officers or servants of the Crown. Their independence means that they cannot be regarded as servants.[219] Yet, being Crown appointees, are they officers? An affirmative answer would mean that the Crown could control the publication and other copyright use of their judgments.[220] So long as that is so, it ought to be concluded that the judges are not officers appointed for the purpose of delivering any particular judgment[221]; accordingly a judgment remains personal to its author for copyright purposes.

It may be that the circumstances in which it is delivered amount to a waiver of any claim by the judge, at least to economic rights.[222] Those who make a business of transcribing and publishing judgments would remain able to claim any transcriber's copyright which may fall to them under *Walter v Lane*[223] and their publisher's right in the format of their edition.

---

218 See above, n.210; the second test was first publication.

219 They can be ordered to undertake work, but not told how to do it; *a fortiori* university teachers and their research: see above, paras 13–06, 13–07.

220 Control could involve suppression or alteration, though, in the latter case, the author would have a right to object to derogatory treatment which doubtless would not be side-stepped by any sufficient disclaimer: see CDPA 1988, ss.80, 82. Even *extempore* judgments recorded by others will attract copyright under the CDPA 1988: above, para.11–34.

221 cf. Laddie et al. paras 36.41 et seq. See generally Taggart (1984) 10 Sydney L.R. 319; von Nessen (1985) 48 M.L.R. 412; Tapper (1985) 11 Monash U.L.R. 78; Monotti [1992] E.I.P.R. 305.

222 See Laddie et al. para.36.45.

223 See above, para.11–34. Most court reporting in England is undertaken privately: see further, Laddie et al. paras 36.46–36.47.

CHAPTER 15

INDUSTRIAL DESIGN

1. BACKGROUND

Industrial designs are primarily those elements incorporated into mass-produced products that aim to enhance their attractiveness by their appearance. Today when so many consumer products are technically very similar, design becomes an important distinguishing factor, often not easily separated in the minds of purchasers and users from trade marks and similar symbols. These latter "signs", however, are protected as indicators of the trade source from which the goods come and not for the addition to appearance as such. Because most consumers use trade marks as a reference point for securing the qualities of goods or services which they have learned to expect (or at least hope to enjoy), there is no easy borderline to be drawn between design and trade mark rights. Yet there is one prime reason from a legal perspective for not treating the two as "converging" (in the sense of intermixing the two types of IPR): by common consent, design elements should be the subject of IPRs only for a limited period, whereas trade marks need to continue for as long as a business continues to use them. 15–01

Intellectual property in industrial designs occupies a midway point between patents and copyright, at the one pole, and trade marks at the other. But like the earth's equator, it is not easy to fix if you only have a compass.[1] Countries have adopted very different stances on the subject[2]:

(1) the protection may be by official registration (in which case, like a patent, it may bind all third parties)[3]; or it may be informal (in which case it will be confined to acts of copying). The former are registered designs (RDs), the latter unregistered design rights (UDRs). NB UDRs may be achieved through copyright or by a separate right—as with the unregistered design rights which are given by the EU and by UK legislation. Copyright and separate UDRs may be allowed cumulatively, or copyright may be excluded, at least in some measure. That is what has happened in current UK law;
(2) the protection may be confined to elements which are appreciated for their appearance; or it may extend to shapes which are assumed for technical reasons.[4]
(3) the protection may depend upon the design being novel, or in other respects different from what has gone before. It may be limited to production-line products or extend to individual items, such as handicrafts.

The UK approach to the subject has shifted with different winds of policy. Notoriously, there was a period (1968–1988) when the traditional registered design was suddenly overtaken by artistic copyright. This extravagance (and that was how much of industry saw it) was then curtailed. In place of copyright came a part-substitution in the form of UK unregistered design right. Our legislators had some hope that this compromise would become a standard for EU intervention on the subject. But it was too complex, and too far removed from any Continental approach to the subject, to achieve this aim. Instead the European Commission evolved its own eclectic model for the European future, introducing a EU RD and a short-term EU UDR. However, as with trade marks, these rights have arrived as alternatives to the national RD systems, so the latter have been in large measure harmonised by Directive. Yet, leaving the matter hopelessly unco-ordinated between different EU states, it has not curtailed other cumulative forms of protection in the various national laws (which could take the form of copyright, national UDR, or unfair competition). It has to be asked whether, in principle, the result meets the constitutional basis for EU

[1] Design rights have been labelled hybrids because they are derived from both patents and copyright: Reichman (1983) Duke L.J. 1143, 31 J.Copyright Soc USA 267.
[2] But it may still be restricted to copying, as in France and Germany until of late.
[3] For European comparisons, see Fellner, *The Protection of Industrial Designs in the EEC* (1985).
[4] The Germans have registered rights separately in decorative and in technical designs, the latter being a form of utility model, for which, see above, paras 3–30—3–35.

intervention—that differences in protection which distort trade in products within the Single Market are being reduced or eliminated. If ever asked, the ECJ would doubtless say that the Designs Directive is a sufficient step in the right direction, which will in time be improved upon. That would be the only way of suppressing the doubt.

Certainly, in Britain since the invasion of EU designs law, the protection of designs has become utterly disparate both in principle and in the morass of detail. The Government should be taking determined steps to simplify objections and eliminate unnecessary differences in scope and operation of the rights. But probably the subject is insufficiently central to business practices for there to be legislative action. It will be left a field after battle to which protectionists and free competitors will return for further inconclusive engagements.

(1) Origins of design registration

The only hope for understanding the present law lies in some outline of its **15–02** tortured history. It effectively begins with a design registration scheme which took recognisable form in the 1830s and 1840s.The memorable aspect of this stage was that it bred protection not only for decorative designs but also for shapes that were essential functional—a distinction of purpose that has been difficult to manage ever since.[5] Initially the rights gave only very short terms of protection, covering the lead-time needed for introducing a newly designed product onto the market. As the law developed, the RD right drew closer to the patent system. The right was treated as good against all the world. It therefore had to be shown to be novel at the priority date of the application. The application became subject to an examination before registration. The maximum term was similar to that for patents.

(2) Copyright Act 1911

The CA 1911 introduced the concept of infringement of an artistic work by **15–03** "reproduction in a material form", including the conversion of a two-dimensional design into a three-dimensional article.[6] In order to sterilise the potency of this new notion in the field of industrial design, s.22 excluded all copyright in designs capable of being registered under the registration system, which were used or intended to be used as models or patterns to be

[5] For the earlier history, see Sherman and Bently, *The Making of Intellectual Property Law* (1999) esp. Pts 2 and 3; Cornish in Cornish et al., *Oxford History of the Laws of England* XIII(2010) Pt V Ch.4. Statutes of 1787-94 provided a pre-cursor by giving minimal protection to designs for calico printing.

[6] To be understood with the co-ordinate principle: infringement may occur by indirect copying of the article legitimately made from the design: see *King Features* case (below, para.15–35, n.137).

multiplied by any industrial process.[7] This had the effect of keeping copyright out of most industrial territory, though its operation did not extend to designs which were originally intended for a non-industrial process, such as comic-strip illustration. Because of this difference the section was eventually judged unsatisfactory, though it continued to be the rule affecting copyright in pre-1957 designs.[8]

(3) Copyright Act 1956

15–04 The CA 1956 set out to eliminate dual protection by copyright as well as design registration on a different, highly complex basis. The essential feature of s.10 was that while copyright now subsisted in designs of all kinds, industrial application of them would not amount to infringement of the copyright if a registered right had been applied for, or if the copyright owner had used the design on industrially produced articles. In the regrettable decision of *Dorling v Honnor Marine*,[9] the Court of Appeal chose to distinguish between designs capable of registration which were subject to s.10, and designs which were not registerable (chiefly because they were functional) and so bore full-term artistic copyright even in respect of industrial products.[10]

(4) Design Copyright Act 1968

15–05 The CA 1956 provision was modified in 1968, by a terse Act,[11] which in essence put off the moment for excluding copyright in industrial applications of a design until 15 years from first authorised marketing of articles bearing the design. Despite the best efforts of Whitford J.,[12] this was held to continue the *Dorling* distinction between registrable designs (now able to

---

[7] For a long period there was little consideration of which designs were capable of registration. Latterly, it was held that, while they might not be registrable because solely functional (below, see para.15–19), they did not lose this quality because in the particular case they were not "new or original": see *Interlego v Tyco* [1988] R.P.C. 343 (JC from Hong Kong); and see *Interlego v Alex Foley* [1987] F.S.R. 283. In the *Tyco* case the point was part of an argument of considerable audacity (which failed). See McGee and Scanlan [2003] J.B.L. 470.

[8] See now CDPA 1988 Sch.1 para.6.

[9] *Dorling v Honnor Marine* [1965] Ch. 1.

[10] If the reason why a design was unregistrable was that it was not novel, this was eventually treated as not giving it full artistic copyright.

[11] Introduced as a Private Member's Bill, it was intended to improve the position of the designs of furniture, jewellery, toys and the like. Its impact on functional design went unappreciated during its hasty enactment.

[12] e.g. *Hoover v Hulme* [1982] F.S.R. 565; over-ruled (quite unnecessarily) by the Court of Appeal in *British Leyland v Armstrong* [1986] R.P.C. 279. The issue was not taken to the House of Lords.

enjoy 15-year copyright) and non-registrable functional designs which had a copyright enduring for the designer's life and 50 years thereafter.[13]

The 1968 Act highlighted the implications of the *Dorling* case and ushered in a merry litigious bonanza. Design copyright was held to exist in the copying of a vast range of industrial products, and indeed for every part of them, whether they were watches or atomic power-stations.[14] It had this swamping effect by virtue of three general principles: (1) that a design was an artistic work irrespective of artistic quality; (2) that an artistic work in two dimensions could be copied by reproduction in three; and (3) that a person who made his own product by copying another's product would indirectly infringe copyright in the production drawings.[15]

(5) *British Leyland v Armstrong*[16]; *Canon v Green Cartridge*[17]

Because this disproportion produced extreme results affecting so much industrial production,[18] the House of Lords were moved to intervene in advance of new legislation. In the *British Leyland* case they had to consider a copyright claim to the design of the exhaust pipes for certain British Leyland (BL) cars, which was being asserted against spare-part manufacturers. Exhaust pipes had the characteristics: (i) that they must assume a given shape in order to fit the particular contours of the underbody; and (ii) that they needed quite regular replacement. The market was accordingly lucrative, and much more so for BL if its licence was needed for all pipes made to its designs.[19] The majority of the House of Lords were attracted by the notion that the sale of a car carried with it an implied licence to use BL designs in the course of repairing the car.[20] But they saw the need to go **15–06**

[13] A distinction labelled by the Whitford Committee, "bizarre": (Cmnd.6732, 1977) para.96. When, in 1974, the House of Lords raised the level of "eye appeal" for a registered design (*Amp v Utilux* (below, para.15–19, n.62)) the effect was to increase the range or functional designs which acquired full-term copyright.

[14] The existence in the then law of an entitlement to conversion damages, as distinct from infringement damages, meant that the material value of precious objects and complex machinery might be payable to a successful claimant. This outrageously oppressive consequence was abandoned in the CDPA 1988, on the Whitford Committee's recommendation (Cmnd.6732, 1977), para.702.

[15] See above, para.12–05. For the law before the CDPA 1988, see Fellner (above, n.3), Ch.1.

[16] *British Leyland v Armstrong* [1986] R.P.C. 279.

[17] *Canon v Green Cartridge* [1997] F.S.R. 817 JC.

[18] An equivalent result was reached under the laws of most Commonwealth countries, causing Thomas J. to cast an anathema upon all (including textbook writers!) who had allowed the law to get so out of hand: "Like ants in the forest, they have constructed a misshapen anthill of enormous proportions which is of no use or value to anyone or anything save other ants and the parasites that feed upon their indulgent labours", etc.: *Franklin Machinery v Albany Farm Centre* (1991) 23 I.P.R. 649 SC (NZ). See Wei (1998) 114 L.Q.R. 39.

[19] The "Euro-defence" of abuse of dominant position (art.102, TFEU ex art.86 Rome Treaty) was dismissed in the litigation in a manner amounting virtually to incomprehension.

[20] Lord Griffiths' interesting dissent went so far as to deny that a design for a functional part could be infringed by three-dimensional, indirect copying. This solution would have prevented much artistic copyright from operating in the sphere of industrial production. The majority judgments are confined to cases of spare parts.

beyond the idea of implied licence[21] and instead imported the land law concept that a person may not derogate from his grant. From this they drew the conclusion that BL could not object to anyone, including a spare-parts manufacturer, using the designs to make things which would go to repairing their cars.

To transplant so basic a notion into a new field raises various uncertainties about its potential, and the decision has since been severely criticised in the *Canon* case as constitutionally unacceptable.[22] Lord Hoffmann, for the Privy Council, considered that a head of public policy ought not to be created by judges in order to modify express statutory rights of property, however much those rights might result in the exercise of monopoly power in the after-market. The Judicial Committee refused to hold that the *British Leyland* doctrine could be applied to the design of cartridges which had regularly to be replaced in laser printers and photocopiers.[23] *British Leyland* was confined to parts needed for occasional repairs. So much apparently could be regarded as an inherent aspect of ownership—the entitlement to keep a thing in repair. Jacob J. has since held that the doctrine cannot apply even in that sphere since the limitations on industrial copyright and the unregistered design right, both in the CDPA 1988, were introduced without an explicit exception for spare parts.[24] Other limitations govern the latter, notably those for "must fit" and "must match" exceptions.[25] The *Canon* decision may also have limited future applications of the *British Leyland* public policy by requiring positive evidence that monopolistic consequences are flowing or will probably flow from enforcement of the intellectual property right.

(6) Copyright, Designs and Patents Act 1988

15–07 The new deal of 1988 was intended to prune the luxuriant jungle of design rights which had grown in the previous 20 years. The principal measures were:

(1) the Registered Design system was amended in various details, including an extension of the maximum period of protection from 15 to 25 years;
(2) the intrusion of artistic copyright into the industrial design field was constrained by seeking to reserve it for 3D objects which themselves could be copyright works (sculptures, works of artistic craftsmanship,

[21] The difficulties with "implied licence" were: (1) how could it extend to protect a parts manufacturer?; and (2) how could its exclusion by express statement to the contrary in the initial contract of sale be prevented?
[22] Above, n.17. See also *Flogates v Refco* [1996] F.S.R. 874; *Creative Technology v Aztech Systems* [1997] F.S.R. 491 CA Sing.
[23] See also *Creative Technology v Aztech Systems* (above, n.22).
[24] *Mars UK v Teknowledge* [2000] F.S.R. 138.
[25] Below, paras 15–40—15–42.

etc.); and at the same time by limiting the term of even these copyrights in the sphere of industrial production to 25 years;

(3) in the hole left by the uprooting of most industrial copyright, the CDPA 1988 Pt III, created the UK Unregistered Design Right, which protects product shapes, whether technical or not, but only for a shortish term—normally 10 years. Coming as it did during the legislative course of the 1988 Bill, the *British Leyland* decision at least had a decided impact on the spare parts question, since they were largely excepted from protection under this UDR.

(7) The Community interventions by Regulation and Directive

The EU Designs Regulation introduced its unitary Registered Design Right, which is in operation from 2003 and forms an alternative to national RDs. By a corresponding Designs Directive, national RDs must adapt to the standards for the EU RD. This intervention, as already mentioned, is stated to have no effect on other forms of protection for designs in national law. For the United Kingdom this means survival of artistic copyright and UK UDR as defined and differentiated by the CDPA 1988. **15–08**

The EU goes one step further by also creating its own EU UDR, three years only in duration and available for designs falling within its RD scheme. Most significantly, therefore, it is not for purely technical designs. This, however, is one of the main objects of UK UDR.

(8) Order of the chapter[26]

We will traverse the regions of this variegated territory in the following order: **15–09**

(1) Registered Designs (RD), concentrating on the principles now common to the EU and the UK RDs;
(2) EU UDR (Unregistered Design Right), as an appendage to RDs;
(3) Artistic Copyright, detailing the extent to which under the CDPA 1988 it gives informal protection to industrial products;
(4) UK UDR under the CDPA 1988 Pt III, noting its unique position in comparison with other design protection schemes in EU states and elsewhere.

2. Registered Designs

Registered design law has been substantially revamped in order to bring into effect the EU Registered Design, i.e. the unified right across the EU **15–10**

[26] For full treatment, see *Russell-Clarke and Howe on Industrial Designs* 7th edn (2005).

prescribed in the EU Designs Regulation. This became operative from 2003[27] and is granted (as are EU Trade Marks) by OHIM (the Trade Marks and Designs Registrations Office of the European Union) in Alicante, Spain. Alongside this EU scheme, the national registration systems continue in operation, as harmonised by the EU Designs Directive.[28] The UK legislation governing the national registered design is still the 1949 Act, but the original remains only as a shell.[29] The substantive flesh and much of the procedural fibre comes from these European instruments. As Europe has already learned from trade mark registration,[30] the meaning which will attach to the dispositions common to EU and national registered designs will increasingly be settled in European institutions and during the processing of EU applications, by Examiners and Appeal Boards of the OHIM, and from them, the General Court (ex. CFI) and, in the ultimate event, the ECJ itself. After registration of the design, national courts will determine issues of validity, infringement and so on, subject always to the reference of questions of interpretation of the EU legislation to the ECJ. In the next paragraphs we concentrate on the legal rights and obligations which apply equally to both forms of registered design right, EU RD and UK RD.

15–11 As already noted, the EU Designs Regulation also establishes a short-term EU Unregistered Design Right, which has to be carefully distinguished from the UK's Unregistered Design Right. These are discussed separately below.[31]

(1) Requirements for a registrable design (validity)

15–12 The new law on registered design abandons many constrictions which had accumulated in the varied laws of EU states on the subject. The range of products for which designs may be registered has expanded, and the right may be applied to products of all kinds in or on which it creates the same overall impression, not just to those for which it is registered.[32] The basic thrust of a registered design is to provide exclusive protection for elements of product design for a maximum of 25 years, after which, in principle, those elements become open to copying by competitors. But designs with such a long life in commerce may in the interim have been built up as trade marks (and in some EU countries there may be full-term copyrights to consider as well), so the 25-year limit may provide no real passport to others. In this

[27] Regulations 6/2002; [2002] OJ L3/1; see Musker, *Community Design Law* (2002), Scanlan and Gale [2005] J.B.L.91.

[28] Directive 98/71/EC. For first experiences, see Schlötenburg [2003] E.I.P.R. 383.; Izquierdo Peris [2006] E.I.P.R. 146.

[29] The latest amendments are introduced into the RDA 1949 by the Registered Designs Rules 1995 (as amended).

[30] Below, Ch.18.

[31] See below, paras 15–31, 15–38—15–56.

[32] See below, para.15–25.

field issues of "cumulation" or "convergence" of rights are with us as never before.

(a) *Product design*

In the European scheme, what is protected is a *design* for a *product*. Incorporation of the design into any product, not just that for which the registration is procured, then falls within the right. Previously the design had to be registered for each product separately.[33] This greater scope could be of considerable significance in practice. Hence everything stems from the following definitions: **15–13**

- *Design:* "the appearance of the whole or a part of a product resulting from the features of, in particular, the lines, contours, colours, shape, texture or materials of the product or its ornamentation".[34]
- *Product:* "means any industrial or handicraft item other than a computer program: and, in particular, includes packaging, get-up, graphic symbols, typographic typefaces and parts intended to be assembled into a complex product".[35]

Accordingly designs are elements of appearance in products. The former UK law required that the design appeal to the eye—a requirement which the courts treated with notable generosity, even though "appeal" suggests some feeling of aesthetic satisfaction which is sparked by seeing. "Appearance" points to much the same characteristic. Recital 11 refers to "features which are shown visibly", suggesting that a similar low level of consumer response to visible features will suffice as under the previous law.[36] In the main the question is whether the appearance has been adopted for technical, rather than any aesthetic or associative reason. This factor is reinforced by exceptions in the new designs law concerning technical designs. To these we come later.[37] While there remains a distinction from the realm of patents secured by the exclusions of technical elements, there can be "cumulation" with the protection of trade marks. Wherever the appearance of the mark is in some measure distinctive of the source of the products, albeit that the visual appeal lies in recognition of the brand, it can be a registrable design.[38] **15–14**

---

[33] For the scope of protection, now much widened, see below, paras 15–25 et seq.

[34] Designs Regulation art.3; Designs Directive art.1; RDA 1949 s.1(2). The old UK formula, "shape, configuration, pattern or ornament" covered much the same ground, though the new reference to texture and materials seems to go further. Even trade marks have not yet extended to "feelies"; cf. below, para.18–20.

[35] Designs Regulation art.3; Designs Directive art.1; RDA 1949 s.1(3).

[36] The reference to "visible" signs creates many uncertainties: see Musker [2003] E.I.P.R. 450.

[37] Below, para.15–19.

[38] Although not where the design incorporates another's distinctive sign: see Designs Regulation art.25(1)(e). See also *Piotrowski v Compagnie Gervais Danone* [2008] E.T.M.R. 27; *Ningbo Beifa v Schwan-Stabilo* [2009] E.T.M.R. 7 and *Business Alliance v VITEC Global* [2009] E.C.D.R. 7.

It is, of course, decades since Andy Warhol and the Pop-Art gang taught us that one man's soup-can is the next woman's screen-print.

15–15 No longer is the product of which the design forms part restricted to one produced by an industrial process, since handicrafts are also included and they are the antithesis of the machine-made. That is one indication of the EU's determination to make the new right an embracing one. Even more is that true of the awkward and indeterminate concept of a "product", which not only covers "items" consisting of packaging and get-up such as bottle shapes and distinctive labels, but also "items" constituted by a graphic symbol or a type-face. What these latter may comprise is a mystery since in this context "item" suggests a thing with a physical form: the sign for a new currency made into a balloon, perhaps? Or alphabet soup in a new visual format? Probably what was meant was that designs could be on any kind of surface. This would include not only wallpaper, curtains and the like (which were within the former UK right), but also things printed on paper and similar surfaces, like paintings, posters, lettering, stamps and transfers. These were largely excluded under the former law, as belonging to the sphere of copyright.[39] It is being suggested by advocates of expansion that the carrying medium need not be permanent, so that computer screen icons and the like may be the subject of registrations.[40] Here is "convergence" of rights plainly at work, since these can also be copyright.[41]

15–16 There will also be some uncertainty over the statement that the design may be for part of an item as well as the whole of it. This avoids the scrupulous approach of the former UK law which required that the design be for a product which was sold separately—a requirement that led to the exclusion of spare part designs for cars, unless they were accessories (like wing mirrors, wheels and accessories) intended for separate sale.[42] On the divisive spare parts issue there is now a different compromise—concerning the scope of the right, rather than its validity—which we will tackle below.[43]

(b) *Novelty and individual character*

15–17 Because an RD is effective against all third parties, and not just against imitators, a registered design is subject to conditions of *novelty* and *individual character*.[44] While these criteria resemble novelty and non-obviousness

[39] The previous exclusion was mainly provided in the Designs Rules r.26 and included not only "printed matter primarily of a literary or artistic character", but also sculptures, plaques and medals. The distinction does, however, survive in relation to artistic copyright: see below, para.15–36.

[40] In *Apple Computer v Designs Registry* [2002] E.C.D.R. 191, Jacob J. found that even the old law did not exclude these. Kur argues that the same result was intended for the EU design and equivalent national law: (2003) 34 I.I.C. 50.

[41] Below, para 20–23.

[42] *Ford Motor's Designs* [1995] R.P.C. 167 HL. See the amended definition of "design" in RDA 1949 s.44(1).

[43] See below, para.15–29.

[44] Designs Regulation arts 5–7; Designs Directive arts 3–5; RDA 1949 s.1B.

in patent law, they are rather less severe and in some respects they are more complex to apply.

First, both matters fall to be judged at the application date for protection, unless the applicant can take advantage of the Paris Convention's six-month period of priority, measured from the first application date in another Convention state.[45] Testing at that date, one asks: was the same design, or one of similar character, already "available to the public" in a broad sense, i.e. published, exhibited, used in trade or otherwise disclosed?[46] The prior art must be a "design" as that is now defined,[47] but it can be a design for any kind of item, and this, as we have seen, includes most forms of artistic work in a copyright sense, including such subjects as a new type-face.[48] The essential question is then judged by the eye of the informed user,[49] who differs from the notional person in other areas of intellectual property law. The informed user is not akin to the person skilled in the art in patent law (and thus is not an average designer) and is more discriminating and better informed than the average consumer in trade mark law.[50]

In deciding what is within the prior art, the following disclosures are nonetheless to be disregarded:[51] **15–18**

(1) disclosures made in confidence to outsiders;
(2) disclosures which could not reasonably have become known in the normal course of business to persons carrying on business in the EEA and specialising in the sector concerned[52]—the "*European limitation*"; and
(3) disclosures made by the designer or a successor in title within the previous 12 months, or by the recipient of information from the designer or a successor, or by someone in abuse of a relation with the designer or successor, in each case during the same 12 months—the "*grace period*".

---

45 Designs Regulation arts 5(1), 6(1); Designs Directive art.6(1); RDA 1949 ss.1B(7), 14(2). For conflicting applications to register, see RDA 1949 ss.1A(2), 11ZB(4), as amended by the Registered Designs Regulations 2003 (SI 2003/550).

46 Designs Regulation art.7(1); Designs Directive art.6(1); RDA 1949 s.1B(5).

47 So it cannot be a human, however iconified by publicity: *Spice Girls' Application* [2000] E.C.D.R. 148.

48 Cf. CDPA 1988 s.53.

49 Cf *Normann Copenhagen v Paton Calvert* [2010] E.C.D.R. 3 where the OHIM Third Board of Appeal held that the informed user is relevant only to individual character and not novelty—an odd conclusion.

50 *Procter & Gamble v Reckitt Benckiser (UK)* [2008] F.S.R. 8 CA, paras 16, 24–28.

51 Designs Regulation art.7; Designs Directive art.6; RDA 1949 s.1B(6).

52 The "sector concerned" in Designs Regulation art.7(1) means the sector which comprises the alleged prior art and is not limited to the sector for which the design was registered: *Green Lane Products v PMS International* [2008] F.S.R. 28 CA. The Court of Appeal arrived at its conclusion based on the language of the Designs Regulation, the travaux préparatoires and common sense.

Compare patent law. There the "prior art" includes whatever is made available freely to a single person anywhere in the world—a formalistic test which greatly reduces the scope for argument about what constitutes an anticipation. Not so with the EU designs law. The following pattern of behaviour is common enough: a design copier goes to a trade fair, picks up another's design ideas and incorporates them into his own products. The very display at the trade fair anywhere in the world will begin to jeopardise the designer's chances of obtaining a registered design in the EU. But since the display is by the designer, at most it only starts the 12 months' grace period running. However, once the rival products are on the EU market, the copyist will have prevented the original designer from registering a design. That will be equally true where the rival products are distributed outside the EU if EU designers regularly monitor the products appearing in that place. At least the rival will not himself be able validly to register the design: his claim to be the designer will be open to challenge.[53]

As to the twin criteria under discussion, novelty goes to the essential sameness to pre-existing designs: are they identical, save for immaterial differences?[54] Individual character, however, is much more in the eye of the particular beholder. One must ask: does the overall impression which the design produces on the informed user clearly differ from the overall impression produced on that notional person by any prior design?[55] Under the former UK law a design was not registrable where its appearance was not material in an aesthetic sense[56] or where the design involved only variants commonly used in the trade.[57]. The test is likely to be rather more severe than formerly, since "individual character" has been given a separate status from novelty as a legal condition. Highly relevant to establishing "individual character" will be the existing design corpus and the degree of freedom of the designer in developing the design.[58]

---

[53] See below, para.15–22.

[54] Designs Regulation art.5(2); Designs Directive art.4; RDA 1949 s.1B(2). Under the previous law differences which were immaterial could not confer novelty.

[55] Designs Regulation art.6(1) and Rec.14; Designs Directive art.5(1); RDA 1949 s.1B(3); *Procter & Gamble v Reckitt Benckiser (UK)* [2008] F.S.R. 8 CA, paras 18–19. The informed user has been identified according to the class of products indicated in the registration: *Atria v HK Ruokatalo* [2008] E.C.D.R. 6; *Wuxi Kipor v Honda* [2009] E.C.D.R. 4; *Woodhouse UK v Architectural Lighting* [2006] R.P.C. 1.

[56] This was understood to exclude designs for parts of products which would never be seen by users (undersides of shower trays), but not parts which would not be revealed until after sale (insides of chocolates). The latter should presumably remain registrable under the new law (cf. *Ferrero's Application* [1978] R.P.C. 473). The Designs Regulation Rec.12, excludes protection of component parts not visible when used or mounted in position.

[57] Despite this restriction, it was held that a design for a coffee-pot could be protected which brought together four features from different pots: *Household Article's RD* [1998] F.S.R. 676. What of the situation in *Sebel's Application* [1959] R.P.C. 12? An old rocking horse was put on an old base and the composite design was not valid. Under the new law the impression could perhaps be of two distinct things, neither of them changed.

[58] Designs Regulation Rec.14. For examples of where the relatively unlimited design freedom has undermined claims to individual character see: *Atria v HK Ruokatalo* [2008] E.C.D.R. 6; *Honda v Kwang Yang* [2008] E.C.D.R. 5; *Holey Soles v Crocs* [2008] E.C.D.R. 8.

(c) *Technical function*

The belief that design protection should be kept separate from rights in technical effects is present in the new European law, but in terms which have been kept obscure, despite the problems being well-enough appreciated. Design registration may not subsist in any features of appearance of a product which are solely dictated by the product's technical function.[59] What type of "merger" doctrine is this? To be excluded from protection, does the design feature have to be adopted because it is the sole manner in which the technical effect can be achieved? That will rarely be the case. Almost always there will be some other shape that will perform the function. Or is it enough for exclusion that the sole purpose of the design feature is to make the item work, rather than to make it attractive to the eye? Decisions under the former law may point to the contrast. In *Cow v Cannon*,[60] the Court of Appeal allowed the registration of a design showing thick ribs on a hot-water bottle which ran in a diagonal direction. The object of the ribs was to act as built-in insulation; but, pointing out that the ribs might be equally horizontal or vertical, the court found that the design was not solely technical. The danger of this approach is that it would take the designer only a couple more registrations covering the obvious alternatives and he or she would have a monopoly on the practicable ways of giving effect to a clever technical idea without having to satisfy the requirements for a patent.[61] Soon enough the House of Lords preferred a wider view of the exception. In *Amp v Utilux*[62] an electrical terminal for a washing machine had a cruciform appearance, which was certainly not the only possible shape for the part. The House judged the matter by the view of the typical purchaser and found that anyone buying a machine that incorporated the terminal would attach no significance to the appearance of the particular terminal but would treat it as a strictly functional element. It was therefore not registrable. **15–19**

Advocate-General Ruiz-Jarabo has given it as his opinion that the exclusion of functional designs applies only where no other shape would achieve the technical result.[63] In *Landor & Hawa v Azure Designs*,[64] Fysh J. agreed with him, pointing to the requirement in the present law that the design be "essential", not merely "necessary", to function and the Court of

[59] Designs Regulation art.8(1); Designs Directive art.7(1); RDA 1949 s.1C(1). Much the same exception existed in the former UK law of registered designs, although it affected only shapes and configurations. The difference is rarely likely to be material. The separate objection that the design was a method or principle of construction has been removed.

[60] *Cow v Cannon* [1959] R.P.C. 347.

[61] A concern that has been dismissed, at least in relation to the UK UDR: *Landor & Hawa,* (below, n.65) at para.25.

[62] *Amp v Utilux* [1972] R.P.C. 103.

[63] *Philips v Remington* [2001] R.P.C. 38, paras 33–34 (contrasting the exclusion of shape trade marks in terms considered to be wider—"dictated" is not part of the formula there); cf. below, paras 18–40 et seq.

[64] *Landor & Hawa v Azure Designs* [2006] F.S.R. 22.

Appeal has upheld this view.[65] The current UK approach has, however, been rejected by the OHIM Third Board of Appeal in *Lindner Recyclingtech v Franssons*[66] largely because of the real risk that monopolies will be granted over technical solutions. Instead, the Board has favoured the previous UK approach, as represented by *Amp v Utilux*,[67] on the basis that it will allow the purpose of the technical function exclusion to be achieved. According to the Board of Appeal in *Lindner* the exclusion "denies protection to those features of a product's appearance that were chosen exclusively for the purpose of designing a product that performs its function, as opposed to features that were chosen, at least to some degree, for the purpose of enhancing the product's visual appearance."[68]

As we shall see, the way in which the exception is interpreted has vital implications for the future of the UK UDR. The exception of solely technical designs applies equally to the EU UDR. So if it rarely affects that right, it is hard to justify continuance of a UK right of longer duration which has largely the same object.[69] If on the other hand, the UK UDR has its own zone of operation, the comparison should be with systems for registering technical novelties, such as utility models, petty patents and short-term patents. These latter rights, as we have noted, already exist in numerous EU countries, but in substantially differing forms.[70]

15–20 Alongside the general exclusion of purely technical designs from the ambit of design registration, there is also an exclusion of so-called "must fit" features of a product, i.e.:

> "features of appearance...which must necessarily be reproduced in their exact form and dimensions in order to permit the product in which the design is incorporated or to which it is applied to be mechanically connected to or placed in, around or against another product so that either product may perform its function".[71]

This is perhaps the clearest case of a design element which is solely functional, so it is not obvious why the separate exception has been included and why then it is limited to "must fit" features which *necessarily* must be exactly reproduced. Perhaps it implies that the general exception of solely technical designs is not just for "must fit" cases. That argument may sustain the *Amp v Utilux* approach to the main exclusion under the new law. Such an interpretation is needed, if designs are not to lead to monopolies in technical products.

---

[65] *Landor & Hawa v Azure Designs* [2007] F.S.R. 9 CA, paras 32–39
[66] *Lindner Recyclingtech v Franssons* [2010] E.C.D.R. 1.
[67] *Amp v Utilux* [1972] R.P.C. 103.
[68] *Lindner* [2010] E.C.D.R. 1, para.36.
[69] Below, para.15–31.
[70] Above, paras 3–31—3–34.
[71] Designs Regulation art.8(2); Designs Directive art.7(2); RDA 1949 s.1C(2). The old law of registered designs contained no separate "must fit" exception.

There is one special qualification of both the general and the "must fit" exception. Registration is after all permitted of design features which allow the multiple assembly or connection of mutually interchangeable products within a modular system.[72] Toy manufacturers convinced EU legislators that they must have special treatment for play-sets which invite users to construct buildings, lay out railways and the like. A Recital pronounces that these elements can be important innovations and "present a major marketing asset".[73] Why these explanations should constitute some difference in kind from connective elements in other products (often excluded for their technical character) goes unexplained. The concession does show how determined lobbying can squeeze special concessions into legislation.

Traditionally, registered designs had been subject to compulsory licensing on the ground of insufficient use in the United Kingdom. This power to override the exclusive right has no place in the new European law. The Crown has however retained its power to use designs upon payment of a reasonable royalty.[74] This in general terms is similar to the Crown use power over patents.[75]

(d) *Public policy and morality*

Registrations are not valid for designs which are contrary to public policy or **15–21** morality, following what is now a standard EU prohibition.[76] Under the old law, the Registrar had a similar discretion, which recently has been applied with distinct caution.[77]

(e) *Proprietorship and dealings: right to be named* **15–22**

The new registered designs law is not subject to any qualification rule which requires the designer or a successor in title to have any personal connection, or to publish first, in any country. Here there is a direct contrast with the qualification conditions imposed on UK unregistered design right.[78]

The law concerning initial entitlement to apply for a registered design has now become quite needlessly complex. The Designs Directive does not deal with the matter, ownership being considered a matter specially suited to national law. Accordingly, for the UK registered design right, the rules from the former law survive.

The commissioner of a design for money or money's worth[79] is the person primarily entitled to apply for registration. If the design is not so created, the

[72] Designs Regulation art.8(3); Designs Directive art.7(3); RDA 1949 s.1C(3)
[73] Designs Regulation Rec.11.
[74] RDA 1949 s.12, Sch.1; cf. above, para.7–50 and below, para.15–30.
[75] See above, para.7–49.
[76] Designs Regulation art.9; Designs Directive art.8; RDA 1949 s.1D.
[77] *Masterman's* (sic) *Design* [1991] R.P.C. 89 ("Highlander" doll with what is beneath sporran held registrable: full monty at p.108.)
[78] See below, paras 15–44, 15–48.
[79] For an instance of money's worth: *Breville v Thorn EMI* (1985) [1995] F.S.R. 77.

right is in the employer of the designer, where it is created in the course of employment. Otherwise the right belongs to the designer.[80] If a person not entitled applies, the registration is invalid whether or not the applicant was *mala fides*.[81] These rules are not the same for copyright, where initial ownership is presumed to be in an employer but not in a commissioner.[82] This difference, which makes it important to determine the matter by express agreement wherever possible, is also mediated by a provision of the CDPA 1988, which exempts from copyright infringement anything done bona fide under an assignment or licence of a corresponding registered design.[83]

Necessarily the Community Design Regulation makes its own disposition on the matter of initial entitlement and it is not the same as that in UK law, so far as concerns designs produced on commission outside employment. For EU RD, an employer is presumptively the person first entitled to a design made by an employee under the employment, but a commissioner is not.[84] On this the national law should be brought into line with the EU RD rule. The judges have residual power to imply a contractual term giving the right to the commissioner where all the circumstances suggest it.[85] At present the legal difference—a curious pitfall for the unwary—needs to be dealt with by an express contractual term.

The right to apply may be transferred by assignment, transmission or operation of law. As with patents, access to the system is open to all, regardless of nationality. The preference accorded to nationals of Paris Convention countries is the six-month priority affecting the question of novelty.

(2) Registration and term[86]

15–23 A UK design registration, as already noted, is effective against the use of the design on any item where it gives no different overall impression.[87] Nonetheless, as of old, it has to be registered for a specified product on which it is

[80] RDA 1949 s.2(1)–(1B). If the design is computer-generated without a human author, the arranger of its creation is treated as author: s.2(4); and cf. below, paras 20–44, 20–45.

[81] *Woodhouse UK v Architectural Lighting* [2006] R.P.C. 1; *Ifejika v Ifejika* [2010] F.S.R. 7.

[82] Above, paras 13–05, 13–06.

[83] CDPA 1988 s.53.

[84] The ECJ has ruled that the Designs Regulation art.14(3) only governs employee produced designs and not commissioned designs. As such, it is for the national court to ascertain whether there has been an assignment of any rights in commissioned designs: *Fundación española v Cul de Sac Espacio Creativo* [2009] E.C.D.R. 19.

[85] cf. above, para.13–12.

[86] RDA 1949 ss.3–3D; Designs Rules (as amended r.14). The equivalent provisions for applying for a Community design will not be detailed here: see Musker (above, n.27), A002–A020. The Hague Agreement for the International Registration of Designs has not been an arrangement in which the UK has participated. However, it was given new form by its Geneva Act of 1999 and the UK was a signatory.

[87] And see further, below, para.15–25.

to be used, and can be registered separately for other products.[88] This will place it within a classification[89] and enable it to be found by searchers, if they know or guess where to look.

Another recent change is that the UK Registry has ceased to conduct an *ex officio* search of prior registrations for designs which are the same or similar and which could therefore lead to an objection to the novel or individual character of the design in the application. Only if a search is requested and paid for will the Registry carry it out.[90] The result may arm an opponent with ammunition to attack the registration; but this is possible only after grant, in proceedings which may be instituted before the Registry or the High Court. Upon grant the design will be officially published. There are limited powers to modify an application during its course, and registration may be made with disclaimers of rights over elements in the design.[91] The right of third parties to obtain a declaration of invalidity of an RD from the Registrar (with appeal to a Registered Designs Appeal Tribunal) is specified in detail. The result may be nullification ab initio or from another date, in whole or in part, or modification of the registration.[92]

The term of a registered design is measured from the date of the application.[93] Under the 1949 Act, the duration was originally a maximum of three periods each of five years. This has been extended to five periods, making a maximum of 25 years.[94] The term thus became broadly equivalent to that being given to industrial applications of artistic copyright.[95]

(3) Property rights

Once granted, a registered design can be transferred by assignment, transmission on death or operation of law, but only in respect of all the subject-matter in it—this is particularly so for EU RDs in order to preserve their unitary character.[96] It can also be licensed and used as security.[97] To have any effect against third parties (save those with knowledge of a prior **15–24**

[88] Registering for particular articles may help in demonstrating similarity to another design.

[89] Classification follows the Locarno Agreement on the subject (1968). With Community designs, OHIM must not change the classification of the products for which the design is registered without offering the applicant a right to comment: *Re Casio Keisanki* [2007] E.C.D.R. 13.

[90] The registrar has power to carry out such searches as he thinks fit: s.3(4).

[91] RDA 1949 s.3B.

[92] RDA 1949 ss.11ZA–11ZC.

[93] RDA 1949 s.3C.

[94] RDA 1949 s.8. Provisions are added, equivalent to those in PA 1977 ss.25(4), 28, allowing the restoration of a registration which has lapsed through non-payment of renewal fees: ss.8(4), 8A, 8B.

[95] See below, para.15–37.

[96] Designs Regulation arts 27, 28; RDA 1949 s.19(1). There are equivalent rights in applications to register: Designs Regulation art.34.

[97] Designs Regulation arts 32, 29; RDA 1949 s.19.

conflicting interest), all proprietary transactions need to be registered. To that extent there is a formal requirement of writing.[98]

(4) Right given by registration

(a) *The test of scope*

15–25 A registered design is now infringed by any unauthorised act which uses the design or any design which does not produce on the informed user a different overall impression, taking into account the degree of freedom of the designer in developing his design. According to the Court of Appeal in *Procter & Gamble v Reckitt Benckiser (UK)*[99] the test is not the equivalent of that which determines whether the protected design has individual character when compared with the prior art.[100] This is because "individual character" requires a *clearly* different overall impression from the design corpus,[101] whereas the infringement test is in less emphatic terms (a different overall impression).[102] The divergence is apparently justified by the need to avoid bestowing monopolies in "routine, ordinary, minor everyday design modifications".[103]

As much in the previous system demonstrates, the real difficulties in design law are reached when it comes to considering the relation between the design and the article (or "item" as it now is) in or on which it is embodied. While a design still has to be registered for a product, infringement is no longer confined to use on the article for which the design is registered.[104] The design may be infringed by use on anything where the overall impression is not different. This may prove to be a difficult test to apply, particularly since the design may affect only part of an article. A test couched in negative terms is an oddity. What, after all, is the synonym for "not different"—the same, similar?

(b) *Wrongful acts*

15–26 The acts which may constitute infringement now comprise a complete list of commercial activities equivalent to those for patents: making, offering,

[98] Designs Regulation art.33; RDA 1949 s.20.

[99] *Procter & Gamble v Reckitt Benckiser (UK)* [2008] F.S.R. 8 CA; see Carboni [2008] 30 E.I.P.R. 111.

[100] Cf. the Austrian Supreme Court which took the opposite view: *T Company v R GmbH* [2009] E.C.C. 3.

[101] See above, para.15–18.

[102] *J Choo v Towerstone* [2008] F.S.R. 19.

[103] *Procter & Gamble v Reckitt Benckiser (UK)* [2008] F.S.R. 8 CA, para 19.

[104] See above, para.15–23. No expert evidence on the comparison is needed except perhaps on technical matters, such as constraints on design freedom: *Oren v Redbox Toy Factory* [1999] F.S.R. 785; *Thermos v Aladdin Sales* [2000] F.S.R. 402; *Procter & Gamble v Reckitt Benckiser (UK)* [2008] F.S.R. 8 CA, paras 4–5.

putting on the market, importing, exporting or use a product incorporating or applying the design; and stocking the product for these purposes.[105]

(c) *Exclusions from protection*

Again following the model of patent law, there is now a list of activities which are excluded from the right, of which the most general are: private and non-commercial acts and experimental purposes.[106] Included is a copyright-related exclusion: reproduction for teaching or citation, provided that the source is named and the act is compatible with fair trade practice and does not unduly prejudice normal exploitation.[107] **15–27**

As to exhaustion of rights, the usual formula is followed. Within the EEA free movement of protected goods is required; but from outside that Area, registered design right is yet one more IPR with which to guard the fortress: it may be used to prevent the entry of goods first marketed by or with the EU right-owner's consent in non-EEA country.[108]

(d) *Innocent infringement*

Where a person innocently infringes a UK RD, damages or an account of profits shall not be awarded.[109] Innocence is assessed at the date of infringement and requires the defendant to show that he was not aware or had no reasonable grounds for supposing that the design was registered.[110] Bizarrely, the legislature did not introduce the same exemption for EU RDs or UDRs.[111] **15–28**

(e) *"Complex products"*[112]

For a quarter-century the most prominent political argument concerning IPRs in industrial designs has concerned the provision of spare parts, above all in the motor industry. Spares take distinctive shapes, some of them reflecting the design features of the thing into which they are inserted (panels for car doors, etc.), some having a purely functional shape (fans and fan-belts, exhaust pipes, etc.). Both kinds of replacements, in the majority of instances, will need to take the same shape (at least in part). To that extent the owner of the thing will not be able to seek spares in other shapes from competing suppliers. If therefore there is an IPR which prevents all save the **15–29**

[105] Designs Regulation art.19(1); Designs Directive art.12; RDA 1949 s.7(2).

[106] The specific cases relate to foreign ships and aircraft temporarily in the UK, and importation of spare parts for their repair, and carrying out the repairs. See Designs Regulation art.20; Designs Directive art.13, RDA 1949 s.7A.

[107] RDA 1949 s.7A(3).

[108] Designs Regulation art.21; Designs Directive art.15, RDA 1949 s.7A(4), see below, para.19–17.

[109] The defence is also available for UK UDR, but is limited to awards of damages: CDPA s.233(1).

[110] RDA 1949 s.24B, inserted into UK law by the Intellectual Property Enforcement Regulations 2006 (SI 2006/1028).

[111] As confirmed in *J Choo v Towerstone* [2008] F.S.R. 19.

[112] Drexl, Hilty and Kur (2005) I.I.C. 448.

original producer from marketing spares, the opportunity for monopoly pricing is at least to some extent present. (Ultimately, given the highly competitive market for products such as cars, consumers may take against a producer precisely because of its charges for spares—but only where that producer stands out from the flock.)

The EU Designs Regulation and (indirectly) the on the Designs Directive have for the moment adopted a pro-consumer approach, principally by limiting what will be treated as infringement of any design for a "complex product", i.e. one composed of at least two components permitting disassembly and reassembly.[113] So far as a registered design (either EU or UK) is concerned, no right can exist in a component part for such a product unless the component is visible during normal use, and unless the component itself is new and has individual character.[114] Even assuming that these hurdles are overcome, it is not infringement of the registered design to use the component to repair the thing so as to restore its original appearance.[115] Other Member States have been allowed to continue design protection of spare parts and many have done so. The Commisson reported (SEC (2004) 1097) that the result was distortion in the after-market particular for vehicles and recommended that they be directed to adopt the same approach as for community designs. Action has not yet been followed.

(5) Crown use

15–30 The Crown is entitled to use (or authorise the use of) a registered design for the services of the Crown.[116] The conditions are similar to those applying to patents. Compensation must be paid unless the Crown had already recorded or applied the design otherwise than in consequence of the registered proprietor's communication before the date of registration.[117] In the case of a EU patent, Crown use is authorised only in relation to essential defence and security needs.[118]

3. EU Unregistered Design Right (UDR)

15–31 Some industries—those dedicated to satisfying the consumer's insatiable appetite for novelty in fashion—change their stock not just annually but even season by season. For them a registered design system is too slow and

[113] Designs Regulation art.3(c); Designs Directive art.1(c), RDA 1949 s.1(3).

[114] Designs Regulation art.4(2); Designs Directive art.3(3), RDA 1949 s.1B(8). For the very similar position regarding the two UDRs, see below, paras 15–31, 15–38—15–43.

[115] Designs Regulation art.110; RDA 1949 s.7A(5) (and for continuation of the prior UK law excluding protection until the EU revisits the issue, see Designs Directive art.12(2)).

[116] RDA 1949 s.12, Sch.1, now amended to include compensation for loss of profit provisions, as with patents; see above, para.7–50.

[117] RDA 1949 Sch.1 para.1(2), (3).

[118] Designs Regulation art.23.

costly and some Continental countries introduced short-term rights to deal with the problem.[119] This has now been replicated for the whole EU by the creation of an EU UDR, with a three-year term, alongside its EU RD.[120] This UDR also has a complementary purpose. Where a design has to be launched as soon as production is possible, yet it will have a life of several years, the EU UDR provides protection during the initiatory stage before the registration is actually applied for. For this there is a one-year grace period between publication of the design and the application for a RD.[121] The informal UDR is meant to provide an adequate bridge, while leaving the registration system to supply the real backing for the longer term. Of course, in countries which allow more extensive informal protection by copyright or a different UDR—as in the United Kingdom—this last effect may only be partial.

The EU UDR arises wherever there is a "design" within the definition of that term for the registration system,[122] which has novelty and individual character.[123] It is infringed by the same kinds of act which constitute infringement of an EU registered design. But since the right arises without any formality, it must in addition be shown that the defendant copied the protected design.[124] The right lasts for three years from the date on which it was first made available to the public.[125] This can be by publishing, exhibiting, using in trade or otherwise disclosing the design anywhere, provided that it could reasonably be known in specialised EU circles (as with the test for novelty and individual character).[126] This may send a defendant in search of revelations by the claimant which it made but has not acknowledged.

The EU UDR may provide a modicum of short-term assistance, particularly in commercial circles of the EU where competitors are expected not to copy. In Britain, it will not be of much significance so long as we keep both artistic copyright for some industrial designs (e.g. surface decorations) and also the UK type of UDR, which, as we shall see, lasts longer and is not fettered by the exclusion of purely technical designs other than those which "must fit". However, there will be cases where all the informal rights are

[119] e.g. the French Law of 1952 protecting fashion designs.

[120] Designs Regulation art.11—the first directly enforceable EU right of intellectual property which is not dependent on any form of prior registration.

[121] See above, para.15–18.

[122] Above, para.15–13.

[123] See above, paras 15–17 et seq.

[124] Designs Regulation art.19(2). A convoluted sentence raises a presumption of copying from similarity, which is rebutted by the defendant showing that a designer made the design by independent work and could "reasonably be thought not to be familiar" with the claimant's design. An example of similarity giving rise to an inference of copying is *J Choo v Towerstone* [2008] F.S.R. 19. A further preference is given to the owner of an EU RD who takes advantage of the ability to have official publication of the registration deferred for 30 months (Designs Regulation art.50).

[125] Designs Regulation art.11(2).

[126] See above, para.15–18. The act could be by any person who has the design from the claimant—for instance, a proposed manufacturer or distributor; but acts which are in breach of confidence, not surprisingly, do not count.

pleaded and the precise scope of each will need to be argued. Then the absurd twists in the present legal maze will become truly apparent.

4. Artistic Copyright[127]

(1) The exclusion of design documents and models

15–32 Under the CDPA 1988, as before, copyright in a drawing arises irrespective of artistic quality, provided that there is sufficient labour, skill and judgment to give originality. It may be infringed by reproducing it in a three-dimensional article; and it matters not whether the act of copying is direct or indirect.[128] However, in s.51, important limitations are introduced to those principles, by cutting out the application of copyright to industrial products which are not themselves capable of being the subject of copyright. The object is to create a separate space for the UK UDR, which forms Pt III of the Act. Section 51 states that the act of making an article from a "design document or model" which records or embodies a design cannot after all constitute infringement. This applies where the design is "for anything other than an artistic work or a typeface". In this provision "design" has a restricted meaning: "the design of any aspect of the shape or configuration (whether internal or external) of the whole or part of an article, other than surface decoration".[129] However, one point should be kept in mind: it is not copyright in the design, but copyright in the design document or model, which is affected by the new limitation.

Section 51 undoubtedly excludes from the sphere of copyright much of what, under the previous law, has been considered to fall within it: blue-prints for pumps, car exhausts or taps must count as design documents for non-artistic works, and this is so whatever the form of record—whether it is "a drawing, a written description, a photograph, data stored in a computer or otherwise".[130] The material thus excluded can only be protected as a registered or an unregistered design, if the conditions governing those rights are met. Previously there was no such limitation and artistic copyright ranged across much of the industrial landscape. A degree of uncertainty infects the *penumbra* of s.51, as can be seen if each of its requirements is further examined.

---

[127] See Laddie et al., Ch.59; Copinger, paras 13.275–13.314.

[128] See above, para.12–05.

[129] For instances which were not just surface decoration: *Wilkinson v Woodcraft Design* [1998] F.S.R. 63 (beading, etc.); *Fulton v Grant Barnett* [2001] R.P.C. 16 (stitching on corners of umbrella case).

[130] The reference to "design models" excludes prototypes and mock-ups for things, provided that those things are not themselves artistic works: a model for a cup may be a sculpture (see below, para.15–34) but it is still a model for a thing incapable of bearing copyright. Contrast a model for a figurine.

(a) *"Design document or model recording or embodying a design for anything other than an artistic work..."*

If the design document is for a piece of jewellery, the design is in many cases for a "work of artistic craftsmanship". It could accordingly be infringement of copyright in the drawing to make up the jewellery from it (direct), or from jewellery made from it (indirect); and in the latter case it would also be infringement of copyright in the jewellery (and the authors of these two copyrights may well be different people: designer and silversmith respectively). **15–33**

The category, "work of artistic craftsmanship", is a limited one, as the House of Lords demonstrated in *Hensher v Restawile*.[131] Copyright is not in this case accorded "irrespective of artistic quality". But among those things which are protected without regard to artistic quality, as well as drawings, are sculpture, engravings and etchings.[132] Thus mats and engraved plates were recently held to constitute engravings and so were not touched by s.51.[133]

In considering the impact of these broad notions, the key is to remember the governing consideration: what is the design *for*?[134] If a document is drawn for the purpose of making a sculpture, an etching or an engraving, then the exclusion of copyright from industrial infringement does not apply.[135] If, however, the design is for something which is not itself an artistic work—such as, designs for the Teletubby dolls beloved of children's television[136]—the mere fact that a three-dimensional model (itself counting as a sculpture) is made as a stepping stone towards final production will not exclude s.51. The intermediate version is not the end, only a means to it. **15–34**

Here we look at the same phrase one step back. Concern shifts to another aspect of the preposition "for". It brings into consideration the intention or purpose for which the design was recorded. Take the classic example—the cartoon character, Popeye, and his merchandising as a doll.[137] Initially the drawings were *for* a comic strip, not for making articles. Read naturally, s.51 would appear not to touch such a case, leaving the merchandising of such a figure to the sphere of copyright (and thus in effect returning to a basic distinction under the CA 1911). However, it would be possible, if strained, to read the section as extending to any subject-matter capable of being **15–35**

---

131 See above, paras 11–17—11–21.

132 None of these artistic works is further defined, save that "sculpture" includes a cast or model. A multi-factorial test for sculpture was approved by the Court of Appeal in *Lucasfilm v Ainsworth* [2010] F.S.R. 10. In that case, the helmets and armour of "stormtrooper" characters from the film "Star Wars" were not protected as sculptures. As such, the drawings used to create these costumes were "design documents" and s.51, CDPA 1988 applied.

133 *Hi-Tech Autoparts v Towergate (No. 2)* [2002] F.S.R. 270. Cf. the other instances discussed in above, para.11–14.

134 Taylor and Dworkin [1990] E.I.P.R. 33.

135 For these types of artistic work, see above, paras 11–13 et seq.

136 *BBC Worldwide v Pally Screen Printing* [1998] F.S.R. 665.

137 *King Features Syndicate v Kleeman* [1941] A.C. 417.

turned into an article. In which case, Popeye and his ilk would be covered by it, so far as concerns the production of articles.

(b) *"Any aspect of shape or configuration ....other than surface decoration"*

15–36 It will be a nice question whether a feature of shape or configuration is for surface decoration, so that a design document embodying it may bear artistic copyright; or whether it is for some other element of shape or configuration, with the consequence that it is excluded by s.51.[138] There is nothing to say that the surface must be flat. The result must, however, be decorative. A circuit diagram for an electronic mixer amounts to "configuration" but it is not decorative, so it falls within s.51.[139] Since the copyright and UK UDR provisions use exactly the same terminology, this interpretation ought to apply equally to copyright. On clothing, colours woven into the fabric, tipping in the knit and welts at the bottom edge were treated as not being surface decoration, whereas embroidery was, because it was added afterwards.[140] An artistic work which corresponded to the shape of an article (a badge) was a graphic design which could exist separately and thus was surface decoration.[141]

(2) The limitation of duration

15–37 In any case where s.51 does not apply to a design, copyright will continue to be infringed by making three-dimensional copies of it. But once any artistic work has been used in industrial production with the copyright owner's authority, the duration of this aspect of the copyright is foreshortened by s.52.[142] It ceases to be infringement to make articles of any description (other than those of a primarily literary or artistic character)[143] which copy the copyright work, after 25 years from the end of the year in which industrially produced articles from the work were first marketed anywhere in the world by or with the authority of the copyright owner.[144] The concept of

[138] In *Flashing Badge v Groves* [2007] F.S.R. 36, it was held that the design document incorporated both a design for an artistic work and a design for something other than an artistic work but that s.51 was relevant only to the latter design.

[139] *Mackie Designs v Behringer* [1999] R.P.C. 717; and cf. the registered design cases, *Sommer-Allibert v Flair Plastics* [1987] R.P.C. 599; *Cow v Cannon* [1961] R.P.C. 236; and note the general reliance on Luxmoore J. *Kestos v Kempat* (1936) 53 R.P.C. 139 at 152.

[140] *Jo-Y-Jo v Matalan Retail* [2000] E.C.D.R. 178; see below, para.15–34. *Lambretta Clothing v Teddy Smith* [2005] R.P.C. 6 CA. The tipping and welts caught by s.51 did not qualify for design right because they were found to be commonplace.

[141] *Flashing Badge v Groves* [2007] F.S.R. 36.

[142] cf. CA 1956 s.10, after its amendment by the Design Copyright Act 1968: both the CA 1956 and CDPA 1988 excluded one application of copyright from infringement; but the period before this happens is now 25, not 15 years; and there is no longer a distinction between designs that could, and could not, be registered.

[143] As defined in the Copyright (Industrial Process and Excluded Articles) (No.2) Order 1989 (SI 1989/1070) art.3(1).

[144] There is no territorial limitation on the place of production: *Lucasfilm Ltd v Ainsworth* [2008] E.C.D.R. 17, [162] and [2010] F.S.R. 10 CA.

"industrially produced articles" continues from the previous law: it requires the design to be applied to more than 50 articles (other than sets) or to non-hand-made goods manufactured in lengths or pieces (carpet, wallpaper, etc.).[145] The section embodies the obligation under the Berne Convention to accord at least 25 years' protection to a work of applied art so far as it is copyright.[146] At the same time it rids copyright of its most egregious excess in entering the realm of industrial property.

Apart from this limitation of term in relation to industrial exploitation, copyright principles apply as before.[147] Qualification extends to persons connected by personal status to prescribed Convention countries—an important contrast, it seems, with unregistered design right. First ownership of a work made under commission belongs to the artist who creates the work (unless there has been an express assignment)—a contrast with both registered and unregistered design right.[148] The artist, moreover, will benefit from the moral right to be identified (subject to the duration limit of s.52) and the right to object to derogatory treatment. These could be of some assistance to designers who are not employees.

5. UK Unregistered Design Right[149]

(1) Subject matter

The CDPA 1988 Pt III, calls this peculiarly UK entitlement simply "design **15–38**
right", but it is now necessary to think of it as UK UDR. The first purpose is to distinguish it from EU UDR—the temporary cover which supports design registration in the manner already explained.[150] UK UDR is a right distinct from a registered design and both may exist in the same design feature cumulatively. UDR is a substitute for artistic copyright over industrial production of shaped articles and the two are not cumulative: where copyright is available it displaces the UDR.[151] It is a hybrid displaying characteristics both of copyright and registered design law. Accordingly one

[145] Copyright (Industrial Process and Excluded Articles) (No.2) Order 1989 (SI 1989/1070) art.3(2).

[146] See the Paris Act of the Berne Convention (1971), art.7(4); Ricketson and Ginsburg, para.9–49.

[147] For designs made before August 1, 1989, the previous law concerning design copyright continued in principle to apply, but subject to a series of restrictions which reduce protection to a level close to that of the UK UDR.

[148] cf. above, para.15–22; below, para.15–48. Note that the designer of material in a design document that has applications precluded from copyright by CDPA 1988 s.51, has no moral right to be identified in those applications; but he does retain a right to object to derogatory treatment: cf. ss.79(4)(f), (g), 80, 81; and see generally, above, paras 12–76 et seq.

[149] See Laddie et al. Chs 40–44; Fellner, *Industrial Designs Law* (1995), paras 2.220–2.269, 3.04–3.53, 5.01–5.75; Howe, *Russell-Clarke on Industrial Designs* 7th edn (2005) Ch.4; Bently and Coulthard [1997] E.I.P.R. 401.

[150] See above, para.15–31.

[151] CDPA 1988 s.236.

must be wary of transposing assumptions from either field without careful examination. Just what it consists of, however, has been the subject of severe remonstrations from the Court of Appeal.[152]

The right arises in an "original design", comprising "any aspect of the shape or configuration (whether internal or external) of an article" or part of an article which is not "surface decoration".[153] Aspects of shape or configuration must relate to the physical manifestation of the article and not be characterised at an abstract level in an attempt to protect the underlying design concept.[154] Surface decoration is left to be the subject of copyright, and the phrase covers 2D designs on 3D articles. To complicate matters, the courts have said that surface decoration can occur in 3D on a 2D surface or as a flat part of a 3D article. To the contrary, there can on occasion be 2D features that count as shape or configuration, as may well occur where the surface has a significant technical function.[155]

In contrast with registered designs, there is nothing to require that the design should be concerned with appearance so as to evoke any kind of attraction in the viewer; nor is there any need for them to be visible in use. Thus prostheses for women who have had a breast removed gain design right.[156] Indeed, one major purpose of the new right is to give relatively short-term, informal protection to technical designs. The right has been recognised in a slurry separator and its components, mobile phone cases, shape elements in transformers and spare parts for vacuum cleaners.[157] Since "design" is not confined to things that a human can see, the layout of a semiconductor chip is included within design right as a specially regulated instance of it.[158] The detailed dimensional shapes for contact lenses could in principle fall within the general scope of the right,[159] though they may face difficulties when it comes to the exclusory conditions mentioned below; so also with vacuum parts.

Could the structure of genetically engineered proteins, which are highly dependent on the manner in which they fold, therefore, attract design right?[160] For such a notion, kites have been flown.[161] However, they may well fail to take off. What an electron microscope can detect is not what Parliament was considering when it employed the term "design" in this context.

---

[152] Jacob L.J. *Dyson v Qualtex* [2006] R.P.C. 31 CA, para.14.

[153] CDPA 1988 s.213(1), (2), (3)(c); see above, para.15–36.

[154] *Rolawn v Turfmech Machinery* [2008] E.C.D.R. 13 para.80; *Virgin Atlantic v Premium Aircraft Interiors* [2009] E.C.D.R. 11 paras 24–25.

[155] *Mark Wilkinson Furniture v Woodcraft Designs* [1998] F.S.R. 63; *Dyson v Qualtex* [2006] R.P.C. 31 CA, paras 74–83.

[156] *Amoena v Trulife* [1995] S.R.I.S. C/72/95.

[157] *Farmers Build v Carier Bulk* [1999] R.P.C. 461 CA; *Parker v Tidball* [1997] F.S.R. 680; *Electronic Techniques v Critchley Components* [1997] F.S.R. 401; *Dyson v Qualtex* [2006] R.P.C. 31 CA

[158] Below, paras 15–53—15–56.

[159] *Ocular Sciences v Aspect Vision Care* [1997] R.P.C. 289 at 423.

[160] A naturally occurring DNA sequence would not pass the requisite test of originality.

[161] Hirde and Peeters [1991] E.I.P.R. 334; Laddie et al. Ch.38.

To qualify for UK UDR, the design needs to be original, while for the registered right it must be novel.[162] Design right, being informal, can be infringed only by copying and "originality" here has its copyright meaning of "not copied".[163] This must be judged as a matter of substance. It is not original to add a previously used cable winder to a handle, if that was no more than mere collocation.[164] Apart from originality in general, it is necessary to consider whether the design is "commonplace in the design field in question at the time of its creation". Such a design is not to be regarded as original for the purpose of UK UDR.[165] This excludes a design which is trite, trivial, common-or-garden, hackneyed or of the type which would excite no particular attention in the relevant art.[166] Compare with this the exclusion from registration of designs which differ from prior art only in "variants commonly used in the trade". A thing could be "commonplace" in a design field, without necessarily being one of the variants used in a trade. Nonetheless, the court will place weight on the number and closeness of other designs.[167] The objective precondition for design right may thus be harder to satisfy than that for registered designs. A design does not become commonplace just because there is an obscure article which is similar to it[168] or if it contains a number of commonplace elements.[169] The exclusion of commonplace designs is thus a requirement of somewhat extended novelty, which probably resembles the twin criteria of novelty and individual character in registered designs law. **15–39**

UK UDR is not restricted to designs applicable to the article as a whole ("any aspect ... of the whole or any part").[170] This phrase has been read inclusively to cover any element that is "discernible" or "recognisable"; it is not correct to treat a feature of the design as visually insignificant by relating **15–40**

[162] cf. CDPA 1988 s.213(1), (4); RDA 1949 s.2(2), (4); above, para.15–17.

[163] cf. EU Designs Directive art.4, above, para.15–18. It does not matter that the design came from abroad: *Ultraframe (UK) v Eurocell Building Plastics* [2005] R.P.C. 7; nor does it have to be marketed in the UK for it to constitute prior use when estimating whether a later design is commonplace: *Dyson v Qualtex* [2005] R.P.C. 19.

[164] *Dyson v Qualtex* [2006] R.P.C. 31 CA, paras 95–96.

[165] This derives from the Semiconductor Topography Directive art.2(2); below, para.15–53. In *Guild v Eskander* [2003] F.S.R. 23, the Court of Appeal recognised that the question is the same as for copyright, subject to the "commonplace" issue. Relatively minor changes may not be enough to confer "originality": *Ultraframe v Eurocell Building Plastics* [2005] R.P.C. 7.

[166] *Ocular Sciences v Aspect Vision Care*, above, n.38: at 429; *Amoena v Trulife*, above, n.156—criticising the view that the test was that for novelty in patent law: *C & H Engineering v Klucznik* [1992] F.S.R. 421.

[167] *Farmers Build v Carier Bulk*, above, n.157. It does not need expert evidence to decide the issue: *Scholes Windows v Magnet* [2002] F.S.R. 43 CA.

[168] *Fulton v Grant Barnett* [2001] R.P.C. 257; Ashby [2001] E.I.P.R. 255. And see *Spraymiser v Rightway Marketing* [2000] E.C.D.R. 349 (design from human figure not necessarily commonplace).

[169] *Rolawn v Turfmech Machinery*, above, n.154, para.89.

[170] cf. the test for infringement, below, para.15–46, and also the position regarding registered designs, above, para.15–26. It is for the claimant to set out in his pleadings what features give rise to design right. This determines the subject-matter which has to be shown to be "original" and infringed: see *Dyson v Qualtex* [2006] R.P.C. 31 CA, paras 121–25.

it to the design of the whole article.[171] However, a method or principle of construction is excluded.[172] This exclusion has been construed narrowly such that designs will not be caught simply because they serve a functional purpose, unless that purpose cannot be achieved by other means.[173] In addition there are two specific exceptions which were included to prevent the new right after all from applying to replacement parts in the cases specified (but not beyond them). These are: "features of shape or configuration which:

(1) enable the article to be connected to, or placed around or against, another article so that either article may perform its function, or
(2) are dependent upon the appearance of another article of which the article is intended by the designer to form an integral part."[174]

15–41 The first of these is a "must fit" exception, broader than the specific exception in registered designs law, but narrower than the exclusion of designs dictated solely by function there.[175] The exception here requires that the article including the design must take its place "so that" one or other article may perform its function. This, however, can happen between components within complex machinery, such as a transformer.[176] It has even been held that one article may be a living organ: thus all those dimensional features of a contact lens which fixed it in place on the surface of an eye had to be discounted in a claim to UK UDR. Moreover, the exception is not confined to the case where only one shape will do.[177]

15–42 The second exception—"must match"—has been added in the same terms to registered designs law.[178] The typical case was thought to be the panel for a car door, and in all likelihood that example is within the exception. The exception must allow for repairs which give "something which was, in aesthetic terms, the same sort of article as he had originally bought".[179] The

[171] *Dyson v Qualtex* [2006] R.P.C. 31 CA, paras 22, 23.

[172] CDPA 1988 s.213(3)(a). For this reason, the stitching on mobile phone cases was excluded: *Parker v Tidball*, above, n.157; as was a generalised design concept for a wide-area mower: *Rolawn v Turfmech Machinery,* above, n.154. Cf. *Fulton v Grant Barnett* [2001] R.P.C. 257, design for an umbrella, providing a distinct result and shape; *Landor & Hawa v Azure Designs* [2007] F.S.R. 9 CA, design for an expanding suitcase was not excluded simply because it had a functional purpose.

[173] *Landor & Hawa v Azure Designs* [2007] F.S.R. 9 CA.

[174] CDPA 1988 s.213(3)(b).

[175] See above, para.15–19.

[176] *Electronic Techniques v Critchley*, above, n.157, cf. *Baby-Dan v Brevi.* The parts do not have to touch: *Dyson v Qualtex* [2006] R.P.C. 31 paras 31–39.

[177] *Ocular Sciences v Aspect Vision Care*, above, n.159, at 425; *Parker v Tidball*, above, n.157; *Dyson v Qualtex* [2006] R.P.C. 31, CA. There comes a point where there is no sufficiently precise correspondence in the fit, e.g. between prosthetic breast and brassiere: *Amoena v Trulife*, above, n.156. Cf. the requirements of essential function in respect of fit in registered designs law: above, para.15–29.

[178] See above, para.15–20. For registered design law this exception has been deprived of much significance.

[179] *Dyson v Qualtex* [2006] R.P.C. 31 CA; Michaels [2006] E.I.P.R. 396.

requirement that the shape or configuration be intended by the designer to form an integral part of something else was included in order to prevent the exception from extending to things intended to be made in sets, such as cutlery or glasses.[180] Whether one design is dependent on the appearance of another article is tested by asking whether it allows for substitution which does not radically affect that appearance.[181]

It must be noted that, because of international obligations or in pursuit of reciprocity, the Secretary of State may make different provision for different descriptions of design or article or exclude acts from the scope of infringement.[182] This allows the special topography right to continue in the form prescribed by EU Directive at the dictation of the United States.[183] **15–43**

(2) Qualification

One important motive in creating a separate UDR in the United Kingdom has been to preclude foreigners from entitlement, in a way that was difficult to introduce while protection was accorded under copyright.[184] **15–44**

The explicit provisions on qualification for unregistered design rights are expressed to relate to the United Kingdom, other Member States of the EU, the colonies and like territories to which Pt 2 may be extended, and countries which accord reciprocal protection to UK designs.[185] "Qualifying individuals" are citizens, subjects or habitual residents of one of these countries; and "qualifying persons" are these individuals together with corporate bodies incorporated in, or carrying on substantial business in, such a country.[186] Qualification also turns on the circumstances in which a design is made. If not made under commission or in employment, the designer must be a qualifying individual (or qualifying person, where the work is computer-generated).[187] In the excepted cases, it is the commissioner or employer who must be a qualifying person.[188] If there is no qualification according to these rules (and there may well not be), then it may arise from first marketing by a qualifying person with exclusive marketing rights in the United Kingdom, its extended territories, or the EU.[189]

In this form, the qualification provisions amount to an attempt by this country to follow the path of reciprocity which it has long since abandoned in established fields of intellectual property, but to which it was led in the

[180] There is, however, no exception for modular connectors in building toys and the like. Cf. above, para.15–20.
[181] *Dyson v Qualtex* [2006] R.P.C. 31 CA, paras 63–64.
[182] CDPA 1988 s.245.
[183] See below, paras 15–53—15–56.
[184] Because of Berne Convention (Paris Act) art.2(4).
[185] These countries are specified by Order under CDPA 1988 s.256.
[186] CDPA 1988 s.217. For an example of the consequences for a foreign claimant, see *Mackie Designs v Behringer* [1999] R.P.C. 717; Spavin [2000] E.I.P.R. 30.
[187] CDPA 1988 s.218; for joint designers, see s.218(3), (4).
[188] CDPA 1988 s.219.
[189] CDPA 1988 s.220.

cognate field of computer chip topography by pressure from the United States.[190]

15–45 The Paris Convention for the Protection of Industrial Property, of which the United Kingdom has been a member for more than a century, has as its object "patents, utility models, industrial designs..." and requires that "industrial property" be understood in its "broadest sense".[191] Accordingly it is arguable that, once the United Kingdom institutes a specific scheme for the protection of industrial designs, even though this does not require registration, it is obliged to provide equal treatment to nationals of Paris Convention states. The Government, it appears, is sufficiently uncertain of its position to have taken power to do this.[192]

(3) Exclusive right

15–46 The scope of design right bears important affinities to copyright, rather than to registered design. However, UK UDR has its own peculiarities. Primary infringement (which occurs irrespective of the defendant's culpability or innocence)[193] consists of reproduction of the design for commercial purposes by either making articles to the design or making a design document in order to make such articles. What must occur is reproduction of the design, that is copying of the design, directly or indirectly, so as to produce articles exactly or substantially to that design.[194] Like copyright, it turns on proof of copying.[195] Nonetheless it is a more difficult test to satisfy than an inquiry to see whether there has been substantial reproduction in the copyright sense. Here there must be at least a substantial taking of the design as a whole: mere similarity is not enough.[196] Much turns on what the design is alleged to be. In the *Klucznik* case,[197] it was for a pig fender of which the only element out of the ordinary was a round tube on top (to stop sows hurting their teats). Aldous J. compared the other party's fender as a whole. Because it

[190] See below, paras 15–53 et seq.

[191] PIP art.1(2), (3). For the obligation to protect industrial designs, see art.5*quinquies*.

[192] CDPA 1988 s.221.

[193] Cf. *Società Esplosivi v Ordnance Technologies (UK)* [2008] R.P.C. 12 paras 52–62, where Lindsay J. held that a commercial purpose requires a particular state of mind of the infringer; further that for s.226(1)(b) the making of the design document must be for the purpose that articles to the design should thereby be enabled to be made.

[194] CDPA 1988 s.226. But where infringement arises from making a design document the articles have to be made exactly to the design: *Società Esplosivi v Ordnance Technologies (UK)*, above, n.193, para.55.

[195] CDPA 1988 s.226(2); *C & H Engineering v Klucznik* (below, n.197) at 428; *Woolley Jewellers v A & A Jewellery (No. 2)* [2003] F.S.R. 15; and see [2004] F.S.R. 47. The functional purpose of the design may make proof of copying difficult: *Ocular Sciences*, above, n.159; *Amoena v Trulife* (above, n.156); cf. Bently and Coulthard (above, n.149). Copying may not be inferred where access to the design article is extremely limited as in *Rolawn v Turfmech Machinery* (above, n.154).

[196] *Guild v Eskander* [2003] F.S.R. 23 CA; *Virgin Atlantic v Premium Aircraft Interiors* [2009] E.C.D.R. 11 para. 31. When the design cannot be perceived by the eye, the test becomes particularly difficult to apply: cf. *Ocular Sciences* (above, n.38) at 424.

[197] *C & H Engineering v Klucznik* [1992] F.S.R. 421.

contained other features, notably an arrangement for stacking, there was no infringement.

Secondary infringement, which can occur only where the defendant knows or has reason to believe that he is dealing with an infringing article, may be constituted by unauthorised importation for commercial purposes, possessing for commercial purposes, and selling, letting for hire, or offering or exposing for sale or hire, in the course of a business.[198]

The right is akin to copyright infringement in that it has equivalent provisions concerning additional damages, delivery up, disposal of infringing articles, exclusion of damages for innocent infringement, exclusive licensees, and joint ownership.[199] There is, however, no right to engage in self-help seizure.

In UK UDR cases, the plaintiff is given one exceptional advantage which is not accorded in copyright. Once he shows that an alleged "infringing article" has been made to a design in which the right subsists or has subsisted at any time, it is for the defendant to prove that the article was made at a time when design right did not subsist.[200] That seems a fair presumption when the duration of the right itself is not in issue and the only question is the date on which the defendant acted. If, however, there is contention over the date on which the plaintiff's design was first recorded, or on which the plaintiff first authorised marketing of articles to the design somewhere in the world—both of which will affect the duration of the right—the defendant is put to proof of matter which cannot be in his own knowledge. The inherent unfairness of the provision might be limited if the plaintiff were first obliged to show that his design was not copied from another source. This at least could oblige him to give details of its creation, if not of its first marketing. It is accordingly desirable that "original" should include this concept. **15–47**

Unregistered design right is subject to Crown use on terms of compensation. The rules are as for UK RDs.[201]

(4) Authorship and first ownership

The rules concerning authorship and first ownership run in tandem with those for UK RDs and differ from those for copyright. This has already been commented upon.[202] If a design is made under a commission for money or money's worth, first ownership is accorded to the commissioner[203]; if that is not the case, where it is made by an employee in the course of employment, it belongs to the employer; failing this, the designer—that is the **15–48**

[198] CDPA 1988 s.227; s.228 applies to UK UDR the same rules concerning importation as have so far operated for copyright: but see above, para.12–29.

[199] CDPA 1988 ss.229–235.

[200] CDPA 1988 s.228(4).

[201] CDPA 1988 ss.240–244, 252.

[202] cf. above, para.15–22.

[203] The amount paid does not have to be adequate: *Farmers Build v Carier Bulk* (above, n.157).

creator—becomes the first owner.[204] If any of these persons are prospective owners of a design still to be created, they may assign their right by agreement in writing, signed by both parties, so as to vest the right on creation in the assignee.[205]

(5) Duration and licences of right

15–49 The period of UK UDR, though more substantial than EU UDR, is nonetheless shorter than that arising under copyright or the design registration system. The main thrust of the UDR is to give protection to functional objects and parts against imitation in the early years of their exploitation. Design right expires 15 years after first recording of the design in a design document or the first making of an article to the design, whichever is earlier; or—a further limitation—if articles to the design are legitimately marketed anywhere in the world within the first five years of recording or making the design, then the period is 10 years from first beginning this activity. The latter circumstance is likely to be the most usual.[206]

Moreover, during the last five years of the right—in most cases, after five years from first legitimate marketing—others are entitled to a licence of right to do anything within the scope of the right, its terms to be settled (if necessary) by the Comptroller, with appeal to the Designs Appeal Tribunal.[207] In exceptional cases, after reference to the Competition Commission and a finding by it that design right is being asserted in a manner contrary to the public interest, the Minister may order (inter alia) that licences of right be available even before the last five-year period.[208] There have been two Reports which have criticised aspects of design copyright exploitation by car manufacturers—reports which were influential in settling the terms of the 1988 New Deal.[209] Now there is legislative machinery for giving effect to the Commission's decisions, whether they relate to patents, copyright, registered designs or unregistered designs.[210] The application for a licence of right in the final five years may be made up to one year before commencement.[211]

15–50 Once the final five-year period is reached, an alleged infringer who

---

[204] CDPA 1988 ss.214, 215. Normally the designer is the person who draws the design, but could conceivably be the person who describes what is to be drawn: *Parker v Tidball* (above, n.157). A person who arranges the production of a computer-aided design is the designer: CDPA 1988 s.214(2).

[205] CDPA 1988 s.223.

[206] CDPA 1988 s.216; Reed [2005] E.I.P.R. 298.

[207] CDPA 1988 s.237; *Bance's Application* [1996] R.P.C. 667. Categories of design may be excluded from this provision by Order, because of a Convention obligation or in order to secure or maintain reciprocal protection of UK designs; the obvious case is the topography right in semiconductor chips; for which see below, para.15–53.

[208] CDPA 1988 s.238.

[209] *Re Car Parts* [1983] F.S.R. 115.

[210] For the equivalent provisions, see CDPA 1988 ss.144, 270.

[211] CDPA 1988 s.247.

undertakes to obtain a licence of right cannot be the subject of an injunction or delivery up order; and damages against him are limited to double the rate of royalty set in the licence of right.[212] In arriving at an appropriate royalty rate, the Comptroller will be seeking to evaluate the design element in the plaintiff's product as a contributory factor both to its development cost and to its success in the market.[213] In some circumstances, as an aid there may be evidence of royalty practices in voluntary licences.

Behind the availability of licences of right may well lurk issues of sub- **15–51** sistence of the right, its terms and first entitlement. Save in infringement proceedings and other actions where they arise incidentally, these issues can be raised only in proceedings before the Comptroller, with only limited rights of appeal to the High Court.[214] The controversial presumption in the plaintiff's favour which arises in relation to "infringing articles" does not seemingly apply in such proceedings, a matter which design copiers would do well to note.

(6) A brief comparison

By way of summary, let us conjure the vision of a table lamp consisting of a **15–52** base modelled as a mermaid and a lampshade in the form of a water-lily. The whole lovely complement could be the subject of a registered design, claiming its novelty in all these aspects of appearance. The design registration could endure for up to 25 years from registration.

Equally the lamp might attract artistic copyright: (1) as a whole, because it had the quality to rank among works of artistic craftsmanship; or because copyright can be traced back to a drawing that was not for an industrial design, but (say) for a book illustration; (2) in part, because one or other element constitutes a sculpture or perhaps an engraving—the base or (particularly if it is moulded) the shade. In these cases the protection will last for 25 years from the first legitimate marketing of products embodying the copyright work.

Such copyright can subsist beside any registered design that there may be. But to the extent that there is copyright there can be no infringement of UK UDR in any element of shape or configuration.[215] There may, however, be elements, such as the bulb-holder, which will at most attract this lesser form

[212] CDPA 1988 s.239. See also *Dyrlund Smith v Turberville Smith* [1998] F.S.R. 403; *NIC Instruments' Application* [2005] R.P.C. 1. Application after expiry of right: *Ultraframe v Eurocell Building Plastics* [2005] R.P.C. 7.

[213] In exercising his discretion as to terms, the Comptroller is given little statutory guidance. Some of the considerations which have been brought to bear on patent licences of right (see above, para.4–25) are treated as germane: *E-UK Controls' Licence of Right* [1998] R.P.C. 833.

[214] CDPA 1988 s.246.

[215] CDPA 1988 s.236; *Guild v Eskander* [2003] F.S.R. 23. Since, thanks to the different rules about ownership of commissioned works, there may be disputes about ownership, the presence or absence of copyright may well fall to be tested.

of protection (with its normal maximum of 10 years, subject to licences of right in the last five years). Moreover, the essentially utilitarian bulb-holder could not attract the lesser design right so far as it was commonplace in the trade, nor so far as its shape was formed to receive the bulb ("must fit"). A registered design can be obtained in the design so far as it is novel and has individual character. In assessing this the 12-month grace period for activities of the designer and his associates must now be remembered. Elements such as the bulb-holder may well be excluded for their technical character and any "must fit" element cannot in any case be protected. During the three-year period allowed for EU UDR, any aspect of the design which could be the subject of a registered right is protected against copying informally under this right.

The super-imposition of forms of protection for industrial designs in the United Kingdom makes the law an absurd maze. It is an area where for a few industries the protection is a useful incentive to make improvements and provide attractive alternatives. Only a relatively small number of registered designs are granted each year for the United Kingdom. Probably a similarly limited range of producers have an interest to rely upon copyright or either of EU DRs. Just because design protection is of such secondary importance the maze is unlikely to be clipped back rapidly to some manageable proportion. It certainly deserves to be.

(7) Topography right[216]

15–53 Finally in this section we reach a juncture where the special demands of computer technology meet more general concerns over the protection of industrial design. The semiconductor chip gives effect to program instructions through a circuitry fixed on semiconductor material in layered form.[217] The familiar ROMs, RAMs and EPROMs that are the basis of software packages are forms of such chips. Their mass-production is frequently the result of major investment in design, so there has been great pressure for legal means to prevent their imitation.

In the United Kingdom, it was likely that, because design copyright under the CA 1956 (as amended) was such an extended notion, the layered circuitry, taken from a design, could be treated as copyright. This was arguable particularly where photography was used to produce the layout. In other countries even this prospect was not open and the sole chance lay in an extension of unfair competition law. The United States, with the largest

[216] See generally Christie, *Integrated Circuits and their Contents: International Protection* (1995); Laddie et al. Ch.58; Chiu and Shen [2006] E.I.P.R.38.

[217] For a clear technical description, Christie (above, n.92), App.A. The design may be constituted on a single layer: *Fulton v Totes Isotomer* [2004] R.P.C. 16 CA.

investments at risk, insisted that there be rapid legislative intervention. Its own Semiconductor Chip Protection Act 1984 created a sui generis right in original "mask" works.[218] At the same time it announced that, if other countries wished their nationals to enjoy this new protection in the United States, they must provide equivalent protection for American mask works in their own territories. The EU, by Directive to Member States,[219] led the scramble to comply with this edict, though it has been far from clear why, in the then state of the computer industry worldwide, it should hasten to confer rights which overall would be of greater benefit to Americans than would the reciprocal benefits in the United States to its own firms.[220]

The obligation under the Directive was originally met in the United Kingdom by Regulations of 1987 creating a "topography right". These have since become a specially conditioned form of unregistered design right.[221] The subject of protection is the pattern fixed, or intended to be fixed, in or upon a layer of a semiconductor product, or in the arrangement of the layers of a semiconductor product; and a semiconductor product is: **15–54**

> "an article the purpose, or one of the purposes, of which is the performance of an electronic function and which consists of two or more layers, at least one of which is composed of semiconducting material and in or upon one or more of which is fixed a pattern appertaining to that or another function."[222]

To acquire protection the topography must be "original", in the same double sense that applies to design right in general.[223]

The basic period of protection is also as for UK UDR. No compulsory licence provision limits the range of topography right.[224] Qualification for it was initially dependent on close reciprocation, for which there are separate lists of countries, including, of course, the United States. This has now changed so as to extend the protection to all citizens or habitual residents of WTO countries.[225] Rules giving first ownership to a commissioner, an employer or otherwise the creator of the design closely parallel those for UK UDR.[226]

---

218 So called from the masking technique which is one method of producing the circuitry on the chip surface. See Ladd et al. *Protection of Semiconductor Chip Masks in the United States* (1986); Rauch (1993) 75 J.P.T.O.S. 93.

219 Directive 87/54; [1987] OJ L24/36.

220 In 1989, a WIPO Treaty on Intellectual Property in Respect of Integrated Circuits was concluded; but lay fallow. The TRIPS Agreement provides for 10 years of protection, on the lines of the US model: see arts 35–39.

221 Design Right (Semiconductor Topographies) Regulations 1989 (SI 1989/1100).

222 Design Right (Semiconductor Topography) Regulations 1989 (SI 1989/1100) reg.2(1).

223 See above, para.15–38.

224 Design Right (Semiconductor Topography) Regulations 1989 (SI 1989/1100) regs 6, 7, 9.

225 Design Right (Semiconductor Topography) Regulations 2006 (SI 2006/1833).

226 For computer-generated design see above, para 15–48, n.204.

15–55 The rules governing infringement are modified in a number of ways. Thus, there is a defence for reproduction of the design privately for non-commercial aims.[227] More significantly, and in direct descent from the US Act, there is a wide-ranging freedom to engage in reverse engineering. It is permissible to reproduce the topography for the purpose of analysing or evaluating it, or analysing, evaluating or teaching the concepts, processes, systems or techniques embodied in it; and as a result of such steps, it is permissible to create another original topography.[228] This in effect substitutes an older test of copyright infringement for the one that currently prevails in that sphere. For topography right, it would seem, the question is how much original work has been done in addition by the alleged infringer, not, as in current copyright law, how much of the old can be traced in the new.[229] Under similar legislation in Australia, it has been held that to shrink the scale of the plaintiff's integrated circuit is merely a reducing operation involving no "intellectual or unique design work". Not surprisingly the defence was not made out.[230]

15–56 It will be appreciated that much of the unregistered design right now introduced in the CDPA 1988 derives from the Topography Regulation. The two main points of difference are the absence from the latter of licences of right in the last five years and the absence from the former of the reverse engineering defence. In these respects the topography right continues to keep its special contours, set according to the American mould.[231]

[227] Design Right (Semiconductor Topography) Regulations 1989 (SI 1989/1100) reg.8(1).
[228] Design Right (Semiconductor Topography) Regulations 1989 (SI 1989/1100) reg.8(1), (4). See also Hart [1989] E.I.P.R. 111.
[229] The onus of making out the defence is probably on the defendant: Christie (above, n.216) pp.147–148, 153.
[230] *Nintendo v Centronics Systems* (1993) 23 I.P.R. 119.
[231] Under CDPA 1988 ss.221(2), 237(3), 245(1).

Part V

TRADE MARKS AND NAMES

CHAPTER 16

COMPETITOR AND CONSUMER

1. UNDERLYING THEMES

This Part focuses upon rights included in the scope of intellectual property, but which are concerned with methods of promoting and selling goods and services. Once more the purpose of legal intervention is to give protection to information. However, trade marks, names and other such signs have a less finite character than the information protected by patents, copyright and confidence. In an economy where most goods and services come from competing enterprises, trade mark owners typically use their marks to distinguish their products and services from others on offer. Their hope is that this will trigger an association in consumers' minds between origin and good value or quality. What consumers understand by the mark will depend on their previous knowledge and experience. **16–01**

Where brands are well-established—and that today means supporting actual trade with heavy and continuous advertising across regions or continents—their valuation as assets will run into billions of pounds.[1] Trade marks and names are accordingly quite as significant in economic terms as patents and copyright; and their impact across industry is far wider. What is critical to bear in mind however was well-expressed by Lewison J. in *O2 v Hutchison*:

> "English law does not, however, protect brands as such. It will protect goodwill (via the law of passing off); trade marks (via trade mark infringement); the use of particular words, sounds and images (via the law

[1] Valuing brands as assets is an important financial service: for methods, see Smith [1990] E.I.P.R. 159; Dalbosco (1997) 31 IP Forum 8; Sykes and King, *Valuation and Exploitation of Intellectual Property and Intangible Assets* (2003); Smith & Parr, *Intellectual Property: Valuation, Exploitation, and Infringement Damages* 3rd edn (2005).

of copyright); and configurations of articles (via the law of unregistered design right) and so on. But to the extent that a brand is greater than the sum of the parts that English law will protect, it is defenceless against the chill wind of competition."[2]

16–02 Two themes underlie the detailed law that is the subject of the following chapters. The first was raised in Ch.1[3] and need not be dwelt upon at length at this point. It is the question, how far should traders be given power to sue to stop the unfair business practices of their competitors? We have already noticed the traditional British reluctance to do more than give protection against promotional tactics that will harm one rival in particular, for instance by passing off goods as his. In varying degrees, the unfair competition laws of most continental European states go further, and the differences have noticeable repercussions when it comes to the "Europeanisation" of specific regimes of intellectual property protection.

The most directly relevant of those regimes concerns the registration of trade marks. European registration systems were substantially reshaped in 1996 by the introduction of a unitary mark for the whole EU (giving rise to a Community Trade Mark or "CTM"). At the same time the national systems of registration—which continue as alternatives to the CTM—were being substantially harmonised by a Directive.[4] Even before the creation of this dual system, some progress had been made towards a harmonised law of unfair competition. Already in 1984, the Misleading Advertising Directive[5] had been passed to harmonise the laws in that area. After years of debate amongst Member States having very different attitudes to the subject,[6] a further Directive on Comparative Advertising was approved and published in the Official Journal in October 1997.[7] This amended the 1984 Directive.[8]

Despite these developments, there remain significant differences between the different European approaches, which are all too easily ignored or underestimated.[9] Some systems—such as the French and Belgian—are based on the principle that, in the vast majority of cases, marks must be registered if they are to enjoy legal protection. There is no additional (and cumulative)

---

[2] [2006] E.T.M.R. 677 at para.7.

[3] See above, paras 1–13 and following.

[4] See below, Ch.18.

[5] Council Directive 84/450, OJ L250/17.

[6] For example, see Schricker (1990) 21 I.I.C. 620; (1991) 22 I.I.C. 788.

[7] Directive 97/55; [1997] OJ LO290/18, giving Member States 30 months to implement its provisions; this has now been replaced by Dir.2006/114, a codified version with numbering changes. Unlike the original provisions on misleading advertising, the rules are intended as maximum standards: the important provision is art.4 (ex-3a(1)) which permits the use of comparative advertising under certain, relatively stringent, conditions.

[8] For more recent proposals to build on the 1984 and 1997 Directives, see Henning-Bodewig and Schricker [2002] E.I.P.R. 271. The 1984 Directive has now been amended further by Directive 2005/29: see below, para.16–20.

[9] See generally, Cornish, *Intellectual Property: Omnipresent, Distracting, Irrelevant?* (2004) Ch.3.

form of action to protect aspects of an actual reputation built up in trade. Such an all-or-nothing approach operates to give industry advance information about what is and what is not protected. Among its disadvantages is that it encourages both legislatures and courts to expand what may be registered and thereby to give early entrants extensive "rights" which they may not have to do anything other than pay renewal fees to maintain.[10] On the other hand, the British and Irish passing off approach allows for a more discriminating balance of interests between first user and subsequent, perfectly honest entrants. It turns on what is actually happening in the marketplace[11]; and the remedies granted can be limited in various ways.[12]

One area in which the tensions are highlighted is that of sports merchandising: the use of team names on scarves, hats and the like is a practice that predates the expansion of trade mark law into areas which in reality are distant from the notion of the trade mark as a badge of origin. Indeed many traders in the United Kingdom (including Mr Reed of *Arsenal* fame)[13] have over the years been encouraged by the sports clubs themselves to sell to fans such indications of allegiance. It is surely disingenuous for people (including Advocate-General Ruiz-Jarabo Colomer in the *Arsenal* case)[14] to argue now that, because the amount of money involved has become large, it must be a trade mark issue, rather than in appropriate circumstances (i.e. where a misrepresentation is being made and that is a question of evidence) one of passing off or possibly unfair competition. The flexibility of the passing off action permits an analysis of what is actually happening in the marketplace[15] rather than the rigid application of a trade mark statute which strains to catch within its purview what is at its core not a trade mark question.

The second and related theme concerns the uses to which trade marks are **16–03**
put and the scope of legal protection that as a result ought to be accorded to them. Over the last century these uses have increased in diversity, which has raised conflicts with policies directed towards the welfare of consumers. The historical section below provides an introduction to the interplay between business demands and legal response in Britain and other countries. Thereafter an attempt is made to present some current controversies surrounding trade mark protection.

---

[10] They must not fail to use it for five years or allow it to become generic in the trade: below, paras 18–69—18–75.

[11] "[P]assing off is closely connected to and dependent upon what is happening in the marketplace. It is a judge made law which tries to ensure, in its own limited way, a degree of honesty and fairness in the way trade is conducted", per Laddie J. in *Irvine v Talksport* [2002] F.S.R. 943 at para.13.

[12] See further, below, para.17–12.

[13] See [2003] E.T.M.R. 227, ECJ.

[14] [2003] E.T.M.R. 227 at para.84: "The great clubs, such as Arsenal ". . . are not mere sporting associations whose aim is the playing of football, but genuine 'emporia' which, with the object of playing professional football, pursue an economic activity of the first order."

[15] "[T]he tort protects against harm to 'deserving' plaintiffs where it is in the public interest that this should happen", Carty, in 7 "Perspectives on Intellectual Property" 31 (2000) at 35.

2. Historical Development

(1) Judicial protection[16]

16–04 As modern capitalism has grown, the drive to sell products and services using some mark, brand or name has invaded more and more fields. Some foods and a few other staples are still sold to the consumer without branding, but the tendency is consistently towards some form of labelling to indicate source. Before industrialisation, there were, of course, instances of traders or trader groups who deployed marks of various kinds to distinguish their products. The hallmarks of goldsmiths and silversmiths and the marks of Sheffield cutlers are English examples which have survived as distinct systems.[17] But the demand for general legal protection against unfair imitation of marks and names is a product of the Industrial Revolution that followed factory production and the growth of canals and railways. That demand has swelled immensely with the development of modern advertising and large-scale retailing. Most advertising teaches the consumer to buy by product mark or house name and keeps reiterating its message in the hope of persuading buyers not to defect to rivals. Trade marks and names have become nothing more nor less than the crux of marketplace competition.

16–05 In English case law demands for legal protection against the imitation of marks and names were made and acceded to from the early years of industrialisation. The courts of equity gave a lead because claimants wanted injunctions. They intervened when one trader represented to the public that he was selling the goods or carrying on the business of another.[18] Soon afterwards, similar actions for damages at common law are found, the action for deceit being made available to a competitor.[19]

That extension bore its own limitation, for deceit required proof of deliberate fraud.[20] The courts of equity, however, being concerned primarily with the injunction (a forward-looking remedy), did not feel the same

[16] See generally Schechter, *The Historical Foundations of the Law Relating to Trade Marks* (1925), Ch.6; Behrendt (1961) 51 T.M.R. 853; McClure (1979) 69 T.M.R. 305; Bently et al, *Trade Marks and Brands* (2008) Ch.1; Cornish et al, *Oxford History of the Laws of England* XIII (2010) Pt V, Ch.6.

[17] British hallmarks are regulated by the Hallmarking Act 1973, as amended in 1998 to comply with EU legislation; also, the Hallmarking (International Convention) Order 2002 (SI 506/2002) recognises and permits the use in the UK of certain hallmarks applied in another Vienna Convention country.

[18] The possibility of such an action seems recognised by Lord Hardwicke L.C. in *Blanchard v Hill* (1742) 2 Atk. 485. He treated the older, obscure case at common law, *Southern v How* (1618) Popham 144, as allowing an action on the case for a fraudulent design "to put off bad cloths . . . or to draw away customers from another clothier" (i.e. a competitor's, as well as a consumer's, action): see Dawson (2003) 24 J.L.H. 111.Thereafter, see *Hogg v Kirby* (1803) 8 Ves. 215; cf. *Longman v Winchester* (1809) 16 Ves. Jun. 269; *Crutwell v Lye* (1810) 17 Ves. Jun. 335.

[19] *Sykes v Sykes* (1824) 3 B. & C. 541 (the basic principle appears to be established already); *Blofeld v Payne* (1833) 4 B. & Ad. 410.

[20] See *Pasley v Freeman* (1789) 3 T.R. 51; *Derry v Peek* (1889) 14 App. Cas. 337 HL.

constraint. Impelled by their sense of the injury that could be caused by passing off, they would enjoin even a defendant who had adopted the mark or name in all innocence: the goodwill at risk was easily characterised as "property", the deception of the public was in itself "fraud".[21] Other potential limitations were bypassed: the common law courts had no scruple in holding it actionable for a manufacturer to supply a retailer with "the instruments of fraud"[22]; or for one trader to pass off goods as another's even if they were not of inferior quality.[23] Westbury as Lord Chancellor insisted that a mark or name could be protected even though the public did not know the producer as such but used the connection with a trade source simply as a sign of quality.[24]

By the 1850s, public agitation about the extent to which food, drugs and other commodities were sold in an adulterated state was beginning to run high. It mixed with the complaints of established competitors that they were being undercut by such practices, by cheap imports that did not declare what they were and by the false imitation of brands, marks and names.[25] To some extent, purchasers found a market remedy—by lending their custom to the new retailing co-operatives.[26] But there were also calls on their behalf for legal protection, the criminal law being envisaged as the principal machinery.[27] **16–06**

Important commercial interests, however, wanted Britain to adopt a system of registering trade marks—after the model, for instance, of the French law of 1857.[28] In part their concern was domestic. The passing off action, though useful, depended on proving in each case that the claimant had a trade reputation with the public. That could sometimes be costly and laborious. If there were a register, the issue could be reduced to the question: was the defendant imitating the mark in a manner liable to deceive? But in part it was from international trade that the demand arose. Prussian and American counterfeiters were said to be passing off their own "Manchester" textiles and "Sheffield" cutlery in various parts of the world.[29] The hope of stopping foreign imitations of British marks seemed to lie in also

[21] *Millington v Fox* (1838) 3 My. & Cr. 338; *Edelsten v Edelsten* (1863) 4 De G.J. & S. 185. But for the adventures of "property" in this subject matter, see below, paras 17–02—17–06.

[22] *Sykes v Sykes* (1824) 3 B. & C. 541; a notion relied on by Aldous L.J. some 175 years later to combat cybersquatting in *British Telecommunications v One in a Million* [1999] 1 W.L.R. 903 CA, at 920.

[23] *Blofeld v Payne* (1833) 4 B. & Ad. 410.

[24] *Hall v Barrows* (1863) 4 De G.J. & S. 150 at 157.

[25] See, e.g. E.W. Stieb, *Drug Adulteration* (1966), Chs 8–11.

[26] See, e.g. G.D.H. Cole, *A Century of Co-operation* (1945); C.R. Fay, *Co-operation at Home and Abroad* 5th edn (1948).

[27] One record of this political activity is the Report of the Trade Marks Bill Select Committee PP 1862 (212) XII.

[28] For this step and its consequences in French trade mark law, see Beier (1975) 6 I.I.C. 285 at 294–298.

[29] See the many complaints in evidence to the 1862 Committee.

establishing a register. Mutual protection of foreigners' marks in Britain could then be offered as a quid pro quo.

16–07 There was considerable "liberal" suspicion of this idea for a new property right: a first entrant might be able to appropriate ways of marking his goods that could pose difficulties for later competitors. The Merchandise Marks Act 1862, which included "forging a trade mark" amongst its prohibitions on the false marking of goods, was solely a criminal statute, and deliberately so.[30] A pattern of considerable moment was thus established: the criminal law was to provide the general machinery against misdescription of wares. The normal principle that any citizen might prosecute was to apply—indeed in the 1862 Act it was encouraged by the old device of sharing the penalty between prosecutor and Crown. But competitors were not to have the weaponry of civil suits to deal with a wide range of misleading trade descriptions. The Merchandise Marks legislation grew in completeness with a revised statute of 1887. This was to continue in force (with amendments) until the Trade Descriptions Act 1968.[31] Its actual enforcement was extremely patchy, for unlike under the neighbouring legislation on food and drugs and weights and measures, local authorities were not placed under any duty to provide inspectors and others who would see to observance. In practice competitors showed little interest in putting their resources to the task.[32]

(2) The Trade Marks Register[33]

16–08 Traders kept up pressure to have the protection of trade marks made more secure. In 1875 the campaign for a registration system succeeded so far as marks for goods were concerned.[34] But the new system acquired from the start a number of characteristics which stamped it as a special privilege conceded with some misgiving:

(1) for the first 30 years of the Register's operation, only a limited range of symbols could be registered as trade marks[35];

[30] See Cornish, above n.16, at 1000–1001.

[31] Enacted in the wake of the Final Report of the Malony Committee on Consumer Protection (Cmnd.1781, 1962).

[32] Occasional prosecutions reached the law reports, e.g. where a name of geographical origin was in issue: see e.g. *Holmes v Pipers* [1914] 1 K.B. 57; *Corke v Pipers*, referred to in *Vine Products v Mackenzie* [1969] R.P.C. 1 at 18–19. The failure of criminal proceedings against the importers of "Spanish Champagne" (see *Bollinger v Costa Brava Co Ltd* [1961] R.P.C. 116 at 119) underlines the standard of proof required. For subsequent developments, see below, para.17–38.

[33] See Bently, above, n.16 and in Dinwoodie and Janis *Trade Mark Law and Theory* (2008) Ch 1; Cornish, above n.16, at 998–1007.

[34] Trade Marks Registration Act 1875; amended in 1876 and 1877 and then incorporated into the Patents, Designs and Trade Marks Act 1883.

[35] In 1875, these were: name of individual or firm specially printed, etc., written signature, distinctive device, mark, heading, label or ticket, to which certain other matter might be added: see s.10, slightly expanded in the Patents, Designs and Trade Marks Acts 1883 and 1888.

(2) registration was not simply a matter of deposit but was subject to an official examination and open to opposition by third parties after advertisement of the application;
(3) not only prior registrations but also prior use of the same mark or one deceptively similar prevented registration.

Critically, there was no obligation to use the mark before registering it.[36] This gave businesses an important measure of security when launching a new product.

For a time it was not clear whether the registrable types of mark could be protected only after registration.[37] But the judges were sympathetic to the view that goodwill acquired through actual trading should be accorded legal protection also. Common law and equity were held still to give relief against passing off, even if it was effected through imitating a mark that might have been registered.[38] The methods of protection became cumulative, not alternative.

Trade mark registration systems may work on different premises: registration may be allowed without any substantive examination for conflicting interests (as in France prior to the changes brought about by the Trade Mark Approximation Directive); as a corollary, protection is made conditional upon registration, so that industry has an official record of all marks already in existence. Until its "Europeanisation" in 1994, the British system continued to build upon its Victorian foundations. The cumulative relation between common law and statutory rights and the existence of a pre-grant examination allowed the categories of registrable marks to be expanded. By the Act of 1905, if there was some inherent objection to a mark (particularly because, being a word, it had some other meaning), this might be overcome upon proof of sufficient use as a trade mark to distinguish the origin of goods: a provision which continues to play a critical role in trade mark registration systems the world over.[39] Furthermore, in 1919 the Register was divided into Pts A and B so that certain marks could be given lesser protection until they had been used enough to overcome all doubts.[40] However, marks used for services were left outside the system until the mid-1980s, thus leaving one whole field exclusively to common law protection. **16–09**

The 1905 Act tied the statutory privilege to actual trading by making non-use for the previous five years a ground upon which a person with an interest

[36] cf. the Lanham Trademark Act of 1946 in the US.

[37] The 1875 Act s.1 (and its amendments in 1876) provided that "proceedings to prevent the infringement of any trade mark" should not be brought unless the mark was registered.

[38] See especially *Great Tower v Langford* (1888) 5 R.P.C. 66; *Faulder v Rushton* (1903) 20 R.P.C. 477, CA. In the USA the existence of common law rights alongside the federal system of registration has also been important, though with somewhat different consequences: see McCarthy, *Trade Marks and Unfair Competition* (3rd edn) Ch.1.

[39] On this see further, below, paras 18–25 et seq.

[40] A scheme given up in the 1994 Act.

could have a mark removed from the register.[41] In a different way, the courts insisted on the same connection: under the 1905 Act, they treated registration as expungeable if the mark had been licensed, for that rendered obscure whether the mark indicated a connection in trade with the registered proprietor or the licensee. They would not consider the registered right as a discrete part of the trader's property to be exploited by him without reference to the public's understanding of its meaning.

16–10 The increasing scale of business organisation in the twentieth century led to many shifts in trading practice. The spread of production, the growth of a popular press with its immense prospects for advertising, the increase of transnational business in successful products and the consequent need to shield high-priced markets against parallel imports from elsewhere were all characteristics of the inter-war years. Brand advertising on a large scale by manufacturers supplemented goodwill that was principally associated with retail outlets, and this only increased the commercial significance of the trade marks around which it revolved. There was considerable pressure to be able to license and assign marks more freely than was possible under the British system. This stemmed from the increased complexity of corporate groupings and the increase in both domestic and cross-border licensing of technology and business "packages". One particular advantage, it was hoped, was that, if the same trade mark was in legally distinct ownership in different countries, the rights could be employed to deter parallel importing.[42] An elaborate and not very satisfactory compromise over assignment and licensing was embodied in the Trade Marks Act,1938,[43] the Act which carried the law through to its Europeanisation in 1994.

16–11 New advertising techniques also led to pressure on the registration system to compensate for the absence of a general unfair competition law. The 1938 Act contained two concessions in this direction.[44] Very well-known trade marks became registrable "defensively" for goods in which the owner did not trade, in the hope of preventing others from annexing any of their notoriety. But the judges treated this arrangement coldly and it had little impact.[45] Owners of Pt A trade marks were also enabled to object to comparative advertising and similar practices which attempted to take the

[41] For the present law, see below, paras 18–69 et seq.

[42] For the fate of this device in recent times, see below, paras 18–119 et seq.

[43] A system of so-called registered users (or licensees) was set up by s.28 and use by such users was deemed to be use by the proprietor; however, the system did not require registration of licences and it remained somewhat unclear what the consequence of non-registration was. For a detailed explanation of the treatment of assignments and licensing in the 1938 Act, see *Kerly* 12th edn (1986) at paras 13.10–13.19 and 13.20–13.34, respectively.

[44] Both following recommendations of the Goschen Committee (Cmd.4568, 1934) paras 73–77, 184–185.

[45] See esp. *Ferodo's Application* (1945) 65 R.P.C. 111; and *Eastex's Application* (1947) 64 R.P.C. 142. Between 1938 and 1974 only 100 defensive registrations succeeded and the Mathys Committee (Cmnd.5601, 1974) para.102, recommended the abandonment of this special form of registration. In the 1994 Act this has come about because of a broader approach to "dilution": see paras 18–99—18–102.

benefit of the advertising without paying for it. Again, some judges found the expansion of the law unpalatable and the provision had an uncertain effect.[46]

In 1974, the Mathys Departmental Committee reported on the system under the 1938 Act in terms of general satisfaction with the British way of doing things.[47] The most significant proposal was to admit service marks onto the register; implemented in 1984.[48] But doubts as to the sustainability of the British system soon began to surface, arising mainly from the use of marks in international, rather than domestic, trade. Transnational businesses want simple, certain and cheap registration without having to apply country by country using systems encrusted with individual idiosyncrasies. Within the EU, both approximating national trade mark systems (which differed in material respects) and introducing a unitary mark for the Single Market became attractive aims. On the world scene, new initiatives were proposed to secure an international system to simplify registration in a number of countries. **16–12**

As a result, extensive changes were introduced into UK law by the Trade Marks Act 1994.[49] This establishes a new regime for trade mark registration and sweeps away the old system, while stating explicitly that "nothing in this Act affects the law relating to passing off".[50] At the same time it allows access to international registration through the so-called Madrid Protocol.[51] The background to these important changes is to be found in developments on both the international and the EU levels.

(3) Trade marks in world trade

(a) *International agreements*[52]

The UK trade mark registration system succeeded largely because of the needs of British exporters. It had proved difficult to negotiate bilateral arrangements with other countries when their nationals could not be offered the protection of a registered right in Britain.[53] The 1875 Act gave British manufacturers the increasingly important hope of protection abroad, and there was then no difficulty in supporting the provisions on trade marks in the Paris Convention on Industrial Property of 1883. These were modest, **16–13**

---

[46] See para.17–83 of the 4th edition of this work.

[47] Cmnd.5601, 1974, esp. para.46.

[48] Trade Marks Amendment Act 1984 (with addenda in 1986); the form of this legislation, introducing separate Acts for goods and service marks, was unduly elaborate and sometimes inconsistent.

[49] The Government's intentions were indicated in the White Paper, *Reform of Trade Marks Law* (Cm.1203, 1990).

[50] TMA 1994 s.2(2); on which see *Inter Lotto (UK) v Camelot* [2004] R.P.C. 186 CA.

[51] See further, below, para.16–14.

[52] See the writings referred to above in nn.16 and 33.

[53] See Schechter, *The Historical Foundations of the Law Relating to Trade Marks* (1925) at 140.

consisting mainly of the principle of "national treatment",[54] and a short period of priority stemming from the filing of a first application in a Paris Convention country,[55] along with an acknowledgment of the independence both of filing and registration in each country.[56]

At no stage has the Paris Convention itself provided any form of international application for registration in a number of countries. But as early as 1891, some Paris participants were prepared to take this step in the Madrid Agreement.[57] This allows an applicant who has registered a mark in his home country to deposit an international registration with an international office (now WIPO). The mark will then be registered in each other contracting State designated by the applicant, unless that state raises an objection, under its national law, within 12 months. Independent national trade marks are thus procured, subject, in the original Madrid Agreement, to the qualification that if the home registration is invalidated within five years, all the international registrations fall victim to this "central attack".

16–14 For countries such as the United Kingdom and the United States, with a full official examination of trade mark applications, the Madrid Agreement in its original form has remained unattractive and its fee structure unacceptable.[58] In 1989, however, a Protocol to Madrid (so called but effectively a new agreement) was negotiated which offered an alternative method of using the Madrid Scheme. This Protocol has attracted British approval and

---

54 See above, para.1–32.

55 For international priority and trade mark applications, see below, para.18–04. The Paris Convention now contains a number of other guarantees (also incorporated in TRIPS). The following must be protected: service marks, collective marks, business names, national emblems, official signs, hallmarks, etc. (arts 6*ter*, 6*sexies*, 7*bis*, 8); marks well-known in a country through their international reputation (art 6*bis*, see below, para.17–17); and competitors against acts of unfair competition (art.10*bis*, see below, paras 16–19, 16–20). There are provisions on infringing imports, remedies and the right to sue (arts 9, 10*ter*).

56 There is no need to file first in a country of origin, validity does not depend on that in a country of origin (cf. below, n.57), and nor does renewal (art.6). However, registration in a country of origin restricts the objections which may be raised in other countries to those listed in art.6*quinquies* B: third party rights, lack of distinctiveness, objections on grounds of morality and public order and unfair competition.

57 Madrid Agreement concerning the International Registration of Marks. At the same time a second Madrid Agreement was also reached, covering the Repression of False or Deceptive Indications of Source of Goods (1891, revised 1911, 1934, 1958; additional act, 1967) to which the UK has not become a party also. The main participants in the original Madrid Agreement have been the non-Nordic countries of Continental Europe and certain North African states.

58 From time to time there have been attempts to bring more of the world's industrial countries into an international application scheme. Notably a Trademark Registration Treaty (WIPO) reached final form in 1974, but in the event attracted few signatories and became a lost cause. The Trademark Law Treaty (WIPO), adopted on October 27, 1994, is a more modest arrangement, designed to secure greater homogeneity in national procedures for trade mark applications, changes of ownership and renewals. It contains some quite significant restraints on national legislation which might otherwise create special difficulties for foreign enterprises—for instance, regarding the need to produce evidence of actual use (see esp. arts 3(7), 11(4), 13(4)).

was given effect by the 1994 Act.[59] The old Madrid countries remain happy with their original arrangement, and it has been necessary to introduce provisions to continue the original arrangements between them, whilst giving the Protocol effect between the old set and the new joiners.

The relaxations of the rigours of the original Madrid Agreement which the Protocol admits include the following. (1) International registration can proceed from a home application, rather than a home registration.[60] (2) The fee basis allows countries with full examining offices to receive charges reflecting the work they do.[61] (3) The hotly contested principle of central attack is modified: if the original application or registration in the home country fails or is held invalid within five years, and the international registration falls in consequence, conversion into national applications of equivalent priority date may occur.[62] (4) The time-limit within which a country may raise its own objections to an international application is 18 months, with possibility of extension to take account of opposition proceedings.[63]

The TRIPS Agreement imposes an obligation on its participant states to **16–15**
apply the Paris Convention standards relating to trade marks.[64] It also cross-refers to those provisions at a number of points, supplements some of them in significant respects and imposes its own obligations in addition. Thus in adopting a broad definition of the signs capable of being marks, it requires trade mark registration to extend to marks for services.[65]

It strikes out on its own in defining the right in a registered mark: this is the exclusive right to prevent unauthorised third parties from using in the course of trade identical or similar signs for goods or services which are identical or similar to those in respect of which the mark is registered and there is a likelihood of confusion; this likelihood will be presumed where both mark and goods or services are identical.[66] Also, TRIPS extends the Paris Convention provision on the protection of well-known marks to service marks and to cases of dilution by use for different goods and services where that use is damaging.[67]

Use may not be made an automatic precondition of registration, though it is to be taken into account in assessing distinctiveness.[68] Removal for non-

[59] See *Kerly* Ch.7. The USA also signed the Madrid Protocol, on November 2, 2002, and now uses the system. See (2002) 92 T.M.R. 1430.

[60] For what constitutes a sufficient domestic basis, see the Madrid Agreement art.1; and for the six-month Paris Convention priority, see art.4(2).

[61] Madrid Protocol art.8.

[62] Madrid Protocol art.9*quinquies*.

[63] Madrid Protocol art.5. See below, para.18–02.

[64] TRIPS art.2(1).

[65] TRIPS art.15.

[66] TRIPS art.16(1). This does not go as far as the provisions in the EU Directive and Regulation: below, paras 18–86 et seq.

[67] TRIPS art.16.

[68] TRIPS art.15(1), (3). On the other hand, the mark has to be published and an opportunity for opposition afforded: art.15(5).

use can occur only after a period of at least three years.[69] The term before renewal of a registration is required must be at least seven years.[70]

While it is proper to require the use of a house mark in addition to a product mark, other incumbrances, such as use with another trade mark, use in a special form or use in a manner detrimental to its capacity to distinguish, are forbidden,[71] as is compulsory licensing.[72] Assignments, moreover, are to be permitted with or without the transfer of the related business.[73] Developing countries have sometimes sought to impose trade mark curbs with a view to controlling technology transfers involving transnational corporations. These hopes were largely in vain and have been curtailed or abandoned. TRIPS has helped to bury them.

(b) *The Community Trade Mark and the EU Trade Mark Approximation Directive*[74]

16–16 The Mathys Committee reported shortly after the United Kingdom joined the then European Economic Community at the beginning of 1973. Already Community law was beginning to affect the national systems for the protection of intellectual property rights. It was clear that the Treaty of Rome imposed significant limitations upon the use of trade marks to prevent the movement of "parallel" (i.e., genuine) goods from one Member State to another. The European Court of Justice was indeed developing a highly sceptical view of the outreaches of trade mark protection and this led to intense debate.[75] One consequence of the court's intervention was to revive an earlier proposal for a Community-wide mark.[76] This in its turn focused attention on the differing regimes operating in the Member States and posed difficult questions. How would conflicts between marks legitimately used in different parts of the Single Market be resolved? What priority should be given to those who would use community-wide media to promote their

[69] TRIPS art.19.

[70] TRIPS art.18. Renewals must be allowed indefinitely.

[71] This prohibition has been used by those arguing against the legitimacy of the trade mark impacts of recent EU anti-tobacco advertising legislation, on the basis that the effect of that legislation is to prevent use of lawfully obtained trade marks: an argument rejected by the ECJ in *R. v Secretary of State for Health Ex. p. British American Tobacco (Investments) and others*, noted at [2002] E.T.M.R. 1244, Judgment, at paras 154–155.

[72] Such licensing would seem to conflict with the prime object of marking, which is to indicate source connections. But it offers a remedy for monopolistic practices, which has tempted even US antitrust jurisdictions.

[73] TRIPS arts 20, 21.

[74] Kur (1997) 28 I.I.C. 1.

[75] See below, para.19–04.

[76] A Working Party, chaired by De Haan, had reported in 1964 but this was published only in 1973, once the EPC was complete: see DTI, *Proposed European Trade Mark* (1973). In 1976 a small group of experts produced a Memorandum on the Creation of an EEC Trade Mark (Bull. E.C. Supp. 8/76). In 1980, when the Commission produced its First Draft for a Regulation, it added a Draft Directive which contained some highly contentious provisions to foster the Single Market concept (see on the two documents, House of Lords, EC Select Committee, Report 1982–1983, p.21). Revised drafts followed (Regulation 1984; Directive 1985) before the final enactments.

products throughout the whole territory or major parts of it? What registration system was best designed to hold the balance between effectiveness and due respect for competing interests, large and small? What place would remain for the legal protection of marks and names on the basis of use rather than registration, where national law so allowed?

Reaching accord took substantial, but not inordinate, time. As already mentioned, a measure requiring the considerable (but not complete) harmonisation of national laws was enacted in 1988 and is in effect in all Member States.[77] In parallel a system for the grant of Community Trade Marks (CTMs) was developed and introduced[78]: in April 1996 the inelegantly-titled Office for the Harmonisation in the Internal Market (Trade Marks and Designs) in Alicante (OHIM or the CTM Registry, for short) opened its doors for CTM applications. In the United Kingdom it was these two EU initiatives, together with adherence to the Madrid Protocol, which led to the Trade Marks Act 1994, an Act which rewrites much of the form and substance of trade mark law as it was known previously.

As with patents, the 1994 Act offers optional routes by which to apply for trade mark registration in the United Kingdom, and indeed it confronts the applicant with even more choices than does the patent system. The entrance doors now open are: **16–17**

(1) At the UK Registry (in Newport), to apply for: (a) UK registration in the old way; or (b) a UK registration using the application as a basis for international registration through WIPO in such Madrid Protocol countries as are designated; or (c) following a Madrid application started in another country, international registration of a UK mark. In all three cases, so far as the United Kingdom is concerned, a UK registration is the object and the rights in it arise under the 1994 Act and are enforceable in the courts of the United Kingdom.[79]

(2) At the CTM Registry, to apply for a CTM which is unitary in effect and is enforceable throughout the EU in accordance with the terms of the CTM Regulation.[80]

Business people seeking trade marks need sophisticated advice.[81] Any judgment on how to proceed must balance the appropriate geographical and economic spread for the particular mark (language is a crucial factor in many cases), the likelihood of objections in various parts of the much larger, **16–18**

---

[77] First Directive (December 21, 1988) [1989] OJ L40/1. The First Directive has now been replaced by Directive 2008/95 but without change to numbering or substance.

[78] Regulation (December 20, 1993) [1994] OJ L11/1; Jaffey (1997) 28 I.I.C. 153.

[79] See below, paras 18–02 et seq.

[80] See below, para.18–11. Also, a CTM application may be made by a UK applicant via the UK Registry, which gives the application a filing date and forwards it to Alicante.

[81] "The entire law of registered trade marks ... has become ever so complicated", per Sir Robin (now Lord Justice) Jacob in the Preface to Kerly's *Law of Trade Marks and Trade Names* 13th edn (2001). The situation has not improved since.

single European market of 27 Member States and comparative costs of national versus regional protection. Preliminary private searching is often advisable to avoid unpleasant surprises later (computerised databases have revolutionised the possibilities).[82] The danger, however, is of the tendency to rush and register whatever one can get away with and argue later about its true validity as a registered trade mark. Examples abound of shape or other non-traditional marks whose presence on the register must raise serious concern in the minds of those wishing for a coherent and justifiable trade mark system with a proper balance between the legitimate interests of traders, their competitors and consumers.

(c) *Unfair competition and consumer protection*

16–19 Over a long period there have been attempts to arrive at a common foundation of unfair competition law within the EU.[83] This goal remains far off: the job is too intricate. Recognising the difficulty of reconciling different national attitudes and legal cultures, the EU Commission notes in its 2001 Green Paper on EU Consumer Protection that it would probably be easier to reach agreement on a framework Directive based on the notion of deceptive and misleading practices than one based on "fair commercial practices".[84]

However, in 1978, the Commission, developing its role in the protection of consumers, produced a draft Directive requiring the harmonisation of laws against misleading and unfair advertising.[85] Originally of very considerable scope, it came under sustained attack. The case put by the British advertising industry was that there existed voluntary mechanisms, such as the Advertising Standards Authority (ASA),[86] which were better able to achieve results than the compulsory sanction of legal regulation.[87] Reflecting the difficulties still felt today, the Directive which emerged was of more modest proportion. In implementing it by Regulation in 1988,[88] the UK Government added to existing legislation on trade descriptions and related matters only in relatively minor ways.[89] Similarly, when the Comparative

[82] In her Opinion in *Céline* [2007] E.T.M.R.80, ECJ, Advocate-General Sharpston notes that "mere ignorance of the existence of [a] trade mark [will not] be sufficient to bring the adoption of the name within the fold of honest practice ... a search in national and Community trade mark registers is not normally particularly difficult or burdensome", at para.55.

[83] See, in particular, the Max-Planck-Institute volumes, Ulmer (ed.), on the legal position in each Member State; Beier (1985) 16 I.I.C. 139; Robertson and Horton [1995] E.I.P.R. 568; Wadlow [2006] E.I.P.R. 433 and 469.

[84] COM(2001) 531, at para.4.2.

[85] See Schricker (1977) 8 I.I.C. 185; but cf. (1991) 22 I.I.C. 788 and esp. [1994] GRUR Int. 586, questioning the wisdom of the severe German approach.

[86] See above, para.2–25.

[87] See HL Select Committee, *Report on Misleading Advertising* (HL, 1978); but cf. Director-General of Fair Trading, *Review of the Self-Regulatory System of Advertising Control* (1978), taking a less sanguine view of self-regulation.

[88] Control of Misleading Advertisements Regulations 1988 (SI 1988/915).

[89] See below, para.17–56.

Advertising Directive[90] came to be implemented in the United Kingdom, the position was adopted that existing regulation did not need considerable amendment to comply.[91]

In a bid to consolidate UK legislation on consumer protection, and to try **16–20**
to harmonise with other EU Member States' legislation on unfair trading, the Consumer Protection from Unfair Trading Regulations 2008[92] (somewhat confusingly, given the acronym for the Civil Procedure Rules, known as the CPRs) implements the EU Unfair Commercial Practices Directive 2005 (2005/29/EC) UCPD) and replaces a number of existing laws,[93] particularly much of the Trade Descriptions Act 1968.[94] The CPRs include a general prohibition against unfair commercial practices which acts as a sweep-up provision where a commercial practice is deemed unfair but does not fall within the other specific offences[95] under the CPRs.

The Business Protection from Misleading Marketing Regulations 2008 (BPRs)[96] both subsume the 1988 Regulations and implement the now consolidated Misleading and Comparative Advertising Directive 2006 (2006/114/EC). The BPRs prohibit business-to-business advertising which is misleading under reg.3, and also govern situations where comparative advertising is permitted.[97]

Despite the powers granted to the OFT and OFCOM under the Communications Act 2003, self-regulation by the advertising industry itself remains the norm in the United Kingdom. ASA plays a central part, regulating both broadcast media advertisements (such as television and radio, using the "Television Advertising Standards Code" and the "Radio Advertising Standards Code", which are produced by the Broadcast

[90] Directive 97/55 [1997] OJ L290/18; now replaced by Directive 2006/114 [2006] OJ L376/21. For a description of how the Directive has altered the way German courts view advertising, see Dominguez Perez (2001) 32 I.I.C. 20, in particular the German Supreme Court decision in "*Compare*", [1999] GRUR Int. 453, which is heralded as a "new stage in the approach", at 51; cf. the German Supreme Court decision in "*Get Champagne, Pay for Sparkling Water*" (2002) 33 I.I.C. 991.

[91] See Control of Misleading Advertisement (Amendment) Regulations 2000 (SI 2000/914), which came into force on April 23, 2000. These Regulations also deal with the protected designation of origin ("PDO") and protected geographical indication ("PGI") rights introduced by EC Regulation 2081/92.

[92] SI 2008/1277.

[93] The CPRs wholly or partially repeal provisions in 23 laws; 12 laws have been repealed outright, for instance, Pt III of the Consumer Protection Act 1987, and 11 have been repealed in part.

[94] e.g., provisions on false trade descriptions (s.1(1) of Trade Descriptions Act 1968) and on false or misleading statements (s.14) would fall within the scope of the UCPD as they apply in business-to-consumer cases. For further information, see the Explanatory Memorandum to Consumer Protection from Unfair Trading Regulations 2008 and the Business Protection from Misleading Marketing Regulations, available on the OPSI website: *http://www.opsi.gov.uk/si/si2008/em/uksiem_20081277_en.pdf*.

[95] The CPRs also define what are considered to be misleading actions (reg.5), misleading omissions (reg.6) and aggressive commercial practices (reg.7). Schedule 1 of the Regulations also lists 31 unfair commercial practices that are strictly prohibited.

[96] SI 2008/1276.

[97] BPRs reg.4.

Committee of Advertising Practice (BCAP)) and non-broadcast media advertisements (such as newspapers and posters, but also online marketing, such as banners and pop-up ads) under "The British Code of Advertising, Sales Promotion and Direct Marketing" (or the "CAP Code"). The OFT, alongside other authorities, has a statutory duty to enforce the CPRs, through various measures of compliance. The ASA and the Codes of Conduct used under the previous consumer protection regime are still considered to be effective and are compatible with the CPRs.

In relation to trade marks, trade names and other distinguishing marks, the CAP Code states that when advertising products or services, advertisers are not to create confusion between their marks and those of competitors. Further, advertisers are not to take unfair advantage of competitors' marks and when making comparisons with identifiable competitors, they should not present products as imitations or replicas of products bearing a protected mark.[98] Similar provisions can be found in the "Radio Advertising Standards Code" and the "Television Advertising Standards Code".

A ground of objection may arise from prejudice to competitors as well as consumers. When upholding a complaint it has received about a misleading or comparative advertisement, the ASA publishes its ruling as a deterrent, based on the negative publicity this is likely to cause (even if for some companies "all publicity is good publicity"). In most cases, advertisers respect such rulings. Also, other media, which have a common interest in upholding ASA's rulings, are likely to refuse any further publication of the advertisement in question.

The OFT (for non-broadcast media) and OFCOM (for broadcast media) usually take action only if either the ASA has referred matters to it or (in exceptional cases) where the relevant body considers that a complaint has not been dealt with adequately by the ASA. In such cases, the OFT and OFCOM have a range of measures at their disposal under the 2008 Regulations and other legislation. For advertisements in the non-broadcast media, the OFT may seek an injunction from the High Court against anyone concerned with publication of the advertisements. For the broadcast media, the 1988 Regulations now refer to the powers granted to OFCOM under s.325(4) of the Communications Act 2003. It is usually a term in any broadcast licence that the broadcaster comply with OFCOM's standard codes (including codes relating to advertising). In the event of breach of such codes by the broadcaster, OFCOM has the power to impose fines and shorten the term of or even revoke the broadcast licence in question.

(d) *Source indications and other naming systems*

16–21 The core consideration in this Part is the use of signs and symbols consisting of words, designs, shapes, colours and the like to indicate the trade origin of goods and services. We live today surrounded by systems for indicating

[98] See ss.19.2, 20.2 and 21.2 of the CAP Code.

specific contacts: telephone numbers, numbers for financial services and state support schemes, names for corporate and unincorporated businesses, special welfare schemes, and so on. Ensuring that specific names and addresses remain distinct within some of these systems has been of such crucial importance that they have had to be regulated. An early instance was the hallmarking of gold and silver objects to underpin the value associated with the purity of the metal and the maker's identity. Until 1985 there was a register of business names where those names differed from those of the natural or legal persons running the enterprise. Company names are subject to approval by the Registrar of Companies,[99] who above all else has been concerned to ensure that identical or very similar names are not adopted by unconnected companies.[100]

The Secretary of State may require a corporate name to be changed if it is the same as or looks too like one already on the Register[101] and an injunction to secure such a change where there is likely to be confusion between the two may also be obtained from a court.[102] To that extent the earlier company has a quasi-proprietary entitlement in its name. But the name is an attribute of the company and cannot be detached from it and dealt with separately. Accordingly this right on its own falls well short of full property. In addressing this issue, the Companies Act 2006 introduced a provision under which the Secretary of State can appoint Company Names Adjudicators who will decide cases where a complaint has been filed under s.69 of the Act. A person (whether natural or legal) can object to a registered company name on the ground that it is the same as a name in which that person has goodwill or that it is sufficiently similar to such a name to mislead people to think that there is a connection between the company and the complainant. However, the Company Names Tribunal has made it clear that the adjudicators may only deal with applications that show "opportunistic registrations" made by the respondent. Any aggrieved applicants

[99] Part 5 of the Companies Act 2006 has replaced existing provisions on company names in the 1985 Act. The 2006 Act introduces certain new rules, e.g. on: (i) the power of the Secretary of State to issue regulations which specify what letters, signs, symbols, accents and punctuation may be used in a company name (s.57); and (ii) the right of a person (whether natural or legal) to object to a registered company name on the ground that it is the same as a name in which that person has goodwill or that it is sufficiently similar to such a name to mislead people to think that there is a connection between the company and the complainant (s.69).

[100] See, for example, *Association of Certified Public Accountants v Secretary of State for Trade and Industry* [1998] 1 W.L.R. 164.

[101] Companies Act 2006 s.67. The Secretary of State must act within 12 months of registration and specify in writing a period within which the company is to change its name: s.68(2) and (4).

[102] See, e.g. *Glaxo v Glaxowellcome* [1996] F.S.R. 388: anticipating the merger of the two drug companies, Glaxo and Wellcome, a squatter registered a company using their conjoined names. He was ordered to surrender it. Also, see *Direct Line Group v Direct Line Estate Agency* [1997] F.S.R. 374. In *Global Projects Management v Citigroup* [2006] F.S.R. 721, Park J. granted summary judgment on Citigroup's counterclaim for passing off and trade mark infringement, even though the registrant had no history of "cybersquatting" but at the time of registration must have known of the announced merger of Citibank and Travelers to be known as Citigroup.

who feel that the respondent's company name is too similar to their own is unlikely to succeed in their complaint, if there is no evidence that the respondent registered the name to either gain money from the applicant or to prevent the applicant from registering the company name. Since the creation on October 1, 2008 of the Company Names Tribunal, administered by the UK Intellectual Property Office, a number of complaints have been brought; the first being an order against Coke Cola Limited, which was required by the Adjudicator to change its name within one month to one which did not fall foul of s.69, because the name was sufficiently similar to that of The Coca-Cola Company Limited, and its use was likely to mislead consumers.[103]

The types of "name-jacking" which occurred in the past were somewhat costly—they needed, for instance, a company or a trade mark registration. Accordingly they would produce blemishes from time to time, but rarely more. However, with the internet, the ease with which domain names can be acquired, and their sudden popularity with businesses and organisations of all kinds, brought a rash of "cyber-squatting"; namely, securing a top level domain consisting of a well-known company's name or mark, or the name of a celebrity, a city, a product, or what have you, purely in order to sell it to the person with the "legitimate" claim to the name, word or other sign.[104] Businesses have complained loudly and persistently about such demands upon them, because the cyber-squatter is able to make his anticipatory bid only because of the renown built up by the targetted firm. It cuts no ice to suggest (as squatters like to) that the enterprise should have been quicker to secure the domain name for itself. For one thing, there are always numerous variants open as domain names. Legitimate businesses cannot be expected to acquire them all.

Some curbs upon cyber-squatting have been found through national litigation. The practice is not really a form of competition, since a squatter will have no intention to trade using the domain name, nor probably to sell it to a competitor who will trade. Nonetheless a standard reaction among judges across the world has been that it can be prevented as a form of unfair competition or passing off. As we shall see, the decision of the English Court of Appeal to this effect in the *One-in-a-Million* case has been widely influential.[105] Of even more interest, however, has been the establishment of novel "cyber-jurisdictions" which order the transfer of domain names from deliberate cyber-squatters to their intended victims. The internet being a

[103] *The Coca-Cola Company's Appln* 0/318/08, December 3, 2008, found on *http://www.ipo.gov.uk/cna/cna-notifications.htm*. As of April 20, 2010 there had been 95 applications brought before the Company Names Tribunal: two were struck out; two were withdrawn; and in the rest the applicant was successful.

[104] A "typosquatter" varies the name in the domain by small spelling or punctuation differences, but stays intent on selling at a price.

[105] Below, para.17–27. Where the domain name holder actually uses it for a website offering goods or services which claim to be the trade mark owner's when they are not, a straightforward case of passing off or infringement of the mark is likely to arise.

network of contractual interrelations, these jurisdictions are established by standard terms to which domain name holders must agree when they register. These international *fora* for settling domain name disputes are dealt with in Ch.20 as part of the discussion of digitisation and its multitudinous consequences for intellectual property.

3. The Purpose of Protecting Trade Marks[106]

(1) Trade mark functions

Trade marks and names perform a variety of economic functions. Discussions of the proper scope for their legal protection often take these functions as a starting point. Let us state them, discuss the economic world they seek to differentiate, and then return to them as tools in arguments about legal policy.[107] **16–22**

Three functions of trade marks may be distinguished:

(1) *Origin function*. Marks deserve protection so that they may operate as indicators of the trade source from which goods or services come, or are in some other way connected;
(2) *Quality or guarantee function*. Marks deserve protection because they symbolise qualities associated by consumers with certain goods or services and guarantee that the goods or services measure up to expectations;
(3) *Investment or advertising function*. Marks are cyphers around which investment in the promotion of a product is built and that investment is a value which deserves protection as such, even when there is no abuse arising from misrepresentations either about origin or quality.

(2) Information versus promotion

Rational judgement and emotional preference intermingle in the many choices confronting consumers. In consequence, trade marks become crucial elements in the process of reaching decisions about what to buy. With the immense growth in the scale of business and the advertising that accompanies it, modern customers rarely have that personal knowledge of **16–23**

[106] There is a growing body of literature on the economics of information which pertains to the following discussion. References to it, and an attempt to extract its relevance to the policy issues surrounding trade marks can be found in Cornish and Phillips (1982) 13 I.I.C. 41; Landes and Posner (1987) 30 J.L. & Econ. 265 and *The Economic Structure of Intellectual Property Law* (2003); Economides (1988) 78 T.M.R. 523; Towse and Holzhauer (eds), *The Economics of Intellectual Property* (2002), IV.

[107] See Schechter (1927) 40 Harv. L.R. 813; Shanahan (1982) 72 T.M.R. 233; Akazaki (1990) 72 JPTOS 255; Dreyfuss (1990) 65 Notre Dame L.R. 397; Martino, *Trade Mark Dilution* (1996); Maniatis in Sterling (ed.), *Intellectual Property and Market Freedom* (1997) p.63.

suppliers which is the hallmark of a village economy. Even so, their interest in source of supply has not in essence changed. Information about origin is only a means towards an end: their main concern is in the quality of what they are buying.

In the case of some goods, part of that quality may be bound up with source in a specific way: as, for instance, when the goods will need servicing and the manufacturer or supplier is looked to for the service. But in a great many cases source, particularly when indicated by a cypher such as a product mark or get-up, does not have even this significance. What it does is to enable the purchaser to link goods or services to a range of personal expectations about quality which derive from previous dealings, recommendations of others, attractive advertising and so on. Nor should it be forgotten that, however persuasively the advertiser may seek to promote this sort of symbol, it retains a neutral character in one sense; once a consumer learns that he does not want particular goods, the mark, name or get-up becomes a significant warning signal.

16–24 It is a basic assumption in a competitive economy that the consumer benefits by being able to choose among a wide range in the quality and price of goods and services. But once a range of alternatives is offered, he can choose rationally only if he knows the relevant differences. Acquiring all the appropriate information is in many cases too time-consuming and costly, so risks have to be taken. This is particularly so over qualities that cannot properly be checked or tested before purchase, but have to be taken on trust. How willing a purchaser is to take the risk of buying something unknown in place of something known will depend on many factors; for instance, how satisfied he is with the known, and how serious the consequences will be for him if the unknown turns out unsatisfactory. It is one thing to experiment with a washing powder, but another with a drug or with decaffeinated coffee.

16–25 The seller's interest is to emphasise qualities (including price) that differentiate his product from those of his competitors. Inevitably, if those differences are in reality slight, he will be tempted to exaggerate them, or to bolster them with appeals to sentiment of one kind or another. There is a strong case for controlling the claims of advertisers in the interests of consumers. The approach may be by persuasion[108] or by legal prohibition. In either case, it will probably aim first to eliminate factual inaccuracies, then points of spurious differentiation and ultimately the more oppressive manipulations of feeling—naked appeals, for instance, to fear or aggression.

16–26 In such laudable pursuits, the continuing importance of being able to distinguish the source of goods and services should not be forgotten. To remove the possibility of differentiation (save for goods that can be tested by inspection) is, indeed, to eliminate the incentive to provide goods of superior

[108] As in the self-regulation systems so characteristic of British business, such as the Advertising Standards Authority: for which see above, para.16–20.

quality.[109] If the consumer cannot trust the information that he receives, he will tend to buy things of lower quality, although overall he may be less satisfied with the results. He may even feel compelled into extraordinary measures in his own defence. To take an extreme but telling example: developing countries have become alarmed by the high price of pharmaceuticals and the amount of advertising—filled with claims difficult to check—which accompanies their marketing. There has accordingly been a temptation to outlaw the sale of drugs by trade mark. Where this has been tried, however, without at the same time giving the state control over quality in the market, suspicion of the efficacy and genuineness of what is on offer soon runs high. So do black-market prices for products still bearing trustworthy trade marks.[110]

A law protecting marks, names and get-up accordingly seems unavoidable **16–27** in a market economy. In various aspects, however, these laws have tended to develop in a manner that may appear to confer power without responsibility. The trade mark owner acquires the all-important right to stop imitations of his indication of source, but his own use is conditioned by few limitations or positive requirements. It is perfectly possible for the public to be taught that a box bearing a particular mark and get-up contains 500 grams of chocolates and then, by discreet expansion of the packaging, for the manufacturer to reduce that amount to 475 grams. Customarily the way of providing against such conduct, if it is shown to mislead the public, is to penalise it through criminal laws, such as those in the United Kingdom against false and misleading trade descriptions; or to enjoin it through laws on unfair competition (if they extend to such cases),[111] but trade mark law does not get involved.

As part of its quality function, should such a trader be deprived of his trade mark, or refused the right to enforce it? The main consequence of doing so would be to open the door to imitators of the mark,[112] thus compounding the existing confusion by the prospect of other imitators. Moreover, when uncovering the deception had led to adverse publicity, there will then be sectors of the public who want the mark to continue in use in order to know what to avoid.

In practice it is difficult to show that conduct of the kind just illustrated is definitely misleading. The qualities indicated by a trade mark are rarely definable with sufficient precision for it to be possible to say that if they are

[109] On this, see especially Akerlof (1970) 84 Q.J. Economics 488; Heal (1976) 90 Q.J. Economics 499 (with reply by Akerlof); Shapiro (1983) 98 Q.J. Economics 659; Meiners & Staaf (1990) 13 Harv. J.Law and Public Policy 911.

[110] The country in question was Pakistan; see UNCTAD Secretariat, "The Impact of Trade Marks on the Development Process in Developing Countries" (TD/B/C/, 6A/C3.3, 1977) at 266.

[111] It would of course be possible to include such powers in trade mark statutes, if it were thought important enough to insist upon.

[112] Theoretically, it would be possible to enjoin the misuser from all uses of the mark in future, not just misleading ones. But that would be extreme.

changed there is definite deception. The best hope of securing more reliable and relevant information for the buying public is by specifying the characteristics that must be given in labelling and advertising (although these can become so detailed and complex as to defeat the purpose of education, as is arguably now the case with advertising in the United States of OTC pharmaceuticals). Marketing which does not comply with the requirements can then be directly penalised or prohibited. To threaten deprivation of trade mark rights will in practice rarely be of assistance.

(3) Functions and rights

16–28 How serviceable, then, is it to distinguish between the origin, quality and investment functions of trade marks, when deciding the proper extent of legal protection for them? In *L'Oréal v Bellure* [2010] E.W.C.A. Civ 535, Jacob L.J. admitted "I am bound to say that I have real difficulty with these functions when divorced from the origin function" (at para.30.) Among those who seek to justify their position by reference to functions, it soon becomes apparent that there is no agreement about what these "functions" are and that disagreements often reflect the underlying commitment of the proponent.

First and foremost, the "origin function" is understood in two quite different ways. Supporters of a limited and cautious approach to trade mark protection tend to argue that the law should concern itself only with the "origin function". By this they mean both the use of marks actually to tell consumers specifically where goods or services come from, and also a looser usage to distinguish one line of goods or services from another on the market, in cases where consumers have no interest in source as such but only as the key to qualities. This approach has been labelled by the late Advocate- General Ruiz-Jarabo Colomer of the European Court as "simplistic reductionism",[113] whatever that may mean!

Radicals who strive for a broader, more "modern", approach, on the other hand, tend to denigrate "origin" theories, by understanding them only to cover the first, specific usage. It can then be said that, plainly, trade mark law covers a second, "differentiation", or "identification" (or "communication") function, which is something more elusive, something as much concerned with the feelings and subconscious appreciations of consumers as with the rational evaluation of information. Because this is already so, goes

[113] At para.46 of his Opinion in the *Arsenal* case [2003] E.T.M.R. 19; referred to by Lewison J. in *L'Oréal v Bellure* [2007] E.T.M.R. 1, in support of his statement that "it is .... now recognised that a trade mark has legitimate functions apart from merely identifying and guaranteeing trade origin. The proprietor of a trade mark has a legitimate interest in protecting the image that the registered mark represents.": at para.99. Cf., Jacob L.J. in *L'Oréal v Bellure* [2010] E.W.C.A. Civ 535: "all advertisements for rival products [to those of famous mark owners] will impinge on the owner's efforts and affects the advertising and investment function of the brand in question. No-one would say such jostling for fame and image in the market should be stopped." (at para.30)

the argument, there is an equal case for protecting the guarantees of quality and, indeed, all investment values which develop in a mark, name or similar sign as an essential element of business goodwill.[114] In Advocate-General Ruiz-Jarabo Colomer's view, a trade mark:

> "acquires a life of its own, making a statement about quality, reputation and even, in certain cases, a way of seeing life. The messages it sends out are, moreover, autonomous. A distinctive sign can indicate at the same time trade origin, the reputation of its proprietor and the quality of the goods it represents, but there is nothing to prevent a consumer, unaware of who manufactures the goods or provides the services which bear the trade mark, from acquiring them because he perceives the mark as an emblem of prestige or a guarantee of quality .... I see no reason whatever not to protect those other functions of the trade mark and to safeguard only the function of indicating the trade origin of the goods and services."[115]

More succinctly, according to Griffiths, "[t]rade marks can gain a 'psychological hold' on the minds of consumers, which gives them a selling power above that of the underlying goodwill".[116]

Arguments along this divide have been with us since the birth of today's advertising practices.[117] The conflicts between them have nowhere been resolved to the complete satisfaction of one side or the other because they address attitudes towards marketing and promotion about which many people are ambivalent. Competitors in developed economies are dependent on these processes for establishing and maintaining market share. Some would claim that today it is often the mark, rather than the product, which has an autonomous image, deriving from the promotional aura; it has even been claimed that this enhances the consumer's rational choice.[118] Yet many observers are repelled by the manipulative persuasion of so much advertising, with its images of glamour and success, or its more or less cynical

[114] Indeed, "differentiation" may well be a sub-set of "quality", rather than of "origin", function. See also Jacob L.J. in *L'Oréal v Bellure* [2010] E.W.C.A. Civ 535: "[these functions] are vague and undefined" (at para.30.)

[115] [2003] E.T.M.R. 19 at paras 46–47. In *the BergSpechte* case, C-278/08 of March 25, 2010 (unreported), the ECJ said: "Those functions include not only the essential function of the trade mark, which is to guarantee to consumers the origin of the goods or services ... but also its other functions, in particular that of guaranteeing the quality of the goods or services in question and those of communication, investment or advertising": at [31].

[116] Griffiths [2001] I.P.Q. 326 at 329.

[117] Carty (1996) 112 L.Q.R. 632; [1997] E.I.P.R. 684.

[118] See, e.g. Kur (1992) 23 I.I.C. 218; Martino, *Trade Mark Dilution* (1996); Mostert, *Famous and Well-known Marks* (1997); McCarthy in Vaver and Bently Ch.11.

appropriation of the shocking and pitiable,[119] particularly when contrasted with its thin or non-existent measure of information.[120]

16–29 Not surprisingly, then, legal systems have taken up different positions between the poles of restricted and extended protection. The matter is complicated by differences in the relationship between registered marks and unfair competition or passing off protection.[121] Jurisdictions under British influence, and to some extent those in the United States as well, have tended in the main towards caution. On the other hand, Continental European jurisdictions, in some cases through an eager deployment of unfair competition rules, have gone a considerable way towards eradicating competitive behaviour which undercuts a market position built through the advertising of brands, whatever form that behaviour takes.

16–30 It is this opposition of attitudes which makes so intriguing the changes in statutory structures within the EU and elsewhere. Over the past 16 years or so, new trade mark laws have taken largely standardised form.[122] Both the CTM Regulation and the TM Directive state as the guiding principle that "the function of [legal protection] is in particular to guarantee the trade mark as an indication of origin" (plainly here, "origin" in a broad sense).[123]

Whilst repeatedly reiterating the principal origin function of trade marks, judgments of the ECJ have made clear that the system also protects the advertising[124] and "investment" functions of marks, the latter usually in the context of so-called parallel imports from outside the EEA. Thus, marks may be used to shore up higher prices for a given product within the EU than outside—a differential that consumers often resent and politicians find

[119] As in the well-known advertisements for the "Benetton" clothing chain.

[120] Note particularly Schechter, *The Historical Foundations of the Law Relating to Trade Marks* (1925). Also, on a more populist level, see Klein, *No Logo* (2000).

[121] A striking example is provided by German approaches to the question of dilution: first, "famous" marks were given wide protection within the registered trade mark law; then this was abandoned in favour of protecting "well-known" marks through unfair competition law: see Schricker (1979) 11 I.I.C. 166; Lehmann (1986) 17 I.I.C. 746; Kur (1992) 23 I.I.C. 218.

[122] As an example of how courts around the world are having to deal with very similar issues arising from these new laws, see the wide-ranging judgment of Andrew Phang J. in *Nations Fitting v Oystertec* [2006] F.S.R. 740 Sing. HC, on the issues raised by registration of shapes as trade marks.

[123] TM Directive Rec.10; CTM Regulation Rec.7.

[124] e.g. *Parfums Christian Dior v Evora* [1997] E.C.R. I–6013 at 6027, although Advocate-General Jacobs considered the advertising function to be a derivative of the origin function (para.42 of his Opinion [1998] R.P.C. 166 at 180–181); cf. *L'Oréal v Bellure* [2007] E.T.M.R. 1 at para.99. See also the potentially far-reaching judgment in *Copad v Christian Dior* [2009] F.S.R. 22 ECJ, which held that a trade mark proprietor can invoke the rights conferred by the mark against a licensee who breaches a provision in a licence agreement prohibiting sales to discount stores if it is shown that the breach "damages the allure and prestigious image which bestows ... an aura of luxury", at [37].

convenient to denounce.[125] There may be reasons justifying the price discrimination—for instance, higher labour or advertising costs—and we will discuss them, together with the state of the law, at a later juncture.[126]

Other issues which have already had to be dealt with by the ECJ[127] include the extent to which there should be protection against dilution[128] and of what are essentially design elements in products.[129] After considering some trade mark judgments of his court, Judge Edward of the ECJ was moved to remark in 2001: "in certain respects, the law of intellectual property has become counter-productive, and in some respects absurd".[130] And four years later Lord Justice Jacob commented of those Court of Justice judgments: "despite all the cases the clear impression one has is that things are less certain than before".[131] As we shall see, little that has happened since would cause either to change his views. **16–31**

[125] See Edward (former Judge of the ECJ) [2001] I.P.Q. 135 at p.139, expressing surprise that the British Consumer Affairs Minister had attacked the ECJ for deciding the *Silhouette* case "precisely in the sense contended for by the United Kingdom Government".

[126] See below, paras 18–119 et seq.

[127] Either on a reference under the EU Treaty art.267 (ex-234) or on appeal from the Court of First Instance (and so originally from OHIM).

[128] See below, paras 18–99 et seq.

[129] See below, paras 18–17 et seq.

[130] Edward [2001] I.P.Q. 135, at 140: "Should a motor manufacturer really be able to come to a court to claim a monopoly in 'fourness' on the basis that there are consumers who might go into a sale room to buy an Audi Quattro and come out by mistake with a Renault Quadra?", referring to *Audi v Deutsche Renault* [1993] E.C.R. I–6227 (but noting that the ECJ left it to the referring court in Germany to decide whether Quadra was an infringement of Quattro, see his n.26).

[131] See the Preface to *Kerly* 14th edn (2005).

CHAPTER 17

COMMON LAW LIABILITY

1. PASSING OFF[1]

The passing off action was first developed to meet a classic case. As Lord Halsbury put it: "nobody has any right to represent his goods as the goods of somebody else".[2] The same has been held of representations about services; and a defendant may also be liable for passing off one class of the claimant's goods as another.[3] His means may consist of misappropriating the claimant's mark, business name or get-up; or he may simply supply his own goods when he receives an order for the claimant's.[4] In all such cases the claimant loses the customer because the latter is misled by a competitor. The seriousness of such a threat is recognised in legal principle: the action will lie even where the defendant is innocent[5]; and relief may be granted without proof of actual damage, but simply because of the likelihood of future injury.[6] This, as we have seen, carries passing off further than most other economic torts.[7] Because it is in this sense a wide-ranging form of liability, the judges have in the past been careful to ensure that it is not applied indiscriminately to analogies which fall outside the classic cases. 17–01

[1] See, generally, Wadlow, *The Law of Passing Off* 3rd rev. edn (2005); *Kerly's Law of Trade Marks and Trade Names* (*Kerly*) 14th edn (2005) Ch.15; Carty, *An Analysis of the Economic Torts* (2001) Ch.8; Morison (1956) 2 Syd. L.R. 50; Cornish (1972) 12 J.S.P.T.L. 126; Gummow (1974) 7 Syd. L.R. 224; Dworkin [1979] 1 E.I.P.R. 241; Naresh [1986] C.L.J. 97; Spence (1996) 112 L.Q.R. 472; Carty, in Dawson and Firth (eds), "Perspectives on Intellectual Property", Vol. 7 (2000) 31. For the history of the action, see above, paras 16–04—16–06.

[2] *Reddaway v Banham* [1896] A.C. 199 at 204, 13 R.P.C. 218 at 224; echoing Lord Langdale M.R. in *Perry v Truefitt* (1842) 6 Beav. 66 at 73. For the latter, see Lord Jauncey, *Reckitt & Colman v Borden* [1990] R.P.C. 340 HL.

[3] See below, para.17–11.

[4] As in *Bostitch v McGarry* [1964] R.P.C. 173.

[5] See below, para.17–22.

[6] See below, paras 17–29—17–35.

[7] See above, paras 2–12.

17–02 This caution is, for instance, expressed in the refusal to treat rights arising from use of a trade mark as giving a fully-fledged right of property in that mark. All that the common law protects through its passing-off action is the goodwill between a trader and his customers which the mark helps to create; there is no property in a name as such.[8] His rights against imitators last only so long as he does not abandon his business; and he cannot by assignment give another trader the power to sue for passing off unless he assigns his business at the same time.[9] Moreover, this principle restricts the tort to injury in the course of trade. One person cannot object if the name by which his house is known is used on the house next door.[10]

17–03 Even if attention is confined to cases where customers are misled, there are forms of unfair competition which do not yet give a competitor a civil right of action. In particular, if one trader misdescribes some physical quality of his own goods in a way that brings in customers, this may well expose him to criminal sanctions and to contractual or even tortious liability to those actually deceived, but not to an action by other members of the trade.[11] One explanation for this may be that none of them suffers in a special degree more than the others. But we shall see that this has ceased to be a categorical point of distinction. In *Erven Warnink v Townend* (the "*Advocaat*" case)[12] the House of Lords accepted that where a group of traders share a reputation in a trade name that describes a type of product, any one of them may sue an outsider who uses it for goods which are not properly so described. For this Lord Diplock offered a broad justification in terms of policy. After noting the wider ambit of criminal offences in the Merchandise Marks Acts and then contained in the Trade Descriptions Act 1968 and associated legislation, he said:

> "Where over a period of years there can be discerned a steady trend in legislation which reflects the view of successive Parliaments as to what the public interest demands in a particular field of law, development of the common law in that part of the same field which has been left to it ought to proceed upon a parallel rather than a diverging course."[13]

---

8 See especially per Lord Parker, *Burberrys v Cording* (1909) 26 R.P.C. 693 at 701; *Spalding v Gamage* (1915) 32 R.P.C. 273 HL, at 284; and see *Singer Mfg v Loog* (1882) 8 App. Cas. 15; *Reddaway v Banham* [1896] A.C. 199 HL; *Star Industrial v Yap* [1976] F.S.R. 256 JC; *Erven Warnink v Townend* [1980] R.P.C. 31 HL; *Harrods v Harrodian School* [1996] R.P.C. 697 CA; *Harrods v Harrods (Buenos Aires)* [1999] F.S.R. 187 CA.

9 See below, paras 17–19—17–21.

10 *Day v Brownrigg* (1878) 10 Ch.D. 294. The same notion is expressed in the requirement of likely damage: see *Street v Union Bank* (1885) 30 Ch.D. 156; *Hall of Arts v Hall* (1934) 51 R.P.C. 398; and see below, paras 17–29 et seq.

11 See above, para.2–18

12 [1979] F.S.R. 397; [1980] R.P.C. 31 HL.

13 [1979] F.S.R. 397 at 405–406. See *Clark v Associated Newspapers* [1998] R.P.C. 261 and *Diageo v Intercontinental Brands* [2010] E.W.H.C. 17 (Ch) in which Arnold J. upheld the claimant's claim for passing off in respect of the defendant's use of the mark "Vodkat" (along with get-up reminiscent of that used on many vodka bottles), holding that as the leading producer of vodka the claimant had been harmed.

Yet on the heels of this encouragement came a warning. In *Cadbury-Schweppes v Pub Squash*,[14] unfair trading was alleged in relation to the defendant's advertising which had adopted the general tenor of the claimant's successful campaign to stress both the masculinity and the nostalgia attending the drinking of lemon squash. But there was no confusion between the trade marks or the get-up of the actual products themselves and so no passing off, Lord Scarman remarking on the importance of not stifling competition by undue redress, and refraining from deciding whether any cause of action could lie in the absence of such confusion.[15] Accordingly there are some difficulties in describing the precise scope of the cause of action: what can be stated categorically is that it depends always on the facts and therefore the value of precedent can be overstated. **17–04**

In the "*Jif Lemon*" case, Lord Oliver elaborated the three elements a claimant must show in order to make a case of passing off: **17–05**

> "First, he must establish a goodwill or reputation attached to the goods or services which he supplies in the mind of the purchasing public by association with the identifying 'get-up' (whether it consists simply of a brand name or a trade description, or the individual features of labelling or packaging) under which his particular goods or services are offered to the public, such that the get-up is recognised by the public as distinctive specifically of the [claimant's] goods or services. Secondly, he must demonstrate a misrepresentation by the defendant to the public (whether or not intentional) leading or likely to lead the public to believe that goods or services offered by him are the goods or services of the [claimant] . . . Thirdly, he must demonstrate that he suffers, or in a *quia timet* action, that he is likely to suffer damage by reason of the erroneous belief engendered by the defendant's misrepresentation that the source of the defendant's goods or services is the same as the source of those offered by the [claimant]."[16]

These three requirements of goodwill/reputation, a misrepresentation leading to deception and damage are the basis of the analysis which follows. Frequent reference is made in judgments also to Lord Diplock's enumeration in the "*Advocaat*" case, of five minimum requirements for the action: **17–06**

> "(1) a misrepresentation (2) made by a trader in the course of trade, (3) to prospective customers of his or ultimate consumers of goods or services supplied by him, (4) which is calculated to injure the business or goodwill of another trader (in the sense that this is a reasonably foreseeable

[14] [1981] R.P.C. 429 PC; and see *Adidas v O'Neill* [1983] F.S.R. 76 SC (Ir.); but cf. *Elida-Gibbs v Colgate-Palmolive* [1983] F.S.R. 95.
[15] [1981] R.P.C. 429 PC, at 490–491.
[16] *Reckitt & Colman v Borden* [1990] R.P.C. 341 HL, at 499; described as the "classical trinity" in *Kerly*, at para.15–005.

consequence) and (5) which causes actual damage to a business or goodwill of the trader by whom the action is brought or (in a *quia timet* action) will probably do so."[17]

However, these requisites are not to be taken as unduly confining the action. It must evolve so as to deal with changes in methods of trade and communication.[18]

(1) The claimant's reputation

(a) *Not just confusion*

17–07 In the normal case of passing off, the claimant has to prove a reputation sufficient for members of the public to be misled by the defendant's conduct into thinking that they are securing the goods or services of the claimant. It is not enough for the public simply to be confused about whether it is getting the claimant's or the defendant's goods: such might be the case, for example, where both start trading at virtually the same time with confusingly similar names[19]; or where a mark will not suggest either of them to the public because instead it carries an association with some third party. The makers of "Evian" water-bottles (for their "Evian" bicycles) could not stop a rival from selling bottles under the same name; the mark on the bottles was likely to be understood as referring to a third party, the marketers of "Evian" mineral-spring water.[20]

Accordingly, the claimant will demonstrate the volume of his sales and advertising expenditure and will supplement this by evidence from traders and the public of the meaning that they attach to the distinguishing features of the claimant's goods or business: saying, for instance, that they have long understood the trade mark "XXXX" to denote goods of the claimant's manufacture. At the end of the day, the claimant must show that it is his goodwill that is being misappropriated by the defendant. Otherwise it may

---

[17] [1980] R.P.C. 31 HL, at 93. See also Lord Fraser at 105–106, who adds that the reputation must be with the English public as the result of trading in England (see below, paras 17–16, 17–17). Lord Fraser's formulation has been regarded as made "in the context of the case he was considering": Ralph Gibson L.J. in *Bristol Conservatories v Conservatories Custom Built* [1989] R.P.C. 455 at 466. Nourse L.J. expressed a decided preference for Lord Oliver's triptych over Diplockian neo-classicism: *Consorzio del Prosciutto di Parma v Marks & Spencer* [1991] R.P.C. 351 at 368–369. But the formulations of Lords Diplock and Fraser were relied upon once more in *Chocosuisse v Cadbury* [1999] R.P.C. 826 CA, e.g. at 830, and *Diageo v Intercontinental Brands* [2010] E.W.H.C. 17 (Ch) at paras 11–15.

[18] As with domain names: *British Telecommunications v One in a Million* [1999] F.S.R. 1 CA.

[19] But a head-start of three weeks was enough to secure an interim injunction against a deliberate imitator in *Stannard v Reay* [1967] R.P.C. 589; cf. *Compatibility Research v Computer Psyche* [1967] R.P.C. 201 (logo for computer dating not sufficiently established in short period of use).

[20] *Evian v Bowles* [1965] R.P.C. 327 and see *Rolls Razor v Rolls (Lighters)* (1949) 66 R.P.C. 137 (suggesting, in the case of each product, "in the Rolls-Royce class").

well be a case of "the unknown seeking remedies against the known".[21] Likewise, the court will not protect a goodwill of only trivial extent.[22]

(b) *Distinguishing feature*

The claimant must have some badge of recognition upon which to found his reputation. Commonly this is a trade mark (whether it be a word, or a symbol such as a logo) or a corporate, business, professional or philanthropic name specially adopted. But it need not be: it may simply be a personal name—in full or abbreviated, actual or assumed[23]; or the name of a place where the person does business; or the "get-up" in which goods or documents are packaged,[24] or, of course, any combination of mark, name and get-up. In one extreme case, the very shape of the product itself (laundry blue with a stick in it) was held to have come to indicate the claimant's goods.[25] In another, extreme in a rather different way, the claimant company was held to have a trading reputation in lemon juice sold in life-size plastic lemons, even though these also bore labels with its mark "Jif"; and the defendants' lemon containers amounted to passing off even though they bore the mark, "ReaLemon".[26] There have been others, which can be kept for later discussion, in which the reference to the claimant is decidedly indirect.[27] However, the tort will not be available to protect the product itself, rather than the goodwill built up through the use of a name or get-up: in *L'Oréal v Bellure*[28] Lewison J. stated categorically: "the smell of a perfume is not capable of being protected by the law of passing off. In other words, the smell does not form part of the protectable goodwill" and "the law of passing off is not designed to protect a trader against others selling the same goods or copied goods."[29] **17–08**

21 Harman J. *Serville v Constance* (1954) 71 R.P.C. 146 at 149.

22 Per Jacob J. in *Hart v Relentless Records* [2003] F.S.R. 647 at para.62.

23 Thus journalists and performers have protected their *noms de plume* and stage names: e.g. *Landa v Greenberg* (1908) 24 T.L.R. 441 ("Aunt Naomi"); *Hines v Winnick* [1947] Ch. 708 ("Dr. Crock and his Crackpots"); *Marengo v Daily Sketch* (1948) 65 R.P.C. 242 ("Kem" the cartoonist); *Sykes v Fairfax* [1978] F.S.R. 312 SC (NSW).

24 This may even consist of the colouring of a container: *Sodastream v Thorn Cascade* [1982] R.P.C. 459 CA.

25 *Edge v Niccolls* [1911] A.C. 693 HL—despite the possible effect of raising the cost of production for any other competitor: see at 709. But that is an unfortunate consequence, avoided in other cases by making it difficult to prove the necessary reputation, e.g. *Williams v Bronnley* (1909) 26 R.P.C. 765; *Hawkins v Fludes Carpets* [1957] R.P.C. 8; *British American Glass v Winton* [1962] R.P.C. 230; *Gordon Fraser v Tatt* [1966] R.P.C. 505; *Jarman & Platt v Barget* [1977] F.S.R. 260 at 272 CA; *Rizla v Bryant & May* [1986] R.P.C. 389; *Hodgkinson & Corby v Wards Mobility* [1995] F.S.R. 169. But note *Combe International v Scholl* [1980] R.P.C. 1; *Weber-Stephen v Alrite Engineering* [1992] R.P.C. 549 SC (SA). See also Evans (1968) 31 M.L.R. 642; Walton [1987] E.I.P.R. 159 cf. now the protection of industrial design by copyright and registered and unregistered design rights: above, Ch.15.

26 *Reckitt & Colman v Borden* [1990] R.P.C. 341; Christie [1990] C.L.J. 403. Although the defendant's mark was very well-known as such in the US, there was evidence that in the UK shoppers took it to be descriptive of the product.

27 See below, paras 17–37—17–40.

28 [2007] E.T.M.R. 1 at para.164.

29 Citing Laddie J. in *Irvine v Talksport* [2002] F.S.R. 943.

17–09 In the case of literary and other artistic works, and of performances, the reputation may lie in the work or performance itself, or in a "character" drawn from either. In this way, subject matter which may have no copyright receives protection: thus for a defendant to suggest that his film was yet another in a successful series concerning the "One-armed Swordsman" was held actionable at the suit of the producer of the series.[30]

17–10 It is the claimant's reputation as a source of goods or services that is in issue. The courts have not required that he make his identity plain by, for instance, giving full name and address. It is enough that a trader uses a mark, name or device of any kind as a cypher by which to teach the public how to get his goods.[31] Nor have the courts required that this connection be of any particular kind: he may be the manufacturer, wholesaler, retailer, selector or distributor of goods.[32] An importer who provides all the advertising, sales and servicing for a product in his own name may well acquire the reputation even against the manufacturer.[33] If the claimant's reputation is sufficient, even to suggest falsely that goods are made under his licence or some other trading arrangement giving him a means of control over them would be actionable.[34]

17–11 Accordingly the starting point for deciding whether there has been a misrepresentation amounting to passing off is the understanding that the claimant has built up with the public. Thus if his mark is used on one product of a particular quality, the defendant may not use the mark in trade for other goods, even if they emanate from the claimant. In *Spalding v Gamage*,[35] for instance, the defendant was held not entitled to sell the claimant's "Orb" footballs as his "New Improved Orb" footballs. But in such cases it has been said that there must be two distinct classes of the claimant's goods: a songwriter could not prevent an early work from being passed off as a new work where the court could draw no clear dividing line in quality between the older and the more recent.[36]

However, where a mark (whether it is a product or a house mark) is built up by an international group of companies, it may well signify the group as

---

[30] *Shaw Bros v Golden Harvest* [1972] R.P.C. 559 SC (HK); cf. *Producers' Distributing v Samuelson* [1932] 1 Ch. 201; below, para.17–44.

[31] *Powell v Birmingham Vinegar* [1897] A.C. 710; 14 R.P.C. 720; *Reckitt & Colman v Borden* [1990] R.P.C. 341; cf. *Politechnika v Dallas Print Transfers* [1982] F.S.R. 529 ("Rubik's cube").

[32] In Hong Kong, reputation as a buyer has been protected: *Penney v Punjabi Nick* [1979] F.S.R. 26; *Penney v Penneys* [1979] F.S.R. 29.

[33] For the problems that arise between rival claimants to a single reputation, see below, para.17–15.

[34] So said in *HP Bulmer v Bollinger* [1978] R.P.C. 79 CA. But a majority of the court refused to believe that the use of "champagne perry" led to the belief either that the drink was champagne or was indorsed by any champagne house.

[35] (1915) 32 R.P.C. 273 HL, and see *Robinson v Wilts United Dairies* [1958] R.P.C. 94 CA; *Colgate Palmolive v Markwell* [1988] R.P.C. 283 CA. The same applies where secondhand goods are called new, or imperfect goods perfect: see *Kerly*, paras 14–115 et seq.

[36] *Harris v Warren* (1918) 35 R.P.C. 217; cf. Dworkin (1979) 1 E.I.P.R. 241 at 245.

a whole, rather than individual members of it. This may limit the opportunity of using passing-off proceedings to prevent the parallel importing of the group's products. To this we return later.[37]

(c) *Secondary meaning*

If the claimant has used a mark or name which has some other connotation for the public, then he faces the special difficulty of establishing that the public does understand the word or symbol to indicate that goods or services come from him. The other meaning may exist quite independently before he starts to trade: it may be a word or phrase which describes the goods or services, in particular or in general, or it may have a geographical significance. The claimant must then establish that his use of the term as an indicator of source has given it a "secondary meaning". How difficult it will be to do this depends on the particular circumstances. If the term precisely describes the product, then the secondary meaning has to be proved up to the hilt. In *Reddaway v Banham*,[38] for instance, the mark "Camel Hair Belting" had just this character. However, as the House of Lords insisted in that case, there is no absolute rule that traders are not entitled to protection if they use such terms. Equally, in the "*Jif Lemon*" case already mentioned,[39] there was surprising but incontrovertible evidence that considerable numbers of the public took a plastic lemon container to indicate the claimant's lemon juice. Other traders' interests are considered to be sufficiently protected by the form of injunction that will be granted. This requires the defendant not to use the descriptive term in such a way as to mislead the public into thinking that it is getting the claimant's goods or services.[40] Where the claimant is the first to develop a market, or has a legal monopoly 17–12

[37] See below, paras 18–119 et seq.

[38] *Reddaway v Banham* [1896] A.C. 199; cf. *Cellular Clothing v Maxton* [1899] A.C. 326; 16 R.P.C. 397, and for further case law, *Kerly*, paras 15–093 et seq.

[39] See above, para.17–08.

[40] *Reddaway v Banham* [1899] A.C. 199 at 221, 231, 234. It may not provide much help to the defendant: see Lord Bridge's regret in the "*Jif*" case [1990] R.P.C. 341 at 402: "The result gives the claimants a *de facto* monopoly of the container as such which is just as effective as a *de jure* monopoly." On the same point, see *British Sky Broadcasting Group v Sky Home Services* [2006] All E.R. (D) 114, where Briggs J. held that "where the existence of a *de facto* monopoly in particular goods or services gives rise to the likelihood that the arrival on the market of a competing or related product will cause confusion in the mind of the relevant section of the public (taking them as you find them), there is an increased risk that the marketing method adopted by the competitor will cause or contribute to that confusion by an implied misrepresentation, in circumstances where but for that monopoly, the same method might not have done. In such circumstances the competitor is not subjected to a free standing duty to distinguish his product from any connection with the monopolist, but only to take such care as will prevent his chosen marketing method from conveying any misrepresentation to the effect that there is such a connection. Separate branding may or may not achieve that result. The adequacy of the steps taken by the competitor to avoid implied misrepresentation will be a question of fact" (at para.82).

of it (for instance, through a patent), the courts show great reluctance to treat the name of the product or service offered as bearing a secondary meaning: "oven chips", "Chicago pizza", "The Gold AM" (for a morning broadcast of "golden oldies") are examples.[41]

The same approach applies to geographical names. The makers of "Glenfield" starch sued a defendant who set up his starch-making business in Glenfield and then used the name as a trade mark. They secured an injunction in similarly qualified terms.[42] Again, where one trader has had the field to himself and has built up quality associations as an element in his get-up—such as different packet colouring for different qualities of cigarette paper—he cannot prevent a second entrant into his market from adopting the same indicators together with a different trade mark.[43]

(d) *Personal names*

17–13 Special considerations apply when the claimant establishes a reputation in a word that is the defendant's personal name. It is the present rule "that a man must be allowed to trade in his own name and, if some confusion results, that is a lesser evil than that a man should be deprived of what would appear to be a natural and inherent right"[44]; but he must act honestly,[45] not setting out deliberately to take advantage of another's reputation. Moreover, the exception is confined to the naming of a business. It does not justify the use of a personal name as a mark for goods, if the result will be confusion with the established reputation of another.[46] In modern

[41] See *McCain International v Country Fair Foods* [1981] R.P.C. 69 CA; *My Kinda Town v Soll* [1983] R.P.C. 407 CA; *County Sounds v Ocean Sound* [1991] F.S.R. 367 CA.

[42] *Wotherspoon v Currie* (1872) L.R. 5 HL 508 HL, where Lord Westbury first used the phrase "secondary meaning" (at 521); cf. the special facts of the "*Stone Ale*" case: *Montgomery v Thompson* [1891] A.C. 217 HL.

[43] *Rizla v Bryant & May* [1986] R.P.C. 389.

[44] Lord Simonds, *Marengo v Daily Sketch* (1948) 65 R.P.C. 242 at 251. See also Lord Greene, M.R., reported at [1992] F.S.R. 1 at 2, 3. But first names and nicknames are not specially privileged: *Biba Group v Biba Boutique* [1980] R.P.C. 413.

[45] Seeking out an individual with an appropriate name in order to lend colour to the imitation of a rival's name is not likely to be found honest. Likewise where the name of a person genuinely associated with an enterprise is nevertheless used as part of a scheme to suggest an association with the claimant which does not exist: as in *Bentley v Lagonda* (1947) 64 R.P.C. 33. A member of a family may not use the family name deliberately to set up a breakaway business: *Tussaud v Tussaud* (1890) 44 Ch.D. 678; *Gucci v Gucci* [1991] F.S.R. 89; *Asprey & Garrard v WRA (Guns) and William R Asprey* [2002] F.S.R. 487 CA.

[46] The distinction was clearly drawn by Romer J., *Rodgers v Rodgers* (1924) 41 R.P.C. 227 at 291, and accepted, e.g. in *Baume v Moore* [1958] R.P.C. 226 CA, and by a majority of the House of Lords in *Parker-Knoll v Knoll International* [1962] R.P.C. 265 at 279, 284, 287. In *Reed Executive v Reed Business Information* [2004] R.P.C. 767 (a case involving a company name), Jacob L.J. referred to Romer J.'s test and commented, at para.112: "no case comes to mind in which it has succeeded. Because the test is honesty, I do not see how any man who is in fact causing deception and knows that to be so can possibly have a defence to passing off." See also, *IN Newman Ltd v Richard T Adlem* [2006] F.S.R. 253 per Jacob L.J. at para.47; cf. Arden L.J. dissenting at paras 99–101.

times most judges have felt that some other mark can be found for goods.[47]

Company names are deliberately adopted in a way that personal names are not (unless they are assumed) and an established business adopting a new name cannot avail itself of the "own name" defence.[48] On the other hand, if a company originally takes its name honestly and then conducts business under it for a period, it will be entitled to continue using it for the business (but not as a mark for goods) as if it were an individual using a personal name.[49] A new company cannot claim this privilege, even if its name is taken chiefly from that of a person, unless it has taken over an existing business and is continuing to use its name.[50]

(e) *Mark becoming descriptive*

A mark may initially be used to distinguish the origin of goods; but if it proves highly successful the public may begin to use it as a generic term for the kind of article to which it has been applied. Marks of this sort—the advertiser's dream so long as they remain within the range of protection—are most commonly associated with products that have some really novel property or technical construction.[51] The company making "Corona" cigars proved that some purchasers treated this as a brand, others as an indication of size and shape. The claimant was entitled to a limited injunction against selling cigars not made by the claimant without making clear that this was so; only if the defendant proved that the word had wholly lost its original meaning, it seems, would he be entirely free to use it. But if the way in which he uses the term makes plain to his customers that he is adopting the descriptive sense, he will not be enjoined.[52] **17–14**

(f) *Concurrent reputation*

If two separate businesses have honestly acquired a reputation in a single mark or name, some of the public may associate it with the one, some with **17–15**

[47] The earlier case law tended to treat the right to one's name as a higher right even in relation to selling goods: see, e.g. *Burgess v Burgess* (1853) 3 De G.M. & G. 896; *Turton v Turton* (1889) 42 Ch.D. 128. A turn in the tide is discernible in Buckley L.J.'s judgment in *Brinsmead v Brinsmead* (1913) 30 R.P.C. 493 at 507–509; but there have been more recent supporters of the older approach: Lord Greene M.R., *Wright v Wright* (1949) 66 R.P.C. 149 at 151–152; Lord Denning, *Parker-Knoll v Knoll* [1962] R.P.C. 265 HL, at 277.

[48] *HFC Bank v Midland Bank* [2000] F.S.R. 176 at 201–202; *Asprey & Garrard v WRA (Guns)* [2002] F.S.R. 487 CA, at para.43: "otherwise a route to piracy would be obvious".

[49] *Parker-Knoll v Knoll* [1962] R.P.C. 265 HL; *Anderson & Lembke v Anderson & Lembke* [1989] R.P.C. 124. But cf. cases where there is a dispute over entitlement to the reputation of a single business: below, para.17–15.

[50] *Dunlop Pneumatic v Dunlop Motor* (1907) 24 R.P.C. 572 HL; *Waring v Gillow* (1916) 33 R.P.C. 173; *Hawtin v Hawtin* [1960] R.P.C. 95; *Fine Cotton Spinners v Harwood Cash* (1907) 24 R.P.C. 533; *Kingston Miller v Kingston* (1912) 29 R.P.C. 289; *Fletcher Challenge v Fletcher Challenge* [1982] F.S.R. 1; *Asprey & Garrard v WRA (Guns) and William R Asprey* [2002] F.S.R. 487 CA.

[51] For instance, in English courts, "Linoleum" was found non-distinctive (*Linoleum Co v Nairn* (1878) 7 Ch.D. 834); but the registration of "Vaseline" as a trade mark survived (*Chese-borough's TM* (1901) 19 R.P.C. 342 CA).

[52] *Havana Cigar v Oddenino* [1924] 1 Ch. 179 CA.

the other, some with both. This has not prevented the courts from holding that each has a sufficient reputation to take action against an outside interloper who attempts to take advantage of it.[53] The same principle has been extended to the case where numbers of manufacturers have a joint reputation in the name for a product with particular qualities. The question, according to the House of Lords, is whether the class of traders can be defined with reasonable precision. The test can be satisfied by showing that a word connotes recognisable and distinctive qualities in goods. All who supply them then share in the reputation[54]; "champagne", "sherry", "Scotch whisky" and "advocaat" have all been held examples.[55] In the first of these instances there were at least 150 shippers, each of whom was entitled separately to sue.[56]

Contrast with these cases of shared reputation, the difficulties that may arise between two traders each of whom has built up an independent reputation quite honestly in the same or a similar mark. If one can show that he has the reputation in a business name for a particular area, the other will not be permitted to use the name in that area, however much he may enjoy a reputation in the name in some other part of the country.[57] But if each has built up his reputation in his own locality and argument arises because both are expanding business into intermediate territory, neither may be able to show that the public there associates the name with him so as to lead to passing off by the other.[58] Likewise if two companies have previously enjoyed a shared reputation through an element of joint ownership, and that connection is severed, for instance, by the nationalisation of one of them.[59]

---

[53] *Dent v Turpin* (1861) 2 J. & H. 139 (single business divided among successors)—a case characterised by Jacob L.J. in *Phones4U* [2007] R.P.C. 83 as one of "tolerated deception", at paras 21–22; *Southorn v Reynolds* (1865) 12 L.T. 75. Neither can sue the other: see below, para.17–15. An association of the trade may have no trading activity on which it can sue in its own right, and there is presently no entitlement to sue in a representative capacity: *Chocosuisse* [1999] R.P.C. 826 CA; cf. the position of members of an unincorporated association: *Artistic Upholstery v Art Forma* [2000] F.S.R. 311.

[54] *Erven Warnink v Townend* [1980] R.P.C. 31. On the nature of the reputation raised in these cases—an issue at the frontier of passing off—see below, paras 17–38, 17–39.

[55] *Bollinger v Costa Brava* [1960] R.P.C. 16; [1961] R.P.C. 116; *Vine Products v Mackenzie* [1969] R.P.C. 1; *Walker (John) v Ost* [1970] R.P.C. 489. See also *Pillsbury Washburn v Eagle*, 86 Fed. Rep. 608 (1898).

[56] "The larger [the class] is, the broader must be the range and quality of products to which the descriptive term used by the members of the class has been applied, and the more difficult it must be to show that the term has acquired a public reputation and goodwill as denoting a product endowed with recognisable qualities which distinguish it from others of inferior reputation that compete with it in the same market": Lord Diplock, *Warnink* case [1980] R.P.C. 31 at 95.

[57] *Cavendish House v Cavendish-Woodhouse* [1970] R.P.C. 234 CA; *Levy v Henderson-Kenton* [1974] R.P.C. 617.

[58] *Evans v Eradicure* [1972] R.P.C. 808; *City Link v Lakin* [1979] F.S.R. 653.

[59] *Habib Bank Ltd v Habib Bank AG* [1982] R.P.C. 1; *Gromax v Don & Law* [1999] R.P.C. 367.

(g) *Geographical considerations*

In the ordinary case, the claimant's reputation lies with the public within the jurisdiction and the defendant's passing off is directed at that public. But English courts have not hesitated to extend their protection to certain aspects of foreign trade: relief will be granted against supplying the "instruments of fraud" in Britain for the purpose of deceiving a foreign populace.[60] **17–16**

A more difficult case arises where the claimant's business is one which is run abroad but has an international reputation which extends to this country. In the past, some courts have insisted that what is in issue is the claimant's reputation with the English public bred from business conducted in England.[61] The proprietor of the internationally known "Crazy Horse Saloon" in Paris was thus unable to enjoin an imitator in London from cashing in on the reputation of the name and "get-up".[62] Some decisions have treated this dividing-line as too categorical. But it was re-affirmed in the "*Budweiser*" case, where the American and Czech enterprises, which each traded under this mark in selling lager in their domestic and other markets, were seeking to launch their own products in Britain at much the same time. The Americans sought to claim prior reputation by virtue of sales in service-base shops to US forces; but the Court of Appeal refused to bring this reputation into account: it did not amount to carrying on a business in the country.[63]

However, under s.56 of the Trade Marks Act 1994, art.6*bis* of the Paris International Convention has been expressly made part of UK law. A claimant must show that it is a Convention proprietor,[64] and that its mark is "well-known" (in the Paris Convention sense) in the United Kingdom. Then, irrespective of whether it carries on business or has any goodwill in the United Kingdom, it may enjoin use of an identical or similar mark, in **17–17**

[60] *Johnston v Orr-Erwing* (1882) 7 App. Cas. 216 HL; *Walker (John) v Ost* [1970] R.P.C. 489; and see Dawson in Firth and Dawson (eds), *Trade Marks Retrospective*, Vol.7 (2000) 57.

[61] See esp. *Erven Warnink v Townend* [1980] R.P.C. 31 at 105, 106, per Lord Fraser; *Anheuser-Busch* case [1984] F.S.R. 413 CA.

[62] *Bernardin v Pavilion Properties* [1967] R.P.C. 581.

[63] *Anheuser-Busch v Budejovicky Budvar* [1984] F.S.R. 413 CA. In another circumstance, it could be enough that a Californian company responded to an unsolicited order from England, for there to be British goodwill: *Jian Tools v Roderick Manhattan* [1995] F.S.R. 924.

[64] i.e. if a natural person, a national or domiciliary of a Convention state (other than the UK—see *Imperial Tobacco v Berry Bros & Rudd* [2001] All E.R. (D.) 447); if a legal entity, having a real and effective industrial or commercial establishment in a Convention state: TMA 1994 ss.55(1), 56(1). PIP art.6*bis* only applies to marks for goods when applied to goods: Bodenhausen, *WIPO Guide to the Paris Convention* (1968), pp.90–91. It may be, therefore, that TMA 1994 s.56 is similarly limited, since it applies to "trade marks entitled to protection under the Paris Convention as a well-known trade mark"; but it at least allows confusing use for goods or services to be taken into account: s.56(2). See Ballatyne [2002] E.I.P.R. 415.

relation to identical or similar goods or services, where the use is likely to cause confusion.[65] Though of wider ambit,[66] the main impact of this provision in the United Kingdom is to override the scruple requiring, for passing off, a business base in the country, which is found in the case law just mentioned.

Two main limitations need to be observed: the first is that "well-known" in the Convention sense requires proof of a substantial degree of recognition, though how high a degree is not defined.[67] This country is unlikely to take as methodical an approach to the matter as the Germans, who require 80 per cent recognition in an adequate market survey[68]; but the courts are likely to think in broadly equivalent terms. Secondly, the Convention requires that the mark be well-known in the country where the injury is occurring, not in some other country. It is, therefore, only an occasional weapon against the "kidnapper" who seeks to appropriate a mark well-known abroad before it is introduced into a particular country. The lack of any Convention obligation relating to a foreign reputation is not a major problem in respect of a market such as the United Kingdom.

(h) *Temporal considerations*

17–18 Again, in the straightforward case, the claimant's reputation arises from trade or business that he has built up and is continuing. If his business has ceased, his reputation may nevertheless survive. He will, however, only be able to succeed if he can also show that he has not abandoned the name or mark[69]; in other words that he intends to do business with it again in the future.[70] So the name-owner may preserve his interest while his business is temporarily closed during a change of premises.[71] The owner of the "Ad-Lib Club" was able to assert its notoriety even though it had been closed for five years (because of an injunction against noise); no alternative premises had since been found in which to re-open it, but that remained his intention.[72] The reputation must survive, however. Use at one period gives no property right of indefinite duration.[73]

[65] Relief is apparently limited to an injunction; but possibly an account or delivery up could be ordered (as of old) by way of support for that order; an application for registration can be objected to on the same ground: TMA 1994 s.5(4)(a).

[66] Introduced into the Paris Convention in 1925, its prime aim was to give well-known but unregistered marks protection in countries which otherwise required registration as a prerequisite. In the UK and elsewhere, the passing-off action largely fulfilled the Convention obligation.

[67] In French "*marque notoire*"; cf. the German distinctions between "famous" and "well-known" marks in relation to dilution onto other products: see above, para.16–29.

[68] See esp. Kur (1992) 23 I.I.C. 218.

[69] *Maxim's v Dye* [1977] F.S.R. 321; *C & A Modes v C & A (Waterford)* [1978] F.S.R. 126.

[70] *Star Industrial v Yap* [1976] F.S.R. 256 JC.

[71] *Berkeley Hotel v Berkeley International* [1972] R.P.C. 673.

[72] *Ad-Lib Club v Granville* [1972] R.P.C. 673; *Sutherland v V2 Music*, [2002] E.M.L.R. 568, noted in Dennis [2002] E.I.P.R. 331.

[73] *Norman Kark v Odhams* [1962] R.P.C. 163 (*Today* as a magazine title held not to survive seven years' non-use).

From the other end of the spectrum, a sufficient reputation through publicity may be shown even before the claimant starts trading. The BBC succeeded in demonstrating such a reputation from the media interest in its "Carfax" traffic information system for cars.[74]

(i) *Dealings in trade reputation*

In different ways the preceding paragraphs have drawn attention to the fact that in a passing-off action what is being protected is the trading reputation built with the public, not some larger and more permanent right of property. This factor becomes specially significant when we turn to attempts to assign and to license "common law" marks. **17–19**

First consider a common occurrence in international trade: a foreign enterprise sets up a distributing agency in Britain[75]; success makes it desirable to manufacture here[76]; eventually the British enterprise, for whatever reason, acquires independence that is economic as well as legal. At different stages the question may arise, which has the better right to the marks and names: foreign "originator" or local trader? A prime issue is: what has the British public been taught to understand by the reputation? If the mark is built up as the original manufacturer's mark and the goods still come from him, then the reputation must be his[77]; but the contrary is true where it becomes known as the importer's or local manufacturer's, however much the originator may have desired and supposed that the mark would remain his.[78] There is no general principle that any goodwill accruing during the co-operation must belong to him at its end[79] and the matter should be specifically dealt with by contract.

If the marks have been transferred together with the business that uses them, then they must belong to the transferee. An extreme case is this: where the marks of a German company's British subsidiary were transferred to an **17–20**

[74] *BBC v Talbot* [1981] F.S.R. 228, a case arguably decided incorrectly on a misreading of earlier cases; but note *My Kinda Bones v Dr Pepper's Stove* [1984] F.S.R. 289.

[75] The agency may not start as a distinct legal entity; or it may be a subsidiary; or it may be an independent entity taking its own commercial risks.

[76] Or add to the product range from local manufacture: cf. *Scandecor* [2002] F.S.R. 122; below, at para.17–21.

[77] e.g. *Imperial Tobacco v Bonnan* (1924) 41 R.P.C. 441 JC (not passing off to import genuine "Gold Flake" cigarettes into India, despite the creation of an exclusive distributorship there); *Sturvenant Engineering v Sturvenant Mill* (1936) 53 R.P.C. 430 (end of market-splitting agreement).

[78] *Oertli v Bowman* [1959] R.P.C. 1 HL (manufacturing licensee); *Diehl's TM* [1970] R.P.C. 435 (distributor's registered mark—unregistered mark should be similarly treated); *Fender Australia v Bevk and Sullivan* (1989) 15 I.P.R. 257; *Medgen v Passion for Life Products* [2001] F.S.R. 496 (exclusive UK distributor, no reference to foreign manufacturer on packaging). In the context of interpreting the duration of a licence to use a mark, see *Harrods v Harrods (Buenos Aires)* [1997] F.S.R. 420.

[79] *Scandecor Development v Scandecor Marketing* [1998] F.S.R. 503 CA.

unconnected entity as a measure of wartime expropriation, the new owner was able to restrain passing off by the German company.[80]

If the original owner believes it advantageous to "transfer" the marks without the accompanying business, he may instead create grave jeopardy: he himself will have abandoned his interest, however much his reputation lingers[81]; the "assignee" will have no reputation of his own on which to sue.[82]

17–21 Before the Trade Marks Act 1938, these sorts of difficulties affected registered trade marks as well as unregistered.[83] The Act accordingly allowed the originator to license (and thus keep ultimate control of) registered marks and to assign them even without goodwill.[84] Now the 1994 Trade Marks Act removes most fetters to licensing of registered marks.[85] The development of the law in this area was reviewed by Lord Niccolls in *Scandecor*.[86] His Lordship concluded that, whilst accepting that under the 1938 Act this would have been "distressingly heretical",

> "[c]ustomers are well used to the practice of licensing of trade marks ... [and] are not to be taken to rely on the protection supposedly afforded by a legal requirement that the proprietor must always retain and exercise an inherently imprecise degree of control over the licensee's activities."[87]

---

[80] *Adrema v Adrema-Werke* [1958] R.P.C. 323; if the two concerns remain connected, the contrary may well be true: if the goods are being imported into the UK from another EU state, the result of the *Adrema* case will now be affected by the EU Treaty arts 34 and 36. If both share the British goodwill, then neither may sue the other for passing off: *Scandecor Development v Scandecor Marketing* [1998] F.S.R. 503 CA (an issue not considered by the House of Lords); cf. *Sir Robert McAlpine Ltd v Alfred McAlpine Plc* [2004] R.P.C. 36, where the defendant construction company was split off from the claimant construction company in 1935 and for over 50 years the market distinguished between the two by reference to the first names "Robert" and "Alfred". When, during a rebranding exercise, the defendant decided to use "McAlpine" alone for trading purposes (although keeping "Alfred" in its corporate name), the claimant successfully sued for passing off, it being held that the parties were co-owners of the goodwill in the name "McAlpine" and by using that name alone, the defendant had "taken steps which suggest that it is the sole owner of the name, and to do that is to affect the value of the name to [the claimant] because it starts to elbow it out—it deprives [the claimant] of some of the value of the name to itself, and it blurs or diminishes [the claimant's] rights" (at para.50). In coming to this conclusion, Mann J. expressly stated that "[t]his is not to invent the tort of misappropriation of goodwill ... It is to recognise that the shared rights to goodwill can be damaged by the co-owner arrogating to himself the use of the name in circumstances where that amounts to a misrepresentation and a partial ouster of the claimant" (at para.49).

[81] See above, para.17–18.

[82] At least until he builds up his own trade: see *Pinto v Badman* (1891) 8 R.P.C. 181.

[83] Hence cases on registered and unregistered marks were decided on a similar basis. *Pinto v Badman* in fact concerned the former. Probably the marks associated with a distinct part of the business could be assigned with that part alone; but this could not give cover to the assignment of one out of several marks with which the assignor labelled a single type of goods: see *Sinclair's TM* (1932) 49 R.P.C. 123; *Kerly* 12th edn, paras 13–02—13–09.

[84] But subject to certain controls no longer relevant under the TMA 1994, discussed in para.17–13 of the 4th edn of this book.

[85] See below, paras 18–14 et seq.

[86] [2002] F.S.R. 122 HL at paras 20–41.

[87] [2002] F.S.R. 122 at paras 38 and 40.

The courts have not, however, been prepared so far to adapt the law affecting "common law" marks in order to bring about a comparable development. In *Star Industrial v Yap*, a company manufacturing "Ace Brand" toothbrushes in Hong Kong stopped importing them into Singapore after an import duty was imposed on them, and it abandoned its business there. The Privy Council held that it could not, three years later, assign its Singapore rights in the mark to a part-owned subsidiary; nor, more than five years later, could it secure relief against passing off by a competitor.[88] It must be said however that the judgment of Lord Niccolls in *Scandecor* gives some encouragement for the proposition that if presented with the right case the courts may now be ready to recognise what actually happens in the marketplace and uphold the validity of licensing of unregistered marks subject to appropriate controls.

To businesses which have not secured registration for a mark, the existing rule may present an unexpected obstacle to a profitable transaction. On the other hand, the rule only emphasises a policy to which the courts have consistently adhered: the passing off action should extend only to the protection of subsisting goodwill; beyond this other traders should be free to use the names and marks that are to their best advantage.[89]

(2) Defendant's representation

(a) *Defendant's state of mind*

Where a defendant is perpetrating the passing off personally, the fact that he does not realise it is no defence to the grant of an injunction. Nineteenth-century Chancery courts had no qualms about imposing their future-regarding remedy even on those who started on a course of business without appreciating its injurious effect. For a long period, however, it was not clear that more than nominal damages would be awarded for the period before notification of the passing off to the defendant.[90] In historical terms passing-off liability derived from the action on the case for deceit, and so could be said to contain the same restriction to intentional and reckless conduct.[91] As a solution, moreover, it resembled the results fashioned for some other forms of intellectual property by precedent or statute.[92] **17–22**

[88] [1976] F.S.R. 256; cf. *Coles v Need* [1934] A.C. 82 JC.

[89] If they do so in a way which misleads consumers into connecting their goods with a former user of the mark, the public interest may be protected through the trade description legislation.

[90] See Lord Westbury L.C. *Edelsten v Edelsten* (1863) 1 De G. J. & S. 184 at 199 (refusing an equitable account or other compensation, while granting an injunction); *Draper v Trist* (1939) 56 R.P.C. 429, esp. at 443 (Goddard L.J.); *Marengo v Daily Sketch* (1948) 65 R.P.C. 242 HL. In favour of substantial damages, e.g. Lord Parker, *Spalding v Gamage* (1915) 32 R.P.C. 273; Greene M.R. in the *Draper* case (at 434); Cairns, *The Remedies for Trade Mark Infringement* (1988).

[91] See above, para.16–05.

[92] See above, para.2–41.

In *Gillette v Edenwest*,[93] however, Blackburne J. held that passing off gives rise to damages regardless of the defendant's state of mind, just as with infringement of a registered trade mark (he took no account of the ability, in the latter case, to consult a public register).[94] So now the only remedy excluded for innocence (in respect of both forms of liability) is equity's account of profits.[95]

Where the defendant has supplied others with products which they then use to perpetrate passing off upon ultimate consumers, he will be liable for the misrepresentation if, in Lord Diplock's phrase, "it is calculated to injure [the claimant] (in the sense that this is a reasonably foreseeable consequence)".[96] It is one thing to put "instruments of fraud" into the hands of a collaborating distributor.[97] It is another to supply packaging intended for the claimant's product, only to have a person down the chain of distribution replace the real thing with a substitute.

(b) *Form of passing off*

17–23 As already noted, it does not matter what means the defendant uses to represent his goods or business to be another's. He may simply supply his own in response to an order for the claimant's, without ever making a positively misleading statement. Or he may imitate the badge which the claimant has used to implant reputation in the public mind. Nor does it matter what misrepresentation about trade is made: falsely to claim to be a manufacturer's authorised agent may be actionable.[98]

Confusion may occur only after sale—for instance, because the goods themselves will only be seen upon removal of packaging, or when taken to pieces, or when some distinguishing tag is seen without accompanying labels. So far, English courts have shown some reluctance to take "post-sale confusion" into account, notably in relation to the "look-alike" elements of get-up.[99] But, at least in Lord Diplock's characterisation of passing off, consequent confusion appears to be a relevant factor. Where, therefore, actual or truly likely injury can be shown to arise in this way it ought to be actionable.

[93] [1994] R.P.C. 279 (innocent importation of counterfeit razor cartridges).

[94] For infringement of a registered mark, see below, paras 18–84 et seq.

[95] See, e.g. the *Edelsten* case (1863) 1 De G.J. & S. 184.

[96] *Erven Warnink v Townend* [1979] F.S.R. 397.

[97] It is in just such a case that the courts have extended the tort to cover English suppliers of counterfeit goods intended for marketing abroad: see above, para.17–16.

[98] *Sony v Saray Electronics* [1983] F.S.R. 302 CA. See also *BT v Planet Telecom* [2002] E.W.H.C. 553 Ch, where the misrepresentation consisted of sending out by fax forms to customers with references to "192" and "directory enquiries"; the judge ordered the defendant to include on the forms the words: "This fax is not from BT. We have nothing to do with BT's 192 directory enquiry service."

[99] *Bostik v Sellotape* [1994] R.P.C. 556 (substitute for "Blu-tak", differently labelled but also coloured blue); cf. *Levi Strauss v Kimbyr* [1994] F.S.R. 335 HC (NZ) (red tag on jeans found confusing after sale); Prescott [1990] E.I.P.R. 241; Karet [1995] E.I.P.R. 3; further, see *BP Amoco v John Kelly*, at para.18–94, on the apparent position now under the TMA 1994.

(c) *Likelihood of confusion*

In a case where there is something to be said in the defendant's favour, the most frequent issue is whether his way of doing business is sufficiently likely to confuse the public. If he has imitated the claimant's mark or other badge exactly, the main question left is whether he has done enough else to dispel the otherwise misleading effect of his imitation: has he said with sufficient prominence "No connection with the claimant"? It is an unusual case in which a trader attempts to do this; even more rarely will he do enough.[100] "Thirsty people want beer not explanations."[101] Despite which, judges and legislators sometimes treat the ability to add distinguishing information as a practical possibility.[102] If the word or sign is unlikely to be taken as being used as a trade mark—for instance, when it is a T-shirt decoration only—a separate reason will exist why there is no passing off.[103] **17–24**

If the defendant's marking or naming is not an exact imitation, the first question is whether he has sailed too close to the wind, or has shown a true mariner's judgment. This has to be decided largely in light of the particular circumstances. But the comparison to be made must be emphasised: it is between the manner in which the claimant's reputation has been acquired in actual trade and the trading practice in which the defendant is indulging or threatens to indulge.[104]

The question is: what impact would the defendant's mark be likely to have on probable customers, given the expectations they already have and the amount of attention that they will pay[105]: they are assumed to be "reasonably well informed and reasonably observant and circumspect".[106] All the **17–25**

[100] One instance is where the defendant is understood to be using the claimant's mark only to indicate that he is selling the same sort of product: "a substitute for 'Yeastvite'", "Claret style", and a host of nicely nuanced variants. On this sort of comparative reference, see below, paras 17–54—17–56.

[101] Lord Macnaghten, *Montgomery v Thompson* [1891] A.C. 217. And see *McDonald's v Burger King* [1986] F.S.R. 45 ("It's not just Big, Mac"—taken to arouse confusing associations with claimant's product); *Neutrogena v Golden* [1996] R.P.C. 473; *Kimberley-Clark v Fort Sterling* [1997] F.S.R. 877.

[102] It was the justification for introducing Pt B to the Register between 1919 and 1994.

[103] *Arsenal v Reed* [2001] R.P.C. 622 (Laddie J.), as to which there was no appeal: [2003] R.P.C. 696 CA, although for curious reasons Aldous L.J. stated that "I am not convinced that his reasoning was correct", at paras 70–71; cf. the position if the mark is registered: below, paras 18–87 et seq.

[104] Compare the test of whether a registered trade mark has been infringed: below, paras 18–82 et seq. In general the principles here discussed apply equally in comparing marks on an application to register and in deciding upon infringement of a registered mark. For greater detail, see *Kerly* Ch.17.

[105] Good examples may be found in the cases concerning newspaper titles: e.g. *Morning Star v Express Newspapers* [1979] F.S.R. 113 (see especially at 117; if "only a moron in a hurry would be misled" the case is not made out); *Morgan-Grampian v Training Personnel* [1991] F.S.R. 267; *Tamworth Herald v Thompson* [1991] F.S.R. 337; *Management Publications v Blenheim Exhibitions* [1991] F.S.R. 550 CA; *The European v The Economist Newspaper* [1998] F.S.R. 283 CA; *Associated Newspapers v Express Newspapers* [2003] F.S.R. 51.

[106] Per Chadwick L.J. in *Bach Flower Remedies* [2000] R.P.C. 513, a description derived from EU law (see below, para.18–38) but which is to the same effect as that applied traditionally in passing off cases.

circumstances in which goods are actually sold, or business conducted, will be considered[107]: will an appeal be made to the same set of customers? Will orders be in writing or by word of mouth? Will there be sales among ill-educated or illiterate customers?[108] Will marks be used in clearly legible and striking form?[109] If the goods themselves can be inspected before purchase, will this reveal a difference in kind?[110] The customer must, moreover, be led to think that the claimant had assumed responsibility for the quality of the defendant's goods or services,[111] not merely that the claimant had sponsored or given financial support to the defendant: as where there is a misrepresentation about sports or arts sponsorship. Thus Harrods department store in Knightsbridge could not object to the Harrodian School being set up in nearby Barnes, when at most this suggested that the store approved or gave some support to it.[112]

Normally the customer will not have the opportunity of seeing the two marks side by side. So, in comparing their visual appearance, it is necessary to allow for imperfect recollection by a person of ordinary memory.[113] A court will concentrate on the aspect of the mark that is most likely to be memorable—the "idea of the mark" as it is sometimes called. Thus, to mark cigarettes "99" was held not to pass them off as "999"; the idea of the latter was triplication.[114] But to use a lion's head on a soap wrapper may well be actionable if someone else is already known for his "Lion" or "Red Lion"

[107] "[I]t is legitimate in assessing the likelihood of confusion to take into account the nature of the goods or services supplied by the defendant. Different considerations apply to bags of laundry blue (*Edge v Niccolls* [1911] A.C. 693), of 'Jif' lemons picked up for a few pence in a supermarket (Reckitt & Colman [1990] R.P.C. 341) than apply to bank loans (*HFC Bank v Midland Bank* [2000] F.S.R. 176 at 185–185), healthcare products (*Hodgkinson & Corby v Wards Mobility* [1994] 1 W.L.R. 1564 at 1575E) or saloon cars (*Lancer TM* [1987] R.P.C. 303 at 325, a trade mark case). In the latter category of case purchases are considered more carefully and the opportunities for confusion accordingly reduced", per Deputy Judge Floyd in *Teleworks v Telework* [2002] R.P.C. 535 at para.12.

[108] e.g. *Edge v Niccolls* [1911] A.C. 693 HL; *Johnston v Orr-Ewing* (1882) 7 App.Cas. 219 HL (yarn for the "natives of Aden and India"); *Bollinger v Costa Brava Wine* [1960] R.P.C. 16.

[109] Think of signs on petrol stations and marks on watches: e.g. *British Petroleum v European Petroleum* [1968] R.P.C. 54; *"Accutron" TM* [1966] R.P.C. 152 at 155.

[110] Thus, in *Island Trading v Anchor Brewing* [1989] R.P.C. 287 "Steam Beer" was enjoined for sales of draught, but not for bottled, beer.

[111] Even evidence of actual confusion does not necessarily show there has been a misrepresentation; all that it shows is "that people make assumptions, jump to unjustified conclusions, and put two and two together to make five", per Lloyd J. in *HFC Bank v Midland Bank* [2000] F.S.R. 176 at 201. The case was described by Jacob L.J. in *Phones 4U* [2007] R.P.C. 83 as "one on its facts. It decided no question of principle": at para.20.

[112] *Harrods v Harrodian School* [1996] R.P.C. 697, CA.

[113] See especially *Aristoc v Rysta* [1945] A.C. 68 HL; and Luxmoore L.J. in (1943) 60 R.P.C. 87 at 108 CA (registration case).

[114] *Ardath v Sandorides* (1824) 42 R.P.C. 50. *Johnston v Orr-Ewing* (1882) 7 App. Cas. 219 HL, provides a good example where the mark is compounded of picture and words. *Lever v Goodwin* (1887) 36 Ch.D. 1 CA, is useful on general get-up. Whether there are similarities in colour may be important in passing off cases, because the actual usages are being compared; cf. the position with a registered trade mark: below, para.18–86.

soap.[115] If phonetic similarity is important, account must be taken not only of the different ways in which customers and sales staff might pronounce a word but also of slovenly speech: consider, for example, the possibilities inherent in "Rysta", when compared with "Aristoc", for stockings[116]; or "Piquant" and "Picot" for cosmetics.[117]

(d) *Descriptive connotation*

Where the key to the claimant's reputation is alleged to lie in a word or other symbol that describes some quality of the goods or services, the defendant may avoid liability by relatively minor differentiation. Thus, in a leading case, "Office Cleaning Association" was held sufficiently distinct from "Office Cleaning Services".[118] There has been much concern to ensure that a claimant is not unfairly enclosing part of "the great common of the English language".[119] Accordingly, whether the action succeeds is likely to depend on proof of actual passing off—proof that there were people who both took the word or phrase as indicating the claimant and were misled by the defendant's imitation; or at least that the defendant adopted his name in the hope of producing this result. In *Phones 4U Ltd v Phone4U.co.uk Internet Ltd*[120] Jacob L.J. held that the question is: "whether what is said to be deception rather than mere confusion is really likely to be damaging to the claimant's goodwill or divert trade from him. I emphasise the word 'really'." That depends on the evidence. **17–26**

(e) *Responsibility upon the defendant*

In the context of passing off, the courts have felt no hesitation in pinning responsibility upon a person who enables the injury to occur.[121] A manufacturer or wholesaler who provides retailers with the means of deception **17–27**

[115] *Hodgson v Kynoch* (1898) 15 R.P.C. 465 (note that the evidence was held to establish passing off but not trade mark infringement).
[116] See *Aristoc v Rysta* [1945] A.C. 68 HL.
[117] *Picot v Goya* [1967] R.P.C. 573.
[118] *Office Cleaning Service v Westminster Cleaners* (1946) 63 R.P.C. 39 HL: Jacob L.J. in *Phones 4U* [2007] R.P.C. 83 summarised the case thus: "where the 'badge' of the plaintiff is descriptive, cases of 'mere confusion' . . . will not count. A certain amount of deception is to be tolerated for policy reasons—one calls it 'mere confusion'", at para.23. For further examples, see *Kerly* para.15–097. Likewise if the claimant's mark is close to a descriptive word, the courts look with care at evidence of actual confusion, particularly if it is secured by a trap order: *Fox's Glacier Mints v Jobbings* (1932) 49 R.P.C. 352 (local use of "glassy mints"). On trap orders generally, see *Diageo v Intercontinental Brands* [2010] EWHC 17 (Ch) at paras 39–45.
[119] Cozens Hardy M.R. *Crosfield's Application* (1909) 26 R.P.C. 837 at 854. For an analysis of the history and modern validity of this concern, see Davis [2002] I.P.Q. 342, which concludes, taking into account the changes wrought by the 1994 Trade Marks Act: "The enclosure of the common which [the] M.R. contemplated with some trepidation as long ago as 1909 seems finally to have come to pass": at 367.
[120] [2007] R.P.C. 83 at para.19.
[121] cf. the position over patents (above, paras 6–17—6–19) and copyright (above, paras 12–18—12–20).

will be liable without proof either that the retailers knew that they were passing off or that actual passing off was taking place.[122]

The general test is whether the passing off is a reasonably foreseeable consequence of the misrepresentation.[123] This test was given an extended reading in a case of "cyber-squatting". The defendants made a practice of acquiring internet top-level domain names which included the names of well-known British companies (*bt.org.*, *marksandspencer.com*, etc.). Each company had then to buy off the defendants if it wanted the name for itself. That was the defendants' main object; neither they nor any other "purchaser" from them could lawfully use the name in trade, e.g. on an advertising website. Even so, there was held to be passing off in threatening to provide others with such an "instrument of fraud".[124] The defendants were ordered to surrender the domain names to those "rightfully" entitled.[125] Much the same result has been reached in other countries.[126]

But the claimant, rather than the defendant, may be primarily responsible for the confusing state of affairs, as when he puts similar labels on products of different quality. In *Champagne Heidsieck v Buxton*,[127] the claimant sold different types of champagne in France and England under similar labels. It was not open to him to say that an importer who brought the French goods into England for resale passed them off. It was for the claimant himself to make the difference plain. This concept would seem to place a particular difficulty in the way of using the passing off action against a parallel importer and in that context we shall return to it.[128]

(f) *Proof of likely deception*

17–28 The claimant is not required to show actual deception in order to succeed, but if he can do so, his case will be much advanced.[129] Likewise he is not obliged to show that the defendant was acting dishonestly.[130] But if there is a

[122] *Singer v Loog* (1882) 8 App Cas. 15; *Lever v Goodwin* (1887) 36 Ch.D. 1 CA; *Draper v Trist* (1939) 56 R.P.C. 429 CA; and see above, para.17–22. It is different when goods leave the defendant in "innocent" condition and a subsequent seller misuses them.

[123] See Lord Diplock, "*Advocaat*" case [1980] R.P.C. 31.

[124] *British Telecommunications v One in a Million* [1999] F.S.R. 1 CA; Osborne [1997] E.I.P.R. 644; Meyer-Rochon [1998] E.I.P.R. 405; cf. *Reality Group v Chance* [2002] F.S.R. 13, where Patten J. questioned whether the "instrument of fraud" analysis in the *BT* case could be applied to an application for a trade mark (although he declined to strike out the claim as unarguable); and *L'Oréal v Bellure* [2008] E.T.M.R. 1 CA, in which Jacob L.J. noted "If what is complained of does not inherently tell a lie, it is not an instrument of deception itself", at para.132. For the domain name registration system, see above, para/16–21; below, paras 20—90. For a different inference of fraud: applying to register a mark after a finding of passing off, *Reality Group v Chance* (sic) [2002] F.S.R. 223.

[125] A questionable procedure when there could be more than one genuine claim—as was the case with *virgin.com*. See also *Global Projects Management Ltd v Citigroup* [2006] F.S.R. 721; *Phones 4U Ltd v phone4u.co.uk* [2007] R.P.C. 83 CA.

[126] See Bettinger (1997) 28 I.I.C. 508.

[127] [1930] 1 Ch. 330; cf. *Champagne Heidsieck v Scotto* (1926) 43 R.P.C. 101.

[128] See below, para.18–119.

[129] See *Kerly* para.15–192.

[130] See above, para.17–22.

question whether the public will be deceived, proof of actual fraud carries him a long way (without being necessarily conclusive): "Why should we be astute to say that [the defendant] cannot succeed in doing that which he is straining every nerve to do?"[131]

There has been little discussion of how many people must likely be deceived.[132] It seems that their number must be "substantial", in the sense of more than de minimis.[133] The courts are prepared to take account of surveys, as long as they are carried out fairly and in accordance with the rules set out by Whitford J. in *Imperial v Philip Morris*.[134] Also, parties are now required to seek permission from the court to carry out a survey "so that consideration can be given to the probative value and cost of the evidence before the bulk of the money is spent."[135] However, most surveys adduced in evidence in both passing off and trade mark infringement over recent years have been criticised in one way or more and their overall contribution to the finding in the particular case must be questionable.[136] Far more useful has been the practice of using the survey as a witness gathering exercise.[137] Clearly there are difficulties in devising investigations that are not biased, particularly if left to the parties; they are also expensive. But they can bring an element of objectivity into an inquiry that otherwise leaves a judge to his own hunch having heard the conflicting views of a large number of witnesses. (An important case management tool now available to judges in passing-off cases is the general power to restrict the number of witnesses who give evidence in court: in *HFC Bank v Midland Bank*[138] the claimant was limited to its 20 best witnesses, later increased to 27.)

[131] Lindley L.J. *Slazenger v Feltham* (1889) 6 R.P.C. 531 at 538 and see *Kerly* paras 15–199 and 15–120.

[132] e.g. *Globelegance v Sarkissian* [1974] R.P.C. 603; *Wienerwald v Kwan* [1979] F.S.R. 381.

[133] Per Jacob J. in *Neutrogena v Golden* [1996] R.P.C. 473 (upheld on appeal). He also noted that "there are always some people who are confused and even when products and names are well-differentiated, mistakes do occur", at 482. The difficulty is that the defendant can, of course, never prove a negative and there can be a tendency for the court to extrapolate from a very limited number of confused witnesses to the public at large (despite the warning of Morritt L.J. in *Neutrogena* [1996] R.P.C. 473, that this is not necessary, at 505); cf. *Premier Luggage v Premier* [2002] E.T.M.R. 69 CA.

[134] [1984] R.P.C. 293 at 302–303.

[135] Per Arnold J. *Diageo v Intercontinental Brands* [2010] EWHC 17, at para.161.

[136] For a detailed review of the use of opinion polls in German trade mark and unfair competition proceedings, see Eichmann, 31 I.I.C. 408 and 530. In Germany the court will frequently direct that an opinion poll be carried out; as noted by Eichmann: "There is no question of determining public opinion by hearing witnesses in German law ... since this would represent an improper exploratory questioning not permitted by procedural law": at 554.

[137] See, for example, *Neutrogena* [1996] R.P.C. 473 CA; *Julius Sämaan Ltd v Tetrosyl Ltd* [2006] F.S.R. 849 at para.64.

[138] [2000] F.S.R. 176; Connor [2000] E.I.P.R. 181 at 183. Regarding the time at which confusion falls to be judged, see *Daimler Chrysler v Alavi* [2001] E.T.M.R. 1069.

(3) Likelihood of damage

(a) *Likely damage*

17–29 Because the "property" is in the goodwill or business of the claimant, and not in his mark, name or get-up, he has to show, if not actual injury, then at least some likelihood of injury that is more than mere imitation. The mark or other symbol, in other words, is not simply a licensable commodity. In "ordinary" passing off between competitors who are selling the same or substitutable products or services, likelihood of damage is the corollary of demonstrating likelihood of confusion. This third element assumes a distinctive role when the case is not one of simple diversion of customers from one rival to another.[139]

(b) *Goods or business not the same*

17–30 In *Walter v Ashton*,[140] the defendant, who had been responsible for a successful sales campaign to sell "Daily Express" bicycles with the co-operation of that newspaper, launched a new campaign to sell "The Times" bicycles, but without having any connection with "The Times". Byrne J. required the existence of a "tangible probability of injury" to the claimant's property and found it thus: the representation that "The Times" had a business responsibility for the sale of the cycles exposed it at least to the risk of litigation and possibly (if the newspaper did not take steps to disconnect its name) even to liability. This test, though occasionally criticised,[141] has often been the touchstone of later cases.[142]

Another form of probable injury is damage to trade reputation from the assumed connection, such as suggesting that a nightclub had begun an escort agency[143] or that the Queen of department stores had stooped to money-lending (as conducted by the defendant).[144] Again, the claimant may be injured by losing the chance to expand his business into the field that the defendant has occupied, if the latter is not restrained. A claimant who sold "Marigold" rubber gloves and the like secured an interim injunction against a defendant who began using the mark on toilet tissues, the claimant stating

[139] For an example of such a case, see the detailed review of the evidence (at paras 42–51) justifying the finding of a "real risk" of harm in *Sir Robert McAlpine Ltd v Alfred McAlpine plc* [2004] R.P.C. 711 per Mann J.

[140] [1902] 2 Ch. 282.

[141] *Harrods v Harrod* (1924) 41 R.P.C. 74 at 78; cf. at 86–87.

[142] The requirement is strongly reaffirmed in *Erven Warnink v Townend* and *Reckitt & Colman v Borden* (see above, paras 17–05 and 17–06).

[143] *Annabel's v Schock* [1972] R.P.C. 838.

[144] *Harrods* case (1924) 41 R.P.C. 74. See also *Hulton Press v White Eagle* (1951) 68 R.P.C. 126.

that he was planning to use the mark upon very similar goods.[145] In contrast, there have been numerous cases in which, because the goods or businesses are not the same, the claimant has failed, either at the interim or the final stage. For instance, the "Albert Hall Orchestra" (organised by Albert Edward Hall) was allowed to continue using this name over the objection of the proprietor of the Royal Albert Hall, there being no actual or reasonable danger of damage.[146] The makers of "Zoom" iced lollipops could not obtain interim relief against the marketing of "Zoom" bubble gum.[147] The night-club "Stringfellows" could not object to oven chips sold by that name.[148]

(c) *Not trading in the same geographical area*

The same considerations apply when the claimant establishes a business reputation in one place and the defendant then sets up a similar business in another so as to suggest that the claimant has opened a new outlet. In *Brestian v Try*, for instance, the claimant had hairdressers' shops in London, Wembley and Brighton; the defendant was restrained from using the same name for hairdressing in Tunbridge Wells. But Jenkins L.J. was careful to find "that damage would probably ensue" because customers might go to the defendant instead of the claimant; and Romer L.J. pointed to evidence that the claimant's credit and reputation might be endangered.[149] Similarly, a business with "Chelsea Man" shops in three cities was held entitled to a country-wide injunction preventing the opening of "Chelsea Girl" outlets, because of its intention to extend business beyond these places.[150] **17–31**

This ought to be the appropriate principle for dealing with cases where a claimant has built up a reputation by business abroad and the defendant imitates him so as to lead customers to believe that the claimant has come to Britain.[151] If there is a tangible risk that the claimant's good name will be hurt by the poor quality of what the defendant provides or adverse publicity

145 *LRC v Lilla Edets* [1973] R.P.C. 560. An extreme example is *Eastman Photographic v Griffiths* (1898) 15 R.P.C. 105 ("Kodak" for bicycles, when cameras were being specially sold for bicycles: the prospect of the claimants actually applying their mark to bicycles seems to have been supposition). Another is *Lego System v Lego M Lemelstrich* [1983] F.S.R. 155 (plastic gardening equipment likely to be associated with the well-known "Lego" toys; defendant's name adopted perfectly properly in Israel and elsewhere).

146 *Hall of Arts v Albert Hall* (1934) 51 R.P.C. 398.

147 *Lyons Maid v Trebor* [1967] R.P.C. 222.

148 *Stringfellow v McCain Foods* [1984] R.P.C. 501, despite persuasive evidence at trial of what seemed to be deception.

149 [1958] R.P.C. 161 CA; and see also *Outram v Evening Newspapers* (1911) 28 R.P.C. 308 (papers of same name in Glasgow and London: no likelihood of pecuniary loss from confusion); *The Clock v Clock House* (1936) 53 R.P.C. 269 (confusion of road houses, the proximity (five miles) being stressed).

150 *Chelsea Man v Chelsea Girl* [1987] R.P.C. 189 CA.

151 cf. the discounting of foreign reputation in *Bernardin v Pavilion Properties* [1967] R.P.C. 581 and *Anheuser Busch v Budejovicky Budvar* [1984] F.S.R. 413 CA.

about him,[152] or if the claimant has plans to come to the United Kingdom which will be jeopardised,[153] these should provide a sufficient basis for his claim. But, despite frequent attempts, it would be a new departure to give such a claimant relief merely because the defendant was taking advantage of his reputation.[154] If the claimant has a reputation in the United Kingdom in advance of any trading, relief may now be available under s.56 of the Trade Marks Act 1994.[155]

(d) *Not trading: other sufficient reputation*

17–32 Professional and charitable institutions may have a reputation that will be protected in passing off proceedings if it is likely to be injured by the defendant's activities. Again courts have been careful to state what it is that creates a tangible probability of injury: in the case of a professional association it may be that the passing off will induce members to leave and potential members not to join[156]; in the case of a charity that regularly appeals for funds, it may be the danger to its reputation, should the defendant ever fall into financial difficulties.[157] Another example is where the Chief Executive of the Countryside Alliance succeeded on the basis of passing off in obtaining an interim injunction preventing the defendant (a former member of the British National Party) from misdescribing himself as a "Countryside Alliance" candidate for a council election,[158] the Court of Appeal reviewing in detail the authorities on charities and professional associations.

(e) *Not trading: sponsorship and personality association*[159]

17–33 The practice of having celebrities lend their names to the endorsement of products or services is an advertising device with a long history. For the

[152] cf. *Annabel's v Schock* [1972] R.P.C. 838 CA.

[153] A nice question is, how definite must the claimant's plan to expand be? What is to be done about the business which tries to secure the name or brand of a transnational company before the latter moves into a particular market? Note that in the *Bernardin* case, the proprietors of the French business had no plans to set up in Britain, so the refusal of relief may well have been correct on the facts.

[154] *Maxim's v Dye* [1977] F.S.R. 321 appears to come close to this; but the defendant did not appear at the hearing; cf. *C & A Modes v C & A (Waterford)* [1978] F.S.R. 126 SC (Ir.), where it was insisted that "goodwill does not necessarily stop at a frontier", but that the claimant's goodwill must nonetheless be liable to be damaged by the passing off. Both decisions were criticised in *Athletes Foot v Cobra Sports* [1980] R.P.C. 343, which held that the claimant must have at least a customer in England. Generally, see *Kerly* at para.15–070, which compares the strict position in the UK with that elsewhere in the Commonwealth.

[155] See above, para.17–17.

[156] e.g. *Society of Accountants v Goodway* [1907] 1 Ch. 489; 24 R.P.C. 159; *BMA v Marsh* (1931) 48 R.P.C. 565; *Law Society v Society of Lawyers* [1996] F.S.R. 739; cf. *British Assoc. of Aesthetic Plastic Surgeons v Cambright* [1987] R.P.C. 549.

[157] *British Legion v British Legion Club* (1931) 48 R.P.C. 555; *Dr Barnardo's v Barnado Amalgamated* (1949) 66 R.P.C. 103; *British Diabetic Association v Diabetic Society* [1996] F.S.R. 1.

[158] *Burge v Haycock* [2002] R.P.C. 553 CA.

[159] See Murumba, *Commercial Exploitation of Personality* (1986) Pt II; Frazer (1983) 99 L.Q.R. 281; Van Caenegem [1990] E.I.P.R. 452; Phillips [1998] E.I.P.R. 201.

most part this kind of sponsorship is arranged by contract, and in the advertising industry it is considered improper to use a person's name without his consent for this purpose.[160] Laddie J. confirmed in *Irvine v Talksport* that the law of passing off in its modern form applies to cases of false endorsement.[161] Consider two cases:

(1) The value in taking the alleged "sponsor's" name lies in his expert knowledge of the product or business in question and it can be shown that his professional reputation will be damaged by the association that is wished upon him. Typically a doctor's name is taken to promote a medicine. In such a case there should be no obstacle to the grant of relief. The bulk of dicta seem to be in favour, though there is no authority clearly in point.[162]

(2) The value in taking the alleged sponsor's name lies either in his own expertise or simply in the glamour of the association; but there is no evidence that any professional reputation will suffer or that there will be any other form of financial loss.[163] It was in this context that Wynn-Parry J. insisted that, for the grant of an injunction, there be "a common field of activity in which, however remotely, both the claimant and the defendant were engaged".[164] In *McCullough v May*, he held that "Uncle Mac", the children's broadcaster, could therefore not restrain the use of "Uncle Mac" as a trade mark for puffed wheat.

The appearance of certainty about this test appealed to some judges as a reason for refusing relief[165]; to others it has seemed unduly mechanical, leading apparently to a denial of relief even where it is likely that the

[160] See above, paras 2–25 and 2–26.

[161] *Irvine v Talksport* [2002] F.S.R. 943, upheld on appeal.

[162] See, e.g. Lord Cairns, *Maxwell v Hogg* (1867) L.R. 2 Ch. App. 307 at 310; Maugham J. *BMA v Marsh* (1931) 48 R.P.C. 565 at 574; Sugerman J. *Henderson v Radio Corp* [1969] R.P.C. 218 at 221. In the old case of *Clark v Freeman* (1848) 11 Beav 112, a doctor, who objected to being associated with a quack medicine, failed to secure an injunction before his case had been put to a jury in a trial at law. But that only reflected the general practice before the Chancery reforms of the 1850s; Lord Langdale M.R. expressly left open the possibility of an injunction after a verdict for the claimant. But cf. *Dockrell v Dougall* (1899) 80 L.T. 556; and see McClelland (1961) 3 Sydney L.R. 525, Mathieson (1961) 39 Can B.R. 409; Treece (1973) 51 Texas L.R. 637.

[163] Exceptionally, the use of a person's name as a sponsor may be found to carry an innuendo that will support a defamation action: the suggestion, for instance, that an amateur sportsman was in fact taking money for his sponsorship: *Tolley v Fry* [1931] A.C. 333 HL. If a popular personality has already contracted exclusively to sponsor another trader's product and this is known, the tort of interfering with business relations might apply.

[164] (1948) 65 R.P.C. 58.

[165] See, e.g. Walton J. *Wombles v Womble Skips* [1975] F.S.R. 488; *Nice and Safe Attitude v Flook* [1997] F.S.R. 14; cf. Millett L.J. *Harrods v Harrodian School* [1996] R.P.C. 697 at 714–715, treating the absence of a common field of activity as highly relevant to the question whether there was a likelihood of confusion.

claimant has, or will, suffer damage.[166] In *Irvine v Talksport*,[167] the decision was described as "discredited".

At root the question remains whether the right to one's own name (and to such other indicia of personality as sound of voice and appearance)[168] deserve to be a full property right. In *Henderson v Radio Corporation*, the Supreme Court of New South Wales considered that a professional dancing couple could enjoin the unauthorised use of their photograph upon a record sleeve without proof of any likely financial loss[169]; the Ontario Court of Appeal has recognised that a professional player may sue for the "appropriation of his personality".[170]

No English court until *Irvine v Talksport* had been prepared boldly to go so far[171] and even this decision has been described as of "limited value" because "where the claimant cannot prove direct loss or damage, the pecuniary sanction for the defendant's wrongdoing will be calculated on the same basis as if the defendant had acted properly in seeking a licence prior to using the claimant's image".[172] The case itself involved an unauthorised use by the defendant of a photograph of the claimant, the well-known Formula 1 racing driver Eddie Irvine, on the front of a brochure advertising the defendant's Talk Radio. The photograph had been manipulated so that it appeared Mr Irvine was carrying a portable radio to which the words "Talk Radio" were added. In finding passing off, Laddie J. emphasised that in his view endorsement is very different to merchandising in that members of the public may not think that the products are in any sense endorsed by the film company or actors in the film: that would be a question of evidence.

17–34 To prove a false endorsement claim, the claimant had to prove: (a) that he had a substantial goodwill (and the witnesses proved this to the satisfaction of the judge by reference to extensive newspaper coverage and other publicity); and (b) that the activities of the defendant gave rise to a false message which would be understood by a not insignificant section of his market that his goods had been endorsed, recommended or approved by Mr Irvine (which was found to have been proved also). Despite the fact that the

166 e.g. in *Henderson v Radio Corp* [1969] R.P.C. 218; *Totalizator Agency Board v Turf News* [1967] V.R. 605.

167 Per Laddie J. [2002] F.S.R. 943 at para.56, having reviewed carefully the authorities in England and Australia.

168 Such as the voice of a well-known actor: *Sim v Heinz* [1959] R.P.C. 75; Lloyd [1961] C.L.P. 39.

169 [1969] R.P.C. 218.

170 *Krouse v Chrysler* (1973) 40 D.L.R. (3d) 15 (claim failed on facts); *Athans v Canadian Adventure Camps* (1978) 80 D.L.R. (3d) 583; for an analysis of these and later cases, see Singer (1998) 15 Can. IPR 65.

171 Upheld by the Court of Appeal [2003] F.S.R. 619; cf. *Lyngstad v Anabas* [1977] F.S.R. 62 (doubt in interim proceedings whether real prospect of the pop-group Abba succeeding at trial in preventing use of their name and likenesses on T-shirts, jewellery, etc.); *Harrison v Polydor* [1977] F.S.R. 1 (no real prospect of preventing use of photos of The Beatles on the sleeve for a recording of interviews with them).

172 Michaels [2002] E.I.P.R. 448 at 449. Note the higher figure awarded by the Court of Appeal: [2003] F.S.R. 619 at paras 97–116.

brochure had been distributed to just under 1,000 people, the judge found that considerable potential long-term damage had been suffered by Mr Irvine, even though the direct loss was negligible in monetary terms. Damages of £2,000 were awarded, there being none for potential long-term injury.[173] On appeal the damages were increased to £25,000, as the amount the evidence showed Mr Irvine would have charged.

The concern which must arise from this case is that because of the way in which damages are assessed, the law provides no real deterrent to those who wish to avoid the need to contract with celebrities they wish to have endorse their product or service but instead are prepared to run the risk that they may be sued, at which point they settle for the amount they would have had to pay had they sought consent. Along with the furore created by the ongoing *Douglas v Hello!*[174] saga, this decision has led to calls for reconsideration of whether there ought to be a specific "personality right" introduced into English law and there will undoubtedly be further attempts in this direction.

Today the use of names and images is frequently, but by no means universally, the subject of a publicity contract with the individual or the organisation which has "manufactured" the fame or been closely associated with it (as in *Irvine v Talksport* where the judge considered the complicated contractual framework involving Ferrari, at para.75). Frequently, the individual gives a company the right to licence and control the quality of the goods bearing the name or image; whether that power is actually exercised is, however, highly variable.

As can be seen from Laddie J.'s concern to emphasise the difference between endorsement and merchandising, English law has steadfastly refused to adopt any embracing principle that a person has a right to his, or her name, or, for that matter to identifying characteristics, such as voice or image.[175] An entitlement simply to demand that such characteristics without more amount to property in personality is rightly regarded as a step too far. Its tendency would be to prevent others from making reference to the person in too varied a range of circumstances to be socially or economically justified.[176] The attempts by the trustees of the Diana, Princess of Wales Memorial Fund to appropriate her name and memory were just a demonstration of how far this process could extend. English courts have signalled clearly that only a much more discriminating approach is justifiable. Certainly greater protection has been afforded to personal privacy than hitherto, by reason of the Human Rights Act 1998.[177] That, however, is itself

[173] [2002] F.S.R. 943.
[174] [2001] F.S.R. 732 CA; [2004] E.M.L.R. (2) 13; [2005] All E.R. (D) 280.
[175] e.g. [2001] F.S.R. 732 CA.
[176] The person might be a municipality, a charity, a university, a government agency; cf. e.g. the use by a business of the NASA logo in *Nice and Safe Attitude v Flook* [1997] F.S.R. 14.
[177] For which, above, see Ch.9.

a more limited thing; and it is the obverse of a right to annexe all value flowing from publicity.

17–35 To some degree, copyright will prevent the misappropriation of various elements of personality. Photographs and extracts from sound or video recordings, if taken without licence for another's advertising or products, may well be sufficiently substantial to amount to infringement of the relevant copyrights or performance rights.[178] The demand for a separate right of publicity goes to cases beyond this range: those where, for instance, advertisers use an imitator to produce a "look-alike" or a "sound-alike" of a political personality or an actress.[179]

The leading commercial jurisdictions in the United States have been active in establishing a "right of publicity" within a common law frame of reference.[180] In doing so they have had to face all the difficulties of attempting to define and delimit a novel exclusive right in intangible subject matter which Brandeis J. famously insisted must be a matter for legislatures rather than case law.[181] With organisations such as the Elvis Presley and Martin Luther King Estates resorting to litigation in pursuit of publicity revenues, it has been necessary to consider to what extent the new right survives the individual him or herself.[182]

These difficulties are doubtless one reason why British judges have not encouraged a right of personal publicity any more than they have welcomed claims to merchandising rights in characters and other signs. If a right against the misappropriation of personality for the purpose of advertising or dressing-up products and services were to be recognised, its conditions would need to be carefully defined by statute. Subject to the *Irvine v Talksport* type of false endorsement claim, however, the British have chosen to limit the misappropriation of personal images to cases of advertising through controls which in the print media are organised voluntarily and which in broadcasting result from a statutory system of approval.[183] This practical approach avoids the excesses that may follow from conferring a private proprietary right in name, appearance and voice.

---

[178] See also below, paras 17–45 and 17–46.

[179] The right of publicity in the US has advanced by virtue of these forms of misappropriation: thus a Jackie Onassis look-alike in an advertisement, and a Bette Midler sound-alike, have both been held actionable; *Onassis v Christian Dior*, 472 N.Y.S. 2d 254 (1984) (affirmed 488 N.Y.S. 943); *Midler v Ford Motor*, 849 F. 2d. 460 (1988).

[180] See McCarthy (1989) 79 T.M.R. 681; Goodenough [1992] E.I.P.R. 55, 90.

[181] In the *INS* case, 248 U.S. 215 (1918) SC (US).

[182] It is extremely difficult to arrive at a reasonable answer to such a question by judicial decision; accordingly some states have intervened with legislation.

[183] See above, paras 2–24 and 2–25. Indeed, this has now led to problems with downloading from the internet where the Advertising Standards Authority considers it has no jurisdiction/role.

(4) The proper scope of passing off[184]

The action labelled passing off is not confined to misrepresentations that the defendant's goods or services are those of a trade competitor. Expansion of the tort is aided by the unspecific terms in which the elements of reputation, confusion of customers and likely damage are indicated in Lord Diplock's five characteristics.[185] A number of key issues deserve to be reviewed, some connected with cases already decided, and others of a more speculative nature. **17–36**

(a) *Nature of the deception*

Trade marks and names, which traders employ as indications of origin, are, so far as customers are concerned, a means of identifying qualities that they more or less consciously link with origin.[186] Because of this, it seems natural to allow passing off to be extended to other indications which give consumers similar information about quality, either *in toto* or in some specific respect. While there have been cases which have confined passing off to misrepresenting indications of origin, a number of other decisions have been more liberal. For instance, the following have been treated as actionable: inserting pages of advertisements into a magazine, thus making it less attractive to other advertisers and exposing the publisher to claims of responsibility for inaccuracy[187]; claiming that pictures of the claimant's products are the defendant's (a trick of newcomers into the building trade)[188]; "misappropriating" commendations from customers of another trader's goods[189]; advertising goods to be "as shown on television", when it was really the claimant's goods that had been shown.[190] Contrast with these the decision (now of doubtful standing) that no action lay against selling one collection of Hazlitt's Essays as the book set for a particular examination, when in fact it was another collection (the claimant's) that was set.[191] **17–37**

---

[184] See Ricketson (1984) U. NSW L.R. (Special Issue) 1; Terry (1988) 51 M.L.R. 296; Morcom [1991] E.I.P.R. 380; Meyer-Rochow (1994) 84 T.M.R. 38; Kamperman Sanders in Sterling (ed.), *Intellectual Property and Market Freedom* (1997) 131 and cf. Kaufmann, *Passing Off and Misappropriation* (1986); Stephens (1990) 99 Yale L.J. 759.

[185] cf. the remark of Romer L.J. below, para.17–44.

[186] See above, paras 16–22.

[187] *Illustrated Newspapers v Publicity Services* (1938) 55 R.P.C. 172; and see *Associated Newspapers v Insert Media* [1991] F.S.R. 380 CA.

[188] *Bristol Conservatories v Conservatories Custom Built* [1989] R.P.C. 455 CA; *John Robert Powers School v Tessensohn* [1995] F.S.R. 947, CA (Sing.); Carty [1993] E.I.P.R. 370.

[189] *Plomein Fuel v National School of Salesmanship* (1943) 60 R.P.C. 219.

[190] *Copydex v Noso* (1952) 69 R.P.C. 38.

[191] *Cambridge University Press v University Tutorial Press* (1928) 45 R.P.C. 335. A similar attitude is to be found in older cases in which the defendant laid claim to prizes, medals or patents properly belonging to the claimant, but the latter could not prove that the public therefore thought that it was getting his goods: see e.g. *Batty v Hill* (1863) 1 H. & M. 264 (where the transient value of the reputation was stressed); *Tallerman v Dowsing Radiant* [1900] 1 Ch. 1; *Serville v Constance* [1954] 1 All E.R. 662. They might be differently decided today: see *Kerly* para.15–127.

17–38 The line between quality and origin is also blurred in cases where claimants share a reputation in a name that is descriptive such as "champagne" or "Scotch whisky": the so-called extended form of passing off. In its "*Advocaat*" decision, the House of Lords refused to confine the kind of description that would suffice to special cases, such as appellations of origin which indicate that a product has physical properties associated with its place of primary production.[192] But there is another, even more striking, respect in which these cases have extended the notion of deception. In the cases concerning the defendant's use of "Spanish champagne", "British sherry" and the like,[193] the addition of the national adjective must have told the cognoscenti that they were getting a substitute; only those who wanted "the real thing" without knowing what it was would not pick up the distinction.[194] Relief was given in order to protect the proper meaning of the words against dilution even by an expression which would confuse only those with little idea of that meaning and so of the claimant's reputation.[195] The Court of Appeal has accepted the sufficiency of this approach and held that it was applicable in a further "champagne" case, where the defendant's product, "elderflower champagne", was a non-alcoholic fruit cordial. The claimant champagne house succeeded on evidence that some people in England would confuse the defendant's product with the wine, and also on the ground that the singularity and exclusiveness of "champagne" would be eroded, leading to "insidious but serious" damage to the champagne houses' interest in the name.[196]

17–39 This latter finding should be linked with certain other cases where an interest outside the normal range of "reputation" has been treated by the courts as a protectable part of business "goodwill". This is the basis on which the Court of Appeal has protected an author's connection with his work, a manufacturer's connection with commendations of his product and a builder's connection with the appearance of his conservatories.[197] The interests in question are such that their misappropriation by a defendant is treated as of itself damaging: proof of loss in trade as the result of confusion among customers is not required. The interests, it could be said, have the

[192] Thus "advocaat" was properly described a liqueur, wherever made, which contained spirit, but not fortified wine. In *Chocosuisse v Cadbury* [1999] R.P.C. 826 CA, this was even extended to "Swiss Chocolate" because of its recognised creamy smoothness. In some desperation, the court's order defined this in terms of the ingredients which secured the quality (percentage of fats, particle size).

[193] See above, para.17–15.

[194] See *Bollinger v Costa Brava Wine* [1961] R.P.C. 116; *Vine Products v Mackenzie* [1969] R.P.C. 1.

[195] See esp. [1969] R.P.C. at 23.

[196] *Taittinger v Allbev* [1993] F.S.R. 641, esp. at 668–670, 674, 678; and see Wadlow Ch.3; *Scotch Whisky Association v Glen Kella* [1997] E.T.M.R. 470. In *Harrods v Harrodian School* [1996] R.P.C. 697 CA, the extension of liability to cases where there is no proof of confusion is rejected by Millett L.J., though accepted by Sir Michael Kerr (dissenting). The injunction also restrained breach of EC Regulation 823/87 on wine labelling; see Carty [1996] E.I.P.R. 629; cf. Murray [1997] E.I.P.R. 345.

[197] See, above, para.17–37.

status of property, in the sense that their taking by others requires to be licensed.[198] Since a pragmatic approach prevails, the judges may accept other interests as entitled to be similarly treated. As already argued, there is a good case for so treating personal attributes of living people—name, likeness, voice and so forth; borrowing them directly or imitating them by means of a look- or sound-alike for advertising and similar commercial purposes should be tortious in itself. A similar argument can also be put in relation to the merchandising of characters and names, though it is inherently less compelling. To this we will return under a separate head below.[199]

The judges are not, however, prepared to allow any wholescale abandonment of the need to show confusion of customers leading to damage in favour of some loosely defined wrong covering cases where all that can be said is that a defendant derives some tangential advantage from imprecise recollection and association. This the Privy Council signalled in the "*Pub Squash*" case, over a general similarity of tone in advertising and packaging.[200] Since that decision, there has been a succession of attempts to base passing off on similarities of packaging get-up where the trade marks used are clearly distinct. Similar blue tubs for baby wipes, similarly ridged pots for "pot noodles", pink pages in newspapers, similarly wrapped digestive biscuits, similar music cover designs[201]—in all these instances, the distinct trade marks were enough to dispel any possible confusion as to source. In *BBC v Talksport*[202] an application to restrain the defendant from describing its broadcast of a sporting event as "live" failed: the judge finding that the BBC had no protectable goodwill in "live broadcasting" or "live coverage of sporting events".

Occasionally, the "look-alike" element in packaging has been held to overstep the line so as to cause likely or actual confusion. Such a case was *Reckitt & Colman v Borden*, where the English public was shown to be very familiar with the plastic lemon as an indicator of the claimant's juice—so familiar that they would not take account of the defendant's attached label giving its own name.[203] But since "look-alikes" are generally quite sophisticated, most escape legal censure. It is not enough that the public calls the established product to mind through some loose form of "association".[204] **17–40**

---

[198] As to which, see below, para.17–44.

[199] See below, paras 17–44 and following.

[200] See above, para.17–04.

[201] *Scott v Nice-Pak* [1989] F.S.R. 100 CA; *Financial Times v Evening Standard* [1991] F.S.R. 7; *United Biscuits v Burtons Biscuits* [1992] F.S.R. 14; *Dalgety Spillers v Food Brokers* [1994] F.S.R. 504; *GMG Radio v Tokyo Project Ltd* [2006] F.S.R. 239. A fortiori, in the case of the product itself: *Cadbury v Ulmer* [1988] F.S.R. 385 ("Flake" chocolate sticks).

[202] [2001] F.S.R. 53.

[203] Above, para.17–08. For a similar outcome, *United Biscuits v Asda Stores* [1997] R.P.C. 513 ("Puffin" biscuits which resembled "Penguin" biscuits).

[204] For the failed attempt to secure protection of registered trade marks against "association" which lies beyond "confusion", see below, para.18–95. Nothing has come of pressure upon the UK Government to extend the protection for look-alikes: see *Hansard*, HL, Vol. 553, cols 78–83. Cf. Annand (1996) 84 T.M.R. 142.

(b) *Nature of the injury*

17–41 The other direction in which the "drink" cases extend concepts concerns the likelihood of damage. "Classic" passing off involves a claimant who is peculiarly injured because it is his exclusive goodwill which is misappropriated. But in the cases concerning a shared reputation it is not necessary to show that the claimant suffers more than others with whom he shares the exclusive *goodwill which is misappropriated.*[205] This carries passing off some way towards providing a general unfair competition action against all misdescriptive promotion of products and services. It would seem no substantial step after these cases to allow any one trader whose goods have a particular quality from objecting when another advertises his goods as having the quality when they do not. In the "drink" cases, it is true, qualities were subsumed within a word describing the product as a whole. But "advocaat" was held properly to describe an egg-and-spirits drink, whereas the defendant's product was composed of egg and fortified wine. A similar outcome might well have been reached if the misdescription had been directly of the contents of the drink, although Arnold J. reiterated in *Diageo v Intercontinential Brands*[206] that not every descriptive term can be protected: "the term must be one which has a reputation and hence gives rise to goodwill."[207]

It would be going further again to give a competitor an action where his product does not contain the quality which the defendant inaccurately claims for his own. This would indeed make the mere fact of being a competitor a sufficient ground for objecting to misleading advertising. This is often permitted in legal systems which have a general concept of unfair competition,[208] and the traditions of other EU states in the matter may eventually exert their own influence upon developments in the United Kingdom[209] where commentators increasingly refer to Continental European notions of unfair competition laws when discussing passing off.[210] The issue has also been raised in the courts: in the Court of Appeal in *L'Oréal v Bellure*[211], Jacob L.J. was trenchant in his rejection of the notion that the common law should, in the words of counsel for the claimants, "move on and embrace" a tort of unfair competition:

> "The rejected complaint [in *Hodgkinson & Corby v Wards Mobility*[212]] shows just how anti-competitive a law of unfair competition would or

[205] See above, para.17–15.
[206] [2010] EWHC 17 (Ch).
[207] [2010] EWHC 17 (Ch) at para.35.
[208] In the US, see Lanham Trademarks Act 1946 s.43(a).
[209] See above, paras 16–19 and 16–20.
[210] For example see the full title of the 3rd revised edition of Wadlow, *The Law of Passing Off: Unfair Competition by Misrepresentation* (2005).
[211] [2008] E.T.M.R. 1 CA.
[212] [1994] 1 W.L.R. 1564, in which a claim for passing off in relation to a look-alike special cushion to prevent sores for immobile users was rejected by Jacob J. (as he then was).

> might be. What one man calls "unfair", another calls "fair". The market involves the interests of traders, their competitors and consumers. They all have different perspectives. An established trader would like the law to hold off all his competitors—and for as long as possible. He would want to prevent all copying of his products—and for as long as possible, preferably indefinitely. He would want as wide a gap as possible between his trade marks and those of others. He would oppose any form of comparative advertising. A newcomer will want to be able to copy—and to improve. He will want to be able fairly to advertise comparatively. And the consumer will want the best deal he can get. He would oppose anything deceptive, but probably nothing else.
>
> So I think there are real difficulties in formulating a clear and rational line between that which is fair and that which is not, once one goes outside the requirement of no deception.
>
> Moreover, the basic economic rule is that competition is not only lawful but a mainspring of the economy... It is not for judges to step in and legislate into existence new categories of intellectual property rights."[213]

No doubt this is not the last word in this area but is certainly clear.

Many would treat competitors and consumers as having the same interest to prevent misrepresentative marketing. Accordingly they would welcome the provision of competitors' actions as an effective method of policing from within an industry. But before accepting this unthinkingly, it is as well to reflect upon the reasons that may in the past have led the judges (including, most recently, Jacob L.J. and Blackburne J. in *L'Oréal v Bellure*)[214] to move with circumspection in this field. Competitors furnished with a right of civil action, which includes the chance of stopping a rival by injunction, have a powerful weapon at their command. Some indication of that power has already been outlined in Ch.2. In the cut and thrust of competitive marketing, the threat of intervening when a rival is launching an advertising campaign can inflict grave injury. That, of course, is justified when the defendant is plainly in the wrong. But there will be many cases when the issue is not easily determined; and others again when the claimant's concern for the welfare of the consumer might seem rather heavily spiced with self-interest. No one can weigh in advance the respective benefits and costs of making the content of each competitor's advertising and labelling the subject of actionable criticism by the rest of his industry. No one can predict how far a penchant for competition by litigation might develop. **17–42**

The British approach to date has been largely to rely upon a set of criminal sanctions aimed directly at protecting the consumer, and, since 1968, enforced principally through the trading standards departments of **17–43**

[213] [2008] E.T.M.R. 1 CA at paras 135–141.

[214] [2008] E.T.M.R. 1 CA. Blackburne J. expressed himself as "in entire agreement with what Jacob L.J.has said on the topics of passing off and unfair competition": at para.167.

local authorities.[215] The procedures of the criminal law do not normally allow for rapid preventive action and they require a high standard of proof. At least in England, competitors are as free as other private citizens to launch such prosecutions. However, it seems that they do so only occasionally when they feel their own interests to be particularly threatened. Accordingly, as these laws operate in their modern context,[216] they provide a reasonably adequate means of combating the serious cases of malpractice. There is certainly some wisdom in the courts' reluctance to give competitors the additional chance of bringing a civil suit, with the inherent danger of self-serving interference that this would import.

(c) *Character merchandising*[217]

17–44 The limited protection currently available for the commercialisation of personality has already been outlined. Here we move to the general issue of merchandising. Again, we should begin with what can be legally protected. Merchandising of fictional characters may make prominent use of images of them. If those images—drawings, photographs, film clips—are copyright material which is owned by the person seeking to assert a right in them, and if they are being copied to a substantial extent without licence, then infringement occurs. However, there is no copyright in a fictional character or a performer's act outside the confines of the particular texts or scenarios in which the character or act is developed. Copyright does not extend to the name Harry Potter, or the character repeatedly played by Charlie Chaplin (who has featured in advertising for IBM products and services), whatever they are made to do or say.

Nevertheless, passing off may sometimes be used in aid of copyright. In *Samuelson v Producers Distributing*,[218] the defendant held out his film as containing a popular revue sketch written by the claimant, when in fact it did not. (If it had, liability in copyright would have arisen.) The claimant's copyright included the exclusive right throughout its duration to authorise filming of the sketch. In granting relief, the Court of Appeal in effect treated this aspect of the property as equivalent to goodwill built up through trade. Romer L.J. pointed out that injunctions granted to restrain "classic" passing off were "merely instances ... of a much wider principle ... that the Court will always ... restrain irreparable injury being done to the claimant's property".[219]

So where a fictional character is put into a new unauthorised book, play or film an action may be grounded on injury to goodwill. A publisher,

---

[215] See above, para.2–24.

[216] See above, paras 16–19, 16–20.

[217] See generally Adams, *Merchandising Intellectual Property* 3rd edn (2007); Carty [2004] I.P.Q. 209.

[218] [1932] 1 Ch. 201. Cf. *Ormond v Knopf* (1932) 49 R.P.C. 634.

[219] *Samuelson* case [1932] 1 Ch. 201 CA at 210. This dictum was used in cases such as "*Champagne*" to justify a broad view of passing off.

impresario or producer who shows that he is likely to lose sales of his own books or theatre seats in consequence will have a cause of action.[220] However, where the character is deployed in some way that does not compete with the publishing or audio-visual business of the original exploiters—as when its name (as distinct from any visual image) is used on T-shirts, toys, sweets, badges or what you will—the difficulty of demonstrating damage or its likelihood stands in the way of a passing off claim. Thus the developers of the children's television characters, the Wombles, could not secure relief against a person using "Wombles" on rubbish skips.[221]

Arguments that the relevant goodwill arises from the public's belief that originators do grant licences and that this acts as a guarantee of quality have been dismissed in cases concerned with the merchandising of a name alone, whether the name is of an entirely fictional character (such as the Wombles), a television character associated with a particular actor (such as Kojak)[222] or a pop group (such as Abba).[223] All these decisions were distinguished by the V.C. in *Mirage Studios v Counter-Feat*[224] on the narrow basis that they were concerned with names rather than copyright material.[225]

Of these instances, the *Abba* case takes us squarely back to the protection **17–45**
of an aspect of personality,[226] and *Kojak* suggests that there is an important intermediate case where actor and role elide to such an extent that the buying public may simply not distinguish between the two. In Australia, the commercialisation of personality has been more readily protected in the latter case as well as the former: the taking of the character, Crocodile Dundee (played by the highly personable Paul Hogan), for use in spoof advertisements was held to amount to a form of passing off.[227] Moreover, in a case concerning toys which were shoddy versions of the "Muppet" characters from *Sesame Street*, an Australian court found (on strong evidence) that the public did think that such toys were made under licence from the originators.[228]

[220] Illustrations are *Shaw Bros v Golden Harvest* [1972] R.P.C. 559 and *Marengo v Daily Sketch* (1948) 65 R.P.C. 242 HL (cartoonist's *nom de plume*).

[221] *Wombles v Wombles Skips* [1977] R.P.C. 99.

[222] *Tavener Rutledge v Trexapalm* [1975] F.S.R. 479 esp. at 485–486; unassociated sweet manufacturer built up substantial trade in "Kojakpop" lollipops; it was entitled to prevent a "licensee" of the owner of the television series from entering the same market.

[223] *Lyngstad v Anabas* [1977] F.S.R. 62.

[224] [1991] F.S.R. 145.

[225] Per Sir Nicholas Browne-Wilkinson V.C.: [1991] F.S.R. 145 at 158.

[226] See above, paras 17–33–17–35.

[227] *Pacific Dunlop v Hogan* (1989) 87 A.L.R. 14; and see *Hogan v Koala Dundee* (1988) 83 A.L.R. 187 (a very broad view of misappropriation of personality); Shanahan (1991) 81 T.M.R. 351; Burley [1991] E.I.P.R. 227; Duxbury [1991] E.I.P.R. 426.

[228] *Children's Television Workshop v Woolworths* [1981] R.P.C. 187: a case in which the claimant did exercise carefully its quality control powers over licensees; and see also *Fido Dido v Venture Stores* (1981) 16 I.P.R. 365; cf. *Lorimar Productions v Sterling ("Dallas")* [1982] R.P.C. 395 SC (SA); *Grundy Television v Startrain ("Neighbours")* [1988] F.S.R. 581. The refusal, in the related aspect of registered trade mark law, to accept that use of a pop star's name suggests a licensing arrangement strengthens the continuing British scepticism: *Re Elvis Presley Enterprises Applications* [1999] R.P.C. 567 CA.

Although an interim injunction application only, the *Mirage Studios* decision[229] of Browne-Wilkinson V.C. examined the Australian authorities and followed this "Muppet" precedent. The defendant (the wonderfully-named Counter-Feat Clothing) had commissioned drawings of turtles with characteristics similar to the claimant's Teenage Mutant Ninja Turtles and was licensing these to T-shirt makers. While no arguable case of copyright infringement was made out for the purpose of interim relief, passing off was found to be arguable: the relevant misrepresentation arose from the evidence that "a substantial number of the buying public now expect and know that where a famous cartoon or television character is reproduced on goods, that reproduction is the result of a licence". (On the other hand, Laddie J. in *BBC v Pally Screen Printing*,[230] a case involving T-shirts with unauthorised pictures of the Teletubbies characters, considered "it is quite possible that members of the public will look at T-shirts bearing this artwork and think no more than it is artwork bearing illustrations of well-known television characters without having any regard whatsoever to the source of supply and without having any regard as to whether or not [they were authorised by the claimants]".)[231]

In *Mirage Studios*[232] Browne Wilkinson V.C. viewed the situation as one where the claimant was merchandising copyright drawings on a large scale and would lose the royalties if the defendants could continue "misrepresenting to the public that his drawings are the drawings of the plaintiffs or are licensed by the plaintiffs". It sufficed to show that the public believed that the Turtle characters would not appear without the claimants' licence. It was not necessary—so he held, though this must surely be controversial[233]—to demonstrate that they would rely on this misrepresentation when buying the products.

17–46 The interim nature of the decision makes it of dubious value as a precedent, although Robert Walker L.J in *Elvis Presley*[234] described it as "very clear and convincing".[235] It is best regarded as a variant of the *Samuelson* case, in which the defendant is condemned for claiming to provide a known copyright work, when in fact he is offering something else.[236]

---

229 [1991] F.S.R. 145.
230 [1998] F.S.R. 665.
231 [1998] F.S.R. 665 at 674.
232 [1991] F.S.R. 145.
233 See Wadlow, Ch.5, contrasting, in particular, the *Fido Dido* case (1981) 16 I.P.R. 365, which calls for proof of a causal relation between the misrepresentation and purchases and the Federal Court of Australia in another case involving the Teenage Mutant Ninja Turtles (*Surge Licensing v Pearson* 21 I.P.R. 228) which found that no evidence was required to show that consumers were misled or deceived: this would not be the position in English proceedings.
234 [1999] R.P.C. 567.
235 [1999] R.P.C. 567 at 582, referring to the somewhat disparaging reference to it by the trial judge (Laddie J.) as an ex tempore judgment on an interlocutory application, he noted that the hearing had lasted three days.
236 See above, para.17–44.

Accordingly, it cannot be taken as instituting any radical departure from the previous law. With a certain reluctance, the Vice-Chancellor accepted the earlier authorities which give no protection to the merchandising of mere names.[237] No British court has yet been prepared to take the major step of saying that names of characters deserve protection, not as indications of origin or of advertising support, but simply as names.

To draw the line at this point may seem unduly cautious—a distinction which has about it a distinct tinge of arbitrariness.[238] It does, however, place a barrier in the way of claims to exclusive rights for any product which bears a name or image popularised by someone else, although of course such protection may now be available through a registered trade mark. For if the law is as wide as that, then potentially the act of publicising or popularising anything would appear to give exclusive rights in all signs and symbols which identify that thing; for a term, moreover, which is unlimited. Who knows whether that right is restricted to the business which does the initial popularisation, or is a piece of property which may be transferred independently; and whether this imports the other rights and liabilities that attach to property. If there is to be such a broad development, it is surely of the kind (following Justice Brandeis) which should be given concrete form in legislation.

English law is more limited in scope than many jurisdictions that actively **17–47** foster a law of unfair competition. In arguing the case for extension, Vaver claimed that this would "reflect the habits of fair commercial men and public expectations, without any recognisable public interest weighing against it".[239] The case can of course be put attractively. The desire to exploit a character on merchandise stems from its success with the public in the original fictional entertainment. For that success the author or performer and his associates are responsible and they claim in effect that merchandising rights should become part of their property.

But the corollary of property is potential market power. The claim to merchandising rights is made at a time when the popularity of the character would give an opportunity to charge monopoly prices if the rights were conceded. Far from there being no public interest against according the rights, there seems to be a strong case for preserving competition. At least the argument is close enough to militate against extending the law by judicial decision. Major additions to copyright are today generally made by Parliament and, as we have seen, this is the way in which some forms of reaping without sowing have recently been made actionable.[240] The same

237 *Wombles* [1977] F.S.R. 99; *Tavener Rutledge* [1975] F.S.R. 479; *Lyngstad* [1977] F.S.R. 62.
238 The matter looks even more casuistic when it is realised that public authorities and personages often secure special protection of their own names and images: see below, para.18–51.
239 [1978] 9 I.I.C. 541.
240 Attempts to include a merchandising right in the CDPA 1988 did not succeed.

ought to apply to the claim to merchandising rights.[241] If such a change were introduced, it would presumably also include merchandising rights in the names and pictures of real people such as pop stars. As already suggested, their claim seems rather stronger.[242]

What ought to be of concern is that someone who does not trade should have the right nevertheless to license. The law should let all competitors come onto the market until such time as one of them shows that the name definitely indicates goods originating from him to a substantial sector of the public. This is partly a question of preventing registered trade mark rights from being too readily acquired—an aspect that will be reviewed later.[243] But if the issue is raised in passing off proceedings, a question of secondary meaning arises, since the character's name has non-trade mark associations.[244] This, equally, deserves to be dealt with by demanding clear proof that the name has nevertheless come to be recognised as indicating a trade connection.[245]

2. Injurious Falsehood[246]

(1) Elements of the tort

17–48 The tort of injurious falsehood is sometimes available to deal with forms of unfair trading that do not amount to passing off. These may consist of false claims to legal rights (including, of course, intellectual property rights) and other false statements, such as disparaging criticisms of a competitor's goods or business. But, in contrast with passing off, at the end of the nineteenth century the courts deliberately confined this tort to those circumstances which were most incontrovertibly unjustifiable. Their caution stands as one of the chief barriers to the adoption of any broad conception of unfair competition.[247]

In *Ratcliffe v Evans*, Bowen L.J. declared written or oral falsehoods to be actionable "where they are maliciously published, where they are calculated in the ordinary course of things to produce, and where they do produce,

[241] Though not, presumably, in copyright legislation, since characters have not been thought an appropriate subject matter for copyright; certainly the Whitford Committee (Cmnd.6732, 1977), para.909, thought an unfair competition law was the appropriate framework for any development, rather than copyright.

[242] See above, para.17–34 et seq.

[243] A battle which appears to have been lost: see below, paras 18–26 and following.

[244] cf. *"Tarzan" TM* [1970] R.P.C. 450.

[245] On this, note the facts of the "*Kojakpops*" case ([1975] F.S.R. 479) where initially there were a number of competitors exploiting the name, but they all faded away save the claimant, who proved very substantial goodwill.

[246] See generally, Wood (1942) 20 Can.B.R. 296; Prosser (1959) 59 Col. L.R. 425; Morison (1959) 3 Sydney L.R. 4; Carty, *An Analysis of the Economic Torts* (2001) at para.17–01; *Kerly*, Ch.18.

[247] For its relation to the registered trade mark system, see below, paras 18–79 and following.

actual damage".[248] This formulation, which encapsulates the tort in its modern form, is broad so far as types of falsehood are concerned, but narrow in its requirement of malice and special damage (the latter being now modified by statute in many cases). Each of these elements calls for separate consideration.

(a) *The falsehood*

The first actionable falsehoods concerned slanders of title to land. In the course of the last century, the tort came to cover other misstatements—especially about property and business—until any falsehood was encompassed; but the requirement of pecuniary damage has served to limit successful claims mainly to falsehoods about property, profession, trade or business. The claimant must show that the statement is false: true statements, however disparaging and harmful, are not actionable.[249] **17–49**

The damaging untruth may arise by implication from what is actually said.[250] To state, for instance, that a man is working for a particular organisation may suggest to the hearer that he is no longer working in his former business and so deprive him of orders.[251] Equally, for a defendant to claim to be the sole agent for particular machinery may imply that the claimant is no longer, or never was, such an agent.[252] If a statement is not explicitly about the claimant, whether it must nevertheless be taken as referring to him depends on the particular circumstances. In this connection, the courts have held that an untrue claim to a title of any kind, or to be an inventor or designer, is a falsehood that may be actionable at the instance of the person properly entitled, which forms a link to what is sometimes called "inverse" passing off.[253] But there must be some reason to associate the statement with the particular claimant, rather than with all traders of his class.[254]

(b) *Malice*

There are occasions when "malice", as a legal term of art, has a broad objective sense, indicating circumstances when a person has done something which has no sufficient justification or excuse; and there have been **17–50**

248 [1892] 2 Q.B. 524 at 527. In the test put forward by Glidewell L.J. in *Kaye v Robertson* [1991] F.S.R. 62 the damage should be "the direct and natural result" of the publication: at 67.

249 The onus of proof, moreover, lies upon the claimant: see *Burnett v Tak* (1882) 45 L.T. 743; *Anderson v Liebig's Extract* (1882) 45 L.T. 757; cf. *Hargrave v Le Breton* (1769) 4 Burr. 2422 at 2425.

250 As in defamation law, in the absence of intrinsic knowledge from which to draw an innuendo, the courts will look for the natural and ordinary meaning (including inferential meaning) which the words would convey to the ordinary, reasonable, fair-minded, reader: *Charleston v News Group* [1995] 2 All E.R. 313 at 317 (Lord Bridge); *Vodafone v Orange* [1997] F.S.R. 34.

251 cf. *Balden v Shorter* [1933] Ch. 427.

252 *Danish Mercantile v Beaumont* (1950) 67 R.P.C. 111. Consider also *Liebig's Extract v Anderson* (1886) 55 L.T. 206.

253 e.g. *Serville v Constance* [1954] 1 All E.R. 662; *Customglass Boats v Salthouse* [1976] 1 N.Z.L.R. 36; [1976] R.P.C. 589 and see above, para.17–37.

254 cf. cases cited above, in para.17–15.

suggestions that this is what the term means in the law of injurious falsehood.[255] But most modern decisions agree that here it refers to the defendant's state of mind. Did he know his statement to be false? Did he act with some "sinister purpose"[256] or (to put it less pungently) some "indirect or dishonest motive".[257] Stable J. has summarised the case law thus: if the defendant knows the statement to be untrue, it is malicious whether or not the defendant intended to benefit himself (or someone else) rather than injure the claimant. If, however, the defendant does believe his untrue statement, but nevertheless he makes it for the purpose of injuring the claimant, that too will suffice.[258]

(c) *Special damage*

17–51 Until Parliament intervened, the courts required proof of special damage—proof, for instance, that property had lost its value, or a business its custom or a source of supply, as a consequence flowing naturally from the false statement.[259] But, in trading cases at least, they did not always restrict this to unequivocal proof that the claimant had lost particular transactions or profits. Where a defendant said in a press report that the claimant had gone out of business, then it might well be sufficient for him to prove that his sales overall had forthwith fallen, if his customers were normally unknown and changing; but not if they were regular and known.[260] What evidence will suffice must depend on the circumstances; a claimant who fails to follow up a reasonable prospect of furnishing concrete proof may severely weaken his case.

Section 3 of the Defamation Act 1952 has abrogated the need to prove special damage if the words in question: (1) were calculated to cause pecuniary damage to the claimant and were published in writing or other permanent form; or (2) were calculated to cause pecuniary damage to the claimant in respect of any office, profession, calling, trade or business, held or carried on by him at the time of the publication.[261] The pecuniary damage must be likely as a natural and probable consequence of the wrongful act.[262]

---

[255] e.g. Lord Davey, *Royal Baking Powder v Wright Crossley* (1900) 18 R.P.C. 95 at 99; and see Newark (1944) 60 L.Q.R. 366.

[256] Harman J. *Serville v Constance* [1954] 1 All E.R. 662 at 665.

[257] Scrutton L.J. *Greers v Pearman* (1922) 39 R.P.C. 406 at 417; *Balden v Shorter* [1933] Ch. 427; cf. earlier, less stringent views: *Royal Baking Powder v Wright*; Crossley (1901) 18 R.P.C. 95.

[258] *Wilts United Dairy v Robinson* [1957] R.P.C. 220 at 237.

[259] *Haddan v Lott* (1854) 15 C.B. 411.

[260] e.g. *Ratcliffe v Evans* [1892] 2 Q.B. 524 CA; *Greers v Pearman* (1922) 39 R.P.C. 406.

[261] This was recommended by the Porter Committee on the Law of Defamation (Cmd.7536, 1952), paras 50–54. A defamatory statement that is in the same form or of the same character as the cases covered by s.3 is actionable in defamation without proof of special damage. The Faulks Committee on Defamation (Cmnd.5909, 1975), paras 584–589, recommended that the distinction between the written and the spoken word should be abolished.

[262] *Lynch v Knight* (1861) 9 H.L.C. 577; *Stewart-Brady v Express Newspapers* [1997] E.M.L.R. 192; *Customglass* case [1976] 1 N.Z.L.R. 36 at 603.

It is not, in other words, a specific part of the requirement of malice, but is akin to the requirement of likely damage in the tort of passing off.[263]

(2) Particular aspects

(a) *Relation to other torts*

If the defendant's statement represents that his goods or business are those of the claimant, it is an injurious falsehood that amounts to passing off. So it is actionable despite lack of malice.[264] If the statement tends to lower the defendant personally in the eyes of right-thinking members of society then it is actionable as defamation: proof of intent to defame is then, in principle, irrelevant; and it is for the defendant to excuse himself by proving the truth of the statement or establishing some other defence such as fair comment on a matter of public interest or one of the forms of privilege. It is not defamation, but only injurious falsehood, to disparage a trader's goods, business or property, save where there is also an imputation of undue "carelessness, misconduct or want of skill".[265] This may, of course, be the innuendo behind a statement about the goods or business. Unless this is so, honest disparagement is not actionable at common law.[266] **17–52**

Because injurious falsehood requires it to be shown that there was a misrepresentation of the truth, it will not be committed if a statement is made in corrected form, and an injunction may be limited to exclude this. In one distasteful example, newspaper reporters broke into the hospital room of an actor who was recovering from a serious head injury. They insisted on "interviewing" and photographing him despite his poor condition. They could be enjoined from publishing the interview as an "exclusive" granted to the paper, since this lie prejudiced the victim's undoubted chances of selling his story later to others. But they could not be stopped from publishing an account and picture which stated truthfully how the material was obtained.[267]

---

263 See above, paras 17–41 and following.

264 An instance where both were successfully pleaded is the *Wilts United Dairy* case [1957] R.P.C. 220.

265 *Linotype v British Empire Type-Setting* (1899) 81 L.T. 331; *Griffiths v Benn* (1911) 27 T.L.R. 346; *Kaye v Robertson* [1991] F.S.R. 62 CA; *CHC Software v Hopkins & Wood* [1983] F.S.R. 241. Each must in consequence be separately pleaded: *A & M Records v Audio Magnetics* [1979] F.S.R. 1 at 9. The distinction nonetheless did not appeal to forthright minds: see Lord Halsbury in the *Linotype* case at 333.

266 Defamation of a private corporation is in principle actionable (*South Hetton Coal v North-Eastern News* [1894] 1 Q.B. 133); but not of a local authority (*Derbyshire CC v Times Newspapers* [1993] A.C. 534 HL).

267 *Kaye v Robertson* [1991] F.S.R. 62 CA: no other cause of action was presented which justified interim relief: there was no trespass to the person merely from a flashlight which caused no reaction; no passing off, because the claimant was not a trader (though he had a story to sell!); and there was no defamatory innuendo clear enough—not even the suggestion that he talking to the Sunday Sport—to justify an injunction until trial. See above, Ch.9.

(b) *False claims of infringement*

17–53 Because intellectual property is protectable by litigation alone, and not also by possession, the ability to assert rights is crucial. And equally, as earlier noted,[268] because it often takes time and expense to assess whether there has been infringement of a valid right, a threat to sue can do immense commercial harm, particularly to a manufacturer whose customers receive the threats. In this connection, the limited scope of injurious falsehood deserves special note. For it is only if a person untruthfully and maliciously asserts to a rival's customers that they are receiving infringing goods that the rival has any cause of action under the general common law. Hence the introduction of the special statutory action for threats of patent, registered design and registered trade mark infringement; and the question whether the same should apply to other threats of litigation. These have already been discussed.[269]

(c) *Comparative advertising*

17–54 Comparison—explicit or implied, specific or vague—lies at the root of modern advertising. Where there is price competition, the cheaper rival may seek to stress similarities in his comparison with the more expensive; where there is not, he may emphasise some point of differentiation, more or less genuine and useful to the consumer. In the absence of passing off, the only weapon which the common law provided against any sort of comparative advertising was restricted to disparagements that amounted to injurious falsehood. And at an early stage of both the modern tort and modern advertising, the courts showed particular reluctance to allow such actions to succeed.

Not only must there be malice and untruth in the comparison, but, where the two are distinct, the misstatement must be about the claimant's goods and not about the defendant's.[270] In *White v Mellin*[271] the House of Lords held it not actionable for a retailer to attach stickers puffing his "own brand" to tins of the claimant's baby food; all the stickers said was that the "own brand" was "far more nutritious and healthful than any other preparation". Lord Herschell, in particular, feared a flood of litigation over the rival merits of products and the deployment of judicial decision as a means

[268] See above, paras 2–93 and following.

[269] See above, paras 2–93—2–96. Note that one effect of emphasising the balance of convenience in proceedings for an interim injunction may be to undermine the requirement of malice in injurious falsehood: see *Jaybeam v Abru* [1976] R.P.C. 308. But cf. *Polydor v Harlequin Records* [1980] F.S.R. 26 CA; *Crest Homes v Ascott* [1980] F.S.R. 396.

[270] *Canham v Jones* (1813) V & B. 218; *Young v Macrae* (1862) 3 B. & S. 264; cf. *Western Counties Manure v Lawes* (1874) L.R. 9 Ex. 218, which was criticised in *White v Mellin* [1895] A.C. 154 HL at 164.

[271] [1895] A.C. 154 HL.

of advertisement.[272] In *Hubbuck v Wilkinson*[273] the Court of Appeal treated even an advertisement purporting to set out the results of chemical tests as no more than a statement that the defendant's paint was equal to, or somewhat better than, the claimant's.

Actions have occasionally succeeded for specific and damaging lies, such as that the defendant's newspaper circulation was 20 times that of any local paper (that is the claimant's).[274] The present test has been stated thus: there must be a real disparagement or untrue statement that a reasonable man would take to be a serious claim.[275] Hyperbolic puffing, in other words, will be discounted for what it is.[276] At the same time, the courts will not give traders freedom to make false statements about their competitors' prices and then say that they did not really mean the statement to be believed: where one chain of electrical stores, Comet, advertised their marked prices as being lower than the promotional prices of a competitor, Currys, the judge found the statement "I charge less than X for the same goods" to be clearly different to the statement that "My goods are better than X's". The latter was a mere puff that was not actionable; the former, on the other hand, was "plainly intended to be taken seriously [by the reasonable consumer] and is likely to be taken seriously".[277] In opposing the claimant's application to extend the injunction against the false statements, counsel for the defendant contended that resort to the courts was an escalation of a price war which should not be encouraged and that there was a risk that legal proceedings would become a tool of marketing policy. Whilst noting that it was to be regretted that the dispute could not be resolved without recourse to the courts, the judge rejected this argument in strong terms and instead found that where there was clear evidence of malicious falsehood the court "should not flinch from granting interlocutory relief if justified on the facts simply because it represents an escalation of a price war".[278] Perhaps judges are becoming more willing than their predecessors to find that the "reasonable man" takes comparisons seriously. But the stress on an objective test should be noted. **17–55**

Prior to the liberalisation of the use of registered trade marks in comparative advertising introduced by the Trade Marks Act 1994, the common law could often be left on one side, because under s.4(1)(b) of the Trade Marks Act 1938, comparative advertising constituted infringement simply **17–56**

[272] [1895] A.C. 154 at 164; an idea stressed in the context of passing off: *Consorzio del Prosciutto di Parma v Marks & Spencer* [1996] R.P.C. 351.

[273] [1899] 1 Q.B. 86; and see *Alcott v Millar's Karri* (1904) 21 T.L.R. 30.

[274] *Lyne v Nicholls* (1906) 23 T.L.R. 86. At the interim stage, the judge will ask whether there was any likelihood of a jury finding the misstatements to be true: *Compaq v Dell* [1992] F.S.R. 93.

[275] *De Beers Abrasive v International General Electric* [1975] F.S.R. 323.

[276] "Advertisements are not to be read as if they were some testamentary disposition in a will": per Whitford J. *McDonald's v Burger King* [1986] F.S.R. 45 at 58.

[277] Per Owen J. in *DSG Retail v Comet* [2002] F.S.R. 899 at 910.

[278] [2002] F.S.R. 899 at 912.

upon proof that a registered mark had been used to "import a reference" to the registered proprietor or his goods, whether that reference was true or false, flattering or disparaging.[279] In its role of consumer protector, the EU has also adopted a Directive on the subject.[280] This takes a circumspect view of permissible comparative advertising which to some degree seeks to curb certain (to the common lawyer) over-protective applications of Continental unfair competition laws to them in the past. The British Government considered that the Directive's terms required no alteration even to our common law principles. That, however, is a question to which we revert when comparing the position on registered marks.[281] But the Directive has not brought about any new dawn for injurious falsehood in comparison cases; instead there have been a number of cases which question whether a claim for injurious falsehood adds anything to a claim of trade mark infringement.[282]

Overall the law seems to have played a surprisingly minor role in the matter. Until relatively recently there was little use made of comparative advertising: very largely a "dog-bites-dog" attitude among advertising agencies and their clients kept "knocking copy" out of the British media. However, in the more aggressive atmosphere of the late twentieth century, such tactics became a regular feature of some industries' advertising and this has continued. This only strengthens the case for returning the law to the discriminating attitude found in the cases on injurious falsehood.

[279] Some judges looked decidedly askance at this departure from the "origin function" of the mark: see esp. *Bismag v Amblins* (1940) 57 R.P.C. 209, where the judges were divided about an advertisement to sell both lines of product compared; and *Aristoc v Rysta* (1945) 62 R.P.C. 65 at 77, 79, 85.

[280] Directive 97/55, amending the Misleading Advertising Directive 84/450.

[281] Below, paras 18–103–18–106. See *Oz v Hutchison* [2007] E.T.M.R. 264, CA.

[282] For example, Jacob J. in both *Cable & Wireless v BT* [1998] F.S.R. 383 at 385 and *British Airways v Ryanair* [2001] E.T.M.R. 235 at paras 9–14.

CHAPTER 18

REGISTERED TRADE MARKS

1. REGISTRATION SYSTEMS

From the initial adoption of a registration system in 1875, the British approach has been to treat common law protection and registration cumulatively, the common law giving protection wherever trading activity justified it and registration providing surer, more straightforward, protection when an official grant had been secured. As already outlined, the aim of the EU system was to make registration easier, either through the national registries or, for a CTM, the Office for Harmonisation in the Internal Market (Trade Marks and Designs) (OHIM).[1] As a consequence, common **18–01**

[1] See generally, Firth, Lea & Cornford, *Trade Marks: Law & Practice* 2nd edn (2006); *Kerly* 14th edn (2005); Morcom, Roughton & Graham, *The Modern Law of Trade Marks* 3rd edn (2008); Phillips, *Trade Mark Law: A Practical Anatomy* (2003). For the CTM, see Gold, Abnett & Farwell (eds), *The Community Trade Mark Handbook* (2001, looseleaf); von Mühlendahl, Ohlgart & von Bomhard, *Die Gemeinschaftsmarke* (1998). On ECJ judgments, see Maniatis and Botis, *Trade Marks in Europe: A Practical Jurisprudence* 2nd edn (2009).

law protection is needed less than when the bar for registration was set much higher under the Trade Marks Act 1938 and its predecessors,[2] although it remains a valuable alternative either where a registration has not been obtained or the registered mark protection is circumscribed in some way.

This chapter is concerned with the registration systems for the United Kingdom and for the EU and with the substantive law which, in large measure, is in common form for both[3]: as has been stated frequently (for example by Advocate-General Jacobs in *Arthur et Felicie*)[4] the parallel provisions of the Directive and the CTM Regulation should be interpreted in the same way. Despite a flood of cases before the Court of Justice (ECJ) and the General Court (GC; formerly CFI) as court of appeal from the OHIM Boards of Appeal, the interpretation of these standard statutory provisions in different Member States continues in many areas to reflect inherited traditions and attitudes of the various countries[5]:

> "[t]he fact is that trade mark law is and the concepts involved are much subtler and more complex than an outsider would, at first blush, expect."[6]

These traditions and attitudes vary at two levels:

(1) *As to the extent to which legal protection of any kind should go.* Some countries have been more willing than others to carry the protection of marks for goods and services beyond the origin function, so as to protect a variety of "investment functions" associated with matters such as dilution, comparative advertising and parallel importation. A strongly protectionist country is likely to have an engrained belief (at least among its judges) in the gullibility of its consuming public and of the need to protect established businesses from encroachments into their markets which play upon this naivety. What other explanation can there have been for the obsessive policing of potential

---

[2] See Annand at pp.112–125, in *7 Perspectives on Intellectual Property, Trade Marks Retrospective* (2000).

[3] For Benelux law, see Evrard and Péters, *La Défense de la Marque dans le Benelux* 2nd edn (2000); the law comprising the national laws of Belgium, Holland and Luxembourg, the uniform Benelux law, the EU Directive, the CTM Regulation and international conventions.

[4] *LTJ Diffusion v Sadas* [2003] F.S.R. 1 at paras 21–28.

[5] The final arbiter of their meaning is the European Court of Justice (ECJ). Interpretation of provisions deriving from the CTM Regulation or TM Directive depends upon them and not upon explanations offered in the UK White Paper or parliamentary debates: *British Sugar v James Robertson* [1996] R.P.C. 281 at 292. In *O2 v Hutchison* [2006] E.T.M.R. 677, the judge noted the scathing criticisms of the GC and the ECJ in *Kerly* but commented "[h]owever well-founded their criticisms may be, it is for the European courts, and not a national judge, to respond to them": at para.63.

[6] per Jacob L.J. in *Reed Executive v Reed Business Information* [2004] R.P.C. 767 at para.128.

misrepresentation under the old German Law against Unfair Competition?[7]

(2) *As to the type of legal protection to be employed.* Even where there is general accord that certain conduct should not be permitted, countries differ over whether to impose liability through underlying principle, such as is provided by a law of unfair competition or (in common law jurisdictions) by torts of passing off and the like, or as a consequence of registering a trade mark; or both. A registered trade mark law which requires almost all protection of marks to be given within it will be likely to strain to impose liabilities which other systems deal with through the inherently subtler medium of tort or unfair competition law.

This difference in attitude remains significant, despite unsuccessful attempts to secure recognition of earlier Benelux trade mark law (which provided expansive, unfair competition-like protection) as a source of interpretation of the EU texts. English courts were early to reject this.[8]

At the same time, the British judges have been scrupulous in acknowledging that the Trade Marks Act 1994 (TMA 1994) is a new law and "should not be assumed to be the same as the old UK law nor to be different from it"[9] (although the House of Lords has noted that "many of the basic concepts in the Directive appear to be the same as, or closely similar to, those which have informed the previous domestic law".[10]) A decision of the Court of Appeal goes so far as to say that "one has to start by forgetting the preconceptions of pre-1994 Act trade mark law".[11] Indeed, where the words of the UK Act differ from those of the TM Directive,[12] English judges have relied consistently on the latter as the authoritative source.[13] Unfortunately, this does not help in the many areas where the legislative provisions or their

[7] Recognised as such by a leading authority: Schricker [1994] GRUR Int. 586, although more recently the case-law of the German Supreme Court has become more liberal. On the 2004 Law against Unfair Competition, see Henning-Bodewig (2005) 36 I.I.C. 421 and Sosnitza (2005) I.I.C. 525.

[8] See Laddie J. *Wagamama v City Centre Restaurants* [1995] F.S.R. 713; discussed below in para.18–94 (concerning likelihood of "association" between marks—a central issue).

[9] per Aldous L.J. in *Philips v Remington* [1999] R.P.C. 809 at 815; also, *Inter Lotto v Camelot* [2004] R.P.C. 186 CA, in which Carnwath L.J. commented that "historical analysis has to be approached with caution": at para.14.

[10] per Lord Walker of Gestingthorpe in *R. v Johnstone* [2003] F.S.R. 748 HL at para.63.

[11] per Arden L.J. in *"ESB" (West (t/a Eastenders) v Fullers)* [2003] F.S.R. 44 CA at para.69, suggesting also that: "If King Canute had been a trade mark agent, the waters of Community law, which Lord Denning depicted as rushing up our native shores, would surely have overwhelmed him by now."

[12] The original TM Directive has been replaced by Directive 2008/95 but the numbering has not changed nor the substance.

[13] e.g. in *Budejovicky Budvar v Anheuser-Busch* [2009] EWCA 1022, Jacob L.J. commented: "Unfortunately the draftsman of the Act got the idea that it would be helpful in implementing the Directive to use different language. It is not. Quite the opposite. At best it wastes everyone's time trying to relate the section to the provision of the Directive which it is implementing. At worst it positively misleads": at para.19.

interpretation by the ECJ are not thought through properly, are inconsistent or are just plain nonsense. The situation in which trade mark law now finds itself has been summarised by the leading English judge in the field thus:

> "European trade mark law seems to have arrived at such a state of uncertainty that no one really knows what the rules are, outside the obviously core case of straightforward infringement (the use of a mark as a trade mark for the defendant's goods which is the same or confusingly similar to a plaintiff's registered mark registered for the same or similar goods). Big brand owners want bigger rights; smaller players, no change or less. The compromises which have emerged have very fuzzy lines."[14]

2. The Process of Registration

18–02 This section outlines the steps involved in applying for a registered trade mark under the TMA 1994.[15] It takes, first of all, the case of an application under national law to the UK Registry. Where an applicant is interested only in the national market, his sole objective will likely be a UK registration. But through UK participation in the Madrid Protocol,[16] those with wider horizons may use an application to the UK Registry (or indeed an existing registration) as the basis for a so-called "International Registration" in Protocol countries. This innovation is dealt with next. Finally, within the EU, it is possible to apply to OHIM in Alicante for a Community Trade Mark that has effect throughout all 27 Member States of the European Union.[17] A simple diagram on p.675 indicates these options and their inter-relationships.

(1) Procedure for a UK application

(a) *Applicants*

18–03 Any person, natural or legal, who has a bona fide intention to use a mark (either himself or by authorising another person to do so) for the goods or

---

[14] per Jacob L.J. in *Boehringer Ingelheim v Swingward* [2008] E.T.M.R. 36 CA at para.2; cf. the view of Dr Simon Ffima that "[a]rguably though, Jacob L.J.'s prognosis is a little too gloomy." [2008] E.T.M.R. Pt 6 at para.E2.

[15] For fuller accounts, see the works cited in n.1 above.

[16] For the genesis of the Protocol, see above, para.16–14. The CTM system also joined Madrid with effect from October 1, 2004.

[17] For the evolution of OHIM, see above, para.16–16. It received applications from January 1996, processing them from April 1, 1996. Trade mark applications may now be filed in any of the 23 official languages (Bulgarian, Irish and Rumanian became official languages on January 1, 2007).

TRADE MARK APPLICATIONS FOR AND FROM THE UNITED KINGDOM

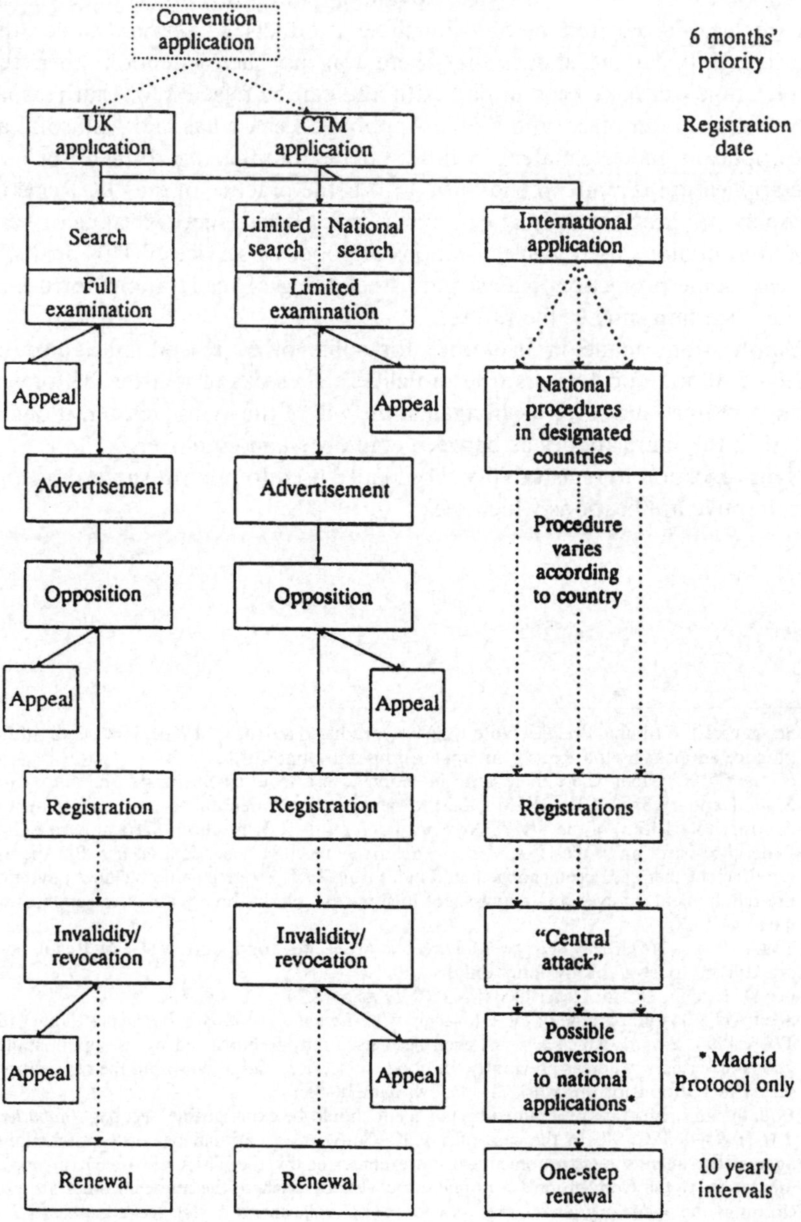

services specified in the application, may apply to the Trade Marks Registry of the Intellectual Property Office to register it.[18] There is no requirement to have used the mark before applying, all that needs to be declared is an intention to use.[19] One of the great advantages of registration is to be able to secure legal protection before launching products or services under the mark.[20] If it can be shown that there was no such intention, then the application will have been in bad faith and can be rejected for that reason, or expunged after registration[21]: the Appointed Person has said: "[i]nsofar as the applicant makes a materially false statement in this regard then I believe the application is made in bad faith."[22] It is the practice of the UK Registry to query applications only in extreme cases or where there is vague or very wide terminology used in specifications of goods or services.[23] This provides at least some protection against pure stockpiling of registrations for use at some uncertain time in the future.

Applications made in bad faith for some other reason must also be rejected. If an importing distributor deliberately seeks to register the foreign manufacturer's mark for itself, against the will of the manufacturer, it ought to fail[24]; the same applies as between employee and employer.[25]

This objection to registrability should also used to prevent succeeding any pre-emptive applications which seek:

---

[18] See generally Tribunal Practice Note 1/2000 (reproduced at App.5 of *Kerly*) for details of the practice adopted by the Registry in applications and oppositions.

[19] cf. the CTM system where there is no intention to use requirement. In its *Bad Faith Case Study* (January 31, 2003), OHIM took the view that an "intention to use" requirement is contrary to art.15(3) of the TRIPS Agreement; cf. on the UK position, *Kerly* at para.8–272.

[20] Federal registration in the USA was until relatively recently dependent on use. But the use requirement there has been changed; and indeed the TRIPS Agreement precludes any prior use requirement, or even any requirement to show use within three years of the application date: art.15(3).

[21] TMA 1994 ss.3(6), 32(3), 47(1); TM Directive art.3(2)(d) (optional); cf. CTM Regulation, art.51(1)(b) (post-grant invalidity only).

[22] per D. Kitchin QC in *Kinder* [2004] R.P.C. 29 at para.23.

[23] See PAN 5/06 and para.40 of the UK Registry's *Manual of Trade Mark Practice*. Under the TMA 1994, a mark which has not even been used may be infringed by use upon similar goods or services, whereas previously the goods or services had to be within the registration: see earlier editions of this work. See below, para.18–05.

[24] Equally, any registration obtained by the agent should be expungeable: see, e.g. *"Sabatier" TM* [1993] R.P.C. 97. In the case of a Paris Convention national or corporation, rights against the agent's registration and use are conferred by the TMA 1994 s.60 (in implementation of the Convention's art.6*septies*); cf. the case where the mark becomes an indication of the agent (e.g. as repairer and source of replacement parts): see, e.g. *Diehl's TM* [1970] R.P.C. 435.

[25] e.g. *"Zoppas" TM* [1965] R.P.C. 381; cf. *Ball v The Eden Project Ltd* [2002] F.S.R. 686, where the court ordered assignment to the company of a mark registered by one of its directors in breach of his fiduciary duty; bad faith does not seem to have been argued.

(1) to stockpile marks because they may be needed at some point in the future undetermined at the time of the application[26];
(2) to misappropriate marks with a strong reputation outside the United Kingdom but not yet used here[27]; and perhaps even:
(3) to acquire without consent other "merchandisable" marks, such as the names of pop stars and film characters, although these are likely to fail as being devoid of distinctive character under s.3(1)(b), for example both "Jane Austen"[28] and "Diana, Princess of Wales"[29] failed for this reason.

However, the ground for refusal does not "require applicants to submit to an open-ended assessment of their commercial morality".[30] Nor will the Registry entertain unsubstantiated allegations of bad faith: it is a serious allegation that must be supported by evidence.[31] In *Chocoladenfabriken Lindt & Sprüngli v Franz Hauswirth*[32] the Court of Justice held that the intention and state of mind of the applicant at the time of the application, although subjective factors, must be considered by reference to the objective circumstances of the case.[33]

After a period when they diverged, the test now applied by both the UK Registry and OHIM is the same.[34] If the applicant has had business dealings with an opponent who has prior use of the mark he is applying for, whether in the United Kingdom or elsewhere, he will certainly have to give good

[26] cf. the CTM system in which "it is entirely left to the applicant to file a list of goods and services as long as he sees fit, i.e. a list exceeding his actual scope of business activity, and try later to expand his activities in order to be able to show genuine use of his CTM or face revocation under Article 50(1)(a) CTMR [s.46(1)(a), TMA 1994] and other sanctions, respectively." Per OHIM First Cancellation Division in *Trillium*, March 28, 2000, commented on and criticised at paras 7–229 and 7–230 of the 13th edn of *Kerly*, and subsequently the scope has been widened, see 14th edn of *Kerly* at paras 8–258—8–262.

[27] A competitor whose mark is being misappropriated may need to bring opposition proceedings in order to demonstrate the bad faith involved: TMA 1994 s.5(4) because of its reference to passing off (which requires goodwill in the UK) is unlikely to be interpreted sufficiently broadly to give comfort in most cases.

[28] SRIS O/198/99 TM Registry.

[29] SRIS O/261/00 TM Registry. See now Ch.3 para.21 of the UK Registry's *Manual of Trade Mark Practice*.

[30] Per the Appointed Person (G.Hobbs, QC) in *Demon Ale* [2000] R.P.C. 345 at 356.

[31] Per the Appointed Person (S. Thorley, QC) in *Royal Enfield TMs* [2002] R.P.C. 508 at 516.

[32] *Chocoladenfabriken Lindt & Sprüngli v Franz Hauswirth* [2009] E.T.M.R. 56 ECJ. The Court of Justice made clear that it was not sufficient in itself for a finding of bad faith that the applicant knew that a third party had been using for a long time an identical or similar mark for identical or similar goods that may be confused with the mark being applied for: the applicant's intention must also be considered (at paras 40 and 41).

[33] Case C-529/07 at para.42.

[34] See Arnold J. in *Hotel Cipriani SRL v Cipriani (Grosvenor Street) Ltd* [2009] R.P.C. 9 at paras 165–202; the judge's finding that the CTM application involved in the case was not made in bad faith was upheld by the Court of Appeal, [2010] EWCA Civ 110 at para.56.

reasons why he is seeking to register the mark.[35] However, courts have refused to interfere with applications where there is a real intention to use the mark on some of the goods included in the specification[36] and a claim of bad faith by reason of wishing to use the mark only in conjunction with others was rejected also.[37]

The practice of trade mark "squatting" has long been known[38]: a mark becomes well-known abroad before it is used in the United Kingdom. An opportunist registers it in advance, expecting then to be bought off by the foreign owner who has built up the reputation.[39] It is desirable that this conduct should be treated as "bad faith" since the concept distinguishes between cases where the applicant for registration does and does not have sufficient ground to make the application.[40]

A more refined issue which goes to bad faith is the question whether the mark is to be used for the goods or services specified or really as a mark for something else. Under the old law, the owners of the famous mark "Kodak" lost their registration of it for clothing, when their only use was to advertise cameras and films on T-shirts.[41]

---

[35] See the judgment of the Benelux Supreme Court in *Intergro v Interbuy* [2003] E.T.M.R. 152 on the bad faith provision in the Uniform Benelux Trade Mark Law, to the effect that it was not necessary for a finding of bad faith that the parties (the applicant and opponent) have a formal or contractual relationship but it was sufficient that the previous use of the mark had been known when commercial discussions took place about possible cooperation.

[36] *Second Sight v Novell* [1995] R.P.C 423. In *Knoll AG's TM* [2003] R.P.C. 175, it was held it would be inappropriate to adopt a strict interpretation of the Act that meant a mark could only be registered for products that were already on the market or would be in the foreseeable future; the applicant was only using the mark on obesity products but intended to use in relation to other pharmaceutical products if it proved commercially successful and, in rejecting the attack on validity, Neuberger J. noted that this was a common and acceptable practice in the pharmaceutical industry (at para.31).

[37] By the Court of Appeal of Northern Ireland in *BP Amoco v John Kelly* [2002] F.S.R. 87.

[38] It is more expensive and laborious than "domain name squatting" but it involves the same parasitic instinct which courts everywhere seek to combat as evidently and inexcusably unfair: see above, para.16–21.

[39] See *Daawat TM* [2003] R.P.C. 187 Appointed Person (G. Hobbs, QC), where the Indian mark was known to the UK applicant (subsequently registered proprietor; the application was to remove for invalidity by reason of bad faith), who wanted to improve his prospects of being appointed an agent or distributor. Also, *Byford v Oliver* [2003] E.M.L.R. 20 and *Ferrero SpA's TMs* [2004] R.P.C. 583 Appointed Person (D. Kitchin QC).

[40] In practice, the issue is likely to be raised most frequently in opposition or invalidity proceedings, and under the CTM only the latter is possible (see CTM Regulation art.51(1)(b)). Owners of famous marks have accordingly campaigned for some form of international register from which national systems would derive proof and so be enabled to reject the application of their own motion at an early stage: although "meeting general resistance", see Kur (2000) 31 I.I.C. 824 at 826.

[41] *"Kodak" TM* [1990] F.S.R. 495; cf. the OHIM Opposition Division decision in *Malibu device*, Decision No.374/2001, where the opponent relied upon earlier registrations for clothing and submitted evidence of use on T-shirts: the decision correctly rejected such use, as clothing distributed at promotional events was merely an instrument for the marketing of "Malibu" drinks; and *Premier Brands v Typhoon Europe* [2000] F.S.R. 767, where Neuberger J. considered such use (on tea caddies) may be understood by the public as promoting Typhoo tea but also might lead to an assumption on the part of the public that the tea caddies were marketed by or with the consent of the makers of Typhoo tea, at 807.

An application must contain: a request for registration, the applicant's name and address, a statement of the goods and/or services to be included in the registration and a "representation" of the mark.[42] If complete it will be given a filing date—a vital factor in determining its claims as against competing applications and uses.[43]

(b) *Priority*

Sometimes independent parties will be seeking the same or similar marks without either of them being able to claim an earlier right from prior use. Then the issue will turn on which application has the earlier filing date, and priority arrangements under the Paris Convention may be important. These allow an applicant[44] in (say) the United Kingdom to claim up to six months' priority from an application in another Convention country.[45] If there has been more than one earlier application, it is the first that counts, subject to the exception that an application which has been abandoned without publication may be discounted.[46] **18–04**

(c) *Classification*

The Trade Marks Register is divided into 45 Classes, 34 for goods and 11 for services, in accordance with the Nice International Arrangement on the subject.[47] This classification is an administrative measure, designed to aid the process of searching. An applicant needs to name all the goods and services for which he wants the registration from the outset, since amendment is only allowed to clarify or narrow the specification.[48] Since many classes are wide, the applicant will often specify the goods or services within a class for which registration is sought. The Registrar has a final power to decide the class in which particular goods or services are to be placed[49] but not to change the class number at the request of the applicant (unless an obvious mistake).[50] **18–05**

[42] TMA 1994 s.32, which also requires a declaration of actual or intended use (unlike under the CTMR). For "representation", see below, para.18–20.

[43] TMA 1994 s.33.

[44] The applicant must have Convention nationality or establishment.

[45] The same principle applies in relation to dependent British territories and to other countries (e.g. Taiwan) with which Britain has a bilateral agreement on the matter; but not in relation to an earlier British application (which may, however, be the subject of a merger under TMA 1994 s.41). See in general s.35, which allows partial priorities to be claimed.

[46] At the UK filing date the earlier application must have been withdrawn, abandoned or refused without publication, without leaving any rights outstanding: TMA 1994 s.35(4), following the Paris Convention art.4C(4).

[47] Originally of 1957 and now in its 9th edn. See TMA 1994 s.34: TM (Amendment) Rules 2006 (SI 3039/2006) implementing the Nice Classification in force from time to time (currently 9th).

[48] See TMA 1994 s.39(2) for the very limited ability to amend applications.

[49] TMA 1994 s.34(2).

[50] *Altecnic's TM Application* [2002] R.P.C. 639 CA: "The fact that the internationally agreed Nice Classification System has been devised to 'serve exclusively administrative purposes' (see, for example, rule 2(4) of the Commission Regulation 2868/95) does not mean that the selection by the applicant of one or more Class numbers in his application for registration has to be ignored in deciding what the application is for": at 648.

Classification does not directly affect the validity or the scope of protection of a mark.[51] It does not, for instance, settle what goods or services shall or shall not be treated as "similar".[52] Under the TMA 1994 (for the first time) a single application may be made in respect of goods or services in different classes, though still with supplementary fees for each class.[53] Moreover, there is provision for filing a single application covering a series of marks which differ only in ways not substantially affecting the identity of the mark.[54]

Broad specifications are now generally acceptable.[55] However, in construing the registration it is the core meaning which should be used.[56]

One important area in which applications are permitted, but were not previously, is retail services.[57] The Court of Justice confirmed in *Praktiker*[58] that the notion of "services" in the TM Directive (and therefore the CTM Regulation also) covers services provided in connection with retail trade in goods, and general wording such as "bringing together of a variety of goods, enabling customers to conveniently view and purchase those goods" is sufficient to identify those services.[59] In *Land Securities v Registrar of Trade Marks*[60] Floyd J. overturned the Registry's refusal to permit registration of trade marks for the services of a shopping centre or mall operator, noting that shopping centres make extensive use of branding to attract as many visitors as possible.[61]

(d) *Search and examination*

18–06 An intending applicant will in all likelihood have a search undertaken for prior conflicting marks. Whether or not this happens, upon receipt with the

[51] However, a reference in the description of goods or services to the classification (as, for instance, "syrups in Class 30") will exclude those goods under another class (as, for instance, syrups constituting jams, which fall under Class 29): *British Sugar v James Robertson* [1996] R.P.C. 281 at 288–290. Classification may also determine the nature of the goods where homonyms are concerned, e.g. "valves" in Class 7 means "engine valves", in Class 9 "electronic valves", and Class 11 "water or fluid control valves".

[52] However, the fact that a registration is limited to a type of goods "within Class X" may restrict the range of goods outside Class X which can be regarded as "similar": see Jacob J. in *British Sugar v Robertson* [1996] R.P.C. 281, below, para.18–91.

[53] TM Rules r.5.

[54] TMA 1994 s.41(1)(c)—this allows variations in script, hyphenation and non-distinctive suffixes, such as model numbers, to be covered in one application, for which only a single fee is payable. In this connection, particularly, the Registry's power to allow division or merger may be useful: TMA 1994 s.41(1); TM Rules rr.19, 20.

[55] PAN 5/06, care still has to be taken in Classes 7, 9, 42, 43, 44 and 45.

[56] *Avnet v Isoact* [1998] F.S.R. 16 (running an internet service for other advertisers is not providing "advertising and promotional services"); applied in *Reed Executive v Reed Business Information* [2004] R.P.C. 767 CA at para.45.

[57] As a result originally of *Giacomelli* [2000] E.T.M.R. 277, OHIM BA; see now UK Registry Practice Amendment Notices, PAN 6/05 and PAN 7/06, applying *Praktiker*.

[58] *Praktiker* [2005] E.T.M.R. 88 ECJ.

[59] In the UK Registry the applicant must identify the type of goods to which the retail services relate, see PAN 6/05.

[60] *Land Securities v Registrar of Trade Marks* [2009] R.P.C. 5.

[61] *Land Securities* [2009] R.P.C. 5 at paras 10-13.

necessary fee, the Registry will conduct a search of identical and similar earlier marks, to the extent that is considered necessary.[62] It will then examine the application in the light of the absolute grounds of objection discussed below.[63] After October 2007, the Registry has continued to examine on relative grounds and report them to the applicant but no longer raises relative grounds as objections to registration. This is left to the opposition stage. If the Registry finds the mark not registrable on absolute grounds, it must inform the applicant and allow representations and, if permitted, amendments.[64]

Once the Registrar is satisfied that the application meets the conditions specified in the Act, it must be accepted, although it has been emphasised (somewhat piously) by the Court of Justice that:

> "examination carried out at the time of application must not be a minimal one; for reasons of legal certainty and good administration, it is necessary to ensure that trade marks whose use could successfully be challenged before the courts are not registered".[65]

The Registry has no discretion in the matter if the application meets the conditions for registrability. Publication of the application follows in the *Trade Marks Journal*. Once this occurs, the file becomes open to public inspection[66]—and capable of use by opponents.

(e) *Opposition*

Any person may then within two months of publication in the *Trade Marks* **18–07**
Journal (now available only online) launch a formal opposition,[67] or in the alternative submit observations informally.[68] An opposition must allege in detail at least one of the substantive grounds of objection, absolute or relative.[69] It must later be supported by evidence, normally in the form of witness statements. There is now provision for disclosure (formerly

[62] On the changes to the official search after October 2007, see below, para.18–11.
[63] For the role of disclaimers, see below, para.18–60.
[64] TMA 1994 s.37(4). Amendment may restrict the specification of goods or services; beyond this, only name and address, errors of wording or copying and obvious mistakes may be corrected: s.39; TM Rules r.18.
[65] *Libertel* [2003] E.T.M.R. 807 ECJ at para.21.
[66] TMA 1994 s.67.
[67] TMA 94 s.38(2); the process is set out in the TM Rules 2008 rr.17–18. The period is extendible only for one month, without payment of a fee. The applicant will receive notice of opposition or observations, and must respond within two months to the former by a counter-statement, leading to the filing of evidence, a hearing (if requested) and a reasoned decision. To encourage settlement, since 2000 there has been provision for a cooling off period, of seven months renewable for a maximum of a further nine months, if agreed between applicant and opponent.
[68] TMA 1994 s.38(3); this may lead to the Registrar reopening the case; cf. the more limited effect of observations under the CTM Regulation art.41.
[69] For which, see below, paras 18–23 et seq.

discovery), although it is rarely used in practice. Although there is power to call and cross-examine witnesses,[70] this also is done rarely.

(f) *Appeal*

18–08 A decision by the Registrar is subject to appeal either to the High Court or, in a relatively inexpensive and quick process,[71] to an "appointed person".[72] Appeals must be notified within one month of the decision.[73] Costs may be awarded in all proceedings and security for costs required.[74] It has been made clear in a number of decisions that the Trade Marks Registry is the tribunal where facts are decided and that appellate courts (including the Appointed Person) will not go behind findings of fact (or hear further evidence) except in exceptional circumstances.[75]

(g) *Registration and term*

18–09 Once an application has succeeded in overcoming whatever objections have been raised to it,[76] it will be registered as of the filing date of the application.[77] From this "date of registration" the right lasts for 10 years and falls due for renewal at 10-yearly intervals[78] for as long as the mark does not become liable to revocation, particularly for non-use, or invalidation. The registration may be voluntarily surrendered, in whole or in part[79]—an important provision in the negotiation of compromises with others who have or want potentially conflicting marks. While the registration continues

[70] TMA 1994 s.69(b).

[71] Hence transfer to the High Court should occur only sparingly: *Levy's TM (No. 2)* [1999] R.P.C. 358 and *Elizabeth Emmanuel TM* [2004] R.P.C. 293 AP (D. Kitchin QC), which rejected an application to refer to the High Court.

[72] A senior lawyer, usually a QC, appointed by the Lord Chancellor: TMA 1994 s.77. From this person, no further appeal lies, though on issues of EU law, questions may still be referred to the ECJ, as by the Appointed Person (D.Kitchin, QC) in *Elizabeth Emanuel TM*; in the resultant judgment, [2006] E.T.M.R. 750, the ECJ accepted that the Appointed Person fulfilled the requirements a judicial body must satisfy in order to refer questions to the court under art.267 (ex-234). Also, rather than hearing it himself or herself, the Appointed Person may refer a case to the High Court if a point of general legal importance is involved: s.76(3); e.g. see *Bud and Budweiser Budbräu TMs* [2002] R.P.C. 747.

[73] TMA 94 s.76.

[74] TMA 94 s.68.

[75] *"Reef" TM* [2003] R.P.C. 101 CA: the appellate court should show "a real reluctance, but not the very highest degree of reluctance, to interfere in the absence of a distinct and material error of principle", per Walker L.J. at 109–110. Also, *Bud and Budweiser Budbräu TMs* [2003] R.P.C. 477 CA, at para.12 per Sir Martin Nourse.

[76] Even after disposal of oppositions, the Registrar may refuse to register the mark if it was accepted in error, TMA 94 s.40(1). The fee for registration must be paid: s.40(2).

[77] TMA 94 s.40(3). However, infringement proceedings can only be initiated after actual registration—though they may claim damages retrospectively; and criminal proceedings under s.92 can only relate to things done after actual registration: s.9(3). Rectification of the Register is permissible only to the limited extent allowed by s.64; the mark itself may be changed only to alter a name or address, if it does not substantially affect the mark: s.44.

[78] For renewal, see s.43, which allows for a request up to six months late, upon payment of a supplementary renewal fee. A trade mark which lapses for failure to renew may be restored under certain conditions: TM Rules rr.29, 30.

[79] TMA 1994 s.45; TM Rules r.26.

it may be amended or otherwise rectified only in strictly limited ways.[80] Registration creates a prima facie case of validity.[81]

One way in which trans-European businesses make use of the EU system, even for their established marks, is by obtaining a CTM registration and then surrendering the equivalent national marks. This they do while retaining the "seniority" of the national mark[82]; and they will do so if the advantages from fee reductions and unified infringement proceedings prove sufficient.

(2) Madrid Protocol: international applications

The United Kingdom joined the Protocol version of the Madrid Agreement concerning International Registration of Marks and its provisions were implemented by statutory instrument in 1996.[83] The complexities which will result from maintaining the old Madrid Agreement for its original countries in parallel with the Protocol for relations between them and the Protocol countries have already been mentioned. Since the United Kingdom only participates in the Protocol, attention here may be confined to it. **18–10**

The Protocol, like the original system, is "closed", in the sense that it can be used only by persons who are vested in a Protocol country or "organisation".[84] Vesting can arise by nationality, domicile or—most importantly—by having a "real or effective industrial or commercial establishment" in a country. The first step is to make a "home" application for the mark.[85] On fulfilling this pre-condition, an international application, in English, French or Spanish, can be made via the Office of Origin (i.e. the national registry where the base application or registration is held) to WIPO as the administrator of the Madrid and Protocol systems, seeking registration in as many other contracting states as are designated.[86] After a formal examination, it is passed to the national offices of those states for treatment in the same manner as national applications there.[87] The national offices have a limited period in which to find the application unacceptable: 18 months or such longer period as it takes to determine an opposition.[88] For this a fee equal to

[80] See TMA 1994 s.44.
[81] TMA 94 s.72.
[82] CTM Regulation arts 34, 35; but subject to attacks on the validity of the prior national marks: see TMA 1994 s.52(2)(b).
[83] Trade Marks (International Registration) Order 1996 (SI 1996/714), now amended by the Trade Marks (International Registration) (Amendment) Order 2000 (SI 2000/138), pursuant to TMA 1994 ss.53, 54.
[84] "Organisation" refers to an organisation of states together, notably the CTM system (which joined with effect from October 2004).
[85] Madrid Protocol art.2. The original Madrid requires a home registration as first base—which created difficulty for a system with full examination such as the British.
[86] Madrid Protocol art.3*ter*. Further designations can be made subsequently as required. One application may cover as many classes of the Nice classification system as are required.
[87] At this point, it remains generally desirable to use a local trade mark agent.
[88] Madrid Protocol art.5. With the opposition addition, this is much longer than the 12 months allowed under original Madrid.

the ordinary national fee may be charged,[89] although some national registries charge much lower fees at the rates of the Madrid Agreement.

There is a limited form of "central attack". If, say, a UK applicant makes an international application for five other countries and then fails to secure or to keep his UK registration within the first five years of the International Registration, then all the other applications-cum-registrations fall as well; but (unlike under original Madrid) they may be transformed into national applications in any of the other countries, holding the priority date of the International Registration for the purpose.[90] Registration lasts for 10 years,[91] and can be renewed with one application to WIPO for all the designated States. Assignments may also be registered centrally as may various formalities, such as changes of name.[92] Advertisement of the "international registration" is undertaken by WIPO in *Les Marques Internationales*; while advertisement to invite opposition to the local designation is made in accordance with the relevant local law.

(3) Community trade marks[93]

18–11 Applications for a CTM are made to OHIM in Alicante[94] (either directly or via a national registry or the Benelux Trademarks Office). In many respects, applications for a Community mark follow a similar course to the UK route, although there is no requirement for a declaration of use or bona fide intention to use.[95] Details will therefore not be given here, but can be found in the CTM Regulation, Title IV (registration procedure), Title V (duration, renewal and alteration), Title VII (appeals) and Title IX (procedure).

Before October 2007, the one substantial difference was the more limited Community system of official search for conflicting earlier marks and other rights: OHIM does not raise with the applicant any earlier national or Community marks as a ground for refusal of the later conflicting application. Relative grounds may be raised only in oppositions: owners of cited CTM registrations/applications are notified, so that they may oppose if they

[89] Madrid Protocol arts 7(1), 8(7), 9*ter*. Original Madrid fees are noticeably lower, and there is some potential for discrimination against those who do not use the international system for their non-home applications; but there are not many such cases.

[90] Madrid Protocol art.9*quinquies*.

[91] Madrid Protocol art.6; the initial registration under Madrid is for 20 years.

[92] Madrid Protocol arts 9, 9*bis*.

[93] See, generally, *Kerly* Ch.6; Gold, Abnett & Farwell (eds), *The Community Trade Mark Handbook* (2001, looseleaf).

[94] The issue of languages has created tensions and produced a complex result. Applications may be in any of the 23 official languages of the EU; and publications of the OHIM and Registry entries will be in those languages. Oppositions and cancellation proceedings must be in one of the Office's working languages: English, French, German, Italian and Spanish: CTM Regulation arts 115–117.

[95] cf. TMA 1994 s.32(3); Form TM3.

wish.[96] In contrast, the UK office continued search and official examination on relative grounds until October 2007.

The range of objections which may be raised encompass rights both in earlier marks in any EU Member State and earlier rights protected through passing-off or unfair competition actions or through other intellectual property and associated rights. When considering an opposition (which at OHIM is always done on the papers alone), the Office has the power to invite the parties to make a friendly settlement[97]—a provision which in the United Kingdom has been reflected to some extent in the "cooling off period" introduced in 2000.

3. Proprietary Interests and Licences

As with the other main forms of intellectual property, registered trade marks are now declared to be a personal property right under English law.[98] Trade marks are protected in law primarily in order that they may serve the function of distinguishing the "origin" of goods and services. **18–12**

There is no limit on the persons who may be co-proprietors of trade marks: no legal relationship or business association has to be demonstrated. Presumptively, co-owners have equal undivided shares in the mark. Each has the right to use the mark personally or through an agent. But the consent of all other co-proprietors is needed in order to license, assign or charge the share.[99]

(1) Assignment

Unlike earlier legislation,[100] the TMA 1994 does not provide for official supervision of assignments of registered UK marks whether with or without goodwill. As noted by Lord Nicolls in *Scandecor*[101]: **18–13**

> "In this image-conscious age trade marks are an important marketing tool. Licensing has become commonplace. The law relating to trade marks has responded to these changing conditions. Restrictions on the sale of trade marks have gradually been eased."

[96] In 2009, 89,969 CTMs were registered and 13,851 oppositions received.
[97] CTM Regulation art.43(4) (and for revocation and invalidity, see arts 56(4), 96(5)).
[98] TMA 1994 ss.2(1), 22 (in Scotland, incorporeal moveable property). This applies also to applications to register, as in general do the other provisions on proprietary effect: s.27. For Community marks as "objects of property", see CTM Regulation arts 16.
[99] TMA 1994 s.23(1)–(4). On bankruptcy, the share passes to the trustee in bankruptcy. In infringement proceedings, after the interim stage, all co-owners must be joined as claimants, or else as defendants: TMA 1994 s.23(5).
[100] See 4th edn of this work at para.17–13.
[101] *Scandecor* [2001] F.S.R. 122 HL at 130.

A written instrument signed by (or on behalf of) the assignor or a personal representative is all that is needed. Details of the assignment will then be registrable (although the document evidencing the assignment need not be adduced provided the assignor and assignee sign the TM16 form) and will be subject to essentially the same rules concerning registration and failure to register as are patents and registered designs.[102]

The mark may be assigned in whole or in part, for all or some of the specified goods or services, or for the use of the mark in a particular manner or a particular locality.[103] These provisions are notably more liberal than those applying to Community marks, for the principle of unity dictates that a CTM can only be dealt with in its entirety and for the whole area of the Community (though it may be the subject of split licensing).[104]

An assignment of either a UK or a Community mark is subject to the over-riding consideration that the use made of it in consequence must not be liable to mislead the public, particularly as to the nature, quality or geographical origin of the specified goods or services[105]:

> "Now it is up to the assignee of the mark, if he does not also acquire the assignor's business, to make with the assignor whatever arrangements may be necessary to ensure that the mark will continue to be indicative exclusively of one source, viz. after the assignment, the assignee."[106]

This controlling device should assume greater significance, now that assignment is relatively uncontrolled in other ways. The matter is discussed below.[107]

---

[102] Registration of an assignment, as of a licence, creates a presumption of validity of the transaction: TMA 1994 s.72. Assignments of Community marks, if not part of a transfer of goodwill, must be in writing signed by both parties: CTM Regulation art.17(2), (3). There are several consequential provisions on assignments, secured interests, execution of judgments, bankruptcy and conflicts with third parties: see arts 17(5), (6), 18–21, 23.

[103] TMA 1994 s.24. There may also be transmission by testamentary disposition or operation of law. These provisions do not derive from the TM Directive.

[104] CTM Regulation art.16, which, subject to further provisions of the Regulation itself, makes them subject to the national law of the state of the registered proprietor's seat or domicile, or otherwise, establishment; failing which, the law of Spain (as seat of OHIM).

[105] TMA 1994 s.46(1)(d), derived from the TM Directive art.12(2)(b); CTM Regulation art.50(1)(c). And note CTM Regulation art.17(4), allowing refusal of registration when a particular objection is apparent on the transfer documents. For an analysis of some of the difficult issues raised by s.46, see *Kerly* at para.13–043—13–056.

[106] Per Lord Nicolls in *Scandecor* [2001] F.S.R. 122 HL at 136–137.

[107] See below, para.18–76.

(2) Licensing[108]

A licence to use a registered mark does not of itself confer any proprietary interest but amounts to a permission to use which prevents any allegation of infringement.[109] However, concurrently with the rights of the registered proprietor, an exclusive licensee is given rights and remedies as though he were an assignee.[110] **18–14**

In principle the TMA 1994 permits licences, like assignments, to be general or limited as to the goods or services covered, the manner of use and the locality.[111] A licence must be in writing, signed by or for the grantor[112]; a requirement which is often ignored, especially where intra-group licensing is concerned. This should not, however, be taken, as between licensor and licensee, to preclude the effect of any oral or implied contract, estoppel or acquiescence.

An important issue under the licensing regime, discussed later, is: in what circumstances could licensing mean that a mark has become liable to deceive and so to be revocable?[113] If it is made a term of an exclusive licence, the licensee may sue an infringer as if he were an assignee.[114] Even without this, any licensee can require the proprietor to proceed against an infringer affecting him; and, upon a lapse of two months without action, he can then sue as though he were proprietor.[115] **18–15**

A trade mark licence may be subject to conditions which have the effect of distorting competition either within the United Kingdom or between Member States of the EU. They are then subject to, respectively, the Competition Act 1998 or art.81 of the EU Treaty, but difficulties are not frequent or standard enough to merit any form of Block Exemption at EU level.[116]

---

[108] See generally Wilkof & Burkitt, *Trade Mark Licensing* 2nd edn (2005).
[109] See *Northern & Shell v Condé Nast* [1995] R.P.C. 117 for obiter comments on the TMA 1994, the decision having been made under the 1938 Act on the basis of the TMA 1994 transitional provisions.
[110] See above, para.18–13.
[111] TMA 1994 s.28; and for Community marks, CTM Regulation art.22.
[112] TMA 1994 s.28(2).
[113] See below, para.18–78.
[114] TMA 1994 s.31, normally requiring joinder of the proprietor as claimant or defendant for stages after interim relief (s.31(4)). There are certain limits on monetary remedies and delivery up: s.31(6), (7); cf. CTM Regulation art.22(4). Exclusivity requires exclusion even of the licensor: TMA 1994 s.29(1).
[115] TMA 1994 s.30; cf. CTM Regulation art.22(3).
[116] See Galandi [1997] E.I.P.R. 723 and *Kerly* at para.16–131.

4. Conditions for Securing Registration: Absolute Grounds

(1) "Trade mark"

18–16 Only a "trade mark" may be registered, and anything which is not a trade mark must be refused registration, or if necessary removed from the register.[117] The TMA 1994 defines a "trade mark" in the same broad terms as the Regulation and the Directive. The term covers:

> "any sign capable of being represented graphically which is capable of distinguishing goods or services of one undertaking from those of other undertakings."[118]

It includes "words (including personal names), designs, letters, numerals or the shape of goods or their packaging".[119] The definition is intended to open to registration as wide a range of potential marks as is practicable.[120] This is effected by three main elements in the definition: "capacity to distinguish", "graphic representation" and "undertaking". In addition, the Court of Justice in *Dyson*[121] held that an application to register a transparent bin, as represented in two drawings by way of example on the application form, was not a "sign" within art.2 of the TM Directive (s.1(1) TMA 1994): "[g]iven the exclusivity inherent in trade mark right [sic], the holder of a trade mark relating to such a non-specific subject-matter would gain an unfair competitive advantage ... it follows that [it] is a mere property of the product concerned" and not a sign.[122]

(a) *Capacity to distinguish*

18–17 The inclusion of capacity to distinguish in the very definition of a trade mark ties the system for the most part to its historic basis: that the law's purpose is to protect marks as, in a broad sense, indicators of origin.[123]

However, the breadth of the definition has meant that many marks which were unregistrable under earlier legislation are now registered. For example,

---

117 TMA 1994 ss.3(1)(a), 47(1).

118 The inclusion of the shape of the goods themselves supports the view that the generic class of "signs", to which all trade marks must belong, is to be read broadly; it is not to be confined to something which is added to or attached to the product by way of representation or point of distinction.

119 TMA 1994 s.1(1); TM Directive art.2; CTM Regulation art.4; cf. the TRIPS Agreement, which is in generally similar terms, but adds specifically, "figurative elements and combinations of colours". For collective and certification marks, see below, para.A2–05.

120 See Explanatory Memorandum to Draft CTM Regulation COM (80) 635; White Paper, *Reform of Trade Marks Law* (Cmnd.1203, 1990), para.2.06.

121 *Dyson Ltd v Registrar of TMs* [2007] E.T.M.R. 34.

122 *Dyson Ltd v Registrar of TMs* [2007] E.T.M.R. 34 at paras 38–39.

123 See equally the relevant Recitals of the Regulation and Directive.

under the former law, the House of Lords refused to treat the shape of the "Coca-Cola" bottle as a trade mark for non-alcoholic beverages in Class 32[124]: it is now registered; so is the shape of the Jif lemon.[125] The danger that, as a trade mark, such a shape will become a "perpetual monopoly"[126] is separately addressed, because a mark has also to pass the "absolute" tests of distinctiveness in s.3 (including those specifically concerned with shape).[127]

Signs are held to lack a capacity to distinguish so as not even to be trade **18–18** marks, not to function as indicators of origin,[128] only in the plainest cases[129]: s.3(1)(a) sets "a low minimum standard".[130] The pre-TMA 1994 case law may still have some marginal relevance to questions of distinctiveness arising under s.3 of the TMA 1994.[131] But the most general of the grounds under that section is that a mark is not to be registered if it is "devoid of any distinctive character". Lack of capacity to distinguish—as an element in the initial definition of what is to count as a trade mark at all—must pertain to objections even more fundamental (and therefore less likely to arise) than "devoid of any distinctive character": an example would be a chemical formula purporting to describe a smell.

This is not to say that "capacity to distinguish" is entirely without sig- **18–19** nificance, although it has been suggested persuasively that there is properly only one test for distinctiveness in s.3(1)(a), (b), (c) and (d) and (3).[132] Most geographical and descriptive words are "capable" of being marks and must be tested for the acquisition of that secondary meaning. But some words must remain totally incapable of ever being marks. Thus "Soap" could never now be registered for soap.[133] More importantly, "Jeryl Lynn" has been held wholly incapable of being a registrable mark, given that for 20 years it had been used in medical biology to describe a manipulated strain of the mumps virus which formed the basis of a successful vaccine.[134] Similarly,

---

124 *Coca-Cola TM* [1986] R.P.C. 421.

125 See *Reckitt & Colman v Borden* [1990] R.P.C. 341 HL, for an example of the difficulty which can arise if one is forced to rely on the uncertain law of passing off to protect such symbols.

126 This was the fear expressed by Lord Templeman in the *Coca-Cola* case [1986] R.P.C. 421 at 457.

127 TMA 1994 s.3(2): below, paras 18–40—18–45.

128 See, for example, *Nichols* [2005] R.P.C. 243 ECJ at para.22.

129 e.g. *Allied Domecq's Application ("AD2000")* [1997] E.T.M.R. 253, although it must be borne in mind that this decision pre-dated both *Baby-Dry* and *Philips v Remington* in the ECJ, on which see below.

130 Per Lloyd J. in *Dualit Ltd's (Toaster Shapes) Applications* [1999] R.P.C. 890.

131 See below, paras 18–29—18–35.

132 See *Kerly* paras 2–072—2–099, which concludes that "capable of distinguishing" must be interpreted in relation to the essential function of a trade mark, to indicate origin; cf. Keeling [2003] I.P.Q. 131, supporting the so-called German theory, that the requirement should be considered in the abstract, without reference to particular goods or services.

133 Per Jacob J. in *Philips Electronics v Remington* [1998] R.P.C. 283 at 299–302, although it could be registered for clothing, for example.

134 *"Jeryl Lynn" TM* [1999] F.S.R. 491. The name was that of the six-year-old from whose throat the research began.

in *Bach Flower Remedies*[135] a mark that originally was capable of distinguishing had become *incapable* as a result of use in a generic sense for particular herbal remedies. Thus, s.3(1)(a):

> "subsumes two sub-categories (A) those signs which have never been capable of distinguishing the goods of one undertaking from those of other undertakings and (B) those which once had the capacity to distinguish but have, through use, ceased to be capable of doing so".[136]

Because of the wide scope of eligible subject matter, there have been many attempts to turn into trade marks what are primary characteristics of products themselves. When these are functional (as with the shape of an electric razor head)[137] the inappropriateness of protection as a trade mark is plain. This should also be the case where the product element is essentially decorative (designs on a picture frame). Likewise for sound and smell trade marks. Despite the attitude of other jurisdictions, the fragrance of a scent cannot be a trade mark within the above definition as it is the essence of the product itself and indeed cannot in any meaningful sense be represented graphically. The smell incorporated in a detergent, however, is a non-essential additive,[138] although the issue still remains whether it functions as a trade mark.

Because the objection excludes the mark from registration at the outset—even where there is very strong evidence that it has acquired secondary meaning—it has been interpreted strictly. That famously descriptive mark, "camel-hair belting", which was long ago protected against passing off because of overwhelming evidence of secondary meaning, should now qualify for registration[139]: the evidence of secondary meaning would satisfy distinctiveness for the purposes of s.3 and there would be no sufficient reason for excluding registration under s.1 because the mark was (utterly) incapable of being an indication of origin.

---

[135] *Bach Flower Remedies* [2000] R.P.C. 513 CA.

[136] [2000] R.P.C. 513 per Chadwick L.J. at 533.

[137] *Philips* [1999] R.P.C. 809, found the primary message conveyed by the shape of the head to be: "'Here is a three headed rotary shaver—from what you see you know how this device works'." For the contrary conclusion in the equivalent Swedish litigation, see *Ide Line v Philips Electronics* [1997] E.T.M.R. 377 (Stockholm DC).

[138] The discussion of smell marks in the USA has drawn this basic distinction: see esp. Elias (1992) 82 T.M.R. 475; and see Burton [1995] E.I.P.R. 378: below, para.18–34.

[139] See above, para.17–12.

(b) *Graphic representation*

The ways in which a trade mark may be infringed include oral use.[140] As one corollary, if a mark consisting of sound or smell can be "graphically represented"[141] (and it has "capacity to distinguish"), it is in principle registrable. (The question then becomes whether on balance the particular sign meets the various criteria of distinctiveness set out in s.3.)[142] However: **18–20**

> "the degree of precision with which the sign is represented must be sufficient to permit full and effective implementation of the provisions of the Act relating to absolute unregistrability (s.3), relative unregistrability (s.5), infringement (s.10) and public inspection of the Register".[143]

Advertising jingles can be written in musical notation,[144] non-musical sounds perhaps can be described ("the roar of a lion") subject to the requirements that the description be clear, precise and objective.

It had been thought that smells could be defined in terms of chemical components or by chromatographical analysis (although this raised the question of how they could be searched for).[145] However, in *Sieckmann*[146] the ECJ found that the requirement of graphic representation was not satisfied by a chemical formula (in the particular case C6H5-CH = CHCOOCH3), by a description in written words (balsamically fruity with a slight hint of cinnamon), by a deposit of an odour sample, or a combination of these.[147] This highlights the fact that the mark must be capable of being understood

---

140 See below, para.18–85.

141 In *Shield Mark* [2004] R.P.C. 17, the ECJ held that a sound mark could be described by written description or musical notation, provided the graphical representation is clear, precise, self-contained, easily accessible, intelligible, durable and objective (which also applies to smell marks, *Sieckmann* [2003] R.P.C. 38 ECJ at paras 47–55).

142 See below, paras 18–23.

143 *Ty Nant Spring Water Ltd's TM Application* [2000] R.P.C. 55 at 56, in the context of an application to register a colour mark with a description which required the use of a spectrophotometer to translate into the colour cobalt blue.

144 Or some written description of that notation: *Shield Mark* [2004] R.P.C. 315 ECJ.

145 In *John Lewis of Hungerford's Application* [2001] E.T.M.R. 1193, an application comprising the words "the smell, aroma or essence of cinnamon" was found by the Appointed Person (G. Hobbs, QC) to lack precision because of the degree of subjectivity it permitted. A graphical representation of an electronic sensory analysis had been rejected by the Registry on the ground that it would be unintelligible to people inspecting the Register, at para.34. This can be compared to the somewhat surprising finding of the Court of Appeal of Northern Ireland in *BP Amoco v John Kelly* [2002] F.S.R. 87 at 98, that a person searching the Register for the claimant's registration of a particular shade of green (Pantone 348C) for vehicle service stations "could readily consult the TM3 application forms" if he were unsure of the precise colour. This must fall foul of the "self-contained" criterion laid down by *Sieckmann* [2003] E.T.M.R. 466. See also Lyons [1994] E.I.P.R. 540 (referred to by the Appointed Person in *John Lewis of Hungerford's Application* at para.52).

146 *Sieckmann* [2003] E.T.M.R. 466 ECJ.

147 *Sieckmann* [2003] E.T.M.R. 466 at para.72.

from the description; it is similarly not acceptable for a 3D mark to be registered with only a description rather than a representation.[148]

Thus, "graphic representation" seems sensibly to be limited to clear and easily determined means of describing sensations which can be appreciated by smell (or, presumably, hearing). For CTMs, OHIM originally manifested a remarkably accommodating attitude: "the smell of fresh-cut grass" was allowed for tennis balls.[149] But now (correctly) it is far more restrictive and in the light of *Sieckmann* should remain so. (Somewhat bizarrely, there have been suggestions that the requirement for "graphic representation" be dropped in the European trade mark systems but it is difficult to see how even the most passionate advocates of "register everything" could justify this further departure from the whole basis of having a register capable of being searched to ascertain what can and cannot be done without infringing another's rights.)

(c) *Undertaking*

18–21 Whereas the previous law required that trade marks had to indicate "a connection in the course of trade", the TMA 1994, following the Directive, refers to the capacity to distinguish goods or services of one undertaking from those of other undertakings. In the course of the Parliamentary debate on the Bill, the Government insisted that this wording (from the Directive) implied that the mark must be used in a commercial context and therefore refused to accept an amendment which would have said so explicitly.[150] All in all, a requirement for a trade connection continues to be necessary.

(2) Absolute and relative grounds

18–22 The grounds upon which an application to register a "trade mark" may be refused are the same as those for the CTM[151] (except for the absence in the latter of a "bad faith" objection). These divide into two main categories:

(1) the *absolute grounds*, which relate to inherent objections to distinctiveness and certain public interest objections; and
(2) the *relative grounds*, which arise because some other trader or proprietor has an earlier conflicting right.

The absolute grounds are by their nature not open to waiver by another person, but the relative grounds are. In general the aim and practice is to

[148] The shape of a "Loveheart" sweet was described but the application refused because it presupposed a knowledge of the product, *Swizzels Matlow Ltd's Application (No.2)* [2000] E.T.M.R. 58.
[149] *Senta Aromatic's Application* [1999] E.T.M.R. 429.
[150] *Hansard*, HL Vol. 552, cols 732–733.
[151] TM Directive arts 3, 4; CTM Regulation arts 7, 8.

apply the objections in only clear cases and so make registration considerably easier at the boundaries.

(3) Absolute grounds: general categories

Section 3 of the TMA 1994 lists the absolute grounds of objection, first in a list of general objections; then in subsections which deal with: (1) shapes of goods; (2) public interest; deceptiveness and illegality; and (3) bad faith on the part of the applicant.[152] **18–23**

(a) *Statutory provisions*

The statutory provisions begin with signs which do not even fall within the definition of a trade mark (s.(1)(a)).[153] As just noted, the main criterion of a trade mark, apart from the need for graphic representation, is its capacity to distinguish the source of goods and services. **18–24**

There follow three categories of trade marks to which absolute objection may be taken[154]:

(1) trade marks which are devoid of any distinctive character (s.3(1)(b)—the "devoid of distinctiveness" objection);
(2) trade marks which consist exclusively of signs or indications which may serve, in trade, to designate the kind, quality, quantity, intended purposes, value, geographical origin, the time of production of goods or rendering of services, or other characteristics of goods or services (s.3(1)(c)—the "descriptiveness" objection);
(3) trade marks which consist exclusively of signs or indications which have become customary in the current language or in the bona fide and established practices of the trade (s.3(1)(d)—the "customary usage" objection).

The need for distinctiveness accordingly operates at three levels: for there to be a trade mark at all, i.e. the need for a *capacity* to distinguish; under the undefined "devoid of distinctiveness" objection; and in relation to the more specific "descriptiveness" and "customary usage" objections. These levels overlap and their operation is cumulative.[155] In practice many challenges have been raised under the "descriptiveness" objection, but there are also important cases under "customary usage" and "devoid of distinctiveness".

---

[152] As to bad faith, see above, para.18–03; cf. CTM Regulation art.38(2), giving the CTM Office power to request a disclaimer as a condition of grant.

[153] See above, paras 18–16—18–21.

[154] All three derive from art.6*quinquies* B.2 of the Paris Convention.

[155] *Postkantoor* [2004] E.T.M.R. 77 ECJ at paras 67 and 85. In the TRIPS Agreement, the obligation to protect trade marks depends upon a definition which is derived from the EU formula; but it omits the category, "devoid of distinctiveness": art.15.1. The same provision permits Member States to require, as a condition of registration, that signs be "visually perceptible"; this has not been included in the CTM Regulation.

Indeed, in certain cases it could be argued that the correct objection was not relied upon[156] and, on appeals from OHIM, the GC (former CFI) appears to have taken the position that as long as, for example, a mark is descriptive, then it is also devoid of distinctive character, which is correct,[157] but also vice versa, which is not.[158]

(b) *Countervailing evidence to show acquired distinctiveness*

18–25 There is another basic consideration to bring into account. As long as a sign qualifies to be a trade mark, the "devoid of distinctiveness", "descriptiveness" and "customary usage" objections are subject to a proviso. If, before the application date, the mark "has in fact acquired a distinctive character as a result of the use made of it",[159] then it shall not after all be refused registration (or subsequently removed under the invalidity grounds in s.47). This "acquired distinctiveness" must be proved by evidence.

In*Nestlé v Mars*[160] the evidence of use submitted in support of a claim for acquired distinctiveness of the mark "Have a Break" was primarily of the trade mark "Have a Break ... Have a Kit Kat". On a reference from the Court of Appeal, whilst confirming that distinctiveness may be acquired by an "essential" part of a composite mark, the Court of Justice held that it is for the national court to assess whether or not that distinctiveness has in fact been acquired on the basis of the following criteria: (a) the market share held by the mark[161]; (b) how intensive, geographically widespread and long-standing the use of the mark has been; (c) the amount invested by the applicant in promoting the mark[162]; (d) the proportion of the relevant class of persons who, because of the mark at issue, identify the goods as originating from a particular undertaking; and (e) statements from chambers of commerce or other trade and professional associations.[163] In *O2 v Hutchison*[164] the question to be answered was characterised thus: "whether, as a result of use of part of the composite whole, the relevant class of persons actually perceive the product or service, designated *exclusively* by the mark applied for, as originating from a given undertaking."[165] Surely this will be very difficult to prove.

[156] "Unravelling the skein formed by ... Articles 2 and 3(1) (a) to (d) of the Trade Marks Directive [TMA 1994, s.1(1), 3] ... is not an obviously easy matter" commented Advocate-General Jacobs (with commendable understatement) in "*Baby-Dry*" [2002] R.P.C. 349 at para.61; see the detailed analysis in *Kerly* at para.2–072.

[157] *Biomild* [2005] E.C.R. I-7975 ECJ at para.19.

[158] *Postkantoor* [2004] E.T.M.R. 77 ECJ at para.70.

[159] TMA 1994 s.3(1) proviso.

[160] *Nestlé v Mars* [2003] F.S.R. 684.

[161] Although the mark in issue was "Have a break", which had no market share in any meaningful sense.

[162] Again, in the context of "Have a break" this would presumably be the amount invested in relation to that mark as opposed to the already registered trade marks "Kit Kat" and "Have a break ... Have a Kit Kat".

[163] [2006] F.S.R. 49 ECJ.

[164] *O2 v Hutchison* [2006] E.T.M.R. 677.

[165] *O2* [2006] E.T.M.R. 677 at para.75.

In the United Kingdom, Lord Parker's well-known guidance nearly a century ago remains pertinent (but increasingly honoured in the breach): the right to register should: **18–26**

> "largely depend on whether other traders are likely, in the ordinary course of their business and without any improper motive, to desire to use the same mark, or some mark nearly resembling it, upon or in connection with their own goods".[166]

Registration should be denied not only where other traders would be under an intolerable burden, but also where they would be hindered or embarrassed.

However, despite the fact that failure to register a particular mark does not keep an applicant out of the market and, as was wisely said (in relation to the pre-1994 law):

> "the power of a trade mark monopoly should not be granted where it would require honest men to look for a defence to an infringement action",[167]

it is evident that the grounds for refusal must be construed narrowly and the over-riding principle is that a mark should be registered unless there is an unequivocal reason for it not to be. However, although *Baby-Dry*[168] states that the presence of a defence in s.11(2)(b) (art.12 of the CTM Regulation) where the third-party use is descriptive should be taken into account in the assessment of whether a mark has the capability of distinguishing required by s.3(1), subsequent cases have made it clear that to do so would be an abdication of the responsibility of the trade mark registries to apply the absolute grounds correctly.[169] Notwithstanding this, there is little doubt that in practice, as Jacob J. (as he then was) commented,[170] the TMA (and the CTM Regulation) has:

> "shifted the balance towards trade mark owners who have the resources and foresight to use the registration system and against the public in general and weaker and less organised companies".

[166] *Registrar v W & G Du Cros* (1913) 30 R.P.C. 660 at 672. In the context of a geographical name, the ECJ has insisted that not only the present, but also the probable future, must be considered: *Windsurfing Chiemsee v Huber* [1999] E.T.M.R. 585 ECJ: see below, para.18–37.

[167] *"Colorcoat" TM* [1990] R.P.C. 511 at 517 per R. Jacob QC; but now it can be contended that the emphasis is the opposite: perhaps "the power of a trade mark monopoly should not be refused merely because it requires honest men to look for a defence".

[168] *Baby-Dry* [2002] R.P.C. 17 ECJ at paras 35–40. Confirmed by Jacobs A.G. in his Opinion in *Doublemint* [2004] R.P.C. 18.

[169] See, for example, *Libertel* [2004] F.S.R. 4 at paras 58 and 59.

[170] *Nichols TM Application* [2003] E.T.M.R. 180 at para.15.

18–27 The permissive attitude applies also to Community marks[171] although there is often a considerable range of objections, absolute and relative (raised in oppositions), to EU applications. As difficult questions of interpretation have been clarified (although frequently not resolved) by judgments of the ECJ and GC, both the liberal and the restrictive excesses of the early years of the bipolar EU system have been abandoned and in general the system has acquired more consistency. However, it remains highly important that the system maintains a balance between protecting the legitimate interests of traders and the public interest in ensuring that obstacles to free competition are given and retained only where justifiable. To do so will help avoid collisions with national courts hearing invalidity claims after registration.

(c) *Indefeasible objections*

18–28 Under the former law it was decided that certain marks were so inescapably descriptive, or geographical, that they could not be registered even if there was conclusive evidence that in trade they were understood to be the applicant's trade mark or were (as it was inelegantly put) "100 per cent. distinctive in fact". Accordingly, as a well-known place "York" was refused for freight containers.[172] This was over-scrupulous; the TMA 1994 leaves the question of distinctiveness in such doubtful cases to be assessed by the Registry and the courts.[173] There is no class of marks having a distinctive character by its nature or the use made of marks within it that is not capable of distinguishing for the purposes of s.1(1) (art.2 of the TM Directive).[174]

The objection that a sign is not even a trade mark, which cannot be overcome by evidence of acquired distinctiveness, is for objections to subject matter which lacks any capability to distinguish at all.[175] Some of these are dealt with specifically in the later sub-heads of s.3—notably that relating to the shape of products. But there will be similar cases, which do not fit within that exception, but which deserve to be excluded because of their ability to keep other traders from marketing something, however it is otherwise marked. Marks claiming fungibles—say a new type of drink or a new fruit—might fall to be excluded in this way, however overwhelming the evidence of their connection on the market with a single source.

On the argument that the name or shape of a patented product should not be permitted to acquire distinctiveness merely by reason of exclusive use

[171] A good example is the highly questionable GC decision in *"Vitalite" (Sunrider v OHIM)* [2001] E.T.M.R. 605, where the appeal was upheld against refusal of the mark for baby foods and for mineral and aerated waters, on the ground that even though "Vitalite" could be read in French as "vitalité", it could not be regarded as being able to designate the intended purpose of the goods, instead it was indirectly evocative of them.

[172] *"York" TM* [1984] R.P.C. 231 HL.

[173] *British Sugar v James Robertson* [1996] R.P.C. 281 at 305; this view is confirmed by *Windsurfing Chiemsee v Huber* [1999] E.T.M.R. 585: see below, para.18–37.

[174] *Philips Electronics v Remington* [2003] R.P.C. 14 ECJ at para.39.

[175] *Philips Electronics v Remington* [2003] R.P.C. 14 ECJ and see above, para.18–17.

during the period of the monopoly, the ECJ in *Philips v Remington*[176] ruled that it did not matter that a particular undertaking had been the sole source of a product for many years and therefore the public had come to associate a particular shape of product with that undertaking only. Rather the issue remains, as it does with all kinds of mark, whether as a result of that use the public has come to view the shape as a trade mark, i.e. as an indication of origin. The national court is left to determine this, without reference to particular pre-ordained percentages.[177] The court also answered in the negative the question posed by the English Court of Appeal as to whether there is a category of marks which is not excluded by art/s.3(1)(b), (c) and (d) and the proviso (art.3(3) of the TM Directive) but which is nevertheless excluded from registration by art/s.3(1)(a) as being incapable of distinguishing.[178]

(d) *"Devoid of distinctiveness"*

(i) **General.** Many marks are inherently distinctive because no meaning other than that they are an indication of origin, at least in the context of marking goods and services, attaches to them. There are many devices, including logos, which have no pictorial content to conjure up other associations. Likewise there are many invented words, like "Kodak" and "Exxon", which have the same naturally distinctive character. The objections now being considered relate, in a variety of ways, to factors that deprive a mark of distinctiveness as a trade mark. **18–29**

Under the head "devoid of distinctiveness" fall objections to distinctiveness that find no place in the two subsequent categories. But it is a separate head of exclusion: it cannot be assumed that marks which are not wholly descriptive, and therefore fall outside the exclusion in s.3(1)(c), are necessarily distinctive.[179] "Devoid"[180] indicates a limited criterion for objection.[181] But it must be remembered that to be a mark at all, the sign must be capable of distinguishing as a trade mark[182] and that question must be answered in

[176] *Philips v Remington* [2002] F.S.R. 955 at paras 57–65.

[177] *Philips v Remington* [2002] F.S.R. 955 at para.62.

[178] The Court of Appeal in "*ESB*" [2003] F.S.R. 44 at para.35 found that this effectively overruled the earlier decision of the Court of Appeal on this issue in *Bach Flower Remedies* [2000] R.P.C. 513 CA.

[179] This would be to "ignore the reality of everyday experience: distinctiveness is a matter of fact and degree", per the Appointed Person (G. Hobbs, QC) in *"Cycling is . . ." TM Application* [2002] R.P.C. 729 at 741.

[180] Only the UK, Ireland, Germany and Greece use this word; the Benelux Act refers to "lack": see *Kerly* at paras 8–048—8–053.

[181] See the German Supreme Court in *Likoerflasche TM* [2002] E.T.M.R. 456: "the standard applied must be generous, that is, any distinctiveness, be it even of the weakest kind will be sufficient to overcome the barrier to protection", at para.15; cf. *Kerly* at paras 8–039—8–053, which, after criticising the ECJ for setting the hurdle too low, concludes that "[m]any of the problems caused by setting too low a standard for distinctive character could be overcome if the ECJ were to state clearly that the basic requirement for registration of any mark is that it must possess a distinctive character, whether inherent or acquired".

[182] *Linde* [2003] E.T.M.R. 78 ECJ at para.47.

the context of the goods or services for which registration is sought,[183] taking into account the presumed expectations of the average consumer.[184]

The objection "devoid of distinctiveness" has been held to cover signs with the potential (capability) to become trade marks, but which need supporting evidence that they are recognised as such.[185] Under this intermediate head may fall signs which are also surnames, image-promoting or laudatory words, letters, numerals, colours and smells. However, merely a lack of imagination or of an element of originality is not sufficient to bring the objection into play: registration of "Das Prinzip der Bequemlichkeit" (The Principle of Comfort) for household and office furniture was allowed,[186] as was "Sat.2" for satellite broadcasting.[187] Also, it is not appropriate to apply to slogans criteria which are stricter than those applicable to other types of sign.[188]

18–30 (ii) **Surnames and Forenames.** An objection which has arisen not infrequently under "devoid of distinctiveness" is to the use of names, particularly surnames: these are "neither automatically eligible nor automatically ineligible for registration".[189] The criteria to be applied in assessing distinctiveness are the same as for all other categories of mark[190]; in other words, there are no special rules applicable to surnames, they may not be refused merely because they appear hundreds of times in the London telephone directory but instead must be evaluated for their distinctiveness. So, the king of rock n' roll's signature, "Elvis Presley", was held to have some little capacity to distinguish from the manner in which it was written, despite the ordinariness of the handwriting.[191] Registration of a name without further limitation means that infringement may occur however the name is written.

Many surnames have another meaning either in English (for example "Walker" and "Read") or another language and, depending on the goods or services applied for, may need to be considered both under the descriptivenesss and the devoid of distinctiveness exclusions. On foreign surnames, it has been emphasised that under the 1994 Act the inquiry, even in relation to

---

[183] *Merz & Krell ("Bravo")* [2001] E.T.M.R. 105 ECJ at para.29.

[184] *Mag Instrument* [2004] E.T.M.R. 71 at para.50.

[185] See *British Sugar* [1997] E.T.M.R. 118; *Windsurfing Chiemsee* [1999] E.T.M.R. 585 ECJ at para.47; *Heidelberger Bauchemie* [2004] E.T.M.R. 1289 ECJ at para.39.

[186] [2005] E.T.M.R.731 ECJ, a judgment criticised by *Kerly* (at para.8–041) as having set too low a threshold for distinctiveness, noting that "it is difficult to comprehend how the laudatory expression 'The Comfort Principle' for furniture could possibly be said to possess *inherent* distinctive character".

[187] [2005] E.T.M.R. 20 ECJ. In *Easynet Group v Easygroup IP Licensing* [2007] R.P.C. 6 the judge dismissed the appeal against the finding of the hearing officer that "easy.com" for a wide variety of goods and services was not exclusively descriptive when looked at as a whole.

[188] *Erpo Moebelwerk* [2005] E.T.M.R. 731 ECJ at para.36; *Nestlé v Mars* [2006] F.S.R. 49 ECJ.

[189] Per the Appointed Person (G. Hobbs, QC) in *"Mister Long" TM Application* [1999] E.T.M.R. 406.

[190] *Nichols* [2005] R.P.C. 243 ECJ at para.25.

[191] *"Elvis Presley" TMs* [1999] R.P.C. 567 CA.

a mark for export goods, remains as to distinctiveness in the United Kingdom.[192] Nonetheless, with the "Europeanisation" of the trade mark system, foreign usage must have increased significance. Obviously, it is imperative that OHIM be even-handed, given that a Community mark is for the entire EU. In judging an application for a personal name, the basic issue remains that of assessing the likelihood of the public treating the mark and its use as an indication of origin, rather than merely a person's name.[193] So it has been held that the more "Elvis Presley" came to be known as the singer's name, the less likely it was that it would be viewed as a *mark* for merchandise:

> "[i]n addressing the critical issue of distinctiveness there should be no *a priori* assumption that only a celebrity or his successors may ever market (or licence the marketing of) his own character. Monopolies should not be so readily created."[194]

Neither modern merchandising practices nor any notion of an inherent commercial right in a natural person's name has been allowed to affect the approach, here as elsewhere.[195]

(iii) **Other cases.** A motley collection of other considerations also fall under "devoid of distinctiveness", for there are many circumstances in honest traders may wish to use some mark or a variant of it.[196] Words which promote the image of a product, however imprecisely, are of this kind[197]: examples include "The Perfectionists" for women's underwear[198] and "XpressLink" for telecommunication devices,[199] and slogans such as "Real People, Real Solutions"[200] and "Best Buy".[201] In "*Companyline*"[202] the ECJ dismissed the applicant's appeal against the CFI's finding that coupling together, without graphic or semantic modification, two words which are customary in English-speaking countries did not confer on the sign a distinctive character. The Court of Justice also found that it was not wrong for the GC to refuse consideration of the alternative objection under the **18–31**

192 *"Al Bassam" TM* [1995] R.P.C. 511 CA.

193 *British Sugar v Robertson* [1996] R.P.C. 281 at 286; *Philips Electronics v Remington* [1999] R.P.C. 809 CA at 819; and see *Car Wheel Trim TM* [1998] E.T.M.R. 584 (German SC).

194 Per Simon Brown L.J. in *"Elvis Presley" TM* [1999] R.P.C. 567 at 598.

195 See above, para.17–33.

196 Trade marks consisting of the shape of products or their packaging have to be judged under this and the next head, after having applied to them the specific criteria relevant to shapes only in s.3(2), which cannot be remedied by evidence of use: see below, para.18–41.

197 Although these may be excluded also under s.3(1)(d): e.g. *"Bravo", Merz & Krell* [2001] E.T.M.R. 105 ECJ.

198 [1997] E.T.M.R. 505.

199 [1999] E.T.M.R. 146.

200 [2003] E.T.M.R. 57 GC.

201 [2004] E.T.M.R. 19 GC.

202 *DKV Deutsche Krankenversicherung v OHIM* [2003] E.T.M.R. 241 ECJ.

descriptiveness head once it had decided that the sign was devoid of distinctive character.[203]

18–32 Letters and numerals raise similar difficulties.[204] However, the threshold for distinctiveness is low and it is not impossible that a single letter could be registered[205]:

> "[w]hen there is no descriptive content of the letter in regard to the products for which registration is sought .... it is then entirely out of the question to deny that letter's distinctiveness [as an indication of business origin]".[206]

In *Sat.2*[207] the Court of Justice held that the mark must be considered as a whole (Jacobs A.G. considered that the numerical element in the mark ensured distinctiveness[208]) and, although it was not unusual and lacked a high degree of inventiveness (surely an understatement), this was not sufficient to exclude distinctiveness, which depends ultimately on the mark's capacity to distinguish the goods or service of one undertaking from those of others.[209] Of course, usually evidence of use as a trade mark of letters and numerals will be given or required.

18–33 Colour has also been treated cautiously in the past. Any registration for a single colour is likely to cover a relatively wide portion of the spectrum (red, blue, etc.) and it could well be that relatively few applications could between them cover all the useable colours for a particular product, thus preventing other competitors from marketing in anything other than a clear wrapper.[210]

---

[203] *DKV Deutsche Krankenversicherung v OHIM* [2003] E.T.M.R. 241 ECJ at para.28.

[204] Likewise Chinese characters: *Yomeishu-Seizo v Sinma Medical* [1991] F.S.R. 278.

[205] See, e.g. the *OHIM Examination Guidelines* para.8.

[206] *Letter "K" TM* [2001] E.T.M.R. 1181 German SC at para.14, remitting the application for further consideration.

[207] *Sat.1 SatellitenFernsehen v OHIM* [2005] E.T.M.R. 20 ECJ.

[208] cf. *BioID* [2005] E.C.R. I-7579, where the Court of Justice agreed with the GC that the mark "BioID.1" would be perceived by the relevant consumer as being an abbreviation of "biometrical" and "identification", and the graphical elements, the full stop ("."), and the registration symbol ("1"), did nothing to help distinguish the goods and services covered by the mark: at paras 68–72.

[209] *Sat.1 SatellitenFernsehen v OHIM* [2005] E.T.M.R. 20 ECJ at paras 40–43. The court found that it is not appropriate to take into account the fact of frequent use of a word or initials, such as "Sat.", together with a number, ".1" or ".2", in the telecommunications (sic) sector to justify a conclusion that such a sign should as a matter of principle be viewed to be devoid of distinctive character under art/s.3(1)(b), at para.44 (although it could be relevant to a descriptiveness finding; followed by the ECJ in *BioID* [2005] E.C.R. I-7975 in overturning the GC's reliance on likely common use in trade to justify a finding of lack of distinctive character, at paras 61–64).

[210] See the view of Maniatis that this concern is overstated: [2002] I.P.Q. 121 at 149; cf. the ECJ in *Libertel* [2003] E.T.M.R. 63: "in assessing the potential distinctiveness of a given colour as a trade mark, regard must be had to the general interest in not unduly restricting the availability of colours": at para.60.

Notwithstanding this, courts in the different Member States have taken widely diverging positions as far as the registrability of colours is concerned.[211] In the United Kingdom, striping for toothpaste (so-called "sandwiches" combining two other colours with the white of toothpaste) was refused registration on the basis that it was devoid of distinctive character. Although the get-ups were novel in the market, it was not accepted that the average consumer would view them as indicating origin[212]; instead, the Appointed Person found that they were likely to be seen as "the arrangement of the product itself, mere decoration or perhaps even as indicating the active ingredients in the toothpaste".[213]

The Court of Justice in *KWS Saat v OHIM*[214] held that the ability of colours to be distinctive without evidence of use is "inconceivable" save in exceptional circumstances, whilst noting that the position becomes stronger when the relevant goods or services are restricted and the relevant market very specific.[215] (Somewhat surprisingly, the GC had held that the colour application for services should be allowed: "services by nature have no colour",[216] but this was not appealed to the ECJ.) As noted in the "*Green & Grey*"[217] judgment, the public are less likely to view a colour as indicating origin than a word or figurative mark.[218] Indeed, in *Heidelberger Bauchemie*[219] Leger A.G. repeated his view, rejected by the ECJ in *Libertel*,[220] that colours per se and in particular a colour combination with no particular arrangement cannot be distinctive or capable of graphical representation. Again the Court of Justice disagreed, reaffirming and expanding the principles established in *Libertel*: the sign must be "precise", "unambiguous" and "durable", and where it is a combination of colours must be "systematically arranged ... in a predetermined and uniform way".[221] So, while steadfastly refusing to declare colours unregistrable without evidence of use, the practical consequence of the Court of Justice's judgments in this area is that significant evidence of use as a trade mark will usually be required.[222]

---

211 See Schulze [2003] E.I.P.R. 55 for a review of the more permissive German decisions, although this was written prior to the *KWS Saat* and *Heidelberger Bauchemie* judgments of the ECJ.

212 *Colgate-Palmolive Co's TM Applications* [2002] R.P.C. 519.

213 *Colgate-Palmolive Co's TM Applications* [2002] R.P.C. 519, per the Appointed Person (Prof. Annand) at 531.

214 *KWS Saat v OHIM* [2005] E.T.M.R. 1016 ECJ.

215 *KWS Saat* [2005] E.T.M.R. 1016 at para.79.

216 [2003] E.T.M.R. 288 CFI at para.42.

217 *Viking Umwelttechnik v OHIM* [2003] E.T.M.R. 196 GC at para.27.

218 See also, *Henkel v OHIM* [2001] E.C.R II-2957 at paras 51.

219 [2004] E.T.M.R. 1289.

220 [2003] E.T.M.R. 807 ECJ.

221 [2004] E.T.M.R. 1289 at para.33.

222 For example, in *Duckham & Co's Application* [2004] R.P.C. 557 TM Registry, the application for the colour green used to colour the applicant's engine oils was rejected on the ground that there was insufficient evidence that trade or end consumers relied on the colour of the applicant's engine oil in order to distinguish its products in the course of trade: at para.101.

18–34 Smell marks face even greater difficulties. When the smell is the main object of the product (as with scent or an air freshener) it should not be capable of being a trade mark at all.[223] Even when it is a secondary additive (detergent, shampoo, notepaper), it is registrable only on very strong evidence of recognition as a trade mark, assuming that in some way the applicant has complied with the "graphical representation" requirements set out in *Sieckmann*.[224] Given that there are likely to be other more evident visual marks used at the same time, it may indeed be very difficult to show that the public has come to consider the smell as an indicator distinguishing source.[225]

(e) *"Descriptiveness"*

18–35 The head, "descriptiveness", set out above, deals with relatively specific indicators of one or other quality of a product or service. Typical cases that have arisen include the following.

18–36 (i) **"Kind, quality, quantity, intended purpose, value . . . the time of production of goods or of the rendering of services, or other characteristics of goods and services.**" The following have been refused registration without use: "Day by Day",[226] "Bonus Gold" for financial investment services; "Automatic Network Exchange" for certain business information; "Coffeemix" for coffee and the like; "Froot Loops" for cereals; "Eurolamb" for that meat; "Poly pads" for saddles, because of "pony".[227]

Again, the objection must be interpreted narrowly: the German Supreme Court allowed registration of the mark "Yes" for cigarettes, etc. noting:

> "[a]s a general rule, the public perceives a sign used as a trade mark in the manner in which it encounters it, and does not subject it to analytic considerations . . . [I]f a word trademark cannot be ascribed a semantic content that primarily describes the goods in question, and if it is otherwise not a usual word in German or a known foreign language that is always interpreted by the public only as such",

it should be registered.[228]

In the United Kingdom, the mark "easy.com" was allowed for a wide

[223] See above, para.18–20.

[224] *Sieckmann* [2003] R.P.C. 38 ECJ.

[225] In the US, where smell marks have been registrable since 1946, the first registration succeeded only in 1990: *Re Clarke*, 17 U.S.P.O. (2d) 1238 (fragrance of plumeria blossoms for embroidery yarn).

[226] *Besnier SA's TM Application* [2002] R.P.C. 260, finding that it might embarrass other traders in milk products.

[227] *"Bonus Gold" TM* [1998] R.P.C. 859; *"Automotive Network Exchange" TM* [1998] R.P.C. 885; *"Coffee Mix" TM* [1998] R.P.C. 717; *"Froot Loops" TM* [1998] R.P.C. 240; *"Eurolamb" TM* [1997] E.T.M.R. 420; *Penny McKinnon's Application* [1999] E.T.M.R. 234 (OHIM—note the necessity to consider various languages there).

[228] (2000) 31 I.I.C. 1036 at 1039.

range of goods and services[229] and "E.S.B." for beer was found to be only indirectly descriptive (meaning Extra Strong Bitter) and therefore fell outside s.3(1)(c),[230] especially bearing in mind that some form of mental activity was necessary in order to work out the descriptive reference.[231]

This decision applied the controversial judgment of the ECJ in the *Baby-Dry* case,[232] which described the purpose of the exclusion as:

> "to prevent registration as trade marks of signs or indications which, because they are no different from the usual way of designating the relevant goods or services or their characteristics, could not fulfil the function of identifying the undertaking that markets them and are thus devoid of the distinctive character needed for that function".[233]

However, the court found in relation to the mark "Baby-Dry" for babies' nappies that, whilst each of the two words "baby" and "dry" may form part of expressions used to describe the function of the goods (as in "these keep your baby dry"), their "syntactically unusual juxtaposition is not a familiar expression in the English language for designating babies' nappies or for describing their essential characteristics".[234] It was "a lexical invention bestowing distinctive power".[235]

This judgment caused some considerable re-thinking on the part of national registries,[236] OHIM and advisers as to the (apparently very low) height of the hurdle to be overcome in s.3(1)(c), but is now generally viewed as the high point of the European Court's liberal attitude to registrability of descriptive marks. The later *Doublemint* judgment[237] indicates a realisation by the Court of Justice that matters had gone too far and needed to be reined in: in refusing registration of "Doublemint" for chewing gum (critically, without evidence of acquired distinctiveness),[238] the court held that there is a public interest[239] that descriptive terms may be freely used by all

[229] [2007] R.P.C. 107, Mann J. found that the "overall impression test" does not require that, in order to avoid a descriptiveness objection, a mark includes some element which is "unusual" or "out of the ordinary" or "extraordinary": at para.32.

[230] *West (t/a Eastenders) v Fuller Smith & Turner* [2003] F.S.R. 816 CA.

[231] [2002] F.S.R. 822 at para.16: a view held by the Court of Appeal to be "not open to criticism": at para.27.

[232] *Procter & Gamble v OHIM* [2002] R.P.C. 369 ECJ, by way of appeal from the GC which had found the mark purely descriptive [1999] E.C.R. II-2383.

[233] [2002] R.P.C. 369 at para.37, although the appeal to the ECJ involved only art/s.3(1)(c) not (b).

[234] [2002] R.P.C. 369 ECJ at para.42.

[235] [2002] R.P.C. 369 ECJ at para.44.

[236] As an example of the impact of the judgment, see *"Top Breeders Recommend It"* [2003] E.T.M.R. 1016, where the Irish Registry's decision to refuse registration of that slogan was (probably wrongly) overturned by the High Court.

[237] *Doublemint* [2004] R.P.C. 18 ECJ.

[238] It must be emphasised, without evidence of use.

[239] Or, more recently, a *general* interest, e.g. *SAT.2* [2005] E.T.M.R. 20 at para.26; the general interest underlying s.3(1)(b), on the other hand, is the need "not to restrict unduly" the availability of signs for other operators who operate in the same field: at para.26.

traders. This is so whether the use by other traders has already occurred or may in the future,[240] and whether it is "commercially essential or merely ancillary".[241] On the other hand, what became evident to the UK Registry after *Baby-Dry* was that it had been imposing too restrictive a view on s.3(1)(c) objections, although it considered quite rightly that the case did not settle the scope of the s.3(1)(b) ground for refusal.[242] What is clear is that descriptiveness and distinctiveness are not mutually exclusive: as found by the Court of Appeal in "*ESB*", "[a] mark may be both distinctive (in that it communicates a message as to the trade origin of the goods to which it is applied) while simultaneously conveying a clear description of those goods".[243]

In the United Kingdom, knowledge of the main European languages is now assumed. At OHIM, the issue of meaning in at least all the EU languages, official and unofficial, is of importance and difficulty.[244] This issue acquired even greater significance with the accession of 10 new Member States in 2004 and a further two in 2007 with all the absolute and relative objections they brought with them; for example, a mark which was previously registrable, e.g. "Viz" for water, presumably became unregistrable because of the languages of the newly acceded Member States; it means water in Hungarian.

18–37 (ii) **"Geographical origin".** As with words describing qualities of the goods or services, the legitimate interests of other traders, present and future, dictate that no one person should acquire exclusive rights in a geographical name without convincing evidence that the name has been appropriated to trade mark purposes by actual use. In *Windsurfing Chiemsee v Huber*,[245] the ECJ refused to confine the scope of this objection to cases where there is a real, current or serious need to leave the mark free for use by others.[246] Rather, if the relevant public, in all the particular circumstances, would (or could later) take use of the name to indicate the locality from which goods come, or in which they were conceived or designed, the objection to registration must in principle arise. Thus, "Chiemsee" for clothing was open to objection, since the Chiemsee is a large and well-known lake in Bavaria.[247] Applying the case in a UK context, the Appointed Person found the

---

240 *OHIM v Wm Wrigley Jr Co ("Doublemint")* [2004] R.P.C. 18 ECJ at para.35.

241 *Koninklijke KPN Nederland v Benelux-Merkenbureau ("Postkantoor")* [2004] E.T.M.R. 771 ECJ at para.102.

242 TMA 1994, s.3(1)(b) was not in issue in the appeal.

243 *ESB* [2003] F.S.R. 816 CA per Pumfrey J. at para.36.

244 cf. *Matratzen Concord* [2003] E.T.M.R. 392 GC, where the word "Matratzen" was found not to be descriptive from the perspective of the relevant public (Spanish-speaking because the application was opposed by the owner of an earlier national Spanish mark), even though it means "mattresses" in German. This cannot be correct.

245 *Windsurfing Chiemsee v Huber* [1999] E.T.M.R. 690.

246 Thus rejecting the German doctrine of *Freihaltsbedürfnis*, raised by the referring court, see Phillips (2005) 36 I.I.C. 389.

247 As to countervailing evidence of use, see above, para.18–25.

registered mark "Nordic" for goods made of wood was not capable of distinguishing without proof of acquired distinctiveness and upheld its removal from the Register.[248] In addition, the geographical word must not be allowed to mislead the public over where the goods or services come from: a company with no business in Switzerland could not therefore register "Swiss Miss" for its chocolate products.[249]

Commercially valuable associations between a place and type of goods or services are not infrequently built up by use of a place name.[250] The association may derive from the physical conditions for production of raw material (for example grapes for wine) or for carrying out a manufacturing process (for example Roquefort cheese) or from an established tradition of local craftsmanship. In these cases, once a number of traders have come to share the use of the name, within the EU they may together be entitled to the special protection now accorded to appellations of origin and indications of source; and one way of achieving this is through the registration of certification marks and collective marks, or alternatively a Protected Designation of Origin or Protected Geographical Indication.[251]

Where this process has only just started, it may be possible for one producer to get such a headstart that no one else could honestly claim to be entitled to use the name. The first user will be entitled to an exclusive registration—but only in special circumstances. Under the pre-1994 law, the producers of "The Glenlivet" whisky not only succeeded in registering that name for whisky, their distillery being in the small Glen Livet; they also succeeded in registering the mark for mineral water before using it on that product, on the basis of evidence that the public would think water so marked not only came from a source in the valley but also from them.[252] The decision emphasises not only the close association between water and whisky as a source of likely confusion but also that other traders could not honestly adopt the particular geographical name. Its thinking, therefore, seems closely in line with the concept of confusing "association" (as to origin) in the TMA 1994.[253]

The question whether a word is to be treated as geographical has to be **18–38**
answered taking into account the presumed understanding of the average consumer of the goods or services concerned, who "is deemed to be

[248] S. Thorley, QC in *Nordic Sauna's TM* [2002] E.T.M.R. 210.
[249] *"Swiss Miss" TM* [1998] R.P.C. 889 CA.
[250] The converse may also apply: in *Alvito Hldgs's Appln* [2008] E.T.M.R. 28, the OHIM Board of Appeal rejected the applicant's appeal against the refusal to register a device mark in which the most most prominent part was the slogan "Not Made in China" on the basis it fell within art.7(1)(c) CTM Reg as being "in an objective way descriptive when taken at face value": at para.18.
[251] Under Regulation 2081/92. See *Kerly* Ch.11.
[252] *"The Glenlivet" TM* [1993] R.P.C. 461.
[253] See TMA 1994 s.3(1) proviso, and s.5(2): below, paras 18–94 and following.

reasonably well-informed and reasonably observant and circumspect".[254] For a UK application, this consumer is presumably a member of the public in the United Kingdom (with all that that entails in terms of parochialism?). Therefore, "*Oberammergau*" would be prima facie registrable for, say, clothing even though it is the name of a Bavarian village well-known in Germany (especially at the time of its world-renowned Passion Play).[255] If the geographical usage is very little known, the word is likely to be treated as invented or to have some other meaning, according to the circumstances. Equally, fanciful uses of place names are permitted: the classic examples have been "North Pole" bananas and "Monte Rosa" cigarettes.[256]

As to countervailing evidence of use of the geographical name as a mark (acquired distinctiveness by the date of the application[257]) under the proviso to s.3(1) (TM Directive art.3(3): CTM Regulation art.7(3)), *Windsurfing Chiemsee*[258] provides important, if somewhat opaque, guidance on the issue generally. Where a geographical (or other descriptive) name (or term) is very well-known as such, proof of trade mark use has to be longstanding and intensive; the more so, if the word has been used to indicate the geographical origin of the category of goods in question.[259] The overall assessment must take account of promotional expenditure on the mark; the proportion of the relevant public who recognise it as distinctive; and statements from chambers of commerce and industry, and other trade and professional associations.[260] While recognising the value of opinion poll evidence, the Court of Justice wisely refused to lay down numerical degrees of recognition as a test.[261]

In *Bach Flower Remedies*[262] Chadwick L.J. referred to the ECJ judgment in *Windsurfing Chiemsee* and said that:

---

[254] *Lloyd Schuhfabrik* [1999] F.S.R. 627 ECJ; *Philips v Remington* [2003] R.P.C. 2 ECJ at para.65; both quoting from *Gut Springenheide* [1998] E.C.R. I-4657 (a misleading advertising case). This standard is one which Jacob J. (as he then was) considered is the same as was traditionally applied in passing off and trade mark infringement cases in the UK, see *British Airways v Ryanair* [2001] E.T.M.R. 235 at para.31.

[255] Although it would not be registrable as a CTM nor, presumably, a German mark.

[256] In *Windsurfing Chiemsee* [1999] E.T.M.R. 585, the ECJ refers to the name of a mountain or lake as an example of this exceptional category; scrupulously, this is said not to include a case where the lakeshore or surrounding area would be thought to be included: paras 33, 34.

[257] *Ecopy* [2003] E.T.M.R. 99 at para.36.

[258] *Windsurfing Chiemsee* [1999] E.T.M.R. 585 ECJ at paras 38–54.

[259] As on the first question in the case ([1999] E.T.M.R. 585), the court rejects any use of the German *Freihaltsbedurfnis* (need to keep free) test as a means of favouring the mark-owner at the expense of other trading interests: judgment, paras 38, 48. In *Think Promotions v All England Lawn Tennis Club* [2006] E.T.M.R. 436, the OHIM Cancellation Division rejected an application to invalidate the tennis club's registered mark "Wimbledon" on the ground that other local traders should be able to use the word.

[260] It should be borne in mind that the assessment for a CTM application should consider appropriate evidence for the part of the EU, which should be a substantial part, in which the absolute objection is present: *"Options"* [2004] E.T.M.R. 554 CFI.

[261] As has done the German Supreme Court, despite the urgings of commentators and parties alike, see Eichmann (2000) 31 I.I.C. 530 at 556.

[262] *Bach Flower Remedies* [2000] R.P.C. 513 at 534.

"in seeking to apply the test, the court is unlikely to be assisted by repetitious evidence from individual consumers ... The task for the court is to inform itself, by evidence, of the matters of which a reasonably well-informed and reasonably observant and circumspect consumer of the products would know; and then ... ask this question: would he say that the words or word identify, for him, the goods as originating from a particular undertaking?"

(f) *"Customary usage"*

Two cases are covered: signs or indications which have become customary: (1) in the current language; or (2) in the bona fide and established practices of the trade. The expression, "signs ... customary in the current language" is not clear, but most likely refers to words and other symbols (such as numbers, letters of an alphabet and punctuation) which have some meaning other than as a trade mark[263] or have become generic. In *Merz & Krell* ("*Bravo*")[264] the ECJ held that where the sign has become customary in everyday language to designate the goods or services covered by the mark it was irrelevant whether it was used as an advertising slogan, an indication of quality or an incitement to purchase. In the United Kingdom, the word "bitter" for beer[265] would fall to be excluded as customary use in trade practice, where the evidence justified the conclusion. Also, where there was before the court evidence of sales over many years of England rugby shirts bearing a red rose design, it was found that a CTM consisting of a similar rose device was invalid on the basis of art.7(1)(d) CTMR (equivalent to s.3(1)(d), TMA 1994) as it had become customary in the trade to use the rose to associate shirts with the England rugby team.[266] **18–39**

[263] It is not clear whether the phrase "of the trade" qualifies "the common language" as well as "the bona fide and established practices"; the repetition of the definite article rather suggests that it does; so may the CTM Regulation art.7(1)(d), which in employing the same expression must be referring to all Community languages; cf. the equivalent ground of revocation, below, paras 18–74, 18–75, which is confined solely to trade usage.

[264] *Merz & Krell* [2002] E.T.M.R. 231, in such a case it is not necessary to consider whether the devoid of distinctiveness or the descriptive objections apply, at para.38. On the corresponding provision in the CTM Regulation see *Alcon v OHIM* [2004] E.T.M.R. 83 GC.

[265] Example given at first instance in *West (t/a Eastenders) v Fuller Smith & Turner* [2002] F.S.R. 822 at 831. On the other hand, there was insufficient evidence to satisfy the court that the term "Extra Special/Strong Bitter" was likely to be abbreviated to ESB (this, in the words of the Court of Appeal, "multi-factorial determination" on the evidence was upheld; [2003] F.S.R. 816 at para.42).

[266] *RFU and Nike v Cotton Traders* [2002] E.T.M.R. 861.

(4) Absolute grounds: specific categories

(a) *Shapes*

18–40 With the growth of design variations as major keys to marketing success, the desire to protect them as trade marks has also increased. Hence the specific inclusion in the definition of a "trade mark" of "the shape of goods or their packaging".[267] If a valid trade mark can be procured for an element of design shape, the protection may continue as long as the registration is renewed and so is not limited in the same way as copyright and design rights in the design elements.

In the past the particular danger of creating a continuing right in design features which may block the legitimate use of similar elements by others has been appreciated by excluding the shape of packaging as well as products from the scope of the trade mark registration system[268]; and, in the law of passing off, by making it very difficult to demonstrate that shape, particularly of articles themselves, has acquired a secondary meaning as an indication of source.[269] In the TMA 1994, a list of shape marks which are inherently objectionable is given in s.3(2).[270] Shapes within this list are treated as are other signs that have no "capacity to distinguish" and so do not qualify as trade marks at all.[271] This list is intended to apply to the shape of packaging as well as products themselves (even though it does not say so).[272]

18–41 Before considering the list of exclusions, the position of other shapes—those not excluded—must be understood. All shapes must satisfy the general tests of distinctiveness, under which inherent objections are balanced against any evidence submitted by the applicant of use as an indication of origin. Shape, just as much as other product ingredients such as colour, patterning or smell, is inherently distinctive as a mark only in exceptional circumstances. Whatever form it takes, it will usually require considerable evidence of use before it can be registered:

> "the relevant public's perception is not necessarily the same in relation to a three-dimensional mark consisting of the shape and colours of the product itself as it is in relation to a word or figurative mark ... Average consumers are not in the habit of making assumptions about the origin of products on the basis of their shape or the shape of their packaging in the

[267] TMA 1994 s.1(1): above, para.18–16; see Henning-Bodewig and Ruijsenaars (1992) 23 I.I.C. 643; Pagenberg (2004) 35 I.I.C. 831.

[268] See above, para.18–17.

[269] See above, para.17–12.

[270] A European precursor of the list is to be found in the Benelux Trade Mark Law art.1(2) though its language is more restricted. For the Benelux case law, see Strowel [1995] E.I.P.R. 154.

[271] See above, paras 18–18, 18–19.

[272] Non-citable Minute of Council and Commission on CTM Regulation art.7(1)(e).

absence of any graphic or word element and it could therefore prove more difficult to establish distinctiveness".[273]

Philips sought to register the shaving-head shape of its "Philishave" electric razors, in which three circular cutters are placed within an equilateral triangle. There was evidence: (1) of widespread, but not universal, recognition of this as an indication of trade source; and (2) of the efficacy of this formation for the design of a three-cutter head. The Court of Appeal accepted that there was no sufficient case to overcome either the "devoid of distinctiveness" or the "descriptiveness" objections (s.3(1)(a) and (b)).[274]

The presence of the excluded list implies that there must be some tempering of the position that, within the registration system, all traders must be left free to choose to sell containers or articles of similar shape.[275] But since labelling exists as the first and obvious technique for distinguishing source, it should only be where secondary meaning is clear from usage that any registration of shape is allowed.[276]

In principle, then, the exclusionary list becomes relevant only when a **18–42**
shape is so well-established as a mark that it is on balance distinctive,[277] although logically one would consider the specific shape exclusions first as they are not capable of being overcome by acquired distinctiveness. In *Unilever v Nestlé*[278] Jacob J. suggested that the acceptance of unusual shapes without proof that they have become indications of origin was undesirable in principle: "Trade mark registries would in effect be acting as design registries if they accept novel or attractive shapes merely on the grounds of novelty or attractiveness"[279] and in *Bongrain SA's TM Application* the same judge, by then Jacob L.J., reiterated:

---

[273] *Procter & Gamble v OHIM* [2004] E.T.M.R. 1176 ECJ at para.36, citing earlier ECJ authorities.

[274] *Philips Electronics v Remington* [1999] R.P.C. 809 CA; Helbling [1997] I.P.Q. 413. See also *Procter & Gamble's Applications* [1999] E.T.M.R. 375 CA (shapes and colours of cleaning product bottles not registrable without evidence of use).

[275] See above, para.18–17.

[276] *Philips Electronics v Remington* [1999] R.P.C. 809 CA, emphasising that each party sold its razors under internationally known word marks. At first instance Jacob J. had referred to the shape as at best "a kind of limping mark" ([1998] R.P.C. 283 at 312), a description which the Court of Appeal considered unhelpful. See also, *Dyson* [2003] R.P.C. 821, where Patten J. upheld the refusal to register the transparent collection bin for the Dual Cyclone vacuum cleaner, noting that he would also have rejected the application under s.3(1)(c).

[277] For a description of what appears to be the liberal German practice in this area, see Strobele (2001) 32 I.I.C. 161; cf. judgment of the German Supreme Court in *Swatch* (2002) 33 I.I.C. 892.

[278] *Unilever v Nestlé* [2003] E.T.M.R. 681.

[279] [2003] E.T.M.R. 681 at para.18.

"[e]ven if the shape of the goods themselves is indeed fancy, that is not enough to entitle the would-be trader in them to registration as a trade mark. (I say would-be because one is here working on the hypothesis of an unused mark)."[280]

This must be correct: a shape which has not been used in trade, although falling within the definition of a "trade mark" in s.1(1), can hardly ever have distinctive character *as a trade mark* so as to fall outside the absolute ground for refusal in s.3(1)(b). If it does, either (highly unusually) by its nature or through nurture (i.e. use as a trade mark prior to the date of application), even then the framers of the legislation were cognisant of the fact that this is a trade mark law and should not give protection to aspects of a product (or its packaging) which: (a) arise from the natural shape of the product itself (e.g. a fruit); (b) are dictated solely by its function (which may be protected by a patent); or (c) comprise only aesthetically pleasing design features for which design law caters. In this respect, the liberal treatment of shape trade mark applications in many Member States (and occasionally OHIM) illustrates a fundamental misconception as to the whole basis of protection under the Directive: distinctive character is not an abstract concept but must be tied very firmly to the subject-matter of the system, trade marks. It is wrong to equate shape marks with words or logos when considering whether a shape mark is devoid of distinctive character. In the real world (one from which the trade mark law world seems to be increasingly divorced), shapes do not function to indicate origin without education or use as such: "[t]he public is not used to mere shapes conveying trade mark significance".[281]

The list of signs unregistrable because they consist exclusively of certain shapes is as follows:

(1) shapes resulting from the nature of the goods themselves;
(2) shapes of goods necessary to obtain a technical result; and
(3) shapes which give substantial value to goods.

Or, in the words of Advocate-General Ruiz-Jarabo Colomer in *Philips v Remington* (see below), "natural, functional or ornamental" shapes.[282]

This statutory formula contains a number of indications that shapes on

[280] [2005] R.P.C. 306 CA at para.27. He then emphasised that he was not saying that a shape of goods could not become a trade mark "by acceptance as such by the public", but in relation to the shape of a cheese "[c]onsumers do not expect to eat trade marks or part of them": at para.28.

[281] per Jacob L.J. in *Bongrain's TM Application* [2005] R.P.C. 306 CA at para.25.

[282] *Philips v Remington* [2001] R.P.C. 745 at 751. Also see Linde [2003] E.C.R. I-3161, which emphasises the public interest aspect to the exclusion (at para.73). In *Unilever v Nestlé* [2003] R.P.C. 651, Jacob J. suggested that therefore this head of exclusion should be limited to naturally occurring shapes rather than artificially created shapes such as the Viennetta ice-cream shape: at para.14. On the registrability of a car grille, see *DaimlerChrysler v OHIM* [2003] E.C.R. II-701 CFI, where the court found the grille for a Jeep registrable because it had a particular and unusual appearance: at paras 46 and 48.

the prohibited list arise only in strictly limited cases: in all cases, the objection must relate exclusively to the listed shape; head (2) turns on the adjective, "necessary", head (3) on "substantial". Moreover, the cases listed are precisely those in which it is least likely that sufficient distinctiveness can be made out. This will serve to give a sense of proportion in considering the list, which employs terms which have potentially broad scope.

(i) **Nature of the goods or packaging.** This first category leads at once into a contemplation of the essence or the identity of things. One can be sure that an apple cannot be registered either for apples or for packaging in the shape of an apple. But what about packaging designed to hold kiwi-fruit safely? What about a pear-shaped balloon? Is its essence just its balloonness, or also its shape? In determining what the goods are, the court should have regard to how they are considered in commercial terms: a picture of a banana for fruit would be objectionable just as much as for bananas.[283] The question should not be determined by the specification of the application. **18–43**

Once the goods are identified, then the registration of a shape which forms only part of them is unlikely to result from their "nature". In the English *Philips Electronics v Remington* case, the goods were found to be electric shavers (rather than either shavers, or three-headed shavers) and the registration of the particular head-formation was not refused under this head.[284]

(ii) **Technical necessity.** This objection overlaps to some degree with the first, and equally suggests the extent to which trade marks are annexing the sphere of design. The law of design protection has long known the exclusion of exclusively technical design, and has, therefore, grappled with the same sort of problem. Is a shape to be regarded as exclusively technical only if no other shape will perform its function (of this there are probably very few examples); or does it cover all cases where function is the main reason for an object having the shape which is claimed as a trade mark? In the two parallel cases at national level over the "Philips" shaver, a majority of the Stockholm District Court took the first, limited view of the exclusionary ground. In England, however, Jacob J. and the Court of Appeal preferred the dissenting view in Sweden, that of Judge Nilsson: where the purpose of the shape is solely to produce a technical result it is not registrable.[285] In its ruling on the reference from the English Court of Appeal, the ECJ also preferred the broader view of the exclusion, finding that provided the essential functional characteristics of the shape are attributable solely to the technical result, it did not matter that the same technical result could be **18–44**

[283] *Philips Electronics v Remington* [1999] R.P.C. 809 CA at 820.
[284] *Philips Electronics v Remington* [1999] R.P.C. 809 CA at 820.
[285] *Ide Line v Philips Electronics* [1997] E.T.M.R. 103, cf. on appeal [1997] E.T.M.R. 377; *Philips Electronics v Remington* [1999] R.P.C. 809.

achieved by a number of other shapes.[286] In yet another attempt to obtain registered trade mark protection for the shape of its three-headed rotary shaver, Philips registered a slight variant of the shape held invalid in the litigation in which the ECJ gave judgment and when that too was held invalid, the Court of Appeal commented:

> "[i]n order to decide whether the shape of the goods in question was necessary to obtain a technical result the court had to consider the mark as a whole. That was how the relevant section of the purchasing public would perceive it. A trade mark was not treated by the public as a mere assembly of component parts."[287]

18–45 (iii) **Substantial value.** The third category seems particularly opaque. It asks the question: assuming that a shape has acquired distinctiveness in the trade mark sense, is that shape somehow so substantial an element in its value that nevertheless registration should be ruled out? In the *Philips* case in England the Court of Appeal, having said that the purpose of the provision is to exclude "aesthetic-type shapes",[288] found that such added value did not result from the shaving-head despite its technical importance.[289] Apart from that consideration, it is easiest to say that there is added value if the shape element can be regarded as a "capricious addition or feature"—say, the incorporation of animal figures into a lamp base. But there will be great difficulty over features of "good" design which, wittingly or (possibly) not, make functional elements at the same time beautiful or at least striking (to consumers? or to art critics?). In *Dualit*[290] the court upheld the refusal of the Hearing Officer to allow registration of the shape of a toaster which had been described as a "design classic" and attracted a significant price premium over competing toasters.

Inevitably, there are questions about the type of value which may be brought into account. Under the equivalent provision of the Benelux law, the Dutch Supreme Court held, in different cases, that the round shape of one biscuit was unregistrable, while the spiral shape of another was

---

[286] [2002] E.T.M.R. 955 at para.84. In *Lego Juris v Mega Brands* [2007] E.T.M.R. 169, relying on *Philips* the Grand Board of Appeal at OHIM dismissed Lego's appeal against cancellation of registration of a Lego brick, noting that "a prior patent is practically irrefutable evidence that the features therein disclosed or claimed are functional": at para.40.

[287] *Philips v Remington* [2006] F.S.R. 537 at para.62 per curiam.

[288] [1999] R.P.C. 809 CA per Aldous L.J. at 822. In *Unilever v Nestlé* [2003] R.P.C. 651, Jacob J. expressed considerable surprise that this objection had not been taken to the "Viennetta" shape, as the appearance is "obviously intended to attract customers as compared with other designs ... being essentially an aesthetic creation": at para.8.

[289] The one point of difference from Jacob J.: cf. *Philips Electronics v Remington* [1998] R.P.C. 283 at 309–310.

[290] Lloyd J. [1999] R.P.C. 890.

registrable.[291] The first shape added too substantial an element of value, there being little distinction of taste between competing products; the second was said to add only to market value, whereas what mattered was "intrinsic" value. Such mysteries, which already haunt our copyright law on works of artistic craftsmanship,[292] seem destined to enshroud trade mark law across the EU for some time to come.

As fluctuating US case law on the same subject shows all too plainly, courts will be drawn into asking why customers buy for the shape: is it because they like it as a shape or because they treat it as a distinguishing sign for a product line? So far as liking it as a shape, their judgment may be affected by aesthetic sensibilities or functional concerns, or these two factors may merge in their minds. It is an issue which arises both initially in considering whether the shape has acquired secondary meaning; and then again if it proves necessary to address the strict exclusion for "substantial value".

(b) *Personality and character merchandising*

English courts have been reluctant to hold that sportsmen, actors, pop stars **18–46**
and the like have an inherent right of publicity in their names, images or voices, and they adopt essentially the same approach to fictitious characters. At root, they continue to recognise only the origin function of trade marks and endorsements. Moreover, there have been differing views as to whether the public assumes that there is necessarily any licensing arrangement in place,[293] let alone one under which the personality or promoter produces or guarantees the quality of the product or service bearing the name. The strenuous, but unsuccessful, attempts to monopolise the name and image of Diana, Princess of Wales, sharpened this attitude in respect of memorabilia.

When Elvis Presley died, he left his estate without any real organisation for exploiting his personality; this came only later. (Today, doubtless, there would have been much closer attention to merchandising.) In the United Kingdom, in consequence, marks could not be registered in Class 3 for his names or signature without actual proof that the public recognised them as the estate's trade mark, rather than merely as an association with their hero.[294] Despite this rebuff, there are many marks on the UK Register that

[291] *Bacony Snack* [1989] E.I.P.R. D–122; *Wokkels* [1986] Ned. Jur. 285. The Benelux Court of Justice ruled that commercial value was the relevant factor in *Burberrys I* [1989] Ned. Jur. 834; [1989] E.I.P.R. D–122; but approved of *Wokkels* in *Burberry II* [1992] Ned. Jur. 567; [1992] E.I.P.R. D–140. So much for precedent in the Benelux system.

[292] See above, paras 11–17.

[293] cf. *Holly Hobbie* [1984] 1 W.L.R. 189 HL, where an awareness of merchandising by the public was accepted, with *BBC Worldwide v Pally Screen Printing* [1998] F.S.R. 665, where Laddie J. refused to accept without evidence that the public would make such an assumption.

[294] *Re Elvis Presley Enterprises' Applications* [1999] R.P.C. 567 CA. Arising under the 1938 Act, it applied the character merchandising case, "*Tarzan*" *TM* [1970] F.S.R. 245 CA. Sid Shaw, who ran an independent business in "Elvisly Yours" memorabilia, had registered that mark already in Class 3. Since this could not be attacked, its similarity gave rise to a conflict which rendered the applications at issue unregistrable.

purport to protect the names and images of well-known personalities; where they are registered for goods with which the average consumer would expect them to be involved and are not likely to be considered mere "image carriers" (e.g. posters, figurines),[295] the mark should survive scrutiny. The problem is likely to arise with licensing activities (and marks registered) in fields remote from the principal activity of the proprietor. In his Opinion in *"Picasso/Picaro"*[296] Advocate-General Ruiz-Jarabo Colomer commented:

> "it is worth making two points about the legitimate protection of names which have earned their owner's prestige. In the first place, when such a name is allowed to be used in a completely different context to that it which its reputation was earned, the greater protection which must be given to marks with a highly distinctive character cannot automatically be claimed. The simple reason for this is that, in that other context, it is very doubtful whether the name gives any information about the commercial origin of the goods or services, at least initially. Secondly, there is a certain general interest in protecting the names of great artists, which represent a universal cultural heritage, from insatiable commercial greed, in order to safeguard their work from trivialisation."[297]

Also, the ramifications of the delphic pronouncements of the ECJ on what kind of use is required for a finding of trade mark infringement remain to be worked out (see below, at para.18–87).

(c) *Public interest*

18–47 Three "absolute" grounds of objection exist by way of protecting general public interests. A mark is not registrable:

(1) if it is contrary to public policy or to accepted principles of morality;
(2) if it is of such a nature as to deceive the public (for instance as to the nature, quality or geographical origin of the goods or services); or
(3) if or to the extent that its use is prohibited by UK or EU law.[298]

18–48 (i) **Public policy or morality.** Of the grounds of objection the public policy or morality ground continues to find an occasional use where it can be said that the mark would offend the generally accepted mores of the time[299]: refusal to register "Jesus" for clothing and other goods was upheld on the basis that "use of it as a trade mark should ... be regarded as seriously

[295] On which see *Linkin Park LLC's Application* [2006] E.T.M.R. 1017 (Appointed Person, Arnold QC).
[296] *Picasso/Picaro* [2006] E.T.M.R. 349 ECJ.
[297] *Picasso/Picaro* [2006] E.T.M.R. 349 at para.AGO69.
[298] TMA 1994 s.3(3), (4).
[299] In *Philips v Remington* [2001] E.T.M.R. 509 Advocate-General Ruiz-Jarabo Colomer suggested the example of "Babykiller" for a pharmaceutical abortifacient: at 516.

troubling in terms of the public interest".[300] In *French Connection v Sutton*[301] Rattee J. expressed considerable distaste for the claimant's registered mark "FCUK". However, affirming the Registry's refusal of an application for "Tiny Penis" for clothing,[302] the Appointed Person (S. Thorley, QC) found that distaste on the part of a section of the public was not sufficient, what was required was that the mark would offend the moral principles of right-thinking members of the public and the mark was refused as likely to offend public decency. It is only in cases where it is plain that an accepted principle of morality is being offended that the registration should be refused:

> "[I]f the goods are calculated to appeal to a certain section of the community such that the choice of distasteful mark is, in that trader's view, calculated to enhance sales, so be it".[303]

(ii) **Likely to deceive.** The most important of these grounds of objection will be the second. Marks which evoke some connotation other than source may not only lack distinctiveness (as already indicated) but may be positively deceptive. Account must be taken of the nature of the trade and its customers in deciding whether the mark will give rise to an expectation that the goods or services will be of a particular quality, be from a particular place ("Highland Spring" from Scotland, for example) or made of a particular material. Thus, "Filet-O-Fish" was refused as descriptive if actually a fillet of fish and deceptive if not. Presumably, as in the past, a mere intention to change a previous connection with goods, as where a manufacturer is deciding for the future to become an importing agent of goods made by another concern, will not be prejudicial. In *Elizabeth Emmanuel*[304] the Court of Justice found that there needs to exist actual deceit or a serious risk that consumers will be deceived and it was not sufficient in itself that a particular **18–49**

[300] per Geoffrey Hobbs QC, Appointed Person, in *Basic Trademark SA's TM Application* [2005] R.P.C. 611 at para.26, referring to art.10 of the European Convention on Human Rights.

[301] *French Connection v Sutton* [2000] E.T.M.R. 341. In *French Connection Ltd's Application* [2007] E.T.M.R. 121, the Appointed Person (R. Arnold, QC) dismissed an appeal against refusal of an application to revoke "FCUK", noting after a thorough review of the authorities the paradox which underlies s.3(3)(a) of the TMA 1994: "refusal to grant an intellectual property right pursuant to such provisions does not prevent the applicant from using the subject-matter of the right in commerce": at para.54.

[302] *Ghazilian's TM Application* [2002] R.P.C. 628. Mr Thorley found "difficult" the question whether the mark would cause outrage: "accepted principles of morality change with time": at 638. In *Application of Kenneth* [2007] E.T.M.R. 111, the Grand Board of OHIM upheld refusal of the mark "Screw You" for various goods marketed in outlets used by the general public but permitted registration for sex toys as "[a] person who enters a sex shop or visits a web site devoted to sex products is, by definition, unlikely to be offended by a trade mark which contains crude, sexually charged language": at para.29.

[303] [2002] R.P.C. 628, at 633. See also *Durferrit v OHIM* [2003] E.C.R. II-1589 CFI, which found that the corrresponding provision in the CTM Regulation does not cover the situation where the applicant acts in bad faith (at para.76).

[304] *Elizabeth Emmanuel* [2006] E.T.M.R. 750 ECJ.

person was no longer associated with the proprietor of a trade mark comprising that person's name:

> "even if the average consumer might be influenced in his act of purchasing a garment bearing the trade mark 'Elizabeth Emmanuel' by imagining that [the designer Elizabeth Emmanuel] was involved in the design of the garment, the characteristics and the qualities of that garment remain guaranteed by the undertaking which owns the trade mark."[305]

18–50 (iii) **Use contrary to law.** The third ground allows objection to be taken to the use of marks in ways that contravene consumer protection legislation.[306]

(d) *State, official and Royal emblems and other indicia*

18–51 As in the previous law, it is not possible, without authorisation, to register various coats of arms, flags, crests and representations of the Royal Family.[307] The flags and emblems of Paris Convention States and of international organisations are similarly treated, in most cases after due notification.[308] Also following from that Convention, official signs and hallmarks which are used in other contracting states to indicate control and warranty, may not be registered for the goods in question or similar goods. Again there has to be due notification.[309] A new s.4(5) has been added to give effect to the Olympic Symbol, etc. (Protection) Act 1995: this prevents the registration without the consent of the British Olympic Association of the Olympic symbol, motto or words such as Olympic, Olympiad and Olympian.[310] Pity the poor Greeks trading from Mount Olympus or flying to the United Kingdom on Olympic Airways!

Royalty may be regarded as the first great merchandisers of their images and connections; the obtaining and brandishing of a warrant to purvey to royal personages has long been recognised as *the* form of snobbish endorsement. Governments and international organisations have not been slow to

---

305 *Elizabeth Emmanuel* [2006] E.T.M.R. 750 ECJ, at para.48. The court stated at para.51 that this was particularly the case where the proprietor had acquired the goodwill of the business formerly carried on by the person whose name it has registered as a trade mark, thereby surely begging the question as to whether it could be deceptive if this were not the position.

306 For which see above, paras 16–19 et seq.; likewise, legislation protecting hallmarks (Hallmarking Act 1973) and names such as "Cognac" and "Champagne" protected by EU legislation (in their case Regulation 823/87 as amended).

307 TMA 1994 s.4. With some foresight, no objection succeeded in *"Queen Diana" TM* [1991] R.P.C. 395.

308 TMA 1994 ss.57–59. There is an exception in respect of international organisations: see s.58(2).

309 TMA 94 ss.57, 59.

310 The Act was amended by the London Olympic Games and Paralympic Games Act 2006, which extends protection to cover any representation in the course of trade that creates a likelihood of association with the London Olympics (and in this context "association" does not require confusion and the Act includes in the groups of word which may lead to "association": "Games", "2012", "gold", "summer", and so on); see Norris [2006] N.L.J. 1465.

follow suit in securing exclusive rights in their names and insignia. Why then should there be such qualms over according general merchandising rights to private claimants? Is it because public bodies are assumed not to take any return for the licensing of their signs, or that, if they do, it redounds to the benefit of the public? Even if true, should this make any difference?

Section 3 ends with the provision dealing with bad faith, already treated above, at para.18–03.

5. Conditions for Securing Registration: The Relative Grounds

The relative grounds concern conflicts between marks and other signs. In the CTM Office they may accordingly be raised only by an opponent; and after October 2007 the same applies in the UK Registry but until then the UK Registry continues its former practice of searching for conflicting registrations and examining them ex officio.[311] The conflicts in question are between the mark applied for and both "earlier trade marks" and "earlier rights". **18–52**

"Earlier trade mark" covers: (1) UK and CTMs with an earlier registration date (after bringing any priority dating into account)[312]; (2) CTMs with seniority derived from an earlier UK mark; and (3) earlier "well-known" marks within the meaning of art.6*bis* of the Paris Convention.[313]

"Earlier right" covers: (1) the entitlement to protect an unregistered right or other sign used in the course of trade (in particular by passing off proceedings); and (2) other entitlements to object, in particular by virtue of the law of copyright, design right or registered designs.[314]

These two types of objection will be discussed separately. It is also necessary to have in mind a number of additional factors which affect the assessment of the objection: consent by third parties, onus of proof, absence of power to require a disclaimer, and (until October 2007) honest concurrent use. These are referred to subsequently.[315]

---

[311] See above, para.18–06. An opponent does not have to be the person entitled to the conflicting right: *"Wild Child" TM* [1998] R.P.C. 455.

[312] See above, para.18–04.

[313] TMA 1994 s.6(1), here includes both UK registrations, international marks (UK) and international marks (EU) under the Madrid Protocol. It also covers an application still being processed but subsequently registered (s.6(2)), since on registration the right dates back to the date of application (s.9(3)). It also includes an expired mark for one year after expiry, unless there had been two years of non-use immediately before expiry (s.6(3), implementing TM Directive art.11(1), but going further). For Paris Convention art.6*bis* protection, see above, para.17–17.

[314] TMA 1994 s.5(4). This would now include Registered Community Designs and Unregistered Community Designs, see above, generally at paras 15–11 et seq. For marks which infringe other rights, see below, para.18–54.

[315] See below, paras 18–58.

(1) Earlier marks

18–53 The relative grounds of objection relating to "earlier trade marks" divide into three types[316]:

Type 1: Where the marks being compared are identical and the goods or services are also identical,[317] no likelihood of confusion need be shown.[318] Because of the identity on both fronts, it is assumed that confusion must be sufficiently likely to raise a bar to registration of the second sign. Because Type 1 gives such embracing protection, its scope is limited and a question for the eye of the judge.[319] Yet difficulties inevitably arise over what is identical: in *LTJ Diffusion v Sadas*[320] the Court of Justice stated that the criterion of identity must be interpreted strictly, whilst bearing in mind the imperfect recollection of the average consumer. This guidance was described by Jacob L.J. in *Reed Executive*[321] as "opaque" and he considered that as a policy issue there is no reason to suppose that the ECJ meant to "soften the edges of 'strict identity'",[322] concluding that there is only identity "if there is both aural and visual identity".[323] The Court of Appeal found that "Reed" and "Reed Business Information" were not identical: the additional words "Business Information" would not "go unnoticed by the average consumer".[324]

Type 2: Where the goods or services are only similar and not identical; or the marks are only similar (for identical or similar goods or services), it must be shown that "there exists a likelihood of confusion on the part of the public, which includes the likelihood of association with

---

[316] There is an equivalent division relating to infringement and authorities in one may be used in the other: see below, paras 18–82.

[317] See *Reed Executive v Reed Business Information* [2004] R.P.C. 767 CA at paras 42–76 for an example of the difficulties that can arise in deciding whether the defendant is using his sign in relation to services identical to those for which the mark is registered; on the facts before the court, Jacob L.J. found that one must identify the core activities of an "employment agency" and then compare that with what the defendant was doing, i.e. operating a searchable jobs advertisement website: these were not identical.

[318] TMA 1994 s.5(1).

[319] Per Pumfrey J. in *AAH Pharmaceuticals v VantageMax* [2003] E.T.M.R. 205 at para.43, finding (probably wrongly) the defendant's signs "VantageRewards" and "VantagePoints" identical to the registered mark "Vantage", at para.44; cf. *Compass Publishing v Compass Logistics* [2004] R.P.C. 809, where it was held that "Compass" and "Compass Logistics" were not identical.

[320] *LTJ Diffusion v Sadas* [2003] F.S.R. 608 ECJ at paras 50–54.

[321] *Reed Executive* [2004] R.P.C. 767 at para.25.

[322] *Reed Executive* [2004] R.P.C. 767 at para.27, although minute and wholly insignificant differences may be ignored (per A.G. Jacobs, [2003] F.S.R. 1 AGO at para.50.

[323] *Reed Executive* [2004] R.P.C. 767 at para.32.

[324] *Reed Executive* [2004] R.P.C. 767 at para.39.

the earlier trade mark".[325] The ECJ has accepted that "association" is one form of "confusion", not an independent concept.[326]

In *Lloyd Schuhfabrik*,[327] the Court of Justice has also stressed that it is for the trade mark office or national court to assess the likelihood of confusion on the basis of a global appreciation, taking into account all factors relevant to the circumstances of the case.[328] It accordingly refused to lay down detailed rules about either the degree of similarity needed between one-syllable word marks or the effect of any given level of public recognition of the earlier mark. Rather it is for the office or court itself to consider whether there is a genuine and properly substantiated likelihood of confusion on the part of an average consumer,[329] "to confuse only the careless or stupid is not enough".[330] The "average consumer" is one who is "reasonably well informed and reasonably observant and circumspect". However, the chance to make a direct comparison is rare, so that imperfect recollection must be given account,[331] bearing in mind that the average consumer's level of attention will vary for different types of goods and services.[332]

It is necessary to consider visual and conceptual similarity, and also whether there is a danger of aural confusion, for that in itself may

---

[325] TMA 1994 s.5(2).

[326] *Sabel v Puma* [1998] R.P.C. 199. The formulation comes from the CTM Regulation (art.8(1)(b)) and TM Directive (art.4(1)(b)), not from the Benelux Trade Mark Act art.13. See below, para.18–95.

[327] *Lloyd Schuhfabrik* [1999] E.T.M.R. 690: "Lloyd" for shoes, opposed by "Loints", also for shoes.

[328] *Lloyd Schuhfabrik* [1999] E.T.M.R. 690 ECJ at para.18. In *Medion v Thomson Multimedia* [2006] E.T.M.R. 164 ECJ, the Court of Justice held that "assessment of the similarity between two marks [LIFE and THOMSON LIFE for the purpose of assessing likelihood of confusion] means more than taking one component of a composite trade mark and comparing it with another mark. On the contrary, the comparison must be made by examining each of the marks in question as a whole, which does not mean that the overall impression conveyed to the relevant public by a composite trade mark may not, in certain circumstances, be dominated by one or more of its components": at para.179. The referring court did not seem to have even considered whether the sign could be viewed as identical to the registered mark. Cf. *Gateway v OHIM* [2009] E.T.M.R. 32 ECJ where the comparison was between "Gateway" and "ACTIVY Media Gateway" and the Court of Justice upheld the view of the GC that they were neither similar nor identical: at para.53.

[329] *Sabel v Puma* [1998] R.P.C. 199; *Gut Springenheide* [1998] I E.C.R. 4657; *Windsurfing Chiemsee v Huber* [1999] E.T.M.R. 585; above, at para.18–37. In *esure Insurance v Direct Line Insurance* [2008] R.P.C. 34 CA, Arden L.J. commented that in analysing the likelihood of confusion on the part of the average consumer "it is difficult to see what is gained from the evidence of an expert as to his own opinion": at para.62; Jacob L.J. characterised the brand expert's evidence as "empty rhetoric" and of no value: at para.76.

[330] Per Jacob L.J. in *Reed Executive* [2004] R.P.C. 767 at para.82.

[331] "[D]ue allowance must be made for the occasions when the person who sees the other use has only a general recollection of the normal and fair use by the proprietor of the trade mark", per Aldous L.J. in *Thomson Holidays v Norwegian Cruise Line* [2003] R.P.C. 586 at para.60, following *Lloyd Schuhfabrik* [1999] E.T.M.R. 690 ECJ, and *Canon* [1999] R.P.C. 117, ECJ.

[332] *Lloyd Schuhfabrik* [1999] E.T.M.R. 690; *"Picasso/Picaro"* [2006] E.T.M.R. 349 ECJ at paras 38–43.

suffice (*Lloyd Schuhfabrik* para.28). Likewise the more distinctive the prior mark has become through use, the more probable that there will be confusion (*Canon* para.18): a proposition that Pumfrey J. labelled as "very surprising" and "perhaps only a presumption of fact".[333] Where both marks are characterised by some unusual or original feature, this also increases that risk[334]; whereas, the presence of a descriptive element will lessen it.[335] All these factors are interdependent and should not be looked at "in separate watertight compartments",[336] instead:

> "The global assessment of all the relevant factors involves an iterative process between all the relevant factors, in particular the similarities in the goods or services and the similarities in the marks. ... Thus, for example, a lesser degree of similarity between the goods or services may be offset by a greater degree of similarity between the marks, and vice versa."[337]

Type 3: In addition, an "anti-dilution" provision operates. A relative objection arises where an earlier identical or similar mark has a reputation in the United Kingdom—or, where it is a Community mark, in the EU—and the use of the later mark without due cause would take unfair advantage of, or be detrimental to, the distinctive character or repute of the earlier trade mark. It should be observed that this type of objection arises not only where there is a danger of confusion, including association (as in Type 2), but also in circumstances more embracing: the ground covers any use of another mark which can be characterised as affecting distinctive character or repute, not only so as to cause detriment to, but equally to take unfair advantage of, that character or repute. Making out such a case where there is no confusion is difficult but not impossible with relevant

[333] In *Reed Executive v Reed Business Information* [2003] R.P.C. 207 at para.103, a sentiment with which Jacob L.J. agreed in the appeal, [2004] R.P.C. 767 at para.83.

[334] *Sabel v Puma* [1998] R.P.C. 199 ECJ; *Lloyd Schuhfabrik* [1999] E.T.M.R. 690 ECJ at para.23.

[335] *Windsurfing Chiemsee* [1999] E.T.M.R. 585 ECJ at para.51; *Reed Executive v Reed Business Information* [2004] R.P.C. 767 at paras 84–85: "It is worth examining why that factual proposition is so—it is because where you have something largely descriptive the average consumer will recognise that to be so, expect others to use similar descriptive marks and thus be alert for detail which would differentiate one provider from another", per Jacob L.J. at para.85.

[336] *esure Insurance v Direct Line Insurance* [2008] R.P.C. 34 CA at para.48 per Arden L.J.

[337] *esure Insurance v Direct Line Insurance* [2008] R.P.C. 34 CA at para.46 per Arden L.J., citing *Lloyd Schuhfabrik* [2000] F.S.R. 77 at para 19. As an example of the application of the "global appreciation" test, in *Fiorelli T.M.* [2007] R.P.C. 18, where the similarities between the marks "Fiorucci" and "Fiorelli" were not great, the judge regarded it as decisive that there was no evidence of confusion despite at least seven years in which both marks had been on the market: at paras 41–42.

proof.[338] This deployment of the registration scheme to protect aspects of "investment function" is further explored below.[339]

Precisely these three Types are applied to the later question, what constitutes infringement of a mark once registered? Each issue—relative objection to registration and infringement—is accordingly treated as one of seniority in entitlement: which of the contestants has the prior right to marks that overlap in one of the three ways? Some of the many difficult issues which arise in interpreting the three Types are accordingly left for the discussion of infringement. Here the footnotes refer the reader forward to the relevant passages.

Article 43(2) of the CTM Regulation provides, and art.10 of the TM Directive requires, that the earlier mark should, if necessary, be shown to have been put to genuine use in the previous five years. In opposition proceedings the Registrar will not refuse to register a mark by reason of an earlier trade mark unless the registered proprietor can show use within the five-year period prior to the advertisement of the later application (where such earlier registration was granted more than five years prior to publication for opposition purposes of the opposed mark).[340]

(2) Earlier rights

In this category the definition of "earlier rights" itself delineates the scope of the objections. In the UK legislation there are two sub-types: **18–54**

Sub-type (1): Where use in the United Kingdom of the mark applied for is liable to be prevented by any rule of law protecting an unregistered trade mark or other sign used in the course of trade. This relates in particular to passing off proceedings and may, therefore, cover conflicts with unregistered marks which are identical or similar, for goods or services which are the same or similar, or other circumstances where the three main requirements for passing off exist: a protectible goodwill or reputation in the country,[341] a relevant misrepresentation

[338] In *Intel Corp v CPM* [2006] E.T.M.R. 1249, Patten J. upheld the Hearing Officer's dismissal of computer company Intel's application for invalidity of "Intelmark" for telemarketing services under s.5(3), holding that "the circumstances must ... justify the conclusion that the character or repute of the earlier mark will actually be weakened in the eyes of consumers by its association through the later mark with a different class of goods or services. Where the differences between the marks and the products or services to which they relate indicate that no real connection will be made ... then that damage cannot occur": at para.56.

[339] See below, para.18–99.

[340] TMA 1994 s.6A, added by reg.4 of the Trade Marks (Proof of Use, etc.) Regulations (SI 2004/946). See Ch.7 para.3.1 of the UK Registry's *Manual of Trade Mark Practice*.

[341] It is not essential to file evidence from the trade or the public to prove goodwill, figures relating to turnover and promotion may be sufficient: *per* Appointed Person (R. Arnold QC) in *Scholl Ltd v Lidl Stiftung*, Unreported July 18, 2006.

and likelihood of damage.[342] Purely local rights are as relevant as those with coverage throughout the jurisdiction.[343]

Sub-type (2): Where use in the United Kingdom of the mark applied for is liable to be prevented by virtue of some other right, in particular a copyright, design right or registered design.[344]

(3) Anti-dilution measures[345]

18–55 Thus, a plethora of objections may be raised on the basis of "earlier trade marks" and "earlier rights" in unregistered marks. The first to acquire rights is entitled to have them protected not only in respect of their "origin" function, but also in respect of other less specific values, including those involved in one or other notion of "dilution".

18–56 One major distinction is between registered and unregistered trade marks. For the most part, the latter give rise to objection only if they qualify to be treated as "earlier rights" and that depends largely upon whether the objector could sue for passing off. This distinction would be straightforward, were it not for the fact that unregistered as well as registered rights may fall to be treated as "earlier trade marks" when they acquire sufficient notoriety to be classified as "well-known" within the Paris Convention.[346] This circumstance should be treated as a special case, for most marks of this degree of fame will be registered in the UK or EU Register. Dilution may cause difficulty here.

"Macy's" is famous throughout America as a department store and, if evidence can show it, will also be "well-known" in Britain for goods that such stores sell.[347] Another applicant, even one with substantial British trade under that mark, could not register it, or any close variant ("Macey", "Maty's"), for any department store goods or services. New York Macy's could oppose identical services, similar goods or services and even dissimilar goods or services if they can show: (1) "a reputation in the United Kingdom" (which, despite sloppy use by the ECJ of the term "well-known mark", rather than the correct term "mark with a reputation", in *Davidoff v Gofkid* (below), calls for a lower level of recognition than being a "well-known mark", but probably includes a trading reputation, even without use,

[342] Within this head will fall the special right given to a principal mark-owner in a Convention country to enjoin use of his trade mark by his British agent, where the use is unauthorised and unjustified: TMA 1994 s.60(4), (5), implementing the Paris Convention art.6*septies*. See *"Travelpro" TM* [1998] R.P.C. 864.

[343] cf. the CTM: below, para.18–68.

[344] As under the previous law: e.g. *"Karo Step" TM* [1977] R.P.C. 255 at 276 (trade name in logo-like presentation an artistic work); *"Oscar" TM* [1979] R.P.C. 173 (picture of the famous statuette); Lyons [1994] E.I.P.R. 21.

[345] See further below, para.18–99.

[346] For the meaning of "well-known" in the Paris Convention, and for a comparison with the various refinements of the same general idea which over time have plagued German jurisprudence, see Kur (1992) 23 I.I.C. 18.

[347] An example sparked by *Macy's TM* [1989] R.P.C. 546.

in the United Kingdom); and (2) the taking of unfair advantage or causing of detriment referred to in s.5(3) of the TMA 1994.

If the mark is not so internationally famous as to be "well-known" in the United Kingdom, then the application can be prevented only by showing a goodwill (i.e. use in the United Kingdom) sufficient to establish a right to prevent passing off.

The other main distinction affecting "earlier trade marks" turns on whether or not there is evidence of a reputation in the United Kingdom, probably (but see above) arising from use. If the marks and/or the goods or services are similar, objection arises where the public is likely to be confused between them even if there has been no use of the earlier trade mark. However, if the earlier mark has a relevant reputation arising from its actual use, the grounds of objection broaden to cover unfair advantage or detriment which would arise from use of the later mark on goods or services.[348] A fortiori, one would suppose, these broader grounds of objection should apply when the marks are being applied to similar goods and services, though this was not clear on the face of the text in the TM Directive (or the TMA as originally enacted). In *Davidoff v Gofkid*[349] the ECJ finessed this problem in surprising fashion, by stating that art.5(2) (ss.5(3) and 10(3) of the TMA 1994 as originally enacted): **18–57**

> "must not be interpreted solely on the basis of its wording, but also in the light of the overall scheme and objectives of the system of which it is a part. Having regard to the latter aspects, that article cannot be given an interpretation which would lead to well-known [sic] marks having less protection where a sign is used for identical or similar goods or services than where a sign is used for non-similar goods or services" (at paras 24 and 25).

Thus, protection must be accorded to marks with a reputation against use of a sign on similar goods or services even if there is no likelihood of confusion but instead an unfair advantage is taken or detriment caused to the proprietor of the earlier mark. Logical though this may be,[350] it is a breathtaking example of judicial lawmaking: despite the words of the provision being clearly (and admittedly) to the contrary, the court required an

[348] For example, in *Aktieselskabet af 21. November 2001 v OHIM* [2009] E.T.M.R. 36 ECJ, the opponent succeeded in preventing registration of "TDK" for clothing by reason of a risk of unfair advantage or detriment in the future to its registered marks for "TDK" in Class 9 (apparatus for recording sound or images).

[349] *Davidoff v Gofkid* [2003] E.T.M.R. 534, art.234 reference from a German court.

[350] See Casparie-Kerdel, [2001] E.I.P.R. 185 for a comparison of US, Benelux and EU laws on this topic. The author questions "why the ECJ, if it recognises the relation between the distinctiveness of [a] trade mark and its scope of protection, is so firmly clinging to the necessity of confusion. In fact the opposite of the court's view is much more plausible: if a mark is very distinctive and has a reputation ... consumers are less likely to be confused, as they will recognise even very small differences between the famous mark and the sign": at 192.

interpretation that it believed was intended. In *Adidas-Salomon v Fitness-World*[351] the Court of Justice then rejected the argument that extending the broader protection to identical or similar goods or services was optional, deciding that once a Member State decided to adopt the TM Directive's optional provision providing broader protection, it was mandatory to include identical or similar goods in its scope. As a result, in the United Kingdom ss.5(3) and 10(3) of the TMA 1994 were amended to this effect by reg.7 of The Trade Marks (Proof of Use, etc.) Regulations 2004.[352]

(4) Other factors

(a) *Public interest*

18–58 As already emphasised, with effect from October 1, 2007 objections on these relative grounds may be made only in an opposition. The Registrar has no residual power to consider the matter in the public interest. Only if an objection can be brought within an absolute ground, such as that the mark is likely to deceive or its use could be prohibited by law,[353] can the Registry refuse an application which it may view as contrary to the public interest.

(b) *Scope of objections*

18–59 There is no onus on the applicant itself to overcome all objections to registration: on the contrary, it is for the Registrar or an opponent to make out a sufficient objection.

At the same time, a moderating technique of the earlier UK law is reduced in effect. This is registration with a disclaimer. (In addition, until October 2007 and the abandonment of Registry examination on relative grounds, there was provision for registration upon proof of honest concurrent use.)[354]

(c) *Disclaimer*

18–60 Until 1994, there had long been a practice of registering marks subject to disclaimers of exclusive right in some part of the whole, or subject to other limitations, and there remain many such entries on the UK Register. In this way the Registry was empowered to give the applicant some part of what it sought, while taking sufficient account of an objection to the distinctiveness or deceptiveness of the mark. The scope of disclaimers and limitations continues to be the subject of extended discussion between Registry and applicant. However, the Registry has no power to impose them (although it may indicate to an applicant that an application will be rejected unless an

351 *Adidas-Salomon v FitnessWorld* [2004] E.T.M.R. 10.
352 SI 2004/946; which took effect on on May 5, 2004.
353 See above, paras 18–49, 18–50.
354 See para.17–59 of the 5th edn. of this work for details. In *Budejovicky Budvar v Anheuser-Busch* [2010] R.P.C. 7 CA, Jacob L.J. suggested that "some doctrine of honest concurrent use needs to be fashioned" in European trade mark law: at para.52.

appropriate amendment to the specification of goods or services is made[355]); they have to be volunteered by the applicant. Notwithstanding this, they are still a valuable method of resolving objections.

It is explicitly stated that the rights in the mark are restricted in accordance with the disclaimer or limitation[356]: **18–61**

> "[a]n applicant who agrees that the rights conferred by registration shall be subject to a limitation is agreeing, in effect, that the use of the mark outside the limitation is not to be treated as an infringement of the mark notwithstanding that such use would, otherwise, fall within section 10 of the Act."[357]

The correct approach is, first, to consider whether the mark is registrable apart from any question of disclaiming[358]; and then, if necessary, to consider whether, after discounting what is disclaimed, enough will remain of independent substance to deserve registration.[359]

(5) Comparison between marks

(a) *The basis for comparison*

Where in fact there has been use of the other mark, it is that actual use which must be compared with any normal and fair use of the mark applied for.[360] **18–62**

Where an opponent is relying not upon the registration but upon an unregistered mark protected by passing off, then the comparison is with the actual reputation of the earlier mark derived from trading. It is necessary for the person claiming the earlier right to show that he has a legal right to prevent use of the mark applied for, in particular because of passing off. This means demonstrating a sufficient reputation with the public and not merely that the public will be muddled about source. It is for the tribunal, rather than witnesses, to determine whether a relative ground of objection is made out. **18–63**

---

355 *Nettec Solutions Application* [2003] R.P.C. 17, Appointed Person.

356 TMA 1994 s.13. "[A]n objection under section 5(2) [on the basis of an earlier right] cannot succeed in a case where the resemblance between the marks is attributable to nothing more than the presence in the earlier mark of an element for which protection has been disclaimed" per the Appointed Person (G. Hobbs, QC) in *Torremar TM* [2003] R.P.C. 89 at para.29.

357 Per Mummery L.J. in *Nestlé's TM Application* [2005] R.P.C. 77 CA at para.33; however note also *L'Oréal v Bellure* [2007] E.T.M.R. 1, where Lewison J. held that an application which claims a particular colour does not thereby disclaim protection against use of other colours: at para.88.

358 *"Superwound" TM* [1988] R.P.C. 272.

359 *"P.R.E.P.A.R.E." TM* [1997] R.P.C. 884: that mark not registrable even with a disclaimer of the word without the full stops.

360 In opposition proceedings the onus is on the opponent: *Oasis Stores* [1998] R.P.C. 631; cf. *Dualit* [1999] R.P.C. 304.

(b) *Factors in the comparison*

18–64 Where words are involved, the proper approach was stated in classic form by Parker J. in *Pianotist's Application*[361]:

> "You must take the two words. You must judge of them, both by their look and by their sound. You must consider the goods to which they are to be applied. You must consider the nature and kind of customer who would be likely to buy those goods. In fact, you must consider all the circumstances; and you must further consider what is likely to happen if each of those trade marks is used in a normal way as a trade mark for the goods of the respective owners of the marks."

Or, to summarise the ECJ in *Sabel v Puma*,[362] there must be a global assessment made which takes into account all relevant factors.[363]

At the same time, Farwell J.'s warning against artifice in the *"Erectiko"* case[364] remains pertinent:

> "I do not think it is right to take a part of the word and compare it with a part of the other word; one word must be considered as a whole and compared with the other word as a whole ... There may be two words which in their component parts are widely different but which, when read or spoken together, do represent something which is so similar as to lead inevitably to confusion."

Or, more succinctly, again from the ECJ, "[t]he average consumer normally perceives the mark as a whole and does not proceed to analyse its various details".[365]

If the mark is not just a word, but a word or words in a given format, a symbol, colour, ideogram, picture, shape or a combination of some or all of these, then the comparison is between the two, taking account particularly of the features which make them memorable. Obviously, if it is only capable of being seen and not spoken, it is only visual comparison that is relevant.

Comparison between goods and services for the purpose of the application procedure follows the same analysis as for infringement, discussed at

[361] *Pianotist's Application* (1906) 23 R.P.C. 774 at 777. There is a family resemblance in the approach to comparison of marks with that in a passing off action: for which see above, paras 17–24—17–25, and indeed in *Asprey & Garrard v WRA (Guns)* [2002] F.S.R. 487 CA, Peter Gibson L.J. accepted that the evidence sufficient to support the finding of passing off was enough to find trade mark infringement under s.10(2): at para.49.

[362] *Sabel v Puma* [1997] E.C.R. I-6191.

[363] In *Nations Fitting v Oystertec* [2006] F.S.R. 740 Sing. HC, Andrew Phang J. concluded that there is no inherent contradiction betweeen the global assessment test on the one hand and the "more specific approach embodied within the English jurisprudence on the other hand. In many ways both were two sides of the same coin": at para.95.

[364] *William Bailey's Application* (1935) 52 R.P.C. 136 at 151–152.

[365] *Sabel v Puma* [1997] E.C.R. I-6191 at para.23.

paras 18–82; although of course with an application one is comparing the mark applied for with the mark registered, whereas with infringement the comparison is the sign as used with the registered mark.

The case law provides a lava-flow of illustrations. Some deal with the issue at the stage of application, others with infringement. In each case the essence of the inquiry is the same. Here are a few: **18–65**

- Registration of "Reef" for promotional or souvenir articles relating to a music group was allowed in the face of opposition by "Reef Brazil" for footwear: the marks were one word against two, in "Reef Brazil" both words were equally distinctive, the respective goods were not so similar as to override these differences, the reputation of the "Reef Brazil" mark in the United Kingdom was not sufficient to tip the balance and the evidence did not show that the relevant retail outlets and customers overlapped.[366]
- The owner of the "Morgan" trade mark registered for women's and children's clothing successfully opposed the application for "Lorna Morgan" for clothing, footwear and headgear. The Appointed Person (R. Arnold, QC) found that, taking into account the reputation of the registered mark and the degree of attention of the average consumer of clothing, the average consumer "might well assume that [goods marked with 'Lorna Morgan'] came from economically-linked undertakings."[367]
- Registration was refused of "Intel-Play" for constructional toy puzzles upon opposition by the proprietor of "Intel", which was widely known and recognised by consumers. The judge upheld the Hearing Officer's finding that the applicant's intended use would without due cause take advantage of and be detrimental to the character and repute of the "Intel" mark, contrary to s.5(3).[368]
- An application to register for nuts a series of four marks each comprising a monkey eating a monkey nut was opposed by the owner of eight earlier marks for the word "Monkies" either alone or with a device. The Appointed Person found that it was not permissible to group together several earlier marks as part of the global appreciation required under s.5(2)(b). Instead the comparison had to be made against each of the earlier marks separately, unless evidence had been submitted that an enhanced distinctiveness had been acquired as a

[366] *Reef TM* [2003] R.P.C. 101, CA (the Court of Appeal considered the extent to which appellate courts should interfere with the Hearing Officer's findings; the judge in the first instance appeal, [2002] R.P.C. 19, had disagreed with the Hearing Officer's finding on trade outlets and customers but the Court of Appeal overruled this, at para.37, per Robert Walker L.J.).

[367] *Oska's Ltd's TM Application* [2005] R.P.C. 525 at para.49.

[368] *Intel v Kirpal Singh Sihra* [2003] R.P.C. 789.

result of a common component in a family of marks. It would not be presumed from the Register.[369]

— The owner of the well-known three-stripes marks for footwear opposed an application to register a 3D mark for a drinks bottle in the shape of a football boot, the design of which included six parallel lines on each side (giving the impression of three stripes). The Appointed Person found that the question of similarity of goods under s.5(3) depended not only on the degree of similarity but on all other factors including the extent of reputation of the earlier mark and dismissed the appeal against refusal. He considered also that the section is intended to prevent "parasitic" use which unjustly draws upon the recollection of the opponent's trade mark in the course of trade in goods bearing the applicant's trade mark (at para.21).[370]

(6) Community trade marks

18–66 The relative grounds affecting the registration of CTMs are largely in the same terms to those for national marks. The consequential difficulties that this presents are considerable. Under the EU system there has from the outset been no ex officio examination on these grounds and everything accordingly depends on oppositions by third parties.[371] The number of oppositions is large and indeed the CFI, to which an appeal from an OHIM Board of Appeal lies on questions of fact as well as law, has heard many cases.

These opponents may succeed by showing a senior mark or right within the three types of objection found also in the TMA 1994. But that earlier mark may be a CTM or a mark registered in any Member State: where it is the latter, OHIM will take into account the likelihood of confusion amongst the relevant public in that particular Member State.[372] Also brought into account are earlier unregistered rights. It was particularly important to the British and Irish, with systems which traditionally obliged many traders to rely on passing off rights for a substantial part of their protection, to secure

[369] *The Infamous Nut Co Ltd's TM* [2003] R.P.C. 126, Appointed Person (Prof. R. Annand), esp. at para.37.

[370] *Inlima's Application* [2000] R.P.C. 661 (S. Thorley, QC); for the similar Spanish decision on the same facts, *Adidas-Salomon v Spanish Patent & Trade Mark Office* [2005] E.T.M.R. 1317. See also, *Smirnoff* [2003] E.W.H.C. 970, where Jacob J. overturned the Hearing Officer's decision to permit the registration of Smirnoff in cyrillic script by a party other than the well-known maker of the vodka.

[371] CTM Regulation art.8. Where the earlier right is a registered mark, owners and licensees are both entitled to oppose.

[372] For example, in *Ferrero v Jordi Tarrida Llopart* [2003] E.T.M.R. 188, the German registration "Mon Cheri" was unsuccessfully relied upon in opposition to the application for "Montxeri": the Board of Appeal considered how the average German consumer would perceive the two marks. In *Lidl Stiftung v Heinz Iberica* [2003] E.T.M.R. 312, it was noted by the Board of Appeal that decisions of the trade mark authorities and courts in the territory in which the earlier right exists "deserve a special consideration": at para.16.

this last ground of opposition; it was heavily resisted by the German Government from a fear that the pre-grant procedure would become hopelessly over-burdened.[373] This has not turned out to be the case and OHIM has functioned efficiently and speedily in the main.

There is, however, one limit to the scope of objections to a CTM, which does not affect national applications to the same extent: non-registered rights which are of "mere local significance" are not brought into account either in opposition or in subsequent invalidity proceedings.[374] They may, however, be asserted against the CTM holder for (in England) passing off in the particular locality until acquiescence has lasted for five years; and even thereafter the CTM owner has no right to stop the earlier user from continuing his marking in the locality.[375] **18–67**

What is to count as merely "local" is not defined. In *Compass Publishing v Compass Logistics*[376] Laddie J. held that:

> "a mark should be considered as having mere local significance . . . if its geographical spread is restricted to substantially less than the whole of the European Union and that, from the perspective of the Community market in the services or goods in question, the mark is of little significance."[377]

At some point, the Court of Justice may find itself wrestling with this question.[378]

6. Revocation and Invalidity

A UK trade mark registration is open to attack on two major fronts: **18–68**

(1) revocation proceedings may be brought in relation to grounds which have arisen since the date of registration—notably because of non-use or because the mark has become descriptive or misleading. A

---

373 See von Mühlendahl (1989) 20 I.I.C. 583; Pagenberg (1989) 20 I.I.C. 595.

374 CTM Regulation arts 8(4), 52(1)(c). There have been a number of oppositions at OHIM based on art.8(4), e.g. by the owners of the appellation of origin "Budweiser Budvar" to the mark "Budweiser" and by the Franklin Mint to registration of a stylised form of the name "Diana", which have failed because the opponent failed to explain to the satisfaction of the Opposition Division the national law on which reliance was being placed, in the latter case the English law of passing off.

375 CTM Regulation art.107.

376 *Compass Publishing v Compass Logistics* [2004] R.P.C. 809.

377 *Compass Publishing* [2004] R.P.C. 809 at para.56; cf. the OHIM Opposition Guidelines Pt 4 para.5.3, which suggests that it should be within a particular country.

378 An earlier "local" right can also provide a defence to an infringement action under the TMA 1994 s.11(3); see below, para.18–112.

revocation order will operate from the date of the application to revoke or the date on which the ground for revocation existed, if earlier[379];

(2) proceedings to have the registration declared invalid may be brought on absolute or relative grounds which existed at the time of registration and which cannot be excused by subsequent events. If they succeed, the registration will be deemed never to have been made.[380]

A Community trade mark is open to attack on equivalent grounds,[381] but because of its unitary character, the objections have to be considered on an EU basis. It remains far from clear what precisely this means. Discussion here will consider the position as it relates to UK trade marks, but will draw attention to this special characteristic of Community marks.[382]

One apparent difference may be noted at once. If an EU ground for revocation or declaration of invalidity is made out, there is no discretion left to the tribunal concerned over whether to take consequent action: it is mandatory.[383] It had been thought that the inclusion of the word "may" in ss.46 and 47 TMA 1994, perhaps following the TM Directive,[384] left to the tribunal some discretion but this appears not to be the case.[385]

(1) Revocation for non-use

18–69 The conception of a trade mark registration as an entitlement dependent upon need—which has always underpinned the UK approach to the subject—has become a major element in the EU system.[386] Accordingly, although under the TMA 1994 the applicant for registration must intend bona fide to use the mark—a requirement already discussed[387]—but not in the CTM system, in both systems after registration the proprietor or a licensee must put it to genuine use within five years if it is not to become vulnerable to attack.[388]

However, it is hard to eliminate stockpiling. In an effort to do so, the US and Canadian systems require positive evidence of use to accompany each

[379] TMA 1994 s.46, implementing the TM Directive arts 12–14.
[380] TMA 1994 s.47, implementing the TM Directive arts 3, 4, 13, 14.
[381] CTM Regulation arts 50, 51.
[382] Since the validity of a mark may be raised in infringement proceedings before national courts, they are obliged to decide such questions: see CTM Regulation arts 50(1), 51(1).
[383] CTM Regulation arts 50, 51—"shall be declared revoked/invalid".
[384] TMA 1994 ss.46, 47—"may be revoked/declared invalid"; TM Directive arts 3, 4, 12—"liable to be revoked/declared invalid". Cf. Annand and Norman p.141.
[385] In *Wing Joo Long Ginseng v Qinghai Xinyuan Foreign Trade* [2009] F.S.R. 13, the Singapore Court of Appeal decided, after reviewing the local and UK case law and views of academic works such as *Kerly*, that there is no residual discretion: at para.157.
[386] TMA 1994 s.50(1)(a) and (b), embodies the TM Directive art.10, so far as it is relevant to the country. For the equivalent provisions in the CTM Regulation, see above, n.78. For a review of the position around the world, see Taylor (1990) 80 T.M.R. 197.
[387] See above, para.18–03.
[388] For licensing, see above, para.18–14.

application to renew the registration. It was initially proposed that there be a similar requirement for Community marks[389]: but protests from European industry led to a much less demanding approach, akin to that which, for instance, already operated in the UK system. However, it does at least place the burden of proving use on the mark owner[390] and the evidence adduced must show that use[391]; in *Philosophy Inc v Ferretti Studio*[392] a single transaction involving 500 bottles sent as samples but marked with a contact name were held insufficient in themselves to constitute "genuine use" when there was no evidence that those samples were sent for the purpose of inducing "sales in real trade".[393] The reversal of the burden of proof is a significant exception to the general presumption of validity upon registration.

(a) *Scope of the ground*

Subject to certain exceptions, a registration is to be revoked for failure by **18–70** the proprietor, or any person with his consent (such as by a licensee),[394] to make genuine use of the mark[395] in the United Kingdom in relation to the specified goods or services:

(1) in the five years from completion of registration[396]; or
(2) in any later uninterrupted period of five years.[397]

[389] See the first Draft CTM Regulation, III/D/753/78, art.43.

[390] TMA 1994 s.100.

[391] In the form of brochures, catalogues, pamphlets, advertisements and the like, together with evidence of the level of sales, see for example *Carte Bleue TMs* [2002] R.P.C. 599; TM Regulation, at 607. "Those concerned with proof of use should read their evidence with a critical eye ... All the t's should be crossed and all the i's dotted" per Jacob J. in *Laboratoire de la Mer TMs* [2002] F.S.R. 790 at para.9. See also *Cocoon/Silk Cocoon* [2003] E.C.R. II-789, CFI, where the court annulled an OHIM Board of Appeal decision which accepted a contention of use without evidence.

[392] *Philosophy Inc v Ferretti Studio* [2003] E.T.M.R. 97 CA.

[393] per Peter Gibson L.J. [2003] E.T.M.R. 97 CA at para.21.

[394] It is not sufficient to merely assert that use was with consent, it needs to be proved: see *Continental Shelf 128 Ltd's TM* [2007] E.T.M.R. 95, TM Registry, where the Hearing Officer noted that acquiescence is not synonymous with consent: at para.14.

[395] In *Anheuser-Busch v Budejovicky Budvar* [2003] R.P.C. 25, the Court of Appeal found that use of a mark in ordinary block capitals constitutes use of a mark registered in a stylised form, being use "in a form differing in elements which do not alter the distinctive character of the mark" under s.46(2). It is interesting to contrast this with the view of Jacobs A.G. in *LTJ Diffusion v Sadas* [2003] F.S.R. 1 at para.A50, that a change of type to one noticeably different to that registered may be sufficient to make the sign merely similar.

[396] i.e. the actual date on which registration is complete, not the "date of registration" which involves a notional back-dating to the date of filing of the application. The CTM Regulation omits reference to the first of these grounds: art.50(1)(a).

[397] TMA 1994 s.46(1)(a), (b). The registration may be revoked on these grounds. Accordingly there is a discretion not to do so where sufficient reason exists: *Glen Catrine's TM* [1996] E.T.M.R. 56. In addition, the grounds themselves allow a mark to be saved where there are proper reasons for non-use: see below, para.18–72. There seems no reason in principle why the same mark may not be registered by the same proprietor for identical goods. The second registration will then have its own five-year term for use to begin; but there will be a question whether initially it is registered in good faith (s.3(6)), or in order to repair the lack of use of the first registration: cf. *Unilever v Cussons (New Zealand)* [1998] R.P.C. 369.

An application to revoke may be made by any person.[398] It is not therefore necessary for an objector to establish any interest in the mark; it is in no one's interest to have unused marks cluttering up the Register. If the objection is made out only for some of the goods or services specified, there will be revocation for them alone.[399] How the specification should be amended if this is the case has been the subject of a number of judgments in the United Kingdom,[400] and now seems to be relatively clear in theory (although application in particular cases undoubtedly will continue to prove difficult). In deciding what is a fair specification of goods having regard to the use made, the court must adopt the attitude of the reasonably informed consumer of the products; in doing so it must inform itself of the nature of the trade and then decide how the notional consumer would describe the use which has taken place.[401] It is important to bear in mind that too wide a specification affects the rights of the public, and indeed in view of s.10(2) is not necessary in order to be fair to the proprietor. As was emphasised in *Cernivet TM*, it is important for the tribunal to identify clearly and accurately the goods for which the mark should remain registered, so that it is appropriate to accept that "a likelihood of confusion shall be presumed" in the event of unauthorised use of an identical sign, referring to both the tenth recital of the Directive and art.19(1) of the TRIPS Agreement.[402]

18–71 It is expressly stated that affixing the mark to goods or packaging purely for export from the United Kingdom is sufficient use.[403] Where the use is in website advertising for a business whose physical location is outside the United Kingdom, the question arises as to whether that suffices to maintain a registration here: the answer must depend on an intention to attract

[398] The same applies to the other grounds for revocation and declaration of invalidity. The application may be made to the Registrar or the High Court, unless the issue is already pending before the latter. The Registrar may refer the application to the court at any stage: TMA 1994 s.46(4).

[399] TMA 1994 s.46(5).

[400] See, for example, *Thomson Holidays v Norwegian Cruise Lines* [2003] R.P.C. 586. For amendment of an application during opposition, see *Nettec Solutions Ltd's TM Application* [2003] R.P.C. 308.

[401] per Aldous L.J. in *Thomson Holidays v Norwegian Cruise Line* [2003] R.P.C. 586 CA at para.31, approving *Decon v Fred Baker* [2001] R.P.C. 293. Applying this test in *"ESB"* [2003] E.T.M.R. 376, the Court of Appeal upheld the finding of the judge at first instance who found (somewhat surprisingly) that "[b]eer drinkers in the main drink either lager or bitter, but not both. There is little overlap of trade marks between those two classes" and therefore revoked the mark except for "bitter beer". Of course, it would be inadvisable for a brewer to rely on this partial revocation to start using the initials ESB on lager.

[402] per the Appointed Person (G. Hobbs QC) [2002] R.P.C. 585 at para.47. Mr Hobbs noted also that judicial authorities in EU Member States are now obliged to interpret their trade mark laws in the light of the wording and purpose of the TRIPS Agreement, referring to the ECJ judgment in *Schieving-Nijstad v Groeneveld* [2002] F.S.R. 346 (a case involving the Dutch "kort geding" procedure, which has attracted much criticism outside that country).

[403] TMA 1994 s.46(2); see *Imaginarium TM* [2004] R.P.C. 594 TM Registry, holding that the fact that both the import and export of the goods was by or with the consent of the registered proprietor did not mean it was other than "genuine use": at para.41.

customers from the United Kingdom.[404] Generally, the extent of use that needs to be proved depends on the market for the relevant goods or services[405] but a small number of genuine, as opposed to "token", sales may be sufficient[406] although a wide specification may be cut back: "[t]hat would leave him with just a small umbra and a correspondingly reduced penumbra".[407] It appears that the genuine use may be on any market and not just to consumers or end-users: in *Laboratoires Goemar v La Mer Technology* the Court of Appeal rejected the contention that minimal sales (of £800 worth of goods bearing the mark over a five year period) to a single UK importer, with no further evidence of any sales on the open market, did not qualify as genuine use.[408] It would seem also that if the proprietor has made genuine efforts to start trading, then to supply goods under the mark on a single occasion, or possibly to make some other definite marketing effort, may amount to use.[409] It may even suffice to show that the mark has been used purely in brochures or advertisements, though such a case should be examined carefully. Use merely to endorse the products of others—for instance, by a chain store or a magazine—would not be enough[410] and nor would giving free samples away on the sale of other, unrelated goods.[411]

So far as concerns UK marks, it is only use of the mark in the United Kingdom that is relevant. But for a Community mark, "use in the Community" is the criterion.[412] This should be read as referring to use in more than one Member State (although an EU Council Minute states that use in one Member State constitutes use in them all for non-use purposes). An EU registration, after all, gives a right of wide scope and should arguably be reserved for marks being used for trade between Member States. It is expressly provided that a CTM may be converted into a national mark where it has been revoked for non-use "in the Community", provided that it

---

[404] *Euromarket Designs v Peters* [2000] E.T.M.R. 1025; *800-FLOWERS TM* [2002] F.S.R. 738 CA (considering the issue under the 1938 Act).

[405] *Ansul v Ajax* [2003] R.P.C. 717 ECJ at para.39.

[406] In *Ansul v Ajax* [2003] R.P.C. 717, the ECJ distinguished between "genuine" and "token" use: genuine use must be real commercial exploitation, at paras 36 and 37: this surely implies use as a trade mark for the goods or services registered, and not for some other purpose: cf. Annand and Norman pp.126–127. The ECJ found that after-sales services may be sufficient (such as selling spare parts or servicing for fire extinguishers already on the market).

[407] per Jacob J. in *Laboratoire de la Mer TMs* [2002] F.S.R. 790 at para.32.

[408] [2006] F.S.R. 49 CA; cf. *Kerly* at para.10–040 and following, which concludes: "We consider that the reasoning of the Court of Appeal is significantly out of step with *Ansul*, *La Mer* and numerous GC decisions, as well as representing a serious retrograde step in this area of the law. The privilege of trade mark registration requires that the trade mark must be put to genuine or real use": at para.10–050.

[409] *"Bon Matin" TM* [1989] R.P.C. 537—a case where genuine preparations to market sufficed, without evidence of actual sales.

[410] *Safeway Stores v HFP* [1997] E.T.M.R. 352; *"Elle" TMs* [1997] F.S.R. 529.

[411] *Silberquelle v Maselli* [2009] E.T.M.R. 28 ECJ, where the proprietor gave away alcohol-free drinks bearing its mark "Wellness" to customers who bought its clothing products.

[412] CTM Regulation art.50(1)(a).

has been genuinely used in the state concerned.[413] This implies that a higher level of use needs be shown in the EU system than in national systems. Of course it has proved difficult to persuade EU tribunals to take any determined line on this. But the matter can equally be raised in a counterclaim before a national court hearing infringement proceedings; and that could be a court in a country where the CTM proprietor had not used the mark.

(b) *Exceptions*

18–72 For both UK and Community marks, there will be no revocation if any of the specified exceptions apply:

(1) there has been use of a mark that differs only in elements which do not alter the distinctive character of the mark registered[414];
(2) there has been a subsequent resumption of use before the application to revoke is made. But here resumption within three months of that application does not count (unless preparations for resumption began prior to knowledge that revocation would be threatened); this enables an attacker to give warning of his intention without inducing a repellent spurt of use[415];
(3) there are proper reasons for non-use.[416] The UK Registry has held that this means any reason that is "apt, acceptable, reasonable, justifiable in all of the circumstances". Thus, where there had been preparations to license the mark but these had been put in suspense by the revocation proceedings, this was held sufficient justification.[417] However, a trader's own business difficulties or ordinary commercial delays[418] will not suffice; production difficulties must be exceptional and generally outside the control of the proprietor.[419]

18–73 It is not an excuse that the mark has been used on similar goods or for similar services. This strictness is appropriate, given that the scope of right

[413] A matter which would be assessed by the national registry considering the application for conversion: see CTM Regulation arts 108–110.
[414] TMA 1994 s.46(2): based on art.5(C)(2) Paris Convention. In *Bud and Budweiser Budbräu TMs* [2003] R.P.C. 477 CA, it was noted by Sir Martin Nourse that "[a] mark may have recognisable elements other than the words themselves which are nevertheless not significant enough to be part of its distinctive character; or, to put it the other way round, the words have a dominance which reduces to insignificance the other recognisable elements": at para.12.
[415] TMA 1994 s.46(3).
[416] TMA 1994 s.46(1)(a), (b); cf. art.19(1), TRIPS Agreement: see *Cernivet TM* [2002] R.P.C. 585, where the Appointed Person (Mr Hobbs QC) considered that difficult questions were likely to arise as to whether "proper reasons" (TM Directive wording) or "obstacles" (TRIPS wording) can arise from "personal circumstances such as illness or impecuniosity": at para.52.
[417] *"Invermont" TM* [1997] R.P.C. 125; *Worth TMs* [1998] R.P.C. 875.
[418] *Nestlé v Zeta Espacial* [2000] E.T.M.R. 226; *Philosophy Inc v Ferretti Studio* [2003] R.P.C. 287 CA at para.25.
[419] *Magic Ball TM* [2000] R.P.C. 439.

granted under the law extends not only to specified goods and services but also to those which are similar. However, use on beer mats has been held to suffice as use in relation to beer.[420]

(2) Mark becoming generic

When a new product appears on the market, and particularly when patent protection eliminates direct competition for some initial period, the producer may find that the mark which he gives it comes to be used as a description of the product itself. Names which have gone through this process to a greater or lesser extent include aspirin, shredded wheat, thermos, hoover, vaseline, tabloid, walkman and formica (most of which are registered in some countries and generic in others). **18–74**

In some cases, the trade mark owner takes regular steps to emphasise that there is a separate generic name for the product, and to encourage those in trade to use the trade mark only for its own products, the generic name for substitutes (as, for instance, "personal audio system" rather than "Walkman").[421] If they take considerable care, then they are likely to be able to show that the distinct meanings remain understood. As well as ensuring that their own usage does not slide in a descriptive direction, they ought actively to pursue others who are careless.[422] They are then likely to have a preservable trade mark which is of great value. If generic use of the mark becomes widespread, however, they may not be able to show a sufficient reputation to support passing off,[423] and equally they may face revocation of their trade mark registrations.

The ground of revocation is that, in consequence of acts or inactivity of the proprietor, the mark has become the common name in the trade for a product or service for which it is registered.[424] Pumfrey J. in *"ESB"*[425] observed: **18–75**

---

[420] *Bud and Budweiser Budbräu TMs* [2002] R.P.C. 747 at para.42, on which the Court of Appeal expressed no view; [2003] R.P.C. 477 at para.33.

[421] cf. the Austrian case in which Sony lost its registration of "Walkman" despite strenuous efforts to protect it against unauthorised use because it appeared in Duden, a German dictionary (4 Ob 269/01i).

[422] A particular danger arises if a trade mark is given a generic description in a dictionary. In the case of a Community trade mark, a dictionary or reference work publisher who has done this can be ordered to indicate in the next edition that the word is a registered trade mark: CTM Regulation art.10. The TM Directive did not require such a provision in the TMA 1994 and none was introduced; it might well have been.

[423] See above, para.17–14.

[424] If a mark was not distinctive at its date of registration, it will be declared invalid ab initio under TMA 1994 s.47; but that ground applies only to non-distinctiveness at that date, not subsequently: see the analysis in *"Spambuster"* [2005] R.P.C. 657 at paras 127–131.

[425] *"ESB"* [2003] F.S.R. 816 at para.44. See also *Alcon* [2004] E.T.M.R. 83, CFI: "BSS" had become generic.

> "I have no doubt that in the same way that a mark can gain distinctiveness after registration, so also it can lose distinctiveness because of the use which is made of it by the proprietor",

although the evidence of use of ESB by other brewers did not support such a finding in that case. However, the question is not only what the relevant trade understands by the mark, but primarily what consumers and end users of it think:

> "[t]he whole aim of the commercialisation process is the purchase of the product by those persons and the role of the intermediary [the trade] consists as much in detecting and anticipating the demand for that product as in increasing or directing it".[426]

In *Hormel Foods v Antilles Landscape Investments*[427] the registered mark "Spambuster" for computer programming was found to have become a common name[428] in the trade for computer programming services to combat spam; the judge holding that the proprietor's failure to take steps to stop this need not be the *sole* but only *a* cause of its becoming a common name in *the trade*.[429]

(3) Mark becoming deceptive

18–76 Just as a mark may lose its distinctiveness after registration by becoming a general description of a product, so it is possible (though doubtless rare) that it will become deceptive through some subsequent event. In the pre-1994 UK law, it was for a long time uncertain what circumstances of this character would justify expunging a registration. Eventually it was settled that only where the registered proprietor had been guilty of "blameworthy conduct" would there be a substantive reason for removing the mark from the register.[430]

Some echo of this approach resounds in the TMA 1994, which gives as a ground for revocation that:

[426] *Björnekulla Fruktindustrier v Procordia* [2004] E.T.M.R. 985 ECJ at para.24.

[427] *Hormel Foods v Antilles Landscape Investments* [2005] R.P.C. 657 Ch.D.

[428] It was held that the words of s.46(1)(c) (the common name) should not be read literally but instead should be interpreted to mean "a common name": at para.167.

[429] *Hormel Foods* [2005] R.P.C. 657 at paras 170 and 171. In *Wing Joo Long Ginseng Hong v Qinghai Xinyuan Foreign Trade* [2009] F.S.R. 13, the Singapore Court of Appeal referred to the *Hormel Foods* case when holding that the burden imposed on the applicant for revocation to show that the mark had become customary in the current language was not easy to discharge: at para.77. The court found it was not enough for the applicant for revocation to show that the mark in question was popular or even the only brand used to market a particular product: at para.66.

[430] *"GE" TM* [1973] R.P.C. 297 at 334 HL per Lord Diplock. See further *New South Wales Dairy v Murray Goulburn* [1991] R.P.C. 144 HC (Aust.); *Riv-Oland v Settef* (1988) 12 I.P.R. 321.

"as a consequence of use made by the proprietor of the registered trade mark or by any third party with the proprietor's consent, such use is liable to mislead the public, particularly as to the nature, quality or geographical origin of those goods and/or services".

This, however, refers only to "use" and so omits the element of moral culpability inherent in "blameworthy".

Obvious examples of what is caught can easily be conceived: for instance, to use a mark incorporating the word "Scottish" if the relevant products are no longer made in that country, or where a mark registered with a limitation that it be used only on elongated products is used for short ones.[431] Such misleading deployments of the mark itself could come about either when it is put to use for the first time, when a change in use occurs, or as a result of an assignment or licensing.[432]

More equivocal issues will arise where public understanding of the mark's **18–77** significance comes from its manner of past use, and where something occurs which misleads as to source (not of itself a factor specifically listed in the ground of revocation).

Consider a Canadian case: "Wilkinson Sword" for razor blades had been promoted in that country as a mark suggesting British manufacture—though this was not something inherent in the mark itself. Deception justifying removal from the Register was held to arise when the mark was assigned to a manufacturing subsidiary for use on blades manufactured in Canada, the assignment being a tool to prevent parallel importation of the British originals. Under the TMA 1994, this ought to be treated as use of the mark by the proprietor or with his consent. The issue in such circumstances would be whether, on the evidence, the public is liable to be misled.[433]

So far as source is concerned, the provision does not refer directly to it as **18–78** a relevant form of deception, but does not exclude consideration of it. It is possible for a mark to become confusing with another only after its registration. As noted above, assignment or licensing of a mark by one enterprise to another has some potential for causing confusion about source. As we have seen, the Registrar has no role to play in ensuring that either type of transaction is proper. However, there are serious hazards in restructuring relationships without clarifying the trade mark position so that it reflects the actual reputation derived from trading.

Scandecor was a successful art poster business whose international operations were centred in Sweden. Its UK marketing subsidiary registered

---

[431] In *Unilever's Application* [1999] E.T.M.R. 406, "Mr Long" was registered for ices, on the condition that it would be used only on elongated products.

[432] As in the complicated chain of events giving rise to *Scandecor Development v Scandecor Marketing* [2002] F.S.R. 122 HL.

[433] *Wilkinson Sword v Juda* (1967) 59 D.L.R. (2d) 418. There is no presumption or requirement that the established connection with a mark is that of a manufacturer, rather than distributor: *Gromax v Don & Low* [1999] R.P.C. 367.

as UK trade marks both a logo incorporating the word "Scandecor" and the word "Scandecor" alone for posters and similar products. Subsequently these marks were assigned to the Swedish parent company, which later became insolvent and its assets were sold to Scandecor Development AB. This company then sued the UK company (still run by one of the originators of the business) for trade mark infringement (and passing off) by reason of its continued use of the word "Scandecor" as part of its company name. Even though the marks had been used by the international company to indicate a connection with Swedish production, the goodwill in Britain was found, in the light of the whole complicated history, to belong to it. Use of the marks by the registered Swedish owner accordingly amounted to passing off. The registration had therefore to be revoked under s.46(1)(d).[434]

In such circumstances there can be no absolutely compelling resolution to the dispute. A different view of the factual situation might have resulted in victory for the Swedish claimant company.

7. Invalidity of a Registered Mark

18–79 The courts and tribunals which determine revocation proceedings also have power to make declarations of invalidity concerning the original registration.[435] If such a declaration is made, the registration will be invalid from the outset.[436] The grounds are accordingly the absolute or relative grounds of objection to an application, and the case for applying them will only arise where an application has wrongly slipped through the initial net and reached registration: obviously, this possibility becomes more important from October 1, 2007 when the Registry ceases ex officio examination on relative grounds. The time to which they refer is that of registration, not any later date.[437] If it were otherwise, the relative validity of marks could be the subject of continual contest as their comparative reputations on the market varied with use.[438]

434 *"Scandecor"* [2001] F.S.R. 122 HL.

435 The substantive grounds are found in TMA 1994 s.47; CTM Regulation art.7; TMA 1994 ss.51, 52. The application may be made by any person; and in the case of a registration in bad faith, the Registrar may apply to the court for a declaration of invalidity: TMA 1994 s.47(4).

436 TMA 1994 s.47(5), (6); CTM Regulation art.54(2); for the consequences, see above, para.18–68.

437 Note, however, the different tenses used in formulating the absolute and relative grounds of invalidity.

438 The danger of such an investigation must increase under the *Canon* principle, which extends the scope of protection as reputation grows: see below, paras 18–91—18–92.

(1) Absolute grounds

So far as the absolute grounds are concerned, those objections to a sign which is a trade mark, but which lacks distinctiveness under s.3(1)(b), (c) or (d) of the TMA 1994, will not operate if there is countervailing evidence that the mark has become distinctive since registration in relation to the specified goods or services, although "care must be used if it is used for that purpose".[439] This qualification introduces the equivalent balancing process to that which applies during the application stage,[440] but with reference to a different period. **18–80**

(2) Relative grounds: acquiescence

As for the relative grounds, no owner of a senior mark or other right can object to a registration after consenting to it.[441] And even without any positive assent, the right to object may be lost through inaction which falls within the limits of statutory acquiescence.[442] This arises only when the person with the prior right has been aware that the later registered mark has been used in the United Kingdom for a continuous period of five years.[443] There is no acquiescence, however, when the later registration is obtained in bad faith: this might occur when a renowned foreign mark has been improperly "misappropriated".[444] Curiously, once an earlier owner has acquiesced, the later owner cannot "oppose" that person's use of its own mark or unregistered right.[445] But there may be proceedings, it seems, to revoke it for (say) non-use or deceptive use. **18–81**

In relation to a CTM, the same rules apply. If the earlier owner has a CTM, the acquiescence relates to any use of the later mark within the EU of which that person was aware; and to any use within the national territory concerned so far as there are earlier national registrations.[446] The rule

---

439 Per Pumfrey J. in the CA in *ESB* [2003] F.S.R. 44 at para.46.

440 See TMA 1994 s.3(1) proviso; and note the power given by the TM Directive art.3(3). A laudatory word like "Treat" did not acquire distinctiveness by evidence that less than 60% of the public treat it as a trade mark: *British Sugar v James Robertson* [1996] R.P.C. 281 at 306.

441 No particular form is required for this consent, which could in an appropriate case be implied from conduct. A person who maintains that he is licensed under a mark, is estopped from seeking its removal from the register: *"Job" TM* [1993] F.S.R. 118.

442 Five years. The rule applies equally in relation to proceedings attacking the use of the later mark. The statutory definition now given to acquiescence in this context must be taken to replace the less definite concepts of acquiescence and laches in equity. See *Kerly* paras 14–190—14–191.

443 Where the objection is by a Convention country principal against conflicting action by an agent (see above, para.18–03), the period of acquiescence is three years: TMA 1994 s.60(6).

444 See above, para.18–03.

445 TMA 1994 s.48(2).

446 TMA 1994 s.48; CTM Regulation art.53: a person who acquiesces may not secure a declaration of invalidity or enjoin use of the mark—a consequence which follows anyway so long as the later mark remains registered: see below, para.18–110.

concerning acquiescence makes registrations noticeably less secure than they would have been with an incontestability rule, for acquiescence will preclude an objection only in cases of clear awareness on the part of the senior right-holder.

8. Infringement

18–82 The typical infringer uses another's registered mark, or some confusingly similar sign, as a trade mark to indicate the source of goods or services. In a market of competitors, if this conduct is not prevented, not only will the mark-owner lose out but consumers will not be able to trust the marks they see and possibilities of product differentiation will disintegrate. Preventing such direct harm remains the prime object in defining infringement and much is quite rightly heard of the "origin" function of marks, both from policy-makers and from courts.[447]

Modern legislators, however, cannot resist calls to expand the range of rights stemming from registration so that it may give protection to some at least of the more controversial elements of value in marks.

18–83 The TMA 1994, drawn in accordance with the TM Directive and influenced by the CTM Regulation, seeks to stretch the ambit of the registration system beyond the protection of source indications. There are provisions both on the dilution of marks with a reputation and on the use of marks in comparative advertising; and these too have penumbra which cast uncertainty over a wide periphery. Their obscurity stems in part from unresolved tensions between the advocates of greater protection for modern advertising and promotion and the European integrationists (well represented in the EU Commission) who wanted to prevent trade marks from acquiring unnecessary power to impede the movement of products and the provision of services within the Single Market.[448]

A particular complication is that the law of infringement laid down in the TMA 1994 for UK marks does not coincide exactly with that applying to CTMs under the Regulation. This section will first discuss the TMA 1994 provisions, noting in the process the extent to which they derive (via the TM Directive) from EU law provisions and are therefore subject to interpretation ultimately by the European Court of Justice. The different extent of rights in a CTM will then be separately outlined.

One important structural aspect of the law is that there is a direct correlation between the relative grounds of objection which a prior trade mark owner may bring against later applications to register[449] and the scope of infringement. It is not a mirror image, since at the application stage, prior

---

[447] See, e.g. the TM Directive Rec.10: "the function of [the protection afforded by the registered trade mark] is in particular to guarantee the trade mark as an indication of origin".
[448] See above, para.16–02.
[449] For which, see above, paras 18–52 et seq.

unregistered rights have also to be brought into account. But to a very substantial extent there is an overlap and much of the case law is transferable from the one sphere to the other: in large measure what is an objection to validity by a person with a "senior" claim will amount to infringement by a "junior". Reference should therefore be made as appropriate to the cases cited above in relation to the registration process.

(1) Infringement of a UK registered mark

The basic definition of infringement is compounded to two elements: (1) the types of use of a mark which can amount to infringement; and (2) the definition of the wrong vis-à-vis the registered mark. **18–84**

(a) *Types of use amounting to infringement*

The list of activities which may constitute trade mark infringement in UK law is now a more extensive one than ever before. The TMA 1994 includes within infringement a use "otherwise than by means of a graphic representation", and so in principle could include renditions of the trade mark (or a close approximation of it) through sound or smell.[450] **18–85**

The most likely forms of infringement involve use of a sign in some material form. The TMA 1994 lists the actions which "in particular" amount to using a sign[451]: affixing it to goods or packaging[452]; trading in goods[453] or supplying services[454] under it; importing or exporting goods under it; using it on business papers[455] or in advertising.[456] There is a form of contributory infringement affecting anyone who applies a mark to material for labelling, packaging, business paper or advertising, and who knows or

---

[450] TMA 1994 s.103(2). This clarification does not apply expressly to CTMs, since it is not included in the CTM Regulation (nor is it in the TM Directive); it might be read into the definition of those trade mark rights as a necessary counterpart to the granting of marks of this character.

[451] TMA 1994 s.10(4), reproducing the same non-exclusive lists in the TM Directive art.5(3): CTM Regulation art.9(2).

[452] But not making packaging to export for use elsewhere: *Beautimatic v Mitchell Pharmaceuticals* [2000] F.S.R. 267; cf. *Irish Distillers v Cooley Distillers* [2009] E.T.M.R., where the High Court of Ireland enjoined the defendant's use of a label similar to the claimant's registered mark for the label of Jameson Irish Whiskey, even though it was used on products for sale to Russia only; the court considering it significant that Russian consumers would pay more attention to the get-up than to the names (which were clearly different).

[453] i.e. offering or exposing goods for sale, putting them on the market or stocking them for these purposes: TMA 1994 s.10(4)(b). "Infringing goods", "infringing material" and "infringing articles" are defined in equivalent terms in s.17: the first of these includes goods proposed to be imported into the UK, other than those which may be imported by virtue of an enforceable EU right: see below, para.19–02.

[454] i.e. offering or supplying the services: TMA 1994 s.10(4)(b); and see s.17(4): "infringing material".

[455] TMA 1994 s.10(4)(d), covering letters, orders and invoices; even perhaps letters containing the actual mark which are sent by customers to an infringing manufacturer or supplier.

[456] The same applies to the CTM: CTM Regulation art.9(2).

has reason to believe that the use is not authorised by the proprietor or a licensee.[457]

Merely to apply for an internet domain name[458] which consists of, or contains, another's mark, is not close enough to the trading activities in this list of itself to amount to trade mark infringement. But use of the domain name in advertising or a business document, including references on the internet itself, will be acts which are capable of infringing the trade mark registration. Likewise, against "cyber-squatters", the Court of Appeal did not hesitate to hold that their conduct (offering to assign, including possible assignment to a third party) creates the likelihood of infringing activity then occurring.[459] It therefore granted anticipatory relief ordering the transfer of the domain names to the various targeted enterprises.[460] The reasons offered for this aspect of the decision are far from persuasive; but the result resembles that reached in courts across the world.[461]

(b) *The wrong to the registered mark*

18–86 The TMA 1994 defines three types of infringement.[462] Through this typology runs a set of distinctions relating to the identity or similarity of marks and of goods or services, which for the most part parallels the relative grounds of opposition and invalidity[463]:

Type 1: It is infringement to use, in the course of trade, a sign identical to the trade mark in suit for identical goods or services to those within the specification.[464] Under this head, unlike the next, it is not necessary to show any likelihood of confusion. For a claimant, accordingly, this is the most straightforward case, though there can easily be questions about whether the marks are identical[465] and whether the goods or services for which the defendant is using the mark fall within

---

457 TMA 1994 s.10(5).

458 Likewise for a company name registration.

459 In *Global Projects Management v Citigroup* [2006] F.S.R. 721, in a trademark threats action brought by the registrant of the *citigroup.co.uk* domain name, Park J. granted summary judgment on Citigroup's counterclaim for passing off and trade mark infringement under s.10(3), even though the registrant had no history of "cyber-squatting" but at the time of registration must have known of the announced merger of Citibank and Travelers to be known as Citigroup.

460 *British Telecom v One in a Million* [1999] F.S.R. 1 CA (and see above, para.17–27).

461 Bettinger (1997) 28 I.I.C. 508.

462 In addition, the special protection accorded a Convention principal against unjustified acts of a British agent (for which see para.18–03, above) can arise in relation to a mark already registered.

463 For which, see above, paras 18–52 et seq.

464 TMA 1994 s.10(1).

465 See the cases cited above, at para.18–53. In *Reed Executive v Reed Business Information* [2004] R.P.C. 767 Jacob L.J. emphasised that "an addition in the defendant's sign to a registered mark may take the case outside one of identity": at para.51.

those specified in the registration.[466] For the latter it is necessary to consider the "core" content of the specification:

A company supplying electronic components and software registered the mark "Avnet" for advertising and promotional services. Aviators Network, the provider of an internet service comprising a discussion forum for aviation and within it a sector where others could advertise products and services, did not infringe the first mark by using and having others use the domain name, *avnet.co.uk*.[467]

Because Type 1 exempts a claimant from the need to prove likelihood of confusion, there is good reason to require that the twin identities are strictly proved[468]: thus words ought to be the same both in spelling and sound.[469]

Type 2: Where there is only similarity rather than identity between goods or services, and/or similarity between the defendant's sign and the plaintiff's mark, then the plaintiff must prove that "there exists a likelihood of confusion on the part of the public, which includes likelihood of association with the trade mark".[470]

Type 3: Over and above this, where a trade mark has a "reputation" in the United Kingdom, it is infringement to use an identical or similar sign, where "the use of the sign, being without due cause, takes unfair advantage of, or is detrimental to, the distinctive character or the repute" of the mark.[471]

At least four patches of obscurity (upon each of which the ECJ has shone what there passes for light) lie within these definitions. They concern: (1) the defendant's use of a "sign"; (2) similarity of goods or services; (3) association as a form of confusion; and (4) the extended protection of marks with a reputation.

(i) **The defendant's use of a "sign".** All three types of infringement require that the defendant use "in the course of trade a sign". It is no longer an **18–87**

[466] In *British Sugar* [1996] R.P.C. 281, Jacob J. refused to find a spread to be a "dessert sauce or syrup" merely because it was occasionally used as such.

[467] *Avnet v Isoact* [1998] F.S.R. 16; cf. *British Sugar v Robertson* [1996] R.P.C. 281 at 293, where (surprisingly and probably incorrectly) regard was given only to "Treat" in the phrase "Robertson's Toffee Treat", leading to a wide finding of identity. Also, *Reed Executive v Reed Business Information* [2004] R.P.C. 767 CA at para.45; obiter, a specification's meaning cannot change its meaning over time (at para.47).

[468] "[O]nly a strict interpretation appears to be consistent with the scheme, history and context of [Arts 4(1)(a) TM Directive on registrability and 5(1)(a) on infringement]"; per Jacobs A.G. in *LTJ Diffusion v Sadas* [2003] F.S.R. 1, at para.AGO32; followed by the Court of Justice [2003] E.T.M.R. 1005 at para.50.

[469] *Reed Executive v Reed Business Information* [2004] R.P.C. 767 CA; cf. *Canon KK v MGM* [1999] E.T.M.R. 1 ECJ, where the marks were "Canon" and "Cannon".

[470] TMA 1994 s.10(2), implementing the TM Directive art.5(1); see further below, para.18–90.

[471] TMA 1994 s.10(3), as permitted by the TM Directive art.5(2); see further below, para.18–99.

explicit requirement that this use be "as a trade mark", although it appears from the *Arsenal* judgment and others of the ECJ[472] that it is only use that affects or might affect the functions of the registered mark that will be enjoined. After an exhaustive review of the authorities, Geoffrey Hobbs QC (sitting as a Deputy High Court judge) summarised the position in *Electrocoin Automatics v Coinworld*[473]:

> "the rights conferred by registration of a trade mark are not engaged (and therefore not infringed) by use of a sign 'other than for the purposes of distinguishing goods and services'. The expression 'distinguishing goods or services' refers to the function which a sign must be able to perform in order to satisfy the general requirement for registration in Article 2 [of the TM Directive/s.1(1) and s.3(1)(a) TMA 1994]."

It is noteworthy that the Court of Justice's judgment in the *Adam Opel* case[474] leaves it once again to the national court to decide whether on the facts the defendant's use on replicas affects the functions of the Opel logo registered for toys by the car company. As the reference from the German court had explained that the average German consumer of the products in the toy industry expected scale models to be realistic and that such a consumer would understand that the Opel logo on Autec's products indicated that it was a miniature replica of an Opel car,[475] the Court of Justice considered that the referring court would have to conclude that the use did not affect the essential function of the trade mark registered for toys.[476] As regards infringement under art.5(2) of the TM Directive (the equivalent of s.10(3) TMA 1994), again the court said it is up to the national court to assess if there has been unfair advantage taken or detriment caused, without giving any advice as to the factors to take into account in making that assessment or commenting at all on whether the factual position as regards consumers' perceptions should be relevant under this provision also.[477] Once more the court refused to grasp the nettle, and say unequivocally (at least in relation to Types 1 and 2) that trade mark infringement requires use by the defendant of its sign as a trade mark.

---

472 [2003] E.T.M.R. 227 at para.51; *Anheuser-Busch v Budéjovicky Budvar* [2005] E.T.M.R. 286 ECJ at paras 59–64.

473 *Electrocoin Automatics v Coinworld* [2005] F.S.R. 79 at para.85, having referred inter alia to *Robelco v Robeco* [2003] E.T.M.R. 671 ECJ, where the Court of Justice observed that protection of a trade mark against uses of a sign other than for the purposes of distinguishing goods or services, on the facts as a corporate name, was not dealt with by the TM Directive at paras 30–35.

474 *Adam Opel v Autec* [2007] E.T.M.R. 500 ECJ.

475 This can be compared to the Court of Appeal in the *Arsenal* case [2003] R.P.C. 696, whose "readiness to generalize from rather thin evidence [on consumers' perceptions] is apparent": Cornish, *Intellectual Property: Omnipresent, Distracting, Irrelevant?* (2004) at p.96.

476 *Adam Opel v Autec* [2007] E.T.M.R. 500 at paras 23 and 24.

477 *Adam Opel v Autec* [2007] E.T.M.R. 500 ECJ at paras 35–37.

Signs may well be used in trade for descriptive purposes or for identification not concerned with origin and to a large extent this is permitted by explicit exception, treated below.[478] For instance, use of the name of the pop group, "Wet, Wet, Wet", registered as a mark, in a book-title would fall within the exception for indications of the actual character of the book itself (as opposed to its trade origin).[479] On the other hand, the third question in the *Adam Opel* case, to which the Court of Justice did give a clear answer, was whether the use could benefit from the defence (or, more properly, limitation) contained in art.6(1)(b) of the TM Directive (s.11(2)(b) TMA 1994) for indications concerning characteristics of products. The Court of Justice considered it could not: "the Opel logo does not in any way indicate the kind, quality or other characteristics of the scale models" and "[it] is merely an element in the faithful reproduction of the original vehicles."[480]

In addition, however, courts have confined infringement to trade mark uses of the mark because this is taken to be inherent in the notion of using a sign in the course of trade. There are indications of this tendency set out below. **18–88**

(1) In the "*Philishave*" shape-mark case, the defendant, Remington, argued (inter alia) that, when they incorporated a similar shaving-head in their product, their use was functional and would not be understood as a trade mark. The point did not need to be decided and Jacob J. left it for consideration on a subsequent occasion.[481]

(2) The Football Association sought to prevent a well-known sweet manufacturer from putting cards in the products which showed England team players in shirts which bore the Association's registered logo. The court refused to find that the sweets were in any meaningful way offered for sale under that sign; so there was no "use in relation to goods".[482]

(3) The French Cour de Cassation refused to find that the slogan "Visa pour le Muscle", when used on printed material, infringed the well-

[478] TMA 1994 s.11(2); below, at para.18–111.

[479] *Bravado Merchandising v Mainstream Publishing* [1996] F.S.R. 208; TMA s.11(2).

[480] *Adam Opel v Autec* [2007] E.T.M.R. 500 ECJ at paras 40–44.

[481] *Philips Electronics v Remington* [1998] R.P.C. 283 at 312 (above, para.18–43); cf. the judge's earlier view that there was no requirement for use as a trade mark: *British Sugar v Robertson* [1996] R.P.C. 281 at 292–293, criticising the concession to the contrary in *Bravado Merchandising* [1996] F.S.R. 208. In *Nation Fitting v Oystertec* [2006] F.S.R. 740, the Singapore High Court concluded in a case involving alleged infringement of a shape mark that there must be use as a trade mark: "such a requirement will also ensure that the legal protection of the rights of registered trade mark holders is so well-justified that it cannot be said that such holders are exploiting what might otherwise be labelled, in effect, as unnecessary or excessive monopoly rights": at para.62.

[482] *Trebor Bassett v Football Association* [1997] F.S.R. 211.

known credit card mark. It held that "Visa" was here used in the sense of a passport.[483]

(4) In dealing with an allegation that one bank's German company name, "Europabank", infringed another bank's registration of that word as a mark for its products and services, the Benelux Trade Mark Court advised that the first bank would infringe the mark only if it used the mark to distinguish the services which it offered. This it would not do merely by giving its business name.[484]

(5) Where the registered marks "Spirit Sun" and "Context Cut" were used by the alleged infringer in the course of oral sales negotiations to refer to a particular cut of gemstone, the ECJ (on a reference from a German court) found that such use did not fall within the concept of use required for a finding of infringement under art.5(1) of the Directive.[485]

(6) The mark "Euro 2000" was registered in Germany for footballs by the governing body of European football, UEFA. When another party wished to use "Euro 2000" on its footballs, it applied for a declaration of non-infringement. The German Supreme Court held that if the relevant public saw the use of Euro 2000 as descriptive or as "a decorative advertising supplement without a reference to a particular enterprise", there would be no infringement as there is no trade mark use.[486]

In these cases, the courts display a natural reluctance to prevent one trader from employing a word or other sign which corresponds to another's mark in circumstances where potential damage and undue misappropriation appear equally slight. They display a firm sense that marks are to be protected for their value as indications of origin.

In an attempt to reconcile the different views in this area, in *L'Oréal v eBay*[487] Arnold J. analysed the judgments of the ECJ, which he said establish that the proprietor of a mark can succeed in a claim under art.5(1)(a) (s.10(1)) only:

[483] *Visa International v Editions Liberna* [1998] E.T.M.R. 380; cf. *CA Sheimer Sdn Bhd's TM Application* [2000] R.P.C. 484, Appointed Person (G. Hobbs QC) where an application to register "Visa" for condoms was refused under s.5(3) on the basis of an opposition by the owners of the well-known "Visa" mark.

[484] *Europabank v Banque pour l'Europe* [1997] E.T.M.R. 143: the relevant provision in the Uniform Benelux Trade Mark Act s.13A; cf. Tanderil [1985] B.I.E. 50.

[485] *Hölterhoff v Freiesleben* [2002] E.C.R. I-4187 at para.16; surely the case is properly analysed as one of comparative advertising; cf. the discussion by Arnold J. in *L'Oréal v eBay* [2009] R.P.C. 21 at paras 283–306, where the judge suggests that, although he would have decided that the use in *Hölterhoff* fell within art.5(1)(a) (s.10(1)), "it would seem clear that the defendant would have had a defence under Art.6(1)(b)"(s.11(2)(b)).

[486] [2006] E.T.M.R. 272 at para.20.

[487] *L'Oréal v eBay* [2009] R.P.C. 21.

> "if six conditions are satisfied: (i) there must be use of a sign by a third party; (ii) the use must be in the course of trade; (iii) it must be without the consent of the proprietor of the trade mark; (iv) it must be of a sign which is identical to the trade mark; (v) it must be in relation to goods or services which are identical to those for which the trade mark is registered; and (vi) it must affect or be liable to affect the functions of the trade mark; in particular its essential function of guaranteeing to consumers the origin of the goods or services".[488]

He concluded that:

> "some of the present difficulty and confusion in European trade mark law would be dispelled if it were recognised that the sixth condition adds nothing to the fifth condition. Once it is shown that the first five conditions are satisfied, then the case falls within Art.5(1)(a) [s.10(1)]. The question then is whether the use in question is saved from infringement by Art.6 [s.11] or Art.7 [s.12]".[489]

However, it is clear from the subsequent judgment of the ECJ in *Google France and Google*[490] that the sixth condition remains an essential component in deciding whether a defendant's activity falls within art.5(1)(a) (s.10(1) TMA).

Where (in relation to Type 3) the mark has a reputation, the consequent liability could encompass a non-trade mark use.[491] Giving a mark a generic description in a dictionary would be detrimental to distinctive character and might possibly be regarded both as a use in trade (as distinct from a "trade mark use") and "being without due cause" in that its character as a mark was ignored. This, however, is to scrape for some equivalent to the explicit "dictionary" protection given to Community marks but omitted from the TM Directive.[492] **18–89**

[488] *L'Oréal* [2009] R.P.C. 21 at para.283.

[489] *L'Oréal* [2009] R.P.C. 21 at para.306.

[490] [2010] E.T.M.R. 30 at paras 76–98.

[491] In *Tesco Stores v Elogicom* [2006] E.T.M.R. 1270, the infringing use under s.10(3) (as well as s.10(2) although the reasoning on this is very questionable) was use as a domain name, e.g. *tescodvd.co.uk*, that was redirected (without the user's knowledge) to a genuine Tesco website, "with the object of capturing part of the traffic of persons browsing the internet and entering Tesco related names in the address bars on their computers in the hope of being taken to Tesco websites" (which in fact they were), at para.34, the judge finding that this was "without due cause" and took "unfair advantage" and that s.10(6) did not apply as it was not an honest practice: at para.38.

[492] CTM Regulation art.10. In *Adidas v Fitnessworld* [2004] E.T.M.R.129 ECJ, it was found that "where ... the relevant section of the public views the sign purely as an embellishment, it does not necessarily establish any link with a registered mark", such that there can be no infringement: at para.40; see the decision of the Danish High Court in *Adidas Intl v FDB* [2006] E.T.M.R. 1220, finding that the four stripes on the defendant's clothing would be seen by customers as an embellishment, at para.72, and noting that "consumers generally will know that Adidas' trade mark consists of exactly three and not any other number of stripes": at para.71.

18–90 (ii) **Similarity of goods or services.** In the TMA 1994, Type 2 infringement extends beyond the goods and services for which the trade mark is registered to those which are "similar", provided also that the public are likely to be confused.[493] Six factors may need to be considered:

(1) the respective uses of the respective goods or services;
(2) the respective users of the respective goods or services;
(3) the physical nature of the goods or acts of service;
(4) the respective trade channels through which the goods or services reach the market;
(5) whether in self-service stores they are found together or apart;
(6) the extent to which the respective goods or services are competitive (for instance, in the eyes of market research companies).[494]

18–91 Applying these criteria, in *British Sugar v Robertson*, Jacob J. found that spreads for bread were not goods similar to dessert sauces and syrups (ice-cream toppings and the like).[495] This restrictive interpretation can now be seen to be incorrect and an assessment of similarity must be made taking into account both the goods or services in question and the strength of the registered mark: a "global appreciation".

Equivalent, and misplaced, caution was shown in resolving a separate problem. Jacob J. held that the question whether goods or services were "similar" was a distinct issue, which had to be settled before turning to the question whether the two marks were confusingly similar. This makes the question of similarity an objective issue, in the sense that no account is taken of the existing reputation of either mark. Somewhat surprisingly, however, in *Canon*,[496] the ECJ held that this too is the wrong approach. In Germany, MGM was seeking to register "Cannon" for films and related services but faced the earlier registration of "Canon" for cameras and various television devices. Responding to a direct question on the legal issue, the court held that:

[493] Jacob J., *British Sugar v James Robertson* [1996] R.P.C. 281 at 294, 295.

[494] Listed by Jacob J. in *British Sugar* [1996] R.P.C. 281 at 296, 297; *Canon* [1999] R.P.C. 117 ECJ at para.17 and following; *Cobra Beer's Application* [2000] E.T.M.R. 638 OHIM BA.

[495] *British Sugar v Robertson* [1996] R.P.C. 281 at 296, 297. As the judge separately found, the registration was specifically for "dessert sauces and syrups in Class 30", yet spreads for bread were in Class 29. If the goods were nonetheless similar, the limitation in the registration would be ineffective, even if it had for any reason been required by the Registry as a condition of registration. This aspect of the decision may lead to it being distinguished as a special case yet more than it has been already. There is no general requirement that in order to be similar the goods or services be in the same class: *Gromax v Don & Low* [1999] R.P.C. 367.

[496] *Canon* [1999] E.T.M.R. 1. In refusing to find similarity, the lower courts in Germany had shown a caution equivalent to that in the English decisions.

> "marks with a highly distinctive character, either *per se* or because of the reputation they possess on the market, enjoy broader protection than marks with a less distinctive character" (at para.132),

although

> "even where a mark is identical to another with a highly distinctive character, it is still necessary to adduce evidence of similarity between the goods and services covered" (at para.133).

Once a mark has been registered, little is left of the traditional common law distinction between the core protection of infringement which was relatively straightforward to prove and a surrounding periphery of passing off which, when the mark was not naturally distinctive, required a strong case to be made out. The two now meld into one and an effect is achieved which has gone a long way to harmonising the different European approaches to the scope of trade mark protection. **18–92**

For that reason, the ECJ has been firm in its opinion that the protection for registered marks which have been used extends to a wider range of goods and services than marks which have not (and thus have no reputation). However, one consequence of this has been to bring oppositions to applications for registration (and indeed claims of invalidity if the mark is already registered) very close to passing-off actions, not just where the senior mark is unregistered, but equally where it is registered for different, but somewhat related, goods. This has imposed considerable burdens on registries and in the United Kingdom the much-heralded abandonment of examination on relative grounds from October 2007 was partly to ease the Trade Marks Registry's burden.

So far as infringement is concerned, the following may occur: a senior mark is not yet very well-known when a junior mark is allowed on the register for dissimilar goods. The senior mark becomes popular: the junior mark comes to be for similar goods, and therefore in principle becomes a Type 2 infringement. So long as the junior mark remains registered, however, UK law provides a defence to an action for infringement of the registration[497] and the senior owner would after all be obliged to sue for passing off. The registration itself would not be open to attack, since no relative ground of objection existed when it was made, and subsequent likelihood of confusion could only in the rarest cases suffice for revocation.[498] **18–93**

(iii) **Likely confusion including association.** In infringement actions of the first two Types the essential comparison is between the claimant's mark as registered and the defendant's actual practice. It is one object of the registration system to provide advance security by foreshortening investigations (by survey, trade or consumer evidence) into actual comparisons as to how **18–94**

[497] TMA 1994 s.11(1). See below, para.18–110.

[498] TMA 1994 s.46(1)(d); above, para.18–76.

the claimant's and defendant's goods or services are marketed. Of course, as in the past, courts consider the features of the markets for the goods or services in question,[499] and, as appropriate, take account of confusion arising in both written and oral usage; consumers' knowledge about origin; the nature of consumers affected, and so on.

On the other hand, the *BP Amoco v Kelly* decision of the Court of Appeal in Northern Ireland[500] suggests that one can now also take into account so-called "initial interest" confusion[501]: surprisingly, it was found sufficient that a motorist travelling at speed along a road may see the defendant's green TOP petrol station from a distance and think it was a BP station before having the opportunity of reading the TOP logo, even though it was accepted that a customer who was confused at the time of buying petrol would have to be "fairly stupid or fairly uncaring".[502] Thus, whereas mere confusion does not suffice for a finding of passing off (as the court noted at para.48), apparently it may (even if fleeting) for trade mark infringement.

What is clear however is that the considerations which arise on a comparison of marks at the application stage are in general terms equally applicable to infringement.[503] Also, it appears from the *Arsenal* case,[504] and others since,[505] that it remains necessary to show that the defendant's use of the mark is "as a trade mark", for the purpose of distinguishing goods or services.[506] Once that is done, in the words of a judgment under the old law, "no amount of added matter intended to show the true origin of the goods"[507] can affect the question whether there is infringement (while it

[499] See *"Picasso/Picaro"* [2006] E.T.M.R. 349, ECJ: "Where it is established in fact that the objective characteristics of a given product mean that the average consumer purchases it only after a particularly careful examination, it is important in law to take into account that such a fact may reduce the likelihood of confusion between marks relating to such goods at the crucial moment when the choice between those goods and marks is made."

[500] *BP Amoco v Kelly* [2002] F.S.R. 87 at para.44.

[501] In *L'Oréal v Bellure* [2007] E.T.M.R. 1, Lewison J. was very dismissive of claimant counsel's written submission alleging "initial interest confusion", noting "there was not a shred of evidence to support it": at para.191.

[502] *BP Amoco* [2002] F.S.R. 87 at para.48.

[503] *Origins Natural Resources v Origin Clothing* [1995] F.S.R. 280; *Neutrogena v Golden* [1996] R.P.C. 473 CA; see above, para.18–53. For survey evidence in different jurisdictions, see Knaak (1990) 21 I.I.C. 372.

[504] *Arsenal* [2003] R.P.C. 144. See also *R. v Johnstone* [2003] F.S.R. 748, where Lord Walker expresses the view that the "likely effect [of the *Arsenal* case] is that the province of trade mark use has annexed a significant part of the no man's land in which elements of distinctiveness and descriptiveness overlap": at para.87.

[505] See the review of authorities in *Electrocoin Automatics v Coinworld* [2005] F.S.R. 79.

[506] In *Céline* [2007] E.T.M.R. 80 ECJ, Sharpston A.G. was of the opinion that "the mere adoption of a company or trade name similar or identical to a registered mark does not constitute use" falling within art.5(1) of the TM Directive (ss.10(1) and (2) of the TMA 1994): at para.35 of the Opinion.

[507] Greene M.R. *Saville Perfumery v June Perfect* (1941) 58 R.P.C. 147 at 162 CA; put slightly differently but to the same effect by Kitchin J. in *Julius Sämaan v Tetrosyl* [2006] 849 at para.52: "The court must consider the likelihood of confusion arising from the use by the defendant of the offending sign, discounting added matter or circumstances. If the sign and the mark are confusingly similar then the defendant cannot escape by showing that by something outside the actual mark itself he has distinguished his goods from those of the proprietor."

would, of course, be relevant to passing off: in *Julius Sämaan v Tetrosyl* trade mark infringement was found but not passing off because the defendant's product was sold in a box and generally from a counter display unit away from other similar products including the claimant's[508]).

This complements the provision (in s.10(2) of the TMA 1994) that "a likelihood of confusion on the part of the public ... *includes* the likelihood of association with the trade mark". This is a factor that has also to be taken into account in considering the relative grounds for refusal, and the discussion here is equally relevant in that context.[509] The concept has been said to derive from Benelux trade mark law as it stood before implementation of the Directive.[510]

However, the Benelux Act referred only to proving similarity (it did not require likelihood of confusion); and the Benelux Court of Justice had ruled that confusion and association, which in Benelux law are separate concepts, were each sufficient to give rise to liability.[511]

In *Sabel v Puma*,[512] the ECJ refused to interpret the Type 2 form of conflict between mark and sign in the Regulation and Directive so as to give "association" a distinct conceptual standing. On the contrary "association" was treated as a sub-set of "confusion". This was considered the correct approach both because of the legislative language and because the origin function of trade marks remains the primary purpose of legal protection and it deserves to be tested by the criterion of likelihood of confusion. **18–95**

Accordingly the senior mark, a drawing of a springing puma, did not give rise to an objection on relative grounds to registration of a junior mark, comprising a springing cheetah with the word "Sabel". No danger of confusion to the relevant public could be found, and it was not enough to find that that public might assume an "association" between the two.

---

[508] *Julius Sämaan v Tetrosyl* [2006] F.S.R. 849 at paras 116–118 on passing off and paras 47–76 on trade mark infringement, ignoring the added matter.

[509] See above, para.18–52.

[510] An unpublished (but well-known) EC Council and Commission Minute records cryptically that " ... 'likelihood of association' is a concept which in particular has been developed by Benelux case law". In *Wagamama v City Centre Restaurants* [1995] F.S.R. 713, Laddie J. refused to consider the Minute because of its non-public nature. Even if it could be given account in English proceedings, it does not resolve how Benelux understandings should be applied to a quite different statutory formulation, however "strange" that difference may appear to Benelux lawyers: cf. Gielen and Strowel [1995] Mitt. d. Patentanwälte 198. In truth the Minute echoed the considerable reluctance among other Member States to adopt the Benelux approach, as the Benelux negotiators recorded: Fürstner and Geuze, ECTA Newsletter, March 1989, 215, referred to in *Wagamama*.

[511] *Union/Union Soleure* [1984] Ned Jur. 72; Würtenberger [2002] E.I.P.R. 20.

[512] *Sabel v Puma* [1998] R.P.C. 199; Davies and Annand (1998) 103 T.W. 18; Gielen [1998] E.I.P.R. 109; Gevers et al. (1998) 106 T.W. 18; Norman [1998] E.I.P.R. 310; Torremans [1998] I.P.R. 295. The issue was first confronted, somewhat dramatically, in *Wagamama v City Centre Restaurants* [1995] F.S.R. 713, where Laddie J. refused to find infringement of the mark "Wagamama" for restaurants by "Rajamama" on any separate ground of "association", though he did find sufficient likelihood of confusion for Type 2. For polarised reactions, see Kamperman Sanders [1996] E.I.P.R. 3, 521; Prescott [1996] E.I.P.R. 317; [1997] E.I.P.R. 99.

The court issued significant guidance on the application of Type 2, both to registration and to infringement. Attention must be directed to "the perception of marks in the mind of the average consumer of the type of goods or services in question". There has to be a "global appreciation of the likelihood of confusion. The average consumer normally perceives a mark as a whole and does not analyse its various details."[513] The court then continued:

> "In that perspective, the more distinctive the earlier mark, the greater will be the likelihood of confusion. It is therefore not impossible that the conceptual similarity resulting from the fact that two marks use images with analogous semantic content may give rise to a likelihood of confusion where the earlier mark has a particularly distinctive character, either *per se* or because of the reputation it enjoys with the public."[514]

However, whether a mark has a strong distinctive character cannot be decided merely on the basis of generalised percentages of recognition of the mark by the relevant public[515]:

(1) Where the registered mark "Freestyle" was registered (after amendment by revocation) for "package holidays", the use by the defendant of the signs "Freestyle Cruising" and "NCL Freestyle Cruising" for cruises was found to be use of a sign identical to the registered mark but the registered mark was considered evocative and not "highly distinctive" (in the sense outlined above). Notwithstanding this, in the light of the facts that both package holidays and cruises are marketed through travel agents, that they are sometimes in the same brochure and that brochures for both are often displayed on the same shelves, it was held there existed a risk that the average consumer "with imperfect recollection of the normal and fair use by the proprietor of 'Freestyle', would conclude that [the defendant's] cruises came from the same company or from an economically linked company".[516]

(2) The registered mark "Viagra" for pharmaceuticals was found to be "extremely well-known" and "a household word". The defendant's proposed use of the sign "Viagrene" on a drink marketed as an aphrodisiac, although superficially a different product to a drug, fell

[513] In *Bud and Budweiser Budbräu TMs* [2003] R.P.C. 477 CA, Lord Walker stated "... 'central message' [of a mark] may not be too bad a paraphrase, so long as it is understood as comprehending the essential 'visual, aural and conceptual' qualities which combine to give a mark distinctive character": at para.47.

[514] *Sabel* [1998] R.P.C. 199 ECJ at 224. For more of the same on the "global appreciation" test, see *Canon* [1999] R.P.C. 117; *Lloyd Schuhfabrik* [2000] F.S.R. 77; and *Marca Mode v Adidas* [2000] E.T.M.R. 723.

[515] *Windsurfing Chiemsee* [1995] E.T.M.R. 585 ECJ at para.52

[516] *Thomson Holidays v Norwegian Cruise Line* [2003] R.P.C. 586 per Aldous L.J. at paras 62–64.

within s.10(2) as use of a similar mark on similar goods (taking all factors into account, the court considered both were designed to appeal to those suffering from impotence).[517]

(3) Although prior to *Sabel*, the registered mark "Wagamama" was infringed under s.10(2) by use of the sign "Rajamama" for identical services. It was held to be "significant that the marks are being used in relation to comparatively inexpensive restaurant services. This is an area where imperfect recollection is likely to play an important role. Furthermore the fact that the [claimant's] mark is quite meaningless means that imperfect recollection is more likely."[518]

(4) Where a member of the Asprey family set up his own business under the trading name "William R Asprey" selling guns and other goods, the owner of the registered mark "Asprey" for, amongst other goods, firearms and ammunition sued for trade mark infringement (and passing off). Summary judgment was given under s.10(1), the trial judge disregarding the "William R" and finding the sign identical to the registered mark, but the Court of Appeal considered this could not stand in view of the then-pending reference to the ECJ in *LTJ Diffusion v Sadas*.[519] On the other hand, the appeal was dismissed against the finding of infringement under s.10(2): the two businesses were located in the same area, they were competing in a similar field of commerce, they used similar methods to promote their products and the defendant used his connection with the Asprey family (from whom the claimant had acquired the business including the registered mark) in his publicity. These factors were found to support both a finding of passing off and of trade mark infringement.[520]

(5) In the United Kingdom, "Ty.phoo" is a renowned mark for tea and was also registered for kitchenware (in respect of which it was much less known). Where the sign "Typhoon" was used for kitchen utensils, it was found that there was no "likelihood of confusion" under s.10(2). Wrongly (in the light of *Canon*), the judge considered the question of whether or not the goods were similar, which he found was the case, to be an issue separate to whether there was a likelihood of confusion.[521]

Just as *Sabel v Puma* and the subsequent ECJ cases require, all these decisions (except, strictly, the last that went wrong on similarity of goods, although the conclusion was correct) looked at the circumstances overall in **18–96**

[517] *Pfizer v Eurofood Link* [2001] F.S.R. 3 at para.58; also finding infringement of the corresponding CTM under art.9(1)(b) CTM Regulation.
[518] per Laddie J. in *Wagamama v City Centre Restaurants* [1995] F.S.R. 713 at 733.
[519] A correct finding in view of the subsequent judgment of the Court of Justice [2003] F.S.R. 609 ECJ.
[520] *Asprey & Garrard v WRA (Guns)* [2002] F.S.R. 487 CA.
[521] *Premier Brands v Typhoon Europe* [2000] F.S.R. 767.

order to determine whether there was, in a genuine and properly substantiated sense,[522] some likelihood of confusion. It was not enough that an average consumer might be attracted to choose goods or services under the second mark because some loose, non-confusing, association might be made to the first. An attempt to re-kindle the former Benelux doctrine to this effect was quashed firmly by the ECJ in *Marca Mode v Adidas*.[523]

However, it has to be acknowledged that much of the difficulty about drawing this distinction between confusion and association stems from a lack of agreement over what is meant in the first place by "confusion" (and the English law view is certainly a broad one). There may remain nuanced differences about the meaning of "confusion", but they are far fewer than those surrounding "association". The latter word is a passport to clever speculation about the possible psychological impact of marking or get-up on this or that social group. Much was made in this context of actions by the owners of the mark, "Monopoly" (for the property board-game) against "Anti-Monopoly"—an anti-capitalistic competing game. In the Dutch proceedings on the subject, the court actually found on the evidence that a significant portion of the public would be confused between the two.[524] It has, however, since been claimed of that decision that consumers could not confuse the two because of their obverse qualities as games; liability should therefore be regarded as arising from a supposed likelihood of association which was distinct from confusion. But why? Anyone with intelligence enough to work out the difference between the games would surely dissociate, not associate; indeed the success of the competing product would surely depend on purchasers realising that it was not the "Monopoly" game.

A good instance of the danger inherent in allowing "association" to float free of "confusion" is provided by the Dutch action alleging infringement of "Isoglass" by "Isover" for building insulation. A survey demonstrated that some 15 per cent of consumers "associated" the two; but then over half that number also associated "Isoglass" and "Rockwool"![525]

18–97 Courts everywhere should bear in mind the need, in developing the European jurisprudence, to adopt a considered approach to protection and intervene only where the claimant faces substantial, rather than fancied, injury.[526] It is important to remember that for every successful claimant there is at least one restrained defendant and that there is a fine line between protecting legitimate interests and enabling unfair competition.

18–98 Because association is stated to be one form of likely confusion, it cannot arise in most cases of comparative advertising. The point of such advertisements is to set the protected products or services apart from those of the competitor making the comparison, in order that the advantages of the

[522] *Marca Mode v Adidas* [2000] E.T.M.R. 723 ECJ at 731–732.
[523] *Marca Mode v Adidas* [2000] E.T.M.R. 723.
[524] *Edor v General Mills Fun* [1978] Ned. Jur. 83.
[525] [1989] Ned. Jur. 836. Given such evidence, the court could scarcely find infringement.
[526] An objective clearly sought in early drafts of the CTM Regulation: see above, para.16–16.

latter can be demonstrated. Once the comparison is made plain,[527] there should be no scope for confusion (as in the "Anti-Monopoly" case cited above?), even though, at least in sycophantic advertising, there is association, rather than dissociation, between the things compared. However, the absolute nature of Type 1 infringement means that comparative advertisements may need to avail themselves of a defence in order to avoid liability.[528]

(iv) **Use of mark identical or similar to a registered mark with a reputation.** The third Type of infringement, where there is use by the defendant of the identical or a similar mark, can arise where: **18–99**

(1) the claimant has a registered mark with a "reputation"; and
(2) the use by the defendant is without due cause,[529] and takes unfair advantage of or is detrimental to, the distinctive character or repute of the mark.

This derives from the CTM Regulation.[530] The alternatives—unfair advantage or detriment, distinctive character or repute—give it a broad scope, since they must be presumed not to be co-terminous. The provision gives protection against "dilution", "tarnishment" and "free-riding" by the use of an established mark on the same, similar or different goods by persons not connected with the proprietor, or, in the words of Geoffrey Hobbs, QC in *Electrocoin*, "cross-pollination".[531]

It draws particular support from art.13A of the Benelux Trade Mark Law, but is also sustained by the manner in which countries such as Germany and France give far-reaching protection against this type of dilution of famous trade marks under their unfair competition laws.[532] Thus under Benelux trade mark law, Colgate could not call a liquid soap product, "Klarein", in view of the famous Dutch gin, "Claeryn"[533]; in Germany it was unfair competition to advertise "IBM Aptiva" computers using the strapline "Get Champagne, Pay for Sparkling Wine"[534] and in France for Yves St. Laurent to use "Champagne" for scent.[535]

---

[527] An initial question is always whether the "comparison" is actually being used to deceive consumers into thinking that they are getting the products compared, rather than the defendant's products.

[528] For which see below, paras 18–103—18–106.

[529] In *Enterprise Rent-A-Car v Eurodrive CarRental* [2005] E.T.M.R. 1379 Laddie J. commented that the meaning of "due cause" would likely need to be interpreted by the ECJ at some point.

[530] CTM Regulation art.9(1)(c); it is permitted in national legislation by the TM Directive, art.5(2). All Member States have taken advantage of the Directive's permission.

[531] *Electrocoin* [2005] F.S.R. 79 at para.100.

[532] In Benelux law unfair competition rights are severely limited in the field of trade marks: see above, para.18–01.

[533] (1976) 7 I.I.C. 420. The two marks were pronounced the same.

[534] (2002) 33 I.I.C. 991 German Supreme Court.

[535] [1994] E.I.P.R. D–74.

The incorporation of such liability within the EU regime makes some sense for Member States where unfair competition laws are substantially precluded from the sphere of trade marks. Whether it was wise to extend national trade mark law in the same way in countries where there is already coverage under these general principles is less clear, as can be seen from the Court of Justice's struggle to arrive at a coherent interpretation.[536] What remains the case is that "dilution"[537] or "tarnishment" should be prevented only in cases where there really is sufficient cause for interfering with the freedom of all traders to promote their goods and services as best they can.

18–100 There have long been those who consider trade mark dilution an insidious and dangerous threat to advertising reputation. In America individual states enacted special statutes to bring diluters to heel.[538] These laws seem not to have made much headway, because they are met with a general scepticism: "Champagne" will survive being applied to scent because the public will appreciate what is going on and will, if anything, think the more and the better of the wine. In 1996, a Federal Trademark Dilution Statute introduced measures against the tarnishment and blurring of trade marks,[539] which proved valuable in dealing with one special problem: that posed by the cyber-squatter who has secured domain names embodying the business names or marks of famous corporations with a view to selling them over at a ransom price.[540] However, in the *Victoria's Secret* case[541] the US Supreme Court held that proof of actual dilution and not mere likelihood of injury was required by the statute, thus setting the evidential burden very high.[542] To remedy this perceived defect, the Trademark Dilution Revision Act was passed in 2006, introducing a less onerous, likelihood of dilution, test in return for narrowing the definition of the type of marks it covers, to only those which have achieved widespread fame among the general consuming public. In amending s.43 of the Lanham Act, the law also provides a definition of dilution by blurring and by tarnishment.

---

[536] For a valiant attempt to reconcile and explain the Court of Justice judgments, see *Whirlpool v Kenwood* [2010] E.T.M.R. 7 CA.

[537] The leading commentator on US trademark law, Professor McCarthy, has commented of "dilution": "No part of trade-mark law I have encountered in my 40 years of teaching and practising IP law has created so much doctrinal puzzlement and judicial incomprehension", in Vaver & Bently (eds), *Intellectual Property in the New Millennium* (2004) at p.159.

[538] Stimulated in particular by Schechter (1927) 40 Harv. L.R. 813, drawing upon German theory; for the history, see *McCarthy, McCarthy On Trademarks and Unfair Competition* 4th edn (2001) Ch.24 Pt 2. Also, see Swann [2002] T.M.R. 585.

[539] The Act added a further case to the unfair competition provisions of the Lanham Act 1946 s.43: see 15 U.S.C. s.1125(c). See Micheletti and Dorfman (2002) 92 T.M.R. 1345.

[540] Since the dilution liability does not require likelihood of confusion, defences cannot centre on the fact that the domain name is not for given goods or services. See the similar result reached in England in *British Telecommunications v One in a Million* [1999] F.S.R. 1 CA; above, para.17–27.

[541] *Victoria's Secret* 537 US 418 at 123 S Ct 1115 (2003).

[542] See McCarthy (2004) 94 T.M.R. 1163 for a critical comparative analysis of the US and EU positions on "dilution" before the 2006 Revision Act.

In the United Kingdom, after initial doubts,[543] it is now clear that there is no requirement to show confusion under s.10(3) (art.5(2) of the Directive)[544] and it has been recognised that the detriment required by the section can occur through either "blurring" or "tarnishing".[545] Previously and without being driven round a statutory assault course of the kind in the TMA 1994, the English courts have used the passing off action against occasional instances of "dilution", such as the application of "Lego" to plastic gardening accessories and "Champagne" to elderflower cordial—cases where some prospect of confusion (in a broad sense) is considered to give rise to a sufficient likelihood of damage.[546] But these have been exceptional instances; hopes that the statutory provision would be reserved for similar cases have been dashed as a Type 3 infringement claim has become almost standard, alongside a more legitimate Type 1 or Type 2 claim. Type 3 infringement exists, after all, mainly in order to give a form of passing off law to jurisdictions such as the Benelux, which normally insist that registration should be the basis of any protection.

Two elements in the statutory wording mean that liability is more readily imposed than hitherto. The first is that a registered proprietor may sue for Type 3 infringement where the mark has a "reputation"; it does not have to be "well-known" or "famous".[547] In emphasising this, the Court of Justice has held also that the reputation need exist only in part of the geographical area for which the registration pertains—as, for instance, Austria[548] or a part of the Benelux.[549] The second is that it is enough to show that a defendant is taking unfair advantage, without showing that the proprietor is suffering detriment. **18–101**

Despite these considerations and the ECJ's "clarification" that it applies to similar as well as dissimilar goods or services, Type 3 ought to be seen in the context of other forms of infringement, and in particular Type 2. Under the latter, where the goods or services are similar, there is infringement only if there is a likelihood of confusion, including association. It cannot be logical that a mark-owner with a reputation has a right of action even where there is no likely harm, just because he has a reputation. The ECJ's solution

543 *Baywatch v The Home Video Channel* [1997] F.S.R. 22 represented the highpoint of this misconception.

544 *Sabel v Puma* [1997] E.C.R. I-6191.

545 *Premier Brands* [2000] F.S.R. 767 at 787.

546 See above, paras 17–38, 17–30.

547 See above, para.17–17.

548 *Pago International v Tirolmilch registrierte Genossenschaft* [2010] E.T.M.R. 5 ECJ; cf the decision by the Benelux Office for IP in *Leno Merken/Hagelkruis Beheer* (January 15, 2010) that use in only one Member State was not sufficient as it would operate as a barrier to trade within the EU, commented on by Khwaja [2010] Trademark World 19.

549 *General Motors v Yplon* ("Chevy"—affectionate nickname for Chevrolets) [2000] R.P.C. 572.

in *Davidoff v Gofkid*[550] recognised the problem but clarified that the Directive (and Regulation) should be interpreted in this way.[551]

18–102 Type 3 can be treated consistently only if the further conditions on which it depends—lack of due cause, unfair advantage or detriment—are given substantial meaning and are not assumed to be present whenever there is "dilution" by use on any products: the *Intel v CPM* [552] case makes clear that it is not enough that the use of the sign merely reminds people of the registered mark:

> "[I]t requires evidence of a change in the economic behaviour of the average consumer of the goods or services for which the earlier mark was registered consequent on the use of the later mark, or a serious likelihood that such a change will occur in the future".[553]

Evidence of confusion (in a broad sense) as to source is the most likely circumstance to satisfy this requirement. It should be sufficient confusion to lead the public to believe that the owner of the mark with a reputation is extending its lines of business; that will occur most readily when the extension is an inherently likely one. There may be other cases of tarnishment, where the trade mark "is sullied or debased by its association with something unseemly"[554]: perhaps the supposed mockery of "Claeryn" gin by "Klarein" liquid soap amounted to an instance.[555] And there may be cases of unacceptable misappropriation of goodwill, which might occasionally fit within the provision: an example is the kind of "free riding" by smell-alike perfume producers condemned in *L'Oréal v Bellure*.[556] What ought not to happen is that the owner of a mark, which has a trading reputation with (say) 50 per cent of the relevant public, should acquire a monopoly on that mark for all trading uses, including passing comparisons of a vaguely associative kind.[557] In *Whirlpool v Kenwood* [558], where the registered (CTM) mark for food mixers comprised a shape that would have been refused

[550] *Davidoff v Gofkid* [2003] E.T.M.R. 534 ECJ.

[551] As a result of *Davidoff* and *Adidas-Salomon v Fitnessworld* [2004] E.T.M.R. 10, the TMA 1994 was amended to delete the dissimilar requirement for Type 3 infringement, by the Trade Marks (Proof of Use, etc.) Regulations 2004 (SI 2004/946).

[552] *Intel v CPM* [2009] E.T.M.R. 13 CJEU at para.32.

[553] *Intel* [2009] E.T.M.R. 13 CJEU at para.77.

[554] per the Third Board of Appeal of OHIM in *Elleni Holding v Sigla* [2005] E.T.M.R. 51 at para.41.

[555] (1976) 7 I.I.C. 420.

[556] *L'Oréal v Bellure* [2008] E.T.M.R. 1 CA, on the basis that the extent of similarity between the registered packaging marks and the defendant's signs was deliberate, the "copied" fragrances were well-promoted, and the extent of similarity permitted the charging of higher prices than for those copycat perfumes not so similar: at paras 151 and 152. Also, [2009] E.T.M.R. 55, ECJ.

[557] This is the approach taken in *Oasis Stores Application* [1998] R.P.C. 634; for a comparative analysis of the issues arising in the Court of Appeal of Singapore judgment in *McDonald's Corp v Future Enterprises* [2005] 1 S.L.R. 177, see Llewelyn & Leong (2005) 16 A.I.P.J. 138.

[558] *Whirlpool v Kenwood* [2010] E.T.M.R. 7 CA.

registration on its own together with a word KitchenAid that, apparently, was not even visible upon searching the register,[559] the Court of Appeal rejected the contention that once an advantage was found it did not need to be "unfair":

> "It is not sufficient to show (even if Whirlpool could) that Kenwood has obtained an advantage. There must be an added factor of some kind for that advantage to be categorised as unfair".[560]

The Court of Appeal was unwilling to draw that conclusion from the Court of Justice's judgment in *L'Oréal v Bellure* that stated baldly:

> "an advantage taken unfairly ... [arises] where [a third] party seeks by that use to ride on the coat-tails of the mark in question in order to benefit from the power of attraction, its reputation and its prestige, and to exploit, without paying any financial compensation and without being required to make efforts of his own in that regard, the marketing effort expended by the proprietor of that mark in order to create and maintain the image of that mark".[561]

The Court of Appeal clearly felt in *Whirlpool* that there is no sufficient case for interfering even more sweepingly with the general freedom of an enterprise to adopt attractive marks whose use will do no evident harm to any other mark:[562] even though it accepted that there would be average relevant consumers who, being design aware, would be reminded of the claimant's mixer when looking at the defendant's,[563] the reminder was not strong enough.[564]

---

559 This is an example of how a strict (some may say unthinking) application by OHIM of the individual registrability provisions can lead to the registration of a shape mark of a sort that the legislation clearly intended should not be allowed on the register (by stating that a distinctive word appears on the shape, although in fact it was not easily visible) and how thereafter through use of that "unregistrable" mark it could acquire a reputation and seek protection under the extended form of Type 3 infringement. Understandably, both the High Court and Court of Appeal recoiled from extending the consequences to a successful action for infringement, notwithstanding the evidence.

560 *Whirlpool* [2010] E.T.M.R. 7 at para.136.

561 *Whirlpool* [2010] E.T.M.R. 30 at para.49. However, in *L'Oréal v Bellure* [2010] E.W.C.A. Civ 535, Jacob LJ concluded that the ECJ judgment means: "the provision [Art.5(2), s.10 (3)] should be read as though the word unfair was simply not there. No line between 'permissible free riding' and 'impermissible free riding' is to be drawn. All free-riding is 'unfair'. It is a conclusion high in moral content) the thought is clearly that copyists, even of lawful products should be condemned) rather than on economic content... I do not agree with or welcome this conclusion – it amounts to a pointless monopoly." (At paras 48-49)

562 Merely because a mark has a substantial reputation does not avoid the need for real, as opposed to theoretical, evidence of detriment or unfair advantage: *Mastercard Int v Hitachi Credit* [2005] E.T.M.R. 85; although this was before both the CJEU judgments in both *Intel* and *L'Oréal*.

563 *Whirlpool* [2010] E.T.M.R. 7 at para.136.

564 *Whirlpool* [2010] E.T.M.R. 7 at para.137.

Also, in Britain there has traditionally not been much sympathy for attempts to stop the deployment of trade marks in parody advertisements,[565] counter-cultural advertising or other forms of critical comment.[566] Strong marks should be able to survive such knocks: they may even emerge the stronger.

18–103 (v) **Comparative advertising.** As already noted, comparison (provided that it is made plain) is the obverse of confusion, and it can certainly be argued that those who seek to protect marks against use in comparative advertising have no complaint that the origins of goods or services are being muddled together. What is at stake is a different annexation of goodwill. In this field the common law offers protection only against injurious falsehood. So it leaves considerable freedom to pursue true, or at least honest, comparisons with the products and services of other traders.[567]

18–104 However, comparative advertising using third parties' registered marks gives rise to particular problems in view of the apparently absolute nature of Type 1 infringement as it will usually involve the use of a third party's mark in exactly the form in which it is registered, therefore constituting use of an identical sign, albeit in relation to the proprietor's own goods or services.[568] Section 10(1) applies to make an infringement any use in trade, even one which does not cause confusion, unless a specific defence/limitation operates. Although in the TMA 1994 s.10(6), there is an exception where the use of a registered mark is "for the purpose of identifying goods or services as

---

[565] cf. *Miss World v Channel Four Television* [2007] E.T.M.R. 66, in which Pumfrey J. granted an interim injunction to prevent the screening of a TV programme called "Mr Miss World" about a transvestite beauty pageant, considering that "it is very likely that this is a s. 10(3) infringement" of the claimant's registered mark "Miss World": at para.43; also, Gredley and Maniatis [1997] E.I.P.R. 412; Spence (1998) 114 L.Q.R. 595; *Felix/Loesje* [1993] I.E.R. 56: "Ooh, that's tarty" (catfood marks) permitted in Netherlands for satirical political cartoon.

[566] See cf. the Dutch cases restraining: (i) a film showing a girl using a "Coca-Cola" bottle in an unusual way (*Coca-Cola/Alicia* [1997] Ned. Jur. 59); and (2) incorporation into the Philips logo of a swastika in an article illustrating the company's wartime activities (*Philips/Haagse Post* [1982] B.I.E. 41).

[567] See above, para.17–54. Injurious falsehood remains the only possibility where comparisons are made by reference to an unregistered mark or other sign outside the scope of the registration system.

[568] As to passing off where similar marks were used, see, e.g. *McDonald's v Burger King* [1986] F.S.R. 45: defendants liable for saying of their "Whopper" burger, "Not just Big, Mac"; nowadays, a case could also be brought under TMA s.10(3).

those of the proprietor or a licensee",[569] Jacob L.J. has recommended the provision should be repealed "as an unnecessary distraction in an already complicated branch of the law".[570] As a result, cases involving comparative advertising are now approached by the courts without regard to the provision.

Much of Continental Europe traditionally viewed comparative advertising **18–105** from a protectionist perspective which held little appeal in Britain. Not only do results of cases still vary between EU countries as in the past, but the differences spurred the EU to enact a Directive on Comparative Advertising (CAD). The initial consumerist bias of the proposal for this Directive was, in its final version, replaced by an attitude much more censorious.[571] Under it, both direct and implicit comparison are permitted in advertising only if: (i) it is for goods or services meeting the same needs or purposes; (ii) it objectively compares one or more material, relevant, verifiable and representative features, which may include price[572]; (iii) it is not misleading, confusing as to source, discrediting or denigrating[573]; and (iv) it does not take unfair advantage of the reputation of a mark, name or designation of origin.[574]

[569] Although it is no longer used, this exception prima facie excused the use of another's trade mark when making comparisons (although it is broader in scope and catches any use of a trade mark for the purpose of identifying genuine goods or services of the proprietor): see, for example, *Wolters Kluwer v Reed Elsevier* [2006] F.S.R. 519, where the unsuccessfully challenged use by the defendant was for the purpose of diverting custom through a reference to the claimant's registered mark; at para.15. However, the elaborate qualification which follows nevertheless imposed liability, if the reference to the proprietor or a licensee: (1) is otherwise than in accordance with honest practices in industrial and commercial matters; (2) is without due cause; and (3) takes unfair advantage of, or is detrimental to, the distinctive character or repute of the mark. Laddie J. pointed out the virtually tautological character of these cumulative strands, but refused to hold that a claimant would succeed merely by showing that the defendant was taking an unfair advantage of the mark at stake: *Barclays Bank v RBS Advanta* [1996] R.P.C. 307 at 313–315, drawing attention to the different formulation of similar tests in TMA 1994 ss.10(3) and 11(2); cf. *L'Oréal v Bellure* [2008] E.T.M.R. 1. Since the sub-section was clearly intended to permit comparative advertising unless it was shown to be unjustifiable, a case of material dishonesty had to be made out which went beyond mere puffery. In the case before him, he refused interim relief to "Barclaycard", when another bank's credit card venture claimed both to have 15 particular advantages and to fare well in a chart of charges which compared eight other credit cards by name, including "Barclaycard".

[570] *O2 Holdings v Hutchison* [2007] R.P.C. 16 at para.58; see also the comments of Pumfrey J. in *PAG v Hawk-Woods* [2002] F.S.R. 723 at para.24, on the scope of this "homegrown" provision which is not derived from the TM Directive.

[571] Directive on Comparative Advertising 97/55/EC; implemented in national law by April 6, 2000. The Directive amended Directive 84/850/EEC on Misleading Advertising. References are to that Directive as amended. See in this context the ECJ judgment in *Pippig* [2004] E.T.M.R. 5.

[572] Special offers have to be clearly dated: see art.3a(2).

[573] The so-called "Bastards" advertisement in *British Airways v Ryanair* [2001] F.S.R. 32, would have fallen within this category; see judgment at para.35.

[574] No statement may present goods or services as an imitation or replica or marked goods or services: see art.3a(1)(h); see *Gillette v LA-Laboratories* [2005] F.S.R. 808 ECJ at para.45. At present in the UK, copyright material may not be inserted in a comparative advertisement without licence: *IPC Magazines v Mirror Group* [1998] F.S.R. 431; but this may be excluded by the Directive: see art.7(1), (2).

In *O2 v Hutchison 3G*[575] Jacob L.J. expressed the view that comparative advertising should not fall within ss.10(1) and (2) where it was not likely to confuse or otherwise jeopardise the origin function of the registered mark:

> "[t]he defendant is in no way using the mark to indicate the trade origin of his goods or services, not even that he is dealing in those of the trade mark owner. There is simply no reasonable need for trade mark law to cover this kind of use. If the comparative advertising is unfair, derogatory or otherwise fails to comply with all the conditions of the [CAD, Comparative Advertising Directive now codified in 2006/114], there are independent mechanisms for dealing with it. That is what the CAD requires. They come into play whether or not the 'victim' of the advertising has a registered mark. There is no need for the law of registered trade marks to get involved with any of this."[576]

In *L'Oréal v Bellure* [2010] E.W.C.A. Civ 535, the same judge held, applying the Court of Justice's replies (particularly paras 75 and 76) on art.3a(1)(g) and (h) CAD, that "even saying, truthfully, that the defendant's product has an essential characteristic (in the instant case the smell) of the trade mark owner's product amounts to saying the product is an "imitation or replica" and so outside the protection of the CAD. I am forced so to conclude...I can actually see no rational basis for such a rule...If, as I think there should be, there is to be reform of the law, this aspect of the CAD should be reconsidered. And in my view, it should be made explicit that telling the truth about a lawful product does not involve any "unfair advantage" (the phrase used in art.3a(1)(g))."

The primary objective of the CAD is to permit honest comparative advertising, there being nothing inherently wrong in informing the public of the relative merits of goods or services by reference to registered marks.[577]

[575] *O2 v Hutchison 3G* [2007] R.P.C. 16

[576] *O2* [2007] R.P.C. 16 at para.33. However, having reviewed paras 55–53 of the ECJ judgment in *L'Oréal v Bellure*, Jacob L.J. in the resumed appeal in the same case, [2010] E.W.C.A. Civ 535, noted that while the Court of Justice stated that "the [comparison lists] use we have to consider is indeed within art.5(1)(a)" [s.10(1)], it then proceeded to require that the national court decide whether such use "is liable to affect one of the functions" of the marks (at para.63), even though the use "is not capable of jeopardising the essential function of the mark which is to indicate the origin of the goods" (para.65). With regret, the learned judge accepted that the Court of Justice considered the [comparison lists] use to be within art.5(1)(a) as it went beyond "purely descriptive" use, commenting "I confess I do not know where [the] line [between permissible and impermissible advertising] is, but this case falls the wrong side of it. Why? Because the Court has said so. It regards the use as affecting the communication, advertising and investment function of the mark." (At para.31)

[577] In *O2 Holdings v Hutchison* [2007] R.P.C. 16 Jacob L.J. observed that there are "some oddities about the CAD. First and foremost is the fact that there is no explicit provision which says that compliance with the Art. 3a [now Art.4] [CAD] conditions [as to a permissible comparative advertisement] is a defence to a trade mark infringement suit. ... One has the uneasy feeling that those responsible for this legislation had but a hazy idea of how various kinds of IP rights could apply to comparative advertising"; at paras 45–46.

The onus of proving non-compliance with the conditions laid down in the CAD lies with the mark-owner whose mark has been taken for comparison. He must show that the advertisement is not in accordance with art.4 of the CAD (although it appears that where there is infringement under s.10(3), this will follow automatically[578]).

Thus, while much comparative advertising will be excluded from infringement by falling within the "descriptive use" defence/limitation contained in s.12(1)(b) (art.6(1) TM Directive), where the advertising does not comply with art.4 of the CAD it will fall foul of the proviso to s.12(1) requiring that such descriptive use "must be in accordance with honest practices in industrial or commercial matters", fall outside the defence/limitation and constitute an infringement.

Inevitably, the requirements contained in the CAD are interpreted dif- **18–106** ferently depending on the historic attitude of the particular Member State to comparative advertising. It is practically impossible for the European Court of Justice to provide such further clarification of them as will prevent evident variations when national courts apply them to particular advertisements. This is most apparent when the diffusion of material—whether in the press, through broadcasting or on the internet—leads to cross-border litigation.[579]

In *British Airways v Ryanair*[580] Jacob J. held that the CAD does not require the TMA to be interpreted any differently to the way it had been previously as it was not intended to amend the TM Directive on which the TMA is based, but more recently the Court of Justice did take into account the former Directive in interpreting the term "honest practices" contained in art.6 of the latter.[581] As a result, in *O2 v Hutchison*,[582] Jacob L.J. accepted that his earlier decision was wrong. More difficult in relation to comparative advertising is the extent of protection afforded particularly to unregistered marks, business names and other signs apart from the registration system. As earlier noted, the tort of injurious falsehood is less protective than s.10(6) was intended to be, requiring proof both of a sufficient falsehood and of malice on the part of the defendant, in the sense of deliberate or reckless conduct, rather than mere negligence.[583] As far as falsehood is concerned, s.10(6) was interpreted robustly so as in effect to impose the same objective

[578] *L'Oréal v Bellure* [2007] E.T.M.R. 1 at para.169: this was despite the fact that the signs used by the defendant which were found to infringe under s.10(3) did not feature in the product comparison list; in this respect the decision must be questionable.

[579] The European Commission has reported on the feasibility of a complaints system for cross-border comparative advertisements but this seems unlikely to come to fruition.

[580] *British Airways* [2001] F.S.R. 32 at paras 24 to 28.

[581] *Gillette v La-Laboratories* [2006] at paras 9 and 42–45; see also, applying *Gillette*, *L'Oréal v Bellure* [2007] E.T.M.R. 1, where Lewison J. found that use in comparison lists for smell-alike perfumes of an identical sign could not be in accordance with honest practices where it took unfair advantage of the distinctive character or repute of the registered trade mark: at para.159.

[582] *O2* [2007] R.P.C. 16 at para.58.

[583] See above, para.17–50; see esp. *Emaco v Dyson Appliances* [1999] E.T.M.R. 903.

test of misleading the public as is laid down for injurious falsehood in *De Beers Abrasive Products v International General Electric*.[584] As to malice, in the context of comparative advertising the test is one of advertising that is contrary to honest commercial practices. This should then be interpreted in the same way as it was previously under s.10(6).[585]

(c) *Scope of infringement: other factors*

18–107 (i) **Positive and negative definitions.** The rights accorded to a trade mark proprietor are determined exclusively by the various types of infringement discussed above.[586]

18–108 (ii) **Time factors.** Registration is backdated to the date of application, but proceedings for infringement may not be begun until actual grant.[587]

18–109 (iii) **Contributory infringement.** The TMA 1994 lays down that a person (such as printer or packager) who actually applies a trade mark will be party to any subsequent infringing use of the mark if he knew or had reason to believe that the application of the mark was not authorised.[588] This could, for example, make an internet service provider which hosts a site containing an infringing trade mark liable for the infringement after notification. However, in *L'Oréal v eBay*[589] Arnold J. found that as a matter of domestic common law eBay Europe was under no legal duty to prevent infringement of third parties' registered trade marks on its auction website.[590]

(d) *Defences, or limitations upon infringement*

18–110 (i) **Conflicts between marks.** The 1994 Act provides that so long as a mark remains registered, use of it in its registered form cannot amount to infringement of any other mark[591] (although it may constitute passing off). The owner of the conflicting mark may still be able to bring proceedings for passing off, if he can make out the requirements of that tort.[592] However, it

584 *De Beers Abrasive Products v International General Electric* [1975] F.S.R. 323, relied upon in relation to s.10(6) in *Cable & Wireless v British Telecom* [1998] F.S.R. 383 at 390; also, see the robust decision in *British Airways v Ryanair* [2001] E.T.M.R. 235.

585 *L'Oréal v Bellure* [2007] E.T.M.R. 1 at para.159. Also, *O2 v Hutchison* [2006] E.T.M.R. 677 at para.170.

586 TMA 1994 s.9(1), (2); *British Sugar v James Robertson* [1996] R.P.C. 281 at 290, 291.

587 TMA 1994 ss.9(3), 40(3). Criminal proceedings under s.92 may only relate to events after actual registration. In *Vitasoy International v The Sunrider Corp* [2007] R.P.C. 29 it was held that the continuous period of five years acquiescence required by s.48 to extinguish a right to obtain a declaration of invalidity ran from the actual date of registration rather than being backdated to the date of application of a mark subsequently registered.

588 TMA 1994 s.10(5).

589 *L'Oréal* [2009] R.P.C. 21.

590 *L'Oréal* [2009] R.P.C. 21 at para.375.

591 In s.11(1). This provision, which does not derive from the TM Directive or CTM Regulation, gives no right which survives opposition or invalidity proceedings. So TMA 1994 s.11(1) appears merely to require a counterclaim, rather than a defence (each carrying the onus of proof). For what it is worth, it would seem to operate in the same way for a CTM: see CTM Regulation art.106(2).

592 This is one effect of the preservation of passing off: see TMA 1994 s.2(2).

may be hard to make out the necessary reputation for passing off in cases where both parties have been trading in overlapping areas from much the same point in time.[593] Alternatively, the later owner may proceed for a declaration of invalidity on the relative ground of a prior mark at the time of registration. The ability to invalidate a registration by showing a prior right at the time of application is subject to the twin limitations of the proprietor's consent to the conflicting registration and subsequent acquiescence in the registration by not objecting to known use.[594]

A different type of consent occurs where it is the proprietor or a licensee who has been responsible for marking particular goods. As already noted in connection with comparative advertising, no accurate and honest use of a mark to identify goods or services as those of the proprietor or a licensee will (or should) infringe. This principle continues to limit the usefulness of trade marks as a means of controlling parallel imports, a matter to which we return later.[595] We will then consider it together with the statutory rule on exhaustion of rights within the EU,[596] and the specific question, how far (as a matter both of UK and of EU law) this provision can justify a recipient of the proprietor's goods or those of a licensee in repackaging them or relabelling them.

(ii) **Legitimate uses of the mark by an unauthorised user.** Certain uses of a mark have always been permitted as legitimate forms of trading. Under the TMA 1994, particularly in cases involving identical marks on identical goods or services,[597] a particular significance attaches to such exceptions (or defences). The Act[598] permits the use, provided it is in accordance with honest practices in industrial and commercial matters, of the following: **18–111**

(1) a person's own name or address[599];
(2) indications of kind, quality, quantity, intended purpose, value, geographical origin, time of production or rendering, or other characteristics of goods or services[600];

---

593 See above, para.17–15.
594 See above, para.18–81; and also the CTM Regulation art.106(1).
595 See below, paras 18–119 et seq.
596 TMA 1994 s.12; CTM Regulation art.13.
597 As with comparative advertising. Use on similar goods or services, or use of a similar mark, first requires proof of a likelihood of confusion and this of itself may prevent a descriptive use of the mark from infringing; no such question arises in relation to an identical mark for identical goods or services: above, para.18–86.
598 TMA 1994 s.11(1), (2). The list applies equally to CTMs: CTM Regulation art.12.
599 This exception is not limited to natural persons: *Anheuser-Busch* [2004] E.C.R. I-10989 ECJ at paras 77–80. In *Asprey & Garrard v WRA (Guns)* [2002] F.S.R. 487 CA, the fact that the defendant company traded under the name "William R Asprey" did not give rise to an own name defence, per Peter Gibson L.J. at paras 42–43 et seq.
600 The equivalent list to that in the absolute grounds of objection: see above, para.18–36.

(3) the mark itself, where this is necessary to indicate the intended purpose of a product or service—in particular, as accessories or spare parts.[601]

According to Chadwick L.J. in *D Green & Co v Regalzone*[602] the purpose of the provision (and art.6(1) of the Directive) is to ensure that:

> "[t]rade mark protection is not available unless the use complained of is likely to be taken as use for the purpose of indicating, or so as to indicate, a connection between the goods in relation to which the use is made and some person having the right to use the registered mark".

As he points out, s.11(2)(b) re-introduces the dichotomy between distinctive and descriptive use that is present in s.3(1)(b) and (c)[603]; in every case, the court must consider, would the average consumer consider the use complained of to be distinctive or descriptive use?[604]

On use of own name, it has been held that:

> "a man may use his own name even if there is some actual confusion with a registered trade mark. The amount of confusion which can be tolerated is a question of degree—only if objectively what he does, in all the circumstances, amounts to unfair competition, will there also be infringement. In practice there would have to be significant actual deception."[605]

The defendant's use in the other two cases may be excepted whether it is purely descriptive or when it involves use of a trade mark as such for some honest descriptive purpose (for example, comparative advertising). On this basis the name of a pop group may be used as the title for a book about them,[606] a mark-owner's own product may be referred to in a comparative

[601] TMA 1994 s.11(2)(c).

[602] *D Green & Co v Regalzone* [2002] E.T.M.R. 241 CA at para.30.

[603] *D Green & Co* [2002] E.T.M.R. 241 CA at para.32.

[604] *D Green & Co* [2002] E.T.M.R. 241 CA at para.34. Although not necessary for the decision overruling the trial judge, which was made under the Trade Marks Act 1938 and the transitional provisions of the 1994 Act, Chadwick L.J. also considered under s.11(2)(b) of the latter Act the potential infringement of the claimant's mark "Spork" by the defendant's use of the term (a combination of spoon and fork) in its correspondence and price lists. He found that trade purchasers (the relevant public) would not take the defendant's use to be of the claimant's mark as the products were described as being produced by Master Plastics, a Danish company, and therefore the use fell within the exclusion from infringement in s.11(2)(b).

[605] *Reed Executive v Reed Business Information* [2004] R.P.C. 767 CA per Jacob L.J. applying *Gerolsteiner Brunnen v Putsch* [2004] R.P.C. 761 ECJ.

[606] *Bravado Merchandising v Mainstream Publishing* [1996] F.S.R. 205.

advertisement[607] and a red rose emblem used on the front of rugby shirts.[608] Even if there is no separate requirement as such that the infringement involve "use as a trade mark",[609] a use by the defendant which is not of this character is the more likely to be excused under s.11[610]: in *L'Oréal v eBay*[611] Arnold J. expressed the view that the correct analysis in such circumstances is that the use falls within art.5(1)(a) (s.10(1)) but is saved by the defence (in that case, the "exhaustion" defence in art.7(1) (s.12(1)). Similarly, in *O2 v Hutchison 3G*[612] Jacob L.J. commented that he could not think of any use of a third party's mark in comparative advertising which would fall outside art.6(1)(b) (s.11(2)(b)),[613] although the use must be "in accordance with honest practices in industrial or commercial matters".[614] It is hard however to see on the strict wording the exclusion from liability contained in s.11(2)(b) applying to decorative use on the front of clothing of a name which turns out to be another's mark.[615]

Such uses of a mark are excused if they are in accordance with honest practices, which should be interpreted objectively,[616] rather than by subjective decision:

> "the defendant must compensate the trade mark owner if he has even unwittingly caused damage by significant, but unintended deception. I think that is what an honest man would do. Moreover the language of the

[607] Previously this gave rise to an overlap with TMA 1994 s.10(6): *British Sugar v Robertson* [1996] R.P.C. 281; cf. *Mothercare v Penguin Books* [1998] R.P.C. 113 CA, but s.10(6) has fallen into disuse as it does not derive from the TM Directive. In *L'Oréal v eBay* [2009] R.P.C. 21 Arnold J. considered that a comparative advertisement would fall within art.5(1)(a) (s.10(1)) where the comparative advertiser used the third party's mark as registered, but could be saved by art.7(1) (s.12(1)), relying on *BMW v Deenik* [1998] E.T.M.R. 348 ECJ.

[608] *RFU and Nike v Cotton Traders* [2002] E.T.M.R. 861, rejecting an argument that the defendant's use falling within art.12(b) of the CTM Regulation (s.11(2)(b)) should be disregarded because it was not "honest" due to the defendant having previously been an official supplier of England shirts: at para.55.

[609] See above, para.18–87.

[610] *British Sugar v Robertson* [1996] R.P.C. 281 at 299, 300, holding that "Treat" in the phrase "Toffee Treat" on the label for a spread would not be taken as a trade mark use (despite the defendant's efforts to achieve this). Also, see *Green v Regalzone* [2002] E.T.M.R. 241 CA.

[611] *L'Oréal* [2009] R.P.C. 21.

[612] *eBay* [2007] R.P.C. 16.

[613] *eBay* [2007] R.P.C. 16 at para.55.

[614] *eBay* [2007] R.P.C. 16 at para.56. Obviously a misleading comparative advertisement that fell outside the CAD would not be honest and Jacob L.J. also expressed the view that "even a non-misleading but disparaging use would now be caught".

[615] cf. *Unidoor v Marks & Spencer* [1998] R.P.C. 275: "Coast to Coast" featured on T-shirts—under the 1938 Act, held not to be "use as a trade mark"; surely a result which would somehow be arrived at under the 1994 Act (despite the ECJ judgment in *Arsenal* [2003] R.P.C. 144 where the use was in the full knowledge that the "Arsenal" name was registered as a trade mark), although the judgment of Arnold J. in *L'Oréal v eBay* [2009] R.P.C. 21 must give rise to some doubt whether common sense would prevail.

[616] "Honest practice in the choice of a name to be used in trade must imply reasonable diligence in ascertaining that the name chosen does not conflict" with another, per Sharpston A.G. in *Céline* [2007] E.T.M.R. 80 at para.55.

provision rather suggests that the actual defendant's state of mind is irrelevant—referring as it does to 'honest *practices*' rather than 'honest use'."[617]

Of these three defences, the third is needed on a regular basis, since traders must be permitted to advertise their films as useable in a "Kodak" camera, or as a replacement cartridge for a "Xerox" copier. However, if the statement being made is misleading (e.g. where a claim of compatibility is being made in circumstances where the product is clearly inferior to the original), the use of the mark would not be honest (which is a duty to act fairly in relation to the legitimate interests of the trade mark proprietor[618]) and could therefore be the subject of proceedings for infringement. Similarly, where the use of the mark is unusually prominent when comparing it with other use in the product line concerned.[619]

18–112 The TMA 1994 adds a different exception for purely local use of an unregistered mark or other sign which is itself protectable as an "earlier right".[620] But the mark or sign must have been in continuous use since a date before the registered mark was used or registered. A person entitled to such an earlier right may take advantage of this defence where his right to protection (most likely against passing off) applies only "in a particular locality", a phrase which it is left to courts to define more precisely. This exception is related to the exclusion of purely local "earlier rights" from the relative grounds of objection to a CTM, where the same question arises.[621] Those whose rights extend to larger areas must take positive steps to attack the registration being asserted against them; and if they fail to act, they risk being held to have acquiesced in that registration.[622]

---

617 *Reed Executive v Reed Business Information* [2004] R.P.C. 767 CA, per Jacob L.J. at para.132, noting that this is also the position adopted in passing off so far as damages are concerned, at para.134. In her Opinion in *Céline*, [2007] E.T.M.R. 80, Sharpston A.G. considered that "a person who contacted the trade mark proprietor (ensuring that his notification was received) could be considered to be acting in accordance with honest practices if, after a reasonable period had elapsed, no objection was made": at para.58.

618 *Gerolsteiner Brunnen v Putsch* [2005] E.T.M.R. 559 ECJ at para.24; cf. Roughton in *Trade Mark Use* (Phillips & Simon (eds), 2005), at p.188, noting that the ECJ "has substituted one word—fairness—for another—honesty."

619 Generally, see *Gillette v LA-Laboratories* [2005] E.T.M.R. 825 ECJ.

620 TMA 1994 s.11(3), rendering into English the gibberish of TM Directive art.6(2). For the equivalent limitation upon a CTM, see CTM Regulation art.107, which—in a form of little-and-large co-existence—allows the defence to continue even after acquiescence by the local right-holder prevents him from objecting to the use of the CTM in his locality.

621 See above, para.18–67.

622 The CTM Regulation art.107 has a similar provision, which continues to operate even when the proprietor of the earlier right has through acquiescence lost his power to prevent use of the CTM in his locality. See *Compass Publishing v Compass Logistics* [2004] R.P.C. 809, where Laddie J. held that "[t]he precise way in which the national legal system gave the objector title to interfere was of no significance": at paras 46–49, rejecting an argument that passing off does not protect non-registered marks, but instead a trading reputation or goodwill, and therefore could not be relied upon.

(2) Exhaustion of right

As noted elsewhere, the concept of exhaustion of right is relevant to genuine goods which emanate initially from an intellectual property owner or associated enterprises (other subsidiaries, licensees, distributors, etc.).[623] Although it also applies to the normal sale of trade-marked products in the domestic market, its particular relevance over the last forty years has been in relation to the parallel importation of goods between different Member States of the EU. In that context, the European Court of Justice has established, through interpretation of the EU Treaty, that the exhaustion of trade mark rights applies on an EU-wide basis, rather than only a purely national one.[624] The expression of this rule in the CTM Regulation and the Trade Marks Directive, applies to exhaustion within a single Member State as well as between Member States; the right may not be asserted "in relation to goods which have been put on the market in the Community [EEA] under that trade mark by the proprietor or with his consent".[625] In addition to the usual "parallel import" situation, this exemption from general liability may also apply to comparative advertising.[626] However, it does not apply: **18–113**

> "where there exist legitimate reasons for the proprietor to oppose further commercialisation of the goods, especially where the condition of the goods is changed or impaired after they have been put on the market".[627]

The consequence is that the courts have some scope for deciding what forms of "interference" with, or other "improper" reference to trade-marked products already put on the market is to amount to an act of infringement. In *Copad v Christian Dior*[628] the ECJ reiterated that damage done to the reputation by cut-price resellers may, in principle, be a legitimate reason to oppose further commercialisation of luxury goods, although not merely due to the presence in a licence agreement of a provision prohibiting sale to discount stores.[629] Similarly, in a parallel imports context the Court of Justice has held that a distributor may not repackage legitimate goods, or label them with a different trade mark, unless the practice complies with the

---

[623] Above, esp. para.1–49.

[624] See below, para.19–04 for fully "international" exhaustion, as it affects products initially marketed outside the EEA, see below, paras 18–119 et seq.

[625] CTM Regulation art.13; Directive art.7; from which comes TMA 1994 s.12. The rule applies equally to goods first marketed within the same State.

[626] See the discussion by Arnold J. in *L'Oréal v eBay* [2009] R.P.C. 21 at paras 289–299.

[627] TMA 1994 s.12(2) following the language of the CTM Regulation art.13 and the Directive, art.7.

[628] *Copad v Christian Dior* [2009] E.T.M.R. 40.

[629] *Copad* [2009] E.T.M.R. 40 at para.59. See also the judgment of the German Supreme Court in *Perfume Tester Bottles* [2009] E.T.M.R. 9 where the onward sale of perfume tester bottles given to retailers by the perfume manufacturer and marked "Not for resale" could not be restrained; the activity did not fall within art.7(2) TM Directive as there was no alteration or impairment of the bottles after they were put on the market: at para.23.

special conditions which the Court of Justice has already laid down for parallel importation from another Member State.[630]

18–114 In the context of parallel importing from elsewhere in the EEA, the ECJ has given two formative decisions:

(1) *in Parfums Christian Dior v Evora*,[631] the claimant perfume house sought to prevent a supermarket chain from advertising genuine "Dior" perfumes in a Christmas promotion alongside other less expensive brands. The court advised that they could not do so unless it could show that such a use of the mark would seriously damage its reputation. Where the advertising followed the customs of the retailer's sector of the trade, sufficient damage could be made out only in quite specific circumstances.[632]
(2) *in BMW v Deenik*,[633] the claimant car company sought to object to the use of its Benelux "BMW" mark by a garage-owner in Holland who specialised in selling second-hand BMWs and in servicing and repairing them. He was not an authorised dealer, but it was alleged that he was holding himself out to be one, or, that, by annexing the aura of high quality associated with the marque, he was infringing the claimant's rights. The European Court indicated that the exhaustion of right principle must apply to the cars, once sold in the EU. No exception to that principle could apply where the trader was informing the public of his wholly legitimate business in BMW repairs, servicing and resales. Only statements designed to suggest that he was an authorised dealer would infringe.[634]

In these decisions, true to its insistence that the "origin" function normally delimits the proper scope of the trade mark right, the court has refused to allow it to become a general prop for marketing strategies merely because they seek to confine the choices of distributors and therefore the

[630] For the case law, see further above, paras 18–04 et seq.
[631] *Parfums Christian Dior v Evora* [1998] R.P.C. 166. The goods were obtained by parallel importation from elsewhere in the EU, but the same principle ought to apply where they are purchased in the home market. For copyright aspects, see Kur (2000) 32 I.I.C. 308.
[632] See now *Copad v* Dior [2009] E.T.M.R. 22, ECJ, and the decision of the Provincial Appeals Court, Zaragoza, Spain in *Clarins Paris v Supermercados Sabeco* [2005] E.T.M.R. 1293, where a retailer which was not a member of the Clarins selective distribution network was restrained from selling Clarins products on the basis of trade mark infringement: the court finding that the products' "luxury image" protected by trade mark law was harmed by sale in "perceptively worse" circumstances than in an authorised dealership: below, at paras 19–20 et seq.
[633] *BMW v Deenik* [1999] E.T.M.R. 339; see also *Volkswagen and Audi v Garage X* [2003] E.T.M.R. 225, where the Swiss Federal Court referred to the *BMW* case and came to the same conclusion, noting that the size of the defendant's signage was normal in the trade.
[634] The same approach had to be adopted in deciding whether there was an act of infringement of Type 2 (likelihood of confusion in use of mark for cars and for servicing them); and in deciding whether any exception arose under the Directive art.6, TMA 1994 s.11(2).

opportunities for consumers. That is not an investment value which the law of trade marks exists to support.

(3) Infringement of a CTM

The "effects of Community trade marks" are determined solely by the CTM Regulation, whereas other aspects of their infringement are in the main governed by national trade mark law.[635] By "effects" the Regulation means the content of arts 9–13, since they are placed under this general heading. These articles cover the rights conferred by a CTM[636]; reproduction in dictionaries[637]; prohibition of unauthorised use of a mark by an agent or representative in whose name it has been registered[638]; defences of honest use[639]; and exhaustion of rights.[640] **18–115**

In the main, EU law corresponds to national law so far as concerns the definition of acts constituting use of the mark[641]; the limitations allowing honest use of name, address, descriptions and indications of intended purpose[642]; and its treatment of comparative advertising.

As noted earlier, the CTM Regulation, unlike in the now ignored TMA 1994 s.10(6), does not have any explicit exception for using a mark to identify the goods or services of the actual proprietor, nor any qualification where such a use of the mark falls outside the sphere of honest trade practices.[643] Of course, the abandonment of reliance on s.10(6) means that the CTM Regulation and the TMA should be interpreted in the same way.

There are two consequential issues which go directly to the competing views of trade mark functions: **18–116**

[635] CTM Regulation art.14; cf. art.97, which brings into account, where appropriate, the private international law of a State; also arts 98–103 on sanctions, provisional measures, jurisdictional conflicts, appeals, and other disputes. Art.14(2) preserves rights under the general civil law and unfair competition law (in common law terms, the torts of passing off, injurious falsehood, etc.). For a comparative perspective, Bastian and Knaak (1995) 26 I.I.C. 149.

[636] CTM Regulation art.9.

[637] CTM Regulation art.10, a special provision, with no equivalent in UK law. It requires a dictionary publisher who has created the impression that a trade mark is a generic name to correct that impression at least by the next edition. Presumably this imposes a statutory duty under EU law, enforceable if necessary by a mandatory injunction.

[638] CTM Regulation art.11, implementing in part the Paris Convention art.6*septies*. This Convention provision is now fully imported into UK law by the TMA 1994 s.60, which also provides the "proprietor of the mark" with the right to oppose the agent's application to register and the right to be substituted as named proprietor. There are certain three-year limitation periods: see s.60(6): see above, para.18–03.

[639] CTM Regulation art.12, see above, para.18–111.

[640] See below, para.18–119.

[641] See above, para.18–86; but note above, paras 18–102, 18–111 et seq.

[642] See above, para.18–111; but note above, para.18–113.

[643] See above, para.18–111. It is not possible to treat TMA 1994 s.10(6) as itself applying to CTMs because it deals with one of their effects. The matter must be entirely a matter for EU law. In this context, the stress in CTM Regulation Rec.10, on "origin theory" may provide an important clue.

(1) Use of a Community mark to identify the proprietor's or licensee's own goods or services in the course of comparative advertising could arguably be actionable in all cases: the reference in the advertisement will be to the very mark for the very goods or services and so in principle an "absolute" Type 1 liability. While there is no direct equivalent to the now redundant homegrown provision, s.10(6) of the TMA 1994, similar issues arise when deciding whether art.12(b) of the CTM Regulation (TM Directive art.6(1)(b); TMA s.12(2)(b)) applies. Although it can be argued that courts should not read art.9(1)(a) of the CTM Regulation in this mechanistic way, the interpretation of the equivalent provisions in the TM Directive by Arnold J. in *L'Oréal v eBay* on the basis of the ECJ authorities would suggest otherwise. On the other hand, in *Toshiba Europe v Katun Germany*[644] the ECJ adopted a commonsense approach to the interpretation of Directive 84/45 as amended (on misleading and comparative advertising) and found that "[a]n advertiser cannot be considered as taking unfair advantage of the reputation attached to distinguishing marks of his competitor if effective competition on the relevant market [for spare parts] is conditional upon a reference to those marks".

(2) Use of a Community mark to identify the goods of the proprietor or a licensee may be objected to where a parallel importer, who has acquired them in a non-EEA country, seeks to bring them into any EEA country from outside. This has been taken by many to be a necessary implication of the "standard exhaustion formula"—for trade marks as much as for rights protecting one or other type of idea. It is a subject of pressing concern, to which we return below.

18–117 As to other aspects of infringement of a CTM, the concepts which leave a considerable range of judgment to courts—questions of what marks and goods or services are similar, of what amounts to confusion (including association), of what dilution of marks with a reputation is unacceptable—are being developed in a "Community" context. There has been consideration of precedents from a variety of Member States, and not (as feared by some) just those of the Benelux. It is for the European Court of Justice to continue maintaining a balance between its interpretations of the CTM Regulation and of equivalent provisions in the TM Directive as they apply in the context of national laws.

18–118 The CTM Regulation contains a set of provisions on jurisdiction to hear infringement actions and related matters, which establish an important precedent for EU forms of intellectual property.[645] Each Member State is required to nominate certain courts as Community trade mark courts of first

[644] *Toshiba Europe v Katun Germany* [2002] F.S.R. 606 at para.54.

[645] These provisions were first drafted in relation to the Community patent (see CPC, Protocol on Litigation, art.14), but have first taken effect in relation to the CTM, which is why they are described here.

and second instance (with further rights of appeal in accordance with general national rules). In the United Kingdom this allows CTM jurisdiction to be exercised in the same courts as deal with national trade mark disputes. These courts alone may try:

(1) infringement proceedings;
(2) actions for a declaration of non-infringement;
(3) actions for compensation for acts done during the application period; and
(4) counterclaims for revocation of Community registrations or for declarations of their invalidity.[646]

The hierarchy of jurisdictions between Member States follows a standard model. In order to secure relief throughout the EU, actions are to be brought:

(a) first, in the Member State of the defendant's domicile or else establishment (if the domicile is not in an EU State);
(b) in the Member State of the claimant's domicile, or else establishment; and failing either;
(c) in Spain (since the Office is there).[647]

The Brussels Judgments Convention[648] is applicable, with certain modifications.[649] In *Prudential Assurance v Prudential Insurance*[650] Laddie J. rejected an argument, based on decisions of the ECJ on art.21 of the Brussels Convention,[651] that an opposition to registration on the basis of prior rights decided upon in one Member State prevents the CTM court in another Member State from hearing an infringement action involving the same marks:

[646] CTM Regulation art.92, the mark being presumed valid unless the defendant puts the matter in issue: art.95(1). For other proceedings involving Community marks, see art.102; the mark must in these cases be treated as valid: art.103. As to sanctions, including interim relief, in the main national law applies; but injunctions against infringements or threats to infringe must be granted unless there are special reasons: arts 98, 99 et seq. For interim relief, courts other than CTM courts may have jurisdiction: art.99(1).

[647] Subject to agreement to submit to another Community trade mark court, or appearance in such a court by the defendant: CTM Regulation art.93(1)–(4). The court empowered under this hierarchy may make interim orders having EU-wide effect: art.99(2). See generally, Curley [1998] Man. I.P.14.

[648] As set out in EU Regulation 44/2001, which has replaced the Convention for all members of the EU (prior to July 1, 2007 it did not extend to Denmark).

[649] CTM Regulation arts 90, 104 et seq. The modifications are spelled out in art.90(2).

[650] *Prudential Assurance v Prudential Insurance* [2002] E.T.M.R. 1013; upheld by the Court of Appeal, [2004] E.T.M.R. 404.

[651] *Prudential Assurance* Applicable to the interpretation of arts 105(2) and (3) of the CTM Regulation.

"opposition proceedings before a national registry (or OHIM) are not to be equated with an action for infringement ... This is not altered by the fact that in this case an appeal lay to the *Cour d'Appel*. The hierarchy through which proceedings pass does not alter the nature of the proceedings."[652]

The relevant CTM court may make orders relating to activity within any Member State, which are enforceable there without further proceedings. This is the essential practical advantage of a CTM registration.[653]

There is a separate jurisdiction given to national CTM courts in respect of wrongful acts occurring in that Member State, but orders are then confined to activities within that territory.[654]

(4) Trade marks and parallel importing

18–119 As we have noted, EU law imposes an exhaustion of trade mark rights throughout the EEA.[655] Accordingly the activities of a parallel importer who operates between one EEA state and another cannot in most cases be controlled by trade mark rights in the country into which he imports. The working out of this general principle has proved particularly difficult in relation to trade marks, but its scope has now been clearly delineated by the European Court of Justice[656]; and it has been encapsulated in both the CTM Regulation and the TM Directive. Subject to certain exceptions, neither a CTM nor a national mark may:

"entitle the proprietor to prohibit its use in relation to goods which have been put on the market in the Community under that trade mark by the proprietor or with his consent".[657]

While this exhaustion rule operates in respect of goods which have been put on the market within the EU, nothing is said explicitly about importing goods from outside into the EEA. Originally it was proposed to introduce into the CTM Regulation a rule of fully international exhaustion, bringing national trade mark rights to an end in respect of marked goods marketed anywhere in the world by the right-owner or with its consent.[658] This was a particularly pronounced expression of the desire to draw trade mark protection back to its origin function. It would have coincided with the scope of rules then operating at the national level in some, but not all, EEA countries. Germany, for instance, had adopted international exhaustion in

[652] [2002] E.T.M.R. 1013 at 1037.
[653] CTM Regulation art.94(1).
[654] CTM Regulation arts 93(5), 94(2). It does not extend to declarations of non-infringement.
[655] Above, para.18–113. For greater detail in the context of the EU Treaty, see below, para.19–02 et seq.
[656] See below, paras 19–04 et seq.
[657] CTM Regulation art.13; TM Directive art.7; TMA 1994 s.12(1); for the exceptions, see below, para.19–09.
[658] See above, para.16–16.

relation to all economically connected enterprises.[659] At the other end of the scale, Italy appears to have permitted marks to act as national barriers, whether they were held by the same or different legal persons (however closely connected) in the countries of export and import.[660]

In the United Kingdom, the law took a midway position, though its scope was far from settled or complete. In *Revlon v Cripps & Lee*,[661] the products of an internationally known corporate group could not be prevented from parallel movement into Britain from the United States. There was nothing about the product (shampoo) which would mislead an ordinary British consumer about the American product's qualities. Accordingly there was neither passing off nor infringement of the mark, as registered under the 1938 Act. On the other hand, if, as in *Colgate-Palmolive v Markwell*,[662] the British consumer would expect, from his prior knowledge of goods sold under the mark at home, that the imported products were of much higher quality than they in fact were, both forms of liability would arise. The position where the foreign marketer was not a subsidiary, but a licensed manufacturer for a limited territory, remained unsettled.

There was considerable pressure from European industry to retain trade **18–120** marks as a means of preventing parallel importing, in cases where no question of internal EU policy arose. The CTM Regulation and TM Directive were accordingly re-drafted in their final, less embracing terms, as set out above. The Commission announced that this text imposes a ring of non-exhaustion around the EEA.[663]

If such a blanket rule was to be, it could easily have been stated. Instead, it was left to be implied, because there was little certainty about what was being agreed or should be agreed when the text was settled.[664]

---

659 See esp. *Cinzano v Java Kaffeegeschäfte* [1974] 2 C.M.L.R. 21 (BGH): Cinzano Germany held not entitled to use its trade mark rights to prevent importation of "Cinzano" vermouth made by Spanish subsidiary or French exclusive licensee, each with taste variations designed to flatter local palates. For the history, Beier (1970) 1 I.I.C. 48. At least some degree of international exhaustion applied under the Benelux system and in the Scandinavian countries, Ireland and Austria, as well as the UK. For a survey of the position before the TM Directive, see Klaka [1994] GRUR Int. 321.

660 See the Survey by Beier and von Mühlendahl [1980] Mitt. d. Patentanwälte 101.

661 *Revlon v Cripps & Lee* [1980] F.S.R. 85 CA.

662 *Colgate-Palmolive v Markwell* [1989] R.P.C. 49 CA. The case sought to distinguish the *Revlon* case, but so far as it is based on the strict territorial conception of marks, it is hard to see that both could stand together.

663 See its statement 94/C340/37 (December 12, 1994). By contrast, the EFTA Court ruled that the issue of international exhaustion remained a matter for each participant state: *Mag Instrument v California Trading* [1998] E.T.M.R. 85 EFTA; Baudenbacher (1999) 22 Fordham Int. L.J. 645.

664 For the range of views, compare, e.g. Beier (1990) 21 I.I.C. 131; Verkade [1992] GRUR Int. 92; von Gamm [1993] WRP 793 (all against the Commission's position); Shea [1995] E.I.P.R. 174; Rasmussen [1995] E.I.P.R. 174; Weekblad 232 (all for); and again Van Bunnen in *Jura Vigilantibus* (1994) 285 (favouring freedom of entry as a result of delictual liability).

The issue is incurably divisive[665]: consumers object to paying high prices for goods which they are told are cheaper in another country and politicians are ready enough to share their concern. From the opposite side, manufacturers point to various reasons why the price differential is justifiable and should be supported by a trade mark right which prevents parallel importation internationally. They may have to invest more in order to launch and maintain a product in the higher-priced market; or it may be of different, superior quality there; or it may not be put on the less developed, cheaper market in the first place if parallel importation is the consequence: ideas of quality guarantee and investment protection underlie such pleas.

18–121 However, one frequent explanation of price differentials for a product as between roughly equivalent markets is the fluctuation of exchange rates—a general risk affecting profitability which has very little to do with the marketing of particular product lines. Yet branding is now a crucial factor in selling virtually all finished products, and trade marks are not protected as any special incentive to production (as are patented inventions or copyright works). Marks serve the primary function of distinguishing origin.[666] It is accordingly hard to accept as a matter of principle that the law should adopt so wide-ranging a protective measure as an undiscriminating non-exhaustion of trade mark rights at the international level.

Nonetheless, in reading art.7 of the Trade Mark Directive[667] as necessarily implying exactly this, the Commission and its Member State supporters found a technique for sealing off "Fortress Europe", operating across most trades as a matter of private right, rather than as a state measure imposed in a trade agreement and open therefore to re-negotiation. The legal question, accordingly, was whether art.7 does indeed achieve this. The Court of Justice gave its answer in *Silhouette v Hartlauer*[668]; and subsequently in *Davidoff* (below) and other cases it has affirmed that this sealing off has been effected in the vast majority of cases.

Silhouette concerned a superior range of spectacle frames, manufactured and sold internationally under the mark "Silhouette" by the Austrian claimants. A batch of the previous season's "Silhouette" spectacle frames were offloaded in Norway and sold on into Bulgaria on condition that marketing would occur only in former Eastern Bloc countries. Through further deals, however, the frames were imported into Austria by the defendant and sold through its chain of outlets, which were no part of Silhouette's distribution system there. If the former Austrian law still applied, an extensive rule of international exhaustion would have protected

[665] See the study, *Economic Consequences of the Choice of Regime of Exhaustion in the Area of Trade Marks* (1999), written by NERA and others for the European Commission in the wake of the *Silhouette* case; cf. Van Melle [1999] E.I.P.R. 63.

[666] A policy which is stated in the TM Directive Rec.10, as the ECJ has repeatedly emphasised: e.g. *CNL-Sucal v Hag* [1990] E.C.R. 3711; *IHT v Ideal Standard* [1994] E.C.R. I-2789.

[667] Together with its equivalent in the CTM Regulation art.12. Both are a reiteration in legislative form of the ECJ's jurisprudence following the *Centrafarm* case, [1974] E.C.R. 1183.

[668] *Silhouette v Hartlauer* [1998] E.C.R. I-4799; cf. Cornish [1998] E.I.P.R. 172.

the defendant. The general question which the Austrian Supreme Court put to the European Court of Justice was accordingly whether art.7 of the Trade Mark Directive, by sufficiently clear implication, required Member States to give up their national doctrine on the subject in favour of the EU law rule laid down in that article. The court, having reworded the question so as to make plain that this was the only question it was deciding, held that indeed there was no room for the continuance of the national law, whatever it might be. If some countries were free to maintain international exhaustion, while others did not, there would be an immediate difficulty in maintaining free movement within the internal market.[669]

As we shall see, the court has limited the rule of exhaustion in the internal market of the EEA so as not to apply where the trade mark function is unavoidably compromised, notably where there has been relabelling or repackaging of goods by a parallel importer which fails to meet the strict limits which the court itself has defined.[670] It must therefore remain open to the court to introduce limits, defined by EU law, to the art.7 rule of non-international exhaustion. There are two directions in which it might in the future still be drawn to impose qualifications upon that rule; after all, *HAG II*[671] illustrates that the court does sometimes change its mind! **18–122**

First, there must remain scope for the mark owner to consent to parallel importation from outside the EEA, since that consent must be binding. Such consent must usually be express, although it may be implied where facts and circumstances "unequivally demonstrate that the proprietor has renounced his right to oppose placing of the goods on the market within the EEA"[672] and cannot be implied from a course of dealing.[673] In *Zino Davidoff v A & G Imports*[674] the ECJ held that such an implication may not be made from the fact that the trade mark owner had not conveyed expressly to all subsequent purchasers his opposition to marketing within the EU. Also, it was irrelevant both that the goods themselves did not carry such a warning and that there was no specific contractual restriction in the conditions of sale. Consent could not be assumed from silence and it was up to the parallel importer to provide the evidence. Obviously, in practical terms this has made extremely difficult parallel importing from outside the EEA as such evidence

[669] Moreover, since national rights and the CTM must be subject to an equivalent rule, and since the CTM is governed exclusively by EU law, it could make no sense to preserve differing national principles for the former: cf. Abbott and Verkade [1998] B.I.E. 111.

[670] Below, para.19–09.

[671] *CNL-Sucal v Hag* [1990] E.C.R. 3711.

[672] per Jacob L.J. in *Mastercigars Direct v Hunters & Frankau* [2007] R.P.C. 24 at paras 16–17.

[673] Although "a positive decision to condone" was found to be sufficient: per Jacob L.J. in *Mastercigars Direct v Hunters & Frankau* [2007] R.P.C. 24 at para.59.

[674] Joined with *Levi Strauss v Tesco* [2002] R.P.C. 403.

is rarely available or accessible.[675] However, in some circumstances competition law may impose its own inhibitions on express notices limiting export to EEA countries. This possibility we explore in the next chapter.[676]

Secondly, at some point the ECJ may decide to follow the precedents currently prevailing in US law on the subject. It could distinguish between cases where the parallel imports are in no relevant way distinguishable from those being sold directly in the home market and cases where the goods are different in quality and home consumers could be confused about them. As already noted, the latter case is one where there is a particular justification for preventing the entry of the parallel imports. In the inevitably rough distinctions to which the law is driven on this question, the line is one that could be used to maintain a reasonable balance of interests. It may be in Europe's longer-term interests that it should move in this direction.

---

[675] See the suggestion of the German Supreme Court that labelling by the trade mark owner should be required to the effect that the goods may not be sold into the EU, discussed in Rosner, [2002] E.I.P.R. 604. For an example of the problems faced by the importer, see *Mastercigars Direct v Hunters & Frankau* [2006] R.P.C. 24 CA, involving the importation of Cuban cigars, and *Sun Microsystems v M-Tech Data* [2010] E.T.M.R. 13, involving the importation into the UK of disk drives purchased in the USA.

[676] Below, para.19–21.

Part VI

THE EUROPEAN DIMENSION AND NEW TECHNOLOGIES

CHAPTER 19

INTELLECTUAL PROPERTY IN THE EUROPEAN UNION

Over the past two decades, world trade has been transformed by the end of the Cold War and by the emergence of rapidly developing industrial economies in both Asia and the former Communist bloc, as well as by the creation of the World Trade Organisation as successor to GATT. The long-standing industrialised states see labour-intensive production moving away, leaving them to count increasingly on their sophisticated skills in servicing, marketing, financing and other intangible assets. For developed and developing countries alike, there are new reasons to attach major importance to the creation of value which intellectual property rights can provide. As a consequence it was possible to include a panoply of protection in the TRIPS Agreement. Indeed, the protection was so broad that it has had to be reined back since and the Doha WTO Ministerial Declaration[1] recognised that the interests of the developing countries had not been catered for sufficiently, in particular in relation to public health. **19–01**

No doubt, full integration of intellectual property regulation on a global scale is likely to be a slow and tortuous process, even if it is accepted as desirable or appropriate (both of which must be open to vigorous debate). Even within so committed an association of states as the EU, movement towards the (supposed) ideal of a standard set of rules applicable on a unitary basis throughout the whole territory has been bumpy and difficult, as so many chapters of this book show. This has often been because intellectual property forms a central barrier along the boundary between fair and unfair competition, and ideas about where that boundary should be drawn undoubtedly vary. These ideas are about basic values which, on being converted into practical policies and legal rules, need to build on shared experiences as well as respect for differences of national attitudes and imperatives.

[1] Adopted on November 14, 2001, see Commission on Intellectual Property Rights Report, *Integrating Intellectual Property Rights and Development Policy* (London, 2002) at p.40.

The EU has been obliged to settle the place of intellectual property in relation to a variety of its quintessential objectives, which include the elimination of: internal restrictions on the import and export of goods; a common commercial policy; an internal market without obstacles to the free movement of goods, persons, services and capital; non-distortion of internal market competition; approximation of national laws required for the functioning of the Single Market; promotion of research and technological development; encouragement of trans-European networks; and the strengthening of consumer protection.[2]

There are points at which details of intellectual property rules have had to adapt to fundamental tenets of the Treaty. One basic guarantee of integration is that there shall be no discrimination on ground of nationality between citizens of Member States.[3] This had a dramatic impact on the performer's right in German law, which was accorded to German nationals wherever they performed, but to citizens of other countries (including other EU Member States) only if the performance took place in a Rome Convention country (as that Convention required). By German law, a British pop singer, Phil Collins, was thus not entitled to the performer's right in a performance recorded in the United States—a non-Rome Convention country—whereas a German singer would have been.[4] The Court of Justice held that he must equally be accorded the right.[5]

1. The Internal Market: "Intellectual Property"[6]

(1) Free movement of goods

19–02 After over 50 years of striving towards a unified internal market, the elimination of price differentials for goods as between Member States still

[2] Treaty of Lisbon art.3. The Treaty of Lisbon (hereafter, EU Treaty), also known as the Treaty on the Functioning of Europe, which incorporated and supplemented the Treaty of the European Union (TEU or Maastricht Treaty) and the EC Treaty (formerly the Treaty of Rome), was signed on December 13, 2007, Cmnd 7310 of January 2008, and entered into force on December 1, 2009.

[3] EU Treaty art.18.

[4] *Collins v Imtrat* [1993] E.C.R. I-5145. In a joined case, Cliff Richard had no right under German law because his performance was recorded in Britain before Germany assumed Rome Convention obligations. Accordingly, he was subject to discrimination under the EU Treaty.

[5] EU law thus affected the scope of the right within its own national territory; no cross-border issue arose over moving goods or providing services. For the impact of the case on implementation of the Directive on Copyright Term, see above, para.11–45.

[6] Of the extensive literature on this topic, Oliver, *Free Movement of Goods in the European Community* 4th edn (2003), paras 8–172—8–237; Keeling, *Intellectual Property Rights in EU Law; Free Movement and Competition Law* (2003). Also, Joliet [1975] C.L.P. 15; Rothnie, *Parallel Imports* (1993); Marenco and Banks (1990) 15 Eur.L.R. 224; Beier (1990) 21 I.I.C. 131; Ullrich in Gijlstra and Murphy (eds), *Competition Law of Western Europe and the USA*, C–491; Loewenheim (1995) 26 I.I.C. 829; *Kerly*, at Ch.16. For the application of the policy to new Member States, see Heath (2004) 35 I.I.C. 776.

remains far off, although brought much closer by the introduction of the Euro at the beginning of 2002. Differences in national tastes and other priorities, differences in the cost of establishing new products in particular parts of the market, differences in the way in which government influences or controls prices in certain sectors (notably pharmaceuticals), fluctuations in currency exchange rates between the Eurozone and other Member States—any one of these may cause understandable price differences. In consequence, parallel (or gray) importation, i.e. buying in a low-cost country and selling in a high-cost country, is likely to occur (and indeed in many ways is encouraged) and that practice may act, within the EU itself, as an adjustment mechanism driving towards price uniformity. The activities of the parallel importer are thus of importance to achievement of the Single Market and have been supported, wherever possible, by EU institutions—not least by the Court of Justice.

In the formative years of what was then called the European Economic Community (EEC), the question soon arose: how far could intellectual property in one Member State (Country Impo) be used to stop the movement into that country of the "same" genuine goods from another Member State (Country Expo)? What was the situation, in particular, when the goods had first been marketed in the other Member State (Country Expo) and had been acquired there by a parallel importer who would take them to Country Impo, only to be met there by proceedings for infringement of the national intellectual property right? Specifically, could the action in Country Impo succeed when the initial marketing in Country Expo was by the owner of the national right in Country Impo, or by a person connected with that owner—through a corporate grouping, manufacturing licence or distribution agreement?

As already outlined in Ch.1, the Court of Justice reached answers which in considerable measure favoured the parallel importer.[7] At the beginning the court applied the Rules of Competition (in arts 85 and 86 of the Treaty of Rome, now arts 101 and 102 EU Treaty); but as time went on[8] increasingly relied upon the principle of the Free Movement of Goods (under arts 30 and 36 Treaty of Rome, now arts 34 and 36 EU Treaty). For an outline of these provisions of the Treaty, the reader should return to the discussion in Ch.1, where in particular their differing scope is noted.

(a) *Preliminary factors*

Over time the Court of Justice has laid down a number of basic tenets concerning the impact of the free movement of goods principle on intellectual property. These can be listed in short order: **19–03**

[7] See above, para.1–51.

[8] The prohibition on measures having equivalent effect to quantitative imports came into effect only in 1970, see Oliver, *Free Movement of Goods in the European Community* 4th edn (2003) at para.6–03.

(1) an action in a national court, founded upon a national intellectual property law, which prevents the importation of goods is a measure "having equivalent effect" to the quantitative restrictions on imports between Member States which are prohibited by art.34.[9]
(2) art.34 can be relied upon directly by a defendant to an intellectual property action. The article therefore overrides the national right unless the latter can be maintained as an exception under art.36;
(3) art.36 obliges the claimant to show: (a) that the right was a provision for "the protection of industrial or commercial property"; and (b) that in the circumstances it does not amount to "a means of arbitrary discrimination nor to a disguised restriction on trade between Member States";
(4) not only patents, trade marks and design rights but also authors' rights, neighbouring rights, database rights, plant variety rights,[10] appellations of origin[11] and even joint rights in geographical denominations[12] are treated as within the notion of "industrial or commercial property".[13] Much has come therefore to turn upon the derogations for arbitrary discrimination and disguised restrictions on trade in the second sentence of art.36, which the court has, by and large, treated as an invitation for judicial policy-making;
(5) some of the most difficult cases have arisen because of the absence or more limited scope of intellectual property rights in Country Expo than in Country Impo. The court has very largely refused to enter

[9] It is with the state's intervention that the free movement policy is concerned, not with any act of an undertaking, such as selling with a prohibition against export: see, e.g. *Bayer v Süllhöfer* [1988] E.C.R. 5249; *Ministre Public v Tournier* [1989] E.C.R. 2521. The latter falls to be considered under the Competition Rules: see below, para.19–14. In certain circumstances it has been held that what at first sight seems to be an undertaking is in fact an emanation of the state and therefore caught by art.34; thus, in *Commission v Federal Republic of Germany* [2002] E.T.M.R. 823, a private organisation administering a quality mark system ("Markenqualität aus deutschen Landen"—Quality mark from the German provinces) was considered by the Advocate-General (Jacobs) to constitute a measure taken by the German State contrary to art.28 (now 34).

[10] As in *Nungesser* [1981] E.C.R. 45.

[11] *Delhaize v Promalvin* [1992] E.C.R. I-3669; cf. A.G. Jacobs in *Commission v Federal Republic of Germany* [2002] E.T.M.R. 823, suggesting that simple geographical indications of source do not constitute industrial or commercial property within art.30 (now 36), at para.42–43.

[12] *Exportur v Lur* [1992] E.C.R. I-5529.

[13] Arguments were made in the 1970s that authors' rights, because of their moral ascendancy, must be treated apart; but that would require finding an even broader exception somewhere within the EC Treaty. In the event they were not distinguished: *Musik Vertrieb Membran v GEMA* [1981] E.C.R. 147; *Dansk Supermarked* [1981] E.C.R. 181. It has been argued, contrary to the court's approach, that "unfair competition" laws should be similarly treated, because they are included within the Paris Convention: see Beier (1990) 21 I.I.C. 131 at 159, 160. This view has not gained acceptance.

upon any critical evaluation of such differences.[14] Until there is a relevant harmonisation Directive, or an EU right becomes a complete substitute, it is for national law in each state to determine the content and scope of the rights and the conditions for obtaining them[15]; and

(6) where EU legislation does express the role of exhaustion within the Single Market it will be interpreted in the sense already developed in the court's decisions on arts 34-36 (ex 28–30).[16]

(b) *Basic rule and its application*

Despite the obscurities of art.36 in relation to intellectual property, the Court of Justice reached a basic proposition on the free movement of goods policy: **19–04**

> "The exercise, by a patentee [or other intellectual property owner], of the right which he enjoys under the legislation of a Member State to prohibit the sale, in that State, of a product protected by the patent [or other right] which has been marketed in another Member State by the patentee [or other owner] or with his consent is incompatible with the rules of the E.C. Treaty concerning the free movement of goods within the Common Market."

What is relevant is consent to the act of first marketing of the specific goods,[17] not to the act of manufacture, whether that occurs within the EU or outside it.[18]

It should be noted at once that, in this formulation, the policy only has its over-riding effect where national law would otherwise empower the right-owner to prevent the parallel importation—so the starting point is always the scope of the national law of Country Impo. Note also that the policy provides a rule of "EU-wide exhaustion"—it operates when the right-owner

[14] See, however, the comment of the late Sir Hugh Laddie on the *Magill* judgment of the ECJ: "Many believe that part, at least, of the ECJ's motivation in effectively emasculating the right was the belief that in this respect British and Irish law was unreasonably out of line with the law of our Continental neighbours. Put it another way, if all Member States of the European Union accorded copyright protection to television ... schedules, would the ECJ have felt able to emasculate it as it did in Magill? I doubt it" [2001] E.I.P.R. 402 at 405.

[15] See, e.g. *Terrapin* [1976] E.C.R. 1039 (scope of protection for well-known marks in Germany); *Nancy Kean Gifts* [1982] E.C.R. 2853 (entitlement of applicant to Benelux design right); *Volvo v Veng* [1988] E.C.R. 6211; and *CICRA v Renault* [1988] E.C.R. 6039 (both concerning design rights applicable to car spare parts); *Thetford v Fiamma* [1988] 3 C.M.L.R. 549 (narrower test of novelty in UK patent law meant patent maintainable there while not in Italy); *Generics v Smith Kline & French Laboratories* [1997] R.P.C. 801 ECJ (generic drug manufacturer infringed patent in course of obtaining authorisation to market after its expiry; remedy could include an injunction ceasing 14 months after expiry). See also *Deutsche Renault v Audi* [1993] 1 E.C.R. 6227.

[16] An example is the exhaustion provision in the Community Trade Mark Regulation, art.12, and the First Trade Mark Approximation Directive, art.7: see above, paras 18–113, 18–120.

[17] It is not enough that other batches of the same product have already been placed on the first market: *Sebago v GB-Unic* [1999] E.T.M.R. 681 ECJ.

[18] *Phytheron v Jean Bourdon* [1997] E.C.R. I-1729 ECJ.

has marketed the goods, or consented to their marketing, in Country Expo and thereby has brought his rights (in Country Impo) to an end; it is not normally concerned with the direct access of the manufacturer or initial distributor in Country Expo to the market in Country Impo.

The Court applied the principle, for instance, to the following circumstances:

- (*Deutsche Grammophon v Metro*[19]: parent and subsidiary.) Records marketed by the French subsidiary of Deutsche Grammophon in France were bought there and exported indirectly to Germany for sale at a price less than that set under the then operating rules for resale price maintenance. Deutsche Grammophon's neighbouring right in the sound recording under German law could not be used to stop those sales, even though their effect was to destroy the maintained price at all retail outlets. France then had no equivalent neighbouring right and no price maintenance system, which may have explained the fact that French prices were much lower than the German. These factors did not, however, affect the outcome, since Deutsche Grammophon had consented to the initial sales by its subsidiaries.
- (*Centrafarm v Sterling Drug*[20]: same right-holder, different subsidiaries in a group.) A urinary infection drug, patented and marketed under the registered mark, Negram, was produced in the United Kingdom by the parent patentee, Sterling Drug, and marketed there by a Sterling subsidiary, registered proprietor of the mark. Its parallel importation into the Netherlands was opposed by Sterling as owner of the equivalent Dutch patent and a different subsidiary as owner of the Dutch trade mark. The Dutch price was much higher, chiefly because of improvements in the exchange rate of the guilder against sterling; but also possibly because the major purchaser in the United Kingdom, the Department of Health, could buy at reasonable royalty rates as a Crown user, and because of the Department's strong assertion of its buying power. These various factors did not justify the use of either the patent or the trade mark to block free movement between Member States: all that mattered was the consent to the United Kingdom marketing by a member of the group.
- (*Dansk Supermarked v Imerco*[21]: manufacturing licence.) Imerco, a Danish firm, commissioned Broadhurst to manufacture china services in the United Kingdom, subject to strict quality standards, for sale in Denmark in celebration of Imerco's fiftieth anniversary. Three hundred sub-standard sets were rejected but Broadhurst were permitted

[19] *Deutsche Grammophon v Metro* [1971] E.C.R. 487.

[20] *Centrafarm v Sterling Drug* [1974] E.C.R. 1147 (patent) and *Centrafarm v Winthrop* [1974] E.C.R. 1183 (trade mark).

[21] *Dansk Supermarked v Imerco* [1981] E.C.R. 181.

to sell them off, subject to the condition that they were not to be brought onto the Danish market. When a parallel importer did just that, Imerco was not permitted to assert its copyright in the designs, nor its trade mark, against their sale; nor could it make a difference that the breach of condition rendered the conduct a form of unfair competition.[22]

- (*Merck v Stephar*[23]: manufacturer operating in unprotected and protected market.) Merck held no patent on a hypertension drug, "Moduretic", in Italy but did have a patent for it in the Netherlands. It marketed the drug in Italy, where a parallel importer acquired it and exported to the Netherlands. Even though *Merck* had had no opportunity at all in Italy to profit from patent protection, the fact that it had itself undertaken the marketing there was treated as exhausting the Dutch patent right.[24]

(c) *Justifications*

These decisions were justified primarily in terms of policy. For example, the Court of Justice said of the subject-matter of *Deutsche Grammophon*: **19–05**

> "If a right related to copyright is relied upon to prevent the marketing in a Member State of products distributed by the holder of the right or with his consent on the territory of another Member State on the sole ground that such distribution did not take place on the national territory, such a prohibition, which would legitimise the isolation of national markets, would be repugnant to the essential purpose of the Treaty, which is to unite national markets into a Single Market."

Underlying this justification is an assumption that, had the product first been sold in Country Impo, the right would thereafter have been treated as exhausted and could not affect subsequent sales.[25] But because that exhaustion was applied only within the domestic market and not internationally, the parallel importer from elsewhere in the EU was discriminated

[22] Specifically, in breach of the Danish Marketing Act of 1974. For the application of similar principles to unfair competition laws, see below, paras 19–11 et seq.

[23] *Merck v Stephar* [1981] E.C.R. 2063. Re-affirmed in *Merck v Primecrown*, below, para.19–08.

[24] Where a product imported into Germany bore the words "Contains aspirin", this could not constitute infringement of the German registered mark "Aspirin" because the products had been put on the market in the UK (where aspirin was a generic term) by a company associated with the German trade mark proprietor: (2000) 31 I.I.C. 349. Thus, as in *Merck v Stephar*, there was no right to be exhausted in Country Expo.

[25] Subsequently, the court seems not to have considered whether the national right was subject to exhaustion. Had it done so in *Sterling Drug*, it would have found that UK patent law had no doctrine of exhaustion (see above, paras 6–15, 6–16). Its result could not, therefore, have depended on discrimination under art.36 (ex art.30); instead there must have been a "disguised" (i.e. unjustifiable) restriction on trade.

against. The Court of Justice might have taken its stand explicitly upon the discrimination provision of art.36 (ex art.30). But it was here dealing with *property*; and art.345 (ex art.222) prescribes that the "Treaty shall in no way prejudice the rules in Member States governing the system of property ownership".[26] Uneasy that it risked trespassing on this special preserve, the court ventured upon legalistic distinctions whose obscurity served only to disguise their essential banality.

The first of these is the supposed distinction between the existence of a right and its exercise:

> "...it is clear from [art.36], in particular its second sentence, as well as from the context, that whilst the Treaty does not affect the existence of rights recognised by the legislation of a Member State in matters of industrial and commercial property, yet the exercise of these rights may nevertheless, depending on the circumstances, be affected by the prohibitions of the Treaty."[27]

Since a right exists to the extent that it can be exercised, this amounted to superior sophistry and the court soon chose to go further (probably in the hope of identifying "existence") by holding that the derogations from free movement permitted by art.36 can be made only "where such derogations are justified for the purpose of safeguarding rights which constitute the specific subject-matter of this property".[28] While the court has from time to time attempted (in particular in the context of an alleged abuse under art.102—ex 82) some elucidation of what the specific subject matter of various intellectual property rights is, in most instances the only real content of this "definition" concerns the scope of exhaustion. For instance:

> "In relation to patents, the specific subject-matter of the industrial property is the guarantee that the patentee, to reward the creative effort of the inventor, has the exclusive right to use an invention with a view to manufacturing industrial products and putting them into circulation for

---

[26] The reference to "property systems" expressed the intention to preserve whatever degree of socialisation existed in Member States. Accordingly, the impact of what is now art.345 (ex art.222) on a conflict between a Treaty policy and national intellectual property was not clear and produced starkly opposed views: see Ladas (1974) 5 I.I.C. 302; Mann (1975) 24 I.C.L.Q. 31; Mak (1975) 6 I.I.C. 29; Waelbroeck (1976) 21 Antitrust Bull. 99; Jacobs (1975) 24 I.C.L.Q. 643; Johannes and Wright (1976) 1 Eur. L.R. 230. More recently, the ECJ reiterated that the right to property must be viewed in relation to its social function, when considering Directive 2001/37 on the presentation and sale of tobacco products: *R. v Secretary of State for Health Ex p. British American Tobacco (Investments*, noted at [2002] E.T.M.R. 1244 ECJ.

[27] *Centrafarm v Sterling Drug* [1974] E.C.R. 1149 ECJ at para.7. The formula has been much recited: Marenco and Banks (1990) 15 Eur.L.R. 224 at 224–225.

[28] *Sterling Drug* [1974] E.C.R. 1149 para.8.

the first time, either directly or by the grant of licences to third parties, as well as the right to oppose infringements."[29]

As a proposition, this too provides little by way of justification or even clarification. It might acquire some substance if it were a statement, made in the light of a comparative study, that all the Member States accepted as a matter of policy that the intellectual property right deserved to cover only first marketing. In fact the position in Member States is not uniform, and anyway differs from one type of intellectual property to another. The proposition, therefore, does little other than reiterate the very policy decision the Court of Justice is seeking to justify.

The most that can be said for the "boot-strapping" character of this core reasoning is that the court is left free to adopt a pragmatic approach to the other related issues reviewed below. This pragmatism is apparent in the examples which follow.

(d) *The "common origin" adventure*

In one spectacular instance in this sphere, the Court of Justice has indeed reversed itself and, whilst the result is now an historical diversion, it is not therefore to be ignored. In 1973, at the height of its determination to free the internal market of intellectual property sub-divisions, the court developed a second principle, the so-called doctrine of "common origin", which was distinct from the principle concerning exhaustion by first marketing with consent. **19–06**

(*Van Zuylen v Hag*[30] ("*Hag I*").) The "Hag" trade mark for decaffeinated coffee, originally held by a single enterprise in Germany and Belgium, had passed in the latter country into entirely separate ownership as a measure of wartime sequestration. The original common ownership of the mark was held to entitle the German producer to market his trade-marked product–either through a distributor (in reality, a parallel importer) or even directly—in the Benelux territories. Reflecting a disdainful view of the purpose and value of marks, the court indicated that other means must be found for informing the Benelux public that they were obtaining the German, and not the Belgian, product.

The decision provoked an outcry from industry, for, if the Court of Justice would go so far, why not apply the same result even to marks of

[29] *Sterling Drug* [1974] E.C.R. 1149 para.9. The specific subject matter of the trade mark was first described as "the guarantee that the owner of the trade mark has the exclusive right to use that trade mark, for the purpose of putting products protected by the trade mark into circulation for the first time, and is therefore intended to protect him against competitors wishing to take advantage of the status and reputation of the trade mark by selling products illegally bearing that trade mark": *Centrafarm v Winthrop* [1974] E.C.R. 1147 ECJ para.8. This was developed further in later cases; see *American Home Products* [1978] E.C.R. 1823 and "*Hag II*" [1990] 1 E.C.R. 3711. It took temerity to attempt such a formulation for copyright, but the GC tried in "*Magill*": [1991] E.C.R. II-485 paras 54–56 and following.

[30] *Van Zuylen v Hag* [1974] E.C.R. 731.

unconnected enterprises in different EU countries which had never had an original connection? That too would liberate the internal market. In the event, the court soon drew back from this further step, holding in "*Terranova*"[31] that common origin was a special case.

Eventually, the court would hear the counter-case between, in effect, the parties to the first *"Hag"* decision, and would reverse itself. Now showing an enhanced appreciation of trade marks as necessary indicators of the source of goods and services, the court held in *CNL-Sucal v Hag GF* ("*Hag II*") that the Belgian business had no right to go into the German market, directly or indirectly, because in that territory the mark designated the German enterprise.[32] The same must apply to imports into Belgium (despite the first decision); it could not be said that the German firm deserved greater protection because it had never lost or changed its rights at home.

The ensuing decision in the *Ideal Standard* case[33] removed the last vestiges of "common origin" by holding that, even where trade marks were split within the EU between separate enterprises by a voluntary assignment, rather than by Government expropriation, this of itself did not entitle either of the consequent owners or parallel importers to go into the other country. However, given the voluntary character of the assignment, that transaction and the surrounding conduct of the parties would fall to be assessed under the Rules of Competition.

The *affaire "Hag"* shows how far the court had progressed in its appreciation of the objectives of intellectual property. For the scope of national laws to be limited by virtue of art.34, it appears that there must generally have been a consensual act in Country Expo bringing about an exhaustion of right in Country Impo which frees parallel imports from possible restraint by reliance on national rights. The main addition to this arises when there is some provision in a national law which disadvantages imported goods in comparison with domestically-produced goods.[34] This attitude is much more scrupulous than in related legal fields where art.36 is held not to apply.[35]

(e) *Absence of consent*

19–07 By necessary implication, if a person other than the right-owner in Country Expo (or someone acting with its consent) placed the goods on the Expo market, there would be no exhaustion of the right in Country Impo.

---

[31] See [1976] E.C.R. 1039.

[32] *CNL-Sucal v Hag GF* [1990] 1 E.C.R. I-3711. Note the eloquent appreciation of the issue by Jacobs A.G.

[33] *IHT v Ideal Standard* [1994] 1 E.C.R. 2789; Gagliardi [1998] E.I.P.R. 371. See also the writings of its *juge rapporteur*: Joliet (1983) 5 N.W.J Int. L. 755; (1984) 15 I.I.C. 21.

[34] As for instance, the less favourable conditions of compulsory patent licences when granted for imports from another EU country than when manufactured in the domestic market: *Allen & Hanburys v Generics* [1988] E.C.R. 1275; *EC Commission v United Kingdom and Italy* [1992] 1 E.C.R. 829.

[35] See below, paras 19–11 et seq.

(*Terrapin v Terranova.*)[36] The owner of "Terranova" and other "Terra" prefix marks (for construction materials) in Germany could assert them against the importation of prefabricated housing made by a British firm and bearing its house mark, "Terrapin". Because there had never been any connection between the firms and the marks had been acquired quite independently in the two countries, the German firm's action could be maintained.[37]

(*Keurkoop v Nancy Kean Gifts.*)[38] The owner of a Benelux registered design[39] for a handbag could object to the importation of bags bearing the design from another Member State into Holland, if they were not marketed in that other country "by, or with the consent of, the proprietor of the right or a person legally or economically dependent on him".[40]

(*EMI Electrola v Patricia.*)[41] The sound recording right in Cliff Richard's recordings had expired in Denmark but not in Germany, where it was still owned by EMI. The defendant, an unconnected company, organised the marketing of its own version of the recordings by a Danish company in Denmark, and it re-purchased them for export to Germany. It was unsuccessful in claiming the freedom to ignore the German right.[42]

(*Pharmon v Hoechst.*)[43] Hoechst held patents on the drug, frusemide, in the United Kingdom and the Netherlands. DDSA obtained a compulsory licence to manufacture and sell the drug in the United Kingdom, subject to a prohibition against export.[44] DDSA nonetheless claimed the right under art.34 to sell the British drug in Holland.[45] Because the manufacturing licence was compulsory, the Court of Justice found that *Merck* did not consent to DDSA's activities and so could still rely upon its Dutch patent.

In *Pharmon* the court repeated its definition of the specific subject-matter of a patent, and held it:

---

[36] *Terrapin v Terranova* [1976] E.C.R. 1039.

[37] The case raised concern over the scope of German trade mark and unfair competition rights: for this aspect, see below, para.19–11. It had also to deal with the separate doctrine of "common origin" of trade marks, on which it is now otiose: see above, para.19–06.

[38] *Keurkoop v Nancy Kean Gifts* [1982] E.C.R. 2853.

[39] Under Benelux Design Law, a person other than the designer could apply for the design unless the designer objected—a common enough formula in intellectual property law. The court treated this rule as a matter purely for national law, and not one which could be the subject of an attack under the proviso to art.36 (ex art.30).

[40] There must be no anti-competitive agreement or concerted practice or co-ordinated registration of the design under separate names in different states, but it was for national courts to assess this.

[41] *EMI Electrola v Patricia* [1989] E.C.R. 79; Strivens [1989] E.I.P.R. 297.

[42] It was this case which provided justification for the Duration Directive, equating (and in many cases extending) the term of authors' and neighbouring rights.

[43] *Pharmon v Hoechst* [1985] E.C.R. 2281.

[44] Granted under the PA 1949 s.41, repealed in 1977.

[45] Direct exports were therefore at issue, but the court considered the case as if they were by a parallel importer.

> "necessary to allow the patent proprietor to prevent the importation and marketing of products manufactured under a compulsory licence in order to protect the substance of his exclusive rights under his patent".[46]

In doing so it referred to *Merck v Stephar*[47] without concern. But its remark appears to cast doubt on the outcome of that case, raising the questions which have so frequently been posed by commentators[48]: if a right-holder had no equivalent right in Country Expo from which to extract a benefit there, why should its mere consent to first marketing deprive it of the enhanced value of the product in Country Impo where it does have a right? Does not the *Merck* decision make it hard for the right-owner to market in Country Expo, since to do so threatens to reduce the Country Impo price towards that in Country Expo? May that not deprive consumers in Country Expo of a novel and desirable product?

19–08 The markedly low prices of patented pharmaceuticals in Spain and Portugal made the problem particularly pressing once those countries passed beyond the transitional stage of their entry into the EU (and the same issues have arisen more recently with the entry of eastern European and other countries). In a case aimed against the export of parallel drugs from Spain to Britain, the manufacturer—again *Merck*—sought to show that its moral responsibility to supply an important drug even to low-profit countries fettered their "consent" as much as if they had been subjected to compulsory licensing. The court, however, refused to alter its position and required that no injunction in Britain should prevent the movement of the patented goods.[49] It did so, despite the fact that, as cases such as "*Hag II*" and "*Ideal Standard*" demonstrate, the Court of Justice by then attached a great deal more significance to the objectives of the different forms of intellectual property than previously.

(f) *Repackaging and relabelling*

19–09 In the sphere of trade marks, some particularly difficult issues arose over repackaging and relabelling with a different mark. These special principles, first developed by the court under arts 30–36 (now 34–36), have been given explicit legislative expression in the Trade Marks Directive and Regulation.[50] In many EU Member States, it is considered an infringement of the

[46] *Pharmon* [1985] E.C.R. 2281, judgment, para.26.

[47] *Merck v Stephar* [1981] E.C.R. 2063.

[48] Led by Joliet [1975] C.L.P. 15. Where statutory licensing powers exist (for instance, under Crown use provisions, or an entitlement only to fair remuneration in copyright), but the licensor has nonetheless entered voluntary licences, it may be that *Pharmon* will apply: cf. *Sterling Drug* [1974] E.C.R. 1149; *Musik Vertrieb Membran v GEMA* [1981] E.C.R. 147.

[49] *Merck v Primecrown* [1997] F.S.R. 237, cf. the opposite conclusion of Fennelly A.G. The decision is criticised by Fernandex Vicin [1996] E.C.L.R. 219; Korah [1997] E.C.L.R. 265; Kon and Schaffer [1997] E.C.L.R. 123; Torremans and Stamatoudi [1997] E.I.P.R. 545.

[50] TM Directive art.7: CTM Regulation art.12, for which see above, para.18–114. Within the EEA (the EU countries plus Iceland, Liechtenstein and Norway), exhaustion of trade marks must apply unless EU law admits an exception.

mark to deal in marked goods which have been re-packed, re-marked or otherwise interfered with, because the mark no longer accurately indicates that the goods come unaltered from the originating enterprise. In the pharmaceutical field, this aspect of the right was turned against parallel importers in two ways:

(*Hoffmann-La Roche v Centrafarm*[51]: repackaging.) The practice in Germany was to supply certain drugs in packages of 1,000, whilst in the United Kingdom sales were in lots of 100 or 250. A parallel importer from the United Kingdom accordingly repacked the smaller lots into the larger, re-using the mark and indicating that it was the importer. Although the essential function of the mark as a guarantee of origin "would in fact be jeopardised if it were permissible for a third party to affix the mark to the product, even to an original product", nonetheless it had to be asked whether a particular assertion of the right amounted to a "disguised restriction on trade". This would after all occur in a case where a new larger pack showed that the original packs had not been interfered with, or where a public authority supervised the repackaging; but to act within this exception, the parallel importer must warn the right-owner in advance and indicate on the packaging what had been done.[52]

In the *Paranova* case, the court restated the conditions under which an importer may repackage goods where that is necessary in order to emulate the manufacturer's own practices in different markets.[53] It adds, as instances of permitted conduct, the fixing of self-adhesive labels to the inner packaging of a product, the addition of new instructions or information, and the insertion of an additional article. The national court must determine whether any of these acts omits information or misleads consumers or does not comply with the manufacturer's method of use or dosage. In long-running joined cases which have been referred to it twice, *Boehringer v Swingward* and *Boehringer v Dowelhurst*, the ECJ has held that the parallel importer must provide reasonable initial evidence that the repackaging has done no damage to the trade mark proprietor but then the burden is shifted to the

[51] *Hoffmann-La Roche v Centrafarm* [1978] E.C.R. 1139. An attempt was made to reverse this decision upon the argument that the exhaustion rule now embodied in the TM Directive art.7, allows exceptions to be made for legitimate reasons. Jacobs A.G and the ECJ refused to upset the earlier decision: *Bristol-Myers Squibb v Paranova* [1996] F.S.R. 225.

[52] In *Pfizer v EurimPharm* [1981] E.C.R. 2913, the parallel importer was held by the court to have satisfied the conditions. See the persuasive criticisms of the requirement for notice put forward by Laddie J. in *Glaxo v Dowelhurst (No. 2)* [2000] E.T.M.R. 415 at paras 117–143, but given short shrift by the ECJ in its response to the resultant reference.

[53] *Bristol-Myers Squibb v Paranova* [1996] I-E.C.R. 3457. However, where the packaging of a pharmaceutical has been specified in a marketing authorisation under Regulation 2309/93 (on the authorisation of medicinal products, including directions on presentation and form of packaging) it is not permitted to repackage, for example to repack 25-item packs into 1 10-item package: *Aventis Pharma v Kohlpharma* [2002] All E.R. (D) 105. See also, *Wellcome v Paranova*, [2009] E.T.M.R. 20, ECJ (December 22, 2008).

proprietor to show that both its reputation and that of the trade mark have been harmed.[54]

The court, however, has no objection to relabelling where the different marks contribute to an artificial partitioning of the internal market, whether or not this is the manufacturer's intention and the conditions prescribed for repackaging are followed.[55] The reputation of the trade mark must not be liable to be damaged[56]; but this does not mean that the manufacturer's own bar code for country of origin must be left on the product—an important factor in the complex battles over the sourcing of parallel imports.[57]

In disposing of the constant stream of relabelling and repackaging cases,[58] the court has faced practices which pose a peculiarly provocative constraint on free movement. It has only been able to provide awkward answers which have not proved easy to apply in subsequent practice and many of the illogical results were identified in the challenging judgment of Laddie J. in *Glaxo v Dowelhurst (No. 2)*.[59] There may, for instance, be various explanations of why different marks were adopted in different countries: different prior rights in each of them, different relations to national languages, and so on. The court's discomfort is marked in its reasoning in subsequent cases. In particular the "existence/exercise" distinction is wrung dry of identifiable content. Indeed it appears that, with pharmaceuticals, to some extent the battleground has moved to questions on the EU product licensing regime.[60]

(2) Rights in performance and other temporary use

19–10 The Court of Justice developed its main doctrine around the primary activities of the parallel importer: the actual importation or the subsequent sale of goods embodying or bearing the protected subject-matter. But intellectual property may be employed against other activities. When these

[54] The extent of harm is left unclear, the court did not adopt the A.G. Sharpston's suggestion that the proprietor needed to show "serious" harm.

[55] So proposed by Jacobs A.G. in *Upjohn v Paranova* [1999] E.T.M.R. 97. In the pharmaceutical field, the European Medicines Evaluation Authority has imposed a requirement of a single mark for the whole EU except in justified cases only (according to the EMEA 35% of trade marks submitted were rejected in 2000 and 2001). The opposition remains vociferous, particularly from the European pharmaceutical industry association EFPIA. For an example of the issues which can arise, see *Doncaster Pharmaceuticals v (The) Bolton Pharmaceutical Co* [2007] F.S.R. 1 CA.

[56] Using the mark in chain-store advertising may be a sufficient injury to its reputation: see *Christian Dior Parfums v Evora* [1998] R.P.C. 166 ECJ and *Copad v Dior* [2009] E.T.M.R. 22 ECJ; above, para.18–114.

[57] *Loendersloot v George Ballantine* [1998] F.S.R. 544 ECJ. In this instance also, the manufacturer's intention is treated by the court as irrelevant. See Clark [1998] E.I.P.R. 328; cf. *Sportswear v Stonestyle* [2007] F.S.R. 33 CA, where the Court of Appeal held that it was not unarguable that art.81 (now 101 EU Treaty) could be used as a shield in a trade mark infringement action involving parallel imports: at paras 40–41.

[58] For an in-depth analysis, see Stothers, *Parallel Trade in Europe: Intellectual Property, Competition and Regulatory Law* (2007, Hart Publishing).

[59] *Glaxo v Dowelhurst (No. 2* [2000] E.T.M.R. 415.

[60] *Aventis Pharma Deutschland v Kohlpharma* [2003] E.T.M.R. 143 ECJ.

too began to be challenged as contrary to Single Market principles, the court showed an essential sympathy for the objectives of intellectual property protection.

(*Coditel v Ciné Vog (No. 1).*)[61] The owner of copyright in the film, *Le Boucher*, granted cinema and television rights in Belgium exclusively to Ciné Vog for seven years. Under another licence, the German television channel, ARD, broadcast the film. The Coditel companies received it off-air and re-transmitted it to their cable subscribers in Western Belgium. Under Belgian law this was an infringement of Ciné Vog exclusive rights for which they claimed damages. Coditel relied on the principle of Free Provision of Services in the Treaty (then arts 59 to 66, now 56 to 62) for the proposition that their conduct could not be a breach of Ciné Vog's rights.

Whilst the court was prepared to treat those articles as overriding the claim if it involved arbitrary discrimination or a disguised restriction on trade,[62] it could find neither in these circumstances. It accepted that the exploitation of performing rights by geographically limited licences was a necessary element in such copyright; and that because broadcasting was organised nationally, any other unit for dividing television rights would be impracticable.[63] Inevitably the case left floating the question, is the movement of goods between Member States really so different?

(*Warner Bros v Christiansen.*)[64] At a stage when a rental right for films had been introduced into Denmark but not yet into the United Kingdom, a Dane purchased in London a video-cassette of the film *Never Say Never Again* and hired it out from his video shop in Copenhagen. The owner of copyright in the film, together with the exclusive manager of its video rights in Denmark, succeeded in obtaining an injunction under Danish copyright law. The Court of Justice found that the Danish rental right applied equally to Danish and to imported videos and, being thus non-discriminatory, art.36 EU Treaty (formerly art.30) allowed the rental right to be asserted against the imports. The court's view that the introduction of rental rights is a proper addition to the range of copyright protection led to the Directive on Rental, Public Lending and Related Rights.[65] In turn the court has upheld the constitutionality of that Directive's imposition of a standard rental right across the EU. Rental is not an activity which conflicts with the right of unfettered disposition guaranteed by the free movement of goods policy.[66]

(*Basset v SACEM.*)[67] At the relevant time, French law did not grant a neighbouring right to a sound recording producer for the public

[61] *Coditel v Ciné Vog (No. 1)* [1980] E.C.R. 881.

[62] There is no express reference to these art.36 (ex art.30) expressions in the articles.

[63] There was a separate question whether the territorial licences were unduly restrictive of competition: see above, para.14–28.

[64] *Warner Bros v Christiansen* [1988] E.C.R. 2605; Defalque [1989] E.I.P.R. 434.

[65] See above, para.10–18 et seq.

[66] *Metronome Music v Music-Point-Hokamp* [1997] E.M.L.R. 93.

[67] *Basset v SACEM* [1987] E.C.R. 1747.

performance or broadcast of a record. However, the composer's reproduction right in music is not limited by any exhaustion upon first sale even in France; instead subsequent uses may be controlled (if notified) through a *droit de destination*. On this basis, the French collecting society for composers, SACEM, charged disco owners and others a supplementary "mechanical reproduction" fee (1.65 per cent of receipts) in addition to its performing right fee (6.6 per cent). It levied this charge equally on records originating from the legitimate producer in other Member States and imported into France. The Court of Justice refused to view the different fees as more than subdivisions of a total charge for a normal exploitation of copyright, a charge which applied indiscriminately to French records and imports and was therefore not contrary to arts 30 to 36 (now arts 34 to 36 EU Treaty).

2. Internal Market: Unfair Competition

19–11 In settling the impact of the free movement of goods policy on the major intellectual property rights, the Court of Justice has inevitably been much influenced by the terms of art.36 EU Treaty. But "intellectual property" shades off into surrounding forms of civil liability. This includes, in the UK approach, such non-statutory liability as that for passing off and breach of confidence; and in Continental European thought it touches at least some aspects of unfair competition. In these spheres, likewise, the free movement policy has produced conflicts with national rights of action and here the court has developed interpretations of art.36 itself which require a balancing of factors. But under art.34 (formerly 28) the weighting of the scales is not the same.

In particular, in the "*Cassis de Dijon*", *Irish Souvenirs* and subsequent cases,[68] the following principle was established: in the absence of common rules relating to the production and marketing of products, obstacles to movement within the EU resulting from disparities between national legislation must be accepted in so far as such legislation, applying without discrimination to both domestic and imported products, may be justified as being necessary in order to satisfy mandatory requirements relating in particular to the protection of consumers and fairness in commercial transactions. In cases before it, moreover, the Court of Justice was not prepared to leave the assessment involved in its application to national courts (as sometimes it will). Since that was a controversial step for it to take, the intensity of its mistrust will be apparent.[69]

[68] *Rewe v Bundesmonopolverwaltung* [1979] E.C.R. 649; *EC Commission v Ireland* [1981] E.C.R. 1625; see generally, Oliver, *Free Movement of Goods in the European Community* 4th edn (2003) at para.8–148.

[69] cf. Schricker [1994] GRUR Int. 586, arguing the need for some deregulation of German Unfair Competition Law, given its relentlessly protective drive at that time.

Illustrations of this principle in operations which border upon intellectual property include the following:

(*Pall v Dahlhausen.*)[70] Dahlhausen produced blood filters in Italy using its Italian mark, "Micropore", and indicating registration of the mark there by the symbol (R). The mark was not registered in Germany and a competitor objected that the (R) might therefore mislead German consumers and competitors, contrary to the Unfair Competition Law of 1909 art.3. Applying "*Cassis de Dijon*", the court found that removal of the (R) would be a disproportionate burden, compared to the very doubtful alleged dangers: consumers were more interested in qualities of the product than place of registration of the mark; and other traders could consult the public register.

(*Verband Sozialer Wettbewerb v Clinique Laboratories.*)[71] Estée Lauder marketed a line of cosmetics under the mark, "Clinique", save in Germany, where an unfair competition objection had been raised: the mark might lead an appreciable proportion of consumers into thinking that the product had medical properties. The firm, obliged to package the goods destined for the German market as "Linique", objected to the additional cost involved. The court, applying "*Cassis de Dijon*", laid prime emphasis on the fact that no objection to the use of "Clinique" arose under the laws of other Member States, and proceeded to hold that the German prohibition displayed unnecessary scruple for consumer protection and human health.

(*Commission v Germany.*)[72] Where German legislation required imported products using the terms "hollandaise" and "béarnaise" to state that it had not been manufactured in accordance with the traditional German recipe, this was found by the ECJ to discriminate in favour of domestic producers and the alternative of domestic producers pointing out that their products were so made was preferable.

(*Industrie Diensten Groep v Beele.*)[73] Dutch unfair competition law would enjoin the slavish imitation of the appearance of a product (pipe housing for ships), where its distinctive shape was not dictated by functional considerations. Here, there being no discrimination between domestic and imported products, the operation of the law was considered justified in the interest of consumer protection and fair trading.

The same principle operates not only in respect of consumer confusion **19–12** over a particular competitor's individual products or identifying marks, but also with names and get-up associated with groups of traders. It has been applied also to descriptions shared at a national or regional level—thus

[70] *Pall v Dahlhausen* [1990] E.C.R. 4827.

[71] *Verband Sozialer Wettbewerb v Clinique Laboratories* [1994] E.C.R. 317.

[72] *Commission v Germany* [1995] E.C.R. I-3599.

[73] *Industrie Diensten Groep v Beele* [1982] E.C.R. 707.

art.34 (ex 28) over-rode the restriction of "Sekt" and "Branntwein" to German products.[74] It has also been held to override a range of other protection measures where trade between Member States is affected. Cases cover rules preventing free gifts as part of sales,[75] rules constraining the advertising of price cuts,[76] and powers conferred on a monopoly corporation to exclude (without the right of appeal) others from markets in attachment products.[77]

The *Cassis de Dijon* principle applies whether or not there is explicit or implicit discrimination operating across a border. The degree to which this might lead to curbs being placed on local unfair competition rules caused the court at one stage to draw back. In *Keck and Mithouard*,[78] a French law making it unlawful to sell off goods below cost as "loss-leaders" was held to be properly applied to imports from Germany. The law was not overtly discriminatory and constituted a "mere selling arrangement". It can nonetheless be very difficult to determine what falls into this amorphous category.

(*Fratelli Graffione v Ditta Fransa.*)[79] In Italy the claimant was ordered not to use "Cotonelle" as a mark for toilet paper and disposable handkerchiefs, lest the public think them made from cotton. It was able to continue to use the mark in France and Spain and parallel importing of the products into Italy then occurred. Here the Court of Justice left it to the national courts to estimate whether the danger of misleading the public was sufficiently serious to justify an injunction against free movement

(*Vereinigte Familiapress v Heinrich Bauer Verlag.*)[80] An Austrian law designed to protect local products forbade the inclusion of crossword competitions for prizes in magazines: its impact was mainly on major publishers in Germany. The Court of Justice held this to be a "mere selling arrangement" and left it for the national tribunal to assess whether, given the desirability of press diversity, the measure was proportionate and non-discriminatory.

19–13 In applying art.34 to cases not within art.36, the court has often evaluated the merits or otherwise of the national rule in its application to the particular case, making much of the equivalent position in other Member States. It has refused to wait for harmonisation measures, sensing doubtless that there are differences of national attitude here which run too deep for any

[74] *Commission v Germany* [1975] E.C.R. 181 (applying Directive 70/50 art.2(3)); and equally the German reservation of the "Bockbeutel" wine bottle to certain national products, when that shape had long been legitimately used for wine in other Member States: *Prantl* [1984] E.C.R. 1299; cf. *Exportur* [1992] I E.C.R. 5529; Cornish [1992] Y.Eur.L. 635.

[75] *Oosthoeks Uitgeversmaatschappij* [1982] E.C.R. 4575.

[76] *GE-Inno-BM* [1990] E.C.R. I-667.

[77] *Regie des Télégraphes v GB-Inno-BM* [1991] E.C.R. I-5941.

[78] *Keck and Mithouard* [1995] 1 C.M.L.R. 101, ECJ; and see *Hönermund* [1994] GRUR Int. 170.

[79] *Fratelli Graffione v Ditta Fransa* [1997] E.T.M.R. 71.

[80] *Vereinigte Familiapress v Heinrich Bauer Verlag* [1997] E.C.R. I-3689.

early bridging. It emerges from the comparative readiness to set aside the interstate operation of over-enthusiastic unfair competition rules, that, give or take the odd false step,[81] the court has been comparatively careful to respect the policy objectives of intellectual property.

Its attitude is in line with the increased awareness of intellectual property as a necessary condition of industrial and commercial prosperity. That it should not change its approach needs to be stressed in the light of the somewhat ominous formulation of its judgment in *Deutsche Renault v Audi*.[82] The validity of a German trade mark comprising a single foreign number ("Quattro" for cars) and its application to exclude imports of the "Espace Quadro", were both challenged as unnecessary extensions of trade mark rights. While insisting that it was for national law to set the bounds on both these characteristics of the industrial property, the court nevertheless spelled out why it thought the law's application to these facts was not excessive. However, the case has not been followed by others in which the court has been provoked into finding excess. Down that road lies incessant second-guessing about the correctness of intellectual property laws, based presumably on intra-EU comparisons. The temptation to open up this difficult route should continue to be resisted.

The Court of Justice's restraint so far has been aided by the willingness of Member States to make progress towards the ideal of unified EU rights, or at least harmonised national laws. That movement has been great over the past 30 years or so and for this the court may have reason to be pleased. However, now it is beset with appeals, for example in the trade marks sphere, to unravel the complexities of newish Regulations and Directives, it may be experiencing some discomfort. But it is well advised to continue bearing in mind the wisdom of Brandeis J.[83] that intellectual property is subject matter too complex to be fashioned out of case law.

3. The Rules of Competition

The EU Treaty makes plain that, complementary though they undoubtedly **19–14**
are, free movement and the fostering of competition are separate objectives, secured by different legal means.[84] The licensing of intellectual property must comply with the Competition Rules, and those Rules have been applied not only to horizontal arrangements to divide markets but also to vertical arrangements which restrict competition in unnecessary ways. We

[81] Most famously, "*Hag I*", above, para.19–06, n.30.
[82] *Deutsche Renault v Audi* [1993] E.C.R. I-6227; see the comment of Edward J. on the case, cited above at para.16–31.
[83] See the *INS* case, 248 U.S. 215 (1918), above, para.1–15.
[84] See above, paras 1–51—1–57. See, for example, Jakobsen & Broberg [2002] E.C.L.R. 127.

have already considered their impact in relation to patent and know-how licences and noted the shifting attitudes which have changed the application of the Rules to that subject matter.

Parallel importation between Member States is undoubtedly one matter which a restrictive agreement may seek to prevent. But the practice is central to the dominant objective of a unified Single Market and that is why the cases just reviewed have mainly been dealt with under free movement policies, notably arts 34–36 on goods. By comparison the Competition Rules pose the difficulty that their application must be related to the impact of the particular trader or concerting group of traders in the relevant market.

The impact of the Competition Rules on internal movement[85] should, however, not be forgotten. For one thing, the Rules operate upon agreements and other actions which do not necessarily involve enforcement through litigation.[86] For another, breach of the Rules may result in investigations by the Commission, fines and the voiding of contracts in national courts. Equally the Competition Rules affect both parallel importation and direct territorial licensing. The two policies lock together over the matter of parallel imports: it was not possible, through use of the exemption powers in art.101(3) (ex 81(3)), for the Commission to approve contractual terms aimed at keeping out the independent transporter of goods around the Community: arts 34-36 settle the overriding importance of such activity and art.101 (ex81) is similarly interpreted.[87]

19–15 However, as the discussion of patent and know-how licensing has already demonstrated,[88] agreements which carve out exclusive territories for manufacturers or their own distributors raise different issues, which are not affected by arts 34–36. Exclusive licences of all intellectual property (including know-how) have to be examined carefully, first to decide whether they create any inhibition on competition at all, and, if they do, whether there are countervailing benefits which would justify their benefitting from art.101 (ex81) (3) exemption.[89]

It is accepted that once an intellectual property right is exploited by means of a licence or some equivalent consensual agreement or arrangement, the effect on trade is properly a matter for competition law. Within the EU, this is so whether the attack is upon an agreement or a concerted practice

[85] For external effects, see below, paras 19–17 et seq.

[86] As in *Nungesser* [1981] E.C.R. 45.

[87] *Nungesser v EC Commission* [1982] E.C.R. 2015. For the position regarding imports from outside the EEA, see below, paras 19–17 et seq.

[88] See above, paras 7–32—7–40.

[89] From May 1, 2004, Regulation 1/2000, [2003] OJ L1/1, imposes on the person claiming the benefit of art.101 (ex81)(3) the burden of proving the conditions are satisfied, whereas previously the Commission had the exclusive power to grant exemptions.

(art.101 (ex81))[90] or goes to the acquisition and exercise of market power (art.102 (ex82)). At both the national and the international level, the general issue is likewise conceded.[91]

Where, however, an intellectual property owner does nothing apart from refusing licences to those who seek them, serious controversy arises, in which the Court of Justice has been embroiled. **19–16**

(*Volvo v Veng*[92]: registered design for car spare parts.) Volvo was registered proprietor in the United Kingdom of designs for the front wings of its Series 200 cars. It was entitled to assert those rights against an independent importer of front-wing panels from elsewhere in the EU. The court considered the relevant market to be that in Volvo spare parts. Volvo accordingly held a dominant position, which it could abuse. This it would do if it refused arbitrarily to supply spare parts to independent repairers, fixed prices for them at an unfair level or gave up supplying them when many cars of the model in question were still in circulation.[93]

(*RTE and ITP v EC Commission* ("*Magill*")[94]: TV programme listings.) In Ireland and Northern Ireland, the public and commercial broadcasting authorities each refused to license newspapers and magazines to print week-long listings of their forthcoming programmes, thus obliging viewers to purchase their own separate periodicals. Under Irish law, as in the United Kingdom, the material was copyright. So Magill, a firm which began independently to publish the week's listings from all channels, was enjoined in the Irish High Court.

The Court of Justice found that the broadcasters were monopoly suppliers of information about their programmes and inferred from the extent to which each authority's broadcasts were received in the other Member State that there was a market for a joint listings magazine which was being denied by the refusal to licence. Exercise of an exclusive right in this fashion could exceptionally constitute a breach of art.102 (ex82). These circumstances were within that exception. Each broadcaster was subjected to a

[90] For an example, see *Intel v Via Technologies* [2003] F.S.R. 574 CA, where it was held (at para.72 per Sir Andrew Morritt V.C.) that a licence term is contrary to art.101 (ex81) if it seeks to regulate the market by controlling not only what is made with the licensed technology but also the use which is made of it after, applying the ECJ judgment in *Windsurfing* [1986] E.C.R. 611.

[91] For UK competition law, see below, App.1 (hardback edition). In the TRIPS Agreement art.40(2) allows for the adoption of measures against "licensing practices or conditions that may in particular cases constitute an abuse of intellectual property rights having an adverse effect on competition in the relevant market"; and note the provisions for consultation between States towards enforcement: art.40(3), (4).

[92] *Volvo v Veng* [1988] E.C.R. 6211.

[93] These forewarnings reflected the considerable battles already fought in Europe between major car manufacturers and competition authorities over spare-parts exclusivity: for which, see above, para.15–06.

[94] *RTE and ITP v EC Commission* [1995] 4 C.M.L.R. 718; [1995] F.S.R. 530; and see *Biotrading & Financing v Biohit* [1998] F.S.R. 109 CA; and see Korah [1997] I.P.J. 395; Greaves [1998] E.I.P.R. 370; Drexl (2005) 35 I.I.C. 788.

compulsory obligation to supply programme content against payment of a reasonable royalty.[95]

This art.102 (ex82) control over monopolists who refuse to license their intellectual property is a weapon which could ultimately be turned upon any enterprise with a major intellectual property success on its hands as the basis for requiring a licence. But although there is not much case law which attempts to define what circumstances will give rise to this "exceptional" jurisdiction, two factors about *Magill* suggest that the intervention is justified only in unusual and special cases.[96]

First, the right which underpinned the broadcasters' position was an extension of copyright to subject-matter (straightforward factual information) which many Member States would consider not to justify intellectual property protection in the first place. In a period when intellectual property rights are being rapidly expanded, it must be wise for competition authorities to retain some ultimate means of curbing their range in egregious cases which, in the scramble to satisfy industrial lobbies, legislatures may not have sufficiently considered.

The other is that in *Magill*, the power over the listings market was an ancillary product of the entire system of broadcasting control. Since that primary market became itself competitive (as has happened with the expansion of scope made possible by digital technology) the broadcasters have clamoured to have their schedules publicised wherever possible. The decision does not stress sufficiently the barrier to entry in the "pre-market" which was the cause of unjustifiably monopolistic behaviour in the "after-market". An adequate emphasis upon this factor would help to identify what it was that made the dominant actors' refusal to license an abuse of their position.

In *Tiercé Ladbroke v European Commission*[97] a refusal to licence for showing in betting shops the copyright in films of horse races was found acceptable under art.102 (ex82) as it did not concern a service which "was either essential for the exercise of the activity in question, in that there was no real or effective substitute, or was a new product whose introduction might be prevented" (at para.131).[98]

A British court has insisted that the *Volvo v Veng* principle defines the norms in intellectual property exploitation and an owner who refuses to grant licences on reasonable terms is not therefore in breach of art.102

[95] In the UK, this solution had already been introduced by statute: Broadcasting Act 1990, s.176, following a Report on the subject by the Monopolies and Mergers Commission (Cmnd.9614, 1985). Jurisdiction under the Act was given to the Copyright Tribunal: see *News Group v ITP* [1993] R.P.C. 173; Laddie et al. paras 14.46–14.48.

[96] See Schmidt [2002] E.C.L.R. 210 for a comparison between EU and US law.

[97] *Tiercé Ladbroke v European Commission* [1997] E.C.R. II 923.

[98] Also, see *IMS Health v European Commission* [2002] C.M.L.R. 58, in which a stay was granted by the GC on the basis that there was an arguable case of abuse under art.82 (now 102 EU Treaty) by reason of a refusal to licence copyright in a so-called "brick structure" used to divide up a country for the purposes of market research.

(ex82); there must be additional monopolistic behaviour of an unacceptable kind, if the *Magill* exception is to prevail.[99] However, it has also been held that *Magill* is not so restrictive as to require that all competition be excluded from all sources before an art.82 abuse is triggered: "[w]ere it otherwise liability under Art.102 (ex82) could be simply avoided by the grant of a licence to an unenergetic rival".[100]

4. Parallel Importation from Outside the EEA[101]

The rapidly changing conditions of world trade have thrown countries into a quandary about the potential of parallel importation, when considered on a global scale. The EU is affected by this as much as others. Large industrial producers likely to be placing their products on advanced and developing markets at differentiated prices have pressed for general barriers which will allow the higher price levels to be maintained. Consumers in those higher priced markets are likely to become suspicious when they find that the same product (or one virtually the same) can be bought more cheaply abroad. There is no easy resolution to the problem.[102] **19–17**

At various stages this book has examined the extent to which intellectual property rights may be used to create barriers to cross-border movement. It has been argued that the justification for deploying them in this way varies with the fundamental purpose of the right. In particular, rights in forms or expressions of ideas—patents, copyright, designs and so forth—are granted essentially as a stimulus to their creation and exploitation. That incentive may be heightened if price differentials between geographical markets can be maintained and the potential profitability of each can thus be extracted.[103] In these cases, there is a good argument for extending the right to cover parallel importation from cheaper markets (if necessary, upon condition that notice of the limitation is given).[104]

---

[99] *Philips Electronics v Ingman* [1999] F.S.R. 112.

[100] per Sir Andrew Morritt, V.C. in *Intel v Via Technologies* [2003] F.S.R. 574 CA at para.49.

[101] See Stothers. *Parallel Trade in Europe: Intellectual Property, Competition and Regulatory Law* (2007, Hart Publishing), pp 331-402; Rasmussen [1995] E.I.P.R. 174; Abbott and Verkade [1998] B.I.E. 111; Cornish [1998] E.I.P.R. 172.

[102] The Commission on Intellectual Property Rights Report, *Integrating Intellectual Property Rights and Development Policy* (London, 2002) recommended that developed countries should maintain and strengthen their legislative regimes to prevent imports of low priced pharmaceutical products from developing countries, whilst developing countries should aim to facilitate parallel imports in their legislation: at pp.41–42. This highlights the essentially politico-economic nature of the parallel imports debate.

[103] Even so, one must speak conditionally; price differentials come about through such external causes as currency shifts, and are scarcely something on which an investor or researcher counts in advance.

[104] If a product is manufactured outside the EEA (and, e.g. marked there), but then sold to an independent trader inside the EEA, it must thereafter be left free to circulate in the whole market: *Phytheron v Jean Bourdon* [1997] E.T.M.R. 211 ECJ; cf. *Re Tylosin* [1977] 1 C.M.L.R. 460; and see *Re Patented Bandaging Material* [1988] 2 C.M.L.R. 359.

19–18 The approach in trade mark law is much more controversial, since marks are protected primarily as symbols for ascertaining the origin of products and to some extent for guaranteeing their qualities when these are associated in the public mind with their source. That moderate position may suggest that, where the mark-bearing goods of an enterprise or group differ in quality between one market and another, it may be reasonable to use trade mark rights to protect each market from parallel importation of the goods from the other. On the other hand, it would not be reasonable to do that when the goods are in no way different and the mark exactly performs its origin-cum-quality function to the extent that policy demands. That, for instance, is the position generally prevailing in the law of the United States.

19–19 However, those who argue for a general measure against parallel importing in world trade demand that marks be recognised as primary marketing tools and that therefore the investment in them be accorded much more embracing legal protection. On this view, trade mark rights should be automatically available to prevent the movement of legitimate goods by a parallel importer into markets for which they are not intended. As we have already seen, the ECJ treats the legal question as having been largely settled by the terms of the First TM Harmonisation Directive art.7 and the Community Trade Mark Regulation art.12. These, it has been held, make it necessary to imply into the statement of the internal exhaustion rule that Member States may not maintain, as part of their own law, a rule of international exhaustion. The court believes that the political choice in favour of using trade marks, both CTMs and national rights, as buttresses of a "fortress Europe", has been expressed clearly by EU legislation.

19–20 At this point, let us pursue a different line of observation. In legal terms, it is not just from an intellectual property law perspective that the matter has to be approached. There is also the question of the impact of the Rules of Competition. It has long been accepted that, for instance, agreements between manufacturers which divide the external market from the EU market can infringe art.101 (ex81). *CBS UK v EMI Records*[105] dealt with the separation of the mark "Columbia" for records. Achieved in 1922, this had the effect of giving the mark in the then EC countries to EMI, and in the Americas to CBS. National trade mark law in the United Kingdom, Denmark and the then West Germany could be used by EMI to prevent imports of CBS "Columbia" records by a CBS subsidiary and an independent importer, and the free movement of goods policy could have no application for the reason that it is stated to operate only upon trade between Member States. But the Court of Justice went on to warn that if the trade mark barrier to entry to any part of the Common Market (as it was then described) was "the subject, the means, or the consequence of a restrictive practice", art.101 (ex81) could be breached; and this might occur if a formally abandoned agreement nonetheless continues to have practical effect.

[105] *CBS UK v EMI Records* [1976] E.C.R. 811; above, para.1–56.

But if the external manufacturer has other marks which he could use, then it is permissible to require him to change the labelling.[106]

It has become clear that art.101 (ex81) can apply to vertical agreements down the chain of distribution which affect parallel importation.[107] In *Javico v Yves Saint-Laurent*,[108] the Court of Justice dealt with an importation of "YSL" products from East Europe, which had been sold there under an express condition that the purchaser was to resell only in Russia and the Ukraine. While this contractual prohibition was not necessarily prohibited under art.101 (ex81), it would be a breach in any case where: **19–21**

> "[the EU] ... market in the products in question is characterised by an oligopolistic structure or by an appreciable difference between the prices charged for the contractual products within the [EU] and those charged outside the [EU] and where, in view of the position occupied by the supplier of the products at issue and the extent of the supplier's production and sales in the Member States, the prohibition entails the risk that it might have an appreciable effect on the patterns of trade between Member States such as to undermine attainment of the objectives of the Common Market."

With leading brands of luxury goods, high prices in EU markets tend to be buttressed by selective distribution systems, and these may create the conditions for breach of art.101 (ex81) under the *Javico* test.[109] Equally the principle could be applied to prohibitions on the re-sale of products protected by patents, copyright and other intellectual property,[110] perhaps by reference to the specific subject-matter discussed above. As this book has been at pains to stress, attitudes towards the practice of parallel importation continue to be as divided as ever and no lasting resolution can be expected to what ultimately is a politico-economic question. *Javico* exhibits an underlying hostility towards restrictions on the practice, which is the opposite of the non-exhaustion policy set for trade marks by *Silhouette* and *Davidoff*, and in relation to non-exhaustion within the EU more recently by

[106] *CBS UK* [1976] E.C.R. 811 ECJ at paras 26–34. See also *Ideal Standard* [1995] F.S.R. 59 ECJ at para.59.

[107] And potentially horizontal agreements also: *Doncaster Pharmaceuticals v (The) Bolton Pharmaceutical Co* [2007] F.S.R. 63 CA, refusing to grant summary judgment for trade mark infringement in relation to parallel imports, Longmore L.J. noting: "If the owner of a trade mark could assign his mark successively to different entities in each EU country [relying on *Ideal Standard*], freedom of movement of goods could be said to be more of an inspiration than a reality. The relevant law is still in the process of formulation": at para.92.

[108] *Javico v Yves Saint-Laurent* [1998] E.C.R. I-1983.

[109] See now *Copad v Dior* [2009] E.T.M.R. 22 ECJ, in which a clause prohibiting sale by a selective distributor to discount stores was upheld, as a matter of trade mark law but without apparent consideration of art.101 issues.

[110] In this connection, one should recall not only the *Nungesser* case [1983] F.S.R. 309 ECJ, but also the decisions of the Commission concerning territorial limits in patent licences for countries outside the EU: *Raymond/Nagoya* [1972] C.M.L.R. D45; *Kabelmetall/Luchaire* [1975] 2 C.M.L.R. D40. See above, paras 7–33 et seq.

Copad v Dior.[111] It is interesting that *Javico* seems to be treated by some as an aberration but nevertheless only time will tell which view is in the end to prevail, although *Copad v Dior* suggests that the latter policy is certainly in the ascendancy?

19–22 The dilemma remains and the Court of Justice will undoubtedly be called upon to revisit it over the years. However, it is only one more instance of problems with the very idea of intellectual property: in broad terms there is a good case for its various instances in the need for particular incentives and protection against unfair imitation. But arguments justifying the exact boundaries between protection and freedom to engage in competition are difficult to state convincingly. The law's actual limits often reflect political and social allegiances of an imprecise kind. When it comes to detail the present intellectual property systems have much about them that is arbitrary. Accordingly, they are with us for better, for worse. The luckiest right-owners emerge very much the richer, many users and consumers are left rather the poorer, but with some enhancement of their opportunities. We do best by continuing to recognise a basic presumption in favour of competition. To it intellectual property operates as an exception which should always need a sufficient justification.

[111] *Copad* [2009] E.T.M.R. 22 ECJ.

CHAPTER 20

DIGITAL TECHNOLOGY: COMPUTERS AND THE INTERNET

The computer holds information in the binary electronic notation of 0s and 1s, so that it can be transferred, stored and manipulated to quite extraordinary degrees. Computers are the basic machinery from which has burgeoned the Knowledge Economy—an overused term which nonetheless conveys something of the remarkable transformation that has come about in industrial production, financial and commercial operations, government, international relations, education, leisure, and most other spheres of existence in developed countries today. Data stores have become huge and they can be searched as never before by keyword or other indicator. Laborious indexing can be by-passed, and copies can be made from a digital source without error and without depleting the quality of the original in any way. Legal regulation of the whole complex presented by the digital revolution is forming and transforming as fast as the technology is expanding. With IPRs the changes have mostly been by way of rough adaptation of existing rights. How far the results have been effective in real terms, how far therefore they have been fair, is a debate that for the moment can only rage. **20–01**

This chapter addresses the many challenges which digitisation sets for intellectual property regimes, which we divide under three heads: **20–02**

(1) *Computer programs*. Computer programs are the digital instructions used to drive the electronic hardware of the computer itself. Computers may come in a variety of forms. There is the popular PC (personal computer), along with the ubiquitous but less well recognised embedded computers contained in devices such as mobile

phones, dvd players, household appliances, automobiles and medical equipment. Programs relevant to PCs will be the basic operating system of the machine and applications for a range of purposes, including word processing, web browsing, financial management and product design. Embedded computing systems, on the other hand, are designed to perform dedicated functions—to allow the dvd to play or the washing machine to operate. We will see that copyright has become the standard IP tool for preventing the copying of most types of programs; but also that patents are coming to be granted for inventive elements in programming, at least where they produce some form of technical effect. In addition, confidence, contract and trade marks have long had a role in protecting programs.

(2) *Computer storage and output.* The ability to store quantities of information in digitised form means that investment goes into accumulations of knowledge from the most mundane compilations to sophisticated treatments which enhance access or reach a level of real originality. This has been reflected in the development of IPRs in databases and has posed for copyright the question of how to deal with novel types of material which have been characterised as "multimedia".

(3) *The internet.* The internet has provided an astonishingly powerful form of networked communication across the globe. As an instrument governed by protocols and agreements over which no government holds direct power, its relation to traditional legal patterns is problematic, and not least in relation to intellectual property, since the rapidity and cheapness with which it can transmit text, images, music, films, and data of every kind poses confrontations between freedom of access and control. As we shall see, some copyright industries find their future in jeopardy and are gaining new types of legal restraint in a desperate hope that these can support technological barriers within the system. How far these can succeed is still highly questionable. Other problems have rapidly appeared. We end the chapter with the outbreak of cyber-squatting which has troubled the spread of domain names as business symbols, looking particularly at the special jurisdictions which internet governance has established by way of reaction, and also the growing use of "adwords" which are increasingly being used to gain a competitive edge when it comes to on-line commercial activities.

1. Computer Programs

20–03 In the 1970s, the arrival of computer products for mass markets—notably personal computers and computer games—put paid to "first generation" notions that functioning elements, and above all computer programs, could be adequately protected within the framework of contracts and associated confidence. While these legal mechanisms have remained vital, they have come to be underpinned, first by copyright in software and now, to an increasing extent, also by patents upon inventive techniques associated with programming.

It is the giants of the industry who are most assiduous in pursuing these objectives. An obverse ideology exists among many who are involved in computing research (not least in universities), and increasingly among smaller enterprises which share an interest and belief in cooperative, rather than competitive, development of the field. The Free Software or Open Source movement has a 20-year history of promoting the concept that contracts which license software should allow recipients to correct, adapt and develop the program and accompanying source material, subject only to an undertaking that alterations to the program will be made available to the public in the same terms. As new versions emerge and are sold or licensed, this will be on terms in the copyright licence which allow for equivalent developments.[1] Since the mid-1990s Linux operating software has become the practical symbol of the movement's success.[2] It has popularised an alternative business model for the industry[3] and has sustained effective political campaigns against the monopolistic potential of IPRs, particularly in the computer industry—but by no means confined to it. Not least in Europe, attempts to extend IPRs meet vehement objection from open source lobbyists.

(1) Copyright in programs[4]

As in the working out of complete copyright works such as films or symphonies, the program which instructs a computer to perform the desired operation often goes through a series of evolutionary steps from preliminary conception to detailed and complex expression. In this process (which varies from case to case) a crucial stage in the conception is the expression of the basic steps to be executed—the algorithm—in the form of a flow-chart or **20–04**

[1] First drafted for the Free Software Foundation by law professors, it was developed into a General Public License (GPL) with several variants. Happily the movement adopted the slogan, Copyleft.

[2] Linux—the brainchild of a young Finn, Linus Torvalds—provides a straightforward foundation platform from which to build in many directions.

[3] Typically the software itself is provided at low cost and returns are amplified by providing services which ensure that it is running satisfactorily for the purchaser's needs.

[4] For the position since enactment of the EU Directive of 1991 on the Legal Protection of Computer Programs (91/250/EEC), see Czarnota and Hart, *Legal Protection of Computer Programs in Europe* (1991); Carr and Arnold, *Computer Software* 2nd edn (1992), Chs 4, 5; Laddie et al., Ch.34; Rowland and Macdonald, *Information Technology Law* (1997); Lai, *Copyright Protection of Computer Software in the UK* (2000); Attridge [2000] E.I.P.R. 563; Karjala (2003) 35 Connecticut LR 435; Bing in Derclaye (ed), *Research Handbook on the Future of EU Copyright* (2009). For a comparison of the current UK, US and Australian position see Lim and Longdin (2009) 40 I.I.C. 374.

other logical flow diagram. Thereafter the statement of instructions in a computer language is relatively unskilled though it may be very laborious. The detailed writing may be in a so-called "high level" language (such as Fortran or Cobol), giving the program in source code. The computer itself then converts this into operational terms of object code, by means of a separate system control program.

20–05 Since the advent of the personal computer, producers of software, some of it the result of very large investment indeed, have been determined to prevent imitations appearing on the mass market and to prevent down-line copying by legitimate purchasers. They turned to copyright as the form of intellectual property most immediately adaptable to their purpose and strove to establish, country by country, that the generation of a program is considered the creation of literary work. In some countries this result was first achieved by court decision.

However, two hazards in particular emerged. First, there was a counter-argument that, at least when the program reaches electronic form, it has become a means of operating the machine and is no longer appropriate subject-matter for copyright protection.[5] This was a particularly damaging view, not least because most programs are now written entirely on computer, rather than first on paper. Secondly, in countries which require for copyright that a sufficient level of originality be shown, there might be no protection for a program involving only humdrum writing skills.[6]

20–06 Partly because of these considerations,[7] there have been contemporaneous attempts to procure legislation specifically incorporating programs into the copyright fold, mainly as literary works.[8] While in the United Kingdom, the judges showed no tendency to resist this deployment of copyright,[9] an Act was nevertheless procured in 1985 which sought to forestall any lapse into apostasy.[10] In the CDPA 1988, that position was re-affirmed and extended. Going even further down the same road, the 1991 Computer Programs

[5] So the High Court of Australia by majority held in *Computer Edge v Apple Computer* [1986] F.S.R. 537, joining in the revival of Davey L.J.'s dictum: "a literary work is intended to afford either information and instruction, or pleasure, in the form of literary enjoyment" (*Hollinrake v Truswell* [1894] 3 Ch. 420; and see *Exxon v Exxon* [1982] R.P.C. 69). But "instruction"? For the opposite view, in the US and Canada: *Apple Computer v Franklin* 714 F.2d 1240 (1984); *Whelan v Jaslow* 797 F.2d 1222 (1986); [1987] F.S.R. 1; *Broderbund Software v Unison World* 684 F.Supp. 1127; *Apple Computer v Mackintosh Computers* (1986) 28 D.L.R. (4th) 178.

[6] See, for instance, the German Supreme Court's decision, *Inkasso-Program* (1986) 17 I.I.C. 681. Now altered by the Computer Programs Directive art.1(3), for which, see para.20–08, below.

[7] For a discussion of the appropriateness of copyright protection for computer programs see Samuelson et al. (1994) 94 Col. L.R. 2308; Reichmann (1994) 94 Col. L.R. 2432; and Ginsburg (1994) 94 Col. L.R. 2559.

[8] Along with international recognition of computer programs as literary works: see now TRIPs art.10(1) and WCT art.4.

[9] Thus there were interim decisions in which copyright protection was assumed: e.g. *Sega Enterprises v Richards* [1983] F.S.R. 73; *Thrustcode v WW Computing* [1983] F.S.R. 502.

[10] Copyright (Computer Software) Amendment Act 1985, applying the CA 1956 to programs as it applied to literary works.

Directive required a standard set of provisions in the national copyright laws of EU States and this was adapted into the CDPA 1988 by amendment.[11] The excruciating gestation of the Directive left it with strange marks, and its subsequent conversion into UK law has added others.

(a) *Existence of copyright*

"Literary work"—which in general is any work that is not dramatic or musical and which is written, spoken or sung—now explicitly includes a computer program and (separately) preparatory design material for a program.[12] The program must be recorded in writing or otherwise; but this is defined to include writing in code, not necessarily by hand, and "regardless of the method by which, or medium in or on which, it is recorded".[13] This is wide enough to embrace storage in a computer. **20–07**

According to the Computer Programs Directive protection extends "to the expression in any form of a computer program" but not to its underlying ideas and principles thus excluding algorithms and programming languages.[14] In *Navitaire v Easyjet*[15] this was held to exclude individual and complex commands from being literary works.

There will still be the general copyright considerations: has there been sufficient labour, skill and judgment to satisfy the requirement that there is an "original literary work"? The mental input may therefore consist in the writing of the program from its first sketching in any detail, through source code to object code.[16] It can also consist in compiling a suite of programs

[11] Copyright (Computer Programs) Regulations 1992 (SI 1992/3233).

[12] CDPA 1988 s.3(1)(b), (c). Unlike the Australian and US legislation, there is no definition of "computer program". Australian courts have interpreted the definition of "computer program" in s.10 of the Copyright Act 1968 (Cth) to exclude macro commands (*Data Access v Powerflex Services* (1999) 202 C.L.R. 1, HC Aust) and to include an editor file and table file used as part of a content management system for websites (*Dais Studio v Bullet-Creative* [2007] FCA 2054, FC Aust). In the United Kingdom, the placing of preparatory material not within "computer program" (as required by the Computer Programs Directive, art.1(1)) but apart, means that the special defences do not apply to the material; but conversely the general "fair dealing provisions" may: see Chalton [1993] 9 Comp.L.S.R. 115. The European Commission has taken the view that treating "preparatory design material" as a separate sub-category does not make the United Kingdom non-compliant with the Directive: Report on the implementation and effects of and effects of Directive 91/250/EEC on the legal protection of computer programs, Brussels, April 10, 2000, p.9.

[13] CDPA 1988 ss.3(2), 178, "writing".

[14] Computer Programs Directive art.1(2) and rec.14. In Case 393/09 *Bezpecnostní Softwarová Asociace v Ministerstvo kultury CR* the Supreme Administrative Court of the Czech Republic has referred a question asking whether "expression in any form of a computer program" includes the graphic user interface: OJ C 11 of 16.01.2010, p.14. The answer should be no, otherwise the underlying ideas and principles will risk being protected.

[15] *Navitaire v Easyjet* [2006] R.P.C. 3.

[16] What is a sufficient working out of an initial idea to count as copyrightable "expression" must be judged in the circumstances; but certainly source code may be copyright: *Ibcos* case (n.55, below) at 296.

together.[17] Very simple programs may fail to embody sufficient "labour, skill and judgment"[18]; but, provided that they are not in substance copied, programs will mostly pass that threshold and be given a breadth of protection proportionate to the intellectual value of their content.[19]

20–08 UK implementation of the Computer Programs Directive has made no alteration to these general principles. Note, however, that the Directive seeks to impose a test of originality for software which requires the program to be "the author's own intellectual creation".[20] For some Commission officials especially, the UK implementation is defective in not introducing this wording.[21] The difference could affect such questions as whether there is copyright in microcode embodying simple functions,[22] or in identification codes for such things as drugs or the controls on a traffic-light system.[23]

The general rules for literary works also apply to questions of authorship, since this is permitted by the Computer Programs Directive.[24] So in UK law, the programmer or programmers will be author or joint authors.[25] Their lives will therefore measure the term of protection, which, however inappropriately, follows the longest-life-plus-70-years rule.[26] Where the work is

---

[17] *Ibcos* (n.54, below), at 290.

[18] The process of converting a program for use on a different computer can be a complex business involving "translation" into a different source code language; this secondary work ought to attract copyright, even where it may also involve adaptation of the first version: cf. *John Richardson Computers v Flanders* (n.52, below) at 518.

[19] cf. *Autodesk v Dyason* [1992] R.P.C. 575, where the High Court of Australia (by majority) found that a locking device needed to gain access to a popular design program had been infringed by an alternative device which, like the first, gave electronic instructions to "turn the key". Pumfrey J. criticised the decision for considering substantiality separately in relation to this small part of a program, and thus justifying protection for copyright in any part of the whole which is needed to make it work: *Cantor Fitzgerald v Tradition (UK)* [2000] R.P.C. 95, para.75.

[20] Computer Programs Directive art.1(3), so provided chiefly in order to oblige the German courts to abandon the high standard of originality which they had adopted in *Inkasso-Program* (for which see n.6, above). At the same time, the introduction of a personal creation test of originality has been seen as a bridgehead against the common law conception; which in turn makes the UK omission provocative.

[21] Of course, the phrase could be read to refer only to a "not-copied" test.

[22] Held to be protected in the US: *NEC v Intel* 645 F. Supp. 1485 (1985).

[23] cf. *Flanders* case (n.48, below); *Computer-Aided Systems v Bolwell* (1989) I.P.D., April 1990, 15.

[24] Computer Programs Directive art.2, which is a moderate concession away from strict author's right theory.

[25] Contributions such as error fixing and setting the functional specifications and parameters of the software were not regarded as contributions to programming: *Fylde Microsystems v Key Radio* [1998] F.S.R. 449.

[26] The Commission's original intention to impose a limit of 50 years' protection was surrendered in order to show that the EU was treating programs as works within the Berne Convention. The Convention was last revised before their inclusion was a practical issue. Accordingly, countries wishing to foster their international protection treated them as if within the Convention pour encourager les autres. Now their protection as literary works under Berne is required by TRIPS art.10(1) and WCT art.4.

created in employment, first ownership must go to the employer, in the absence of a contrary contractual arrangement.[27] In all other cases the ownership trail starts with the author. If he or she is commissioned to write the program, there may be an implied undertaking (if there is no express term) to assign the right.[28]

(b) *Exclusive rights*[29]

The CDPA 1988 takes an embracing approach to the exclusive rights in a program (and equally to works stored as data in a computer)[30] by defining "copying a work" to include storing the work in any medium by electronic means. This includes the making of copies which are transient or are incidental to some other use of the work.[31] The Computer Programs Directive is more specific, but probably goes little further: it requires the exclusive right to cover any permanent or temporary reproduction of a program[32] by any means and in any form, in part or in whole,[33] to be authorised, including loading, displaying, running, transmission and storage. Programs have been the foremost form of digital record to have proved pre-eminently copiable. It is this capacity savagely to undermine major investment by developers of software that has driven the copyright in copies to a point where it virtually overlaps with the notion of performance (without, however, being tied to any concept of public availability). **20–09**

So far as dealings in copies are concerned, particularly in relation to parallel importation across State boundaries, it is in the Computer Programs Directive that the EU has sought to enshrine in national copyright laws its formula for intra-EEA exhaustion, together with extra-EEA non-exhaustion.[34]

---

[27] The importation of this convenient presumption appears the thin end of a disruptive wedge for authors' rights theorists. The Directive restricts it to the "economic" rights. This is of no importance to UK law, since there are no moral rights in computer program copyright: see paras 12–74, 12–81, above.

[28] See para.13–12, above.

[29] See generally, Copyright Law Review Committee, (Australia), *Final Report on Computer Software Protection* (1995); Drexl, *What is Protected in a Computer Program?* (1994); Bandey, *International Copyright in Computer Program Technology* (1996).

[30] See paras 20–37 et seq., below.

[31] CDPA 1988 s.17(1), (2), (6), which anticipated the requirements of the Computer Programs Directive on the matter: see art.4. The Act thereby pushes the notion of "reproduction" to the very boundary of passing uses and approaches those associated with performance: some uses of random access memory (RAM) involve only fleeting retention of computerised information. A computer game console with an infringing program on it temporarily becomes an infringing article within the definition of secondary infringement in s.27: *Sony Computer Entertainment v Ball* [2005] F.S.R. 9.

[32] For the difficulties about transmission of data as part of an online service, see CDPA 1988 s.24(2).

[33] Whatever this may imply, UK law operates in accordance with its general test of substantial taking of the "work"; see paras 12–06, above and 20–10, below.

[34] See para.12–27, above. Its precursor in the matter was the Semi-Conductor Topographies Directive 87/54 art.5(5).

(c) *Substantial taking*

20–10 Major commercial programs are, almost inevitably, subject to direct, line-by-line copying. The software industry has had to tackle not only those who make a business of piracy but also private corporations, professional practices, government organisations and educational establishments which clone multiple copies of programs from a single purchase. It is the disparity between the costs of originally producing programs and those of direct accurate copying which has so much strengthened the political argument for their protection.[35]

Copyright also covers selective, altered, summarised and otherwise varied versions of a work, where it still involves substantial reproduction of the original. Indeed, it is explicitly provided that adaptation, as an act of infringement, includes making an arrangement, an altered version or a translation (from one language or code to another) of a program.[36] Since programming is a sphere in which, for many reasons, derivation in some sense may be occurring in the course of evolving new programs, there is endless scope for argument about what should amount to infringement. Successful programs invite the challenge of more or less competitive variants. With a form of protection as ubiquitous as copyright, it is particularly difficult to distinguish the inexcusably predatory from the acceptably competitive.

20–11 On this most central of all issues, the Computer Programs Directive has relatively little to contribute—mercifully, since the essential judgment must be specific to each case and can only be made by courts. The question whether the program itself is infringed—as distinct from issues about copyright in related output, such as screen displays of "menus" and games–is likely to turn either upon analysis of actual program content (at the level of lines of source or assembly code), or else upon analysis of those elements which together make up the program. In copyright terms, these latter elements, often characterised as a compilation, form the "sequence, structure and organisation" of the program. If that can be said to have been re-created in another program, a finding of infringement may follow, even in the absence of line-by-line copying. Some warning against too readily assuming that structure is protectable subject matter occurs in the Computer Programs Directive which specifies that "expression" alone is protected, and not underlying ideas and principles, "including those which underlie its interfaces".[37]

The proposition that protection does not extend to underlying ideas and principles has been left unstated in the UK implementation,[38] for the

---

[35] So also for all digitally recorded material; see paras 20–52 et seq., below.

[36] CDPA 1988 s.21, amended to comply with the Computer Programs Directive art.4(b).

[37] art.1(2); and see *Powerflex Services v Data Access* [1997] F.C.R. 490, FC Aust; *Creative Technology v Aztech Systems* [1997] F.S.R. 491, CA Sing. For user interfaces, see paras 20–23 et seq., below

[38] It is in the Directive only for the avoidance of doubt: Rec.13.

understandable reason that it is already there as a matter of common law principle applicable to the entire field of copyright.[39] Thus *Nova Productions v Mazooma Games*[40] considered whether certain visual aspects and functions used in a computer game, when copied by an imitator (but without copying the underlying code), would amount to substantial taking. Kitchin J. at first instance held (against the claimant) that:

> "They are ideas which have little to do with the skill and effort expended by the programmer and do not constitute the form of expression of the literary works relied upon."[41]

The Court of Appeal upheld this view.[42]

In the United States, the Copyright Act of 1976 sets out the dichotomy.[43] **20–12**
In applying it to computer program cases, courts there showed the world what differences of attitude can emerge:

> (*Whelan v Jaslow*[44]: dental laboratory program.) The claimants held the copyright in a program, "Dentalab", for organising the business of dental laboratories. The defendants, previously involved in commissioning and marketing that program, then prepared a similar program, "Dentcom", in a different computer language (BASIC, rather than EDL), which could be used on personal computers. The Third Circuit Court of Appeals upheld infringement. Line-by-line copying did not have to be shown. It sufficed that there were step-by-step similarities in the listings of the source code covering particularly significant subroutines. These were referred to as similarities of "structure".
>
> In rejecting an argument that all elements of "structure" must be excluded from consideration as mere "idea", the Court proferred the generalisation that "the purpose or function of a utilitarian work would be the work's idea, and everything that is not necessary to that purpose or function would be part of the expression of the idea".[45] Aiding the business of a dental laboratory was "idea", but how this was worked out in any particular program was expression, a crucial indicator being that

[39] It is applied, for instance, in *Ibcos* (n.54, below) esp. at 305, with the embellishment that "general" ideas are precluded, while "specific" ideas are not: at 291–292.

[40] *Nova Productions v Mazooma Games* [2006] R.P.C. 14. As the judge noted, it is not relevant to assess how far the defendant's borrowing amounted to a substantial part of his own product: see above, para.12–06.

[41] *Nova Productions v Mazooma Games* [2006] R.P.C. 14 at [247]. See also [248].

[42] *Nova Productions v Mazooma Games* [2007] R.P.C. 25, CA, [44] per Jacob L.J.

[43] Copyright Act 1976 s.102(b): "In no case does copyright protection for an original work of authorship extend to any idea, procedure, process, system, method of operation, concept, principle, or discovery, regardless of the form in which it is described, explained, illustrated, or embodied in such work."

[44] *Whelan v Jaslow* [1987] F.S.R. 1 (C.Apps., 3d Circ.).

[45] Derived from Learned Hand J.'s dictum on the subject (para.12–06, above), this nonetheless went as far in favour of liability as "what is worth copying is worth protecting".

various non-infringing dental laboratory programs were competing on the market.[46]

(*Computer Associates v Altai*[47]: computer job scheduling.) The defendants' "Oscar" program, which controlled the order of computing tasks, contained an interface component which allowed use with different operating systems. The claimants alleged that this element had been added by unlawful copying from its "Adapter" program.[48] Here, rejecting *Whelan*, the Court refused protection, applying an apparently scrupulous legal test. It first analysed the "levels of abstraction" of the claimant's program, starting from its final expression in object code. It retraced and mapped the program designer's steps back from implementation to formative conception.[49] It was then in a position to exclude from consideration those elements taken from the public domain and those which could be expressed only in one way (elements dictated by "efficiency" and by "external factors",[50] where expression must be regarded as confounded into idea—the "merger doctrine"). It thus arrived at a "core of protectable expression" and on the facts the defendant was found not to have taken this.[51]

20–13 The learning process evident in these and other US decisions has had a variable impact in English courts:

(*John Richardson Computers v Flanders*[52]: labelling and stock-taking program for pharmacies.) The defendant programmer, who had previously written an application program for the claimant, produced a competitive program in a different computer language from the claimant's and the claimant did not contend that detailed programming had been taken. Rather, as in *Whelan*, there was said to be infringement in building the program as a whole from various sub-units—the routine and

---

[46] [1981] F.S.R. 1 at 19, 21–22. For US views highly supportive of embracing protection, see Clapes and Daniels (1992) 9 No. 11, Comp. Lyr. 11; Miller (1993) 106 Harv. L.R. 977.

[47] *Computer Associates v Altai* 982 F. 2d 693 (1992) (C.Apps. 2d Circ.); Karjala (1998) 68 Brooklyn L.R. 519.

[48] It was first added by an ex-employee of the claimants, who did infringe. When the defendants found out, they removed his work and had the element reprogrammed independently.

[49] Again, the starting point is Learned Hand J.'s dictum. Subsequently, in *Gates Rubber v Bando* 9 F.3d 823 (1993), the Tenth Circuit CA, identified six levels: from main purpose and program architecture through modules and algorithms to source code and finally object code. Only the last two would almost always be protected, those in the middle being a matter of judging the particular case.

[50] i.e. "incidents, characters or settings which are as a practical matter indispensable...in the treatment of a given topic": *Atari v North American Philips* 672 F. 2d 607 at 616. The *Whelan* judgment equally emphasises the need to exclude such matters: see [1987] F.S.R. 1 at 18–20.

[51] For US views supporting this caution, see e.g. Karjala [1994] E.I.P.R. 13, 58; (1994) 13 U. Dayton L.R. 975; Gambrell, Hamilton and Hood (1994) 11, No.7, Comp. Lyr. 9. The majority of Federal Circuit Courts continue to show allegiance to the *Computer Associates* formulation. Inevitably, however, in the constant stream of American case law differences have emerged over its application.

[52] *John Richardson Computers v Flanders* [1993] F.S.R. 497.

information order for entering drugs, codes for doses, pre-printing options for labels, best day's stock control, etc. Ferris J. concluded that he should undertake the "abstraction, filtration and analysis" process prescribed in *Computer Associates*, though he found it difficult. Curiously, he then concluded that in the whole program there were 17 apparently similar elements, but that of these only three constituted infringement, all of them aspects of the display to the user of the program.[53]

(*Ibcos Computers v Barclays Mercantile*[54]: packaged "suite" of accounting programs for agricultural dealership.) In factually quite different circumstances, Jacob J. held that UK copyright law did not demand a search for a "core of protectable expression", and he rejected the very concept of a "merger" of expression into idea, of which increasing use had been made in US decisions.[55] The claimant's program was found infringed by "over-borrowing". In the particular circumstances this was demonstrated partly by identifying copying of specific lines of code (the judge refusing to believe the programmer's protestations that he had not started from the claimant's program) and partly by transferring structures from the claimant's program.

(*Cantor Fitzgerald v Tradition (UK)*[56]: several employees of the claimant wrote a bond-broking program for them which became an important part of their armoury as inter-dealer bond brokers.) The employees then went to Tradition to build up a rival business. Starting from a version of the claimant's program, they produced a program for Tradition in three months in which only at most 3.3 per cent of the claimant's code was found to have been copied. Pumfrey J. recognised that there could be infringing copying at the levels of the "architecture" of a program—its overall structure, and its allocation of functions between various programs; and compilation in detail (at which level alone he found instances of infringement). He derived no assistance from the notion of "over-borrowing" and instead drew from the continuing theme in classic authorities—the need to show taking of a substantial part of the whole work, judged by the skill, labour and judgment which went into the element alleged to have been infringed.[57]

(*Navitaire v easyJet Airline*[58]: internet bookings program.) The airline easyJet became dissatisfied with the bookings program supplied to it by Navitaire, and contracted with Bulletproof to produce its own program

[53] For this see paras 20–23, 20–24, below.

[54] *Ibcos Computers v Barclays Mercantile* [1994] F.S.R. 275; see Grewal [1996] E.I.P.R. 454. Applied in *Cantor Fitzgerald v Tradition (UK)*, n.54, below.

[55] [1994] F.S.R. 275 at 289–291. Note the Whelanesque flourish, mentioned in n.44, above. "What is worth copying is worth protecting" is, however, disparaged as a means of jumping to a conclusion.

[56] *Cantor Fitzgerald v Tradition (UK)* [2000] R.P.C. 95.

[57] See above, n.19.

[58] *Navitaire* [2006] R.P.C. 3.

by way of replacement, a principal requirement being that the user interfaces—particularly that for day-to-day bookings and that for long-term changes to flight schedules and the like—should be as close as possible to that of the Navitaire system. The claimant did not contend that there was textual copying of its coding. It sought instead to build its case around the achievement of the same "look and feel" in the resulting screens and in the output of recorded bookings. Pumfrey J. acknowledged that there could be infringement in taking an idea that was sufficiently detailed. But he gave particular attention to the provisions of the Computer Programs Directive which excluded languages and the ideas underlying interfaces from the protection of programs as literary works.[59] He was accordingly reluctant to find infringement in the adoption of the "business logic" of the program. It was necessary to consider not only the degree of detail in any copying but also whether the relevant skill and knowledge was of its nature the subject of copyright—and not, for instance, skill and knowledge for the production of a machine or the confection of a pudding.[60] He accordingly found infringement only in minor elements in the program as a whole.

(*Nova Productions v Mazooma Games*[61]: computer video game for playing pool.) The claimant produced a computer video game based on pool and alleged that the defendants' games infringed copyright in the computer programs as literary works. The defendants had not copied the source code of the claimant's program, but there existed some similarities in appearance and function, namely: the presence of a power meter, a visual indication of the direction of the shot, the ability of the cue to rotate around the cue ball, a plain view of the pool table and the values associated with particular pockets. The Court of Appeal upheld the decision of Kitchin J. at first instance that the defendants had not infringed because they had not copied the program code or architecture, but had only copied ideas.[62]

20–14 The *Ibcos* judgment is right to point out some essential differences between British and American copyright doctrine. The former, deploying its strictly limited requirement of "originality", has not hesitated to protect compilations of information against copying, even where there is little real

[59] Computer Programs Directive, recs 13–15 art.1(2). The collection of commands was characterised as a computer language and for that reason excluded from protection: para.92.

[60] paras 125–128, relying upon Lord Hoffmann's identification of two types of idea lying outside copyright—ideas unconnected with the literary, dramatic, musical or artistic nature of the work; and ideas that are not original or so commonplace as to form no substantial part of the work: see *Designers Guild v Russell Williams* [2001] 1 W.L.R. 2416, 2423.

[61] *Nova Productions v Mazooma Games* [2006] R.P.C. 14; [2007] R.P.C. 25, CA.

[62] *Nova Productions* [2007] R.P.C. 25, CA, paras.31–45 per Jacob L.J. (Lloyd L.J. and Sir Andrew Morritt in agreement).

scope for alternative expression.[63] Likewise it has not feared to trespass on the territory of the "functional".[64]

Nonetheless the caution exhibited in *Computer Associates* is not without its resonances for the assessment of "substantial taking" under UK law. That judgment focuses very firmly on the quality of what has been reproduced. Indeed all pronouncements on the subject underscore the importance of considering, in one direction, the unusualness, and, in the other, the ordinariness, of what is being taken. So standard programming, even if copied, may be given little weight, whereas a truly ingenious structural device may be found to infringe even when subsequently varied quite considerably. Long ago, it was held that a simple picture of a hand pointing to a square on a ballot paper could be copyright, even though its whole purpose was to tell the voter where to put a cross; but for such a simple, functional work only very close imitation would infringe.[65]

It is true that the UK experience with copyright in industrial design **20–15** established that the protection extended to the purely functional. However, as the Court of Appeal has stressed, what is necessarily functional should not for that reason be accorded any special weight in reaching a final judgment on whether there has been substantial taking of a drawing or other work which is accorded artistic copyright.[66] It remains to be seen whether an equivalent approach can be built into the assessment of literary "copying". As *Cantor Fitzgerald* confirms, the courts look to see if a defendant who is conversant with the claimant's work (whether he admits this or his denial is not believed) has nonetheless in large measure produced his own work, as distinct from disguising his borrowings from the claimant. *Navitaire* and *Nova Productions* show how difficult it can be to make out a case of infringement in a whole program, when there have been no direct borrowings of code, but only similarities in end results.

[63] Hence the protection of street directories and TV programme scheduling: for which see para.11–09, above; cf. especially the *Feist* case there mentioned. Commissioner Bangemann, however, did not hesitate to assure the European Parliament that the merger doctrine was a general component of European copyright laws (Session, April 16, 1991, p.83). How long can the British maintain their peculiarity in the matter?

[64] As in the protection of grid layouts for a competition (*Express Newspapers v Liverpool Daily Post* [1985] 3 All E.R. 680) and engineering drawings against 3D reproduction. This contrasts notably with the US doctrine stemming from the classic *Baker v Selden* 101 US 99 (1877) (no copyright there in accounting forms); *Rosenthal v Kalpakian*, 446 F.2d. 738 (1971).

[65] *Kenrick v Lawrence* (1890) 25 QBD 99; on which, see the *Ibcos* case (n.55, above), at 290–291.

[66] *Johnstone Safety v Cook* [1990] F.S.R. 161 (traffic cones). The scope of such copyright is in any case much reduced under the CDPA 1988: see para.15–32, above.

(d) *Exceptions*

20–16 (i) **Back-up copies.** The Computer Programs Directive, and hence the CDPA 1988, entitles lawful users of a program to make "necessary" back-up copies.[67] Making back-ups of programs as well as stored data is widely considered a matter of sensible practice; so it can only be hoped that what is "necessary" will be given reasonable scope. A contractual clause seeking to over-ride the entitlement is void.[68] In addition, in order to correct errors in a program or for any other purpose "necessary for ... lawful use", there is power to copy or adapt the program; but this may be excluded by a contractual term which after all prohibits such interference and so sends the user back to the manufacturer or supplier for debugging and other maintenance.[69]

20–17 (ii) **Decompilation and other reverse analysis.** During the personal computing revolution of the last 20 years, the industry's leaders have explored, with varying degrees of commitment, the possibility of maintaining "closed" systems in which they would produce and maintain an entire complex of software, covering not only the basic input-output systems (BIOS) which link all other programs to the hardware, but programs for external connections and application programs of all kinds (word-processing, spreadsheets, etc.). Equally a buoyant explosion of independent producers, both of PCs and of programs for them, have competed to supply a host of alternatives, ranging from the directly competitive to the wholly complementary. In the early 1980s, IBM established its personal computer as the dominant product and the great bulk of programs came to be written to operate on this machine. Not only had other software producers to ensure compatability with the IBM PC-BIOS but also computer producers (such as, in Europe, Olivetti and Bull) had to provide a BIOS which would function accurately with such programs. While IBM fostered this development,[70] Apple was able to build up a second, more closely tied, system.

---

[67] Computer Programs Directive art.5(2); CDPA 1988 s.50A. At least under the Act, a "lawful user" can be not only a licensed purchaser but any successor in title or other reasonably anticipated user (employee, agent, inspector, etc.). Initially the Government insisted that even the question of back-up be left to contractual terms; a "back-up" power was doubtless normally to be implied—or possibly imposed as "non-derogable" under *British Leyland v Armstrong* (for which, see para.15–06, above). See also, CDPA 1988 s.56(2) on the implied transfer of back-up and adaptation rights to subsequent transferees of a copy.

[68] Computer Programs Directive art.9(1); CDPA 1988 ss.50A(3), 296A; not affecting agreements made before January 1, 1993: Copyright (Computer) Regulations 1992 (SI 1992/3233) reg.12(2).

[69] Computer Programs Directive arts 5(1), 9(1); CDPA 1988, ss.50A(2), 50C; but cf. Directive Rec.17; Smith (1990–91) 7 C.S.L.R. 148.

[70] At first, IBM published its BIOS source and object code (which made this a de facto standard); later it was choosier about how much program information it released, being obliged to give more by a competition dispute with the EU Commission which was settled on terms (EC Bulletin 10–1984). The subsequent confrontation over the content of the Computer Programs Directive expressed a renewed concern by IBM to prevent interoperability with its products.

All in all, the range of consumer choice spiralled. The EU, looking to assist a European computer industry in third place behind the American and Japanese, saw the importance of open systems in which programs supplied from different sources are "interoperable". The technical key to interoperability has lain in the ability of the outsider to have access to the structure of the technical interface of software to which a connection is desired. For the interface is a set of electronic keys which, so far as structure is concerned, must be precisely emulated, in order to secure co-operation between programs. **20–18**

After a contortionate wrestle, the campaign for interoperability succeeded to a significant extent in Europe.[71] Even so, major providers may choose to reveal in full only the object code of their programs, keeping the source code a guarded secret. For an outsider to secure knowledge of the interface information in that code, it was in some cases necessary to engage in the tedious and often only approximate business of "decompilation".[72] This required the conversion of machine code by means of a disassembly program back to a level which gave partial access to the source code. No automated system existed, however, from which to recapture the full source code. Indications which explained the intent behind the succession of steps could not be recovered because these comments would not have been transmitted into the machine code.[73] Without them, it requires highly skilled and laborious work even to approximate source code. It can, however, be done sufficiently well to provide both substitute and complementary programs and this ability has been vital to the way in which the industry has developed to date.

That is the crucial significance of art.6 of the Computer Programs Directive, which eventually took a comparatively broad form.[74] The article was intended to give the industry immediate guidance on what decompilation was permitted, so as not to leave the issue to the vagaries of case law in **20–19**

---

[71] And has recently been given a boost by the decision of the General Court (ex. CFI) in *Microsoft v Commission* [2007] 5 C.M.L.R. 11 where refusal to licence interoperability information that would allow competitors to produce work group server operating systems compatible with Windows operating system was held to be an abuse of dominant position. For a discussion see: Byrne (2007) 2 J.I.P.L.P 324; Batchelor [2008] C.T.L.R. 17; Dizon [2008] C.T.L.R. 213; Penny and Edwards [2008] Ent. L.R. 77; and Subramanian (2010) 5 J.I.P.L.P. 245.

[72] Particularly in the production of compatible BIOS's. In other cases, it suffices to engage in "black box" techniques—test runs, communication line traces, storage media dumps, etc. These now receive some protection (see para.20–17, above). In any case, they are distinct from decompilation in that they do not require the making of a copy of a version of the program by disassembly.

[73] Johnson-Laird (1992) 5 Software L.J. 331; (1994) 19 U. Dayton L.R. 843.

[74] For an analysis of the proposals for narrower and wider drafting of the Directive, see Vinje in Lehmann and Tapper (eds) *Handbook of European Software Law* (1993); cf. Hart [2006] E.I.P.R. 361. Even so, it does not permit all forms of interoperability which explains the resort to competition law in the *Microsoft* case (n.71, above), where art.102 TFEU (ex. art 82 TEC) was treated as of higher rank than art.6 of the Computer Programs Directive.

the various jurisdictions.[75] It is essential to keep in mind the special circumstances in which the issue arises. Decompilation will become significant if it leads to the writing and production of a program which is not itself an infringement of the program decompiled. If it can be shown that the final product infringes then it can itself be attacked; in support of that, decompilation for the purpose of writing such a program cannot fall within the exception provided by art.6.[76]

Decompilation is concerned with clear, line-by-line, copying and so does not raise questions about "substantial taking" of the kind discussed above. Those who argued against any exception took their stand partly on the difficulties of demonstrating infringement in rewritten final products.[77] They claimed that they must be able to object to the one step in the evolution of those products which unequivocally involved straightforward copying. Their opponents riposted that other copyright works could be consulted and drawn upon in order to follow instructions or to make other works, provided that the results were not themselves infringements.[78] From this perspective it was merely a peculiarity of computer technology that a single copy had to be made before the step of consultation could take place.

20–20 The actual exception now inserted in the CDPA 1988 is an adapted version of art.6 of the Computer Programs Directive. It might have been more discreet to tread this bloody and treacherous battlefield exactly in the footsteps of the Directive; but our valiant draftsman struck out for himself.[79]

Under the new s.50B of the CDPA 1988 it is not infringement of copyright for a lawful user to decompile a program for a "permitted objective", provided that a set of limiting conditions are satisfied. A term in an agreement, which seeks to prevent such decompilation, is void.[80] On the other hand, the defence of fair dealing for purposes of research or private study has no application to decompilation[81] (though it remains relevant to

---

[75] Thus, while it may be that "of course, an individual owner could interface his program with that of another" (per Jacob J., *Ibcos* case (n.54, above) at 290), that does not settle how much can be reproduced in a search for interface specifications. Nor is it clear how far taking one copy at that stage could lead to an award of damages including losses from the competition of a non-infringing program: cf. para.2–45, above.

[76] Computer Programs Directive art.6(2)(c); CDPA 1988 s.50B(3)(d).

[77] See esp. Lake et al. [1989] E.I.P.R. 43; Hart [1991] E.I.P.R. 111; Miller (1993) 106 Harvard L.R. 977.

[78] See, esp., Colombe and Meyer [1990] E.I.P.R. 79, 325; Karjala (1994) 19 U. Dayton L.R. 975; Vinje [1994] E.I.P.R. 364.

[79] Following the modern approach to European texts, Pumfrey J. has said that either the language of the British draftsman embodies the Directive's requirement, or it is a mistransposition into UK law: *Navitaire v easyJet Airlines* [2006] R.P.C. 3, para.88.

[80] CDPA 1988 ss.50B(4), 296A; the contract must have been entered after January 1, 1993: Copyright (Computer Programs) Regulations 1992 (SI 1992/3233) reg.12(2).

[81] CDPA 1988 s.29(4).

any other computer use which otherwise would constitute infringement).[82] The section departs from the Computer Programs Directive at two basic points. It defines "decompiling" as converting a copy of a computer program expressed in a low level language into a version in a higher level language; or, incidentally while doing so, copying the program.[83] Moreover, eschewing entirely the concocted term, "interoperability", it defines the "permitted objective" of decompilation as: obtaining the information necessary to create an independent program which can be operated with the program decompiled or with another program.[84]

Of the limiting conditions, three are in the nature of corollaries to the basic definitions. The sole permitted purpose is to create an independent interoperable program; so (1) the information obtained must not be used for any other purpose; in particular (2) it must not be used in a program which infringes that decompiled[85]; nor (3) must it be supplied to any other person for a different purpose. Beyond these are two factors which are inherently adapted to provoke controversy: **20–21**

(a) the lawful user must not have the necessary information "readily available to him"; and
(b) the lawful user must not decompile more than necessary to achieve the permitted objective.

Condition (a) will not be satisfied where the details of technical interfaces have been accurately published, for instance, with copies of the program: but in that case, who would wish to engage in the tedious treasure-hunt of

[82] The Computer Programs Directive and its implementation set other conundrums about the relationship of the specific provisions to the general law: as for instance the preservation in Computer Programs Directive art.9(1) of other intellectual property rights and those concerning unfair competition and trade secrets. Where a contractual term is specifically declared void, it would be strange indeed for a court to find that its purported obligation nonetheless arose under an equitable duty to preserve trade secrets: see Dreier [1991] E.I.P.R. 319 at 325.

[83] The Computer Programs Directive wisely avoids any comparison in the level of languages. The UK section may not apply to a "hex dump", which is the conversion of object code in binary form into hexadecimal code—not itself a higher level language.

[84] This is clearer than the Computer Programs Directive in defining the types of interoperable connection.

[85] This is expressed over-emphatically in both the Computer Programs Directive and CDPA 1988 s.50B(3)(d) as use "to create a program which is substantially similar in its expression to the program decompiled or to do any act restricted by copyright". The first is necessarily included in the second, and it is quite unclear what, if anything, may fall only within the second; so the "or" makes no appreciable sense.

The Computer Programs Directive (art.6(3)) spells out the limits which the Berne Convention (art.9(2)) places upon national exceptions to the reproduction right: decompilation must not conflict with normal exploitation or unreasonably prejudice the right-holder's legitimate interests (mysteriously, these are put in reverse order). CDPA 1988 s.50B makes no mention of this: rightly, since it must be taken to exemplify the Berne proposition.

decompilation? How far it also covers a case where the right-holder will provide details for a charge is entirely unsettled. But a decompiler who fails first to inquire whether the information is available and on what terms puts himself at risk.[86]

Condition (b) may create some hazard for those who have to search around a program for interface structures, bearing in mind that they may have been scrupulously hidden. A decompiler ought not to be held to have acted improperly unless it becomes clear that he went fishing for other things using interoperability as a pretext.[87]

20–22 In addition to the provision allowing this limited measure of decompilation, s.50BA of the CDPA 1988 also stipulates that it will not be an infringement to observe, study or test the functioning of a program in order to understand the underlying ideas and principles of any element in it—not just interface elements—and s.296A makes terms seeking to restrict such acts void.[88] Section 50BA covers acts, such as running the program, which fall outside decompilation and acts as a reasonable complement to the decompilation section.

(e) *Screen displays*

20–23 We move here to elements in the complex of computing which are closely allied to programs, but (at least for copyright purposes) must be considered something apart. The displays on a screen provide the crucial elements of the "graphic user interface" (GUI). They are the keys which allow the user to instruct the computer what is wanted of the programs being run. The immense spread of computer usage, and the progress towards "open", mixed programming, make it vital that this process should be made as simple and easily memorised as possible. Nevertheless, each user builds up a fund of knowledge about a program or programs which turns upon familiarity with particular displays and their operation. At this stage of the evolving technology (as is typical of such developments),[89] the lack of standard usage may still tie the user to the system he or she knows.

At present, therefore, new software competitors may in effect need to emulate the screen displays of leading programs if they are to make much headway in the market. In the United Kingdom the issue in copyright law has so far been considered only in passing. There are, however, signs that displays may be treated either as literary, artistic or film works (depending

[86] See Krocker [1997] E.I.P.R. 247.

[87] cf. Walker L.J., *Pro Sieben v Carlton UK TV* [1999] E.M.L.R. 109, 127.

[88] Implementing Computer Programs Directive art.5(3). Previously, the only transposition of art.5(3) was s.296A but following criticism of the UK by the Commission for failing properly to implement this obligation the Copyright and Related Rights Regulations 2003 (SI 2003/2498) introduced s.50BA.

[89] Compare car driving, as did the US Court in *Apple v Microsoft* 24 U.S.P.Q. 2d 1081, 1088–1089 (1992).

on their content), which give exclusive copyright protection.[90] If this is so, it is irrelevant that the programming to achieve them is quite different.[91] Moreover, it has been held that registered designs for GUI icons are available.[92] That form of protection may become accepted throughout Europe through EU Designs law and its national counterparts.[93]

In the United States the issue provoked a rash of litigation, which has turned in favour of defendants as courts have come to appreciate the tying effect on users. Apple, for instance, failed in claims against Microsoft.[94] Lotus failed to protect the menu command hierarchy of its "1–2–3" spreadsheet against Borland, who replicated it (using its own code) and provided for the transmission of the user's own Macros[95] from the Lotus sheet.[96] In both decisions much emphasis was placed (following *Computer Associates v Altai*) on filtering out unprotectable elements which were functional, unoriginal or indispensable in the circumstances, or which produced mergers of expression into idea. There is no mistaking the strong antipathy which the courts felt towards so extended a reach for this new and strange application of copyright protection. **20–24**

As already noted, UK copyright law lacks any principle which places "functional" elements beyond copyright, just as it has no general concept of fair use to call in aid. But, as already noted, similarities which are functional may be discounted in deciding whether there has been taking at all and in assessing whether that taking is substantial. If courts here were to become as **20–25**

[90] In the *Flanders* case (n.52, above), Ferris J. correctly distinguished a screen display as a product of the program, distinct from the program itself. He considered that the display might itself be a photographic work or a film; and that it might reproduce a drawing so that if copied there would be indirect infringement of copyright in the drawing: at 527. In the *Navitaire* case (n.58, above) Pumfrey J. accepted that screen displays or aspects thereof could be protected as literary or artistic works and that there had been limited infringement in this respect. In the *Nova Productions* case (n.61, above) the Court of Appeal accepted that screen graphics may be artistic works and that series of screen displays may be films, although on the facts no infringement was found. The argument that screen displays may be dramatic works has not met with success: *Nova Productions* (n.61, above). See also *Powerflex Services v Data Access* (1997) 37 I.P.R. 436; Jew [1997] E.I.P.R. 732.

[91] As Ferris J. recognises in *Flanders*, similarity of displays does not prove that the program to produce each is the same. But this appears to be ignored in the finding that the program was infringed by three interface elements because they were the same in their presentation to the user: see Karjala [1994] E.I.P.R. 58, 63–64.

[92] *Apple Computer v Designs Registry* [2002] R.P.C. 191, a decision under the pre–2002 law overturning earlier practice.

[93] Above, paras 15–12 et seq. See Kur (2003) 34 I.I.C. 50.

[94] *Apple v Microsoft* 35 F 3d. 1435 (1994), refusing a broad "look-and-feel" approach (of *Whelan* parentage) in favour of a scrupulous analysis to exclude non-protectable elements (out of *Altai*); leading to the conclusion that what was sought to be protected was functional and therefore not the subject of copyright: see Neville (1996) 61 Missouri L.R. 203.

[95] i.e. chains of commands which the user has linked so that all will be performed upon a single instruction.

[96] *Lotus Development v Borland International* 49 F. 3rd 807 (1995), affirmed by the Supreme Court (4–4).

indignant as their American counterparts about claims of this nature, they might well use these limitations robustly.[97]

If the claims could be said to affect trade between EU countries, there might also be a prospect of challenging the assertion of copyright as anti-competitive. Conceivably, the practice might amount to abuse of a dominant position, under art.102 of the TFEU (ex. 82 TEC), because restrictions on an "aftermarket" are gained through controls obtained in the "foremarket". The "*Magill*" case has settled that, in extreme circumstances, art.102 may apply even to refusals to license intellectual property to a competitor and nothing else.[98]

(2) Patents for computer programs[99]

(a) *Patentable subject matter*

20–26 The exclusion of computer programs "as such" from the scope of the EPC in 1973 reflected a widespread view in the early computer industry and among researchers in the field; but that was before the age of mass production of micro-processors which was about to burst upon it.[100] It stood alongside schemes, rules or methods of performing a mental act, playing a game or doing business, all of them precluded, but only "as such". Software was open to protection by trade secrets law, contract and (soon enough) copyright.[101] But since the 1990s, there has been ever-growing pressure from the giants of the computer industry to underpin all other IP in the field with patents for inventions. On a world scale, the movement has been powered particularly by the readiness of the US Patent Office and courts to allow patents for programs as such and for business methods, at least where they are underpinned by computer software as their vital element.

20–27 Some willingness to explore accommodations within the EPC framework was indicated by the EPO when it amended its Guidelines in 1985.[102] The change made it clear that that Office would allow claims involving use of a program if overall the invention made a contribution to an art that was technical. The scope of what has since been accepted and what is still excluded has become ever more clouded, but there has undoubtedly been

---

[97] There now seems little scope to apply the concept of non-derogation from grant in this context: see para.15–06, above; and see *Creative Technology v Aztech Systems* [1997] F.S.R. 491, CA Sing.

[98] See para.19–16, above.

[99] Beresford, *Patenting Software under the EPC* (2000); Bakels and Berrit, *Patentability of Computer Programs* (2000); articles by Ghidini and Arrezo, Pila, Hilty and Geiger, and Weyand and Haase in (2005) 36 I.I.C. 159, 173, 615, 647.

[100] Before the EPC took effect, UK courts showed a distinct readiness to allow patents for the programming of computers, even if it resulted in the processing of digital information without affecting the production of a distinct product: see *Burroughs' (Perkins) Application* [1974] R.P.C. 147. But the French Patent Law of 1968 had excluded such patents.

[101] Above, paras 20–04 et seq.

[102] Guidelines, C IV 2.2. See Sherman [1991] E.I.P.R. 85, and for wider comparisons, Hoffmann et al. [1988] E.I.P.R. 355; [1989] E.I.P.R. 7; Daehwan Koo [2002] I.P.Q. 172.

some growth in what is allowable. As a result, there is an obvious difficulty about cumulation with copyright. But institutions such as the European Commission are prepared to treat the two as essentially complementary.[103] In its view, copyright protects detailed expression of particular programs in source and object code. Patents should be available for more fundamental techniques, which can be deployed in a range of programming, but subject to the general requirements of novelty, inventive step and industrial application.

In a Draft Directive on the issue, the Commission joined those who are concerned to foster the ever-growing software industry and believe that the monopoly opportunities of patents are needed to attracting investment in a field. That opinion was vehemently opposed by those who hold that the resultant monopolies would be seriously damaging. In this the loud hostility of the Open Source software movement towards invasive domination of the industry through patents on programs and business methods was particularly prominent. In the event the Commission withdrew its proposal, leaving it to patent offices and courts within the EU to pursue their own course.

It cannot be pretended that EPO tribunals and UK courts have reached an interpretation of the exclusion of computer programs "as such" that is pellucid or wholly consistent. In the *Aerotel* and *Macrossan* cases[104], the Court of Appeal has at least endorsed a schema for approaching the question of a program's patentability. The four steps are the following: (1) construe the claim in question; (2) identify the actual contribution to the art; (3) ask whether it falls solely within the excluded subject-matter; and (4) check whether the actual or alleged contribution is technical in nature. During the 1990s, much attention was given to the question whether the invention relating to the program has a "technical effect" or "technical character" and the Court's schema emphasises how important that remains. **20–28**

Straightforward examples of what constitutes "technical effect" can be taken from EPO case law: **20–29**

(1) (*Koch and Sterzel*[105]: program governing the operation of a technical device.) A claim was held patentable to X-ray apparatus controlled by a computer program so as to secure optimal exposure without overloading the X-ray tube. It sufficed that "technical means" were involved as well as the mathematical method or algorithm, which was characterised as "non-technical". It was not necessary to show that invention lay exclusively or largely in the technical, rather than the non-technical domain—a matter of prime significance to other, less easy, cases.[106]

---

[103] For the Draft Directive to harmonise national law on the patentability of computer implemented inventions: COM (2002) 92; 2002 OJ C151.

[104] For which see below, para 20–32.

[105] *Koch and Sterzel* [1988] OJ EPO 19.

[106] See also *Sohei Ford Management System* [1996] E.P.O.R. 253.

(2) (*Vicom's Application*[107]: computer operating program in an industrial technique.) Likewise a claim is patentable to a computer so programmed (or provided with hardware) as to be able to process digital images in accordance with a given mathematical procedure expressed as an algorithm. The program had been developed for the computer-aided design (CAD) of engineering and similar products, and the application was upheld once the claim was amended so as to cover only uses which started with a computerised image; the original claim was for less specific methods of using the algorithm. This was allowed because the claim went to the general functioning of the computer, rather than to an application designed to execute particular tasks. With this amendment the Board of Appeal could accept that it was sufficiently "directed to a technical process". At root, what mattered was that CAD is a widely used and most valuable aid to product design. Again the decision was a leading development.

(3) (*IBM's Application*[108]: program for placement of windows on screen.) The program dealt with a manner of affecting the display on a computer screen, which enabled one window, when obscured by another, to be brought forward or alongside the other window. The case was novel in that claims were allowed not just to a computer when so programmed but also to a product which held the program on any medium, including the internet. While a claim merely to the method of programming would remain a computer program as such, the "potential technical character" possessed by a disk or tape of the program existed in its capacity for downloading into a computer. In consequence the program as sold commercially could be a direct infringement of the claim, thus making a supplier liable without having to satisfy the conditions for "indirect" infringement.[109] In that decision can be sensed a willingness to interpret the exclusion of computer programs narrowly, so that European patent law could to some degree emulate the liberal practice of the US Patent Office.[110]

In all these cases the program directly affected the operation of a piece of equipment in what can be considered a technical manner. This included a computer itself, making the decisions important where the program was some part of an operating system. One consequence is that, much as it may be detested by computing specialists whose instincts are communal rather than competitive, the patent system already operates in the territory which most interests them.

---

[107] *Vicom's Application* [1987] OJ EPO 14.

[108] *IBM's Application* [2000] E.P.O.R. 301, TBA; and see *IBM/Computer program products II* [2000] E.P.O.R. 219.

[109] See above, para.6–17.

[110] For the continuing influence of this political factor, see *Aerotel* (n.129, below), at paras 14–15.

The cases may be contrasted with decisions of English courts concerning claims which either involve types of traditional mental activity or human judgement: **20–30**

(4) (*Gale's Application*[111]: new method of calculating square roots.) The applicant's essential discovery was of a computerised method of calculating square roots by eliminating division and restricting multiplication to specified binary functions. This could be given form in the electronic circuitry of a read-only memory (ROM) and the claim was to a ROM carrying the relevant controls. Aldous J. was prepared to accept the claim; but the Court of Appeal refused the application for its very apparent reference to mathematical procedures for producing numbers. The Court refused to accept in such a case that embodiment in a ROM made the program patentable, where it would not be if expressed purely in mathematical terms or was contained on a floppy disk for insertion in a computer. Such a distinction, according to Nicholls L.J. would be nonsense.[112]

(5) (*Fujitsu's Application*[113]: physical analysis; human judgment.) The Court of Appeal rejected a claim to a computer programmed to convert data concerning the structure of two crystals into data representing the physical layout of the crystal structure that would have been obtained, by combining the original two structures in such a way that the two selected atoms, the two selected lattice-vectors and the two selected crystal-faces were superimposed. This was held unpatentable because the whole operation revolved around the computer program and there was no technical contribution, as in *Vicom*.[114] Further, in obiter, the court held that the claim left it to the operator to select what data to work on, how to work on it, how to assess the results and which results to use. The process was abstract and the result of the use of it undefined. What was produced was not an inevitable result of taking a number of defined steps but was determined by the personal skill and assessment of the operator. This amounted to a method of performing mental acts which involved no sufficient technical contribution.

---

111 *Gale's Application* [1991] R.P.C. 305. Similarly, in the EPO a claim was refused for a program to run on conventional hardware which would replace difficult expressions in a text with comprehensible synonyms: *IBM/Text Clarity* [1990] OJ EPO 384; German and Australian courts have refused a word-processing program which enabled a user to write Chinese characters: see *CCOM v Jiejing* [1993] F.S.R. 315; XZB 29/89 (1993) 24 I.I.C. 124.

112 [1991] R.P.C. at 325–6.

113 *Fujitsu's Application* [1997] R.P.C. 608, CA; and see *Speech Analysis Apparatus* [2002] 33 I.I.C. 343, German SC; *Hutchins' Application.* [2003] R.P.C. 264: computer program giving guidance to paramedics on performing heart-lung resuscitation—not patentable (UK IPO, not applying *Pension Benefits*, below n.116).

114 The Court of Appeal in *Symbian v Comptroller-General* [2009] R.P.C. 1 at [42] expressed doubts about whether the conclusion reached in *Fujitsu* is consistent with *Vicom* and *Gale*.

(6) (*Merrill Lynch's Application*[115]: analysis of stock market data.) The application program was for use in an automated market for shares. It analysed customers' orders to buy and sell against given criteria; if the criteria were satisfied, the transaction was executed automatically. The Court of Appeal held this unpatentable because the operation that resulted was a legal transaction, not a technical effect. In doing so, it was held wrong to consider whether the inventive step being claimed for the invention lay solely in the program (i.e. the excluded subject matter). That approach would lead to an undue level of exclusion from the patent system.

20–31 The cases most evidently on the borderline of "technical character" concern claims to the processing of information for some business or informational end which is useful, but results in "information" rather than a "product" in the ordinary sense of a manufacture. It is in this extensive category that the US practice became much readier to allow patents than in Europe.[116] The two decisions of Technical Boards of Appeal which follow are of this kind, and have caused great controversy in seeking to airbrush out any real substance from art.52(2)(d) and 53(2), while keeping issues of technical means or effect for the general requirements of novelty and non-obviousness.

(7) (*PBS Partnership*[117]: pension benefit system.) Claims to software for operating an employer's pension system in which the amounts due to pensioners are calculated by reference to a set of standard factors, including actuarial averages of the life-span of all the employees involved. The patent claims were in two groups: the first were to methods of making the calculation; the second to "apparatus" (i.e. computers) programmed to execute the method. The method claims were held to be proximate to the mere making of the calculation and accordingly were computer programs as such. However, the claims to apparatus were not, because, on the issue of "computer program as such", there should be no consideration of whether the technical element (operation of the computer) was the contributing factor to "invention". That factor, however, did remain germane in assessing whether there was an inventive step in the particular instance and on that distinct ground the "apparatus" claims failed. In reaching this result the Technical Board of Appeal assumed that the programmer skilled in the art would have "knowledge of the concept and structure of the improved pensions benefit system and of the underlying

[115] *Merrill Lynch's Application* [1989] R.P.C. 561, CA.

[116] Although the generous US approach may be curbed depending on what the US Supreme Court decides in *Re Bilski*, on appeal from the Court of Appeals for the Federal Circuit: 545 F 3d 943 (2008).

[117] *PBS Partnership* [2001] OJ EPO 441, TBA.

schemes of information processing as set out for example in the present method claims".[118]

(8) (*Hitachi/auction method.*[119]) Claims both to a computer as programmed and a method of programming a computer were made to the conduct of a Dutch auction: i.e. an auction in which the auctioneer names a high price, reduces it until he receives a bid and then calls for bids over the first bid until he reaches a highest offer. By stating with each bid not just a "desired price" but also a "maximum price", a mode was provided for resolving which of multiple bids at the same "desired price" should be preferred. The advantage of automation was that it could eliminate time-lags that would otherwise occur, particularly if potential bidders were not all together. Taking the approach in the *Pension Benefits* case one step further, the Technical Board of Appeal refused to distinguish between the two types of claim that had been separately treated in the earlier decision: claims to the computing apparatus as programmed, and claims to the method of causing the apparatus to function. Both types of claim had a sufficiently technical character to be in principle patentable inventions despite the exclusions in the EPC art.52(2), (3). Thus, for instance, claims to a data transmission system for television programmes which could allow the viewer to know the content being broadcast by various channels passed this test simply because it was to operate by means of a standard teletext system.[120] Only an abstract set of instructions fell to be treated as a "computer program as such". But again, the Board nonetheless found the claims obvious. It concluded that even the adaptation introduced into the auction to deal with equal bids was a modification of a business scheme (the form of the auction) which solved no technical problem, but instead sidestepped it. So it became the approach of the Technical Board of Appeal most directly concerned with this field (3.5.1) that, in assessing the validity of a claim involving a computer program, or method of programming a computer, only the technical features delineated in the specification would be taken into account—above all in testing inventive step.[121] As later decisions specify, functional objectives such as marketing ploys,[122] rules for games of chance,[123] business methods

[118] Reasons for Decision, para.8.

[119] *Hitachi/auction method* T258/03; [2004] OJ EPO 575, TBA.

[120] *Matsushita/transmission system* (T679/04) [2007] E.P.O.R. 18.

[121] Two decisions thereupon came to be treated as formative: *Comvik/two identities* (T641/00) [2004] E.P.O.R. 10; *Ricoh/order management* (T172/03) (unpublished).

[122] *Spende/entry ticket* (T1482/05) [2008] E.P.O.R. 35; *West Direct/telemarketing* (T588/05) [2010] E.P.O.R. 12.

[123] *IGT/electronic multi-play poker* (T336/07) [2008] E.P.O.R. 18; *Konami/video game device* (T1793/07) [2009] E.P.O.R. 103; *Nintendo/Gamemachine and storage medium* (T12/08) [2009] E.P.O.R. 31. Note the similar approach (under art.52) in *Cranway v Playtech* [2010] F.S.R. 3.

of calculating loan contract prices or opening accounts,[124] or assessment of the environmental impact of a product,[125] are not themselves to be regarded in deciding what is inventive.

(9) What is being sought is technical information about the solution to problems of, for instance, the formation or transmission of signals, receipt, storage retrieval, processing structuring or outputting it's functional data. In an inventive step assessment, if such matters were not present, there would be nothing that could count as an invention and the claim would be rejected. In cases where there was a mixture of technical and non-technical elements, it was a matter of judgment whether the former differed from the prior art enough to amount to invention. This would be judged by the "problem–solution approach". The Boards now require that, in assessing inventive step, the difference between the prior art and the claimed invention be assessed having regard only to directly technical features of the claim—and not, for instance to psychological influences upon users of the program. On that approach, in *British Telecommunications/data selection systems,*[126] a claim was treated as obvious when it consisted of a method of sorting the content of large databases and presenting the results in a visual form that enabled a user to evaluate it more easily and efficiently. There was in this no direct technical improvement of change over the prior art and the claim had to be treated as no more than a "presentation of information"—a conclusion that takes one back to the list of subject matter excluded from what is patentable.[127] The decision may be contrasted with *Microsoft/Clipboard Formats,*[128] where claims that enabled format changes on clipboards were held both novel and inventive because the techniques related directly to improvements in computer operating systems (as equally in example (3) above).

20–32 This style of rationalisation by EPO Appeal Tribunals did not, however, go without challenge, particularly from the English Court of Appeal.[129] In *Aerotel* and *Macrossan,*[130] the Court of Appeal conducted a review of the case law which is, above all, highly critical of the reasoning in the new line in

[124] *King/loan system* (T1284/04) [2009] E.P.O.R. 11; *Citibank/integrated account* (T368/05) [2007] E.P.O.R. 54.

[125] *Toshiba/environmental impact estimation* (T1029/06) [2010] E.P.O.R. 13.

[126] *British Telecommunications/data selection systems* (T1143/06) [2010] E.P.O.R. 11.

[127] EPC arts 52(2)(d), 52(3). See to similar effect, the refusal by Mann J. of claims to the improvement to electronic programme guides by providing that the interface at its first step be automatically linked to the second step, and so on: *J Gemstar v Virgin* [2009] EWHC Civ 3068.

[128] *Microsoft/Clipboard Formats* (T424/03) [2006] E.P.O.R. 40.

[129] Judges of the German Federal Supreme Court indicated that they too did not accept the downgrading of EPC arts 52(2), (3): see *Symbian v Comptroller-General* [2009] R.P.C. 1 at [31].

[130] *Aerotel v Telco, Macrossan's Application* [2007] R.P.C. 7, CA.

EPO Board decisions led by examples (7) and (8). The Court did not accept that the exclusion of programs "as such" should be confined to abstract sets of instructions. Earlier decisions of the Court itself were to the contrary—including those in examples (4)–(6) above. More than that, the approach "would seem to open the way in practice to the patentability in principle of any computer program".[131] In the Court of Appeal's view (approving the practice of the UK Intellectual Property Office) the correct approach is the following strategy:

(1) Properly construe the claim;
(2) Identify the actual contribution;
(3) Ask whether it falls solely within the excluded subject matter—meaning not just the exclusion of computer programs, but equally of discoveries, scientific theories and mathematical methods; schemes, rules and methods for performing mental acts, playing games or doing business; and presentations of information—all of them "as such";
(4) Check whether the actual or alleged contribution is actually technical in nature.[132]

The Court of Appeal also criticised EPO jurisprudence for transferring the question of whether there is technical character to the general tests of novelty and obviousness. Why does it matter at which stage the issue is raised, since each turns at root on assessment of what factors are to be regarded as "technical"? Even for those inventions which are beyond the scope of the art.52 exclusions as such, the general tests of novelty and inventive step have to be met, though the results are likely to be the same whether or not art.52 can be dealt with by simply rules about the form of the claim, rather than its content. The main objective of the *Pension Benefits* approach was probably political—to find an interpretation of art.52(2) that narrows the gap between the then highly liberal US and the restricted European systems. Then it could no longer be asserted that Europe and its computer industries were unduly hamstrung by a provision introduced into the Convention back in the dark age of 1973. (Even this, it may be said, is a curious argument, since the nationality of patentees does not affect the right to apply in different systems. It would be very different if US patentees could have their European patents granted according to US law; but that is emphatically not the case.)

While maintaining that issues of technical character still required resolution under art.52(2), rather than just art.56, the Court of Appeal nonetheless drew distinctions on much the same lines. In *Aerotel* it allowed claims

[131] *Aerotel v Telco, Macrossan's Application* [2007] R.P.C. 7, CA at [115].
[132] On how far the fourth step overlaps with the third, see, e.g., Kitchin J. *Astron Clinica v Comptroller-General* [2008] R.P.C. 14 at [49].

to a computerised networking of telephone exchanges in a novel layout, which would permit a call to continue as long as an account remained in credit. This involved a new physical combination of hardware. In *Macrossan*, the claims were to an automated method of acquiring the documents necessary to incorporate a company by interactive communication with the person seeking to do so. They were refused as a plain example of a pure business method. In deciding those cases, the Court of Appeal regarded it as high time for the essential questions of interpretation of the EPC to be put to the Enlarged Board of Appeal of the EPO. In a spirit of friendly, but by no means provincial, co-operation, it dared to formulate (upon its own motion) the questions that it would like to see put. The Technical Board of Appeal of the EPO chiefly engaged in these cases (3.5.1) sought to write *Aerotel* off as lèse-majesté,[133] but the issue continued to fester. Applying *Aerotel,* the UK IPO took the view that computer programs were patentable only where they affected the technical functioning of apparatus outside the computer on which they were to run—a decidedly broad view of the exclusion of computer programs as such. Soon enough a challenge to that practice reached the Court of Appeal, which instead decided, in *Symbian v Comptroller-General,* that a program was patentable if it made a technical difference to the running of any computer including that on which it was being used.[134] In a diplomatic but forceful judgment, Lord Neuberger refused to find a settled line of jurisprudence supporting the patentability of any claim in either the "computer as programmed" or the "method of programming form". He emphasised the great difficulty of giving clear meaning to the terms of the EPC on the subject and pointed to TBA decisions before and after *Pension Benefits* and *Hitachi* which appeared to take other approaches. In particular, in *Gameaccount*, the Technical Board of Appeal 3.2.4 considered that the EPC could not have been intended to reduce the question of the scope of exclusions by art.52(2) purely to a matter of the form of claims, which could therefore easily be satisfied.[135] That Board took the view that, whenever the invention consisted in a mixture of technical and non-technical elements, it was necessary to decide in the particular circumstances whether the technical elements were of sufficient significance to place the case beyond the exception. Following the request for an Enlarged Board review made by the Court of Appeal in *Aerotel*, one President of the EPO announced that there was no sufficient disagreement in TBA decisions to warrant the step; but the next President decided after all to make the reference.[136] The Enlarged Board has now refused to find any

[133] *Duns Licensing/sales activity* (T154/04) [2007] E.P.O.R. 38.

[134] *Symbian v Comptroller-General* [2009] R.P.C. 1.

[135] *Gameaccount* (T1543/06) June 29, 2007 EPO (Unreported).

[136] Case G 3/08; for the tense politics surrounding the reference, see *President's Reference/ Objection to Member of EBA* [2009] E.P.O.R. 10. The *President's Reference* [2009] E.P.O.R. 9, contains a review not only of the diverse EPO decision-making but also of the unsuccessful attempts to remove "computer programs" from art.52 during the negotiation of EPC 2000.

sufficient disagreement between the TBA's decisions to provide it with jurisdiction in the matter.[137] Where there have been apparent divergences, it sees only continuities. For the future, the question of a sufficient technical step will be dealt within under the heading of obviousness. Whether Boards of Appeal consider that they may now extend the scope of that notion so as to allow patents for wider ranges of computer programs remains shrouded in mystery.

In the meantime, there are signs that both the English judges and the EPO Tribunals are conceding a certain amount of ground. Thus in England, Lewison J. has helpfully listed the types of case in which it is likely that a claim will be accepted despite PA 1977 s.1(2): (1) where it affects a process carried on outside the computer; (2) where it operates at the level of the architecture of the computer; (3) where it results in the computer being made to operate in a new way; (4) where it increases the speed or reliability of the computer; and (5) where it overcomes a perceived problem in the computer, as distinct from merely side-stepping it.[138] In the EPO, there has been some renewed acknowledgment of the *Gameaccount* alternative.[139] Whatever resolution may come from the Reference, the whole imbroglio demonstrates the egregious folly of creating a set of parallel jurisdictions which lack an overarching body with powers to determine final appeals.

(b) *Scope of rights*

As already indicated, patents for computer programs raise considerable tensions among software creators, especially over the freedom to take the work of others and improve or adapt it. Fundamentally opposed attitudes come into direct confrontation on the issue. The patent system already contains its exemption for further research on any invention, where the research is concerned with the invention claimed rather than something different; and it is reasonably clear that in Europe (as opposed to the United States) this defence can extend to commercially sponsored research, though not to the commercialisation of successful results. However, there is no defence to patent infringement for decompilation activities directed at discovering the structures of a program in order to secure interoperability.[140] Thanks to the Computer Programs Directive of 1991 (after an intense fight), these already apply to copyright in programs. There would seem to be a case a fortiori where wider, more basic, rights are being conferred by a patent. **20–33**

137 (G3/08) Opinion of May 12, 2010, strictly interpreting EPC, art.112.
138 *AT&T Knowledge's Patent* [2009] F.S.R. 19; *Cranway v Playtech* [2010] F.S.R. 2.
139 See, e.g., *Citibank/integrated account* (T368/050) [2007] E.P.O.R. 54.
140 Draft Directive, above, n.103, which relied upon the disclosure requirement in patent law to demonstrate any patented barrier to interoperability—a sanguine view indeed.

(c) *Business methods, presentations of information, playing a game*[141]

20–34 The US decision that there is no barrier in the law to patents upon business methods induced a snowstorm of applications in this category.[142] Many of them were granted in the lax US manner but are highly unlikely to survive any challenge in court. In reality it is only those which involve implementation by computer program that are at all likely to be enforceable. The significant rule in that country has been that patents are permissible for computer programs which produce purely informational results and involve no technical means other than the ability to use the program on a standard computer. In Europe, where business methods and, by their side, the performance of mental acts "as such" are not patentable, it appears that the meaning of these other categories is shaped by the decisions on what computer program patents are permissible. But the point of exclusion, so far as general propositions can be made to have any real precision, appears in Europe to be somewhat more severe.

The requirement of technical character, on which it will be difficult ever to expect a truly uniform view among examiners and judges, is called for in the EPO. That Office currently takes the view that the real significance of technical character lies not in any exclusion by category but in the assessment of inventive step in the particular circumstances. On the broader issue of the value or otherwise of extending patents into a territory already covered quite usefully by copyright it may be possible to return a clearer verdict from business surveys and the like. They should certainly be undertaken. The field is of high economic importance to Europe's future.[143]

2. Stored Content and Output

(1) Databases

(a) *Copyright originality*

20–35 To shift from computer programs to input and output of information is to open up very different prospects. The storage of data in computers and other electronic servers is a highly significant element in digital information

[141] See, e.g. Daehwan Koo [2002] I.P.Q. 172; Chandra (2002) 5(4) J.W.I.P. 545; O'Sullivan [2004] E.I.P.R. 340; Gonzalez [2004] E.I.P.R. 331; Jänich (2004) I.I.C. 376.

[142] *State Street Bank v Signature Financial* 149 Fed. 3d 1368 (1998); *AT & T v Excel Communications* 172 Fed 3d. 1352 (1999). The CAFC held that there was no general bar on patents for business methods and that grants could be made for any invention that is "useful, concrete and tangible". Trenchantly criticised by Thomas [2000] I.P.Q. 27; but followed in Australia in *Welcome Real-Time v Catuity* [2001] F.C.A. 405; Ricketson [2003] I.P.Q. 79. In *Re Bilski*, the US Supreme Court has upheld that approach, while reserving the power to exclude claims that are evidently non-technical (Decision of June 30, 2010).

[143] In a brief overview, the *Gowers Review* supports the current position in European law, so far as it can be detected: paras 4.109–4.122.

systems. Yet it is unclear how far, in many legal systems, the twin steps of storage and extraction attract copyright protection. To create digital files of a hundred medical journals or a national art collection or the daily business of world stock exchanges is a costly business and an investment which could be shattered by free access for re-copying. If control is not possible, the investors will become prey both to pirates who are looking to create rival services and to those who want to extract material for their own benefit (and perhaps that of a surrounding circle) without payment.

Where the material on the base is itself copyright that is in the hands of the database provider (say, a publisher or record producer), that enterprise is protected already against extractions which involve making a computer copy, even if it is only on a transient basis. More difficult are the cases of enterprises that collect information, including works which are not their copyright, for provision to subscribers. These providers act like anthologists or directory compilers or cataloguers. Traditionally, if they contributed sufficient skill, judgment and labour to this compilation process, albeit entirely through collecting and recording mundane data, they were treated in UK law as themselves having copyright in their database. Their right was infringed only if there was substantial reproduction (or other taking) of their contribution. They had rights against the pirate who took the whole base and against many who for commercial purposes extracted some significant part in order to re-utilise it, perhaps in re-edited form. But the hacker who extracted small amounts of the total, even if what he took (financial details, say, or a photograph) was itself a protected work, would not infringe the copyright in the database.

The importance of databases as a commercial phenomenon in their own right has found expression in the Database Directive.[144] This has been incorporated into UK law from January 1, 1998 and affects both pre-existing and new databases.[145] The legal need for it is accentuated by the hard fact that most Member States refuse to abandon their test of originality in copyright, which requires a protectable work to be the product of personal intellectual creativity. The Dutch Supreme Court, for instance, held that the compiler of a dictionary will have copyright in the words selected for entry (as distinct from the definitions supplied) only if there is shown to be sufficient individuality in choosing them. In similar spirit, the US Supreme Court ruled against copyright in a white pages telephone book **20–36**

[144] The introduction of the Directive's rights coincided with a sudden rise in the number of new database companies in Europe, but that rise has not since been sustained and was probably one result of dot.com mania: see Maurer, Hugenholtz and Onsrud (2001) 294 Science 789; European Commission's Report. See also Ginsburg in Dreyfuss et al. *Expanding the Boundaries of Intellectual Property* (2001), Ch.3.

[145] Directive on the Legal Protection of Databases, March 11, 1996 [1996] OJ L77/20. Implementation in UK law is by the Copyright and Rights in Databases Regulations 1997 (SI 1997/3032—hereafter "Database Regs"). For database copyright these amend the CDPA 1988. For the *sui generis* right of the database maker, the Regulations themselves prescribe the law in Pts III and IV and associated Schedules.

which lists all subscribers. In Canada, the same exclusion has been applied to a yellow pages book, which categorises subscribers by business type.[146]

(b) *The Database Directive*

20–37 (i) **Copyright in the Compilation.** The Database Directive engages in a highly elaborate strategy in order to by-pass this difficulty. First, it defines what is meant by a database: "a collection of independent works, data or other materials arranged in a systematic or methodical way and individually accessible by electronic or other means".[147] Then it allows copyright in a database (as distinct from its contents), but only on the basis of authorship involving personal intellectual creativity.[148] This is a new limitation, so far as common law countries are concerned, and one that may foreshadow a raising of the standard of originality throughout UK copyright law. Intellectual judgment which is in some sense the author's own must go either into choosing contents or into the method of arrangement.[149] A selective dictionary will doubtless be a clearer case for copyright than the classificatory telephone directory, but each may have some hope; the merely comprehensive will be precluded—that is the silliness of the whole construct.

Where this copyright arises, it is an author's right. Accordingly it will last for life plus 70 years; so a couple of youngsters should be on the production team (with their "personal intellectual contributions" carefully recorded).[150] The author's right will be available under the Berne Convention to Americans and others entitled to national treatment. The right covers a comprehensive list of copying and like activities, and of public communication and similar steps.[151]

---

[146] For these cases, see para.11–10, above.

[147] Database Directive art.3; CDPA 1988 s.3A(1). For a discussion of the breadth of this definition see Derclaye (2002) 5 Jnl. W. Int.Prop. L. 281; Aplin, *Copyright Law in the Digital Society* (2005), pp.44–52.

[148] Database Directive art.3(1); CDPA 1988 ss.3(1)(d), 3A(2). The UK distinguishes between "databases" and "tables or compilations other than a database", with the result that the new test of originality applies to the former and the old test of "labour, skill and judgment" applies to the latter. Given that the vast majority of compilations will fall within the definition of database there are likely to be few non-database compilations and so the disparity in originality tests should not have a pronounced effect. See *Football Dataco v Brittens Pools* [2010] E.W.H.C. 841 Ch.

[149] Where rules prescribe a particular form of expression, or constrain the exercise of human choices this will undermine any independent intellectual effort: *Telstra Corp. v Phone Directories* [2010] F.C.A. 44, FC Aust.

[150] Note that the inability to identify authors of a database may make establishing originality impossible: *Telstra Corp. v Phone Directories* [2010] F.C.A. 44, FC Aust.

[151] Database Directive art:5; and for the exceptions which Member States may adopt: art.6; in the CDPA 1988 this follows from characterising an original database as a literary work. A contract which deprives a person of the freedom to abstract material outside the scope of this copyright is void: CDPA 1988 s.50D. See *Navitaire v easyJet* [2006] R.P.C. 3 at [275].

(ii) **Database right.**[152] In addition there is a separate *sui generis* right given to the maker of a database (the investor who initiates it) against extraction or re-utilisation of the contents of the database.[153] Five essential points may be highlighted: **20–38**

(1) the right applies to databases whether or not their arrangement justifies copyright and whatever the position may be regarding copyright in individual items in its contents;[154]
(2) the focus upon contents, rather than organisational structure, is intended to give a right where the contents have been wholly or substantially taken out and re-arranged (generally by a computer) so as to provide a quite different organisation to essentially the same material—a re-organisation which would not necessarily amount to infringement of copyright in the original arrangement.[155] This, however, is not to discount the relevance of structural arrangements of the material;[156]
(3) the database has to be the product of substantial investment. It cannot, for instance, consist merely of different works collected together on an ordinary music CD.[157] In some European States, there were early decisions that website files of articles, news items or advertisements from the continuing numbers of a paper or magazine would constitute a database.[158] The question has now become intertwined with the issue of whether the investment has been made in creating the informational material, as distinct from constructing the database;
(4) the right protects "extraction" and/or "re-utilisation" of the whole or a substantial part, evaluated quantitatively and qualitatively, of the contents. "Extraction" here means the permanent or temporary transfer of contents to another medium by any means or form; and "re-utilisation" means making the contents available to the public by any means.[159] It is expressly stated that repeated and systematic

---

[152] For recent writing on a fast-changing subject, Davison, *Legal Protection of Databases* (2004); Derclaye, *The Legal Protection of Databases* (2008); Derclaye (2005) 36 I.I.C. 2; Waelde [2006] I.P.Q. 256; Galli (2006) 37 I.I.C. 452; Hugenholtz website: *http://www.ivir.nl/files/database/indiex.html.*
[153] By Rec.41, Database Directive the "maker of the database" is the person who takes the initiative and the risk of investing, not any sub-contractor (cf. the *A & M Records* case, para.13–10, above).
[154] See Database Directive, Recs 38–40, 45, 46.
[155] See Database Directive, Rec.38; and see Cerina (1993) 24 I.I.C. 579.
[156] See, e.g. Berlin CA, June 9, 2000.
[157] See Database Directive, Rec.19: such a collation would give no compiler's copyright either.
[158] e.g. Munich DC, September 18, 2001; March 18, 2002.
[159] Database Directive art.7(2) and see Recs 40–41; Database Regs reg.12. see further below, para.20–43. Cf. the ruling on the scope of the the publisher's right in typographical format: *Newspaper Licensing Agency v Marks & Spencer* [2003] 1 A.C. 551, HL.

extraction of insubstantial parts of a database can constitute infringement;[160]

(5) The right lasts for 15 years from completion of the database, or 15 years from its becoming available to the public during that 15-year period.[161] However, further substantial investment in additions, deletions or alterations starts time running afresh.[162] This means in effect that a living database has indeterminate protection, just as does a copyright textbook from regular editions containing revised material.[163]

20–39 The *sui generis* right has its place in the Database Directive because there is no harmonised law of unfair competition as between EU States by which undue misappropriation of information could be attacked.[164] The five essential elements in the right constitute some attempt to define what is to count as unfair. Database right goes beyond copyright (points (1) and (2)), yet it confines protection to substantial investment in a roughly proportionate way (points (3)–(5)). Accordingly, it seeks the sort of balance that was, for instance, so signally lacking when the United Kingdom engaged in its extraordinary experiment with copyright in industrial designs (1968–1988).[165] Even so there are uncertainties about how that balance is to be achieved, some of which have now been ruled upon by the ECJ.

20–40 From the outset courts around the EU had difficulty in deciding what is an adequate minimum investment to justify this form of protection. One source for the *sui generis* right was the "catalogue" protection in Nordic copyright statutes, which is given for a short term to collections of data as such. The "catalogue" right was limited in various ways and courts in those countries showed some tendency to lean in favour of treating the *sui generis* right under the Directive as similarly limited.[166]

20–41 In *British Horseracing Board (BHB) v William Hill*,[167] the ECJ has adopted a parallel ruling, which affects the existence of the right, rather than just its infringement. BHB, the claimant, maintains a large, costly database concerned with horseracing across Britain as part of its management of the

160 Database Directive art.7(5).

161 Database Directive art.10(1), (2).

162 Database Directive art.10(3). For verification, see Rec.55; this seems to have been wrongly omitted from the Database Regs reg.17(3).

163 See below, para.20–42.

164 See Database Directive Rec.6. The *sui generis* right will be accorded to nationals, habitual residents and companies of non-EU countries only where there is a Community agreement, based presumably on sufficient reciprocity. This necessarily assumes that the new right does not already fall within the unfair competition provisions of the Paris Convention art.10*bis*. The contrary could be argued, not least in a TRIPS dispute settlement proceeding.

165 For which, see paras 15–05—15–06, above; Laddie [1995] E.I.P.R. 253.

166 Hence the reference to the ECJ from courts in Finland and Sweden (below, n.171).

167 *British Horseracing Board (BHB) v William Hill* [2004] E.C.R. I–1045, ECJ. See Aplin [2005] I.P.Q. 52; Davison and Hugenholtz [2005] E.I.P.R. 113; Derclaye [2005] Eur. L.R. 420; Kur, Hilty et al. (2006) 37 I.I.C. 520. For application of the judgment by the CA, see [2005] R.P.C. 35; Masson [2006] E.I.P.R. 261.

industry. Details of entries and results at race meetings are constantly being added. This information is sold to two companies, who are then entitled to distribute it under their own contracts with bookmakers and others. The defendant, the United Kingdom's largest betting firm, obtained the information in this way for publicising each day's racing programs in its betting shops. However, when it set up an internet betting service, partly based on this source of information, the BHB relied upon its database right to demand a separate charge. Laddie J., at first instance, found for the BHB, deciding, inter alia, that the database right was not limited to the appropriation of the database more or less as a whole.[168] In this he was assisted by the Directive's provision that repeated and systematic extraction or re-utilisation of insubstantial parts amounts to substantial taking.[169] Laddie J. was prepared to find infringement either on that ground or on the basis that the takings were substantial. The Court of Appeal, however, considered that these and other issues must be referred for interpretation by the ECJ. At the same time, references were made from courts elsewhere in the EU in which database right claims were also being made in relation to internet betting, the subject-matter being the fixture lists of English football associations.

The Court's ruling on these cases has very substantially truncated the **20–42**
scope of the *sui generis* database right. Identifying the object of the right as the promotion and protection of investment in data "storage" and "processing" systems, it drew a fundamental distinction between investment in creating the information in the first place and investment in storing and processing it in the database. To claim database right it was necessary to show substantial investment in the latter in both qualitative and quantitative terms. In relation to the case in suit, the listing and checking of horse and rider details for each race were activities belonging to the former category—they were concerned with creating the information, not with storing it.[170] There was accordingly no substantial investment that qualified for database right. Nor could there be in football fixtures listings put out by professional associations of clubs.[171] The same outcome has since been reached in the Netherlands in respect of an estate agent's list of properties which it is marketing for clients.[172] The same may be true of a land registry which sets up a database to give the prices at which different titles have been sold, when the information is a by-product of the registration of transfers of title. A contrasting case may be a commercial service which takes the price information from the land registry site and adds information from other sources

[168] In argument this was inelegantly expressed as a need to show a taking of the "database-ness" of the database.

[169] Directive art.7(5); Database Regs reg.12.

[170] *BHB v Wm Hill* (above, n.170), paras 31–40 et seq. Cf. the approach to originality for copyright databases in *Football Dataco* (above, n.148) at [74] and [84].

[171] *Fixtures Marketing v Oy Veikkaus*; *Fixtures Marketing v OPAP*; *Fixtures Marketing v Svenska* (judgments given by the ECJ contemporaneously with that in *BHB v Wm Hill*, above).

[172] *Zoekallehuizen.nl v NVM* (Arnhem CA, July 27, 2006).

about (say) the period that each property was on the market or the difference between asking price and sale price. There will surely be cases where it is difficult to assign expenditure to acquiring the information as distinct from placing it in a database.

20–43 Where the collection and storage investment is substantial, database right will still arise. For there to be infringement, there has to be a substantial extraction or utilisation, including in that repeated takings that are in themselves insubstantial. Both "extraction" and "re-utilisation" rights have been broadly construed by the ECJ, neither being limited to direct acts nor, in the case of "re-utilisation", the first making available to the public of the database contents.[173] What is substantial depends both on the quantity of what is taken and its quality. In the *BHB* case, the ECJ held that quality is to be judged by referring back to the elements of investment which give rise to the existence of the right in the first place. This, rather than the value of the extracted material itself, is the measure to be assessed—a somewhat strained distinction.[174] On the facts of *BHB* and the associated cases it was easy to decide that there could be no infringement, even assuming the existence of database right. As to the provision about repeated extractions of insubstantial content, the Court was careful to insist that this would constitute infringement only if it allowed the defendant to:

> "reconstitute and make available to the public the whole or a substantial part of the contents of the BHB database and thereby seriously prejudice the investment made by BHB in the creasion of that database".[175]

An infringer in one of these senses will escape liability only if: (i) there is fair dealing by way of illustration for teaching or research—a defence open only to those who are already lawful users[176]; or (ii) certain exclusions relating to parliamentary and judicial proceedings and other public administration apply[177]; or (iii) control by the Copyright Tribunal of licensing schemes and collective licensing of database rights can be relied upon. As to the first of these, it is unacceptable that the defences should not be as embracing as those available against claims to copyright infringement.[178] As to the last, the Tribunal's jurisdiction is defined in terms corresponding to those for copyright.[179] Beyond this lie the corrective measures which may be taken against abuse of dominant position under art.102 of the TFEU (ex art.82 TEC). The "*Magill*" case authorises the imposition of compulsory licences where, exceptionally, it is found that intellectual property is being licensed

[173] Case 304/07 *Directmedia Publishing GmbH v Albert-Ludwigs-Universitat Freiburg* [2009] C.M.L.R. 7; Case 545/07 *Apis-Hristovich EOOD v Lakorda AD* [2009] 3 C.M.L.R. 3.
[174] *BHB v Wm Hill* (above, n.167) at [71].
[175] *BHB v Wm Hill* (above, n.167) at [91].
[176] Database Regs reg.20(1).
[177] Database Regs reg.20(2).
[178] See Kur et al. (2006) I.I.C. 551, 556–7.
[179] Database Regs reg.24.

only on unacceptable terms.[180] This power could prove to be of some significance in relation to database right, where the owner refuses any licence at all or offers terms so extravagant as to have the same effect. This may be particularly important where the database owner has exclusive access to the data, there being no special treatment of such "single source" information in the Directive as it finally emerged in the legislative process. Since the Directive preserves the operation of other types of intellectual property and related rights to databases, cases that do not satisfy the *BHB* criteria for the *sui generis* right could, where appropriate, be protected as trade secrets. Recalling older British attitudes favouring "sweat of the brow" copyright in the compilation of information, courts in the United Kingdom might take a wide view of what constitutes database copyright satisfying the requirement of personal intellectual expression inserted into the law by the Directive.[181] That however might run against the division laid down by the Directive between copyright and *sui generis* right in databases. Where Member State systems that have an unfair competition law covering slavish imitation, it is equally doubtful whether their courts should fill the gaps by reference to this cause of action.

As it was obliged by the Directive to do, the European Commission issued a Report in December 2005, on the experience with the right. With remarkable frankness, it noted that there was no evidence from practice that introducing the right had encouraged any increase in database production, whereas in the United States, where there is no equivalent protection, their number has grown strikingly. Given the cautionary effect of the *BHB* and associated judgments, the most likely consequence is that the law will be left in its present convoluted and uncertain form. That perhaps is a reasonable outcome, given that, as a matter of political reality, the law will not be completely withdrawn. The real mistake was in introducing the right in the first place without careful assessment of the need for it and identification in some detail of the situations which really called for it.[182]

(2) Computer output

Where a computer is utilised to produce material that is recognisable as a "work" in any copyright sense, the question of copyright in that output can also arise. According to the Whitford Committee: **20–44**

> "the author of the output can be none other than the person, or persons, who devised the instructions and originated the data used to control and

[180] *RTE v EC Commission* [1995] E.C.R. I-743; *IMS Health v Commission*, above, para.19–16. Even in the absence of intellectual property rights, a refusal by a sole source provider to licence data may be anti-competitive: see *Attheraces v British Horseracing Board* [2007] E.C.C. 7, CA, although the Court of Appeal found on the facts that this was not the case.

[181] This has not happened so far: see *Football Dataco* above, n.148.

[182] See Kur et al., above, n.178.

condition the computer to produce the particular result. In many cases it will be a matter of joint authorship."[183]

This analysis may fit expectations when an individual or an organisation is responsible for its own data and program. The outcome can be secured by express assignment, or, if it has to be assumed from the circumstances, by an assignment implied by a court.[184] It is a solution which preserves the essence of copyright even in this strange territory, and so accords with the tenets of an author's right approach to the subject.

Abandoning any such purism, however, the CDPA 1988 introduced the "computer-generated work—a work produced "in circumstances such that there is no human author".[185] Dazzled by ideas that computer-aided design and computer-aided manufacture (CAD/CAM) were lighting a road towards industrial and informational productions from the "intelligence" of computers, Parliament felt that this precautionary intervention was needed. Where it can be said that there was no human author, but where a software house is commissioned by a client to provide the program, it may well be reasonable for the client to assume that it holds copyright in the output.

20–45 The copyright in a computer-generated work endures for 50 years from making the work[186] and is accorded initially to "the person by whom the arrangements necessary for the creation of the work are undertaken".[187] These rules make plain the borrowing from ideas affecting the older neighbouring rights, particularly in films. But their transposition to this new field is less than happy. As between the provider of a database (such as Lexis) and a user who extracts information from it, who undertakes the arrangements for creation? Perhaps this is a case of joint authorship, as the Whitford Committee suggested—but is there really a "common design"? "Computer-generated works" have been part of the law for several years, but the uncertainties about when a human author can and cannot be identified remain as great as ever. In international circles the concept has been greeted with scepticism—partly because the idea is antipathetic to "authorship" and partly because there is no rush of actual cases where investment would otherwise go unprotected. The experimental concept has not so far proved successful and some consider that it should be abandoned.[188] But the next generation of advances of computing techniques—towards such fascinations as neural networks—may give it a usefulness that

---

183 Cmnd.6732 (1977) paras 514, 515; see also National Commission on New Technological Uses of Copyrighted Works (CONTU), Final Report 43–46; Davison and Hugenholtz [2005] E.I.P.R. 113; Geiger [2006] E.I.P.R. 366.

184 cf. similar implications in the program cases: para.20–08, above.

185 CDPA 1988 s.178.

186 CDPA 1988 s.12(3).

187 CDPA 1988 s.9(3); for the exclusion of moral rights, ss.79(2), 81(2).

188 e.g. Tapper, in Lehmann and Tapper (n.74, above), at 150.

is currently hard to guess at.[189] It is probably better at the moment to wait and see.

(3) Multi-media: program and content mixed[190]

In the 1980s the cabled linking of computers to provide email services and access to databases grew apace. These extraordinary capacities were harnessed to form the internet, which originated as an electronic network designed to disperse defence information and so to guard it from central attack. Scholars were soon enticed by the ready exchange of ideas that it offered; others with interests and obsessions, high and low, were drawn to its frenetic interchanging of information across continents. By the early 1990s, the World Wide Web blossomed within it. As ever in the history of education, entertainment and culture, a new technology for the expression of ideas soon enough began to be commercialised. The super-highways for information supplied by the internet now attract those who will supply only upon payment and who deal in products attractive enough to find customers at a price. **20–46**

Digital technique is the same whatever information is being recorded. It may be retrieved as written text, graphic display, moving images, spoken words, music or other sounds. So long at least as digital recording is not compressed for purposes of transmission, it can be endlessly reproduced without loss of quality. It may be transmitted in hard form, as in a CD-ROM, but equally it may be displayed from a computer's random access memory (RAM) or downloaded onto its read only memory (ROM).[191] Users can interact with it in many novel ways: stopping it, asking questions of it, going down particular tracks of interest, ordering and paying through it. The result of these diverse possibilities has been labelled multi-media and it poses interesting issues for copyright laws which were drafted for more rigid and separate methods of production and distribution. These we may relate to traditional copyright concepts.

(a) *Work*

Works which otherwise qualify under our definitions of literary, dramatic, musical and artistic works are nonetheless copyright for all that their fixation or recording occurs in digital form; likewise with sound recordings and films. However, the range of material which may be combined together in digital recording (as in a multi-media product) is such that the result may not easily fit into any one of these relatively limited categories. **20–47**

Where, for instance, does one place an electronic encyclopedia which can illustrate its basic text by films, recordings of music and of animal sounds,

---

[189] See Laddie et al., paras 43.71 et seq.

[190] Stamatoudi, *Copyright and Multimedia Works* (2002); Aplin, *Copyright Law in the Digital Society* (2005).

[191] Cf. *KK Sony Computer Entertainments v Stevens* [2005] H.C.A. 58 (H.C., Australia).

and which offers the user the capacity to re-draw and re-colour artistic works? Like songs and films before it, such a compendium can be conceived as a coalescence of different copyrights. In so far as it is a film, as well as constituting an accumulation of contributory copyrights, the digitised encyclopedia will also be a work in itself. But large parts of it may not produce moving images; the whole (or perhaps those parts) may therefore not fit within the definition of film. What the electronic editor does in assembling the whole seems akin in skill and judgment to the work involved in creating a printed encyclopedia and so ought to qualify for literary copyright, and, in appropriate cases, musical and artistic copyright as well. A court would seek to find copyright in any substantial work of this kind so as to be able to stop substantial unauthorised borrowing. If there proves to be difficulties over this, it may be necessary to add some inclusive form of definition to the statute.[192]

20–48 As with other forms of collated material, what is described as "editorship" may at one extreme call for highly sophisticated judgment and at the other be no more than indiscriminate assemblage, of the same order as choosing the titles for a newsagent's shelves. Legal systems use different tests of originality in order to settle where exactly copyright begins on the line between these poles. The common law approach takes a liberal view, but even it will exclude matter which fails to embody any sufficient labour, skill and judgment.[193]

The investment needed to put together factual information which is complete, rather than significantly selective, can be very considerable where the material is being collected in digital form. It is the rapid development of such databases, and the prospect that they could be commercially hijacked, that led to the EU's Database Directive with its double tier of rights. Despite its considerable complexity, it provides an ample basis for protecting investment in digital compilations.[194] Accordingly there seems to be no urgent case for protecting multi-media works in a category of their own.

(b) *Author*

20–49 Copyright law already has a highly flexible notion of authorship which operates on twin planes: where a work within a particular category (literary, musical, etc.) results from the joint planning of two or more creators, they become joint authors of a single work; if that is not the case, successive work can create successive copyrights. Where the works are in different categories (words and music of a song), or where a first work is in some way re-worked (translated, put into a comic strip, etc.) a succession of distinct copyrights is

[192] In 1994, New Zealand attempted this by defining "compilation", a form of literary work, to include compilations of works and/or other data of any kind. "Work" covers the same broad range of matter as in the CDPA 1988.

[193] See para.11–06, above.

[194] See para.20–37, above.

generated, each with its own authors, on whose lives the various terms will depend.[195] In detail these rules may vary between legal systems, thus bringing marginal divergences in their train. But because copyright interests can be collected into a single hand for purposes of exploitation (by means of assignment, exclusive licensing or a presumption in employment), the law operates with considerable subtlety. There seems no strong reason for distinguishing multi-media products from other material equally complex in its constitution, such as operas and films.

Computer technology allows developments in the electronic treatment of material at a wholly new level. First, a program may be written to operate upon automatically recorded data so as to produce interpretations which have the appearance of a new work: the generation of weather reports from continual atmospheric monitoring is the common example; automatic translation will prove to be another. It has been with such instances in mind that the UK legislation has introduced the concept of a computer-generated work, for products which have no sufficiently identifiable author. As we have seen, the character of this right is in the nature of a long-stop.[196] It has not as yet been taken up in most other legal systems, since it dispenses with authorship as the prime justification for copyright protection. That caution is possible partly because it is not yet clear that there is any strong demand in practice for protection of this sort of material. In most cases it is possible to assign authorship to some person or persons.

Secondly, programming can allow interaction by a person who receives material, so as to add to it or alter it, and this step can occur not only when a further commercial service (such as a database) is being generated but also when an individual user receives it. The circumstances in which this technique might be employed seem vast. Accordingly, the actual conditions in which intervention might confer significant added value on the original are still very hard to predict. As problems emerge an adequate legal solution can probably be fashioned within copyright law. It is hard to see that any *sui generis* alternative would produce surer justice, and as always it would be immensely cumbersome and time-consuming to develop.

(c) *Adaptation*

A digitised encyclopedia or other databank may well draw pre-existing works directly into its content, either in their original form or with alterations. The step of putting material into digital form for the first time, as also of transferring it from one digital bank to another, amount to copying within the right of reproduction. The immense new capacity for combining and modifying works of all kinds may indeed give their first form a merely conditional quality but it will enjoy copyright nonetheless. **20–50**

The relevant copyright test to apply to an adaptation is whether the result

[195] See para.11–06, above.
[196] See para.11–22, above.

still contains a substantial reproduction of the original work.[197] This requires judgment and so leaves scope for considerable argument. One particular problem may prove to be the endless divisibility of digitally recorded material: for what, then, is the *work* from which assessment starts? Nonetheless the test seems as appropriate to this medium as to others, such as a film or broadcast. A rule which would instead ask whether there had been sufficient addition or re-fashioning to create a "new work", might result in fewer claims, but it would be at least as uncertain in operation.[198] On the other hand, a rule which imposed liability for any provable borrowing, even when nothing of the original ultimately remained, would be unduly severe.

At present, there is much concern about the amount and complexity of "permissions" work for putting together elaborate digital collections. Mixed with it are complaints about the unreasonably high demands of copyright owners, when asked to grant licences. Some multi-media projects have been abandoned, so it is said, in the face of such intransigence. The essential difficulty is that regular markets for the material are only slowly emerging, and owners have suspicions still to be overcome. It is a problem, however, for which a market solution would seem wholly appropriate. Electronic shops of copyright material are open with prices in their windows. Much photographic and other design material is available in this form. If a market fails to come into being, it would be possible for the law to subject owners of copyright works to statutory licensing requirements. But why should such a solution be imported for multi-media works, if it does not also apply to films or broadcasts?[199]

(d) *Moral rights and digital manipulation*

20–51 The ease with which digitised material can be transformed is likely to raise difficulties in the sphere of moral rights. These can be over the failure to identify the author or one of the authors, or the false attribution of authorship, or the integrity of the original work and most of all in that intermediate territory where alterations have been made.

As for the original author's concern to protect the integrity of his creation, the moral right against derogatory treatment supplies a reasonable basis for intervention. How it should be exercisable in a digital environment has been discussed already.[200] It may be recalled that in the United Kingdom the writing of computer programs has been considered so technical an activity as to warrant the exclusion of moral rights in relation to them.[201] That is a difficult proposition, since programs are constantly being worked upon by others in order to eliminate bugs, to add new uses and for many

[197] See para.12–06, above.
[198] cf. the fate of such a test in relation to lampoons: para.12–10, above.
[199] There would in any case be grave difficulties in distinguishing such types of work, one from another.
[200] See para.12–83, above.
[201] See para.12–81, above.

other intrinsically valuable purposes. Indeed it is the basic thrust of the Free Software initiative to encourage such serial collaboration as a necessary ethos for program development. But there will be cases where the intervention proves harmful because poor quality work can easily reduce the value of the whole. There is thus a case for treating egregious cases of harmful intervention as an attack on the integrity of the program, since it will go to its very core. The problem is no different from that over translation, which is for the most part a valuable activity but in the wrong hands can be seriously damaging. That too is currently outside the bounds of the moral right of integrity in UK law. Both deserve to be brought within. At least with digital copyright material other than programs, whether the medium is a hard copy or an internet source, the general principles concerning moral rights apply.

3. Material on the Internet

(1) Introductory

(a) *The internet and copyright*

This section treats the most inflamed issue in current intellectual property.[202] **20–52** With extraordinary ease and accuracy, the internet provides for the storage, identification and distribution of literary, artistic, musical and audio-visual material held in digital format. Its interactive capacities are remarkable, making a simple operation of searching, cross-linking, ordering, altering and many things else. Once accessed via a website, chatroom, email service or social networking site, material can be transmitted over and over again without loss of quality. The internet organises electronic transmission, mainly by cable, from the site where the material is held for a content provider on the server of an internet service provider (ISP). It moves via a maze of intermediate telecommunication servers to an access provider for a user and thence to that user.

So far as concerns IPRs in the material, electronic copying—some of it **20–53** ephemeral, some temporary, but some long-lasting—occurs all along the internet chain from uploading to delivery; and, subject to variations between systems over purely transient copying, this provides a first legal basis for asserting copyright control at many points. Equally, thanks to the act of

[202] For a most useful survey of the IP issues, see WIPO, *Intellectual Property on the Internet: a Survey of Issues* (2002). Chs 1 and 2 discuss the development and expanding commercial usage of the internet. Ch.3 raises questions of impact of various aspects of IPRs, not all of them discussed in any detail in this presentation of issues. See generally, Lessig, *Code and Other Laws of Cyberspace* (1999); *The Future of Ideas* (2001); Edwards and Waelde, (eds) *Law and the Internet* 3rd edn (2009); Lloyd, *Information Technology Law* 5th edn (2008); Smith, *Internet Law and Regulation* 4th edn (2007); Gringras, *Laws of the Internet* 3rd edn (2008).

making the material available, a new form of "performing right" has been introduced, which is constituted by communicating material to the public by making it available for individuals to order it where and when they choose. But the position is far more complex and controversial than that. Digital media exist in hard forms, such as CDs, CD-ROMs and DVDs, and the ease and accuracy of this technology has led to a great spate of piratical copying. The same dangers for the record, film and publishing industries arise on the internet, where hard copy ceases to be the major means of transmission. The current copyright industries, some of them dominated by a few international firms, are desperately insisting that their very doom is at hand. Certainly they are under considerable threat.

20–54 At the same time, these industries are looking to see what potential the brave new internet world may have in store for them. After all electronic management may give them control over their works with far greater precision than used to follow from traditional copyright, in which infringement occurred only at points of manufacture, sale, rental and specified public use. Potentially the internet could restrict access for every use desired by a consumer. If users can only get to the material by a password, a decryption device or some other barrier, and if the material can be controlled after access as well, then the whole relationship can be the subject of a range of contractual conditions, precisely modulated. They get much more exactly what they pay for: for each use a micro-payment. Such a result sounds the very model of economic efficiency.

20–55 There are many who in their turn fear that, particularly where the only access to certain material is on a single site, such novel methods of electronic control will become a serious inhibition on freedom of information and expression.[203] The spectre is of conditional access on highly restrictive terms. The very prospect has inspired concern among policy analysts for the future of those users of copyright material who are exempt from liability for infringement by virtue of some defence of fair or private use. It also offers an ethical weapon to large numbers of computer enthusiasts who set up their own free systems of distributing copyrighted work without paying for it each time and who devise programs and other techniques for un-picking the electronic locks and badges that encase legitimate material. The battle of wills and wits that is ensuing has no predictable outcome, especially for digital music and films. One aspect of the internet's commercial future thus hangs precariously in the balance, dependent first and foremost on technology versus counter-technology, but in second place on legal provisions which outlaw illegitimate attacks while striving to sustain legitimate operations.

---

[203] The charge was set in the much wider context of the controls over freedom on the internet by Boyle, *Shamans, Software and Spleens* (1996) and Lessig, *Code and other Laws of Cyberspace* (1999). In relation to copyright interests the themes are developed by Lessig in *The Future of Ideas* (2001), Chs 11, 14. See also Litman, *Digital Copyright* (2001).

(b) *Copyright and adjunct protection*[204]

Our first task will be to consider the relevance of traditional copyright enforcement among those legal provisions. There are two aspects: first, there is material that has been placed on the internet without copyright authorisation and so is illegitimate from the outset; and secondly, material that is owned or licensed but is not made available for free access and use by others. Since the internet is alive with possibilities for informing individuals how and where to obtain copyright material without paying for it, there are many questions in the copyright complex about participatory infringement. **20–56**

However, alongside copyright and distinct from it are measures that aim to prevent the undermining of material available at protected sites with conditional access, both at the sites themselves and then when it is released on limited terms. Here we reach rules which seek to outlaw "circumvention means", programs and other keys which would allow free access to gated sites or would undermine time-bars, copying-bars or other limits implanted in released material or operating so as to affect it from outside. Likewise we are concerned with rules which protect the integrity of DRM (Digital Rights Management) systems by, for instance, attacking the accounting records which they keep, or removing watermarks or fingerprints implanted in the material.

(c) *Legislative moves*[205]

In seeking enhanced legal powers, the copyright industries have concentrated attention at the international level, as well as the national and (for Europe) the regional. The TRIPS Agreement was negotiated too early to deal with Internet issues. But by 1996, WIPO had secured the signing of two "digital agenda" treaties. As already noted, the WIPO Copyright Treaty (WCT) (covering authors' rights in the Berne Convention sense)[206] and the WIPO Performances and Phonograms Treaty[207] (WPPT), required those who would join them to provide a right of communication to the public, and **20–57**

[204] See Litman, *Digital Copyright* (2001); Mazziotti, *EU Digital Copyright Law and the End-User* (2008); Stokes, *Digital Copyright Law and Practice* 4th edn (2009); MacQueen in Edwards and Waelde (above, n.202); Wiese [2002] E.I.P.R. 387. For famous scepticism about copyright in the internet world, John Perry Barlow, repr. in Hugenholtz (ed.), *Future of Copyright in a Digital Environment* (1996), p.169. Barlow's concern was for the earnings of composers, artists and other creators in the future.

[205] See Stamatoudi and Torremans (eds), *Copyright in the New Digital Environment* (2000); Ficsor, *Law of Copyright and the Internet* (2002); Reinbothe and von Lewinski, *The WIPO Treaties 1996* (2002).

[206] The WCT was first proposed as a Protocol to the Berne Convention but ended merely as a "special agreement" allowed under Berne but placing no obligations on Berne States to ratify it.

[207] Above, para.10–38. The two Treaties came into force in 2002. A third convention on a related right in databases was abandoned in face of US scepticism.

in rather preliminary terms to deal with circumvention means and interference with DRMS, but they can be regarded as no more than a first step.[208]

In 1998, the United States enacted its Digital Millennium Copyright Act (DMCA) which embraced a number of compromises between internet interests and copyright holders and also paid some attention to the future of copyright exceptions in an electronic system that might otherwise bypass them. The EU interventions in the same territory followed. They have already woven their way into the book, notably in Ch.11, since they also involved a degree of harmonisation of the copyright laws of Member States beyond the Directives of 1991–1996. The E-Commerce Directive limits the responsibilities of ISPs for copyright infringement, as it does for other types of liability (defamation, pornography, etc.) arising from content which they are hosting or holding for transmission. The InfoSoc Directive requires various elements which make up authors' rights and related rights to be defined in ways which cover internet deployment. It introduces limits on the exceptions to copyright infringement which can exist in national law (thus providing only a rough approximation); and it lays down specific requirements for control of circumvention means and DRMS infractions. The E-Commerce Directive has been implemented in UK law[209]; as has the InfoSoc Directive.[210]

(d) *Private international law and procedure*

20–58 Until the world eliminates all conflicts of substantive law and jurisdiction affecting copyright material on the internet, the issues of private international law and procedure remain acute and plans for dealing with them proliferate.[211] One school of thought argues, by general analogy to the satellite broadcasting solution in the EU, that normally the applicable law governing internet placement and transmission should be the law of the Host ISP's operation.[212] Users would thus have a clear point of reference in determining what licences are necessary. The opposite school of thought

[208] Typically, the scope was restricted by suspicions between the interest groups. Notably, while the WPPT gives international recognition to a variety of rights for performers and record producers, the US film industry relentlessly opposed according to performers any right in fixed versions of audio-visual performances. Record producers by contrast accepted that there be such a right, supported by an entitlement to equitable remuneration in respect of the rental right: see art.9. Subsequent attempts to resolve this have failed.

[209] Electronic Commerce (EC Directive) Regulations 2002 (SI 2002/2013). In addition, the Conditional Access to Services Directive (98/84/EC)—dealing with the provision of devices which allow access to broadcasts and similar services, such as Pay-TV—is given effect by the Conditional Access (Unauthorised Decoders) Regulations 2000 (SI 2000/1175); see further, para.20–77, below.

[210] Copyright and Related Rights Regulations 2003 (SI 2003/2498). On the InfoSoc Directive, see generally, Hugenholtz [2000] E.I.P.R. 499; Hart [2002] E.I.P.R. 58.

[211] Neither the E-Commerce Directive nor the InfoSoc Directive deals with the problems. More generally, see the WIPO Survey (n.202, above), 113–130.

[212] See above, paras 11–27, 14–26.

distances the satellite solution as a regional arrangement between responsible operators, quite unlike the utterly unregulated condition of the internet.[213] Accordingly it is necessary to leave liability to be settled on a multi-country basis against the whole range of ISPs.[214] Only in this way can it be ensured that hosts do not take their business off to "havens" with only very limited copyright laws.[215] The argument over international liability underlies all that will be said about the position in the United Kingdom.

(2) UK law and its amendment

From both a legal and a technical perspective, a useful primary division is between illicit and legitimate content. The first question, in other words, is whether, at the moment when content is placed on an internet site a copyright infringement occurs. Much else flows from that distinction. **20–59**

(a) *Illicit material*

(i) **Initial infringement.** Material may be illegitimately placed on the internet by a content supplier, with the deliberate intent of infringing, or it may arise from ignorance or mistake, as where the supplier is unwittingly exceeding a limited licence. The infringer may be copying from a traditional source, such as a book or record; or there may be a transfer from another internet site—as where one newspaper proprietor lifts the main headlines from a rival's paper on its website[216]; or the code-constructing elements of one website are lifted for use in another[217]; or material may be extracted by an internet search engine in order to give a reasonably detailed indication of contents in its own indexing system. **20–60**

In the United Kingdom the liability of the content provider and host falls to be considered both under the "reproduction" and the "performing" rights. The content provider infringes by its own act of copying and by authorising the Host ISP's computer to make its copy.[218] It is the ISP's machine which makes the copy and that equally amounts to primary infringement by copying. So far as concerns reproduction, the CDPA 1988

[213] See Dreier in Hugenholtz, *Future of Copyright in a Digital Environment* (1996) and Ficsor, *Law of Copyright and the Internet* (2002); Sterling *World Copyright Law* 3rd edn (2008).

[214] For the US position, e.g. see *National Football League v Prime Time* 24, 211 F.3d 10 (2 Cir. 2000).

[215] See generally papers by Lucas, Ginsburg, Dinwoodie and Austin, WIPO forum on PIL and IP (2001); and by Lucas and Dreyfuss & Ginsburg, ALAI, Proceedings 2002; Mankowski (2001) 32 I.I.C. 290; Kur [2002] E.I.P.R. 175; Guibault, *Copyright Limitations and Contracts* (2002); Burrell and Coleman, *Copyright Exceptions: the Digital Impact* (2005); Torremans in Derclaye (ed.), *Research Handbook on the Future of EU Copyright* (2009).

[216] As was occurring in the *Shetland Times* case (below, n.222).

[217] As in Gringras' example (above, n.202 at para.4.9.6.3.4): in constructing a website, a set of instructions (written as a Java applet) is copied without licence in order to make the site-holder's logo turn like a globe.

[218] *Sony Music Entertainment v Easyinternetcafe* [2003] F.S.R. 48. See Strowel in Stamatoudi and Torremans, *Copyright in the New Digital Environment* (2000), p.131.

pushed the concept a considerable distance by making even transient and incidental copying suffice.[219] The real issues for UK legislation relate to the scope of counterbalancing exceptions—which ought to be correspondingly broad.[220]

20–61 Following the InfoSoc Directive art.3, liability arises from communicating a copyright work to the public,[221] an activity which includes copyright material in an on-demand service or other interactive service.[222] Any site which is open to access by the public, whether for free or for payment, is responsible for communicating to the public. Users of peer-to-peer services have also been held to be communicating works to the public, as have operators of websites that provide not only the links to content, but also the technical means of assembling and downloading that content.[223] A Host ISP, however, is unlikely to be communicating to the public where their role is essentially passive and they are not responsible for the content.[224]

There has been some discussion internationally of whether the communication to the public right accords the copyright holder one element in an "access right" of potentially wider scope, but the bulk of copyright experts seem disinclined to accept such a concept.[225] The person who gains access is typically an "end-user" consumer and it is no part of copyright tradition to impose liabilities upon recipients, as distinct from producers and distributors. As we shall see, there is some breach in that tradition in respect of

---

[219] CDPA 1988, s.17(6), above, para.12–23. See also *R v Gilham* [2010] E.C.D.R. 5. cf. generally, Spoor in Hugenholtz, *Future of Copyright in the Digital Environment* (1996) p.67. Because copying is so inclusively defined, there is little need to consider whether providing or hosting internet content can amount to infringement by first publishing copies of works (under s.18). Is making internet content available to users the issuing of copies to the public? More likely s.18 is confined to the delivery of material embodiments, such as books, records and films. This is even clearer in the case of the rental right, since rental requires return of the thing rented (s.18A). Most of the acts of secondary infringement are probably not relevant to internet activities for the same reason.

[220] See below, paras 20–73 et seq.

[221] This right has been the subject of several references, although in the context of onward transmission of television broadcasts to television sets via a central antenna: see *SGAE v Rafael Hotels SA* [2006] ECR I-11519; and the pending references in Case 403/08 *FAPL v QC Leisure* OJ C 301 of 22.11.2008, p.19 and Case 136/09 *Organismos Sillogikis v Divani Acropolis Hotel* OJ C 141 of 20.06.2009, p. 32.

[222] CDPA 1988 s.20. An on-demand service is an "interactive service for making a work available to the public by electronic transmission in such a way that members of the public may access the work from a place and at a time individually chosen by them." This new definition, together with that of broadcasting, incorporates the exclusive right to engage in communication by cable. See *Polydor v Brown* [2005] E.W.H.C. 3191. Under the original version of the CDPA 1988 cabling was held to extend to internet transmissions in *Shetland Times v Wills* [1997] F.S.R. 604, CS, OH.

[223] See *Roadshow Films v iiNet* [2010] F.C.A. 24, FC Aust (users of "BitTorrent"); and *Twentieth Century Fox Film v Newzbin* [2010] E.W.H.C. 608 (Ch), para.125 (a website which enabled films to be located, assembled and downloaded via the Usenet service).

[224] See *Roadshow Films v iiNet* [2010] F.C.A. 24, FC Aust.

[225] See ALAI, *Adjuncts and Alternatives to Copyright* (2001), pp.281–372.

"circumvention means", but that needs to be faced explicitly, rather than smuggled in under cover of anything as obscure as an access right.[226]

As part of the "horizontal effects" of the E-Commerce Directive, an exception has been introduced against imposing pecuniary relief upon innocent hosts.[227] The objective is to provide a European equivalent to the "Notice and Take Down" procedure of the DMCA in the United States. This procedure is in constant use to notify ISPs that they must remove a site which they are hosting because the site contains infringing or other unlawful material. This most summary of procedures is capable of abuse and error, and protection in the United States has been provided in two ways: (i) by allowing the site-owner a right to object before "take-down"; and (ii) by preventing the site-owner from bringing proceedings against the ISP after the event—for instance, for breach of their contract to keep the site available. **20–62**

In the United States, the bulk of ISP interests had agreed to the legislative scheme before its enactment. Europe has not yet progressed so far. The Directive lays down the primary rule: an ISP is not liable so long as it does not have actual knowledge of the illegal activity or information[228]; and so also after notice is received,[229] provided that it expeditiously disables access to the site. Arrangements are evolving in each EU Member State to establish the safeguards needed for a full "Notice-and-Take-Down" schemes.[230] The UK Government, for some time, favoured a voluntary approach through an industry code. However, the recently introduced Digital Economy Act 2010 takes a legislative "carrot and stick" approach by leaving room for voluntary industry codes, provided these are approved by OFCOM, and where none have been approved, obliging OFCOM to introduce their own. Where such codes exist, ISPs are obliged to notify subscribers of infringing activities and provide copyright infringement lists to owners. As well, the Secretary of State and OFCOM may place obligations on ISPs to adopt **20–63**

[226] An additional ambiguity arises with the current fashion for re-casting exemptions and defences as rights, since these then become "access rights" accorded to the user, not the copyright owner.

[227] Article 14, which is linked to a provision preventing Member States from imposing any obligation to monitor the content of the site: art.15; transposed by Electronic Commerce Regulations 2002 (SI 2002/2013), reg.19. A person may be acting in part as content provider, and in part as host—for instance where an information and comment site provides space for contributions by outsiders.

[228] So far as concerns damages, the ISP must not have knowledge of facts or circumstances from which the illegal activity or information is apparent. In Joined Cases 236/08 to 238/08 *Google France v Louis Vuitton; Google France v Viaticum; Google France v CNRRH* Judgment of the Court (Grand Chamber) March 23, 2010 the ECJ at para.114 ruled that art.14 of the E-Commerce Directive, read together with Rec.42, applies where "the role played by that service provider is neutral, in the sense that its conduct is merely technical, automatic and passive, pointing to a lack of knowledge or control of the data which it stores."

[229] As to adequate notice, cf. the US decisions under the DMCA, *ALS Scan v RemarQ* 239 F. 619 (4 Cir., 2001); *Hendrickson v eBay* 165 F. Supp 2d 1082 (2000).

[230] Further guidance is contained in Rec.46 of the E-Commerce Directive, which requires that freedom of expression and related national procedures be respected.

technical measures to reduce copyright infringing activities.[231] The provisions apply broadly to ISPs that provide access to internet services and not simply to Host ISPs.

20–64 (ii) **Search engines and other connection services.** Searching on the World Wide Web is a digital service that is as extensive as it is rapid and cheap. In large measure, using a search engine to identify sites and pages does not lead to copyright infringement for it turns on the recognition of keywords, domain names and the like.[232] In straightforward cases the user is simply taken to the home page of each site that is contacted by a link to it. However, there are other situations where an element of unfairness enters and these can raise interesting legal issues.

20–65 (iii) **Deep linking.** One concerns the practice of deep linking, where one site contains a link to another at a particular page within its contents. One likely form of commercial damage is that the link bypasses the home page of the second site on which advertising appears. In *Shetland Times v Wills*,[233] one newspaper linked to specific items in another by giving the precise headlines used by the other on its own website. In interim proceedings, this activity was found likely to constitute copyright infringement. Was there a substantial taking? Perhaps so, if all the headlines from an edition of a paper were treated together.[234] But the general requirements of copyright infringement have to be applied and linking can certainly be organised without any such borrowing of "expression".[235] Short of that, an objection under UK law could be sustained only if there were an infringement of a database right[236] or if consumers were being misled about source so as to constitute passing off. In countries with a broader conception of unfair competition liability, there may be greater scope for legal intervention.[237] The effect of imposing liability would be to cut down one means of usefully providing

231 See clauses 3–16 of the Digital Economy Act 2010 c.24 inserting ss.124A–124N of the Communications Act 2003.

232 See below, paras 20–90 et seq.

233 *Shetland Times v Wills* [1997] F.S.R. 604; as to the wrongful act, see n.216, above.

234 This, however, is not how the judge apparently approached the matter.

235 As in the US example, *Ticketmaster v Tickets.com* (2003) WL 21406289 (CD Cal, 2003): one site permitted to link its visitors to another's ticketing service. For opposing attitudes taken by courts in European countries and the US, see Garotte [2002] E.I.P.R. 184. For the position in the US see Effross (1998) 49 South Carolina L. Rev. 651; Jackson (1997) 49 *Fed. Comm. L. J.* 731; Wassom (1998) 49 Case Western Reserve L. Rev. 181.

236 See generally, above, paras 20–38 et seq.; Case No. IZR 259/00 (July 3, 2003), German Supreme Court (2004) 35 I.I.C. 1097 and *Danske Dagblades Forening v Newsbooster* [2003] E.C.D.R. 5, Denmark City Court. Cf. *Algemeen Dagblad v Eureka Internetdiensten* [2002] E.C.D.R. 1., Dist Ct Rotterdam.

237 See, e.g. *StepStone v UK OfiR, Financial Times*, January 18, 2001 (Germany); but cf. *PCM v Kranten.com, Financial Times*, August 22, 2000 (Netherlands). The Higher Regional Court of Cologne, October 27, 2002, refused to find infringement of either copyright or database right where links to specific pages of online versions of newspapers were provided by a search engine. The online versions of the paper were provided free and so this linkage was characterised as "normal".

leads to other sources of information. So there is wisdom in the scrupulous approach of English law.

(iv) **Framing.** Mistakes about source are more likely to arise, as is substantial taking from the copyright contents of a site, in the cognate practice of framing. Here the actual layout, or at least the information, that is provided on one site is taken to another and placed within a different frame with its own name and logo, advertising, links and so on. Parasitic appropriation of this kind is unlikely to go unremedied in any system. Certainly in Germany, the extraction and utilisation of extracts from a medical dictionary in an electronic form was held to constitute infringement both of the copyright in the database and the sui generis database right, when the material was placed within the defendant's own frame.[238] **20–66**

(v) **Peer-to-peer systems.**[239] Different again are cases where additional services are part of an internet information package. The MP3 player for recorded music allows CD or other digital recording to be compressed to a degree which enables rapid transfer of its contents without significant loss of quality. Likewise with DVD for films. Famously, Shawn Fanning's Napster website provided free software for peer-to-peer (P2P) connections between its users. The users could each list through Napster the material that they were willing to transfer directly to others, thanks to the Napster software held on its server. In California, Napster's service was held to constitute both vicarious and contributory infringement of copyright works, which were being provided free but without licence from the copyright owner.[240] That decision led to a proliferation of other P2P providers in which many sought to add services of their own to the software by which others could connect, thus bolstering arguments that their package was not solely for copying unlicensed copyright material. The hope was that the package could be treated as a mechanism by which downloaders could engage in legitimate or illegitimate conduct as *they* chose. The manufacturers could then be treated as not involved in vicarious or contributory infringement—an argument based on the well-known decision of the Supreme Court in *Sony v Betamax*.[241] When MGM studio brought proceedings against the P2P enterprises, Grokster and Stream Cast, the lower courts accepted this argument. But the Supreme Court itself distinguished between situations such as arose in *Sony*, where the manufacturer of the equipment simply knew that there would be both types of use, and the typical P2P case where **20–67**

---

238 *Medizinsches Lexicon I*, Hamburg DC, July 12, 2000. See also *Derpoet.de*, Cologne DC, May 2, 2001.

239 Grosheide (2002) 33 I.I.C. 586, 698; Sheill [2005] 15 Ent. L.R. 63; [2005] 15 Ent. L.R. 107; Akester [2005] E.I.P.R. 106; Nasir [2005] Ent. L.R. 50; [2005] Ent. L.R. 82; Akester and Lima [2006] E.I.P.R. 576.

240 *A & M Records v Napster*, 239 F.Supp 3d 1004 (9 Cir., 2001). The appellate court restricted interim relief to cases where the right-owner proved title to the copyright. The result allowed Napster to linger on before its demise in bankruptcy proceedings.

241 380 F 3d 1154 (1984).

there was proof that the supplier's actual purpose or intent was to cause the infringing activity. In the latter case, there would be contributory liability.[242]

If equivalent proceedings were launched in the United Kingdom, there would be little doubt that both the provider and the recipient of transmitted material would be making unauthorised internet copies and so would be infringing. Accordingly, the equivalent questions about liability to those under US law would primarily be: (i) was the P2P supplier also a primary infringer as one who authorised these infringements?[243] and (ii) was the supplier secondarily liable for transmitting the material by means of a telecommunications system.[244] The outcome of any case is likely to turn on the structure of the particular P2P operation and the extent to which it is part of a larger service.[245] If it could be shown that it was merely facilitating cross-access on the internet to material which might or might not be infringing, there might well be an analogy to the case of the manufacturer of the twin-deck tape recorder. Taking a strictly limited view of "collaborative" liability, the House of Lords, in *CBS Songs v Amstrad*,[246] held that the provider of a machine for copying audio material from tape to tape was not liable for authorising infringement, nor for any form of economic tort, such as conspiracy or incitement.[247] In that case, the supplier had no control over the uses, legitimate or illegitimate, to which the recorder might be put in that case and the evidence that it had incited users to infringe copyright was relatively slight. In Australia, the Sharman group, which marketed KaZaa P2P software there, were found liable for authorising copyright infringement, in the sense that they "facilitated" it.[248] Sharman's own publicity showed that 2.4 million users had obtained KaZaa software just in one week. There was evidence that the great bulk of users did in consequence obtain illicit copies of recordings, that website warnings not to infringe were known by Sharman to have little effect, and that Sharman's publicity encouraged users to join the file-sharing revolution against the major record

[242] *MGM Studios v Grokster* 545 US 913 (2005). The liability related to ss.501–513 of the US Copyright Act 1977, but turned in part on common law concepts: see Ganley [2006] E.I.P.R. 15 and Heyman (2006) 37 I.I.C. 31.

[243] For which concept, see above, paras 12–18 et seq.

[244] Under CDPA 1988, s.24(2), which would require proof of knowledge or reason to believe that an infringing copy would be made from the transmission. For this a copy in RAM might well suffice.

[245] In considering vicarious (i.e. primary) infringement the *Napster* court took a view, generous to the copyright owners, that liability arose: (i) because Napster's contract gave it power to terminate a user's account, so that it continued to retain control over activities; and (ii) because Napster had a sufficient financial benefit through the attraction of customers to it. What attention an English court would pay to these considerations has not been tested, but a conclusion against liability is possible: Haftle and Daniels [2001] Ent. L.R. 107.

[246] *CBS Songs v Amstrad* [1988] A.C. 1013.

[247] Above, paras 2–13—2–17.

[248] See above, paras 12–18—12–19. For similar proceedings against KaZaa in the Dutch Supreme Court, see *Buma/KaZaa*, HR December 19, 2003, AMI 2004 9.

companies.[249] In England, the same tendency to look at the preponderance of the evidence concerning knowledge, and indeed, incitement in deciding whether to distinguish *CBS v Amstrad* is already apparent in a case concerning the Messiah computer games console[250] and was made explicit by the recent decision in *Twentieth Century Fox Film v Newzbin.*[251] In *Newzbin,* the defendants operated a website on the Usenet system which permitted their subscribers easily to locate and reassemble files such that they could download films. Kitchin J. held that the defendants had authorised their subscribers' infringing activities because they operated a facility which went beyond indexing and categorisation and which actively facilitated and encouraged the downloading of copyright films. Indeed, rather than installing some kind of filtering system, the defendant had encouraged their editors to identify links to commercial films. As to P2P providers of the usual type, it is hard to imagine an English court reaching a different decision from that of the Australian Federal Court in *Kazaa.*[252]

The *Napster* and *Grokster* judgments in the United States became **20–68**
bleeding images much paraded in the campaigns to preserve the internet as an unfettered instrument of free exchange, which would at the same time place the music industry giants in jeopardy.[253] It is unlikely that, either in the United States or Europe, copyright law will be amended to provide exemption for P2P software providers.[254] Instead, the cat-and-mouse activities involved in chasing both providers and P2P users are increasing and the pressure to involve ISPs in this game is mounting,[255] raising difficult questions around when ISPs have an obligation to intervene and their

---

[249] *Universal Music v Sharman* [2005] F.C.A. 1242. FC Aust. See also *Cooper v Universal Music Australia* [2006] F.C.A.F.C. 187, Full Ct FC Aust which held that operating a website structured to permit ready access to unauthorised music files via hyperlinks constituted authorisation.

[250] *Sony Computer Equipment v Owen* [2002] E.C.D.R. 298, a case arising under CDPA 1988 s.196, for which see below, para.20–79 n.289.

[251] *Twentieth Century Fox Film v Newzbin* [2010] E.W.H.C. 608 (Ch).

[252] Bolstered by the fact that in *Newzbin* (above, n.251), Kitchin J. at para.95 regarded the decisions in *Cooper v Universal Music Australia* [2006] F.C.A.F.C. 187, Full FC Aust and *Roadshow Films v iiNet Ltd (No.3)* [2010] F.C.A. 24, FC Aust as "entirely consistent" with English principles on authorisation liability.

[253] See, e.g. Lessig, *The Future of Ideas*, (2001), esp. pp.194–196.

[254] Despite calls to the contrary: see e.g. Netanel (2003) Harv. J. L. & Tech. 1 who argues for an exemption for non-commercial P2P use and the imposition of levies on digital equipment and services.

[255] In the UK see clauses 3–16 of the Digital Economy Act 2010 c.24 inserting ss.124A–124N of the Communications Act 2003, discussed above at para.20–63. In Ireland see the voluntary "three-strikes" protocol adopted by Eircom (the largest ISP), the legitimacy of which, from a data protection perspective, was considered in *EMI Records (Ireland) v Eircom* [2010] I.E.H.C. 108. In France there is the controversial "graduated response" legislation—Law 2009–669 of June 12, 2009 favouring the Diffusion and Protection of Creation on the Internet: see Strowel (2009) WIPO Journal 76.

(sometimes conflicting) duties to preserve privacy.[256] In the meantime, new P2P providers spring from their holes around the internet skirting. Blocking one outlet seems to provoke 10 times the tunnelling elsewhere, in respect not just of music but equally of films and of other material. Guerilla tactics give positive delight and put pressure on the record and film industries' leaders to change their whole mode of business. To the extent that they become obliged to supply legitimate versions of more and better material through competitive subscription services, the benefits to consumers are obvious.

20–69 (vi) **Transmission of illegitimate material.** Initially some leaders of the copyright industries pressed the case for imposing strict liability on all who transmitted infringing and other wrongful material on the internet, whether as hosts or as mere conduits. That would indeed have given highly effective cover. Telecommunication corporations, a powerful counter-lobby, resisted the claim as wholly unreasonable, claiming that their position was simply analogous to a mail carrier. In the upshot, as we have seen, host ISPs and certain other intermediaries were dealt with by imposing liability only on notice and failure to react.[257]

As for the intermediate transmitters, no liability attaches in any case where the transmission is nothing more than as a conduit.[258] As the InfoSoc Directive chooses to express it in art.5(1), there is an exemption for temporary acts of reproduction which: (i) are transient or incidental; [259] (ii) are an integral and essential part of a technological process; (iii) have as their sole purpose to enable either: (a) a transmission of the work in a network between third parties by an intermediary: or (b) a lawful use; and (iv) have no independent economic significance.[260] This formulation may appear unduly elaborate and cautious. However, it reached its final form only after the European Parliament had recommended that the exemption should be

---

[256] *Promusicae v Telefónica de España SAU* [2008] E.C.D.R. 10: ECJ ruled that the E-Commerce, InfoSoc and Enforcement Directives, along with Directive 2002/58 on private and electronic communications did not require Member States to obligate the disclosure of personal data in order to protect copyright, but that any transposition of those directives had to strike a balance between rights of property (copyright) and privacy. To the same effect see: Case 557/07 *LSG-Gesellschaft zur Wahrnehmung von Leistungsschutzrechten v Tele2 Telecommunication* OJ C 113 16.5.2009, p.14.

[257] Above, para.20–62; Strowel in Stamatoudi and Torremans (above, n.218).

[258] See E-Commerce Directive art.12 and Electronic Commerce Regulations 2002 (SI 2002/2013) reg.17.

[259] According to the ECJ ruling in *Infopaq International v Danske Dagblades Forening* [2009] E.C.D.R. 16, para.64, "transient" requires that the duration of storage is "limited to what is necessary for the proper completion of the technological process in question" and the process must be automated so that "it deletes that act automatically, without human intervention, once its function of enabling the completion of such process has come to an end."

[260] CDPA 1988, s.28A, covering injunctive as well as pecuniary relief and criminal sanctions. The scope of s.28A is the subject of a pending reference to the ECJ in Case 403/08 *FAPL v QC Leisure* OJ C 301 of 22.11.2008, p.19.

cut back so as to cover only lawful uses—a move that would have rendered it of only vestigial relevance.[261]

(vii) **"Caching" by the access provider and user.** Even at the end-points of an internet transmission, a copy is made, so in UK law there would in principle be a basis for liability when the material has come from an illegitimate source. In order to overcome delays in retrieving material from an original site, particularly when it is wanted repeatedly by the same or different users, their representatives, the access providers use facilities for holding the information in a "cache" on their own server (sometimes called a "mirror cache"). This extended retention was argued by copyright owners to be distinguishable from mere conduit transmission—a step which should justify liability and so a charge for the privilege. That argument, however, has been rejected in Europe and elsewhere. Access providers are exempt, under the E-Commerce Directive art.13, from liabilities which might otherwise arise over the automatic, intermediate and temporary storage of information solely for this purpose. This is subject to "Notice-and-Take-Down" conditions of the kind which also apply to Host ISPs. Since there is also a danger that cached material will not contain the latest version on the original site, there are also obligations to comply with industry practice on updating content and on technology for obtaining data on the use of the information.[262] **20–70**

(b) *Legitimate material*

(i) **Constrictions on transmission and use.** Copyright in much of the material which is placed on the internet belongs to the content provider or has the licence of the copyright owner. Where, in consequence, access to the site is unlimited and the whole intention is to make the content available to anyone who may be interested, there must be at least an implied licence allowing its transmission and its downloading for anticipated uses. One enterprise provided software to another as "shareware" which the latter was entitled to bundle with its own software and distribute over the internet. It was held to have an implied licence to do so, but only in its entire, unaltered form.[263] **20–71**

If the site-holder has imposed a limit upon access by password or other gateway—in order to secure a fee, or to restrict the range of recipients, or for any other reason—it is the technical constraint which in large measure gives the protection. Copyright is needed only against those who hack a way

[261] An added complication is that mere conduits are also exempted from pecuniary remedies and criminal sanctions, thanks to the "horizontal provisions" of the E-Commerce Directive art.12 and Rec.45, as implemented in the Electronic Commerce Regulations 2002 (SI 2002/2013) reg.17. These limit the exemption to storage and transmission where the ISP does not initiate the transmission, select its receiver or select or modify content. The storage must be automatic, intermediate and transient, solely for the transmission in a communication network and stored no longer than reasonably necessary for the purpose. These conditions largely overlap with those in CDPA 1988 s.28A.

[262] Electronic Commerce Regulations 2002 (SI 2002/2013) reg.18.

[263] *Trumpet Software v OzEmail* [1996] 18(12) I.P.R. 69.

round that barrier. It is now widely accepted that, in general, where technical barriers are instituted they should be supported. The WIPO Treaties of 1996 accordingly require national systems to protect electronic rights management information, which identifies the work and the terms and conditions of its use; and to prevent circumvention of technological protection measures.[264] There are, however, controversial issues about the perimeters of this common ground.

20–72 Whether it is permissible to place material on the internet may turn on whether the person who does so owns the copyright in electronic exploitation or has a licence for it. Many copyright owners have been chary of granting electronic publishing rights, for fear that they will undermine their traditional forms of marketing. In many contracts written before the mid-1990s, the position was left unclear because the possibility went unappreciated. English courts will approach the matter as one of interpreting the particular language of the grant.[265] There may be some inclination, where the terms permit it, to exclude from the grant what the parties could not have contemplated; but there is no rule to this effect, as there is in some Continental copyright laws. In many countries, as electronic newspapers have come on stream, this has been a particularly acrimonious issue between journalists and proprietors.[266]

20–73 (ii) **Exceptions for users.**[267] Every copyright system provides exceptions to the general scope of the rights. The countervailing justifications for them in UK law, and the way in which they are expressed, have already been explored in Chs 12 and 14 and the preceding sections of this chapter. With advances in copying technology, many of these exceptions are attacked by the copyright industries as unfair deprivations of potential earning capacity. Supporters of property rights argue the case on the basis that electronic recording now makes it cheap and easy to grant licences for copyright use, where previously this would have been slow and invasive: accordingly market conditions are now able to operate and should therefore be allowed to govern. Putting it in down-to-earth terms, major copyright owners fear that exceptions which have the position of the individual user as a starting point will come to undermine their commercial prospects in the new digital

[264] WIPO Copyright Treaty arts 11 and 12; WIPO Performances and Phonograms Treaty arts 19 and 20.

[265] If the term specifically assigns or grants a licence of rights including those arising in future through novel technical developments, it has in the past been taken at face value: *Campbell Connelly v Noble* [1963] 1 All E.R. 237. Cf. post-internet approaches in the US: *New York Times v Tasini* 121 S.C. 2381 (2001), US SC; *Greenberg v National Geographic Society* 244 F. 3d 1267 (11 Cir., 2001)

[266] See, e.g. Lindner [1998] E.I.P.R. 410.

[267] In addition to the references in n.215 above, see ALAI 1998, *Exceptions and Limitations to Copyright;* Dam (1999) 28 J.Leg. St. 393; Marks and Turnbull [2000] E.I.P.R. 201; Perritt [2003] E.I.P.R. 1; Dreier and Hugenholtz in Dreyfuss et al. (eds), *Expanding the Boundaries of Intellectual Property* (2001), Chs 12 and 14; and Janssens in Derclaye (ed), *Research Handbook on the Future of EU Copyright* (2009).

world. Many copyright laws, for instance, provide an exception for private use.[268] The UK Act, which proceeds more circumspectly by means of its categories of "fair dealing" and other nominate defences, also allows protection for a certain range of cases which justify the same fears—at least to some degree.

Are these fears nonetheless exaggerated? Are they not being expressed mainly as a pretext for upsetting the present balances of interest which the defences represent? Mutual suspicion between owner and user interests runs high. In drafting its InfoSoc Directive, the Commission began from a relatively uninvasive position which would have left the terms of exemptions to national legislators so far at least as the refinements of definition were concerned.[269] The European Parliament, however, was whipped by horror stories of the mass piracy of records, films and the like[270] into a protective frenzy, and a discomforted Commission and Council found themselves arguing for a middle way. The final outcome saw constraints on the scope of exceptions and limitations but these nonetheless specified many of the categories to be found in those European laws (like the German and British) which already contain detailed lists.[271] **20–74**

Any exception admitted by national law is to be conditioned by the Berne-TRIPS constraints,[272] encapsulated in the "Three-Step Test": (i) exceptions can only be for certain specific cases[273]; (ii) they must not create conflict with the normal exploitation of the subject-matter; (iii) nor must they involve use in a manner which unreasonably prejudices the right owner's legitimate interests. The test is now a mantra of international copyright law. However it needs to be interpreted in the light of the not inconsiderable exceptions which were in existence in many national systems in 1967 when the test first appeared in the Berne Convention and were not thereafter altered. There remains also the issue whether the formula merely sets the criteria which Member States must observe in formulating **20–75**

---

[268] In Europe, countries which have such a defence have nonetheless introduced levies on equipment and recording media, such as tapes, by which to some degree to compensate right-owners for private copying. The UK has long resisted the introduction of such a private interest "tax".

[269] But see below, para.20–82.

[270] These belong to the category of illegitimate takings and are accordingly irrelevant to the problem of exceptions. The EP chose to introduce some high-sounding recitals about the social virtues of the exceptions, but it wanted to curtail them.

[271] For a discussion of the success of harmonising exceptions see Commission Report on InfoSoc Directive (November 11, 2007) and querying whether the InfoSoc Directive strikes the right balance between rightholders and users see *Green Paper on Copyright in the Knowledge Economy* (2008) and the subsequent Commission Communication on the Green Paper (October 19, 2009).

[272] See above, para.10–26; Ricketson [1999] I.P.Q. 56.

[273] The two international Agreements say "certain special cases", which some argue imposes a higher standard. Whichever phrase is used, its scope is perplexing, since it was introduced into Berne for the reproduction rights at a time when most Member States had general exceptions for private use or for fair uses or dealings. "Special/specific" cannot therefore be understood in the sense of requiring a decision separately upon each case, as may arise with compulsory licences for patents: cf. TRIPS arts 30, 31a.

exceptions or whether it must be made a distinct element in the substantive law of the State.[274]

20–76 (iii) **Technical barriers, their circumvention and exceptions: Digital Rights Management (DRM).**[275] Questions about what activities on the internet require authorisation from the copyright owner raise two kinds of issue: first, about access to the material at a right-owner's or licensee's website; and secondly concerning uses made of the material once it has been downloaded. In the past, many of the actual concerns raised by the exceptions to copyright have related to the second situation: multiple reprography for classes and choirs, quotations in published reviews, news stories taken over by one newspaper from another. With the internet, much more turns on the initial access and this heightens the clash of interests at stake, because the content provider may impose contractual or technical barriers in the way of obtaining the copyright material. As a result both the initial downloading and the subsequent deployment call for consideration.

The provider of a DRM system may set out contractual conditions to which a person seeking access must agree (by "click-on") before gaining access to the material. Unless there are arrangements for electronic negotiation, the terms offered will ordinarily be in standard form: take or leave. What if those terms seek to take away from the user a freedom which falls within one of the fair dealing or related exceptions in the national law? Suppose that they insist upon a payment before a scholar makes a permanent copy of even the smallest part of a work; or a fee for any quotation in an examination paper; or specific permission before using any part for criticism or review or for reporting current events?

20–77 One novel question is whether the exceptions should be raised to the level of guaranteed rights of access and use, which cannot be bypassed by contractual provisions more protective of copyright owners. In the past, it has often been assumed in British and other copyright systems that exceptions do have this character, though there has been only very occasional contest about it. If that is so, why should the approach change under a digital system? Why should not the former balances of interest continue under the new technology? Can it really be that, because there are the means of requiring payment, every transaction, no matter what its justification, should lead to a payment if the right-owner so wishes? What is the sense in imposing any limit on the duration of copyright itself, if contractual limits

[274] See Mason [1997] E.I.P.R. 636; Rosenblatt (1997) 13 Comp. L. & S. Rep. 307; Quaedvlieg (1998) 29 I.I.C. 420; Vinje [1996] E.I.P.R. 431, [1999] E.I.P.R. 192.

[275] Goldstein [1997] Wisc. L.R. 865; Reidenberg (1998) 76 Tex. L.R. 553; Samuelson and others (1998) 13 Berk, Tech.L.J. 1239 et seq.; ALAI 1998, *Limitations and Exceptions to Copyright*, esp. papers by Spoor, Guilbault, Ginsburg, Sirinelli; ALAI 2001, *Adjuncts and Alternatives to Copyright*, Sect. ID2; Guilbault, *Copyright Limitations and Contracts* (2002); Dusollier (2003) 34 I.I.C. 62; Besek (2004) 27 Col. J.L.A. 385; Ottolia (2004) 35 I.I.C. 491; Barczewski [2005] E.I.P.R. 165; MacCulloch [2005] E.I.P.R. 176; Akester and Akester [2006] E.I.P.R. 159; Ciro and Fox [2006] E.I.P.R. 329; von Lewinski (2005) 35 I.I.C. 844.

can be imposed whether the material is still in copyright or not? On the other hand, if the limitations upon contractual restrictions are to be guaranteed against reversal by contract, why should the same effect be attainable simply by a technical barrier? Why should such a barrier be supported by legal bans on means to circumvent the access bars? In the evolution of the InfoSoc Directive such questions took a long time to attract serious attention.[276]

While that Directive was still in gestation, broadcasters and others succeeded in acquiring a separate form of protection through a Conditional Access Directive of 1998.[277] It has already been incorporated into the technical protection provisions of the copyright legislation of 1998.[278] These stand beside the amendments which flow from the InfoSoc Directive and which are outlined below.[279] It is worth noting, however, that the new rights are given not just to broadcasters and cable-casters, but also to those, like ISPs, who provide an information society service from the EU; it is the investment in these various services which is being protected. Accordingly, as with the copyright in broadcasts, it is not relevant to consider whether there is copyright in the material being accessed or whether an exception to copyright applies. The only question is whether the access has been authorised.[280] The right accordingly has some potential, where the material is not otherwise available, to create a form of perpetual monopoly. How serious this will prove must turn on the frequency with which all access can be blocked. The problem resembles the monopoly potential of database rights.[281]

The provider may build into its site an access control, such as encryption **20–78**
or scrambling of the material or it may adopt a content control mechanism which is designed, once material has been downloaded into a user's computer, to limit use, e.g. by restricting the number of times a recording can be played, or the period of retention in ROM or the ability to burn it onto a CD. Electronic checks of both kinds will have their desired effect so long as no counter-device is at hand to circumvent the protection. It is, however, copy control which provokes many users to react instinctively against a provider having the power still to control what they have acquired.[282] Rental

[276] Cf. the hot debate in the US over a proposed art.2B for the Uniform Commercial Code, which aimed to regulate e-commerce, and the subsequent introduction of similar provisions into the law of individual States. For its relevance to Europe see, e.g. Grosheide and Boele-Woekli (eds), *Europees Privaatrecht 1998* (1998), Pt II (Samuelson and Opsahl, MacQueen et al., Guibault, Grosheide).

[277] Directive 98/EC [1998] OJ L320/54. Note the complementary Council of Europe Convention on Conditional Access of 2000.

[278] By Conditional Access (Unauthorised Decoders) Regulations 2000 (SI 2000/1175), amending CDPA 1988 ss.297A and 298.

[279] Paragraphs 20–79—20–80.

[280] See the pending ECJ references in Case 403/08 *FAPL v QC Leisure* OJ C 301 of 22.11.2008, p.19; and C-429/08 *Murphy v Media Protection Services Ltd* OJ C301 22.11.2008, p.27 which ask, inter alia, in what circumstances is there use of an illicit device within the meaning of the Conditional Access Directive.

[281] Above, para.20–38.

[282] See, e.g. Litman, ALAI 2001 (above, n.275) 456.

of things (including copyright-protected copies) has widespread social acceptance, but that has yet to be built up for its close relative, the electronic copy with technological control. This animus may defeat all the hectic search to find truly impenetrable technical means. It is the impending failure of the technology which makes the legal back-up measures so potentially significant.

20–79 The InfoSoc Directive's eventual provision on the subject, art.6,[283] became during the legislative process so twisted by conflicting demands as to resemble Laocoon wrestling with the serpents. Legislation should never be so hideously contorted, but there it writhes. Even in the CDPA 1988, the United Kingdom had made important provisions against breaking security devices of various sorts.[284] The UK provisions implementing the Directive enhance the civil and criminal law armoury required against "circumvention means". But in order to deal with unfair consequences, there is power to introduce exceptions, if that becomes a political necessity in the future.[285] The provisions were much delayed by controversy, and took effect in late 2003.

Save for computer programs,[286] the former s.296 has been expanded to meet the anti-circumvention requirements of art.6(1). The reach is indeed broad. Copyright is the starting point of s.296ZA to the extent that copies of a copyright work must be issued or made available to the public[287] with the copyright owner's authority and with effective technological measures applied to them.[288] Liability then is imposed on "any person who does anything which circumvents the measures, knowing or having reason to believe, that is the effect of what he is doing".[289] This covers anyone who infiltrates a web source and anyone who breaks instructions placed within the transmitted material in order to limit the use of the copy. It can therefore apply to a consumer-user as much as a trader. Against all such persons there is a right of action equivalent to that for copyright infringement; but it is given not only to the copyright owner concerned but to any other person who is distributing the copyright material with authority.[290]

283 As explicated in Recs 51–53 and the legislative history of the Directive.

284 See above, para.14–23.

285 See below, para.20–82.

286 Programs continue to be governed by the Computer Programs Directive: InfoSoc Directive, arts 1 and 11, and Rec.50. But for this exclusion, the anti-circumvention rules could well have displaced the provisions on decompilation to secure interoperability in the earlier Directive (for which, see above, paras 20–17—20–22). Since many circumvention devices, products or components are programs, the distinction is likely to prove important.

287 Including making available through interactive contact under CDPA 1988 s.20 (above, para.20–61).

288 "Effective technological measures" are broadly defined in s.296ZD and in particular cover both access control and copy control.

289 Section 296ZA(1). "Copyright" is to be read as including rights in performances, publication right and database right: s.296ZA(7).

290 CDPA 1988 s.296ZA(2)–(6), which contain various adaptations of enforcement provisions. For steps taken in other European countries; von Lewinski (2004) 35 I.I.C. 844.

Separately, in implementation of the InfoSoc Directive art.6(2), the same persons are given rights against those who (broadly speaking) engage in supplying anti-circumvention devices or services commercially. Devices (including products or components) are caught provided that any other purpose they may have is limited in its commercial significance; and even then that is no excuse if the primary design was as a circumvention device.[291] Business services are caught when their purpose is circumvention and the wrong includes not only providing the service but promoting it or a product.[292] Commercial suppliers of such devices and services would also be made criminally liable.[293] **20–80**

A second technological approach on which copyright holders pin current hopes is the development of bots and crawlers and the like which can patrol the vast ranges of the World Wide Web. There they will discover where material, originally legitimate, is being misused by others who have no authority. To do this right-owners must watermark or fingerprint their copies in a way which will allow them to be traced into other people's hands. That process will fail if the watermarks can be removed or side-stepped in some other way. Rights which buttress these controls, should they become efficient practical tools, are therefore required of Member States by art.7 of the InfoSoc Directive.[294] The CDPA 1988 therefore provides copyright owners and distributors with civil rights of action against those who remove or alter digital rights management information ('DRM'), where the person doing so, knows, or has reason to believe, that he is inducing, enabling, facilitating or concealing copyright infringement.[295] **20–81**

The principal exceptions allowed by the InfoSoc Directive are identified in art.6(4) as the following: **20–82**

(i) the exception for reprography where there is fair compensation (art.5(2)(a))—this will continue to be provided by the encouragement given in the CDPA 1988 to voluntary arrangements through collecting societies such as CLA and DACS[296];

---

[291] The current law is already interpreted so as to disregard possible non-infringing uses in a small proportion of cases: *Sony Computer Equipment v Owen* [2002] E.C.D.R. 286. In all likelihood a similar attack could be mounted on a DeCSS program for decrypting DVD versions of films: as, notoriously, in the US: *Universal City Studios v Reimerdes* 111 F.Supp. 2d 294 (2000).

[292] CDPA 1988 s.296ZC.

[293] CDPA 1988 s.296ZB.

[294] See also Recs 54–57.

[295] CDPA 1988 s.296ZE. A number of supplemental provisions resemble those in the anti-circumvention provisions.

[296] Copyright Licensing Agency, Designers and Artists Copyright Society. See above, paras 13–54 et seq. and para.14–15. The incentive comes from the small-scale exemption of s.36, which operates where no voluntary scheme is in place.

(ii) the exception for copying by public libraries and similar institutions (art.5(2)(c))—dealt with in detail by the CDPA 1988, s.37–43, as somewhat amended[297];

(iii) the exception for ephemeral recordings for broadcasts (art.5(2)(d))—as in the CDPA 1988 s.68[298];

(iv) the exception for copying broadcasts by social institutions, subject to fair compensation (art.5(2)(e))—as included within the CDPA 1988 s.72.[299]

(v) the exception to both the reproduction right and public communication right for illustration for teaching or scientific research (art.5(3)(a))—now dealt with by the fair dealing exception for private study and non-commercial research[300];

(vi) the exception for the disabled (art.5(3)(b))[301]; and

(vii) the exception for public security and reporting of official proceedings (art.5(3)(e))—dealt with in numerous sections of the CDPA 1988.[302]

20–83 In all these cases, the InfoSoc Directive art.6(4), encourages the right-owner to provide a voluntary mechanism so that users can benefit from the exception or limitation which should operate in their favour. In default—and this is the supposed spur—each State is *obliged* to take what are described as "appropriate measures" to make sure that a person entitled to copy, supply or receive copyright material is not prevented from doing so by effective technological measures.

The exception for reproduction by individuals for private, non-commercial use, again subject to fair compensation (art.5(2)(b)),[303] is dealt with on similar lines, which also insist that, in offering voluntary measures, the rightholder shall be entitled to limit the number of copies being made.

20–84 Article 6(4) and its related Recitals[304] are the product of a lobbying battle of considerable proportions. It accordingly contains comforting but vague phrases which represent a concession one way and then the other. Copyright critics spend much time arguing for a balance of interests, and here is an attempt actually to determine the weighting to be applied. But the chosen method is to rely upon incentives for voluntary action. Nothing more is said about what voluntary arrangements will suffice. What would be sufficient steps to allow the user to benefit from his exception? How, by way of return,

297 Above, paras 12–43 and 14–15.

298 Above, para.12–48.

299 Above, para.12–47.

300 Above, para.12–39, 14–14.

301 Above, para.12–54. See also the Copyright (Visually Impaired Persons) Act 2002.

302 Above, para.12–50.

303 Currently the subject of several pending references to the ECJ: see Case 387/09 *EGEDA v Magnatrading* OJ C 312 19.12.2009, p.18; Case 476/08 *SGAE v Padawan* OJ C 19 24.1.2009, p.12; and Case 462/09 *Stichting de Thuiskopie v Mijndert van der Lee* OJ C 24 30.1.2010, p.38.

304 Recs 45 and 51–53. See Dusollier (2003) 34 I.I.C. 62.

should the user be obliged to show that he only used the material for the permitted purpose? When should a government intervene with compulsory measures? Will they in their turn not have to satisfy the questions which arise over voluntary measures?

These are vital, but puzzling, issues in the numerous Member States which have general exceptions for private use (covering photocopying, home recording and the like). The admission of these exceptions justifies the statutory levy on equipment and/or recording media which acts as a rough compensation for the surrender of rights. The UK approach, by contrast, fails to take the initial step of creating any general exception to copyright liability for private use.[305] Much private use remains a wrongful act. It is simply left to right-owners to do what they can about it. In these cases there is no copyright exception and so no basis for a levy providing compensation for the loss. This certainly limits the relevance of art.6 in the UK context. But limited provisions do exist. Private researchers and students may engage in fair dealing. People are free to record broadcasts privately for the convenience of "time shifting". **20–85**

These and other exceptions could give rise to claims by a person who says that he is an entitled to digital material but is barred by conditions to access. A student, for instance, might insist that he needs to see and take a copy of material on a site without paying a subscription or other charge. The same might happen with a book reviewer who wants material for a review that he is writing. Can either insist that there be an arrangement allowing them free access, upon proof of their credentials? Should right-owners be placed under an obligation to provide simple mechanisms for individuals to establish their bona fides? If they do, should they be able to make some charge, even at low, regulated, rate? The UK Government is not keen to find answers to such practical problems beforehand. Ministers have the power to act under art.6(4) when a sufficient case for statutory backing emerges as the result of a complaint.[306] As it stands that is scarcely an immediate threat to right-owners who push their exclusive rights aggressively, untouched by the winds of popular disapproval. **20–86**

The course of UK copyright legislation has led to a complex balance between economic activities which require a copyright owner's licence and those which are unconditionally or conditionally free. This is achieved partly through the definition of sufficient taking and other basic concepts of the law of infringement and partly though the elaborate patterning of defences. It is of course desirable that parliamentary enactments (or now EU legislation) should settle the boundaries, so far as general prescriptions can achieve this. To a significant degree, judges will be left to determine their **20–87**

[305] See above, paras 14–11 et seq. Section 6(4) gives its protection only to lawful users. This must include those entitled to the benefit of an exception, as well as those who have satisfied the conditions of a limitation.

[306] Section 296ZE An early complaint was from those who conduct encryption research: see CDPA 1988 s.296ZA(2).

real scope. But a law which allows little scope for judges to rely on more fundamental considerations, shows its weaknesses at moments when a new technology emerges. Never has this been more apparent than with the internet, because of the unequivocal revolution which it is creating across the gamut of informational media.

20–88 The main contrast is not, however, with authors' rights systems, despite their preference for a defence of private use, expressing a deep-seated antipathy against intrusion into personal freedom and privacy. It is with the robustly constitutional tradition of the United States, which has kept a general doctrine of fair use as part of its common law inheritance. This leaves to judges a broad power to balance the incentive benefits of copyright protection against other social and moral claims for free access, derivation and transmission of works.

With the internet, American courts have had, for instance, to decide the following:

- — Were the various "private" uses facilitated by Napster and its successors through providing P2P software connections justified? It was held that they were not, since the participants were in many cases gaining free what otherwise they would buy.[307]
- — Was a purchaser of a copy of a work (say a CD) allowed to access a copy of the work placed on the My MP3 website by its operator, in order to allow the first purchaser to play the work through a computer at a different place? The purchasers were held not to be engaging in fair use, because of the ease with which false notifications of initial purchase could be given. Accordingly the website provider could not shelter behind their blamelessness.[308]
- — Where DVD versions of films were copy-protected by a program (CSS), could a website itself provide a simple "free software" program (DeCSS) by which to circumvent it, when one purpose of DeCSS was to avert controls in DVD players which confined them to playing copies of the film purchased in the same country or region? Because this was not the only use to which DeCSS would be put, the fair use claim failed.[309]
- — Could a search engine take digital copies of photographs from other websites in order to display them as low-definition "thumbnails" on their service? They could, because no one could reconstitute the photographs from the thumbnails. But to provide a link to a page from which the actual photographs in digital form could be downloaded free did not lead to fair use copying; the commercial interests

[307] Above, para.20–67.

[308] *UMG Recordings v MP3.com* 92 F. Supp 2d 349; 109 F.Supp.2d 223 (2000, SDNY). The principle for assessing damages meant that they were likely to be massive.

[309] *Universal City Studios v Reimerdes* (above, n.289).

of the photographer were too immediately jeopardised by the practice.[310]

In US law some direction is given to judicial decision-making by prescribing four factors which must be brought into account in different circumstances: the extent to which the defendant's purposes differs from that of the copyright owner; the nature of the work; the amount taken in relation to the whole; and the degree of interference with the owner's own commercial prospects. During the enactment of the Copyright Bill 1988 in the United Kingdom, a proposal to introduce a general qualificatory provision on the same lines as the US defence of "fair use" was not permitted to become part of copyright legislation. Now UK judges are regularly assessing the proportionality of a host of relevant considerations in deciding whether the outcome of cases are consistent with the European Convention on Human Rights. There must therefore be a strong case for them to have an equivalent power over the scope and range of copyright. The types of consideration involved are of basic importance and many have to do with the freedoms open to individual users. Yet, as the US examples suggest, what is required is a precise ruling on how far an exception should stretch and that is something which is often better handled by courts than by legislatures of whatever variety. **20–89**

4. Domain Name and "Adword" Disputes[311]

(1) Internet addresses

As E-commerce has grown, the internet has become a virtual space in which unfair trading with marks, brands and business names is likely to take place.[312] To some extent the structure of the system causes old dangers of public confusion to appear in new forms. Of these the most prominent has been the outbreak of "cyber-squatting" associated with top-level domain names. **20–90**

The addressing system of the internet operates through the assignment of binary numbers to websites, web pages, email addresses and so on, each item having a Uniform Resource Locator (URL). For easier comprehension these are often given to users in mixtures of letters and numbers. At the primary stages of location, words or abbreviations are the most frequent form, and

[310] *Kelly v Arriba* 280 F. 3d 934 (9 Cir., 2002).

[311] Bettinger et al., *Domain Name Law and Practice* (2005); Lindsay, *International Domain Name Law* (2007); Greenberg and Speres (2010) 5 J.I.P.L.P. 268.

[312] See above, para.16–21. For recent instances in English courts, *French Connection v Sutton* [2000] E.T.M.R. 341; *Radio Taxicabs v Taxi Services* [2004] R.P.C. 19; *Global Prospect Management v Citigroup* [2006] F.S.R. 39; *Phones 4u v Phone4u.co.uk* [2007] R.P.C. 5, CA; *Tesco Stores v Elogicom* [2007] F.S.R. 4.

nowhere more so that in the Top-level Domain (TLD: <usco.com>, <britcorp.co.uk>). During the early stages of constructing the World Wide Web as part of a general internet, the agency given the power to organise the registration of TLDs (from 1992–1998, the Internet Assigned Number Authority (IANA)) admitted domain names without any geographical suffix, but through a rough division of activities: <.com> for commercial organisations, <.net> for networks, <.org> for other organisations. Recently, <.biz> for business, <.info> for information and certain restricted TLDs were added. All these were available to users from any country. <.int> has been restricted to international bodies. And, given the American generative power behind the system, <.edu> for education, <.gov> for government and <.mil> for the military were reserved for those from the United States. In other countries, national agencies were accorded power to grant domains which were indicated by a geographical suffix (a gTLD): as in <.uk>, <.de>, <.fr> and the media-friendly <.tv>; for Tuavala. The expansion of gTLDs continues steadily.[313]

20–91 No matter how similar domain names may appear, in internet terms a single digit apart makes all the difference. Domain name registers have been constructed on the basis of first come, first served. Inevitably therefore there has been a scramble for attractive domain names, which has been complicated by the fact that <prince.com> and <prinz.com> can each be held, and by persons entirely unconnected. In many cases the competition has been between persons who have good reason to want the particular verbal form. It is necessarily increased by the fact that domain names, unlike trade marks, are not limited to particular goods or services in trade. Indeed, domain names are used by many who are not trading at all. The names may lead to websites or chatrooms for enthusiasts for (or critics against) anything or anybody under the sun.

20–92 The internet is an extraordinary pathway to the sharing of ideas of innumerable kinds. As a result, there are many closely similar names which a registrant can have unless exactly the same is already registered. Partly, however, the scramble involves those who seek to grab a name with some commercial or celebrity status so that it can be sold on to the person or firm or other organisation with the status. Early tales of very large sums being made out of such cyber-squatting brought a cloud of operators eager for similar pickings, which were to be made on the modest outlay of a registration fee.[314] The result was a cyber-market in domain names, only part of which involved the operations of identifiable cyber-squatters. Against them, however, established individuals and organisations were insistent that there should be some form of effective recourse.

20–93 In 1998 ICANN (Internet Corporation for Assigned Numbers and

313 See the list in Chapman and Holmén [2006] E.I.P.R. 315.

314 Registrations are, however, renewable on payment. So a firm which faces a cyber-squatter may choose to sit the temporary blockage out. On the other hand, squatters may watch for the failure of "legitimate" holders to re-register and jump in themselves.

Names) became the registrant body for the major generic TLDs (<.com>, <.org>, <.int>, etc.). All who register domain names and those who take over their registrations do so under a contractual relationship which gives ICANN power to vary the terms in various ways. Accordingly it was able to establish relations with other independent bodies for adjudicating disputes over domain name registrations and to bind registrants to accept this jurisdiction. The process is governed by its Uniform Domain Name Dispute Resolution Policy (UDRP) and Rules.[315]

The adjudication service which has come to be used most widely is that of WIPO.[316] If a domain name holder is found disentitled under that Policy to retain it, in most cases the registering body will be ordered to transfer it into the name of the complainant. In practice the proceedings are conducted entirely over the internet, the adjudicators being appointed from a published list of independent experts from round the world.[317] A complaint can usually be dealt with within three months and is mostly cheaper than litigation in court. There is provision for either a one-person or a three-person tribunal, the latter at either party's request; but there is no appeal within the system. However, if litigation is begun within 10 days of receiving an order that the domain name is to be transferred or removed, then the order will be stayed for the duration of the litigation and will be subject to its outcome.[318]

In only three years there have been many thousands of complaints han- **20–94**
dled through this system and it has been accepted rapidly by business communities. Even those who abhor the conversion of the internet into a business medium have mostly directed their ire elsewhere than towards this novel juridical device.

The phenomenon—and it deserves that name—is fascinating on two counts. It has generated substantive rules, through its case law, as well as the policy itself. The policy encourages a synthetic approach by empowering panels to apply "any rules and principles of law that it deems applicable".

---

[315] Much therefore turns on the precise construction of the service. For the state of play, see, e.g. WIPO Survey (above, para.20–52, n.200), 54–58 and Willoughby (2009) 4 J.I.P.L.P. 714. For the evolution of the UDRP, Maher (2002) 33 I.I.C. 924.

[316] Other UDRP services are currently provided by the National Arbitration Forum (NAF) and in China, the CPR Institute. The recent additions to gTLDs (<.biz>, etc.) have been subject to the UDRP, with some special transitional provisions. A few national domain name registration authorities have adopted the UDRP. Others, such as the UK body, Nominet, which issues the <.uk>; domains, have set up their own adjudicatory panels, largely on the same lines as the ICANN UDRP, but with some interesting variations in the grounds for intervention: see Bettinger (above, n.311). Note that following the Digital Economy Act 2010, ss.124O-Q was inserted into the Communications Act 2003, granting the Secretary of State certain powers over internet domain registries where they misuse internet domain names or do not have adequate arrangements in place to deal with complaints in connection with internet domain names.

[317] The adjudication service nominates the panellist or panellists in most cases, but there are provisions in Supplemental Rules for challenge by the domain name holder (i.e. the alleged cyber-squatter).

[318] As to the very limited conditions which can justify an unsuccessful complainant's second complaint concerning the same domain name, see, e.g. Cases D2000–0703, D2000–1490.

Equally it is built upon procedural arrangements which strive to provide justice which is fair, as well as being rapid and cheap. Three substantive conditions, laid down in the UDRP, define what the complainant must show:

(i) the domain name must be identical or confusingly similar to a trade mark in which the complainant has rights;
(ii) the respondent must have no rights or legitimate interests in the domain name; and
(iii) the domain name must have been registered and be used in bad faith.

20–95 While these principles are a reflection of a shared approach in most legal systems to deliberately wrongful misrepresentation of indications of source, it does not follow the precise rules of any one legal system. Fundamentally that is because the comparison which has to be made is in essence different. In a dispute over the use of trade marks or names, the claimant is usually concerned to show misrepresentation relating to the defendant's use of the mark on the same or similar goods or services.[319] But a domain name is not tied to trade in anything in particular or indeed to any obligation to use it.

The boldest cyber-squatters offer no apology for acquiring the domain name simply in order to sell it to the enterprise or person whose name is being taken in vain.[320] Others may offer an excuse from a range of ingenious justifications. Deciding how far these must be treated as genuine is a recurrent reason why UDRP adjudication can be far from straightforward. Some of these pleas we shall see as we examine the three conditions in more depth.[321]

20–96 First, *the claimant's right to a mark and confusion with it*.[322] It is accepted that the right may arise through protection of a trading reputation (by passing off or unfair competition) as well as by registration. But a panel may look carefully at claims where the mark is, for instance, descriptive. Evidence for this, which complainants may be coy about revealing, may appear from the fact that applications to register the mark have not been made or are not progressing.[323] The claimant may succeed where a case of unfair competition or passing off can be shown to exist, for example, from long established or heavily advertised trade or other activity. It is over such matters that the scheme is at its most eclectic: the result is a supra-national body of precedent which is rapidly burgeoning.

[319] Where the law goes further and gives a wider remedy against dilution onto dissimilar goods or services, that is based on proof of the claimant's actual trading reputation and the damage that is likely to flow from the dilution.
[320] They may of course offer it on a site selling domain names—no doubt hoping for another cyber-squatter to buy it.
[321] Against such conduct, a Panel may make a declaratory order, which may help to drive away an unjustified complaint.
[322] The right may be that of a licensee as well as a mark-owner.
[323] D2000–0193 (*f1.com*).

It is also accepted that such "common law rights" may be those of celebrities, such as pop stars, authors and sportsmen, since they will at least have rights in the primary goods or services which they are involved in offering.[324] It is sometimes said that this goes further than, for instance, English law, which has been reluctant to protect a celebrity's ability to endorse the goods or services of others.[325] But that is to forget that a domain name is not tied to the making and marking of particular goods and services. Most of the celebrities who have succeeded under the UDRP have a "trade" connection with the primary goods (books, records, films) or services (singing, modelling, footballing) which make them famous. Whether the same can be said of municipal authorities or other public bodies which claim rights in the name of their town or region is much more questionable, even if they hold a mark registration.[326] One issue is who should be allowed to succeed (particularly in securing a transfer of the domain name) when there are several potential complainants.[327] **20–97**

As to probability of confusion, the global character of the internet poses various problems. Who are the public who are likely to be confused by a domain name? It has been held to be any group of substantial size within a country as well as a region or language group. The issue has arisen particularly over "gripe sites" for airing complaints about well-known enterprises and individuals. Any American knows that *walmartsucks.com* is unlikely to lead to an official Walmart site, but will Greeks, Ethiopians or Phillippinos? Some panellists take the view that because the internet is global, there is a relevant danger of confusion.[328] Others consider this far-fetched.[329] Since there is no appellate jurisdiction to settle the difference, only resort to national litigation, or an alteration of the present UDRP, could take the matter further. It is scarcely satisfactory that the result of a particular case can so evidently depend upon the choice of panellist or panellists. **20–98**

Secondly, *a right or legitimate interest of the respondent*. The UDRP states that the respondent can make this out by showing: (i) that he has used the domain name, or made genuine preparations to use it, for a genuine website; (ii) that he or it is commonly known by the name; or (iii) that he is making a **20–99**

[324] WIPO D2000–0235 (*jeanettewinterson.com*): the respondent, lecturer in a certain university, was seeking a percentage of the author's royalties as his price. He held a clutch of similar domains. See also D2000–0210 (*juliaroberts.com*); D2000–0794 (*sade.com*); cf. D2000–0596 (*sting.com*), where there was no evidence to support the complainant's position.

[325] At least until recently: above, paras 17–33—17–35.

[326] As in WIPO D2001–0505 (*barcelona.com*). This was ordered to be transferred to the City of Barcelona. At least in this instance the City held a number of trade mark registrations. There have been discussions about whether the UDRP should have separate rules to cover such names but no action has been taken. Another contentious area which is hard to regulate is the use of descriptive words. Pharmaceutical companies have been acquiring the generic names of their drugs as domains in order to attract attention via search engines.

[327] WIPO, in its second review of the Process, recommended that no extension to geographical names in general should be introduced.

[328] See, e.g. WIPO D2000–0584 (*dixonssucks.com*); WIPO D2002–115 (*bayersucks.org, etc.*).

[329] e.g. WIPO D2002–0857 (*asdasucks.com*).

legitimate non-commercial or fair use of the domain name, without intent, for commercial gain, to divert internet users or tarnish the complainant's mark. Justifications under one or other of these heads play prominent parts in contested UDRP cases, but they need to be more than unsupported assertions. Some of the submissions are dismissed as disingenuous or fantastic. This may well be the fate of assertions that the name is the nickname of the respondent or a family member,[330] or is the name of some event, individual or character associated somehow with them.[331] The same may happen when a claim to be running a business is not shown to have any substance.[332]

20–100 Where the respondent asserts an intention to set up a site commenting on the complainant—by way either of adulation (a fanclub) or of criticism (a commercial gripesite, political opposition)—it is particularly important to recognise any genuine claim to freedom of expression, given its status as a human right. Claims of that kind deserve very careful attention.[333] They can scarcely be sustained where a respondent has collected an array of domain names, which he is offering to the targeted enterprises in order to save them from the domain falling into the hands of someone else who might actually set up a site for spoofs, parodies, complaints, exposés or denunciations.[334]

20–101 Thirdly, *bad faith both in registering and using*. Here the policy makes explicit that "use" has a broad meaning. It covers situations where: (i) the domain name has been obtained primarily for the purpose of selling it to the complainant or a competitor for a sum exceeding out-of-pocket costs[335]; (ii) where the registration is in order to prevent the complainant from reflecting its mark in that domain name or to disrupt its business; and (iii) where it was registered in order to try to divert internet users to the respondent's website by creating a likelihood of confusion. Each of these types of use has in turn been read inclusively. Under (i), advertising the domain as being for sale on an auction website can satisfy the condition.[336] Under (ii), it is not necessary to show that the complainant has been deprived of all possible domains. Evidence that it has appropriated many of them merely reinforces the proof of mala fides.

20–102 Under (iii), there is a difficult question: when, in the process of discovering a website, then clicking on to it and scrolling its pages, can sufficient probability of confusion be said to arise? A search engine looking for

---

330 One respondent asserted (without proof) that he had changed his own name to "Oxford University": D2000–0308 (*oxforduniversity.com*).

331 In D2000–0847, the respondent had purchased <madonna.com>; for $20,000. When subject to complaint by the singer, he claimed to be negotiating to transfer the domain name to the Madonna Hospital for Rehabilitation, Lincoln, Nebraska; but he was not believed.

332 e.g. D2001–0907 (*talalabugazaleh.com*).

333 However, high rhetoric and prolixity do not necessarily carry the day: e.g. WIPO D2000–1838 (*celinedion.com*).

334 e.g. D2000–0636 (*natwestsucks.com*).

335 Or for free education at a university: D2000–0366 (*uwyoming.com*, etc.).

336 D2000–0596 (*dodialfayed.com*).

the main word in the gTLD may produce a great splay of sites. Internet users soon learn that many of them will not be an "official" site. Their true nature will generally be clear from the home page at the site itself, or sometimes only by moving further into the site. If users are led by the name to what turns out to be a comment site which is judged to be a legitimate outlet for opinion, this cannot be a bad faith holding of the name. On the other hand, if the site proves to be a sales outlet for other goods than the complainant's, the temporary uncertainty between finding the site and perusing it is likely to be treated as showing bad faith. Here too there are uncertainties and inconsistencies at work.

UDRP jurisdiction has been heavily used in its early years: WIPO alone **20–103**
has handled some 17,500 cases since 1999.[337] Across the world established businesses have readily accepted the results. Of a handful of critical analyses, some raise issues of real concern, particularly that some panellists have been unduly ready, either to accept the complainant's account of the situation or to stretch the terms of the policy beyond any acceptable limits.[338] It is true that the only means of questioning a decision is to bring proceedings in an appropriate national court, and that has happened only on a handful of occasions.[339] The phenomenon of "reverse hijacking" has been acknowledged as a hazard: inevitably some complaints will turn out to be illegitimate attempts, based on fabricated evidence or wholly unjustified assertions, to oblige domain holders to pay up or suffer transfer. Panels have been given power to declare against a complainant. Respondents rarely seek to have them exercise their powers and much more rarely still is a finding against a complainant successful.[340]

On balance, however, the confidence which the policy has generated seems justified.[341] The jurisdiction deserves comparison with the other "internal" solution to disputes which the internet is generating: the Notice-and-Take-Down procedures for controlling improper content on the internet by requiring site-closure or changes through the intervention of the Internet Service Provider.[342] In the United States at least this is proving one method of mass action against copyright and other infringement which is affecting the balance of power between right-owners and their opponents. It too is capable of over-enthusiastic application: for instance where a site is closed down even though it makes legitimate material available as well as material that infringes copyright (or is defamatory or pornographic, etc.).

337 This includes cases under the cognate policies which it handles. See *http://www.wipo.int/amc/en/domains/statistics* for details.

338 e.g. Mueller, *Rough Justice* (2001); Lipton (2005) 40 Wake Forest L.R. 1361; cf. Geist (2002) 27 Brook. J. Intl. L. 903, where the statistical analysis of outcomes fails to bring into account the distinction between contested and uncontested complaints.

339 Arguably there should be an appeal system within the UDRP itself; but that is likely to be resisted since it would complicate a simple and cheap procedure.

340 See Mueller, above, n.338.

341 See Kur, *UDRP: a Study* (2002).

342 Above, para.20–62.

20–104 The two schemes use the internet to police its operation, with effects for the system across the globe. Both open prospects of mass action which cannot be expected of litigation through national court systems. They affect very different sorts of internet operator. Notice and Take Down is typically aimed at free sharing: the P2P site which provides access to music, films and the like without having to pay the right-owner's subscription to an authorised service. The root intention is not to make money (though that may become a indirect motivation). Many free sharers find it simplest to submit to the take down and to set up again under a new name. The domain name appropriator, on the other hand, is in the business of selling particular names and will have no chance of regaining his asset if it is transferred away to a person entitled to object to a bad faith operation. That is why the UDRP and like jurisdictions are in practice so much more contentious; and why the need to oversee the fairness of the adjudicative process will remain important as long as this form of name-squatting persists.

(2) Adwords

20–105 Search engines enable users to navigate through the vast quantities of information available on the internet and, on the back of this tool, search engine operators, such as Google and Yahoo!, have built advertising business models. One of these models is selling advertising keywords, i.e. "adwords", which are purchased by businesses so that whenever a third party carries out a search including the keyword/s, an advertising link to the website of the business will appear in a separate section of the search results page (known as a "sponsored link"). Advertisers will pay for use of the adword each time a user clicks on the sponsored link and is taken to the advertiser's website (known as a "cost per click" basis).[343] Trade mark proprietors have objected to search engine operators selling adwords that correspond to their registered trade marks, particularly where the purchasers of adwords are selling counterfeit, non-legitimate or competing goods. This issue has been considered in the United Kingdom in *Wilson v Yahoo! UK*.[344] The case involved the sale of adwords which corresponded to the claimant's Community trade mark "Mr Spicy", registered for certain foods and food services. When the words "Mr Spicy" were typed into the search engine, sponsored links to the websites of Sainsbury's supermarket and Pricegrabber.com would appear. The defendants sought summary judgment against the claimant, which was granted by Morgan J. The judge held that the defendants had not used the trade mark and that, assuming

---

[343] More than one person can purchase an adword. The position in which a sponsored link is listed in the search results page will depend on how much a person is willing to pay "cost per click".

[344] *Wilson v Yahoo! UK* [2008] E.T.M.R. 33; see Vranaki [2008] Comm. Law 135.

they had, not in a way that affected its ability to function as a badge of origin.[345]

The decision in *Wilson v Yahoo! UK* is by no means the definitive word on this issue,[346] not least because of the recent ECJ ruling in the joined *Google France*[347] cases, along with references to the ECJ from the English High Court in *L'Oréal v eBay*[348] and *Interflora v Marks & Spencer*.[349] The claimants in the *Google France* cases brought actions against the search engine operator for its adwords service. They complained that the sale of adwords corresponding to their trade marks was leading to sponsored links to businesses that either sold counterfeit products or were competitors of the claimants. The Cour de Cassation referred several questions to the ECJ, including some which essentially asked whether Google France was liable for trade mark infringement. The ECJ ruled that an internet referencing service provider (such as Google France) which stores, as a keyword, a sign identical with a trade mark and organises the display of advertisements on the basis of that keyword does not use the sign within the meaning of art.5 of the Trade Marks Directive or art.9 of the CTMR Regulation but rather allows its clients to use the signs.[350] However, the court further ruled that the advertisers who use keywords identical to registered trade marks to advertise identical goods or services in the context of an internet referencing service are liable for infringement within art.5 of the Trade Marks Directive or art.9(1)(a) of the CTMR Regulation where an average internet user cannot ascertain whether the advertiser is a third party or economically linked to the trade mark proprietor.[351] In other words, although operating an adwords system is not unlawful per se, users of the system may well be infringing trade marks, in which case the overall viability of the system is likely to be undermined. 20–106

[345] *Wilson v Yahoo! UK* [2008] E.T.M.R. 33, paras 58–66.

[346] Somewhat optimistically, Google changed its adword policy in the UK and Ireland from May 5, 2008 as a result of this decision so that it no longer blocks keywords that correspond to registered trade marks. Google does, however, block the use of trade marks in the sponsored link. For details see *Interflora v Marks & Spencer* [2009] R.P.C. 22.

[347] Joined Cases 236/08 to 238/08 *Google France v Louis Vuitton; Google France v Viaticum; Google France v CNRRH* Judgment of the Court (Grand Chamber) March 23, 2010. For a discussion pre-ruling see Shemtov [2008] E.I.P.R. 470; Ventose (2010) 5 J.I.P.L.P. 74; post-ruling see Singleton (2010) 174 C.L. & J. 203.

[348] *L'Oréal v eBay* [2009] R.P.C. 21.

[349] *Interflora v Marks & Spencer* [2009] R.P.C. 22.

[350] *Google France* cases (n.347, above), paras 55–59.

[351] *Google France* cases (n.347, above), para.30.

CHAPTER 21

INTELLECTUAL PROPERTY IN BIOTECHNOLOGY

1. INTRODUCTION

(1) A half-century of modern biotechnology

Biotechnology has become a new and challenging technique for established industries and for specialist entrants. Crops may be genetically manipulated at every level from the specific variety to the genus or species, in order to improve their commercial qualities or to make them resistant to insects or diseases or herbicides which can then be used on surrounding weeds. The environmental dangers that their release may engender remain a cause of public anxiety, however much politicians may back manufacturers. Yet improvements in yield may be a great boon to poor countries, so long at least as the new plant materials are not unduly expensive and are not unfairly tied to a need to buy new stock each year because the material is not capable of self-reproduction. **21–01**

Animal stock can likewise be improved. The cloning of the whole animals has raised scientific interest and horrified sections of the public. The growing of organs for transplantation, even into humans, promises an answer to the shortage of natural products taken from bodies. More generally, research into the causes, diagnosis and treatment of diseases and other conditions is leading to discoveries of their genetic origins and some knowledge of how complex the issues of causation can be. Just as the industries themselves are in a process of remarkable evolution, so intellectual property is also having to adapt in major ways. This chapter concentrates primarily on the impact of human genetics on IPRs, above all on the patent system. So it is in the nature of a case study.

(2) Biological basis[1]

21–02 Biotechnology is the "engineering" of genetic material towards practical ends such as medical and veterinary advances, modified crops and improved animal breeds. It has been built up from a series of great biological revelations of our era: first, in 1953, Crick and Watson's unravelling of the structure of DNA (deoxyribonucleic acid) as the informational basis for all the proteins required by living matter; then the experiments in the period 1970–1973 which demonstrated bacterial enzymes capable of cutting DNA at specific sites and also the splicing of DNA segments into foreign DNA to create *recombinant* molecules with altered functions; and in our own time the mapping of the human genome, which emerged in 2001 in draft form after a decade of massive research—in its latter stages nakedly competitive.

Crick and Watson in Cambridge, just ahead of Linus Paulin in California, demonstrated the celebrated double helix of DNA, made up from the four bases: adenine (A); cytosine (C); guanine (G); and thymine (T). These bases are held together by hydrogen bonds in complementary pairs: A with T, C with G. Each species of animal and plant has its own genetic identity in its DNA, the whole constituting its genome. In complex cells (eukaryotes), parts of the DNA strands are genes, which act as biological instructors to the whole entity, and parts are non-functional. The coding sequence of genes are called exons (for expressed regions), whereas their untranslated intervening sequences are known as introns.

From the 1960s genetic science set out to locate genes along the DNA strands of a genome; and to determine how they could be made to express their cognate proteins, since it is by proteins that many biological changes are affected in a life-form. Above all, the aim has been to discover their functions as codes for biological effects around the whole genome, since from that may come medical benefits in the form of diagnoses and therapies, improvements in animals and plants and the transplantation of genes and even organs from one species to another.

For some time the process of identifying genes was difficult and laborious, even though an increasing number of research teams undertook the work

[1] For a more complete introduction, directed to IPR debates, see Nicol (2005) 29 Melbourne U.L.R. 809.

around the world.[2] In the 1970s, recombinant DNA technology emerged. DNA is first *transcribed* by separating the two strands of the double helix. The enzyme, RNA polymerase, then binds to one strand, the coding strand, and synthesises an RNA (ribonucleic acid) which is complementary to the strand of DNA. Splicing of this RNA to remove introns gives rise to mRNA (messenger RNA). The mRNA produced can then be used to synthesise complementary DNA (cDNA) using the enzyme, reverse transcriptase. The cDNA molecules can be inserted into vectors that are efficiently expressed in other hosts such as bacteria, plants and animals.

As the cDNA is produced from mRNA, which has been stripped of introns, the cDNA does not contain introns. Accordingly it is a laboratory construct. In a suitable host cell cDNA can be made to express a protein—the gene product which is coded for by the gene. That however is a considerable simplification, for, as is now appreciated much more clearly, proteins take differing shapes, depending in part on the effect of particular SNPs (single neucleotide polymorphisms) which occur elsewhere in the DNA. In the 1980s progress in identifying genes picked up and indeed led to the first therapeutic products of genetic engineering,[3] as well as genetic modification of plants and animals with significant commercial potential.[4] These developments furnished the first biotechnological patents worth fighting about.

(3) The HGP and its politics

From 1990 the Human Genome Project (HGP) began as an immense research collaboration between public researchers in the United States and Europe. Genes and gene fragments came to be identified in larger quantities. A spate of patent applications on the DNA sequences and part sequences followed, together with many attendant claims for their cloning and expression as proteins. The utility of these inventions tended to be vaguely identified as, for instance, "a scientific probe for the discovery of genes or expressed sequence tags". A second wave of applications has followed as the human genome map speeded up towards its draft publication. The change of pace grew out of a scientific difference of opinion about how the mapping should proceed. Public sector contributors to the HGP continued their steady, detailed analysis. Led by Dr Craig Venter, proponent of a more rapid analytic approach (the whole genome shot-gun),[5] a group of **21–03**

---

[2] See further below, paras 21–06 et seq.

[3] Such as the protein, t-PA (an anti-blood clotting factor) which was litigated in *Genentech v Wellcome Foundation* [1989] R.P.C. 147 CA; and erythropoeitin litigated in various countries, including the UK: see *Kirin-Amgen v Hoechst Marion Roussel* [2006] R.P.C. 9 HL.

[4] See, for example, the cases discussed below, paras 21–10, 21–11.

[5] This random sequencing method involves breaking the entire genome into hundreds of thousands of random clones. After each clone is sequenced, the fragments are reassembled into their proper order using pattern-recognition software.

collaborators spun away from the HGP to set up commercial rivals with private finance.

A bitter controversy has existed ever since over the relative achievements of the two camps. The Clinton-Blair Declaration of February 2001, which in effect introduced publication of the first drafts of two versions of the human genome map, awarded the victor's crown to neither. What was apparent by that date was the extensive use that was being made of the US and European patent systems to mark out monopoly positions along the genetic chain that might lead to medical advances. By the end of 1999, the corporation behind the Venter initiative, Celera, had filed US applications for some 6,500 "preliminary patents" over partial sequences of the human genome. Other biotechnology corporations were following suit. In Europe, there were signs of the same phenomenon, though they were more modest in scale.[6]

The advance of genetics since the 1990s shifted the frontiers of the rapidly evolving discipline. In particular, much of the former hard labour of identifying genes, their associated proteins, the receptors through which they enter cells and the pathways they pursue, has ceased to be a matter of laboratory searching. Genome maps are now available for various animal and plants and the number is mounting rapidly. Computational genetic searches, for such matters as gene identification between different species of animal, and for variations in the genetic make-up of individuals through automated micro-arrays, are increasing the role of bio-informatics using giant computers. Knowledge of the biological function or functions of individual genes allows changes in cell types and tissues to be monitored, showing, for instance the presence of tumours or susceptibilities to cancer.[7]

(4) Public and private research in biotechnology

21–04 The cost of biotechnological research is mostly very large and from the early stages investors turned to IPRs—and above all to the patent system—in the hopes of underpinning their investment. Much of the work was done in universities and public research institutes, and the prospects for biotechnological inventions became a motivating factor in establishing and building up their own Technology Transfer Offices. In one form or another in the United States, Europe and the Far East, the funding was by Government, research charities, interested industries and venture capitalists. Accordingly their attitudes towards commercial returns and patenting have varied widely. Many in academic science and medical research have shown a deep-seated antipathy towards exclusive rights that prejudice free and

[6] See below, para.21–20.

[7] Typically this is achieved by high-throughput screening in which a microarray of nucleic acid probes is immobilised on a solid substrate, each probe having the ability to bind to its cognate partner in given mRNA in a complex mRNA expression mixture.

immediate access to basic knowledge of biological functioning.[8] However, the march of commercial investment in biotechnology has become inexorable. The result is at present a diverse industrial structure. The odds on striking a truly valuable product or test are still long. Some leading pharmaceutical producers have remained chary of the risks, though now they are entering parts of the field. A few specialist biotech operations are already very profitable, and beside them are a phalanx of companies which are themselves prospectors or provide specialist services to others. At all levels, patents are being sought, often in the hope of income from licensing to others. To an increasing extent this is being backed by threats of litigation and actual suits.

A longer-term aim, particularly for small ventures, is to be bought out by a major firm. In that process any patent holding is likely to be assessed for its potential rather than its achievement. Likewise, for those which attain stock exchange listing as a public company, patents may well be read as important indicators, perhaps affecting share prices in a measure often out of proportion to their actual significance. As "dot-commery" demonstrated all too starkly, most speculators have a primitive notion of what IPRs are for and so exaggerate them as signs either of success or of failure. They may regard patents as guarantees that health services will buy the products; they may treat the very instigation of legal proceedings for revocation as a reason for depressing share prices. In politics, the level of appreciation may be not much more sophisticated. Patents may be welcomed not as an incentive for actual R & D, or the eventual improvement in life-form products and the associated growth of employment, but rather as a simple, immediate stimulus to the market in shares and would-be confidence in the national economy.

(5) Growth of patents for biotechnological inventions[9]

The relatively advanced state of biotechnology in the United States means **21–05** that there is more gene patenting there at present than in other countries. However it is estimated that more than 5,000 applications were made to the EPO in 2000, of which 40 per cent were for micro-organisms, plants and

[8] See Nuffield Council on Bioethics, *The Ethics of Patenting DNA* (2002); Royal Society, *Keeping Science Open* (2003); Eisenberg (2002) 77 Ac.Medicine 1381.

[9] See Ducor, *Patenting the Recombinant Products of Biotechnology* (1998); Grubb, *Patents for Chemicals, Pharmaceuticals and Biotechnology* 4th edn (1999); Warren-Jones, *Patenting Recombinant DNA* (2001); Schatz (1998) 29 I.I.C. 2; ; Bostyn [1999] I.P.Q. 1; Breyer (2000) 28 J. L, Med and Science 23: Holman and Munzer (2000) 85 Iowa L.R. 735; Laurie (2001) June, Sc. & Pub. Affairs 10; Gitter (2001) 76 NYU L.R. 1623; Kirby (2001) Aust. I.P.J. 61; Nicol and Nielsen (2001) 23 Sydney L.R. 347; Barton (2002) 33 I.I.C. 779 ; OECD, *Expert Workshop on Genetic Inventions, IPRs and Licensing Practice* (2002); Dutfield, *Intellectual Property rights and the Life science Industries* (2003); Australian Law Reform Commission, *genes and Ingfenuity* (2004); WHO, *Genetics, Genomics and the Patenting of DNA* (2005); Nicol, above n.1; Berman and Dreyfuss, (2006) 53 UCLA Law *Review* 871; Rimmer, *Intellectual Property and Biotechnology* (2008).

animals; while 60 per cent were for human and animal DNA sequences, or for new gene therapies and medicines, or for both. In 1997, the figure was only some 2,000 applications. It takes time for those applications to work through, some being abandoned and some rejected in the examination process. There are, however, signs that relatively few of them are blossoming into granted patents.[10]

Nonetheless the level of patenting activity has induced widespread concern. The wave of mistrust is widespread and timely. The protest comes not just from utopians who seek some pre- or post-industrial world for the exploration of new science. It expresses the belief of genetic researchers that substantial space must be left for basic discoveries because they need to be shared at once by all who contribute to the great and growing corpus of knowledge.[11] This would leave the patent incentive for private capital to those developments that are proximate to medical and other procedures of practical benefit.

The antipathy against patents at every step has been in part provoked by the expansion of patent systems to accommodate production monopolies over pharmaceuticals and agro-chemicals in general. Patents are undeniably one foundation of industrial structure in those fields. That development has contributed notably to the "proprietorial" belief that patents are an economic tool which should be applied to "everything under the sun made by man". Particularly in IPR circles, chemical substances made up in the laboratory have become increasingly patentable for their medicinal properties; so why not treat artificially reconstituted genetic material in the same way? The analogy can seem straightforward. It is summed up in the view that industrially produced genetic material or other gene-based product involves nothing other than chemical molecules, and so is the same as pharmaceuticals or weedkillers or the like.

We need to distinguish two issues. First, should there be any patent protection at all for life-forms? Secondly, if so, who should benefit from broad patents, who from narrow patents, and who should be left out? In an industry as disparate as biotechnology, much is made to turn on the second issue, but the first cannot be ignored. The questions appear to pull apart. But note their capacity to elide. However they are approached (e.g. on the question of how discovery is to be distinguished from invention) the tendency is to admit that there must be some role for patents. The need to induce private organisations and individuals to engage in costly, speculative research is too great to ignore. Once that admission is made, the competition to be able to patent sets in and much of the argument becomes over the capacity of the system to maintain acceptable boundaries between competitors.

---

[10] See below, para.21–20.

[11] This has been the prevalent, but by no means the only, approach within the Human Genome Project. See Sulston and Ferry, *The Common Thread* (2002).

2. Patent Systems and Bioethics

The proper use of patents and other IPRs in relation to genetic research has created an absorbing and difficult debate. Ethical arguments are invoked, but from perspectives which may embrace normative standards of many varieties. They may derive from religious teaching, philosophical idealism, epistomelogical perceptions, environmental imperatives, social and cultural specificities, economic and other utilitarian desiderata or the experience embodied in rules and procedures of legal systems. Obviously these include the standard consequentialist justifications for the patent system: that innnovation is a necessary economic desideratum and it is encouraged by the incentive of exclusivity and the information flow that patent systems provide.[12] **21–06**

In 2002, the Nuffield Council on Bioethics produced a Discussion Paper on *The Ethics of Patenting DNA* which concentrated much of its attention on the capacity of legal norms already embedded in patent laws to react to assertions that patents were being granted for the wrong research, or for too many overlapping claims, or for monopolies which were disproportionate to their inventive contribution as disclosed in the patent. This may appear to have little to do with ethical debate,[13] but only if that notion refers to one or other set of idealistic norms. Here we shall try to follow the practical lead which the Nuffield Paper provides, since it seems appropriate to a book about the operations of intellectual property systems from their legal foundations.

Many of the issues to be discussed address the fundamental division between a theory of the patent system as strictly a mechanism for enhancing socio-economic functioning at a national, regional or global level, and a theory which retains some place for rewarding individual intellectual contribution. The first prefers to grant core rights to one person, however arbitrary that result may be, because of the unique efficiency of individual ownership as an incentive to realising technological potential. The second is much readier to recognise comparative claims of contributors or to insist upon free exchange of information as part of a competitive environment unimpeded by the IPRs.

We start therefore with two basic principles of European patent law which have evolved over two centuries of experience. The first concerns its limitation to the protection of inventions, as distinct from discoveries, which is marked by the need to show a sufficiently proximate technical application. The second turns to the exclusion from patentability of inventions which it would be contrary to public policy or morality to exploit commercially.

---

[12] In reviewing the EU Biotechnology Directive of 1998, the European Commission emphasises the importance of these objectives in maintaining a European biotechnology industry which can compete with the American: Report (below, n.25).

[13] cf. Crespi [2002] CIPA Journal 255, placing emphasis on the value of the legal inheritance.

(1) Discovery and invention

21–07 Patent laws everywhere protect "invention", as distinct from "discovery, scientific theory or mathematical method", as the EPC expresses it.[14] At what point along a line of research does an addition to scientific knowledge become sufficiently connected with functional outcomes to rank as invention, rather than discovery? The question has become acute in connection with the mapping of the human genome. There it is enmeshed with the basic dislike of treating humans (and so their genetic make-up) as the subject of property rights, an inclination which simply does not have the same force for most people when it comes to animals, let alone plants.[15]

We have no difficulty in treating basic scientific analyses which trigger a whole new field of technical endeavour as real turning points in the march of science—as with Crick and Watson's demonstration of the helical structure of DNA. The basic scientist will enjoy the fame of the discovery. It may lead to academic advancement, honours and prizes, the status and authority of a major contributor to human understanding. But that of itself does not explain why patents are reserved for subsequent, more practical, applications of basic theory. A variety of answers can be posited, none of them entirely satisfying:

(1) All scientific advances emerge from a base of pre-existing knowledge. The continuing process of theoretical investigation and experimental testing demands that each contribution, once published, should be open to others to build upon, because the free exchange of knowledge is too great a value to be compromised by inhibitions on its immediate adoption for all purposes.[16]
(2) Basic knowledge may have manifold practical applications. Therefore to grant IP over it (and particularly a patent, with its effect against all third parties) could furnish commercial monopolies of inordinate compass, conferring the power to control other people's activities as well as to extract financial returns on a scale that could be utterly disportionate, even when constricted by the maximum patent term.[17]
(3) Scientific knowledge of natural phenomena of all kinds is in a sense waiting to be discovered, and there will be moments when a number

[14] EPC art.52(2); PA 1977 s.1(2); TRIPS Agreement art.27; cf. above, para.5–54.
[15] Note, however, the position taken by a bare majority of the Canadian Supreme Court that the older expression "manner of manufacture" excludes all higher life forms (including plants and seeds) from patentability: *Harvard College v Commissioner of Patents* [2004] 2 S.C.R. 45; cf. the same court's view (this time by bare majority the other way) that claims to genes, vectors and plant cells are to be allowed and that they are infringed by using the cells to grow plants: *Monsanto Canada v Schmeiser* [2004] 1 S.C.R. 902.
[16] The same value leads to a generous exception for experimental use in European patent law (but not in the US): see below, para.21–18.
[17] Often enough the time gap between basic perceptions and practical results will be longer than the patent period. That seems equally likely with the medical potentials of genes.

of leaders in a science compete to solve a particular puzzle. To reward the first to produce a convincing analysis with a patent that would apply to all subsequent practical applications would provide a wholly inappropriate market opportunity, which among other things could impose undesirable constraints on investors in those developments. A patent system may be based very largely on a competitive incentive to all would-be risk takers, but it cannot obliterate all concern for justice to individuals.

(4) The present approach obliges scientists and their collaborators to carry through their work to the applied stage before the patent incentive becomes available to them. The system thus strives to ensure that the social and economic potential of the science is derived from it sooner rather than later, and that is a prime objective of its very existence.

Those who nonetheless favour the commodification of knowledge tend towards a broad interpretation of "invention" at the expense of "discovery". Thus in medicinal chemistry, it became common after World War II to treat as patentable the disclosure of a novel organic molecule whose practical value lay purely as a research step.[18] The compound could be claimed as an intermediate in the manufacture of other compounds which in turn might well prove to have direct medical uses, even though these were not yet known.[19] It was this attitude, a consequence of the pharmacological revolution of the post-World War II decades, which raised the prospect of early patenting of human genetic material so as to cover even partial indicators of the presence of genes, when they began to be identified (notably ESTs—expressed sequence tags).

The position which the European Community eventually reached in 1998 was not to remove genetics from patentable subject matter (though certain categories of subject matter, which could embrace biotechnological invention, such as plant and animal varieties, remained outside the frame).[20] According to the long-contested Biotechnology Directive: **21–08**

[18] Above, paras 5–21 et seq.

[19] In the UK, see *Smith's Applications* [1971] R.P.C. 31; thus the issue is one on which any Herchel Smith Professor should be cautious in expressing criticism!

[20] Directive art.4, following EPC art.55(b). At the same time, the exclusion of essentially biological processes for producing plants and animals is confined to crossing and selecting (see the Directive art.2(2)). This makes an interesting comparison with the Supreme Court of Canada's decision (by a close majority) to refuse, under the Canadian Patent Act 1952, to allow claims to the Harvard Oncomouse (see below, para.21–10). While the fertilised mouse ovum, manipulated to increase its susceptibility to cancer, would have been patentable, a claim to the mouse thereafter bred in a surrogate mother did not fall within the term "manufacture or composition of matter". The decision can thus be understood narrowly; but there can be little doubt that the majority saw such difficulties arising out of such an extension of the system as to require that first there should be legislative change. Their view may therefore boost the campaigning of objectors.

(1) The fact that an invention concerns either a product consisting of or containing biological material or an associated process is expressly declared not to place it outside the scope of patenting; in particular it may concern biological material isolated from its natural environment by a technical process, as distinct from its occurrence in nature: art.3(1).
(2) To this there is one categorical exception: the human body, at the various stages of its formation and development, cannot be patented; this includes the simple discovery of one of its elements, including the sequence or partial sequence of a gene: art.5(1).
(3) Nonetheless there may be a patent for an element isolated from the human body or otherwise produced by means of a technical process, including the sequence or partial sequence of a gene, even if identical to a natural element: art.5(2).

Behind the third of these propositions lies the view that stripping back the DNA helix to RNA and its translation into cDNA involves an artificial chemical process. It gives a chemical substance that is not the same as that which occurs in nature.[21] Accordingly, so it is argued, there is patentable subject-matter distinct from living matter in its natural state for two reasons: because a laboratory process has intervened, and because the result is chemically different. In any case, the Directive does not even require the second factor of chemical change. It is enough to make an element isolated from the body by a technical process. From this it may be assumed that there does not have to be anything inventive about carrying out the process.

These distinctions have been sufficient to convince the European Court of Justice, which accordingly upheld the EU's power to enact the Biotechnology Directive.[22] To those who are suspicious of the on-march of patenting in biology, the distinctions remain specious. The genetic structure of the human body remains part of it even after the reconstitution as a cDNA sequence. On this view "a sequence or partial sequence of a gene" which is first declared unpatentable (art.5(1)) cannot become patentable under art.5(2), since that provision still treats it as "a sequence or partial sequence of a gene". It has been widely assumed that human cDNA sequences are in principle patentable by virtue of art.5(2) to the extent that they are produced by a technical process. So far as the United Kingdom is concerned, however, there are statements in *Kirin-Amgen v Hoechst Marion Roussel* which suggest that claims to DNA sequences without qualification

[21] See above, para.21–02.

[22] *Netherlands v European Parliament and Council* (2002) 33 I.I.C. 722. While under no legal obligation to do so, the terms of the Directive were brought within the EPC by amendment to the Implementing Regulations, see esp r.23(b)–(e). Numerous Member States failed to implement the Directive in time, since they had to face heated controversy at home. In 2004, the Commission brought default proceedings and most then fell into line, though not always following the precise terms of the Directive.

are to "discoveries". This must either be because they are already known in the natural world or because they are to be treated as information about the natural world, rather than a practical product or process.[23] What remains unclear is how far that objection is independent of the two questions of whether sufficient information is supplied to overcome any difficulty in knowing the possible ways of making the product of the sequence; and of whether practical values for the sequence have been sufficiently identified.

As to the second of these, there must be an adequate description of the "industrial application" of the claimed sequence.[24] An increasing concern that patents were being admitted into the sphere of basic research, which had no immediate prospect of practical application, led the US Patent Office to insist that the claimed utility for such patents must be "specific, substantial and credible". The EPC contains equivalent provisions. Where it is not otherwise obvious, a specification must indicate explicitly the way in which the invention is capable of industrial application[25]; a requirement that has been strongly endorsed by the English Court of Appeal as part of the need to show industrial *applicability*.[26] Particularly notable was the TBA's decision in *Tymogenetics/Haematopoietics cytokine receptor*.[27] What was required was a sufficiently "sound and concrete technical basis" for the skilled person to recognise that the invention's contribution could lead to practical exploitation in industry. The "concrete benefit" had to be "immediate", rather than one which the skilled reader would have to establish by a research programme. But it was only necessary to show that the disclosure would lead to a "profitable use" in the broad sense of showing how it could be used in industrial practice to solve a given technical problem so as to provide a real as opposed to a theoretical possibility of exploitation.[28] In the application in question, Zcytorl, was identified as a member of

---

[23] See esp. Lord Hoffmann, [2005] R.P.C. 9 at [76, 77], applying *Genentech's Patent* [1989] R.P.C. 147; above, para.5–56; see Rimmer, above, n. (8 CHECK) Ch. 4. For a comparison with the patenting of computer programs, see *Aerotel v Telco*[2006] EWCA 1007at [34–37]. According to Jacob L.J., to define the precise detail of a gene sequence may go beyond "discovery": "Columbus 'discovered' America, but those who in due course mapped it would not normally be said to have 'discovered' the detail they put on their maps."

[24] Ng-Loy (2002) 33 I.I.C. 393; Nicol (2005) 29 Melbourne U.L.R. 809.

[25] EPC Regulations (2000), reg.42(1)(e). Any reference to nucleotides or amino acids must give a sequence listing according to a prescribed list: EPC Regulations (2000) reg.30(1). The EU's Biotechnology Directive (98/44/EC) Rec.23, requires indication of a function for any gene sequence and that is accepted by the EPO (Guidelines IV 4.6). The Commission maintains that these provisions are adequate: Report on the Implications of Patent Law in Biotechnology and Genetic Engineering (COM (2002) 545.

[26] *Eli Lilly v Human Genome Sciences* [2010] EWCA Civ 33, discussed above, para.5–53. See also the UKIPO's Examination Guidelines of Applications relating to Biotechnological Inventions.

[27] *Tymogenetics/Haematopoietics cytokine receptor* [2007] E.P.O.R. 2; see also *ICOS/ Transmembrane receptor* [2000] OJ EPO 275.

[28] See the conclusion in *SmithKline Beecham's Opposition* (T 604/04), finding a sufficient case to have been made out through research that had shown receptors that were clearly of interest to the pharmaceutical industry as well as to theoretical scientists interested in exploring unknown characteristics of the molecule claimed. See also *Salk/steroid/thyroid receptors* (T 338/00).

a haematopoietin receptor family that had a role in the proliferation, differentiation or activation of immune cells. This indicated a possible role for its ligands in therapeutic conditions associated with the immune system. While no experimental evidence was given, computer-aided studies of tissue distribution of Zcytorl expression were disclosed which supported an educated guess that was reasonably credible (and was confirmed by later experimentation—a factor which in such cases it seems difficult entirely to discount). This was more than a "vague" or "hypothetical" suggestion without indication of any practical application.[29].

3. Patentability: Public Policy and Morality

(1) Justiciability

21–09 The EPC precludes the grant of patents upon inventions the commercial exploitation of which would be contrary to public policy or morality.[30] It is only with biotechnology that this inhibition has come to have a serious dimension. Since patents only give the right to prevent the activities of others, and impose no obligations on the patentee in relation to its own activities, the grant or refusal of a patent cannot be any direct substitute for these controls. Many would argue (and in particular those with commercial interests in the relevant technology) that moral and public policy objections should play no part in the question of grant.[31] At least, so it is said, patent office examiners lack any expertise to form the appropriate judgment, so some other body should do so.[32] Moreover, it is pointed out that applications concerning inventions with considerable potential for the relief of human suffering can become embroiled in costly and long-lasting proceedings which reflect bitter, irresoluble conflicts of ideology. These, so the case goes, would be better avoided, leaving the patent system to the technical business of protecting novel inventions.

Convenient as this outcome would be to those looking to recoup large

[29] As in *Max-Planck/phosphotase* [T870/04) For the impact of inventive step and scope of claims on this root issue, see below, para. 21–15.

[30] Above, para.5–83. The present form of words derives from TRIPS art.27(1), which puts the matter positively by indicating, as grounds for the exception, the necessity "to protect human, animal or plant life or health or to avoid serious prejudice to the environment, provided that such exclusion is not made merely because the exploitation is prohibited by . . . law".

[31] e.g. Nott [1993] E.I.P.R. at 85–86; so also the initial decision in *Oncomouse* (below, nn.32, 33).

[32] So far as the EPC structure is concerned, decisions are open to wide-scale review before and after grant by the EPO. Further flexibility is added by the fact that any designated country can reject the consequent national patent on grounds (possibly religious) which seem sufficient within that territory. Thus judges may be involved as much as technical examiners; and they form judgments on a great range of moral and social issues within general rules of law. Cf. Black (1998) 61 M.L.R. 621.

investments in research and development, it seems disingenuous to view the patent system as some morally neutral form of state aid in recognition of the cleverness of inventors. Patents provide an incentive to the introduction of novel technology within a generally competitive economy; and they survive to the extent that industries consider them necessary. The state, as granting authority, cannot disclaim responsibility for the inventions for which it grants protection. It should not hide behind the negative character of the patent right in order to avoid deciding whether a particular idea is inherently too repellent or dangerous to deserve this form of incentive. The power to refuse a patent on grounds of public policy or morality may need to be used cautiously. It is an appropriate step only where all the significant uses of the information are objectionable, and not only where some are. But the objection is rightly contained in the law and courts should not interpret it out of existence.[33]

(2) Morality: genetic animal design

In Europe, the *Harvard/Oncomouse* proceedings before the EPO brought the issues into sharp focus. The application claimed a mouse or other non-human mammal, bred after being genetically manipulated to introduce abnormal sensitivity to carcinogenic substances and stimuli. Thus it was a significant tool in cancer research. The Board of Appeal required the Examining Division to balance the moral and environmental factors involved by a utilitarian calculus.[34] The Division then held that the patent should be granted.[35] Of the objections to grant,[36] it was acknowledged by the Board that the experimental animals were likely to suffer; on the other hand there was little danger in this case of incalculable environmental damage since the animals could not reproduce their artificial genetic make-up.[37] Of the advantages of the invention, the animals were considered highly useful in a form of experimentation indispensable to medical research. It was the importance of this consideration which justified the patent grant. **21–10**

[33] See further, Beyleveld and Brownsword, *Mice, Morality and Patents* (1993); *Patenting Human Genes* (1997) and (2002) I.P.Q. 97.

[34] [1990] OJ EPO 476. This became the basis for the exclusion from patentability in the Biotechnology Directive (98/44/EC) art. 6(2)(d) of processes for modifying the genetic identity of animals which are likely to cause them suffering without any substantial medical benefit to man or animal, and also animals from such processes. This exclusion was not made out against a claim to the breeding of cows to produce a higher milk yield: *Bundesband deutscher Milchviehzüchter v Greenpeace Germany* (EPO, March 4, 2010)

[35] [1992] OJ EPO 589; cf. the refusal of the Canadian Supreme Court (by majority) to permit the patenting of the same invention: *Commissioner of Patents v Harvard College* [2002] S.C.C. 76.

[36] Various objectors filed observations for consideration during examination. Many of their views were canvassed again in the opposition proceedings before the EPO which were finally disposed of only in *Harvard/transgenic animals* [2005] E.P.O.R. 31, TBA. By then the claims had been limited to mice, there being no evidence of utility in other rodents.

[37] The opposite is already true of some biotechnological advances—and accordingly an issue of concern for the future.

(3) Public policy: GM plants[38]

21–11 The outcome in *Oncomouse* was an honest attempt at resolving a difficult and sensitive issue.[39] It was strengthened by the appellate decision in *Plant Genetic Systems*,[40] which rejected an opposition by Greenpeace to a patent for the genetic encoding of crops with a resistance to certain weedkillers. The decision accepted in principle that the protection of the environment fell within the concept of public policy.[41] But the Board of Appeal required that there be sufficient evidence that the environment would be damaged. The suggestions that crops might be transformed into weeds, that the herbicide resistant gene might be spread to other plants or that the eco-system might be damaged, had here raised only possible hazards and that was not sufficient. It may well be that today a stronger case could be made out on just these lines.

As to objections on the ground of morality, the test was said to be: would exploitation of the invention be contrary to conventionally accepted standards of culture inherent in European society and civilisation? Survey and opinion evidence among particular groups (in this case, Swedish farmers) would not necessarily settle the question; nor would the fact that some EPC states permitted exploitation of the invention. In the Board's view, the mere fact that genetic manipulation was used did not render an invention immoral. Traditional selective breeding also brought about genetic alteration and genetic intervention and that had long been treated as acceptable.

(4) Ethical objections: human tissue[42]

21–12 The most emotive issues, inevitably, relate to human tissue and its manipulation. In *Howard Florey/Relaxin*,[43] the EPO allowed a patent for the genetic engineering of DNA from a pregnant woman's body so as to produce human H-2 relaxin. The patient concerned had consented to the procedure, so the objections had to be put on grounds that went beyond any concern for her personal autonomy. Grant of the patent was opposed on moral grounds of sweeping generality: that the procedure involved the patenting of human life, the abuse of pregnant women, the return of slavery, the sale of women piecemeal to industry, etc. The objections, which have their foundation in a substantial philosophical and sociological literature,

---

[38] See Straus in Vaver and Bently Ch.9.

[39] A provision to much the same effect was included in the Directive on Biotechnological Inventions, below, para.21–13.

[40] *Plant Genetic Systems* [1995] E.P.O.R. 357.

[41] At the same time, the Board stressed the necessity of regulatory bodies with the responsibility of testing the safety and environmental acceptability of new substances and processes; and it made plain that the patent system cannot be regarded as a substitute for such investigative procedures.

[42] Eisenberg (2000) 49 Emory L.J. 783; (2002) 8 Boston U J Science & Tech. 190.

[43] *Howard Florey/Relaxin* [1995] E.P.O.R. 541 at 551.

were treated with little sympathy or comprehension. In particular, the DNA, once extracted and treated, was characterised, not as "life", but as a substance carrying genetic information which can be used to produce proteins that are medically useful. The patent grant was therefore maintained.

A similar attitude was displayed over another question. Where a medically useful substance has been developed from genetic material provided by a particular donor, must the donor's informed consent to its use for commercial purposes be secured before a valid patent can be granted for an invention derived from the material? There is no positive requirement in the EPC for this consent, although the Biotechnology Directive, Recital 26, states that such a donor must have had an opportunity of expressing that consent "in accordance with national law". The Recital was made the basis of an attack on the validity of a cancer diagnosis claim, it being asserted that the immorality of failing to secure this consent amounted to a denial of the donor's human rights under national law, so that the patent involved an infraction of EPC 2000 art. 53(a). A TBA refused to accept that the Recital intended this consequence, even though it apparently accepted that consent to all potential uses of human material may be regarded as fundamental. Instead it said that patent law was not the appropriate framework for the imposition and monitoring of such a requirement.[44] In other words consent was not a moral imperative of such overriding signficance that the sanction of refusing a patent should be applied whenever when it had not been obtained. It would have been more transparent to say so.

(5) Clarification by directive

In the hope of drawing a more precise line around the range of the patent **21–13**
system in relation to human and animal life forms, the EC's Directive on Rights in Biotechnological Inventions[45] prescribes that they shall not be granted for:

(1) processes for cloning humans[46];
(2) processes for modifying in humans their germ-line genetic identity (i.e. the inheritable gene characteristics);
(3) uses of human embryos for industrial or commercial purposes; and

---

[44] *University of Utah/breast cancer susceptibility* (T-1213/05) at [48-52, 58] (2008). The TBA's language used was taken by analogy from the Opinion of Jacobs Adv.-Gen to the ECJ in (C 377/98) *Netherlands v European Council and Parliament* (below, n. ..CHECK)

[45] 98/44/EC. The Directive has become part of UK law as PA977, Sch.A2, and it has been adopted into the EPC by Implementing Regulation Rule, 23d: [1999] OJ EPO 437(now EPC 2000 Regulations reg.26–30) The constitutional power to enact it has been accepted by the ECJ: *Netherlands v European Parliament and Council* (C377/01) [2001] E.C.R. I-7079.

[46] Notoriously, the EPO managed to grant a cloning patent to Edinburgh University with claims that could (at least in English) be taken to cover humans. On discovery of the ambiguity this was quickly corrected by amendment to exclude human material.

(4) processes for modifying the genetic identity of animals which are likely to cause them suffering without any substantial medical benefit to man or animal, and also animals resulting from such processes.[47]

The drafting of these exclusions was the product of long and heated argument, but they go very little beyond the EPO's case law, which in turn probably reflects widespread public opinion. In the cases of cloning and modifying germ-line identity, the objections are an aspect of ethical condemnations of the very activities themselves. The objection to patenting is therefore to using the commercial stimulus of an exclusive property right to encourage those activities. The commercial use of embryos reflects wider concerns over embryological practices, particularly relating to human infertility, once they become the subject of a profit motive, and above all when they lead to the birth of children. Objection to the use of animals in genetic experiments, often expressed in the heightened rhetoric of animal rights, requires, according to this disposition, a balancing of consequential advantages.

(6) Human stem-cell research

21–14 One acute confrontation over the morality of patenting has been presented by the extraction of embryonic stem-cells (eSCs) from fertilised human *ova*. Research involving stem cells in "adult" form has been pursued since the 1970s, but "adult" cells are limited in their capacity to convert into other cell types. In their first manifestation in living matter, stem cells are totipotent—capable of developing into any cell type, but, as they divide, for a short period after fertilisation they remain pluripotent—still capable of developing into many cell types. Their extraction at that stage is claimed to be particularly valuable in the search for tissue that could be used in treating patients suffering, for instance, from burns, osteoporosis, heart attack, diabetes, hepatitis, and degenerative conditions such as muscular dystrophy, Alzheimer's or Parkinson's disease. Human eSCs are typically obtained from eggs that have been fertilised in the laboratory during in-vitro treatment (IVF) of couples experiencing difficulty with pregnancy. The fertilised eggs not needed for the treatment will have to be destroyed and to many scientists their use instead to supply eSCs for research makes good utilitarian sense. But some religious and other moralists regard as completely unacceptable a positive intervention which, while securing the eSCs, destroys the nucleus. They argue therefore that the step must prevent patenting by virtue of art.53(a) of the EPC, backed up by the more specific provision in the Biotechnology Directive that excludes patents for "uses of human embryos for industrial or commercial purposes".

So long as there exists no generally accepted technique for obtaining

[47] Article 6, and see Recs 35–45.

human pluripotent stem cells other than as a side-advantage of IVF treatment, this irresolvable clash of philosophies will remain highly controversial. The European Commission has at its disposal an expert European Group on Ethics in Science and New Technologies (EGE) which, as the Biotechnology Directive notes, may reach opinions about human genetic research that is relevant to the question of property rights.[48] In a Report of 2002, the EGE concluded that there was no ethical obstacle to patentability attached to processes involving human eSCs whatever their source.[49] In the *Edinburgh Patent*,[50] an Opposition Division of the EPO was abusively critical of this Report to a degree that suggested that its members were impelled by deeply ingrained beliefs about the sanctity of human life from the moment of conception.[51] The claims in question concerned a research technique for keeping stem cells separate from other types of cell so as to prevent them from being overgrown or supplanted. Neither description nor claims referred to the method of obtaining the stem cells in the first place. The applicant proved willing to amend the application so as to confine its scope explicitly to non-human cells. Its further processing accordingly went on to other questions. But the hostility of the Division showed that one stream of opinion in the EPO favoured a reading of the legislative texts which excluded claims to any exploitation of eSCs, where they were initially obtained from fertilised human nuclei.

The EPO soon faced the same essential issue in *WARF*, which was a claim, not to a research procedure, but to a broad range of eSC cultures which complied with specified criteria relating to durability without change.[52] The proposed patent sought to cover the scientific breakthrough and pioneering invention which opened up a new and exciting field of research having great potential for promising medical therapies and other applications. The questions addressed to the Enlarged BA concerned the exclusion of patents on a ground of morality or public policy (EPC art.53(2)) and the amplification (in the Biotechnology Directive art. 6(2)(c)) that "patents are not to be granted for uses of human embryos for industrial or commercial purposes".[53] The Board began from the position that the commercial exploitation of human embryos had never been regarded as

[48] Biotechnology Directive 98/44 art.7.

[49] Report No.16, May 7, 2002.

[50] Opposition to EP 0695351; see Laurie [[2004] E.I.P.R. 591

[51] See Laurie [2004] E.I.P.R. 59; Cornish in Gruppo Espagnol de la AIPPI, *Estudios sobre Propriedad Industrial e Intellectual y Derecho de la Competencia* (2005), p.283; Plomer [2006] CIPA J. 594; Crespi [2006] E.I.P.R. 569; Rimmer (2008) (above, n.8 Ch. 9.

[52] *Wisconsin Alumni Research Foundation (WARF)* (T1374/040) [2009] E.P.O.R. 15. The EnlBA held that it, rather than the ECJ, was the final jurisdiction with power of interpretation of the EPC reg.28, even though that rule adopts the EU Biotechnology Directive, art.6, as part of EPC law:

[53] See EPC Regulations reg. 28(formerly reg.23(d)); see also PA 1977 Sch A2 para. 3. The *WARF* decision, although concerned with a technology for further research, did not consider whether it was only for a discovery or involved no industrial susceptibility, nor whether it failed to disclose directly practical effects.

patentable; to do so would be an affront to human dignity.[54] Referring to various hints that could be found in the evolution of the Directive, it pronounced that "the intention of the legislator" was to preclude patents relating to eSC cultures, where the only method of extraction for further laboratory cultivation *in vitro* involved destruction of a fertilized ovum and so was "embraced" within the invention.[55] It did not make any difference that this was only an underlying assumption; nor that the claims made no reference to the technique for obtaining the cultures; nor that other, different techniques might later be discovered which did not involve the destruction of embryos. The decision by no means settles all issues relating to the patentability of eSC inventions. The UK is a country where, under the informed guidance of the Human Fertilisation and Embryology Authority, stem cell research has been enabled to blossom. A British court, left to itself, might well be reluctant to follow the ruling of the Enlarged Board in *WARF*, if the issue were to arise on an application to the UK Intellectual Property Office for a national patent.[56] More likely, however, the issue of interpreting the Biotechnology Directive itself will be tested by questions to the ECJ arising out of national litigation, since this is already under way.[57] The outcome of that process, one way or the other, would have a binding effect on UK Courts.

4. Patents and Human Genetics

21–15 In addition to the issues just discussed concerning the general ambit of the patent system, complaints are now levied against forms of "over-patenting" in the sphere particularly of human genetics. A series of concerns arise:

(1) that in this field the requirements of novelty and inventive step will be underplayed;
(2) that patentees may be granted rights disproportionately extensive to the invention disclosed; (this may be the effect of so-called "reach-through claims" (RTCs));
(3) that the space for R & D will become severely constricted where too many closely related patents are granted to different firms, each of which then has an interest in pressing for royalties or restrictions on the way the invention is used (so-called "royalty-stacking");
(4) that the exceptions for experimental and similar uses are too narrow; researchers, both in the public sector and in industry, are unduly

[54] *WARF* [2009] E.P.O.R. 15 at [13]. The Board refused to adopt a limited definition of "embryo" by confining it to those at least 14 days old: see [19-20].
[55] *WARF* [2009] E.P.O.R. 15 Regulations [21] et seq.
[56] For the persuasive but not binding effect of EnlBA decisions, see, e.g. Lord Neuberger M.R. *Symbian v Comptroller-General* [2008] EWCA 1066 at [33-36].
[57] See *Brüstle v Greenpeace* (C-34/10).

inhibited in pursuing programmes which will advance knowledge in the field of a protected invention;

(5) that, more generally, anxieties arise of the use of genetic patents to restrict the availability of diagnostic tests and other medical advances by coupling high charges with restrictions requiring material to be sent to a facility run by the patentee or under an exclusive licence.

Each of these is explored in the following paragraphs.

(1) Novelty and inventive step

The standards which restrict patent rights to significant technical advances are, first, the requirement of novelty over what is already known and, secondly, the need to establish an inventive step over the prior art known at the priority date of the patent. Examining patent offices test applications by these criteria and they should act as the main filter in the system as a whole. It is understandable that at the early stages of a complex new technology patent applications will seem strikingly original and it is only as the procedures become familiar that an accepted idea of what should be allowed begins to establish itself. **21–16**

All patent offices feel some responsibility towards their applicants not to reject their proposals even before, in most cases, they reach the market. It is widely considered that the US Patent Office treats the threshold of non-obviousness as a low one and that accordingly it is accepting applications for inventions in genetics that would not pass muster elsewhere, including the EPO. That criticism is a prominent strand in the Nuffield Council on Bioethics' Discussion Paper, *The Ethics of Patenting DNA*. The paper argues that these standard tests of patentability are the best chance of reaching a moderate and acceptable role for the patent system in fostering the introduction of genetic diagnosis, therapy and medicinal products. While in particular it attacks American laxity, the paper demands equally firm treatment of the matter elsewhere. In particular it emphasises that much genetic experimentation today is dependent on computerised matching of DNA patterns. The scale of computer power needed is formidable, but the procedure itself is repetitious. It may well be hard to see what is inventive about the result.[58]

In the 1970s, when British courts were assessing patents upon microbiological processes and products for medicinal purposes, many judges took a generous view of non-obviousness, even when they felt it necessary to express some scepticism about the theoretical justification for the outcome. Thus Lord Diplock once remarked:

[58] The requirement of industrial applicability must also be satisfied: e.g. *Zymogenetics/Hematopoietic cytokine receptor* [2007] E.P.O.R. (2)12; *Universaity of Utah/breast cancer susceptibility* [2008] E.P.O.R. See also above, para.21-08.

> "The task . . . calls for the exercise of technical proficiency and is laborious and very costly, for the odds against success are large. It is not easy to see what inventive step, as distinct from the mere exercise of proficiency and practice, is involved in this kind of research, but the result of success in it is a new product useful to humanity which does not exist in nature. If such research is to be encouraged in a competitive society, the monetary rewards of success must be assured to those who undertake the expense; and the means of doing so in this and in most other countries with comparable social systems is by according to the successful discoverer of the new product the controlled and limited monopoly granted for inventions under the national patent laws."[59]

In relation particularly to the bioinformatics of genetic investigation, it may be hard to see what inventive step is present in the work that leads to the claimed invention.[60] In the United States it is currently assumed that novel genetic information must be taken to be non-obvious; and some urge that Europe must not be more severe in its standards, since European industry will be prejudiced.[61] As the BRCA cases illustrate, however, those who suffer from a finding of obviousness (or any other ground of objection) may well be from outside Europe. In any country where the industry is likely to gain as much or more from new entrant firms as from established successes (and that may well be the case for European biotech companies) the argument for loosely conceived rights rings hollow.

(2) Industrial susceptibility

21–17 The second area of concern brings us to a meeting point of a number of doctrines in patent law which have, more or less recently, become part of the preconditions for validity. They have emerged principally from the long campaigns to make pharmaceutical chemistry, with its considerable dependence on organic matter, as open to patenting as inanimate productions and processes of engineering and electronics. As we saw in general terms at an earlier stage, patent systems have come to apply in all these spheres the same assumption to initiating or pioneering inventions. If an inventor demonstrated a first use for a thing, whether it was a machine, a mineral or living matter, he was entitled to patent it. This had the

[59] *American Cyanamid (Dann's) Patent* [1971] R.P.C. 425 at 451; cf. also *Beecham Group's (Amoxycillin) Application* [1980] R.P.C.261, CA, where Templeman L.J., dissenting, would have refused the application because of doubts resembling Lord Diplock's.

[60] cf. *Genentech v Wellcome Foundation* [1989] R.P.C. 147 CA: the patent concerned the location and reproduction of a protein, t-PA (an anti-blood-clotting agent), by recombinant DNA technology. The broad claims were, in various forms, for all methods of producing t-PA by the technology. A majority of the Court of Appeal characterised such claims as obvious. Purchas L.J. viewed them as purely for discovery.

[61] For a survey of approaches to the issue, relating particularly to the Tripartite discussions of the EPO, JPO and USPO, see Schertenleib [2003] E.I.P.R. 125.

consequence that, so long as the patent lasted, the monopoly extended to the thing, whatever it was used for, even where later its use for a different and novel purpose was demonstrated. The European Parliament has objected to the application of this principle in the field of genetic knowledge;[62] but a TBA of the EPO has refused to take up this restrictive idea, finding that it has no authority to depart from a rule affecting the grant of patents in general in order to take account of its effects on particular technologies.[63] It should be recalled that claims for substances, as distinct from claims for methods of deploying them, were the first means by which the prohibition on patents for methods of medical treatment came to be side-stepped. To that end patentees were also allowed to take advantage of the doctrine of selection patents; they were also permitted to hold claims to first medical uses of known substances; and subsequently they secured grants over subsequent medical uses by the rigmarole of the "Swiss-form claim" to a pharmaceutical preparation.[64]

Transferring these notions to genetic research leads to claims for genetic material itself, and to associated cellular characteristics, which equally apply to all known or proposed uses. These "reach through claims" are, indeed, supplemented by provisions of the Biotechnology Directive which attach additional "reach through" effects to certain types of claim. Thus a claim to biological material possessing specific characteristics also covers versions retaining those characteristics which are propagated or multiplied in divergent form; and a claim to a process for producing such material covers material directly obtained from the process where the propagation is in divergent form.[65]

A much discussed example is Human Genome Sciences' US patent on the CCR5 receptor.[66] Receptors are protein products which form pathways by which certain genetic material enters a cell or attaches to its surface. HGS's claimed value for CCR5 was as a cell-surface receptor potentially useful in anti-inflammatory therapy. French researchers soon afterwards demonstrated that CCR5 was the route by which the HIV/AIDS virus enters a cell. The HGS patent appears broad enough to cover any deployment of the CCR5 receptor. The patentee may therefore demand that any third party secure a licence for any invention which employs it—notably in an HIV therapy.

It is now accepted in Europe that the early, voluminous applications to protect partial sequences of genes went beyond the acceptable scope of the patent system. In pharmacology in general, there may be some case for

[62] See its Resolution P6 TA (2005) 0407 (October 26, 2005).

[63] *University of Utah/breast cancer susceptibility* (T1213/05) at [52-53] (2008). In particular, the TBA refused to accept that it should use socio-economic criteria in order to decide on the scope of what subject matter is patentable.

[64] For the recent history of this curious piece of judicial legislation, see above, paras 5–22, 5–73–75.

[65] Directive 98/44/EC art.8.

[66] See, e.g. Nuffield Report (above, n.8), paras 4.9–4.10.

allowing the initial patentee a reach-through claim, thus extending the right for some distance into uses which also depend upon subsequent research. For one thing, the first to get to an actual product will bear the expense of convincing government authorities that it is safe to administer it to humans. That procedure may require much higher expenditure than is needed to secure licences for later improved versions. But here the patent is over material at the stage when it is only an experimental contribution towards a final, useful result. It is that result which is likely to constitute the truly significant practical outcome and it may well provide the most "inventive" of all the contributory steps. What then is the justification for allowing earlier contributors to the whole development a right that stretches beyond the industrial application demonstrated for the contribution? The way in which claim practice has been permitted to develop for pharmaceuticals in general has extensively deployed the concept of a claim to a substance, either for its discovered advantages (as with selection patents) or for its newly discovered uses (as with first and subsequent medical use claims).[67] In relation to intermediate step claims over genetic material, there is a good case for restricting the claim to the discovered use so to impose an appropriate limit on scope.[68]

(3) "Anti-commons" that impede R & D

21–18 Research on genetic material, particularly if it is directed towards discovering diagnostic tests for illness or dysfunctional conditions, or if it is working towards a form of gene therapy or medicinal product, is likely to follow a relatively constricted number of promising pathways identified by prior research. Because of the inherent complexity of chopping away the undergrowth on any one of them, a number of separate entities, some academic, some commercial, may be working on different stretches of the course. There are certainly examples already where a profusion of patentees have clustered along a line of development. A potential investor seeking to come in alongside those already there may have to face paying royalties to some or all of these predecessors. Leading geneticists fear that soon there will be more such situations.

The result has been pictured as an "anti-common", where a knowledge domain, initially public, is becoming criss-crossed with small-holder gates, making it in practice too toll-laden to cross.[69] Would-be contributors to further R & D are accordingly driven off to other, less obstructed, highways or byeways. The most obvious barrier will arise from too many jostling demands for royalties. Even stout defenders of the patent system admit that, while cases of three to five separate licences are manageable, when the

[67] For which, see above, paras. 5-23/27.
[68] White [2002] CIPA Journal 89, 134; not accepted by Crespi, [2002] CIPA Journal 89 255.
[69] See esp., Heller and Eisenberg (2000) 280 Science 698; the obverse idea to that was sparked by Hardin (1968) 162 Science 1243: "Freedom in a commons brings ruin to all".

"royalty stack" comes from 8, 12 or even 15 sources, insurmountable blocks may have been erected. They obstruct the very incentive which is supposed to flow from the discipline of private ownership, when contrasted with the anarchy of a shared "common".

Any solution is rendered problematic by the high level of investment required and by the new and shifting nature of the biotechnology industry, which lacks experience and standards for reaching agreement on royalty shares, where some acceptable split is the way forward that is likely to reach the goals of new forms of treatment. Scrambles for IP ownership are likely to accompany the sudden upsurge of a new industry and in the past the emergent markets have provided the discipline which leads to economically valuable results and actual revenue. It may, however, be that, in relation to genetic medicine, the blockages will become so serious that there must be some intervention by public authority.

One cure, already within the structure of UK patent law, is the granting of **21–19** compulsory licences, or—where the provision will be for services of the Crown (including government health services)—reliance on the Crown use provisions.[70] One ground for a compulsory licence is that refusal of a licence on reasonable terms under one patent is preventing the exploitation of another invention provided that the second invention must be important technically and economically. Accordingly it is a solution that presents itself only when two inventions have progressed some distance down their paths to success.

Certain other grounds might conceivably be relevant in particular circumstances. Even then, British experience teaches that the costs of securing compulsory licences from unwilling patentees can be very expensive and long-drawn-out. There is an apparent contrast here with the Crown use provisions, which require no preliminary approval, but only the payment of compensation to the patentee. Beyond these powers, at present there is only the prospect of resort to competition law criteria and procedures. These are necessarily constrained. It is, after all, within the proper purposes of the patent system that a patentee should be entitled to refuse to license at all or to demand such royalty as he thinks he can secure from his position of market exclusivity.

As to the transactional complexities of numerous dealings, the market in other complex fields—notably at the moment, telecommunications—has generated "one-stop shops": licences of patents and other IPRs are packaged and made available to all developers, often in the form of a standard for a type of product. But where patents are involved, one person's standardisation is the next person's patents pool. Patents pools used to be routinely condemned under competition laws as a means by which industry leaders would themselves exchange patent licences on inventions which netted the entire industry; but at the same time they would refuse to allow

[70] Above, paras 7–41—7–50.

new entrants to join the swim. In the complexities of today's new technologies, competition authorities have come to recognise that patent pools may sometimes be advantageous, notably when the standard which the patents underpin are made open (albeit at a price) to newcomers. Whether the conditions of genetic R & D are such that these patent packages would become well-established and convenient remains speculative. At present there are few signs that the industry is anything like stable enough to take to collaborative patent management. So the danger of competitive royalty stacking appears serious. It adds fuel to the case for accepting, at the examination stage only those applications with clear claims to real inventive advance.

(4) Research tool patents and experimental use

21–20 In science generally, novel methods of investigation emerge which become widely used research techniques. They are deployed for studies which are not seeking any improvement of the method itself but are pursuing an independent line of inquiry for which the method is the accepted procedure. These methods are "research tools" in the common usage of the term. A quarter century ago in biotechnology, the introduction of recombinant DNA technology provides one example.[71] Another is the highly ingenious identification of PCR (polymerase chain reactor). This provided the main tool for multiplying DNA from samples, which has been central to genetic science ever since. The patent on it led to licensing at high commercial rates and that behaviour has been a considerable irritant to scientists who would rather see limited budgets go on other spending. The irritation has not, however, led to attempts to curb the full effect of the patent—for instance, through compulsory licensing or competition law controls.

The present European law admits exceptions both for private, non-commercial use and experimental use.[72] A scientist working alone without commercial funding is the archetype of the private user; and he or she could claim a right to free use of a patented research tool. That would, of course, only be of value where no physical material, such as a biological sample, has to be obtained from the patentee or a licensee. The private use exception has led to relatively wide reading of the experimental use exception, so as to include commercial work. This contrasts with the US position, where any exception is confined to private study and does not even include unsponsored university research.[73] However, as is generally accepted, the exception

[71] The inventors, Calder and Boyers, patented the invention in the US (though not in countries where no grace period operated to discount revelations at scientific meetings). It was licensed to all comers at a low royalty by the University of California—an outcome widely accepted as reasonable. The contemporaneous evolution of the hybridoma technique of producing monoclonal antibodies, discovered by Milstein and Köhler, was not patented.

[72] See generally, above, para.6–11 In relation to biotechnological patenting, see Rimmer (above, n.8) Ch.6.

[73] *Madey v Duke University*, 307 F.3d 1351 (Fed.Cir., 2002).

only applies to research that is on the subject matter of the patent itself, aiming to extend knowledge about it by improvement or variation.[74] Hence the exception is not available for the use of research tools in the sense just discussed.

There are stages in research, where an intermediate thing or substance is produced in the course of a particular line of development, and these are in a sense research tools. As already mentioned, to be patentable these must have sufficient industrial applicability.[75] If they do gain protection, others may pursue research involving their use under the exceptions for private use or for experimental purposes so long as the work is to discover more about their characteristics or potential. This is of great significance in medical genetics, particularly as work approaches the stages of providing an actual diagnostic test or therapy. The German Supreme Court has decided that the experimental use exception covers clinical trials on human patients, where it is to discover further medical applications or to provide more information on effects of treatment. This is so even where a separate purpose is to improve the health of the patients, and it can apply where tests are done in a number of separate hospitals.[76] The end-point of exemption will be reached, only when the trials are unlikely to produce further information but are merely repeating and substantiating what is already known.[77] The approach harmonises with one view of the incentive role of the patents, which recognises that the system must encompass not only the initial stages of invention, but also extend to additions, modifications and improvements of all kinds (provided that they are inventive). In that way, it can operate against any tendency of the first patentee to sit back on its laurels and inhibit progress by others.

The interpretation also provides a balance of interests which has some appeal. The subsequent researcher is free to undertake follow-on work within a reasonably broad compass. If that work itself results in invention, then the researcher will have a second patent to bring to the negotiating table, both for cross-licensing with the first inventor and for seeking a return from third-party users. The one danger then is that multiple royalty demands may inhibit yet further research by others.[78] If the experimental work is not successful, the second researcher will have gained nothing that impedes the commercial progress of the first.

---

[74] See *Monsanto v Stauffer* [1985] R.P.C. 515 CA; *Schütz v Werit* [2010] EWHC 1623 (pat).

[75] Above, para.6–11. In this context note the refusal in the US of a patent claiming five ESTs from maize leaves as molecular markers for mapping the maize genome as a whole: these were treated as merely hypothetical possibilities: *Re Fisher*, 421 F 3d 1365 (2005) CAFC.

[76] *Klinische Versuche I and II* [1997] R.P.C. 623; [1998] R.P.C. 423; above, para.6–11.

[77] For this distinction, see *Monsanto v Stauffer* [1985] R.P.C. 515 CA. Note now the special extension of protection to tests for obtaining medical marketing approval: above, para.6–11.

[78] Above, para.21–17.

(5) The causes of anguish

21–21 In recent years health care providers have been particularly alarmed by the assertive manner in which the biotechnology company, Myriad Genetics of Utah, has deployed its patents on two diagnostic tests for susceptibility to breast cancer.[79] The first identifies mutations in the BRCA1 gene on chromosome 17; the second does the same for the BRCA2 gene on chromosome 13.[80] The initial evolution of the patents is a complex story, which raises in striking form the question, should a patent go only to the person who makes the last connecting step across a line of stones put in place by a number of research teams. That, however, is a side issue here.

For better, for worse, the patents were granted to or acquired by Myriad Genetics in the US, through the EPO and in other countries (albeit that their validity remained open to contest after grant). Myriad (now with its partner, University of Utah) has insisted that the diagnostic test be administered only in its own laboratories at a price which could impose a severe burden on health authorities, insurers and private patients.[81] Part of its stated justification was its fear that in other hands the test would be inadequately applied. Simpler versions of the test were developed by doctors in various countries and they wanted to be able to use them under licence from Myriad.[82] This was not just because the licence fee ought to be less but also because the results can be tied closely to the care of the patient, who could well be found likely to develop breast cancer but could not (as yet) be given a medical regime which would reduce the danger by a reasonably simple measure.[83]

The example brings home the reach that patent rights may have over advances in genetics. The claims in the BRCA1-gene patents were not just for test procedures involving the gene, but also, in "reach-through" fashion, for the gene itself (after DNA re-combination). More precisely these latter claims were for the gene in various discovered mutations and also in its normal form.[84] How far these involved serious overreaching depended on the course of further knowledge about the gene. While a few diseases (such as Huntington's Chorea and cystic fibrosis) derive from defects in a single gene, it is becoming clear that the full genetic story behind many others is elaborate and may involve multiple interactions and overlapping, the influence of SNPs and much else. A patent over a single gene may prove to

[79] See Rimmer, above, n.8, Ch.7; Verbeure, Matthijs and Van Overwalle (2006) 14 Eur.J. Human Genetics 26.

[80] For comments on the specifications, Crespi in OECD papers, above, para.21–05.

[81] The test is performed on a sample of skin tissue, and is therefore not excluded from patentability by EPC 2000 art. 53(c): *University of Utah/mutation* (T666/05) at [78-79] (2008).

[82] For an instance, see Rimmer, above n.71, at 27–28.

[83] Complete mastectomy is invasive, costly and not without its own complications.

[84] The question of what activity by an unauthorised person actually amounts to infringement of these claims is a problematic one, raising the issue when does that person "make the patented product" in the sense of PA 1977 s.60.

set up a barrier against its use in a quite distinct genetic procedure for a different medical condition which is worked out only subsequently. One of the lessons which has come from breast cancer research is that the BRCA1 and BRCA2 genes are the source of the carcinoma in only a very small percentage of all cases. It seems that, in its initial excitement, Myriad Genetics believed it had found the single cause. Its subsequent behaviour may have stemmed in part from disappointment at learning that this was not so. The patents had a potential capacity to block diagnostic and curative tools for other things than breast cancer, particularly given the inclusion of the normal gene in the claim. As with many patents involving gene material, the prospect of multi-functional complications makes for an eventual pile-up of patents and a "royalty stack". That is a first reason why they have been regarded with suspicion.

In any event, Myriad's determination to keep diagnostic testing for the two genes for itself triggered attacks upon the patents. In Europe, the patents one granted came under immediate opposition from the Marie Curie Institute of France and other opponents who included the Dutch and Austrian governments. Of the BRCA1 patents, one was rejected in opposition proceedings and another was reduced in scope to such an extent that the opponents could claim that it no longer constituted a hindrance to the implementation of diagnostic tests in research and health care institutions. The course of its BRCA2 patent was deflected by a rival patent granted to Cancer Research UK. These outcomes suggest that the EPO is applying the criteria of patentability and adequate disclosure scrupulously to subject matter of this type. The dangers of over-reaching demands from patentees are thereby reduced. In the US certain Myriad patents have been held invalid on the ground that they were for the fundamental natural state of DNA in the human body or for information encoded by it. Sweet DJ refused to recognise any distinction between native DNA and DNA reconstituted by standard recombination techniques.[85] In the EU, however, the Biotechnology Directive art.5(2) has undercut such argumentation. It provides that an element isolated from the human body or otherwise produced by means of a technical process, including the sequence or partial sequence of a gene, may constitute a patentable invention, even if the structure of that element is identical to that of a natural element. This has been treated as legally conclusive by the TBA which decided *University of Utah/mutation*.[86]

Ideas about developing the reach and scope of a medical procedure **21–22**
concering a malignant condition that occurs frequently in developed economies. Myriad Genetics' interest in requiring samples to be sent to its laboratories carries the implication that it wishes to control further developments in the field. Accordingly it has to be asked whether the patent

[85] *Association for Molecular Pathology v USPTO*, March 31, 2010, decided, rather remarkably, in favour of an application for summary judgment; appeal by patentees to the CAFC expected.

[86] *University of Utah/mutation* (T666/05) at [74–76] (2008).

monopoly should put to this end. It would be possible to limit the economic effect of such a patent by resort to compulsory licensing. Under UK law (now conditioned by the requirements of TRIPS art.31), a licence might be imposed when an applicant could demonstrate that the UK public is not being supplied with the patented diagnostic test on reasonable terms, or that the establishment or development of commercial or industrial activities is being unfairly prejudiced.[87] Aternatively, a government department could employ Crown use powers to set up versions of the diagnostic tests by itself or someone it authorises.[88] Under competition law, the authorities of the United Kingdom or the EU might accept that the attempt to "appropriate" future research development would constitute an exceptional use of patent rights towards an unacceptable end. At least so far as further research is concerned, provided that a reasonably broad interpretation of the experimental use exception is maintained, much work on the patented genes could be justified without needing Myriad's licence. Unlike in the United States, where any such exception appears more clearly than ever to be confined to strictly non-commercial work, Europe could prove a readier home for this research. Governments, after all, profess great concern that patent laws should encourage local industries (though they are often less ready to examine how far it is that foreign enterprises will be the real beneficiaries). They ought at least to take note of the legal difference in the research exception on the two sides of the Atlantic,[89] and the advantages that the European approach contains for biotechnological companies and services here.

For a decade, the remarkable development of genetics towards a new era in medicine, has been subject to patenting strategies which aim to establish dominant strongholds over the routes to commercial returns. The motives for this have been quite closely related to the incentive aims of patent systems. No one denies that the costs of gene research are extremely high; or that it is only by paying them that there is real hope of improved health care. But governments and major charities have played such a significant role in the investment required that it becomes difficult to decide how readily patents should be available, particularly to private industry engaged in aspects of the whole development. Any answer will prove pragmatic. The best hope probably lies in adhering to the conceptual framework which has evolved for patent systems over two centuries of always contentious development. There are signs now, at least in Europe, that this advice, given from various sides with increasing stridency, is beginning to be heeded.[90] If it can become a standard approach, then the system will have proved itself mature enough to adapt to a new technology which has an extraordinary potential for human good.

[87] But subject to the various conditions of PA 1977 ss.48A–50, outlined above, para.7–44.
[88] Above, paras 7–49, 7–50.
[89] Above, para.21–18.
[90] See, e.g. the statistics on EPO applications in the field.

5. Other IPRS and Genetic Knowledge

As it became apparent that the Human Genome Project might lead to patents claiming whole genes and fragments, a search began for some form of entitlement more moderate in impact than a patent which could still serve as a means of recompensing the investment, at least in part, and therefore of making it worthwhile. There was discussion among scientists and policy makers in various countries of some form of "copyright" which might require a person availing himself of a knowledge base to pay a royalty for access but which would not keep him from it. This would have been a sui generis solution which would have come to depend on the cost effectiveness of the licensing involved—an equivalent problem which arises in relation to statutory and compulsory licences of exclusive rights such as patents and copyright. In UK law, almost uniquely, it was possible to advocate the adaptation of the British Unregistered Design Right to this end.[91] The intellectual step was perhaps not great, but the likelihood of it actually being allowed by courts has always seemed slender. So far, none of these ideas has gained real momentum. **21–23**

In Europe, there is a different right which has at least some immediate prospects for IPR protection—the sui generis database right, discussed in the previous chapter.[92] Introduced at the behest of publishers, its impact on the collection of data of all kinds in scientific research went virtually unnoticed during the passage of the EU's Directive of 1996 on the subject.[93] Yet it may apply to any of the large, computerised collections of genetic information which are now proliferating.[94] Since "database" is defined broadly to include "other material", apart from works and data, it is arguable that it also covers collections of physical material, such as genetic samples.[95] The investment involved can easily be characterised as "substantial" and regular taking of information from it will probably satisfy the test for infringement by extraction or re-utilisation. For those, including the sources financing the HGP, there is therefore a right which comes into existence without formality and is good against "copying". It is therefore necessary for those who wish the information contained in the database to be open to all who wish to consult it to make their waiver of rights apparent.

[91] See Laddie et al., Ch.38; above, para.15–37. Cf. the proposal for a short-term registration right, partly exclusive and partly non-exclusive, as with UDR: Holman and Munzer (2000) 85 Iowa L.R. 735.

[92] Above, paras 20–35 et seq.; and see Lipton [2003] E.I.P.R. 139.

[93] It is, however, the concerns of scientists about locking up scientific data for commercial exploitation which has been largely responsible for the failure to secure a similar right in the US: see, e.g. Reichman and Samuelson (1996) 50 Vand. L.R. 51. One consequence is that US firms cannot claim European database rights in any field: see above, para.20–39, n.38.

[94] For IPRs in bioinformatics, see esp. Rimmer (2003) 34 I.I.C. 31.

[95] The one proviso is that the material be organised in a systematic or methodical way and be individually accessible by electronic or other means: Database Directive (9/96/EC) art.1. Rec.17, however, makes no reference to the prospect.

With a project as complex and international as the HGP it has been vital to set out this freedom of access as a contribution to science with utmost clarity, given the inclination to behave in contrary mode which can so easily develop among collaborators.

If a collection of material does not fall within the definition of a "database", then its collectors can prevent disclosures and uses from it only if they can show that they have copyright in a literary work which is being substantially taken, or that they have imposed obligations to keep the information confidential. Of these routes, a contract clearly specifying the limitations upon disclosure or use is the most straightforward approach, but it may not bind third-party recipients.

6. Derived Cell-lines and Participation

21–24 There are many other illustrations of how close the relationship can be between genetic material in physical form and knowledge about its structure. In relation to patenting, special arrangements for accessing biological samples have had to be introduced in order to meet the criterion of adequate disclosure, in cases where the industry cannot otherwise obtain access to starting material.[96] Cell-lines which have an identifiable physical source can all too easily produce legal contests, not merely over the propriety of using the material without informed consent, but over sharing the proceeds of exploitation—an area which is close to the realm of IPRs. Famously, John Moore was held entitled in principle under Californian law to sue in respect of the multiplication and treatment of a cell-line from his spleen for medical purposes, where he had not been sufficiently informed of the experimentation and commercialisation which in fact occurred. That case did not establish that he had any intangible property right in his own body and elements taken from it, which would give him any share in a patent on the successful treatment, or even a right to a royalty for being the source of the cell-line. As currently conceived in most systems, patents are for inventors, not for those who in any other sense make the invention possible. Certainly there is no express entitlement in the European patent system. However, in the EU's Biotechnology Directive, Rec.26 requires that, where an invention is based on human biological material and a patent application is made, the person concerned should have opportunity to express free and informed consent to the application. The Recital was a concession to those who treat consent issues of this kind as an important ethical consideration, and it has no operative counterpart in the Directive itself. In any case, there is no indication that this provision is meant to have greater effect on the outcome of the application than does the current "paternity" requirement in patent

[96] Above, para.5–89.

law to identify the inventor in the specification.[97] There are those who believe strongly that the law should change so as to afford not just personal recognition (where that is desired) but a share in income generated.[98]

A parallel desire to spread the shares in income generated by protected inventions is currently being pressed, not so much in favour of individuals who form a single source, as in favour of communities from which biological source material is derived. The medicinal qualities of certain plants is part of the inherited knowledge of many third-world communities. It may well provide the clue from which purified, perhaps genetically manipulated, versions or variations can be produced by developed country research teams and turned into highly profitable patented drugs. Campaigns by developing countries and their supporters to provide a right of communal property in such developments now have a real political profile at the international level.[99] Equally this is true for genetically enhanced food sources that have a traditional origin and for cultural works based in folklore. Solutions, other than those that arise through voluntary arrangements and the following of enlightened example, are difficult to devise. There are often questions about which group exactly is the traditional source; there are, inevitably, questions about how any legally binding obligation would be determined and how it would be distributed and for what purposes. **21–25**

These are important issues for the developing world, which will scarcely affect IPRs in the United Kingdom itself. But they return us to basic issues about the proper purposes of intellectual property itself. In its manifestations which relate to fostering new technological and cultural ideas and material, the foremost instances of these rights focus upon the mental activity of making the invention or creating the work. Other rights, it is true, are given to investors who bring about the commercial exploitation of the ideas. Nonetheless the systems do not confer intangible property, and so the potential for earning, upon those who provide precedent ideas any more than they do on those who merely manage research, development or marketing for enterprises other than their own. Under capitalism they must earn for the services or things that provide. Now come claims, within the very frame of mutual concessions towards increased world trade, that some who provide preliminary data for modern technical developments should share in revenue from successful industrialised exploitation.

It is an interesting idea, which people of conscience link to their desire to provide some relatively immediate return to developing countries for technology prospects of which they for once have been the supplier. TRIPS has obliged them, after all, to adopt first-world IP standards mainly for the benefit of first-world corporations active in their territories.[100] The idea does, **21–26**

[97] Above, para.4–09.

[98] Beylefeld and Brownsword, above, para.21–09, n.31; cf. Laurie, *Genetic Privacy* (2002) Ch.6.

[99] For a full assessment of the debates, see the Commission on IPRs (UK Department for International Development), Integrating IPRs and Development Policy (2002) Ch.4.

[100] See above, para.7–42.

however, break with the basic assumption that IPRs have a narrow focus, etched by an economic determinism which places its trust in constant technical development as the key to richer and more varied life chances for all. It departs likewise from the belief that property rights—concentrated where possible in a single exploitative individual or enterprise—will lead to the extraction of the greatest value from resources, intellectual as well as material, through market forces. Arguments about controlling intellectual resources, about sharing them only on terms, are today increasingly at the centre of our visions for ordered and stable civil societies. IPRs are an important way in which those arguments are expressed. That is why the limits placed upon them in law and its practice, and through technology itself, are also of great importance. This has been a book about how those legal confines are set, and should be adapted, in one developed country which is now part of an expanding economic union. From that rather practical perspective, we hope that it has contributed to larger, more fundamental, debates.

INDEX

New Patterns: Process and Change in Human Geography

Michael Carr

Nelson

Thomas Nelson and Sons Ltd
Nelson House
Mayfield Road
Walton-on-Thames
Surrey KT12 5PL
United Kingdom

First published by Thomas Nelson and Sons Ltd 1997

I(T)P® Thomas Nelson is an International Thomson Publishing Company
I(T)P® is used under licence

ISBN 0-17-438681-8
NPN 9 8 7 6 5 4 3 2 1

Typeset in 9.5/12 pt Stone Serif and Franklin Gothic
Printed in Great Britain by Hobbs the Printers

Publication team:
Acquisitions: Roda Morrison, Steve Berry
Administration: Jenny Goode
Editorial Management: Simon Tanner-Tremaine
Freelance Editorial: Melanie McRae
Marketing: Jane Lewis
Production: Liam Reardon
Concept Design: Mark Callaghan
Design and Illustration: Hardlines

Contents

List of illustrations

To the reader

Although this text has been written specifically for advanced level and degree foundation studies in Geography, it is also suitable for those concerned with the contribution the subject makes towards an understanding of many of the current issues and problems which face the world and its peoples.

A systematic approach is taken beginning with population, since people lie at the heart of all human geography. Here, as elsewhere in the text, interactions between people and the environment are explored with a view to bringing out locational aspects and the resultant distribution patterns and spatial relationships which occur.

In this approach and through the balance of themes covered, the text remains true to the human geography tradition. Also fundamental to it is an awareness of the rapid changes which are taking place in the world today and out of which emerge important issues and problems of concern to geographers and others in related disciplines. Hence emphasis throughout the text is on change and the processes underlying it. Since the first text was published, issues of social and spatial justice, of sustainability and concern for the environment from local to global, have become increasingly central to geographical debate. These issues are discussed throughout the text. Increasingly globalisation of economic activity is one of the most important changes which occurs today; this and its implications are also addressed.

Case studies are introduced throughout the text, since we must go beyond generalities to the implications they have for particular people and places. These are an important and integral part of the book.

The introductory quotes at the beginning and concluding comments at the ends of the chapters are features new to this edition. The concluding comments are not a summary of the contents of the respective chapters but, like the quotes, are included to provide a guide to further study sources and a basis for discussions.

It is assumed that the reader will have at hand an atlas, without which it would be difficult to appreciate sufficiently the locational and spatial aspects raised in many of the discussions and which are central to geographical understanding.

Michael Carr
Homerton College
Cambridge 1997

Personal acknowledgements

I am very conscious of and grateful for all the help and support I have been given in the course of completing this text. My thanks go especially to the following: the late Gus Caesar and also Emrys Jones for the grounding in geography I was privileged to receive from them; to my colleague and friend, Mike Younger, for his kindly advice and encouragement; to Steve Berry at Thomas Nelson, for his continuous support and patience with me; to Melanie McRae, for her expert editing and friendly, stimulating persistence on my behalf; and to Simon Tanner-Tremaine and others at Thomas Nelson involved with this text.

Above all, I should like to acknowledge the patience and support of my wife, Zena, to whom with love, together with our now extended family, I dedicate this text.

Michael Carr
Homerton College
Cambridge 1997

Acknowledgements

The author and publishers wish to thank these publishers for kind permission to use their material as a basis for the following:

Figure 7.5 – *The Atlas of African Affairs*; Figure 31.2 – *The Ecologist*; Case study 20.1 – *The Far Eastern Economic Review*; Figures 8.2, 20.7, 28.7, 31.10, 32.5, 32.6, 32.8, 32.11, Case studies 2.1, 19.3, 24.1, 27.3, text pages 153, 203, 336, 371, 416 – *The Financial Times*; Figures 5.3, 14.18, 15.6, text page 48 – *Geofile*, Stanley Thornes Publishers; Figures 10.2, 16.1, 20.11, Case studies 2.2, 9.3, text page 97 – *The Geographical Association*; Figures 10.2, 16.1, 20.11, Case studies 2.2, 9.3 – *Geographical Review*, Philip Alan Publishers; Figures 10.4, 10.5, text page 409 – *The Guardian*; Figures 6.5, 6.6, 9.2 – *Human Development Report*, Oxford University Press; Case study 28.3, text pages 151, 182 – *The Independent*; Figure 14.17, text page 173 – The Institute of Employment Research, University of Warwick; Figures 8.1, 8.5, text page 16 – *New Internationalist*; Figures 5.6, 10.3, 14.16, Case study 2.1 – OPCS; Figure 12.2, text pages 442, 446 – The Royal Geographical Society; Figure 15.15 – *The Times*; Figures 32.4, 33.13, 33.15 – *Third World Guide*; Figure 15.17 – *The Town Planning Review*; Figures 2.6, 2.7, 5.7 – UNFPA; Figure 14.23, Case study 5.3, text page 184 – University of Zimbabwe; Figure 20.4, Case study 20.1, UNIDO; Figures 15.1, 15.3, text pages 193, 269 – *Urban Studies*; Figures 2.3a, 2.3b, 2.5, 2.10, 2.12, 2.13, 2.14, 2.16, 6.7, 8.3, 20.3, 24.2, 33.16, Case study 2.1 – *World Development Report*, Oxford University Press; Figures 1.4, 5.10, 8.7, 9.4, text page 369 – World Resources Institute, Oxford University Press

The author and publishers wish to thank Tony Stone Images for permission to reproduce the photographs by Barry Lewis, Bill Heinsonn, Hilarie Kavanagh and Robert Frerck on the cover.

CHAPTER 1

Population geography and the quality of life

'Numbers, densities and qualities of the population form the essential background for all geography. Population is the point of reference from which all other elements are observed and from which they all singly and collectively derive significance and meaning.'

WRIGLEY

The basics of population geography

Population distributions and densities

Much of the data used in population geography are collated by demographers – specialists in population studies. Demographers are essentially concerned with the enumeration (counting of heads) of population and changes in population structure, whereas geographers have been mainly interested in aspects of population distribution and density, including changes in these over time (Figure 1.1). Geographers examine the ways in which population densities are related to the environment and its resources from one place to another, because these factors influence the capacity of any environment to support its population. We can use skills and the available technology to maximise the environment's resources, thereby supporting ourselves and improving standards of living.

Among other factors, the rate at which resources can be increased is related to the structure and state of society at any given time and is also related to outside influences. The mix of factors which affects the density distributions of populations and changes appears to be complex. The main factors are highlighted in Figure 1.3.

Qualities of life

Geographers have focused increasingly on the wide variations in the quality of life of different people, even though population distributions and densities and their changes remain at the core of population geography studies. Key factors are access to basic necessities – clean water, food, housing, health care and other welfare provision – and to basic human rights.

Population growth and environmental issues

Aspects of population and quality of life are inevitably linked to other world concerns, particularly the need to safeguard the environment and its resources, which are vital to the support of a continually increasing world population. Between 1950 and 1990, world population had doubled to five billion and is projected to reach eight billion by the year 2025 AD (Figures1.2 and 1.4). Such a rate of increase places considerable strain on environments and has led to serious damage, reducing the capacity of certain environments to sustain the indigenous population.

Geographers are making an important contribution to an understanding of these issues. This section of the text deals with the basics of population geography and also focusses on other issues which affect the quality of life.

Location, distribution and characteristics of population e.g. nutrition and health levels, sex, age, ethnic composition, natural increase rates.

↓

Changes in distribution over time resulting from regional differences in rates of natural increase and net migration rates.

↓

The relationship of population to the environment and its resources from which people gain a living.

↓

Population migration and urbanisation as processes related to the comparative development of countries and their societies.

NOTE: Information about the population of a country is gained largely from taking a periodic census.
The amount and kinds of information obtained varies from one country to another as does its reliability.

***Figure 1.1** Components of population geography*

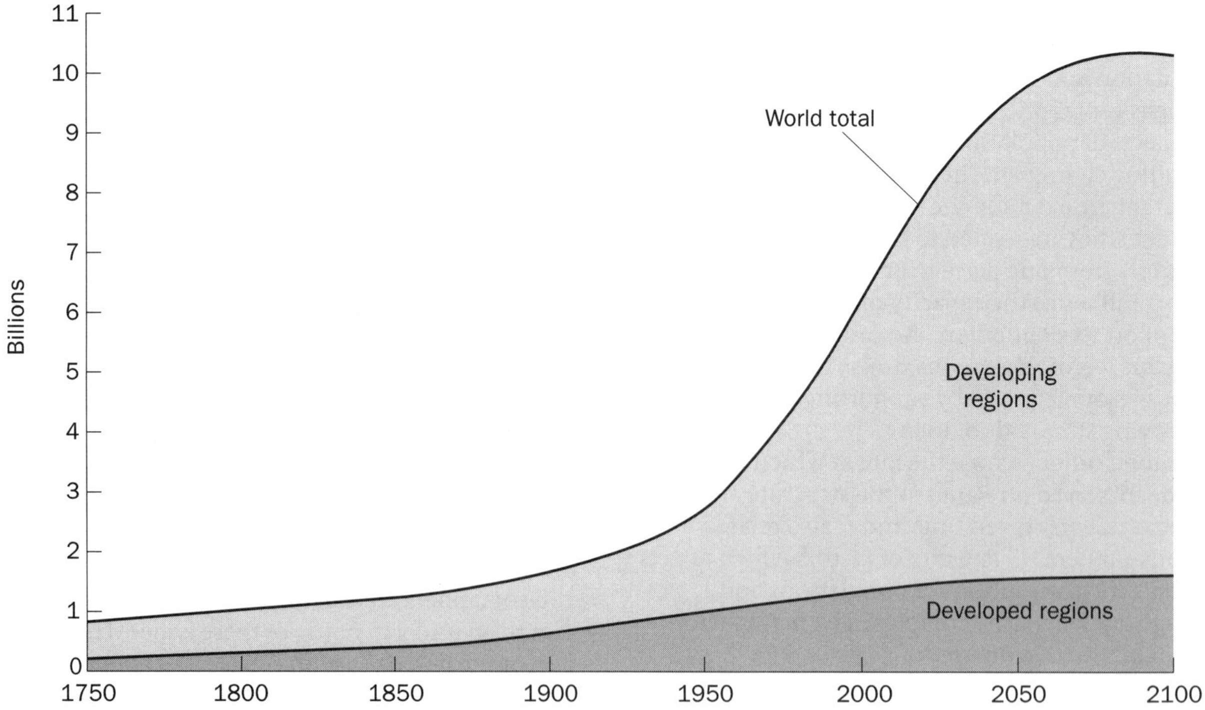

[SOURCE: Thomas W Merrick et al, *World Population in Transition, Population Bulletin*, Vol. 42, No. 2, 1986]

***Figure 1.2** Population growth 1750 – 2100*

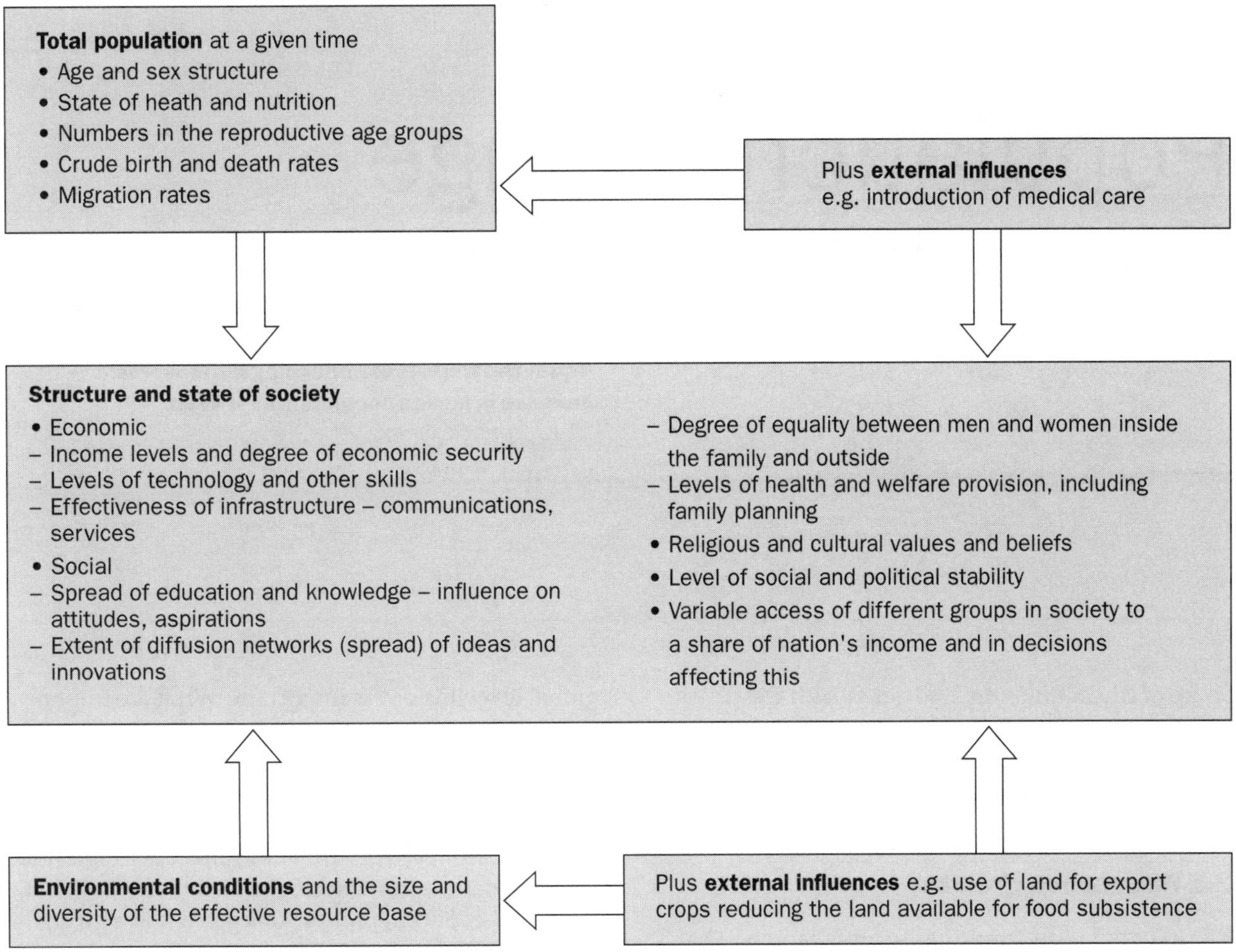

Figure 1.3 *Factors which affect density, distribution and change*

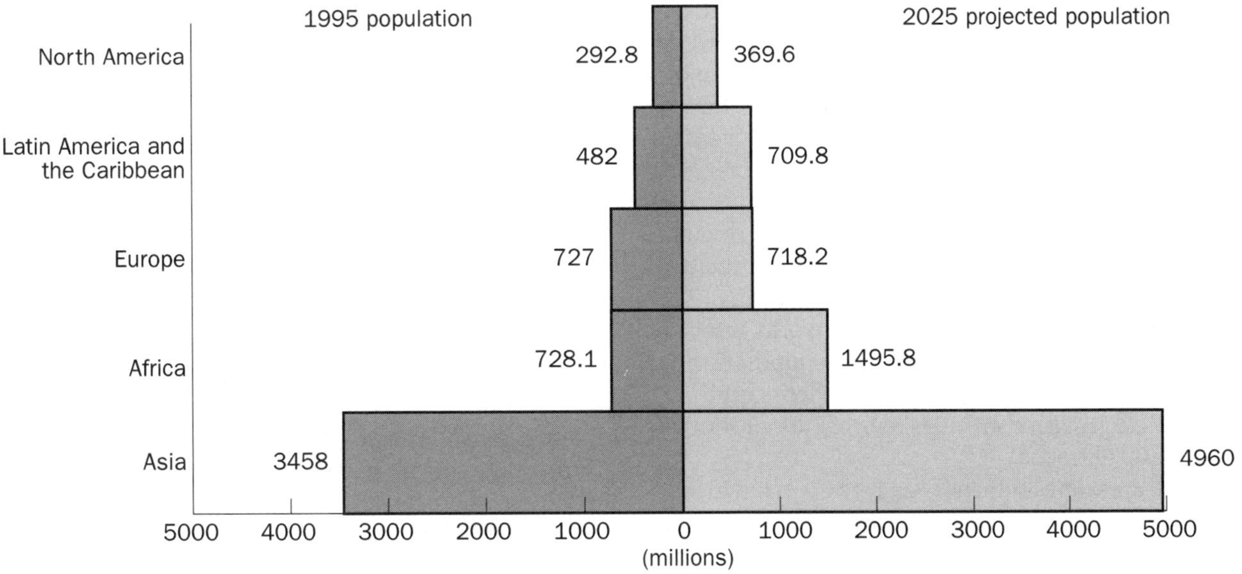

[SOURCE: World Resources 1996]

Figure 1.4 *Population trends 1990 – 2100*

2

CHAPTER 2

Population change through time and space

'Today the world is experiencing the most rapid increase in human population ever seen.'

World Resources 1994 – 1995, World Resources Institute, 1994

Some of the main terms associated with the continued growth in world population numbers and variations in rates of population change across the world are identified in Figure 2.2.

2.1 Population growth

World population continues to grow rapidly. The present level of 4.8 billion is projected to rise to six billion by the year 2000 AD. Although the overall rate of growth is slowing down, the actual numbers per year is still increasing. In the mid-1980s the estimation was 75 million a year, but by the turn of the century it is likely to be 90 million a year. It is thought that the actual numbers added each year to the world's population will not decrease before 2025 AD.

There is considerable variation in rates of population growth across the world (Figure 1.4). At the two extremes of the spectrum are the economically advanced countries in the developed world, which have anxieties about a decrease in the population, and the lesser developed countries, where rapid population growth continues to bring about serious anxieties (Figure 1.3).

There are some countries, such as China, which warrant particular attention because of their sudden transition from a high growth rate to a marked decline in growth due to a fall in birth rate.

Factors which affect population growth

At a national level migration becomes a relevant factor which influences population growth, but at a global level it is not as important. What are important are the differences between mortality and fertility rates, the base size of the population and the age structure of the population because this influences the number of women in the reproductive (child-bearing) age group. These direct demographic influences are in turn closely related to the political and socio-economic conditions present at a given time in a particular region or country(Figure 2.4).

2.2 Types of population change

The cause of rapid population growth

Although fertility rates remain significantly higher than mortality rates, they are falling. The number of children born per woman is decreasing but the number of women of child-bearing age (15 – 50 years) has increased more rapidly. This is a consequence of past rapid growth rates; the children of one generation are the parents of the next.

Rapid population growth is only a problem for lesser developed countries. Despite some decline, fertility rates in a number of countries remain relatively high and the proportion of women of child-bearing age continues to increase (Figure 2.7). Even in China where fertility rates have fallen to a level on a par with advanced countries, such is the size of the base population of 1 135 million and the still youthful character of its age structure, that the increasing number of women of reproductive age will continue to lead to marked population increases (Figure 2.1).

Women of child-bearing age as a % of all women		Fertility rates	
1965	45	**1970**	5.8
1991	56	**1991**	2.1

Figure 2.1 *China's child-bearing population*

The cause of declining population growth

However, a fall in population is a concern for advanced industrialised countries such as western Europe, the United States and Japan. Due to an ageing population with a steady mortality rate and a falling fertility rate, the population is not able to replace itself. The fertility rate needs to be above 2, that is, more than two children on average for every woman of child-bearing age. In the USA and Sweden the fertility rate is 1.9 and as low as 1.3 in Italy and 1.5 in Spain. The problem will be aggravated as the proportion of women in the reproductive age drops as the population structure becomes progressively more aged, unless there is a reversal in trend and the birth rates begin to rise again.

Ultimately it is hoped that developing countries will follow the demographic trend of the industrialised nations where the fall in fertility rates is slowing down population growth. Except in countries such as China and Singapore, where the governments have deliberately adopted a widespread family planning campaign, this has not happened rapidly enough. There are signs that fertility rates are declining in other developing countries but the momentum of population growth has not yet been checked (Figure 2.3).

Measures of mortality

Crude death rate: deaths per 1000 population in a particular year

Infant mortality rate: number of deaths of children under 1 year old (i.e. in the first year of life) per 1000 live births in a particular year

Life expectancy: expectation of life at birth; this is the average number of years that would be lived by a group of persons born in the same year

Measures of fertility

Crude birth rate: the number of births in a year per 1000 of the population

General fertility rate: the number of births in a year per 1000 women of normal reproductive age (usually taken as within the 15 – 44 age group)

Child-women ratio: ratio of children under five years old to women of child-bearing age (usually taken as 15 – 49 for this measure)

Natural rate of increase: the difference between the crude birth and death rates per 1000 of the population in any one year

Replacement rate: is attained when there are just sufficient children born in any one year to balance the number of people who die in that year

Age-sex structure: the pattern created when people are grouped by age

- The size of each group repesents the number of people in any given age-range usually classed in five-year groups: 0 – 4, 5 – 9, 10 – 14, etc.
- Each five-year group is also divided by sex into males and females
- Age-sex structure of a given population is usually represented by a population pyramid which is constructed by representing the five-year age groups on the vertical scale and males and females on the horizontal scale

Dependency ratio is a term frequently linked to the age structure of the population. The population is divided into the *non-economically active age groups*, usually taken as those under 15 years and over 65 years, and the *economically active*, usually taken as those between 15 to 64 years. The dependency ratio is then worked out as a percentage by dividing the number of non-economically active by the number of working age and multiplying by 100.

Figure 2.2 *Population change: terminology*

	Crude birth rate per 1000		Crude death rate per 1000		Total fertility rate		Life expectancy
	1970	1991	1970	1991	1970	1991	1991
Low income countries							
Ethiopia	43	50	20	21	5.8	7.5	48
Bangladesh	48	34	21	13	7.0	4.4	51
India	41	30	18	10	5.8	3.9	60
Average	39	30	14	10	6.5	3.8	62
Middle income countries							
Bolivia	46	36	19	10	6.5	4.8	59
Botswana	53	36	17	6	6.9	4.8	68
Brazil	35	24	10	7	4.9	2.8	66
Average	38	28	13	10	5.7	3.7	64
High income countries							
Singapore	23	18	5	5	3.1	1.8	74
UK	16	14	12	11	2.4	1.8	75
USA	18	16	10	9	2.5	2.1	76
Average	18	13	10	9	2.4	1.8	77

[SOURCE: World Development Report 1993]

a Selected countries

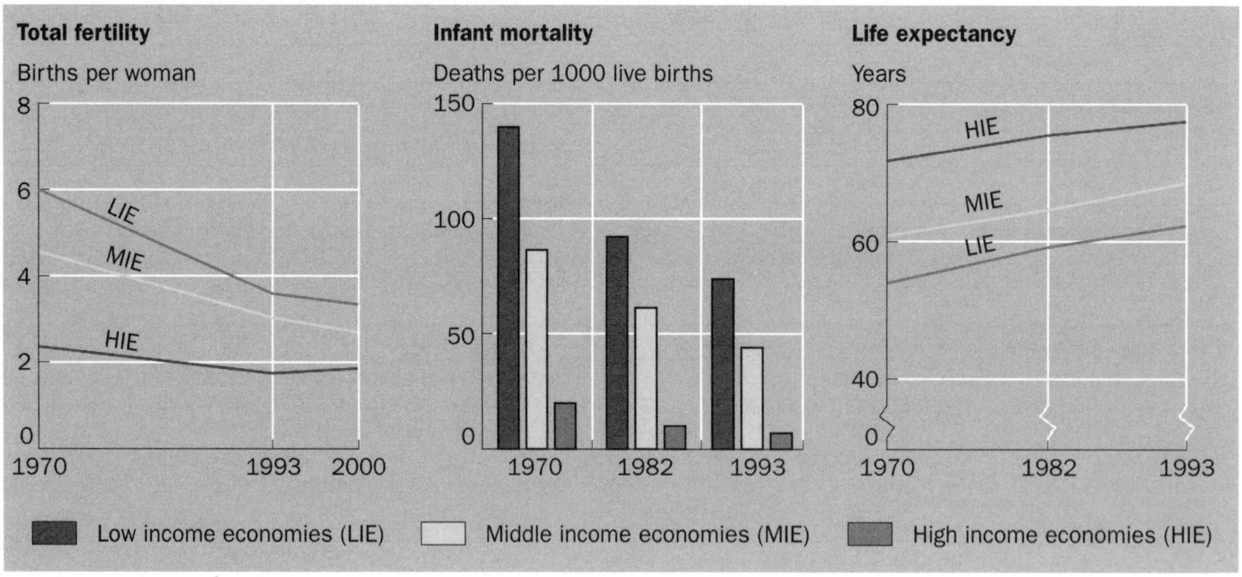

[SOURCE: World Development Report 1995]

b Type of economy

Figure 2.3 Demographic indicators

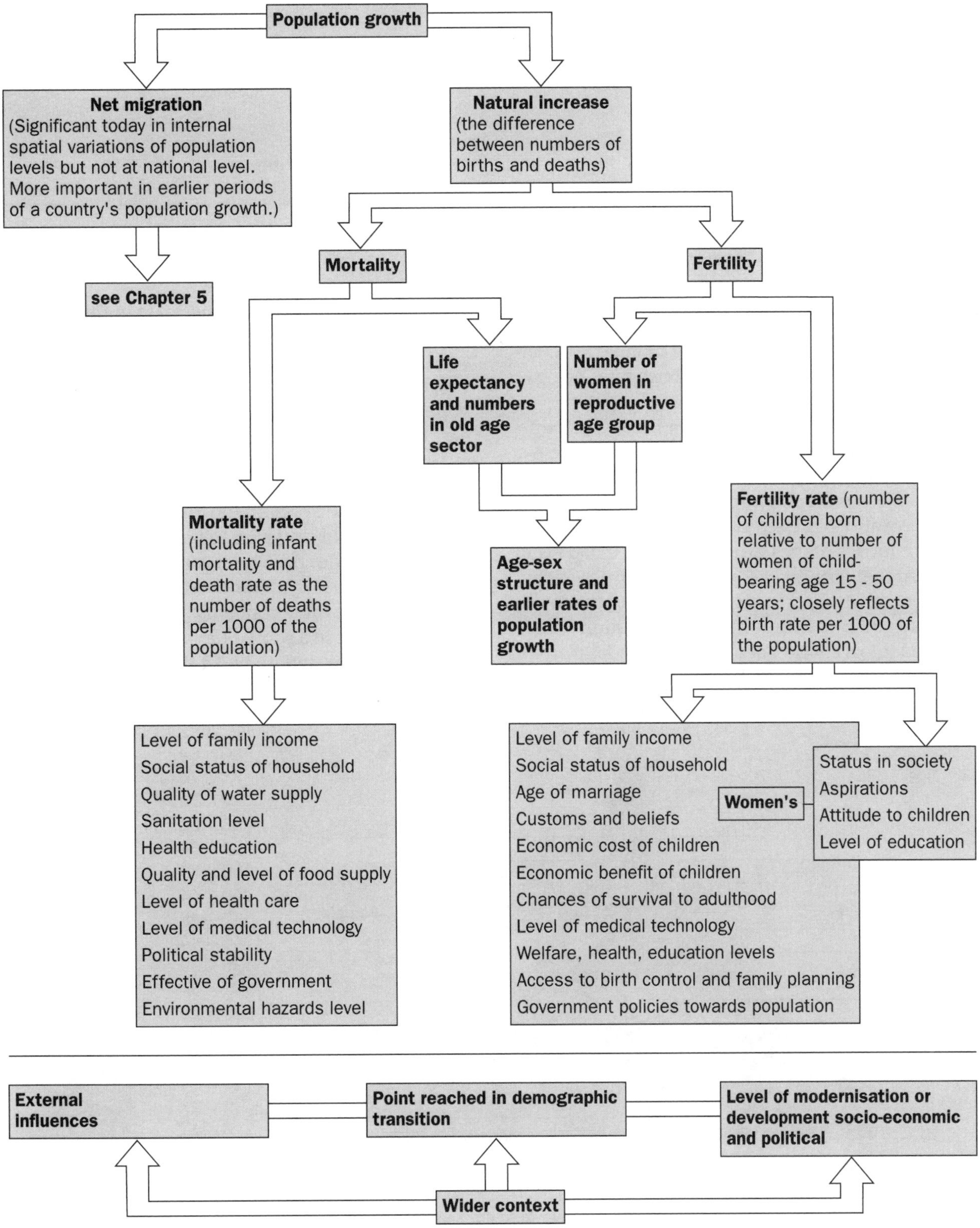

Figure 2.4 *Factors which influence population growth*

	Women of child-bearing age as a % of all women		Fertility rates	
	1965	1991	1970	1991
Low income countries	46	51	6.0	3.8
Middle income countries	45	49	5.0	3.2
Advanced high income countries	42	49	3.9	2.1
World	46	50	5.0	3.3

[SOURCE: World Development Report 1993]

Figure 2.5 *Percentage of women of child-bearing age and fertlity rates*

2.3 **Non-replacement of population**

Over the last decade, an increasing number of developed countries are anxious about birth rates being too low and the population ageing too rapidly (Figure 2.6). In addition in Western European countries such as Sweden, France and Germany, there is a fear of declining population numbers. Some of the countries of southern Europe, such as Spain and Italy, have also expressed growing concern. (Because of the influence of the Catholic religion, it had been expected that fertility rates would remain above the replacement level.) Japan is anxious about too low a birth rate, despite already having 123 million people crowded into a country about the size of California and three quarters of which is mountainous.

Psychologically, an actual decrease in the population is seen to weaken a country's security and position in the world. There is also the very real concern about the cost of supporting an ageing population, which taxes the economic system and puts comparatively little back. A survey carried out in 1990 by Japan's Ministry of Finance indicated that the concern was for both the social welfare costs of an ageing population and for the declining number of young and working-age people. There would be a serious decline in economic and social vitality and a major labour shortage.

To overcome these concerns, Japan, Sweden and other countries in a similar demographic situation are taking active steps to boost the birth rate again.

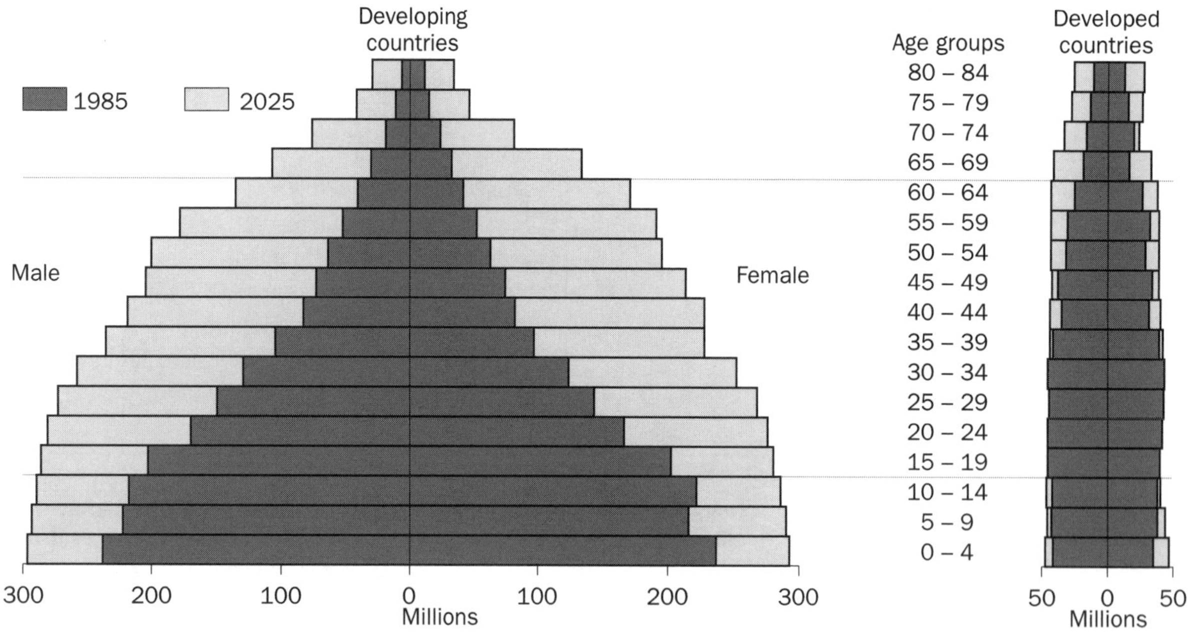

In 1985, 37% of the total population of the developing world consisted of children below the age of 15 and only 4% were 65 years or older. By contrast, the developed countries' population of children under 15 was 22% of the total, with 11% 65 years or older.

[SOURCE: *Population and environment: the challenges ahead*, UNPFA 1991]

Figure 2.6 *Population age pyramids 1985 and 2025*

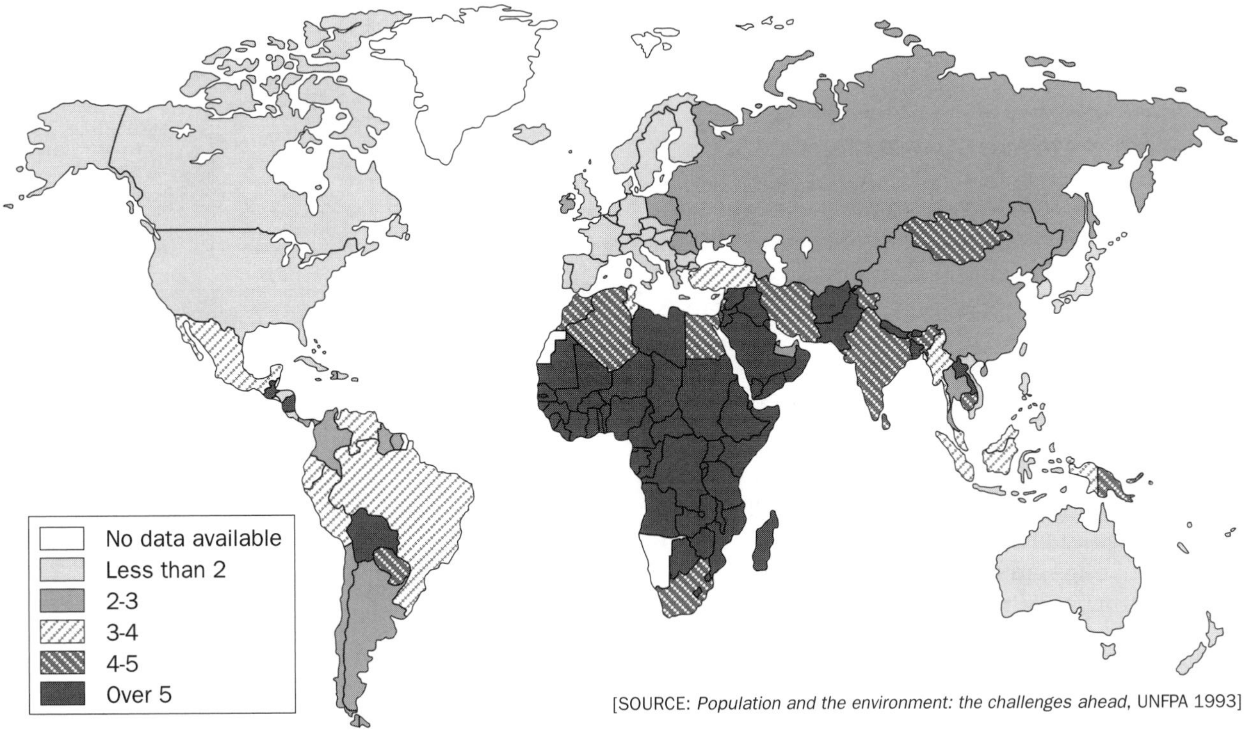

[SOURCE: *Population and the environment: the challenges ahead*, UNFPA 1993]

Figure 2.7 *Total fertility rates 1990 – 95*

Fall in fertility rates

Socio-economic influences

Better health and welfare provision, which has brought about a marked fall in infant mortality rates, and improved pre-natal care meant that there was less need to have a number of children. This was a feature of western European countries from the turn of the century and, more recently, in southern Europe.

There are other influences associated with the socio-economic changes of modernisation. Better education and the emancipation of women have led to later marriages and more time spent by women in a career outside the home. This has reduced the number of years in marriage when children could be born, the first children on average being born much later. The desire for smaller families, easier access to birth control methods and abortion facilities also influenced the birth rate. While higher incomes and greater leisure facilities have influenced couples who do not want a number of children in the family, recent research has shown that it is concern for the future of the children which also motivates couples to stop producing more than two children.

The high cost of living is also a deterrent. In the UK and Japan, the extremely high cost of housing delays the time of having children in a marriage and reduces in the income available to raise them. The physical and emotional cost of child-rearing and of education are also more likely limits on family size than hindrances to careers or a preference for leisure and consumer goods.

Most quoted reasons	Percentage of respondents
High cost of child care	37%
High cost of education	30%
Physical and emotional burdens of child-rearing	25%
Lack of household space	16%
Hindrance to careers	14%

[SOURCE: *Look Japan*, October 1990]

Figure 2.8 *Why Japanese families are having fewer children*

While the the level of response is likely to vary from one advanced industrial society to another, what is felt by Japanese couples appears to be broadly replicated elsewhere. (Figure 2.8)

Government policies

It follows that if the cost of living and the cost of raising children limits family size, then government policies towards taxation and family welfare are also significant influences on how many children a couple will have. In the UK for example, it is claimed that high levels of taxation, insufficient family benefit payment and too few creche and nursery facilities deter couples from having more than one or two children. Where governments have taken active steps to encourage a rise in the birth rate, the results have been positive. Sweden, for example, has reversed the downward trend in the birth rate by such measures as offering childcare allowances and paid leave from work for both parents when a child is expected. Between 1975 and 1987 the number of children per woman had risen from 1.65 to 1.84. In Singapore, since 1987, couples with three or more children have been given an annual tax break of $5 500, which had helped to increase the number of children per couples from 1.5 to 1.9 by 1990.

Decline in the reproductive age sector

Once fertility rates fall over time, the population begins to age and fewer women fall into the reproductive age groups. As the age structure becomes top heavy in the low stationary phase of demographic transition, there are fewer women to bear children. Thus, if birth rates are to be reversed then the number of children per woman of reproductive age must be increased. It becomes more important for governments to provide the incentive for couples to increase the size of the family.

Mortality rates

Better health care, better nutrition and improved environmental conditions have been important factors in bringing about a fall in the death rate to the level now experienced in developed countries and with this, a marked rise in the life expectancy age. However, the ageing of the population is also a critical factor itself on mortality rates, offsetting the effect of health and environmental improvement.

An increase in the ageing sector of the population increases the mortality rate. The older a person is, the greater likelihood of that person dying. Thus, the greater the proportion of the population in the old age sector (over 65), the higher the death rate for the population as a whole. The fall in mortality rates brought about by improved living conditions is thus countered by an increasing proportion of aged in the population.

Mortality rates are no longer dropping in the developed world; they seem to hover at around nine per 1000, a level now being reached by a number of developing countries. In some countries, the death rate now exceeds that of some developing countries. For example, Sweden and Norway in the early 1990s had death rates of 11, whereas Sri Lanka with its youthful age structure had a death rate of six, and Brazil eight per 1000.

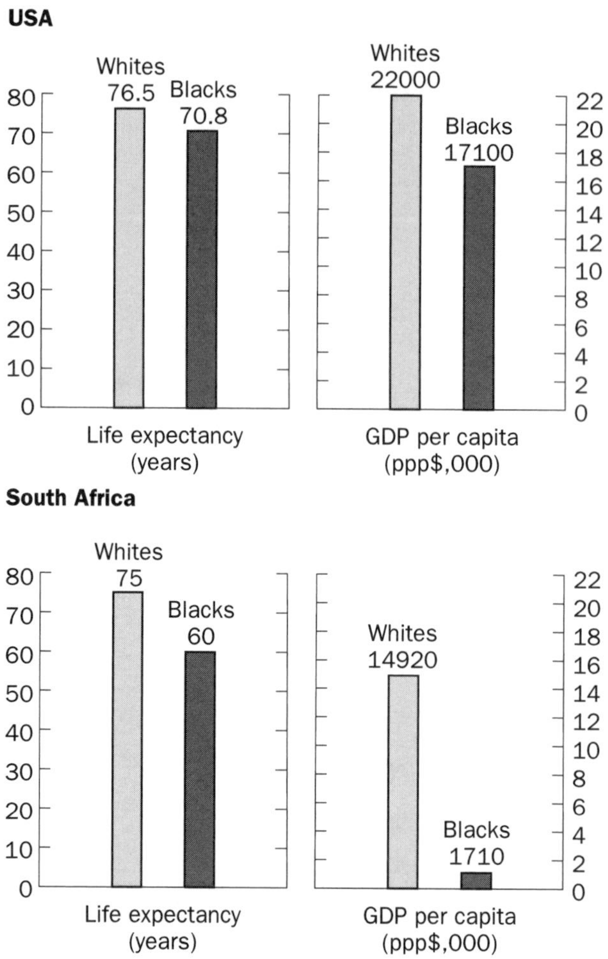

Figure 2.9 *Variations in life expectancy and per capita GDP between the white and black population in the USA and South Africa*

Variations in mortality rates within a population

Research into mortality rates also shows significant variations within any population. Men in general have a lower life expectancy than women. Mortality rates are higher amongst people on lower incomes and in manual occupations because they have less access to good health care and live in poorer environmental conditions than higher income groups. Research has shown that high rates of heart disease are concentrated in the old heavy industrial areas of the UK and in inner city areas. Lung cancer is also more prevalent in industrial and densely populated areas with higher than average levels of air pollution.

Studies in the USA have shown that mortality levels are higher amongst coloured ethnic groups than amongst the white population (Figure 2.9). Black Americans, for example, can probably expect to die six years sooner than white Americans. Evidence indicates that this is largely due to poorer living conditions – 31% of all black families live below the poverty line as against 9% of white families. Evidence from Britain and France indicates that relative disadvantaged health and environmental conditions have a similar effect on mortality rates for ethnic minorities.

Any further reductions in mortality rates depends on more help for the poorest in society. Thus, to reduce mortality rates requires much more financial investment in medical research and other measures to reduce heart and cancer related illnesses. Much greater investment is needed to improve the living and welfare conditions of the poorest in society. Government policies related to distribution of budget finances, for example, are important influences on mortality rates.

The effects of an ageing population on an economy

The ageing of Europe's population poses big challenges for the state and the market place.

Key points about ageing in Europe

1 In Western Europe 15% of the population is over 65 years of age i.e. 50 million.
2 Average European woman of child-bearing age produces only 1.7 children, insufficient to replace the population. Italy has the lowest figure.
3 80% of Europeans believe those in work have a duty through contributions and taxes to ensure older people have a decent standard of living.
4 Economic growth rates of up to 1.5% are needed if pensions are to rise with earnings.
5 Public health spending for people aged over 65 years is four times higher per capita than that for those under 65 years.

Increase in the dependency ratio

As a population ages, more people have to be supported by a diminishing number in the working sector. It has been claimed that in economic terms, once a person reaches 45 years old he or she begins to take more out of the economy than he or she contributes. The imbalance between contribution and extraction steadily widens with age. Most elderly people have made their contribution earlier in life as members of the working sector and are thus entitled to support on humanitarian and social grounds in their old age. Many elderly people continue to make positive contributions to society. Nevertheless, the financial burden of an increasing old age sector remains very real. The aged need care and support and this places a great strain on social services and health care, which in most developed countries, are largely funded out of public finance.

Increase in the social burden

The greatest impact will be in Germany where the population will decline by 15 million between 1995 – 2030.
By 2030 the proportion 20 years or younger will have declined from 20% of the population to 16%, while those over 65 years wll have climbed from 16% to 20%. People between these age groups, having to contribute most to support the elderly, will have decreased from 46% to 38% of the population. Alarmed by the anticipated costs of supporting this 'exploding' pensioner population, the German government increased employees social insurance contributions, raised the retirement age and reduced the level of pensions.

The social security burden grows as more people become dependents rather than producers. Each elderly person has fewer relatives, on average, to care for him or her. The growth in the number of people over 75 years old as part of this aged sector (men older than 65; women older than 60) will continue right up to 2002 AD.

In the UK there is serious concern that pension levels cannot be maintained as more people become eligible for a state pension. Equally, the burden on health and welfare services is placing a great strain on finances. As a consequence, successive Conservative governments have encouraged people to join private pension schemes and to opt out of the National Health Service by joining the private health care organisations such as BUPA.

Uneven distribution of the social burden

People who are sufficiently wealthy tend to retire to the coast or rural areas, making the imbalance between age groups even greater in such areas. For example, the south coast districts in the UK have elderly populations of more than 30%, placing a heavy strain on social and health services in these districts, so much so that some districts are actively discouraging any further increase in the elderly.

The poor amongst the elderly are often found in rundown inner city areas, in old housing with poor provision of basic amenities. Providing for and improving the quality of life for the elderly in these disadvantaged areas is one of the greatest needs in society.

There may also be an over-concentration of elderly in the depopulated rural areas. Many of the younger, more mobile and more affluent members of these regions have moved away to areas with better amenities and employment opportunities. Note, for example, the disproportionate number of elderly in the rural interior of Wales and parts of Scotland in the UK, and in the more remote areas of inland Japan.

Possible effect on economic competition
A recent series of articles on whether or not Europe can successfully hold its competitive position in the world noted that the ageing of Europe's populations has an enormous impact on the economies of countries and their international competitiveness.

Newly industrialising countries such as China and Brazil would gain from economic change as in the first half of the twenty-first century they would have a much younger population than Europe, Japan and North America. A greater proportion of the Gross Domestic Product of these latter countries will have to be diverted to social spending on the elderly rather than towards investment in economic growth.

Demographic restructuring could alter patterns of consumption, production, employment and innovation
There will be a much tighter labour market despite the increase in labour-saving technology. The number of younger people will decrease. Older staff will be employed for a longer period with a possible rise in the retiring age. People who are not working but are of working age will be pressured to return to work, especially women who had left their employment to have children.

Businesses will have to cope with changes in demand patterns as the number of older consumers increase and younger ones decrease. 'Third age' consumers are seen as a distinctive group, keen to spend more on leisure, holidays and health care. Their housing requirements are different from those of younger couples. Already some companies concentrate on building retirement complexes which incorporates dwelling units, leisure and care facilities. Retired people make up a significant proportion of the market for the marina complexes that are becoming a feature of river, lake and coastal areas throughout Western Europe as well as in parts of the United States and Japan.

Many people of middle and higher incomes are making private provision for their welfare as it becomes evident that the state is less able to take on this role. This will boost the financial services of those companies which offer personal pensions.

2.4 The falling growth rate in newly industrialised countries

There is emerging concern amongst the more mature newly industrialising countries about falling population rates. For example, in 1983 Lee Kuan Yew, the Prime Minister of Singapore, became involved in the 'great marriage debate', which gave rise to a suggested policy by the government of Singapore. Because there was a growing number of unmarried graduate women and those married were having fewer children, it was felt that there would be a decline in the intellectual quality of the population and its business vitality. However, the proposed preferential treatment for graduate women and mothers, suggested by the government to encourage a greater number of marriages and larger families, was opposed on grounds of discrimination against the less educated majority.

By 1986 concern had intensified because the average number of children had fallen below the population replacement level of two per family – a trend which, if continued, would lead to a population decline within twenty years. (Ironically the problem had partly arisen because of the earlier highly successful government family planning programme initiated in 1966 to control the growth of Singapore's population, a policy of 'Stop at Two' with severe penalties if couples had more than two children.) Since 1987 tax breaks have been given to raise the birth rate from 1.5 to 1.9 by 1990.

Without immigration or an increase in the birth rate, the government fear that economic growth will be slowed. An abundance of adaptable labour had been one of the bases for Singapore's highly successful industrialisation, which attracted multi-national companies to set up the more labour-intensive industries, such as assembly electronics and textiles. It is thought that increased productivity through more technological investment and the reorganisation of production methods will be needed if the labour supply declines. However, these may incur costs greater than those of other industrialising countries, such as India and Brazil, which still have relatively cheap labour available.

2.5 Too rapid population growth in developing countries

In tropical African countries and in some Asian and Middle East countries, populations are growing faster than food supplies. This is often accompanied by an increase in the incidence of famine and environmental degradation. Recently, in certain

Latin American countries, some resurgence of growth in the already high birth rates has occurred as more women enter the reproductive age range. For example, Bolivia's crude birth rate remains high at 35 per thousand in 1993, compared to 46 per thousand in 1965, while the infant mortality rate has fallen from 160 to 73 over the same period.

Mortality and life expectancy

The decline in infant mortality rate and increase in life expectancy are useful measures of falling mortality rates in those developing countries which have entered a period of rapid population growth. (Figures 2.10 and 2.11)

Environmental conditions and western influence

In developing countries mortality rates are still influenced by environmental conditions, more so than by the degenerative effects of ageing. Environmental conditions include level of food supply (nutrition), water supply, sanitation, health care and endemic disease, such as malaria and sleeping sickness. The fall in mortality rates and especially in infant mortality levels between the 1950s and 1960s, has been largely attributed to western intervention, which had significantly improved welfare and environmental conditions.

There has been a notable reduction and, in some cases, an eradication of some of the epidemic diseases which used to sweep through populations, bringing with them increases in the death rate. This reduction is linked to the increased level of contact with western populations, leading to immunisation against earlier killer diseases such as malaria, smallpox, tuberculosis and measles.

Improved diets and better health care through improved sanitation and the quality of water supplies have also brought about a marked fall in the mortality rate. Life expectancy has thus been increased. For example, as late as 1960 in India, average life expectancy was as low as 40 years of age, but in just over 20 years it has increased to 55 years of age and is now approaching 60 years.

In recent years, due to cutbacks in the funding of social programmes and the increased resistance of some disease carriers to preventive measures, there has been a disturbing upsurge again in certain diseases, particularly in the incidence of malaria. Every year it is estimated that 100 million people contract the disease, but the actual number of reported cases is only 10 million a year, of which 80% are in Africa, south of the Sahara. In some areas this has led to an increase in infant and child mortality rates, reversing the former downward trend. The increase is also associated with the widespread refugee movements during famine and civil war, bringing non-immune people into infected areas or infected people into previously malaria-free areas. Increases in uncontrolled breeding sites due to wider irrigation and forest clearance for agriculture, as in Amazonia, have also contributed to the resurgence of malaria.

The marked slowing down in the fall of mortality rates is also a result of a failure to eradicate poverty and malnutrition amongst the poorest sectors of the population, both in less fertile rural areas and in growing squatter settlements in the cities. In Bangladesh, for example, the infant mortality rate in slum city areas remains as high as 140 per thousand

	Child mortality		Life expectancy at birth (years)	
Region	1975	1990	1975	1990
Sub-Saharan Africa	212	175	48	52
India	195	127	53	58
China	85	43	56	69
Other Asia and islands	135	97	56	62
Latin America and the Caribbean	104	60	62	70
Middle East	174	111	52	61
Advanced Countries	21	11	73	76
World	135	96	60	65

[SOURCE: World Development Report 1993]

Figure 2.10 Changes in child mortality and life expectancy by demographic region, 1975 – 1990

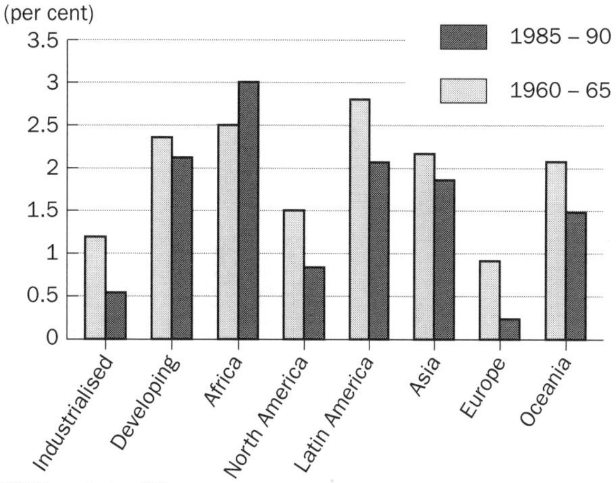

NOTE: excludes CIS
[SOURCE: United Nations Population Division, World Population Prospects 1990, New York, 1991]

Figure 2.11 Average annual population growth rates, 1960 – 65 and 1985 – 90

as against a national average of 114 per thousand. There are similar variations in life expectancy.

Educational influences

In addition to western influence reducing mortality rates, the educational level of mothers also seems an important factor (Figure 2.12). The more informed the mother, the more likely are the children in the family to be immunised against diseases. More care is also given to sanitation, basic health care and the cooking and preparation of food.

In a different context, education is also important in extending life expectancy amongst adults. A better education leads to better employment and income, enabling the quality of living to be significantly raised.

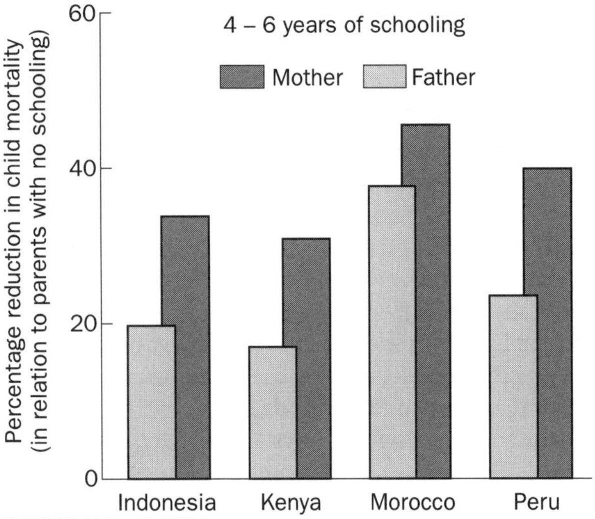

[SOURCE: Hobcraft 1993]

***Figure 2.12** Child health depends more on the mother's than on the father's schooling*

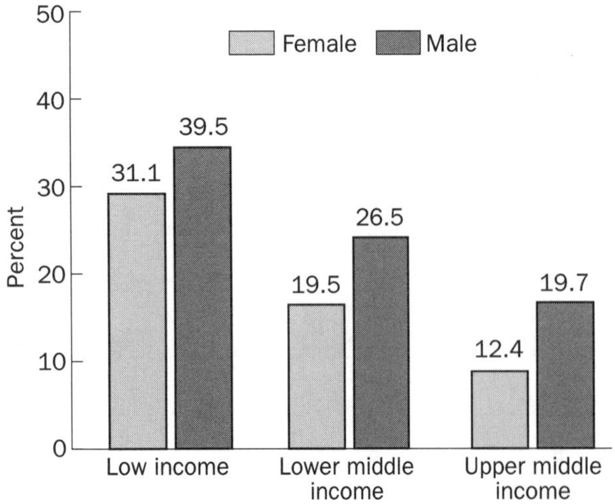

NOTE: Adult mortality is the probability at age 15 of dying before age 60, expressed as a percentage.
[SOURCE: World Development Report 1990]

***Figure 2.13** Adult mortality in the developing world*

Status and spatial variations in mortality rates

Average figures of mortality rates obscure significant variations between groups. There is a direct link between the level of income and adult mortality rate as there is also to infant mortality rates.

There are also important spatial variations across a country. Because urban populations have better access to health and welfare facilities, mortality is lower than in rural areas. The most striking feature to emerge from a detailed investigation of patterns of mortality in less developed countries is the geographic diversity rather than the uniformity of mortality rates. Degree of accessibility is a key feature. The more remote the area, the shorter the life expectancy and the higher the mortality rate.

	Water		**Sanitation**	
	Urban	**Rural**	**Urban**	**Rural**
All developing countries	85	60	76	40
Least developed countries	61	45	45	15

[SOURCE: World Development Report 1993]

***Figure 2.14** Percentage of population with access to water, access to sanitation, 1991*

As regards variations between countries, the extent of government commitment towards raising food, health and other welfare levels is crucial. This depends not only upon the attitudes of governments towards the level of priority given to the quality of life, but also the finance available to them.

Birth and fertility rates

Fertility rates remain highest in Africa, while in Latin America which up to 1975 had a similar rate to Africa, fertility rates have fallen sharply. They have also dropped over much of Asia, with China having an exceptional downward trend (Figure 2.7). It is expected that the population growth rate will stabilise in Latin America and Asia by the year 2000. In Africa, because the current high fertility rates are bringing an increasing number of women in to the child-bearing age, the momentum of growth will be maintained up until the year 2025, making tropical Africa unique.

Within any one continent there are sharp national and regional variations. For example, among the East African countries the crude birth rate from 1985 to 1990 averaged around 42 per thousand, but in Malawi it has remained persistently high at 53 per thousand, showing little decline since the late 1960s. In Latin America the birth rate now averages approximately 26 per thousand, but in Cuba it is as low as 16 per thousand, while in Bolivia it remains relatively high at 36 per thousand. In Asia, similar variations are evident. A number of countries such as Sri Lanka, Thailand and Korea have levels at between 22 per thousand to 18 per thousand, but Bangladesh and Pakistan, like some Middle East Muslim countries remain relatively high at around 34 per thousand, double that of some other Asian countries.

Factors which affect fertility rates

Attempts have been made to identify why rates remain persistently high in some parts of the developing world, while in others they have been successfully lowered.

Bongaart's fertility model

Bongaart's general observation is that factors which affect fertility can be divided into natural factors and the deliberate control of fertility by married couples through family planning methods (Fertility transition model).

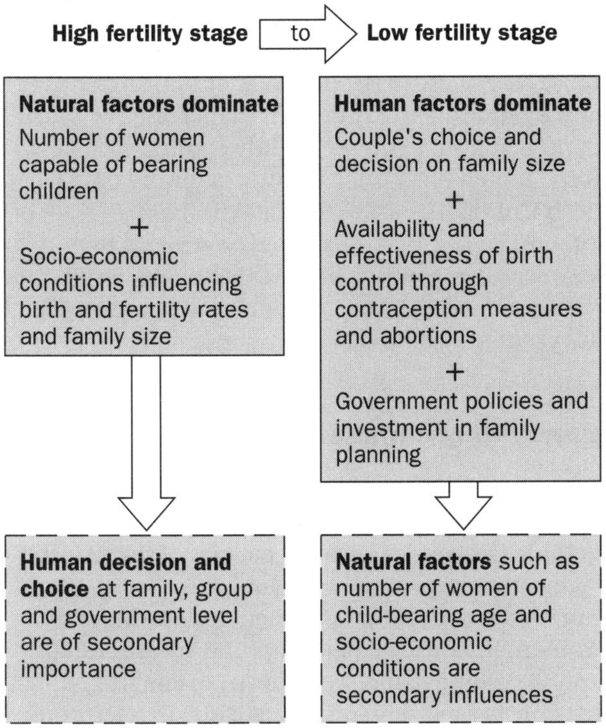

[SOURCE: based on Bongaarts J *A Framework for Analysing Proximate determinants of Fertility, Population and Development Review*]

Figure 2.15 *Fertility transition*

Where fertility rates remain high, natural factors dominate, two of which are the proportion of married females in the population and the duration of the period after birth when a woman cannot conceive.

The most important human control methods of fertility are using contraception and induced abortion. Bongaart identifies a fertility transition, the rate of which is affected by the rate at which human control of fertility takes over from natural control. Such a transition is experienced by those developing world countries which have achieved a marked fall in birth and fertility rates. In each country, for example in China, Singapore, Thailand, Costa Rica and Sri Lanka, there has been widespread acceptance of family planning methods (Figure 2.16).

However, other factors also influence natural and human fertility control. Natural factors are influenced by the age structure of the population, poverty and the low status and education of women (Chapter 9). Human fertility control is stimulated by rising incomes, education, a positive government policy and investment in family planning.

UNFPA report 1992

In formal education, UNFPA continued to support the integration of population and family life education in the curricula of primary and secondary schools. Most countries are still in the early stages of this process. Only Botswana, the Seychelles and Zimbabwe have introduced population or family life education in more than half of their primary schools; and only Botswana, Burkino Faso, the Central Africa Republic, Gambia, Mauritius, Senegal, Sierra Leone and Zimbabwe have achieved similar levels of integration at the secondary level.

[SOURCE: United Nations Population Fund]

Tropical Africa needs more labour

Birth rates are falling everywhere in the world but the fall is slowest in Africa. This is because Africa is underpopulated due to the nineteenth century slave trade and the rural to urban depopulation. Imposition of a moneyed tax meant that many were forced to seek some cash income in the cities, causing a severe shortage of labour on farms. Consequently more children were needed to help cultivate the land and livestock, and to do the chores around the household. Beyond this it was felt that the larger the number of children, the more were likely to survive and provide economic security in old age.

Having children seems to be a logical response to the loss of labour in an export economy. Studies, for example in Burkina Faso, indicate that the main problem is not shortage of land or drought, but that there are not enough people to raise agricultural production. In any country the rich can invest and reinvest their capital producing greater and greater profits but the poor can only produce children.

Poverty encourages a high fertility rate

Poverty implies a lack of educational opportunity, especially for women. Women are very much tied to tradition and cannot escape from the twin tasks of raising children and looking after the household. Both World Conferences on Populations in 1974 and 1984 emphasised the eradication of poverty and better educational opportunity as essential steps towards couples' acceptance of birth control and family planning.

Fertility and equality

It is not just the wealth of a nation that influences whether or not people will choose to have fewer children. Far more important is the distribution of that wealth to individual families.

	per capita GNP ($)	% wealth owned by richest 10%	Total fertility rate
Kenya	370	45.4	6.4
Sri Lanka	470	43.0	3.3
Venezuela (1991)	2730	33.0	2.7

[SOURCE: *New Internationalist* 1987]

Better education would overcome traditional attitudes

Without better opportunities and better education, couples are subject to tradition as was shown by the strong opposition to contraception by Muslim nations at the recent World Population Summit in Cairo (1994). Saudi Arabia actually boycotted the summit. Muslin countries still have a very high birth rate. In addition, the tradition of early marriages extends the period of a woman's child-bearing age.

Government policy on family planning is influential

Most governments in developing countries have shown the need for some family planning and birth control, and have introduced a form of family planning programme but the degree of commitment towards family planning is usually inadequate. In India, although $500 million is devoted to family planning and welfare, political parties do not include family planning as part of their ideology because it is unpopular with many voters, and to reduce the growth of population may in future reduce the number of potential supporters. There is also the financial cost of family planning programmes to consider. Between the 1980s and early 1990s when many developing countries had an increasing debt problem, it has been the social welfare programmes which suffered cutbacks.

Political attempts to impose family planning are also unproductive since it removes from couples the right to choose how many children they will have. Apart from imposed controls in certain communist countries, such as China, the most notable reaction to attempts to impose a birth control programme was seen in India, when in the 1975 – 77 emergency under Sanjay Gandhi, local officials were enlisted to fulfil sterilisation quotas.

The political will to increase family planning needs to be linked to consultation with prospective parents. Dramatic falls in fertility rates can occur in these circumstances, as in Bangladesh, where fertility rates have fallen by 20% between 1970 and 1991 from seven children to 5.5 children. The recent Cairo Population Summit has placed great emphasis on promoting family planning in consultation with the people. Governments need to raise the standard of living and education so that couples may be in a position to make an informed and favourable decision which satisfies their needs as well as the requirements of any planning policy.

Once this happens, birth and fertility rates do fall significantly, bringing population growth under control. Thailand has one of the most successful family planning programmes in the world, which relies on the use of the media, economic incentives and community involvement to increase the use of contraception. Perhaps the only country to sucessfully implement a forced family planning policy has been China. Its success was due to a particular set of circumstances. However, there now seems to be some reversal towards a higher birth rate despite the coercion used to try to get couples to comply with government demands.

Concluding comment

The Cairo Conference took great strides by focussing on individual needs instead of demographic targets. At Cairo the nations of the world agreed that governments should give special attention to the education of women, the health of women, the survival of infants and young children and the empowerment of women to enable couples to achieve their reproductive goals and determine freely and responsibly the number and spacing of their children.

If governments ensure that this basic package of social policies and reprodcutive health services is in place, the Cairo census implies that they will make great strides toward greater social equity and reduce high rates of population growth.
(Sinding S W and Fathalla MF reflecting on the 1995 International Conference on Population and Development).

[SOURCE: Populi, December 1995, United Nations Population Fund]

Thailand is the home of one of the most successful and effective family planning programs in the world. The program relies on the use of the media, economic incentives, and community involvement to increase the use of contraception.

Thailand's striking approach stresses the immediate practical benefits from lower fertility and uses methods that mix humor and audacity. The program is run by an NGO, the population and Community Development Association (PDA), with the support of the Ministry of Public Health.

The Community Based Family Planning Services (CBFPS), a PDA program, was initiated in 1974 and now reaches more than 16 000 villages and 17 million people – one-third of the nation's population. The key message links population growth to low standards of living and family planning to economic gains. To convey this message, taboos surrounding birth control had to be broken down. Birth control carnivals, games, condom-blowing balloon contests, raffles, village fairs, and weddings have served as occasions for promoting family planning joyfully. Vasectomy marathons are held on Labor Day and on the king's birthday. In 1983 a team of forty doctors and eighty nurses performed a record breaking 1190 vasectomies during the one-day festival. The PDA also delivers free, convenient and efficient vasectomy services in clinics and mobile units. Between July 1980 and June 1984 it performed 25 412 vasectomies.

Registered family planners may also rent cattle for ploughing their fields – family planning buffaloes – at half the regular price. They are encouraged to market some of their products through the CBFPS at prices about 30 per cent higher than regular middlemen offer and to buy fertilizer and seeds at 30 per cent below local market prices.Under a similar program villagers who practice contraception may have their goods transported to the marketplace at a discount or may receive free piglets.

In 1985 about 60 per cent of all Thai couples practised some form of birth control. The total fertility rate fell from 6.1 in 1965 – 70 to 2.8 in 1985, as against an average 4.1 for lower-middle income countries.

[SOURCE: World Development Report 1990]

Figure 2.16 *Family planning, buffaloes and vasectomy festivals in Thailand*

case study

2.1 **Britain's ageing population**

Where the elderly live

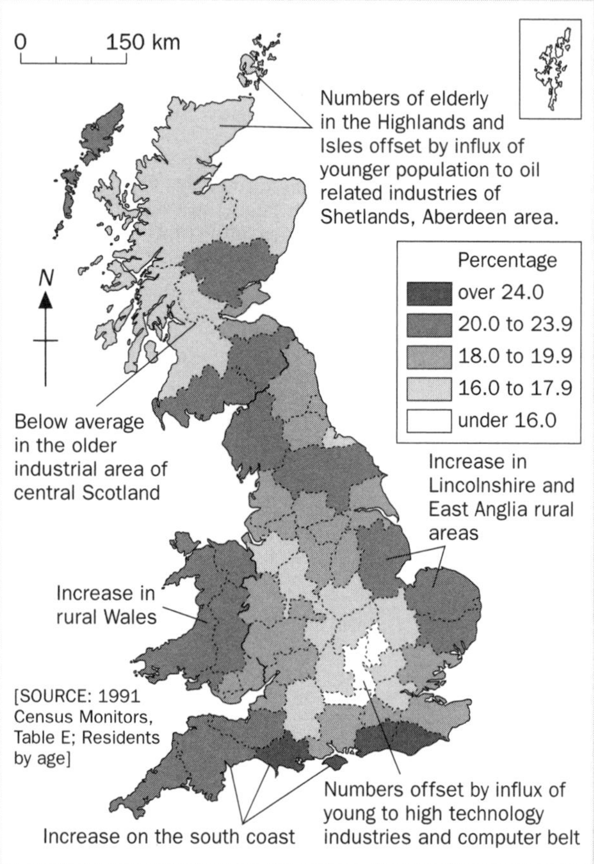

Persons of pensionable age and over as a proportion of all residents, 1991

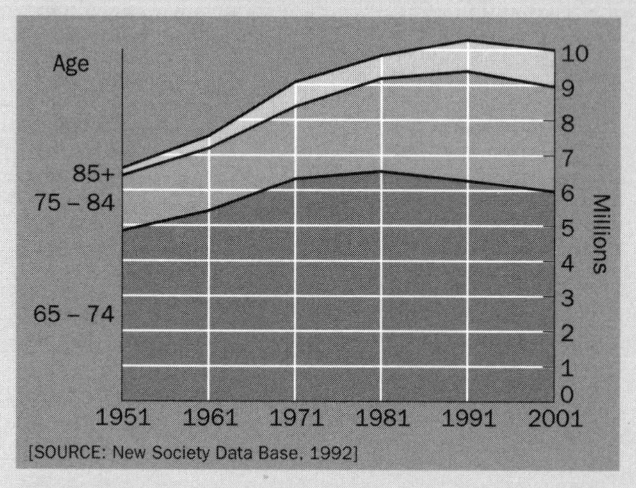

The growing elderly

Burden per person aged 15 – 64 years

1980=100	2000	2010	2020	2030	2040
France	101	105	117	129	133
Germany	112	119	131	157	162
Italy	102	109	120	135	143
UK	98	101	106	118	117
Japan	112	133	138	136	150
US	97	100	118	133	132

Trends in social expenditure

The distribution pattern in the UK reflects the retirement move to what are termed 'counties of leisure' in southern and eastern coastal England, north and west Wales and along the England-Scotland border areas. (Although the upturn in migration activity of the retired is not marked in terms of total migration pattern, it does have a significant effect on the distribution of the elderly population.)

The pattern in rural areas is also affected to some extent by the outward migration of the younger population due to restricted work opportunities as in rural Wales, for example.

What the map does not show is the spatial variation in the proportion of elderly within the major urban conurbations and cities. Migration leads to higher proportions on the rural fringes, but there are also significant numbers of the poor elderly in inner city areas, especially in local authority council housing and sheltered homes. Due to poverty this particular elderly sector is unable to move to a more pleasant environment. These elderly people are especially affected by the stresses of inner city living (Chapter 14).

The pattern is also influenced by the fact that certain areas, especially older industrial regions, have a poorer health record due to a legacy of the toll exacted by heavy manual labour in the earlier years and poorer living conditions. This is shown in the 1991 Census, with parts of South Wales, central Scotland and northern England having a higher than average proportion with limiting long-term illnesses increasing mortality rates.

Some dominant factors

As in other developed countries, the ageing of Britain's population is due to a number of factors:

- Decreased birth and fertility rates since the 1950s have progressively reduced the numbers coming into the lower age sectors, so making the population pyramid more top-heavy.

- At the same time, longer life expectancy resulting from higher standards of living and better health and social care facilities have also helped to increase the numbers in the old age sectors above 65 years.

1981

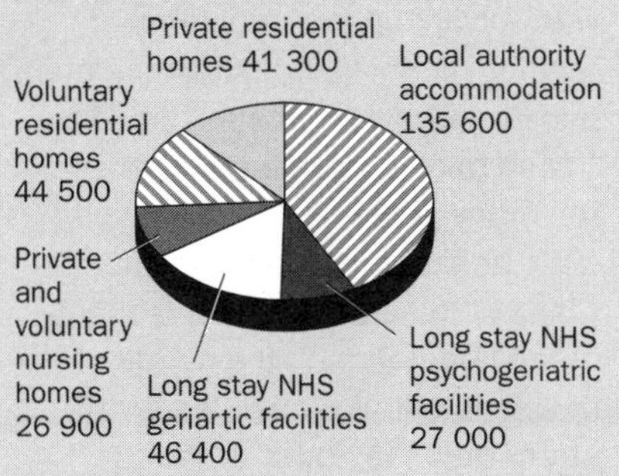

1991

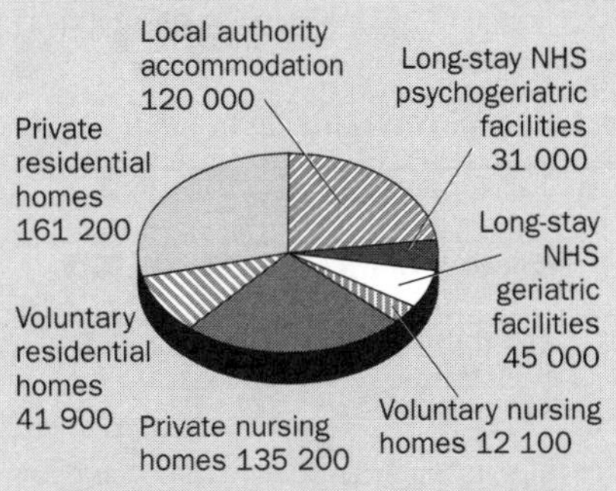

[SOURCE: Champion M *Population Matters* 1993]

Places in long-term care for elderly, chronically ill and disabled in the UK

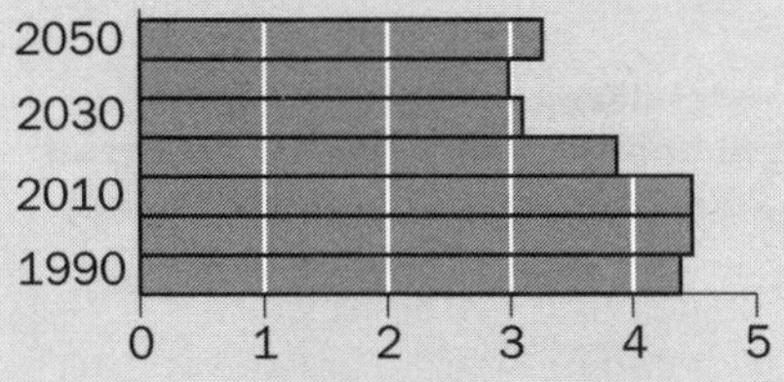

Trends in the dependancy ratio
The ratio of the number of working age 15 – 64 years to support each person over 65 years of age is decreasing.
[SOURCE: *Financial Times* 8.3.94]

Increased social costs and market demand of an ageing population

- On the whole, shorter working hours, more leisure and recreational facilities including longer holidays with visits to rural and coastal areas have also contributed to greater life expectancy.

	1970	1991
Crude birth rate per 1000	16	14
Women of child-bearing age as a percentage of all women	45	48
Total fertility rate	2.4	1.8
Crude death rate per 1000	12	11
Life expectancy (years)	71	76

[SOURCE: World Development Report 1993]

Key demographic indicators

Age group	Percent in age group		Percent change
	1981	1991	
Under 16	22.3	20.3	-6.5
16–64/59	59.9	61.3	4.6
65/66 and over	17.8	18.4	5.5
Total	100.00	100.00	2.3

[SOURCE: OPCS (1992b) Table 6]

Age structure of the UK population 1981 – 91

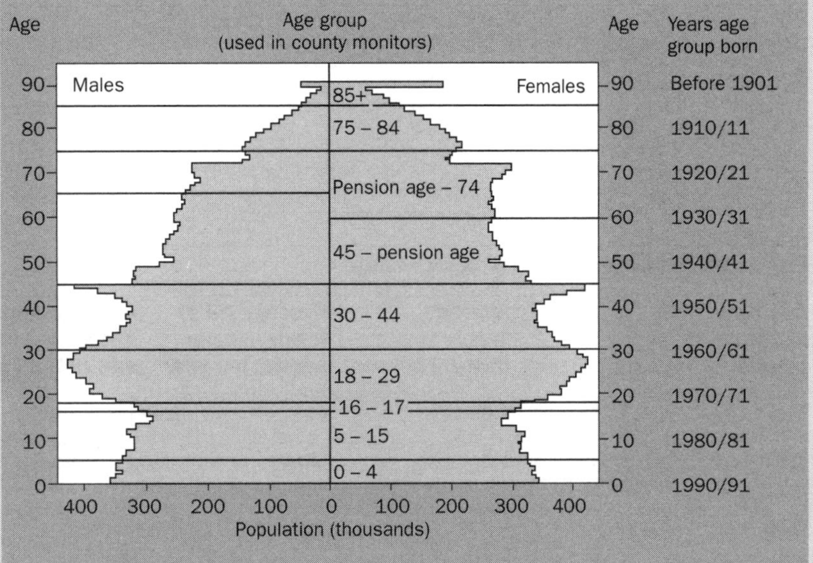

[SOURCE: *The Geography of Age, Geographical Review*, January 1994]

Population pyramid of England and Wales, 1991

case study

2.2 China: Demographic change under a Marxist ideology

'China is a country in the primary stage of socialism, being populous and underdeveloped. People use limited rustic ideas and traditional concepts and customs of childbirth inherited from the old society, such as 'the bigger the family the more prosperous, and the more children the greater the happiness.'

PIZ POPULATION, *FAMILY PLANNING* 1990 BEIJING

The ideology

The government redefined production to include both production of material goods and reproduction of human beings - planned production of human beings is needed as well as planned development of economy

'Social production itself is of a twofold character on the one hand the production of the means of subsistence of food, of clothing, of shelter and the necessary tools, and on the other, production of human beings themselves, the propagation of the species.'

Liu Zheng, *Problems of China's Population Growth in Jingi Yanjiu*,1979

Potential for simultaneously achieving these twin goals was conceived to be one of the unique strengths of the socialist mode of development and identified by Engels, one of the founders of Marxism. Policy implemented by chairman Mao in China to his death in 1976 and continued by successors: State planning versus the right of individual choice but collective commitment to well being of China's people.

China's One Child Policy

In the 1970s, Zou Enlai, preparing for the four modernisations, listed birth control as the major priority. In the 1970s it was a strong campaign of three reproductive norms 'later, longer and fewer': limit of two children with four years between and later marriage at 23 – 25 years.

Despite support for a free market economy as the way forward to quadruple GNP by 2000 AD, Deng Xiaobing, leader in 1979, saw strict imposition of birth control as fundamental to its success, hence the 'one child policy'. The government was convinced that problems of feeding, clothing, housing education and employing population could be traced to one common problem – too many people!

The goal of family planning in China is to suit the size and quality of the population to the needs of development of productive forces, strengthen the power of the country, and lift it out of poverty and backwardness.

Beijing 1990

Projected scenarios relating to basic needs

Projected scenarios if did not impose this policy

Average births percouple		Population figure Year 2000	Number of increase Over 1979
3	Rate above imposed policy	1 414 million	444 million
2.3		1 282 million	312 million
2.0		1 217 million	247 million
1.5		1 125 million	155 million
1.0*	* 'One child' policy	1 050 million*	80 million*

Projected scenarios related to basic needs

Average births per couple		Average arable land (mu per person)	Average Jin of foodgrain per person per year	Average number of children entering primary school annually 1996 – 2000 (millions)	Total nurturing expenses incurred (100 million yuan)
3	Over one child	1.05	618	1.8	9763
2.3		1.16	682	1.4	6864
2		1.22	718	1.3	5434
1.5		1.32	777	0.9	3410
1	One child policy	1.42	833	0.7	1760

[SOURCE: Croll E *The Simple Child Family*]

The 'one child policy' has been ruthlessly imposed. Every district had set its own birth rate control targets and appointed committees to monitor each couple's family planning. The couples were visited, and contraception and abortion enforced. Each couple received a 10% income bonus if they kept to one child, plus free welfare and education. If they exceeded one child, 10% tax and other penalties were imposed. This practice was embodied in the 'construction' and marriage law in 1980 and was allied to strict control on migration to large cities to ensure that agricultural production targets were kept and to prevent problems of over urbanisation.

This policy was more successful in urban areas and easier to enforce. In the remote rural areas, however, it ran counter to the economic need for family labour and security in old age (in that an old age pension scheme was needed). Where the policy was not enforced, there was a noticeable rise in births in the later 1980s. In rural areas in particular, there were too few people to support an ageing population.

China's rapid progress through the demographic transition means that it enjoys advanced levels of demographic development but at an early stage of economic development.

China's rapid demographic transition, 1949 – 1990

- **Demographic factors**
  Changing rates of natural increase together with changing age structure and total population affect future numbers in the reproductive range. Low rates of natural increase plus an ageing population leads ultimately to nil growth. It is estimated that China will reach this by 2025 (originally aimed at 2000).

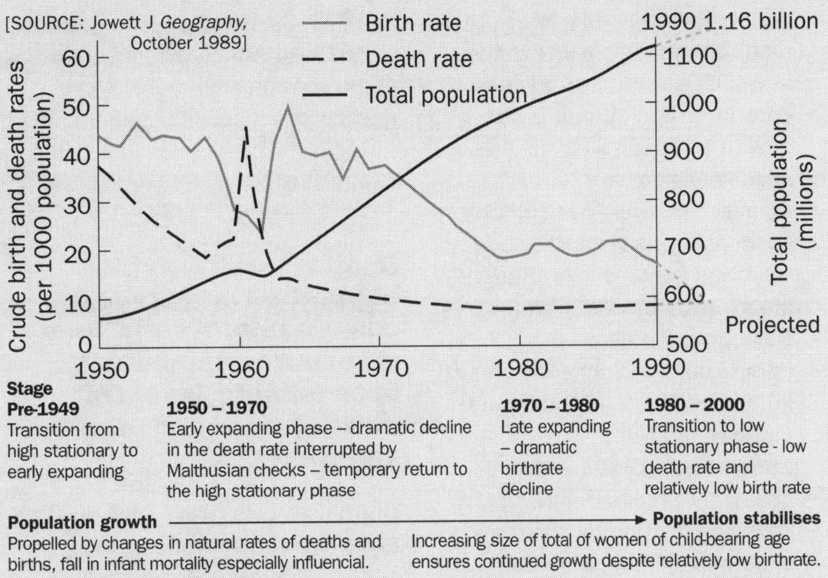

Crude Birth & Death Rates (per 1000 population)

- **Socio-economic factors**
  1949 The Communists took over an economy and society ravaged by a century of imperial decline, natural disasters, foreign invasion and civil war, thus Malthusian checks were still operating to delay demographic transition. Before the Communist Revolution, life expectancy on average was as low as 36 years.
  1949 – 1970 Planned economic development together with a rich resource base led to 10% annual growth rate in the economy. Agriculture and rural industry remained the main base of the economy. Much of population remained rural therefore social development was limited despite the changed ideology. A very successful health care programme and better nutrition brought a marked fall in the death rate especially in infant mortality. Family planning was little used up until the 1960s, therefore birth rates remained high.
  (**1958 – 1962** A 'demographic disaster' was experienced during this period, with 25 to 30 million more deaths and 30 to 35 million fewer births. The 'Great Leap Forward Programme' failed due to political mismanagement and low grain production, and weakened the infrastructure. Widespread famine caused a temporary decline in fertility but a baby boom when the economy recovered.)
  1970 – 1980 Continued economic development with more balanced growth and some introduction of private enterprise raised the level of agricultural production. Increased urban development was seen, with some industrial growth. More social change favoured a slight decrease in birth rate. An increasingly stringent family planning programme with increased availability of contraception and abortion hastened a fall in the birth rate.
  1980 – 1990 Economic growth slowed due to inflation and a trade imbalance. The burden of

population size and a return to a rigid command economy in the late 1980s restricted private enterprise and output. Urban growth was controlled, as was social development toward smaller families. The rigid 'one child' policy had brought about a relatively low birth rate. By 1990, life expectancy was 70 years.

- **Government policy**
  Prior to communism there was little health care and no family planning policy.
  1950s – mid-1960s A primary health care programme brought down the death rate. The family planning voluntary birthrate remained high.
  1970s There was strong encouragement to family planning -*wan, xi, shao*, (later marriage, longer between births, fewer children). Between 1970 and 1979, the birth rate was halved.
  1979 – 1990 The imposed family planning programme, the 'one child' policy caused resentment. The birth rate rose again into the late 1980s.

Spatial variations in population density and change reflect variations in resource opportunity, accessibility, levels of development and ethnic variations.

The density pattern is broadly inverse to the rate of natural increase pattern. The most economically advanced area is associated with social advancement and rising incomes, therefore a natural inclination to smaller families enables government family planning to be more readily implemented.

Large cities are more economically advanced and therefore more demographically advanced than rural areas. For example, the birth rate is 16 per thousand in Shanghai and 32 per thousand in Tibet, which is remote and under ethnic influence.

North-east regions are more advanced and have lower natural rates of increase than other areas apart from Sichuan in the south-west.

The poorer and more remote rural areas, especially where dependent on agriculture, are less accessible to government control and education, and more economically dependent on a large family to provide agricultural labour. They are also more tied to tradition. Birth rate and levels of literacy are closely and inversely related.

Regional disparities, 1992

GDP Distribution by sectors % 1994	
Agriculture	21
Industry	47
Services	32
% Urban population	
1980	19
1994	29

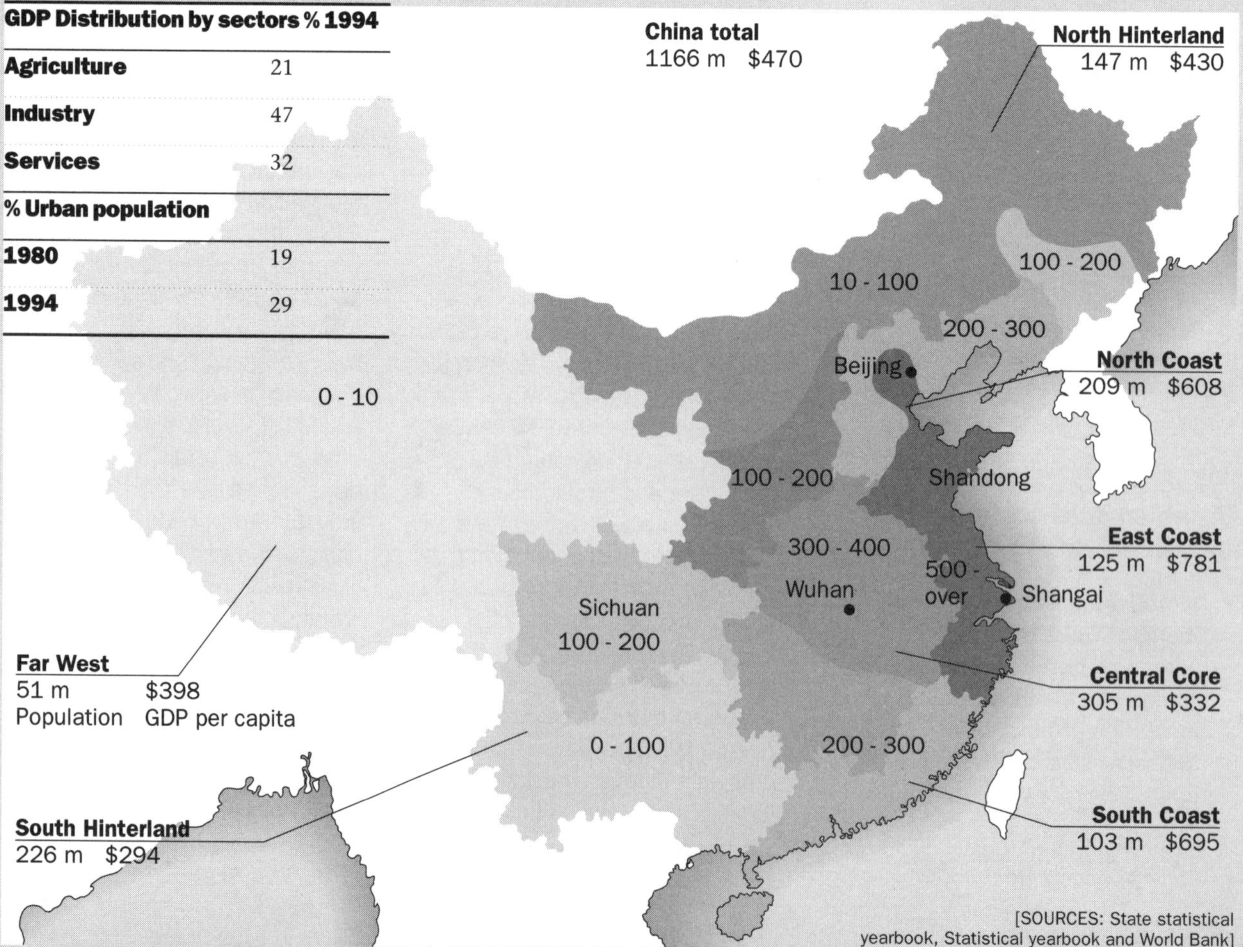

case study

2.3 Tanzania: Population and change

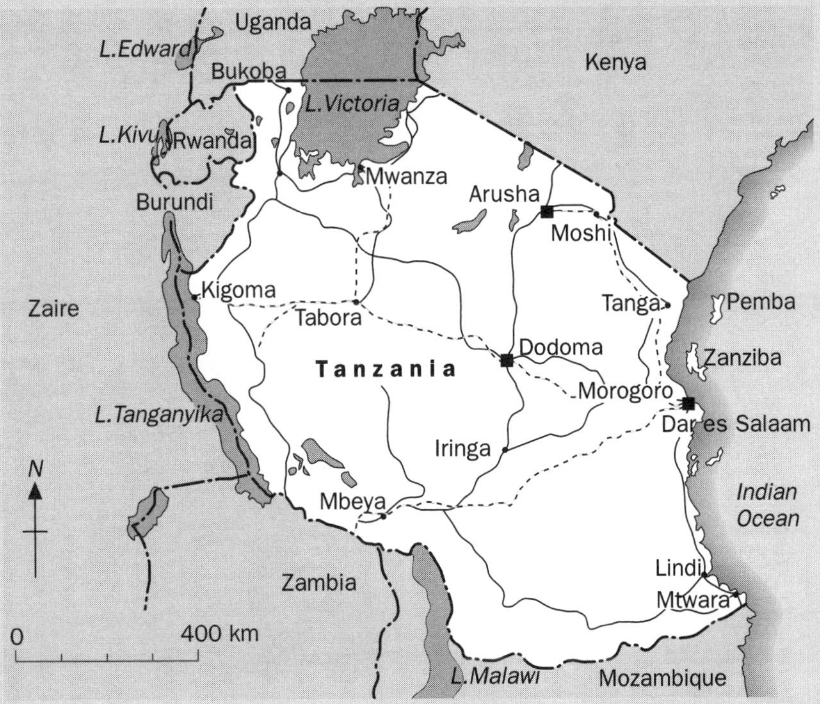

Tanzania

Population and other basic indices

	1965–70	1990–95
Crude birth rate	52.4/0000	43.1/0000
Crude death rate	21.0/0000	13.6/0000
Life expectancy	44 yrs	52 yrs
Infant mortality rate	135/0000	85/0000
Population growth	3.3% annually	3.0%
Total population	10 mill (1960)	29.6 mill (1988)
Urbanised population	5%	24%
Gross domestic product per capita	1598$(US)	620$(US)
Total gross domestic product	790 mill $(US)	4688 mill $(US)
Percentage derived from agriculture	46%	57%
Calorie intake per capital daily	1832	2021

Demographic structure and influences

- Population indices, a youthful age structure and increased numbers in reproductive age range indicate that Tanzania is still in the early expanding phase. Birth rates remain high while death rates have fallen. However, there are signs of a fall in the birth rate, indicating that the country is about to enter the late expanding phase. It will to some extent be offset by an increase in the number of women of child-bearing age. The population is not projected to stabilise until 2045 AD, leaving Tanzania with severe problems in terms of limited economic development.
  - Attitudes and values are still linked to the traditional culture which favours a desire for large families with limited urbanisation and modernisation influences.
  - External influences have brought better health care and a fall in the death rate together with longer life expectancy.
- In some ways Tanzania's stage within the demographic transition model reflects that of tropical Africa in general and is subject to a combination of similar factors:

i Limited socio-economic development means that much of the population is dependent on the rural sector and on subsistence agriculture.
- Large families are needed for labour and security in old age.

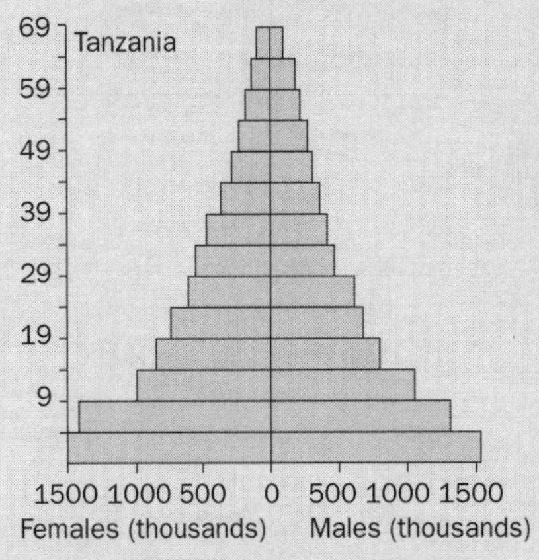

Population pyramid for Tanzania, 1990

ii Government policies towards population growth since independence 1962 have been modified.

- A Socialist government from 1964 encouraged large families and population growth believng this good for the agricultural economy and increasing military manpower. It was also felt that Tanzania had the space and resources to support a larger population growth, thus there was no family planning programme. Better food supplies and primary health led to a marked fall in death rate and in the infant mortality rate. Along with the higher birth rate, this ensured a higher rate of natural increase with further projected growth (Fertility rate 1965 – 70 = 6.5 and 1985 – 90 = 7.1)
- Economic difficulties, debt, pressure on population of resources and world agency pressures to adopt a family planning programme have led to a reversal of policy towards family planning. There has been active encouragement to reduce family size but no penalties to enforce this. Education on family planning and use of contraception is still very limited. The birth rate is not falling fast enough but latest estimates show a growth in population, although it is still less than projected for 1989 – 90 (actual 2.8% annually as against 3.1 projected; female literacy 18% in 1970 and now 88%).

iii Some fall in the birth rate is encouraged by a marked increase in female literacy, aiding the spread of birth control measures and increased urbanisation and modernisation.

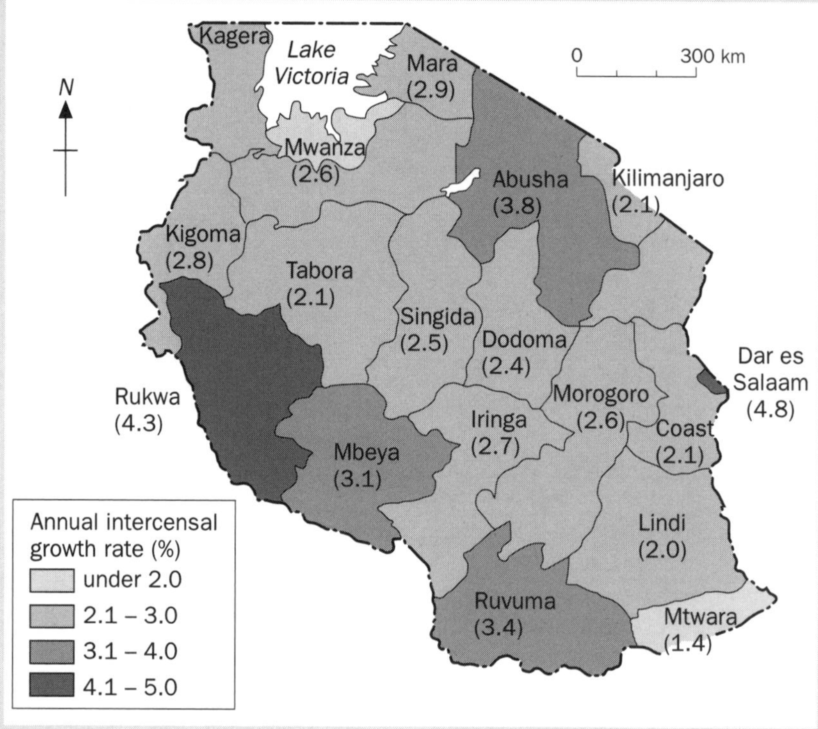

Annual average intercensal population growth rate by region, 1978 – 1988

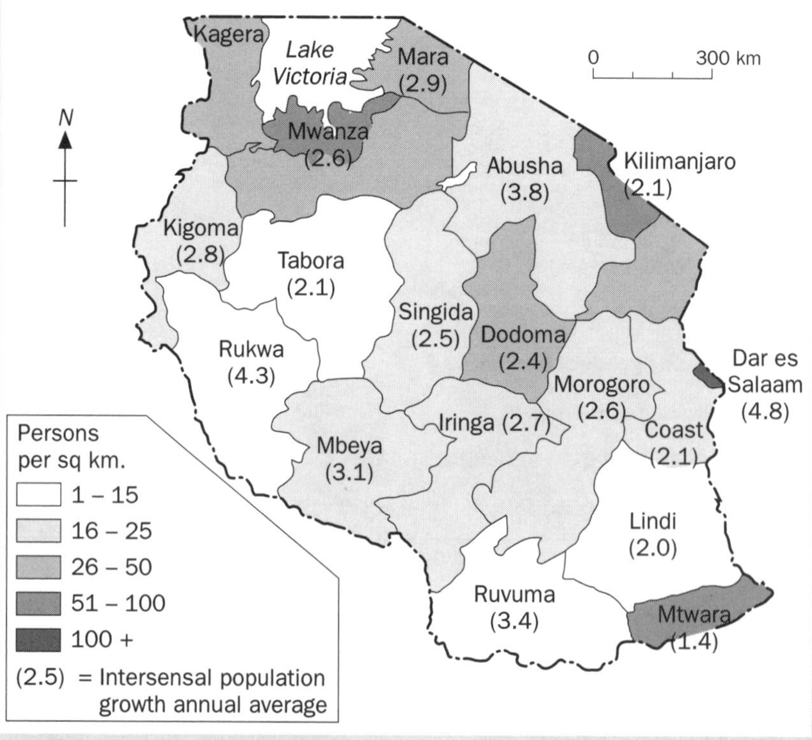

Annual average intercensal population growth rate by region, 1978 – 1988

Change to 1990s in economic base and policies

- A Socialist ideology had been adopted, with the emphasis on agricultural self-sufficiency and development. The Ujamaa policy was d eveloped to concentrate a dispersed rural population into large, planned, nucleated villages which would form the social and economic units. The land was to be farmed collectively. The policy was, however, resisted by most people, and production declined or stagnated. Allied to government mismanagement, this led to serious economic problems and international debt at a time when people really needed support.
- Tanzania was under pressure from the International Monetary Fund which controlled aid and loans. President Myinji, who succeeded President Nyerere, has had to instigate economic reform with a shift away from socialist planning to more market-based development. **The Three Year Economic Recovery Programme** (1986) was initiated with its harsh budget of increased taxation and cutbacks on government expenditure. It has affected the poorest, but has also reduced government interference in economic production and led to a recovery of export crop production. Plantation estates were denationalised and handed back to private owners in a number of cases (e.g. Brooke Bond Tanzania).
  Coffee, tea (mainly in the southern Highlands) and cloves (mainly on Pemba island) are the main export earners; cotton, sisal and cashew nuts are also important.
- Much of the agriculture is still subsistence, but food crop output, especially maize, has grown. Other subsistence crops are cassava, bananas and plantains.
  Agricultural expansion, however, is not keeping pace with population growth and the country will experience severe problems if the growth is not regulated.
- Manufacturing accounts for less than 6% of GDP and Tanzania has few minerals. There is a large phosphate mine which supplies a fertiliser plant at Tanga. Manufacturing has declined due to the inefficient state running of the plants. Small private businesses are being encouraged under the recovery programme and these are proving successful.
- Nevertheless, the bulk of the population will remain dependent on agriculture and agricultural exports to pay off debts (takes 50% of export revenue) and to pay for imports. An expansion of industry and tourism are needed to diversify the economy. Pemba and Zanzibar islands are important for trade, tourism and cloves.
- The distribution of population is consistent with the better rainfall areas where agriculture is concentrated, especially around Lake Victoria where fishing is important, and the areas accessible to main coastal ports (Dar es Salam and Lindi). Dodoma is the new planned capital, located nearer the centre of country. Urbanisation is relatively low but increasing.

3

CHAPTER 3

Population trends and the modernisation process

'To forecast demographic trends, we rely on what has happened in the past, mainly noting the experiences of the industrialised countries of western Europe and North America. Despite limitations in the data available, demographers have recognised a general pattern in the way crude birth and death rates have changed in these countries over time. It has also been noted that this change is closely related to the processes of development which these countries have undergone.'

THIS DEMOGRAPHIC TRANSITION PATTERN COULD ALSO BROADLY BE EXPERIENCED BY THE LESSER DEVELOPED COUNTRIES, AS THEY BECOME MORE ECONOMICALLY DEVELOPED AND MODERNISED.

3.1 The demographic transition model

The demographic transition model was developed by Notestein in 1945. His model, based on demographic studies of North America and Western Europe, was put forward in four parts; three were descriptive and the fourth offered an explanation for the demographic transition cycle as described.

He defined three stages within the demographic transition cycle of population growth – slow, rapid and slow. The middle stage is now commonly divided, giving four phases in all. Countries were broadly envisaged as passing successively through each stage, the change being brought about by the cumulative effects of the socio-economic advances of the modernisation process (Figure 3.4b).

The effects of modernisation on demographic change

The effects of this modernisation on the course of demographic change were summarised by Notestein as follows:

- The demographic revolution which takes a country out of the high stationary phase is

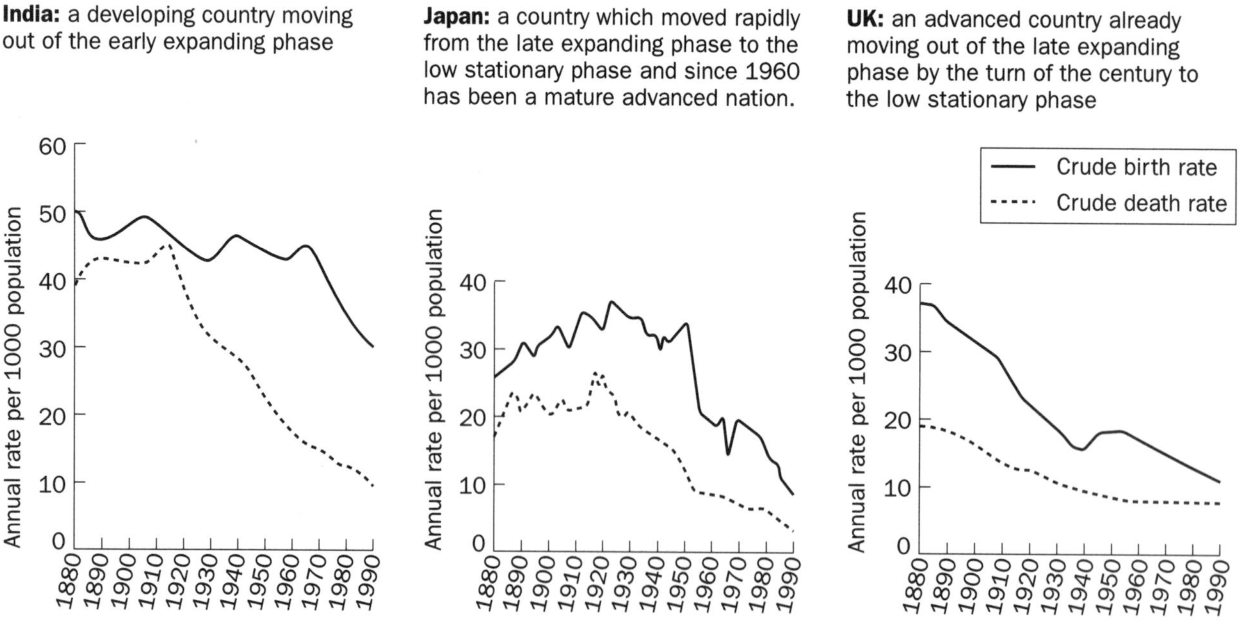

Figure 3.1 Demographic transition for India, Japan and the UK, 1880 – 1990

initiated by a permanent and continuous decline in mortality.

- This decline in mortality is caused by the cumulative influences of the agricultural, industrial and sanitary revolutions which lead to better food supplies, an improvement in the standard of living in general, and improvements in public health.
- Rapid population growth results from the widening gap between declining death rates and unchanging birth rates.
- However, fertility (birth rate) decline eventually follows because the social and economic supports to high fertility (e.g. the need for labour in rural farming) are removed. The new way of life associated with rapid urbanisation leads to the use of contraceptive methods to control fertility.

As and when death and birth rates are both under control, the population cycle finally enters a stage of very slow growth – the low stationary phase.

However, growth of population numbers is not simply a function of the difference in birth and death rates as outlined in the transition cycle. It is also dependent upon the size of the population to which the birth and death rates relate, and upon the age-sex structure of the population (Figures 3.2 and 3.3). These factors influence the rates at a given time and affects succeeding trends, in particular, influencing the number of women of child-bearing age.

	Natural increase (%)	Population (million)	Annual addition (million)
Group 1			
Nigeria	3.0	99	2.97
Tanzania	3.0	25	0.75
Senegal	3.0	8	0.24
Group 2			
Brazil	2.0	151	3.00
Mexico	2.0	83	1.66
Colombia	2.0	33	0.17
Group 3			
Jamaica	1.0	2	0.02
Mauritius	1.0	1	0.01
Group 4			
UK	0.2	58	0.12
Austria	0.2	8	0.01

Figure 3.2 *Effect of base populations on annual addition for countries with similar natural rates of increase, 1991*

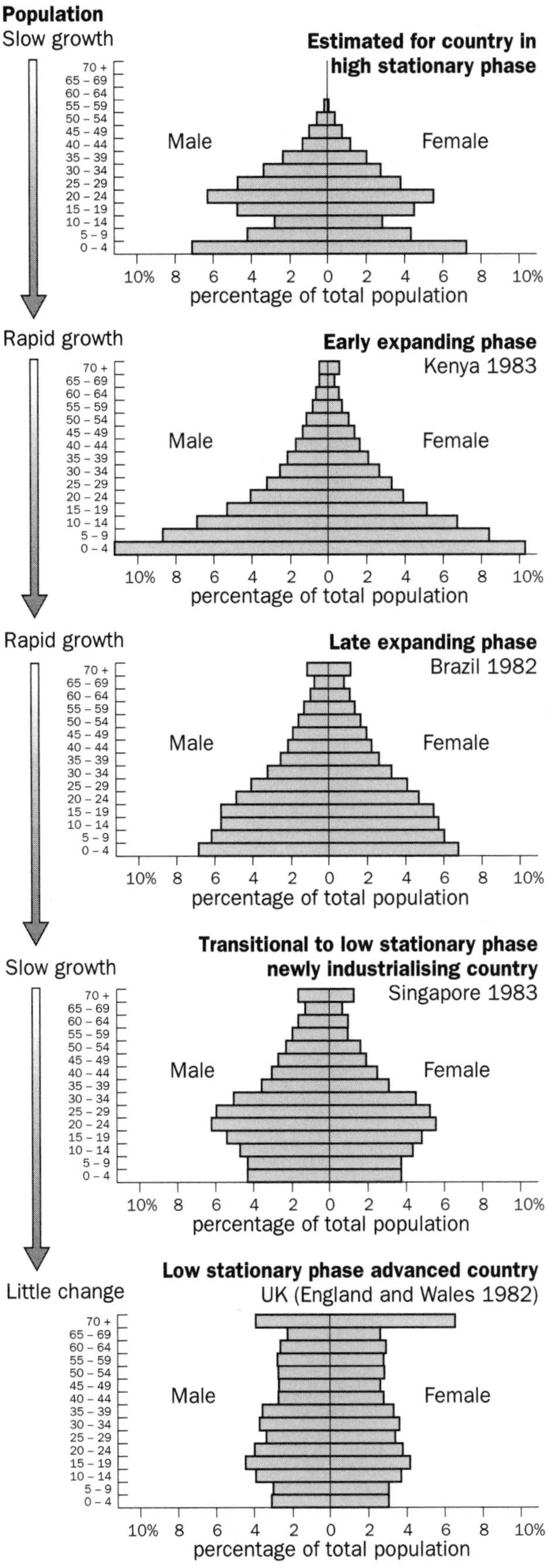

Figure 3.3 *Age structure pyramids for different phases of demographic transition*

3.2 Economic development and the demographic transition model

Economic development leads to industrialisation and urbanisation and, along with the socio-political changes, is seen by Notestein as the main driving force behind population change. The demographic transition cycle may therefore be closely linked to models of economic change (Figure 3.4).

Rostow's Stages of Economic Growth

Like the demographic transition cycle, Rostow's stages of economic growth is based on changes in North America and western Europe. The conditions which underlie each of Rostow's economic changes are also those which support each stage of the demographic cycle.

The characteristics of Rostow's traditional society phase forms the base for stage 1, the high stationary phase of the demographic cycle. The conditions associated with the preconditions for take off and take-off itself underlie stage 2, the early expanding phase. The late expanding phase of population change is characterised by Rostow's drive for maturity. There is also a link between the high mass consumption stage and the low stationary phase of the demographic cycle (Figure 3.4a).

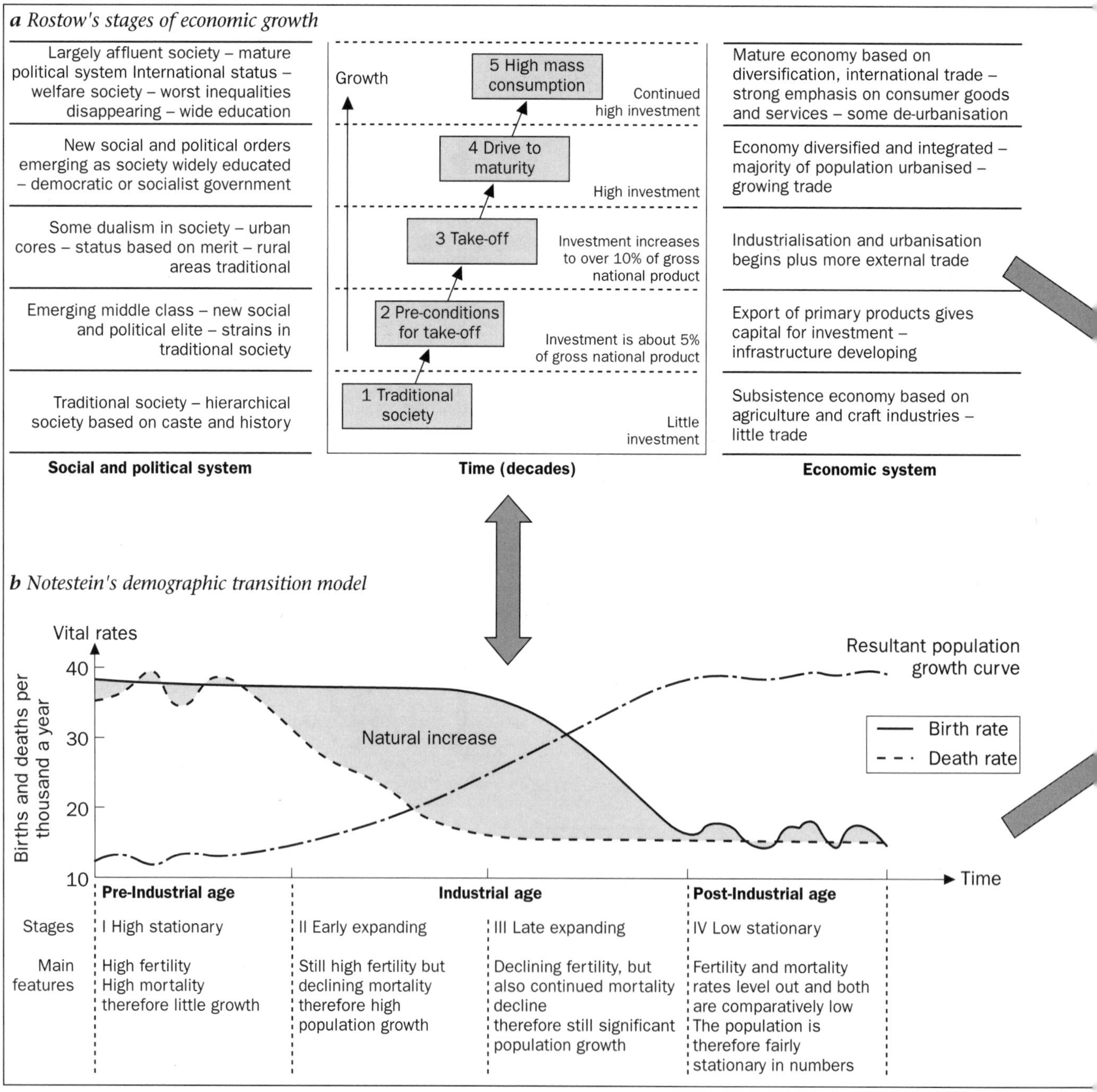

While these broad correlations are useful in highlighting some of the important factors behind population change, when studying the experiences of particular countries, especially within the developing world, they can at best provide only a limited explanation.

Myrdal's Cumulative Causation Process

The demographic transition cycle could also be linked to Myrdal's cumulative causation process, which is complementary to the Rostow model of development. Myrdal's model introduces the concept of unbalanced regional growth, adding an important spatial dimension to the pattern of development (Figure 3.4c).

According to Myrdal's causation process, economic change is initiated in an advantaged region which develops with industrialisation and urbanisation, making it the core region. The peripheral areas remain relatively under-developed. The forces for economic development have an uneven effect and, in its more extreme form, can create a kind of dualism with the core region advanced and peripheral regions remaining largely in the traditional society phase of Rostow's economic growth model.

Figure 3.4 *Demographic transition cycle in relation to models of economic change*

Economic Development/Demographic transition over time

Economic development - Improved living conditions thus mortality rates decline with rapid population growth occurring **Cumulative causation** - Leads to further industrialisation and rapid urbanisation, leading to some further fall in mortality rates but now also a fall in fertility rates as the necessity for large families is removed and birth control measures are adopted. But population continues to grow as the young age structure brings more women into the reproductive age group for a time **Diffusion spreads economic growth effects from the core regions into the rural areas** - Bringing a fall in mortality rates followed by a fall in fertility rates leading to a slowing down of population growth across the whole country **With a mature advanced economy and an ageing population structure** - Together with a low mortality and fertility rate population growth is at a low level or even halted

c Myrdal's model of cumulative causation

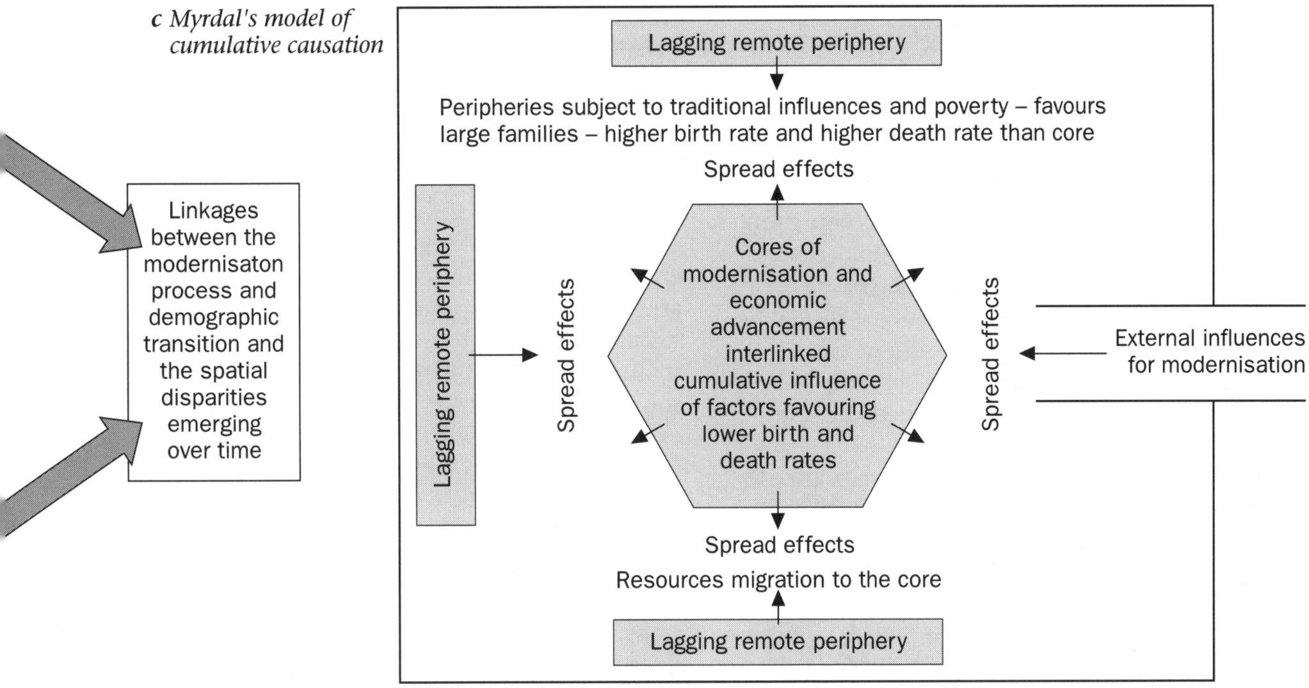

Regional imbalance – growing and lagging regions - Growth cores are based on centres of initial and derived advantages supported by external influences for modernisation. These are 'fed' labour and resources from the surrounding areas including the lagging remote peripheral regions. Nearer areas to the increasingly urbanised core(s) are positively influenced by the spread of modernisation processes through diffusion and dispersion from the core(s)

NOTE: Such a scheme as this is of some relevance in contrasting the stage of demographic transition and modernisation reached by different countries as well as being particularly appropriate to the situation in one country. Note also the limitations of the models used - especially their Euro-centred approach which is less relevant today in a developing world context particularly where the prevailing political ideology is not capitalist-based.

Regional differences in the rate of demographic transition are linked to regional differences in the rate of economic development. The importance of this concept of core-periphery balance is that the core region is likely to advance most rapidly through the demographic cycle. It is here that the forces for economic change are most concentrated and effective. Demographic change is much slower in the more remote areas. Different parts of the country are therefore at different stages of the demographic cycle as in the case of Brazil, for example (Case study 3.1). Just as economic development is uneven, so is demographic change.

Core and outer regions are not independent of each other. Interaction occurs between them. While the core region may drain outer regions of their resources (a strong rural-urban migration occurs which 'feeds' the core region), there are reciprocal though slower 'spread' effects, with the diffusion of some modernisation outwards from the core towards the lagging peripheral regions. As there is some spread of economic development and change into other regions, so there will be a diffusion of forces which will stimulate demographic change, helping to take these lagging regions into the later stage of population transition. However, the demographic structure here is also bound to be modified by the loss of much of the younger rural population to the urbanising core.

Criticism of these Euro-centred models

These models are now being crtiticised as being too Euro-centred, that is, based on western experience and a western perspective. They are also based on a capitalist system of development which is driven by market forces which aims to maximise profits. Countries in the western world have broadly followed the pattern of change outlined in these models.

The models do, however, have some relevance to the developing world situation because, until the period of post-war independence, much of the developing world was influenced by the capitalist system and subjected to European influences. Since the 1950s into the 1970s, a number of developing world countries sought to industrialise along a similar pattern to western Europe and North America. Rostow and Myrdal-type influences continued to play a strong role in determining the economic pattern in these newly independent countries. A number of governments supported by western advisers and agencies have sought to hasten their countries' progress through the demographic transition cycle by adopting family planning programmes based on western guidelines.

Recently it has been found that development policies based on western experience have their problems. For most developing world countries these do not raise the standard of living for the masses nor do they solve their problems of rapid population growth. The circumstances of developing world countries differ in a number of ways from those in the western world. The failure to acknowledge these differences underlines the limitations of the demographic transition model as an explanatory framework for current trends in developing countries, though it can be used as a descriptive tool.

3.3 The demographic transition model: its limitations

Classification

Chung (1970) and other writers have classified countries on the basis of the stage reached in the demographic transition cycle. Chung saw western European countries, the USA and the Soviet Union as having entered the final stage of development by the 1960s, while a number of Latin American countries, such as Brazil, were still entering the late expanding phase. Most countries of tropical Africa and some in south-east Asia, such as Bangladesh, were seen as entering the early expanding phase. By the 1990s the majority of countries had progressed further through their demographic transitions. Some of the newly industrialising countries, such as Singapore, appeared to be entering the low stationary phase, while China and Brazil were approaching the end of the late expanding phase. Other tropical countries, including much of Africa and some middle and south Asian countries, seem fixed in the early expanding phase with an insufficient fall in fertility rates, following the fall in mortality rates which took them into the early expanding phase. Only limited transition had taken place.

The varied experiences of individual countries

However, while for purposes of discussion it may be useful to classify the demographic situations of particular countries in terms of stages reached in Notestein's demographic transition model, the demographic experiences of individual countries do appear to vary significantly from this.

'The demography of historical societies was both more varied and more complex than had been previously thought.'

Developing countries may follow a different rate and pattern of demographic transition from developed countries. Compared to western countries, which seem to have already passed through their transition cycles, the trends for developing countries in the process of transition are different because of their unique circumstances.

Outside intervention

Developing countries have suffered considerable intervention from other nations, which affected both their population structures and character of economic development. Recent technological advances have influenced mortality rates and, to some extent, fertility rates. Both the pattern and pace of demographic change are thus likely to be different from the demographic transition model, though the idea of a country passing through stages of a demographic cycle remains very useful.

Wood, in his critical review of the explanatory framework supporting the model, comments that the fall in mortality rates for developing world countries in the post-war period was much more rapid than had earlier occurred in North America and Europe. For a number of developing countries, mainly in Africa and the Middle East, this has not yet been complemented by a really significant fall in the fertility rate which succeeded declines in mortality in the west.

The rapid fall in the mortality rates of developing countries has come about largely because of health measures and medical technological advances introduced from Europe and North America. They have particularly affected infant mortaility rates, but were not accompanied by the socio-economic changes needed to prompt a decline in fertility rates. In Europe, the fall in child and infant mortality tended to reinforce the need for the advantages of family limitation. Without the required social and economic development, fertility rates in the developing world could not respond quickly enough to slow down population growth as has happened in the west. This has significantly contributed to the 'population explosion' in the developing world.

Cultural differences

Cultural contexts are different, and also affect patterns of demographic change in developing countries. These influence the way societies view the family status and role of women. For example, under Islam, a faith followed by a fifth of the world's population, the family is regarded as the most important social grouping and there are strict ideas about the nature of family life. Early marriage of women and large families are favoured. Government interference in the matter of family size has been frowned upon, complicating family planning programmes.

Some Islamic countries, such as Iraq and Iran, have encouraged increases in family size in order to expand the country's population and its influence in the Middle East relative to other religious groups, in particular, to the Jewish population of Israel. As a result, birth rates remain high in most Islamic countries, despite some western-style development. This contrasts markedly with some socialist countries, such as Cuba and China, where religion is second to the ideology of the state and in which government-sponsored family planning programmes have been instrumental in the sharp decline in the birth rate. Family planning programmes have also been implemented in some Muslim countries where the Muslim population is less dominant, such as Turkey and Indonesia.

The influence of government policies

Government policy-making decisions, particularly those concerned with the economy and the provision of welfare and other services, also affect demographic change (Case study 2.1). They influence the resource base of a country, its infrastructure and welfare provision, and significantly affect the rate of population growth.

It has been shown that poverty and lack of educational opportunity are two important factors which contribute to high fertility rates in some developing countries. On the other hand, where development policies aim to improve the living standards of the poor who form the major part of the population in most developing world countries, then the desire and need for a large family is reduced. Corbridge indicated that the best spur to family limitations is to reduce inequalities and poverty and improve the lot of women (Chapter 9). Derek Brown, looking at policy attempts to limit family size in India, also notes that correlation between female education and smaller healthier families is '*startlingly obvious, and amazingly neglected*'.

Decision-making by women

The principal factors which affect family size are the desires and decisions of individuals. Where these decisions have been considered, the emphasis has been on the dominance of men in the marital partnership and in society at large. Many recent studies, however, point to the crucial role of women's status and aspirations. It has been assumed that in developing countries, as in Victorian England, large families occur because the man desired it and the woman had little choice. Studies show that, traditionally, women in developing countries have also desired large families as status.

Social constraints on women in traditional society mean that it is only through motherhood and home life that status can be achieved. There is growing evidence that as women become more emancipated, better educated and have the opportunity to contribute in other ways to society, their desire is for a smaller family. This has contributed significantly to the fall in fertility rates in the post-war western world.

As their status increases in society, women tend to marry at a later age. A world fertility survey in 1985 showed that younger women who had received more education than their older counterparts also desired smaller families, though the number of children wanted varied from one part of the world to another (Figure 3.5).

	As stated by mothers aged 45–49	**As stated by daughters aged 15–19**
Africa	7.8	6.6
Asia and the Pacific	4.9	3.3
Latin America	5.5	3.3
Middle East	5.9	4.2

Figure 3.5 *Ideal family size*

Concluding comment

While the demographic model can provide a broad descriptive framework, its use as an analytical framework, even when allied to the processes of economic development and modernisation underlying it, are somewhat limited.

- There are weaknesses in the demographic basis of the transition model itself.
- The approach is Euro-centred, weakening its use in relation to the lesser developed countries.
- Any attempt at analysis must take account not only of the effects of economic development and modernisation processes, but also of the cultural context within which this occurs. Government policy decisions and the aspirations of individuals, particularly the emerging aspirations and influence of women in society, should also be considered.

case study

3.1 **Brazil**

Regional aspects of demography

The interior – north/centre west
Least developed – sparse population, most at subsistence level.

Birth and death rates remain high limited natural increase. But since 1960s efforts to develop interior including new capital Brasilia, led to in migration and therefore population increase. Emerging centres contrast with rest of interior.

North-east
Apart from the coastal region much of the population lives at subsistence level.

While birth and death rates remain high inland, on the more developed coast death rates have fallen due to better medical facilities and higher incomes there is a marked natural increase overall.

South-east
The most industrialised region.

Marked contrast demographically between richer well educated minority and improvished masses.

But generally birth and death rates are lower that in the north-east and interior but there is still a significant natural increase.

South
Many western European settlers e.g. Dutch, German – highly commercialised mixed economy – agriculture and industry.

Demographic structure is similar to developed countries but less so in the coffee lands bordering the south-east.

Density distribution and main migration flows

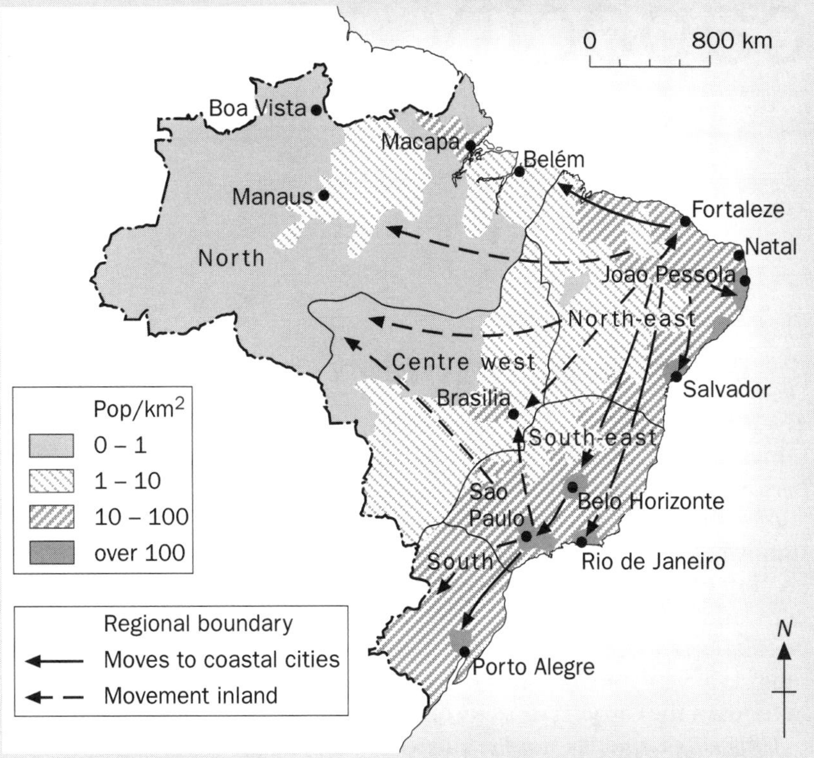

Note: Regional constrasts in economic development and opportunities have led to strong migration flows to the more industrialised south-east and other coastal regions. This is only partly compensated for by a counter settler flow to the interior. Thus migration also affects the population structure of different regions.

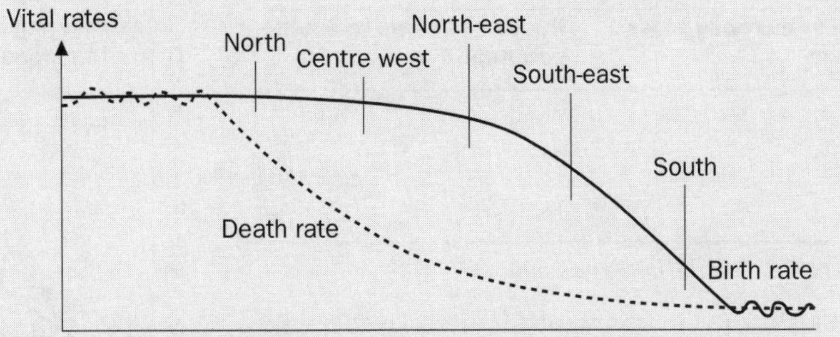

Suggested position of each region along the demographic transition cycle

4

CHAPTER 4

Population density, distribution and carrying capacity

'In a planet in which the history of this century has been marked by technological progress, it does not seem possible that the scientific and technical aspects of food production have failed to meet the needs of its inhabitants.'

INSTITUTO DEL TERCO MUNDO, THE WORLD –9 A THIRD WORLD GUIDE 1995 – 96

4.1 Density and carrying capacity

The most elementary index of population distribution is that of crude density, that is, the number of persons per unit area, usually expressed per square kilometre. As the index of population distribution simply relates people to an area of land, taking no account of the capacity of that land to support the population or the standard of living at which the population expects to be supported, the crude density index is of very limited value. Density should be seen in terms of the carrying capacity of the land.

Carrying capacity is an ecological concept. It is used to identify the number of livestock which an area of grazing land can support, for example, but it has proved useful too in the study of human population. A population can, in theory, expand at an exponential rate soon doubling, as shown in Figure 4.1.

Rate of increase % per annum	Number of years to double population
2	35
3	23
4	18

Figure 4.1 *Population expansion*

In reality, as environmental limits take effect, the exponential curve for any living species will level off. The point at which this occurs will vary from one species to another and from one kind of habitat to another. It will depend on the food requirements of the species and on its environmental conditions. These will include the amount and dependability of the food supply in any habitat, and such factors as climatic conditions, the threat of predators and competition from other species for the same food supply (Figure 4.2).

Once the population has reached the uppermost limit for a particular habitat, growth will level off and the population stabilise. Any temporary increase in population due to unusually favourable conditions, such as a good growing season for vegetation and wildlife, will ultimately be wiped out through natural checks and outmigration when conditions return to normal. Conversely, any temporary deterioration in conditions, for instance, a prolonged drought, will also bring about the operation of natural checks and outmigration, as seen when livestock and human populations occupy marginal land.

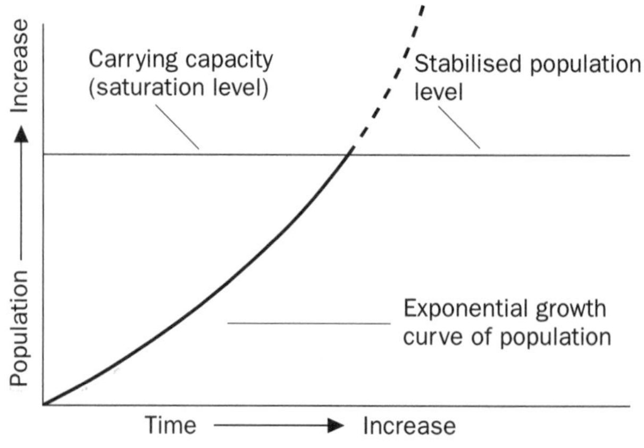

Figure 4.2 *The effect of carrying capacity on population over time*

Where such natural checks and outmigration are in evidence over a period of time, this is an indication that the carrying capacity of that particular environment has been reached. For human populations this means that there is enough food for survival but not for optimum growth and any slight unfavourable change in environmental conditions could be disastrous. Today there are undoubtedly populations in this situation, notably in the drier areas of Africa. Survival carrying capacity can be associated with two other concepts, optimum carrying capacity and tolerance capacity.

Optimum carrying capacity occurs when numbers are below the survival carrying capacity, allowing for adequate nutrition and individual growth. In effect for human populations, it allows for a rise in the standard of living and so, is similar to the concept of optimum population used by demographers.

Amongst any population, quality of living is not simply a matter of material well-being. This applies as much to animals as to human beings and with them, the term tolerance capacity is used. Stresses of high density living for instance, may lead to feelings of dissatisfaction and depression, encouraging migration to areas with more tolerable conditions. Thus, tolerance capacity is a useful concept which relates to the urban overcrowding of populations.

4.2 **Optimum, over- and underpopulation**

While optimum population as a term is synonymous with optimum carrying capacity, over- and underpopulation refer to both the carrying capacity and also to the standard of living at which the population can be supported. Thus overpopulation occurs where a reduction in numbers would lead to a rise in the standard of living for the remaining population, by releasing some resources for investment in further development. Underpopulation occurs where an increase in numbers would enable more efficient use of resources, again leading to a rise in the standard of living.

Overpopulation

High densities of population may lead to situations of overpopulation, but overpopulation may also occur where densities are low. For example, in harsh environments such as desert margins, basic resource support is so limited that even a small increase in population can lead to overpopulation. Alternatively, in the same kinds of environment, prolonged drought may reduce the resource support for an existing population. However, if outside agencies intervene by bringing in basic food supplies or the technology to increase local resources, such as sinking wells to increase the water supply for irrigation or livestock, then a situation of overpopulation can be remedied.

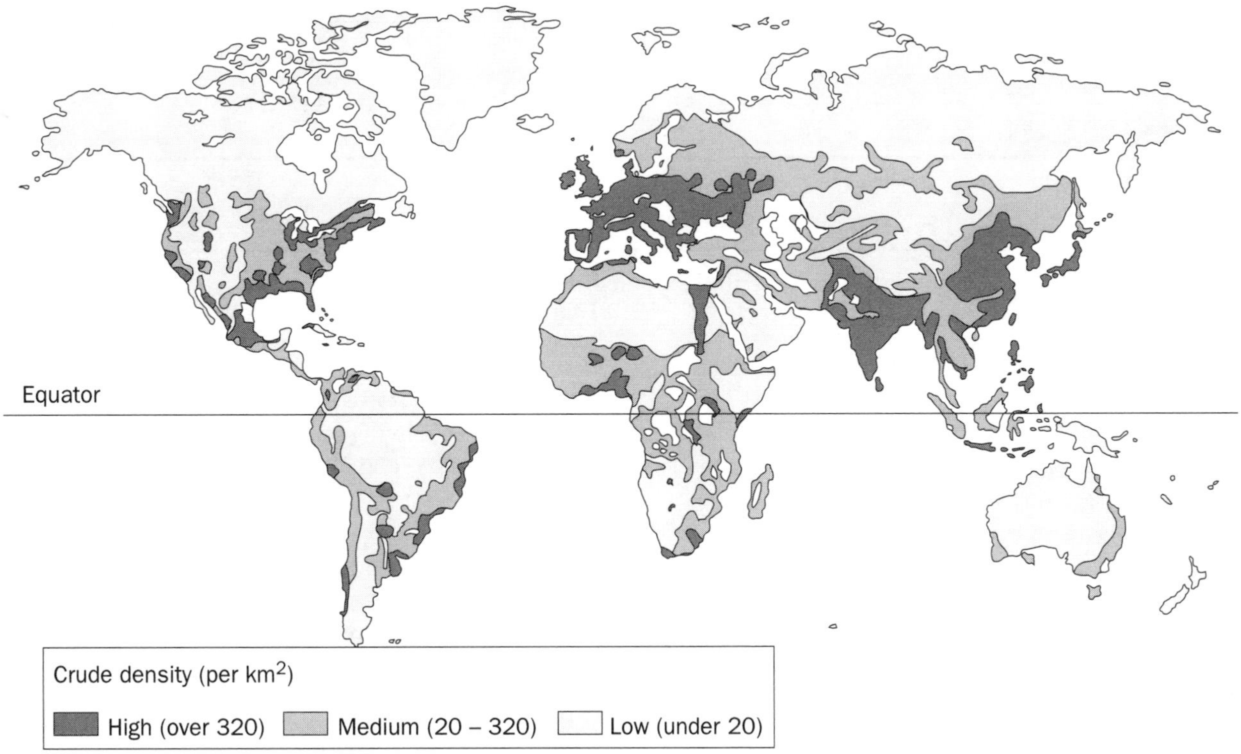

Figure 4.3 *Population density distribution*

In developed countries, capital, technology and knowledge have helped along with the use of more local and international resources; they have allowed the increasing population densities to be supported at improved living standards. Yet overpopulation may still occur. While material standards may be maintained, overconcentration causes other stresses which lower the quality of life. The level of population has gone beyond tolerance capacity. A check on population growth or active decentralisation away from congested regions would improve the quality of living.

Different situations in which overpopulation currently occurs are illustrated in Figure 4.4. These examples also show that situations are never static and that overpopulation itself is a relative term, not only in the locational sense, but also within the dimension of time.

Figure 4.4 *Different situations of overpopulation*

Some basic indicators

Indicators	**Chad**	**Bangladesh**	**Hong Kong**	**Netherlands**
Population (mill.)	6.3	120.4	5.8	15.1
Birth rate 1000	44	35	13	13
Death rate 1000	18	12	6	9
Natural increase % per annum	2.7	2.2	0.8	0.6
Crude density per sq. km	4.0	803	5599	366
Income				
Gross national product per capita in dollars	210	220	16 060	20 950
Growth rate of economy % per annum	3.2	2.1	5.4	1.7
Food				
Calorie intake per capita as % of minimum requirements	73	88	125	129
Employment %				
Primary	83	59	1	5
Manufacturing	5	13	35	22
Services	12	28	64	78

[Sources for 1993-95]

Profile of overcrowding

Chad

Low density and low standard of living

Harsh desert margin environment – pastoralism – cultivation in watered areas

Drought disasters lead to forced outmigration

Emergency food relief – longer-term improvement through secure water supply and better agriculture.

Netherlands

High density at a high standard of living

Ranstaadt example of overcrowded urban living – social-psychological pressures and inner city problems – long distance commuting.

Solution sought through decentralisation – green belt and other planning controls.

Bangladesh

High density – low standard – crowded population onto alluvial lowlands – mass depend on subsistence rice farming

Flood/typhoon hazards

Relief and rise in living standard sought through the Green Revolution and birth control (Case study 23.3).

Hong Kong

High density – rising incomes but extreme overcrowding on limited site – urban high-rise blocks

Island site spreading to mainland – dependent on industry and trade – rising prosperity

Overcrowding exacerbated by earlier refugee influx from China and Vietnam

Relief sought through control on immigration – planned new town and tunnel linkage on New Territory mainland.

Underpopulation

Underpopulation usually occurs where, despite the resource potential to support a higher density, a region is unattractive when compared with more settled areas. It may be that the area is a frontier region awaiting development or a longer settled area which has lost its population to more attractive areas.

Frontier regions

The more remote areas of Australia and Siberia have rich mineral and other resources awaiting development, but one of the problems is attracting enough labour. People are reluctant to move from the more favourable urbanised areas into these harsh environments. By improving communications, including light passenger planes, and by offering very high wages, some labour is attracted but it is usually only temporary. Population numbers remain low.

A similar problem has been recognised in Brazil, where an extreme population imbalance exists between the heavily settled coastal regions, particularly the South-East and the sparsely populated interior, including Amazonia (Case studies 14.3 and 28.5). In an effort to attract people into the interior, the new capital of Brasilia was created in the 1960s, 960 km from the coast. It was made a focal point for a network of highways which link the interior and coastal regions. It was hoped that this would provide a basic infrastructure to encourage the spread of the settlement and development to areas around Brasilia and further afield.

Brasilia itself now has a population of around one million people. However, it is only the area immediately around the city that has attracted further settlement and development, partly in response to the expanding market for foodstuffs and other produce created by the capital. Brasilia has, to some extent, produced a counter-effect on surrounding areas, encouraging rural depopulation to the new capital in the hopes of employment and a better standard of living.

Brazil has recently adopted a wider and more comprehensive regional development programme for the interior, involving Amazonia and the plateau interior. In addition to extending the major highway network, further secondary growth points to promote rural development are being set up.

Underpopulation as a result of depopulation

Underpopulation also exists in settled regions such as the rural peripheries in the advanced countries of Western Europe. In the UK, wages are on an average lower and unemployment higher in the peripheral South-West, rural Wales and the Highlands of Scotland, than for the rest of the country, except in the older declining industrial areas.

Resultant outward migration becomes self-perpetuating unless something is done to stem the flow. Fewer people mean a decreasing demand for services. The lower level of services reduces the viability of the community and encourages further outmigration (Section 13.4; Case study 24.4).

4.3 Factors which influence density distributions

The population - resource - technology relationship

While the concept of carrying capacity does indicate that there is a close relationship between population numbers and the resources available to these numbers, another important element needs to be added to the relationship, namely, the level of technology available (Figure 4.5).

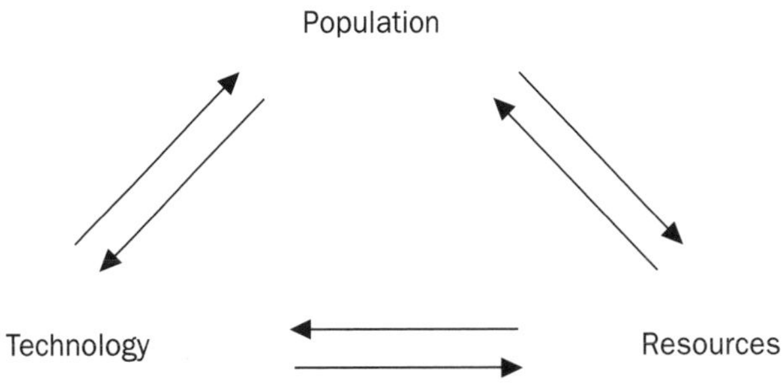

Figure 4.5 *The population-technology-resources relationship*

It is evident that the level of technology available will influence the extent to which resources can be tapped and used to support a population. However, the level of technology available also influences the size of the resource base and the size of the population which has to be supported by that resource base. For example, new techniques of birth control influence the birth rate and through this, the rate of natural increase. Advances in medical care and the eradication of diseases can lower the death rate and also influence the natural rates of increase and thus population numbers at any given time.

The basic population-resource-technology relationship is a dynamic relationship which effects changes in density distributions over time. The whole development process as it affects a country is about this very thing.

Figure 4.3 shows density distributions in a real world situation.

The population resource relationship is more complex in real world situations (Figure 4.6) than shown in Figure 4.5.

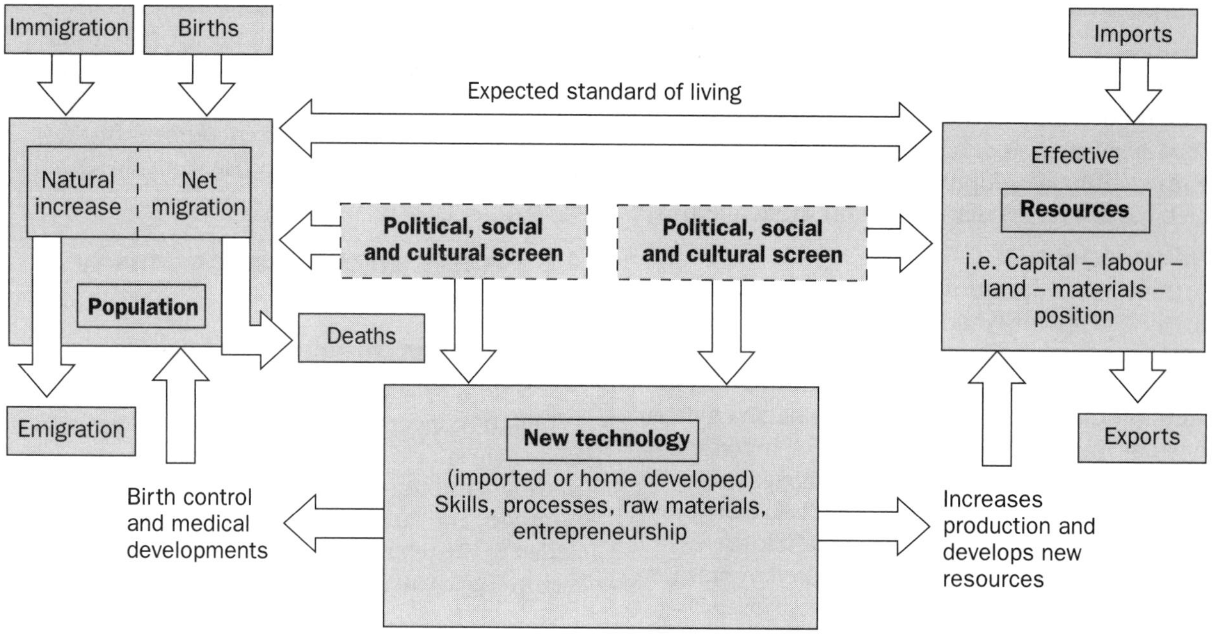

Figure 4.6 *Population, resource, technology relationships*

- What is involved under each of the basic terms – population, resources and technology – needs to be defined.
- The standard of living expected by a population is also important. Where given a certain resource and technology level, a population is 'content' to live at subsistence level, more people can be supported than if a higher level of living was demanded. In the latter case, more resources would be needed per head and therefor fewer people would be supported.
- Cultural and political factors are also important. If birth control is frowned upon in a particular culture, for example, this will affect the birth rate. Political decisions influencing the allocation of finance can affect both resource exploitation and population numbers. If finance is diverted to non-productive military expenditure, this reduces the amount available to develop the resource base, as is seen in some countries in Africa, such as Mozambique. Conversely, where a country pursues a policy of neutrality, as in the case of Switzerland, a greater proportion of income is available for resource development.
- External influences directly affect each of the basic elements in the population-resource-technology relationship. The influence of outside medical aid to the developing countries affects population numbers. Import of resources by advanced countries has expanded their resource base and has had an adverse effect on the resource base of those developing countries from which the imported resources had come. On the other hand, the green revolution technology introduced into certain developing countries has increased their food supplies.

4.4 Regional variations in population density distributions

Every country has a varied density distribution pattern. This is partly a reflection of the initial uneven distribution of natural resources, including differences in location and accessibility. It is also a result of the effect of development on different parts of a country, including the influence of technological changes over time, government policy decisions, population pressures, and the effects of external events.

Contrasting sparsely populated lagging regions and densely populated growth cores

Various development models, including Myrdal's cumulative causation model, may be used to readily identify lagging peripheral regions (Figure 3.4). These regions are initially sparsely populated and, in time, continue to lose out to the contrasting growth core through government neglect and depopulation. Within the UK, the western and northern upland periphery falls into this category, as does the Amazon region in Brazil (Case studies 11.1 and 28.5).

In contrast, development models may also be readily used to identify the main growth core regions which have benefited from initial resource and locational advantages. They would attract investment and favourable government treatment,

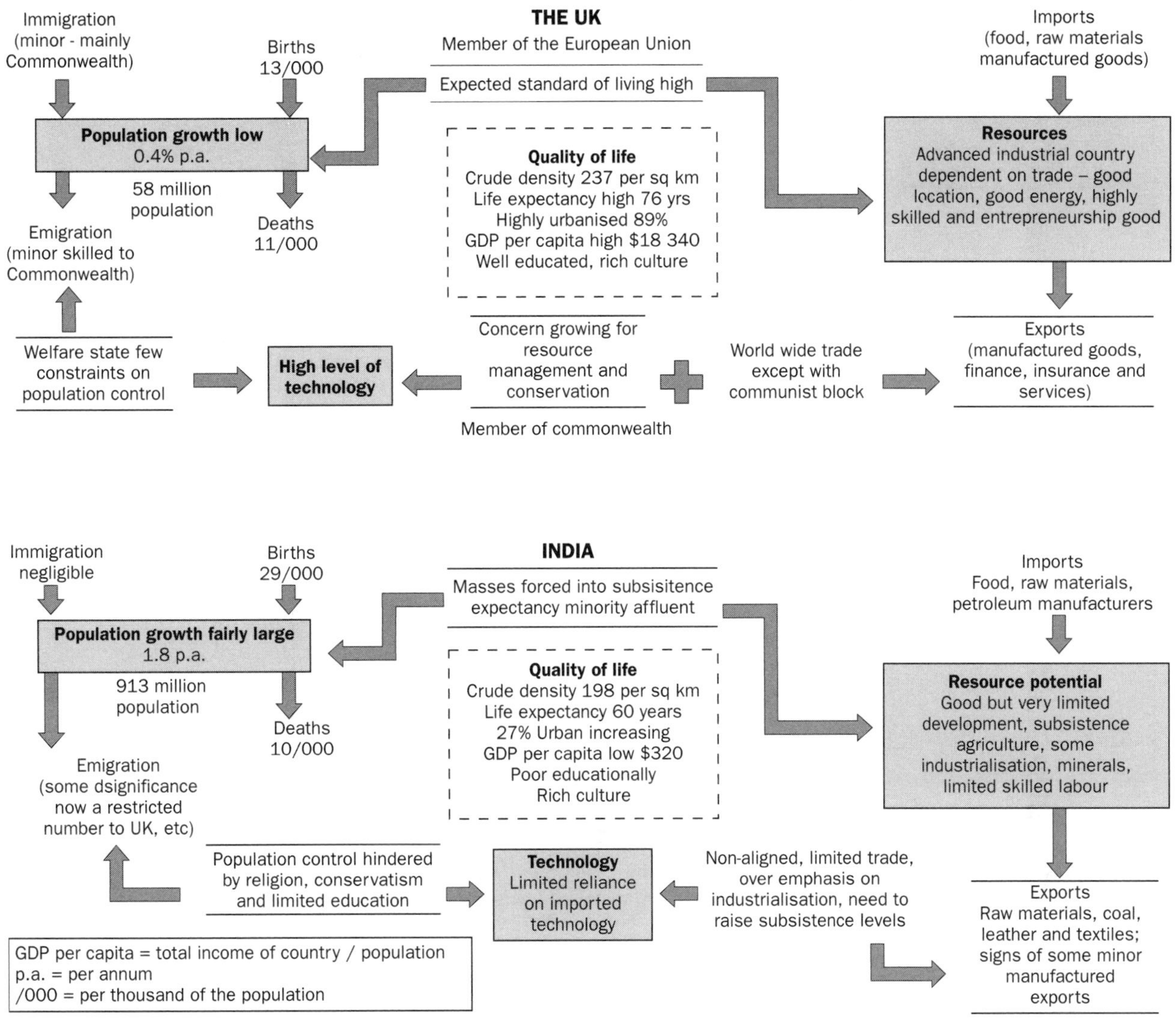

Figure 4.7 *The UK and India: population, resource, technology relationships*

which would lead to both a cumulative growth in economic activity and high population growth over time. These regions would thus become densely populated. The south-east London region, the metropolis and capital of the UK, is clearly one such growth core region (Case study 4.2). Its equivalent in Brazil is the South East region, which centres on two metropolitan areas: Rio de Janeiro and São Paulo.

Regions of changing fortune over time

Besides these lagging and growth core regions, there are other regions which, as a result of a combination of changes in the population, resource, technology and policy factors present in the development process, have either declined or become new growth centres. Their place in the pattern of regional variations has thus changed over time (Figure 4.8).

Core regions which are now in decline or stagnating, are usually still relatively densely populated areas, but some of the factors which were originally responsible for their growth have now fallen away and a decline in their economic bases has occurred.

Declining regions in advanced countries

The most common examples of declining regions in advanced countries are old industrial regions which were originally built up on coal and other mineral resources which have now been exhausted. As a result the heavy industry based upon these resources have declined (Case study 4.2).

Such regions have also suffered from the emergence of heavy industrial areas overseas, based on new and cheaper mineral and power sources. These have attracted the investment which at one time would have gone to the established and now declining heavy industry areas. Furthermore, the older industrial areas present a negative image to potential investors, with their derelict landscape and social problems of unemployment and growing

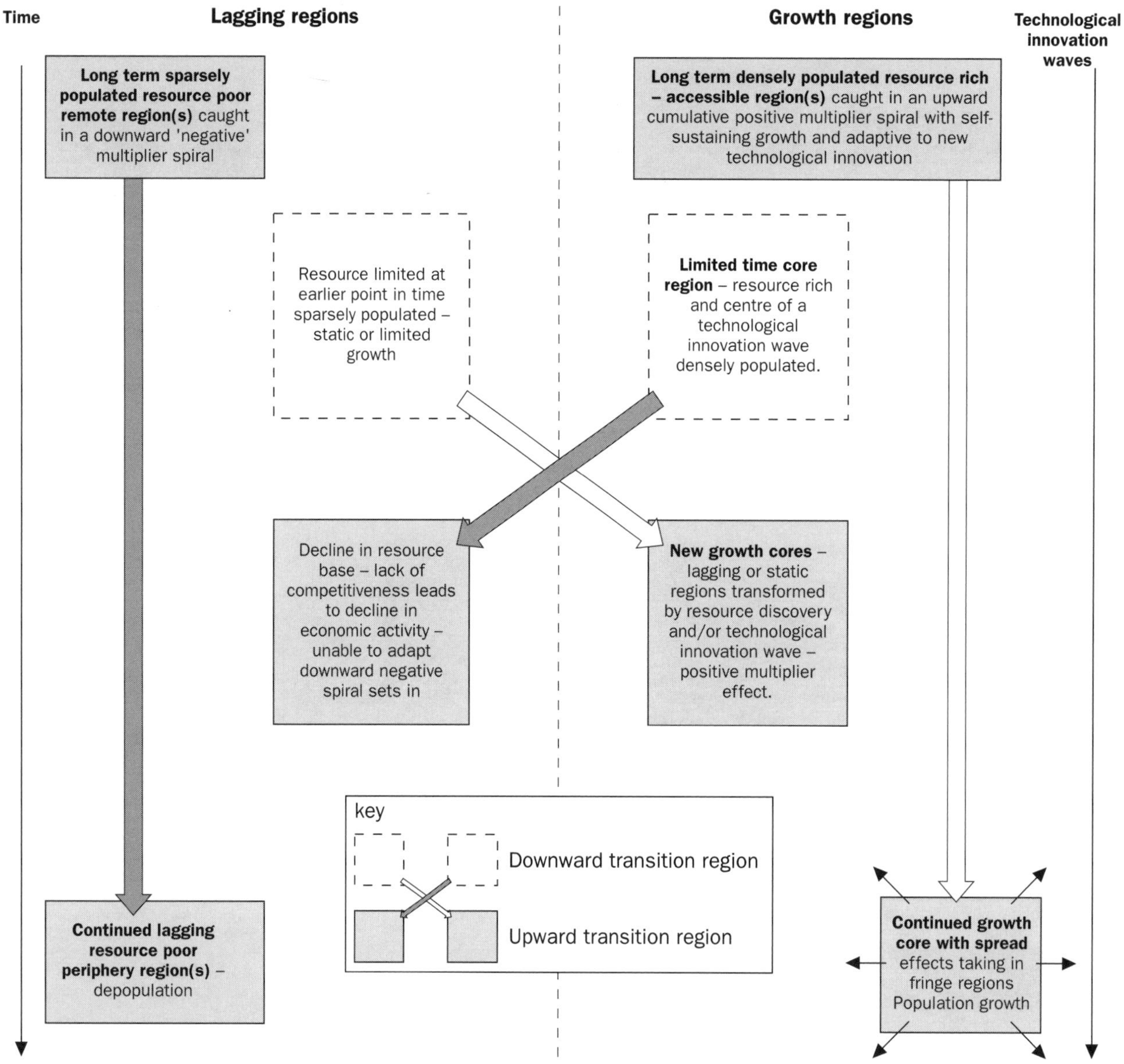

Figure 4.8 Lagging, growth and changing intermediate regions over time

poverty. Governmental attempts to rejuvenate these areas are usually insufficient and simply slows down the decline, unless an area attracts new technological and innovative investment, as seems likely in South Wales. Within the rest of the UK, the old industrial regions in the North remain depressed and lag behind the prospering and expanding South-East.

Declining regions in the developing countries

Just as the advanced countries have these once prosperous but declining regions, so developing countries also exhibit them. However, the cause of their change in fortune tends to be different.

The most easily recognised regions are the boom areas, which were based on some resource exploitation and which failed to attract long-term industrial growth. The Katanga copper belt region of the Congo is at present in decline, partly as a result of falling world copper prices but also because of political instability in the region. In North-East Brazil, the coastal region flourished as a growth region for a time under a Portuguese sugar plantation economy during the seventeenth and eighteenth centuries, exporting sugar, molasses and rum to Europe. The region declined with the expansion of sugar production in the southern United States and the Caribbean. Today, North-East Brazil is a problem region with widespread poverty and a flagging economy.

More recently, a second kind of declining or stagnating region has been identified in the developing world, where the problem is not so much one of a declining resource base but of the pressure of over-population allied to a lack of political investment to reduce this population pressure. Chapman, in his study of regional variations in India, classifies the whole of the densely populated Ganges valley in this category. Here the sheer pressure of population is outstripping the agricultural resource base in the rural areas, while the tremendous influx of population from these impoverished rural areas outpaces the capacity of Calcutta to absorb it. Calcutta has been further disadvantaged by the decline in its jute industry when the partition of India cut the city off from its hinterland which supplied the jute raw material but now forms part of Bangladesh.

New growth regions with an increasing population density

Technological innovation or identification of new resources, in conjunction with favourable government policy support, may encourage the emergence of new growth regions as a country develops. These attract populations which, along with growing economic activity, set up a positive cumulative growth spiral.

Since the 1960s within advanced countries, there has been a fundamental shift in the bases of economies away from heavy industry and consumer durables manufacturing to a dependence on services, high technology and information-based industries (Chapter 20). These have tended to be located away from the congested older industrial areas and near more accessible, spacious and environmentally friendly sites, in more ruralised regions. Thus, new growth sunbelt regions are emerging, attracting more economic activity and an influx of population.

In the United States, California in the west and Florida in the south are the fastest growing regions. In the UK, sunbelt growth is mainly adjacent to the established growth core of the south-east and represented by growth corridors either side of major motorways: west along the M4, south along the M3, north along the M1 into the Midlands and along the M11 into East Anglia (Case study 4.2).

In a number of cases this growth has been encouraged by the respective governments, partly to reduce pressure on the established growth region and also to attract foreign and home investment to ensure a prosperous new economic base for the twenty-first century. Motorway and other transport investment ensures increased accessibility to and from the new growth regions, while more flexible planning regulations and favourable financial incentives by national and local government bodies encourage private investment. Cumulative growth is thus encouraged.

New growth regions in the developing countries

In developing countries, new growth regions are a result of innovative changes as part of the development process, private and public investment and favourable government development policies. In newly industrialising countries, manufacturing growth has not only been encouraged in established growth centres, but also in new centres where the presence of resources has attracted investment and development, using new and established technologies. Chapman has noted the rapid growth of the established Bombay region since the introduction of nuclear power and petrochemical industries, which use newly developed offshore oil finds. There has also been new dynamic growth in the south of India, centred on Madras and Hyderabad. New aerospace and other high technology industries are being developed by joint cooperative ventures between multinational corporations and the Indian government. In Venezuela, the Cuidad Guayana development was established as a new growth centre, exploiting hitherto untapped iron ore and bauxite deposits and the vast hydro-electric potential of the tributaries of the Orinoco River.

While most new growth centres which attract an increasing population density are based on industrial and service sector expansion, they may also be based on improvements in agriculture. This is usually engendered by new techniques and the opening up of rural areas through a better infrastructure in access to markets. The green revolution in northern Punjab, which gave rise to new strains of higher yielding wheat and an extension of the area under irrigation, has made this region one of dynamic growth and growing prosperity, enabling it to support a higher density of population than before (Case study 4.1).

Concluding comment

Regional variations in population density may be explained within the improved framework of the population-resource-technology schema. It needs to be noted that the pattern is not static, but changes with variations in the rate of natural increase in population from one region to another and because of the effects of migration, some regions losing population, others attracting migration. This is, in turn, affected by changes in regional rates of economic development and of the economy as a whole.

case study

4.1 India: Population distribution and regional inequalities

India has sharp regional variations in its population distribution, which may be explained in terms of the population-resource-technology relationship. Variations in the pace of change are responsible for the growth and lagging regions identified here.

The densely populated but lagging east – the Ganges Valley and Calcutta

Victim of its own historical success

- Rural economy – The fertile Ganges valley with monsoon rain and river always supported a dense rural population. Rice is the staple crop. A settled traditional agriculture is practised on small plots, but tenants are exploited by landlords. There is a large mass of landless labourers. Poverty is still acute, however, the emerging middle class peasantry benefited from the Green Revolution. There is a high population density, poverty and strong traditional caste system hold back progress
- Until 1911 Calcutta was the capital of India and large metropolis centre. It lost its capital status to Delhi. At independence, it lost much of its hinterland to Bangladesh and was cut off from its jute sources. Even though its main industry is in decline, it is still a strong commercial centre and has diversified industry. Progress is also held back by the vast migration influx from rural areas. There are many slum shanty areas of poverty.
- Damador is the main industrial region, rich in coal, iron and other minerals. Even though the central government pushed for development, the advance did not affect its neighbouring regions, Damador had few economic links with them.

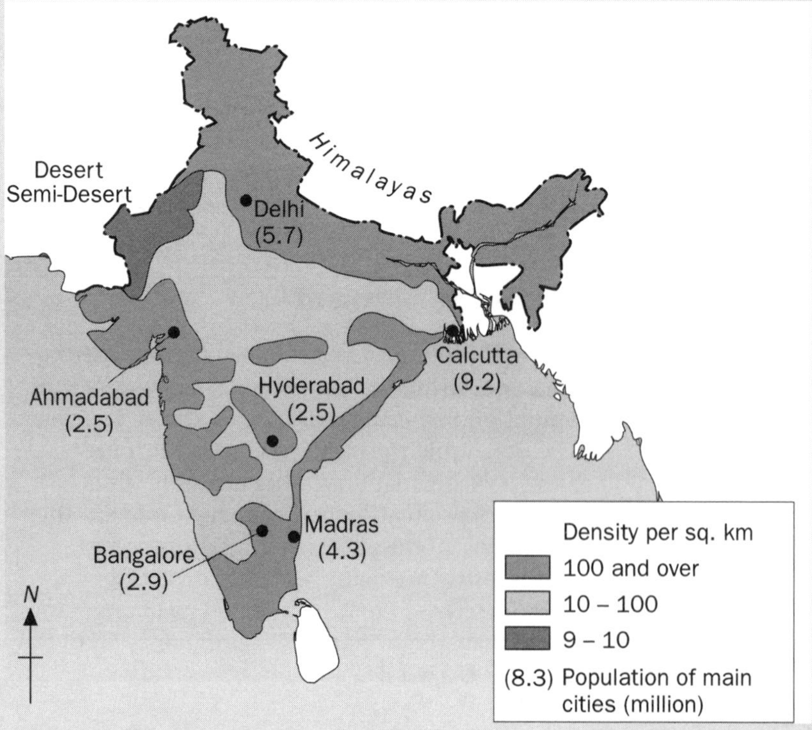

Population distribution in India

Growth regions

- **North-west: densely populated urban core and a green revolution dynamic agricultural core**
- Rural 'miracle' food basket of India is in Punjab and Haryana. It benefited most from the 'green revolution'. The peasantry prospered, with wheat yelds trebling under new strains and irrigation extensions. The holdings were larger than the rest of India and communities more commercially orientated than elsewhere. Urban links and infrastructure encourage a market economy. There was also a remittance of monies from Punjab minorities in the UK.
- Delhi is the fastest growing city in India. It is a capital and has a strong commercial and diversified base. There is prospering market demand which spreads to surrounding areas.
- **West: two dynamic urban cores and a linked hinterland**
- The west is strongly based more on urban core regions than rural prosperity. Bombay and linked cities of Pune (Poona), Thane (Bombay's satellite new town) and Ulhasanagar form the strongest industrial region in India. Prosperity was based initially on the excellent harbour, colonial trade links and flourishing cotton textiles, fed by the Deccan cotton region. New industrial diversification – textiles, heavy and light engineering, vehicles, petrochemicals based on offshore oil and nuclear power – has helped to

develop a strong infra-structure, spreading prosperity.

Ahmadabad is the other younger core and is a major textile and growth centre. Prosperity declines inland as the Deccan region is too dry for agriculture.

- **South**
  Prosperity is based on both agriculture and urban-based activities.
- A rural economy is based on rice on wetter coastal lowland, while diverse cropping occurs inland. The region has been reasonably successful in adopting the 'green revolution'. There has been rural advancement with a developing infrastructure and market opportunities.
- Initially based on textiles, the urban centres at Madras and Hyderabad are now boosted by the new domestic and craft industry and a growth in high technology. There is also an aeronautical industry based in these regions.

  The urban system and infrastructure is expanding along the coast.

Special: North-East

The north-east practises its own cultures and is rather separate from the Ganges heartland. It is at an intermediate stage of economic growth with Assam the most advanced area. The border states are unsettled.

Regional inequality contrasts indicators

What is most significant is the way in which regional patterns correlate over so many indicators: lower rates of urbanisation, poorer agriculture, slower growth in industry and poorer infrastructure all combine in some poorer areas. The reverse occurs in richer areas.

Inequalities have, if anything, increased. There is no mechanism for reducing inequalities, since the central government is relatively weak and the local state government stronger.

Rural population numbers and the contribution of agriculture to the GDP do not match. About 70% of the population is rural but agriculture contributes only 30% of the national GDP.

[SOURCE: Chapman G *Change in the South Asian Core*, 1992]

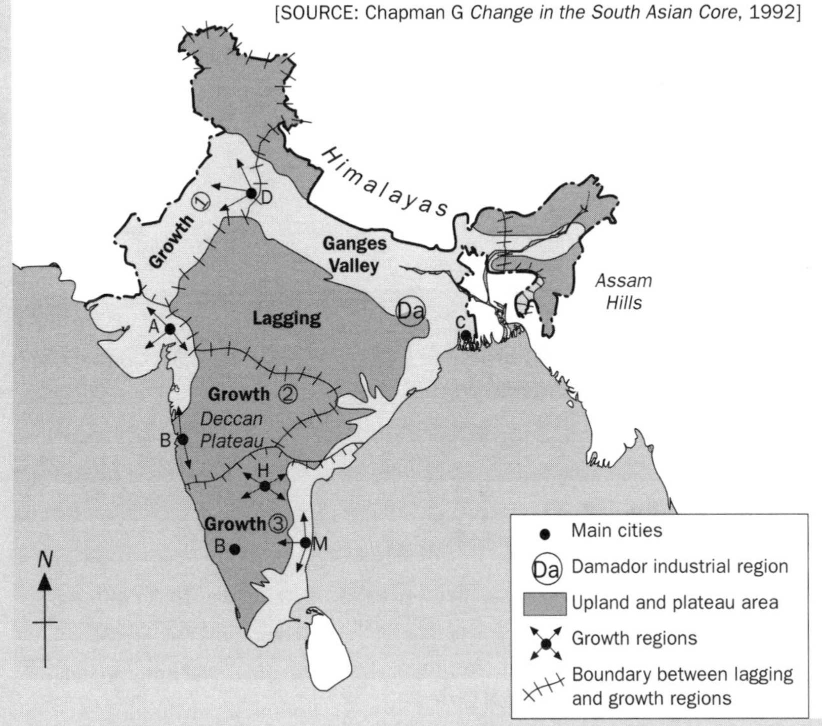

Economic regions in India

Basic indicators	(1991)		(1961–81)	(1985)	(1986)	(1983)
Growth regions	Popul mills	Urban %	GDP per capita (annual growth)	Popul % below poverty line	Villages electrified %	Villages with all weather roads %
North-West	101.2	28	1.5	23	79	47
West	116.2	34	1.5	30	93	42
South	193.9	27	1.3	33	81	42
Lagging region:						
East	377.6	18	0.0	45	54	19

Inequality indicators

case study

4.2 UK: Population distribution and regional inequalities

Though economically more advanced than India, regional variations in population distribution in the UK also reflect the influence of resources and technology. Changes over time in this relationship help to explain regional inequalities, including a core growth and lagging areas.

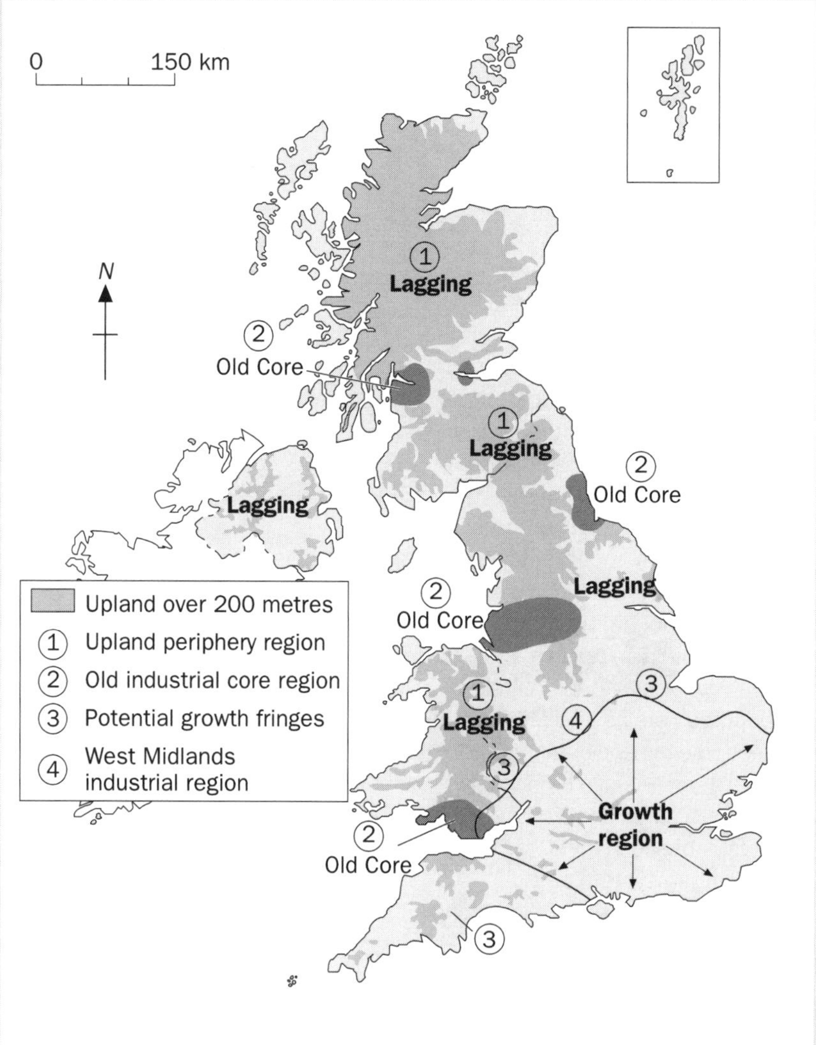

Economic regions in UK

The growth core and spreading 'golden zone' from London and the south-east

(i.e. East Anglia, South Midlands, the M4 west and M3 south corridors)

- The greatest initial resource was London's location on the Thames estuary, facing the continent. The UK's incorporation into the EU and completion of the Channel Tunnel remain significant factors in its growth.
- London has exerted a strong long-term influence as the capital and centre for administration and finance. The area is of national and international importance, setting off a cumulative causation and multiplier effect. It is the hub of a national route network. Its expanding population provides a prosperous market, helping towards making it the greatest entrepreneurial centre in the UK.
- It has benefitted from a shift in economy from heavy industry to lighter, service industry, including banking and insurance, especially since the mid-1930s. The focus is now on high technology industry and further service growth.
- Prosperity has spread, especially since the 1960s. Peoples' desires and higher core costs led to a decentralisation of population and economic activity into the more spacious rural areas, particularly along the M4 and M3 growth corridors and north into East Anglia.

Lagging regions and a transitional growth fringe

1 The Upland rural periphery: Scottish Highlands, Uplands and Pennines

The poor physical resource base and remoteness account for the sparse population. Its lack of mineral resources made the highland areas lagging regions ever since the Middle Ages. Depopulation is a continuous trend, despite government assistance through Development Boards and some resucitation as leisure areas for the more populated urban regions. The designation of much of the upland periphery as National Parks ensures little future growth in population, except where external influence prompts growth e.g. Aberdeen in Scotland as a base for offshore North Sea oil operations.

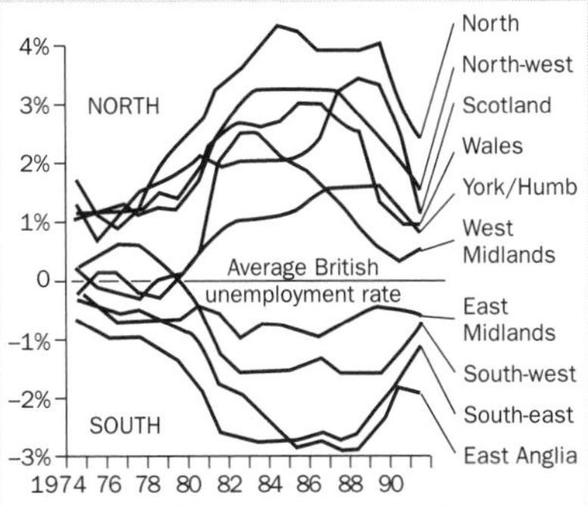

Regional unemployment differentials

2 Old industrial cores aided to encourage regeneration and prevent downward spiral: Scottish Central Lowlands, South Wales, North East and North West

- The high population densities are a result of the coal and iron-ore resource base for heavy industry which developed during the industrial revolution. This was aided by port access. The focus on technology and enterprise led to continued prosperity until the 1920s, when these areas suffered a decline due to a diminishing resource base and a decrease in UK competitiveness with foreign heavy industry products.
- The area failed to attract enough new growth and service industries, despite government development assistance grants to counter heavy industrial decline.
- Nevertheless large urban bases and regional administrative and commercial functions stabilised the population to some extent. The two bridges which link South Wales to the M4 corridor may ensure its revival. The North-East is the most dynamic of the old northern cores, attracting foreign investment and service growth.

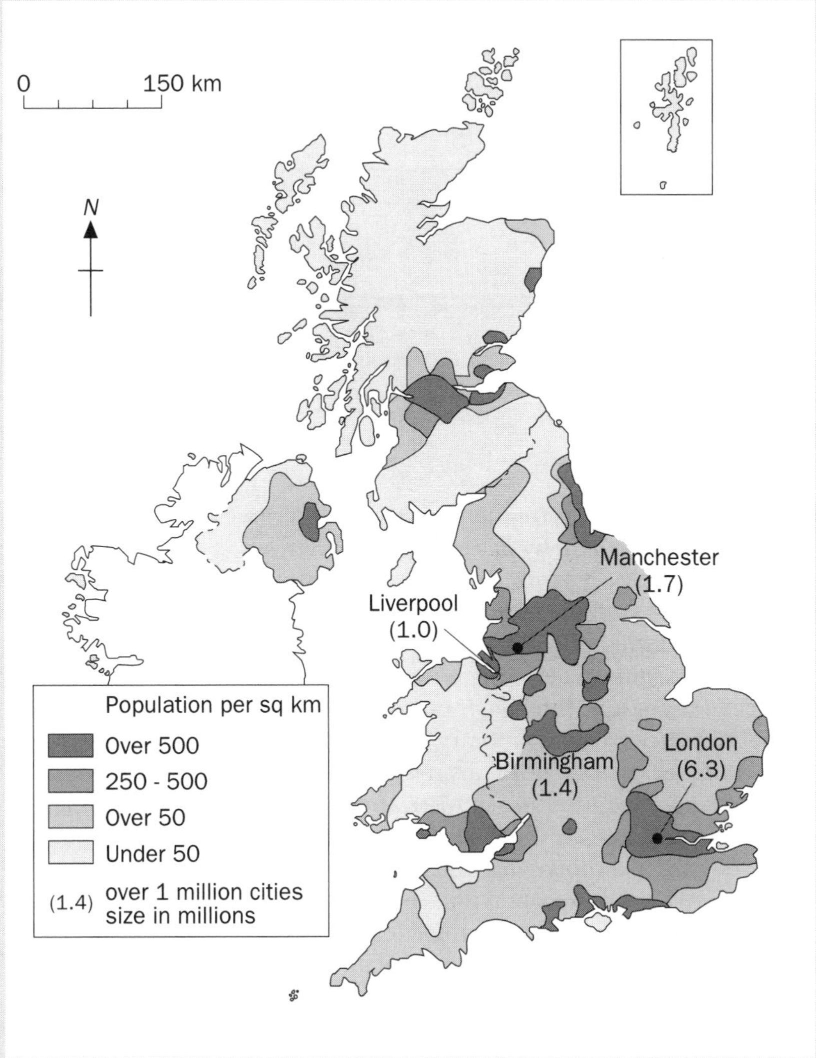

Population density distribution in the UK

3 Fringe of growth regions-potential for future growth

- East Anglia and East Midlands, as part of lowland Britain, have comparatively fertile loam soils and moderate rainfall with sunny summers. These regions are favoured for agricultural prosperity and as market centres. East Anglia is the fastest growth area in the UK aided by the electrification of rail lines for commuter growth and science park developments. The East Midlands and West Midlands established engineering and automobile industrial areas are also being revived by high technology and service growth.
- The south-west was part of the more remote upland fringe until recently. Now with lower cost, rural setting and developing motorway and commuter train links, it attracts both retirement and working households, service and high technology growth, as well as tourists.

5

CHAPTER 5

Migration and urbanisation

'Migration is a phenomenon as old as mankind.'

JAN PRONK – EUROPEAN POPULATION CONVENTION 1993

The term 'migration' is frequently used to describe any kind of movement by people, but most writers concerned with population studies agree that its use should be restricted to ***moves which involve a permanent change of residence.*** (The United Nations constitution defines 'permanent' as a change of residence which lasts more than a year.) It does not encompass temporary movements. Such things as pastoral nomadism, seasonal movement of labour, commuting to work and tourism, are not classified under the heading of migration, since they are of a short-term and temporary nature and involve a return to a previous location (Case study 23.2). These are better termed 'circulatory movements' and are dealt with in later chapters.

Permanent migrations can be classified in three ways:

- cause of the move, whether voluntary, from choice, or involuntary, as a result of being forced out of the area.
- the distance over which the migration occurs, the main differentiation being between international migrations where national frontiers are crossed and those internal to a country. This internal kind of move is further divided between localised and longer inter-regional migration.
- the type of area from and to which the migration occurs.

On the basis of these criteria, an overall classification of the different kinds of migration can be made.

Figure 5.1 *A basic classification of migration*

Cause	**Distance**		
Voluntary	**International** (across national frontiers)	**Internal to a country** *Regional*	 *Local*
	Overseas – Continental	rural – rural rural – urban urban – rural urban – urban frontierwards	rural – rural rural – urban urban – rural intra – urban (i.e. within an urban area)
Involuntary	*International*	*Regional*	*Local*
	Overseas – Continental		

5.1 Patterns of migration

International patterns

The main directions of international migrations for recent times are shown in Figure 5.2. There have also been many shorter migrations across national boundaries. However, much of it has been of an involuntary nature; refugees, for example, fleeing from natural disasters or war zones, such as over a million Rwandans crossing into Zaire.

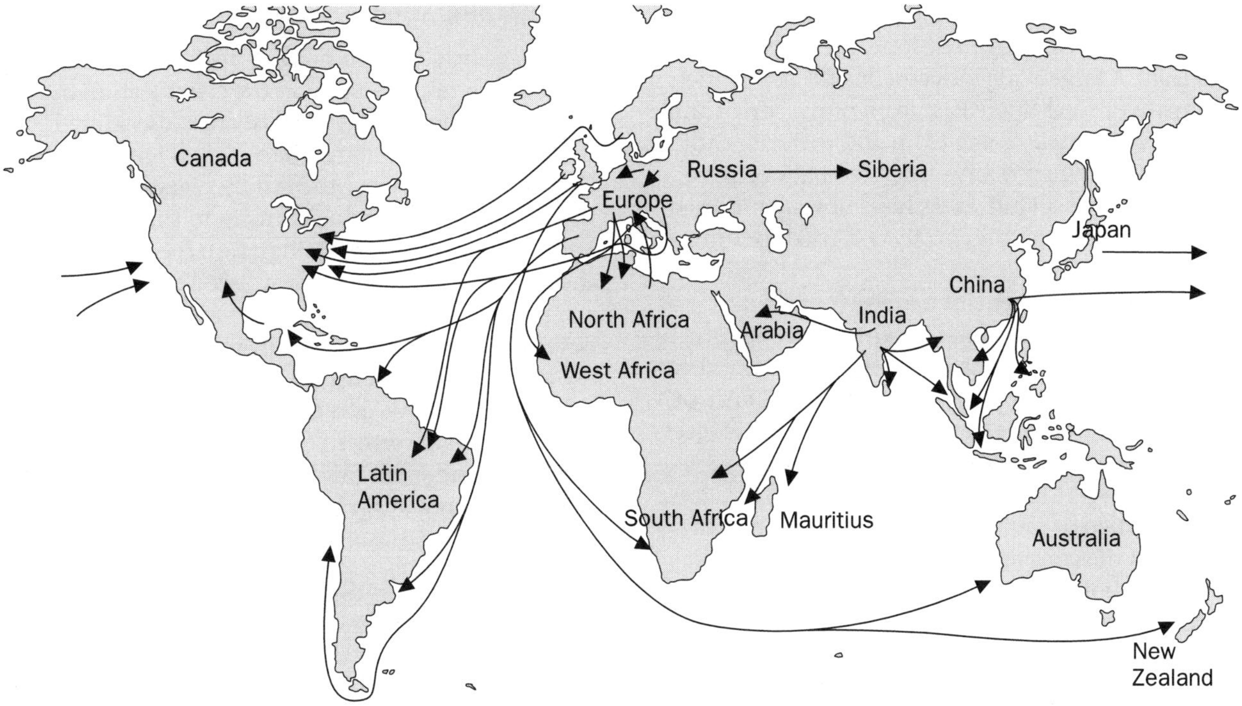

Figure 5.2 *Main world migrations since the beginning of the twentieth century*

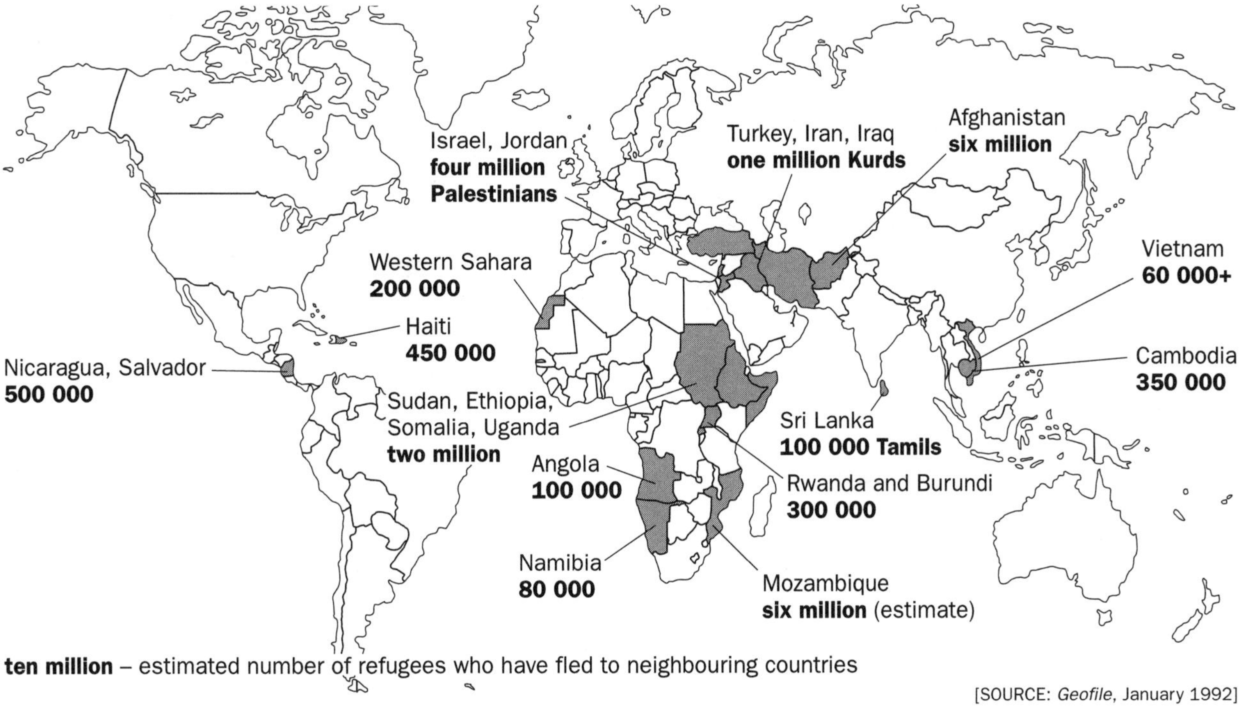

[SOURCE: *Geofile*, January 1992]

Figure 5.3 *Forced population movements, 1991*

Most international migration in recent years has been of an involuntary kind. Besides the waves of refugees already mentioned, there are even larger numbers of people who migrate out of economic necessity; poverty drives them to seek work in other countries. This international migration is mainly, but not entirely, a move from the poorer southern hemisphere to the more affluent north. The largest stream is from Mexico to the USA. Of the eight million people who entered the United States in the last decade, half came from Mexico. In addition, in 1990 alone, one million Mexicans tried to cross the border illegally (Figure 5.4).

Another lesser migration has been from poor areas in north Africa into Europe, mainly to France and Italy. A large-scale movement into the oil-rich countries of the Middle East from north Africa and south Asia virtually came to an end with the Gulf War in 1991, when many either fled back or were repatriated. Most Gulf states have now abandoned policies which were previously designed to bring in labour from outside.

Most refugee movement has been between developing countries, some in central America and in south and south-east Asia. By far the largest numbers of refugees have moved between countries in Africa. For example, from 1986 to 1991, six million refugees fled from the civil war in Mozambique into neighbouring African countries. In Malawi, refugees mainly settled in camps south of Lilongwe, making up 11% of the country's eight million population. They have put a great strain on an already impoverished economy.

Today, only the smaller international flows of skilled and educated people are seen as beneficial to receiving countries. All other movements, whether of refugees or of those seeking work, are seen largely in terms of the problems they create and the threat they pose to the livelihood of established residents.

This contrasts with the approach towards migration which geographers have adopted in the past: *'Geographers have traditionally regarded migration as a spatial reallocation of human resources.'*

Consequently, most countries have recently tightened up immigration laws to cut down on immigration, with the exception of professional and skilled personnel to whom, in contrast, greater incentives are being offered.

'Whilst demonstrating concern for the continuing migration of unskilled labour from Mexico, the United States government is actively seeking highly qualified scientists. New immigration laws passed in November 1990 were specifically designed to make it easier for professional people to enter the United States. The law tripled the number of visas allocated to such people to 140,000.'

[SOURCE: Elizabeth Walls, *Geofile*, January 1992]

The trend towards reduced international migration is further reinforced by a redirection policy and more finance being allocated to improve conditions in forwarding countries, thus reducing the incentive to migrate. Surveys indicate that most would-be migrants would prefer to stay in their own country if employment was available and local conditions were politically stable.

Internal migration

It is possible to find, in most countries, all the classic types of migration shown in the classification in Figure 5.1. The most important are those related to the major metropolitan urban cores (Figure 5.5; Case study 14.2). Over the last 25 years, however, there has been a growing contrast in the character and direction of internal migration for countries in the developing world and advanced countries.

The scale of migration is much greater in developing countries. It usually involves people in the lower income groups who are looking for manual and unskilled work, and is overwhelmingly directed towards the large growth cities from the surrounding rural areas and small towns. On a smaller scale, there is also some migration to frontier areas which are being opened up in some countries (Case study 28.5).

Rural-urban migration in the Third world constitutes the last phase in a great human revolution; it completes the urban transition . . . The magnitude of it, the sheer number of people involved in it, is without precedent in human history.

[SOURCE: Gugler J *Internal Migration in the Third World, Population Geography: Progress and Prospects*]

In advanced countries the scale of internal migration has declined and increasingly involves middle-income groups and not the lower paid. It is predominantly from the main metropolitan centres to the surrounding rural areas and smaller towns (Figures 5.6). There is also some reversal of

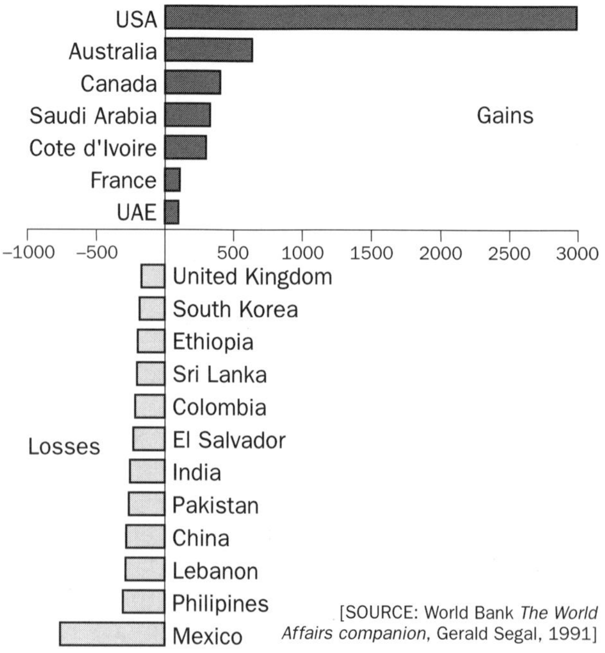

[SOURCE: World Bank *The World Affairs companion*, Gerald Segal, 1991]

***Figure 5.4** Major net international migration, 1985 – 90 (in thousands)*

the depopulation of the rural periphery regions which had occurred all through the nineteenth and twentieth century. In some of these areas, there is small selective in-migration of mainly professional and retired people who are escaping the pressures of urban living (Chapter 12).

5.2 **Migration: towards an explanation**

Push-pull mechanisms

Given the complex pattern of migration and the variety of influences at work, it is not surprising that it has proved difficult to provide a satisfactory framework or model within which to explain these various kinds of migration. One of the most basic explanations sees migration as a response to a simple push-pull mechanism. Negative factors in the losing area are seen as forcing or encouraging people to move in response to a pull of better opportunities, whether real or perceived in the receiving area.

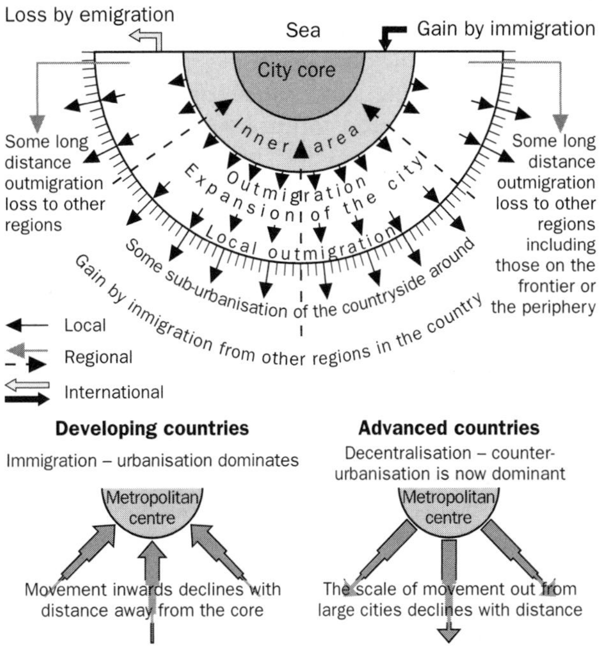

Figure 5.5 Patterns of internal migration associated with main urban metropolitan regions

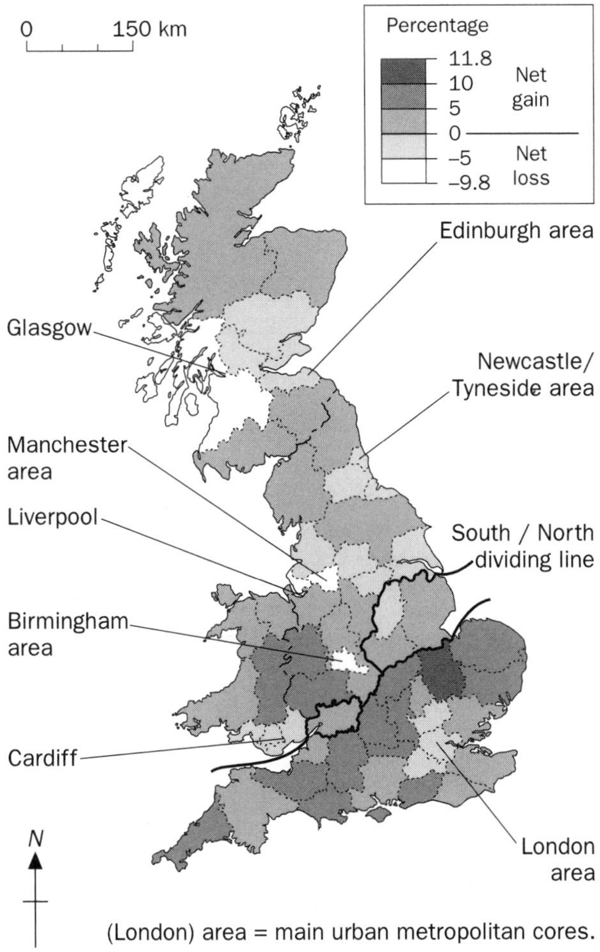

The figures show that, over the last ten years, the rural districts of England and Wales enjoyed the fastest population growth in both percentage terms and, when compared to districts with far larger populations, in the actual increase in numbers of people living there. Extending the picture to include Scotland, the more remote, mainly rural districts gained about 365 000 people over the decade, an increase of 6.1 per cent.
Some of the biggest contributions suffered major losses of population. London's head count was down by nearly 320 000 (five per cent) and that of other principal cities by 370 000 (8.7 per cent). The largest cities in non-metropolitan countries also lost 3.6 per cent of their population.'

Type of district	South		North	
	000s	%	000s	%
Total	+485.4	+1.71	-689.2	-2.51
Greater London				
Inner boroughs	-147.0	-5.89	-	-
Outer boroughs	-171.5	-4.08	-	-
Metropolitan				
Principal cities	-	-	-369.7	-8.69
Other districts	-	-	-371.9	-4.30
Non metropolitan				
Large cities	-58.7	-3.29	-72.1	-4.00
Small cities	+8.6	+0.84	+2.4	+0.30
Industrial areas	+49.1	+1.89	-91.0	-1.9
Districts with new towns	+102.4	+8.86	+30.6	+2.04
Resort, port and retirement	+152.6	+5.77	+20.9	+3.03
Urban and mixed urban/rural	+282.1	+3.76	+36.6	+1.63
More remote, mainly rural	+240.8	+7.25	+124.9	+4.64

NOTES: South is defined as the south-east , south-west, East Anglia and east Midlands regions. North is the remainder of the country.
'–' = no cases.
[SOURCE: calculated from OPCS 1991a and RGS 1991]

Figure 5.6 Decentralisation and counterurbanisation trends in the United Kingdom, 1981 – 1991

In considering factors associated with push-pull mechanisms, some distinction has to be made between forced migration where the migrant has little or no choice, and voluntary migration, where the prospective migrant does have some choice.

Adding a decision-making element

Recent studies have tended to give more weight to the process by which individual households and groups decide whether or not to move. Gulger's research into rural-urban migration revealed how important discussion is within households and in the community. Thus migration is not simply a response to a group of external factors, but it is also a conscious decision that is made.

Lee, in his theory of migration, does focus on the decision-making process. He sees the individual, family or group, as making a decision to move in the light of a range of factors, in the home area at one extreme, and in the contemplated prospective receiving areas at the other. Lee also introduces the idea of there being a number of real and perceived personal and environmental obstacles which have to be overcome before migration takes place. The longer the distance of the contemplated move, the greater are the real and perceived obstacles which need to be overcome. Initial moves thus tend to be over a limited distance (Figure 5.8).

Faced with making the kinds of decisions which are outlined in Lee's theory, some families and individuals will be in a better position to move than others. Circumstances make them highly mobile in contrast to those who are immobile. The reason for staying or leaving are summarised in Figure 5.9.

Consequences of migration

The consequences of moving will vary according to the nature and volume of the migrations which have occurred, and will vary from one particular situation to another (Figure 5.9).

Figure 5.7 Factors which affect migration

Forced migration
'The decision in many cases is driven by necessity as much as by choice.'

Area of origin
Wars / Persecution
Breakdown of economies
Environmental catastrophies

Distance has some influence but necessity may overcome the friction of distance

Receiving areas
Frequently movement to the nearest area which is likely to accept migrants and provide relief

Voluntary migration
'There is always pull as well as push as migrants move in search of a better life.'
'Migration is a sign of wide disparities in economic and social conditions between origin and destination'

Area of origin
Population exceeds the capacity of the economy to support it.
Decreasing employment opportunity.
Income uncertain or too low.
Level of commercial and public services and amenities are poor – below or perceived as below the level in receiving areas.
Life chances and security considered as uncertain.

Receiving areas
Has or perceived as having better employment opportunities in the formal and informal sectors.
Better or perceived better commercial and public services and amenities.
Considered to have more security and better life chances.

Improvements in transport and personal mobility encourage migration.
More information available through the media and personal contacts.

'Migration decisions are about family security and long-term life chances, rather than simply a maximisation of income'
'Images through the global communication media and social networks strengthens the 'pull' of richer countries (and areas)'

[SOURCE: *The State of the World Population*, UNFPA 1993]

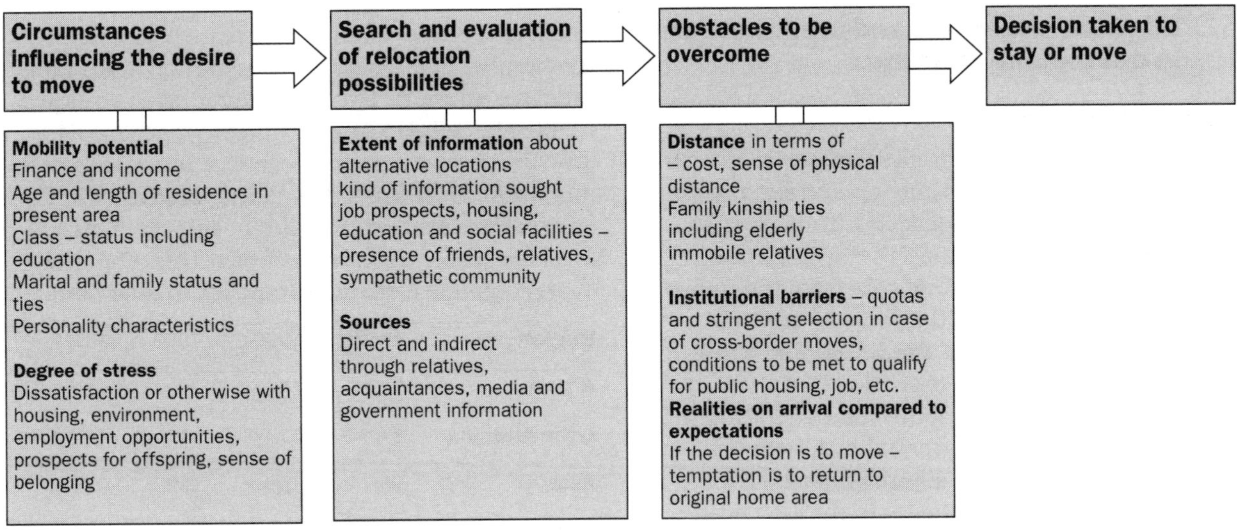

Figure 5.8 *The decision-making process and its influences*

Consequences for receiving areas

	Voluntary migration		**Forced migration**
	Poorer and less skilled	**Educated and skilled**	**Families, women and children**
Demographic	Builds up the reproductive sector in the population as well as adding to the population thus continued population growth.	Adds to population but unlikely to increase birth rate as more educated and favour smaller families.	May greatly add to absolute numbers but unlikely to increase the birth rates.
Social	May add a new ethnic dimension creating area concentrations with own culture. May bring in new ideas and self help but may put a lot of strain on social services and infrastructures.	More likely to integrate with the existing population and promote local initiatives.	Unlikely to integrate with resident population. Will retain own culture.
Economic	May provide a valuable labour source but if influx is too great, an unemployment problem is created. Likely to further create an informal sector in the economy.	Brings ideas and skills plus more consumer demand.	Severe pressure put on poorer economies but it may be providing a labour source.

Consequences for sending areas

	Voluntary migration		**Forced migration**
	Poorer and less skilled	**Educated and skilled**	**Families, women and children**
Demographic	May relieve population pressure as majority of migrants are part of the younger reproductive sector of the population, but if rural areas affected, then birth rate may remain high for residue of reproductive population. Thus fall in and ageing of the population may not be as much as expected.		Depending on size of migration it will accentuate the fall already brought about by the disaster causing the refugee outflow.
Social	Feedback of information and return of some migrants loosens traditional social structures and values and encourages a more outgoing and materialistic outlook.		Break up of family and community life.
Economic	Relieves population pressure but the loss of the able-bodied younger sector may lead to a fall in the productivity of the land and create a severe labour shortage.	Very detrimental as takes away the educated and skilled manpower needed for further development. This shortage may deter outside investment.	May relieve population pressure but also takes away people needed to restore the economy.
Political	Lessens local allegiances and may allow domination by outside forces.	Removes the effective political voices needed in the democratic process.	Likely to prolong political instability.

Figure 5.9 *Consequences of migration for receiving areas and for sending areas*

5.3 Migration, mobility and urbanisation in developing countries

Types of migration

Apart from circulatory movements associated with seasonal changes in agriculture or land exhaustion, and forced migrations associated with inter-tribal wars and the slave trade, most of the migration flows in the developing world date from the time of European intervention and colonisation.

At present, migration in the developing world, both within and between countries, is of a far greater volume and importance than migration in the developed world. This may at first seem surprising, since mobility and the capacity for people to move are much better in the advanced countries than in developing countries. Because the bulk of the world population is in the developing world, however, there are many more potential migrants and the need to move is much more forceful. Whereas most people in the developed world move to improve their standard of living and out of a desire to do so, most developing world migrants move for survival and employment. Compulsory migration is seen in large-scale refugee movements, in seasonal and longer term labour migrations and in the flight from rural poverty to the cities.

Much attention is focused on rural to urban movement and on the process of urbanisation well advanced in Latin America and parts of Asia, and gathering momentum in Africa. While urbanisation is a central focus as far as internal migration goes, refugee movements across national borders dominate international migrations. These migration flows within and between countries are illustrated in Case studies 5.2 and 5.3.

Urbanisation

Urbanisation is closely linked to the modernisation or development process. The further a country progresses along the path of development, the more important and dominant cities become in the total life and economy of that country. ***Urbanisation has been defined as 'becoming more urban' and in this process, four interlinked characteristics can be identified.***

Population numbers
An increasing proportion of the population can be found in cities with conversely fewer in rural areas. In the first stages of urbanisation, this is a result of large-scale migration from the countryside into the city, as is currently evident in Africa and on the Indian sub-continent, for example. At a later stage, much of it is due to natural increase in the city as the number of people in the reproductive age range increases and rural to urban migration slows down. In most large Latin American cities for example, growth is now due more to natural increase than in-migration. Over time, this natural increase will slow down as better education and health care is made available under urban conditions. This often leads to an acceptance of and a desire for smaller families.

Region	1950	1970	1990	2015
Africa	3	16	59	225
Latin America	17	57	118	225
Asia	58	168	359	903
Europe	73	116	141	156
North America	40	78	105	148

[SOURCE: World Resources 1996 – 97]

Figure 5.10 *Population in cities with more than one million residents, by region, 1950 – 2015*

	1970	1990	2000 (Projected)
Nigeria	20	35	43
Ghana	29	33	38
Kenya	10	24	32
Zimbabwe	17	28	38
Zambia	30	56	65
Ivory Coast	27	47	55

Figure 5.11 *Urban population as a percentage of total population for some African countries*

Shift in economy
Urbanisation also implies a shift in the economy towards urban-based activities associated with manufacturing and services. These include public services, such as administration and welfare, and commercial services of a variety of kinds, including retailing, financial, leisure and transport provision. Rural activities, in particular agriculture, become less important.

The nature of society
An urbanised society is more materially oriented as there is a shift towards a moneyed economy. Lifestyle is based on secondary contacts through work and wider social activities. Attitudes are increasingly influenced by the media and by more contact with the outside world.

	Agriculture	Industry	(Manu-facturing)	Services
Nigeria	37	38	(-)	26
Ghana	53	17	(10)	29
Kenya	27	22	(12)	51
Zimbabwe	20	32	(26)	49
Zambia	16	47	(36)	37
Ivory Coast	38	22	(21)	40

(*Manufacturing is a subset of Industry)

Figure 5.12 *Distribution of GDP per sector by percentage, 1991*

Urban behaviour

Urbanisation is increasingly seen as a dynamic force in society. The values and behaviour patterns recognised as urban are spread beyond the cities into surrounding rural areas as they become increasingly bound up with the economy and life of the city.

> The world over, rural populations have been drawn into the urban nexus. Subsistence farmers have come to produce for urban markets ... They have become subject to political control exerted from urban centres ... Throughout the world today, most rural dwellers know what it is like to sell and buy in markets and shops, they can see what a school certificate can do for the future of a child, have listened to first hand accounts of those who work in the city.
>
> [SOURCE: Gugler J *Internal Migration in the Third World, Population Geography: Progress and Prospects*]

Causes of developing world urbanisation

The influence of colonialism which changed tropical countries and brought them into an industrial capitalist system and a world economy underlies the process of urbanisation in the developing world . While great cities had existed in older civilisations, most of the large cities of the developing world today are based on the administrative role initiated by earlier colonial powers and on economic activities which tie them into the world trading and economic system.

The pull of the cities is inextricably tied to inequalities, heightened and intensified by a colonial system which focused wealth in the cities and drained the rural areas of much of their resources. Since then, the disparity between the urban cores and more peripheral areas has been intensified by the policies of national governments which favour economic growth in the major city core regions, to the neglect of rural areas, and by the increasing dependence of developing countries on outside trade and investment through the major city regions.

> There is no way in which the process of urban development can be understood in isolation from the processes that generate inequality ... These inequalities within the third world have contributed to the forms which have emerged. In the absence of such wide inequalities in access to resources the phenomena we describe would be very different.
>
> [SOURCE: Alan Gilbert, *Cities, Poverty and Development* 1992]

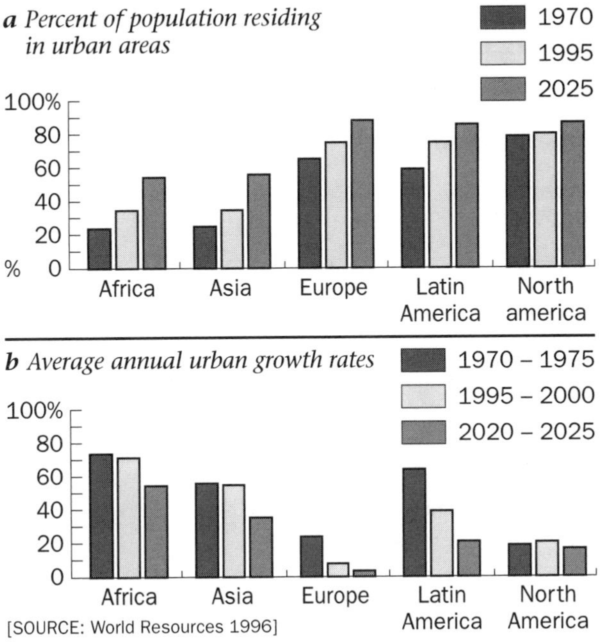

Figure 5.13 *The dominance of developing world urbanisation*

5.4 **The pace of urbanisation**

Since 1800 urbanisation had dramatically gathered momentum in advanced countries, but since the 1950s it has shifted to the developing countries. In 1800, 50 million people lived in cities but today the number is over two billion (Figure 5.14). Over 45% of the world's population are now urban dwellers and the continued upward trend of urbanisation indicates that in five years time this will rise to over 50%. Most will be in cities of over a million people, with the largest cities in the developing world showing a dramatic increase in size (Figure 5.15). Mexico City, one of the largest world cities, has already doubled in size in the last twenty years to 20 million and by the year 2000, will have a population of 26 million (Case study 11.3).

	Population (millions)	Average annual growth rate 1990–95 (%)
Tokyo, Japan	26.8	1.41
Sao Paolo, Brazil	16.4	2.01
New York, USA	16.3	0.34
Mexico City, Mexico	15.6	0.73
Bombay, India	15.1	4.22
Shanghai, China	15.1	2.29
Los Angeles, USA	12.4	1.60
Beijing, China	12.4	2.57
Calcutta, India	11.7	1.67
Seoul, Rep of Korea	11.6	1.95
Jakarta, Indonesia	11.5	4.35
Buenos Aires, Argentina	11.0	0.68
Tianjin, China	10.7	2.88
Osaka, Japan	10.6	0.23
Lagos, Nigeria	10.3	5.68
Rio de Janeiro, Brazil	9.9	0.77
Delhi, India	9.9	3.80
Karachi, Pakistan	9.9	4.27
Cairo, Egypt	9.7	2.24
Paris, France	9.5	0.29
Metro Manila, Philippines	9.3	3.05
Moscow, Russian Federation	9.2	0.40
Dhaka, Bangladesh	7.8	5.74
Istanbul, Turkey	7.8	3.67
Lima, Peru	7.5	2.81

Figure 5.14 *World's twenty-five largest cities, 1995*

There seems a clear link between general population growth and the rate of urbanisation. A study of developing world countries in 1992 indicated that the 48 countries with the fastest population growth had an average annual urban growth of 6.1% while the others averaged 3.6%.

Urbanisation is also linked to the rate of industrial and service expansion in the economy, since these are mainly urban-based activities and thus offer employment opportunities to would-be migrants. This link is clearly illustrated in some African countries (Case study 5.3).

Such has been the pace of urbanisation in developing countries that it has actually outstripped the capacity of cities to provide jobs. Authorities have also been unable to provide enough essential services such as housing, health and education. In the face of the growing problems in the largest cities, there have been calls to halt the flow of migrants into the cities. Apart from this being impracticable, there is plenty of evidence that despite the problems, most migrants are better off than they would be in the rural areas which they had left. If the problems in the cities are to be solved then most authorities and international agencies accept that the pace of urbanisation must be slowed. This can only occur if conditions in rural areas are improved, reducing inequalities of opportunity between these areas and the cities, thus giving would-be migrants more incentive to stay.

5.5 Urbanisation in Africa

Although Africa is the least urbanised continent, having only 30% of its population in cities as compared to 70% in Latin America, the pace of urbanisation has markedly quickened since 1970. It now has one of the fastest rates of urbanisation, averaging 6% per annum for all cities, but as high as 8.5% for the largest cities of over one million in size (Figure 5.15). If present trends continue, the size of the urban population in Africa will double in the next ten years. However, the rate of urbanisation varies significantly from country to country, depending on how important manufacturing and service activities have become in the economy. It is generally higher for west African and east African countries (Figure 5.11).

Rural to urban migration

Motivation

The essential motivating force behind rural to urban migration is the imbalance in opportunities between rural areas and the city and, in particular, employment and earning prospects. A substantial body of research over the last thirty years confirms that most people migrate for economic reasons. Pressure of population on land in Africa and insufficient investment in alternative economic activities to farming, have pushed many into migration. This has been accentuated where, as in the Sahel belt, drought and civil war have occurred (Case study 7.1). In contrast in a number of African countries which have become independent, the draw of employment prospects in the towns has been enhanced because the passing of minimum wage legislation has led to a rise in earnings.

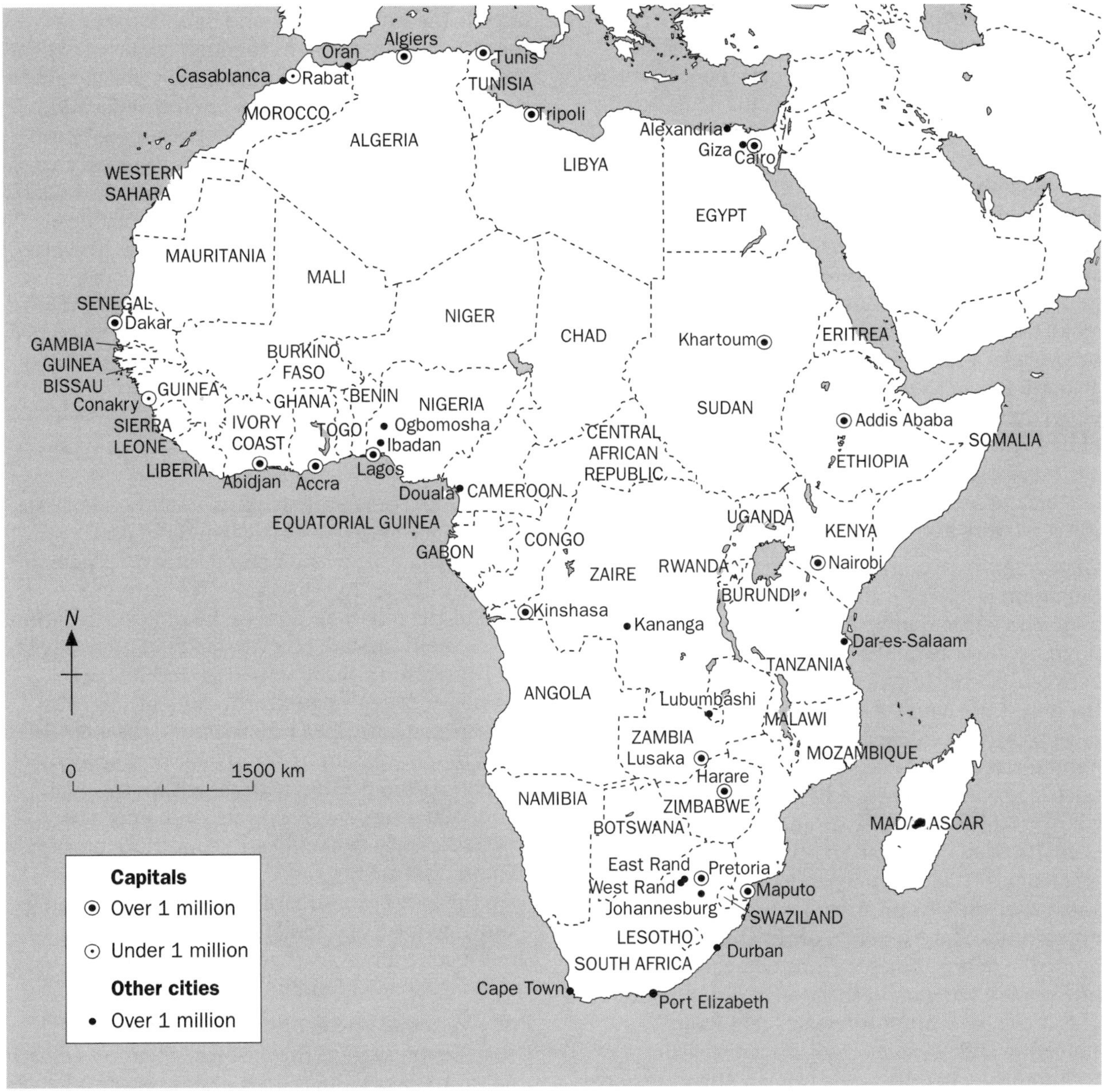

Figure 5.15 *Main urban centres in Africa*

In addition to better economic prospects, cities also offer better facilities than rural areas, including better health care, education and training prospects. Prospects of better education prospects for their children is becoming an increasingly important influence on African parents who see this as the main key to future success. The better the education, however, the less likely young adults are to look to the countryside as a place to live. For those in the rural areas who gain some educational qualifications, 'going to town' becomes the norm, and it is assumed by their family and friends that this is what they will do.

Studies have shown that the support of relatives and friends is a potent force in contributing to the decision to migrate and also in helping towards its success by giving further support when migrants reach the city. Relatives and friends look for job opportunities and provide accommodation. Gugler, from studies of migrants coming to Enugu in Nigeria, concluded that *'the relative success of most migration is due in a large part to the fact that it is embedded in social relations'*. The extended family act as an agent of migration. Information from previous migrants who have kept in touch with their home area or who periodically return there, is also important.

Direction of migration

Most movements are to the large cities or mining areas with their urban centres, but it is not always a straightforward movement (Case study 5.3). In the case of migrants just generally looking for work, Udo has shown that many move to the nearest sizeable city and if unable to find a job, may return home for a few months before trying again at a much larger city over a greater distance. Others may move straight on to the capital city without returning home. In the case of labour migrations to mining areas, this is usually an established line of movement and successive migrants from the same local area will follow the same route as their predecessors, either on short-term contracts or over longer periods of two years or more. This may even be across national boundaries as in the case of migrating labour from neighbouring countries into South Africa to work in the mines.

Character of migration

Migration is selective on the basis of age, sex and socio-economic standing. The largest number of migrants come from the young adult age range between 16 and 35 years of age. This age range has the fewest ties with the local area and the greatest incentive to move, except when civil war or some natural catastrophe occurs. People of all ages then flock to urban areas which they deem safer than the countryside and where assistance might be found.

In Africa, male migration is still dominant as women have had less independence to move, particularly in Muslim areas. There are also fewer job opportunities for women in urban areas. Most are limited to doing domestic work, or are pressurised into petty trading or prostitution in order to survive. This is changing as more females get a basic education and play a more prominent role in communities. Besides single women, there are now an increasing number who are divorced or separated from their husbands. In Latin America and parts of south-east Asia where women have greater social standing and there has been an expansion of job opportunities for women in service industries, the number of women migrating to urban areas now matches the number of men. Until industrialisation increases in African countries, however, men are likely to continue to outnumber women in movements to the city. The most prominent movement of women in Africa is that of married women moving with their children to join their husbands who have secured a more permanent job and somewhere for the family to live.

Generally, the more educated and skilled a person is, the more likely that person is to migrate. With education, people are better informed of areas outside their own locality and have both the incentive and aspirations to move. Moreover, their chances of obtaining employment in the city are much higher than are those with little education and training. An unfortunate consequence of this selective aspect of migration is that the local area loses the people most likely to bring the beneficial changes in rural areas needed to stem the tide of movement to the cities. These people are likely to maintain contact with their home area, but are unlikely to resettle there until they retire. By then, the status they have gained through career advancement in the city will also ensure respect and social standing in their local rural community.

Consequences of urbanisation

Demographic

Unlike some urban areas in Latin America and Asia, such as Sáo Paulo and Rio de Janerio in Brazil and Bombay in India, where natural increase is now the dominant factor in urban growth, migration remains the essential cause of the urban population explosion in Africa. The natural rate of increase of the population already settled in the city is a secondary, though significant, influence. Fertility rates are generally lower than in rural areas but are offset to some extent by the greater proportion of the population in cities who are within the reproductive age group. It is also influenced by lower mortality rates as health conditions are better than in rural areas.

In the long term, urbanisation is likely to lead to a slowing down of population growth in Africa, since it contributes to social changes which encourage smaller families.

Positive social and economic effects

Urbanisation hastens the modernisation process for the country as a whole and it brings people into contact with more jobs as well as better health, education and welfare facilities (Section 3.2).

Urbanisation is not as much a disruptive influences on family life as it appears to be in some literature. While important changes do occur, the transition is gradual. Links with relatives and the local rural community continue. Even after migrants have been permanently settled in the city, they still regard the original rural locality as their real home.

Once in the city, studies show, the migrant does adapt to conditions, frequently settling close to kin or friends from the same home locality. They share information and give support to one another in coping with problems. At work, links may also be developed with colleagues. For example, in the towns of the Zambian Copperbelt and in West Africa there may even be corporate kinship and other organisations where people meet regularly to exchange news about the home rural area and conditions at work. Few suffer the sense of isolation which is suggested by some writers, or disillusionment with the reality of city life compared to their expectations of it. Surveys of migrants in Ghana indicate that for two thirds, conditions in the city were as they expected them to be. With better communications and more contact with urban areas, prospective migrants have a much more realistic view of urban conditions than in the earlier phases of urbanisation.

Employment

Today it is recognised that there are two sectors of employment. ***One is the formal sector of labour working in established factories, businesses and government employment under some form of contract and protected by employment legislation which helps to control wage levels and conditions of working.*** Major parts of this sector are the large factories owned by multi-national companies which involve considerable outside capital investment, technology and expertise, combined with plentiful labour in the large cities of the developing countries (Sections 17.3 and 20.6). Without some level of training and education, entry to this formal sector of the labour market is very difficult.

However, in many cities the labour engaged in the formal sector is outnumbered by those in the ***informal sector which Castelles and Portes define as any activity in which labour is 'unprotected'.*** It covers a vast range of activities, including small family firms which use their own labour in such diverse activities as the making of clothing and leather goods, to supplying parts on subcontract for big multinational companies (Section 20.7). At the other end of the scale are the vast number of petty street traders, individuals engaged in illegal taxi services, people doing menial chores such as cleaning shoes and others scavenging on the garbage heaps to recycle waste. It is estimated that as many as two-fifths to two-thirds of employment in the large cities is in this informal sector. In Ghana, for example, the figure is 65%.

In the Mathare Valley, an informal settlement of 200 000 people (the largest in Nairobi). About 80% of informal employment is in trading and half is by women. One quarter of activities are in the open air and most others are in sheds. Little infrastructure is available and only 10% of informal enterprises have electricity. It is hard for informal entrepreneurs to get credit and less than one quarter have security of tenure. Earnings are on average four times above the minimum wage in Nairobi and more may be brought in from part-time employment in the formal sector.

In the face of rising unemployment, international agencies and governments such as Kenya's are advocating active promotion of the informal sector as a way of reducing the undoubted poverty which does exist in developing world cities. Since many migrants also send money back to dependents in the rural areas, expansion of employment in the informal sector would indirectly help to relieve poverty in the rural areas. Conditions in this sector are unregulated, however, and wages are significantly below the minimum level in the formal sector.

Detrimental effects of urbanisation

Insufficient employment opportunities

Job opportunities cannot be expanded fast enough. Although housing and other service facilities are increasing, especially in Latin America, they are not sufficient. The actual planning and administrative frameworks within which authorities are trying to deal with the problems of rapid urbanisation are quite unsuitable in relation to the size and complexity of it.

There is growing unemployment as well as pollution and health hazards, some of which are directly attributable to informal efforts to set up small businesses and other activities to maintain a living. The waste from these activities is either tipped into cesspits or runs down the alleyways in the poorer inner quarters or spontaneous settlements on the periphery.

Shortage of housing

In Addis Ababba, 85% of the population live in what the United Nations defines as 'informal settlements', that is, shelters built illegally by migrants and lacking basic facilities. In Luande, the figure is 70% and for Dar es Salaam, 60%. Erastus Mutheira, the Kenyan Cooperative Bank manager, has estimated that Kenya's major urban centres need 260 000 housing units to meet basic housing needs. To date, public agencies have built only 10 000, and private companies are building few units that the lower income bracket can afford (Section 14.5).

Infrastructure problems

The sheer growth of large urban centres has created severe infrastructure problems (Section 15.7). As the city grows, the journey to work for many poorly paid workers who live in spontaneous settlements at a distance from industry and employment in the central area, takes increasingly more time. Bus services are infrequent, unreliable and comparatively expensive. Highways become clogged with traffic, increasing economic and social costs to workers and businesses. Many people spend four to five hours a day travelling to and from work. This situation is seen in large cities such as Lagos, Nairobi and, outside of Africa, in Mexico City and São Paulo.

Effect on rural areas

Over-urbanisation also has detrimental effects on rural areas in such things as the loss to the cities of the youngest, most able-bodied and educated people. Urban migrants have less money to remit back to family and other relatives in the countryside because of unemployment and rising costs in the large cities .

Towards a solution

A recent World Bank Report examined the problems of tropical Africa and suggested the following points as part of an urban strategy which would help to bring problems under control.

An overhaul of administrative and planning structures

Many planning structures are legacies from an earlier colonial period and cover an inadequate administrative area because urbanisation has spread beyond the old administrative boundaries. Different departments of central government compete with each other or are unaware of what is being done by other departments, making comprehensive and coordinated planning difficult. There is also a need to reform rating and taxation laws to bring in more income to fund urban improvements. In particular, the richest minority need to be targeted to provide a greater contribution to city budgets.

Realistic servicing

Many migrants to the city are highly motivated and have higher expectations of what the city should provide for them, compared to what it is realistically feasible. On the other hand, many authorities have in the past concentrated on the wrong type of housing and servicing. Construction has been of a higher standard and price than the vast majority can afford. Until recently, the government's response to spontaneous housing development on land illegally occupied, has been to bulldoze them down as, for example, in Zimbabwe. This was usually followed by comprehensive redevelopment of the site with housing which the poor could not afford (Figure 14.23).

More recently, a more realistic and service approach has been adopted whereby the local authority or government supply the site foundations and services but the occupiers do the building on a self-help basis. In this way costs are kept down, and construction is more rapid and of a kind suitable to people's needs. People are more directly involved and are more motivated to continue improving the settlement as well as acquiring a greater sense of collective identity. Areas can later be upgraded to receive other services such as schools, shopping centres and clinics.

Two obstacles have to be overcome if this is to be successful. Firstly, for many developing world countries and cities, provision of services is regarded as a function of political patronage so that particular spontaneous settlements are singled out for upgrading because the people there either do or will support the party in power with their vote. Such discrimination is likely to foster inequalities and resentment. Provision of site and services should be on the basis of need and not political patronage. Secondly, there is the need to ensure that people have secure tenure of the land on which their houses are built, else they will not have the incentive to improve them.

Employment

While efforts continue to be made to expand the formal sector of city economies, employment in and expansion of the informal sector should be encouraged, since activities in this sector are labour-intensive, the cost of job creation is low, and local materials rather than imported ones are often used. Encouragement of small businesses also affects local initiatives in a positive knock-on effect. Regulations need to be relaxed and low cost credit provided to stimulate such expansion (Section 20.7).

Slowing down the rate of rural to urban migration

This will help to keep existing urban problems at a more manageable level. National and regional planning policies need to give more attention and finance to improving conditions and opportunities in the countryside, to persuade more people to stay in rural areas. Some governments are developing a more balanced strategy in their planning, with more capital being invested in agricultural improvement schemes and in local market towns to encourage small-scale industry and commerce. This is evident, for example, in Zimbabwe (Case Study 7.3). The main obstacle to more rural development is that effective power still rests with a small powerful elite who live mainly in the large urban centres. This powerful elite is motivated by self-interest, by the effective lobbying of big business, and by other powerful lobby groups with vested interests in the city but not in the rural areas.

The huge burden of foreign debt carried by most developing world governments and the structural realignment strategies imposed by international agencies, such as the International Monetary Fund, have drastically curtailed the aid and finance needed for effective development of rural areas (Chapter 33).

5.6 Migration and counterurbanisation in developed countries

The role of counterurbanisation is particularly important in developed countries. This is a central theme in Chapter 12 and the succeeding chapter. Case study 5.1 is also relevant.

Concluding comment

Large-scale overseas migration has ended. However, in Africa, civil wars and natural disasters continue to cause mass forced migration across national borders, bringing with them, problems which require international assistance if they are to be solved.

As regards internal migrations, while urbanisation intensifies in developing countries, counterurbanisation is characteristic of advanced countries. These contrasting movements reflect the different staged each has reached in the modernisation process.

case study

5.1 The USA: migration

White migration

- 1800 – 1910 (40 million from Europe) to 1890 mainly from west Europe – some forced by disasters (Irish potato famine in 1840) and wars. Most seeking new opportunities.
- Settled initially in 'North East Sea Board' to work in industry and on the land. As the West was opened up and population increased by births and immigration, movement was westward to Mid-West and onward to California, aided by railways at close of nineteenth century
- Later immigration from Europe more selective, some refugees but flow restricted by quota and slowing down of population growth in Europe. After 1945, 9 million came.
- Recent internal migration to 'Sunbelt' of west and south – for retirement and to new industrial growth and out of a desire to move out of large cities.

Consequences

- Brought capital, expertise and labour to open up the continent
- Money resources and products shifted back to Europe helped further growth of the country
- Rich cultural and political mix
- Rising living standards except for poor whites in rural backwaters of South Appalachia and inner cities.

Black migration

- 1750 – 1850, 15 million slaves from West Africa mainly to the South plantations.
- After the Civil War (1860) and abolition of slavery, many moved to industrial cities in the North - peak reached 1910 - settled in inner cities - black ghettos.
- Since 1945 move west to large metropolitan centres of California e.g. San Francisco.
- Recent counter-migration back to south attracted by oil and technology boom on the Gulf coast and psychological pull of the South.

Consequences

- 27 million (11% of total population) increasing as higher fertility rate than whites.
- Rich labour resource for the south and industrial cities.
- Rich contribution to United States culture.
- Offset by racial tension, discrimination, plight of black inner city ghettos.

White migration

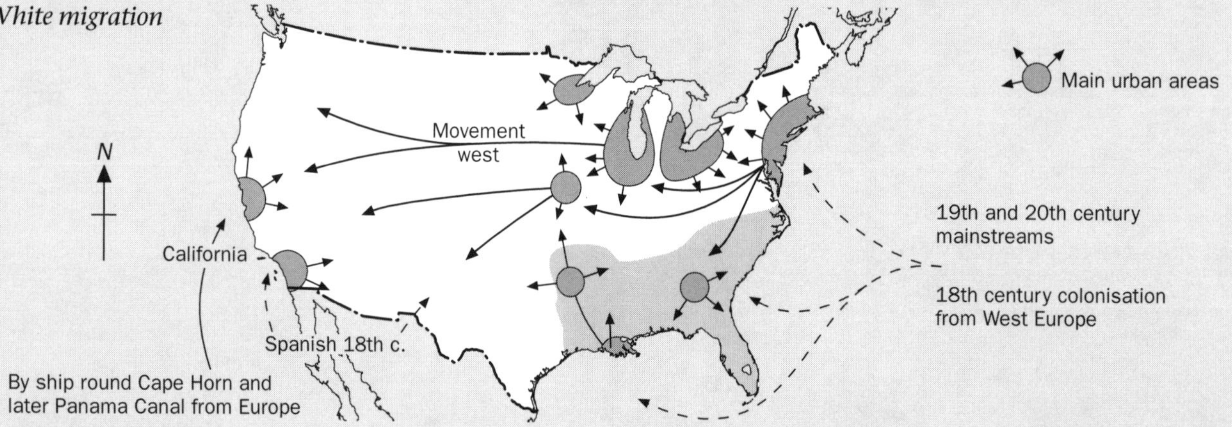

Black migration

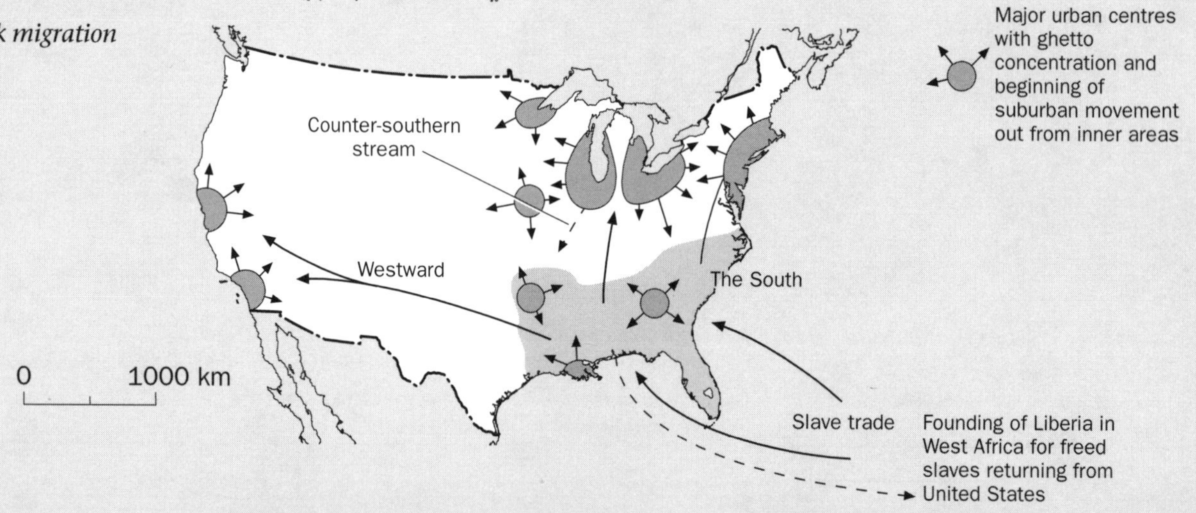

Recent migration trends

- West to California and south to the Gulf States, partly a flow of retired people to warmer areas but much is due to more job opportunities.
- Decentralisation from the large cities to the outer fringes and beyond but the 1992 census shows a slowing down of decentralisation trends over the last decade

	Metropolitan	Non-metropolitan
North-east	3.1	5.6
Mid-west	2.7	-1.8
South	17.4	4.6
West	23.9	14.2
Total USA	11.6	3.9

Population change for metropolitan and non-metropolitan areas by region and percentage 1980 - 1990

- Recent immigration amounting to 8 million mainly from Mexico and Puerto Rico to the South and West to work in agriculture but with also many moving to the cities. There were lesser flows from Europe, North Africa and Asia.

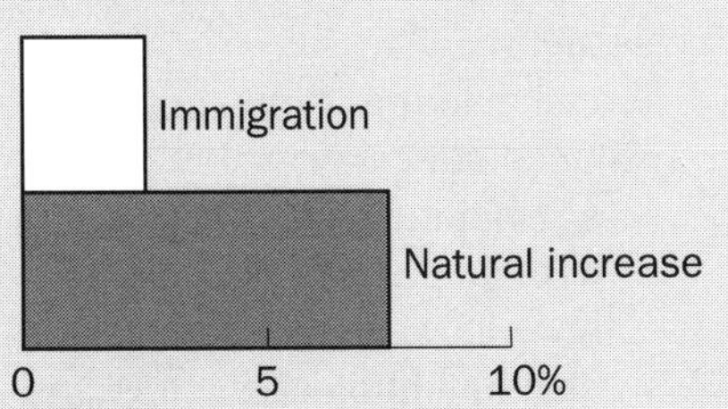

Relative contribution of natural increase and immigration to population increase in the USA, 1980 – 1990

Recent migration trends

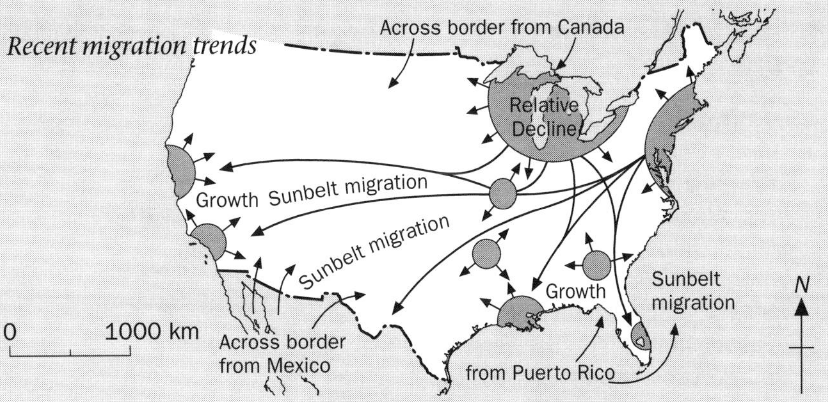

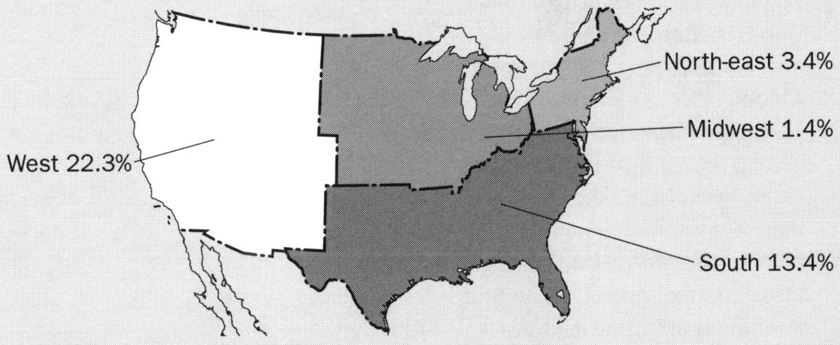

The shift in population from the north-east and mid-west to the south and west by regional population percentage change 1980 – 1990

North-east		**South**	
New York	+ 3.5	**Jacksonville**	+ 17.9
Philadelpia	+ 6.1	**Houston**	+ 2.2
Baltimore	– 6.4	**Dallas**	+ 11.3
Boston	+ 2.0	**Memphis**	– 5.5
Washington	– 4.9	**San Antonio**	+ 19.1
		Phoenix	+ 24.5
		Columbus	+ 12.0
Average change	– 2.4	**Average change**	+ 11.6
Midwest		**West**	
Chicago	– 7.4	**Los Angeles**	+ 17.4
Detroit	– 14.6	**San Diego**	+ 26.8
Milwaukee	1.3	**San Francisco**	+ 6.6
Indianapolis	+ 4.3	**San Jose**	+ 24.3
Average change	– 4.7	**Average change**	+ 19.2

Relative population change for the twenty largest cities taken by region, 1980 – 1990

case study

5.2 Africa: Migration and mobility trends

Migration from and to overseas

Slave trade

- Great effect on population change and pattern especially in West Africa. 20 million Blacks transhipped to Americas and across Sahara by Arab slave raiders. Another 40 million died in associated inter-tribal warfare. Result: 1850 population back to 1650 proportions of 100 million. Depopulation left sparsely settled belts, e.g. middle West Africa
- Disrupted development in Africa. In sixteenth century, Africa had as progressive an economy and culture as rich as that in Europe and the Mediterranean. Slave trade caused loss of labour and abandonment of agricultural land. Barter trade by Liverpool ships, etc. engaged in trade brought in cheap goods which adversely affected home craft industries e.g. textile and metal working

Asians arrived in the late nineteenth century as traders and businessmen to East Africa but Indians also came to South Africa to work on sugar plantations adding to the ethnic mix and also bringing economic benefits.

With the independence of east African states many whites left e.g. Uganda and Zimbabwe because of an uncertain future, leaving more land for Africans but depriving the new states of much needed skills and businesses. The expulsion of Asians from Uganda in the early 1970s was also a similar loss.

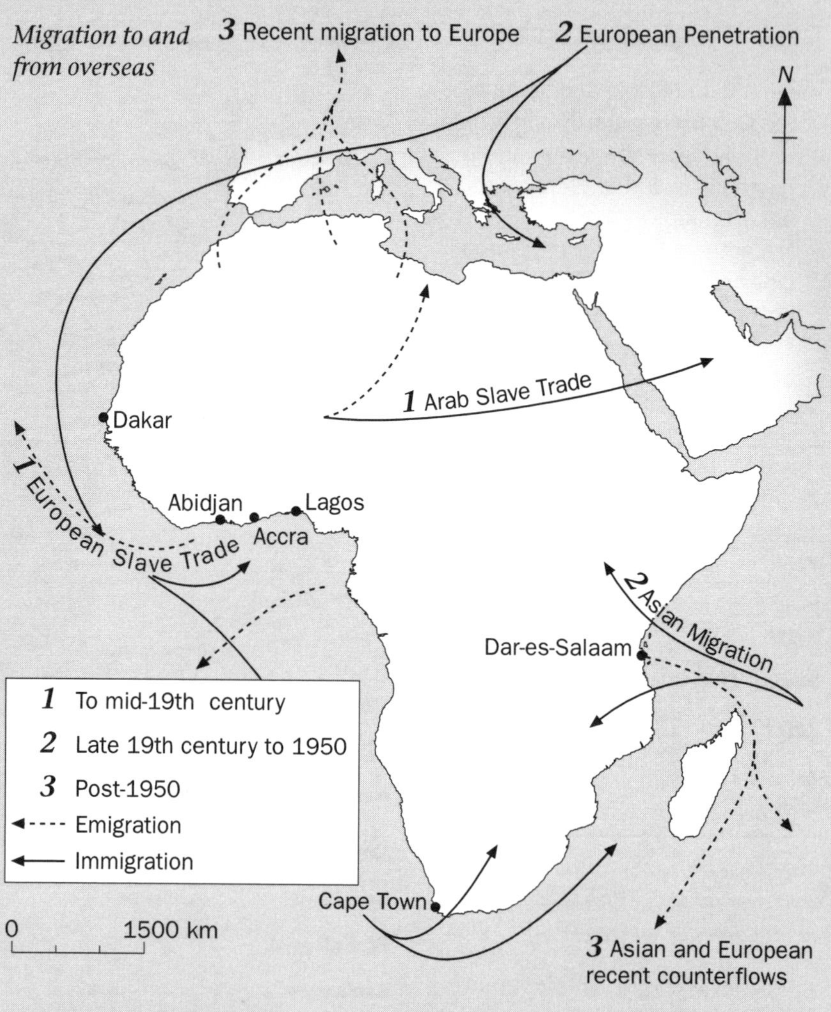

European penetration

- Settlement only in climatically favourable highlands of east Africa and South Africa.
- Brought some benefits opening up areas – some education and health measures but on balance African geographers Udo and Mabogunge claimed it was detrimental, disrupting economic and social development and making Africa subservient to European modernisation to provide minerals and agricultural products in exchange for industries which undermined Africa's traditional home industries.
- Communication network developed not to serve Africa but European needs – geared to coastal outlets.
- Some of the best land taken over for plantations and in East and South Africa by White settlers.
- Racial discrimination under colonialism
  - Against indigenous black population
  - After independence reverse discrimination against Asians and whites leading to counter-migration flow 1960s onwards from east Africa

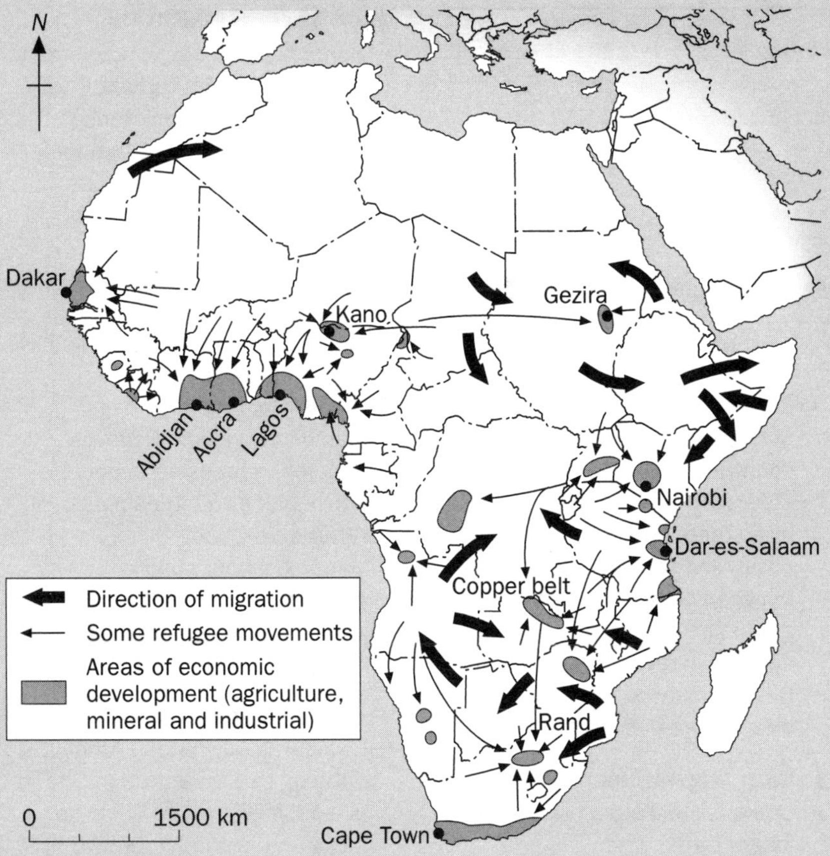

National and frontier migration

- Apartheid in white dominated South Africa – greatest economic progress occurred here using mineral and other resources to build up a modern economy which the black population is only just beginning to share.
  Recent abolition of Apartheid laws and moves to political independence will give the black, coloured and Asian populations more freedom. Mass of black population still likely to suffer economic discrimination and poverty.

Recent black outmigration

- Most has been from former colonies in North Africa (mainly Tunisia, Morocco and Algeria) to Western Europe in response to work opportunities there. In 1990 there were 2.1 million including dependents mainly in France, Italy and Germany. It has relieved population pressures and there is some economic benefit to north African countries in the return of remittances to relatives.
- Migration of young educated people to train overseas has a mixed effect some return with their skills but some are lost to other countries.
- Africa has lost an estimated one third of highly educated labour in recent decades 'causing development bottlenecks'.

Regional migration and urbanisation

Rural to urban migration

- Not as urbanised as other con-tinents but the pace is quickening mainly due to pressure of population on rural areas with insufficient land to go round and hopes of employment and further advancement in towns (Case study 5.3).
- Inequalities between urban and rural areas since colonial times increasing wealth centred on the cities – after independence government policies favoured urban-based activities and rural areas neglected.
- Pressures occur on good subsistence farmland e.g. Kikuyu areas in Kenya highlands (density 300 per sq km) – fragmentation of holdings, soil impoverishment, declining crop yields fuelled by high birth rates in rural areas and backward farming methods.
- Pressures in marginal areas heightened by harsh environmental conditions including periodic drought e.g. Okore highlands Uganda, Mali in west Africa, Communal Lands in Zimbabwe.
- Some of the best land is under commercial farming increasing land shortages among peasants.
- As education spreads among young Africans they turn away from rural life towards perceived opportunities in the cities. Relieves pressure on rural areas and some cash sent home to pay taxes, for education, etc. but may create problems in towns e.g. Lagos due to insufficient jobs, housing and services for numbers coming. Since most migrants are in the younger reproductive age, population growth increases in urban areas.

	Population (million)	% Urban	% Urban growth (1990-95)
East Africa	207	20	5.8
Cent. Africa	75	33	4.7
North Africa	147	45	3.5
South Africa	45	47	3.3
West Africa	206	35	5.4

Urbanisation indicators – 1992

Refugee movements

Causes

- It is difficult to distinguish economic and political causes. Economic disparities typically exist alongside political apprehension and violence.
- Africa had 5.2 million refugees outside their own countries; 1 million from Mozambique were in Malawi, 500 000 from Liberia in Guinea, 500 000 from Angola in Zaire and 2 million from Sudan, Ethiopia and Somalia in each other's countries. As many again were refugees in their own countries. Two thirds are women and children.

Consequences

- Though regarded as temporary residents many have been in refugee camps for over a year and some will never go back.
- Such large-scale displacement puts great strain on receiving countries which already have severe economic problems. It may create political instability, social and ethnic conflict between indigenous and refugee groups and severe environmental damage in receiving areas. Development is hindered and inequalities intensified.

Labour migrations

- Some is circulatory but others longer term.
- Search for employment and cash wage are main reasons.
- Biggest is from neighbouring countries to South Africa mining areas – male dominated. Valuable source of labour but disrupts family life and farming back home-compensated to some extent by cash remittances.

Rural to rural migration

- Nomadic circulatory movements are declining. Movement from overpopulated subsistence farming to plantation, timber and road construction sites remains strong – some long term, some seasonal.
- Cote d'Ivoire has 30% migrant population from neighbouring countries working on largely foreign-owned coffee, cocoa, rubber plantations and on diamond workings. Relieves population pressure in poorer surrounding countries plus cash returns.
- Valuable labour supply in receiving areas but there can be ethnic clashes especially in times of recession.

'Frontier' migration

- Comparatively little in Africa but opening of Gezira area in Sudan is a case of new growth area migration and in Zimbabwe in the south-east there have recently been new irrigation area settlements.
- In Sub-Sahara Africa, in one third of countries women make up half migrants – mainly but not exclusively younger people – age is no barrier in refugee movements

case study

5.3 **Harare: rural – urban migration**

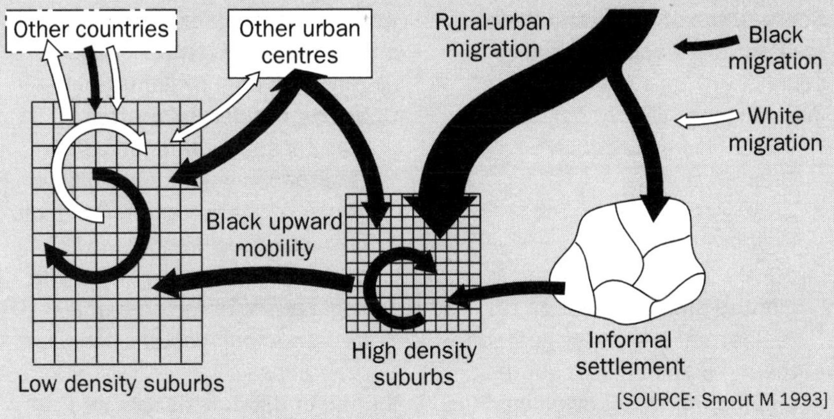

Generalised migration flows in relation to a post-colonial city including intra (within) urban movements.

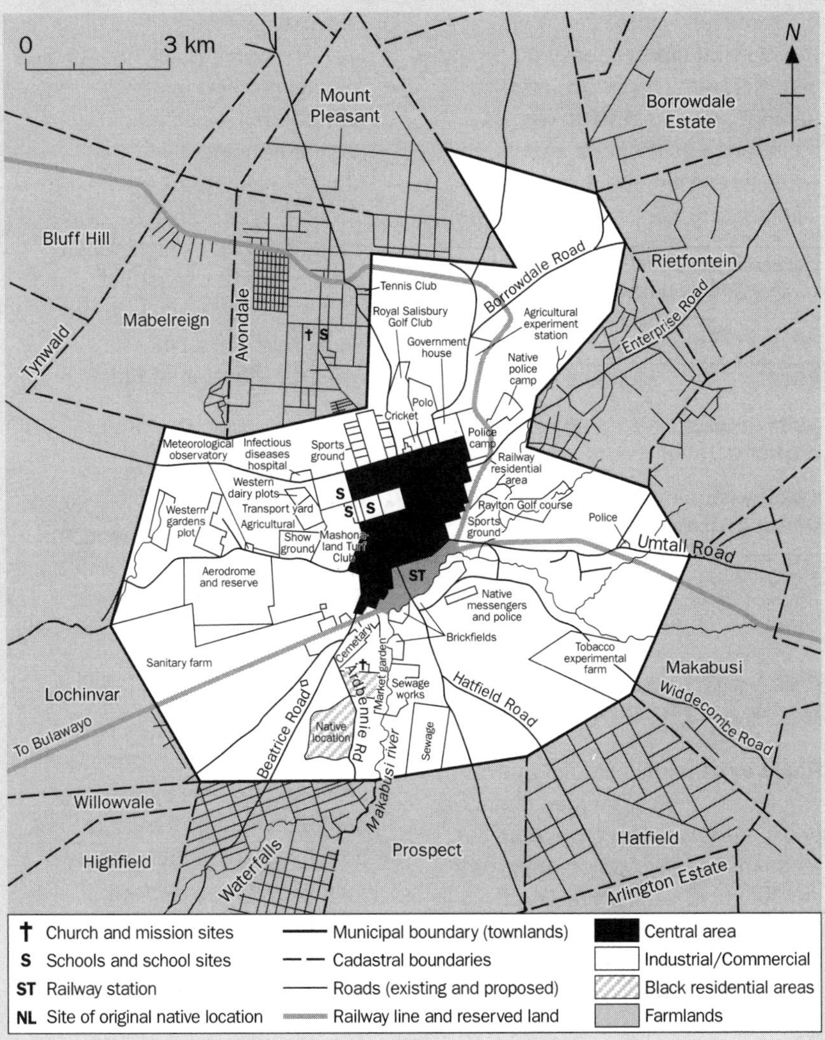

The colonial city – Harare 1930

Stages in Urban migration

- **Colonial times** – migration influenced by the need for black labour in town and controlled by legislation. Need to pay hut and other taxes 'forced' migration of black labour to towns to work as domestic servants and labourers but controlled influx by legislation
- **War of Liberation late 1970s** – political instability in rural areas led to influx into towns which offered security
- **Post-independence** – migration free of legislation controls and thus determined largely by market forces and population pressure in rural areas. Expansion and hope of jobs in town 'pulled' in migrants and harsh rural conditions pushed them.

Factors influencing the founding and growth pattern of Harare

Founded in 1890 by pioneer column of white settlers moving north under Rhodes from South Africa. Originally named Fort Salisbury

Sited here because of:

- Ample water from Mukuvisi River
- Close to hill (kopje) a defensive site
- Reliable rainfall plus 1 500 metres,height made climate cooler and free from malaria
- Highveld fertile area around
- Close to gold deposits in Mazowe 30 km north
- By 1899 linked by telegraph and rail to Beira port (Mozambique) and Cape Town (South Africa)

Present land-use pattern strongly influenced by early decisions.

- Present CBD based on administrative and commercial centre of 1890 settlers
- Layout of main part of town (market by 1930 municipal boundary) planned 1894 large plots and wide streets. Immediate area to north of centre laid out as large residential plot for officials and well to-do residents – now known as the Avenues.
- Edge of Avenue in arc to west, north, north-east became institutional lands – education, hospitals, agricultural research station and recreation area.
- Land to south of centre reserved for railways – attracted service industries, light manufacturing with more land available for later industries.
- Further south land reserved for black residential areas but later some of the land was developed as separate suburbs, for Asians (e.g. Belvedere), low income 'Whites' (e.g Waterfalls), white railway employees (Lochinvar). Decided therefore present high density suburbs and most African settlement would be to the south.
- Low density white settlement in north. Early days land outside municipal boundary – privately owned farms bought up by land speculators – land sold to white settlers in large plots as land plentiful and cheap plus local authorities decreed minimal one acre size plots – bungalow built on spacious plots (stands) – north limited to white settlement.

  Thus the structure of Harare to 1980 was largely determined by early colonial administrators.

Segregation of Black and White residential areas reinforced by subsequent legislation to time of independence 1979.

1908 – Urban Location Ordinance

1930 – Native Accommodation Registration Act

1969 – Land Tenure Act

Limited black population to residential areas designated for them – high density suburbs of small uniform hut dwelling units and close to town men's hostels. (Black domestic workers could live on white employers plots)

Residential land allocation insufficient – African squatter settlement grew up outside town boundary – as the town expanded some bulldozed and replaced by high density black residential areas.

Harare from 1890 – Steady increase to 310 360 population by 1960

Basic data:	
1969	386 400 population
1982 (annual growth 8%)	658 400 population
1989 (with Chitungwiza)	1.5 million population

Attractions as capital of Zimbabwe, main service and industrial centre (48% of all manufacturing), educational and recreational centre.

Post-colonial city of Harare – 1980 onwards

Rapid expansion included rise in employment opportunities mainly in public services and commerce but some in industry but job opportunities have not kept pace with rapid influx and rise in population – Harare has a serious unemployment problem, desperate shortage of affordable housing, insufficient welfare provision and serious transport difficulties especially as many African residential areas are distant from employment centres.

Changing residential pattern

'Typical segregated residential landscapes of a colonial city no longer exists in Harare. While the physical structure and location of residential areas reflects the segregation of the past, the racial composition has changed dramatically.'

Spread of Black residents into formerly White reserved areas began even during liberation wars as Whites left out of fear and uncertainty.

- Higher income Black households moved into low density northern suburbs but number limited by cost of housing
- Most movement has been into cheaper areas close to former designated black high density housing and close industry and work e.g. Waterfalls in south and Mabelreign in north.

Current distribution of Black households

- Formerly designated high density Black areas in city
- Filtration into areas formerly reserved for White households – filtration slowed because of rising prices of houses.
- Dormitory areas outside the town especially Chitungwiza

  The policy of the post-independence government has been to bulldoze all illegal informal settlement and replace by purpose-built high density serviced housing. Largest outside town boundary is Chitungwiza l(approximately 250 000). It is on the site of a former township and former illegal squatter areas and is a result of decision in 1970 not to build houses for blacks in

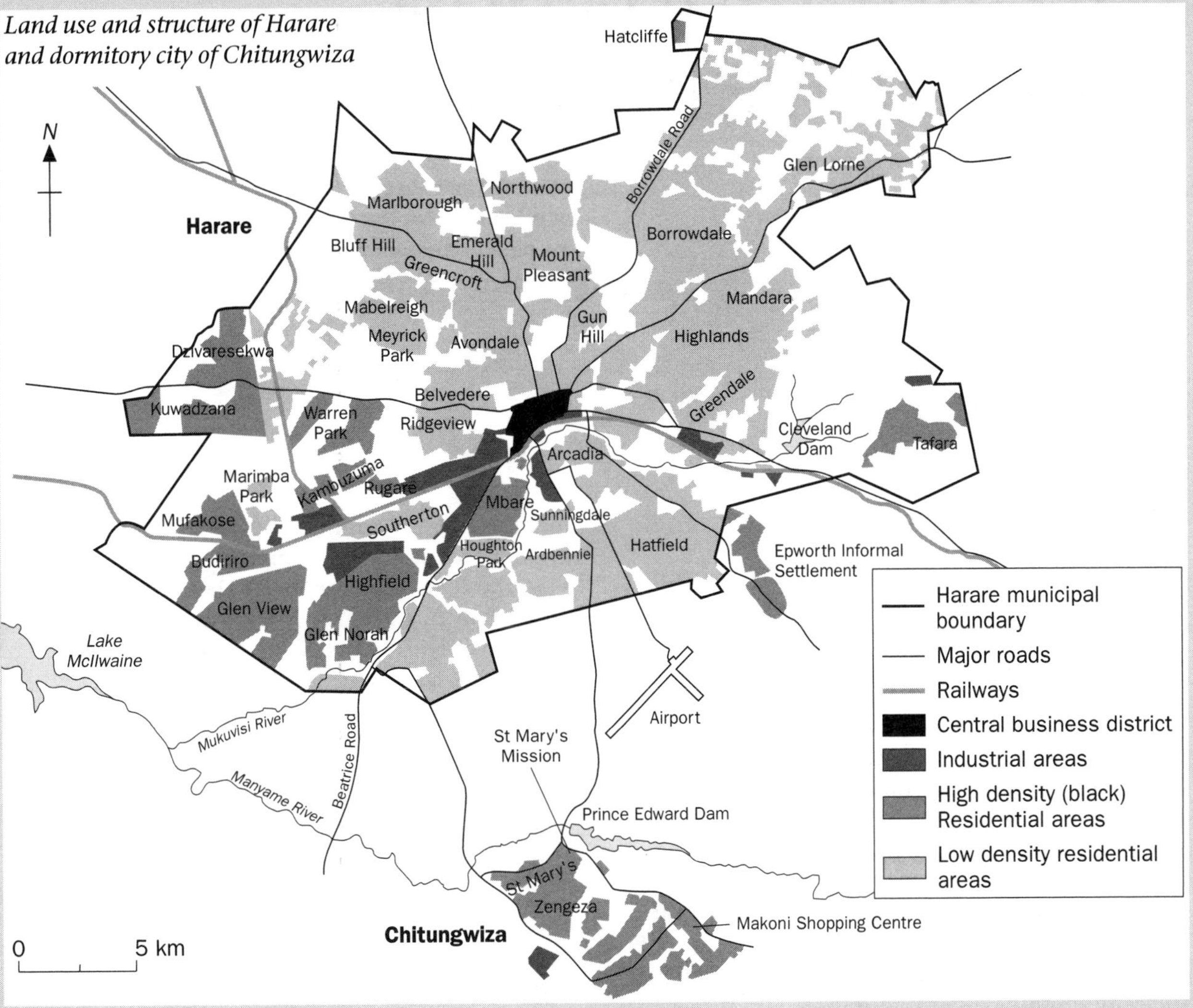

Harare but new towns on communal land areas away from white residential areas. In 1970 Chitungwiza had 15 000 population but by 1982 this had risen to 172 000. It has high density housing with service provision but despite financial incentives and 'growth centre' status, it is too far from Harare to attract enough industry and services. Most workers have to travel 25 km to Harare for work and transport inadequate.

- Illegal residence – drastic shortage of affordable housing (60% of black workers earn too little to afford rent) – many lodge in high density housing areas – on many plots illegal dwellings have been added – 40% of African workforce in city are in such 'lodgings' Outside of boundary most illegal settlement has been bulldozed but Epworth in the south-east left as been there long time, decided by government to upgrade it and provide basic services. Some absentee landlords have divided plots into single room dwellings – people themselves built schools and clinic.

(S Cummings p. 172 *Harare*)
[Based on extracts from L Zinyama, D Tevera and S Cummings (ed), *Harare – The Growth and Problems of the City*, University of Zimbabwe 1993]

6

CHAPTER 6

Development and underdevelopment

The relationship between population and development is one of the central themes in human geography, but its meaning has changed over the last four decades.

6.1 **Economic development**

Up to the 1970s 'development' was taken to mean 'economic development'. A country needed to be developed in order to support its population at a progressively better standard of living as measured in material terms. Unfortunately, the focus of economic development was not centred on the individual needs of people but on production and economic advancement through industrialisation, along broadly the same lines as those followed by the advanced industrial countries of the west. In particular, the newly independent countries of the developing world, encouraged by western technical assistance, saw industrialisation as the key, not only to economic advancement but also to increasing their international political prestige.

One of the most influential models for economic development was that propounded by the economic historian W.W. Rostow during the 1950s and published in 1960 as *The Stages of Economic Growth: a non-communist manifesto*. It was based on historical data which covered economic change in 15 countries, mainly in Western Europe but also including the USA, which Rostow considered to be at the most advanced stage of development (Figure 3.4).

Based on his findings, Rostow maintained that all societies or countries in the world could be located at some point along a progress, marked by five stages – from traditional society through to the stage of high mass consumption. The key stage happened over approximately two decades when a 'take-off' occurred in economic growth, propelling the country into more or less automatic growth. For 'take-off' to occur, he identified three important requirements:

- In the economy there had to be a rise in surplus funds available to invest in further economic growth. The rise needed to be in the order of from 5% to over 10% of national income.
- A substantial manufacturing sector needed to develop which would be the stimulus or 'engine' for further economic growth.
- There needed to be changes to the political and social structures of a country to fit in with and facilitate this economic growth.

Rostow's writings were very persuasive. For lesser developed countries his model of economic growth offered a clear path to progress, following the lead of Western countries which had already reached or approached the stage of mass consumption in which a high standard of living could be enjoyed. However, while the drive to achieve industrialisation and higher income has been relatively successful for some developing countries, notably newly industrialised countries in South-East Asia such as South Korea, Singapore and Malaysia, for others it has been less successful (Figure 6.1; Case studies 20.1 and 20.2). The disadvantages of copying the western pattern of economic progress as outlined by Rostow had become painfully obvious by the beginning of the early 1970s.

- The majority of the population remained impoverished (Figure 6.1). In many developing countries, especially in Africa and Latin America, the mass of the population have received relatively few benefits while an elite minority enjoyed the bulk of the country's new found wealth.

Country type	High income		Middle income		Low income	
Examples	**Netherlands**	**Japan**	**Saudi Arabia**	**Mexico**	**Bangladesh**	**Mozambique**
Indices						
GNP per capita ($) – (1991)	18 780	26 930	7820	3030	220	80
Growth in GNP (1981 – 91)	1.6	3.6	–3.4	–0.5	1.9	–1.1
Distribution of productions (1991)						
Agriculture	4	3	7	9	36	64
Indust.	32	42	52	30	26	16
(Manuf.)	(20)	(25)	(7)	(22)	(9)	–
Services	64	56	41	61	48	21
Energy consumption (kg of oil equiv) – 1991	5147	3552	4886	1383	57	59
Supporting measures						
Urbanisations (% of population) – 1991	89	77	78	73	17	28
Level of adult illiteracy (% of population) – 1991	Fraction	Fraction	38	13	65	67
Life expectancy (years) – 1991	77	79	69	70	51	47

[SOURCE: Extracts from World Development Report 1993]

- GNP = gross national product = approx. means a country's income including receipts from abroad
- Indust. covers mining, manufacturing, electricity, water and gas.
- Manuf. covers manufacturing only but it is a sub-group of indust.

Figure 6.1 Some basic indices of economic development

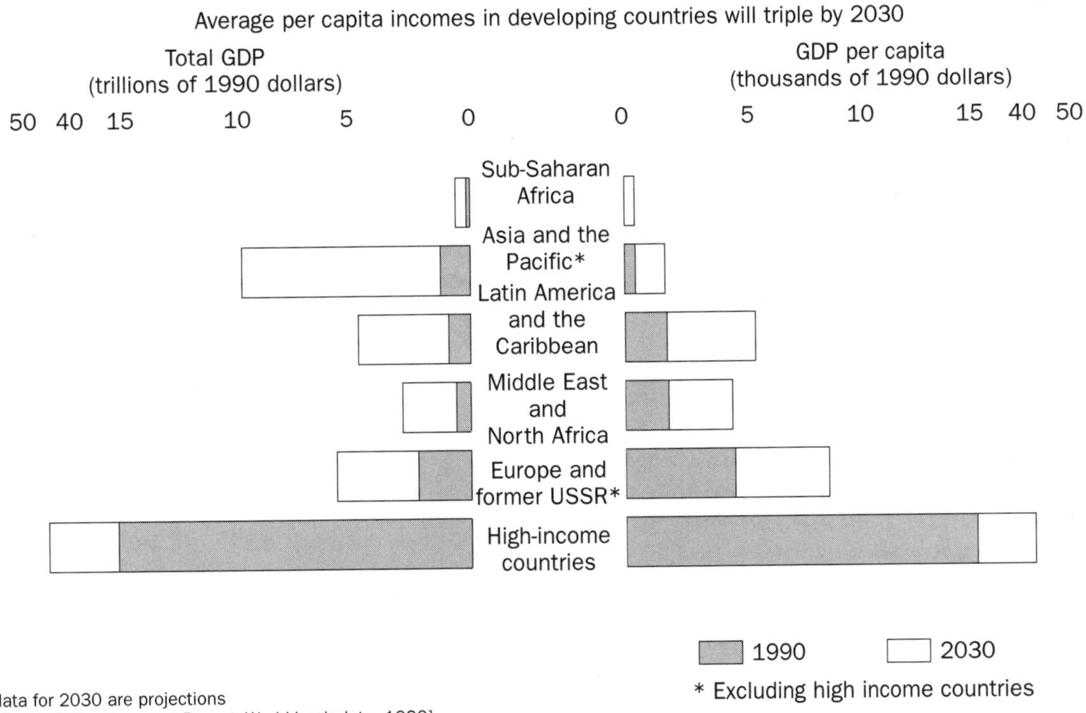

NOTE: data for 2030 are projections
[SOURCE: *World Development Report*, World bank data, 1992]

Figure 6.2 Total GDP and GDP per capita in developing regions and high-income countries, 1990 and projected 2030

- Development strategies based on the Rostow model have heightened regional inequalities in a country. They have produced or intensified a dual economic structure in which a prospering market-oriented and industrialised core contrasts sharply with lagging regions. This leaves a periphery which is still tied to a traditional economy, drained of resources and labour by the prospering core.
- The dependency under colonialism has been replaced by another kind of dependency upon the industrialised western countries, creating what has become known as neo-colonialism. Political independence has been gained but economic dependence still ties developing countries to the West.

Poverty, inequality and dependency despite economic development

For developing countries the way to achieve the surplus needed for take-off and industrialisation was to concentrate on the export production of either agricultural raw materials or minerals needed by the west and industrialising Japan. The profits could then be used to invest in the technology and expertise required to both industrialise and at the same time increase export production, to generate further money surpluses for economic growth. The result of this has been outlined by Mabogunge in his critical analysis of this kind of development process (Mabogunge A L *The Development Process – a spatial perspective,* 1980):

- Export growth and industrialisation became focused in certain favoured areas, usually around the major port or ports of export which received most of the investment and technology for development. These areas expanded industrially and commercially leading to rapid urbanisation and a flood of population from the countryside in search of low wage labour. The vast majority, including many unable to obtain work, have been forced to live in poor conditions, receiving few of the benefits of the growing prosperity of the core, while foreign investors and a small elite section of the population have gained an increasingly large share of the wealth generated.
- While the core has been swept towards a western style economy, much of the rest of the country has lagged behind. It remained, as it were, in the traditional society stage of Rostow's model, except that some if its land, resources and a significant part of its working population has been used to provide the raw materials and labour for the industrialising core. Consequently in these lagging and peripheral regions, less land is available for food production and less labour to work it. The rural population remains at a very low standard of living with poor access to basic health and other welfare care (Figure 3.4c).
- The dependency of these developing countries on the advanced countries of the west has continued as industrialisation has only been possible with foreign investment and technical help, and on the expectation that the west would continue to buy the exports of raw materials and minerals to provide the revenue needed by developing countries.

'By the end of the 1960s it became clear that development as economic development was not having the expected wide ranging effect on the standards and conditions of the majority of individuals in many Third World Countries. If anything, the relative position of the masses worsened vis a vis that of the elite. Widespread poverty and destitution became visible, tangible and compelling' (Mabogunge).

The concept of development had to change

'Development' could no longer be seen only in terms of raising the average per capita income of a country. There had to be a focus on the basic needs of people, especially on reducing the poverty level of the masses by ensuring that a bigger share of the country's income was invested in meeting their basic needs. There had to be an emphasis on what became known as 'distributive justice', ensuring amongst people a more equal access to the country's wealth, goods and services, including health, education and other welfare services (Figure 6.3).

As the inequalities in developing countries and the plight of the masses became increasingly evident at the beginning of the 1970s, it coincided with increasing anxieties in the advanced industrial countries about environmental pollution and the fear of global resources being rapidly depleted.

The linking of distributive justice within developing countries to the world north-south divide and the solving of world environmental problems

To an important extent, the United Nations Conference on the Human Environment in 1972 signalled a change in what was regarded as development. The increasing focus on equity and social justice in the distribution of a country's income and services amongst its people was highlighted, as was the issue of a more equal, international distribution of resources between the richer and poorer nations, between the North and the South.

Because the economies of the developing world grew under an economic process based on western economies and had become increasingly bound up with the world economic system, it was realised that there could not be any worthwhile redistribution of wealth within these countries without also these

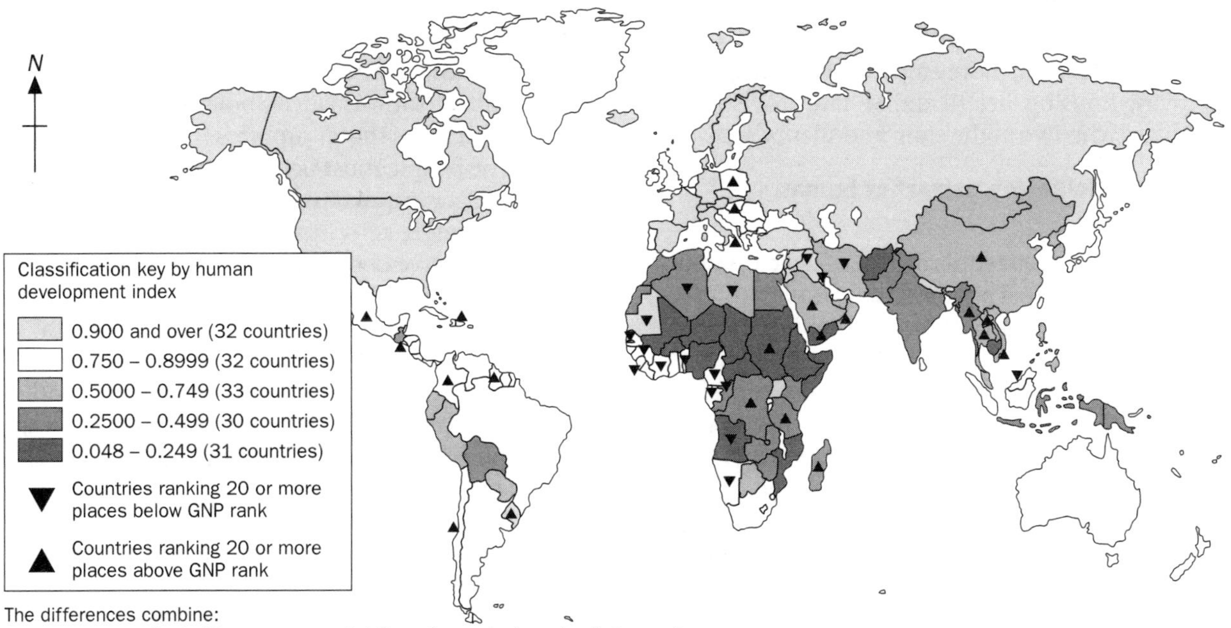

The differences combine:

- adjusted income per capital (based on actual purchasing power)
- educational attainment (Adnet literacy measure plus average years of schooling per capita)
- life expectancy

and is compared to classification based on economic development only (as measured by GNP)

[SOURCE: A Rogers *A new map of world development*, Geographical Review, 1992]

Figure 6.3 *Differences in development based on 'a human development' index*

same countries receiving a more equitable share of the world's wealth as a whole. For instance, disadvantageous trading patterns and the terms on which investment loans had been made to developing countries by western banks and other agencies to foster industrialisation, had contributed to the growing debt of these nations. Trying to repay the interest on these debts had increasingly deprived a number of developing countries of a large share of their national income which was desperately needed to meet the basic needs of the deprived masses and generate further development in which they could share (Chapters 32 and 33).

While advanced countries were significant contributors to serious environmental problems, such as air pollution and deforestation as a result of increasing consumption and inappropriate use of the world's resources, it was realised that the environmental problems in the developing countries were largely those resulting from poverty. The solution to these environmental problems was thus tied up with eradicating poverty. This could only be done if new strategies of development were adopted. Development now had taken on a much wider meaning and it had to be centred on the individual needs of people. Economic development was encapsulated into the wider spectrum of human development.

6.2 Human development

Meeting basic human needs and distributive justice

Human development has shifted the purpose of development to that of meeting human needs, and away from the old style economic development centred on the transformation of a country's economy. It emphasises human security, trying to ensure that an individual's basic needs, of which the most essential are food, water and housing, are met. It goes further to also include access to adequate health, education and other welfare services (Figure 6.4; Chapters 7 and 8).

International government and non-government agencies have encouraged the governments of developing world countries to increasingly direct their development policies towards achieving human development (Figure 6.4). While economic development remains a central part of new development strategies, since this raises the revenue and incomes to meet individual needs, the emphasis is on a more balanced development in which the needs of rural areas are given much more prominence. Whereas in the 1950s and 1960s the larger share of investment went to the prospering core, rural development programmes for peripheral areas are now generally receiving much more of the investment funding as, for example, in India's and Brazil's development programmes.

In the main cities, more emphasis is being given to improving housing, health and welfare provision for the masses who live in the slum and shanty sectors.

People participation as part of human development

Despite the declared reorientation of development strategies, the United Nations, in its *Human Development Report* of 1993, noted that progress towards alleviating poverty among the masses and removing inequalities in the developing world has been limited (Figures 6.4, 6.5 and 6.6). *'More than a billion of the world's people still languish in absolute poverty and the poorest fifth find that the richest fifth enjoy more than 150 times their income'*.

The reasons why further progress has not been made over the last two decades are numerous, but central to the failure has been a lack of sufficient will amongst governments. On the one hand, in most developing countries governments have not redirected enough funding to alleviate poverty in their countries. On the other hand, governments of the wealthier advanced countries in the more prosperous North have been unwilling to redistribute sufficient of their excessive share of the world's wealth to the poorer South (Section 33.3).

The United Nations Development Programme Agency concludes that if progress is to be made, the mass of the people must be given the right to have a say in the decision-making about the development process and more active participation in it. Without access to effective political power the masses will continue to languish in poverty.

People participation is thus becoming a central part of human development strategies. It coincides with a surge of democracy across former communist areas in Europe and within a number of developing world countries where authoritarian governments are being replaced by popularly elected leaders. There is a growing determination by people to participate at local and national level in the events and processes that shape their lives.

Human development in meeting basic needs must include the right to vote and participate. The masses themselves are in the best position to know what their needs are and have the experience to contribute towards the ways in which these can best be met.

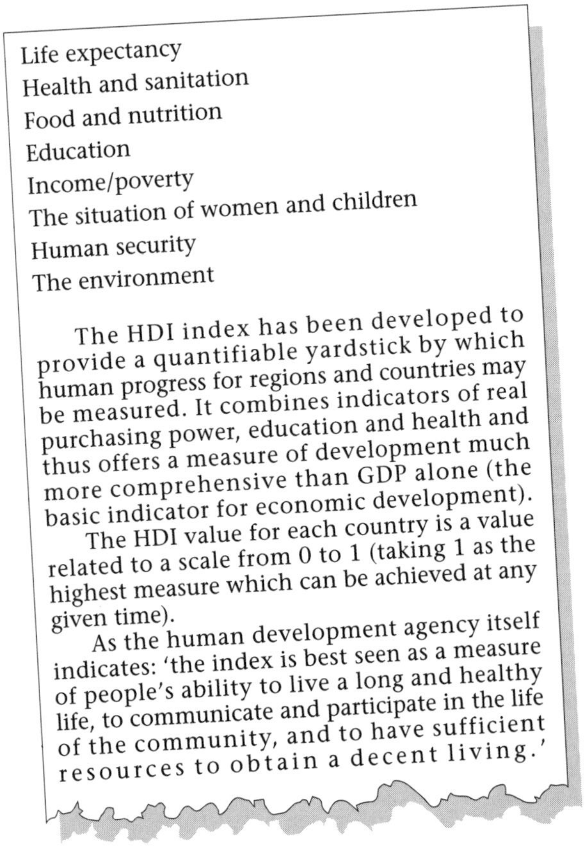

Life expectancy
Health and sanitation
Food and nutrition
Education
Income/poverty
The situation of women and children
Human security
The environment

The HDI index has been developed to provide a quantifiable yardstick by which human progress for regions and countries may be measured. It combines indicators of real purchasing power, education and health and thus offers a measure of development much more comprehensive than GDP alone (the basic indicator for economic development).

The HDI value for each country is a value related to a scale from 0 to 1 (taking 1 as the highest measure which can be achieved at any given time).

As the human development agency itself indicates: 'the index is best seen as a measure of people's ability to live a long and healthy life, to communicate and participate in the life of the community, and to have sufficient resources to obtain a decent living.'

Figure 6.4 *Human development indices making up the HDI, United Nations Development Programme Agency (human development report)*

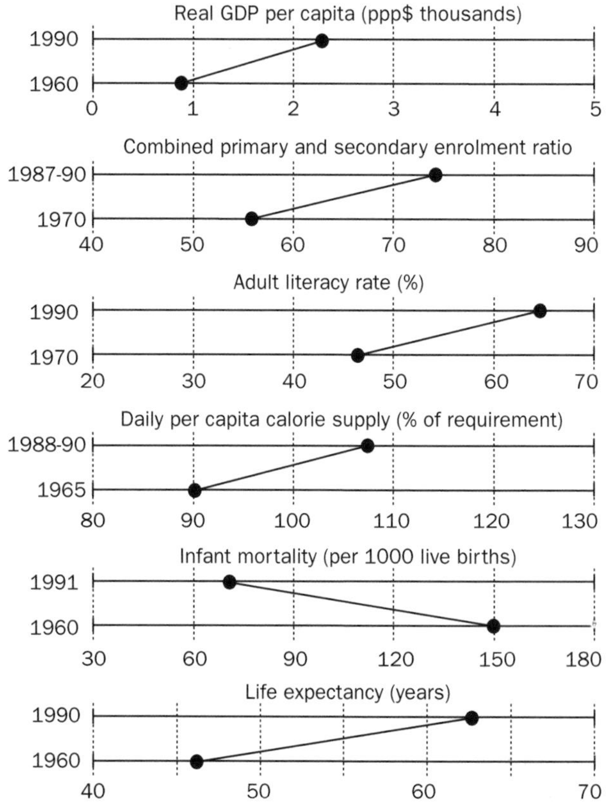

[SOURCE: Human Development Report, 1993]

Figure 6.5 *Human development progress in developing countries*

Developing countries Balance sheet of human development – developing countries HDI indices

Progress		Deprivation
• Average life expectancy increased by over one-third during the past three decades; 23 countries have achieved a life expectancy of 70 years and more.	Life expectancy	• Of the 300 million people above the age of 60, only 20% have any form of income security.
• In the developing world, more than 70% of the population has access to health services. • Nearly 60% of the population has access to sanitation.	Health and sanitation	• About 17 million people die every year from infectious and parasitic diseases, such as diarrhoea, malaria and tuberculosis. • More than 80% of the 12–13 million HIV-infected people are in the developing world, and the cumulative direct and indirect cost of AIDS during the past decade was around $30 billion.
• Between 1965 and 1990, the number of countries that met their daily per capita calorie requirements doubled – from about 25 to 50.	Food and nutrition	• Some 800 million people still do not get enough food.
• Primary school enrolment increased in the past two decades – from less than 70% to well over 80%. In the same period, secondary enrolment almost doubled – from less than 25% to 40%.	Education	• Nearly one billion people – 35% of the adult population – are still illiterate, and the drop-out rate at the primary level is still as high as 30%.
• In south and east Asia, where two-thirds of the developing world's population live, the GNP growth averaged more than 7% a year during the 1980s.	Income and poverty	• Almost one-third of the total population, or 1.3 billion people, are in absolute poverty.
• During the past 30 years, infant and under-five morality rates were more than halved.	Children	• Each day, 34 000 young children still die from malnutrition and disease.
• The secondary enrolment ratio for girls increased from around 17% in 1970 to 36% in 1990.	Women	• Two-thirds of illiterates are women.
• With the end of the cold war, developing countries no longer have to serve as proxies for superpower rivalry, and in 1990, about 380 000 refugees returned to their homelands in Asia, Africa and Latin America.	Human security	• Internal conflicts afflict some 60 countries, and about 35 million people are refugees or internally displaced.
• The percentage of rural families with access to safe water has increased from less than 10% to almost 60% during the past two decades.	Environment	• The rate of tropical forest destruction is about the equivalent of one soccer field per second. • More than 850 million people live in areas that are in various stages of desertification.

Industrialised countries Balance sheet of human development– industrial countries HDI indices

Progress		Deprivation
• In 1960, life expectancy was more than 70 years in only 12 countries. Now, it is more than 70 years in all industrial countries.	Life expectancy and health	• Nearly two million people are HIV-infected, and the direct and indirect cost during the 1980s was $210 billion.
• The tertiary enrolment ratio more than doubled between 1965 and 1990.	Education	• More than one-third of the adults lack any upper secondary or higher education.
• The per capita GNP grew at an annual rate of 2.4% between 1965 and 1990.	Income and employment	• The average unemployment rate is about 7%, and a quarter of the more than 30 million unemployed have been out of work for more than two years.
• Social security expenditures now account for just under 15% of GDP.	Social security	• About 100 million people live below the poverty line.
• Women now account for more than 40% of total employment.	Women	• Women hold fewer than 10% of parliamentary seats.
• There are now five library books and more than one radio for every person, and more than one telephone and one television set for every two people. One in three people reads a newspaper.	Social fabric	• There are more than 15 suicides, more than 100 drug crimes and more than 15 deaths from road accidents per 100 000 people. • The number of divorces is now one-third the number of marriages contracted, and well over 5% of households are single-parent homes.
• Energy requirements per unit of GDP fell by 40% between 1965 and 1990.	Population and environment	• People in industrial countries make up about one-fifth of world population but consume ten times more commercial energy than people in developing countries, and they account for 71% of the world's carbon monoxide emissions and 68% of the world's industrial waste.

[SOURCE: Human Development Report *Trends in human development*, 1993]

***Figure 6.6** Human development progress based on HDI indices, 1993*

Achieving human development goals

The United Nations Development Programme Agency offers guidelines towards formulating human development strategies which will contribute towards solving world poverty and inequalities:

- use money saved on defence cuts resulting from the end of the Cold War between the communist and western blocs, to finance human development and encourage developing world countries to divert money from armaments to meet basic human needs. It is estimated that if this was done, universal literacy and primary basic health care and safe drinking water for all could be achieved by the year 2000 AD
- increase human security by preventive diplomacy through new regional and international alliances for peace
- invest in human capabilities through better education, better health and training skills, so that people can work productively and creatively (Figure 6.7)

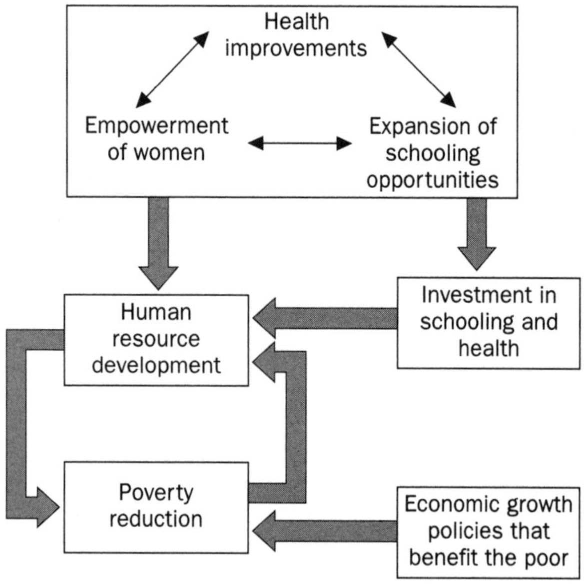

Especially in the poorest countries, policies that accelerate income growth and reduce poverty make it possible for people to afford better diets, healthier living conditions, and better health care. Policies to expand educational opportunities, particularly for girls, help households to achieve healthier lives by increasing their access to information and their ability to make good use of it. When all policies are combined they create a virtuous circle in which reduction of poverty and improvements in health reinforce one another'.

[SOURCE: *Households and health*, World Development Report 1993]

Figure 6.7 Mutually reinforcing cycles: reduction of poverty and development of human resources

- ensure that the income from generated growth is distributed fairly and wisely
- give everyone a chance to participate –
  (i) in productive and remunerative employment
  (ii) liberate private enterprise and make markets more accessible to everyone
  (iii) support small-scale enterprise and informal employment through reforming the credit system and by tax incentives
  (iv) create an efficient service economy
  (v) encourage labour-intensive technology to provide more jobs and lower capital costs
  (vi) extend employment safety nets through better unemployment benefits and creation of public works programmes to help absorb the unemployed.

It remains to be seen whether or not countries are willing to adopt and encourage human development programmes along these guidelines but with variations to suit their particular circumstances.

Human development and solving environmental problems

Proper husbanding of the world's resources and management of environments have become linked with human development strategies. The term 'development' has thus become more comprehensive still, so that another type of development is increasingly prominent, that of sustainable development.

Sustainable development is not simply a matter of environmental concerns being incorporated into the concept of development. The term 'sustainable' clearly implies development to meet current needs and a responsibility for ensuring that opportunities are provided for future populations to meet their needs too. The moral obligation of policy makers and participants in the development process is not only to the present generation but also to future generations.

6.3 Sustainable development

'Sustainable development' as a term was brought into common use by the World Commission on Environment and Development (the Bundtland Commission) in its 1987 report, *Our Common Future*. Five years later, at the 1992 Rio de Janeiro *Earth Summit* conference, a programme for action to avert global environmental disaster was outlined, based on the underlying principle of sustainable development.

The basic concept of sustainable development is that it meets the needs of the present generation while leaving the same or an improved resource

base as a bequest for the future. The needs of future generations are thus not compromised while satisfying those of the present. Thus both economic and environmental or ecological considerations must be covered in planning policies.

The relationship between human development and the environment is two-way. On the one hand, the environment itself contributes to human welfare and well being, for example provision of safe water and healthy air quality. It provides the essential resources needed to meet human needs. On the other hand, if in the process of making economic progress the environment is damaged through, for example, soils being degraded and exhausted, the water table lowered and water resources depleted or ecosystems destroyed, then future economic progress will be jeopardised (Case studies 21.1 and 28.4).

Economic development and care for the environment are not incompatible

Some writers have tried to indicate that there is a stark choice between either further economic growth and progress, or protecting and sustaining the environment. Recent authoritative guides (for example, *World Development Report 1992*, the World Bank) have indicated that this premise is false. It has largely arisen because many of the current world environmental problems have been blamed on the richer nations over-exploiting the world's resources in the rush towards ever higher standards of living and mass consumption, leading to serious pollution problems, ozone depletion and global warming. These are what are called the 'loud emergencies' in the environment, created by the affluence and extravagance of advanced countries – 'loud' because they are the centre of media attention.

While there is some truth in this, it does not mean that further economic progress has to be sacrificed, but rather that technologies and methods must be found which can be used to increase production while at the same time ensuring proper long-term management of the environment and its resources. The costs and benefits of doing this must be incorporated into the profit and loss accounting of businesses. There are already signs that this reorientation of business planning is occurring, for example, the move to 'greener' farming and the greater investment being made in renewable energy resources. The World Development Report of 1992 emphasises that the gains from adopting a more environmentally friendly development strategy are high and the costs in foregone income modest where appropriate policies are adopted. Governments do need to intervene to achieve sustainable development but the emphasis should be on incentives for businesses to adopt appropriate policies rather than for governments to impose regulatory controls.

Within developing countries further economic growth is seen as imperative if environmental problems are to be tackled since poverty is one of the greatest threats to the environment.

The poverty - environment link

Poverty reduces people's capacity to use resources in a sustainable manner and it intensifies environmental pressure.

The poor are forced to forego the needs of the future to meet the needs of the present.

[SOURCE: Brundtland Report, World Commission, 1987]

Poverty is the greatest single cause of environmental damage in the developing world; it is a major contributor to water pollution, land degradation, erosion and deforestation. In contrast to the 'loud emergencies' associated with the richer nations, these are the 'silent emergencies of poverty'. Eradicating poverty and promoting human development will lead to fewer pressures on the environment for two basic reasons: that people will have the income, education, insight and participation in decision-making to adopt sustainable development strategies; that rising incomes and better education are the central keys to reducing the population growth and resultant population pressure which are so damaging to the sensitive environments of the tropics.

Concluding comment

Sustainable development incorporates economic development, human development and the proper management of the environment and its resources. Moreover, it does so in relation to the needs of the present generation and to those of future generations. This poses a daunting challenge which developing countries in particular will find hard to meet.

China, with the largest population in the world and now a rapid rate of economic growth, provides a key example of how difficult the road is to sustainable development. While in a number of areas making progress towards this goal (Case study 6.1), it still holds on to a Communist regime in which individuals have only a limited say on policies and decisions. Yet, as has been noted earlier, greater individual participation is essential if real progress is to be made towards sustainable development.

case study

6.1 China: the challenge of sustainable development

The challenge

Population pressure

- The population of 1.15 billion is projected to grow to 1.3 billion by the year 2000. Present annual growth is 17 million at a rate of 1.4%. Birth rate is down to 20.8 per 1000 with death rate at 7 per 1000. Life expectancy is 71 years. If the fertility rate falls, population will stabilise at 1.7 billion by 2050 and then be set to fall.
- The population is rapidly urbanising. Urban population now represents 25% (297 million) of the total population, but 90 million of this was added since 1982. Beijing has an annual natural increase of 8% compared to a national average of 1.4%. Urbanisation will bring serious problems socially and environmentally, including pressure on land for increased food supplies. Only 10% of China is cropland, an average of only 0.08 ha per person.
- An ageing population in rural areas will hinder the capacity of agricultural areas to feed the towns.

Rapid economic development with lagging environmental controls

- China's economy has experienced an average 9% annual growth since 1980, with rapid industrialisation. Industrialisation has an annual growth of 11% compared to 5% in agriculture with insufficient emphasis on environmental controls to meet the associated problems. Although much of the industrial growth is in coastal zone cities, especially in the south, there is also rapid expansion of light and consumer industries in rural areas, for example, brick and tile making.
- With the rapid economic development, energy consumption increased by 200% between 1970 and 1990. China is the third largest consumer of energy in world; 80% is derived from coal, leading to serious environmental pollution, especially as production methods are inefficient. Schemes to increase energy from other sectors are also leading to problems, for example, the Three Gorges project controversy in relation to loss of 23 800 ha of cultivated land and need to resettle 1.1 million people.
- Expansion and intensification of agriculture to meet population needs has led to land degradation especially in the west where low and unpredictable rainfall occurs. Much of the land is of difficult, steep, sloping terrain; desertification and soil erosion is extensive here. Soil erosion is also present in the wetter areas in the east, where flood and drought is cyclic.

Pressure on a fragile environment

- Half of China's territory is arid or semi-arid, mainly in the west and north-west and is therefore particularly open to soil erosion and desertification.
- About 65% of the land is of sloping, or mountainous terrain and cultivation occurred without adequate protection. The loess areas on the middle basin parts of the Juang (Yellow) and Changiang (Yangtze) Rivers are particularly susceptible to erosion.
- The monsoonal climate regime can also bring severe flooding to the same river basins.
- About 7% of China is coastal wetland with a delicate ecosystem. In the past, China had seen this simply as wasteland to be reclaimed for agriculture or industry.

Overuse of basic resources: water, forests and fish

- Demand for water is soaring in all sectors, including agriculture which currently takes 87% of all water used. Most expansion is likely to be in residential and industrial sectors, shortages becoming acute in drier North China. About 50 cities have severe water shortages.
- The demand for wood exceeds supply. Most of the virgin forest has disappeared, due mainly to clearance for agriculture and wood fuel. Illegal felling is widespread.
- Together with Japan and the states of the former USSR, China accounts for one third of the world's fishing. Coastal fishing has declined due to sea pollution and over-fishing.

Agriculture

Soil erosion is serious and increasing amounts of land are eroded, rising from 125 million ha in 1985 to 162 million ha by 1993. Protection against erosion is practised only on 34% of cropland. Desertification has increased from 156 000 ha a year in 1970, to 210 000 ha in the 1990s.
About 7 million ha of irrigated land are affected by salinisation. Intensification of agriculture has led to a rapid increase in the use of chemical fertilisers and herbicides. This caused pollution run-off to enter the existing water courses.

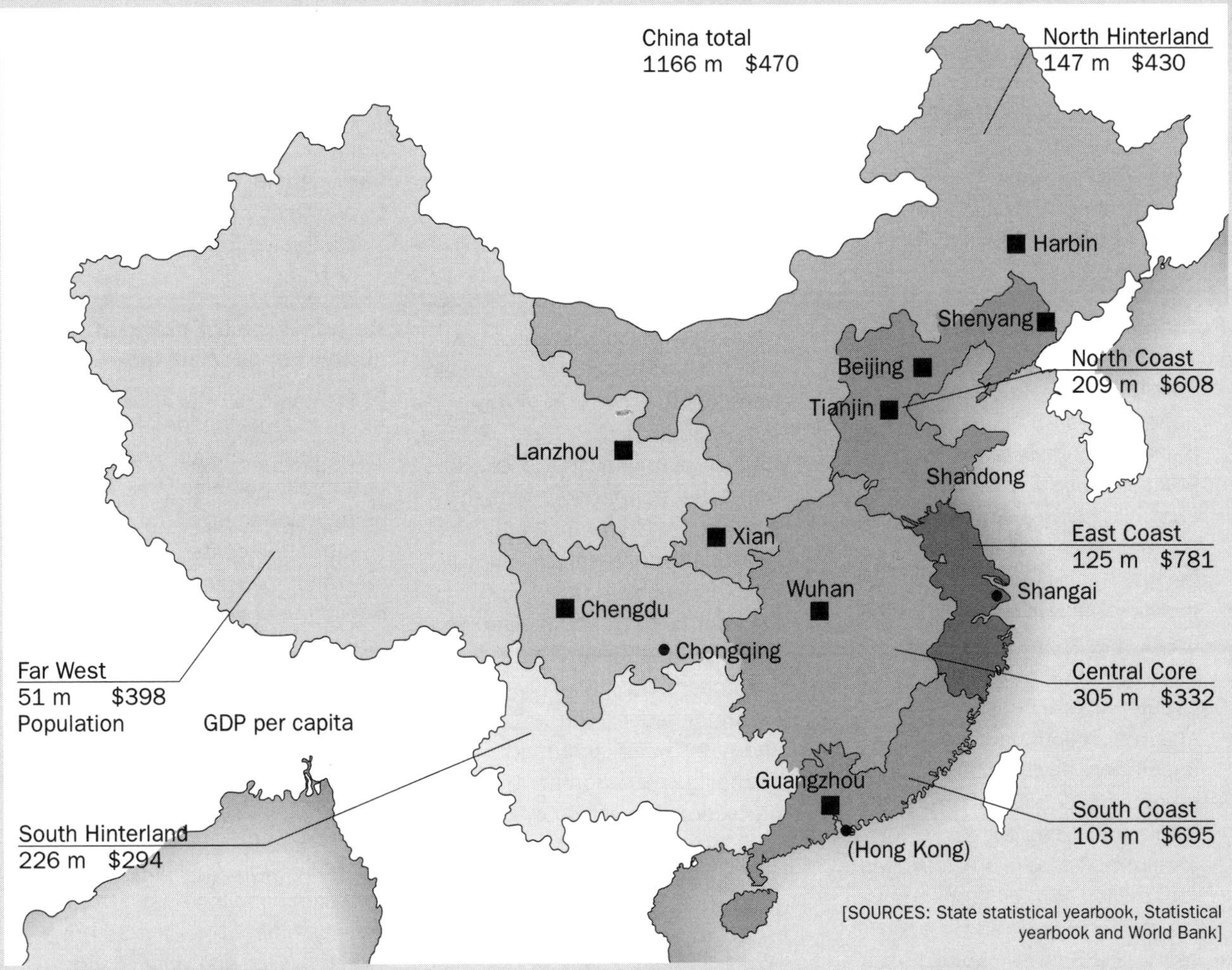

Population and GDP per capita by region

Industrial and urban pollution

The use of coal as a major energy supply, together with insufficient controls, led to serious air pollution. The increase in the size of cities and expansion of vehicle use added to urban pollution. Beijing records one of the highest urban pollution levels in the world. About 26% of all deaths in China are due to chest or lung illnesses, five times higher than in the USA. Pollution is a significant factor.

Decrease in finite basic resources

The loss of agricultural land, forest areas, over-consumption of water and depletion of fish stocks have already been highlighted. Although China is rich in coal and other mineral resources, stocks are being rapidly depleted not simply because of rapid rise in demand but also due to inefficiency in processing and use of materials plus insufficient regard to using substitute materials.

'Environmental problems are looming as perhaps the most worrying consequence of China's "double digit growth" of 13% over the last two years.'

FINANCIAL TIMES 26.8.94

Progress towards sustainable development

Professor Li indicates that China is backward in protecting its environment and huge investment is

required. *'Although the central government is doing a great deal to improve environmental consciousness, it has met a lot of resistance at the grass roots'.*
In 1991–2021: "Policy Choices of China's Economic Development" – Chinese Academy of Social Sciences 1994 –

Population partly under control

- Population growth is now largely under control. Stringent family planning controls have been in practise since 1970, with the one child policy since 1980. Population control is helped by a general desire to limit family size in cities, but it is less so in rural areas. The sheer size of the reproductive sector of the population and better health ensures a continued rise in population, however.
- Huge displacement of rural labour into cities poses problems. There is an estimated 100 million surplus farm labourers (15 million are added each year). The urban economy needs to continue to expand to absorb this surplus, but this increases the size of cities, bringing other problems of housing and infrastructure shortages.

Proper management of environment and its resources

- There is a need to make up for 'lost time'. From 1950 to 1970 there was little regard for environmental management. The economic policy, the *Great Leap Forward*, caused environmental havoc. Famine and natural catastrophes of 1959 and 1961 caused 30 million deaths. Four million hectares of cultivable land were lost to erosion and desertification.
- Attitudes changed in the 1970s. China agreed to resolutions at the first UN Conference on Human Environment and set up the National and Local Environment Protection Agencies in 1972. The Environment Protection Law of 1978 was strengthened in 1989.
- There has been increased spending on environment protection from 0.7% to 0.9% of GNP, but even the government recognises the need for 1.5% of the GNP to control current environment degradation.
- Some management measures have been improved. The biggest emphasis is not on changing energy sources but more on the efficient use of energy, for example, replacing outdated coal boilers. There is greater rural use of windpower and biogas.
- Measures against soil erosion include sand break forests for 8 million ha. Stereoagriculture is practised on the slopes combining forests and mixed farming.

Regulations for pollution control on all new industries

Regulations are being introduced slowly e.g. in Guandong where industrial expansion is rapid, new potentially polluting industries are being made to pay 30% of total construction costs to the local environment bureau to pay for the regulation of environment measures.

Planning controls are being more strictly enforced to reduce pollution but legislation and enforcement are not yet keeping pace with the speed of industrial expansion.

Urban pollution is increasing especially from coal-burning emissions and increased traffic density. Main ways forward are a switch over to natural gas and stricter emission controls.

7

CHAPTER 7

The food crisis and basic health care

'In developing countries, one person in three lives in poverty. Even basic social services primary health care, basic education, safe drinking water and adequate nutrition – are not available to more than one billion people. In the industrial world, about 100 million people are still below the official poverty line, though social safety nets help protect them.'

HUMAN DEVELOPMENT REPORT, 1995

7.1 Malnutrition and world food supplies

We need protein and energy foods together with certain vitamins and minerals to survive. Proteins are vital for body building and carbohydrates for energy. If carbohydrate intake falls below minimum, the body will divert some of the protein intake to make up for this deficiency. If protein and carbohydrate food intake is adequate, vitamin and mineral needs will also be met by the food consumed.

Since the carbohydrate intake is so critical, this is generally the nutrition measure used to show differences in diet and food intake levels from one part of the world to another. It is measured in calories.

Variations between countries and within countries

Figure 7.1 shows how calorie intakes vary across the world. People in more advanced countries have more than their proportion of the world's food; overeating causes more food problems than malnutrition. In contrast, there are many lesser developed parts of the world where malnutrition is a severe problem.

The direct link between food level intake, on the one hand, and vital population rates as indicated by mortality and life expectancy rates, on the other, is indicated in Figure 7.2

Poverty, not a world food shortage, is the cause of malnutrition. The main source of carbohydrates is cereals and thus levels of world production and distribution of cereals relative to demand are critical.

Despite the huge increases in the world's population through the twentieth century, there is more than enough food being produced to adequately feed the world. Record levels of production in rice, wheat and coarse grains, such as millet and barley, have consistently been reached (Figure 7.3). There have even been cutbacks in planting among major producers in the western world for fear of an over-supply (Chapters 21 and 22). Because of the uneven distribution of food, however, it is still estimated that 20% of the world's population is suffering from serious malnutrition and starvation. These populations do not consume enough food and because of poor health, are susceptible to many diseases, especially in the tropical regions.

The uneven distribution of food is due to a number of factors, including poor transportation networks and poverty. The problem is particularly acute in parts of south Asia, especially Bangladesh, and in tropical sub-Saharan Africa, where the average per capita food consumption continues to fall (Case study 23.3).

There are parts of the developing world where dramatic improvements have been made (Chapter 22). A notable case is that of India with one of the largest populations in the world. Per capita food consumption is rising, and from being a net importer of food, India is now a net exporter. During the famine of 1987 – 88 in the Maharashtra region, due a failure in the monsoon rains, India was able to use part of its own 30 million emergency reserve of wheat to relieve distress. Unlike parts of sub-Saharan Africa, such as Somalia and the Sudan, India does not have to rely on international emergency aid.

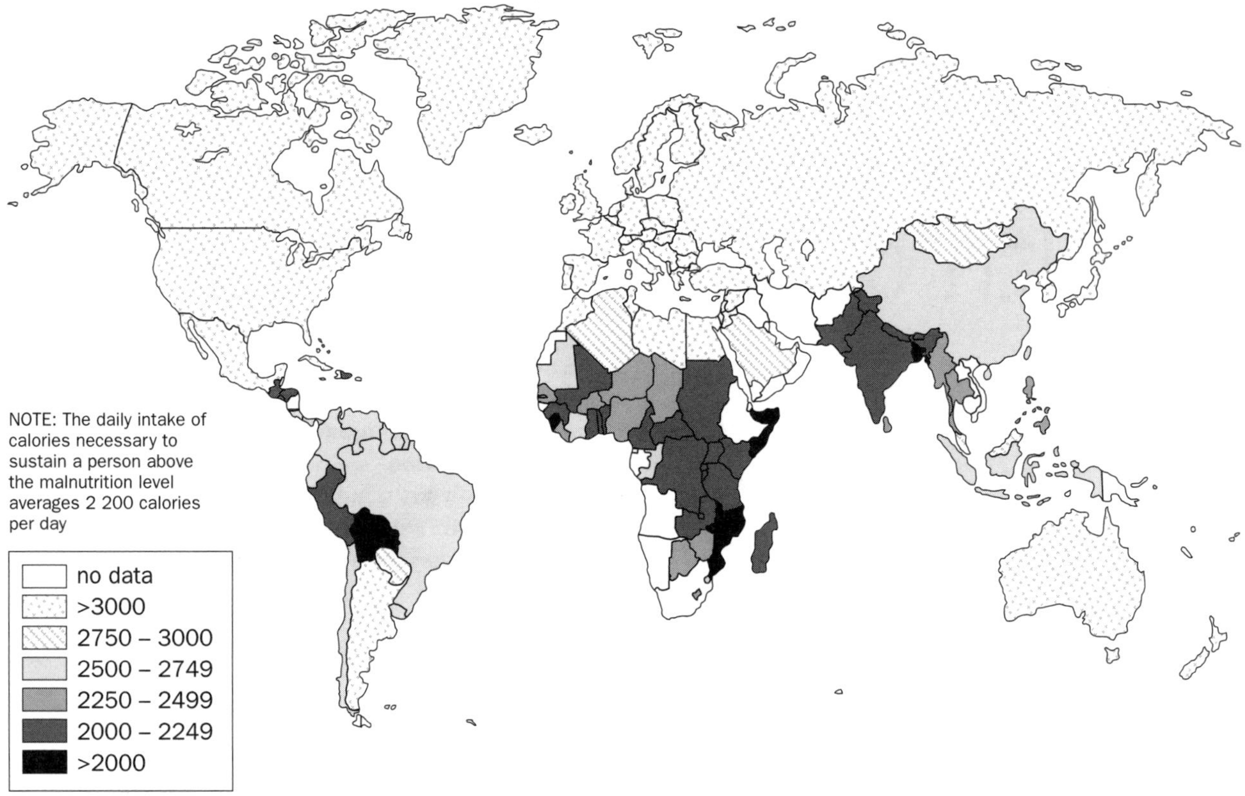

[SOURCE: Food and Agriculture Organisation (FAO) Production Yearbook, 1990, 44, FAO, Rome]

Figure 7.1 Average daily calorie intake per capita, 1990

	Daily calorie intake (per capita) 1992	Infant mortality rates (per 1000 live birth)	Life expectancy (at birth)
Low income countries	**2406**	**64**	**62.0**
Ethiopia	1610	117	47.5
India	2395	80	60.5
Bangladesh	2109	106	55.6
Kenya	2075	61	55.7
Middle income countries	**2860**	**40**	**66.0**
Egypt	3336	64	63.6
Bolivia	2100	73	59.4
Malaysia	2884	13	70.8
Mexico	3181	35	70.8
Industrialised countries	**3409 (1990)**	**8**	**77.0**
Italy	3549	8	77.5
UK	3149	7	76.2
Japan	2956	4	79.5
USA	3671	9	76.0

NOTE: The minimum daily calorie intake to prevent malnutrition is officially estimated at 2200 calories.
[SOURCE: World Development Report 1995, World Bank, 1995]

Figure 7.2 Infant mortality and life expectancy rates in relation to average daily calorie intake for selected countries, 1992

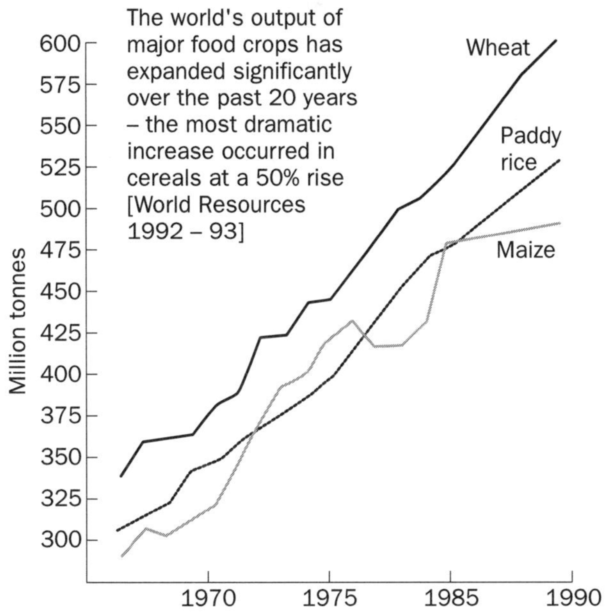

Figure 7.3 *World production of major cereals, 1970 – 1990*

Figure 7.4 shows the factors which affects the current food crisis in Africa. It also addresses the following two issues: why, in a world which produces more than enough food there is still widespread malnutrition and periodically serious famines; and why some of the previously poorest countries have managed to make dramatic progress towards eliminating poverty and widespread malnutrition, while others, especially those in sub-Saharan Africa, are actually deteriorating.

7.2 **Population growth and the environment's resources**

There seems to be a direct relationship between the rate of population growth and the ability of the environment to sustain that growth in those countries which suffer the most from malnutrition and famine. A popular explanation for the food crisis is that population growth is outstripping food supplies. This certainly appears to be the case in a number of African countries, such as the Sudan and

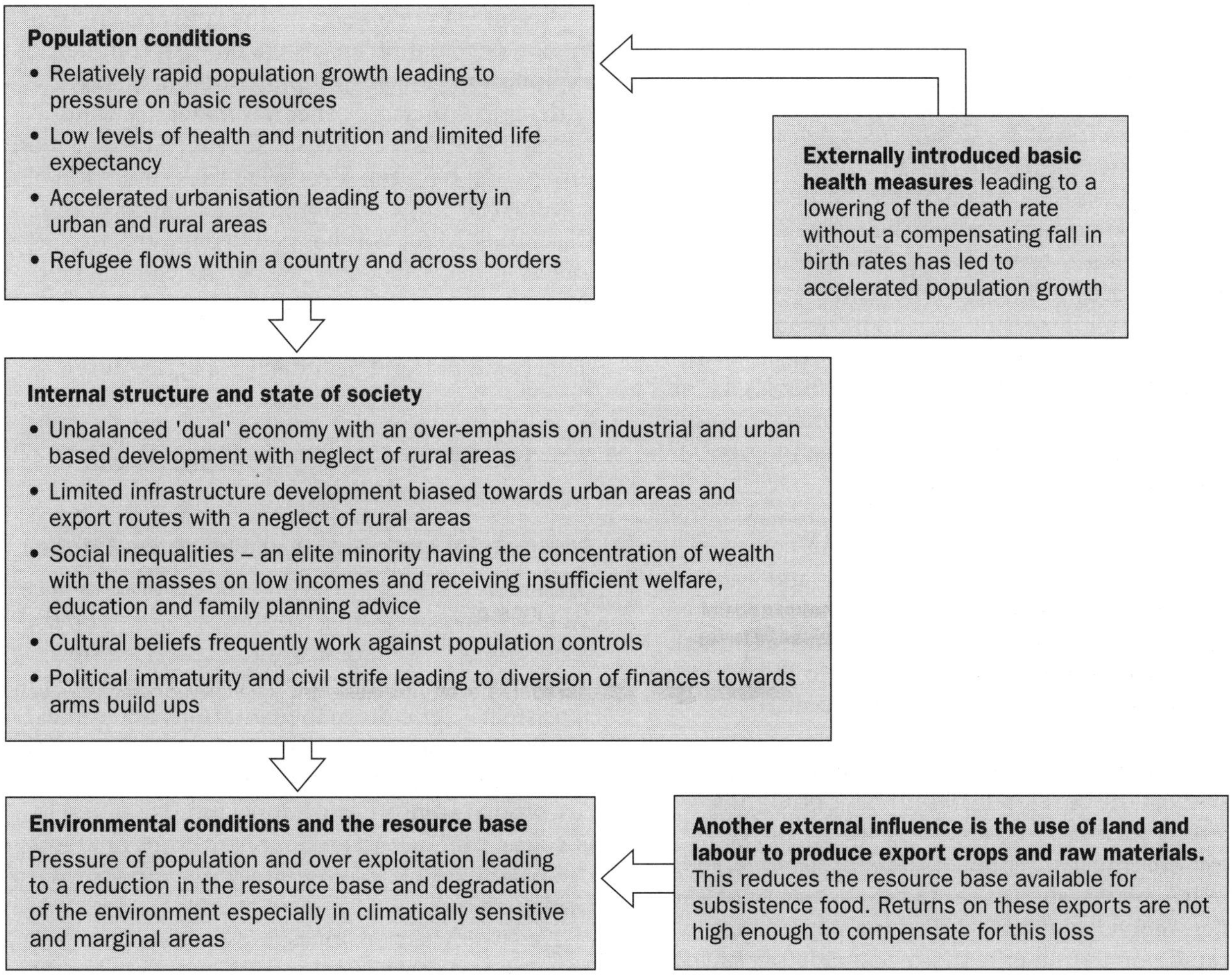

Figure 7.4 *Factors which affect levels of malnutrition and famine in parts of the developing world, especially in Africa*

Ethiopia, where the annual rate of population growth at between 3% and 4% is amongst the highest in the world, and where serious famine has recently occurred due to crop failure and a breakdown in food supplies (Case study 7.1).

The theories of Malthus and Boserup

In 1798 Malthus produced his *Essay on the Principles of Population*, in which he stated that the growth in numbers would always keep the mass population's living standards at subsistence level. While the 'passions between the sexes' would remain constant, leading to population in a geometric ratio (that is, 1, 2, 4, 8,16, etc.), the limit to increasing food supplies for them would be set by the limited amount of new land available for cultivation, so that food supplies would only increase in an arithmetic ratio (that is, 1, 2, 3, 4, etc.). Thus population would tax resources to such an extent that the natural and positive checks of famine, pestilence, war and higher mortality rates among the weak and the diseased would prevail. This pressure would only be offset by a conscious reduction in early marriages among the more educated in society and a voluntary restraint from intercourse.

Ester Boserup challenged this assertion in 1965 in her publication of *The Conditions of Agricultural Growth*. She pointed out that much of the world has escaped the misery which Malthus predicted. Population pressure, far from being the cause of demographic catastrophe, has been the driving force behind agricultural innovation and the greatest incentive for increasing agricultural production. Agriculture has expanded to meet the needs of an increasing population. Because of technological and social progress and new discoveries, much of the world has been able to balance population needs and food supplies.

There still remains clear evidence, however, that Malthusian checks do operate in some countries. It is especially so in the drought-ridden and war-torn areas of parts of Africa like the Sahel, which border the Sahara and stretches from West Africa through to the Sudan and Ethiopia, and also in Mozambique where civil war has devastated the country (Case study 7.2).

The famines and food crises in Africa and other parts of the developing world have brought a strong revival of interest in Malthus' theory. A neo-Malthusian school of thought has emerged, led by writers such as Paul Ehrlich, author of *The Population Bomb*, but while it is accepted that rapid population growth is a contributory factor, it is not itself the cause of the food crisis.

Malthus-type arguments increasingly allied to fears for the environment

This is particularly in those parts of the world where the ecological balance between humans and nature is precarious. This is especially noticeable in regions where the environment is fragile because of the uncertainties and unreliability of climate, and the natural infertility of the soil. Due to population increase, population pressures in such sensitive environments have brought about widespread environmental degradation. This has further reduced the capacity of the environment to support its population. Degradation of the environment is seen, for example, in the destruction of the natural vegetation through overgrazing and clearance of woodland for agriculture and fuel (Case study 27.6). This has increased the uncertainty of rainfall and contributed to droughts in the Sahel region, while clearance of forest areas on upland watersheds has led to disastrous flooding in Nepal and Bangladesh (Case study 23.3). Extending cultivation into marginal areas with poor soils and unreliable rainfall has also increased soil erosion and crop failure.

Pressure of population on the land and environmental degradation are also to do with commercial exploitation, largely to supply external markets with agricultural and other raw materials. Land which might have been used for much needed food production has been diverted to the production of commercial crops and raw materials (Section 23.6; Case study 23.6). This has had two important effects. It has reduced the area of agricultural land available to feed the expanding population, and it has forced some of the population off existing land on to marginal land unsuitable for agriculture.

7.3 The influence of colonialism and neo-colonialism

Commercial exploitation of the tropical world

Under colonialism, the economic development of much of the developing world was centred on the provision of raw materials and markets for the western world. Labour was diverted away from subsistence agriculture to plantations and mines, leaving food production largely in the hands of the women and elderly in the villages.

Colonial administrators introduced taxation to encourage farmers to produce cash crops or to force them to migrate to plantations, mines and towns to work for wages.

The infrastructure, including the transport network and siting of colonial towns, was also organised to encourage efficient administration of the colony and the export of materials rather than to meet the needs of the indigenous population. The legacy is seen in the predominance of coastal cities and the focus of transport networks on them as, for example, in Latin American countries such as Brazil or in African countries such as Mozambique.

A dual economy developed in a number of countries, with one part having a more westernised and developed economy due to outside investment. Other parts of these countries, usually the more remote areas, were neglected and remained under a traditional subsistence economy with the indigenous culture largely intact. Over time these neglected regions have lagged further and further behind the core region, leading to serious regional inequalities (Case study 7.3). Most of the poverty and malnutrition can be seen in these lagging areas as, for example, in the north-east and interior of Brazil, in contrast to its developed south.

Neo-colonialism

While independence has brought freedom from political domination by western powers, much of the tropical world remains economically tied to the advanced countries. A number of African countries, for example, Sierre Leone, Ghana and Zambia, remain dependent on a narrow range of exports to the advanced countries.

Former colonies are also increasingly dependent on the investment of large overseas multinational corporations. These exert a considerable influence on the pattern of economic development in the young national states. It is thus claimed that the restrictions of colonialism have been replaced, to some extent, by a neo-colonialism. Much of the land and labour is still geared to the production of export crops and raw materials for the benefit of multinational corporations and the advanced countries. Much of the profit from exports goes overseas to the shareholders in these large corporations rather than providing much needed finance to improve subsistence agriculture and the growing of food crops for the rapidly expanding urban populations in tropical countries.

A number of countries have become less self-sufficient in food production and increasingly dependent on food imports because of the concentration on exports and neglect of domestic agriculture. The World Food and Agricultural Organisation estimates that the rate of decline in food self-sufficiency in sub-Saharan Africa is so marked that food imports will have trebled from 1980 to the year 2000. Some of these imports will be in the form of food aid but much of it has to be paid for and this is increasing the financial strain on poor countries. This increases their international debt burden (Figure 7.5).

7.4 **The problem of debt**

Unfavourable terms of trade increases the cost of food and basic imports. Over the post-war years, terms of world trade have been consistently against developing countries. Prices of cash crops and raw materials have not been rising as fast as the costs which have to be paid for imported fuels and manufactured goods from advanced countries. Developing countries thus have less money to pay for food and other imports, forcing them to apply for foreign loans, thereby increasing the debt burden. They are unable to settle earlier loans and cannot even meet the interest due on them.

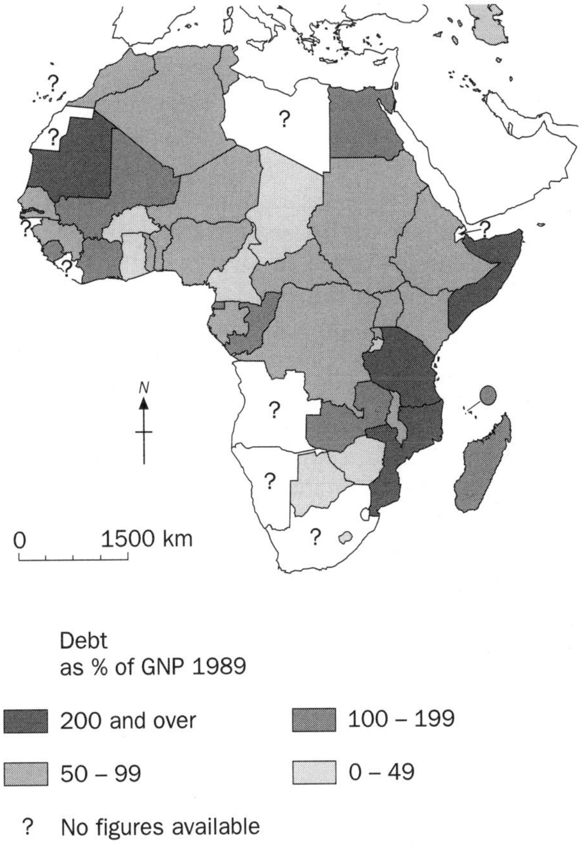

[SOURCE: *The Atlas of African Affairs*, 1994]

Figure 7.5 *Foreign indebtness in Africa (expressed as a percentage of each state's Gross National Product)*

Poorer developing countries have insufficient funds to raise food output, partly because of the size of their international debt. Aid and loans received from foreign investors are increasingly outweighed by the interest payments which have to be made to the richer developing countries. The World Bank estimates that the South (the developing countries) are making a net transfer of 20 billion dollars a year to the North (the advanced countries). Since the end of the 1980s, the International Monetary Fund

(IMF) has been working with some of the world's major banks to solve developing world debt.

In return for cancelling some of this debt and extending the period over which loan interest and repayments have to be made, the IMF and other institutions have set conditions which particular developing countries have to meet. These are aimed at making them economically more efficient and reducing their budget deficits. Some of the ways in which developing countries have tried to do this, however, are by cutting back welfare programmes, reducing subsidies on food prices and raising levels of taxation. The poor have been hardest hit by these measures and their living standards have dropped even further. In the short term, conditions have worsened as a result of outside intervention.

It has been claimed that debt and imposed restrictions by the IMF are leading to worsening conditions in sub-Saharan Africa and the poorer parts of south Asia, and that they are also choking off two decades of progress in Latin American countries. For example, hunger and disease are once again on the increase in Andean countries and in the lagging north-eastern and interior areas of Brazil.

The World Development Report for 1990 states that the contrasts in poverty and national wealth are more striking in Latin American and Caribbean countries than anywhere else. Despite the fact that average per capita incomes are five to six times higher than in sub-Saharan Africa, nearly one fifth of the population in Latin America and the Caribbean live in poverty and suffer from hunger. While recognising the role of external influences in bringing this about, World Bank officials also emphasise the role of developing world governments, particularly their failure to reduce the gross inequalities among the people in their countries.

7.5 Political immaturity in low income countries

It is no coincidence that some of the worst famine areas in Africa are in countries where civil war rages and there are clashes between neighbouring states. These clashes arise out of tribal or ethnic divisions or ideological differences between powerful groups as, for example, in Somalia and Mozambique. Other clashes arise when dictatorial governments try to extend their power into neighbouring countries. Funds are diverted to military expenditure and away from food production. Civil war has brought about a breakdown in economies, disrupted food supplies and reduced participating countries to bankruptcy (Case study 7.1).

Political instability and breakdowns in economies cause large-scale displacement of populations within countries and across national borders, adding to the problem of feeding the masses. This is evident in Africa and was also seen in the Middle East during the Gulf War when two million refugees fled across the border into Jordan during the occupation of Kuwait by Iraq. Concerted international aid was required to avoid the threat of famine for these refugees.

The pursuit of western-style development and the over-concentration on manufacturing and service development in the urban sector of the economy have been major problems in some developing countries (Case study 20.2). Raising food output has been neglected. Where more balanced development programmes have been adopted, as in India, agricultural productivity has been raised and severe malnutrition reduced. In the 1990s investment in rural development programmes has been widely seen as a key to solving the developing world food crisis. Bangladesh, for example, is committed to investing half of its development funds in rural development. Such investment can lead to raising food production and reducing the widespread drift of rural people into urban areas where poverty and hunger remains a problem in the shanty areas (Case study 23.3).

Food pricing policies have discouraged farmers from producing food for sale. A number of writers have emphasised that rural development programmes will not succeed unless prices of food are sufficiently high to encourage farmers to produce. In the past, governments have deliberately kept the price of foodstuffs down to help wage earners in the urban sector. This was done partly to gain political support from the growing urban masses, but also to keep down wage demands, thereby ensuring a cheaper labour supply. By manipulating the pricing system, governments have interfered with supply and demand so that during food shortages, the prices have not been allowed to rise sufficiently to encourage farmers to produce more supplies for the market.

7.6 Towards food security and the elimination of malnutrition

Controlling population growth

Until recently a lot of emphasis was placed on controlling population growth to reduce the pressure on the environment and its resources. Although there is evidence that rates of population growth are slowing down, it is clear that this will not be fast enough to have any appreciable effect within the next 40 to 50 years. Family planning programmes and population control take time to work and, though important, can only have an appreciable effect over the long term. Population experts have indicated that over the next 50 years the population to be fed from the earth's food supplies will more than double, regardless of the success or failure of any present efforts to control population growth. This is essentially because the present population of the developing world is dominated by children who, as they reach adulthood, will greatly enlarge the future reproductive sector of the population. This will sustain population growth despite any successes of family planning programmes in reducing fertility and birth rates (Chapter 2).

Reducing poverty and expanding food production are the essential keys to solving the problem. Widespread malnutrition which affects 20% of the world's population is due to a failure to expand food production itself in areas of need, and a failure to provide ways for people to earn sufficient to purchase their food and other basic needs.

But to allow this to happen there needs to be some progress towards tackling the root cause at the heart of most world problems – the gross inequalities between people which result from from the ways in which political, economic and international levels are organised.

Within countries, the gross inequality is between one sector and another. Certain disadvantaged sectors are systematically denied the ability and income to support themselves due to a legacy of history and impoverishment of rural areas. At an international level, the gross inequality is that between the poorer South (the poorer developing nations) and the affluent North (the richer advanced nations) (Figure 33.18).

The political will to eradicate these inequalities is needed. At a national level there are moves towards more democratic government in some developing countries and a switch towards an emphasis on the development of rural areas where most of the poorest live. This, for example, has been a key feature in India's successful progress towards reducing hunger and the threat of famine. Amongst African countries, rural development is a key feature of Zimbabwe's development programme (Case study 7.3).

Internationally, efforts are being made towards a greater liberalisation of world trade which, it is hoped, may benefit developing countries. There are also attempts to address their debt to advanced countries and replace short-term aid by longer-term schemes, which will improve the livelihoods of the rural poor (Chapters 32 and 33).

Concluding comment

Strategies for sustainable food security for all must take into account all the policies that affect the three-fold challenge of shifting production to where it is most needed, securing the livelihoods of the rural poor, and conserving the environment and its resources to allow for sustainable development.

case study

7.1 **Crisis in Africa**

'Famine signifies an exceptional event – a collective catastrophe of such magnitude as to cause social and economic dislocation. It generally results in abnormal levels of destitution, hunger and death. It can lead to complete disintegration of work and subsistence and can greatly disrupt customary norms of morality and social behaviour. If hunger can be likened to a disease, famine constitutes its epidemic state – the multiplication of existing conditions of inequality, poverty and malnutrition into a crisis of massive proportions.'

[Arnold D *Famine*, 1988]

Causes

Famine is provoked by a failure in the production and supply of food. Immediate abnormal events such as drought, flood, locust plague and war may be the catalyst, but there are deeper causes. These bring people to such a low level of subsistence and health that these abnormal events can plunge them into famine.

Deeper contributory factors

- **a population growth** that is too rapid. The annual growth rate in tropical Africa averages approximately 3% and is outstripping food supplies.
- **declining soil fertility** and environmental degradation, particularly in low rainfall areas. This can be brought about by overcropping, overgrazing and deforestation caused by burning and the increasing need for fuel-wood. Extending the zone of deforestation. Environmental degradation has hastened run-off and accelerated soil erosion. Together with climatic fluctuations, this has extended the spread of desert conditions into former arid areas of grassland and bush.
- **poor farming methods** due to poverty, lack of knowledge, insufficient access to land and insufficient government funding.
- **poor infrastructure**, making the distribution of food difficult during famine and insufficient access during normal periods.
- **unequal distribution of wealth** with too much land in the hands of the elite.

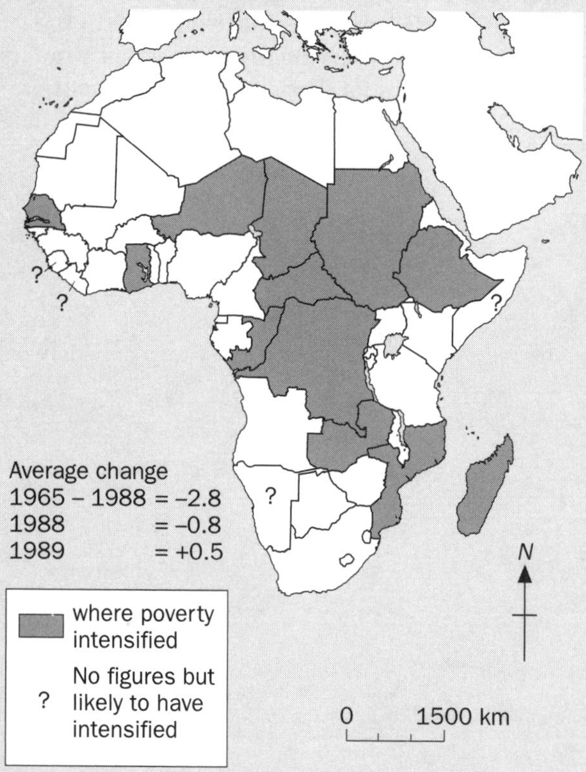

Poverty intensifies in tropical Africa

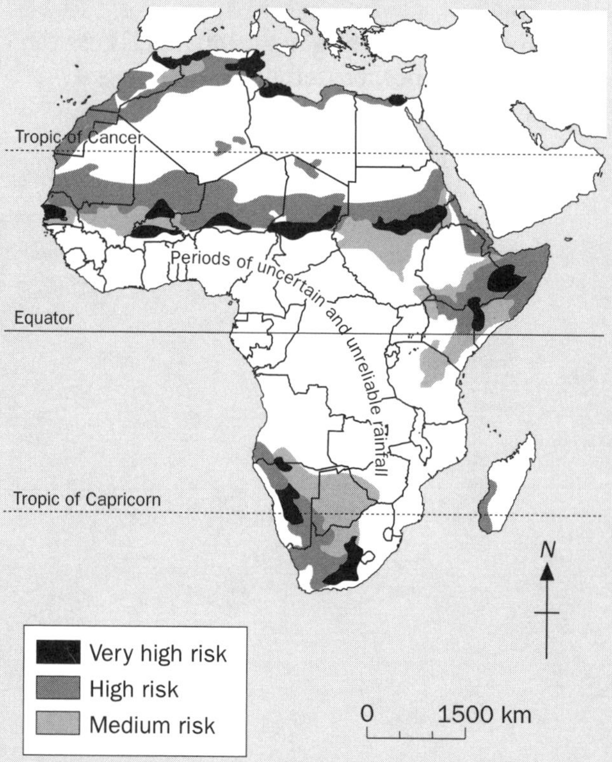

Desertification

- **unbalanced government policy** with too much emphasis on urban-based growth and cash crop exports.
- **lack of emergency food supplies** and contingency plans.
- **political instability** which leads to the disruption of economic systems and military overspending.
- **insufficient external support** and aid for development and emergencies.

Long-term solutions

- **Reverse environmental degradation** through widespread conservation measures.
- **Direct funding and expertise to rural development.**
- **Distribute land and wealth more equally.**
- **Encourage greater political stability and participation through democracy.**
- **Develop long-term external relationships for aid and support.**

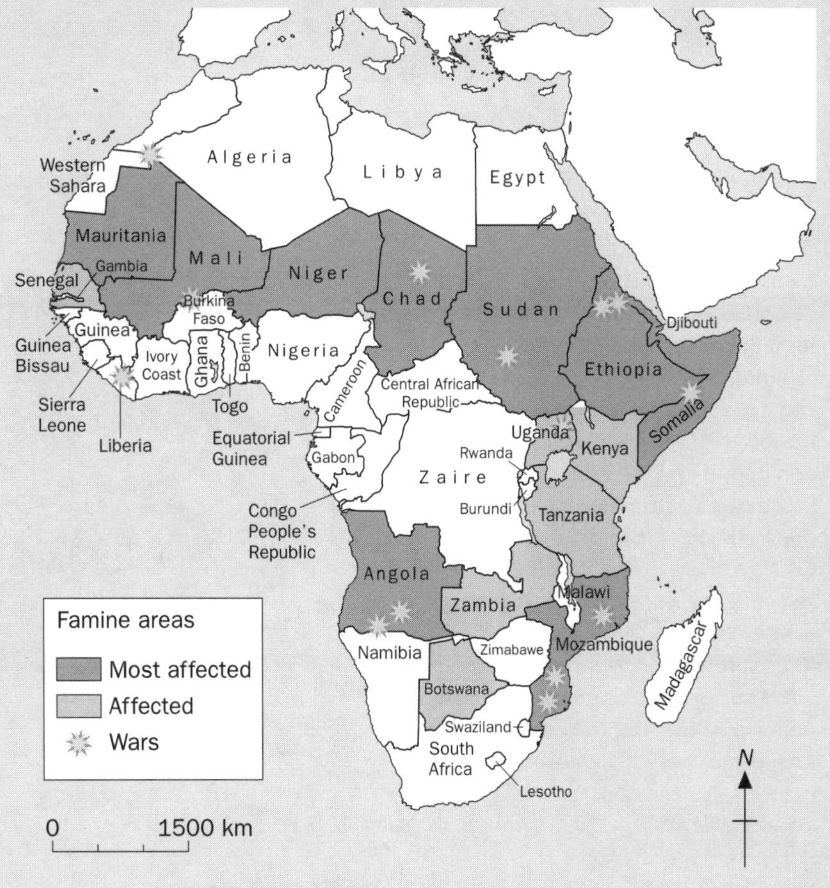

Tropical Africa: famine areas and loction of major wars

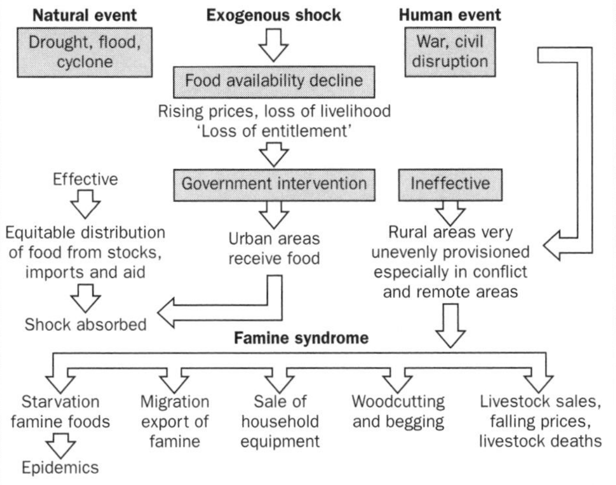

Under African conditions, where a very high proportion of the people are poor and undernourished, the famine syndrome rapidly develops. If they are deprived of food by drought or conflict, or a combination of these, farmers are forced to sell off their livestock and then their meagre household goods, turn to traditional famine foods and finally migrate to the cities or relief camps.

The development of the famine syndrome

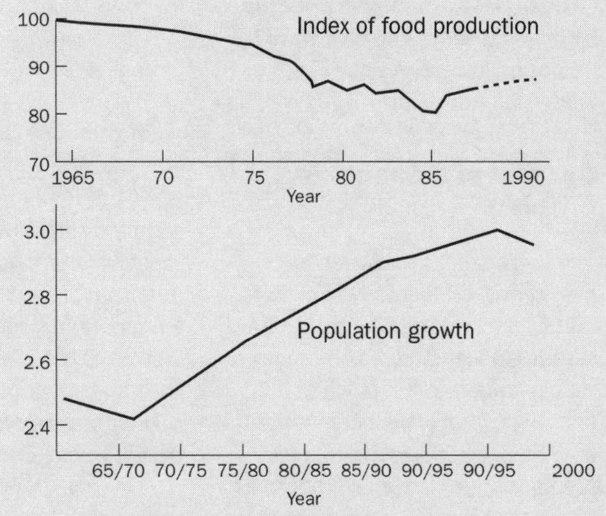

[SOURCES: World Resources 1988 – 89; International institute of Environment and Development; World Bank Report, 1990]

Food production, population and growth

case study

7.2 **Ethiopia: recurrent famine**

The problem

Ethiopia has a population of 47 million, the third largest in tropical Africa, and an average annual growth rate of 3.3%. It is one of the poorest African countries. Food production has fallen by 11% compared to 1980.

Population growth is outstripping food supplies, with recurrent famine; there were six in the last two decades. This mainly affected the north of the country and semi-arid coatal lowland areas.

Extreme environmental degradation is leading to rapid soil erosion and a loss of fertility, reducing the possibility of reversing adverse trends. Populations lpressures are increasing.

The situation is aggravated by the policies of the Marxist Lenin government which came into power in 1974. It has pursued a policy of development which favours the urban sector and export of commercial crops, spending on unproductive prestige schemes and a large military build up.

The economy was also affected by internal strife and civil wars by liberation groups in Eritrea and Tigray, for example.

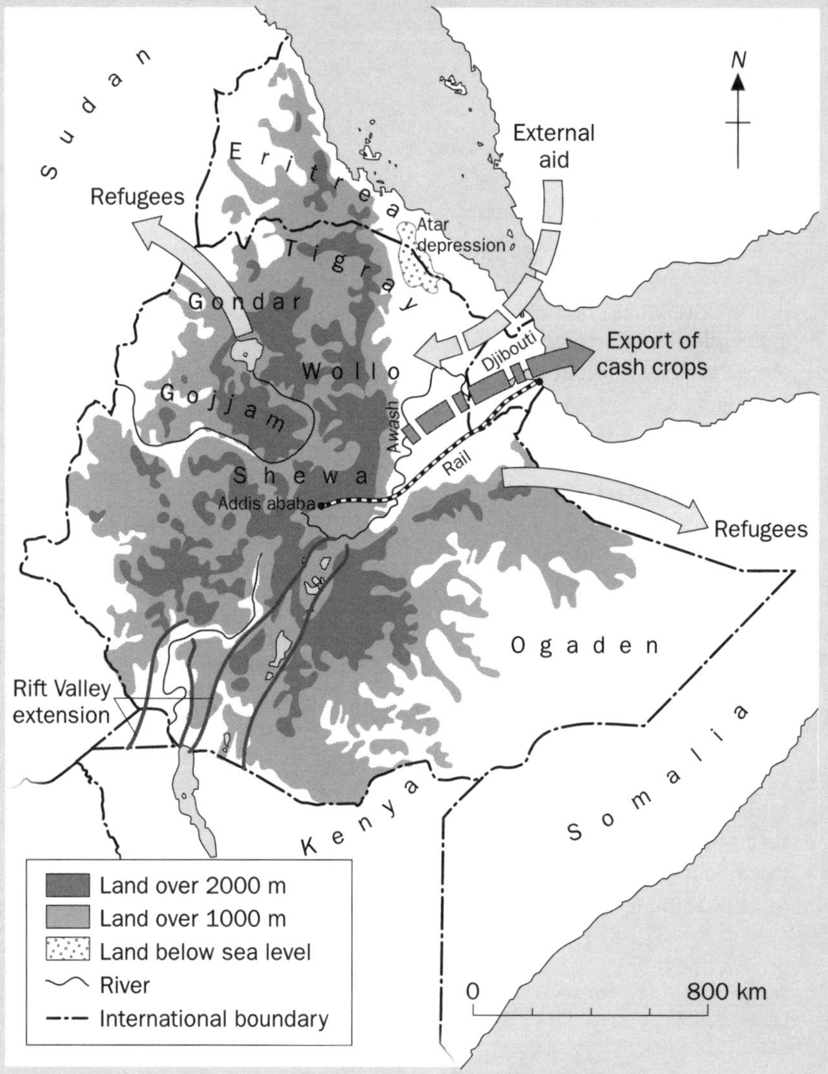

Ethiopia

Causes of a deepening problem

The increasing population is pressuring the sensitive environment. Much of the country is heavily dissected highland. The monsoon rain is adequate but much of it is lost due to run-off. Also, most of the land belongs to a few elite, leaving the peasants with small fragmented holdings. Livestock grazing and increasing deforestation accelerates soil erosion.

On the drier lowland coastal areas, pastoral nomads have been forced out from the wetter Awash River by commercial irrigation for sugar and cotton to areas where overgrazing was already occurring.

The government is unsympathetic to the needs of the rural population. The inequalities left over from the imperial regime have not yet been corrected by the socialist government. The forced rural resetlement from the north to the south has been unsuccessful.

There is too little external aid partly due to the West's suspicion of Marxist ideals and a lack of the means of communications to distribute aid. Some of the aid is diverted to the black market. There is a desperate need for long-term support and to reverse environmental degradation.

case study

7.3 **Zimbabwe: towards food security and rural development**

General

Zimbabwe, with a population of 10.4 million, is one of the more advanced African states. Even here population growth rate remains high at between 2.8% and 3.1% annually, but it has the capacity to support this growth. Although the north-west and south-east have low and unreliable rainfall and relatively poor soils, the rest of the country including the Highveld central belt has more reliable rainfall and better soils.

The Highveld was occupied by white settlers in the colonial period beginning in the 1890s and is now the most prosperous region economically. (Harare, the present capital, has a population of approximately 1.4 million.) It contrasts with the poorer communal land areas allocated to the African peasants. There is a strong regional disparity between the white 'commercial areas' and the communal lands.

Since independence the socialist black African government has tried to redress the balance but is still heavily dependent on the commercial export sector (tobacco, cotton, ferro alloys and other metals, including gold) and investment from outside, including multinational companies.

The country is landlocked and relies on export routes through neighbouring countries, including South Africa.

The problem

A crucial problem for the government (under President Mugabe) has been trying to reduce the widening gap between population growth and food supplies.

Special attention has been given to reducing poverty and food shortages in rural areas. Because of shortage of finance due to overseas debt and a continued reliance on the commercial sector developed under colonialism, the government has had to move slowly to redress some of the worst distortions left over from a white settler colonial economy.

The most notable imbalance is the income difference between, on the one hand, the remaining white population and an emergent black African 'middle class' in the towns and the commercial farming areas, and on the other hand, the majority of the black population. Some are in low-paid employment in the towns, in mining and on commercial farms, but most are in the communal lands (4 million) and rely mainly on subsistence agriculture with a small amount of cash cropping, plus remittances from relatives in the commercial sector. These communal areas are the poorest and most overcrowded which, because of low and unreliable rainfall, are the hardest hit in drought periods, such as that of 1991 – 92.

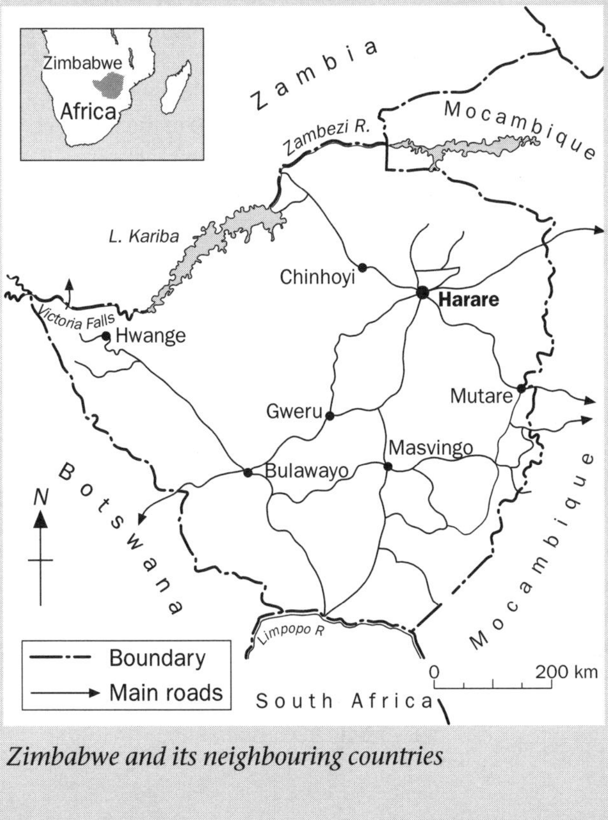

Zimbabwe and its neighbouring countries

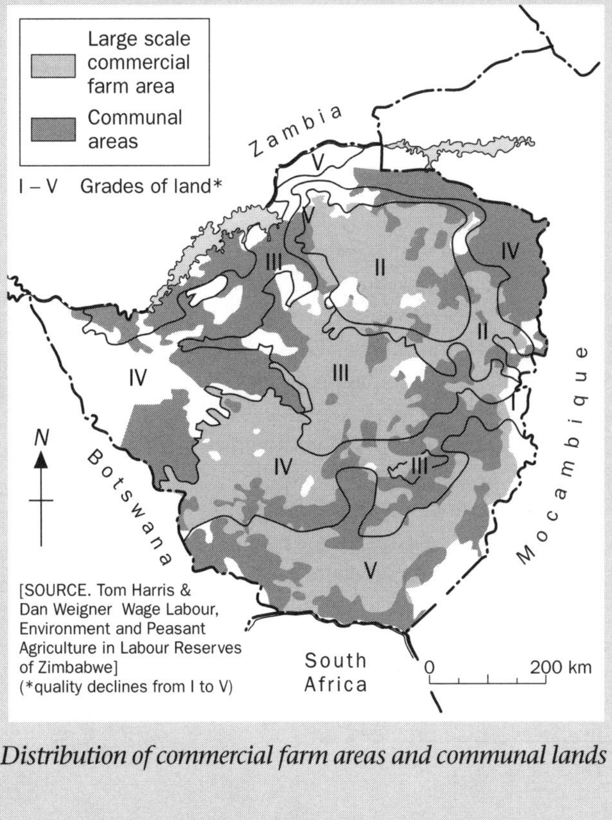

Distribution of commercial farm areas and communal lands

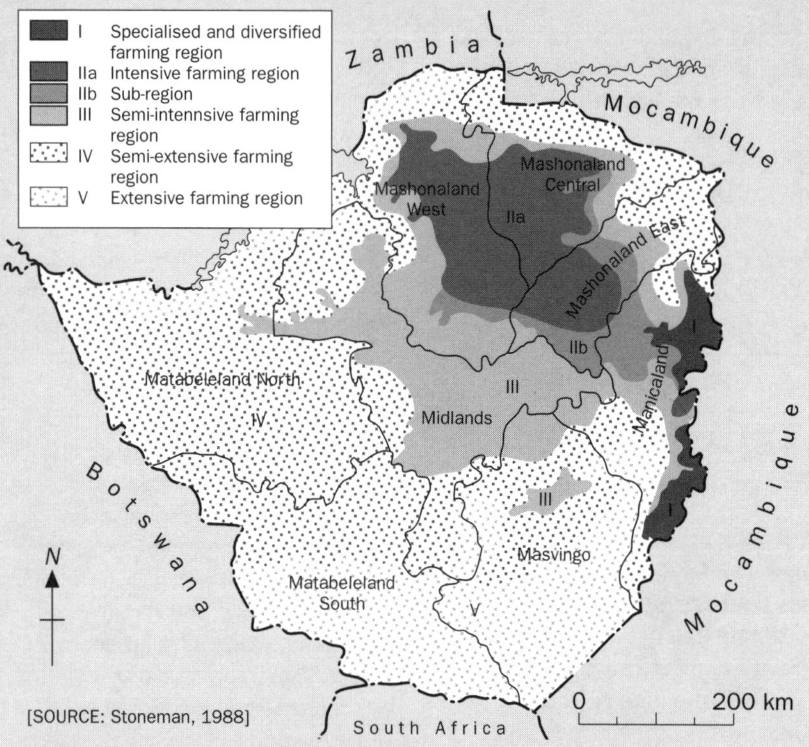

Farming regions based on rainfall, reliability, soil quality and type

The agricultural sectors

The socialist government inherited a 'dual structure' economy.

A large-scale commercial sector, dominated by white farmers, occupies the better watered land in the east and north-east of the country and produces cash crops of maize, tobacco and cotton, using advanced farming techniques, mechanisation and black labour. Nearer Harare, dairying, fruit and vegetables are also important. Other commercial areas are located in parts of the highlands in the east. Further south, a drier area is given over mainly to commercial ranching near Bulawayo, but also includes irrigated areas which concentrates on sugar production, such as the Hippo Valley. This sector covers 32% of the land, much of which is considered under utilised but provides essential export revenue. It also provides employment for a large yet diminishing black labour force.

In contrast are the 'communal lands', formerly the Tribal Trust Lands, reserved for the black rural population and mainly devoted to subsistence agriculture. Because most of the male population is away as migrant labour to supplement family incomes, most of the work is left to women, the young and the elderly, except at planting and harvesting times. Each family is usually allocated a 5 to 6 hectare fragmented holding on which to grow maize, millet or vegetables. There is also access to the communal grazing lands for draught animals and other livestock, mainly cattle and goats. Cultivation methods are traditional and, until recently, there was little outside advice or financial assistance. Some cash crop production is now encouraged but has only been successful in areas accessible to markets. The government is beginning to establish collection depots in more remote areas.

Two serious problems have arisen largely due to increasing pressure of population: a relative increase in rural poverty and widespread land degradation due to over-exploitation of the land, especially in the more vulnerable areas with uncertain rainfall and poor soils. Exhaustion of existing cultivated lands, expansion into marginal areas, overgrazing and deforestation in search of building timber and fuelwood, have led to widespread soil erosion, further reducing crop yields.

The solution

Land redistribution and resettlement

Up until 1990, the government has been limited by the Independence Agreement on how much land could be transferred from the white commercial sector to the black rural peasants. By 1990, approximately 3 million hectares had been bought, upon which 40 000 of the intended target of 162 000 have been settled. Some of the land redistribution is for cooperatives but more commonly in a resettlement scheme, each family is given 5 to 6 hectares plus communal grazing rights. Some cash cropping is encouraged with the provision of loan credit, support services and access to a marketing depot. These resettlements and other African farmed areas are now making a significant contribution to Zimbabwe's cash crop output, especially in maize and cotton production, for example, providing half of the 1990 maize delivery to the Marketing Board. However, the resettlement scheme is behind schedule and much more needs to be done.

In the drier south, irrigation schemes are also being initiated to raise output.

Transfer of population

Transfer of surplus population takes place from communal areas to the towns to work in the growing service and manufacturing sectors. There are already problems of unemployment and an acute housing shortage in urban areas. Thus the extent to which this can contribute to relieving population pressure in the communal land areas is currently very limited.

CARD (Co-ordinated Agricultural and Rural Development)

Possibly the most promising policy is that of the Coordinated Agricultural and Rural Development programmes in the communal lands. The aim is not to impose western-style development, but ' to use a development in partnership with peasant farmers to improve the existing economic base and way of living.

The emphasis is on a comprehensive package to improve agriculture on existing land, to introduce conservation measures and to improve the quality of life through better health, sanitation and on improved water supply. Infrastructures are also improved and, where needed, the settlement pattern is re-ordered. Attention is given to the promotion of rural industries. Women are important contributors to redevelopment schemes not only because of their involvement but because it is estimated that 20% of communal households are headed by women.

As part of a CARD programme, a German team is working with the communal population in the Gutu district, for example, to reduce the cultivated area, improve yields on the better land, improve grazing land using a paddock system and carry out an agro-forestry programme. **It is seen as a linked programme:**

Increased yields on a reduced area -> Fewer draught animal needed -> Excess livestock sold plus improved herds -> More cash income to invest in better methods -> Improved ecological balance -> Sustainable development.

SADCC and external influences

Zimbabwe as a pivotal state has joined with its neighbours to form the trading and economic bloc of SADCC (South African Development Co-ordination Conference) now joined by South Africa. Zimbabwe exports manufactured goods and surplus maize stock ensuring food security in Botswana and Zambia, for example. It is itself dependent on foreign markets, investment, aid and expertise from outside the country, however.

At present the country is suffering from a serious balance of trade problem and a shortage of foreign currency, which limits the import of manufactured goods, including capital equipment and machine parts needed to improve output in its different economic sectors.

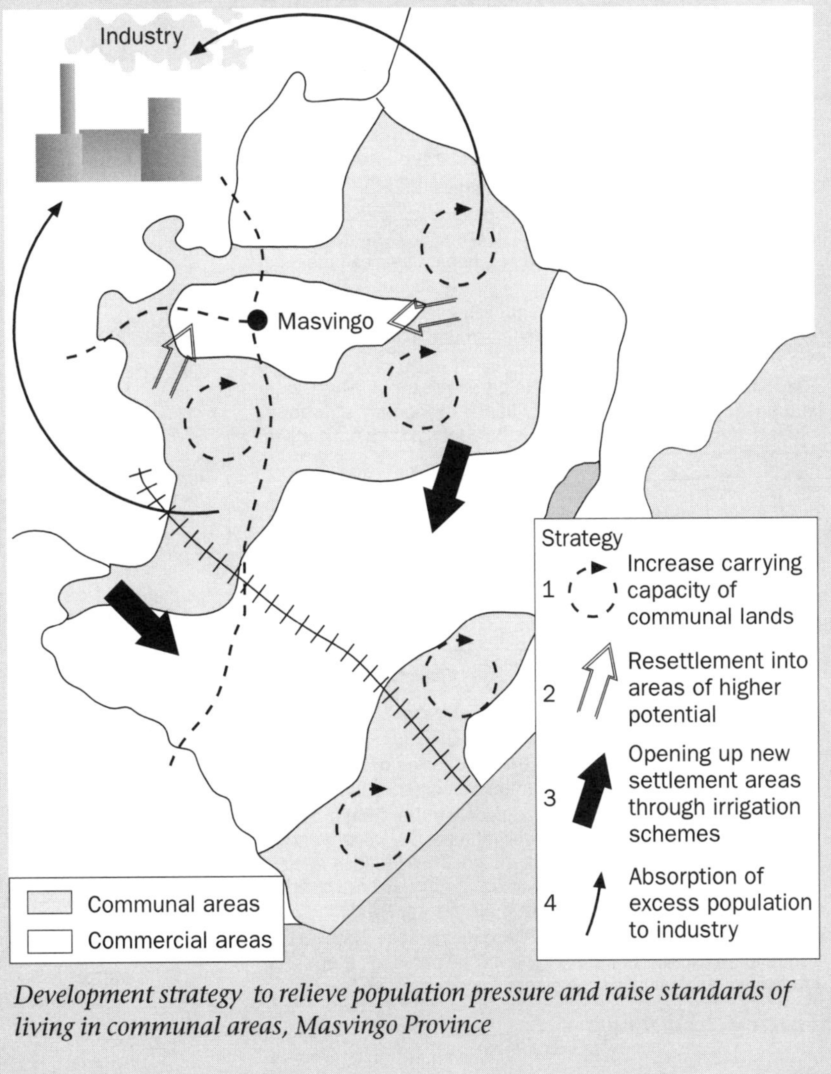

Development strategy to relieve population pressure and raise standards of living in communal areas, Masvingo Province

8

CHAPTER 8

Poverty and health

'World Bank public declarations over the past thirty years have pointed to constant improvements in the health sector of the Third World. But "improvements" in health in many countries have slowed down or stopped altogether as of the early 1980s.'

THE WORLD – A THIRD WORLD GUIDE 1995 – 96

8.1 **The problem**

Poverty and hunger are clearly linked to health. The malnutrition which results from poverty makes the population more susceptible to disease which is the main cause of higher mortality in developing countries. Other important factors include diseases associated with contaminated water and poor sanitation (Figure 8.1).

Proper hygiene and sanitation is at least as important as clean water in combatting the worst water- and dirt-related diseases.

Oral-faecal diseases

Examples: diarrhoeas and dysenteries, including cholera, E. coli diarrhoea, salmonellosis, giardiasis, amoebic dysentery: enteric fevers such as typhoid; poliomyelitis, hepatitis A; ascariasis, trichuriasis.

Disease toll: 5 million children under the age of five die annually of dehydration caused by diarrhoea; around 100 million people suffer diarrhoea at any one time.

Prevention: Sometimes the bug is carried in the drinking water and passed on that way but dirty hands or food are at least as often to blame. Washing is very important.

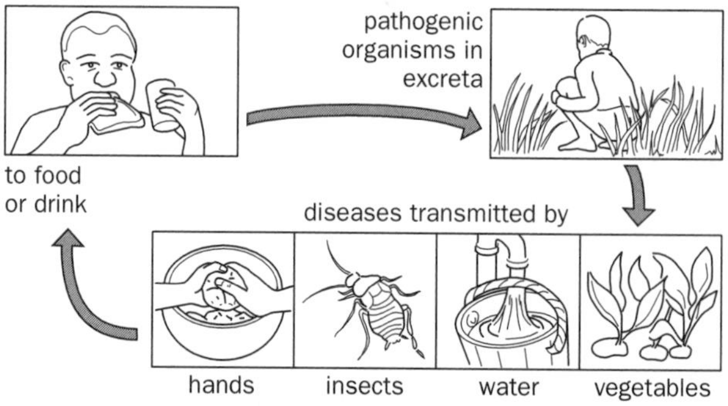

Water-based diseases

Examples: schistosomiasis (bilharzia), transmitted by water snails; guinea worm (dracumculiasis), transmitted by water flea.

Disease toll: 200 million people suffer from the lassitude of schistosomiasis, mostly those living near slow-moving bodies of water; 10 million suffer from guinea worm and are out of action for the painful weeks of the worm's emergence throught the skin.

Prevention: Avoid wading in the water or imbibing it; clear the snails or fleas from the water source; strain drinking water.

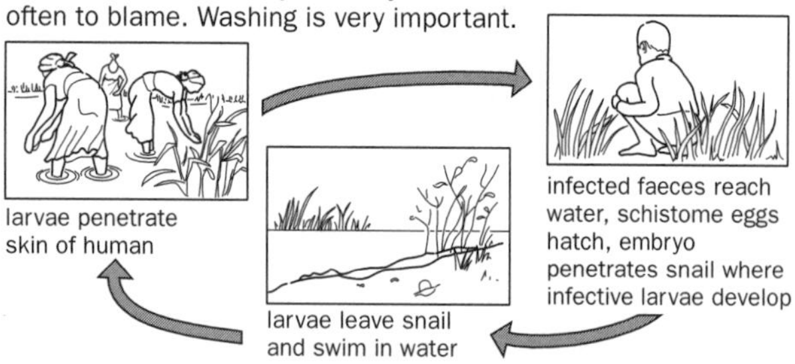

Water insect-related diseases

Examples: malaria, sleeping sickness, river blindness, yellow fever. All are spread by flying insects – certain species of fly and mosquito – which breed in or bite near water.

Disease toll: Each year 800 million people suffer from malaria, one of the most pervasive and debilitating of the world's economic diseases. It kills one million children under two in Africa each year. One million people suffer from river blindness (onchocerciasis) carried by blackfly, of which 340000 are already blind.

Prevention: The vectors – the flies and mosquitos – have to be controlled by spraying and drainage: or the parasites they carry eradicated by eliminating the disease in humans.

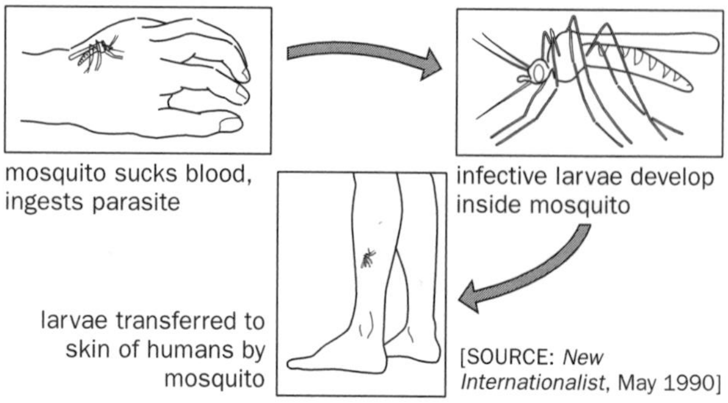

[SOURCE: *New Internationalist*, May 1990]

Figure 8.1 *Killer Bugs*

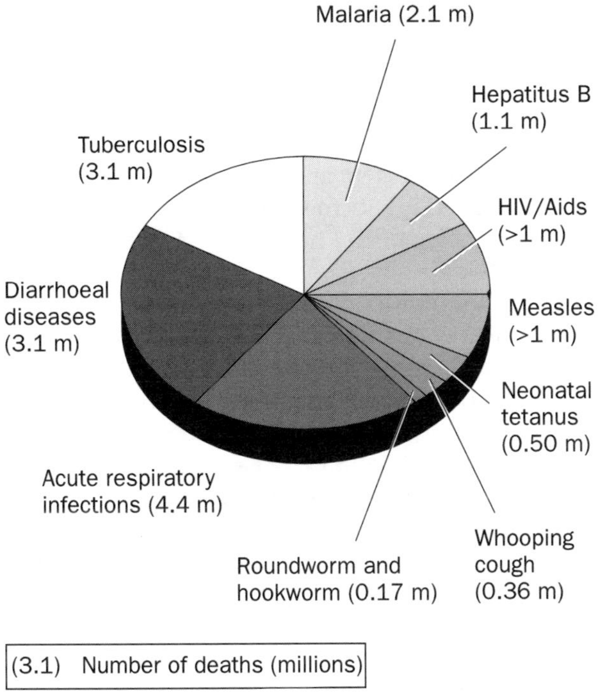

[SOURCE: *Financial Times* 20.05.96]

Figure 8.2 *The ten biggest infectious killers in 1995*

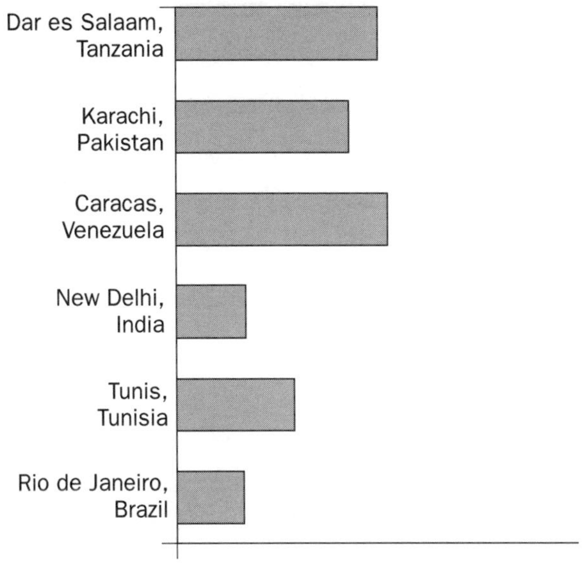

NOTE: Squatter housing is defined as the per cent of the total housing stock in an urban area that is currently occupying land illegally.

[SOURCE: World Bank, 1993]

Figure 8.3 *Squatter housing as a percentage of total housing stock for selected cities, 1990*

Causes

An estimated 25 000 people die every day through not having access to pure drinking water. Disease-carrying insects, such as mosquitoes and various species of fly, breed in contaminated water and poor sanitary conditions. Malaria, carried by mosquitoes, is widespread (Figure 8.2); it affects up to 400 million people and causes the death of five million each year. Malaria and diseases associated with dehydration and diarrhoea are particularly responsible for the high infant mortality rates in a number of developing countries. In Bangladesh, for example, which has one of the highest infant mortality rates in Asia (108 per 1000), 29% of infant deaths are associated with diarrheal diseases directly related to the poor quality and poor management of water. One of the recent disease infections associated with contaminated water, has been the cholera epidemics in South America and Africa in 1991 and 1992. African countries reported a nine-fold increase in the incidence of the disease in 1991 compared with previous years. Nigeria was particularly badly affected.

The eradication of poverty and inequality lies at the heart of progress on health care. Poor housing conditions, another major cause of poor health, is particularly effective in the crowded shanty-type settlements in some cities of the developing world (Figure 8.3). Poor ventilation and overcrowding lead to respiratory diseases and tubercolosis.

8.2 **Solutions**

The basis of the health problem lies in the unequal distribution of and the wrong kind of the health care provided. Much of the limited funds for health care is centred on the wealthier people in the cities, while the poorer rural areas are neglected. For example, in Peru, two thirds of the doctors practise in the capital Lima while in the rural areas there is only one doctor for every 10 000 people.

Most of the health care spending goes on hospital care and curing rather than on the prevention of disease. International agencies, such as the World Health Organisation (WHO) and the United Nations Children's Fund (UNICEF), believe that the way to reduce widespread disease and lower mortality rates is through preventative measures. Countries are encouraged to adopt programmes of primary health care similar to the Chinese Health Model (Case study 8.1). This can only be achieved if there is continued International Community Aid and a commitment to Primary Health Care by governments of developing countries. This should include:

- a programme for health care
- a family planning programme since high fertility rates would put pressures on health services, reducing the benefits of any attempt at community health care
- development of an infrastructure network to enable health care to reach more remote areas

The UN International Drinking Water Supply and Sanitation Decade was launched to provide 'water and sanitation for all by 1990'. This ambitious target was never realisable and 300 million more people lacked sanitation in 1990 than in 1980. But in percentage terms there has been some progress, especially with water: 50% of people in rural areas now have an adequate water supply compared with only 30% ten years ago.

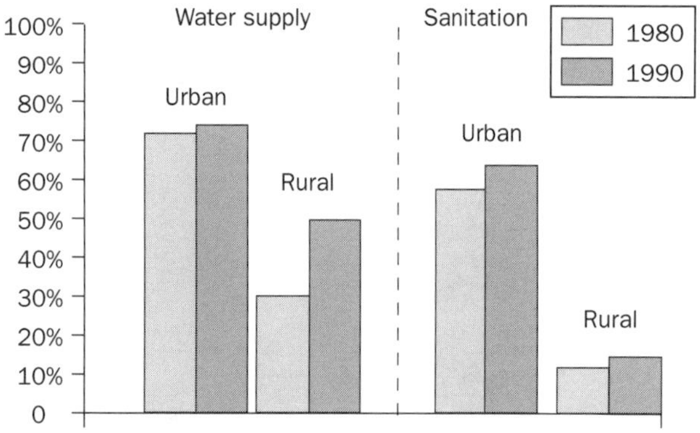

Figure 8.4 *Some progress*

- an education campaign to persuade the poorer people to avail themselves of any facilities provided and change their personal habits. For example, it has been observed in Bangladesh that villagers may shun a piped water supply, preferring to walk to a polluted well supply because, traditionally, it is not only a source of water but also of gossip.

Barefoot doctors wage war on Brazil's other child killers'

'The brutal killing of eight street children in Rio recently thrust Brazil into the headlines, but many more children are being claimed by a lower-profile killer. Victims of a woeful lack of basic sanitation and inadequate food, 30 000 die each year in the country's impoverished north east for want of minimum health care'.

But 'one of the country's poorest states is showing that with political will it is possible to improve the situation.

In just three years the north eastern state of Ceara has slashed infant mortality rates by a third through a cheap and simple project of door to door basic health care'.

Although the health agents, (visiting door to door, many of them semi-literate young women), are paid by the state government, they are chosen by the communities.

'Success has bred acceptance and the new governor has expanded the scheme to 7300 agents attending 4 million people.'

[SOURCE: Christina Lamb *Financial Guardian* 1993]

Primary Health Care must involve the people at a local level. It requires their support and participation. The success of the Chinese Primary Health Care Programme has been largely due to the decentralisation of health care from centralised and bureaucratic control to involvement at village level, using simple techniques and locally trained people.

Where these policies have been adopted, progress has already been made. Since 1978 for example, International Community Aid, using affordable low technology child survival techniques such as mass immunisation programmes and oral rehydration therapy (ORT), has brought about a unique public health revolution in countries willing to cooperate.

Countries committed to Primary Health Care programmes such as Sri Lanka, Cuba and Costa Rica have particularly benefited. Over the developing world, 60% of young children are now immunised as opposed to only 5% in 1970. Much more still needs to be done, however. Current progress is already under threat due to growing debt and inflation, resulting in cuts in public spending (Figure 8.5) and political instability. The problems are noticeable in Central America, for example, where much progress had been made.

Change in proportions of government spending between 1972 and 1986

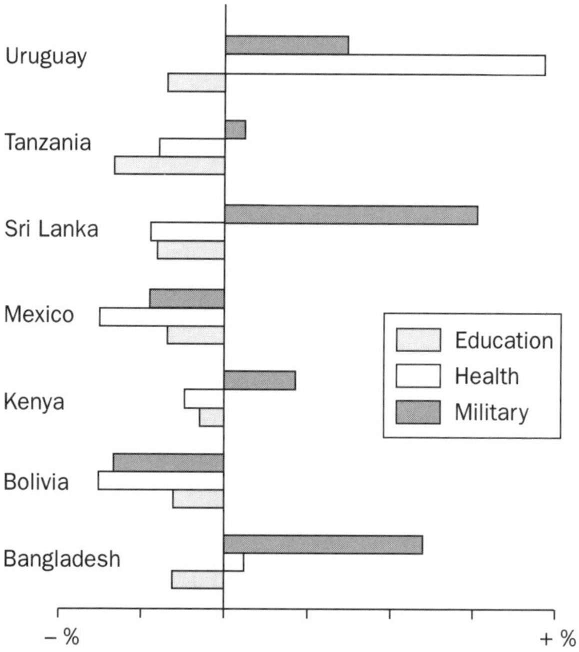

Third World governments have been forced by the debt crisis and IMF policies to cut their public spending. But they have all too often done this by cutting health and education, while spending more on arms.

[SOURCE: *New Internationalist*, 1989]

Figure 8.5 *Social spending slashed*

8.3 Health in advanced countries

Stress and over indulgence

While the high level of health care enjoyed by the people of advanced countries contrasts starkly with those in the developing world, advanced countries are not without health concerns albeit of a different character and scale to those of the poorer nations.

Life expectancy and mortality rates have reached a plateau within advanced countries. While great progress has been made in preventative medicine, ill health associated with the stress and over indulgences of modern life remains a problem (Figure 8.7).

In developed countries, the smoking of tobacco is rated as the main single cause of death. For example, it is estimated that in Europe between 500 000 to 800 000 die each year from smoke related conditions. Amongst every 1000 young males, only one will die from murder, six by death on the roads but 250 will die from tobacco smoke, mainly through lung cancer.

The second most serious health problem is that of heart and liver failures due to stress and over indulgence. In contrast, the much feared AIDS disease (Acquired Immune Deficiency Syndrome) is a relatively minor cause of death in terms of numbers. It poses a serious potential threat, however. In 1990, only 204 000 cases were reported world wide but by the end of the decade, the death toll is likely to be 400 000, mainly in sub-Saharan Africa and Europe.

While there are concerns over health hazards from over-use of pesticides, toxic gases and the dumping radio active waste, the number of people affected is relatively small. However, as with many diseases and other health hazards in developed countries, much of the ill health from cancer and heart and liver failure is preventable. It is largely a matter of commitment to adopt the necessary health care measures. The same is true of the more recent threats from AIDS and pesticide and toxic poisoning. Despite increased awareness from the influence of pressure groups and media coverage, commitment has not improved significantly as yet.

Unequal access to health care

While most people in advanced countries do enjoy better health care than those in developing countries, there is still a disadvantaged sector who find it difficult to obtain basic health care. Most disadvantaged are to be found in the rundown inner city areas of large conurbations. Frequently, ethnic minorities suffer, but the elderly and single parent families are also affected (Section 14.2; Case study 14.2).

In 1991, 20% of American children were living in poverty and, according to official reports, this was linked mainly to the increasing number of single parent households, especially in inner city areas.

'In inner city areas only about one half of young children had been immunised against measles, mumps and rubella as against 70% in the nation as a whole.'

Concluding comment

Clearly there needs to be progress generally on health care, but as has been emphasised throughout this section on population and the quality of living, the eradication of poverty lies at the heart of any such progress.

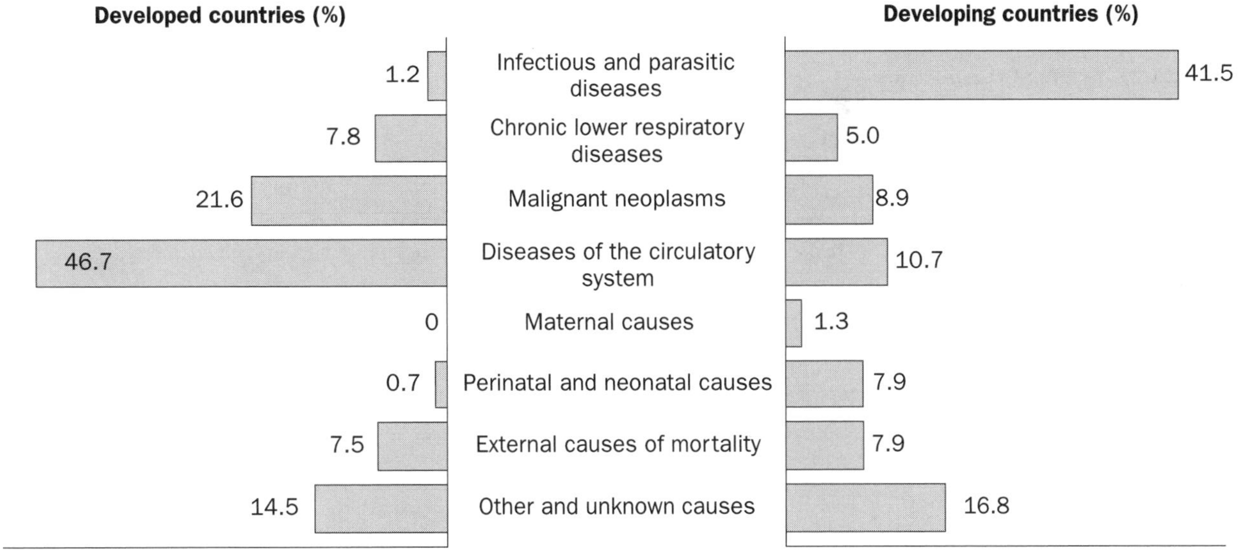

[SOURCE: World Resources 1996]

Figure 8.7 Causes of death in developed and developing countries, 1993

case study

8.1 China's primary health care

'China's remarkable performance owes as much to safe drinking water, improved sewage disposal and other sanitation measures as to broad immunisation cover and mass campaigns against parasitic diseases. It has much to do with the provision of basic health care and affordable drugs to even the remote parts of the country. It reflects the successful drive to reduce fertility and to increase through the age of first delivery (of a child) as well as great efforts to provide eduction on health and nutrition. And it would have been impossible without a safety net that among other things guaranteed minimum food rations for even the poorest people.'

WORLD DEVELOPMENT REPORT, *SOCIAL SECTOR POLICIES*, 1990

'It teaches us an important general lesson – large improvements in health care can be achieved if there is a broad and lasting commitment.'

'Social progress is not merely a by-product of economic development. Policies matter – the need is for strong government intervention based on long-term commitment to social progress.'

The Chinese health care model

Pre-1949, China's mortality and poor health figures attested to the wide occurrence of poverty and suffering. By 1956, however, under a Communist regime, China had virtually eradicated the most prevalent communicable diseases and built up a strong preventative network in both urban and rural areas across the whole country.

Success was based on four health care principles, which together became known as the *Chinese Health Care Model*, now regarded as a possible guide to community health schemes in other countries.

- The same type of health care for all
- Prevention to receive priority
- Uniting of Western and traditional medicine
- Community participation in health care including:
- mass campaigns in which all people are production units in ridding the country of disease carriers
- mass health education
- 'Barefoot Doctor' policy i.e. a part-time health worker chosen by and responsible to the community to undertake general health care. (However, from the 1980s, private doctors and hospitals were also encouraged).

Indices of health progress	1965	1990
Infant mortality	90	27 per 1000
Daily calories per capita	1926	2630
Population per physician	1600	1000
Primary education	–	98%
Life expectancy	23	70
Birth rate	38	21 per 1000
Fertility rate	6.4	2.3

Health indices

9

CHAPTER 9

Inequality between men and women

'In the world of women there are few developed nations.'

SEAGAR J AND OLSEN A *WOMEN IN THE DEVELOPED WORLD*, 1986

'What we do see is that everywhere women have less power, less autonomy, more work, less money and more responsibility. Women have a smaller share of the pie. Women in richer countries have a higher standard of living than do women in poorer countries, but nowhere are women equal with men.'

'Women are the world's largest excluded group.'

HUMAN DEVELOPMENT REPORT, 1993

Although the United Nations declared the decade of 1975 – 1985 the 'United Nations' Decade for Women', progress towards equality with men remains slow. Women constitute half the world's population and do 65% of the work hours undertaken, but they receive only 10% of the world's income and own less than 1% of the world's property.

Much of the literature is about inequality and exploitation of women in the developing world, but inequality is also marked in advanced countries.

9.1 **Women in advanced countries**

In most advanced countries women are deemed to have equal rights and opportunities, but in reality, much open and indirect discrimination occurs.

Women are largely disregarded but indispensable to the economy

In the planning of economies and the management of the environment, little regard has been given to the views and needs of women, since it has been assumed that their role in society is restricted to the home. The literature provides a male-centred view of the world, in which men are the producers in the economy and organisers of society while women play a purely reproductive and supporting role.

Since the end of World War II, an increasing number of women have taken on part-time or full-time paid employment and are indispensable to the running of the economy. An increasing number of women are entering the workforce in Britain. In 1971, women formed 32% of the workforce; 30% of married women went out to work. In 1991 in comparison, women formed 36% of the workforce; 42% of married women went out to work (Case study 9.1).

The participation of women in public life has also dramatically increased. Some women hold prominent positions, despite the difficulties they faced when seeking access to wider opportunities.

'In Britain as elsewhere it was clear that by the 1970s that as firms were relocating their activities the existence of 'pools' of potential female employees who would provide a low cost and many believed tractable and dextrous labour force was acting as an important element attracting firms to new towns and suburbs, old industrial and rural areas, all of which had low rates of female employment.'

[Bowlby S *Feminist Geography and the Changing Curriculum*, 1992]

The difficulties and problems

Although half the women aged between 18 and 64 years have paid work, most are in lower paid jobs. The average wage for women is significantly less than that for men. The problem is particularly acute for women in inner cities who work in small businesses, often run under 'sweat shop' conditions, as in the garment-making and electrical assembly work in the East End of London and inner Birmingham. Others are forced into unskilled work such as office cleaning or shop work, usually because:

- Laws related to pay and conditions are insufficiently enforced.

- Choice of work is limited due to women being less mobile than men. Women are more reliant on public transport but because of fare increases, they have to take jobs nearer home. A recent survey in Peterlee, a new town in north-east England, indicates that difficulties over transport are the main reasons why women have had to accept lower paid local work.
- Choice of jobs is limited because the hours which many women are available for work are controlled by home and family responsibilities.
- In most countries, a low priority is given to the provision of nursery and child-minding facilities which would enable more women to go out to work and accept a wider choice of jobs.

'A recent survey of social attitudes in Britain (in Social Trends 1987) revealed that in 72% of households where both partners were in full-time employment, women continued to do most of the domestic work. The acceptance of a woman's right to work outside the home does not yet appear to have translated itself into a sense of egalitarianism in the allocation of tasks within the home.'
[SOURCE: McDowell L *Life without father and Ford – the new gender order of post Fordism*, 1991]

Women have limited access to leisure facilities and fewer opportunities to participate in a range of public activities, partly because of the more limited employment opportunities but also because of active discrimination.

This reinforces the dominantly patriarchal forms of social organisation as, for example, in politics and planning. If greater equality is to be achieved, it requires a fundamental change in the political and social organisation of society to allow women an equal voice in the decision taking processes.

9.2 **Women in developing countries**

'They are the providers of food, fuel and water and often of the whole family income – the sustainers and developers of their families, communities and countries. The fate of women is a critical determinant of whole societies.'
[SOURCE: Snyder E]

Comparative evidence shows that the socio-economic position of women in the developing world is worsening, despite the increasing efforts of international and private agencies. In addition to the widely held traditional view of women as 'second class citizens' whose main role is to bear children, governments over recent years have cut back on the welfare and educational expenditure which was beginning to improve conditions for women. These cutbacks are part of the governments' efforts to cope with their growing debts and budget deficits (Case study 9.2).

Initiatives for progress

An increasing number of initiatives are being taken to reverse the worsening trend. For example, womens' movements are lobbying for the International Convention on the Elimination of All Forms of Discrimination Against Women to be incorporated in national government legislation. As a result of strong lobbying, this Women's Convention was incorporated into the 1991 Colombian Constitution. As in advanced countries, however, there remains a large gap between the equality cited in legislation and the actual position of women in the real life of a country.

The achievement of greater equality and more opportunity for women is linked to wider issues, such as poverty in the developing world and the

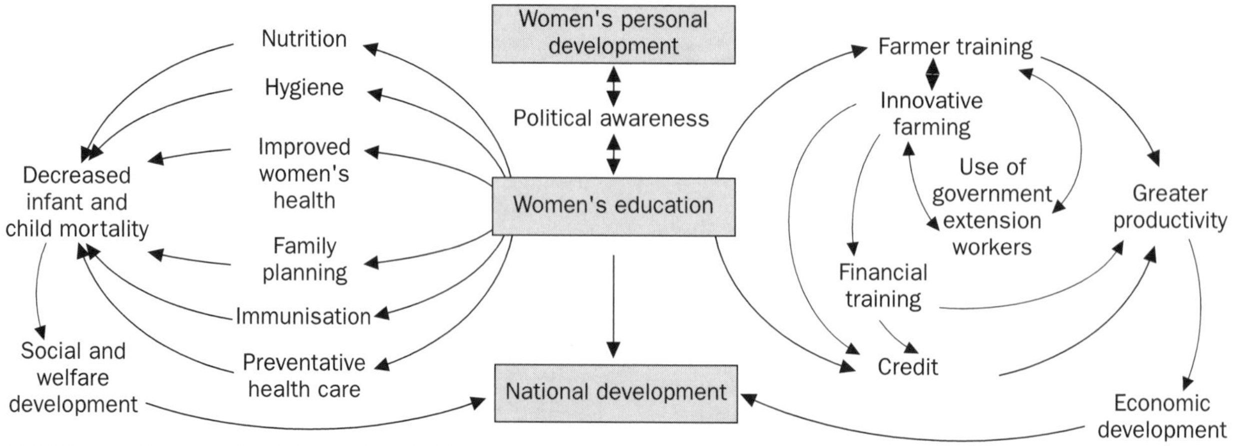

[SOURCE: Angela Browne and Hazel Barrett *Women's Education in Sub-Sahara Africa, Geographical Review 17*, 1994]

***Figure 9.1** Links between women's education and aspects of development*

environmental degradation, which destroys the basic resources upon which sustainable development depends. Consequently, women's movements at all levels increasingly focus on the contribution women can make to resolving these kinds of problems. The new international movement, DAWN (Development Alternative With Women For a New Era), is an example. The Chipco Andolan Movement in India is led mainly by women and is aimed at preventing further destruction of local forests which most households depend upon for wood fuel. Saving the forests would also prevent increased water run-off and further soil erosion.

Advancing the position of women

The cause of women needs advancement on three interrelated fronts:

Meeting the needs of individuals

Better basic health care reduces the risks associated with child bearing. Sixteen and a half million illnesses result from child birth and half a million women die in child birth each year. Women in developing countries have more pregnancies than women in developed countries but poorer pre-natal and post natal health care.

Progress in health care means greater government commitment and funding and also allowing women more say in family size. A recent World Fertility Survey of the most populous countries found that women would have two fewer children than at present if the decision was left to them.

Studies show that the focus of governments and international agencies regarding women's health has been directed towards birth and fertility control in an effort to reduce population growth. Other aspects of women's health remains neglected, in particular, the effects of hard labour. Many women have to combine child bearing with heavy household chores, working in the fields or on assembly lines in factories.

Improving women's education raises their awareness, self confidence, and their ability to engage in decision making. It has been shown, for example, that where educational opportunities are increased, child bearing is delayed to a later age. Women also have a better understanding of family planning and basic health care.

Significant progress in the proportion of girls with being given primary education has been made since the 1960s, but the proportion of girls having access to secondary and higher education is less (Figure 9.2). This reflects the subordinate role which women play and the overwhelming influence of men in decision making in society.

Equal rights and equal access to opportunities

Equal rights and equal access to opportunities differs between rural and urban areas. In rural areas it is generally acknowledged that women bear a greater labour load than men. In respect of survival tasks for the houshold, they do most of the cultivation of food crops, the collecting of wood fuel and the carrying of water. On average, it is estimated that over a year, women in Tanzania do 3069 hours of work compared to 1829 hours by men.

Advances in agriculture have tended to lengthen the working day for women. Better and more accessible land has in some areas been given over to cash crops and women have to work more marginal land at a greater distances from the village. This involves more time walking to the fields and lower yields in return for their efforts.

Despite their involvement in cultivating the land, women's rights to land ownership have been restricted. *'Under colonialism traditional inheritance laws and communal rights to land which once allowed access by women have been replaced by title deed systems which by law or custom restrict land ownership to man.'* (Women and Environment in the Third World). After independence when land reform measures and cooperative movements were

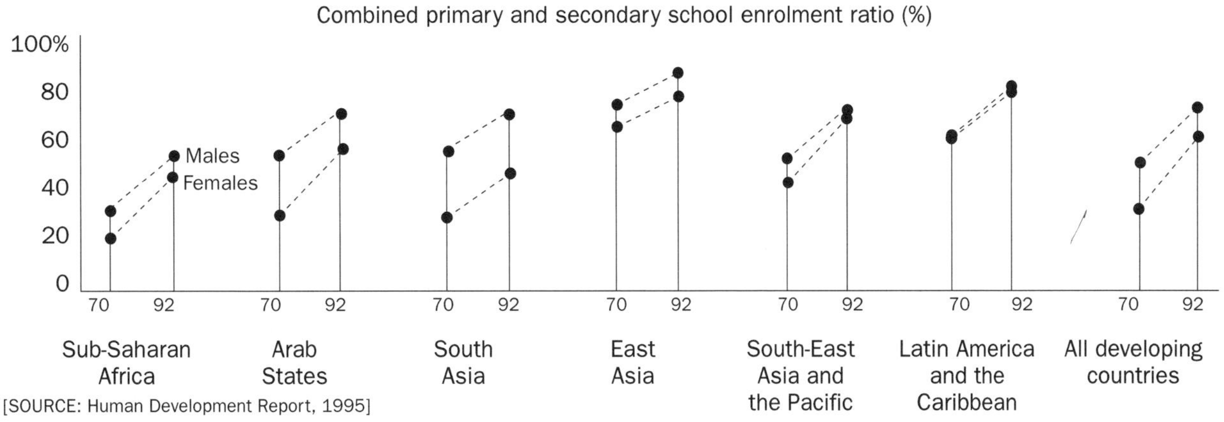

***Figure 9.2** Schooling for males and females, 1970 and 1992*

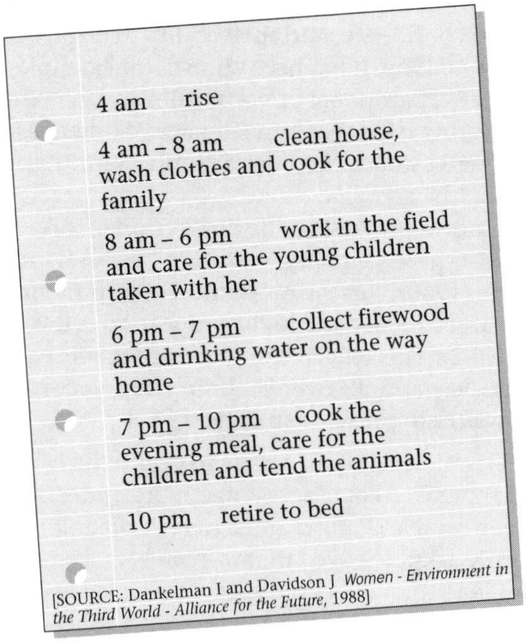
4 am rise

4 am – 8 am clean house, wash clothes and cook for the family

8 am – 6 pm work in the field and care for the young children taken with her

6 pm – 7 pm collect firewood and drinking water on the way home

7 pm – 10 pm cook the evening meal, care for the children and tend the animals

10 pm retire to bed

[SOURCE: Dankelman I and Davidson J *Women - Environment in the Third World - Alliance for the Future*, 1988]

Figure 9.3 *The day's work for a female Indian agricultural worker*

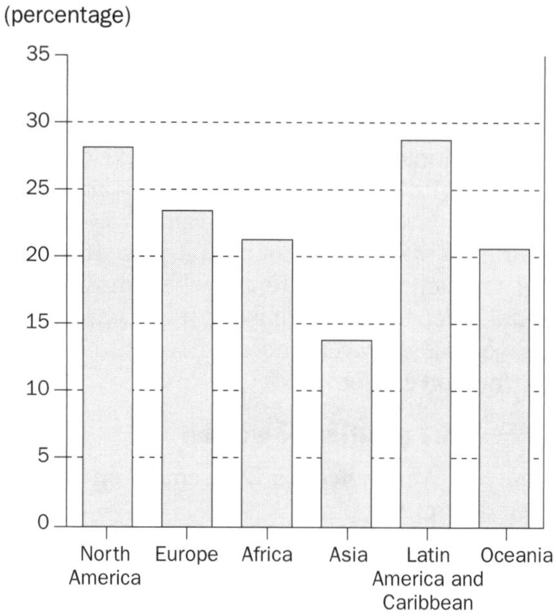

[SOURCE: World Resources 1994 – 95, 1994]

Figure 9.4 *Households headed by women*

introduced, women's land rights were also largely ignored. With the introduction of rural development programmes, women have had little say, despite their long experience of working the land. Now demands for rights to land ownership and participation in decision making are growing. For example, these demands are central to the Rural Association for Progress, concerned with new rural development strategies in the south of Zimbabwe.

While work is as heavy for women in urban areas as in rural areas, the nature of it is different. Many women have to engage in petty trading and other activities to support the household. In newly industrialising countries many women work long hours on factory assembly lines for significantly lower wages than men doing equivalent work.

Access to housing is a crucial issue in urban areas. Increasingly, the emphasis is on self-help strategies to solve the acute shortage. Housing projects are organised on the basis that households would secure ownership or tenure of a plot, basic services would be installed, then households would proceed to build their own homes. Women-headed households have frequently been excluded from such projects due to their subordinate positions in terms of education, income and job security. Applicants usually have to show evidence of an income greater than the lowest 10% of households. Most women, however, receive lower wages than men and fall into the lowest 10% bracket. Many have no job security and therefore cannot get a loan with which to secure a plot site on a housing scheme. Because of poor education, many women are unable to cope with completing the forms or producing the relevant documents needed by the housing authorities.

Following the UN Decade for Women 1975 – 1985, there have been a number of international conferences to ascertain what is needed to bring about more effective progress in developing countries and improve the conditions for women. A policy initiative, known as *Forward Looking Strategies*, has been formulated and includes the fundamental principle that effective development requires the integration of women in development both as agents and beneficiaries. Moser and Peake list a number of reasons why women should be offered a more active role, both at local and national level.

- As individuals they have an equal right as men to policy formulation and implementation.
- Being more involved than men in the day to day life of the community, they have a clearer idea of what improvements are needed.
- It is estimated that around one third of all households are headed by women, either because men are away seeking work or have deserted the family (Figure 9.4).
- More active involvement in development would overcome the apathy and lack of confidence women may feel as a result of the long-standing subjugation and subordinate role imposed on them.

Women as agents of change

The need for women to be involved as agents of change is well illustrated in sub-Saharan Africa, where there is a crucial need for a long-term solution to the food crisis and periodic famines. Policies will not succeed here unless women are actively involved, since it is estimated that they are responsible for 60% of the food produced. They have the best understanding of traditional agriculture and local environmental conditions. In the past, development agencies have imposed methods which have destroyed the traditional system of agriculture.

In the case of the urban sector, one of the crucial needs is to find a solution to the growing squatter housing problem. Research has shown that while local authorities have assumed that men play the dominant role in neighbourhood provision, it is women who have taken the most active part in community management. Women are now more actively involved in politics at a national level. For example until recently, the Prime Ministers of both the Philippines and Pakistan were women.

An international movement, Women in Development (WID), has emerged with international support, but such movements can only be effective if their aims are implemented at a local level. Two such efforts are horticulture initiatives: one is the Golcutta Settlement horticulture initiative in Ethiopia, a joint venture between the Revolutionary Ethiopian Women's Association and the Food and Agricultural Organisation, and the other is supported by the Gambia government, in which a number of garden cooperatives, largely involving women growers, have been set up to supply tourist areas with fruit and vegetables (Case study 9.3).

Concluding comment

Progress towards a greater involvement by women in the development process is still slow.

- Many international agencies and government organisations still cling to the idea that the public domain should be left to men and the domestic to women.
- Most women themselves do not seek a more prominent role in the development process.

case study

9.1 Japan: women and progress towards equality

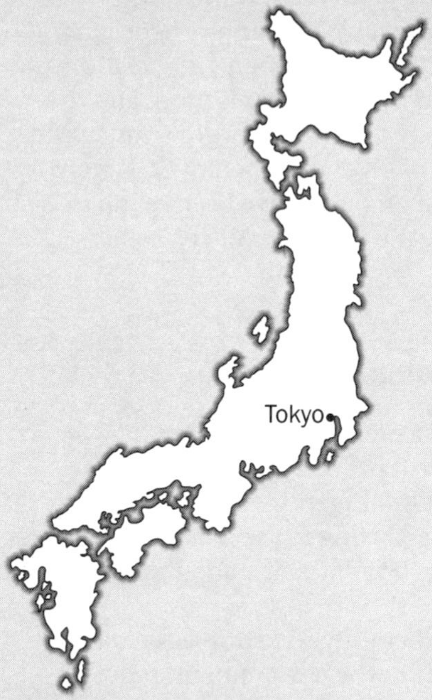

Kinko Sato is only the fifth female public prosecutor in Japan. 'Today,' she says, 'women cannot argue that socially they are in a weaker position than men. They have to grasp what equality is, and understand the difference between discrimination and differentiation.'

1943	Born in Tokyo
1958	Graduated in law from the University of Tokyo
1960	Appointed public prosecutor, Tokyo District Public Prosecutors Office
1970	Research Fellow at Radcliff
1972	Institute and the Law School at Harvard University
1976 – 1977	Served as a representative of the Japanese government at the 31st and 32nd UN General Assemblies
1978 – 1981	Councillor to Prime Minister's Office
1987 –	Board member at NHK (Japan Broadcasting Corporation)
1988	Member of the Japan Association of Corporate Executives.

Historical background

Traditionally women occupied a subordinate role. Their influence was limited to the home and child rearing. Before 1945 the extended family was the norm with the wife being dominated by her husband's parents, in particular her mother-in-law. In rural areas women were expected to work in the fields, in addition to undertaking home duties. In urban areas, the traditional division of roles between men and women was upheld; men dominated work and life outside the home.

Since the end of World War 2 in 1945, there has been progress towards more equality but reality has lagged behind the equality granted by legislation.

Legal equality

Under the new constitution of 1945, all discrimination on the basis of sex, creed, race, social status and family origin was outlawed.

Important progress was made during the United Nations *Decade for Women 1975 – 85* when organisations campaigned to gain equal status for women and increase public awareness of women's rights. In 1980 inheritance laws were altered to increase the inheritance rights of women from one third to half their husbands' property. There was also a break-down in the traditional sex-based division of work with more and more women doing work outside the home as an integral part of their lives. The Equal Opportunities Employment Bill 1986 encourages employers to conform to the principle of equal rights and opportunities.

Progress in reality

Work outside the home

Over 40% of the employed work-force is now female, amounting to 16.7 million. Of these, two-thirds are married, indicating some break-down in the traditional role of men and women. Increasing shortage of labour is likely to bring more women into the workforce, yet the opportunity for advancement of women is limited. Only 7% of administrative and managerial posts are held by women.

Public life

Increasingly since the 1950s women have had greater indepen-dence and freedom. They are now very active in local affairs, such as parent teacher associations, neighbourhood cooperatives and environmental movements. There is also much more opportunity for leisure and educational activities. Participation in national public life is very limited despite newer parties such as the Japan Socialist Party which encourages more women candidates. Japan's largest party, the Liberal Democrat Party, has actively discriminated against women seeking parliamentary seats. Overall, only 2% of the seats are held by women. However, women increasingly influence policy via pressure groups and the ballot.

Home life

Although not the chief decision maker, women have traditionally been dominant in the running of the household and in child rearing. These roles are more important than in other advanced countries because men in Japan spend more time at work and much of their leisure time with work colleagues rather than with the family. (Men devote only 3.4 hours weekly to family matters compared to 22 hours by women.) Despite greater independence, the woman's role in the management of family finance and children's success in an increasingly competitive education system has increased.

Although the traditional division of roles between men and women is disappearing, with more women going out to work, this is not in any sense matched by men taking on more domestic responsibility.

'Despite the lip service paid to equality, women are still subject to overt and hidden discrimination.'

TAMURA R *A YEAR FOR WOMEN*, *LOOK JAPAN*, JANUARY 1990

Summary

Japanese society is today progressing towards greater maturity, albeit rather belatedly, in such areas as equality between the sexes, women's participation in society and legally guaranteed equality in employment opportunities for men and women. Says Sato, 'The days are gone when women can say they are in a socially oppressed position. However, the number of women who can compete with men on an equal footing and display their competence to the full is still small. Problems remain in our society. Today, the only chance women have to compete without handicap is in examinations; there women can exhibit their competence to the full.'

[SOURCE: Kinko Watanabe *Equality Differentials*, *Look Japan*, October 1993]

case study

9.2 **Nepal: women and equality**

General

Nepal, with a population of 10 million, is a remote Hindu kingdom situated between Tibet and India. The northern region forms part of the Himalayas and is very sparsely populated. The central region is a heavily dissected zone which includes the capital of Katmandu. The south covers part of the Ganges valley and is the most populated area. The Ganges drains most of the country.

The population mainly depends on peasant agriculture on fragmented holdings. Nepal is one of the world's poorest countries with a per capita income of only 180 US dollars (1991). The continued population pressure (growth rate 2.5% per annum), with rising food and wood fuel demands, is exhausting the land. This, combined with heavy seasonal rainfall on steep slopes, has led to serious soil erosion problems.

Cultural factors

- The Hindu religion relegates women to a subordinate role.
- Married women and widows have no rights to property or land.

Demographic measures (1990/91)	
Crude birth rate	38/1000
Crude death rate	13/1000
Total fertility rate	4.6
Female life expectancy	51 years

Educational indicators for women (1990)	
Enrolment in primary school	43% of those eligible
Enrolment in secondary school	17% of those eligible
Literacy rate for 15 – 24 age group	15%

- Within the household women occupy a subordinate role and have little influence over the household's economic resources or finances.

Economic factors

- From the age of 10 most females are only valued for what they can contribute economically and as child bearers.
- They work at least 40% more hours than men dividing their time between:
  - helping on the land, carting manure, breaking the soil down, planting and weeding, tending the vegetable garden and small livestock,
  - carrying water and wood, the latter from increasing distances due to widespread deforestation,
  - at home cooking, washing, spinning and weaving
  - bringing up children.

Family conditions

Birth and fertility rates are among the highest in the world due to early marriages (average age is 17 years old), the cultural and economic value placed on children and the absence of widespread birth control (only 13% have access to birth control methods). The strain of a large family, a heavy work load and limited medical facilities result in a low life expectancy.

Limited educational opportunity

Despite international aid and a campaign to raise educational standards, primary school enrolment for women is between 40% and 50% less than for men. Except among higher cast Hindus, and in towns, few woman go on to secondary education. Consequently, literacy rates are lower and the opportunity for advancement very limited. While men are increasingly migrating from rural areas to better opportunities in the towns, women are 'anchored' at home, caring for the family and working the land.

Improvement for women

The improvement in the lot of women appears to be linked to greater urbanisation. Women living in Katmandu and the area around have greater educational opportunity and more independence than those in the more remote rural areas. However, at present only 10% of the population is urbanised.

Location of Nepal

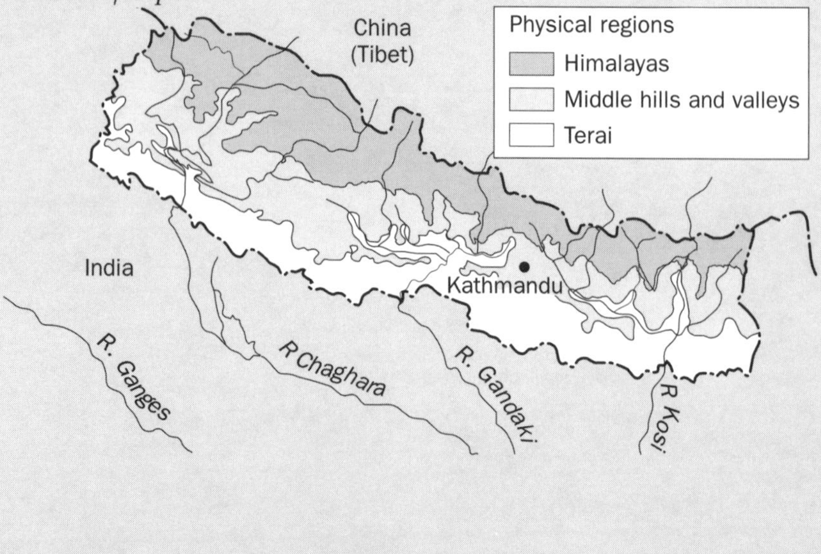

case study

9.3 Gambia: women and the development of the agricultural economy

General

Gambia is one of the smallest African states, (population one million). Its economy is dominated by agriculture, on which 80% of the population are dependent. Until the late 1980s export of groundnuts provided 90% of Gambia's export earnings, providing a narrow and precarious base to the economy due to periodic drought and fluctuating world prices for groundnuts (e.g. 1977 output = 132,000 tonnes but 1985 = 55,000; while world prices in 1981 = $623 per tonne in 1983 it was $349).

The severe economic problems associated with these fluctuations led the government to call in foreign expertise and, with the help of the International Monetary Fund, initiate an economic recovery programme.

Diversification of the economy with aid from abroad was seen as the solution to be achieved through expansion of tourism, diversification of agriculture and infrastructure improvements to support tourism and agriculture.

Location of schemes

[SOURCE: Barrett H R and Browne A W, *Women's Horticulture in the Peri-urban Zone of Gambia, Geography* No. 319, 1988]

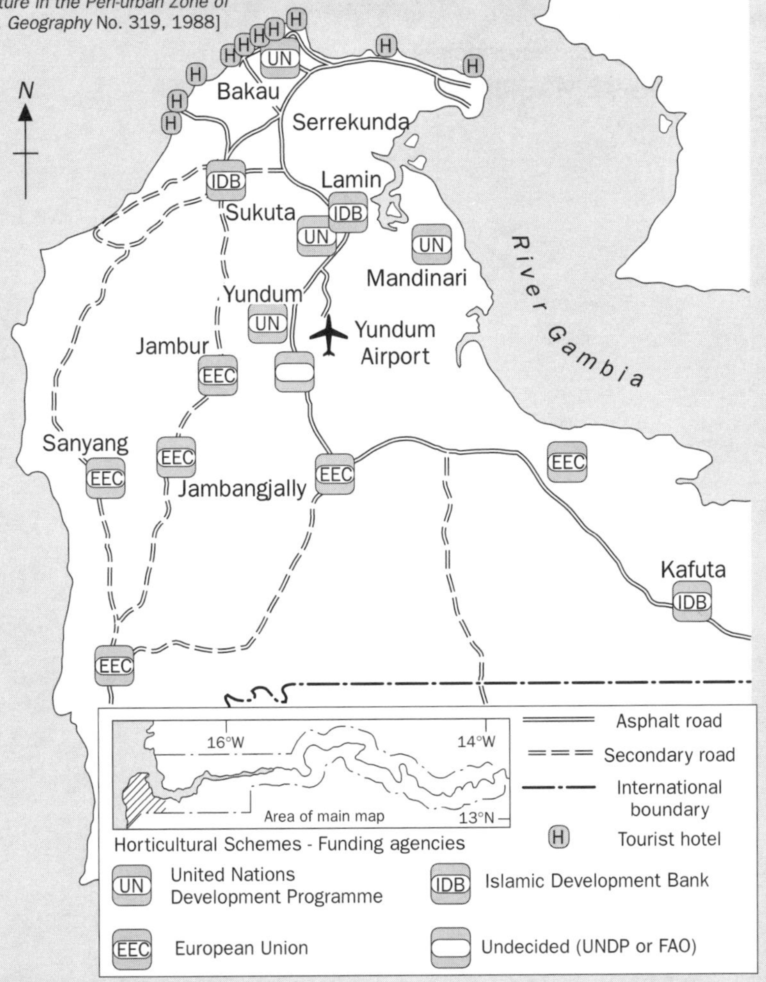

The role of women in agriculture

Traditionally, men grew the cash crops (mainly groundnuts) while women grew the food crops such as rice and vegetables. The Gambian government, already committed to a more direct role for women in the development process, decided to involve them in horticultural cash crop production. This was based on women's village cooperatives to grow vegetables for the tourist market and export. Since 1987 a series of cooperatives have been set up in the 'peri-urban' zone, close to the urban and tourist markets, to the international airport of Yundum and with easy access to road routes.

The horticultural schemes

The horticultural schemes were initially funded by external agencies and, with the guidance of a horticultural adviser from the Ministry of Agriculture, were run by women's cooperatives. The marketing of crops was through Citro Products, a subsidiary of the Gambia Produce Marketing Board. Irrigation was provided to ensure all the year-round crop production. However, there has been some disquiet as to the economic and environmental sustainability of certain schemes.

The Sukutu scheme (started in 1987)

A 15 ha. site was clear-felled leaving the ground with little protection. Five hectares was allocated for communal cash crops which used a borehole and overhead sprinkler irrigation, saving labour time. The other 10 ha. has been divided between the 230 women of the cooperative as their individual vegetable plots. Cash crops produced are mainly potatoes, tomatoes, aubergines, chilli peppers, okra and salad crops.

Loans to develop the site have been paid off and individual earnings are between £12 and £15 a year. However, this is not enough return to meet overheads or to replace equipment. Also clear felling and a lowering of the water table may lead to environmental problems in the near future.

Smaller schemes funded by the EU

The smaller schemes cover 1 ha to 2 ha and only 20 women are involved in the cooperative. More tree cover has been left and the use of manual irrigation from wells has reduced the amount and cost of water extraction. The schemes are thus more economic and more environmentally friendly, as well as easier to manage than the Sukutu scheme, but the amount of work per unit yield is much greater.

Issues arising

- There has been greater involvement by women in the decision making and running of the schemes, but the smaller schemes involve intensive labour in addition to other work and for comparatively small returns. The larger schemes involve less work but may not be sustainable beyond the short term.
- Outside agencies may provide inappropriate advice in relation to local environmental conditions. The financial terms laid down may make it difficult for coopera-tives to succeed.
- More use needs to be made of women's environmental knowledge. Traditionally, tree cover has been left to provide shade for crops and help maintain soil moisture.

10

CHAPTER 10

Ethnic and racial inequalities

There is growing international concern over the problems associated with discrimination against and unfair treatment of ethnic groups by the dominant group within state or society. However, any discussion of this needs to be based on the ***characteristics which***, with time, ***have distinguished one ethnic/racial group from another. These are***:

- ***Racial – distinction by physical characteristics, including build, appearance and colour***
- ***Ethnic – development of a distinctive culture and way of life, including language, attitudes, values and beliefs***
- ***Territorial space – occupation of, interaction and identification with a particular territory over a period of time.***

10.1 The nature of racial and ethnic discrimination

Discrimination and injustices have always occurred. With increased migration, contact between racial groups intensified, bringing with it increased discrimination and injustices. Most countries contain more than one racial ethnic group. In some countries, such groups have been assimilated or exist peaceably as a plural society. For example, until the migration of New Commonwealth people into the UK after the Second World War, incoming migrants had been largely assimilated into the population. In Malaysia, Chinese and Indian groups have retained much of their distinctive cultural identities but generally coexist as a plural society (Case study 10.4). In some countries, however, tension and conflict has emerged as one group tried to dominate and discriminate against another. Although there are many examples of this in the world today, only those where widespread violence and civil war occur are given international attention, as in the case of South Africa and Israel.

10.2 Causes of racial/ethnic discrimination and inequalities

Tension is heightened where the group which is discriminated against seeks to retain its separate identity and resists assimilation. Discrimination against coloured ethnic groups in some of the larger cities of the UK, for example, is partly as a reaction to their desire to retain distinctive cultural identity through the residential areas they choose to live in and that they favour their own places of worship.

Belief of dominant groups in their superiority to other ethnic groups is an important factor in exploitation. Such discrimination is not only between people of different colour; it also occurs amongst people of similar physical make-up. For example, some black African tribes annihilated the indigenous hunting and gathering tribes, such as the Hottentot, in southern Africa in the latter half of the century. Recently, the Iraq government actively discriminated against the Kurds in northern Iraq (Figure 10.1).

The search for a Kurdestan homeland

The Kurds number more than 20 million, the largest nation in the world without a state. As minorities within Iraq, Turkey and Iran, they have suffered a decade of oppression and are now resorting to extreme measures to secure an independent homeland. The most extreme element is the Syrian-backed PKK Marxist movement in northern Turkey; with 10 000 armed fighters, it is waging a guerilla war against Turkey. In contrast, moderate elements, in conjunction with the United Nations, are seeking a peaceful settlement. In northern Iraq, for example, the Kurds are under the protection of the United Nations and have secured some autonomy.

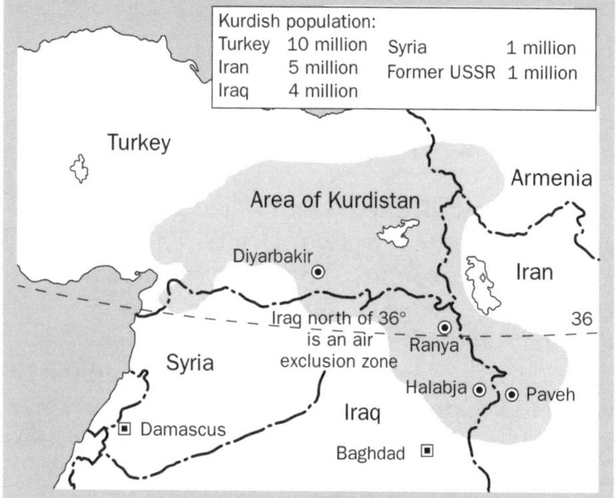

Figure 10.1 The search for a Kurdestan homeland

The question of land rights is an important element in most cases of racial and ethnic tension because access to land is fundamental to basic needs. For the invaders, territory was sought for material resources and for political acquisition. For the indigenous people, however, land has always held much more than material significance (Case study 10.1). It not only provides basic material needs, but holds deep spiritual significance. This point is frequently missed by authorities who arbitrate on territorial disputes, when those in authority come from a culture with different norms and values to that of the indigenous group.

Marginalisation of subjugated groups is not only a result of discrimination against them but may itself be a cause of continued discrimination even after political subjugation has disappeared.

In the course of losing land to invaders, subjugated groups have frequently been relegated to poorer marginal lands, resulting in poverty and inequalities of various kinds. During the colonial period the colonising power frequently settled and progressively developed the best resourced land and neglected the poorer periphery which, because of its marginal character and lack of investment, progressively lagged behind the prospering core region. After independence, economic inequality between the core and periphery has remained, with much of the indigenous group still suffering poverty and discrimination (Case study 7.3).

Exploitation of labour of the ethnic groups is also an important contributory factor in discrimination. Black slave labour was exploited in the New World on plantations in southern United States and Central America. Today in South Africa most of the black population are still relegated to the lowest paid and most menial jobs in the mines, in factories, on commercial farms and in domestic employment.

The denial of equal rights is a central feature of discrimination. In some cases it may include no right to vote and thus no representation in regard to the policy making and decision taking institutions of a country. This makes it virtually impossible for victimised groups to gain redress and equality except perhaps through violent protest and armed struggle.

More commonly, denial of equal rights comes from denial of equal access to basic rights, in particular, equal access to a share of society's basic resources (Chapters 7 and 8). Dominated groups frequently suffer poor basic amenities in the form of housing, health and educational facilities. This may not be a result of legislation discriminating against them but because of the way market forces and powerful pressure groups work to deny access. It is frequently stated, for example, that both in the United States and the UK, ethnic minority groups are discriminated against in the housing market in terms of availability of mortgages and by agents being persuaded not to deal with ethnic minority families wanting to purchase homes in predominantly white neighbourhoods (Case study 14.2).

Much more significant is that ethnic minorities are frequently forced to live in deprived areas, such as inner city areas and townships where the provision of facilities is poor. Because of low income, it is difficult to move to better neighbourhoods and enhance the standard of living (Section 14.2).

Active discrimination causes resentment and alienation, making it more difficult to absorb groups into the mainstream of the society.

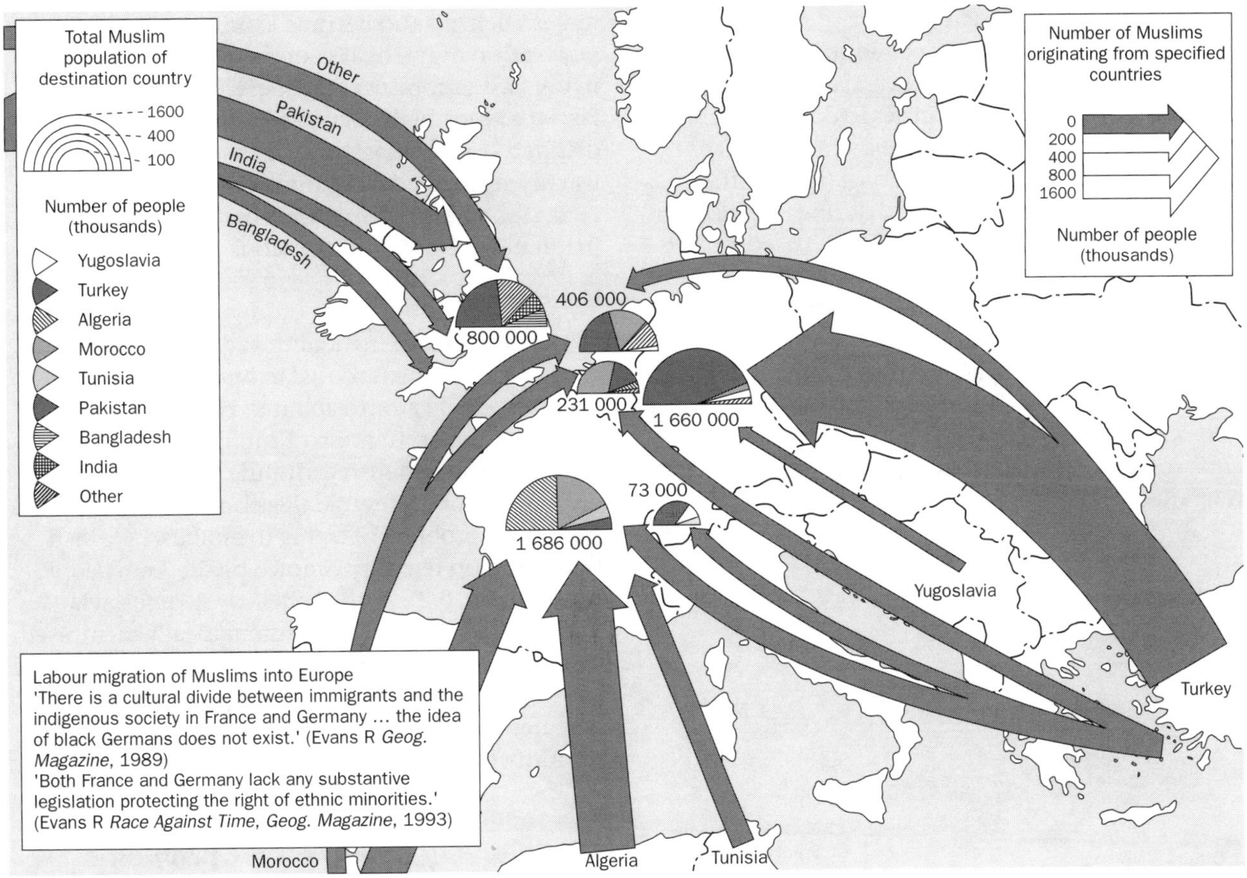

***Figure 10.2** Origin of Europe's Muslim population*

10.3 **The historical dimension**

Colonialism

Many, though not all cases, of racial discrimination in the world today have their roots in colonialism. In the process of colonisation, Britain and other European nations subjugated the native peoples and broke up existing domestic economies and ways of living (Case study 10.4).

Both the resources and labour of a colonised area were used to foster capitalist economies based on industrialisation and trade. The colonies were seen as providing the agricultural products, minerals and other raw materials which were needed and the native people were exploited as cheap labour.

Where the indigenous population was too small in number or was unsuitable, labour was imported, usually from another developing country either through the slave trade or as indentured labour. This has led to more mixed populations, exploitation by the colonising power and racial tension between imported labour and indigenous groups. For example, there have been clashes between the black African population in Natal province in South Africa and the Indian population brought in to work on sugar plantations.

Legacies of colonialism

Ethnic and racial inequalities do not cease when a former colonial area becomes independent. The United States was one of the first countries to gain its independence from European colonial ties but racial discrimination against the black population and the depleted Indian population has continued. Similarly, in parts of Africa and in South America, exploitation and discrimination against black and Indian people remains.

Colonialism has now been replaced by neo-colonialism – the continued domination of former colonial areas and their people in the developing world through economic pressure from western industrialised countries which still exploit their resources and labour. Multi-national corporations are frequently seen by developing world people as the means through which neo-colonialism operates. It has thus become difficult for the now politically independent countries to reorientate their economies to allow for the breakdown of the inequality developed under colonialism. However, the continuation of ethnic and racial inequality may also to some extent be the result of inappropriate policies and problems created by post-independence governments (Case study 20.2).

Post-war labour migrations

During the post-war years of economic expansion in western countries, there have been large labour migrations from poorer countries to do the lower paid and frequently unskilled jobs which could not be filled from the resident workforce (Figure 10.2). The greatest movement occurred during the 1960s in western Europe, but since the early 1970s, economic recessions and tighter immigration controls have greatly reduced these flows. Much of the migration was from former colonies, as in the case of New Commonwealth minorities to the UK and Algerian minorities to France (Figure 10.3). Labour migrations also came from other countries in southern Europe and around the Mediterranean, particularly Turkish migration into Germany, Belgium and Switzerland.

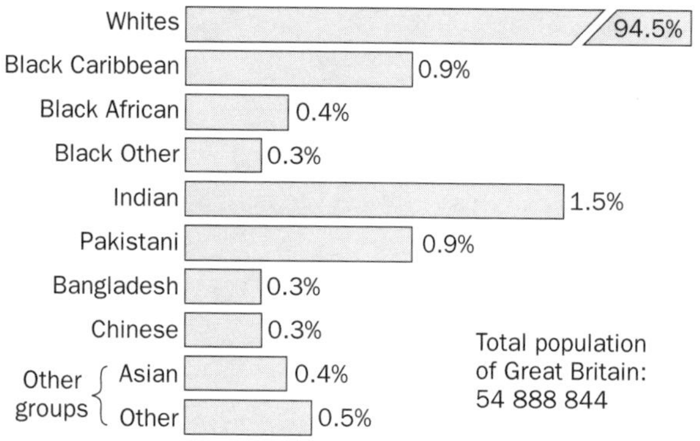

[SOURCE: OPCS 1991]

***Figure 10.3** Total population of Great Britain including minority groups, Census 1991*

The United States too has had large labour migrations from Mexico and Puerto Rico, in particular. Migration occurred over a long period but had increased since the 1970s, especially from Central American countries and Mexico. By 1991 there were 24 million Hispanic speaking people in the United States and by 2000, it is estimated this will have reached 35 million, overtaking black Americans as the largest racial minority in the country. Many of the minorities live in the inner city areas of large conurbations in the south-west of the country (one-third of the population of Los Angeles is of Hispanic origin) (Case study 5.1).

Refugee movements

Throughout history, refugee movements have occurred in response to repression by authoritarian governments, wars and natural disasters, such as famine. In some cases the move is temporary, with the majority of people returning to their home countries when conditions improve. Some refugees remain behind and become assimilated into the population of the host country, as in the case of many East Europeans who fled to the West from fascist governments. Some refugees retain their distinctive identities, however, and are usually segregated from the indigenous population. As segregated minorities they may be subject to inequalities and discrimination.

Historical disputes

While much racial inequality may be based in colonialism, some is rooted in historical disputes between ethnic groups about territorial rights, or as a result of the occupation of a territory by another state. The Palestine-Israel dispute and the resulting discrimination in the West Bank and Gaza strip were part of the problem of trying to establish a Jewish homeland on territory claimed by the Arab people (Case study 10.2). In the break-up of Yugoslavia, minority groups are being systematically victimised by the dominant occupying groups. The break-up of the former Soviet Union has also led to territorial disputes between the emergent states in which minority groups are being unfairly treated.

10.4 Solving racial/ethnic problems

It is in the relationship between one ethnic group and another that feelings of prejudice, attitudes of superiority and acts of discrimination will continue to occur. Acts of discrimination on the basis of racial or ethnic differences may decrease over time, for a number of reasons:

- the decline of empires and with it, colonialism. This has been followed by the break-up of the Communist bloc in eastern Europe and the Soviet Union, leading to the creation of more independent states (Figure 10.4). The domination of territories and their people by a stronger power has been reduced.
- the increased desire of people to participate in the processes that shape their lives. This is seen in the democratic transition in many developing countries, the collapse of many socialist regimes and the world-wide emergence of peoples' organisations. People are demanding an effective say in government and the decisions which affect them.
- the growing influence of international organisations to find and address the inequalities which exist within and between countries. They also deal with problems which hinder the improvement of the underprivileged and disadvantaged groups.

[SOURCE: *Financial Guardian*, 1992]

Figure 10.4 *Alignment of former Soviet Republics*

- the growing force of public opinion. Improved communication across the globe and increased contact between people is facilitated by personal mobility.
- an increasing realisation of the interdependence between different countries as more nations are integrated into a world system. Disputes arising from inequalities and exploitation of one group by another can spill over into other areas and disrupt the world economy.
- an increasing emphasis on resolving disputes through discussion, often with the help of external mediators rather than through violence or armed struggle (Figure 10.5). With the increased technological development of weapons, including germ warfare and nuclear weapons, it is necessary for peaceful solutions to be found.

Concluding comment

Looking at the world today progress appears slow, but since the end of the Second World War, evidence of progress is more clearly seen.

'Our world is still of difference ... many ethnic minorities still live a separate nation within their own countries ... and political and economic democracy is still a reluctant process in several countries ... but many new windows of opportunity are opening.'

HUMAN DEVELOPMENT REPORT, 1993

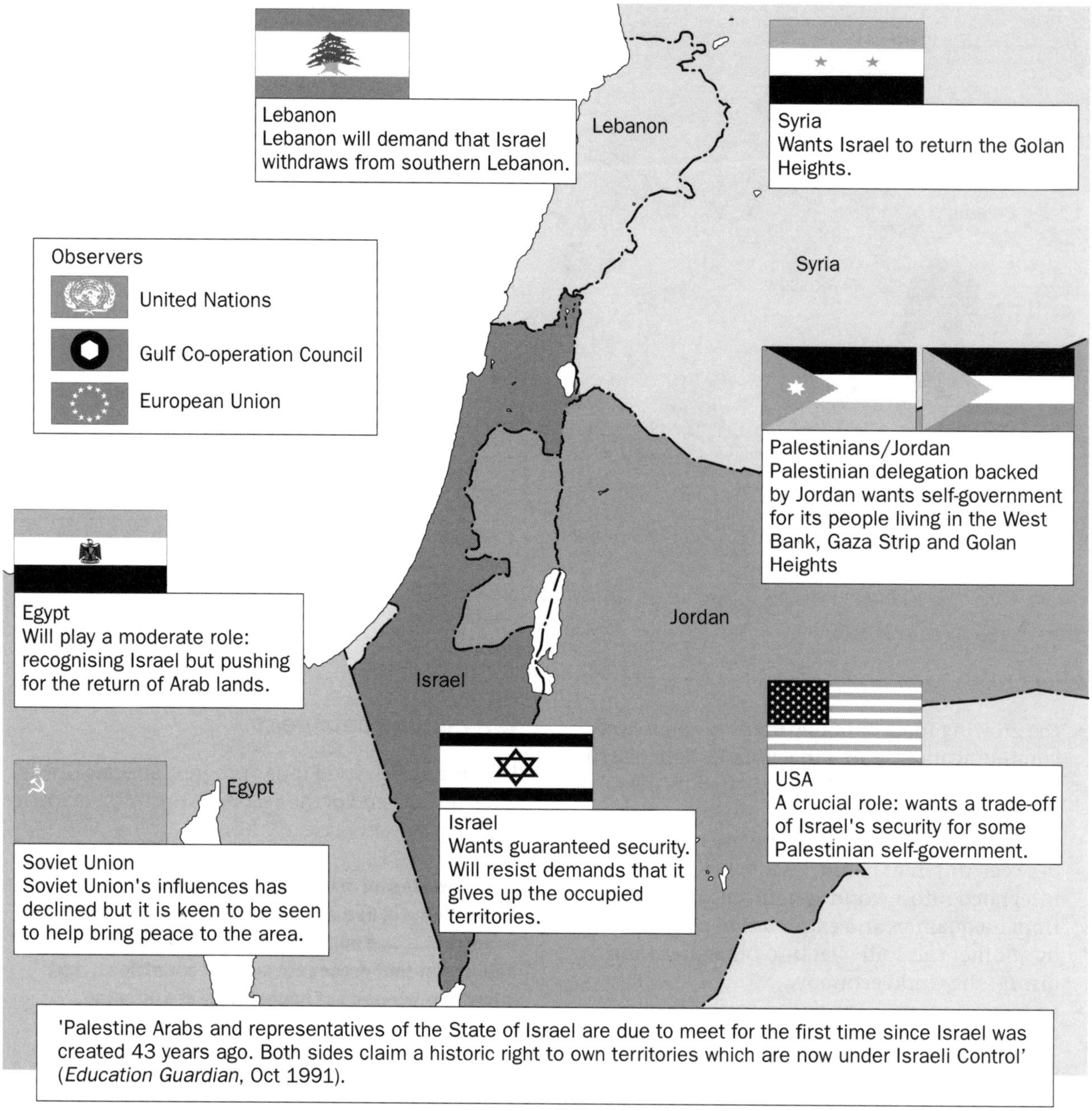

Figure 10.5 *Look who's talking*

case study

10.1 Australia: its underprivileged minority

The indigenous inhabitants

The aboriginal population has been described as 'aliens in their own lands'. With the coming of the white settlers to Australia in the late eighteenth century, much of the aboriginal population was decimated by attacks, disease and unhealthy diets. Attempts to 'christianise and civilise' with mission schools and clinics between 1820 and 1840 largely failed because the cultural gap was too great. Between 1860 and the 1920s, government efforts were negative in terms of its attempts to assimilate the aboriginal population through government protection and reservation land, handouts of food, blankets and medicines. Since the 1930s, more positive attempts were made through the Aboriginal Department to provide for families and communities, recognising the right of aboriginal groups to a separate identity. However, the position of the relatively large number of part aborigines was particularly difficult.

Distribution	
New South Wales and Capital Territories	60 231
Victoria	12 611
Queensland	61 269
Western Australia	37 788
Tasmania	6 712
North Territory	34 739
Total	227 645
(Total Population of Australia)	17.6 million

Aboriginal population distribution

Cultures apart

Before the arrival of the white settlers, the aboriginal population comprised over 300 small tribal groups, each with its own customs and language, in a territory to which the group had a deep spiritual attachment through ancestral links. Their existence was semi-nomadic, based on hunting and gathering and adapted to a harsh, inhospitable environment. Attitudes and beliefs, particularly in relation to land and material possessions, is in stark contrast to the rather material culture of the white population, one of the reasons for the difficulty of assimilation of the aboriginals in the new Australia.

The aboriginal population is commonly understood to occupy the more remote outback of the interior but there are significant numbers in the towns, such as Darwin and Sydney (about 25% are in state capital cities). Their urban life style is different from those in the bush, but they are both 'underprivileged'.

The underprivileged minority

In a land with one of the highest average per capital incomes and a mass consumption society, the majority of Australian aboriginals are said to live in developing world conditions of poverty, overcrowding, disease, high infant mortality, poor education, alcoholism, violence, racial prejudice and high unemployment. They frequently have to exist on government handouts.

Infant mortality rates are four times that of Australian whites; one in four dies before the age of 30. The aborigines suffer from poor diets and associated diseases, only 4% have education beyond 15 years old and unemployment is nine times above the national average.

Aboriginal settlements are frequently without running water, sewerage systems, proper roads and other facilities. People in the towns live in the worst slums, such as in Redfern, Sydney.

Without equal rights

Until 1966 the aboriginal population had no rights to citizenship or a right to vote. Until 1988 they had no rights to their ancestral lands outside of the reserves. The areas which were set aside as reserves are threatened by white economic exploitation, for example, by mining companies as in the Northern Territory.

Threatened loss of cultural roots

There is a threat of the loss of human dignity and cultural roots, particularly amongst the younger aboriginal people who are more susceptible to white material influences. Many have lost their cultural identity and faced with racial prejudice and antagonism, cannot find acceptance within a white culture. They thus occupy a 'grey' area between cultures, with little sense of identity or purpose, making them more open to social dangers, such as alcoholisms.

Struggle for recognition and land rights

From the mid-1960s there has been an increasingly organised and effective movement amongst the aborigines for fairer treatment and a recognition of their claims to ancestral territory. The Federation of Land Councils is seeking the return of lands.

[redacted]

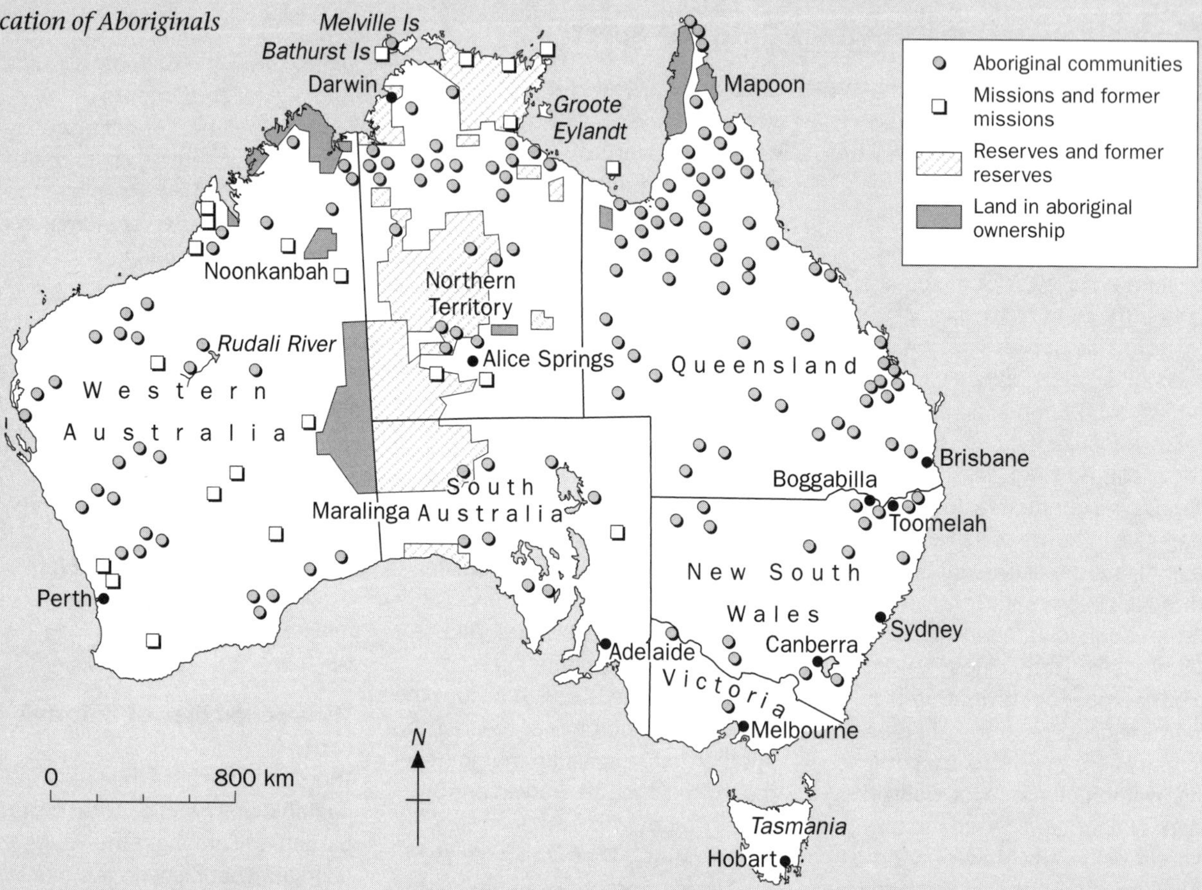

Location of Aboriginals

In 1988 the Prime Minister, Bob Hawke, met with aborigines at Barunga in the Northern Territory and declared a government intention to sign a treaty within two years which recognised aboriginal right to territory. He offered compensation for losses, right to self-determination and self-management with a national elected body to oversee aboriginal affairs. Since then, considerable progress has been made towards recognising aboriginal territorial rights. Under the new Labour government of 1993, Prime Minister Keating promised to give the Aboriginal issue a high priority.

State and federal progress

Much of what needs to be done regarding land rights has, until recently, been left to the State governments. Policies have varied. The Northern Territory and South Australia have made the most progress.

In Northern Territory, a 1976 Land Rights Law did recognise aboriginal claims to land which has helped to restrict mining exploration in that area. In South Australia, land rights to 10% of the state have been recognised. Ayers Rock, an important symbolic location, was handed back in 1986. the aborigines are likely to receive compensation and royalties over use of land by mining, tourist and other commercial ventures.

In respect of federal recognition, a historic court ruling 1992 recognised for the first time that native title rights could exist if the indigenous inhabitants had maintained 'close and continuing association with a piece of land' but established white settler land acquisitions are not affected. In 1994, a Native Title Tribunal was set up through which aborginals could challenge claims which affected their tribal areas. The tribunal mainly relates to crown lands in Australia.

More importantly still, a Social Justice package is being set up to address and redress the current disadvantages of aboriginal people.

case study

10.2 **Israeli and Arab tensions**

Because of its history and position as one of the world's cross roads, the Middle East has been a region of conflict between different culture groups and nations. This has been heightened by the intervention of outside super powers and, in recent times, as the source of an important part of the world's oil.

Basic facts

There are 4.6 million people in Israel and 1.5 million in the occupied territories. The Arabs make up 38% of these at present, but because of a higher birth rate than the Jewish and a decline in Jewish immigration, Arabs are likely to make up the majority of the population by 2000 AD.

There are strong religious and cultural differences between the Jewish 83% and the 38% Arabs, who are mainly Moslem.

Israel's economy has been seriously weakened by continued conflict. It is dependent on outside financial assistance from Jews in other parts of the world.

The futures of both Israel and Palestinian economies are interpendent and Arab population growth poses a serious problem for the future.

As current Middle East peace talks indicate, the solution to the Israel-Palestinian problem is tied up with solutions to other Middle East problems, including world wide acts of terrorism by extremist groups.

Root of the conflict

Both the Jews and the Arabs have historical claims to the territory now occupied by Israel since both are descendants of the Semitic people who occupied the territory during the times referred to in the Old Testament. Jewish connections were strongest under King David who united the Jewish tribes of Israel. The kingdom came to an end with the Roman occupation and the dispersion of the Jews after 133 AD, when Jews could no longer live in Jerusalem.

The Palestinians, as descendants of the Canaanites and Philistines, have always inhabited the area. Their Arab links were forged during the Arab conquest of the Middle East, bringing with it the religion of Islam. Since the sixteenth century, Arab control was lost to the Turkish Ottoman Empire until World War 1.

Outside interventionist policies have contributed to the conflict. The West's intervention in the Middle East dates from the Crusades of the eleventh and twelfth centuries, prompted by the regard for Jerusalem and the surrounding areas as the place of origin of Christianity. Later intervention was also politically and economically motivated, as the Middle East was seen as an essential pivot to the Western powers' empire-building aspirations and as a crossroads for essential trade routes.

After the break up of the Ottoman Empire at the close of World War 1, Britain and France held mandates over the Ottoman territories in the Middle East but provisionally recognised the territories as independent states. Britain held the mandate over Palestine.

However, as a result of the Balfour Declaration in 1917, the British made two incompatible promises in respect of the Palestine territory: independence for the Arabs occupying Palestine and favouring a Jewish homeland in Palestine provided nothing was done to 'prejudice the rights of the Arab population'.

Developing tension and conflict between Israel and the Arabs

The state of Israel was eventually set up but Arab claims and efforts to set up a state of Palestine was thwarted by the world depression and persecution of Jews in Europe in the 1930s. During this time, Jewish persecution, especially by the Nazis in Germany, led to a flood of Jewish immigrants into Palestine, creating tension with the Arab population living there. By 1946 600 000 Jews lived in Palestine, making up one-third of the population.

In 1947 the United Nations favoured a partition of Palestine into separate Jewish and Arab states. The Arabs rejected this since they were offered only 43% of the territory and had 70% of the population.

In 1948 the British mandate over Palestine came to an end and the state of Israel was created. There followed a series of conflicts between the new Jewish state of Israel and the Palestinian and other Arab neighbouring groups.

In 1967, following the Six Day War, Israel occupied the Arab territories of the West Bank, the Golan Heights and the Gaza strip (insert map) to try to secure its borders. Contrary to United Nations Convention, the Israeli government has pursued a policy of settling the occupied Arab territories with Jewish groups.

SInce then there has been sporadic conflict between Israel and Arabs in the occupied territories and with neighbouring Arab states.

Arab Palestinians, supported by the Palestinian Liberation Organisation, have adopted a policy of active resistance and non cooperation in the occupied territories.

A peace process is underway to settle the disputes over territory and Arab rights, but progress towards Palestine self-government and a separate Palestine state are hindered by Israel's hardline attitude and continued Arab civil unrest, fuelled by Arab extremist groups.

Discrimination against Arabs in Israel

Within Israel, Arabs are excluded from occupying 92% of the territory. People in Arab-controlled local authorities receive only one quarter the expenditure per capita on services, compared to people in Jewish municipalities. Arabs occupy mainly the lower paid manual jobs.

In occupied territories Arabs have been losing land and water rights to Jewish settlers. Quotas are set on agricultural production and the majority are dependent on commuting into Israel for lower paid jobs.

Towards a solution

In 1994 a peace treaty between Israel and the Palestinian Arabs, represented by the Palestine Liberation Organisation, was begun. The right of Palestinians to a state was recognised. Israel has already withdrawn from the Gaza strip which is now under Palestinian administration and negotiations in respect of the other occupied territories are under way. However, this is complicated by the Jewish settlements which have been established there. The fledgling Palestine state will require extensive aid from the West to build up an infrastructure and economy. This aid is currently being channelled through the World Bank, but any future economy will of necessity involve economic cooperation with Israel as well as neighbouring Arab states.

Israel has also begun to establish diplomatic relations and negotiate peace treaties with its Arab neighbours: Syria, Lebanon and Jordan. Again, economic cooperation is essential, particularly over water supplies, since the main river sources cross the national boundaries. There is preliminary negotiation over joint ventures on tourism, for example. A shared electricity grid and a canal which links the Dead Sea, Red and Mediterranean Seas, together with hydro-electricity generation, are also under discussion.

However, the assassination of the former Prime Minister Yitzhak, continued terrorist action by Hamas and other extremist Palestinian groups, with reprisals to these attacks by Israel threatens the Middle East Peace process. The recent election in 1996 of the 'right wing' Binyamin Netanyatu as Israel's Prime Minister may also slow down the peace process. An emergency summit of the 21 Arab leaders has declared that Israel should honour its commitment to withdraw from occupied territories.

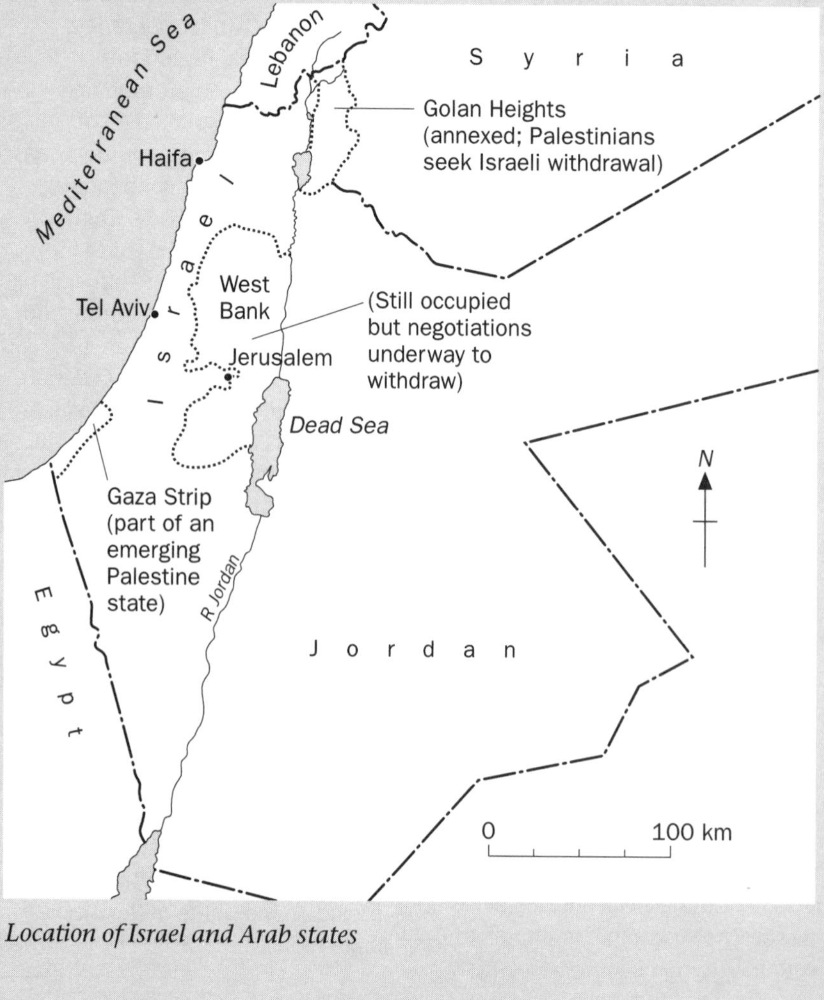

Location of Israel and Arab states

case study

10.3 South Africa: its racial mosaic

Migration and the present racial mosaic

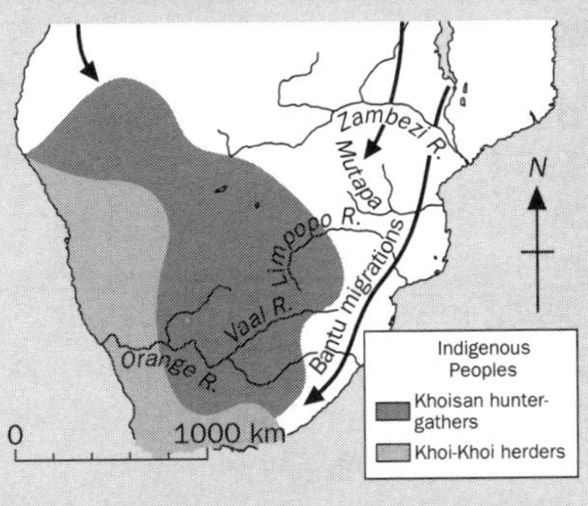

Southward migration of Zulu and Bantu

The present black majority of people in South Africa are not indigenous but are colonisers like the white settlers. Because of population pressure and of territorial ambitions, they subjugated and pushed the indigenous inhabitants, including the Hottentot, westward into the drier inhospitable Kalahari region.

The Africans who pushed southwards clashed with Europeans who were penetrating inland from the Cape.

Following earlier Portuguese settlement on the coast further north, the Dutch established fuelling and trade depots in southern Africa, including Cape Town, in 1652. The Dutch were followed, in the eighteenth century, by the English and later also by the Germans and the French.

In the nineteenth century, as part of the scramble for Africa, the Europeans pushed inland. The Dutch Boers founded the Orange Free State and the Transvaal. Many more people followed in the diamond and gold rushes, occupying land and subjugating the Africans. Many black people were pushed onto 'reserves' and were used as cheap labour on farms, as domestic servants and in the mines.

The Asian element in the population has its origin in the indentured labour brought in to work in the sugar plantations in Natal.

The 'coloureds', who make up the balance of the population, resulted from some intermixing among the white settlers, the black African population and the immigrant Asian labour.

The origin of Apartheid

Discrimination by the white minority against the black, coloured and Asian populations was rooted in the history of settlement and economic development of South Africa. It was part of a wider domination associated with the opening up of the world to trade, colonising and empire building by the Europeans. In Africa, it dated from the initial phase of slave trading, followed by the scramble for colonies in Africa during the nineteenth century.

In South Africa, racial discrimination was deliberately incorporated into state policy with a view to retaining white rule and privileges. It was also seen as a way of providing labour for a capitalist economy. In the post-war years it had been reinforced because of the sense of insecurity felt by the white minority ruling group as colonies around them gained independence.

Discrimination has taken a range of forms. Apartheid was the imposition of rigid social and spatial segregation of different racial groups. An Apartheid policy was officially instigated in 1948, when the Afrikaaner (Dutch and German descendants) Nationalist Party came to power.

Two-scale levels continued to exist up to the 1994 elections despite the recent official dismantling of the laws of Apartheid.

Former black reserves had been termed 'homelands' for black Africans, some of which were recognised as independent states (inset map) but most were fragmented, on the poorest land and have a high population density.

In the major cities Africans were excluded from white areas and were relegated to townships on the edge of or beyond the city. Conditions are very poor in the townships.

The black population had no voting rights outside the homelands and had an average income one seventh that of the white population. Most black households suffer poor living conditions with fewer welfare, education, and sporting facilities than the white population.

The dismantling of Apartheid

Pressure to end Apartheid was put on the South African government by outside countries through trade sanctions, withdrawal of some foreign investments and by pressure groups. Possibly the most influence had been exerted through organised opposition from the black majority population in South Africa itself, supported by liberal elements amongst the white population and the 'front line' states, such as Zimbabwe and Botswana.

Within Africa, armed action against apartheid came from the African National Congress group (ANC) and the Zulu-dominated Inkatha movement. These and other groups, such as the Trade Union movement and the Church, have also exerted peaceful resistance through consumer boycotts and strikes.

The dismantling of apartheid had gathered pace since 1989 when President Botha was replaced by the more liberal President De Klerk. Many detainees were released, including Nelson Mandela, leader of the ANC who later was elected president. The ANC and other movements have been officially recognised.

The South African government had dismantled Apartheid completely by 1994. In 1991 the Convention for Democratic South Africa (CODESA) was set up with the main black African movements jointly with the government, working towards establishing a non-racial multi-party democracy. There is a sharing of political power, with the black population being given voting and other basic rights.

Province	Population (as at 30 June 1995)	GGP (Gross Geographical Product – 1991)	as a % of GDP
Northern Province	5.40 m	R10.5 bn	3.8%
North West	3.35 m	R15.5 bn	5.6%
Gauteng	7.05 m	R103.9 bn	37.4%
Mpumalanga	3.01 m	R23.3 bn	8.4%
Northern Cape	0.74 m	R5.9 bn	2.1%
Free State	2.78 m	R17.6 bn	6.3%
KwaZulu/Natal	8.71 m	R41.5 bn	14.9%
Western Cape	3.72 m	R38.5 bn	13.9%
Eastern Cape	6.48 m	R21.0 bn	7.6%

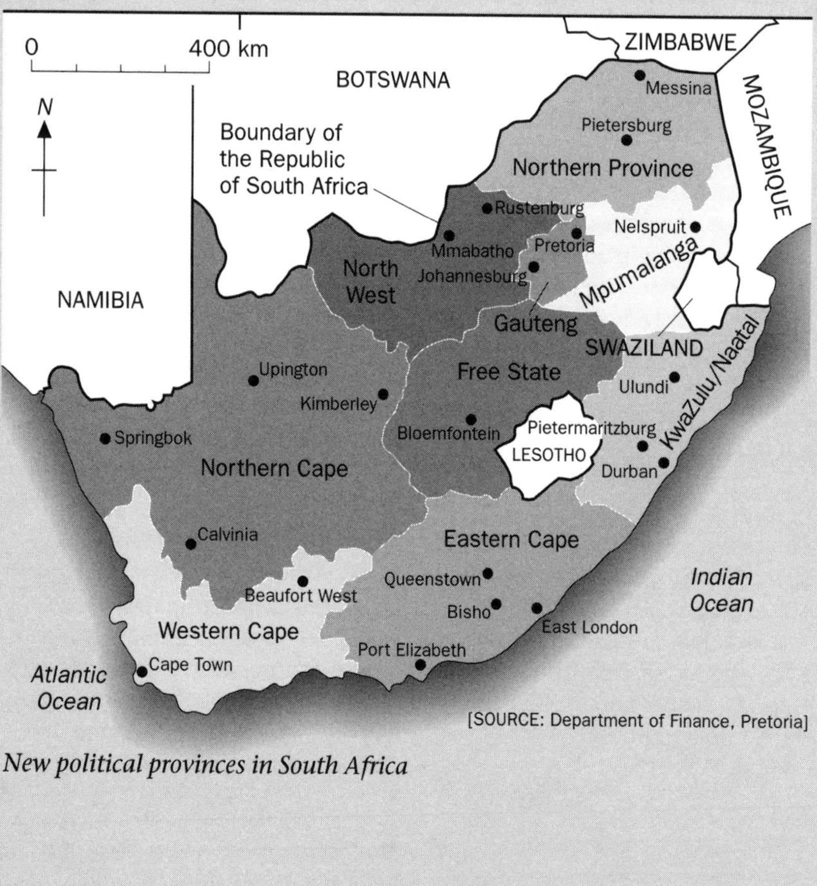

[SOURCE: Department of Finance, Pretoria]

New political provinces in South Africa

Parts of Apartheid which had been dismantled include the Separate Amenities, Group Areas, Population and Land Acts legislation.

Democratic elections, May 1994

'After more than 300 years of white supremacy the white minority has finally, irrevocably and peacefully surrendered power at the ballot box to the country's black majority'. All adults have the vote and the election brought in a Government of National Unity with Nelson Mandela as President and with F.W. de Klerk, the former white prime minister, as a Deputy President.

The former African 'homelands' have been abolished and the country has been divided into nine provinces, each with its own provincial government. Only in the province of the Western Cape does the white dominated National Party hold a majority.

Apartheid and political inequality have gone but a strong social and economic inequality will remain. 'The fear is that a Latin American model will emerge of a handful of rich white and black and a seething mass of poverty and unemployment just out of sight in the townships'. Conditions remain desperate for the vast majority of the black population. For example, 47% of the economically active cannot find work in the formal sector.

The intent is to end social and economic inequalities. However, it is difficult to see how sufficient finance and active cooperation can be created for the fulfilment of African aspirations as set out in the government's adopted Reconstruction and Development Programme. Its aims are to meet basic human needs, develop human resources, build up the economy and turn the state and society into a true democracy. For example, the scale of the task is indicated by the intent to increase housing construction from the 1992 level of 50 000 houses to an annual level of 300 000 over the next five years and to provide ten years of compulsory education for all children.

African material expectations may be too high relative to the economy's ability to meet those expectations.

There is also clear evidence that this may be frustrated because population increase may outstrip the growth in the economy which in 1995 and 1996 was a modest 3%. It is estimated that a sustained growth of 6% to 8% is needed to match population growth and help raise the standard of living for the mass of the black population.

1991	**%**
Blacks	74
Whites	15
Coloureds	9
Asian origin	3
Total	38 million

NOTE: a) the above excludes the large black migrant labour force from other African states and living in hostels.
b) as the birth rate of non-white population is significantly higher their majority is increasing.

Racial composition as officially classified

case study

10.4 **Pluralism in Malaysia**

For almost two centuries three main ethnic groups have co-existed in Malaysia. Of the 19 million population, 50% are Malays (or Bumiputeras), recognised as the indigenous people under the constitution when Malaysia became independent in 1957. The Chinese make up 33% of the population and the Indians 26%, with other very small ethnic groups in the north and on the islands.

During the nineteenth century, both Chinese and Indians were encouraged to immigrate by the British colonial government; the Chinese to work in the mines and the ports, and the Indians to work on the rubber plantations. There is rivalry among the groups. Until 1970 the Malays had only a small share of the total national income but had special privileges in access to education and public sector employment since independence.

The different ethnic groups have by tradition dominated different economic sectors, with the Malays mainly in agriculture but also more recently in the public services. The Chinese have been prominent in commerce, industry and mining, and the Indians in the rubber industry and the professions.

There are a number of probable reasons for the peaceful co-existence in Malaysia.

Under British colonial rule, all groups had to co-exist and at independence, all groups were granted citizenship. Although ethnic differences have dominated domestic politics, a democratic system has allowed clashes to be peacefully resolved. For example, under the New Economic Policy of 1970 the Malays have increased their share of national income to 30%, at the expense foreign investors rather than other ethnic groups. Greater equity is also guaranteed under the 1991 National Development project.

Malaysia's rapid economic advance grants opportunities to all ethnic groups and reduces tensions.

CHAPTER 11

Settlement patterns and change

For some purposes it is useful to distinguish between urban and rural settlements but because there are close links between settlements in any area, it is important also to see the settlement pattern as a whole. This is done here in two ways: firstly, by considering the sorts of settlement patterns which may develop and secondly, through use of the central place concept, the relationship which links settlements into a functioning system.

Rural settlement is then briefly discussed and the rest of the section is devoted to various facets of urban areas which increasingly dominate both the overall form of settlement patterns and also the structure of society.

11.1 **Factors which influence settlement patterns**

Any pattern reflects not only current influences but also past influences and the physical constraints which operated as the settlement pattern developed. These formative influences are summarised in Figure 11.1, noting that though the nature of these may vary, they still continue to influence the way the pattern is changing today. They have affected the initial siting of settlements, their situation relative to other settlements, the way they have developed and the transport network which links them.

In remote areas of difficult terrain and with harsh climatic conditions, settlement patterns are thin.

What settlements there are, are closely related to the few locations which are accessible and offer more favourable physical conditions than surrounding areas. A well structured and closely linked settlement pattern is unable to develop. With time population may be lost to areas of greater opportunity so that some of the smallest settlements, individual homesteads and small hamlets may disappear altogether. This may be illustrated in Case study 11.1, but is a common feature of all peripheral highland regions. Even where there is some impetus for growth, such as the development of a mineral resource, it tends only to affect one or two settlements and not the settlement pattern as a whole. For example, in the Australian outback, Alice Springs has recently expanded because of a growth in tourism but it has little effect on the isolated settlements around.

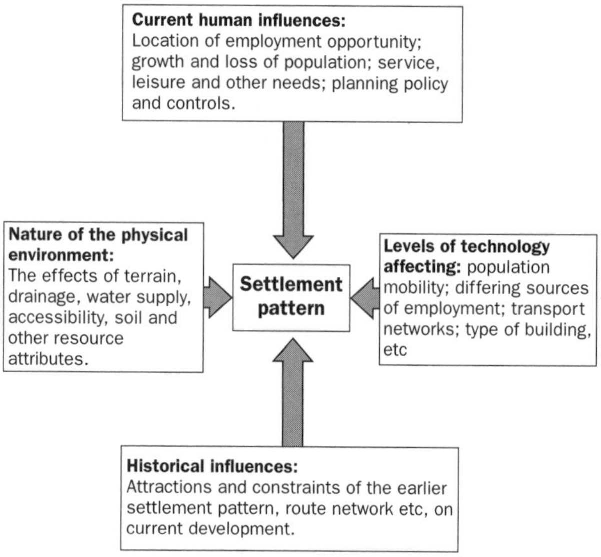

Figure 11.1 Factors which affect the shape and form of settlement patterns

Where physical conditions are favourable to settlement, a more structured and fuller settlement pattern can develop over time. It is possible to recognise a hierarchical arrangement within the settlement pattern beginning with the towns which act as regional centres, passing down through villages, then to hamlets and finally to farms and other individual dwellings. If the area is uniformly favourable, it may also be possible to recognise order too in the special arrangement of settlements, though local variations and physical conditions may produce some modifications. This type of pattern is typical for agricultural areas, such as East Anglia.

Where the economy of a region is dominantly urban-based, the settlement as a whole is strongly permeated by urban influences, with town suburbs infringing upon the rural areas and dormitory settlement in the nearby villages. The main features in this settlement pattern are that of decreasing intensity with distance from the major urban centre and disruption of the hierarchy with the urban population component swamping the lower order of rural settlements. Because of the fear of too much urban sprawl, the settlement pattern is also increasingly controlled by planning policy decisions. These include issues such as maintaining a green belt to separate the town from the countryside and designating those villages where some dormitory growth may be allowed, as opposed to those protected from further expansion by conservation orders.

Physical conditions and past historical influences in the case of urban-dominated patterns tend to be overshadowed by the current influences. Although differentiated by scale, areas dominated by the largest conurbations do exhibit many of the features of areas centred around smaller but still dynamic urban centres, such as Cambridge (Case study 11.2).

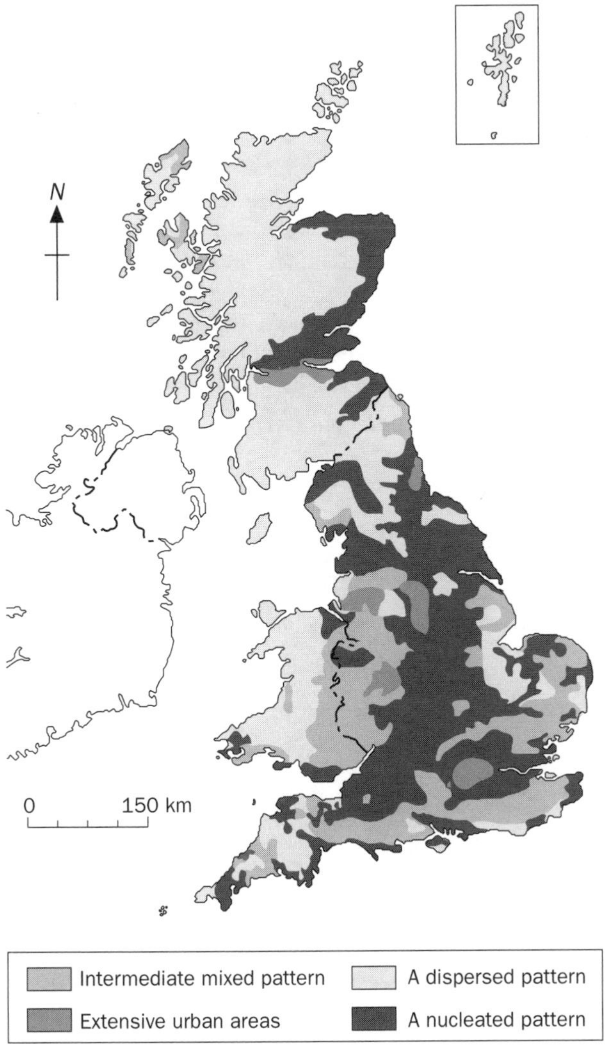

Figure 11.2 Types of rural settlement in Britain

11.2 Understanding settlement patterns

The earliest studies of rural settlement related it to geology, the morphological layout of individual settlements and physical landscape, since historically these were held to significantly determine the settlement pattern in an area. It was only during the 1950s that attention shifted towards theoretical models of settlement patterns and more recently, the influence of these models on planning policies for rural settlement.

The traditional approach

Under the pressures of modern living, with its advances in technology, spread and acceleration of communications and the increasing erosion of the countryside by urban influences, the character of rural settlements is changing (Chapter 12). It is possible to recognise certain fundamental features, both in the pattern of settlements and structure of communities which have persisted over a long period. These are most apparent in the areas furthest away from our large cities but also remain significant features, even in areas where settlements are rapidly being transformed into dormitories for the masses who commute into the city for work.

Nucleation and dispersion

In seeking to clarify rural patterns geographers have traditionally distinguished between nucleated and dispersed settlements. The highland in the west of Britain, for example, is generally characterised by a dispersed settlement pattern and the eastern scarplands and lowlands, by a nucleated one. Other areas, such as the Midlands, are a mixture of the two (Figure 11.2). Examples of dispersed and nucleated patterns are given in the following case studies. In these cases, as elsewhere, the pattern has become increasingly modified by external influences. In the Teify Valley (Wales), for example, uneconomic and remote upland marginal settlement has been abandoned and second home buyers and tourist services have intruded into others lower down. In lowland areas, like County Durham, the spread of cities into the countryside exercises an all-pervasive influence, which goes beyond the extension of the built up areas and dormitory extension to villages. It has had deep effects on the character of communities and the structure of society in hitherto rural settings.

Central Place theory and the pattern of settlement

The order of size, spatial distribution and inter-relatedness of settlements within a region are the key issues of the theories about settlement patterns, most notably the central place theory as expounded by Christaller and others (Figure 11.3).

Figure 11.4 illustrates a simple functional interdependence of settlements within a hierarchy. The farms and smaller settlements depend on nearby Cottenham and Cambridge itself for such things as weekly shopping and secondary education. Cottenham, like other villages and the smaller settlements, depends on Cambridge for more specialist services, such as hospital treatment and entertainment. However, the whole Cambridge region looks beyond to London, a still higher order centre, for certain very special services, such as opera and first division football, entertainment and very specialised shopping, such as as at Selfridges and Harrods department stores. In London the choices and quality of goods and services on offer are much greater than in Cambridge.

This dependency relationship exists because of the inability of smaller settlements further down the hierarchy to provide some of the more specialist services required by their populations. It would not be viable for anyone to set up specialist services in a small settlement centre; not enough people would use this service to make it a worthwhile, profitable venture. Hence the more expensive and less frequently required goods and services are made available at large centres where the resident population provide a market demand which is further reinforced by people coming in from the smaller settlements.

When discussing places as services centres, the term 'central place' is used. Hence central place theory is concerned with settlements of service centres – places where goods and services are offered and bought, either by the public coming to the centre or the supplier going to the consumer.

For urban centres, the most important part of the catchment area is the population of the centre itself, as a Lincolnshire shopping survey illustrates in Figure 11.5. Also within any one town, in addition to the main centre – the central business district – there is a hierarchy of sub-centres for the provision of lower order goods and services for the people who live within reach of them. These are part of the total pattern of service centres, completed by other sub-centres within the region, around the central city, which is at the head of the service centre hierarchy.

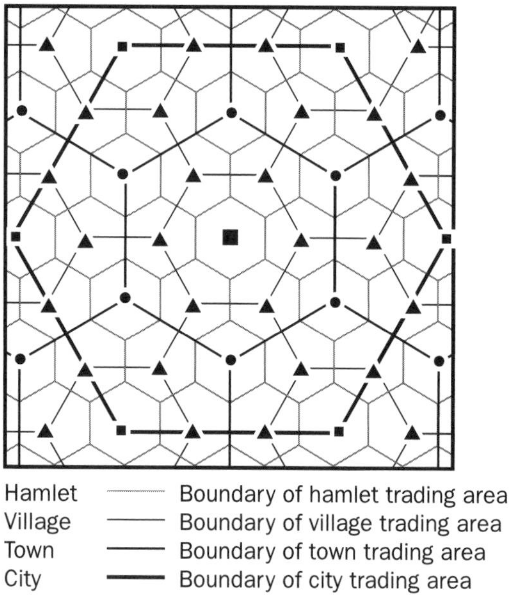

Figure 11.3 *Christaller pattern*

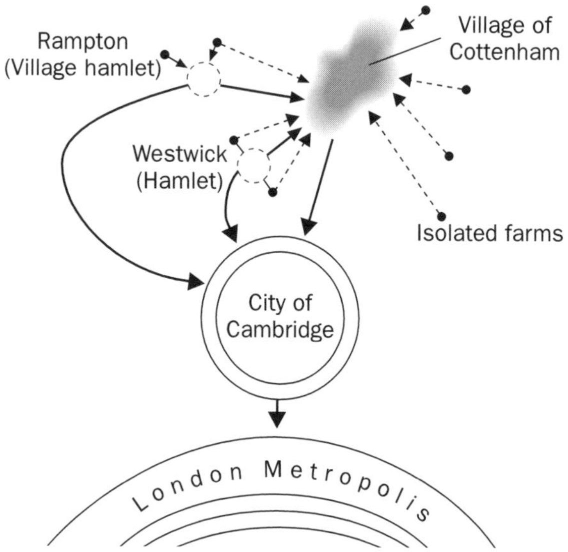

Figure 11.4 *A simple functional interdependence of settlements*

	Distance from town centre				
	Lincoln	up to 8 km	8 – 16 km	over 16 km	Total
Number of shoppers	284	63	38	15	400
Expressed as a percentage	71.0	15.8	9.5	3.8	100

[SOURCE: Dalton R et al *Sampling Techniques in Geography*, 1975]

Figure 11.5 *A Lincolnshire shopping survey*

Central Place theory

The ***centrality of a place refers to its functional importance***. This clearly depends on the number and variety of goods and services it provides for the people who reside there, and the area around.

Threshold population is the minimum number of people needed to support any good or service outlet established at a central place. The frequency with which a good or service is required and its cost determines the size of the threshold needed to support one outlet. For example, if a good is bought at any one time by only a few people out of all the potential buyers in an area, then the threshold population will need to be large to ensure that there are sufficient customers.

The minimum range of a good or service is defined by the distance of the boundary needed to enclose the threshold population for the outlet which provides it. The maximum range of a good or service is the furthest distance measured in time and cost over which either a customer would be prepared to travel to obtain it or a supplier travel to provide it.

The concept of range or **sphere of influence** is closely related to the cost of a good or service. For something cheap and frequently required, such as a daily newspaper, people will not expend much time or money travelling to obtain it. The range, therefore, of a lower order good like this one is small. Because of this and the fact that most people in an area will buy that good, nearly all central places, including villages, will have shops and outlets which sell low order goods, such as newspapers, sweets, cigarettes and groceries. In contrast, high order goods of a larger range are those which cost more and which are not required very frequently, hence people will be prepared to travel a longer distance for them. The catchment area or hinterland for such a good or service must be sufficiently large for this type of outlet. While every central place will have lower order outlets, only the larger central places will have the higher order ones.

Spheres of influence for a good or service, or a combination of these, may be mapped to show the relationship between the relative extent of urban fields and their respective central places. This is illustrated in Figure 11.6 for the island of Hokkaido in Japan. The catchment or hinterland boundaries have also been drawn for the dominant cities. . What is already clear is that the sphere of influence for a central place declines in intensity with increasing distance from it. The greater the variety or goods and services surveyed, the more complete the relative picture of the pattern of spheres of influence.

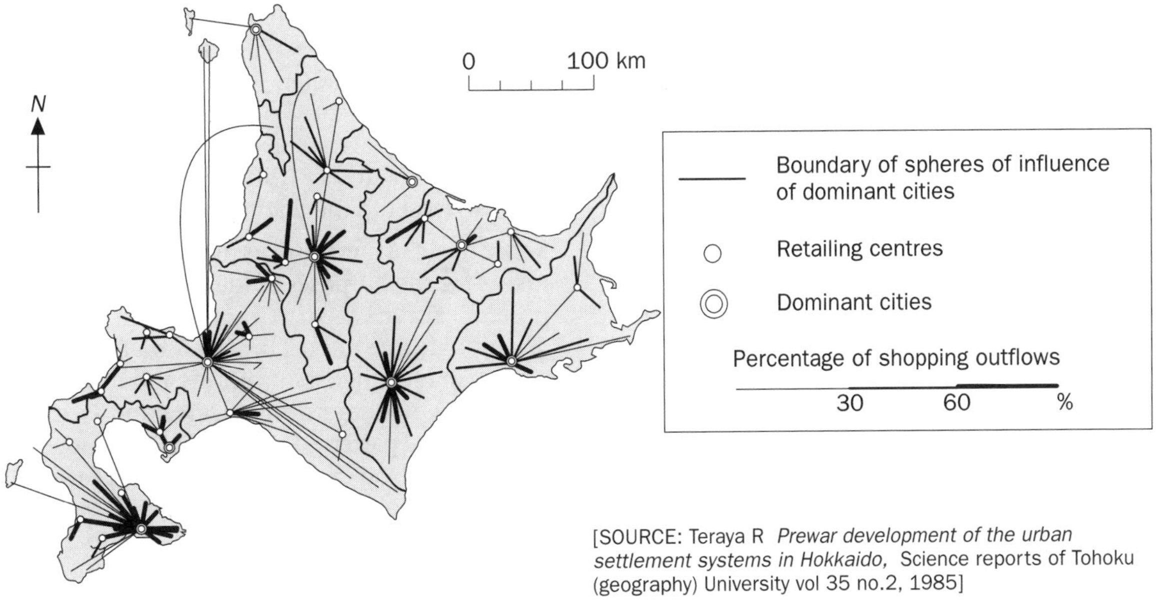

[SOURCE: Teraya R *Prewar development of the urban settlement systems in Hokkaido,* Science reports of Tohoku (geography) University vol 35 no.2, 1985]

Figure 11.6 *Network of cities, towns and villages in Hokkaido by consumer purchasing*

Settlement form	Distance apart (km)	Population	Tributary area size (km^2)	Population
Market hamlet (Markort)	7	800	45	2 700
Township centre (Amstort)	12	1 500	135	8 100
County seat (Kreistadt)	21	3 500	400	24 000
District city (Bezirksstadt)	36	9 000	1 200	75 000
Small state capital (Gaustadt)	62	27 000	3 600	225 000
Provincial head capital (Provinzhaupstadt)	108	90 000	10 800	675 000
Regional capital city (Landeshaupstadt)	186	300 000	32 400	2 025 000

[SOURCE: Ullman E L *American Journal of Sociology* 46, 1941]

Figure 11.7 *The urban hierarchy in SW Germany (after Christaller)*

The Central Place hierarchy and classification of settlements

Within any region the hierarchy of central places can be established by classifying each central place according to the highest order good or service it supplies. At the apex of the hierarchy will be the largest central place in a region, with a catchment area not only large enough to support more than one outlet for all the orders of goods and services present in a centre smaller than it, but also at least one outlet for each of the higher order goods and services not present in these smaller centres. Below this leading central place, the hierarchy progressively descends to the lowest order (Figure 11.7). It follows that at each level in the hierarchy, a central place will support an order of outlet not present in central places of lower levels and also all the types of outlets evident in these smaller central places.

From his studies in south Germany, Christaller was able to show that within a Central Place hierarchy there was not only regularity in the size order of places and the number of places found at each level of the hierarchy, but also regularity of the spatial distribution of central places for any one level and between different orders of central places.

When attributing only a service site function to places, Christaller termed the resultant theoretical hierarchy and spatial order pattern as a K3 system. Any central place at one order level required within its catchment area three times the population of a central place of the next lower order. Christaller envisaged a hierarchy or central places such that a number of them rose in a geometric progression from the highest to the lowest order. The geometric progression for a K3 system would involve the following sequence: 1, 2, 6, 18, 54, 162, etc. He also suggested the K4 system, based on the transportation function the centre might provide and a K7 system, based on its administrative function.

In respect of the spatial network formed by a hierarchy, he saw this as a hexagonal pattern with every place at one hierarchical level being equidistant from the others at that level. To minimise the number of central places so that they were equidistant from one another required them to be at the corner of equilateral triangles which together formed the hexagons. Such an arrangement meant there would be no overlap of trade areas and the smaller hexagons would pack or nest within the larger hexagonal areas in a way conforming with the K3 principle.

It was left to Lösch to incorporate the K4 and K7 networks with the K3 model into a total settlement system. Clearly a network which incorporated the marketing, administrative and transport functions was closer to reality than any single type of network proposed by Christaller. To achieve the composite network, Lösch rotated superimposed K3, K4 and K7 networks to allow for what he called 'city rich' and 'city poor' areas within the system, since he felt this was closer to the distribution pattern in reality.

Some basic underlying assumptions

Just as for the purposes of identifying certain principles of his theory Christaller tried to disentangle one important function from the rest, he also made other assumptions about an area. These included regarding the area upon which a central place pattern developed as a homogeneous plain (an isotropic surface), with equal ease of travel in any direction away from the centre. He also assumed free market competition in that both supplier and customer would make decisions entirely on economic grounds.

The limitations of Central Place theory

To avoid any unwarranted and superficial criticism of Christaller's work, it is necessary to emphasise that, as with other theories, Central Place theory is not meant to have universal validity, nor does it offer a total explanation of a settlement pattern in any region. Its purpose is to identify some of the salient elements in certain types of patterns and some of the factors which might lie behind them. It is to be regarded as one of the tools available when seeking to describe and understand particular patterns in the world. It is up to the potential user to decide whether the theory would be of use in a particular situation or not.

While, for example, the Central Place theory would be a useful analytical tool in the study of a region where the marketing function is important in the economics of settlements, it clearly would be of very limited use if a settlement pattern were dominated by industry. For example, Dickinson, working at the same time as Christaller in the 1930s, identified a central place type pattern in the agricultural region of East Anglia where towns were important market centres. However, in an industrial region such as the north-east of England, the market function was submerged beneath manufacturing influences and therefore central place theory would be of very limited use.

Even when a potential user has identified the region as being amenable to a central place type of analysis, as for example in the case of Coquetdale, Northumberland (Figure 11.8), it is important that as analysis proceeds, some of the underlying assumptions made by Christaller should be relaxed to allow the modifying effects of reality to come into play. For example, starting from the assumption of an isotropic plain may lead to some identification of a regular hierarchical network, but recognition of irregularities in the terrain of the area is needed to help understand why distortions from the

Figure 11.8 *Classification of settlements in Coquetdale*

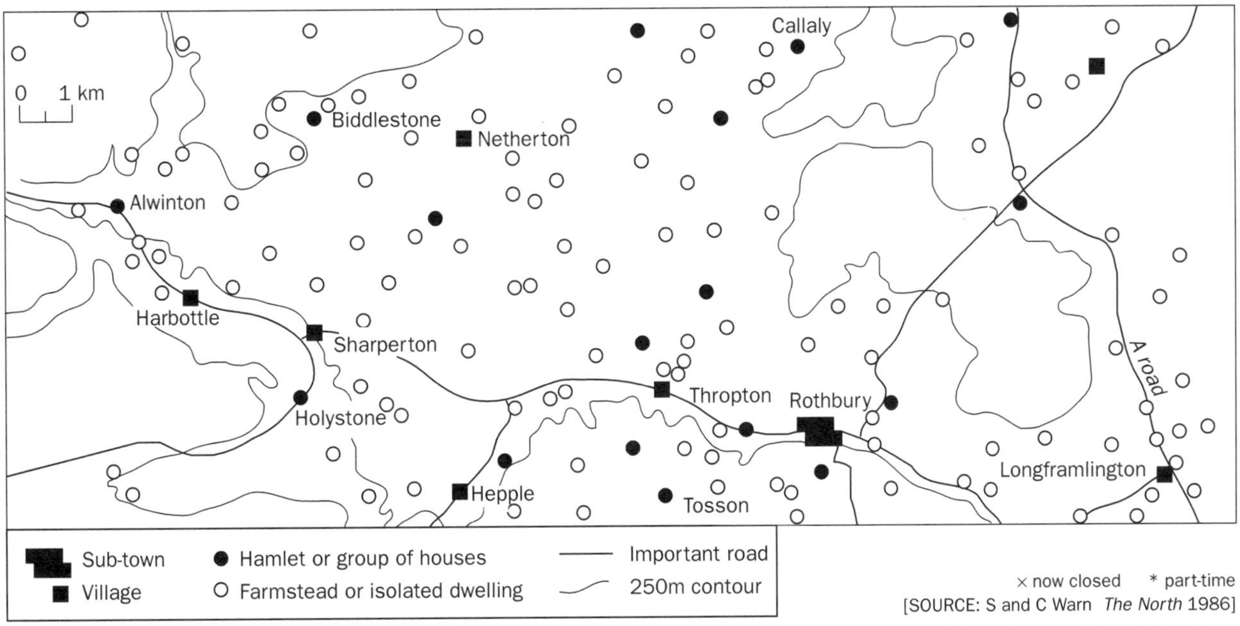

× now closed * part-time
[SOURCE: S and C Warn *The North* 1986]

	Telephone	PO Box	Pub	Post Office	Shop	First school	Village hall	Library	Church	Chapel	Nurse	Doctor	Clinic	Bank	Middle school	Hospital	Petrol	Garage	Solicitor
Alwinton	1	1	1		1				×										
Biddlestone	1	1							×										
Callaly	1	1				×	1												
Harbottle	1	1	1	1		1	1		1	1		1							
Hepple	1	1		×		×			×										
Holystone	1	1	1			×													
Longframlington	1	1	3	1	4	×	1	1*	1		1*		1*				1		
Netherton	1	1	1	1		1	1										1		
Rothbury	1	1	7	1	36	1	2	1	2			3		2	1	×		2	1
Sharpeton	1	1		1															
Snitter	1	1																	
Thropton	1	1	2	1	4	1	1		2									2	
Tosson	1																		

theoretical hexagonal pattern occur. It would also be necessary to recognise that distortions will occur because total free competition does not exist and people are motivated by social and attitude influences, as well as by economic considerations.

However, even given user awareness, there are progressively fewer situations in which Central Place theory can offer a useful framework. Times have changed since Christaller formulated his theory and therefore the underlying circumstances which affect settlement patterns are different.

Demand patterns for services and goods have altered because of affluence, changes in taste and preferences and greater mobility, enabling people to travel further to do their shopping and obtain other services. Technological progress has also brought changes in the ways in which provision of goods and services are organised and located. For example, to obtain benefits of economies of scale, provision of services is centralised into fewer and larger units, such as the hypermarkets and supermarkets now located away from town centres.

Because larger centres are now more accessible and offer a greater variety of goods and services, these are attracting customers away from smaller centres. Smaller towns are losing some of their functions to larger towns even for lower order goods and services, such as weekly shopping. At village level, other losses occur, such as the closing of primary schools, pubs and shops.

Increased government intervention, through planning measures and other legislation, has also interfered in the operation of the market forces which help to shape the central place system. Witness, for example, the effect of locating a planned town of the size of Milton Keynes with a quarter of a million people within the East Midlands settlement pattern. Other planning decisions affect such things as out-of-town shopping centres and the future growth of various settlements around the town.

Despite these recent changes, Central Place theory does have some value as an analytical tool. It can still help identify more clearly the role of settlements as places of trade and exchange and the extent to which this has influenced the nature of the settlement pattern in a region. It also helps to identify some of the important principles or concepts inherent in settlements which function as central places. Concepts such as threshold population, range of a good and frequency of demand are useful in their own right apart from any central place theory. It also encourages us to think of individual settlements in their wider context and to seek some order in the spacing and interrelatedness of settlements.

Applying central place theory as a planning tool

Cloke, in his study of rural settlement planning, has seen a definite link of post-war planning with Central Place and other related concepts. Through the implementation of planning policies, then, Central Place theory has had an influence on the pattern and development of rural settlements since the 1950s. Although this has not been as strong over recent years, its influence is still apparent, both in advanced and developing countries. Cloke identifies, in particular, the influence of the following concepts:

- acceptance of the existence of hierarchial settlement patterns along the lines outlined in central place theory
- the notion of service thresholds
- the effect of economies of scale, that is, the cost advantage of concentrating the supply of services in the larger scale centres on the basis that the cost of providing each additional unit of a service decreases with increasing scale of output
- the growth centre concept which includes the notion of spread effects to benefit the surrounding area. Planners have used this as a reason for concentrating investment in services at a limited number of favoured centres which can act as poles of growth for their surrounding areas, including the smaller rural settlement.

The use of these concepts was particularly evident in the development plans of the 145 planning authorities in Britain in respect of the 1947 Town and Country Planning Act. According to Cloke, many authorities assumed that settlement patterns in their areas were broadly similar to the central place theory pattern (Figure 11.9). Consequently, a 'key settlement' policy was adopted under which certain key higher order settlements were identified and targeted for the investment needed to increase the provision of services in rural areas. By this it was hoped to:

- promote growth in the more remote rural areas
- reduce or reverse rural depopulation by creating centres of intervening opportunities
- achieve the most efficient and cost effective pattern of providing rural services
- concentrate services in areas of greatest need.

Thus within the identified settlement hierarchy, selected centres would be designated for 'a comprehensive concentration of housing, employment, services and facilities' in order to provide for needs of the key settlement and its surrounding area.

Despite criticisms of key settlement type policies and their limited success through into the 1970s, elements of it still apply. A number of authorities have retained the key policy settlement in a more flexible and modified form; the structure plans

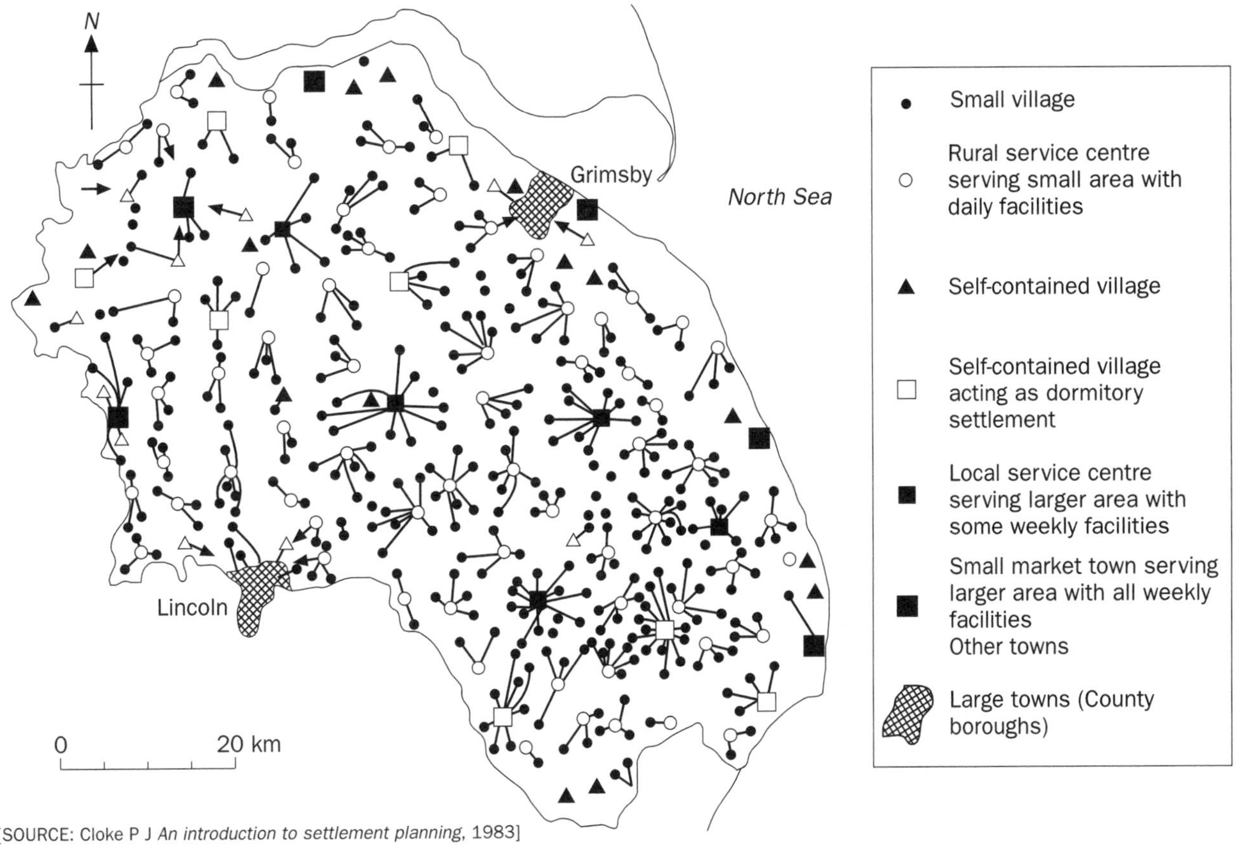

[SOURCE: Cloke P J *An introduction to settlement planning*, 1983]

Figure 11.9 *The rural settlement hierarchy for Lindsey, Lincolnshire, as set out in Lindsey County Council's development plan, 1955*

replaced the earlier development plans. Settlements are still seen as part of a tiered hierarchy and are categorised in a ranking classification in terms of planning and further development. The revised structure plan for Cambridgeshire (1989) for example, categorises rural settlement into 'rural growth locations' and 'other settlements. However, in authorities where the settlement pattern is generally sparse and rural depopulation is a significant problem, the key settlement approach has recently been replaced by the opposite policy of 'dispersal of growth' in an effort to maintain viable communities (Case study 11.2).

Application of central place concepts is not limited to planning in advanced countries. It is increasingly evident in the rural development policies of a number of developing countries where there is a need to slow down rural depopulation and prevent rapid growth of major cities. Planners have sought to either identify or set up growth centres in rural areas where investment might be allocated to provide better services for surrounding areas and employment opportunities.

For example, in Cuba an aim of the state since 1959 has been to promote a more even geographical pattern of development. Therefore, the growth of provincial towns in the 20 000 to 200 000 population range has been encouraged. At the next level down, villages have been regrouped into 'rural new towns' (communidades). Each has been developed with its own food and clothing stores, nurseries, primary schools, clinic, social centre, bookshop and cafes. By 1982, 382 communidades had been established.

In certain areas in Zimbabwe and Tanzania, rural settlement has been reorganised according to central place theory. Certain centres have been designated as higher order centres to serve the surrounding smaller settlements and act as growth and marketing collection points. For example, within the coordinated and rural development programme of Zimbabwe, this approach is being used in some communal land and resettlement areas such as in the Masvingo province.

11.3 **Rank Size rule and urban primacy**

While the Central Place theory focuses on the regularity of the size hierarchy within a settlement system and the regularity in its spatial pattern, the ***Rank Size rule, as developed by Zipf, is concerned solely with the size relationship. Under it the ideal***

theoretical relationship is expressed thus: if all the settlements of a country or region are ranked according to their population size, the size of the settlement will be inversely proportional to their rank. Thus for example, the population of the second largest settlement will have a population half of the largest one, while the third ranked one will have a population one-third the size of the largest settlement, and so on. The relationship may be expressed as: the population (Pn) of the nth settlement in the ranking will be 1/nth of the largest settlement (P).

When plotted on an arithmetical graph, the ideal rank size distribution would appear as a steep, downward-sloping smooth curve but when plotted logarithmically, it would appear as a straight line sloping at 45° (Figure 11.10).

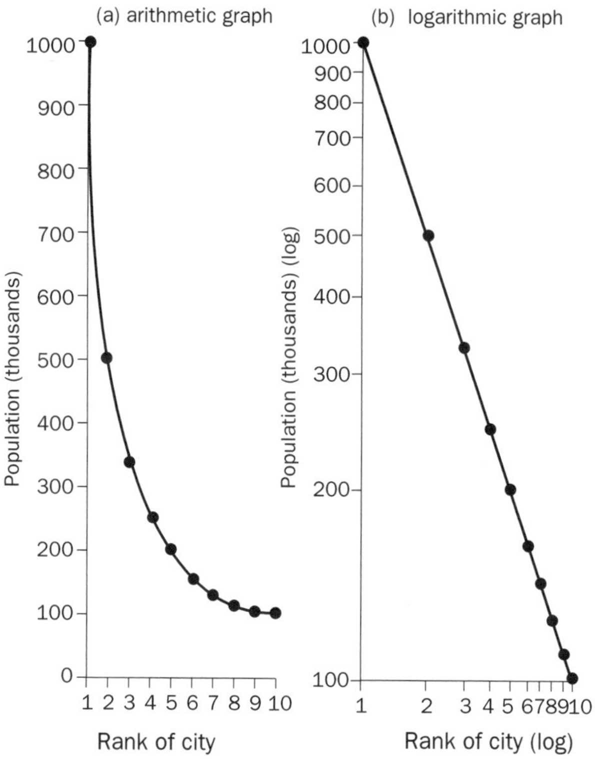

Figure 11.10 *The rank size rule*

Applying the Rank Size rule

In reality, a close correlation of any settlement size distribution in a country to this ideal rank size rule is unlikely because of the variety of influences at work over time. The size distribution tends to become distorted the more developed a country is. However, the rank rule provides a useful guide against which to examine and compare actual rank size in the real world, such as that shown for the region of Hokkaido in Japan (Figure 11.11). Because this area is less industrialised and less developed than other regions of the country, its settlements have a closer similarity to the rank size rule than those of the other regions. However, even in Hokkaido there are significant deviations from the ideal and the size distribution pattern on the graph can be seen to have changed over time.

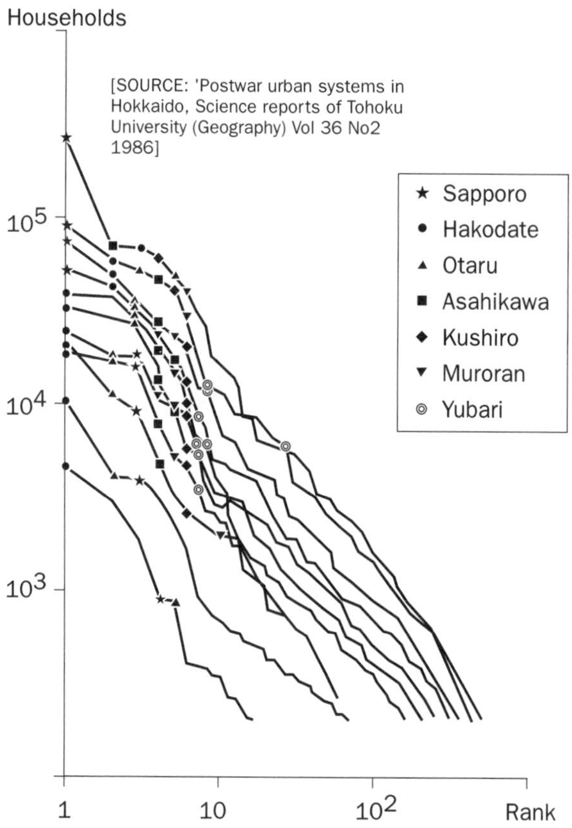

Figure 11.11 *Changes of rank size distribution of Hokkaido settlements, 1879 – 1976*

Urban Primacy

Jefferson and others made comparisons and studied the existence of urban primacy in a country. ***In urban primacy, the largest city or town in a country or region is well over twice the size of any other, so much so that the primate city dominates the urban system in terms of its population size and its political, administrative and economic importance.*** It is thus a gross exception to the rank size rule.

While Urban Primacy is particularly characteristic of countries in the developing world, it may also be found in certain countries of the developed world. Examples of the former are Lima (Peru), Mexico City (Case study 11.3), Seoul (South Korea) and Havana (Cuba), and of the latter, London (UK), Paris (France) and Tokyo (Figure 11.12 and Case study 11.3).

It is difficult to generalise about the conditions which lead to the development of urban primacy but broadly, it is to do with the initial advantages which

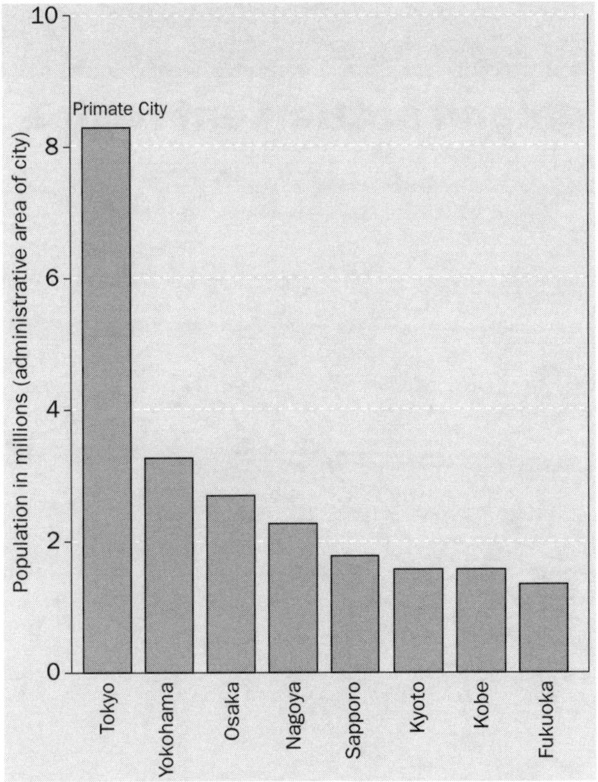

***Figure 11.12** Relative size of main cities in Japan*

site location may give, together with historical circumstances and the cumulative and agglomerative magnetism for further disproportionate growth which a primate has over time.

Primate cities today attract the interest of geographers because of their importance and because of the serious problems which arise as a result of their excessive growth. Primate cities tend to develop serious diseconomies, such as severe traffic congestion and escalating land prices, as well as serious housing shortages. Problems are particularly acute for the disadvantaged sectors of society, including those in the older inner areas of the primate city and those on the periphery, whether as in the advanced world living in rundown estates or in the developing world, in sprawling shanty areas.

There are problems generated beyond the bounds of the primate city. Urbanising influences are spread around a considerable area as population and activities move by choice or are forced out of the city to the periphery, creating commuter dormitories, business parks and secondary growth centres. At its extreme, urbanisation of the surrounding areas may be so strong as to begin to link the primate city and other cities in a region into one vast urbanised belt `– a megalopolis, as in the case of the spread of Tokyo along the Pacific belt of Japan to join up with Nagoya and Osaka, creating what has become known as the Tokkaido megalopolis.

The other problem is the effect of excessive growth of the primate city on regional inequalities across a country. The primate city at the centre of the core growth region absorbs so much of the country's investment and attracts population and economic activities away from other regions, especially those on the periphery. It is thus a contributory factor to the problem of regional inequality. Problems of lagging peripheral regions cannot be satisfactory dealt with without also addressing the problem of excessive growth of the primate city at the core.

Concluding comment

There are various ways in which settlements may be classified. None is comprehensive and the decision on which classification to adopt clearly depends on the purpose for which it is required. Classifications by their very nature are generalisations and 'creatures of their time' while settlements and settlement patterns are unique to the area in which they occur and are changing.

case study

11.1 **Glen Lyon, Scotland: a highland settlement region**

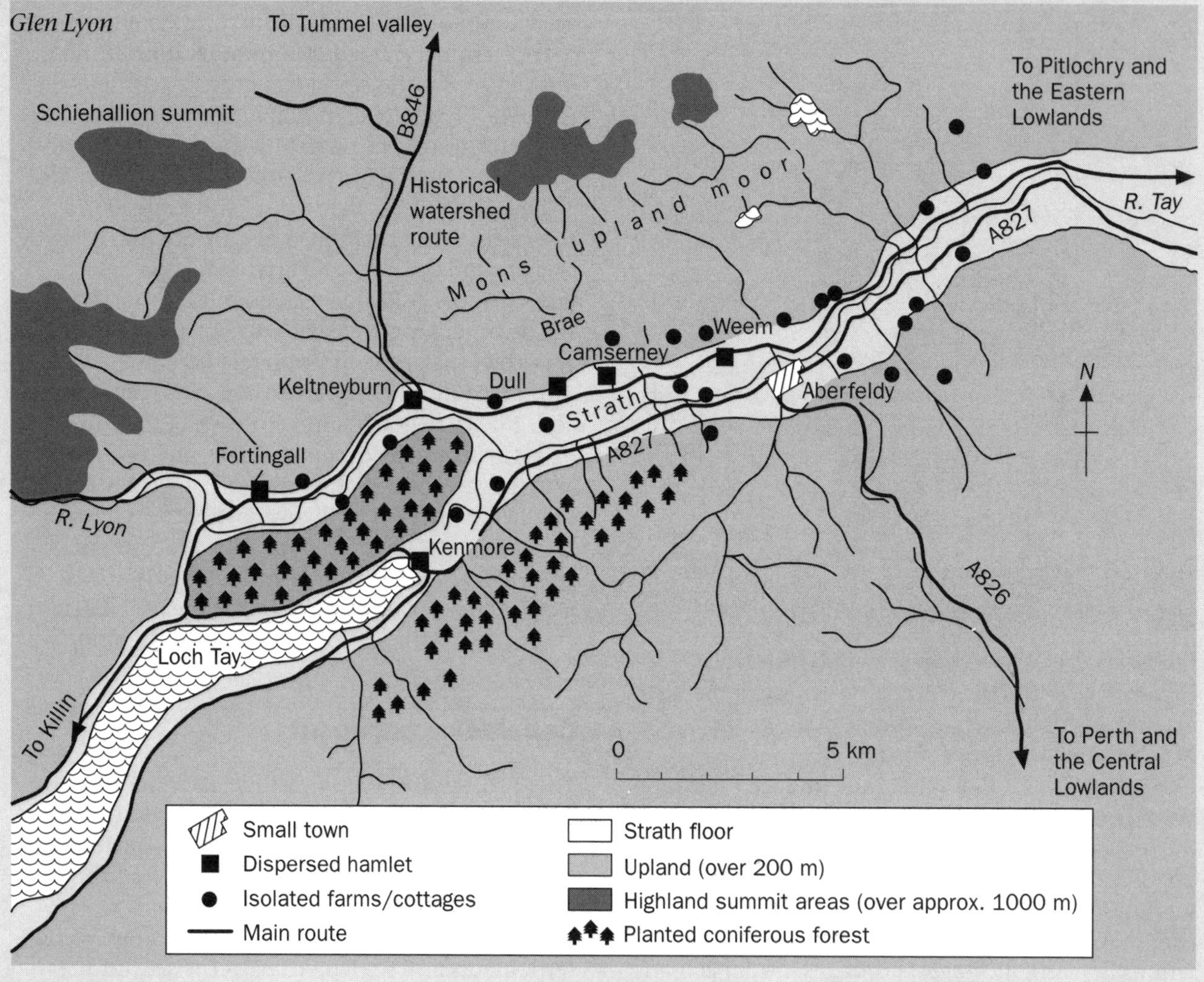

Characteristics

Glen Lyon shows a sparse linear settlement pattern along the lower valley edge, apart from the small market centre of Aberfeldy at a route node and bridging point.

Settlement units are of marginal viability, based on primary occupations, such as agriculture and forestry, but are now heavily reliant on external support socially and economically through subsidies, grants and tourism. The population is temporarily swollen in the summer, including second home occupancies.

Factors which affect the settlement pattern

The physical environment

The harsh dissected highland above the valley areas repels settlement; it is infertile, poorly drained, and much of of is with difficult access. Climatic conditions are uncertain. It is wet, with over 1270 mm precipitation, and experiences hard winters and frequent storms. The terrain is acidic, rough and poorly drained.

Settlement concentrates on the accessible valley edge with its more fertile soils and milder climate; most of it is on the sunny south-facing side. Avoidance of the valley floor is due to the liability of flooding.Settlement decreases westward into the Highland proper.

Aberfeldy's location is favoured by a bridging point and focal position, a dry terraced site and a sheltered aspect.

Human and historical influences

Apart from the emergence of Aberfeldy (in the eighteenth century) and some depopulation, especially from higher marginal settlements, the pattern has little altered since the fifteenth century.

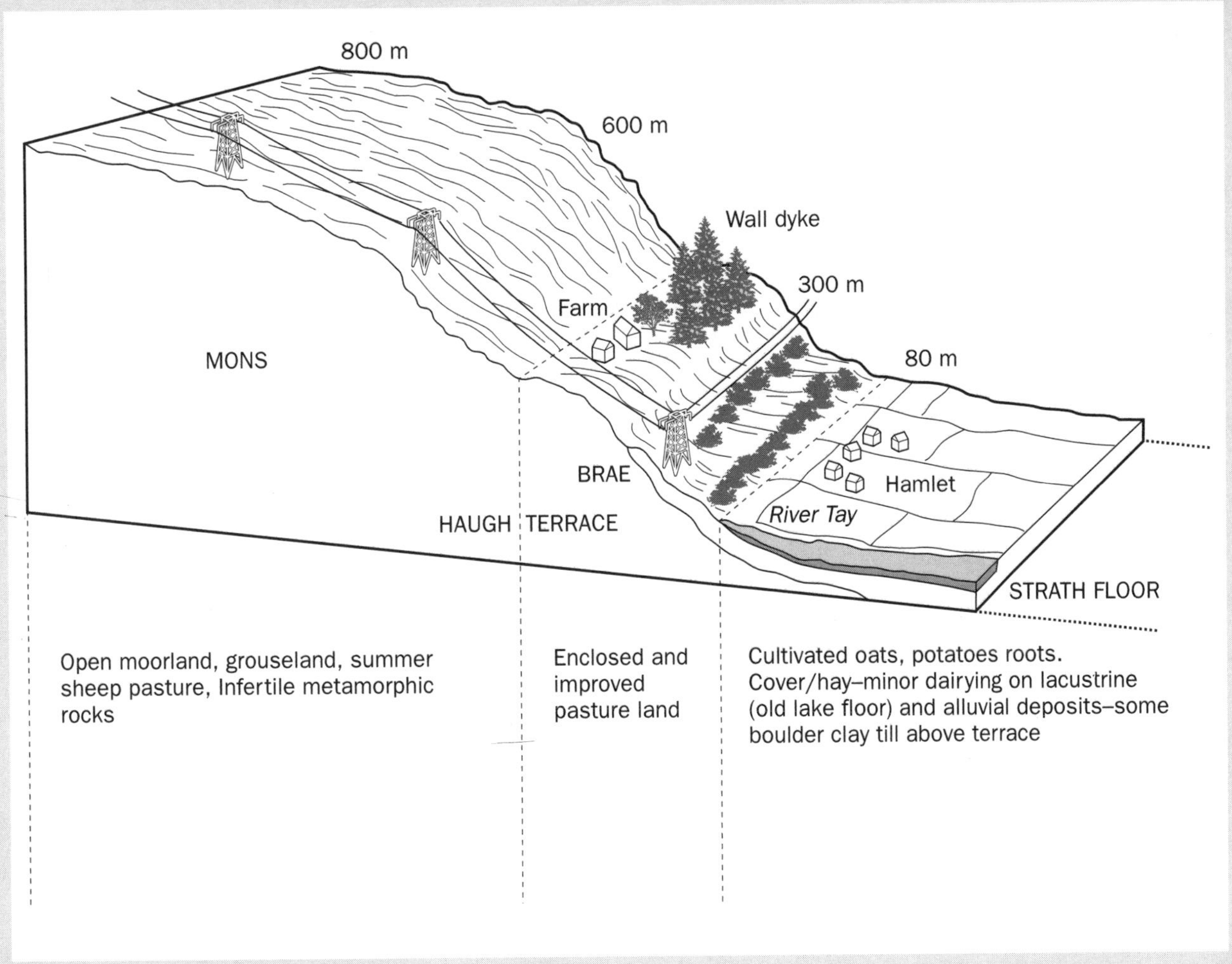

Glen Lyon: the physical environment

Phase 1

- Celtic settlement from the west with some later Nordic infusion from the east
- a self sufficient agriculturally based economy with Weem of ecclesiastical and military prominence.

Phase 2

- a clan feudal system to the mid-eighteenth century
- summer grazing on the upper slopes and peat for fuel; mixed farming on lower slopes, water mills for local craft work
- drove road links to outside world.

Phase 3

- depopulation following Jacobite rebellion causing the break up of clans
- conversion of upland to sheep runs and grouse moors.

Phase 4

- twentieth century rise of Aberfeldy following railway link of 1856
- marginal hillfarming, forestry, hydro-electric schemes and tourism supports sparse settlement.

An interrupted and truncated settlement hierarchy

Recent trends

Aberfeldy

Though a significant local shopping centre for the surrounding Highland settlements, Aberfeldy, is too isolated to develop into a higher order centre. It is anticipated that the people will travel to the growing regional centre of Perth for more durable goods. Aberfeldy is highly dependent on tourist expenditure thus the aim is to increase its attraction by upgrading the central area. Some addition to the retirement population is expected and land has been allocated for 50 or more houses. However, the population is not expected to rise much beyond its current level of 2000.

Glen Lyon

Especially in Glen Lyons, the key issue is how to arrest rural depopulation and maintain basic services for the small rural communities. Planners had the choice of targeting key rural settlements to develop them as 'regional community foci', or a dispersed strategy policy to preserve all the communities. They took the latter option, encouraging housing addition and some conversions within existing settlements. The main need is for more low cost housing, especially for the younger local population and to arrest the decline in jobs by diversifying agriculture through more tourism and adding craft and light industry centres to certain farm holdings and settlements. (Taymouth Castle is to be allowed to develop as a timeshare complex and a ski centre to the north of Drumochter.) However, like limited afforestation, this has to be done sensitively as most of the area is protected for its scenic value and fragile environmental and ecological importance.

case study

11.2 Cambridge: a dynamic settlement pattern

Characteristics

Cambridge shows a well settled and well defined pattern influenced by terrain and drainage, increasingly submerged beneath the invasion of urban dormitory influences.

It shows strong viable community structures. The fenland is still primarily agricultural, but other areas are under urbanisation pressures, having sometimes dual community structures, even in 'limited villages' which are protected by planning.

Cambridge has a controlled size of 110 000 and an overspill to dormitory villages of 1000 to 2000 in size. Controlled villages comprise approximately 200 to 600 inhabitants.

Factors which affect the settlement pattern

The physical environment

The pattern of settlement is still apparent but is increasingly overshadowed by human influences, especially with suburban and dormitory spread from the city.

The physically favourable areas for settlement are the chalklands to the east and south, the fen edges and the boulder clay plateau, together with greensand outcrops to the west. These areas offer generally firm, well-drained sites with a water supply along the springline or from wells. There are also good access routes.

Areas negative to settlement are the low-lying fenland and the Cam floodplain.

The early nodal growth of Cambridge has occurred on the river terraces of the River Cam and the chalk spurs which approach close to the original bridging point of the river.

Human and historical influences

Phase 1: to mid-nineteenth century

- settlement had its economic base in agriculture
- fertile fen edge soils and rich fenlands once they were drained
- chalkland and plateau favoured mixed farming
- Cambridge had a dual function as a long-established market town and ecclesiastical/university centre.

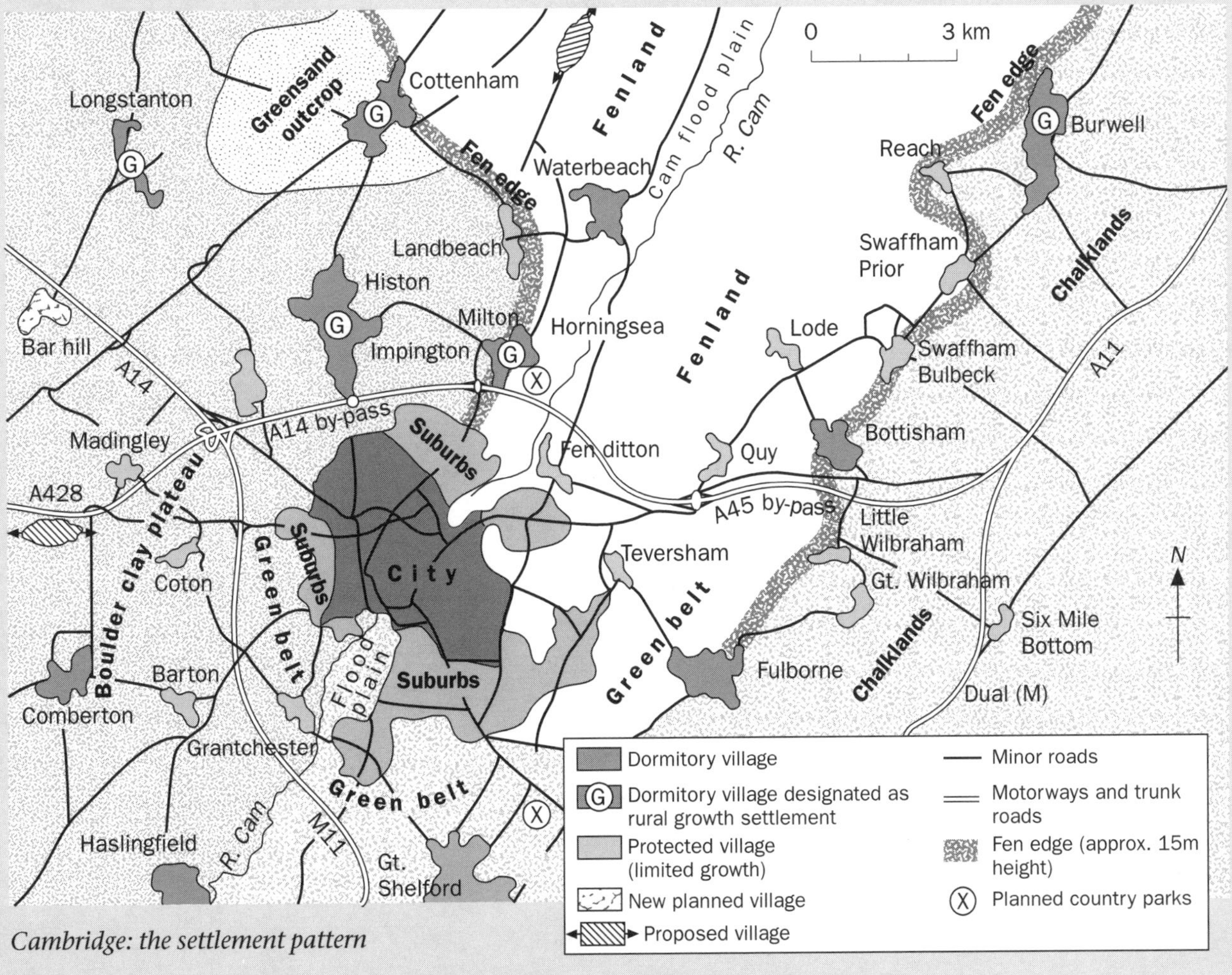

Cambridge: the settlement pattern

Phase 2: 1875 to 1945

- suburban growth of Cambridge takes in nearby villages e.g. Cherry Hinton, through ribbon development
- some town industry but Cambridge still has a strong agricultural base.

Phase 3: 1945 to present

- continued suburban pressure controlled by planners
- greenbelt and limited villages
- dormitory and light industrial growth in others
- London commuter influence to south.

Planning policy and future trends

(Revised Structure Plan 1989 and Rural Strategy Plan 1992)

- Constrain growth to the south of Cambridge where there is already too much pressure due to the combined pull of Cambridge and in migration of London commuting population.
- Cambridge is under substantial growth pressure because of high technology business and office expansion due to the prestige of location in the city, research and university links, language schools and other educational expansion. Tourism also brings in over three million visitors a year. Controlled growth is to be allowed mainly on the northern edge of the city near to the existing science park and in 'growth villages' north of the greenbelt, including two new villages on the A45, east of Cambridge and on the A10, towards Ely. These areas are to include housing and business parks.
- Growth is particularly encouraged to the north of the county in the fens which has stagnated economically due to the relative decline in agriculture. (Under the EU CAP policy, a further 27 800 ha will be taken out of cultivation in the 1990s.) High technology, light industry and service expansion is to be encouraged away from Cambridge to fen towns e.g. Ely and Wisbech, together with some tourism and recreational expansion e.g. a country park has been developed at Milton near Cambridge and water and nature study recreation centres in the fens.
- To the east of the county, growth in market towns along the A1 corridor has already occurred because of London overspill expansion in the 1950s and 1960s. With the upgrading of the A1 and the trunk road construction between this and the M1 to link the Midlands to the east coast ports, self sustaining growth is likely.

However, any expansion will be constrained by the need to maintain the historical character of Cambridge and its greenbelt and to safeguard land designated as environmentally sensitive and/or of high grade agriculturally. Land liable to flooding should also be avoided.

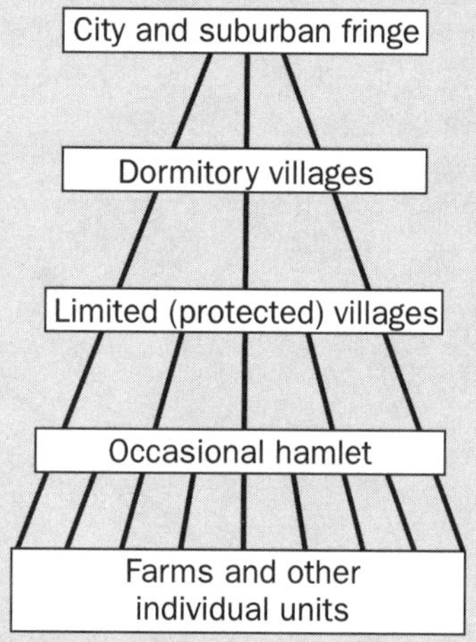

A well-defined and ordered settlement hierarchy (modified by planning intervention)

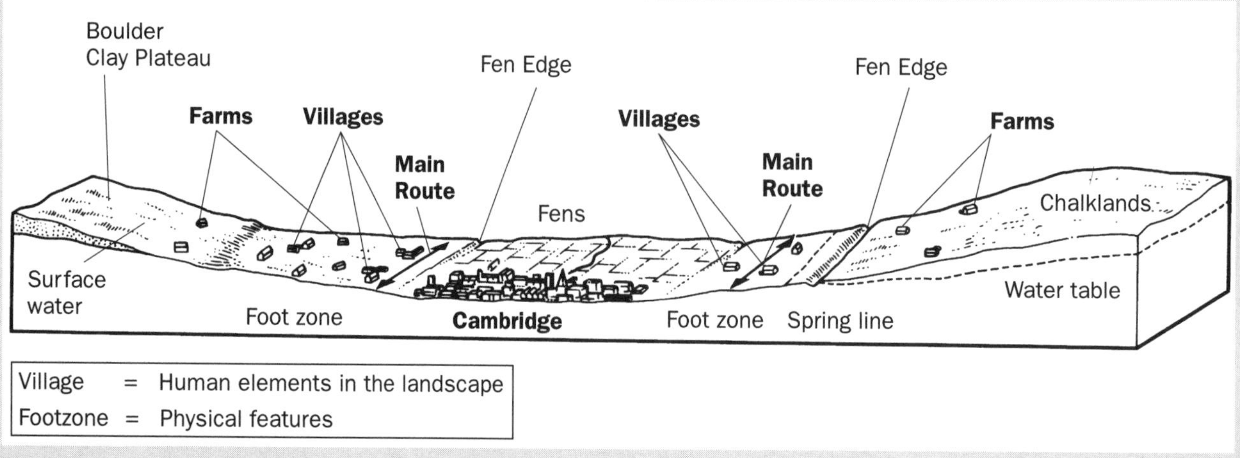

Cross-section relating settlement to physical features in the landscape

case study

11.3 Mexico City and Tokyo: two primate cities

Mexico City

Mexico City is located in a fertile plain with a moderate climate and is at the focus of routes coming off the adjacent plateau. It was the centre of the Aztec empire before the coming of the Europeans. The city then stood on an island in a lagoon, which was later drained.

History

After the Spanish Conquest, Mexico City was made the heart of the colonial empire and administrative centre. This continued after Mexico became independent in 1821. Since then, it has attracted much of the commercial and industrial growth as well as being the cultural centre.

The route network hinged around Mexico City but by 1930, it only had a population of 1.3 million, despite already being the primate city. Its greatest growth came with the rapid urbanisation since the 1950s as Mexico became more industrialised and the rural population was drawn into the city itself.

Current situation

Mexico City has a population of 33 million (including the built areas beyond its administrative boundary), one-third of the country's population, and is overwhelmingly dominant in every way. It generates one-third of the country's gross domestic product and has two-fifths of its manufacturing, partly because of its market size and cumulative attractions. As the cultural heart of the country it has an increasing tourist industry.

Problems

Severe diseconomies have set in because of the city's rapid growth and size. The government has been unable to provide the necessary expansion of service and housing (an estimated 75% of housing is substandard). Its pollution problems are the worst of any city in the world, particularly because of traffic and industrial exhaust and gas emissions. The government are attempting to decentralise activities away from Mexico City but as yet, no alternative growth pole has been set up.

Tokyo

Tokyo is situated in the most extensive fertile plain in Japan, at the head of Tokyo Bay, with access to coastal and shipping routes. It is located in the Pacific Belt, the most prosperous region of Japan.

Location of Mexico City and the primary road network

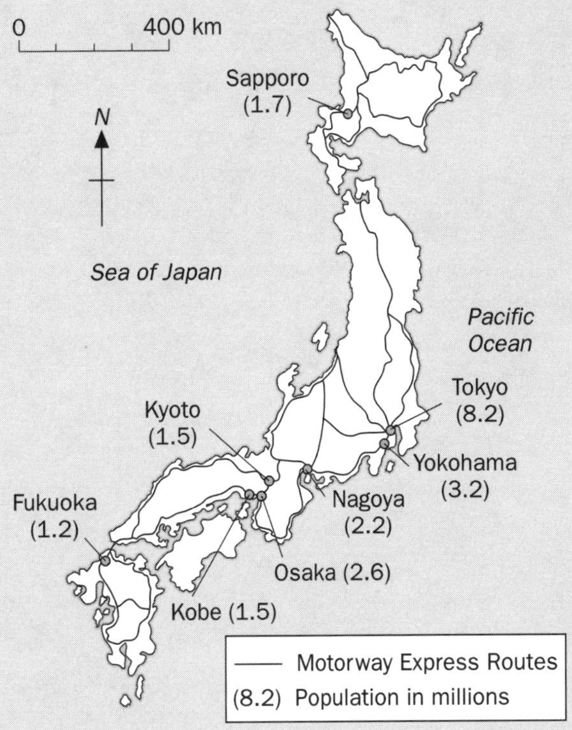

Location of Tokyo and the motorway express network

[redacted]

History

Effective political power was transferred to Edo (later called Tokyo) in 1603 and since then, it was consciously developed as the effective administrative, commercial and economic heart of Japan, at the expense of other regions and cities. The transport network was developed around it.

As early as 1700, Tokyo's population had reached 1 million. At the Meiji Restoration in 1869, it became the official capital and the centre of Japan's industrialisation and modernisation programme. As this progressed, Tokyo's dominance in every sphere increased because of its cumulative attraction.

Current situation

Tokyo is overwhelming dominant because of the cumulative effect of Japan's post-1945 prosperity boom and because of the increasing internationalisation of the city. Greater Tokyo has now spread to dominate the area within a 50 km radius, with its population of approximately 30 million people, giving it a tremendous market pull. It has one-third of Japan's manufacturing and an even greater share of its commerce and services. Tokyo is the third financial capital of the world and an international cultural centre.

Problems

Severe diseconomies have set in. For example, astronomical land prices, congestion and housing shortages have prompted planned decentralisation of the population and economic activities to satellite cities. Osaka has been promoted as a second international city to act as a counter magnet.

12

CHAPTER 12

Decentralisation and change

'Whilst the pace of urban population growth was accelerating in the third world, the urbanisation process at least in terms of the concentration of population into large agglomerations appeared to be going into reverse in the first world – a population turnaround was occurring.'

CHAMPION A G *COUNTERURBANISATION*, 1989

12.1 Decentralisation in developed countries

Settlement patterns are never static for any length of time. In western countries, change has been dominated by the flow of people into cities, leading to the emergence of large conurbations and metropolitan areas as it is doing today in developing countries.

While until recently, inward flow dominated in western countries there was also some counter movement of people out of the cities.

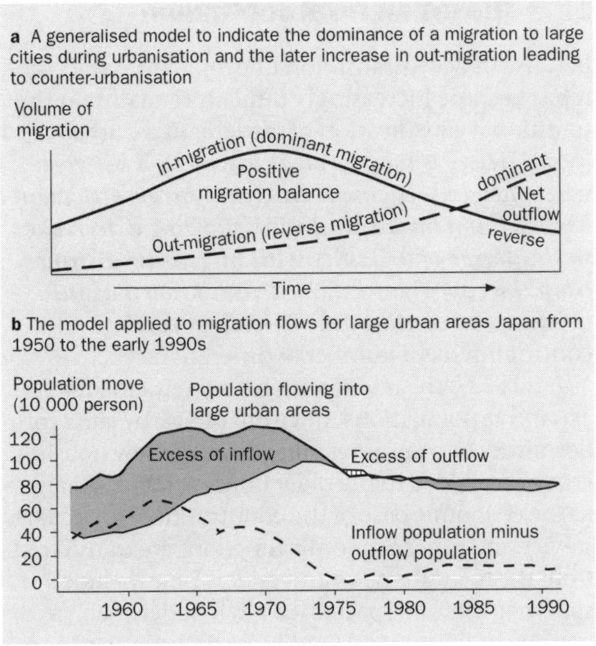

Figure 12.1 Inward flow replaced by outward migration from large cities

Population change, 1981-91, by type of district, south and north of Great Britain separately.

Type of district	South		North	
	000s	%	000s	%
Total	+485.4	+1.71	– 689.2	– 2.51
Greater London				
Inner boroughs	– 147.0	– 5.89	–	–
Outer boroughs	– 171.5	– 4.08	–	–
Metropolitan				
Principal cities	–	–	– 369.7	– 8.69
Other districts	–	–	– 371.9	– 4.30
Non-metropolitan				
Large cities	– 58.7	– 3.29	– 72.1	– 4.00
Small cities	+8.6	+ 0.84	+ 2.4	+ 0.30
Industrial areas	+ 49.1	+ 1.89	– 91.0	– 1.90
Districts with new towns	+ 102.4	+ 8.86	+30.6	+ 2.04
Resort, port & retirement	+ 152.6	+ 5.77	+ 20.9	+ 3.03
Urban and mixed urban/rural	+ 282.1	+ 3.76	+ 36.6	+1.63
Remote, mainly rural	+ 240.8	+ 7.25	+ 124.9	+ 4.64

NOTES: 'South' refers to the south-east, south-west, east Anglia and east Midlands regions.
'–' = no cases.
Losses are greatest for large cities.
[SOURCE: Calculated from OPCS (1991a) and RGS (1991), *Geographical magazine*, January 1992]

Figure 12.2 Counterurbanisation in the UK, 1981 – 1991

a The gradient of the urban-rural continuum

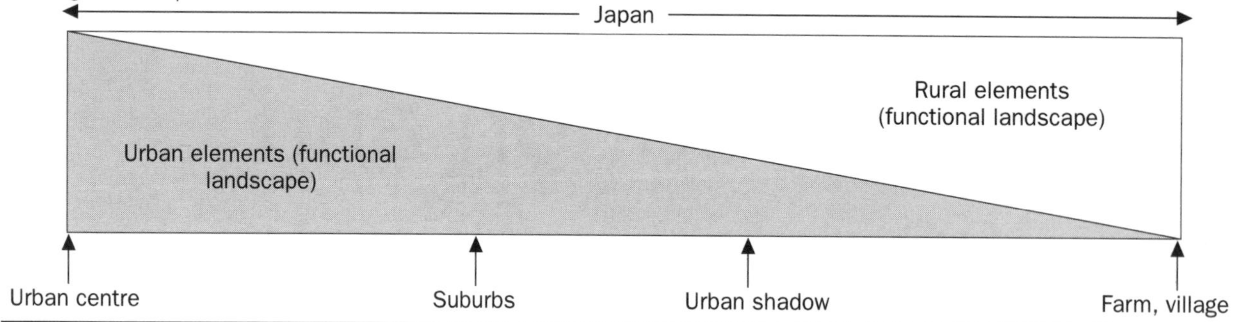

Type of space	**A**	**A**	**B**	**C**	**D**	**E**	**F**
	Urban	Suburban	Urban shadow	Peripheral	Highly agricultural	Remote	Self-employment
Landscape	U + r	U + R	u + R	R	R	R	U + R
Employment structure	U + r	U + r	U + R	U + R	u + R	U + R	U + r
Type of off-farm employment	⟵ Commuting to city jobs ⟶ highest - degree of intensity - lowest			← Daily wage labour →		← Seasonal → migratory work	← Self- → employment

b Type of space

U : Dominant urban element
R : Dominant rural element
u : Minor urban element
r : Minor rural element

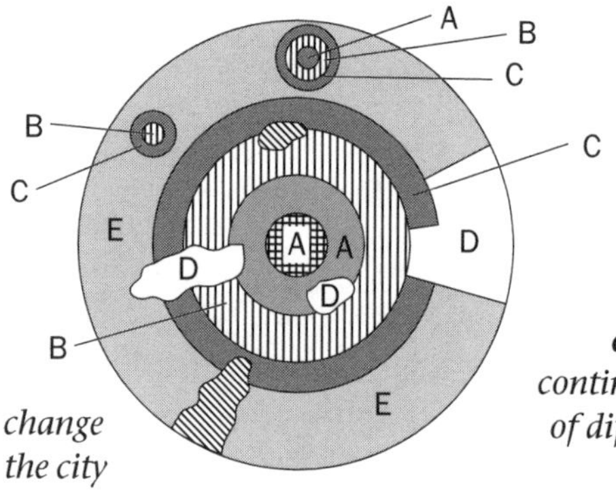

c Model of the urban-rural continuum and the distribution of different types of rural space around a metropolis

***Figure 12.3** The urban-rural continuum and the change in landscape and occupations with distance from the city*

Studies of such counter-urbanisation in the USA and Western Europe have shown that during the 1960s and 1970s, this decentralisation trend had become dominant; more people are leaving the cities than moving into them. Thus the earlier urbanisation trend has been reversed and despite some slowing down of this reversal in the early 1980s, it has continued bringing marked changes to the pattern of settlement in the countryside, especially around the larger cities. (Case study 11.2).

Even around the turn of the century when movement into the cities was still in progress, Ebenezer Howard, who became one of the leaders of the 'Garden City' movement wrote that *'while the age in which we live is the age of the great closely compacted overcrowded city, there are already signs that for those who can read them, of a coming change so great and momentous that the twentieth century will be known as the great exodus from the city.'*
(Ward A *Old prophets of new city regions, Town and Country Planning,* Dec. 1990)

12.2 The urban-rural continuum

Because of decentralisation of people from the cities, it has become increasingly difficult to maintain the traditional classification of settlement as 'urban' and 'rural'. ***There is now no clear distinction between where urban settlement ends and rural settlement begins, but a broad gradation showing a decrease in the degree of urbanity with increasing distance from the city*** (Figure 12.2). ***This is known as the urban-rural continuum.*** The urban-rural continuum has a number of different facets.

It includes the rate at which rural settlements expand as populations move out of nearby cities into dormitory or commuter villages and as new housing estates are added to the older housing fabric. Changes to the economic base of the countryside also occur as service and other economic functions are transferred from the town to the countryside. These include supermarkets and specialised retail outlets, such as boutiques. Offices and light industry have also been attracted to a more rural location because of its more pleasant environment and cheaper land.

Important social changes are affecting rural communities which are subjected to the incursion of urban households. The traditionally close community ties tend to be broken down and a more complex social structure is created, sometimes of a broadly dual nature with not infrequently tension occurring between the older established villagers and the newcomers.

The increasing recreational needs of city dwellers are resulting in more land being taken from farming and put to leisure use, hence the increasing number of areas designated as country parks and allocated to golf courses. Farmers are also converting buildings to craft and leisure activities, prompted by the decline in the profitability of agriculture and government incentives for using farm land for other purposes.

Indices	Characteristics in rural areas
Population per acre	Low
% change in population 1951 - 61, 1961 - 71	Decrease
% total population: over 65 years	High
% total population: male 15 - 45 years	Low
% total population: female 15 - 45 years	Low
Occupancy rate: % population at 1.5 per room	Low
Households per dwelling	Low
% households with exclusive use of: (a) Hot water (b) Fixed bath (c) Inside WC	High
% in socio-economic groups: 13/14 farmers	High
% in socio-economic group: 15 farm workers	High
% residents in employment working outside the rural district	Low
% population resident for < 5 years	Low
% population moved out in last year	Low
% in-/ out-migrants	Low
Distance from nearest urban centre of 50 000	High
Distance from nearest urban centre of 100 000	High
Distance from nearest urban centre of 200 000	High

[SOURCE: Cloke P J *An index of rurality for England and Wales, Regional Studies II*, 1977]

Figure 12.4 *Index of rurality*

Impact of changes is related to distance from major cities

The extent of changes is related to distance away from the major cities. As would be expected, change decreases in intensity with distance, but as studies have shown, the effect of decentralisation of people and activities from large cities is still felt across settlements in the more remote areas. For example, one third of the increase in the number of residents in the highlands and islands of Scotland between 1971 and 1981 was due to the migration from England and Wales, many of them self employed and from the larger cities. Robinson attributes these moves to *'a conscious social distancing (on the part of the movers away) from metropolitan work structures, consumption patterns and life styles'.*

Thus the rural-urban continuum can now be said to stretch from the largest cities to the most remote rural areas. There are a number of measures of the intensity of change over distance, of which perhaps the most well known is Cloke's ***index of rurality*** (1977) shown in Figure 12.4.

The index is derived by combining a range of socio-economic measures or variables, giving absolute urbanity at one extreme and absolute rurality at the other. Using a five-fold classification, he produced a map of England and Wales based on the index of rurality (Figure 12.5). In addition, it highlighted those areas most under pressure from the outward movement of people and urban traits from the major conurbations.

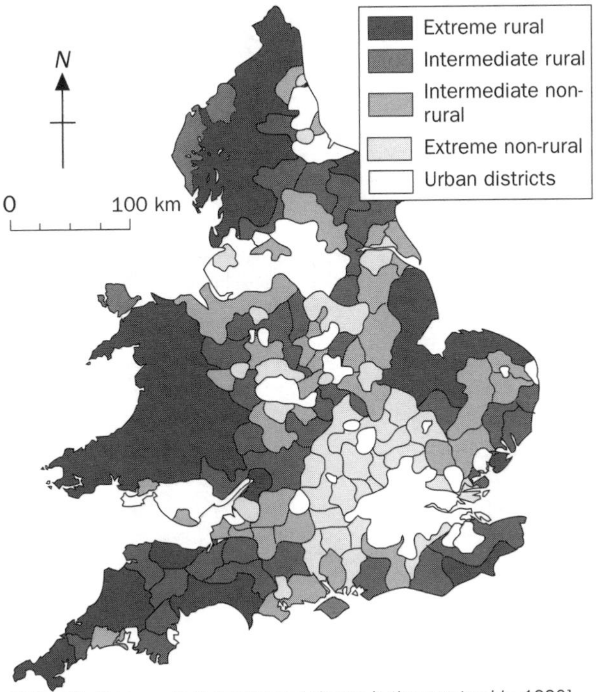

[SOURCE: Robinson G M *Conflict and change in the countryside*, 1990]

Figure 12.5 *Rurality in England and Wales, 1981*

12.3 Intensification and spread of the decentralisation process

Decentralisation develops over a number of phases or stages in which different factors vary in importance. A complex interplay of related factors influences decentralisation trends (Figure 12.6). Some have been evident for a long period. Others are more recent. As cities initially develop some activities are pushed to the fringe, but later there is a movement to create suburbs, which extends the city into the rural area and engulfs the existing fringe. Any further fringe development would occur on the edge of the suburbs. During the later part of the twentieth century, people and economic activities have relocated from the city to these sub-urban fringes, thus invading of the countryside. Fringe zones, older and newer suburbs and some urbanisation of the countryside beyond exists around most sizeable cities.

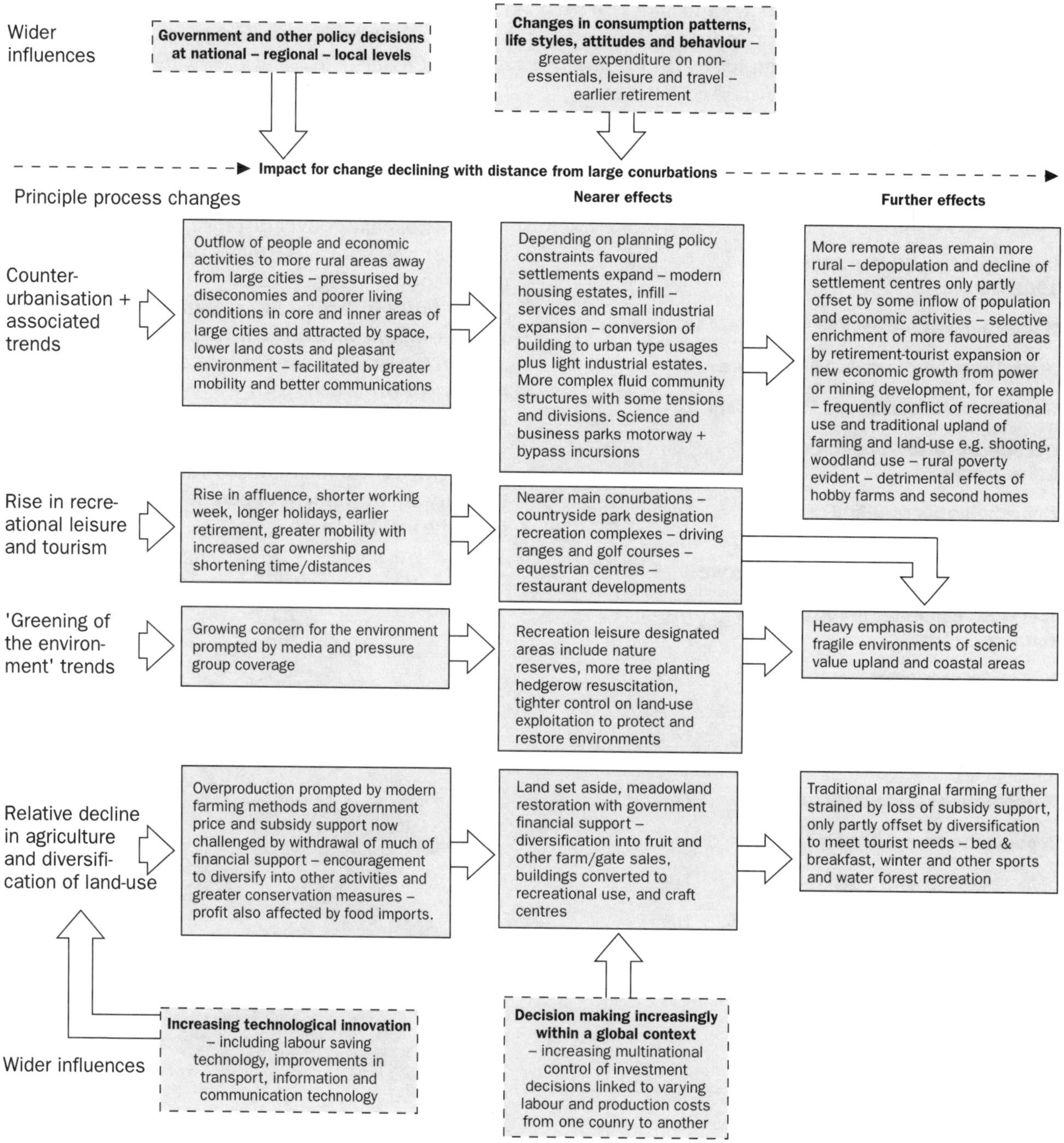

Figure 12.6 Factors and processes which alter the settlement pattern and socio-economic base of the countryside

The rural urban fringe

The rural urban fringe is the zone of transition between the built up area of the city and the surrounding countryside. Within it, urban activities have begun to encroach on the rural landscape showing an intermixed land use pattern. The rural urban fringe tends to be marked by those land usages either unable to afford a more central location or needing to be isolated from the main built up area of the city. At the turn of the century these included cemeteries, sewage works and isolation hospitals, together with playing fields. In addition, detached houses and villas built by business people who looked for a more rural location and affordable space, were also a feature.

Before green belt restrictions were placed around cities, this rural urban fringe would have been engulfed by the next phase of expansion of the city and incorporated within it (Figure 16.3). Conzen, Whitehand and others who studied the successive rings of suburban development round the older core and inner areas of cities, have identified a number of fringes now encapsulated with in the built up area, each fringe marking a stage of standstill before the next phase of city expansion (Figures 12.7 and 12.8).

Today extension of the urban rural fringe extends beyond the Green Belt and because of this and other planning restrictions, it is unlikely to be incorporated into the city in the future. However, considerable pressure and change continues to occur on the existing rural urban fringe, particularly around major cities (Case study 12.1).

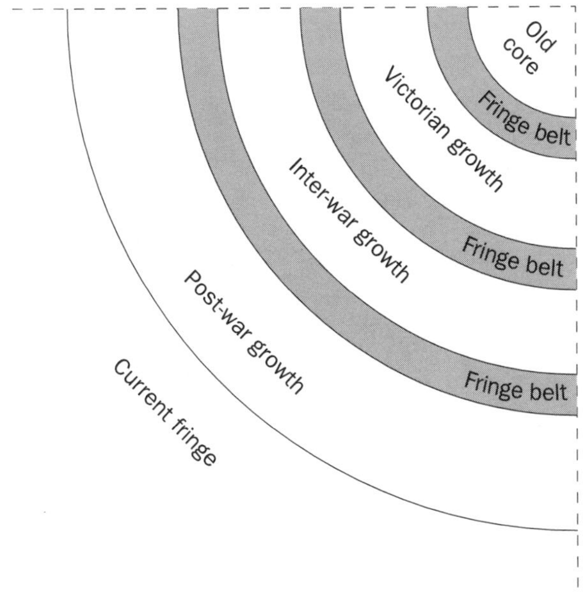

Figure 12.7 *A model of fringe belts*

The suburbanisation phase

The suburbanisation phase is defined as the decentralisation of people, employment and services from the inner and central areas of cities and their relocation towards the margins of the built up area, a process which has led to the build up of suburbs and the extension of the city over a larger area. Suburbanisation is a process which has been happening since the medieval period and which greatly intensified since the last quarter of the nineteenth century.

In the nineteenth century suburbs were built mainly for the wealthier middle classes who moved away from overcrowded living conditions and the increasing mass of the poor in the inner areas of the city. They were drawn by the more spacious environment of the countryside in which they could build large homes in large garden plots. Improvements in transport with the extension of the rail network around the largest cities increasingly enabled business people to live in rural surroundings yet commute to their work places in the city.

From the 1930s there was a mass escalation in the process of suburbanisation as mobility was increased with improved bus services and greater car ownership. Higher levels of income and aspirations towards home ownership encouraged many clerical and skilled workers to move to the suburbs. Cheaper home ownership and mass building construction enabled more families to realise their dream of a house and garden in a semi rural setting.

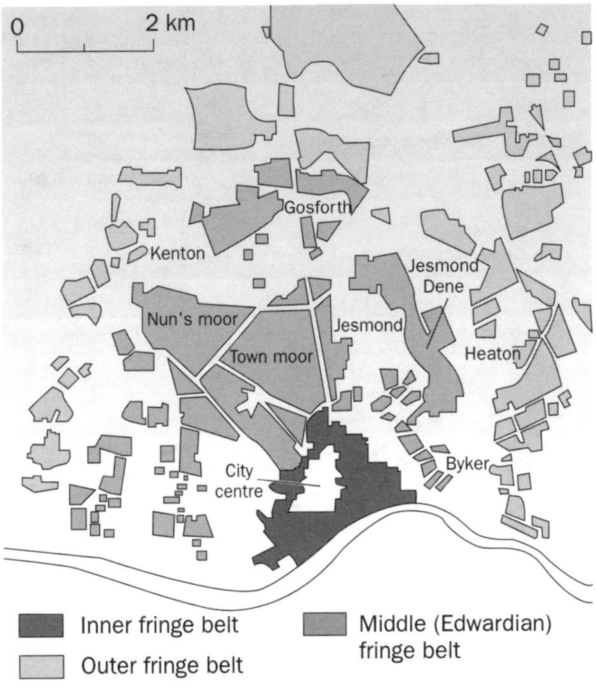

Figure 12.8 *Newcastle upon Tyne, 1965: an example of early fringe belt development*

The vast spread of interwar suburbia surrounding the older parts of large cities in England and to some extent, other West European countries and the USA, are evidence of this revolution in home ownership.

After the Second World War the process of suburbanisation continued but in a less active manner, as the further sprawl of cities in to the countryside was controlled by tight greenbelt restrictions on building. Furthermore, post-war suburbs tend to have a more diversified land use. They include large local authority housing estates as people were moved out of slums and other substandard housing in inner cities (Figures 14.6). Businesses have also followed labour out to the newer suburbs with the construction of light industrial estates and office parks. More recently, supermarkets and hypermarkets have moved, attracted by cheaper sites, motor way access and expanding market demand in outer suburban and fringe areas (Section 15.5).

Throughout the period of suburbanisation, the spread of housing and other urban land usages has enveloped the older rural villages and hamlets, incorporating them into the fabric of the city. Much was destroyed, but evidence of the earlier rural landscape remains in the village church and pub, in former country mansions and in labourers' cottages, now much desired because of their distinctive character and links with the past (Case studies 11.2 and 14.1).

The stages by which the countryside has passed from being completely rural to becoming the urban fringe, and then through suburban spread to being incorporated as part of the built up area of the city is illustrated in the development on the south-eastern edge of metropolitan London since the second half of the nineteenth century to the mid-twentieth century (Figure 12.9).

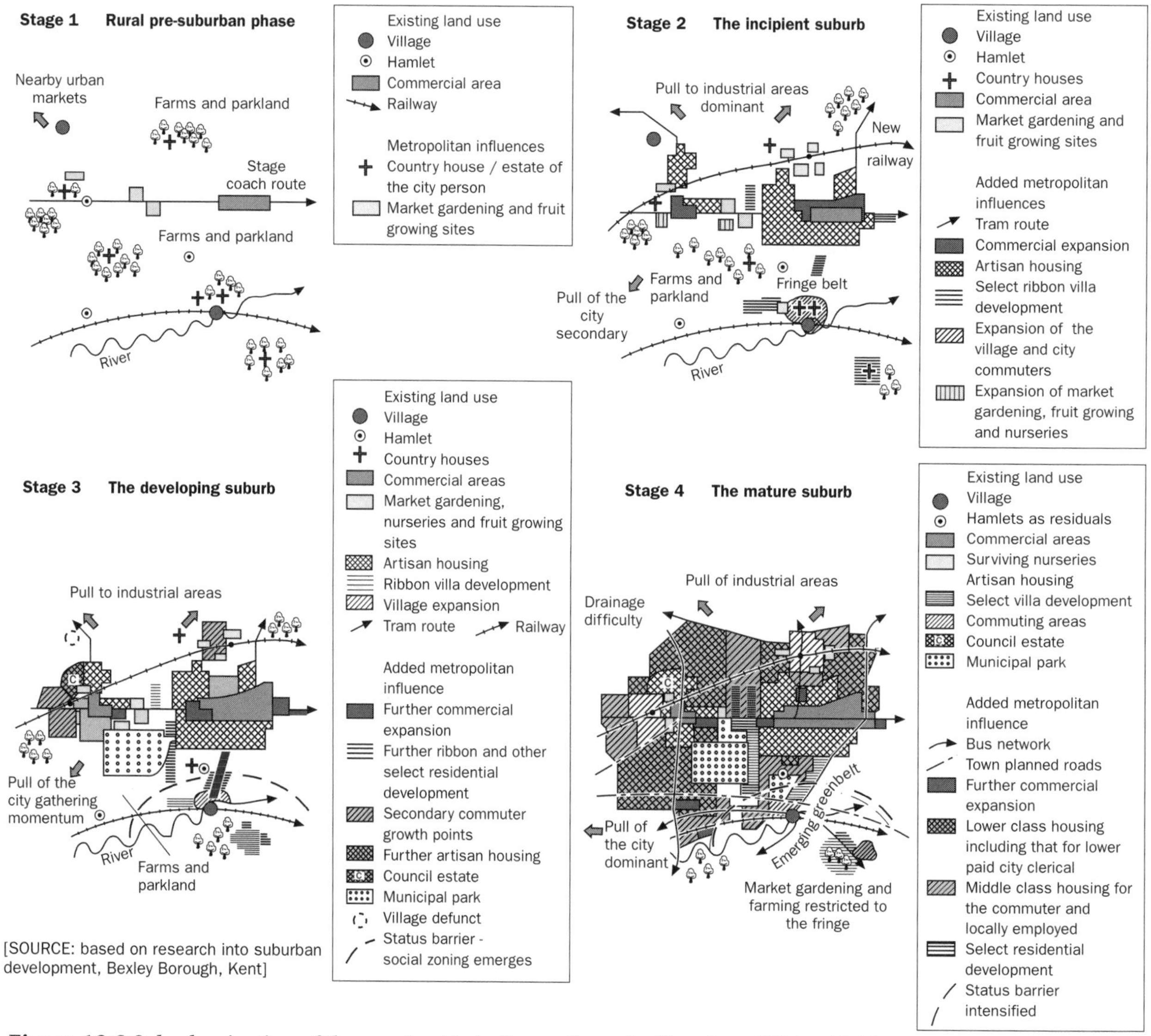

***Figure 12.9** Suburbanisation of the countryside to the south-east of London, 1880 – 1945*

Suburbanisation of the countryside or counter-urbanisation

Since the 1960s, outward movement from the city has been physically detached from it, thus preventing urban spread. The effect therefore on the countryside has been quite different. The countryside is changed but not engulfed by the city. Moreover, decentralisation which has leapfrogged the green belt is more tightly controlled by the planning regulations which are incorporated into county structure plans and rural strategy policy documents.

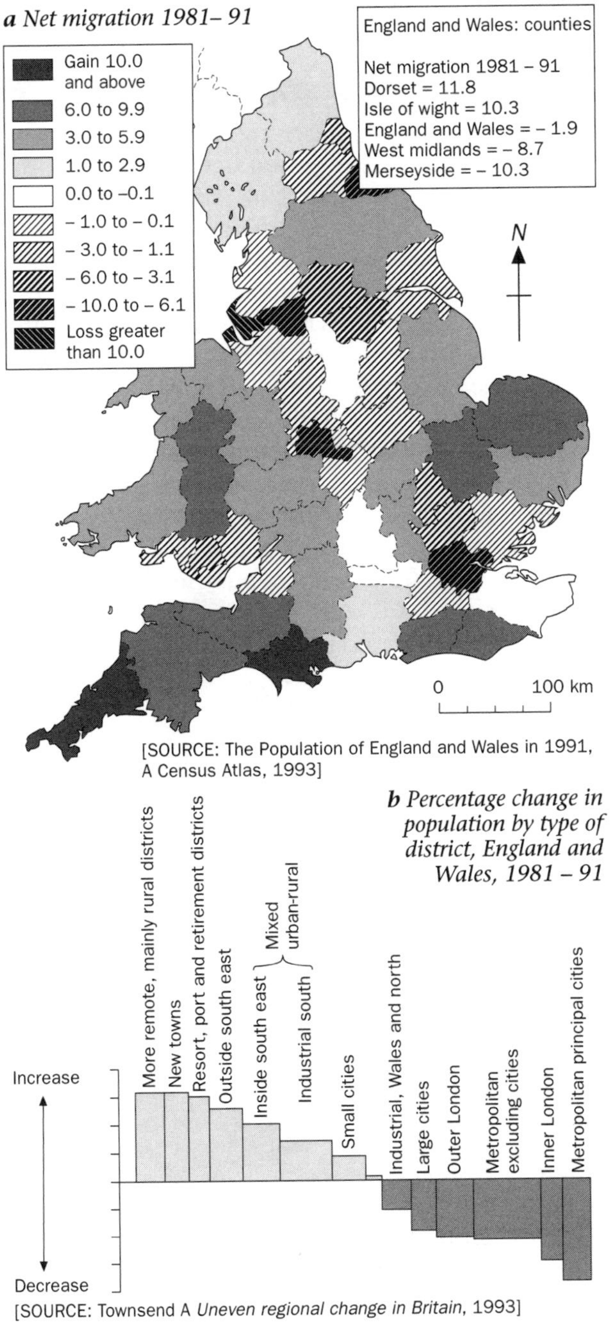

[SOURCE: The Population of England and Wales in 1991, A Census Atlas, 1993]

[SOURCE: Townsend A *Uneven regional change in Britain*, 1993]

Figure 12.10 *Migration and population change in England and Wales, 1981 – 91*

The scenario is further complicated by other movements which affect rural areas, such as the continued movement of some people from these rural areas to the cities in search of further education and employment. There is also movement between different rural areas. An additional and more important trend is the increasing volume of temporary movement of people from the cities into the countryside for leisure and holidays.

The decentralisation of people and activities into the countryside from the cities has loosely been described as 'suburbanisation of the countryside'. More recently the term 'counter-urbanisation' has been used because of the growing dominance of this decentralisation trend and its distinction from the suburban spread, which was essentially part of the urbanisation process which added to the growth of cities.

This switch from urbanisation to counterurbanisation can be measured by comparing the rate of population change for metropolitan areas against those for rural and non-metropolitan areas (Figure 12.10). The table for England and Wales indicates that it is the smaller towns and rural areas which have the greatest positive percentage change. This is also the case for other countries of Western Europe and the USA. Urbanisation has been replaced by counterurbanisation (Figure 12.10).

12.4 Counterurbanisation: more than people moving to the countryside

The reversal of trends is about more than the outflow of people into the countryside, just as the process of urbanisation is more than the movement of people into the cities. Urbanisation was associated with industrialisation and a change in the way of life of the people 'swept' up in it. So also, counterurbanisation is linked to the decentralisation of economic life away from the city and the de-industrialisation process which now affects western countries as service activities, information and high technology enterprises replace traditional industries as the 'engine of the economy'.

Keinath, in his study of counterurbanisation in the USA (1985), emphasises this decentralisation of economic life towards the periphery and especially towards the more rural environment of the sunbelt states, such as Florida and California (Case study 5.1; Section 15.5). Newby shows the same for counter-urbanisation in the UK – *'for the first time since the industrial revolution technological change is allowing rural areas to compete on equal terms with towns and cities for employment.'*

As part of this trend in the UK, Hall writes of the transformation of the countryside into a *'golden belt'* westward from London to as far as Devon, Dorset and Somerset, and north-west and north-eastward towards Oxford and Northampton and into East Anglia. In East Anglia there has been a *'proliferation of new houses, new housing estates, new roads and motorways, superstores and business parks stretching past the provincial centres of Cambridge and Norwich and enveloping the once sleepy market towns such as Woodbridge, Diss and King's Lynn'.*

Counter-urbanisation is thus very different in character from the decentralisation of people into the rural fringe of cities, creating dormitory settlements from which they commute daily back into the city. Some of this still happens, but according to Berry, counter-urbanisation represents a conscious decision on the part of peoples and families involved in it 'to turn their backs on the city' and both live and work in a rural environment.

12.5 Counterurbanisation: its effect on the overall settlement pattern

A less defined pattern of settlement

Despite counterurbanisation, it is too soon to talk of the demise of the large city. Large cities are still seen as the main foci of economic activity into the twenty-first century, especially as the role of the largest cities, such as London, Tokyo and New York, is global as well as national. However, the term 'city region' which links the area around the city to it as a functioning whole, is beginning to lose its meaning. The traditional pattern of population and economic concentration separated by more sparsely populated rural areas is giving way to a more dispersed pattern in which the functional unit is no longer the city region, but a much wider and less defined area.

This new type of area consists of an interconnected settlement network based on complementary functional relationships, rather than the hierarchial system of settlements described in Central Place theory, with the one large settlement dominant at the head of the hierarchy. However, in the new pattern not every settlement will be equally successful so that a very varied pattern of population can be expected. Planning measures too affect the pattern.

A decline in agriculture also changes the basis of rural areas

The traditional rural settlement pattern is disappearing and farming will no longer provide the fundamental basis for rural life as it has done in the past. The erosion of rural life and landscape has been occurring since the 1950s and has been accelerating. The transformation is not solely the result of the counter-urbanisation process; it has also been due to the decline in the importance of agriculture itself. For example, within the UK the amount of land devoted to agricultural production fell by 265 000 ha from 1986 to 1990 and official estimates of further losses to 1995 are at 150 000 ha, with the loss of another 25 000 jobs in agriculture and the related food processing industries.

Where counterurbanisation trends are dominant, the agricultural base will be largely replaced by economic activities decentralised from the city and the new service and information-based enterprises now being set up in rural areas (Figure 12.11). Attempts by farmers to diversify into non-agricultural activities, such as leisure provision for city people and those families moving out to the countryside, will be of some significance but much less important (Section 29.4; Case study 29.3).

In more remote areas, especially upland areas, the economic outlook appears bleak. Some compensation for the fall in agricultural income may be gained from seasonal tourism but this will be limited. In the UK it is estimated that the gross income per household gained from a bed and

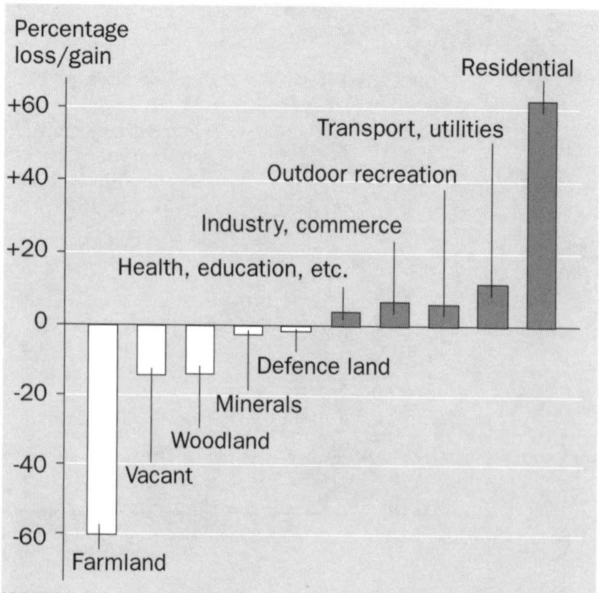

[SOURCE: Council for the Protection of Rural England from DOE figures]

Figure 12.11 Land use change in rural areas in England, 1960 – 1990

breakfast supplementary activity, which is the principal source of income from tourism, is only £3000 per year per farm household. This is not nearly enough to compensate for the fall in agricultural income. Conservation activities, afforestation and other schemes are unlikely to make up the deficiency even with government support.

Concluding comment

Rural areas may be divided into two main categories, though because of the rural urban continuum, the division is not clear cut.

One category includes those accessible areas where counterurbanisation forces are transforming the settlement pattern and way of life (Case studies 11.2 and 4.2).

The other category includes those more remote areas where, without substantial government support, depopulation will continue and counter-urbanisation flows will be too weak to prevent the decline in the economic base of the settlements which are affected. With this decline in population and economic income, the local infrastructure of transport, welfare and other services cannot be adequately supported, so that small settlements will ultimately disappear. This continues a trend already evident on the upland margins and other remote areas in western countries. (Case studies 11.1 and 24.4).

case study

12.1 Pressures and opportunities on the western urban-rural fringe of London

A policy for the urban fringe

'Until the 1960s the urban fringe has been one of the forgotten areas of planning – neither town nor country it has fallen between the traditional spheres of planning activity' (Pryce G *The Planner*, 1992).

Today it is an essential component of urban life and for the most part it fulfils functions directly related to urban life. Its proximity to towns and cities has often been the cause of its gradual degradation and results in it attracting intense pressures for change and development. There is intense conflict and competition for limited space.

Following a circular from the Ministry of the Environment in 1983, a more positive approach has been advocated in respect of the Green Belt. Positive management should help to restore and enhance the landscape, promote recreational uses, especially for the local population, and to safeguard agricultural and woodland areas by restricting public access.

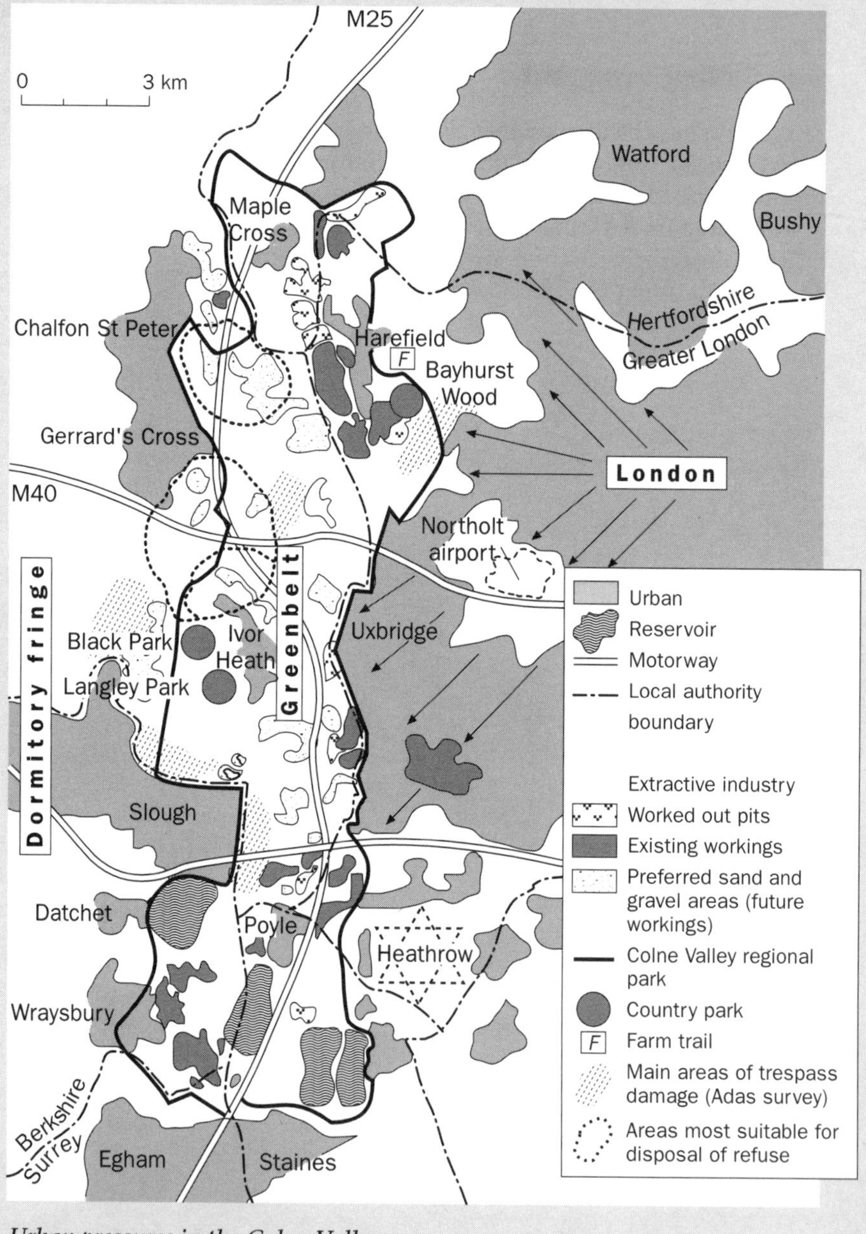

Urban pressures in the Colne Valley

Urbanisation pressures

The undisciplined growth of London and its dormitory satellites in the interwar period brought with it increasing pressure. The improvement of rail and road transport networks and the increasing realisation of home ownership aspirations exacerbated urbanisation.

Green belt legislation was initiated in 1938 to control the spread of London and was incorporated in Abercrombie's 'Greater London Plan in 1944, but it came too late to prevent the urban fringe intrusion into the Colne Valley through, for example, gravel workings, sewage stations and landfill waste site. However, it did control residential building.

Pressure for housing, especially in the 1960s to 1980s period, led to further substantial dormitory spread immediately west of the Green Belt, for example, at Slough.

To this was added the increasing popularity of out-of-town sites for offices, light and service industries and retail complexes as, for example, in the vicinity of Gerrards Cross.

The building of the M25 orbital motorway around London, through the Colne Valley, together with the M4 and M25 increased the pressures on the fringe.

The growing traffic on the motorways and increasing air traffic from Heathrow added to environmental and air pollution, while water areas were affected by waste disposal seepage.

Throughout the postwar period demands on the green belt area by public utilities, such as schools, and increased recreation needs for golf, riding and water sports, for example, have added to the pressure.

The Colne Valley Regional Park

In 1965 there was a proposal to convert a 40 sq. mile swath of mixed land use, including prime development land and other land severely depleted by mineral and gravel extraction, into the Colne Valley Regional Park. It was the nearest continuous belt of open country to London and a target for further road development, power and pipelines, sewage and scrap metal yards. The area lies in the Colne Valley; through it runs the Grand Union canal. The area was already disrupted by the lines of the M4, M40 and the M25.

The park was inaugurated in 1969 and involved liaison between 11 local authorities and national bodies, like the Countryside Commission. In 1982 the Colne Valley Groundwork Trust was set up to coordinate the work, financed largely by the local authorities which had areas in the park.

Much of the area is under private ownership. The most formidable task was reclaiming the huge mineral workings and land which had been scarred by gravel works. The owners and volunteers contributed to the reclamation. The landscape has been improved by tree planting, woodland management, improved footpath access, restoration of the canal and the development of water-based recreation and nature reserves.

Schemes within the regional park

- Black Park – 500 acres of woodland with walking, riding and cycling paths; a lake for boating, fishing and swimming and nature reserves
- Park Lodge Farm – near Uxbridge;a working commercial farm of 532 acres with a sheep flock and a dairy herd, seventeenth and eighteenth century buildings and an interpretative and educational centre together with farm trails
- Staines Moor water meadows – a wildfowl sanctuary and a site of special scientific interest
- Chiltern open air museum near Chalfont St Peters
- The Grand Union Canal with its towpath walk, car parks and pubs.

Current and proposed urban pressures

Despite green belt restrictions, the M25 has stimulated demand for land for more housing, offices, services and out-of-town retail centres.

Plans are in hand to use more land for motorway improvements to reduce traffic congestion, for example, widening the M25 to four lanes by 1997 and in parts, creating a 14-lane super highway. This would attract extensive gravel and aggregate material workings in the area.

Plans to build a fifth terminal at Heathrow may be resurrected, which would extend into the Colne Valley and add to the existing air and noise pollution.

Railtrack has plans to build a satellite station for London next to the M25, together with a huge car parking terminal.

Conclusion

Already there is conflict between the growing recreational needs of the urban population, agricultural needs and the need for environmental and wildlife protection. Tension is likely to increase and add to the existing conflict between the differing recreation needs on water and land areas.

Land-use mixture on the urban fringe

- Urbanised – completed urban development including all residential, office, manufacturing, transport uses and public utilities (24% increase 1949 to 1982)
- Disturbed – the region is in the process of change , for example, quarrying, rubbish dumps, bare ground, land being restored and construction land
- Neglected – low-intensity agriculture; horse pasture, stable and other sheds, scrub, weed-infested land sometimes deliberately neglected in the hope of speculative development but also as a result of urban vandalism, derelict sites, dying woodland and derelict quarries, for example, quarry farm. (30% increase 1949 to 1982)
- Traditional agricultural activities– farming landscape, small fields, mixed farming, hedges, animal grazing, regional type building. for example, Stocker's Farm
- New agricultural activities – arable 'prairies', modern factory-like buildings, battery houses, extensive views with little visual, recreational or wildlife quality, for example, Woodoaks Farm (17% decrease in both types of agriculture 1949 to 1982)
- Amenity – woodland, water and playing fields, for example, publicly accessible Rickmansworth Aquadrome, private amenities, for example, Lynsters lake fishing.

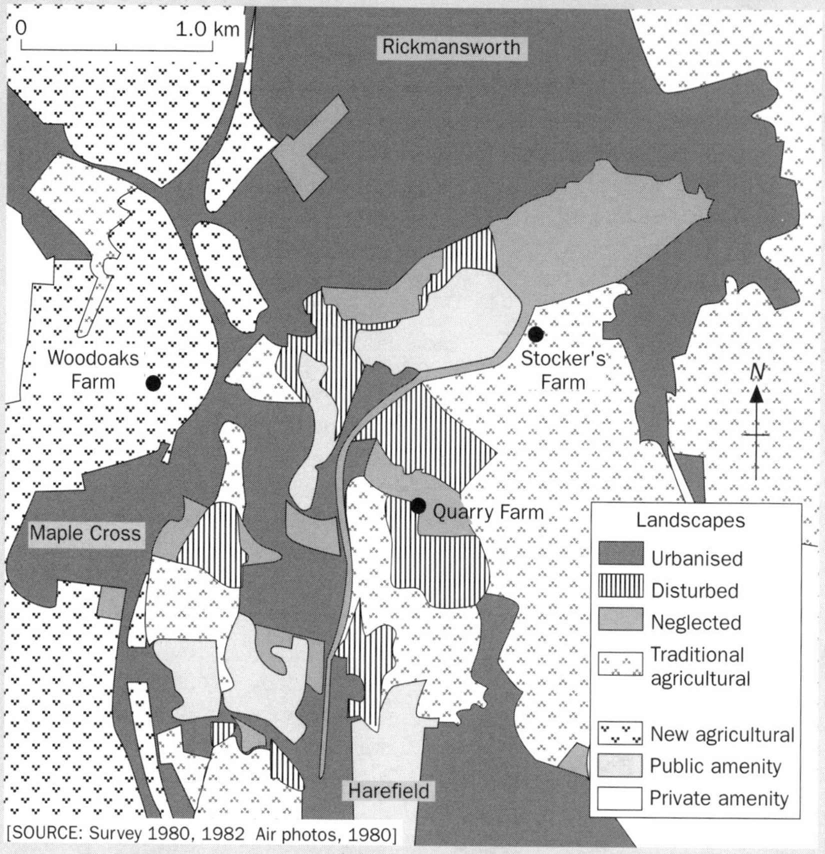

Landscape types in the rural-urban fringe, Rickmansworth (Hertfordshire)

13

CHAPTER 13

Changing economic and social geography of rural areas

13.1 A typology of rural communities

Life in a rural community is frequently contrasted with living in a city. In sociology, the idea of a rural community based on everyday neighbourly contact and an accepted order of society, is set against the more impersonalised urban living, where status depends upon achievement rather than inheritance. Tonnies' characterisations of the ideal rural community (*gemeinschaft*) and of urban living (*gesellschaft*) are perhaps the most well known. However, a simple classification of this kind tends to hide the variety and complexity evident in all but the most remote communities. Mass media, better transport and greater mobility have taken urban aspects of living into the countryside.

Many people work in the town and live in the countryside, and many towns dwellers have retired there. Thus rural communities contain a mixture of newcomers and old established families who still have some links with the land. Social institutions have as a consequence become more varied in the more accessible rural communities, in particular, in dormitory villages close to larger cities.

Something of Tonnies' *gemeinschaft* however remains in the more isolated rural areas; it is that of kinship. Rees, commenting on the reasons for stability and immobility amongst Welsh upland communities, states that '*the solidarity of the family, the bonds of kinship and the individual status among his neighbours – all ties him to his locality and makes life incomplete elsewhere.*'

In contrast, in areas within reach of cities, a dual social structure frequently develops, with middle and working class groups having their own separate social organisations. This division seems to be growing more significant than hitherto recognised division of newcomers and established villages. However, both characteristics may be present, making a social and spatial mix of the community even more complex.

Given this complexity and the variety of rural communities, it is evident that Tonnies' simple description of the rural community is quite inadequate. Mitchell has recently suggested a four-fold classification of rural communities based on, firstly, the extent to which rural communities may be receptive to outside influences and secondly, upon the extent to which there is evidence of an integrated community feeling. While the four typologies may be somewhat different in the developing world, the two criteria of degree of openness to outside influences and extent of community feeling may also provide a basis for classifying rural communities (Figure 13.1).

There is one set of external influences over which rural communities have only limited control and which are increasingly affecting the structure of the community. These are the actions and policies of the various central and local government institutions. For example, to prevent rural areas near towns from being swamped by dormitory spread, planning legislation protects some rural settlements from any dormitory development while others may be designated as suitable for it. Great efforts have been made through various measures,

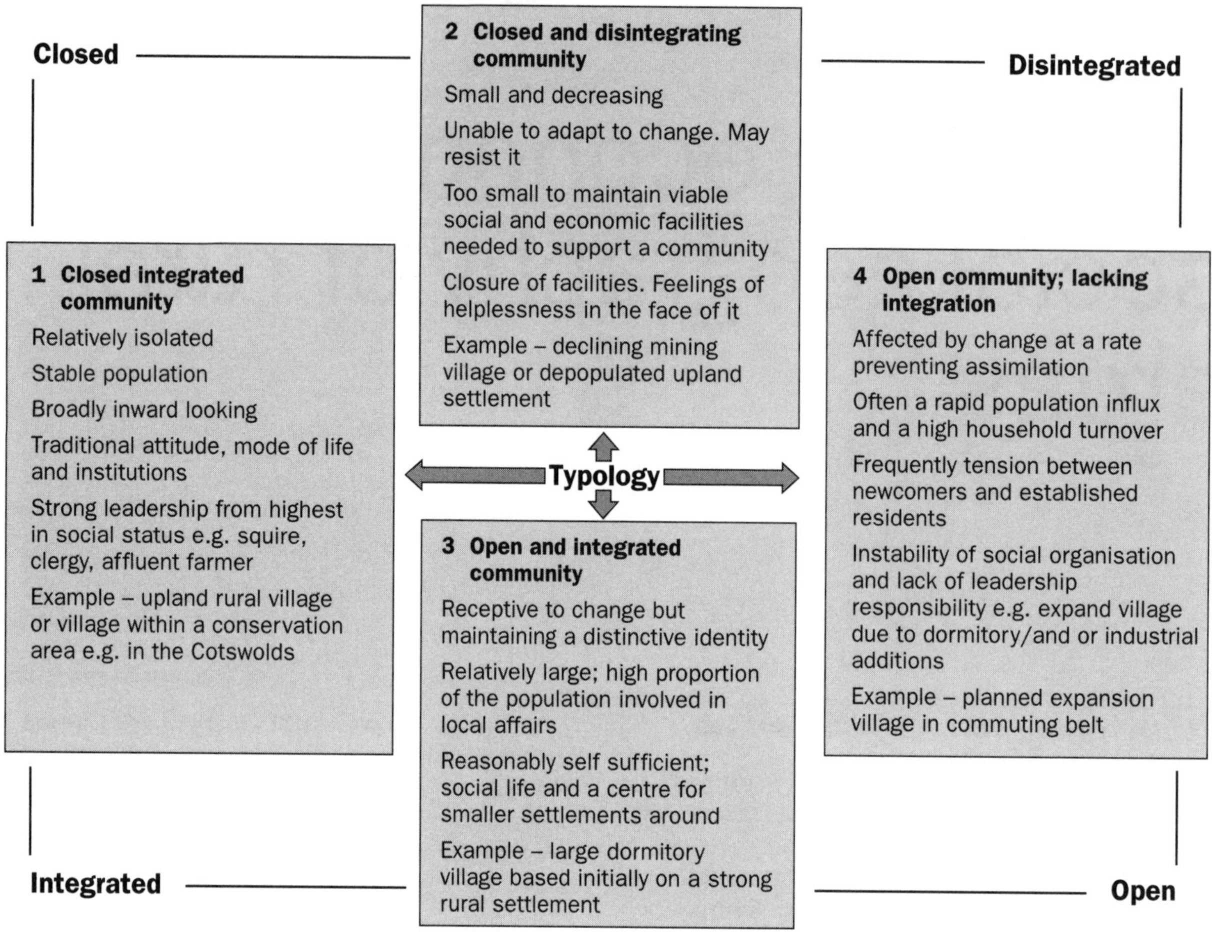

Figure 13.1 *A typology of rural communities*

such as subsidising agriculture and social services, to maintain the viability of rural life and small communities in the more remote rural areas.

Thus with time, rural settlement patterns and the social geography of the communities living in the settlements tend to become more complex.

13.2 Community structure and a sense of identity

Modernisation influences

Some of the changes which affect rural settlements are not limited to rural settlements but also affect urban residential areas. One of these is the increasing frequency with which households move their place of residence. It is now estimated that on average, one fifth of all households move each year. This increased turnover is bound to have an important influence on the structure and social cohesion of a population in an area, including those in rural communities.

Allied to this trend and partly accounting for it, increased car ownership and improved transport networks have increased mobility so that a larger proportion of the working population can live at some distance from their place of work.

Increased mobility has also encouraged people to look for services outside their local area of residence in order to have greater choice at a more competitive price. Hence, the ties to the community area of residence are weakened and the number of small shops and local services have declined in most rural settlements and urban neighbourhoods.

The infiltration of populations into rural settlements

The effect of increased migration from urban areas out to surrounding rural areas is most evident from the accretionary growth of small suburban type housing estates on the edge of the village and the infill of back areas by small closes of executive-type housing (Case study 13.1). Less evident but also an important indicator of change is the gentrification and modernisation of existing houses and cottages by new occupants. Some farm houses and land have also been taken over by newcomers for what is now called 'rural retreating' and later retirement in many cases.

In coastal and scenic areas the influx may also be evident in the form of retirement bungalows and

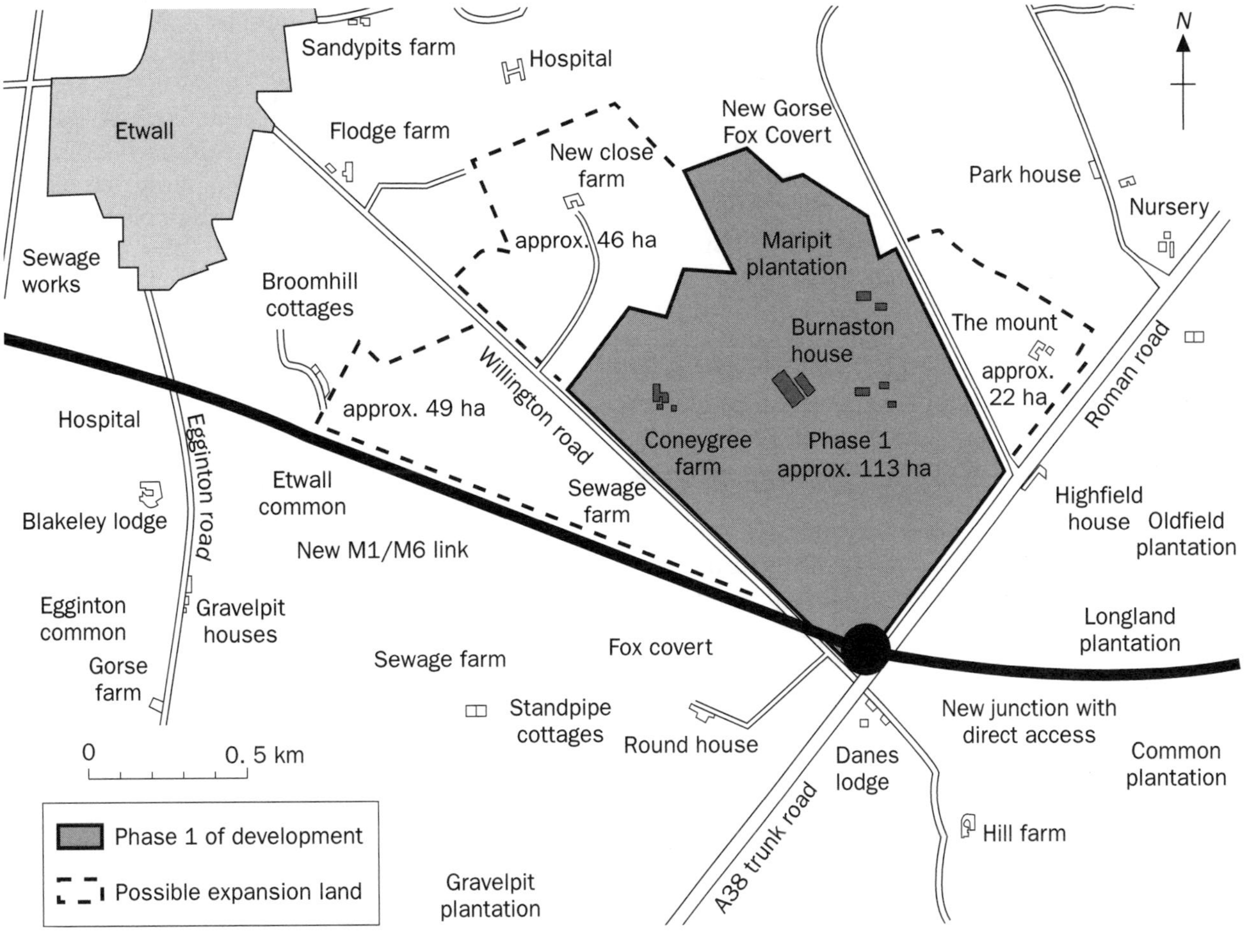

Figure 13.2 The new Toyota car plant in a rural location between Burton on Trent and Derby in the East Midlands

more recently, the appearance of retirement complexes which offer warden support and other services. These tend to overshadow the phenomenon of second homes which was so prominent up to the 1980s.

In certain cases the introduction of a particular economic activity may bring a rapid and marked change to the character of rural settlement in affected areas, as for example, in the offshore drilling in the Shetlands, affecting the opening of an open cast coal mine, or the building of a large factory, such the Toyota plant near Derby in 1992 (Figure 13.2).

The kind of people who move is important

The selectivity of people within migration flows and the scale of the influx are crucial to the character of social change. More people moving in will clearly affect the demand for services, such as schooling and medical care, as well as shopping and other commercial services. The nature and scale of the increased demand will also be influenced by the age composition of the newcomers, their life style and socio-economic status.

The effect of an influx of older and retired people

In some areas there has been an inflow of more elderly retired but still mobile households, while at the same time there has been an outflow of younger people, usually because of poor job prospects, lack of affordable housing and limited recreational activities. This has a detrimental effect on settlements in more remote areas, such as upland Wales and the Scottish Highlands, for example (Case study 11.1) and in smaller villages in other less accessible areas. The situation is similar in the rest of the European Union and in the USA. The loss of younger families may lead to the closure of the village school and the local shop. Incoming elderly may not compensate for the loss of trade but may require additional welfare facilities.

Once established, the new residents may resist further change to the character of a settlement, perhaps seeking designation of it as a 'conservation' area as in the Wiltshire village of Castle Combe. *'Here the modern world has not just passed by, it has been forced back by a tide of conservatism and conservation.'*

[SOURCE: *The Independent* 27.1.93]

An influx of younger families can lead to more activities and a rapid expansion of the village

There are villages close to larger towns which have been 'swamped' by an influx of younger families in the broad middle income band. These villages have expanded dramatically, including new school premises, an expansion in other services and voluntary activities (Case study 13.1). Usually these are settlements which had been targeted for growth by the planning authorities as commuter pressures build up, while neighbouring settlements may be protected or any growth limited to small infill. Where such rapid expansion occurs, the character of both the settlement and the community may change dramatically. Despite the urbanite influx, established rural families still play a significant part in the life and ordering of the village. For example, the remnants of the formerly dominant farming sector may still be represented on the parish council, along with representatives of the new dormitory population, as studies have shown. (Moseley M J (ed), *Social issues in rural Norfolk*, 1978.)

Provided that the pace of influx is not too rapid, the scale of it not too large and the newcomers socially mixed, the more likely it is that the service base of a rural settlement will be maintained and the life of the community will evolve rather than be disrupted. However, recent studies show that much also depends on the prime motivation of migrants in moving away from the city into the surrounding countryside.

Kinds of newcomers

Incoming households can be classified into two groups: community migrants and reluctant migrants. Community migrants are 'true' counter-urbanisation migrants. They have deliberately chosen to give up city life and live in a rural settlement because they perceive it as a more satisfying lifestyle for them and their families. These people are likely to participate in the life of the village and feel a sense of identity with the community.

Reluctant migrants would prefer to live in the city and its suburbs but have been forced out to cheaper housing in the surrounding rural areas because they cannot afford city prices. They are

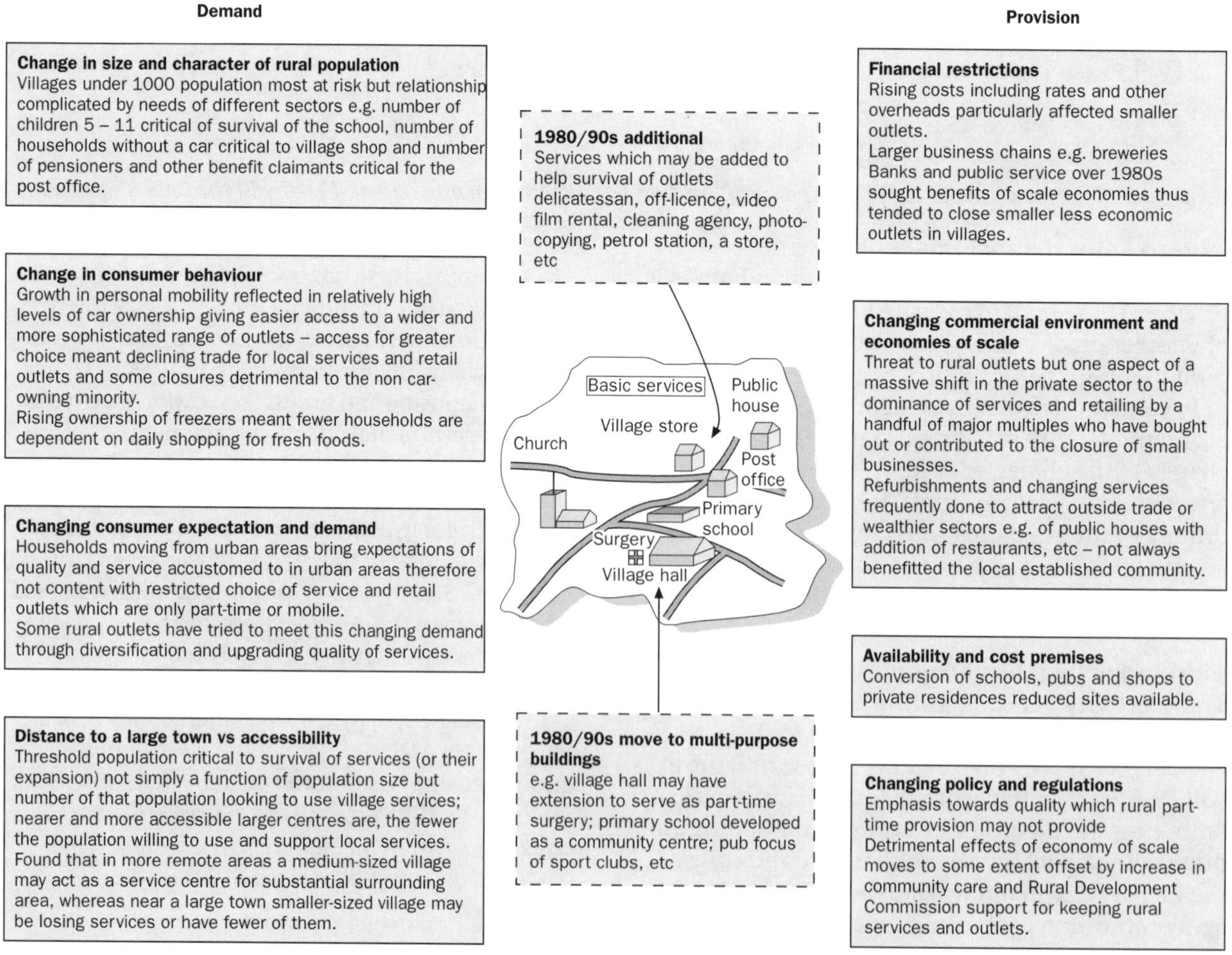

Figure 13.3 *Major related influences on changes of service provision in rural villages*

likely to use the village as a dormitory and continue to use the services and recreational facilities in the city. They tend to take little part in village community life and feel little sense of belonging. As soon as they can afford it, they are likely to move back into the city.

Measuring the strength of community and identity

Martin Shaw, in his study of six Norfolk villages, used three broad measures in assessing the social cohesion within a community and the strength of community feeling.

- the sense of local identity – a sense of belonging and of identity with the village and acceptance by other residents
- a willingness to become involved in events and activities as assessed by observed levels of participation or perception of residents who are or who feel involved in village events
- a common attitude of mind -- the extent to which residents share a common view of the quality of life in the village.

[SOURCE: *Social implications of village development, Social issues in rural Norfolk*, Moseley M J, 1978]

Shaw found that residents who were established and, in particular, who had lived all their lives in the village, scored highest. More importantly amongst the 'newcomers', he was able to demonstrate that the 'community migrants' scored more highly that the 'reluctant migrants'. He and Pahl, who has studied the Hertfordshire commuter belt, also indicated that middle income families are more likely to be involved in the community than lower income families.

However, the social cohesion is not only dependent on the mix and character of resident households, but also on the strength of the service and activities base of a rural settlement (Figure 13.3) since the proportion of residents using facilities generally depends on this.

If more of the residents use the facilities and activities, then through contact, the greater will be the sense of identity and belonging. From surveys taken in various villages, the existence of a primary school seems the most important single influence in this respect. Parents meet up when taking children to school and the village school is frequently the catalyst for other community activities, such as an annual fête, for example. Fulbourn (Cambridge), one of the case examples, refects this well (Case study 13.1).

There have been continued additions to facilities and the list of social and recreational activities. For example, in 1992 – 93, a bowls and tennis club and another playgroup was formed. Six more shop premises were built; two provide financial services and others ranged from a beauty treatment parlour to interior design and flower shops.

The influence of planning policies

The policies of planners is also significant in relation to the community structure and a sense of identity in a rural settlement. Where a key settlement approach encourages over-rapid expansion of certain villages, it may be difficult to maintain the cohesion which previously existed in these communities, since there is insufficient time for newcomers to be absorbed. The rapid influx of the newcomers may also be resented by the established residents. A division may occur, giving rise to a dual structure with a feeling of 'them and us' which is often difficult to break down.

13.3 Rural problems

To date, too much rural planning policy has been dominated by economic issues, with too little regard for the effect of planning decisions on the social structures of rural settlements.

There is downside to change in rural areas

Village schools are still closing, and for the 15 per cent of rural families without use of a car, access to medical facilities, shopping and other services is difficult. Pockets of real poverty persist.

There are also areas, such as Mid-Wales or parts of Cornwall, which are quite untouched by "development" and where de-population, though nothing like as serious as in much of rural France, is prevented only by substantial direct and indirect government aid, mainly to farmers.

Above all, rurally concerned bodies such as the RDC draw attention to the inability of local people to afford to buy houses as prices rise with the competition from 'incomers.'

[SOURCE: Bridget Bloom, *The Rural Revolution, Financial Times*]

A number of studies have increasingly highlighted the need for more consideration of disadvantaged households in rural communities – the elderly, families on low income, the disabled and the less mobile. Rural deprivation has been overshadowed by the larger issues of deprivation in the inner city areas but there is increasing recognition of and concern for rural deprivation. It is now a key issue both in the UK and elsewhere in the western world, as well as in developing countries.

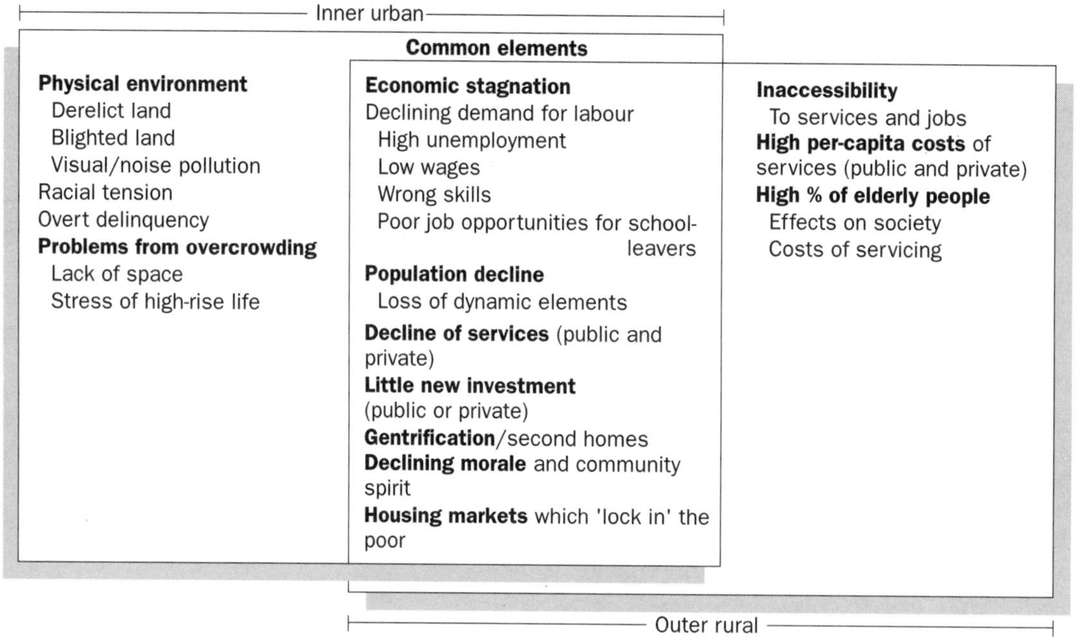

Figure 13.4 Common elements between inner urban and rural deprivation

Rural deprivation

'Unlike urban deprivation which is concentrated in large areas of run-down property and visibly apparent physical decay, rural deprivation is spread more thinly' (Gilg, A. *Rural geography*, 1985). Thus until recently, rural deprivation has received comparatively little attention. As Gilg points out, there are similarities between it and inner city urban deprivation, which seems to indicate that rural deprivation is not simply a function of rurality but to do with the more general aspects of a nation's social structure (Figure 13.4). In other words, there are common forces at work which promote both rural and urban deprivation.

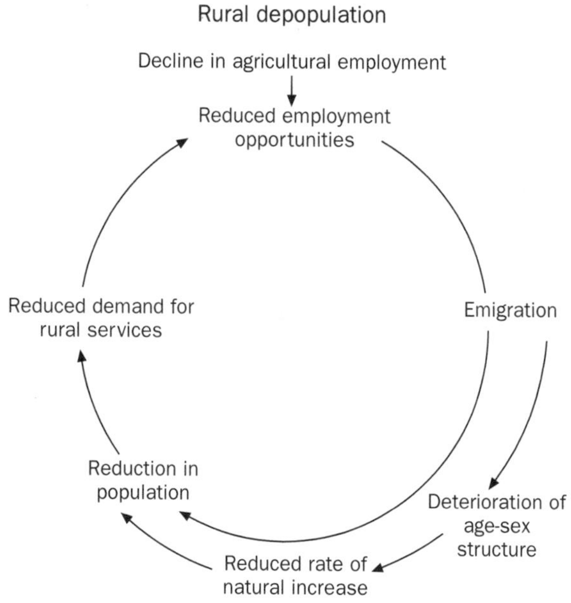

Figure 13.5 The cyclic nature of rural decline

Rural deprivation is further accentuated by the problem of accessibility in sparsely populated and sometimes remote rural areas.

It is further exacerbated by the increasing tendency to concentrate employment and services in the larger rural centres of population. Although these influences affect all the population in more remote settlements, the increased costs and inconvenience bear most heavily on the already disadvantaged. Moreover, the increasing tendency in certain countries to allow market forces to have a strong play in deciding the allocation of services, transport provision and employment opportunities, has worked against the needs of the disadvantaged sector of the rural population (Figure 13.5), a sector already under-represented on councils and other public bodies which decide policy and public funding allocations.

The scale of the problem has until now been underestimated because disadvantaged households tend to be more widely scattered than those in urban areas. It is now recognised that in the USA there are as many as 11 million people in rural areas with incomes below the poverty threshold; this amounts to almost 40% of the nation's poor.

Housing issues

The quality of rural housing and variable opportunity of access to existing housing stock across different social groups is a critical factor in rural deprivation.

Housing a central problem
One of the chief deterrents to living where they are, is the lack of affordable rural housing for young home-makers. Prices have been affected by the demand for weekend holiday cottages by middle-class town dwellers. Thus, provision of affordable housing remains one of the most pressing infrastructural needs if communities are to retain the potential for economic revitalisation. (*Rural Focus*, Issue 2, 1992, p. 2)

Because of the rather romantic view of rural life held by many people, a significant amount of poor rural housing has not received much attention. Yet it has been a problem in many countries over a long period. Before the Second World War, many houses in Western Europe lacked basic amenities, such as running water and electricity. Since then, this proportion has dwindled, partly due to more rigorous regulations and partly due to improved incomes, thereby allowing households to carry out improvements.

In the UK, around 5% of housing is classed as unfit for habitation, a higher proportion than in city areas. The percentage rises in more remote areas, such as rural Wales and Cornwall. It is the rural poor who live in this substandard housing. Most breadwinners amongst these are likely to be employed in agriculture where income levels are generally lower than in most urban-based occupations. In the UK some of this substandard housing is part of the 'tied cottage' system, whereby farm workers are housed in property which belongs to the farm or landed estate, the accommodation going with the job. These workers until recently also faced the additional threat of eviction if they lost their jobs or reached retirement age.

A bigger and more widespread problem is the differential access to housing from one income group to another. People on low incomes have suffered from the general rise in the prices of rural housing through the postwar years and increases in rural wage levels fail to keep pace. The chances of poorer paid local workers buying a home of their own have been further weakened by the influx of house purchasers who move out of the city and the rise in second home ownership by the wealthier group. In addition, under the more restrictive policies of central government in the UK over the 1980s and early 1990s, fewer local authority houses have been built for rental, while at the same time the number of existing houses to rent have been reduced by the sale of houses to tenants.

The private sector has largely concentrated on building houses for the middle and upper ends of the housing market as this capitalised on the limited land available for building. Thus the actions of both public and private sectors in the rural housing market have conspired against those of low income.

Homelessness is on the increase
The recent four-year changes (1987 – 91) have been much more effective. Rural homelessness increased systematically faster than urban,. In non-rural areas, homelessness rates slightly more than doubled in this period; in deep rural areas, they more than trebled.

Over the last decade homelessness increased throughout the country. In the early 1980s the increase was greater in the provincial urban areas, including the metropolitan districts. Since 1986, the rural areas have experienced a much faster increase.

Rural Development Commission, 1992

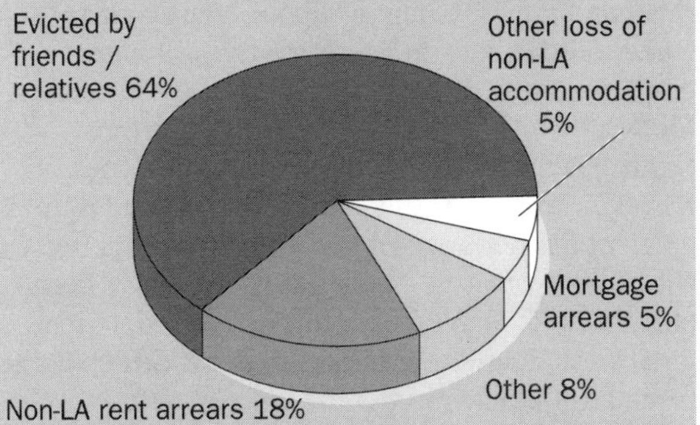

[SOURCE: Rural Development Commissison, *Homelessness in Rural Areas*, 1992]

Figure 13.6 *Main reasons for homelessness*

The increasing shortage of housing for those on low incomes, the elderly and first time buyers, has been highlighted in a number of reports. For example in 1989, the rural development unit of the Scottish Development Agency indicated that the number of families on the waiting list for rural housing in Scotland had increased by 40% in the first half of the 1980s, while homelessness had gone up by 83%.

Shortage of housing has undoubtedly been a contributory factor to the increased migration of young married couples out of their local rural area to better paid jobs and improved prospects of housing in the towns. This exodus is particularly serious for the smaller rural communities where depopulation has been a serious problem for many years (Case study 11.1). The fall in the reproductive sector of the population may mean that the threshold population is no longer there to support certain services such as the local school, the church, the village shop and bus service. The loss of these has in many cases hastened depopulation, encouraging the resident population to leave and deterring potential newcomers.

The shortage of affordable housing and housing to let is now being more seriously addressed across countries in the European Union. The UK, for example, is encouraging local authorities to set aside land for low cost housing and financial support for low income families to help to purchase. Housing associations are also being encouraged to provide accommodation for the disadvantaged amongst the rural population.

Employment and opportunity deprivation

In more remote regions away from decentralising influences, insufficient employment opportunities and poor rates of pay are an integral part of the deprivation cycle in rural areas and thus require some mention here (Figure 13.5).

While accurate data on rural employment is hard to collect because of the seasonal nature of some employment, such as the practice of casual employment and the use of family labour, there is clear evidence that even on a conservative estimate, employment in the primary sector, mainly accounted for by agriculture, has fallen over the last twenty years by an average of 2% to 3% annually. The trend continues, due to the greater mechanisation and more efficient methods in farming and to the reduction in the number of farms. Many small farms have been absorbed into larger farm estates or, as in upland marginal areas, abandoned because a living can no longer be had from them (Section 24.6; Case study 24.4).

In many rural areas the fall in employment opportunities in the primary sector has not been compensated by a sufficient expansion of opportunity in other sectors, such as tourism and recreation (Section 29.4; Case study 29.3). Moreover, the difficulty of finding employment has contributed to the comparatively low wage levels in agriculture and other primary occupations, such as forestry, when compared with wages in the more urban-based sectors, such as manufacturing.

Some writers highlight the need to increase the trend of decentralisation of office and manufacturing jobs out of the cities into rural areas, to provide more varied and better employment opportunities. Frequently, however, rural workers do not have the qualifications or relevant experience to compete for these jobs with people who are moving out of the city. In any case, more remote rural areas, where employment opportunities in agriculture are least, are not attractive to businesses moving out of the city since access and transport facilities are not adequate.

There are a range of agencies which offer incentives to firms to move into the rural peripheral regions, including in Western Europe the EU with its regional and social funds initiative, but so far, only limited success has been achieved.

However, for certain firms, the existence of a pool of cheaper labour has encouraged them to set up assembly branch plants in rural areas not too far from a large city. For example in Japan, where there has been an increasing shortage of labour in urban areas throughout the 1980s and early 1990s, this has been a major incentive for the setting up of assembly plants in rural areas. It is one of the major reasons why the island of Kyushu has emerged as the second most important region to the Tokyo area for the semi-conductor industry. Other attractions included cheaper land and a cleaner environment.

With time, this decentralisation of office and manufacturing employment may well replace the primary sector as the main source of jobs for rural families but so far, only the lower paid in rural areas close to towns have benefited from these decentralisation trends.

13.4 An emerging rural north-south divide in the UK?

The Rural Development Commission set up to contribute towards solving some of the problems that change is bringing to rural areas suggests that a broad north-south divide is emerging.

South of a line from The Wash to the Bristol Channel (the line which traditionally divides the country into upland and lowland Britain), change is resulting in the emergence of an adaptable self-sustaining economy and thriving settlements. Here decentralisation of economic activity from urban areas into the countryside and some diversification of activities on farms is more than compensating for the decline in agriculture and the loss of jobs in this sector. At the same time the movement of people from large towns into the countryside is ensuring the survival and growth of the social structure and service base of rural settlements.

In contrast, north of this Wash-Bristol Channel line and especially in the upland areas of Cumbria, Northumberland, the Peak District, North Lancashire, Devon and Cornwall, decentralisation of activities and people from towns has been insufficient to compensate for the decline and loss of jobs in agriculture. Consequently, not only is the rural economy declining but so are settlements.

The key to this north-south divide is accessibility. To the north and west of this line, upland areas are considered too inaccessible and too remote from markets and clientele to attract enough new economic activity. This is seen as the key problem but others include inadequate roads and transport, a sparse population, a poor infrastructure, inadequate water supplies, sewage and electricity and unsatisfactory community services.

To remedy these problems and reduce rural deprivation in these areas, they have been designated as Rural Development Areas (Figure 13.7). They qualify for particular grant aid and advice support to attract new growth, either from within the communities by encouraging regeneration schemes, or from outside.

Enclaves of deprivation even in the prosperous south

Whilst the north-south divide is a useful one, it masks the fact that even within the 'prosperous south' there are pockets of rural deprivation and stagnation. These are usually in areas furthest from urban influences and so, to the would be investor or mover, are less attractive than those rural areas which are closer to towns and better serviced by transport and other facilities. Such pockets are to be found in the arable lands of Lincolnshire and Norfolk, in the 'marshland' areas, such as Romney Marsh and in parts of Shropshire and Hereford along the Welsh borders.

Equally to the north of the Wash-Bristol Channel line there are rural areas of prosperity, particularly areas whose environment and historical links make them attractive to the wealthy retired and to business people. The area around Richmond and Harrogate in North Yorkshire and much of rural Cheshire are particularly attractive. Easy access to the motorway network is also a factor in creating these rural 'golden areas of the north'.

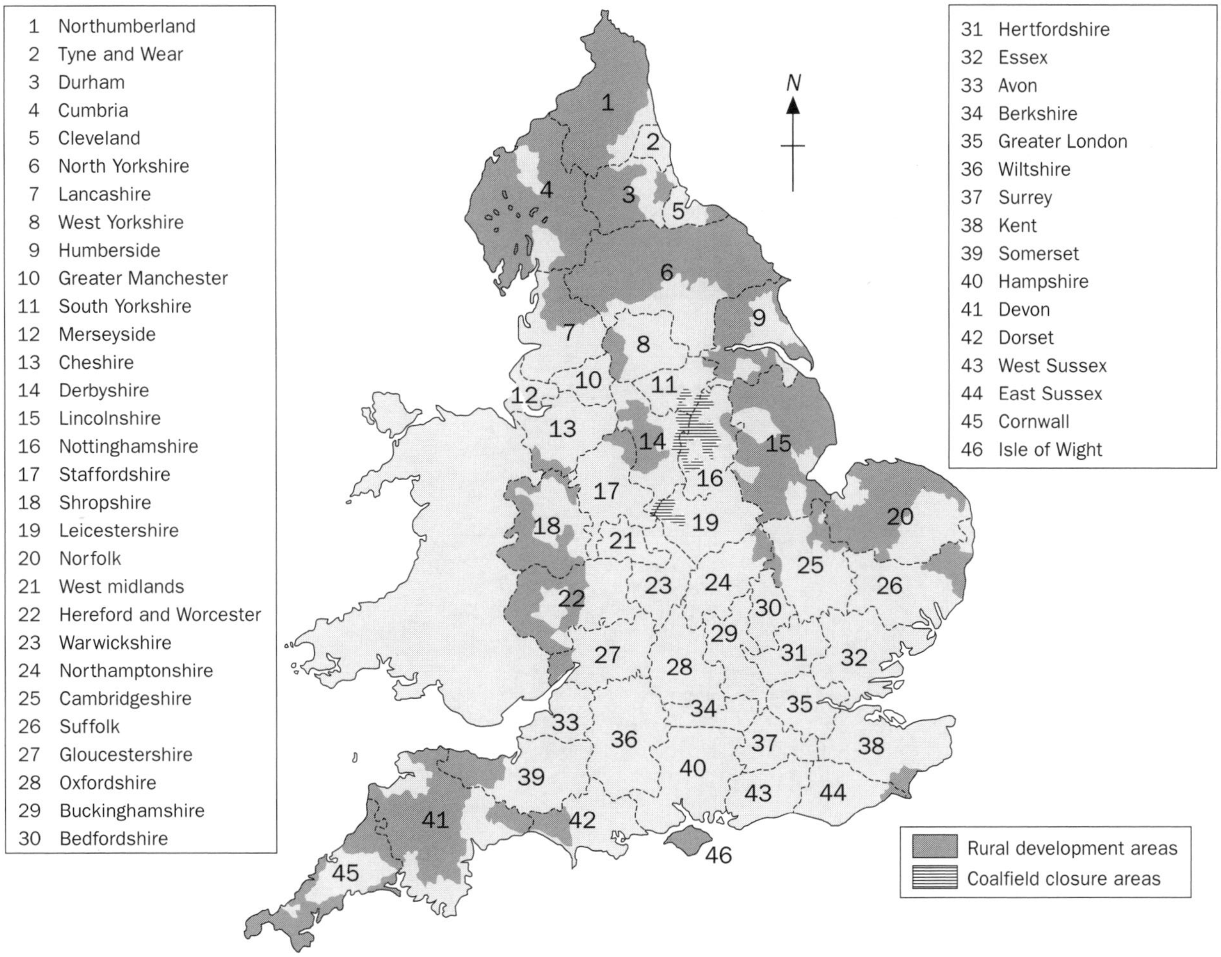

Priority areas

To concentrate its resources on those areas of England with the most significant rural problems, the Rural Development Commission designated the 27 rural development areas in 1984. These areas are populated by some 2.5 million people, roughly one in 20 of the population of England.

In 1990, the two East Midlands coalfield closure areas were given status to reflect the dramatic effects of job redundancies from pit closures in these areas.

Each priority area has access to funds through a rural development programme prepared by a local committee, to represent a consensus view of local solutions to local problems. They aim to achieve co-ordinated and integrated action focused on that particular priority area.

Figure 13.7 *Rural Development Areas*

The rural coalfield and mining areas

There is a tendency in the literature on changes in rural areas to overlook the fact that in other countries of Western Europe, there are rural areas which, since the industrial revolution, have not had their economic and social roots in agriculture but in mining. These areas have suffered problems of decline since the 1960s. This has recently intensified due to the further rapid decline in the coal industry (Section 27.4; Case study 27.1). In the UK areas include West Durham and West Cumbria. Now however, the problem of growing unemployment and decline has spread to the hitherto prosperous mining areas of the East Midlands (Case study 13.2) and South Yorkshire. Apart from economic decline, these regions have the additional problem of derelict land and environments scarred by mining activity, making them unattractive to alternative economic activity.

These areas too need special economic assistance. In 1990, in association with the Coal Board, the Rural Development Commission set up two Rural Coalfield Areas covering the East Midlands and South Yorkshire. These receive special financial assistance to revive their economies and communities by attracting new business as well as regenerate the environment and heal the scars of the industrial revolution. However, the legacy of this industrial history is also capitalised upon as one of the bases for regeneration. For example, the disused canals built to carry coal and other materials are being renovated and bought back into use for leisure holidays. Craft museums and working coalmines are also being set up as attractions for people from the large conurbations and for the growing number of tourists from abroad.

Concluding comment

Counterurbanisation and other modernising influences are bringing fundamental changes to the structure of rural communities and rural economies. In the process, increasing inequalities and associated rural problems are emerging. The dispersed nature of these makes them less obvious than those of large cities and consequently it is only recently that these rural problems have begun to be seriously addressed.

case study

13.1 **Cambridge: the rural fringe**

The three villages lie immediately to the east of Cambridge and were historically sited on a dry foot zone area between the chalklands to the south and east, and fingers of poorly drained fen land to the north. They have developed around ancient core settlements which date back to at least the thirteenth century. The residues of this early settlement are now conservation areas.

The villages are under severe commuter expansion pressure being within easy access of Cambridge and within commuting distance of London with easy access to the M11 motorway and Cambridge station. Estate development from the built up area of Cambridge has been held back by the Green Belt, acting as a buffer to the west of the villages. (Recent applications have been made for permission for housing and supermarket development on part of this Green Belt.)

The villages are in an area classified by planners as an 'area of constraint' because parts are within the Green Belt and the rest is high-grade agricultural land or areas of sensitive environment, including nature reserves. Fulbourn is the dominant village with a good range of facilities and to some extent acts as a service area base for the neighbouring Wilbrahams.

Fulbourn

Fulbourn is a 'limited rural growth village' with a population of 4732. It is one of the inner 'necklace' villages around Cambridge. Apart from some nineteenth century linear development north from the core to the station, most of the development since the 1930s has been westward towards Cambridge. The development is roughly divided between local authority housing to the south and private housing to the north. Some small links with agriculture remain, but most of the working population are employed in Cambridge.

It has a wide range of facilities including four food shops, chemists, six other retail outlets, agricultural sales, small industrial estate, health centre, dentist, community centre and a variety of other services together with a good range of active social and sports clubs. Extensive enlargement and upgrading of recreation ground facilities has recently occurred.

Location of Fulbourn, Great Wilbraham and Little Wilbraham

Fulbourn: social geography profile revealed in 1991 census returns

Population change 1981 = 4139 / 1991 = 4732

Household unit (1981 in brackets)		**Tenure**		**House type**	
Family with children	27.5% (39.2)	Owner occupied	70.4%	Detached	39.4%
Pensioners – single & couple	28.7 (31.8)	Council rented	16.9%	Semi-detached	31.1%
Others	43.8 (29.0)	Other rented	12.7%	Terrace	23.1%

Migration: in 1981, 8.9% had come in the previous year and in 1991, 16%

Great Wilbraham

Great Wilbraham is a 'group village' with very limited growth. It has a population of only 610. The village dates back to the thirteenth century and shows very limited development as it has not been on main drainage until recently. It is linear in form. Although it still has agricultural links, it contains a number of retired townspeople and some who are employed in Cambridge.

Facilities are limited but there is quite a strong community identity. The small primary school has recently moved into new premises. There is a recreation ground and village hall used by a number of social and sports clubs. But there is only one general shop and post office combined.

Little Wilbraham

Little Wilbraham is an 'infill only village', with a population of 368. It is a small linear settlement, more a hamlet than a village in character and lies on the fen edge, close to Great Wilbraham. It dates back to the Middle Ages. It still retains its agricultural character and is attractive to retired professional and business people.

There is some community feeling but very few facilities - no shop, open play space but no recreation ground and no school, the church has recently been reprieved from threat of closure. Neighbourly and informal support services exist for the less advantaged.

Population change 1981 = 613 / 1991 = 610

Household unit (1981 in brackets)		**Tenure**		**House type**	
Family with children	27.7% (34.8)	Owner occupied	69.2%	Detached	0 48%
Pensioner: single/couple	32.8% (35.3)	Council rented	19.0%	Semi-detached	27.9%
Others	39.5% (29.9)	Other rented	11.8%	Terrace	20.7%

Migration: in 1981, 9.8% had come in the previous year and in 1991, 6.7%

Great Wilbraham: social geography profile revealed in 1991 census returns

Population change 1981 = 355 / 1991 = 368

Household unit (1981 in brackets)		**Tenure**		**House type**	
Family with children	17.2% (27.1)	Owner occupied	58.1%	Detached	45.8%
Pensioners – single & couple	45.2% (43.8)	Council rented	20.6%	Semi-detached	29.4%
Others	37.6% (38.5)	Other rented	11.8%	Terrace	14.7%

Migration: in 1981, 14.7% had come in the previous year and in 1991, 6.8%

Little Wilbraham: social geography profile revealed in the 1991 census returns

case study

13.2 Measham: a declining coalmining village

Problems following colliery closure

Revival means overcoming problems that are typical of other coalfield communities whose collieries have also closed.

High unemployment

1In 1981, coalmining in the rural coalfield area employed 8000 people, making it the largest employer for males in the area. The closure of the mines and other traditional industries, such as textiles and hosiery, meant that by 1987, 34% of all economically active males in Measham were unemployed.

Depopulation

As jobs disappeared, so did young people who looked for employment elsewhere. A 3% reduction in population, together with unemployment, meant a drop in spending power in the village.

Shops began to close

Faced with a reduced range of local choice, shoppers started to travel out of the village to nearby shopping centres, which exacerbated the problems of retailing in Measham. Retailers lost the incentive to invest, adding to the village's downward spiral as a shopping centre. By May 1990, more than ten shops in the high street and the adjoining road were vacant.

The physical environment

Paradoxically, as local road traffic declined, traffic speeds through the village have increased. Despite the availability of a by-pass HGVs thundered along the high street, affecting the quality of life of the inhabitants.

Housing

Local estate agents confirm that the pattern of economic decline and environmental deterioration within Measham led to a lack of interest in it by local developers. As with the retailers, house builders showed an unwillingness to invest. Despite the need for new residential development, even before the recession, the local housing market lacked vitality.

Plans for regeneration

Two workshops were held in the village hall on the evenings of July 5 and August 9, 1990. Residents were invited to discuss what they liked and disliked about their village, and what they would like to see changed. Three main problem areas were highlighted by residents: housing and other development, jobs and the village environment.

Development

Residents accepted the need for new housing but wanted it to be developed in scale with the village and not to swamp it. They wanted low-cost, low-density housing, together with job-creating small workshops and more retail outlets housed in existing vacant shops. They were particularly concerned

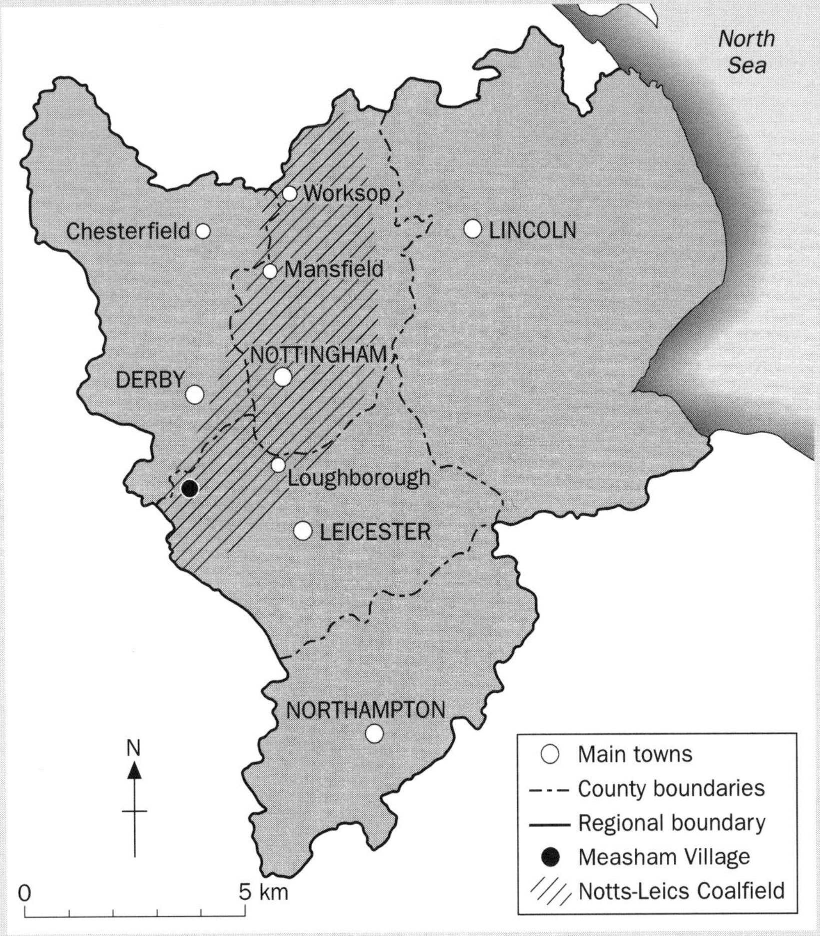

Measham: its location

that developers should utilise the existing fabric of the village with infill building rather than creating new sprawling developments.

Job creation

It was hoped that new development would create jobs, but the residents also wanted training programmes, particularly for the young. Measham stands on the banks of the Ashby Canal with an interconnecting system of towpaths and walkways. This potential asset inspired an ambitious vision of creating a tourism honeypot, based around a museum, craft shop, canalside pub, restaurants and the canal itself as a conduit for visiting canal boats and other leisure craft. The work of rebuilding the village would partly depend on the finance from tourism.

Environmental improvements

Most residents expressed concern over the through-traffic problem. The stream of heavy goods vehicles emphasised the high street's run-down state. An action plan for Measham has been drawn up but has to be implemented. It is being backed by the commission and other public and private bodies.

14

CHAPTER 14

Urban places – people in the city

'Each urban place is a very dense concentration of people and homes, plus their attendant work-places, centres of trade, entertainment and recreation and the many facilities and utilities needed to service all these.'

JOHNSTON R J *SPATIAL STRUCTURES*, 1973

14.1 Spatial inequalities

Without people and their needs there would be no urban places. The structure and functions of towns and cities have developed with time in response to these needs. Thus it is people who initiate the interest in urban studies. In looking at the social geography of the city, in particular, housing patterns, many geographers have been concerned that the needs of some groups or classes are much better served than those of others. The wealthy not only have access to the most favoured housing areas, but have much better service provision than the poor, be they shanty dwellers in some developing world city, like Calcutta, or slum dwellers in an inner city slum or ghetto of a city, such as New York. Social inequalities are mirrored in unequal access to space and desirable locations, so that spatial and social inequality go together.

As a result, a number of geographers have adopted a more radical approach in urban geography and a concern for welfare geography. Bunge was so struck by the inequalities from his study of Detroit that he adopted rather emotive terms for his division of the city and emphasised the ways in which the poorer income groups and ethnic minorities of the city were being 'exploited' by the rest of the city, particularly by the elite business, entrepreneurial and professional classes who occupied his 'city of superfluity' – pleasant suburbs and rural dormitory areas (Figure 14.1).

This concern for social inequalities and for what Harvey calls 'social justice in the city' is not new. It lies at the core of urban structure models which dominate in urban geography and which were originated by Burgess and Park, two eminent sociologists who studied the social problems of Chicago during the 1920s. They identified some of the important processes which still help us to understand the way in which cities are residentially zoned and why inner city areas are characterised by special types of social problems, such as poor housing, racial tension, and social deprivation.

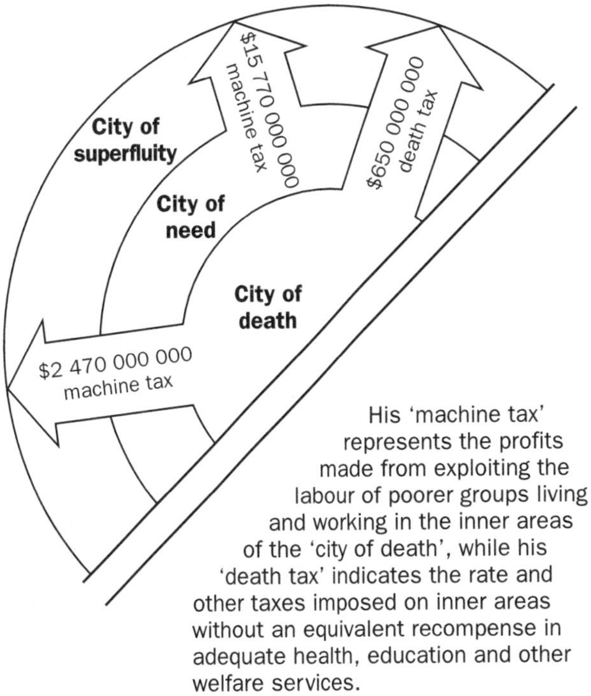

Figure 14.1 *Bunge's view of exploitation and inequality in the city*

The concentric ring model – Burgess and Park

In the process of collecting data about social conditions in Chicago during the 1920s, Burgess and Park were able to identify something of the structure of the city. At the time the city was experiencing mushroom growth due to the influx of migrants who were attracted by booming industries and job opportunities.

Burgess and Park were able to recognise some of the processes in which the population was being spatially differentiated into housing zones. The terms used by Burgess for the zones he identified not only indicate the unequal struggle between different groups for housing space, but also the desire of most groups to escape from the worst areas near the centre of the city.

Residential structure

a The model

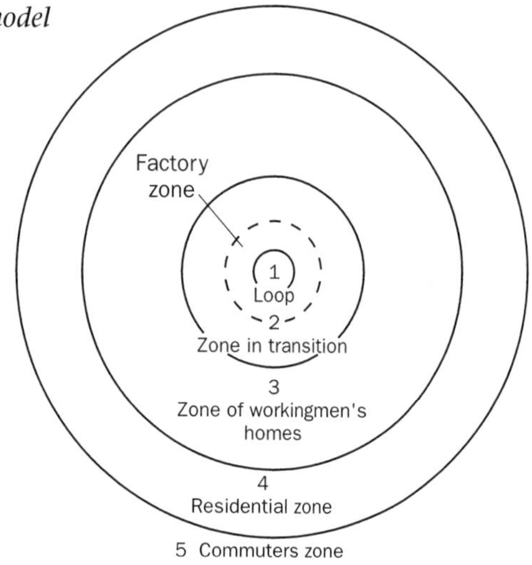

b Applied to Chicago

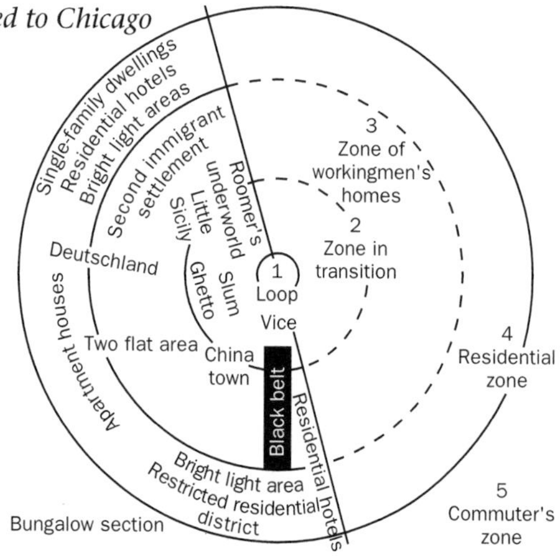

Figure 14.2 Burgess' model of the city

With reference to Figure 14.2, the following is the city's residential structure as seen by Burgess and Park.

1 'Within the central business district (the loop) is the 'main stem of 'hobohemia, the teeming rialto of the homeless migratory man of the middle west'
2 In the zone of deterioration, including the central business district, are always to be found the so-called 'slums' and 'bad lands'
3 A third area is inhabited by the workers in industry who have escaped the area of deterioration
4 Beyond this zone is the 'residential area' of high class apartment buildings of exclusive 'restricted' districts of single family dwellings
5 Still farther out beyond the city limits is the commuters' zone – suburban areas or satellite cities – within thirty to sixty minute ride of the CBD.

Factors which underlie this residential structure

Generally common aspirations but variations in income lead to a sorting out of different income groups. This movement to the periphery has been sought by people from all walks of life. Beginning with the most well-off, suburbanisation has moved, with time, progressively down the social scale as real incomes have risen and better transportation has increased mobility, allowing home and other work-places to be at some distance from one another. Disadvantaged groups trapped by circumstance remain in decaying inner city areas, both in the old and the new world. They are unable to move either because they cannot afford it or because they are being discriminated against in the housing market.

Processes of invasion, succession and segregation have occurred. Burgess was concerned with the influx of people into the city and the problems associated with the dynamic growth of the city which ensued from this continued influx. From his studies he emphasised the still important processes of invasion and succession, concentration and deconcentration which occurred as incoming migrants sought to live close the city centre, the economic, social and political heart of the community. With continued invasion, frequently by poorer ethnic minorities, established residents who could afford to moved out into the suburbs and nearby countryside, commuting from there to work in the city. In Burgess' terms, written in the mid-1920s, the newcomers went into '*the areas of deterioration which were not many years ago the zone inhabited by independent wage earners and within the memories of thousands of Chicagoans, contained the residence of the best families.*'

The effect of these processes over time as the city grows by accretion shows a historical process in action. ***The city grows outward by a process of accretion*** as particular groups or classes segregate themselves from other groups whose life style is very different and considered inferior.

The 'under classes' and the problem areas of the inner city and the periphery

Incoming families sought security and identification with their own groups in inner areas but were also relegated to these locations because they could not afford to live in better housing areas further out, nor could they afford the cost of travelling into inner areas where most of the job opportunities were. Ultimately, as they established themselves in the city, Burgess saw many families like those before them moving out. However, certain groups were forced to stay in inner areas which physically deteriorated with time and were 'invaded' by commercial use overflowing from the bulging CBD or downtown area. Ghettos developed where particular ethnic minorities concentrated. Other disadvantaged groups found in the zone of deterioration were the aged and unemployable, as well as transients who occupied lodging houses and apartments. In this twilight or transition zone, vice, violence and disease flourished in the 1920s.

Similar problem areas can be found today in the world's larger cities but they are not confined to inner areas. They are now also found on the periphery. In the developing countries these include shanty areas sited on marginal land normally unsuitable for building, such as the steep slope behind Rio de Janeiro in Brazil, or low-lying areas liable to flooding. In advanced countries they take the form of large, low-cost housing estates, frequently including high rise blocks, built hurriedly on the edge of cities to meet housing shortages in the 1950s and 1960s. Much of it, such as that at Speke, outside Liverpool, was built by local authorities to house the homeless, including those from inner slum clearance areas. Unfortunately, the sheer size of estates, the psychological pressures of high-rise living, faulty building, isolation from familiar surroundings and too few social amenities have resulted in many of these becoming serious problem areas. More recently, here and on the continent, rising unemployment has aggravated the problem.

Alternative models

Since Burgess and Park, others have produced alternative models of city structure. ***Like the concentric ring model, they are ecological models in that they incorporate the same ecological processes of establishment around a core, together with accretion, invasion, succession, deconcentration and adaptation by new groups, of the existing areas they have occupied.***

While differing in form from the concentric ring model, other ecological models are variations upon it rather than new structures. All incorporate the idea of different classes of residential areas based upon inequalities of opportunity and access between one group and another. The same broad processes are recognised as shaping the form of the city.

Hoyt sector model

Hoyt introduced the idea of sectors to Burgess' concentric rings in the zonation of urban places (Figure 14.3). This was in part based on the idea of unequal access to the city, with main routes being favoured, thus attracting wholesale and manufacturing activity along them with low-class housing for the workers next to the zone. Part of it was also based on the recognition that once a certain class of residential area had been established in a city, it would over time attract accretionary growth of similar residential housing, thus extending the zone out as a sector.

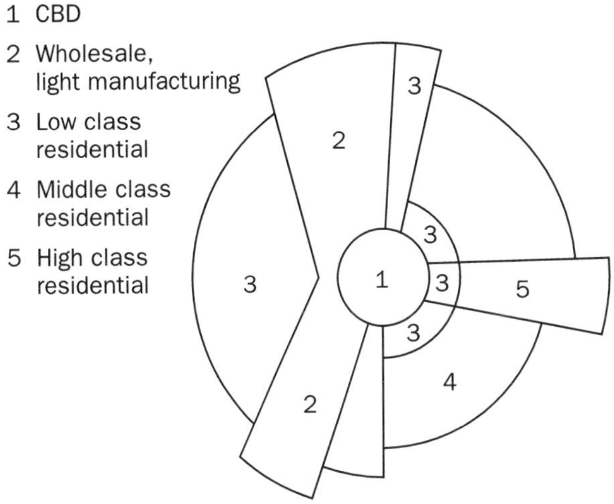

Figure 14.3 *Hoyt's sector model of urban structure*

Ullman and Harris multi-nuclei model

Ullman and Harris recognised that growth might occur around the main Central Business District and also round sub-centres (Figure 14.4). Working as they were at a much later date than Burgess and Park or Hoyt, they were also able to incorporate industrial and commercial suburbs as well as peripheral residential growth, as some usages could not find sufficient space nor afford the cost of development at the centre of the city.

Mann's model for British cities

Mann has attempted to use the ideas of Burgess and Hoyt in constructing a model which could be applied to British cities (Figure 14.5). In addition, he allowed for the effects of westerly prevailing winds, encouraging higher income groups to live upwind of the smoke and grime from industry near the centre. He also allowed for the rather different housing sectors present in British towns compared with their American counterparts.

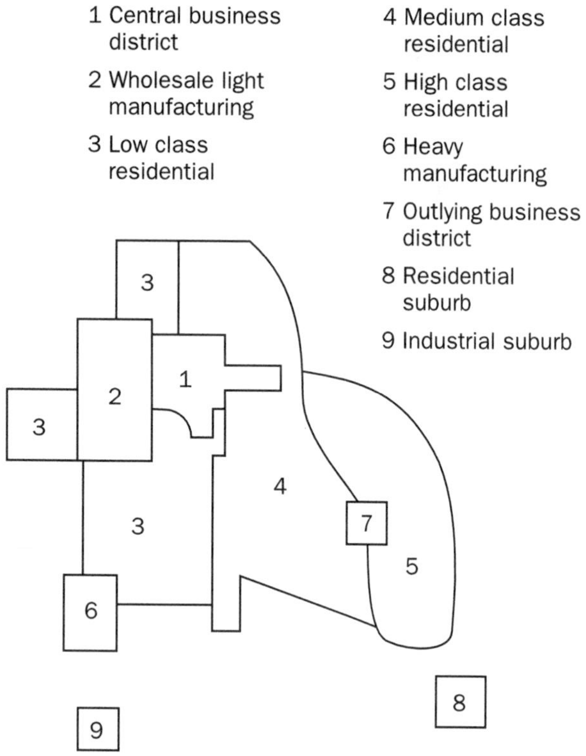

Figure 14.4 *Harris and Ullman's multiple nuclei model*

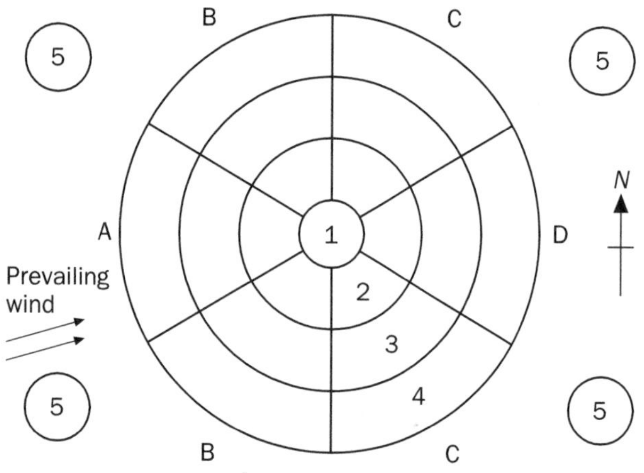

CBD
1 Transitional zone
2 Zone of small terrace houses in sectors C and D:
3 large old houses in sector A
4 Post-1918 residential areas, with post-1945 development mainly on the periphery
5 Commuting distance 'dormitory' town
A Middle class sector
B Lower middle class sector
C Working class sector (and main council estates)
D Industry and lowest working-class sector

Figure 14.5 *Model of a British city (based on Hoyt and Burgess)*

The limitations of these models

'Unrealistic' assumptions

As in the case of Central Place Theory discussed in Chapter 11, model makers had to make certain assumptions which are not necessarily accurate in reality, for example, the assumption that the city developed on a flat (isotropic) surface with accessibility equal in all directions away from the centre of the city. This does not occur in reality.

Differences of terrain,drainage patterns and the presence of barriers such as a coastlines lead to distortions of the generalised model when applied to real world cities, as seen for example in Burgess and Park's application of their concentric model to Chicago (Figure 14.2 b).

There is also some assumption that the location of a particular type of residential zone is based on the varied ability of different income groups to pay for the most desirable locations. The less wealthy have to accept the less desirable locations which higher income groups do not want.

In reality, however, other factors may be at work. For example, local authorities may purchase land for the development of housing in more desirable locations, such as semi-rural areas on the edge of the city. This may then be allocated to lower income groups which other wise could not afford such a location. Such an event happened after the Second World War when local authorities moved lower income families out of slum housing in the older inner areas of cities to new estates on the outskirts (Figure 14.6).

Transport conditions have changed

When these models were formulated, most income groups were reliant on public transport and this limited the distance they could live from the city centre which provided most of the employment opportunities and services. Since the 1950s, car ownership has spread to all income groups enabling all but the most disadvantaged groups, to live at greater distances from the centre, so producing much more urban sprawl and dormitory settlements beyond the main built-up area of the city.

Congestion in central areas and the development of ring roads and by-passes have on the one hand relatively reduced accessibility to city centres and on the other, improved access to peripheral locations, making the latter increasingly desirable for retailing, warehousing and lighter industries. As work opportunities have moved to the periphery of cities, housing estate developments have followed, making the residential structure pattern of cities more complex.

Figure 14.6 Local authority housing developments in Nottingham showing locations in all distance zones away from the centre

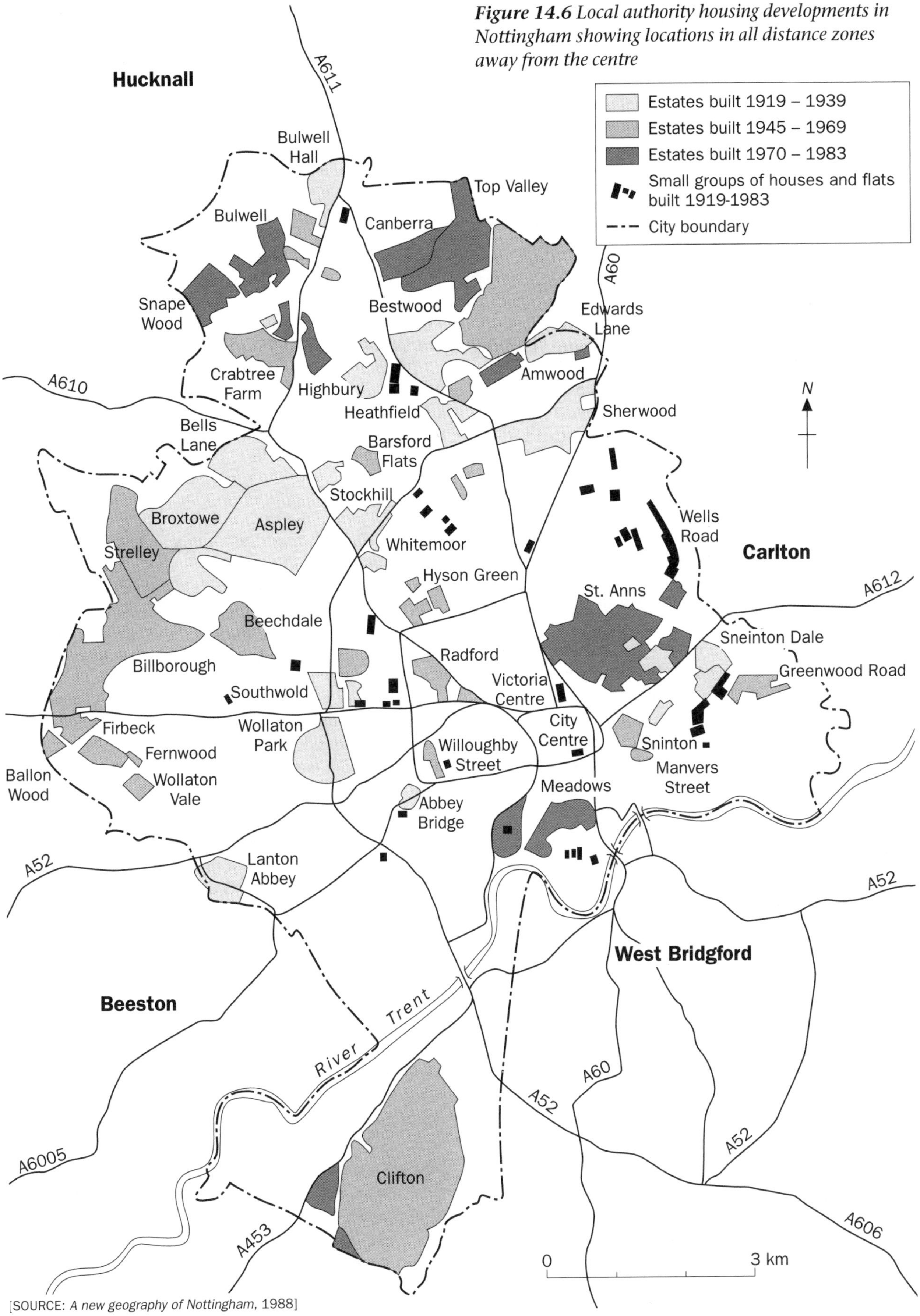

[SOURCE: *A new geography of Nottingham*, 1988]

Government intervention in the allocation of land

In the construction of their models, the authors have assumed that economic and social factors have operated freely in influencing residential zoning. However, since the turn of the century, location of housing and economic activities have been subject to planning and other legislative controls. This again has modified the residential structuring of cities as has already been noted in the case of the location of local authority housing, for example.

Have the ecological models outlived their usefulness?

There has been a tendency to fit a particular city to one of the structural patterns described in the ecological models outlined above. As will be already apparent, it is highly unlikely that any model will be a good fit. Circumstances have changed and new influences have 'distorted' the structural pattern of cities. The models produced by Hoyt, Ullman-Harris and Mann have been modifications of the concentric rings model produced by Burgess and Park in order to produce a generalised model more in keeping with how cities were developing. The important points to note when examining the relevance of these models to present day situations are that:

- Some element of the concentric rings zonation centring on a CBD, is retained in the later succeeding models because there remains the tendency for ring zonation in the structure of many cities today. Sector and multi-nuclei elements in turn are to be found in many present day patterns.
- Although cities may not any longer resemble the pattern of any particular model, they do still reflect the main processes highlighted by the creators of these ecological models. For example, Burgess' and Park's emphasis on the segregative tendencies of different ethnic groups and of different income groups remains true today, as does the influence of the process of invasion and succession. Cities still grow by accretion on their margins, though today, redevelopment of older inner areas is also important in the way city structures develop.

Hoyt's emphasis on sector development along routes is very significant still. Harris-Ullman's concentration on multi-nuclei development is evident today, especially as sub-centres develop on the margins of cities.

In order to understand and explain present city structures there is a continual need to search for generalisations about the spatial patterns of cities and to identify the main forces and processes which work to produce those patterns.

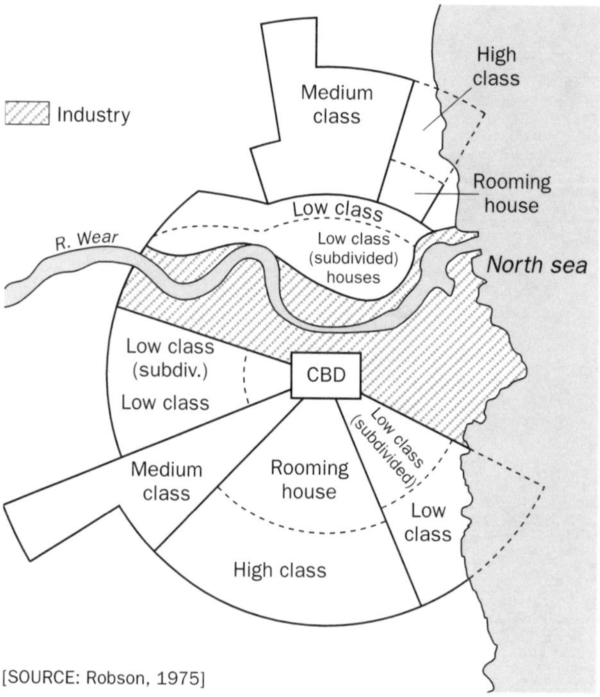

Figure 14.7 Patterns of residential segregation in Sunderland, 1963
Robson's model for Sunderland (1963) reflects elements of both the Burgess and Hoyt models but also indicates modifications to take account of the influence of the River Wear and Sunderland's coastal position

The earlier ecological models remain useful guides to both the patterns and processes underlying them, provided one is not studied to the exclusion of others and it is recognised that in any particular situation, in addition to the processes identified as important in the models, there may also be other local and more recent factors at work (Figure 14.7).

Below are further and more recent generalisations about city structures, based to some extent on the earlier models but also including the influence of additional and more recent factors. Figure 14.8 is a generalisation for a common type of western city. Figure 14.9 relates to cities in developing countries where colonial influences have modified the initial pre-colonial pattern and the segregation of the white minority population and the indigenous population has been an important element in the pattern. As seen in the case of Harare (Case study 5.3), while in post-colonial times this segregation is being broken down with many wealthier indigenous households now moving into formerly exclusively white areas, its influence on the actual physical structure of residential patterns remains very apparent.

An additional feature which distinguishes city structures in developing countries from those in the developed world, is the occurrence of tracts of

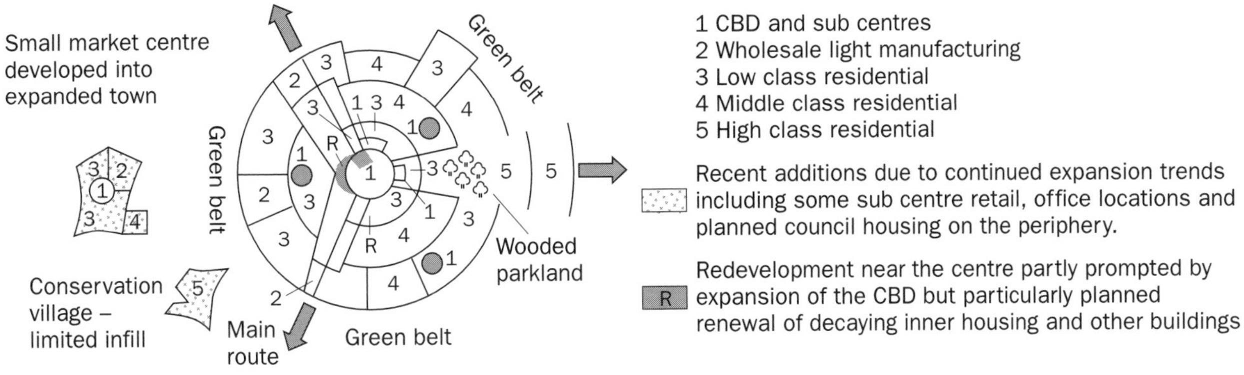

Figure 14.8 A moderately-sized Western city

informal housing ('shanty' areas) on the edge of large cities. This is a product of very rapid urbanisation and the inability of governments to provide sufficient housing. Thus poorer households are forced to occupy land illegally on the periphery.

Social Area Analysis

When the main concern is for the distribution of different social groups within a city rather than for examining residential structure as a whole (which would include such features as housing characteristics and the type of households occupying the housing), a social area analysis approach is frequently preferred to the use of city structure models.

In this approach, pioneered by the American sociologists Shevky, Williams and Bell, ***a series of social indicators are combined as a means of classifying social areas and the spatial pattern of these for any particular city.*** Census data is generally used as the source for the selected indicators which can be mapped for each defined census area (usually, in Britain by electoral wards, or by enumeration districts if a more detailed map is required).

While there are various ways in which indices may be combined, a common approach is that used by Murdie (Figure 14.10). In order to produce a social area analysis model as the basis for studying social area patterns, the factors (variables) which influence a family or household's residential location have been grouped as three contributory components, each of which, when mapped, produces a regular spatial pattern.

- The socio-economic status component, including the occupation of the head of household, when mapped tends to produce a sector pattern
- The effect of the stage reached in the life-cycle component produces a ring pattern
- The ethnic or segregation component exhibits a nucleated pattern with 'alike' households wanting to locate together in the same area.

These sector, ring and nucleation components, when superimposed onto a map of the physical characteristics of the city, results in a generalised structure of the city showing its major social areas.

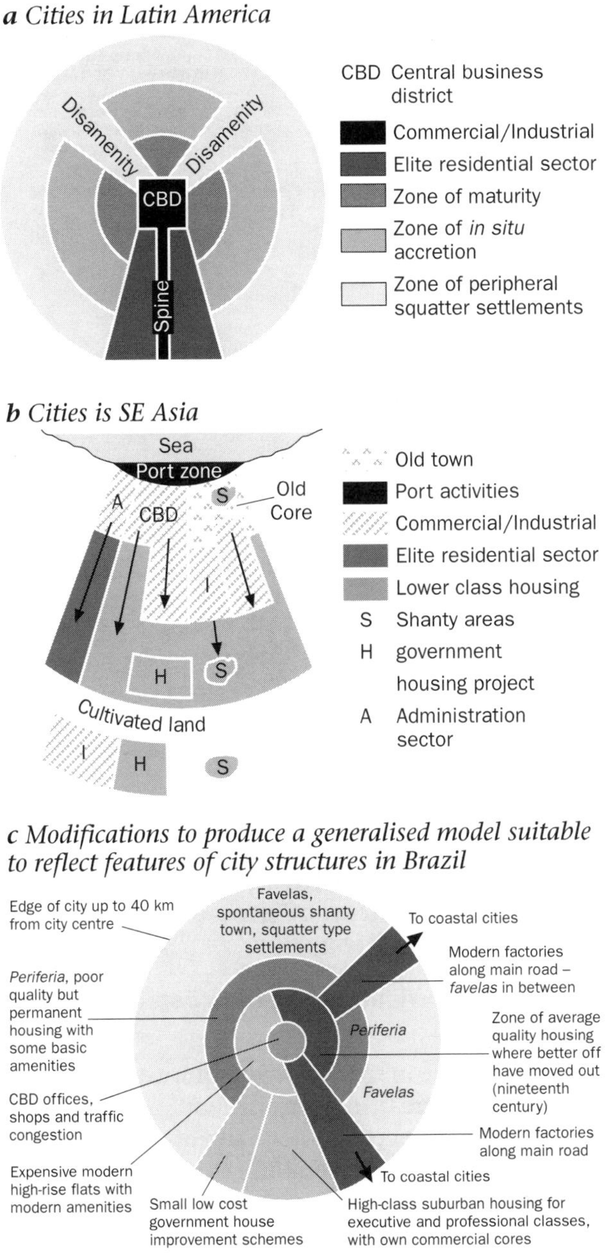

Figure 14.9 City structure models for the developing world

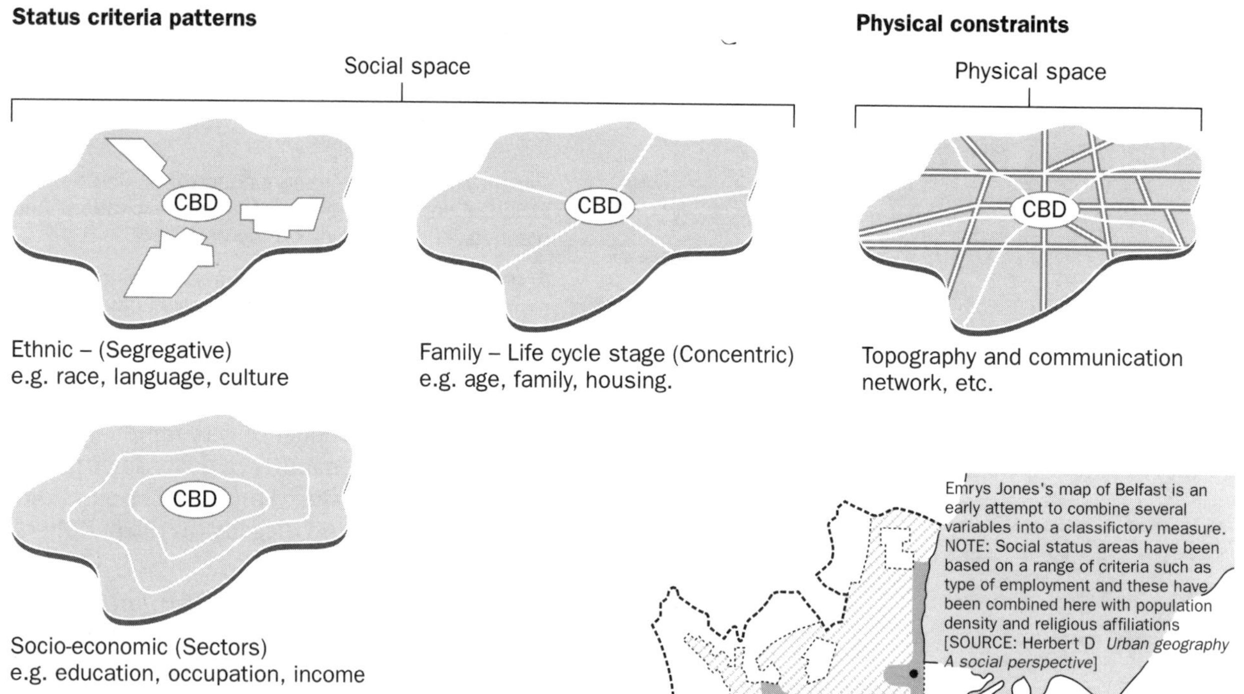

Figure 14.10 Social area analysis model showing the 3 social space components and the physical space map onto which they can be superimposed

The social area analysis approach has yielded useful generalisations in a variety of situations where it has been applied, including those for different cultures. It is a more flexible approach than that based on the classical ecological models of Burgess and Park and others. In each situation, it is based on data derived from a survey of households in that particular situation. Therefore, the generalised social areas map reflects the actual social geography of that particular town or city more thoroughly and accurately than a model-based city structure map (Figure 14.11).

An open factors approach

In some situations, especially where the city being studied does not readily lend itself to these more generalised approaches, a more basic and subjective approach might be appropriate. In this case, some of the underlying processes already identified within the ecological models and social areas analysis approaches may be combined with other factors, such as the constraints on patterns of growth imposed by the physical environment, to provide the kind of framework indicated in Figure 14.10. Once the residential structure for any particular city or town has been mapped on the basis of field survey or other data, the framework can then be used as an analytical tool in analysing the residential structure map (Figure 14.12 and Case study 14.1)

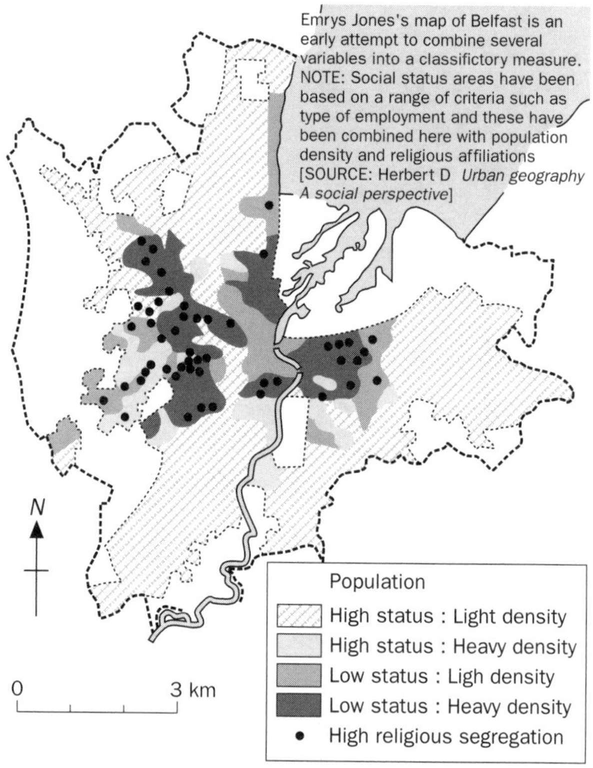

Figure 14.11 Social regions in Belfast

14.2 Dualism and the spatial concentration of the poor in western cities

Increased polarisation between deprived and other groups

A central theme in the recent literature on urban society is an increasing concern about polarisation, with the gap between the poor and other income groups continuing to widen since the 1970s. The number of households classed as deprived has also considerably increased and they have become more spatially concentrated and segregated from other households (Figure 14.13).

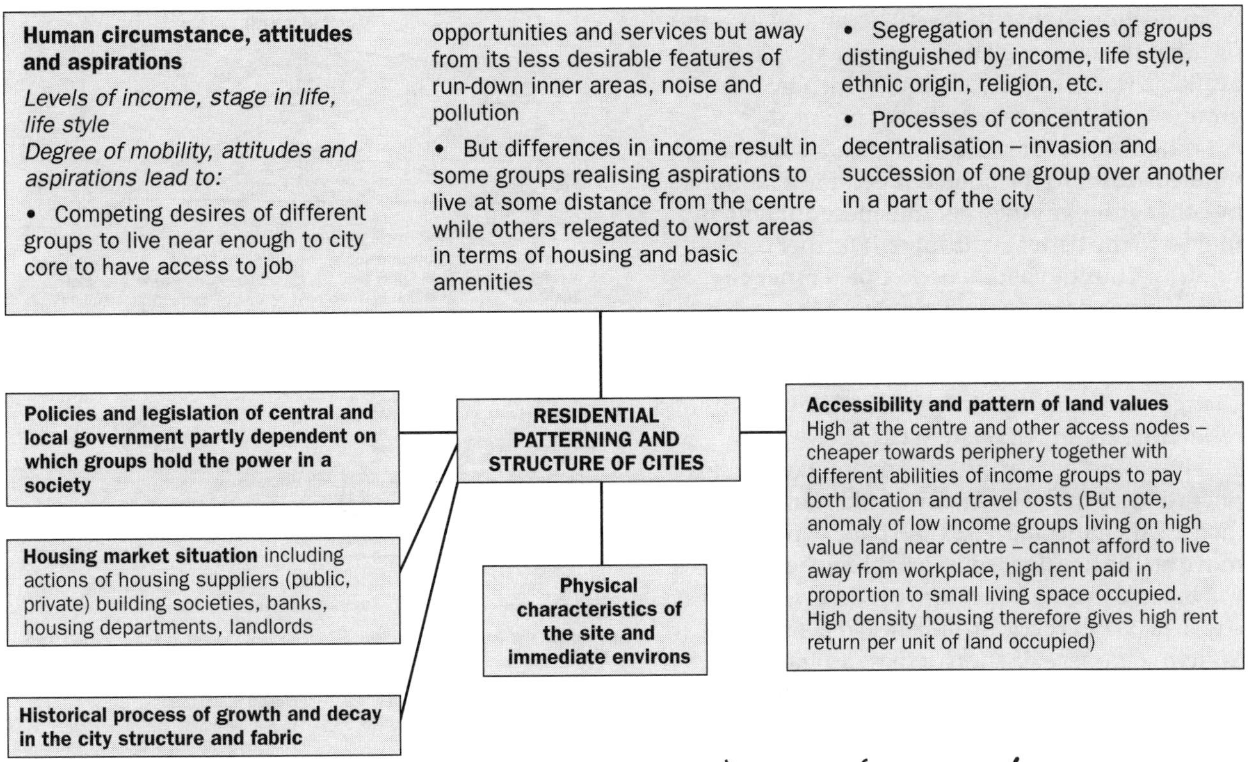

Figure 14.12 *Residential patterning and structure of cities*

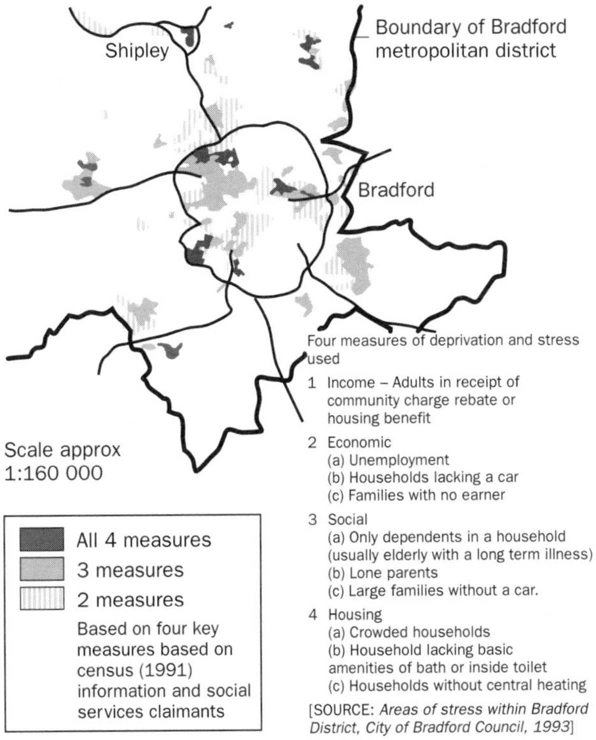

Figure 14.13 *Areas of deprivation in the Bradford (Yorkshire) district, 1991*

In the USA concentration continues to be in the older run down inner-city areas and is especially pronounced in large metropolitan cities, such as New York and Chicago. In some countries of Western Europe including the UK, localised concentrations occur in inner-city areas and also on rundown council estates on the edge of large cities, for example Meadowhall Estate, west of Newcastle, Drumchapel Estate on the edge of Glasgow, and Holmewood Estate in Bradford (Case study 14.2).

The problems of ethnic minorities

In the inner-city areas a significant number of the most deprived households are found amongst the ethnic minority households. For example, a recent study of deprivation in Utrecht, one of The Netherland's major cities, showed that in general, unemployment had risen from 5% in 1980 to 18% in 1990, but amongst ethnic minority groups it had risen to 40%. Although the problems of deprivation and those of ethnic minorities have become closely linked, poverty affects both majority white and minority groups.

Reasons for continued deprivation

The identification of disadvantaged groups and deprived inner-city areas is not new. It was central to the work of Burgess and Park back in the 1920s and 1930s and is a prominent element in their concentric rings model. Much of their explanation for the concentration of poor households in inner areas remains valid today: the perceived need to be close to whatever work opportunities might be available in the central area (though today these are far more limited than in the 1920s and 1930s); the fact that the only available accommodation available was inner city housing which no other group wanted because of its poor physical condition and poor facilities. This housing was 'filtered' down to the poor as it became abandoned by other groups as they became more affluent and moved to the better environment further out in the suburbs. Thus the poor had occupied inner city housing by a process of invasion and succession.

However, these influences have been increasingly overshadowed since the 1970s by fundamental changes in the mechanisms which have determined residential zoning in western cities.

It was assumed that even the poorer households once resident in the inner city would gradually increase their income levels and have opportunity to move up the housing ladder, enabling them to move to a better dwelling away from the deprived inner city-area (via the cycle of affluence) (Figure 14.14). In Western Europe realisation of these aspirations by poorer households was enhanced by a general rise in wage levels and economic expansion after the Second World War and also by changes in government policies aimed at producing a more equitable society. In the UK a mortgage subsidy was introduced to encourage house ownership and local authority housing built to let at subsidised rents, much of it on land in the outer suburbs. There were also slum clearance schemes to replace much of the older unfit Victorian terrace housing of inner city areas by new dwelling units, albeit in high rise buildings which were later to have their own problems.

Since the 1970s the decline of employment opportunities, brought about by the restructuring of western economies after the decline of manufacturing and changes in government housing policies, have severely reduced the chances of lower income households improving their quality of living. To the contrary, an increasing number find themselves worse off and increasingly cut off from the mainstream of the urban economy and the opportunities which hitherto has existed for them.

They have become trapped in areas of deprivation. ***There has emerged what are becoming known as the 'modern poor' or the 'underclasses' and with them the emergence of a 'culture of poverty' linked to a 'cycle of poverty or deprivation'***(Figure 14.14). The origin of the terms emerged from the study of deprived American inner-city areas and in particular, black ghetto areas in the large cities. These terms and concepts have been increasingly used in the wider context provided by the recent intensification and increase in poverty in almost all large western cities, including those in western Europe.

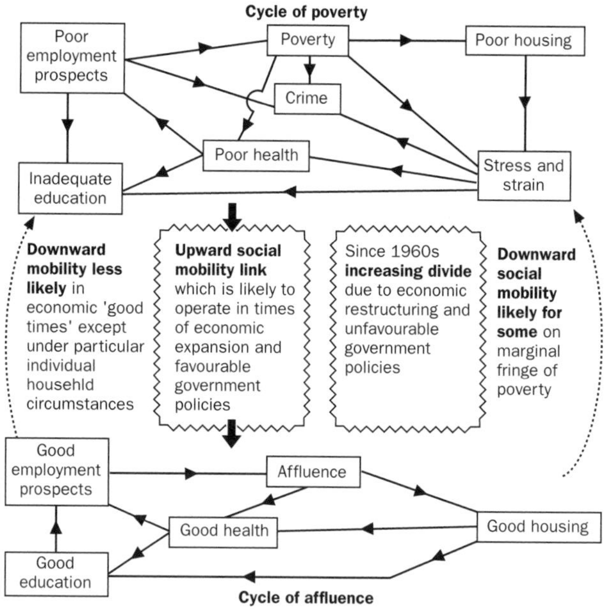

Indicators of poverty and wealth

In the absence of direct income measures from the Census of Population, it is necessary to make use of proxy indicators of poverty and wealth.
Other research shows that three key correlates of low income are: no car, no owned home and no job. The following proxy indicators relating to these three key correlates and aspects of socio-economic structure are utilised in the analysis:

Poverty indicators

1 unemployment rate
2 % households with no car
3 % of households in rented accommodation
4 inactivity rate for 20 – 59 year olds
5 % of working age males inactive
6 % of working age females inactive
7 % economically active in SEG class C: semi-skilled and labourers –SEGs 6, 7, 10, 11, 15
8 % economically active in SEG class D: no occupation – not included in SEGs 1– 5

Wealth indicators

1 % households with two or more cars
2 % households from social classes 1 and 2
3 % economically active in employment
4 % of adults highly qualified
5 % employed residents with higher qualifications
6 % economically active in SEG class A: professionals and managers – SEGs 1, 2, 3, 4, 13

It is useful to have indicators which measure slightly different dimensions, since poverty and wealth are themselves multi-dimensional

[Evidence from Census of Population 1991 and 1981; *Geography of poverty and wealth*, Anne Green Institute of Employment Research, 1994]

Figure 14.14 *Cycle of poverty (deprivation) and the cycle of affluence*

Cycle of poverty or deprivation

This is a concept which is largely, though not exclusively, linked to inner city problems. It offers some explanation of how the problems had arisen. The cycle of poverty involves a continuous process which transmits relative poverty from one generation to another and which makes escape from deprivation very difficult. In the vast majority of cases this arises from the way the economic system in a capitalist society operates. Certain occupational groups are given very low incomes which makes for a low standard of living, including poor housing (since they cannot afford any better). The poor environment may produce stresses and strains in the household and poor health amongst household members. In turn, this affects the educational and other prospects of younger members of the family. The school and neighbourhood may lack the resources and skilled people needed to improve conditions for the young who are caught in this cycle of poverty. They tend to leave school early with insecure job prospects.

This deprived group is particularly vulnerable during an economic recession. It is adversely affected when industry is modernised, rationalised and relocated away from inner city areas as happened in most western countries after the Second World War. Poor conditions and poor prospects encourage criminal activity and lack of interest in the neighbourhood environment, discouraging outside investment and incentives to improve it. On the contrary, the neighbourhood becomes even more run down and an adverse image of it is created, discouraging inward movement of all but the desperate households who have no where else to go.

The cycle of poverty is thus characteristic of the underclasses and is also increasingly concentrated in particular areas of the city and in certain housing estates on the edge of some cities.

Cycle of affluence

The cycle of affluence, the counterpart to the cycle of poverty, allows households of reasonable and higher incomes to improve their lifestyles and become upwardly socially mobile, especially in times of economic expansion. Adults who plan to start a family may progressively migrate to better housing areas. However, in times of social unrest and recession, these groups will have the influence to protect their locations and social positions against the needs and perceived threat from the 'underclasses', making it even more difficult for them to escape their cycle of poverty.

Increasing concentration of poverty 1981–1991

The extent of poverty, 1981 – 1991

- In general, fewer LADs (Local Authority Districts) had one or more constituent wards represented in the 'top' decile group of the national distribution of wards on poverty and wealth indicators in 1991 than in 1981. This is indicative of a trend towards a somewhat greater spatial concentration of poverty and wealth over the decade to 1991.
- Neighbourhoods characterised by extreme poverty are concentrated in a smaller number of LADs than are neighbourhoods of extreme wealth.
- Patterns of spatial clustering of extreme poverty wards, and changes in such patterns, vary between cities. For example, in Birmingham there was an increase in spatial clustering of high unemployment wards in the inner city between 1981 and 1991, while in Newcastle upon Tyne the trend was towards greater dispersal – as high unemployment levels became more extensive on selected outer estates.

The intensity of poverty

- In order to capture the localised severity of poverty or wealth within an area, a measure of intensity was calculated as the mean of the 'highest three' ranked wards on an indicator.
- Many of the'pockets' of most intense poverty are in the largest cities.

[SOURCE: Anne Green, *The Geography of Poverty and Wealth*, Institute of Employment Research, University of Warwick, 1994]

Recently the idea of a 'dualistic' city in which a distinct divide exists and which deprived households find it increasingly difficult to cross, has been added to the debate about the increasing social polarisation. The concept of 'dualism' has spatial connotations. Recent census data from a number of West European countries and the USA indicate that the 'modern poor' are increasingly concentrated in particular areas of the city, increasing the concentration of poverty. Some writers have criticised the 'dualistic city' concept as being too simplistic, pointing to the fact that areas of deprivation are not themselves concentrated together in one part of the city but may occur in a number of locations, including on the outer edge of cities as well as near the central core. This is evident from the location pattern of neighbourhood rioting which has occurred in large cities since the 1970s.

Nevertheless, the idea of a 'dualistic city' remains useful because the conditions under which the 'underclasses' live and their attitudes, norms and expectations are increasingly disparate from those of the more fortunate majority of urban society.

Studies show that the ***culture of poverty which characterises deprived groups*** is primarily not of their own making, but arises from the policies and circumstances which have resulted in their exclusion from the usual opportunities and entitlements present in society.The consequences of this are all too evident in almost all major cities in the western world: rioting, race conflict, rising crime rates and an increase in the number of single parent households.

Moreover, there is concern that unless tackled by appropriate action from outside agencies in close cooperation with members of the deprived groups, there will be an increase in the number of urban poor and a continued downward spiral for those caught up in the culture of poverty, ultimately resulting in a breakdown in urban society as a whole. At present these problems are not being tackled because the necessary political will is not there and insufficient resources are being made available.

14.3 Recent influences which bring more high status groups back into the city

Historical enclaves

From the nineteenth century the general trend has been for higher status households to locate in the outer suburbs and surrounding countryside away from the city centre. However, enclaves of high status housing have continued to exist in inner areas where, for historical reasons, a location has prestige and an exceptionally favourable environment. The most obvious examples are closes of housing within a cathedral setting, such as the Minster Yard at Lincoln, or those overlooking a historical garden or city park ,especially where it has been planned as an integral part of an important architectural development, as in the case of Queens Square and the Crescent at Bath (Figure 14.15). Such areas today are protected against redevelopment by conservation measures. Similar areas also exist in developing world cities such as The Avenue immediately north of the centre of Harare (Zimbabwe) (Case study 5.3).

Although there is some tendency for such housing to be taken over by high status professional services, such as that of solicitors, or to be divided into flats, much of it may remain occupied by high income households, especially those associated with the professions.

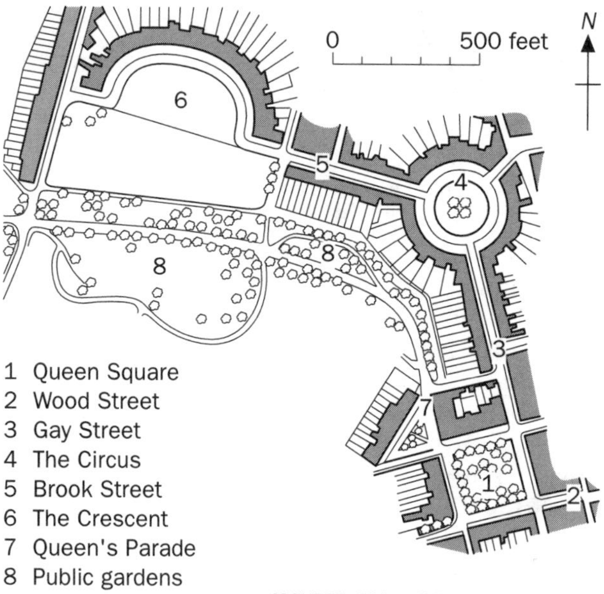

[SOURCE: Gibbon F *Town design*, 1962]

Figure 14.15 *High status housing near central Bath*

Gentrification and multi-purpose redevelopment schemes

Peter Hall, in a notable article, *Forces reshaping urban Europe* (*Urban Studies*, 1993), has identified the major economic developments which are now bringing back other high status groups into central areas, leading to the displacement of some lower income households. In particular, he highlights the following influences:

- As economic production becomes more internationalised, there will be a growth of (major) central service nodes to manage the space economy. Access to information both by face to face contact and the new information technologies favours those cities which are already strong information-gathering and dissemination centres, especially those with global status. These include cities with government offices, universities, financial services and media services. Expansion of these services and the growth of companies will create growing employment opportunities with high status and high salaries, attracting an increasing number of managerial, professional and other well qualified people wanting to live close to the heart of the city.
- Another drawing force creating both employment opportunities and reasons for living close to the heart of the city is the expansion of cultural and educational services, including museums, theatres, galleries and entertainment facilities.
- Employment is also being created by the expansion of a range of personal services, partly to cater for the needs of the increasing number of high status workers and business people and the general increase in the demand for leisure activities. These would include hotels, sports clubs and urban tourism.

Hall points to these as growth sectors in a period when manufacturing has been replaced by information-based high technology and services as the economic basis of cities. He emphasises that much of the routine office, retail and service activities have been decentralised to the periphery of cities, where sites are cheaper, access better and space more plentiful. Consequently, the lower paid routine office and other employment opportunities have been decentralised, inducing workers and their families to move out too. City central areas have been increasingly taken over by these new high status service sectors which require highly skilled well-educated personnel, many of whom are in the 20- to 30-year age range, either single or recently married without a family but with both partners in well paid jobs.

While many employees commute in, a significant number of those working in the growth service sectors want to live close to the city centre. Various surveys have shown that they are attracted by the lively environment generated in the city and want to live close to the workplace to avoid both the cost and inconvenience of commuting and also because the nature of their work may demand unconventional working hours. The closeness to communication centres such as main line stations and node stations for tube services, is important, as are the attractions of entertainment, restaurants and other facilities available in a city. The dwelling units on offer are attractive and, in the case of new developments, easy to service and with modern conveniences.

A number of the new high status living areas provided for this sector of the market are part of multi-purpose redevelopment schemes in the hearts of cities. These have been built by property developers or consortiums in association with local authorities to meet the needs of the new service sectors. The most well known area in the UK is London Docklands. Waterfront locations are particular attractive but others include old hospital sites and derelict small industrial sites (Figure 15.11).

Gentrification – a process which occurs in certain inner city areas where old, substandard housing is bought and modernised and occupied by middle class and wealthy families.

The increasing demand by these higher-paid single and younger married households for accommodation close to the heart of the city has also led to the gentrification of certain older inner city housing originally built for the lower paid as, for example, the Lea Bank area in inner Birmingham and certain inner Paris locations (Case study 16.2). These are usually streets of nineteenth century terrace housing close to city centres. There is not a sudden dramatic takeover but a gradual piecemeal social upgrading of an area as more of the housing is bought by couples who, with increasing salaries and frequently also with the help of local authority improvement grants, refurbish and improve old housing. Demand and modernisation generally pushes up the price of housing, encouraging older and lower paid households to sell up and move out. As gentrification spreads, the affected neighbourhood becomes 'fashionable' and more higher income households move in, refurbishing dwellings until the whole area becomes upgraded. Such upgrading improves the 'tone' of the neighbourhood and may also lead to improvements in the environment and of shopping and other services, including the local school. All of this adds to the attraction to upwardly mobile higher income households.

One of the most notable features of the development of these high status areas, whether through gentrification or total redevelopment, is that such areas frequently exist alongside some of the most deprived housing neighbourhoods of the inner city (Case study 16.2). Part of the London Docklands, for example, backs on to council housing in Tower Hamlets, where some of the most serious deprivation in the inner London area occurs. Thus the two ends of the social polarisation which occur because of economic restructuring, are starkly and visibly evident.

14.4 **Ethnic minorities in cities**

Recent studies indicate that, despite some signs of dispersion, in western countries ethnic minorities are still mainly concentrated in large cities. For instance, Anne Green, on the basis of the 1991 census figures for the UK concludes that 'minority groups are disproportionately concentrated in London, the principal cities and metropolitan areas' (*The geography of poverty and wealth*, 1994). However, the pattern for the different minority groups is not the same (Figure 14.16). Black and Bangladeshi populations are more concentrated in inner London while there are more Indians in outer London, indicating that the latter are more dispersed than the Black and Bangladeshi populations. Pakistani minority groups are over represented in the large cities of the Midlands and the North (Figure 14.16).

Looking at distribution patterns within the main cities and metropolitan areas, ethnic minorities are predominantly to be found in inner areas where the greatest concentrations of poverty and deprivation occurs (14.17). However, it is important to note that there are more white people in inner areas classed as 'deprived' than ethnic minority people.

In the USA, though, there are broad similarities to the UK pattern in the distribution of ethnic minority groups; the distribution in the USA assumes a much greater significance because ethnic minorities make up a larger proportion of the total population. In 1991 it was just over one quarter of the population, a significant rise on the figure for 1981. This was due to a greater rate of natural increase amongst the ethnic population than the white population, and to the continued immigration of Hispanic and Asian people (Figure 14.18).

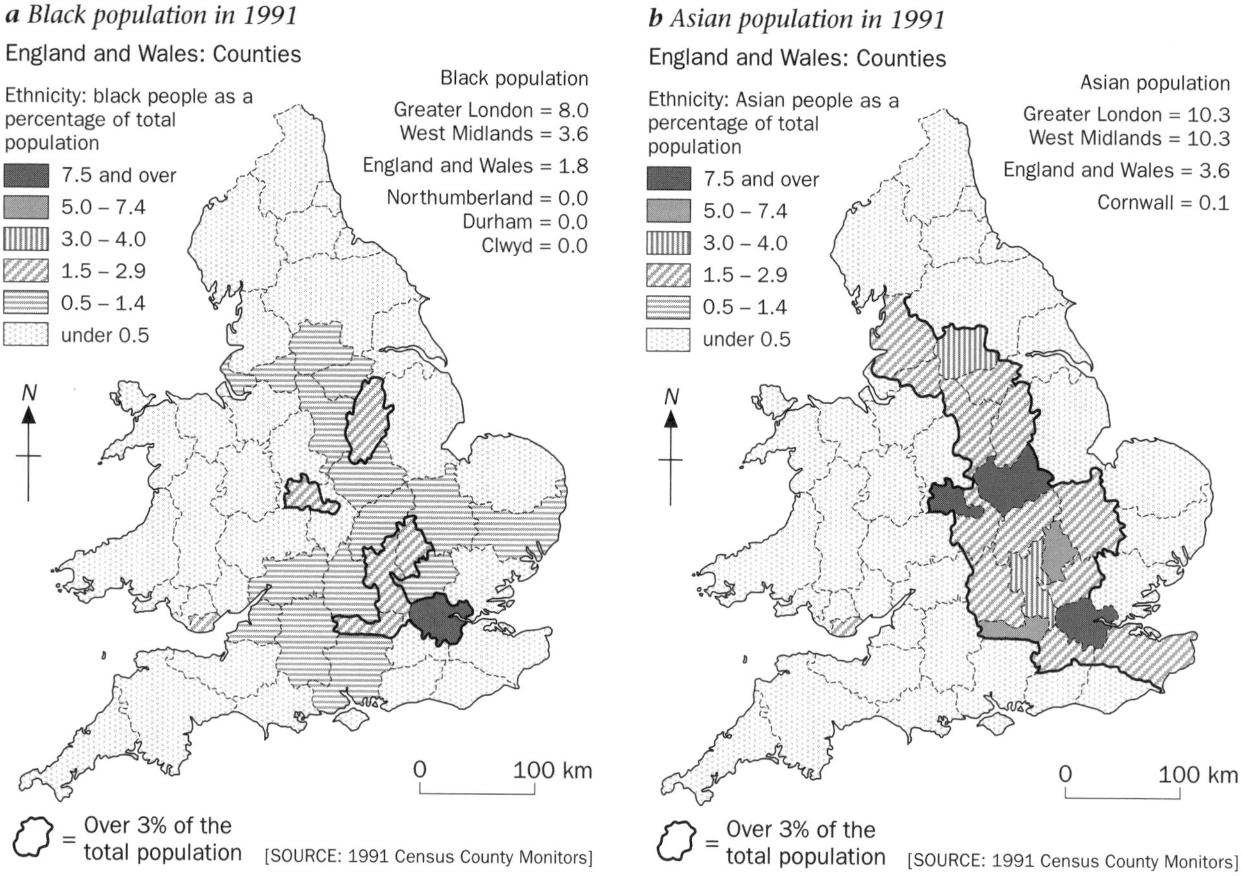

***Figure 14.16** Distribution of Asian and Black populations in the UK, 1991*

Two-thirds of the ethnic minority populations are in the large metropolitan areas (Figure 14.18), with the greatest gains since 1981 being in Los Angeles on the west coast where an increase of 20% occurred, followed by San Diego, Dallas-Fort Worth, Chicago and Washington. However, New York continues to have the largest minority population.

Because of the expected continued higher trend in natural increase and some continued immigration, the proportion of ethnic minority populations in the large cities in the USA is likely to continue to increase.

As in the UK, there are distinctive differences in the distribution pattern of one main ethnic group compared to another. The Hispanic population is most represented in the large cities of the south and west. Although there has been some migration of black people from the north to the metropolitan cities in the west and south, most of the black population is still to be found in the north with the next highest in the south.

Why the large metropolitan areas?

In the case of ethnic minority groups in the UK, the concentration arises from the initial main wave of immigrants coming in principally from the Caribbean and the Indian subcontinent in the period 1948 – 68. Driven by poverty, unemployment and overpopulation in their own countries, they were attracted to the large conurbations, especially to London, by job opportunities at a time when there was an acute shortage of labour for the lower paid semi- and unskilled jobs in manufacturing and service occupations. These lower paid jobs were unattractive to the majority of the working white population at a time of expanding job opportunities in the post-war boom period.

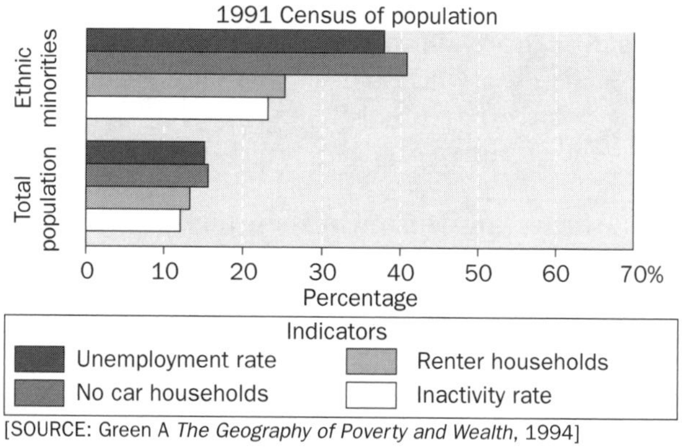

[SOURCE: Green A *The Geography of Poverty and Wealth*, 1994]

***Figure 14.17** Relative proportion of ethnic populations residing in 'extreme' poverty wards by selected indicators in England and Wales*

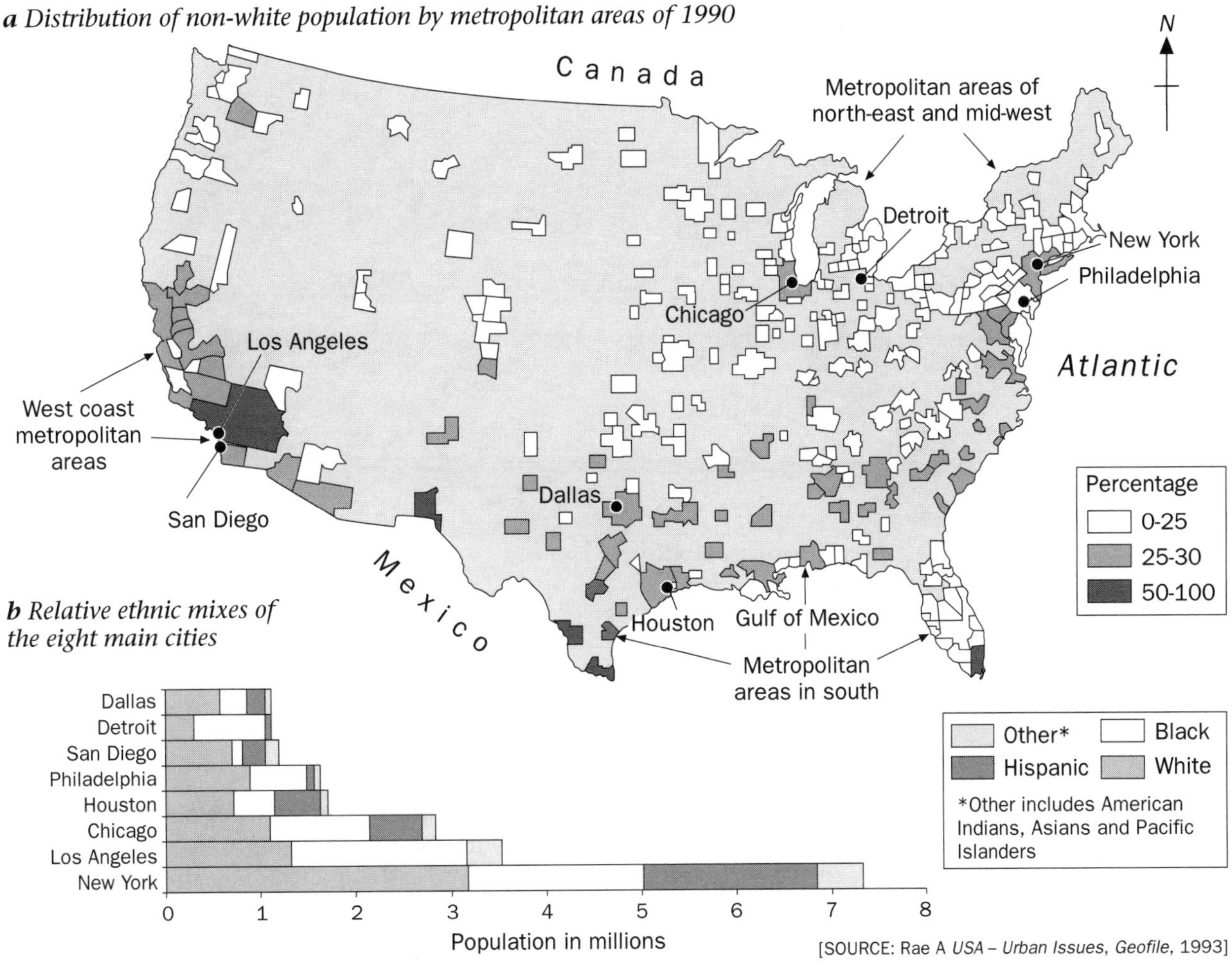

Figure 14.18 *Distribution of ethnic populations in metropolitan areas of the USA*

Immigrants were also drawn to the UK because, as part of the British Commonwealth, they had ties with the mother country and could identify with it. Also, in order to overcome the labour shortages in the UK people were actively encouraged to migrate from other Commonwealth countries by the British authorities up to the early 1960s.

Once the first influx of migrants were settled in the large conurbations, a chain migration operated. Much of the knowledge of places and perceived opportunities gained by later migrants came from letters and other news fed back to home areas by the earlier New Commonwealth entrants and this reinforced the attractions of the large conurbations. In addition, it was natural that later migrants should be drawn to areas where people of their own kind were already settled since there they would feel at home, more secure and could receive the support needed while they found jobs and settled in to a new situation. Not only was there a growing segregation from the white population, but also segregation between different ethnic groups. For example, in terms of people coming from the Caribbean islands to London, a significant number from the Dominica and St Lucia are to be found in Notting Hill and Paddington, while people from Granada are concentrated in Hammersmith and Ealing.

Because of the growing problems associated with the influx of New Commonwealth immigrants and the fall in job vacancies by the early 1960s, further growth in the numbers of ethnic minority groups in the large conurbations have largely been due to the arrival of the dependents of people already here and increasingly to the effect of natural increase; the proportion of those born in this country as a percentage of the total ethnic minority population has been steadily rising. A significant number are now third generation citizens.

Another increasingly important factor for the concentration of ethnic minorities in a few principal cities is the failure of ethnic minorities to disperse to other areas and become assimilated into the main body of the population as was initially

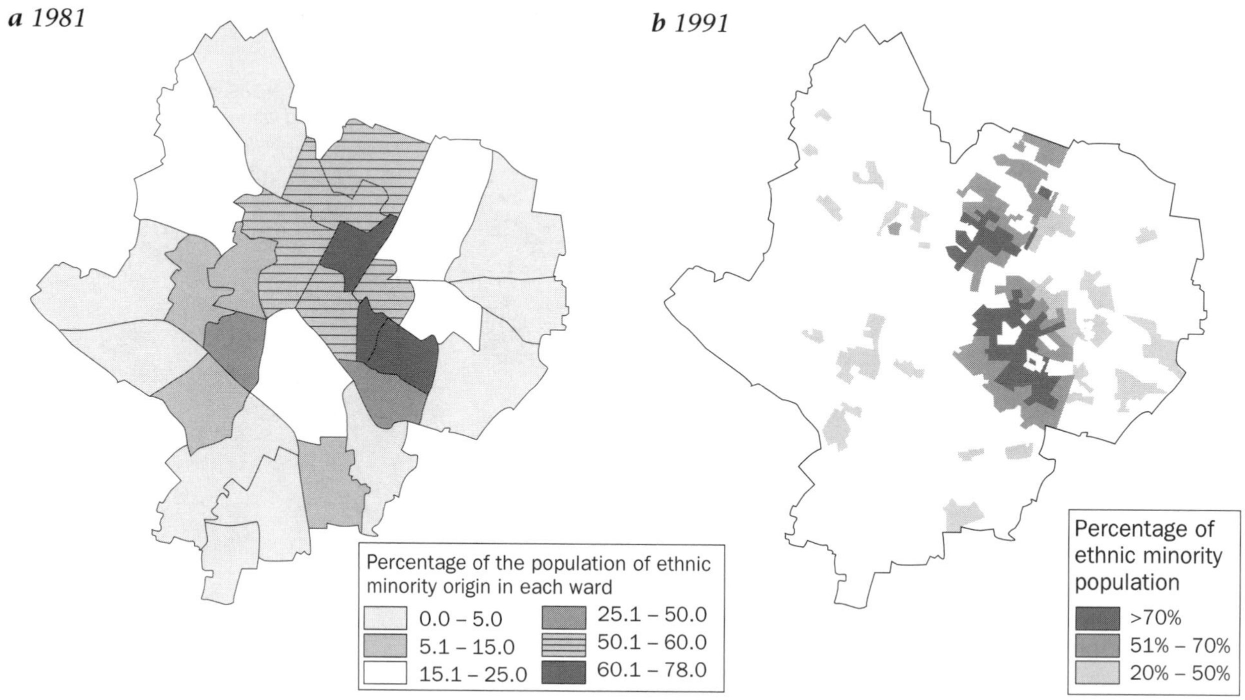

[SOURCE: Survey of Leicester 1983 and research information group, Leicester County Council]

Figure 14.19 Distribution of ethnic population in Leicester 1981 and 1991

anticipated would happen (Figure 14.19). This failure is partly due to the conscious decision of ethnic minority groups to largely stay together and partly due to external circumstances which prevent or discourage dispersion and assimilation, despite the efforts made to improve opportunities for ethnic minorities, even as in the case of education, through a policy of positive discrimination.

Both in respect of other Western European countries and the USA, similar reasons may be put forward for the concentration of ethnic minorities in the large cities.

> 'Historically, immigrants have tended to settle in either traditional port of entry areas or where large concentrations of ethnic groups were already located. Native born minorities have mainly travelled well-worn migration paths where the chance to be near friends and family often took precedence over economic opportunities.'
>
> [SOURCE: Frey W H *The New Urban Revival in the United States*, 1993]

The 'port of entry' and in general points of entry are particularly evident in the distribution of the Asian and Hispanic ethnic minorities in the USA. Hispanic migration, for example, is particularly concentrated in cities in the south-west and along the border with Mexico, where much cross border migration has occurred (Figure 14.18).

However, in the case of the black population in the USA with its origins in the slave trade in the eighteenth and early nineteenth century, the historical factor, internal migration patterns and the effect of the natural increase rate are of added significance. Following the end of the civil war in 1865, earlier migration was from the south to growing metropolitan centres in the north-east and mid-west where rapid industrialisation provided job opportunities. More recently, with the decline of older established manufacturing in these regions, there has been a reverse flow to the south and moves to the other 'sunbelt' metropolises, such as Los Angeles in the west where the new high technology and other modern industries have rapidly expanded along with low paid service sector jobs (Case study 5.1).

Why the concentration in inner areas of large cities and metropolitan areas?

Practically all studies to do with the distribution of ethnic minorities have emphasised the concentration of ethnic minorities mainly in the inner residential areas. Historically, there has been some spread as numbers have increased, but this largely reflects the growth in the total built-up area of metropolises. The inner area has been correspondingly enlarged as suburbanisation of the wealthier white households has spread into surrounding areas. The central area dispersion of ethnic minorities may be pronounced in particular directions, frequently those where older industries were sited and therefore less attractive and rated lower than other inner suburb areas (Case study 14.2).

The reasons for the presence of deprived groups in inner areas generally apply

Many of the reasons for the concentration of ethnic minorities in inner areas have already been highlighted in the earlier discussion on the concentration of deprived groups in general in inner areas. There is a danger in assuming that all ethnic minority households fall into this deprived sector of the population. However, even in these inner areas a significant number continue to live there but have incomes and a quality of living significantly above the poverty line.

The loss of potential leadership of the elite amongst ethnic minorities

There are also a growing number of better educated ethnic minority households with relatively high incomes from businesses or the professions to be found in outer suburban residential areas. In the UK this is particularly evident amongst the Indian and Chinese minority groups. Massey and Denton, in their study entitled 'American apartheid,' point to an increasing elite minority of black people now living in the higher status outer suburban areas with aspirations more akin to those of wealthier white people than to the majority of black people consigned to the poorer inner areas. They point to a growing cleavage between the dispersed elite and the rest (a feature already evident in large African cities following independence).

This is another reason why the majority of ethnic minority households remain concentrated in the poorer inner areas. With better educated and increasing incomes, more fortunate ethnic households have left the inner areas, depriving inner area populations of the voice and effective influence needed if the conditions and opportunities in inner areas are to be fundamentally improved.

Denial of access to most of the housing market is a crucial factor

The key feature as to why most ethnic minority households are concentrated in inner areas is their very limited access to the housing market. Most are on low incomes and are thus excluded from the main part of the housing market, largely being limited to the rented sector of the market and very low cost housing, both of which are concentrated in the older inner areas of the large cities. With little opportunity of improving incomes, there is equally little opportunity of moving out of inner areas. Once denied full access to the housing market other consequences follow, making it difficult for ethnic minority households to move.

> 'Housing markets are central to individual social and economic well being because they distribute more than shelter; they also distribute a variety of other resources that shape and largely determine one's life chances. Along with housing, residential markets also allocate schooling, peer groups, safety, jobs, insurance costs, public services, home equity and ultimately wealth. By tolerating the persistent and systematic disenfranchisement of blacks (and other ethnic minority groups) from housing markets we send a clear signal to one group that hard work, individual enterprise, sacrifice and aspirations don't matter; what determines is the colour of one's skin.
>
> Residential segregation remains and from this follows a host of deadly ills that continue to undercut and overwhelm the progress achieved in other areas.'
>
> [SOURCE: Massey D and Denton N *American Apartheid*]

Apart from being unable to afford better housing, there are other obstacles to be overcome. Massey and Denton, in reflecting on the effectiveness of the Fair Housing Act (1968) in the USA, which was designed to make discrimination in the housing market against coloured ethnic minority groups illegal (and the strengthening of the act 1988), indicate how in practice, discrimination continues to operate because the law is not effectively enforced. The reason is the failure of public and collective political will to ensure its enforcement.

Even in Chicago where the authorities have led the nation in fair housing legislation and in efforts to enforce it, segregation remains with little change having occurred over the last ten years. The same is generally true in the UK.

Here, however, there is the added dimension of much greater provision of local authority housing, which should allow more dispersion of households from inner city areas and decrease segregation, since provision is directed to those on low incomes with no discrimination against ethnic households and much of the housing is now on outer city estates. In practice, few ethnic households are to be found on these outer estates. This is mainly because most ethnic applicants apply for inner area council housing as they want to stay near their own kind, be close to facilities provided and would feel insecure on outer estates, fearing possible racial harassment. As a consequence, despite most households now having lived sufficiently long in an area to have the same chance as white households of applying for council housing, their success rate in gaining accommodation is on average half that of white applicants (Case study 14.2).

Investigations have also shown that many who qualify to be on the housing list do not in fact apply. This is partly because they do not know how to and partly because they feel uncomfortable about applying through the system. There is also some evidence of more self-help support groups in ethnic minority dominated inner housing areas.

The wish of most ethnic minority households to remain segregated from the majority white population

Much of the discussion so far has centred on indirect discrimination against ethnic minority groups and the circumstances operating to keep them residentially segregated. There is also a powerful inbuilt desire to remain segregated. minorities wish to retain their cultural identities and religious and social practices, the strength and influence of family and kinship ties, the opportunity to share and retain their particular language. There has also developed other features which encourage ethnic minority households to remain in these areas. These include the provision of services specifically designed to meet their needs, ranging from retail shops, financial services, community centres, to places of worship and schools in which the majority of students are from the ethnic community and in which norms and values familiar to the community will be encouraged.

The effect of marked changes in public policies

There is a move from efforts to assimilate ethnic minorities to acceptance of a plural society. There has also been a marked change in public policy in the UK. Up to the 1970s efforts were directed towards giving ethnic minority households equal rights and support services to enable them to be gradually assimilated into the mainstream of society. Ethnic minority groups saw this as directed and controlled by the white majority and not basically responding to the wishes of the ethnic minority groups. Thus efforts at assimilation were resisted. Since the 1970s there has been a marked shift in public policy towards that of giving 'parity of esteem' and a recognition of the right of ethnic groups to maintain their cultural practices as long as these do not conflict with the laws of the land. Agencies and cooperation groups have therefore been set up to ensure that this happens. Public policy is supporting segregation indirectly by encouraging ethnic groups to retain their cultural identities. Distinctive identities are further heightened by the increased emphasis amongst younger elements in the ethnic minorities towards positive discrimination against the majority white population and those public services they perceive as being white-dominated .

Thus in the UK what is essentially a plurist society is developing, in which ethnic minorities are not only retaining their own cultural identity but also their own distinctive residential areas. This is also the case in other western European countries and in the USA, although the extent of it and reasons for it may vary in their relative importance.

14.5 **Housing and the poor in developing world cities**

A worsening situation

Despite increased efforts by the poor themselves and by governments to improve housing conditions in the cities, the scale of the housing problem in developing countries increased throughout the 1980s. In Addis Ababa, for example, 85% of residents live in what the United Nations calls 'informal settlements'. In Luanda, the figure is 70%, in Dar es Salaam, 60% and in Bogota, 59%. Bombay is India's wealthiest city, but half of its 11 million residents live in slums, with 350 000 sleeping on the streets'. This was partly a result of the sheer increase in numbers due to the continued influx of migrants and the rate of natural increase in the cities. It was also a result of a fall in real incomes as economic conditions worsened during the 1980s and faulty government financial planning led to spiralling inflation and increased unemployment. For example, research has shown that in Lima and Mexico City, real wages fell by over 50% while land and building material costs more than doubled. In addition, the spread of poor housing further into

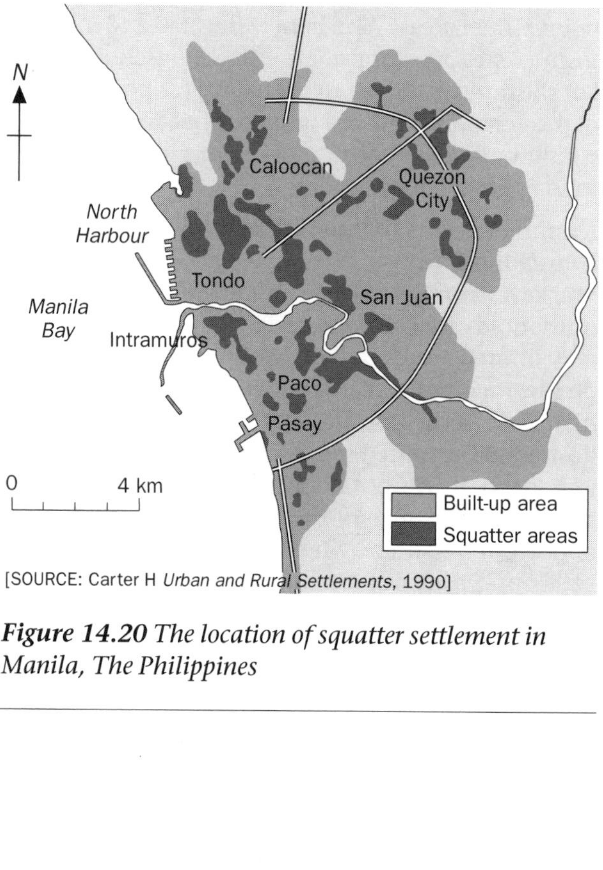

Figure 14.20 The location of squatter settlement in Manila, The Philippines

the rural areas around cities led to marked increases in travelling costs to work for the majority of those who had jobs in the formal sector.

Provision of housing thus remains one of the most crucial issues for the governments of nearly all of the developing countries. For example, it is estimated that Kenya's urban centres require at least 260 000 dwelling units annually to meet the housing needs of its growing urban population. Public agencies have been unable to build more than 10 000 a year on average and private construction businesses add few additional affordable units.

The location of housing for low income groups

Attention is largely centred on the burgeoning mass of ***spontaneous or informal self-help housing*** (***loosely termed shanty housing***) on the fringe of large cities. While fringe developments dominate in terms of area covered, the distribution of high density dwellings for low income groups is complex (Figure 14.20). In Latin American cities, for example, there are old slum tenements near the city centre and also older spontaneous housing nearby, marking the first influx of migrants during the 1950s. Distribution of self-help housing is also influenced by poor terrain and drainage conditions, since families desperate for shelter which is accessible to work opportunities have been prepared to occupy areas in cities deemed unfit for settlement by middle and higher income groups. Spontaneous settlements have thus grown on steep slopes in Rio de Janeiro, for example, and swampy land near the harbour in Manila, the capital of the Philippines.

However, as the price of land has escalated in the large cities, the poor have been increasingly dispersed to the fringes and frequently into the countryside at some distance from the cities. Thus the poor continue to be marginalised. As has been seen earlier in the example of Harare in Zimbabwe, even where governments have introduced formal housing schemes, most of these tend to be in the form of satellite settlements some distance away from the city and employment (Case study 5.3).

Forms of housing available to the poor

More than half the housing in the large cities is of the ***informal or spontaneous type built by the poor themselves*** but the proportion varies from one country to another according to social, economic and political circumstances. While the amount of conventional housing available is very limited, the renting sector is important. For example, in

Turner suggested that each income group within a city tends to make different 'trade offs' between three basic needs* of opportunity, security and identity.
The 'bridgeheader' newcomer has as a priority, a job, and will accept poor housing and lack of security. The 'consolidator', becoming well established in the city, looks also for security of plot tenure and better quality housing. For the middle-income earner, security and quality of housing take priority over accessibility to work as s/he can afford to travel a distance.

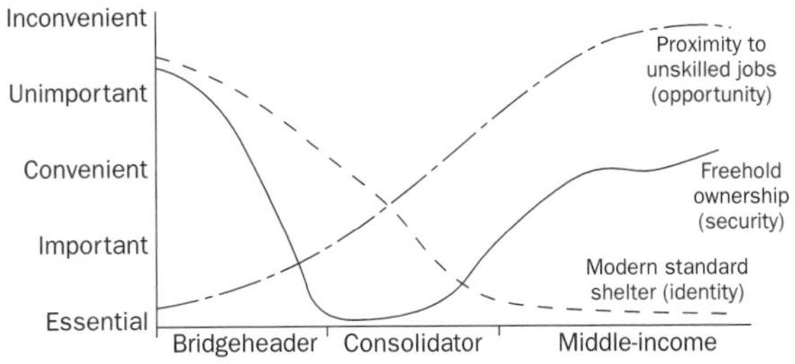

The housing prorities of middle-income groups, consolidators, and bridgeheaders

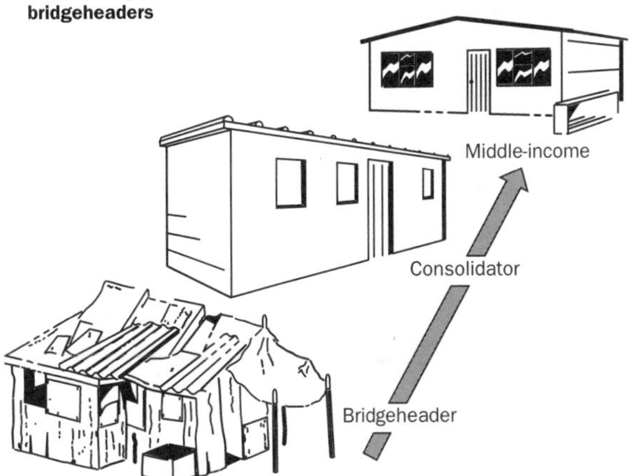

[SOURCE: Turner J F C *Freedom to Build*, 1972]

Figure 14.21 *Quality of housing occupied and progressive changes in aspirations*

Calcutta and Bombay more than 50% of households are in rented accommodation and a similar situation exists in most large Latin American cities. Many tenement and other lhousing units have been subdivided and rooms let to provide income for the landlord or main tenant, particularly in the inner areas of cities. There is also much illegal building of shacks and other shelters at the rear of dwelling unit, plots which are within easy reach of city employment. Access to possibilities of employment is of prime importance, especially for recent arrivals to the city (Figure 14.21) and many turn to those relatives or friends with housing in the city who are willing to allow them to build a shelter on part of their plot or offer a room.

Even within spontaneous settlements there is a lot of evidence of self-built units being extended and part let to other families to increase income and often provide the money needed to upgrade and further develop housing units.

	Casa-blanca	Atenas	Britalia	San Antonio
Age of settlement (years)	9.5	12.1	2.9	9.2
Percentage of households who are renters	42	43	28	43
Services and utilities score	12	15	6	11

[SOURCE: Gilbert and Gugler *Housing the urban poor, Cities, Poverty and Development*, 1992]

Figure 14.22 *Age, renting and servicing of Bogota`s barrios (Colombia)*

Informal, spontaneous or self-help housing

This is the most extensive housing in most large cities. The character and standard of self-help housing varies enormously from the most rudimen tary shelter to a brick or cement block building of a number of rooms and connected to all main services. The quality of the surrounding environment also varies from one totally lacking in community facilities to one well serviced by tarred roads and provided with schools and clinics, for example.

Nairobi's Slum Valley (Kenya)

Environmental conditions

Very few people in Mathare Valley own the shacks they live in. In most cases the owners are the original builders of the dwellings, who have now moved out and become rentiers. The shacks themselves are built with access only to alleys, many of them so narrow that two people can pass each other only with difficulty. Many of the alleys which run up and down the valley side are deeply gullied. They become rivers when it rains, rushing down to the main river, which in turn floods its banks, driving people living too close to the valley floor out of their homes.

Retail services

There are large numbers of goats and hens. There are tiny shops everywhere: these may begin, at the humblest, with a woman sitting on a scrap of plastic with half a dozen rotten tomatoes for sale. At the top end of the scale, there may be a semi-permanent stall.

Unimproved 'shanty dwellings'

The facts are rather basic: a family will normally have a space about half the size of the kitchen of a semi-detached home or flat in Europe. Its floor will normally be mud. It may or may not have a small hole for a window. The construction will be of mud and wattle, or perhaps the bashed-out sides and bottoms of oil drums. Families buy their water from a man with a tap, and use public latrines which smell and leak.

No security of tenure – eviction and land speculation by landlords

Now that Christmas is over, it is likely that a programme of evictions will begin in the valley, and involve many of the women in the group: private landlords – not the city or government – want their tenants out, so that they can add more of the three- and four-storey buildings which are creeping down toward the river.

A family in every 10ft by 4ft room makes these even more profitable than shacks. Ten thousand people are likely to be affected – they will move from mud and tin shacks to plastic huts instead. Mrs Munro's work can reach very few of those, but nobody is shocked. Evictions are routine.

[SOURCE: *The Independent* 28.12.1994]

The great variety in types of self-help housing make definitions and classifications difficult. Turner, who has made extensive studies of housing in the developing world and especially in Lima for example, notes that ***few self-help houses are wholly constructed by the households who occupy them.*** In Lima, he estimates that on average not more than a quarter of the dwelling is built by the family; the rest of the building is contracted out.

Drakakis-Smith and others focus on the way the land has been occupied rather than on the character of the dwelling. ***The common element underlying all areas of spontaneous housing is that the land on which it stands has been acquired illegally and is land which had no planning permission and little by way of site services. Hence the use of the term 'pirate urbanisation'*** to describe such settlement growth. In the 1960s and 1970s, unoccupied public or private land was invaded and simply built on. More recently, land without planning permission is informally purchased and built on in the hope that with time, occupation will be recognised as legal with security of tenure following and mains service provided.

The other distinguishing element is that as the various terms used to describe self-help housing suggests, the initiative has generally come from the group who occupy the land and not some outside body. There is some element of self-help in the construction of the dwellings as well as in the provision of essential facilities.

The descriptive terms 'shanty', 'slum' or 'squatter' area, have gradually faded out of use because their implications as descriptive terms are misleading.

The first two terms imply very poor quality housing, yet many areas have been upgraded to provide substantial and well serviced dwellings. The term 'squatter' implies occupation of land in defiance of the authorities. In many cases the occupation is tolerated by the authorities who may also assist financially in upgrading the housing units and the settlement area as a whole.

Government responses towards self-help housing

Clearance and renewal

Until the 1960s the common policy towards invasion of land and the construction of self-help housing was to force the people off the land and clear it with bulldozers (Case study 5.3). The shortage of housing was to be met by conventional housing schemes, the extent of these depending on the availability of finance and the political ideology of the particular government involved. The reasons behind the policy were generally that it was seen as a way of deterring migration away from the countryside and slowing down a rate of urbanisation with which governments were unable to cope. The self-help housing was also regarded as unsuitable and unhealthy. For newly independent governments, large expanses of shanties and slum housing were regarded as conveying the wrong image to other countries, especially to western countries. For example, in 1970 President Kenyatta defended the clearance of squatter areas in and around Nairobi by arguing that he did not want Kenya's capital turned into a shanty town.

In many newly independent countries what was regarded as adequate housing was largely based on western ideas, many of those in planning having been trained in western countries. There was little regard for what the poor, given their circumstances, regarded and accepted as reasonable housing.

Removal was also often linked to policies of segregation. Frequently land had been occupied and developed close to established middle and higher income housing and thus was seen as a threat to the status and value of established housing areas. In this sense, the policy was in line with segregative tendencies in western countries. While in colonial times residential zoning in cities was based on race and ethnicity, under independence, zoning was increasingly based on income and ability to pay.

> 'Today zoning, income and government housing projects maintain residential segregation on the basis of class not only in Latin America but throughout the non-socialist world.'
>
> [SOURCE: Alan Gilbert and Josef Gugler *Cities, Poverty and Development*, 1992]

Clearance was also done to protect private ownership of land, especially since the wealthy minority were able to exercise political influence and the growing shortage of land within the city boundaries led to the possibility of large speculative profits as prices rose.

A typical site-and-service scheme in Kuwadzana
Funded by the US Agency for International Development (UUSAID), it lies about 12 km west of the city along the Bulawayo Road. Over 7000 plots have been provided since 1984. Beneficiaries were supposed to be low-income households with a income of $175 per month. A maximum of 25.5% of income was to be considered for loan repayments over 30 years and beneficiaries were given loans of between $2500 and £3000, depending on their incomes, to purchase building materials and to pay labour costs for construction. They were expected to complete a four-roomed core house of a least 48 m^2 within 18 months. Beneficiaries were given the choice of using registered private builders, municipal-controlled building brigades, or establishing their own building co-operatives. Government has, since 1983, been advocating the use of the last two methods in the construction of low-income urban housing. (Note: $ = Zimbabwe dollars)

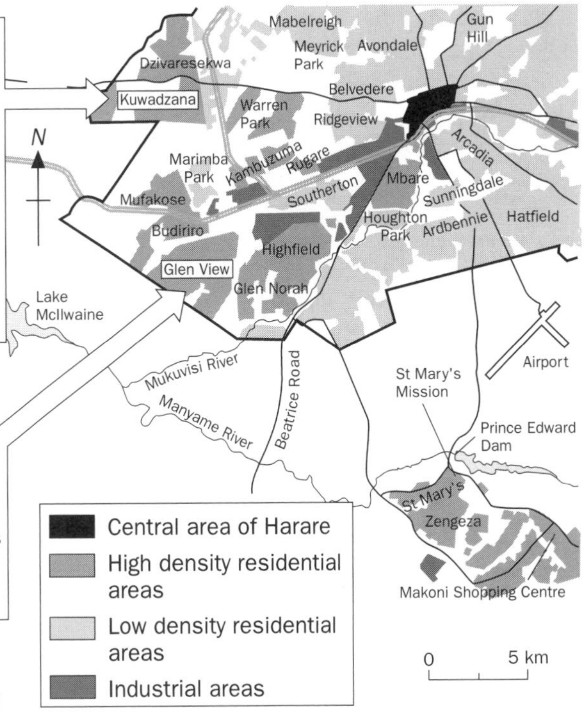

One of the strategies pursued in the provision of low-income housing in the post-independence era has been that of aided self-help schemes. Since the late 1970s public-sector low-income housing projects have concentrated on the provision of serviced plots, with or without some form of wet-core or core housing unti. Over 7000 serviced plots of 200 m^2 each with ablution facilities only were allocated in **Glen View in the early 1980s** and the beneficiaries were supposed to complete a whole house in 10 years. Title would be passed to the beneficiary once the house was completed.

[SOURCE: Zinyama I et al (ed) *Harare – The Growth and Problems of a City*, 1993]

Figure 14.23 *Typical starter 'site and service' schemes, Harare, Zimbabwe*

Frequently land needed for some public work programme or other use had also been illegally occupied.

Removal programmes have in more recent times been heavily criticised. Governments have been unable or unwilling to build sufficient conventional housing to replace the number of self-help units which had been demolished, let alone meet the needs of incoming families. The rent on purpose-built dwelling units, whether in the form of high rise apartments or low rise dwelling units, was generally beyond the means of the vast majority of low paid workers for whom they were intended. Government housing programmes seemed to have only been successful in Hong Kong, Singapore and Saudi Arabia, where governments have financed building programmes on a sufficient scale to meet housing needs and workers with the expansion of the economy, could generally earn enough to pay the rents charged for dwelling units.

Zimbabwe: Inadequacies of an earlier policy of 'slum' clearance and conventional house building approach and the swing towards a 'self-help, site and service approach

Since 1985 a total of 56 000 units were built in rural and urban areas by both the public and private sectors. This give an average annual production of 18 667 housing untis, which falls far short of the required 162 500 units per year for Zimbabwe.

There is a new school of thought which argues that in developing countries such as Zimbabwe sub-standard housing should be regarded as part of the existing housing stock. It is argued that developing countries, because of their weak economies, cannot allocate enough money for the construction of new houses. Many more sub-standard houses are upgraded into standard houses than new standard houses constructed. There is, therefore, a call on governments of developing countries to tailor their policies towards the provision of more land for low-income people to enable them to build sub-standard housing which can be upgraded later.

[SOURCE: Musindo M Chenga *Provision of housing in Zimbabwe – a national view, Harare – The growth and problems of a city*, 1993]

Often housing schemes to rehouse clearance families were developed too far away from work locations, involving residents in costly journeys to work. Moreover, the sense of community and mutual support engendered in the self-help housing areas were lost.

The most common reaction of the displaced population was to either move into areas of self-help housing not cleared or to invade more land and start up another self-help scheme. In the case of those families relocated in renewal schemes, large numbers had to sublet to pay the rent and this led to overcrowding and a deterioration in the quality of the housing. Many others sold their homes or the tenancy to higher income families, as was the case in the massive favela removal programme which took place in Rio de Janeiro during the early 1970s and in Manila in the 1960s.

Removal programmes on the whole therefore did little to improve the conditions of the poor and were motivated less by an interest in them than in clearing the land for prestige developments or speculative profits.

Rent control

In some countries, though not directly related to the specific issue of self-help housing, rent control was used as a tool to ensure more affordable housing for the lower paid. This policy was adopted in Mexico, for example, where the majority of low paid workers occupy rented accommodation. While offering some protection to the poor, studies have shown that rent control discouraged landlords from spending on maintenance of their properties, leading to deterioration in living conditions for the tenants. Rent control also discouraged private building of units for letting, leaving many without the chance of accommodation. Rent controls are thus only effective in the short term.

Site and service and upgrading programmes

During the 1970s it was gradually accepted that most developing world governments could not build sufficient homes and thus some kind of self-help policy had to be implemented. The swing towards supporting self-help housing programmes was also strongly influenced by major outside agencies, such as the World Bank which provided some external funding help for them (Figure 14.3).

There was also the gradual realisation in planning circles that western standards, in respect of housing and western solutions to national housing shortages, were inappropriate in the case of most developing countries. Moreover, support of self-help housing schemes were increasingly regarded by governments as the most economical way to be 'seen to be doing something' about housing the lower paid who form an ever increasing proportion of the populations in cities. It was also a response to political unrest among the poor in some countries and posed a growing threat for revolutionary groups to infiltrate self-help housing areas and use them as bases from which to attempt the overthrow of the established government.

However, support for self-help programmes has not been uniform. Whether an area receives financial help and government sponsored upgrading, depends on a variety of factors. These include such things as the political influence which committees from within the self-help areas can wield and whether or not the political party in power needs the votes of residents. It also depends on the position and age of an area. For example, a self-help area too close to higher income residential areas or on land which might at some future date be needed for another purpose, is less likely to receive support than one in an area which does not pose such difficulties.

Gilbert and Gugler identify two general types of upgrading policies: one, the upgrading of existing settlements and secondly, policies to ease the development of new settlements under site and service schemes.

In upgrading existing housing areas, three main steps are generally taken. Firstly, authorities provide basic services which are absent, such as water, sanitation, an electricity supply, schools and clinics, together with improved paths and roads. This usually also involves some improvement in the layout of the area to allow the installation of services.

House owners are then given security of tenure of their plots either by being given the opportunity to purchase the plot or lease it. Credit and advice may be made available to help them to improve and extend the dwelling unit.

> 'At its best a sites and service programme would offer a family a plot of land, gradual servicing, access to credit, advice on construction and materials, all at a price not beyond the family budget. The security afforded would allow consolidation to take place and community action programmes to be introduced.'
> [SOURCE: Alan Gilbert and Josef Gugler *Cities, Poverty and Development*, 1992]

Where new land is involved, a 'site and service' approach is usually adopted. The land is given or purchased by the authorities, divided into plots and sold or allocated to families with a secure lease ensured. The plots are then supplied with basic services and the residents left to build their own dwelling units according to what they can afford. As incomes are improved, so families can gradually improve their housing (Figure 14.23).

Central to each type of self-help programme is the need to ensure that households have secure ownership or tenure of the plot of land they occupy, because without this there would be no incentive for households to improve and upgrade their dwelling units.

By the mid-1970s there were 80 proposed or completed schemes in 27 countries. However, the impact of self-help schemes has had only a limited impact on the housing problems of the poor. Such schemes assume that households have sufficient income to pay for some improvements themselves. Many have not; it benefits those in regular formal work and with the chance to improve their income over time. It is thus divisive, creating a division between those households who can move up the income and housing ladder and those with no hope. Moreover, it takes out of some areas those with initiative who may sell up their improved residence and move to a better housing area.

In addition to these criticisms, a number of self-help programmes have failed because they have been poorly administered and wasted money. Many local authorities have not been enthusiastic towards the policy and have fallen behind the planned scale of the self improvement programme initially adopted. Perhaps most telling of all has been the increasing realisation by the World Bank and other involved agencies that a number of governments were using a self-help housing policy as a panacea for all housing problems, rather than tackle some of the critical obstacles which stand in the way of helping and ensuring that the mass of the poor have adequate shelter. A number of writers on this issue have pointed to the fundamental need for urban reform, an end to land speculation which is putting the cost of land and housing beyond the reach of many low earners and a reform in the taxation system to ensure that the poor are not unfairly burdened and the rich minority pay more to help finance housing programmes for the low paid.

Concluding comment

Gilbert and Gugler suggest that 'sites and service schemes are both necessary and inevitable, but there can be no avoiding more radical changes which will redistribute the resources of the city and increase the rate of public service provision and job creation' (*Cities, poverty and development*). The call for similar radical changes is also seen in Western cities. Here the number of deprived households is smaller but their right to more social justice and an equitable share of the city's resources is no less urgent.

case study

14.1 Cambridge: the generalised residential structure

The residential structure of Cambridge is based on an 'open' factor approach, but also demonstrates some of the processes identified in the ecological models and social areas analysis approach. It shows growth by accretion.

Apart from older village cores absorbed by accretion, there is a general progression outward from mainly nineteenth century residential development around the core and extending along routes from the centre to more recent development in the periphery. It demonstrates growth by accretion, though minor, infill and redevelopment has occurred since the 1960s.

Higher income residential development attracted by proximity to university, favourable semi-rural setting and main route northward.

University development to west of core along riverside terraces since Medieval period; extended by accretion to present layout. In turn, attracted other compatible land uses, e.g. independent schools, government research centres.

Physical and historical constraints influence location of the core. Core developed around river crossing and route focus on it; overlooked by a defensive point; attracted initial administrative commercial and religious activities, forming nucleus from which modern commercial centre developed.

University proximity and later planning influences attracted higher income residential development from late nineteenth century. Once established, the more elite residential setting attracted later higher income residential development growth by accretion.

Expansion absorbs earlier discrete 'villages' of Newnham and Trumpington, including their small 'sub-centres'; expansion influenced by main A10 route south.

NOTE: the 'satellite' suburbanisation in the countryside around beyond the Green Belt is high to middle income in character.

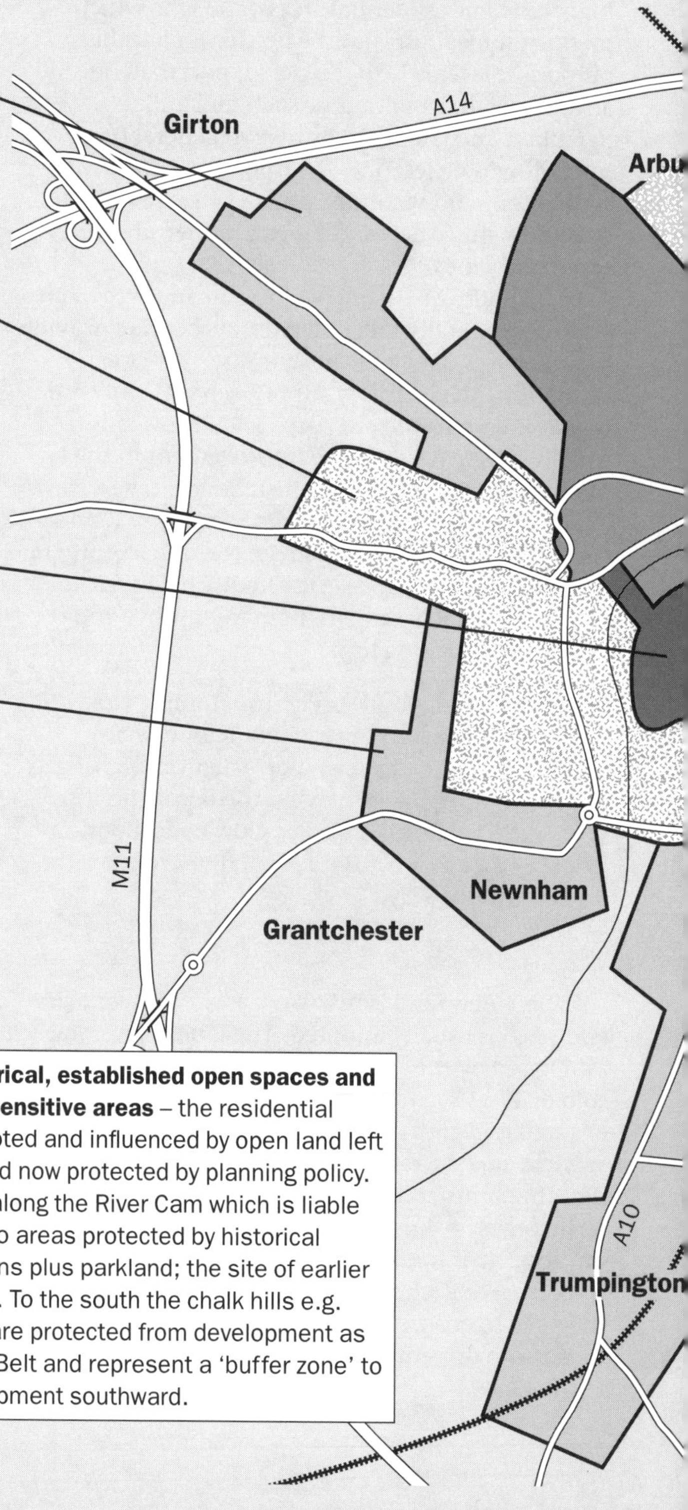

Influence of historical, established open spaces and environmentally sensitive areas – the residential structure is disrupted and influenced by open land left in earlier times and now protected by planning policy. It includes areas along the River Cam which is liable to flooding but also areas protected by historical parks and commons plus parkland; the site of earlier halls and grounds. To the south the chalk hills e.g. Gog Magog hills, are protected from development as part of the Green Belt and represent a 'buffer zone' to residential development southward.

Apart from some commercial and light industrial development to the east, there is a Science Park and other commercial development on available land with access to by-pass roads and the motorway, especially towards the A14. This is attracting middle-income housing in suburban villages e.g. Milton.

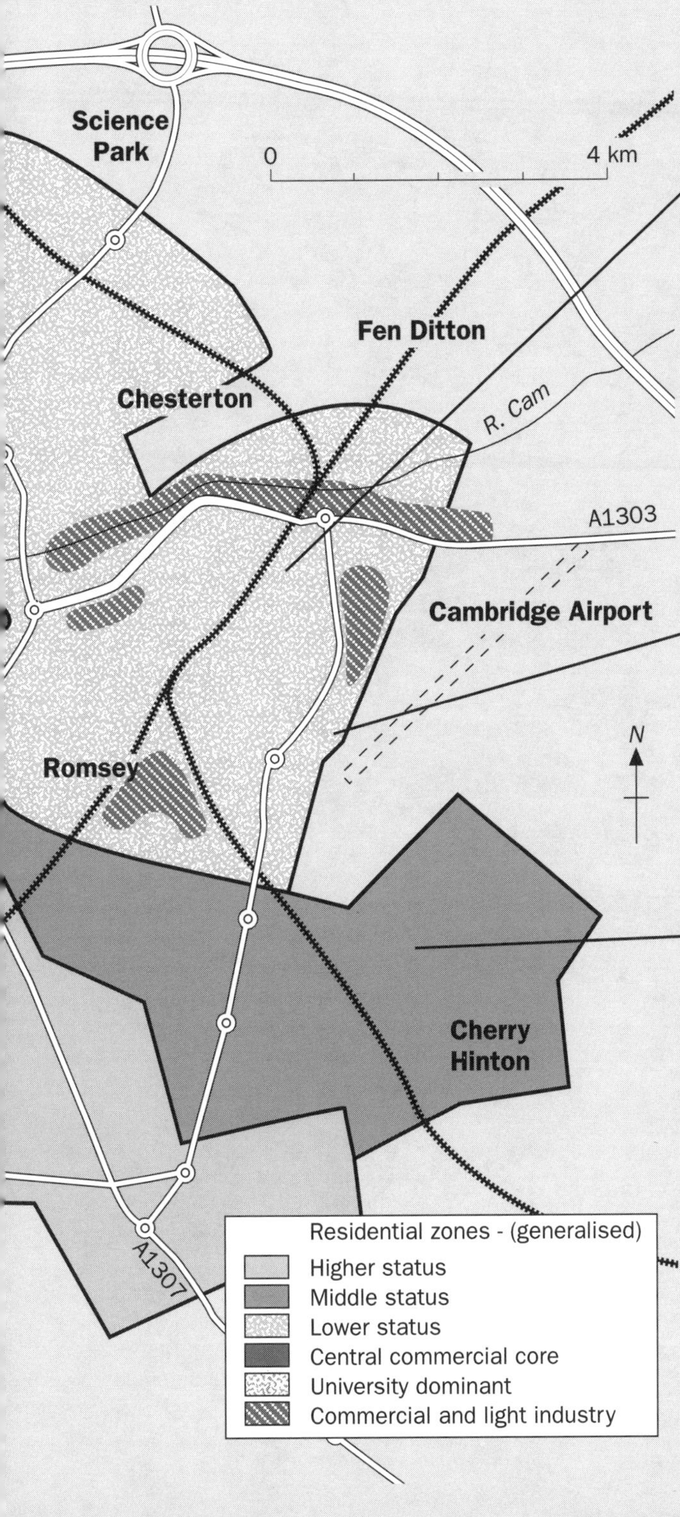

Lower status housing

Inner area and inner suburbs – mainly nineteenth century terrace housing associated with coming of the railway and development of some industry on a small scale alongside; less desirable more low-lying area unattractive to higher income groups but close to work for lower income groups. Included accommodation for domestics and service workers in the university and colleges. Originally rented but much now also owner-occupied with a range of income groups, from elderly pensioners to young professional couples. Areas in Romsey Town show evidence of gentrification (refurbishment by incoming 'better off').

Much of outer lower status suburbs represent local authority housing built mainly during post-war period for lower income groups in Chesterton and North Arbury; location reflects availability of land and an area less attractive to private builders and to the university. It is also evidence of segregative tendencies. (Little council development to the west as considered undesirable on this 'more prestigious side' of Cambridge where most of the land is owned by the university and colleges).

Middle status

A mixed area but mainly occupied by households in the broad middle, income band; small areas of nineteenth century 'middle class housing' conveniently developed around the station and along more major routes leading out of town. Most housing is inter-war with small areas of council housing along the inner ring-road but much of it is now owner-occupied and improved. Attractive to middle income groups as area gives good access to town and has a semi-rural feel with some open park areas. Cherry Hinton village to south-east 'engulfed' by post-war expansion to become an integral part of outer suburbs; infills of more recent housing evident mainly for the middle income group.

case study

14.2 **Bradford: multiple deprivation in 1991**

Bradford demonstrates multiple deprivation at ward level in inner city wards and in fringe wards, where large local authority housing occurs.

Problems accentuating social stress and deprivation

Bradford is a city in the industrial north based primarily on old manufacturing industries, especially textiles and engineering, until 1961. It was badly affected by the decline in manufacturing since the late 1970s.

In 1961, 60% of the workforce was employed in manufacturing, compared to 32% in south-east England. The loss of the employment base is shown by the continual rise in unemployment levels: 13% of the total workforce was unemployed 1993, 21% of them in the 16 – 24 year age group.

Extensive areas of nineteenth century housing are deteriorating in physical quality and lack modern amenities. They were originally associated with industrial expansion until the First World War.

There are large stretches of vacant industrial land. More than 60% of the factories have closed and multi-storey woollen mills have proven costly to convert to other uses.

Despite considerable local initiatives, authorities are failing to replace lost jobs in industry. Expansion has been into new high technology and information industries and services. About 80% of the service sector simply meets the needs of the local economy. The area is unattractive to new financial insurance and leisure sectors, despite some expansion of tourism.

There is a relatively high proportion of ethnic minorities, especially Asian, who formed 15% of the total population in 1984 (62 000).

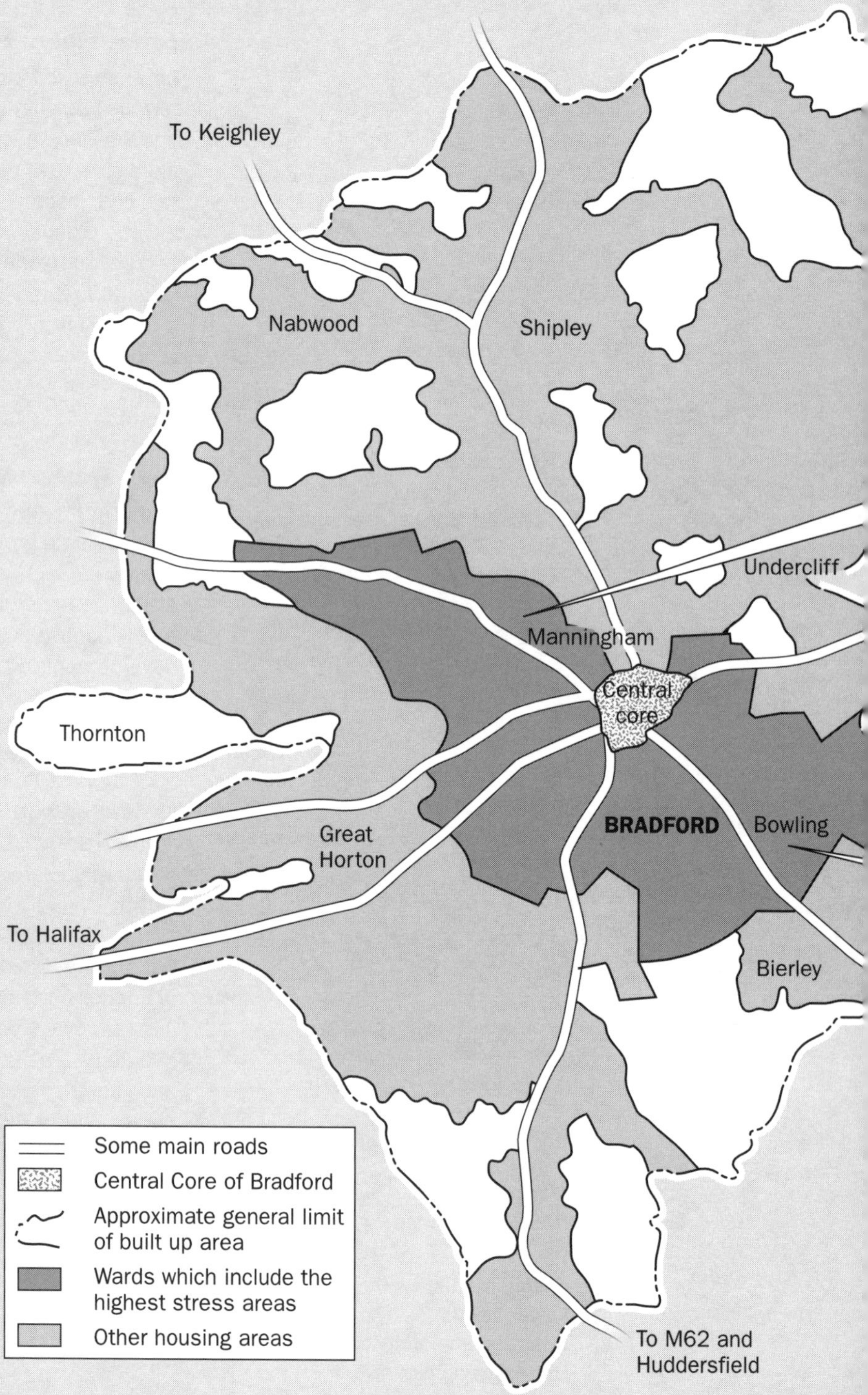

Bradford: example wards and areas of deprivation

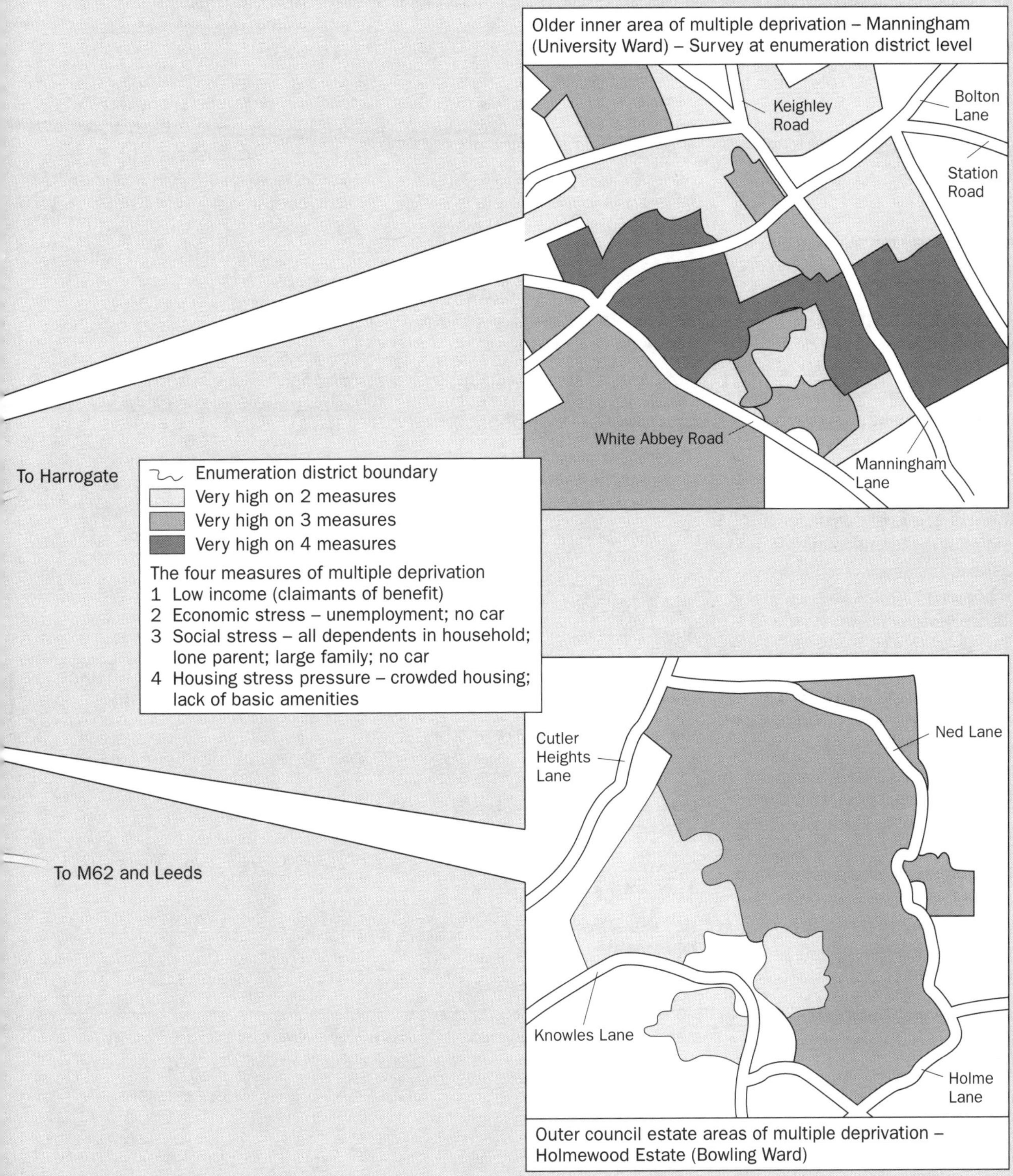

The projected ethnic population increase is to 91 000 by 1996, largely through natural increase. There is more chance on average of ethnic minorities suffering poverty problems, increasing the incidence of multiple deprivation in Bradford.

Other indices of deprivation

Outside of the city centre, the highest recorded crime rate has been in inner areas and on council estates already identified as areas of multiple deprivation.

The three wards of Little Horton, University and Tong contain areas of multiple stress. These are also areas with higher death rates (one-third above national average) and have double the percentage of low weight babies compared with rural wards.

Three-quarters of Bangladeshi residents (the largest minority), half the Pakistani and half of the African-Caribbean minorities live in areas of multiple stress (Indians are more dispersed). This concentration is partly due to most of the populations being in low paid work and discrimination against ethnic minorities in the job market, despite efforts to reduce this.

Along with the economic and urban problems faced by many cities, the Bradford district is also facing the largest increase in population of any metropolitan district, particularly in inner areas where land and resources are already under severe pressure.

Origins of multiple stress at national level – the wider context

At national level, the general restructuring in the economy led to economic hardship.

Successive governments failed to effectively address the underlying causes of the stress, that of the progressive withdrawal of economic and welfare support, lack of self-help policies and the withdrawal of Assisted Area status, which led to a decline in the house building programme for households of low income.

General social stress leads to a breakdown in marriages and an increase in single parent families.

Reasons for the concentration of multiple stress and deprivation in older inner areas and outer council estates

Households on low incomes become concentrated in the low-cost or rented sector housing areas as they have no access to better housing. They are also isolated here, as those households who acquire more income, move out.

The natural increase is greater in these areas. The average family size is 5.1 in inner areas and the projected population increase from 464 000 in 1984 to 480 000 in 1996, puts pressure on services and housing, exacerbating the problems of multiple stress areas. For example, much of the housing pressure will be in the inner city.

Environmental problems are concentrated here. In inner areas, housing is adjacent to declining industrial areas and outer housing estates have insufficient community facilities, contributing to a downward spiral. The declining rate of income makes it difficult for councils to service these areas.

A culture of apathy has developed due to high unemployment, housing and environmental pressures. Personal feelings of stress lead to hopelessness, which stifles initiative. '*There seems little doubt that the poverty, isolation and unemployment in many areas of Bradford create an undercurrent of depression and stress which saps people's energy, taking the heart out of their lives*' (*The changing face of Bradford*, City of Bradford Metropolitan Council, 1984).

(percentages)	Areas of multiple stress	Other areas	Bradford district as a whole
Claimants of benefit % of adults	47.5	19.6	24.6
No car % of households	68.9	34.4	40.7
Lone parent % of households with dependent with children	27.0	11.9	15.1
Crowded – more than 1 person per room	24.4	6.4	9.9
No central heating % of households	51.0	33.9	37.0
Ill and no car % of pensioners	39.7	23.0	25.6

Measures of deprivation and comparative levels in areas identified as areas of multiple stress compared to other areas of Bradford and the district as a whole

case study

14.3 Rio de Janeiro: its changing urban structure and growing dualism

Growth

Until 1960, Rio de Janeiro was Brazil's capital and main city. The new inland capital of Brasilia replaced it and São Paulo overtook it as the largest industrial and commercial centre. However, Rio de Janeiro remains an international metropolis with a population of approximately 10 million and a diversified economic base, ranging from major industries to finance and commerce. It is still the major port of the country.

Founded by the Portuguese in the mid-sixteenth century, Rio is located on an alluvial lowland fronting the great natural harbour of Guanabara Bay but backed by steep hills. It was initially an export centre for primary products and received a major stimulus by the discovery of gold in the neighbouring state of Minais Gerais in the eighteenth century. As the economic heart of the Brazilian colony shifted from the north-east to the south-east, Rio de Janeiro became its focus, with the capital transferred from Salvador to it in 1763.

By 1900 it had a population of 800 000 and grew rapidly to 3 million by 1950, to almost 10 million in 1991. From the central area a diversified range of industry has spread mainly northward along the coast but also with new industrial centres inland. Commercial and financial activities remain focussed on the central area with some limited spread south along the coast and inland, displacing low income settlement in the transitional zone, for example, from Lapa.

However, high income residential areas remain mainly central.

Growth slowed to 8% annually by 1980. By 1990 there was more growth by natural increase than migration.

Urban structure 1987

Rural-urban fringe

Beyond the main commuting zone for Rio de Janeiro; decentralisation of economic activity; rapid growth of low income settlement including favelas.

Newer outer suburbs

Main population growth occurred here; newer industrial centres such as Nota Iguacu and Dugue de Caxias; good axial routes; infrastructure poor; mix of low income housing.

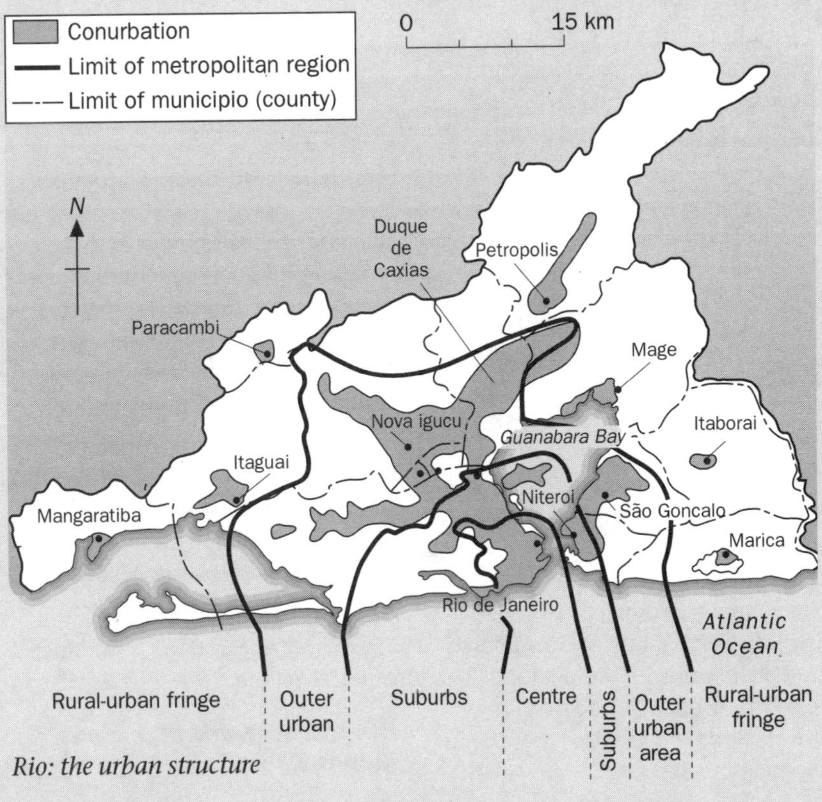

Rio: the urban structure

Older suburbs

Growth from early twentieth century onwards with a rise of traditional and new industry and a good infrastructure; to the north – lower class residential; south fronting beach – higher class residential area.

Centre

Historic core; now the CBD, industrial port complex and high class residential areas together with cultural centres; redevelopment occurring.

Segregation of social classes and dualism

There is a widening gap between the contrasting fortunes of the mass of low income families and the middle to high income elite minority, creating a stark dualism and 'widening' spatial segregation as low income families are forced away from central areas to the fringe.

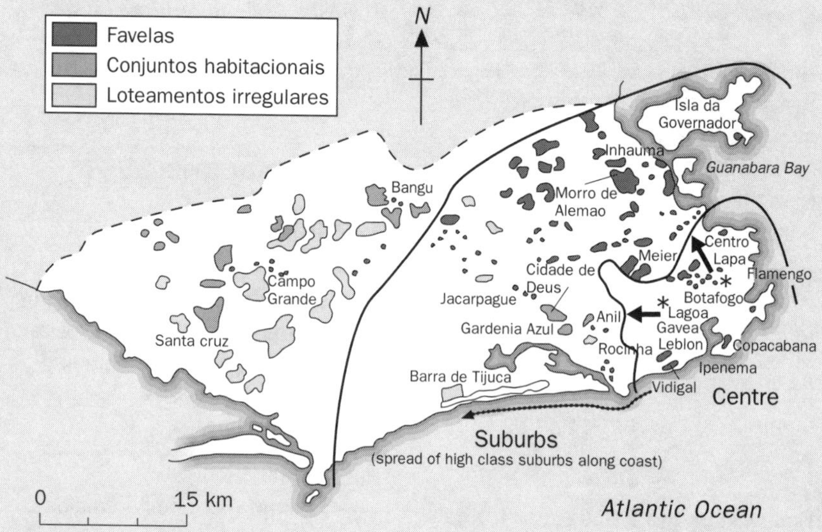

(*: Decentralisation of low income households leaving central areas for high income residents)

Location of low income settlements

Low income households

The favelas (informal settlements)

Officially defined as settlements of 60 or more households in informal accommodation, the favelas lack formal organisation and basic services. The inhabitants have no legal entitlement to the land. About 1 million (17% of the population) live in the favelas. Rocinha, with 80 000 people, is one of the largest. The authorities continue to clear older inner ones when land is required for redevelopment or they are too close to spreading high class areas. By now most of the favelas are accepted and authorities work with residential associations to upgrade them and provide some basic services. Rocinha, for example, has paved streets with lighting and commercial services. However, little has effectively been done for newer favelas and the greatest growth has been in the suburbs.

Conjuntos habitacionais

This area comprises officially built, low cost housing mainly set up in the 1970s for low paid workers, including those displaced by the clearance of favelas. The estates, each built to accommodate 38 000 people, house approx 1 million in conditions little improved from favelas. Physical deterioration and influx of more migrants and some favela infill leads to worsening conditions. Access and infrastructure are comparatively poor.

Lotfeamentos irregulares

This section is made up of informal housing built on illegally sold government land. It suffers poor conditions with few services.

Street dwellers

There are over 600 000 homeless street dwellers.

Central area and high class suburbs

The central area and high class suburbs have received the bulk of the infrastructure investment for residential areas.

To the west of the central area, about 122 sq km, has been cleared and redeveloped as a focus for high class residents. Inland areas have been left to low income households. The coastal stretch had been reserved for the spread of high class suburbs from the central area, with beach access and pleasant environs. It is linked to the city centre by a four-lane highway.

There has been further residential planning based on clusters of high rise luxury apartments. The blocks are enclosed and security guarded. It comprises two commercial cores of offices, shops, restaurants and entertainment. They are effectively self-contained and isolated from the mass of low income housing areas.

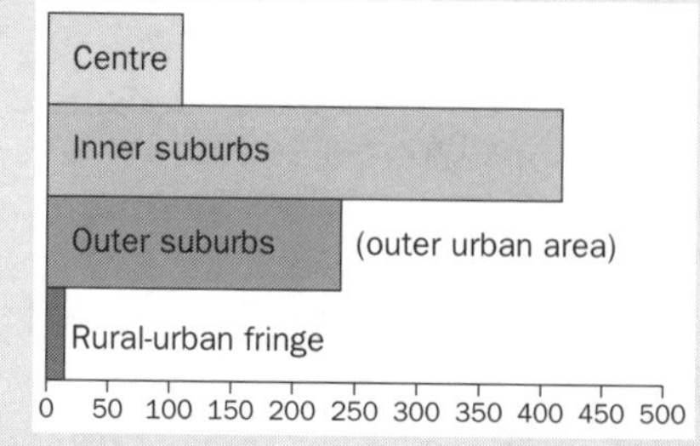

Number of favelas for each zone, 1991

15

CHAPTER 15

The economic basis and infrastructure of cities

'Historically, cities have been driving forces in economic and social development. As centres of industry and commerce cities have long been centres of wealth and power. They also account for a disproportionate share of national income.'

WORLD RESOURCES 1996

15.1 **Economic activities in cities**

The more developed a country, the more its economic activity is located in and around urban centres. For a variety of reasons, the tertiary (service) and manufacturing activities which increasingly dominate the economy, require an urban location. Most of the market demand for goods and services is increasingly located in urban areas. As nodal or route centres, towns provide much of the infrastructure required by manufacturing and services, including an adequate transport network.

The linkages which are needed between a variety of activities draw them to a common urban location. This encourages further expansion, making the city an even more attractive location. ***A process of cumulative causation may thus be set in motion, diversifying and strengthening the economic base.*** Even where a city is noted for one particular activity, such as motor manufacturing or as a resort, the range of other activities also present is quite extensive.

The larger the city, the greater the amount and diversity of economic activity to be found there. This is increasingly noticeable as countries become more economically integrated and communication systems are made more efficient. It is also promoted by the locational decisions of the increasing number of multinational companies which dominate the international economy. The largest cities lie at the key nodes of a large communication network, characterised by high speed trains, international airports and super telecommunications highways.

As key nodes and with a strong and diversified economic base, the largest cities attract the head offices of multinational companies and international agencies and a range of other linked businesses.

New York as a 'metropole'

'Today the New York region is one of the planet's premier world cities. It is home to the largest conglomerate of service firms in the world, including seventy per cent of USA advertising companies, forty per cent of security industries, a major conglomeration of insurance firms and large shares of the nation's accounting, legal and other businesses. It stands at the apex of the national and international banking hierarchy.

It is a 'global front office' and an example of a world city that is seated at the cross roads of control functions of the national and global economy.'

[SOURCE: Bosman J and de Smidt M *The Geographical Formation of International Management Centres in Europe, Urban Studies*, 1993]

On the basis of the degree of internationalisation and strength of their economic bases, there has been a recent classification of European cities into a four-fold hierarchy (Figure 15.1), with London and Paris clearly dominant. It is forecast that Berlin will join these cities in the near future, following the advantages accruing from the unification of Germany and the prospective addition of East European countries to the European union.

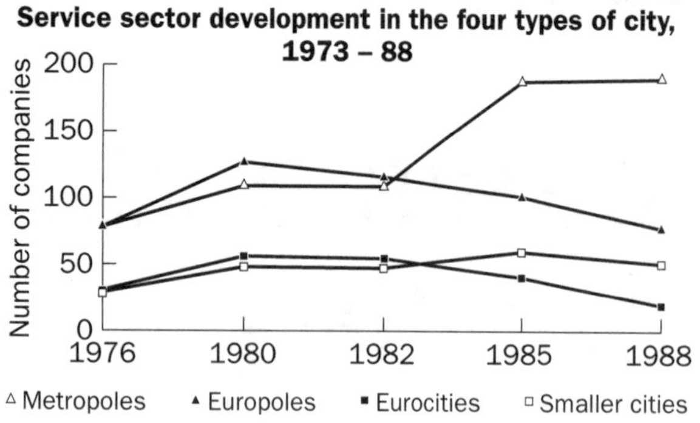

Metropoles – characterised by a high population figure exceeding one million and a high degree of concentrations of different kinds of international functions e.g. London; Paris

Europoles – at least 500 000 in population size and with a range of international functions e.g. Amsterdam; Brussels; Dusseldorf; Copenhagen

Eurocities – smaller but still with some international functions

[SOURCE: Meijer M *The growth and decline of European Cities, Urban Studies*, 1993]

Figure 15.1 *The changing urban hierarchy in Europe*

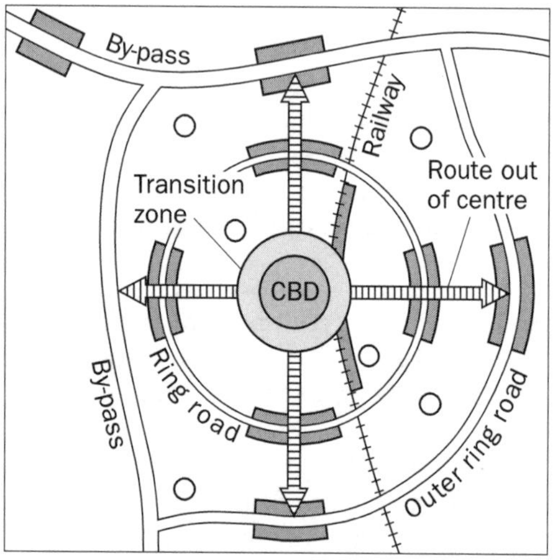

○ Sub-centres of retail and other service activities
▒ Central Business District
▓ Other favoured locations for economic activity
— Main road arteries

NOTE: Locations are all shaded areas of the diagram

Figure 15.2 *The location of economic activity in a typical town or city*

Location of economic activity in the city

The locational pattern of economic activity in a city is quite complex, given its functional diversity. However, it is possible to identify certain favoured locations in and around the Central Business District, along main routes leading out from the centre, at route modes on the periphery, particularly where ring roads around the city intersect with routes leading out from the centre and at service sub-centres in certain residential areas. These can be schematically represented as shown in Figure 15.2 and in Case study 15.1 (Nottingham).

However, the functional pattern for any particular city will vary according to local circumstances. It may deviate where a town or city is dominated by some specialist function. The higher the city is in the urban hierarchy, the more specialist and international functions dominate the central area, relegating the economic uses to locations outside the centre and even to the rural urban fringe. As space is at a premium in the centre, 'edge cities' may also emerge in the suburbs with a mix of economic activities similar to those at the centre of cities further down the urban hierarchy (Figure 15.3).

15.2 Location of tertiary (service) activities

Accessibility is the key to the location of retail, office and other service activities. They must be located where they can best serve the needs of the population dependent on them and where the work force can easily commute from the residential areas around.

In the classical models of city structure, the Central Business District (CBD) and the transitional area around it are identified as the most accessible location in the city. (In recent urban studies there has been some tendency to replace the term CBD and transition zone by widening the use of the term CBD to cover a 'core' where CBD usages dominate and a 'frame' where CBD usages are present but do not exceed half the total land use.) These are the most sought after locations, with different usages competing with each other for sites. Within this competitive situation the usages most likely to occupy a central location will be those which can most profit from it, since these will be able to outbid other uses, relegating them to a position progressively further out from the city centre.

A.C.Nelson defines an 'edge city' as

1. Having at least five million sq. ft. of office space
2. At least 600,000 sq. ft. of retail space
3. A population higher during the working day than at other times
4. A locally recognised place of work. Shopping and entertainment.
5. An area which 30 years ago was predominately rural or low density residential in nature.

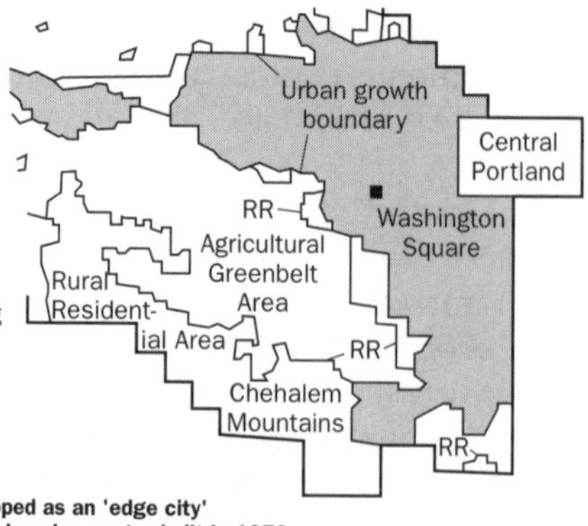

Washington Square developed as an 'edge city' beginning with a regional shopping centre built in 1970.

[SOURCE: Nelson A C *Disamenity influences of edge cities on ex-urban land v Values, Urban Studies*, 1993]

Figure 15.3 *Washington Square, Portland, Oregon, USA*

Commercial activities, like high order retailing, banks, other financial institutions and certain office activities, are thought to profit most from a central location. These activities dominate the core or centre of large cities, with lesser order uses and those requiring large site areas being pushed out to other locations. Residential usage is the least profitable and therefore in city structure models residential zoning makes up the outer rings or sectors of land used.

This process of land use sorting with service activities dominating the CBD is demonstrated in the bid rent curve diagram in Figure15.4.

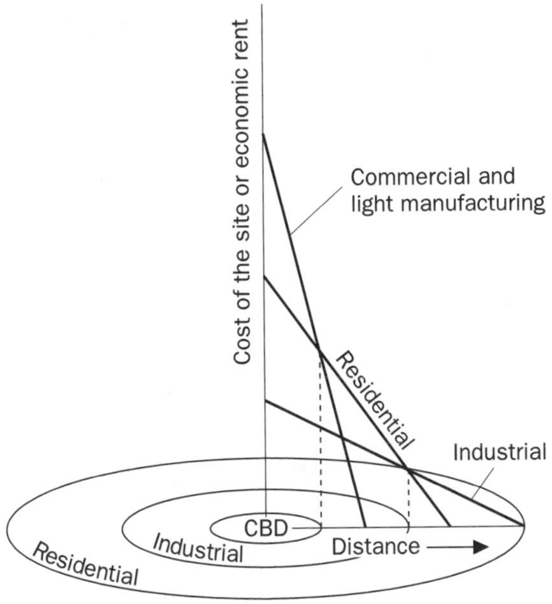

Figure 15.4 *Bid rent graph and resultant ring zoning*

The central area today is not necessarily the most accessible location. Others occur along access routes into the centre and increasingly at nodal points out towards the edges of the city where these routes cross ring roads. While the latter increases the number of accessible locations on the periphery, the accessibility of the CBD is being reduced through increasing traffic congestion. Its attraction as a potential site is also being reduced by soaring rents and rates.

Paradoxically, more widespread car ownership, while contributing to city centre congestion, has increased customer mobility and favoured out-of-town shopping and service expansion. The increasing dispersion of population away from older inner residential areas towards the suburbs and dormitory settlements in the countryside, has also favoured peripheral locations.

Of the activities in a periphery rather than a city centre location, those requiring comparatively large site areas are most attracted, since land is cheaper and more plentiful on the fringe of the city. These include super and hypermarkets, warehouses and certain kinds of light industry, such as furniture assembly. City centre locations are therefore increasingly left to those specialised activities with high turnover and profit margins, which require only a limited amount of space and which need to maintain linkages with similar activities. This is particularly well illustrated by financial institutions.

The concentric arrangement suggested by the simple bid-rent curve needs to be modified to reflect current location patterns for tertiary activities (Figure 15.5).

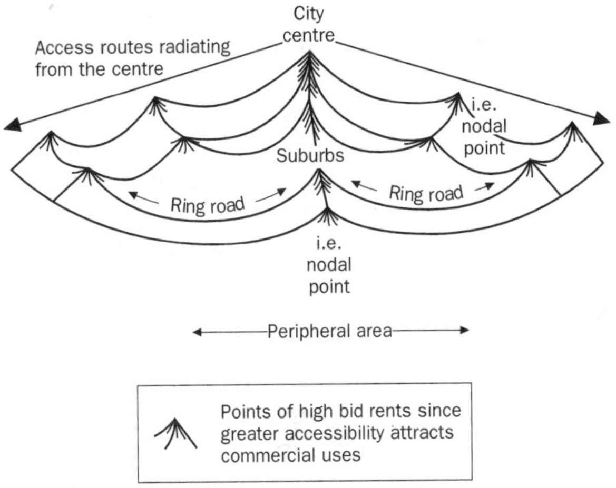

Figure 15.5 *Bid rent curves for a city based on varied accessibility*

15.3 The Central Business District

The Central Business District usually developed around the historical core of the town. Its location has been influenced by physical circumstances, such as a dry site overlooking the bridging point across a river. As the town grows, the CBD expands around this core, frequently extending for a way along the main access routes into the centre. However, with present day pressures and changes in methods of retailing and servicing, part of the old CBD or part of the transitional zone nearby may be re-developed to produce a second and new planned core. Some cities, therefore, have two centres of contrasting appearance, in effect, a dual CBD.

Cambridge, for example, has an established CBD and the more recently constructed Grafton Centre to the north of the old CBD, but within easy walking distance of it. The Grafton Centre, like the CBD, includes department stores such as Debenham's, specialist shops as well as some convenience shops. It is now in the process of being expanded.

Functional concentrations within the CBD

In larger cities where the demand for central area functions is high, it is possible to identify two ways in which some spatial sorting out can occur.

Firstly, ***specialist retailing activities*** need to attract custom off the street and thus generally occupy the ground floor of buildings which face the main thoroughfare. The upper floors are usually occupied by offices which, while needing a central location, do not require constant contact with the general public. Away from the centre where rents are not so high, office and retail activities may occupy the ground floor of buildings.

Secondly, ***clustering of the same functional activity or of linked activities may occur,*** as is shown for Nottingham town centre (Case study 15.1). For example, civic administration may have become clustered around a historical site, such as a castle or market place and the financial quarter in an old merchanting area. Once established, the reputation of an area for a particular activity tends to attract more of the same and ensure its continued importance. However, other clustering of linked activities which need quick personal contact and which may be visited by the same clientele, does occur. One of the best examples of such clustering is that of solicitors, estate agents and insurance offices which may be concerned with a common business such as the sale of a house. In Sheffield, for example, solicitors and some estate agents have taken over the Georgian houses in Paradise Square behind the cathedral but still close to the city centre.

Other clustering occurs because an activity benefits from the large flow of customers drawn to the area. Despite competition between retail outlets located together in the area, each attracts sufficient trade from the large number of potential customers and makes a greater profit than it would be likely to do if sited on its own.

In the streets which lead off the major thoroughfares, rents and rates are lower than on the main frontages. These side streets therefore attract highly specialised shops, such as antiques or rare books, and serve a restricted clientele rather than depending on passing custom. Some low-order retail services, such as sweet shops and small cafes, may also be found off the main street, simply because their turnover is insufficient to pay the higher rents on a main street location. They rely on customers to turn down the street from the main pedestrian thoroughfares.

Service and light industry activities with lower profit margins per unit area and comparatively large areas, tend to be pushed to the margins of the CBD and into the transition zone. A number of such activities can be identified: grocery supermarkets, discount stores, betting shops, second-hand goods shops, spare part sales, small warehouses, printing firms and bingo halls. They may be intermixed with older housing areas, some awaiting redevelopment, others adapted for commercial usage.

However, in smaller cities, particularly in historical market towns, such spatial concentration and sorting may not occur (Figure 15.6). This partly reflects the smaller number of outlets of any one kind needed to serve a much reduced catchment area. It also indicates less pressure on central sites and therefore lower rents. It may also be that historical constraints, such as old buildings conservation measures and ancient street networks, have encouraged only a piecemeal development of CBD functions in a central core. These smaller central business districts are more difficult to define and less susceptible to general description. Each tends to have a character of its own.

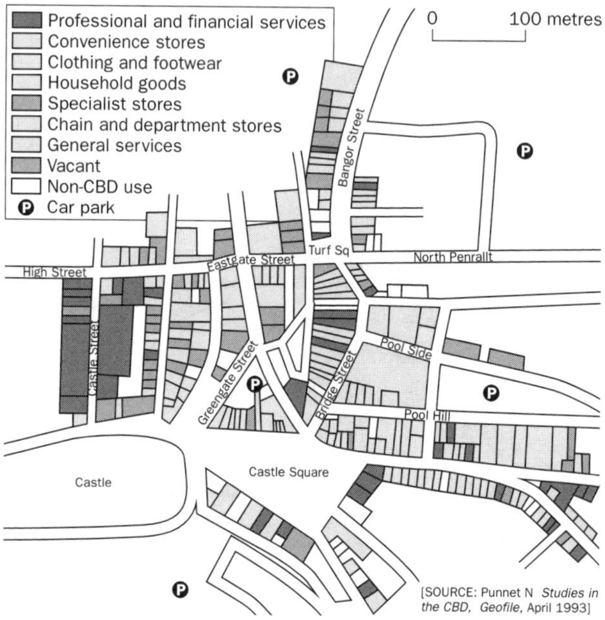

Figure 15.6 *Land use in central Caernarfon, Wales*

The changing CBD

Because of the increasing cost and shortage of land in the centre of cities, older buildings of one or two storeys have increasingly been replaced by new multi-storey developments, including skyscraper blocks in some of the largest cities such as New York and Tokyo. Hence the CBD can now be identified as much by the distinctive height of its skyline as by the concentration of commercial activity within it.

With continued expansion of cities and economies, such has been the pressure on CBDs that more comprehensive redevelopment has frequently taken place (Figure 15.7; Case studies 15.1 and 16.2). This is because there is a limit to the modification

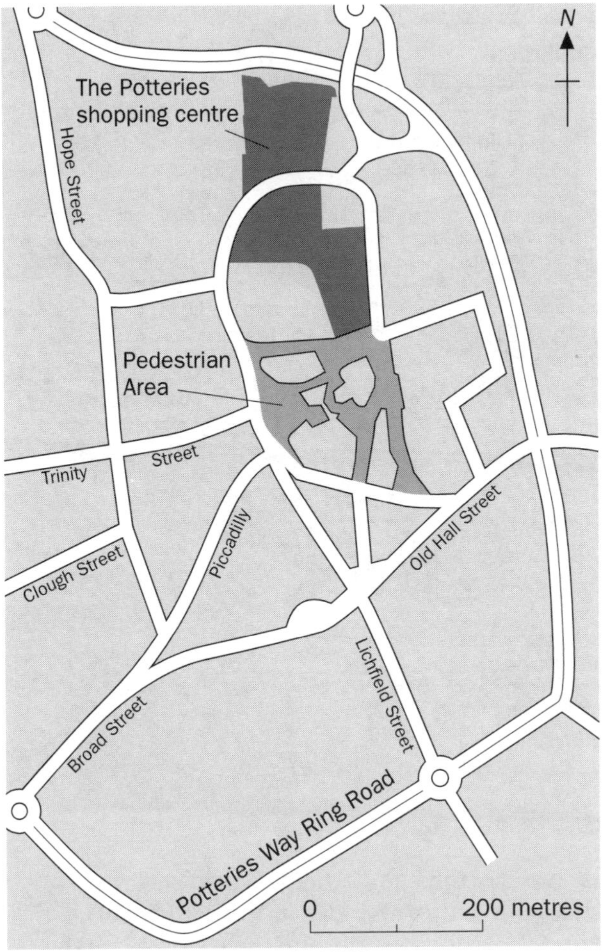

[SOURCE: Kivell P *Land and the city*, 1993]

Redevelopment prompted by:

- poor layout and run down nature of the shopping centre including a number of vacant small shop sites
- need to meet competition from new out of town retail and commercial centre
- better serve needs of The Potteries with approximately half million population.

Redevelopment had three main features:

- the new Potteries Shopping Centre adjacent to the main bus terminal; the centre covers 2.2 ha and has an associated indoor market. The new covered shopping mall has 31 000 sq metres of covered retail spaces around modern landscaped malls with a naturally lit atrium and a large food hall. There are parking facilities for 1200 cars.
- extensive pedestrianisation of prime shopping streets and some landscaping and street furniture, including some seating, give a more attractive and safer shopping environment.
- pedestrianisation would not have been possible without a new traffic management scheme – a new ring road encircling almost the entire city centre, creation of one-way streets, new car parks and a revised public transport system with a new bus terminal.

Figure 15.7 *Redevelopment of the centre of Hanley (Staffordshire)*

that can be made to an existing town plan and existing buildings. Redevelopment has included the building of large under-cover shopping precincts and a redesigning of the street layout to segregate pedestrian and vehicle flows (Section 16.2).

In addition, a number of usages commonly found in the CBD have found it more convenient and as profitable to locate outside the CBD, leaving it for the highest profit-making concerns, such as banks and other financial institutions and large department store.

15.4 **The transitional zone**

In earlier times, as Burgess' city structure model shows, much of the transitional zone was occupied by housing and industry. Working class neighbourhoods grew up next to the factories (Figure 14.2). Today, however, transitional zones tend to be more diversified. They now include commercial activities which have overflowed from the CBD as well as some vacant lots and derelict sites which await redevelopment. More recent additions have been multi-storey car parks and temporary car parking on vacant ground to serve the needs of workers, shoppers and others who use the nearby CBD.

The transitional zone may vary from one part to another depending on whether expansion pressures on the CBD are occurring or not. Evidence from studies of American cities show that pressures are greatest on those parts of the transitional zone adjacent to higher status areas, since these attract offices, new hotels and speciality shops seeking a more favourable environment. In contrast, in lower status areas of the transitional zone, dilapidated housing may be intermixed with incoming uses, such as bars, bingo halls and discount stores. Elsewhere in the more static parts of the transitional zone, small-scale industry may still persist.

Many of the older small-scale works and warehouse premises are characterised by frequent change of use, as some small businesses go bankrupt and other new enterprises take over. These are frequently seed-bed industries, that is, new businesses being set up in some expanding sector of the economy, such as electronics and computing. The rents are cheaper and smaller premises can be found in the transitional zone attracting new firms which, if successful, may then move out to larger premises on the edge of the city. This type of change is particularly noticeable in the inner transitional zone of old industrial cities, such as Birmingham and Manchester in the UK and Boston in the USA.

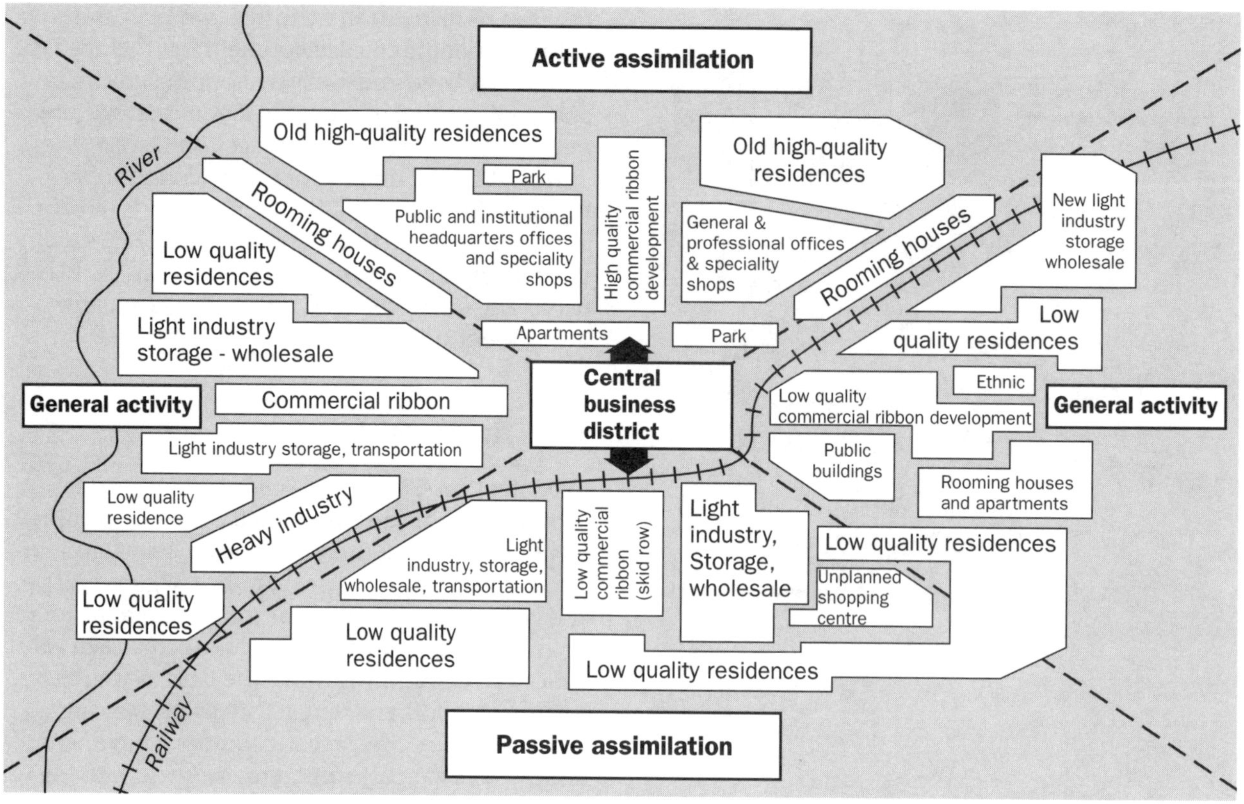

Figure 15.8 Land uses in the transitional zone around the CBD

The varied rate of change and use from one part of the transitional zone to another has been summarised in the generalised pattern of land use shown in the Figure 15.8 and is indicated in the case of Castle Boulevard to the west of Nottingham city centre.

15.5 **Commercial activity in the suburbs and on the edge of the city**

Sub-centres occur outside the CBD to serve local catchment areas. They vary in size but it is possible to recognise some hierarchical order, beginning with the corner ship which provides everyday needs, such as newspapers and groceries for the immediate neighbourhood, through to small shopping parades with a wider catchment area and sub-centres equivalent in size to the CBD of a small town. Such entries include the usual convenience shops and also local branches of banks, estate agents, insurance offices and more specialist shops.

Some of the more important sub-centres for Nottingham are shown in Case study 15.1. Some are of local 'shopping parade' importance while district centres have a much wider catchment area. Good accessibility in relation to the local population served is the main location factor. Some centres, such as Beeston and Netherfield, had begun as shopping centres for independent settlements around Nottingham city and then, along with the settlement itself, had been incorporated into the city as it expanded. New retail centres are established with suburban growth, such as at Trowell Road. The greatest change has been the emergence of the supermarket stores and hypermarkets, some adjacent to established sub-centres.

The other important change has been the disappearance of many small shops, including the general corner shop which was quite important in the inter-war and immediate post-war years. These smaller shops have been unable to compete with the lower prices and range of goods on offer at the larger stores.

Dominance of the large supermarket chains

The retail revolution has seen 750 supermarkets come and 10 000 small independent shops go in twenty years.

Just 2% of British food outlets now account for 52% of food retail sales. Three supermarket companies control 40% of the £25 billion a year food sector. Tesco owns 24% of food sales space in the south-east metropolitan area.

[SOURCE: Vidal J *Sceptred Isles, The Guardian* 5.11.94]

Many retail chains have closed their smaller branches and concentrated sales on large reorganised stores. Perhaps the best example of this are the cooperatives which at one time would have had shops on most small shopping parades but now have branches only in the larger centres.

More recently, the viability of smaller shops has been threatened by the increased sales of food and other convenience goods on petrol station forecourts. From selling only a limited range, the bigger petrol forecourts now offer a sales range as large and competitive as the small supermarket. Moreover, their extensive opening hours, some providing service 24 hours of the day, give these outlets an added advantage over the smaller corner and parade shop.

15.6 Out-of-town shopping centres and offices

The increasing location of certain tertiary activities on the margins of cities or in the nearby countryside has been one of the outstanding features of recent urban development. This includes shopping complexes centred on a supermarket or hypermarket and wholesale services and offices.

The out-of-town development is basically due to the rapid advancement of tertiary activities, relative to manufacturing in the growth of the economy. As people have become more affluent, a greater proportion of their income is spent on retail goods and services. Consequently, there has been a marked rise in demand for premises which could not be fully met in central areas where space is both limited and costly. Other locations had been sought, most notably on the margins of cities where reasonably priced land is available and where new ring roads and other improvements in transport have made such sites increasingly accessible. These and other factors summarised in Figure 15.9 help to explain such growth.

As regards retailing, a distinction should be made between supermarkets, hypermarkets, retail parks (Figure 15.1) ***and regional shopping centres,*** whether associated with central area redevelopment schemes or out-of-town locations (Case study 15.2). Differences of size basically distinguishes supermarkets from hypermarkets. Hypermarkets have a minimum area of 2500 square metres, at least 15 check-out points and, while specialising in food, may offer a variety of other goods and services. The parking area is at least three times the size of the retail selling area and may include a petrol station and kiosk. The whole complex is usually located on a good access route 3 km to 6 km from the town centre, for example, Chandler's Ford in south Hampshire.

Regional shopping centres, like the Parly Deux near Versailles in France, are located outside established urban areas and are defined as a shopping complexes. Again, good accessibility is essential. Brent Cross, though not strictly outside London, is classed as a regional shopping centre because of the number of retail outlets it contains. It is near the junction of the M1 motorway and the North Circular road in north-west London.

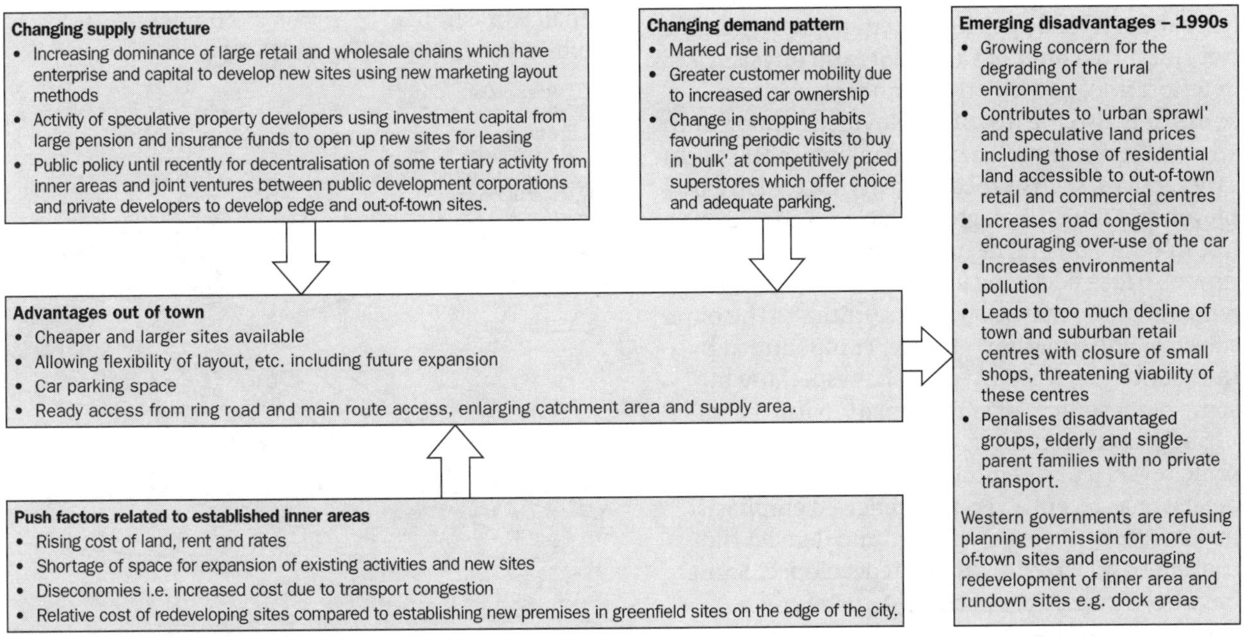

Figure 15.9 *Factors which influence the growth of peripheral and out-of-town centres*

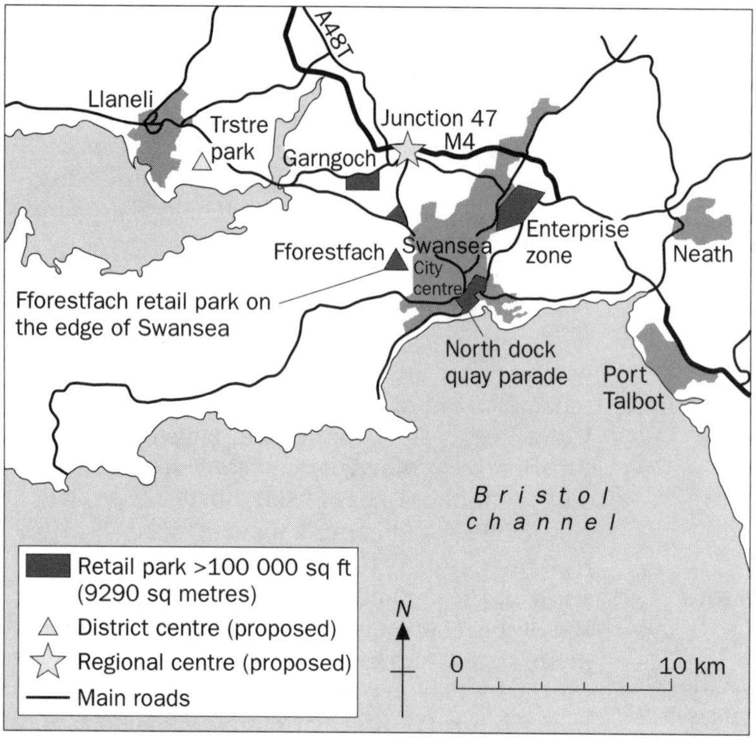

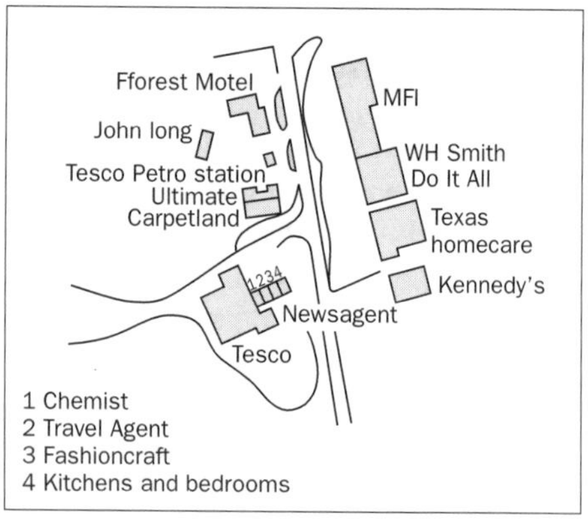

Plan of Fforestfach Retail Park showing Tesco's supermarket, other large stores and a motel – located along a main road going west out of Swansea

Figure 15.10 *Edge-of-town and out-of-town development in Swansea*

Examples of wholesale and warehouse developments outside of urban centres includes the relocation of the London Covent Garden vegetable market at High Elms and its Paris equivalent at Rungis, close to Orly airport and on a main autoroute from Paris.

Over dispersion

Inner city areas including some parts of established CBDs have recently declined so much that there are fears about over dispersion of tertiary activities. It is not simply a matter of vacant lots and physical deterioration, particularly of inner transitional zones, but also the loss of employment opportunity and rate revenue with which to maintain the necessary services, such as roads and lighting. Many people among the poorest groups have no choice but to live in poor housing near the centre of cities and now also face declining job prospects with the removal of too many job opportunities to the outer suburbs. The situation is further compounded by the economic recession which has especially hit some older sources of employment in inner areas.

Such have been the concerns that there is now some reversal of decentralisation policies and this reversal has recently received renewed emphasis. Inner areas are being revitalised and derelict industrial sites and wharf areas also redeveloped. Some have been classed as Special Enterprise Zones, allowing subsidies and other inducements to be offered to attract services and some employment back into the city. Rundown and derelict areas such as the Don Valley in Sheffield have also received some Regional European funding. Similar policies are now being followed in other European countries as well as in America.

Leisure and retailing activities are particularly prominent on many redeveloped sites (Case study 16.2). There is an emphasis on an intermixture of use, including also some residential units, offices, small workshop units as well as conference and exhibition facilities (Figure 15.11).

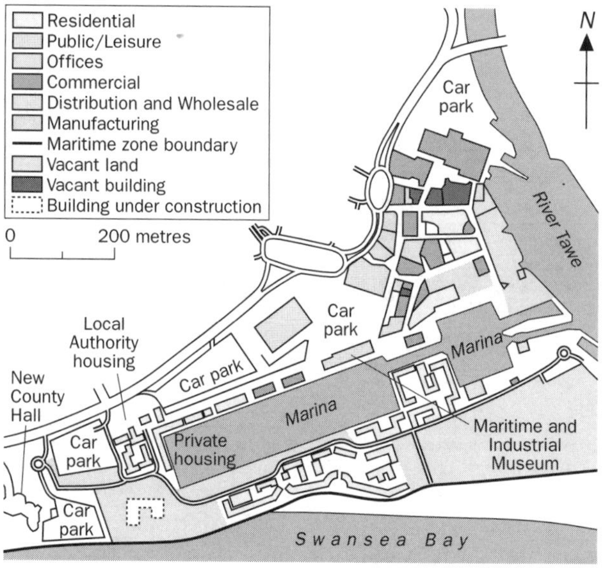

Figure 15.11 *Redevelopment in Swansea waterfront*

15.7 Manufacturing and its location within the city

As city size increases, so does the variety of its manufacturing and its occurrence in several distinct locations. This can often be attributed to some form of cumulative causation wherein once once industry is established and the city prospers, more activity is attracted to it until a stage is reached when, to an important extent, growth is self-sustaining (Figure 15.12). Although small cities may decline through failure of some specialist industries, such as heavy metals or chemicals, large cities never do. They may go through periods of difficulty and reorganisation of their economic base, as with large conurbations such as Tyneside and Merseyside, but they continue to grow or at least to survive (Case study 17.1).

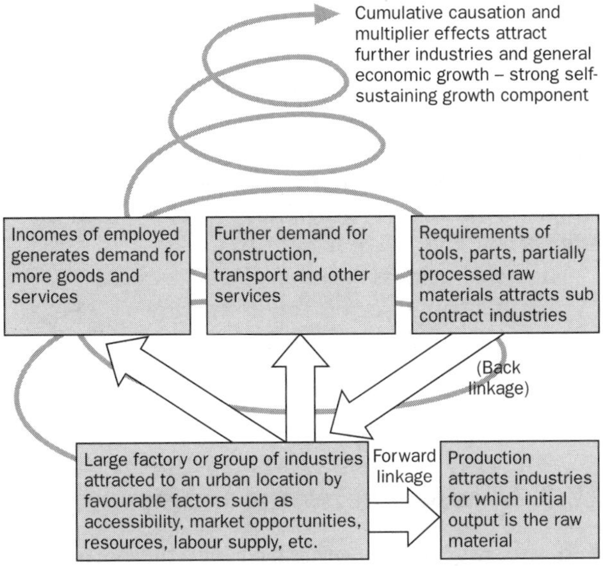

Figure 15.12 *Cumulative growth to self-sustained growth*

As cities have grown, the locational pattern of industry, like that of service activities, has become more complex. In the beginning industry would be concentrated around the initial core of the city and nearby along a waterway, rail line or some other land route which provided the cheapest transport for the raw materials needed and the finished product. With time, shortage of land, congestion, other problems associated with older industrial areas, the development of rapid road transport and technological changes have led to the decentralisation of industry. Established industries have moved out and together with new industries occupied more peripheral locations. Although there has been some recovery and return of small industry to the inner areas of cities, the overall trend has remained one of decentralisation.

Despite the greater complexity of intra-urban patterns of industry it is still possible to identify some of its salient features. These are diagrammatically summarised in Figure 15.13 and illustrated in Case study 15.1. Many of the processes which have influenced urban industrial location in developed countries over a much longer period of time are also evident in the developing world (Case study 14.3).

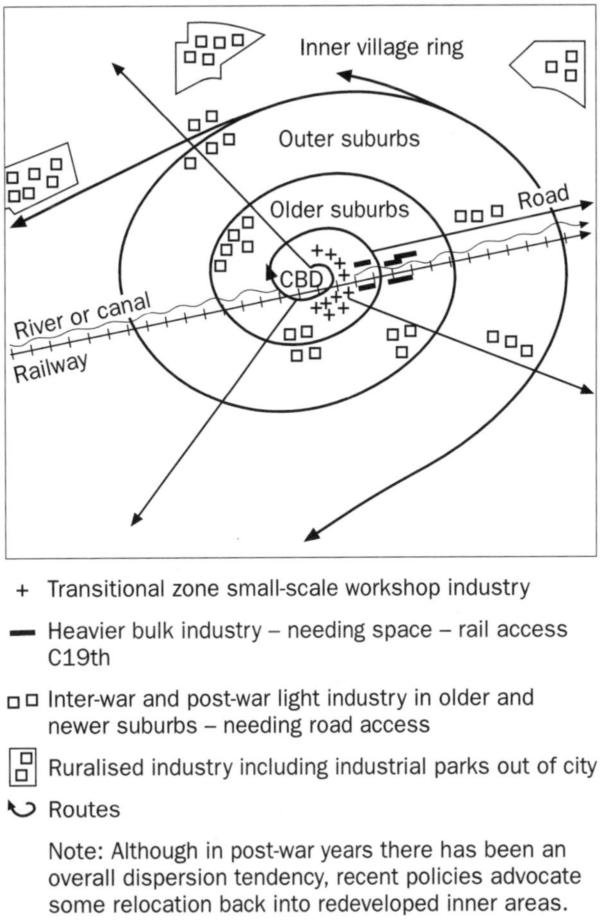

Figure 15.13 *Industry in the intra-urban setting*

Central locations for industry

The oldest industrial zone is usually situated around the CBD of the city. It may include a mixture of small and large firms, many in old and dilapidated buildings, some close to railway termini and canal basins which used to serve them (Case study 15.1). There may also be a considerable number of small new industries set up in converted housing or in factories of the former older industries. There is frequently quite a high turnover amongst smaller businesses as some fail while others expand and require larger premises. The older inner area is therefore one where new industry may be spawned as well as the scene of the former industry on which the city initially depended.

The reasons for the original location of this older industry near the centre are varied. Initially the zone around the CBD would be the fringe zone around the then small city giving good locational access, cheap sites for development and a ready labour supply. Until the end of the nineteenth century there was no compelling reason for industry to move out. Today some industry, especially small-scale industry remains, particularly where close links are needed with activities located in the CBD area and with other workshops in the production process. This is the case, for example, with bespoke tailoring, printing and craft manufacturing, such as jewellery or small precision tools.

In the transition zone too, small rented accommodation is available close to the city centre and nearby warehouses, reducing the need for a canteen for workers, parking and storage space – all factors which are important to businesses with little capital. Such premises are attractive to 'seed bed' industries, that is, small industries which arise from new technologies and which use an adaptable labour force available at central locations. Seed bed industries include electronics, scientific instruments and pattern making as, for example, in Little Sheffield on the western margin of Sheffield's CBD and initially the location of the early cutlery and small metals industry.

In respect of heavy industry such as iron and steel or timber works established near rail sidings and canal docks, the zone frequently extended radially out from the inner site alongside the railway and canal. Industry was attracted because of access to raw materials and markets, and also by vacant and cheaper level land along the valley next to the railway or canal access. This could be seen along the Don Valley below the centre of Sheffield and long the canals near the centres of Birmingham and Tyneside.

Such a pattern was typical in North America and Europe and is today also seen in developing countries where urbanisation and industrialisation have occurred this century, as in the case of Rio de Janeiro in Brazil (Case study 14.3). In respect of heavy industry, capital investment in buildings, equipment and other factors may maintain the location there despite the growing disadvantages associated with an ageing site and a change in transport methods. Hence industrial inertia may be an influential factor in the present siting of old heavy industry towards the inner area and centre of cities.

Suburbanisation of industry

In general there has been a marked suburbanisation or decentralisation of industry. This has gathered momentum and is now affecting large cities all over the world. Some of this change is due to the relocation of industry from inner sites, some of it branch factory establishments by national and multinational companies and the rest new industry to meet changing tastes and a growing demand. Computer and other information technology related industries are particularly prominent. Keeble, in his study of the north-west London suburbs, found for example that whereas in 1914 there were only a handful of firms, by 1960 there were many which employed nearly a quarter of a million people altogether.

Most industry in the suburbs is of a lighter kind, located on purpose-built industrial or trading estates segregated from other land uses though often close to residential and retail areas. Buildings are single storey incorporating office space planned with car parking provisions and other services. They can be found in the older inter-war suburbs as well as in newer ones and more recently, on the rural fringe surrounded by green fields or located on the edge of a village (Case study 14.1).

The new business parks on the edge of cities and in the rural fringe contain an admixture of uses. Industry is usually present but of secondary importance to commercial offices and warehousing (Case study 15.3).

15.8 **Transport networks and movement**

In discussing the economic basis of cities particular emphasis has been placed on accessibility and the effect of developments in transport on the pattern of economic activity (Chapter 31).

Their influence on residential patterns has been equally significant allowing, for example, the increasing separation of residence and workplace and with it, suburbanisation and dormitory growth. While communications have a direct influence on location, communication networks warrant attention, as the pattern of traffic which flows along them between different parts of the city helps to show how it functions. For example, commuter flows indicate the link between residence and workplace and shopping trips and service centres, including the CBD. Thus through a study of the transport network we see the city as a functioning system, its different parts not only interrelated but also interdependent. Any urban transport network has to be capable of catering for a range of traffic, each competing with the other for travel space. Also it has to cater for many different patterns of journey. It is commonly assumed that the most used routes are those to and from the city centre, but surveys show that cross traffic in larger cities is even greater. There is also 'all through' traffic flow as well as that along link roads.

Given all this volume of traffic and the complexity of journey patterns, a very flexible mode of transport is required. Hence the increasing emphasis on roads and motor vehicles though other secondary types of transport are still of significance. For example, suburban underground and rail facilities in large cities such as London and Tokyo are vital in helping to carry commuters to and from work.

So rapid has been the growth in the volume of traffic, that much of the planning since the war has been concerned with solving the problem of too much traffic in cities. This has also been associated with safeguarding the rights of pedestrians and cyclists who make up the bulk of movements over short distances in a city. For example, a quarter of the journeys of under 1.5 km in the City of London are by foot.

Cities in the developing world are beginning to face similar problems, but because of the rapid rate of urbanisation and the shortage of finance, problems are likely to become even more acute than in western cities. Newly industrialising countries are beginning to devise comprehensive transport strategies but lesser developed countries, such as Colombia and Bangladesh, have not yet begun to seriously deal with the growing problems of severe traffic congestion in their large cities, for example.

From traffic chaos to thinking about transport planning

Bogota, the capital of Colombia, has grown by 4.5% annually over the last ten years and now has a population of 6.3 million. It has one third of Colombia's expanding industrial base. The demands on its transport network have thus greatly expanded but little has been done to systematically upgrade it.

'Roads have been widened and flyovers thrown up haphazardly'. The number of vehicles has increased to 600 000 but because of the poverty of most of the population, 90% of passenger journeys are by public transports. A rapid transit system has been regularly debated but in 1994 the transit project for a metro line north to south combined with an east to west busway still remains only on paper.

[SOURCE: Kendal S *Bumper stickers cannot fix unruly, dirty and unlovely Bogota, Financial Times* 9.10.94]

Improvements to city transport systems

Accommodation of motor vehicle traffic

This has involved complete systems of ringways and by-passes to divert through traffic away from the city centre and facilitate cross-city traffic movement (Figure 15.7). There is usually an inner ring road for local traffic and an outer ring road particularly to allow traffic to bypass the most built up areas of the city. There may also be freeways of dual carriageway proportions into the heart of the city, the traffic gaining easy access by clover leaf type junctions where the freeway intersects ring roads (Figure 15.14).

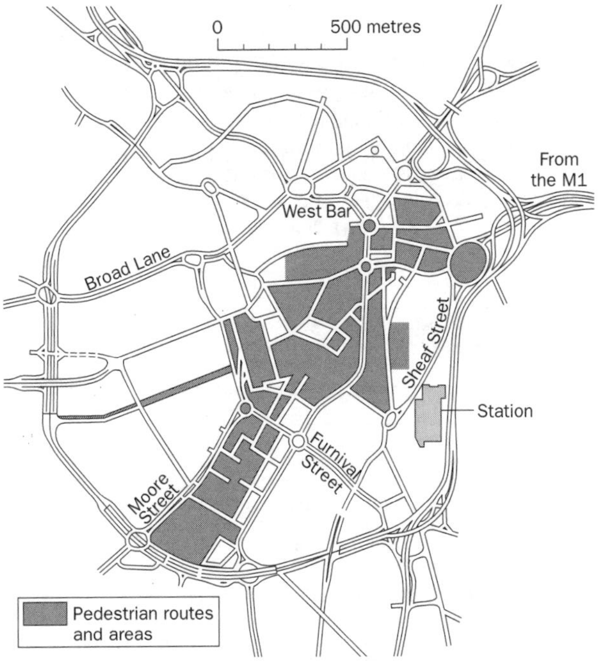

Figure 15.14 Sheffield's central traffic system and pedestrian routes

These kinds of improvement may bring benefits but they are economically and socially costly. Valuable urban land has been used up, housing cleared to make way for motorways and communities divided by new routes crossing through the middle of residential areas. There is also the problem of increased noise and high levels of pollution from exhaust fumes (Figure 15.15). Frequently it is the poorer housing areas which are most seriously affected while it is businesses and the more affluent car-owning sectors of society who benefit most. For example, London's Westway – a six-lane dual cariageway – has been carved right through North Kensington and Paddington's poorer housing areas and prompted the following observations: *'The construction of a new motorway is a type of modern parable using public funds to make life easier for the rich and harder for the poor.'*

[SOURCE: *The Times* 11.07.94]

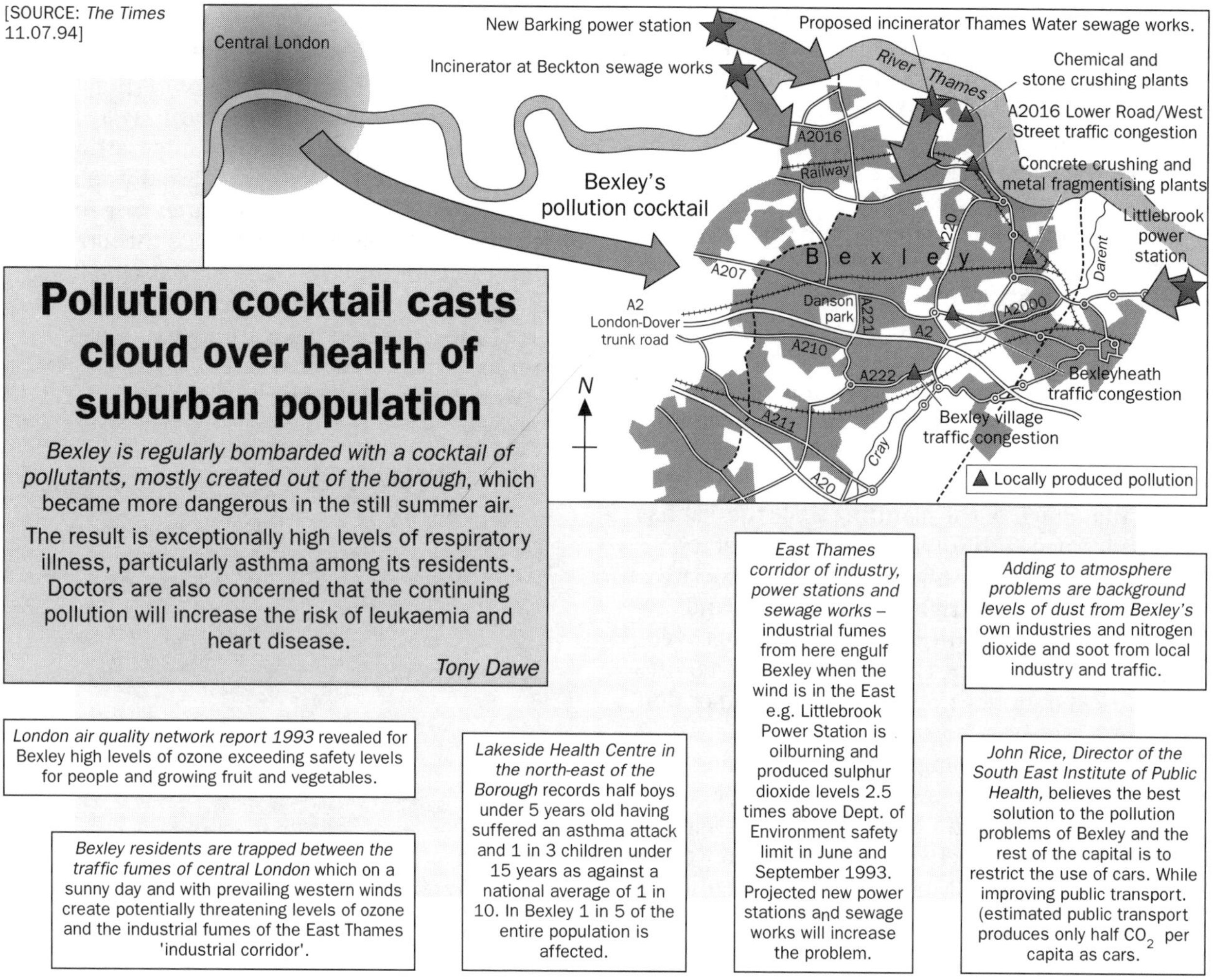

Pollution cocktail casts cloud over health of suburban population

Bexley is regularly bombarded with a cocktail of pollutants, mostly created out of the borough, which became more dangerous in the still summer air.

The result is exceptionally high levels of respiratory illness, particularly asthma among its residents. Doctors are also concerned that the continuing pollution will increase the risk of leukaemia and heart disease.

Tony Dawe

East Thames corridor of industry, power stations and sewage works – industrial fumes from here engulf Bexley when the wind is in the East e.g. Littlebrook Power Station is oilburning and produced sulphur dioxide levels 2.5 times above Dept. of Environment safety limit in June and September 1993. Projected new power stations and sewage works will increase the problem.

Adding to atmosphere problems are background levels of dust from Bexley's own industries and nitrogen dioxide and soot from local industry and traffic.

London air quality network report 1993 revealed for Bexley high levels of ozone exceeding safety levels for people and growing fruit and vegetables.

Lakeside Health Centre in the north-east of the Borough records half boys under 5 years old having suffered an asthma attack and 1 in 3 children under 15 years as against a national average of 1 in 10. In Bexley 1 in 5 of the entire population is affected.

John Rice, Director of the South East Institute of Public Health, believes the best solution to the pollution problems of Bexley and the rest of the capital is to restrict the use of cars. While improving public transport. (estimated public transport produces only half CO_2 per capita as cars.

Bexley residents are trapped between the traffic fumes of central London which on a sunny day and with prevailing western winds create potentially threatening levels of ozone and the industrial fumes of the East Thames 'industrial corridor'.

Figure 15.15 *Sources of pollution for an outer suburb of London metropolis*

Increased parking space is also needed in the city. Frequently this is in the transitional zone next to the CBD using up land which may be needed to provide more housing for lower income groups.

Alternative transport provision

Until recently the needs of those walking or cycling in the city have been given comparatively little attention, but further measures have followed on from the idea of helping those on foot by providing some pedestrian precincts and subways under busy roads. Now a number of pedestrian ways are being weatherproofed, as well as some being built above ground level. In highly congested areas like The Bank in London, conveyor belts are also being installed over short distances.

Increasingly for town centres, traffic systems are being devised to give preference to pedestrians and to separate pedestrian traffic from all wheeled traffic, as in the case of Cambridge which because of its university, has an unusually high density of cycle traffic (Figure 15.16).

To increase road safety and deter the use of private cars in towns as a whole, preference is increasingly given to cyclists. While the Netherlands has long had its cycleways they are a recent innovation in most European cities. In the UK the new town of Milton Keynes has an extensive network of cycleways (Case study 16.3). Now older cities such as Nottingham are also developing networks (Figure 15.17). These link residential areas to workplaces and shopping centres, to park and ride car parks on the city outskirts and to rail stations, providing a way of integrating cycle use with node points where vehicle users reach the city.

For longer journeys the main alternative to private cars has been the extension and improvement of suburban and underground rail networks, as can be seen in the case of London. This is also happening in a number of large cities in the developing world. In Hong Kong, a complete new system has been installed and the network is to be further extended to link the new planned international airport on Lantau Island to Kowloon and other main urban concentration on the main island (Figure 15.18).

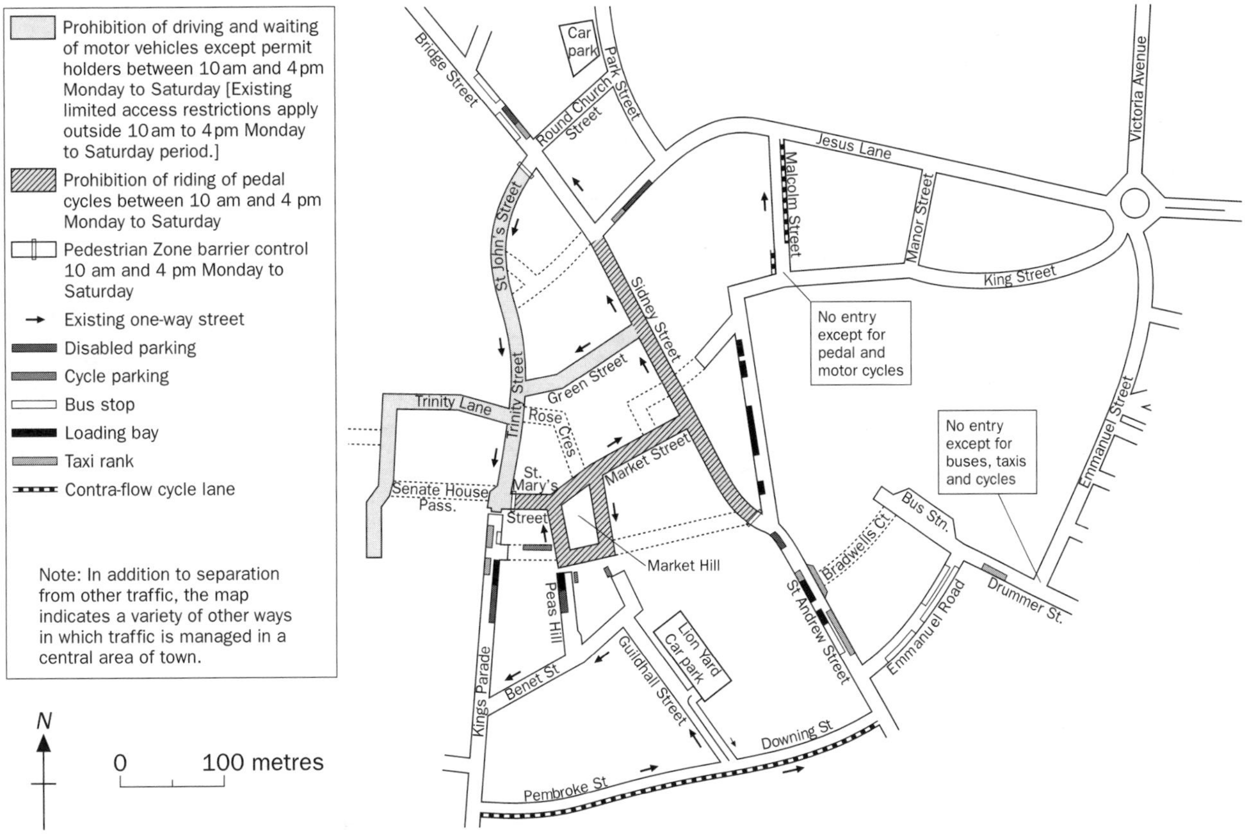

Figure 15.16 *Cambridge centre: the pedestrian zone scheme*

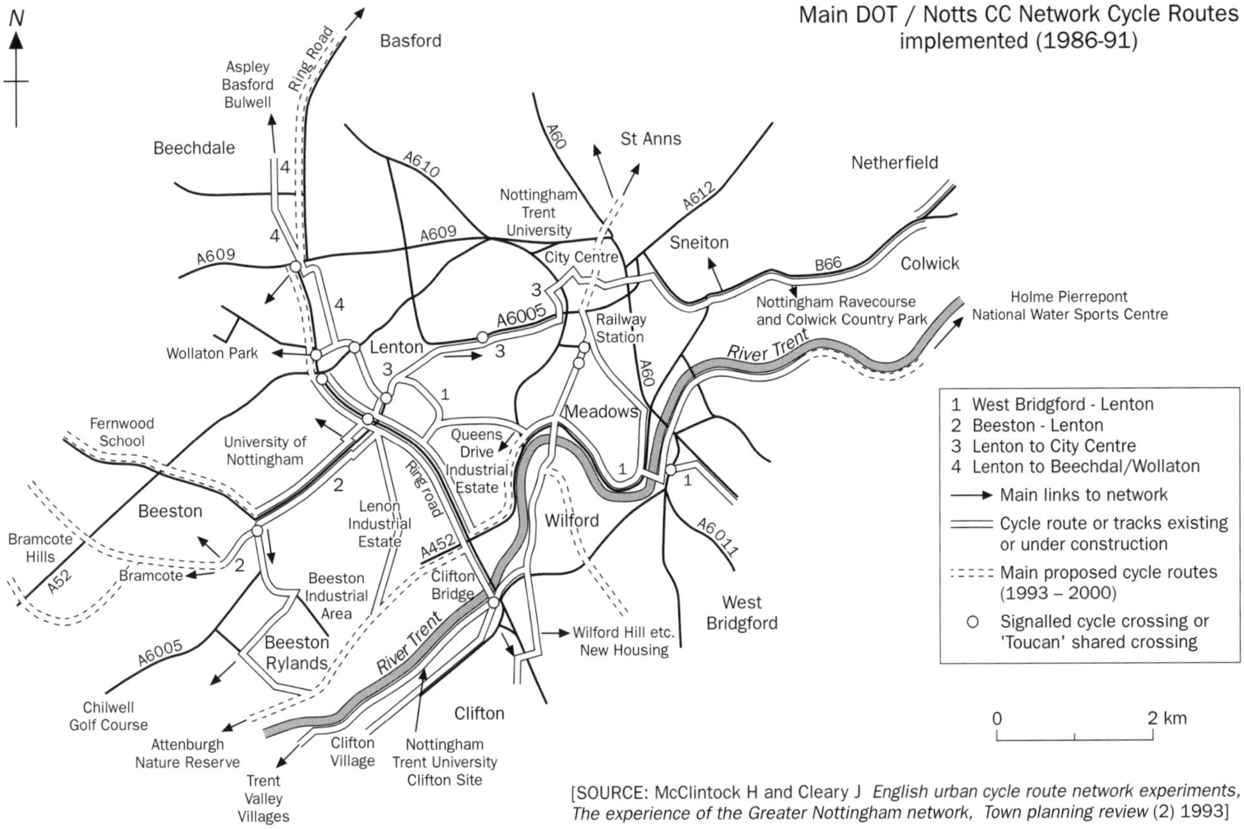

[SOURCE: McClintock H and Cleary J *English urban cycle route network experiments, The experience of the Greater Nottingham network, Town planning review* (2) 1993]

Figure 15.17 *Greater Nottingham cycle route network*

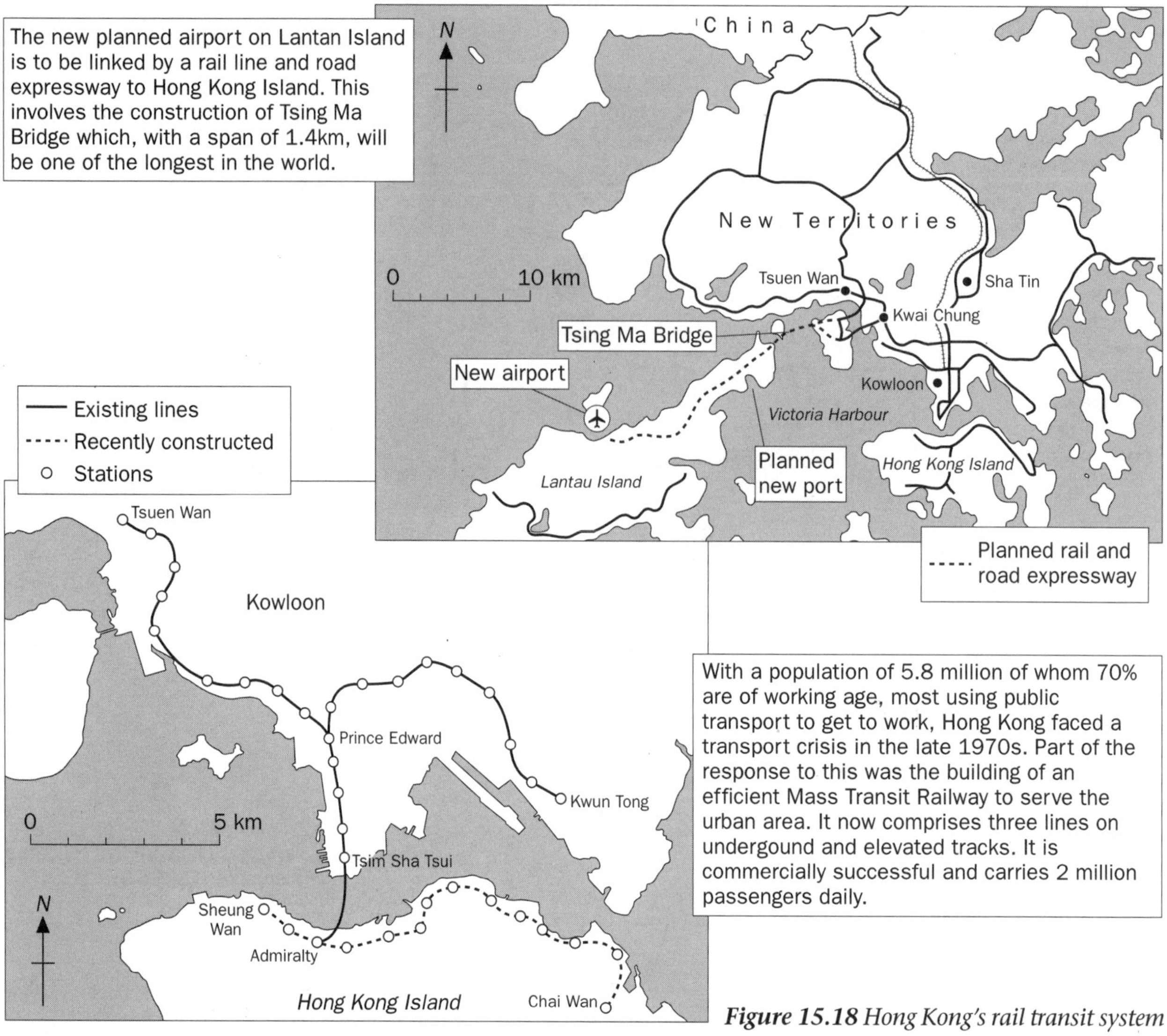

Figure 15.18 *Hong Kong's rail transit system*

More attention is also being given to the introduction of super tramways and other means of rapid transit along the main transport arteries in major cities. The super tram system installed in Manchester has been very successful and one is in the process of construction in Sheffield along part of the Don Valley, linking the city centre with the Meadowhall regional shopping and main suburban areas.

Concluding comment

In conclusion, it can be seen that great efforts are being made to cope with the increased traffic in towns but perhaps the biggest contribution to a long-term solution will be a further decentralisation of employment and service facilities, bringing them into closer proximity to residential areas. This together with increased home working, will perhaps not only reduce the need for people to travel by car into the more congested central areas but also reduce the amount of freight which must be transported across the city. However, decentralisation may ultimately transfer traffic congestion to the outskirts of cities unless there is also a move to more mixed land use in new developments so that residence, workplace and service and leisure provision are within walking distance of each other. In a number of new business park and edge city developments this policy is already being followed as in the 'fourth generation' extension of the Aztec West business park at Junction 16 on the M5, six miles west of Bristol.

case study

15.1 Nottingham: The location of services and industries

City centre

Nottingham is the regional centre for the East Midlands and among the top ten retail centres in the country. In 1994 it had 720 000 sq ft of convenience shopping and 2 million sq ft of comparative shopping.

The location is based on the historical core and is the crossing point on the River Trent. Formerly linear in shape, lying east to west, it has been extensively redeveloped with major additions of the recently built Victoria and Broad Marsh shopping malls. This CBD has a new north-to-south axial trend.

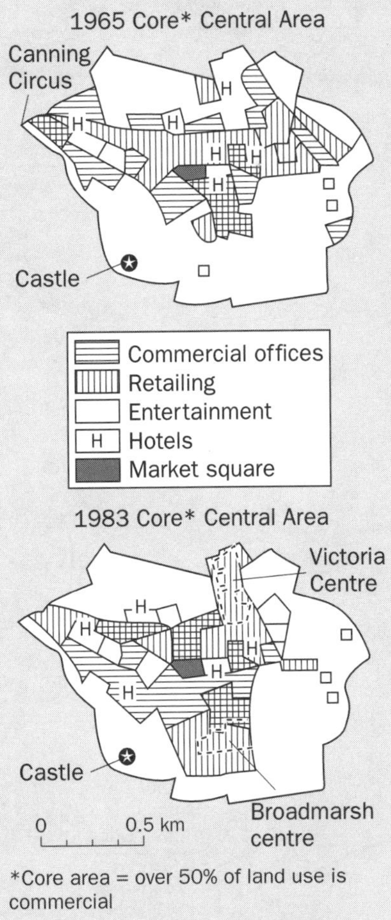

Major land uses in the core and frame areas of Nottingham's city centre, 1965 and 1983

Suburban and out-of-town services

While the prosperity of the CBD has been maintained, services have expanded relatively quickly in out-of-town centre locations. This expansion and the location of services have been mainly influenced by:

- a growth in population and purchasing power in the suburbs
- greater mobility with increased car ownership and the lines of accessibility, especially along major routes and at node points including established service centres
- availability and price of land variations
- the policy of the council favouring areas underserved and with expanding populations e.g. Trowell Road.

The most notable trend has been the expansion of super stores and hypermarkets, some adjacent to existing centres such as Arnold, but others in selfstanding locations e.g. on former Wilford Power Station: in 1994 it had 944 000 sq ft of super and hypermarket shopping.

Currently the policy is moving against out-of-town shopping centres to preserve the viability of town and suburban retail centres.

Post-war prosperity of the East Midlands catchment area and better accessibility to Nottingham, especially off the M1 motorway, has led to expansion of the CBD and rising land prices, forcing out industry warehouse/wholesale and residential land use. High rise developments are significant.

The core has been increasingly taken over by commercial offices, specialist retailing and entertainment functions. Since the 1970s retailing expansion has been greater in the suburbs and town fringe.

Land use has become increasingly segregated e.g. commercial offices to the south-west of Market Square.

CBD uses have expanded into the transition zone, especially during the 1980s, including government offices and large superstores. Car park provision has had to increase.

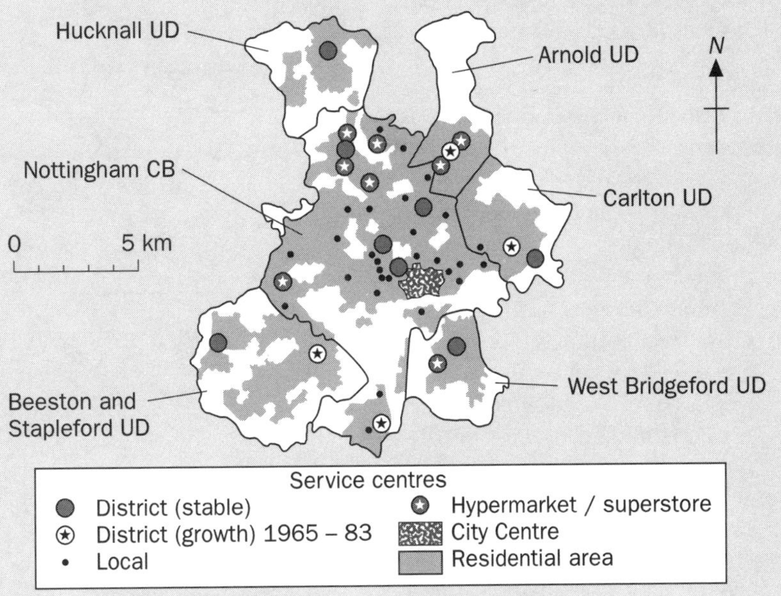

Changing pattern of service centres in the Nottingham conurbation

Industrial structure and location

Nottingham has a diversified industrial base but no heavy capital industry.

The main industries apart from electrical engineering, date back to the mid-nineteenth century, and textiles much earlier. The lace and knitwear industry was very prominent to the 1920s but declined since. Bicycle, pharmaceutical and tobacco industries have remained prominent; electrical engineering has made the most rapid advance. There is a whole range of industries including small and large businesses such as boots (pharmaceutical), Players (tobacco), Tube Investments (Raleigh) and Plessey (engineering).

Since the 1970s the importance of industry has declined in favour of the service sector but because much of it is in the consumer durable and light consumer sectors, the industrial base has weathered the 1980s recession better than most other cities. Manufacturing employment has fallen from 63 700 (1984) to 52 000 (1991) but services have expanded.

Influences on the locational pattern

- historical locations including textiles and Boots in inner area. Plants set up by individual entrepreneurs e.g Colwick Industrial Estate to the west set up by Colwick (typewriters) in 1917.
- line of Trent River Valley – south-west to east and tributary valley of Leen trending from the north – provided vacant land, water and a routeway including access to railway. Today it remains prominent as the cleared old industrial and power site is used for new industrial estates.
- smaller historical industrial centres e.g. Hucknall (Rolls Royce) and Beeston are now enveloped by the spread of Nottingham. Plessey built a business park at Beeston on land adjacent to established works.
- Local Authority locational policy for establishment of inter-war and post-war industrial estates on vacant land e.g. coalmining sites and railway land such as Colwick Railway Sidings. It also favoured small workshop and business complexes in redevelopment inner area e.g. Meadows, south of Town Centre (Core).
- road access is increasingly vital e.g. the building of Clifton Bridge opened low-lying land in Sherwood to the north and the western ring road and M1 are drawing new light industry to them.

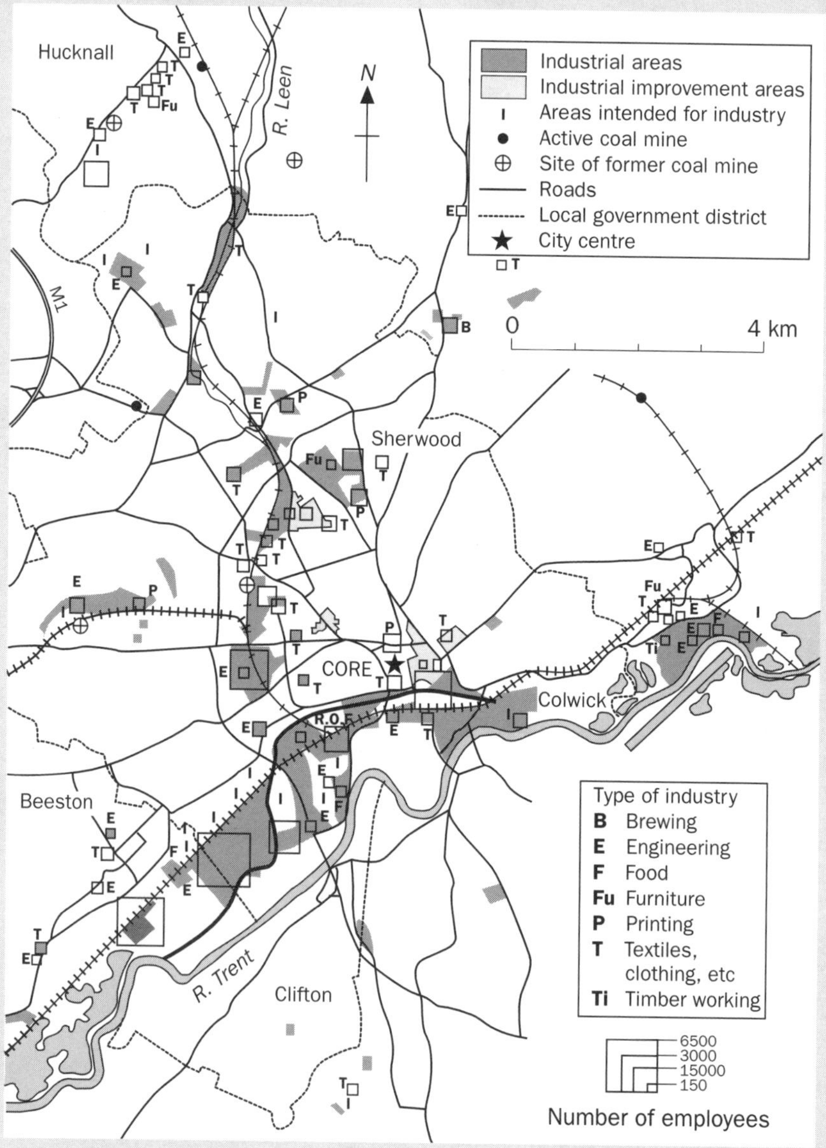

Industrial areas and employment at larger establishments (early 1980s)

case study

15.2 Merry Hill and Meadow Hall: major out-of-town retail centres

Merry Hill, Dudley

The site lies within an area in the West Midlands under Special Enterprise zone status, thus planning approval was readily available. Moreover, the site was derelict industrial land.

Development began in 1984 with retail warehouses, to which has been added a Carrefour (Asda) superstore and smaller shopping units under cover. In 1988 a ten screen cinema was built nearby. The retail shopping was extended further bringing in Marks and Spencer as a major lead retail department store.

However, access is not good. The centre is several miles away from a motorway and local roads have had to be used, leading to congestion and some traffic pollution.

Since 1992 it has been taken over by another property company. Being at the centre of the West Midlands urban region, its catchment area is very profitable.

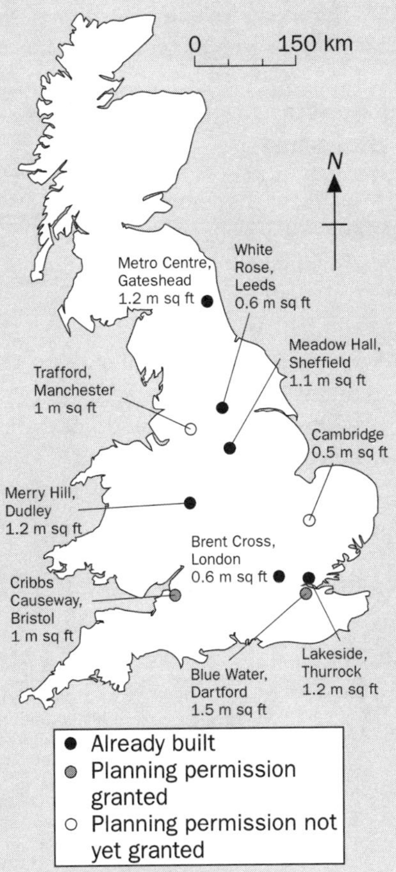

Shoppers are increasingly forsaking high streets and traditional town centres for vast, out-of-town shopping centres built on sites that are legacies of Britain's industrial past. There, shoppers decant in enormous parking lots and head indoors, where the atmosphere is warm, bright, safe and synthetic – complete with patrolling security guards and slashing fountains.
[*The Independent* 18.11.91]

Meadow Hall, Sheffield

Meadow Hall was developed on derelict industrial land in the Don Valley, three miles out of Sheffield City Centre in the early 1990s. It is adjacent to the M1 motorway and thus, unlike Merry Hill, has excellent access to serve much of South Yorkshire and part of the East Midlands regions. The M18 link is also near via the M1. The estimated catchment area has a population of 9 million.

Approval for Meadow Hall was based on seeing it as a key to help generate the decaying Lower Don Valley and to some extent it has succeeded. However, fears for its detrimental effect on the Sheffield Centre retail trade has proved well founded, as the centre is in decline.

It contains a large range of retail services under cover including leading department store. Substantial leisure amenity provision is also envisaged.

A change of policy

Since 1993 the Department for the Environment has discouraged schemes for out-of-town shopping centres partly to safeguard the environment but as the article indicates, also to protect established retail centres from losing trade and decaying.

case study

15.3 Swindon: industrial business parks

'Home' to a range of nationally and internationally known concerns originally noted for railway engineering – finally closing 1987. Now a diversified base but with engineering, electronics and distribution firms outstanding e.g. Motorola, Intel, Emmerson, Electrics (USA) Honda car industry, a national Royal Mail distribution centre, Gallileo air data base networks, W H Smith and Reader's Digest publishing distribution, Allied Dunbar financial services.

Business Parks

The term 'business park' originally indicated a self-standing greenfield site development offering new standards of space and environment quality with good access for industrial and office users. First originating in the USA in the 1960s the concept spread to other countries and the term covers almost any new development for business whether on greenfield or redeveloped sites within the city. During the 1980s most of the Business Park area was given over to industrial users but by the early 1990s around 70% was for offices and other commercial uses.

The term now loosely covers any developments from small suburban industrial estates such as surrounding Heathrow and the urban park recently developed at Chiswick, London, to very large parks of over 100 acres for which the term is most appropriately used e.g. the 650 acres King's Hill Development (West Malling, Kent) with 318 million sq foot of space when complete. The first phase has USA style flex buildings, single storey for industrial and office users and will have on-site amenities – restaurants, leisure and educational plus some housing.

Requirements

A green environment may be desirable but a commercially suitable location offering cost savings will win hands down. Some urban sites may be preferred to greenfield sites. Of paramount importance are good access spaces, reasonable rent, access to skilled educated and access to a variety of amenities.

Locational advantages of Swindon

- An excellent central position on the M4 growth corridor
- Excellent communications by rail, motorway and air (close to Heathrow)
- Plenty of space including redeveloped railway land and agricultural land around.
- Lower cost than competing centres of London, Reading and Bristol
- Active and cooperative support from Thamesmead borough, Wiltshire council and the Great Western Enterprise private sector agency. But no public subsidy or grant aid. However liberal planning regulations and openness to all kinds of small and large businesses.
- Initially a good range of skilled educated labour available with a traditional basis in engineering plus a good range of entrepreneurship but now a shortage of labour.
- Pleasant residential areas within easy commuting distance.
- Very good infrastructure and diversified commercial and industrial base offering excellent linkage and ancillary support.

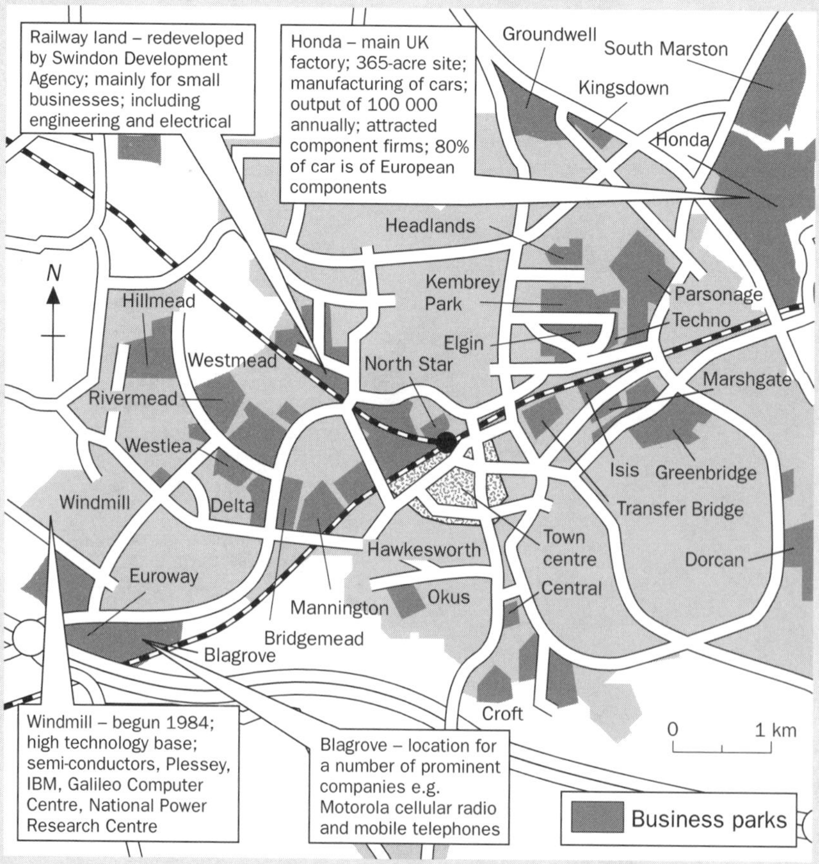

Industrial and business park locations in Swindon

16

CHAPTER 16

The form and future shape of the modern city

'As urban life has expanded and been diffused ever widely, the form which cities have taken at various periods and in different cultural contexts have not remained constant.

Hence there is considerable interest in unravelling the contributions which successive technological and social situations have made to the morphology of cities.'

JOHNSON J H *URBAN SOCIETY AND URBAN FORM*, *URBAN GEOGRAPHY*, 1972

16.1 The character of change, morphological periods and fringe belts

From what has already been shown in earlier chapters, it is evident that the form and shape of the city is never static. Change has taken place throughout history, but it has not been at an even rate. ***Change tends to occur in cycles, with a rapid growth period followed by a time of minor change and consolidation and each growth period having its own physical character in the nature of town design and building style.*** Because each period has its own distinctive character, they have been defined as morphological periods. The contribution that each period makes to the form and shape of a city is thus distinctively evident on the ground.

Morphological period

A morphological period is any period in the cultural history of an area which creates distinctive material forms in the cultural landscape to suit the particular socio-economic needs of its society. These forms survive in varying degrees in the current landscape as residual features of their particular period.

Morphological periods have been prompted by items of rapid economic and technological change, such as those associated with the industrial revolution. These economic and technological changes in turn prompt population movements which also affect city growth. In a time of rapid change there is not only outward expansion of the city to accommodate new and expanded needs, but also considerable modification of the already built area, since the older forms of street layout and buildings may no longer be suitable.

Technological changes in transport are particularly influential since they increase the mobility of people and the ways in which freight is transported. Greater mobility enables the spread and functional zoning of cities, as the separation of residence from places of work and service provision becomes increasingly feasible. The effect of the railways on cities is clearly evident in that part of a city's morphology which had been created in the nineteenth century, as is the advent of motor transport on the morphology of the inter-war phase and the more recent post-war developments.

The current morphology and form of any urban place depends, to some extent, on how old it is. The older the city, the greater the number of morphological (historical) periods which have contributed to its makeup. New towns such as Milton Keynes in the UK and Brasilia, the interior capital of Brazil, are a product of the present, but older cities like London or Rio de Janerio are products of a number of morphological periods. In inner areas, the street plan and some buildings pre-date even those phases of the nineteenth century – inter-war and post-1945 – which have made the greatest contribution to the shape of cities in the developed world.

When looking at cities it is possible to recognise from the shape and style of buildings and the nature of the street plan which historical phase contributed most to the character of a city. However, it is difficult to pick out a growth clearly, partly because succeeding development adds further accretionary growth onto the fringes of a city and may bring some redevelopment and adaptation to existing areas. Furthermore, every period of growth tends to throw certain usages out to the fringe, such as sewer and gas works, mental hospitals, allotments and playing fields (Chapter 12).

Fringe belt

The fringe belt is a belt-like zone which originates from the temporarily stationary or very slowly advancing fringe of a town. It is composed of a characteristic mixture of land use units initially seeking a peripheral location.

Each morphological period tends to have its fringe belt which, during the following phases of expansion, gets filled in with new development and encapsulated into the city. Thus, besides the usual zonation of cities, it is possible to recognise old fringe belts of mixed use which mark the outer limits of a city or town at different phases in its development (Figures 12.7 and 12.8).

Phases of growth and fringe development may also be seen in cities of the developing world but here the morphological form of cities is frequently complicated by colonial and post-colonial influences which have introduced elements of a 'western' cultural form to many cities. Sometimes indigenous and external influences may be spatially separated, giving a distinctive dual structure to the city, as in the case of Bombay in India and Kano in Nigeria. It is more usual to find that influences are mixed, though there may be distinct native and European quarters.

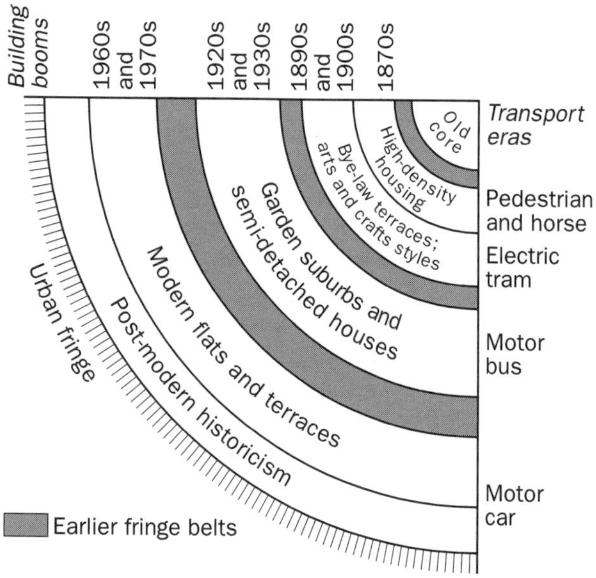

[SOURCE: Whitehand T W R *Development cycles and urban landscapes, Geography,* 1994]

Figure 16.1 *Model of Western city development – an innovation/building cycle model*

More recently, continued pressures have brought redevelopment in the centre and the spread of suburbs (Case studies 11.2 and 14.1). Thus many of the larger cities in a developing world such as Rio de Janerio and Mexico City have newer areas, including high rise development, which make them very reminiscent of modern cities in the developed world (Case study 14.3). Unlike the latter, there has been the additional development of shanty areas both on the edge and further in where difficult terrain hitherto deterred building.

Whitehand has recently produced simple models of a typical development of a western city which encapsulates the contribution of different morphological periods and fringe developments and also the era of transport innovation which contributed to them (Figure 16.1).

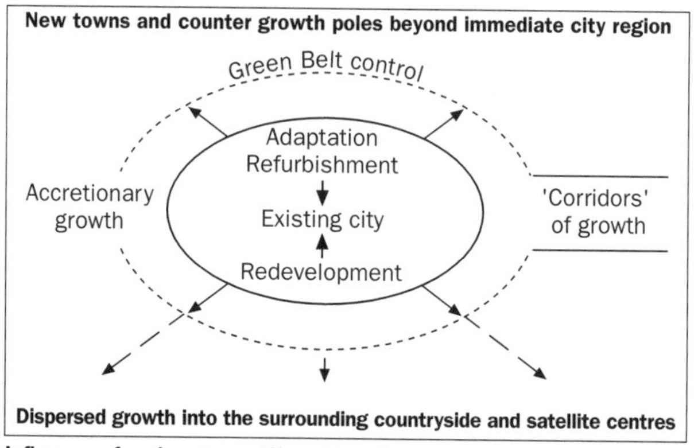

Influences for change
- Expanding demand and changes in demand for housing, retail and other services, business offices, manufacturing premises, infra-structure, such as transport, car parks, etc.
- Technological changes including changes in modes of transport, ways in which goods and services are provided requiring different building design, etc.
- Growing diseconomies within the existing city due to ageing and physical deterioration of buildings, congestion and environmental degradation, and rising land prices
- Changing aspirations, attitudes and 'fashions' e.g. as to residential preferences, regard for different locations, building design, changes in priorities.

Historical constraints to change
- Existing form of road and street layout
- Form of existing buildings
- Areas and buildings protected by conservation orders.

Types of change
- Physical constraints to change
- Form of terrain and drainage some areas conducive to change, others barriers to change.

Human constraints on change
- Amount of finance available
- Planning regulations and zonation as to permitted use of different areas
- Pressure groups for various reasons opposed to the change envisaged e.g. environmental groups, neighbourhood groups and vested interest groups, such as chambers of commerce.

Agents of change
- 'Governments' through policy and financial decisions of national and local level
- Decisions by business on amount, location and type of development
- Decisions by land-owners on sale of land and conditions of use of the land
- Speculators in land, building and service provision ahead of demand
- Decisions by individual entrepreneurs and architects, etc.
- Decisions by the public as individuals or member of a group organisation e.g. housing association cooperative, etc.

Figure 16.2 *Main trends in the changing form and shape of the city – Constraints, influences and agencies in relation to change*

Past constraints

During the twentieth century the pace of modernisation had so quickened that simple accretionary growth and adaptation of existing buildings in towns were no longer sufficient to meet the changing needs of society. Consequently, wholesale redevelopment of older and even comparatively recent city areas and the spread of cities are evident, as is the development of new kinds of cities. To some extent these are based on the Garden City movement which started in the 1930s with the work of Ebenezer Howard and other pioneers.

However in established cities, change still has to take place within the constraints left by the past. The existing built form of a city, including the street plan and general layout which make up the morphology or physical structure of a city, cannot simply be swept aside. Apart from pressure from conservation groups, the existing built form represents a massive financial investment, some of which must continue to be used where possible. Thus to understand the nature of present change we do need to have some regard for the past (Figure 16.2).

16.2 Adaptation, renewal and redevelopment in existing cities and conurbations

Until comparatively recently, pressures for change in already established and built up areas were mainly accommodated by changing the use of buildings and refurbishing them, as for example, in the conversion of large dwelling houses on the edge of CBDs into offices for small businesses. Similarly, old industrial buildings and warehouses have been converted to other uses, as in the case of those on disused dockland and riverside sites, such as at the mouth of the River Orwell at Ipswich, Suffolk.

Such adaptation still occurs today, especially in conservation areas where buildings and their surroundings are protected, as in Le Marais District in the city of Paris (Case study 16.2). However, the pace of modernisation in the 1950s and 1960s was such that tracts of inner city areas and Central Business Districts were subject to total redevelopment. It was considered too costly to renovate and amongst planners and architects the ideal was for 'new forms' to be created to suit a new age of expansion.

By the 1970s some of the weaknesses and problems of a policy of wholesale clearance and redevelopment were becoming evident, including the break up of communities and the faulty design and construction of much the new building that had taken place in the haste to meet the housing shortages of the post-war years. While redevelopment of city centres was happening, wholesale clearance and rebuilding came to an end in inner city areas.

Much more emphasis was placed on revitalising inner city areas through encouraging local authorities, private individuals and communities to refurbish existing buildings and improve the local environment. The public were also encouraged to contribute towards local area schemes (Case study 16.1) and the formulation of structure plans for the future pattern of city development rather than simply accept what public authorities decided. This emphasis on cooperation and partnership has continued to be the main basis of more recent initiatives towards renewal and redevelopment. Much greater private investment and entrepreneurship has also been encouraged with government funding playing a secondary role. This is evident in the development in Enterprise Zones and in the larger areas under the care of Development Corporations.

Redevelopment of derelict tracts also takes place. Up to the end of the 1970s most of the concern was for the older decaying areas of cities. However, in the 1980s it became apparent that a significant amount of the earlier redevelopment and the new areas built on the edge of the cities to house lower income families displaced from the inner city areas or newcomers to the city, was also in a state of deterioration and contributed social problems. Thus currently much of the change in cities is concerned with renewal and redevelopment of these areas, often with a return to the small-scale mixed types of development more characteristic of the earlier growth of cities and which are more user-friendly and socially acceptable. (Case study 16.1)

Cities in the developing world

Cities in the developing world have faced more serious problems because of the much more rapid rate of urbanisation and expansion that occurs. Much redevelopment takes place both in established built up areas and in the mass of spontaneous settlement spread at the edge of large conurbations. However, the scale of this redevelopment is likely to be even greater than in the developed world, provided the finance can be found to undertake it. (Case study 14.3).

16.3 Dispersed growth and the development of new and expanded towns

Where urbanisation has passed its peak there is a natural movement of people away from overcrowded cities into the countryside. It had begun in Western Europe at the turn of the century and gathered momentum in the inter-war years when improvements in road transport and rising affluence among ordinary people led to the rapid spread of suburbs around major cities. This continued into the post-war years and is evident in the sprawl of outer suburbs and in the dormitory growth of villages in the nearby countryside (Chapter 12).

Green Belts

Green Belts are areas of open and low density land use surrounding existing settlements where further urban extension is to be strictly controlled (Case study 11.1). ***They were created following the 1947 Town and Country Planning Act. The Green Belt for Greater London was already designated by 1946 under the Abercrombie Plan*** (Case study 12.1). Although they have largely been upheld, the Green Belt policy has come under increasing pressure as influences on the outer edge of cities themselves have increased. Consequently, there has recently been some relaxation of planning controls to allow some development on greenbelt land, especially where growth corridors from major conurbations have been identified (Figure 16.3).

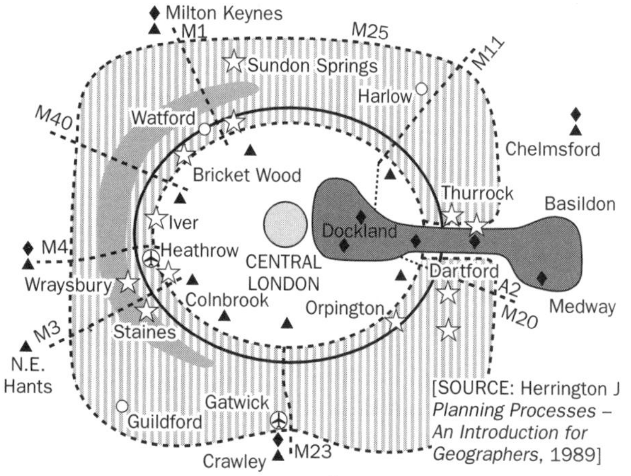

- - - Main radial roads
Metropolitan Green Belt
Areas where development is encouraged
...... Dockland / M25 links
Areas with sustantial developments commitments:
♦ Industry / Distribution
▲ Offices / Retailing
☆ Proposed shopping 'megacentres' (>500 000 sq.ft)
Area under pressure for development

The Green Belt round Greater London and urban pressures on it. The government encouraged East Thames Growth Corridor extending out from the London docklands is also indicated.

Figure 16.3 *The Green Belt around London*

Greenbelt restrictions imposed on the further growth of built up areas and the Town and Country Planning legislation of the late nineteenth century exerted pressure on the villages and small towns immediately beyond the greenbelt.

This pressure, combined with that on the older areas in cities, forced governments to adopt a more positive approach which would actively encourage decentralisation away from major cities. It needed to be planned towards locations which could readily absorb and benefit from such growth. ***New towns were developed on greenfield sites in the country or adjacent to small settlements, as in the case of Harlow and Stevenage which were built to accommodate some of London's over-spill.*** These towns (Case study 16.1) were laid out along the guidelines pioneered by Ebenezer Howard and others, which itself was responsible for the Garden City of Letchworth.

In addition, a number of small market towns in need of further growth and better economic prospects were identified to receive overspill from London and other large cities under the ***Expanded Towns Act of 1953. For example, some of the older market towns of East Anglia, such as St Neots, Haverhill and Huntingdon, have been expanded to take in overspill population from Greater London, together with some businesses.***

Despite the individual success enjoyed by certain new and expanded towns, overall the policy has only been partially successful in relieving pressure on the largest conurbations. For one thing, insufficient employment opportunities were available and some of the new towns were too close to a main conurbation. Many who lived in new and expanded towns continued to commute back to work in the large cities and this has placed a severe strain on the transport network. It has also encouraged the continued setting up of offices and expansion of factories in the conurbations, despite the planning restrictions against them.

As a consequence in the UK and elsewhere in Europe, a second generation of new towns were planned, this time sufficiently far from established conurbations to be independent of them and large enough to act as counter-magnets to them. They would eventually generate further growth without government support and financial aid. The best known of these second generation new towns in the UK is Milton Keynes in Buckinghamshire which was designated in 1967 (Case study 16.3). In a number of ways, Milton Keynes marked the transition phase towards the future town which may take a widely dispersed form, with housing and business areas being separated by green leisure zones and open spaces.

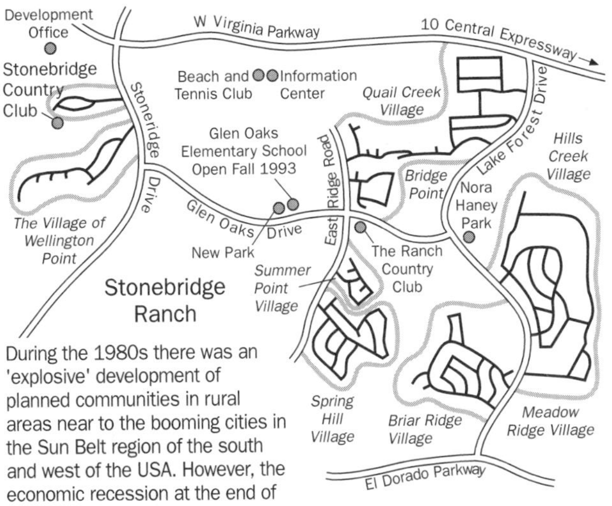

During the 1980s there was an 'explosive' development of planned communities in rural areas near to the booming cities in the Sun Belt region of the south and west of the USA. However, the economic recession at the end of the 1980s reduced the housing market drastically and a number of developers went bankrupt with the 'planned' communities unfinished.

Stoneridge Ranch is succeeding and is located one hour's drive north of Dallas. It covers over 6000 acres and has a planned capacity of 27 500 residential units and 91 million square feet of commercial space.

It is designed to be a self-contained community for middle and higher income families. It has its own country club, a tennis complex, sites for schools and retail and other service provision.

[SOURCE: Waddell P *Dallas: Will surburban dispersion ever cease? Built Environment* Vol 20]

Figure 16.4 *Plan of an ex-urban new town development near Dallas, Texas, USA*

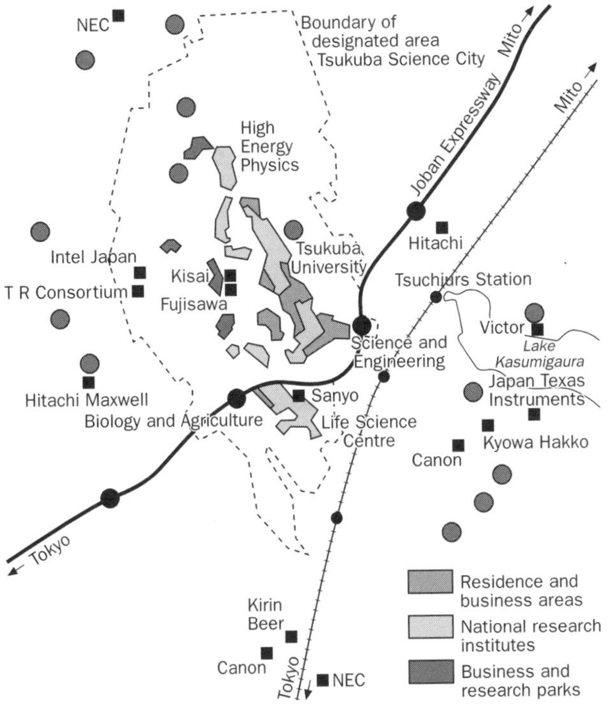

The city is 60 km north-east of Tokyo and 40 km north-west of Narita International airport. It was originally planned in the 1960s but still in the process of expansion. In 1989 it had a population of 278 000 including Suburban District. By 1990 it had 30% of all Japan's national research agencies. However, it was only in the 1980s that it began to attract private investors as opposed to public funding.

Figure 16.5 *The structure of Tsukubu Science City and some of the associated high technology industries*

Despite consortiums of private developers proposing a range of schemes for new towns, there are unlikely to be any designated in the UK in the near future because the government's concern is to arrest the decline of the central and inner areas of the older conurbations (Case study 16.1). The prosperity and attraction of the new towns has over recent years been seen as diverting much needed investment away from attempts to revive and, where necessary, redevelop inner areas in the established towns and cities.

However, elsewhere in other advanced countries, such as the USA (Figure 16.4) and Australia, there are a number of privately developed 'instant cities'. Some of them have been designed to meet the growing trend for people to retire to sunbelt regions or coastal areas. Rising incomes, increased leisure and comparatively lower costs of travel have also increased the demand for second home ownership, which is also swelling the market for new city locations.

Another trend associated with current progress is the emergence of ***new science cities for research and the new computer and information technology industries (Figure 16.5)***. For example, as part of its regional development policy, the Japanese government has encouraged the setting up of technopolis cities in each prefecture. These new cities, in addition to research and information technology sites, also include housing areas and a full range of amenities.

Corridors of growth

In a period of rapid economic expansion there is a tendency for cities to expand along major routeways because these provide the advantage of good accessibility to the core of the city and good linkages with other urban centres and markets. ***Growth is particularly active along a route corridor which links two urban growth poles.*** This is evident, for example, along the M4 which links London to Bristol, and in the rapid growth along the M27 which links Southampton and Bournemouth along the south coast. This growth is driven by market forces as private investors and businesses seek the greatest profit-generating locations. The government's role is essentially that of attempting to control this growth, so as to preserve something of the rural environment and prevent the corridor from becoming an almost continuously built up area.

In areas where the economy is stagnating, a decay of settlement and the spread of dereliction as factories close, governments may provide funding and support to promote a corridor of growth. This is already evident in South Wales along the M4 from Newport to Swansea and on a smaller scale, in the

Lower Don valley between Sheffield and Rotherham, which is being redeveloped by a designated Urban Development Corporation. Recently the government has promoted a counter growth corridor to the M4 corridor west of London. Consequently, an East Thames growth corridor is being planned, extending from London Docklands eastwards either side of the Thames. It is hoped that this will revive areas along the Thames which have declined with the closure of the older dock area and the processing industries dependent on the port. The opening of the Cross Channel tunnel improved trade and links with the continent and, it is felt, will help provide self-sustained growth once the East Thames corridor has been established.

Dispersion and new towns in the developing world

Although for some time decentralisation policies have been adopted in the Western world, reinforcing the spontaneous de-urbanisation which has also occurred, it is only really since the 1970s that such policies have been widely adopted in the developing world. Planned suburban dispersion, dormitory growth and new towns are characteristics of most developing countries. Botswana, like a number of African and other countries, has planned and developed a new capital city (Case study 16.3). These new cities are largely designed to take pressure off existing metropolitan areas and to promote alternative growth poles to provide for a more balanced distribution of population and economic development across the country. In Botswana, until the 1960s there was no urban system, since the country was sparsely populated and largely dependent on pastoralism. Gabarone is one of a number of new towns established to form the basis for more diversified economic development and modernisation.

In contrast, South Korea is one of a number of newly industrialising countries in south-east Asia with an already well developed urban system which is rapidly advancing to the stage of economic maturity. A major programme of planned dispersion of further growth away from Seoul, the capital, has been undertaken by establishing a series of new towns at some distance away from Seoul, as well as promoting growth in established settlements along the growth corridors.

South Korea, like other developing countries, such as Brazil and India, is taking on decentralisation policies similar to those adopted earlier in developed countries. However, developing countries may run into the same problems with continued expansion of the primate city due to self-sustained growth through natural increase amongst the population already resident. There is also the likely problem of siting future growth too close to the capital, as with the first new towns built around London. Thus urban sprawl could continue. There is evidence in the developing countries that greenbelt restrictions placed on large cities to prevent further development have been overtaken by other events, with the city continuing to sprawl and take up much of the greenbelt areas.

Concluding comment

With time the shape and nature of cities have changed in response to the needs of society. These changes have been on the one hand conditioned by the existing form of the city and on the other hand, by the opportunities and constraints of the available technologies and prevailing planning controls. Within established cities the influence of the past is still prominent despite redevelopment and recent outward growth. The more dispersed form of future urban landscapes is already becoming evident in the new towns and other planned settlements taking shape in the countryside beyond, both in developed and developing countries.

case study

16.1 The UK: changing government policy in relation to the form of cities

Phase 1 – 1946 to 1967: the provision of housing

- **The government was faced with a serious housing shortage following the Second World War** and the decay of inner city areas, along with bombed sites which needed redevelopment.
- **The proposed solution was:**
  - **a** clearance and rebuilding in inner city areas mainly of council housing and high rise blocks
  - **b** new council estates on the edge of cities
  - **c** transfer of many households to new towns and expanded towns.
- **The policies under the main Comprehensive Development Area Act (1947) and The New Towns Act (1946) and Expanded Towns Scheme (1952) have been of only limited success as:**
  - **a** serious housing shortages remained
  - **b** too little regard was given to social and employment provision
  - **c** communities were uprooted and disrupted.

Phase 2 – 1967 to 1977: greater emphasis on social and economic provision and on refurbishment rather than wholesale redevelopment of older inner areas

- **New and Expanded Towns policies continued** but much more emphasis was given to social amenity provision and encouraging industry and businesses to replace to provide more jobs.

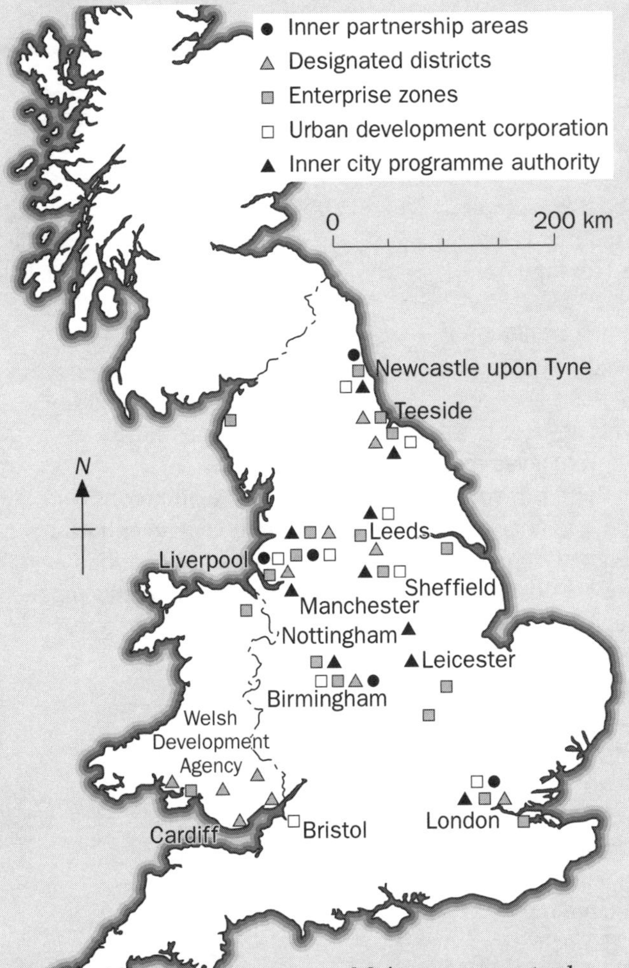

Main government urban initiatives 1977 - 1990, England and Wales

New towns in England

In respect of inner areas, the emphasis was on grant provision to enable local authorities, private landlords and owner occupiers to improve their properties and add basic amenities rather than demolish old properties. Local authorities were also given grants to improve the local environment. This was mainly done by designating small inner areas as General Improvement Areas (GIAs, 1969) and by defining Housing Action Areas (HAAs, 1974) where need was especially urgent.

- **Problems remained in the outer post-war estates and the New and Expanded Towns** as insufficient funding was provided and physical defects also became apparent.

  In the inner areas the schemes were too small and funding limited. Gentrification was encouraged since higher income individuals and bought old properties cheaply, receiving considerable grant aid to refurbish them. This deprived the poor of some much-needed housing.

  The Comprehensive Community Action Programme to coordinate service provision made only limited progress.

Phase 3 – 1977 to 1990: away from new town initiatives towards more comprehensive programmes for older inner areas and refurbishment of run-down post-war housing areas

- **The Policy for Inner City** White Paper saw the inner areas as problem regions and emphasised combined environmental, social and economic programmes. The key role was given to economic investment and economic revival which would prompt new physical redevelopment and upgrading, including the provision of housing. Public investment in New Towns was to be wound down and any further development left largely to private investment but with some government encouragement.
- **The Development of the Environment was given the co-ordinating role to produce whole inner city Enhanced Urban Programmes:**

a Under the Inner Urban Areas Act 1978 the government undertook Inner City partnership with local authorities and voluntary organisations to redevelop inner areas and granted more funding. This was taken up by London Dockland authorities, Salford and Newcastle, for example. 'Designated districts' were also identified for funding under the Act.

Industrial Improvement Areas were designated for public funding to improve basic services and the physical environment, so attracting private investment which would receive tax- and rate-saving concessions.

b Urban Development Corporations were designated government sponsored agencies in 1981 to take over and regenerate whole tracts of derelict land, especially associated with old industrial and dockside areas which had declined. The first were created for London Docklands and Merseyside and later, others were added e.g. Trafford Park (Manchester) and the Don Valley (Sheffield).

c **Other measures were designed to promote private initiatives** on a smaller scale by reducing financial costs and easing administrative controls for private developers.

i Enterprise zones were created since 1980 in the inner city and in other areas which needed new commercial and industrial investment e.g. Telford and North West Kent.

ii In 1986 Inner City Initiatives was launched to create Task Forces to deal with selected small areas with acute unemployment and social problems as at Toxteth-Ganby (Liverpool), a scene of rioting and ethnic conflict. The aim was to try out new approaches to resuscitate these areas.

iii These initiatives were allied to a New City Grant scheme to foster redevelopment and refurbishment of individual sites.

- **There was considerable success in regenerating areas** but the number of jobs created was limited.
- **The Central Government increasingly took over initiatives from local authorities** thus alienating them and reducing the input of local experience and expertise.

Phase 4 – 1990 to the Present - Policies in Place continued but a Return to Partnership with Local Authorities along with the Private Sector - increasing emphasis on entrepreneurship, limited 'pump priming' funding and efficient generation of private investment.

- **In 1991 the City Challenge** Scheme was created to encourage local authorities to compete for funding for regeneration projects. Money was available on the basis of the comparative merit of schemes offered and evidence of a clear link with private enterprise initiatives, as for example in the successful bid to improve the west end of Newcastle.
- **The 'Heartland of Birmingham'** project was not accepted under the City Challenge Scheme but has been given Urban Development Corporation status for funding.
- Though New Town Development Corporations have been wound down, **the Commission for New Towns will continue** for another ten years to finalise the scale and transfer of remaining assets to the private sector. Apart from a suggested East Thames Growth corridor initiative, the government is to leave any new settlement development to the private sector. However, with increased concern for the environment and with past evidence of diversion of growth and people from the established older conurbations, new settlement schemes will be strictly controlled and limited.
- **The whole urban programme is to be brought under one government agency** – The Urban Regeneration Agency' – as urban redevelopment and renewal in the past has suffered from an uncoordinated and piecemeal approach.
- Despite significant financial input from European Regional Development funding and other aid from the European Union policies, the biggest weakness remains that of too little funding for urban redevelopment and renewal. The recent economic recession has highlighted even more starkly how governments continue to fail to meet the needs of the lower income sector of society.

case study

16.2 Paris: refurbishment, renewal, redevelopment and conservation

Aim

Paris was to be renewed to maintain its status and prestige as the national capital and cultural centre for Europe and possibly the future 'capital' of Europe. The most marked change occurred in the south and east. It redressed the balance between the east and west but benefited the better off and displaced the poorer population further out.

Need

- Decaying and unfit buildings from earlier morphological periods on high priced land could be redeveloped for higher economic returns.
- There is continued pressure for space in Paris as the country's route focus, political and administrative capital, and commercial heart of France. However, the needs are changing, with increased emphasis on service and leisure provision.
- To support government policies to divert commercial growth from the west to the east of central Paris.
- The technological change in transport and design makes established buildings and areas to some extent obsolete.

Management of change

Management takes place by a combination of private and public enterprise and investment, within the framework and constraints of the 1967 and 1976 Structure Plans for Paris and conservation measures instituted under the Loi Malraux of 1962.

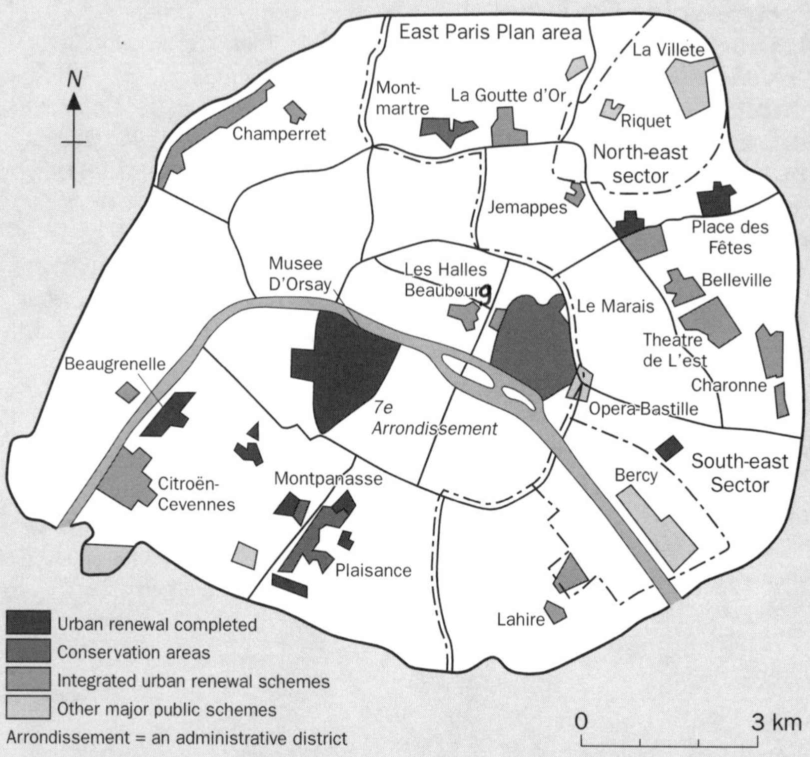

Location of redevelopment, renewal and conservation schemes

Redevelopment and renewal

General

Large-scale redevelopment has taken place in the south and east and is still in progress in much of the east and north.

Mixed development

Mixed redevelopment and renewal, especially of Les Halles, has taken place. Les Halles is a site of a mid-nineteenth century wholesale market, covering a 32 ha. It is also a lively noisy quarter for small businesses and traders, all night cafes and brothels sited in narrow streets with rundown tenement blocks.

There was much controversy as to how to redevelop the site, which was finally cleared in 1971. Part of it was redeveloped with a new Metro underground station as a major interchange between metro systems. Another area was redeveloped as The Forum, a major underground shopping centre on four levels, which attracted shoppers and tourists, groups of youths, migrant workers and the homeless. Above ground redevelopment included green open space, an international hotel and concert hall, some of the site has been residentially redeveloped. Nearby is the Hologe district with 750 dwelling units which have not been cleared but refurbished and upgraded.

However, only a third of the original residents can afford to reoccupy the area; the remainder have been re-housed further out of Paris. As in the London Docklands redevelopment lower income locals have been displaced by more wealthy incomers.

Non-residential schemes

Culture schemes

The Beaubourg Arts Centre is a popular culture and arts centre built in 1977 on the site of old tenement blocks which had been demolished in the 1930s.

The Gare-D'Orsay Impressionist Museum opened in 1987 in the old railway station.

In 1990, a third opera house was built at Bastille, replacing an area of rundown housing.

Mixed use

A leisure, entertainment and educational (science and music) complex with a large green park is located on an old abbatoir site.

Large-scale development of offices and commercial buildings in the outer arrondissements are on sites of demolished factories and commercial buildings, for example, as at Montparnasse and Gare du Lyon where the government built a new Ministry of Finance headquarters, partly to encourage private industry and commercial investment in the area.

New growth poles were designated at Bercy in the south-east and La Villette in the north-east to direct growth from the central area and promote corridors of growth out into the suburbs.

Residential development

Almost a quarter of the housing in the City of Paris has been redeveloped or refurbished since 1968.

During the 1970s – 80s, large-scale residential redevelopment took place in the southern sector, consisting mainly of new apartment blocks, much of them to serve the needs of employees of nearby new commercial developments as at Montparnasse.

In the east there has been extensive slum clearance and replacement by local authority apartment developments, for example, the tower blocks at Place de Fetes and Belleville where nineteenth century housing occupied by African immigrant labour was cleared and replaced by medium-rise public housing in landscaped grouds.

Recent more sensitive redevelopment has taken place in the east for mixed social housing plus some upgrading and gentrification of smaller units.

The least development has taken place in the west where the residences are already of higher quality.

Conservation constraints and conservation areas

- The seventh Arrondissement on the left bank has many public buildings and fashionable shopping streets.
- Marais was drained and developed in the fifteenth and sixteenth centuries by the nobility and clergy, who built imposing mansions and public buildings. The buildings eventually decayed and were later subdivided as an artisan craft area. The mansions have now been restored and the houses and hotels refurbished. High gentrification had taken place, making Marais one of the most sought after residential locations in Paris.
- Montmartre is an old hill village centre, containing a jumble of streets, Sacré Coeur cathedral and the bohemian quarter. It is retained mainly as a tourist attraction.

case study

16.3 Milton Keynes: the last of the second generation of new towns in the UK

Milton Keynes was established as a counter-magnet growth town to London in a pleasant, well-located environment, providing a mixture of housing, services and employment opportunity. Once established, it was hoped that it would generate self-sustained growth with an inflow of private investment.

Structure

Commissioned in 1967 Milton Keynes was to be built around and incorporate three existing small towns, including Bletchley and 13 villages in Buckinghamshire. One hour's drive from London it is centrally placed in the national transport network.

It covered 18 000 acres of land under the Milton Keynes Development Corporation which, with over £2 billion of government finance, has over 25 years laid out the city on an American-type open road grid and within each grid planner for a balanced mix of housing, retail, social and leisure amenities. The road grid network was lined with a pedestrian and cycle network of 'Redways' to separate it from car traffic and allow easy connections across the town.

The Corporation initially provided housing, commercial buildings and amenities but the intention was to let or sell premises and land to private developers. The area was well provided with open spaces, parks, lake and waterways and 13 million trees and shrubs.

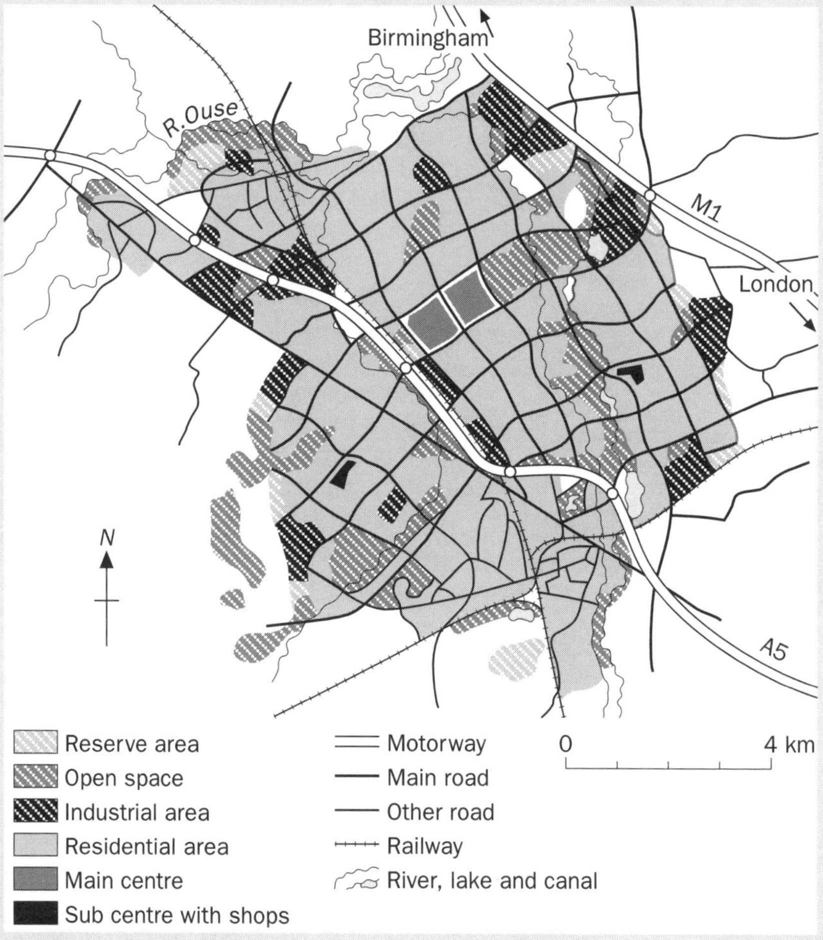

Planned layout

Success of Milton Keynes

Residential success

The town had grown from an initial population of 40 000 to 155 000 by 1994 and has land left to house another 50 000. One third of the population today have moved from London; the area now attracts people from surrounding regions and from abroad as foreign companies have invested in it.

In response to a survey, 75% of residents indicated their satisfaction with their way of life and prospects in Milton Keynes:

'I came here fourteen years ago because housing was cheap and there was work. I would never go back to Southall (London). This is marvellous for the kids.'

Manual worker

'I am very happy with the lifestyle here. I live in a village in the country but am in the office in ten minutes. I can always park. I can drive to Heathrow (airport) in one hour and also door to door to London in one hour.'

Office manager

Business success

Having attracted a good balance of business investment, Milton Keynes survived the recent economic recession better than most large cities, with unemployment at 7% (1992) below the national average. Up to 1992 companies had invested an estimated £3 billion in Milton Keynes locations.

There are over 2500 companies in the town, mainly employing each less than 100 employees. The largest is the Abbey National Building Society with 3500 employees. About 200 of the companies are foreign. Overall, 21% of the employment is in manufacturing, the remainder is services and finance, for example, Argos mail order and, Volkswagen national distribution centre.

Half the foreign companies are American, including Unisys which provides network information and servicing systems marketed over Europe. One-quarter are Japanese, including Alps Electrics which produces electrical mechanical components for Sony and Panasonic. Alps chose Milton Keynes out of a range of possible locations across Europe.

Reasons for Milton Keynes as a business location

- it is centrally placed to serve the UK and Europe, being relatively close to Heathrow and Luton airports and central to the motorway network
- it has plentiful land at reasonable prices, lower than London or Birmingham
- it has a good mixture of relatively cheap housing
- it is located in a pleasant open environment attractive to workers and with a good provision of amenities
- there is ease of movement around Milton Keynes – average car speed in London equals 10mph but in Milton Keynes the average is 40 mph.

A city of enterprise

Although it is in a pleasant rural environment, Milton Keynes has encouraged and attracted technological advances. It has the largest urban cable television network in the country, spearheads energy efficient homes and commercial building and has a 600-acre ' energy park' with the largest energy saving houses and offices. It is the site of the new National Energy Centre, Odyssey, with an exhibition hall and an 'energy-saving theme park'.

Milton Keynes hosts the largest Open University in the world which has been a pioneer in distance learning for mature students. It is now also a leading institution in business management and overseas ventures. The town also serves De Montfort University's pioneering Computer Campus, together with other applied courses.

Although Milton Keynes has excellent sports provision, its centre lacks sufficient cultural entertainment provision, but it is expanding as a retail centre. There are plans to expand cultural facilities.

case study

16.4 Gaborone: a new town and new capital for Botswana

A country of new towns

All Botswana's cities are new towns. Before independence in 1966 the largest settlements were villages of around 10 000 people. Gaborone was planned as the new administrative centre and capital. Since 1970 other new towns have been built, the most recent being Maun in the north-west of the country.

Location

Gaborone is in the south-east, on the main strategic north to south route through the country from Zimbabwe and Zambia to South Africa. This route runs through the eastern strip of the country which contains 70% of the population. Much of the remainder of the country is desert or swamp.

Site

It was sited adjacent to the old village settlement of Gaborone on level dry land and next to the River Natwani to provide a water supply.

Too successful

Originally planned for 20 000 people and laid out with allocated sites for government offices and commercial activities, economic development and urbanisation have been so rapid that a revised plan had to be drafted to allow for a population of 92 000. Already by 1992 the population had expanded to 138 000, leading to extensive squatter settlements on land not yet developed.

Botswana's increasing international importance

Originally the economy was based on pastoralism but since the 1980s the economy has boomed with the exploitation of its mineral wealth, especially diamonds, nickel, copper and manganese. Tourism is also being expanded. As a result, the transport network and international links are being upgraded, including a new international airport at Gaborone. Gaborone is consequently gaining in importance as a centre for commerce, with consumer and other industries being introduced.

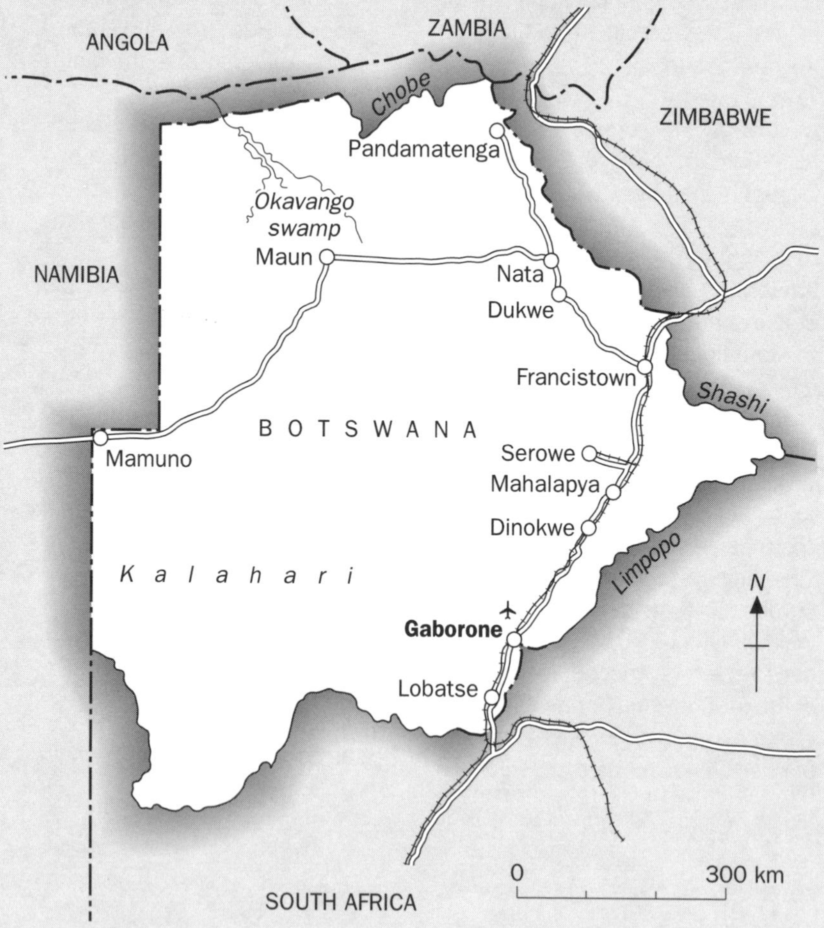

Location of Gabarone

CHAPTER 17

Manufacturing and industry

'Manufacturing has always been a necessary human activity ever since the first fashioning of a plough or spear from the branch of a tree.'

DAVID M SMITH

17.1 The manufacturing process: industrialisation

Industry as a term, besides referring to manufacturing, can also be used to refer to other economic activities, such as mining, construction and public utilities, including gas and electricity supplies. ***Here manufacturing industry is discussed, that is, the making of a product under factory conditions. Various inputs (factors of production) such as raw materials, power, labour and capital are brought together in the production process from which there emerges an output – the product*** (Figure 17.1).

Frequently the output of one manufacturing industry becomes one of the raw materials of another. Steel, for example, is used to make car bodies and is therefore one of the inputs needed by the automobile industry. The market for many industries is another industry and only certain manufacturing firms, such as those concerned with food processing and furniture making, sell directly to the public. Such industries are referred to as consumer industries.

It is usual to divide manufacturing into heavy and light industry, consumer manufacturing being part of the latter. This simple division is to some

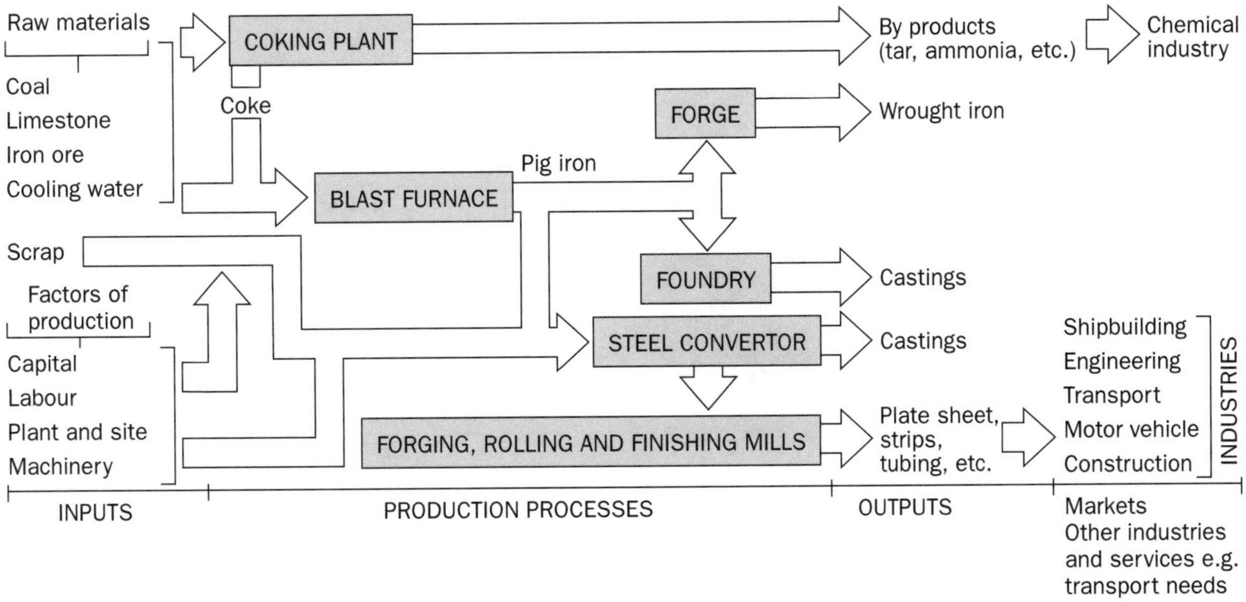

Figure 17.1 Simplified production flow for iron and steel

extent based on the weight of inputs and output but also involves the notion of heavy industry as the basic manufacturing sector upon which many lighter industries depend. Consequently, countries which try to industrialise have given special attention to the development of a heavy industrial sector, even when only a few natural advantages of raw materials and power resources, for example, were available and the capital investment needed was in short supply. Once underway, further industrialisation led to development of a variety of lighter industries in response to both the needs of already established industries and the demand for goods by an increasingly affluent population. Other factors too played their part, such as the acquiring of entrepreneurial skill, investment capital and an improvement in infrastructure facilities.

The main features associated with this industrialisation process are shown in Figure 17.2. The principal feature of the locational pattern which arises from it is the concentration of most of the manufacturing into a few locations as, for example, in the case of India which has undergone rapid industrialisation since the 1950s (Case study 17.2).

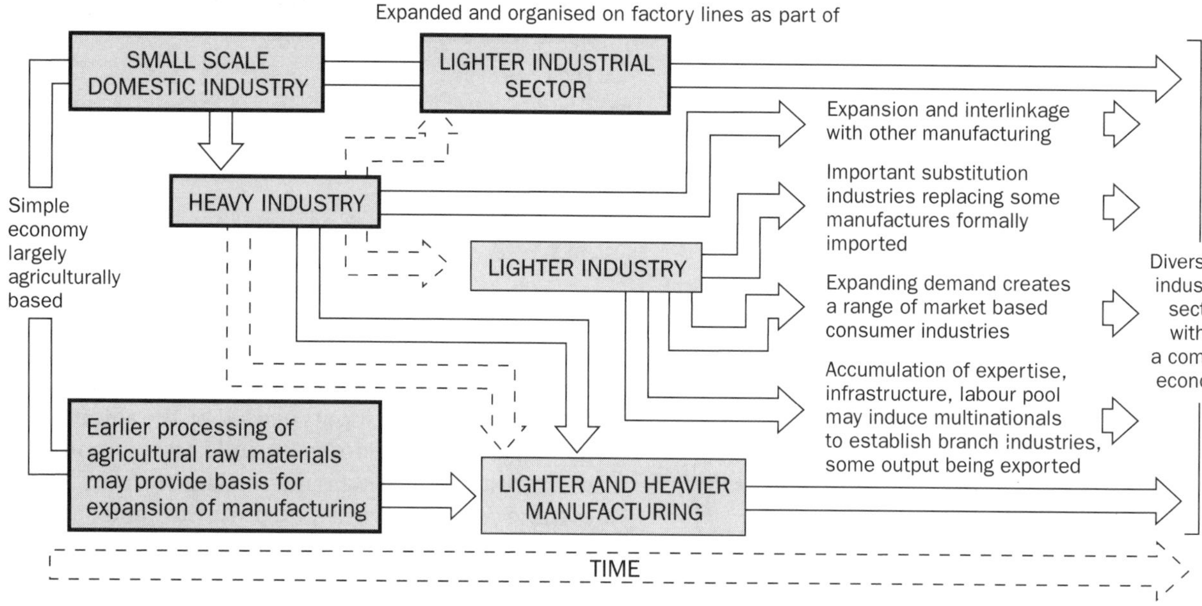

Figure 17.2 Industrialisation in a developing country

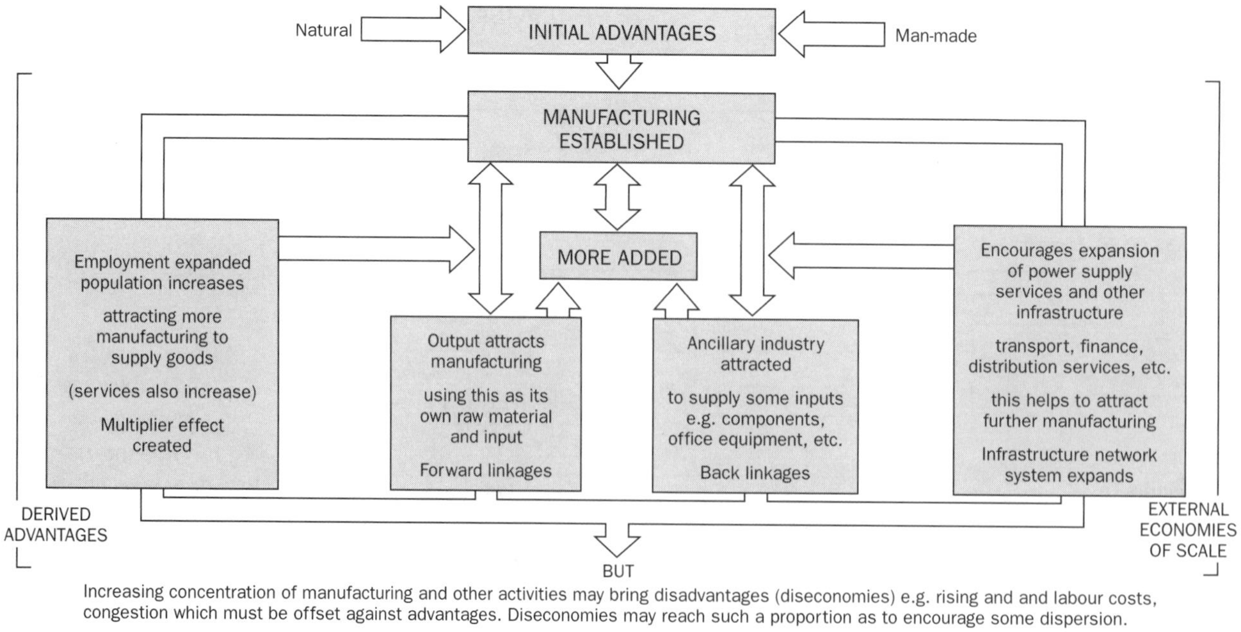

Figure 17.3 The cumulative causation process leading to the growth of manufacturing and other economic activities at a location

The cumulative causation process: concepts and mechanisms associated with it

Agglomeration
Agglomeration is the clustering together and association of economic activities in close proximity to one another. Such agglomeration can lead to associated firms and businesses enjoying benefits of external economies of scale, since agglomeration encourages expansion and improvements in the infrastructure and provision of services in that location. Agglomeration also facilitates beneficial linkages between the associated activities.

External economies of scale
These are cost advantages arising from sources outside the firm or business as a result of characteristics and attributes of the particular location. These could include access to an already available skilled labour supply, availability of ancillary industries and services which are needed and an efficient transport network. Such provisions in effect enable a firm to save on costs because it does not have to lay out some of its own capital to provide them.

Internal economies of scale
The cumulative causation process may well increase the profitability of a firm in a location and encourage it or its head office to expand production through increasing the scale of the firm's operations or investing in more efficient production methods which decrease unit costs (that is, reduce the cost of each unit of production). For example, the cost of research and design which is a fixed cost could be spread among more units of production thus reducing the cost per unit. Adoption of assembly line methods may also reduce unit costs as mass production takes place.

Linkages
These are contacts and flows of information and materials between firms which can occur more easily and cheaply where the firms are in close proximity. Three kinds of linkages are generally recognised:

- Backward linkages – from one firm to other firms which supply it with raw materials, components, goods and services needed in its production processes and activities.
- Forward linkages – with its customers which take its products or services.
- Sideways or horizontal linkages – with other firms involved in the same processes or production e.g. collaboration with other firms on research, exchange of information or marketing of products.

Multiplier
In a multiplier, the setting up of an activity in a location directly or indirectly triggers off additional economic activities and further employment is generated. These activities can be directly related to economic activity initially set up or may also include the provision of services and products to the employees and their households. Sometimes firms may also be attracted by the pool of female labour created by households which move into an area.

17.2 Complex locational influences which affect concentrations of industry

Manufacturing tends to occur as concentrations in particular locations as the industrialisation process of a country progresses (Case study 17.2). Although present patterns of manufacturing do indicate some tendency to dispersion, this is still towards particular locations producing, in effect, new forms of concentration, such as science parks and axial bands of industry along major routeways. Thus both the older established concentrations and the newer ones which occur beyond the major industrial conurbations are characterised by agglomerative tendencies (Case studies 15.1 and 15.3).

Agglomeration of manufacturing is primarily associated with the process of cumulative causation (Figure 17.3). The expansion or decline of any industrial concentration is also influenced by a whole range of wider forces operating at both the national and international level, and interlinking with any cumulative causation process (Figure 17.4 and Case studies 17.1 and 17.2). To account for concentration of industry, the explanatory framework must thus be broadened to include the more localised forces of cumulative causation and also these wider national and international influences. These wider influences are becoming increasingly important as large multinational corporations make locational decisions within an international context.

The cumulative causation process: features and mechanisms

A number of writers, including Myrdal, have identified a kind of cumulative process to answer why manufacturing along with other economic activity is mainly concentrated in a few growth centres in a country (Figures 3.4, 17.3 and Case study 17.1). (While the positive operation of the cumulative causation process will lead to further growth, there is also ample evidence from the decline of older industrial centres in advanced

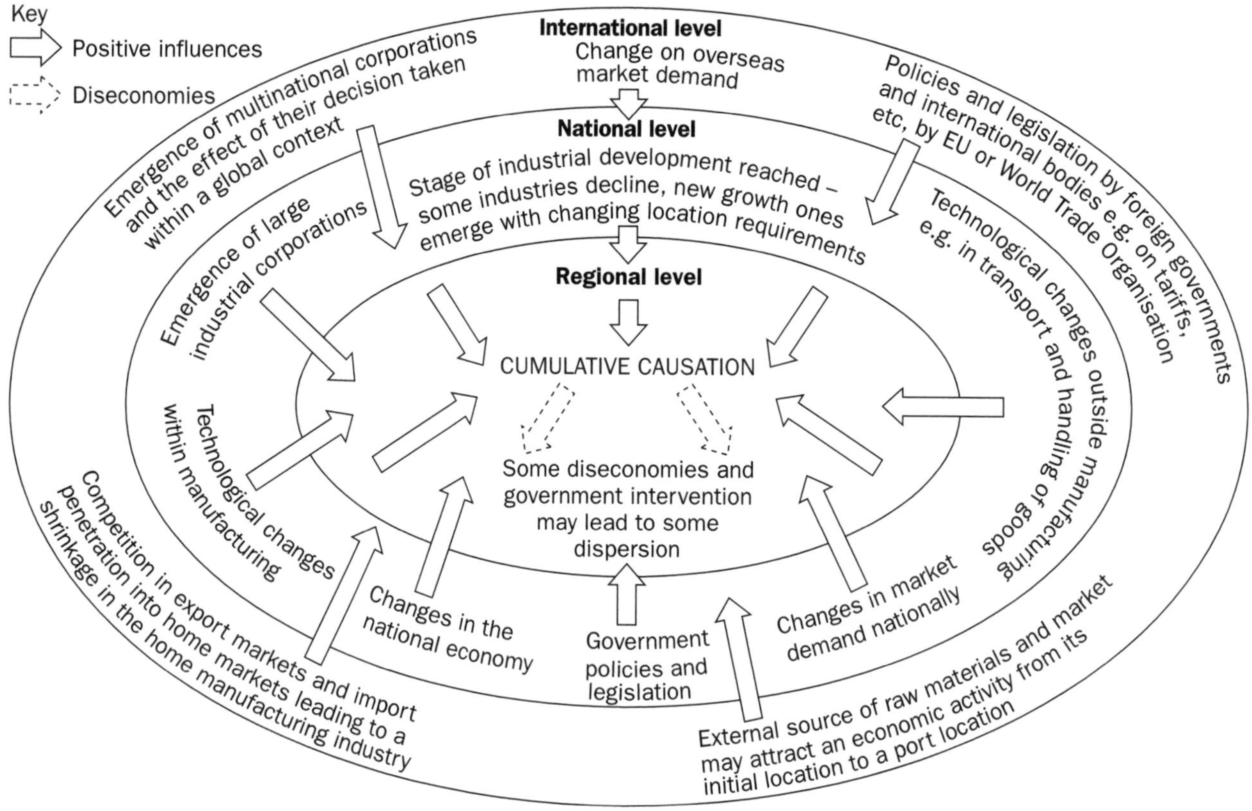

Figure 17.4 Cumulative causation and other influences on manufacturing outlined in this chapter

countries that the process, reinforced by wider influences unfavourable to growth in those centres, can operate in reverse, leading to deindustrialisation and decline.) ***The cumulative causation process is seen as three stages***:

- ***Initial advantages*** possessed by that location which attracts manufacturing to it. These could be both natural and man-made advantages. For example, raw materials such as coal and iron ore may be present, or the location could be favourable, such as a coastal region with sea access, or the centre may already be established as an important commercial and administrative centre at a focus of routes.
- ***A second stage*** of rapid manufacturing growth when derived advantages flowing from the earlier concentration of manufacturing reinforce initial advantages and lead to a multiplier effect.
- ***A final stage*** may be reached in which so much concentration has occurred that problems arise, leading to some dispersion of manufacturing to the periphery of the region or further afield. As indicated above, it may also be due to changes in external circumstances which work against a particular manufacturing centre.

Over-concentration of manufacturing

If growth continues over-concentration can occur, leading to what are called ***diseconomies***. These not only raise the cost of manufacturing but they also involve a social cost to the community which may require considerable public expenditure if the situation is to be ameliorated (Figure 17.5).

All large concentrations of manufacturing experience diseconomies. However, the point at which this leads to some dispersion of industry depends on the extent to which economies of scale savings are eroded away. There is a point at which an alternative site is looked for, but some firms do remain in a location for a length of time after this point has been reached. This is the result of an ***inertia*** factor at work; plant owners do not want to write off the capital they have invested in building plant and machinery on the old site, nor may they wish to leave the pool of skilled labour that has been acquired over a long period of time.

However, much of the dispersal of industry which has occurred has been over a short distance so that firms have been able to shed the effects of diseconomies and yet retain some of the benefits of close proximity to the established growth centre. However, the actions of multinational corporations which control much of industry today and those of government have also led to dispersion of operations further afield.

Figure 17.5 *Over concentration leads to diseconomies of scale and increasing costs*

17.3 The role of multinational corporations

Changes have been taking place within the organisation of manufacturing which greatly affect its distribution pattern. Despite the continued existence of many small-scale industries, most modern manufacturing, whether expressed by value or volume of output, is under the control of large corporations. Such corporations, many of which are multinational, control a range of manufacturing and have branch plants in the parent country and abroad.

There are at present about 37 000 multinational companies with 170 000 affiliated concerns across the world. However, 1% of these own half the total investment made in the world. They exercise a great influence on the world economy. Dicken indicates that multinational corporations are the most important single force creating global shifts in economic activity through their locational decision-making.

For example, almost half of Canada's manufacturing employment is in foreign-owned plants, particularly those owned by large corporations with headquarters in the USA. In India, much of the investment expansion of industry comes from foreign investment, including link-ups with domestic firms and branch plants as, for example, in the Japanese link-ups to expand the motor cycle and motor vehicle industry.

Another way of expressing the worldwide spread of multinational corporations is to show the location patterns of a particular industry. The Japanese Matsushita Electrical Industrial Company Ltd, which trades under the brand names of National Panasonic, Technics and Quasar, produce a wide range of products in consumer electronics, industrial equipment, business machines, home appliances, lighting equipment, systems, products, electrical components, motors and batteries. It has branches all over the world. In all, there are around 110 manufacturing departments in different parts of Japan, employing 107 000 people and 39 manufacturing companies overseas employing another 33 000. In 1990 its total sales was valued at $US 47.5 billion, of which $20.7 billion was foreign sales (Figure 17.6).

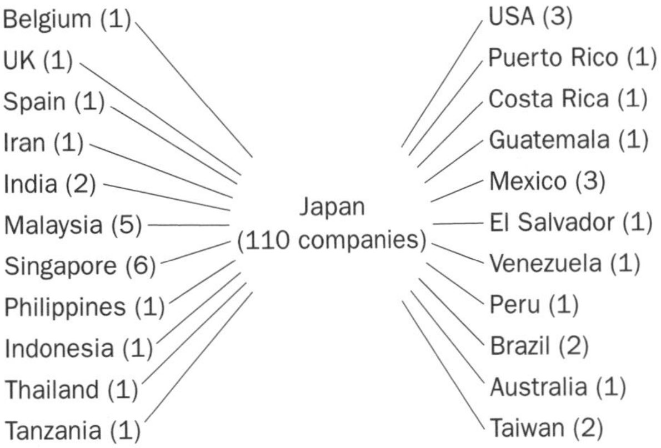

Figure 17.6 *Branches of the Matsushita electronic corporation*

Manufacturing on a large scale under corporate ownership can be seen as a further development of a process begun during the Industrial Revolution. With advances in technology much larger capital investment in specialised machinery and plants have been required, together with highly organised research, sales and administration, catering for world as well as home markets. Only large companies and corporations have the capital and expertise to make many of the types of products on the scale which present market demands require.

By operating on such a large scale these corporations can achieve important ***internal economies of scale, leading to a decrease in the average cost per unit of output as the quantity of output or volume increases.*** Average costs tend to decrease with an increase in the scale of operations.

The general reasons why this occurs are related to four important cost components: specialisation, discount on bulk purchase of raw materials, vertical integration which links all processes together on a production line and the possibility of standardisation. For example, in a small firm one person may have to do several jobs, but in a large firm one person can specialise in a job and thereby be that much more efficient and produce more output per hour than the non-specialist who has to spend time moving from one job to another.

The decisions of large corporations involved with locating branch plants will be different from those of an individual small firm. For one thing, larger factories mean larger sites, access to more raw materials and more infrastructure. While large corporations may have the capital to develop industry in new locations, it is usually more economic to locate within or near the established large centre which can provide the necessary infrastructure linkages, size of labour and other requirements. There have been instances, however, where a corporation has set up a new growth centre particularly when tapping a mineral source or locating on a new deep water coastal site, as in the case of multinational oil corporations. Whether at an established or new centre, the location of branch plants by multinational corporations will attract further growth, contributing to the cumulative causation process. For example, the growth of Aberdeen as a result of North Sea oil operations has brought with it further expansion from support companies being set up, service backup and other infrastructure developments. However, more recently as the oil production has levelled out, the multiplier has to some extent operated in reverse.

The scale of operations undertaken by multinational corporations also has other implications for the location of industry. Whereas the board of a single firm can consider a location solely on the needs of the one plant, the board of a multinational corporation, when setting up a branch plant or contemplating closing one down, must consider it in the context of the corporation's whole operations.

Multinational corporation

This is a large business organisation which operates in a number of countries. About 60% are concerned largely with manufacturing and the remainder mainly with services, such as insurance and banking. Most have their headquarters in the advanced industrial countries, mainly in the USA, the UK and Japan. The number of multinationals centred on the newly industrialised countries is increasing e.g. in South Korea, Taiwan and Malaysia. Most multinationals, though noted for a particular type of product or service, are concerned with a range of activities. (The term ***Transnational Corporation*** is sometimes used as an alternative term of Multinational Corporation.)

It is also quite common for a multinational corporation to shut down a plant in an established area even though that plant might be making a profit, and open up a branch plant elsewhere where better proximity to the market and lower labour costs ensure greater profits. Examples include the Ford Motor Corporation reducing its capacity in the USA and the UK and opening up new factories in the cheaper production areas of Spain and Brazil.

17.4 The influence of governments and supranational public bodies

National governments

During the post-war years governments have been preoccupied with two major concerns in relation to manufacturing. One was to do with the problems arising from over-expansion and concentration in new industrial areas and the decline of older ones. The other was to ensure the build up of certain basic and strategic industries, such as iron and steel and chemicals. More recently governments have been also concerned about establishing a sound base in information and technology related industries, as these are seen as vital to the success of the economy as a whole (Chapter 19).

Regional industrial policy in the UK

In the UK the first comprehensive attempt to tackle the problem of over-expanding and declining regions stemmed from the Royal Commission into the Distribution of Industrial Population and the associated Barlow Report in 1940. The report linked the loss of jobs between the wars in old industrial areas, such as the north-east and south Wales, to the over-concentration of job opportunities in the South East and Midlands, both of which had attracted the new market orientated growth industries in the economy, such as the motor vehicle industry and electrical engineering. Under the Distribution of Industry Act of 1945 which followed the Barlow Report, older depressed industrial areas which had already been granted special area status during the 1930s were given further assistance as Development Areas. Loans, grants and tax concessions were made to industries willing to locate there. Perhaps the most significant action by the government was the decision that all planned industrial development in excess of 5000 square feet would require an Industrial Development Certificate (IDC). The government could therefore withhold an IDC to prevent expansion in a growth area where there was already too much industry and thereby direct industry into depressed or marginal areas which required more employment opportunities and a more balanced economic base.

In practice, the large business corporations, such as ICI and Ford, frequently made a compromise agreement and accepted some direction to development areas in exchange for being allowed some modest expansion in the more prosperous regions of the South East and the Midlands. The Ford Motor Company, for example, based in England at Dagenham in Essex, agreed to open a new assembly plant in the North West at Ellesmere near Liverpool, and in return was allowed to expand operations at its main Dagenham plant.

The use of assisted area status and other regional policy initiatives has changed over the last two decades. In the 1980s under the Thatcher Conservative government, a regional policy was less evident since a free market approach to the economy was favoured and the economy itself was buoyant enough to favour most manufacturing locations. However, so severe has been the recent recession from 1980 to 1993, that the Major government has adopted a number of regional and other policy initiatives not only to help old industrial areas but also the most severely affected areas of hitherto prosperous regions, such as the Midlands and the South East. For example, in 1993 two areas of London, the Isle of Wight and the Isle of Thanet in Kent, have been given assisted area status (Figure 17.7).

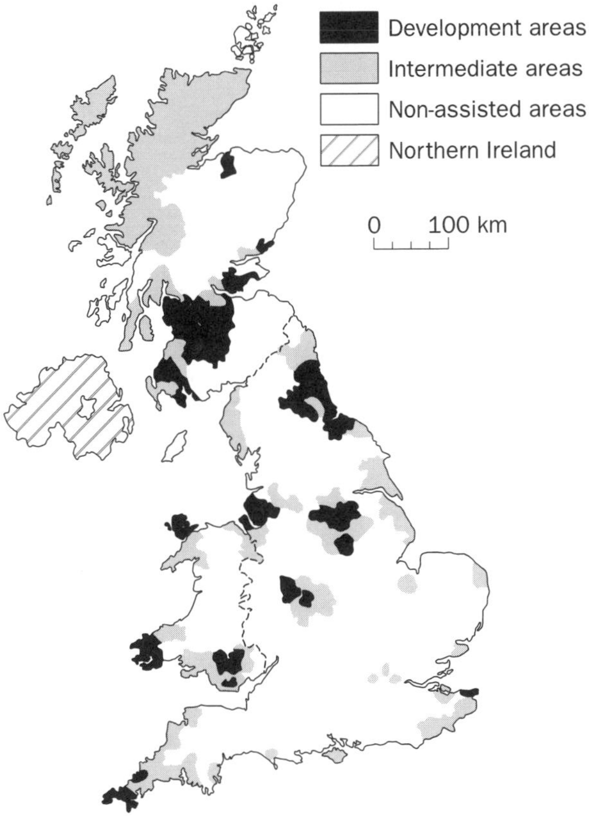

Figure 17.7 *Regional policy in Britain: assisted areas July 1993*

There are also a whole range of other government actions which influence the location of manufacturing and other economic activity. The Welsh and Scottish Development Agencies have for example achieved considerable success in attracting foreign investment and branch plants to their respective regions. Major infrastructure investment in new roads has been significant. A range of new initiatives have also been adopted to help regenerate and attract some new manufacturing to 'run down' areas, in particular inner city and dockside areas (Chapter 15).

Ensuring a secure manufacturing base for the country

Most governments have in the past taken certain vital industrial sectors into public ownership in order to obtain a measure of control over them (Case study 19.1).

In the UK most of the iron and steel industry was nationalised and the government had a significant stake in the shipbuilding, aerospace and motor vehicle industries. However, over the last decade the iron and steel industry has been privatised and government investment in other industries much reduced, as has also occurred in a number of other countries, particularly recently in eastern Europe. Even so, governments still exercise a significant direct influence on vital industries should they wish to exercise it. This influence has recently been most keenly felt in government decisions not to rescue ailing manufacturing plants, as in the British government's decision not to help keep open the Swan and Hunter shipyard on Tyneside nor the Ravenscraig steel plant in Scotland. These industries had been initially located under the government's former policy to locate new plants to help arrest industrial decline in old industrial areas.

Supranational bodies

Regional blocs

National economies and particular economic activities are now increasingly affected by the policies and actions of regional blocs (Chapter 32), such as the widening European Union (EU), the Asia Pacific Economic Co-operation (APEC) group of countries and the North American Free Trade Agreement

(NAFTA) group of Canada, the USA and Mexico. Increasing co-operation and liberalisation of trade within these groups widens the choice of locations for firms wanting to set up within the region as in the case of the multinational group Samsung setting up production complexes to tap the European and North American markets (Case study 17.3).

In the case of the EU, policies related to manufacturing activities have through recent years become increasingly interventionist both in terms of protecting European companies from outside competition, using import quotas and tariffs, and by regulating the output of key industries within the EU. For example, output from iron and steel plants is strictly controlled. This has been a factor in the closure of uneconomic plants such as Ravenscraig in Scotland and has inhibited the setting up of new plants by more efficient producers.

The EU has also a positive influence on economic activity through the provision of Regional Development Fund grants and loans from the European Investment Bank to encourage the setting up of new plants in areas needing regeneration, such as the Ruhr in Germany, where assistance has been granted to the Emscher Valley Park scheme to attract science and technology based industries together with service activities.

With the creation of the Single Market in 1993 for the EU, it is anticipated that manufacturing corporations will be encouraged to rationalise their activities into fewer and larger plants to take advantage of economies of scale, so reducing costs and increasing their competitiveness. More rapid dissemination of research and development findings is also envisaged and this too will have consequences for the choice of manufacturing locations as companies modernise existing manufacturing activities and introduce new products.

International institutions

At an international level, a whole range of institutions also affect the scale, character and location of economic activity. For example, conditions attached to the financial aid and loans given by the World Bank and the International Monetary Fund (IMF) to developing countries are currently directly affecting national economies (Sections 33.3 and 33.4). A number of countries have been persuaded to adopt drastic economic restructuring programmes which have reduced the protection and support given to domestic industries and opened them to the effects of outside competition. This has led to rationalisation and the closure of uncompetitive plants in some industries. For example, retrenchment in Zimbabwe has severely affected the textile industry leading to the closure of some factories such as the one at Gweru and to serious unemployment.

The World Trade Organisation (WTO), which on 1 January 1995 replaced Gatt as the international body concerned with the regulation and liberalisation of world trade following the recently completed Uruguay Round of talks, is likely to have a strong influence on the world economy. Participants are already committed to a liberalisation of the world economy, allowing market forces a greater influence on the location and scale of economic activity. Countries are for example already committed to the dismantling of trade barriers which hinder the movement of agricultural products and textiles. While this will adversely affect less efficient producers it should lead to the further expansion of the more efficient ones.

Supranational bodies along with multinational corporations will directly and indirectly exercise a steadily increasing influence as co-operation, interchange and interpendence are set to increase in the economic sectors.

Concluding comment

Until comparatively recently, industrial location theory was the starting point for explaining the locational pattern of manufacturing. However, it is of very limited value in explaining the tendency of industry to agglomerate, whether in established locations or in the newer types of locations now evident.

The concept of cumulative causation and associated processes provide a more useful context in which to study these agglomerative tendencies of manufacturing. However, there is also increasingly the need to take account of the decision-making influence of the multinational corporations which now control manufacturing, and of governments operating both individually and collectively.

case study

17.1 Coventry: the cumulative causation process and other influences on manufacturing

Cumulative causation: agglomeration, linkage and multiplier effects

- **Initial advantages**
  Coventry has a central location between London and the industrial North. The West Midlands was one of cradles for the Industrial Revolution. Coventry was a medieval silk trade centre but then changed to 'cottage industry', producing watches and clocks and sewing machines. Bicycles and early vehicle manufacture took place using a wealth of entrepreneurial and labour skills.
- **Derived advantages**
  Entrepreneurial expertise and early engineering experience led to Coventry being an early centre for motor vehicle manufacture. The period between the 1900s and 1930s benefited from linkages with general expansion in the West Midlands.
- **Agglomeration: linkage and multiplier effects**
  Expansion of car ownership inter-war and post-war provided stimulus for modernisation and rationalisation of factory assembly lines. Fewer, larger firms moved to larger sites on the outskirts. More components were supplied by outside firms, many in Coventry e.g. Lucas, car bodies, etc. and others in the West Midlands area.

  Since the late 1970s there has been contraction of employment and a fall in production. Rover declined as a producer but Jaguar was taken over by Ford (USA) and Peugeot-Talbot by French PSA. Half of the 42 000 employed population are in component firms in Coventry supplying the 'motor vehicle industry'. About 120 of Jaguar component suppliers are in Coventry and the West Midlands.

  The area also benefited from its central place on the motorway network and available pool of skilled labour.

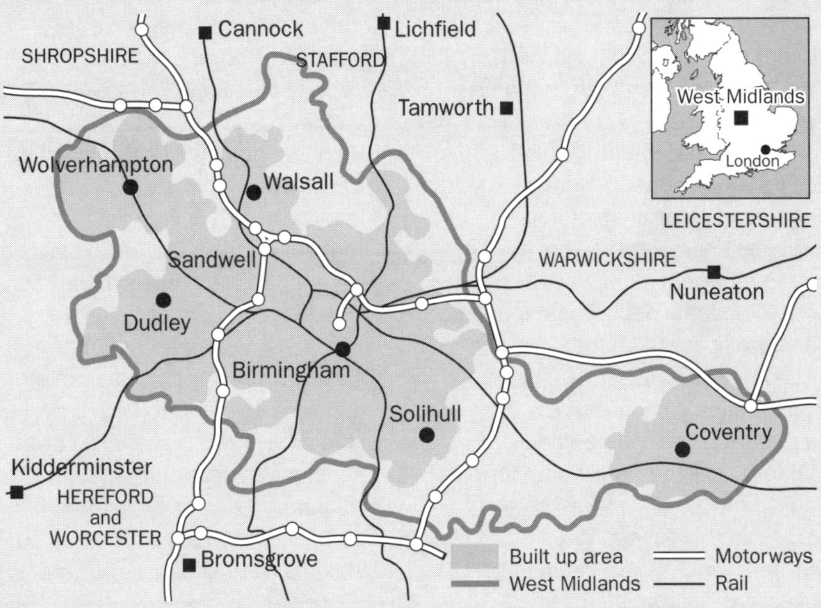

Location within the West Midlands region

Wider national influences

Markets in the rest of the UK and overseas engineering and motor vehicle industries are particularly susceptible to fluctuations in the national economy. As a result, there was a rapid decline during the late 1970s to mid-1980s, followed by recovery.

The government exerted influence through:

- general policies on industrial location and taxation changes affecting consumer market.
- providing financial support and encouragement to firms such as Rover. Leyland linked up with foreign companies in joint ventures. Now over half of Coventry's large manufacturing firms are foreign-owned, including most of the motor vehicle assembly.
- granting Assisted Area status to Coventry in 1984, significantly encouraging an influx of new investment, including Ford's take-over of Jaguar (1984). The inflow of services increased employment.
- upgrading the motorway network, which encouraged competition within Coventry's industry e.g. new M6 – A14 link to east coast ports.

Wider international influences

A significant part of motor vehicle and other production is for overseas markets e.g. 46% of Jaguar's 1990 production was exported to the USA, Peugeot-Talbot Ryton plant supplies European as well as UK markets. Thus the prosperity of Coventry's industry is very much dependent on conditions in the world economy and international competition. In the 1980s, it was adversely affected by overseas competition especially from expanding Japanese manufacturers.

Since a number of plants are foreign-owned, location and organisational decisions depend on outside policy for companies e.g. PSA (France) decided Peugeot-Talbot should be largely an assembly place ('screw driver' factory) at Ryton, most components being imported from France.

Currency exchange rates influence Coventry industry's competition overseas e.g. during the late 1980s, the low value of the pound against the dollar made exports to USA cheaper and influenced international and EU trade agreements.

Deindustrialisation – rationalisation recovery

Coventry went through a sharp phase of deindustrialisation along with the rest of the UK during the late 1970s to mid-1980s. This was followed by a recovery wherein industry was rationalised with better productivity. There was some recovery in employment but more in services than in manufacturing.

Dominance of engineering and motor vehicle production but

there are currently signs of some diversification with expansion of the service sector and two clusters of new industry.

- Service influx e.g. Barclays Bank complex (1500 employees), Land Registry – rents are one-third those of London, plus labour pool, good accessibility to London.
- High technology industry is linked to Warwick University Science Park which specialises in industrial design, etc. therefore serving and linking to established industry.
- Textile garment infant industry, since 1980s, employs a pool of female Asian labour (2500) available as a result of the influx of Asian male labour into the motor vehicle and engineering manufacturing industry, thus acting as an indirect multiplier.

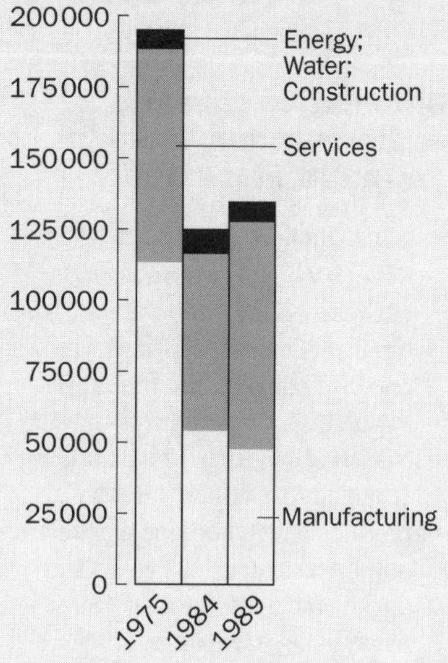

Changes in employment structure

Name	Employment	Types of Manufacturing
Jaguar	9984	Motor vehicles
GPT (Coventry)	5556	Electrical engineering
Peugeot Talbot	5383	Motor vehicles
Rolls Royce	3921	Mechanical engineering
Courtaulds	3026	Manmade fibres
Dunlop	2601	Transport equipment
Rover	2018	Motor vehicles
Massey Ferguson	1924	Mechanical engineering
Alvis	878	Mechanical engineering
Matrix Churchill	640	Mechanical engineering
Motor Panels	601	Motor vehicles
Torrington Co.	549	Motor vehicles
Carbodies	471	Motor vehicles
Lucas Industries	427	Electrical engineering
Sandvik	414	Metal manufacture

Dominant manufacturers, 1990 – Coventry

case study

17.2 India: its major industrial regions

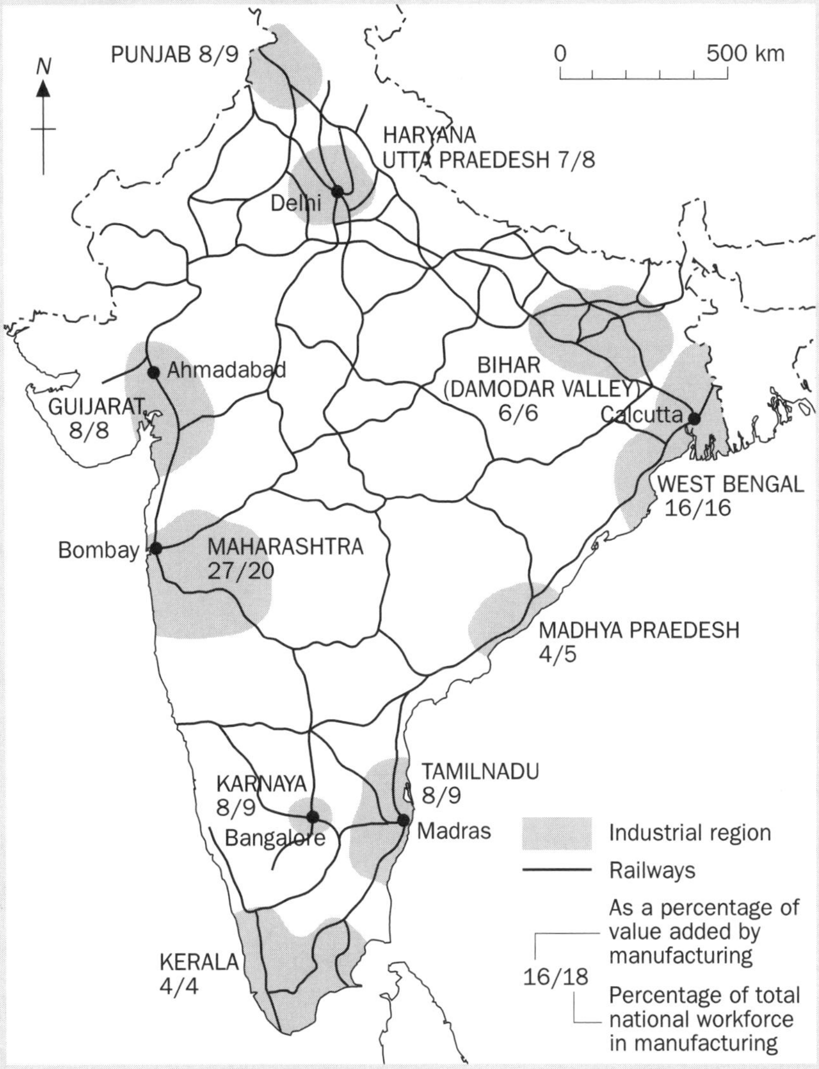

Major industrial regions

Character, locational influences and major industrial regions

Maharashatra (Bombay, Pune and other cities)

This is the leading industrial region which is continuing to expand. Originally dominated by textile production, it now has a very diversified industrial base – dyed and printed fabrics, electrical, mechanical engineering, mini steel production plant, petro-chemicals, durable and everyday consumables e.g. food processing, cigarettes.

This region is aided by good port and overseas access, proximity to the Deccan cotton growing region and cumulative advantages, including a growing domestic market (Bombay alone has 5 million population), a varied labour pool, business and administrative expertise. It has head offices of some of India's biggest companies, a good infrastructure including oil, nuclear and HEP supplies and an international reputation.

However, increasing diseconomies are leading to decentralisation of industry to the surrounding cluster of cities, including Ulhasanger, Bombay's planned satellite city.

West Bengal (Calcutta, Hooghlyside)

This area has lost its industrial lead to the Bombay region because the Marxist government of the state has not facilitated modernisation of infrastructure (e.g. power failures and transport congestion pose severe problems), and outside investors feel it a risky region for investment due to state controls and labour unrest. Even established companies are diverting new plants to other regions e.g. IBF to South India where there is a more liberal state government and more reliable power supplies.

Despite these problems, West Bengal remains the second most important industrial region with a very diversified industrial base, including various textile ventures ranging from jute to synthetic textiles, hand and factory loom production, engineering, machinery and vehicle production, oil refining and petrochemicals and a whole range of consumer products e.g. Bata shoes.

This region is historically favoured as a port and commercial centre with access to India's major jute growing region. Cumulative advantages include a large market (Calcutta alone has 11 million population but per capita purchasing power is low compared to Bombay), a very large labour pool, external scale economies (although now also severe diseconomies), and the port of Haldia.

Bihar (Damador)

Bihar is the main focus of India's heavy industry, based on local coal, iron ore and HEP power. Expansion was favoured by the initial Tata family investment followed by heavy state investment. The region is still the major steel producing area with Jamshedpur a main centre, but has now diversified into chemicals, heavy engineering, brickmaking, locomotives, tool industries and radio production.

Much of the heavy industry plant is now old and the investment has not been made available to modernise it. The region has suffered in the current recession and production has fallen off. Despite its importance, the region is not well linked to other areas. Rationalisation and modernisation are needed for further growth to occur.

Utta Praedesh and Haryana (including Delhi)

Already an important region, this area has the potential for further growth. The focus is Delhi, India's capital, with 5 million population. It has a highly diversified industrial base with the main emphasis on light industry, including consumer durables. One of the major manufacturing belts in the region is the Faridad-Ballabgarh area which has 9000 small and large factories, employing 120 000 with a very diverse range of products from needles to earth moving equipment and an array of component manufacturers e.g. Auto Pins now produces a range of components from leaf pins to seat belts.

The Delhi area currently suffers from increasing diseconomies of high land prices, power shortage and traffic bottlenecks together with political unrest.

Other regions

- **Guijarat (Ahmadabad)** is expanding with an export bias having port access, important for petro-chemicals and diversified textile production e.g. Arvind Mills produce blue denim and cotton shirting materials for export.
- **South India,** including Madras and the Bangladore regions, throughout the 1980s has benefited from the government policy of some regional decentralisation of industry and outside investment. Comparative political stability, lower land prices, cheaper labour and reliable power supplies together with infrastructure links have also been favourable to industrial development. Madras has diversified industries; Kerala has important textiles and processing industries. However, the Bangladore region has had the greatest expansion, being a focus for the aeronautics industry, chemicals, electrical industry and an emergent high technology industry as well as some traditional small-scale production e.g. silk carpets. A number of large national companies have established branch plants here.
- **Punjab** is one of the most prosperous agricultural regions of India and thus has a range of associated industries e.g. fertilisers, agricultural machinery and milling. It is also one of India's leading textile centres including cottage and factory carpet manufacture.
- **Madhya Pradesh** is of relatively modest importance with a diversification of industries mainly for the regional market and much of it on a small scale.

Structural organisation of India's industrial economy

Lowest: village and household

This level is based mostly on hand labour with little capital and a localised market e.g. textiles and metal working. The government has encouraged expansion at this level to strengthen the rural sector.

Middle: small scale with limited technology

Located in urban areas, this level receives government aid via the 'Small Industries Development Organisation' – light industrial estate units to let. The sector employs 30% of manufacturing labour and produces varied products for the local market but with increased subcontracting to large industry. This sector is increasingly important for manufacturing components to support the expansion of larger companies e.g. in the early 1980s India's developing television industry relied on imports for 90% of its components but by the early 1990s, 80% came from home suppliers.

This sector is an important supplier to the agricultural sector e.g. of hand tools and pumps. Until recently the government has strongly protected it from overseas competition.

Largest: large-scale industry

Found only in major cities, this sector takes advantage of scale economies. It is increasingly concentrated on new sites specifically for industry. Large corporations diversify and establish branch plants, especially in the west and south

- Private enterprise e.g. Tata or IBF dominant in electrical, vehicle and machine tools – consumer goods

- Government and public ownership – iron and steel, non-ferrous metals, heavy engineering – some privatisation now occurring
- Mixed ownership – aluminium, chemicals, road and sea transport.

Expansion of the industrial economy

With a population of 943 million, the potential domestic market is very large but unlike China, the Indian industry as yet has not been able to significantly tap its domestic market. This is partly because the majority of the population are too poor and partly due to the government's failure in managing the economy effectively enough to improve incomes.

Until 1992 the government has kept much of the heavy industry in state ownership which has been inefficient and has exercised tight controls on the private sector. It has over-protected existing industry but at the same time imposed taxes on good products, thus raising their prices. Through industrial licenses especially to foreign firms, the government has controlled and hindered the establishment of new businesses. However, under the present government, a programme of liberalisation is slowly being embarked upon which should allow more industrialisation, including branch plants from overseas companies.

Shortages of finance and infrastructure weaknesses are also a hindrance. By the early 1990s India had severe overseas debt problems, a budget deficit and inflation which drastically cut back the capital available for industry and infrastructure improvements. At the same time the debt problem and stock market scandals severely discouraged further investment from overseas. The government has now embarked on a programme of restructuring to readdress the economic imbalance.

On the positive side, many overseas corporations recognise the potential of India's home market and India as a low cost production base for manufacturing for overseas sales. Link-ups have already taken place and with deregulation, foreign firms will invest in branch plants in India. For example, joint ventures include Maruti scooter producers with Suzuki (Japan), Peico Electronics with Phillips (Holland), IBF with Siemens (Germany) for washing machine production.

Indian firms are acquiring increasing expertise, investing more in research, diversifying and looking to export-led growth e.g. Tata Enterprises now has diversified from heavy industry and textiles into computers and telecommunications, automobile production and service industries.

case study

17.3 The South Korean Multinational Corporation: Samsung invests in an electronics complex at Wynyard in Cleveland, 1994

A global investment programme to establish regional manufacturing centres round the world

Samsung is the world's fifth biggest electronics group, with plants already at Tijuana (Mexico) to serve the North American market and a planned complex in Shanghai (China) to serve Asian markets, for example. The corporation sought a base to serve the European market. Having considered locations in Portugal, Germany, France, Spain and the UK (VCR production already took place at Barcelona in Spain and colour televisions at Billingham in Cleveland in the UK), the UK Wynyard (Cleveland) location was chosen.

Factors favouring Wynyard location over other possible European locations (Mr Cham Bea, Managing Director of Samsung UK)

- Already good experience of labour productivity at Samsung plant at Billingham and planned to establish European servicing centre at Telford UK.
- Good bridgehead into European markets and the UK markets including the Silicon Glen high technology belt in Scotland.
- Good infrastructure – UK government had invested heavily in 1970s and 1980 in the motorway network for the North East, including tunnel link for A19 dual carriageway east coast route.
- Korea familiar with English as a second language.
- UK government and other financial incentives including tax concessions; good co-operation from bodies involved.
- Samsung will also have links with other development planned for Wynyard Estate.

Role of government and local authority incentives in attracting the Samsung investment

- Since the late 1970s the Conservative government have been creating a 'climate' favourable to inward foreign investment to revive declining old industrial regions such as the North East. Local Authorities equally offered financial incentives and liberal planning legislation to attract investment.
- Various quasi public and public bodies were involved, for example:
  - –North Development Company to attract inward investment and economic regeneration in the North East and Cumbria
  - –Teesside Development Corporation.
- Financial incentives – £58 million of regional selective assistance by the government; £5 million each from Cleveland County Council and Teesside TEC; £1.8 million EU funding.

Planned Electronics Complex at Wynyard – A £450 million investment covering 400 acres and offering 3000 jobs

Production is to include

1 million computer monitors

1.3 million micro-wave ovens

1/4 million facsimile machines

1/4 million personal computers

3 million monitor tubes

Semi-conductor wafers and televisions.

The market targeted is the UK and other EU countries.

Multiplier effect

Cleveland County Council envisages 2000 more jobs will be created by multiplier effect e.g. attract plastic injection and wiring system production which will provide components.

Part shift of North East from traditional heavy industry which have declined to a service and consumer, electronics based economy

- Cleveland (Teesside) is still important for steel, chemicals and oil refining but lost half its employment in this sector during 1981 to 1991, up to 18 000 jobs.
- It gained 16 500 in the service sector.
- There are already electronics and consumer industries in the region including plants by other Asian multi-nationals in the region e.g. Nissan's car plant near Sunderland, and Fujitsu is a semi-conductor plant at Newton Aycliffe, Durham.

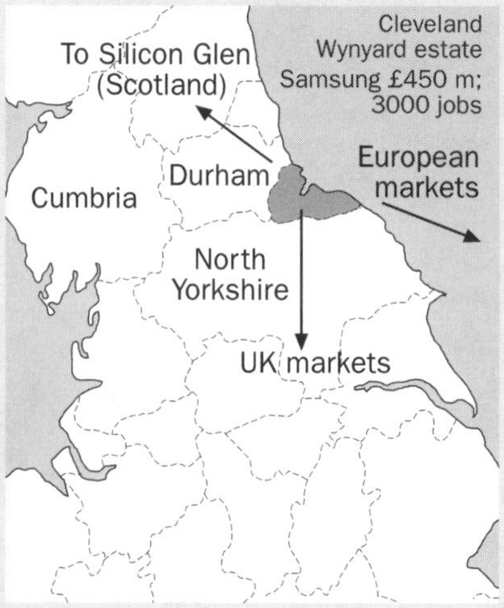

Location of the corporation

18

CHAPTER 18

Industrial Location Theory – a critical review

Until recently classical location theory was used as an explanation for the location of an individual firm or industry. While many of the widespread forces for change identified in the previous chapter may have limited the value of such theory, it is still important because there have been attempts to update it, thus bringing theory closer to reality.

18.1 Weber's Least Cost Theory

Basic principles

Classical location theory is rooted in economics and was much influenced by the German economist, Alfred Weber. In the search for the best location for a firm, Weber focused on a least cost approach, seeing the most favourable location as the one where costs could be minimised. To him the most important costs were transport costs, but he also took into account the supporting or offsetting effects of the cost of labour, together with what he termed agglomerative (concentrating) and deglomerative (dispersion) costs.

To focus attention on these central influences, Weber neutralised the effects of secondary influences, by making certain assumptions along lines similar to other classical location theorists. These assumptions included free competition, all decision-making to be based solely on economic reasoning and the existence of an isotropic (uniform) plain. As analysis proceeded, these assumptions could be relaxed to allow for the effects of secondary influences.

Weber saw the identification of a least cost location as a resolving of competing location pulls – on the one hand, that of raw material sources and on the other, the pull of a market location. These he saw as occurring at fixed points rather than spread over an area, except for certain raw materials which were to be found everywhere, such as air and water. These he termed ubiquitous and therefore of no consequence in deciding a firm's location.

To resolve the problem of opposing locational pulls, Weber developed a ***material index*** as the central feature of his least cost theory. Taking the transport cost of raw materials and the finished product as a function of weight per unit and distance over which it had to be transported, the material index for a firm could be obtained by dividing the weight of localised raw materials needed for one unit of output by the weight of that unit of output. Where the answer was greater than one, the weight of raw materials is greatest and the firm concerned is dealing with a weight-losing product, as is the case with iron and steel for example. In this case the industry would be drawn towards a raw material rather than a market location.

Conversely, if the material index is less than one the product is a weight-gaining one as for example in the case of brewing where water is added during processing and the product has to be bottled for shipment. In this case the pull would be towards the markets. The higher the material index the greater the pull towards a raw material location. Once the index drops below one, the more potent the location to market pull. However, as indicated earlier, labour cost considerations and/or agglomerative and deglomerative influences could modify the result. If sufficiently important and operating in a counter manner to the material index, these other cost factors could in fact result in an opposing location to that decided on the material index alone. Examples of different situations and locations for a firm are indicated in Figure 18.1.

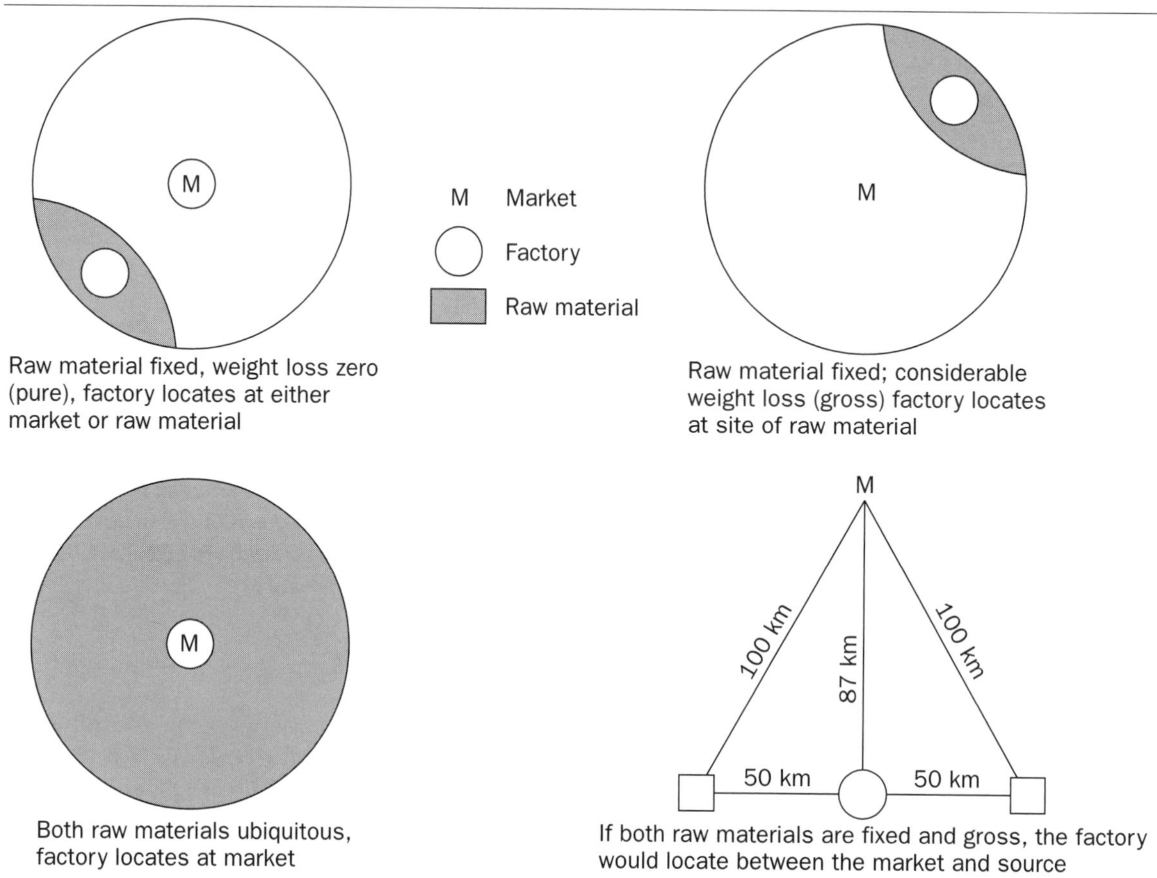

Figure 18.1 *Factory locations as determined by raw material and market pulls*

The isodopanes (equal combined transport cost lines) progressively decrease in the direction of the raw material source indicating the cheapest location for a factory i.e. towards this source and enclosed by the '5' value isodopane line.

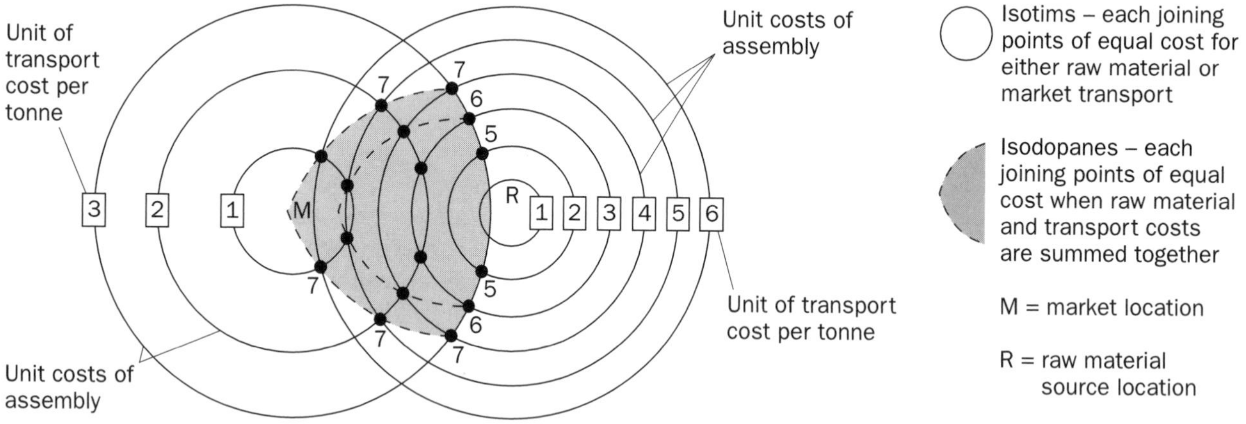

Figure 18.2 *Assembly and delivery costs related to a market and a raw material source*

In order to identify points of least cost for a manufacturing firm Weber devised a useful technique involving isotim lines and isodopanes (Figure 18.2). Each isotim line connects points of equal transport costs. Isotim lines can be drawn to show how transport assembly costs change with distance from raw material sources on the one hand and on the other, how delivery charges change with distance from market. In the simplest case in which a firm deals with only one source of raw material and one market there would thus be two sets of isotim lines. On the basis of where these intersect, it is possible to construct the isodopane lines, each joining points of equal transport cost over all. From these isodopane lines the least cost location can be found.

However, in reality there may not only be a number of raw material sources and markets but also cost lines for access to a labour pool as well. Thus reaching any diagrammatic solution using isotim and isodopane lines can be a complex process. Add to this the influence of agglomeration which firms might enjoy through locating close together rather than each in its own location and the complexity increases. Weber himself recognised no less than fourteen different locational types resulting from the influence of different combinations of transportation costs, labour costs and agglomeration economies.

Use and limitations

While Weber's is a useful approach in that it identifies certain basic influences, its value is now limited – partly because of certain inherent weaknesses in the theory and also because circumstances have changed since the turn of the century when Weber first formulated it.

Weber's material index was too crude a measure – transportation costs are not directly proportional to distance and not equal for given weights of materials. More important still, transport costs are rarely a basic criteria for the location of a firm today. Although varying from one kind of firm to another it is estimated that on average, transport costs make up only 5% to 12% of a firm's total cost.

By concentrating too much on minimising costs, Weber's theory fails to identify the revenue aspects of a firm's operation which also directly affects the profitability of a firm. The theory, therefore, gives an unbalanced approach to the question of location.

The agglomerative and deglomerative influences already identified in earlier discussions on cumulative causation now occupy a far more central position in location decisions than allowed for by Weber. Furthermore, some of the secondary influences suppressed in the assumptions Weber made, also have an important effect. Political, social and other human considerations, including imperfect knowledge of situations, are all recognised today as significant in deciding the location of a firm or a branch plant.

18.2 Lösch's Market Area or Profit Maximisation Approach

Having felt that Weber had overemphasised the cost factor, and unrealistically seen a market as a point rather than a demand spread over an area, Lösch sought to draw attention to the marketing factor and the idea of maximum profits related to sales revenue. Thus he held production costs constant in his initial analysis and indicated the optimum location for a firm as being where the largest possible market area could be monopolised or controlled. However, it should be noted that revenue would fall off with distance from the point at which the firm chose to locate in the market area, because of the cost of transporting the product to the consumer. One could initially envisage a simple revenue cone covering the market area, as shown in Figure 18.3.

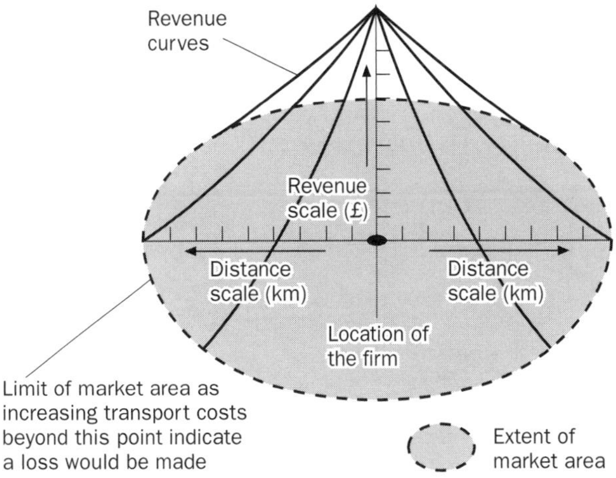

Figure 18.3 *The revenue cone for a firm*

The market demand factor would encourage firms in any one industry to disperse across a region so that each could have control of its own market area. However, Lösch saw that firms from different industries could also benefit from agglomerative economies by congregating together at the same location in any one market area.

While Lösch emphasised a different approach to that of Weber, some of Lösch's simplifying assumptions were similar, such as perfect competition and rational economic decision-making, and thus the theory suffers similar defects. Moreover Lösch's calculation of market demand was too crude and ignored many of the difficulties an entrepreneur would encounter in trying to estimate demand as a basis for a locational decision. The market-orientated approach does have some validity for consumer industries such as brewing, furniture assembly and baking in this sense. Thus to some extent it complements Weber's Least Cost Theory which is more suited to heavier industry.

18.3 The Spatial Limits Model

If the best of Weber's Least Cost Model could be combined with the best of Lösch's Profit Maximisation Model a better model could be formed. Later alternative approaches, such as that by D M Smith, attempt to do this. However, it is accepted that an entrepreneur is unlikely to have full knowledge of the facts needed for a firm to be located at its optimum point.

Once it is accepted that firms may be located in other than the optimum location, not one but a range of possible locations are evident. This can be illustrated from Smith's simple model of industrial location which introduces the idea of spatial margins, locations outside of which would result in the firm making a loss, but inside which the extent of profit-making based on the difference between costs and revenue would vary according to the location chosen (Figure 18.4).

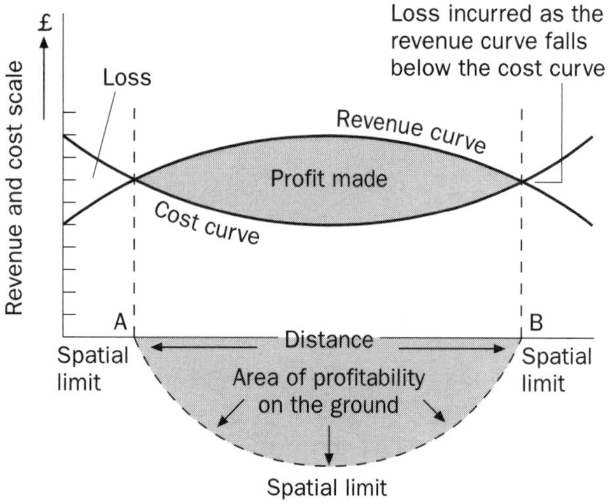

Figure 18.4 *Revenue/cost curve for a firm indicating spatial limits to a profitable location*

It is accepted then that entrepreneurs may choose locations which will satisfy them because reasonable profits can be made though they may not be the 'optimum' profit maximisation locations. Once this is recognised we have entrepreneurs as '***satisfiers***' instead of '***economic optimisers***', which lies at the basis of earlier location theory. Entrepreneurs can then be seen as consciously allowing other factors than economic ones to influence their decision making, for example environmental and social considerations.

These spatial margins models, by allowing for a range of possible sub-optimum locations and the influence of non-economic factors in the decision making process, are more realistic than the earlier classical location models out of which they grew. However, they still have the weakness of concentrating on the location of a single firm and the actions of individual entrepreneurs. Yet as we have seen in an earlier section, much of the industry is under the control of large organisations, including varying degrees of state ownership in some countries.

18.4 **The behavioural approach – locational decision making**

This approach emphasises the way an individual or groups of individuals reach decisions. It takes into account the perception they have of situations and such things as the way their attitudes and values affect decision making. While earlier behavioural work was concerned with the individual entrepreneur and the single firm, more recently much has been about the corporate decision making process in the large scale multi-plant, multi-functional and multinational organisations which control much of industry.

In pursuit of the specific goals sought for the corporation as a whole, the decision about the location of one branch plant (the equivalent of the single firm), is but a small part of the decision making process as a whole. It is but one of the decisions which need to be made about setting up a particular branch plant. Others would include the nature of the product to be manufactured, the way production should be organised and the scale of size of the plant. Such considerations as well as the overall goals of the organisation must have a bearing on the question of location. (Figure 18.5).

Moreover, while a large industrial organisation is essentially motivated by a search for profits, its goals cannot be wholly divorced from political and social considerations. This is clearly indicated in Gold's diagram in which decisions about location are seen as part of the overall investment process and as one of the four product decisions which have to be made about any contemplated new branch plant and industrial output overall. It will be noted that many of the wider influences discussed in the previous section are now given a place in a general framework. The character of the people involved and the kinds of decision making procedures pursued have an important bearing on the ultimate choice of locations for branch plants.

Even within large corporations, with all their expertise and communication technology, the search began with the local and familiar, and that decisions were made within the limited context of a highly parochial and partial schema. Further, quick and satisfactory solutions rather than optimum solutions were sought. Personal preference also played an important part in the decision making.

It would thus appear from recent studies that the kind of wider behavioural approach outlined by Gold and others, is more likely to provide a fuller and more realistic context for the study of industrial location than the earlier narrowly based and theoretical models. Already the behavioural approach is under heavy criticism for centring attention only on the decisions of entrepreneurs and management, having little regard to the role of labour and the needs of society.

18.5 **Towards a more radical view**

Reisser and others concerned with the welfare and prosperity of society as a whole deplore any approach which centres on business and its goal of maximum profits. Reisser points out, for example, that the massive monopolies which increasingly control much of economic activity not only continue to search for profit maximisation (though ultimately accepting less than this), but do so by increasingly manipulating consumer demand through such mechanisms as media advertising. Thus for many industrialists it is not so much a matter of responding to a market demand but of creating that market demand.

The 'risk taking' which in the ideology of capitalism justifies the owner and shareholders receiving a much greater share of the revenue from the sale of goods than the workers whose labours have helped to produce those goods, is stated by critics of the capitalist approach as now very much reduced. State support for industry by way of subsidies and grants, price support systems and the like have seen to this. Thus workers are entitled to a greater share of business income as well as a share in decision taking.

Whether one supports such criticism or not, it has to be accepted that the needs and interests of workers as well as of society in general, should have a place in the study of economic activity. Trade union activity as representative of labour and intervention by the state in the location and organisation of economic activity in the interests of society as a whole mean that these other voices already have an important place (whether directly or indirectly) in decision making procedures. Hence any change in the way geographers approach the question of location must recognise the important parts which government and trade unions play. Some of these additional influences will be seen in the study of selected industries.

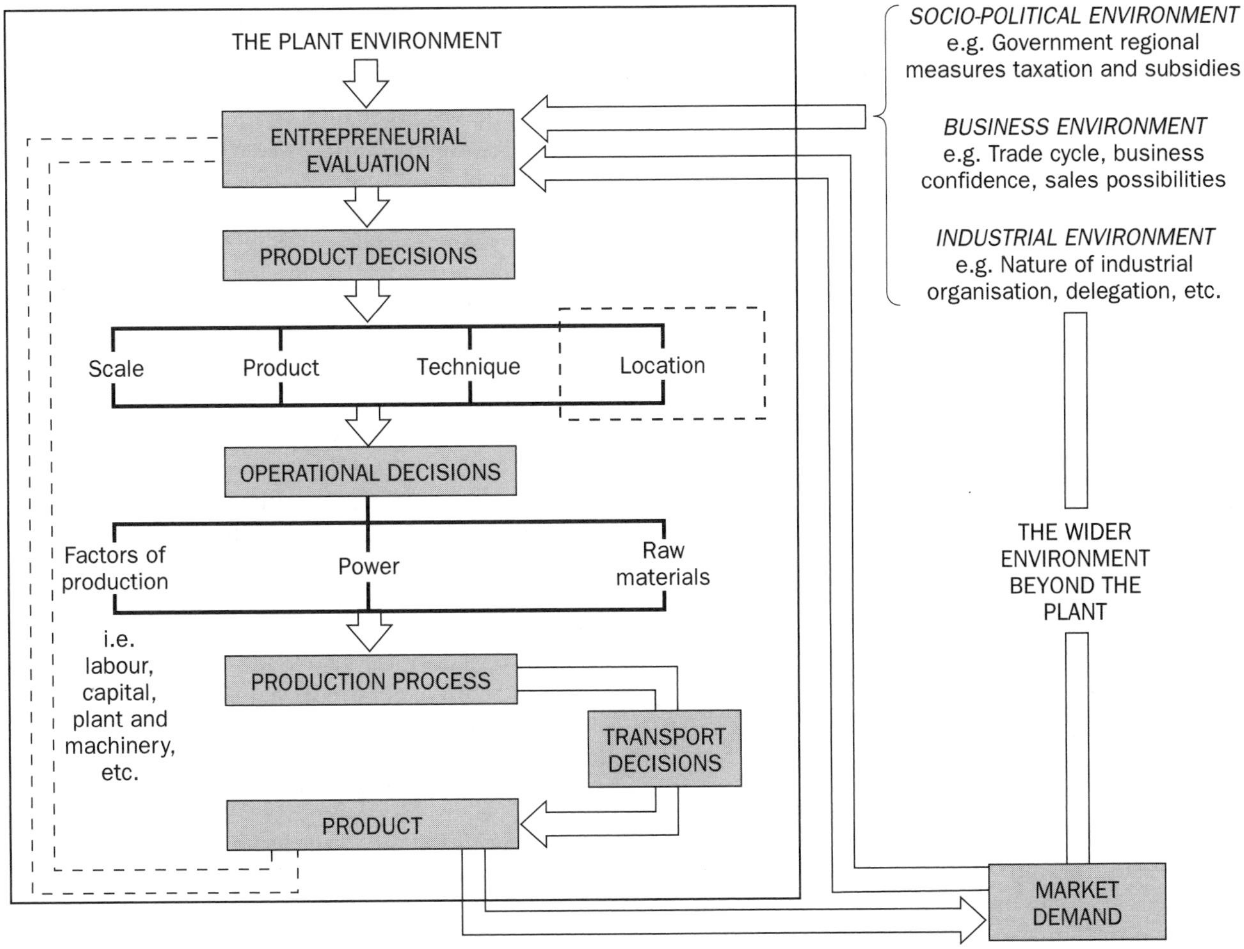

Figure 18.5 *Location decisions as part of the total investment process (based on Gold)*

19

CHAPTER 19

The changing pattern of selected industries

A study of a few different industries will help to show how the relative importance of locational factors differs from one industry to another and also how changes over time occur, bringing shifts in the distribution of an industry. It can also emphasise why earlier location theory, though still of some value, is being replaced by a more dynamic and comprehensive approach.

19.1 Changes in the UK iron and steel industry

The iron and steel industry, perhaps more than any other, has been used to illustrate the validity of Weber's Least Cost Theory. Being a weight losing industry, its material index is greater than one, resulting in a location pull towards raw materials. This was initially towards fuel sources of charcoal and later coal. As technological developments reduced fuel requirements, the shift has been towards iron ore sources. For example in the case of the UK this was partly to the Jurassic ore fields of the East Midlands but also increasingly to coastal locations where imported ores could be brought in. Other influences were also significant and in particular instances, resulted in some small works remaining on coalfield sites or being orientated towards markets.

The structure and distribution pattern of the industry has undergone further significant changes since the 1950s. While access to raw materials remains important, the changes that have taken place have had more to do with market competition and the policy decisions of the large corporations which, together with governments, now control much of the world's iron and steel making. This is illustrated in Case study 19.1.

Changes 1950 – 1973

In the 1950s, though some steel was being made in electric arc furnaces using scrap, most was produced in oxygen steel furnaces using pig iron from iron smelting works. In iron smelting, approximately three and three quarter tonnes of raw material were needed to produce one tonne of pig iron and since iron ore was the largest single item, this was the strongest single influence on the location of industry. This accounts for the two major types of location on the low grade Jurassic ore fields and near to or on tidewater locations, where high grade ore could be imported and which required less fuel in smelting than home ores. (A few works due to inertia factors remained on coalfield locations e.g. Consett, Durham.)

In 1967 the bulk of the iron and steel industry was nationalised as the British Steel Corporation (BSC). In future, government policies and investment plans would play an important role in the structuring and distribution of the industry. While the BSC in its Ten Year Development Strategy Paper (1973) saw the medium-term outlook for world steel as promising, it faced severe competition from cheaper overseas producers. The major producer was Japan, where the steel industry was being rapidly expanded and which was capturing more of the world markets. Developing countries such as Brazil, India and South Korea were also emerging as significant steel producers. They had the advantage of invested foreign capital and skill being combined with rich domestic ore resources and cheaper labour costs.

1973 – 1990 Further rationalisation against a background of world overcapacity

In order to be competitive the BSC saw it as essential to follow the same kind of development strategy already proving successful in Japan, namely, to take advantage of recent technology developments and concentrate production in a few larger integrated works in coastal districts though not necessarily on tidewater sites. During the 1970s BSC concentrated its bulk steel production on five main integrated coastal district sites giving increased economies of scale which would help reduce costs per unit output and make the industry more competitive. Costs were further reduced by using mainly fuel-saving rich foreign ores imported to deep water sites in bulk carriers, together with an increasing import of coke for the smelting of that iron ore, but only two of the five integrated works were actually on tide-water locations, that is, Port Talbot and Lackenby, Redcar. Of the others, Llanwern relied on iron ore brought 80 km from Port Talbot while the two more inland sites at Ravenscraig and Scunthorpe were dependent on ore brought from specially constructed ore terminals at Hunterston and Immingham.

However, rationalisation also meant contraction closure of older and smaller inland iron and steel works such as Ebbw Vale, Shotton and Consett. Even though some as individual works might still be operated at a profit, in the total plan of the corporation most were seen as uneconomic. The corporation closed 23 inland works between 1973 and 1980 which, together with modernisation of remaining works, resulted in a reduction of the workforce from 336 000 to 162 000 in 1980. Since then a further 100 000 jobs have been lost in the steel industry with severe problems to towns particularly dependent on steel works, such as Corby.

While a substantial number of finishing mills were retained inland, only small specialised steel works using scrap and electric furnaces were left open. These, like some in the private sector such as Hatfields at Sheffield, had a capacity of a few hundred thousand tonnes a year and were competitive for a limited range of specialised products, such as alloy steels. The electric arc method was a rapid, flexible and cost effective process, scrap was within easy reach and locations also had a pool of highly skilled labour.

During the 1970s world steel markets did not develop as expected. Instead, at a time when steel production capacity was being rapidly expanded, home demand dropped dramatically due to the economic recession and a fall in UK's share of overseas markets. Steel consumption at home peaked in 1973 and then fell back to its level of 1950 (Figure 19.1). (The motor vehicle industry reduced steel consumption from 1.6 million (1967) to 0.62 million tonnes (1980). Also, cheaper foreign steel import trebled during the 1970s.).

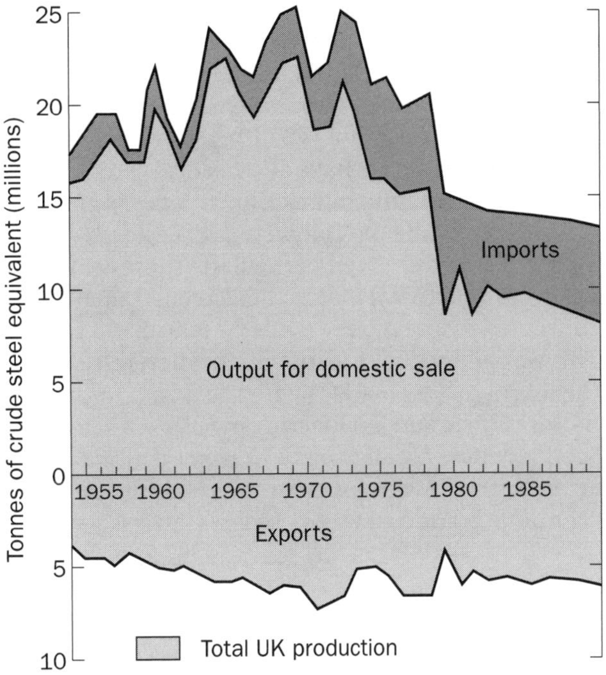

Figure 19.1 *Steel production, imports and exports for the UK, 1954 – 90*

Despite some recovery in the world economy during the 1980s, the basic problem of overcapacity remained. The world steel industry in 1982, had the capacity to produce 650 million tonnes but world consumption was only 400 million tonne. Furthermore, production continues to expand amongst new lower cost producers in the developing world where in contrast to the general trend, demand had risen 50% in the 1970s. With the security of an expanding home market certain of the new developing world producers are in a good position to penetrate world markets: the Pohang Steel Corporation of South Korea now exports steel plate and strip to Japan.

Faced with these problems of excess capacity and increasing overseas competition, the BSC has had to drastically revise its plans for the industry. However, Britain is part of the EU and so subject to the EU agreements, the Davignon Plan of 1977 was a major one aimed at further rationalisation of the industry in Western Europe.

The effects of BSC's revised policy in conjunction with measures announced for the European Union as a whole, have been to continue the locational trends evident all the way through the post-war years, namely, closure of more small, uneconomic plants inland and a concentration on even fewer progressively more efficient integrated coastal plants.

The difference from earlier policies is that greater efficiency means not only further modernisation and re-organisation of the management structure of the industry but also reducing the capacity of the remaining coastally oriented plants. Work forces have been further reduced, raising productivity per person from 14 human hours per tonne of steel in 1980 to four human hours in 1984. New fuel saving and other techniques have also been adopted. More money has gone into research and marketing.

However, while the Llanwern and Lackenby-Redcar plants have been particularly successful in raising productivity, the smaller Ravenscraig plant continued to lose money (£40 000 000 in 1983 – 84). This was partly due to its poorer location inland and the loss of nearby markets with the slump in the motor vehicle and engineering industries in Scotland. Ravenscraig had been kept open so far to avoid further unemployment in the region, but on economic grounds it was closed in 1994.

An additional feature has been the financial assistance given to cushion the effects of closure and rationalisation. Both the British government and the European Union have put a great deal of effort into financing new industry into declining steel areas. This has met with variable success, one of the more successful locations being Corby.

The British steel industry has undergone further reshaping and restructuring in the 1990s. It is now a profitable industry and one of the world's lowest cost producers. It is looking to expand its share of an expanding world market and through joint ventures transform itself from a national to a globalised industry by the twenty-first century (Case study 19.1).

Figure 19.2 *The automobile production system*

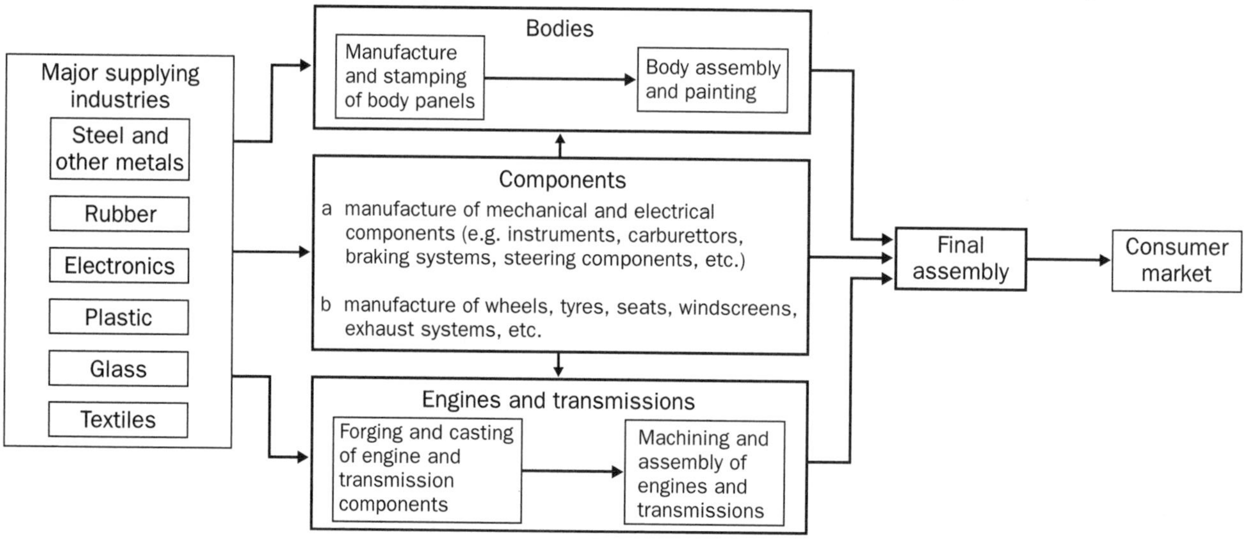

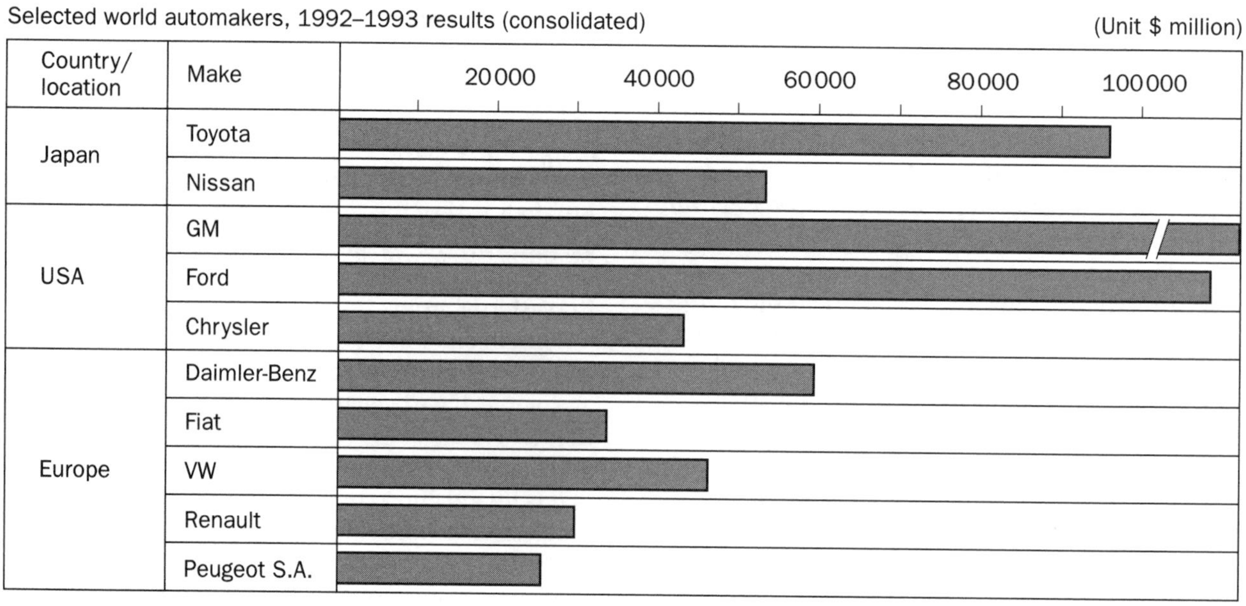

Figure 19.3 *Sales of leading automobile manufacturers, 1993*

19.2 The motor vehicle industry: a barometer for change

A global industry dominated by a few multinational industries

The motor vehicle industry, both in terms of value of production and numbers employed, is one of the most important world industries. It is essentially an assembly industry supported by a vast range of component suppliers (Figure 19.2). It is dominated by a few multinational industries operating increasingly at a global scale. The ten leading producers, such as Ford, General Motors and Toyota, supply approximately 80% of the world market (Figure 19.3). In contrast, until recently, component supplies came mainly from medium- to small-sized firms but now well-known multinational companies, such as Bosch and Siemens, are emerging as main component suppliers.

Production remains concentrated in advanced countries

Despite the expansion of motor vehicle assembly and production in certain developing countries, most notably South Korea (Case study 20.1), the industry is still overwhelmingly located within advanced countries (Figure 19.3) because this is where 90% of market demand occurs (Figure 19.4). There is one car to 1.3 people in the USA while in Brazil, for example, it is one to 12.1 people.

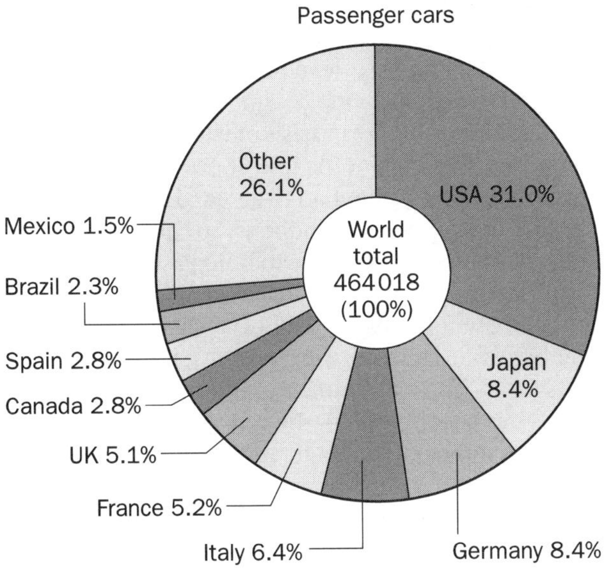

Figure 19.4 *Number of passenger cars in use in selected countries, 1992*

While expansion of demand has slowed down in advanced countries to about 3% per annum, it is rising on average by 10% in the developing countries. However the market in the developing world is likely to remain small except in the most progressive newly industrialising countries in South East Asia. Market expansion is held back by low incomes and by poor infrastructures since the road capacity to cater for more vehicles is lacking, especially in heavily urbanised regions.

Changes in the organisational structure of the industry are reducing its regional concentration

The industry being an assembly industry is market orientated and component suppliers are in turn drawn towards countries where the assembly plants occur. However, the organisational structure of the industry and the geography of its production are undergoing marked changes, making it difficult to generalise about locations and distribution patterns.

Since the 1960s change and rationalisation have been characteristic of the industry, but the current changes are probably the most fundamental yet. After further rapid expansion during the 1980s, a marked fall in demand due to the recent world wide recession has triggered a restructuring of the industry world wide.

Organisational change

Fordist mass production

The early years of the motor vehicle industry were characterised by many small firms, each producing their own models in limited numbers at a comparatively high cost to supply a limited market. As early as 1913 the Ford Motor Company developed mass production of a 'people's car' which was cheap enough for many to afford. ***Ford introduced the assembly line method of production in which components could be brought together and assembled on a moving assembly line into the finished car. Each worker on the line performed a narrow, specialised and repetitive task. The aim was to set up very large assembly plants to enable economies of scale to operate and produce a limited range of standard models at a price which created and further expanded a mass market.***

Small companies could not compete and either went out of business or were bought by the large manufacturers which had adopted the Ford mass production methods (Figure 19.5).

Although some companies such as Ford itself produced some of the components in-house, the large mass producers in general relied on a host of component suppliers competing with one another to gain orders. To reduce costs of transport and maintain contact with the large assembly plants, component suppliers tended to locate within reasonable proximity, thus motor manufacturing complexes developed, such as that at Detroit in the USA and in and around Birmingham in the UK.

Characteristic	Fordist Mass production	Lean production
Technology	Complex, but rigid, single-purpose machinery using standardised components. Heavy time and cost penalty involved in switching to new products	Highly flexible methods of production using modular component systems. Relatively easy to switch to new products
Labour force	Very narrowly skilled professional workers design products but production itself performed by unskilled / semi-skilled 'interchangeable' workers. Each performs a very simple task repetitively and in a pre-defined time and sequence	Multiskilled workers operate in teams. Responsibilities include several manufacturing operations plus responsibility for simple maintenance and repair
Supplier relationship	Distant relationships with suppliers, both functionally and geographically. Large inventories held at assembly plant 'just in case' of disruption to supply	Very close relationships with a functionally tiered system of suppliers. Use of 'just in time' delivery systems encourages geographical proximity between customers and suppliers
Production volume	Extremely high	Extremely high
Product variety	A narrow range of standardised designs with only minor product differentiation	Increasingly wide range of differentiated products

Figure 19.5 *Comparisons between Fordist 'mass production' and the more recent 'lean production' characteristics*

Increasingly since the 1960s, as the industry became more competitive, manufacturers sought lower cost component suppliers over a wider area and the close proximity linkages have begun to break down helped by improved means of transport and lower transport costs. Nevertheless until the 1970s the industry remained broadly organised along Fordist lines.

However, this production system has been increasingly challenged by the 'lean production' system (Figure 19.5), pioneered and developed by the major Japanese motor manufacturers, especially Toyota. These have expanded so successfully and rapidly that by the end of the 1980s Japan had overtaken the USA as the leading world producer. While Japanese producers have benefited from a protected and expanding home market, their success in overseas sales has been based to an important degree on the efficiency of the 'lean production' method which has until very recently improved the quality and price competitiveness of Japanese-produced cars compared to American and European-produced cars.

The Lean Production method

It is not easy to define what is meant by 'lean production', but it essentially combines some of the best benefits of mass production with changes which produce flexibility in working and production. This allows a reduction in costs per unit and a marked improvement in quality of product while at the same time providing a wider range of products to meet changing demand and preferences. The word 'lean' implies in addition that lean production uses less of everything compared to the older mass production method: as Womack, Jones and Roos stated in *The Machine That Changed the World* (1990), *'half the human effort in the factory, half the manufacturing space, half the investment in tools, and half the time needed to produce a new product'.*

This method involves a change in the relationship between the manufacturer and component supplier and a change in the relationship between capital and labour in the production process compared to the Fordist method of mass production. Under the latter, large American and European firms worked on short-term contracts with many component suppliers. Looking for lowest cost producers they would switch from one supplier to another to achieve this. In contrast, the Japanese 'lean production' approach has been to develop a long-term relationship with a first tier of suppliers on a basis of trust and strict guarantee of quality at the lowest possible cost. Moreover, the supplier had to agree to a just-in-time method of supply of components so that manufacturers did not have to hold vast stocks of components. Emphasis was also on first tier suppliers providing whole sub-assemblies, such as engines, gear boxes and transmission systems, thus reducing costs for the motor manufacturer. When a change of model has been required, the sub-assembly supplier also bore some of the design and investment costs, again reducing the manufacturer's expenses.

The first tier suppliers would be supported by many second and third tier suppliers of components with which to make up the sub-assemblies (Figure 19.6).

In respect of the capital-labour relationship on the assembly line, automation of assembly increasingly using robots was allied to team work, with workers trained to take on a range of tasks on the assembly line. Each team is encouraged to work together to produce as efficiently as possible with the emphasis

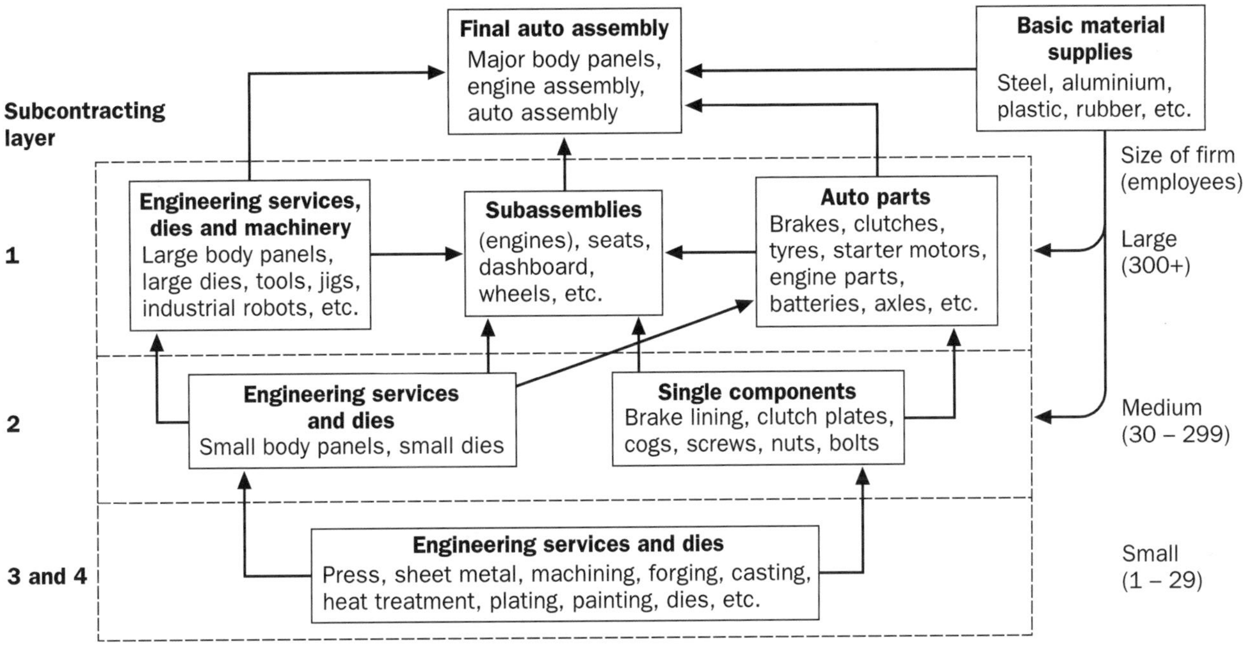

Figure 19.6 *Tiers of components and parts suppliers in the Japanese automobile 'lean production' system*

on productivity and quality. In return, workers are encouraged to feel part of the firm, to offer ways of improving production and have been guaranteed long-term employment, good pay and other benefits. To prevent demarcation of task problems which have occurred under Ford mass production, workers were either non-union members or all belonged to one union. Flexibility of work practices was thus possible.

Collaboration and joint ventures between major producers

In the face of increasingly successful Japanese penetration of world markets and changing market demand, both the American and European major producers have had to reappraise and change their organisational structures to become more efficient and competitive. This has meant increasing collaboration and joint ventures with Japanese manufacturers and each other in the design and production of new models. It has also meant a decision to either adapt or adopt 'lean production' methods.

At the same time, manufacturers have had to preserve and extend their scale of production to survive in an increasingly competitive global market. Thus during the 1980s further mergers have occurred reducing the number of major producers. As a consequence the UK, one of the leaders in the motor manufacturing industry, no longer has a British-owned firm; production is by subsidiaries of American, French and Japanese multinationals. In 1994 for example, Japanese firms accounted for 25% of UK production and the Nissan company was the UK's leading vehicle exporter.

However, changes in the structure of the motor vehicle industry and in its locational pattern are not simply a response to Japanese competition and changing levels and types of market demand. They are also related to the regulatory controls, policies and actions of governments and technological changes which occur within and outside the industry.

The role of governments

State policy

Since the automobile industry plays a central part in the manufacturing sector of advanced economies, government intervention has been important. Some West European governments have a direct stake in industry, for example, the French government in Renault and the Italian government in Fiat and until 1989, the British government in the Rover group. Apart from this direct participation (now of decreasing importance), there are two key aspects of state policy which continue to affect the decisions of the multinationals dominating the industry.

The first aspect is the extent to which governments allow foreign firms access to their domestic markets via direct imports or through the setting up of production plants in the country. The second is the kind of support a government gives to domestic producers and the extent to which it discriminates against foreign firms.

Governments pursue a mixture of the two but the balance varies. Both the USA and the UK have encouraged access by foreign firms and treated them equally with domestic producers. This is one of the reasons why these two countries have the largest number of foreign-owned plants and strong collaborative and joint ventures between domestic and foreign firms. It is now being extended to include the setting up of foreign components and parts plants. Germany has granted access to foreign firms but discriminated against them in favour of domestic producers while France gives only limited access and also discriminates against foreign firms. Japan is perhaps the most protective of its domestic markets and interventionist in favour of its domestic producers.

Historically, advanced countries have protected their domestic markets by tariff barriers, tariffs being as high as 30% to 50% on vehicle imports. In the post-war years this has meant foreign firms adopting a policy of establishing branch plants inside the countries with expanding market demand in order to access these markets. Today only Australia levies high tariffs; other advanced countries have moved towards favouring non-tariff barriers including negotiating voluntary quota agreements to limit foreign imports and a host of indirect limits, such as strict regulations on safety and exhaust emission controls which require production modifications by firms on cars destined for particular export markets.

Local content and export promotion

Other important influences have been policies in respect of local content and export requirements related to foreign production plants. Where foreign production plants have been set up governments have been anxious to safeguard domestic plants and to ensure a beneficial multiplier effect on the economy and jobs. Thus granting permission for the setting up of a foreign plant has been subject to the manufacturer agreeing to a substantial percentage of the required parts and components coming from domestic suppliers. In the EU an ultimate of 80% local content is to be demanded.

This local content is also a feature now being emphasised by developing countries such as Brazil, Mexico and China where foreign multinationals have increasingly sought to establish branch plants because of comparatively low costs of production. Initially plants were little more than 'screw driver' factories assembling imported kits or parts. However, governments are now pursuing vigorous import substitution policies under which they would like to see the whole process of manufacture, including the making of components and parts, taking place in the host country. India, Brazil and Mexico are looking at a 50% local content level to expand employment opportunities and increase the value added from production and lead to vehicle exports.

Concessions and incentives to attract foreign firms

Governments want to encourage foreign investment. In advanced countries this would offset the general decline in industry and the effects of recession. In developing countries it is seen as essential to increasing industrialisation.

Inward investment can provide much needed employment and act as a stimulus to the economy. Increased competition from foreign firms in domestic markets can also pressurise domestic producers to become more productive and efficient. This was a policy followed under the Thatcher government in the UK in the 1980s when financial and other incentives such as more flexible regularity conditions were provided in order to encourage foreign firms into the country.

Within a country there is equally fierce competition at a regional level to attract foreign investment. It is estimated for example that in the USA, $325 million was recently spent by the state of Kentucky to persuade Toyota to locate its new motor vehicle plant there rather than elsewhere. In the UK Nissan was lobbied by 53 local organisations before it finally decided on Washington (Tyne and Wearside) as the location for its new plant. The arrival of a large new vehicle production plant can give a significant boost to a regional economy. Such are the ancillary, linkage and multiplier effects that it is estimated for every job created in the car industry, 40 more jobs are created with in the economy.

The growing influence of supranational governments

Increasingly however, policies towards foreign imports and establishment of branch plants in countries are influenced by the joint policies and regulations of countries which act as economic blocs. The EU single market and its continuing enlargement with the entry of more countries are having a profound effect on the decisions of multinational companies. The EU is of particular significance since it is now the single largest market for motor vehicles. For Japanese plants locating in the UK, it is seen as a launch pad for accessing the EU single market.

The recent agreement between the USA, Canada and Mexico leading to the formation of the North American Free Trade Area will also be of great significance (Case study 32.1). Mexico with its low labour costs and ready access to the rich North American market is already attracting the attention of multinational producers.

The geography of production

It will already be apparent that the major changes in the structure of the motor vehicle industry and the influence of governments are, along with market demand, the most important factors to influence the current distribution pattern of the motor vehicle industry.

At a global level

The most noticeable feature to affect the global pattern is the decision of the main producers to structure their operations on a global scale (Case studies 19.2 and 19.3). Locational decisions both in respect of the siting of major assembly plants and other operations will be made at the global level. This, to an increasing extent, will also be the case in respect of link-ups with major component suppliers.

Major Japanese automobile manufacturers are already organised along global lines (Case study 19.2). By 1994 a quarter of Nissan's and one third of Toyota's production was overseas. Some of the cars produced were actually being imported back into Japan. Major American corporations, General Motors and Ford, have recently announced sweeping restructuring of their operations. For example, Ford has merged its separate North American and European operations into one single operation to be known as Ford Automotive Operations (Case study 19.3). This will reduce management overheads, rationalise research and technical operations and enable greater bulk purchase of autoparts, leading to estimated savings of two to three billion dollars a year. This will make Ford more globally competitive in world markets but will also have important implications for the locational pattern of its operations.

Major European producers such as BMW and Renault are similarly integrating their operations along global lines. It has been indicated that this will also force major component suppliers to reorganise their operations along global lines with the closure of smaller uneconomic component plants.

The global pattern of automobile production thus needs to be set against this move by the major producers to set up global scale operations. American and Japanese multi-national companies are likely to continue to dominate world production. Assembly plants are likely to be reduced in number but enlarged in size to gain economies of scale and savings on unit costs. Toyota for example in 1995 announced an expansion of its plant near Derby and a doubling of output to meet the entire needs of the European market. Plants will continue to be located mainly in the advanced countries where market demand is highest.

The number of assembly plants set up as joint ventures between multi-national companies is likely to increase. Most will be in North America and Western Europe. Despite some moves towards deregulation and great collaboration, the Japanese government is unlikely to encourage the establishment of many joint venture plants in Japan. However, as a step towards establishing their own automobile industries, developing countries such as China and Brazil are likely to encourage more joint ventures of domestic firms with established multi-national automobile manufacturers.

There clearly is a trend towards the establishment of branch plants in lower cost areas especially where suitable cheap labour is available. (Labour costs represent 20% – 30% of total production costs in automobile assembly plants.) Some will be in southern and eastern Europe but an increasing number are being set up in newly industrialising countries, especially in South East Asia where Japanese companies are most active (Figure 19.7).

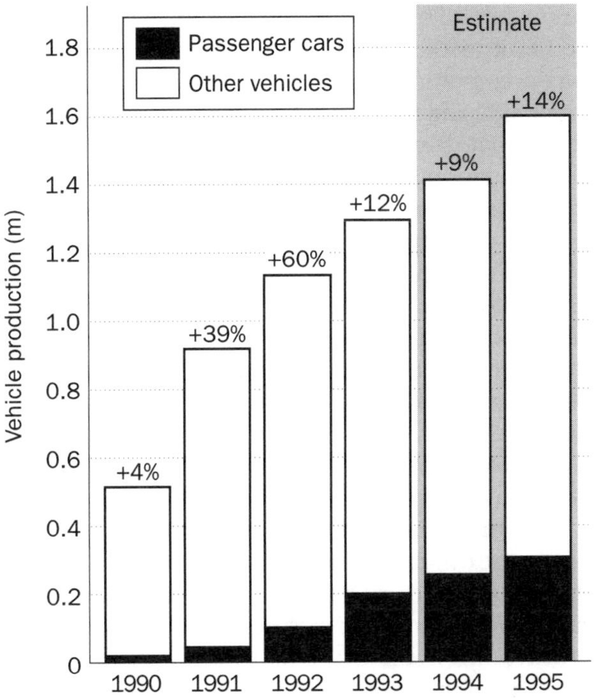

***Figure 19.7** The car industry in China – further expansion planned but foreign participation to be limited*

While established multinational corporations dominate, other multi-national corporations are emerging within the newly industrialising countries (Figure 19.8). These are likely to gain an increasing share of the world market since they can combine the latest technology with relatively low production costs. At present it is only South Korea but already Malaysia is looking to become a significant world exporter of automobiles.

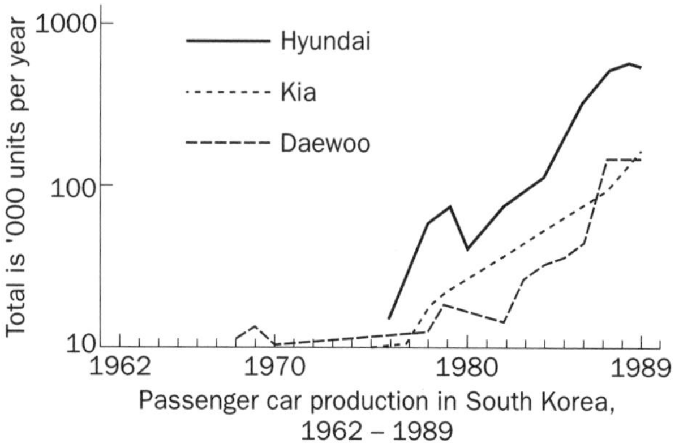

Figure 19.8 Expansion of production by South Korea's 'multinational' automobile manufacturers and the direction of vehicle exports

At a national level

A locational pattern of production is now less evident within the major producing countries due to decentralisation and rationalisation trends.

In recent years as a result of technological changes, a slump in home demand and foreign penetration of domestic markets in European countries and America, multinational corporations have had to rationalise and restructure established plants and re-negotiate their relationship with parts suppliers. Uneconomic plants have been closed and others reorganised along 'lean production lines'. The number of components and parts suppliers have been reduced with a first tier of sub-assembly suppliers established at a distance from older locations. Thus while some automobile manufacturing remains in the older established centres their importance has been greatly reduced with a large level of job loss occurring (Case study 17.1). Between 1987 and1990, General Motors closed seven plants, reducing its output by 1.3 million.

Within all the major advanced countries except Japan, the distinctive regional concentration of automobile manufacturing has broken down. It is not only due to a process of closures, rationalisation and restructuring in these regional centres, but also due to the establishment of plants, mainly by foreign countries in new locations with no previous experience of the motor industry. In the UK for example, Japanese companies have located plants in former heavy industrial areas such as the North East and South Wales and the East Midlands near Derby. Thus with the exception of the Honda plant near Swindon, plants are located at sites where plentiful labour was available, there was no history of labour militancy related to the car industry, land costs were comparatively low and financial incentives were available.

Consequently, the combined effect of closures in established automobile areas and the locating of new foreign-owned plants is decentralisation, though some vestiges of the former regional concentration of the automobile industry remains.

In Japan, however, the broad pattern of production has not changed a great deal (Case study 19.2). The tightest regional concentration remains centred in Toyota City with a looser concentration in the Tokyo region. There are three reasons why the pattern of production in Japan has not experienced the same decentralisation trends evident in the USA and West European countries.

- Japan's automobile industry is much younger and thus the locational pattern already reflected the recent influences which have affected the older patterns in the USA and Western European countries.
- Japanese multinational companies have mainly chosen to push new production overseas rather than locate new branch plants elsewhere in Japan. The continued rise in the value of the yen against other currencies has further intensified this trend towards offshore locations.
- There has been little inward investment by foreign companies which may have gone towards branch plant location in greenfield sites outside present producing areas.

It has also been the organisational policy of the major Japanese companies to locate in a new regional concentration in the USA, in a belt running south from the former Great Lakes concentration into Tennessee and Kentucky. Lower labour costs and cheaper sites combined with good accessibility have drawn most Japanese investment in new assembly plants into this belt. These Japanese-owned assembly plants have also begun to attract around them branch plants of their main component suppliers in Japan. Thus some new complexes of automobile production are emerging. The same tendency is evident in South East Asian countries such as Malaysia. In Europe, however, Japanese companies have tended to use established domestic components suppliers for their new branch plants and thus there is not the same tendency for new automobile manufacturing complexes to emerge.

19.3 The emergence of high technology industries

The micro-electronics industry: part of a new industrial revolution

The electronics industry, along with the emergence of the bio-technology industries and new materials and new energy sources, forms the basis of what is widely described as a new industrial revolution. Unlike the earlier industrial revolution its locational core is not in Western Europe but in the major Pacific Rim countries of the USA and Japan. Despite the numerous innovations associated with individuals and some companies in the EU, Europe has only a supporting, though significant, role.

The geographical pattern of this new wave of industry is different and more complex than earlier established industries and is associated with the role of the new high technology and information industries in the globalisation of industries for without them, corporations could not operate internationally.

The character of high technology industries

Today's high technology and information industries are based on a series of dramatic steps made in micro-electronic technology over the last three decades beginning with the development of transistors and semi-conductors in the late 1940s. This was followed in the 1950s by the invention of the integrated circuit whereby a number of transistors could be linked in a single silicon chip. By the early 1970s a number of complicated solid state circuits could be incorporated on a single, small chip to create a micro-processor. This dramatically increased the power of the electronic components into which they were incorporated as well as progressively decreasing their size and that of the vast range of products using these components, such as pocket calculators, computers, industrial robots and guided missiles.

It is difficult to be definitive about high technology industries, partly because they form part of the broader range of electronic industries and also because new ones are being constantly developed. At the heart of the high technology group lie the semi-conductor industry, computers and related software products, but there are many others. High technology and information industries can be broadly divided into a components sector and the products sector incorporating these components (Figure 19.9).

Structural characteristics

High technology and information industries are extremely capital intensive and have a larger than average proportion of highly skilled and highly educated personnel in professional, scientific and engineering posts – on average around 25% compared to 5% for manufacturing as a whole. The rest of the workforce is largely semi- and unskilled, mainly female and concerned with assembly work, though automation of the basic assembly stages is rapidly increasing.

High technology industries are also characterised by rapid growth rate since the 1970s, growth rate averaging over 10% annually (Case studies 19.4 and 19.5). With its future potential for growth it has attracted a large amount of public interest and government support. In all advanced countries and in the more progressive newly industrialising countries such as South Korea, further investment in the high technology sector is seen as essential to the future well-being of a country. This is because of its own potential for further growth and its application in other sectors of industry as well in offices and other services.

Initially there was hope that employment opportunities in this sector might offset losses in other sectors of advanced countries, but while some opportunities exist they are insufficient to compensate. Moreover, much of the basic assembly processes in which most employment opportunity occurs is being moved offshore to developing countries where labour is cheaper (Figure 19.10).

The computer, micro-electronic and allied industries comprising this growing sector are also characterised by ***dual structure***. While a few multinationals dominate the mass production end concerned with component manufacture and the making of mainstream products such as computers,

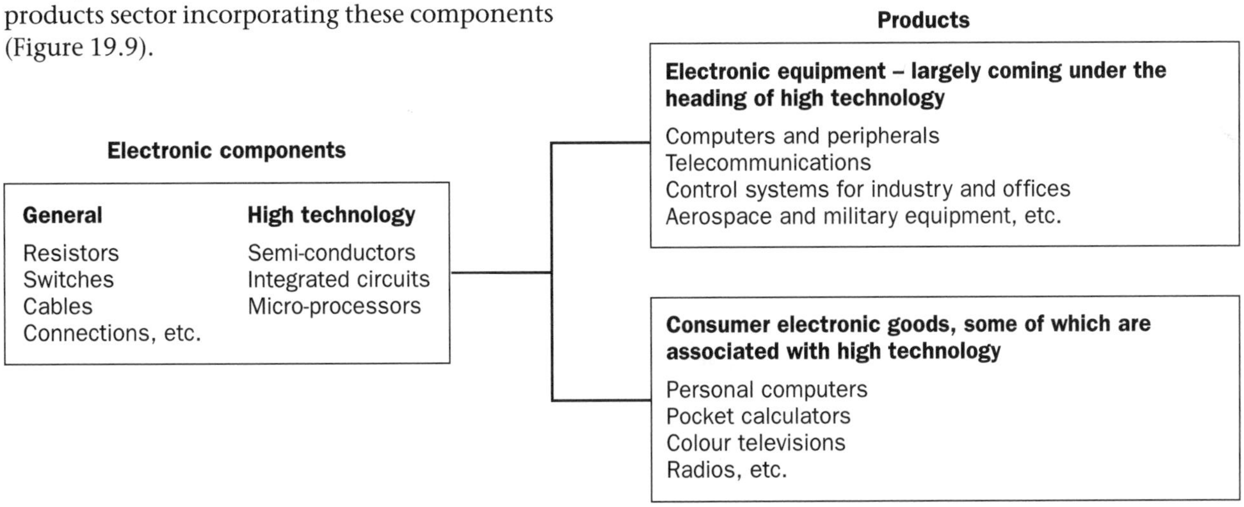

Figure 19.9 The structure of the electronics industry and the high technology industries in it

there are a vast range of smaller businesses. The most notable of these are those at the forefront of high technology innovation and concerned with research and design, together with the production of sophisticated software and specialised customised products. As an innovative and dynamic industry, there is the constant spawning of seedbed firms, many formed by university research graduates in association with the providers of the venture capital needed to support high risk innovation. Because it is an infant industry with rapid growth and change, there is a rapid turnover of small businesses – some coming in, others going bankrupt while others are merged into larger companies and a few flourish to become multinational corporations, such as Apple and Software.

However, while many small companies represent individual entrepreneurship, many others are closely linked to multinationals which control the 'heavier end' of the industry as indicated in the case of the Silicon Valley complex of industries in California and those in Silicon Glen in Scotland (Case studies 19.4 and 19.5). Apart from frontline innovative enterprises, many financially backed by those large corporations, there is a large range of smaller component and support industries acting as subcontractors to the large multinationals.

Locational pattern

All branches of the industry initially tended to be located in reasonable proximity because the small scale of enterprises and the linkage of one process of the industry to another made this possible and necessary. However, increasingly the different requirements of the basic component production and the assembly end of the industry from those of the research and design, software production and high quality customised product sectors, have led to a spatial separation of these two parts of the high technology and information industry. As a result production has become globally organised.

Spatially a global industry with a clear geographical separation between different stages of the production process

'The most significant characteristic of the semi-conductor industry is not simply that its markets are global but rather that its production is organised globally.

The electronics industry was the first to which the label 'global factory' was applied because of its early use of offshore assembly.

'It is in the semi-conductor industry that a spatial hierarchy of production at the global scale is most apparent with clear geographical separation between different stages of the production process. It is overwhelmingly the assembly stages that have been partly relocated to certain developing countries. In general, the higher level design R & D and more complex stages of production have tended to either remain in the firm's home country or to be established in other developed countries where the necessary labour skills and physical infrastructure are more readily available.'

[SOURCE: Dickens P *Global Shift*, 1992]

Like the automobile industry, the assembly side of the semi-conductor, micro-processor and also computer industries have been increasingly oriented to the cheaper locations both in the advanced and developing countries. Here plentiful and amenable semi-skilled labour is available along with cheaper land sites, supportive and flexible planning regulations and financial and other incentives from local and central governments which compete to attract them to a particular location.

As with the automobile industry, this globalisation has also been encouraged by the need to get inside markets to avoid tariff and quota restrictions on imports and by the intense competition between multinationals requiring a reduction in unit production costs for survival and expansion.

This is clearly indicated in the locational pattern for the Japanese and American producers which dominate world markets (Figure 19.10) and for the new producers, such as the South Korean Samsung conglomerate (Figure 19.11; Case study 17.3).

Three types of location are evident:

- those in South East Asia, especially China, Malaysia and Thailand and the more advanced 'tigers' such as South Korea and Singapore
- more ruralised areas in advanced countries, such as the South in the USA where cheap labour is available as a result of decreased employment opportunities in agriculture
- old declining industrial areas such as the North East of England where unemployment is high, costs economic and government incentives are available to attract newer industry as a way of reindustrialising and revitalising a region.

The needs of the more specialised innovative end of the industry are quite different and consequently, so is the locational pattern.

For successful growth of this sector of the high technology industry the following factors need to be present:

- generation of new technological knowledge, access to it, and the means of disseminating this to enable further innovation to occur and its use to be adopted in industry.

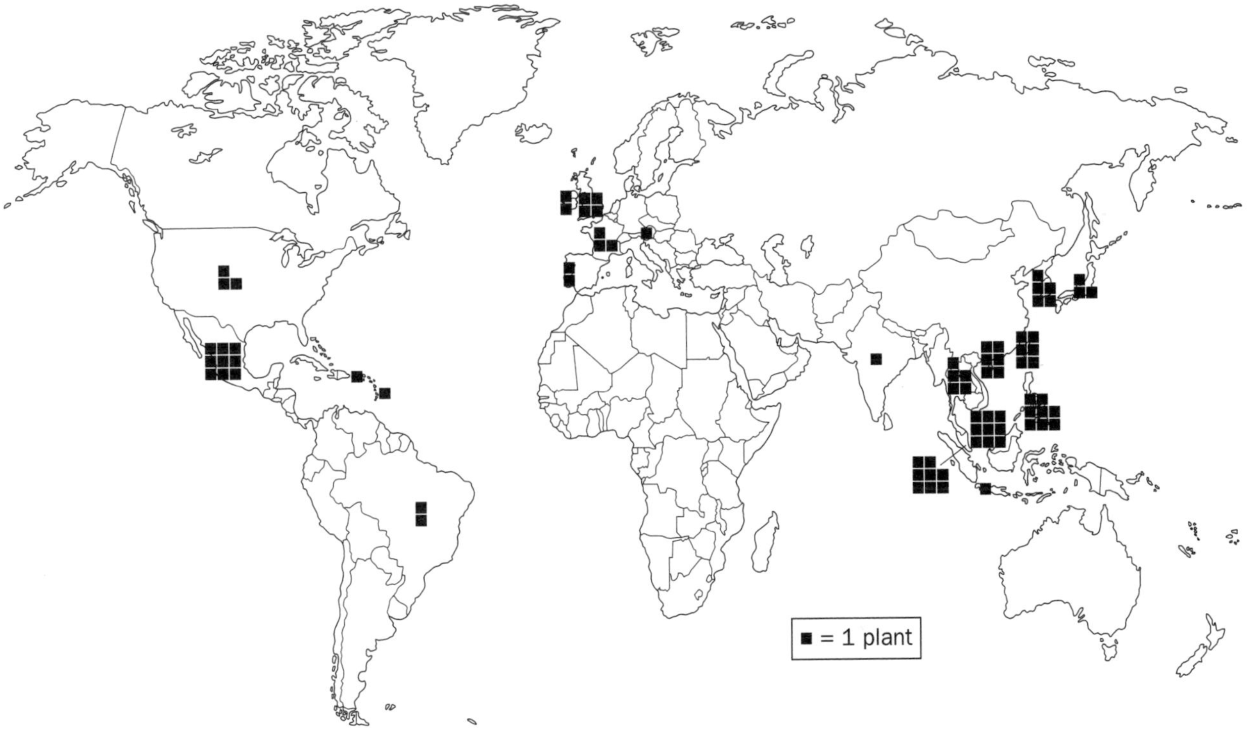

Figure 19.10 *The distribution of US semi-conductor assembly plants*

- evidence of a demand for further innovation. Much of this initially came from the needs of defence and the aerospace industry.
- availability of venture capital to finance technological developments in what is a high risk sector. Venture capital comes from a number of sources, such as university and government funding, reinvestment of profits from earlier successful ventures in the industry, and now increasingly from outside businesses, including multinationals.
- access to a pool of highly skilled and educated personnel, including young, well-qualified graduates in science technology, business and other fields.
- a pleasant and stimulating environment, both for those employed in the industry and their families. Hence semi-rural environments and science parks with good links to a major city are favoured locations.
- good accessibility not only for business purposes but also for social reasons such as the need for services, good schooling and leisure activities.

There are three major types of locations which meet these needs:

The first location includes major metropolises such as London, Tokyo and Paris. Hence the greatest amount of advanced high technology economic activity is associated with metropolises, though some have been more successful than others.

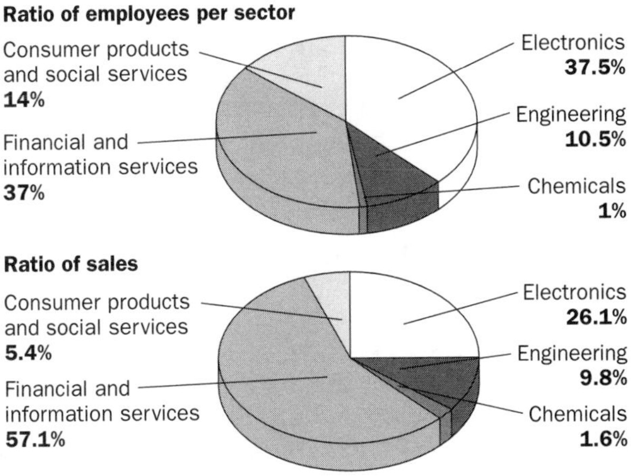

A diversified multinational producing consumer electronics, ships, machinery and petro-chemicals but also having an important banking and services sector.

The semi-conductor division is the main source of earning for the company.

The different sectors – 1994

Samsung faces fierce competition and price cutting amongst multinationals in this field.

The stakes are high for Samsung Electronics as it anxiously awaits a decision from Washington on whether the US will impose dumping duties on semi-conductors.

The world's largest manufacturer of semi-conductor memory chips establishing large assembly plants in Cleveland (North East England), China, Thailand and Mexico.

Samsung has forged alliances with other chipmakers to reduce production costs e.g. with the Japanese multinational Toshiba.

The group's strategic importance to South Korea may force the government to support it with increased subsidies loan and other aid for research and investment if dumping duties seriously threaten profits.

Figure 19.11 *Samsung – South Korea's largest conglomerate*

While some of the industry continues to flourish in inner metropolitan areas, especially small seedbed firms in old converted premises or new workshop units, the major part is in the 'new industrial space' along growth corridors leading away from within a semi-rural environment. The M4 corridor west of London is a typical example.

Another type of location is of self-standing new growth areas associated with particular universities with outstanding research facilities and reputations and located in rural areas with good accessibility. An example of this is Silicon Glen in California (Case study 19.3). Cambridge Science Park in the UK, though smaller in scale, is of a similar genre. These new growth areas developed out of university and private entrepreneurship, particularly linked with the initiative of certain individuals. Once momentum for growth was acquired, the prestige and importance of the area also drew in expertise, capital and firms from within the host country and also globally.

A third type of location also exists, namely, the planned growth centre. The high technology industry is seen as an important tool in regional planning to counter overgrowth in core regions and stimulate growth in lagging regions. Consequently, there are the planned technopoles illustrated by the Japanese technopole programme (Figure 16.5).

Also noting the success of the earlier spontaneous new high technology growth areas, universities, private enterprise and local authorities have planned and developed their own science parks, technopoles and even science cities with varying degrees of success.

Silicon Glen in Scotland, for example, has until recently prospered (Case study 19.4) whereas Akademgorod near Novosobirsk planned by Krushchev in the 1950s as a future catalyst for economic growth in Russian Siberia, has failed as a regional development project through surviving as a research centre.

Concluding comment

Each of the three industries considered can be said to represent three important stages in the development of an industrial economy.

The iron and steel industry developed as a basic industry of the ***first industrial revolution***. Despite radical changes and rationalisation, it still remains fundamental to an economy. For example, it provides important material for the construction industry and essential inputs for other industries, such as the automobile industry.

The automobile industry brought a transport revolution in the 1920s, the 1930s and the post-war years which has had wide repercussions on the structure and locational pattern of other industries as well as on settlements. It also heralded a ***second industrial revolution*** based on oil as the new energy source and on a new organisation of industry; an organisation based on the mass production assembly line introduced by Ford. Again the automobile industry remains central to modern economies.

The high technology and information industry is seen as heralding a ***new industrial revolution. It is seen as one of three contemporary revolutions***:

- there is this ***technological revolution***, to them 'at least as momentous historically as the two industrial revolutions based on the discovery of 'new sources of energy' such as, steam using coal and oil.
- ***the formation of a global economy***, that is, the structuring of all economic processes on a planetary scale and an economy working 'as a unit in world wide space be it for capital, management, labour, technology, information or markets'.
- ***the emergence of a new form of economic production and management*** which Castell and Hall call 'informational'. The basis of it is that 'productivity and competitiveness are increasingly dependent on the generation of new knowledge and on the access to, and processing of, appropriate information.'

If the economies of mature industrial countries are to prosper and meet the growing competition from the rapidly developing newly industrialising countries typified by the 'Asian Tigers', it is essential they are at the forefront of this technological and informational industrial revolution.

case study

19.1 UK iron and steel industry: its current structure in EU and world contexts

British Steel now one of most efficient producers in Europe with productivity greatly improved.

Continued job losses are likely as, even if demand recovers, new technology reduces labour needs and lower costs e.g. Port Talbot Works introduced computerised controls of steel production reducing waste and enhancing efficiency. In the 1960s the works had 17 000 employees; in 1994 it had 4200.

Competing against cheaper imports, British Steel will concentrate on special steels for particular markets and expand exports e.g. they produced 3 million tonnes of steel for Toyota, SA plant in Turkey to supply 45% of this new work's car body panels.

By product grouping	£m
Uncoated strip products	955
Coated strip products	918
Sections and plates	931
Tubular products	3900
Stainless products	–
Other steel products	74
Total finished products	3 268
Semi-finished products	237
Total steel industry products	3 505
Markets by destination by turnover value	
UK	2 233
Rest of Europe	1 223
Other areas	735
Total	4 191

British steel production by turnover value, 1994

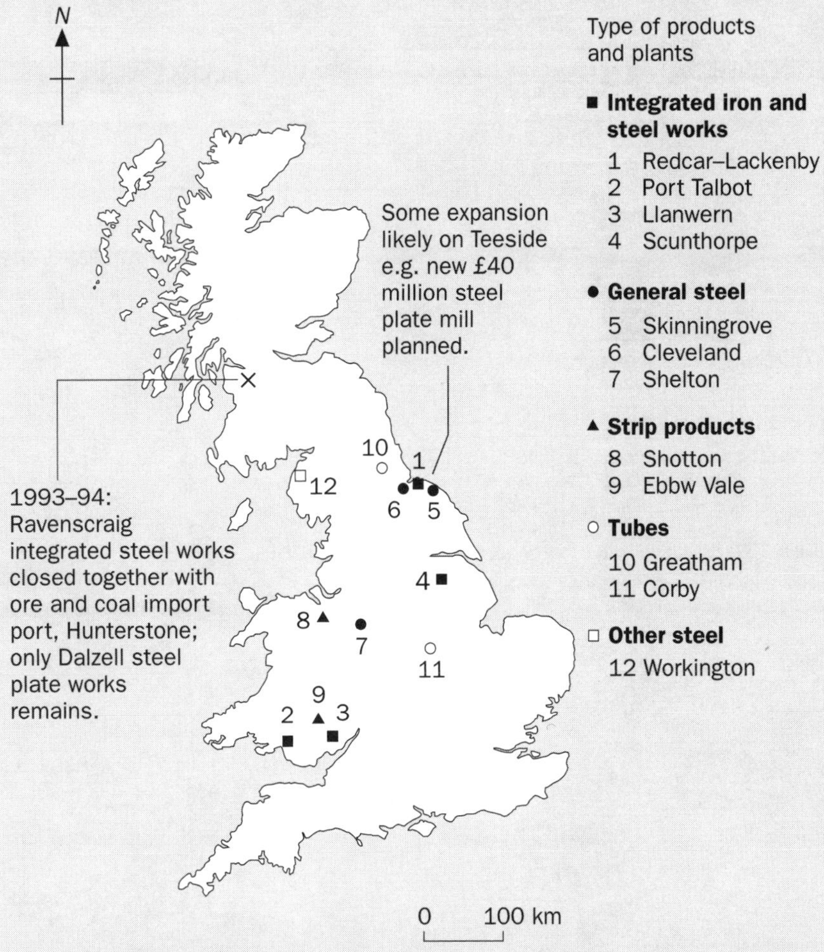

Location of British Steel Industry 1994

European Union, 1994: the problem of over-capacity

The EU total capacity is 170 million tonnes; an excess capacity goes up to 30 million tonnes. The EU aims to get agreement amongst steel producers to cut production by between 19 and 26 million tonnes to bring production more in line with market demand. This, along with some restriction on imports, would stop a fall in prices which is contributing to non-viability of some producers (Eastern Europe also has over-capacity).

Since 1992 the EU has been trying to devise a new plan to replace the Davignon Plan to control steel products. The EU Competition Commissioner tried to get producers to agree to a deal involving protection from cheap imports, monitoring of steel demand, forecast demand to match production to demand and voluntary agreement for cuts in production scheme. Even though this scheme was not accepted in 1994, there is still hope for voluntary agreements. The main problem has been the refusal of state-protected

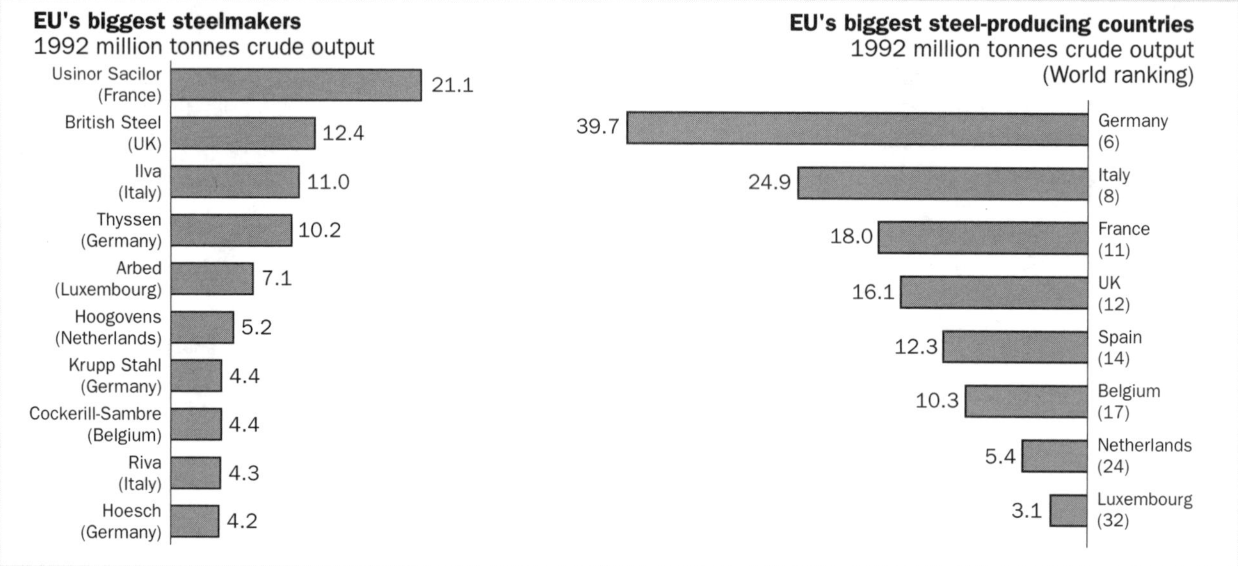

EU's biggest steelmakers and steel-producing countries, 1992

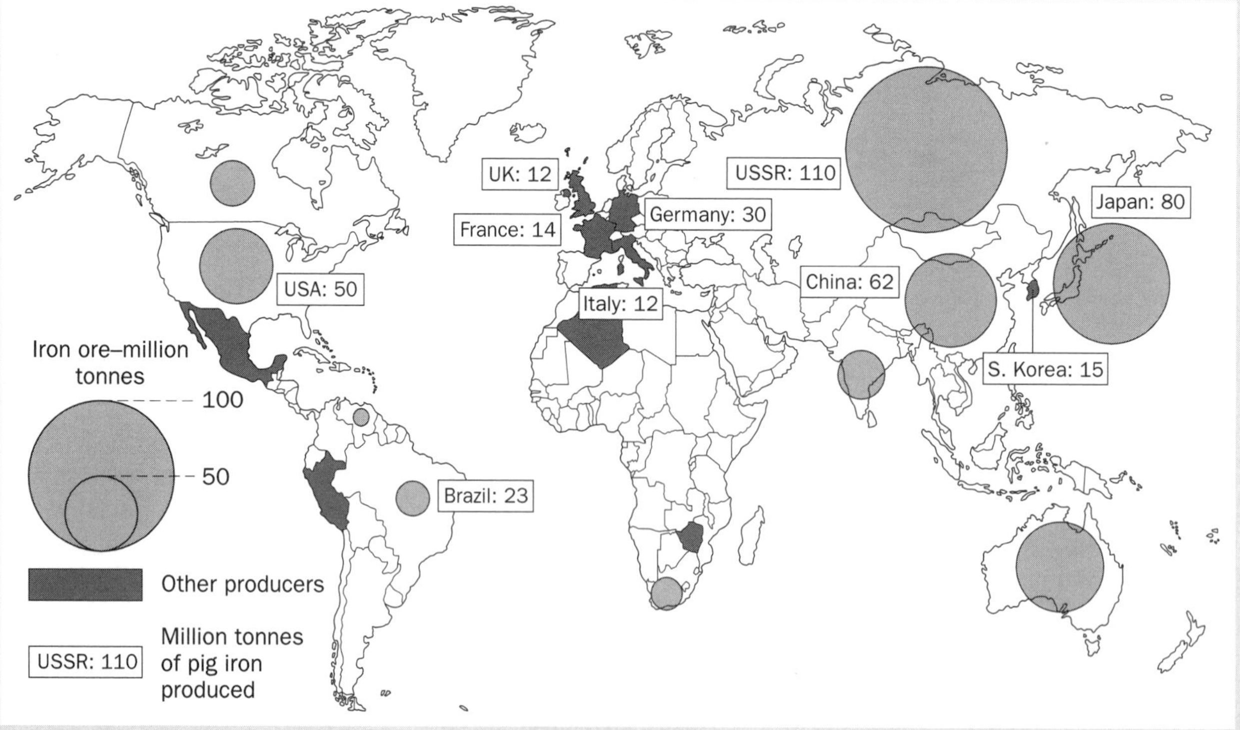

Main pig iron and steel producers, 1990

producers to cut production e.g. Spain agreed to close an older integrated plant at Anzio in exchange for a new modern steel plant at Sastaso but so far has failed to do so. De-industrialisation in Europe, even without recession, has reduced demand in EU countries and EU producers are having difficulty competing against lower cost producers in world markets.

World context

World steel demand is still steadily rising. Older industrialised countries still provide the main market which, in 1993, consumed 297 million tonnes against 135 million tonnes in the developing world. However, the demand trend is shifting towards the industrialising developing countries, especially in Asia. Here market expansion rate is greatest including India and China.

However, world production and capacity have expanded in excess of demand due to over investment capacity in the advanced countries in the 1980s and the rapid expansion of new producers in the developing world of China, South Korea and Brazil.

New producers have the advantage that not 'held back' by older works as in advanced countries where they cannot afford to lose capital invested in older plant, nor adopt new technology wholesale. New producers with the help of foreign investment and new technology can have the most cost efficient plants, with the added advantages of local or cheaply imported raw materials at the lowest prices, cheaper labour costs, cheaper land and less environmental control.

South Korea: an example of a newly industrialised country producer

South Korea was a negligible producer until 1967 but is now a leading world producer based on an expanding home market and competitive export, state support and foreign investment, and as a late entrant, was able to adopt the most modern cost efficient production methods. It is therefore a cheap producer e.g. the main producer Pohang Iron and Steel just bought Corex technology from Voest Alpine (Austria) to reduce iron-ore directly to hot metal with 20% saving on costs.

In the advanced world increasing efforts have been made to rationalise and explore niche markets. Most progress has been made by smaller specialist producers e.g. Nucor in south USA has the fastest expansion in the USA, based on mini mills, new technology, risk taking and cheap locations.

Future trends: the globalisation of the steel industry

- The world market for steel is expanding especially demand from China and other developing countries. Their share of world consumption has risen to 30% (1994) from 20% (1988).
- National interest in steel production has meant a significant part of the industry has been under state ownership and unlike other industries such as chemicals and motor vehicles, multinational companies have not emerged. However, increasing privatisation has allowed companies to be more competitive and have greater productivity. To tap expanding overseas markets, the steel industry needs globalising. The first step was the joint venture between British Steel, LTV Steel (USA) and Sumito Steel (Japan) to form the new Trico Steel in 1994. Trico was to tap expanding markets in China and other developing countries. This may lead to the first multinational steel corporation.
- Technological advances have been rapid to lower costs and produce a greater range of steels for specific markets e.g. an ultra-light steel for car bodies. Mini mills have greater flexibility than large integrated works and now produce one third of world steel. Their share is likely to expand but large integrated works will remain dominant for some time as their productivity and flexibility increases.

case study

19.2 Japan: its car industry with reference to the Toyota Corporation

Location of the Japanese car industry

General locating factors

The car industry is concentrated mainly in the Nagoya and Tokyo regions, close to much of the home market and major export outlets. Initially it developed in the Tokyo region with the Nagoya region developing later, based on existing skills and business interests in cycle and small engineering workshops, the presence of an adaptable labour force and an expanding home market. Cumulative and agglomerative advantages for these regions followed, e.g. linkages to component suppliers, access to research institutes and government agencies.

Modern line assembly methods requiring more space led to dispersion of assembly plants to the periphery of the producing regions but still within easy reach of component suppliers and markets. (Most minor producing regions are also well linked by rail and road to the major home markets.)

Decline in exports

Exports have been declining since 1986 mainly because Japanese manufacturers have increasingly pushed more production offshore into East Asia, North America and Europe to more readily access overseas markets and also because costs of production have been rising in Japan compared with overseas locations.

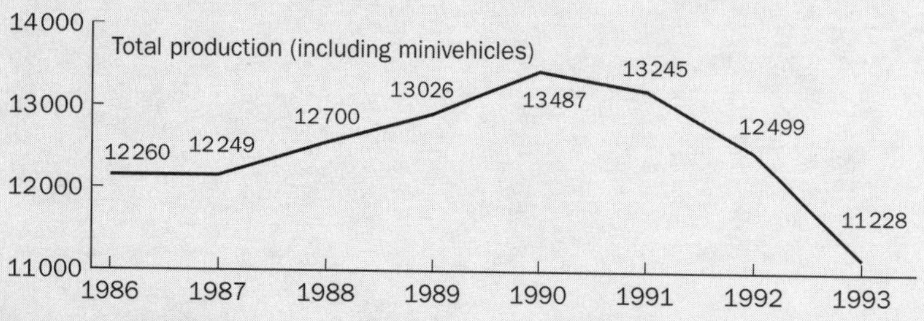

Production affect by recent recession

Exports for 1993 were 5 million, down 11% on 1992. As a consumer industry the automobile industry is sensitive to upturns and downturns in the economy. There is currently excess capacity and Japanese producers are re-organising production to meet other markets not only from established producers but also from South Korea.

The Toyota Corporation

Factors which influenced regional localisation

- The Toyota motor company grew out of the Toyada weaving and corn industries which included many small craft and engineering firms in the 1930s. The family-based concern then moved into steel and aircraft manufacture. By the 1950s, they had the basis for expansion into a large

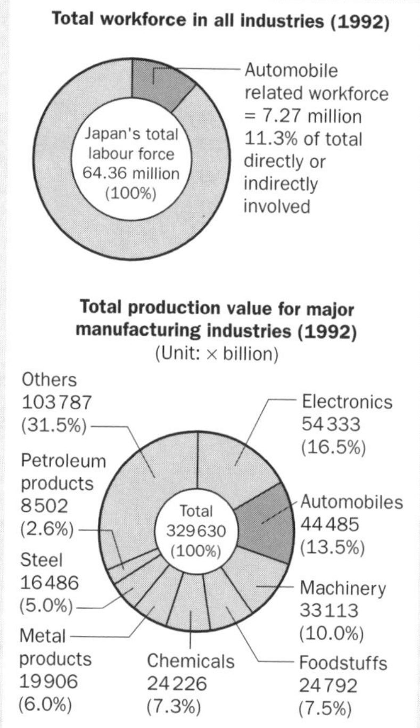

Japan's leading industries

corporation. Although concentrating on automobile manufacture, the corporation has diversified into other activities e.g. prefabricated buildings.

- The company adopted a policy of high investment to maintain technological advance which had the backing of 50 Japanese banks. It was the first corporation to develop the 'lean production system', including the just-in-time principle.
- It is organised as one mammoth production system centred on one head office and has good labour relations. The management and labour are united on goals.
- Toyota was given government financial backing and protected by restriction on foreign imports. It has links overseas with General Motors, sharing design and research.
- Toyota City is the sixth largest industrial city in Japan and lies approximately 250 km south of Tokyo. About 90% of its workforce is connected with the motor industry. With production of 3 million vehicles a year it is the country's largest producer and now has an expanding number of overseas subsidiaries and collaborative ventures.
- A labour force is readily available, the company previously being sited in an agricultural region with a large adaptable workforce who are reliable and hardworking. In turn, the company provides security of employment, housing, some shopping facilities, health and recreation provision.
- An expanding home demand with the increasing affluence of post-war years is a major influence. Toyota City commands a central position in the Pacific Industrial Belt where most of the demand is.
- There is close communication and information links with the Tokyo region. The research, secretariat and sales force are in Tokyo itself. The excellent communication network and infrastructure includes export points.
- The company has space and facilities for mass production. It was initially centred on the small town of Koromo; its local authority was influential in attracting Toyota Motors to the site in the 1950s. Plenty of land was available cheaply, a dam was built to supply adequate water; parking and other facilities were added, a new highway was built and a rail line extension encouraged.
- Toyota also has a production plant in Kyushu and an autopart plant in Hokkaido.

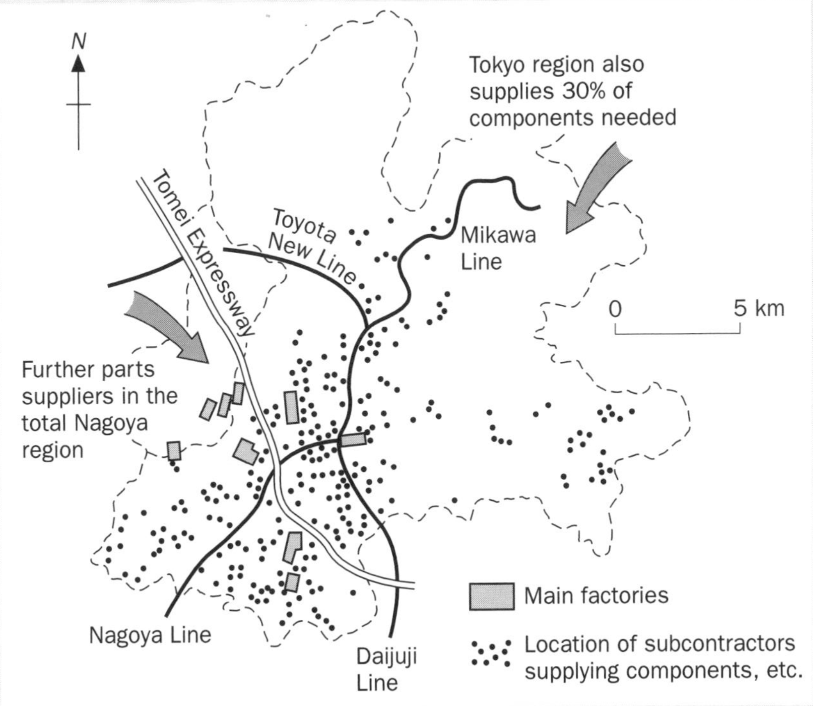

Tokyo City and the Toyota Motor Corporation

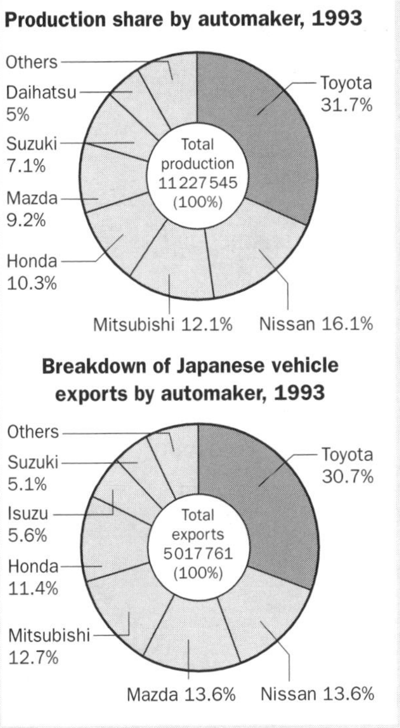

Relative importance of Toyota motor corporation in Japanese automobile production

Toyota's mid-term global business plan

- to increase overseas production from 890 000 units to 1 350 000 by 1996; an increase of 50%. In the USA output has been doubled from 200 000 to 400 000 units and in the UK from 37 000 units to 100 000 units in 1994.
- to promote exports from overseas bases. e.g. from USA bases back to Japan and to Taiwan, Europe, Canada and Middle East; from UK to other European countries.
- to promote complementary auto parts supply scheme in ASEAN, taking advantage of regional strengths
- to have design centres overseas co-operating with Toyota's Research and Development centres in Japan
- global procurement system for autoparts and materials, including actively searching for new suppliers and promote design in projects. Toyota expects its parts and material supplies from overseas suppliers to its major production bases in 10 countries, including Japan, to increase from 6.3 billion dollars (1992) to 9.7 billion dollars (1996). It will also extend its Toyota Supplier Support Centre. New facilities in North America are to supply regions outside North America to encourage improvement in cost efficiency, quality and just-in-time delivery
- global co-operation with overseas automakers including joint sales agreement in Japan e.g. Volkswagen and GM Cars in Toyota (Duo) retail sales outlets main overseas tie-ups in capital and operations with GM in USA; joint new United Motor Manufacturing (NUMM) in western USA and a joint venture in Australia and with Volkswagen in Germany and Renault in a joint venture in Colombia.

1993	Total
North America	532 788
Latin America	2 638
Europe	49 455
Asia	161 899
Middle East	2 147
Oceania	58 732
Africa	81 056
Grand total	888 715

Overseas production by region, 1993

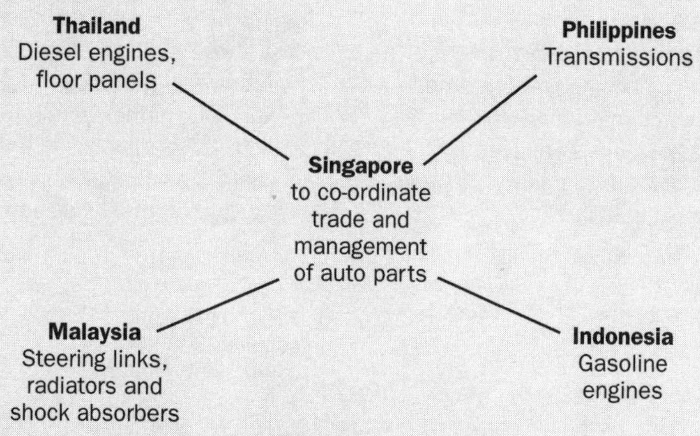

Auto part branch plants overseas as part of Toyota's Global Procurement system

case study

19.3 Ford: its restructuring and ambitions to become a global car company

What is involved

- Ford is planning to move to a single set of processes and systems throughout: its product development, manufacturing and supply and sales activity.
- Ford is re-organising itself along global product lines based on five vehicle programme centres (VPCs); four in North America and one in Europe

Example of effect of this restructuring: the nearest to a one-model world car has been the Mondeo produced for both American and European markets:

- Assembly plants in Genk (Belgium), Kansas City (USA) and in Mexico
- Engine plants in Bridgend (UK), Cologne (Germany), Cleveland (USA) and Chihuana (Mexico)
- Manual transmissions – Halewood (Merseyside UK) and Cologne, electronically controlled gear box (US)
- After a global search common component producers were chosen to supply both European and American 'Mondeo' assembly plants.

A world wide structure

Supporting the world wide product development process based on the VPCs, Ford's manufacturing, purchasing and marketing will each become integrated world wide. An automotive strategy office will co-ordinate strategic planning.

Why restructure

For the first time in its history it is seeking to become a global corporation, breaking down the national and regional barriers that have blocked its drive to create common vehicles for the world market.

All the world's car makers face the same challenge of trying to improve the efficiency of their enormous investment programmes while at the same time producing a greater diversity of products.

They must increase the speed by which they bring products to the market while jumping into emerging markets.

They must squeeze their massive materials purchasing bills by moving to global sourcing for parts and systems.

Problem of integrating its joint ventures and a world wide system

- owns 25% of the Japanese Mazda company
- integration of Latin American operations where jointly owns Autolatina with Volkswagen.

Any integration of these joint ventures into the Ford world wide system will require the cooperation of the foreign companies involved in these joint ventures.

Factory sales

worldwide 000 units	**1993**
Cars USA	1950
Cars Canada	128
Total cars	**2077**
Trucks USA	1876
Trucks Canada	126
Total trucks	**2002**
Total US & Canada	**4078**
Germany	831
UK	422
Spain	211
Taiwan	114
Mexico	91
Australia	127
Japan	53
Other	37
Total overseas	**1886**
Total worldwide factory sales	**5964**

Revenue (loss)

by region $m	**1992**	**1993**
Canada	(200)	(91)
USA	(400)	1500
Europe excl Jaguar	(647)	(407)
Europe inc Jaguar	(1288)	(960)
Latin America	211	459
Asia Pacific and other	148	50
Total foreign automotive	**(1129)**	**(542)**
Financial services worldwide	1043	1600

Ford Corporation: revenue and sales

case study

19.4 The Silicon valley, California: a crucible of the high technology industry

Silicon Valley has a guaranteed place in history as the original industrial core of the revolution of information technologies

Location of Silicon Valley

Most of the key inventions in Micro-electronics and computing were made here

↓

e.g. Integrated circuits and the Planar Process to produce them

↓

e.g. Micro-processor

↓

e.g. Personal computer

Key stages in the development of Silicon Valley

- Background of innovation in electronic engineering from early 1920s at Stanford University
- Stimulated further by World War II technology demands and advances and the setting up of the Stanford Industrial park in the 1950s with university research graduates encouraged to set up businesses there
- 1960s: growth of micro-electronics and semi-conductor firms and further spin off innovations; support of government finance to serve military and aerospace space needs together with private venture capital crucial to expansion
- Growing international reputation plus launch of personal computing and associated software in 1970s
- Growing domination of computer side 1980s; continued innovation and expansion even through recession of late 1980s; 35% growth.

Basic factors fundamental to success

- Entrepreneurial research, innovation and dissemination; with leading individuals to stimulate protégés to further developments; initially from Stanford University and later Berkeley and other local universities; reputation of valley attracted more from outside
- Availability of government finance and high risk venture capital
- Continued availability of highly qualified work force
- Strong social and professional networking to share ideas and stimulate further innovation; a creative synergy (information) culture emerged
- In earlier phases: access to cheap West Coast ethnic labour significant e.g. Hispanic and Vietnamese
- Initially pleasant working environment and good access to San Francisco metropolis
- Strong links with industry and continued rapid growth in market demand.

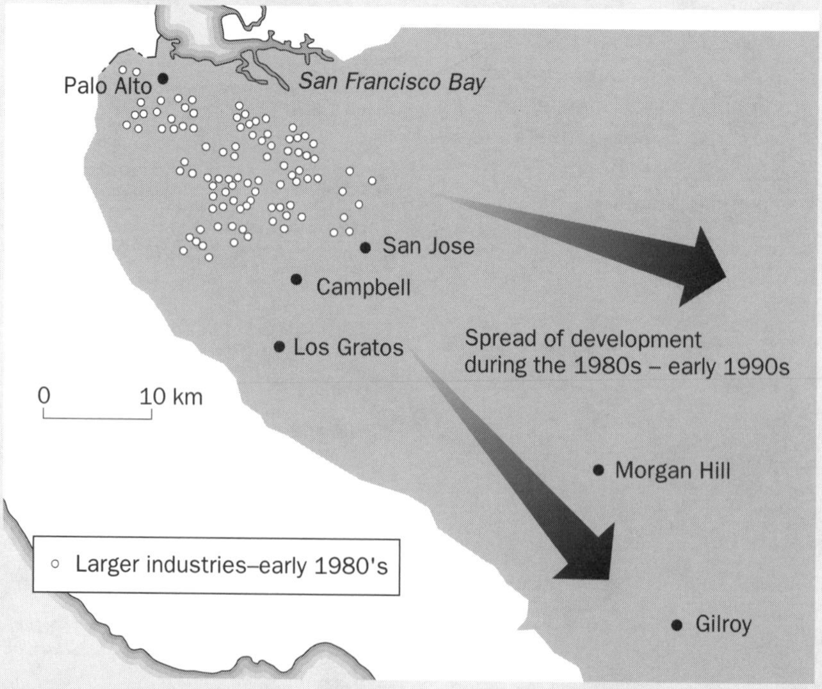

Silicon Valley in Santa Clara country

Growing diseconomies and a darker side

- Original agricultural pleasant environment now highly urbanised and spreading; spiralling land prices, destruction of environment, road congestion and even chemical ground contamination
- High social stress culture
- Increasing social segregation and inequality between high achievers and families and the lower paid semi-skilled group increasingly spatially and socially marginalised.

Economic structure

- Electronics manufacturing ranges widely but broadly it is based on the semi-conductor/integrated circuit related production, computers, especially personal computers, and software production with computing and software now dominant. More automated, less skilled assembly production has now moved out to cheaper locations in the USA such as Texas and abroad. Singapore Silicon Valley concentrates on research and design and high quality customised production, for example.
- Direct supporting services such as financial, computer business services and consultancies
- Other activities including construction services, leisure consumer and production services for what is now a highly urbanised region.

Scale of production

- Now internationalised; in the early 1980s it was dominated by small companies with less than five workers; innovative and of high calibre. As Silicon Valley gained in importance and prestige outside corporations were attracted to collaborative ventures and branch plants, including Japanese Corporations. Initial small ventures also grew into international companies for example Apple, Internet, Hewlett & Packard, Software.
- Larger companies employing more than a 1000 each and given below indicate range of production and types of firms with main locations (though now spread further east and south from this concentration).

case study

19.5 Silicon Glen, Scotland: a high-technology growth centre or a low-cost assembly area?

Location decisions are taken globally

'Mr John Ward, the resident director of IBM in Scotland and chairman of the SEF, says that intensified global competition means that a multinational plant in Scotland must compete for survival against other plants in the same group. Mr Ward acknowledges that multinationals will make strategic decisions according to their own interests.'

[SOURCE: Monitor USA Consultancy report]

Structural weaknesses

- Silicon Glen is largely an artificial creation. The government encouraged inward investment from global companies which regard Scotland as a relatively low-cost manufacturing base for the European Union market. However, these companies have not brought in research and development facilities to stimulate further growth.
- After a good average growth of 18% through the 1980s, little growth occurred and employment has levelled off since 1989.
- Scottish subcontractors and component suppliers provide only 12% of components. Thus the general impact on the economy is weakened.
- There is insufficient integration between companies, universities and investors, such as venture capitalists. Thus the network present in Silicon Valley California, is not present in Scotland and Silicon Glen lacks the ability to respond to market opportunities.

The shift from smokestack to electronic industries – a success story

'Elegant electronics factories set in landscaped parkland, producing personal computers, mobile telephones of microchips, have replaced smokestack industries such as steel and shipbuilding as the mainstay of Scotland's manufacturing industry.

For the government, the Scottish electronics industry is one of its successes of industrial policy. It accounts for 40 per cent of Scotland's exports.'

[SOURCE: *Financial Times* 2.2.94]

Scotland – trends in electronics compared to non-electronic industries

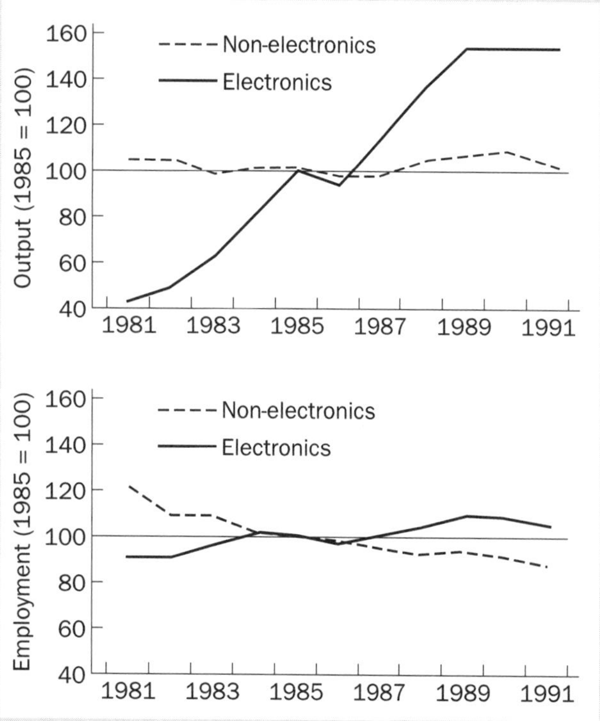

Multinationals with branches in Silicon Glen

The top high-technology employers

Company	Location	Products	Employees
IBM	Greenock	PCs & monitors	2 300
Motorola	East Kilbride	Semiconductors	2 000
Motorola	Bathgate	Cellular phones	1 600
NCR	Dundee	Auto teller machines	1 600
Digital	Ayr	Workstation & PCs	1 550
National Semi	Greenock	Microchips	1 300
Hewlett-Packard	S. Queensferry	Telecoms	1 000
NEC	Livingston	Semiconductors	850
Compaq	Erskine	PCs	700
JVC	Kilbride	Televisions	700
Digital	S. Queensferry	Wafers	559
Mitsubishi	Haddington	Televisions	514

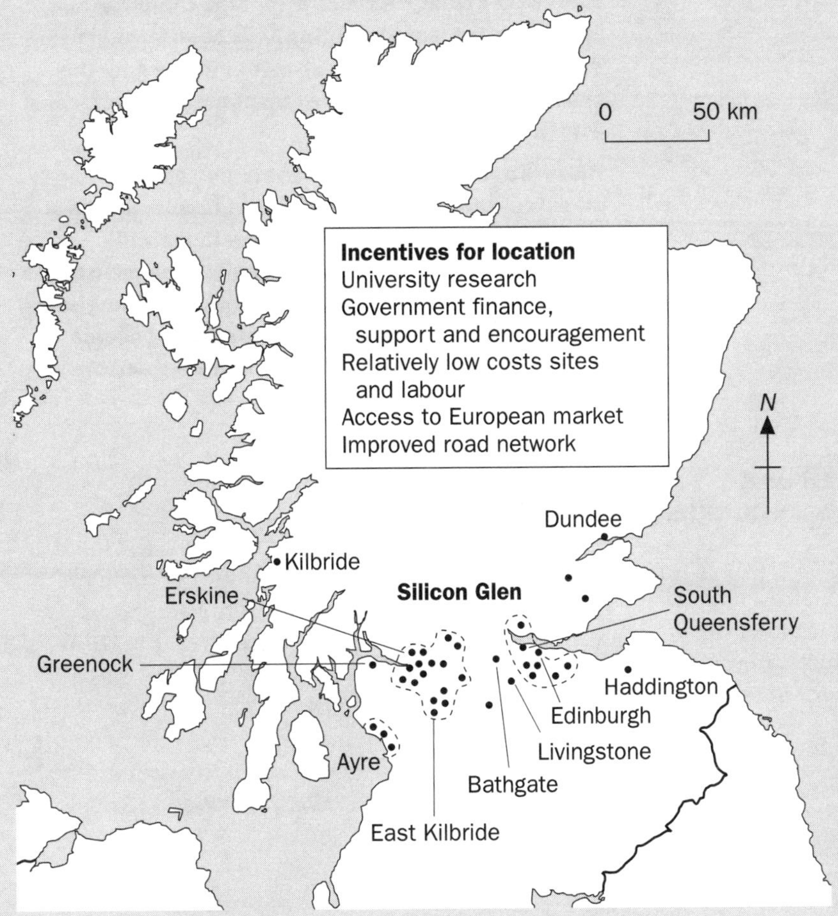

Location of firms in Silicon Glen

Evidence for further growth

- The stagnation of output may be simply a consequence of the general recession in the late 1980s and early 1990s. Exabyte, which makes computer tape systems, is opening a factory in Falkirk to employ 100. Compaq is taking on 250 extra staff.
- Local branches of multinationals now are co-operating with one another and indigenous companies through a Scottish Electronics Forum (SEP).
- There is strong high technology research in local Scottish universities, such as Strathclyde.

The government needs to alter its approach. Too much emphasis has been placed on encouraging inward movement of firms to create jobs and too little on financing and encouraging research and development and new products. The government need to persuade multinationals to put down deeper roots and encourage innovation through indigenous companies.

20

CHAPTER 20

Global manufacturing

Many of the changes which affect the character and importance of manufacturing have been introduced in the previous chapter. This chapter will consider the changing importance of the manufacturing sector as a whole.

There is a relative decline in the importance of manufacturing both within the world economy and in the national economies of the older industrial countries due to the much more rapid expansion of the service sector (Figure 20.1). Fundamental changes are also taking place within the manufacturing sector itself, both in the nature of manufacturing and the way it is spatially organised.

20.1 Tertiarisation or the increasing dominance of services in economies

Dickens, in his discussion of *Global Shift – The Internationalisation of Economic Activity*, shows the increasing importance of services in a number of ways: by share of gross domestic product, of employment, of trade and of foreign investment in services.

'One of the most significant developments of the last few decades in the global economy has been the rapid growth of service industries ... Services account for the largest share of gross domestic product in all but the lowest income countries. They are increasingly the major source of employment in all the developed market economies and in many developing countries as well ... During the 1980s international trade in commercial services accelerated to become an important driving force in its own right in the global trading system. The services sector has also been attracting an increasing share of the world foreign direct investment ... services now account for a larger share of direct foreign investment, for the leading industrialised countries as a whole, than manufacturing industry.

[SOURCE: Dickens P *Global Shift*, 1993]

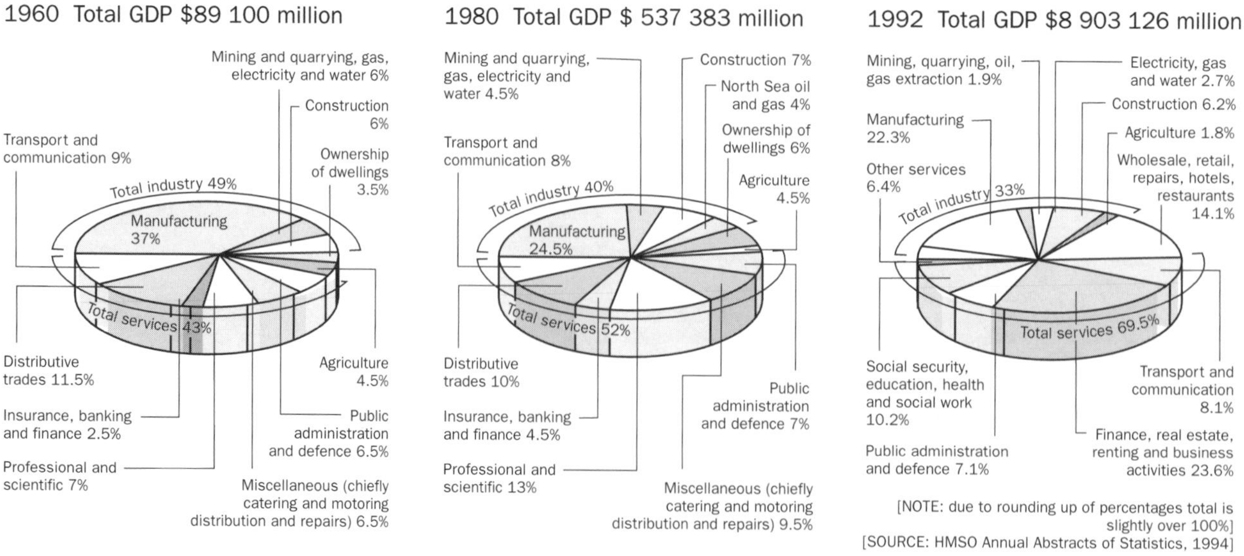

Figure 20.1 Change in the UK economy, 1960, 1980 and 1992

	Agriculture	Industry	Services
Average for Low Income Countries	28	34	36
Average for Middle Income Countries	10	36	52
Average for High Income Countries	3	32	65

NOTE: Industry consists mainly of manufacturing but also includes mining and the public utilities – gas, electricity and water
[SOURCE: based on World Development Report, 1996]

Figure 20.2 *The structure of production as percentages of GDP, 1994*

Services expansion marks the transition from an industrial to a post-industrial society. It is a 'natural' step in the process of modernisation (Figures 20.1 and 20.2).

With increasing affluence and educational advancement there is a limit to demand for material goods. Although new consumer goods may continually be brought onto the market, like high technology products such as personal computers and home entertainment systems, an increasing proportion of household income is spent on services to improve the quality of life as seen for example in the increased expenditure on leisure and recreation. ***However, changes in household expenditure only accounts for consumer services.***

Expansion has been even more rapid in the other service sectors, that of ***producer services*** (generally classified as the quaternary sector). Producer services largely meet the needs of businesses including manufacturing companies, and those of government. These services include finance, banking, insurance, marketing and advertising, commercial law, research and design, and management consultancies, but may also include a range of other activities such as warehousing and freighting. Expansion in producer services is related to the increased internationalisation of economic activity including global manufacturing and the impact of advances in high technology and information technology, for example, in international financial transactions.

Whereas changes in manufacturing have led to spatial dispersion of manufacturing activity both globally and nationally, producer services are characterised by a high degree of concentration in new major world metropolises. Paris and London for example have by far the greatest concentrations in Europe and their share is increasing (Figure 33.9). There are emerging international or super cities which form the service nodes, managing and linking together the different parts of an increasingly complex global economy.

'The spatial dispersion of production, including its internationalisation, has contributed to the growth of centralised service nodes for the management and regulation of the new space economy. To a considerable extent the weight of economic activity over the last fifteen years has shifted from production places to centres of finance and highly specialised services'
[SOURCE: Hall P *Forces Shaping Urban Europe*, Urban Studies, 1993]

Reasons for concentration are associated with the initial and cumulative advantages of large cities, including a highly sophisticated infrastructure, the presence of the highly skilled and specialised personnel, the prestige of the city and the possibility of the close personal contact and proximity still needed between producer services and their major clients, such as the head offices of multinational companies and government departments. Modern information technology also makes it possible to centralise producer services, so gaining economies of scale. As is evident in most cities, branches of services are closing and activities being concentrated in fewer but larger centres.

20.2 **Relative decline of manufacturing**

'Relative decline in manufacturing activity should not be confused with absolute decline – manufacturing output continues to increase'.

While services have expanded more rapidly than manufacturing, manufacturing output worldwide has continued to increase. Despite increases in the newly industrialising countries, most is still in the older established industrial countries (Figure 20.3). These countries are likely to dominate world manufacturing for the foreseeable future. Allowing for short-term recessions, output of manufacturing has continued to rise in the industrialised countries though employment has fallen (Figure 20.3). While declining employment is a serious social and economic problem, it is not a true indicator of the state of manufacturing itself. The level and value of manufacturing output are more objective indicators. These have continually risen.

Manufacturing is fundamental to economies, both providing products and goods for the home market and for external trade. An important proportion of service activity and employment is directly related to and dependent on the manufacturing sector. Thus while accepting that there has been a shift towards a service-based economy, governments in advanced countries are increasingly seeing the need to arrest the relative decline in manufacturing.

	1971	1991
	(in $ millions)	
Low/Middle Income Countries Example of Middle Income (Newly Industrialising Countries)	**243 973**	**1 090 664**
Korea	1 180	77 821
Brazil	10 421	90 062
Mexico	8 697	63 784
High Income Countries Examples of High Income (Advanced Industrial Countries)	**603 564**	**3 397 192**
Japan	73 342	970 484
Germany	70 888	467 900
Italy	29 093	241 346

[Based on *Structure of Manufacturing*, World Development Report, 1994]

***Figure 20.3** Value added in manufacturing, 1971 and 1991*

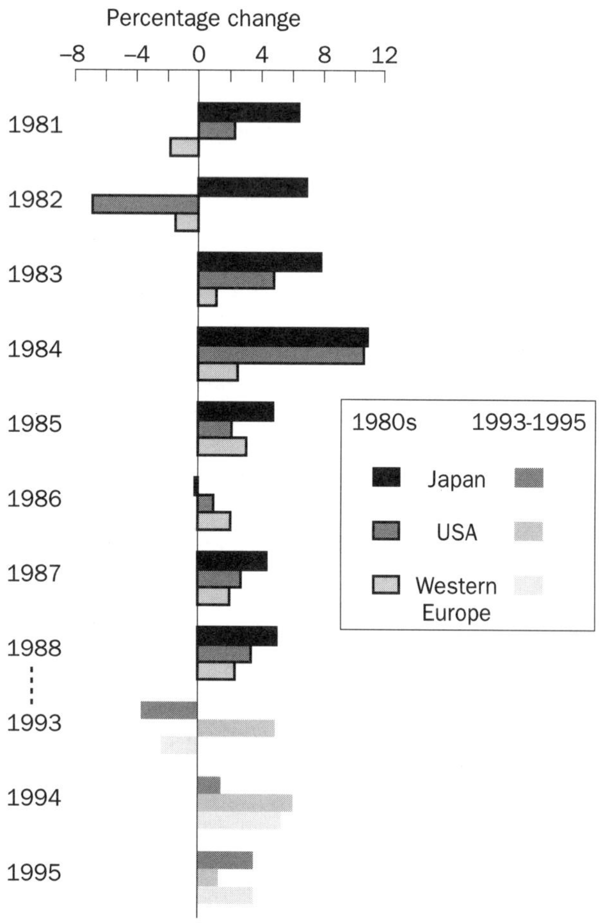

[SOURCE: based on *Industry and Development: Global Report*, UNIDO 1987]

***Figure 20.4** The differential manufacturing performance of the USA, Western Europe and Japan since the 1980s*

20.3 A global shift: de-industrialisation and restructuring in advanced countries

Fundamental changes taking place in the manufacturing sector can be summarised under three related headings.

Manufacturing on a global scale

Manufacturing is increasingly being organised on a global scale as multinational companies command an increasing larger share of production. At this global level two important spatial shifts have also occurred.

From the 1950s to 1970s the most important was the emergence of Japan as one of the world's leading manufacturing countries vying with the USA as a world economic superpower. Most adversely affected were countries of Western Europe, particularly the UK and the USA. Their share of world manufacturing output and trade in manufactured goods fell (Figure 20.5).

	Rank *			Share of world manufacturing output (%)*		
	1963	**1987**	**1994**	**1963**	**1987**	**1994**
USA	1	1	1	40.3	24.0	24.9
Japan	5	2	2	5.5	20.4	16.9
West Germany	2	3	3	9.7	10.1	10.3 (Germany)
France	4	4	4	6.3	5.4	4.9
UK	3	5	5	6.5	3.3	3.8
Italy	6	6	6	3.4	2.2	4.8

* Market economies only
[SOURCE: *World Development Report*, UNIDO, Industry and Development]

***Figure 20.5** Shifts between the older industrialised countries: changes in manufacturing production, 1963 – 94*

Since the 1970s newly industrialising countries, especially those of South East Asia, Brazil and Mexico, have become increasingly important. While these and other emergent newly industrialising countries are taking an increasing share of world manufacturing output, a significant amount of this can simply be seen as an extension of manufacturing in the advanced countries, since it represents direct foreign investment by multinationals based in the advanced countries. For economic reasons these multinationals have chosen to transplant some stages of the production process to the developing countries. However, the more mature of the newly industrialising countries, such as South Korea, also now have their own multinationals, producing for the home market and competing for world markets. These are reversing the investment process by investing in branch plants in the advanced countries such as the USA and the UK. Globalisation of manufacturing is thus taking on another dimension.

There are many reasons for these global shifts as a summary of the forces behind the Japanese economic miracle illustrates (Figure 20.6), but at the core of it lies the concept of ***comparative advantage***, that is, that ***areas will produce those items in which they have the greatest ratio advantage over other areas.*** This means that an area will specialise in the production of those goods which it can most efficiently and cost effectively produce. In the 1960s and 1970s ***comparative advantage*** shifted towards Japan and away from other advanced industrial countries. For some aspects of manufacturing, the comparative advantage has now moved in favour of the newly developing countries.

Newly industrialising countries have a number of advantages over older industrial areas leading to lower production costs – lower labour costs, cheaper sites, lower business taxation rates and more relaxed environmental controls. These lower costs combined with foreign capital investment and 'know how' particularly favoured the setting up and transfer to these countries of labour-intensive industries and the assembly line stage of production in some consumer durable industries, such as television production.

Re-industrialisation and restructuring

Changes are so fundamental that some writers increasingly view advanced economies as being at the threshold of another industrial revolution. The key to this lies in a wave of new inventions and innovations associated with the new information and other high technologies. Where industrial progress is seen as taking place as a series of waves coinciding with the onset of new technological systems, each wave being separated by a decline in the rate industrial activity and periods of recession

A new technological system is emerging based on inventions and innovations associated with information technology, bio-technology, materials technology, energy technology and space technology.

Re-industrialisation

New technology leads to a whole range of new industries and products which lie at the cutting edge of the new industrial revolution. Because of the comparative advantage the advanced countries have over the newly industrialising countries in these new industries, it is these industries which are seen as vital to the future economic well-being of advanced economies. The rate of growth in these new industries is appreciably greater than in other manufacturing industries.

New industries represent the re-industrialisation component of current changes in the manufacturing sector, leading to the spatial reorganisation of industry. They are located in the technopoles and

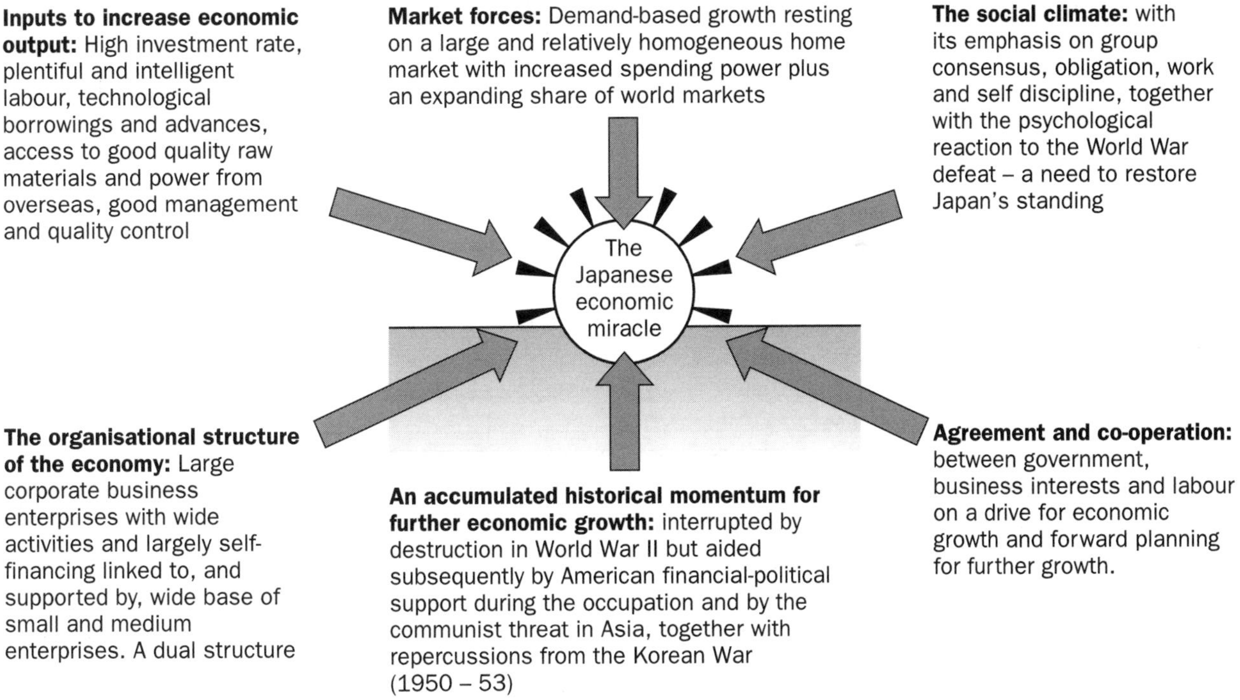

Figure 20.6 *Factors behind the Japanese 'economic miracle' giving it a comparative advantage over earlier industrialised countries*

science parks in pleasant environments within and in the rural surroundings of large conurbations and in 'sunbelt' regions, rather than in old industrial core regions (except where government policies and financial aid have decreed a new science park be located) (Figure 16.5; Case study 15.3).

However, since some assembly plants of the electronics industries which use the new technologies have been based in industrial declining areas as a result of collaboration between large multinational corporations and government agencies, some re-industrialisation can be said to have occurred here too (Figure 20.7).

Although Scottish manufacturing is growing more quickly than in the UK as a whole, forecasters point out that almost all the growth is in advanced technology while most other sectors show little growth or are declining.

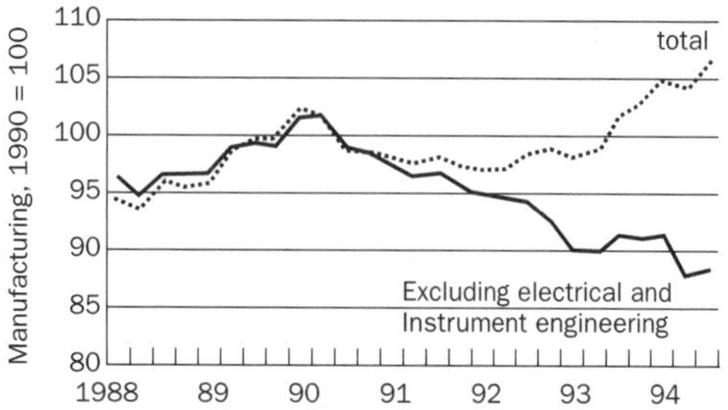

The Fraser of Allander Institute, Scotland's best known economic forecasting body, pointed out that although manufacturing output in Scotland is growing more quickly than in the UK as a whole, almost all the growth is in just one sector, electronics, while most other sectors show little growth or are actually declining, but the economy was not dragged down by heavy industry because its steel, shipbuilding and heavy engineering industries are a shadow of what they were. The economy also benefited from expansion in North Sea oil activity.

[SOURCE: *Financial Times* 7.4.95]

Figure 20.7 *Domination of the 'chip' economy in central Scotland*

Restructuring

'Not only does the emergence of new technological systems lead to the emergence of a new range of products, services, systems and industries in its own right – it also affects directly or indirectly almost every other branch of the economy ... the changes go beyond specific product or process technologies and affect the input cost structure and conditions of production and distribution throughout the system.'

[Freeman C *The Challenge of the New Technologies*, 1987]

Increased automation in both the organisation of industry and processes in manufacturing are leading to important changes within established industries (Chapter 18). The most apparent is the increased output which can be obtained with fewer workers. There has been a marked decrease in employment levels with redundancies and early retirement in almost every branch of manufacturing. This to some extent accounts for higher productivity levels per worker left in employment.

£16 million of technical advancement in British steel at Corby – Northants.

'British Steel still Corby's second biggest employer (with 1200 employees) has invested £16 million over the past two years in making its tube making operations the most technically advanced in Europe.'

[SOURCE: Special Report *Investing in Corby, Daily Telegraph* 16.9.94]

New techniques and better control of processes can also lead to savings in other areas, such as more efficient use of energy supplies and raw materials and better quality controls leading to less waste and a higher standard of product. Thus industry is more cost effective and overall productivity increases.

Restructuring in established industries is also due to other influences. For example, as industry becomes more globalised and dominated by multinational companies, industrial organisation also changes because of mergers, takeovers and collaboration between companies. Although these have been occurring for some time, their scale and frequency have accelerated since the 1970s and increasingly involved companies based in different countries, further adding to the globalisation process (Figure 20.8).

Another important aspect frequently associated with mergers and takeovers is the increasing extent to which expansion of manufacturing in advanced countries is related to direct investment from overseas multinational corporations (Figure 20.8). It is estimated that in 1993 approximately 20% of manufacturing expansion in the UK was due to foreign investment. The proportion is even higher in respect of the older industrial areas where generous government assistance and concessions have made these areas particularly attractive to foreign investors.

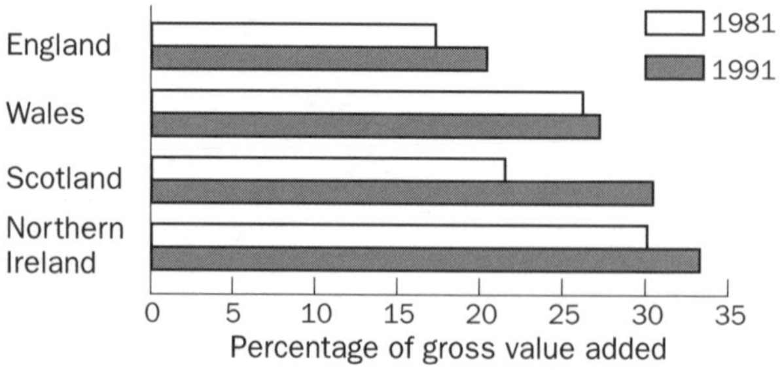

[SOURCE: *CSO Regional Trends*, 1993]

Figure 20.8 *Gross value added by manufacturing by foreign enterprises in Great Britain 1981 and 1991 – expressed as a percentage*

In addition to these trends towards rationalisation, modernisation and concentration of production into larger more efficient units within a globally organised framework, observers note two other different trends, particularly related to changes in the nature of market demand in advanced countries.

As the market has become more affluent and sophisticated a significant sector of the customer market has become more discerning, requiring a greater choice and customised products of quality and up-to-date design rather than mass produced goods. Thus in some sectors of the consumer industries there is a move away from a standardised product to more flexible production systems, allowing for shorter runs of more distinctive goods and updating of the product as consumer tastes and fashions change. The results of these changes are seen for example in the wide variety of brands and makes of the same basic good on supermarket shelves and the introduction of improved versions of different models of cars and electronic products such as home computers and televisions.

While much of this more customised production may be undertaken by the large manufacturing corporations, changes in market demand provide many niches in the market for small companies. Thus the number of small companies which concentrate on customised high quality products, especially for the upper end of the market has increased, making particular components or accessories needed by large companies a more customised product.

Deindustrialisation

Deindustrialisation was initially defined as an absolute loss of jobs in industry, but it has recently had a broader meaning to include the increasing displacement of manufacturing by service activities in the economy (Figure 20.10).

However, the process of deindustrialisation is not uniform across the whole range of manufacturing. It tends to be both region and industry selective. The greatest losses initially occurred in the staple industries, such as iron and steel, heavy engineering, shipbuilding and textiles, adversely affecting older industrial areas where these industries were most heavily concentrated. Closures in these industries came at a time when coalmining was also declining in a number of these regions (Case study 27.1). Deindustrialisation also spread to the consumer durable industries, particularly since the late 1970s, affecting regions such as the West Midlands which until then had prospered (Figure 20.11; Case study 17.1). Now measures in terms of declining employment opportunities, deindustrialisation in varying degrees is affecting all branches of manufacturing.

Shifts in the relative importance of different sectors of industry in a nation's economy and global shifts of each sector over time

The importance of different manufacturing sector changes as per capita incomes rise

Basis of the cycle

Time → **Stage 1** → **Stage 2** → **Stage 3**

Most dynamic section → Light consumer industries → Heavy capital intensive industries → Engineering and related industries + High technology industries

Relative importance of factors

Stage 1	Stage 2	Stage 3
Relatively low incomes limited market	**Rising incomes strong market**	**High incomes; wide market demand**
+ plentiful cheap labour	+ labour more expensive	+ labour expensive and skilled / highly skilled
+ limited capital	**+ greater capital accumulation**	**+ high capital accumulation**
+ limited infrastructure	+ increasing infrastructure	sophisticated infrastructure
+ limited technology	**+ technological progress**	**+ advanced technology base**

NOTE: The income driven product cycle not only helps to explain changes with time as a nation matures economically but also how, as the more maturing nations lose competitiveness in one sector, this is taken over by the next wave of industrialising nations. Hence currently the industrial sector of mature advanced countries (e.g. USA, UK) is dominated by Stage 3 industries, the first wave of NICS (e.g. South Korea, Taiwan) by Stage 2 (and now moving towards Stage 3) and the latest wave of NICs (e.g. China, Thailand, Mauritius) by Stage 1 industries.

Figure 20.9 The income driven product cycle

Causes of deindustrialisation

Loss of competitiveness

Earlier declines affecting manufacturing were mainly attributed to declining competitiveness in the face of newer producing countries. For older staple industries in advanced countries, costs were relatively high due to uneconomic locations and growing diseconomies associated with outdated factories and machinery, higher labour costs and restrictive practices compared to the newer producing countries. In some cases costs of power and raw materials were also higher as the older producing countries continued to rely on coalfields and mines which were becoming exhausted and costly to work. Loss of competitiveness and shift of some sectors of industry to the new industrialising countries has been summarised in the Income Driven Product Cycle (Figure 20.9).

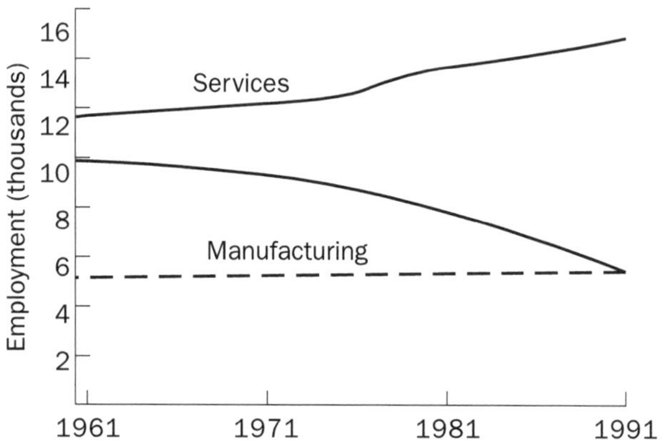

Figure 20.10 Employment in manufacturing and services

Technological change

In 1994 the European Commission's White paper on Growth, Competitiveness and Employment emphasised that the loss in manufacturing jobs in Western European countries was due more to technological changes in industry than loss of comparative advantage to the newly industrialising countries. Rapid increase in automation and computer control of production lines together with industrial robots drastically reduced the demand for labour. Greater capital investment in technology has led to a rapid rise in productivity. Output is increasing but employment continues to fall. Job losses have been greatest amongst unskilled labour since it is the tasks performed by unskilled labour which can most readily be automated. As technology becomes more sophisticated, the effects of 'technological redundancies' will also be increasingly felt amongst the skilled and educated work force .

More rapid expansion of the service sector

Deindustrialisation, within the wider meaning of the term, is also due to the rapid expansion of services compared to manufacturing, leading to services replacing manufacturing as the 'engine of the economy' in advanced countries (Section 20.1).

20.4 **Newly industrialising countries**

Rates of manufacturing growth amongst countries in the developing world are extremely variable. Some, like the smaller central African states such as Uganda, have had comparatively little growth

	1979 000s	**1984 000s**	**1989 000s**	**1992 000s**	**% change 1979–84**	**% change 1984–89**	**% change 1989–92**
a Great Britain							
Manufacturing	7 107.0	5 326.0	5 129.0	4 247.0	–25.1	–3.7	–17.1
Services	13 260.0	13 541.8	15 320.0	15 159.0	+2.1	+13.1	–1.0
Other	2 240.0	1 977.5	1 779.0	1 484.0	–11.7	–10.0	–16.6
Total	**22 611.0**	**20 845.9**	**22 227.0**	**20 890.0**	**–7.8**	**+9.7**	**–6.0**
b West Midlands region							
Manufacturing	985.0	709.2	668.0	554.0	–28.1	–5.8	–17.1
Services	1 071.0	1 103.9	1 230.0	1 251.0	+3.1	+11.4	+1.7
Other	185.0	167.8	156.0	128.0	–9.2	–7.0	–17.9
Total	**2 241.0**	**1 981.0**	**2 054.0**	**1 933.0**	**–11.6**	**+3.7**	**–5.9**

The figures indicate deindustrialisation at **a** the national level and **b** the regional level as exemplified by the West Midlands region, one of the most prosperous regions in the 1960s and 1970s. Note that the general trend is distorted by the recession of 1989 – 92.
[SOURCE: Regional Development *Geography in the UK* No. 347 Vol 80, 1995]

Figure 20.11 Employment change 1979 to 1992

whilst others, such as Brazil, South Korea and Taiwan, have experienced so much growth that they are important exporters of manufactured goods. Overall annual growth rates averaged 6% to 8% from 1960 to 1980 but since then, with the exception of the newly industrialised countries of South East Asia, growth has slowed. Despite this decline, the average contribution of manufacturing to economies in the developing world has now risen to a quarter of their gross domestic output. However, their share of world manufacturing output remains small.

'Essence of industrialisation for developing countries today consists as much in an enhanced production capability of traditional and domestic goods as in the acquisition of know how in technology, design, manufacturing and marketing at all levels of distribution for new products which are demanded by the world at large.'

[SOURCE: United Nationals Industrial Development Organisation Report 1993, 1994]

The increase of the developing world's share of international trade in manufactured goods is even more significant. This has risen faster than manufacturing output, from 7% in 1970 to 17% in 1990. However, over 80% of this output is from Asian countries. The newly industrialised countries of South East Asia dominate the manufacturing output of the developing world, taking manufactured exports as the main measure. However, in most developing countries a significant proportion of manufacturing expansion has been directed to meeting the needs of the domestic market rather than export markets, as for example in the case of Brazil and Mexico, both of which have very large home markets.

Identifying the new industrialising countries

Selecting the countries which fall under the heading of newly industrialising countries has become problematic for a number of reasons.

- 'Industrialising' is a term used to denote expansion of manufacturing and also the general rate at which a country is developing. It is associated with increases in the general standard of living and an improved quality of life.
- Some countries generally regarded as part of the developed world such as Spain, Greece and Portugal have been included under the category of Newly Industrialising Countries because, on the basis of the indices used, they can be equated with developing countries.
- There are now certain South East Asian countries, such as South Korea, Taiwan, Hong Kong and Singapore, which are classed as Newly Industrialising but whose economies and standard of living now begin to match those of the older advanced industrialised countries.

Identification of Newly Industrialising countries depends on the criteria used. In 1979 OECD used the following criteria:

- a fast growth on the absolute level of industrial employment and its share of total employment
- a rising share of world exports in manufactures
- a fast growth in real per capita income such that there is a successful narrowing in the gap with advanced industrial countries.

While the first two criteria are direct measures of the rate of growth manufacturing, the last is to do with the general rise in the standard of living equating industrialisation with rate of development.

Two tiers of Newly Industrialising Countries were initially identified by the World Bank in the early 1970s. The first tier was seen as composed of the first wave of developing countries, concentrating on industrialisation and the second, a later wave of younger industrialising countries. It follows that the distinction between the countries in each tier is not only one of date but also one of different levels of industrialisation. The first tier of NICs has a more developed and diversified manufacturing base than the second tier. This is a useful distinction as will be seen when the character of manufacturing is considered.

A more objective classification

To resolve the confusion resulting from the wider interpretation of industrialisation as including stage of development of a country, it would be legitimate to limit the indices used to those strictly concerned with manufacturing expansion. ***Thus to qualify as a Newly Industrialising Country it could be suggested that a country should meet at least two of the following three criteria identified above on the basis of classifications made by OECD and Chowdbury and Islam.***

- ***the manufacturing sector's share of GDP should be at least 20%***
- ***its share of total employment should be at least 20%***
- ***the share of manufactures in visible exports should be at least 50%.***

(Note that while excluding human development criteria as a basis of classification, these become significant when considering the factors which influence the rate of manufacturing growth (Chapter 6).)

Variations and the spatial distribution of manufacturing

Some important observations on the spatial distribution of manufacturing amongst the developing countries can be made.

- On a range of measures the 'four Asian tigers' – South Korea, Taiwan, Singapore and Hong Kong – stand out as having the most impressive manufacturing sectors not only in terms of share of GDP and employment but also their very high share of exports. The 'Four Asian Tigers' are the only countries to have maintained a high rate of manufacturing growth throughout the 1970s and 1980s.
- Brazil and Mexico, while matching South Korea in size of manufacturing output, only maintained a rapid rate of growth through the 1970s. Through the 1980s the manufacturing sector has stagnated, largely due to debt and inflation problems in these countries.
- While expansion of manufacturing stagnated in Latin American and African countries over the 1980s, it was rapid in the case of the second wave of South East Asian countries comprising of Thailand, Indonesia, Malaysia and China. These are emerging as important manufacturing countries and exporters. In terms of size of output, China is ahead of the others.
- India meets only one of the basic criteria, that of a significant exporter of manufactured goods. Its continued rate of manufacturing expansion and absolute size of manufacturing output justify its inclusion among the ranks of NICs.
- There are other interesting individual inclusions. As the size of the Gross Domestic output indicates, Mauritius has a small economy but expansion of manufacturing has matched that of the newly industrialising South Asia group. However, expansion is much narrower, being mainly related to the setting up of an industrial-free zone to attract foreign investment mainly in textile manufacture, using until recent shortages, a readily available and relatively low-cost labour supply. Export of textile garments predominantly to EU countries has replaced sugar as the main export. The case of Mauritius is illustrative of a number of smaller economies which come into the category of a Newly Industrialising Country (NIC) on the basis of a growing but narrow specialised manufacturing sector, largely externally financed and producing for export.

20.5 Factors which influence the rate of growth in the manufacturing sector of NICs

As Figure 20.12 and Case studies 20.1 indicate, rates of growth of manufacturing depend upon a combination of internal and external factors. Of the latter, the state of the world economy and its rate of expansion exercise an overriding influence.

Internal conditions

The size and variety of the energy and resource base

This has been important in the case of Brazil and more recently in the case of China and India. These countries have large energy sources, important mineral deposits and agricultural resources. On the one hand, these energy and mineral resources have to some extent favoured the setting up of a domestic heavy industry such as iron and steel and on the other hand, processing industries for export. However, this has only been achieved with the use of external technology and to some extent, external financing and tariff protection for infant heavy industries. The capital cost of setting up a large iron and steel plant in a developing country such as Brazil in the late 1970s for example, was estimated as 20% higher than establishing one in an industrialised country.

While having some energy and raw material resources, the more successful Newly Industrialised Countries of South east Asia, such as South Korea and Taiwan, are relatively poorly endowed and yet have achieved very successful manufacturing expansion. On balance, other internal factors seem more vital than a rich and varied domestic energy and resource base.

The role of government

Most studies of successful NICs have emphasised that the policies and actions of government are of paramount importance because they strongly affect so many factors vital to the successful expansion of the manufacturing sector.

From an inward to an outward looking economic policy as industrialisation progresses

The 1993 – 94 Report by the United Nations Industrial Development Organisation (UNIDO) in examining links between industrialisation and trade, notes that the most successful Newly Industrialising Countries initially embarked on an ***'import substitution industrialisation' strategy based on state intervention and foreign aid. The state supported infant industries by giving them a protected home market in which prices above the***

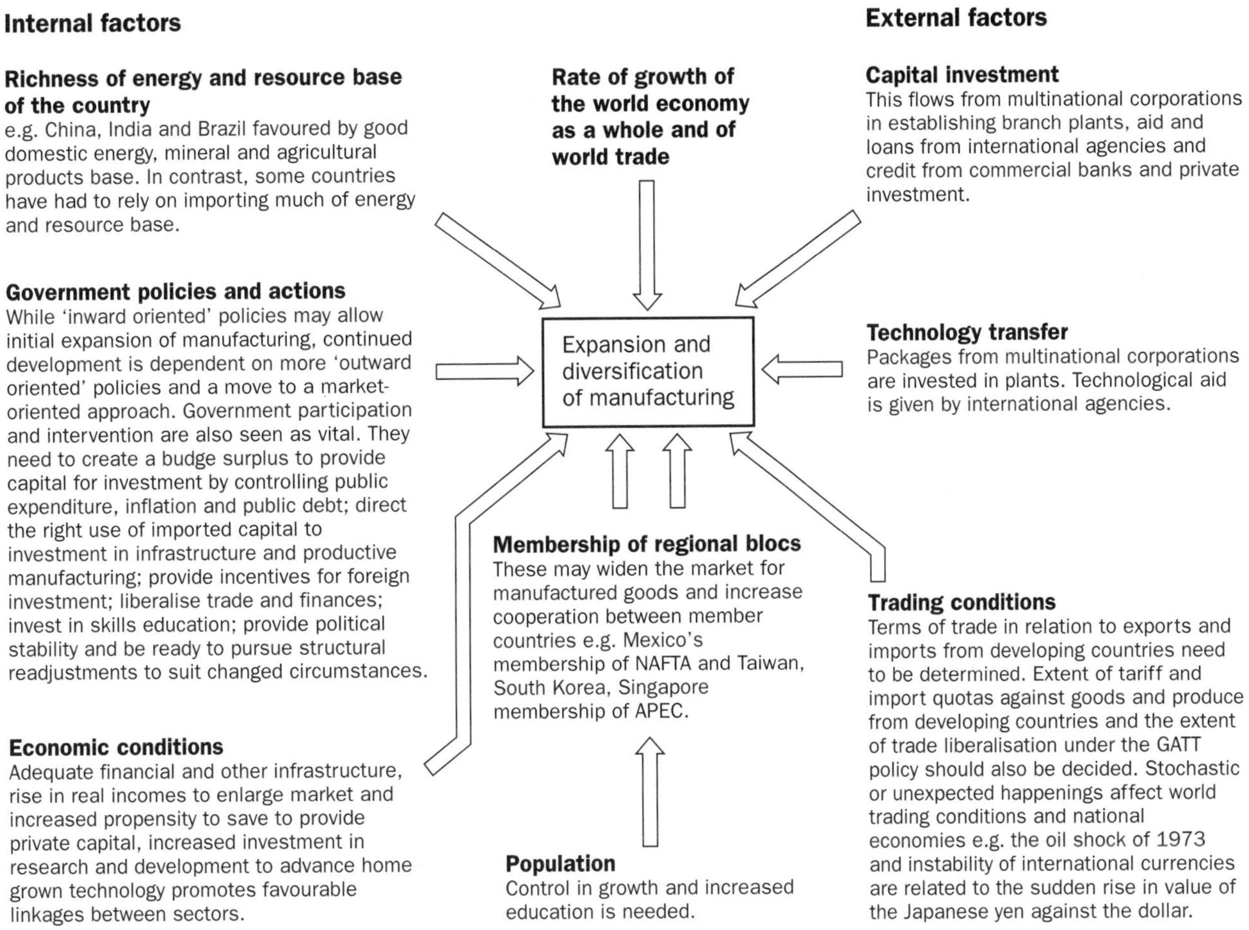

Figure 20.12 Keys to development of the manufacturing sector in newly industrialising countries

world market levels could be charted because foreign competition was kept out through quotas and tariffs on foreign goods. Infant export industries were also encouraged through the granting of export subsidies. The Report emphasises that industries, once established, had then to be gradually exposed to market forces to ensure their long-term efficiency and development.

In practice, however, no government entirely deregulates its economy, leaving market forces alone to shape the form of the country's manufacturing sector. In the 1970s and 1980s, for example, South Korea adopted the type of strong outward oriented policy advocated by the United Nations Industrial Development Organisation (UNIDO). However, it was selective in the type of multinational manufacturing investment it wished to encourage in order to protect its own multinationals, such as Hyundai and Samsung.

The UNIDO Report stresses that governments will also need to exercise other policies without which no long-term industrialisation programme can succeed. These include ensuring political stability in the country which will help to attract outside investment and providing a complementary rural development programme including agricultural reforms. Improvements in the country's infrastructure and ensuring the 'human capital formation' needed are also important (Figure 6.6). Human capital investment implies both provision of a suitable labour supply and such things as development of an education system capable of providing the skills and expertise needed as the manufacturing sector is expanded.

Rural development and modernisation of agriculture

Successful industrialisation programmes have usually been preceded by agricultural reforms which have produced a more modernised and market-oriented agriculture sector. To some extent this has happened in Brazil and Mexico but it is better illustrated from South East Asia. Here the drive to attract external investment for expanding the manufacturing sector had been preceded by agricultural reforms beginning from 1979. This released land back into individual peasant ownership and encouraged changes towards a market-oriented agricultural system.

[SOURCE: D R Philips *Geographical Review*, October 1989]

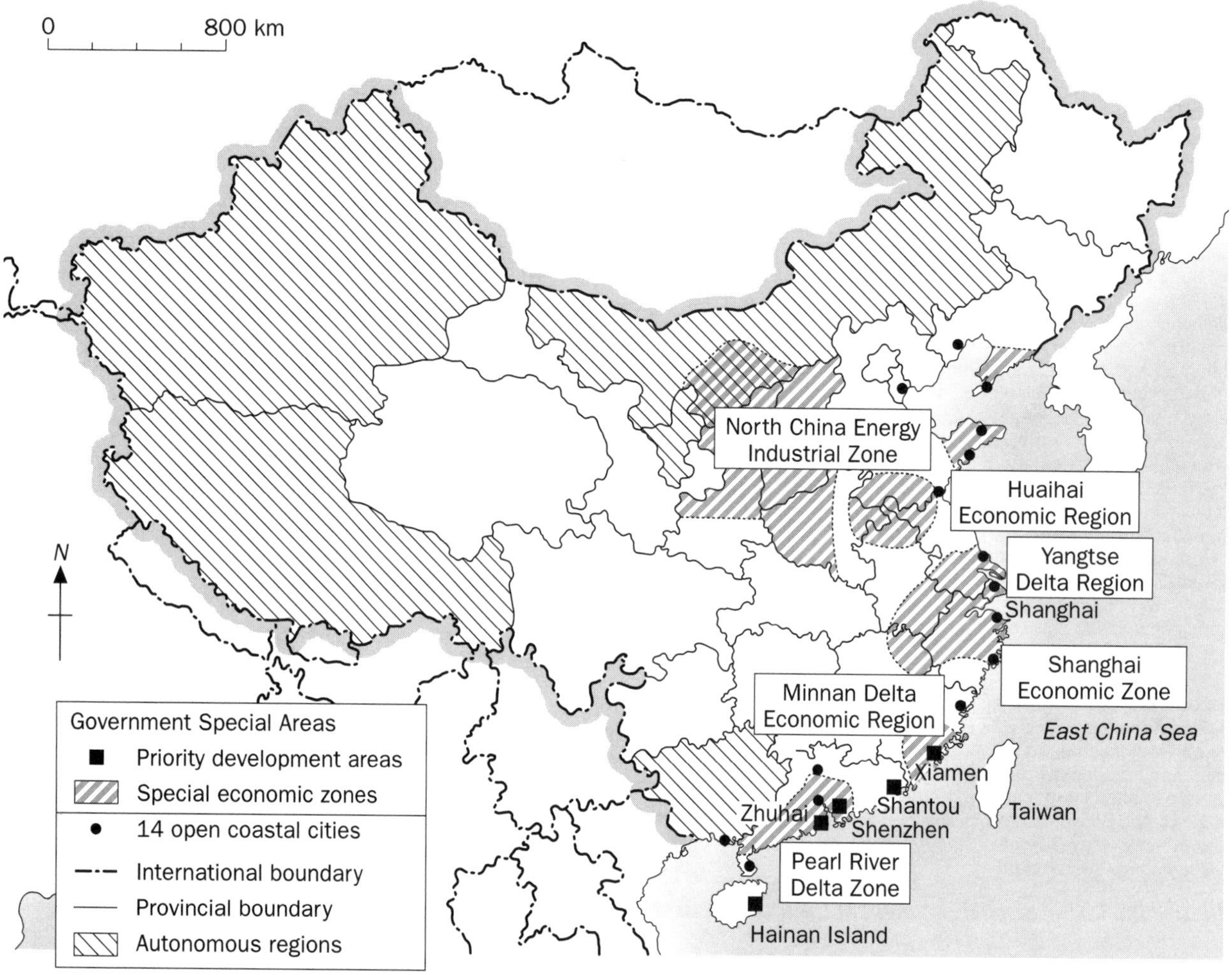

1 The development of special economic zones and open cities was one of the major strategies under the seventh five-year plan 1986 – 90 to promote rapid industrialisation. (Recently there have been fears of overindustrialisation in the coastal regions. The wish to spread economic development inland has led China in its current five-year plan to nominate special economic zones inland.)

2 Shenzen since 1980 has become a major industrial centre increasing in population from 30 000 to 3 million, the work opportunities drawing in people from the surrounding Guangdong Province and other ports of China (In 1992 the average income per head in Shenzen was approximately £420 compared with the average of £70 in rural parts of China).

***Figure 20.13** China's Special Economic Zones, Priority Development Areas and Open Cities with special reference to Shenzhen*

3 Shenzen's rapid growth has been due to
- China's 'Open Door Policy' towards outside investment with financial and other incentives offered
- a plentiful labour pool – adaptable but cheaper than in the more mature NICs of South East Asia e.g. Hong Kong nearby (rents and labour costs are half that in Hong Kong)
- a coastal location for import of manufacturing inputs and export of manufactured goods
- closeness to Hong Kong with much financial investment coming from there and expansion of industry into Shenzen from here as well as from multinational companies from Japan and other advanced countries.

4 Shenzen has a great number of foreign multinational plants mainly for assembling processed raw materials and components e.g. a wide range of electrical goods such as televisions and video cassette recorders, clothing, hardware, plastics, food, drink, footwear – much of it for export. Now it is beginning to attract component supplier plants as well as generate home based businesses.

Modernisation of agriculture has released labour off the land into nearby industry as has occurred for example in the rapidly industrialising Guandong province in the south-east of China (Figure 20.13). The plentiful and adaptable labour supply has provided an important incentive for foreign multinationals to invest in branch assembly plants in Guandong province.

Agricultural modernisation has also increased the demand for agricultural machinery, fertilisers and consumer goods as incomes have risen in rural areas. The market incentive has encouraged farmers to save and branch out into small-scale industry.

Modernisation of agriculture is also vital to provide the surplus food needed in the towns as the industrial and urban population expands, as well as providing industrial crops and other agricultural produce for processing into agricultural goods.

Incentives to attract foreign investment

Governments are in competition with one another to attract foreign investment for industrial expansion. Apart from encouraging a ready supply of adaptable labour it is important wage costs are initially kept down and unionisation subdued to prevent labour unrest and increasing costs. In Thailand wage costs are on average 40% below those in Korea and this is a powerful incentive for foreign companies to invest in establishing assembly line branch plants there. In China, since 1980, union activity has been regulated in the Special Economic Zones established to attract foreign manufacturing (Figure 20.13).

One of the most important measures used by developing countries to attract foreign investment and stimulate export industries has been the setting up of Export Processing Zones (EPZ) in which special concessions are provided, such as the import of goods and materials on a duty-free basis. Within the EPZ the infrastructure and services needed for manufacturing are provided and sometimes restrictions on the proportion of foreign ownership of assets which may be allowed are waived. Special Economic Zones is another term given to enclaves of areas set aside as privileged zones for manufacturing and exports. Hong Kong and Singapore are free trade zones, but manufacturing for export is restricted to a number of industrial estates.

While most EPZs are in South East Asia they also occur in other parts of the developing world especially in countries around the Caribbean. Mexico has in effect established an EPZ zone along its border with the USA through its Border Industrialisation Programme, centred on towns such as Ciudad Juarez and Tijuana. Mexico has waived its duties on imports of materials and components from the USA as long as the endproducts are exported. These concessions, along with a plentiful cheap labour supply and close proximity to the USA have been a powerful incentive for American multinational companies to invest in electrical and other assembly plants in this Border Industrialisation Zone. By the late 1980s there were around 1400 manufacturing plants which employed over 310 000 Mexican workers. The recent formation of the North American Free Trade Association bringing Mexico, the USA and Canada together, will provide a further stimulus to development in the Border Zone.

Management of state finances

If finance is to be made available for the development of infrastructure, for investment in 'human capital formation' and in manufacturing, it is important for governments to pursue prudent and balanced financial and other economic policies. In particular, excessive expenditure on grandiose unproductive schemes and military equipment has to be avoided. In most African states as well as in some other developing countries, such expenditure and other mismanagement of funds has contributed to their severe debt problems (Case study 20.2). High rates of inflation through loose monetary policies have also occurred. In 1993 for example, debt servicing amounted to 42% of Brazil's GDP and inflation was rampant. These financial 'drains' undoubtedly contributed to the fall in the rate of manufacturing growth from almost 12% annually in the 1970s to below 3% in the early 1990s. Since then Brazil has made strenuous efforts to reduce its budget deficit, slow down the money supply and stabilise prices. Brazil hopes that such measures will help to put the country on a stable footing and restore confidence amongst the international investors which the country needs for further industrial expansion. A recent resumption of growth in the economy would suggest these measures are working.

Conditions for 'Human Capital' formation and a growth in national incomes

Investment in population control programmes and in education and welfare developments have been a strong part of government policies amongst successful industrialising countries in South East Asia. Too rapid population growth puts an normous financial drain on both state and private family budgets, preventing the accumulation of surplus financial capital for investment in both human and economic development. High population growth rates is one of the greatest hindrances to progress in Zimbabwe, Kenya and other African states.

In contrast in South East Asia, countries such as Malaysia, Singapore and Taiwan have brought population under control and embarked on educational programmes with the intention of raising the general level of skills amongst labour and through higher education and research programmes, to produce the trained technical, management and entrepreneurial personnel needed to reduce reliance on foreign companies.

While cheap labour is an incentive to multinational corporations to invest in branch plants over time, it is essential that incomes rise to provide both the incentive to the workforce and also to a viable domestic market for manufactured goods as occurred in Japan's transition to an advanced industrial country. There is evidence in Taiwan and the other advancing South East Asian countries that an increasing proportion of consumer manufacturing is for the home market. Rising incomes also increase the incentive for families to save, so increasing the amount of private funds available for investment. For example, in Malaysia as incomes have been raised, domestic savings have risen from 25% of GDP in the 1970s to 34% between 1980 and 1990. It is at a similar rate in China. In contrast in Latin America and Africa, where incomes remain very low for the mass of the population, the home market for everyday consumer goods remains limited and the saving ratio to GDP very low.

Improving industrial skills and the expertise in finance, marketing, shipping and trading

Where a developing country looks to basing its economy on a successful manufactured exports strategy, UNIDO emphasises that the market price of internationally traded goods is largely determined not by production costs but by distribution and marketing costs. For example, in a survey of brand named products made in EPZ zones in Sri Lanka and China, the average ratio between the factory gate price and the retail price in the market place was 1:12. Thus to compete successfully in world markets NICs need distribution and marketing expertise. The South East Asian NICs are not only adept at producing relatively cheaply but are also skilled at efficiently and economically marketing their products abroad through their own large trading companies with a world wide sales network and expertise in selling, buying, brokering, financing and shipping. As a developing country seeks to expand and diversify its manufacturing sector, this must also be accompanied by a growth of expertise in these complementary fields of distribution and marketing.

External influences

World economic and trading conditions

During the 1960s and 1970s the world economy expanded substantially and while the Oil Shock of 1973 caused a temporary slow down in world trade, this too expanded significantly. With the expansion in the world economy, investment funding from manufacturing expansion was more readily available and markets for manufactured goods expanded. Through the 1980s a number of world economic problems became acute, including the world debt problem and increasing moves towards protectionism, discriminating against imported manufactured goods. As a consequence, conditions remain difficult for further industrialisation outside of the newly industrialising countries of South East Asia.

During the first part of the 1990s there have been mixed indications as to whether or not conditions will improve. Since 1994 the advanced countries have begun to pull out of recession; thus the demand for manufactured goods from the developing countries may improve and with it, the flow of investment. The successful Uruguay round of GATT talks and the setting up of the new World Trading Organisation (WTO) to implement more equitable and liberal trading conditions also gives cause for some optimism (Chapters 32 and 33).

At the same time there is increased instability of currency exchange rates. In particular, the marked decline in the value of the dollar against the Japanese yen is a serious problem as the dollar is the leading world currency.

IMF and other international agencies constraints

Financial and technical aid from international agencies during the 1960s and 1970s were significant influences towards promoting manufacturing in South East Asia and Latin America but since the 1980s the role of international agencies has changed to that of a constraining influence (Chapter 33).

Writing at the close of the 1980s, Broad and Kavanagh in an article, *No more NICs* (Far Eastern Economic Review), described the international environment as no longer favourable for the emergence of any more Newly Industrialising Countries. Their evaluation was not only based on the world debt problem and growing protectionist trends amongst advanced countries. It was also based on the fact that international agencies have imposed severe economic restructuring strategies on a number of developing countries and these have led to increased levels of taxation and reduced public spending in these countries. Under these circumstances it is unlikely that internally generated internal financial capital will be available for the further development of manufacturing. Countries undergoing such economic restructuring are not attractive to outside investors. It is significant that the recently emerging Newly Industrialising Countries are countries which do not have serious and unmanageable external debt problems.

However, while in the short term the internal restructuring forced on a number of developing countries by the World Bank, IMF and other external agencies may be seen as a deterrent to further industrialisation, in the long term these tighter controls may be seen as beneficial, allowing for long-term balanced economic growth.

The role of regional trading blocs

While the new World Trading Organisation aims to increase and expand world wide trade which should benefit NICs, the growth of regional economic groupings is viewed with some concern, especially as trade within regional groups such as the EU, APEC and NAFTA now amounts to 50% of total world trading. The fear is that each regional trading bloc may discriminate against outside countries to protect its member countries against foreign competition but members may keep individual developing countries (Section 32.4).

The role of foreign multinational companies

Much has been made of the role of multinationals in promoting manufacturing development in the developing countries. Undoubtedly their role is essential in the early phase of manufacturing and governments have gone to great lengths to attract the multinational companies, including setting up special economic zones and free cities which offer particular incentives. However, significant qualifications must be made about the role of multinationals (Figure 20.14). The strategy of foreign multinational corporations is global and based on generating the highest profit. It is significant that as developing countries mature industrially, much more stringent controls are put on the participation of foreign multinationals. Governments tend to support the development of the country's own manufacturing firms and multinationals and create domestic research and technical expertise to reduce dependence on foreign multinationals.

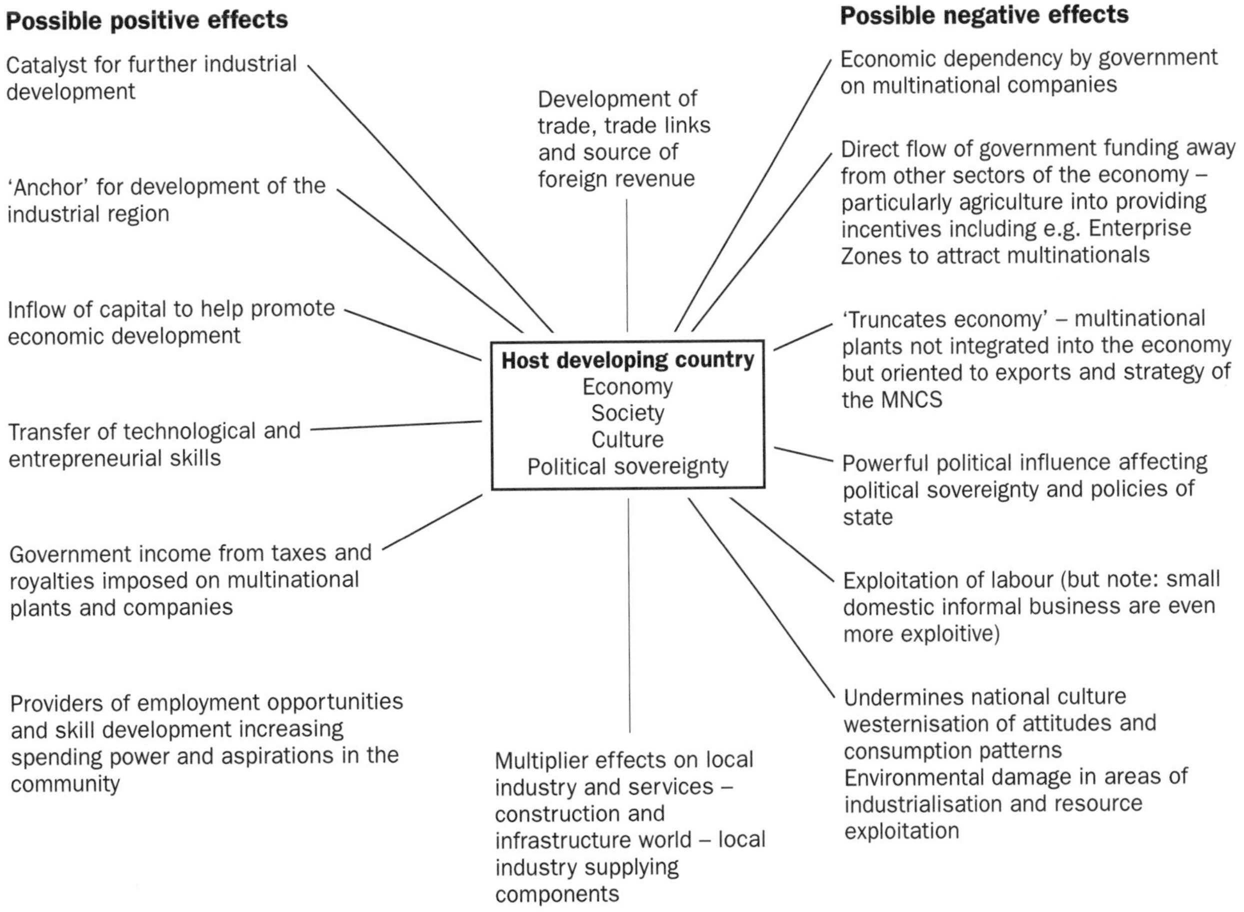

Figure 20.14 Impact of multinational (transnational) corporations on host developing countries

20.6 Types of manufacturing

Small businesses

This informal sector of manufacturing is the longest established, since most developing countries have always had small craft industries in villages and cities to supply everyday needs. Also, certain specialist crafts such as metal working and pottery making have had a market in neighbouring countries too.

While some of the indigenous craft was lost due to the cheap import of substitute goods during colonial times, much survived, particularly in the rural areas. There has been a revival of small business with political independence, increasing population numbers and rising demand, but most of it is now centred in the towns. Some governments recognising this as an important source of goods at affordable prices and an important provider, now give official financial support and protection. India, for example, has encouraged the growth of co-operatives to help small family concerns and under the Small Industries Development Organisation, has set up district centres which offer technical, financial and other business advice to small firms. Under its Development Plans the manufacture of 600 products is exclusively reserved for small firms. Significantly these now include more sophisticated products such as electronic and light engineering products as well as the traditional products of food and clothing (Case study 17.2).

Small-scale industry has many advantages: the ratio of employed to capital investment is much higher than in large scale industry, there is increasing labour opportunities and it uses minimum capital. Also products can be tailored to meet the needs of limited local markets and output can be adapted to suit changes in demand. This sector is therefore seen as increasingly important in the diversification of the economy of developing countries.

Processing for export

Processing or semi-processing of primary products from agriculture, mining and forestry ready for export is another sector of the export industry. Some processing is needed either because of the perishable nature of the product in its raw state or because its reduction in bulk makes for cheaper transport costs. The size of the processing sector depends on the type and volume of primary products. Most countries have a narrow range of such products often one being the dominant, for example, copper from Zambia, sugar from the Caribbean islands, cocoa and certain minerals from Ghana.

Since independence, developing countries have tried to reduce dependence on a narrow range of exports because of fluctuating world demand and prices and production levels are controlled by foreign-owned multinational companies. Since these exports earn much needed foreign currency and are an important sector in the economy, processing of primary products for export remains very important. However, where feasible, governments are now demanding that an increasing proportion of primary products are fully processed before export. This puts them into the category of manufactured products, raises their export value and provides more revenue and employment in the producing country. Brazil, for example, now smelts a significant proportion of its own iron-ore to make iron and steel, and Malaysia increasingly more of its own rubber products factories.

Import substitution and capital-intensive industries

Apart from the further development of small–scale industry and the extension of some processing into manufacturing, developing countries have sought to widen their industrial base sufficiently to reduce imports of foreign manufactured goods. Further industrialisation is also a way of modernising the country and increasing its world prestige.

However, there have been serious problems: insufficient finance, technical know-how, suitable labour skills and inability to compete with foreign produced manufactures in some areas. Early efforts at industrialisation over-emphasised intensive capital industries such as iron and steel and heavy engineering or production of modern durable consumer goods which only a limited and more affluent sector of the population could afford. This diverted finance and expertise away from economically more viable and important areas in the economy, such as agriculture and small-scale industry (Case study 20.2).

Some countries, notably Brazil, Mexico, India and some South East Asian countries, such as Taiwan and Korea have succeeded. However, development has relied heavily on government support, foreign technology and investment, frequently from the kind of large multinational corporations of which the newly independent states in the world are politically so critical. This newer industrial growth can be broadly divided into import substitution light industries and heavy capital industry.

Light industry tends to be centred on consumer goods such as foods, drinks, tobacco, textiles and clothing, the manufacture of which does not require complex technology and is labour intensive relative to the amount of capital invested. Much of it is in branch plants established by foreign companies attracted by lower labour costs, weak union organisation of labour and expanding markets. Textiles have particularly been seen as one of the ways of extending manufacturing. As for other products, much depends on the size of the home market available and the potential for export. It is therefore not surprising that import substitution industries have expanded most in countries with large populations, for example India, Brazil and Nigeria (Case studies 17.2 and 20.2). Many developing countries have a population of less than 10 million and this is a serious handicap to any significant industrialisation.

Where light industries have developed they have attracted other industrial growth by a process of cumulative causation and have been able to expand to gain more economies of scale. This has attracted more investment, raised the quality of products while maintaining prices at a competitive level. It has also given a base for growing exports to other countries. The range of consumer goods is now being extended in the most successful countries to include durable consumers, such as motor vehicle assembly and electrical goods as in Brazil, Singapore, Taiwan and South Korea (Case study 20.1).

While most countries have tried to develop heavy basic industries under the protection and direct involvement of governments, only a few countries have done this successfully. In most countries insufficient raw materials, power resources, finance and the limited size of the home market have meant that these industries have operated at a continuous loss whatever their prestige value.

Where home markets are large, the country has important raw materials of its own or can import these cheaply and is established enough to have sufficient support infrastructure and skilled labour, capital intensive industries have been established successfully, ranging from iron and steel, to other metals, chemicals and heavy engineering. India has an important iron and steel industry centred on the Damodar valley where iron-ore, coal, and hydro-electric power are available. The Middle East countries are developing important petro-chemical industries based on plentiful oil supplies and finance gained from the export of oil. South Korea has been in a position to import raw materials to add to its own to make it a significant iron and steel, shipbuilding and marine engineering producer.

Unfortunately, in a number of these industrialising nations the recent world recession and over-extension of foreign borrowing have led them into massive foreign debt. This has brought inflation and economic disruption at home and a serious reappraisal of the role of industrialisation in the economy; Nigeria, Brazil, Mexico and Argentina are some of the nations with massive debt problems. Perhaps out of this may come more securely based policies which take into account the capacity and needs of the domestic home market and the need to put economic viability before political expediency.

20.7 Models of industrialisation

The more mature Newly Industrialising Countries such as South Korea and Taiwan have successfully industrialised broadly along lines followed by the advanced industrial countries. They now have a sophisticated and diverse industrial base oriented towards export as well as serving an increasingly large and affluent home market. However, attempts by other countries to industrialise along similar lines have ended in failure, notably the topical African states. For reasons already outlined in Case study 20.2, it is unlikely that further continued attempts to industrialise along western lines will succeed. Nor is it desirable that every country should follow the same development path.

Certain advanced countries such as New Zealand and Australia have already followed a rather different development path to that of West European countries. While having a significant industrial sector, New Zealand and Australia still have strong primary sectors which provide the major part of their export earnings because their main comparative advantage lies with the primary sector.

For most African countries and others such as Bangladesh and Peru, their comparative advantage lies with agricultural and mineral production. It makes economic sense for any industrialisation programme to complement rather than replace the primary sector within the economy and as the main export earner. Most attention needs to be given to rural development programmes in order to produce a prosperous economic primary commercial sector and to reduce the over rapid flow of population from rural to urban areas which cannot sustain influx.

It may be useful to think of two possible alternative models of industrial development, which might be labelled as a South East Asia type model and an African type model (Figures 20.15 and 20.16).

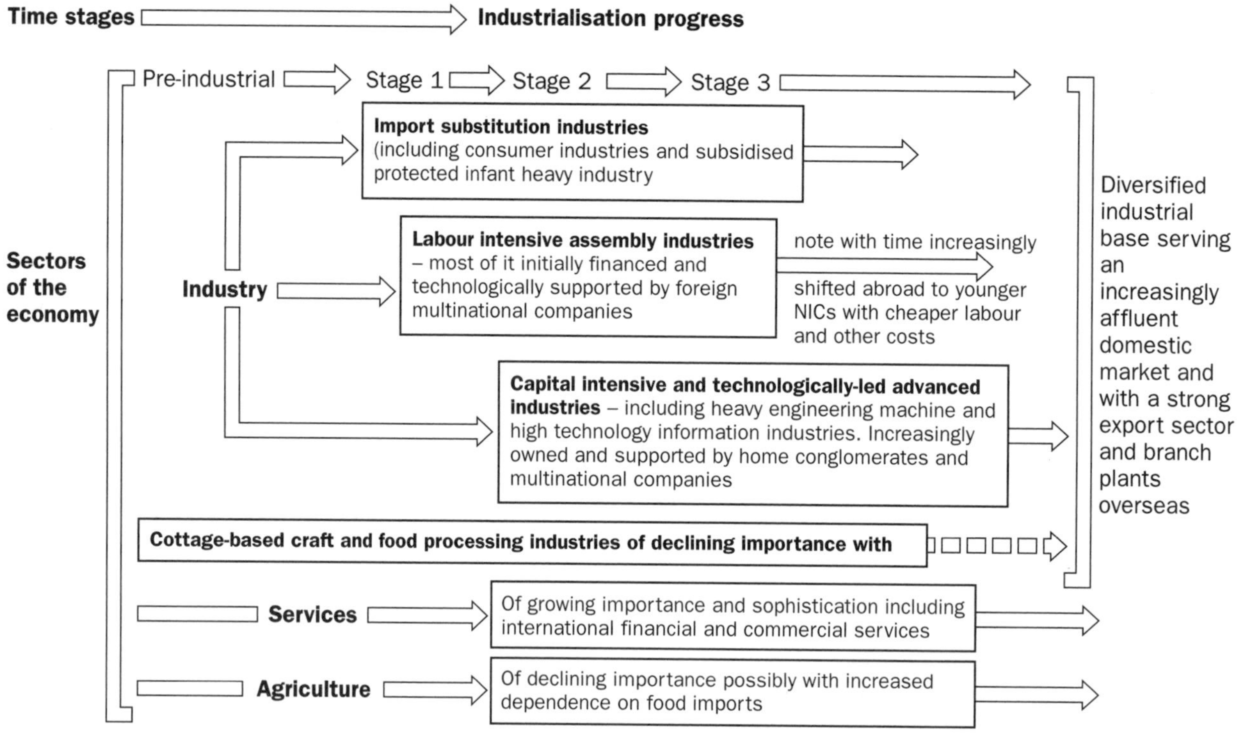

Figure 20.15 South East Asia model

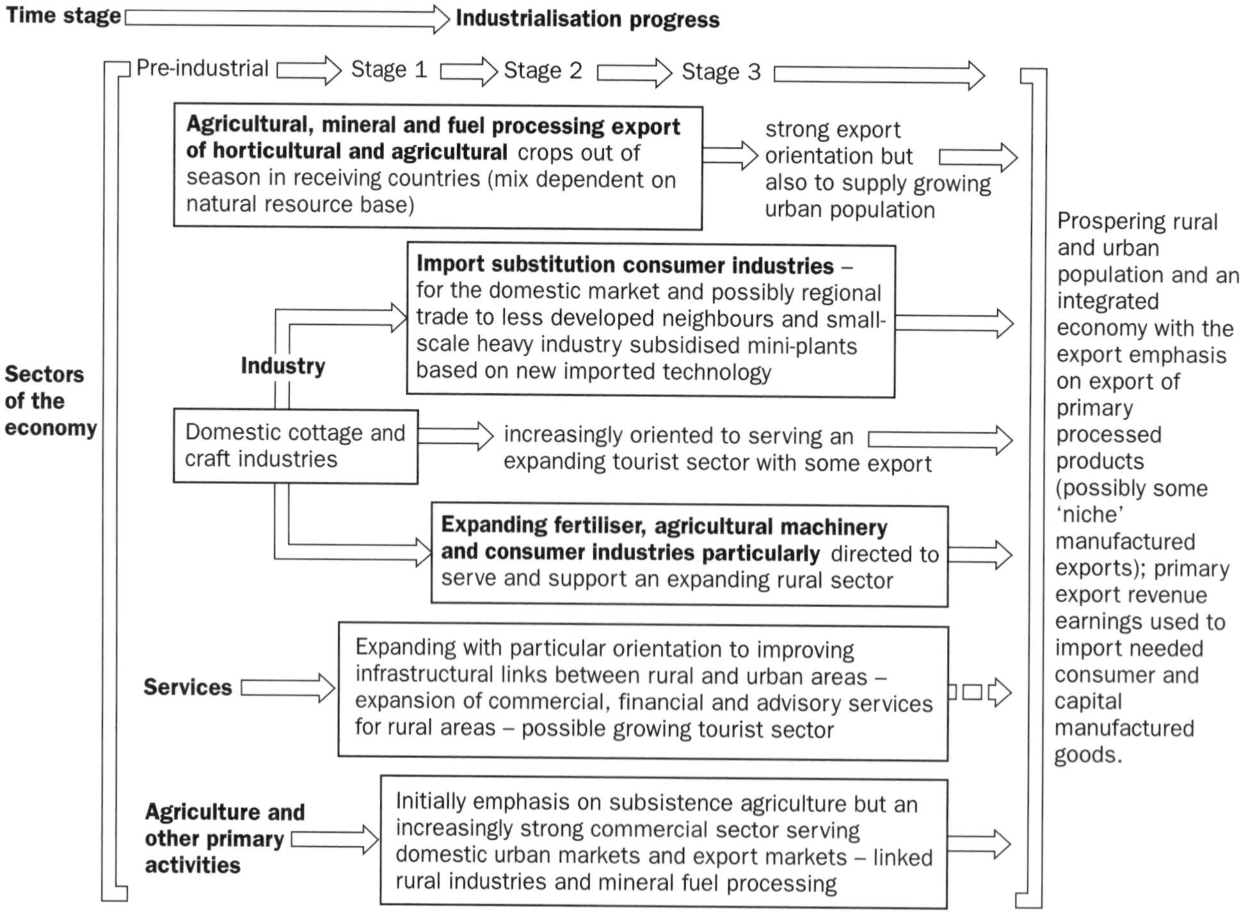

Figure 20.16 The African model

20.8 The location of manufacturing

The most dominant feature of the pattern of industry in the countries in the case studies, is its concentration into a few centres (Case studies 17.2, 20.1 and 20.2).

The largest concentrations of population have attracted the most industry. These are the centres which offer the largest markets and they have advantages arising from cumulative causation and agglomeration effects. Where coastally situated, they have the added advantage of an export point which attracted earlier processing industries and the growth of an infrastructure.

In the case of ports and their surrounding areas, the concentration of manufacturing has been enhanced by governments, in some cases nominating the port and coastal area as an Export Processing Zone or Special Economic Zone (Figure 20.13).

However, there are other centres based on a narrow and more specialist range of factors, in particular, the presence or access to raw material and power. Examples include the petro-chemical industry located at oil refining centres which have access to local oil supplies, e.g. at Maracaibo in Venezuela and copper smelting at Kitwe in Zambia.

In longer established industrial regions such as south-east Brazil, the process of deconcentration or dispersion is beginning to take place. The reasons are similar to those in the developed world that is, increasing diseconomies where industry is heavily concentrated and government directives both to relieve pressure on heavily congested regions and to generate alternative growth centres in areas requiring more employment opportunities.

Much dispersion tends to be only to the edge of cities with such features as industrial trading estates and greenfield site factories becoming common as, for example, on the edge of São Paulo in Brazil and Singapore.

Large ports and capital cities are particularly attractive locations to manufacturing, but new growth poles are also evident in most of the NICs. A notable example is Ciudad Guayana in Venezuela where access to iron-ore, bauxite, local timber and hydro-electric power potential, together with navigable river access provided a good basis for industrial development. This, it is hoped, will aid general growth in the southern part of the country and reduce pressure on Caracas and other centres in the north.

20.9 Industrialisation and environmental problems

The conflict between economic growth and the need to safeguard the environment

A substantial amount of the damage being done to the environment in developing countries is associated with population pressures and over exploitation of the land (Case study 6.1). However, there are growing concerns about the adverse affects of industrialisation, especially where this is rapid as in Thailand for example.

Country	Environmental damage as a percentage of GNP
Nigeria	17
Indonesia	17
Madagascar	16
Mexico	12
Brazil	10
USA	4
Germany	4
Japan	2

* No national figures are available to identify the specific proportion of these general percentages that can be attributed to industrial environmental damage.

[SOURCE: Pearce D W and Atkinson G *Are National Economies Sustainable?*, Discussion paper, 1992]

***Figure 20.17** Economic cost of environmental damage*

Environmental pressures resulting form over-rapid industrialisation in Thailand

Equally there is an uneasy acceptance that many economic development projects have paid too little attention to the long-term sustainability of their natural resource base; that laws and regulations have been weighed in favour of the unscrupulous, rather than the conscientious, and that a fair distribution of the wealth derived from Thailand's natural resources and industrial progress is as distant a prospect as ever.

Population in Bangkok

The most potent images of rapid growth are to be found in Bangkok itself. As industrialisation has continued apace, the economic relations of the country have become progressively oriented upwards the capital city, to the extent that over 75% of Thailand's factories dealing with hazardous chemicals are now located within

Bangkok's hinterland. The growth of private transport has been equally phenomenal, and the city is fast becoming choked with traffic.

The problems are the hallmarks of four decades of rapid, uncontrolled and largely unplanned growth. As in all developing cities, the urban underclasses are suffering the most and carry the least political clout, but the problems are beginning to affect everyone. Here is an extract taken from a letter written by one concerned woman in Bangkok:

'Once fertile farmlands have been turned into factory sites, beaches and forest reserves have become tourist resorts, paralysed traffic has become a way of life, the air has become heavy with industrial smoke in Bangkok, and there would be more natural disasters to contend with as nature takes her revenge on us.'

[*The Bangkok Post*, 26 November 1989]

[SOURCE: Hewitt T et al (ed) *Industrialisation and Development*, 1992]

Environmental damage is much more likely in developing countries than in advanced countries, because legislation safeguards are less strict and developing countries lack sufficient capital and advanced technology to ensure industrial processes are environmentally clean. In the developing world three dimensions of environmental degradation are evident:

Environmental degradation arises from industry itself, not only in terms of the amount of air, water and ground pollution generated but also through the destruction of countryside and coastal environments. This occurs both as a result of the spread of industrial sites and the development of the infrastructure, such as road networks needed to service them. Environmental damage is especially serious where heavy industries such as iron and steel and chemicals are involved, since these are high energy users and produce harmful and in some cases, toxic waste.

Industrialisation is usually accompanied by over rapid urbanisation and all its associated problems. This is well illustrated from the massive expansion of Bangkok largely as a result of Thailand's rapid industrialisation over the last decade and the over-concentration of industrial development in the Bangkok region. Such over-concentration is repeated in a number of developing countries: greater Lagos in Nigeria, Mexico City and the São Paulo region in Brazil, for example.

In some cases industrialisation is supported by exploitation of resources further inland which causes damage to the environments. In Indonesia for example there is widespread destruction of tropical forest areas to support the timber industry and in India, exploitation of coal and iron ore in the Damador valley for its steel industries (Case study 17.2). While resources are needed for industry there is not the legislation or enforcement needed to ensure responsible their responsible development.

It is frequently argued that much of this environmental degradation is due to the actions of foreign multinational companies, but as reports indicate, governments and environmental agencies in the developing countries bear the main responsibility for safeguarding the environment. It is only recently that these governments have begun to develop coherent environment management policies and there is even more difficulty assembling the will and finance needed to enforce them.

Much of the spur towards better environment management has come from the 1992 Rio *Earth Summit*. It was also at this summit that a number of developing countries pointed out that speedy economic development was vital to eliminate the widespread poverty in the developing world. Most of these governments are now showing a conscious awareness of the urgency to balance the need for further economic development with the need for more environmental safeguards in the interests of future sustainability.

Concluding comment

Trends and prospects in the manufacturing sector for different world regions to the year 2000

As the economies of the developed countries have recovered from the recent recession, industrial activity has accelerated. For example, in the USA manufacturing activity was vigorous and broadly based with general purpose machinery and information-processing among the fastest growing industries.

After years of industrial decline, considerable progress has been made in Eastern Europe, with manufacturing activity playing an important part in the improvement of production. In contrast, most member states of the Commonwealth of Independent States are still in deep recession.

In the case of developing countries, the gap between the least developed countries and those that are fast moving towards the status of NICs, is widening.

Prospects for the least developed countries are not encouraging. Their capacity utilisation and labour productivity remain low.

case study

20.1 South Korea: a successful newly industrialising country

South Korea is a maturing industrial economy, rated alongside France in terms of the strength and diversification of its economy.

General

South Korea has a population of 44 million with 40% within Seoul and the commuting area around. A per capita income of $8500 gives manufacturing a strong domestic market base, supporting an export-oriented strategy. For example, in 1994 home car sales were one and a half million, supporting expanding car exports and overseas assembly plants.

In 1994 economic growth accelerated again to 8% and is forecast to continue.

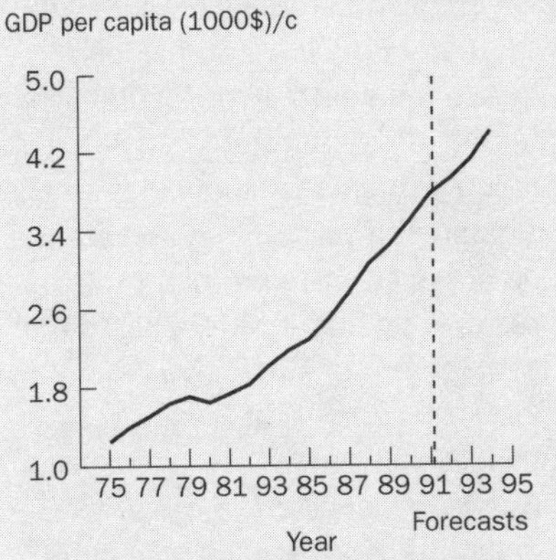

[SOURCE: UNIDO Report, 1993 – 94]

Economic growth – gross domestic product per capita (1000 US$)

Diverse and strong manufacturing sector

'*It makes not only ships but cars, electronic goods, petro-chemicals, cement, tyres, textiles and a wide range of products between.*'

[SOURCE: Focus South Korea, *Times* 8.3.95]

It is the world's largest shipbuilder, third in memory chip production, fourth in ethylene production and sixth in cars.

Industrial structural change (index of value added: 1980 – 100)

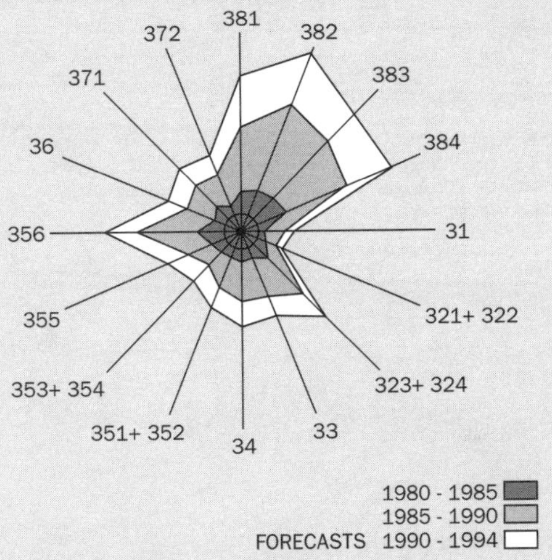

ISIC Code	(Industries)
31	(Food products)
321, 322	(Textiles)
323, 324	(Leather)
33	(Wood and furniture)
34	(Paper and printing)
351, 352	(Chemicals)
353, 354	(Petroleum and coal)
355	(Rubber product)
356	(Plastic product)
36	(Non-metal mineral products)
371	(Iron and steel)
372	(Non-ferrous metals)
381	(Metals products)
382	(Non-electrical machinery)
383	(Electrical machinery)
384	(Transport equipment)

Relative growth of industrial sectors

Change in industry

South Korea is increasingly moving to capital intensive, technologically and skill oriented industries and globalised industrial activities, together with joint ventures and co-operation with overseas companies. Although Korea has many small and medium-sized industrial firms, manufacturing is dominated by multinational conglomerates such as Samsung, Hyundai and Daewoo, with smaller conglomerates such as Lotte (food, ice cream and soft drinks) and Kumho (petro-chemicals, tyres and an air line). The big conglomerates are further diversifying.

For example, Samsung deals in construction, heavy machinery, high technology and electrical products. Over 30% of its value comes from overseas plants. It is also entering the car industry and has its own banking, shipping and trading arm.

Links between government and industry

There are strong links between government and industry, with the government using an interventionist but supportive policy. It gives tariff protection and financial aid to industry embarking on rapid maturation so that a more open economic policy can be adopted. Industries are therefore able to compete under freer market conditions. The government itself has a stake in industry. For example, it owns Pohang Iron and Steel one of the largest steel producers in the world, supplying steel to shipbuilding and the car industry. By 1998 output will have expanded to 28 million tonnes annually.

Industrial production index (1980 – 100)

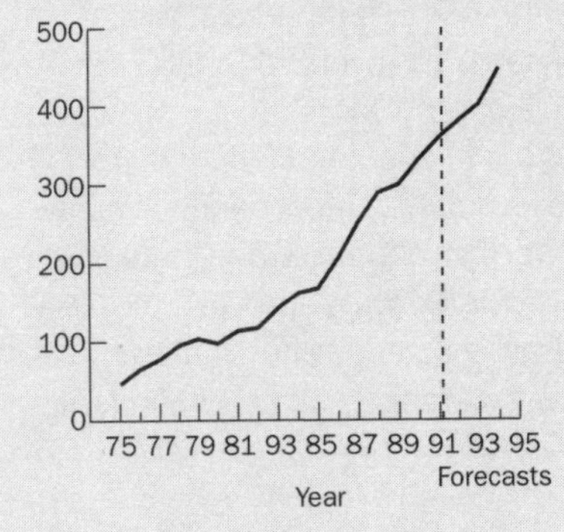

[SOURCE: UNIDO Report, 1993 – 94]

Growth in industrial production

Industry	Products	Target date for commercialisation
Automobiles	Electric car	1996
Bioengineering	Advanced waste treatment	–
	Alternatives to chloro-fluorocarbons	–
Computers	Multimedia computers	1994
	Neural networks	1997
	Voice recognition	2000
Consumer electronics	Television monitors	1993
	Television transmission	1994
	Flat panel displays	1997
Energy	Light-water nuclear reactor	2001
Manufacturing	computer integration	1996
	Intelligent manufacturing	2000
Materials	Alloys and polymers	1997
Medicine	Genetically engineered DNA	1993
	Herbally based biotechnology	1996
	Genetically engineered drugs	1997
Telecommunications	Advanced switches (ATMs)	1996
	Digital network (ISDN)	2001

[SOURCE: *Far Eastern Economic Review* 8.4.93]

New products targeted by the Republic of Korea for commercialisation, 1993 – 2001

Factors favouring industrial success

In the late 1960s take-off was based on a favoured South East Asia coastal location, cheap, adaptable and educated labour supply, government support and an inflow of foreign capital and technology, especially from Japan and the USA.

As the economy has matured, success was increasingly dependent on Korea itself providing a highly educated and skilled technical and managerial personnel supply, its own innovative sector and an increasingly affluent home market which supported the government's move to increasing export orientation within a more democratic system under President Kim. The industrial sector is supported by an increasingly sophisticated financial and commercial sector.

The location of industry

Industry is oriented towards the capital region of Seoul in response to the large market there, large labour supply, pool of expertise, infrastructure and government linkages, together with other agglomerative advantages.

However, diseconomies and growth have led to decentralisation and dispersion to coastal sites and along the main highways going south. There is for example the Kia motor corporation's new 600 000 annual unit capacity plant on reclaimed land in Asan Bay, south-east of Seoul. Government-planned new towns and technopoles are part of this dispersion.

This has led to a broad 400 km axis of growth southward to link up with major port and coastal locations in the south, in particular with the port of Pusan. Here heavier industry, such as shipbuilding (e.g. Hanshin shipyards), iron and steel, and chemicals are prominent. Pressure on Pusan is leading to the development of a massive new industrial complex at Kwang Yong Bay further west.

As costs increase in Korea more labour intensive assembly sectors of industry will be shifted overseas to China and Thailand, together with branch plant locations in western markets in the USA, its main trading partner, and in the EU.

case study

20.2 Nigeria: Failure of African industrialisation

Potential unfulfilled

Although manufacturing output is small compared to leading SE Asian NICs, Nigeria was the leading manufacturing country in tropical Africa. Even so, manufacturing is only 8% of the country's GDP.

Nigeria has a potentially rich resource base. In agriculture, it was a leading producer of palm oil, cocoa, rubber from the coastal belt and cotton and leather from the north. The rich oil and gas deposits in the Delta region and offshore makes it the sixth world producer, providing 95% of the country's exports. Other mineral wealth includes tin, columbite (Jos Plateau), coal and iron-ore.

There is a basic infrastructure developed from colonial times, in particular the rail network which extends inland from the major ports e.g. Lagos.

The population of 110 million (35% urban) gives a large potential market but purchasing power is as yet very limited as per capita income is only $250.

Location of industry

The main industrial core is in the Lagos region with industry spreading inland along the railway as Lagos itself has become increasingly congested. The reasons for this are typical for this type of location. Until recently Lagos was the political capital. It remains the main port outlet and economic region with the largest market area in Nigeria. It is also a nodal point of the country's communication infrastructure.

Port Harcourt, the centre of the delta oil industry, is the focus of a smaller industrial core, but beyond this, the country has only industrial cities. Many are located in the more prosperous south and most are

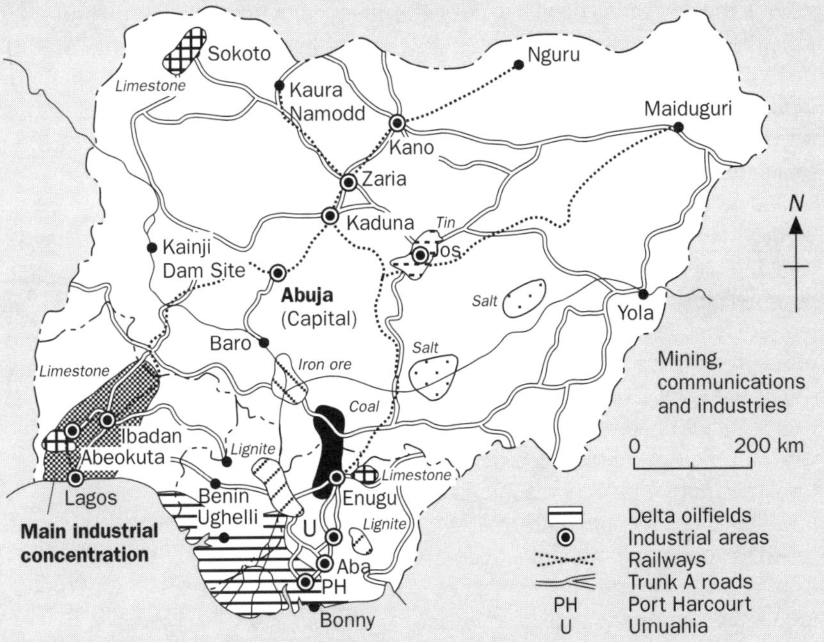

[SOURCE: Udo R K *A comprehensive geography of West Africa*]

Location of manufacturing

state capitals. However, there are important centres in the north such as Kano, the centre of the cotton and livestock region of Nigeria, and Jos, a centre for tin mining.

A key location factor for almost all industrial cities is location on the main rail routes which extend inland from the coast as these remain the main transport arteries.

Initial expansion

Since independence in 1960, there was an initial phase of rapid expansion in manufacturing. Based largely on import substitution, industries were protected from foreign competition. The mainstream consumer industries included food, drink, textiles, plastics, pharmaceuticals, vehicle and radio assembly.

Along with some large-scale industry, iron and steel, oil refining and chemicals also experienced expansion. As in consumer industry, there was some foreign multinational participation but shares in companies were tightly limited by Nigeria Enterprise Production Decrees.

Agricultural processing for export also saw initial growth. The traditional small-scale and cottage industry continued in the towns and rural areas.

Towards the end of the 1970s there were plans to make Nigeria the economic hub of Sub-Saharan Africa. The boom of prosperity was based on oil and 500% was added to the value of manufacturing from 1977 – 82. However, the strategy and oil basis of the economy was collapsing by the mid-1980s amid widespread political unrest and a series of military coups.

Collapse of the economy since the mid-1980s

The dependency on oil for export income and government revenue to finance the economy was exposed with the collapse of world oil prices in 1985.

Since the 1970s, agriculture, the other basis of the economy, had been neglected in favour of oil and industrial expansion. Plantations have been disbanded and 90% of agricultural production was controlled by smallholders using outdated methods. They were 'starved' of credit, fertilisers, and revenue for new machinery. There was a rural labour shortage with increased urban migration and employment by the oil industry. Export earnings from agricultural products fell away, with insufficient supplies of agricultural raw materials for home industries. Food production, therefore, failed to keep pace with population expansion and Nigeria became a net food importer. Roads and other rural infrastructure fell into disrepair. Market demands for goods fell due to increased poverty.

Government debts increased, with no coherent financial and economic programme. Currency was overvalued with severe inflation and mounting international debts of $33 billion, using up 25% of export earnings to finance it.

A rapid population growth of 3.3% annually and over urbanisation made matters worse.

Corruption and inefficient management in parts of the industrial sector but especially government-owned industry also contributed to the problem. Operating costs of manufacturing plants were on average 30% higher than in advanced countries and South East Asia.

Rectifying the situation

Under the Restructuring Programme which had been forced on governments since 1986, promises of reforms were made and some undertaken, but a coherent programme has not been carried through. Nigeria's own Manufacturing Association are highly critical of the government's lack of progress.

There are some moves towards a market economy and financial reforms. The currency has been devalued, subsidies removed and more restrictions placed on imports of consumer goods to try to restore the economy.

Promises to privatise state-owned firms were not fully carried through. For example, the National Oil Company remains, thus inefficiencies will continue.

The need to revitalise agriculture and repair infrastructure is not yet seriously underway. A reorientation of industrial strategy based on agro-industry links depends on it and a sound use of oil revenues to rebuild the economy.

Above all, moves towards political democracy and building up 'human capital' has been promised by the military ruler, President General Abucha, but has not yet been undertaken.

Some slight improvement in the short term is forecast by UNIDO but no substantial progress can be expected until after the year 2000, as reforms will not have a significant effect for some years.

Industrial structural change (index of value added: 1980 – 100)

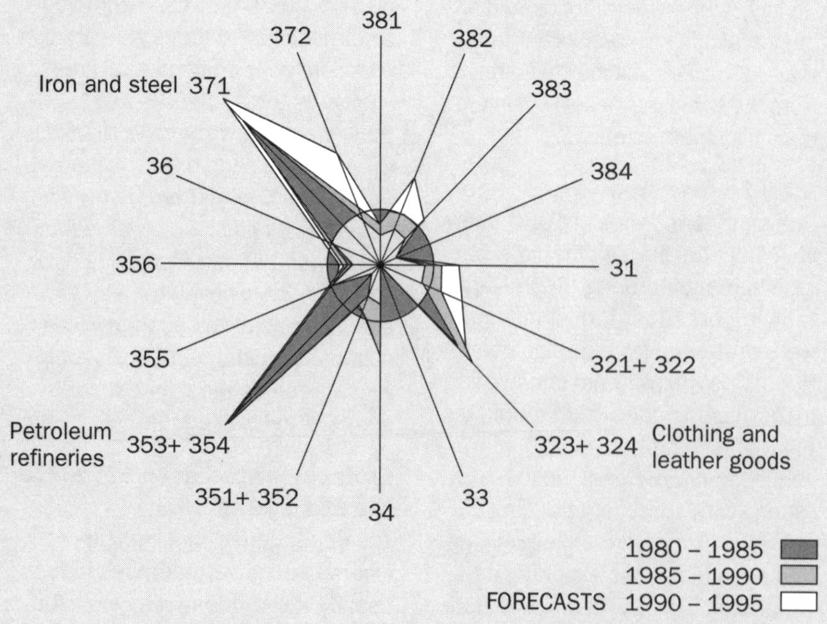

Change in industrial production for different manufacturing sectors, 1980 – 95

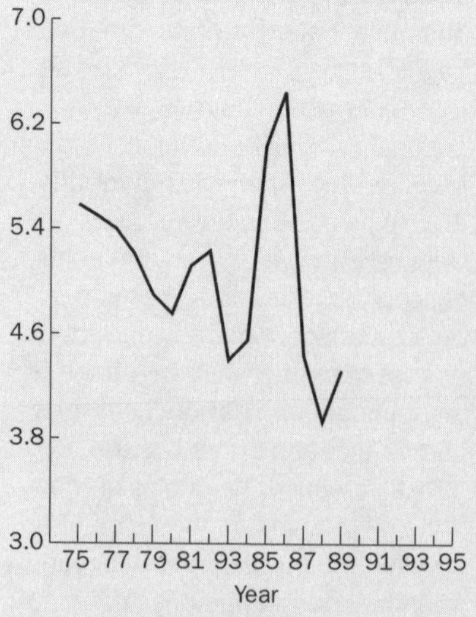

Manufacturing's share of GDP, 1975 – 90

CHAPTER 21

The basis of agriculture

The geographer is mainly concerned with the distribution of different kinds of farming and the reasons for their changes. One of the related issues to consider is whether or not sufficient food can be made available for the continuously growing world population. This involves, amongst other things, examining how different kinds of farming can be made productive, particularly those in tropical regions. Other questions include whether increases can be achieved without damaging the environment or the fabric of society in rural areas.

21.1 **The farming system**

A systems approach to agriculture has gained favour over recent years, partly because it highlights inter-relationships touching on some important agricultural issues, but also because central to systems is the idea of process and change, which is fundamental to understanding farming patterns today. Except subsistence agriculture in which the farmer cultivates for his family's needs (Figure 21.1), it is important to see farming as composed of two linked parts or subsystems (Figure 21.2). The production subsystem comprises the group or groups of farms and the marketing subsystem is responsible for processing, packing and marketing the produce. This may be controlled by the farmer or company running the farm but more often by an independent marketing organisation.

Since production and marketing subsystems are usually separate, adequate transport links are required between them as well as between the marketing organisation and the ultimate consumer of the farm produce. In addition to movement of produce to market, there is also movement of inputs or resources to help grow crops or rearing livestock. Some are natural environment inputs – climate, soil, and land inputs. Others are human inputs, some involving transport of materials to the farm as well as on the farm itself, for example, fertilisers, labour and machinery. Efficient and cost effective transport is therefore another part of the total farming system. A farming system consists of much more than the land on which the food or agricultural raw materials are produced. It is also to do with efficient marketing and transport facilities.

Figure 21.1 A simple subsistence farming system

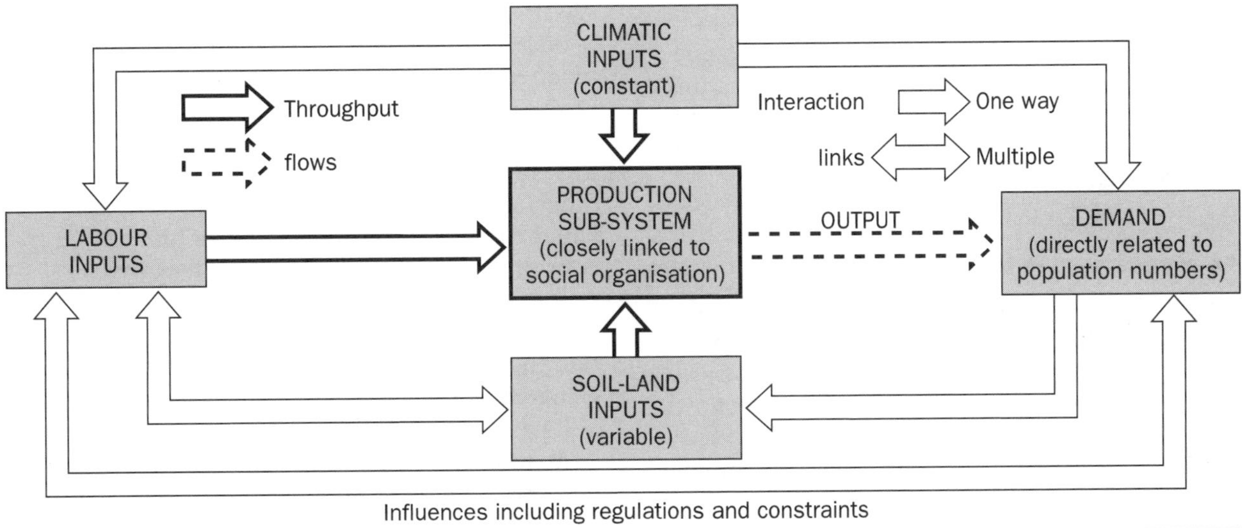

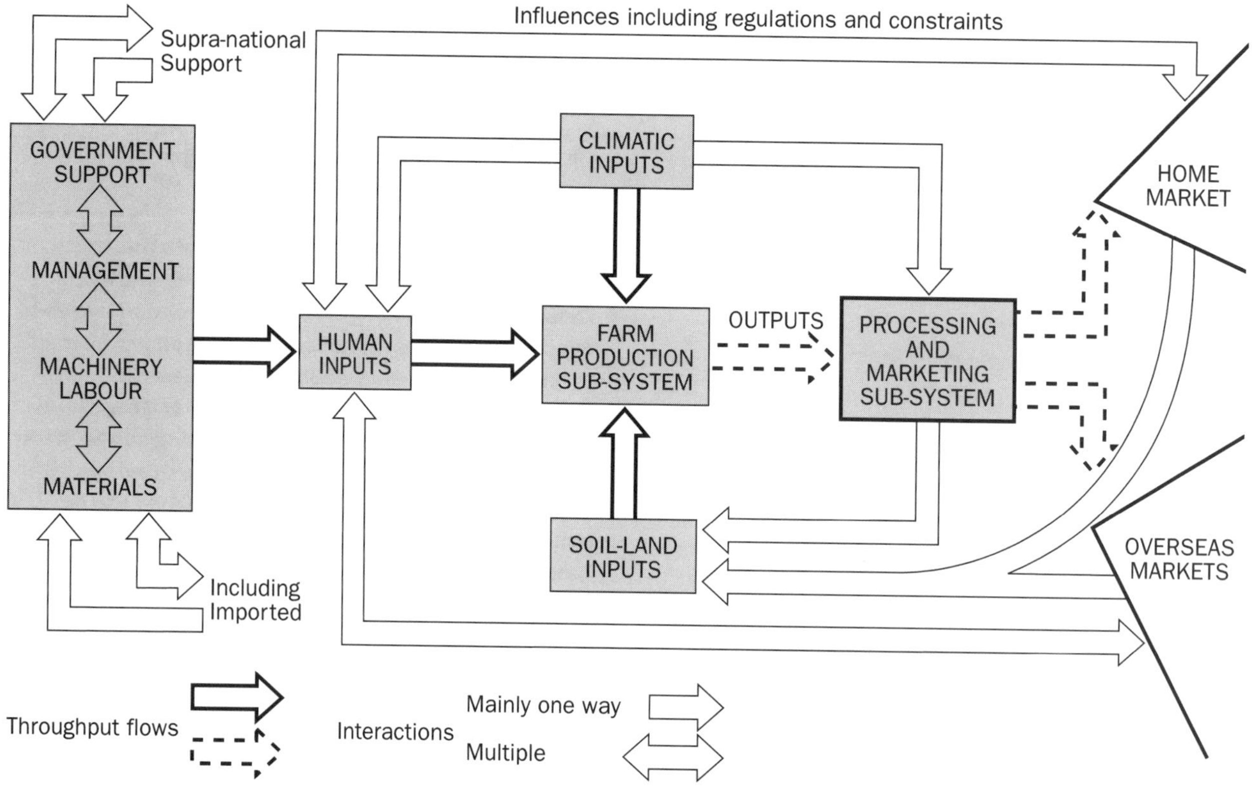

Figure 21.2 The complex commercial farming system

Apart from giving a more comprehensive view of agriculture at any given time, a systems context is valuable because it emphasises the movements, processes and inter-relationships through which one part of farming is affected by and affects the rest.

21.2 **Assessing its efficiency**

Until recently, the developed world has been inclined to measure the efficiency of any production and marketing system in terms of its financial profitability, that is, the amount by which input costs (including production, transport, processing and other marketing costs) are exceeded by the revenue gained by selling the produce output. However, this is only a partial measure of the system's efficiency. It does not give an adequate measure of environmental costs, for example the extent to which farming practices maintain or increase soil fertility.

An assessment in terms of ecology

Energy flows and food chains

Using an ecological approach, inputs and outputs from a human agricultural system can be measured like any natural ecosystem in terms of energy flows passing through it. Inputs can be measured in terms of solar and 'people' energy and output measured in millions of calories.

The throughputs of energy can be seen as food chains. Different types of farming are represented by different food chains. One kind of food chain is that for arable farming in which crops are grown to be directly consumed. Livestock farming is represented by different and longer food chains, in which the crops or grasses grown are first eaten by livestock; these in turn provide the produce for human consumption. Arable farming has only one stage in the food chain while livestock or pastoral farming has two (Figure 21.3). Different kinds of farming can therefore be seen as a series of food chains.

The relative efficiency of two or more farming systems can be measured by comparing the amount of energy output with the amount of energy input required to produce that output for each food chain. Inevitably, as energy flows through the food chain some of it is lost in a variety of ways, but the loss is greater for some types of food chains than others. In the case of food chain A in Figure 21.3 where tillage crops are produced for human consumption, much of the energy remains as output because there is only one stage in the food chain. In the case of food chain B for livestock farming, there are two stages in the chain and there is therefore a greater chance that energy will be lost as it passes through each stage.

Apart from emphasising the much greater efficiency of crop farming over livestock farming,

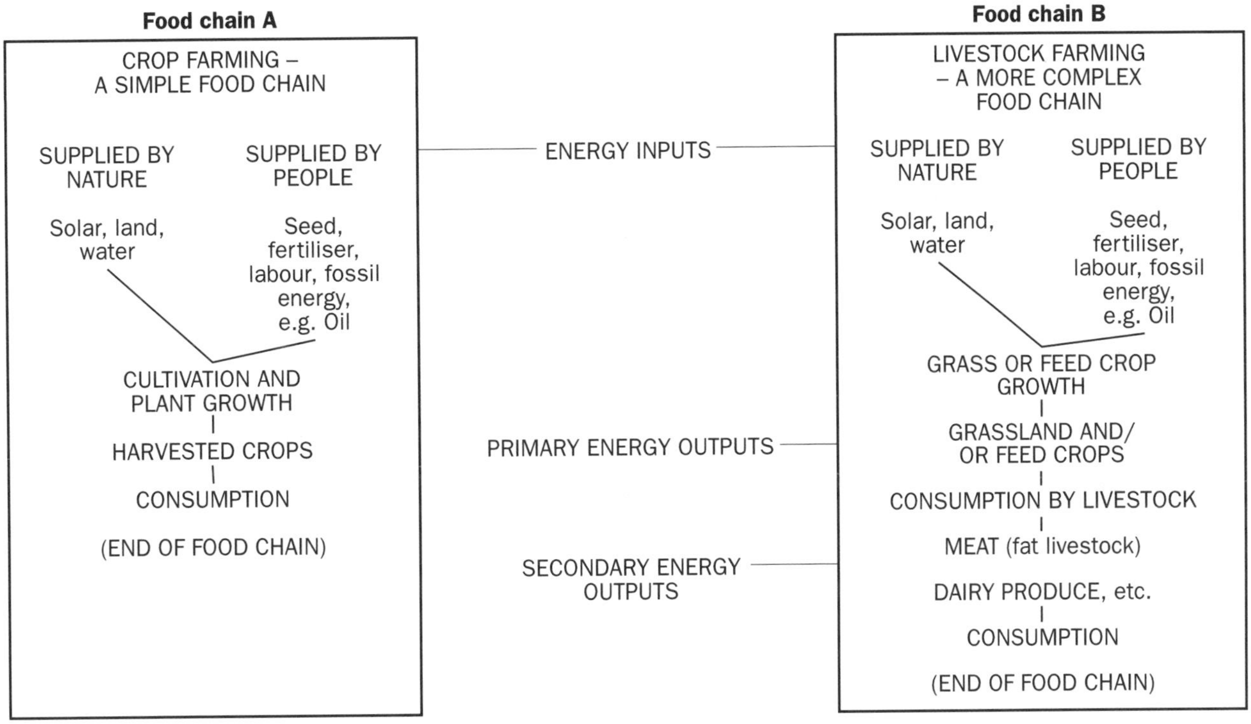

***Figure 21.3** Two food chains compared*

regarding systems as food chains also highlights where energy losses occur in the total farming process. It can therefore indicate ways of making farming more efficient.

Frequently, when considering the food needs of people in the developing world, emphasis is on developing higher yielding strains of crops increasing inputs of fertilisers and machinery. While these may benefit they are difficult and costly to implement. Much more of the energy input would be saved and the amount of food effectively increased if greater attention was given to more efficient methods of harvesting, storing and processing agricultural products. Since the latter could be achieved relatively cheaply, the benefits to the poorer parts of the developing world would be significant.

To the importance of the percentage of energy balance at the end of the food chain, must be added its nutritional value. Meat and fish are richer in protein than food crops and this partly explains why there is so much livestock farming despite its apparent inefficiency in terms of large inputs needed relative to the output of energy produced. Certain crops are also relatively rich in protein and can to some extent substitute for meat and fish. These include pulses, such as peas and beans, which have the added advantage of restoring nitrogen content to the soil when used in crop rotation. More recently, attention has been given to the soya bean plant. Its acreage has increased rapidly in areas like southern USA and the more humid parts of the Asian Steppes and China. Also, a number of agricultural research institutions have been established to develop other high yielding strains of protein-rich pulses and cereals.

Unfortunately scientific advances like these and other changes in the kind of food eaten in the developing world are hindered by conservative market demand – traditional food being preferred or more acceptable for cultural and religious reasons.

Measures of efficiency also need to take account of the effect that pressures for increasing food supplies and agricultural raw materials have on the 'health' of the environment. If the land is not kept in good health, yields can rapidly decline.

21.3 Efficiency and the environmental impact

The effects demand for food and agricultural raw materials have on the environment can be illustrated by examining the nutrient flow within a farming system. The nutrient output consumed as human food is only one of a number of nutrient flows within an agrosystem (Figure 21.4).

Nutrient flows are brought into farming systems both through nature's own activities and by human input, such as applying manures and fertilisers. These nutrients are mainly held in the soil as a nutrient bank. The nutrient bank is also renewed from plant remains left in the field after harvesting and from livestock droppings. Nutrients can be taken directly from the atmosphere by plants; legume plants for example are able to fix nitrogen from the atmosphere.

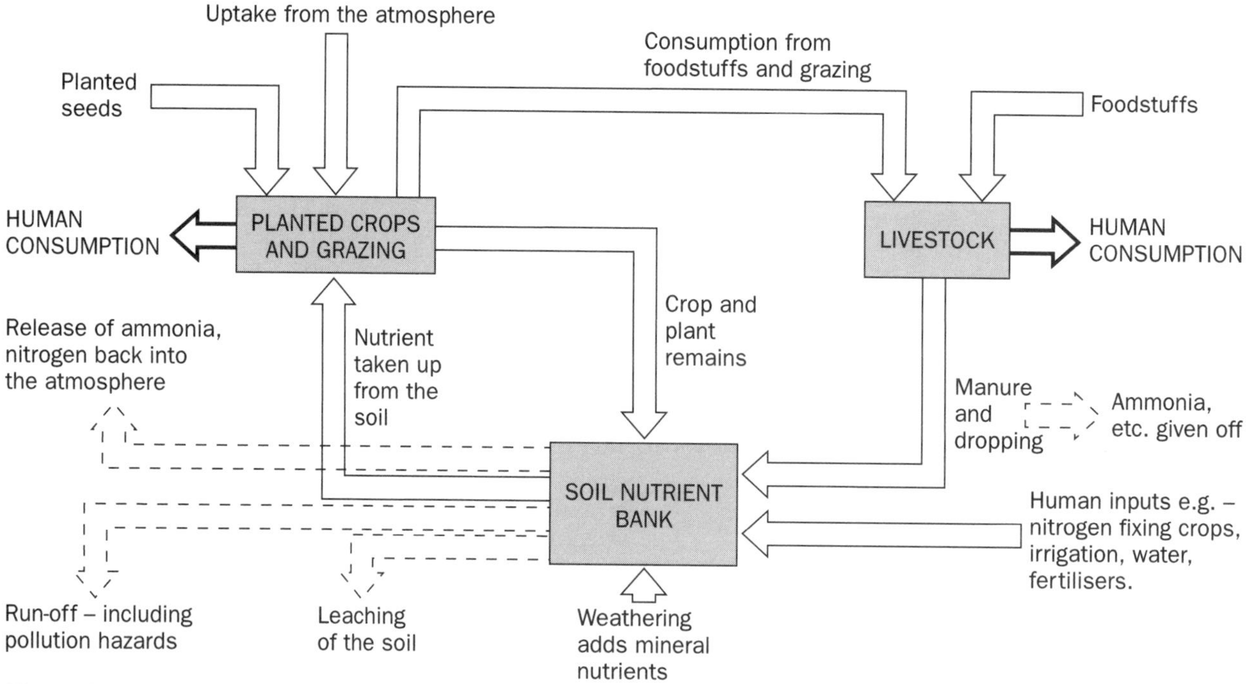

Figure 21.4 Simple nutrient flows in an agro-system

Nutrients are lost out of the system by direct output in the form of harvested crops and livestock produced and through natural processes such as leaching through water percolating down through the soil and surface run-off. Nutrients are also lost through other surface processes, breaking down and removing the soil itself along with the nutrients it contains. Just as good farming practice can reduce this loss, bad farming practices can accelerate and in extreme cases lead to soil erosion by wind blow, and sheet and gully erosion by water run-off (Figures 21.5 and 21.6). Farming should therefore be assessed according to how well it maintains and builds up the soil nutrient bank, since this is an essential requisite for the soil's fertility and yield.

There are many examples of the results of bad farming practice which, in areas with difficult climatic conditions lead to severe soil erosion and loss of nutrients at a rate nature is unable to replace. Overcropping and overgrazing where too little is put back into the soil and too much taken out are common causes. In the old cotton belt of the southern USA, for example, a series of exceptionally dry years combined with poor farming practices under the share cropping system led to the Dust Bowl phenomenon. In some areas it totally destroyed the soil's fertility.

In tropical regions where torrential rains of the hot, wet season alternate with a hot, dry season when wind blow as well as water can be a potent erosion force, soil erosion is also a severe problem (Case study 21.1). This is especially so where there is pressure of population, ignorance or poverty or commercial greed.

For example, overgrazing by the cattle of the Masaai around water-holes in East Africa has led to breakdown of the soil and widespread gully erosion. Also widespread clearance of land and monoculture by Europeans, as for example in the coffee lands of South East Brazil and other tropical regions, have had equally disastrous results.

The effects of these kinds of bad farming practices are now clearly recognised and measures have been taken to remedy them. These include diversification of agriculture and adoption of multi-purposes schemes such as that of the Tennessee Valley Authority in the USA.

However, with modern farming practices there are less obvious but equally serious ways in which the nutrient bank and the environment in general can be harmed. For example, market demand and government subsidies such as those given under the EU Common Agricultural Policy, have led to the spread of intensive arable farming on to hills, areas formerly under permanent grassland or a natural vegetation cover. This has led to a significant increase in soil erosion (Case study 21.2).

Over-use of fertilisers and insecticides, while over the short term increasing yields, can lead to harmful chemicals being carried away in solution and with these, some of the soil nutrients. These enter lakes and water courses creating widespread pollution (Case study 21.3). Over-use of herbicides and insecticides can also have detrimental effects on wildlife and on human health through contamination of food and drinking water.

CAUSES
Poor farming and other detrimental land-use practices accelerate natural processes of erosion by wind and water in climatically vulnerable areas and places of steep terrain. Soil erosion increases at a rate exceeding that at which natural processes and human inputs can renew the soil structure and cover.

Climatically vulnerable areas
due to low unreliable rainfall, seasonal drought, intense storms e.g. continental interiors, tropical savanna, monsoon and equatorial areas

Areas of steep terrain
with limited vegetation to check surface run-off

Poor land-use practices
Deforestation for timber or fuel
Overgrazing
Monoculture
Poor rotational practice
Little fertilising
Ploughing down steep slopes

These arise from over-exploitation of land due to population pressure, poverty, conservative farming tradition or deliberate commercial policy of short-term gain i.e. greed

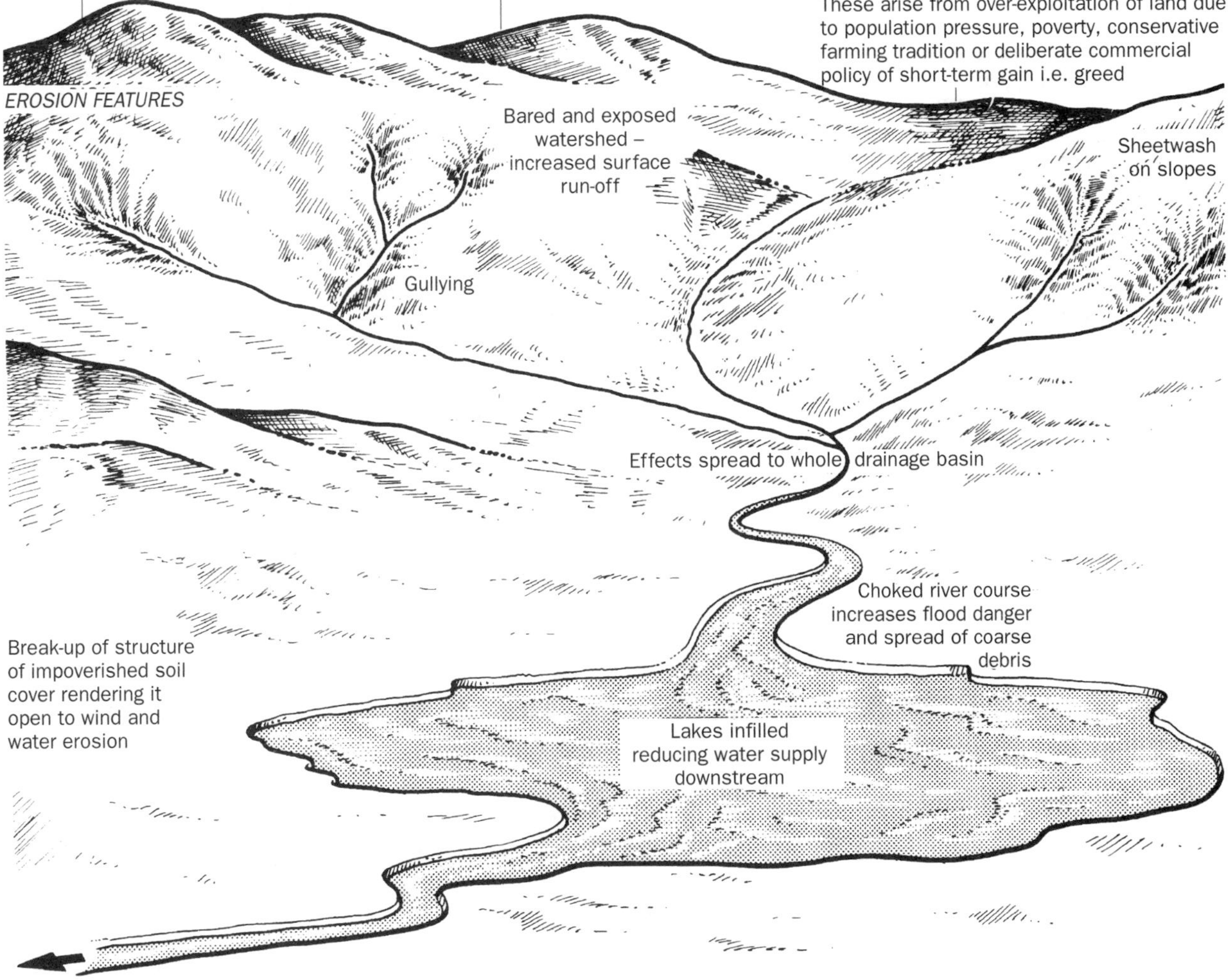

PREVENTIVE MEASURES
These must cover the whole drainage basin as misuse in one area affects the whole basin.

a Direct measures
Afforestation, control of livestock numbers, responsible cultivation practices e.g. adequate humus inputs, windbreaks, good drainage, suitable rotation, diversified farming.

b These are not likely to occur without more comprehensive measures
Advisory and education services to disseminate good practices, adequate finance provision, responsible population policies, alternate employment to reduce pressure on the land, conservation legislation especially to protect watershed areas.

Figure 21.5 *Soil erosion: causes, erosion features and preventative measures*

A better understanding of nutrient cycles and overall ecological conditions will encourage better farming practices which will maintain and even improve agricultural productivity. It can improve the land drainage, soil and other environmental resources upon which agriculture depends. Fortunately in recent years a greater awareness of the need for a more sensitive and conservation minded approach to land has become evident. There are also more legislative controls to enforce better conservation measures.

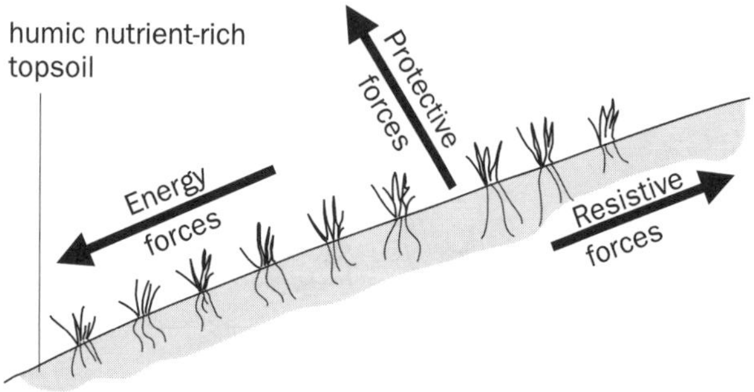

Energy forces – amount available to detach and transport soil particles.
Resistive forces – help over come energy forces. Resistive forces depend on soil properties as influenced by nature and human inputs.
Protective forces – neutralise energy forces and are related to human influence on vegetation cover and land-use.

[SOURCE: Whitlow R *Land degradation in Zimbabwe*, 1988]

Figure 21.6 *A model of a soil erosion system which could provide a framework for the study of soil erosion in a particular region or locality*

21.4 A classification of agricultural regions based on farming systems

There are a number of existing classifications of farming systems, one of the most well known by Whittleseys, which is based on five criteria. These are: crop and livestock combinations, methods employed, intensity of use of labour – capital – organisation, method of disposal of farm products and the kinds of buildings and structures necessary to carry on the agricultural activities.

Although now somewhat dated, Whittlesey's classification has proved useful, but it is not a sufficiently genetic classification, that is, one which leads to some identification of the factors indicating why one area has a different kind of farming from another. However, if the basis of classification is extended using the systems approach this enables us to see that the character of any farming is determined by the demand for its output and the kinds of physical and human inputs needed to use that output (Figure 21.7).

Output demand

The demand factor is the most influential because without the demand there would be no agriculture. This must therefore form the basis of a world classification of farming types. The simplest kind of demand is a subsistence demand, in which the farmer and his family consume their own produce, except for any surplus which may be sold locally to provide cash to meet other household needs such as paying taxes. The other is commercial demand in which farming is essentially geared to production for sale on the market, in other words, cash farming. By its very

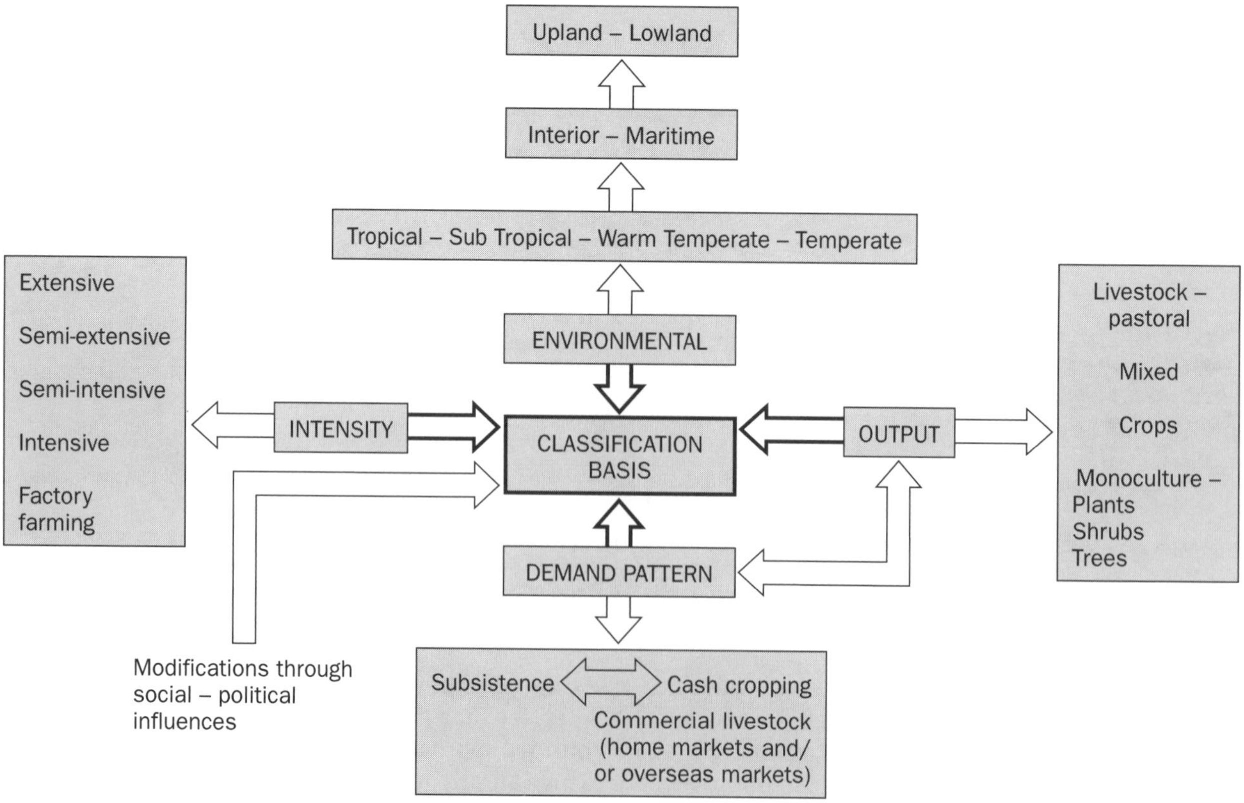

Figure 21.7 *A classification basis for farming systems*

nature it involves separating the production from the marketing aspect, the two frequently being run by separate businesses, though in plantation farming a business corporation may have overall control, from growing the crop to marketing the produce.

Human input factors – intensive and extensive farming

Just as the demand has led to the basic division of farming types into subsistence farming on the one hand and commercial farming on the other, consideration of the human aspect leads to a further subdivision within these two groups. This is on the basis of the intensity with which human inputs are applied, leading to a division into intensive and extensive farming.

Terms associated with the economics of agriculture

Intensive farming systems

Systems with relatively high levels of inputs i.e. capital inputs (machinery, fertilisers, etc.) and labour inputs per unit area farmed, the intention being to achieve high yields per unit area.

[NOTE: High yields may also be encouraged by favourable soil and climatic conditions.]

The actual unit combinations of inputs can vary from one intensive farming system to another, e.g.

- Traditional rice agriculture – the emphasis is on a high level of labour inputs (combined with natural fertiliser application on fertile alluvial soils and a monsoon climate regime) – capital inputs are relatively low. Labour productivity is high because yields per worker are high.
- Horticulture may combine high levels of both capital and labour inputs. Again labour productivity will still be high.
- Factory farming (intensive rearing of livestock indoors) combines very high relative levels of capital input with relatively low levels of labour inputs as most processes and tasks are automated. Labour productivity is exceptionally high because output per unit area is very high in relation to the number of workers employed.

Extensive farming systems

Systems with relative low levels in inputs i.e. both capital and labour inputs per unit area farmed and yields per unit area are also relatively low. However the actual total size of land holding is usually very large so total output may also be high (though yield per unit area is low).

Combinations of inputs vary:

- Commercial grain farming in temperate continental interiors combines comparatively higher inputs of capital with relatively very little labour input per unit area. Because total output is high compared to labour employed, labour productivity will be high.
- In contrast, tropical subsistence shifting agriculture combines relatively high inputs of labour compared to very little capital inputs per unit area. Because yields are low per unit area cultivated and much of the tribe's land area is left fallow in any one year, total output is exceptionally low. Thus labour productivity is also low.

[NOTE: There is some tendency to confuse labour (or employment or worker) productivity with per capita output. Per Capita Output is the output per head of population living in an area or country. Its most common use is related to per capita output of food.]

Intensive farming is defined by the ratio of labour, capital and other inputs to the available land area. The simplest form is intensive subsistence rice farming in South East Asia, where large amounts of labour energy are invested on small plots to obtain as high a yield as possible. More complex are the commercial intensive system such as market gardening in which a high amount of technology, fertilisers and labour are invested per unit of land area to obtain maximum yields.

At the other end of the scale, ***extensive farming occurs where land is sufficiently plentiful for the producer to think in terms of overall returns across the whole land holding and not primarily in terms of yield per unit area.*** Because of the amount of land at his disposal, the farmer will instead concentrate on keeping his cost per unit area as low as possible. Moderate or low yields may result, but if the total unit acreage is large, overall profits can be high. This is the case with sheep ranching in areas such as central Queensland. Extensive grain farming on prairie lands in the USA and Canada is similar, except that capital inputs will be higher by way of fertilisers and the use of machinery. It is more difficult to find examples of extensive subsistence agriculture. Shifting agriculture may be termed as extensive despite the fact that only part of the tribal territory is cleared of cultivation at any one time. The amount of labour input is low and so relatively are yields.

Social and political influences

The intervention of government and other institutions is becoming increasingly important in agriculture as in other spheres. It is strongest in socialist countries such as China, Cuba and Tanzania. Policies adopted towards agriculture depend not only upon the kind of political ideology prevailing in a country but also attitudes and values held by different

	Temperate		Warm Temperate to Sub-Tropical		Tropical	
	Extensive	**Intensive**	**Extensive**	**Intensive**	**Extensive**	**Intensive**
Livestock (Chain B)	Sheep (wool) C Australia Cattle (beef) W USA	Dairying New Zealand, Denmark, Netherlands, UK, S E Australia	Sheep (wool) S & SE Australia, Veld – S Africa Cattle Texas – New Mexico	Dairying N Japan S E USA S W Australia	CATTLE (Beef, Hides) N E Brazil, Amazonia, Orinocco Lowlands, Queensland – Australia	
	Upland sheep (meat) S New Zealand	Factory farming (Pigs, Poultry, Dairying) W Europe, USA	Sheep & goats Mediterranean	Factory Farming Poultry Dairying e.g. California		Dairying Kenya, Zimbabwe
	* nomadic reindeer herding Finland		* nomadic pastoralism – N Africa, Middle East		* nomadic pastoralism – Sahara, Savanna – Africa	
Mixed (Livestock and tillage) (Chains A and B)	Mixed W European Lowlands, St Lawrence Lowland, S E Australia, Tasmania, Corn belt – USA		Mixed (Cotton, tobacco with Livestock) S E USA (Wheat, Leys and Sheep) S Australia, S Brazil, C Chile Budapest Lowlands		MIXED (Maize, Millet, Legumes, Cattle) C Africa, C Brazil Uruguay	
		* peasant small-holdings C Europe, Appalachians	* peasant smallholdings S Europe – Cereal Olives, Fruit, Sheep, Goats		semi-subsistence Food crops, Livestock Cash crop e.g. Coffee E Africa, Andes.	
Tillage crops (Chain A)	Arable (cereals, roots) W Europe lowlands e.g. Fenlands	Horticulture Netherlands, E coast USA			Maize, Tobacco, Cotton, Fruit Zimbabwe, S Brazil	Rice Thailand, Burma, Japan Wheat (irrigated) N Punjab
		Mkt gardening Netherlands, E coast USA, Urban Europe			• Shifting Agriculture Upland S E Asia C W Africa, Amazon Bush Fallow C Africa	Sedentary Hoe (Millet, etc. Rice & Veg) S China
Monoculture Plants, Trees, Shrubs (Chain A)	Grain Prairies, Pampas, Russian steppes	Fruit (e.g. Cider apples) UK Viticulture France	Grain Prairies, Veld – S Africa Steppe	Rice S USA Cotton S. Russia	Plantations (Coastal & accessible inland areas) Sisal, Sugar, Pineapple, Rubber, Cacao, Palm Oil, Coconut, Bananas, Coffee, Tea, Cotton	*Rice Monsoon Asia

Figure 21.8 A classification of farming systems

societies concerning the relative national importance of farming. These can influence both the input and output sides of farming systems. For example with regard to inputs, grant aid and tax concessions to farmers on purchase of machinery and other capital inputs encourages more mechanisation and lower labour inputs. Price support schemes as a guaranteed price for the produce whatever happens to the market price encourages farmers to maintain or even expand output. In the UK, both policies have helped to maintain for example, hill farming in marginal areas such as the Welsh Uplands and the Lake District. Under a free market economy such farming would most likely have been uneconomic.

Paradoxically, the strongest personal preference element seems to be in marginal farming areas. It is epitomised in the hill farmer of upland areas in Western Europe for example and in a different way, by the subsistence cultivators of tropical lands.

Physical inputs – climate, soil and vegetation

Climatic influences seriously limit the type of agriculture which can be practised in particular parts of the world. For this reason there is a broad similarity between patterns on a climatic map of the world and one showing the different types of agriculture. The same remains true at a more regional level, for example, in the USA (Case study 21.4).

The prime influence on other climatic factors affecting agriculture is solar energy. This determines the daily duration and intensity of insolation received, the temperature regime and wind systems. Combined with these, solar energy also influences the amount of precipitation and evapo-transpiration in any locality and thus, its effective precipitation.

Solar energy and precipitation play a dominant role in influencing the character of the soil and vegetation, which also affect the type of agriculture that can be practised in any given locality. While vegetation is of minor importance as a factor, except perhaps in livestock grazing on natural pasture, once the land has been cleared for farming, soil is of direct importance. Apart from river alluvium and wind-borne loess, the main zonal soils of the world are largely determined by climatic conditions and therefore, by incorporating an index of climate in the classification we are also taking account of the effect of soil type.

The resulting classification

Figure 21.8 has as its frame side the type of output from the system as classified above, together with the type of food chain to which it is related. Across the top are broad environmental divisions based on latitude belts. Within this outer frame have been inserted the scale of inputs ranging from intensive through to extensive input combinations. Finally, within the matrix boxes a subdivision into subsistence systems and commercial systems has been made.

This is a simplification of the systems which actually exist. All classifications are bound to be generalisations, omitting some of the less important and more localised types.

The application of this type of classification system and the factors which underpin it can be seen in the agricultural regions for the USA, a country largely lying within the temperate latitudes, and Zimbabwe, a country within the tropics. (Case studies 21.4 and 7.3).

case study

21.1 Zimbabwe: soil erosion and land degradation at a national level

Whereas in temperate areas, soil erosion and land degradation are a consequence of market forces and attitudes adopted by commercial farmers and governments, in the tropics much erosion and land degradation arises from land shortage, extreme population pressure and lack of awareness. Potential for erosion and degradation is heightened by greater climate extremes and poorer soil structure in tropical areas compared to areas in temperate latitudes.

Fluvial erosion is dominant in the sub-humid climatic condition of Zimbabwe. The effects of rain splash and run-off, both sub-surface and surface, are felt. Aeolian or wind erosion is more localised but has occurred in the south-west especially in recent drought years.

The problem

In parts of Zimbabwe, the problem is so severe that they are 'running out' of soil. In many areas soil is being lost at the rate of 40 tonnes per hectare per year. On soils unprotected by thick vegetation and on long uninterrupted slopes the problem is even worse. Accelerated soil erosion due to growing pressures on the land from human and livestock populations is particularly widespread in communal lands. In many cases erosion is threatening to undermine major rural development programmes. In some areas within just ten years soil depth may become insufficient to grow the staple crop, maize. Even major dam sites are vulnerable in the longer term, putting domestic water supplies at risk and frustrating efforts to extend irrigated cropping.

On a national scale, the value of nutrient loss in eroded soil, related to the cost equivalent of fertilisers amounts to millions of dollars a year.

Causes

The most serious problem is in communal lands. While 80% of commercial farmlands suffer little erosion because they are in areas less prone to erosion and the farming system leads to generally appropriate land-use management, much of the communal land area suffers soil erosion with over 25% of the area seriously eroded. The causes are mainly associated with their conditions.

Overpopulation leads to and combines with unsuitable farming practices in ecologically fragile areas because of a combination light sandy soil and low unreliable rainfall which occurs in short heavy torrential downpours. This encourages sheetwash rilling and gullying, especially on steep slopes in widespread granitic inselberg areas where surface run-off is increased.

The Land Tenure System under colonialism, particularly the Land Apportionment Act of 1931, relegated the majority of black African population to 'communal lands' in physically marginal land. This led to overpopulation.

Rapid population growth e.g. 3% annually 1981 – 1991, exacerbated population pressure on communal lands despite increased movement of the African population to the towns. Since 1982 'Resettlement Schemes' instigated by the government have been insufficient to lessen population pressure in communal lands.

Unsuitable and poor land management practices are conducted.

On cropland, initial clearance of savanna woodland and increasing clearance of watershed areas for woodfuel encouraged rapid surface run-off. In the communal lands the common practice of late planting left soil exposed which, together with shallow ploughing and limited manuring, left a loose soil structure especially susceptible to erosion in the early part of the rainy season (November – December).

Increasing population pressure led to the cropping area being extended into dry, sandy, marginal and stream park cultivation which encouraged erosion, collapsing banks and silting up of rivers. Cultivation of the headwaters of the Sabe River in the south east and extension on to steeper land in Mangwende Communal Land led to extensive gully erosion as many fields and plough furrows were aligned up and down slopes with no container ridges to steady the run-off.

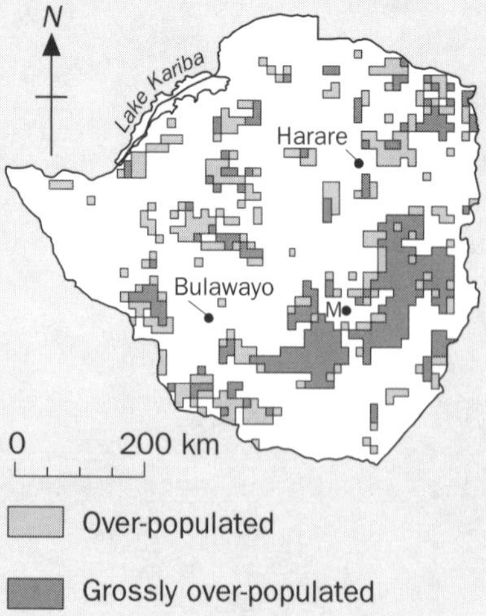

Overpopulated areas

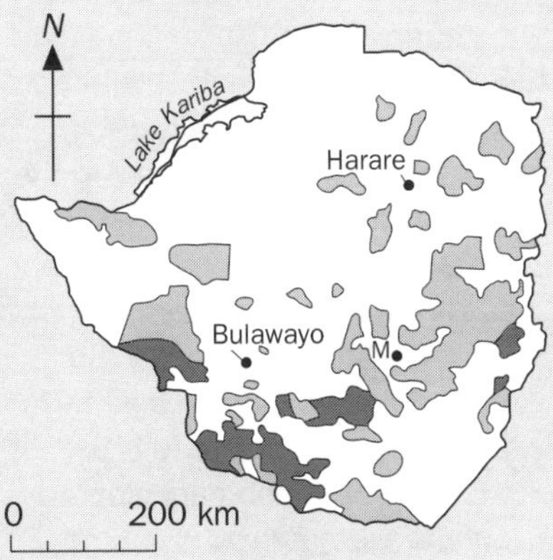

Very overgrazed

Bare

Overgrazed regions

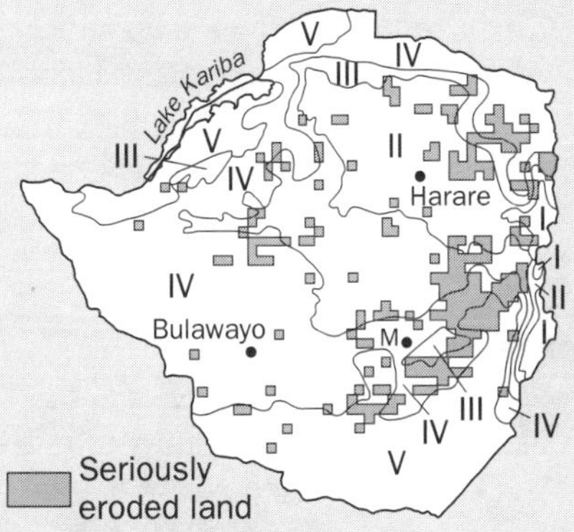

Seriously eroded land

I, II, III, IV and V = Natural regions as defined by Agritex

[SOURCE: Whitlow *Land Degradation in Zimbabwe*, Report for Department of Natural Resources, 1988]

Seriously eroded land in Zimbabwe

Nearly half the communal lands are rated as bare to overgrazed with livestock numbers generally in excess of capacity. Sheet erosion is encouraged. Prominent gullying erosion also occurs along cattle tracks and around water holes and dipping tanks where, in the wet season, several thousand cattle may converge weekly causing excessive trampling and overgrazing.

Towards conservation

Erosion is not a serious problem on commercial farmlands. In the early decades of the twentieth century inappropriate and exploitative cultivation methods caused serious erosion. After the Commission of Enquiry of 1939, subsidies were made available for conservation work and there was improved extension and farm planning. There is now a high level of conservation awareness leading to mechanical measures to prevent erosion (e.g. contour ridges), crop rotation and proper tillage. This not only maintained soil structure and reduced erosion but improved yields.

Conservation measures in communal land areas requires various measures.

A basic need is to reduce population pressure but in the short term little can be done e.g. Matabeleland North recommended a carrying capacity of 3.2 km^2; in 1993 it was still 15.9 km^2. The movement of population out of communal areas makes matters worse. Towns are already showing signs of overcrowding with high levels of unemployment evident. Resettlement schemes have been introduced in which three million hectares of white commercial farms were acquired to resettle 40 000 families from communal lands. However, little was done to relieve pressure and in resettlement areas, soil erosion is emerging as a problem. The extension into the Zambezi lowland which had been cleared of tse tse fly also suffers from overgrazing and soil erosion.

The Ministry has a goal to extend family planning services to all parts of the country but in communal areas adoption is very limited.

Conservation measures

Outwardly Zimbabwe now has a strong conservation policy with an increasing awareness shown of the soil erosion problem. Agritex (Department of Agricultural, Technical and Extension Services of Ministry of Lands, Agriculture and Rural Settlement) now pursues vigorous soil conservation programmes to control woodland clearance and reduce overgrazing and over cultivation, with extensions officers in the field and financial support from the government and external agencies. They have had some success but an insufficient advisory service and finances to comprehensively tackle the problem. It has been especially difficult in the more remote rural areas where farmers cling to traditional methods.

Periodic drought adversely affects soil structure and reduces finances available to adopt better tillage and grazing methods. Ideally any communal land areas need a comprehensive conservation programme e.g. at Wedza District (Mashonaland East) – a reafforestation programme, a new growth point to introduce other economic activities, rotation paddocks for cattle with improved breeds, more boreholes aiding irrigation and some diversification of agriculture with improved tillage. Crop rotation and conservation tillage are encouraged, with contour terracing, cover mulching to protect surfaces and reduced ploughing. Housing, education and family planning programmes have also been adopted.

case study

21.2 **UK: soil erosion on the South Downs**

While not as serious as in regions such as the South Eastern Appalachians in the USA where land is steeper and seasonal rainstorms of greater intensity, soil erosion on the South Downs has become a matter of concern. On a lesser scale, it mirrors most of the factors associated with water-induced erosion in regions of the world where it is a major problem.

Potential vulnerability

- Steeply sloping land on the dip slope dissected by dry valleys increases slope erosion potential and encourages in-channelling of run-off slopes of 5% – 25%.
- Shallow rendzina soils not more than 25 mm thick with horizons typically of 70% silt developed from post-glacial loess; head soils developed on chalk.
- Persistent spells of autumn rainfall includes heavy intensive rainstorms of 30 mm – 60 mm over 24 hours.

Rainfall (mm) Sept – March	Soil loss m³
1987 – 88 – 739	13 229
1988 – 89 – 324	4
1989 – 90 - 621	9402
1990 – 91 – 469	1527
1991 – 92 – 298	112

Periodic incidence of erosion

Human-induced water erosion

- While the area was pastureland up to World War 2 (1939 – 45), little soil erosion was recorded. Some downland was ploughed up during the war for food cereals. Even in 1960 most of the slope area was described as 'unsuitable' to permanent cultivation. It comprised largely permanent grassland and scrub.
- By the late 1970s most of the land which was not too steep or exposed was ploughed up and under cereals. In the 1980s land as steep as 20% was arable.

Incidences of soil erosion increased from the late 1970s when much of the land was put under autumn-sown cereals. This left land bare or thinly sown and open to severe rainstorms which, in turn, gave way to rilling and gullying with heavy run-off. Flooding and deposition of mud on the lower slopes affected the nearby urban areas.

- Soil erosion occurs also in other susceptible hill areas of the UK e.g. the new red sandstone friable soils on hill slopes of Devon.
- Wind erosion of peat soils occurs on Fenland around the Wash in dry spring when open land is prepared for the spring sowing of beet, vegetable and cereal crops.
- Contributory factors:

1. amalgamation of fields; loss of hedgerows and earth banks
2. intensification with no crop break or icy periods
3. loss of organic content helping soil aggregation – cultivation to a fine tilth seed bed laying it open to erosion
4. compacting by increasingly heavy machinery up slope; once the soil is saturated surface run-off and rilling is encouraged
5. allowing built-up area to spread into South Downs increased surface run-off; liability of flooding.

- Economic forces and government subsidy policies affected the causes. High cereal prices in the 1970s and 1980s and EU subsidies encouraged the spread of arable cultivation.
- Farmers attributed the cause to winter storms and not their farming methods. They were unwilling to change their practices.
- Local government and central government response was initially ineffective, showing too little concern.

Responses

- The building of earth dams at the foot of the Downs and above housing areas e.g. above Portislade after 1987, helped to prevent flooding. However, they did not prevent erosion. These measures were also judged as too costly e.g. in 1988, £150 000 was spent on one large dam and three small ones by Adur District Council.
- Since the 1980s, a change in EU policy has returned land to pasture in a set aside scheme, Grants and inducement payments were offered to farmers; some areas were designated as Environmentally Sensitive Area (ESA).

Monitored area of the South Downs

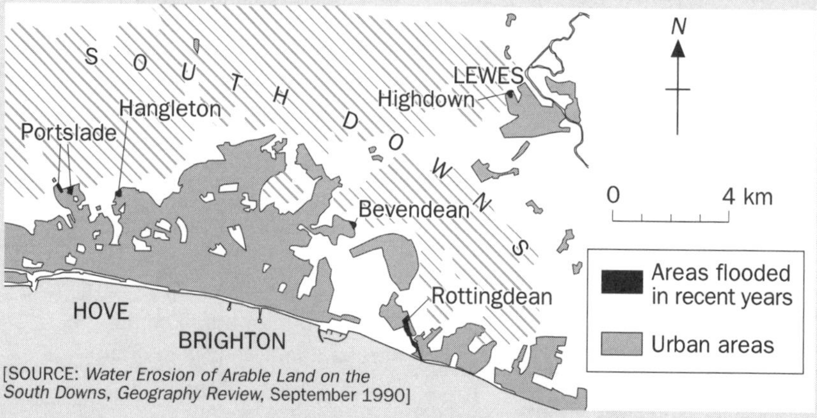

[SOURCE: *Water Erosion of Arable Land on the South Downs, Geography Review*, September 1990]

case study

21.3 The pollution effects of intensive farming

Intensified mechanised agriculture in lowland England and other lowland arable areas of Western Europe has not only led to some destruction of wildlife habitats and 'spoilation' of scenery but to serious pollution problems, particularly the 'nitrate problem'.

What is the 'nitrate problem'?

Together with sewage effluent and slurry spread on land, the greatly increased application of nitrogen-rich inorganic fertilisers to farmland has led to a serious increase in nitrate levels in surface waters through direct run-off and soil leaching. This has two adverse effects:

- increased nitrites in drinking water derived from surface and ground water sources
- eutrophication of lakes, reservoirs and rivers through nitrogen enrichment causing rapid plant and weed growth and algae blooming on the water surface. This cuts out light penetration and reduces the oxygen content of the water, adversely affecting fish stocks and other aquatic life.

Underlying causes

- governments encouraging increase of agricultural production through financial and other incentives
- relative cheapness of nitrogen fertilisers in relation to additional output profit generated
- higher fertiliser application required by new cereal varieties and recently introduced industrial crops e.g. oil seed rape
- more frequent ploughing releases nitrates by bacterial process of mineralisation.

Reducing the problem

Indirect reduction

Since the mid-1980s fears of over-production of food and other agricultural products led to measures to reduce acreage under certain crops and livestock numbers.

- 1984 EU threshold controls and milk quotas: farmers received guaranteed prices only up to a specified quantity
- 1988 Set Aside Regulations: up to 15% of arable land was taken out of production
- Farm Diversification Schemes with grant support and a Farm Woodland Scheme were implemented.

These measures reduced crop acreage and thus the amount of nitrates entering surface and ground water supplies.

Increasing public pressure and political lobbying

With fears for public health from the effect of herbicides and fertilisers on food sold in shops and 'contaminated' water, environmental groups campaigned against pollution of the countryside.

This led to the UK's Nitrate Sensitive Area Scheme in 1991, which was introduced in areas at risk of concentrations of nitrates in drinking water and ground and surface water pollution above EU safe level guidelines. If a farmer voluntarily takes up either the Basic Scheme or the Premium Scheme Compensation, he will receive payment. The Basic Scheme limits inorganic and organic fertiliser application, demands a cover crop to avoid bare land in winter and restricts grassland ploughing. The Premium Scheme requires arable land conversion to grassland and woodland with larger compensation payments.

In 1991 Nitrate Advisory Areas were set up, particularly near hedges and water courses, to encourage good farming practice which would help reduce nitrate application.

Later in 1991 an EU Directive on Nitrates made it mandatory for countries to control water nitrate levels. Vulnerable areas have to be identified and farmers have to adopt good practices of the kind outlined under the Nitrate Sensitive Area scheme.

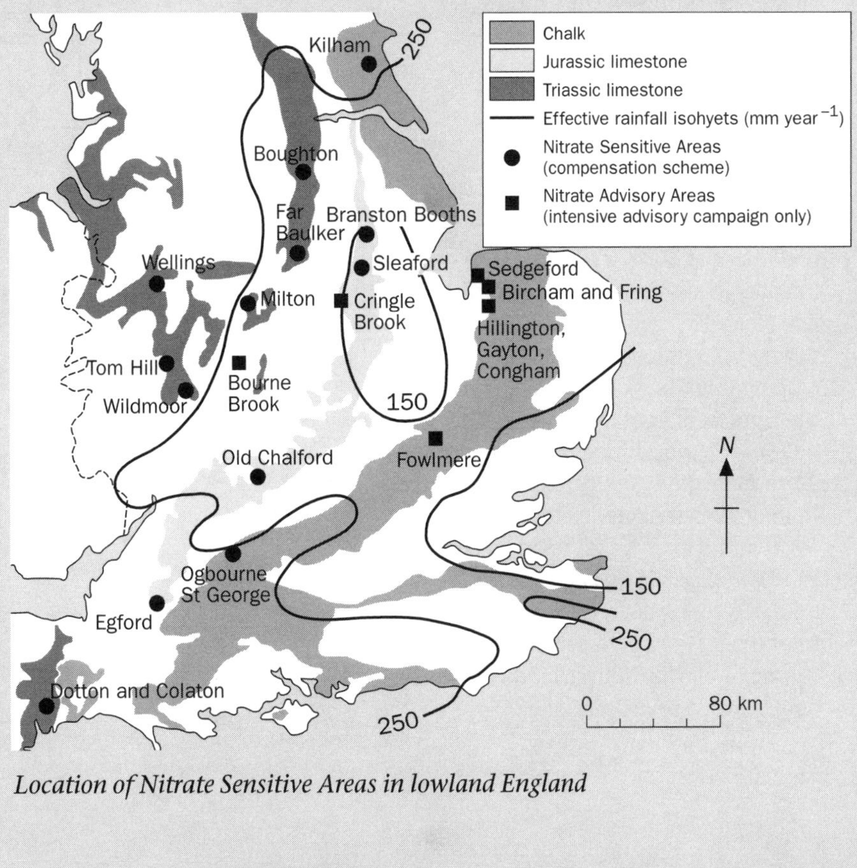

Location of Nitrate Sensitive Areas in lowland England

case study

21.4 USA: agricultural regions and formative influences

About 57% of the USA is farmland but only 15% is under crops. Since 1980 output has only risen by approximately 6% mainly because of fears of overproduction. However, yields per unit area have gone up by a larger percentage e.g. cereals by 18% (1980 – 92). In addition to supplying a home market of 260 million people, the country is a significant exporter of agricultural produce, by value marking up 10% of total exports e.g. soya beans, maize and meat products.

Physical influences

'It must be recognised that the ultimate control of the pattern (of agricultural regions) is not human but natural.'

Climatic controls exercise the major influence on the boundaries of the main belts. From north to south, temperatures control margins of belts, e.g. spring wheat's northern limit is set by frost hazard (but newer strains with a shorter growing period pushed the limit further north). Cotton's northern limit is 200 frost free days.

Decreases in rainfall east–west control margins e.g. the hay, corn and cotton belts end at 500 – 625 mm and wheat at 300 – 375 mm (but irrigation in dry areas can overcome this limit).

Climate regimes also influence crop-pest limits. For example, as the Bureau of Agriculture indicates boll weevil pest affecting cotton did more to diversity the cotton belt than any other single factor.

Within the main belts, regional and local variations in soil and terrain help determine changes in agricultural production. In Mississippi, for example, alluvial bottom lands in the south favour soya bean cultivation.

The mountainous terrain of the Rockies limits livestock ranching to the west.

Government influences

Historically, government influences are strong. For example, family ownership and farm sizes are influenced by the Homestead Act of 1962, emphasising the quarter section of 106 acres as the basic unit. There are also Acts related to the building and pattern of transcontinental railways, government programmes for the recovery of agriculture and conservation following the 1930s depression. TVA in the South controls production of certain crops and encourages crop rotation and diversification.

For 60 years the main government influence has been through its five-yearly Farm Bill which currently provides £12 billion a year of support to agriculture through three main methods:

- The Commodity Programme (and Conservation Programme) to aid conservation and prevent overproduction gives support prices to agricultural crop and livestock in return for land taken

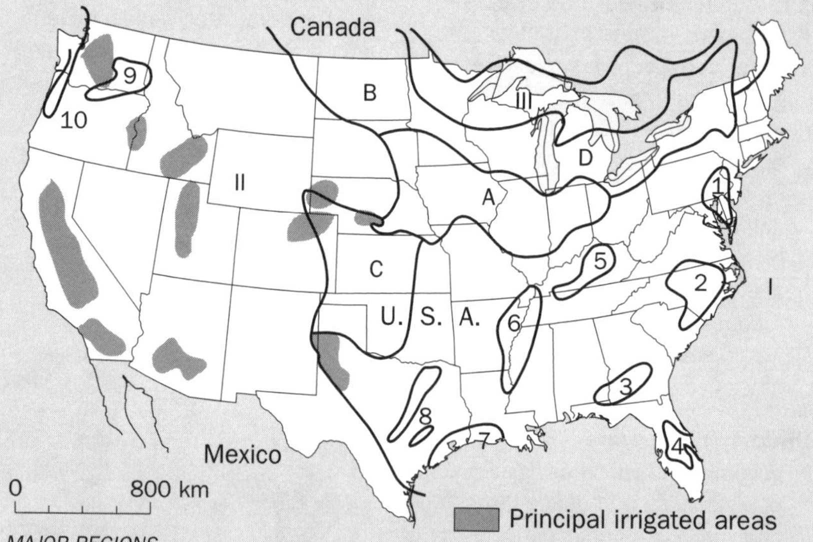

MAJOR REGIONS
A *Corn belt* (cash: beef cattle, hogs, corn, soyabeans,; feed; corn, hay, oats)
B *Spring wheat region* (with barley, oats, flaxseed, rapeseed, cattle)
C *Winter wheat region* (with grain sorghum, cattle)
D *Dairy region* (with other livestock, specially crops)

SECONDARY REGIONS
1 *South-east Pennsylvania – Delmarva* (dairy, poultry, hogs, vegetables)
2 *Carolina-Virginia tobacco region* (with hogs, corn, soyabeans, cotton)
3 *Georgia-Alabama Coastal Plain peanuts region* (with hogs, pecans, cotton, corn)
4 *Florida citrus region* (with vegetables, cattle)
5 *Kentucky Bluegrass and Pennyroyal tobacco regions* (with cattle, hogs, horses, wheat, corn)
6 *Mississippi Alluvial Valley* (soybeans, cotton, rice, cattle)
7 *Texas-Louisiana Gulf Coast* (rice and cattle)
8 *Texas Black Prairies sorghum region* (with hogs, cattle, cotton, corn)
9 *Columbia Basin wheat region* (with barley, peas, lentils)
10 *Willamette Valley-Puget Sound* (dairy, fruit, vegetables)

OTHER AGRICULTURAL AREAS
i *South and East* (crop and livestock farming interspersed with wooded areas, some of which are pastured)
ii *Western Livestock Ranching region* (cropland limited mainly to small irrigated areas. Surrounding areas of grassland, open forest, brush and semi-desert grazed by beef cattle and some sheep)
iii *Northern Fringe* (minor areas of marginal agriculture advancing and retreating)

Agricultural regions

out of production (currently 60 million acres withdrawn from family production). Since it requires the farmer to produce established crops, it tends to operate against change in response to changes in market demand. Therefore it preserves existing regional specialisation.

- The Disaster Programme is designed to alleviate flooding and drought.
- There is control on export subsidies, such as on wheat, maize, soya bean and meat.

As a result of the1995 Debate on the Farm Bill, the current system benefits large farmers but not rural communities. Some parties want the Farm Bill replaced by an innovative rural programme to import rural infrastructure, business and education. However, a strong farm lobby is against change.

Historical factors

Opening up lands with westward colonisation in the second half of the nineteenth century revealed the full extent of potential agricultural land available.

The rail network was established for agricultural produce to reach home markets especially in the industrialising north-east and later west coast cities. Regional specialisation for exports occurred in lake and coastal ports.

Expansion and specialisation was influenced by expanding urban markets in the country and expanding demand overseas, especially in industrial countries of Western Europe e.g. beef, wheat from the interior via lake ports and from the south cotton, sugar and tobacco through the gulf ports.

Economic technological factors

The main factors are home and overseas market demand, an efficient transportation system, technological advances in machinery, a plentiful land supply and regional specialisation based on comparative advantage.

Within physical constraints, the main determinant in the type of farming is not farmers' decision-making, but the markets as set by the great food processing and retail companies and exporting firms. While most land is still under family ownership, only 12% of the value of agricultural produce sold goes to the farmer; the rest goes to the agricultural businesses which supply farms with machinery, fertiliser and other inputs, and to the distributors, including food processors and supermarket chains.

Labour has always been relatively scarce. To utilise large land area units available, emphasis has been on capital inputs and utilisation of technological advance in mechanisation, herbicides and fertilisers. New varieties of crops and livestock breeds have increased. Adoption of irrigation has also been an important feature.

The most important recent changes in agricultural regions have been the result of changes in market demand and technological advances in methods and new varieties. The most striking included a great increase in intensive poultry production in the North East since market demand for white meat has expanded. Soya bean acreage in the Corn Belt and Mississippi lowland has expanded, as has the demand for soya bean oil for consumption and as livestock feed. Grain sorghum growth too in southern and central Great Plains to supply intensive livestock feed lots are increasingly established there.

Detailed spatial changes occur as farmers increasingly move over to contract farming to supply a narrow specialised range of agricultural products, specified by food processing or supermarket chains to which the farmers are contracted.

22

CHAPTER 22

Von Thunen's 'Isolated State' theory

22.1 **An economic approach**

Much of agricultural geography has been concerned with patterns on a regional and more localised scale and was based in Von Thunen's 'Isolated State' theory, which is concerned with how land-use patterns change with distance from a centrally located market. It particularly helps to highlight how changes in supply and demand relative to cost and price variations are reflected in spatial changes in land-use within the area serving a market.

22.2 **The theory**

Johanne Henrich Von Thunen's theory was both rooted in ideas from the classic economic theory of his day and based on data gained from running his own estate, including cost accounting over many years.

Underlying assumptions including change

At the centre of Von Thunen's theory is the concept of the 'Isolierte Staat' – the idea of an isolated state in which there is only one market, that is, the central city and around it an extensive plain of tillable land of uniform physical character. The market is served by one mode of transport – horse and cart. The farmers occupying the land supply the central city and adjust their resources so as to meet any changes in demand.

Von Thunen made these assumptions to hold constant a number of the factors which normally contribute to the diversity of farming at a regional level, such as changes in soil fertility. Assumptions, however, would ultimately have to be relaxed to allow these factors some part in an explanation.

Von Thunen also assumed farmers would respond to changes in the market situation. His was not the static theory some writers would have us believe. On the contrary, one of the greatest values of Von Thunen's work is not his visual presentation of concentric rings of different land-use round the central market (Figure 22.1) but the fact that changes in market demand will bring ripples of change throughout the pattern of farming around the market, as well as in the nature of the farming system characteristic of each zone of land-use. This he illustrated in a number of ways, the most commonly quoted being the effects of a secondary market introduced into a region and of another form of transport, namely water transport, in addition to the horse and cart.

Of much greater importance is Thunen's discussion of how the agland, that is, the cultivated land and its zones of land-use, would be extended as increasing population in the central city forced the demand for agricultural foods to increase. Change lies at the heart of Von Thunen's theory and this is what makes his work of direct relevance to current discussions on farming patterns and systems.

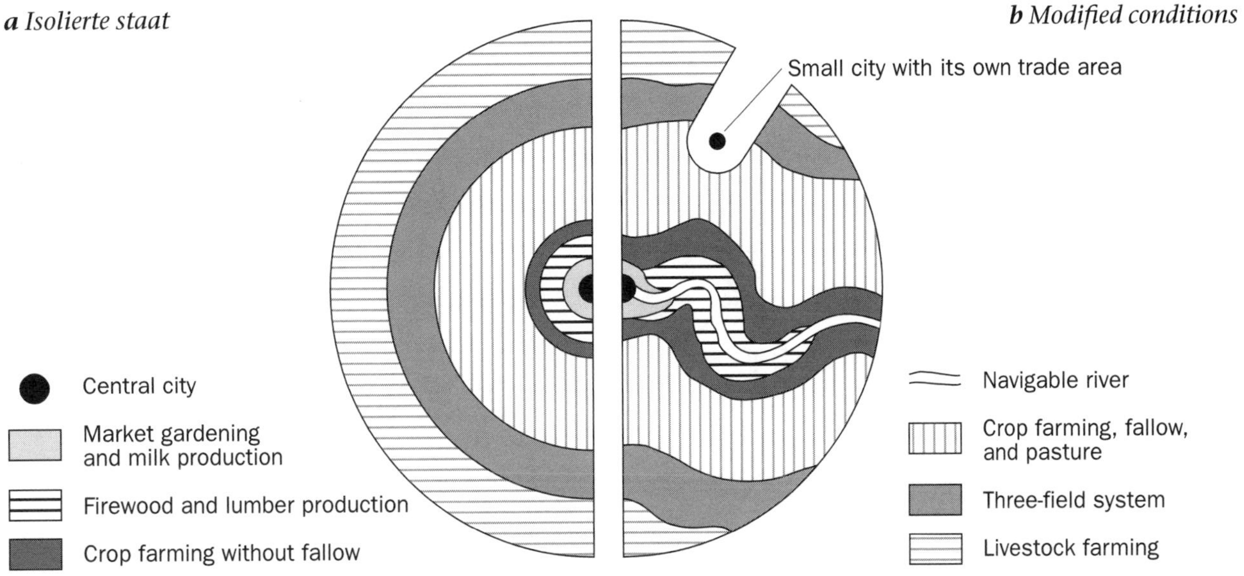

Figure 22.1 The location of agricultural production after Von Thunen

Principles

The central relationships Thunen emphasised were to do with three variables (factors): ***distance of farms from the market, the price received by farmers for their products and economic rent.***

The relationship between distance and market price is simple. The price a farmer obtained for any unit of his product was equal to its price at the market minus the cost of transporting it to the market. Thus the nearer the farmer was to the market the greater his returns from the sale of his produce. These high returns from land near the market and the greater competition for such land raising its price, encouraged farmers to make the most use of the land. Thus land-use tended to be the most intensive near the market and decreased in intensity with distance away from it. A further factor leading to less intensive use of land away from the market was that as transport costs increased with distance, so farmers could not afford to put the other amounts of inputs into farming which were necessary to give higher yields.

The other factor of economic rent was concerned with returns which could be obtained by putting land to a particular use. The return of economic rent could be calculated by subtracting production and transport costs from the revenue obtained from selling the produce at the market.

Formula: $V - (E + T) = P$

Where **V** is the value of revenue from the product, **E** is the production cost and **T** transport cost, while **P** is the net return profit or economic rent.

Since the market revenue or price on any product varied as did production and transport costs, so would the returns or economic rent. Thus a farmer out to make maximum profits would choose that crop or combination of agricultural produce which would give the best economic rent.

However, for any one crop or other produce, the economic rent gain on it would fall with distance from the market. While other costs and the price at the market remained constant, transport costs would rise. There would be diminishing returns with distance, until a point would be reached when it was not worth using the land for that crop. The margins of cultivation would have been reached. This is illustrated in Figure 22.2 for certain sample crops.

Patterns of land-use round the market

The pattern of land-use was dependent on the relative returns which each agricultural product could command with distance from the market. At any particular distance those agricultural products giving the highest returns would relegate other usages to an outer zone. The zonations are not only distinguished by differences in what is produced but also by the system under which production occurs. Different combinations of inputs were used and different kinds of crop rotations were adopted both to maximise returns and maintain the land in a state of good fertility.

The scale of farming also has changed, becoming more extensive with distance from the market, because to compensate for increased transport costs of getting produce to market for inputs to the farm such as seed, fertiliser and labour, the farmer had to

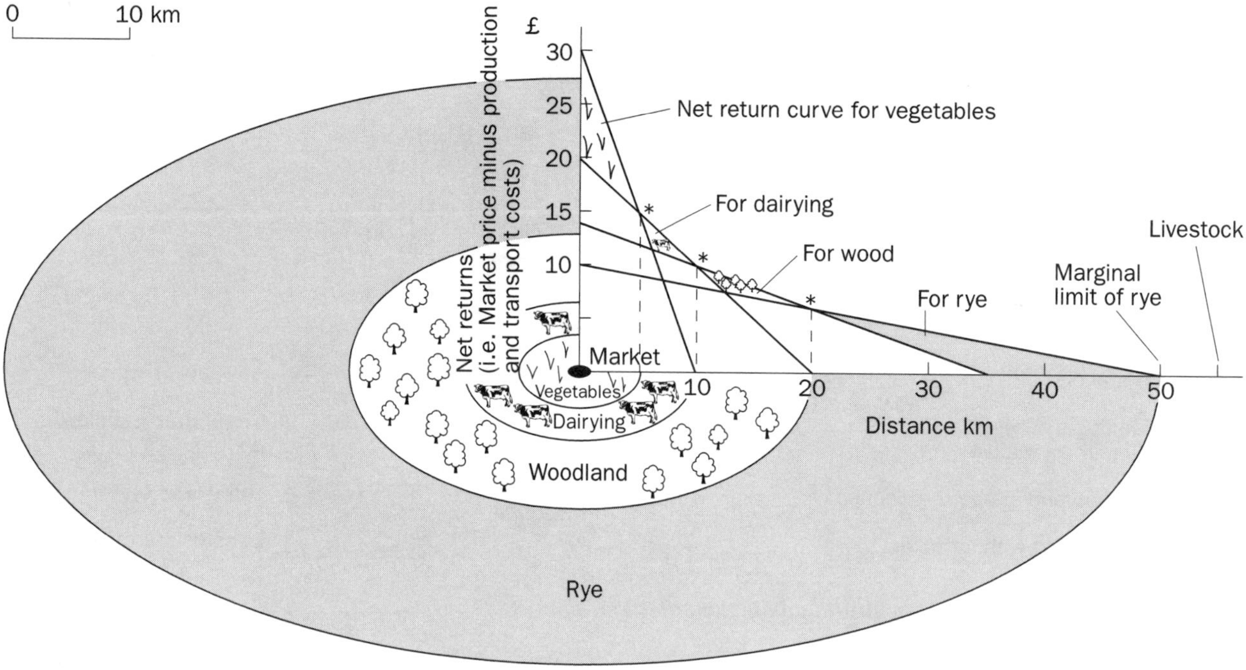

NOTE: * Point of intersection of the two net revenue curves indicates the distance from the market at which it is profitable to change land use in favour of that product giving the higher return.

Crop or product	Market revenue or price (V)	Production cost per hectare (E)	Return without transport cost (V-E)	Transport cost per km (T)	Marginal limit of crop or product (km from the market)
Vegetables	60	30	30	3.00	10
Dairying	45	25	20	1.00	20
Wood	24	10	14	0.40	35
Rye	15	5	10	0.20	50

Figure 22.2 Declining returns (economic rent) with distance from market for selected land uses

cut down on the amount of some inputs purchased. This inevitably led to lower yields per unit of area of land farmed. However, the farmer could still maintain his overall profit by farming more land. This was possible because land was both cheaper and more plentiful away from the market – hence farms were larger.

The main features of each zone starting with that nearest the market were as follows:

- Intensive dairying and market gardening – fresh milk and vegetables are required constantly in the city. Given their perishability and the slow means of cartage they had to be produced close to the market. Prices therefore had to be high enough to make it profitable for farmers close to the market to go in for dairying and market gardening rather than any other land-use. Thus in effect dairying and fresh vegetable production gave the highest returns and therefore yielded the highest economic rent.
- In Von Thunen's time wood was also needed constantly for fuel, building and other purposes. Silviculture for wood production then occupied the second zone because of this need and because of the cost of transporting such a bulky good.
- Beyond the woodland lay three zones in which rye from which bread was made was one of the most important crops.

The difference between the three zones lay in the system under which rye and associated crops, such as flax, were cultivated. To offset distance cost and maximise returns, the type of crop rotation varied and the intensive land-use declined from the nearer to the outer of the three zones.

- At the outermost edge of the cultivated land came an area of livestock farming. Livestock for meat was sent on the hoof thus saving transport costs, while such products as cheese and butter were small in bulk and therefore relatively cheap to transport compared to the favourable price received for them on the market.

However, apart from the way zonation occurred, the other important point to note is that the extent and location of the zones changed over time. Demand for any agricultural product varied and hence the price changed. Also, costs varied, thus economic rent changed for one product as against another. Therefore as a farmer at any one location would respond by changing to that crop or combination of agricultural products which would give the highest returns, thus the limit of each zonation would fluctuate with time.

What generally happened over a period of time was that the margins of farming were pushed outward. As population increased, demand for food and other agricultural produce rose, pushing up market prices, making it profitable and necessary to extend the margins of farming. More land was brought under cultivation – the agland (farmed area) was extended and the limits of each zone in it also pushed outwards as rippling effects of rising demand were felt through the entire farming area.

Eventually there would be a point where all the needs of a region's population could not be met from the land around and some agricultural product had to be imported. In effect the outer limit of the agland was extended to take in land beyond the state. Hence some writers have seen present zonations at a much larger scale as a reflection of the continuing influence of the basic principles which Von Thunen outlined in this theory. For example, the extensive wheatlands of the prairies of North America are seen as part of the outer zone of agriculture which serves West European markets.

22.3 The value of Von Thunen's work

Times and methods of farming have changed but some of the important principles recognised by Von Thunen remain. It matters not that we can no longer recognise concentric zonation around a central market except in the simplest of farming economies, usually those under subsistence agriculture in the tropics and in some Mediterranean lands (Figure 23.5). As Von Thunen himself pointed out, even in his time there were modifying influences – a number of markets had to be served not one, transport methods and accessibility varied and outside competition made inroads into the potential markets, threatening home produce. Physical variations also interrupt the postulated ideal zonation of land-use. Thus today we should not expect a simple zonation pattern in any region but only some semblance towards one .

Distance from market does still influence the relative location of different crops and particular agricultural products. There is still for example a tendency for liquid milk production and market gardening to be dominant only where there is quick access to markets, albeit that technological advances have distorted the actual location pattern showing locations both physically close to the market and others further away. Extensive farming of non-perishable crops such as grain is mainly carried out at a further distance from markets. While some cereal growing does take place in Western Europe for example, the bulk of the grain supplies come from extensive producers like those of the American prairies.

It is of interest and instructive to consider the pattern of the agricultural regions of the USA and Zimbabwe given in Case studies 21.4 and 7.3. Zimbabwe in particular demonstrates some affinity with Von Thunen's model. Intensity of farming does decrease with distance from the main market of Harare, the capital, but note also the influence of climatic patterns on the zonation.

Further, as Von Thunen indicated, any particular crop can still be grown under different farming systems with the production inputs including land being altered to compensate for other increased costs. For example, wheat is intensively cultivated under a mixed arable system in the lowlands of Western Europe such as East Anglia with high yields per unit area, whereas the same crop is grown under a monoculture system and much more extensively in the poorer lands of the continental interiors. Here lower yields are compensated for by lower production costs, especially labour, and by a much larger size of farm holding. Again the keeping of beef cattle can be done under a more intensive mixed system including some stall feeding as in the north-east USA and English Midlands, or under extensive ranching as in Queensland, and on the pampas of South America where the farming system is very different. In each case the different producers are reacting in the most appropriate way to general market conditions as well as to the economic and physical conditions of the particular region in which they find themselves.

Moreover, changes in market demand brought changes in methods and the overall pattern of farming, as it still does today. Von Thunen demonstrated quite clearly that as population rose the growth in demand could only be met in two ways: firstly, the yields could be increased on existing agricultural lands by improvements in farming and secondly, new land could be taken in with successive zones of cultivation being pushed progressively outwards. Both are very much in evidence today, prompted by rapidly rising demand. In the developing world this comes from a sheer increase in the number of mouths to be fed, as in India and China, while in the developed world it is prompted by rising affluence.

The forwardness of Von Thunen's thinking is further emphasised if we conclude with some brief observations on the second and much less publicised part of his text '*The Isolated State*'. Although social and political influences are more important today, he discusses them in this second part. He discussed for example how a natural (just) wage could be arrived at and made the point that capital spent on working class education is repaid at ample interest by the workers' higher productivity. He brings in other current issues in farming such as the effects of increased taxation and of competition from imports. Thus Von Thunen not only saw humans as economic beings making rational decisions in response to changes in supply and demand, but also as part of society and subject to its social and political influences.

Concluding comment

Von Thunen recognised change as a fundamental fact of life; he lived in a period of change. These were part of wider changes which had been going on for some time, part of a modernisation process which continues to the present, both in the developed and developing world. Change in systems and patterns of farming are part of this process.

23

CHAPTER 23

Tropical farming systems

'Agriculture in tropical countries is not simply about food production; it produces income for the rural poor who depend on agriculture.'

[PAARLBORG R AN EXTRACT FROM THE POLICY STATEMENT MADE AT *A VISION FOR FOOD AGRICULTURE AND THE ENVIRONMENT*, WASHINGTON DC INTERNATIONAL CONFERENCE, JUNE 1996]

23.1 Subsistence farming and peasant farming

Nowadays, most types of subsistence farming incorporate some form of cash sales partly because of the need for money to pay taxes, for education and to purchase goods. However, there are still many traditional farming systems where the prime objective is production of food for the household's own use, with any sale of produce secondary to this. This would still generally be regarded as a form of subsistence agriculture though sometimes referred to as peasant farming or peasant agriculture. The close relationship between subsistence and peasant farming is noted in Michael Watts' definition of subsistence agriculture.

Subsistence agriculture
A subsistence agricultural system is a complex of functionally related resources and human practices through which a group (a household, a village, a society) secures food for its reproduction through its own effort, typically by the direct exploitation of the environment (Nietschmann, 1973). The primary objective is food, whether from hunting, fishing, horticulture or agriculture. Subsistence normally refers to production for use (i.e. use values) as opposed to production for exchange, but food may circulate within social networks for ritual ceremonial and reciprocal exchange purposes, and some food may be sold on the open market (i.e. realise exchange values). Subsistence agriculture without market involvement of any sort is referred to as a tribal or 'primitive' economy, whereas household subsistence producers with some form of production for sale, and some degree of surplus production over needs, are *peasants*. Subsistence agriculture is often seen as a form of cultural adaptation by which social groups adapt to and regulate the ecosystems of which they are part. Self-sufficient, internally regulated subsistence systems are becoming rare in the modern world, as the expansion of the market and production for exchange erodes 'pure subsistence' and what is seen by many as the ecological stability and rational utilisation of complex tropical *ecosystems*.
[SOURCE: Johnston R J et al *Dictionary of Human Geography*, 1994]

23.2 Shifting agriculture

Despite its declining importance, it is estimated that approximately 200 million people are still dependent on some form of shifting agriculture. Shifting agriculture is practised extensively in the tropics, taking up about one-third of the world's cultivable soils. The systems vary from one continent to another and within one continent, from region to region (Figure 23.1).

Characteristics

Before rising population pressures and increasing shortage of land combined to force some modification in the system practised, shifting agriculture in its classical form was extremely well adapted to the environmental conditions in which it occurred. Following clearance of a small area of

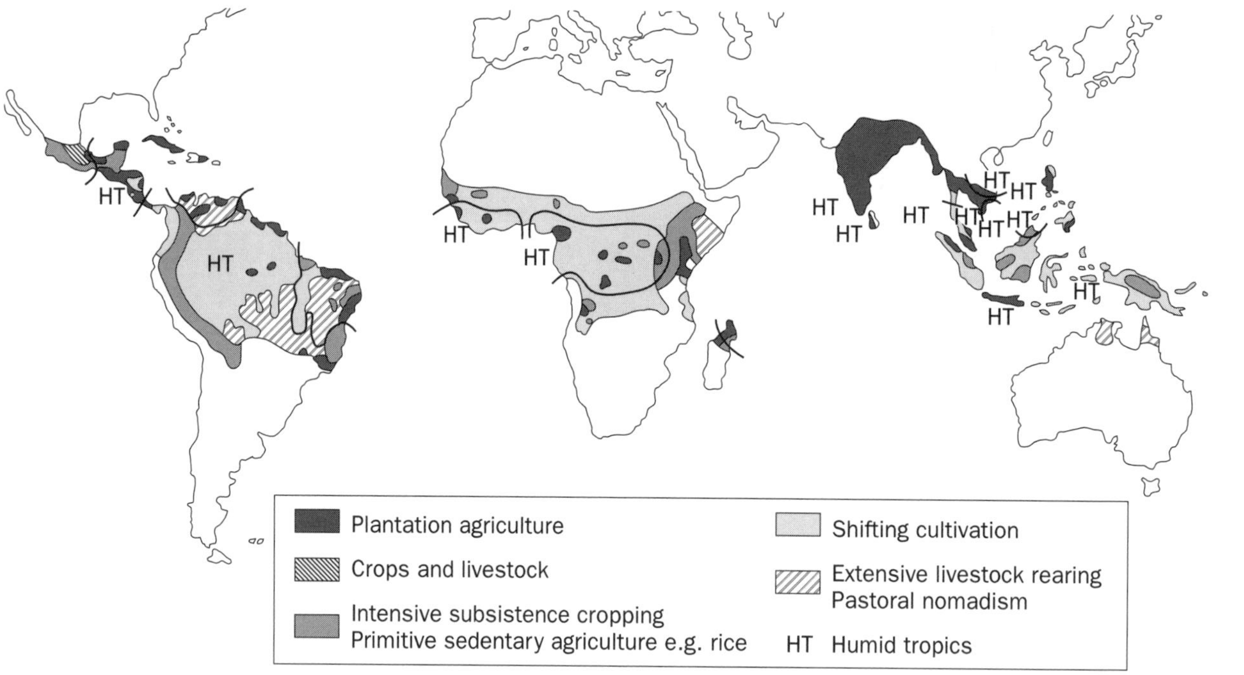

Figure 23.1 *Land use patterns in the humid tropics*

tribal territory and its use for a number of years, the clearings and settlements were abandoned for a long period, somewhere in the region of 20 years, to allow the natural regeneration of vegetation and a restoration of fertility before the soil was used again.

Yields were low and methods were, in economic terms, inefficient, compared to other systems. Supplemented by hunting and gathering, shifting agriculture was sufficient to maintain a small population given a plentiful supply of land.

The whole practice of shifting agriculture is closely bound up with the cultural traditions of a tribe and the individual groups which practise it. Despite the low level of agricultural output achieved, much human energy and a substantial proportion of the output were regularly diverted to satisfy social obligations and towards observing tribal rituals. No serious modification of it could take place without having repercussions on the culture of the people practising it (Case study 23.1).

Change has social and environmental implications

Today, however, this traditional way of living is under threat. In some locations such as Thailand its practice has been made illegal because it is considered incompatible with other uses of the forest land where it is practised and detrimental to the environment. In other areas, outside influences and the increasing population numbers which have to be supported are drastically changing it both as an agricultural system and as a way of life.

There is, however, growing realisation that modernisation of tropical agriculture has brought social problems for indigenous rural populations and in many areas, deterioration of the environment. Some reassessment of traditional agricultural methods is being made, taking into account their worth and the problems which arise from growing population pressures and from exposure to outside market and monetary forces. There is interest in modifying traditional agricultural methods in ways which will actively involve the indigenous peoples themselves rather than replacing traditional methods with a system imposed from outside irrespective of its environmental effects.

23.3 Pastoral nomadism and semi-nomadism

Though of declining importance, pastoral nomadism is still significant in the semi-humid tropics where conditions are unfavourable to crop growing. The classic definition of the term nomadism is that by Richthofen (1908).

Nomadism occurs in desert, savanna and steppeland regions when the whole tribe migrates with the herd according to marked seasonal variations in rainfall and in search of the basic fodder requirements of cattle, sheep, goats and camels. Individual families own no land, but the territory is held communally by the group. No cultivation of crops is undertaken, the group depending on what their livestock can provide apart from some occasional barter.

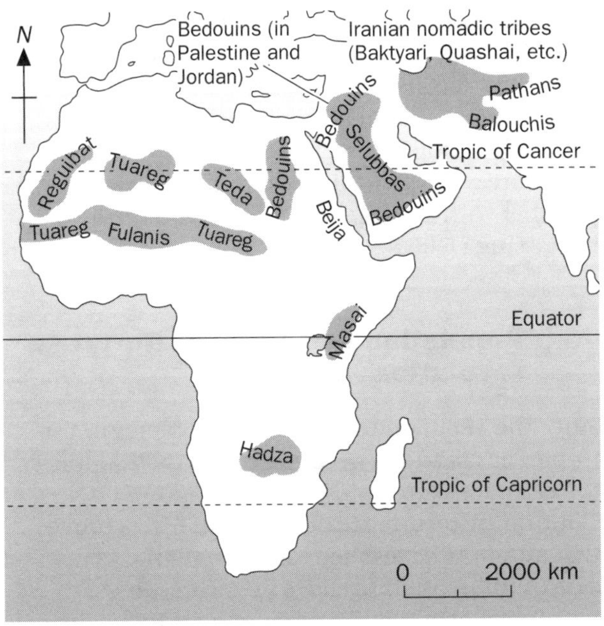

Figure 23.2 *Distribution of nomadic pastoralists in the tropics*

Such a definition would fit the old way of life of the Bedouin nomads on the Sahara fringes, the Khirghiz of the Asiatic Steppe and the Maasai of the East African Plateau (Figure 23.2). In these and other cases, external influences and pressures are leading to a breakdown of the traditional way of life. Pure nomadism as described by Richthofen no longer exits.

Migration across national frontiers like those of the Fulbe or Fulani of West Africa has been made illegal. Nomads every where have been encouraged or coerced into adopting a more settled way of life. There is considerable controversy not only over the manner in which this has been and is still occurring (Case study 23.2). There is increasing evidence that the changes not only violated the rights of many nomadic people but were based on unproven assumptions as to the environmental damage the nomadic way of life caused in semi-arid regions. What is clear is that there can be no return to the traditional way of life. The nomadic people have all to varying extents been constrained within nation state boundaries and drawn into a commercial world based on money.

23.4 **Subsistence rice culture**

The staple food grain for half the world's population including Monsoon Asia

Most of the population living in the wet tropics particularly in Monsoon Asia depend upon rice as their staple food crop. China and India, with the world's largest populations, 1220 and 914 millions respectively, produce half of the world's rice which is used almost exclusively for home consumption (Figure 23.3). Rice is essentially a subsistence crop, at the basis of a farming system almost as ancient as shifting agriculture.

Apart from internal domestic trade to meet needs in the rapidly growing towns, rice is commercially important only to Vietnam and Thailand in the tropics, although rice is also of some commercial importance to countries such as the USA, Australia, France and Italy where it is grown under irrigation. The main areas in the USA are the Gulf Coast and Southern California; in Australia, the Murray-Murrumbidgee basin; in Italy, the Valley of the Po and in France towards the mouth of the Rhone.

Japan has traditionally been seen as one of the main subsistence rice regions, but today rice is grown intensively, increasingly using modern methods and mainly as a cash crop to be sold on the home market. The bulk of Japan's population is now urbanised, with approximately two-thirds in the Industrial Pacific Belt centred on Tokyo, Kobe and Osaka. Only a small proportion of the rice grown is consumed on the farms.

Just as with shifting agriculture, rice farming systems vary from region to region, but the broad distinction is that between unirrigated upland rice, frequently grown as well by shifting agriculturists in Monsoon Asia, and lowland rice or paddy which is grown under irrigation and gives a much higher yield. This is the rice which supports the high concentrations of rural populations on the alluvial valleys and coastal plains of India, China and other monsoon countries.

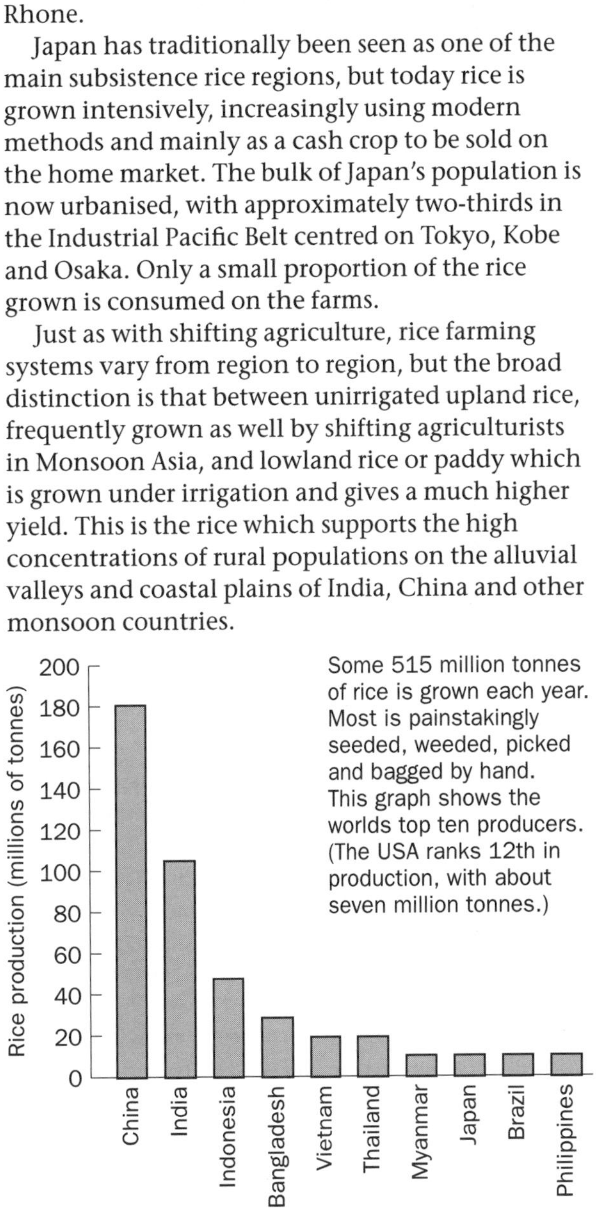

Figure 23.3 *Rice production and distribution by country*

Varieties of rice within each of these two broad divisions have increased with the new hybrid varieties developed as part of the Green Revolution. New hybrids have not only complicated farming patterns in traditional areas such as the Ganges plain in India, but also extended the crop's climatic limits, since some of the new varieties require a shorter growing period and can withstand more severe conditions than established types of paddy. For example, in Japan rice can be grown as far north as Hokkaido in temperate latitudes, while the shorter growing season required allows a more widespread use of multi-cropping. Thus both in terms of area under cultivation and total yields, rice is more important than ever.

Conditions and characteristics of paddy farming systems

Paddy farming is an intensive farming system (Case study 23.3), farming units being small, frequently under one hectare and fragmented into scattered strips, except where land reforms have led to some consolidation and rationalisation, as in Japan and China. Labour inputs are high, a heavy dependence being placed on unpaid family labour with limited hired help. In relation to this high labour intensity, capital inputs such as fertilisers and insecticides are limited. All these inputs are carefully regulated by the marked seasonal rhythm which controls rice cultivation.

Climatic inputs are loosely generalised as those of a monsoon regime, that is, high temperatures and a marked seasonal incidence of rainfall. Wherever temperatures exceed 20°C in the growing season and there is an abundant supply of moisture, rice can be grown. Figure 23.1 shows the increasing area under rice in the equatorial coastlands of West Africa and Brazil. The length of growing season needed varies with the types of rice, ranging from three to eight months.

Although alluvial lowlands such as the Mekong River Basin in Vietnam are eminently suitable, rice is reasonably tolerant of soil conditions. As long as the soil is moisture-retentive, rice will grow in both medium and heavy soils where the land is naturally level or has been terraced to allow flooding of paddy fields in the growing season and the general control of the water supply.

These physical conditions combined with a high labour input per unit of cultivated area underlie the intensive nature of the system. Yields from each unit area under rice vary considerably. It is much higher in the more mechanised rice growing areas beyond the tropics, such as the Gulf Coast of the USA, than in the traditional rice lowlands of South East Asia. This is generally because more advanced countries make use of larger amounts of capital inputs like fertilisers and herbicides. These more scientific methods help to give yields as much as eight to ten times those in subsistence rice areas. The more widespread use of new hybrid varieties together with more capital inputs is markedly improving yields.

23.5 Population pressure and the green revolution

Since the 1960s one of the major problems in the tropics has been the need to expand food supplies to keep pace with rapid population growth. Continuing recurrence of famine in Africa prove that attempts have failed here but in Asia, as the case of India, attempts have met with success. Expansion of world rice production principally in Monsoon Asia, has been little short of spectacular. In the 1950s and 1960s India had a widening food deficit and was dependent on increasing food imports. By 1986 – 88 when there was a recurrence of drought, India had not only expanded food output to keep pace with population growth but had stored sufficient buffer stocks to last through the drought.

Much of the expansion of rice production has been attributed to the effects of the Green Revolution, though recent studies have also indicated the associated role of market forces which encourage commercialisation of agriculture and hasten the adoption of the Green Revolution.

The Green Revolution

The term 'Green Revolution' is widely used but far from clearly understood. While most people connect the term with the introduction of high-yielding varieties (HYV) of certain food crops, particularly wheat and rice, the nature of the Green Revolution is far more complex. Three distinct meanings can be attached to the term:

- a breakthrough in plant breeding that produced high-yielding food grains
- a package of technology, including fertiliser, insecticide, implements, water control and HYV seed
- an agricultural development strategy in which the application of technology to Third World agriculture is central to the problem of increasing food production.

[SOURCE: Dixon C *Rural Development in the Third World*, 1990]

Although pioneered by American researchers in Mexico to improve yields of wheat and maize, the Green Revolution has come to be particularly associated with improving rice yields in Monsoon Asia. Its express purpose was to raise rice output to combat what was then seen as a possible world catastrophe due to a population explosion in Monsoon Asia.

Over the 1960s and 1970s its most effective impact was felt in India and Pakistan, but the new high yielding varieties of rice are now planted in most areas where rice is grown under irrigation (Case study 23.4). Farmers in the tropical world wishing to plant the new strains had to adopt a whole package of new measures, such as addition of artificial fertilisers to the soil, a carefully controlled water supply and the use of insecticides and herbicides to control pest and diseases.

Where the package was adopted spectacular increases in yields have been recorded. The world rice harvest doubled between 1967 and 1992. In Indonesia output trebled from 15 to 48 million tonnes. Although much of this is due to the new varieties giving higher yields now levelling off at ten tonnes a hectare, it is also due to two and three crops being possible on irrigated land because the growing season has been shortened from 160 to 110 days.

The impact of the Green Revolution

A success in terms of expansion of output

The Green Revolution has undoubtedly been a resounding success in terms of increase of output and saving Monsoon Asia from the threat of famine as population growth threatened to outstrip the land's carrying capacity. However, measured in other terms, its degree of success is debatable.

Environment

Its adoption has been criticised on health and environmental grounds because of the damaging effects of too much artificial fertiliser and herbicide application to the land. Intensification of irrigation without adequate drainage (Case study 23.4) and its extension into unsuitable soil area have damaged soils.

Less benefit for poorer farmers and landless households

Initially designed to help the poorest farmers, in effect it helped mostly the rich and middle income farmers who could afford the package of measures needed to implement the Green Revolution. Many poorer farmers could not afford it and of those who attempted to adopt it, many ran into debt and had to sell their land to wealthier neighbours. The landless gained relatively little as those farmers who prospered most out the Green Revolution began to adopt some mechanisation.

Socio-economic effects on rural communities

Apart from its unequal economic impact, the Green Revolution is said to have undesirable social effects on village communities. The already dominant rural elite minority have gained even more power and influence. The orderly social structure and cohesion of village life has been strained and altered with the poorer becoming increasingly resentful of the elite minority.

However, recent studies have indicated that earlier criticisms were probably over extreme. Although the Green Revolution may have widened the disparity between the rich and the poor in rural areas it merely contributed to a trend set in motion by other changes, such as the growing commercialisation of agriculture and increased urban links which mainly benefited richer landowners.

'Many of the changes currently under way in rural areas – growing inequalities, rising landlessness, the breakdown of traditional society – are best understood as part of the wider process of agrarian change and agricultural commercialisation. The role of the Green Revolution has often been to ameliorate the negative consequences of these developments, not to promote them' (Rigg 1989).

Adoption largely restricted to areas under irrigation

One important limitation in the impact of the Green Revolution is that the new strains of rice can only really be effectively planted in lowland areas where irrigation can be used to control the supply of water (Case study 23.4). Only one third of Asian wet rice areas have reliable water supplies during the growing season.

Too little attention given to other food crops

While much attention has been focused successfully on developing new high-yielding strains of rice and wheat. According to the United Nations Research Institute for Social Development, not enough attention has so far been given to improving other crops, especially those rich in protein such as peas, beans and other pulses. Yet ironically the diet of most people in the tropics is seriously lacking in protein content.

Too little attention to storage and effective distribution of food crops

A good deal of research has shown that the real problem is not an overall shortage due to insufficient production but losses of a significant part of harvested crops through poor storage and the difficulty of distributing the right balance of food to where it is needed. Finance should be made available to improve distribution and marketing methods.

The FAO recognise the need for a second Green Revolution in which the aim would be to produce even higher yielding strains of rice and wheat and other crops which could be grown in a way less harmful to the environment. The Institute aims to achieve this improvement in a way more friendly to the smaller and poorer farmers and which will acknowledge traditional farming methods and practical realities, such as the limited finances available at this level. Thus future progress will be significantly different from those of the first Green Revolution. It will be more of a rural evolution than revolution.

The Green Revolution – the next step forward

In Asia

- Trial higher yielding hybrids raising yields in irrigated rice areas from a maximum of 10 tonnes to the hectare to 12.5 tonnes.
- Develop hybrids suited to the rain-fed rice growing areas which would treble yields from the present one tonne per hectare.
- Cross breed to produce a hybrid, the seed from which can be used for the next year's planting, reducing costly purchase of seed each year.
- Reduce the concentration on wheat; focus on other crops such as lentils and peas which will also benefit farmers in drier areas.
- Replace costly and harmful pesticides by natural predators. Natural predator adoption in Indonesia (third largest rice producer) reduced pesticide use by 65% with no decrease in yields.
- The use of fertiliser is vital otherwise the soil breaks down under constant rice cultivation. Reduce costs and harmful effects of artificial fertilisers by more crop rotation to recycle nutrients and by using green manuring.
- Reduce labour input by using 'alternative technology' such as a simple scoop to remove harmful snails off rice plants and a milling machine driven by burning rice hulls.
- A wider dissemination and greater involvement of small farmers includes educational programmes.

In Africa

While Asian and Latin American countries benefited from the Green Revolution it has, until recently, not been to the advantage of African farmers. In the 1960s and 1970s in Africa, the concentration was on technology and crops which could only effectively be used by commercial farmers in lowland areas under irrigation. Many small farmers live in drier and upland areas of low natural fertility and have insufficient money to buy fertilisers or irrigate crops. Much of the responsibility to improve agriculture rests with the International Institute for Tropical Agriculture. Since the mid-1980s, IITA has changed its strategies to more effectively meet small farmer needs and help solve Africa's food crisis.

- Adopt a more comprehensive approach using new hybrids and farming systems which take into account social problems. Involve the peasant farmers, especially the women who do most of the cultivating (Case study 9.3).
- Research into a wider crop range of maize, rice and other grains such as millets, legumes (soyabean and cowpeas) and roots such as yams and cassavas, a staple crop in much of tropical Africa. The aim is not for maximum yield and fertiliser-hungry hybrids but for disease-, pest- and drought-resistant strains.
- Maintaining crumb soil structure is essential in kaolite clays common in Africa. Based to some extent on traditional farming methods, the IITA advocates non-tillage cultivation, hand clear land and rotation of crops with no return to the bush by combining nitrogen fixing velvet beans, maize and cow peas, mulching and green manuring, for example.
- Agroforestry and multi-storey cropping is encouraged as in smallholding gardens near dwellings such as gallery palms, sheltering plantains (bananas) and at ground level, roots and vegetables.

Agrarian change is more than the impact of a Green Revolution

The effects of the Green Revolution must be seen in the context of and related to wider changes that have been occurring in tropical regions. Some of these have already been noted.

International debt structural adjustment programmes and government policies towards rural development and agriculture

As can be seen from Case study 7.3, agricultural change is dependent on the degree of priority given to rural development and the kinds of rural policies adopted by governments, including attitudes towards land reform and agricultural financial policy decisions. However, these have been severely affected by international debt problems and structural readjustment.

Under freer markets, smaller farmers are being driven back to subsistence farming or abandoning their lands as they cannot compete with the growing number of agri-businesses and large scale co-operatives which operate more efficiently using modern methods and economies of scale.

Under the economic restructuring pressed on developing countries by the World Bank and the International Monetary Fund as a condition of further financial assistance, most governments have felt obliged to reduce aid to agriculture and open it to more outside foreign competition (Section 33.4). In the face of greater market competition the large agribusinesses and cooperatives have been more successful than peasant farmers in raising productivity. Large scale concerns have the capital to invest in more efficient methods and can benefit from economies of scale. Many small farmers are being driven back to subsistence farming or are abandoning their smallholdings.

In Brazil, for example, in the case of the large-scale Coplan cooperative with 538 cotton and coffee growers and located south of São Paulo, withdrawal of government subsidies in the 1980s led to a drive for greater efficiency and an end to corruption. Productivity was raised by using more technologically advanced methods involving the use of high-yielding hybrid, large fertiliser inputs and more automation. The greatest advances in productivity have occurred in the large enterprises which concentrate on soya bean production. In the early 1980s, the ten million hectares under soya beans yielded 15 million tonnes but by 1994, this had risen to 23 million tonnes. Soya is now Brazil's most valuable agricultural export, comprising 40% by value.

In contrast while the Brazilian government has aided the large-scale producers by selling or donating land to them, the number of landless peasant families had increased to five million by the late 1980s. In the face of growing rural unrest the government made land reform a key policy in 1988. By 1994, however, land reform legislation still remained incomplete and reallocation of land has been very limited. For example, in the north-east, only 3000 of the 350 000 peasant households awaiting allocation had been given holdings.

The actions of most governments are severely conditioned by international debt and currently, the associated structural readjustment programmes enforced on them by the World Bank and other external agencies.

The role of aid donors and providers of credit

External governments and agencies also exercise a positive influence for the expansion of agricultural production, just as major aid donors and credit suppliers do, without which few governments in the tropics could run rural development and agricultural programmes. Increasingly the efforts of these agencies and voluntary organisations are moving away from large-scale schemes towards small-scale ones which effectively involve local communities in decision-making. Many of these schemes are proving to be successful without disrupting traditional social structures and cultural values (Case studies 23.5 and 9.3).

The role of market forces

Probably the most potent force for change has been market forces. Increasing urbanisation, better access to markets and the build-up of the necessary commercial infrastructure have been powerful stimuli to expand production. Given sufficient profit incentive, subsistence farmers, other small-scale producers and those with larger holdings will adopt the measures needed to raise output.

Now there is a further market incentive. Large multinational and other commercial companies are setting up processing plants and marketing organisations to link up with farmers often through local co-operatives to expand cash crop production.

Population control

International agencies and governments have expressed serious concern about food supplies keeping pace with population growth in the developing world (Chapter 7). Because of the younger structure of populations in most of the tropics, substantial population growth will continue over the short term into the next century. Any attempt to expand food production must be matched by a comprehensive rural development programme which also aims at promoting health, education and family planning. The other need is advancement in the greater equality and status of women, which is necessary for social reasons and because in many tropical countries women play a major role in agriculture (Chapter 9).

The next step for expanding food production

The opportunity for a further expansion of agricultural output by expanding the margins of cultivated areas in the tropics is severely limited. The serious land degradation already occurring on the margins indicates that the limits of farming have already been over extended (Case study 21.2). Also, competing demands for land in established areas will lead to an actual reduction in the cultivable land available. Thus expansion of output must come from greater productivity per unit area farmed and this will need to be done with less labour than presently available in Monsoon Asia and elsewhere.

23.6 Tropical commercial farming

The character of tropical cash crop farming has changed substantially in the post-colonial period. Previously most of it was under European control to supply export markets in Western Europe and other parts of the developed world. Much of it is now under the control of the indigenous peoples with an increasing proportion of the agricultural output being absorbed within the tropics as populations increase, incomes rise and more and more people move into the towns.

Nationalisation and land reform measures have led to increasingly more land being taken from Europeans and returned to the local people. Some of this is still organised on plantation lines; much of it is linked to co-operatives or farmed as small cash crop holdings. Commercial livestock farming in the tropics, however, still remains largely in the hands of white landowners or controlled by foreign companies in association with the governments concerned.

23.7 Commercial livestock farming

In tropical areas experiencing savanna conditions and where Europeans have settled, livestock farming has become important, for example beef rearing in North Australia. The Llanos area of the Orinocco Plains in Venezuela and Colombia is a region where strenuous efforts are being made to re-establish cattle ranching as part of a more general attempt to assist rural development and bring about a more balanced population distribution.

The market for livestock produce is increasingly to be found within the tropics. Population and demand are growing here. In the West, tropical livestock produce has to compete with much greater supplies from temperate farming areas and more protective tariff quota measures to help home livestock producers.

23.8 Cash crop farming in the tropics

The growing participation of small farmers in expanding urban markets

Cash cropping in the tropics and sub-tropics is usually associated with plantations but plantation agriculture has declined. It is being replaced by an extension of cash crop farming on native small holdings and medium-sized enterprises, under the control of local people with strong government support as in Malaysia, where rubber production was once dominated by European-owned and managed plantations. Most rubber now comes from the small holding sector and even in the reduced estate sector most estates are owned and managed by non-Europeans (Case study 23.5).

Peasant farmers increasingly need a cash income as they are drawn into a money economy and there is a growing domestic market to be served. In the humid savanna belt of Africa *'the popularity of high yielding crops such as manioc, maize and yams in the lightly to moderately populated humid savanna zone is not simply a matter of adequately provisioning the producer societies with food. Increasingly over the last few decades these food crops have been produced in surplus for the national market.'* Integration of the traditional farming system into the market economy and extension of what is meant by cash cropping to include cash sale of staple food crops are both important.

While demand overseas for tropical foods and agricultural raw materials may fluctuate and competition for these markets has been intensified, it is still very substantial. Many tropical countries rely on earnings from agricultural exports to pay for essential imports. Thus while home markets may be increasingly important, cash farmers will have to continue to compete in these overseas markets with plantation crops produced under European management.

Plantation and estate cash cropping

Despite its declining contribution, the plantation or estate system as it is now sometimes called, still remains important. Plantations were initially established to supply developed countries with certain luxury foods, beverages and raw materials which could only be produced under tropical conditions but which established farming systems were unable to produce in sufficient quantity or of a consistently high quality. As they needed large areas of land with accessibility to shipment points, plantations were established on thinly settled islands and coastal locations.

The classic definition of a ***plantation*** is that by Waibel (1933): *'The plantation is a large-scale agricultural and industrial enterprise producing high value vegetable products, usually under the management of Europeans; and involving great investment in labour and capital equipment.'* Plantations were usually monoculture, producing only one crop, so as to gain benefits from specialisation and large-scale operations. The amount of processing of the crop before shipment varied with the crop, bananas clearly requiring no processing while rubber requires a considerable amount, as does sugar.

However, the character of plantations has changed. Cultivation methods now take account of maintaining soil fertility and cropping patterns having been diversified. Cocoa and oil palm are now intercropped in Ghana and Nigeria, while in the states of Parana and São Paulo in Brazil, livestock farming is associated with some coffee fazendas.

Advantages	Disadvantages
High quality products due to better management and more scientific methods	Much of revenue goes out of the country
Of a scale to meet rising demands in advanced countries for tropical agricultural products	Unfair competition for smallholders wanting to develop cash farming, especially as much of the marketing system is controlled by the multinationals
Opened up new areas and aided overall development	Initially over-exploited and exhausted land under monoculture Reliance of region on export of narrow range of agricultural products, neglect of basic food crops and economic dependency on importing countries
Provision of infrastructure including communication and port outlets	Reliance of region on export of narrow range of agricultural products, neglect of basic food crops and economic dependency on importing countries
Some diffusion of new techniques, encouragement of cash crop farming in area around	Disruptive and divisive of indigenous social system – leading to a dual system, firstly of areas under some plantation / western-orientated system based on money income, with import of other ethnic labour and secondly, other usually remoter areas under old subsistence systems and a traditional culture
Cash income for workers encourages local market economy	

Figure 23.4 *The plantation system – for and against*

Larger plantations characteristically include facilities for the workers and their families such as schooling and medical facilities. In addition, many have garden patches on which to grow staple food crops and many owners allow some cash cropping to supplement plantation wages. In some areas this helps maintain a labour supply which might otherwise be attracted by higher wages in the city as, for example, in Malaysia (Case study 23.5).

The value of the plantation system as opposed to smaller systems under non-European control has been a subject of considerable debate in recent years. The pros and cons are summarised in Figure 23.4 and on balance it seems that essentially for social and political reasons, the plantation system will continue to decline though its final demise is a long way off. This is illustrated in the banana industry. The banana is both an important food and export crop.

The role of transnationals in the banana industry

It is indicative of the expanding food consumption in the tropical regions themselves that of the 45 million metric tonne of bananas or plantains, less than 20% enters world trade. Despite some expansion of small-scale producers, trade is dominated by large transnational companies such as Geest which controls all the transport and marketing of bananas from the Caribbean Windward Islands. American transnational companies such as Del Monte, Dole and Chiquite (formerly United Fruit) dominate commercial growing in the Central Republics of Latin America to such an extent that their influence on the economies and politics of these countries is very strong.

While providing much needed employment and export earnings for the Caribbean countries, there is increasing evidence the influence of these transnationals seriously distorts the economies of the countries in which they operate and increase damage to the environment (Case study 23.6).

The economies of scale achieved by large-scale production under the plantation system and their dominance of world trade is also making it difficult for small-scale growers to expand their share of the market. Efforts are being made by governments in banana producing countries to achieve a greater influence on production and trade through the setting up of a Union of Banana Exporting Countries (UBEC). However, internal arguments, political instability and insufficient finance and expertise have largely prevented these countries from adopting a more radical approach against the multinationals. The stand taken by the European Union against the 'dollar banana' exporting companies gaining a greater share of the European market, the largest in the banana trade, has done more to protect the smaller producers (Case study 23.6).

Cash cropping under a smallholding system combining subsistence farming

Cash cropping in association with subsistence agriculture is often regarded as a recent phenomenon but in fact it has a long history under a variety of traditional systems. These range from some form of rotational fallowing of plots around a settlement to permanent plot cultivation. For example, in the savanna belt of West Africa cotton and groundnuts are characteristic cash crops within a rotational fallowing system. Jute is an important cash crop in the settled intensive farming system of peasant cultivation in the delta region of Bangladesh. Tree crops such as oil palm have long provided additional income to smallholders in the rain forest belts of both Africa and South East Asia (Figure 23.5).

In contrast to plantations, most smallholdings on which some cash crops are grown are usually under five hectares and rely mainly on family labour, hiring of labour placing a considerable burden on the farmer who has little spare finance to pay for it. Nevertheless there are richer farmers or landlords in every region, who either rely on hired labour or let out part of their holdings under some tenancy or share cropping arrangements.

Despite the increasing variety of systems under which small-scale cash cropping takes place, many writers have commented on the prevalence of a common pattern akin to the infield and outfield system at one time present over much of peasant Europe. There is a circular arrangement to land-use around a village or smallholding, with the intensity of cultivation declining with distance for reasons similar to those outlined by Thunen in his 'isolated state'. The village or farm is the place where produce must be brought from off the land and inputs of labour and fertiliser also have to be got out from the village or farm to the land where it is needed. Consequently the nearest land, including house gardens, is the most intensively cultivated and kept fertile by the addition of waste material and dung from the settlement. A second zone further away is less intensively cultivated because of the greater time required to get to and from it. Occasionally the land may be manured by putting cattle on it following harvesting. On the outer rings, scattered clearings may be periodically made in the bush or forest and cultivated more extensively on a rotational bush fallow basis. After it has been cropped for a number of years it is allowed to return to bush so that natural processes may restore its fertility (Figure 23.5).

The increasing shift to small-scale commercial farming

While a combination of some cash cropping with subsistence farming is an important feature of the changes currently taking place within tropical agriculture, the expansion of small-scale commercial farming is even more evident. Here the

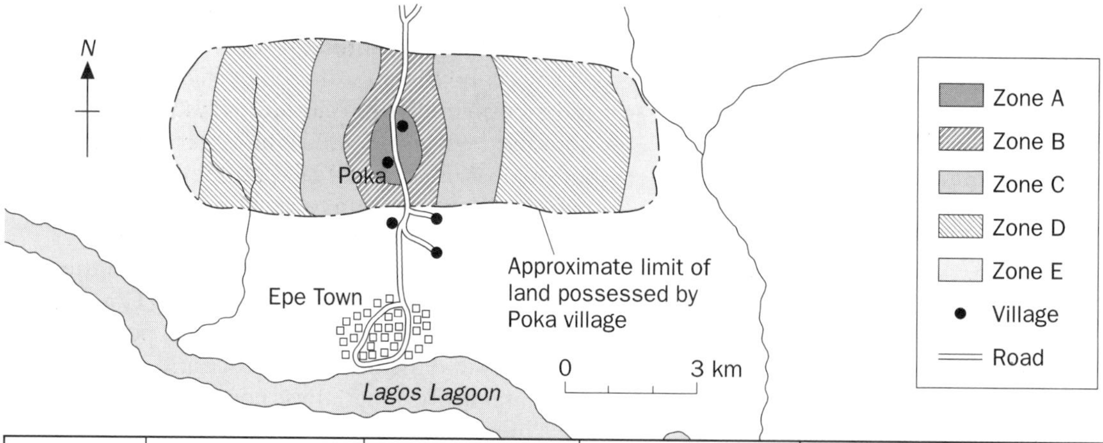

	Zone A	Zone B	Zone C	Zone D	Zone E
INTENSITY	PERMANENT with multi-cropping	SEMI-PERMANENT 1 yr crops and 1 yr fallow or 2 – 3 years. crops and 1 yr fallow multi-cropping or inter-cropping	PERMANENT peasant plantations	ROTATIONAL BUSH FALLOW 3 yrs crops (in succession) + 3–5 yrs fallow some forest	FOREST ZONE gathering
MANURE	MANURED	MANURED	—	—	—
PLOTS	TINY	0.2 ha	up to 4.0 h	up to 1.0 h	
CROPS	SUBSISTENCE yams, peppers, vegetables and fruit trees	SUBSISTENCE cassava, maize and melons	CASH tree crops: kola nut, rubber and some cocoa; other crops, cassava, maize and cocoyam	CASH cassava and groundnuts, maize and melons	SUBSISTENCE firewood oil palm hunting and tiny plots of food crops
SETTLEMENT	PERMANENT VILLAGE	—	—	SOME TEMPORARY FARM SHELTERS	SEMI-PERMANENT BUSH CAMPS

Figure 23.5 Land use round Poka, SW Nigeria

Advantages	Disadvantages
Integrated with the general agricultural economy	Yields and quality generally lower
Utilises traditional farming methods, together with some modernisation. The emphasis is on family labour	Supplies are less reliable as farmers switch according to market prices
Provides a much needed cash income and helps to integrate rural and urban sectors of the economy and society	Some neglect of basic food crops therefore necessitating some import of these
Adaptable and flexible: can withstand market fluctuations better than plantations being able to switch more between food and cash crops	Uneven and dispersed distribution of smallholdings makes provision of marketing and other infrastructure difficult and expensive. Diffusion of new techniques also difficult
Better adapted to tropical environmental conditions	Until recently government neglected needed support for agriculture in favour of industrialisation

Figure 23.6 *Smallholding cash crop farming – for and against*

main purpose is cash crop production commonly using family labour. Food production for the household is secondary to this. In the most favourably located areas such as those near capital cities and airports, small-scale intensive commercial agriculture and horticulture employing outside labour and modern techniques is also becoming important. For example, Zimbabwe has a rapidly expanding horticulture industry in the area around the capital not only supplying Harare but also exporting out-of-season vegetables, flowers and fruit by air to European markets.

It is becoming increasingly difficult to generalise about small-scale production in tropical countries. The commercial farming sector is increasingly geared to serving expanding urban markets within the producing countries themselves, although agricultural exports will still be important to a number of economies. In a dualistic sector, however, the small-scale producers are gaining ground over the plantation and estate production. In some countries as in Malaysia (Case study 23.5), government policy explicitly favours the small producers but in others, including the Caribbean countries, foreign multinational companies and emerging large domestic companies still have control of the largest proportion of the best lands in large estates.

Concluding comment

'Agriculture is the best motor of growth for developing countries' ... 'Asian countries such as Taiwan and South Korea built industrial development on rapidly growing agriculture, unlike African countries where industry was promoted at the expense of agriculture.'

[SOURCE: Pinstrup Anderson, Director of the International Food Policy Research Institute, *Financial Times* 13.6.95]

case study

23.1 New Guinea: the Chimbu agricultural systems

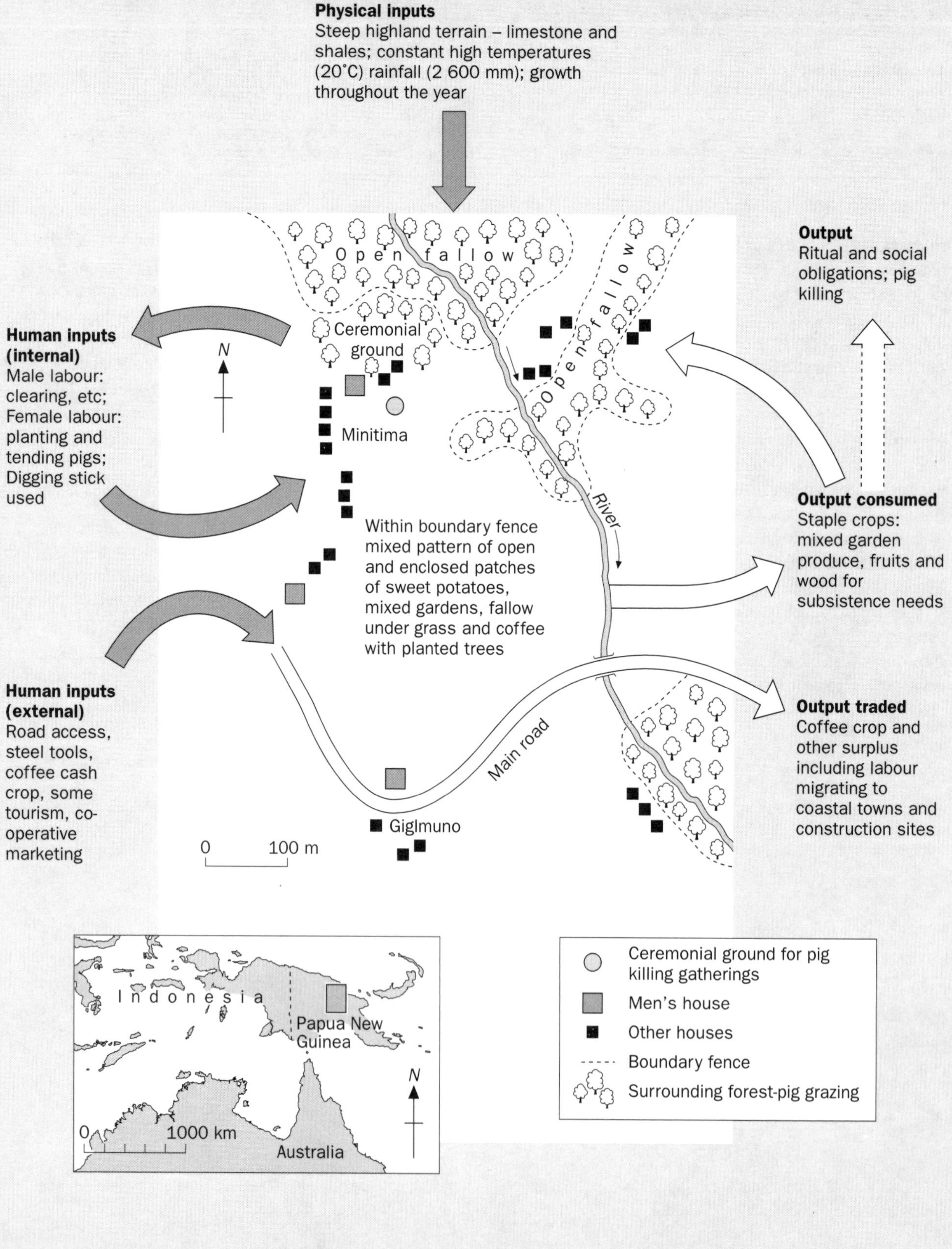

Main economic and social characteristics

Land and food crops

Land is held communally but cultivated by individual families on a 6 – 8 year cycle followed by fallow. Mixed 'garden' – intercropping of staple foods of yam and cassava with taro beans, green vegetable and sugar cane; supplemented by bananas and other tree fruits.

Dominance of the pig killing cycle in their culture and way of life

800 pigs are grazed and fattened for periodic ceremonial gathering kills and to meet social obligations. Pig production is the fundamental basis of interpersonal and group relations.

Traditional features

Traditional tension between food and pig production as pig population encroaches on crop land.

Increasing pressures and tensions

Competition for land between food and cash crops.

Increased medical facilities caused rising population pressure from 100 to 200 per sq. km; this is overtaxing land, shortening fallow period, causing soil exhaustion and erosion.

Incompatibility of the traditional way of life with an imported money economy and outside job opportunities.

Externally introduced features

Introduction of a coffee cash crop and market sale of surplus food with outside advice and through an introduced co-operative system.

Additional income from entertaining tourists with tribal dances and other customs, etc.

case study

23.2 Fulani pastoralism: a changing way of life

Basic characteristics of Fulani pastoralism

The way of life and wealth of the Fulani pastoralists are based on livestock. They have traditionally migrated seasonally with herds of cattle, sheep and goats. The general direction has been eastward across the Savanna, after harvest and with the onset of the dry season, southward, away from the drier Savanna onto stubble land in search of pasture. In exchange for use of the Hausa people's farmland, the fertility of the soil was annually renewed by the manure droppings of the livestock. The relationship was thus mutually beneficial to the two groups.

To supplement the staple diet based on milk, the Fulani sold butter and other milk products in the local markets in exchange for corn, rice, tea and coffee.

Periodic drought and rinderpest could decimate herds and now increasing population pressure and the extension of farmland under irrigation has so reduced the opportunities for migration that apart from the Bororo, most Fulani are semi- or permanently settled, growing crops as well as keeping livestock.

The changing economy and way of life of the Goshi – Fulani of the northern Cameroons

The Goshi, a clan of the Jafun Fulani, adopted a settled way of life earlier than most other groups. Originating from the Kano region, they had by the 1920s settled in the Bamenda Grasslands, living alongside farming groups. Migration of livestock was limited to short distance moves.

The Goshi have had links with Europeans from this time with veterinary and cattle control officers advising on stock and grazing. After the Second World War strong support and encouragement from the Cameroon government and external agencies helped to improve breeds and pasture including fodder for the dry season. The ultimate aim was to settle the Fulani on cattle ranches or produce beef for a growing population and urban market.

The Goshi people have increasingly been drawn into a moneyed economy – grazing cattle for rich urban-based owners, regularly marketing cattle in the commercial centre and port of Doula. Cement dwellings are replacing traditional ones. The more wealthy own vehicles, using cash purchases for imported tinned food and clothing. There has also been some drift of Fulani youth to the towns.

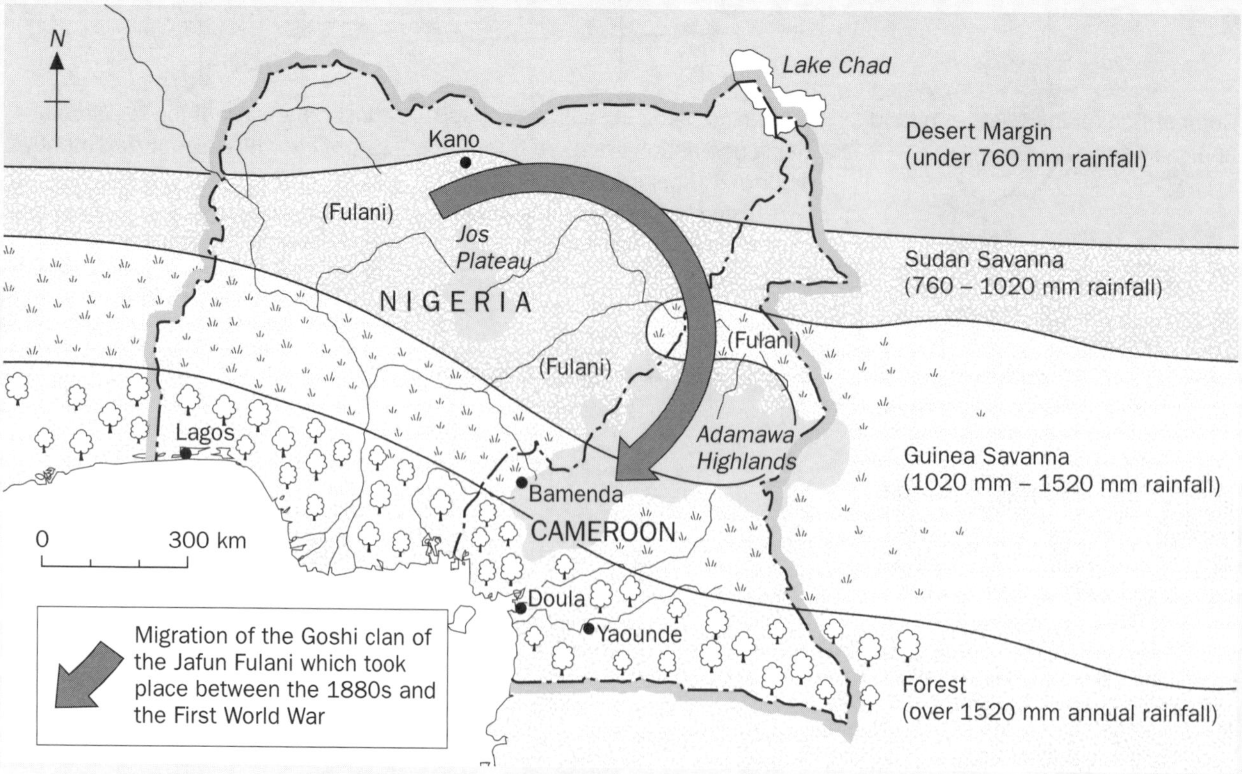

Cattle Fulani in Nigeria and Cameroon

case study

23.3 Bangladesh: the rice culture

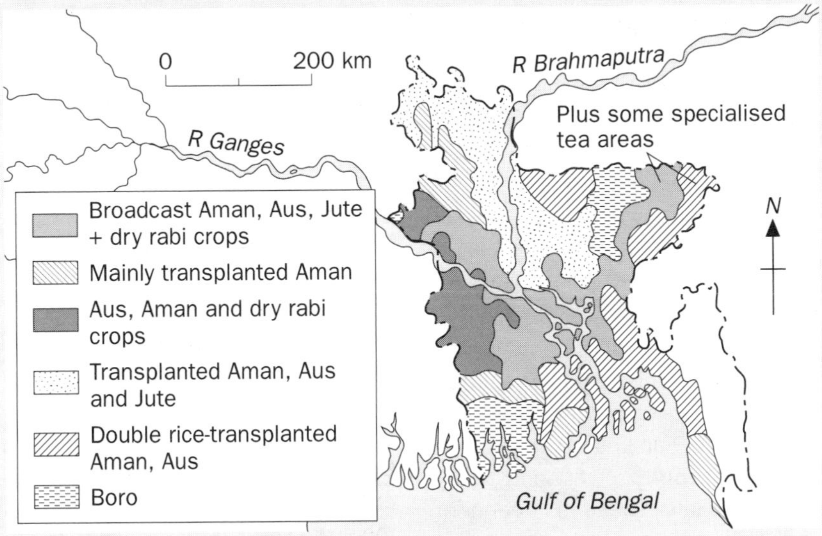

Agricultural regions

Rice is the dominant crop in all the farming systems in Bangaldesh except for shifting subsistence and tea in the Chittagong Hills. There are three main seasonal crops of rice: aman, aus and boro.

Although mainly a subsistence crop, there are cash sales to help meet debts, social obligations and buy essentials. The amount of other cash cropping depends on physical conditions, size of holding and tenancy conditions; land let out on a share crop basis by absentee landlords may have significant cash cropping.

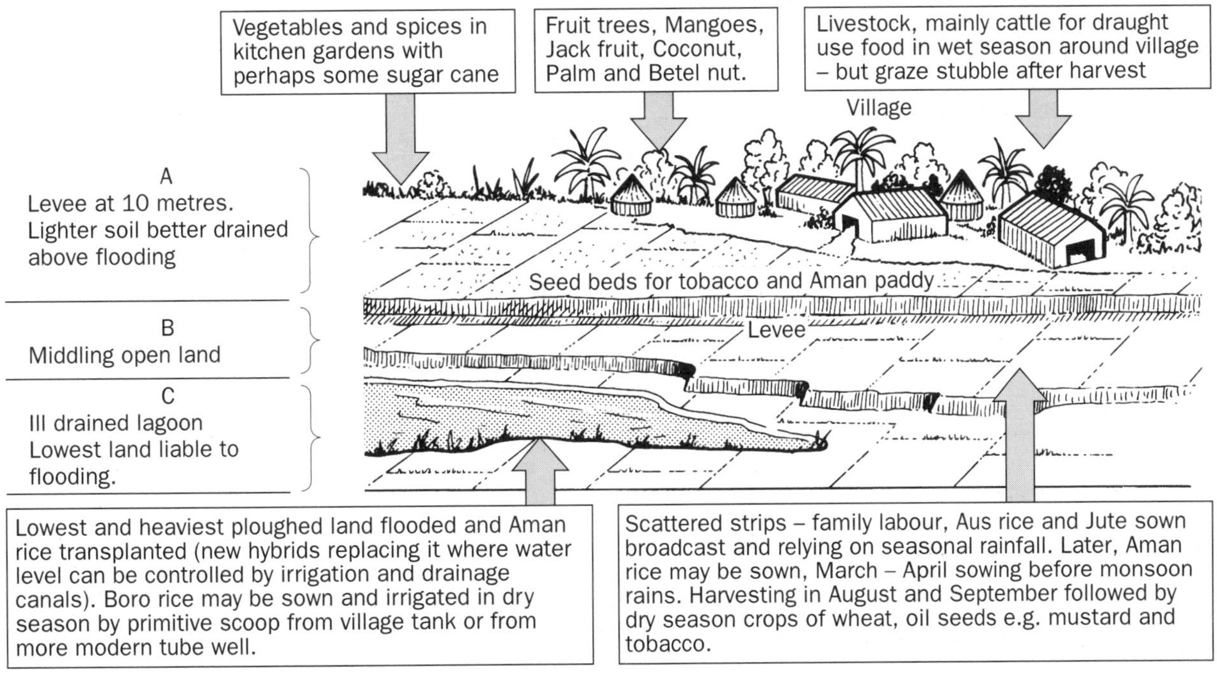

Month	March April May	September March
Season	Pre-monsoon Wet season	Dry season
Levee crest homestead and gardens	Cattle in yard mangoes, vegetables	Repairing and thatching green coconuts, Betel nuts
Middling open land	Sugar cane, Aus paddy, Jute	Aus seed bed, wheat, tobacco, mustard
Lower heavier land	Grazing, Aman and Boro rice (flooding)	Grazing, sweet potato and tomatoes

Agriculture in a village on the Lower Delta region

Increasing agricultural output

With a population of 117 million (1994), Bangladesh is one of the world's poorest countries, having a per capita income of only $220. Three quarters of the population are dependent on agriculture which also provides half the country's GDP. Thus any improvement in standards of living is dependent on increasing agricultural output especially of rice, the staple food.

Since 1971 when Bangladesh had to import 30% of its food needs, output of agriculture has improved by 25% but it is not keeping pace with population growth. The annual rate of growth is currently 1.8% giving an estimated increase of population to 132 million by the year 2000.

Pressure of population and very low living standards in rural areas have led to a rapid increase in urbanisation. If current rates continue, the percentage of the population in urban areas will rise from the present 20% to 37% in twenty years time. Cities do not have the resources or employment to support such a rise (there are already 134 million in urban shanty areas). Thus improvements in the rural sector are needed to stem urbanisation.

Ways of increasing output

Application of the Green Revolution has brought with it increased benefits. Planting of the new hybrid varieties of rice have been the main reason why output of rice has increased since 1971 but further output is also dependent on other factors.

More consolidation of holdings is needed, many are under one hectare in size, and may be fragmented into as many as 20 separate strips.

Much of the land is concentrated into the hands of an elite rural minority of landlords with half of rural households effectively landless. Thus more land reform is needed, but without more rural credit and extension workers to advise, reform may not raise food output.

Adequate and controlled water supplies are vital to monsoon agriculture. The government, with the support of the World Bank, has embarked on a comprehensive Flood Action Plan based on a principle of controlled flooding. Agriculture in the delta is dependent on the flood waters of the Ganges-Brahmaputra-Meghana River systems which seasonally floods half the land with water and riverine silt. This annually replenishes the land's fertility. However, excessive uncontrolled flooding as in 1988, brings devastation.

The lower delta can also suffer from cyclones and the associated tidal wave surge inland brings devastation and salination of the land by sea water. Measures are being taken to control the incursions but as yet with only limited success.

Extension of irrigated land is needed. At present only a quarter of land can be irrigated in the dry season. Diesel pumping of ground water could irrigate one million more hectares. Better canal distribution of river water is needed such as the Ganges-Kabak Scheme which irrigates 90 000 ha. in the Kush district, for example. However, river-derived schemes are dependent on water from India. At hill margins tube wells can tap ground water allowing double cropping such as in the northern district of Dinajpur.

Adequate drainage must also be ensured otherwise intensification of irrigation produces hard panning, increased soil salinity and declining yields.

Other issues

Improvements in agriculture and the rural sector in general are dependent on resolving other important issues. Endemic internal political instability and poor relations with India and Pakistan hinder progress and money is diverted to military 'build-ups'. Good relations are essential, especially with India, as it controls the rivers which feed Bangladesh.

Practically the whole of Bangladesh's Development Programme is reliant on outside financing by the World Bank and other agencies. The country is also running a serious budget deficit and 17% of export income goes towards servicing overseas debt. Thus Bangladesh has little money for further agricultural developments.

Between 1947 – 71 the rural sector was neglected with no institutional systems to organise rural improvements. Since then these have received more attention but progress has been limited as the monitoring of the Rural Development Policy Initiatives begun in 1982 shows. The aim was to set up local urban centres of around 12 000 population, each called 'thanas', to provide the catalyst for rural development with local involvement. The local administration would work towards providing health, education, a much-needed family planning programme, more services and local industry and agricultural improvements. Only limited progress has been made because of insufficient finance and control by bureaucrats in alliance with the local landlords.

Bangladesh faces other serious environmental problems, some of which affect agricultural improvements. For example, the Farrakka Barrage scheme in India designed to resolve Calcutta's water problem has adversely affected the drier west of Bangladesh, reducing irrigation in the dry season and causing uncontrollable flooding in the wet season.

Serious deforestation in the hill area of the country also detrimentally affects river regimes. The coastal waters in the Bay of Bengal are amongst the most polluted in the world, from industrial waste and sewage outflow seriously affecting fish stocks already heavily depleted by over-fishing. The Asian Development Bank has launched a $5 million clean-up programme.

Conclusion

Expansion of staple rice production is essential but there is only limited opportunity to expand the margins of cultivation. Thus increased rice output only comes from greater productivity which in turn is closely tied to effective water control and land reform.

Measures are being taken to slow down population growth but these need to be intensified to reduce pressure on food supplies. In turn, expansion of alternative sources of employment are needed to reduce rural population pressure. Despite some progress the Bangladeshi have not been able to formulate a viable, balanced and sustainable strategy for raising the quality of life of the masses.

case study

23.4 Pakistan: contrasting fortunes in irrigated land

Location

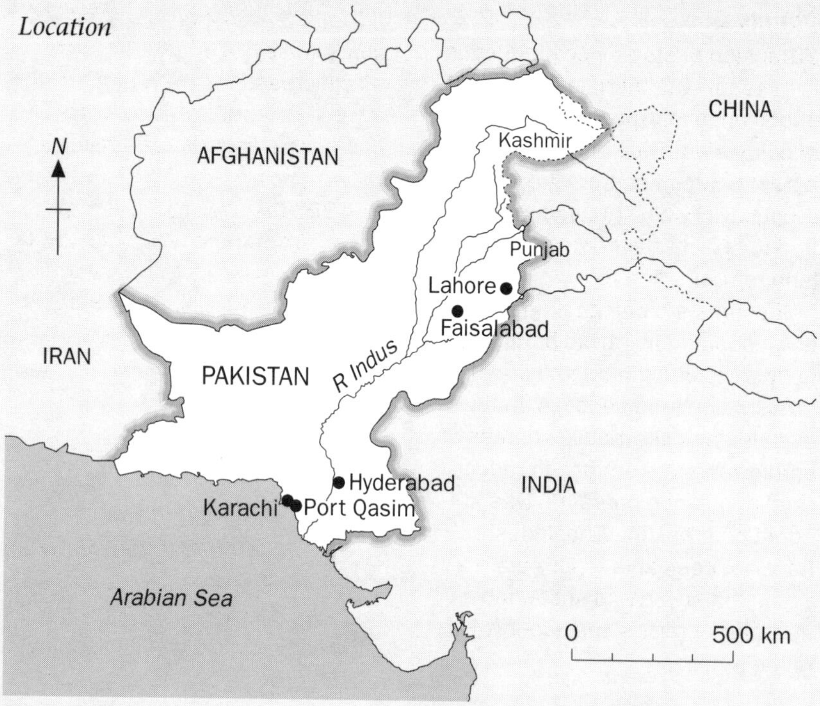

General

Pakistan is located on the Indus Plain and fed by waters from the mountains to the north. Agriculture contributes 22% of GDP and employs nearly 50% of the workforce. It is vital to the country's economy, providing 70% of its export earnings. With very little rainfall, 80% of its agricultural output comes from irrigated lands. Irrigation schemes based on the Indus have been extended to the maximum limit possible. The main crops are wheat, rice, sugar cane and cotton.

Pakistan has benefited greatly from the Green Revolution which, along with irrigation, greatly expanded agricultural output. However, the main beneficiaries were the large landowners, many of whom are absentee landlords; they could afford water, credit, fertilisers, new hybrid seeds and more mechanisation. Small farmers have had to continue using traditional methods with limited cash crops for sale.

Agricultural crisis

Agriculture is now in crisis due to deforestation in the mountains which led to increased flooding of the Indus. For example, in 1992 nearly half a million hectares of the cotton crop was lost in the Punjab.

Due to mismanagement, significant areas of irrigated land are suffering from water logging and salination.

In 1995 a World Bank Report indicated that Pakistan's irrigation system was operating under 40% of efficiency because of poor maintenance, leading to silting and clogging of the canal system and abuse of the system by large landowners.

Because of non-collection of a significant proportion of the water charges, income is below running costs. Thus the system is in financial crisis.

Poorer farmers on the tail-end of the canal system suffer most as they cannot afford alternative tube well water.

Successful small schemes in the Northern Mountains with some cash crop expansion

In contrast to the crisis on the Indus Plain, there are successful small schemes in the northern mountainous region. For example, the dry mountain valleys round Gilget under the Aga Khan Support Programme plus Canadian and UK financial aid, glacier meltwater-fed irrigation has been increased by 50% for village projects. There are over 1800 village organisations with 100 000 members. Training of village specialists has occurred and in addition to their own savings, villagers can borrow another 35% credit.

Average holdings are one hectare, traditionally growing wheat on terraced field strips with some livestock and poultry. Now with more irrigation, apples, apricots and seed potatoes are also being produced for cash sale via the Gilgit Marketing Association.

About 13 million trees have been planted to check soil erosion and to provide fuel. Livestock provide essential manure.

Apart from essential irrigation expansion and the co-operative marketing organisation, the other key to success uses the Chinese-built Karakoram Highway to link the mountain region southward with Islamabad and outside markets.

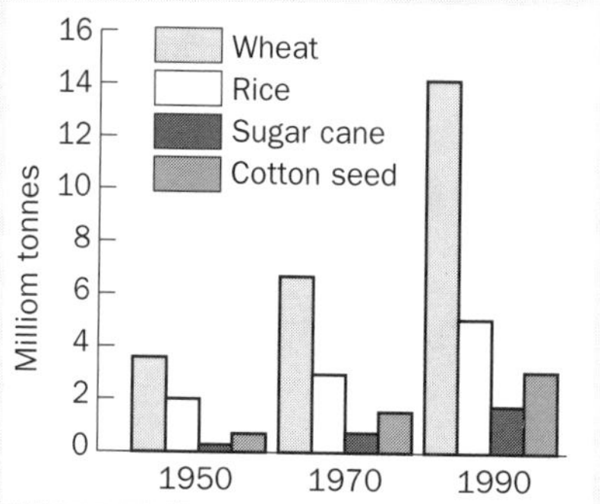

Agricultural production statistics, 1950 – 90

case study

23.5 Malaysia: rubber production

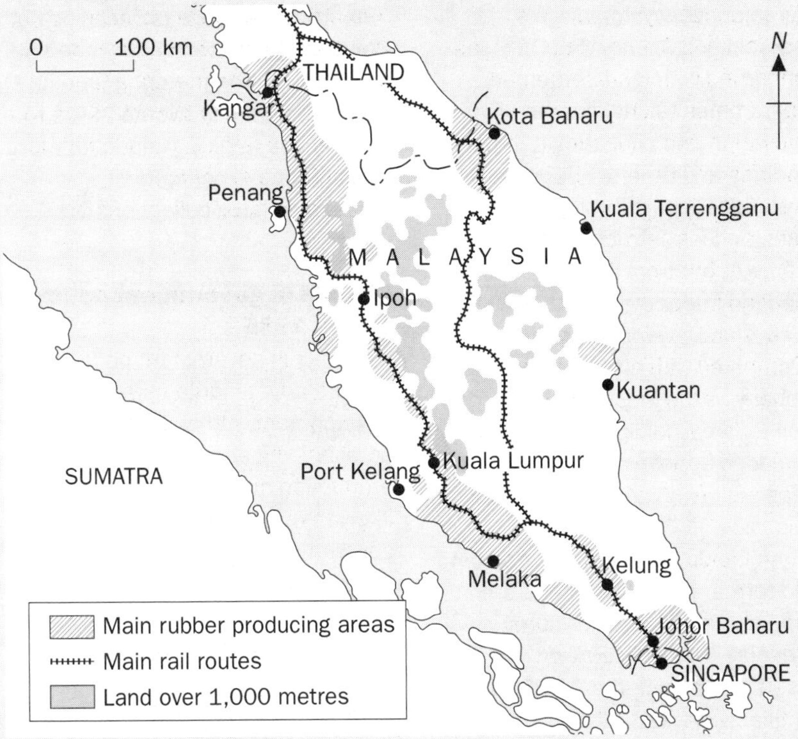

Rubber production

Conditions influencing development of rubber production to 1970s

Physical inputs

Malaysia has constantly high temperatures 25˚C and 30˚C. It also has a seasonally well distributed rainfall of more than 2500 mm, especially in the west.

Land was initially plentiful. The undulating coastal lands were favoured as good drainage is needed. The land is also tolerant of a variety of soils.

Human inputs

Malaysia is subject to historic colonial and continuing British interest through finance, entrepreneurship and expertise and research. It also now enjoys local Chinese and Malaysian investment.

The labour force comprises imported Tamils and Chinese together with indigenous Malaysian.

The infrastructure and port outlets were already established by the British for the tin mining sector. The government stimulates production, especially for smallholdings. Cooperation in the Association of Natural Rubber Producers helps Malaysia to keep a world share of the market despite competition from synthetic rubber.

Production 1993	1000 tonnes	Share
Malaysia	1500	27%
Indonesia	1370	25%
Thailand	210	22%

Share of world rubber production

Place in world markets

There has been a spectacular recovery in world rubber prices. They rose by 40% between 1994 – 95 largely due to China increasing imports by 50% but even this rise did not lead to significant expansion in Malaysia output. Recent price increases led to only marginal growth in output because it was still cheaper to produce outside Malaysia.

In 1995 the new International Rubber Agreement (INRA) sought to stabilise market prices through holding rubber stocks to provide rubber producers with steadier economic conditions.

Rubber is of declining importance in the Malaysian economy

There has been a significant expansion of industry; manufactured goods, especially high technical products, have replaced agricultural commodities and tin as the leading export products by value (1993).

Transistors and valves	15%
Crude petroleum	13%
Tropical woods	11%
Vegetable oils	6%
Rubber	5%

Export products by value, 1993

While rubber production declined from 1.6 million tonnes to 1.0 million tonnes by 1994, palm oil has been experiencing a boom and replaced rubber as the most important output on both small holdings and plantation estates. Malaysia is the leading world producer with a 55% share; palm oil covers 2 million hectares, expanded from 6.3 (1994) to 7.5 million tonnes 1995 (and an anticipated 9 million by the turn of the century).

Until 1994 world rubber prices were in decline (like tin) whereas demand for palm oil expanded and prices rose (oil palm vying with soya bean as the main vegetable oil product).

Indonesia and Thailand can produce natural rubber more cheaply as there is more plentiful land available, labour costs are approximately 60% less (Malaysian rubber producers losing labour to better paid manufacturing jobs) and Indonesia and Thailand governments subsidise fertiliser costs, for example.

In the 1960s plantation owners and managers who were pushed out of Malaysia brought expertise to Indonesia.

Smallholder production of rubber

Smallholdings now provide 70% – 80% of Malaysia's rubber output (and also dominate in its palm oil output) with 1.8 million ha of rubber on mainly one to two hectare holdings.

Since 1970 the Malaysian government has pursued a new economic policy to eradicate poverty and restructure society. In the agricultural sector this was represented by a deliberate movement away from plantation agriculture and a pressurising of foreign companies to leave.

Through a series of five-year plans until 1991 Malaysia pursued a rural development policy which, while allowing Malaysia ownership of plantations, favoured smallholders development in the rubber industry (RISDA) and helped subsistence padi rice smallholders. It encouraged consolidation of fragmented holdings, new village and township development and application of Green Revolution techniques.

A major agency, Malaysia's Federal Land Agency (FELDA), was concerned with land settlement programmes taking more land into cultivation and allocating it to the landless and others. FELDA has given full support through credit loans and infrastructure, for example, but from 1991 its role has changed under the 1991 – 95 sixth Malaysian Development Plan.

Compared with plantation workings, rubber was the most important cash crop for smallholdings but it is now exceeded by palm oil. Old rubber trees are being steadily replaced by palm oil.

Smallholdings on established land and former plantation areas are supported by various national agencies. Under FELDA's resettlement scheme 715 800 families were settled on smallholdings and block schemes by 1994. Earlier FELDA schemes included clearance of land and allocation of 4-ha plots, two-thirds in subsistence crops (rice and vegetables) and the rest in cash crops, namely rubber. In the 1980s 10 – 15 families were allocated to each block of land.

Plantations are still significant but increasingly need to hire foreign labour as there is a growing shortage of Malaysian labour. About 7% of rubber production cost is labour. Nearly all the plantations are now Malaysian-owned with Chinese prominent. They still practise largely monoculture.

Plantation acreage is declining but yields are significantly increased by new strains. The maturing time has been cut from eight years to five to six years so latex is yielded for more years. Some experiments to mechanise latex collections are underway.

Change in government policy, 1991 – 1995

A change in government policy favours private large estate development. Although the smallholding share of rubber production may decline, it is still likely to remain dominant. The government is now looking for increases in agricultural productivity rather than smallholding expansion.

Smallholding production is seen as being less efficient than private estate enterprise which could achieve scale economies. Smallholders cannot afford to adopt new methods to compete on world markets and are more reluctant to advance techniques. Their families are younger and increasingly reluctant to remain in farming thus forming an outflow to city jobs.

There is less land for resettlement and it is becoming more costly to resettle people on smallholdings.

The Malaysian government now favours manufacturing expansion more than agriculture and is rapidly industrialising the economy.

case study

23.6 Bananas: the main issues in world trade

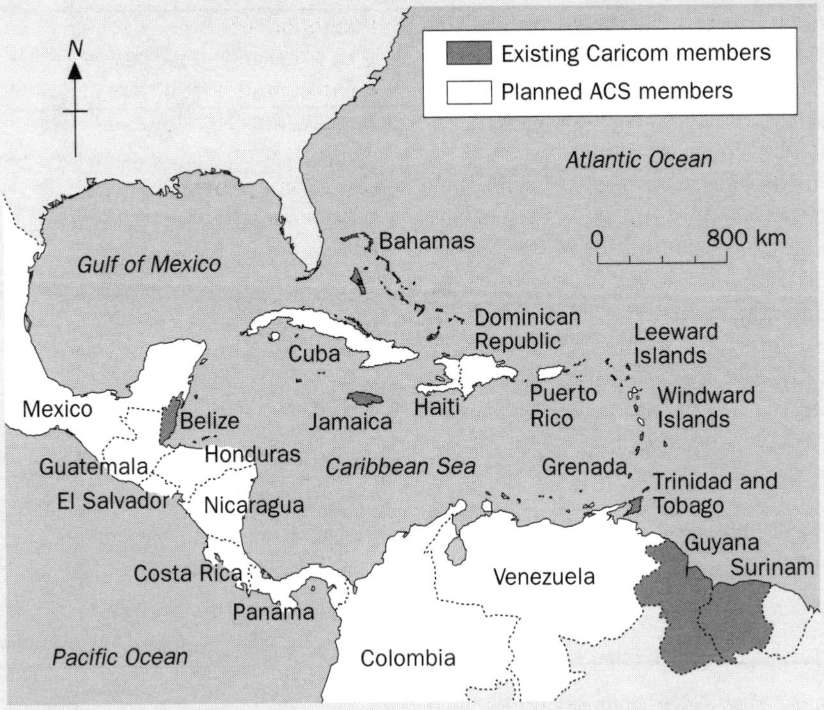

The Caribbean trading bloc

Main source of bananas entering world trade

While bananas are grown in most tropical countries with a humid climate of around 200 cm of rainfall annually and Asian countries are the leading producers, world trade is largely centred on the Caribbean region (with smaller contributions from the Philippines, West Africa and the Canary Islands).

Caribbean production is divided into two groups: dollar 'bananas' from the Central American Republics and Colombia with production controlled by the large American multinational companies and mainly grown under the large plantation system on cleared lowland areas and ACP (African Caribbean Islands and Pacific) bananas grown in former colonial areas, such as Jamaica, Belize and the Windward Islands as well as in Surinam, Cameroon and Ivory Coast.

Bananas are mainly grown on smallholdings but the marketing is through transnationals, especially the Dutch based Geest corporation.

The dollar banana countries can produce more cheaply than ACP banana areas and have the largest share of world trade but ACP areas enjoy a protected position in the European market.

Environmental impact of over-concentration – the case of Costa Rica

'The banana industry is one of the principal environmental problems in Costa Rica. It is not just an environmental problem but also its a human rights and sociological problem as well.' Costa Rica is a leading banana exporter in the Caribbean region and second in the world to Ecuador.

There has been large scale clearance of forest areas. Since the 1980s, expansion of the banana plantation area exceeded that of the declining beef ranching areas in Costa Rica. This caused ecological loss of forest area and natural wild life.

Banana growing requires large fertiliser input and is exhaustive of soil. Estates are abandoned as fertility declines. Since 1979, 90 000 ha has been abandoned along the Caribbean coast. Farmers shift production to cleared land on the Pacific coast.

Abandonment is also associated with 'booms' and slumps in the banana trade.

Intensive use of fertilisers and pesticides, including types now banned in the USA, led to some poisoning of land and water courses (irrigation trenches flushed as part of cultivation took millions of tonnes of contaminated soils into waterways, adding to chemicals escaping through the water run-off).

About 25% – 30% of Costa Rican lowland is now seriously affected. There has been a decline of fish stocks in rivers and in Caribbean coastal waters; half a million fish were found dead in July 1990 in the canal areas of the banana producing region. Also, 90% of the coral reef off Costa Rica's Caribbean coast is dead as a result of pesticide run-off and sedimentation mainly from banana plantations. The Tortuguera national park in Costa Rica also suffers from these problems.

Governments have encouraged the expansion of plantation and other cash crops and have not adopted sufficiently stringent environmental safeguards.

[redacted]

ACP production	'Dollar' production
Physical conditions	**Physical conditions**
a Hilly mountainous area in main	a Main areas on large lowland areas
b Limited land available	b Transnationals able to buy up large areas
c Greater hurricane damage e.g. Jamaica banana crop wiped out by hurricane Gilbert 1989.	c Richer alluvial soil plus methods of cultivation give 18–24 tonnes/acre
	d Less hurricane damage as outside main tracks of cyclones
Economic conditions	**Economic conditions**
a Mainly small farm production (e.g. 25 000 growers Windward Islands)	a Large plantation system most owned by American multinationals
b Family labour	b Hired labour – low wages with little union protection on conditions and rights
c Relatively low technology hand cultivation and packing	c Combined with more mechanisation in land preparation, sorting, packing, etc.
d Higher cost fertiliser input and higher shipping costs due to smaller volume handled	d Larger volume production sites lower costs

ACP Caribbean production versus 'dollar' Central America production

Environmental problems also rest with small ACP farmers. Boom times and the Geest expansion policy encouraged clearing of more hill land for cash crops, causing erosion and contamination through greater fertiliser use. Bananas have shallow root systems and do not anchor the soil well.

Economic and social effects of banana production

The economic returns to the host countries are limited. It is estimated for example, that Honduras receives only 16% of the profits from the banana trade; the rest stays overseas, mainly with transnational companies.

The narrow dependence on export crops distorts the economy of some Caribbean producers and exposes them to world price and trade fluctuations as trends in banana production and trade show. For example, St Lucia, Dominica, St Vincent's economies depend on the banana trade for their survival. St Vincent bananas account for 85% of export earnings.

Pressure and the influence of the Geest Corporation hinders diversity into other cash crops such as fruits and vegetables. The economy of the [St Vincent] archipelago is in the hands of transnationals that also control tourism, the banana plantations and financial centre.

The focus on export crops made nearly all of the Caribbean countries dependent on imports for food. An increasing percentage of basic food supplies is imported. Costa Rica has a 30% food import dependency and St Vincent, 113%.

Since much of the land is controlled by multinationals, too little land is left for the rural population especially as population growth is relatively high. These conditions contribute to poverty and migration to towns.

Governments have so far given very little support to lift the low wage levels and encourage union movement. The labour exploitation thus encourages out migration and urban flow.

CHAPTER 24

Temperate farming systems

24.1 The importance of farming and its changing basis

An importance much greater than its actual contribution to national incomes

Temperate lands are mainly made up of developed countries (Figure 24.1). Farming systems are principally commercially based though varying in scale, intensity of production and types of output. Much of the output is oriented to domestic markets since temperate countries are predominantly urbanised, but a significant proportion does enter world trade. Thus most farming is influenced by conditions within the home country and also by world demand and trade in agricultural products. Through recent years, major economic and political policy changes have taken place both at a national and international level and these in turn are bringing important changes to the structure and output of the agriculture sector in temperate countries.

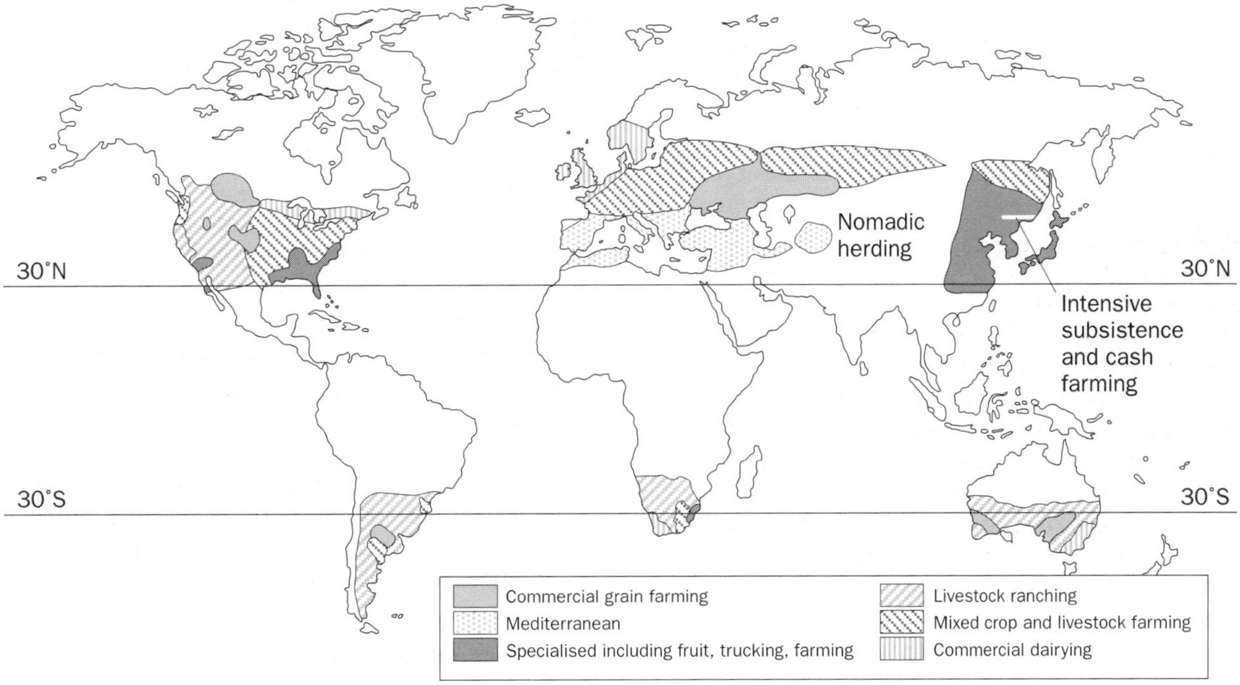

Figure 24.1 *Types of temperate farming systems*

Measured in terms of the contribution of agriculture to the national wealth of temperate countries, such changes would initially appear relatively unimportant (Figure 24.2). In all countries, even for those such as Canada, Australia and Denmark which are significant exporters of agricultural produce, agriculture contributes less than 10% to the national income. In reality the importance of agriculture is much greater than this measure indicates.

As a Percentage	Agriculture	Industry	Services
France	3	29	69
UK	2	41	57
Australia	3	29	67

[SOURCE: World Bank Development Report, 1995]

Figure 24.2 *Distribution of GDP across economic sectors*

Food is a basic necessity and the more a country can produce for itself, the greater the sense of security. Two world wars since the turn of the century which seriously threatened food supplies for most temperate countries, have intensified the feeling that a country should be as self-sufficient in food as possible even if a significant proportion could be imported more cheaply from abroad. Hence government policies towards agriculture since 1945 have been influenced by this self-sufficiency drive.

As great a self-sufficiency as possible is also seen as desirable to reduce the amount paid out on food imports and help the trade balance of payments. While temperate countries have to import those agricultural products which can only be produced under tropical conditions, concern is expressed in respect of imports of temperate agricultural products. For example in the case of the UK, the food and drink sector made up 42% of the country's trade deficit in 1993 and of this, over half were food and drink products from European countries with similar climatic conditions to the UK. Thus the general view was that 'these could just have easily have been produced in the UK.' Despite this oversimplification which ignores a range of factors such as differing costs and prices between home produced and imported products and the politics of trade, it is a view strongly held amongst the farming sector and a number of those in government.

Historically, the agricultural sector has made a much greater contribution than in recent times and many of the principal figures in governments have come from highly influential and rich farming families. While the economic contribution of agriculture to national income has declined, the strength of the farming lobby and voice in national affairs has not declined to anything like the same degree. In France, the UK and the USA, the farming lobby remains very powerful. It is also supported by the rural ties which many urban families feel and the holding of idealised positive images of the countryside and rural life.

The influence of the farming lobby is also felt within the European Union: the financial aid given to the rural sector up to the CAP reforms in 1992 was four times that given to the industrial sector, while the number of families dependent on agriculture for a living was a quarter of those dependent on industry.

Interestingly the idealised view of the countryside and rural life held by pressure groups in urban areas has recently led to a divergence from general support for agriculture. As agriculture has become increasingly intensified and industrialised with the advent of agribusinesses, large farming enterprises have been seen as a threat to the countryside and traditional farming. Powerful preservation and conservation groups have emerged to exercise a strong constraint on the expansion of agricultural production. Sympathy of such preservation groups remains only with the small farmers who are still viewed as the guardians of traditional rural life.

Thus self-sufficiency arguments, the strength of the farming lobby and growing concern for the countryside, have all combined to give agriculture a much greater prominence than economics alone would warrant.

Recent changes in the structure and organisation of agriculture

Physical conditions and technological advances

While physical conditions continue to exercise a significant influence on the distribution and limits to different kinds of farming systems, technological innovations have reduced their influence. New strains of crops which are climatically more tolerant for example, have been produced, allowing the economic margins of cultivation to be extended, as seen in the northward expansion of wheat farming in Canada. More sophisticated machinery is now available which can tackle terrain hitherto considered too steep for cultivation.

The most effective influences for change are increasingly changes in the supply and demand for agricultural products and the policy decisions made by individual governments and even more so, by trading blocs and international organisations such as GATT.

Changing market influences

Within the market place two important trends can be seen:

Rise in food demand

There is the continued rise in world demand for basic food commodities and other agricultural products. As a consequence, agricultural output has expanded to meet this demand by greater intensification to raise yields, greater specialisation, and expansion of the scale of operations to benefit from economies of scale. Generally, small and increasingly uneconomic farms have declined in numbers (Figure 24.3; Case studies 24.1 and 24.4). Those which survive have mainly done so because of government subsidies and through diversification into non-farming activities to provide alternative incomes. Agriculture is increasingly dominated by large farms and agribusinesses with a high degree of capital investment, strong business management and the latest technology.

Percentage of agricultural land for each farm size category, 1993

Farm size (ha)	Percentage
<10	2.1
10 – 19	3.3
20 – 49	12.3
50 – 99	19.8
100 – 199	24.7
200 – 300	12.7
>300	25.3

[SOURCE: Agricultural Census]

Figure 24.3 *Farm size category and agricultural land use in England*

The nature of market demand

Domestic markets within the industrialised countries are increasingly dominated by the large food processing firms and supermarket chains. These require from farmers large quantities of particular agricultural products at a consistently high quality. Over 60% of UK agricultural production is done on contract farming to food processing firms and supermarket chains. While this is most apparent in livestock, fruit and vegetable production, it is also the case for industrial crops such as oilseed rape and for part of the cereal crop output. Farmers with smallholdings find they cannot produce the output needed nor the consistent quality required.

Individual consumer demand has also changed partly due to increased affluence, taste and changed modes of living but also due to strong advertising by food firms and retail chains. The demand for basic foods has decreased in industrialised countries. There is now an increased demand for convenience and processed foods as well as for greater variety of choice including newer exotic foods. Farming has had to increasingly change to meet these changes in demand. For example, in the dairy industry demand for liquid milk has declined and the demand for yoghurt products soared. The greatly increased demand for poultry has led to a vast expansion in the broiler industry sector of agriculture.

Yet a further change in market demand is bringing important changes to the structure of farming and the nature of outputs. This is the expanding demand for industrial crops, such as oilseed rape and soya crops. For example, oilseed rape introduced into the UK only in the early 1970s, is now the third most important crop for arable farmers and has effectively changed cropping patterns and rotational systems on farms (Case study 24.1).

GATT and changing world trading conditions

The basic purpose of the Uruguay Round of discussions between countries of the world was to liberalise international trade including that in agricultural commodities (Figure 32.6). The general agreement was for a steady move towards freer trade and more equitable opportunity amongst countries. This can only be achieved by particular countries lowering prices and other financial support for their farming sectors, and lowering tariffs and the level of quota restrictions on the trade in agricultural commodities. Such moves are already having far reaching consequences for the farming sectors of temperate as well as tropical countries. Farmers are increasingly exposed to free market conditions. Thus only the most competitive will survive and each will specialise in a crop or other output for which the greatest comparative advantage is held. Under more open competition, the large specialist farmer will be generally better placed than the small farmer who cannot benefit from the advantage of scale economies.

The GATT agreement has had a marked influence on government policies and support for agriculture. It was one of the reasons making reform of the European Unions CAP policy inevitable.

The effects of the CAP reforms and UK policy

The effects of the CAP reforms and UK policies towards agriculture are further expanded in Case studies 24.1 and 24.4. The case studies examine in an interrelated way the complex factors which influence European farming.

CAP reforms have not yet substantially reduced the financial support for European agriculture but have significantly shifted support from agricultural production to direct aid to farmers. This, together with the integration of environmental protection measures, is having a major influence on the organisation of farming operations and the economics underlying them. The original CAP policy and individual government policies which guaranteed prices for selected crops and livestock operations, led farmers to go for maximum output by increasing inputs to raise yields and enlarging operations to achieve economies of scale.

The shift away from price support for particular commodities to direct aid, allied to changes in the set-aside policy and associated environmentally oriented measures, accelerated a change in farming already being brought about by falling prices over the 1980s for a range of commodities and increasing debt problems. There was a shift away from a 'maximum output' strategy to profitable farming by reducing the amounts of inputs and therefore input costs but maintaining as far as possible advantages of scale economies.

Individual governments have joined forces to delay the process of the shift away from support prices which had encouraged over-production and excessive costs for the taxpayers. Thus the shift to cost efficient farming has been delayed. For example, the EU Commissioner leading the 1992 CAP reform had pressed for a reduction of 36% in the support price for cereals, but the UK campaigned successfully for a reduction of only 26%.

The Green Pound
This is used to translate support prices set by the EU into sterling. Successive devaluation of sterling in relation to the Green pound since 1993 have in effect increased payments received by British farmers.

There are growing indications that the reforms were insufficient and another round of reforms are needed. Because of the way they have been operated and improved trading conditions and prices for a range of commodities during 1993 – 95, the reforms allied to other influences have adversely affected the small farmers most. However, larger farmers will also need to reorganise their farming operations further. In particular, they need for them to reduce the fixed capital liabilities resulting from substantial borrowing to cover their operations. Continuing reductions in direct price support mean that high fixed costs will be increasingly difficult to cover.

Environmental considerations

Environmental considerations are increasingly important. Much of the credit is given to pressure groups persuading governments and supra-national bodies to bring in legislation and controls for farmers to adopt more environmentally friendly measures but much of the change can be attributed to the changing economic situation facing the agricultural sector. For example, the introduction of set-aside regulations at present bringing 15% of arable land out of production, was mainly due to the need to cut agricultural output closer to the levels of demand and reduce the enormous financial burden on the EU budgets of storing surplus produce. Relatively generous payments have persuaded farmers to accept the environmental measures.

These difficult economic conditions and reduced price support for particular agricultural outputs have encouraged farmers to stop cultivating marginally productive lands, much of which is classed as of important scientific and ecological interests. Thus valuable ecosystems and natural habitats such as wetlands and downland grasslands have been restored.

A reduction in the application of environmentally damaging artificial fertilisers and pesticides was already beginning to occur before legislative measures and regulations were practised. Farmers, in order to remain profitable, needed to reduce input costs and fertilisers and pesticides represent an important proportion of those costs.

Thus while recognising the significance of environmental arguments, their relative importance needs to be put into perspective. What is without dispute is that environmental considerations have become an integral part of farming policies in most advanced countries (Case studies 21.2 and 21.3).

From the farming sector itself
A more realistic mood at the annual meeting of the UK's National Farmer's Union
'This new mood accepts that government does not owe farmers a living; that there is not enough cash around to guarantee such security anyway even if there was a shortage of food which there is not. It recognises that this is an age in which expectations of market forces and expanding free trade dominate political thinking. It is acutely aware that alongside this it is necessary to show that farmers care for the environment.'

[SOURCE: Richardson D extract from *Agriculture Faces Up to the Inevitability of Change*, *Financial Times* 16.2.93]

Today the current shift is towards integrated crop management which is sufficiently important to be laboured *'The Quiet Revolution'*. However it still incorporates some of the long standing tenets which underpin agriculture in the advanced industrial countries, such as ensuring national food supplies and continued support for the farming sector.

The Quiet Revolution

The EU is now accepting 'a commitment to a concept of viable agriculture that is environmentally and socially acceptable and ensures the continuity of supply of wholesome affordable food, whilst conserving and enhancing the fabric of the countryside for future generations.'

[SOURCE: *Financial Times* 11.4.95]

24.2 **Farming on the urban fringe**

One of the problems facing agriculturists in the heavily populated industrial countries is the loss of good farming land due to continued urban sprawl.

Land-use on the urban fringe is very mixed (Case study 12.1). The area around the city is an unstable shadow or fringe zone, which moves outwards as urban pressures successfully result in the incorporation of more and more land into the city. There is an intermingling of land-use, involving an irregular transition from farm to non-farm land. It is also characterised by land speculation, with land values fluctuating and ownership changing. Agricultural land also falls into disuse under urban pressures and financial speculation on its change to urban use.

Some dairying, market gardening and soft fruit growing are still done in open land, especially in those parts of the fringe further away from built up areas and where physical conditions are suitable, for example, the Central and Imperial valleys of California with proximity to San Francisco and Los Angeles. Here alluvial bottom land, a Mediterranean climate and irrigation facilities all favour intensive production for urban markets. This is also the case with the Lower Rhône valley in France just above Marseilles, a city of over one million people.

Because building land is so much more valuable than agricultural land, it is not surprising that given the continued pressure for expansion of large cities, agricultural landowners have sold out to the urban developer and speculator. However, it is less easy to appreciate why much land on the urban fringe is falling into disuse, in particular, land trapped within the urban fringe (Case study 12.1).

Types

A decline in horticulture but an expansion of 'factory farming'

Some activities usually associated with land close to an urban market have declined in importance, including market gardening and horticulture. This is due to a variety of reasons – increased fencing costs, damage to crops from trespassers and vandalism, labour problems with alternative better paid factory jobs usually being available, increased competition with cheaper fruit and vegetables brought in from elsewhere. Some of these difficulties have also led to a decline of pastoral farming on moorland areas close to industrial cities such as Manchester, Leeds and Sheffield.

However, intensive livestock production under cover and in conditions similar to factory assembly line production has increased. Factory farming is helping to meet the rising demand for meat, poultry and eggs from supermarket chains, and it makes more efficient use of sites which are expensive and costly to maintain. There is also greater security where stock can be housed behind locked doors. In addition, the latest production techniques including quality control can be applied indoors to make the most economic use of the labour which is employed and ensure the combination of steady production and high quality.

Factory farming now covers a range of activities – broiler chicken rearing, battery hen production, deep litter method of pig production, calf rearing for veal and fully automatic dairies with stall feeding all the year round. All these activities have expanded in industrialised countries. In the USA, for example, it is estimated that 200 000 diary cows are kept within the Los Angeles Metropolitan area and stall fed from feed brought in peanuts and citrus waste, while pig and poultry rearing has intensified close to London.

24.3 **Market gardening, horticulture and fruit growing: its changing character**

Market gardening, or truck farming as it is known in the USA, is concerned with the intensive cultivation of vegetables, fruit and flowers on open land. Horticulture has tended to be used as a term for even more intensive growing of these under nursery conditions, where much of the land is under greenhouse or some other protective cover, such as cloche and polythene sheeting. However, the distinction between the two terms has tended to disappear. More and more market gardeners have intensified cultivation by making use of a similar method to those in nurseries while increasingly more vegetables are being grown under open field systems on arable farms, under contracts with canning and freezing firms.

Market gardening, apart from factory farming, is probably the most intensive type of cultivation with a very high ratio of inputs to each land unit area utilised and a high value output. It has generally been noted as labour intensive, especially in the case of indoor cultivation. For example, labour represents 50% of the costs in the rapidly expanding mushroom growing industry.

In absolute terms, however, the amount of labour used has declined, partly because labour has become increasingly expensive but also because of the use of labour-saving technology, such as roto-cultivators, automatic sprinklers and harvesting machines. The whole market gardening scene has become increasingly capital intensive and this is the most outstanding feature of the industry today.

Besides labour-saving devices, there has been the introduction of other costly inputs, such as polythene and other cover to extend the growing season, oil-heating of greenhouses, and a much greater amount and variety of fertiliser and other conditioning media to improve soil conditions. There is also much more capital invested in processing, packaging and marketing the crops to provide as high and consistent a quality as possible.

Thus the character of market gardening is changing in response to a variety of influences. These include expanding markets for quick frozen produce, other technological advances, higher labour costs and increasing competition from overseas. For example, Mediterranean and tropical areas with natural environmental conditions are on the whole more favourable and offer cheaper labour .

Market gardening and fruit growing in the UK

Market gardening and fruit growing are limited to lowland regions predominantly in the southern half of the country (Case study 24.3). Growing areas are fairly close to coasts and estuaries, allowing oceanic influences to moderate climatic conditions. Despite increasing artificial ways of protecting crops from adverse weather and extending the growing seasons, climatic influences remain very important. The mild winters and early springs, together with reliable rainfall experienced in areas such as Cornwall and the Vale of Evesham are still significant. So too are terrain, drainage and soil conditions. This is illustrated from the presence of fruit growing on lower slopes to avoid the frost pockets which occur in valley bottoms in late spring; also, intensive market gardening on the rich peat fens around the Wash is an example. Physical conditions remain important because every effort to create artificial conditions is costly; there is therefore a limit to how much can be done if the grower is not to price himself out of the market.

Market access also remains important, but speedier and improved methods of transport together with quick freezing have allowed a greater dispersion of market gardening and fruit production away from traditional areas, such as those on the south coast and in Somerset. A more dispersed distribution is also due to the trend for some vegetables, such as peas, early carrots, brassicas and runner beans, to be grown as field crops e.g. in East Anglia. Here various companies offer growing contracts to farmers, together with an assured price for the product which is then quick frozen or canned by the companies. Frequently the freezing and canning plants are located on the coast so that fish products may be similarly processed, again making for economies of scale. Expansion has also been greatly expanded due to increased demand for frozen products with most households now having a deep freeze as well as a fridge.

Despite these dispersion trends, certain concentrations of market gardening persist, even though technological developments have reduced some of the advantages these locations initially enjoyed. For example, there is rhubarb growing in the Leeds area, raspberry growing in the Dundee area, cherry orchards and hops in Kent and cider orchards in Herefordshire. Such regions have gained a reputation for a particular type of produce, have accumulated experience and expertise and have invested capital in buildings, equipment and marketing outlets – all favouring the continuation of each particular speciality in the established area. In some cases some form of co-operative organisation has also been built up to keep costs competitive. For example, the Nursery Trades Ltd (Lee Valley) was initially set up to serve growers in the Lee Valley but now has members as far afield as Oxford and Suffolk.

However, at the present time UK growers are suffering severe competition. Regions such as the Canary Islands (tomatoes), Southern France (early vegetables) and even Kenya (orchids), which enjoy more favourable and reliable weather conditions as well as cheaper labour costs, are now being offered cheaper freight rates to market their produce through shops and supermarket chains in this country. French and Dutch growers are also being more heavily subsidised by government grants and price support arrangements than growers in this country. For example, Dutch glasshouse growers have lower heating costs than their opposite numbers in the Vale of Evesham and on the south coast.

In 1989 the British Government introduced a Horticulture Buildings and Replanting Grant Scheme to help existing producers but take-up has been small. Growers feel that the government should address the more central problems of the influx of produce from other EU and overseas countries and give more assistance in marketing home-grown produce.

Recent changes affecting EU growers as a whole

One of these is the increasing demand for a higher and more uniform quality of output. This is particularly being imposed by the large multiple retail chains which now take over 50% of market garden produce. Emphasis is on taste, freshness, strictly graded size and biologically approved growing conditions. EU regulations reinforce these quality controls. In Holland there has been a 90% reduction in chemical inputs since 1990 and an emphasis on natural insect predators to control crop pests.

Better quantity and quality control is driving out smaller producers and favouring large co-operative enterprises most of which import some produce from overseas during the out-of-season period to maintain a contract flow to retail multiple chains.

For example, Hassy Carrot Growers was set up in 1988 at Whitehall Farm in the Cambridgeshire fens by eight co-operative groups to grade, pack and market carrots under contract to supermarket chains. Hassy Carrot Growers guarantee a 'soil to supermarket' supply within 24 hours and have an annual output of 25 000 tonnes a year, including some imported produce.

Outdoor acreages have fallen in less favourable areas. For example, in Kent apple growing areas on higher, less fertile ground liable to frosts are being 'grubbed up'.

The other important influence has been changes in demand for certain produce and demand for new kinds of produce. For example, demand for tomatoes and cucumbers has declined while demand for peppers, aubergines and asparagus have expanded. In the Netherlands the production of tomatoes fell from 605 million tonnes to 499 million tonnes between 1990 – 94, while the production of peppers increased from 143 to 228 million tonnes over the same period.

The harder times resulting from increased competition and more discerning consumer demand are further intensified by overproduction in the EU, producing a glut of some produce such as tomatoes, apples and soft fruits at the height of the season. Consequently prices fall markedly. Thus, the area under intensive market gardening and fruit orchards is steadily being reduced.

Truck farming and fruit growing in Mediterranean and sub-tropical areas

In continental size countries such as the USA and Australia, sheer distance to market becomes an important cost factor. To some extent this is offset by improved methods of transport and technological developments, such as refrigeration and more favourable climatic conditions enjoyed by Mediterranean and sub-tropical areas compared with those in the UK and other areas of Western Europe. Major fruit and truck farming regions in warm temperate to sub-tropical latitudes enjoy a constantly warm and sunny climate and have irrigation facilities to ensure water through the growing season as, for example, Florida and California and the Murray-Murrumbidgee valley of South Australia.

24.4 Dairying: an intensive form of pastoral farming

In this type of farming the main activity is the production of liquid milk either to be sold as such in urban markets or processed for sale as cream, butter, cheese, yoghurt and dried milk products. The proportion of liquid milk sales has fallen in recent years while that of processed milk products has risen significantly (Figure 24.2).

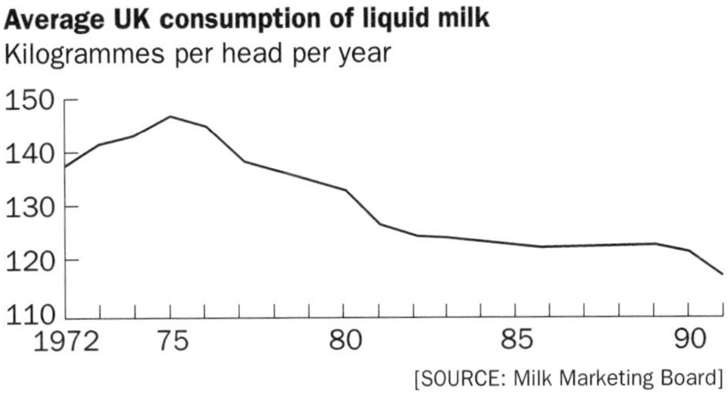

Figure 24.4 Falling milk consumption, 1972 – 92

Like market gardening, dairying is usually regarded as intensive in nature, there being a high ratio of inputs (capital, labour, fertiliser, etc.) to each unit area farmed and an emphasis on obtaining maximum yield per head of dairy cattle kept. As with market gardening, the degree of intensity varies – from a factory-type system in which dairy cattle are stall-fed all the year round (as in large cities such as Los Angeles), to an all-the-year-round open grazing system in regions such as North Island, New Zealand, where holdings reach an average size of 250 hectares (Case study 24.2).

The locational pattern is somewhat similar to market gardening being influenced to an important extent by similar conditions. Liquid milk production, like fresh vegetables and fruit, needs to be within easy reach of large urban markets either immediately in the vicinity of urban centres or a few hours away. Greater London receives its liquid milk from as far away as the West Country as well as from nearer areas such as North Essex.

Where dairying takes place beyond daily freight distance of markets, liquid milk has to be processed into some form that will keep, be in market demand and stand the cost of transport. For Western European markets, regions include nearer countries such as Denmark, the Netherlands and Switzerland (supplying the large population of industrial regions) and distant ones, such as New Zealand and South East Australia, which may be as much as 30 days in shipping distance from West European markets. Yet refrigeration and other technical developments still allow them a share in this market.

Dairy production has been increasingly influenced by government policies and the extent of financial support offered. Dairying has enjoyed strong support in the case of EU countries and main exporters, such as New Zealand (Case study 24.2). However, since the late 1980s there has been a major shift away from protective and financial support and increased exposure to world market forces. While undoubtedly accelerated by the recent GATT world trading agreement, reduced support was already in evidence because governments were finding it too expensive.

Under the EU's CAP reforms, dairy producers are still subject to quotas, price support has decreased and protection from overseas imports is gradually declining. Within the UK the most radical step has been the abolition of the government's Milk Marketing Board which for over 60 years has controlled prices paid to dairy farmers and the collection and marketing of milk. This has been replaced by Milk Marque, a co-operative venture, which it was hoped 80% of dairy farmers would join. Since its start of operations in 1994 far fewer have joined, since they are now free to alternatively contract their milk sales to other milk processing companies, such as the multinational corporations of Nestlé and Unigate.

While free to seek the highest prices, the abolition of the Milk Marketing Board does also mean more exposure to market forces and greater uncertainty. There is already evidence that small and less efficient dairy farmers are selling their quota allowance to larger dairy farming units and abandoning dairying altogether.

Dairying in New Zealand

New Zealand is one of the world's most important dairying countries with 80% of its production concentrated on North Island (Case study 24.2). Its pre-eminence stems from the last part of the nineteenth century when refrigeration in 1882 and faster steamships brought the UK and other West European markets in its reach. Very favourable physical conditions, efficient production methods, together with strict government controls and support enable producers in this region to still maintain an important share of these traditional markets as well as penetrating new ones such as Japan, where increased affluence and changing tastes have created a rapidly expanding market for dairy produce.

The recent experiences of the New Zealand producers demonstrate both the difficulties now facing agricultural producers and the need to be able to respond quickly to the marked changes in trading conditions which are becoming characteristic of the 1990s. At the heart of these are changes in internal government agricultural policy and the world market place.

A reduction in government intervention and financial support

Up to the early 1960s government support for the New Zealand dairy industry was limited to research, free advisory services and marketing through the Dairy Board. Since 1963 the government introduced a policy of giving subsidies to raise agricultural exports in the face of increased competition in overseas markets from the European Union and the USA. It was also vital to increase exports to offset increasing balance of payments problems.

In 1984 the Labour government abandoned the protectionist and interventionist policy in favour of allowing market forces to shape the agricultural sector. The dairying industry thus went through a painful adjustment having to cut farm input costs and co-operatives increase the efficiency of their dairy processing plants.

In 1988 the Dairy Board also withdrew from its pricing control, bringing government support approximately back to its pre-1960s level, that is, to a continued but improved research and advisory service and strong advertising support for overseas sales.

World market conditions

Since over 90% of dairy produce is exported and it makes up 20% of the value of New Zealand's exports by value, any changes in world trading conditions are important. The most significant has been the greater liberalisation in world trade brought in by the 1993 GATT agreement. This has been welcomed by New Zealand producers since it will not only mean lower tariff and barrier quotas set up by the EU and other countries, but will prevent what it regarded as the unfair dumping of subsidised surplus dairy products on world markets by its main competitors, the EU countries and the USA.

The other important market changes have been shifts in the nature and amount of demand away from CIS countries to Latin America, for example

(Figure 24.5). There has been some expansion of demand for butter and cheese with Britain still the main market for the former, but the greatest increase in demand has been for casein, other specialised milk protein products and in milk powder products, the latter particularly to growing markets in South East Asia and Latin America. While Europe remains an important market, the emphasis seems to be swinging to the emergent markets in developing countries.

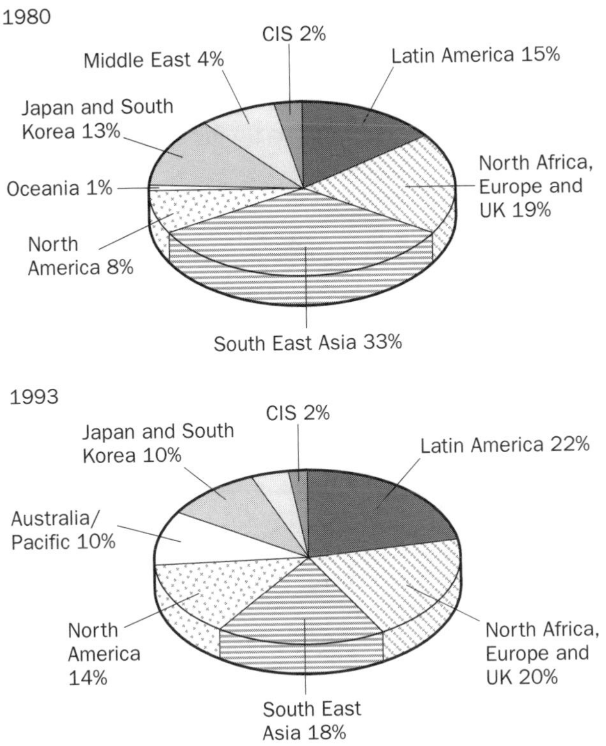

Year ended 31 March
New Zealand Dairy Board rules
CIS = Commonwealth of Independent States

Report of Chairman New Zealand Dairy Board 1995
'*Looking at the global scene it is hard to recall a time more propitious for the New Zealand Dairy Industry*' ... He warned of the damaging effects to European agriculture of the CAP price support system. Outside Europe he noted countries were following New Zealand's deregulatory lead ... '*We can expect to see declining exports from Europe, balanced by increases in export production in New Zealand, Australia and within three to five years, the United States.*'

Figure 24.5 *Destination of New Zealand dairy production exports by world region 1980 and 1993*

Over the last two years the dairy industry in New Zealand has prospered (Figure 24.6). With relatively low costs, excellent organisation through its co-operative systems, perhaps the most advanced research and advisory support and now a stable low inflation economy in New Zealand, the dairy industry is well placed to increase its world market share.

Milk production and utilisation for New Zealand 1987 – 93

Product	**1989–90**	**1992–93**
	million litres	
Production		
Total milk production	7 302	8 050
Utilisation		
Milk sent to dairy factories	7 868	7 629

*New series, includes milk sold for processing only.
[SOURCE: New Zealand Dairy Board]
NOTE: There are presently 16 co-operative dairy companies, which operate around 40 dairy factories for the production of manufactured dairy products.

Figure 24.6 *Changes in milk and dairy factory production, New Zealand, 1987 – 93*

24.5 **Commercial cereal farming – wheat**

Wheat is the dominant cereal in temperate lands and is also found in drier areas of Monsoon Asia, such as Pakistan. Although generally associated with the interior steppe and prairie lands, wheat is grown under a variety of physical conditions and under both intensive and extensive systems. For example in East Anglia it is produced as part of a mixed arable system on farms averaging around 600 hectares in size, whereas in the drier Soviet steppelands of Kazakhstan it was commonly grown under monoculture on state farms averaging 27 000 hectares in size.

One of the reasons why wheat is found under a variety of conditions is the widespread demand for it as a staple food. Another is the many kinds of wheat available, each tolerating differing environmental conditions. The two broad types are winter wheat and spring wheat. Winter-sown wheat is favoured where conditions are milder but spring-sown wheat has to be grown where winters are severe. Winter wheat is lower in gluten content than spring wheat and therefore the flour made from it is softer. The gluten content of winter wheat makes it ideal for bread. It is the spring wheat grown in the surplus-producing interior continental regions of the old world which enters most into world trade.

With the GATT world trade agreement and moves by governments to reduce financial support for wheat growers, competition between the main deporting countries such the EU countries, USA, Canada, Australia and Argentina will significantly increase.

Currently the demand for wheat is expanding and world prices for different wheats have risen in 1994 and 1995. However, wheat yields are levelling off and there is some concern about a world short-fall in relation to predicted demand. Present levelling out of yields contrasts with dramatic increase in yields since the 1960s, which were largely brought about by increasing application of chemical fertilisers and sowing of new higher yielding strains of wheat (Figure 24.7). The increase in yield for every tonne of fertiliser supplied has steadily diminished since the late 1980s, making further intensification through increasing inputs less profitable. There is also the environmental argument against increased chemical fertiliser and herbicide inputs.

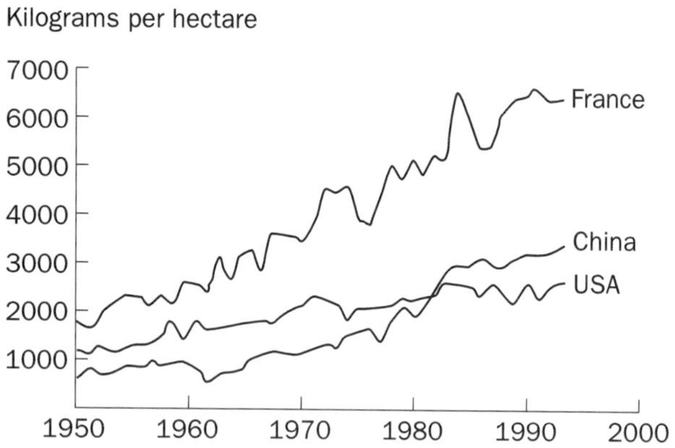

[SOURCE: USDA]

Figure 24.7 Change in wheat yields

	(000 tonnes) 1993
CIS (formerly Soviet Union)	59 823*
China	105 005
USA	65 374
India	56 762
France	29 324
Canada	27 825

[SOURCE: based on *Philip's Geographical Digest* 1996 – 97]
(* Figure based on reported output for main CIS states, Russia's share of 42 480 is a reliable figure but output figures from other states are at best estimates – the total output is likely to be higher but less than the 1990 figure)

Figure 24.8 World wheat production, 1990

An increase in world output is likely to come from diverting land from other uses to wheat growing. In the developed world there is considerable pressure from the EU and wheat growers for governments to reduce the proportion of land which has had to be taken out of production, so that some of this can be used to increase wheat output. It is a demand supported by livestock producers since wheat is an important part of livestock feed. Increased output might result in lower market prices which would also benefit countries which import wheat, such as former Russia, the world's leading wheat producing country (Figure 24.8).

Russia and the CIS remain the world's wheat producing region

While being the most important growing region, Russia has not been a major exporter; most of what is produced is consumed at home. Since the break up of the Soviet Union and following droughts in the southern marginal areas of the wheat belt, Russia had to import some wheat to feed its population.

A broad geographical division can be made between wheat growing lands in the west where winter wheat is grown with little surplus for other regions; and lands to the east of the Volga River, mainly in Siberia (Figure 24.9), where spring wheat is grown under more extensive conditions and mainly for shipment back to the heavily populated industrial areas in the west.

Wheat growing areas coincide with the wooded steppelands and the Steppes proper, where an undulating terrain of well-drained, loamy chernozem soil favours cereal growing under mechanisation. These regions also provide the necessary climatic conditions. Wheat requires an average of 100 growing days to mature but further north in the continental interior where summer days are longer, a fast maturing variety requiring as little as 60 days can be sown. The most favourable climate is in the west as temperatures are higher, the growing season longer and precipitation more reliable (though falling off rapidly southward towards the Black Sea).

Wheat requires an effective rainfall of between 380 – 760 mm including moist conditions for its germination and early growth, some precipitation to swell the wheat ears during the ripening period but a dry harvesting spell. Increasingly to the east these conditions are not met. The severe winters restrict production to spring-grown wheat. Severe frost to the north limits growth in that direction and in the south and eastward, rainfall is less reliable both in amount and incidence.

Wheat growing has been much longer established in western areas such as the Ukraine than in the east and the land is used more intensively. Most wheat is still grown on large collective farms averaging around 6000 hectares and worked by 400 or so families. A greater range of crops is grown than further east and farm units are more diversified with pigs and cattle integrated into the farm system.

Diversification was partly a response to deteriorating soil conditions arising from too much monoculture, but increasingly it was partly due to a more varied demand for food and other agricultural products as urbanisation and industrialisation increased, as for example in the Ukraine and Moscow regions.

In the west, nearly all the wheat output is marketed in the producing areas until recently via the state-run marketing system but now increasingly commercially. To the east of the Volga, conditions are markedly different with farming becoming increasingly extensive the further east one goes. Kazakhstan and West Siberia are now the great surplus-producing regions upon which the industrialised regions are vitally dependent. These regions have only been opened up under State Plans since 1954 – 61, when the rising population and declining yields further west required a rapid increase in food output.

As a result, the state initiated the 'virgin and idle lands campaign' to open up the fertile steppelands of Siberia. Several thousands of volunteers from European Russia and other regions to the west were encouraged by the state to settle in these frontier regions to the east. The regions were divided up into huge state farms averaging 27 000 hectares and supporting 4000 people. These were highly mechanised and state-financed with workers being paid wages on piece rates. Output per worker is high but yields per unit area much lower than further west or on wheat growing areas of Western Europe. Initially, despite the unreliability of climatic conditions, the rich virgin soil helped make wheat growing a success.

However, increasing problems have emerged, including increasing fertilisers and other inputs to offset deteriorating soil conditions. Recently determined efforts have been made to move away from the near monoculture characteristic of much of the main wheat belt of the Kazakhstan and West Siberia, to more diversified systems including better crop rotation and more attention to livestock production.

Despite variations caused by adverse weather conditions, output in Russia and the other CIS states has remained generally static since the break up of the Soviet Union. Until economic reforms are completed there is little hope for an expansion of output despite the pressure of demand in the country.

24.6 **Marginal farming**

Marginal farming tends to be discussed both in economic and physical terms.

Economic margins of farming

For Von Thunen, marginal farming occurred on the outer periphery of the city state where, whatever the method of farming adopted, the farmer had difficulty in covering his costs and making a living. Many problems were associated with the distance from the central market. Despite the farmer's efforts to compensate for increased transport costs by cutting down on other costs and farming extensively, there came a point where farming was no longer viable. Beyond this point the land was

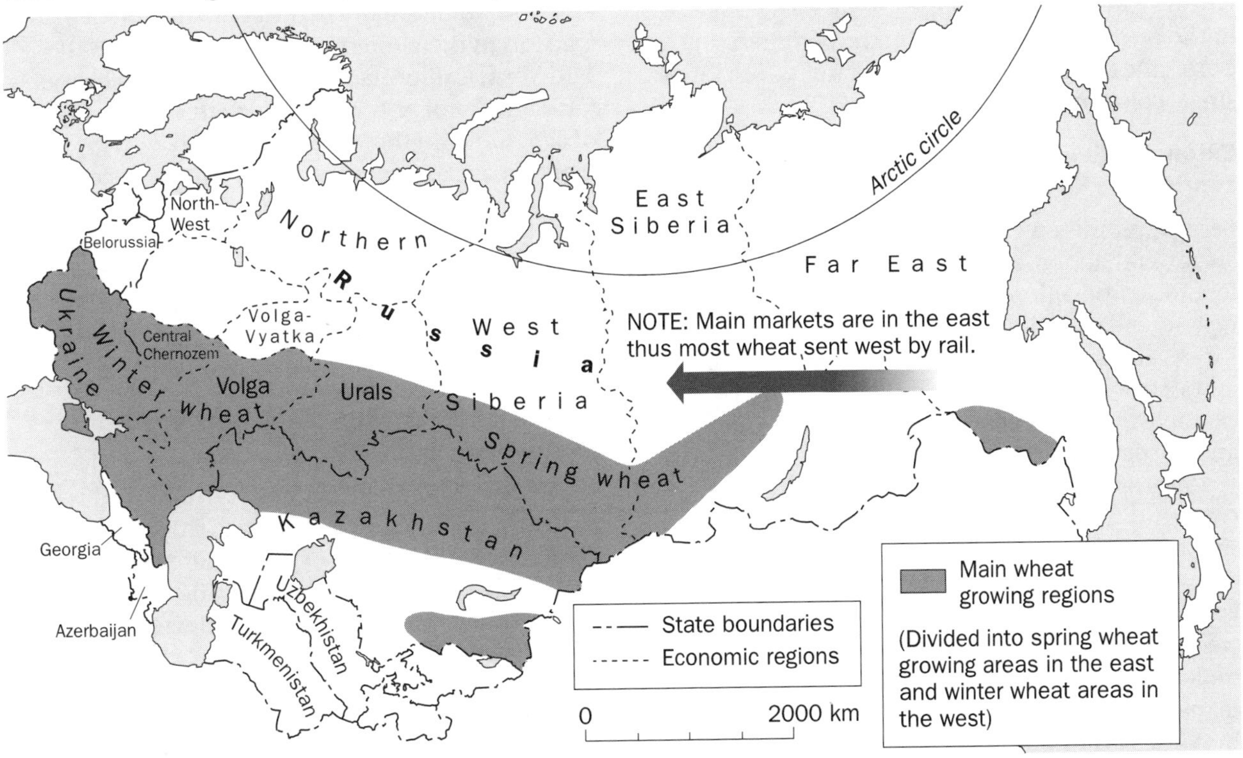

Figure 24.9 Main wheat growing belt of Russia and other states in the Commonwealth of Independent States (CIS)

not worth farming (Chapter 22). Today, isolation from market remains an important factor in deciding the marginality or otherwise of farming.

Apart from the ultimate margin beyond which no kind of farming will occur, there are also economic margins to each kind of farming system. Thereafter it will be replaced by another kind from which profits can be made. These and the outermost margin are not fixed, but change in response to changes in the circumstances controlling them.

Falling transport costs for example will clearly allow the outer economic margin of farming to be pushed even further out, with more land being taken in for farming, and each zone of farming being pushed outwards. A subsidy on some costs will have a similar effect. Rising revenue due to an increased demand and rising prices, would also encourage farmers to move out to the margin and take in more land. This was the case with wheat farming in South Australia in 1880 – 1920. The opposite will occur if costs rise or prices fall.

Physical margins to farming

As demand for agricultural products increased so there was the temptation to push agriculture into regions with harsh physical conditions of one sort or another. Remoteness combined to make the costs of farming high and return on investment in time, labour and money, uncertain. Every continent has its physical margins for farming as in the case of wheat growing on the steppes of the USSR, but also in the tropical regions. Here on the periphery, economic margins and physical margins fuse into a single concept of marginality.

Extensive livestock production in the continental interior

Because returns on extensive livestock production are lower than those from cereal growing, extensive livestock production has been forced into marginal regions where the rainfall is too low and unreliable for cereal growing. These are the semi-arid grasslands and steppe scrubland of the continental interiors, for example the High Plains of western North America and the drier pampas region of South America.

Uncertain physical conditions, relatively poor communication links to markets, yet an abundant supply of land dictate that the only profitable way to manage livestock ranching is along extensive lines. For example, sheep ranches which concentrate on wool production are commonly 50 000 hectares to a million hectares in size with the latter running as many as 100 000 sheep, at around one head per 10 hectares. Beef cattle ranges may extend from 6000 to 20 000 sq km. In the driest areas, such as the Basin Ranges of western USA, there may be only one head of cattle for every 40 hectares. Returns per unit area are therefore low and in order for an enterprise to be profitable it has to be very large. Generally, the larger the better, with the limit decided by the area which can be effectively controlled under one management.

Labour and capital inputs per unit area are very low once the initial capital investment in fencing, water supplies and buildings has been made. Because quite a lot of the uncertainties have now been taken out of livestock ranching these large enterprises are guaranteed a profit but in the earlier years climatic hazards, such as drought or an over severe winter, frequently meant bankruptcy, as for example during the 1930s, the Dustbowl era.

Beef and wool production are not limited to extensive pastoral systems. Today, more of both is produced on mixed farming systems in areas of more reliable rainfall and milder climatic conditions, for example beef fattening in the USA, south and Mid-West and wool production in New Zealand. Because of this increasing competition and an extension of irrigation and water supply schemes, the simple regional patterns of extensive livestock production have been changing since the 1950s. This can be illustrated from beef cattle fattening and rearing in the USA.

Before the 1950s the most common situation was for cattle to be reared on the drier ranges of the Western Plains and taken east to the Corn Belt for fattening. Today many of the cattle are fattened on feed lots in the Western Plains itself or sent to the Mid-West, California and the south. This is because fattening is not only associated with a diversification of agriculture in these regions but also with growing markets, as California and the south have become increasingly industrialised and have higher shares of the country's population.

The nature of the livestock industry and the conditions underlying it is further illustrated in Case study 24.5, Texas, one of the chief cattle regions of the USA.

Marginal hill farming – an extensive form of pastoralism in the UK

About one third of Britain's agricultural land is in fact suitable only for hill farming. This is land defined by the Ministry of Agriculture as of such a nature as to be only fit for the rearing of livestock and not their fattening. The official size of holdings gives little indication of the amount of land actually needed to support the number of sheep necessary to make an upland farm viable, for the size given usually takes into account only the enclosed land, which may be anything from 24 hectares up to

1000 hectares if it is run by an estate company. In addition, large areas of open moorland are used for summer grazing. The enclosed land is mainly used for permanent pasture on which to winter the stock and grow summer grass for silage. Because of the increasing costs of labour, little of the lower land is now used for winter feed crop growing such as kale, turnips and oats, as was formerly the case.

At the present time, these hill farms account for half of Britain's sheep population as well as a significant number of its beef and dairy cattle. (The monthly milk cheque is one of the few sources of regular income which many of the small hill farmers have.) Their direct contribution to British farming is small, by value only about 7%.

Hill farming remains important for two basic reasons: it is still considered the most valuable way of using the upland margins of Britain, providing not only a vital income to isolated rural settlements but also helping to maintain the social viability of the communities at a time when depopulation of highland fringes threatens their existence. Secondly, upland farms are the main suppliers of sheep for fattening on lowland farms and provide some of the young cattle stock. They therefore make an important contribution to the success of the mixed farming system on neighbouring lowland areas, such as those in the West Midlands and Central Scotland.

However, because of problems, the number of hill farms is declining (Case study 24.4). There are more part-time farmers making up their income in a variety of ways. For example, it is estimated that about one third of Lake District farms offer tourist facilities, such as bed and breakfast and camping or caravan sites. Many hill farmers and others in the household take on outside jobs, either seasonally or through the year in such things as forestry and hotel work because the farm alone cannot provide a living.

Efforts have been made to improve the lot of hill farming. Ever since the Hill Farming Act of 1945, grants and subsidies have been available under which buildings and land have been improved, and price supports given. This has been continued under the auspices of the EU through the European Fund for Regional Development.

Although hill farming is regarded in Brussels as a special case, requiring extra support if it is to be viable, the amount of support is being reduced both by the EU and the government. Following cuts in 1992, hill farmers received an annual premium of £18.75 per sheep from Brussels but the British government also cut its Hill Livestock Compensatory Payment per sheep from £8.75 to £6.50. It is thought that such cuts will halve profit margins for hill farmers despite some improvements in livestock market prices in the last two years. Most hope is seen through such measures as amalgamation of uneconomic holdings, improvement of moorland by drainage schemes, reseeding of permanent pastures, closer co-operation in the use of machinery and in marketing and an improved advisory and insurance service to avoid heavy financial loss during very hard winters.

It would seem that in the future here and elsewhere in Western Europe – such as the Alps and the South of Italy, where the nature of hill farming is different – the trend is likely to be one of decline.

Concluding comment

A panel organised by the UK Minister for Agriculture made the core recommendation that Europe's farmers must compete globally. They should be paid the world market price for the food they grow, without price guarantees. If followed, it would lead to a continued fall in the number of people working on the land and the amalgamation of small- and medium-sized holdings.

Support for the poor, more remote rural regions heavily dependent on agriculture should continue but in the form of help for new non-farming employment or direct income support.

By the end of the twentieth century, due to a subsidy driven revolution in agriculture, 20% of farm land may not be needed for food production and a small but growing number of farmers are being paid to be conservers and restorers of landscape rather than growers of crops and producers of meat.

case study

24.1 CAP reforms and exposure to more competition

Mr Swift – 39-ha. mixed farm with cereals and vegetables, Lancashire Plain
Most of Mr Swift's crops do not qualify for CAP support. '*I'm not ashamed to say I have been living on charity for the last six months.*' He has only stayed in business because of a sympathetic bank manager and relies on the part-time help of friends and hired machinery to cultivate and harvest his crops. '*I'm not really making a living just paying the bills.*' He is having to look for other part-time employment.

Mr Bedlam – a 1423-ha. cereal holding in lowland Gloucestershire
Mr Bedlam has one of the most profitable holdings at £491 per ha. He is enlarging his holding to 3000 ha. to gain more economies of scale and is diversifying, for example, to grow rape for a planned bio-diesel plant and selling straw to the new South East Electric 20MW electricity generating plant which runs on burnt straw. He is also enlarging his grain drying unit to contract dry grain for neighbouring farmers.

Mr D Lloyd – a small mixed livestock farm, Wales
Mr Lloyd, having to look for alternative income, has accepted government grants to help develop holiday cottages on his farm.

Mr T Kallahoe – 300 ha. near Copenhagen, Denmark
Mr Kallahoe is adding 200 ha. to his holding, has diversified by renting out some land for hunting and is growing Christmas trees on 182 ha.

Mr McCarthy – Country Kildare, Ireland
Mr McCarthy has low profits on his 200-ha. holding of £150 a hectare (compared to the cereal large farm of Mr Bedlam in lowland England with £491 profit per ha.), due to high costs and difficult weather conditions. He has accepted the early retirement pension offer to over 55 years of age farmers under the CAP reforms.

Mr A Peck – 400 ha. in Cambridgeshire, part of the 'grain belt'
In 1993 Mr Peck raised profits by 23% because of continued if reduced CAP support, cuts softened by the devaluation of the 'Green pound' which effectively increased sterling cereal prices. He also paid £13 500 for 60 ha. in the set-aside scheme. Under the British government March budget he received 40% tax allowance on new farm equipment. The prevailing low interest rates reduced borrowing costs but he is looking to reduce input costs to be able to compete effectively.

R J Earl – pig farmer, Kent
Mr Earl is selling pigs at 90p per kilogram but it costs him £1 a kilogram to rear them. Pork prices receive no CAP support. '*We are tightening our belts but cannot go on in this situation for long.*'

Mr F Ringo – 150 ha. in Northern France lowland area
Mr Ringo has reduced agro-chemical inputs from £319 ha. to £187 with no significant loss of yield. He is growing bio-fuel crops on his set-aside land as well as rape for the diesel petrol additive. Some of his wheat and sugar beet is sold on contract to an ethanol producing plant.

CAP reforms have not aided struggling small farmers as much as was intended.

Larger farmers are cutting costs, enlarging holdings and diversifying.

[SOURCE: based on extracts from *Financial Times* farming reports 29.11.93 and 17.7.94]

case study

24.2 New Zealand: dairy farming

Characteristics and farm organisation

- Cattle graze out all year
- Rotational grazing using mobile electric fencing
- Paddocks – heavy fertiliser input and pest sprayed. Two resown each year with rye grass
- Other cropping – one fifth of paddocks shut off for hay and silage; Kale and soft turnips winter strip grazed. barley for pig feed
- Livestock – 90 Jersey herd – 50 000 gallon annual output sent to Rongotea butter plant. Return skim milk for intensive veal calf fattening together with 200 pork bacon pig fattening unit
- Family farm of 150 ha subdivided into paddocks each with piped water

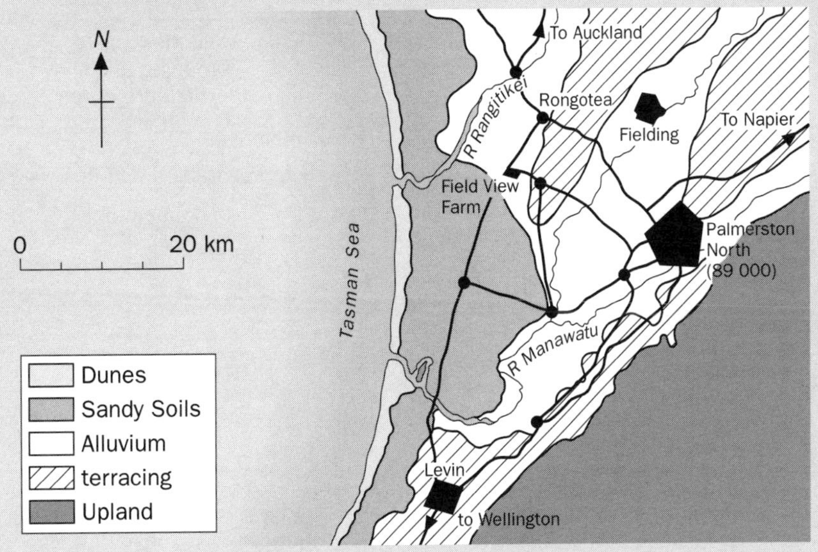

Location of Field View Farm, Manawatu area

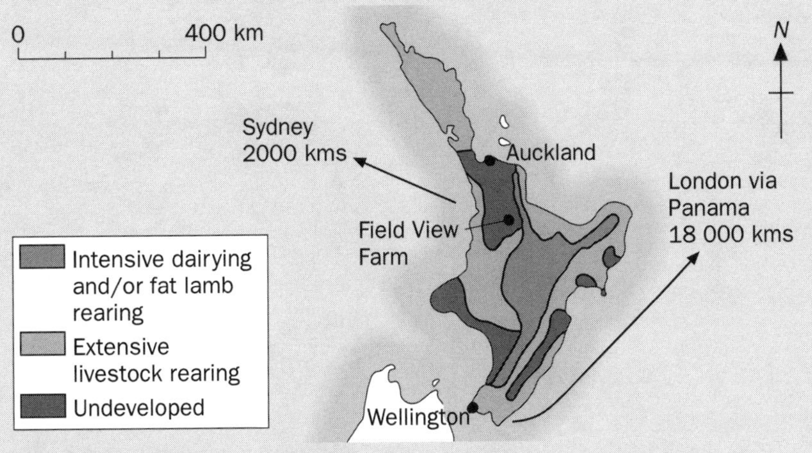

Types of farming in North Island

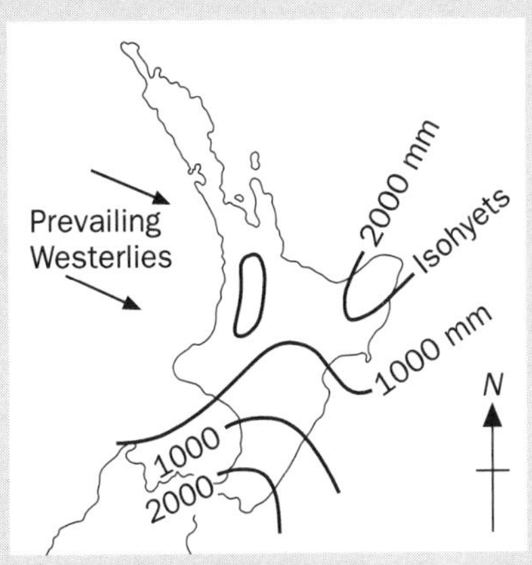

Climate of North Island

Factors affecting the farming system

Human and economic inputs

- Investment and expertise of family unit
- Processing and marketing organisation – Manawatu Dairy Co-operative – giving economies of scale advantages and competitive strength. Butter, cheese, dried milk – mainly for export via Wellington. Over 90% of New Zealand dairy produce is exported.
- Dependent on export markets – EU restrictions led to greater dependence on other markets e.g. Japan, USA, though UK still significant. With government financial support taken away now open to world competition but since 1990 to 1994 dairy exports risen 60% by value.
- Government and research support – Local – Palmerston University, Artificial Insemination Centre. National – Herd Improvement Society, Dairy Research Institute. Price and quality control – via Government's Dairy Products Prices Authority and Dairy Production and Marketing Board. Since 1984 government subsidy support declined and Dairy Board no longer controls prices.

Physical inputs

- Undulating terrain with gravel alluvial soils suitable for pasture
- Climate – prevailing westerlies bring well distributed rainfall all the year
- Mild winters and warm summers also help to ensure good outdoor grazing throughout the year

case study

24.3 Market gardening

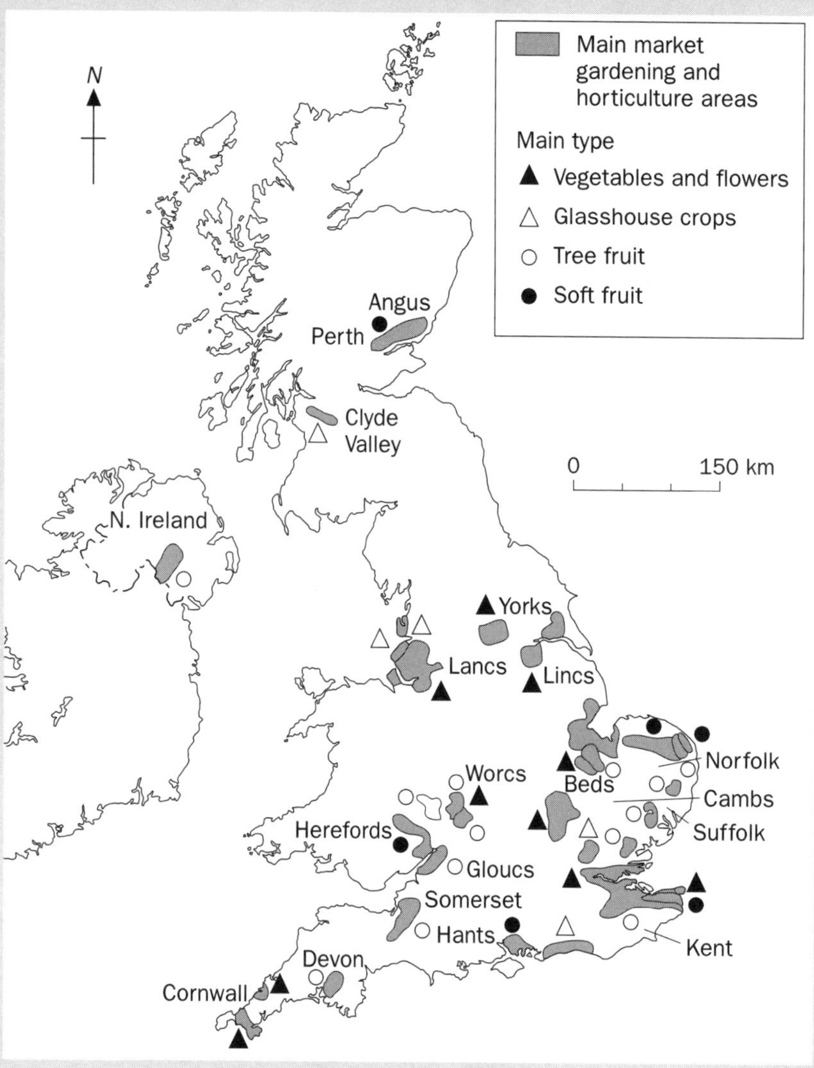

Distribution of market gardening and horticulture

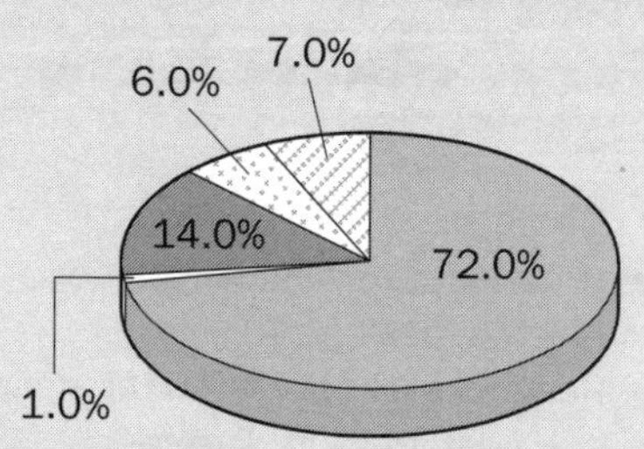

a Percentage of area

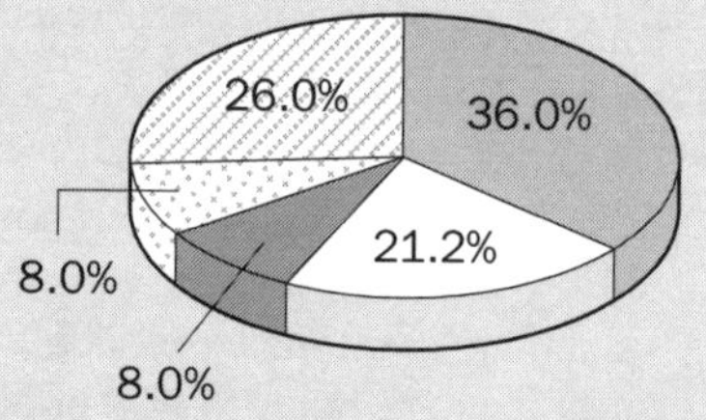

b Percentages of value

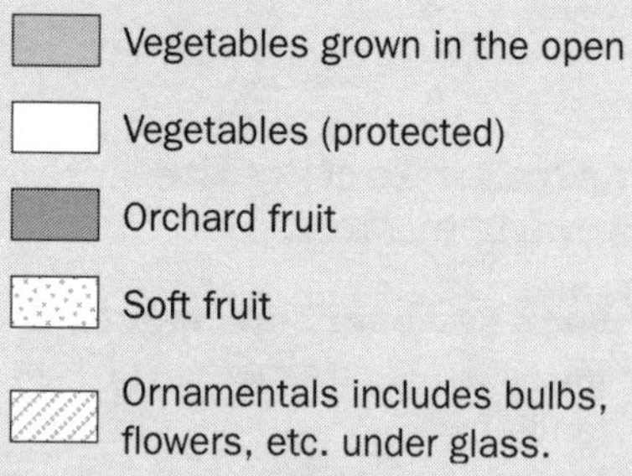

Percentage amongst different types of market garden and horticultural produce based on agricultural census, 1988

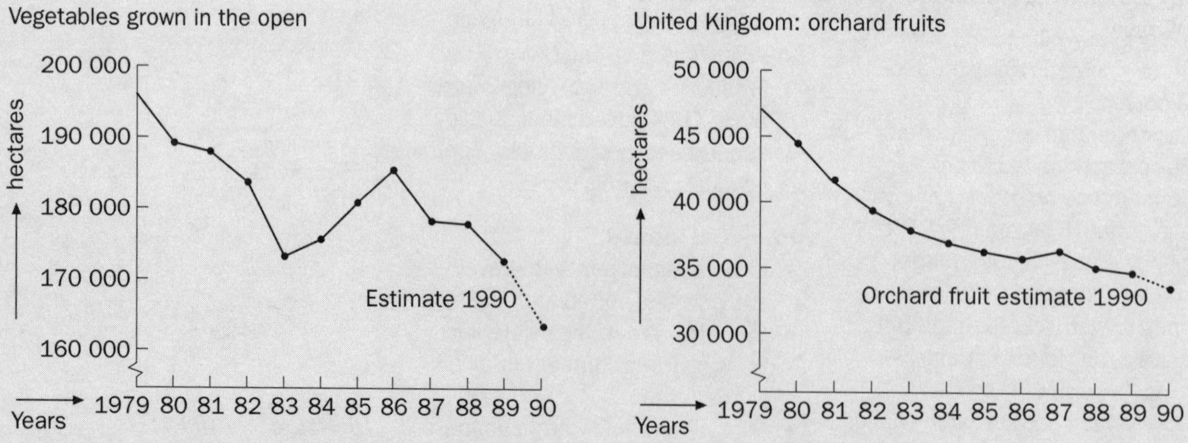

Fall in field crop areas, 1980 – 90

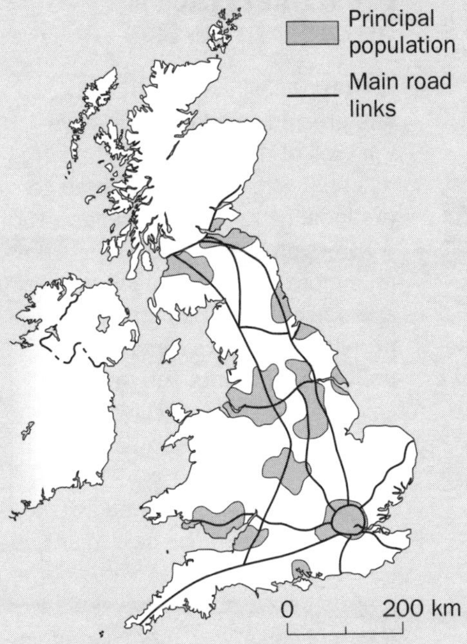

Principal population concentrations and some main road links

Human and economic factors

Historical accumulation of expertise and investment for specialist crops

Extent of government support

Growing and marketing associations

Market demand and proximity – for salad veg., Fruit and flower products

Freezing, canning areas

Factors affecting the distribution of market gardening and fruit production

Technological developments in freezing, transport, etc. protective covering seed, fertiliser and water supply control

Competition from continental and overseas suppliers

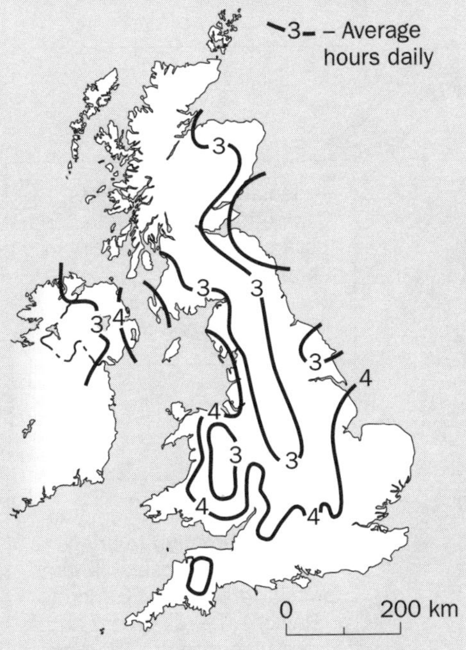

Sunshine

Mild damp weather favouring early growth and maturing of crops

Average to above average days of sunshine

Level or undulating terrain but above frost pockets

Well drained light to medium soils

Physical factors

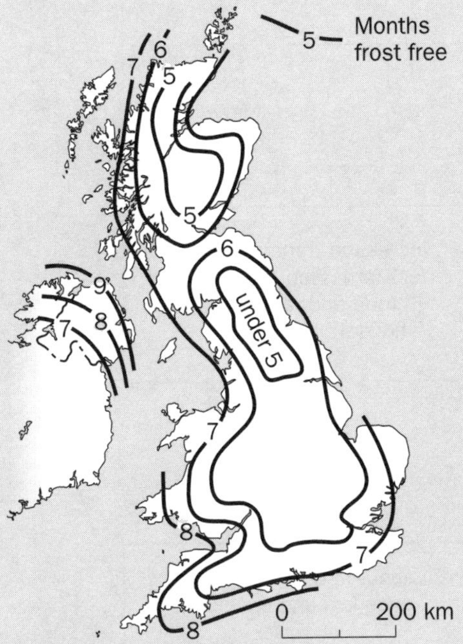

Frost free period

Factors influencing the distribution

case study

24.4 UK: hill farming and its problems

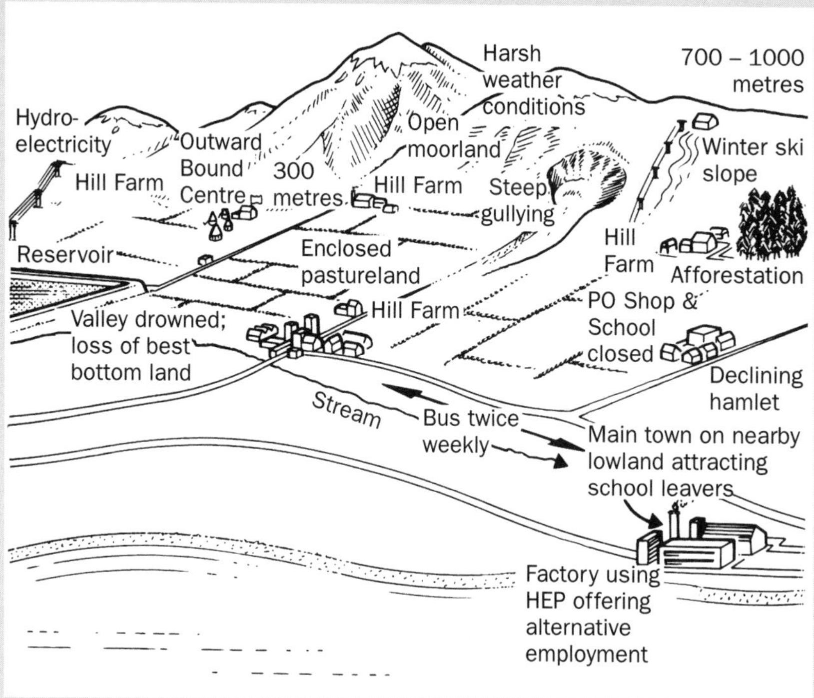

Hill farmers face a struggle to survive

Mr R Howells has a hill farm of 720 hectares on Myndd Caeru above Port Talbot, South Wales. The farm has been in the family for three generations; he keeps 2500 sheep and 50 cows on it. He reckons he makes little more than the Welsh farmer's average of £7000 a year, half of it from the financial support of the EU premium payments and the British government's own Hill Livestock Compensatory payment.

[Based on extract *Financial Times* 24.11.93]

'It may not be many years down the road before we will be paid to sit here and look after visitor people. May be we will be paid to keep a few dozen sheep to give them something to look at.'

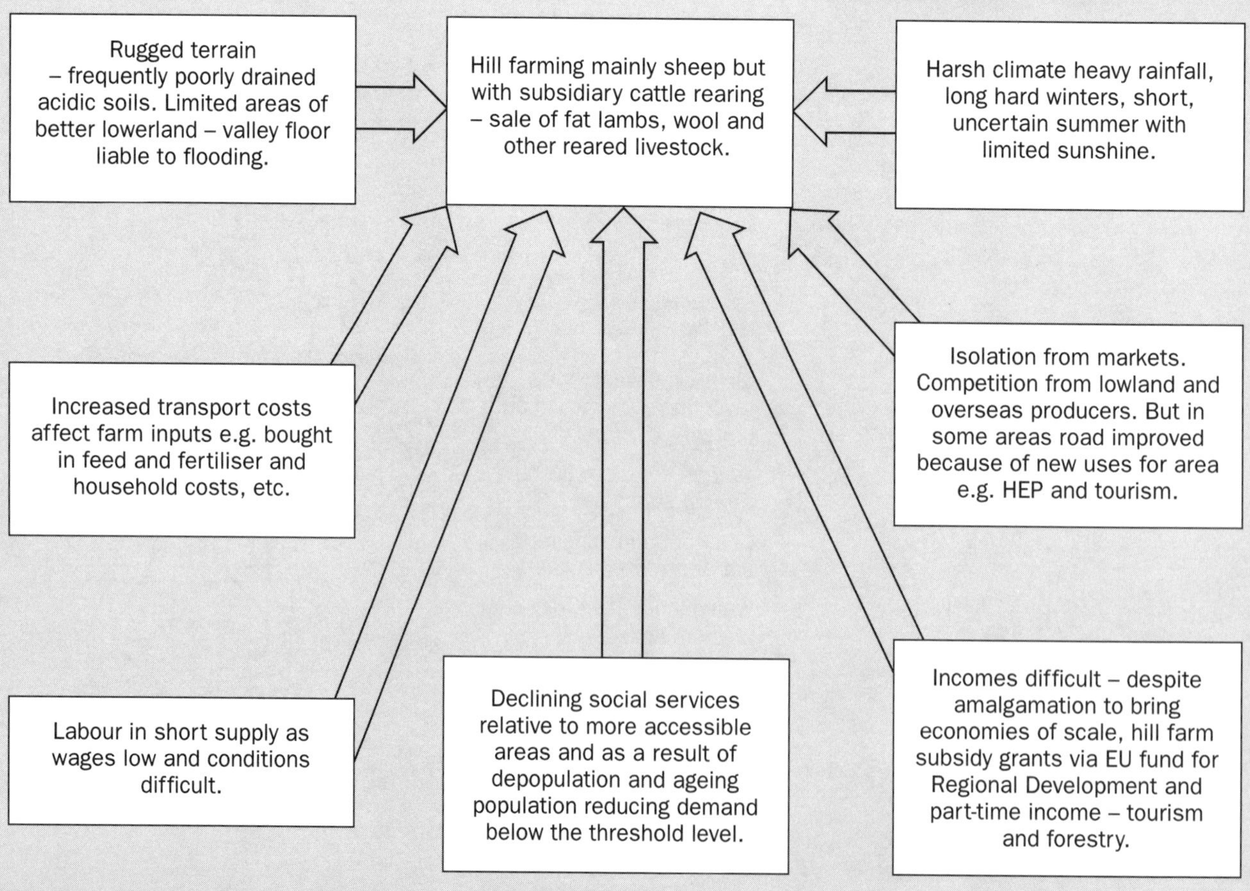

Physical, economic and social conditions affecting hill farming

Mr D Norman – sheep farmer based on Knottrigg in the Lake District.

In 1992 his profit from a flock of 900 sheep was £1632 while his wife made £6000 from bed and breakfast letting to tourists.

[SOURCE: Based on extracts *The Independent* 9.2.92]

The wider importance of hill farming

The National Farmer's Union estimates that for every £1000 earned by a hill farmer, £2500 is earned by supporting industries in transport and supply of inputs to the farm, for example.

The hill farmer is vital to maintaining the upland landscape which attracts the tourist income for local communities. The farmers' view is if they had to give up hill farming the local economy would suffer. The hill pastures would revert to scrub, stone walls would crumble, shops would close and many villages would be depopulated.

Tourism currently brings £250 million a year into the Lake District economy, for example, and hill farming is fundamental to the attractions of the Lake District. This is also a view held by the National Trust which owns one third of the land. To keep hill farmers, it is considering offering its tenants a negative rent, that is, paying them to tenant the land.

The hill farms supply 60% of the breeding stock needed by lowland farmers. Also for many, buying hill sheep for fattening on the lowland pastures is integral to their farming operations.

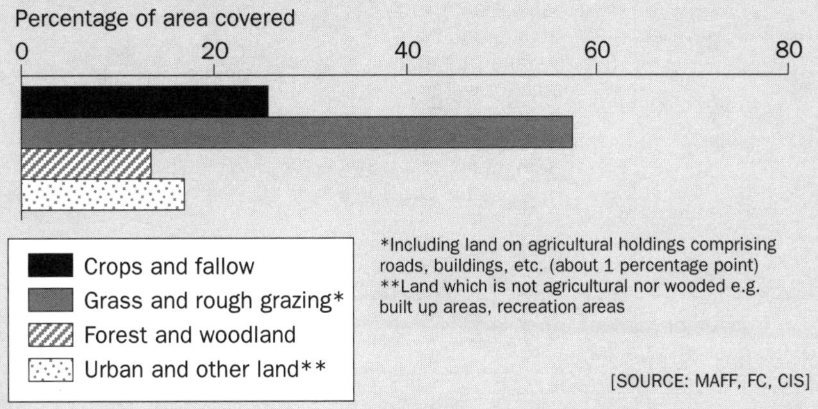

*Including land on agricultural holdings comprising roads, buildings, etc. (about 1 percentage point)
**Land which is not agricultural nor wooded e.g. built up areas, recreation areas

[SOURCE: MAFF, FC, CIS]

Land use in the UK, 1993

case study

24.5 Texas, USA: extensive cattle rearing and beef production

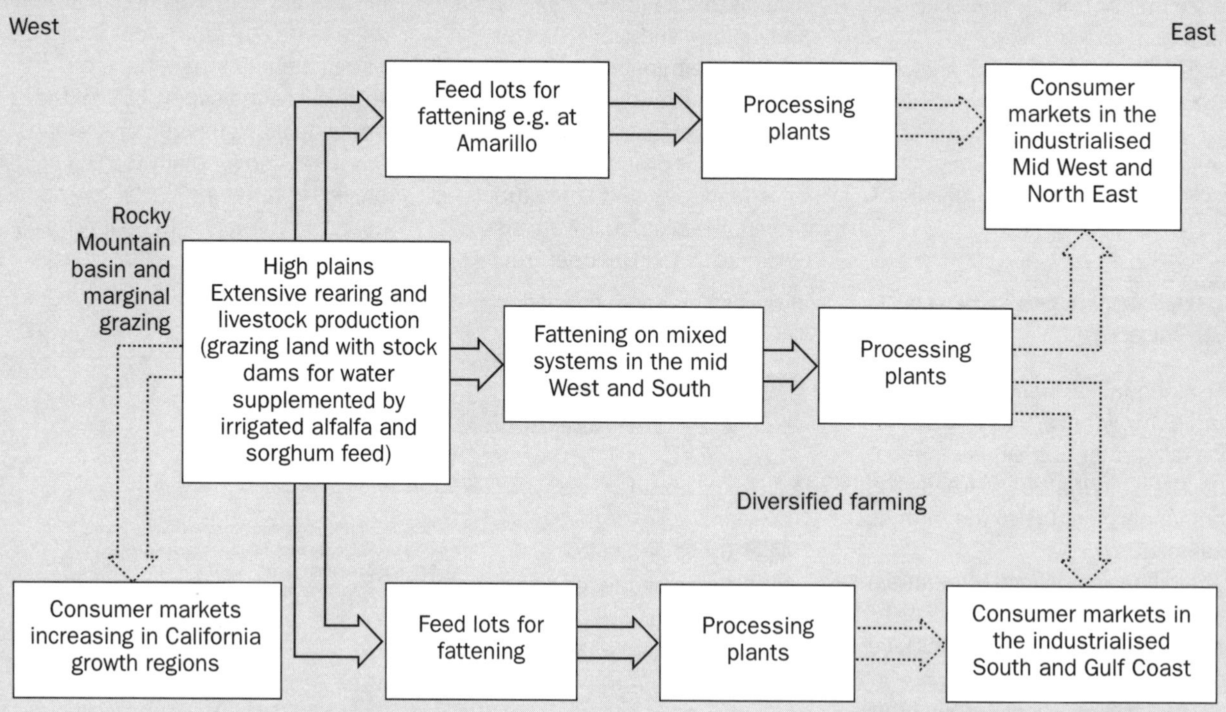

The USA beef fattening system based initially on cattle rearing in the Texas high plains

Location of 06 Ranch near Alpine and of Amarillo area

A beef fattening lot , Amarillo area, Texas

Five million cattle coming off the High Plains to the west are fattened in feed yards with capacities from 1000 to 80 000 cattle each. Stock feed lots use sorghum feed, which is replacing wheat in marginal areas. Most sorghum growing requires irrigation especially in marginal areas – 728 000 ha are planted. The feed yards both supply 14 regional processing and packing plants and ship a further 50 000 – 75 000 head weekly to mixed fattening systems further east.

Rearing livestock production, the 06 Ranch, north of Alpine, south-west texas

The ranch covers 350 sq km extending into Davis Mountains foothills. Cattle graze in the traditional way but grazing is improved by adding more waterholes.

The climate is one of extremes – floods, droughts, blizzards and tornadoes; 'softer' seasons are short.

Yearling steers and calves are raised and sold by contract to the companies which own fattening lots in Oklahoma. Herds of British and mixed breeds, including Brahma, are rounded up in the fall and shipped by rail.

CHAPTER 25

The nature of resources and their use

'We hardly know the planet there are countless gaps in our understanding and in our ability to compute both the cost of environmental damage and the cost of inaction. The world's environmental data base is incomplete and of variable quality.'

ATLAS OF PLANET MANAGEMENT, 1994

25.1 **Definitions**

Resource: a concept employed to denote sources of human satisfaction, wealth or strength. Labour, entrepreneurial skills, investment funds, fixed capital assets, technology and cultural and physical attributes may all be referred to as resources of a nation.

[SOURCE: Johnston R J (ed) *Dictionary of Human Geography* 1994]

Resource is a term applicable to a wide range of environmental attributes which are of potential use to man either directly as an input to the agricultural or industrial economy or indirectly by exchanging the resource for monetary assets.

[SOURCE: Cook J A *Resource Assessment in Africa, Geography* 1979 No. 283 – Vol. 64, Part 2]

Johnston's more comprehensive definition of resources emphasises the importance of human resources with those arising from the use of environmental or physical attributes to which Cook's more limited definition directs attention. Human and environmental resources are closely linked because human resources are needed for the development of environmental resources.

25.2 **Renewable and non-renewable resources**

Environmental resources are commonly divided into those considered to be ***renewable and non-renewable. Renewable resources are those which naturally regenerate within a human defined time***

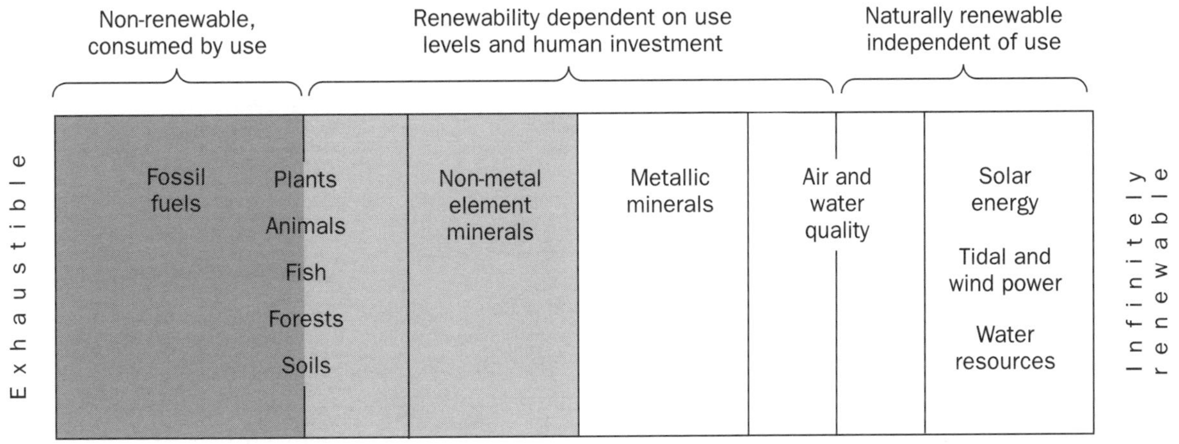

[SOURCE: Rees J *Natural resources, economy and society*, 1989]

Figure 25.1 *Continuum of natural resources*

span to provide new supplies of those resources. Non-renewable, such as minerals and land, have taken millions of years to form and therefore in human terms, are fixed in the supply available.

In reality, however, the distinction is not as clear cut and resources are increasingly being classified in terms of degree of renewability within what Rees (1989) sees as a 'use-renewability continuum' (Figure 25.1). At one extreme of the continuum are infinitely renewable resources, irrespective of how it is used by humans, e.g. solar energy and tidal power. At the other extreme are resources which, as they are used, cannot be replaced, e.g. fossil fuels. In between these two extremes are resources, the renewal of which depends on the rate at which they are used, how they are managed (including concern for the rate at which the biological ones, such as the soil and plants, regenerate) and the extent to which recycling or substitution of them can occur (e.g. metallic minerals).

The continuum approach is helpful; it raises issues of rate of use and management of the environment, issues central to the current debate on sustainable development.

Figure 25.2 Factors affecting the development of a particular resource 'body'

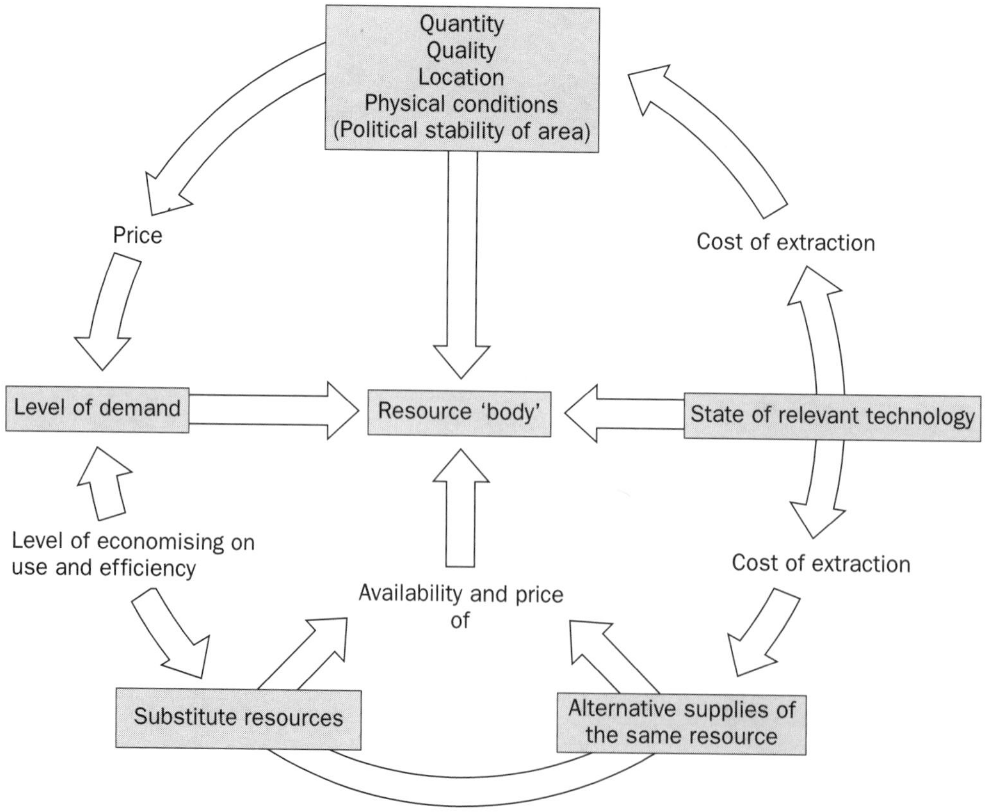

25.3 **Potential vs usable resources**

Although an environmental resource is defined as something of potential use to humans, at any one point in time the essentially important resources are those which can be and are actually being used. These are but a small part of the total potential which exist in the environment. Many resource areas are as yet unexplored and unassessed. Others, though known to exist, cannot at present be used, either because they are not financially worthwhile or we do not have the technology to make them viable. North Sea oil and gas resources were known to exist in large quantities over fifty years ago, but only since the 1970s has a rise in world prices and advances in technology justified extraction of oil and gas in the very difficult physical conditions of the North Sea (Figure 25.2; Case study 27.3).

Resources shortage: concerns and effects

Despite the many resource discoveries being made and a continual advance in technology, it was feared demand would outstrip available world resources. Although some resources such as water are renewable, most are regarded as non-renewable; they are considered finite and once used, cannot be replaced. Concern grew following the publication in the early 1960s of *Limits to Growth* by the Club of Rome because of the oil crisis of the 1970s. The 'energy crisis' as it is called, is familiar to us all and was accompanied by rising energy costs (Case study 27.1).

Along with the threat of exhaustion of valuable resources is an increasing concern for the environment. In extracting resources and using them, some irreparable damage is being done to the environment. Extraction of coal and minerals leaves scars on the landscape, while the processing and consumption of them leads to pollution in rivers, in coastal areas, on the land and in the atmosphere. Thus concern for proper resource management and conservation includes a careful monitoring of resource extraction and concern for the direct and indirect effects of resource use on the environment (Case study 6.1).

A third issue is that of equity of distribution of the world's usable resources. *'It can be believed that (some) natural resources, the heritage of poor countries are being consumed by the rich countries, denying the poor any real hope for better living conditions'*. Takeover of land by transnationals to exploit resources when the land has traditionally been the home of indigenous peoples, should also be considered.

It is important that economic needs are balanced against arguments for environmental conservation. However, the matter of equity of distribution is morally a clear-cut issue if not readily attainable in practicable terms.

25.4 **Supply and demand**

Why the world will not run out of power and mineral resources

Resource and energy crises are not new. Throughout history humanity has faced them at different periods and within the very crisis itself, has been the spur to its solution and also the beginnings of another phase of material progress. This was the very basis of the Industrial Revolution.

Tapping more of the same resource and the development of alternatives

Towards the end of the eighteenth century the advanced economies of Western Europe, and in particular Britain, faced two major crises. One was the using up of available woodland which was the major source of building material as well as of the charcoal which provided their only means of smelting iron-ore. The other was the exhaustion of coal supplies since much of the surface coal had been used and due to flooding, there was no way of extracting the coal at deeper levels. The steam engine provided the power for the pumps and coal-winding gear needed for deeper mining and the invention of a way to process coal into coke provided an alternative fuel to charcoal for smelting the iron-ore. This in turn eased the demand on wood as a building material since iron could now also be used.

Thus further discoveries and technological breakthroughs can make available more of the same resource and can enable one resource to be replaced by another.

Recycling

More recently there is another way to increase the quantity of resource, namely, recycle the product made from it (Case study 25.1). For example, scrap replaces some iron-ore input in the steel industry. Recovery of waste is also recycling. Due to technological advances it is now possible to recover mineral content from the residue dumped from earlier mining operations, as is happening for example in areas of earlier lead and tin mining.

Up to the 1980s only about 10% of household and industrial waste was recycled but with a greater awareness of conservation and the health hazards of waste dumping, the percentage recycled has markedly increased.

However, the proportion recycled is still very much related to the cost in proportion to the price of the original raw materials. For example in the case of paper, a very significant increase in the price of wood pulp during 1994 and 1995 has led to a sharp increase in the amount of paper recycled and prices paid for it. Still, the amount of waste continues to grow.

Until very recently the consumption of raw materials and the proportion of products recycled has been governed largely by market forces and the associated underlying concept of progressive economic development which has continually raised levels of consumption (Figure 25.3). It is most clearly demonstrated by the economic history of advanced industrial countries but now also characterises developing countries, especially the newly industrialising countries of South East Asia.

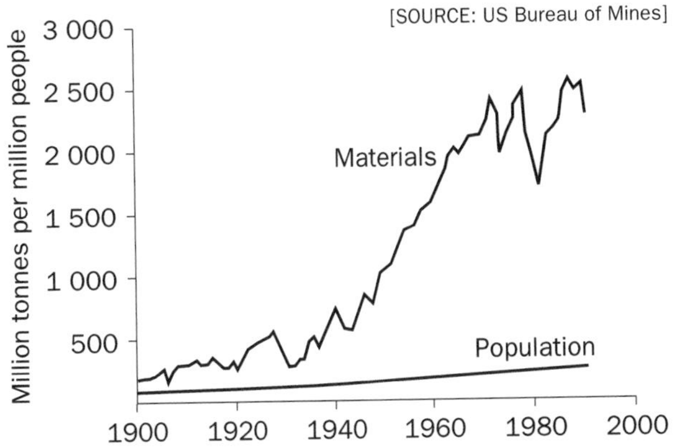

Figure 25.3 *A comparison between the rates of population growth and materials consumption in the USA, 1900 – 91*

25.5 Equity and management of the environment

That there is unequal distribution of the world's resources is self evident and there is increasing pressure from governments of developing countries for some redress. As governments become better organised, especially with the formation of regional blocs such as SADC (southern African regions), this pressure will become progressively more effective.

Where tapping of resources in developing countries is being negotiated by external businesses, usually by multinational companies, there is also the question of inequality of bargaining power. In the past, TNCs (Transnational Corporations) have been able to negotiate very lucrative agreements with leaders of national governments who have found themselves in contractually inferior bargaining positions or been ready to accept personal financial inducements to accede to a deal. For example in the case of Namibia which contains rich deposits of lead, cadmium, zinc, diamonds and uranium, TNCs in combination with the South African government were able to get lucrative mining rights and a plentiful cheap labour supply from the black homelands.

However since the 1970s, governments have a greater share of the revenues from developing a resource and greater control over production. Commonly also, governments insist on some processing of the resource before export by the foreign company, so providing more work in the developing country and higher export revenue. This has been particularly noticeable in the case of the OPEC oil exporting countries, such as Saudi Arabia.

Even so, such is the wealth and power of large transnational companies, that in general they still retain the advantage in any negotiating situation, particularly where a government of a developing country is narrowly dependent on export of primary resources.

Exploitation of a resource deposit frequently involves displacement of local peoples with very little choice or compensation given. One of the most publicised examples has been the displacement of Australian aboriginal tribal groups from their territories in North West Australia as a result of mining operations (Case study 26.1). Similarly, there is the problem of the displacement of indigenous groups as a result of logging and mining operations in tropical rainforest regions, such as Amazonia (Case study 28.5).

Exploitation and processing of a resource also has environmental implications. These are not restricted to peoples affected in developing countries but apply also to resident populations in localities in advanced countries where a company is proposing to exploit a resource. There have been many battles over opencast coal mining or quarrying for example, in both the UK and the USA. Local populations have to bear the cost in terms of loss of environmental amenity, increased noise and possible health hazards. However, affected groups in advanced countries are legally and financially more able to oppose any intended development than are groups in developing countries.

Environmental questions related to fairness are not restricted to exploitation of a resource. Increasingly hazardous waste resulting from the processing and use of a resource in advanced countries has been dumped in locations in developing countries where laws relating to the disposal of hazardous waste are less strict. Their respective governments, desperate for more foreign exchange revenue, see contracts with waste disposal firms as a means of acquiring more revenue. Greater conservation of the resources from which waste is generated together with more recycling of waste products or the use of alternatives would help to contain and in time, reduce it.

The moral and environmental argument of equity thus cannot be divorced from the market forces of supply and demand which have so far dominated the extent to which resources are being exploited and used.

25.6 Creating a sustainable materials economy; greater use of secondary materials

Why conserve, repair and recycle?

There is a need for greater equity and conservation of the environment. The fewer resources exploited for the use of advanced countries, the more there will be for people in developing countries and the less the environmental damage and hazards to which they are exposed (Section 6.3).

The damage to the environment is great. Damage occurs not only during the extraction of resources but also in their processing and the disposal of waste products associated with the '*immense but rarely noticed complexes of mines, smelters, petroleum refineries and chemical plants, logging operations and pulp mills*'. It is estimated that mining, for example, currently removes 28 billion tonnes of soil and rock annually, a greater amount than that removed by natural processes. In the USA the four primary production industries of paper, plastics, chemicals and metals produce 71% of toxic emissions and disposal of waste from the associated products in landfills contributes to poisoning of ground water and surface water.

Such industries also use up considerable amounts of energy. Processing of raw materials is the biggest single consumer of energy. Mining and smelting alone consume around 10% of the energy used in the world. Potential energy is also lost by waste disposal. For example, while incineration of municipal solid waste can be used as a supplementary supply of energy, the recycling of such waste effectively saves three to five times that amount of energy by reducing the need for making new products.

Young and Sachs also advance a jobs creation argument for more repair and recycling. For example, they point out that official studies show that whereas disposal of one million tonnes of waste by landfill will create 600 jobs and by incineration 80 jobs, recycling of this same amount of waste will create 1600 jobs. Repairing products for further use and recycling are becoming significant job creation areas of advanced economies. In the USA for example, employment in auto repairs rose by 45% between 1970 and 1992, while that in manufacturing of new vehicles rose only 3% over the same period. While increased automation reduces the labour needed in vehicle manufacturing, vehicle repair work by its very nature is labour intensive.

The 1980 recession also brought a long-term change of attitude to new car purchase; despite economic recovery over the last two years, new car purchases have failed to regain earlier levels. Probably, many car owners having had opportunity to weigh up the costs of maintaining a car longer against purchase of a new vehicle have now decided to keep their cars longer.

Changing the pattern of materials consumption

If values and patterns of consumption are to change, persuasion through morality and protection of the environment are not enough. Economic pressure will also be needed. Young and Sachs advocate the following economic measures to reduce the rate of raw materials consumption:

- extraction and use of raw materials should be taxed not subsidised
- reform the tax system so that all industries have to cover the full environmental costs of their activities instead of leaving the public to settle the bill
- the public and commercial companies should pay the full cost of disposing of their waste rather than be subsidised, as is commonly the case.

Young and Sachs feel that by raising prices there would be strong incentive not to degrade the resource base in the first place. *'Market forces need to be aligned for rather than against materials efficiency'* but the commercial lobby in favour of the status quo remains strong.

Achieving a change of attitude

Evidence supports the likelihood of significant moves in this direction but falls far short of pointing to a complete change of policy (Case study 25.1). However desirable the change on grounds of equity and responsible management of the environment, the economic cost would be too great.

However, attitudes are changing and measures increasing to conserve resources and protect the environment. Legislation on exploiting resources and disposal of waste is much stricter than it was ten years ago. In the UK for example, a lower tax on unleaded petrol has encouraged car manufacturers to produce vehicles which are more fuel efficient.

Greater efficiency in the use of resources is probably most evident for energy resources, initially prompted by the oil crisis of the mid-1970s but increasingly so by the strength of the environmental and health arguments for it (Chapter 27). Over the last twenty years new energy-efficient lighting, insulation and heating and air conditioning systems have been introduced into homes and offices. Technological advances have enabled great energy savings to be made in the manufacturing sector. It is estimated that these savings amount to 75% of the total energy used in 1970.

As to the possibility of resource efficiency groups succeeding against vested business interests, the case of transport in the USA is frequently quoted. In 1991 a coalition of community development, civil rights and environmental groups combined with local governments to replace 'highways bills' with the Intermodal Surface Transportation Efficiency Act. This forced transportation agencies to move away from a concentration on highways building and adopt an integrated approach to transport systems as a whole, in conjunction with development and air quality planning.

Concluding comment

The economist Herman Daly sees developing an ecologically sound economy as presenting tremendous opportunities: *'In the materials economy, as with energy and water, the key to the shift will be a change in values, a new emphasis on quality over quantity. Instead of defining success as getting the most materials, we need to move to a new standard: getting the most from materials.'*

[SOURCE: *The Steady State Economics*, 1991]

case study

25.1 USA: recycling progress and salient influences

Some progress

Recycling is gaining ground. In 1988, there were 1000 recycling programmes but by 1994, this had risen to 5000 covering 85 million of the total 250 million. The kind of recycling varies with the type of waste.

Percentage recycled	
Aluminium cans	65%
Steel cans	25%
Paper	25%
Glass	20%

However, two thirds of solid waste still goes to landfill;16% is incinerated.

The USA has the highest amount of waste per capita in the world. On average every person discards 3.6 lb a day, a result of a mass consumer high spending society. The per capita amount is double that of the average for advanced countries. One third of solid waste comes from the 'packaging' of products.

The proportion of waste recycled varies regionally depending on extent of state legislation support for it. Seattle for example with its 'pay as you throw' programme, recovers 45% as against the 17% USA average.

Observations

P Bailey, National Recycling Coalition

'Recycling works and it makes economic sense even when material is plentiful. Recycling glass required less energy than making it from sand. Recycling steel is cheaper than mining ore.

Recycling is where the environment and economy meet. It is becoming an integral part of business and industry.'

J Garbarino, in charge of the recycling centre, San Rafael California

'We've got to do it right, create local markets, make recycling a natural part of the economy so that it becomes part of our lifestyle.

Of all the environmental concerns that have come up through the years, this is the most personal. People are uncertain what they can do about saving whales or the rainforest but they can recycle their waste every day of their lives.'

Emerging influences

The relative costs of new products and waste disposal as against recycling varies from product to product; paper and steel can be recycled as cheaply as new production but oil less so. In New York it is estimated that recycling costs $240 a tonne as against $200 as landfill waste. The relationship is not constant, for example, a rise in the cost of raw paper pulp encouraged recycling.

A shortage of landfill sites is a pressing factor in the USA. This is particularly serious in the heavily populated East Coast region, where it is estimated there will be no landfill sites available by 2000 AD. Nationally, 80% of the present sites will be closed by then. The western states have more landfill space.

There is a growing consciousness of waste and environmental concerns both for ground and air pollution. Local and national organisations pressing for and organising recycling programmes are increasing, helped by reader media coverage. The government oversees progress through the Environmental Protection Agency.

The extent of legislation encourages and enforces recycling. Seattle is the most progressive city. It instituted a 'public pay the full cost' policy for waste disposal. Its 'pay as you throw programme', charging 815 dollars a month per 30 gallon waste container, covers the cost of waste collection and recycling. Collections are done by firms which make a profit by selling the 'recyclables'. In 1988 Florida passed the Solid Waste Management Act, ordering all its counties to ensure that 30% of waste is recycled by 1994.

The markets for recycled products are increasing. A significant amount is exported for recycling, for example, Taiwan relies on USA waste paper. There are also a growing number of recycling firms in the USA, including Evergreen Oils (Newark), Ford Howard Corporation (Paper) and Dejo Shoes (Portahead region).

Location of USA and Canada

26

CHAPTER 26

Mineral exploitation

26.1 The nature and development of mineral deposits

Mineral deposits represent non-renewable resources, important for industries dependent on them and for the region in which mining occurs. Some regions have only a fleeting prosperity and once the mineral deposit is exhausted, they are abandoned. Ghost towns and old workings, as in the gold rush areas of Kalgoorlie (Australia) and the Yukon (Alaska), are all that remain of the short boom period.

However in other cases such may be the size of deposits and other favourable factors, for example, availability of power and an accessible location, that mining leads to further development, attracting lasting settlement. This has further multiplier effects, resulting in a region having a large and diversified economic base with sufficient momentum to maintain growth even after the initial mineral workings have been exhausted. For example, the Rand gold mining area where mining began in the late nineteenth century is now one of the world's major industrial regions. At its heart lies Johannesburg, a large metropolis of 1.5 million people, where economic growth is likely to continue even when gold mining is no longer possible.

Factors which affect mineral development

Of the factors which determine the fate of mining areas, some are geological, such as the size and quality of the deposit; others are economic, such as its location relative to prospective markets and costs of development compared to alternative source areas. Yet others are political and social. Warren summarises it as: *'the geography of mining is the response of an enterprise to the known geological facts, though conditioned by the availability of capital and labour, by political considerations, planning controls and very importantly by the legacy from past patterns'.*

However, situations change. For example, a mineral deposit which at one point was not worth mining or which may have been abandoned because mining was no longer viable may at a later date be worth exploiting. Demand may have risen causing a rise in market price, making it possible to cover higher mining costs, or new techniques may have been developed, reducing mining costs. Old tin mining areas in Cornwall have been re-opened as a result of such changes in circumstance.

Mineral classification

The classification by Blunden is useful to the geographer since it groups minerals according to their physical or chemical characteristics and on the basis of their locational occurrence. The basic division is as follows:

- Ubiquitous non-metallic minerals, e.g. gravel, limestone, etc.
- Localised non-metallic minerals, e.g. salt, potash, china-clay, etc.
- Non-ferrous metals, e.g. copper, bauxite, tin, etc.
- Ferrous metals, e.g. various kinds of iron-ore
- Carbon and hydro-carbon fuels, e.g. oil, coal.

26.2 Ubiquitous non-metallic minerals

Materials used in the building and construction industry dominate this group. They include gravel and brick clays which, because of their widespread (ubiquitous) occurrence and low unit value, are unable to stand the cost of transport over any appreciable distance. Thus they tend to be exploited close to their markets. There are many workings where suitable outcrops of the parent materials occur. Depending to some extent on the size of the market served, workings tend to be on a small scale, though some may be extensive as, for example, with the brick clay workings at Peterborough and Bedford which serve the Midlands and Home Counties of the Lee Valley gravel workings, north of London.

The location of cement works in the UK shows the dispersion of workings for the chalk/limestone and clay needed as raw materials and their association with the alignment of geological outcrops in which these occur. Recent changes in the locational pattern of cement works also reflect other factors which affect the industry and therefore, whether potentially workable deposits will be quarried or not. In particular, restrictions on expansion of some workings and opening of new ones reflect environmental concerns. Greater restrictions on workings in the South East compared to other regions have significantly altered the locational pattern of workings in this country.

Because workings are open-cast, large scale extraction may pose particular problems – stripping of over-burden and dumping of waste scars the landscape; pits are liable to flooding. In the case of brick-making, atmospheric pollution may be caused and in general, heavy lorries cause congestion and possibly some damage to local roads. However, increasingly tight planning controls and the growing influence exercised by environmental groups do today ensure a sympathetic location of extraction sites and proper reclamation of worked over land. An unattractive site may be turned into a community asset providing storage and recreational facilities. It is difficult for example to know what would happen to the mountains of waste created by modern living were not disused quarries and other kinds of pits available as dumping areas, the infill later being reclaimed as land for agriculture or light industrial building. On a much larger scale, the old gravel workings along the flooded gravel pits of the Lee Valley for example, have been linked by walkways and grassed areas to provide the Lee Valley Regional park, a major recreational outlet for the population of Greater London and for the growing numbers in the commuter belt through which the park runs (Case study 29.1).

26.3 Localised non-metallic minerals

Because they are so localised and less plentiful than those in the ubiquitous non-metal group, this group of minerals has a higher unit value than the ubiquitous class of minerals and can therefore stand the cost of transport over longer distances. In general they are the raw materials of more specialised industries. Potash and salt for example are used in branches of the chemical industry, while china-clay is an important ingredient in the finer side of the pottery industry and in papermaking.

While providing employment opportunities and prompting some infrastructure development in a region, together with limited ancillary activities, only in a few cases does the exploitation of localised non-metallic minerals provide the basis for sustained industrial growth. Much depends on other factors such as the availability of a plentiful water supply, power supplies and proximity to outlet points for the manufactured product. In the case of the chemical industries of Cheshire and Teesside, these other factors were present in that both are near coalfields and have close links to a sizeable home market and port outlets, for example. The latter also allowed the import of other raw materials as the region's industries became more diversified. Consequently, industrial growth did occur.

In contrast, exploitation of china-clay in Cornwall where there are no coalfield sites and no large market areas close to hand, while important to the region because of other limited employment opportunities, has not led to any appreciable industrial growth. The china-clay is either sent out by road to the potteries of North Staffordshire or the paper works in the London region and elsewhere, or exported from the ports of Par and Fowey.

With increasing demands in the paper industry where china-clay is used to give a sheen to paper, the china-clay industry has expanded considerably since the 1930s. Apart from large deposits in Georgia (USA), the Cornwall deposits are said to be the only major source of kaolin (china-clay). The companies involved in working this deposit have initiated large-scale schemes for extending the workings.

Because of the environmental implications, heightened as it is by the location of the main area of workings around St Austell on the borders of the Dartmoor National Park, there has been widespread opposition to plans to extend workings. The case of the Lee Moor workings illustrate the sort of compromise which is reached to reconcile economic needs with responsible management of an environment.

26.4 Non-ferrous metals

This group includes a wide range of minerals from precious metals like gold, silver and uranium to metals essential to modern industry such as tin, bauxite and copper. While the USA and the former Soviet states have large deposits of most of these minerals, most other industrial countries are heavily dependent on imports, mainly from developing countries or Australia and Canada.

Supplies are sensitive to changes in the level of world prices and demand and there have been serious fluctuations since the 1960s (Figure 26.1). These have badly affected the economies of those countries such as Chile, Peru, Zaire and Zambia which are dependent upon a narrow range of exports in which metals figure prominently. For example, copper from the Copper Belt makes up over 70% by value of Zaire and Zambia's exports.

This chart contains a weighted price index for the 50 product groups covered. The weights are the values of production in 1993

This chart shows a weighted index of production for the 50 product groups covered. The weights are the values of production in 1993

[SOURCE: Crowson P *Minerals Handbook* 1994 – 95, 1994]

Figure 26.1 *World price changes in relation to mineral production, 1979 – 93*

Fluctuations on the world commodity market are due to a number of causes, including economic recession in importing countries, availability of more favourably priced substitute materials and the discovery and exploitation of new sources of a mineral. For example, rich deposits of manganese and uranium are now being exploited in Gabon in Central Africa and further explorations have uncovered deposits of barytes, lead, zinc, copper and smaller deposits of gold and diamonds. These and large ferrous deposits or iron-ore are also likely to be exploited once the railway is extended inland from the coast.

Two important developments have been new techniques enabling a much larger scale of working, including viable access to deposits of poorer mineral content hitherto considered uneconomic to mine, and more semi-processing of the mineral before export. Both have significant implications for the countries concerned. While more mechanisation would reduce demand for labour; a larger scale of working does help to maintain the existing work-force and attracts ancillary activities such as power and maintenance services, giving a multiplier effect and attracting more labour to the area. Processing of the mineral also generates more employment opportunities as well as raising the unit value of the mineral before export, thereby increasing the revenue to be gained by the producing country as well as providing much needed foreign exchange and capital for other developments in the economy. Some of these cumulative advantages are illustrated in Figure 26.2.

As former colonial territories have gained independence, they have adopted measures to gain an important controlling stake in the country's resources and to raise the level of revenue earned by adopting a greater degree of processing before export. However, there is a limit to how far this can go, as developing countries on the whole need the capital and expertise from foreign investment and the activities of the large multinational companies which tend to dominate export resource development in the newer countries, as for example in Namibia and Sierra Leone.

26.5 Ferrous metals

Iron is one of the most common minerals and most countries which produce iron and steel also have iron-ore deposits of one kind or other. However, as home resources have become depleted and iron and steel production has expanded, iron has increasingly entered into world trade. Of the major industrial nations, only the former Soviet Union has sufficient domestic deposits; all others import large amounts of iron-ore. Although the USA is an important importer, its dependence on world trade is much less than Japan and the major West European producers, such as Germany and the UK.

Trade in iron-ore has also increased because the development of bulk ore carriers has made it economic to transport iron-ore over longer distances. Also, better mining and processing techniques have enabled the concentration of the ore by pelletisation or some other method, reducing the amount of waste in iron-ore carried by these bulk carriers.

Leading exporters are those countries still in the process of industrialising and in which large workable deposits have recently been discovered. Certain countries such as Canada, Australia, Brazil and India have risen in the ranks of world production to become foremost exporters. Australia and India are important suppliers to the Japanese iron and steel industries and together with Canada and Brazil, also ship ore to the USA and Western Europe.

Except where ores are in relatively remote locations, major exporters are also developing important iron and steel industries themselves. So iron exports only represent a proportion of the iron-ore actually mined. Advanced countries depending on iron imports must invest in further exploration for new supplies, For example Japan, the country most dependent on iron imports, has invested heavily in Brazil. Foreign investment has also been made in new regions such as Gabon and Mauritania.

It is magnetite and haematite ores which mainly enter world trade, as these kinds of deposits contain sufficient iron content to make export worth while. Both occur on a large scale and can be worked by open-cast methods. Magnetite has the highest iron content, varying between 70% and 45%. That worked in Kiruna and Gallivare in North Sweden and exported via Narvik (Norway) and Lulea (Sweden), for example, has a 60% iron content, while those in Mauritania at Fort Gourand in the Sahara and shipped out via Port Etienne are of 65% iron content.

At present, haematite ores with on average a lower content than magnetite enter most into world trade. For example, the bulk of Brazil and Australia's deposits are of this kind. Because of their lower iron-ore content, the development of pelletisation methods to reduce the waste before shipment has been particularly important for the various kinds of haematite ore being exploited.

Australia is now the world's major exporter of iron-ore and by volume of production, is exceeded only by the Soviet Union. The Pilbara area is Australia's main iron-ore region (Case study 26.1).

Foreign investment by multinationals in Australia

Foreign-based multinational companies such as RTZ (Rio Tinto Zinc) have invested heavily in the development of Australian resources. This is partly because of the variety and size of mineral deposits available, particularly in Western Australia and in Queensland. Australia is also a politically stable area

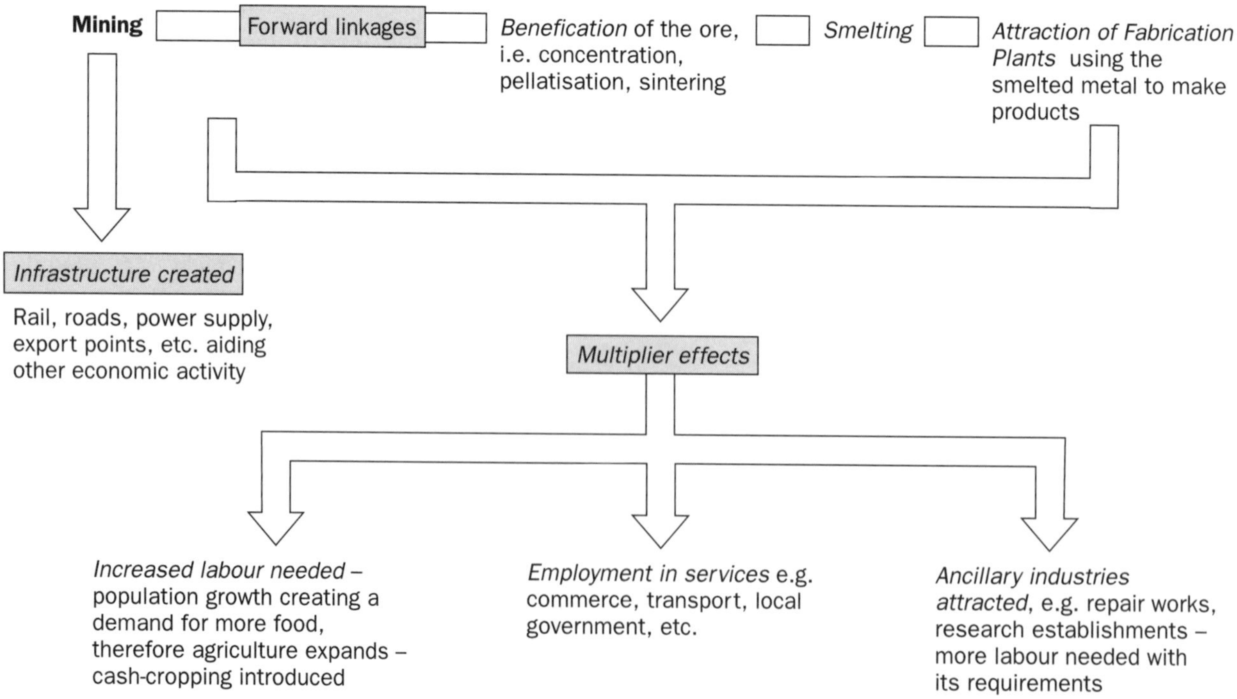

Figure 26.2 Possible development effects of mineral exploitation

and allied to the developed world, so it is unlikely to nationalise the assets of foreign companies. These advantages, together with the availability of high technology skills in the country, make it more attractive for investment than the developing countries located in less stable regions such as Africa and Latin America.

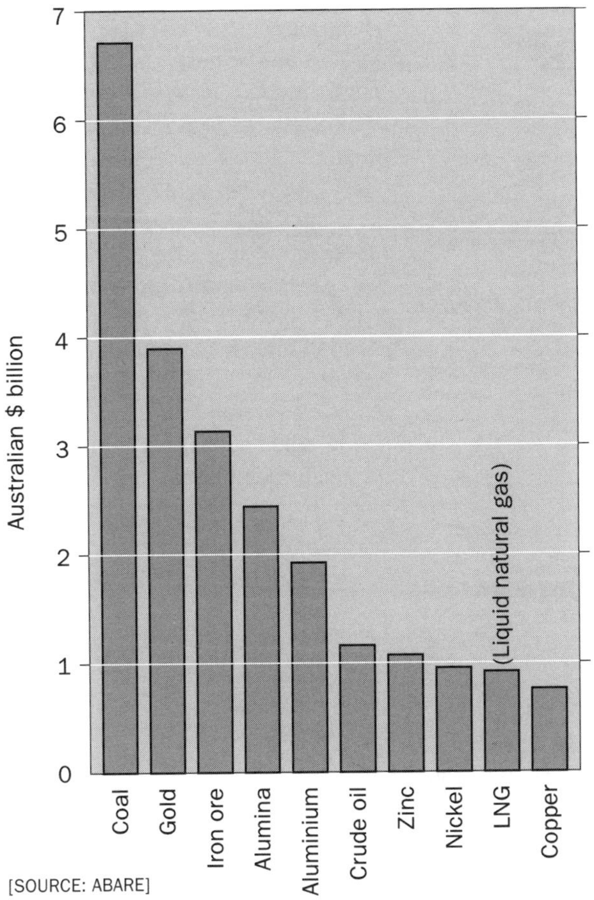

[SOURCE: ABARE]

Figure 26.3 *Australia: value of mineral resources exports, 1991 – 92*

Australian Aboriginal rights

While future mineral developments and manufacturing associated with these may to an important extent depend on economic factors and the policies of multinational companies and governments, there are other factors of an environmental and social nature. The largest is to do with the rights of the Aboriginals (Case study 10.1).

In Australia one of the most intractable problems is that a number of the biggest mineral discoveries in Western Australia and Queensland have occurred on land reserved for the Aboriginals. For example, some of the largest uranium deposits are in the Alligator River region, including part of the Arnhem Land Reserve. Any exploitation affects the rights of the Aboriginal and in the case of uranium, may pose grave environmental risks, including the danger of polluted rainwater run-off.

The Australian government has made positive moves to recognise Aboriginal rights to their tribal territory. In 1993 the Australian High Court gave aboriginal people title to large tracts of territory, in what became known as the 'Mabo' ruling, despite the opposition of agriculture and mining interests. This will make it much more difficult for large corporations to gain access to the large mineral deposits as yet untapped, particularly in Western Australia, the Northern Territory and Queensland which contain the greatest reserves but also where much of the aboriginal territories are situated. There has been some reconciliation between Aboriginal rights and commercial interests.

Concluding comment

'Even without resource sparing policies, the cumulative effect of increasing reserves, more competition among suppliers, and technology trends that create substitutes suggests that global shortages of most non-renewable resources are unlikely to check developments in the early decades of the next century.' (*World Resources*, 1994 – 95)

Three matters of major concern are:

- *'that exploitation of the minerals of the developing world have been mainly in the interests of the consuming nations of the developed world and not always consistent with the development needs and objectives of the Third World'* (*Geography of the Third World*, 1996)
- the impact on the environment of mining and the refining of metals will be of increasing concern in both the decision-making of bodies granting planning permission and of business corporations seeking it
- land rights of ethnic minority groups will be of growing importance where mining corporations seek to exploit mineral deposits.

case study

26.1 **Pilbara Region, Western Australia: iron ore mining**

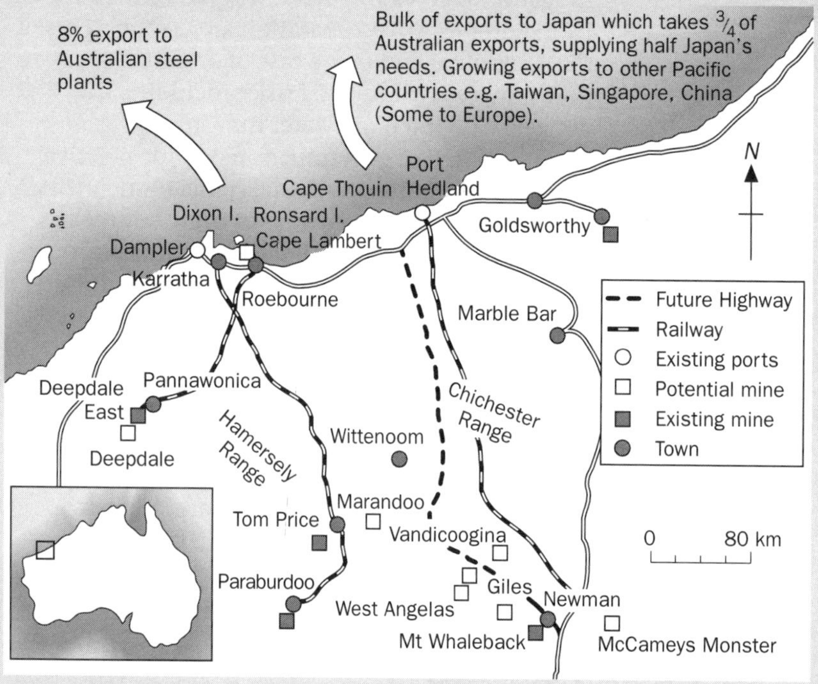

Location of iron ore mining and associated development

Importance

The mining industry provides half the region's total employment. The Pilbara region supplies 90% of Australia's iron-ore output but due to the recent world economic recession, the region is working under capacity. It has a capacity of 100 million tonnes annual output.

CRA Corporation's Hammersley mines alone produced 48 million tonnes in 1994.

Social injustice

As in other cases when big business and multinationals begin to exploit a region, it can have unfortunate consequences for the indigenous population. In this case the territorial right of the Aboriginals and their way of life have been affected. However, there are signs now of a more sympathetic awareness of this problem as elsewhere, e.g. in south-west Namibia.

Factors influencing exploitation

Large scale iron-ore deposits were identified before World War II in the Hammersley and Ophthalmia ranges but they were too remote and expensive to mine compared to deposits elsewhere, such as south-east Brazil.

Market demand and capital was available in the 1950s when Japan became a major iron and steel producer, urgently requiring increasing amounts of iron-ore. Mitsui Company along with Australian companies provided the huge financial outlay required.

With regard to the infrastructure, the power communication network was costly in this remote area. It is estimated that two thirds of investments costs are to do with infrastructure installations.

Aided by technological developments, bulk ocean ore carriers lowered sea transport costs, though rail haul to the coast is long. Transport is helped by bulk ore trains of 1700 tonnes capacity each.

Benefication plants at the mine sites reduced waste in the ore transported. Also some palletisation occurred at port before export.

A 480-km rail link was developed inland as were deepwater ports at Port Hedland and Dampier.

Water and power were costly compared to Labrador and Venezuela, for example. Power was based on imported oil and coal. The North West offshore gasfield is a possible future source of power.

Labour is extremely costly (despite being a capital intensive industry). High wages and other incentives are needed to attract labour to this remote area. Townships with amenities were recently developed, partly aided by tourism in this part of Western Australia.

World Reserves by percentage	
Former USSR	36.5%
Australia	15.8%
Canada	7.1%
India	5.1%

World Mine Production 1991–92 by percentage	
Brazil	19.2
Australia	14.3
China	18.7
Ukraine	7.8
Russia	8.7
USA	18.7

Australian iron-ore in a world context

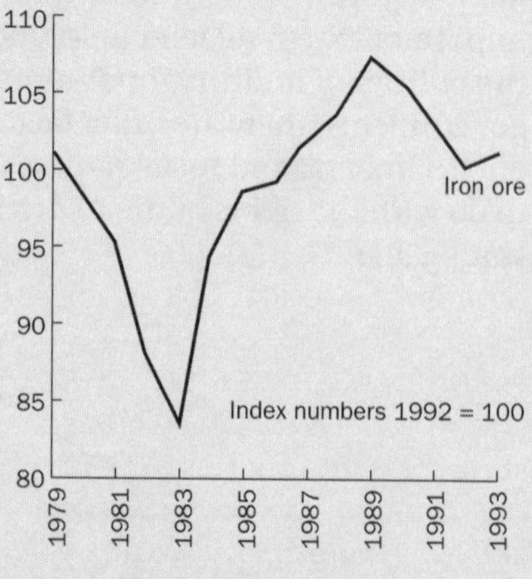

[SOURCE: *Minerals Handbook*, 1994 – 95]

World production 1979 – 93

27

CHAPTER 27

Energy

'Each and every society's capability of development or indeed its ability to survive depends on continuing access to energy in appropriate forms and quantities at acceptable levels of cost.'

COOK E *MAN, ENERGY AND SOCIETY*, 1976

27.1 Rates of economic development and energy use

There is a close relationship between the rate of economic development and the amount of energy used. For the world as a whole, the average annual increase since 1860 has been just over 2%, although it accelerated to around 5% per annum in the period 1945 – 73. Since then the rate has fallen back to around 2% and is forecast to continue into the twenty-first century. Although the anticipated predominant use of the fossil fuels, such as coal, oil and gas, is likely to raise serious environmental issues, there is unlikely to be a world energy shortage. However, the balance of demand will change. Per capita rate of growth is slowing down in the advanced countries but accelerating amongst developing countries (Figure 27.1). These countries have three quarters of the world's population but use only a third of the world energy production.

Developing world energy consumption has doubled since 1970 and is forecast to double again to 2050. In 1994 the industrialised countries' share of world energy consumption fell below 50% though per capita consumption still remains very high at about eight times that for the developing world.

The relative decline in the share of advanced countries and the shift in favour of the developing countries can broadly be linked to the different stages of economic development reached. In terms of Rostow's stages of economic development, advanced countries have moved beyond the stage of rapid economic development and industrialisation to a post-industrial phase of more efficient energy use. In contrast, most developing countries are either entering or are in the phase of rapid economic development and industrialisation when energy consumption is accelerating (Figure 3.4).

	1992	
Region	**Energy use (exajoules)**	**Per capita (gigajoules per person)**
	(percentage share)	
Industrial World	**253 (64.5)**	**207**
North America	99	351
Western Europe	63	167
Central Europe	67	161
Indus. Australasia	23	160
Developing World	**139 (35.5)**	**33**
China	39	33
Developing Asia	47	27
Africa & Middle East	31	36
Latin America	22	49
World	**392 (100)**	**72**

Columns may not add up to totals due to rounding.
[SOURCE: Flavin C and Lenssen N *Power Surge*, 1995]

***Figure 27.1** World primary energy use by region, 1992 in relation to per capita income*

O'Dell has shown this relationship between energy use and economic development, that is, the rate of increase (decrease) as a function of the stage of economic development. In analysing this relationship he points out that use of energy is not simply a matter of changes in demand but also of the relative price of energy at particular points in time (Figures 27.2 and 27.3).

For example, in the period 1950 to 1973, world consumption accelerated to an average increase of 5% annually. O'Dell attributes this to almost all the world's nations being at stages of development when economies were either going through or entering their most heavily energy intensive periods and the price of energy in real terms was falling. This was led by a decline in the price of oil (Figure 27.3). *'Cheap energy was one of the bases for the revolution in rising consumer expectations.'*

In the west, main manufacturing industries, motor vehicles, household consumer durables, iron and steel and petro-chemicals were energy intensive. At the same time consumer per capita energy use rose with the rise in car ownership, increased number of commuting and leisure journeys and improved home comforts through central heating, instant hot water, fridges and electrical household goods, such as vacuum cleaners. In the CIS and other East European countries much of the expansion was associated with the rapid expansion of heavy industry and public transport. A number of the developing countries were moving into a phase of expanding energy use because of government policies to copy the west and industrialise rapidly to achieve economic development. In turn this brought rapid urbanisation which itself led to further increased energy consumption (Figure 27.2).

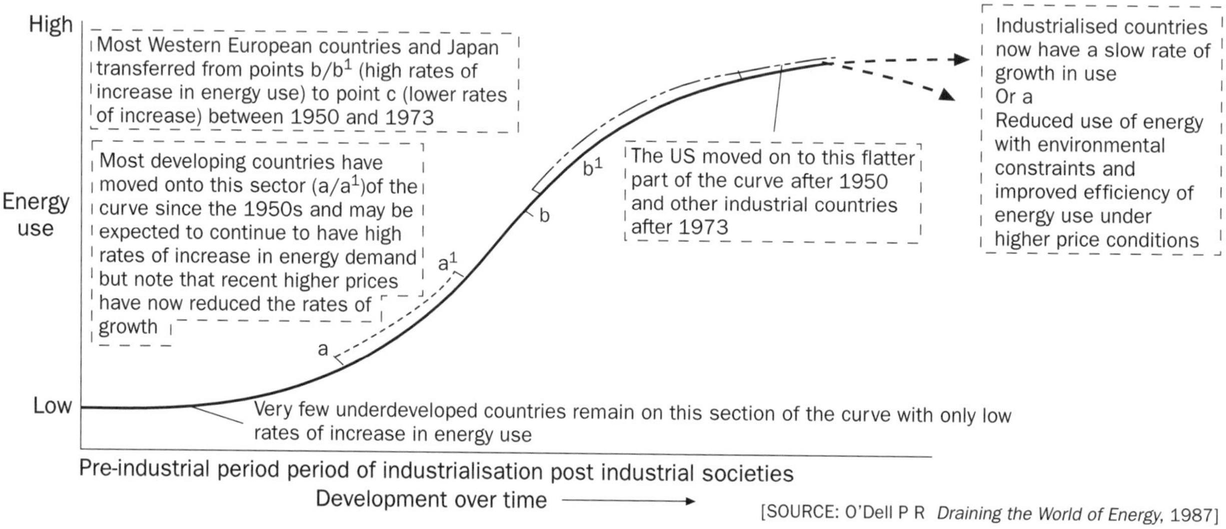

[SOURCE: O'Dell P R *Draining the World of Energy*, 1987]

Figure 27.2 *The relationship between energy use and economic development and the position of developing and advanced countries on the relationship curve*

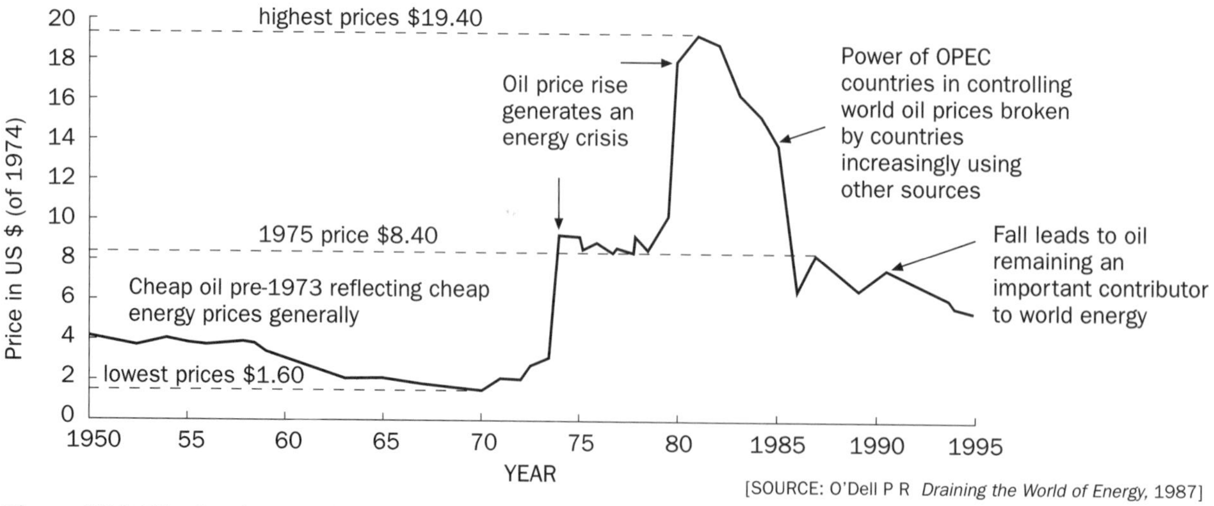

[SOURCE: O'Dell P R *Draining the World of Energy*, 1987]

Figure 27.3 *Oil price changes 1950 – 95*

27.2 Energy prices, energy consumption and the impact of the 1970s oil crisis on world energy

The influence of energy price changes on energy demand is dramatically illustrated in the world oil crisis of 1973 to 1976 when the action of the OPEC countries led to a sudden and unexpected rise in the price of oil, triggering a short-term world energy crisis. Countries which had become dependent on import of cheap oil from the Middle East and other OPEC countries were unable to switch quickly to other energy sources. Thus the sudden increase in the price of fuel triggered a rise in costs in industry, transport and household heating bills (Figure 27.3).

Advanced countries such as Japan were seriously affected economically and psychologically since the oil crisis exposed their vulnerability to and dependence on Middle East oil. Comparatively developing countries were even more seriously affected since a number were unable to pay the increased prices without further borrowing. Thus the oil crisis badly affected their economies and also increased their international debt problems. The oil crisis had four important consequences:

- It prompted a search for energy savings especially amongst advanced countries.
- It intensified the search for alternative sources of oil to reduce dependence on OPEC countries. The rise in oil prices made it economic to exploit deposits in locations which, because of difficult physical conditions, had previously been too costly, notably in Alaska and the North Sea. In the process, large natural gas deposits were discovered and are making an increasing contribution to energy needs.
- It made countries look more to alternative sources of power, particularly renewable energy sources (Figures 27.5, 27.6 and 27.7).
- It accelerated the search for technologies to increase energy efficiency and access new sources of power.

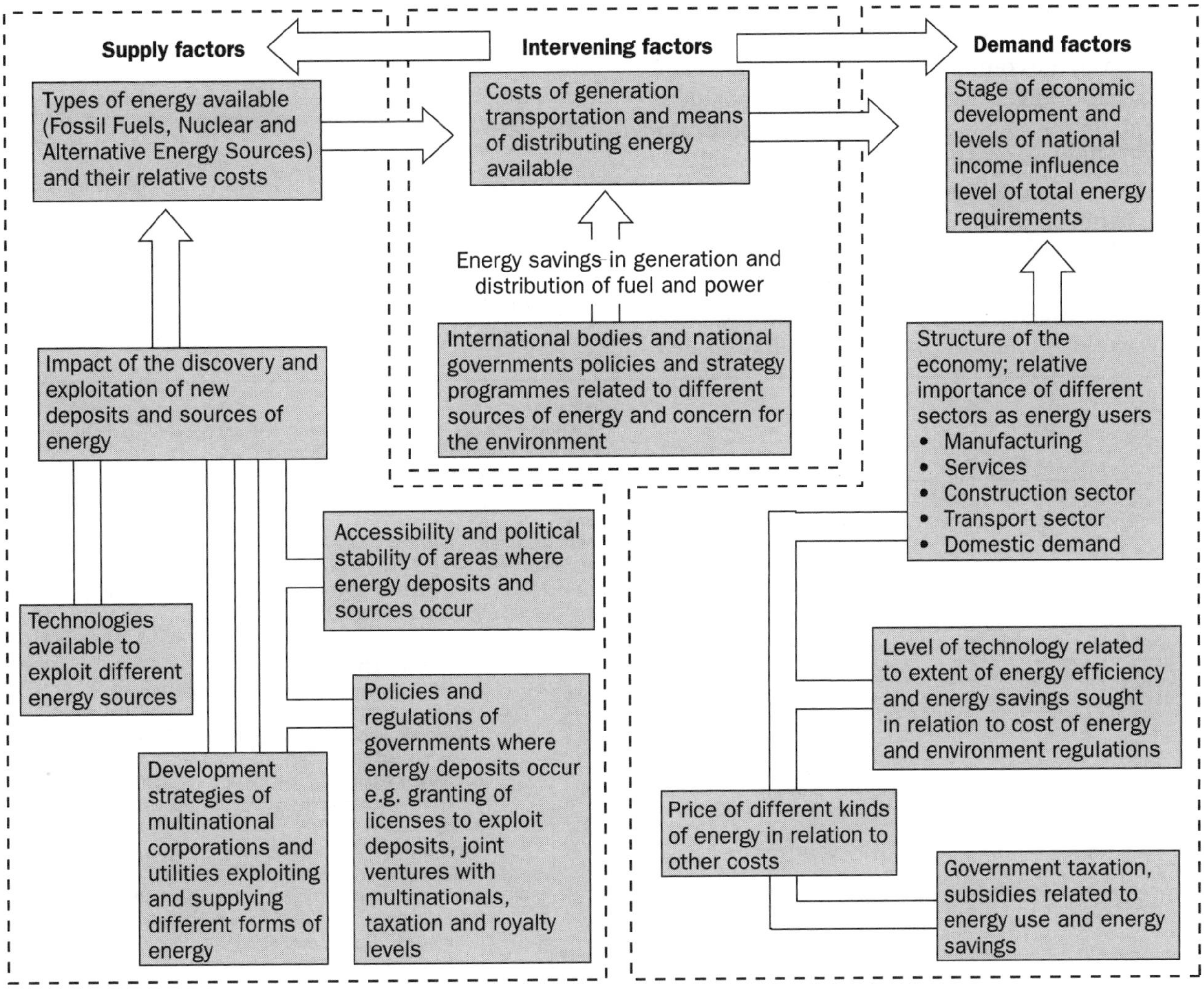

Figure 27.4 *Factors influencing the supply and demand for energy*

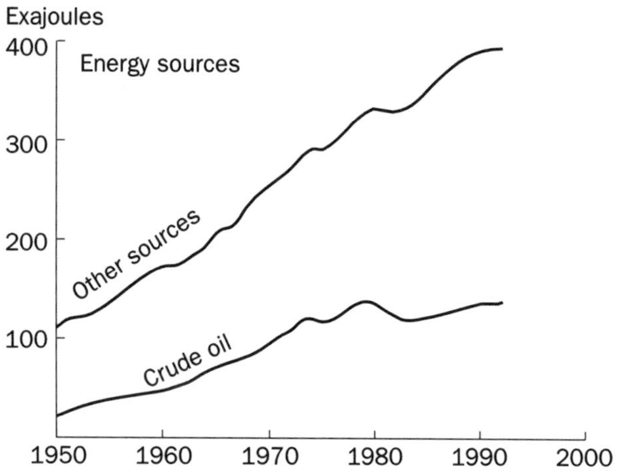

Figure 27.5 *Relative contribution of oil to other sources in changes in world energy supply, 1950 – 92*

As a result of the rise in energy prices, increased energy efficiency in industry, offices, transport and homes, and the growing impact of energy conservation programmes, the rate of growth in world energy use has decreased since the mid-1970s to 2% per annum.

However, the contribution of different sources of energy has changed (Figure 27.6). While fossil fuels will remain the main source for the foreseeable future, the contribution of coal has fallen and while oil remains important, the contribution of natural gas is rising significantly (Figures 27.7). Within the developing countries, biomass (mainly wood fuel) still provides 36% of the total energy used and it provides virtually all the fuel used by 2.5 billion people – 45% of the world's population living largely in rural areas.

Overall, the developing world's share of energy is rising since countries are at or entering stages of economic development of relatively intensive energy use while the share of advanced countries is falling as they are entering a post-industrial phase of energy efficiency. Even so, their share per capita is disproportionately high reflecting yet another measure of the inequalities between the world's 'rich North and poor South'.

It follows also that on a per capita basis '*the industrialised countries contribute a disproportionate share of the impact of fossil fuel consumption on the global commons (environment)*' though developing world use of biomass also has serious environmental implications.

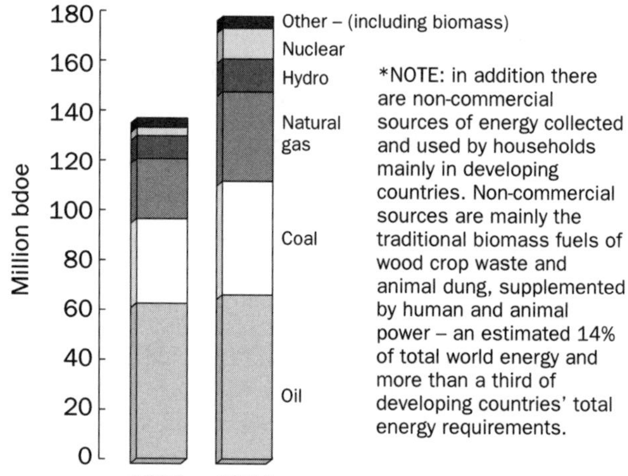

[SOURCE: *Energy in Profile*, 1995]

Figure 27.7 *Relative changes in sources of commercial energy* according to supply and demand, 1980 – 94*

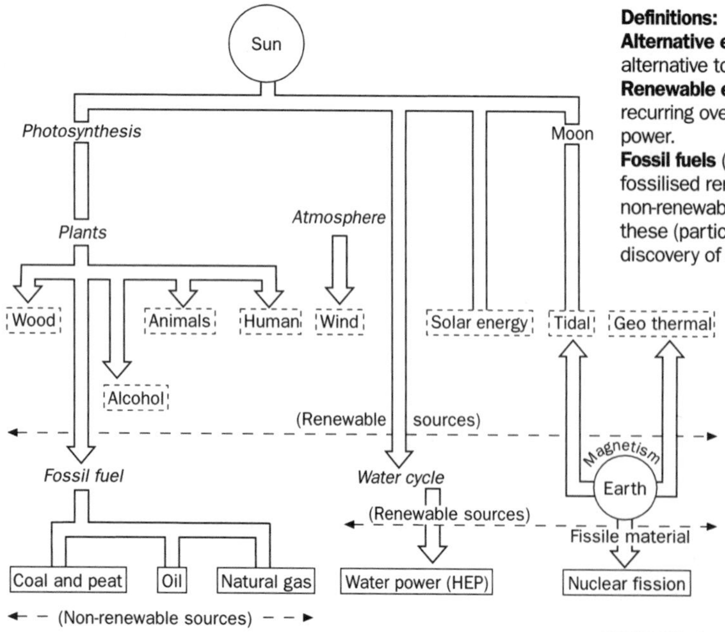

Figure 27.6 *Energy sources*

Definitions:

Alternative energy is 'renewable sources of energy which offer an alternative to fossil fuels and nuclear power'

Renewable energy is infinite energy sources which are of a 'flow nature' recurring over time e.g. precipitation the renewable basis of hydro-electric power.

Fossil fuels (non-renewable energy) are combustible materials made from fossilised remains e.g. lignite, peat, coal, oil and natural gas. These are non-renewable in the sense that once deposits have been exhausted these (particular) deposits cannot be renewed. However, the continuing discovery of new deposits can extend the world's reserves of fossil fuels.

Other related terms:

Primary energy is energy derived from renewable resources such as the sun, wind and wood and directly from fossil fuels i.e. natural gas, oil and coal.
These should be distinguished from –

Secondary energy e.g. petrol, coke, manufactured gas and electricity which is derived from the processing of primary energy.

Thermal electricity is electricity generated in thermal power stations which make electricity by boiling water to make steam which turns the generators. These are conventional power stations using fossil fuels such as coal, oil and natural gas. Thermal electricity generation also includes nuclear power stations which use thermal neutrons.

[SOURCE: Small J and Witherick M *A modern dictionary of geography*, 1995]

An extraordinarily wide range of environmental degradation is associated with fossil fuel production, transport, and use. Local effects include land degradation from strip-mining of coal and the disposal of deep-coal mine tailings, and from oil and gas production and transport in fragile environments; freshwater pollution from acid mine drainage, oil refinery operations and improper disposal of used petroleum products; marine pollution from oil spilled or deliberately flushed out of tankers; and air pollution from fossil fuel combustion (sulphur dioxide and particulates), refinery operations (toxic emissions), coal combustion (dust and soot), and industrial and automobile fuels (urban smog). Regional effects include acid precipitation, primarily from coal and oil combustion, with its impact on monuments; buildings; forests and other vegetation; soil and lakes. In addition, there is the potential global impact of climate change driven by greenhouse gases such as carbon dioxide, a product of all fossil fuel combustion, and methane emitted during the production, transport, and use of natural gas.

[SOURCE: *World Resources 1994 – 95*, 1994]

27.3 **Impact of the Eco Shock**

While the economics and politics of oil dominated world energy changes between the mid-1970s and the mid-1980s, since the late 1980s energy markets have been increasingly shaped by the realisation of growing environmental problems and responses to them.

Disasters, examples of which increasingly highlight a world environmental crisis

- 1986 – Explosion at the Chernobyl nuclear plant in the Ukraine sending a radio-active plume across much of Central and Western Europe – hastened the scaling down in the projected growth of nuclear energy – numerous planned nuclear power stations abandoned.
- 1989 – The wrecking of the oil tanker the Exxon Valdez left an extensive oil slick in the ecologically fragile Prince William Sound off Alaska, highlighting both oil pollution problems and the still major place of oil in world energy consumption, contributed to the growing move towards more environmentally friendly sources of energy.
- 1992 – a series of droughts across North America and in Africa and abnormal weather conditions in other parts of the world, together with prominent statements from government agencies and scientists brought the public face-to-face with the problem of 'global warming' as the atmosphere absorbed heat from the growing amounts of trapped carbon dioxide and other gases. Much of these came from the increasing amount of fossil fuels being generated and used in industry, offices, homes and different modes of transport. A consciousness of the problem of global warning has been a major factor in increased legislation to rescue air pollution and the growing emphasis on achieving greater energy efficiency.

Exploitation of energy resources and the use of energy cause considerable environmental damage on land, in the waters and in the atmosphere. A series of events over the last decade have brought environmental issues right to the forefront of the energy debate. They have increased public concerns on different kinds of energy and have forced governments and commercial interests to take action.

While single events served to highlight environmental problems, increased environmental concern can be traced to at least three other strong and continuing influences:

- Technical advances were made which enabled environmental effects to be more accurately measured. These included major improvements in satellite reconnaissance from the air, making it much easier to locate and measure the extent of environmental damage and more accurate data on past climate trends and current rates and causes of global warming.
- There was a very significant growth in the number and influence of environmental pressure groups such as 'Green Peace' which operates on an international scale to link and mobilise public opinion. Ready platforms for disseminating concerns were provided by the press and more potently, through television coverage with on-the-scenes reporting reaching a continually expanding audience across the globe.
- The number of official agencies concerned with enforcing environmental legislation was growing as was the amount of attention given to the problem by government bodies and commercial concerns. The USA government passed 'The Clean Air Act' in 1972 and subsequently most advanced countries and some developing countries passed similar acts, setting air quality standards and control on emissions in to the atmosphere. As a result, by the late 1980s key pollutant emissions in new cars were 90% – 95% less than for cars produced in the early 1970s and there was a similar scale of reductions of sulphur dioxide emissions from new power stations.

However, the world measure of sulphur dioxide emissions was down by only 26% and that of nitrogen oxides (car exhaust fumes being a major contributory factor) by only 15%. Much of the saving brought about stricter pollution controls was offset by the continued rise in the total amount of world energy being produced. One of the best methods of control is a reduction in the rate of world energy increase through greater energy efficiency. Better use of energy generated would reduce the demand for additional energy.

A turning point – The Rio Earth Summit of 1992

The United Nations 'Earth Summit' at Rio de Janeiro in 1992 was convened to initiate global action for a clean up of the environment and stabilise it for the next century. The issue of energy was on the agenda, particularly in relation to the threat of global warming. One of the main intentions was to set global deadlines for curbing harmful gaseous emissions from vehicles, power stations and factories. As a result of the summit meeting, 106 participating nations signed an agreement to submit action plans to stabilise greenhouse gas concentrations in the atmosphere, the plans to be enforced from 1994 onwards.

Increased funding has been devoted to energy saving projects and more research has been done into renewable energy technologies. The biggest stumbling block to greater progress is the reluctance of governments to significantly reduce subsidies which actually encourage fossil fuel burning and their failure to impose a carbon tax which would discourage the use of these fuels. This is particularly so in developing countries where energy consumption is rising the fastest.

Even in the OECD countries which have more active pollution control and energy saving programmes, carbon dioxide emissions are forecast to rise slightly over the 1990s. However, the efforts vary from one country to another. The Netherlands and Denmark for example do have effective programmes which shift the emphasis away from coal and oil and include a ban on nuclear energy generation in favour of a greater use of more environmentally friendly natural gas and renewable energy.

Greater energy efficiency

There is a growing belief that the most effective way of reducing the detrimental environmental effects of energy generation and use is by a drive towards greater energy efficiency. Greater energy efficiency would reduce harmful gaseous emissions into the atmosphere, emissions into the soil and water and reduce the rate of growth in energy consumption. Studies increasingly indicate that there is enormous potential for energy savings and that over a comparatively short time the cost of achieving these would be recouped. Where energy savings have been instituted there is significant evidence of an overall reduction in costs. The major opposition to increasing energy efficiency comes from vested interests and lack of will. Also, while energy efficiency can be built into new plants, new machinery, new means of transport and appliances, it may be costly to convert established plant and equipment. Within developing countries there is also the basic difficulty of raising the large initial capital outlay needed.

However, the overall structure of the economy must also be considered. As advanced countries have deindustrialised and moved away from energy intensive heavy industries towards a service-based economy and high technology information-based industries, then their economies have become more energy efficient overall. In contrast as developing countries industrialise, their economies are likely to be less energy efficient. On average from 1973 to 1991, the energy use in developing countries expanded 28% faster than did their economies.

Examples of energy conservation through better energy efficiency

As energy costs rose from 1973 to 1988 and governments and businesses became increasingly conscious of environmental issues, so there have been greater efforts across both the public and private sectors to increase energy efficiency.

For example in the production of iron and steel, the introduction of continuous casting in integrated works reduced the amount of fuel needed per unit of steel production. Energy savings were also improved with the increased switching of a proportion of steel making to smaller, more energy efficient electric arc furnaces. Savings were also made in the production of goods and buildings by replacing energy intensive materials with alternative materials. For instance, steel in automobile bodies has been increasingly replaced by plastics and lighter metals such as aluminium and the amount of steel in office construction reduced by a third compared with 30 years ago.

In the case of the energy, heating and lighting used in factory buildings, huge savings have been made through 'cogeneration' of both heat for the buildings and electricity to drive machinery and provide lighting rather than using separate sources. In the home, wall insulation and double glazing reduces heat loss and thus the energy needed to heat the home.

Improvements in energy generation and transmission of electricity

There have also been marked savings during the actual generation and distribution of electricity. Modern power stations now require less fuel to generate the same amount of electricity, both reducing harmful gas emissions and saving on fossil fuels.

> **Demand for energy efficiency is focusing on the generators**
>
> **More efficient modern power plants**
> What privatisation may do is open up the generation side of the market for new, more efficient technologies. Nearly all of the plant being built or proposed today is based on combined cycle gas-fired turbines (CCGT) which achieve greater efficiency levels than conventional coal-fired plants. It has also raised the profile of combined heat and power (CHP), which has potential efficiency levels of more than 80 per cent.
>
> [SOURCE: *The Electricity Industry, Financial Times Special Supplement* 25.4.91]

Transmission and distribution of energy is undergoing rapid improvements through such technological advances as replacing conventional iron core transformers by amorphous metal transformers, representing a saving of 70% – 90% electricity previously lost as electric power passes from the generating station to the consumer. This and other technological advances have also made it economic to transmit electricity over increasingly longer distances.

Plans are now advanced to link national grid networks together to produce continental grid networks, transferring energy from one national grid to another. More integration will enable a more efficient use of different energy sources as well as more effectively meeting changing levels of demand. In turn because of this wider network, countries will have great flexibility on what sources and amounts of energy to use to meet their energy budgets.

Alternative energy sources

Yet another important way to reduce the demand for conventional forms of energy is through the increased use of alternative energy sources. Outside of developing countries where biomass fuels are extensively used, alternative energy sources are still making a very small contribution to world energy needs (Figure 27.6).

27.4 **Coal**

Production and consumption

There are still vast world reserves of economically recoverable hard and soft coal and despite concerns about detrimental effects of coal mining and coal-powered electricity generating plants on the environment, it is likely to remain an important energy source well into the twenty-first century. Already considerable progress has been made towards creating 'clean coal' power generation, so markedly reducing the harmful effects of gas emissions from power plants.

World production continues to increase (Figure 27.8). For example, hard coal production rose by 109 million tonnes from 1993 to 1994 to a level of 3565 million tonnes, while consumption went up by a similar amount to 2546 million tonnes (Figure 27.8). Production and consumption of soft brown coal and lignite also remained steady at around 1100 million tonnes.

Changes in world production of hard coal, 1980 – 94

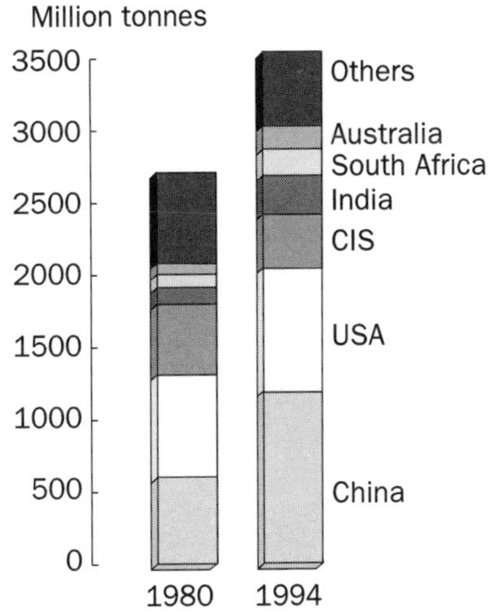

Coal consumption, 1994

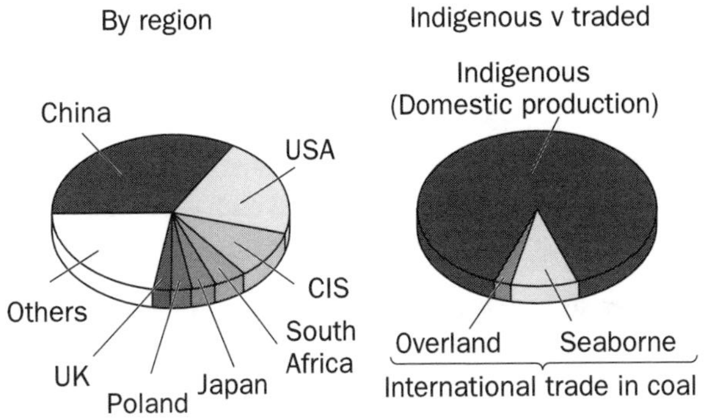

Total: 35465 million tonnes

Figure 27.8 *Coal production, consumption and sources*

Expansion of consumption was largely due to an expansion of demand in South East Asia where new power plants are being built to meet rising energy needs as economic growth gathers momentum with increasing industrialisation. China is one of the world's main coal producers; it is the largest consumer with coal currently meeting around 75% of the country's energy needs. Other South East Asia industrialising countries have to rely to an important extent on coal imports mainly from Australia and the USA which have surplus production (Figure 27.9). However, the advanced industrial countries still rely on coal for about a quarter of their energy needs; the USA is self-sufficient (Case study 27.5) but West European countries are importing an increasing amount, despite having large coal reserves.

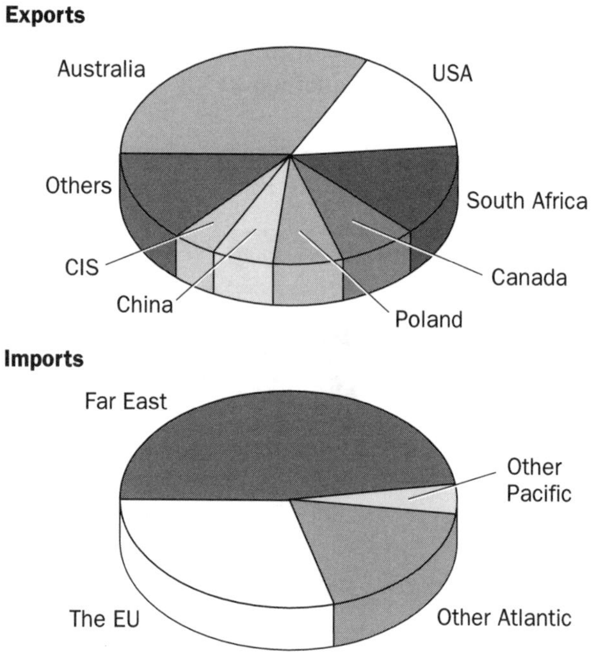

Total trade: 407 million tonnes

Figure 27.9 *World trade in coal*

Coal makes only a minor contribution to the energy requirements of the developing countries. However, its share may expand beyond the present 10% as industrialisation increases and capital becomes available to exploit the considerable reserves which are known to exist .

Factors affecting mining and production

The distribution of mineable reserves, whether by shaft mining or open-cast methods is very uneven. Although the relative importance of factors affecting whether deposits will be exploited or not varies from one location to another, the following factors affect most decisions about working a deposit.

Location and mode of occurrence

Like oil, coal deposits vary in quality and mode of geological occurrence. This, together with their location relative to markets, greatly influences whether a deposit will be worked or not.

The easiest to work and therefore the cheapest to extract is near the surface because it can be strip mined. Although costs have increased since it has become the responsibility of the mining operator to restore the landscape scarred by open-cast mining, it is still cheaper to work than deeper coal. Technological advances in machinery have also made it possible to work on a much larger scale. Open-cast mining is on the increase, particularly in the western USA where the Navajo mine near Farmington, New Mexico, is one of the largest in the world (Case study 27.2).

The rest of the world's coal is extracted by shaft mining, but as the ore accessible seams are worked out, these are at increasing depths, making working more expensive. Most of the mining is now on the concealed part of coalfields with a consequent closure of old pits on the exposed field, loss of jobs and the decline of mining settlements. This is seen in the eastward shift of coal mining on the fields along the eastern flank of the English Pennines though even here coal mining has significantly diminished over the early 1990s (Case study 27.1).

Fortunately low grade coal such as brown coal and lignite also occur near the surface and if deposits are large and close enough to a market then they will be worked. Most low grade coal is consumed in thermal power stations. For example, lignite from the Tula field in the Kasnoyansk in Siberia is extracted to supply power to Moscow.

Relative price of alternative sources of coal and fuel

Other factors such as the price of alternative coal supplies and that of competing fuels such as oil and gas also affect whether or not the coal will be mined. Cheap imported coal and North Sea oil and gas for example have severely affected the profitability of the coal mining industry in the UK (Case study 27.1). The USA has nearly a quarter of the world's coal reserves and the depletion of its reserves of oil and gas and the rising price of imported oil during the first half of the 1970s have greatly stimulated the extension of coal mining in western USA (Case study 27.2).

Such is the abundance of coal in China relative to other sources of power, that China intends to base much of its massive industrial expansion on utilisation of its coal resources despite the distance of the main world coalfields in the north-west from the main markets in the south-east of the country (Case study 6.1). At present almost 40% of train freight consists of coal transhipments. The government is negotiating with a large American Corporation to build a 900 km coal slurry pipeline to transport coal from the coalfields to the main consuming area in the Gaundong Province in the south-east and to export ports.

Location of market and size of demand

The main markets for coal are thermal power stations, steel and metallurgical industries. Demand is thus greatest in the advanced industrial countries and the rapidly industrialising countries of South East Asia.

Environmental costs and the cost of 'clean coal' technology

Amongst the different forms of fuel used for power generation, it is generally agreed that coal has the most detrimental effects. While ground pollution is a serious hazard, the greatest objection to the use of coal has arisen from its contribution to air pollution and global warning.

Environmental arguments have had an important influence in limiting the increase in coal powered thermal stations in Western Europe in favour of expansion of the cleaner gas-fired power stations (Figure 27.10). However, amongst other major consumers, even though there has been a serious response to the demand for a reduction in pollution from coal-fired power stations, the use of coal has continued to expand. There is a growing tendency towards clean coal generation but this is costly and progress will depend on how prices compare against the alternative use of oil and gas fuel. At present gas-fired generation is cheaper while oil-fired generation is about the same and also itself poses environmental problems.

27.5 The importance of the oil industry

The dimensions of the oil industry are somewhat different to those for coal. Despite the search for new oil and alternative energy sources following the oil crisis of the early 1970s, most industrial countries continue to depend on oil imports, especially from the Middle East. Discovery and continuing development of the vast North Sea oil and gas deposits have reduced this for the EU countries, especially the UK, but the USA and Japan in particular, will continue to be dependent on oil imports, although these countries have widened their sources throughout the 1980s and early 1990s. Newly Industrialised countries such as South Korea and China, have now also become net importers.

While oil is being replaced to some extent by natural gas and other alternative sources as a source of electric energy (Case study 27.1), there are areas in which oil supplies will remain critical for the foreseeable future. These are in transportation (in the forms of diesel oil, jet fuel and petrol) and as the main basis for the petro-chemical industry which is the source of many products such as plastics, artificial fibres and various chemicals. Like fuel oil, these products are vital to modern economies.

Oil imports are equally critical to many lesser developed countries, particularly in tropical Africa. In the future their importance is likely to increase as transportation and industry expand. Already while oil consumption is rising only slowly amongst the mature industrialised countries, it is rising more steeply in tropical countries, notably in Latin American and South East Asia.

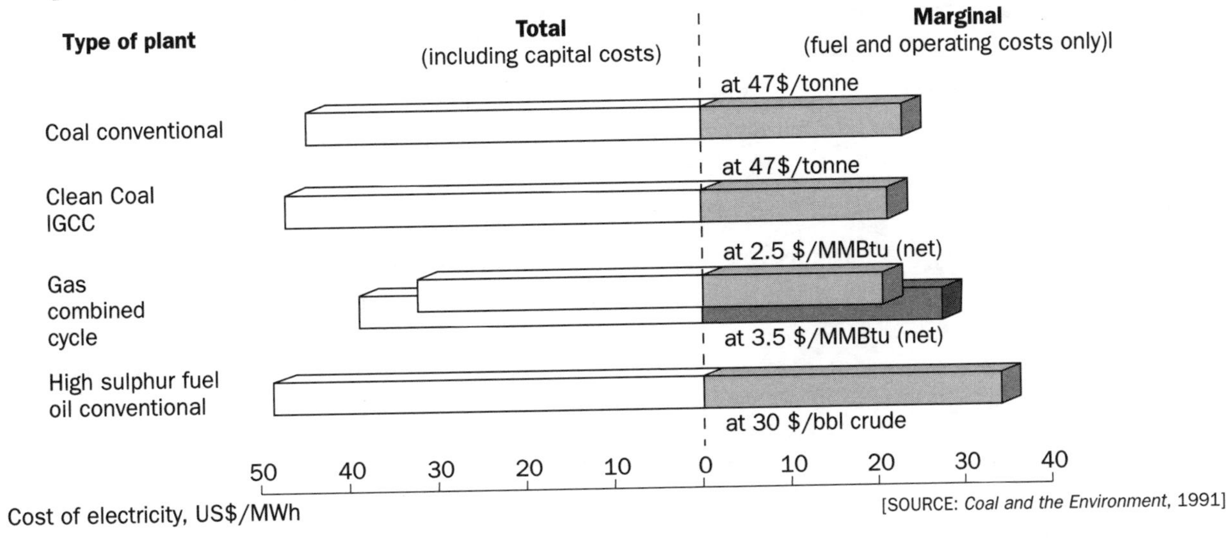

Figure 27.10 Relative costs of different kinds of thermal power generation

Production, trade and consumption

Oil is a finite resource yet known and proven world reserves have been increasing significantly, rising from 625 billion barrels in 1973 to 1004 billion in 1993. New fields are being discovered and as technology improves, established reserves have been substantially increased for a number of fields, including those in the North Sea. Much exploration is offshore though significant finds are also being made in more remote inland areas such as Amazonia. There is little likelihood of the world running out of oil in the foreseeable future. Future production is likely to depend on a range of other factors including the relative cost of exploiting the oil, its market price compared to alternative energy sources and world politics (Case study 27.3).

Petroleum occurs in porous sedimentary rocks which are interbedded with non-porous rocks, thus trapping the oil and associated gas. Gently folded rock providing anticlines in which the oil and gas concentrates, present the most favourable conditions and these occur in certain parts of the world such as the Middle East and in off-shore basins such as those now being developed in the North Sea, on the edge of the Mexican Gulf and off parts of South East Asia. Oil also occurs in the oil shales such as those in the Athabasca basin of Canada

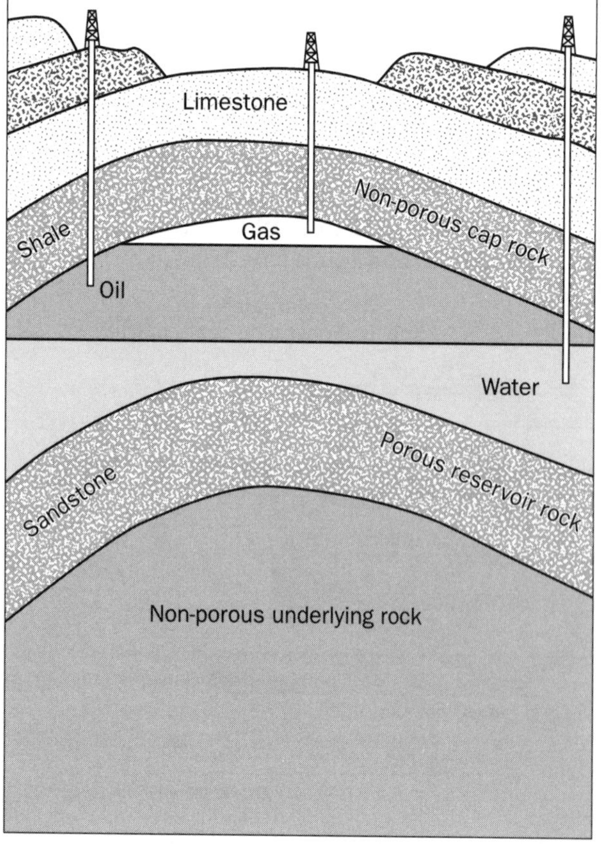

Figure 27.11 Oil and petro-chemicals

Three quarters of the world's oil reserves are to be found in the OPEC countries and half in the Middle East (Figure 27.12). Saudi Arabia alone has a quarter of world oil reserves and as a leading world producer and exporter, exercises an important influence on the world economy. Apart from the CIS countries, the industrialised world has relatively few reserves. More reserves exist in the non-OPEC developing countries; for example, significant finds have recently been made off the Malaysian coast and in the Philippines. The increase in these non-OPEC countries is largely due to the efforts of western oil companies which are trying to reduce their dependence on OPEC supplies.

Total: 1004 billion barrels, at 1 January 1994

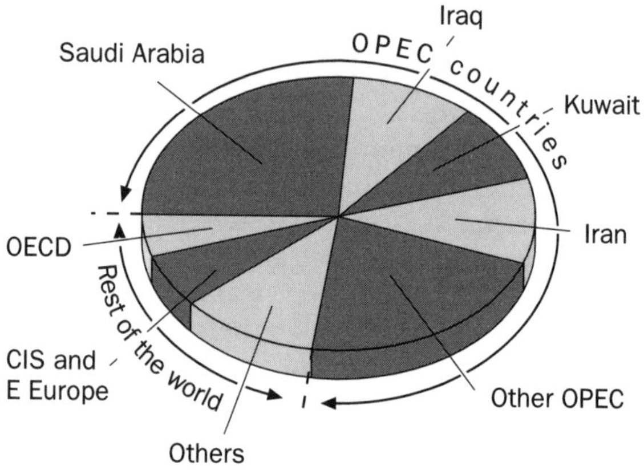

[SOURCE: *Energy in Profile*, 1994]

Figure 27.12 Proven oil reserves

The OPEC countries produced 40% of the world's oil in 1994 with Saudi Arabia amongst the three top world producers and continuing to expand production, while in the USA and the FSU (Former Soviet Union countries) production has continued to decline (Figure 27.13). Because of the embargo on Iraq oil trading since the Gulf War, this country has temporarily lost its position as an important oil producer. Conversely Kuwait, having had its oilfields destroyed in the Gulf War, is now regaining importance. Amongst Latin American producers, the leading countries of Mexico and Venezuela are expanding production. With regard to North Sea production, recent developments of new fields such as the Scott field and 'redevelopment' of established fields led to record production levels in 1995 (Case study 27.3). While modest in terms of percentage of world production, this increase is important to the economies of the European Union countries, in particular the UK and Norway.

Production – 1993 (million barrels a day)

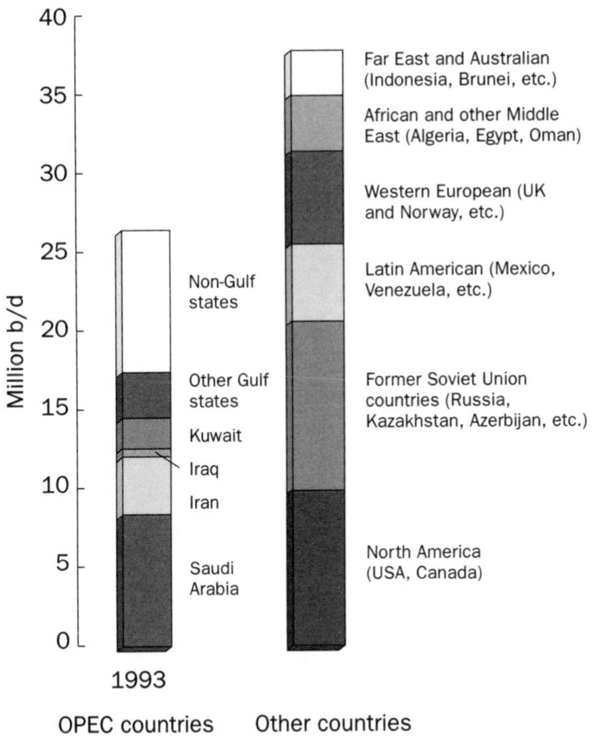

Figure 27.13 *Oil production, 1993*

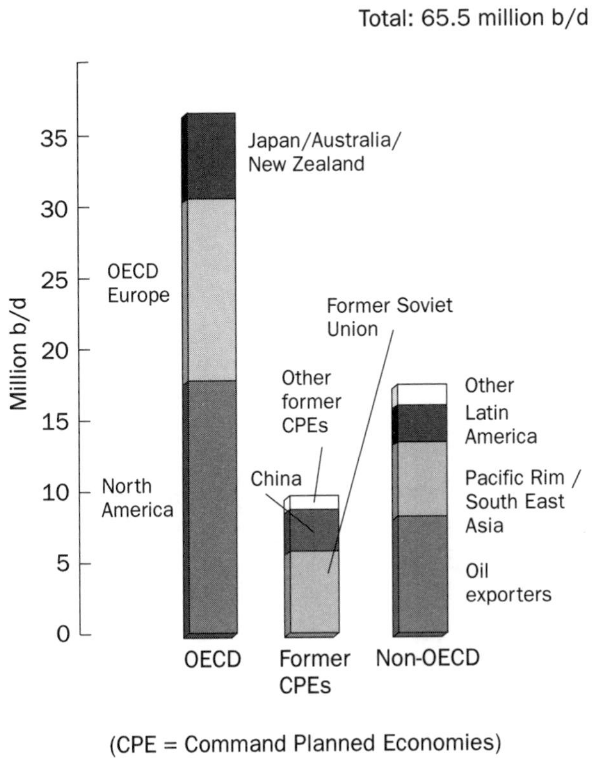

[SOURCE: *Energy in Profile*, 1994]

Figure 27.14 *World demand – 1993 (million barrels a day)*

World demand is expanding slowly at an estimated rate of 1.5% per annum, a level predicted to continue to the year 2000. The bulk of world consumption is in the advanced countries, 70% in the transport sector. Despite expansion of demand in the newly industrialising countries, the pattern of consumption will continue to be dominated by the USA, Japan and the other OECD countries.

Since many oil resources are far from oil markets, transportation and trade in oil are vital aspects of the oil industry. Over 60% of the world's crude oil is transported by sea though transport by oil pipeline from producing areas to shipping point or on-shore oil refinery is also a vital link in the transportation chain. Despite the drop in production in the former Soviet Union, there is still also an important movement of oil by pipelines into Western Europe. This is likely to increase again as western oil companies negotiate production deals with the now independent countries, such as Azerbijan.

Shipment by sea was revolutionised by the introduction of bulk oil carriers in the late 1960s. The Large Crude Carriers (VLCCs) account for about half of the oil transported by sea today. Because of the economies of scale associated with these bulk carriers, freight costs have fallen dramatically; for example, between 1970 – 74 freight costs fell from 60% to 5% of the cost of acquiring crude oil and shipping it from the Arabian Gulf to Western Europe. However, there has been severe environmental costs associated with the introduction of bulk carriers. Environmental disasters due to major oil spillages resulting from the grounding and break up of certain bulk oil carriers testify to this.

The world trading pattern in oil is dominated by OECD countries as the main importers and the OPEC countries as the main exporters (Figure 27.14). This reflects the fact that domestic production falls far short of demand while OPEC countries have a large surplus, home markets for oil being as yet very limited. The USA together with Japan, Germany, France, Italy and South Korea account for two thirds of imports. Since the early 1970s exports from OPEC countries have fluctuated considerably, reflecting the sensitivity of oil trade to political upheavals, economic recessions and price changes. Following the oil crisis of the early 1970s, oil exports from OPEC countries rose again to 90% of world trade in 1979 but fell back to 60% in 1985. Since then their share has gradually increased but they have faced increasing competition from non-OPEC countries, in particular Norway and Mexico. As the former Soviet Union republics become politically more stable and their economies reorganised, exports from this region will expand.

NOTE:
Total World Trade Flow = 32 million barrels a day; thickness of flow lines is proportionate to percentage of total flow.

Figure 27.15 *World oil trade flows, 1993*

Since the 1980s there has been surplus world oil capacity in relation to demand and as a result, OPEC countries have had to accept a sharp fall in oil prices with drastic consequences for their oil revenues. Since oil is a key source of revenue, this fall has had a serious effect on the economies of OPEC countries.

The petro-chemical industry and its location

Vast oil refining petro-chemical industries have developed based on the exploitation of crude oil and gas. They supply the world with a range of items considered vital to modern living including fuels, plastics, artificial fibres, a range of fertilisers and heavy chemicals, bitumen for road surfacing, protein foods and a host of other products (Figure 27.16).

Because so many derivatives are associated with oil it has proved more economic in the past to locate both refining and the petro-chemical industries at points of entry into the consuming countries. Hence most large ports such as Rotterdam, Antwerp and Southampton have an oil-refining and heavy chemicals sector. These are usually locationally distinct from other port activities and at a distance from any residential areas because of the obnoxious character of petroleum refining and the heavy chemicals industry and also because of the potential risk associated with it. However, there are other factors involved such as the need for large sites both for the plants and marshalling yards adjacent to them, the need for large water supplies and coastal access to dispose of treated effluent. While the industry is capital intensive, a large financial outlay being needed to establish the plant and associated infrastructure, it is not labour intensive and therefore access to labour is not a significant locational factor.

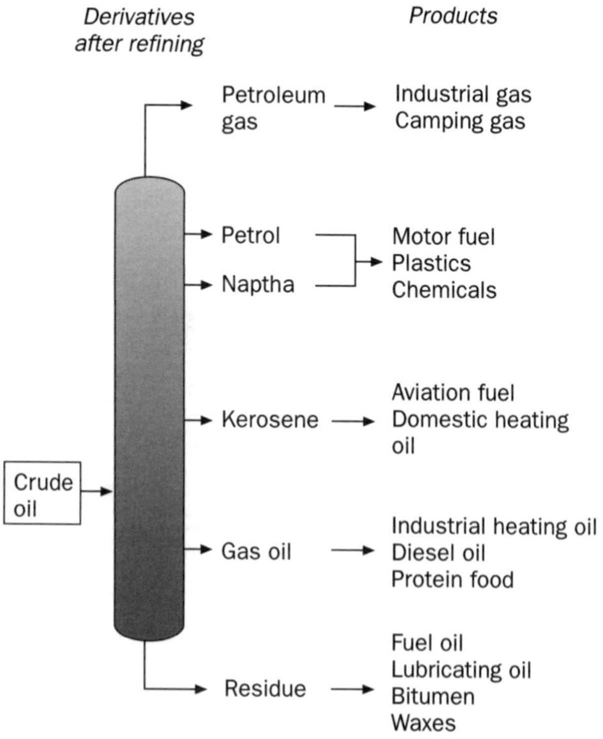

Figure 27.16 *Products of crude oil refining*

Apart from the need of a coastal location where oil or natural gas can readily be brought ashore or imported, the industry does require access to a good communication network both by rail and road for the shipment of varied products to their distinctive markets. Road transport with the use of economic bulk road carriers and the construction of a national motorway network in advanced countries, has become increasingly important.

During the 1950s and 1960s as demand for oil and gas products expanded and the size of ocean bulk oil carriers increased to over 100 000 tonnes, new deep-water coastal locations were sought outside of the established port complexes which neither had the necessary deep-water anchorages to accommodate bulk carriers nor the site space for large scale petro-chemical complexes. In some cases new sites were developed close by as at Marseilles and Rotterdam, further down the estuary, or a short way along the coast where both deep-water access and large sites were available on drained alluvial flats. In a number of cases totally new sites were developed at some distance from established ports. In some, multiple usage was developed, iron and steel or aluminium smelting also being established at the same coastal site. In the UK, Teesside provides an example of the latter while Milford Haven in Pembrokeshire was an example of a one purpose development for oil-refining and petro-chemicals.

During the economic recession, which deepened at the end of the 1970s, the petro-chemical industry in most advanced countries suffered from over-capacity. Consequently a number of these new large specialist complexes such as Milford Haven are being closed. In contrast, the oil-refining and petro-chemical industry was expanded in some of the oil producing countries, since overall, higher prices can be gained from refined products than from the export of crude oil or natural gas in liquified form. During the 1970s rising oil prices enabled OPEC countries to finance developments in this field. Pressure was also exerted on oil companies to invest more in refining in the producing countries. Also, as state companies have been founded to share in the exploitation of oil and gas resources, these have been financially supported by the state to process some of their own oil and gas production. Consequently oil and petro-chemical complexes have been expanded at established export points and at new shipment points including those for oil pipeline terminals.

Such developments are mirrored in other oil exporting countries such as Algeria, Mexico and Venezuela. However, expansion is limited due to current world over-capacity in oil-refining and petro-chemicals. Thus despite this trend towards more oil-refining in exporting countries, oil-refining and petro-chemicals measured by output remain overwhelmingly concentrated in the developed countries since they still supply the main markets.

Following a significant rationalisation in the oil-refining and petro-chemical industry during the 1980s to reduce over-capacity, world capacity in 1993 was back to its level at the end of the 1970s but the regional pattern has changed (Figure 27.17). The USA and the former Soviet Republic countries retain the largest share but some of the share of Western European countries has been lost to refineries in the Middle East, the Far East and Australia.

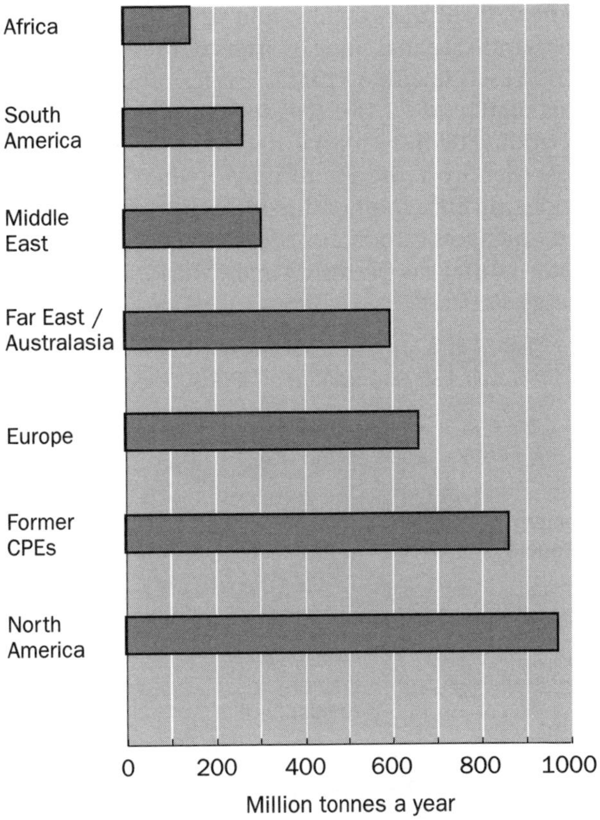

[SOURCE: *Energy in Profile*, 1994]

Figure 27.17 *World oil refinery capacity by region, 1993*

One of the biggest problems facing the oil-refining and petro-chemicals industry is the cost of upgrading refinery facilities to meet environmental legislation requiring cleaner products such as oxygenated gasoline, low sulphur diesels and cleaner waste emissions. This and the sluggish growth in demand in relation to capacity is likely to prevent any further significant changes in the pattern of the industry to the end of the twentieth century.

27.6 Natural and liquified gas – a major primary energy source

> 'Even as reliance on natural gas grows during the next decade, one of its most important features will become apparent; it is the logical bridge to what some scientists believe will be our ultimate energy carrier-gaseous hydrogen produced from solar energy and other renewable sources.'
> [SOURCE: Flavin C and Lenssen N *Power Surge*, 1995]

Until recently natural gas production has generally been regarded as an adjunct of oil production, since it is found associated with oil deposits and was extracted as part of the general development of an oil field. Continued exploration since the early 1970s indicate that three quarters of these reserves is 'non associated gas', that is, gas found separate from oil (Figure 27.18). This and the rapidly expanding demand for natural gas as the fossil fuel most friendly to the environment (when burnt producing little sulphur dioxide or nitrogen oxide and much less carbon dioxide than oil or coal), has made natural gas the third largest world primary energy source.

By region, 1993

Total: 135 000 milliard m^3 @ 9500 kcal/m^3

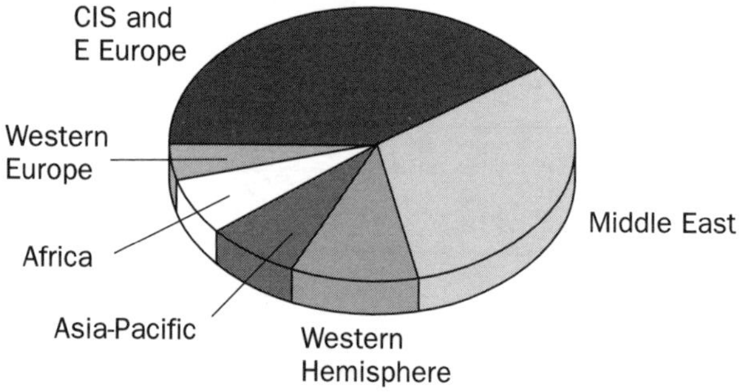

[SOURCE: *Energy in Profile*, 1994]

By country – 1990 (exajoules)

CIS	2100	**Saudi Arabia**	200
Iran	700	**USA**	200
Argentina	300	**Algeria**	125
Canada	300	**Iraq**	125
United Arab Emirates	225	**Venezuela**	125
		Norway	100
Qatar	200	**Indonesia**	100

[SOURCE: *Power Surge*, 1995]

***Figure 27.18** Proven reserves of natural gas, 1993 and 1990*

As technological advances have improved the efficiency of gas turbines, this has given gas an advantage in power generation so that its contribution to electricity supplies has expanded rapidly in recent years (Case study 27.1). There is also now in every country a complex system of natural gas pipelines which supplies gas heating and cooking systems. It is the most important source for heating for example in the Netherlands which, in addition to supplies from its own major offshore gas fields, imports natural gas from other North Sea fields and overland from Russia and Algeria. Natural gas is also likely to make a major contribution to transportation needs in the near future. One of the most important recent technological advances to widen its uses has been the development of the gas-powered fuel cell which can be made to all sizes, from power plant scale to a fuel cell to fit under a car bonnet.

There is no shortage of gas. At current rates of consumption proven reserves will last 60 years and new reserves are still being discovered although at increasing distances from the major markets. In 1993, 40% of proven gas reserves were in the former Soviet Union countries with another 30% in the Middle East, half of which was in Iran. Still the number of countries with known reserves continues to increase, including countries such as Argentina with few other energy sources (Figure 27.19).

In Europe, Norway and the Netherlands have giant gas fields and the UK also significant reserves, mainly offshore. The world's largest producers are the former Soviet Union countries and the USA (Figure 27.18). Here reserves are only 4% of the world total but production has been expanded to reduce dependence on imported oil and nuclear fuels for energy needs (Figure 27.20). Production in Western Europe has been expanding, the greatest increase being in the UK with 14 new fields initiated in 1993 (Case study 27.1).

Transportation is a key aspect of the gas business, fields being generally remote from markets. Most gas is transported by pipeline. For long distances, the gas is super cooled to a liquid state to reduce its volume to 1/600th of its original gaseous form. Liquified natural gas (LNG) can also be transported overseas by special tankers.

Most gas is consumed in the producing countries. Only 16% was exported in 1993 but the proportion is likely to increase if the costs of liquifying and transporting natural gas can be further reduced. The CIS are the largest exporters, mainly by pipeline to Germany and other EU countries.

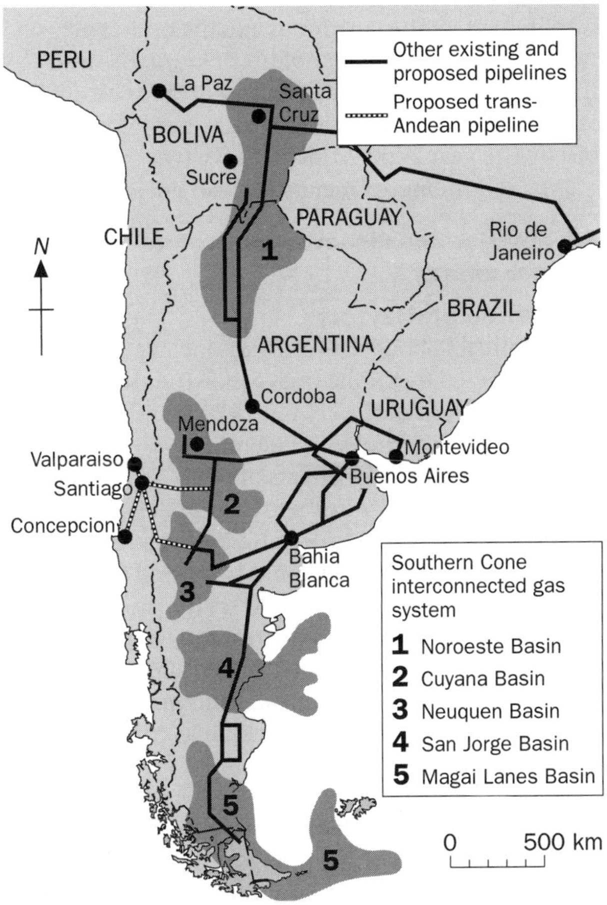

Argentina has major gas fields, the Noroeste Basin extending into Bolivia. These gas fields will make an increasing contribution to Argentina's energy needs and to those of her neighbours. For example trans-Andean gas pipelines are scheduled to be completed in 1997 to supply new gas power plants to be completed between 1998 – 2001. These are likely to replace existing coal- and oil-fired plants and lead to the delay of hydro-plant building as capital costs for these are much greater than for gas-fired plants. The main pipelines will be to Santiago, the capital, where a new environmental law operative in 1997 will force coal-fired plants and industries to switch to gas. Another gas pipeline spur will supply Concepcion, a centre for the pulp and paper industry, steel and fish meal plants.

***Figure 27.19** The importance of natural gas fields in supplying southern Latin American countries with power*

By far the most important market for liquified natural gas carried by sea is Japan since, though a major energy user, Japan has few energy resources of its own (Figure 27.22). The LNG trade is mainly centred on the Asia-Pacific region, two thirds of exports going to Japan from Indonesia and other surrounding countries such as Brunei, Malaysia and Australia. These also supply South Korea, the other major South East Asia importer. Another important development has been the emergence of Algeria as an important exporter. Algerian LNG mainly goes to France and USA. LNG trade is likely to make up an increasing proportion of the world trade in natural gas as more countries switch to a greater reliance on it as an energy and fuel source.

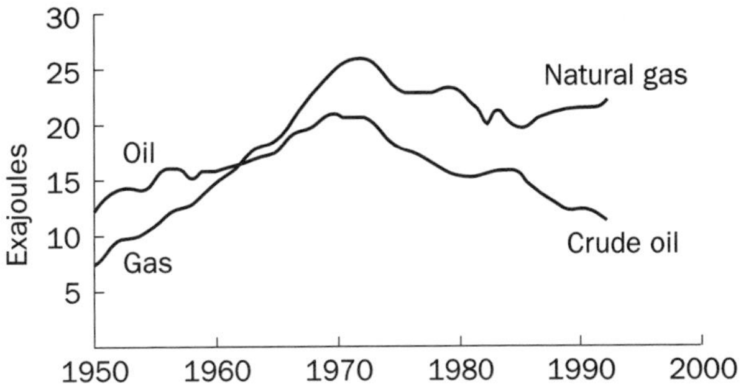

[SOURCE: *Annual Energy Review*, US Depot of Environment, 1993]

***Figure 27.20** Changes in crude oil and natural gas production, USA, 1950 – 93*

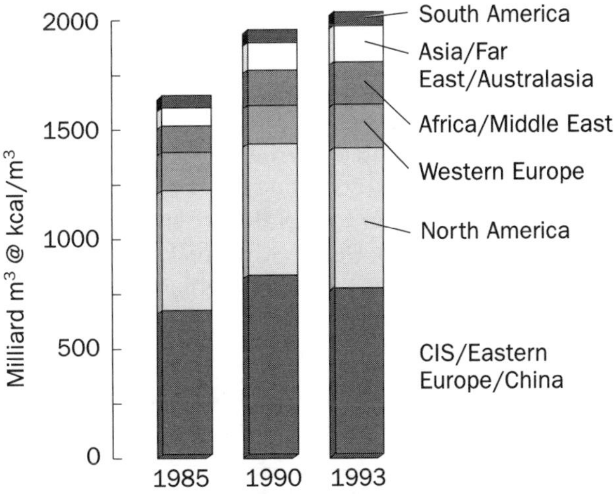

*Excludes reinjected/flared gas and shrinkage due to the extraction of NGL.

***Figure 27.21** The continued rise in gas production, 1985 – 93*

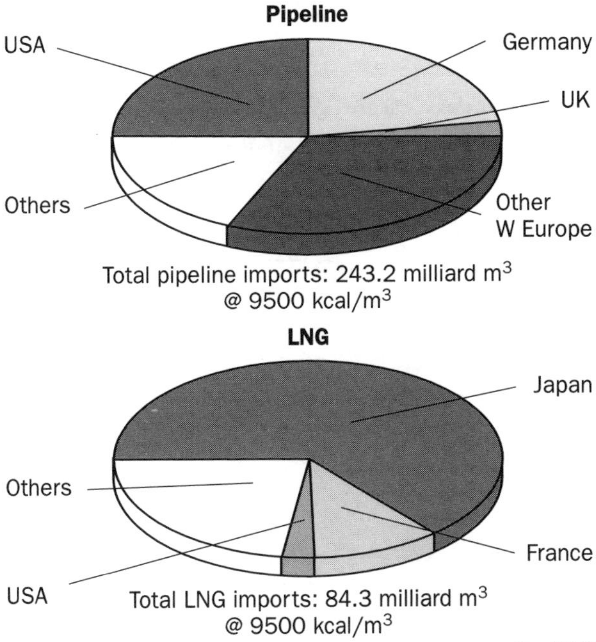

[SOURCE: *Energy in Profile*, 1994]

***Figure 27.22** Imports of natural gas, 1993*

27.7 **Nuclear energy**

Importance decreases in the developed world but expands in South East Asia

The contribution of nuclear to world energy supplies rose from 8% in 1980 to 17% by 1995, but its future as a source of energy is uncertain. Expansion has significantly slowed down from that originally forecast and its share of the world market is set to decline to between 13% to 15% by the year 2015. The reasons for the deceleration particularly in developed countries are two-fold: there is increasing public opposition to expanding nuclear energy further and there is also the commercial factor. In the changing energy climate, alternative sources are seen as more commercially viable and more risk-free.

Expansion of nuclear energy has been halted in advanced countries except in France and Japan which have very limited alternative domestic sources of energy and continue to see nuclear energy as a major contributor to their future energy requirements (Figure 27.23). Despite the break up of the Communist Bloc, nuclear energy remains significant in Eastern Europe notwithstanding the ageing of its nuclear reactors and continued fears of nuclear accidents. However, it is in South East Asia that most of the expansion of nuclear energy is planned. This is to help meet the enormous expansion in energy needs which occur as standards of living rise and industry rapidly expands. South Korea for example still relied on imported oil for half its energy in 1990 but by the year 2000, hopes to have two thirds of its energy requirements met by nuclear energy.

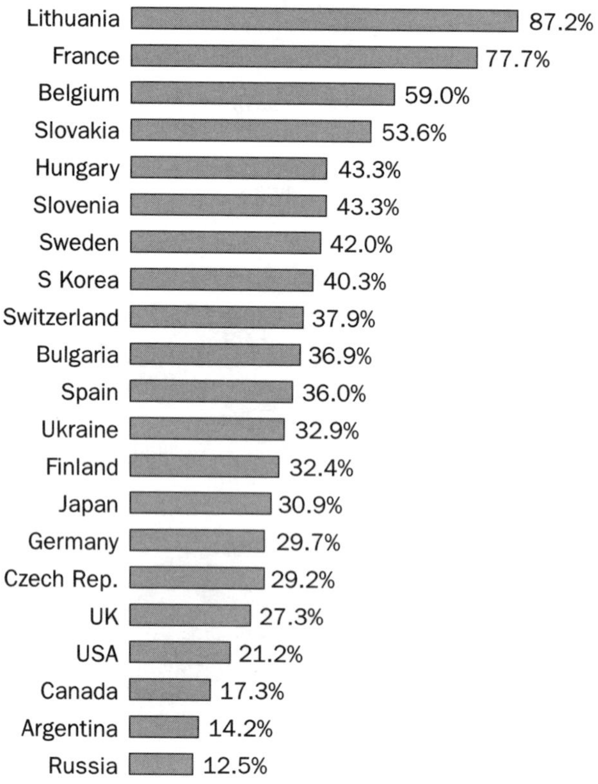

[SOURCE: IAEA (International Atomic Energy Agency)]

Figure 27.23 *Nuclear share of total electricity by major producers generation during 1993*

Advantages and disadvantages of developing nuclear energy

Environmental factors

Uncertainties about the future of nuclear energy were triggered by public fears following the Seven Islands accident in the USA in 1979 and the even more serious Chernobyl accident in 1986. In the case of Chernobyl, the effects of radio-active matter escaping into the atmosphere are still being felt and it is feared that if an accident involving a reactor blaze occurred, radiation could be carried into the water table and contaminate rivers for thousands of square kilometres around the reactor. Despite these particular incidents and media magnification of the dangers in developed countries, nuclear reactors so far have had as good a safety record as conventional power plants.

How to safely dispose of nuclear waste and decommission redundant reactors are causing the most concern, not only amongst environmentalists but also for governments and those in the nuclear industry itself. In the past, nuclear waste had been stored in barrels and some dumped at sea. For example, it is estimated that the Barents Sea near Russia contains two thirds of the radio-active waste dumped into the world's oceans. Amendments to the International Conventions on Marine Waste Option Disposal at sea have suspended disposal at sea until the year 2005. Land disposal is now the only option, either at the surface in concrete-like bunkers which can be monitored, or deep underground as suggested at Sellafield in the UK and the Gorleben salt mine in Germany. Because of fears of seepage especially if earth tremors occur, no agreement has been reached. Similarly in the USA no agreement has been reached on a permanent disposal site.

Some of the waste can be reprocessed to provide more nuclear power and less ultimate waste as is successfully happening at the Thorpe reprocessing plant near Sellafield. However, not all the waste can be reused in this way; thus the problem of permanent disposal remains.

Decommissioning of ageing reactors is now becoming a serious problem in terms of cost and on environmental grounds. High levels of radiation present in shutdown reactors mean that dismantling procedures are complex and costly and have to be spread over 100 years. So far in the UK decommissioning has begun at Berkeley power station in Gloucestershire and Trawsfyndd in Wales.

However, nuclear plants produce very little polluting gaseous emissions during operation compared to conventional stations and are held to be less intrusive in the landscape.

Economic issues

Economic arguments against further expansion of nuclear energy capacity have mounted as the generating industries have increasingly passed into the private sector and away from state ownership (Case study 27.1). Under the latter, capital expenditure was less governed by economic viability and running costs were subsidised. In investigating possible options for increasing generating capacity, private utilities are considering

- low capital costs
- power plants for which planning permission can be readily gained
- short lead times from the beginning of construction to the plant becoming operational
- power plants that can be flexibly used according to short-term fluctuations in the demand for electricity.

Gas-fired plants which have been increasingly favoured can fulfil these requirements but nuclear reactors cannot. They are very expensive to build. They frequently involve long and costly complex planning enquiries as for example in the building of the Sizewell B reactor in Suffolk which took 13 years to construct compared to four years for the gas-fired power plant at Killingholme on the River Trent in Nottinghamshire (Case study 27.1). Nuclear plants are inflexible, being mainly suitable for supplying base load into the grid system, that is, meeting the basic demand level as against seasonal increases in demand.

Added to this, is the decrease in the expansion of energy needs in the west largely due to the emphasis on increasing energy efficiency and the suspension of nuclear programmes.

However, these short- to medium-term economic arguments must be seen in terms of the world energy scene. Over the foreseeable future world energy needs will continue to rise, particularly amongst the newly industrialising countries. It is estimated that expansion of fossil fuel sources will be insufficient to meet expanding demand and that renewable energy sources in the short- and medium-term cannot be expanded sufficiently to bridge the gap. Thus nuclear expansion is seen as a necessity, especially where the scale of the rise in market demand warrants large installations to meet base load requirements. Flexibility in supply can be met by allying expansion of nuclear capacity with smaller installations of gas or other conventional power stations and development of renewable energy sources. This is the policy now being adopted by South East Asian countries where the greatest rise in world energy needs is occurring. Capital costs will be very heavy but planning time can be speeded up with less environmental opposition than would be anticipated in the west. Moreover, technological research is increasingly improving the safety aspects of nuclear reactors and bringing down operating costs.

The location and siting of nuclear power stations

The prime factors in the location of nuclear power stations are safety, location near abundant water and an expanse of level site. Coastal and other waterside sites away from population concentrations are thus more favoured (Case study 27.4). However, the location pattern in Eastern Europe is mainly inland but still on water side locations. Most plants are well away from large cities but as safety factors were not stringent as in the West, some nuclear plants have been built relatively close to particular cities, such as Minsk and Volvograd, to provide them with heat and power.

Apart from schemes to supply power to particular areas, electricity generated from nuclear reactors is fed into national grid networks. Thus markets have only a limited effect on the siting of reactors. Although disposal of exhausted reactor fuel presents a problem, its small volume makes it possible to transport it over large distances either by rail or road at off-peak times, thus reducing the risk of accidents.

The general pattern of location is unlikely to change in the near future as existing locational influences are likely to remain and there is a tendency to locate new reactors adjacent to old ones, as in the case of the Sizewell B plant. This is because agglomerative advantages can be gained from utilising an established infrastructure and ancillary support services.

27.8 Renewable energy sources

Contribution to world energy needs

Because of the limited resources of coal and oil and reservations about the expansion of nuclear energy, the search for alternative sources has intensified since the 1970s. Interest, research and investment in renewable energy resources has gathered further impetus with the increasing realisation of the negative effects of fossil fuels on the environment (Figure 27.24). However, apart from hydro-electricity

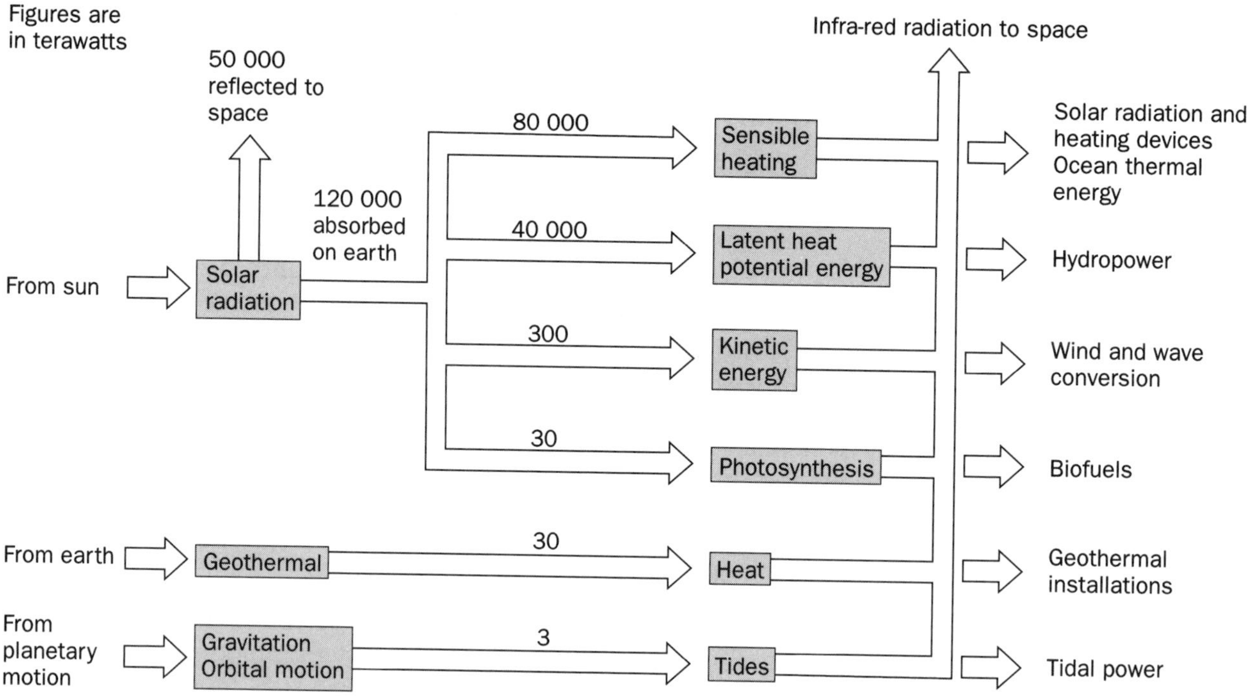

[SOURCE: Twidell and Weir *Renewable Energy Resources*]

Figure 27.24 *Sources of renewable energy and energy flows*

which contributes 6% of the world's commercial energy needs, renewable energy sources contribute only 2% to current needs. The World Energy Council in 1993 envisaged that despite their enormous potential, renewable energy resources would still only contribute 4% of world commercial energy needs by 2020. Half of this is likely to be from biomass sources. However, for certain countries the figure would be significantly higher.

There are formidable obstacles to any large-scale expansion of renewable energy sources. One is the much greater amount of investment needed; the World Energy Council estimates that 'ecologically driven' energy projects will require $2400 million of investment up to the year 2020, while to produce the same equivalent increase in energy from conventional sources would require only $930 million of investment. Nevertheless, most governments are sponsoring research and investment into renewable sources.

Although technological advances are reducing the unit costs of electricity produced by the different renewable sources, prices are in general significantly higher than the price of electricity produced by conventional means. Most governments are currently having to subsidise renewable energy production to keep the cost to the consumer at a reasonable level. (Figure 27.25). Also, renewables are not free from environmental problems. For example, wind farms occupy large land areas, are visually intrusive in the landscape and are noisy. The planned tidal barrages on the Severn and the Mersey estuaries in the UK have met with strong opposition, in particular because of their disruption of wildlife habitats (Case study 27.5).

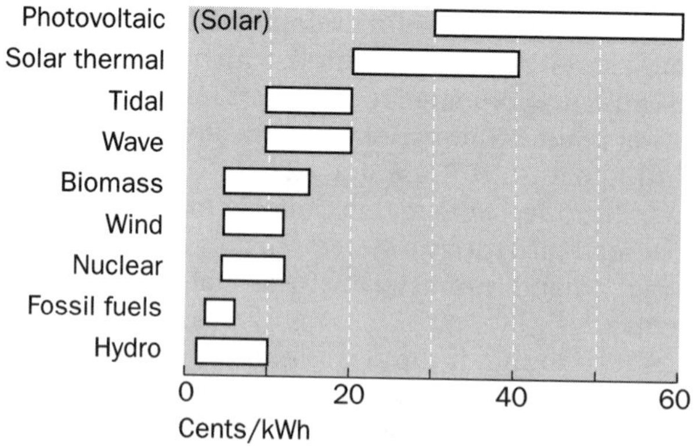

NOTE: Ranges from small scale plants (e.g. PV) installed close to end use to large scale central power plants (e.g. nuclear, fossil fuel) where distribution costs are not included.

Figure 27.25 *Cost of electricity from renewable sources relative to fossil fuels*

Wood fuel – 'the poor man's oil'

If non-commercial consumption of energy is considered then biomass is the fourth largest world energy source. It is the only source of fuel for heating and cooking for half the world's population, principally in the developing world. Wood fuel is by far the largest source; other biomass sources used are charcoal, straw, rice husks, other crop residues and animal dung. Wood is being used at an unsustainable rate and efforts to slow down the rate and encourage planting of fast growing species of trees such as eucalyptus have so far met with limited success (Case study 27.6).

However, while developed countries see renewables as alternative sources which will supplement conventional ones, it is likely that for developing countries the newer renewable energy sources such as solar energy, wind turbines and biomass, will be seen as essential to meet expanding needs, especially in rural areas. Future development is likely to be in the form of many small-scale schemes, meeting local needs and aiding the spread of electrification in rural areas.

Water power

Relative importance

Despite the vast potential of hydro-electric power, it actually contributes only a small proportion towards the world's energy needs. In 1991 it contributed one fifth of the world's electricity but only 6% of the total primary energy supplies. Nevertheless, hydro-electricity output has doubled in the last twenty years mainly because of schemes completed in the developing world which now has 37% of the world's installed capacity.

While the USA, Canada and Russia are the leading countries for hydro-electricity output, its contribution is relatively more important for those parts of the world which have few or limited oil, gas and coal reserves. These include much of South America where apart from Venezuela with large oil supplies and Argentina with recent large gas finds, hydro-electricity provides around three quarters of the electricity needed. It is also important to tropical African countries and parts of South East Asia. For some developed countries such as Switzerland, Norway and Sweden which have physical conditions favouring hydro-electric schemes, it is the major source of energy.

Energy from hydro-electricity has the advantage over energy based on coal, oil and natural gas in that it is based upon a renewable resource. (However, the problem of silting in reservoirs can effectively reduce the amount of water available.) It is also a clean and highly efficient source of energy. Whereas oil and coal have an efficiency of only 30%, hydro-electricity is 80% to 90% efficient, efficiency being based on that proportion of input which can be effectively used as energy. Per unit of output capital costs are much higher, hydro-electric schemes being very costly to install. For this reason, despite lower running costs, countries have only invested in schemes which have the best prospects.

Many of the world's largest potential sites are in remote and sparsely populated areas, for example on the upper reaches of the Amazon in South America. This raises the costs of the scheme, materials and labour being very costly to transport, and effectively puts the potential site out of reach of market demand. However, the distance over which electricity may be transmitted without too much loss in the process is being steadily increased. Up to the 1960s it was only possible to transmit electricity economically over 300 km, whereas by the 1970s it had been extended to 800 km.

This technological advance has been an important factor in large-scale hydro-electric schemes in some parts of Africa and Latin America. For example, the Cabora-Bassa scheme on the lower Zambezi in Mozambique was set up to supply power to Mozambique and to South Africa, which helped finance the scheme. Long distance transmission of energy is also contemplated for the Niger Dams project at Kainji, Jebba and Shiroro in Nigeria and for the largest single scheme in the world now recently completed at Itaipu on the Parana River. This will supply one fifth of Brazil's electricity needs as well as much of that of neighbouring Paraguay.

Hydro-electric power schemes can be be divided into two basic types: those solely constructed to generate electricity and multi-purpose schemes which supply power and are also designed for additional purposes such as the control of seasonal flooding, provision of irrigation water and to aid navigating by ensuring a consistent water level (Case study 28.4). In some cases, lake or reservoir schemes can also lead to an expansion of fishing. This is especially important in tropical regions where much of the malnutrition amongst people is due to protein deficiencies. Both types of schemes can also provide an added tourist attraction.

The factors which influence the development of hydro-electric schemes are outlined in Figure 27.26. Future development of large-scale schemes is in doubt due to growing opposition on environmental and social grounds. Schemes in remote mountain areas have a drastic impact in such environmentally sensitive areas, while schemes in lowland areas in addition to their environmental implications usually mean the drowning of settlements and displacement of communities. The Three Gorges Scheme on the Chaing Jian (Yangtze) River in China and that on the Narmada River in India have run into strong national and international opposition. Despite this, China has still embarked on the Three Gorges Scheme which will take 15 years to complete.

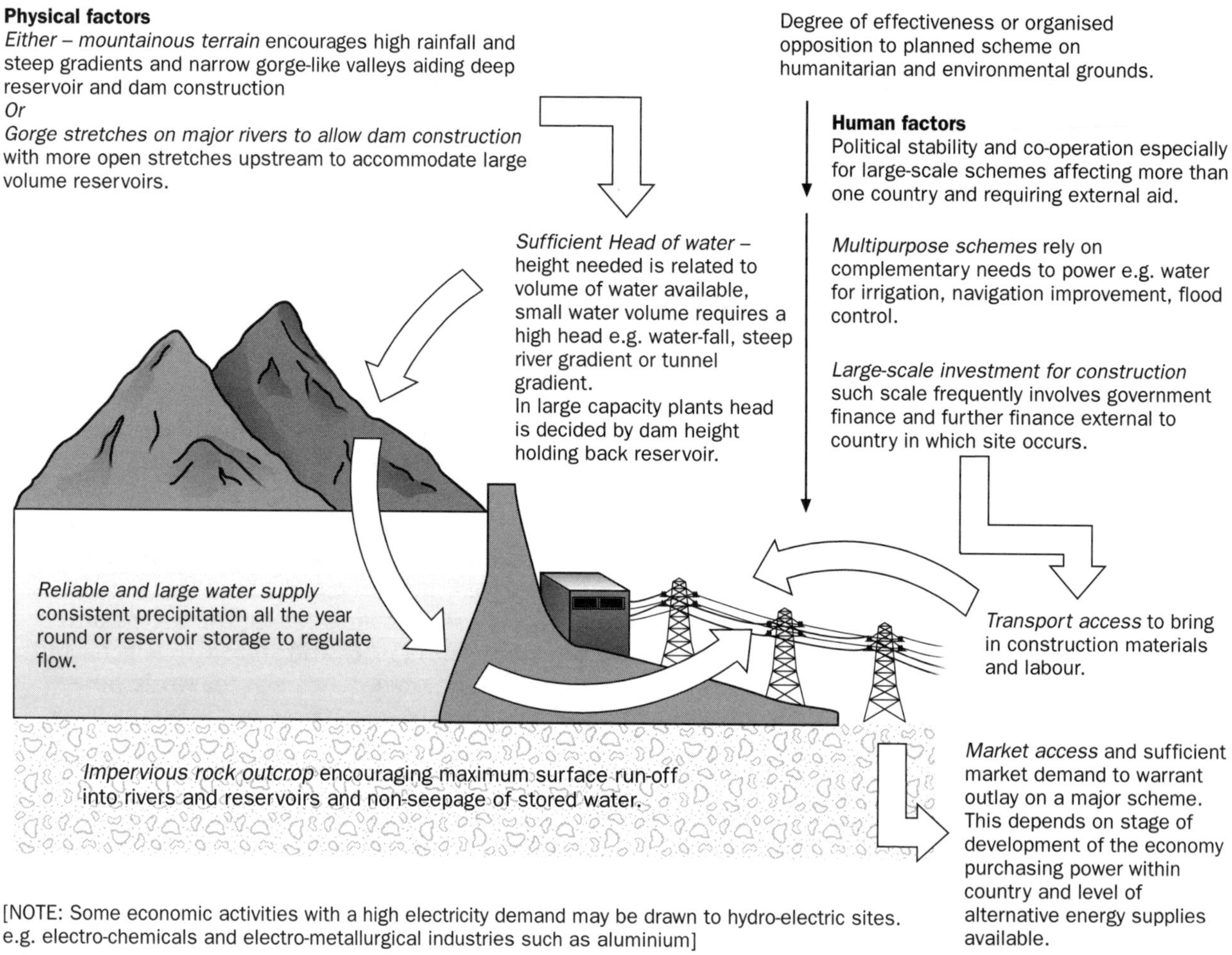

Figure 27.26 Factors affecting the location and implementation of HEP schemes

It may be that the future of hydro-electricity lies with the development of small schemes to serve local areas as is now happening in parts of China. Micro-hydro schemes, generating less than 100 kilowatts and requiring no reservoir storage, are increasing rapidly in number to serve small rural communities, especially in India and China. However, most of the power now being generated comes from multi-purpose, large-scale schemes. These are of vital importance to the current and future development of the economies of Africa where there is a desperate need to increase food output, and to expand rural economies and industry to raise living standards.

Multi-purpose schemes in Africa

In Africa large-scale developments are multi-purpose, particularly combining provision of irrigation water with increasing energy supplies. Since the rainfall over much of Africa is seasonal and unreliable and the energy supplies are in very short supply, various countries exploited some of the major rivers flowing from the heart of the continent. Fortunately where these rivers break through the high plateau rim suitable sites are available. Others occur where crystalline block uplands are encountered by rivers, giving deep gorge sections.

A number of schemes have been developed in each of Africa's major rivers including the Nile, the Zambezi and the Niger. These have largely been externally financed and much of the technical skills needed were imported, since African countries have neither the capital nor the skills to undertake such large-scale developments. For example, most recently a hydro-electric and irrigation plant is to be developed in Angola on the Kwando River using Brazilian and Russian financial and technical aid, but plans for this have had to be shelved because of the civil war in Angola. While not the largest, the Aswan Dam project in Egypt (also involving the neighbouring parts of the Sudan) is one of the most established schemes. It highlights both the advantages and problems which can result from the impact of this type of scheme on the economy and social conditions in the countries concerned.

27.9 Other renewable energy sources

Direct solar energy

Solar heaters have been in use for a long time in sunny climates to supply hot water and central heating for buildings. Over the last ten years their use has been further extended into temperate climate areas, mainly as a summer supplement to other sources of energy. For example, a number of houses in most West European countries have solar heating panels in the roof. Germany promoted a 'One Thousand Roof' programme in 1990 and recently upgraded it to 2500 roofs. Switzerland, a leader in developing renewable energy, hopes to install a solar system in every village by the year 2000.

Until relatively recently there have been formidable technological and financial obstacles to overcome before solar energy could be seen as a viable alternative energy source on a large commercial scale. Costs have been progressively reduced especially with advances in the production of photovoltaic cells. Over the past twenty years the costs of solar electricity using this method have fallen by a factor of four.

Most photovoltaic power devices produce energy in small quantities for a variety of purposes such as rural electrification schemes in developing countries power supplies for instrumentation and telecommunications and power for consumer goods such as watches and calculators.

Mixed Messages

'Perhaps the best example of a new approach to solar electrification is in the Dominican Republic where 2000 homes have been solarised in the last nine years largely by the efforts of Enersol a US non profit group', with a credit scheme for participating households.

Since 1990 similar organisations have been started elsewhere e.g. China, Sri Lanka and Zimbabwe. But the vast majority of the developing world's population would not be able to afford even this easier credit system.

[SOURCE: Flavin C and Lenssen N *Power Surge*, 1995]

With further technical advances and failing costs, photovoltaic cells are beginning to be used for more large-scale applications. A number of multinational corporations are involved in research and expanding the world market for solar powered cells, including BP Solar and Siemen's, the world's leading producer of PV cells in 1993.

Most governments have subsidised expansion of solar energy. Ultimately it may be possible to meet up to a fifth of the world's electricity demands from solar energy without the need for storage.

Biomass and biogas

Such is the rate of consumption of biomass in the developing world, that it cannot be currently considered in practical terms to be renewable (Case study 27.6). However, in the developed world the very limited use made of biomass is sustainable.

In the forest products industries wood waste is widely used to fuel steam turbine systems. However, steam turbines are expensive and inefficient for the usually small-scale use of biomass. Thus gas turbines are used for electricity generation. The Shell Corporation is trialling a larger 30 MW gas turbine power plant in Brazil fuelled by biomass from a eucalyptus plantation. If successful, it could expand the potential of biomass energy using planted fuelwood plantation or energy crops such as sugar cane, sugar beet and rape seed.

Most biogas is being produced using animal manure, crop waste and industrial and household waste. In the USA 8400 MW of biomass energy based on these kind of sources is already being produced, equivalent to the electricity from 10 nuclear power stations. Denmark has a countrywide system of biomass plants mainly using animal manure.

In the UK following the government's recent invitation for subsidy bids to expand renewable energy, it is anticipated that bids will come from companies wishing to establish large municipal incinerators which fuel combined heating and power plants serving whole urban districts.

Although biomass energy is more expensive to produce than fossil fuel energy, with continued government subsidy its contribution is likely to increase in the developed world because it can make use of waste materials or land not needed for other purposes. It also gives little pollutant emission. While there is some production of liquid biofuels as substitutes for oil-based diesel or petrol, costs are too high for biofuels to be a serious alternative in the near future.

Wind energy

Wind has been widely used in more remote rural areas where other forms of electrification are not available, especially in Australia and the USA. There is now much research into its use on a wider scale in both developing countries and developed countries. While some new wind generators are sophisticated, machinery for harnessing the wind can be simply built at a modest cost. This is particularly important for poorer rural areas of the world.

On a small scale the main advances have been in producing small wind machines of light weight which can be easily erected. These have generating capacities of 5 kW to 100 kW. For example, the Intermediate Technology Development Group, in investigating ways of providing simple energy generators for the developing countries, have designed a machine with a rotor diameter of about 7 m and of improved operating efficiency. This is now being manufactured in Kenya at a modest cost for use in agricultural areas.

One of the problems of depending on wind as a primary energy source is that wind varies from day to day. Storage batteries for the current generated will greatly improve the reliability of wind power. Furthermore, their use is being extended into such things as providing electricity for production of fertilisers, aerating ponds on fish farms and desalination of seawater.

Apart from its increasing potential for small-scale needs, much more research is going on into the contribution it can make to multi-energy systems for use in isolated and island communities where small wind turbines are used in conjunction with diesel generators and as an additional energy supply to national grid systems. Outside of open plains, highland and coastal sites provide useful locations, being more exposed to the wind than sheltered sites. The Italian government have already embarked on the development of wind energy farms. The one at Fiume Santo on the north-west Sardinian coast consists of ten aero-generators. Energy farms like this one can be used to supply power to a particular district or supply electricity into the general grid.

The expansion of wind generated energy has been limited mainly because costs are not yet economic compared to traditional energy sources and also because of environmental opposition to them. The most favourable locations are in areas with a high scenic value. Wind farms take up large land areas and are visually intrusive. One solution may be to locate them in shallow water offshore. A demonstration wind farm has already been constructed offshore in Denmark which, after California, has the largest investment in wind turbines. California has the world's largest concentration mainly because of high tax incentives to invest in them in the early 1980s.

The UK now has a number of wind farms, the most recent being opened in Carno in mid-Wales, 1996. Development of wind energy is part of the Department of Energy's alternative energy programme. They estimate that it should be possible to generate the equivalent of 10% of the country's current electricity consumption from wind turbines. Large wind turbines are being designed with capacities ranging from 10 kW to 5 MW (5000 kW).

Geothermal energy

Geothermal energy is the natural heat of the earth's crust stored in rock and water within the earth. This energy can be extracted via natural channels in the earth's crust or by drilling wells to tap concentrations of steam at high pressures and at depths shallow enough to be economically justified. The steam is led out through pipes and can be either used directly for heating purposes or to drive electricity generating turbines, so providing a source of power.

Geothermal fields are fairly widespread in the world, most notably near the surface in areas of earthquake and volcanic action. Large fields, however, have also been found at much greater depths underlying the thick layers of sedimentary rocks across continental areas and the ocean floor. It is estimated that one third of the CIS is underlain by exploitable geothermal energy. Generally it is at a depth of more than 20 km, making it uneconomical to exploit at present.

Fracture zones in unstable areas of the earth's crust, such as around the Pacific edge and the Mediterranean, New Zealand and the Rift Valley, allow steam and water to circulate, carrying some of the earth's heat to the surface. Where it is available, the simplest and cheapest use of geothermal energy has been for direct heating purposes. The steam can be led directly into pipes either to heat domestic houses or for the growing of crops in greenhouses. Geothermal heat has been developed on a local scale in areas as far apart as Iceland and New Zealand. One of its great advantages is that direct heating by geothermal energy is half the cost of oil-fired heating.

Because of high capital costs and the technological problems involved, world interest in geothermal energy as a power source was negligible until the 1950s when intensive exploration activities then led to the commissioning of geothermal power stations in New Zealand, Japan, the USA and Iceland.

A United Nations conference on New Sources of Energy in 1961 helped to further publicise the benefits and potential of geothermal energy. Since then a number of countries have been actively involved in developing geothermal energy programmes. In developed countries geothermal sources are likely to remain secondary, but in some developing countries where the shortage is chronic, utilisation of gethermal supplies may help to meet the short-term energy gap until larger capital-intensive schemes can be developed.

Within the developing world the Philippines is the leading producer of geothermal energy. In 1994 it produced 1053 MW of steam from nine geothermal plants, about half that produced in the USA (the world's number one producer), but twice that of Mexico, the third ranked producer. Although the Philippines' location astride shifting continental plates and its 200 active and dormant volcanoes pose a serious natural disaster threat, it has also given it one of the highest potentials for geothermal energy. It is estimated that current geothermal output could be expanded by four times.

Other countries round the Pacific 'Ring of Fire' are also developing geothermal energy. Japan for example is expanding its geothermal programme while Indonesia's geothermal production is likely to exceed that of the Philippines by the year 2000.

There is small production of geothermal energy in African countries along the Great Rift Valley where the potential is high. It has for example been possible to economically tap supplies near the surface in the Olkaria area where underground water from Lake Naivasha to the north percolates along surface layers into the heat zone. However, the high capital costs developing geothermal energy are an obstacle to further significant development. Capital costs are more than twice that of oil-fired stations, but operating costs are very much lower and the life of geothermal stations is much greater. For East African countries, expansion of geothermal supplies would also reduce the present dependence on imported oil.

Energy from the oceans

Although the oceans offer enormous potential, tidal and wave power are at present the least developed of renewable energy sources currently used. Tidal schemes are dependent on a large enough tidal range. There are a few schemes around the world and others are being considered on tidal estuaries or inlets where tidal barrages can be constructed. One of the largest schemes in operation is at La Rance in France which has operated successfully since the mid-1960s. Much further development of tidal power is hampered by the high capital investment needed, the long construction time needed and the potentially severe impact on the environment around possible sites (Case study 27.5).

Wave power using the oscillation of the waves has only so far been successful on a very small scale despite the many experiments to construct larger schemes. Small floating devices have been made for flashing warning lights on buoys. There are also now a number of small 'shoreline generation' wave power schemes in operation, feeding electricity into the grid system, for example in Norway and on the island of Islay in Scotland.

The best potential for larger scale wave power generation would be from large floating devices several kilometres out to sea, but large scale offshore devices are unlikely to become economic until into the next century.

27.10 Energy transition in the developing countries

The energy crisis

Apart from oil-rich nations, most of the developing countries are chronically short of commercial energy supplies both for domestic needs, industry and the rural sector. Yet if these countries are to achieve economic and social progress, an adequate energy supply is a basic necessity. At present, while richer nations are consuming commercial energy at an average rate of 5 tonnes of coal equivalent per head, consumption amongst the poorer nations is barely 0.25 tonne equivalent.

This low consumption reflects a number of disturbing facets about developing nations (Case study 27.6). A number of the poorer nations are not well endowed with energy resources. Apart from limited hydro-electricity potential this applies to much of sub-Saharan Africa. Where there is potential there is insufficient finance and technical expertise available to develop it.

Consequently, there is heavy reliance on imported oil for electricity and for the transport system of a country. Since the 1970s the rising price of oil placed an increasing strain on oil importing countries as a whole, but particularly on the poorer nations. The steep rise in oil prices came at a time of world recession when export of the agricultural goods and other raw materials which paid for all imports was becoming increasingly difficult. The recession thus had a serious effect on the economic stability of these countries. Without the continuance of international aid and loans a number of countries, such as Bangladesh, Uganda and Tanzania would be bankrupt.

The demand for commercial energy however is also low compared to demand in developed countries. This partly reflects low levels of industrialisation in the developing countries and the underdevelopment of agriculture. Most of the energy needed for agriculture must be supplied by human labour and draught animals. Also, the low demand for commercial energy reflects the fact that most people rely on traditional supplies (wood fuel, farm waste and animal dung) for domestic needs, rather than on commercial energy sources such as gas and electricity. Outside of the newly industrialising countries, traditional sources of energy make up 65% of energy supplies. In some African countries wood and animal dung contribute as much as 90% of all energy needs.

Nor are these simply the main sources for rural populations. The increasing urban sector is also chiefly dependent on wood fuel for cooking and heating. As populations continue to rise, more firewood is being burnt than can be replenished. Consequently much woodland is disappearing. Increasing amounts of animal dung are also being burnt in an effort to meet requirements.

As a result of the destruction of woodland and the diversion of much needed animal dung to maintain soil fertility, serious environmental problems are arising. More of the land is open to soil erosion and the increased seasonal flooding in the south of Bangladesh, for example, is being attributed to the more rapid surface run-off of water now that much of the woodland has been cleared on watershed areas.

Towards solutions

It is only over the last decade that developing nations have attempted to formulate comprehensive energy policies and intensify the search for exploitable home energy sources in order to lower their dependency on imported oil and cut down on the use of wood and animal dung (Case study 27.6).

In some regions hydro-electric schemes have been developed with outside financial and technical aid. Mozambique for example has linked up with South Africa and other developed countries outside of Africa, to develop the Caborra Bassa dam on the lower Zambezi. Generally most of the emphasis is being placed on exploration for oil and gas and coal reserves.

Oil and gas reserves are the most significant, since oil supplies half as much energy as its coal equivalent, is easily stored and is more versatile in its uses (Figure 27.19). However, while important discoveries are being made, especially in shallow offshore waters, costs of development are very high. Also, many poorer countries simply do not have the infrastructure necessary for supplies to be used across the country as a whole, especially in the rural areas, where the main need is likely to be.

Useful though oil and gas discoveries may be, other sources of energy are obviously required, such as the uses of wind generators and simple direct solar heating devices. Considerable research is also going on into the treatment of farm waste and animal dung to produce gas which can be used for domestic heating and cooking, and yet leave the residue suitable for spreading on the land to maintain soil fertility.

Probably the greatest contribution may be made through devising more efficient ways of using traditional fuels; at present most cooking is done on open fires which is very wasteful of wood fuel. Widespread efforts are being made to replant areas with species of quick growing timber as a means of replenishing depleted forest and woodland sources. All this depends on finance, basic technical skill and persuading the indigenous population to adapt some traditional habits.

Concluding comment

The energy problems of the industrialised nations, serious though they are, pale in comparison to those facing most of the world's developing countries. The 'energy crisis' of the rich countries may merely be the initial trauma of converting to a leaner, but adequate and certainly healthier energy diet. But for most developing countries, the existing energy situation is more one of debilitatingly inadequate nutrition, virtually a condition of energy starvation.

[SOURCE: Smith V and Knowland K *Energy in the Developing World*, 1980]

case study

27.1 UK: the energy industry

Location of power stations in England and Wales

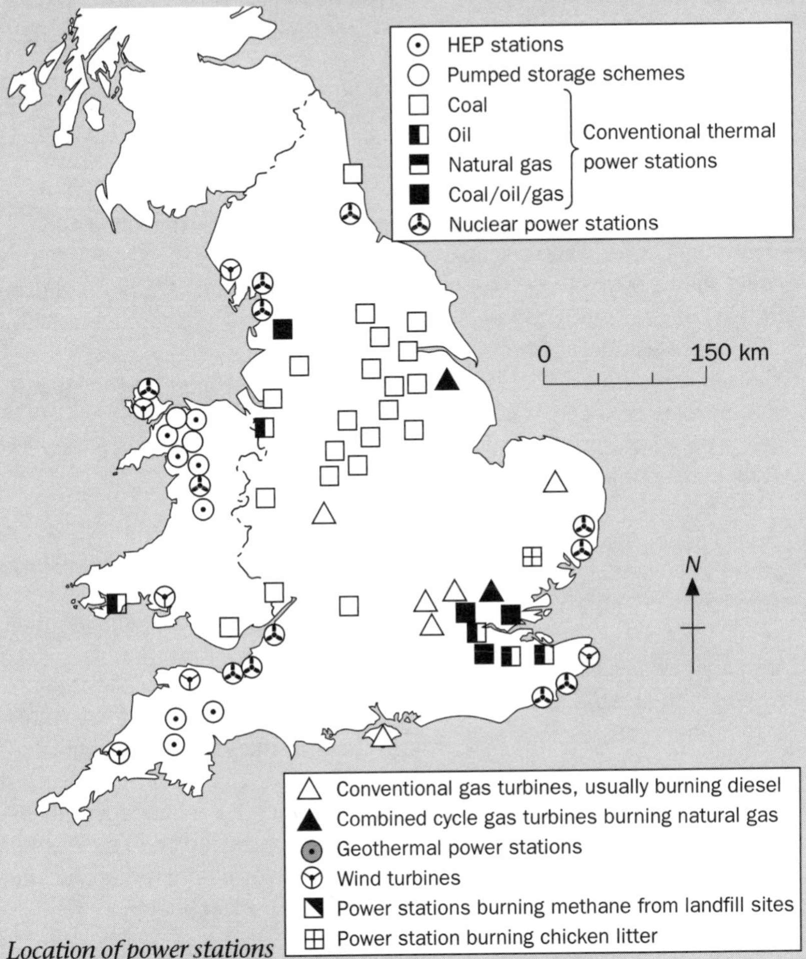

Location of power stations

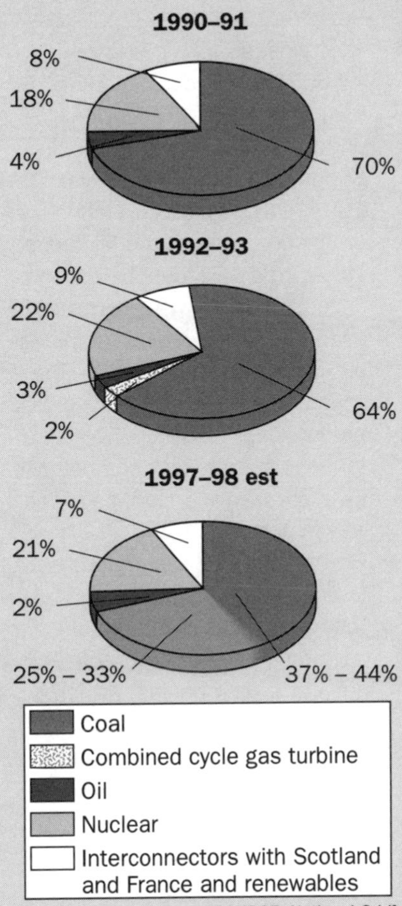

[SOURCE: National Grid]

Fuel sources for electricity in England and Wales

The factors influencing power plant locations

- The distribution pattern linked to coastal or river valley sites shows a common need for large supplies of water. For some it is also linked to supplies of fuel e.g. coal imports or gas or oil piped ashore. Coastal and river floor locations are also linked to the need for large level sites.
- Different types of fuel-powered stations also reflect particular needs:
  - nuclear plants need to be located away from large concentrations of populations for safety reasons
  - HEP plants in heavy rainfall highland areas for steep gradients and sufficient water head
  - coal-fired plants need to be reasonably close to a coalfield (or import port) to reduce freight costs of coal e.g. concentration in the lower Trent valley on the Derby/Notts/South Yorks coalfield.
- While the pattern shows some correlation with large markets this is 'historical' rather than a current need as electricity can be fed and economically transported on the grid network.

Coal in decline

Declining coal production in Western Europe

- While still making a major contribution to energy needs, coal production has fallen since the 1950s. In 1990 coal still provided 40% of electricity generation in the European Union but coal production had fallen 30% since 1973 as imports rose 300%. The decline in the UK is similar to that in France, Germany and Belgium, the other major West European producers.

- Between 1961 to 1992, 26 pits were closed with the loss of 44 000 colliery jobs. A further nine pits and 8600 jobs went during 1992 to 1994. By the time British Coal was privatised in 1994, only 30 pits were left in production, most in the Midlands. These produced 40 million tonnes of coal mainly for power generation while open-cast mines produced 16 million tonnes. The government were subsidising coal production by approximately £1 a tonne to try to keep it competitive. Even so, 17 million tonnes of coal was imported in 1994.
- For the 'sell off,' five regions were created and buyers were guaranteed a certain amount of sales for a limited period to the electricity-generating companies, National Power and Scottish Power. Management, trade unions and business consortiums have been involved in the 'buy up'.
- There has been a drive to cut costs to try to make coal competitive against imports and other sources of fuel.

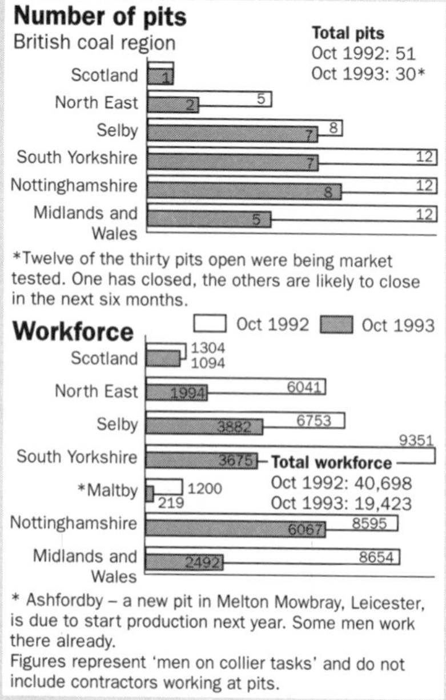

Coal in decline

Reasons for the decline in coal production

- Since the 1950s coal production costs have been rising as easier worked seams were exhausted and wage rates rose, particularly due to union pressure. British Coal increasingly automated operations to increase productivity and closed uneconomic pits causing rising unemployment.
- British coal has been undercut by cheaper coal imports from Australia and the USA. In 1992 coal imports cost 100 – 120 pence per gigajoule of energy while home-mined coal was 185 – 150 pence.
- Energy needs have been levelling off with the small rises being met from fuels other than coal.
- Because of conventional coal-fired generator's contribution to air pollution and the UK's commitment to cut emissions, coal-powered generation is being reduced. Both nuclear and gas are 'clean air' generators. Gas generators are cheaper to build and can produce electricity at a lower unit cost.
- In 1994 – 95 there was overcapacity compared with demand for electricity and because of increasing energy efficiency, demand is unlikely to substantially increase in the near future.

Consequences of the decline in coal production

- Serious unemployment on the coalfield areas is particularly devastating for settlements e.g. Grimesthorpe (South Yorkshire) where economy rests almost completely on coal.
- A negative multiplier effect exacerbates unemployment. Firms supplying the coal industry through maintenance contracts and coal freighting and firms in the settlements reduce demand for retail goods, entertainment, etc.
- Sheer speed of closures made it difficult to put alternative work opportunities in place. Where alternative jobs were found these were frequently unskilled and lower paid.
- Social stress and family and community break-up increased. With the loss of status, husbands depend on women to find jobs.
- A rise in crime is felt as the younger generation have little hope of work.

Some positive aspects

- The closure of mines reduced environmental pollution and led to land reclamation with greening of the area.
- It prompted grants to alleviate problems leading to infrastructure improvements and other public works.
- For a minority, redundancy money and retaining led on to successful self-employment or other skilled jobs and better health.

Case experience of effect on communities of coal mine closures

Cotgrave in Nottinghamshire

The mine was opened in 1964 and at its peak employed 2000. It expanded an agricultural village of 300 to a small mining town of 8000. When the pit was closed in 1994, 600 miners lost their jobs. The effect on Cotgrove went beyond job loss – *'the pit was the social glue of the town – everything revolved round the pit – we lived, worked and socialised together'. 'Men are becoming house husbands, women becoming bread winners.'*

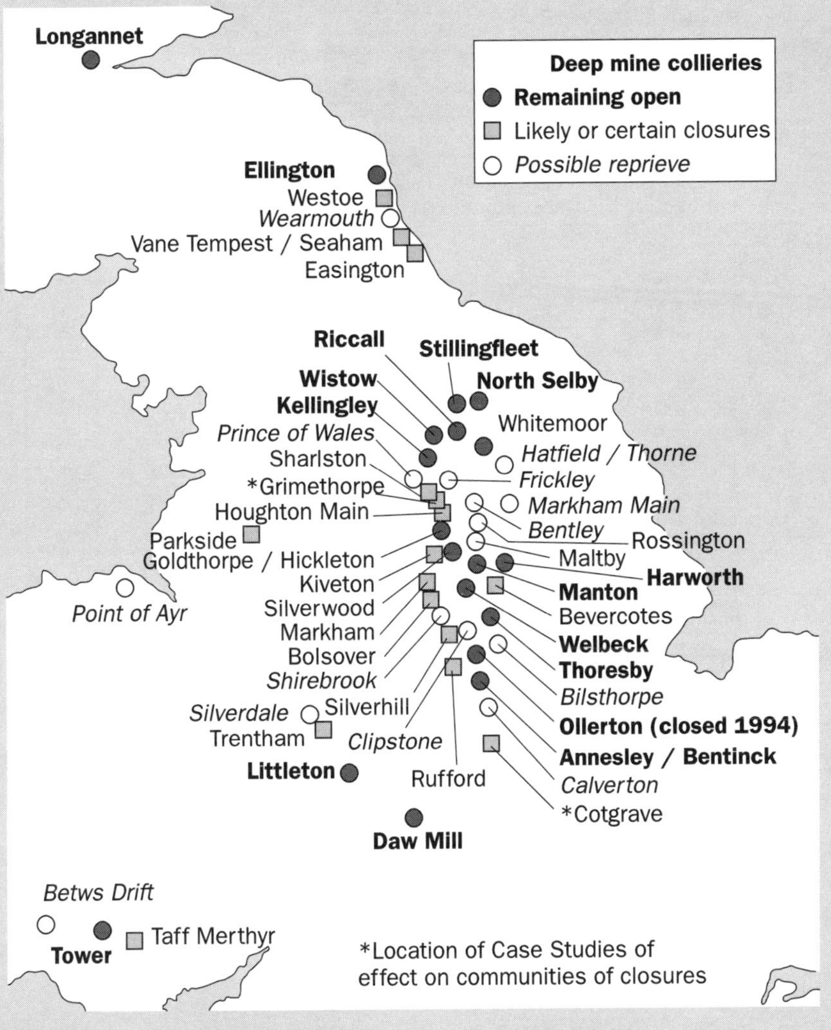

Possible future of Britain's pits 1993

Since Cotgrave is in the Midlands which has a diversified economy, many ex-miners have found alternative employment albeit at lower wages. Unemployment in 1994 was officially running at 9%.

The area has gained Assisted Area status, thus attracting grants from the EU as well as government and local authority assistance. The £400 000 grant from the Coalfield Area Fund enabled the building of industrial units on the edge of town for small business 'start-ups' and for the renovation of the leisure centre. The New Deal for Nottinghamshire County Initiative has provided job training, job creation schemes, environmental improvements and a new traffic management scheme. British Coal and Rushcliffe District Council have redevelopment plans for the colliery site for industrial or leisure development since it has good communication links.

Although community unity has gone, alternative employment has been found for most miners who wish to carry on working. Also, environment and infrastructure improvements have been made which would not probably have materialised without the pit closure.

Grimesthorpe, South Yorkshire

A more desperate situation exists here where there is little alternative employment available. It is not well located to attract new enterprises, being four miles away from Barnsley on a 'cul de sac' road.

The pit closed in 1934 with the loss of 2500 jobs and by 1994, only 5% had obtained alternative employment. The community of 3500 has become a 'benefit dependent community' which has had its self-confidence and choices taken away. There is apathy and loss of sense of community. Training schemes are in place and the Acorn community centre has been set up with a range of community support initiatives but most families may have to move to have any chance of employment.

The future outlook for coal

There are plentiful reserves of coal (600 million tonnes in the UK) but any increase in output depends on:

- the relative pricing of coal against other alternative fuels
- changes in the total demand for energy and the price of energy
- further development in 'clean coal technology' to make coal more environmentally acceptable (see Case study 27.3 for oil and gas).

The dash for gas

- This is essentially a 1990s phenomenon based on expansion of gas supplies from the UK's North Sea oil and gas fields with the prospects of further supplies.
- Technological advances in gas-fired generators and the cost of natural gas compared to other fuels have made them the best economic proposition. They provide a flexible supply of energy.
  - They combine gas cycle-turbine technology and can be built in a range of sizes up to 340 mega-watts.

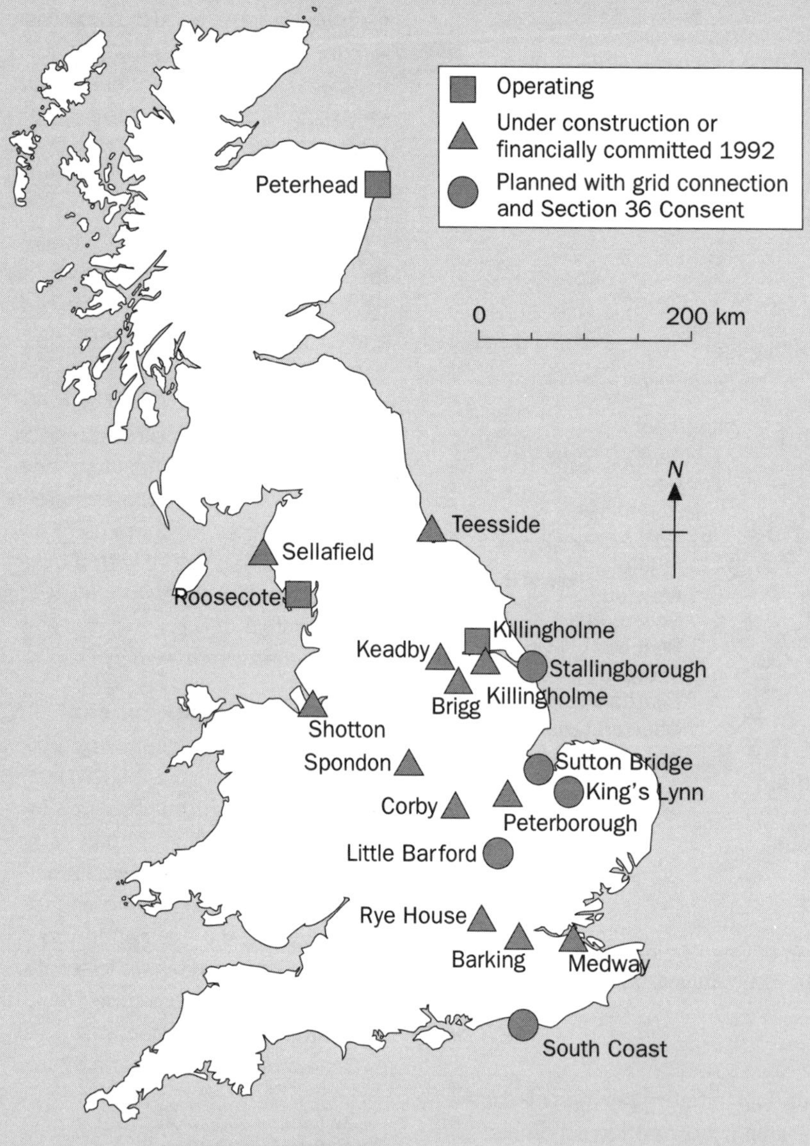

Gas-fired power stations in the UK

- They are economically and quickly built and thus responsive to changes in energy demand compared to building nuclear and coal-fired plants.
- They can be built on smaller sites since no fuel stock space has to be provided which facilitates planning permission, reduces site costs and intrusiveness into the landscape.
- They are more environmentally friendly than coal with only half the CO_2 emissions.
- They can accommodate daily and seasonal changes in electricity demand.

The more debateable aspects of the 'Dash for Gas'

- The price of gas may rise.
- Reserves of gas are emitted and the UK may have to rely on imports within 20 to 30 years.

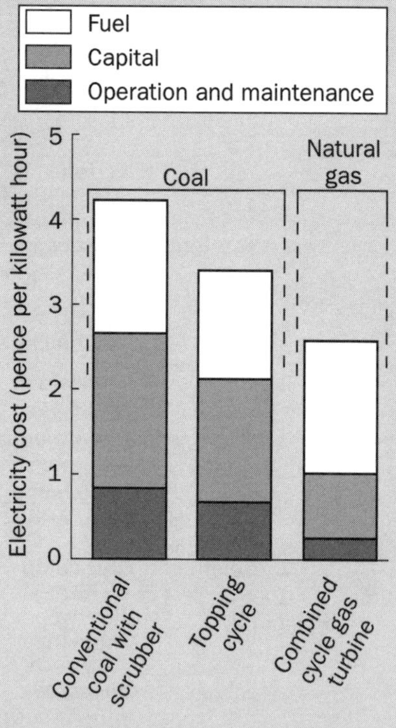

Generating costs of coal versus natural gas

- Being in the hands of a wide range of companies it is thus less easy to regulate future supplies.
- Each company needs to negotiate for supplies of gas and a market for the electricity produced e.g. Peterhead gas-fired plant owned by Scottish Power takes its gas from the off-shore Miller oil and gas field and Scottish Power itself feeds the electricity into its own power system.

Expansion of nuclear energy comes to an end

A significant but uneconomic contributor to UK energy needs

- The nuclear energy industry, run by Scottish Nuclear and Nuclear Electric (now combined as British Energy), contributed 23% of electricity in 1994, up from 16% in 1989 – 90.

- With the decision not to go ahead with the planned Sizewell C and Hinkley Point C plants and the decommissioning of older nuclear plants, nuclear energy's contribution to electricity supplies will decline, with a forecast contribution of only 1% by the year 2020.
- Production has been uneconomic as capital costs have been very heavy and the cost per unit of electricity at 5.2 p to 3.1 p (higher than gas- and oil-fired stations) has only been achieved through a massive subsidy from a 10% levy on all electricity sold.

Reasons for initial expansion

- It was originally forecast that nuclear power stations would produce power at a cost little different from a coal-fired station.
- The British government, up to 1995, has backed expansion and given massive subsidy support.
- A rapid of growth in energy needs was forecast in the 1960s which could not be met only from fossil fuels.
- It was expanded to reduce dependence on oil imports in the years before North Sea oil was developed.
- The rising cost of home-produced coal promoted expansion.
- It is a clean energy producing little air pollution.
- Until recently the UK was a world leader in nuclear technology.

Reasons for the halt to nuclear energy expansion

- Environmental fears concerning the effects of nuclear accidents and disposal of radio-active waste have persisted and been backed by a powerful lobby and public doubts about the safety of nuclear plants.
- The decision to halt expansion has been taken ultimately on economic grounds:
  - there is not in the foreseeable future sufficient expansion of demand to warrant further expansion.
  - energy prices have fallen, making nuclear fuelled energy even less economic per unit of production.
  - it is cheaper and more flexible to invest in gas-fired stations where most of the emphasis is. A new nuclear plant would cost 5 – 10 times more than a gas-fired one. Gas is cheaper per unit of electricity.
  - electricity can be imported more cheaply as needed from French nuclear stations and increasing emphasis is being put on expansion of renewable energy sources.
  - disposing of nuclear waste is not only environmentally difficult but enormously costly as is the decommissioning of nuclear power stations.

The future

- *'Britain's nuclear era comes to an end ... Britain's nuclear power faces extinction following the decision by British Energy, the soon to be privatised nuclear company to abandon plans to build any new generating plants.'* [*The Independent* 12.12.95]
- Older plants will have to be decommissioned; Berkeley and Trawsfyndd have already been closed and the rest will follow by 2020 probably only leaving Sizewell B (opened in 1995). All the costs of decommissioning are estimated at £18 billion.
- The privatisation sale is likely to realise only £2.5 billion; when Sizewell C alone cost £2.3 billion to build.
- France and Japan have looked to the longer term and are continuing to expand nuclear energy output (Nuclear energy contributes 75% of generating needs in France). These countries do not have extensive reserves of fossil fuels such as the UK has and do not want to be dependent on imports and unpredictable price changes. In any case, nuclear energy does not contribute to global warming. Also, running down will mean the UK may lose its nuclear expertise and opportunities to sell this to countries such as South Korea and Taiwan which plan to build nuclear plants.

Other energy sources

- Oil is a vital part of the UK's total energy sector in providing for transport and industrial needs. It contributes around 30% to 35% of total energy but only 3% of electricity production because of its relatively higher cost to gas and it is a 'dirty' form of energy.
- HEP and other renewables together with imports by grid and cable from Spain and France, account for approximately 7% of needs. While the government is committed to advancing new renewable sources of energy even by 2000 this will supply only 2% to 3% of electricity needs.

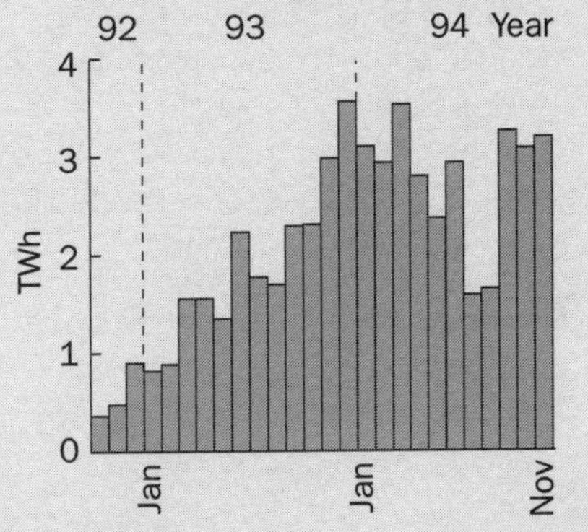

Nuclear energy monthly output from CCGTs

case study

27.2 The contribution of coal to United States power

US power a mixed bag for electricity generation

Rich in resources, the USA generates electricity in many ways; hydro-power is a major factor on the west coast, fuel oil in the north-east, natural gas in some Gulf states and in California, nuclear in the east, and coal nearly everywhere. Even so, some regions may suffer shortages of electricity in extreme weather. Planners hope 'megawatts,' power saved by conservation, will help delay a crunch.

The revival of the United States coal industry

Contribution to energy requirements

Although coal has been mined in the USA from the early eighteenth century it was not until the 1880s that coal replaced wood as the major fuel source. By the mid-1920s, 70% of the United States fuel and energy needs were met from coal, as they were cheaper and easier to transport than coal. Now however, production of coal is once again being expanded with a record 800 million tonnes being mined in 1980. By 1990 production of hard coal had risen to 80 million tonnes. The USA also produced 83 million tonnes of lignite and brown coal. Despite this output level, coal still supplies only one quarter of United States total energy requirements – a measure of the great expansion of energy requirements over the post-war years. (Some coal is also exported to Japan and Western Europe.)

Reasons for the revival in coal output

There are a number of reasons why coal output has doubled since 1960. One is the sheer growth in energy demand. Others are the uncertainties of the political situation in the Middle East, the major source of imported oil, and fears about future energy supplies. This led to President Carter's Energy Plan in 1974 in which he emphasised the need to expand home energy supplies, in particular a greater use of the country's plentiful coal reserves. This has become more feasible because the rise in oil and gas prices has left coal as a cheaper alternative and further mechanisation of open-cast coalmining has reduced the unit cost of extraction. However, since the mid-1980s oil and gas prices have fallen.

Why is open-cast mining now so much more important?

Apart from the increased need for coal, the reasons for the greater exploitation of reserves by open-cast methods include important improvements in the size and efficiency of strip mining equipment. This has greatly increased the output per day in open-cast areas to 28 tonnes, double the average for deep mining and an important factor in view of increasing wage costs for deep mining. Other factors include better labour relations in the newer western fields and fewer health hazards with strip mining. Anti-pollution laws, including the 1970 Clean Air Amendment Act, have favoured the use of low sulphur coals, the main type produced by open-cast mining methods, despite the fact that more is needed to produce the same energy, for many low sulphur coal deposits are relatively low in heat value.

Importance of coal in power generation

Coal provides the bulk of the fuel for power generation in the USA though the contribution of gas-fired stations has recently increased. Fears over the safety of nuclear power have limited expansion of nuclear stations. However, the greater running costs of thermal stations and the fact that nuclear is non-polluting of the atmosphere, together with continued rising demand, may see some renewal of the nuclear power programme.

Regional differences in total power generation reflect differences in demand, most consumption being in the urban and manufacturing metropolises.

It also to some extent reflects location of power sources. For example hydro-electricity is more important in the Rocky Mountains and the West where conditions favour hydro-electricity production.

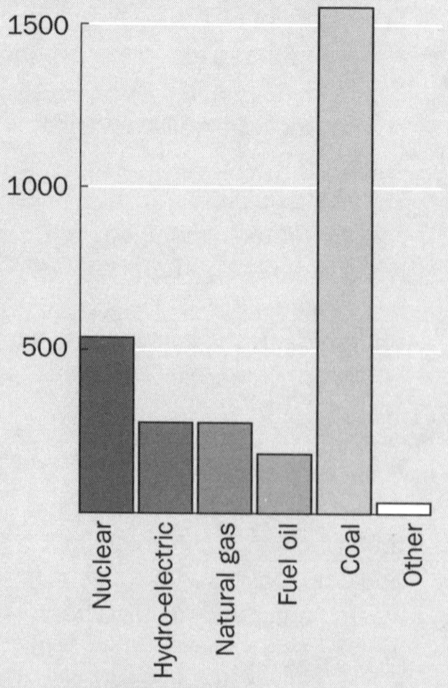

Total US electricity generation (billion kilowatt-hour)

Distribution of coal fields and coal slurry pipe lines to the main urban and industrial markets

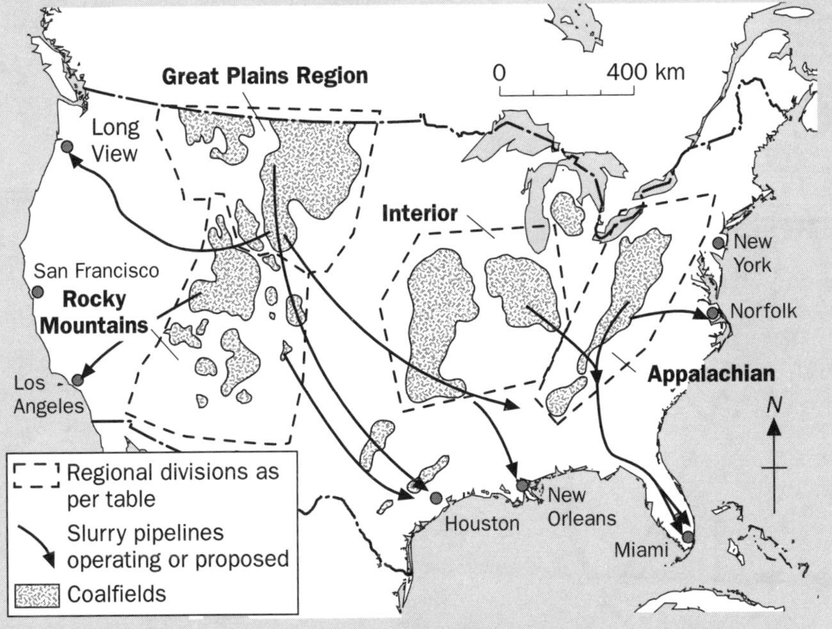

Regions	1970 (million tonnes)	1980 (million tonnes)	1990 % open cast	1990 (million tonnes)
Appalactia	337	466	40%	–
Interior	67	124	45%	– not available
Rocky Mountains and Great Plains	34	260	92%	–
Total	603	824	–	861

Increasing importance of western open cast coal fields and open cast mining

As can be seen from the map, the coal resources are widely distributed. East of the Mississippi, coal is obtained by underground mining and increasingly from open-cast mining, while to the west, nearly all production is from open-cast mines. Apart from the general rise in production the most important changes have been the much greater reliance on open-cast mining in the areas west of the Mississippi and the increased importance of the low sulphur coal deposits in these areas. There has thus been some swing in emphasis away from the Appalachian Region, traditionally the most important producer. Appalachia however still retains its lead in total production.

The Powder River Basin, Wyoming

Open-cast coalmining – a new energy frontier in the west

Economic aspects of coal exploitation in Powder River Basin

- **Expanding demand**
  In home markets mainly for power stations, e.g in the Houston growth area and Chicago. Export demand from Japan.
- **Favourable conditions**
  The basin has huge reserves of 60 billion tonnes of bituminous reserves near the surface. It is amenable to low coast mechanised open-cast mining.
  The coal is low in sulphur content making it attractive to users who are under pressure to comply with clean air legislation.
- **Problems**
  There is a long market haul both to home markets and export points.
  Coal is of lower calorific (heating) value than that of the main eastern coalfields.
  The infrastructure and labour supplies are limited, as Wyoming was mainly cattle country until recently.
  In an areas of special environmental attractions.
- **Development**
  Powder River Basin was developed from 1969. It had 12 strip mines by 1980 with a further 20 planned. Output rose from 7 million tonnes in 1970 to 80 million tonnes in 1980.
  Labour was attracted by high wages.
  Coal is shipped by trains 1 km long each with a 12000 tonnes capacity.

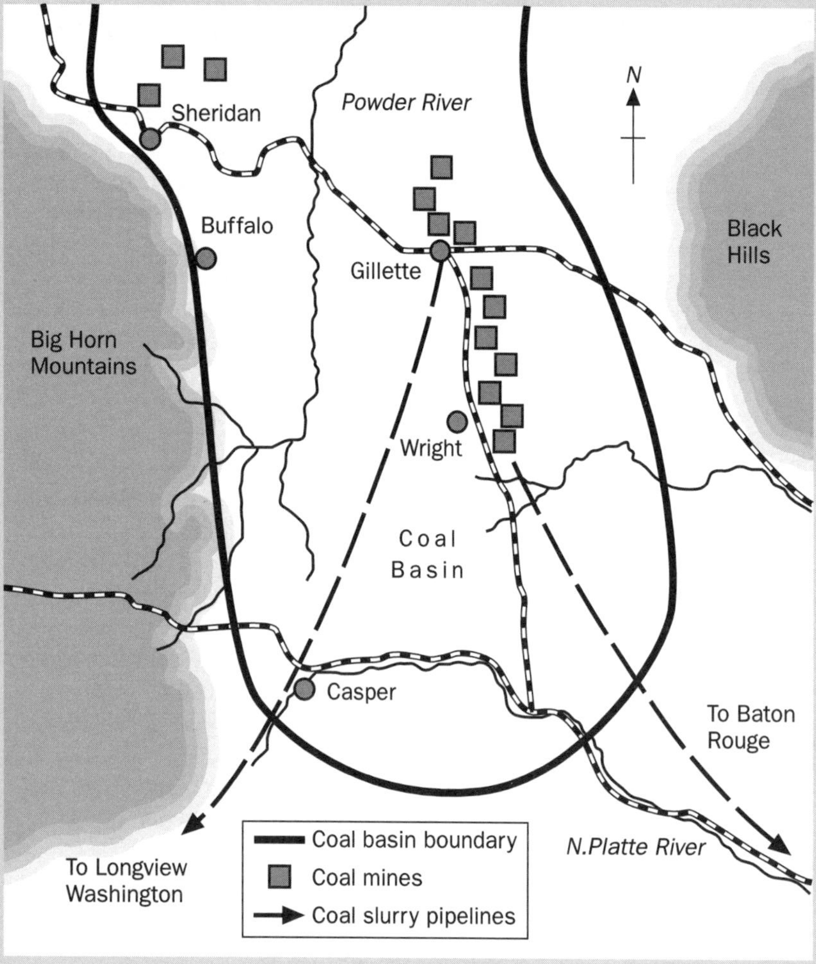

Powder River Basin

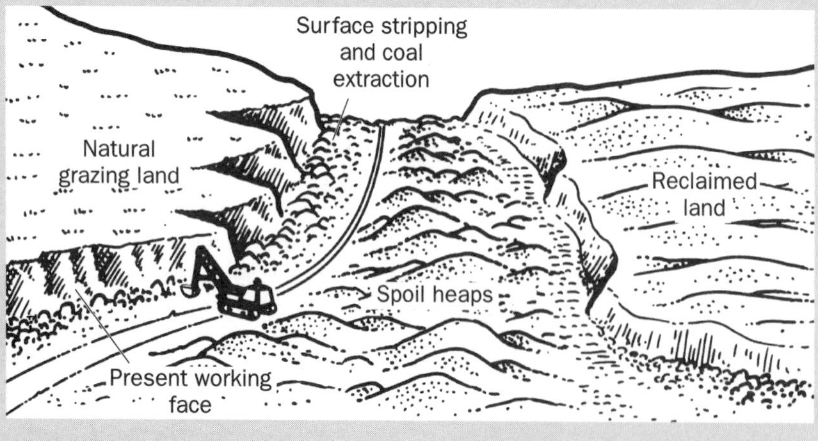

Open-cast strip mining

Social and environmental issues

- **Population pressure**
  Labour influx was caused by a 41% rise in population between 1970 – 80. This put severe pressure on limited amenities such as housing, leisure facilities, etc. The town of Gillette has grown from 4000 in 1969 to 14 000 in 1980, for example. 'Boom frontier' conditions are causing the break up of the established cattle country rural communities.
- **Environmental pressures on cattle country and the national parks**
  There is opposition from cattle ranchers and environmentalists as strip mining destroys large areas of grazing and creates soil heaps and slurry lakes. Legislation has been passed to ensure companies reclaim land but new land is still susceptible to erosion due to drought, severe winters and heavy grazing.
- **Pollution hazard**
  Coal mining poses a hazard to water courses and the air including emissions of Texaco and Mobil plants near Buffalo which convert coal into synthetic fuel.
- **Pressure on water supplies**
  In a region where drought may occur there is pressure on water supplies. Heavy demand by increased population has already led to a falling water table. Further demand for slurry transport will add to the problems.

case study

27.3 **North Sea oil and gas**

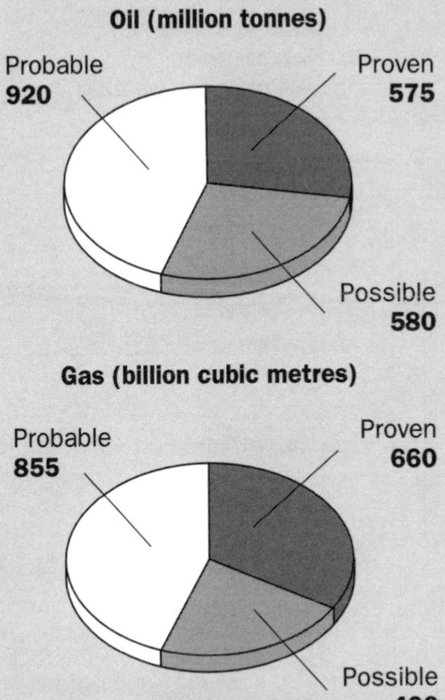

[SOURCE: *Financial Times* 4.9.95]

Remaining UK oil and gas reserves, 1995

Stages in development

Stage 1

Following the important discoveries in the late 1950s of a large gasfield near Groningen in the Netherlands (and smaller developments across the border in Germany), exploration was intensified off-shore in the North Sea where gas and oil deposits were already known to exist. Despite the difficulties created by the uncertain sea and weather conditions, a number of major companies such as Shell sought exploration concessions. Gas was first exploited and piped ashore to Easington (Humberside) in 1967 and later Bacton (Norfolk) from the West Sole and Leman fields in the southern sector of the North Sea. These ashore supplies were linked into a national distribution network focused on the Canvey Island–Leeds axis and thus coal gas was replaced by natural gas.

Stage 2

Oil development then followed. The first was from the Ekofisk field in the Norwegian sector, the oil being pumped ashore at Teesside since to lay a pipeline to a terminal in Norway would have been very much more difficult and expensive. Other finds followed, the largest development being that of the Brent field, 160 km from Shetland at a depth of about 150 m of water. This oil is piped ashore at Sullom Voe in the Shetlands where an oil complex was developed in the mid-1970s.

Stage 3

Oil production reach an initial peak of 2.5 million barrels a day in 1985. From this, production was forecast to decline due to the falling price of oil compared to relatively high extraction costs in the North Sea field. In 1990 production declined to 70% of peak output.

However, lowering costs of development and further exploration finds have led to a resurgence of output which, until 1994, was 2.6 million barrels a day. New fields, like the Lyell field 300 miles north-east of Aberdeen, have come on stream. Norway has also expanded production but at a slower rate. Still, Norway is now the world's second largest oil exporter following Saudi Arabia.

Stage 4

Expansion of the gas production by the late 1980s supplied 25% of the UK's energy needs. The first gas fields in the south of the North Sea are still significant but are past peak production. Gas reserves elsewhere have been developed, including from the Frigg and Brent fields in the north. The UK also takes gas from the Norwegian sector. The plan to link the UK into the continental gas pipeline network by a pipeline from Bacton in Norfolk to Zeebrugge in Belgium are very significant as a route for exporting gas to the continent or importing it from there, depending on supply, demand and relative prices.

Factors encouraging further development during the 1990s

- The North Sea fields are maturely understood, reducing risks of exploration. Apart from European companies, American companies are actively joining in further exploration.
- The success rate of exploration drillings is among the highest in the world – now standing at 1 in 4 of drillings as against a world average of a 1 in 20 rate of success.
- New finds are being made of small fields in the North Sea and the margins west of the Shetland show good potential.
- New technologies are being developed making tapping of deeper and difficult fields more viable.
- Although oil prices have fallen, exploration and running costs have decreased by 20% – 30% compared to the mid-1980s.
- The UK government has adopted a stable oil tax policy and facilitate the licensing and exploration.
- There is demand in Western Europe, especially for natural gas.

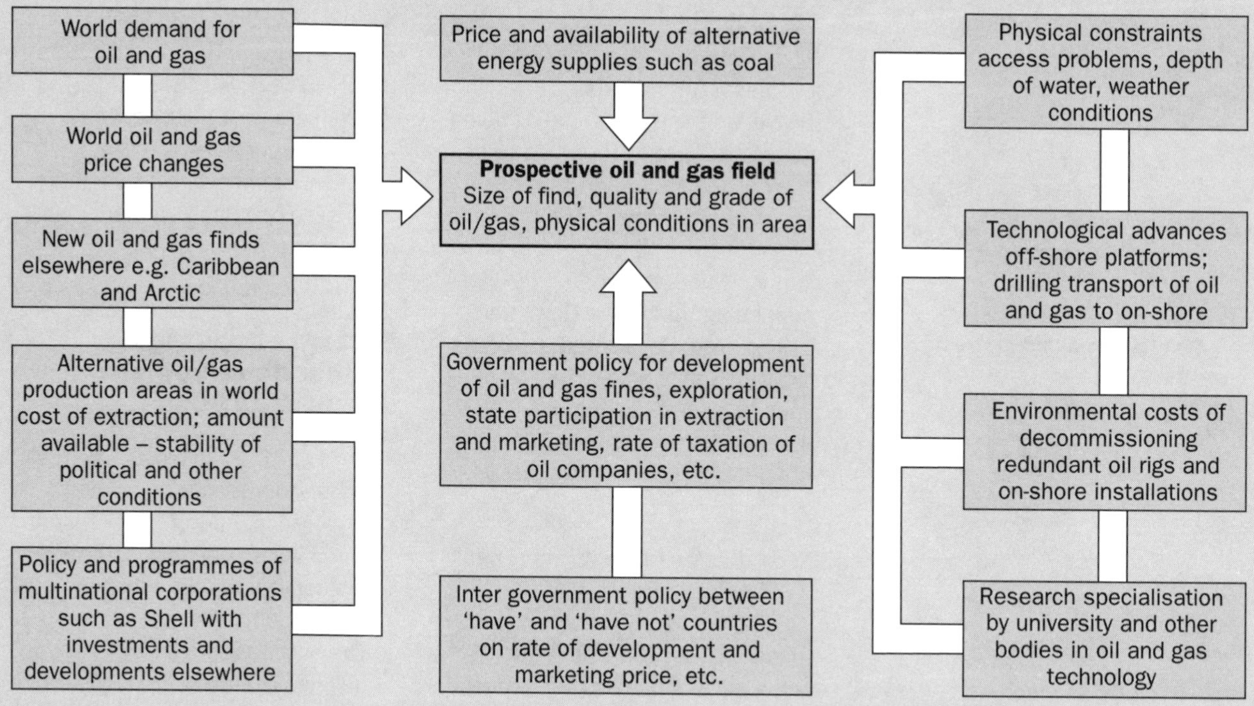

Factors influencing development

One of a number of offshore developments taking place around the world

Because North Sea oil and gas finds are at the centre of one of the heartlands of the Western world, developments here have tended to overshadow equally important developments elsewhere. The North Sea fields are but one of a group of off-shore developments which are taking place around the world. There are others, for example around the Caribbean, off the coast of West Africa, in South East Asia and in particular off China, where rapid economic advancement and a population of 1000 million are creating unprecedented energy demands.

It is likely that finds in these off-shore regions will ultimately exceed those in the North Sea.

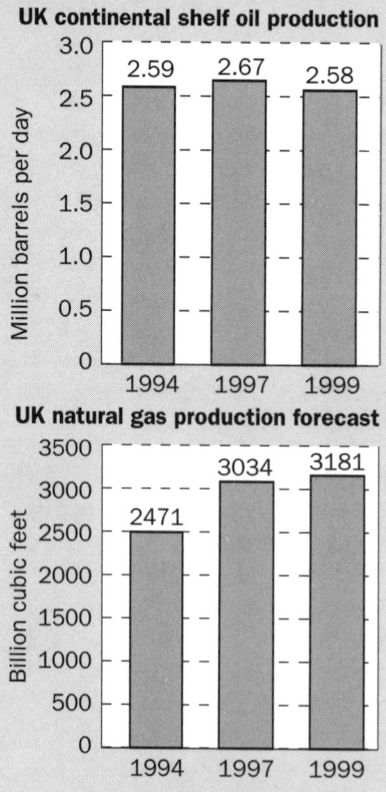

Shelf oil and gas production

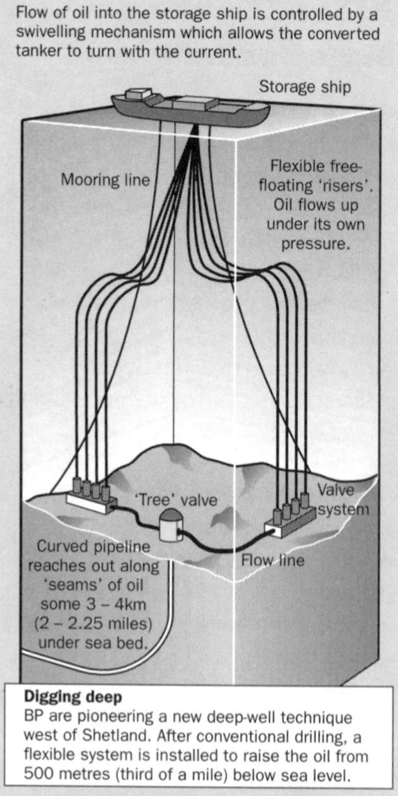

New technologies for developing fields in the harsh conditions west of the Shetlands

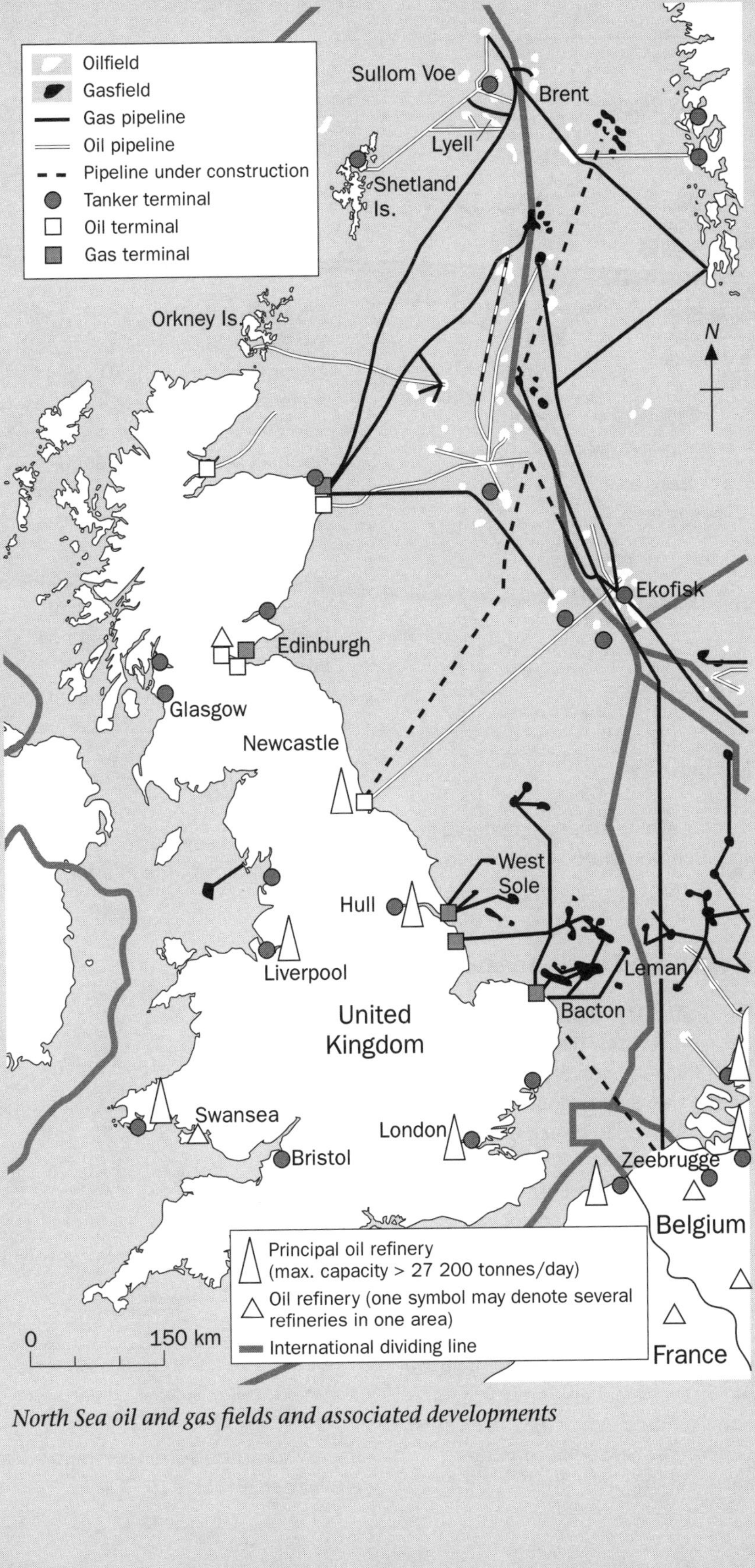

North Sea oil and gas fields and associated developments

case study

27.4 France: nuclear energy for three quarters of its energy needs

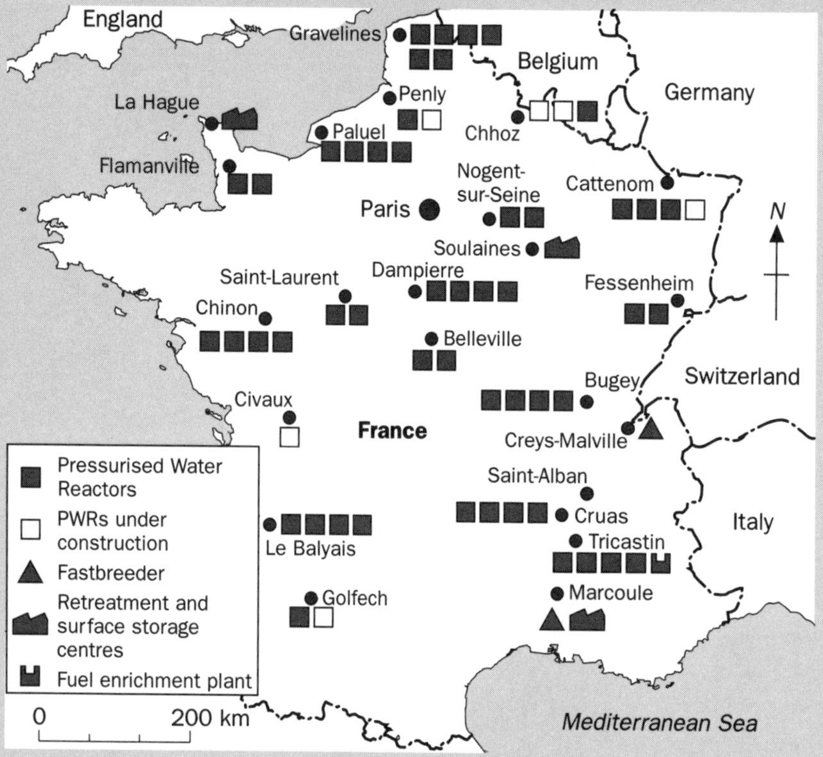

Distribution of present and planned nuclear industry

1975 New energy strategy

The world oil crisis caused a major re-evaluation of France's energy strategy in 1975 when, under a new national energy plan designed to reduce dependence on imported oil, it was decided:

- to embark on a massive expansion of nuclear energy
- to diversify towards more use of renewable energy especially solar and thermal energy
- to accept that only a modest expansion of hydro-electricity was possible due to limited site potential and environmental objections to further schemes
- that because of the relative cost of coal-fired power and the detrimental effects of gaseous emissions, coal would play only a secondary role
- that strong emphasis should be placed on more efficient use of energy.

Continued dependence

By 1990, 30 nuclear stations had been built widely distributed but with concentrations on the Loire and Rhône rivers and coastal sites in the north. Access to ample water supplies was a crucial location factor.

Despite environmental concerns about over dependence on nuclear energy, the government intends to continue to rely on it for 80% of France's energy needs and to export surplus nuclear electricity to neighbouring countries where deregulation of electricity markets provide good opportunities. About 12% is currently supplied to bordering countries, including the UK.

Electricité de France also looks to exporting its expertise and nuclear equipment to Asian countries as they expand their nuclear energy capacities.

Safety concerns

- Although there is concern about the safety of nuclear reactors the crucial concern is how to dispose of nuclear waste.
- The Electricité de France are opening a new reprocessing plant at La Hague (Brittany) to deal with 800 tonnes of waste.
- After much controversy and opposition the decommissioned superphenic reactor south of Lyons, the world's largest has been recommissioned as a research reactor in the quest for more efficient nuclear energy production.
- A poll in 1993 revealed that 80% of the French population were satisfied to see nuclear energy as the main source of energy.

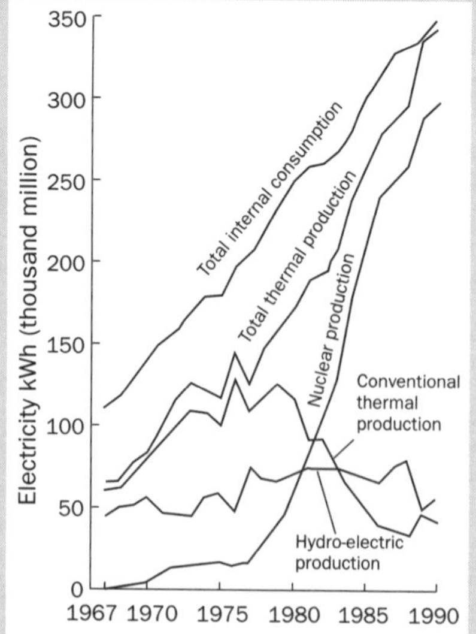

Conventional thermal production includes coal, oil and gas. [SOURCE: *Electricité de France*, 1991]

Energy sources used for electricity production, France, 1967 – 90

case study

27.5 The Mersey barrage tidal power project

The proposed Mersey Barrage would be two miles upstream from Liverpool's centre and would be 1.5 miles along. Forty six sluice gates and 28 turbines are proposed with two locks to allow shipping upstream. A road along the barrage across the estuary would be of great benefit to Merseyside. However, after subsidising research into the scheme the government has halted support. The scheme is unlikely to go ahead before 2000 for a number of reasons including:

- Capital costs would be unlikely to pay a return on money invested in them. Although they are cheap to run, the cost of building the barrage is three times that of an equivalent coal, oil or gas power station. The Mersey Barrage Company planning the scheme wanted a guaranteed price of 6.75 p per kilowatt hour, about three times the market price of electricity in 1991.
- The 3000 ships sailing up the estuary beyond Liverpool port to smaller ports inland and up the Manchester Ship canal would have to negotiate an extra set of locks, causing delays. During the building of the barrage navigation would be severely disrupted. Ports and shipping interests have therefore opposed the scheme.
- Mudflats exposed at low tide are an important wildlife habitat providing rich feeding grounds for thousands of migratory wading birds. If the barrage is built, water levels upstream will only fall by half the level under current tidal regimes, so a smaller area of flats will be exposed for a shorter time (mudflats below the barrage will not be affected).

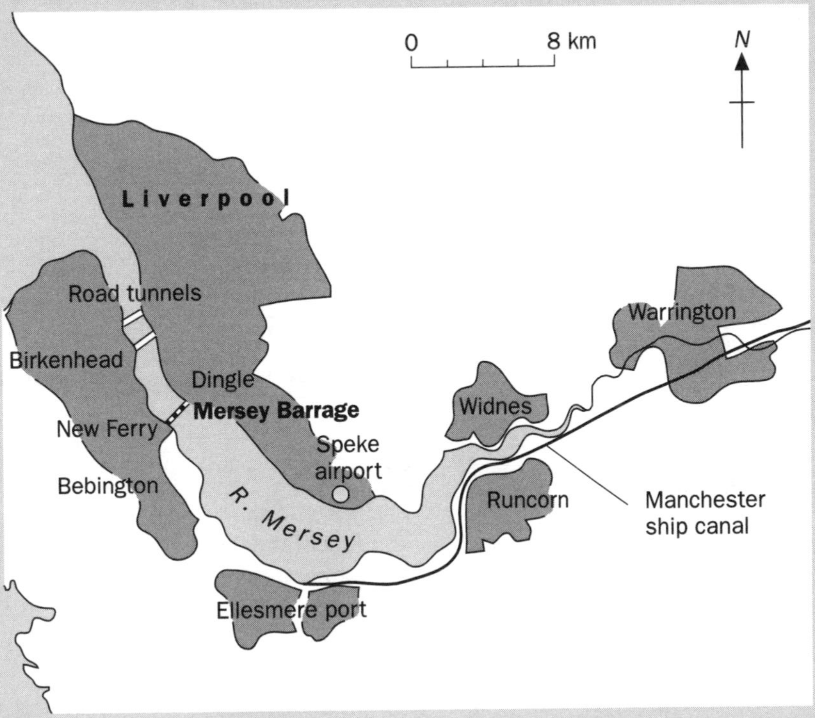

Location of proposed barrage

case study

27.6 Tanzania: the twin energy dilemmas facing poorer developing countries

The dominant 'subsistence energy' sector

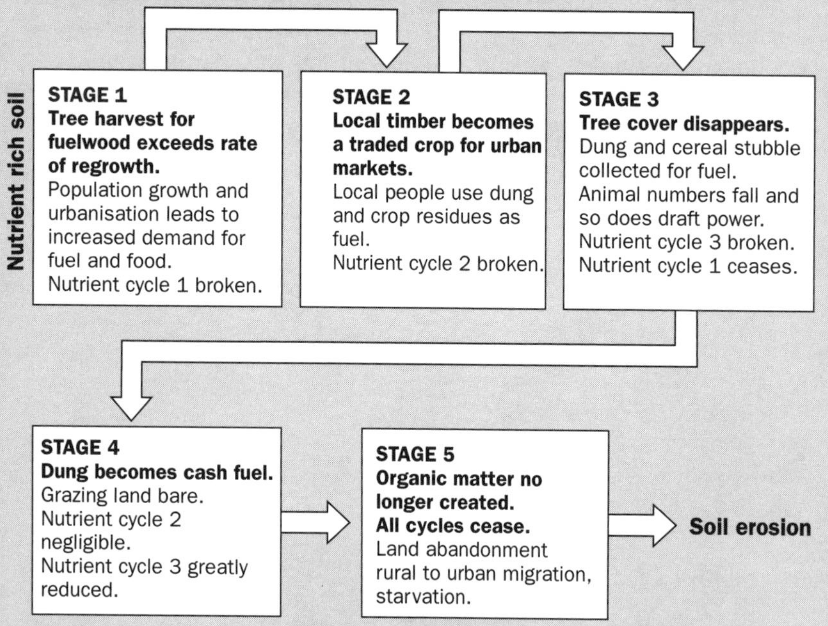

Stages in land degradation due to demand for fuel

More than 90% of the energy consumed occurs in this sector and overwhelmingly from rural households together with most of the population in the growing cities. Wood fuel is an essential subsistence requirement for cooking and heating. Demand has doubled in the last ten years and is now at an unsustainable rate leading to widespread deforestation and environmental degradation.

Although Tanzania is classed as having a 46% woodland cover, 130 000 hectares annually are being lost through clearance for wood fuel and more agricultural land. On average only 9000 hectares are being replanted. Most wood is being collected by rural households; with clearance near agricultural villages they are having to spend a longer part of the day walking further distances for wood which increases the burden on households.

Most of the 33% of the population in urban areas also depend on wood or charcoal for basic cooking and heating. As this has to be brought from increasing distances the cost rises, taking an increasing share of already very low incomes.

The Tanzanian government has made some commitment to reducing the rate of wood clearance and to more replanting but this is as yet far too little to counter the rising demand for wood fuel, especially as population is increasing at 3% annually and the rate of urbanisation at double this rate.

Some progress has been made to make more efficient use of wood fuel by designing more economic stoves. However, until there is a comprehensive rural development programme and a rise in incomes in urban areas, the problem of deforestation and environmental degradation and the burden on poorer households will remain.

The small commercial energy sector

The commercial energy market is very small, much of it being in transportation. It continues to rely overwhelmingly on imported oil, which swallows up 26% of the value of exports (another 32% is absorbed by servicing the international debt which past oil imports have helped to create). The continued high level of oil imports is a serious drain on the country's foreign exchange reserves. This deprives the economic sector of capital to finance development of potential domestic resources of commercial energy and economic development, which would enlarge the energy market by making domestic schemes more viable. An inflation rate still around 25% and World Bank demands for a reduction of government spending and economic restructuring as a condition for further loans and aid, increase the problems in the short term.

Paradoxically, the World Bank also recognises that Tanzania has sufficient potential commercial energy resources to make it independent of oil imports. However, there is little hope in the short term of developing these sufficiently due to the high costs involved and too small a market demand.

There are huge coalfields in the extreme south in the Ruaha basin east of Lake Malawi but only the Songwe field is being developed, with two mines providing an output of only around 150 000 tonnes annually. The coalfields are too remote from the main markets in the north e.g. it is over 1000 miles to Dar es Salaam.

Like the Zambezi, the Great Ruaha river and its tributaries flowing off the granitic plateau in gorge sections, offer good hydro-electric potential. Only three sites have been developed so far, providing energy equivalent to less than a third of that generated at Kariba on the Zambezi. The best potential site is at the Stiegler's gorge but this lies in the Selous Game Reserve where any development would have serious environmental implications.

Natural gas has been discovered off the north-east coast and a small field developed near Songo Island. Since the gas fields are relatively close to the most populated coastal area, development would be very beneficial but there is too small a commercial market at present.

In the long term, Tanzania's best hope may be in developing these sources as part of a co-ordinated energy programme for southern African as Tanzania is part of the SADDC (South African Development Co-ordination Conference) regional group.

Population	2.8 million (forecast 33 million by 2000 AD), 3.2% annual growth rate
Urban	33% of the population
GDP	\$90 (1993) from \$111 (1992)
Employment	Agriculture 85%, Industry 5%, Services 10%.

Indicators of poverty, population pressure and underdevelopment

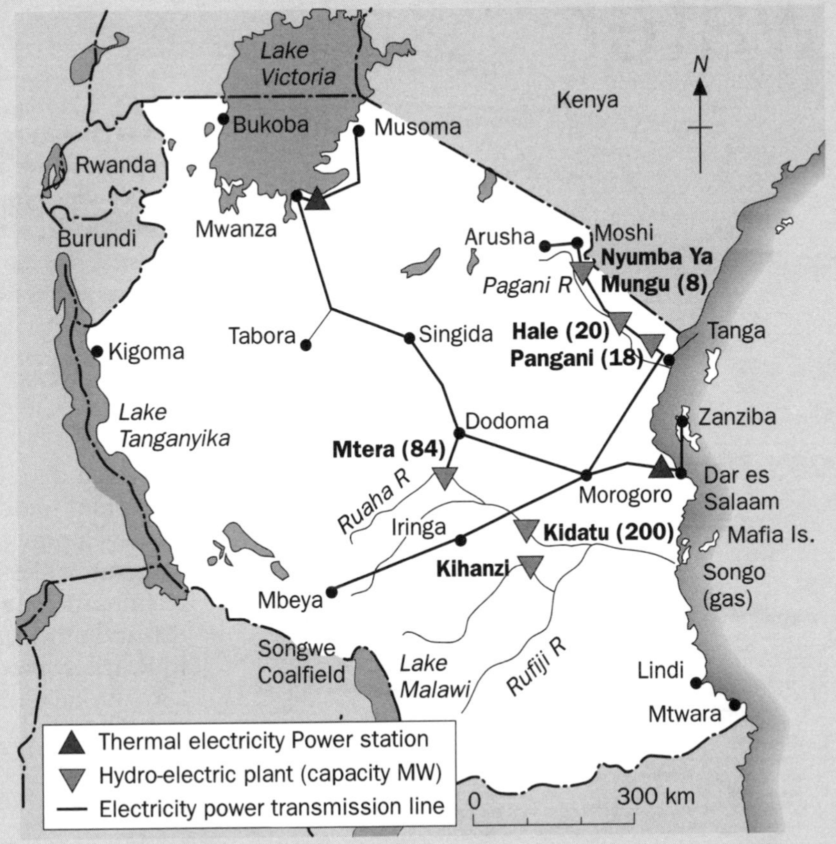

Developed commercial energy sources

CHAPTER 28

Fishing, forestry and water

These primary resources have provided for some of our basic needs but today, demand is outstripping supply. Unless measures are taken to ensure better management of these primary resources, they will diminish and the environmental damage already evident as a consequence of over-exploitation will escalate.

28.1 **Fishing**

'The unthinkable has come to pass. The wealth of oceans, once deemed as inexhaustible, has proved finite, and fish once dubbed the "poor man's protein" have become a resource coveted–and fought over–by nations.'

[Pratt M *'Diminishing Returns'*, *National Geographic*, November 1995]

Marine and fresh-water fishing remains an important source of protein. This is particularly so for developing countries where fish already provide something like 20% of protein needs. In addition to its importance as a direct food supply, many smaller fish and other organisms such as krill are industrially processed for animal feed and agricultural fertiliser.

1 **USA/China**: Former threatens latter with possible trade sanctions over failure to bring fishermen into line with United Nations driftnet ban
2 **Alaska**: US fishermen set up blockade in support of demands for greater compensation following poor pink-salmon seasons due to the Exxon Valdez oil-spill disaster
3 **Ecuador**: Conflicts within national industry between commercial operations and traditional small-scale fishing
4 **Caribbean**: Poaching by the region's local industry and illegal fishing by Japan, Russia, Taiwan, USA and Venezuela
5 **Patagonian Shelf**: Illegal fishing by Taiwanese and South Koreans; Argentinian gunboat sinks Taiwanese vessel after hot pursuit
6 **South Georgia**: Illegal fishing by Russians and Chileans in 200-mile zone
7 **USA/France**: Former accuses latter of refusing to honour international agreements to conserve bluefin tuna
8 **Flamish Cap/Grandbanks**: Canada arrests the Kristina Logos, with Portuguese crew sailing under Panamanian flag, for fishing banned sizes of flounder, cod, plaice and redfish
9 **ICCAT area**: Stock depletion from over-fishing by ICCAT members and from illegal fishing by non-parties to ICCAT, the international agreement to protect Atlantic tuna stocks
10 **Senegal**: Local industry protests that it is threatened by illegal fishing by European Union vessels
11 **Ireland**: Irish accuse Spain of illegal fishing in European Union conservation zone
12 **Bay of Biscay**: British, French and Spanish fishermen in dispute, sometimes violently, over methods used to catch tuna
13 **Channel Islands/Isles of Scilly**: Disputes between British and French lead to French trawlers' being excluded from rich lobster and other shellfish grounds
14 **Scotland**: Fishermen attack Russian trawler, destroying £250 000-worth of cod
15 **Smutthulet area**: Iceland and Norway in dispute over Arctic rights in this so-called Escape Hole region outside control of Norway and Russia

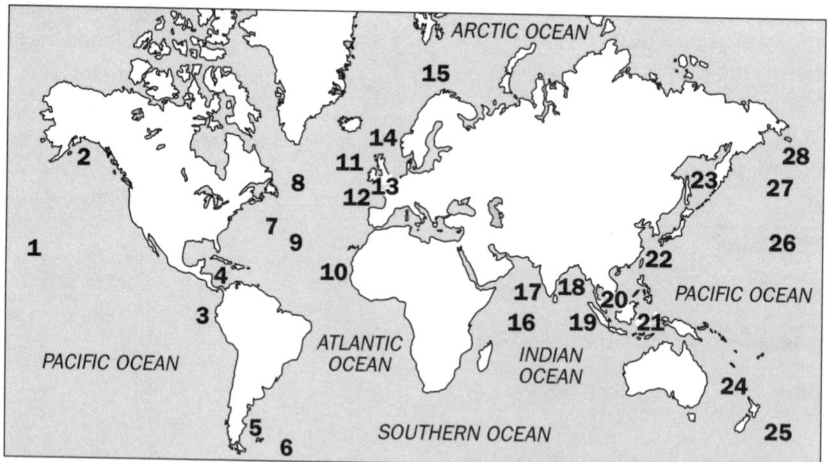

16 **BIOT area**: Japanese longliner caught fishing illegally in British Indian Ocean Territory
17 **Kerala**: Traditional small-scale fishing under threat from area's emerging industrialised operations
18 **Bay of Bengal**: Pirate attacks on shrimp trawlers
19 **Straits of Malacca**: Malaysia confiscates illegal surimi trawlers
20 **China/Vietnam**: Long-standing dispute over rights exacerbated by Vietnamese arrests of Chinese vessels; each accuses the other of illegal fishing
21 **Indonesia/Taiwan**: 10 Taiwanese boats with 100 crew detained for allegedly fishing with improper licenses
22 **China/Taiwan**: Poaching and piracy by both; reports of violent clashes leading to injuries and sometimes deaths
23 **Peanut Hole**: Russia fires at Japanese vessels for encroaching into its Exclusive Economic Zone
24 **New Zealand**: Dispute with foreign fleets over bluefin stocks, especially over Japanese fishing
25 **Chatham Rise**: New Zealand protests against illegal fishing, especially off Chatham Rise; also seizes Ukrainian and Russian vessels in hoki fishery
26 **North Pacific**: Six North Pacific Andromous Fish Commission vessels sighted driftnetting illegally
27 **Bering Sea**: Poaching by non-parties to international agreements: South Korea and Taiwan especially criticised
28 **Donut Hole**: Russia accuses USA of illegal fishing in Bering Sea; China, Japan and South Korea also reportedly involved in illegal operations

[SOURCE: Research by Indrani Lutchman, Fisheries Officer World Wide Fund for Nature (WWF) UK]

Figure 28.1 Fishing disputes, clashes, poaching and piracy over the past year 1993 – 94

Over recent years advances in fish farming or mari-culture have attracted considerable public attention, but the bulk of the demand must be met from conventional fisheries-established fishing grounds. It is thus vital that the fish stocks of these are carefully managed to ensure maximum future yields. This requires some idea of market demand in relation to the fish stock which it is economically viable to take. A knowledge of the physical and ecological conditions under which the various kinds of fish and associated life forms live and reproduce is also needed.

While freshwater fishing is locally and regionally important, particularly in the vicinity of large fresh-water bodies such as the Rift Valley lakes like Lake Victoria in Africa and in ponded areas in South East Asia, the vast bulk of the fish eaten or processed into animal feed comes from the ocean.

Factors affecting the level of fishing and fish stocks in the oceans

Ocean areas vary in their productivity

Different parts of the ocean vary in their productivity. Ecologically, the richest areas occur where upwellings of deep water happen along the margins of continents, such as that off the Peruvian coast and along parts of the Iceland–Faroes ridge. Here are nutrient-rich areas with plentiful phytoplankton (plant life) on which the zooplankton (minute animals) feed and which, in turn, support the fish at higher levels in the food chain. The most important fishing grounds are to be found along the continental shelf where the water is at depths of 200 m or less, allowing for light and oxygen to penetrate. These conditions, along with nutrients partly carried by rivers and derived from the nearby land, encourage an abundance of plankton and therefore plentiful supplies of fish.

Productivity is lowest in the ocean deeps and also comparatively low in tropical waters where a thermolayer occurs between the warm surface water and the cold deeps, inhibiting the functioning of the nutrient cycle. Though somewhat higher in the temperate and sub-polar waters, there are marked seasonal variations in productivity.

Any major expansion of world fishing grounds is likely to be around the continental shelf including areas of upwelling waters. Also, economic methods of fishing the deeper oceans for new species of fish and smaller livestock, such as krill in the southern oceans are being considered.

Interruption of the food chain

It is usual to divide marine life into pelagic life, which lives above the floor of the ocean, mainly in

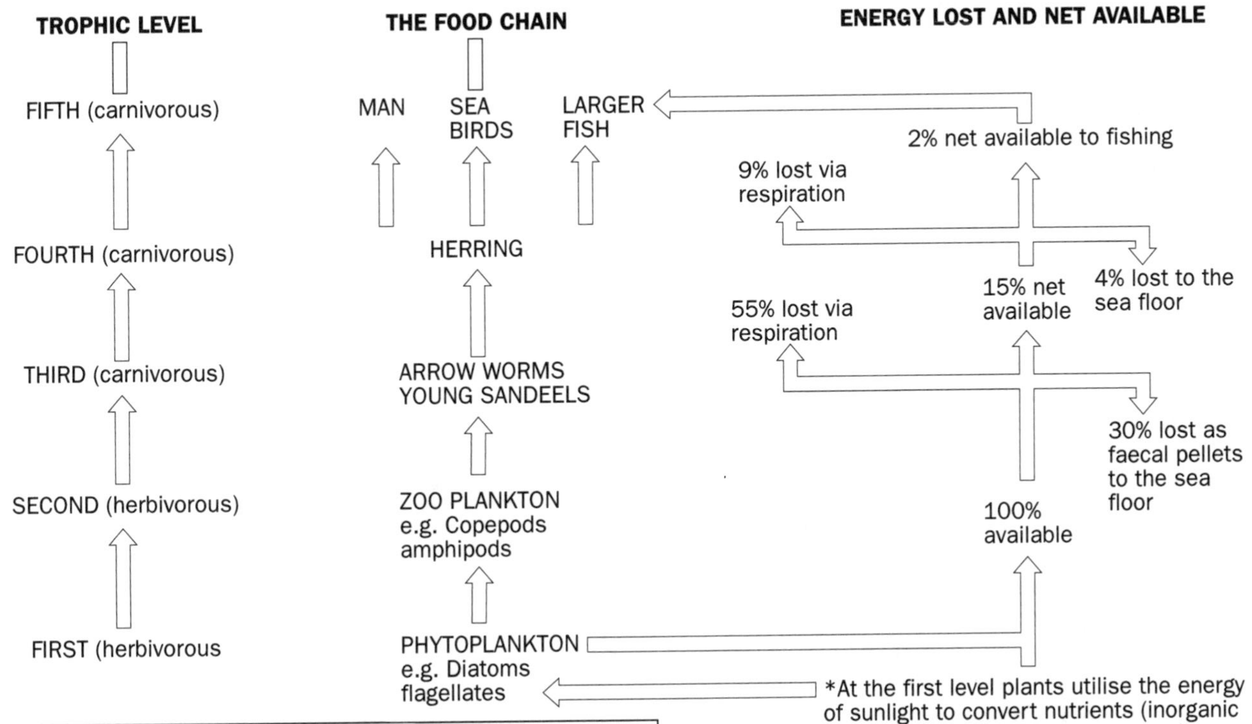

NOTE: As with other food chains, the relative efficiency of the food chain can be assessed in terms of the proportion of the initially convertible energy (100%) left at the end of the chain. In the case of the food chain of the herring this is only 2% and even some of this will be lost to sea birds and larger fish which also consume herring.

Figure 28.2 Food chain for the herring

the surface layers of the oceans, and benthos life such as flat fish and crustaceans which live on the ocean bottom, principally the floor of the continental shelf. Herring is a typical pelagic fish, while cod and plaice are the most common benthos fish. Each is supported by a food chain and any interruption of it by either natural events or human activity can be serious (Figure 28.2).

A change in physical conditions may for example drastically reduce the amount of phytoplankton and in turn, the zooplankton upon which fish feed. For example, the once abundant anchovy off the Peruvian coast have been markedly reduced due to a change in current flows, affecting upwelling and mixing of cold water with warmer surface waters and therefore the amount of plankton available to anchovy (Case study 28.1).

Changes in the conditions off-shore have also been brought about by pollution and by reclamation of coastal wetland areas where some fish breed and feed. These problems are particularly evident off heavily populated coast areas such as those off Western Europe and California, but are increasing off the coast of China and other rapidly industrialising South East Asian countries. There have also been grave ecological consequences from oil spillages such as that associated with the sinking of the oil tanker, the Exxon Valdez, in Prince William Sound, Alaska, one of the richest fishing areas in the world.

Overfishing

Overfishing reduces the amount of fish left to carry on the reproductive cycle essential to the level of future fish stocks in the ocean. The amount of fishing should not be determined by the total number of fish available, that is, by the standard crop, but by the rates of production amongst the various fished stock. The production of fish potentially exploitable depends on a level of fishing which allows for maximum reproduction and provides conditions encouraging fish to mature to the best marketable size.

Major fishing nations, including Japan, the CIS, Peru and China, have paid more attention to the economics of market demand than to the need to leave sufficient fish for maximum reproduction levels to be maintained (Figure 28.3). Where over-fishing is combined with a change in the natural conditions affecting fish population, the results can be very serious. For example, the Peruvian fishing industry was rapidly developed after the Second World War to make Peru one of the world's leading fishing nations by the 1960s – only to be followed by a catastrophic decline from which the country is only now recovering (Case study 28.1).

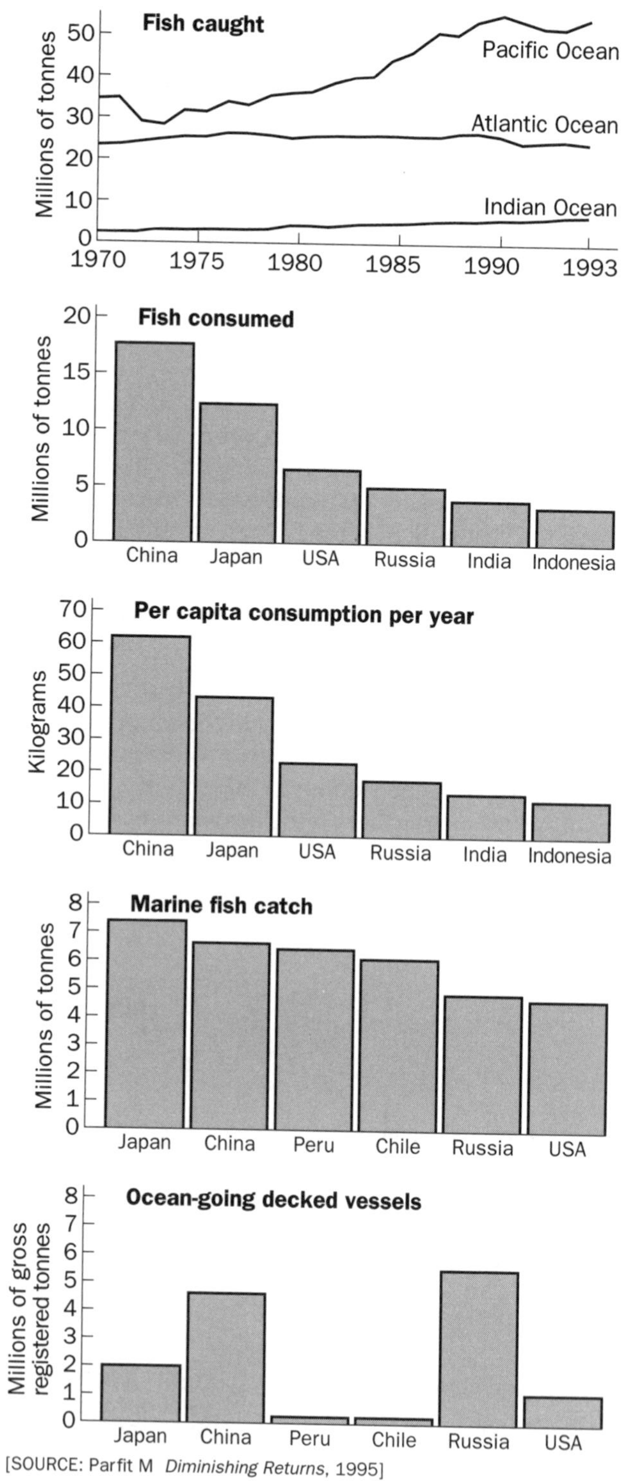

Figure 28.3 Fish catches from major oceans and the world's leading fishing and consuming nations, 1992

The major commercial fishing nations, including EU countries such as Spain and the UK, have over-fished their own coastal and deepwater fishing grounds and increasingly penetrated those of other nations as well as the wider oceans beyond territorial waters (Figure 28.1).

Increasingly developing countries with rich offshore fishing grounds are selling access to these grounds to the richer commercial fishing nations. Namibia for example has a joint venture with a Spanish fishing company worth $44 million dollars. China, now the second largest fishing nation after Japan, has negotiated agreements with 12 nations for access to their territorial waters.

At the same time as rights of access are being sold off, dependence on fishing for a livelihood in developing countries, such as Senegal, are encouraging the local populations to expand their own operations and enter export markets. The net result has been a spread in the problem of overfishing. Also, much of the catch has been diverted away from local markets and from the people most in need. Vietnam, for instance, plans to more than double its fish exports by the end of the decade to a value of around $900 million a year.

Overfishing is now evident in most of the world's major fishing grounds for a number of reasons:

- a continued rise in world demand as population increases.
- as demand exceeds supply with world production having peaked at 78 million tonnes, the price of fish has increased encouraging over-exploitation, including illegal fishing, frequently for immature fish, affecting future breeding stocks (Figure 28.4).
- quotas and controls imposed within territorial waters have diverted pressure to fishing grounds beyond territorial controls. Off the Grand Banks of Nova Scotia a bitter dispute occurred between Canada and Spain in 1994 over Spanish trawlers allegedly overfishing on the edge of the Grand Banks (Figure 28.1).
- very significant technological advances have increased the scale of fishing operations. There are now powerful 'industrial fleets' with freezer trawlers and factory ships, able to operate for long periods out at sea using the latest tracking and catching devices.
- despite warnings of a decrease in marine catches in the 1970s and 80s, the fishing industry continued to expand. The World Food and Agricultural Organisation indicated that the world fishing fleet doubled between 1970 to 1990 so that it now has twice the capacity currently needed. This has been encouraged because of rising prices of fish and because governments, while imposing quotas on fish catch, were at the same time subsidising the fishing fleets to help them modernise and operate.

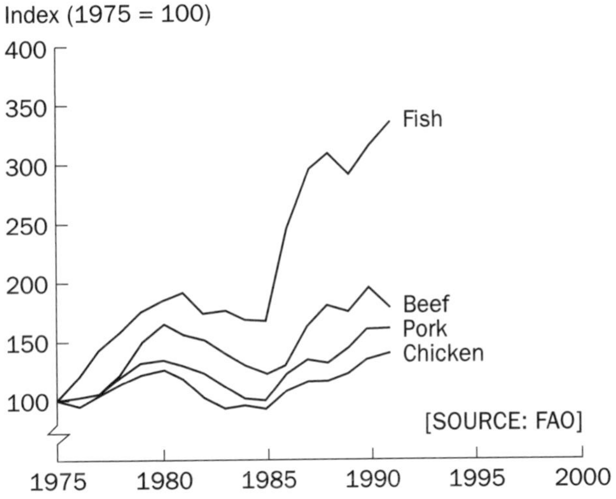

Figure 28.4 *Comparison of fish, beef, pork and chicken export prices, 1975 – 91*

Fencing the oceans

As a consequence of the boom in fishing in the 1960s and 1970s and the fierce competition over fishing the grounds, there was increasing pressure to curtail free access to the world's fishing regions. As part of the Third United Nations Conference on the Law of the Sea in 1974, governments agreed to establish a zone of 200 nautical miles wide within which a coastal country has sole rights to natural resources. Access by other nations to it could only be by negotiation. This exclusive economic zone (EEZ) took in most of the ocean's productive fishing grounds. Nearly all coastal countries have now laid claim to EEZs.

Since then there have been other international conferences on the Law of the Sea investigating global management and development of fish stocks and a range of other issues which were agreed. This included an action programme of planning, management and development of fisheries, development of aquaculture, international trade in fish and fish products and promoting fisheries to alleviate undernourishment amongst the world populations.

However, difficulties in implementing a successful policy can be seen from efforts by EU countries to achieve an acceptable policy relating to the North Sea and north-east Atlantic fishing grounds which fall within a joint EEZ zone.

The most successful policy of management is judged to be one where, besides the usual combination of closed season, restricted areas, size limits, species restrictions, quotas and restrictions, there is also local community control and individual involvement, as in Japan. As early as 1901 for example, Japan passed a Fisheries Law in which the government delegated control of local fishing grounds to local Fishing Cooperative Associations which organised all coastal fishers and enforced control over the fisheries. This has worked comparatively well. The fishers have the security of knowing how much they can harvest each year, can concentrate on operating in an economic manner and have a vested interest in maintaining fish stocks at healthy levels.

Implementing a consensus about fishing and management of the open ocean beyond EEZ zones is even more problematic and as yet there is no general agreement on how this can be achieved. The most helpful way forward appears to be to pay greater attention to ocean ecosystems as integrated units rather than consider the effects of overfishing on particular species of fish. When overfishing of a particular species occurs for example, this affects the population and diversity of other organisms linked to that species in an ecosystem, that is, predators, competitors and prey. Thus all parts of the ecosystem need to be studied in relation to each other.

The concept of the Large Marine Ecosystems has now been developed. LMEs are defined as ecologically coherent areas of the ocean about 200 000 sq. km in size. So far 49 have been identified, covering most of the world's commercial productive fisheries. The LME covering the continental shelf fishing grounds off north-east USA is most often studied. It has been shown here that overfishing did reduce the amount of ground fish but not the total finfish biomass, as sand eels, dogfish and skates grew in numbers to replace ground fish. This clearly indicates the need to diversify fish catch within a LME and reduce the catch of one particular species. With wider understanding of LMEs and better management of fish stocks, it is estimated that a world fish take could be doubled and still be sustainable. This could go a long way towards meeting the protein needs of populations in poorer countries.

Likely shorter term prospects

At present there is little hope of extending fishing in the conventional fishing regions, and the greatest potential probably lies in responsible expansion of fishing of the suitable but lesser used waters of the south-west Atlantic and north-west Indian Ocean. It is also estimated that some 15 million more tonnes might be added by harvesting other kinds of fish and marine life. Already some hitherto little marketed fish, for example those related to cod at the top of the food chain such as coley, are being exploited and are increasingly common on the fish sales counters at supermarkets. As regards the deepwater high seas resources, catch costs would be high, thus only high value fish such as tuna will be worth exploiting.

Smaller organisms, including zooplankton are now being successfully exploited. These occur earlier in the food chain therefore they provide higher productivity fishing as less of the primary productivity energy has been lost. The Russians and the Japanese have developed large suction retrieval and processing methods, enabling mid-water trawling of lantern fish and shrimps for example, which congregate in large shoals at several hundred metres down. With the decline in the whale population in the Southern Ocean and waters around Antarctica, the krill plankton on which whales feed has increased so much that it is now economic to harvest them. This is currently at the rate of 10 million tonnes a year and it could rise to 50 million tonnes. Careful management, however, is needed as krill are the food for a variety of marine life in these waters.

Smaller marine species are largely processed into livestock feed for chickens, pigs and cattle and therefore indirectly add an important extra source of protein to world diets. This could be particularly important in the future in helping to solve protein deficiencies amongst the poorer countries. Apart from extending the range of harvesting to a greater variety, another way of increasing fish, shellfish and other marine life, including edible seaweed and other plants, is by fish farming or mari-culture.

Fish farming or aquaculture (mari-culture)

Aquaculture now accounts for 20% of the total of fish harvested. It is mainly concerned with freshwater species; only 5% is reared under saltwater conditions. Output has doubled in the last ten years. The World Food and Agricultural Organisation is looking for output to double again in the next 15 years, partly to compensate for depletion of ocean fish stocks, but particularly to help meet the basic protein needs of growing populations in developing countries.

Fish farming has been practised for centuries in South East Asian countries where fish is part of the staple diet. Over 80% of world output comes from Asia, much of it for local consumption. China is by far the largest producer with half of all fish farmed. Freshwater carp are reared in ponds at low cost, while milk fish and mullet are kept in coastal ponds linked by open water. However, since fish are subject to more stress under artificial rearing, the number of species which can be farmed in this way is limited.

Expansion and environmental concerns

A number of developing countries are looking to tilapia, a white tropical fish which can grow quickly and is herbivorous, like most fish farmed in tropical countries. The FAO is encouraging this type of fish farming in Asia, Africa and Latin America, both to supply local needs and also for export to advanced countries to earn foreign revenue. Jamaica for example already supplies 5000 tonnes of tilapia annually to the UK and the USA has begun to import tilapia. Markets are also expanding in the more mature Newly Industrialising Countries of South East Asia, such as South Korea.

Japan and other South Eastern Asian countries are developing marine polyculture, especially on low wetland coasts with access to tidal water. Mangrove swamp areas offer particularly nutritious environs due to rapid decomposition of plant life under tropical conditions. Here a variety of fish and shellfish are being reared in the same ponds. However, extension of fish farming in coastal areas also leads to clearance of some mangrove swamps and wetland areas which are the sanctuary, nursery and breeding grounds of many kinds of wild fish. Thus some aquaculture such as shrimp farming is at the expense of oceanic fisheries.

Inland areas also offer important opportunities, especially large inland lake areas. In Africa for example, lakes such as Lake Malawi and Lake Victoria have over centuries attracted fishing village settlements. Both on natural lakes and artificial lakes such as Lake Kariba, fish farming is being encouraged. Shrimp fishing for example is now a flourishing industry on Lake Kariba.

In western countries intensive production of high value species is being rapidly developed, particularly as the price of fish increases and ocean stocks become depleted. Attention is on species such as salmon, sea- and freshwater trout which under controlled conditions and intensive feeding will quickly mature. For example, 60 000 tonnes of farmed salmon are now being marketed annually in the UK.

Aquaculture and harvesting of fish under natural conditions are not entirely separate activities. Small fry can be caught under natural conditions and introduced into enclosed areas to be reared under farming conditions. Similarly, efforts have been made to release artificially reared young fry into open water in an effort to increase fish stocks, but so far with limited success.

Fish farming in Fiji

Coastal villages have access to sea fishing but inland villages due to poor communications have difficulty obtaining fish. Thus the FAO, supported by Japanese Aid funding, established a South Pacific Aquaculture Scheme in the late 1980s. Under this, 500 fish farms have been developed for inland villages, with the villagers digging their own 500 sq. metre ponds. Initial fish food and tilapia fry are provided from a hatchery on Viti Levu island. The fry mature within 5 – 6 months, allowing two harvests a year. The villages have now developed the traditional Chinese method of combining poultry with fish farming, the chickens and ducks helping to fertilise and enrich the pond for the fish to feed. Villages are now looking beyond simply feeding themselves to marketing the surplus.

[SOURCE: *Financial Guardian* 17.12.91]

28.2 **Forestry**

Although there are important woodland areas in middle latitudes and locally important forestry industries exist, such as those in the Black Forest of Germany and the eucalyptus woodlands of Australia, the main forest belts are those of the humid tropics in the equatorial and monsoon regions and those of the cold temperate high latitudes in Northern Canada and Eurasia (Figure 28.5). Important extensions of these occur in lower latitudes where mountainous terrain experience similar climatic conditions to that of the northlands.

Because of the extensive need for paper and other timber products in industrial countries, forested areas are principally seen as sources for such products. This has led to over-exploitation of forests and insufficient concern for the other uses of these areas, in particular as human and animal habitats. The contribution of forested areas to the oxygen balance of the earth's atmosphere and their effects on world climate have also been insufficiently understood. Now with a growing awareness of the destruction of forested areas, particularly in the tropics, and the wider issues involved in proper management of forest lands, more attention is being given to the conflicting demands made on the world's reserves and the replenishment of this important resource.

Forest industry

The total tree harvest exceeds three billion cubic metres a year but half of this is consumed as fuelwood, mainly in developing countries. The other half is labelled as commercial or industrial roundwood which provides the feedstock for a number of products broadly divided into paper and paperboard products, wood-based panels (mainly plywood and chipboard) and sawnwood, used in the construction and furniture industry (Figure 28.6).

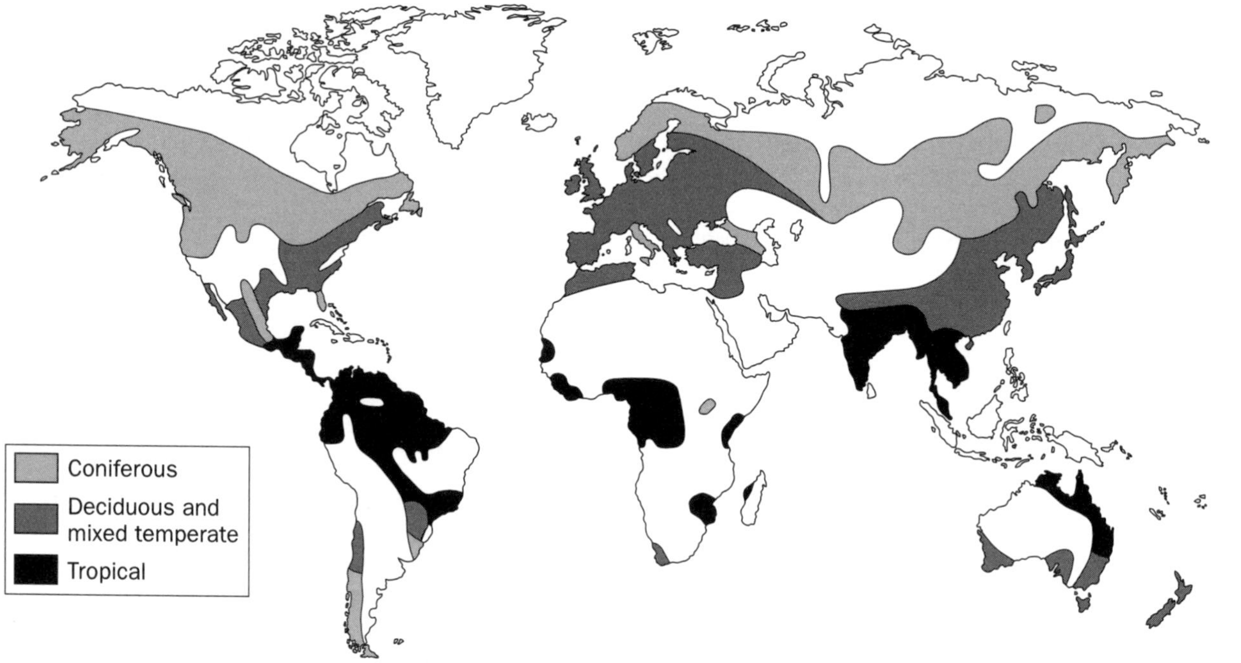

Figure 28.5 *Main forest areas of the world*

Demand is dominated by the industrialised countries which takes about 70% of all commercial roundwood (Figure 28.6). However, demand is rising fastest in the developing countries, especially the Newly Industrialising Countries in Asia and Latin America, reflecting the relationship between per capita consumption and rate of economic development (Figures 28.7).

Consumption of the different categories of forest products varies considerably. The rate for sawn wood has levelled off but that for wood panel and paper products has continued to expand (UK paper). Wood panelled products such as plywood and fibre board have steadily replaced sawn timber in the construction industry since they are cheaper. While the demand for wood pulp has expanded, an increasing proportion of paper is made from recycled products. Today about 40% of the materials going into paper and paper board products is recycled materials, reflecting the effect of environmental pressures to conserve forested areas and improvements in the techniques and economics of recycling.

Much of the commercial or industrial roundwood comes from temperate forest areas as the production figures for forest products indicates (Figure 28.8). However, there is a significant shift towards increasing production in the developing world. Indonesia and Brazil are emerging as major producers (Case study 28.2). This shift is also reflected in the increasing globalisation of the forestry industry as major timber corporations invest in developing countries

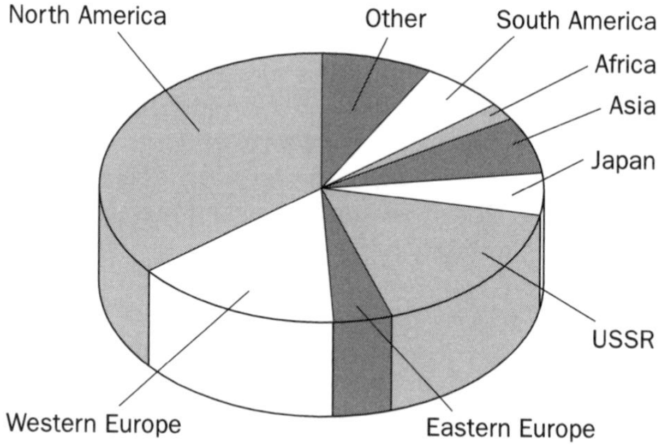

[SOURCE: FAO Yearbook 1990]

Figure 28.6 *Consumption of industrial roundwood by region*

The three leading consuming regions compared to a representative selection of other regions

Advanced Countries		**Newly Industrial Countries**	
North America	310	Mexico	39
Japan	230	Chile	38
European Union	162	Brazil	30
		China	18
		India	4

NOTE: Level of per capita consumption reflects level of economic development
[SOURCE: *Financial Times* 17.5.94]

Figure 28.7 *The paper and paper board by product consumers 1993 (000 tonnes per capita)*

and embark on joint ventures with timber companies there where costs are lower. However, production is still dominated by advanced countries.

Paper (mill. tonnes)		Wood pulp (mill. tonnes)	
USA	69.5	**USA**	55.5
Japan	24.6	**Canada**	23.6
Canada	16.6	**Japan**	10.4
China	14.1	**Russia**	10.4
Germany	11.9	**Sweden**	10.1
Russia	10.2	**Finland**	9.0
Finland	8.7	**Brazil**	4.4
Sweden	8.2	**Germany**	3.0

Roundwood–Coniferous (logs, sawn timber, etc) (mill. cubic metres)		Roundwood–Broad Leaved (Mainly tropical) (mill. cubic metres)	
USA	345	**India**	243
Russia	327	**USA**	135
Canada	164	**Indonesia**	172
China	134	**China**	142
Sweden	44	**Nigeria**	96
Brazil	42		
Finland	39		

[SOURCE: *Phillips Digest*, 1992]

Figure 28.8 *Forestry products and leading countries*

Softwood coniferous forest belts

Distribution

The present distribution of coniferous forest is largely controlled by climatic factors (including altitude) and patterns of past exploitation. Coniferous evergreen species are able to withstand cold and drought, are adapted to a short growing season and can survive on poor sandy soils such as those of coastal dunes. This explains the location of certain large tracts such as the sandy areas of the southern USA. The main commercial species are pines, firs and spruces but within these groups certain species are favoured because of particular qualities, such as quick growth, straightness of trunk and can be used either as timber or pulp (poorer trees being used for the latter). Amongst the commonly known species are the white pine, the Douglas fir and the Norwegian spruce. In the southern hemisphere the Parana and Radiata pines are particularly important. Because of the warmer and more moist climates in countries such as Chile and New Zealand, coniferous woods mature more quickly. Chile in particular is extending planted areas of Radiata pine and rapidly expanding its forest industry. (Within Brazil planted eucalyptus tracts are being extended to increase softwood supplies.)

Unlike deciduous woodland and tree species in the tropical rainforest, conifers occur in essentially pure stands with little undergrowth clutter, thus making exploitation of them easier. Increasingly today many of these pure stands are a result of replanting programmes initiated to bolster the world's depleting reserves of softwood timber, particularly along the earlier exploited southern margins of the coniferous belt in Eurasia and North America.

Management and conservation

In the past conservation has generally been synonymous with the preservation of existing forest lands and the wildlife dependent upon it. Today it is recognised that much of the world's forested areas must be managed in such a way as to provide an increasing amount and variety of uses.

Leisure use of forested and other national areas for recreation has greatly expanded and is highly profitable. With regard to present resource use, it is estimated that the demand for pulp-based products will double in the next 50 years, putting increasing pressure on raising the timber yields in any given areas.

Forest preservation

As a way of resolving difficulties between the two main groups of protagonists – conservationists and commercial users – most countries have adopted a common policy of identifying certain forest lands as primarily areas for the support and maintenance of wildlife and the natural habitat upon which it depends, while also trying to ensure responsible use of the remainder.

In the early 1900s the USA, largely through the initiative of Theodore Roosevelt, established National Parks such as the Yosemite Valley and National Monument Parks in the western USA. Finland today also has a comprehensive programme of nature reserves covering approximately one million hectares, much of it forest land. These provide recreational areas, though their use has to be carefully monitored to prevent detrimental effects both to the habitat and its wildlife.

Management of other forest areas

Outside of preservation areas, forests managed for commercial purposes under public or private ownership are still subject to legislation to protect wildlife. In addition, timber stands on watershed areas are protected from wholesale felling or clearance from other uses, such as overgrazing which kills young saplings and destroys most of the undergrowth. If this happened, the resultant increased water run-off could lead to serious soil erosion as in the USA Appalachian region at the turn of the twentieth century.

With respect to timber extraction, in all major timber producing countries of the northern hemisphere, emphasis is on farming timber rather than exploiting the forest land. In Finland timber is seen as a rotation crop with the government carefully overseeing the amount of timber felled, ensuring this is balanced against replanting. As land is cut over, it is drained, ploughed, enriched with fertiliser and replanted. Trees are carefully selected from the most suitable species and nurtured until strong enough to be moved to their planting situations. Advisory services ensure careful management until the trees are mature enough for felling. Clear felling over limited tracts is the usual method as this not only increases timber yields but allows easier replanting cycles. Thus with improved management methods, it is estimated that Finland has doubled its timber yields without reducing forest stock.

In the USA, clear felling is more difficult because much of the commercial timber is on upland watershed land. Whether clear felling occurs or not depends on factors such as the age and composition of the trees, the slope of the land, type of soil, the amount and intensity of rainfall and the species and type of wildlife affected. In many locations only selected fellings are possible under forest management. It is estimated that the USA, at present dependent on a third of its needs being supplied by Canada, could be self-sufficient in timber and even a net exporter within the next ten years.

Acid rain

One of the most difficult problems affecting all kinds of woodland is air pollution, particularly in industrial countries. In Central Europe for example, acid rain caused by sulphurous and other fumes carried in the wind and bringing precipitation to forest lands, is having such a serious effect it is estimated that about a quarter of woodland in West Germany is damaged beyond recovery. This is a far more of a problem than ground pollution from water contaminated by effluent from timber mills or other industrial usages close to forest lands. Acid rain requires legislation of a much more comprehensive nature than that directly concerned with the forest land itself.

More effective use of timber

Responsible management of timber resources must also require the efficient use of the timber once it is cut. Thus, in the case of timber needed for the construction industries, much of the sawn timber output is being replaced by reconstituted timber from the grinding up of whole trees to reduce waste. Powerful glues are then used to reconstitute and remould them to the consumer's needs. More effective recycling programmes for waste paper and other products are also important to enable the re-use of resources.

Tropical forests

Natural conditions affecting exploitation

There are important differences between softwood coniferous forests and the tropical forests of monsoon and equatorial lands (Figure 28.5). Tropical forests are dominated by hardwoods and there is a much greater variety of species with few pure stands of any one particular type of tree. This makes extraction of commercial timber difficult.

Commercial exploitation of the most sought after hardwoods such as teak, ebony and mahogany is hindered by species being scattered throughout a forest tract, among other conditions. Felling and transportation to assembly points for larger distance shipments is made difficult by the close packing of trees and secondary growth. Conditions under foot are frequently swampy and much of the forest lands are away from any natural access routes such as navigable rivers. The hot, humid climate also reduces the efficiency of labour and is detrimental to the health of people who work and live in remote logging areas away from medical and other amenities. It is thus not surprising that until relatively recently, commercial exploitation of tropical forest lands has been very limited, taking place mainly where access to navigable coasts and rivers or road and rail transport was available.

Deforestation and forest degradation

Land clearance and domestic fuel demand

Whereas coniferous forest management has been centrally concerned with over-exploitation of the timber for commercial purposes without sufficient regard for other uses, future supplies and the effect on wildlife, in most tropical regions the biggest problem has been the destruction of many areas to meet local domestic needs for agricultural or grazing land. As populations have increased, more and more land has been cleared. Overgrazing in marginal areas of the forest as in West Africa and Latin America led to the continual pushing back of forest margins (Case study 28.5).

Perhaps the greatest loss however has been through the use of wood as the major fuel in all tropical areas where woodland occurs.

Commercial logging

Commercial logging has significantly increased since 1980 contributing to deforestation and forest degradation. The area of tropical timber plantations has increased from 18 million to 40 million hectares, nowhere near enough to compensate for the area being lost to logging of primary forest areas (Figure 28.9).

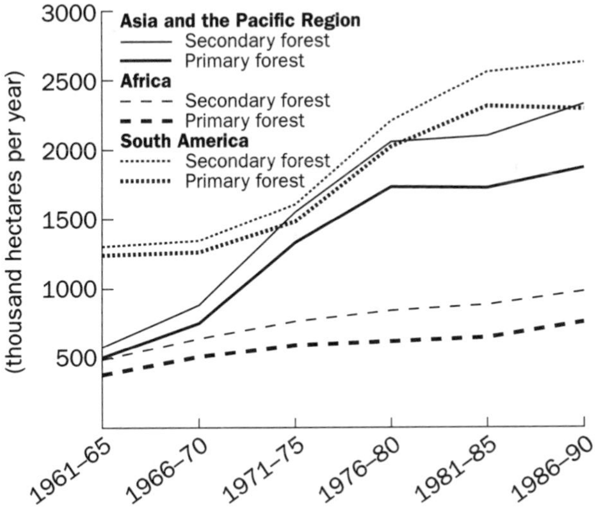

[SOURCE: Food and Agriculture Organization of the United Nations (FAO), 1993]

Figure 28.9 *Tropical forest area logged*

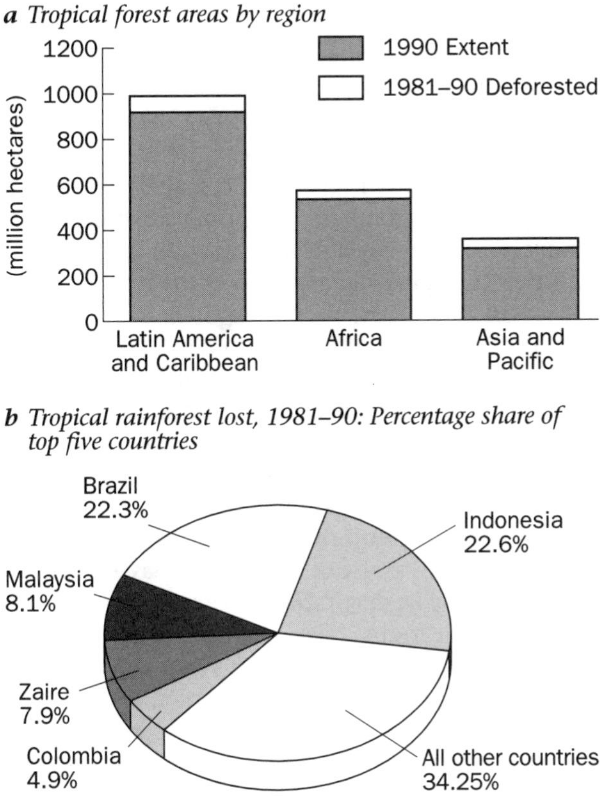

[SOURCE: Food and Agriculture Organization of the United Nations (FAO), 1993]

Figure 28.10 *Changes in forest areas*

A United Nations survey of tropical forests completed in 1993, show tropical forests have been shrinking at an average annual rate of 0.8% (Figure 28.10). Highest rates are in Asia and Central America which have the lowest surviving areas of tropical forest mainly due to clearances for agriculture. In addition, degradation and fragmentation of forest is proceeding at a rate equal to deforestation.

Increasing exploitation for export

While wood may also be used commercially in countries, increasingly tropical woods are being felled for export to developed countries. Brazil and India are important producers; the leading exporters are Indonesia, Malaysia and Nigeria. The main importers are Japan, followed by the EU and USA.

Because of the growing world demand for tropical timber and the increasing attention given to the possibility of setting up plantations to supply pulp for paper and allied industries, strenuous efforts are being made to ensure future supplies and regulate world trade and prices. In 1983 an International Tropical Timber Agreement was signed to promote trade in timber and ensure sustainable use and conservation of forests. Malaysia for example is worried that her timber stocks will be depleted as logging exceeds reafforestation. The main problem is to get sufficient co-ordination between consumers and producers to ensure that logging and reafforestation programmes can be arranged. Insufficient investment funds for replanting programmes is the main stumbling block. The World Bank estimate approximately two million hectares of replanting is needed over the next five to ten years. Tree plantations rather than replacement of felled timber in existing forest areas, are favoured as newly developed, quick-maturing species can then be planted. At present most of the timber comes from selective felling of mature trees in mixed topical forests.

The other major task has been to promote more timber processing in the producer countries. Developing countries want to stop or severely restrict export of sawn timber as processing before export raises the value of timber products and increases employment. In addition to lower costs, developing countries have fewer environmental controls on processing methods, though this is now changing. In 1993 the Indorayan pulp and rayon plant in northern Sumatra (Indonesia) was forced to close for a period following a chlorine leak into a river.

Increased processing in producer countries is well exemplified in Indonesia, one of the leading timber producer countries. Under the country's second and third year plans not only has there been a major expansion of lumbering, but an increasing number of factories have been established at the ports to produce plywoods and veneers. Most of the industry is concentrated on Kalimantan and also now in Sumatra, since the heavily populated islands such as Java and Bali have been largely cleared of rainforest (Case study 28.2).

Other resources from tropical forests

Unlike coniferous forest areas mainly for timber or pulp, tropical forests are rich in many other products needed in a modern world. It is estimated that a quarter of the medication issued on prescription in modern societies is based on materials coming from tropical rainforest plants or animals. Plants, roots and insects contain properties which are now commercially used in the treatment of cancer, leukaemia and various nervous disorders.

Other specialist materials from tropical forests are used in industry. Latex, gums, camphor, resins, dyes and oils come from forests and plantations in South East Asia, West Africa and Latin America.

Any discussion about future use of tropical forests must therefore consider the multitude of uses to which forest and associated plants can be put and take into account the ecological implications.

Reconciling demand and conservation

Today the world is faced by two major and to some extent conflicting dilemmas in relation to tropical rainforests: producing more timber for local and export needs and proper conservation and management of forests.

While the needs of overseas markets are quite different from those of local populations increasingly desperate for wood for basic heating and cooking, the solution to both appears to be the establishment of woodland plantations of single species. Total reliance on natural regeneration of already exploited natural rainforest is unrealistic, given the scale of demand and the time it takes for regeneration.

Planting of eucalyptus trees has increasingly been seen as a solution, though in more arid areas the cassias tree is more suitable, maturing within five or six years. India, Zimbabwe and Zambia, is faced with an increasing shortage of wood at a time when population and demand are increasing. Consequently, afforestation programmes have been increasingly concerned with encouraging planting of quick-maturing species, in particular, the eucalyptus tree which is indigenous to Australasia.

There is however considerable debate on the wisdom of relying too much on the monoculture of eucalyptus over wide areas. The return to agro-forestry in which trees can be intercropped with field crops allows food and fuel to be produced from the same land.

The case of Amazonia

Wider issues are highlighted in debate on the future of the Amazon rainforests. A succession of controversial government measures passed since the 1950s encouraging exploitation of many other resources in addition to timber. Large areas of the rainforests are being cleared with serious consequences which are likely to be very difficult to reverse. Up to the 1950s, incursion into the rainforest, while bringing about a considerable reduction in the numbers of Indians through the spread of disease and disruption of their traditional ways of life, had not seriously affected the extent of the forest and its delicate ecological balance. However, exploitation has escalated as the Brazilian government has begun to look to the Amazon region as the last major resource frontier to the overcrowded lands of the impoverished north-east. Multinational investment companies overseas have added to pressures as better technology and improved transport bring the potentially rich and diverse resources of the Amazon forest within economic grasp (Case study 28.5).

International trade in timber products

Forest products are the third most valuable commodity to be traded internationally after oil and gas, but only about 15% of total timber production enters international trade, as major producers such as the USA have their own large domestic markets.

The main exporters are producers with relatively small populations and limited home consumption, for example, Canada and Scandinavian countries. Together they provided nearly half the world's exports in 1990. Since then their share has declined with the increase in exports from developing world countries such as Indonesia, Malaysia and Brazil.

Trade has declined in industrial roundwood. This is mainly in high value hardwoods such as mahogany and teak from tropical producers such as Nigeria in Africa and South East Asian countries such as Malaysia, with the Japan and European Union countries as the main markets. Sawnwood trade is mainly from coniferous forest regions in Canada and Scandinavia to neighbouring countries. Unprocessed wood is also traded as woodchips for pulping. Japan is the dominant market, mainly importing hardwood from northern Australia and softwood from the west coast of the USA. However, there has been a significant increase in woodchip exports from Chile and New Zealand where the area under fast-growing plantations is increasing.

Trade in processed products is still focused on the advanced countries as the main markets. Different suppliers dominate in the case of each product. Indonesia is now the main world exporter of panels (mainly plywood) but Canada and the Scandinavian countries dominate the trade in paper, mainly to neighbouring countries. The most significant change in pulp trade has been the increased export share taken by Brazil and Chile, though Canada remains the main exporting country.

Rationalisation and globalisation in the timber industry

Traditionally the timber industry has been highly fragmented but as with most industry, rationalisation has occurred at two levels. Firstly, processing plants have increased in size; many smaller and older plants are being closed. Secondly, mergers and acquisitions are occurring between companies both domestically and internationally. Large international conglomerates with investments in a number of countries are beginning to dominate the industry, making investment and locational decisions at a global level.

Rationalisation is a response to increasing competition especially among pulp and paper companies which require more economies of scale to reduce costs. It is also made possible by technological advances in the industry. New pulp mills coming on stream in the 1990s will have capacities of 350 000 to 500 000 tonnes, about double those constructed in the 1970s.

Since 1993 good profits provided the capital for acquisitions and mergers. For example, in 1995 the Finnish companies of Repola and Kymenne merged to form the largest European forestry products business. Two of the largest USA companies, Kimberley Clarke and Scott Paper have also merged. These larger corporations are also buying up smaller companies to extend their geographic reach into markets. At the same time these enlarged conglomerates are investing in tropical timber-producing areas which supply an increasing proportion of the world's pulp.

Location of plants – increasingly in the timber-producing countries

Because of the bulky nature of timber and its comparatively low unit cost, first processing stages are located close to lumbering regions. However, other locational factors are important – power for the milling and pulping of timber, large amounts of water and access to markets. Waterside sites with hydro-electric facilities are particularly favoured locations, as is evident in the large number of plants found on fall-line situations behind which the forested shield plateaux occur and in front, either navigable lake or river routes are located, for example, along the margins of the Canadian Shield in the Great Lakes region of Canada-USA and the Baltic Shield in Sweden and Finland. Here the fall-line comes close to navigable river estuaries and the coast. Other locations occur at the foot of mountainous upland into which coastal inlets have penetrated, as in British Columbia and Washington-Oregon in western North America.

Until recently, location of paper board and cellulose fibre industries using pulp in the timber-producing regions largely depended on the size of the home market and the nearness of other markets. In the case of USA-Canada, the size of the USA market favoured large integrated plants in which linkage of pulp to the pulping mills provided important economies of scale, including the use of waste products as fuel to reduce power costs, for example, in the case of the Thunder Bay works on the shores of Lake Superior in Ontario.

The trend is generally towards location of all processes in the timber-producing countries and the closure of many of the small mills in timber-importing countries such as the UK. This shift is seen for example in the expansion of production of paper products such as newsprint, wrapping and packaging board in Finland and Sweden to serve the UK market and as a corollary, the closure of branch plants in this company. The exception to such closures are plants which utilise waste paper and other materials. These are both located on the source of raw materials and the market.

28.3 Water supply and control

Water is a basic human necessity. Amongst simpler societies obtaining water or controlling it requires a constant physical effort and therefore it is appreciated as a precious commodity. Amongst advanced industrial societies a constant supply of water is usually taken for granted – a matter of simply turning on a tap. With further expansion of domestic, industrial and agricultural usage, anxieties are being expressed about demand outstripping supplies. Danger of existing supplies being polluted is another worry, with greater industrialisation and use of chemicals in agriculture.

The Spanish Water Crisis

This is Spain's fourth consecutive year of drought ... since 1992 rainfall has been at less than 30% average: reservoirs are at 10% and falling

Restrictions in water use are in force all over the south causing inconvenience and hardship to town dwellers and threatening farmers with ruin.

Spain's struggle for water is political. The government's National Hydrographic Plan has been meandering through parliament, for more than three years, dammed into sluggish backwaters by the refusal of the country's water rich regions to allow transfer of the precious resource.

Farmers beseeched Andalusian authorities in Seville to give money to improve the infrastructure – 40% of water is lost through leaky pipes.

There is fear in the south that residents will be made to suffer to keep tourists happy

[SOURCE: *A Terrible Thirst in Torremolinos, The Independent* 26.4.94]

The issue is how water should be managed in a mainly dry country. As consumption has risen with expanding populations and enlarged agricultural areas under irrigation water has become increasingly scarce.

[SOURCE: *Water gets Political in Very Dry Spain, Financial Times* 28.7.94]

Given the finance and knowledge, people can do much to manage water supplies but ultimately they are dependent upon the rate at which water is supplied and replenished through the hydrological cycle and the drainage basin systems (Figure 28.11).

Control and use of water in the UK – an example of a developed country

Most of the UK's water supply is taken from surface waters in rivers and lakes but there is increased attention to underground aquifers, especially in south eastern England where the scarpland topography of alternating outcrops of porous rocks, such as the chalklands, and of impervious underlying softer clays provide favourable conditions for underground water to accumulate.

One of the problems in the UK is that most of the precipitation falls on the uplands whereas the greatest demand is in the heavily industrialised and urban regions of the lowlands. Water stored in upland reservoirs has to be transferred by pipe and surface channels to areas of demand. Until the 1960s, however, most of the transfer was from individual reservoirs to particular demand centres, making it difficult to transfer water away from areas with a surplus to those where demand was either increasing too rapidly or where occasional drought periods cut back supply.

New larger Regional Water Authorities were set up by the Water Authorities Act of 1973 to co-ordinate and control water supplies and manage associated features such as industrial waste disposal, pollution and flood control, together with inland fisheries and water recreation. Within the boundaries of these larger Regional Water Authorities there has survived a number of 'water supply only' companies serving local areas, such as The Cambridge Water Company within Anglia's region. In 1989 under a new Water Act, water services were placed under ten new privatised regional water companies (Case study 28.3). River and groundwater regulatory and conservation functions were taken on by the National Rivers Authority (NRA). The NRA obtains much of its funding from the Regional Water Authorities by selling licenses for water abstraction from surface and ground water supplies and for allowing effluent returns.

River pollution worsened 1980 to 1990

A survey by the National Rivers Authority of the rivers of England and Wales in 1990 indicated that overall 500 to 1000 miles of rivers were of poorer quality than in 1980. By region, rivers had improved in the Trent, Southern, Welsh and Wessex regions but had declined in six with the worst falls in the South West and Thameside. Sewage works and farms have been generally to blame.

The 1989 Water Act required the NRA to ensure 'statutory water qualities' are met. The government has put forward a scheme whereby within three to five years from 1993, rivers would reach these quality objectives. Discharges from sewage works and by industry are covered by 'consents' – legal agreements between the discharger and the NRA. The 'consents' will be tightened to ensure quality objective. But most farms are not covered by these. Farms at present can only be prosecuted if they break anti-pollution regulations or an act of pollution can be proved. The NRA wants every farm which could possibly pollute rivers to be covered by a waste plan.

Apart from control of water pollution and concern for conservation the water industry faces two other major problems: how to meet the growing demand for water and yet ensure sustainability and flood control. Increased variability in seasonal weather conditions and the possibility of longer term climatic changes bringing hotter and drier summers have increased these problems. Ensuring good quality water is a shared responsibility between the NEA and RWAs. The NRA is concerned about ensuring long-term sustainability of water resources nationally;

a

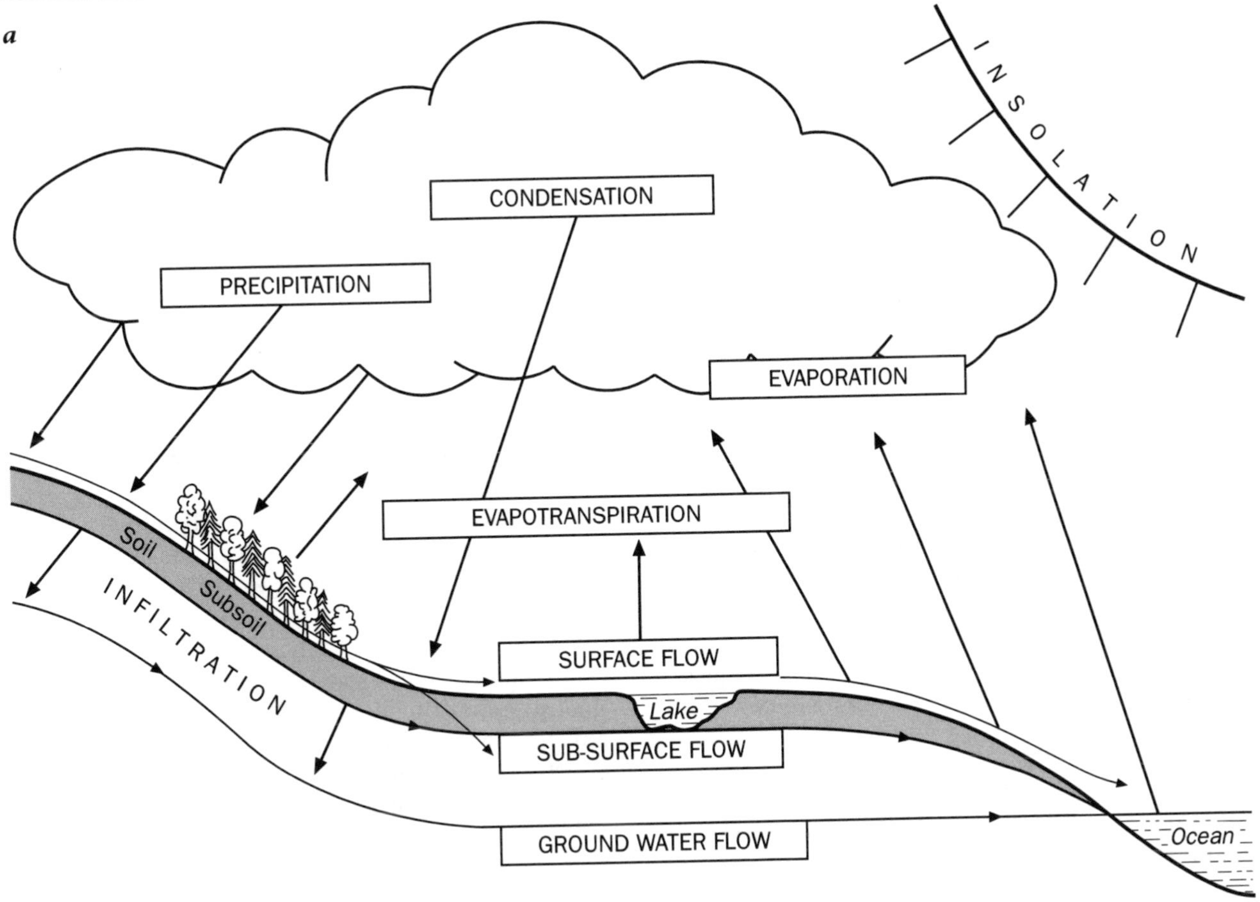

b

The throughput of water in the cycle is determined not only by physical conditions such as amounts and seasonal intensity of precipitation, evaporation rates, as well as vegetation cover, soil and geological conditions acting as storage elements, but also by storage of water in reservoirs and the amount and time of abstraction of water for various usages – agriculture, industrial and domestic.

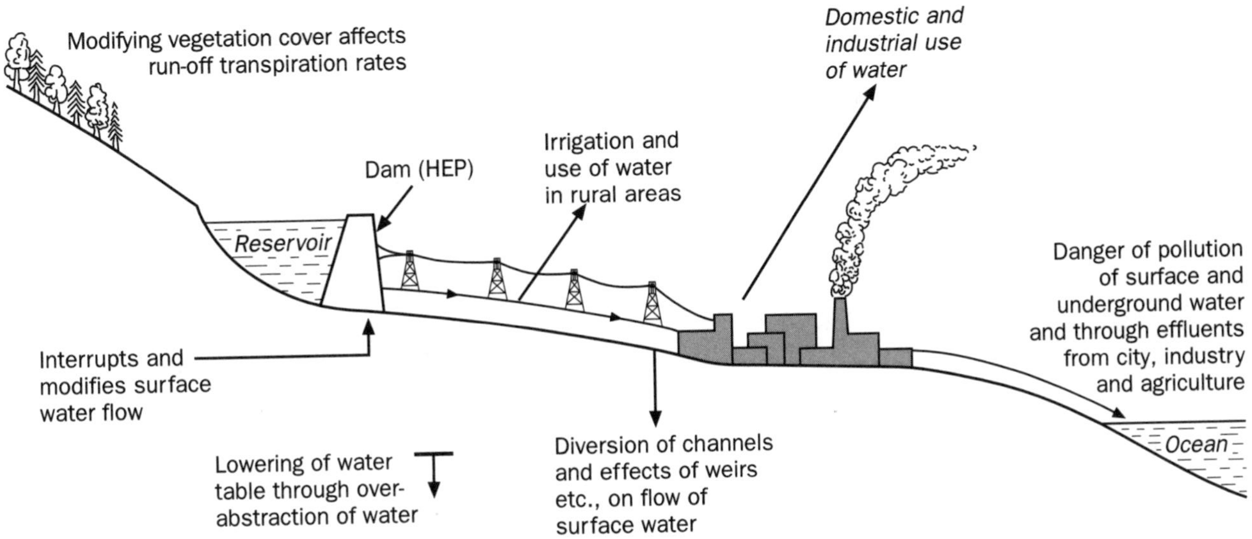

***Figure 28.11** **a** Hydrological cycle **b** and human impact on the cycle*

RWAs are only responsible for ensuring water supplies within their own regions. Flood control covering both coastal flooding from sea incursions and river flooding essentially is also the responsibility of the NRA.

Ensuring water supplies

Cryer, in a recent article which discusses at length the Changing Responses to Water Resource Problems in England and Wales concludes that *'there will be a forecast shortage in the water industry's basic resource in the south and east because of population increase, increasing demand for water, possible climatic change and because it (i.e. the water industry) is approaching the limits of the resource in some areas'* and that *'there needs to be a balanced approach between demand – and supply – side over time with perhaps demand management leading the way to buy time for supply schemes to be planned, approved and developed'* (*Geography* Part 1, 1995).

How the UK industry is meeting the challenge is outlined in Case study 28.3.

Control of flooding

Causes – a combination of abnormal weather and increased human activity in areas at risk

Abnormally heavy rainfall, sea incursions or rapid snowmelt when the ground is still frozen are the main causes of flooding. Effects of these have been heightened by the increasing concentration of population and economic activity in vulnerable areas, such as river flood plains and low coastal areas. As increasingly more land is built over, this reduces the area for water infiltration and hence increases surface run-off. Thus under heavy storm conditions or rapid snowmelt, water quickly reaches river courses via surface drains and culverts, causing an abnormal rise in river levels and flooding of low-lying land. This was illustrated on a small scale round Chichester in Hampshire in January 1994 and on a much larger scale with disastrous consequences along the Mississippi River Basin (USA) in the summer of 1993 and along the Rhine and Meuse valleys in northern Europe, in February 1995.

Coping with floods

While river engineering (straightening of river channels, raising bank levels and building second channels to divert flood water) can reduce flood risks, the general conclusion is that there is a limit both in terms of capital outlay and engineering to what can be done. However, better planning controls and land management to reduce development in vulnerable areas will help.

While localised river flooding occurs in the UK, most widespread flooding has come from North Sea surges. These are most destructive where the surge inland at high tide is confined to estuaries and holds back river flow so that flooding occurs along tidal stretches and also inland on low-lying land adjacent to the lower swollen river reaches. The effects of such flooding have become widespread as lowland around the North Sea is gradually sinking relative to sea level, due to isostatic adjustment following the last ice age. High tide at London Bridge for example has been rising by about 0.73 m a decade.

Consequently, sea defences and river embanking has been done throughout history both in the UK and across the North Sea, most notably in the Netherlands. Until the recent construction of the Thames Barrier, completed in 1983, much of Central London and boroughs lying east along Thameside, were still liable to serious flooding at least once every 50 years (Figure 28.12).

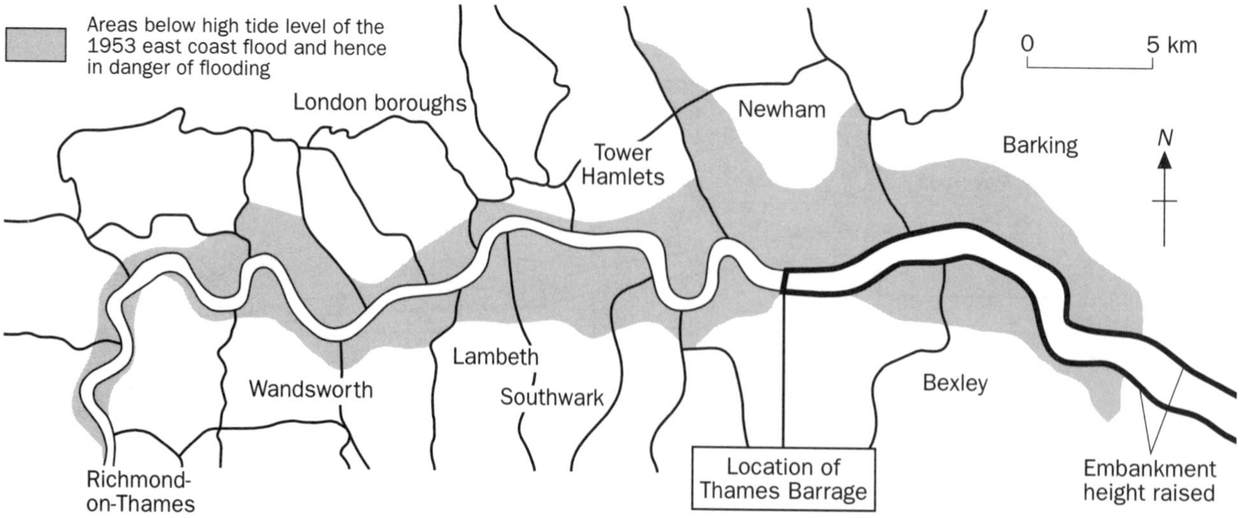

Figure 28.12 The Thames Barrier

The Thames Barrier cost £730 million, a small price compared with the estimated £3.5 billion destruction flooding would have caused in damage to property and disruption of transport and other services.

Problems of water supply and control in the developing world

A world crisis

> The wars of the next century will not be over politics or oil but water. This warning comes from the World Bank as supply is increasingly outstripped by demand. We are running out of something no one can live without.
> [SOURCE: Extract from *The Water Bomb, The Guardian* 8.12.95]

The rivers over which there is international dispute include:

- The Nile which flows through ten countries (most politically unstable) and supplies nearly all Egypt's water but Egypt has only so far signed a water treaty with the Sudan.
- The Tigris/Euphrates, the headwaters of which are controlled by Turkey through a scheme which includes 33 dams. Countries downstream, like Syria and Iraq, depend on the Euphrates and have ambitious plans to extend irrigation and water use overall.
- The Mekong which rises mainly in Thailand and flows through Laos and Vietnam. Like Thailand, they are industrialising and extending the areas under irrigation. There are already disputes on how to manage the river and no agreement has yet been reached (Case study 28.4).

Political tensions over the use and management of water are mounting across the developing world, particularly where the world's largest rivers cross a number of countries. Problems are becoming more acute because of the rapid increase in the demand for water and the fear of demand outstripping supply. Over recent years this has been readily recognised in Africa where periodic drought, desertification, population pressure and famine have received international attention.

Tragic as problems are in Sub-Saharan Africa, both the World Bank and the world's Food and Agricultural Organisation point to shortage and management of water as a problem on a truly international scale, going far beyond arid and semi-arid regions to now embrace other climatic regions in the tropics, including much of monsoonal Asia and Latin America. Neither is the crisis limited to the world's poorest countries; it is increasingly affecting the rapidly industrialising countries, such as Mexico and Thailand.

A human demand and management crisis

While there are periodic variations in climatic conditions which can accentuate the shortage of water, most experts agree the problem is human induced. According to a 1995 FAO report, world demand for water has doubled in 21 years, mainly in the developing world. A number of reasons are suggested for this.

- With the continued expansion of the world's population, people demand more food, which demands more water.
- The new high yielding varieties of staple crops such as rice and wheat, promoted as the most efficient way to feed more people, demand more water than traditional varieties. Additionally, much is wasted.
- Both the World Bank and FAO agree that the 'agricultural drought' will also worsen because as wealth and industry increase in the expanding cities of the developing world, agriculture will be denied some of its essential water.
- The problem is further exacerbated by the pressure of the World Bank and international agencies and the policies of the developing countries to expand export sectors as a way of raising foreign revenue and paying off international debt under agreed Structural Readjustment programmes. These export initiatives result in high unit use of water. The water, for example, is used for irrigated flowers and other out-of-season horticultural crops being developed by a number of African countries such as Kenya and Zimbabwe for export, new mining and industrial operations by transnationals, expansion of tourism, including eco-tourism in tropical countries (Case studies 28.4 and 30.1).

Attaining water security

After pointing out that only a relatively small proportion of the world's rainfall can be accessed to provide water and that 75% is used in agriculture mainly for watering crops, Lean and Hinrishen show two complementary ways of approaching the problem:

Firstly, supplies can be increased by building more dams and reservoirs. However, they rule out large-scale schemes which were common in the 1960s and 1970s because of the problems involved. The emphasis should be on many small local reservoir and dam schemes as a part of comprehensive rural development schemes for local communities. It is essential that the local community be fully involved in the planning, decision-making and implementation of schemes if they are to succeed (Case study 23.4).

The main emphasis should be on conservation of water and a more efficient use of what is available. At present, for example, only one third of irrigation water actually reaches the crops to help them grow. Repairing and improving irrigation channels could cut wastage by 40% (Case study 23.4). Use of overhead sprinklers as for example in Israel, can reduce loss by 70% but because of cost, this is unlikely to happen on a wide scale in the near future. However, through more effective advisory education and work on local schemes, much can be done to ensure more effective use of irrigation water and safe water for communities.

A further problem is population increase in the major fertile river basins of monsoon Asia and an extension and intensification of agriculture has made the problem of flooding progressively more serious. Only recently have comprehensive conservation and flood control systems for total river basins been adopted as, for example, in the case of the Brahmaputra basin to cope with the flood problem in Bangladesh (Case study 23.3).

Concluding comment

- The worst news is that the pressures of human numbers and over-consumption of the earth's resources are still increasing.
- Damage to the land, pollution and destruction of habitats are proving intractable under this relentless pressure.
- However, many nations are now making major efforts to conserve forests, water and land, improve health and access to birth control, and conserve and recycle resources.

case study

28.1 Peru: changing conditions in the fishing industry

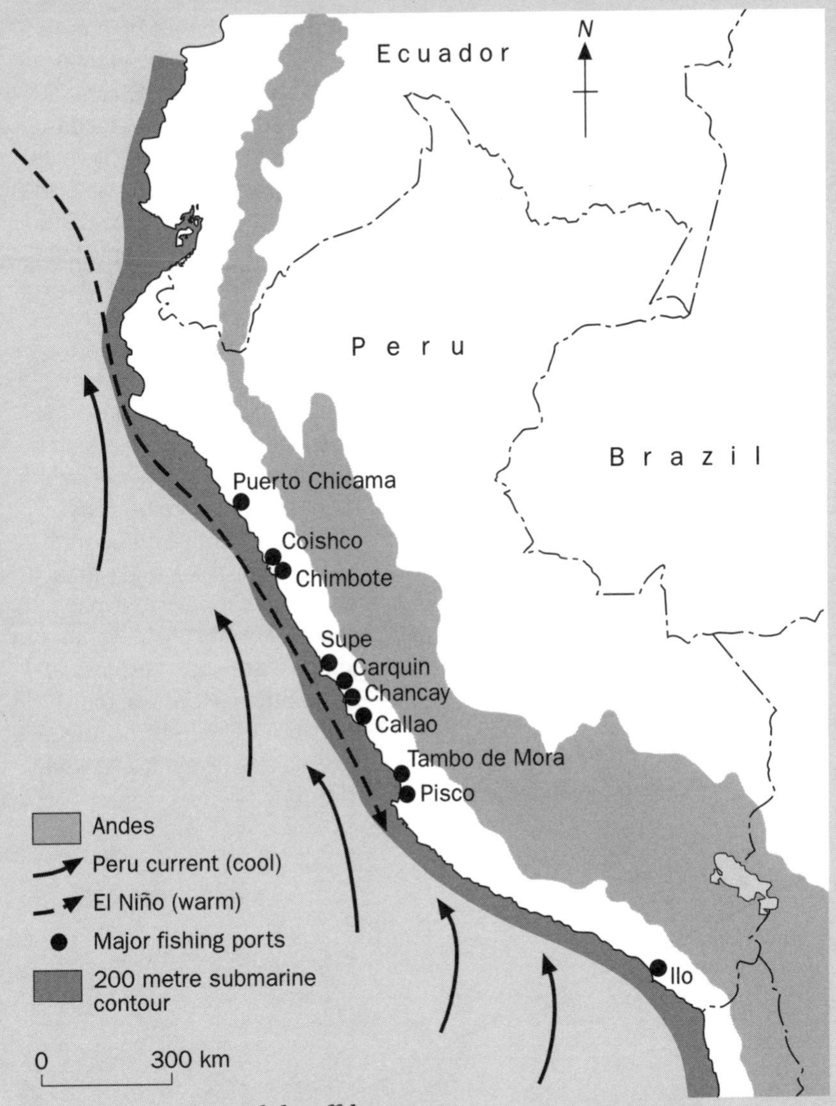

Major fishing ports and the offshore zone

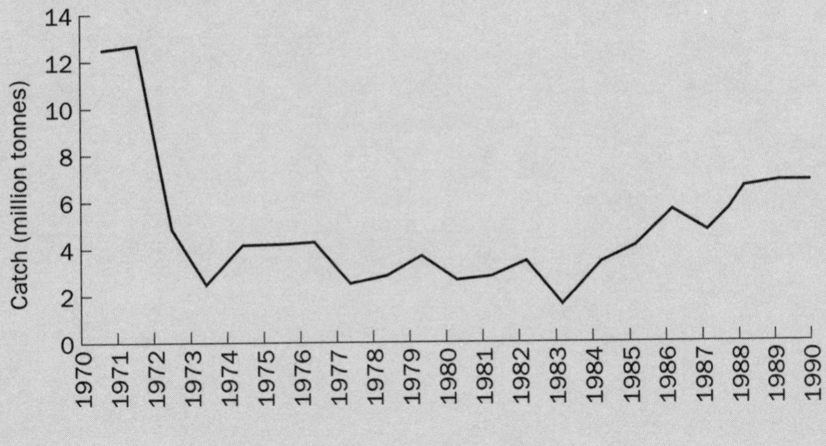

Peru's fish catch 1970 – 90

Influence of physical conditions

- The continental shelf extends for 150 km off the coast.
- Upwellings of water occasioned by the cool Humbolt current made the area rich in nutrients and plankton, which normally supports many species of fish, especially anchovy and tuna.
- The disastrous extension of warm water 'El Niño' from the north brought conditions alien to plankton resulting in a rapid decline in fish numbers. This contributed to a depression in Peru's fishing industry. Favourable physical conditions returned but other incursions of El Niño are likely, as occurred in 1991 – 92.

Influence of human conditions

- Peru developed into one of the world's leading fishing nations from the 1950s, largely on the basis of abundance of fish off-shore, absence of controls on fishing, a rising demand over-seas for fish meal and nitrate fertiliser, decline in competition due to overfishing e.g. off the USA Pacific coast, and foreign investment in the fishing fleet and processing plants on-shore.
- The catch reached a record 9 million tonnes in 1954 and it rose to 12.5 million tonnes, only to plunge to 2.7 million tonnes by 1980. While incursions of El Niño were partly responsible, experts consider overfishing the most serious threat.

- Overfishing by Peru and other nations, including indiscriminate catching of young stock by seine netting to process for fish meal and fertiliser, contributed to a rapid decline in the industry through the late 1970s.
- Peru has now taken measures to build up stocks through stricter regulations, including a two to three month closed season and trying to enforce a 320 km off-shore limit against foreign fleets e.g. of Japan.
- Peru is now the third largest producer of fish and fish stocks. Catches continue to fluctuate according to changes in physical conditions. In 1993 – 94 fish catch was up by 50% on the previous years but in 1995 fell back again.
- Experts warn anchovy and sardine stocks are being stretched to the limit. There is a pressing need to diversify fishing to reduce pressures on anchovy and sardine stocks. In deeper waters beyond the continental shelf, there are ample fish stocks, especially of horse and jack mackerel. To fish in deeper waters requires much investment in modern trawlers and finding markets for the new fish catches.

Importance and structure

- Fishing and the fish processing industry are vital to the economy. Fish are an important source of protein in a country with limited meat supplies. Fish meal and other fish-based fertilisers are important for increasing agriculture productivity. In 1993, 8.4 million tonnes of fish were landed and 1.3 million tonnes of fish meal produced. Fish meal and products are the second most important export by value following copper, the main markets being China and the USA.
- The industry is partly privatised and partly nationalised but the aim is total privatisation. The state concerned, Pescaperu intends to sell off its 20 fish meal and four fish oil refineries. Production is being expanded in the private sector e.g. new plants at Matarani Port in the south.

  There are joint ventures with foreign companies e.g. with a Japanese company to expand tuna fishing and a joint venture to expand frozen hake exports to EU countries. However, the Peruvian fleet needs modernising to be able to diversify and work efficiently.

case study

28.2 Indonesia: timber production and factors affecting the industry

Distribution of tropical forests

Next to Brazil, Indonesia has the largest surviving area of tropical forest at 144 ha. Of this, 66 million is classed as productive forest, mainly in Kalimantan.

Location of timber production

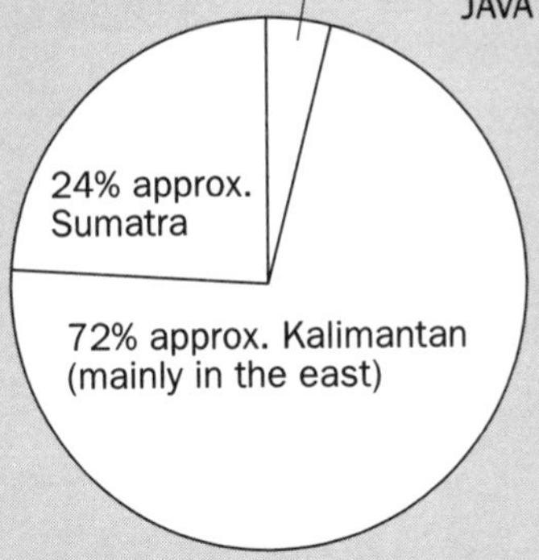

Availability of timber stands

Much has been lost through clearance for agriculture but in 1993, a government reassessment of the remaining forest areas planned 66 million ha. to be available for selective logging, 30 million to be cleared for agriculture and settlement and 48 million to be left untouched as National Park areas or to protect upland watersheds.

Continued expansion of home demand

Indonesia has a large and expanding population of 193 million (1994) with rising incomes (GDP per capita $670 US). Along with continued industrialisation this will increase domestic demand for timber products.

Expansion of exports

Indonesia is looking to expand exports of forest products further. These rose from $1.5 billion in 1986 to $3.5 billion in 1991. Timber products are the most important exports by value next to oil and textiles. Export of logs has been banned. Indonesia is now the world's leading exporter of plywoods.

Panel wood, pulp and paper exports are rising. The main market is Japan followed by other South East Asian countries e.g. Taiwan and South Korea. The USA and EU countries are significant but less important markets.

Technological advances and changes in production methods

Traditional methods have been replaced by mechanisation and cost effective methods of felling and processing. The size of operations has been scaled up to reduce costs. There has been a dramatic expansion of both logging (mainly of Meranti and Iquan species) and processing with plants mainly located at coastal ports.

In addition to expansion of plywoods, the industry is planning to expand pulp production from the 1993 figure of 1.5 million tonnes to 14.5 million by the year 2005 and paper from 3.2 million to 7.2 million over the same period.

Increasing foreign investment

The government is keen to retain development in the hands of Indonesian conglomerates such as Barito Pacific Timber but has encouraged joint ventures and given some logging concessions to foreign companies. Barito Pacific Timber, for example, has concluded deals with the Malaysian timber corporation CASH (Kuala Lumpur) while the Japan Pulp and Paper Company has invested in Indonesia, as have USA companies.

[redacted]

Government influence

Although there has been emphasis on expansion, the government is exercising increasing controls on the conditions under which this is done:

- stricter control on illegal logging which is a major problem
- an emphasis on selective felling with recent moves to strip clearance leaving alternate strips of forest untouched
- an expanded programme of tree planting to provide renewable plantations for pulp and paper products
- reduction in the practice of shifting cultivation.

The biggest problems remain the need for much more effective enforcement of legislation and the will to increase tax revenues from the timber industry to finance management and conservation programmes.

Increasing pressure from environmental groups and local people

Much of the pressure for conservation has come from outside but within Indonesia, environmental groups are becoming more effective. Also, there is growing opposition to commercial logging from indigenous groups as it threatens their land and way of life e.g. in 1993 inhabitants of Yamdena and Siberut islands won a reprieve for their forests.

case study

28.3 The UK water industry: matching supply and demand

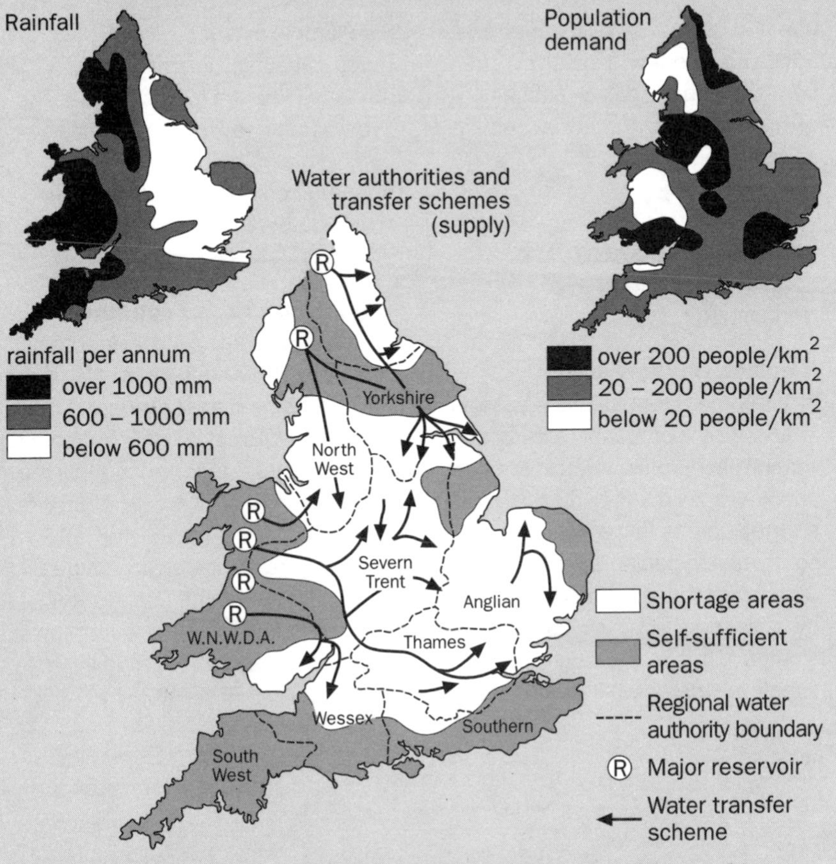

The normal relationship of rainfall distribution, supply and demand in England and Wales

The mid-1990s water crisis situation

The demand for water continues to increase

Water consumption has increased by 70% in the last 30 years and is forecast to rise by 1.5% annually into the twenty-first century. Domestic usage has gone up because of changes in personal habits (more baths) and widespread installation of washing machines and dishwashers – a dishwasher uses 70 – 115 litres of water per programme. There has been a ten-fold increase in the use of garden sprinklers in the last 30 years.

While industrial usage has tended to decline with de-industrialisation, commercial and service usage has expanded, for example, car washes have proliferated.

Abstraction by agriculture for over-head irrigation has also increased. The NRA's report in 1991 on 'Demand and Resources of Water Undertakers' state that demand will outstrip supplies in Yorkshire, Midlands, South East and East Anglia, certainly by 2020 and proba-bly by 2000 unless measures are taken to contain the rise in demand.

Unpredictable climate conditions

Because of climatic changes, the Department of the Environment predicted in 1991 that areas of the UK could face '*many consecutive years of water shortage and frequent drought*'. In future, wetter winters would benefit water resources in general but warmer summers with longer growing seasons and increased evaporation would lead to greater pressure on water resources, especially in the south and east of the UK.

'In 1990 – the hottest summer on record – over 40 rivers in Great Britain either suffered low flows or dried up. In March 1991 more than 20 million people were affected by water restrictions, many for the third year running. In March 1991 groundwater supplies in some areas were at their lowest on record.' [*In Hot Water, Geographical Magazine*, 1992]

Domestic water usage

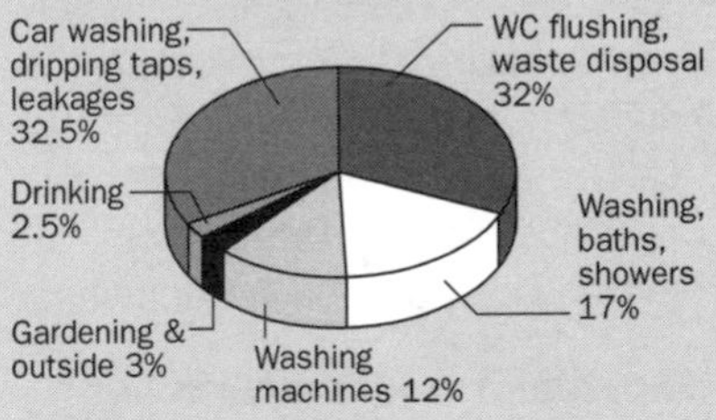

Water use in the UK
millions of litres/day

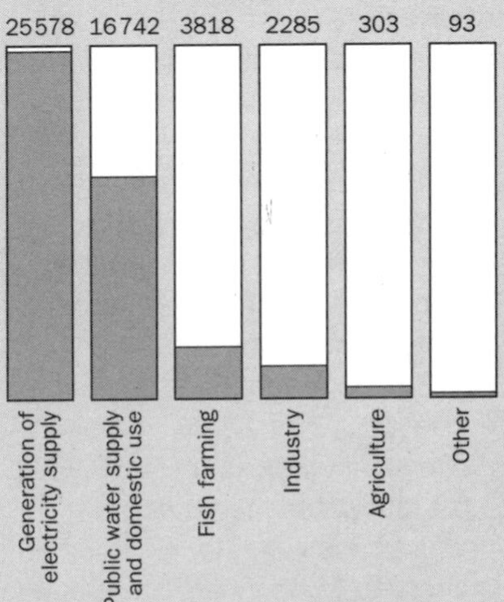

[SOURCE: *The Independent* 22.8.95]
England serviced by water companies, Scotland serviced by local authorities, Northern Ireland serviced by unitary Water Executive

Domestic water usage in the UK

Towards a solution

More effective supplies

Private water companies have been accused of squandering precious water resources in allowing one third of the supply, 826 million gallons every day, to escape from faulty mains. Some work has been done to replace leaky pipes. The water companies have spent £4 billion reducing leakages on average from 35% to 30% since 1989. To produce a totally leak-proof system would cost as much as £20 billion and much of this cost would fall on the customer – the charge would be too high.

For London, Thames Water have completed a deep new 80 km tunnel ring main around London to replace old surface mains. This was operational in 1996 and supplies half London's water.

New reservoirs are being constructed e.g. at Broadoak in Kent and at Testwood in Hampshire.

Short- and medium-term 'demand management' – the need for a conservation strategy

Domestic consumers and industry until recently have never regarded water as a limited resource. Effective savings could be made through cutting down on non-essential use and recycling water e.g. in Sweden domestic water is recycled to flush toilets. There needs to be 'effective consumer education'.

Extend metering so that instead of a flat rate water charge as at present based on rateable value of properties, households would pay for what they use. Trials in the Isle of Wight indicate metering would cut use by 10% but installing metres is costly and would be divisive, penalising low income families.

Raise costs for industrial and agricultural users.

Long-term solution: a national water grid network?

A national transfer

In 1992 the National Rivers Authority resurrected a proposal to transfer water from surplus areas in the north and Wales via rivers and canals to shortage areas in the south and south-east including East Anglia. Currently transfers already exist but the proposals would virtually create a national grid to spatially balance supply and demand. It would mean for example extending the Kielder Reservoir supply further south, through Yorkshire to East Anglia. The Yyrnwy Reservoir in Wales would be deployed and the Craig Goch Reservoir enlarged to transfer into the Wye-Severn rivers and by canals into the Thames.

Objections to the scheme

- The cost would be enormous, at £400 – £600 million in development cost for each 100 million litres of water transferred as against a reservoir supply the same amount at a cost of £50 – £250 million.
- There are strong environmental objections – large-scale water transfer would effect water flows and habitats, affect food chains and spread disease.

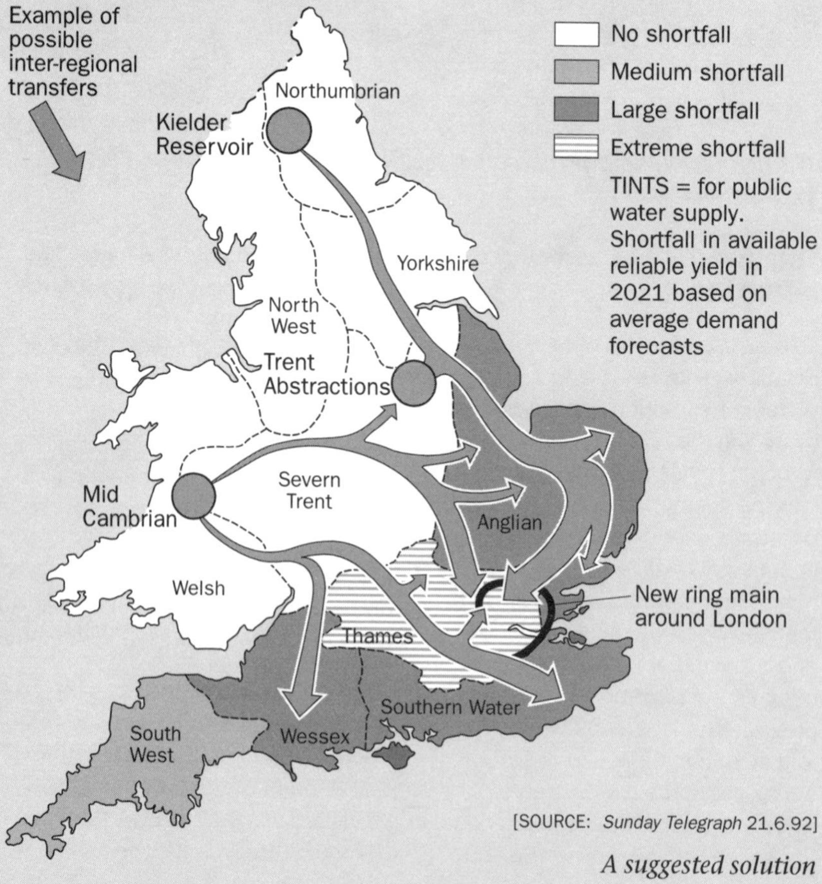

[SOURCE: *Sunday Telegraph* 21.6.92]

A suggested solution

case study

28.4 The water crisis in Thailand

'The Water Crisis has not been created by a reduced supply but by increased demand and management weaknesses.' The crisis reflects some of the concerns and issues over water current in much of the developing world.

Physical context

In terms of annual amount, Thailand would appear to have adequate rainfall. However, the monsoonal climate regime has distinct wet and dry seasons requiring regulation of river flows and water conservation for the dry season. An additional problem is the variability in the timing and amount of monsoonal rainfall.

Thailand is fed by rivers rising in the highlands to the west, north and east with extensive fertile alluvial lowlands to the south. An important problem is that rivers like the Mekong cross national boundaries with other countries such as Cambodia, Laos and Burma (Myanmar), also competing to abstract water from them. Thus further demands on the water systems requires sensitive and difficult political negotiations with neighbouring countries.

Water supplies have been regulated by an increasing number of dams and reservoirs mainly in the headwater tributaries of the Mekong and Ping rivers. However, some of the main schemes are multipurpose to supply both water and hydro-electricity with power supply requirements, at times clashing with water needs.

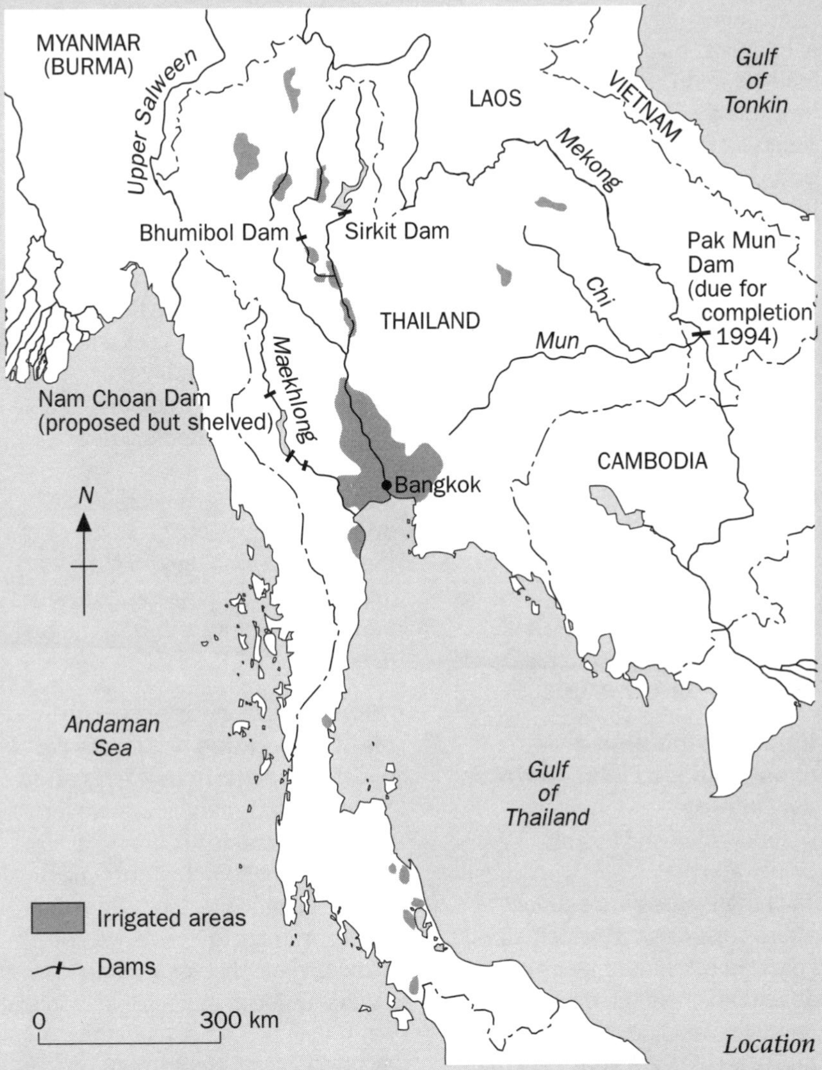

Location

Human context

An expanding population and prospering economy increases the demand for water

The population has grown from 31 million to 58 million in 1994 but growth has slowed markedly with economic advancement. The biggest problem is rapid urbanisation; 23% of the population is now urban and it continues to increase. Bangkok now has a population of 6 million. This is putting an increasing strain on all infrastructure, including water and power. With a per capita GDP of $2410 and an economic growth rate of 8% annually (1994), consumption per head is also rising.

Industrialisation is rapid, again increasing infrastructure demands. Agriculture has greatly expanded and is putting most of the pressure on water supplies.

In the past, an adequate supply of 'cheap' water has been assumed

User groups have regarded water as a free resource and have largely been shielded from conflicts over its use and the costs. For example, agricultural use of water for irrigation is heavily subsidised with returns insufficient to cover running costs, let alone the capital costs of reservoir building, etc. This has encouraged some wasteful and inefficient use of water.

In the cities recent arrivals are faced by escalating costs of water and sewage. Both in the countryside and the towns it is questionable whether the poorer masses could pay a realistic economic price for water. Again there is the fundamental question as to whether supply should be based on need or on cost, treating water as a good and not a basic need.

Linked causes of the current water crisis

Upland catchment area changes have reduced water availability

Deforestation and clearance for timber and agriculture in the upland catchment areas have critically altered hydrological systems. Forested catchment areas could absorb and hold the monsoonal rainfall, evening out the river flow and extending the season of natural supply of water for agricultural use, particularly for the major paddy culture of the lowland areas to the south. The 53% forest cover in 1961 has been reduced officially to 29% (unofficially to 15%), accelerating surface run-off and loss of water in the wet season so that more reservoirs have had to be built for irrigating crops.

Increased upland dry cropping of maize and cassava has taken water previously available to lowland farmers.

Greatly expanded demand for water by the agricultural sector

Since the rural sector takes 90% of the water this is clearly the most critical sector. The irrigated area has been expanded from 462 000 ha. in 1980 to 718 000 ha. by 1991, 55% growth and hence a greatly increased demand for water.

The change to 'Green Revolution' high-yielding varieties demanding more water and better water management than traditional staple rice, has exacerbated the rise in demand.

Double cropping of rice and other dry season cropping has extended the irrigated area. Increased irrigation has increased waste since traditional attitudes to water remain.

Competing management to meet expanding demands for hydro-electricity and irrigation

The dam and reservoir system for supplying water is not controlled by the Royal Irrigation Department but by the National Electricity Generating Board. Water is released over the dams to meet the rising demand for electricity. Much more is lost in this way during the wet season than is needed by the farmers, instead of water being conserved in the reservoirs for dry season irrigation. As a result, insufficient water leads to protracted crises in seasons of lower than normal rainfall, as in 1994.

Expanding urban and industrial demand

At present urban domestic demand makes up only 4% of total national needs and industrial demand, 6%. However, demand is rising rapidly due to the increased pace of industrialisation, an increasing middle class with more extravagant water demands per head and a very large and increasing poor sector in the slum areas as yet without a reliable basic water supply and sewage system.

An expanding tourist industry is making extravagant demands

There is growing opposition to the priority being given to the tourist industry which the government wants to encourage. For example, the proliferation of golf courses which are heavy users of water is taking water away from agriculture.

How to solve the water crisis

The problem caused by lower than average rainfall is short term and will be naturally solved by a return to normal or higher than normal rainfall. The longer-term human issues need to be addressed.

Better management and an extension of the multipurpose dam and reservoir system

There clearly is room for better management especially in reconciling power and irrigation needs.

More dams should be built, but this is increasingly difficult due to strong environmental opposition. For example, the Namchoan Dam scheme was successfully stopped in Kanchanbura Province in 1988.

Viable sites have already been developed and other possible sites are too heavily populated. Other possible sites require agreement with neighbouring states. There is some suggestion of a dam on the upper Salwen river inside Burma and diverting water south into the Ping River system.

Encouraging more efficient use of water in agriculture and reducing demand

The price of water could be increased but many farmers could not afford it. It might increase rural to urban migration, exacerbating problems there. The government has a strong Rural Development Programme to further raise revenues from cash crops, reduce urbanisation and encourage decentralisation of industry into the country to give more balance to rural economic development.

A shift away from water-demanding crops towards dry land crops should be encouraged. However, the agricultural system in the alluvial lowlands is based on rice culture and it would be difficult to switch.

There are increased advisory services on conserving water and better management; these need to be extended.

Increase and ration water supplies to urban areas and industry

This sector only takes 10% of all water and there are already restrictions in force. Raising prices would fall most heavily on the poor.

Use less hydro-electric power to allow conservation of water for irrigation in the dry season

This is difficult as demand is increasing and alternative sources could be more costly. However, Thailand like other South East Asian countries, is looking to develop nuclear energy and is exploring for more oil and gas.

Conclusion

Finding ways through the water crisis is likely to increase conflict between farmers and the growing urban commercial sector. It is also likely to become more of a political issue inside Thailand and for Thailand in its relations with neighbouring countries.

case study

28.5 **Pressures on the Amazon Basin**

Time

Situation prior to increasing pressure from the 1950s – delicately balanced ecological system
High rainfall, humidity, temperatures and isolation. Rapid growth favoured – high biomass production. Rapid nutrient cycling but most nutrients near surface. Soil protected by dense vegetation cover and ground litter. Close integration of diverse flora and fauna. Highly susceptible to any disruption.

Wider implication of climate and vegetation linkages
Half of atmospheric moisture generated from the rainforest itself except on savanna margins. Destruction of cover could both significantly reduce precipitation and affect wider world heat balance and atmosphere's oxygen content.

Human occupance
Indigenous Amerind (Indian) groups fitted into ecological system – low population pressure due to cultural controls on population fertility, recognition of group territories and subsistence economy of shifting cultivation, hunting and collecting. More intensive cultivation on seasonally inundated soils of Lower Amazon flood plain.

External exploration limited historically
Brief rubber collection boom, collecting of nuts, quinine bark trade limited and centred on ports.

Manaus
Made a freeport (1966) to encourage trade and development

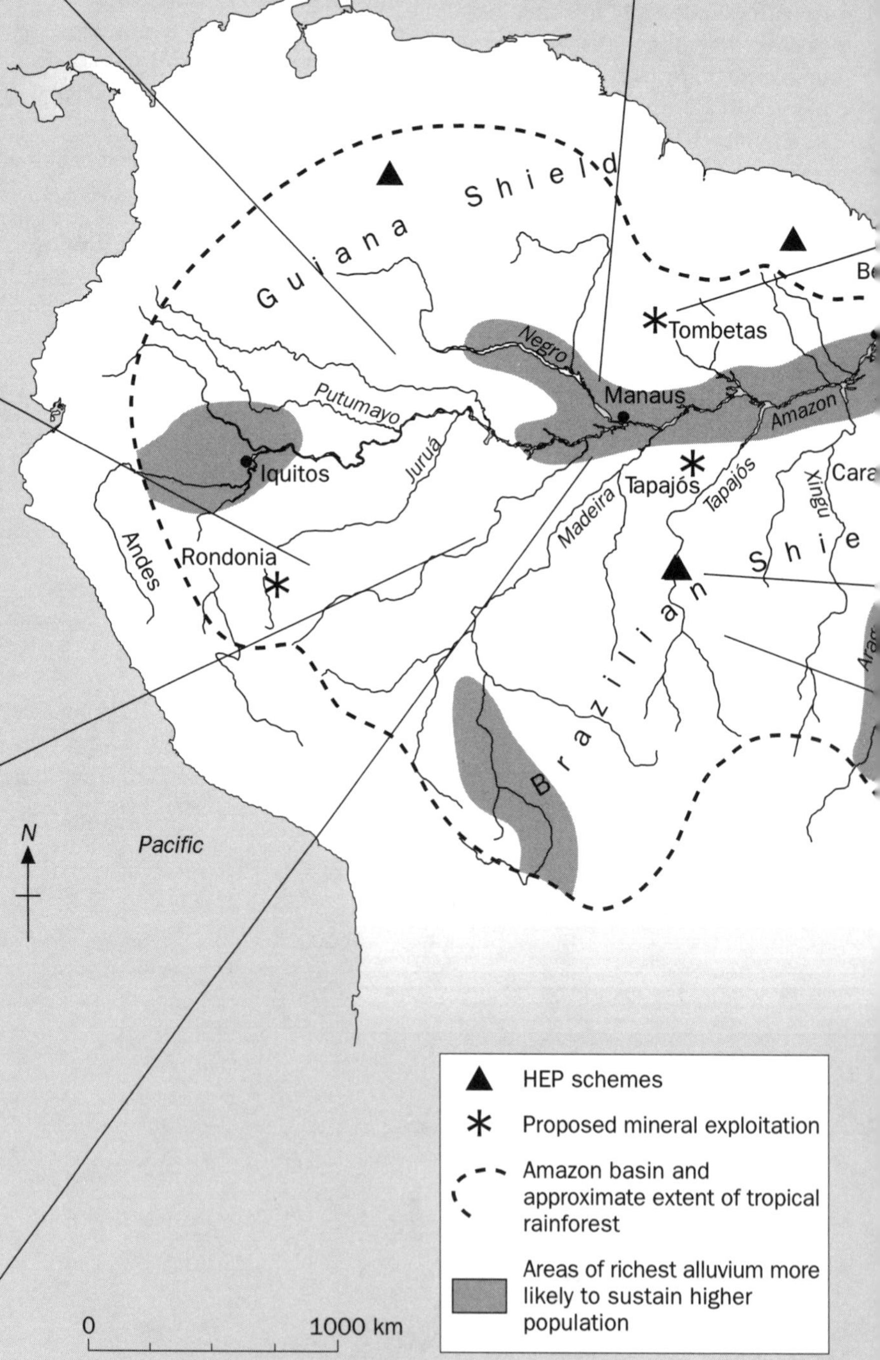

Recent pressures

Causing loss of forest cover – soil erosion – poorer secondary cover with lower timber yield – probably detrimental effect on rainfall and wider atmospheric conditions – reduction of wildlife and indigenous population (1 million 1900, now only 50 000) – loss to modern society – of their culture and herbal knowledge. Since the 1970s indigenous Indian groups have set up their own organisations for protection of their tribal areas and for the right to self determination. Brazilian government is increasingly sensitive to world opinion.

Mineral power developments

Surrounding forest cleared e.g. Tucuruni, Trombetas

Cattle ranching

$2\frac{1}{2}$ million ha. of cover cleared by fire – seeding gives grazing for only 12 years – soil exhaustion and erosion – especially on forest margins.

Atlantic

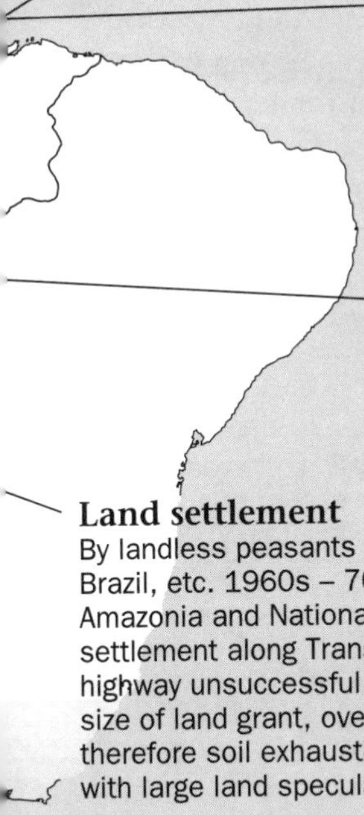

Jari Lumbering

From 1950s – project now covers 2.1 million ha. Forest cover cleared, replanting by faster growing Asian Gmelina and Honduras pine stands with claims these were ecologically efficient. Project not a success but since 1990 revitalised under a Brazilian consortium now concentrating on growing eucalyptus stands for cellulose pulp. From a modernised processing plant looks to exports of 320 000 tonnes by 1998.

Land speculation by multinationals

Aided by recent government policy favouring large concerns and highway developments e.g. 1974 Polamazonia government policy.

Land settlement

By landless peasants from North East Brazil, etc. 1960s – 70s operation Amazonia and National Integration – settlement along Trans-Amazonia highway unsuccessful due to small size of land grant, over-farmed therefore soil exhaustion and friction with large land speculators.

Building of highways

Under 1960s revitalisation programme and the SUDDAM regional development government agency providing avenues of penetration for exploitation of resources and settlement. One of largest development schemes Polonoreste programme begun in 1982 – focused on Rondonia with designated areas of colonisation under along highway construction routes.

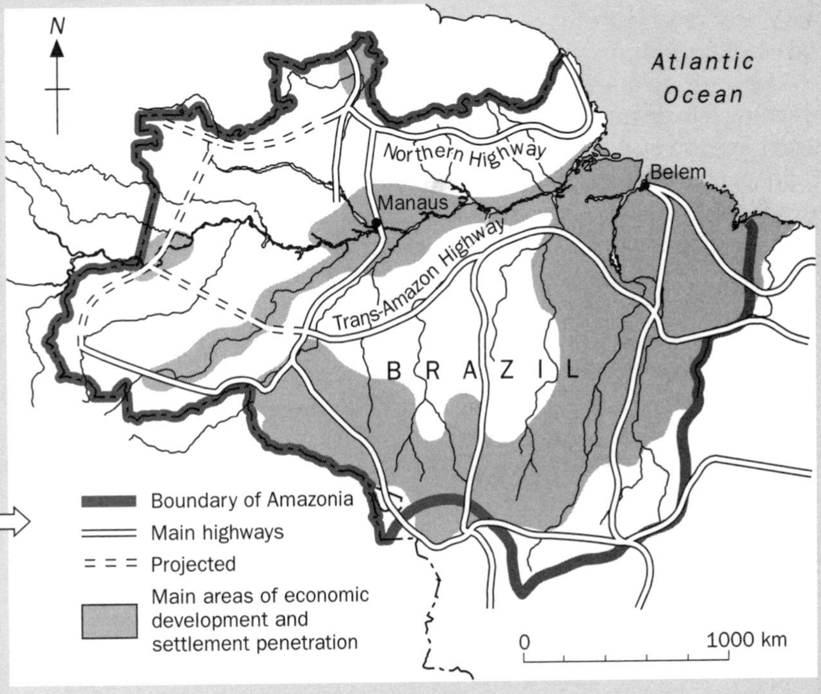

Road building and settlement penetration

CHAPTER 29

Leisure, recreation and tourism – a growth sector in consumer services

'The distinction between leisure, recreation and tourism is very blurred.'

29.1 Its growth and implications

Leisure, recreation and tourism now occupy a central place in both human and environmental geography. In post-industrial societies leisure activities, including tourism, take up an increasing amount of time. Leisure provision is also an increasingly, important sector of the economy and increasingly more space is given to it.

The spatial implications of increased leisure time stretch along a continuum embracing every spatial scale (Figure 29.1) from the local area to remote rural areas and globally, as ever increasing numbers take holidays abroad at increasing distances.

Not only are many more places involved in meeting leisure needs but increased leisure needs also have increasing implications for the management of environments. Providing for leisure needs can enhance environments in some cases and provide income for their protection. However, ever increasing leisure demands have created serious concerns about the capacity of environments to meet these needs. Thus concepts such as 'honey pot' sites, carrying capacity, sustainable tourism and green tourism are becoming central to studies of leisure, recreation and tourist activities.

Environmental concerns are not only to do with pressures on the physical environment but also the pressures on host communities in areas where leisure activities have been intensified say, through the setting up of a major theme park in close proximity to a rural community as for example Alton Towers theme park near to Alton village in Staffordshire. Thus leisure activities are central to sustainable development centring around how the current needs of society at large can be met without compromising the ability of future generations to meet their own needs.

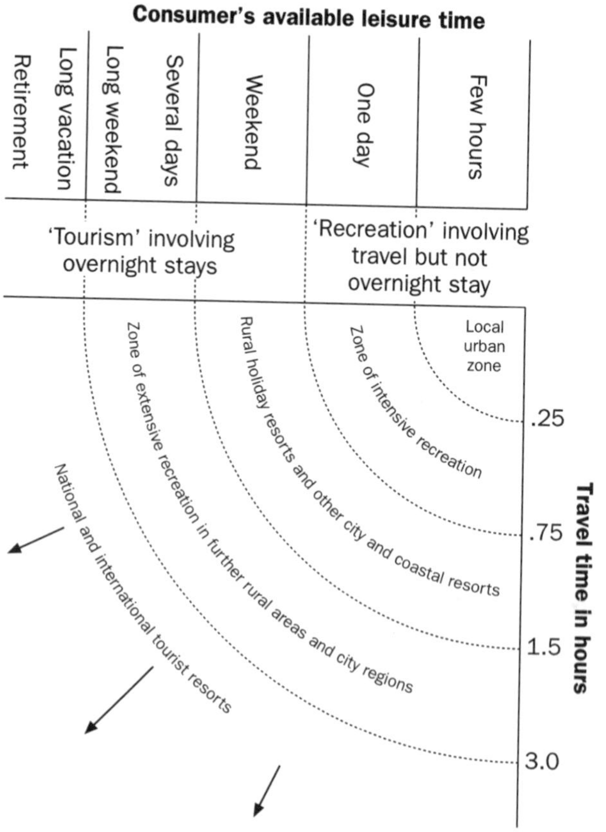

Figure 29.1 The Recreation/Tourism Spatial Continuum

Some benefits and problems of recreational activity and tourism for rural environments

Some benefits

Landscape conservation has become an increasingly important form of heritage protection. Although this dates back to the designation of America's Yellowstone National Park in 1872, the national park movement is still progressing and most countries now have a wide range of lesser designations covering many types of landscape. Landscape is of crucial importance to rural tourism but, equally, visitor use is vital to the landscape conservation industry. Visitor use brings political benefits, can bring economic gains, and can provide jobs in maintaining and repairing traditional landscapes worn by recreational activities.

Nature conservation, like landscape conservation, is a stated goal of most modern governments. It is, however, an expensive process. Rural tourism can provide money for conservation. Visitors are prepared to pay to see nature: most reserves and many national parks successfully charge for entrance. How far charging can be extended is a much discussed point in conservation circles.

The historic built environment can benefit from rural tourism in two ways. Many historic properties now charge for admission in order to maintain their fabrics and surrounding gardens and parklands. Secondly, there are important buildings from the past which have become redundant e.g. castles and churches. The tourist industry can usually use these redundant buildings profitably and imaginatively: they can become attractions in their own right.

Environmental improvements such as village paving and traffic regulation schemes, sewage and litter disposal can be assisted by tourism revenues and political pressures from tourism authorities. These help develop pride of place, important in retaining existing population and businesses, and in attracting new enterprises and families.

Smaller settlements in the countryside have been at greater risk and are unable to support the many services which now require larger threshold populations. Rural tourism can help these smaller settlements survive, because smaller places have a special attraction for visitors. However, careful management of visitor numbers is needed.

Small fishing communities are suffering badly from dwindling fish stocks, quota restrictions and international bans on some activities. A number of these communities can successfully diversify into sports fishing, bird and seal watching, and coastal sightseeing. Some environmental groups claim potential revenue from whale and dolphin watching could exceed revenue from catching whales for meat.

Some problems

The environmental threat. Rural tourism operates within sensitive natural environments. Some of the most attractive tourist destinations have the most sensitive environments. These include sea and lake shorelines, wetlands, high mountain areas and polar areas. The problems of tourist pressure on such environments is well known. The peace, quiet and authentic nature of the countryside can also be seriously compromised. To avoid these problems skilled management of the countryside is needed but management of the order required is as yet rarely available.

The socio-cultural threat. Just as the influx of large numbers of visitors can disrupt the natural world, visitors impinge upon the small-scale, static, and well ordered socio-cultural world of the rural community. Earnings patterns change, success-failure relationships are altered; power structures are challenged. More fundamentally, sociologists have long recognised that the impact of 'advanced' cultures on 'traditional' cultures almost always brings change to the traditional culture and not in the other direction.

The housing question. In some successful rural tourism areas – in the Canadian Rockies, in South-West England, in part of the Alps – tourism has reduced accommodation for local people. Small communities rarely have very much surplus housing. Also, if they are to retain character they must not expand too much or too rapidly. Visitor demand has three main effects. Housing can be taken over for visitor accommodation, usually in the self-catering sector. Second homes are purchased by city people and often rarely used, bringing little economic benefit to the local community. Housing is purchased as retirement homes by holidaymakers who 'fall in love' with their holiday areas.

The incoming entrepreneur. For reasons which will be discussed later, many local farmers and businesses do not decide to enter the tourism market when opportunities present themselves. Surveys show that, in extreme cases, up to 80% of tourism-related businesses in small towns and villages are owned, managed or controlled by incoming or non-local entrepreneurs. In some respects, incomers can provide a valuable transfusion of contacts, capital and skill but they can also present problems. They may be insensitive to local tradition, cultures, working practices and architectural styles. They may use non-local suppliers for goods and services. They may repatriate their profits and capital gains out of the area.

Traffic congestion. Usually road traffic, but in some cases sea and air traffic, can be a major problem if an area is successful in attracting tourists. Narrow roads can easily be choked by traffic both inside and outside settlements, parking becomes an issue, non-tourism business can suffer and, in extreme cases, emergency services cannot make urgent calls. The attractiveness of the area as a destination can decline, taking it down-market. There can be side effects on landscape and nature conservation. Traffic management techniques and better use of public transport can help, but the funds and skills necessary are not usually available.

[SOURCE: Organisation for Economic Cooperation and Development (OECD) in Tourist Policy and International Tourism 1994]

In the past, much leisure activity was informal but increasingly it is being dominated by commerce. Informally organised leisure is being converted into products and services traded by large and small companies, like any other commercial product and service. Through the media and other advertising, the commercial sector can manipulate and shape consumer tastes and fashions, segmenting the leisure market according to age, lifestyles and income groups. Leisure complexes are built by business corporations to provide a range of recreational activities and shops from which the fashion clothing and equipment for particular activities can be bought. Theme parks, frequently incorporating characters and activities associated with popular television series films, are being built in increasing numbers. Heritage, craft and antique centres multiply as visiting these becomes popularised.

In a number of developed countries leisure provision is the fastest growing sector of the economy (Figure 29.3) and is a key to the regeneration of old inner city areas, derelict industrial areas and water-fronts, as well as a way of restoring the economic viability of declining rural areas. On a global scale, a number of developing countries have seen tourism as an alternative way to industrialisation to bring about economic development.

Leisure and tourism is estimated to be the greatest source of employment and is attracting an increasing share of capital investment from multinational corporations and governments. On the basis of present trends, world tourism is expected to double in value within the next ten years (Figure 29.2). At a national level, leisure provision is also the most rapidly growing sector in terms of income earned in a number of advanced countries, including the USA and the UK. In the UK for example in 1993, about 1.5 million jobs were in the leisure and tourism industry and it contributed about 5% of the national GDP (Figure 29.3). It is estimated by the British Tourist Authority that leisure expenditure will have risen by 30% from 1992 to 1997.

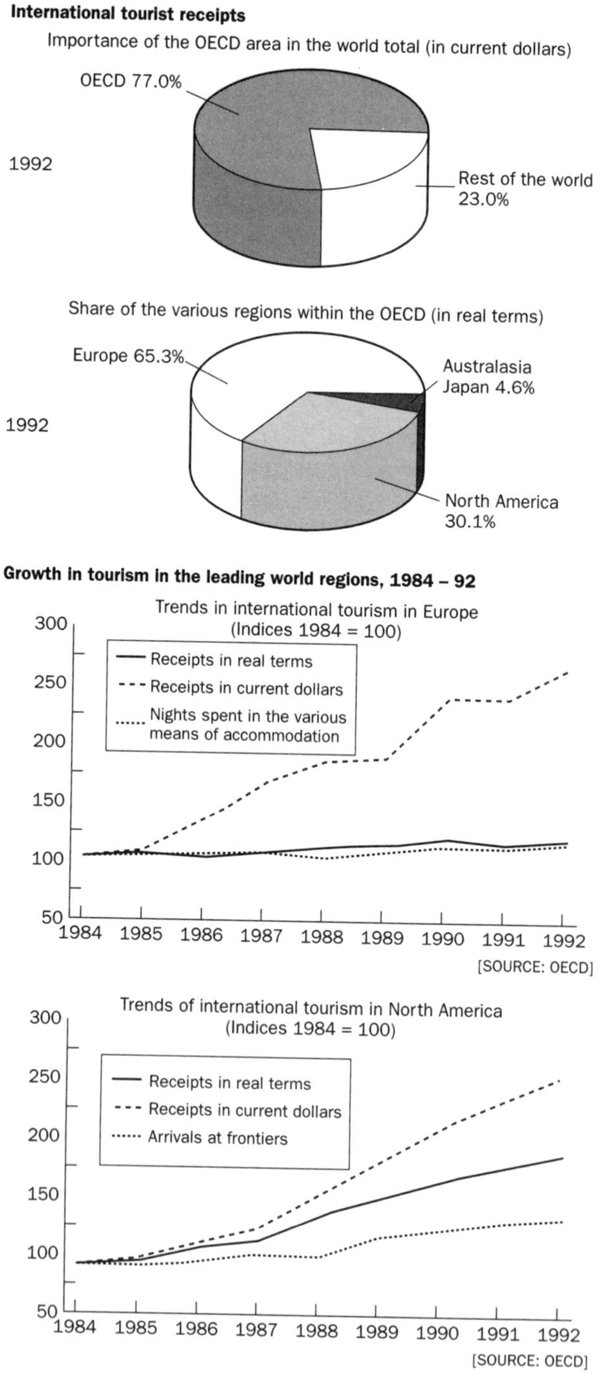

Leading countries in terms international tourism receipts, 1993

1	USA	$56 501 mn	**4**	Spain	$19 425 mn
2	France	$23 410 mn	**5**	Austria	$13 566 mn
3	Italy	$20 521 mn	**6**	UK	$13 449 mn

Figure 29.2 World tourism, 1992

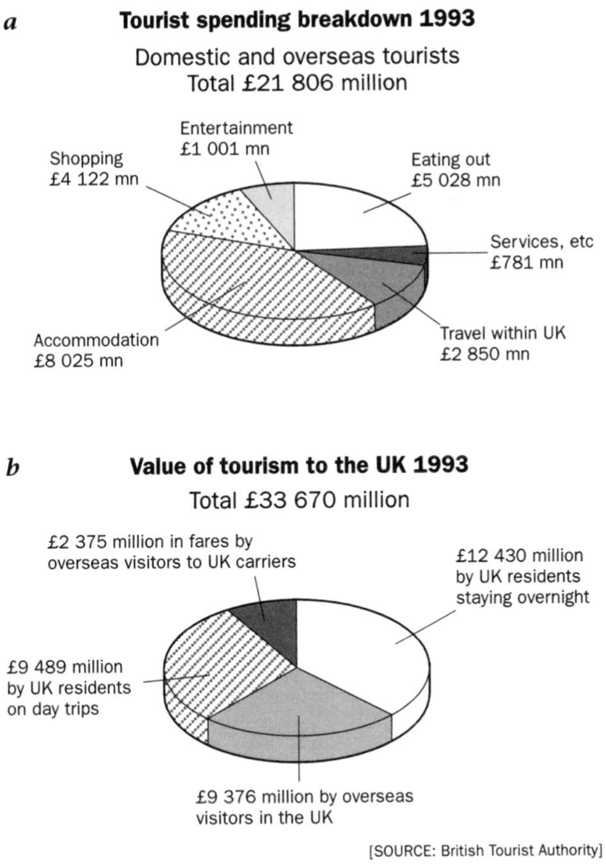

Figure 29.3 *Contribution of tourism to the UK economy, 1993*

The nature of leisure and forces shaping the growth in leisure time and leisure activities

Leisure is concerned with the time people have outside working hours and sleeping. It involves feelings such as gaining pleasure and a sense of experiences. It is also linked to health, time for leisure being regarded as essential to a person's well-being and providing a break from the pressures of everyday living. So important is leisure to the quality of life that access to leisure time is now regarded as a basic human right; for example, it is part of the United Nations' *Universal Declaration of Human Rights* and increasingly seen by governments as providing 'preventative medicine' to the pressures of everyday living.

Leisure, leisure activities and leisure industries have become increasingly important throughout this century, especially since the 1950s in developed countries and more recently in some developing countries such as Taiwan, Singapore and South Korea in South East Asia. Some of the reasons for the growing importance of leisure are known – a shorter working week, longer paid holidays, a rise in disposable income, greater mobility and changing attitudes towards leisure and rising expectations across society.

Like other types of consumption, the leisure market and people's leisure needs have been shaped and fuelled by mass advertising, changing fashion and speculative provision of leisure opportunities by commercial organisations and public bodies. This is not only in terms of actual provision of leisure activities but also in the provision of clothing and equipment deemed to be desirable for such activities as seen for example in fashions for outdoor clothing and footwear for walking and sports activities, or the spectacular growth in the mountain bike market and the number of four-wheel-drive vehicles.

Governments and other public agencies have also played an important part in generating leisure activities. Most local authorities now have their own leisure departments, including regional tourist boards and national tourist authorities which promote and help finance leisure activities and also compete for a share in the leisure industry as a way of bringing in more revenue and providing more jobs.

Improvements in communications and a range of technological advances which free people more from work and decrease the length of time spent on household chores, have also encouraged the growth in leisure time. At the same time a host of technological advances have influenced, changed and enhanced the type of leisure activities which people can participate in, from television, access to teletext and the increase in personal computers, to technological advances in leisure provision itself, such as leisure complexes which include artificial playing pitches to 'state-of-the-art' theme parks and heritage centres.

Variations in access to leisure time and leisure activities

The actual amount of leisure time and the types of leisure activities in which people engage vary considerably across societies, between societies and from one culture to another. Studies show that leisure time and leisure activities vary between different age groups and associated position in the life cycle and according to sex and socio-economic status. It also varies according to residential location, opportunities in remote rural areas being fewer than in a large city, for example.

Providers of leisure in the commercial, voluntary and public sectors recognise these variations and target particular segments of it. Tourist companies, for example, target different age sectors, such as holidays for the over 55 age groups and for the 18 to 30 age groups. Recently, local authorities have been particularly concerned to target the unemployed and elderly, providing special concessions and facilities to increase leisure opportunities for these groups.

Preferences in leisure also vary across cultures. However, as contact between cultures increases observers have noted a move to greater homogeneity with the growth of 'mass culture' as a result of the mass media and an ever greater volume of international travel. The main trend includes a spread of western attitudes towards leisure, with sectors of developing world society adopting consumption patterns, general values and lifestyles of western countries.

Unequal access to leisure time and opportunities for leisure activities across societies can vary because some groups are disadvantaged. Given right to leisure is now accepted as a basic human right; inequality of access is of increasing concern. Despite efforts of governments to widen access, as the gap between the poor and rich widens within societies and between different societies, so the inequalities of access to leisure time and opportunities also widen. Participation in most leisure activities depends on the amount of disposable income available to households and levels of education available. The latter affects awareness of and appreciation of what is on offer by way of leisure opportunities. Within western societies it is the poor, elderly, the unemployed and certain ethnic minorities in inner urban areas who are generally most disadvantaged. However, poverty, isolation and absence of sufficient leisure facilities are also characteristic of some rural areas, especially in more remote locations.

While in general the amount of time for leisure and access to leisure facilities have been increasing in developed countries, for many people in the developing world leisure time has decreased. In many rural areas, simply to subsist requires effort throughout most of the waking hours, while with increased industrialisation many poorer people in urban areas are subject to sweated labour conditions in factories, working excessively long hours for low wages. This sense of deprivation may be heightened as host populations come into contact with a growing number of relatively wealthy and privileged tourists as tourist destinations and the scale of tourism increases in the developing world.

Recreation and tourism as subsets of leisure

Recreation is usually defined as the activities which people engage in outside of home during part of their leisure time. This covers a vast range of activities from the more passive drive out in the countryside to mountain climbing. While such home leisure pursuits as gardening, knitting or making models may involve activity, they do not fall under the heading of recreation as defined above.

Tourism is a part of leisure and recreation but involves those activities requiring travelling from home and at least one overnight stay but less than a year. According to the World Tourism Organisation's definition, in addition to holidaying, tourism would also include travel and overnight stay for the purposes of visiting friends or relatives, or undertaking business or more specialised journeys, such as going on a pilgrimage (Figure 29.4). The wider inclusion of such activities under tourism is associated with the fact that these make use of the same facilities as holiday tourists such as the use of travel agents, airlines and hotel accommodation. Thus, in any statistical analysis on the importance of tourism to the economy or employment structure of a country, it would be difficult to isolate the impact of holiday makers from these other travellers. Also, visiting friends and relatives and some aspect of business trips and pilgrimages may include elements of pleasure and relaxation.

Figures in millions	UK residents		Overseas visitors	
	Trips	Spending	Trips	Spending
Holiday	54.9	£8 425	8.4	£3 848
Business	9.7	£1 730	4.7	£2 419
To visit friends or relatives	21.6	£1 630	4.1	£1 458
Other	4.7	£645	2.3	£1 651
All purposes	90.9	£12 430	19.5	£9 376

[SOURCE: British Tourist Authority]

Figure 29.4 *Purpose of tourism 1993*

A considerable amount of attention has been given to international tourism but domestic tourism is of more importance to most developed countries, in terms of volume and income generated. For example in 1993 the number of tourist nights spent away from home by UK residents was double that of overseas visitors and their spending was also greater (Figure 29.5). In the USA the proportion was even higher. There are, however, a number of developing countries such as Kenya, Mauritius and certain Caribbean countries where tourists predominate.

Recreation and tourism are but subsets of leisure as a whole and tourism, an extension of recreation. When looking at the organisation and spatial pattern of leisure activities, it is difficult to isolate quantitatively how much is a response to the leisure needs of the local or regional population as opposed

Figures in millions	Trips	Nights	Spending
UK Residents	90.9	376	£12 430
Overseas visitors	19.5	185	£9 376
Total	110.4	561	£21 806

Figure 29.5 Volume and spending of tourists in the UK, 1993

to provision for tourists. Both in varying degrees tend to make use of the same facilities, apart from hotel and other overnight accommodation for visitors. It is broadly possible to distinguish whether a place or area has a predominate function as a tourist location as for example in the case of the Costa del Sol region of Spain or Goa in India. Beyond this, most towns and areas are multifunctional in relation to recreation and tourism consumers.

29.2 Internal tourism

Urban-based leisure, recreation and tourism

Given that in developed countries most of the population live in urban areas and large cities are a major focus for tourists, it is not surprising that urban-based recreation and tourism are much more important than rural recreation and tourism in terms of numbers involved and of economic measures, such as numbers employed and receipts. However, types of leisure activity are highly varied and complex, since leisure users include the local population, day visitors and tourists.

In smaller cities most leisure provision is devoted to the everyday needs of the local population and is mainly provided by small businesses, voluntary bodies and the local authority. As the scale of the city increases, so the scale of leisure provision increases and day and tourist visitors become an increasingly large segment of the market being served.

A leisure tourist urban hierarchy

As with central places services in general, it is possible to classify cities and towns into a hierarchy based on the order and scale of leisure provision and the market served (Figure 29.7). At the top are the international cities such as London, Paris and Rome, receiving millions of tourists annually and serving an intensely populated and wide regional hinterland (Figure 29.6). People commute to work in the cosmopolitan core and depend upon the city for much of their leisure and recreational needs. Below these are cities principally of national and regional importance but also with particular historical and cultural characteristics to attract overseas tourists (Figure 29.7). Within the UK, Edinburgh, Bath, Stratford, York and Cambridge would fall into this category (Case study 29.1).

The local leisure catchment area may be considerably smaller than some of the cities in the third rank order – that of regional centres such as Liverpool, Manchester and Birmingham which serve regional rather than tourist leisure markets (Figure 29.8). However, a number of these are trying to break into the international and domestic tourist market under strategy planning and urban regeneration schemes. Below these are a host of smaller cities with no particular attraction to tourists and in which the structure of leisure provision is overwhelmingly directed at meeting the leisure and recreational needs of the local population (Figure 29.9).

City	Millions of visitor nights	City	Millions of visitor nights
London	c. 20	Vienna	4.6
Paris	16	Munich	2.6
Rome	5.6	Amsterdam	2.5
Madrid	5.5	Brussels	2.4
Athens	4.7	Copenhagen	2.1

[SOURCE: Shaw G and Williams A *Critical Issues in Tourism*]

Figure 29.6 International visitor nights in large cities, 1990

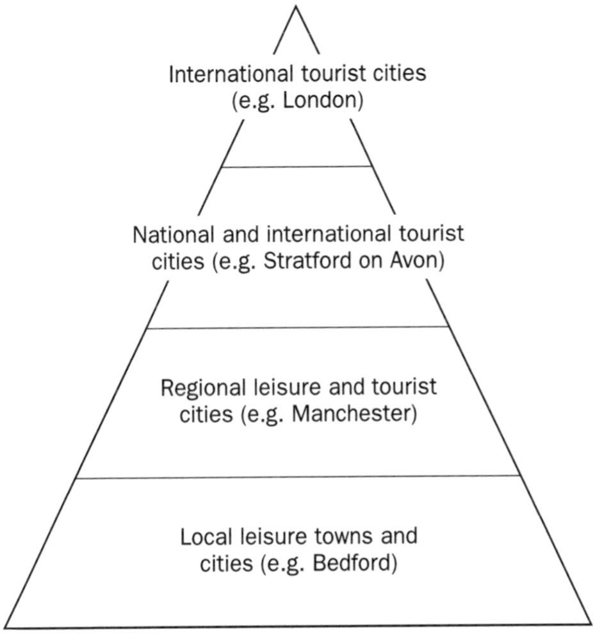

Figure 29.7 The leisure, tourist urban hierarchy

Rank	City/Town	1993 Nights (mn.)
Hierarchy level		
International	1 London	67.6
National or Regional	2 Edinburgh	4.5
	3 Glasgow	3.0
	4 Oxford	2.7
	5 Birmingham	2.6
	5 Brighton/Hove	2.6
	7 Cambridge	2.5
	7 Manchester	2.5
	9 Bournemouth	1.9
	10 Bristol	1.4
	11 York	1.3
	12 Bath	1.2
	12 Liverpool	1.2

[SOURCE: British Tourist Authority]

***Figure 29.8** Ranking of cities by order of visitor nights*

The general spatial structure of leisure provision for smaller cities

Leisure provision in smaller cities tends to be concentrated in the central area or dispersed to the periphery, though each neighbourhood may have some everyday leisure provision such as the local pub, social clubs, a local library and a local park with limited play and sports facilities. The central area contains entertainment, leisure facilities and leisure sales outlets requiring little space, such as a cinema, theatre, restaurants sportswear shops, etc. Recreational activities taking up more space are mainly on the periphery where land is more plentiful – leisure centres, sports pitches, garden centres and small 'country parks' usually focused on or aligned to some natural feature such as a lake, a stretch of river or a local woodland (Figure 29.9).

The organisational structure for urban tourism

In looking at larger cities higher in the hierarchy which are important centres for longer distance day and tourist visitors and also at major regional leisure centres, there is an increasing tendency to focus on the city as a tourist leisure centre in which

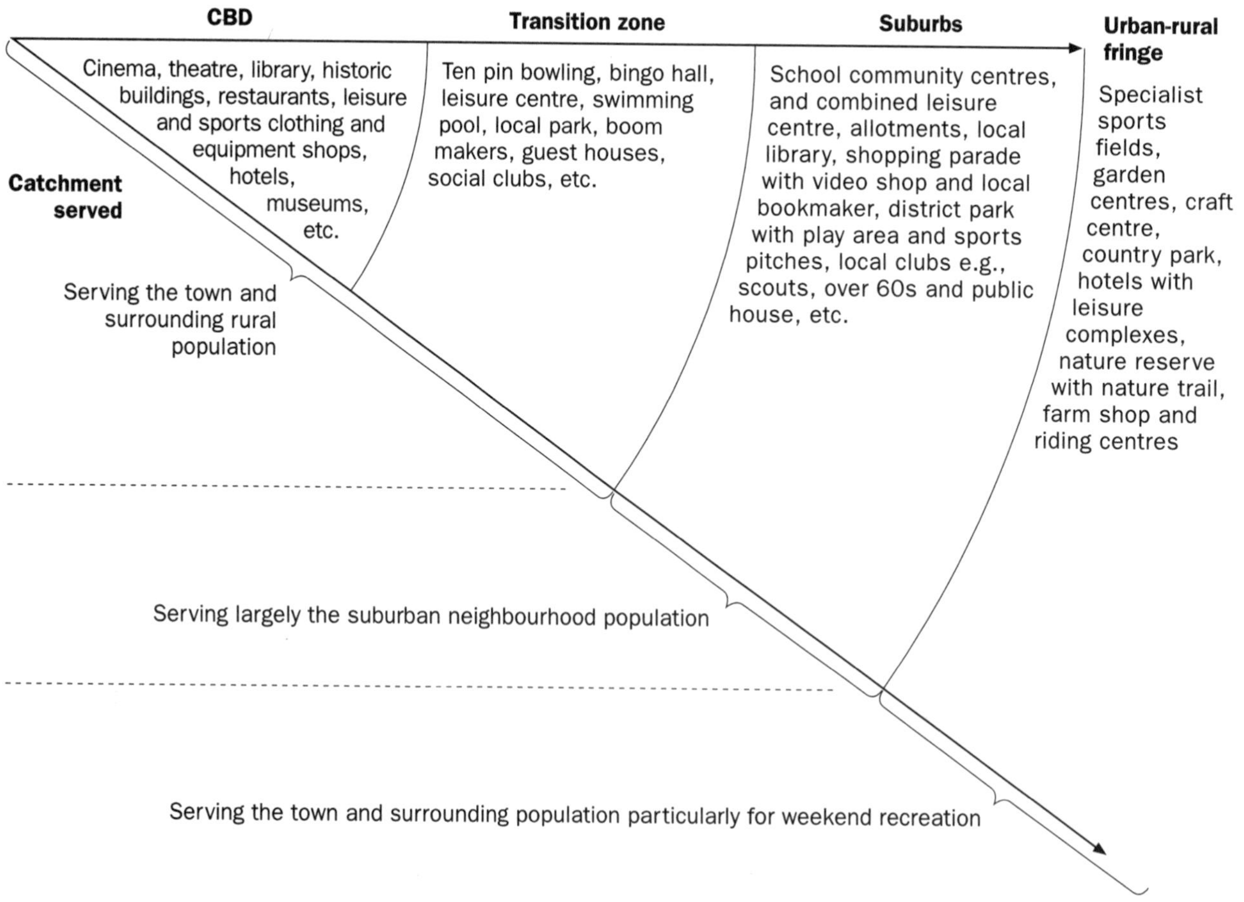

***Figure 29.9** Leisure provision location in a typical small- to medium-sized city*

primary tourist facilities can be identified (Figure 29.10), Supporting these are necessary secondary elements used by the tourist or leisure visitor but also serving the population at large, such as shopping and catering facilities. Finally, there are the conditioning or enabling elements such as the tourist information centre and parking facilities, without which the visitor would find it difficult to access and take part in the primary leisure activities on offer (Case study 29.1).

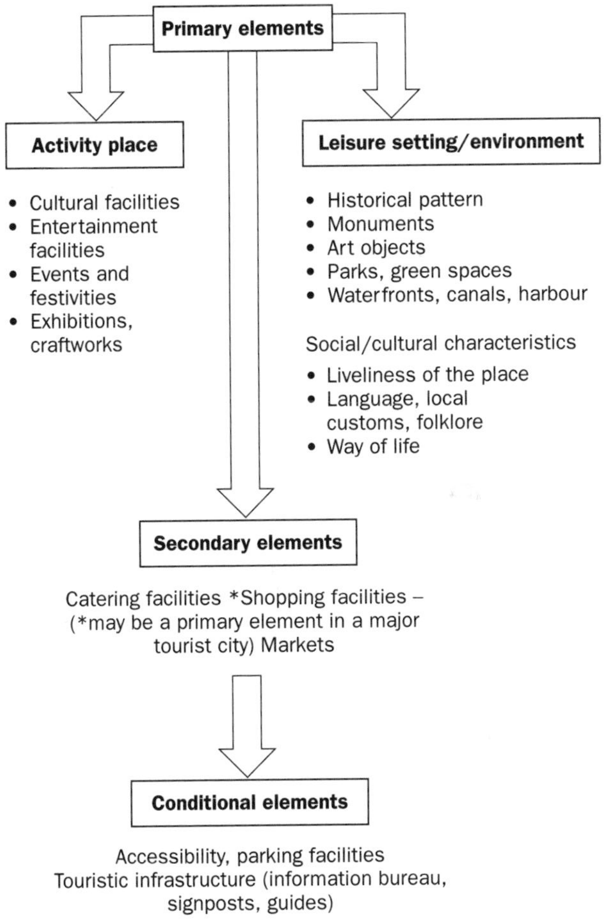

[SOURCE: Jansen-Verbeke M and Dietrorst A *Leisure, Recreation and Tourism: a geographic view of integration*, 1987]

Figure 29.10 *Organisational structure of the tourist city*

This type of approach allows a systematic consideration of the supply side of urban tourism and focuses on direct sources of tourist income and employment from the primary elements and also gives some appreciation of indirect income and employment created through the visitors' use of secondary and facilitating elements. For example, tourist use of car parking provides additional revenue and employment beyond that generated by other users such as office workers and shoppers. The impact of recreation users on a city's economy and employment is thus more fully appreciated.

The tourist city within the wider leisure city

Once some order is imposed on the structural elements of urban tourism, it is also possible to generalise about the spatial pattern of it, including the location of these structural elements and the spatial network of leisure consumer flows as leisure users move around the city to participate in leisure activities.

Geographers recognise a locational pattern consisting of a core, usually the central area of the city and nodes of other leisure and tourist activity linked to the core by leisure-tourist corridors down which supporting services may spread, such as restaurants, kiosks, gift shops, book shops and sportswear outlets. Where the city has a waterfront or a distinct historical centre separate from the current CBD, these may be seen as further nodes, having importance as sub-cores as, for example, in the case of a large coastal resort such as Brighton.

Tourist and long-distance day visitors use a much more restricted area of the city than local leisure users who have much more extensive knowledge of the city and a greater variety of recreational and leisure needs. Equally, while tourists may be drawn to particular attractions during their stay, for local people the surrounding region has many other attractions, especially at weekends.

We can envisage, therefore, a 'tourist city' used both by tourists and locals and encompassing it, a much larger 'leisure city' (Case study 29.1).

In historical cities the tourist city generally focuses on the central area where this has grown around the historical core, as for example, Cambridge and York. Where the present CBD has developed away from the old historical core, the present tourist city is likely to develop around the old core and not the current CBD. For example, in Lincoln the present CBD lies in the valley bottom but the tourist city is clearly centred on the site of Roman Lincoln on the plateau edge to the north. Around the historical attraction of the cathedral and castle the 'Bail' has been developed as a tourist shopping, eating and accommodation area. The City Council have enhanced this 'tourist city' by further attractions, such as a medieval Christmas fair and the conversion of a nearby redundant army barracks and mental hospital into a Museum of Lincolnshire Life and a craft and art centre, respectively. A corridor of tourism stretches down the medieval Steep Hill to link the tourist city with the present CBD.

The benefits and costs of urban tourism and leisure

The importance of leisure and tourism is now widely recognised also in terms of the growing contribution made to the local and wider regional economy. Almost every city is developing a strategy to enlarge and manage the range of leisure facilities on offer. This sector is seen as in the regeneration of cities, particularly where the contribution of industry has declined as for example, Manchester. It is also a major tool in the growing emphasis on reversing counterurbanisation flows and revitalising 'decaying' cities including many small market towns. The Conservative Conference in Blackpool (1995) highlighted revitalisation of towns as an important swing of policy away from rural to urban 'enhancement'.

Apart from direct benefits to the economy, expansion of leisure facilities can help justify infrastructure improvements generally needed and raise the profile of the city to attract investment in other areas of the commercial sector, such as in offices and distribution facilities.

Leisure and tourist provision is not without its costs. For example, it is estimated that providing tourist services such as additional parking, information centres and litter collection for tourists and other visitors costs each Cambridge resident £3 annually. Tourism causes further traffic congestion and pressure on local facilities, such as town centre cafes, for example, which are also used by local residents. Tourist expansion may also contribute to rising prices in shops, entertainment outlets and the cost of car parking. Hence there is an increasing 'anti-tourist' feeling amongst the local population which tourist authorities are having to address. In extreme cases such as the international tourist city of Venice, pressure of tourism is contributing to depopulation of central areas.

There is also growing realisation of pressure on the environment in terms of increased noise, pollution wear on the urban fabric, and of unsympathetically developed tourist attractions in and around the urban area. In some cases conversion of old buildings to leisure uses has removed parts of a city's historical legacy. However, tighter planning controls are ensuring that the outer historical character is preserved, as for example in the case of the conversion of industrial premises, warehouses and redundant churches into leisure, craft and shopping centres e.g. the Hollywood night club in an Ipswich converted Victorian warehouse.

Thus the value of tourism to the local economy and upkeep of historic buildings and other sites has to be balanced against the social and environmental problems it may bring. In 1991 the English Tourist Board and an Employment Department Group issued a White Paper on *Tourism and the Environment* which has provided the basic guidelines for local authorities in their attempts to manage urban tourism. Similar strategies for the management of urban tourism are also being developed in other European countries.

Tourism and the environment: maintaining a balance – some main guidelines

- Establish tourist thresholds for existing tourism resources in terms of their carrying capacity.
- Control traffic congestion by positive rerouting of through traffic and local traffic, more use of traffic calming measures, pedestrianisation of intense tourist areas and provision of more park-and-ride schemes.
- In intense tourist cities such as Canterbury, cease promoting the city as a 'day trip centre' but encourage longer stay visitors who bring more money to the economy. Promote more out-of-season tourism through winter break promotions and extend the tourist season by putting on high profile arts, entertainment and sporting events.
- Consider increased admission charges to historic buildings such as cathedrals and other heritage sites to help cover upkeep and renovation costs.
- Promote and manage alternative tourist attractions and nodes away from the present tourist core to relieve pressure on the core and help economically rejuvenate other sites and areas in the city.
- Promote public awareness of and involvement in tourism and publicise more the benefits of tourism to the economy and improvement of city infrastructures and facilities which also serve resident population needs.

[SOURCE: Based on the Report by the English Tourist Centre and Employment Department Group, 1991]

The contribution of tourist and leisure developments to urban regeneration

Until the 1980s tourism was neglected as a major contributor to urban regeneration but evidence of its effects on helping to revitalise decaying centres and areas in North American cities such as Baltimore, have increasingly led national and local governments in Europe to see it as a major policy tool.

The English Tourist Board launched a 'revitalise inner cities and industrial environs' campaign in 1981 which included attracting leisure tourists and also conferences and business tourism, in conjunction with local authority and private business initiatives. Growing financial support from national government funding and European Regional Development grants encouraged a range of projects from Urban Heritage Parks and Industrial Museums to specialist sports complex developments and conference-hotel-exhibition centres. Efforts were linked to effective high profile marketing strategies such as the 'Glasgow Miles Better' campaign.

Major cities such as Manchester, Sheffield and Birmingham have made tourism development a central priority rather than a subsidiary factor in urban regeneration. In 1989 a 'Vision for Cities Campaign' covering a five-year programme was launched, intensifying the focus on tourism and leisure as a means of particularly revitalising inner city areas. The results of this initiative between public and private enterprise have been impressive in terms of infrastructure improvements and physical and environmental reconstruction. However, the actual beneficial effects on the local economy, long-term job creation and improvement in the quality of life for local residents in the improved areas are less evident.

The multiplier effect within the economy varies according to the type of leisure tourist project. Hotel development, creation of urban leisure trails and museums have only a very limited impact. Multipurpose developments like the Birmingham International Centre and the Albert Docks Marina development in Liverpool create more jobs and attract further private development such as shops and restaurants around them, so having some multiplier effects. However, a significant amount of the profit generated may not benefit the local economy if the private enterprises involved are multinational or national business corporations. While resuscitation of rundown areas and infrastructure improvements may generate greater local pride in a city, there is only limited evidence of spread benefits to other parts of the city. Perhaps some of the investment directed to tourist revitalisation might have gone towards more basic needs, such as more affordable housing, more local service and welfare provision and restoration of local job opportunities through support of small industries, local shops and businesses.

Thus tourist and leisure initiatives are divisive in terms of the benefits brought to urban society. Although there has been increasing attention paid to more new housing being included in development schemes, with some attention given to the needs of the resident population, much of the private housing development is in the higher price range and attracts incoming professional and business people rather than being affordable by local households.

29.3 The decline of the traditional seaside resort

Emergence of the English seaside resort

While the Mediterranean and Florida coastal resorts are part of the mass tourism scene, dependent to an important extent on international tourist flows, the traditional seaside resorts characteristic of the UK coastline were created to cater for domestic tourism (Case study 30.1). However, over the last 40 years they have been in relative decline (Figure 29.11).

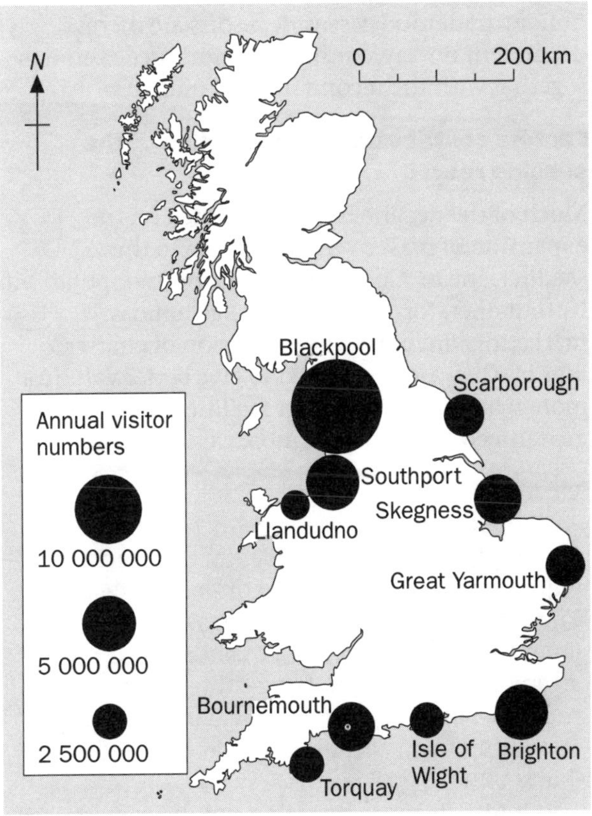

Figure 29.11 *Major seaside resorts*

Seaside resorts such as Scarborough and Brighton developed from the mid-nineteenth century with the railways and the fashion for seaside visits among the middle classes. A 'stay by the sea' was not only seen as a relaxation but also good for one's health. Taking in the sea air, strolling along the front and on the pier and the occasional bathing in sea water were recommended.

It was not until the late 1870s that falling rail prices, the granting of bank holidays and later, a week's annual holiday, enabled the working classes from industrial cities to visit the seaside. Initially it was for day trips but by the inter-war period factories were closing down for one week and the annual holiday by the sea became the highlight for most families.

Other familiar human attractions now typical of seaside resorts such as Skegness, were added to the attractions of the sea, sand and fresh air, together with boarding houses and later, caravan and chalet developments to accommodate the growing influx.

After being virtually closed down during the Second World War, seaside resorts experienced a temporary revival in the immediate post-war period since the late 1950s have been in decline. As late as 1972, seaside tourism accounted for an 82% share of domestic holidays of over four night's stay, but by 1993 only for 58% of a much reduced domestic holiday trade. Today seaside resorts are increasingly dependent on day visitors and short break tourism together with the second holiday trade.

Factors contributing to the decline of the seaside resort

Much of the decline has been blamed on the expansion of mass overseas tourism to the Mediterranean 'Costa del Sol' locations popularised by tour operators through package holiday marketing, including the expansion of charter flights. They are considered to give better value for money holidays with better facilities and guaranteed sunshine in a more exotic location.

> Once upon a time, Britain's seaside towns bustled with holidaymakers wearing silly hats and eating ice cream, taking donkey rides on the beach and enjoying the endless array of off-beat attractions. That was before the Spanish Costas, the traffic jams, the dirty beaches and the noisy games arcades. Today, the empty guesthouses, derelict theatres, boarded-up shops and crumbling piers are a pitiful reminder of the golden age of Britain's 'bucket-and-spade' resorts.
>
> It is little surprise then that holidaymakers continue to desert Britain's resorts, choosing instead the more exotic shores of southern Europe where they can get better value, modern facilities and more reliable weather.
>
> [SOURCE: Hutchings C *Pier Pressure, Geographical Magazine*, September 1995]

Other significant factors include:

- greater affluence of both the middle and working classes enabling them to travel further afield. Also, the relative decline of industry and the closing of factories brought an end to the mass flow of workers' families from the industrial cities such as Manchester and the cotton mill towns to places such as Blackpool for which these 'works holiday' crowds formed the basis of the holiday trade.
- more education and the media exposing the mass of the population to wider holiday horizons.
- the 'catch on' effect through diffusion of the overseas holiday experience and the 'keep up with the Jones' syndrome, popularising the fashion and status symbol of holidaying abroad.
- as tourist income declined, local authorities of sea-side resorts have found it increasingly difficult to maintain basic services, such as litter collections and street lighting, and upgrade the infrastructure.
- especially since the 1980s there has been the growing alternative attraction and development of countryside tourism and of inland attractions, such as theme parks and heritage trails and an increasing interest in sports activities and walking in national park areas, for example. According to a Countryside Commission Report there were 590 million visits to the British Countryside between April to September 1993 as against 90 million to the coast.
- until recently there has been the lack of a coordinated policy towards reversing the decline of seaside tourism. In particular, the need to coordinate the development of hinterland tourist attractions with revitalisation of the resort itself has not been recognised. Nor has an effective promotion and marketing strategy been developed.

Efforts to revive seaside resorts

Some resorts have been able to compensate to some extent by expanding and developing other functions such as office and light industry development, expansion of higher education institutions, including language schools, and their growing function as retirement towns. The most successful of these have been south coast resorts such as Bournemouth and Brighton, within easy access of London and also attracting some growth as dormitories to London. Others, such as the resorts further north like Skegness and Scarborough, are less accessible and without the potential to attract much alternative growth.

These resorts have been dependent on grant aid and their own initiatives to reverse the decline in tourism. In 1992 for example, three smaller resorts collaborated with certain other European resorts to establish the 'Restore Project', backed by European Commission money. Experiences have been pooled and ways of regenerating coastal resorts explored. This has been followed up by the Resort Regeneration Pilot Project covering selected resorts, such as the small resorts of Redcar and Saltburn on the North Yorkshire coast and the wider region of the Costa Brava in Spain.

There must be a well thought out strategic plan at local and regional level to cover the long and the short term. Regeneration will require extensive refurbishment and infrastructure improvement in the resort itself and additional leisure and recreational activities currently in popular demand such as theme parks, heritage and nature trails. There is a greater need to attract more short break visitors.

There is some evidence of resort regeneration. Brighton for example is regarded as having 'reinvented itself' by upgrading accommodation and facilities, promoting itself as a centre for market day trips and as a national and international conference centre. In conjunction with the local authorities, North West Water Authority have undertaken a clean up of the coastal stretch fronting Blackpool, while with the help of a government grant of £21 million, Blackpool's local council has undertaken a major refurbishment of the Central Promenade as well as trying to market its traditional character to overseas tourists. The small Durham seaside resort of South Shields illustrates efforts resorts are making to 'repackage' and market themselves as bases for exploration of the region around; it has for example, a Catherine Cookson Summer Fair, since the novelist had set much of her writing on locations around South Shields.

Resorts with little else to offer beyond seaside tourism have tried to highlight their advantages for the traditional family seaside holiday while at the same time updating and widening their image by adding more modern recreational facilities and promoting the 'green tourism' and historical attractions of the rural and undeveloped coastal areas around.

While to some extent recent trends would support the view that *'seaside towns are a national resource and do have a future'*, given the proliferation of alternative holiday venues abroad and a continued fall in real costs of overseas travel, the traditional seaside resort is unlikely to regain its former position as a magnet for mass domestic tourism.

29.4 Leisure activities and tourism in the countryside

Its importance

Leisure use of the countryside is a mass activity involving over half of the population and is of enormous value to the nation: access to and enjoyment of the countryside delivers great personal and social benefits.

Observations show that for the vast majority of England recreation forms a natural and harmonious component of the legitimate activity of the countryside. It delivers considerable economic benefits, which are increasing.

Recreational enjoyment should be seen as one of the prime purposes of countryside policy, reflecting society's relationship with this aspect of its heritage rather than as a 'secondary add on' to the countryside's purposes as a producer of food, fibre, timber, minerals, etc.

[SOURCE: *The Environmental Impact of Leisure Activities on the English Countryside*, The Countryside Commission, April 1995]

Why rural recreation and tourism has grown

Demand related factors

- increased levels of education correlate with an increase in outdoor recreation, eco-tourism, and special interest holidays.
- over the last 20 years there has been a booming interest in both a nation's historic and natural heritage.
- a move in favour of things 'authentic' as a counter to television, videos and factory-produced goods. It is also regarded as a REAL experience (i.e. rewarding, enriching, adventurous and learning).
- rural areas epitomise 'peace and tranquillity' and an environment in which to relax and 'switch off'.
- it is seen as providing for the individual as against mass consumption.
- it is seen as healthy as opposed to the growing health concerns over too much 'sea, sand and sun'.
- an ageing but active population together with early retirement has greatly increased rural leisure demand, including out-of-season demand. In 1995 half the 60 – 65 age range had retired, many with occupational pensions, giving disposable income.

Supply related factors

- improvements in and the relative cost of transport and communications, including computer booking, fax and credit card technology.
- increased marketing and development of rural attractions by both public and private sector bodies.
- 'green issues', many associated with rural areas have an increasingly higher profile and this has been seized upon by marketing agencies as a 'selling point'.
- great improvement in outdoor clothing and equipment, including popularising of the outdoor fashion styles.

Since its remit as a non-departmental body sponsored by the Department of the Environment, the Countryside Commission aims to conserve and enhance the English countryside and help people enjoy it. Similar support for the expansion of recreational use of the countryside is also expressed by the Rural Development Commission, which advises the government on the social and economic development of the countryside and also works to promote development. Like the Countryside Commission, its advocating of the expansion of rural recreation is set within the context of it being done in a responsible and managed way with due regard for the care and enhancement of both the social and physical environment.

The importance of leisure in the countryside is echoed on a much wider scale across the developed countries in the recent OECD's publication on *Tourism Policy and International Tourism in Advanced countries* (1994) in which 'Tourism Strategies and Rural Development' is the selected theme. The thriving growth of rural tourism (along with the environmental issues it raises) is set against and contrasted with the decline in the relative importance of agriculture, until recently, the economic foundation for rural areas.

It is difficult to know whether or not rural leisure activities in developing countries follow a similar trend to developed countries, as there are as yet relatively few studies on leisure. A study related to Zimbabwe would suggest there are significant variations to do with cultural differences and lower income levels, though some trends are similar; for example, the popularity amongst urban dwellers of simply visiting the nearby countryside to enjoy the scenery and greater tranquillity it affords and the increasing growth in sporting activities (Case study 30.2).

A mass activity

Studies which incorporate results from other research provide a much more objective view of rural leisure activities. This is displacing some of the many statements based on subjective observation and generalisations sweepingly made on *'evidence from a comparatively small number of celebrated and oft quoted locations or areas'*.

Spending leisure time is a mass activity with over half the population visiting the countryside at least once a year and 40% on average, once a fortnight. About 590 million day visits to the English countryside were made between April and September in 1994. However, the proportion of visitors is significantly greater among higher and middle income groups than the lower income groups. This is partly due to higher income groups being better informed and having more disposable income and partly due to different preferences and attitudes to leisure across social groups; a greater proportion of lower income households favour more home- and urban-based leisure.

Although there has been little further growth in total numbers since the late 1970s, the amount of leisure spent in the countryside has gone up as has participation in a variety of sporting activities. The 1995 study of the spending patterns of households in Britain indicates that over 12 months the amount spent on leisure rose by 12% and on average it was about equal to what a household spends on food.

In addition to the vast number of day visitors, in 1993 tourists spent 76 million holiday nights in the countryside, staying mainly in villages and small rural towns. Over half of the 17 million overseas tourists visiting Britain spent some time in the countryside, ranking it as one of the country's major attractions for them. Clearly tourism and leisure are a major feature of the rural scene.

A markedly uneven pattern across the countryside

The spatial pattern of leisure is highly polarised. Over half of day visits are to areas within five miles of home, largely within the rural fringe of urban areas. One in eight visits are within one mile of home. While 53% of visitors use the car, a surprising 38% go on foot.

The other intensely visited locations are the popular 'honeypot' sites further afield, such as the Lake District with 15.8 million visitors in 1993 and more local beauty spots such as Box Hill in Surrey (Case study 29.3). Compared to these polarised and contrasting locations of intense visitor activity, the rest of the countryside is lightly visited (Figure 29.13). Numbers decrease with distance from the major cities but with moderate magnets for higher leisure activity at a particular attraction such as a lake area or countryside park, which offer a variety of leisure activities. For example in the rural East Midlands, Rutland Water and the area around attracts nearly one million visitors a year.

Why do people visit the countryside?

An OECD report (1994) lists a wide variety of reasons why people visit and holiday in the countryside (Figure 29.14). Walking is by far the most popular activity followed by eating or drinking out, visiting friends or relatives and taking

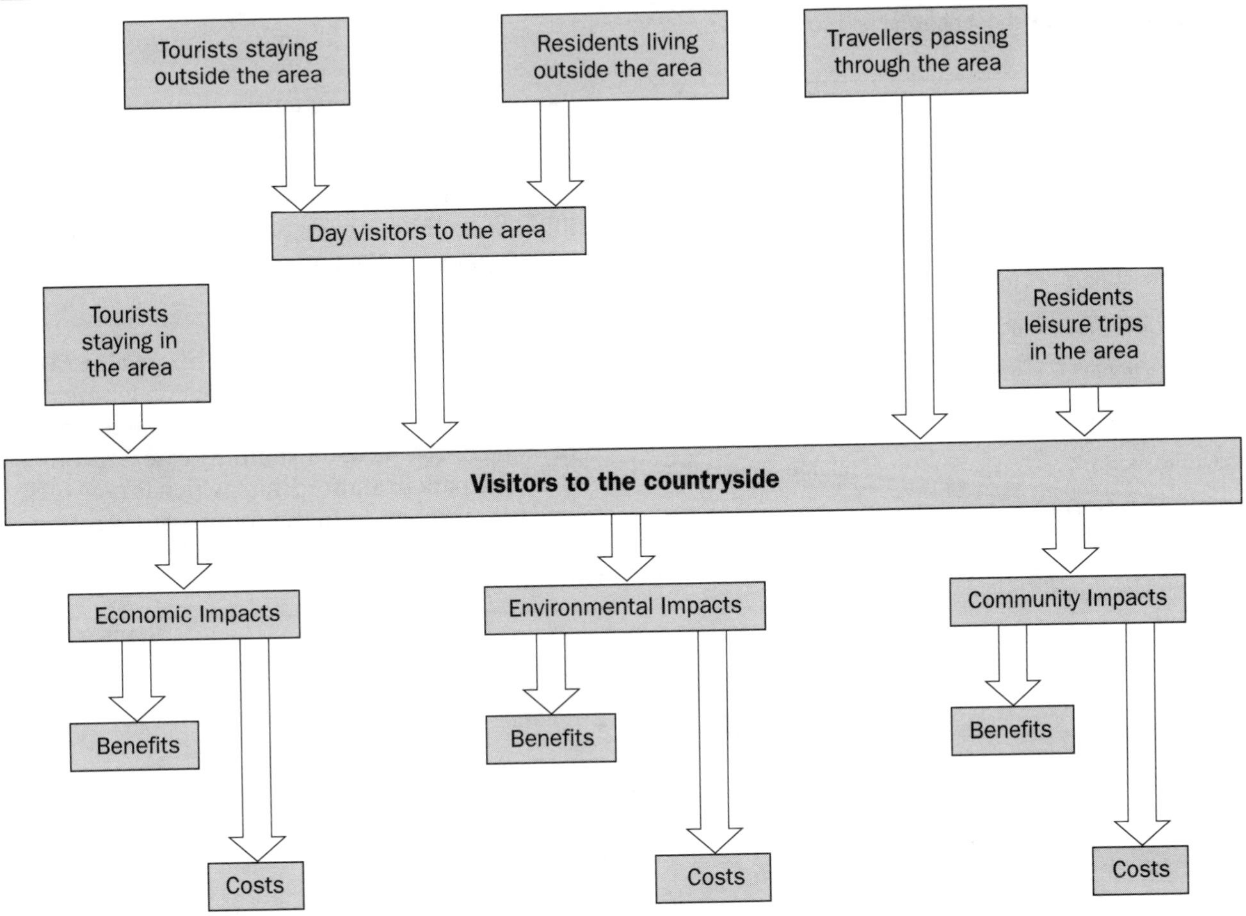

Figure 29.12 *A framework for identifying types of visitors to the countryside and their impact*

Holiday tourism

Destination	Trips (m)	Nights (m)	Spending (£m)
Cumbria	2.4	10.2	370
Northumbria	1.6	6.3	160
Yorkshire & Humbs	5.6	22.4	690
North West	4.5	16.8	615
Heart of England	3.8	13.1	430
East Midlands	4.3	16.7	500
East Anglia	5.8	25.1	760
London	2.7	8.4	350
West Country	10.8	61.8	2 070
Southern	5.8	24.0	730
South East	4.3	16.7	530

Figure 29.13 *Variation in distribution of UK visitors in England by region, 1994 (includes both urban and countryside visits)*

part in outdoor sports. It is thus not surprising that much of the effort of public bodies has gone towards maintenance and establishment of footpaths and creating attractive environments in which to enjoy walking, picnicking and taking part in an outdoor hobby such as bird watching or some sports activity (Case study 29.2).

Much of the emphasis of the Countryside Commission, local authorities and other bodies such as the Sports Council and English Nature has gone towards creating country parks, nature reserves and planting woodlands, many of them in close proximity to large urban areas (Case study 12.1). In the case of regional parks, care has been taken to link these by suggested walks and nature trails to already established countryside attractions, such as the nearby village with its pub and church to the local river, lake or canal (Case study 29.2). In proportion to annual public spending on facilities, it is estimated that private businesses spend about 12% on building new commercial attractions such as golf courses.

Overall, the 'top ten' most popular countryside activities are:

walking	216 million visits (37%)
eating or drinking out	67 million (11%)
taking part in outdoor sports	66 million (11%)
visiting friends or relative	60 million (10%)
leisure attraction/place of interest	33 million (6%)
going for a drive or picnic	29 million (5%)
pursuing a hobby or pastime	25 million (4%)
cycling or mountain biking	25 million (4%)
watching sport	13 million (2%)
going to a place of outdoor entertainment, e.g. fete/open air concert	13 million (2%)

[SOURCE: UKDVS, 1993]

Figure 29.14 *Leisure in the countryside of Britain Survey, 1993*

Still more golf courses but are they needed?

Criticisms include

It is clear local voices are not being heard. Aylesbury Vale County council in Buckinghamshire gave permission for 22 new golf courses in 1992, despite the fact that only 1 in 7 people in the area said they actually wanted more.

And market forces seem to be the only players in this game. In an article in the September 1992 issue of The Planner, Dr Terry Marsden of the University of Hull explained that because of the general lack of local or strategic planning policies, the interests of landowners and developers often tend to marginalise most other claims on the countryside. In other words, if market forces are relied upon in the siting of golf courses, it seems that the local people are invariably left out.

In South Wales, the Caerphilly Golf Club has been granted permission to extend its 14-hole course over Caerphilly Common, despite massive opposition from residents. Construction work has already blocked walkways and bridleways.

The public would seem to agree. A recent survey conducted in Buckinghamshire indicated a desire, not for more golf courses, but more access to informal leisure activities such as bridleways, footpaths and picnic areas.

[SOURCE: Sue Wheat *Playing Around with Nature*, Geographical Magazine, August 1993]

'A course can improve degraded landscapes ... golf courses can work as unofficial nature reserves – linking and creating habitants and protecting sensitive sites'.

In Britain 3 million people regularly golf and 10 million are golfers to some degree. Currently there are 2200 courses – 274 built since 1985.

Safari and theme parks

However, spending is highly concentrated into a few locations and so the local impact on leisure activity and the economy and environment can be very marked. The most outstanding case is Alton Park theme park in Staffordshire which is now the most visited attraction in the country supplanting both Madam Tussaud's (London) and the Tower of London (Figure 29.15).

		Thousands
1	Alton Towers, Staffordshire	2 618
2	Madame Tussaud's, London	2 450
3	Tower of London	2 332
4	St Paul's Cathedral, London	1 900
5	Natural History Museum, London	1 700
6	Chessington World of Adventures	1 495
7	Thorpe Park, Surrey	1 327
8	Science Museum, London	1 277
9	Blackpool Tower	1 250

[SOURCE: British Tourist Authorities]

Figure 29.15 *Top attractions charging admission in 1993*

The impact of leisure and tourism on the countryside

Recent Countryside Commission findings indicate that the impact of leisure and tourism on the countryside is more positive than negative. '*It is possible to accommodate and even increase the quantity of recreation activity without detriment to the environmental quality of the countryside by deploying relevant expertise and management measures.*' (Countryside Commission Report, April 1995)

Even given the growing debate about sustainable development and increasing concern for the environment, the general trend is towards encouraging more use of the countryside for leisure and tourism. It is not motivated solely by the need to accommodate the growing demand but also because of the overall benefits it can bring to rural economies and if properly managed, the contribution it makes towards maintaining and even enhancing rural environments, as in the case of construction of Rutland Water and the Lee Valley Park (Case study 29.2). Certainly in the vicinity of cities, planting of woodland, creation of nature reserves and parks together with footpath maintenance are helping to offset the damage and loss done to the countryside through the intensification of agriculture and the encroachment of suburban spread and industry.

The impact of leisure and tourism activities is uneven, since these activities tend to be concentrated mainly on urban fringes and further afield at localities offering particular attractions. Impact effects also depend on numbers and the type of visitors in terms of age, level of awareness and amount of disposable income. It is also difficult to isolate the effects of leisure and tourism from the effects of other agents of change, such as the increased 'suburbanisation of the countryside' and the increasing numbers who choose to retire to the countryside.

While the direct effects may be reasonably obvious, indirect effects due to the multiplier are sometimes very difficult to detect and quantify. A number of researchers have pointed out that the amount of change brought about by leisure and tourism in any area can only effectively be measured if it is known what the area was like earlier: there are few in-depth earlier studies of rural areas available against which to measure change.

Bearing in mind these reservations, it is useful to see the impact as of two kinds, namely socio-economic and environmental (Figure 29.16).

The observed benefits

A significant amount of income is brought to rural areas – about £3000 million in 1993 for the UK, a third of which was from tourists. From this gross figure must be deducted 'leakages' such as income going to commercial businesses with headquarters based outside the rural area in question, but balancing this should also be the addition of indirect income, such as investment attracted

Type of impact	Benefits	Costs	Level affected by
Economic	Local income Jobs Support for local services Support for local activities Diversification of the economy Improved external profile	Additional infrastructure/services Congestion Competition for labour Displacement of other activities	Nature and scale of visitors Strength of local economy Local linkages Tourism infrastructure provision
Environmental	Support for heritage sites Support for natural sites Greater awareness of landscape, wildlife, heritage in visitors Reuse of redundant buildings	Damage to sites and paths Disturbance and loss of flora and fauna Pollution e.g. air, water, visual, light, noise Litter Development pressure for tourist facilities Development pressure for infrastructure	Nature and scale of visitors Strength of local economy Local linkages Tourism infrastructure provision
Community	Social contact Stimulus of new people and ideas Awareness of local customs and traditions Increased demand for local entertainment and crafts Support for wider range of shops and leisure facilities	Conflict between residents and visitors Competition for housing and other resources Debasement and change in local culture and traditions Influx of temporary/permanent outsiders attracted by tourism Anti-social behaviour Undesirable or inappropriate provision	Number, seasonal and spacial distribution of visitors Characteristics of visitors Robustness and strength of local traditions and community

Figure 29.16 Economic, social and environmental impact of visitors and tourist on the countryside benefits and costs

as a result of tourism or recreation. However approximate the figure, the contribution is very significant.

One of the main reasons for wishing to expand the rural leisure industry is the contribution it can make to job creation and to the diversifying of employment opportunity, especially for the younger, who are most likely to leave rural areas. Job opportunity ranges from work in services such as retailing, transport and hospitality, to providing further work for those in established rural activities, such as farming, forestry and fishing. Leisure provision is particularly seen as supporting agriculture in more remote and marginal upland areas but it is also of importance in farm diversification schemes nearer to urban areas.

In 1994 farm attractions had the fastest growth amongst types of leisure visits for the fifth consecutive year, up by 6% to 8.3 million visits. In the UK a farm survey revealed that 20% of all farmers received some significant income from leisure activities. In Germany, Switzerland and Austria, the figure is higher. In 1991 for example, Austrian farmers provided over a quarter million accommodation nights for tourists.

Certainly leisure and tourism have helped the retention of rural services, enhanced cultural and entertainment opportunities for the local community and even the survival of small communities in more remote areas. The recent completion of the road bridge from the Scottish mainland to the Isle of Skye owed much to the anticipated toll revenue from tourists using it. In Cornwall the reversal of the preceding depopulation trend since 1971 is attributed largely to the economic stimulus experienced from the continued expansion of tourism and the growth in the retirement population.

An important social effect of increased leisure and tourism reported from a number of countries, including Spain, Greece, France, Ireland and Britain, is the more enhanced role given to women in rural society. For example, many farmers' wives were restricted to being unpaid helpers with some farm tasks. They have now taken a dominant role in providing for the leisure needs of visitors in bed-and-breakfast accommodation and organising farm shop sales. Women have also seen opportunities in entrepreneurial roles and in being actively engaged on local bodies for advising on matters to do with tourism and the countryside.

In respect of conservation and management of the environment, a surprising range of beneficial effects have been attributed to the increased use of the countryside for recreation and leisure. These range from the preservation and expansion of rural crafts and customs to the restoration and preservation of historic buildings and ground where sympathetic conversion to leisure use or the charging of admission fees have been of vital importance. Even in respect of the landscape itself, increasing emphasis is being placed on the contribution which leisure income can make to the cost of preservation and maintenance of the countryside including National Park areas.

Possibly even more importantly, increased interest in the countryside as a national heritage and place of tranquillity in contrast to the suffocating pressures of urban living, has raised the profile of rural areas in political debate and the amount of public funding and legislation directed towards protection and enhancement of the countryside. Since 1971 there has been a 500% increase in the membership of voluntary organisations connected with conservation, management and preservation of the rural environment and its wildlife.

A number of researchers have traced stages in the changing social attitudes amongst people in the USA towards national park areas. Although the English National Parks owe much more to human influence, a similar but later trend in attitude has been observed. From 1945 to 1960 the USA national parks such as the Yellowstone National Park were viewed as 'national playgrounds' but during the 1960s there was growing concern for them as 'natural wildernesses' and for their protection from too much encroachment. In 1964 the Wilderness Act was passed, severely restricting access to much of the area covered by National Parks, with the emphasis on preserving their wilderness state by keeping them 'roadless'. Nevertheless, from the 1970s as also in the case of the English National Parks, the number of visitors has dramatically increased. They have had to be accommodated through a careful management policy which acknowledges the right of the public to enjoy the countryside but also recognises the need to sustain and preserve the rural environment. This mirrors the combined but opposing attitudes towards and interest of the public in rural areas.

The problems of increased leisure and tourism

The environmental threat posed by increased recreational activity is seen to be at its greatest in those areas which paradoxically offer the greatest attraction but which are also the most sensitive to human interference. These include sea and lake shores, wetlands and upland areas. The sources of environmental damage are well publicised, for example:

- intensive winter skiing and climbing leading to erosion, landslips and rock falls along with the loss of rare plant and wildlife habitats
- the increased volume of walking, riding, mountain bike riding and four-wheel vehicle driving along foot paths and bridle ways leading to excessive erosion and damage to stone walls
- increased noise and litter, disturbing the tranquillity and aesthetic appearance of the countryside and disturbing wildlife.

While the problems are real and significant, surveys have shown the problems to be exaggerated. Most of the rural area is inaccessible mainly because it is privately owned or physically too remote from any access route. In respect of areas which are accessible to the public, any severe damage is highly localised. For example, Countryside Commission monitoring has revealed that only 1% of public rights of way have suffered any damage. On most affected routes such as the Cleveland and Pennine Ways, damage is limited to the equivalent of 15% of the route and is repairable. Over the 3500 sites of designated Scientific Interest, there were only 18 reports of any environmental or wildlife damage in 1993 due to recreational activity. While there has been a very significant increase in traffic on rural roads, surprisingly less than 2% is attributed to leisure traffic; most is due to commuting and increased economic activity. Nevertheless, there are localised incidences of severe congestion at the height of the summer season and on bank holidays, such as at Ambleside in the Lake District and around Dovedale and Castleton in the Peak National Park. The Countryside Commission states that any potential threat to the environment from the growth in leisure activity can be resolved through cooperation and skilled management.

Any detrimental social and economic effects on rural communities and the rural economy are limited. They are amenable to solution through consideration of the feelings and needs of the affected communities, cooperation, careful planning and proper management of leisure activities. The most serious problem is seen as the disruption which a significant growth in tourism and recreational activity can bring to the ordered life of a community and its traditional economic base. The influx of new business people from outside and intervention by bodies such as the English Tourist Board and the district planning authority can challenge local power structures and reduce the effective voice of the local community in matters affecting it.

A growing and underlying problem has been lack of cooperation between different bodies and with local communities in the management of rural leisure growth, resolving of problems and conflicts of interest. It was only in 1995 that farming, wildlife and countryside organisations met to jointly cooperate in finding a solution to the problems of hill farmers, including ways of increasing their incomes through catering more for leisure visitors and tourists (Case study 29.3).

Management and promotion of sustainable recreational tourist activity in rural areas

Management has to be concerned with two central aspects: to encourage further growth in rural recreation and tourism for more leisure opportunity, and to diversify and improve rural economies and manage this growth in a manner which is sustainable in the interest of rural communities. The OECD suggest the following central points in any management strategy and at a more specific level, these are practised by particular organisations concerned with leisure and the countryside.

Management guidelines

There is a need to understand and relate to the leisure and tourism market in terms of its size, different types and its demands. Allied to this is the need to inform, influence and win markets through information giving and marketing campaigns using public sector agencies such as the regional tourist boards and by liaisoning with private sector agencies, such as travel agents.

Planning and management needs to be conducted within an 'environmentally sustainable enterprise milieu', covering:

- effective planning and conservation legislation
- construction of regional and local sustainable rural strategies which take account of the area's strengths and weaknesses, the opportunities it offers and the likely threats to the community and environment posed by any growth in rural leisure opportunities in the area
- guiding the type and amount of public sector and private sector investment
- an ongoing assessment, evaluation, monitoring and reviewing of the effectiveness of strategies adopted and in particular, responding to community and environmental concerns.

Effective leadership should be provided to ensure effective and considerate responses to community and individual reactions to recreation and related matters, to promote new initiatives and to ensure that effective management does actually occur.

case study

29.1 **Cambridge: urban tourism and leisure**

'Cambridge is no longer a cosy university-cum-market town. It is an international city defined by its academic brilliance, innovation and as a tourist destination. The latter has been one of the main influences on its identity and sense of place over the past 20 years. That influence, however, has been both good and bad.' [Cambridge Tourism Strategy Review, 1995]

Tourism affects so many aspects of life in Cambridge that it cannot be ignored or treated in isolation.

The Cambridge Structure Plan (1991 – 2000) regards Cambridge as the major tourist centre and the engine of tourism for the rest of the region and thus an important contributor to economic growth. Green tourism is supported, environmental problems recognised. However, selective development and positive management are needed.

Tourism and the tourist city

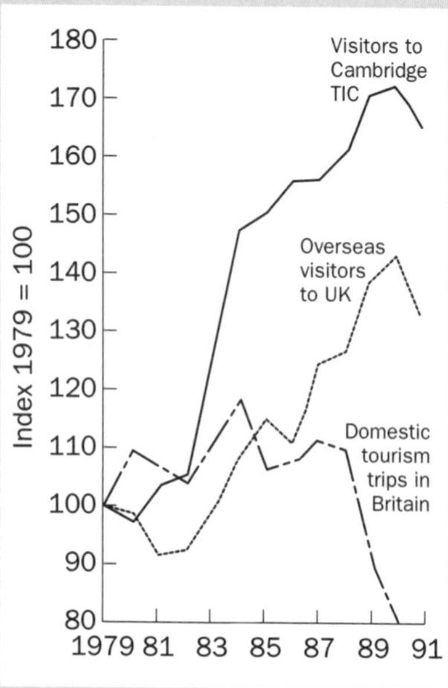

The growth of tourism, 1979 - 91

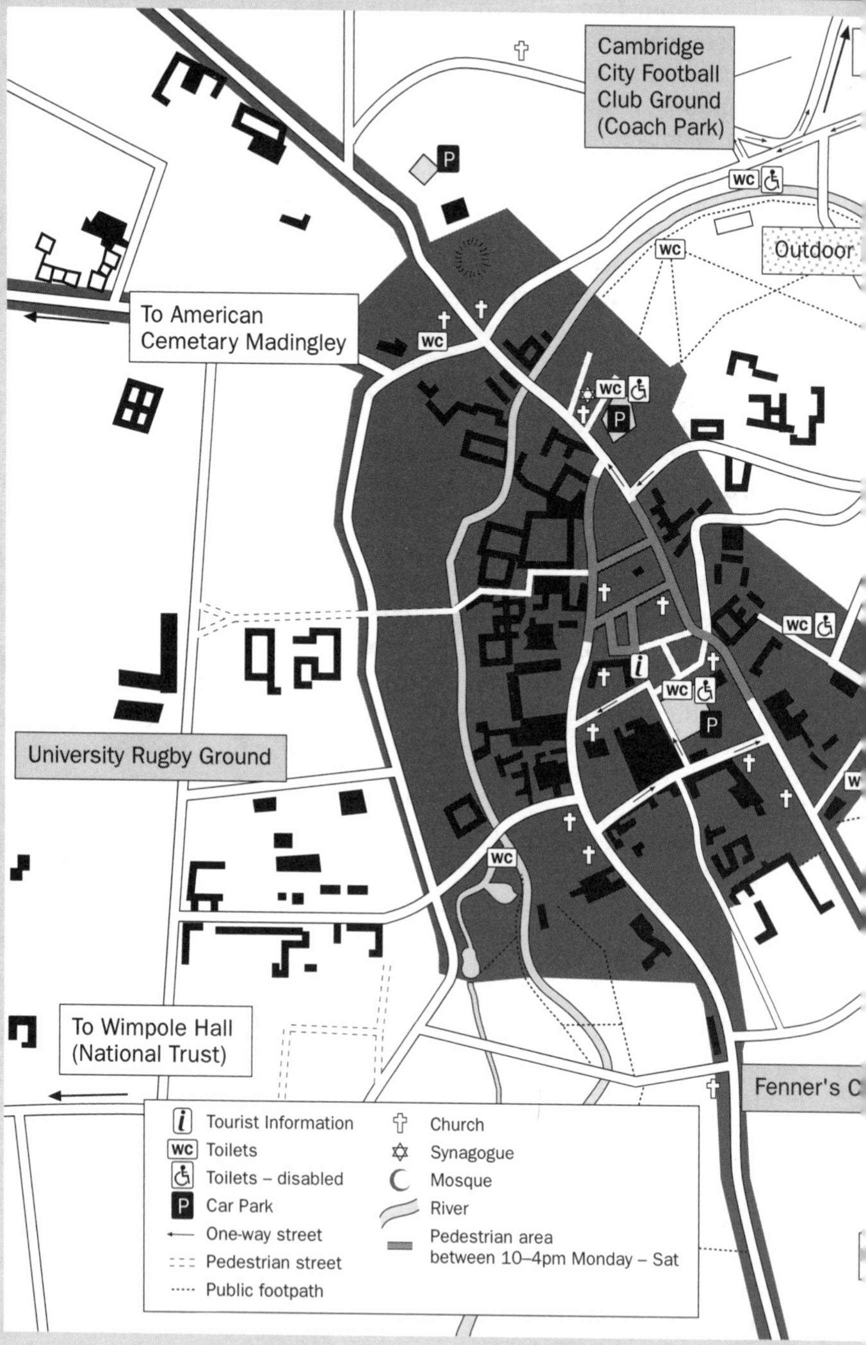

Cambridge: examples of supporting infrastructure for tourist and leisure users

Importance

Cambridge had 3.4 million visitors in 1994; 38% were from great Britain and 62% overseas (half from Europe). Two thirds were day visitors and for others, average length of stay equalled 1.3 days. They spent £195 million in the city, mainly on shopping, food, drink and accommodation. They support 6 650 jobs directly and indirectly. In addition there are 20 000 short-stay students. Tourism is highly seasonal, the peak being between April to September.

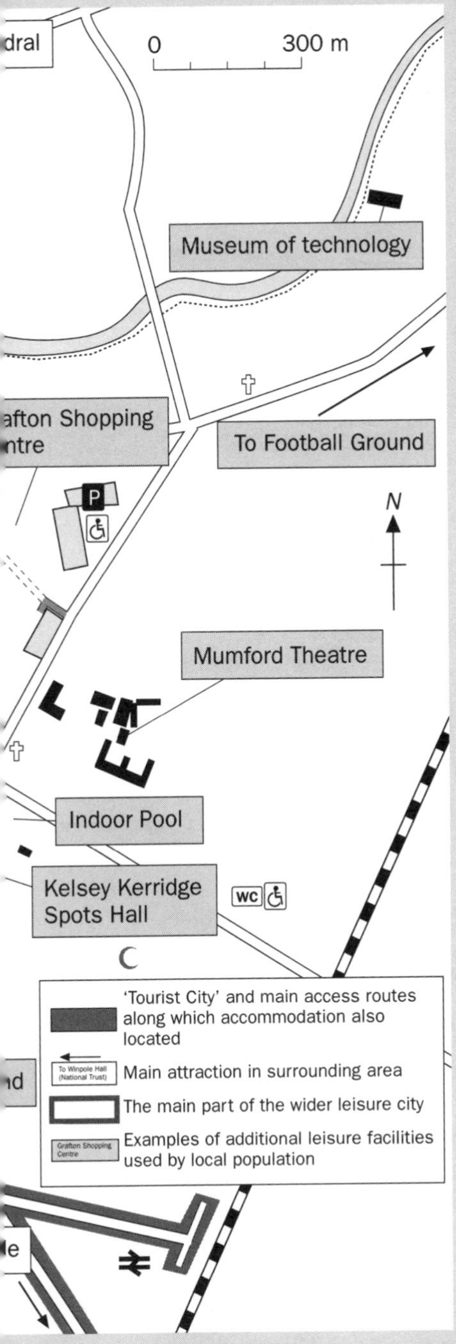

The most popular area visits are Duxford Imperial War Museum, Ely Cathedral, Wimpole Hall, Farm (National Trust) and the American War Cemetery (Madingley).

A strategy for tourism

About 80% of the local population see the benefits of tourism to the city but favour greater management of it. The main strategy is to reconcile '*competing needs of residents, visitors and environment*'.

- conserve (protect, enhance) the local life, beauty, character of Cambridge and its area.
- ensure a satisfying and enjoyable experience for visitors.
- support a prosperous industry for long-term benefit.
- ensure reinvestment by the industry in infrastructure on which tourism depends.

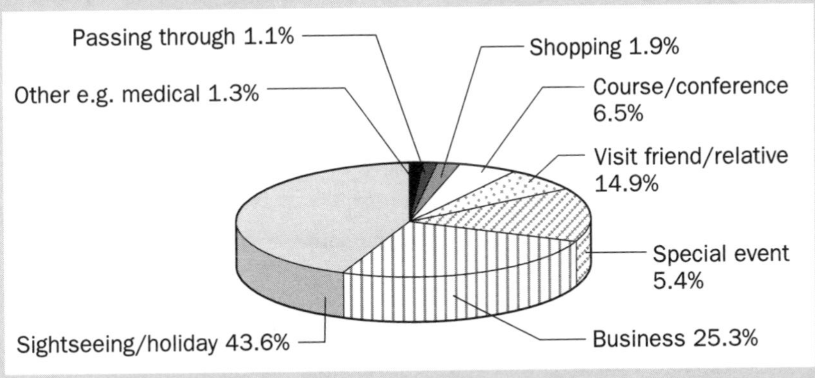

Reasons for visit of people at hotels and guest houses, 1994

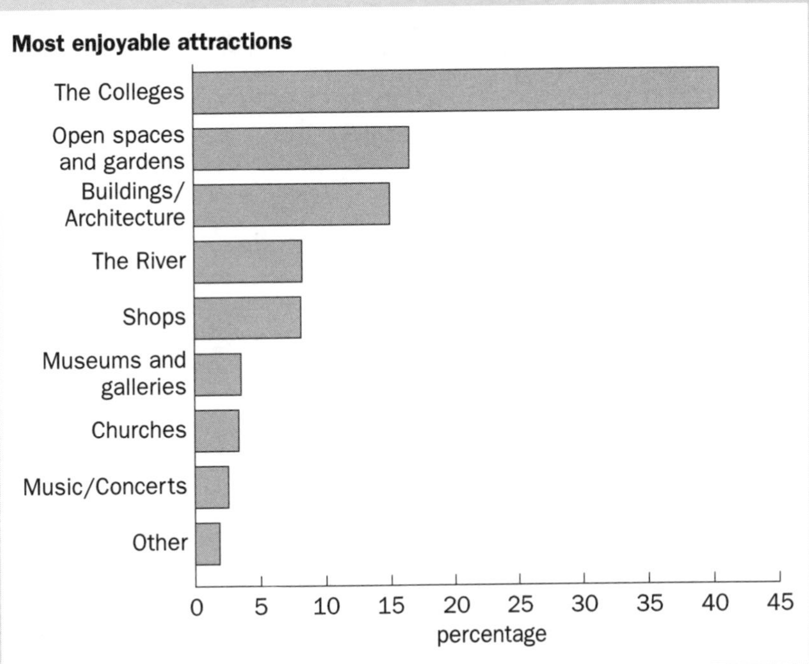

Attractions most enjoyed by staying visitors, 1994

A wider impact

Tourists to Cambridge are selective in their visits to surrounding attractions. Day visitors tend not to venture beyond the 'tourist city' and the 'Guide Friday' bus tour starting from the station.

Most liked features	%	Most disliked features	%
Colleges and buildings	39.7	Traffic, parking streets	15.0
Atmosphere	11.1	Crowds and tourists	6.2
Shopping	7.0	Signposting	3.4
People	5.5	Expensive	3.1
Parks and gardens	4.2	Public transport	2.1
River and punting	4.1	People	1.8
Scenery	4.0	Dirty and noisy	1.8
Quiet and car ban	3.4	Bikes	1.7
Entertainments	2.7	Paying at colleges	1.6
Cleanliness	1.7	Entertainments	1.3

Visitors' top ten likes and dislikes, 1993 – 95

Benefits	Problems
Spending on goods and services	Congestion of people and vehicles
Creates and supports jobs	Disturbance
Supports services used by residents	Wear and tear on buildings and spaces
Raises Cambridge's international profile	Increased public service costs
Promotes contact between cultures	Development pressures
Adds lively cosmopolitan atmosphere	Change of identity and sense of place
Supports conservation	

For Cambridge the issue now is: how can tourism be accommodated through management of supply, demand and its direct impact in a way that ensures sustainability of both the industry itself and Cambridge as a green and civilised city? It is this conflict that the strategy tries to resolve.

Tourism in Cambridge: benefits and problems

The wider leisure city for the local population

The local population, in addition to using the facilities covered by the tourist city, makes use of leisure facilities over a much wider sphere. These include commercially-run activities and a range of public and voluntary facilities, some of which are emphasised as popular venues by the City Council. They offer discount entry tickets e.g. Abbey and Parkside swimming pools, Cambridge Lakes Golf course, Cambridge United Football Ground, Kelsey Kerridge Sports Hall, Cambridge Corn Exchange entertainment, Folk Museum and Flambard Wine Bar.

Grafton Shopping Centre, a sub-centre to the CBD is little used by tourists but heavily used by local people for shopping and leisure.

Leisure facilities on the rural fringe comprise a wide range, from garden centres such as Scotsdale to golf courses, Milton 'Country Park' and pubs and restaurants unknown to 'tourists'.

Such leisure usage supports a greater percentage of workers than tourism and requires a wider infrastructure. It is difficult to quantify since leisure use is integrated with commuting and other uses.

The Cambridge Tourist Strategy Review (1995) also recognises that future demand for leisure is expanding in line with population growth and changes in the age structure of that population.

case study

29.2 Lee Valley Regional Park: leisure space for Greater London

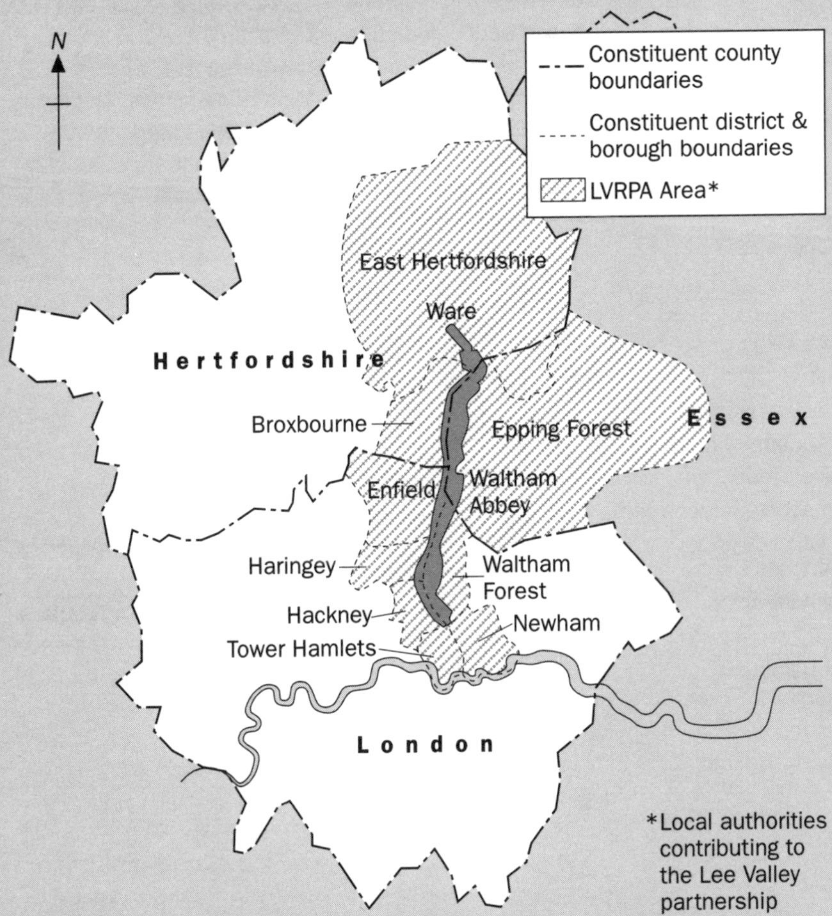

Location

Aim

In 1944 Abercrombie saw it as creating a leisure area for Londoners and rescuing the Lee Valley from years of neglect – **1966 'Lee Valley Regional Park Act'** – the main purpose was to counter the pressures of the expanding metropolis for the development of land for housing, industrial and other purposes and to take a positive approach towards providing opportunities for recreation sport and entertainment and enjoyment of leisure.

Present character

It is a narrow corridor of land and water 23 miles south to north adjacent to the River Lee, hemmed in by urban and industrial development to the south and on its western boundary but with a more rural character in the north and east.

The strategy as seen in 1986 Lee Valley Park Plan – after two decades the Park is still incomplete and the public see it in parts rather than as an entity. As well as providing recreational centres it is intended as a regional reservation of open space – a mosaic of farmland, wildlife habitats, playing fields and spaces offering a wide range of opportunities for land-based outdoor activities from sports to picnicking, nature study, walking, riding and cycling. Particular assets include waterways, flooded gravel and canal towpath.

Lee Navigation Towpath is the only continuous link through the park; access to parts of the Park are poor and need to be improved.

The 1986 Plan addressed several issues:

- conserve existing attractive landscape and give comprehensive landscape treatment to poorly restored gravel workings, glasshouses and chalets; landscape diversity is to be a feature
- improve access especially for walkers and cyclists, horseriders; car access relatively easy and series of parks provided
- range of recreational activities available but a greater emphasis than in the past on open space; opening the Park up to the public for informal recreation
- nature conservation; a range of sites important as nature reserves
- heritage interpretation – has industrial heritage in malt, timber, chemical, explosive and glasshouse industries and a countryside heritage. There are too few interpretive and information facilities offered to visitors interested in heritage sites. Authority will develop visitor centres on heritage themes e.g. recreate a glasshouse nursery, and maltings plus self-guided heritage trails.
- on-going and improving management of the Park.

[redacted]

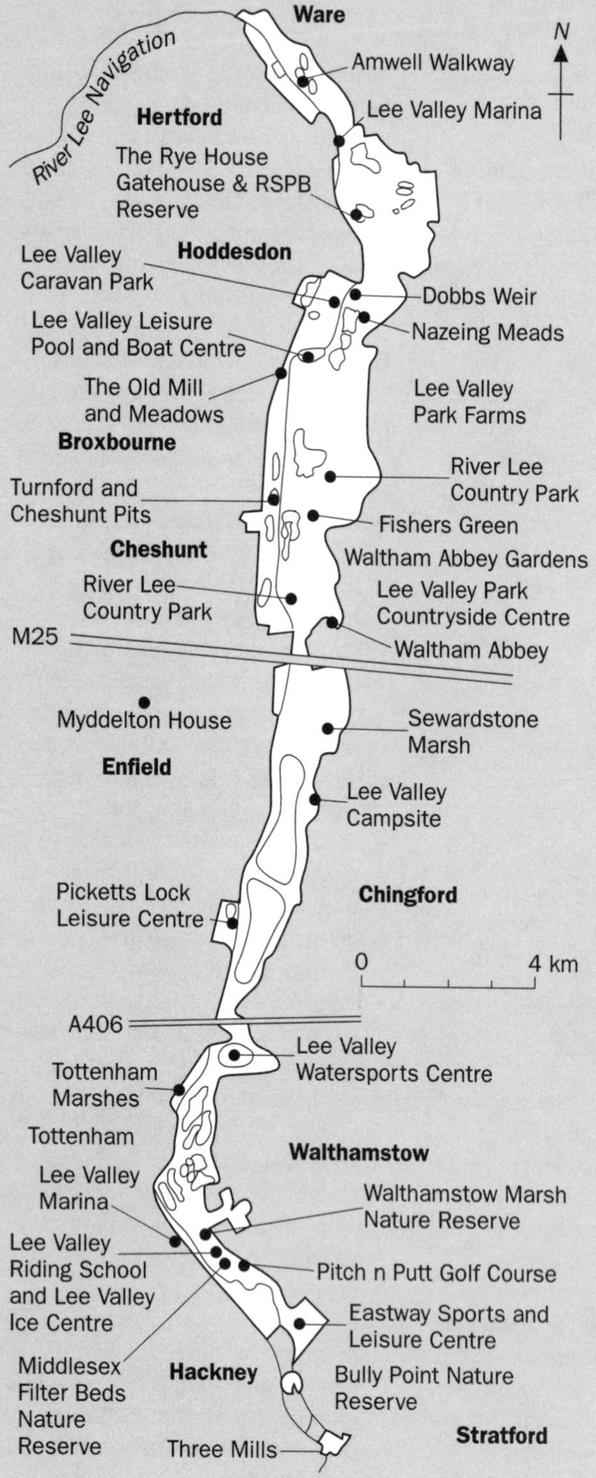

The Lee Valley Park and its facilities

Examples of centre facilities

'Something for everyone' – Leisure, Sports Centres with range of sports facilities, a cycle circuit of 1.6 km, ice skating centre, riding centre, watersports centre, leisure pool, canal boats, countryside centre, angling, a holiday park, countryside and heritage guide, Myddleton House Gardens, 18 hole golf course, a marina, holiday accommodation park – model farm.

1992 – 93 (percentages and total numbers)

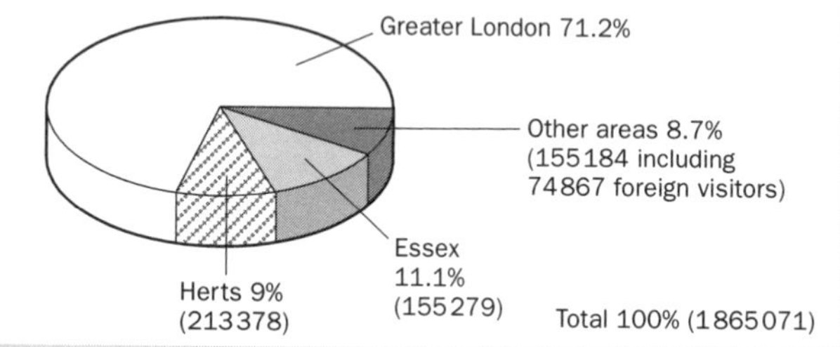

Influx of users

Outdoor activities 1992–93	% of visitors
Walking/rambling	27.2
Cycling	6.9
Golf	8.2
Tennis	7.9
Football	5.4
Fishing	3.8
Others include running, rugby, athletics, bowls	

Outdoor leisure activities regularly visited by population sampled in Lee Valley	% of visitors
Cinema	24.3
Art galleries	12.3
Theatres	20.9
Museums	32.7
Theme parks	21.2
Zoos/safari parks	21.5
Stately homes	25.3
Other places of historic interest	32.2
Other places of natural interest	34.5

case study

29.3 Lake District National Park

National Parks context

Definition

According to National Parks and Access to the Countryside Act 1949, a national park is

- an 'extensive' area of beautiful and relatively wild country in which, for the nation's benefit and by appropriate national decision and action (government policy), the characteristic landscape beauty is strictly preserved
- access and facilities for public open air enjoyment
- wildlife and building and places of architectural and historical interest are suitably protected
- established farming use is effectively maintained.

On-going management

- Each park has a National Park Authority (NPA) but local authorities also have their usual statutory authority inside the park boundary.
- Each NPA produces Structure Plans and subsequent reviews in respect of policy and management, in association with local authorities and landowners. Plans need approval of Department of the Environment, Department of National Heritage, and the Countryside Commission.
- The main task of NPA is to be a 'persuader and negotiator' on use of the park – accommodating a variety of uses of the park and ensuring its sustainability and environment quality. Pressures on the Parks are growing and the NPA needs to negotiate over these, inform and resolve conflicts.

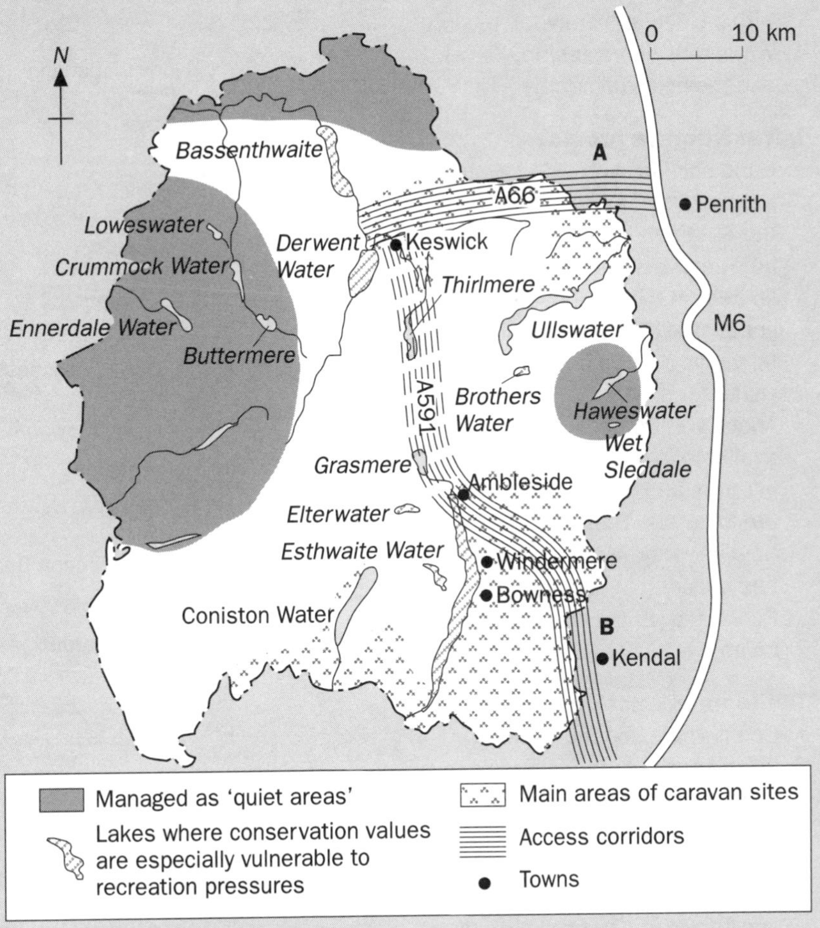

Lake District National Park in Cumbria, North-west England

The Lake District National Park

- The Park was established in 1951 covering approximate 3000 sq km and a resident population of only 42 000 overall.
- It is an outstanding area of upland and lake scenery and a lesser known western coastal belt.
- The main towns are Keswick, Windermere and Ambleside but Kendal and Penrith are closely linked and considered part of the Lake District.
- The west coast just outside the Park was important for coal and iron and steel industries. These have declined but offer industrial heritage sites. In the Park itself upland farming and tourism are the main bases for the economy.

Leisure – tourism aspects

Numbers and location of visitors

- A survey in 1993 estimated the number of visitor days at 15.8 million with a quarter drawn from the large conurbations to the South (e.g. Manchester and Liverpool) and East (e.g. Newcastle). Most came for informal leisure and recreation activities such as walking and sightseeing. About 80% come by car or coach including a significant number of overseas.
- The visitors are unevenly spread being heavily concentrated on the central area from Lake Windermere to Derwent Water

with particular 'honeypot' foci on Windermere, Ambleside, Keswick and the lakeside nearby.

Infrastructure provision

- Good access is provided via the M6 and from this the A591 from the South and A66 from the West but within the Park, access is limited. At the peak season it is congested due to restrictions of terrain and lakes and volume of visitors.
- About 10 000 bed spaces are available, a quarter of which are in farms and guest houses; many are in hotels. There is growing time share provision (now 10% of bed spaces). In and around the Park are a variety of caravan and camp site.

The main attractions

- Countryside, mountains and lakes have substantial public access to open fells, woodlands and lake shores with a dense network of footpaths available; the most important specific sports activities are climbing and water based activities such as sailing.
- There are a variety of specific countryside and historical attractions e.g. Lake District Country Park and Wordsworth's Cottage in Ambleside.
- Towns such as Windermere and Ambleside together with villages are attractions in themselves with a wide range of tourist related shops, activities and facilities.

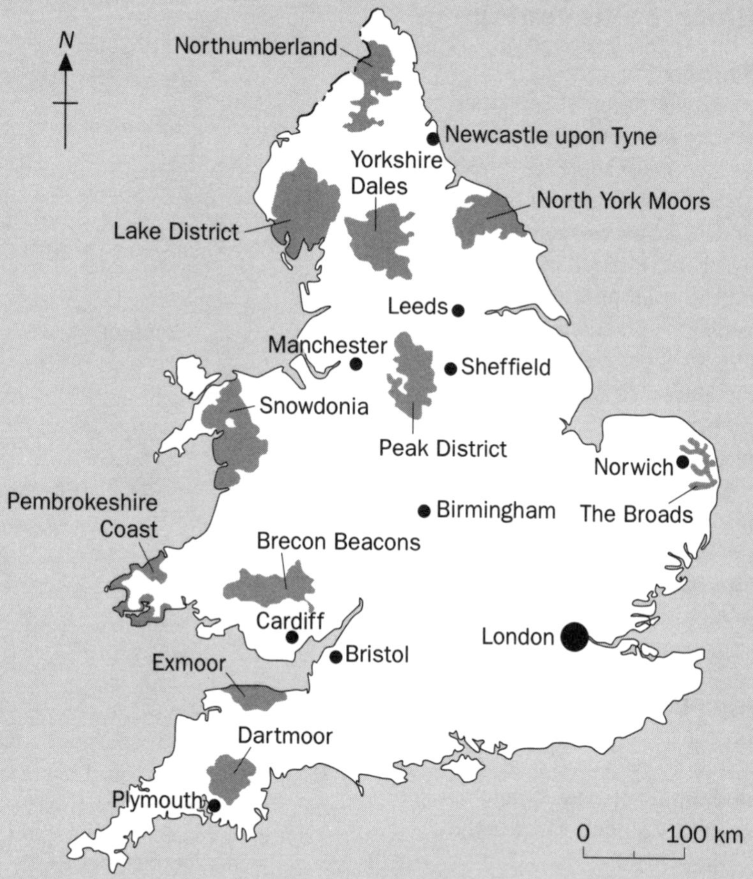

National Parks in England and Wales

Contribution of leisure and tourism in the Lake District

Leisure and tourist expenditure

This is estimated at £262 million – 40% from tourists using hotels and guesthouses but only 12% from day visitors. Of all the expenditure 23% is in shops and 22% in catering outlets.

Actual direct local income

This is estimated at £51 million a significant part of the local economy with 50% of farms receiving some income from leisure and tourism.

For Cumbria as a whole – employment

About 10% of the workforce is directly engaged in leisure and tourism, the percentage being higher inside the National Park boundary. Over 20 000 direct and indirect jobs have been created.

Tourism and leisure activities

These help to support local services such as public transport, a wider range of shops and facilities.

Environmental and community impact

In respect of local communities

- Shopping provision has become very focused on tourism needs in many areas but especially in Ambleside and Bowness possibly to the detriment of local resident needs. It tends also to raise prices of everyday goods in shop.
- Congestion is felt at the height of the season in 'honeypot' sites; traffic pollution and noise lowers the quality of life for local residents.
- Competition for property for holiday cottages, tourism and second home buying contributes to high price of housing and shortage for local buyers/renters.

In respect of environment

- The adverse impact is concentrated at certain locations, mainly along lake shores and valley heads in the central area – footpath erosion and litter are the worst problems, together with traffic congestion – the demand for parking outstrips capacity in some areas. On some lakes such as Windermere, there is a problem of conflict of use and some pollution.
- Problems could be ameliorated by greater management and larger maintenance-inputs but resources available are limited.
- Tourist-leisure income and interest do contribute importantly to safeguarding the overall character of the environment and maintenance and restoration of historic and otherwise redundant buildings.

Management policies

- Disperse visitor pressures spatially by promoting attractions in more peripheral areas e.g. the western side of Lakes and the nearby coast scenery, industrial heritage sites and visits to Sellafield Nuclear Plant.
- Promote winter and off-season breaks to reduce peak season pressure.
- Zone the Park to reduce conflict of use. Set aside parts of the park as 'quiet areas' for those wanting tranquillity and peace. Protect the central and northern uplands from vehicle access wherever possible; access will be by footpath. Increased demand for caravanning and applications from landowners and farmers for site development is limited to 7000 ceiling capacity and to designated parts of the lakes.
- Improve A591, A66 access routes plus parking capacity; limit lorry access.
- Educate and inform the public on responsible use.
- Give more priority to local resident needs.

CHAPTER 30

Global tourism

'There is likely to be a continued increase in mass tourism but the tourist will seek out new venues and new kinds of objects to gaze upon.'

SHAW G AND WILLIAMS A M *CRITICAL ISSUES IN TOURISM*, 1994

30.1 The world's largest industry

According to the World Travel and Tourism Council (1992) tourism has become the world's largest industry on virtually all economic measures – gross output, value added, capital investment, employment and tax contributions. Today it accounts for 12% of all consumer spending and 7% of the world's jobs. Its significance both in terms of size and impact tends to be underestimated because it is such a diversified and fragmented industry. However, its importance varies from country to country both in the developed and developing world. For some, such as Denmark amongst the advanced countries and Ethiopia and Bangladesh amongst the developing countries, for a variety of reasons it makes only a very limited contribution to the economy. For others such as the USA, the UK, Switzerland, Kenya and Bermuda, it is very significant. It is the largest 'commodity' in international trade for a number of countries – Greece, Italy, Spain, Switzerland and most of the Caribbean countries. Tourism is the largest single employer in the USA, the UK, Australia, Canada, Japan, France, Brazil and the Bahamas.

Elements of the tourism industry

Tourism resources
- Natural resources
- Human resources

General and tourism infrastructure
- Means of communication and travel
- Social installations
- Basic installations
- Telecommunications

Receptive facilities
- Hotels, guest houses, towns and villages
- Condominiums
- Complementary residences
- Residences for receptive personnel
- Food and beverage installations

Entertainment and sports facilities
- Recreational and cultural facilities
- Sports facilities

Tourism reception services
- Travel agencies
- Hotel and local promotional offices
- Information offices
- Car hire
- Guides, interpreters

[SOURCE: Sessa A *Elements of Tourism Economics*, 1993]

Tourism supply is a result of all those productive activities including provision of goods and services required to meet tourism demand and which is expressed in tourist consumption.

While the importance of tourism may vary from country to country, what is apparent is that almost every country would like to expand its tourist sector. Especially since the 1970s, a continually increasing number of countries, most of them developing countries, have become important 'players' in the global tourist industry.

> Most travel professionals and government officials feel tourism is at least benign, and at best, one of the most positive contributors to local and regional economies ever conceived. It seems that everyone wants tourists – and the more of them the better. They spend hard cash, solve local unemployment problems by employing relatively unskilled workers, and developers and their financial backers pump millions of dollars into the economies of growing destinations.
>
> [SOURCE: Theobald W F (ed) *Global Tourism – The Next Decade*, 1994]

The growth of mass global tourism

Global tourism as we know it today developed from the 1950s and was mainly focused on Mediterranean resorts. From there it has spread to the USA and the Caribbean and since the 1980s, to developing world countries and to long haul destinations in Australia and New Zealand. In 1965 there were 144 million international tourists; now there are over 400 million (Figure 30.1). Most are from West European countries. Although significant, the number from the USA is a surprisingly smaller fraction of domestic tourist numbers, mainly because the USA is big enough and varied enough to cater for most holiday needs. The Japanese are increasingly holidaying abroad and numbers from developing countries, though rising, are still small, estimated at less than 10% of total numbers.

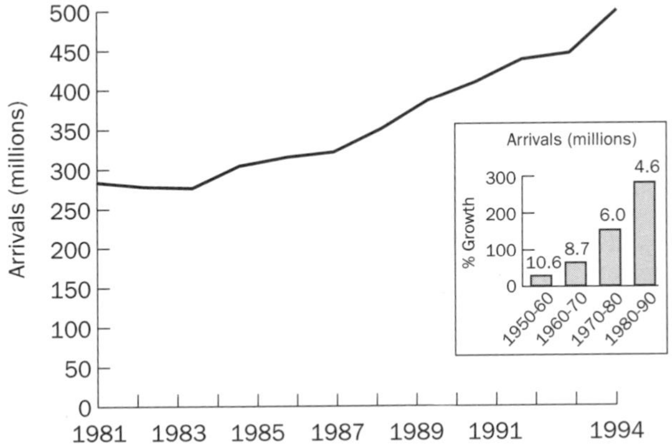

NOTE: World Travel and Tourism anticipate number of International tourists will almost double in 15 years reaching 937 million by the year 2010. By the mid 1990s world tourism 23% faster than the world economy as a whole.

[SOURCE: World Travel Organisation]

Figure 30.1 Growth trends in international tourism by arrivals world-wide, 1981 – 94

With the advent of mass tourism the character of tourists changed from the traditional individuals seeking travel and new cultural experiences to standardised consumers of 'sun, sea and entertainment' and in the winter, 'sun, snow and ski slopes'. Shaw and Williamson see tourism as yet another facet of the mass consumption society and the tertiarisation of the world economy. The suppliers, in response to an increasingly universal style of passive and active leisure needs brought about by the media, advertising and increasing contact between societies, have provided the standard package holiday at an affordable price and guaranteed quality. As the demand for overseas package holidays increased, so tour operators could benefit from scale economies, bringing the price down even further in real terms and within affordable reach of more and more people.

The main characteristics of mass tourism

- The sheer numbers involved mean that the tourism product has to be offered under conditions of mass production
- There is a growing level of expenditure on consumer goods associated with tourism, i.e. surf boards for the beach holiday and skis and skiing accessories for the winter holiday
- A few producers dominate particular markets; Disney in the world of theme parks, and travel companies such as Thomson and Neckermann in the world of package holidays in Europe
- Producers take the lead in developing new tourism attractions, whether opening up new mass destinations such as Thailand, the Gambia and Turkey, or in designing new theme parks such as Euro-Disney
- By and large, mass tourism products are little differentiated: the Mediterranean beach holiday offers much the same mix of architecture, facilities, food and drink and entertainment whether it is located in Turkey, Greece or Spain.

[SOURCE: Shaw G and Williams A M *Critical Issues in Tourism*, 1994]

> Successful growth of tourism in the period following the Second World War has indeed been price led, based on the tour operator's ability to deliver inaccessible warm climate destination's at prices affordable by the vast majority of people in North Europe and North America. To do this operators needed to achieve economies of scale on charter flights and a large allocation of resort hotels at low rates from hoteliers dependent on low wage levels and favourable exchange rates. As a result tourists are given 3-star quality at prices that would hardly pay for a guest house in their own countries.
>
> [SOURCE: Theobald W F (ed) *Global Tourism – The Next Decade*, 1994]

It is useful to group factors accounting for the growth of international tourism into demand and supply factors and the intermediate facilitating factors which bring demand and supply together (Figure 30.2).

There is also the smaller but significant alternative tourism, for which the formative factors are rather different. These are niche tourist markets giving particular kinds of travel experiences different from those in the standard package holidays and are designed to meet individual and small group needs. There are an increasing number of specialist tour operators serving this niche market.

Alternative tourism

It is now commonplace to find reference to a set of new (or even post-modern) forms of tourism promoted as flexible and individually centred (in contrast to the rigid and packaged mass or old tourism) and offered by small tour companies as 'designed' or customised tours.

New tourism involves market niches and a new A – Z of tourism has emerged including academic, adventure, anthro, archaeo, eco, ethnic, nature, scientific, wildlife and so on, together with less formalised 'back packing' and travelling.

[SOURCE: Munt I *Third World Tourism – A Great Escape?, Town and Country Planning*, 1992]

Supply factors

- Total package available to suit consumer tastes leaving little for the tourist to do except book, pay and enjoy.
- Provision of adequate infrastructure in receiving countries e.g. upgrading and increase in capacity of Malaga airport on the Costa del Sol and dual 'carriage way' of the N21 coastal road linking resorts.
- A range of tourist resorts on offer providing quality accommodation at reasonable prices, entertainment, beach facilities and provision for other tourist needs such as a wide variety of eating places and drink establishments, some in the traditional or pseudo-traditional style of the local culture but many in the familiar western style of the tourist's own country.
- Optional excursions and experiences in response to increasing demand for some change from the beach, pool, hotel experience – including development of new attractions such as the theme park.
- An ever widening range of destination choices as tourists tire of the established but 'worn' mass tourist destinations especially those around the Mediterranean, e.g. Goa on the west coast of India was marketed from 1987 as a mass tourist destination at a cost comparable to the Mediterranean tourist resorts due to the starting up of charter flights, the building of the familiar western tourist hotels and to the facilities combined with a cheap supply of labour. Yet Goa also offered the 'exotic' experience increasingly sought.
- Increased catering for all year round tourism to meet the second holiday, short break demand with cheap off-season packages including longer stays for the retired wishing to avoid the 'harsh' winters back home.

Intermediate linking factors

- More political stability in the world in general.
- Emergence of the large-scale tour operators such as Cooks and Thomson Holidays able to provide mass package holidays at increasingly cheaper real prices – largest operate in an integrated way across the total tourist spectrum from travel agent shop to leasing or owning charter planes to controlling hotels in tourist destinations. Ability to advertise widely to inform potential customers as to what is on offer and influence demand.
- Development of air charter plane travel and later jet travel offering comfort, increasingly speedier travel at lower real prices. Advent of the jumbo jet and larger fuel tank/range capacity allowed economies of scale to operate on short haul flights and over long distance flights, bringing long haul flights into the cheap charter flight bracket. Charter travel costs are now lower in real terms than ten years ago.
- A revolution in communications between demand and supply via teletext, computer screen, fax and phone. Use of credit card speeded up transactions and made booking and paying for a holiday easier together with further expenditure while on holiday.

Demand factors

The level of demand is sensitive to the effects of economic recession, to changing fashions and popularity of particular holiday destinations (e.g. 1984 – 90 package holiday trade from the UK to Spain fell 30%). Also sensitive to sudden political instability at any holiday destination.

- Rise in disposable incomes with an increasing proportion spent on leisure.
- Increased leisure time with the 'shorter working week' and increased weeks with paid holiday.
- Rising expectations and aspirations in respect of holiday experiences with overseas locations being regarded as exotic and different with guaranteed sun, sand and entertainment at what is regarded as an affordable price (fed by media images and tourist brochures).
- As population age structure matures there is a higher proportion of the population with more leisure time due to early retirement and with occupational pensions providing more disposable income.

Figure 30.2 Factors influencing the growth of mass tourism

30.2 Global tourism: spatially concentrated or polarised

Global tourism is concentrated spatially by country and within countries on particular areas (Figure 30.3). Urry (1990) attributes this to the way the big tourist operators have *'signposted the potential tourist's gaze'*. Since the 1950s the 'tourist image makers' in Europe have largely promoted beach and ski holidays. There are only a limited supply of locations which can provide the desired conditions. The pattern of location of mass tourist destinations is largely determined by three factors:

- availability of the combination of natural conditions desired by the potential tourist and fostered by multinational tour operators
- a location sufficiently close to market demand for the destination to be affordable
- a location where the necessary large scale of infrastructure and facilities have been built.

1992 Source of tourists for selected destinations (by millions)

Destination	Sources	
Spain (total = 53 mill)	France	12.0
	Portugal	10.5
	Germany	7.5
	UK	6.1
	Sweden	3.4
UK (total = 17 mill)	France	2.3
	Germany	2.1
	USA	2.3
	Ireland	1.3
	Neths	1.1
Mexico	USA	87%
Bermuda	USA	84%
Australia (total = 2.4 mill)	Japan	0.52
	New Zealand	0.48
	UK	0.26
	USA	0.27

Figure 30.3 Mass tourist destinations

Global tourism is largely concentrated around the Mediterranean and at locations in the USA. Other major destinations include the Alpine region of Western Europe (Switzerland and Austria) which has a double tourist season of winter ski holidays and summer mountain and lake scenery holidays.

The UK stands rather apart from other destinations since it has no guaranteed summer sun and only limited winter skiing; its attractions and marketing are based on a combination of historical heritage and historical links, varied scenery within short travelling distances and proximity to major market demand countries. Canada has spectacular scenery attractions and is close to the major USA market.

Travel survey: Visits to UK fail to counter growth in departures

Holiday exodus costs Britain £4.5 bn a year

British travellers

- to France and Spain
- on holiday
- in the summer
- spent £363 per visit
- stayed on average 11 nights
- mainly aged 25 – 55

The bad news for the Exchequer is that Britons travelling abroad spend £4.5 bn more while away than their foreign counterparts do while here, £14.5 bn as opposed to £9.92 bn.

It has not always been so, however. Prior to 1981 the reverse had been the case, though since then the gap in expenditure has widened mirroring the growing number of Britons going abroad.

The number of visits overseas by Britons now outstrips those by foreigners to Britain by nearly two to one, 40 million visits abroad compared to 21 million coming here.

However, the fact that we tend to spend on average £363 each time, while our foreign counterparts fork out £467, explains why the gap in expenditure is considerably less than the number of visits might suggest.

[SOURCE: *The Independent* 9.11.95]

Within countries the pattern of tourism is very uneven, being concentrated on a few major areas. For example, the Spanish Balearic islands have 47 bed spaces per sq.km whereas Spain has only two. This concentration is determined by the three conditions for the successful development of a mass tourist resort area noted above, including accessibility. Once established, the resort area benefits from the scale economies of agglomeration bringing down costs and prices charged to tourists.

The location pattern within a familiar conceptual framework

It is possible to view the spatial pattern of mass tourism within the same familiar context used for the spatial pattern of other economic activities.

Certain locations benefit from initial comparative advantages and to these are added derived advantages as the locations are developed. A cumulative causation process is thus set in motion, leading to the concentration of tourist activity in a few locations. However, as with the concentration of any economic activity, with time diseconomies begin to set in prompting some decentralisation of tourism to areas around and search for alternative tourist 'growth poles', a search initiated by the major tourist operators.

A product cycle for the tourist industry

Changes in fashion and demand within the main tourist markets in Europe and North America can set up diseconomies. Thus the growth and relative decline of older tourist centres should also be seen within the context of the product cycle. The tourist looks for a new kind of experience including some of the familiar ingredients which the tour operator supplies at an affordable price. Since the mid-1980s there has been an extension of mass tourism to new long distance and more exotic destinations such as Florida and East African countries like Kenya (Case study 30.2), and most recently, destinations such as Goa in India, Thailand and Australia. These destinations had hitherto been reserved for 'elite tourism' since the price was beyond the reach of the mass tourist.

Development of charter flights using long haul jumbo jet aircraft have effectively brought these further destinations within affordable reach of the mass tourist market. Enlargement and development of resorts through the collaborative efforts of large-scale tourist operators and the government and private sector in the host countries have brought scale economies, lowering the prices at the resort without sacrificing quality. Hence these long distance mass tourist destinations are very competitively priced compared to older Mediterranean resort areas. However, having suffered some decline in tourist numbers, older resorts are responding to this new competition in ways similar to those adopted in the case of old industrial regions and declining town centres – refurbishment, modernisation, environment 'clean-up' and enhancement, and creating a new image for themselves through high profile marketing.

Global tourism is characterised by market segmentation

The major tourist market demand arises from the advanced countries because their populations have the disposable income and desire to travel abroad for their holidays. However, volume of demand in any individual country is also determined by population size, the variety of opportunity for tourism inside the country itself.

When examining in more detail the actual global flow of tourists it is clear the market is highly segmented. Main tourist destination countries are dominated by flows from nearby countries. For example, Canada and Mexico depend on tourist demand from the USA while Mediterranean countries are dependent mainly on tourists from the UK, France and Germany. The majority of the seven million Japanese tourists travelling abroad go to nearby South East Asian countries or Australia. This is largely to do with keeping travel costs to a minimum but is also associated with tourists feeling that nearby countries are more familiar. Tourist operators concentrate on and develop the market for a few tourist destinations as this is more cost effective.

However for receiving countries, dependence on a very limited segment of the market has drawbacks. For example, recession in a main market demand country can severely reduce the flow of tourists from there. If a major tourist company in one of the sending countries decides to withdraw or curtail its operations in the tourist resort destinations in a country, this too can have a serious effect. Spain, Italy and Greece have over recent years lost some of their percentage share of tourists from their major West European markets. As a result, now efforts are made to reduce over-dependence on a limited part of the market. New markets are cultivated, such as in Scandinavia and Eastern Europe.

30.3 The resort destination life cycle and the impact of mass tourism

On the basis of what has happened to the earlier developed tourist areas, Briggs has produced a useful life cycle model for tourist resorts which may be applied more widely to tourist regions (Figure 30.5). He traces the development of a tourist resort from its infancy when only a few visitors arrive, drawn by the particular attractiveness of this location. Facilities gradually improve on a small scale to meet visitor needs, as was the case for example of Benidorm on the Costa Blanca in the early 1950s. Then simply a small fishing village bordered by fine sandy beaches and with warm sunny summers, it attracted a few tourists. By the 1970s it had developed into a sprawling modern resort of high rise hotels with all the facilities desired by the mass tourist. By the 1980s it had reached Brigg's stage of 'consolidation' with maximum capacity reached. By the late 1980s Benidorm had begun to stagnate and decline in importance. The Spanish government, supported by European funding and in collaboration with the private sector and major tour operators has taken steps to rejuvenate Benidorm and other centres as tourist resorts (Case study 30.1).

While Spain and other established Mediterranean tourist regions such as Greece illustrate the full tourist region life cycle, other regions in the world can be identified as having passed through only part of the cycle. Kenya may already have reached the

Economic

Positive	Negative
Increases gross domestic product directly and indirectly via multiplier Taxes on tourism increases government revenue Increased foreign exchange earnings Creates employment including in unskilled occupations Helps fund new infrastructure and facilities which locals can also use Stimulated economic activity in other sectors – local craft revival, manufacturers, services and agriculture May act as seed bed for entrepreneurship with spin-offs into other sectors	May divert government expenditure from other needy areas of the economy Requires government expenditure on tourism Overdependence on outside agencies and some external control on the economy Income reduced by 'leakages' or outflows Overstretches infrastructure Spread effects limited and may therefore increase regional inequalities between tourist growth areas and lagging periphery Diverts labour and resources away from non-tourist regions and may particularly affect peripheral areas leading to outmigration to tourist resort opportunities Labour unskilled and seasonal Foreign personnel dominate managerial and higher paid posts reducing opportunities for locals

Social

Positive	Negative
Cultural exchange stimulated with broadening of horizons and reduction of prejudices amongst tourist visitors and host population May enhance role of women in society and status as opportunity for goals in tourism created and outlook widened Encourages education Encourages travel and mobility and social integration	May cause polarisation between population in advancing tourist regions and lagging areas, creating a 'dual society' Breakdown of traditional family values creates material aspirations Breakdown of families due to stress between younger generation affected by imported culture as opposed to older members of household Social pathology including an increase in prostitution, drugs and petty crime

Cultural

Positive	Negative
May save aspects of indigenous culture due to tourist interest in them Contact with other cultures may enrich domestic culture through new ideas and customs introduced Encourages contact and harmonious relations between people of different cultures	Impact of commercialisation may lead to pseudo-cultural activities to entertain tourist and at extreme may cause disappearance of indigenous culture Mass tourism may create antagonist reactions from host population concerned for traditional values, etc

Environment

Positive	Negative
Improved landscaping and architectural standards in resort areas including increased local funding for improvement of local housing, etc Promotes interest in monuments and historic buildings and funding to conserve and maintain them May induce tighter environmental legislation to protect environment Establishment of nature reserves and national parks plus growing tourist interest in it protects areas from economic and building encroachment	Poor building and infrastructure development – tourist complexes do not integrate with local architecture Destruction of natural environment and wildlife habitat – marine coastal and inland Excessive pressure leads to air, land and water pollution and breakdown in water supplies, etc

(Based on a World Tourist Organisation classification)

Figure 30.4 *Impact of mass tourism on a region or country*

stage of stagnation, having gone through the cycle in a much shorter period than the Mediterranean resort areas (Case study 30.2). Florida is now well into the development stage with as yet little sign of stagnation. For example, package holidays from the UK to the USA quadrupled between 1986 to 1990 to 472 000, while package holiday visits to Spain fell from 4.7 to 2.8 million.

a Tourist Area/Resort Life Cycle Model

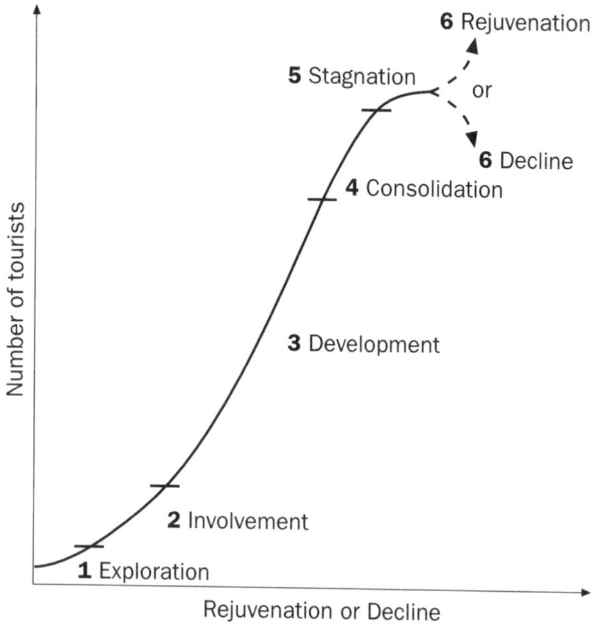

b Stages in the development of a tourist area or resort

1 **Exploration**: small number of visitors attracted by natural beauty or cultural characteristics – numbers are limited and few tourist facilities exist.
2 **Involvement**: limited involvement by local residents to provide some facilities for tourists – recognisable tourist season and market areas begin to emerge.
3 **Development**: Large numbers of tourists arrive, control passes to external organisations and there is increased tension between locals and tourists.
4 **Consolidation**: tourism has become a major part of the local economy, although rates of visitor growth have started to level off and some older facilities are seen as second-rate.
5 **Stagnation**: peak numbers of tourists have been reached, although the resort is no longer considered fashionable and turnover of business properties tends to be high.
6 **Decline** or **rejuvenation**: attractiveness continues to decline, visitors are lost to other resorts, and the resort becomes more dependent on day visitors and weekend recreationalists from a limited geographical area – long-term decline will continue unless action is taken to rejuvenate the area and modernise as a tourist destination.

Figure 30.5 Development of a tourist area or resort

A number of locations may be recognised as possibly in the very early stages of the life cycle, though they may be deliberately limited by the government to niche or select tourist development to avoid the problems associated with mass tourism. The Zimbabwe government for example rejected mass tourism, having seen its results in Kenya but because of its desperate need of foreign currency, it has allowed a limited number of package tours to Victoria Falls (Case study 30.2) and is now selectively developing other potential sites such as the area around the Great Zimbabwe Ruins, a World Heritage site in the south of the country. Some Latin American countries such as Guyana and Chile may be placed in the very early stages of the cycle with much by way of scenery and culture to offer, but as yet attracting relatively few tourists who must travel by expensive scheduled air flights.

Factors contributing to the relative decline of established mass tourist areas

The established Mediterranean region and its resorts are no longer the only ones offering the benefits of a major tourist region. New mass resort destinations are now available, for example the Turkish coast and Eliat in the East Mediterranean and Florida in the USA. Tourists have a wider choice and may thus change to these newer centres. The uniqueness of older centres has worn off and newer centres are perceived as better value for money, including long haul destinations.

The concept of what constitutes an enjoyable value for money holiday has changed. Increasing numbers of tourists now take their cars abroad for more mobility, choice and camp or rent accommodation. France, which is conveniently located in respect of ferry routes and more geared to these types of holiday, has benefited whereas Spain has been less successful, attracting only 1.8 million independent UK tourists in 1990 compared to France's 3.1 million.

Newer tourist destinations, in particular Florida, offer a greater variety of holiday experiences, in particular, theme parks as well as sand, sun and the sea. Long haul destinations, such as Goa are more exotic destinations and seem to have more status amongst friends and neighbours.

The swing away from the coastal resort based package holiday has also been affected by demographic factors. The generation now taking family holidays (25 – 45 years age group), took the Mediterranean holiday for granted in their teens, are used to foreign travel and feel more confident than their parents about trying something different.

Florida – Capital of the Theme Park World

Florida is the capital of the theme park world, home to Disney World, the Disney theme park, Universal Studios and Sea World; it will be joined in 1999 by Universal's Islands, a $26 billion venture between Rank Organisation, the UK leisure and entertainments group and MCA. Disney is also planning to spend an estimated $750 million on a wild animal theme park in Florida.

The 'Drawing Power' of Florida and its Theme Parks

It is the old honeypot theory and it works. People go out there for a week and they go somewhere different every day (Mr B Richards of Tourism Research and Marketing).

[SOURCE: *Financial Times* 16.8.95]

Ageing of older resorts makes them less attractive. They are less able to meet the rising expectations of tourists. Hotels built in the 1970s are in need of refurbishment; decor and facilities are below the quality of those in newer resorts. With 'price cutting wars' and higher labour costs as wages rise, there have not been the profit margins allowing upgrading of facilities. The same applies to the infrastructure, entertainment and other services offered at the resort itself. The host population and workers may be less welcoming to tourists as numbers reach saturation capacity for the resort.

Deterioration in the atmosphere and environment of established resort areas is further emphasised by the increased environmental awareness of the potential tourists, engendered by increased media cover given to environmental and health matters. Established resort areas, especially around the Mediterranean, have acquired both a real and exaggerated reputation for poor standards of hygiene and safety in hotels are associated with overcrowding of resorts and beaches, half finished hotels and dusty construction sites. The environment and atmosphere have been spoilt by uncontrolled spread of building along coastlines and pollution of coastal waters through waste discharge.

As package tour prices have fallen, this has let in large numbers of younger tourists whose style of holidaying is focused on the pool and beach during the day and the bar and disco at night. This has increased the unattractiveness of established resorts for families and older couples who traditionally make up much of the package holiday market. As a result, increasing numbers have deserted the familiar but overdeveloped tourist areas for newer alternative tourist areas.

30.4 Rejuvenating older resort areas

As tourists and tour operators move to other holiday destinations or other types of holidays, the established tourist areas remain. Tourism is too important to the economy and the livelihood of the local people to allow it to decline (Case study 30.1). Strategies have thus to be developed to enable the earlier mass tourist regions to survive and remain competitive. Over the last two or three years, policies for rejuvenation and their effects are increasingly evident across the Mediterranean region and in older winter Alpine ski resorts where stagnation and decline have threatened.

Policies have been centred on a number of interrelated elements: finding new markets, upgrading and refurbishing resort facilities, tighter environmental controls and more careful sympathetic zoning of any new developments, provision of new and more varied sports and other activities, promoting the heritage and other attractions of areas in the hinterland of coastal tourist regions and designating some areas as nature and conservation areas to prevent the sprawl of tourist developments and enhance the attractiveness of the region. All of these are evident in Spain's attempt to maintain its position as one of the world's leading tourist regions (Case study 13.1).

Effects

The experiences of older resort areas would appear to offer valuable lessons for countries where mass tourism is only just beginning to take hold, in particular, for developing world countries which see the tourist industry as an important source of revenue and a way of advancing economic development. These lessons include avoiding overdependence on particular tourist markets and on tourism at the expense of other sectors of the economy, such as advancement of agriculture and industry. Countries should also try to avoid too much external control of their tourist industry. However, collaboration with external tour operators is still essential if a country is to reach customers and market its tourism in the advanced countries which currently have around 90% of the international tourist market.

There is an essential need to maintain and enhance the quality of tourist destinations, manage the environment with sensitivity and pay due regard to the needs and wishes of host communities. There is also a need to see the benefits of tourism spread beyond the locality of the tourist resort or area into the wider region, linking up with and complementing other sectors of the economy.

However, it is apparent in some parts of the developing world that some of the serious problems evident in the older Mediterranean resort areas are already evident. Further, because of the greater cultural gap between western and tropical societies and the more fragile nature of tropical environments additional problems have emerged (Case study 30.3).

30.5 Increasing developing world involvement in tourism

An increasing number of developing countries want a share of the world's fastest growing market (Figure 30.9). While tourism in the developing world is increasing rapidly, only China, Mexico and Hong Kong appear among the world's top 20 tourist countries on the basis of number of arrivals. Although many of the poorer countries may have the natural and cultural potential to attract tourists, they lack the finance, expertise and infrastructure needed for any significant expansion of tourism. Some also suffer from remoteness and political instability (Case study 30.2).

(World Tourism Organisation)

Year	Thousands
1990	454 800
2000	637 000
2010	937 000

Figure 30.9 *Projected growth in international tourism arrivals*

The economic benefits of a tourist industry are readily apparent from established tourist countries, such as Spain, and within the developing world. However, in the case of countries such as Kenya where a mass tourist industry has already been established, the problems which have ensued were either not envisaged or were accepted as an inevitable price to be paid.

Countries such as Zimbabwe, hope to avoid its detrimental effects by more careful management and tighter control of the industry. Others hope to earn badly needed foreign exchange without at the same time destroying their natural resource base by embracing eco-tourism, currently the fastest growing segment of the world tourist industry (Case study 30.3).

Concluding comment

It is inevitable that tourism will greatly expand in the developing world as a whole and that an increasing number of countries will be involved in it. The more meaningful debate will centre round whether these countries are able to avoid the problems of mass tourism of the type all too evident today by concentrating on alternative tourism.

Given however, that as incomes rise more and more people in the developing world itself will be seeking recreation, leisure and tourism, a whole new set of opportunities and potential problems are also on the horizon. The experiences of countries in the developed world in meeting needs and accommodating the pressures may well provide valuable lessons for developing countries in the not too distant future.

case study

30.1 Spain: the location and changing character of tourism with reference to the Costa del Sol

Spanish tourist industry is promoted through the State Turespaña, part of the Ministry of Commerce, but all the regional governments have their own departments dealing with the development of tourism in their areas.

Importance

Costa Del Sol's contribution to Andalusia

Until the development of tourism, Andalusia's economy was dependent on agriculture. This, however, offered limited returns due to a long history of overexploitation and erosion of the land, with too little investment from frequently absent landlords. The infrastructure was also poorly developed. Most of the wealth was centred on Seville, the region's capital.

Currently the region still has a relatively high unemployment rate (3 × the European Union average) and a Gross Domestic product only 40% of European average. Andalusia lagged behind the rest of Spain for centuries.

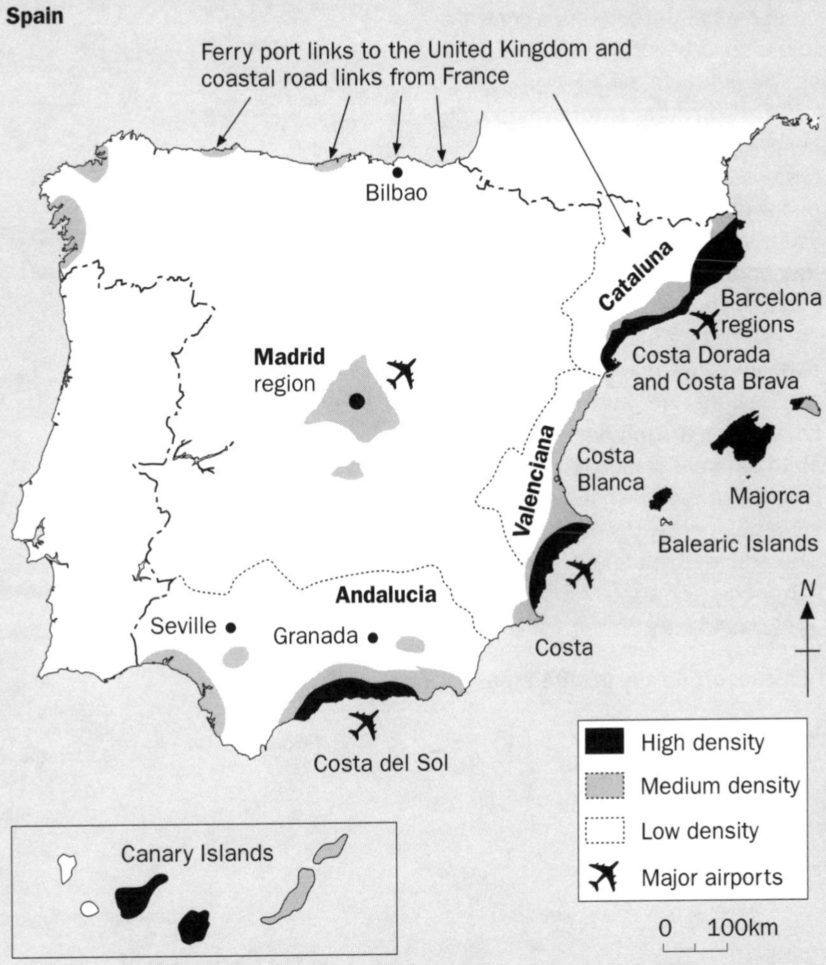

Spatial polarisation of tourism in Spain

Spain: number of visitors, 1993

Visitors	(mills)	Receipts (mill $)	Countries of tourists (1993)	(% of total)	Contribution to the economy (1993)	% of GDP compared to other sectors
1984 – 43	931 658	7 716	France	21.1	Direct tourist income	8.3*
1991 – 53	494 964	19 004	Portugal	19.8	Total services	63.5
1992 – 55	330 710	21 034	Germany	15.2	Construction	8.7
1993 – 57	263 351	23 524	UK	13.1	Industry	24.1
1994 – 61	400 000*	26 808	Benelux	6.3	Agriculture	3.7
(*approx 8% of world total)			Italy	3.5	(*Tourism is significantly more important than the figure suggests as it contributes indirectly also to the service, construction and industry sectors)	
			Scandinavia	2.9		
			Others	18.1		

Agriculture and tourism account for most of region's income but prosperity at the coast is a contrast to the poverty and lack of infrastructure in the interior.

The region suffers from inadequate communications. Until recently, farming concentrated on olive, vine and wheat production, inadequate water supply and an inadequately trained workforce.

Tourism brought a measure of prosperity to the coast and more job opportunity, mainly in unskilled occupations. However, it drained labour from the interior with abandonment of land. Economic benefits of tourism have not spread inland; the potential of Seville and Granada areas not been developed.

Over-concentration of tourism on the Costa del Sol east and west of Malaga led to overdevelopment of the coast and abandonment of traditional fishing activities. There has been some development of horticulture to supply hotels. Investment will lead to a more diversified economy and development inland.

By % of tourists staying in each region

Cataluña	25.6	Coastal tourist regions estimated generates 80% of tourist income in Spain
Valenciana	15.6	
Andalusia	14.2	
Balearic Islands	17.0	
Canaries	13.6	
Madrid region	7.1	

Relative importance of regions, 1993

Saturation, stagnation and environmental stress

The Costa del Sol has a tarnished image. Between 1986 and 1990 there was a decline in number of tourists by 2 million.

Environmental pressures on the Costa del Sol

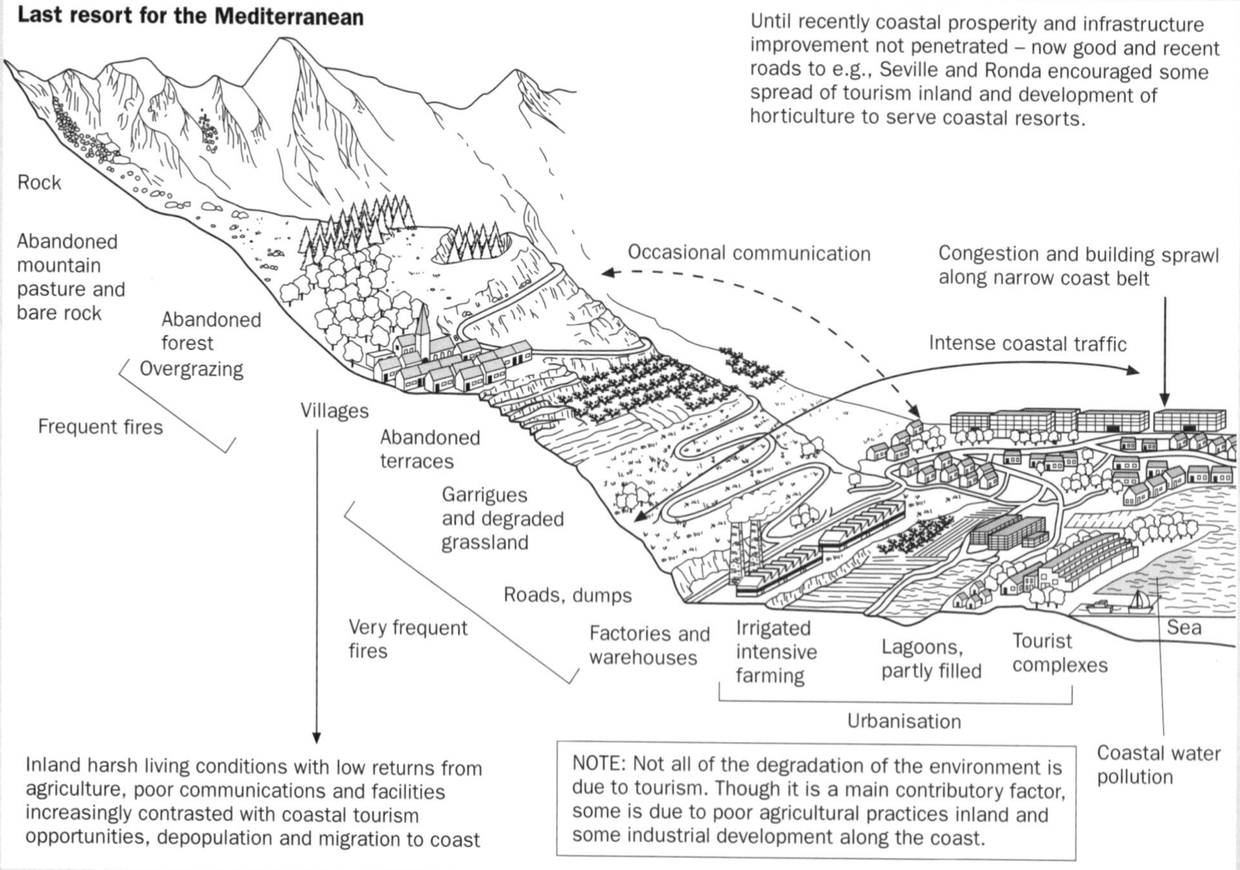

Successful regeneration in the 1990s for Spain including Costa del Sol

After a short 'stagnation' period at the end of the 1980s when the future of the package holiday sector seemed in doubt, the tourist industry in Spain had recovered and continued to expand in the 1990s due to a combination of circumstances.

A continuous rise in numbers and receipts from tourism to 1994 with tourism accounted for 20% of GDP that year. It also accounts for 10% of total employment (800 000 direct jobs and 540 000 indirectly.

The recession of the late 1980s helped to stabilise wage rates and prices. Cost and exchange rate movements helped remove the threat of Spain pricing itself out of the tourist market. The value of the peseta 1990s declined against German and French currencies reducing costs for tourists.

Yugoslavia, Israel and Egypt diverted tourists back to Spain during the 1990s political upheaval.

New markets promoted by the Spanish Tourist Department compensated for some loss from traditional markets such as the UK.

Although the package tourist business continues to underpin the Spanish tourist industry, national and regional governments are taking steps to diversify the types of tourism on offer.

New marketing strategies have been developed to improve image, promote other areas, and other types of tourism such as green tourism and artistic heritage tourism. It promoted the northern Cantabrian coast, established National Parks, and inland centres such as Madrid, Seville, Granada and Cordoba.

EU regional funding and government grants were used to improve established coastal resorts and types of package holidays on offer.

There has been direct investment on improving infrastructure, updating and increasing attraction of promenades, shopping precincts, insertion of parks, flower displays and clean up of beaches e.g. £111 million was invested in the Balearic Islands. Hotels were refurbished.

More water sport, adventure sports and theme parks were added. Special holiday packages have been promoted, such as golf holidays and a new marina at Magaluf (Majorca).

Stricter controls on noise pollution and new developments have been encouraged. High rise development has been curtailed and natural zones conserved to prevent sprawl.

case study

30.2 **Tourism in Africa**

Kenya: saturation point?

Attractions

- scenic – combination of fine sandy beaches and coral coastline, with Savanna wildlife parks and snow-capped mountain peaks
- sunny climate with temperature 26°C all year round
- perceived as a different exotic location enhanced by television and films
- African culture especially Masaai who are perceived as friendly people.

A mass tourist destination

The first charter flights were in the early 1960s but mass tourist development only occurred in the 1980s, with safari excursion days inland of Mombassa. The development of larger 707 Boeing jumbo jets with greater long range fuel capacity allowed economies of scale plus lower prices which compared favourably with Mediterranean resorts.

Foreign tour companies combined with hoteliers to provide western-style hotel quality stretching from south of Mombassa to Malindi on the coast, with development of hotels in Nairobi. Roads inland to game parks were improved.

Strong marketing and advertising by Kenya improved tourism.

Benefits

By the late 1980s tourism had overtaken coffee as Kenya's major export earner; in 1990 it equalled 43% of export earnings.

Tourism was an employer in both the formal and informal sector e.g. informal souvenir sellers en route inland to safari parks.

It helped to pay for infrastructure improvements shared by Africans on the coast and around Nairobi. The international airports at Mombassa and Nairobi were developed. A completely new water supply project for Mombassa was undertaken.

Increasing problems

- Population pressure in Kenya is intense. Investment in tourism did not benefit the poorer majority sufficiently. They needed investment in rural development and slums around Nairobi.
- At least 40% of tourist revenue earnings 'leaked' outside to airlines and travel companies.
- Environmental pollution is seen on the coastline and degradation of the Savanna ecosystem in national parks.
- Most jobs are unskilled and low paid.
- Culture clashes and the less acceptable aspects of western living were felt. Drugs and petty crime increased.
- The increase in crime led to a fall in tourist numbers since 1990.

Source of tourists falling numbers

In 1992 the number of UK visitors fell 70%. Some tour operators dropped Kenya from their package brochure and charter flights were cut. Kenya now has taken measures to regenerate tourism.

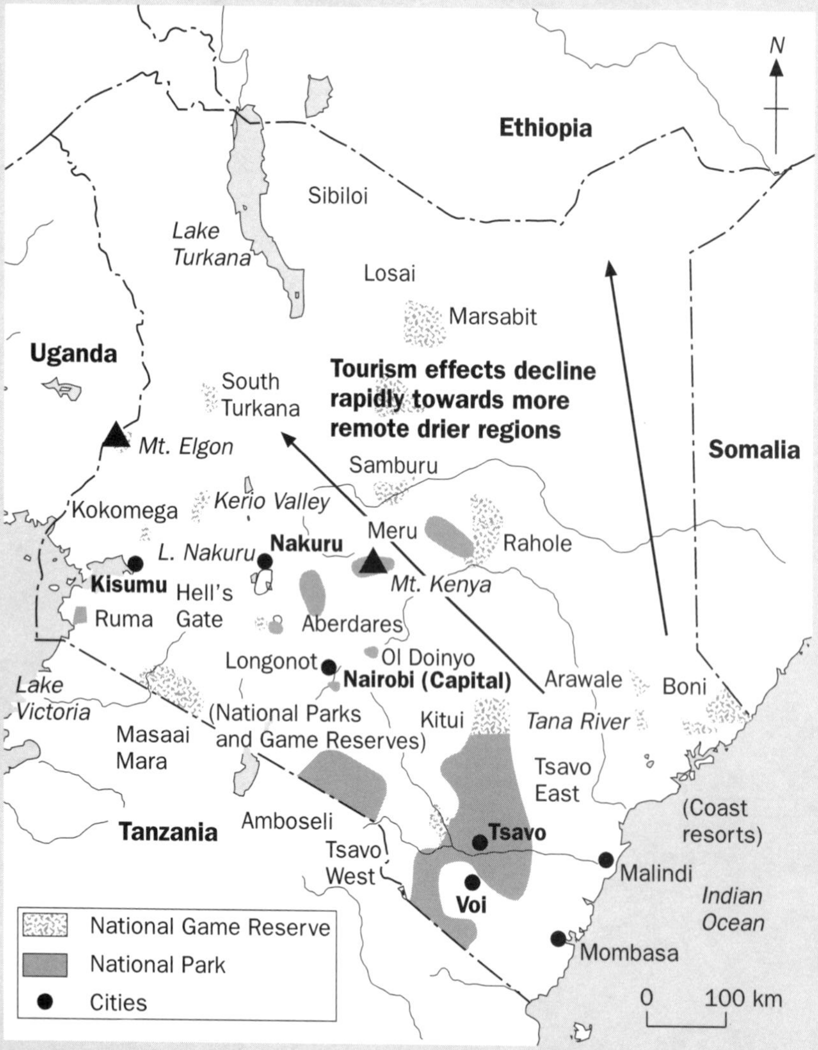

Kenya: its tourist attractions

Zimbabwe and its major recreational destinations

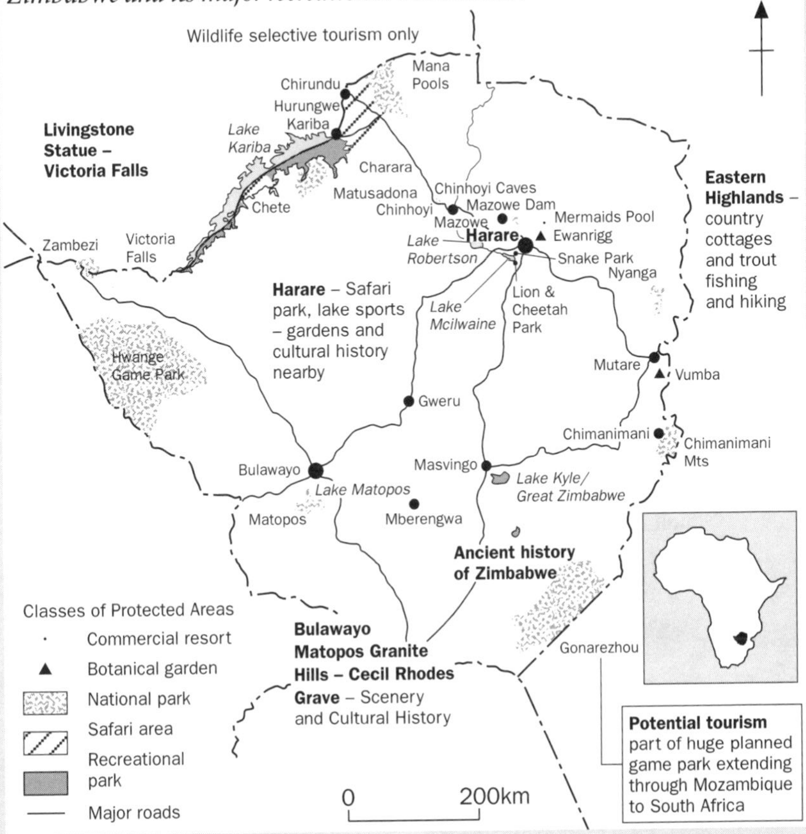

Zimbabwe: from involvement to the development stage

Selective tourism

Development of tourism was delayed by the War of Independence and a period of instability to the mid-1980s. Since then, growth in the tourist industry has accelerated. It now rivals Kenya as tropical Africa's main tourist destination helped by:

- scenic and other natural attractions, fascinating history and culture
- development of a good basic infrastructure linking main tourist regions to Harare and Bulawayo where most tourists stay
- the government's promotion of selective tourism to gain economic benefits without the problems of mass tourism
- 'upmarket' tour operators who promoted it as a special unspoilt experience.

Benefits

- earnings now amount to £53 million annually, a major currency earner
- tourism provides direct employment to 60 000
- infrastructure benefits local population around major tourist centres with some growth in their economies
- there is potential for further growth if tourism is carefully managed.

Problems

- the government is short of funds to develop tourism, yet does not want external control of it
- there is a fear tourism may direct investment away from other basic needs where drought and insufficient facilities are a problem.

Ethiopia: remains at the early exploration stage

Ethiopia has natural and cultural potential for tourism but lacks the infrastructure, investment capital and political stability needed. See Case study 7.2 for map.

Potential

Ethiopia has the most extensive archaeological ruins in Africa outside Egypt, a unique and varied culture, a moderate (sunny) climate, wildlife, breath-taking scenery and people whose cultures and traditions predispose them to welcoming guests.

It lacks

- a political stability, which deters tourism
- a positive media image; images of famine and poverty deters tourists
- development outside of Adis-Ababa; the necessary infrastructure and facilities
- capital
- investment and charter flights, increasing the costs.

What type of tourism may develop?

Despite the need for foreign currency and the potential to expand tourism, Ethiopia is not to move towards mass tourism.

It may develop 'alternative tourism' involving local communities in developing 'eco-tourism' which will benefit the local population, sustain the environment and keep within the socio-cultural carrying capacity.

case study

30.3 Eco-tourism in Belize

Basis of assessment

To be truly sustainable any form of tourism should:

- meet the needs of the host population in terms of improved living standards in both the short and long term
- satisfy the demands of a growing number of tourists and continue to attract them in order to meet this first aim
- safeguard the natural environment in order to achieve both of the preceding aims.

Aim

The government aimed to make conservation and tourism synonymous in Belize. It has declared its commitment to balanced and environmentally sound tourism by promoting eco-tourism.

- Government tourism aims at smaller scale projects where possible under Belize ownership and retaining maximum added value for the country while respecting its traditional eccentric social fabric.

Attractions

- the longest coral barrier reef in the western hemisphere and 450 beautiful cayes (very low lying islands) which are a 'paradise for snorkellers and scuba divers'
- extensive coastal mangrove swamps backed by wetland savanna and some of the best preserved rainforests in the world, each offering their own unique ecosystems
- the beautiful Mayan mountains with fine archaeological remains of the ancient Mayan civilisation
- a friendly people welcoming tourists
- tropical warmth
- political stability and relative safety for visitors

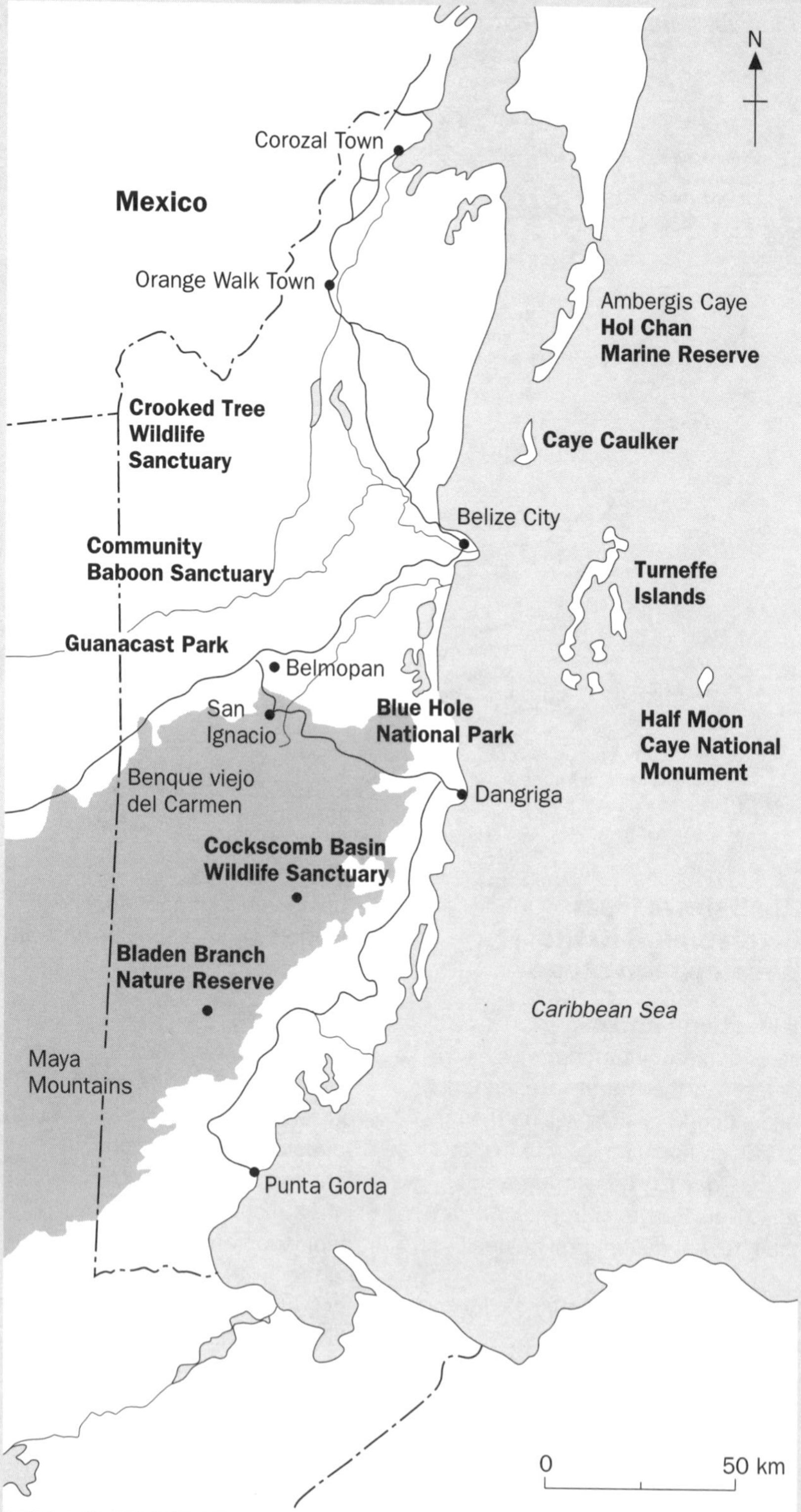

Location and features

- a contrast to the alternative Mexican coastal resorts such as Cacun which have been unsympathetically overdeveloped
- within 2 hours flying times of the USA Gulf towns such as Houston, Miami and New Orleans.

Development of tourism

The government encouraged tourism as an important foreign exchange earner as the country was narrowly dependent on primary exports – agricultural products and timber. Agriculture still accounts for 40% of GDP and 70% of export earnings.

Significant expansion occurred from 1980 with the most visitors coming from USA. From tourist receipts of $8 million in 1981 the figure had risen to approximately $80 million in 1990 with 190 000 tourists a year. Tourism is now the next most important foreign currency earner to agriculture. The rate of expansion is sensitive to economic recessions in the sending countries but on average exceeds 10% annually.

It remains mainly small group tourism involving the higher income discerning traveller with holidays tailor-made to needs.

In respect of the needs of the local community, tourism has provided jobs and helped to stimulate the economy but is controlled from outside the country with the consequent leakage of profits to external companies. Land prices are inflated on the coast, 90% of recent development has been foreign-owned. Initially hotels were small and locally owned but the large overseas hotel chains are beginning to move in.

Ambergires, the main tourist centre, is showing signs of over development with inflated prices and serious sewage and water problems.

There is some evidence of successful local community tourist initiatives e.g. the Sandy Beach Lodge hotel and cultural centre has been developed by the Sandy Beach Women's Cooperative at Hopkins Village.

Evaluation

A quarter of the country has been set aside as natural reserves or National Park areas where 'slash and burn' agriculture and logging are banned while tourism is supposed to be strictly controlled.

However, conservation has been developed in an uncoordinated, haphazard manner. The largest single area covers 200 000 acres in the Rio Brava area. The conservation programme lacks purposeful planning.

More successful ventures include the Cockscomb Reserve preserving 100 threatened jaguars and the Community Baboon Sanctuary for the threatened Black Howler Monkey species – both owe much to individual initiative.

There are some signs of tourist related damage e.g. damage to Hol Chan Marine Reserve coral, decline in conch and lobster as it is being overfished to meet expanded tourist market, ad hoc tourist groups visiting nature reserves with inadequate guidance and supervision.

The government stripped part of Caye Caulker caye to make a landing strip, destroying nesting sites and threatening the local water supply.

The greatest threat is currently to the mangrove swamp belt along the coast, some of which is being drained and infilled for development.

Summary

Tourist numbers are manageable but there are signs that the eco-tourist development is leading to some of the same kind of problems arising from conventional tourism.

There are clearly measures to safeguard unique tropical environments and wildlife from uncontrolled tourist developments. An invasion of slash and burn subsistence agriculture families from nearby Guatemala and Salvador as refugees and a threatened expansion of logging currently pose larger problems than an expansion of alternative tourism.

CHAPTER 31

Transport modes and networks

'The adequacy of infrastructure helps determine one country's success and another's failure in diversifying production, expanding trade, coping with population growth, reducing poverty or improving environmental conditions ... but it has to expand fast enough to accommodate growth.'

WORLD DEVELOPMENT REPORT 1994

31.1 Their central and changing importance

Transport routes, networks and the ways used to convey goods, people and information along them are fundamental to the functioning of society. With time, people in any one place have come to increasingly depend on the world outside for a variety of goods and services and for the exchange of ideas and information. Decisions and events in the world are conveyed by a variety of communication means and influence people's lives wherever they are.

It is often said that transport creates 'utilities of place' in that one of its prime functions is to move surplus raw materials and goods from one place to where there is a need for them, so increasing their value and encouraging more economic activity. As time has progressed, areas have increasingly specialised on those types of economic activity for which they have been most suited, relying on the sale of their surplus in that specialised production and activity to pay for goods and services brought in from outside. This increasing specialisation and dependence on other areas has only been possible because of continuously improving means of transport and communications.

Much of the present exchange is in the form of raw materials and goods and also in people and services. For example, London and New York are financial centres with intricate telex-satellite, telephone and cable links linking these centres constantly to every part of the world (Figure 33.8). Still, the intensity of exchange of information and services within a country between one part and another is no less important.

Faster and cheaper means of transport and communication have led to what is known as space-time convergence. In terms of time and cost of contact, places in the world have come closer together – the globe has become smaller. Events taking place in different parts of the world can for example be conveyed by satellite and shown on televisions as they happen. Again people and air freight, for example, can be conveyed overnight from London to different parts of the world.

Technological changes have brought about this space-time convergence, in particular, those occurring since the 1960s, such as jet air travel and advanced telecommunications.

Competition between different modes of transport has also as a result been intensified. On land, road transport has gained over rail. At an international level, air travel has begun to replace ocean shipping for passenger travel and some specialist freighting, though carrying of bulk freight is still by sea transport because of its relative low cost.

31.2 Transport on land

Travel and freight by road

Movement by road is increasingly becoming the most important form of land transport. This is largely a reflection of its convenience and flexibility, compared to rail and inland waterway transport. No other form of transport can offer a service directly from point of origin to destination. Part of the convenience of road transport is due to the comprehensive road network available, while the rapid expansion of motorways has provided the basic framework linking major cities. These feed into the rest of the network giving direct access by road to almost every house and place of business whether it be a farm, office, warehouse or factory.

Furthermore, road transport is also the most flexible mode of transport in terms of the amount of goods or passengers carried. The largest juggernaut lorries are capable of carrying loads of 40 tonnes and motorway buses over 50 passengers, but there are also small vans available to carry a few hundredweight of freight and it is common to see cars containing only one person.

Technological changes which have contributed to this increased flexibility have also been important in speeding up road transport and yet at the same time improving on fuel economy. Saving of time helps to reduce costs in terms of human hours needed to complete a journey and releases the vehicle in a quicker time for further work. It is also additionally beneficial in that quicker transport has extended the area which can be covered from one distribution point in a given time. The number of depots is being reduced and they are increasingly placed near motorway junctions to take further advantage of time savings, as for example in the case of the M1 – M62 motorway exchanges near Leeds and Manchester. These are larger depots and therefore also enable economies of scale to occur by handling more goods with a given amount of labour and equipment.

Planned expansion - weighing up the cost

Most countries are proposing a further expansion in their road and motorway networks as demand continues to expand. Growth of traffic for example on the UK's motorways was forecast in 1990 to expand by between 20% to 30% in the next decade. Already motorways such as the M25 and M62 are carrying significantly more traffic beyond their forecast capacities, leading to delays and heavy wear and tear, resulting in extensive on-going road repair programmes and causing even more delays.

At the beginning of the 1990s in a series of reports including the *'Roads for Prosperity'* White Paper, the British government launched a £12 billion programme to expand and improve the national road network (Figure 31.1). There are two important constraints: how such a massive expansion will be funded and the environmental costs of it.

In a major switch of policy in the early 1990s, the Conservative government committed itself to significant private funding of much of the expansion, as for example in the case of a planned new east coast route from Cambridge north to Hull, York and Newcastle. The cost would be recouped for example in the case of certain planned orbital roads, such as the West Midlands north of Birmingham, by toll charging.

Critics of further road building point to trends in the past which show that as soon as road building takes place there is a rapid rise in traffic, nullifying much of the beneficial planned effects. Their call is for an integrated transport network involving all the different modes of transport rather than planning each mode as a separate entity.

On a wider scale, there is a massive expansion scheme to expand and integrate more fully the road network across the whole European Union as a necessary condition for closer economic union under the Maastricht Treaty of 1991 to 1993 (Figure 31.2).

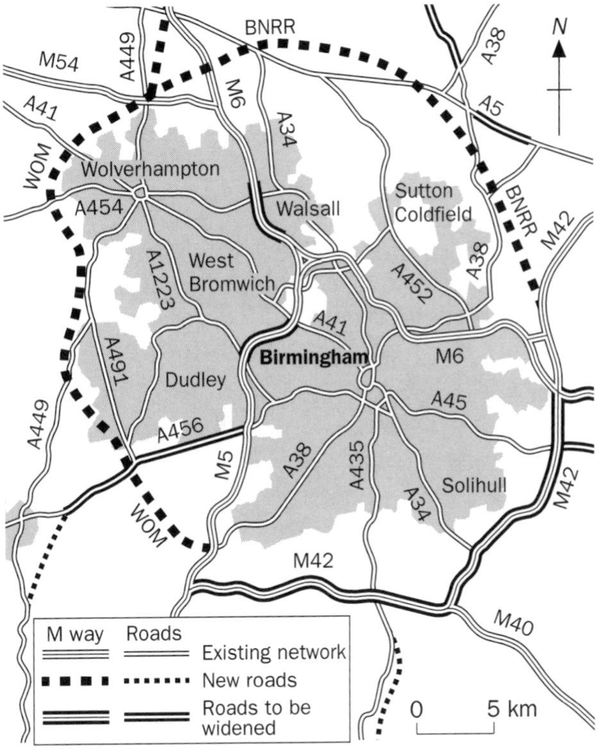

- Britain's first toll motorway, the 33-mile long Birmingham Northern Relief Road (BNRR), will form a 6 – 10 lane bypass to the M6. Probable cost: £400 million.
- The Western Orbital motorway (WOM) probably a toll road, linking the BNRR with the M5/M42 via green belt land. Has already sparked development rush. Probable cost £500 million.
- M42 Widening: full details to be published. Estimated cost: £200 million.
- M6 widening: Proposed width: 8 lanes. Estimated cost: £1 billion.
- The development of the full Birmingham orbital scheme will demand many other smaller road schemes. Councils are pressing for new slip roads, realigned junctions, link roads and interchanges. Bypasses proposed for Brownhills, Burntwood, Clayhanger, Fazely, Massive Hamshall rail freight terminal will need access roads.

***Figure 31.1** The new orbital road around Birmingham*

Apart from the cost factor and the questionable prediction of the economic benefits which would ensue, there is mounting criticism of road expansion plans within the UK and across the rest of the European Union on environmental grounds. Since 1983 in the UK, all motorway and trunk road proposals have been subject to environmental assessment under set procedures. However, environmental groups argue that the procedures are inadequate and inconsistently applied.

English Heritage and English Nature estimate that the planned road expansion programme will for example affect 160 sites designated as of Special Scientific Interest, 800 ancient monument sites and that for every 1 km of new dual carriageway road built, 120 000 tonnes of road stone will be required. Apart from the loss of agricultural land under new roads, much additional landscaping either side a new road will take up more land.

31.3 Rail transport – losing ground to roads

While the greatest expansion has taken place in road transport, considerable developments have also occurred to help maintain the competitiveness of the railways for certain kinds of freighting. Ironically, in most developed countries this has partly been achieved by reducing the rail network, with the closure of many branch lines and improvement of the track between major cities and between industrial areas. In the UK, the Beeching Report of 1963 led to the first post-war major rationalisation of the network to help make it more commercially viable. More recently still, the Serpell Report (1983) has recommended further rationalisation.

The Beeching Report recommended other changes to improve the viability and competitiveness of the main trunk network. Faster diesel locomotives were developed and electrification extended out along the main lines to keep pace with the extension of the commuting area taking place around the larger cities. On the passenger side it was the suburban lines and main regional commuting lines such as the London to Brighton line which carried the bulk of the passenger traffic and were therefore the lines most viable.

The greatest developments have occurred to take further advantage of those kinds of freight for which rail has always been preferred to road, namely heavy bulk materials and products, such as coal and iron-ore. Units of wagons can be assembled and specialist bulk handling sidings set up near raw material sources, factories and power stations. Freightliner trains and freightliner depots have been perhaps the most notable developments (Figure 31.3).

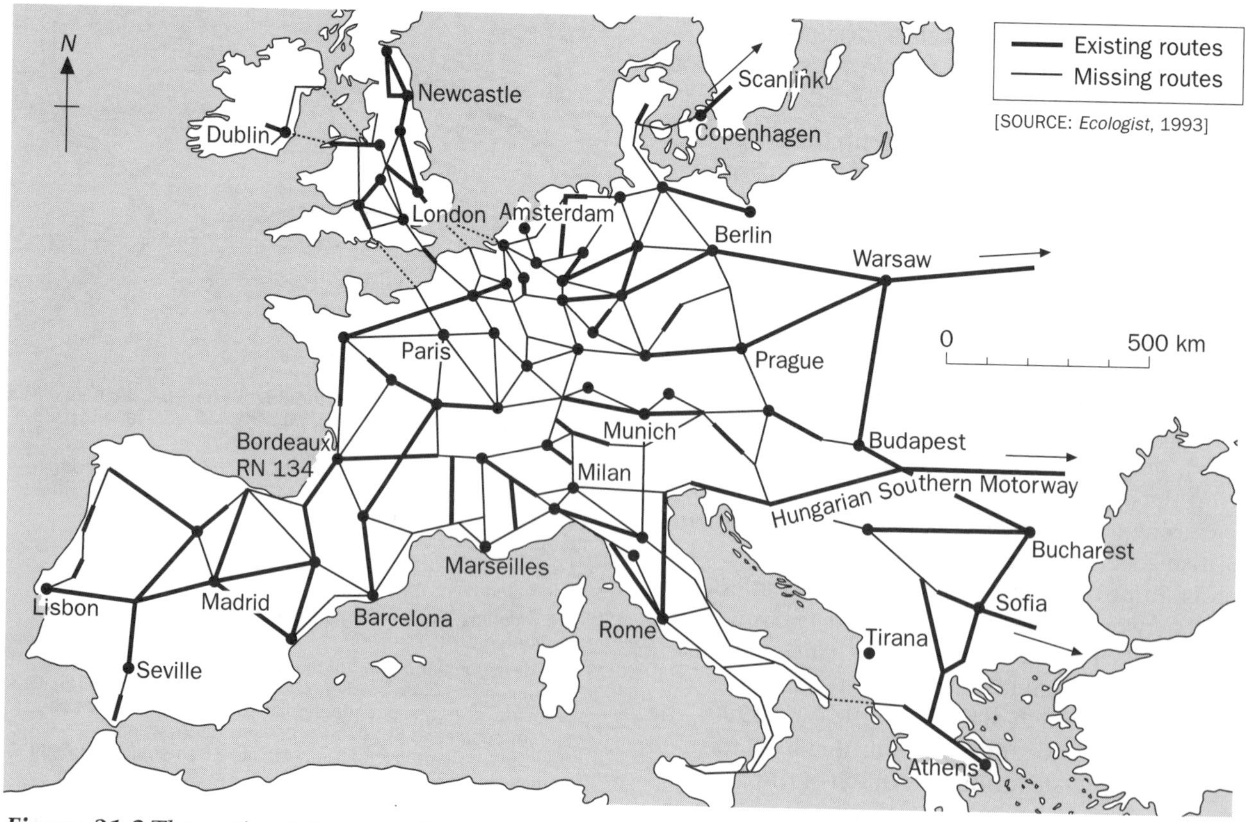

Figure. 31.2 The continental main road route network (1992) and missing links proposed to complete it

The freightliner system in this and other developed countries, including the USA, is also closely linked with the container revolution, whereby large containers of standard size can be loaded with packed freight at an assembly depot and transhipped using mechanical handling equipment. It can thus be transferred from one mode of transport to another quickly and cheaply, either from a lorry onto a rail truck or from the rail truck or lorry onto a ship at the dock. Containerisation has particularly expanded since 1965 for by then, cost savings by using containers progressively exceeded the investment cost in specialised equipment and the sidings which are needed to handle the containers.

The advantages of containers are that they allow quicker turn arounds of rail wagons, lorries, ships and aircraft, so enabling them to be used more frequently in a given time. The amount of labour needed to handle goods is also reduced and there is less loss through breakage and possible theft of goods. Because goods are transhipped more quickly and efficiently, containerisation also reduces the amount of warehousing needed for stock to meet customer orders.

Overcoming barriers to widen the network

As economic activity becomes increasingly internationalised and there are ever greater volumes of movement of goods and people between countries, so the limitations of transport networks developed to primarily serve national economies and needs become increasingly more obvious. Limitations are further emphasised by the fact that even within a country there has been little conscious effort on the part of governments and business concerns to integrate different modes of transport to produce an infrastructure where one mode of transport complements another. Competition not complementarity marks the development of different modes of transport since the nineteenth century.

The movement of European countries towards a single common market and economic integration has belatedly prompted governments to overcome serious barriers to movement and trade. Historically there have been formidable natural barriers to European integration, ranging from the English Channel separating the UK from the rest of Europe, to the formidable barriers of the Alps and the Pyrenees separating Austria and the southern Mediterranean countries from the northern countries of Europe. Equally, the water masses round the Baltic state separated Denmark from Scandinavian countries and these from mainland Europe. Distance and physical barriers also separate newer members on the periphery such as Greece and Turkey from the European Union's economic heartland.

Since the early 1990s better transport links and a more integrated transport network are increasingly being seen as a crucial key to the success of the European Union. Steps are being taken to overcome some of the major physical barriers and to produce an integrated transport infrastructure which will reduce the present dominance of a congested road network (Figure 31.4). Not only will rail transport be given greater prominence but more intermodal transport will be promoted by a greater complementarity between modes.

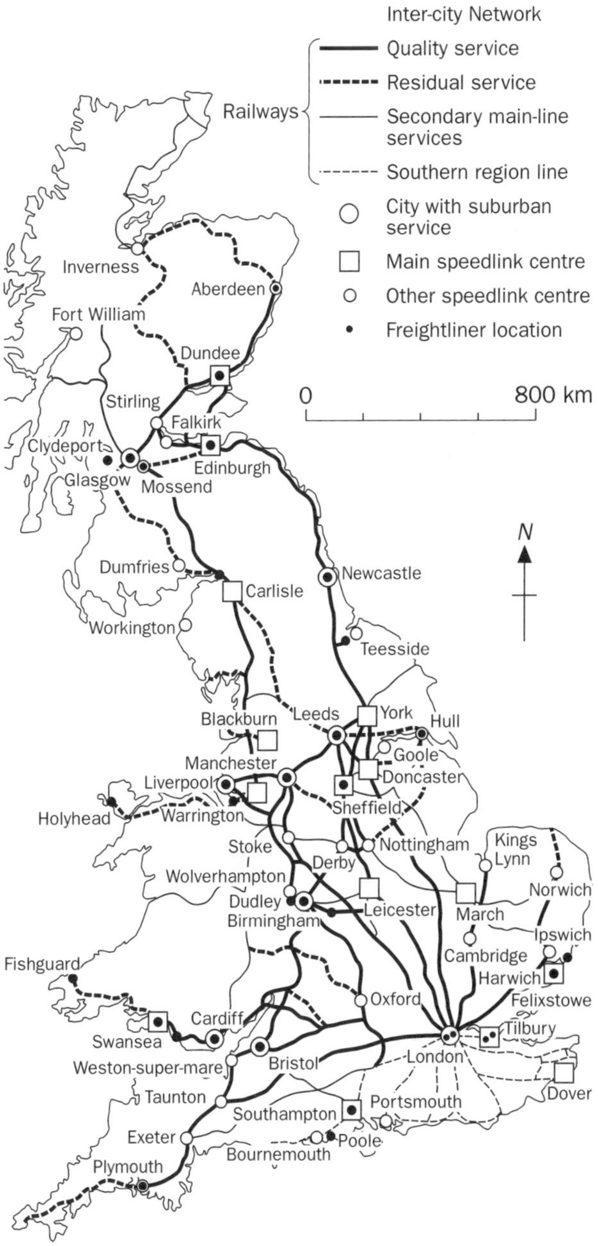

Figure 31.3 Rail network and freightliner d…

The Channel Tunnel – the first link

The first great step towards a more integrated network was the building and completion of the Channel Tunnel by 1994, for the first time giving a continuous link between the UK and its continental European neighbours. As Case study 31.1 indicates, it is not only physical barriers which have to be overcome; for the link to be successfully exploited, serious technological and logistical problems involving the incompatibility and limited efficiency of networks either side the physical barrier also have to be resolved.

The Channel Tunnel has an effect on the areas either side of it and is ultimately part of an integrated European Transport network, optimistically due for completion around the year 2010. The transport context is widened to a vast economic and political intra-national regional scale (Case study 31.1).

Looking at the plans for a European integrated transport infrastructure which links peripheral countries such as Greece, Portugal and Ireland to the 'golden heartland' has again raised a dilemma. It is questionable whether such an infrastructure

The need

- Following a considerable period of European-wide strategic policy vaccuum, transport infrastructure has now been recognised as the key to closer economic and social integration.
- The increasing internationalisation of business, the growth of manufacturing techniques such as 'just-in-time' and increased personal mobility within a single European Common market have given added urgency to the issue of increased accessibility.
- Neil Kinnock, the European Commissioner for transport estimated in 1995 that congestion was costing developed countries 2% of their Gross Domestic Product annually.
- Most transport networks still serve only national needs. Railways are struggling to cope with inherited incompatible systems of electric power supply and incompatible signalling and operations systems. There is no common policy on road tolls, etc. The skies are congested with no effective linked air control system.

Creation of a European Transport Network Scheme (TEN)

The European Union in 1995 launched a project for integrating road, rail, sea and airlinks over the next 15 years at a cost of $381 billion. The aims are to:

- reduce congestion on the busy routes in the heart of Europe
- link the periphery countries such as Portugal and Greece more closely to the core of the European Union
- reduce the relative heavy dependence on roads; at present 75% of passenger and 70% of freight is by road.

There are 14 schemes within the project with $1.8 billion already allocated to feasibility studies, loan guarantees, interest rate subsidies and in exceptional circumstances, grants over the next four years. Schemes cover such ventures as completing high speed rail links e.g. Paris to Strasbourg, motorway links e.g. between Bulgaria and Greece, creation of a single system of air traffic control across the European Union (at present there are 22 information systems). To enable further integration of rail and road transport and switch traffic from roads to railways, all countries are being committed to deregulating the railways and separating management of rail infrastructure from operations. There will be much more competitive access to use of the railways. There is to be a particular emphasis on developing intermodal transport with goods going part of the route by road but the main long distance hauls by rail.

Other programmes towards a more integrated system

- A Maritime Strategy Document in 1996 was drawn up to promote more movement of goods by coastal traffic through port improvements, simplifying paper work and upgrading the image of coastal freighting.
- Improved and more integrated public transport system – Research is underway into a 'Citizen's Network' by improving the infrastructure as a whole, facilitating physical interchanges at any transfer or change of transport point, more efficient information through tickets for different modes of transport and joint time tabling of services.

Crucial to the success of an integrated transport infrastructure programme which needs to reduce the present predominance of road transport is persuading governments to ensure road hauliers and private motorists bear the full cost of use of the road network at the point of use. This would encourage a switch to other modes of transport for all or parts of journeys.

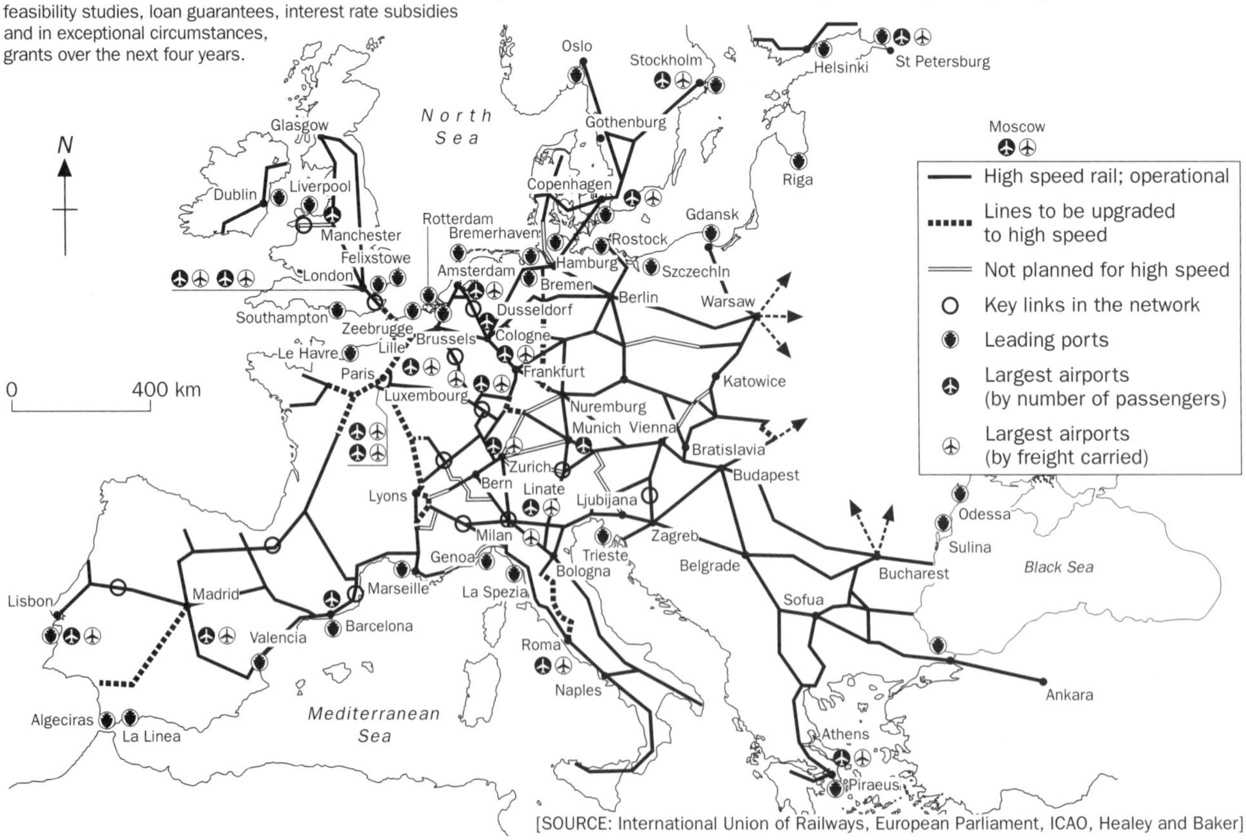

[SOURCE: International Union of Railways, European Parliament, ICAO, Healey and Baker]

Figure 31.4 An integrated transport infrastructure for EU countries

will in fact stimulate economic development in the periphery; rather, it may actually increase the dominance of the heartland (Figure 31.4).

Much depends on other factors such as the relative cost and quality of labour, land and other costs in the periphery compared to the heartland. How much investment European agencies and governments put into improving the total infrastructure on the periphery and the inducements initially given to attract new business makes a difference. As greatly increased investment by multinationals in the North East of England and South Wales of the UK show, for example, such measures, if allied to improved transport links, can raise levels of economic activity. However, whether without grants and subsidy support peripheral regions could compete with the core has yet to be seen since neither the European Union nor national governments have committed themselves to improving transport links to peripheral regions.

31.4 **Inland waterways**

Inland waterways in Western Europe and North America are an important part of the transport network linking in with the rail network and at the point of shipment with sea links between countries. Water transport is slow compared with road and rail, but very useful for carrying bulk cargo such as coal, timber and grain for which time of transport is not important. Because waterways cost less to maintain and running costs of barges and other inland shipping are less, this is a cheaper form of transport than road or rail (Figure 31.5).

Just as efforts have been made to improve land transport, schemes are in hand in a number of countries to extend and improve the inland waterway network. In the USA one of the most significant advances was the opening of the St Lawrence Seaway to allow ocean-going shipping to reach the Great Lakes and, therefore, into the heart of the continent.

In Western Europe the most important system is based on the Rhine, since its hinterland extends into the Benelux countries, France, West Germany and Switzerland. It is used to carry bulky raw materials, non-perishable foodstuffs and low value goods. Together with its linking canal systems and navigable tributaries, the Rhine waterway is one of the world's major transport networks. Its importance to bordering countries is to some extent indicated by the comparative freight totals, though waterway transport is not limited solely to the Rhine system.

The Rhine waterway with its tributary rivers the Moselle, Main, Necker, Sambre, Meuse, Scheldt and linking canals has at its outlet to the North Sea the major world port of Rotterdam (Case study 31.2). In addition, major river ports have been established on the Rhine itself, which have attracted industries reliant on raw materials imported via the waterway and using also the road and rail links which follow the valley routes along which the waterways flow. Industries are diverse and include iron and steel, heavy engineering, oil refining, petro-chemicals, chemicals, paper, textiles and food processing.

The importance of the Rhine waterway is even greater since the Rhine-Marne Danube Canal links it into the Danube waterway which flows into the Black Sea and the Rhine-Marne Canal links it into the Rhone riverway which flows into the Mediterranean.

The significance of inland water transport has been increased not only by the deepening and widening and the building of more canal links, but also by improvements in the freight carriers themselves. Trains of barges drawn by modern high power diesel tugs have a greatly increased carrying capacity compared to the older type river barges. The main stretches of the waterway are capable now of carrying barges of 1500 tonne capacity.

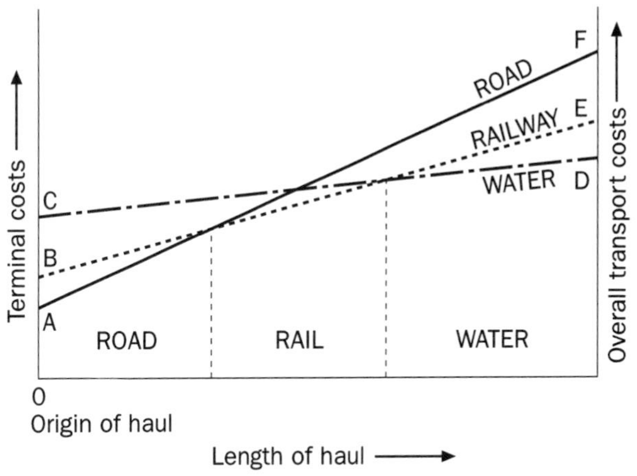

Fixed (terminal) and variable (line-haul) costs of three major transport modes. Terminal costs are indicated on the vertical axis (OA, OB and OC for road, rail and water transport respectively) and increases in variable costs are shown by the gradients of the lines AF (road), BE (rail) and CD (water).

[SOURCE: Tolley R and Turton B *Transport Systems, Policy and Planning*, 1995]

***Figure 31.5** Comparative costs of road, rail and water transport taking into account terminal costs at the point of origin of the journey and overall costs in relation to distance*

31.5 Sea transport

Factors affecting the pattern of shipping routes

The volume and flow patterns of sea and ocean shipping are essentially a reflection of the locations of supply and demand for raw materials, semi-processed and processed products and manufactured goods. With increasing competition from air traffic, passenger traffic, except on cross-ferry and coastal routes, is of decreasing importance.

The pattern of shipping routes is also influenced by variations in the physical environment. Technological developments, while overcoming some of the limitations imposed by physical constraints, have also heightened others. For example, modern large bulk carriers ranging from 80 000 to the largest oil tanker at over 200 000 tonnes, can only berth at deepwater ports and are too large to pass through the Suez and Panama Canals. Hence these mainly use the Cape of Good Hope route.

The influence of basic physical constraints is also evident from the direction of the world's major shipping routes. Shipping avoids the severe weather and icy conditions of high latitudes. The shape and position of the major land masses are also significant. For example, shipping moving between Japan and Western Europe must pass through the Panama or Suez Canals or take the Cape route round the tips of Africa and South America.

The configuration of coastlines is also important in funnelling ocean-going traffic into particular sea lanes, such as the English Channel passage, and in limiting the locations suitable for ports. Deep estuaries leading into highly developed and populous regions are particularly favoured, but some of the largest bulk carriers have to off-load at more remote locations giving deepwater anchorage. The cargo then has to be moved along the coast to consuming areas.

In addition to the development of bulk carriers, the other important technological development of recent times has been the widespread adoption of containerisation and roll-on roll-off facilities. Containerisation of cargo into containers of standard size has enabled much of the handling to be done mechanically with a consequent saving of labour. Break of bulk en route is also avoided because cargo can be assembled at inland depots as well as at the ports, containers being transferred to shipping and, at the other end of the sea journey, back onto lorry or rail before being finally unpacked at the destination.

Roll-on roll-off facilities perform a similar function; road vehicles together with their loads can be driven onto the ship or cross-channel ferry and then driven off at the end of the sea journey. This is an increasingly important component of cross-channel freighting between the UK and other EU countries. It is also important for other short sea crossings, for example between Germany and the Scandinavian countries. There is even a cross Atlantic link with barges coming down the Great Lakes in Canada-USA being transferred to ocean carriers and then being mechanically unloaded at Rotterdam-Euroports to carry on the journey up the Rhine waterway with cargoes such as coal, iron-ore and grain.

Such recent developments are but the latest in a series of technological developments which have transformed the nature and volume of ocean-going traffic.

The top six ports by volume of trade handled
This favours bulk handling ports such as Sullom Voe (oil and gas) and Tees-Hartlepool (iron and steel, chemicals, etc). By value south and east coast ports such as Southampton and Felixstowe would figure more prominently).

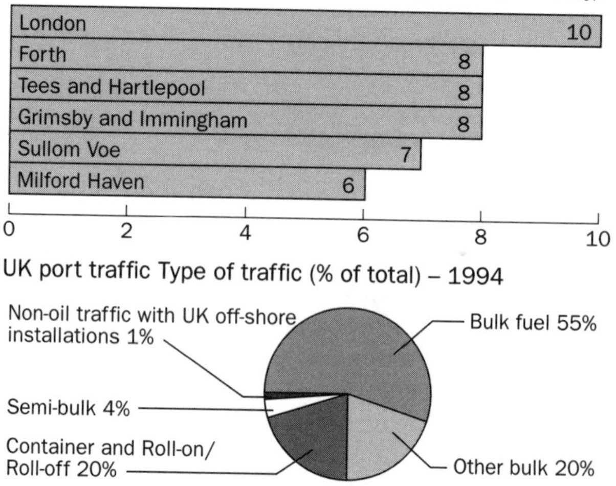

The leading ports of the UK and type of traffic handled

- Since 1990 British ports have undergone major reorganisation and modernisation facilitated by two government measures. In 1989 abolition of the national dock labour scheme which had led to restrictive labour practices making handling costs significantly higher than in rival continental ports such as Rotterdam and Amsterdam. Privatisation of larger 'trust ports' (under self governing organisations set up by Act of Parliament).
- This has made the ports more competitive to capitalise on strong export growth especially with the Continent since 1992. Growth of 14% 1994 took exports to 178 million tonnes and total port volumes to 538 million tonnes – a post-war record.
- Overall growth in the port sector shows a strong shift to the south and east of the country mainly due to the creation of the single European market and growth of European trade. Container ports such as Tilbury, Felixstowe, and Southampton with deepwater berths have particularly expanded.
- Growth has been aided by improved motorway standard links to the ports.
- The larger modernised ports can benefit from economies of scale and many smaller ports are unlikely to survive as cargo handling ports.

Figure 31.6 *Top UK ports*

Port development

All these developments – the economic advancement of countries and therefore the increased amount of trade – have had a substantial impact on sea terminals, ports and harbours. As the size of shipping and volume of traffic have increased and technological developments have occurred, so the nature of port facilities has had to change. Many small ports have declined and traffic is being concentrated in fewer ports, including some new specialised deepwater ports serving particular industries or other activities (Figure 31.6). These include for example the deepwater berth at Immingham on Humberside serving the Scunthorpe Steel Works.

In older port areas on large estuaries, or with large harbourage, there has been a gradual extension of dock facilities downstream as more specialised handling facilities, more dock space and deep anchorages have been required. In some cases, as in the Port of London, this has meant the abandonment of older outdated wharfage upstream. On the Thames, Hays Wharf and other docks have now been abandoned, awaiting redevelopment as part of the London Dockland Enterprise Zone and a number of the trades, including container handling, are centred downstream at Tilbury. Some trade has also been lost to the fast expanding port of Felixstowe further north on the Suffolk coast.

Across the channel, Rotterdam's extension including Europoort on the Rhine outlet, illustrates the stages of development which occur with time of ports serving a thriving hinterland and having to be adapted to meet the changing character of ocean shipping. Such changes are to be found in many parts of the world. Bird (1963) in his study of UK seaports, has postulated a model of port growth — 'Anyport' — within the context of which the development of particular ports such as that of Rotterdam-Europoort can be studied (Case study 31.2).

Coastal trade

While most of the discussion on ports and shipping is centred on overseas trade in raw materials, food and other goods, for most nations with a coastline, coastwise trade and short passage to neighbouring countries are of considerable importance. Ferry and small ship traffic is mainly concerned with freighting, but because of its economic cost, passenger transport remains significant. For certain crossings, because of increased affluence and mobility, it has increased. For example, there is the growing tourist trade between the UK and the continent and within Western Europe itself, with many tourists taking their own cars by ferry over the different channel crossings.

As regards coastal traffic, one of the countries where this has always been important is Japan. In the mid-1970s just over half of all the freight shipped from one part of the archipelago to another went by sea, as against 35% by road and 14% by rail. Today the proportion has declined but coastal trade still remains very significant. As would be expected, the shipping is mainly used for low value bulk cargoes but a significant amount also includes ***entrepôt trade, that is, goods brought in from overseas to major ports such as Yokohama and redistributed to other points along the coast***.

In the developing world, ferry, coastal and sea transport, measured by volume, is not as important as in developed countries. However, relative to needs, it is even more important in some areas because it may provide the only major kind of transport apart from expensive air travel, which is beyond the means of the mass of the population and too expensive for the transfer of all but high value goods. This applies for example, to the people and economies of the South Pacific, as well as to populations around the major lake shores such as Lake Victoria in East Africa.

31.6 **Air transport**

Major expansion of both passenger and freight traffic

The world-wide growth in air traffic, both at an international level and within regions, for the conveyance of passengers and certain kinds of bulk high value freight has greatly accelerated during the post-war years.

Since the early 1970s passenger and freight traffic have been growing at an annual average rate varying between 6% to 9%. The Association for European Airlines for example reported a growth of 7% annually in passenger traffic and 11% in freight traffic between 1990 and 1994 on the domestic and international routes of European airlines. The sheer scale of operations associated with this growth is indicated by the fact that these airlines carried 520 million passengers in 1994 and approximately 8 million tonnes of freight. The rate of growth is even greater in the Far East, a reflection of the pace of general economic growth in this part of the world. The increasing importance of air transport is also indicated by the large modernisation and expansion programmes at many of the world's largest airports, and the building of new international airports such as the Kansai International airport in Japan.

Airports are seen as a means of capturing an increasing proportion of air traffic business and as a powerful spur to economic growth in the region around the airport. Airports are catalysts for economic growth, especially for the large 'gateway' or 'hub' airports. Hub airports act as gateways for international flights but also as gathering or changing points for passengers either to or from internal flights or en route internationally to another destination. Kansai airport for example is part of a multipurpose programme to develop the Osaka-Kobe region as an internationally important economic region which would relieve pressure on the capital region of Tokyo.

One of the most important changes allowing airlines to capitalise on greatly increased market opportunities, has been the gradual deregulation of airlines from international and government control. Until the early 1980s fares and standards of service on airlines were largely controlled by The International Air Transport Association. Deregulation has allowed lower fares and much greater competition. This has also been followed by government deregulation. For example, in 1993 the European Commission deregulated EU flights leading to much more open competition on European routes. Competition, however, favours the largest airlines; numerous smaller airlines have been taken over or forced to close. Some survive within niche markets, for example, short business flight routes or by charter deals with tour operators, as in the case of UK Airlines and Monarch airlines.

Since domestic flights are still dominated by home-based airlines, there have also been moves for inter-continental commercial alliances between large airlines, such as that recently agreed between the German Lufthansa airline and America's largest airline, United Airlines, giving each access into the other's country and allowing passengers to use two airlines on the one ticket.

Thus as with other economic activities, privatisation, rationalisation, modernisation and greater globalisation are characterising air transport developments as markets enlarge and expand. However, some developing nations are subsidising unprofitable infant airlines to enable them to get established because a sound airline network is seen as vital to the future of the country, as in the case of Air Zimbabwe.

At the smaller end of the market, the development of the helicopter has captured the attention of the public with the role it plays in such ventures as North Sea oil operations. The further development and improvement of light aircraft, including the small jet executive and other specialised aircraft have an increased role for comparatively short journeys, often from small local airports. However, for regions with very difficult terrain, scattered communities and poor land communications, these aircraft, run largely by small operators, are essential to the economic and social life of the region concerned, as for example in the Canadian Northlands and the tropical forest lands of Central and South America.

Limitations of air transport

The outstanding advantages of air travel are its speed, the vast distances which can be covered, its directness and the improved accessibility it gives to remote and difficult locations. There is, however, not quite the freedom of the air, for movement has to be along designated flight corridors and countries place political restrictions on their air space.

Routes are not now so constrained by adverse physical conditions, as jet aircraft fly at stratosphere levels above the atmosphere's weather. However, it still seriously affects thousands of light aircraft which provide vital links to small and remote communities in different parts of the world. Also, all aircraft, despite modern radar and other devices, are affected by weather conditions in the vicinity of take-off and landing points – fog, for example, remains a hazard.

Despite its advantages, air transport is limited in the volume of passenger and freight traffic it can carry because it remains the most expensive form of transport. Aircraft have a small pay-load capacity relative to their total weight and the fuel carried and therefore to the costs involved. Aircraft also have a high depreciation cost and a high operating expenditure. They are, therefore, generally used by passengers who wish to economise on time and can afford the comparatively high fares. However, intense competition between airlines on the busiest routes, including rapidly expanding tourist charter flight lines, has resulted in decreasing fares. This has particularly stimulated further expansion of demand from the tourist trade. However, it has also resulted in highly complex air fare structures, with business executives paying far more than passengers on Apex, Stand-by, or Charter flight rates.

As has been noted, freighting by air is increasing. Air transport is suitable for the carriage of commodities with a low bulk yet high value. These include such things as postal mail, parcels, spare machine and vehicle parts, high value electrical equipment and high value livestock such as race horses, as well as increasing trade in high priced, out-of-season fruits and cut flowers. Orchids and carnations for example are flown from Kenya to the USA and Western Europe at out-of-season periods.

Airport location

Modern airports are not only very costly to build and maintain, but require a very large area of land. The advent of larger, faster jet aircraft like the jumbo jet, has limited the number of sites available for large airports. Runways now need to be over 3000 m long and more are needed as the volume of air traffic continues to increase. Large areas too are needed for infrastructure facilities such as arrival and departure terminals, customs warehouses, maintenance hangars, etc.

Airport areas must also be at locations having good access to the main population centres which generate the demand for air traffic (Figure 31.7). Yet increasing environmental concern, particularly associated with the noise jet aircraft make on approach routes and when taking off or landing, puts further constraints on available sites. The tendency now is to locate airports at an increasing distance from the major population centres yet linked to them by fast connecting communication services as illustrated by Birmingham International Airport.

Figure 31.7 *Main airports and services in the UK*

Because of costs, the amount of land involved and environmental concerns, the trend is not to build new airports on greenfield sites to cope with increasing demand but to extend existing airports. For example, plans to build another London airport to the east of the capital to relieve pressure on Heathrow have for the time being been dropped in favour of building a new fifth terminal at Heathrow and extending the use of Stansted. However, as the current planning enquiry into a possible fifth terminal shows, there is also increasingly effective environmental opposition to extending existing large airports. The concern is not simply for the enlargement of the airport itself but also the infrastructure developments needed to serve the catchment area around and the property development boom that expansion is likely to bring. Similar problems occur with the recent decision to build another runway at Manchester Airport.

The arguments appear to revolve around the accrued economic benefits which would come from a new terminal being built and the social and environmental disbenefits which may result (Case study 31.3).

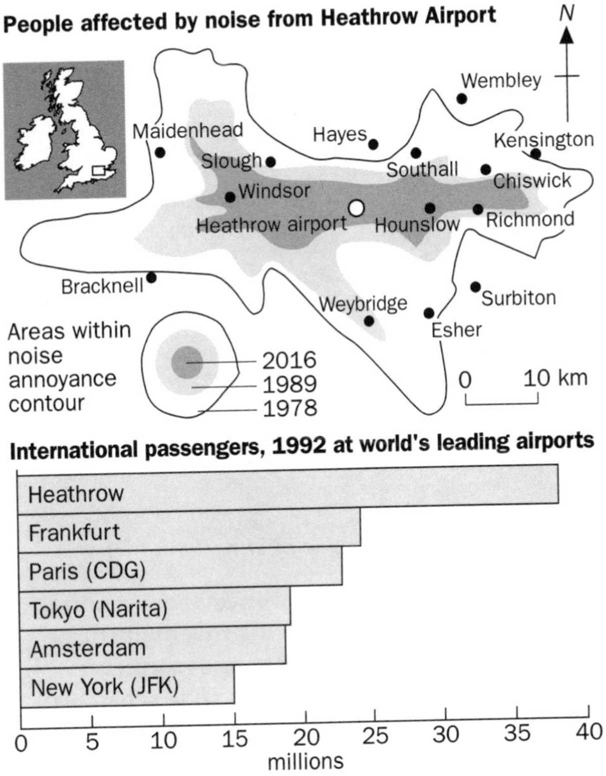

Figure 31.8 *Controversy over the further expansion of Heathrow – its current size and noise effect on surrounding areas*

31.7 Telecommunications and the Information Revolution

> 'Both the time and relative cost of transporting materials, products and people have fallen dramatically as the result of technological innovations in the transport media. However such developments have depended to a considerable degree on parallel developments in telecommunications technology.'
>
> [SOURCE: Dicken P *Global Shift – The Internationalisation of Economic Activity*, 1992]

Through the postal, telephone, telegraph and radio services, most people in the developed world and limited numbers in developing countries had been long accustomed to a transportation network which could convey information. The transistor radio and television have increased access to information, even to villages in remote areas of the tropical world. Today further rapid technological advances are bringing a telecommunications and information revolution with immense implications for the lives of ordinary people and their political and economic future.

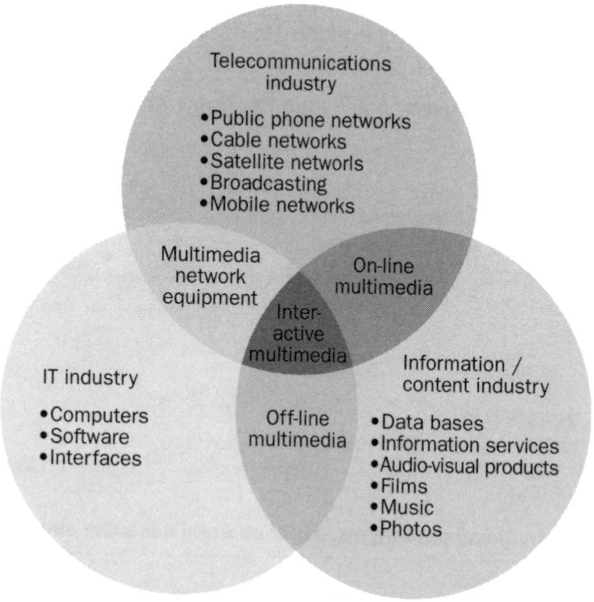

Figure 31.9 The converging information society

Already some of its spatial effects are becoming evident, the most notable being that of further spatial convergence. The speed and manner in which information, transactions and exchange of ideas can take place have brought output and receiving areas together in effect into 'one place or neighbourhood', though physically they may be in different regions of the world (Figure 31.9).

A massive increase in the volume of exchange which can take place is occurring along the global telecommunications network as a result of a range of technological advances including fibre optic cabling and enlarged satellite capacities. However, the impact of this information and communications revolution is very uneven, both across societies and between countries. The differing spatial penetration rates reflect differences in the general rate of economic development, particularly between the high and low income countries.

The cumulative effect of telecommunications advances is to reinforce and strengthen existing global communications patterns since the advances are market driven (Figure 31.10). They strengthen the global importance of the advanced countries and of core economic centres and metropolises, which are the nodes of this emerging telecommunications network (Figure 33.9). The emerging importance of the maturing Newly Industrialising countries in South East Asia is also reflected in the intensification of their links with this global network while low income countries lag behind.

a Top 10 countries by minutes of outgoing international traffic, 1992

Country	Cum total (%)
USA	24.8
Germany	34.8
UK	41.7
France	47.3
Switzerland	51.0
Italy	54.6
Japan	57.7
Hong Kong	60.5
Netherlands	63.2
Belgium	65.5
Total	80.3

b Top international routes, 1993

USA/Canada
USA/Mexico
USA/UK
Hong Kong/China
USA/Germany
Switzerland/Germany
Germany/Austria
USA/Japan
Germany/France
Germany/UK

c Top international routes among developing countries, 1992

World rank	From	To
7	Hong Kong	China
8	China Hong	Kong
73	Singapore	Malaysia
74	Saudi Arabia	Egypt
89	Malaysia	Singapore

[SOURCE: *Financial Times* 13.10.95]

Figure 31.10 Leading telecommunication sources and links

On a national scale, while politicians emphasise the emergence of an interactive super information highway in the USA, carrying information, entertainment and services such as banking and shopping into all homes and linking businesses, the World Bank emphasises the lack of an even basic adequate telecommunication network in low income countries (Figure 31.11). There is a growing need but an inability to fulfil the need. For example, registered waiting lists for a telephone connection in low income countries were at 27% of installed capacity in

1994 with the estimated waiting time as long as 10 years at present rates of installation. In contrast, advanced countries and the more mature Newly Industrialising Countries of South East Asia are in the midst of a mobile telephone 'revolution' which is transforming the nature of business transactions in the market place. Within the emerging Asia Pacific region, the number of mobile telephone subscribers was at 10.3 million in 1994 and the forecast is for 74 million subscribers by 2000 as costs fall and networks are extended internationally with the move to digital systems.

Minutes of outgoing International Telephone Traffic (MITT) per inhabitant in selected countries, 1991

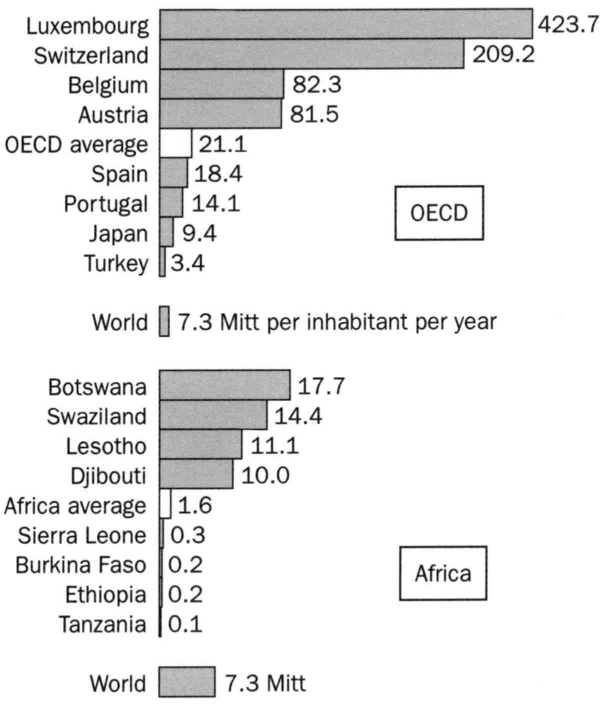

***Figure 31.11** The contrast in the density of outgoing international telephone traffic between selected OECD countries and African countries*

Already multinational business consortia are competing to establish a terrestrial and satellite mobile communications system which will 'allow people to make and receive calls from any point on earth using the same multipurpose handset'. The World Bank sees the unfulfilled demand for telecommunications in parts of the developing world as a severe hindrance to businesses, especially for those seeking to compete in international markets. Studies have shown that the quality of telecommunications is critical to generating exports and attracting foreign investment. For example, with 500 million people in 1995, Sub-Saharan Africa had only 3.5 million telephone lines, of which 60% were in South Africa. The World Bank and IMF, as part of their readjustment strategy for Africa, are pressing governments to privatise state-owned telecommunications industries and develop telecommunications as a matter of urgency. Governments have yet to agree on intra-Africa link-ups and strengthening international links. A current plan to set up the continent's own broadcasting satellite is held up by wrangles as to its location.

A mesh of integrated networks from local to global scale

Telecommunications networks can be viewed like transport networks in the sense that there are local and regional networks meshed within the wider national and international networks. For example, within companies there are now networks based on personal computers able to handle ever more sophisticated software, together with wireless telephonic and high speed communication links, shaping exchanges within the company and its dealings with other businesses and organisations outside. The personal computer work stations are the basis of the system; they are hooked together by telecommunications and hardwire links to form local and wider area networks (Lans and Wans) sharing and exchanging data and linked to printers and computer-based fax machines. Much of companies' external business is now done by fax, e.mail, and electronic trading. Financial transactions also now mainly take place via the computer-based network.

While increasing numbers of smaller companies and individuals are accessing the international network, only the larger corporations and governments have the resources to fully utilise its growing capacity. Their functioning depends on it. Dickens for example, points out that the USA multinational corporation Texas Instruments with 50 plants located in 19 different countries, relies on a satellite-based communication system to '*coordinate on a global scale its production planning, cost accounting, financial planning, marketing, customer services and personnel management*'.

International telecommunication networks are essential in other spheres. Weather forecasting can now be done within a global context and space satellite observation and telecommunication links are vital to early warning of abnormal weather conditions, such as the occurrence and passage of typhoons and hurricanes. Again the International Maritime Satellite Organisation (Inmarsat) has developed a world-wide maritime communications system to guide and control the movement of maritime traffic.

The Internet

The development of the Internet is perhaps making the public realise the global impact of the information and telecommunications network. The Internet information highway can be accessed over the public telephone link using a modem attached to a personal computer to cheaply gain access to a bewildering array of information from around the world as well as exchange information with the estimated other 50 million users of Internet, most of whom live in the USA and Europe. It is estimated that users are logging on currently at the rate of 1 million a month.

It is a network which has grown without any overall planning and regulation, initially in the USA as a way for scientists, technologists and academics to exchange information and ideas via computer networks. Link-ups were then made to computer networks within the UK and Europe. By 1994 the national computer networks of 72 countries were fully connected to the Internet which, though not complete, now stretches virtually around the globe. The major determinant of the actual physical layout of the Internet are the location of the super computer centres into which users can be linked by leased telecom lines.

Increasingly governments and businesses are seeing the potential of the Internet. The use of the Internet is being facilitated by the establishment of the World Wide Web making it easier to access information and also providing a means by which individuals, organisations and businesses can put their pages and data bases on to the Internet. The Web is the means by which newspaper publishers can place their electronic newspapers on the Internet for access by users and is also increasingly the means by which companies are promoting their products and wares (Figure 31.12).

The rapid growth of the Internet is some indication of the pace at which the international information and telecommunications super highway is developing. One of the most important aspects of this development is broadening the transmission bands on the highway to facilitate the transmission of multimedia information, combining computer text with audio and video sound and images.

Of even greater urgency is the extension of the network into low income and other developing countries which, until very recently, have been virtually excluded from this telecommunications revolution. The importance of their participation in a global information network was stressed at The Earth Summit in 1992.

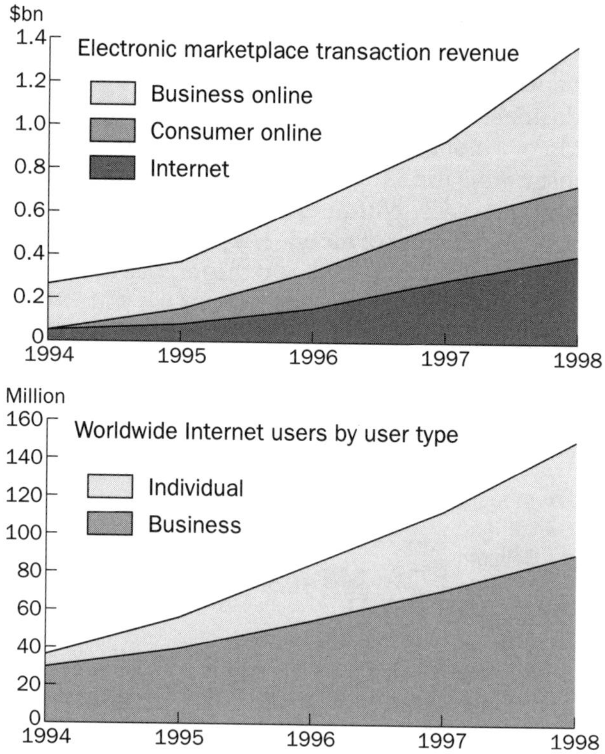

[SOURCE: *Financial Times* 26.2.96]

Figure 31.12 *Commerce on the Net*

For the first time ever electronic mailing and conferencing were widely used by non-government organisations (NGOs) to exchange information and coordinate lobbying efforts in relation to the work of the Summit. Significantly also during the Summit, NGONET was established as part of Internet to 'promote global information sharing and the networking process' in relation to environment and development issues. It was specifically concerned with the information needs of groups in the developing world, including indigenous groups, women's groups and 'grass roots' organisations.

Bissio in *Cyberbase and the 'disabled' of the global village*, emphasises the importance of 'a bottom up' approach so that communities can use the information highway to communicate with each other as well as convey their views to policy-makers and defend them from others outside the communities.

Modern telecommunications may in time become a powerful tool not only for promoting the rights of disadvantaged groups but also in encouraging more balanced and sustainable development since it provides one of the means by which communities at the grass roots can participate in the development process.

31.8 Transport – Communications and development

The importance of an adequate integrated transport and communications network to a country's economic, social and political life is indicated by the percentage of national income spent on transport. Investment in transport is regarded as a priority not only at government levels but also by the general public.

As a country develops and specialisation and diversification becomes a feature of the economy, so the need for transport is increased. For example, in its formative years the industrial revolution in Western Europe was accompanied by a revolution in transport with development of a canal and then an increasingly dense rail network. Today Western Europe is in the throes of another major reshaping of its transport networks.

Transport and economic development

While development of transport has historically been seen as a response to demand, it is also clear today that the relationship is two-way. Where accessibility to an area containing resources is improved, development will be further stimulated. There are many examples of this happening. The development of the motorway network in the UK, for example, has prompted further growth of economic activity in the vicinity of motorway junctions.

However, embarking on a programme of transport development does not automatically lead to further growth. The current demand and a realistic level of future demand must be assessed. Over-investment in transport can lead to insufficient finance being left over for developing the actual resources and economic activities for which the transport network is intended. Brazil, for example, has been criticised for over heavy investment in grandiose highway schemes such as the Trans-Amazonian highway and neglecting the needs of the thousands of settlers encouraged to take up plots of land in the vicinity of the highway.

In the past, transport networks have developed in a piecemeal fashion since there was no overall planning. Each development was usually a response to some sporadic event or some specific economic social or political force. The opening up of a mining area or the clearance of land for commercial agriculture was accompanied by the building of a transport route, as for example in the case of rail lines developed in West Malaysia to link tin mines and rubber plantations to ports.

With time, if economic growth and spread of settlement occurs, some integration of one mode of transport with another will occur, such as feeder roads built to the main rail lines which in turn link to a port outlet. However, deficiencies will be present. The network will be a response to market demand forces and a variable population distribution with most demand being in the densely settled areas while others will be inadequately served.

A model for transport development

Even allowing for deficiencies in networks, there have been a number of attempts by geographers to idealise the way in which a transport network may develop over time in relation to the economic development of a country. One of the most well known is that by Taaffe, Morrill and Gould for the economic growth of an underdeveloped country, in which they saw the improvement of internal accessibility through the expansion of a transportation network as a critical factor.

For many developing countries colonialism and the exploitation of primary products for export were the major forces leading to the initial development of a transport network. Thus the sequence of development is seen as starting with routes leading inland from the ports and ultimately on to the development of an integrated network, including major nodal points inland and at the ports. In the network, the most important primary routes could be identified as those linking the major population and economic centres, with secondary and minor routes linking much of the remaining areas of the country to them. Thus the network could be regarded as a system along which the flows of materials, goods and people reflected the interdependence of different areas within the country and its external links through trade and travel.

Factors affecting the development of a transport network

Human factors

The model essentially sees the development of the transport network as a response to the way economic growth occurs (Figure 31.13). This does make it useful as a context for analysis of the way transport networks develop, but the relationship is not a simple one. Apart from the influence of other types of factors, certain kinds of economic activity require a different level and pattern of transport from others. Development based on primary resources requires a more basic network than one where the economy is more diversified.

Again, though the density of the network will vary spatially according to population density, demand is also determined by income levels – the higher the average per capita income level, the greater the transport network density. Alluvial lands in Monsoon Asia may have the highest concentrations of population, but the poverty of the mass of the population together with a greater dependence on subsistence farming, limits transport development. Network densities are greatest in the populated industrial regions of developed countries – in areas such as the north-east USA and the industrial triangle of Western Europe centred on the Ruhr (Case study 31.1).

At the other extreme, however, even sparsely populated areas may require a basic network, and measured per head of the population, may be greater than the level of demand based on purchasing power would warrant, as is the case in the less populated areas of Australia. This emphasises the fact that transport provision is not solely decided on economic grounds. It is also guided by social and political requirements.

Physical factors

Besides human factors, the other most influential set of forces determining the nature of the transport network is that of the physical environment.

The natural resource of an area exerts an influence, since the level and character of economic activity as well as population numbers are to some extent determined by the resources in an area. A more direct relationship is evident where the discovery of minerals in an otherwise harsh and difficult physical environment will lead to the building of a transport artery, as in the case of iron ore development in the desert area of Mauritania (North Africa) (Case study 26.1).

Some positive aspects of the environment may, however, have a negative effect. This is increasingly so where areas are designated as Areas of Natural Beauty and safeguarded by conservation measures. There have been a number of cases where this has so far either delayed motorway construction or caused deviation from a planned route. In the UK the parallel route to the M62 was scheduled to run through the Derbyshire Peak District but its construction has been prevented by the action of conservationist groups and the government's reappraisal of the necessity for it. Recently there have been attempts to prevent construction of a Newbury by-pass.

Difficult physical conditions do generally deter the development of an integrated transport network. The sheer size and shape of a country are obvious but

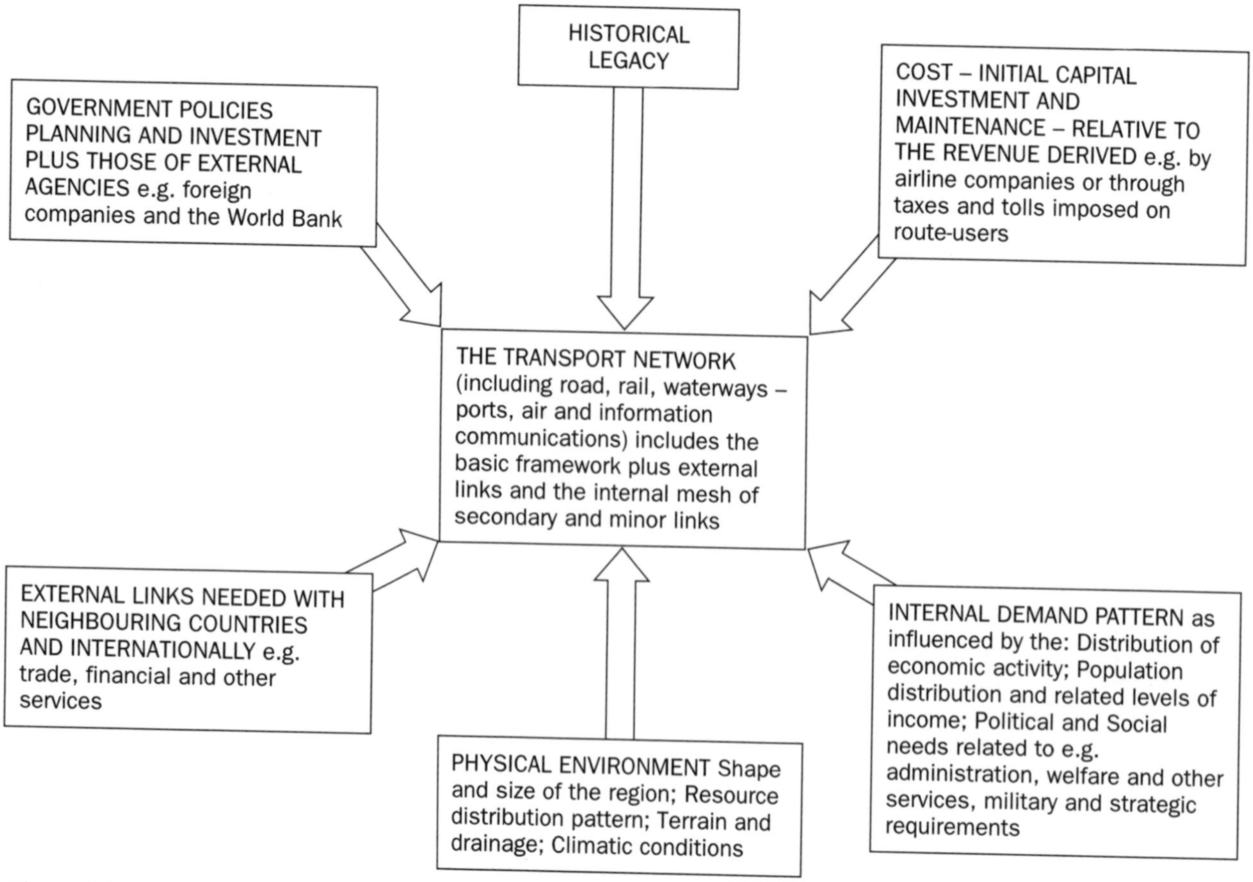

Figure 31.13 Factors influencing the development of a transport system

important influences. The vast distances in Australia for example make transport costs high while the heavily indented coast of Japan directly affects the cost and shape of the network.

The most widespread effects are exercised by difficult terrain, whether it be marshland and ice regions as in North Siberia or the mountainous uplands as in Central Europe and down the west coast of the Americas. Such regions exercise a two-fold influence. They deter settlement anyway and reduce the demand for transport, but also they make the building of the network extremely costly. Also, mountainous areas have adverse weather conditions making the maintenance of routes costly.

However, if the demand is there, adverse physical conditions will be overcome. One of the clearest illustrations of this is the comprehensive network which exists in Switzerland despite its mountainous nature.

In areas of more favourable terrain, networks are generally more efficient, directly linking areas of greatest population and economic activity as seen in the north-west European lowlands and in the Pampas region of Argentina and Paraguay.

Transport planning

In the modern world the organisation of the economic, social and political life of a country is very complex and governments have increasingly found it necessary to exercise some control over development. Since transport is so important a factor in this development, it is not surprising that it is subject to close planning legislation and direct government investment.

Achieving a balanced and optimum network suited to the needs of a country is fraught with problems. Investment needs in this sector must be balanced against investment needs in other sectors, such as agriculture, industry and welfare. In the past over-investment in transport has occurred in some newly independent countries, with too little investment in stimulating economic activities which could make use of the new routes.

One of the most major criticisms of newly independent countries is that larger transport schemes do little for the mass of the people engaged in the rural sector where subsistence farming is combined with some cash cropping. These people cannot afford motorised transport and their essential needs are to do with carrying materials and produce on the farm, from the farm to the roadside and then from the roadside to a local market or co-operative centre.

In Kenya surveys have shown that the greatest need is for improved ways of carrying small loads of 10 to 140 kg in weight over short distances of between 1 and 25 km. The vast bulk of this kind of carrying is still by human porterage, bicycle and animal cart over rough tracks unsuitable for the usual motorised vehicles. International agencies are therefore increasingly trying to direct aid, loans and national government expenditure into intermediate transport technology which would be of direct help to people in the rural sector. It is such things as improvements in bicycle design, mass production of cycle trailers and three-wheel push carrier trikes, better ox and bullock cart design, and at a motorised level, motor cycle carriers and tractor transport, which are needed. In India the nearest thing to a vehicle for the masses is a bicycle, since 1 in 4 households have one – well over 100 million in all.

Improved public transport and other motor transport to the local market town and to reach schools, trading stores and clinics are amongst the other vital needs.

All these basic improvements on the lower order of the network and modes of transport require integrating into a larger scale network, linking larger centres together and the country to the outside world.

Concluding comment

- Much of the chapter has of necessity been concerned with individual modes of transport and communication but emphasis has also been placed on the need to see these as part of an integrated network and a national level and on a global scale.
- At this time of rapid technological change and globalisation of communications, the poorest nations are being increasingly left behind. Without urgent attention being given to improving infrastructures in these countries, it is difficult to envisage any marked improvement in the quality of life for the mass of people living there. Without this, there cannot be an end to the periodic outbreaks of civil war and other political conflicts which in turn negate many of the efforts towards improving the quality of life for the poorest and also threaten general global stability.

case study

31.1 The Channel Tunnel: towards a highspeed integrated continental rail system

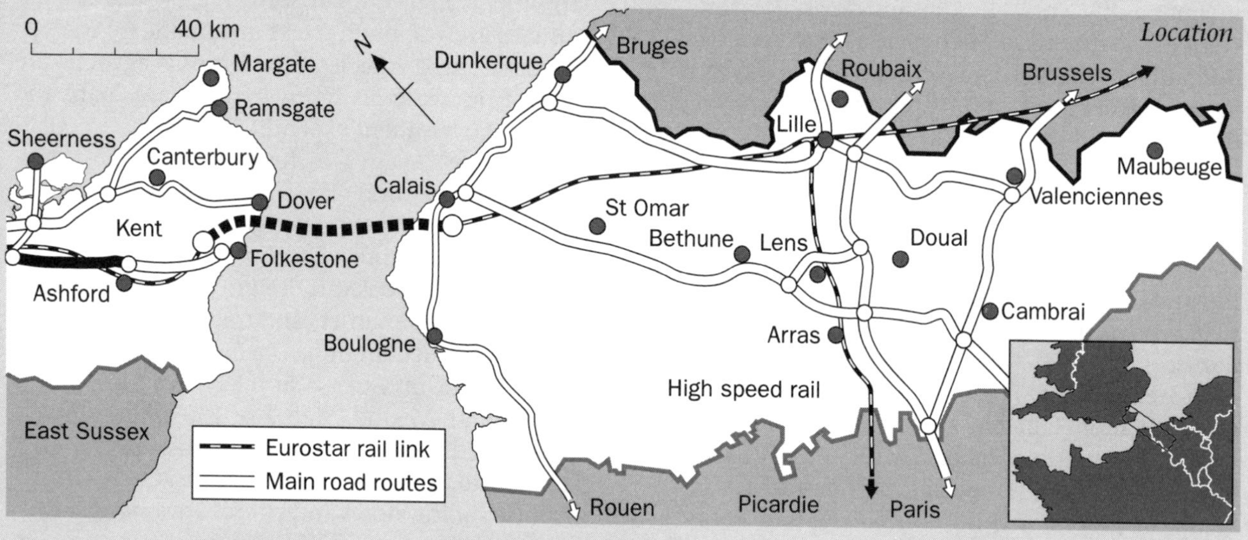

The Channel Tunnel was opened in 1994 at a cost of £106 billion, double the original estimate. It is forecast it will carry 30 million passengers and 15 million tonnes of freight annually. Within 250 km around the terminals it covers much of the European Union's 'golden belt' economic heartland.

Competition for passenger and transport business between the railways, the ferries, air and road services

The rail companies have great expectations for the cross-channel route. It promises a reversal of the decline in rail travel experienced since the end of the Second World War.

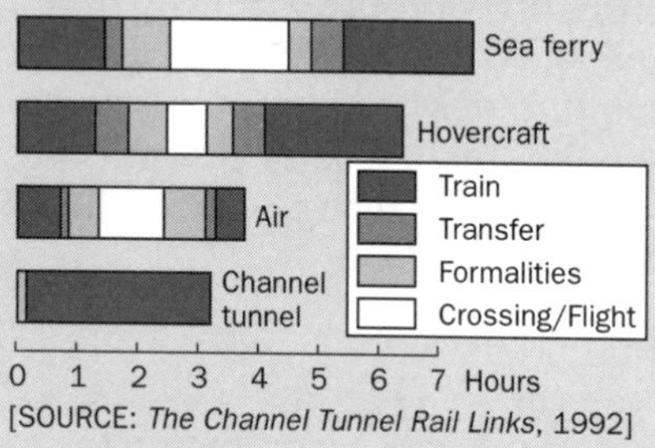

[SOURCE: *The Channel Tunnel Rail Links*, 1992]

Comparative journey times

Potential benefits

- It can deliver passengers straight into the core of cities.
- It can handle large volumes of passenger and freight traffic .
- The tunnel and its fast rail links will boost traffic also on the entire feeder lines network in the UK.
- Electrified rail lines are less polluting and more energy efficient than road and air transport.
- Fast travel at 125 – 160 mph will allow passengers to travel 620 miles in one day. The new high speed link will halve journey times to and in Europe.

Limitations

- There is as yet no fast track built into the UK. Eurostar uses existing lines but the service will be extended to Swansea and Glasgow.
- The track loading gauge is smaller in the UK than on the continent limiting much of the use of continental rolling stock on the UK network.
- At the initiation of the service, only 7% of cross-channel freight went by rail wagon. There is thus much marketing to be done to raise the level to any significant extent.

Progress so far

- Passenger traffic by Eurostar is expanding – trains to Paris are 70% – 80% full but those to Brussels are only 30% full. Car and passenger numbers on the Shuttle services are expanding, aided by aggressive price concessions.
- Almost half the tunnel's capacity will be taken up by freight. Rail Freight Distribution estimates it can capture a quarter of the cross-channel freight traffic. Of the 1200 companies approached in the first major marketing campaigns, deals have been agreed with 900. This includes e.g. a deal to transport Ford motor components from factories in the UK to assembly plants in Spain. Rail freight times significantly undercut times by roads e.g. Liverpool to Stuttgart is 28 hours by rail against 48 by road, Cardiff to Paris 15 as against 18 hours.
- On the UK network it is estimated freight will be increased from the current 2 million tonnes a year to 9 million by the year 2000. A new fast rail freight network is being developed by Rail Freight

Potential rail freight services via the Channel Tunnel

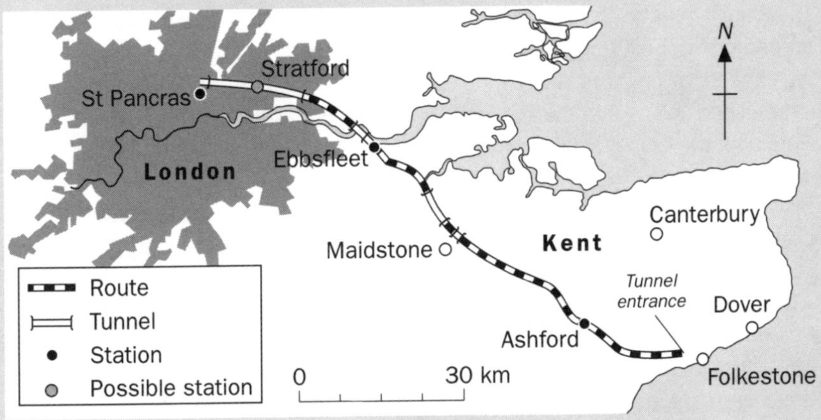

The agreed route 1994 – 95

Distribution to provide efficient loading and a fleet of new loader wagons have been built. There are new Euroterminals at Willesden, Birmingham, Liverpool, Cardiff, Middlesborough and private sector terminal initiatives e.g. at Daventry and Doncaster.

The London to Channel Terminal Rail Link

The benefits of the Channel Tunnel link to the continent have been significantly limited by the failure to build a high speed rail track to London similar to that already in Paris. The Eurostar high speed trains have to use the already congested main North Kent commuter line, adding 30 minutes more to the London-Paris route, extending the total time to 3 hours.

The delay is due to an extended political debate on the route, lack of integrated planning and public and environmental group opposition to suggested routes.

Environmentalists were particularly concerned in case the route went through the ecological habitats of the Medway and Thames marshes. They were concerned about its impact on the Downs and ancient woodland areas such as that near Cobham.

The effect of a new route on house prices adjacent to the route was also considered. Probably the delay itself and uncertainties as to the route have created significant 'house price and planning blight'.

The final decision on the route was made in 1995 and the adverse impact is likely to be less than feared because of the use of tunnelling in sensitive areas and avoidance of the Thames-Medway marshes. The route will generally run along the line of the existing main road and rail routes but cut under the Thames at Dartford to terminate at St Pancras.

Much will be done to reduce the adverse environmental impact of the terminal area through extensive landscaping, moving and replanting a 12-acre wood and discrete disposal of tunnel rubble at the base of the sea cliffs.

Response of the ferry services to competition

The response of the major ferry companies has been to cut prices further and to improve the efficiency of services. In cooperation with the Dover Harbour Dock Authority, dock handling facilities have been greatly improved.

The Ferry Services in 1994 handled 2.89 million tourist cars, 142 000 coaches and 1 million freight trucks.

By offering more facilities and comfort (restaurants, shopping on board, shorter embarking times, etc) they hope to remain viable.

Competition with air traffic

The Channel Tunnel is only a threat to air passenger services over journeys of up to four hours. The cost of the tunnel route is competitive for business travellers and it claims greater efficiency, service and is time saving.

It also claims to avoid the inconvenience of longer taxi or tube journeys from the city to the airport and a long checking-in time.

Possible benefits to Kent

The immediate impact on employment is less than forecast. It was hoped construction and infrastructure developments associated with the tunnel would provide between 6800 to 12 900 jobs in the area around; the estimate is now down to only 2000 additional jobs as the tunnel and single European market have led to significant loss of jobs in the cross-channel services.

Businesses have been hesitant to set up until the benefits of the tunnel are proven. Still, there is expansion of business parks at nodes along the route e.g. Ashford, Maidstone and Crossways at Dartford.

It has not improved the employment blackspot of north-east Kent where in 1994, unemployment was running at 17%. The area has recently gained Assisted Area status but there is no direct link to the Channel Tunnel terminal.

Kent is already the next most important tourist destination after London for visitors from the continent. The tunnel link will give a further boost to the tourist industry.

Some of the present traffic congesting roads in Kent may be reduced by more use of the rail link. Road flows in Kent increased 71% between 1980 – 91 as against a national increase of 37%.

Economic effects of the Tunnel in France

The French have been much better prepared to benefit from the tunnel. A high speed rail link was already established linking into the TGV network near the tunnel at Lille, with direct through-routes to Paris and Brussels. There is only one change at Lille to other European destinations such as Barcelona and Turin.

The focus for the region of Nord-Pas de Calais is Lille, centre of the old industrial region. It is trying to shed its image as a 'grimy nineteenth century mining and textile centre'. Around the new Unralille TGV terminal a vast office, commercial and shopping complex has been built. Now only half an hour from Brussels, Lille is hoping to attract 'satellite' public and other ancillary agencies as rents and land are cheaper than in Brussels.

Initiatives such as tax breaks are being offered to attract businesses. For example, Coca-Cola have established a large factory in Dunkerque and a satellite based Euro-teleport operation has been set up at Roubaix.

Calais also benefits. Close to the tunnel terminal the 90 000 square metres Cite' de l'Europe office, shopping and entertainment complex has been built. It is estimated 3000 more jobs have been created in the Calais area.

British Rail and the expansion of intermodal transport in Europe

While the EU has sanctioned major road network development, it is favouring a more integrated transport approach to reduce expansion of rail and air traffic further. Intermodal transport involves a switch of mode of transport on a freight journey but without the necessity of unloading the freight load at a change of mode point. On the continent, intermodal traffic has risen steeply from 15.4 billion to 20.1 billion tonnes between 1988 and 1993. Most of this combines road and rail transport, the switch from one to the other being either by transferring containers, putting standard truck trailers on to low platform rail wagons or 'piggy back' transfer of the whole road truck and its load.

British Freight Distribution is looking to substantially increase its intermodal transport capacity – currently most is via Le Shuttle services through the tunnel.

case study

31.2 Europoort, Rotterdam: the 'anyport' concept

Stages in the development of 'Anyport'

1. Primitive port established – at a place on the estuary where a harbour can be easily built adjacent to firm ground on which the town develops.
2. Marginal quay extension – need and establishment of quays begins to outstrip town growth.
3. Marginal quay elaboration – pressure for growth but area contained.
4. Dock elaboration – wet docks are built further downstream where water is deeper and more space available on-shore to which road and rail connections are built. Thus increased size of ships and greater volume can be met.
5. Simple lineal quayage – docks quays need to be modified and extended to accommodate larger vessels.
6. Specialised quayage – needed for particular bulk cargoes as well as for container and roll-on roll-off traffic.

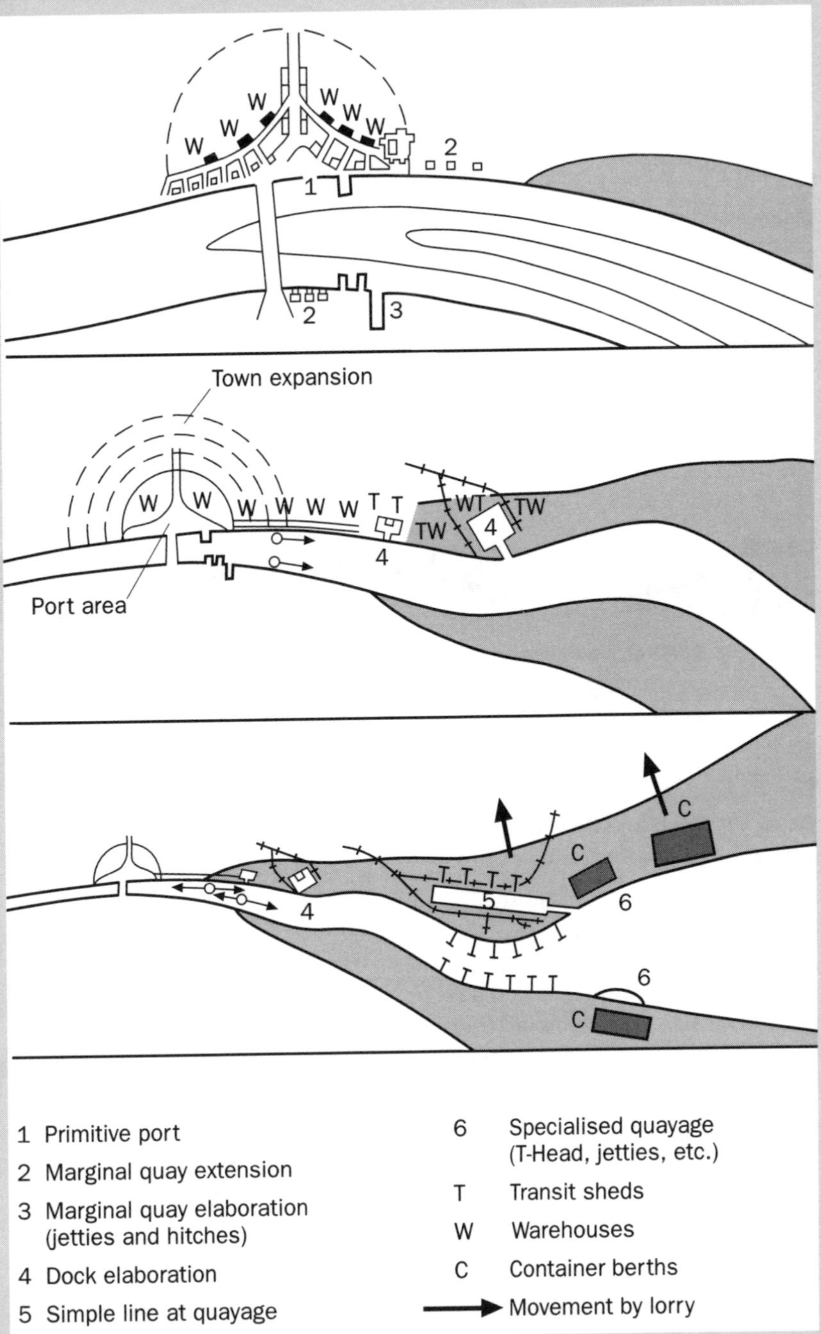

The 'Anyport' concept

Rotterdam – Europoort

1. Originally a medieval fishing village, by the eighteenth century with increasing Dutch overseas development it had become an important port.
2. In 1872 a new waterway had to be cut to accommodate larger vessels. Its importance increased with development of hinterland including the Ruhr and Lorraine. Docks were developed on the south bank at Waalhaven.
3. Trade was boosted by the EU formation in 1958 and bulk/container traffic especially increased oil trade. New channel and Europoort-Botlek Development formed.
4. The most recent development reclamation for industrial sites and quays were at Maasvlakte. The upper harbour was modified to take container traffic.
5. Presently it is a leading world port with waterways as well as fast rail and road links through the hinterland. It has important entrepôt trade (redistribution to other ports). It is one of world's leading industrial complexes – heavy industrial petro-chemicals and food processing. However, it does suffer pollution and congestion problems.

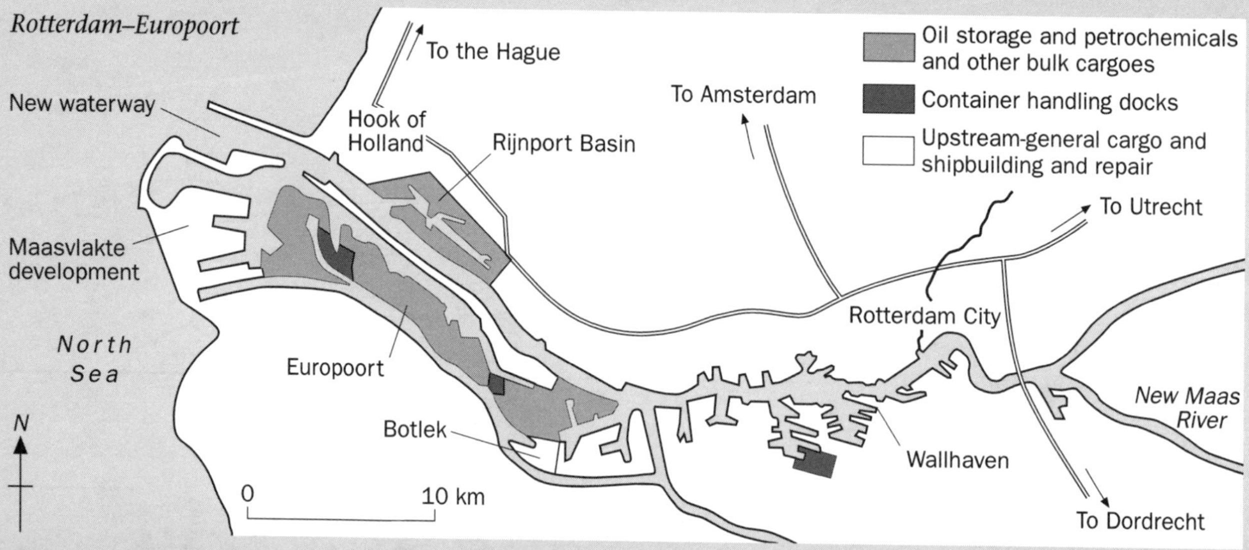

case study

31.3 Controversy over the further expansion of Heathrow airport

The need and justification as seen by the BAA (British Airports Authority)

- Expansion of passenger traffic requires a new terminal if Heathrow is to maintain its competitive lead. Over 52 million passengers used Heathrow in 1994, a third en route to other destinations and the fifth terminal is needed to cope with an additional forecast 30 million passengers.
- If it is not built, these customers will be lost to expanding continental airports such as Schiphol and Frankfurt.
- The land to be used will not extend the airport perimeter since existing land, at present occupied by a sludge works, between the runways will be used.
- The infrastructure is already being further developed to carry traffic from the airport to London e.g. new underground and fast rail link plus widening of the M25.
- Aircraft noise is unlikely to be any more than at present as constant engine and other technological advances are reducing aircraft noise.
- Heathrow is a major generator of economic activity and job growth in the region. At present Heathrow directly employs 8000 people and the new terminal will add another 6000. Office commercial and infrastructure growth around the airport currently provides 60 000 jobs.

Opposition to building a fifth terminal

- The Planning Enquiry into a fifth terminal starting on 16 May 1995 had already received 10 000 letters, 90% objecting to the terminal. The 22 local authorities in the area around also objected. Much of the opposition is organised by a strong lobby HACAN (Heathrow Association for Control of Aircraft Noise).
- Objections are largely on the grounds of increased aircraft noise, much greater traffic congestion on approach roads and the increased danger of aircraft accidents.
- Objections are also on the wider grounds that 'Terminal five sounds like just another terminal. It isn't. It's a whole new airport.' As such it is bound to bring much more pressure for further developments to the west of London where costs, congestion and pressures are already high.
- The Airport Policy Consortium would rather see consideration given to a new airport east of London in line with government policy to regenerate the East Thames corridor.
- Excess passenger growth should also be diverted to Gatwick and particularly Stansted which has spare capacity, land and an already established infrastructure linking it to London and other regions.

CHAPTER 32

The importance of trade to the global economy

Trade is more than the mere exchange of goods and services. In the modern world, trade more often than not sows the seed for growth and development. Here we refer to growth as additions to general well being whereas development is the improvement in the general welfare and quality of life. Trade also provides the knowledge and experience that makes development possible. In turn trade provides the capital goods that are indispensable to economic growth. Trade brings together the knowhow as the means and vehicle for the dissemination of technical knowledge and transmission of innovation.

CHO G *TRADE, AID AND GLOBAL INTERDEPENDENCE*, 1995

32.1 A definition

Trade as an engine of growth towards more global economic integration

International trade has a very important role in fostering the economic growth and development of nations. It is one of the 'engines' of growth but more than this, it is the prime means by which countries can be drawn into an increasingly integrated world economy (Chapter 33). Thus for the developing countries increasing participation in world trade would appear to be essential.

This is a theme particularly emphasised since the early 1970s when the United Nations sought to establish a New International Economic Order (NIEO) which would '*eliminate the widening gap between the developed and the developing countries and ensure steadily accelerating economic and social development*' (part of the UN General Assembly resolution April 1974).

Twenty years on after all the efforts of individual countries to pursue more progressive economic policies to liberalise trade including the recent Uruguay Gatt Round of 1994, four fifths of the world's trade is still dominated by a core of advanced countries. Developing countries with 90% of the world's population, still account for less than 20% of international trade. Little progress towards a New International Economic Order appears to have been made.

However, while advanced countries continue to dominate, the trade of Newly Industrialising Countries has increased dramatically and with it, their pace of economic development. The four Asian tigers (Singapore, Hong Kong, Taiwan and South Korea), have combined a drive towards a more market-driven economy with an increasingly export-orientated strategy. In the late 1980s these four countries accounted for 77% of all manufactured exports from developing countries. While the North Asian countries' (including Japan) share of world trade expanded from 8% in 1960 to 20% in 1992, North America's share fell noticeably from 46% to 32% and Western Europe's share remained constant (Figure 33.3).

In contrast, the poorest countries have fallen further behind (Figures 32.1 and 32.2). The volume of world trade has risen dramatically over the post-war years to a value twelve-fold in real terms compared to that before 1950, but the share of poorer countries remains below 5%. Their failure in gaining an equitable share of world trade is both a symptom of the poverty of their economies and a cause of them.

Development groups (World Bank Classification)	1983 Percentage world share	1983 Average annual growth 1980 – 1993 by %	1993 Percentage world share	1993 Average annual growth 1980 – 1993 by %
High Income Economies	78.3%	5.1	75.8%	5.8
Middle Income Economies	17.5%	4.2*	19.2%	3.0*
Low Income Economies	4.2%	6.4	5.0%	6.5
(when China and India are excluded)	(1.2%)	(1.4)	(1.7%)	(– 2.6)
World total	100%	5.2	100%	5.1

(*Upper Middle Income only given in World Bank figures)

Figure 32.1 *Proportion of world merchandise trade 1993 and average annual growth 1980 – 93*

Figure 32.2 *Rise in the value of visible trade*

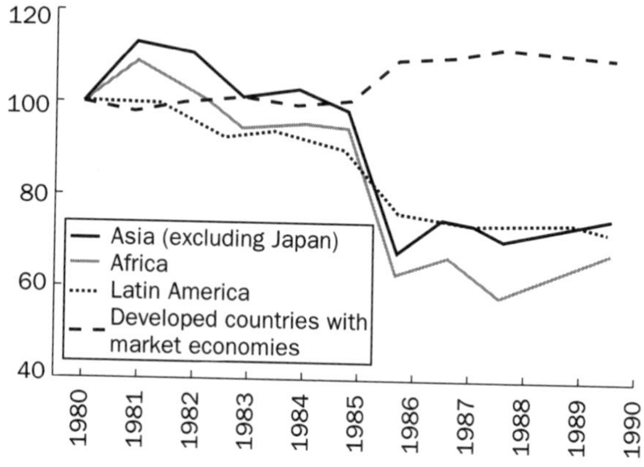

Terms of trade

'Terms of trade' refer to the relationship between the unit value of a country's imports and the unit value of its exports. If we analyse this relation over a period of time, we can see the changes in the buying capacity – or 'purchasing power', of a country's exports. If the Terms of Trade are falling, as is the case with the Third World regions shown in this chart – it means that each year fewer foreign products can be bought with the revenue made from the region's exports. This might be because the value of the region's imports has grown comparative to that of its exports, or simply that the products for export have lost value in relation to those imported.

This chart makes it possible to compare changes in the industrialised countries' Terms of Trade, with changes in those of the Third World. The Third World is represented in regional blocks in order to make the trend easier to observe.

[SOURCE: *Third World Guide 93/94*, 1994]

Figure 32.3 *Changing terms of trade, 1980 – 90*

Factors influencing the structure and pattern of international trade

Comparative advantage and complementarity

Classical theory on international trade has as its basis the concept of ***comparative advantage*** first postulated by Ricardo in 1817. ***It suggests that different regions will specialise in producing those goods and services for which each is best endowed.*** Each region will then trade some of these goods and services with other areas in order to obtain those goods and services which it needs but for which it is not particularly favourably endowed. Despite the complexity of the world economy, the concept remains important.

Exchange brings in also the idea of ***'complementarity'*** suggested by Ullman in 1956 to help explain the spatial interaction between places as evidenced by the flow of goods and services and the movement of people between them. ***Complementarity implies a supply and demand relationship between places in the sense that one place must want what the other has and the other place be willing to supply it.***

Year	Combined index for all primary commodities	Manufactured goods
1986	104	120
1990	127	158
1993	111	157

NOTE: It is clear primary commodities price changes have continually underperformed compared to price changes for manufactured goods – contributory to developing countries exporting primary commodities, experiencing unfavourable terms of trade.

Figure 32.4 *Indices of prices of primary commodities relative to manufactured goods 1986–1993*

Trade between the industrialising countries of Western Europe and their colonies in the nineteenth century would appear to illustrate these concepts of complementarity and comparative advantage. Western Europe imported raw materials and tropical foodstuffs and in exchange, exported manufactured goods to the colonies. However, the circumstances under which it took place ignored some of the basic rules which Ricardo and others saw as part of the theory of international trade: it was not a mutual arrangement freely entered into by partners of equal status and on equal terms, which would mutually benefit each party. It was a trading arrangement dictated by the European countries primarily for their benefit, with the colonies playing a subordinate role which brought them only very limited benefit and distortion of their economies. The historical legacy of this ***trade dependency*** is one of the reasons why the poorer tropical countries today fail to command a larger share of world trade; for most there is still dependency on a narrow range of primary exports mainly to the advanced countries of Western Europe and North America on unfavourable terms of trade (Figure 32.4).

Trade dependency
This occurs when a developing country is so reliant on its advanced economy trading partner(s) that any changes in their economic policy or economic condition could have a severe effect on the developing country's economy. It also implies that the advanced country or countries dominate the trade partnership and exercise an influence over the developing country's economic policy.

Until the 1970s the advanced economies dominating world trade enjoyed a clear comparative advantage in terms of manufacturing output and in tradable services (Figure 32.5). While raw material endowments had declined, other ***factor endowments*** of capital, skills, technology and entrepreneurship had increased. To these were added advantages of economies of scale and agglomeration as production and service provision became increasingly concentrated into large corporations and multinationals to reduce costs and increase competitive advantage (Figure 32.3). The advanced countries dominated world trade, but it was a trade largely conducted among themselves. This negates the idea of complementarity in that the USA, Western Europe and Japan had broadly similar economies.

Top 100 companies

Country	Number of companies	Country	Number of companies
Europe	**19**	**Japan**	**27**
UK	6	**Asia-Pacific**	**4**
Switzerland	5	Australia	1
Germany	4	Hong Kong	1
Neth / UK	2	Singapore	1
Sweden	2	South Korea	1
USA	**50**		

[SOURCE: *Financial Times* 25.1.96]

Figure 32.5 *The dominance of the advanced economies as the base for the world's leading companies 1995*

Factor endowment
The term refers to factors of production and how relatively endowed a country or region is with these. Factor endowment relates to the production of both goods and services. The most basic factors or inputs are land, capital and labour. But in respect of today's production of goods and services, a wide range and number of inputs are included under the term 'factor endowment'. These include strategic location, raw materials, quantity and quality of labour, capital, levels of technology, management and entrepreneurial skills and levels of education.

The influence of the size and character of market demand and competition

Others factors influencing the pattern of world trade are location of market demand and competition. Level of per capita Gross Domestic Product is highest in advanced economies and it is here that the demand for tradeable goods and services is highest. In low income countries a large proportion of income is spent on the basic necessities of food, clothing and shelter. In contrast, in high income countries a high proportion of income is spent on higher order manufactured goods and services. Moreover, within sophisticated economies a choice between competing products and services is also required. Hence as long as there is access to the market, imported goods and services compete with home-produced goods and services for buyers. This is evident today in the range and choice of cars and electrical products on offer in the markets of the advanced countries, for example, as it is in the range of capital goods on offer to businesses.

Mobility of endowment factors and the emergence of Japan and Newly Industrialising Countries as players in world trade

Classical trade theory assumes that endowment factors conveying comparative advantage on a place or country are fixed. A factor such as land is fixed but some factors are mobile and can be transferred from one location to another and from one country to another. These include capital, technology, and technical and entrepreneurial skills. Thus as Dickens emphasises *'comparative advantage is not simply 'given'; it is created and recreated by human action'* (Dickens P, 1992). It changes with time.

Even by the 1960s the older advanced economies of Western Europe and USA were beginning to lose some of their comparative advantage in certain branches of manufactured goods. These included heavy industries such as iron and steel, chemicals and shipbuilding and staple consumer goods industries such as textiles. While in the case of heavy industries it was partly attributable to a run down of raw material endowments (e.g. coal and iron ore), it was much more due to a loss of competitiveness in relation to other factor inputs, such as labour costs, technology inputs and outdated management.

Conversely, Japan was gaining comparative advantage, combining high productivity and competitive pricing due to highly skilled reasonably priced labour with the use of advanced technology, good management and import of raw materials and energy fuels. Further supported by an increasingly large and protected home market, Japanese companies since the 1960s have become powerful players in world trade (Figure 32.7).

However, since the 1970s Japan has been joined by and experienced increasing competition from its neighbours, the 'four Asian tigers', Singapore, Hong Kong, Taiwan and South Korea. The first two have also become increasingly important participants in the world trade of services, especially those related to finance. The advance of these Newly Industrialising Countries and, more recently, others such as Indonesia, Malaysia, Brazil and Mexico, can partly be explained by increases in their 'comparative advantage'. This was initially due to a transfer to them of factor inputs from outside combined with internal factor inputs, of which the most important has been a plentiful supply of adaptable and trainable labour at a cost significantly below that for labour in the advanced economies.

Foreign multinational companies have played the key role in transferring capital and technological expertise to these Newly Industrialising Countries and in combining it with a plentiful supply of labour to produce a range of manufactured goods largely for export. However, the comparative advantage of the 'four Asian tigers' has also been increasingly enhanced by their governments' positive attitude to multinational investment and a drive to advance their economies on the basis of an export-oriented strategy combined with fostering their own transnational companies and building up a strong human and physical infrastructure. Not only are these Asian transnational corporations, such as Samsung of South Korea, now important exporters of manufactured goods but also increasingly are transferring capital by direct foreign investment to other developing countries and to advanced countries (Case study 20.1).

32.2 The influence of multinationals on the structure and pattern of world trade

> Transnational corporations dominate international markets in most tradeable goods and services ... Transnational corporations can be a source of modern management and technical skills as well as the critical (international contract and marketing networks) and domestic (manufacturing techniques and disciplines) elements needed to enter world markets on an equal footing with foreign competitors.
>
> [SOURCE: *Industrial Development*, Global Report, UNIDO 1995]

It is difficult to obtain precise figures on the percentage of world trade and foreign investment flows that can be attributed directly to the activities of multinational corporations, but a UN Commission on Transnationals in 1991 estimated that the leading 500 companies in the world accounted for 70% of world trade and 80% of direct private investment as well as controlling 30% of the world's GDP.

Manufacturing is but one part of multinational activity. There are important multinational institutions engaged in services such as the United States Manhattan Chase Bank. Other multinationals are huge conglomerates engaged in a range of diversified economic activities (Section 17.3). Amongst the most important of these are the Japanese 'sogo-shosha' conglomerates such as Mitsubishi and Sumito, spanning commercial, financial and industrial activities. These have set up the global investment and marketing framework which has increasingly helped Japanese companies to export and operate at a global level since the 1960s. It would be impossible for manufacturing multinationals to operate without the accompanying support of an internationalisation of a whole range of services such as information technology, financial services, advertising and transportation.

Decision-making on the location of economic activity is done at a global level with a view to minimising costs and maximising market access and market share. Consequently, rather than the location of all activity being within one country and export from here to overseas markets, different parts of the production process have been spatially separated and dispersed across national boundaries or branch activities located at points of lowest cost or location of most appropriate access to the market being served.

This increasing internationalisation of the different operations of multinationals has greatly increased the flow of goods and services across national boundaries. The direction of overseas investment gives a good indication where their global economic activity is located and in turn, where the major contributions to the flow of goods and services are originating. Dickens emphasises that contrary to popular thinking *'transnational investment is still concentrated primarily in the developed market economies'* even though the degree of cross-border investment has increased substantially and become more complex. For both European and Japanese multinationals, the USA is the main target for investment both in services and manufacturing. Western Europe as the second most important region, has regained ground since the formation of the European Union single market in 1992. Both USA and Japanese multinationals increasingly see the advantage of penetrating the single market. Since the early 1980s, 80% of foreign investment from multinationals based in the USA and Europe has been in the developed world, as has 40% of Japanese investment.

Thus the overseas activities of multinationals continues to reinforce the dominant role of the advanced countries in world trade.

When considering the direction of the 20% to 25% of multinational foreign investment which has gone to developing countries since the mid-1970s, between 1975 to 1985 the largest volume went to Latin America and the Caribbean mainly because of USA multinational investment in Brazil and Mexico. However, since the mid-1980s East and South East Asia has become the fastest growing concentration of foreign multinational investment. In particular, this region took 23% of all Japanese foreign investment in 1994 to 1995. This and other foreign investment is no longer restricted largely to the Hong Kong, Taiwan, South Korea and Singapore but has and is increasing substantially in China and other Newly Industrialising Countries such as Indonesia, Thailand and Malaysia. Hence the progressively important place of the Newly Industrialising Countries in world trade is supported by the direction of foreign multinational investment.

In contrast, Africa's share of private foreign investment fell from 6.7% in 1975 to 3.5% in 1985, a measure of the unattractiveness of African countries to the foreign investor due to political instability and limited investment opportunities. However, as economic restructuring gathers more pace and with the emergence of a new independent South Africa, there are signs in the mid-1990s that multinational investment is increasing again.

32.3 The influence of GATT and WTO, its successor

The limited role of GATT up to the Uruguay Round

The basis for the conditions under which world trade has operated since the end of the Second World has been the Bretton Woods agreement under which (General Agreement on Trade and Tariffs) was established in 1947 to encourage free and multilateral trading between countries. In particular, GATT was aimed at trying to find ways of reducing tariffs and non-tariff barriers put up by countries to protect domestic producers from too much outside competition and which hindered trade in goods and services.

However, from the start the influence of GATT was limited since essentially only trade in manufactured goods was covered. Trade in agricultural and other primary commodities as well as trade in services was excluded. In a series of GATT rounds to 1970, significant progress was made in cutting tariffs on a series of products which helped to liberalise trade in manufactured goods (Figure 32.6). Tariffs were reduced on average from 40% to 25% but from the early 1970s, further progress was hindered by a growing tide of protectionism both among developed and developing countries as a consequence of world economic recession and increased competition in world markets.

Nevertheless, at the Tokyo Round 1973 – 79, there was agreement to reduce industrial tariff levels further with particular reference to helping export of manufactured goods from developing countries. Despite talk of introducing codes of practice in relation to the imposition of non-tariff barriers such as subsidies for home-produced goods and imposition of quotas on imports, little progress was made in this direction.

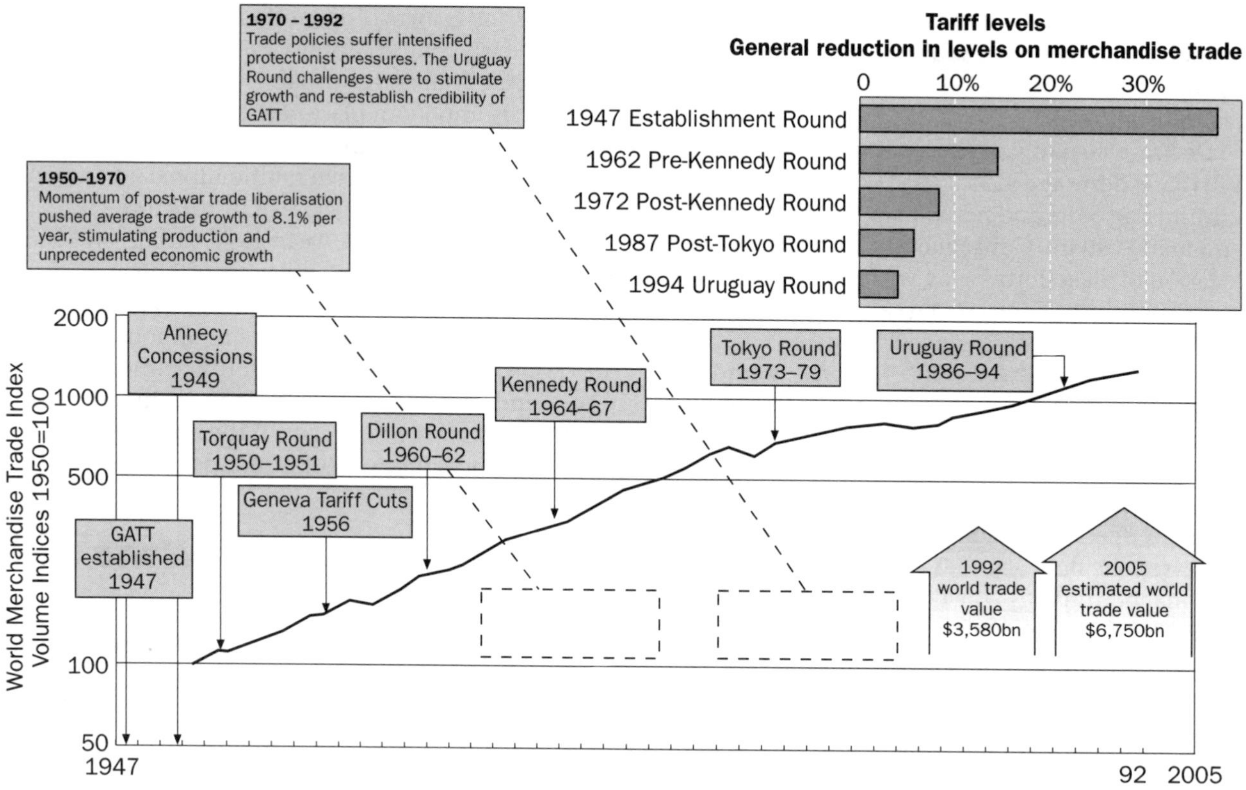

[SOURCE: Based on *Financial Times* 16.11.95]

Figure 32.6 *Progressive liberalisation of trade up to the major Uruguay round*

Expansion of world trade was being significantly hindered by the continued imposition of tariff and non-tariff barriers by all countries. While this did affect the advanced economies it was particularly hard on the developing countries, especially those whose export trade was in primary commodities since they were not subject to the terms of GATT. The position of these developing countries was further worsened due to the fluctuating price of primary commodities and a general price fall relative to the world price of manufactured goods; terms of trade thus moved against them.

Recent studies indicate that if protective barriers were lifted, exports from developing countries would rise by about 10%. Small wonder that through the 1980s developing countries were pressing for a much greater liberalisation of trade which was seen as a spur to economic growth. In addition to growing pressure from individual countries, their cause was also forwarded through UNCTAD (United Nations Conference on Trade and Development). This had been created in 1964 largely at the instigation of developing countries to press for transfer of funding from the North to the South for further development and to give them greater access to world trade. Pressure for further liberalisation of trade was also coming from developed countries.

The Uruguay Round marks a turning point

The GATT Uruguay Round conducted from 1986 to 1994 is likely to have far reaching effects on the nature and level of world trade. It goes much further than any earlier round towards liberalising trade. In addition to trade in manufactured goods, for the first time trade in agricultural goods, other primary products and trade in the growing service sector were covered. A new powerful multilateral trading organisation, the WTO (World Trading Organisation) has also been set up to monitor the implementation of agreements made and settle trade disputes.

In detail the agreements are complex but the broad points and their likely effects include:

- a further progressive reduction in tariffs on industrial goods by the advanced countries. Over 40% of manufactured imports will enter duty free. This will make easier access to world markets for exporters in industrial goods, of particular benefit to Newly Industrialising Countries and to established exporters. Because of increased market competition it should lower prices to consumers.
- Farm subsidies and import barriers to agricultural goods are to be cut over six years. Subsidies on agricultural exports which have particularly been

used by the USA and EU countries are to be cut by 35% in value. This could increase world prices and benefit efficient exporters of agricultural produce but it could increase the price of food imports which would hit poorer countries hard.

- For the first time basic ***fair trade principles*** such as non-discrimination, are to be applied to trade in a range of services such as financial services, telecommunications and air services. Individual countries have pledged to open their markets in services.
- A whole range of other measures were also agreed especially relating to non-tariff barriers, such as implementation of anti-dumping measures and technical obstacles to trade such as different standards and regulations from one country to another.

On the face of it the Uruguay Round is thus a major step towards liberalisation of world trade. However, although developing countries signed the Uruguay Agreement, misgivings were expressed as to the extent they would benefit compared to the advanced countries. A number of countries such as Brazil and India felt the advanced countries had wielded undue influence and that once again the advanced countries would be the main beneficiaries. For example, companies in advanced countries would now have freer access to the growing and potentially lucrative service sector in the developing countries while 'infant' domestic service industries would be unprotected and unable to compete.

The lowering of barriers in advanced countries was also less in effect than appeared on paper. A report in 1995 by the United Nations Food and Agricultural Organisation on the effects of the Uruguay Round to some extent confirmed these fears. It estimated that the GATT deal will lead to a rise in world agricultural trade of 9% but that this will benefit developed countries rather than the world's poorest countries. Developing countries are likely to see their food import bills rise and preferential access to markets in many developed countries shrink.

However, a GATT study estimates that as measures take effect over time, the merchandise or manufactured exports from developing countries will rise by 37% once the Uruguay benefits are fully phased; a rise much greater than that for the advanced economies of the USA and the EU which is estimated only at around 8%.

Another factor of major concern for international trade and for the trade prospects of poorer developing countries is the emergence of regional trading blocs. Under article XXIV of GATT, formation of customs unions and free trade areas are permitted. Within their boundaries there should be free trade and the compatibility of these regional trade areas with world-wide trade, hinges on the degree of their openness to non-members. In practice, the formation of regional trading blocs is seen as having taken a large proportion of trade out of the international trading arena, thus favouring member countries and discriminating against non-members (Figure 32.7).

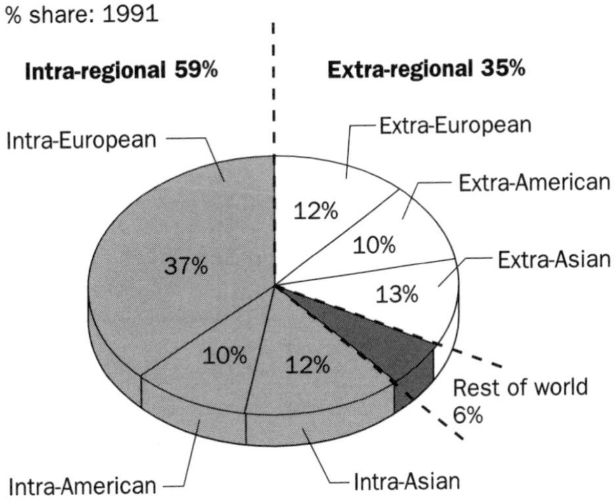

Figure 32.7 *World intra-regional and extra-regional trade*

32.4 Regional integration and its impact on global trading

The number of regional trading blocs increased significantly during the time the GATT Uruguay Round was being negotiated (Figure 32.8). There were in addition a large number of bilateral trading agreements made usually between neighbouring countries. Some observers have seen this increase in regional integration as a reaction to the difficulties encountered at the Uruguay talks in reaching agreement. For example, for a long period it was uncertain as to whether the USA, the world's leading trading nation, would sign. There was thus a fear of a relapse towards protectionism, so countries sought to join trading blocs to guarantee access to their main markets.

There are several types of regional integration models, from loose arrangements for fostering free trade among member countries as for example in the case of APEC, to that aimed at complete economic integration, as in the case of the European Union (Figure 32.9). Some countries belong to more than one regional trading bloc as for example those of Latin and Central America. Marked recent developments have been the enlargement of regional blocs, for example the EU and alliances

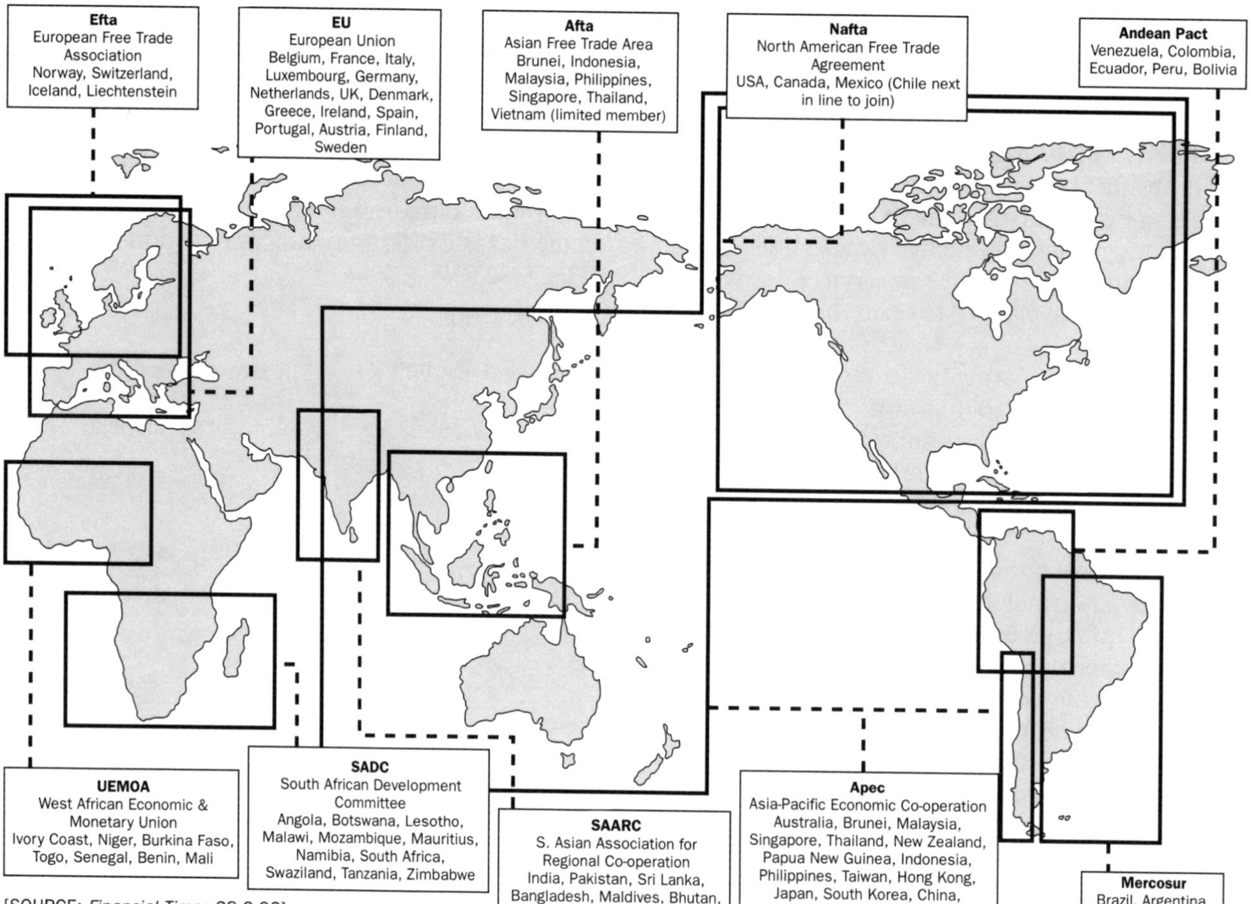

[SOURCE: *Financial Times* 28.2.96]

Figure 32.8 *The main regional trade groups*

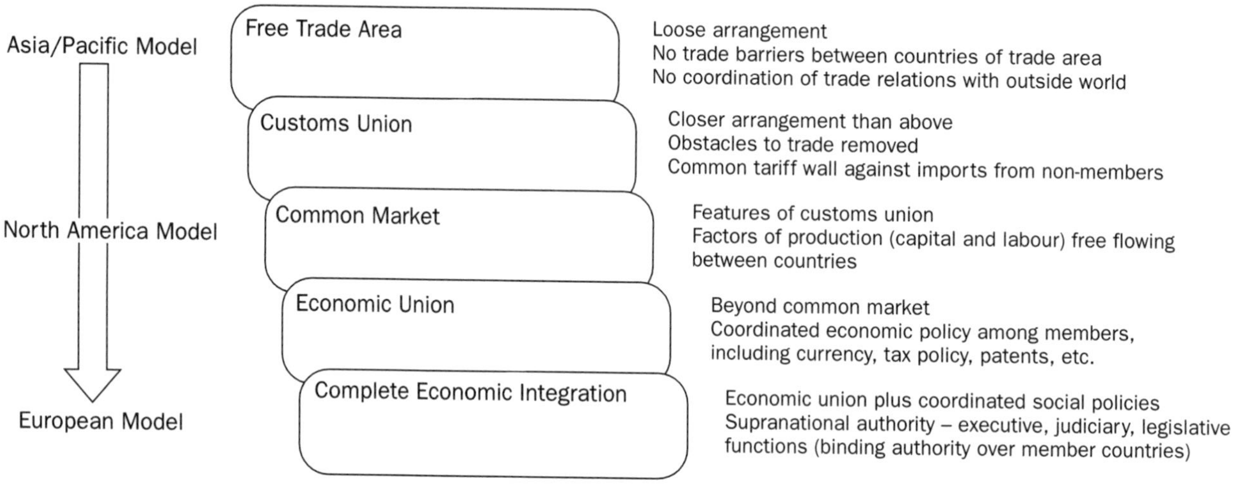

Figure 32.9 *Models of economic integration*

between regional blocs to form much larger free trade areas (Figure 32.9). The formation of NAFTA (North American Free Trade Association) is seen by its members, the USA, Canada and Mexico, as the first building bloc to a total Americas (Western Hemisphere bloc) by the year 2005. Such moves have prompted the view that rather than regional trading blocs hindering the moves towards global free trade promoted by the Uruguay Round and the formation of the WTO, regional integration represents a commitment to the principle of free trade rather than the old inward looking protectionism. Regional trading blocs are from this view point seen as the ***'building bricks' upon which global free trade can be built.***

Figure 32.10 The European Union at 1995 and further countries aspiring to membership by the early twenty-first century

Although there are various types of regional integration, the general aims are to promote more trade between its members, to generate a greater amount and share of external trade and raise the standards of living of the populations of member states. Internally the greatly enlarged markets promote greater economic activity and a greater scale of production, allowing for the benefits of economies of scale, reducing costs and making prices competitive. Greater price competitiveness also gives an advantage in export markets. As a much larger entity a regional trading bloc has more effect than individual members in negotiating on trade-related matters with other countries and external bodies.

The benefits and costs to member countries may vary according to the relative size of their economies, to the level of development reached and how well endowed they both are in terms of resources and human capital. Thus in the case of NAFTA, the USA is seen to gain most while there are some anxieties as to whether the benefits to Mexico will exceed costs (Case study 32.1). Within the European Union, lesser developed peripheral countries such as Portugal and Greece are set to gain but it is the core economies such as those of Germany and France which are gaining most (Figure 32.10). However, benefit disparities can be reduced by a deliberate policy of aid and economic assistance which will compensate *'losers in the process of market integration'* as seen for example in the pattern disbursement of regional development funds and technical assistance in the EU. It is frequently these compensatory flows which, as much as freer access to members' markets, attracts less developed countries to seek membership of a regional trading bloc.

The greatest benefits all round seem to occur where blocs contain one or more countries with strong economies and leadership. These can provide the core economic basis for the bloc and direction and cohesion to the policies adopted. Where the bloc consists of entirely developing economies, regional integration seems less successful as for example in the case of both SADC (South African Development Conference) and CARICOM (The Caribbean Community) (Figures 32.11 and 32.12).

	GDP/GNP ($bn)	Population (million)
Nafta		
Mexico	333.85	89.54
US	5 950.70	252.69
Canada	569.65	27.44
Central American Common Market		
Guatemala	10.50	9.47
El Salvador	5.97	5.38
Honduras	3.18	5.26
Nicaragua	1.97	4.13
Costa Rica	6.53	3.1
Panama	5.49	2.47
Caricom	**12.57**	**5.42**
Andean Pact		
Venezuela	60.43	20.25
Colombia	41.69	33.61
Ecuador	12.68	10.74
Peru*	45.26	22.45
Bolivia	6.06	7.61
Mercosur		
Brazil	394.19	156.28
Paraguay	5.69	4.52
Argentina	228.78	33.1
Uruguay	11.40	3.13
Chile†	**37.89**	**13.6**

There are aspirations towards a total Americas Free Trade area by 2005.
Caricom members: Antigua, Barbados, Guyana, Jamaica, Trinidad and Tobago, Grenada, Dominica, St. Lucia, St. Vincent, Monsterrat, St. Kitts-Nevis-Anguilla, Belize

*Membership suspended temporarily †Likely to seek Nafta accession

[SOURCE: *Financial Times* 19.11.93]

***Figure 32.11** Regional blocs in the Americas and their relative economic strengths expressed by GDP and population size*

With the entry of South Africa in 1995 SADC has been strengthened economically. South Africa has 75% of the total GDP of the new enlarged SADC.

Aspirations

'*South Africa will actively encourage the movement to create a new form of political and economic interaction*' (Foreign Minister Nzo, South Africa). Members see the need to change the thrust of development by establishing competitive export oriented industries and by the implementation of a regional trade treaty ultimately allowing free movement of goods, services and capital across member states.

Reality

- Political tensions: original members were frontline states opposed to South Africa before independence, there is still internal political instability in some states e.g. Angola, Zimbabwe objects to South Africa probably displacing it as leader of SADC.
- Most economies are largely agriculturally based with small national incomes, reliant on international aid and having severe international debt problems.
- Countries have still maintained complex tariff and trade regulations against external competition and it will take a long time to dismantle these.
- As the more advanced and efficient producer South Africa may dominate the flow of goods from it to other members may undercut their less efficient industries e.g. this is already apparent in respect of the textile and footwear industries of Zimbabwe
- Limited trade with other members, dependent on narrow range of commodity exports to the advanced countries

	G.D.P (per capita)	Main Exports (% of total)	Export links (% of total)
Angola	$610	petroleum (91%)	USA (55%), EU (25%)
Tanzania	$110	coffee(25%), cotton(20%)	EU (55%)
Malawi	$210	tobacco (66%)	EU (43%), USA (17%)
Zambia	$420	copper (81%)	EU (33%), Japan (29%)
Zimbabwe	$570	tobacco(22%), minerals(25%)	EU (41%)
Botswana	$2790	precious stones	mainly advanced countries
South Africa	$2670	precious metals(26%)	EU (51%), USA (12%)
Mozambique	$60	data not available	

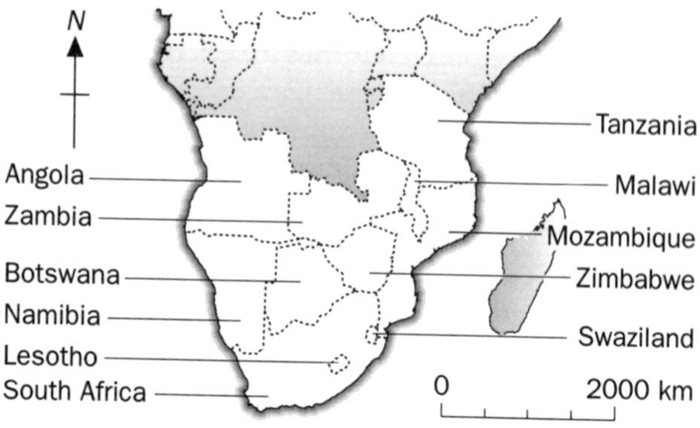

***Figure 32.12** The limitations of regional integration between developing countries as illustrated from SADC*

If the benefits of regional integration between developing countries which are at a similar stage of development are limited, it is understandable that free trade agreement should be sought as part of a bloc including advanced countries. Apart from giving secure and stable access to a sizeable market, it is likely to encourage greater investment flow to the developing country, not only from businesses corporations in the member advanced countries but also from outside, as economic growth as part of a bloc gives wider investment opportunities. Transfers of technological and management are also encouraged. These are certainly benefits seen by Mexico as part of NAFTA and by lesser developed countries in the looser APEC link-up.

Are regional trading blocs detrimental to global trading?

The existence of the three major trading blocs (NAFTA, EU and Pacific APEC) and others of lesser importance has not led to greater fragmentation of world trade. While the flow of intra-regional trade has certainly increased, it has been within the context of a growing volume of world trade in general (Figure 32.2).

Apart from regionalisation leading to freer trade between members within blocs, the growing move to extend blocs and the link-up arrangements between blocs indicates a trend to free trade rather than protectionism. GATT also saw it as easier to negotiate further moves to free trade with blocs rather than a host of individual countries. Nevertheless, there is some discrimination against non-members. A strengthening of the powers of the new World Trade Organisation to prevent discriminatory practices is seen as the best way forward given that regionalisation is becoming an increasingly important feature and influence on the structure and pattern of world trade.

Concluding comment

'*The renewal of confidence in the multilateral trading system that came with the decision to set up the WTO and the assurance of continued trade liberalisation are undoubtedly principal factors in revitalising trade led growth.*' (Chairman of WTO, 1995)

case study

32.1 The implications of NAFTA (North American Free Trade Agreement)

Basis of the Agreement

Signed in January 1994 between the USA, Canada and Mexico, the agreement allows for the gradual ending of tariff barriers and most other barriers over a ten-year period. There is a commitment to liberalise trade in services and to facilitate investment flows between the countries. Mexico undertook to deregulate the chemical and financial sectors but not the basic energy sector. The North American Development Bank with funds of $3 billion was set to supply credit for encouraging economic expansion.

The general consensus is that the agreement will benefit all participants but that Mexico will have the most to gain because three quarters of its trade is with the USA and Canada and with an economy only one twentieth of that of the USA, it has significantly less to offer other members.

	GDP ($ billion)	Population (million)
USA	$5 392 bn	251.5 m
Canada	$570 bn	26.6 m
Mexico	$238 bn	86.2 m

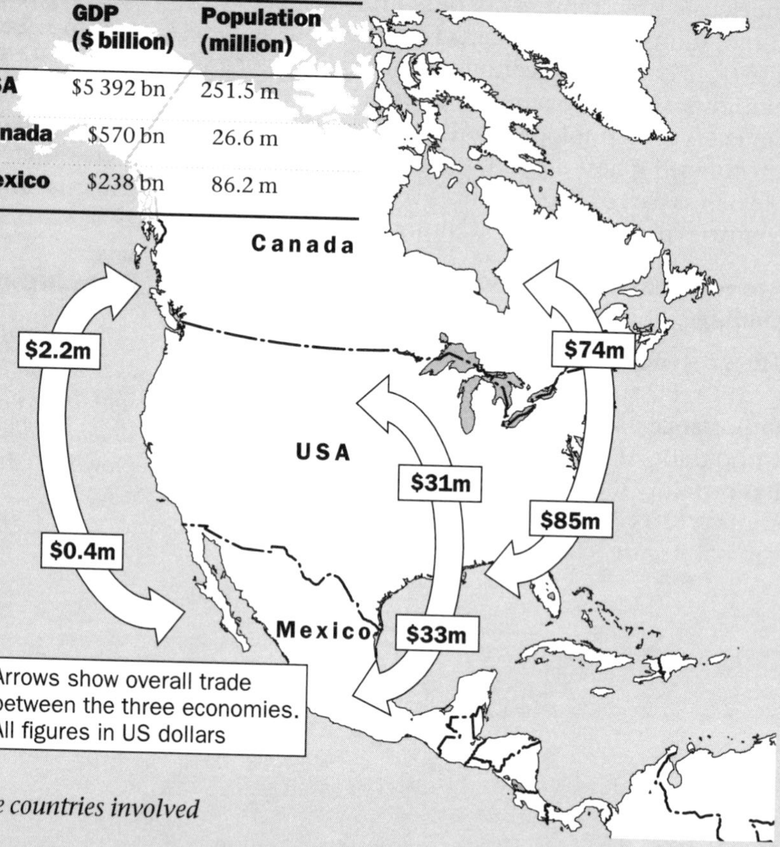

The countries involved

Implications for Mexico

President Salinas supported the agreement as he saw this as a means to boost trade, increase the flow of investment into Mexico and help stabilise the serious financial debt problem and unstable currency. (The IMF had to grant a $10.3 billion loan in 1995 to help restore financial stability.) It would also encourage the economic reforms already begun to increase productivity and the competitiveness of business in the wider global market place. However, there is also fear of too much USA domination.

Implications for the USA

The USA already had a free trade agreement with Canada for four years and a lot of investment flow into the country, so much so that 40% of Canada's manufacturing employment is in foreign-owned plants mainly belonging to USA companies. The new agreement is likely to reduce cross-border disputes such as that arising recently from soft grain 'dumping' in USA markets by Canadian producers. While investment opportunities will be increased in Mexico in the short term, the gains for the USA are more political, in that the agreement is likely to bring more economic and political stability to Mexico and make it easier to control the flow of illegal immigrants across the border into the USA.

Implications for Canada

As yet, while the USA is by far Canada's biggest trading partner, Canada's trade with Mexico is limited. Since the agreement Canadian companies have seen the increased potential of the Mexican market and investment opportunities. Cereal and other foodstuff exports to Mexico for example rose 37% in 1992.

Implications for countries outside NAFTA

The greatest concern has been expressed by Caribbean and other Latin American countries which have strong trade links with the USA, that trade and investment will be diverted from them to Mexico. The United States International Trade Commission estimated Caribbean countries are likely to have a third of their trade with the USA diverted. NAFTA has also for example introduced incentives which will shift investment in textile and apparel manufacture away from Caribbean subsidiaries to Mexican plants.

33

CHAPTER 33

Trade, aid, debt and global inequalities

'The growth of international manufacturing activity and of international trade in manufactured goods however is only possible with the parallel development of 'circulation activities', notably the production and trade in a whole variety of commercial, financial and business services.'

DICKEN P *GLOBAL SHIFT*, 1993

'Threats to the sustainable use of resources comes as much from inequalities in people's access to resources and from the ways in which they use them as from the sheer numbers of people.'

ELLIOT J A *WORLD CONSUMPTION AND ENVIRONMENT DEVELOPMENT*, 1994

33.1 Visible trade

Recent growth in trade and regional variations in growth

Growth in merchandise trade has varied since the mid-1980s but has generally exceeded growth in world output, some indication of increasing global integration (Figure 33.1). Growth in 1994 accelerated to 9%, the best for 20 years, though variable from one region to another. China and Hong Kong for example experienced 18% to 20% growth while that for Germany and the USA was relatively modest at 6%, reflecting differences in rates of general economic growth. Apart from the continued prominence of the South East Asian economies, other recent encouraging signs have been some trade recovery by Latin American countries, up by 15% in 1994 and by Eastern and Central European countries which are in transition from state to market economies. Albeit from a very low base, Eastern Europe increased its external trade by 20% in 1994 mainly through increased trade with the European Union. However, there was little increase for the Commonwealth of Independent States, where economic conditions remain very difficult. There are slight signs of growth in individual countries in sub-Saharan Africa but as a whole the continent lags behind the rest of the world (Figure 33.2).

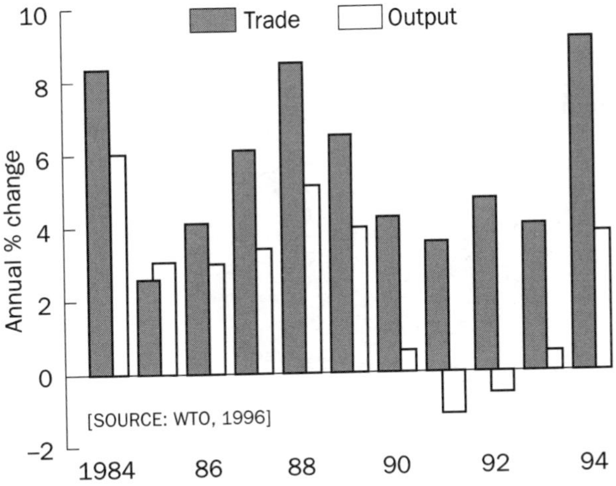

Figure 33.1 Volume of world merchandise trade and output

Dominant trade flows

World trade flows are overwhelmingly dominated by the advanced countries, the EU, USA and Japan (Figure 33.3). Another striking feature is the importance of trade among European Union countries. This amounts to more than half of their total trade and far outweighs the European Union's trade with Japan and the USA. However, apart from Japan, which has built up a significant trade surplus on the bases of an assertive export strategy and protection of its home market, the leading trading nations tend to have deficits with the value of imports exceeding exports (Figure 33.4). This is compensated to some extent by a stronger performance in invisible trade in services including financial dealings, so that there are not serious balance of payments problems, unlike a number of poorer developing countries which experience deficits on both visible and invisible trade.

Share of world merchandise trade

	Exports (%)		Imports (%)	
	1986	**1992**	**1986**	**1992**
North America	19.1	21.2	27.0	23.1
EU*	20.7	20.7	19.2	21.5
Japan	12.6	12.3	7.3	7.9
Asia**	14.6	19.8	14.2	21.2
Latin America	5.7	5.5	5.0	5.8
Middle East & Africa	8.1	9.0	8.7	7.8
Other	19.2	12.6	18.5	12.8

*Excluding EU intra-trade **Excluding Japan and re-exports from Hong Kong

Figure 33.2 The changing balance within GATT, 1986 – 92

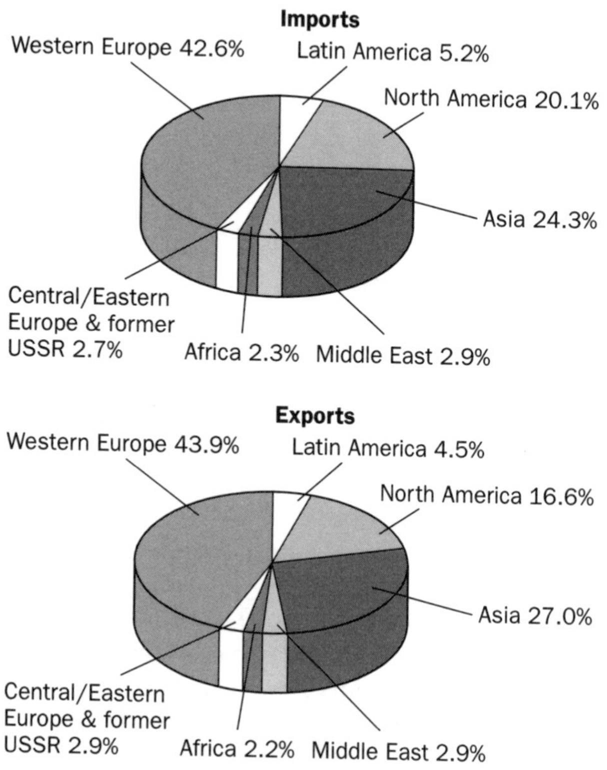

Figure 33.3 World merchandise trade by region, 1994 (based on value)

Year	USA	Japan	Germany	France	UK
1980	–25 481	+2 125	+8 720	–13 419	+3 353
1985	–112 522	+61 601	+28 580	–5 726	–3 850
1991	–73 436	+113 683	+23 060	–10 139	–17 990
1992	–42 062	+632	+43 016	–13 094	–2 085

[SOURCE: *IMF – International Financial Statistics*, 1992]

Figure 33.4 Balance of payments situation for leading countries, 1980 – 92 ($ US millions)

Balance of trade
This refers to the relationship between the value of visible exports and the value of visible imports for any country. Where the value of imports exceeds that of exports the country is said to have a trade deficit or an adverse balance of trade. Conversely, where the value of exports exceeds that of imports the country enjoys a trade surplus or a favourable balance of trade.

Balance of payments
This refers to the relationship between payments of all kinds made from one country to the rest of the world and its receipts from all other countries. It thus takes into account both visible trade and invisible trade. Where payments exceed receipts the country experiences a deficit in its balance of payments or an adverse balance of payments. Where receipts exceed payments then the country enjoys a surplus or favourable balance of payments.

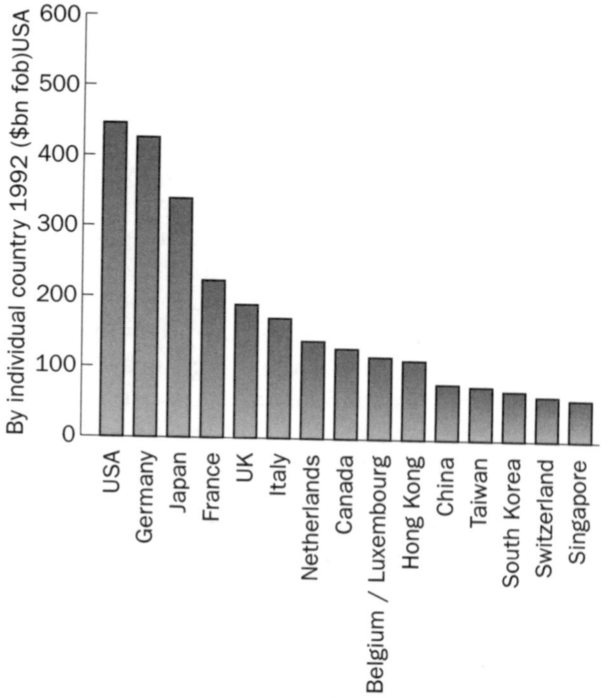

Figure 33.5 Top 15 world exporters by value of trade, 1992

While the advanced economies continue to dominate merchandise trade, East Asian NICs are increasingly prominent (Figure 33.3). By the year 2000 the 'tripolar' structure of world trade based on the USA, Japan, and the European Union, may be replaced by a four-cornered structure with China (by then including Hong Kong), Taiwan, Singapore and South Korea and Asian countries providing the new fourth building block on which the pattern of world trade will be built.

The changing composition of merchandise trade

The value of world merchandise trade rose to $4000 billion in 1994 as compared to $1080 billion of trade in services. The most notable feature of merchandise trade is the increasing proportion of manufactured goods compared with primary commodities and energy fuels (Figure 33.6). In 1994 manufactured goods made up 73% of world visible trade compared to 62% in 1963.

This partly reflects the expansion of world manufacturing in general and its globalisation as a result of the policies of multinational corporations. It also reflects a greatly reduced relative share of energy fuels as countries have sought to reduce reliance on oil imports and pursued policies of energy conservation through improved energy efficiency measures. It is too a measure of the increased proportion of world manufacturing output consisting of capital and technological intensive production of high value goods rather than energy intensive manufacturing of heavier staple products such as iron and steel. This partly accounts for the reduced share of raw material commodities as does increased use of substitutes.

The reduced share of food products in world trade is a reflection of expansion of agricultural production in advanced countries to increase food self-sufficiency. It also shows that there is a higher proportion of market demand for consumer goods and services as incomes rise.

Trade in office and telecommunications products has particularly accelerated, in line with the growing importance of this sector in world manufacturing as a whole. Between 1993 to 1994 information-high technology trade increased 20%, exceeding automotive products and transport equipment.

The changing composition and structure of world merchandise trade reflects changes in the global economy as a whole. However, the actual composition of trade varies country by country. For advanced countries and the more mature Newly Industrialising Countries, trade in manufactured goods dominates but for lesser developed countries, trade in a narrow range of primary commodities or energy fuels make up much of their exports e.g.

Commodity / Country	Food, beverage and tobacco	Raw materials	Fuels	Chemicals	Manufactured goods	Machinery and transport equipment	Miscellaneous	Total value (US $ million)
USA								
Imports	5.4	2.7	10.6	5.1	31.6	37.6	3.6	553 497
Exports	9.2	5.7	2.5	9.8	27.5	40.8	5.0	447 330
Japan								
Imports	16.9	10.4	17.4	7.4	26.2	21.6	9.4	274 742
Exports	2.1	0.7	0.5	5.4	19.8	71.4	1.6	395 600
Germany								
Imports	9.7	4.4	7.5	8.3	33.2	34.5	2.2	408 454
Exports	5.1	1.8	1.3	12.3	27.1	49.6	1.5	430 388
France								
Imports	10.1	3.5	8.6	10.8	21.5	34.8	0.3	238 908
Exports	14.9	2.5	2.4	13.4	27.1	39.3	0.3	231 941
UK								
Imports	10.7	3.7	5.6	9.0	29.5	42.8	1.3	221 318
Exports	8.1	1.7	6.4	13.6	19.6	48.0	1.9	190 099

***Figure 33.6** Exports and imports by commodity 1990 for the five leading trading nations (US $mill)*

Middle East oil-exporting countries. Exports go mainly to advanced countries. In return, manufactured goods are received from these countries and the East Asian NICs.

33.2 Invisible trade – growing trade in services and financial transactions

'A GATT 1993 report expresses criticism of some countries for over concern for widening gaps in merchandise trade. It indicates this as clearly inappropriate because services are an important and growing part of countries' trade.'

Invisible exports are the income earnings of a country arising from the payments made by other countries for services provided. Conversely, the invisible imports of a country are payments made by that country for services provided by other countries. These are classified as tradable or producer services and include banking, insurance, shipping, expenditure by visiting tourists and interest earned on investments and loans made overseas. Daniels emphasises that producer services supply business and government organisations rather than individual consumers. They include:

- Information processing services e.g banking, marketing, insurance, accountancy, property management, advertising, technology.
- Goods related services e.g. distribution, transport management, infrastructure maintenance and repair of communications equipment.
- Personal support services e.g. welfare, leisure provision, catering, personal, travel and accommodation.
- Factor services covering earnings from assets held outside the country e.g. various types of investment, share purchases, loans, etc.

A faster growing sector than visible trade

There has been a faster growth in trade in producer services than in merchandise trade since services for most countries now generally form the largest sector of the economy. Advanced countries dominate world trade in services (Figure 33.7). Almost half of imports and exports in services are generated by the USA, France, the UK, Germany and Japan. About 80% of trade in services is generated in just 20 countries amongst which are included some of the Newly Industrialising Countries such as Singapore, Hong Kong, Mexico as well as South Africa. The latter tend to specialise in providing producer services for neighbouring developing countries, helping their economic development.

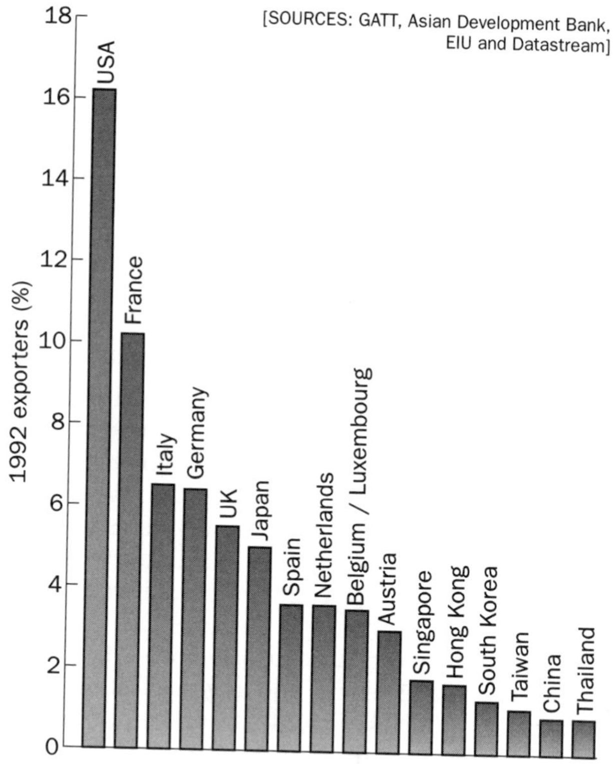

Figure 33.7 World trade in commercial services

A classification of countries prominent in trade in services

On the basis of the relative importance of trade in services, four types of countries can be identified:

- Advanced countries with good factor endowment across the full range of producer services, having an accumulation of expertise, advanced information and other technology, established external links to markets, multinational corporations specialising in service provision, core centres of international prestige and a large domestic market for producer services.
- Countries with a strength and reputation in producer services compensating for limited factor endowment in manufacturing e.g. Singapore, Hong Kong and smaller off-shore centres such as Jersey.
- Countries generating foreign revenue from providing a particular producer service on the basis of special factor endowments. The most notable examples are countries for which tourism is a major export earner (e.g. Spain, Kenya and the Seychelles).
- Lesser developed countries not generating revenue from producer services but for which outgoing debt and interest payments represent a major drain on the economy and foreign earnings.

Sectors of greatest expansion in services

While trade in services as a whole is expanding, the two sectors showing greatest expansion are tourism and information processing services (Chapter 30).

In 1970 information services, comprising the handling of data including telecommunications and professional, technological and financial services, made up a quarter of services trade. By 1990 its share had risen to 40%. This does not include multinationals trading in services through branches or affiliates established in countries overseas.

The rise in information services trade is partly related to the globalisation of manufacturing under the organisation of the manufacturing multinationals.

'As these have proliferated globally so too have the major banks, advertising agencies, legal firms, property companies, insurance companies. The internationalisation both of manufacturing and of these business service activities have become mutually reinforcing.'
(Dickens, 1993)

The manufacturing multinationals generate and need the support of business services to function but so do governments and other official agencies as contact and transactions need information services. The information and telecommunication revolution has increased the capability, speed and relative lower cost of information service provision and in turn, the demand for these services.

Liberalisation of trade in services and deregulation of service markets by an increasing number of countries has also allowed business corporations to access overseas markets hitherto closed to them. Businesses which up to the 1970s largely concentrated on domestic markets have also seized the opportunity for cross-border trade to sustain their profit growth.

Geographical concentration of businesses engaged in Information Services

Trade in information services is more geographically concentrated than for any other type of trade (Figure 33.8). It is dominated by the core international cities of New York, London and Tokyo. Beneath these are a tier of well-established secondary cores and a third tier including centres in developing countries such as Singapore, Hong Kong, São Paulo and Bombay. Up to 28 cities practically control all the world's information service transactions and much of the other trade in services since the headquarters of all the major providers in the global service trade are located in the core centres in the USA, the European Union and Japan.

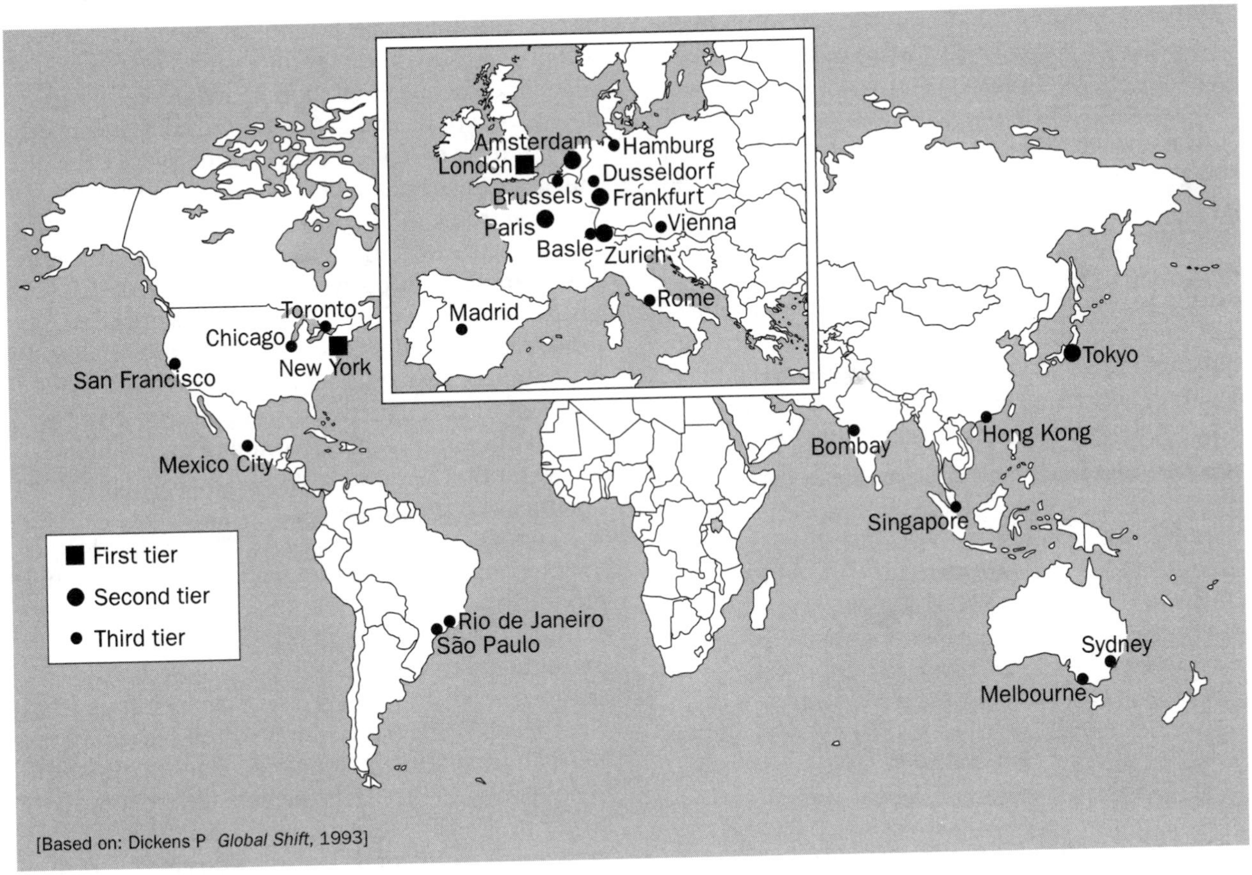

Figure 33.8 *Hierarchy of core centres of the international provision of information services*

The first tier dominance of London and New York arises from their historical prestige as great commercial centres which has also given an accumulated expertise in producer services, in turn attracting further growth. The emergence of Tokyo is associated with Japan's rise since the 1960s to that of a world economic superpower, but it is only since the 1980s that it has become an international centre. Second and third order centres have arisen as a result of the growing number of businesses specialising in particular services of general commercial importance.

The heart of these cores are the financial institutions such as commercial banks and stock exchanges dealing in commodity exchanges, currency transactions and international share and security dealings. Around these gather internationally important businesses dealing in related services such as insurance, accountancy and advertising as they need close contact with financial institutions. Agglomeration of leading businesses leads to the cumulative dominance of these core information service centres.

World flows of financial capital

Cross-border capital flows can be divided into those generated within the private sector and those controlled by public bodies, such as governments, voluntary agencies and international institutions of which by far the most important are the International Monetary Fund (IMF) and the World Bank.

As would be expected, private sector capital flows and information services largely emanate from the core centres. Private capital flows fluctuate but were estimated at $600 billion for the year 1994. About $157 billion of this went to developing countries mainly to Newly Industrialising Countries where market opportunities were greater and anticipated earnings higher than in poorer countries (Figure 33.11). China alone received one third of the direct investment going to developing countries.

Share of world equity market capitalisation (%)

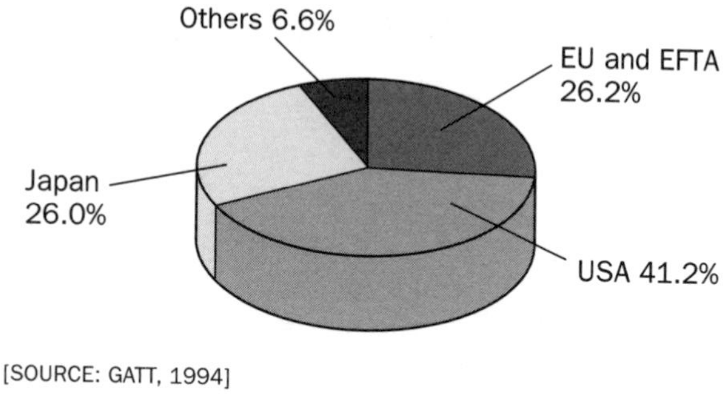

[SOURCE: GATT, 1994]

Figure 33.9 Dominance of USA, EU and Japan in world equity (share) markets

Capital flows to developing countries

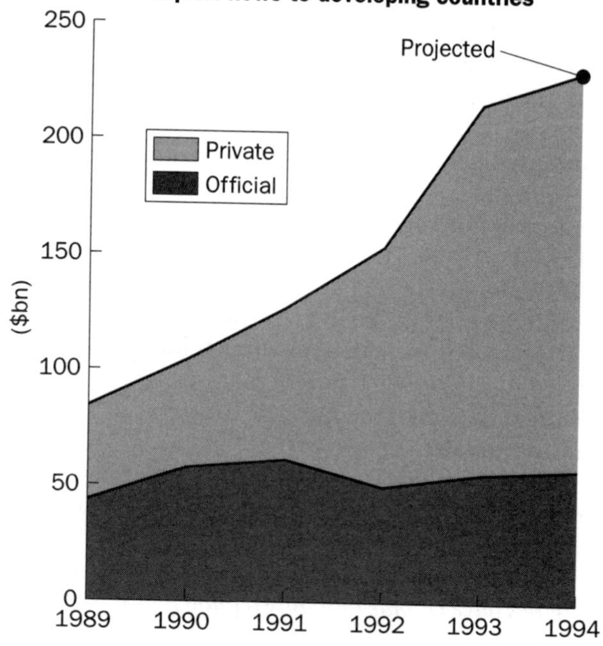

[SOURCE: World Bank]

Figure 33.10 Private and official capital flows to developing countries

Private capital flows have become more complex as new forms of financial products such as 'junk bonds' and 'trading in futures' are added to established ones, such as direct corporate investment, share or equity dealings, bond purchases and bank flows. Growth in capital flows is linked to increased globalisation of manufacturing and services, the much greater ease of global financial transactions with electronic trading and transfer of funds and the increasing interest in overseas market opportunities. For example, large professionally managed institutions controlling pension funds or clients' funds can now switch these around globally almost instantaneously to take advantage of changes in different financial markets. Computerisation and internationalisation of telecommunication links allows trading 24 hours a day and increasingly larger volumes of transactions.

In respect of direct corporate investment (FDI), the most important feature has been the increasing proportion directed to services compared to manufacturing. Although this corporate investment largely concerns flows between the advanced countries, the share of developing countries is rising but it is mainly investment in the Newly Industrialising Countries. Trading in shares or equity markets reflects the same trend, helped by recent progressive deregulation of financial markets allowing foreign institutions for the first time to trade in these markets (Figure 33.9).

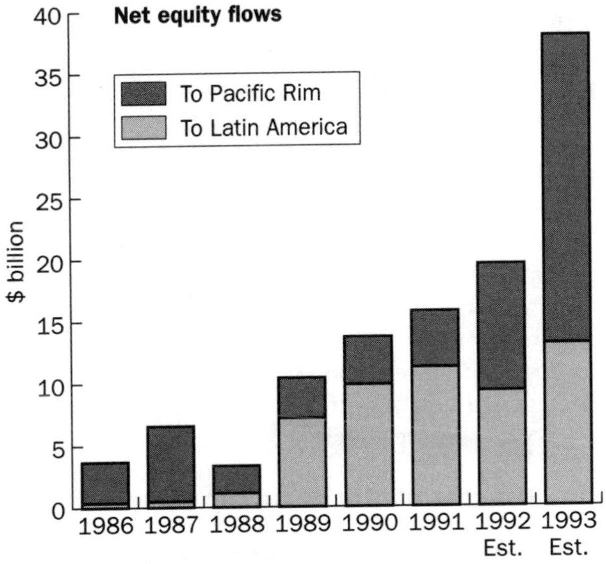

[SOURCE: Baring Securities]

Figure 33.11 The dramatic increase in equity flows to the Pacific Rim and Latin American developing countries' emerging markets

33.3 Aid and its effect on developing countries

Official flows of finance to developing countries are significantly below the level needed

Apart from private sector flows of finance, developing countries and the transitional economies of Eastern Europe and the CIS receive substantial assistance via official aid flows in the form of grants, loans and technical assistance. Net official development aid amounted to $56 billion in 1993, 10% less than the previous year, reflecting continuing difficult economic conditions in donor countries, including relatively high levels of unemployment. Advanced countries are the major donors and have tended to cut back on their donations. During the 1990s this has averaged just above 0.3% of GDP compared with the internationally agreed target of a minimum of 0.7% of GDP needed from donor countries if aid is to effectively help raise standards of living. In 1995 at a World Bank Social Summit, countries reaffirmed to strive for 'the fulfilment of the agreed target of 0.7% of GDP for overall **official direct aid** (ODA)', but this is unlikely. Indeed, major diversion of official aid to eastern Europe, Russia and other CIS republics, means substantially less aid is going to least developed countries, such as Bangladesh and sub-Sahara African countries. Though private flows of finance to developing countries now significantly exceed official aid amounts ($94 billion as against $56 billion of ODA in 1993), the least developed countries also receive less than 2% of these private flows. Official aid remains the principal source of external finance as least developed countries are considered high risk and low return areas for the private investor.

Forms of ODA (Overseas Direct Aid)

There are of two principal types of foreign official aid: bilateral and multilateral aid. Both involve transfer of funds as loans and grants and of resources including technical assistance of various kinds (Figure 33.12). Loans are offered at concessional rates (less than commercial rates of interest) and over longer repayment periods.

	By amount ($ million)	Percentage of GDP		By percentage of GDP
Egypt	4988	(15.2)	Mozambique	69.2
India	2747	(1.1)	Nicaragua	47.6
China	1954	(0.4)	Tanzania	33.8
Indonesia	1854	(1.6)	Bhutan	25.4
Israel	1749	(2.8)	Malawi	22.6
Turkey	1675	(1.6)	Jordan	22.2
Bangladesh	1636	(7.0)	Burundi	21.6
Pakistan	1226	(2.7)	Rwanda	21.5
Ethiopia	1091	(16.5)	Lesotho	20.5
Tanzania	1075	(33.8)	Chad	20.2

[SOURCE: *The World – A Third World Guide* 1995 – 96]

Figure 33.12 *Main recipients of official aid (ODA), 1991*

Bilateral aid is the direct transfer of aid between one government and another but a significant part may be as ***tied aid*** requiring the recipient country to use the transferred funds to purchase goods and/or services from the donor country.

Multilateral aid is the indirect transfer of funds and resources to recipient countries via an international agency. The principal international agencies are the World Bank and International Monetary Fund set up at the end of the Second World as part of the Bretton Woods agreement to restore orderly world economic growth and trade, and assist economic development in lesser developed countries. There are also numerous other official agencies involved in multinational aid, such as the Inter-American Development Bank, the African Development fund and OPEC. Recently, an increasing amount of multilateral aid has been conditional on the recipient countries meeting certain requirements; the most controversial of these have been the Structural

Adjustment programmes imposed by the IMF and World Bank on recipient countries. These have had a major effect on the internal economic and social policies of developing countries.

Emergency aid from official sources has risen sharply in the 1980s and 1990s from $300 million dollars in the 1980s to $3.2 billion in 1993. Some was in response to natural disasters such as earthquakes and drought, but most was in response to wars in various parts of the world – Africa, Central America, Yugoslavia and in Central America – for peace keeping, aid to refugees and other humanitarian needs. Some of these breakdowns in global security have been at least partly attributed to the failure of richer countries to provide sufficient effective on-going aid and more equitable opportunities for the lesser developed countries to improve the standard of living of their people through economic development and trade.

Non-government aid

There are also significant aid flows from non-government organisations (NGOs) such as Oxfam, the international Red Cross, Community Aid Abroad and World Vision. Most of these are centrally concerned with humanitarian and environmental objectives. Most aid is directed to on-going humanitarian and other development projects specifically targeted on community level work with community participation. Although less than one twentieth of that from official government and international sources, NGO aid has been continuously rising and is regarded by many observers as more effective per unit of aid given.

Effectiveness of official aid questioned

The effectiveness of official aid is being increasingly questioned (Figure 33.13). It has been concluded

A negative view of aid

- Postpones governments coming to grips with economic restructuring, including balanced urban and rural development programmes and needed financial reforms.
- Leads to aid dependency
- Much aid gone into large-scale schemes which have had disastrous social and environmental consequences and led to increasing problems of over urbanisation
- Aid flows are uncertain and changes of donor policies can disrupt economic and human development
- Tied and conditional aid can lead to the transfer of inappropriate technology and skills
- Aid can support undemocratic governments intent on staying in power and pursuing self-aggrandisement policies
- Aid is ineffective in helping further real development when used to service interest on loans and debt or solve balance of payment problems
- Encourages indebtedness

Other related problems reduce the effectiveness of aid such as:

- Inefficient or corrupt use of loans by the governments of recipient countries
- Political instability either in the recipient country or neighbouring countries
- External conditions limiting the effectiveness of aid e.g. high rates of interest on loans, world recession, adverse terms of trade and barriers to the export trade of developing countries.

A positive view of aid

- It can provide external resources for investment in development which would not otherwise be undertaken. Is most effective when combined with balanced and informed policies both on the part of the donor and recipient government e.g. in helping South Korea to develop its infrastructure and initiate an export-oriented strategy
- As NGOs (non-government organisations) have demonstrated aid, including suitable technical assistance, can be very effective if combined with local participation in small-scale schemes. These should cover not only economic but also human welfare development leading to self-sustaining development. Official agencies have recently reoriented policies more towards this approach
- Emergency aid in time of natural or human disasters
- Grants with no ties provide more effective aid than loans which require interest payment and ultimate repayment of the loan, particularly in the case of the poorest countries
- Aid is more effective where the circumstances and conditions in recipient country have been thoroughly understood before aid is given and when with the cooperation of the recipient government the use of the aid can be monitored.

Aid can be more effective where:

- There is political stability and democratic accountable governing
- It is within the context of a balanced development programme including attention to rural development and a reduction of inequalities
- External conditions are more favourable including world economic stability, liberalisation of trade, fairer terms of trade and a stabilisation of commodity prices.

Figure 33.13 Aid: a negative and positive view

that aid has done more harm than good to countries most in need of assistance. It is difficult to assess how much the adjudged failure is due to the actions of the external funding agencies and external circumstances, and how much due to the misguided policies of the governments in receipt of this aid. Aid has benefited most Newly Industrialising or middle income countries where the resource base and level of human capital alongside balanced government policies have encouraged economic growth. For one reason or another the poorest countries have simply not reached the threshold where cumulative economic growth and a rise in the standard of living can take hold.

Looking at criticism of ODA, a major problem has been that three quarters of all aid during the 1980s was bilateral aid and much of tied aid. When aid is tied, its value is reduced in the eyes of the recipient government because it cannot be spent as it sees most appropriate. Also, as it must be spent on goods and services from the donor country, there is a strong measure of self-interest by the donor and the recipient country is placed in a greater state of dependency, so undermining its autonomy. The cost of goods and services may also be greater than if the recipient country was free to 'shop around'.

One illustration of problems associated with tied aid is the Pergau Dam affair involving bilateral agreements between Malaysia and the UK. The British government promised project aid to the level of half the cost of the huge Pergau dam scheme in the northern state of Kelantan and scheduled for completion in 1995. The British National Audit office report (1993) stated the British government had agreed aid despite aid officials indicating the dam project was not economically viable. Local Malaysian opposition to the scheme on environmental grounds and the likely disruption to local communities had also been ignored. Two leading British multinational firms (Balfour Beatty and Cementation International) in partnership with a Malaysian company, Kerjaja Binan have the contract to build the dam. In 1994 strained diplomatic relations between Malaysian and British government developed due to a press statement that the bilateral aid was also linked to Malaysia granting British firms defence contracts.

Multilateral aid has been most criticised because the largest sums have been directed towards prestige schemes concerned with economic development, with little or no regard for social welfare and the environment. Both the multilateral agency and the recipient government bear joint responsibility for this. The World Bank itself admitted its 'social and environmental record has been staggeringly bad'. A World Bank official said of its work during the 1960s and 1970s:

'the effects of its work include massive logging in the Amazon (associated with its support of the Trans-Amazonian Highway), dams that are already silting up; heavily polluting coal power schemes that have left the traditionally poor destitute and vast tracts of land unusable.' [*The Guardian* 22.8.94]

In a two-volume analysis by the World Bank on relations between the World Bank and Tanzania, the writers indicate that $1 billion had been spent in the 1960s and 1970s to support President Nyerere's *'poorly thought out socialist experiment'* which had had disastrous consequences for the economy and the population's welfare.

Aid re-think countered by structural readjustment demands

Since 1987 the World Bank has drastically reappraised its approach, moving away from supporting economic development and large-scale schemes towards a greater emphasis on basic human needs of shelter, health, nutrition, education and the environment. In 1994, 17% of its budget was spent on social issues, more than spent on industrial development. Twice as much was spent on restoring and improving the environment as on energy schemes for developing countries.

However, the World Bank and IMF insist on countries accepting structural adjustment programmes in return for aid to help solve their international debt problems. Strategic adjustment programmes have in the short term adversely affected the welfare and standard of living of the poorest sector of the population in the developing countries. Currently the World Bank is following two contradictory policies.

33.4. Aid, indebtedness and structural adjustment programmes

The emerging debt problem

The problem of chronic indebtedness essentially unfolded during the 1970s and though affecting nearly all the developing world, it has proved most intractable in the least developed countries (Figures 33.14 and 33.15). The causes of it are bound up with access to an over-abundant supply of 'cheap money' during the 1960s and 1970s, both in the form of private flows from commercial banks and similar institutions and official supplies of aid. Awash with surplus funds, private institutions were only too willing to lend and invest money at what were then favourable rates to the developing countries, with insufficient regard as to their creditworthiness and the viability of the schemes on which the money was spent. Equally, there was insufficient monitoring of official aid flows. The World Bank estimated that the volume of international bank lending from commercial and official institutional sources already rising throughout the 1960s, rose by an unprecedented 800% between 1970 to 1980.

Total long-term debt payment of developing countries, 1980–1994

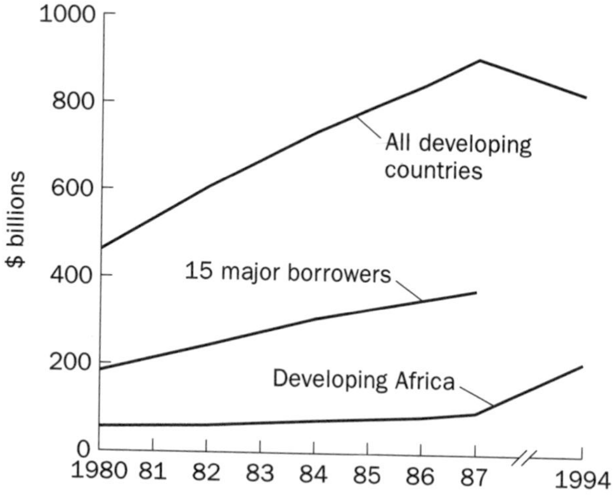

Ratio of total debt service to export of goods and services 1975–1994

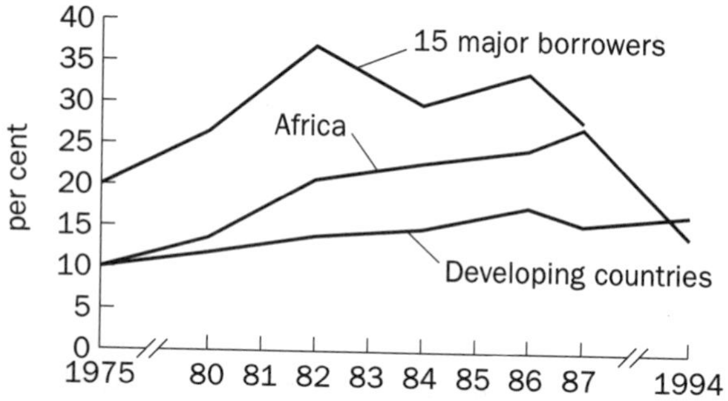

[SOURCE: *Third World Guide*, 1993–94]

***Figure 33.14** Debt of developing nations*

A significant proportion of the borrowed funds went on increasing consumption rather than productive investment, on projects which were economically non-viable, military spending, financing oil imports and some was lost through corruption. As a result, overall returns on investment were too low to allow servicing and repayments of debts. The situation was exacerbated by the world oil crisis of the early 1970s, leading to a steep rise in the price of oil imports which developing countries could not meet by sufficient returns on exports; this in turn led to chronic balance of payment problems.

	By total ($ millions)	Debt service as a ratio of exports		By debt service as a ratio of exports
Brazil	121 110	23	Cambodia	103
Mexico	113 378	44	Guinea Bissau	93
Indonesia	84 385	32	Algeria	71
Russia	78 658	4	Zaire	48
India	76 983	25	Afghanistan	42
China	69 321	10	Paraguay	40
Argentina	67 569	34	Uganda	40

[SOURCE: World Development Report 1994]

***Figure 33.15** Leading external debt countries, 1992*

Rising world interest rates on further borrowings in the late 1970s and early 1980s together with deteriorating terms of trade increased developing world debt problems. By the mid-1980s it was clear that a number of developing countries were not in a position to service debts, let alone repay them, and their economies were in danger of collapse with grave repercussions for global stability. The threat of wider repercussions was heightened because the chronically indebted countries included least developed countries and also larger Newly Industrialising Countries such as Mexico, Brazil and Venezuela.

Debt rescheduling and structural adjustment

A major break-through came with the Brady Initiative in 1985 which attempted to deal with commercial debts. The World Bank agreed to financially support the rescheduling of debt repayments over a longer period with a reduction in debt servicing. However, this was in return for the country concerned adopting a structural adjustment programme and measures to pay back the debt and attract further foreign direct investment. Costa Rica, the Philippines and Mexico were among the countries accepting these conditions.

In respect of bilateral debt, under a Toronto agreement governments could cancel a third of the debts being paid back at commercial rates or adopt a longer repayment period at concessional rates of interest. A variety of policies were adopted for multilateral debt, including some debt write-off, rescheduling of debts and further loans to help countries over a difficult transitional period. This too was conditional on indebted countries accepting major structural adjustment under IMF and World Bank supervision.

Debt for Nature Swap

With increasing concern for the environment, indebted governments have been encouraged to agree to some environmental project in return for debt relief or rescheduling. For example, a number of NGOs* have bought up part of a country's debt in exchange for agreement to an environmental project e.g. in 1987 Conservation International bought up some of Bolivia's debt in return for Bolivia locally funding the Ben Biosphere Reserve. In addition, official agencies such as the Inter American Bank are also now involved in debt or nature swaps. In 1991 Brazil agreed to $100 million of swaps.

(*Non-government organisation)

Structural adjustment – its effects

'Structural adjustment was the centre piece of the Baker Plan (instigated by the USA under President Reagan at an IMF/World Bank meeting 1985). World Bank and IMF funds to assist the indebted countries make their interest payments were promised on condition that 'economic policies along Reaganomic lines – privatisation of state enterprises, an end to subsidies, opening the economy to foreign investment' were adopted ... in addition to the standard IMF requirements of currency devaluation, a reduction in government borrowing, control of the money supply and decontrol of wages and prices.' (*The Third World Guide* 1995 – 96)

The policy-making of the IMF and World Bank is essentially controlled by the advanced countries as the largest subscribers. The many structural adjustment programmes now in place mainly amongst the developing countries but also transitional economies accepting funding, combine what has been described as the short-term 'shock therapy' decreed by the IMF to remedy balance of payments problems and the World Bank's 'long term structural programme' to open up the economy to market forces. In 1988 the two institutions set up a Structural Adjustment Facility (SAF) which allowed officials, including consultants and technical experts, to supervise more closely and ensure implementation of structural adjustment programmes (SAPs). By 1992 a quarter of all World Bank lending was under SAP conditions, giving it a significant measure of control over the economic and financial policies of 70 developing world countries. This in effect increased their external dependency and reduced their autonomy.

While restructuring programmes have led to a number of countries adopting financial reforms and initiatives to increase exports and economic progress as measured by a rise in GDP output, these have been at great cost to the poorer sectors of society. Tight control of public spending has meant the removal of food subsidies and reduction of expenditure on welfare and education. Opening the economy out to market forces and increased foreign investment has also meant that less efficient local producers have been unable to compete, leading to closures and an increase in unemployment and hardship.

Continuing debt problems

Even amongst Newly Industrialising Countries where foreign investment has been increasingly attracted and economic growth is occurring, crises have continued to occur, as in the case of Mexico where the financial crisis of 1994 required an extra-ordinary aid package to rescue the country's economy. This has prompted observers to question whether the continuing debt problem is the crucial issue or whether it is internal weaknesses associated with poor implementation of reforms, continuing mismanagement of the economy and lack of political will.

In the case of the least developed countries measures taken to solve the debt crisis have palpably failed. They have been inadequate and inappropriate. The Sub-Sahara African debt crisis for example has worsened and arrears of debt interest repayment continue to mount. From the early 1980s to 1994 total debt has more than doubled (Figure 33.16). Both the World Bank and IMF admit that policies so far have failed. Two thirds of the total loans made by IMF and the World Bank in 1994 to the Sub-Sahara African countries returned to the IMF and World Bank to service earlier debt loans. Further, the World Bank report for 1996 shows that after interest and other repayments by developing countries, the bank is taking more in funds from developing countries than it lends.

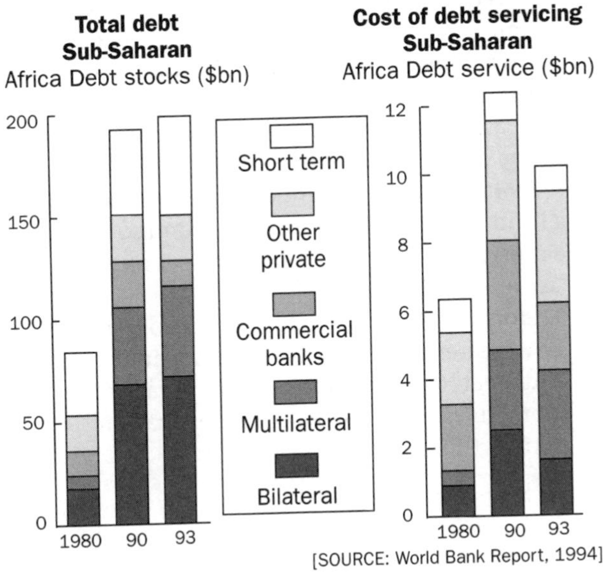

Figure 33.16 Africa's debt problem, 1980 – 93

The IMF and World Bank are now looking at a radical rescue package for the world's 40 poorest countries. It essentially involves creating a new funding facility out of reserves and making this available to the least developed countries so that they can pay the interest on multilateral debt and each part of the debt itself as payment became due. However, this radical new plan would be dependent on debt relief action also being agreed by other creditors, including individual governments which had granted bilateral aid. Further, it would be tied help, conditional on poor countries implementing World Bank policies.

Yet the IMF and World Bank do already have adequate reserves to solve the debt problems of the world's poorest countries: this is a necessity if they are to have any hope of sustainable economic progress. Critics argue if massive emergency rescue packages can be organised for better-off countries such as Mexico and Russia why not also for the poorest countries.

> Kenneth Clarke, Chancellor of the Exchequer, has been at the forefront of the drive to develop a \$5.6 bn – \$7.7 bn (£3.6 bn – £5 bn) six-year plan to cut payments by developing countries on their debt to international institutions. He has won wide acceptance for his suggestion that the IMF should sell a small part of its gold reserves and use the income from reinvesting the proceeds for debt relief.
>
> [SOURCE: *Independent* 16.9.96]

Oxfam urges that African (and the other least developed) countries require a rescue plan on the scale of the Marshall Aid Plan launched at the end of the Second World War to restructure the ruined economies in war-torn Europe. Oxfam put a plan forward at a recent G7 Summit of leading industrial countries, covering:

- increased aid flows, double those at present i.e. up to the 0.7% of GDP agreed by the richer countries in 1945 and in 1995 but not implemented
- a fund to help the processing of commodity exports and the reduction of protectionist barriers to exports
- a reform of structural adjustment programmes to give greater protection for domestic industries and greater attention to human welfare through more investment in health and education
- a strengthening of the UN role in aid and peace keeping.

There is a necessity for action along the lines suggested by the Oxfam policy document. Beyond solving the debt problem, it points to wider issues to do with fairer trade opportunities and basic human welfare. Cooperation with, rather than imposed intervention in the internal affairs of developing countries is the underlying tone of the suggested plan. Further, domestic governments are seen as having a major part to play in moderating the negative effects of market forces.

Concluding comment

World economic growth since the 1950s has been impressive as has the growth of world trade but the benefits have not been equally shared. They have largely gone to the advanced countries though a limited group of former developing countries are also increasingly sharing in these benefits. In contrast, the least developed countries have had to be content with the 'left-overs'. In relative terms they have fallen further and further behind. In a world where market forces hold dominant sway this is inevitable because competition is unequal. The already large economies have the greater accumulated factor endowments to allow them to gain a progressively larger share of world markets.

The IMF, World Bank and other international agencies were initially set up to specifically promote transfer of funds and resources from the richer advanced countries to the developing countries. However, they have failed in their tasks of assisting the economic development of the least developed countries and lessening world inequalities.

Underlying this failure is the unwillingness of the advanced countries to meet the minimum level of resource transfer to which they initially agreed. It is also the failure of some governments in developing countries to responsibly manage both what resources were transferred to them and their own internal physical and economic resource base.

Out of crises however, comes hope. The governments of advanced countries and international agencies are faced with situations which force upon them changes of policy. From within the developing world the voice of local communities is being more effectively articulated and heeded by their own governments and the world outside. Recent international summits and actions have indicated that the issues of inequality, basic human rights and sustainable development are being more urgently addressed to remedy the distortions increasing global integration has brought (Figure 33.17).

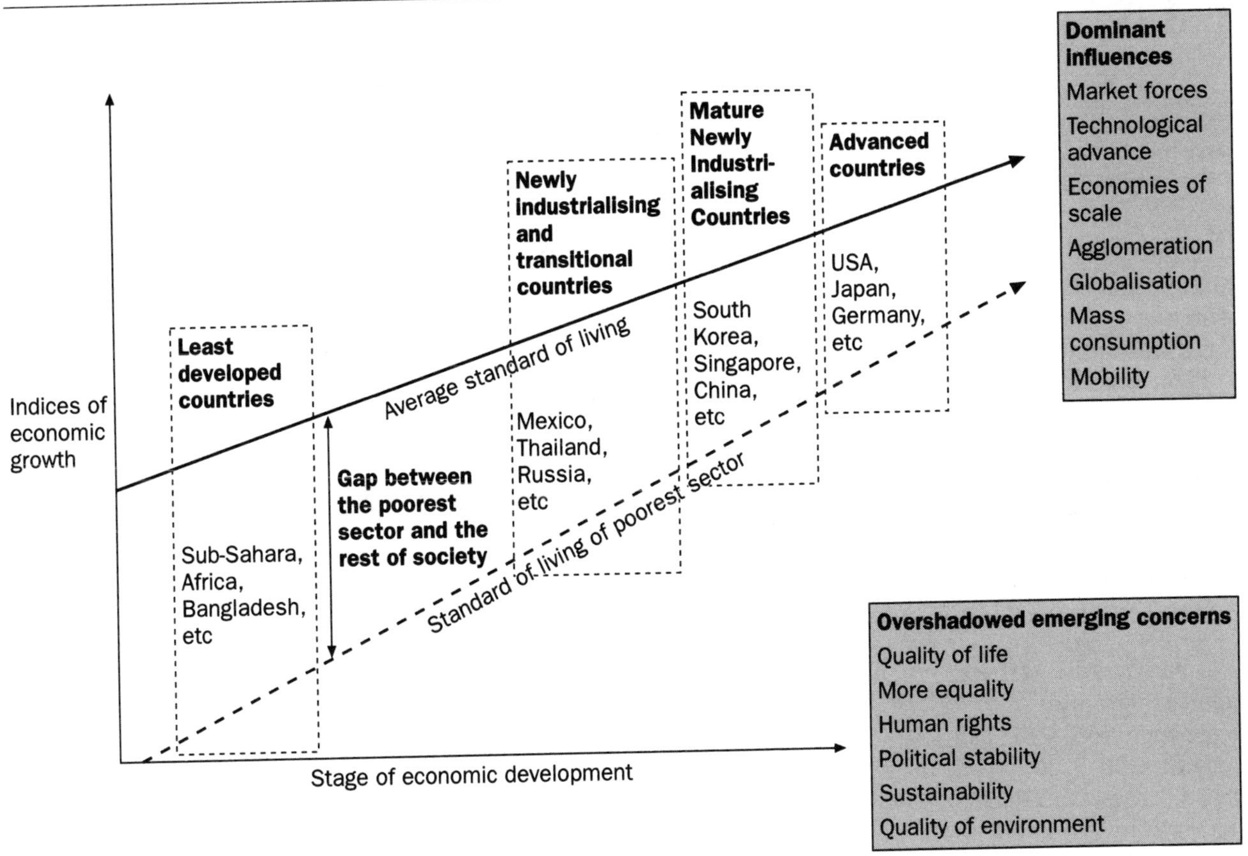

Figure 33.17 *The distortions of global integration*

Epilogue

'Globalisation … opens new opportunities for sustained economic growth and development of the world economy, particularly in developing countries … it also permits countries to share experiences, to learn from one another's achievements and difficulties.'

'At the same time, the rapid processes of change and adjustment have been accompanied by intensified poverty, unemployment and social disintegration … environmental risks have also been globalised.'

'The challenge is how to manage these processes and threats so as to enhance (and spread) their benefits and mitigate their negative effects on people.'

[SOURCE: Extract from the *Declaration and Programme of Action* made at the World Summit for Social Development, UN, 1995]

Index

NOTE:
Page numbers in **bold** denote the main entry,
page numbers in *italic* denote a figure, and
page numbers underlined denote a case study.